Worldwide Guide to Equivalent Irons and Steels

Paul M. Unterweiser
Staff Editor
Manager, Publications Development

Marilyn Penzenik
Project Coordinator

AMERICAN SOCIETY FOR METALS
METALS PARK, OHIO 44073

Library of Congress Cataloging in Publication Data
American Society for Metals
Worldwide guide to equivalent irons and steels.
Includes index.
1. Steel alloys--Handbooks, manuals, etc.
I. Title.
TA478.A32 1979 669'.142 79-24216
ISBN 0-87170-088-3

PRINTED IN THE UNITED STATES OF AMERICA

Introduction

Worldwide Guide to Equivalent Irons and Steels inaugurates a new series of basic reference books, the Engineering Handbook series, compiled and published by American Society for Metals. It is fitting that *Worldwide Guide* be first of the projected series, if only because of the universal demand for a guide to equivalent alloys that can be used to advantage in leading industrial nations and in nations throughout the world whose industrial potentials are in varying stages of development. Inasmuch as irons and steels are by far the leading constructional materials, it is equally appropriate that this introductory volume be devoted to these important materials, substantively assisting in their identification and selection and in the selection of equivalent and/or alternative alloys and alloy products.

To the best of our knowledge, there are several innovations to which the current compilation can lay claim. It is the first to encompass the specifications and designations of as many as 34 standards organizations, representing 18 nations. To this has been added the product of one international and three continental specification groups. It is also the first to present so thorough and comprehensive a selection of ferrous alloys and alloy products, cast and wrought. All of the common mill (wrought) and foundry (cast) products are represented. In it, as arranged in seven major sections, can be found six major alloy families of cast irons, seven of cast steels, and eight of wrought steels. These can be identified by section in the table of contents.

Finally– and perhaps most important– this volume introduces a more realistic concept for the presentation of alloys and alloy products that facilitates the reader's selection on the bases of chemical composition, product form, and nominal mechanical properties. It marks a departure from some practices of routinely citing equivalents and alternatives which, in many instances, prove to be little more than approximations and may fall short of the requirements established for fabrication and end use.

This approach to selection underscores a truism too often ignored, namely, that ultimate selection rests with the reader. Only he can satisfactorily equate a selection with the requirements that fulfill his needs. Bear in mind that individual requirements relating to product form, heat treatment or temper, cost, fabrication and end use may, and often do, vary considerably even when the identical alloy composition is selected. Accordingly, it is essential that the reader– before attempting to make full use of *Worldwide Guide*– first familiarize himself with the details and instructions set forth in the section on "Format and Guidelines for Use", given on the following page (page iv). The ground rules for using the *Guide* most efficiently and effectively are neither simplistic nor overly demanding. When observed, they lead to development of a skill. And in common with most useful and rewarding skills, performance tends to improve with practice.

Format and Guidelines for Use

General Description. The *Guide* is arranged in seven sections according to major alloy families, beginning with cast irons, followed by cast steels, and concluding with wrought steels. The types of alloys given in each of the sections are listed by generic name (e.g., cast irons, wrought stainless steels) in the table of contents (page vii) and on a title page preceding each section. The so-called "running heads" which appear at the top of each sectional page are, of necessity, foreshortened (e.g., cast high alloy steels). Specification numbers are listed in full in the index, beginning on page 563 which has been arranged in alphanumeric sequence.

Page Format. Data entries on individual pages follow a six-column arrangement which, reading from left to right, lists alloy specification number, designation, country of origin, product form(s), chemical composition, and mechanical properties. Of the six columns, only the last two – composition and mechanical properties – warrant further clarification.

Composition. Chemical composition is given in conventional weight percent for each of the chemical elements cited in the specification. Weight percent of each element, either a number or range, *precedes* the chemical symbol for the element to which it applies. Thus, 2.2-2.8 Si, 0.4-0.8 Mn, 3.5-3.8 C describe the weight percentages of the three elements – silicon, manganese and carbon – listed in the specification for the alloy described. Because these are iron-base alloys, the remainder element is iron, whether so stated or implied. Some specifications, notably among those relating to certain cast products, do not specify chemical composition other than carbon content, because alloy selection is based almost exclusively on mechanical properties. Thus, reflecting the original specification, these alloy listings show mechanical properties, and chemical composition other than carbon content is not given.

Mechanical Properties. Property values are preceded by a *condition* (e.g., as-cast, annealed, stress relieved) for which the values, as given in the specification, are applicable. In some instances, the specification values may be arrived at by mutual agreement of supplier and purchaser; in such instances, the condition is described as "as agreed".

Condition is followed by *product size,* that is, the sectional dimension (or range of dimensions) of the product to which the property values are applicable. This dimension most commonly refers to a diameter and is given in inches (no parentheses) followed by millimeters (in parentheses), the metric equivalent. Thus, 0.312 (7.94) diam indicates a diameter of 0.312 inches or 7.94 millimeters. Some specifications do not cite a specific product size but rather indicate an upper limit in size to which property values are applicable; others state that property values are common to all sizes. These stipulations are noted in the columnar listing.

Product size is followed by *mechanical property values,* again expressed in both English and metric units, where applicable. In sequence, the property values given apply to tensile strength, TS; yield strength, YS; and elongation, El. Elongation may be expressed as a percentage in 2 in. or 50 mm, or as a function of specimen diameter or section, e.g., elongation x 4D. Typically, property values are shown as follows: 53 (365) TS, 28 (193) YS, 30 El – indicating a tensile strength of 53 ksi (no parentheses) or 365 MPa (in parentheses), a yield strength of 28 ksi (no parentheses) or 193 MPa (parentheses), and an elongation of 30%. In countries that use the metric system exclusively, only the metric values appear in specifications; this is reflected in the specific listings.

Again, as noted previously under composition, certain specifications refer to mechanical properties but do not list chemical composition other than carbon content, primarily because selection is predicated on these properties.

Rationale. In this *Guide,* all alloys are listed in order of *descending carbon content,* whether that content is expressed as a single value, a range, or— as is common with certain cast products— as total carbon (TC) or carbon equivalent (CE). (Even those alloys whose specifications do not provide a complete chemical composition do, fortunately, indicate a carbon content— frequently expressed as total carbon (TC) or carbon equivalent (CE.) Other elements listed in the composition follow in fixed order, depending on the class of alloys dealt with. This arrangement generally serves as a mechanical sorter, whereby comparable or equivalent alloy compositions are drawn to within close proximity of each other on any given page or series of pages, thus facilitating identification of equivalent alloy compositions. When equivalent compositions have been identified, other factors such as country of origin, product form(s), and mechanical properties can be readily identified and compared.

Thus, when the carbon content of an alloy of interest is known or can be reasonably approximated, selection can be made by careful review of a page or, at most, several pages of the *Guide.* When the specification number of the alloy is known, or if that of a similar alloy is known, then reference to the index is all that is required to locate the specific alloy (and accompanying data) in the *Guide.* Again, it will be found that this alloy is located within reasonably close proximity to other alloys that are comparable or equivalent.

Common Abbreviations and Symbols

diam	– diameter or thickness of test specimen
TS	– tensile strength
YS	– yield strength
El	– elongation; a percentage in 2 in. or 50 mm
$<$	– less than
$\leq$	– up to and including
$>$	– greater than
$\geq$	– greater than and including
max	– maximum
min	– minimum
°C	– degrees Celsius
°F	– degrees Fahrenheit
h	– hour, hours
in 4D	– referring to elongation, a gage length 4 times the specimen diameter
OD	– outer diameter

Frequently, in the chemical composition, the percentage for an element will be given as a multiple of the carbon content, for example 10 x C.

Contributor Standards Organizations

Nation or Organization	Standards Organization, Abbreviation
Australia	AS
Belgium	NBN
Canada	CESA, Standard of Defense, CSA
Denmark	DS
Europe	AECMA, EURONORM
Finland	SFS
France	AFNOR, AIR, NFA
Germany	DIN
India	IS
International Organization for Standardization	ISO
Italy	UNI
Japan	JIS
Mexico	NOM, DGN
Norway	NS
Pan American	COPANT
South Africa	SABS
Sweden	SIS
Switzerland	VSM
Turkey	TS
United Kingdom	BS, DTD
United States	AISI, AMS, ANSI/ASTM, API, ASTM, Federal, Military

Contents

CAST IRONS

CAST IRONS

specification number	designation	country	product forms	composition	mechanical properties (see page iv for explanation)
MIL-C-60625		US	Sand castings	4.3–4.5 **CE**	
ASTM A 159	Grade G 1800	US	Sand castings	4.25–4.50 **CE**, 2.80–2.30 **Si**, 0.50–0.80 **Mn**, 0.25 **P**, 0.15 **S**	**Annealed**: all **diam**, 18 (135) **TS**
ASTM A 159	Grade G 2500	US	Sand castings	4.0–4.25 **CE**, 2.40–2.00 **Si**, 0.60–0.90 **Mn**, 0.20 **P**, 0.15 **S**	**Annealed**: all **diam**, 25 (170) **TS**
ASTM A 159	Grade G 3000	US	Sand castings	3.90–4.15 **CE**, 2.30–1.90 **Si**, 0.60–0.90 **Mn**, 0.15 **P**, 0.15 **S**	**As agreed**: all **diam**, 30 (205) **TS**
ASTM A 319	Grade I	US	Sand castings	3.81–4.40 **CE**	
IS 3355	Grade 1	India	Castings	3.81–4.40 **CE**	
ASTM A 278	Class No. 80	US	Sand castings	3.80 **CE**, 0.25 **P**, 0.12 **S**	**Stress relieved**: 0.88 (22.4) **diam**, 80 (550) **TS**
ASTM A 278	Class No. 70	US	Sand castings	3.80 **CE**, 0.25 **P**, 0.12 **S**	**Stress relieved**: 0.88 (22.4) **diam**, 70 (485) **TS**
ASTM A 278	Class No. 60	US	Sand castings	3.8 **CE**, 0.25 **P**, 0.12 **S**	**Stress relieved**: 0.88 (22.4) **diam**, 60 (415) **TS**
ASTM A 278	Class No. 55	US	Sand castings	3.8 **CE**, 0.25 **P**, 0.12 **S**	**Stress relieved**: 0.88 (22.4) **diam**, 55 (380) **TS**
ASTM A 278	Class No. 50	US	Sand castings	3.8 **CE**, 0.25 **P**, 0.12 **S**	**Stress relieved**: 0.88 (22.4) **diam**, 50 (345) **TS**
ASTM A 278	Class No. 45	US	Sand castings	3.80 **CE**, 0.25 **P**, 0.12 **S**	**Stress relieved**: 0.88 (22.4) **diam**, 45 (310) **TS**
ASTM A 278	Class No. 40	US	Sand castings	3.80 **CE**, 0.25 **P**, 0.12 **S**	**Stress relieved**: 0.88 (22.4) **diam**, 40 (275) **TS**
ASTM A 159	Grade G 4000	US	Sand castings	3.7–3.9 **CE**, 2.10–1.80 **Si**, 0.70–1.00 **Mn**, 0.10 **P**, 0.15 **S**	**As agreed**: all **diam**, 40 (275) **TS**
ASTM A 159	Grade G 3500	US	Sand castings	3.7–3.9 **CE**, 2.20–1.80 **Si**, 0.60–0.90 **Mn**, 0.12 **P**, 0.15 **S**	**As agreed**: all **diam**, 35 (240) **TS**
ASTM A 319	Grade II	US	Sand castings	3.51–4.10 **CE**	
IS 3355	Grade 2	India	Castings	3.51–4.10 **CE**	
SIS 14 01 10	SIS 0110–00	Sweden	Castings	2.2–2.8 **Si**, 0.4–0.8 **Mn**, 3.5–3.8 **C**	**As cast**: all **diam**, (100) **TS**
ASTM A 159	Grade 3500c	US	Sand castings	3.50 min **TC**, 1.30–1.80 **Si**, 0.60–0.90 **Mn**, 0.15 **P**, 0.12 **S**	**As agreed**: all **diam**, 35 (240) **TS**
IS 6331	Grade 15	India	Castings	3.40–3.70 **TC**, 2.30–2.80 **Si**, 0.50–0.80 **Mn**, 0.25 **P**, 0.15 **S**	**As-cast**: (13) **diam**, (187) **TS**
SIS 14 01 15	SIS 0115–00	Sweden	Castings	2.0–2.6 **Si**, 0.5–0.8 **Mn**, 3.4–3.7 **C**, 0.5 **P**, 0.15 **S**	**As cast**: all **diam**, (150) **TS**
ASTM A 159	Grade 3500b	US	Sand castings	3.40 min **TC**, 1.30–1.80 **Si**, 0.60–0.90 **Mn**, 0.15 **P**, 0.12 **S**	**As agreed**: all **diam**, 35 (240) **TS**
ASTM A 159	Grade 2500a	US	Sand castings	3.40 min **CE**, 1.60–2.10 **Si**, 0.60–0.90 **Mn**, 0.15 **P**, 0.12 **S**	**As agreed**: all **diam**, 25 (170) **TS**
SIS 14 01 20	SIS 0120–00	Sweden	Castings	1.8–2.4 **Si**, 0.6–0.8 **Mn**, 3.3–3.6 **C**, 0.35 **P**, 0.15 **S**	**As cast**: all **diam**, (200) **TS**
SIS 14 07 37	SIS 07 37–01	Sweden	Castings	1.6–2.8 **Si**, 0.05–1.0 **Mn**, 0–2.5 **Ni**, 3.2–4.0 **C**, 0.02–0.08 **Mg**, 0.08 **P**, 0.02 **S**	**Annealed or quenched and tempered; normalized**: all **diam**, (700) **TS**, (450) **YS**, 3 **El**
SIS 14 07 32	SIS 07 32–03	Sweden	Castings	1.6–2.8 **Si**, 0.05–1.0 **Mn**, 0–2.5 **Ni**, 3.2–4.0 **C**, 0.08 **P**, 0.02 **S**	**Annealed or quenched and tempered; normalized**: all **diam**, (600) **TS**, (400) **YS**, 5 **El**
AMS 5316A		US	Castings	3.2–4.0 **TC**, 1.7–2.5 **Si**, 0.8 **Mn**, 0.08 **P**	**As cast**: all **diam**, 80 (552) **TS**, 60 (414) **YS**, 2 **El**
SIS 14 07 27	SIS 07 27–02	Sweden	Castings	1.6–2.8 **Si**, 0.05–1.0 **Mn**, 0–2.5 **Ni**, 3.2–4.0 **C**, 0.02–0.08 **Mg**, 0.08 **P**, 0.02 **S**	**Annealed or quenched and tempered; normalized**: all **diam**, (500) **TS**, (350) **YS**, 7 **El**
AMS 5315A		US	Castings	3.2–4.0 **TC**, 1.7–2.5 **Si**, 0.8 **Mn**, 0.08 **P**	**Ferritize annealed**: all **diam**, 60 (414) **TS**, 45 (310) **YS**, 10 **El**
SIS 14 07 17	SIS 07 17–02	Sweden	Castings	1.6–2.8 **Si**, 0.05–1.0 **Mn**, 0–2.5 **Ni**, 3.2–4.0 **C**, 0.02–0.08 **Mg**, 0.08 **P**, 0.02 **S**	**Annealed**: all **diam**, (400) **TS**, (250) **YS**, 28 **El**
SIS 14 07 17	SIS 07 17–12	Sweden	Castings	1.6–2.8 **Si**, 0.05–1.0 **Mn**, 0–2.5 **Ni**, 3.2–4.0 **C**, 0.02–0.08 **Mg**, 0.08 **P**, 0.02 **S**	**Annealed**: all **diam**, (380) **TS**, (250) **YS**, 30 **El**
SIS 14 07 17	SIS 07 17–15	Sweden	Castings	1.6–2.8 **Si**, 0.05–1.0 **Mn**, 0–2.5 **Ni**, 3.2–4.0 **C**, 0.02–0.08 **Mg**, 0.08 **P**, 0.02 **S**	**Annealed**: all **diam**, (350) **TS**, (220) **YS**, 32 **El**
ASTM A 319	Grade III	US	Sand castings	3.20–3.80 **CE**	
IS 3355	Grade 3	India	Castings	3.20–3.80 **CE**	

CAST IRONS

specification number	designation	country	product forms	composition	mechanical properties (see page iv for explanation)
SIS 14 05 13	SIS 05 13–00	Sweden	Castings	0.3–0.6 **Si**, 0.3–0.6 **Mn**, 1.5–2.5 **Cr**, 3.0–5.5 **Ni**, 3.2–3.6 **C**, 0.3 **P**, 0.15 **S**	**As cast**: all **diam**, (490) **TS**, (270) **YS**
BS 4844 Part 2	Grade 2B	UK	Castings	0.3–0.8 **Si**, 0.2–0.8 **Mn**, 1.5–2.5 **Cr**, 3.0–5.5 **Ni**, 0.5 **Mo**, 3.2–3.6 **C**, 0.3 **P**, 0.15 **S**	**Stress relieved or annealed and stress relieved**
BS 4844 Part 2	Grade 2E	UK	Castings	1.5–2.2 **Si**, 0.2–0.8 **Mn**, 8.0–10.0 **Cr**, 4.0–6.0 **Ni**, 0.5 **Mo**, 3.2–3.6 **C**, 0.30 **P**, 0.15 **S**	**Annealed or annealed and stress relieved**
IS 4771	Type 1a NiLCr 34/550	India	Castings	3.2–3.6 **TC**, 0.3–0.6 **Si**, 0.3–0.6 **Mn**, 1.5–2.5 **Cr**, 3.0–5.5 **Ni**, 0.5 **Mo**, 0.3 **P**, 0.15 **S**; rem Fe	**Sand cast**
IS 4771	Type 1b NiHCr 34/600	India	Castings	3.2–3.6 **TC**, 1.5–2.2 **Si**, 0.3–0.6 **Mn**, 7.5–9.5 **Cr**, 4.0–6.0 **Ni**, 0.5 **Mo**, 0.3 **P**, 0.15 **S**; rem Fe	**Sand–cast**
SIS 14 01 25	SIS 0125–00	Sweden	Castings	1.5–2.1 **Si**, 0.6–0.8 **Mn**, 3.2–3.5 **C**, 0.25 **P**, 0.15 **S**	**As cast**: all **diam**, (250) **TS**
IS 6331	Grade 20	India	Castings	3.20–3.50 **TC**, 2.00–2.30 **Si**, 0.60–0.90 **Mn**, 0.15 **S**, 0.20 **P**	**As–cast**: (13) **diam**, (235) **TS**
ASTM A 159	Grade G 4000d	US	Sand castings	3.10–3.60 **TC**, 1.95–2.40 **Si**, 0.60–0.90 **Mn**, 0.85–1.25 **Cr**, 0.40–0.60 **Mo**, 0.10 **P**, 0.15 **S**	**As agreed**: all **diam**, 40 (275) **TS**
IS 4771	Type 2 CrMoHc 34/500	India	Castings	3.1–3.6 **TC**, 0.3–0.8 **Si**, 0.4–0.9 **Mn**, 14.0–18.0 **Cr**, 0.5 **Ni**, 2.5–3.5 **Mo**, 0.30 **P**, 0.15 **S**; rem Fe	**Sand–cast**
IS 6331	Grade 25	India	Castings	3.10–3.40 **TC**, 1.90–2.30 **Si**, 0.60–0.90 **Mn**, 0.15 **P**, 0.15 **S**	**As–cast**: (13) **diam**, (274) **TS**
SIS 14 01 30	SIS 0130–00	Sweden	Castings	1.3–1.8 **Si**, 0.7–0.9 **Mn**, 3.1–3.3 **C**, 0.15 **P**, 0.10 **S**	**As cast**: all **diam**, (300) **TS**
BS 4844 Part 3	Grade 3B	UK	Castings	1.0 **Si**, 0.5–1.5 **Mn**, 14.0–17.0 **Cr**, 0–1.0 **N**, 1–3.0 **Mo**, 0–1.2 **Cu**, 3.0–3.6 **C**, 0.1 **P**	**As cast**
IS 6331	Grade 35	India	Castings	3.00–3.30 **TC**, 1.80–2.10 **Si**, 0.70–1.00 **Mn**, 0.10 **P**, 0.15 **S**	**As–cast**: (30) **diam**, (343) **TS**
IS 6331	Grade 30	India	Castings	3.00–3.30 **TC**, 1.80–2.20 **Si**, 0.60–0.90 **Mn**, 0.12 **P**, 0.15 **S**	**As–cast**: (20) **diam**, (304) **TS**
SIS 14 01 35	SIS 0135–00	Sweden	Castings	1.1–1.5 **Si**, 0.8–1.0 **Mn**, 3.0–3.2 **C**, 0.10 **P**, 0.10 **S**	**As cast**: all **diam**, (350) **TS**
ANSI/ASTM A 476		US	Sand castings	3.0 **TC**, 2.50 **Si**, 0.08 **P**, 0.05 **S**	**As cast**: all **diam**, 80 (550) **TS**, 60 (415) **YS**, 3 **El**
ANSI/ASTM A 395		US	Sand castings	3.00 **TC**	**Annealed**: all **diam**, 60 (415) **TS**, 40 (275) **YS**, 18 **El**
MIL–I–24137	Class A	US	Sand castings	3.0 **TC**, 2.5 **Si**, 0.08 **P**	**Annealed**: all **diam**, 60 (414) **TS**, 45 (310) **YS**, 15 **El**
ASTM A 439	Type D–2B	US	Sand castings	3.00 **TC**, 1.50–3.00 **Si**, 0.70–1.25 **Mn**, 2.75–4.00 **Cr**, 18.00–22.00 **Ni**, 0.08 **P**	**Stress relieved**: all **diam**, 58 (400) **TS**, 30 (205) **YS**, 7 **El**
ASTM A 439	Type D–2	US	Sand castings	3.00 **TC**, 1.50–3.00 **Si**, 0.70–1.25 **Mn**, 1.75–2.75 **Cr**, 18.00–22.00 **Ni**, 0.08 **P**	**Stress relieved**: all **diam**, 58 (400) **TS**, 30 (205) **YS**, 8 **El**
DIN 1694	Grade GGG–NiMn 137–0.7652	Germany	Sand castings	3.0 **TC**, 2.0–3.0 **Si**, 6.0–7.0 **Mn**, 12.0–14.0 **Ni**	**As cast**: all **diam**, (392) **TS**, (215) **YS**, 10 **El**
DIN 1694	Grade GGG–NiCr 20 3–0.7661	Germany	Sand castings	3.0 **TC**, 1.7–3.0 **Si**, 0.7–1.5 **Mn**, 2.5–4.0 **Cr**, 18.0–22.0 **Ni**	**As cast**: all **diam**, (392) **TS**, (215) **YS**, 6 **El**
TS 551	DDOK–NiMn 137	Turkey	Castings	3.0 **TC**, 2.0–3.0 **Si**, 6.0–7.0 **Mn**, 12–14 **Ni**	**Austenitized**: all **diam**, (392) **TS**, (215) **YS**, 10 **El**
TS 551	DDOK–NiCr 203	Turkey	Castings	3.0 **TC**, 1.7–3.0 **Si**, 0.7–1.5 **Mn**, 2.5–4.0 **Cr**, 18–22 **Ni**	**Austenitized**: all **diam**, (392) **TS**, (215) **YS**, 6 **El**
NF A 32–301	S–NM 13 7	France	Castings	2.0–3.0 **Si**, 6.0–7.0 **Mn**, 0.2 **Cr**, 12.0–14.0 **Ni**, 3.0 **C**, 0.5 **Cu**, 0.08 **P**	**Normalized**: all **diam**, (390) **TS**, (210) **YS**, 15 **El**
NF A 32–301	S–NC 20 3	France	Castings	1.5–3.0 **Si**, 0.7–1.25 **Mn**, 2.5–3.5 **Cr**, 18.0–22.0 **Ni**, 3.0 **C**, 0.5 **Cu**, 0.08 **P**	**Normalized**: all **diam**, (390) **TS**, (210) **YS**, 7 **El**
ISO 2892	S–NiMn 13 7	ISO	Sand castings	2.0–3.0 **Si**, 6.0–7.0 **Mn**, 0.2 **Cr**, 12.0–14.0 **Ni**, 0.5 **Cu**, 3.0 **C**, 0.080 **P**	**As cast**: all **diam**, (390) **TS**, (210) **YS**, 15 **El**

CAST IRONS

specification number	designation	country	product forms	composition	mechanical properties (see page iv for explanation)
ISO 2892	S–NiCr 20 3	ISO	Sand castings	1.5–3.0 **Si**, 0.5–1.5 **Mn**, 2.5–3.5 **Cr**, 18.0–22.0 **Ni**, 0.5 **Cu**, 3.0 **C**, 0.080 **P**	**As cast**: all diam, (390) **TS**, (210) **YS**, 7 **El**
AS 1833	Grade AS 1833/S–NiMn 13 7	Australia	Castings	3.0 **TC**, 2.0–3.0 **Si**, 6.0–7.0 **Mn**, 0.2 **Cr**, 12.0–14.0 **Ni**, 0.5 **Cu**, 0.080 **P**	**As agreed**: all **diam**, (390) **TS**, (210) **YS**, 15 **El**
AS 1833	Grade AS 1833/S–NiCr 20 3	Australia	Castings	3.0 **TC**, 1.5–3.0 **Si**, 0.5–1.5 **Mn**, 2.5–3.5 **Cr**, 18.0–22.0 **Ni**, 0.5 **Cu**, 0.080 **P**	**As agreed**: all **diam**, (390) **TS**, (210) **YS**, 7 **El**
BS 3468	S–NiMn 13 7	UK	Castings	2.0–3.0 **Si**, 6.0–7.0 **Mn**, 0.2 **Cr**, 12.0–14.0 **Ni**, 0.5 **Cu**, 3.0 **C**, 0.080 **P**	**As cast**: all diam, (390) **TS**, (210) **YS**, 15 **El**
BS 3468	S–NiCr 20 3	UK	Castings	1.5–3.0 **Si**, 0.5–1.5 **Mn**, 2.5–3.5 **Cr**, 18.0–22.0 **Ni**, 0.5 **Cu**, 3.0 **C**, 0.080 **P**	**As cast**: all diam, (390) **TS**, (210) **YS**, 7 **El**
IS: 5787		India	Castings	3.0 **TC**, 3.0 **Si**, 0.08 **P**, 0.05 **S**	**As cast**: all **diam**, (386) **TS**, (290) **YS**, 3 **El**
SABS 937	Grade ASG–2A	South Africa	Castings	1.00–2.80 **Si**, 0.70–1.50 **Mn**, 1.00–2.50 **Cr**, 18.0–22.0 **Ni**, 3.0 **C**, 0.080 **P**	**As cast**: all **diam**, (375) **TS**, (205) **YS**, 8 **El**
SABS 937	Grade ASG–2B	South Africa	Castings	1.00–2.80 **Si**, 0.70–1.50 **Mn**, 2.0–3.5 **Cr**, 18.0–22.0 **Ni**, 3.0 **C**, 0.080 **P**	**As cast**: all **diam**, (375) **TS**, (205) **YS**, 6 **El**
SABS 937	Grade ASG–3A	South Africa	Castings	1.00–2.80 **Si**, 1.80–2.40 **Mn**, 0.50 **Cr**, 21.0–24.0 **Ni**, 3.0 **C**, 0.080 **P**	**As cast**: all **diam**, (375) **TS**, (195) **YS**, 20 **El**
SABS 937	Grade ASG–4A	South Africa	Castings	4.5–5.5 **Si**, 1.0–1.5 **Mn**, 1.00–2.50 **Cr**, 18.0–22.0 **Ni**, 3.0 **C**, 0.080 **P**	**As cast**: all **diam**, (375) **TS**, (205) **YS**, 10 **El**
DIN 1694	Grade GGG–NiCr 202–0.7660	Germany	Sand castings	3.0 **TC**, 1.7–3.0 **Si**, 0.7–1.5 **Mn**, 1.0–2.5 **Cr**, 18.0–22.0 **Ni**	**As cast**: all **diam**, (372) **TS**, (206) **YS**, 8 **El**
DIN 1694	Grade GGG–NiSiCr 20 42–0.7665	Germany	Sand castings	3.0 **TC**, 3.5–5.5 **Si**, 1.0–1.5 **Mn**, 1.0–2.5 **Cr**, 18.0–22.0 **Ni**	**As cast**: all **diam**, (372) **TS**, (215) **YS**, 10 **El**
DIN 1694	Grade GGG–Ni22–0.7670	Germany	Sand castings	3.0 **TC**, 1.7–3.0 **Si**, 1.8–2.4 **Mn**, 21.0–24.0 **Ni**	**As cast**: all **diam**, (372) **TS**, (206) **YS**, 20 **El**
TS 551	DDOK–NiCr 202	Turkey	Castings	3.0 **TC**, 1.7–3.0 **Si**, 0.7–1.5 **Mn**, 1.0–2.5 **Cr**, 18–22 **Ni**	**Austenitized**: all **diam**, (372) **TS**, (206) **YS**, 8 **El**
TS 551	DDOK–NiSiCr 2042	Turkey	Castings	3.0 **TC**, 3.5–5.5 **Si**, 1.0–1.5 **Mn**, 1.0–2.5 **Cr**, 18–22 **Ni**	**Austenitized**: all **diam**, (372) **TS**, (215) **YS**, 10 **El**
TS 551	DDOK–Ni 22	Turkey	Castings	3.0 **TC**, 1.7–3.0 **Si**, 1.8–2.4 **Mn**, 21.0–24.0 **Ni**	**Austenitized**: all **diam**, (372) **TS**, (206) **YS**, 20 **El**
NF A 32–301	S–NC 20 2	France	Castings	1.5–3.0 **Si**, 0.7–1.25 **Mn**, 1.0–2.5 **Cr**, 18.0–22.0 **Ni**, 3.0 **C**, 0.5 **Cu**, 0.08 **P**	**Normalized:** all **diam**, (370) **TS**, (210) **YS**, 7 **El**
NF A 32–301	S–NSC 20 5 2	France	Castings	4.5–5.5 **Si**, 1.0–1.5 **Mn**, 1.0–2.5 **Cr**, 18.0–22.0 **Ni**, 3.0 **C**, 0.5 **Cu**, 0.08 **P**	**Normalized:** all **diam**, (370) **TS**, (210) **YS**, 10 **El**
NF A 32–301	S–N 22	France	Castings	1.0–3.0 **Si**, 1.8–2.4 **Mn**, 0.5 **Cr**, 21.0–24.0 **Ni**, 3.0 **C**, 0.5 **Cu**, 0.08 **P**	**Normalized:** all **diam**, (370) **TS**, (170) **YS**, 20 **El**
AS 1833	Grade AS 1833/S–NiSiCr 20 5 2	Australia	Castings	3.0 **TC**, 4.5–5.5 **Si**, 0.5–1.5 **Mn**, 1.0–2.5 **Cr**, 18.0–22.0 **Ni**, 0.5 **Cu**, 0.080 **P**	**As agreed:** all **diam**, (370) **TS**, (210) **YS**, 10 **El**
AS 1833	Grade AS 1833/S–Ni 22	Australia	Castings	3.0 **TC**, 1.0–3.0 **Si**, 1.5–2.5 **Mn**, 0.5 **Cr**, 21.0–24.0 **Ni**, 0.5 **Cu**, 0.080 **P**	**As agreed:** all **diam**, (370) **TS**, (170) **YS**, 20 **El**
ISO 2892	S–NiCr 20 2	ISO	Sand castings	1.5–3.0 **Si**, 0.5–1.5 **Mn**, 1.0–2.5 **Cr**, 18.0–22.0 **Ni**, 0.5 **Cu**, 3.0 **C**, 0.080 **P**	**As cast**: all **diam**, (370) **TS**, (210) **YS**, 7 **El**
ISO 2892	S–NiSiCr 20 5 2	ISO	Sand castings	4.5–5.5 **Si**, 0.5–1.5 **Mn**, 1.0–2.5 **Cr**, 18.0–22.0 **Ni**, 0.5 **Cu**, 3.0 **C**, 0.080 **P**	**As cast**: all **diam**, (370) **TS**, (210) **YS**, 10 **El**
ISO 2892	S–Ni 22	ISO	Sand castings	1.0–3.0 **Si**, 1.5–2.5 **Mn**, 0.5 **Cr**, 21.0–24.0 **Ni**, 0.5 **Cu**, 3.0 **C**, 0.080 **P**	**As cast**: all **diam**, (370) **TS**, (170) **YS**, 20 **El**
AS 1833	Grade AS 1833/S–NiCr 20 2	Australia	Castings	3.0 **TC**, 1.5–3.0 **Si**, 0.5–1.5 **Mn**, 1.0–2.5 **Cr**, 18.0–22.0 **Ni**, 0.5 **Cu**, 0.080 **P**	**As agreed:** all **diam**, (370) **TS**, (210) **YS**, 7 **El**
BS 3468	S–NiCr 20 2	UK	Castings	1.5–3.0 **Si**, 0.5–1.5 **Mn**, 1.0–2.5 **Cr**, 18.0–22.0 **Ni**, 0.5 **Cu**, 3.0 **C**, 0.080 **P**	**As cast**: all **diam**, (370) **TS**, (210) **YS**, 7 **El**

CAST IRONS

specification number	designation	country	product forms	composition	mechanical properties (see page iv for explanation)
BS 3468	S–NiSiCr 2052	UK	Castings	4.5–5.5 **Si**, 0.5–1.5 **Mn**, 1.0–2.5 **Cr**, 18.0–22.0 **Ni**, 0.5 **Cu**, 3.0 **C**, 0.080 **P**	**As cast**: all **diam**, (370) **TS**, (210) **YS**, 10 **El**
BS 3468	S–Ni22	UK	Castings	1.0–3.0 **Si**, 1.5–2.5 **Mn**, 0.5 **Cr**, 21.0–24.0 **Ni**, 0.5 **Cu**, 3.0 **C**, 0.080 **P**	**As cast**: all **diam**, (370) **TS**, (170) **YS**, 20 **El**
COPANT 832	FGA Ni Cu Cr 15–6–3	COPANT	Castings	3.0 **TC**, 1.0–2.8 **Si**, 0.5–1.5 **Mn**, 2.5–3.5 **Cr**, 13.5–17.5 **Ni**, 5.5–7.5 **Cu**, 0.12 **S**	**Stress relieved or annealed**: all **diam**, (207) **TS**
ASTM A 436	Type 2b	US	Sand castings	3.00 **TC**, 1.00–2.80 **Si**, 0.5–1.5 **Mn**, 3.00–6.00 **Cr**, 18.00–22.00 **Ni**, 0.50 **Cu**, 0.12 **S**	**Stress relieved**: all **diam**, 30 (205) **TS**
ASTM A 436	Type 1b	US	Sand castings	3.00 **TC**, 1.00–2.80 **Si**, 0.5–1.5 **Mn**, 2.50–3.50 **Cr**, 13.50–17.50 **Ni**, 5.50–7.50 **Cu**, 0.12 **S**	**Stress relieved**: all **diam**, 30 (205) **TS**
COPANT 832	FGA Ni Cr 20–3	COPANT	Castings	3.0 **TC**, 1.0–2.8 **Si**, 0.5–1.5 **Mn**, 3.0–6.0 **Cr**, 18.0–22.0 **Ni**, 0.5 **Cu**, 0.12 **S**	**Stress relieved or annealed**: all **diam**, (201) **TS**
NF A 32–301	L–NUC 15 6 3	France	Castings	1.0–2.8 **Si**, 0.5–1.5 **Mn**, 2.5–3.5 **Cr**, 13.5–17.5 **Ni**, 3.0 **C**, 5.5–7.5 **Cu**	**Normalized**: all **diam**, (190) **TS**, 1 **El**
NF A 32–301	L–NC 20 3	France	Castings	1.0–2.8 **Si**, 0.5–1.5 **Mn**, 2.5–3.5 **Cr**, 18.0–22.0 **Ni**, 3.0 **C**, 0.5 **Cu**	**Normalized**: all **diam**, (190) **TS**, 1 **El**
AS 1833	Grade AS 1833/L–Ni Cu Cr 15 6 3	Australia	Castings	3.0 **TC**, 1.0–2.8 **Si**, 0.5–1.5 **Mn**, 2.5–3.5 **Cr**, 13.5–17.5 **Ni**, 5.5–7.5 **Cu**	**As agreed**: all **diam**, (190) **TS**, 1 **El**
AS 1833	Grade AS 1833/L–Ni Cr 20 3	Australia	Castings	3.0 **TC**, 1.0–2.8 **Si**, 0.5–1.5 **Mn**, 2.5–3.5 **Cr**, 18.0–22.0 **Ni**, 0.5 **Cu**	**As agreed**: all **diam**, (190) **TS**, 1 **El**
ISO 2892	L–NiCuCr 15 6 3	ISO	Sand castings	1.0–2.8 **Si**, 0.5–1.5 **Mn**, 2.5–3.5 **Cr**, 13.5–17.5 **Ni**, 5.5–7.5 **Cu**, 3.0 **C**	**As cast**: all **diam**, (190) **TS**
BS 3468	Grade L–NiCr 203	UK	Castings	1.0–2.8 **Si**, 0.5–1.5 **Mn**, 2.5–3.5 **Cr**, 18.0–22.0 **Ni**, 0.5 **Cu**, 3.0 **C**	**As cast**: all **diam**, (190) **TS**
DIN 1694	Grade GGL–NiCuCr 15 63–0.6656	Germany	Sand castings	3.0 **TC**, 1.0–2.8 **Si**, 1.0–1.5 **Mn**, 2.5–3.5 **Cr**, 13.5–17.5 **Ni**, 5.5–7.5 **Cu**	**As cast**: all **diam**, (176) **TS**
DIN 1694	Grade GGL–NiCr 20 3–0.6661	Germany	Sand castings	3.0 **TC**, 1.0–2.8 **Si**, 1.0–1.5 **Mn**, 2.5–3.5 **Cr**, 18.0–22.0 **Ni**	**As cast**: all **diam**, (176) **TS**
COPANT 832	FGA Ni Cu Cr 15–6–2	COPANT	Castings	3.0 **TC**, 1.0–2.8 **Si**, 0.5–1.5 **Mn**, 1.75–2.5 **Cr**, 13.5–17.5 **Ni**, 5.5–7.5 **Cu**, 0.12 **S**	**Stress relieved or annealed**: all **diam**, (172) **TS**
COPANT	FGA Ni Cr 20–2	COPANT	Castings	3.0 **TC**, 1.0–2.8 **Si**, 0.5–1.5 **Mn**, 1.75–2.5 **Cr**, 18.0–22.0 **Ni**, 0.5 **Cu**, 0.12 **S**	**Stress relieved or annealed**: all **diam**, (172) **TS**
ASTM A 436	Type 6	US	Sand castings	3.00 **TC**, 1.50–2.50 **Si**, 0.5–1.5 **Mn**, 1.00–2.00 **Cr**, 18.00–22.00 **Ni**, 1.00 **Mo**, 3.50–5.50 **Cu**, 0.12 **S**	**Stress relieved**: all **diam**, 25 (170) **TS**
ASTM A 436	Type 2	US	Sand castings	3.00 **TC**, 1.00–2.80 **Si**, 0.5–1.5 **Mn**, 1.5–2.5 **Cr**, 18.00–22.00 **Ni**, 0.50 **Cu**, 0.12 **S**	**Stress relieved**: all **diam**, 25 (170) **TS**
ASTM A 436	Type 1	US	Sand castings	3.00 **TC**, 1.00–2.80 **Si**, 0.5–1.5 **Mn**, 1.5–2.5 **Cr**, 13.50–17.50 **Ni**, 5.50–7.50 **Cu**, 0.12 **S**	**Stress relieved**: all **diam**, 25 (170) **TS**
NF A 32–301	L–NUC 15 6 2	France	Castings	1.0–2.8 **Si**, 0.5–1.5 **Mn**, 1.0–2.5 **Cr**, 13.5–17.5 **Ni**, 3.0 **C**, 5.5–7.5 **Cu**	**Normalized**: all **diam**, (170) **TS**, 2 **El**
NF A 32–301	L–NC 20 2	France	Castings	1.0–2.8 **Si**, 0.5–1.5 **Mn**, 1.0–2.5 **Cr**, 18.0–22.0 **Ni**, 3.0 **C**, 0.5 **Cu**	**Normalized**: all **diam**, (170) **TS**, 2 **El**
AS 1833	Grade AS 1833/L–Ni Cr 20 2	Australia	Castings	3.0 **TC**, 1.0–2.8 **Si**, 0.5–1.5 **Mn**, 1.0–2.5 **Cr**, 18.0–22.0 **Ni**, 0.5 **Cu**	**As agreed**: all **diam**, (170) **TS**, 2 **El**
ISO 2892	L–NiCuCr 15 6 2	ISO	Sand castings	1.0–2.8 **Si**, 0.5–1.5 **Mn**, 1.0–2.5 **Cr**, 13.5–17.5 **Ni**, 5.5–7.5 **Cu**, 3.0 **C**	**As cast**: all **diam**, (170) **TS**
ISO 2892	L–NiCr 20 2	ISO	Sand castings	1.0–2.8 **Si**, 0.5–1.5 **Mn**, 1.0–2.5 **Cr**, 18.0–22.0 **Ni**, 0.5 **Cu**, 3.0 **C**	**As cast**: all **diam**, (170) **TS**

CAST IRONS

specification number	designation	country	product forms	composition	mechanical properties (see page iv for explanation)
BS 3468	Grade L–NiCuCr 1562	UK	Castings	1.0–2.8 **Si**, 0.5–1.5 **Mn**, 1.0–2.5 **Cr**, 13.5–17.5 **Ni**, 5.5–7.5 **Cu**, 3.0 **C**	**As cast**: all **diam**, (170) **TS**
AS 1833	Grade AS 1833/L–Ni Cu Cr 15 6 2	Australia	Castings	3.0 **TC**, 1.0–2.8 **Si**, 0.5–1.5 **Mn**, 1.0–2.5 **Cr**, 13.5–17.5 **Ni**, 5.5–7.5 **Cu**	**As agreed**: all **diam**, (150) **TS**, 2 **El**
DIN 1694	Grade GGL–NiCuCr 15 62–0.6655	Germany	Sand castings	3.0 **TC**, 1.0–2.8 **Si**, 1.0–1.5 **Mn**, 1.0–2.5 **Cr**, 13.5–17.5 **Ni**, 5.5–7.5 **Cu**	**As cast**: all **diam**, (147) **TS**
DIN 1694	Grade GGL–NiCr 20 2–0.6660	Germany	Sand castings	3.0 **TC**, 1.0–2.8 **Si**, 1.0–1.5 **Mn**, 1.0–2.5 **Cr**, 18.0–22.0 **Ni**	**As cast**: all **diam**, (147) **TS**
NF A 32–301	L–NM 13 7	France	Castings	1.5–3.0 **Si**, 6.0–7.0 **Mn**, 0.2 **Cr**, 12.0–14.0 **Ni**, 3.0 **C**, 0.5 **Cu**	**Normalized**: all **diam**, (140) **TS**
AS 1833	Grade AS 1833/L–Ni Mn 13 7	Australia	Castings	3.0 **TC**, 1.5–3.0 **Si**, 6.0–7.0 **Mn**, 0.2 **Cr**, 12.0–14.0 **Ni**, 0.5 **Cu**	**As agreed**: all **diam**, (140) **TS**
ISO 2892	L–NiMn 13 7	ISO	Sand castings	1.5–3.0 **Si**, 6.0–7.0 **Mn**, 0.2 **Cr**, 12.0–14.0 **Ni**, 0.5 **Cu**, 3.0 **C**	**As cast**: all **diam**, (140) **TS**
DIN 1694	Grade GGL–NiMn 137–0.6652	Germany	Sand castings	3.0 **TC**, 1.5–3.0 **Si**, 6.0–7.0 **Mn**, 12.0–14.0 **Ni**	**As cast**: all **diam**, (137) **TS**
SIS 14 05 23	SIS 0523–00	Sweden	Castings	1.0–2.8 **Si**, 1.0–1.5 **Mn**, 1.0–2.5 **Cr**, 18.0–22.0 **Ni**, 0.5 **Cu**, 3.0 **C**	
SIS 14 07 76	SIS 07 76–03	Sweden	Castings	1.5–3.0 **Si**, 0.7–1.25 **Mn**, 1.0–2.5 **Cr**, 18.0–22.0 **Ni**, 0.5 **Cu**, 3.0 **C**, 0.02–0.08 **Mg**, 0.080 **P**, 0.020 **S**	
SIS 14 07 72	SIS 07 72–00	Sweden	Castings	2.0–3.0 **Si**, 6.0–7.0 **Mn**, 12.0–14.0 **Ni**, 0.5 **Cu**, 3.0 **C**, 0.02–0.08 **Mg**, 0.080 **P**, 0.020 **S**	
TS 551	DDOL–NiMn 137	Turkey	Castings	3.0 **TC**, 1.5–3.0 **Si**, 6.0–7.0 **Mn**, 12.0–14.0 **Ni**	
TS 551	DDOL–NiCuCr 1562	Turkey	Castings	3.0 **TC**, 1.0–2.8 **Si**, 1.0–1.5 **Mn**, 1.0–2.5 **Cr**, 13.5–17.5 **Ni**, 5.5–7.5 **Cu**	
TS 551	DDOL–NiCuCr 1563	Turkey	Castings	3.0 **TC**, 1.0–2.8 **Si**, 1.0–1.5 **Mn**, 2.5–3.5 **Cr**, 13.5–17.5 **Ni**, 5.5–7.5 **Cu**	
TS 551	DDOL–NiCr 202	Turkey	Castings	3.0 **TC**, 1.0–2.8 **Si**, 1.0–1.5 **Mn**, 1.0–2.5 **Cr**, 18.0–22.0 **Ni**	
TS 551	DDOL–NiCr 203	Turkey	Castings	3.0 **TC**, 1.0–2.8 **Si**, 1.0–1.5 **Mn**, 2.5–3.5 **Cr**, 18.0–22.0 **Ni**	
IS: 5788		India	Castings	3.00 min **TC**, 2.50 **Si**, 0.08 **P**	**Annealed**: all **diam**, (290) **TS**, (193) **YS**, 18 **El**
SABS 937	Grade ASG–6A	South Africa	Castings	1.5–2.6 **Si**, 3.75–4.50 **Mn**, 0.20 **Cr**, 21.0–24.0 **Ni**, 2.9 **C**, 0.080 **P**	**As cast**: all **diam**, (410) **TS**, (205) **YS**, 25 **El**
ASTM A 439	Type D–2C	US	Sand castings	2.90 **TC**, 1.00–3.00 **Si**, 1.80–2.40 **Mn**, 0.50 **Cr**, 21.00–24.00 **Ni**, 0.08 **P**	**Stress relieved**: all **diam**, 58 (400) **TS**, 28 (195) **YS**, 20 **El**
ASTM A532	Class II type C	US	Sand castings	2.8–3.6 **TC**, 1.0 **Si**, 0.5–1.5 **Mn**, 14.0–18.0 **Cr**, 0.5 **Ni**, 2.3–3.5 **Mo**, 1.2 **Cu**, 0.10 **P**, 0.06 **S**	**As cast or as cast and stress relieved or hardened or hardened and stress relieved or annealed**
SIS 14 04 57	SIS 0457–00	Sweden	Castings	1.5–2.2 **Si**, 0.3–0.6 **Mn**, 8.0–10.0 **Cr**, 4.0–6.0 **Ni**, 2.8–3.3 **C**, 0.3 **P**, 0.15 **S**	**As cast**: all **diam**, (610) **TS**, (490) **YS**
IS 4771	Type 1b NiHCr 30/550	India	Castings	2.8–3.3 **TC**, 1.5–2.2 **Si**, 0.3–0.6 **Mn**, 8.0–10.0 **Cr**, 4.0–6.0 **Ni**, 0.5 **Mo**, 0.3 **P**, 0.15 **S**; rem Fe	**Sand cast**
BS 4844 Part 3	Grade 3E	UK	Castings	1.0 **Si**, 0.5–1.5 **Mn**, 22.0–28.0 **Cr**, 0–1.0 **Ni**, 0–1.5 **Mo**, 0–1.2 **Cu**, 2.8–3.2 **C**, 0.10 **P**	**As cast**
BS 4844 Part 2	Grade 2D	UK	Castings	1.5–2.2 **Si**, 0.2–0.8 **Mn**, 8.0–10.0 **Cr**, 4.0–6.0 **Ni**, 0.50 **Mo**, 2.8–3.2 **C**, 0.30 **P**, 0.15 **S**	**Annealed or annealed and stress relieved**
SIS 14 05 12	SIS 0512–00	Sweden	Castings	0.3–0.6 **Si**, 0.3–0.6 **Mn**, 1.5–2.5 **Cr**, 3.0–5.5 **Ni**, 2.7–3.3 **C**, 0.3 **P**, 0.15 **S**	**As cast**: all **diam**, (550) **TS**, (320) **YS**

CAST IRONS

specification number	designation	country	product forms	composition	mechanical properties (see page iv for explanation)
IS 4771	Type 1a NibCr 30/500	India	Castings	2.7–3.3 **TC**, 0.3–0.6 **Si**, 0.3–0.6 **Mn**, 1.5–2.5 **Cr**, 3.0–5.5 **Ni**, 0.5 **Mo**, 0.3 **P**, 0.15 **S**; rem Fe	**Sand cast**
BS 4844 Part 2	Grade 2A	UK	Castings	0.3–0.8 **Si**, 0.2–0.8 **Mn**, 1.5–2.5 **Cr**, 3.0–5.5 **Ni**, 0.5 **Mo**, 2.7–3.2 **C**, 0.3 **P**, 0.15 **S**	**Stress relieved or annealed and stress relieved**
MIL–I–24137	Class C	US	Sand castings	2.7–3.1 **TC**, 2.0–3.0 **Si**, 1.9–2.5 **Mn**, 0.50 **Cr**, 20.0–23.0 **Ni**, 0.50 **Cu**, 0.15 **P**	**Solution annealed**: all diam, 50 (345) **TS**, 25 (172) **YS**, 20 **El**
ASTM A532	Class II type E	US	Sand castings	2.6–3.2 **TC**, 1.0 **Si**, 0.5–1.5 **Mn**, 18.0–23.0 **Cr**, 1.5 **Ni**, 1.0–2.0 **Mo**, 1.2 **Cu**, 0.10 **P**, 0.06 **S**	**As cast or as cast and stress relieved or hardened or hardened and stress relieved or annealed**
NF A 32–301	S–NM 23 4	France	Castings	1.5–2.5 **Si**, 4.0–4.5 **Mn**, 22.0–24.0 **Ni**, 2.6 **C**, 0.5 **Cu**, 0.08 **P**	**Normalized**: all **diam**, (440) **TS**, (210) **YS**, 25 **El**
AS 1833	Grade AS 1833/S–NiMn 23 4	Australia	Castings	2.6 **TC**, 1.5–2.5 **Si**, 4.0–5.0 **Mn**, 0.2 **Cr**, 22.0–24.0 **Ni**, 0.5 **Cu**, 0.080 **P**	**As agreed**: all **diam**, (440) **TS**, (210) **YS**, 25 **El**
ISO 2892	S–NiMn 23 4	ISO	Sand castings	1.5–2.5 **Si**, 4.0–4.5 **Mn**, 0.2 **Cr**, 22.0–24.0 **Ni**, 0.5 **Cu**, 2.6 **C**, 0.080 **P**	**As cast**: all **diam**, (440) **TS**, (210) **YS**, 25 **El**
BS 3468	S–NiMn 234	UK	Castings	1.5–2.5 **Si**, 4.0–4.5 **Mn**, 0.2 **Cr**, 22.0–24.0 **Ni**, 0.5 **Cu**, 2.6 **C**, 0.080 **P**	**As cast**: all **diam**, (440) **TS**, (210) **YS**, 25 **El**
ASTM A 439	Type D–4	US	Sand castings	2.60 **TC**, 5.00–6.00 **Si**, 1.00 **Mn**, 4.50–5.50 **Cr**, 28.00–32.00 **Ni**, 0.08 **P**	**Stress relieved**: all **diam**, 60 (415) **TS**
DIN 1694	Grade GGG–NiSiCr 30 5 5–0.7680		Sand castings	2.6 **TC**, 5.0–6.0 **Si**, 0.5 **Mn**, 4.5–5.5 **Cr**, 29.0–32.0 **Ni**	**As cast**: all **diam**, (392) **TS**, (235) **YS**, 1 **El**
TS 551	DDOK–NiSiCr 3055	Turkey	Castings	2.6 **TC**, 5.0–6.0 **Si**, 0.5 **Mn**, 4.5–5.5 **Cr**, 29.0–32.0 **Ni**	**Austenitized**: all **diam**, (392) **TS**, (235) **YS**, 1 **El**
NF A 32–301	S–NSC 30 5 5	France	Castings	5.0–6.0 **Si**, 1.0 **Mn**, 4.5–5.5 **Cr**, 28.0–32.0 **Ni**, 2.6 **C**, 0.50 **Cu**, 0.08 **P**	**Normalized**: all **diam**, (390) **TS**, (240) **YS**, 1 **El**
AS 1833	Grade AS 1833/S–NiSiCr 30 5 5	Australia	Castings	2.6 **TC**, 5.0–6.0 **Si**, 0.5–1.5 **Mn**, 4.5–5.5 **Cr**, 28.0–32.0 **Ni**, 0.5 **Cu**, 0.080 **P**	**As agreed**: all **diam**, (390) **TS**, (240) **YS**
ISO 2892	S–NiSiCr 30 5 5	ISO	Sand castings	5.0–6.0 **Si**, 0.5–1.5 **Mn**, 4.5–5.5 **Cr**, 28.0–32.0 **Ni**, 0.5 **Cu**, 2.6 **C**, 0.080 **P**	**As cast**: all **diam**, (390) **TS**, (240) **YS**
BS 3468	S–NiSiCr 3055	UK	Castings	5.0–6.0 **Si**, 0.5–1.5 **Mn**, 4.5–5.5 **Cr**, 28.0–32.0 **Ni**, 0.5 **Cu**, 2.6 **C**, 0.080 **P**	**As cast**: all **diam**, (390) **TS**, (240) **YS**
ASTM A 439	Type D–3A	US	Sand castings	2.60 **TC**, 1.00–2.80 **Si**, 1.00 **Mn**, 1.00–1.50 **Cr**, 28.00–32.00 **Ni**, 0.08 **P**	**Stress relieved**: all **diam**, 55 (380) **TS**, 30 (205) **YS**, 10 **El**
ASTM A 439	Type D–3	US	Sand castings	2.60 **TC**, 1.00–2.80 **Si**, 1.00 **Mn**, 2.50–3.50 **Cr**, 28.00–32.00 **Ni**, 0.08 **P**	**Stress relieved**: all **diam**, 55 (380) **TS**, 30 (205) **YS**, 6.0 **El**
SABS 937	Grade ASG–5A	South Africa	Castings	1.5–2.8 **Si**, 0.5 **Mn**, 2.5–3.5 **Cr**, 28.0–32.0 **Ni**, 2.6 **C**, 0.080 **P**	**As cast**: all **diam**, (375) **TS**, (205) **YS**, 7 **El**
DIN 1694	Grade GGG–NiCr 30 3–0.7676	Germany	Sand castings	2.6 **TC**, 1.5–2.8 **Si**, 0.5 **Mn**, 2.5–3.5 **Cr**, 28.0–32.0 **Ni**	**As cast**: all **diam**, (372) **TS**, (215) **YS**, 7 **El**
DIN 1694	Grade GGG–NiCr 30 1–0.7677	Germany	Sand castings	2.6 **TC**, 1.5–2.0 **Si**, 0.5 **Mn**, 1.0–1.5 **Cr**, 28.0–32.0 **Ni**	**As cast**: all **diam**, (372) **TS**, (206) **YS**, 13 **El**
TS 551	DDOK–NiCr 303	Turkey	Castings	2.6 **TC**, 1.5–2.8 **Si**, 0.5 **Mn**, 2.5–3.5 **Cr**, 28.0–32.0 **Ni**	**Austenitized**: all **diam**, (372) **TS**, (215) **YS**, 7 **El**
TS 551	DDOK–NiCr 301	Turkey	Castings	2.6 **TC**, 1.5–2.0 **Si**, 0.5 **Mn**, 1.0–1.5 **Cr**, 28.0–32.0 **Ni**	**Austenitized**: all **diam**, (372) **TS**, (206) **YS**, 13 **El**
NF A 32–301	S–NC 30 3	France	Castings	1.5–3.0 **Si**, 1.0 **Mn**, 2.5–3.5 **Cr**, 28.0–32.0 **Ni**, 2.6 **C**, 0.50 **Cu**, 0.08 **P**	**Normalized**: all **diam**, (370) **TS**, (210) **YS**, 7 **El**
NF A 32–301	S–NC 30 1	France	Castings	1.5–3.0 **Si**, 1.0 **Mn**, 1.0–1.5 **Cr**, 28.0–32.0 **Ni**, 2.6 **C**, 0.05 **Cu**, 0.08 **P**	**Normalized**: all **diam**, (370) **TS**, (210) **YS**, 13 **El**
AS 1833	Grade AS 1833/S–NiCr 301	Australia	Castings	2.6 **TC**, 1.5–3.0 **Si**, 0.5–1.5 **Mn**, 1.0–1.5 **Cr**, 28.0–32.0 **Ni**, 0.5 **Cu**, 0.080 **P**	**As agreed**: all **diam**, (370) **TS**, (210) **YS**, 13 **El**

CAST IRONS

specification number	designation	country	product forms	composition	mechanical properties (see page iv for explanation)
AS 1833	Grade AS 1833/S–NiCr 30 3	Australia	Castings	2.6 **TC**, 1.5–3.0 **Si**, 0.5–1.5 **Mn**, 2.5–3.5 **Cr**, 28.0–32.0 **Ni**, 0.5 **Cu**, 0.080 **P**	**As agreed**: all diam, (370) **TS**, (210) **YS**, 7 **El**
ISO 2892	S–NiCr 30 1	ISO	Sand castings	1.5–3.0 **Si**, 0.5–1.5 **Mn**, 1.0–1.5 **Cr**, 28.0–32.0 **Ni**, 0.5 **Cu**, 2.6 **C**, 0.080 **P**	**As cast**: all **diam**, (370) **TS**, (210) **YS**, 13 **El**
ISO 2892	S–NiCr 30 3	ISO	Sand castings	1.5–3.0 **Si**, 0.5–1.5 **Mn**, 2.5–3.5 **Cr**, 28.0–32.0 **Ni**, 0.5 **Cu**, 2.6 **C**, 0.080 **P**	**As cast**: all **diam**, (370) **TS**, (210) **YS**, 7 **El**
BS 3468	S–NiCr 301	UK	Castings	1.5–3.0 **Si**, 0.5–1.5 **Mn**, 1.0–1.5 **Cr**, 28.0–32.0 **Ni**, 0.5 **Cu**, 2.6 **C**, 0.080 **P**	**As cast**: all **diam**, (370) **TS**, (210) **YS**, 13 **El**
BS 3468	S–NiCr 303	UK	Castings	1.5–3.0 **Si**, 0.5–1.5 **Mn**, 2.5–3.5 **Cr**, 28.0–32.0 **Ni**, 0.5 **Cu**, 2.6 **C**, 0.080 **P**	**As cast**: all **diam**, (370) **TS**, (210) **YS**, 7 **El**
COPANT 832	FGA Ni Cr 30–3	COPANT	Castings	2.6 **TC**, 1.0–2.0 **Si**, 0.5–1.5 **Mn**, 2.5–3.5 **Cr**, 28.0–32.0 **Ni**, 0.5 **Cu**, 0.12 **S**	**Stress relieved or annealed**: all **diam**, (172) **TS**
COPANT 832	FGA Ni Cu Cr 30–5–5	COPANT	Castings	2.6 **TC**, 3.0–6.0 **Si**, 0.5–1.5 **Mn**, 4.5–5.5 **Cr**, 29.0–32.0 **Ni**, 0.5 **Cu**, 0.12 **S**	**Stress relieved or annealed**: all **diam**, (172) **TS**
ASTM A 436	Type 4	US	Sand castings	2.60 **TC**, 5.00–6.00 **Si**, 0.5–1.5 **Mn**, 4.50–5.50 **Cr**, 29.00–32.00 **Ni**, 0.50 **Cu**, 0.12 **S**	**Stress relieved**: all **diam**, 25 (170) **TS**
ASTM A 436	Type 3	US	Sand castings	2.60 **TC**, 1.00–2.00 **Si**, 0.5–1.5 **Mn**, 2.50–3.50 **Cr**, 28.00–32.00 **Ni**, 0.50 **Cu**, 0.12 **S**	**Stress relieved**: all **diam**, 25 (170) **TS**
DIN 1694	Grade GGL–NiCr 30 3–0.6676	Germany	Sand castings	2.6 **TC**, 1.0–2.0 **Si**, 0.4–0.8 **Mn**, 2.5–3.5 **Cr**, 28.0–32.0 **Ni**	**As cast**: all **diam**, (166) **TS**
DIN 1694	Grade GGL–NiSiCr 30 5 5–0.6680	Germany	Sand castings	2.6 **TC**, 5.0–6.0 **Si**, 0.4–0.8 **Mn**, 4.5–5.5 **Cr**, 29.0–32.0 **Ni**	**As cast**: all **diam**, (147) **TS**
TS 551	DDOL–NiCr 303	Turkey	Castings	2.6 **TC**, 1.0–2.0 **Si**, 0.4–0.8 **Mn**, 2.5–3.5 **Cr**, 28.0–32.0 **Ni**	
TS 551	DDOL–NiSiCr 3055	Turkey	Castings	2.6 **TC**, 5.0–6.0 **Si**, 0.4–0.8 **Mn**, 4.5–5.5 **Cr**, 29.0–32.0 **Ni**	
AMS 5395A		US	Castings	2.50–3.00 **TC**, 2.00–3.00 **Si**, 1.90–2.50 **Mn**, 0.50 **Cr**, 20.00–24.00 **Ni**, 0.30 **Mo**, 0.15 **P**, 0.05 **S**	**As cast**: 0.250 **diam**, (345) **TS**, (172) **YS**, 15 **El**
IS 4771	Type 1b NiHCr 27/500	India	Castings	2.5–2.9 **TC**, 1.5–2.2 **Si**, 0.3–0.6 **Mn**, 8.0–10.0 **Cr**, 4.0–6.0 **Ni**, 0.5 **Mo**, 0.3 **P**, 0.15 **S**; rem Fe	**Sand cast**
SIS 14 04 66	SIS 0466–00	Sweden	Castings	1.0 **Si**, 0.5 **Mn**, 24.0–30.0 **Cr**, 2.5 **C**	**As cast**: all **diam**, (440) **TS**, (250) **YS**
NF A 32-301	L–NSC 20 5 3	France	Castings	4.5–5.5 **Si**, 0.5–1.5 **Mn**, 1.5–4.5 **Cr**, 18.0–22.0 **Ni**, 2.5 **C**, 0.5 **Cu**	**Normalized**: all **diam**, (190) **TS**, 2 **El**
NF A 32-301	L–NC 30 3	France	Castings	1.0–2.0 **Si**, 0.5–1.5 **Mn**, 2.5–3.5 **Cr**, 28.0–32.0 **Ni**, 2.5 **C**, 0.5 **Cu**	**Normalized**: all **diam**, (190) **TS**, 1 **El**
AS 1833	Grade AS 1833/L–Ni Si Cr 20 5 3	Australia	Castings	2.5 **TC**, 4.5–5.5 **Si**, 0.5–1.5 **Mn**, 1.5–4.5 **Cr**, 18.0–22.0 **Ni**, 0.5 **Cu**	**As agreed**: all **diam**, (190) **TS**, 2 **El**
AS 1833	Grade AS 1833/L–Ni Cr 30 3	Australia	Castings	2.5 **TC**, 1.0–2.0 **Si**, 0.5–1.5 **Mn**, 2.5–3.5 **Cr**, 28.0–32.0 **Ni**, 0.5 **Cu**	**As agreed**: all **diam**, (190) **TS**, 1 **El**
ISO 2892	L–NiSiCr 20 5 3	ISO	Sand castings	4.5–5.5 **Si**, 0.5–1.5 **Mn**, 1.5–4.5 **Cr**, 18.0–22.0 **Ni**, 0.5 **Cu**, 2.5 **C**	**As cast**: all **diam**, (190) **TS**
ISO 2892	L–NiCr 30 3	ISO	Sand castings	1.0–2.0 **Si**, 0.5–1.5 **Mn**, 2.5–3.5 **Cr**, 28.0–32.0 **Ni**, 0.5 **Cu**, 2.5 **C**	**As cast**: all **diam**, (190) **TS**
BS 3468	Grade L–NiSiCr 2053	UK	Castings	4.5–5.5 **Si**, 0.5–1.5 **Mn**, 1.5–4.5 **Cr**, 18.0–22.0 **Ni**, 0.5 **Cu**, 2.5 **C**	**As cast**: all **diam**, (190) **TS**
DIN 1694	Grade GGL–NiSiCr 20 43–0.6667	Germany	Sand castings	2.5 **TC**, 3.5–5.5 **Si**, 1.0–1.5 **Mn**, 1.5–4.5 **Cr**, 18.0–22.0 **Ni**	**As cast**: all **diam**, (176) **TS**
NF A 32-301	L–NSC 30 5 5	France	Castings	5.0–6.0 **Si**, 0.5–1.5 **Mn**, 4.5–5.5 **Cr**, 29.0–32 **Ni**, 2.5 **C**, 0.5 **Cu**	**Normalized**: all **diam**, (170) **TS**
AS 1833	Grade AS 1833/Ni Si Cr 30 55	Australia	Castings	2.5 **TC**, 5.0–6.0 **Si**, 0.5–1.5 **Mn**, 4.5–5.5 **Cr**, 29.0–32.0 **Ni**, 0.5 **Cu**	**As agreed**: all **diam**, (170) **TS**

CAST IRONS

specification number	designation	country	product forms	composition	mechanical properties (see page iv for explanation)
ISO 2892	L–NiSiCr 30 5 5	ISO	Sand castings	5.0–6.0 **Si**, 0.5–1.5 **Mn**, 4.5–5.5 **Cr**, 29.0–32.0 **Ni**, 0.5 **Cu**, 2.5 **C**	**As cast**: all **diam**, (170) **TS**
TS 551	DDOL–NiSiCr 2043	Turkey	Castings	2.5 **TC**, 3.5–5.5 **Si**, 1.0–1.5 **Mn**, 1.5–4.5 **Cr**, 18.0–22.0 **Ni**	
BS 4844 Part 1	Grade 1A	UK	Castings	0.5–1.5 **Si**, 0.2–0.8 **Mn**, 2.0 **Cr**, 2.4–3.4 **C**, 0.15 **P**	**As cast**
BS 4844 Part 1	Grade 1B	UK	Castings	0.5–1.5 **Si**, 0.2–0.8 **Mn**, 2.0 **Cr**, 2.4–3.4 **C**, 0.5 **P**	**As cast**
IS 4771	Type 2 CrMoLC 28/500	India	Castings	2.4–3.1 **TC**, 0.30–0.80 **Si**, 0.40–0.90 **Mn**, 14.0–18.0 **Cr**, 0.50 **Ni**, 2.50–3.50 **Mo**, 0.30 **P**, 0.15 **S**; rem Fe	**Sand–cast**: all **diam**; **Hardened**; **Annealed**
AMS 5394A		US	Castings	2.40–3.00 **TC**, 2.00–3.20 **Si**, 0.80–1.60 **Mn**, 1.70–2.40 **Cr**, 18.00–22.00 **Ni**, 0.50 **Cu**, 0.25 **P**, 0.003 **Pb**, 0.15 **S**	**Stress relieved**: all **diam**, (379) **TS**, (221) **YS**, 5 **El**
MIL–I–24137	Class B	US	Sand castings	2.4–3.0 **TC**, 1.8–3.2 **Si**, 0.8–1.5 **Mn**, 1.7–2.4 **Cr**, 18.0–22.0 **Ni**, 0.50 **Cu**, 0.20 **P**	**Solution annealed**: all **diam**, 55 (379) **TS**, 30 (207) **YS**, 7 **El**
BS 4844 Part 3	Grade 3A	UK	Castings	1.0 **Si**, 0.5–1.5 **Mn**, 14.0–17.0 **Cr**, 0–1.0 **Ni**, 0–2.5 **Mo**, 0–1.2 **Cu**, 2.4–3.0 **C**, 0.10 **P**	**As cast**
BS 4844 Part 1	Grade 1C	UK	Castings	0.5–1.5 **Si**, 0.2–0.8 **Mn**, 2.0 **Cr**, 2.4–3.0 **C**, 0.15 **P**	**As cast**
AMS 5393 C		US	Castings	2.4–2.8 **TC**, 1.5–2.8 **Si**, 0.8–1.6 **Mn**, 1.7–2.4 **Cr**, 18.0–22.0 **Ni**, 0.5 **Cu**, 0.30 **P**, 0.003 **Pb**, 0.12 **S**	**Stress relieved**
ASTM A532	Class II type A	US	Sand castings	2.4–2.8 **TC**, 1.0 **Si**, 0.5–1.5 **Mn**, 11.0–14.0 **Cr**, 0.5 **Ni**, 0.5–1.0 **Mo**, 1.2 **Cu**, 0.10 **P**, 0.06 **S**	**As cast or as cast and stress relieved or hardened or hardened and stress relieved or annealed**
BS 4844 Part 3	Grade 3D	UK	Castings	1.0 **Si**, 0.5–1.5 **Mn**, 22.0–28.0 **Cr**, 0–1.0 **Ni**, 0–1.5 **Mo**, 0–1.2 **Cu**, 2.4–2.8 **C**, 0.10 **P**	**As cast**
BS 4844 Part 2	Grade 2C	UK	Castings	1.5–2.2 **Si**, 0.2–0.8 **Mn**, 8.0–10.0 **Cr**, 4.0–6.0 **Ni**, 0.5 **Mo**, 2.4–2.8 **C**, 0.3 **P**, 0.15 **S**	**Annealed or annealed and stress relieved**
ASTM A532	Class II type B	US	Sand castings	2.4–2.8 **TC/ CE**, 1.0 **Si**, 0.5–1.5 **Mn**, 14.0–18.0 **Cr**, 0.5 **Ni**, 1.0–3.0 **Mo**, 1.2 **Cu**, 0.10 **P**, 0.06 **S**	**As cast or as cast and stress relieved or hardened or hardened and stress relieved or annealed**
ASTM A 439	Type D–5B	US	Sand castings	2.40 **TC**, 1.00–2.80 **Si**, 1.00 **Mn**, 2.00–3.00 **Cr**, 34.00–36.00 **Ni**, 0.08 **P**	**Stress relieved**: all **diam**, 55 (380) **TS**, 30 (205) **YS**, 6 **El**
ASTM A 439	Type D–5	US	Sand castings	2.40 **TC**, 1.00–2.80 **Si**, 1.00 **Mn**, 0.10 **Cr**, 34.00–36.00 **Ni**, 0.08 **P**	**Stress relieved**: all **diam**, 55 (380) **TS**, 30 (205) **YS**, 20 **El**
DIN 1694	Grade GGG–NiCr 35 3–0.7685	Germany	Sand castings	2.4 **TC**, 1.5–2.8 **Si**, 0.5 **Mn**, 2.0–3.0 **Cr**, 34–36 **Ni**	**As cast**: all **diam**, (372) **TS**, (217) **YS**
DIN 1694	Grade GGG–Ni 35–0.7683	Germany	Sand castings	2.4 **TC**, 1.5–2.8 **Si**, 0.5 **Mn**, 34.0–36.0 **Ni**	**As cast**: all **diam**, (372) **TS**, (206) **YS**, 20 **El**
TS 551	DDOK–Ni 35	Turkey	Castings	2.4 **TC**, 1.5–2.8 **Si**, 0.5 **Mn**, 34.0–36.0 **Ni**	**Austenitized**: all **diam**, (372) **TS**, (206) **YS**, 20 **El**
TS 551	DDOK–NiCr 353	Turkey	Castings	2.4 **TC**, 1.5–2.8 **Si**, 0.5 **Mn**, 2.0–3.0 **Cr**, 34.0–36.0 **Ni**	**Austenitized**: all **diam**, (372) **TS**, (215) **YS**, 22 **El**
NF A 32–301	S–N 35	France	Castings	1.5–3.0 **Si**, 1.0 **Mn**, 34.0–36.0 **Ni**, 2.4 **C**, 0.050 **Cu**, 0.08 **P**	**Normalized**: all **diam**, (370) **TS**, (210) **YS**, 20 **El**
NF A 32–301	S–NC 35 3	France	Castings	1.5–3.0 **Si**, 1.0 **Mn**, 2.0–3.0 **Cr**, 34.0–36.0 **Ni**, 2.4 **C**, 0.50 **Cu**, 0.08 **P**	**Normalized**: all **diam**, (370) **TS**, (210) **YS**, 5 **El**
AS 1833	Grade AS 1833/S–Ni 35	Australia	Castings	2.4 **TC**, 1.5–3.0 **Si**, 0.5–1.5 **Mn**, 0.2 **Cr**, 34.0–36.0 **Ni**, 0.5 **Cu**, 0.080 **P**	**As agreed**: all **diam**, (370) **TS**, (210) **YS**, 20 **El**
AS 1833	Grade AS 1833/S–NiCr 35 3	Australia	Castings	2.4 **TC**, 1.5–3.0 **Si**, 0.5–1.5 **Mn**, 2.0–3.0 **Cr**, 34.0–36.0 **Ni**, 0.5 **Cu**, 0.080 **P**	**As agreed**: all **diam**, (370) **TS**, (210) **YS**, 7 **El**
ISO 2892	S–Ni 35	ISO	Sand castings	1.5–3.0 **Si**, 0.5–1.5 **Mn**, 0.2 **Cr**, 34.0–36.0 **Ni**, 0.5 **Cu**, 2.4 **C**, 0.080 **P**	**As cast**: all **diam**, (370) **TS**, (210) **YS**, 20 **El**

CAST IRONS

specification number	designation	country	product forms	composition	mechanical properties (see page iv for explanation)
ISO 2892	S–NiCr 35 3	ISO	Sand castings	1.5–3.0 **Si**, 0.5–1.5 **Mn**, 2.0–3.0 **Cr**, 34.0–36.0 **Ni**, 0.5 **Cu**, 2.4 **C**, 0.080 **P**	**As cast**: all **diam**, (370) **TS**, (210) **YS**, 7 **El**
BS 3468	S–Ni 35	UK	Castings	1.5–3.0 **Si**, 0.5–1.5 **Mn**, 0.2 **Cr**, 34.0–36.0 **Ni**, 0.5 **Cu**, 2.4 **C**, 0.080 **P**	**As cast**: all **diam**, (370) **TS**, (210) **YS**, 20 **El**
BS 3468	S–NiCr 35 3	UK	Castings	1.5–3.0 **Si**, 0.5–1.5 **Mn**, 2.0–3.0 **Cr**, 34.0–36.0 **Ni**, 0.5 **Cu**, 2.4 **C**, 0.080 **P**	**As cast**: all **diam**, (370) **TS**, (210) **YS**, 7 **El**
ASTM A 436	Type 5	US	Sand castings	2.40 **TC**, 1.00–2.00 **Si**, 0.5–1.5 **Mn**, 0.10 **Cr**, 34.00–36.00 **Ni**, 0.50 **Cu**, 0.12 **S**	**Stress relieved**: all **diam**, 20 (140) **TS**
COPANT 832	FGA Ni 35	COPANT	Castings	2.4 **TC**, 1.0–2.0 **Si**, 0.5–1.5 **Mn**, 0.10 **Cr**, 34.0–36.0 **Ni**, 0.5 **Cu**, 0.12 **S**	**Stress relieved or annealed**: all **diam**, (138) **TS**
DIN 1694	Grade GGL–Ni 35–0.6683	Germany	Sand castings	2.4 **TC**, 1.0–2.0 **Si**, 0.4–0.8 **Mn**, 34.0–36.0 **Ni**	**As cast**: all **diam**, (137) **TS**
NF A 32–301	L–N 35	France	Castings	1.0–2.0 **Si**, 0.5–1.5 **Mn**, 34.0–36.0 **Ni**, 2.4 **C**, 0.5 **Cu**	**Normalized**: all **diam**, (120) **TS**, 1 **El**
AS 1833	Grade AS 1833/L–Ni 35	Australia	Castings	2.4 **TC**, 1.0–2.0 **Si**, 0.5–1.5 **Mn**, 0.2 **Cr**, 34.0–36.0 **Ni**, 0.5 **Cu**	**As agreed**: all **diam**, (120) **TS**, 1 **El**
ISO 2892	L–Ni 35	ISO	Sand castings	1.0–2.0 **Si**, 0.5–1.5 **Mn**, 0.2 **Cr**, 34.0–36.0 **Ni**, 0.5 **Cu**, 2.4 **C**	**As cast**: all **diam**, (120) **TS**
BS 3468	Grade L–Ni 35	UK	Castings	1.0–2.0 **Si**, 0.5–1.5 **Mn**, 0.2 **Cr**, 34.0–36.0 **Ni**, 0.5 **Cu**, 2.4 **C**	**As cast**: all **diam**, (120) **TS**
TS 551	DDOL–Ni 35	Turkey	Castings	2.4 **TC**, 1.0–2.0 **Si**, 0.4–0.8 **Mn**, 29.0–32.0 **Ni**	
ASTM A532	Class III type A	US	Sand castings	2.3–3.0 **TC**, 1.0 **Si**, 0.5–1.5 **Mn**, 23.0–28.0 **Cr**, 1.5 **Ni**, 1.5 **Mo**, 1.2 **Cu**, 0.10 **P**, 0.06 **S**	**As cast or as cast and stress relieved or hardened or hardened and stress relieved or annealed**
IS 4771	Type 3 HCrNi 27/400	India	Castings	2.3–3.0 **TC**, 0.2–1.5 **Si**, 1.5 **Mn**, 24.0–28.0 **Cr**, 1.2 **Ni**, 0.6 **Mo**, 0.3 **P**, 0.15 **S**; rem Fe	**Sand–cast**; **Hardened**
IS 4771	Type 3 HCr 27/400	India	Castings	2.3–3.0 **TC**, 0.2–1.5 **Si**, 1.5 **Mn**, 24.0–28.0 **Cr**, 0.5 **Ni**, 0.6 **Mo**, 0.3 **P**, 0.15 **S**; rem Fe	**Sand–cast**: all **diam**; **Hardened**; **Annealed**
SIS 14 08 64	SIS 08 64–03	Sweden	Castings	0.8–1.4 **Si**, 0.2–0.6 **Mn**, 2.3–2.8 **C**, 0.01 **P**, 0.03–0.18 **S**	**Quenched and tempered**: all **diam**, (800) **TS**, (600) **YS**, 4 **El**
SIS 14 08 62	SIS 08 62–03	Sweden	Castings	0.8–1.4 **Si**, 0.2–0.6 **Mn**, 2.3–2.8 **C**, 0.01 **P**, 0.03–0.18 **S**	**Quenched and tempered**: all **diam**, (700) **TS**, (530) **YS**, 5 **El**
SIS 14 08 56	SIS 08 56–00	Sweden	Castings	0.8–1.4 **Si**, 0.2–0.6 **Mn**, 2.3–2.8 **C**, 0.01 **P**, 0.03–0.18 **S**	**As–cast**: all **diam**, (600) **TS**, (380) **YS**, 8 **El**
SIS 14 08 54	SIS 08 54–00	Sweden	Castings	0.8–1.4 **Si**, 0.2–0.6 **Mn**, 2.3–2.8 **C**, 0.01 **P**, 0.03–0.18 **S**	**As cast**: all **diam**, (500) **TS**, (300) **YS**, 11 **El**
SIS 14 08 52	SIS 08 52–00	Sweden	Castings	0.8–1.4 **Si**, 0.2–0.6 **Mn**, 2.3–2.8 **C**, 0.01 **P**, 0.03–0.18 **S**	**As cast**: all **diam**, (400) **TS**, (240) **YS**, 16 **El**
SIS 14 08 15	SIS 08 15–00	Sweden	Castings	0.8–1.4 **Si**, 0.2–0.6 **Mn**, 2.3–2.8 **C**, 0.01 **P**, 0.03–0.18 **S**	**As cast**: all **diam**, (320) **TS**, (190) **YS**, 22 **El**
SIS 14 08 14	SIS 08 14–00	Sweden	Castings	0.8–1.4 **Si**, 0.2–0.6 **Mn**, 2.3–2.8 **C**, 0.010 **P**, 0.03–0.18 **S**	
MIL–C–60653	Grade 80	US	Sand castings	2.50–2.75 **Si**, 0.40 **Mn**, 2.30–2.50 **C**, 0.025 min **Mg**, 0.08 **P**, 0.02 **S**	**Annealed**: all **diam**, 170 (1172) **TS**, 80 (552) **YS**, 3 **El**
MIL–C–60653	Grade 60	US	Sand castings	1.70–2.00 **Si**, 0.90–1.25 **Mn**, 2.30–2.50 **C**, 0.025 min **Mg**, 0.08 **P**, 0.02 **S**	**Annealed**: all **diam**, 80 (552) **TS**, 60 (414) **YS**, 5 **El**
MIL–C–60653	Grade 50	US	Sand castings	2.50–2.75 **Si**, 0.40 **Mn**, 2.30–2.50 **C**, 0.025 min **Mg**, 0.08 **P**, 0.02 **S**	**Annealed**: all **diam**, 65 (448) **TS**, 48 (331) **YS**, 18 **El**
TS 551	DDOK–NiMn 234	Turkey		2.2–216 **TC**, 1.9–2.6 **Si**, 4.0–4.4 **Mn**, 22.0–24.0 **Ni**	**Austenitized**: all **diam**, (412) **TS**, (176) **YS**, 25 **El**
BS 4844 Part 3	Grade 3C	UK	Castings	1.0 **Si**, 0.5–1.5 **Mn**, 17.0–22.0 **Cr**, 0–1.5 **Ni**, 0–3.0 **Mo**, 0–1.2 **Cu**, 2.2–3.0 **C**, 0.10 **P**	**As cast**
ANSI/ASTM A 602	Grade M 8501	US	Castings	2.20–2.90 **TC**, 0.90–1.90 **Si**, 0.15–1.25 **Mn**, 0.02–0.15 **P**, 0.02–0.20 **S**	**Quenched and tempered**: all **diam**, 105 (725) **TS**, 85 (585) **YS**, 1 **El**

CAST IRONS

specification number	designation	country	product forms	composition	mechanical properties (see page iv for explanation)
ANSI/ASTM A 602	Grade M 7002	US	Castings	2.20–2.90 **TC**, 0.90–1.90 **Si**, 0.15–1.25 **Mn**, 0.02–0.15 **P**, 0.02–0.20 **S**	**Quenched and tempered**: all **diam**, 90 (620) **TS**, 70 (480) **YS**, 2 **El**
ANSI/ASTM A 602	Grade M 4504	US	Castings	2.20–2.90 **TC**, 0.90–1.90 **Si**, 0.15–1.25 **Mn**, 0.02–0.15 **P**, 0.02–0.20 **S**	**Quenched and tempered**: all **diam**, 65 (445) **TS**, 45 (310) **YS**, 4 **El**
ANSI/ASTM A 602	Grade M 3210	US	Castings	2.20–2.90 **TC**, 0.90–1.90 **Si**, 0.15–1.25 **Mn**, 0.02–0.15 **P**, 0.02–0.20 **S**	**Annealed**: all **diam**, 50 (345) **TS**, 32 (220) **YS**, 10 **El**
ANSI/ASTM A 602	Grade M 5503	US	Castings	2.20–2.90 **TC**, 0.90–1.90 **Si**, 0.15–1.25 **Mn**, 0.02–0.15 **P**, 0.02–0.20 **S**	**Quenched and tempered**: all **diam**, 75 (250) **TS**, 55 (380) **YS**, 3 **El**
ANSI/ASTM A 602	Grade M 5003	US	Castings	2.20–2.90 **TC**, 0.90–1.90 **Si**, 0.15–1.25 **Mn**, 0.02–0.15 **P**, 0.02–0.20 **S**	**Quenched and tempered**: all **diam**, 75 (250) **TS**, 50 (345) **YS**, 3 **El**
IS 5789		India	Castings	2.2–2.7 **TC**, 1.5–2.5 **Si**, 3.75–4.5 **Mn**, 0.20 **Cr**, 21.0–24.0 **Ni**, 0.08 **P**	**Annealed**: all **diam**, (451) **TS**, (206) **YS**, 27 **El**
ANSI/ASTM A 571		US	Sand castings	2.2–2.7 **TC**, 1.5–2.50 **Si**, 3.75–4.5 **Mn**, 0.20 **Cr**, 21.0–24.0 **Ni**, 0.08 **P**	**Annealed**: all **diam**, 65 (450) **TS**, 30 (205) **YS**, 30 **El**
DIN 1694	Grade GGG–NiMn 23 4–0.7673	Germany	Sand castings	2.2–2.6 **TC**, 1.9–2.6 **Si**, 4.0–4.4 **Mn**, 22.0–24.0 **Ni**	**As cast**: all **diam**, (412) **TS**, (176) **YS**, 25 **El**
ASTM A532	Class II type D	US	Sand castings	2.0–2.6 **TC**, 1.0 **Si**, 0.5–1.5 **Mn**, 18.0–23.0 **Cr**, 1.5 **Ni**, 1.5 **Mo**, 1.2 **Cu**, 0.10 **P**, 0.06 **S**	**As cast or as cast and stress relieved or hardened or hardened and stress relieved or annealed**
NF A 32–101	Ft 40 (B, C, D, S)	France	Castings	5.0 **Si**, 1.5 **Mn**, 1.7 **C**	**As agreed**: all **diam**, (400) **TS**
NF A 32–101	Ft 35 (A, B, C, D, E, S)	France	Castings	5.0 **Si**, 1.5 **Mn**, 1.7 **C**	**As agreed**: all **diam**, (350) **TS**
NF A 32–101	Ft 30 (A, B, C, D, E, S)	France	Castings	5.0 **Si**, 1.5 **Mn**, 1.7 **C**	**As agreed**: all **diam**, (300) **TS**
NF A 32–101	Ft 25 (A, B, C, D, E, S)	France	Castings	5.0 **Si**, 1.5 **Mn**, 1.7 **C**	**As agreed**: all **diam**, (250) **TS**
NF A 32–101	Ft 20 (A, B, C, D, E, S)	France	Castings	5.0 **Si**, 1.5 **Mn**, 1.7 **C**	**As agreed**: all **diam**, (200) **TS**
NF A 32–101	Ft 15 (B, C, D, E, S)	France	Castings	5.0 **Si**, 1.5 **Mn**, 1.7 **C**	**As agreed**: all **diam**, (150) **TS**
NF A 32–101	Ft 10 (D, E, S)	France	Castings	5.0 **Si**, 1.5 **Mn**, 1.7 **C**	**As agreed**: all **diam**, (100) **TS**
BS 1591	SiCr 144	UK	Castings	14.25–15.25 **Si**, 0.50 **Mn**, 4.0–5.0 **Cr**, 1.4 **C**, 0.25 **P**, 0.10 **S**	
BS 1591	Si 10	UK	Castings	10.00–12.00 **Si**, 0.50 **Mn**, 1.2 **C**, 0.25 **P**, 0.10 **S**	
BS 1591	Si 14	UK	Castings	14.25–15.25 **Si**, 0.50 **Mn**, 1.0 **C**, 0.25 **P**, 0.10 **S**	
BS 1591	Si 16	UK	Castings	16.00–18.00 **Si**, 0.50 **Mn**, 0.8 **C**, 0.25 **P**, 0.10 **S**	
ASTM A 536	Grade 120–90–02	US	Castings		**Quenched and tempered or normalized and tempered**: all **diam**, 120 (825) **TS**, 90 (620) **YS**, 2.0 **El**
DIN 1693 Sheet 1	Grade GGG–80–0.7080	Germany	Sand cast		**As cast or heat treated**: all **diam**, (800) **TS**, (500) **YS**, 2 **El**
ISO 1083	Grade 800–2	ISO	Sand castings		**As cast**: all **diam**, (800) **TS**, (480) **YS**, 2 **El**
AS 1831	Grade AS 1831/800–480–2	Australia	Castings		**As agreed**: all **diam**, (800) **TS**, (480) **YS**, 2 **El**
NF A 32–201	FGS 800–2	France	Castings		**As agreed**: all **diam**, (800) **TS**, 2 **El**
UNI 4544–74	GS 800–2	Italy	Castings		**Spheroidized**: all **diam**, (800) **TS**, (480) **YS**, 2 **El**
BS 2789	Grade 800/2	UK	Casting, nodular		**As agreed**: all **diam**, (800) **TS**, (460) **YS**, 2 **El**
SFS 2113	GRP 800	Finland	Castings		**As cast**: all **diam**, (800) **TS**, (500) **YS**, 2 **El**
SABS 936	Grade SG 80	South Africa	Castings		**As cast**: all **diam**, (785) **TS**, (490) **YS**, 2 **El**
ASTM A 220	Grade 90001	US	Sand castings		**As cast**: all **diam**, 105 (725) **TS**, 90 (620) **YS**, 1 **El**

CAST IRONS

specification number	designation	country	product forms	composition	mechanical properties (see page iv for explanation)
DIN 1693 Sheet 1	Grade GGG-70-0.7070	Germany	Sand cast		**As cast or heat treated**: all **diam**, (700) **TS**, (440) **YS**, 2 **El**
ISO 1083	Grade 700-2	ISO	Sand castings		**As cast**: all **diam**, (700) **TS**, (420) **YS**, 2 **El**
AS 1831	Grade AS 1831/700-420-2	Australia	Castings		**As agreed**: all **diam**, (700) **TS**, (420) **YS**, 2 **El**
NF A 32-201	FGS 700-2	France	Castings		**As agreed**: all **diam**, (700) **TS**, (420) **YS**, 2 **El**
UNI 4544-74	GS 700-2	Italy	Castings		**Spheroidized**: all **diam**, (700) **TS**, (440) **YS**, 2 **El**
COPANT 827	FMNp 70002	COPANT	Castings		**Oil tempered and quenched**: all **diam**, (700) **TS**, (550) **YS**, 2 in 45 mm **El**
BS 2789	Grade 700/2	UK	Casting, nodular		**As agreed**: all **diam**, (700) **TS**, (400) **YS**, 2 **El**
SFS 2113	GRP 700	Finland	Castings		**As cast**: all **diam**, (700) **TS**, (440) **YS**, 2 **El**
BS 3333	P 690/2	UK	Castings		**Malleabilized**: (15) **diam**, (690) **TS**, (540) **YS**, 2 **El**
AS 1832	Grade AS 1832/690-2	Australia	Castings		**As agreed**: all **diam**, (690) **TS**, (540) **YS**, 2 **El**
ASTM A 536	Grade 100-70-03	US	Castings		**Quenched and tempered or normalized and tempered**: all **diam**, 100 (690) **TS**, 70 (485) **YS**, 3.0 **El**
DS 11 303	0708	Denmark	Castings		**As cast**: (25) **diam**, (690) **TS**, (440) **YS**, 2 **El**
TS 519	DDTS-70	Turkey	Castings		**Quenched and tempered**: (12) **diam**, (686) **TS**, (539) **YS**, 2 **El**
JIS G 5704	Class 5	Japan	Castings		**Graphitized**: all **diam**, (686) **TS**, (510) **YS**, 2 **El**
NF A 32-703	MP 70-2	France	Castings		**As cast**: all **diam**, (686) **TS**, (490) **YS**, 2 **El**
ISO/R944	Grade A	ISO	Sand castings		**Oil quenched and tempered**: (15) **diam**, (686) **TS**, (539) **YS**, 2 **El**
DIN 1692	GTS-70	Germany	Sand castings		**Non-decarburized-annealed, quenched and tempered**: (12) **diam**, (686) **TS**, (539) **YS**, 2 **El**
JIS G 5502	Type 5	Japan	Castings		**Annealed or as agreed**: all **diam**, (686) **TS**, (441) **YS**, 2 **El**
NS 11 301	NS 11 370	Norway	Castings		**As cast**: all **diam**, (686) **TS**, (441) **YS**, 3 **El**
SABS 936	Grade SG 70	South Africa	Castings		**As cast**: all **diam**, (685) **TS**, (440) **YS**, 3 **El**
ASTM A 220	Grade 80002	US	Sand castings		**As cast**: all **diam**, 95 (655) **TS**, 80 (550) **YS**, 2 **El**
COPANT 827	FMNp 65003	COPANT	Castings		**Oil tempered and quenched**: all **diam**, (650) **TS**, (430) **YS**, 3 in 45 mm **El**
TS 519	DDTS-65	Turkey	Castings		**Tempered perlite**: (12) **diam**, (637) **TS**, (421) **YS**, 3 **El**
ISO/R944	Grade B	ISO	Sand castings		**Oil quenched and tempered**: (15) **diam**, (637) **TS**, (421) **YS**, 3 **El**
DIN 1692	GTS-65	Germany	Sand castings		**Non-decarburized-annealed**: (12) **diam**, (637) **TS**, (421) **YS**, 3 **El**
TS 519	DDTB 65	Turkey	Castings		**As cast**: (9) **diam**, (608) **TS**, (401) **YS**, 4 **El**
DIN 1692	GTW-55	Germany	Sand castings		**Decarburized-annealed**: (9) **diam**, (608) **TS**, (401) **YS**, 7 **El**
DIN 1692	GTW-65	Germany	Sand castings		**Decarburized-annealed**: (9) **diam**, (608) **TS**, (401) **YS**, 4 **El**

CAST IRONS

specification number	designation	country	product forms	composition	mechanical properties (see page iv for explanation)
DIN 1693 Sheet 1	Grade GGG–60–0.7060	Germany	Sand cast		**As cast or heat treated**: all **diam**, (600) **TS**, (380) **YS**, 3 **El**
ISO 1083	Grade 600–3	ISO	Sand castings		**As cast**: all **diam**, (600) **TS**, (370) **YS**, 3 **El**
AS 1831	Grade AS 1831/600–370–3	Australia	Castings		**As agreed**: all **diam**, (600) **TS**, (370) **YS**, 3 **El**
NF A 32–201	FGS 600–3	France	Castings		**As agreed**: all **diam**, (600) **TS**, (370) **YS**, 3 **El**
UNI 4544–74	GS 600–2	Italy	Castings		**Spheroidized**: all **diam**, (600) **TS**, (370) **YS**, 2 **El**
BS 2789	Grade 600/3	UK	Casting, nodular		**As agreed**: all **diam**, (600) **TS**, (350) **YS**, 3 **El**
SFS 2113	GRP 600	Finland	Castings		**As cast**: all **diam**, (600) **TS**, (390) **YS**, 3 **El**
SABS 936	Grade SG 60	South Africa	Castings		**As cast**: all **diam**, (590) **TS**, (390) **YS**, 4 **El**
DS 11 303	0707	Denmark	Castings		**As cast**: (25) **diam**, (590) **TS**, (390) **YS**, 2 **El**
JIS G 5704	Class 4	Japan	Castings		**Graphitized**: all **diam**, (588) **TS**, (392) **YS**, 3 **El**
NS 11 501	NS 11 560	Norway	Castings		**As cast**: all **diam**, (588) **TS**, (353) **YS**, 4 **El**
NF A 32–703	MP 60–3	France	Castings		**As cast**: all **diam**, (588) **TS**, (392) **YS**, 3 **El**
JIS G 5502	Type 4	Japan	Castings		**Annealed or as agreed**: all **diam**, (588) **TS**, (392) **YS**, 2 **El**
ASTM A 220	Grade 70003	US	Sand castings		**As cast**: all **diam**, 85 (585) **TS**, 70 (485) **YS**, 3 **El**
NS 11 301	NS 11 360	Norway	Castings		**As cast**: all **diam**, (580) **TS**, (392) **YS**, 5 **El**
BS 3333	P 570/3	UK	Castings		**Malleabilized**: (15) **diam**, (570) **TS**, (420) **YS**, 3 **El**
AS 1832	Grade AS 1832/570–3	Australia	Castings		**As agreed**: all **diam**, (570) **TS**, (400) **YS**, 3 **El**
ASTM A 220	Grade 60004	US	Sand castings		**As cast**: all **diam**, 80 (550) **TS**, 60 (415) **YS**, 4 **El**
ASTM A 536	Grade 80–55–06	US	Castings		**As agreed**: all **diam**, 80 (550) **TS**, 55 (380) **YS**, 6 **El**
COPANT 827	FMNp 55004	COPANT	Castings		**Oil tempered and quenched**: all **diam**, (550) **TS**, (360) **YS**, 4 in 45 mm **El**
BS 3333	P 540/5	UK	Castings		**Malleabilized**: (15) **diam**, (540) **TS**, (340) **YS**, 5 **El**
AS 1832	Grade AS 1832/540–5	Australia	Castings		**As agreed**: all **diam**, (540) **TS**, (320) **YS**, 5 **El**
TS 519	DDTS–55	Turkey	Castings		**Tempered ferrite**: (12) **diam**, (539) **TS**, (353) **YS**, 5 **El**
JIS G 5703	Class 5	Japan	Castings		**Carburized**: (14) **diam**, (539) **TS**, (343) **YS**, 3 **El**
JIS G 5704	Class 3	Japan	Castings		**Graphitized**: all **diam**, (539) **TS**, (343) **YS**, 3 **El**
ISO/R944	Grade C	ISO	Sand castings		**Oil quenched and tempered**: (15) **diam**, (539) **TS**, (353) **YS**, 4 **El**
DIN 1692	GTS–55	Germany	Sand castings		**Non–decarburized–annealed**: (12) **diam**, (539) **TS**, (333) **YS**, 5 **El**
TS 519	DDTB–55	Turkey	Castings		**As cast**: (9) **diam**, (510) **TS**, (333) **YS**, 7 **El**
BS 3333	P 510/4	UK	Castings		**Malleabilized**: (15) **diam**, (510) **TS**, (310) **YS**, 4 **El**
AS 1832	Grade AS 1832/510–4	Australia	Castings		**As agreed**: all **diam**, (510) **TS**, (290) **YS**, 4 **El**
DIN 1693 Sheet 1	Grade GGG–50–0.07050	Germany	Sand cast		**As cast or heat treated**: all **diam**, (500) **TS**, (320) **YS**, 7 **El**

CAST IRONS

specification number	designation	country	product forms	composition	mechanical properties (see page iv for explanation)
ISO 1083	Grade 500–7	ISO	Sand castings		**As cast**: all **diam**, (500) **TS**, (320) **YS**, 7 **El**
AS 1831	Grade AS 1831/500–320–7	Australia	Castings		**As agreed**: all **diam**, (500) **TS**, (320) **YS**, 7 **El**
NF A 32–201	FGS 500–7	France	Castings		**As agreed**: all **diam**, (500) **TS**, (320) **YS**, 7 **El**
UNI 4544–74	GS 500–7	Italy	Castings		**Spheroidized**: all **diam**, (500) **TS**, (320) **YS**, 7 **El**
COPANT 827	FMNp 50005	COPANT	Castings		**Oil tempered and quenched**: all **diam**, (500) **TS**, (320) **YS**, 5 in 45 mm **El**
BS 2789	Grade 500/7	UK	Casting, nodular		**As agreed**: all **diam**, (500) **TS**, (310) **YS**, 7 **El**
SFS 2113	GRP 500	Finland	Castings		**As cast**: all **diam**, (500) **TS**, (330) **YS**, 7 **El**
JIS G 5703	Class 4	Japan	Castings		**Carburized**: (14) **diam**, (490) **TS**, (304) **YS**, 4 **El**
JIS G 5704	Class 2	Japan	Castings		**Graphitized**: all **diam**, (490) **TS**, (304) **YS**, 4 **El**
NS 11 501	NS 11 550	Norway	Castings		**As cast**: all **diam**, (490) **TS**, (294) **YS**, 5 **El**
NF A 32–703	MP 50–5	France	Castings		**As cast**: all **diam**, (490) **TS**, (323) **YS**, 5 **El**
ISO/R944	Grade D	ISO	Sand castings		**Oil quenched and tempered**: (15) **diam**, (490) **TS**, (314) **YS**, 5 **El**
JIS G 5502	Type 3	Japan	Castings		**Annealed or as agreed**: all **diam**, (490) **TS**, (343) **YS**, 7 **El**
SABS 936	Grade SG 50	South Africa	Castings		**As cast**: all **diam**, (490) **TS**, (345) **YS**, 7 **El**
DS 11 303	0727	Denmark	Castings		**As cast**: (25) **diam**, (490) **TS**, (340) **YS**, 7 **El**
NS 11 301	NS 11 350	Norway	Castings		**As cast**: all **diam**, (490) **TS**, (343) **YS**, 7 **El**
ASTM A 220	Grade 50005	US	Sand castings		**As cast**: all **diam**, 70 (485) **TS**, 50 (345) **YS**, 5 **El**
ASTM A 220	Grade 45006	US	Sand castings		**As cast**: all **diam**, 65 (450) **TS**, 45 (310) **YS**, 6 **El**
ASTM A 220	Grade 45008	US	Sand castings		**As cast**: all **diam**, 65 (450) **TS**, 45 (310) **YS**, 8 **El**
ASTM A 536	Grade 65–45–12	US	Castings		**As agreed**: all **diam**, 65 (450) **TS**, 45 (310) **YS**, 12 **El**
COPANT 827	FMNp 45007	COPANT	Castings		**Oil tempered and quenched**: all **diam**, (450) **TS**, (280) **YS**, 7 in 45 mm **El**
TS 519	DDTS–45	Turkey	Castings		**Tempered ferrite**: (12) **diam**, (441) **TS**, (294) **YS**, 7 **El**
JIS G 5703	Class 3	Japan	Castings		**Carburized**: (14) **diam**, (441) **TS**, (265) **YS**, 6 **El**
JIS G 5704	Class 1	Japan	Castings		**Graphitized**: all **diam**, (441) **TS**, (265) **YS**, 6 **El**
ISO/R944	Grade E	ISO	Sand castings		**Oil quenched and tempered**: (15) **diam**, (441) **TS**, (275) **YS**, 7 **El**
DIN 1692	GTS–45	Germany	Sand castings		**Non–decarburized–annealed**: (12) **diam**, (441) **TS**, (294) **YS**, 7 **El**
JIS G 5502	Type 2	Japan	Castings		**Annealed or as agreed**: all **diam**, (441) **TS**, (294) **YS**, 10 **El**
BS 3333	P 440/7	UK	Castings		**Malleabilized**: (15) **diam**, (440) **TS**, (270) **YS**, 7 **El**
AS 1832	Grade AS 1832/440–7	Australia	Castings		**As agreed**: all **diam**, (440) **TS**, (250) **YS**, 7 **El**

CAST IRONS

specification number	designation	country	product forms	composition	mechanical properties (see page iv for explanation)
BS 4772		UK	Pipe		**Centrifugally cast**: (80–100) **diam**, (420) **TS**, (300) **YS**, 10 **El**; **Not centrifugally cast**: all **diam**, (420) **TS**, (300) **YS**, 5 **El**
NBN I 06–002		Belgium	Pipe		**As cast**: all **diam**, (420) **TS**, (300) **YS**, 10 **El**
BS 2789	Grade 420/12	UK	Casting, nodular		**As agreed**: all **diam**, (420) **TS**, (250) **YS**, 12 **El**
CESA S 61	Grade 60	Canada	Castings		**As cast**: all **diam**, (415) **TS**
ANSI/ASTM A 48	Class No. 60A	US	Sand castings		**As cast**: 0.25–0.50 **diam**, 60 (415) **TS**
ASTM A 220	Grade 40010	US	Sand castings		**As cast**: all **diam**, 60 (415) **TS**, 40 (275) **YS**, 10 **El**
ASTM A 536	Grade 60–40–18	US	Castings		**Annealed**: all **diam**, 60 (415) **TS**, 40 (275) **YS**, 18 **El**
ANSI/ASTM A 716	Grade 60–42–10	US	Pipe		**Centrifigally cast**: all **diam**, 60 (415) **TS**, 42 (290) **YS**, 10 **El**
NS 11 301	NS 11 342	Norway	Castings		**As cast**: all **diam**, (412) **TS**, (274) **YS**, 15 **El**
SABS 936	Grade SG 42	South Africa	Castings		**As cast**: all **diam**, (410) **TS**, (275) **YS**, 12 **El**
SIS 14 01 40	SIS 0140–00	Sweden	Castings		**As–cast**: all **diam**, (400) **TS**
SFS 3345	GRS 40	Finland			**As cast**: (10–30) **diam**, (400) **TS**
BS 4622		UK	Pipe		**Centrifugally cast**: (≤300) **diam**, (400) **TS**
DIN 1693 Sheet 1	Grade GGG–40–0.7040	Germany	Sand cast		**As cast or heat treated**: all **diam**, (400) **TS**, (250) **YS**, 15 **El**
DIN 1693 Sheet 1	Grade GGG–40.3–0.7043	Germany	Sand cast		**As cast or heat treated**: all **diam**, (400) **TS**, (250) **YS**, 18 **El**
ISO 1083	Grade 400–12	ISO	Sand castings		**As cast**: all **diam**, (400) **TS**, (250) **YS**, 12 **El**
AS 1831	Grade AS 1831/400–250–12	Australia	Castings		**As agreed**: all **diam**, (400) **TS**, (250) **YS**, 12 **El**
NF A 32–201	FGS 400–12	France	Castings		**As agreed**: all **diam**, (400) **TS**, (250) **YS**, 12 **El**
UNI 4544–74	GS 400–12	Italy	Castings		**Spheroidized**: all **diam**, (400) **TS**, (250) **YS**, 12 **El**
COPANT 828	FG 400	COPANT	Castings		**As cast**: (13) **diam**, (400) **TS**
SFS 2113	GRP 400	Finland	Castings		**As cast**: all **diam**, (400) **TS**, (250) **YS**, 15 **El**
DIN 1691	Grade GG–40–0.6040	Germany	Sand castings		**As cast**: (30) **diam**, (392) **TS**
DS 11 301	GG 40	Denmark	Castings		**As cast**: (30) **diam**, (392) **TS**
TS 519	DDTB–45	Turkey	Castings		**As cast**: (9) **diam**, (392) **TS**, (226) **YS**, 12 **El**
NF A 32–701	MB 40–10	France	Castings		**Decarburized**: all **diam**, (392) **TS**, (245) **YS**, 10 **El**
DIN 1692	GTW–45	Germany	Sand castings		**Decarburized–annealed**: (9) **diam**, (392) **TS**, (225) **YS**, 12 **El**
JIS G 5527		Japan	Pipe: centrifugally cast		**Annealed**: all **diam**, (392) **TS**, 15 **El**
JIS G 5526	Class 1	Japan	Pipe: centrifugally cast		**Annealed**: all **diam**, (392) **TS**, 5 **El**
JIS G 5526	Class 2	Japan	Pipe: centrifugally cast		**Annealed**: all **diam**, (392) **TS**, 5 **El**
JIS G 5526	Class 3	Japan	Pipe: centrifugally cast		**Annealed**: all **diam**, (392) **TS**, 5 **El**
JIS G 5502	Type 1	Japan	Castings		**Annealed or as agreed**: all **diam**, (392) **TS**, (255) **YS**, 15 **El**
DS 11 303	0716	Denmark	Castings		**As cast**: (25) **diam**, (390) **TS**, (250) **YS**, 15 **El**
ANSI/ASTM A 48	Class No. 55A	US	Sand castings		**As cast**: 0.25–0.50 **diam**, 55 (380) **TS**

CAST IRONS

specification number	designation	country	product forms	composition	mechanical properties (see page iv for explanation)
SABS 936	Grade SG 38	South Africa	Castings		**As cast**: all **diam**, (375) **TS**, (245) **YS**, 17 **El**
JIS G 5703	Class 2	Japan	Castings		**Carburized**: (5–9) **diam**, (372) **TS**, (186) **YS**, 8 **El**
NF A 32–702	MN 38–18	France	Castings		**As cast**: all **diam**, (372) **TS**, (245) **YS**, 18 **El**
NS 11 301	NS 11 338	Norway	Castings		**As cast**: all **diam**, (372) **TS**, (235) **YS**, 20 **El**
ISO 1083	Grade 370–17	ISO	Sand castings		**As cast**: all **diam**, (370) **TS**, (230) **YS**, 17 **El**
AS 1831	Grade AS 1831/370–230–17	Australia	Castings		**As agreed**: all **diam**, (370) **TS**, (230) **YS**, 7 **El**
NF A 32–201	FGS 370–17	France	Castings		**As agreed**: all **diam**, (370) **TS**, (230) **YS**, 17 **El**
UNI 4544–74	GS 370–17	Italy	Castings		**Spheroidized**: all **diam**, (370) **TS**, (230) **YS**, 17 **El**
DS 11 303	0715	Denmark	Castings		**As cast**: (25) **diam**, (370) **TS**, (240) **YS**, 17 **El**
BS 2789	Grade 370/17	UK	Casting, nodular		**As agreed**: all **diam**, (370) **TS**, (230) **YS**, 17 **El**
SFS 2113	GRP 370	Finland	Castings	2.3 **Si**, 0.3 **Mn**	**As cast**: all **diam**, (370) **TS**, (250) **YS**, 20 **El**
ASTM A 47	Grade 35018	US	Castings		**As cast**: all **diam**, 53 (365) **TS**, 35 (240) **YS**, 18 **El**
ASTM A 338	Grade 35018	US	Sand castings		**As cast**: all **diam**, 53 (365) **TS**, 35 (240) **YS**, 18 **El**
JIS G 5702	Class 4	Japan	Castings		**Graphitized**: all **diam**, (363) **TS**, (216) **YS**, 14 **El**
TS 519	DDTB–40	Turkey	Castings		**As cast**: (9) **diam**, (353) **TS**, (196) **YS**, 10 **El**
ISO–R942	Grade A	ISO	Sand castings		**As cast and annealed**: (9) **diam**, (353) **TS**, (196) **YS**, 10 **El**
DIN 1692	GTW–40	Germany	Sand castings		**Decarburized**: (9) **diam**, (353) **TS**, (196) **YS**, 10 **El**
SFS 3345	GRS 30	Finland	Castings		**As cast**: (8) **diam**, (350) **TS**
SFS 3345	GRS 35	Finland	Castings		**As cast**: (10–30) **diam**, (350) **TS**
SABS 1034	Grade 350	South Africa	Castings		**As cast**: (20–30) **diam**, (350) **TS**
BS 309	W 410/4	UK	Castings		**Malleabilized**: (9) **diam**, (350) **TS**, (190) **YS**, 10 **El**
AS 1832	Grade AS 1832/410–4	Australia	Castings		**As agreed**: (9) **diam**, (350) **TS**, (190) **YS**, 10 **El**
DIN 1693 Sheet 1	Grade GGG–35.3–0.7033	Germany	Sand cast		**As cast or heat treated**: all **diam**, (350) **TS**, (220) **YS**, 22 **El**
COPANT 829	FMNf 35012	COPANT	Castings		**As cast**: all **diam**, (350) **TS**, (210) **YS**, 12 in 45 mm **El**
CESA S 61	Grade 50	Canada	Castings		**As cast**: all **diam**, (345) **TS**
ANSI/ASTM A 48	Class No. 50A	US	Sand castings		**As cast**: 0.25–0.50 **diam**, 50 (345) **TS**
ASTM A 47	Grade 32510	US	Castings		**As cast**: all **diam**, 50 (345) **TS**, 32 (225) **YS**, 10 **El**
ASTM A 338	Grade 32510	US	Sand castings		**As cast**: all **diam**, 50 (345) **TS**, 32 (224) **YS**, 10 **El**
JIS G 5501	Grade 6	Japan	Castings		**Annealed**: (15–30) **diam**, (343) **TS**
DIN 1691	Grade GG–35–0.6035	Germany	Sand castings		**As cast**: (30) **diam**, (343) **TS**
DS 11 301	GG 35	Denmark	Castings		**As cast**: (30) **diam**, (343) **TS**
TS 519	DDTS–35	Turkey	Castings		**Tempered ferrite**: (12) **diam**, (343) **TS**, (196) **YS**, 12 **El**
JIS G 5702	Class 3	Japan	Castings		**Graphitized**: all **diam**, (343) **TS**, (206) **YS**, 10 **El**
NF A 32–701	MB 35–7	France	Castings		**Decarburized**: all **diam**, (343) **TS**, (215) **YS**, 7 **El**
NF A 32–702	MN 35–10	France	Castings		**As cast**: all **diam**, (343) **TS**, (225) **YS**, 10 **El**

CAST IRONS

specification number	designation	country	product forms	composition	mechanical properties (see page iv for explanation)
DIN 1692	GTS–35	Germany	Sand castings		**Non–decarburized–annealed**: (12) **diam**, (343) **TS**, (196) **YS**, 12 **El**
DS 11 302	0816	Denmark	Castings		**As cast**: (19) **diam**, (340) **TS**, (210) **YS**, 12 **El**
BS 310	B 340/12	UK	Castings		**Malleabilized**: (15) **diam**, (340) **TS**, (200) **YS**, 12 **El**
AS 1832	Grade AS 1832/340–12	Australia	Castings		**As agreed**: all **diam**, (340) **TS**, (200) **YS**, 12 **El**
SFS 2113	GRP 340	Finland	Castings	2.1 **Si**, 0.1 **Mn**, 0.050 **P**	**As cast**: all **diam**, (340) **TS**, (220) **YS**, 22 **El**
TS 519	DDTB–35	Turkey	Castings		**As cast**: (9) **diam**, (333) **TS**, 6 **El**
JIS G 5703	Class 1	Japan	Castings		**Carburized**: (5–9) **diam**, (333) **TS**, (167) **YS**, 5 **El**
DIN 1692	GTW–35	Germany	Sand castings		**Decarburized–annealed**: (9) **diam**, (333) **TS**, 6 **El**
COPANT 828	FG 250	COPANT	Castings		**As cast**: (13) **diam**, (330) **TS**
COPANT 828	FG 300	COPANT	Castings		**As cast**: (13) **diam**, (330) **TS**
NS 11 501	NS 11 533	Norway	Castings		**As cast**: all **diam**, (323) **TS**, (186) **YS**, 14 **El**
COPANT 829	FMNf 32010	COPANT	Castings		**As cast**: all **diam**, (320) **TS**, (190) **YS**, 10 in 45 mm **El**
TS 519	DDTB–K 38	Turkey	Castings		**As cast**: (9) **diam**, (314) **TS**, (167) **YS**, 15 **El**
JIS G 5702	Class 2	Japan	Castings		**Graphitized**: all **diam**, (314) **TS**, (186) **YS**, 8 **El**
NF A 32–702	MN 32–8	France	Castings		**As cast**: all **diam**, (314) **TS**, (206) **YS**, 8 **El**
ISO/R943	Grade B	ISO	Sand castings		**Quenched and tempered**: (15) **diam**, (314) **TS**, (186) **YS**, 10 **El**
DIN 1692	GTW–S38	Germany	Sand castings		**Decarburized–annealed**: (9) **diam**, (314) **TS**, (167) **YS**, 15 **El**
ANSI/ASTM A 48	Class No. 45A	US	Sand castings		**As cast**: 0.25–0.50 **diam**, 45 (310) **TS**
DS 11 302	0815	Denmark	Castings		**As cast**: (19) **diam**, (310) **TS**, (190) **YS**, 10 **El**
BS 310	B 310/10	UK	Castings		**Malleabilized**: (15) **diam**, (310) **TS**, (190) **YS**, 10 **El**
AS 1832	Grade AS 1832/310–10	Australia	Castings		**As agreed**: all **diam**, (310) **TS**, (190) **YS**, 10 **El**
JIS G 5501	Grade 5	Japan	Castings		**Annealed**: (8–15) **diam**, (304) **TS**
SABS 1034	Grade 300	South Africa	Castings		**As cast**: (20–30) **diam**, (300) **TS**
COPANT 829	FMNf 30006	COPANT	Castings		**As cast**: all **diam**, (300) **TS**, (210) **YS**, 6 in 45 mm **El**
DIN 1691	Grade GG–30–0.6030	Germany	Sand castings		**As cast**: (30) **diam**, (294) **TS**
DS 11 301	GG 30	Denmark	Castings		**As cast**: (30) **diam**, (294) **TS**
ISO/R943	Grade C	ISO	Sand casting		**Quenched and tempered**: (15) **diam**, (294) **TS**, 6 **El**
DS 11 302	0814	Denmark	Castings		**As cast**: (19) **diam**, (290) **TS**, 6 **El**
BS 310	B 290/6	UK	Castings		**Malleabilized**: (15) **diam**, (290) **TS**, (170) **YS**, 6 **El**
AS 1832	Grade AS 1832/290–6	Australia	Castings		**As agreed**: all **diam**, (290) **TS**, (170) **YS**, 6 **El**
ASTM A 126	Class C	US	Sand castings		**As cast**: all **diam**, 41 (285) **TS**
COPANT 828	FG 200	COPANT	Castings		**As cast**: (13) **diam**, (280) **TS**
JIS G 5501	Grade 4	Japan	Castings		**Annealed**: (4–8) **diam**, (275) **TS**
CESA S 61	Grade 40	Canada	Castings		**As cast**: all **diam**, (275) **TS**
ANSI/ASTM A 48	Class No. 40A	US	Sand castings		**As cast**: 0.25–0.50 **diam**, 40 (275) **TS**
JIS G 5702	Class 1	Japan	Castings		**Graphitized**: all **diam**, (275) **TS**, (167) **YS**, 5 **El**
ISO–R942	Grade B	ISO	Sand castings		**As cast and annealed**: (9) **diam**, (275) **TS**, 7 **El**

CAST IRONS

specification number	designation	country	product forms	composition	mechanical properties (see page iv for explanation)
SFS 3345	GRS 25	Finland	Castings		**As cast**: (6) **diam**, (270) **TS**
BS 309	W 340/3	UK	Castings		**Malleabilized**: (9) **diam**, (270) **TS**, 7 **El**
AS 1832	Grade AS 1832/340–3	Australia	Castings		**As agreed**: (9) **diam**, (270) **TS**, 7 **El**
DIN 1691	Grade GG–26–0.6026	Germany	Sand castings		**As cast**: (30) **diam**, (255) **TS**
SABS 1034	Grade 250	South Africa	Castings		**As cast**: (20–30) **diam**, (250) **TS**
DIN 1691	Grade GG–25–0.6025	Germany	Sand castings		**As cast**: (30) **diam**, (245) **TS**
DS 11 301	GG 25	Denmark	Castings		**As cast**: (30) **diam**, (245) **TS**
NS 722	SjG–25	Norway	Castings		**As cast**: (30) **diam**, (245) **TS**
ISO/R 943	Grade A	ISO	Sand castings		**Quenched and tempered**: (15) **diam**, (243) **TS**, (206) **YS**, 12 **El**
ASTM A 278	Class No. 35	US	Sand castings		**Stress relieved**: 0.88 (22.4) **diam**, 35 (240) **TS**
SFS 3345	GRS 20	Finland	Castings		**As cast**: (4) **diam**, (240) **TS**
CESA S 61	Grade 35	Canada	Castings		**As cast**: all **diam**, (240) **TS**
ANSI/ASTM A 48	Class No. 35A	US	Sand castings		**As cast**: 0.25–0.50 **diam**, 35 (240) **TS**
JIS G 5501	Grade 3	Japan	Castings		**Annealed**: (4–8) **diam**, (235) **TS**
COPANT 828	FG 150	COPANT	Castings		**As cast**: (13) **diam**, (230) **TS**
DIN 1691	Grade GG–22–0.6022	Germany	Sand castings		**As cast**: (30) **diam**, (215) **TS**
ASTM A 126	Class B	US	Sand castings		**As cast**: all **diam**, 31 (215) **TS**
ASTM A 278	Class No. 30	US	Sand castings		**Stress relieved**: 0.88 (22.4) **diam**, 30 (205) **TS**
CESA S 61	Grade 30	Canada	Castings		**As cast**: all **diam**, (205) **TS**
ANSI/ASTM A 48	Class No. 30A	US	Sand castings		**As cast**: 0.25–0.50 **diam**, 30 (205) **TS**
SABS 1034	Grade 200	South Africa	Castings		**As cast**: (20–30) **diam**, (200) **TS**
DIN 1691	Grade GG–20–0.6020	Germany	Sand castings		**As cast**: (30) **diam**, (196) **TS**
DS 11 301	GG 20	Denmark	Castings		**As cast**: (30) **diam**, (196) **TS**
NS 722	SjG–20	Norway	Castings		**As cast**: (30) **diam**, (196) **TS**
SFS 3345	GRS 15	Finland	Castings		**As cast**: (4) **diam**, (190) **TS**
ISO 2892	L–NiCr 20 3	ISO	Sand castings	1.0–2.8 **Si**, 0.5–1.5 **Mn**, 2.5–3.5 **Cr**, 18.0–22.0 **Ni**, 0.5 **Cu**	**As cast**: all **diam**, (190) **TS**
BS 3468	Grade L–NiCr 303	UK	Castings	1.0–2.0 **Si**, 0.5–1.5 **Mn**, 2.5–3.5 **Cr**, 28.0–32.0 **Ni**, 0.5 **Cu**	**As cast**: all **diam**, (190) **TS**
BS 3468	Grade L–NiCuCr 1563	UK	Castings	1.0–2.8 **Si**, 0.5–1.5 **Mn**, 2.5–3.5 **Cr**, 13.5–17.5 **Ni**, 5.5–7.5 **Cu**	**As cast**: all **diam**, (190) **TS**
JIS G 5501	Grade 2	Japan	Castings		**Annealed**: (4–8) **diam**, (186) **TS**
DIN 1691	Grade GG–18–0.6018	Germany	Sand castings		**As cast**: (30) **diam**, (176) **TS**
ASTM A 278	Class No. 25	US	Sand castings		**Stress relieved**: 0.88 (22.4) **diam**, 25 (170) **TS**
CESA S 61	Grade 25	Canada	Castings		**As cast**: all **diam**, (170) **TS**
ANSI/ASTM A 48	Class No. 25A	US	Sand castings		**As cast**: 0.25–0.50 **diam**, 25 (170) **TS**
BS 3468	Grade L–NiSiCr 3055	UK	Castings	5.0–6.0 **Si**, 0.5–1.5 **Mn**, 4.5–5.5 **Cr**, 29.0–32.0 **Ni**, 0.5 **Cu**	**As cast**: all **diam**, (170) **TS**
BS 3468	Grade L–NiCr 202	UK	Castings	1.0–2.8 **Si**, 0.5–1.5 **Mn**, 1.0–2.5 **Cr**, 18.0–22.0 **Ni**, 0.5 **Cu**	**As cast**: all **diam**, (170) **TS**
SABS 1034	Grade 150	South Africa	Castings		**As cast**: (20–30) **diam**, (150) **TS**
DIN 1691	Grade GG–15–0.6015	Germany	Sand castings		**As cast**: (30) **diam**, (147) **TS**
DS 11 301	GG 15	Denmark	Castings		**As cast**: (30) **diam**, (147) **TS**
NS 722	SjG–15	Norway	Castings		**As cast**: (30) **diam**, (147) **TS**
ASTM A 126	Class A	US	Sand castings		**As cast**: all **diam**, 21 (145) **TS**
ASTM A 278	Class No. 20	US	Sand castings		**Stress relieved**: 0.88 (22.4) **diam**, 20 (140) **TS**
ASTM A 667		US	Castings		**Centrifugally cast**: all **diam**, 20 (140) **TS**
ASTM A 74	Class A	US	Sand castings	0.75 **P**, 0.15 **S**	**As cast**: all **diam**, 21 (140) **TS**

specification number	designation	country	product forms	composition	mechanical properties (see page iv for explanation)
ANSI/ASTM A 48	Class No. 20A	US	Sand castings		**As cast**: 0.25–0.50 **diam**, 20 (140) **TS**
BS 3468	Grade L–NiMn 137	UK	Castings	1.5–3.0 **Si**, 6.0–7.0 **Mn**, 0.2 **Cr**, 12.0–14.0 **Ni**, 0.5 **Cu**	**As cast**: all **diam**, (140) **TS**
DIN 1691	Grade GG–14–0.6014	Germany	Sand castings		**As cast**: (30) **diam**, (137) **TS**
CESA S 61	Grade 20	Canada	Castings		**As cast**: all **diam**, (135) **TS**
DIN 1691	Grade GG–12–0.6012	Germany	Sand castings		**As cast**: (30) **diam**, (117) **TS**
COPANT 828	FG 350	COPANT	Castings		**As cast**: (13) **diam**, (106) **TS**
COPANT 828	FG 100	COPANT	Castings		**As cast**: (13) **diam**, (100) **TS**
JIS G 5501	Grade 1	Japan	Castings		**Annealed**: (4–50) **diam**, (98.1) **TS**
DIN 1691	Grade GG–10–0.6010	Germany	Sand castings		**As cast**: (30) **diam**, (98) **TS**
DIN 1691	Grade GG–10.9–0.6011	Germany	Sand castings		**As cast**: all **diam**, (98) **TS**
DS 11 301	GG 10	Denmark	Castings		**As cast**: (30) **diam**, (98) **TS**
NS 722	SjG–35	Norway	Castings		**As cast**: (30) **diam**, 343 **TS**
NS 722	SjG–40	Norway	Castings		**As cast**: (30) **diam**, 392 **TS**
NS 722	SjG–30	Norway	Castings		**As cast**: (30) **diam**, 294 **TS**

CAST CARBON, LOW ALLOY, AND HIGH STRENGTH STEELS

CAST CARBON STEELS

specification number	designation	country	product forms	composition	mechanical properties (see page iv for explanation)
ASTM A 532	Class I, type A	US	Sand castings	0.8 **Si**, 1.3 **Mn**, 1.4–4.0 **Cr**, 3.3–5.0 **Ni**, 1.0 **Mo**, 3.0–3.6 **C**, 0.30 **P**, 0.15 **S**	**As cast, quenched or annealed**
ASTM A 532	Class I, type C	US	Sand castings	0.8 **Si**, 1.3 **Mn**, 1.1–1.5 **Cr**, 2.7–4.0 **Ni**, 1.0 **Mo**, 2.9–3.7 **C**, 0.30 **P**, 0.15 **S**	**As cast, quenched or annealed**
ASTM A 532	Class I, type D	US	Sand castings	1.0–2.2 **Si**, 1.3 **Mn**, 7.0–11.0 **Cr**, 5.0–7.0 **Ni**, 1.0 **Mo**, 2.5–3.6 **C**, 0.10 **P**, 0.15 **S**	**As cast, quenched or annealed**
ASTM A 532	Class I, type B	US	Sand castings	0.8 **Si**, 1.3 **Mn**, 1.4–4.0 **Cr**, 3.3–5.0 **Ni**, 1.0 **Mo**, 2.5–3.0 **C**, 0.30 **P**, 0.15 **S**	**As cast, quenched or annealed**
ANSI/ASTM A 597	Grade CD–2	US	Castings	1.40–1.60 **C**, 1.00 **Mn**, 1.50 **Si**, 11.00–13.00 **Cr**, 0.70–1.20 **Mo**, 0.40–1.00 **V**, 0.025 **P**, 0.025 **S**, 0.70–1.00 **Co**	
ANSI/ASTM A 597	Grade CD–5	US	Castings	1.35–1.60 **C**, 0.75 **Mn**, 1.50 **Si**, 11.00–13.00 **Cr**, 0.70–1.20 **Mo**, 0.40–0.60 **Ni**, 0.35–0.55 **V**, 0.025 **P**, 0.025 **S**, 2.50–3.50 **Co**	
SIS 14 21 83	SIS 21 83–02	Sweden	Castings	1.10–1.35 **C**, 11.0–14.0 **Mn**, 0.8 **Si**, 0.10 **P**	**Solution annealed**
MIL–S–22141B	1C–52100	US	Investment castings	0.95–1.10 **C**, 0.25–0.55 **Mn**, 0.20–0.80 **Si**, 1.30–1.60 **Cr**	
ASTM A 732	Grade 15A	US	Investment castings	0.95–1.10 **C**, 0.25–0.55 **Mn**, 0.20–0.80 **Si**, 1.30–1.60 **Cr**, 0.040 **P**, 0.045 **S**, 0.60 other elements, total	
ANSI/ASTM A 597	Grade CA–2	US	Castings	0.95–1.05 **C**, 0.75 **Mn**, 1.50 **Si**, 4.75–5.50 **Cr**, 0.90–1.40 **Mo**, 0.20–0.50 **V**, 0.025 **P**, 0.025 **S**	
IS 4896	Grade 3	India	Castings	0.90–1.20 **C**, 0.50–1.00 **Mn**, 0.75 **Si**, 0.80–1.50 **Cr**, 0.050 **P**, 0.050 **S**	**Annealed, normalized, tempered, or normalized, tempered, or hardened, tempered, or annealed, hardene, tempered**
ANSI/ASTM A 597	Grade CO–1	US	Castings	0.85–1.00 **C**, 1.00–1.30 **Mn**, 1.50 **Si**, 0.40–1.00 **Cr**, 0.30 **V**, 0.025 **P**, 0.025 **S**, 0.40–0.60 **W**	
IS 4896	Grade 2	India	Castings	0.55–0.70 **C**, 0.50–1.00 **Mn**, 0.75 **Si**, 0.80–1.50 **Cr**, 0.20–0.40 **Mo**, 0.050 **P**, 0.050 **S**	**Annealed, normalized, tempered, or normalized, tempered, or hardened, tempered, or annealed, hardened, tempered**
BS 3100/1956	Grade C	UK	Sand castings	0.55–0.65 **C**, 0.80–1.5 **Cr**	**Annealed and normalized and tempered or annealed and hardened and tempered**
ANSI/ASTM A 487	Class 14Q	US	Sand castings	0.55 **C**, 0.80–1.10 **Mn**, 0.60 **Si**, 0.20–0.30 **Mo**, 1.40–1.75 **Ni**, 0.03 **V**, 0.040 **P**, 0.045 **S**	**Quenched and tempered**: all **diam**, 120 (825) **TS**, 95 (655) **YS**, 14 **El**
ASTM A 487	Grade 14Q	US	Castings	0.55 **C**, 0.80–1.10 **Mn**, 0.60 **Si**, 0.40 **Cr**, 0.20–0.30 **Mo**, 1.40–1.75 **Ni**, 0.03 **V**, 0.50 **Cu**, 0.04 **P**, 0.045 **S**, 0.10 **W**	**Quenched and tempered**: all **diam**, 120 (825) **TS**, 95 (655) **YS**, 14 **El**
ANSI/ASTM A 487	14Q	US	Castings	0.5 **C**, 0.80–1.10 **Mn**, 0.60 **Si**, 0.20–0.30 **Mo**, 1.40–1.75 **Ni**, 0.030 **V**, 0.040 **P**, 0.045 **S**	**Quenched, tempered**: all **diam**, 120 (825) **TS**, 95 (655) **YS**, 14 **El**
ANSI/ASTM A 597	Grade CS–5	US	Castings	0.50–0.65 **C**, 0.60–1.00 **Mn**, 1.75–2.25 **Si**, 0.35 **Cr**, 0.20–0.80 **Mo**, 0.35 **V**, 0.025 **P**, 0.025 **S**	
IS 2707	Grade 2	India	Castings	0.50–0.60 **C**, 1.0 **Mn**, 0.60 **Si**, 0.25 **Cr**, 0.15 **Mo**, 0.40 **Ni**, 0.30 **Cu**, 0.050 **P**, 0.050 **S**; 0.80 other elements, total	**Annealed or normalized and tempered**: ≤ (100) **diam**, (700) **TS**, (370) **YS**, 8 **El**
BS 3100/1760	Grade B	UK	Sand castings	0.50–0.60 **C**	**Annealed or normalized and tempered**: all **diam**, (695) **TS**, (370) **YS**, 8 **El**
SIS 14 16 06	SIS 16 06–02	Sweden	Castings	0.5 **C**, 0.7 **Mn**, 0.5 **Si**, 0.040 **P**, 0.040 **S**	**Annealed**: all **diam**, (570) **TS**, (300) **YS**

CAST CARBON STEELS

specification number	designation	country	product forms	composition	mechanical properties (see page iv for explanation)
MIL-S-15083B	Class 80-40	US	Sand castings	0.50 **C**, 0.90 **Mn**, 0.80 **Si**, 0.05 **P**, 0.06 **S**	**Annealed or normalized and tempered or quenched and tempered**: all **diam**, 80 (552) **TS**, 40 (276) **YS**, 17 **El**
MIL-S-22141B	1C-6150	US	Investment castings	0.45-0.55 **C**, 0.65-0.95 **Mn**, 0.20-0.80 **Si**, 0.80-1.10 **Cr**, 0.15 min **V**	**Annealed, quenched and tempered**: all **diam**, (1310) **TS**, (1172) **YS**, 4 (4xD) **El**
ASTM A 732	Grade 12Q	US	Investment castings	0.45-0.55 **C**, 0.65-0.95 **Mn**, 0.20-0.80 **Si**, 0.80-1.10 **Cr**, 0.15 min **V**, 0.04 **P**, 0.045 **S**, 1.00 other elements, total	**Quenched and tempered**: all **diam**, 190 (1310) **TS**, 170 (1170) **YS**, 4 **El**
ASTM A 732	Grade 4Q	US	Investment castings	0.45-0.55 **C**, 0.70-1.00 **Mn**, 0.20-1.00 **Si**, 0.04 **P**, 0.045 **S**; 1.00 other elements, total	**Quenched and tempered**: all **diam**, 125 (860) **TS**, 100 (690) **YS**, 5 **El**
BS 3100/1956	Grades A and B	UK	Sand castings	0.45-0.55 **C**, 0.80-1.2 **Cr**	**Annealed and normalized and tempered or annealed and hardened and tempered (Grade A only)**: all **diam**, (695) **TS**, 7 **El**
IS 4896	Grade 1	India	Castings	0.45-0.55 **C**, 0.50-1.00 **Mn**, 0.75 **Si**, 0.80-1.20 **Cr**, 0.050 **P**, 0.050 **S**	**Annealed, normalized, tempered, or normalized, tempered, or hardened, tempered, or annealed, hardened, tempered**: all **diam**, (690) **TS**, 10 **El**
MIL-S-81591	1C-1050	US	Investment castings	0.45-0.55 **C**, 0.70-1.00 **Mn**, 0.20-1.00 **Si**, 0.040 **P**, 0.040 **S**	**Annealed**: all **diam**, 90 (621) **TS**, 50 (345) **YS**, 20 **El**
MIL-S-22141B	1C-1050	US	Investment castings	0.45-0.55 **C**, 0.70-1.00 **Mn**, 0.20-1.00 **Si**	**Annealed**: all **diam**, (620) **TS**, (344) **YS**, 20 (4 x D) **El**; **Quenched and tempered**: all **diam**, (861) **TS**, (689) **YS**, 5 (4 x D) **El**
ASTM A 732	Grade 4A	US	Investment castings	0.45-0.55 **C**, 0.70-1.00 **Mn**, 0.20-1.00 **Si**, 0.04 **P**, 0.045 **S**; 1.00 other elements, total	**Annealed**: all **diam**, 90 (620) **TS**, 50 (345) **YS**, 20 **El**
BS 3100/592	Grade C	UK	Sand castings	0.45 **C**	**Annealed, annealed and normalized, normalized and tempered, or hardened and tempered**: all **diam**, (540) **TS**, (294) **YS**, 14 **El**
BS 3146 Part 1	CLA1: Grade C	UK	Investment and precision castings	0.45 **C**	**Annealed, annealed and normalized, normalized, normalized and tempered, or hardened and tempered**: all **diam**, (540) **TS**, (275) **YS**, 15 **El**
SAE Automotive J435a	Grade 0050 B	US	Castings	0.40-0.50 **C**, 0.50-0.90 **Mn**, 0.80 **Si**, 0.050 **P**, 0.060 **S**	**Quenched and tempered**: all **diam**, 100 (689) **TS**, 70 (483) **YS**, 10 **El**
JIS G 5111	Class 5, SC Mn 5	Japan	Castings, pipe (centrifugally cast)	0.40-0.50 **C**, 0.90-1.00 **Mn**, 0.50-0.80 **Si**, 0.040 **P**, 0.040 **S**	**Normalized and tempered**: all **diam**, (686) **TS**, (392) **YS**, 9 **El**; **Quenched and tempered**: all **diam**, (736) **TS**, (539) **YS**, 9 **El**
IS 2707	Grade 1	India	Castings	0.40-0.50 **C**, 1.00 **Mn**, 0.60 **Si**, 0.25 **Cr**, 0.15 **Mo**, 0.40 **Ni**, 0.30 **Cu**, 0.050 **P**, 0.050 **S**; 0.80 other elements, total	**Annealed or normalized and tempered**: ($\leq$100) **diam**, (620) **TS**, (320) **YS**, 12 **El**
JIS G 5111	Class 5, SCC 5	Japan	Castings, pipe (centrifugally cast)	0.40-0.50 **C**, 0.50-0.80 **Mn**, 0.30-0.60 **Si**, 0.040 **P**, 0.040 **S**	**Normalized and tempered**: all **diam**, (618) **TS**, (294) **YS**, 9 **El**; **Quenched and tempered**: all **diam**, (686) **TS**, (441) **YS**, 9 **El**
BS 3100/1760	Grade A	UK	Sand castings	0.40-0.50 **C**	**Annealed or normalized and tempered**: all **diam**, (615) **TS**, (325) **YS**, 12 **El**
SAE Automotive J435a	Grade 0050 A	US	Castings	0.40-0.50 **C**, 0.50-0.90 **Mn**, 0.80 **Si**, 0.050 **P**, 0.060 **S**	**Normalized, normalized and tempered**: all **diam**, 85 (586) **TS**, 45 (310) **YS**, 16 **El**
ANSI/ASTM A 487	DN	US	Castings	0.40-0.50 **C**, 0.50-0.90 **Mn**, 0.80 **Si**, 0.03 **V**, 0.04 **P**, 0.045 **S**	**Normalized, tempered**: all **diam**, 80 (550) **TS**, 40 (275) **YS**, 17 **El**
ANSI/ASTM A 487	Class DN	US	Sand castings	0.40-0.50 **C**, 0.50-0.90 **Mn**, 0.80 **Si**, 0.03 **V**, 0.04 **P**, 0.045 **S**	**Normalized and tempered**: all **diam**, 80 (550) **TS**, 40 (275) **YS**, 17 **El**

CAST CARBON STEELS

specification number	designation	country	product forms	composition	mechanical properties (see page iv for explanation)
ASTM A 487	Grade DN	US	Castings	0.40–0.50 **C**, 0.50–0.90 **Mn**, 0.80 **Si**, 0.35 **Cr**, 0.50 **Ni**, 0.03 **V**, 0.35 **Cu**, 0.10 **Mo+W**, 0.04 **P**, 0.045 **S**, 0.10 **W**	**Normalized and tempered**: all **diam**, 80 (550) **TS**, 40 (275) **YS**, 17 **El**
SFS 358		Finland	Castings	0.40 **C**, 0.70 **Mn**, 0.50 **Si**, 0.040 **P**, 0.040 **S**	**Annealed or normalized**: all **diam**, (570) **TS**, (300) **YS**, 15 **El**
AMS 5331C		US	Sand castings	0.38–0.46 **C**, 0.60–1.00 **Mn**, 0.50–0.90 **Si**, 0.65–1.00 **Cr**, 0.30–0.45 **Mo**, 1.65–2.00 **Ni**, 0.35 **Cu**, 0.025 **P**, 0.025 **S**	**Annealed, hardened, and tempered**: all **diam**, 200 (1379) **TS**, 180 (1241) **YS**, 5 **El**
AMS 5330A		US	Investment castings	0.38–0.46 **C**, 0.60–1.00 **Mn**, 0.50–1.00 **Si**, 0.65–1.00 **Cr**, 0.30–0.45 **Mo**, 1.65–2.00 **Ni**, 0.35 **Cu**, 0.025 **P**, 0.025 **S**	**Annealed, hardened, and tempered**: all **diam**, 200 (1379) **TS**, 180 (1241) **YS**, 5 in 1 in. **El**
SIS 14 21 20	SIS 21 20–23	Sweden	Castings	0.38–0.45 **C**, 1.10–1.40 **Mn**, 0.30–0.60 **Si**	**Quenched and tempered**: all **diam**, (700) **TS**, (450) **YS**, 12 **El**
SIS 14 21 20	SIS 21 20–21	Sweden	Castings	0.38–0.45 **C**, 1.10–1.40 **Mn**, 0.30–0.60 **Si**	**Normalized**: all **diam**, (600) **TS**, (400) **YS**, 12 **El**
SIS 14 21 20	SIS 21 20 21	Sweden	Castings	0.38–0.45 **C**, 1.10–1.40 **Mn**, 0.30–0.60 **Si**	**Normalized**: all **diam**, (600) **TS**, (400) **YS**, 12 **El**
SIS 14 21 20	SIS 21 20–21	Sweden	Castings	0.38–0.45 **C**, 1.10–1.40 **Mn**, 0.30–0.60 **Si**	**Normalized**: all **diam**, (600) **TS**, (400) **YS**, 12 **El**
ASTM A 487	Grade 6Q	US	Castings	0.38 **C**, 1.30–1.70 **Mn**, 0.80 **Si**, 0.40–0.80 **Cr**, 0.30–0.40 **Mo**, 0.40–0.80 **Ni**, 0.03 **V**, 0.50 **Cu**, 0.04 **P**, 0.045 **S**, 0.10 **W**	**Quenched and tempered**: all **diam**, 120 (825) **TS**, 95 (655) **YS**, 12 **El**
ANSI/ASTM A 487	6Q	US	Castings	0.38 **C**, 1.30–1.70 **Mn**, 0.80 **Si**, 0.40–0.80 **Cr**, 0.30–0.40 **Mo**, 0.40–0.80 **Ni**, 0.030 **V**, 0.040 **P**, 0.045 **S**	**Quenched, tempered**: all **diam**, 120 (825) **TS**, 95 (655) **YS**, 12 **El**
ANSI/ASTM A 487	Class 6Q	US	Sand castings	0.38 **C**, 1.30–1.70 **Mn**, 0.80 **Si**, 0.40–0.80 **Cr**, 0.30–0.40 **Mo**, 0.40–0.80 **Ni**, 0.030 **V**, 0.04 **P**, 0.045 **S**	**Quenched and tempered**: all **diam**, 120 (825) **TS**, 95 (655) **YS**, 12 **El**
ASTM A 487	Grade 6N	US	Castings	0.38 **C**, 1.30–1.70 **Mn**, 0.80 **Si**, 0.40–0.80 **Cr**, 0.30–0.40 **Mo**, 0.40–0.80 **Ni**, 0.03 **V**, 0.50 **Cu**, 0.04 **P**, 0.045 **S**, 0.10 **W**	**Normalized and tempered**: all **diam**, 115 (795) **TS**, 80 (550) **YS**, 18 **El**
ANSI/ASTM A 487	6N	US	Castings	0.38 **C**, 1.30–1.70 **Mn**, 0.80 **Si**, 0.40–0.80 **Cr**, 0.30–0.40 **Mo**, 0.40–0.80 **Ni**, 0.030 **V**, 0.04 **P**, 0.045 **S**	**Normalized, tempered**: all **diam**, 115 (795) **TS**, 80 (550) **YS**, 18 **El**
ANSI/ASTM A 487	Class 6N	US	Sand castings	0.38 **C**, 1.30–1.70 **Mn**, 0.80 **Si**, 0.40–0.80 **Cr**, 0.30–0.40 **Mo**, 0.40–0.80 **Ni**, 0.03 **V**, 0.04 **P**, 0.045 **S**	**Normalized and tempered**: all **diam**, 115 (795) **TS**, 80 (550) **YS**, 18 **El**
IS 7899	Grade 6N, 6Q	India	Castings	0.38 **C**, 1.30–1.70 **Mn**, 0.80 **Si**, 0.40–0.80 **Cr**, 0.30–0.40 **Mo**, 0.40–0.80 **Ni**, 0.04 **P**, 0.045 **S**	**Normalized and tempered**: all **diam**, (790) **TS**, (550) **YS**, 16 **El**; **Quenched and tempered**: all **diam**, (830) **TS**, (660) **YS**, 11 **El**
VSM 10697	GS–60/10553	Switzerland	Castings	0.37–0.43 **C**, 1.0 **Mn**, 0.030 **Si**, 0.40 **Cr**, 0.25 **Mo**, 0.50 **Ni**, 0.030 **P**, 0.030 **S**	**Annealed or normalized**: all **diam**, (600) **TS**, (300) **YS**, 15 **El**
MIL–S–22141B	1C–4340	US	Investment castings	0.36–0.44 **C**, 0.60–0.90 **Mn**, 0.20–0.80 **Si**, 0.70–0.90 **Cr**, 0.20–0.30 **Mo**, 1.65–2.00 **Ni**	**Annealed, quenched and tempered**: all **diam**, (1378) **TS**, (1241) **YS**, 5.0 (4xD) **El**
MIL–S–22141B	1C–4140	US	Investment castings	0.35–0.45 **C**, 0.70–1.05 **Mn**, 0.20–0.80 **Si**, 0.80–1.10 **Cr**, 0.15–0.25 **Mo**	**Annealed, quenched and tempered**: all **diam**, (1241) **TS**, (999) **YS**, 5.0 (4xD) **El**
MIL–S–22141B	1C–8640	US	Investment castings	0.35–0.45 **C**, 0.70–1.05 **Mn**, 0.20–0.80 **Si**, 0.40–0.60 **Cr**, 0.40–0.70 **Mo**, 0.15–0.25 **Ni**	**Annealed, quenched and tempered**: all **diam**, (1241) **TS**, (999) **YS**, 5 (4xD) **El**
ASTM A 732	Grade 10Q	US	Investment castings	0.35–0.45 **C**, 0.70–1.00 **Mn**, 0.20–0.80 **Si**, 0.70–0.90 **Cr**, 0.20–0.30 **Mo**, 1.65–2.00 **Ni**, 0.04 **P**, 0.045 **S**, 1.00 other elements, total	**Quenched and tempered**: all **diam**, 180 (1240) **TS**, 145 (1000) **YS**, 5 **El**

CAST CARBON STEELS

specification number	designation	country	product forms	composition	mechanical properties (see page iv for explanation)
ASTM A 732	Grade 8Q	US	Investment castings	0.35–0.45 **C**, 0.70–1.00 **Mn**, 0.20–0.80 **Si**, 0.80–1.10 **Cr**, 0.15–0.25 **Mo**, 0.04 **P**, 0.045 **S**, 1.00 other elements, total	**Quenched and tempered**: all **diam**, 180 (1240) **TS**, 145 (1000) **YS**, 5 **El**
AMS 5338B		US	Investment castings	0.35–0.45 **C**, 0.75–1.00 **Mn**, 1.00 **Si**, 0.80–1.10 **Cr**, 0.15–0.25 **Mo**, 0.25 **Ni**, 0.35 **Cu**, 0.04 **P**, 0.04 **S**	**Normalized, tempered, hardened and tempered**: all **diam**, 175 (1207) **TS**, 160 (1103) **YS**, 3 in 1 in. **El**
MIL-S-22141B	1C-Nitralloy 135M	US	Investment castings	0.35–0.45 **C**, 0.40–0.70 **Mn**, 0.20–0.80 **Si**, 1.40–1.80 **Cr**, 0.30–0.45 **Mo**, 0.85–1.20 **Al**	**Quenched and tempered**: all **diam**, (930) **TS**, (689) **YS**, 8 (4xD) **El**
ASTM A 732	Grade 3Q	US	Investment castings	0.35–0.45 **C**, 0.70–1.00 **Mn**, 0.20–1.00 **Si**, 0.04 **P**, 0.045 **S**; 1.00 other elements, total	**Quenched and tempered**: all **diam**, 100 (690) **TS**, 90 (620) **YS**, 10 **El**
JIS G 5111	Class 4, SC Mn Cr 4	Japan	Castings, pipe (centrifugally cast)	0.35–0.45 **C**, 1.20–1.60 **Mn**, 0.30–0.60 **Si**, 0.40–0.80 **Cr**, 0.040 **P**, 0.040 **S**	**Normalized and tempered**: all **diam**, (686) **TS**, (412) **YS**, 9 **El**; **Quenched and tempered**: all **diam**, (736) **TS**, (539) **YS**, 13 **El**
BS 3146 Part 1	CLA 8	UK	Investment and precision castings	0.35–0.45 **C**	**Normalized and tempered**: all **diam**, (540) **TS**, (275) **YS**, 15 **El**
MIL-S-22141B	1C-1040	US	Investment castings	0.35–0.45 **C**, 0.70–1.00 **Mn**, 0.20–1.00 **Si**	**Annealed**: all **diam**, (517) **TS**, (330) **YS**, 25 (4 x D) **El**; **Quenched and tempered**: all **diam**, (689) **TS**, (620) **YS**, 10 (4 x D) **El**
ASTM A 732	Grade 3A	US	Investment castings	0.35–0.45 **C**, 0.70–1.00 **Mn**, 0.20–1.00 **Si**, 0.04 **P**, 0.045 **S**; 1.00 other elements, total	**Annealed**: all **diam**, 75 (517) **TS**, 48 (330) **YS**, 25 **El**
MIL-S-81591	1C-1040	US	Investment castings	0.35–0.45 **C**, 0.70–1.00 **Mn**, 0.20–1.00 **Si**, 0.040 **P**, 0.040 **S**	**Annealed**: all **diam**, 75 (517) **TS**, 48 (331) **YS**, 25 **El**
ASTM A486-74	Grade 120	US	Castings	0.35 **C**, 0.05 **P**, 0.06 **S**	**Quenched and tempered**: all **diam**, 120 (827) **TS**, 95 (655) **YS**, 14 **El**
ANSI/ASTM A 486	Class 120	US	Sand castings	0.35 **C**, 0.05 **P**, 0.06 **S**	**Quenched and tempered**: all **diam**, 120 (825) **TS**, 95 (655) **YS**, 14 **El**
UNI 7316-74	Fe G 74-1	Italy	Castings	0.35 **C**, 1.35–1.75 **Mn**, 0.80 **Si**, 0.25–0.55 **Mo**, 0.50 **Cu**, 0.035 **P**, 0.035 **S**, 0.10 **W**	**Quenched and tempered**: all **diam**, (730) **TS**, (590) **YS**, 13 **El**
UNI 7316-74	Fe G 74-2	Italy	Castings	0.35 **C**, 1.0 **Mn**, 0.80 **Si**, 0.40–0.80 **Cr**, 0.15–0.30 **Mo**, 0.40–0.80 **Ni**, 0.035 **P**, 0.035 **S**	**Quenched and tempered**: all **diam**, (730) **TS**, (590) **YS**, 13 **El**
ASTM 201-66	Grade C	US	Castings	0.35 **C**, 0.050 **P**, 0.050 **S**	**Normalized and tempered, quenched and tempered**: all **diam**, 90 (621) **TS**, 60 (414) **YS**, 22 **El**
ASTM A486-74	Grade 90	US	Castings	0.35 **C**, 0.05 **P**, 0.06 **S**	**Normalized, normalized and tempered, quenched and tempered**: all **diam**, (621) **TS**, (414) **YS**, 20 **El**
ANSI/ASTM A 486	Class 90	US	Sand castings	0.35 **C**, 0.05 **P**, 0.06 **S**	**Normalized or normalized and tempered or quenched and tempered**: all **diam**, 90 (620) **TS**, 60 (415) **YS**, 20 **El**
IS 7899	Grade 3N,3Q	India	Castings	0.35 **C**, 1.35–1.75 **Mn**, 0.80 **Si**, 0.25–0.55 **Mo**, 0.04 **P**, 0.045 **S**	**Normalized and tempered**: all **diam**, (620) **TS**, (410) **YS**, 18 **El**; **Quenched and tempered**: all **diam**, (720) **TS**, (590) **YS**, 15 **El**
UNI 7316-74	Fe G 63-1	Italy	Castings	0.35 **C**, 1.35–1.75 **Mn**, 0.80 **Si**, 0.25–0.55 **Mo**, 1.0 **Cr+Ni+Cu+W**, 0.04 **P**, 0.045 **S**	**Normalized and tempered**: all **diam**, (620) **TS**, (410) **YS**, 16 **El**
UNI 7316-74	Fe G 63-2	Italy	Castings	0.35 **C**, 1.00 **Mn**, 0.80 **Si**, 0.40–0.80 **Cr**, 0.15–0.30 **Mo**, 0.40–0.80 **Ni**, 0.50 **Cu**, 0.04 **P**, 0.045 **S**, 0.10 **W**	**Normalized and tempered**: all **diam**, (620) **TS**, (410) **YS**, 16 **El**
ASTM A 732	Grade 6N	US	Investment castings	0.35 **C**, 1.35–1.75 **Mn**, 0.20–0.80 **Si**, 0.25–0.55 **Mo**, 0.04 **P**, 0.045 **S**, 1.00 other elements, total	**Normalized and tempered**: all **diam**, 90 (620) **TS**, 60 (415) **YS**, 20 **El**

CAST CARBON STEELS

specification number	designation	country	product forms	composition	mechanical properties (see page iv for explanation)
BS 1504–161	Grade 540	UK	Castings	0.35 **C**, 1.10 **Mn**, 0.60 **Si**, 0.25 **Cr**, 0.15 **Mo**, 0.40 **Ni**, 0.30 **Cu**, 0.050 **P**, 0.050 **S**	**Austenitized**: all **diam**, (540) **TS**, (280) **YS**, 13 **El**
BS 3100/592	Grade B	UK	Sand castings	0.35 **C**	**Annealed, annealed and normalized, normalized and tempered, hardened and tempered**: all **diam**, (495) **TS**, (265) **YS**, 18 **El**
DTD 5199		UK	Investment and precision castings	0.35 **C**	**Annealed, annealed and normalized, normalized, normalized and tempered or hardened and tempered**: all **diam**, (490) **TS**, (245) **YS**, 15 **El**
BS 3146 Part 1	CLA1: Grade B	UK	Investment and precision castings	0.35 **C**	**Annealed, annealed and normalized, normalized, normalized and tempered, or hardened and tempered**: all **diam**, (490) **TS**, (245) **YS**, 20 **El**
ASTM A356–75	Grade 1	US	Castings	0.35 **C**, 0.70 **Mn**, 0.60 **Si**, 0.035 **P**, 0.030 **S**	**Normalized and tempered**: all **diam**, 70 (485) **TS**, 36 (250) **YS**, 20 **El**
ANSI/ASTM A 486	Class 70	US	Sand castings	0.35 **C**, 0.90 **Mn**, 0.80 **Si**, 0.05 **P**, 0.06 **S**	**Normalized or normalized and tempered or quenched and tempered**: all **diam**, 70 (485) **TS**, 36 (250) **YS**, 22 **El**
ASTM A 27	Grade 70–36	US	Castings	0.35 **C**, 0.70 **Mn**, 0.80 **Si**, 0.05 **P**, 0.06 **S**	**Annealed or normalized or quenched and tempered**: all **diam**, 70 (485) **TS**, 36 (250) **YS**, 22 **El**
ASTM A 356	Grade 1	US	Castings	0.35 **C**, 0.70 **Mn**, 0.60 **Si**, 0.035 **P**, 0.030 **S**	**Normalized or tempered**: all **diam**, 70 (485) **TS**, 36 (250) **YS**, 20 **El**
ASTM A486–74	Grade 70	US	Castings	0.35 **C**, 0.90 **Mn**, 0.80 **Si**, 0.05 **P**, 0.06 **S**	**Normalized, normalized and tempered, quenched and tempered**: all **diam**, 70 (483) **TS**, 36 (248) **YS**, 22 **El**
MIL–S–15083 B	Class 70–36	US	Sand castings	0.35 **C**, 0.05 **P**, 0.05 **S**	**Annealed or normalized and tempered or quenched and tempered**: all **diam**, 70 (483) **TS**, 36 (248) **YS**, 22 **El**
DGN–B–352	Class 49–25	Mexico	Castings	0.35 **C**, 0.90 **Mn**, 0.80 **Si**, 0.050 **P**, 0.060 **S**	**Annealed, normalized, normalized and tempered, quenched and tempered**: all **diam**, (483) **TS**, (248) **YS**, 22 **El**
CSA G28	70–36	Canada	Castings	0.35 **C**, 0.75 **Mn**, 0.80 **Si**, 0.04 **P**, 0.04 **S**	**Full annealed, normalized, normalized and tempered, quenched and tempered**: all **diam**, (483) **TS**, (248) **YS**, 22 **El**
ASTM A 27	Grade 70–36	US	Castings	0.35 **C**, 0.70 **Mn**, 0.80 **Si**, 0.40 **Cr**, 0.20 **Mo**, 0.50 **Ni**, 0.30 **Cu**, 0.05 **P**, 0.06 **S**	**Annealed, normalized, normalized and tempered, quenched and tempered**: all **diam**, 70 (483) **TS**, 36 (248) **YS**, 22 **El**
ASTM A 27	Grade N–2	US	Castings	0.35 **C**, 0.60 **Mn**, 0.80 **Si**, 0.05 **P**, 0.06 **S**	
ASTM A 27	Grade N–2	US	Castings	0.35 **C**, 0.60 **Mn**, 0.80 **Si**, 0.40 **Cr**, 0.20 **Mo**, 0.50 **Ni**, 0.30 **Cu**, 0.05 **P**, 0.06 **S**	
ASTM A 487	Grade 9Q	US	Castings	0.33 **C**, 0.60–1.00 **Mn**, 0.80 **Si**, 0.75–1.10 **Cr**, 0.15–0.30 **Mo**, 0.50 **Ni**, 0.03 **V**, 0.50 **Cu**, 0.04 **P**, 0.045 **S**, 0.10 **W**	**Quenched and tempered**: all **diam**, 105 (725) **TS**, 85 (585) **YS**, 16 **El**
ANSI/ASTM A 487	9Q	US	Castings	0.33 **C**, 0.60–1.00 **Mn**, 0.80 **Si**, 0.75–1.10 **Cr**, 0.15–0.30 **Mo**, 0.03 **V**, 0.04 **P**, 0.045 **S**	**Quenched, tempered**: all **diam**, 105 (725) **TS**, 85 (585) **YS**, 16 **El**
ANSI/ASTM A 487	Class 9Q	US	Sand castings	0.33 **C**, 0.60–1.00 **Mn**, 0.80 **Si**, 0.75–1.10 **Cr**, 0.15–0.30 **Mo**, 0.03 **V**, 0.04 **P**, 0.045 **S**	**Quenched and tempered**: all **diam**, 105 (725) **TS**, 85 (585) **YS**, 16 **El**

CAST CARBON STEELS

specification number	designation	country	product forms	composition	mechanical properties (see page iv for explanation)
IS 7899	Grade 9n, 9q	India	Castings	0.33 **C**, 0.60–1.00 **Mn**, 0.80 **Si**, 0.75–1.10 **Cr**, 0.15–0.30 **Mo**, 0.04 **P**, 0.045 **S**	**Normalized and tempered**: all **diam**, (620) **TS**, (410) **YS**, 18 **El**; **Quenched and tempered**: all **diam**, (720) **TS**, (590) **YS**, 14 **El**
ASTM A 487	Grade 9N	US	Castings	0.33 **C**, 0.60–1.00 **Mn**, 0.80 **Si**, 0.75–1.10 **Cr**, 0.15–0.30 **Mo**, 0.50 **Ni**, 0.03 **V**, 0.50 **Cu**, 0.04 **P**, 0.045 **S**, 0.10 **W**	**Normalized and tempered**: all **diam**, 90 (620) **TS**, 60 (415) **YS**, 20 **El**
ANSI/ASTM A 487	9N	US	Castings	0.33 **C**, 0.60–1.00 **Mn**, 0.80 **Si**, 0.75–1.10 **Cr**, 0.15–0.30 **Mo**, 0.03 **V**, 0.04 **P**, 0.045 **S**	**Normalized, tempered**: all **diam**, 90 (620) **TS**, 60 (415) **YS**, 20 **El**
ANSI/ASTM A 487	Class 9N	US	Sand castings	0.33 **C**, 0.60–1.00 **Mn**, 0.80 **Si**, 0.75–1.10 **Cr**, 0.15–0.30 **Mo**, 0.03 **V**, 0.04 **P**, 0.045 **S**	**Normalized and tempered**: all **diam**, 90 (620) **TS**, 60 (415) **YS**, 20 **El**
ANSI/ASTM A 597	Grade CH-13	US	Castings	0.30–0.42 **C**, 0.75 **Mn**, 1.50 **Si**, 4.75–5.75 **Cr**, 1.25–1.75 **Mo**, 0.75–1.20 **V**, 0.025 **P**, 0.025 **S**	
JIS G 5111	Class 3, SC Mn Cr M 3	Japan	Castings, pipe (centrifugally cast)	0.30–0.40 **C**, 1.20–1.60 **Mn**, 0.30–0.60 **Si**, 0.30–0.70 **Cr**, 0.15–0.35 **Mo**, 0.040 **P**, 0.040 **S**	**Normalized and tempered**: all **diam**, (736) **TS**, (539) **YS**, 9 **El**; **Quenched and tempered**: all **diam**, (834) **TS**, (637) **YS**, 9 **El**
JIS G 5111	Class 3, SC Mn M 3	Japan	Castings, pipe (centrifugally cast)	0.30–0.40 **C**, 1.20–1.60 **Mn**, 0.30–0.60 **Si**, 0.20 **Cr**, 0.15–0.35 **Mo**, 0.040 **P**, 0.040 **S**	**Normalized and tempered**: all **diam**, (686) **TS**, (392) **YS**, 13 **El**; **Quenched and tempered**: all **diam**, (736) **TS**, (490) **YS**, 13 **El**
JIS G 5111	Class 3, SC Cr M 3	Japan	Castings, pipe (centrifugally cast)	0.30–0.40 **C**, 0.50–0.80 **Mn**, 0.30–0.60 **Si**, 0.80–1.20 **Cr**, 0.15–0.35 **Mo**	**Normalized and tempered**: all **diam**, (686) **TS**, (441) **YS**, 9 **El**; **Quenched and tempered**: all **diam**, (785) **TS**, (588) **YS**, 9 **El**
JIS G 5111	Class 3, SC Mn Cr 3	Japan	Castings, pipe (centrifugally cast)	0.30–0.40 **C**, 1.20–1.60 **Mn**, 0.30–0.60 **Si**, 0.40–0.80 **Cr**, 0.040 **P**, 0.040 **S**	**Normalized and tempered**: all **diam**, (637) **TS**, (392) **YS**, 19 **El**; **Quenched and tempered**: all **diam**, (686) **TS**, (490) **YS**, 13 **El**
JIS G 5111	Class 3, SC Mn 3	Japan	Castings, pipe (centrifugally cast)	0.30–0.40 **C**, 1.00–1.60 **Mn**, 0.30–0.60 **Si**, 0.040 **P**, 0.040 **S**	**Normalized and tempered**: all **diam**, (637) **TS**, (373) **YS**, 13 **El**; **Quenched and tempered**: all **diam**, (686) **TS**, (490) **YS**, 13 **El**
JIS G 5111	Class 3, SCC 3	Japan	Castings, pipe (centrifugally cast)	0.30–0.40 **C**, 0.50–0.80 **Mn**, 0.30–0.60 **Si**, 0.040 **P**, 0.040 **S**	**Normalized and tempered**: all **diam**, (549) **TS**, (275) **YS**, 13 **El**; **Quenched and tempered**: all **diam**, (637) **TS**, (392) **YS**, 13 **El**
ANSI/ASTM A 597	Grade CH-12	US	Castings	0.30–0.40 **C**, 0.75 **Mn**, 1.50 **Si**, 4.75–5.75 **Cr**, 1.25–1.75 **Mo**, 0.20–0.50 **V**, 0.025 **P**, 0.025 **S**, 1.00–1.70 **W**	
MIL-S-22141B	1C-4335M	US	Investment castings	0.30–0.38 **C**, 0.60–1.00 **Mn**, 0.50–1.00 **Si**, 0.65–1.00 **Mo**, 0.14 **V**	**Annealed, quenched and tempered**: all **diam**, (1378) **TS**, (1241) **YS**, 5.0 (4xD) **El**
MIL-S-22141B	1C-8735	US	Investment castings	0.30–0.38 **C**, 0.30–0.70 **Mn**, 0.20–1.00 **Si**, 0.35–0.90 **Cr**, 0.15–0.40 **Mo**, 0.35–0.75 **Ni**	**Annealed, quenched and tempered**: all **diam**, (1378) **TS**, (1241) **YS**, 5 (4xD) **El**
ASTM A 487	Grade 10Q	US	Castings	0.30 **C**, 0.80 **Si**, 0.55–0.90 **Cr**, 0.20–0.40 **Mo**, 1.40–2.00 **Ni**, 0.03 **V**, 0.50 **Cu**, 0.04 **P**, 0.045 **S**, 0.10 **W**	**Quenched and tempered**: all **diam**, 125 (860) **TS**, 100 (690) **YS**, 15 **El**
ANSI/ASTM A 487	10Q	US	Castings	0.30 **C**, 0.80 **Si**, 0.55–0.90 **Cr**, 0.20–0.40 **Mo**, 1.40–2.00 **Ni**, 0.030 **V**, 0.040 **P**, 0.045 **S**	**Quenched, tempered**: all **diam**, 125 (860) **TS**, 100 (690) **YS**, 15 **El**
ANSI/ASTM A 487	Class 10Q	US	Sand castings	0.30 **C**, 0.80 **Si**, 0.55–0.90 **Cr**, 0.20–0.40 **Mo**, 1.40–2.00 **Ni**, 0.03 **V**, 0.04 **P**, 0.045 **S**	**Quenched and tempered**: all **diam**, 125 (860) **TS**, 100 (690) **YS**, 15 **El**

CAST CARBON STEELS

specification number	designation	country	product forms	composition	mechanical properties (see page iv for explanation)
ASTM A 487	Grade 4QA	US	Castings	0.30 **C**, 1.00 **Mn**, 0.80 **Si**, 0.40–0.80 **Cr**, 0.15–0.30 **Mo**, 0.40–0.80 **Ni**, 0.03 **V**, 0.50 **Cu**, 0.04 **P**, 0.045 **S**, 0.10 **W**	**Quenched and tempered**: all **diam**, 115 (795) **TS**, 95 (655) **YS**, 15 **El**
ANSI/ASTM A 487	4QA	US	Castings	0.30 **C**, 1.00 **Mn**, 0.80 **Si**, 0.40–0.80 **Cr**, 0.15–0.30 **Mo**, 0.40–0.80 **Ni**, 0.030 **V**, 0.040 **P**, 0.045 **S**	**Quenched, tempered**: all **diam**, 115 (795) **TS**, 95 (655) **YS**, 15 **El**
ANSI/ASTM A 487	Class 4QA	US	Sand castings	0.30 **C**, 1.00 **Mn**, 0.80 **Si**, 0.40–0.80 **Cr**, 0.15–0.30 **Mo**, 0.40–0.80 **Ni**, 0.030 **V**, 0.040 **P**, 0.045 **S**	**Quenched and tempered**: all **diam**, 115 (795) **TS**, 95 (655) **YS**, 15 **El**
ANSI/ASTM A 487	Class 13Q	US	Sand castings	0.30 **C**, 0.80–1.10 **Mn**, 0.60 **Si**, 0.20–0.30 **Mo**, 1.40–1.75 **Ni**, 0.03 **V**, 0.040 **P**, 0.045 **S**	**Quenched and tempered**: all **diam**, 105 (725) **TS**, 85 (585) **YS**, 17 **El**
ASTM A 487	Grade 13Q	US	Castings	0.30 **C**, 0.80–1.10 **Mn**, 0.60 **Si**, 0.40 **Cr**, 0.20–0.30 **Mo**, 1.40–1.75 **Ni**, 0.03 **V**, 0.50 **Cu**, 0.04 **P**, 0.045 **S**, 0.10 **W**	**Quenched and tempered**: all **diam**, 105 (725) **TS**, 85 (585) **YS**, 17 **El**
ASTM A 487	Grade 4Q	US	Castings	0.30 **C**, 1.00 **Mn**, 0.80 **Si**, 0.40–0.80 **Cr**, 0.15–0.30 **Mo**, 0.40–0.80 **Ni**, 0.03 **V**, 0.50 **Cu**, 0.04 **P**, 0.045 **S**, 0.10 **W**	**Quenched and tempered**: all **diam**, 105 (725) **TS**, 85 (585) **YS**, 17 **El**
ANSI/ASTM A 487	13Q	US	Castings	0.30 **C**, 0.80–1.10 **Mn**, 0.60 **Si**, 0.20–0.30 **Mo**, 1.40–1.75 **Ni**, 0.030 **V**, 0.040 **P**, 0.045 **S**	**Quenched, tempered**: all **diam**, 105 (725) **TS**, 85 (585) **YS**, 17 **El**
ANSI/ASTM A 487	4Q	US	Castings	0.30 **C**, 1.00 **Mn**, 0.80 **Si**, 0.40–0.80 **Cr**, 0.15–0.30 **Mo**, 0.40–0.80 **Ni**, 0.030 **V**, 0.040 **P**, 0.045 **S**	**Quenched, tempered**: all **diam**, 105 (725) **TS**, 85 (585) **YS**, 17 **El**
ANSI/ASTM A 487	Class 4Q	US	Sand castings	0.30 **C**, 1.00 **Mn**, 0.80 **Si**, 0.40–0.80 **Cr**, 0.15–0.30 **Mo**, 0.40–0.80 **Ni**, 0.030 **V**, 0.040 **P**, 0.045 **S**	**Quenched and tempered**: all **diam**, 105 (725) **TS**, 85 (585) **YS**, 17 **El**
IS 7899	Grade 5N, 5Q	India	Castings	0.30 **C**, 1.00–1.40 **Mn**, 0.80 **Si**, 0.40–0.80 **Cr**, 0.15–0.25 **Mo**, 0.40–0.80 **Ni**, 0.04 **P**, 0.045 **S**	**Normalized and tempered**: all **diam**, (720) **TS**, (480) **YS**, 16 **El**; **Quenched and tempered**: all **diam**, (720) **TS**, (590) **YS**, 14 **El**
IS 7899	Grade 10 N, 10Q	India	Castings	0.30 **C**, 0.80 **Si**, 0.55–0.90 **Cr**, 0.20–0.40 **Mo**, 1.40–2.00 **Ni**, 0.04 **P**, 0.045 **S**	**Normalized and tempered**: all **diam**, (690) **TS**, (480) **YS**, 16 **El**; **Quenched and tempered**: all **diam**, (860) **TS**, (690) **YS**, 14 **El**
ASTM A 487	Grade 10N	US	Castings	0.30 **C**, 0.80 **Si**, 0.55–0.90 **Cr**, 0.20–0.40 **Mo**, 1.4–2.0 **Ni**, 0.03 **V**, 0.50 **Cu**, 0.04 **P**, 0.045 **S**, 0.10 **W**	**Normalized and tempered**: all **diam**, 100 (690) **TS**, 70 (485) **YS**, 18 **El**
ANSI/ASTM A 487	10N	US	Castings	0.30 **C**, 0.80 **Si**, 0.55–0.90 **Cr**, 0.20–0.40 **Mo**, 1.40–2.00 **Ni**, 0.03 **V**, 0.04 **P**, 0.045 **S**	**Normalized, tempered**: all **diam**, 100 (690) **TS**, 70 (485) **YS**, 18 **El**
ANSI/ASTM A 487	Class 10N	US	Sand castings	0.30 **C**, 0.80 **Si**, 0.55–0.90 **Cr**, 0.20–0.40 **Mo**, 1.40–2.00 **Ni**, 0.03 **V**, 0.04 **P**, 0.045 **S**	**Normalized and tempered**: all **diam**, 100 (690) **TS**, 70 (485) **YS**, 18 **El**
ANSI/ASTM A 487	Class 13N	US	Sand castings	0.30 **C**, 0.80–1.10 **Mn**, 0.60 **Si**, 0.20–0.30 **Mo**, 1.40–1.75 **Ni**, 0.03 **V**, 0.040 **P**, 0.045 **S**	**Normalized and tempered**: all **diam**, 90 (620) **TS**, 60 (415) **YS**, 18 **El**
IS 7899	Grade 4N,4Q	India	Castings	0.30 **C**, 1.00 **Mn**, 0.80 **Si**, 0.40–0.80 **Cr**, 0.15–0.30 **Mo**, 0.40–0.80 **Ni**, 0.04 **P**, 0.045 **S**	**Normalized and tempered**: all **diam**, (620) **TS**, (410) **YS**, 18 **El**; **Quenched and tempered**: all **diam**, (720) **TS**, (590) **YS**, 15 **El**
ASTM A 487	Grade 13N	US	Castings	0.30 **C**, 0.80–1.10 **Mn**, 0.60 **Si**, 0.40 **Cr**, 0.20–0.30 **Mo**, 1.40–1.75 **Ni**, 0.03 **V**, 0.50 **Cu**, 0.04 **P**, 0.045 **S**, 0.10 **W**	**Normalized and tempered**: all **diam**, 90 (620) **TS**, 60 (415) **YS**, 18 **El**
ASTM A 487	Grade 1Q	US	Castings	0.30 **C**, 1.00 **Mn**, 0.80 **Si**, 0.35 **Cr**, 0.50 **Ni**, 0.04–2.0 **V**, 0.50 **Cu**, 0.25 **Mo+W**, 0.04 **P**, 0.045 **S**	**Quenched and tempered**: all **diam**, 90 (620) **TS**, 65 (450) **YS**, 22 **El**
ASTM A 487	Grade 2Q	US	Castings	0.30 **C**, 1.00–1.40 **Mn**, 0.80 **Si**, 0.35 **Cr**, 0.10–0.30 **Mo**, 0.50 **Ni**, 0.03 **V**, 0.50 **Cu**, 0.04 **P**, 0.045 **S**, 0.10 **W**	**Quenched and tempered**: all **diam**, 90 (620) **TS**, 65 (450) **YS**, 22 **El**

CAST CARBON STEELS

specification number	designation	country	product forms	composition	mechanical properties (see page iv for explanation)
ASTM A 487	Grade 4N	US	Castings	0.30 **C**, 1.00 **Mn**, 0.80 **Si**, 0.40–0.80 **Cr**, 0.15–0.30 **Mo**, 0.40–0.80 **Ni**, 0.03 **V**, 0.50 **Cu**, 0.04 **P**, 0.045 **S**, 0.10 **W**	**Normalized and tempered**: all **diam**, 90 (620) **TS**, 60 (415) **YS**, 20 **El**
ANSI/ASTM A 487	13N	US	Castings	0.30 **C**, 0.80–1.10 **Mn**, 0.60 **Si**, 0.20–0.30 **Mo**, 1.40–1.75 **Ni**, 0.030 **V**, 0.040 **P**, 0.045 **S**	**Normalized, tempered**: all **diam**, 90 (620) **TS**, 60 (415) **YS**, 18 **El**
ANSI/ASTM A 487	1Q	US	Castings	0.30 **C**, 1.00 **Mn**, 0.80 **Si**, 0.04–0.12 **V**, 0.040 **P**, 0.0450 **S**	**Quenched, tempered**: all **diam**, 90 (620) **TS**, 65 (450) **YS**, 22 **El**
ANSI/ASTM A 487	2Q	US	Castings	0.30 **C**, 1.00–1.40 **Mn**, 0.80 **Si**, 0.10–0.30 **Mo**, 0.030 **V**, 0.040 **P**, 0.045 **S**	**Quenched, tempered**: all **diam**, 90 (620) **TS**, 65 (450) **YS**, 22 **El**
ANSI/ASTM A 487	4N	US	Castings	0.30 **C**, 1.00 **Mn**, 0.80 **Si**, 0.40–0.80 **Cr**, 0.15–0.30 **Mo**, 0.40–0.80 **Ni**, 0.030 **V**, 0.040 **P**, 0.045 **S**	**Normalized, tempered**: all **diam**, 90 (620) **TS**, 60 (415) **YS**, 20 **El**
ANSI/ASTM A 487	Class 4N	US	Sand castings	0.30 **C**, 1.00 **Mn**, 0.80 **Si**, 0.40–0.80 **Cr**, 0.15–0.30 **Mo**, 0.40–0.80 **Ni**, 0.030 **V**, 0.040 **P**, 0.045 **S**	**Normalized and tempered**: all **diam**, 90 (620) **TS**, 60 (415) **YS**, 20 **El**
ANSI/ASTM A 487	Class 2Q	US	Sand castings	0.30 **C**, 1.00–1.40 **Mn**, 0.80 **Si**, 0.10–0.30 **Mo**, 0.003 **V**, 0.040 **P**, 0.045 **S**	**Quenched and tempered**: all **diam**, 90 (620) **TS**, 65 (450) **YS**, 22 **El**
ANSI/ASTM A 487	Class 1Q	US	Sand castings	0.30 **C**, 1.00 **Mn**, 0.80 **Si**, 0.04–0.12 **V**, 0.04 **P**, 0.045 **S**	**Quenched and tempered**: all **diam**, 90 (620) **TS**, 65 (450) **YS**, 22 **El**
IS 7899	Grade 2N, 2Q	India	Castings	0.30 **C**, 1.00–1.40 **Mn**, 0.80 **Si**, 0.10–0.30 **Mo**, 0.04 **P**, 0.045 **S**	**Normalized and tempered**: all **diam**, (590) **TS**, (360) **YS**, 20 **El**; **Quenched and tempered**: all **diam**, (620) **TS**, (450) **YS**, 20 **El**
IS 7899	Grade 1N, 1Q	India	Castings	0.30 **C**, 1.00 **Mn**, 0.80 **Si**, 0.07–0.15 **V**, 0.040 **P**, 0.045 **S**	**Normalized and tempered**: all **diam**, (590) **TS**, (380) **YS**, 20 **El**; **Quenched and tempered**: all **diam**, (620) **TS**, (450) **YS**, 20 **El**
ASTM A 487	Grade 1N	US	Castings	0.30 **C**, 1.00 **Mn**, 0.80 **Si**, 0.35 **Cr**, 0.50 **Ni**, 0.04–0.12 **V**, 0.50 **Cu**, 0.25 **Mo+W**, 0.04 **P**, 0.045 **S**	**Normalized and tempered**: all **diam**, 85 (585) **TS**, 55 (380) **YS**, 22 **El**
ASTM A 487	Grade 2N	US	Castings	0.30 **C**, 1.00–1.40 **Mn**, 0.80 **Si**, 0.35 **Cr**, 0.10–0.30 **Mo**, 0.50 **Ni**, 0.30 **V**, 0.50 **Cu**, 0.04 **P**, 0.045 **S**, 0.10 **W**	**Normalized and tempered**: all **diam**, 85 (585) **TS**, 53 (365) **YS**, 22 **El**
ANSI/ASTM A 487	1N	US	Castings	0.30 **C**, 1.00 **Mn**, 0.80 **Si**, 0.040–0.12 **V**, 0.040 **P**, 0.045 **S**	**Normalized, tempered**: all **diam**, 85 (585) **TS**, 55 (380) **YS**, 22 **El**
ANSI/ASTM A 487	2N	US	Castings	0.30 **C**, 1.00–1.40 **Mn**, 0.80 **Si**, 0.10–0.30 **Mo**, 0.030 **V**, 0.040 **P**, 0.045 **S**	**Normalized, tempered**: all **diam**, 85 (585) **TS**, 53 (365) **YS**, 22 **El**
ANSI/ASTM A 487	Class 2N	US	Sand castings	0.30 **C**, 1.00–1.40 **Mn**, 0.80 **Si**, 0.10–0.30 **Mo**, 0.03 **V**, 0.04 **P**, 0.045 **S**	**Normalized and tempered**: all **diam**, 85 (585) **TS**, 53 (365) **YS**, 22 **El**
ANSI/ASTM A 487	Class 1N	US	Sand castings	0.30 **C**, 1.00 **Mn**, 0.80 **Si**, 0.04–0.12 **V**, 0.04 **P**, 0.045 **S**	**Normalized and tempered**: all **diam**, 85 (585) **TS**, 55 (380) **YS**, 22 **El**
ASTM A 732	Grade 5N	US	Investment castings	0.30 **C**, 0.70–1.00 **Mn**, 0.20–0.80 **Si**, 0.05–0.15 **V**, 0.04 **P**, 0.045 **S**, 1.00 other elements, total	**Normalized and tempered**: all **diam**, 85 (585) **TS**, 55 (380) **YS**, 22 **El**
ANSI/ASTM A 487	BQ	US	Castings	0.30 **C**, 1.00 **Mn**, 0.60 **Si**, 0.03 **V**, 0.04 **P**, 0.045 **S**	**Quenched, tempered**: all **diam**, 80 (550) **TS**, 36 (250) **YS**, 22 **El**
ANSI/ASTM A 487	Class BQ	US	Sand castings	0.30 **C**, 1.00 **Mn**, 0.60 **Si**, 0.03 **V**, 0.04 **P**, 0.045 **S**	**Quenched and tempered**: all **diam**, 80 (550) **TS**, 36 (250) **YS**, 22 **El**
ASTM A 487	Grade BQ	US	Castings	0.30 **C**, 1.00 **Mn**, 0.60 **Si**, 0.40 **Cr**, 0.25 **Mo**, 0.50 **Ni**, 0.03 **V**, 0.50 **Cu**, 0.04 **P**, 0.045 **S**, 0.10 **W**	**Quenched and tempered**: all **diam**, 80 (550) **TS**, 36 (248) **YS**, 22 **El**
SIS 14 15 05	SIS 15 05–02	Sweden	Castings	0.3 **C**, 0.7 **Mn**, 0.5 **Si**, 0.040 **P**, 0.040 **S**	**Annealed**: all **diam**, (520) **TS**, (260) **YS**
ANSI/ASTM A 487	B	US	Castings	0.30 **C**, 1.00 **Mn**, 0.60 **Si**, 0.03 **V**, 0.04 **P**, 0.045 **S**	**Normalized, tempered**: all **diam**, 70 (485) **TS**, 36 (250) **YS**, 22 **El**

CAST CARBON STEELS

specification number	designation	country	product forms	composition	mechanical properties (see page iv for explanation)
ANSI/ASTM A 487	BN	US	Castings	0.30 **C**, 1.00 **Mn**, 0.60 **Si**, 0.03 **V**, 0.04 **P**, 0.045 **S**	**Normalized, tempered**: all **diam**, 70 (485) **TS**, 36 (250) **YS**, 22 **El**
ANSI/ASTM A 216	WCB	US	Castings	0.30 **C**, 1.00 **Mn**, 0.60 **Si**, 0.04 **P**, 0.045 **S**	**Annealed, or normalized, or normalized, tempered**: all **diam**, 70 (485) **TS**, 36 (250) **YS**, 22 **El**
ANSI/ASTM A 487	Class B and BN	US	Sand castings	0.30 **C**, 1.00 **Mn**, 0.60 **Si**, 0.03 **V**, 0.04 **P**, 0.045 **S**	**Normalized and tempered**: all **diam**, 70 (485) **TS**, 36 (250) **YS**, 22 **El**
ANSI/ASTM A 216	Grade WCB	US	Sand casting	0.30 **C**, 1.00 **Mn**, 0.60 **Si**, 0.04 **P**, 0.045 **S**; 1.00 max, other elements, total	**Annealed or normalized or normalized and tempered**: all **diam**, 70 (485) **TS**, 36 (250) **YS**, 22 **El**
ASTM A 487	Grade B, BN	US	Castings	0.30 **C**, 1.00 **Mn**, 0.60 **Si**, 0.40 **Cr**, 0.25 **Mo**, 0.50 **Ni**, 0.03 **V**, 0.50 **Cu**, 0.04 **P**, 0.045 **S**, 0.10 **W**	**Normalized and tempered**: all **diam**, 70 (485) **TS**, 36 (248) **YS**, 22 **El**
ASTM A 216	Grade WCB	US	Castings	0.30 **C**, 1.00 **Mn**, 0.60 **Si**, 0.40 **Cr**, 0.25 **Mo**, 0.50 **Ni**, 0.03 **V**, 0.50 **Cu**, 0.04 **P**, 0.045 **S**	**Annealed, normalized, normalized and tempered**: all **diam**, 70 (485) **TS**, 36 (250) **YS**, 22 **El**
NOM-B-356	Class WCB	Mexico	Castings	0.30 **C**, 1.00 **Mn**, 0.60 **Si**, 0.040 **P**, 0.045 **S**	**Annealed and normalized or normalized and quenched**: all **diam**, (483) **TS**, (248) **YS**, 22 **El**
ASTM A-660-75	Grade WCB	US	Pipe, centrifugally cast	0.30 **C**, 1.00 **Mn**, 0.60 **Si**, 0.040 **P**, 0.045 **S**	**As agreed**: all **diam**, 70 (483) **TS**, 36 (248) **YS**, 22 **El**
ANSI/ASTM A 660	Grade WCB	US	Pipe: centrifugally cast	0.30 **C**, 1.00 **Mn**, 0.60 **Si**, 0.04 **P**, 0.045 **S**	**Annealed**: all **diam**, 70 (483) **TS**, 36 (248) **YS**, 22 **El**
JIS G 5151	Class 2	Japan	Castings	0.30 **C**, 1.00 **Mn**, 0.60 **Si**, 0.040 **P**, 0.040 **S**	**Annealed, normalized, quenched, tempered**: all **diam**, (481) **TS**, (245) **YS**, 19 **El**
JIS G 5202	Class 2	Japan	Pipe: centrifugally cast	0.30 **C**, 1.10 **Mn**, 0.60 **Si**, 0.040 **P**, 0.040 **S**	**Annealed, normalized, quenched, tempered**: all **diam**, (481) **TS**, (275) **YS**, 19 **El**
BS 1504-161	Grade B	UK	Sand castings	0.30 **C**	**Annealed or normalized or annealed and normalized**: all **diam**, (480) **TS**, (245) **YS**
UNI 7316-74	Fe G 49-1	Italy	Castings	0.30 **C**, 1.0 **Mn**, 0.50 **Si**, 1.0 **Cr+Cu+Mo+Ni+W**, 0.04 **P**, 0.045 **S**	**Annealed, normalized or normalized and tempered**: all **diam**, (480) **TS**, (245) **YS**, 18 **El**
BS 1504-161	Grade 480	UK	Castings	0.30 **C**, 0.90 **Mn**, 0.60 **Si**, 0.25 **Cr**, 0.15 **Mo**, 0.40 **Ni**, 0.30 **Cu**, 0.050 **P**, 0.050 **S**	**Austenitized**: all **diam**, (480) **TS**, (245) **YS**, 20 **El**
DGS 8081		UK	Sand castings	0.30 **C**, 0.80-1.00 **Mn**	**Annealed and normalized**: all **diam**, (460) **TS**
JIS G 5152	Class 1	Japan	Castings, tube (centrifugally cast)	0.30 **C**, 1.00 **Mn**, 0.60 **Si**, 0.040 **P**, 0.040 **S**	**Annealed, normalized, quenched and tempered**: all **diam**, (451) **TS**, (245) **YS**, 21 **El**
ASTM A 352-76	Grade LCB	US	Castings	0.30 **C**, 1.00 **Mn**, 0.60 **Si**, 0.04 **P**, 0.045 **S**	**Normalized and tempered or quenched and tempered**: all **diam**, 65 (450) **TS**, 35 (240) **YS**, 24 **El**
ANSI/ASTM A 352	LCB	US	Castings: ferritic	0.30 **C**, 1.00 **Mn**, 0.60 **Si**, 0.04 **P**, 0.045 **S**	**Quenched, tempered**: all **diam**, 65 (450) **TS**, 35 (240) **YS**, 24 **El**
ASTM A 27	Grade 65-35	US	Castings	0.30 **C**, 0.70 **Mn**, 0.80 **Si**, 0.05 **P**, 0.06 **S**	**Annealed or normalized or quenched and tempered**: all **diam**, 65 (450) **TS**, 35 (240) **YS**, 24 **El**
ANSI/ASTM A 352	Grade LCB	US	Sand castings	0.30 **C**, 1.00 **Mn**, 0.60 **Si**, 0.04 **P**, 0.045 **S**	**Normalized and tempered or quenched and tempered**: all **diam**, 65 (450) **TS**, 35 (240) **YS**, 24 **El**
SAE Automotive J435a	Grade 0030	US	Castings	0.30 **C**, 0.70 **Mn**, 0.80 **Si**, 0.050 **P**, 0.060 **S**	**Annealed, normalized, normalized and tempered, quenched and tempered**: all **diam**, 65 (448) **TS**, 35 (241) **YS**, 24 **El**
MIL-S-15083 B	Class 65-35	US	Sand castings	0.30 **C**, 0.70 **Mn**, 0.80 **Si**, 0.05 **P**, 0.06 **S**	**Annealed or normalized and tempered or quenched and tempered**: all **diam**, 65 (448) **TS**, 35 (241) **YS**, 24 **El**

CAST CARBON STEELS

specification number	designation	country	product forms	composition	mechanical properties (see page iv for explanation)
DGN–B–352	Class 46–24	Mexico	Castings	0.30 **C**, 0.90 **Mn**, 0.80 **Si**, 0.050 **P**, 0.060 **S**	**Annealed, normalized, normalized and tempered, quenched and tempered**: all **diam**, (448) **TS**, (241) **YS**, 24 **El**
CSA G28	65–35	Canada	Castings	0.30 **C**, 0.75 **Mn**, 0.80 **Si**, 0.04 **P**, 0.04 **S**	**Full annealed, normalized, normalized and tempered, quenched and tempered**: all **diam**, (448) **TS**, (241) **YS**, 24 **El**
ASTM A 27	Grade 65–35	US	Castings	0.30 **C**, 0.70 **Mn**, 0.80 **Si**, 0.40 **Cr**, 0.20 **Mo**, 0.50 **Ni**, 0.30 **Cu**, 0.05 **P**, 0.06 **S**	**Annealed, normalized, normalized and tempered, quenched and tempered**: all **diam**, 65 (448) **TS**, 35 (241) **YS**, 24 **El**
ASTM A 27	Grade 60–30	US	Castings	0.30 **C**, 0.60 **Mn**, 0.80 **Si**, 0.05 **P**, 0.06 **S**	**Annealed or normalized or quenched and tempered**: all **diam**, 60 (415) **TS**, 30 (205) **YS**, 24 **El**
MIL–S–15083B	Class B	US	Sand castings	0.30 **C**, 0.60 **Mn**, 0.60 **Si**, 0.05 **P**, 0.05 **S**	**Annealed or normalized and tempered or quenched and tempered**: all **diam**, 60 (414) **TS**, 30 (207) **YS**, 24 **El**
CSA G28	60–30	Canada	Castings	0.30 **C**, 0.75 **Mn**, 0.80 **Si**, 0.04 **P**, 0.04 **S**	**Full annealed, normalized, normalized and tempered, quenched and tempered**: all **diam**, (414) **TS**, (207) **YS**, 24 **El**
ASTM A 27	Grade 60–30	US	Castings	0.30 **C**, 0.60 **Mn**, 0.80 **Si**, 0.40 **Cr**, 0.20 **Mo**, 0.50 **Ni**, 0.30 **Cu**, 0.05 **P**, 0.06 **S**	**Annealed, normalized, normalized and tempered, quenched and tempered**: all **diam**, 60 (414) **TS**, 30 (207) **YS**, 24 **El**
MIL–S–15083 B	Class CW	US	Sand castings	0.30 **C**, 0.70 **Mn**, 0.07 **P**, 0.06 **S**	**Annealed or normalized and tempered or quenched and tempered**: all **diam**, 55 (379) **TS**, 27 (186) **YS**, 15 **El**
AMS 5328A		US	Investment castings	0.28–0.36 **C**, 0.60–1.00 **Mn**, 0.50–1.00 **Si**, 0.65–1.00 **Cr**, 0.30–0.45 **Mo**, 1.65–2.00 **Ni**, 0.35 **Cu**, 0.025 **P**, 0.025 **S**	**Annealed, hardened, and tempered**: all **diam**, 180 (1241) **TS**, 160 (1103) **YS**, 5 in 1 in. **El**
AMS 5329B		US	Sand castings	0.28–0.36 **C**, 0.60–1.00 **Mn**, 0.50–0.90 **Si**, 0.65–1.00 **Cr**, 0.30–0.45 **Mo**, 1.65–2.00 **Ni**, 0.35 **Cu**, 0.025 **P**, 0.025 **S**	**Annealed, hardened, and tempered**: all **diam**, 180 (1241) **TS**, 160 (1103) **YS**, 5 **El**
VSM 10697	GS–30 NiCrMo 8 5 V 95	Switzerland	Castings	0.27–0.33 **C**, 0.60–1.00 **Mn**, 0.30–0.50 **Si**, 1.10–1.40 **Cr**, 0.30–0.40 **Mo**, 1.80–2.10 **Ni**, 0.030 **P**, 0.030 **S**	**Quenched and tempered**: all **diam**, (950) **TS**, (800) **YS**, 10 **El**
VSM 10697	GS–30 NiCrMo 8 5 V 8 5	Switzerland	Castings	0.27–0.34 **C**, 0.60–1.0 **Mn**, 0.30–0.50 **Si**, 1.10–1.40 **Cr**, 0.300–0.400 **Mo**, 1.80–2.10 **Ni**, 0.030 **P**, 0.030 **S**	**Quenched and tempered**: all **diam**, (850) **TS**, (700) **YS**, 12 **El**
VSM 10697	GS–52/1.00551	Switzerland	Castings	0.27–0.33 **C**, 1.0 **Mn**, 0.30–0.50 **Si**, 0.40 **Cr**, 0.25 **Mo**, 0.50 **Ni**, 0.030 **P**, 0.030 **S**	**Annealed or normalized**: all **diam**, (520) **TS**, (260) **YS**, 18 **El**
IS 2708	Grade 3B	India	Castings	0.26–0.35 **C**, 1.20–1.70 **Mn**, 0.30–0.60 **Si**, 0.050 **P**, 0.050 **S**; 1.00 max, other elements, total	**As agreed**: all **diam**, (700) **TS**, (490) **YS**, 12 **El**
IS 2708	Grade 3A	India	Castings	0.26–0.35 **C**, 1.20–1.70 **Mn**, 0.30–0.60 **Si**, 0.050 **P**, 0.050 **S**; 1.00 max, other elements, total	**As agreed**: all **diam**, (620) **TS**, (370) **YS**, 13 **El**
AMS 5334C		US	Investment castings	0.25–0.35 **C**, 0.60–0.95 **Mn**, 1.00 **Si**, 0.35–0.65 **Cr**, 0.15–0.30 **Mo**, 0.35–0.75 **Ni**, 0.35 **Cu**, 0.04 **P**, 0.04 **S**	**Normalized and tempered**: all **diam**, 150 (1034) **TS**, 125 (862) **YS**, 5 in 1 in **El**
AMS 5336B		US	Investment castings	0.25–0.35 **C**, 0.40–0.80 **Mn**, 1.00 **Si**, 0.80–1.10 **Cr**, 0.15–0.25 **Mo**, 0.25 **Ni**, 0.25 **Cu**, 0.04 **P**, 0.04 **S**	**Normalized, tempered, hardened and tempered**: all **diam**, 150 (1034) **TS**, 125 (862) **YS**, 5 in 1 in. **El**
MIL–S–22141B	1C–4130	US	Investment castings	0.25–0.35 **C**, 0.40–0.70 **Mn**, 0.20–0.80 **Si**, 0.80–1.10 **Cr**, 0.15–0.25 **Mo**	**Annealed, quenched and tempered**: all **diam**, (1034) **TS**, (792) **YS**, 7.0 (4 x D) **El**

CAST CARBON STEELS

specification number	designation	country	product forms	composition	mechanical properties (see page iv for explanation)
MIL–S–22141B	1C–8630	US	Investment castings	0.25–0.35 **C**, 0.65–0.95 **Mn**, 0.20–0.80 **Si**, 0.40–0.60 **Cr**, 0.15–0.25 **Mo**, 0.40–0.70 **Ni**	**Annealed, quenched and tempered**: all diam, (1034) **TS**, (792) **YS**, 7 (4xD) **El**
ASTM A 732	Grade 14Q	US	Investment castings	0.25–0.35 **C**, 0.65–0.95 **Mn**, 0.20–0.80 **Si**, 0.40–0.70 **Cr**, 0.15–0.25 **Mo**, 0.40–0.70 **Ni**, 0.04 **P**, 0.045 **S**, 1.00 other elements, total	**Quenched and tempered**: all **diam**, 150 (1030) **TS**, 115 (795) **YS**, 7 **El**
ASTM A 732	Grade 9Q	US	Investment castings	0.25–0.35 **C**, 0.40–0.70 **Mn**, 0.20–0.80 **Si**, 0.70–0.90 **Cr**, 0.20–0.30 **Mo**, 1.65–2.00 **Ni**, 0.04 **P**, 0.045 **S**, 0.60 other elements, total	**Quenched and tempered**: all **diam**, 150 (1030) **TS**, 115 (795) **YS**, 7 **El**
ASTM A 732	Grade 7Q	US	Investment castings	0.25–0.35 **C**, 0.40–0.70 **Mn**, 0.20–0.80 **Si**, 0.80–1.10 **Cr**, 0.15–0.25 **Mo**, 0.04 **P**, 0.045 **S**, 1.00 other elements, total	**Quenched and tempered**: all **diam**, 150 (1030) **TS**, 115 (795) **YS**, 7 **El**
JIS G 5111	Class 2, SC N Cr M 2	Japan	Castings, pipe (centrifugally cast)	0.25–0.35 **C**, 0.90–1.50 **Mn**, 0.30–0.60 **Si**, 0.30–0.90 **Cr**, 0.15–0.35 **Mo**, 1.60–2.00 **Ni**, 0.040 **P**, 0.040 **S**	**Normalized and tempered**: all **diam**, (785) **TS**, (588) **YS**, 9 **El**; **Quenched and tempered**: all **diam**, (981) **TS**, (784) **YS**, 9 **El**
JIS G 5111	Class 2, SC Mn Cr M 2	Japan	Castings, pipe (centrifugally cast)	0.25–0.35 **C**, 1.20–1.60 **Mn**, 0.30–0.60 **Si**, 0.30–0.70 **Cr**, 0.15–0.35 **Mo**; 0.040 **P**, 0.040 **S**	**Normalized and tempered**: all **diam**, (686) **TS**, (441) **YS**, 13 **El**; **Quenched and tempered**: all **diam**, (736) **TS**, (539) **YS**, 13 **El**
JIS G 5111	Class 2, SC Si Mn 2	Japan	Castings, pipe (centrifugally cast)	0.25–0.35 **C**, 0.90–1.20 **Mn**, 0.50–0.80 **Si**, 0.040 **P**, 0.040 **S**	**Normalized and tempered**: all **diam**, (588) **TS**, (294) **YS**, 13 **El**; **Quenched and tempered**: all **diam**, (637) **TS**, (441) **YS**, 17 **El**
JIS G 5111	Class 2, SC Mn 2	Japan	Castings, pipe (centrifugally cast)	0.25–0.35 **C**, 1.00–1.60 **Mn**, 0.30–0.60 **Si**, 0.040 **P**, 0.040 **S**	**Normalized and tempered**: all **diam**, (588) **TS**, (343) **YS**, 16 **El**; **Quenched and tempered**: all **diam**, (637) **TS**, (441) **YS**, 16 **El**
JIS G 5111	Class 2, SC Mn Cr 2	Japan	Castings, pipe (centrifugally cast)	0.25–0.35 **C**, 1.20–1.60 **Mn**, 0.30–0.60 **Si**, 0.40–0.80 **Cr**, 0.040 **P**, 0.040 **S**	**Normalized and tempered**: all **diam**, (588) **TS**, (373) **YS**, 13 **El**; **Quenched and tempered**: all **diam**, (637) **TS**, (539) **YS**, 17 **El**
ASTM A 732	Grade 2Q	US	Investment castings	0.25–0.35 **C**, 0.70–1.00 **Mn**, 0.20–0.60 **Si**, 0.04 **P**, 0.045 **S**; 1.00 other elements, total	**Quenched and tempered**: all **diam**, 85 (585) **TS**, 60 (415) **YS**, 10 **El**
ASTM A 732	Grade 2A	US	Investment castings	0.25–0.35 **C**, 0.70–1.00 **Mn**, 0.20–0.60 **Si**, 0.04 **P**, 0.045 **S**; 1.00 other elements, total	**Annealed**: all **diam**, 65 (450) **TS**, 45 (310) **YS**, 25 **El**
MIL–S–22141B	1C–1030	US	Investment castings	0.25–0.35 **C**, 0.70–1.00 **Mn**, 0.20–1.00 **Si**	**Annealed**: all **diam**, (448) **TS**, (310) **YS**, 25 (4 x D) **El**; **Quenched and tempered**: all **diam**, (586) **TS**, (413) **YS**, 10 (4 x D) **El**
MIL–S–81591	IC–1030	US	Investmest castings	0.25–0.35 **C**, 0.70–1.00 **Mn**, 0.20–1.00 **Si**, 0.01 **P**, 0.04 **S**	**Annealed**: all **diam**, 65 (448) **TS**, 45 (310) **YS**, 25 **El**
AMS 5335C		US	Sand castings	0.25–0.33 **C**, 0.60–0.95 **Mn**, 0.50–0.90 **Si**, 0.40–0.90 **Cr**, 0.15–0.25 **Mo**, 0.40–1.10 **Ni**, 0.35 **Cu**, 0.025 **P**, 0.025 **S**	**Normalized, tempered, hardened and tempered**: all **diam**, 165 (1138) **TS**, 150 (1034) **YS**, 8 **El**
BS 3100/1456	Grade B2	UK	Sand castings	0.25–0.33 **C**, 1.20–1.60 **Mn**	**Hardened and tempered (oil or water)**: all **diam**, (695) **TS**, (495) **YS**, 13 **El**
BS 3146: Part 1	CLA2: Grade B	UK	Investment and precision castings	0.25–0.33 **C**, 1.20–1.70 **Mn**	**Normalized, normalized and tempered or hardened and tempered**: all **diam**, (695) **TS**
BS 3100/1456	Grade B1	UK	Sand castings	0.25–0.33 **C**, 1.20–1.60 **Mn**	**Normalized, normalized and tempered or hardened and tempered**: all **diam**, (615) **TS**, (370) **YS**, 13 **El**

CAST CARBON STEELS

specification number	designation	country	product forms	composition	mechanical properties (see page iv for explanation)
VSM 10697	GS–28 CrMo 12 5 V 95	Switzerland	Castings	0.25–0.30 **C**, 0.80 **Mn**, 0.30–0.50 **Si**, 2.80–3.20 **Cr**, 0.40–0.60 **Mo**, 0.50 **Ni**, 0.030 **P**, 0.030 **S**	**Quenched and tempered**: all **diam**, (950) **TS**, (800) **YS**, 10 **El**
VSM 10697	GS–28 CrMo 12 5 V 8 5	Switzerland	Castings	0.25–0.30 **C**, 0.80 **Mn**, 0.30–0.50 **Si**, 2.80–3.20 **Cr**, 0.40–0.60 **Mo**, 0.50 **Ni**, 0.030 **P**, 0.030 **S**	**Quenched and tempered**: all **diam**, (850) **TS**, (700) **YS**, 12 **El**
BS 1504–623		UK	Castings	0.25 **C**, 0.30–0.70 **Mn**, 0.75 **Si**, 2.5–3.5 **Cr**, 0.35–0.60 **Mo**, 0.40 **Ni**, 0.30 **Cu**, 0.040 **P**, 0.040 **S**	**Normalized and tempered, or hardened and tempered**: all **diam**, (620) **TS**, (370) **YS**, 13 **El**
BS 1504–623		UK	Sand castings	0.25 **C**, 2.50–3.50 **Cr**, 0.35–0.60 **Mo**	**Hardened and tempered (air or oil)**: all **diam**, (615) **TS**, (370) **YS**
BS 3100/1461		UK	Sand castings	0.25 **C**, 2.50–3.50 **Cr**, 0.35–0.60 **Mo**	**Hardened and tempered**: all **diam**, (615) **TS**, (370) **YS**, 13 **El**
DTD 5229		UK	Investment and precision castings	0.25 **C**, 2.5–3.5 **Cr**, 0.35–0.60 **Mo**	**Annealed and hardened and tempered**: all **diam**, (615) **TS**, (460) **YS**, 13 **El**
ANSI/ASTM A 487	CQ	US	Castings	0.25 **C**, 1.20 **Mn**, 0.60 **Si**, 0.03 **V**, 0.04 **P**, 0.045 **S**	**Quenched, tempered**: all **diam**, 80 (550) **TS**, 40 (275) **YS**, 22 **El**
ANSI/ASTM A 487	Class CQ	US	Sand castings	0.25 **C**, 1.20 **Mn**, 0.60 **Si**, 0.03 **V**, 0.04 **P**, 0.045 **S**	**Quenched and tempered**: all **diam**, 80 (550) **TS**, 40 (275) **YS**, 22 **El**
ASTM A 487	Grade CQ	US	Castings	0.25 **C**, 1.20 **Mn**, 0.60 **Si**, 0.40 **Cr**, 0.25 **Mo**, 0.50 **Ni**, 0.03 **V**, 0.50 **Cu**, 0.04 **P**, 0.045 **S**, 0.10 **W**	**Quenched and tempered**: all **diam**, 80 (550) **TS**, 40 (275) **YS**, 22 **El**
ASTM A 643	Grade B1	US	Castings	0.25 **C**, 1.15–1.50 **Mn**, 0.60 **Si**, 0.40 **Cr**, 0.45–0.60 **Mo**, 0.45–1.00 **Ni**, 0.03 **V**, 0.50 **Cu**, 0.035 **P**, 0.035 **S**, 0.10 **W**	**Normalized and tempered quenched and tempered**: all **diam**, 80 (550) **TS**, 50 (345) **YS**, 22 **El**
ANSI/ASTM A 643	Grade B, class 1	US	Sand castings	0.25 **C**, 1.15–1.50 **Mn**, 0.60 **Si**, 0.45–0.60 **Mo**, 0.45–1.00 **Ni**, 0.035 **P**, 0.035 **S**	**Normalized and tempered or quenched and tempered**: >2 **diam**, 80 (550) **TS**, 50 (345) **YS**, 22 **El**
JIS G 5151	Class 22	Japan	Castings	0.25 **C**, 0.50–0.80 **Mn**, 0.60 **Si**, 1.00–1.50 **Cr**, 0.90–1.20 **Mo**, 0.040 **P**, 0.040 **S**	**Annealed, normalized, quenched, tempered**: all **diam**, (549) **TS**, (343) **YS**, 16 **El**
SFS 357		Finland	Castings	0.25 **C**, 0.70 **Mn**, 0.50 **Si**, 0.040 **P**, 0.040 **S**	**Annealed or normalized**: all **diam**, (520) **TS**, (260) **YS**, 18 **El**
NF A 32–053	F C–M	France	Castings	0.25 **C**, 1.50 **Mn**, 0.50 **Si**, 1.00 **Ni**, 0.040 **P**, 0.035 **S**	**As cast**: all **diam**, (520) **TS**, (260) **YS**, 16 **El**
ASTM A352–76	Grade LCC	US	Castings	0.25 **C**, 1.20 **Mn**, 0.60 **Si**, 0.04 **P**, 0.045 **S**	**Normalized and tempered or quenched and tempered**: all **diam**, 70 (485) **TS**, 40 (275) **YS**, 22 **El**
ANSI/ASTM A 487	AQ	US	Castings	0.25 **C**, 0.75 **Mn**, 0.60 **Si**, 0.03 **V**, 0.04 **P**, 0.045 **S**	**Quenched, tempered**: all **diam**, 70 (485) **TS**, 30 (207) **YS**, 24 **El**
ANSI/ASTM A 487	C	US	Castings	0.25 **C**, 1.20 **Mn**, 0.60 **Si**, 0.03 **V**, 0.04 **P**, 0.045 **S**	**Normalized, tempered**: all **diam**, 70 (485) **TS**, 40 (275) **YS**, 22 **El**
ANSI/ASTM A 487	CN	US	Castings	0.25 **C**, 1.20 **Mn**, 0.60 **Si**, 0.03 **V**, 0.04 **P**, 0.045 **S**	**Normalized, tempered**: all **diam**, 70 (485) **TS**, 40 (275) **YS**, 22 **El**
ANSI/ASTM A 352	LCC	US	Castings: ferritic	0.25 **C**, 1.20 **Mn**, 0.60 **Si**, 0.04 **P**, 0.045 **S**	**Quenched, tempered**: all **diam**, 70 (485) **TS**, 40 (275) **YS**, 22 **El**
ANSI/ASTM A 216	WCC	US	Castings	0.25 **C**, 1.20 **Mn**, 0.60 **Si**, 0.04 **P**, 0.045 **S**	**Annealed, or normalized, or normalized, tempered**: all **diam**, 70 (485) **TS**, 40 (275) **YS**, 22 **El**
ANSI/ASTM A 487	Class C and CN	US	Sand castings	0.25 **C**, 1.20 **Mn**, 0.60 **Si**, 0.03 **V**, 0.04 **P**, 0.045 **S**	**Normalized and tempered**: all **diam**, 70 (485) **TS**, 40 (275) **YS**, 22 **El**
ANSI/ASTM A 487	Class AQ	US	Sand castings	0.25 **C**, 0.75 **Mn**, 0.60 **Si**, 0.03 **V**, 0.04 **P**, 0.045 **S**	**Quenched and tempered**: all **diam**, 70 (485) **TS**, 30 (205) **YS**, 24 **El**
ANSI/ASTM A 643	Grade A Class 1	US	Sand castings	0.25 **C**, 1.20 **Mn**, 0.60 **Si**, 0.045 **P**, 0.045 **S**; 1.00 other elements, total	**Normalized and tempered or quenched and tempered**: >2 **diam**, 70 (485) **TS**, 40 (275) **YS**, 22 **El**

CAST CARBON STEELS

specification number	designation	country	product forms	composition	mechanical properties (see page iv for explanation)
ASTM A 27	Grade 70–40	US	Castings	0.25 **C**, 1.20 **Mn**, 0.80 **Si**, 0.05 **P**, 0.06 **S**	**Annealed or normalized or quenched and tempered**: all **diam**, 70 (485) **TS**, 40 (275) **YS**, 22 **El**
ANSI/ASTM A 216	Grade WCC	US	Sand casting	0.25 **C**, 1.20 **Mn**, 0.60 **Si**, 0.04 **P**, 0.045 **S**; 1.00 max, other elements, total	**Annealed or normalized or normalized and tempered**: all **diam**, 70 (485) **TS**, 40 (275) **YS**, 22 **El**
ANSI/ASTM A 352	Grade LCC	US	Sand castings	0.25 **C**, 1.20 **Mn**, 0.60 **Si**, 0.04 **P**, 0.045 **S**	**Normalized and tempered or quenched and tempered**: all **diam**, 70 (485) **TS**, 40 (275) **YS**, 22 **El**
ASTM A 643	Grade A 1	US	Castings	0.25 **C**, 1.20 **Mn**, 0.60 **Si**, 0.40 **Cr**, 0.25 **Mo**, 0.50 **Ni**, 0.03 **V**, 0.50 **Cu**, 0.045 **P**, 0.045 **S**, 0.10 **W**	**Normalized, quenched and tempered**: all **diam**, 70 (485) **TS**, 40 (275) **YS**, 22 **El**
ASTM A 487	Grade C, CN	US	Castings	0.25 **C**, 1.20 **Mn**, 0.60 **Si**, 0.40 **Cr**, 0.25 **Mo**, 0.50 **Ni**, 0.03 **V**, 0.50 **Cu**, 0.04 **P**, 0.045 **S**, 0.10 **W**	**Normalized and tempered**: all **diam**, 70 (485) **TS**, 40 (275) **YS**, 22 **El**
ASTM A 487	Grade AQ	US	Castings	0.25 **C**, 0.75 **Mn**, 0.60 **Si**, 0.40 **Cr**, 0.25 **Mo**, 0.50 **Ni**, 0.03 **V**, 0.50 **Cu**, 0.04 **P**, 0.045 **S**, 0.10 **W**	**Quenched and tempered**: all **diam**, 70 (485) **TS**, 30 (205) **YS**, 24 **El**
ASTM A 356	Grade 5	US	Castings	0.25 **C**, 0.70 **Mn**, 0.60 **Si**, 0.40–0.70 **Cr**, 0.40–0.60 **Mo**, 0.035 **P**, 0.030 **S**	**Normalized and tempered**: all **diam**, 70 (485) **TS**, 40 (275) **YS**, 22 **El**
ASTM A 352	Grade LC2	US	Castings	0.25 **C**, 0.50–0.80 **Mn**, 0.60 **Si**, 2.00–3.00 **Ni**, 0.04 **P**, 0.045 **S**	**Normalized and tempered, or quenched and tempered**: all **diam**, 70 (485) **TS**, 40 (275) **YS**, 24 **El**
ASTM A 216	Grade WCC	US	Castings	0.25 **C**, 1.20 **Mn**, 0.60 **Si**, 0.40 **Cr**, 0.25 **Mo**, 0.50 **Ni**, 0.03 **V**, 0.50 **Cu**, 0.04 **P**, 0.045 **S**	**Annealed, normalized, normalized and tempered**: all **diam**, 70 (485) **TS**, 40 (275) **YS**, 22 **El**
ANSI/ASTM A 352	LC2	US	Castings: ferritic	0.25 **C**, 0.50–0.80 **Mn**, 0.60 **Si**, 2.00–3.00 **Ni**, 0.040 **P**, 0.045 **S**	**Quenched, tempered**: all **diam**, 70 (485) **TS**, 40 (275) **YS**, 24 **El**
ANSI/ASTM A 352	Grade LC2	US	Sand castings	0.25 **C**, 0.50–0.80 **Mn**, 0.60 **Si**, 2.00–3.00 **Ni**, 0.04 **P**, 0.045 **S**	**Normalized and tempered or quenched and tempered**: all **diam**, 70 (485) **TS**, 40 (275) **YS**, 24 **El**
ASTM A 356	Grade 5	US	Castings	0.25 **C**, 0.70 **Mn**, 0.60 **Si**, 0.40–0.70 **Cr**, 0.40–0.60 **Mo**, 0.035 **P**, 0.030 **S**	**Normalized or tempered**: all **diam**, 70 (485) **TS**, 40 (275) **YS**, 22 **El**
NOM–B–356	Class WCC	Mexico	Castings	0.25 **C**, 1.20 **Mn**, 0.60 **Si**, 0.040 **P**, 0.045 **S**	**Annealed and normalized or normalized and quenched**: all **diam**, (483) **TS**, (276) **YS**, 22 **El**
ASTM A–660–75	Grade WCC	US	Pipe, centrifugally cast	0.25 **C**, 1.20 **Mn**, 0.60 **Si**, 0.04 **P**, 0.045 **S**	**As agreed**: all **diam**, 70 (483) **TS**, 40 (276) **YS**, 22 **El**
ANSI/ASTM A 660	Grade WCC	US	Pipe: centrifugally cast	0.25 **C**, 1.20 **Mn**, 0.60 **Si**, 0.04 **P**, 0.045 **S**	**Annealed**: all **diam**, 70 (483) **TS**, 40 (276) **YS**, 22 **El**
CSA G28	70–40	Canada	Castings	0.25 **C**, 1.20 **Mn**, 0.80 **Si**, 0.04 **P**, 0.04 **S**	**Full annealed, normalized, normalized and tempered, quenched and tempered**: all **diam**, (483) **TS**, (276) **YS**, 22 **El**
ASTM A 27	Grade 70–40	US	Castings	0.25 **C**, 1.20 **Mn**, 0.80 **Si**, 0.40 **Cr**, 0.20 **Mo**, 0.50 **Ni**, 0.30 **Cu**, 0.05 **P**, 0.065 **S**	**Annealed, normalized, normalized and tempered, quenched and tempered**: all **diam**, 70 (483) **TS**, 40 (276) **YS**, 22 **El**
JIS G 5152	Class 21	Japan	Castings, tube (centrifugally cast)	0.25 **C**, 0.50–0.80 **Mn**, 0.60 **Si**, 2.00–3.00 **Ni**, 0.040 **P**, 0.040 **S**	**Annealed, normalized, quenched and tempered**: all **diam**, (481) **TS**, (275) **YS**, 21 **El**
UNI 3608–74	G 20 MoCr 52	Italy	Castings	0.25 **C**, 0.80 **Mn**, 0.50 **Si**, 0.40–0.60 **Cr**, 0.45–0.65 **Mo**, 0.035 **P**, 0.035 **S**	**As agreed**: all **diam**, (480) **TS**, (275) **YS**, 20 **El**
UNI 7316–74	Fe G 49–2	Italy	Castings	0.25 **C**, 1.20 **Mn**, 0.50 **Si**, 1.0 **Cr**+**Cu**+**Mo**+**Ni**+**W**, 0.035 **P**, 0.035 **S**	**Annealed, normalized or normalized and tempered**: all **diam**, (480) **TS**, (275) **YS**, 18 **El**
DGS 8081		UK	Sand castings	0.25 **C**, 0.50–0.90 **Mn**	**Annealed and normalized**: all **diam**, (460) **TS**

CAST CARBON STEELS

specification number	designation	country	product forms	composition	mechanical properties (see page iv for explanation)
IS 3038	Grade 2	India	Castings	0.25 **C**, 0.50–1.00 **Mn**, 0.20–0.50 **Si**, 0.40–0.70 **Mo**, 0.040 **P**, 0.045 **S**	**As agreed**: (25) diam, (460) **TS**, (250) **YS**, 17 **El**
BS 3100/1398	Grade A	UK	Sand castings	0.25 **C**, 0.4–0.7 **Mo**	**Annealed or annealed and normalized**: all **diam**, (460) **TS**, (275) **YS**, 18 **El**
JIS G 5151	Class 11	Japan	Castings	0.25 **C**, 0.50–0.80 **Mn**, 0.60 **Si**, 0.45–0.65 **Mo**, 0.040 **P**, 0.040 **S**	**Annealed, normalized, quenched, tempered**: all **diam**, (451) **TS**, (245) **YS**, 22 **El**
JIS G 5152	Class 11	Japan	Castings, tube (centrifugally cast)	0.25 **C**, 0.50–0.80 **Mn**, 0.60 **Si**, 0.45–0.65 **Mo**, 0.040 **P**, 0.040 **S**	**Annealed, normalized, quenched and tempered**: all **diam**, (451) **TS**, (245) **YS**, 21 **El**
NFA 32–051	E 23–45–M	France	Castings	0.25 **C**, 0.50 **Si**, 0.040 **P**, 0.040 **S**	**Annealed, normalized, or quenched and tempered**: all **diam**, (450) **TS**, (230) **YS**, 22 **El**
SIS 14 13 05	SIS 13 05–02	Sweden	Castings	0.25 **C**, 0.7 **Mn**, 0.5 **Si**, 0.040 **P**, 0.040 **S**	**Annealed**: all **diam**, (450) **TS**, (230) **YS**
SFS 356		Finland	Castings	0.25 **C**, 0.70 **Mn**, 0.50 **Si**, 0.040 **P**, 0.040 **S**	**Annealed or normalized**: all **diam**, (450) **TS**, (230) **YS**, 22 **El**
ISO 3755	Grade 23–45	ISO	Sand castings	0.25 **C**, 0.040 **P**, 0.040 **S**	**As cast and annealed or normalized or normalized and tempered or quenched and tempered**: all **diam**, (450) **TS**, (230) **YS**, 22 **El**
NF A 32–053	F CI–M	France	Castings	0.25 **C**, 0.80 **Mn**, 0.50 **Si**, 0.45–0.65 **Mo**, 0.040 **P**, 0.035 **S**	**As cast**: all **diam**, (450) **TS**, (230) **YS**, 18 **El**
NF A 32–053	F CZ–M	France	Castings	0.25 **C**, 0.80 **Mn**, 0.50 **Si**, 2.5–4.0 **Ni**, 0.040 **P**, 0.035 **S**	**As cast**: all **diam**, (450) **TS**, (230) **YS**, 18 **El**
NF A 32–053	FB–M	France	Castings	0.25 **C**, 1.20 **Mn**, 0.50 **Si**, 1.00 **Ni**, 0.040 **P**, 0.035 **S**	**As cast**: all **diam**, (450) **TS**, (230) **YS**, 16 **El**
ASTM A 356	Grade 2	US	Castings	0.25 **C**, 0.70 **Mn**, 0.60 **Si**, 0.45–0.65 **Mo**, 0.035 **P**, 0.030 **S**	**Normalized and tempered**: all **diam**, 65 (450) **TS**, 35 (240) **YS**, 22 **El**
ASTM A 352	Grade LC1	US	Castings	0.25 **C**, 0.50–0.80 **Mn**, 0.60 **Si**, 0.45–0.65 **Mo**, 0.04 **P**, 0.045 **S**	**Normalized and tempered, or quenched and tempered**: all **diam**, 65 (450) **TS**, 35 (240) **YS**, 24 **El**
ASTM A 217	Grade WC1	US	Castings	0.25 **C**, 0.50–0.80 **Mn**, 0.60 **Si**, 0.35 **Cr**, 0.45–0.65 **Mo**, 0.50 **Ni**, 0.50 **Cu**, 0.04 **P**, 0.045 **S**, 0.10 **W**	**Normalized and tempered**: all **diam**, 65 (450) **TS**, 35 (240) **YS**, 24 **El**
ANSI/ASTM A 352	LC1	US	Castings: ferritic	0.25 **C**, 0.50–0.80 **Mn**, 0.60 **Si**, 0.45–0.65 **Mo**, 0.040 **P**, 0.045 **S**	**Quenched, tempered**: all **diam**, 65 (450) **TS**, 35 (240) **YS**, 24 **El**
ANSI/ASTM A 217	WC1	US	Castings	0.25 **C**, 0.50–0.80 **Mn**, 0.60 **Si**, 0.45–0.65 **Mo**, 0.040 **P**, 0.045 **S**	**Normalized, tempered**: all **diam**, 65 (450) **TS**, 35 (240) **YS**, 24 **El**
ANSI/ASTM A 352	Grade LC1	US	Sand castings	0.25 **C**, 0.50–0.80 **Mn**, 0.60 **Si**, 0.45–0.65 **Mo**, 0.04 **P**, 0.045 **S**	**Normalized and tempered or quenched and tempered**: all **diam**, 65 (450) **TS**, 35 (240) **YS**, 24 **El**
ASTM A 356	Grade 2	US	Castings	0.25 **C**, 0.70 **Mn**, 0.60 **Si**, 0.45–0.65 **Mo**, 0.035 **P**, 0.030 **S**	**Normalized or tempered**: all **diam**, 65 (450) **TS**, 35 (240) **YS**, 22 **El**
ASTM A 426	Grade CP1	US	Pipe: centrifugally cast	0.25 **C**, 0.30–0.80 **Mn**, 0.10–0.50 **Si**, 0.44–0.65 **Mo**, 0.50 **Ni**, 0.50 **Cu**, 0.045 **P**, 0.045 **S**, 0.10 **W**	**Normalized and tempered**: all **diam**, (448) **TS**, (241) **YS**, 24 **El**
MIL–S–870B		US	Sand castings	0.25 **C**, 0.50–0.75 **Mn**, 0.20–0.60 **Si**, 0.20 **Cr**, 0.40–0.60 **Mo**, 1.00 **Ni**, 0.30 **Cu**, 0.05 **P**, 0.05 **S**	**Annealed or normalized and tempered**: all **diam**, 65 (448) **TS**, 35 (241) **YS**, 20 **El**
UNI 3608	CG 20	Italy	Castings	0.25 **C**, 0.80 **Mn**, 0.50 **Si**, 0.035 **P**, 0.035 **S**	**As agreed**: all **diam**, (440) **TS**, (235) **YS**, 22 **El**
UNI 7317–74	G22 Mn3	Italy	Castings	0.25 **C**, 1.0 **Mn**, 0.60 **Si**, 0.035 **P**, 0.035 **S**	**Normalized**: all **diam**, (440) **TS**, (235) **YS**, 21 **El**; **Tempered**: all **diam**, (440) **TS**, (235) **YS**, 21 **El**
UNI 3608	G 20 Mo 5	Italy	Castings	0.25 **C**, 0.80 **Mn**, 0.50 **Si**, 0.40–0.60 **Mo**, 0.035 **P**, 0.035 **S**	**As agreed**: all **diam**, (440) **TS**, (245) **YS**, 20 **El**

CAST CARBON STEELS

specification number	designation	country	product forms	composition	mechanical properties (see page iv for explanation)
UNI 7317–74	G 22 Ni 10	Italy	Castings	0.25 **C**, 0.80 **Mn**, 0.60 **Si**, 2.0–3.0 **Ni**, 0.035 **P**, 0.035 **S**	**Normalized and tempered**: all **diam**, (440) **TS**, (275) **YS**, 21 **El**
UNI 7317–74	G 22 Mo 5	Italy	Castings	0.25 **C**, 0.80 **Mn**, 0.60 **Si**, 0.45–0.65 **Mo**, 0.035 **P**, 0.035 **S**	**Normalized and tempered**: all **diam**, (440) **TS**, (235) **YS**, 21 **El**
BS 1504–161	Grade A	UK	Sand castings	0.25 **C**	**Annealed or normalized or annealed and normalized**: all **diam**, (430) **TS**, (215) **YS**
BS 3100/592	Grade A	UK	Sand castings	0.25 **C**	**Annealed, annealed and normalized, normalized and tempered, or hardened and tempered**: all **diam**, (430) **TS**, (230) **YS**, 22 **El**
BS 3146 Part 1	CLA1: Grade A	UK	Investment and precision castings	0.25 **C**	**Annealed, annealed and normalized, normalized, normalized and tempered, or hardened and tempered**: all **diam**, (430) **TS**, (215) **YS**, 22 **El**
BS 1504–161	Grade 430	UK	Castings	0.25 **C**, 0.90 **Mn**, 0.60 **Si**, 0.25 **Cr**, 0.15 **Mo**, 0.40 **Ni**, 0.30 **Cu**, 0.050 **P**, 0.050 **S**	**Austenitized**: all **diam**, (430) **TS**, (230) **YS**, 22 **El**
ASTM A 352–76	Grade LCA	US	Castings	0.25 **C**, 0.70 **Mn**, 0.60 **Si**, 0.04 **P**, 0.045 **S**	**Normalized and tempered or quenched and tempered**: all **diam**, (415) **TS**, (205) **YS**, 24 **El**
ANSI/ASTM A 487	AN	US	Castings	0.25 **C**, 0.75 **Mn**, 0.60 **Si**, 0.03 **V**, 0.04 **P**, 0.045 **S**	**Normalized, tempered**: all **diam**, 60 (415) **TS**, 30 (207) **YS**, 24 **El**
ANSI/ASTM A 352	LCA	US	Castings: ferritic	0.25 **C**, 0.70 **Mn**, 0.60 **Si**, 0.04 **P**, 0.045 **S**	**Quenched, tempered**: all **diam**, 60 (415) **TS**, 30 (205) **YS**, 24 **El**
ANSI/ASTM A 487	Class A and AN	US	Sand castings	0.25 **C**, 0.75 **Mn**, 0.60 **Si**, 0.03 **V**, 0.04 **P**, 0.045 **S**	**Normalized and tempered**: all **diam**, 60 (415) **TS**, 30 (205) **YS**, 24 **El**
ASTM A 27	Grade U–60–30	US	Castings	0.25 **C**, 0.75 **Mn**, 0.80 **Si**, 0.05 **P**, 0.06 **S**	**As cast**: all **diam**, 60 (415) **TS**, 30 (205) **YS**, 22 **El**
ANSI/ASTM A 216	Grade WCA	US	Sand castings	0.25 **C**, 0.70 **Mn**, 0.60 **Si**, 0.04 **P**, 0.045 **S**; 1.00 max, other elements total	**Annealed or normalized or normalized and tempered**: all **diam**, 60 (415) **TS**, 30 (205) **YS**, 24 **El**
ANSI/ASTM A 352	Grade LCA	US	Sand castings	0.25 **C**, 0.70 **Mn**, 0.60 **Si**, 0.04 **P**, 0.045 **S**	**Normalized and tempered or quenched and tempered**: all **diam**, 60 (415) **TS**, 30 (205) **YS**, 24 **El**
ASTM A 487	Grade A, AN	US	Castings	0.25 **C**, 0.75 **Mn**, 0.60 **Si**, 0.40 **Cr**, 0.25 **Mo**, 0.50 **Ni**, 0.03 **V**, 0.50 **Cu**, 0.04 **P**, 0.045 **S**, 0.10 **W**	**Normalized and tempered**: all **diam**, 60 (415) **TS**, 30 (205) **YS**, 24 **El**
ASTM A 216	Grade WCA	US	Castings	0.25 **C**, 0.70 **Mn**, 0.60 **Si**, 0.40 **Cr**, 0.25 **Mo**, 0.50 **Ni**, 0.03 **V**, 0.50 **Cu**, 0.04 **P**, 0.045 **S**	**Annealed, normalized, normalized and tempered**: all **diam**, 60 (415) **TS**, 30 (205) **YS**, 24 **El**
NOM-B-356	Class WCA	Mexico	Castings	0.25 **C**, 0.70 **Mn**, 0.60 **Si**, 0.040 **P**, 0.045 **S**	**Annealed and normalized or normalized and quenched**: all **diam**, (414) **TS**, (207) **YS**, 24 **El**
ASTM A–660–75	Grade WCA	US	Pipe, centrifugally cast	0.25 **C**, 0.70 **Mn**, 0.60 **Si**, 0.04 **P**, 0.045 **S**	**As agreed**: all **diam**, 60 (414) **TS**, 30 (207) **YS**, 24 **El**
SAE Automotive J435a	Grade 0025	US	Castings	0.25 **C**, 0.75 **Mn**, 0.80 **Si**, 0.050 **P**, 0.060 **S**	**Annealed, normalized, normalized and tempered**: all **diam**, 60 (414) **TS**, 30 (207) **YS**, 22 **El**
ANSI/ASTM A 660	Grade WCA	US	Pipe: centrifugally cast	0.25 **C**, 0.70 **Mn**, 0.60 **Si**, 0.04 **P**, 0.045 **S**	**Annealed**: all **diam**, 60 (414) **TS**, 30 (207) **YS**, 24 **El**
ANSI/ASTM A 487	A	US	Castings	0.25 **C**, 0.75 **Mn**, 0.60 **Si**, 0.03 **V**, 0.04 **P**, 0.045 **S**	**Normalized, tempered**: all **diam**, 60 (414) **TS**, 30 (207) **YS**, 24 **El**
ANSI/ASTM A 216	WCA	US	Castings	0.25 **C**, 0.70 **Mn**, 0.60 **Si**, 0.04 **P**, 0.045 **S**	**Annealed or normalized or normalized, tempered**: all **diam**, 60 (414) **TS**, 30 (205) **YS**, 24 **El**
ASTM A 27	Grade U–60–30	US	Castings	0.25 **C**, 0.75 **Mn**, 0.80 **Si**, 0.40 **Cr**, 0.20 **Mo**, 0.50 **Ni**, 0.30 **Cu**, 0.05 **P**, 0.06 **S**	**Annealed**: all **diam**, 60 (414) **TS**, 30 (207) **YS**, 22 **El**

CAST CARBON STEELS

specification number	designation	country	product forms	composition	mechanical properties (see page iv for explanation)
JIS G 5151	Class 1	Japan	Castings	0.25 **C**, 0.70 **Mn**, 0.60 **Si**, 0.040 **P**, 0.040 **S**	**Annealed, normalized, quenched, tempered**: all **diam**, (412) **TS**, (206) **YS**, 21 **El**
IS 4491	Grade 2	India	Castings	0.25 **C**, 0.50 **Mn**, 0.60 **Si**, 0.050 **P**, 0.050 **S**; 0.80 other elements, total	**Annealed**: all **diam**, (400) **TS**, (215) **YS**, 22 **El**
BS 3100/1617	Grade B	UK	Sand castings	0.25 **C**	**Annealed or normalized**: all **diam**, (400) **TS**, (215) **YS**, 22 **El**
NFA 32–053	FA–M	France	Castings	0.25 **C**, 1.00 **Mn**, 0.50 **Si**, 0.040 **P**, 0.040 **S**	**As cast**: all **diam**, (380) **TS**, (200) **YS**, 18 **El**
ASTM A 27	Grade N–1	US	Castings	0.25 **C**, 0.75 **Mn**, 0.80 **Si**, 0.05 **P**, 0.06 **S**	
DGN–B–352	Class C25	Mexico	Castings	0.25 **C**, 0.90 **Mn**, 0.80 **Si**, 0.050 **P**, 0.060 **S**	
NOM–B–141	Class W–C1	Mexico	Castings	0.25 **C**, 0.50–0.80 **Mn**, 0.60 **Si**, 0.45–0.65 **Mo**, 0.040 **P**, 0.045 **S**	
ASTM A 27	Grade N–1	US	Castings	0.25 **C**, 0.75 **Mn**, 0.80 **Si**, 0.40 **Cr**, 0.20 **Mo**, 0.50 **Ni**, 0.30 **Cu**, 0.05 **P**, 0.06 **S**	
NF A 32–055	FC 2–M	France	Castings	0.23 **C**, 1.50 **Mn**, 0.50 **Si**, 2.5–4.0 **Ni**, 0.03 **P**, 0.03 **S**	**Quenched**: all **diam**, (450) **TS**, (230) **YS**, 18 **El**
UNI 7316–74	Fe G 42	Italy	Castings	0.23 **C**, 1.0 **Mn**, 0.50 **Si**, 1.0 **Cr + Cu + Mo + Ni + W**, 0.04 **P**, 0.045 **S**	**Annealed, normalized or normalized and tempered**: all **diam**, (410) **TS**, (205) **YS**, 22 **El**
SIS 14 22 25	SIS 22 25–25	Sweden	Castings	0.22–0.29 **C**, 0.50–0.80 **Mn**, 0.30–0.60 **Si**, 0.90–1.20 **Cr**, 0.15–0.25 **Mo**, 0.30 **Ni**	**Quenched, tempered**: all **diam**, (882) **TS**, (682) **YS**, 8 **El**
BS HC 9		UK	Castings: aircraft quality	0.22–0.34 **C**, 0.30–0.80 **Mn**, 0.30–0.60 **Si**, 0.50–1.30 **Cr**, 0.20–0.70 **Mo**, 0.50–3.0 **Ni**, 0.40 **Cu**, 0.025 **P**, 0.025 **S**	**Annealed, hardened and tempered**: all **diam**, (880) **TS**, (700) **YS**, 8 **El**
SIS 14 22 25	SIS 22 25–25	Sweden	Castings	0.22–0.29 **C**, 0.50–0.80 **Mn**, 0.30–0.60 **Si**, 0.90–1.20 **Cr**, 0.15–0.25 **Mo**, 0.30 **Ni**, 0.035 **P**, 0.035 **S**	**Quenched and tempered**: (<25) **diam**, (880) **TS**, (690) **YS**, 8 **El**
VSM 10697	GS–25 CrMo 4 V 80/1.7218	Switzerland	Castings	0.22–0.29 **C**, 0.50–0.80 **Mn**, 0.30–0.50 **Si**, 0.90–1.20 **Cr**, 0.15–0.30 **Mo**, 0.50 **Ni**, 0.030 **P**, 0.030 **S**	**Quenched and tempered**: all **diam**, (800) **TS**, (600) **YS**, 11 **El**
SIS 14 22 25	SIS 22 25–24	Sweden	Castings	0.22–0.29 **C**, 0.50–0.80 **Mn**, 0.30–0.60 **Si**, 0.90–1.20 **Cr**, 0.15–0.25 **Mo**, 0.30 **Ni**	**Quenched, tempered**: all **diam**, (784) **TS**, (588) **YS**, 10 **El**
SIS 14 22 25	SIS 22 25–24	Sweden	Castings	0.22–0.29 **C**, 0.50–0.80 **Mn**, 0.30–0.60 **Si**, 0.90–1.20 **Cr**, 0.15–0.25 **Mo**, 0.30 **Ni**, 0.035 **P**, 0.035 **S**	**Quenched and tempered**: (<63) **diam**, (780) **TS**, (590) **YS**, 10 **El**
VSM 10697	GS–25 CrMo 4 V 70/1.7218	Switzerland	Castings	0.22–0.29 **C**, 0.50–0.80 **Mn**, 0.30–0.50 **Si**, 0.90–1.20 **Cr**, 0.15–0.30 **Mo**, 0.50 **Ni**, 0.030 **P**, 0.030 **S**	**Quenched and tempered**: all **diam**, (700) **TS**, (500) **YS**, 14 **El**
SIS 14 22 25	SIS 22 25–23	Sweden	Castings	0.22–0.29 **C**, 0.50–0.80 **Mn**, 0.30–0.60 **Si**, 0.90–1.20 **Cr**, 0.15–0.25 **Mo**, 0.30 **Ni**, 0.035 **P**, 0.035 **S**	**Quenched and tempered**: (<63) **diam**, (690) **TS**, (490) **YS**, 12 **El**
SIS 14 22 25	SIS 22 25–23	Sweden	Castings	0.22–0.29 **C**, 0.50–0.80 **Mn**, 0.30–0.60 **Si**, 0.90–1.20 **Cr**, 0.15–0.25 **Mo**, 0.30 **Ni**	**Quenched, tempered**: all **diam**, (686) **TS**, (490) **YS**, 12 **El**
VSM 10697	GS–25 CrMo 4 V 60/1.7218	Switzerland	Castings	0.22–0.29 **C**, 0.50–0.80 **Mn**, 0.30–0.50 **Si**, 0.90–1.2 **Cr**, 0.15–0.30 **Mo**, 0.50 **Ni**, 0.030 **P**, 0.030 **S**	**Quenched and tempered**: all **diam**, (600) **TS**, (400) **YS**, 16 **El**
SIS 14 22 25	SIS 22 25–21	Sweden	Castings	0.22–0.29 **C**, 0.50–0.80 **Mn**, 0.30–0.60 **Si**, 0.90–1.20 **Cr**, 0.15–0.25 **Mo**, 0.30 **Ni**, 0.035 **P**, 0.035 **S**	
SIS 14 22 25	SIS 22 25–21	Sweden	Castings	0.22–0.29 **C**, 0.50–0.80 **Mn**, 0.30–0.60 **Si**, 0.90–1.20 **Cr**, 0.15–0.25 **Mo**, 0.30 **Ni**	

CAST CARBON STEELS

specification number	designation	country	product forms	composition	mechanical properties (see page iv for explanation)
ASTM A 352	Grade LC2-1	US	Castings	0.22 C, 0.55–0.75 Mn, 0.50 Si, 1.35–1.85 Cr, 0.30–0.60 Mo, 2.50–3.50 Ni, 0.04 P, 0.045 S	**Normalized and tempered, or quenched and tempered**: all diam, 105 (725) TS, 80 (550) YS, 18 El
ANSI/ASTM A 352	LC2-1	US	Castings: ferritic	0.22 C, 0.55–0.75 Mn, 0.50 Si, 1.35–1.85 Cr, 0.30–0.60 Mo, 2.50–3.50 Ni, 0.040 P, 0.045 S	**Quenched, tempered**: all diam, 105 (725) TS, 80 (550) YS, 18 El
ANSI/ASTM A 352	Grade LC2-1	US	Sand castings	0.22 C, 0.55–0.75 Mn, 0.50 Si, 1.35–1.85 Cr, 0.30–0.60 Mo, 2.50–3.50 Ni, 0.04 P, 0.045 S	**Normalized and tempered or quenched and tempered**: all diam, 105 (725) TS, 80 (550) YS, 18 El
NF A 32-055	18 CD 2 05-M	France	Castings	0.22 C, 0.90 Mn, 0.60 Si, 0.4–0.65 Cr, 0.45–0.70 Mo, 0.040 P, 0.040 S	**Normalized**: all diam, (500) TS, (300) YS, 18 El
JIS G 5201	Class 2	Japan	Pipe: centrifugally cast	0.22 C, 0.040 P, 0.040 S	**Annealed, normalized, quenched, tempered**: all diam, (481) TS, (275) YS, 20 El
JIS G 5102	Class 2	Japan	Castings	0.22 C, 0.040 P, 0.040 S	**Annealed, normalized, quenched and tempered**: all diam, (481) TS, (275) YS, 20 El
NFA 32-053	FB1-M	France	Castings	0.22 C, 1.50 Mn, 0.50 Si, 0.5–2.0 Ni, 0.040 P, 0.035 S	**As cast**: all diam, (450) TS, (230) YS, 18 El
JIS G 5202	Class 1	Japan	Pipe: centrifugally cast	0.22 C, 1.10 Mn, 0.60 Si, 0.040 P, 0.040 S	**Annealed, normalized, quenched, tempered**: all diam, (412) TS, (245) YS, 21 El
JIS G 5201	Class 1	Japan	Pipe: centrifugally cast	0.22 C, 0.040 P, 0.040 S	**Annealed, normalized, quenched, tempered**: all diam, (412) TS, (235) YS, 21 El
JIS G 5102	Class 1	Japan	Castings	0.22 C, 0.040 P, 0.040 S	**Annealed, normalized, quenched and tempered**: all diam, (412) TS, (235) YS, 21 El
MIL-S-23008B	Hy 100	US	Sand castings	0.22 C, 0.55–0.75 Mn, 0.50 Si, 1.35–1.85 Cr, 0.30–0.60 Mo, 2.75–3.50 Ni, 0.20 Cu, 0.020 P, 0.015 S	**Quenched and tempered**: all diam, 100 (689) YS, 18 El
NF A 32-055	FC-M	France	Castings	0.2 C, 1.50 Mn, 0.50 Si, 1.0 Ni, 0.035 P, 0.035 S	**Normalized or quenched**: all diam, (520) TS, (260) YS, 16 El
NF A 32-855	FB-M	France	Castings	0.2 C, 1.20 Mn, 0.50 Si, 1.0 Ni, 0.035 P, 0.035 S	**Normalized or quenched**: all diam, (450) TS, (230) YS, 16 El
NF A 32-055	20 DS-M	France	Castings	0.2 C, 1.0 Mn, 0.60 Si, 0.40–0.70 Mo, 0.040 P, 0.040 S	**Normalized or quenched**: all diam, (450) TS, (250) YS, 21 El
BS HC 10		UK	Castings: air craft quality	0.2–0.3 C, 0.30–0.80 Mn, 0.30–0.60 Si, 0.50–1.30 Cr, 0.20–0.70 Mo, Annealed, hardened and tempered: all diam, (	**Annealed, hardened and tempered El**
BS HC 8		UK	Castings: aircraft quality	0.2–0.3 C, 0.30–0.80 Mn, 0.30–0.75 Si, 2.5–3.5 Cr, 0.40–0.70 Mo, 0.40 Ni, 0.020 V, 0.40 Cu, 0.025 P, 0.025 S	**Annealed, hardened and tempered**: all diam, (1150) TS, (940) YS, 5 El
BS HC 7		UK	Castings: aircraft quality	0.2–0.3 C, 0.30–0.80 Mn, 0.30–0.705 Si, 2.5–3.5 Cr, 0.40–0.70 Mo, 0.40 Ni, 0.020 V, 0.40 Cu, 0.025 P, 0.025 S	**Annealed, hardened, and tempered**: all diam, (880) TS, (700) YS, 8 El
BS HC 6		UK	Castings: air quality	0.20–0.30 C, 0.30–0.6 Mn, 0.30–0.75 Si, 2.90–3.50 Cr, 0.40–0.70 Mo, 0.400 Ni, 0.020 V, 0.30 Cu, 0.020 P, 0.020 S	**Annealed, hardened and tempered**: all diam, (850) TS, (600) YS, 8 El

CAST CARBON STEELS

specification number	designation	country	product forms	composition	mechanical properties (see page iv for explanation)
DTD 5219		UK	Investment and precision castings	0.20–0.30 **C**, 0.9–1.2 **Cr**, 0.25–0.80 **Mo**	**Annealed and hardened and tempered**: all **diam**, (685) **TS**, (460) **YS**, 11 **El**
JIS G 5111	Class 1, SC Cr M 1	Japan	Castings, pipe (centrifugally cast)	0.20–0.30 **C**, 0.50–0.80 **Mn**, 0.30–0.60 **Si**, 0.80–1.20 **Cr**, 0.15–0.35 **Mo**, 0.040 **P**, 0.040 **S**	**Normalized and tempered**: all **diam**, (637) **TS**, (392) **YS**, 13 **El**; **Quenched and tempered**: all **diam**, (686) **TS**, (490) **YS**, 13 **El**
JIS G 5111	Class 1, SC Mn 1	Japan	Castings, pipe (centrifugally cast)	0.20–0.30 **C**, 1.00–1.60 **Mn**, 0.30–0.60 **Si**, 0.040 **P**, 0.040 **S**	**Normalized and tempered**: all **diam**, (539) **TS**, (275) **YS**, 17 **El**; **Quenched and tempered**: all **diam**, (588) **TS**, (392) **YS**, 17 **El**
IS 2708	Grade 2	India	Castings	0.20–0.26 **C**, 1.20–1.70 **Mn**, 0.30–0.60 **Si**, 0.050 **P**, 0.050 **S**; 1.00 max, other elements, total	**As agreed**: all **diam**, (540) **TS**, (330) **YS**, 16 **El**
ASTM A 643	Grade D2	US	Castings	0.20 **C**, 0.40–0.70 **Mn**, 0.60 **Si**, 1.50–2.00 **Cr**, 0.40–0.60 **Mo**, 2.75–3.90 **Ni**, 0.03 **V**, 0.50 **Cu**, 0.020 **P**, 0.020 **S**, 0.10 **W**	**Normalized and tempered or quenched and tempered**: all **diam**, 115 (795) **TS**, 100 (690) **YS**, 13 **El**
ASTM A 487	Grade 7Q	US	Castings	0.20 **C**, 0.60–1.00 **Mn**, 0.80 **Si**, 0.40–0.80 **Cr**, 0.40–0.60 **Mo**, 0.70–1.00 **Ni**, 0.03 **V**, 0.15–0.50 **Cu**, 0.002–.0006 **B**, 0.04 **P**, 0.045 **S**, 0.10 **W**	**Quenched and tempered**: all **diam**, 115 (795) **TS**, 100 (690) **YS**, 15 **El**
ANSI/ASTM A 487	7Q	US	Castings	0.20 **C**, 0.60–1.00 **Mn**, 0.80 **Si**, 0.40–0.80 **Cr**, 0.40–0.60 **Mo**, 0.70–1.00 **Ni**, 0.03–0.1 **V**, 0.15–0.50 **Cu**, 0.002–0.006 **B**, 0.04 **P**, 0.045 **S**	**Quenched, tempered**: ≥2.5 (63.5) **diam**, 115 (795) **TS**, 100 (690) **YS**, 15 **El**
ANSI/ASTM A 487	Class 7Q	US	Sand castings	0.20 **C**, 0.60–1.00 **Mn**, 0.80 **Si**, 0.40–0.80 **Cr**, 0.40–0.60 **Mo**, 0.70–1.00 **Ni**, 0.03–0.10 **V**, 0.15–0.50 **Cu**, 0.04 **P**, 0.045 **S**, 0.002–0.006 **B**	**Quenched and tempered**: all **diam**, 115 (795) **TS**, 100 (690) **YS**, 15 **El**
ANSI/ASTM A 643	Grade D, class 2	US	Sand castings	0.20 **C**, 0.40–0.70 **Mn**, 0.60 **Si**, 1.50–2.00 **Cr**, 0.40–0.60 **Mo**, 2.75–3.90 **Ni**, 0.020 **P**, 0.020 **S**	**Normalized and tempered or quenched and tempered**: >2 **diam**, 115 (795) **TS**, 100 (690) **YS**, 13 **El**
IS 7899	Grade 7N, 7Q	India	Castings	0.20 **C**, 0.60–1.00 **Mn**, 0.80 **Si**, 0.40–0.80 **Cr**, 0.40–0.60 **Mo**, 0.70–1.00 **Ni**, 0.03–0.10 **V**, 0.15–0.50 **Cu**, 0.002–0.006 **B**, 0.04 **P**, 0.045 **S**	**Quenched and tempered**: (63.5) max **diam**, (790) **TS**, (690) **YS**, 14 **El**
ANSI/ASTM A 487	Class 12Q	US	Sand castings	0.20 **C**, 0.40–0.70 **Mn**, 0.60 **Si**, 0.50–0.90 **Cr**, 0.90–1.20 **Mo**, 0.60–1.00 **Ni**, 0.03 **V**, 0.040 **P**, 0.045 **S**	**Quenched and tempered**: all **diam**, 105 (725) **TS**, 85 (585) **YS**, 17 **El**
ASTM A643	Grade C3	US	Castings	0.20 **C**, 0.40–0.80 **Mn**, 0.60 **Si**, 2.00–2.75 **Cr**, 0.90–1.20 **Mo**, 0.50 **Ni**, 0.03 **V**, 0.50 **Cu**, 0.035 **P**, 0.035 **S**, 0.10 **W**	**Normalized and tempered or quenched and tempered**: all **diam**, 105 (725) **TS**, 85 (585) **YS**, 15 **El**
ASTM A 643	Grade D1	US	Castings	0.20 **C**, 0.40–0.70 **Mn**, 0.60 **Si**, 1.50–2.00 **Cr**, 0.40–0.60 **Mo**, 2.75–3.90 **Ni**, 0.03 **V**, 0.50 **Cu**, 0.020 **P**, 0.020 **S**, 0.10 **W**	**Normalized and tempered or quenched and tempered**: all **diam**, 105 (725) **TS**, 85 (585) **YS**, 15 **El**
ASTM A 487	Grade 8Q	US	Castings	0.20 **C**, 0.50–0.90 **Mn**, 0.80 **Si**, 2.00–2.75 **Cr**, 0.90–1.10 **Mo**, 0.03 **V**, 0.50 **Cu**, 0.04 **P**, 0.045 **S**, 0.10 **W**	**Quenched and tempered**: all **diam**, 105 (725) **TS**, 85 (585) **YS**, 17 **El**
ASTM A 487	Grade 11Q	US	Castings	0.20 **C**, 0.50–0.90 **Mn**, 0.60 **Si**, 0.50–0.80 **Cr**, 0.45–0.65 **Mo**, 0.70–1.10 **Ni**, 0.03 **V**, 0.50 **Cu**, 0.04 **P**, 0.045 **S**, 0.10 **W**	**Quenched and tempered**: all **diam**, 105 (725) **TS**, 85 (585) **YS**, 17 **El**
ASTM A 487	Grade 12Q	US	Castings	0.20 **C**, 0.40–0.70 **Mn**, 0.60 **Si**, 0.50–0.90 **Cr**, 0.90–1.20 **Mo**, 0.60–1.00 **Ni**, 0.03 **V**, 0.50 **Cu**, 0.04 **P**, 0.045 **S**, 0.10 **W**	**Quenched and tempered**: all **diam**, 105 (725) **TS**, 85 (585) **YS**, 17 **El**
ANSI/ASTM A 487	11Q	US	Castings	0.20 **C**, 0.50–0.80 **Mn**, 0.60 **Si**, 0.50–0.80 **Cr**, 0.45–0.65 **Mo**, 0.70–1.10 **Ni**, 0.030 **V**, 0.04 **P**, 0.045 **S**	**Quenched, tempered**: all **diam**, 105 (725) **TS**, 85 (585) **YS**, 17 **El**

CAST CARBON STEELS

specification number	designation	country	product forms	composition	mechanical properties (see page iv for explanation)
ANSI/ASTM A 487	12Q	US	Castings	0.20 **C**, 0.40–0.70 **Mn**, 0.60 **Si**, 0.50–0.90 **Cr**, 0.90–1.20 **Mo**, 0.60–1.00 **Ni**, 0.030 **V**, 0.040 **P**, 0.045 **S**	**Quenched, tempered**: all **diam**, 105 (725) **TS**, 85 (585) **YS**, 17 **El**
ANSI/ASTM A 487	8Q	US	Castings	0.20 **C**, 0.50–0.90 **Mn**, 0.80 **Si**, 2.00–2.75 **Cr**, 0.90–1.10 **Mo**, 0.03 **V**, 0.04 **P**, 0.045 **S**	**Quenched, tempered**: all **diam**, 105 (725) **TS**, 85 (585) **YS**, 17 **El**
ANSI/ASTM A 487	Class 8Q	US	Sand castings	0.20 **C**, 0.50–0.90 **Mn**, 0.80 **Si**, 2.00–2.75 **Cr**, 0.90–1.10 **Mo**, 0.03 **V**, 0.04 **P**, 0.045 **S**	**Quenched and tempered**: all **diam**, 105 (725) **TS**, 85 (585) **YS**, 17 **El**
ANSI/ASTM A 643	Grade D, class 1	US	Sand castings	0.20 **C**, 0.40–0.70 **Mn**, 0.60 **Si**, 1.50–2.00 **Cr**, 0.40–0.60 **Mo**, 2.75–3.90 **Ni**, 0.020 **P**, 0.020 **S**	**Normalized and tempered or quenched and tempered**: >2 **diam**, 105 (725) **TS**, 85 (585) **YS**, 15 **El**
ANSI/ASTM A 643	Grade C, class 3	US	Sand castings	0.20 **C**, 0.40–0.80 **Mn**, 0.60 **Si**, 2.00–2.75 **Cr**, 0.90–1.20 **Mo**, 0.035 **P**, 0.035 **S**	**Normalized and tempered or quenched and tempered**: >2 **diam**, 105 (725) **TS**, 85 (585) **YS**, 15 **El**
NF A 32–053	FC2–1–M	France	Castings	0.20 **C**, 0.80 **Mn**, 0.50 **Si**, 1.0–2.0 **Cr**, 0.3–0.60 **Mo**, 3.0–4.0 **Ni**, 0.040 **P**, 0.035 **S**	**As cast**: all **diam**, (700) **TS**, (500) **YS**, 12 **El**
ASTM A 643	Grade C2	US	Castings	0.20 **C**, 0.40–0.80 **Mn**, 0.60 **Si**, 2.00–2.75 **Cr**, 0.90–1.20 **Mo**, 0.50 **Ni**, 0.03 **V**, 0.50 **Cu**, 0.035 **P**, 0.035 **S**, 0.10 **W**	**Normalized and tempered or quenched and tempered**: all **diam**, 95 (655) **TS**, 75 (515) **YS**, 18 **El**
ANSI/ASTM A 643	Grade C, class 2	US	Sand castings	0.20 **C**, 0.40–0.80 **Mn**, 0.60 **Si**, 2.00–2.75 **Cr**, 0.90–1.20 **Mo**, 0.035 **P**, 0.035 **S**	**Normalized and tempered or quenched and tempered**: >2 **diam**, 95 (655) **TS**, 75 (515) **YS**, 18 **El**
ANSI/ASTM A 426	CP5	US	Pipe: centrifugally cast	0.20 **C**, 0.30–0.70 **Mn**, 0.75 **Si**, 4.00–6.50 **Cr**, 0.45–0.65 **Mo**, 0.030 **P**, 0.030 **S**	**Normalized and tempered**: all **diam**, 90 (621) **TS**, 60 (414) **YS**, 18 **El**
NOM–B–141	Class C5	Mexico	Castings	0.20 **C**, 0.40–0.70 **Mn**, 4.00–6.50 **Cr**, 0.75 **Si**, 0.45–0.65 **Mo**, 0.040 **P**, 0.045 **S**	**Normalized and annealed**: all **diam**, (621) **TS**, (414) **YS**, 18 **El**
NOM–B–141	Class C12	Mexico	Castings	0.20 **C**, 0.35–0.65 **Mn**, 8.00–10.00 **Cr**, 1.00 **Si**, 0.90–1.20 **Mo**, 0.040 **P**, 0.045 **S**	**Normalized and annealed**: all **diam**, (621) **TS**, (414) **YS**, 18 **El**
ASTM A 426	Grade CP9	US	Pipe: centrifugally cast	0.20 **C**, 0.30–0.65 **Mn**, 0.25–1.00 **Si**, 8.0–10.0 **Cr**, 0.90–1.20 **Mo**, 0.50 **Ni**, 0.50 **Cu**, 0.030 **P**, 0.030 **S**, 0.10 **W**	**Normalized and tempered**: all **diam**, (621) **TS**, (414) **YS**, 18 **El**
ASTM A 426	Grade CP5	US	Pipe: centrifugally cast	0.20 **C**, 0.30–0.70 **Mn**, 0.75 **Si**, 4.0–6.5 **Cr**, 0.45–0.65 **Mo**, 0.50 **Ni**, 0.50 **Cu**, 0.030 **P**, 0.030 **S**, 0.10 **W**	**Normalized and tempered**: all **diam**, (621) **TS**, (414) **YS**, 18 **El**
BS 1504–629		UK	Castings	0.20 **C**, 0.30–0.70 **Mn**, 1.0 **Si**, 8.0–10.0 **Cr**, 0.90–1.2 **Mo**, 0.40 **Ni**, 0.30 **Cu**, 0.040 **P**, 0.040 **S**	**Hardened and tempered**: all **diam**, (620) **TS**, (420) **YS**, 13 **El**
BS 1504–625		UK	Castings	0.20 **C**, 0.40–0.70 **Mn**, 0.75 **Si**, 4.0–6.0 **Cr**, 0.45–0.65 **Mo**, 0.40 **Ni**, 0.30 **Cu**, 0.040 **P**, 0.040 **S**	**Hardened and tempered**: all **diam**, (620) **TS**, (420) **YS**, 13 **El**
UNI 3608–74	X G 15 CrMo 5	Italy	Castings	0.20 **C**, 0.80 **Mn**, 0.75 **Si**, 4.0–6.5 **Cr**, 0.45–0.65 **Mo**, 0.035 **P**, 0.035 **S**	**As agreed**: all **diam**, (620) **TS**, (410) **YS**, 16 **El**
UNI 3608–74	X G 15 CrMo 9	Italy	Castings	0.20 **C**, 0.80 **Mn**, 1.0 **Si**, 8.0–10.0 **Cr**, 0.90–1.20 **Mo**, 0.035 **P**, 0.035 **S**	**As agreed**: all **diam**, (620) **TS**, (410) **YS**, 16 **El**
ASTM A 217	Grade C5	US	Castings	0.20 **C**, 0.40–0.70 **Mn**, 0.75 **Si**, 4.00–6.50 **Cr**, 0.45–0.65 **Mo**, 0.50 **Ni**, 0.50 **Cu**, 0.04 **P**, 0.045 **S**, 0.10 **W**	**Normalized and tempered**: all **diam**, 90 (620) **TS**, 60 (415) **YS**, 18 **El**
ASTM A 217	Grade C12	US	Castings	0.20 **C**, 0.35–0.65 **Mn**, 1.00 **Si**, 8.00–10.00 **Cr**, 0.90–1.20 **Mo**, 0.50 **Ni**, 0.50 **Cu**, 0.04 **P**, 0.045 **S**, 0.10 **W**	**Normalized and tempered**: all **diam**, 90 (620) **TS**, 60 (415) **YS**, 18 **El**
ANSI/ASTM A 217	C5	US	Castings	0.20 **C**, 0.40–0.70 **Mn**, 0.75 **Si**, 4.00–6.50 **Cr**, 0.45–0.65 **Mo**, 0.04 **P**, 0.045 **S**	**Normalized, tempered**: all **diam**, 90 (620) **TS**, 60 (415) **YS**, 18 **El**
ANSI/ASTM A 217	C12	US	Castings	0.20 **C**, 0.35–0.65 **Mn**, 1.00 **Si**, 8.00–10.00 **Cr**, 0.90–1.20 **Mo**, 0.04 **P**, 0.045 **S**	**Normalized, tempered**: all **diam**, 90 (620) **TS**, 60 (414) **YS**, 18 **El**

CAST CARBON STEELS

specification number	designation	country	product forms	composition	mechanical properties (see page iv for explanation)
JIS G 5102	Class 4	Japan	Castings	0.20 **C**, 0.040 **P**, 0.040 **S**	**Annealed, normalized, quenched and tempered**: all **diam**, (618) **TS**, (431) **YS**, 17 **El**
JIS G 5151	Class 61	Japan	Castings	0.20 **C**, 0.50–0.80 **Mn**, 0.75 **Si**, 4.00–6.50 **Cr**, 0.45–0.65 **Mo**, 0.040 **P**, 0.040 **S**	**Annealed, normalized, quenched, tempered**: all **diam**, (618) **TS**, (412) **YS**, 17 **El**
BS 1504–629		UK	Sand castings	0.20 **C**, 8.00–10.00 **Cr**, 0.90–1.20 **Mo**	**Hardened and tempered (air or oil)**: all **diam**, (615) **TS**, (420) **YS**
BS 3100/1463		UK	Sand castings	0.20 **C**, 8.00–10.00 **Cr**, 0.90–1.20 **Mo**	**Hardened and tempered**: all **diam**, (615) **TS**, (420) **YS**, 13 **El**
BS 1504–625		UK	Sand castings	0.20 **C**, 4.00–6.00 **Cr**, 0.45–0.65 **Mo**	**Hardened and tempered (air)**: all **diam**, (615) **TS**, (420) **YS**
BS 3100/1462		UK	Sand castings	0.20 **C**, 4.0–6.0 **Cr**, 0.45–0.65 **Mo**	**Hardened and tempered**: all **diam**, (615) **TS**, (420) **YS**, 13 **El**
NF A 32–055	15 CDV 4 10–M	France	Castings	0.20 **C**, 0.80 **Mn**, 0.60 **Si**, 0.80–1.20 **Cr**, 0.85–1.15 **Mo**, 0.15–0.30 **V**, 0.035 **P**, 0.035 **S**	**Normalized**: all **diam**, (600) **TS**, (350) **YS**, 15 **El**
IS 7899	Grade 8N, 8Q	India	Castings	0.20 **C**, 0.50–0.90 **Mn**, 0.80 **Si**, 2.00–2.75 **Cr**, 0.90–1.10 **Mo**, 0.04 **P**, 0.045 **S**	**Normalized and tempered**: all **diam**, (590) **TS**, (380) **YS**, 18 **El**; **Quenched and tempered**: all **diam**, (720) **TS**, (590) **YS**, 15 **El**
ASTM A 643	Grade C1	US	Castings	0.20 **C**, 0.40–0.80 **Mn**, 0.60 **Si**, 2.00–2.75 **Cr**, 0.90–1.20 **Mo**, 0.50 **Ni**, 0.03 **V**, 0.50 **Cu**, 0.035 **P**, 0.035 **S**, 0.10 **W**	**Normalized and tempered, quenched and tempered**: all **diam**, 85 (585) **TS**, 55 (380) **YS**, 20 **El**
ASTM A 487	Grade 8N	US	Castings	0.20 **C**, 0.50–0.90 **Mn**, 0.80 **Si**, 2.00–2.75 **Cr**, 0.90–1.10 **Mo**, 0.03 **V**, 0.50 **Cu**, 0.04 **P**, 0.045 **S**, 0.10 **W**	**Normalized and tempered**: all **diam**, 85 (585) **TS**, 55 (380) **YS**, 20 **El**
ASTM A 356	Grade 10	US	Castings	0.20 **C**, 0.50–0.80 **Mn**, 0.60 **Si**, 2.00–2.75 **Cr**, 0.90–1.20 **Mo**, 0.035 **P**, 0.030 **S**	**Normalized and tempered**: all **diam**, 85 (585) **TS**, 55 (380) **YS**, 20 **El**
ANSI/ASTM A 487	8N	US	Castings	0.20 **C**, 0.50–0.90 **Mn**, 0.80 **Si**, 2.00–2.75 **Cr**, 0.90–1.10 **Mo**, 0.030 **V**, 0.040 **P**, 0.045 **S**	**Normalized, tempered**: all **diam**, 85 (585) **TS**, 55 (380) **YS**, 20 **El**
ANSI/ASTM A 487	Class 8N	US	Sand castings	0.20 **C**, 0.50–0.90 **Mn**, 0.80 **Si**, 2.00–2.75 **Cr**, 0.90–1.10 **Mo**, 0.03 **V**, 0.04 **P**, 0.045 **S**	**Normalized and tempered**: all **diam**, 85 (585) **TS**, 55 (380) **YS**, 20 **El**
ANSI/ASTM A 643	Grade C, class 1	US	Sand castings	0.20 **C**, 0.40–0.80 **Mn**, 0.60 **Si**, 2.00–2.75 **Cr**, 0.90–1.20 **Mo**, 0.035 **P**, 0.035 **S**	**Normalized and tempered or quenched and tempered**: >2 **diam**, 85 (585) **TS**, 55 (380) **YS**, 20 **El**
ASTM A 356	Grade 10	US	Castings	0.20 **C**, 0.50–0.80 **Mn**, 0.60 **Si**, 2.00–2.75 **Cr**, 0.90–1.20 **Mo**, 0.035 **P**, 0.030 **S**	**Normalized or tempered**: all **diam**, 85 (585) **TS**, 55 (380) **YS**, 20 **El**
ASTM A 389	Grade C24	US	Castings	0.20 **C**, 0.30–0.80 **Mn**, 0.60 **Si**, 0.80–1.25 **Cr**, 0.90–1.20 **Mo**, 0.15–0.25 **V**, 0.04 **P**, 0.045 **S**	**Normalized and tempered**: all **diam**, 80 (552) **TS**, 50 (345) **YS**, 15 **El**
ANSI/ASTM A 389	C24	US	Castings	0.20 **C**, 0.30–0.80 **Mn**, 0.60 **Si**, 0.80–1.25 **Cr**, 0.90–1.20 **Mo**, 0.15–0.25 **V**, 0.040 **P**, 0.045 **S**	**Normalized, tempered**: all **diam**, 80 (552) **TS**, 50 (345) **YS**, 15 **El**
ANSI/ASTM A 389	Grade C24	US	Sand castings	0.20 **C**, 0.30–0.80 **Mn**, 0.60 **Si**, 0.80–1.25 **Cr**, 0.90–1.20 **Mo**, 0.15–0.25 **V**, 0.04 **P**, 0.045 **S**	**Normalized and tempered**: all **diam**, 80 (550) **TS**, 50 (345) **YS**, 15 **El**
JIS G 5102	Class 3	Japan	Castings	0.20 **C**, 0.040 **P**, 0.040 **S**	**Annealed, normalized, quenched and tempered**: all **diam**, (549) **TS**, (353) **YS**, 18 **El**
JIS G 5151	Class 23	Japan	Castings	0.20 **C**, 0.50–0.80 **Mn**, 0.60 **Si**, 1.00–1.50 **Cr**, 0.90–1.20 **Mo**, 0.15–0.25 **V**, 0.040 **P**, 0.040 **S**	**Annealed, normalized, quenched, tempered**: all **diam**, (549) **TS**, (343) **YS**, 13 **El**
JIS G 5201	Class 12	Japan	Pipe: centrifugally cast	0.20 **C**, 0.040 **P**, 0.040 **S**	**Annealed, normalized, quenched, tempered**: all **diam**, (520) **TS**, (353) **YS**, 18 **El**
NF A 32–055	15 CD 5 05–M	France	Castings	0.20 **C**, 0.80 **Mn**, 0.80 **Si**, 1.0–1.5 **Cr**, 0.45–0.65 **Mo**, 0.040 **P**, 0.040 **S**	**Normalized or quenched**: all **diam**, (500) **TS**, (300) **YS**, 18 **El**

CAST CARBON STEELS

specification number	designation	country	product forms	composition	mechanical properties (see page iv for explanation)
JIS G 5201	Class II	Japan	Pipe: centrifugally cast	0.20 **C**, 0.040 **P**, 0.040 **S**	**Annealed, normalized, quenched, tempered**: all **diam**, (490) **TS**, (314) **YS**, 20 **El**
SIS 14 21 72	SIS 21 72–21	Sweden	Castings	0.20 **C**, 1.50 **Mn**, 0.30–0.60 **Si**	**Normalized**: all **diam**, (490) **TS**, (290) **YS**, 18 **El**
SFS 369	G–17 CrMo 55	Finland	Castings	0.20 **C**, 0.50–0.80 **Mn**, 0.60 **Si**, 1.0–1.5 **Cr**, 0.45–0.55 **Mo**, 0.4 **Ni**, 0.3 **Cu**, 0.3 **Cu**, 0.040 **P**, 0.040 **S**	**Annealed**: all **diam**, (490) **TS**, (270) **YS**, 20 **El**
SFS 365	G–20 Mn5	Finland	Castings	0.20 **C**, 1.50 **Mn**, 0.60 **Si**, 0.30 **Cr**, 0.40 **Cu**, 0.035 **P**, 0.035 **S**	**Normalized or annealed**: all **diam**, (490) **TS**, (290) **YS**, 18 **El**
SS 14 21 72	SS 21 72–21	Sweden	Castings	0.20 **C**, 1.50 **Mn**, 0.30–0.60 **Si**, 0.03 **Cr**, 0.04 **Cu**	**Normalized**: ($\leq$63) **diam**, (490) **TS**, (290) **YS**, 18 **El**
ANSI/ASTM A 487	Class 11N	US	Sand castings	0.20 **C**, 0.50–0.80 **Mn**, 0.60 **Si**, 0.50–0.80 **Cr**, 0.45–0.65 **Mo**, 0.70–1.10 **Ni**, 0.03 **V**, 0.040 **P**, 0.045 **S**	**Normalized and tempered**: all **diam**, 70 (485) **TS**, 40 (275) **YS**, 20 **El**
ANSI/ASTM A 487	Class 12N	US	Sand castings	0.20 **C**, 0.40–0.70 **Mn**, 0.60 **Si**, 0.50–0.90 **Cr**, 0.90–1.20 **Mo**, 0.60–1.00 **Ni**, 0.03 **V**, 0.04 **P**, 0.045 **S**	**Normalized and tempered**: all **diam**, 70 (485) **TS**, 40 (275) **YS**, 20 **El**
ASTM A 487	Grade 11N	US	Castings	0.20 **C**, 0.50–0.80 **Mn**, 0.60 **Si**, 0.50–0.80 **Cr**, 0.45–0.65 **Mo**, 0.70–1.10 **Ni**, 0.03 **V**, 0.50 **Cu**, 0.04 **P**, 0.045 **S**, 0.10 **W**	**Normalized and tempered**: all **diam**, 70 (485) **TS**, 40 (275) **YS**, 20 **El**
ASTM A 487	Grade 12N	US	Castings	0.20 **C**, 0.40–0.70 **Mn**, 0.60 **Si**, 0.50–0.90 **Cr**, 0.90–1.20 **Mo**, 0.60–1.00 **Ni**, 0.03 **V**, 0.50 **Cu**, 0.04 **P**, 0.045 **S**, 0.10 **W**	**Normalized and tempered**: all **diam**, 70 (485) **TS**, 40 (275) **YS**, 20 **El**
ASTM A 356	Grade 6	US	Castings	0.20 **C**, 0.50–0.80 **Mn**, 0.60 **Si**, 1.00–1.50 **Cr**, 0.45–0.65 **Mo**, 0.035 **P**, 0.030 **S**	**Normalized and tempered**: all **diam**, 70 (485) **TS**, 45 (310) **YS**, 22 **El**
ASTM A 217	Grade WC5	US	Castings	0.20 **C**, 0.40–0.70 **Mn**, 0.60 **Si**, 0.50–0.90 **Cr**, 0.90–1.20 **Mo**, 0.60–1.00 **Ni**, 0.50 **Cu**, 0.04 **P**, 0.045 **S**, 0.10 **W**	**Normalized and tempered**: all **diam**, 70 (485) **TS**, 40 (275) **YS**, 20 **El**
ASTM A 217	Grade WC6	US	Castings	0.20 **C**, 0.50–0.80 **Mn**, 0.60 **Si**, 1.00–1.50 **Cr**, 0.45–0.65 **Mo**, 0.50 **Ni**, 0.50 **Cu**, 0.04 **P**, 0.045 **S**, 0.10 **W**	**Normalized and tempered**: all **diam**, 70 (485) **TS**, 40 (275) **YS**, 20 **El**
ASTM A 217	Grade WC4	US	Castings	0.20 **C**, 0.50–0.80 **Mn**, 0.60 **Si**, 0.50–0.80 **Cr**, 0.45–0.65 **Mo**, 0.70–1.10 **Ni**, 0.50 **Cu**, 0.04 **P**, 0.045 **S**, 0.10 **W**	**Normalized and tempered**: all **diam**, 70 (485) **TS**, 40 (275) **YS**, 20 **El**
ANSI/ASTM A 487	11N	US	Castings	0.20 **C**, 0.50–0.80 **Mn**, 0.60 **Si**, 0.50–0.80 **Cr**, 0.45–0.65 **Mo**, 0.70–1.10 **Ni**, 0.030 **V**, 0.04 **P**, 0.045 **S**	**Normalized, tempered**: all **diam**, 70 (485) **TS**, 40 (275) **YS**, 20 **El**
ANSI/ASTM A 487	12N	US	Castings	0.20 **C**, 0.40–0.70 **Mn**, 0.60 **Si**, 0.500–0.90 **Cr**, 0.90–1.20 **Mo**, 0.60–1.000 **Ni**, 0.030 **V**, 0.040 **P**, 0.045 **S**	**Normalized, tempered**: all **diam**, 70 (485) **TS**, 40 (275) **YS**, 20 **El**
ANSI/ASTM A 217	WC4	US	Castings	0.20 **C**, 0.50–0.80 **Mn**, 0.60 **Si**, 0.50–0.80 **Cr**, 0.45–0.65 **Mo**, 0.70–1.10 **Ni**, 0.040 **P**, 0.045 **S**	**Normalized, tempered**: all **diam**, 70 (485) **TS**, 40 (275) **YS**, 20 **El**
ANSI/ASTM A 217	WC5	US	Castings	0.20 **C**, 0.40–0.70 **Mn**, 0.60 **Si**, 0.50–0.90 **Cr**, 0.90–1.20 **Mo**, 0.60–1.00 **Ni**, 0.040 **P**, 0.045 **S**	**Normalized, tempered**: all **diam**, 70 (485) **TS**, 40 (275) **YS**, 20 **El**
ANSI/ASTM A 217	WC6	US	Castings	0.20 **C**, 0.50–0.80 **Mn**, 0.60 **Si**, 1.00–1.50 **Cr**, 0.45–0.65 **Mo**, 0.040 **P**, 0.045 **S**	**Normalized, tempered**: all **diam**, 70 (485) **TS**, 40 (275) **YS**, 20 **El**
ANSI/ASTM A 389	Grade C 23	US	Sand castings	0.20 **C**, 0.30–0.80 **Mn**, 0.60 **Si**, 1.00–1.50 **Cr**, 0.45–0.65 **Mo**, 0.15–0.25 **V**, 0.04 **P**, 0.045 **S**	**Normalized and tempered**: all **diam**, 70 (485) **TS**, 40 (275) **YS**, 18 **El**
ASTM A 356	Grade 6	US	Castings	0.20 **C**, 0.50–0.80 **Mn**, 0.60 **Si**, 1.00–1.50 **Cr**, 0.45–0.65 **Mo**, 0.035 **P**, 0.030 **S**	**Normalized or tempered**: all **diam**, 70 (485) **TS**, 45 (310) **YS**, 22 **El**
ANSI/ASTM A 346	CP11	US	Pipe: centrifugally cast	0.20 **C**, 0.30–0.80 **Mn**, 0.60 **Si**, 1.00–1.50 **Cr**, 0.44–0.65 **Mo**, 0.030 **P**, 0.030 **S**	**Normalized and tempered**: all **diam**, 70 (483) **TS**, 40 (276) **YS**, 20 **El**

CAST CARBON STEELS

specification number	designation	country	product forms	composition	mechanical properties (see page iv for explanation)
MIL–S–15464B	Class 1	US	Sand castings	0.20 **C**, 0.50–0.80 **Mn**, 0.20–0.60 **Si**, 1.00–1.50 **Cr**, 0.40–0.60 **Mo**, 0.50 **Ni**, 0.50 **Cu**, 0.05 **P**, 0.05 **S**	**Normalized and tempered or annealed, normalized and tempered**: all **diam**, 70 (483) **TS**, 40 (276) **YS**, 20 **El**
NOM–B–141	Class W–C5	Mexico	Castings	0.20 **C**, 0.40–0.70 **Mn**, 0.50–0.90 **Cr**, 0.60–1.00 **Ni**, 0.60 **Si**, 0.90–1.20 **Mo**, 0.040 **P**, 0.045 **S**	**Normalized and annealed**: all **diam**, (483) **TS**, (276) **YS**, 20 **El**
NOM–B–141	Class W–C6	Mexico	Castings	0.20 **C**, 0.50–0.80 **Mn**, 1.00–1.50 **Cr**, 0.60 **Si**, 0.45–0.65 **Mo**, 0.040 **P**, 0.045 **S**	**Normalized and annealed**: all **diam**, (483) **TS**, (276) **YS**, 20 **El**
ASTM A 426	Grade CP11	US	Pipe: centrifugally cast	0.20 **C**, 0.30–0.80 **Mn**, 0.60 **Si**, 1.0–1.5 **Cr**, 0.44–0.65 **Mo**, 0.50 **Ni**, 0.50 **Cu**, 0.030 **P**, 0.030 **S**, 0.10 **W**	**Normalized and tempered**: all **diam**, (483) **TS**, (276) **YS**, 20 **El**
ASTM A 389	Grade C23	US	Castings	0.20 **C**, 0.30–0.80 **Mn**, 0.60 **Si**, 1.00–1.50 **Cr**, 0.45–0.65 **Mo**, 0.15–0.25 **V**, 0.04 **P**, 0.045 **S**	**Normalized and tempered**: all **diam**, 70 (483) **TS**, 40 (276) **YS**, 18 **El**
ANSI/ASTM A 389	C23	US	Castings	0.20 **C**, 0.30–0.80 **Mn**, 0.60 **Si**, 1.00–1.50 **Cr**, 0.405–0.65 **Mo**, 0.15–0.25 **V**, 0.04 **P**, 0.045 **S**	**Normalized, tempered**: all **diam**, 70 (483) **TS**, 40 (276) **YS**, 18 **El**
JIS G 5151	Class 21	Japan	Castings	0.20 **C**, 0.50–0.80 **Mn**, 0.60 **Si**, 1.00–1.50 **Cr**, 0.45–0.65 **Mo**, 0.040 **P**, 0.040 **S**	**Annealed, normalized, quenched, tempered**: all **diam**, (481) **TS**, (275) **YS**, 17 **El**
JIS G 5151	Class 32	Japan	Castings	0.20 **C**, 0.50–0.80 **Mn**, 0.60 **Si**, 2.00–2.75 **Cr**, 0.90–1.20 **Mo**, 0.040 **P**, 0.040 **S**	**Annealed, normalized, quenched, tempered**: all **diam**, (481) **TS**, (275) **YS**, 17 **El**
BS 1504–621		UK	Castings	0.20 **C**, 0.50–0.80 **Mn**, 0.60 **Si**, 1.0–1.5 **Cr**, 0.45–0.65 **Mo**, 0.40 **Ni**, 0.30 **Cu**, 0.050 **P**, 0.050 **S**	**Normalized and tempered**: all **diam**, (480) **TS**, (280) **YS**, 17 **El**
IS 3038	Grade 4	India	Castings	0.20 **C**, 0.50–0.80 **Mn**, 0.60 **Si**, 1.00–1.50 **Cr**, 0.45–0.65 **Mo**, 0.040 **P**, 0.045 **S**	**As agreed**: (25) **diam**, (480) **TS**, (270) **YS**, 17 **El**
UNI 3608–74	G 15 CrMo 55	Italy	Castings	0.20 **C**, 0.80 **Mn**, 0.50 **Si**, 1.0–1.5 **Cr**, 0.45–0.65 **Mo**, 0.035 **P**, 0.035 **S**	**As agreed**: all **diam**, (480) **TS**, (275) **YS**, 18 **El**
BS 3100/1398	Grade B	UK	Sand castings	0.20 **C**, 1.0–1.50 **Cr**, 0.45–0.65 **Mo**	**Annealed or annealed and normalized**: all **diam**, (480) **TS**, (275) **YS**, 17 **El**
BS 1504–621		UK	Sand castings	0.20 **C**, 1.00–1.50 **Cr**, 0.45–0.65 **Mo**	**Annealed or annealed and normalized and tempered**: all **diam**, (480) **TS**, (275) **YS**
BS 3100/4242	Grade B	UK	Sand castings	0.20 **C**, 1.0 **Mn**, 0.45–0.65 **Mo**	**As required**: all **diam**, (460) **TS**, (275) **YS**, 18 **El**
BS 3100/4242	Grade A	UK	Sand castings	0.20 **C**, 1.10 **Mn**	**As required**: all **diam**, (430) **TS**, (230) **YS**, 22 **El**
JIS G 5202	Class 11	Japan	Pipe: centrifugally cast	0.20 **C**, 0.30–0.60 **Mn**, 0.60 **Si**, 0.45–0.65 **Mo**, 0.035 **P**, 0.035 **S**	**Annealed, normalized, quenched, tempered**: all **diam**, (382) **TS**, (206) **YS**, 19 **El**
ANSI/ASTM A 487	Class 11Q	US	Sand castings	0.20 **C**, 0.50–0.80 **Mn**, 0.60 **Si**, 0.50–0.80 **Cr**, 0.45–0.65 **Mo**, 0.70–1.10 **Ni**, 0.03 **V**, 0.04 **P**, 0.045 **S**	**Quenched and tempered**: all **diam**, 105 (275) **TS**, 85 (585) **YS**, 17 **El**
NOM–B–141	Class W–C4	Mexico	Castings	0.20 **C**, 0.50–0.80 **Mn**, 0.60 **Si**, 0.50–0.80 **Cr**, 0.45–0.65 **Mo**, 0.70–1.10 **Ni**, 0.040 **P**, 0.045 **S**	
MIL–S–23008B	Hy 80	US	Sand castings	0.20 **C**, 0.55–0.75 **Mn**, 0.50 **Si**, 1.35–1.65 **Cr**, 0.30–0.60 **Mo**, 2.50–3.25 **Ni**, 0.020 **P**, 0.015 **S**	**Quenched and tempered**: all **diam**, 80 (552) **YS**, 20 **El**
NF A 32–055	Z 15 CD 5 05–M	France	Castings	0.19 **C**, 0.80 **Mn**, 1.0 **Si**, 4.0–6.0 **Cr**, 0.40–0.70 **Mo**, 0.035 **P**, 0.035 **S**	**Normalized or quenched**: all **diam**, (630) **TS**, (420) **YS**, 16 **El**
IS 3038	Grade 1	India	Castings	0.18–0.28 **C**, 1.10–1.60 **Mn**, 0.50 **Si**, 0.050 **P**, 0.050 **S**	**As agreed**: (25) **diam**, (540) **TS**, (300) **YS**, 18 **El**
BS 3100/1456	Grade A	UK	Sand castings	0.18–0.25 **C**, 1.20–1.60 **Mn**	**Normalized, normalized and tempered or hardened and tempered**: all **diam**, (540) **TS**, (340) **YS**, 16 **El**
DTD 5209		UK	Investment and precision castings	0.18–0.25 **C**, 1.20–1.70 **Mn**	**Normalized, normalized or tempered or hardened and tempered or at discretion of founder**: all **diam**, (540) **TS**, (325) **YS**, 13 **El**

CAST CARBON STEELS

specification number	designation	country	product forms	composition	mechanical properties (see page iv for explanation)
BS 3146: Part 1	CLA2: Grade A	UK	Investment and precision castings	0.18–0.25 **C**, 1.20–1.70 **Mn**	**Normalized, normalized and tempered or hardened and tempered**: all **diam**, (540) **TS**
VSM 10698	GS–20 Mn 5 V 48/1.5053	Switzerland	Castings	0.18–0.23 **C**, 1.00–1.40 **Mn**, 0.30–0.50 **Si**, 0.40 **Cr**, 0.25 **Mo**, 0.50 **Ni**, 0.030 **P**, 0.030 **S**	**Normalized**: all **diam**, (475) **TS**, (255) **YS**, 20 **El**
VSM 10697	GS–45/104.43	Switzerland	Castings	0.18–0.23 **C**, 1.00 **Mn**, 0.30–0.50 **Si**, 0.40 **Cr**, 0.25 **Mo**, 0.50 **Ni**, 0.030 **P**, 0.030 **S**	**Annealed or normalized**: all **diam**, (450) **TS**, (230) **YS**, 22 **El**
VSM 10698	GS–45/1.00446	Switzerland	Castings	0.18–0.23 **C**, 1.00 **Mn**, 0.030–0.50 **Si**, 0.40 **Cr**, 0.25 **Mo**, 0.50 **Ni**, 0.030 **P**, 0.030 **S**	**Annealed or normalized**: all **diam**, (445) **TS**, (225) **YS**, 22 **El**
DIN 17245	Grade GS–C 25	Germany	Castings	0.18–0.23 **C**, 0.50–0.80 **Mn**, 0.30–0.50 **Si**, 0.30 **Cr**, 0.050 **P**, 0.050 **S**	**Quenched and tempered or normalized**: all **diam**, (441) **TS**, (245) **YS**, 22 **El**
DIN 17245	Grade GS–22 Mo 4	Germany	Castings	0.18–0.23 **C**, 0.50–0.80 **Mn**, 0.30–0.50 **Si**, 0.30 **Cr**, 0.35–0.45 **Mo**, 0.040 **P**, 0.040 **S**	**Quenched and tempered**: all **diam**, (441) **TS**, (245) **YS**, 22 **El**
VSM 10698	GS–20 MnMo 5 3 V 55	Switzerland	Castings	0.18–0.22 **C**, 1.00–1.40 **Mn**, 0.30–0.50 **Si**, 0.4 **Cr**, 0.20–0.30 **Mo**, 0.5 **Ni**, 0.030 **P**, 0.030 **S**	**Quenched**: all **diam**, (540) **TS**, (395) **YS**, 18 **El**
VSM 10697	GS–20 MnMo 5 3 V 52	Switzerland	Castings	0.18–0.22 **C**, 1.0–1.4 **Mn**, 0.30–0.50 **Si**, 0.40 **Cr**, 0.20–0.30 **Mo**, 0.50 **Ni**, 0.030 **P**, 0.030 **S**	**Quenched and tempered**: all **diam**, (520) **TS**, (350) **YS**, 18 **El**
VSM 10698	GS–20 MnMo 5 3 V 52	Switzerland	Castings	0.18–0.22 **C**, 1.00–1.40 **Mn**, 0.30–0.50 **Si**, 0.40 **Cr**, 0.20–0.30 **Mo**, 0.50 **Ni**, 0.030 **P**, 0.030 **S**	**Quenched**: all **diam**, (510) **TS**, (345) **YS**, 18 **El**
VSM 10698	GS–20 Mn 5 V 50	Switzerland	Castings	0.18–0.22 **C**, 1.00–1.40 **Mn**, 0.30–0.50 **Si**, 0.40 **Cr**, 0.25 **Mo**, 0.50 **Ni**, 0.030 **P**, 0.030 **S**	**Air quenched**: all **diam**, (490) **TS**, (295) **YS**, 18 **El**
VSM 10698	GS–20 CrMo 910 V 60/1.5418	Switzerland	Castings	0.18–0.20 **C**, 1.00–1.40 **Mn**, 0.30–0.50 **Si**, 0.40 **Cr**, 0.20–0.30 **Mo**, 0.50 **Ni**, 0.030 **P**, 0.030 **S**	**Quenched**: all **diam**, (590) **TS**, (490) **YS**, 16 **El**
NF A 32–055	15 CDV 9 10–M	France	Castings	0.18 **C**, 0.70 **Mn**, 0.60 **Si**, 2.0–2.75 **Cr**, 0.90–1.20 **Mo**, 0.15–0.50 **V**, 0.040 **P**, 0.040 **S**	**Normalized**: all **diam**, (600) **TS**, (350) **YS**, 15 **El**
NF A 32–055	15 CDV 9 10–M	France	Castings	0.18 **C**, 0.80 **Mn**, 0.60 **Si**, 2.0–2.5 **Cr**, 0.90–1.10 **Mo**, 0.040 **P**, 0.040 **S**	**Normalized or quenched**: all **diam**, (550) **TS**, (275) **YS**, 17 **El**
BS 1504–622		UK	Castings	0.18 **C**, 0.40–0.70 **Mn**, 0.60 **Si**, 2.0–2.75 **Cr**, 0.90–1.2 **Mo**, 0.40 **Ni**, 0.30 **Cu**, 0.050 **P**, 0.050 **S**	**Normalized and tempered**: all **diam**, (540) **TS**, (325) **YS**, 17 **El**
BS 3100/1398	Grade C	UK	Sand castings	0.18 **C**, 2.0–2.75 **Cr**, 0.9–1.20 **Mo**	**Annealed or annealed and normalized**: all **diam**, (540) **TS**, (325) **YS**, 17 **El**
IS 3038	Grade 5	India	Castings	0.18 **C**, 0.40–0.80 **Mn**, 0.60 **Si**, 2.00–2.75 **Cr**, 0.90–1.20 **Mo**, 0.02 **Al**, 0.040 **P**, 0.045 **S**	**As agreed**: (25) **diam**, (510) **TS**, (300) **YS**, 17 **El**
SFS 370	G–16 CrMo 99	Finland	Castings	0.18 **C**, 0.50–0.80 **Mn**, 0.60 **Si**, 2.0–2.5 **Cr**, 0.90–1.10 **Mo**, 0.40 **Ni**, 0.30 **Cu**, 0.040 **P**, 0.040 **S**	**Annealed**: all **diam**, (490) **TS**, (270) **YS**, 20 **El**
SIS 14 22 23	SIS 22 23–03	Sweden	Castings	0.18 **C**, 0.7 **Mn**, 0.6 **Si**, 0.7–1.1 **Cr**, 0.5–0.7 **Mo**, 0.4 **Ni**, 0.3 **Cu**, 0.040 **P**, 0.040 **S**	**Annealed, normalized**: all **diam**, (490) **TS**, (274) **YS**, 20 **El**
ASTM A 217	Grade WC9	US	Castings	0.18 **C**, 0.40–0.70 **Mn**, 0.60 **Si**, 2.00–2.75 **Cr**, 0.90–1.20 **Mo**, 0.50 **Ni**, 0.50 **Cu**, 0.04 **P**, 0.045 **S**, 0.10 **W**	**Normalized and tempered**: all **diam**, 70 (485) **TS**, 40 (275) **YS**, 20 **El**
ANSI/ASTM A 217	WC9	US	Castings	0.18 **C**, 0.40–0.70 **Mn**, 0.60 **Si**, 2.00–2.75 **Cr**, 0.90–1.20 **Mo**, 0.04 **P**, 0.045 **S**	**Normalized, tempered**: all **diam**, 70 (485) **TS**, 40 (275) **YS**, 20 **El**
MIL–S–15464B	Class 3	US	Sand castings	0.18 **C**, 0.40–0.70 **Mn**, 0.60 **Si**, 1.00–1.50 **Cr**, 0.40–0.60 **Mo**, 0.50 **Ni**, 0.15–0.25 **V**, 0.50 **Cu**, 0.05 **P**, 0.06 **S**	**Normalized and tempered or annealed, normalized and tempered**: all **diam**, 70 (483) **TS**, 40 (276) **YS**, 20 **El**
MIL–S–15464B	Class 2	US	Sand castings	0.18 **C**, 0.40–0.70 **Mn**, 0.20–0.60 **Si**, 2.00–2.75 **Cr**, 0.80–1.10 **Mo**, .50 **Ni**, .50 **Cu**, 0.05 **P**, 0.05 **S**	**Normalized and tempered or annealed, normalized and tempered**: all **diam**, 70 (483) **TS**, 40 (276) **YS**, 20 **El**

CAST CARBON STEELS

specification number	designation	country	product forms	composition	mechanical properties (see page iv for explanation)
NOM-B-141	Class W-C9	Mexico	Castings	0.18 **C**, 0.40–0.70 **Mn**, 2.00–2.75 **Cr**, 0.60 **Si**, 0.90–1.20 **Mo**, 0.040 **P**, 0.045 **S**	**Normalized and annealed**: all **diam**, (483) **TS**, (276) **YS**, 20 **El**
ASTM A 426	Grade CP22	US	Pipe: centrifugally cast	0.18 **C**, 0.30–0.70 **Mn**, 0.60 **Si**, 2.00–2.75 **Cr**, 0.90–1.20 **Mo**, 0.50 **Ni**, 0.50 **Cu**, 0.030 **P**, 0.030 **S**, 0.10 **W**	**Normalized and tempered**: all **diam**, (483) **TS**, (276) **YS**, 20 **El**
UNI 3608–74	G 14 CrMo 9 10	Italy	Castings	0.18 **C**, 0.80 **Mn**, 0.50 **Si**, 2.0–2.75 **Cr**, 0.9–1.20 **Mo**, 0.035 **P**, 0.035 **S**	**As agreed**: all **diam**, (480) **TS**, (275) **YS**, 18 **El**
UNI 3608–74	G 14 CrMoV 9 10 2	Italy	Castings	0.18 **C**, 0.80 **Mn**, 0.50 **Si**, 2.0–2.75 **Cr**, 0.90–1.20 **Mo**, 0.15–0.25 **V**, 0.035 **P**, 0.035 **S**	**As agreed**: all **diam**, (480) **TS**, (275) **YS**, 18 **El**
BS 1504–622		UK	Sand castings	0.18 **C**, 2.00–2.75 **Cr**, 0.90–1.20 **Mo**	**Annealed or annealed and normalized and tempered**: all **diam**, (480) **TS**, (275) **YS**
SIS 14 13 06	SIS 13 06–02	Sweden	Castings	0.18 **C**, 1.1 **Mn**, 0.60 **Si**, 0.3 **Cr**, 0.3 **Cu**, 0.035 **P**, 0.030 **S**	**Annealed**: all **diam**, (402) **TS**, (216) **YS**, 25 **El**
NFA 32–051	E 20–40–M	France	Castings	0.18 **C**, 0.50 **Si**, 0.040 **P**, 0.040 **S**	**Annealed, normalized or quenched and tempered**: all **diam**, (400) **TS**, (200) **YS**, 25 **El**
SFS 355		Finland	Castings	0.18 **C**, 0.70 **Mn**, 0.50 **Si**, 0.040 **P**, 0.040 **S**	**Annealed or normalized**: all **diam**, (400) **TS**, (200) **YS**, 25 **El**
ISO 3755	Grade 20–40	ISO	Sand castings	0.18 **C**, 0.040 **P**, 0.040 **S**	**As cast and annealed or normalized or normalized and tempered or quenched and tempered**: all **diam**, (400) **TS**, (200) **YS**, 25 **El**
MIL-S-22141B	1C–4620	US	Investment castings	0.15–0.25 **C**, 0.40–0.70 **Mn**, 0.20–0.80 **Si**, 0.20–0.30 **Mo**, 1.65–2.00 **Ni**	**Annealed, quenched and tempered**: all **diam**, (827) **TS**, (689) **YS**, 10.0 **El**
ASTM A 732	Grade 11Q	US	Investment castings	0.15–0.25 **C**, 0.40–0.70 **Mn**, 0.20–0.80 **Si**, 0.20–0.30 **Mo**, 1.65–2.00 **Ni**, 0.04 **P**, 0.045 **S**, 1.00 other elements, total	**Quenched and tempered**: all **diam**, 120 (825) **TS**, 100 (690) **YS**, 10 **El**
ASTM A 732	Grade 13Q	US	Investment castings	0.15–0.25 **C**, 0.65–0.95 **Mn**, 0.20–0.80 **Si**, 0.40–0.70 **Cr**, 0.15–0.25 **Mo**, 0.40–0.70 **Ni**, 0.04 **P**, 0.045 **S**, 1.00 other elements, total	**Quenched and tempered**: all **diam**, 105 (725) **TS**, 85 (585) **YS**, 10 **El**
MIL-S-22141B	1C–8620	US	Investment castings	0.15–0.25 **C**, 0.65–0.95 **Mn**, 0.20–0.80 **Si**, 0.40–0.60 **Cr**, 0.15–0.25 **Mo**, 0.40–0.70 **Ni**	**Annealed, quenched and tempered**: all **diam**, (723) **TS**, (586) **YS**, 10 (4xD) **El**
BS 3146 Part 1	CLA6	UK	Investment and precision castings	0.15–0.25 **C**, 0.40–0.70 **Mo**	**Annealed and hardened and tempered**: all **diam**, (615) **TS**, (370) **YS**, 18 **El**
DGS 6081		UK	Sand castings	0.15–0.25 **C**, 0.5–1.0 **Mn**, 0.40–0.70 **Mo**	**Annealed and normalized**: all **diam**, (460) **TS**, (275) **YS**
BS 1504–240		UK	Sand Castings	0.15–0.25 **C**, 0.40–0.70 **Mo**	**Annealed or annealed and normalized**: all **diam**, (460) **TS**, (245) **YS**
ASTM A 732	Grade 1A	US	Investment castings	0.15–0.25 **C**, 0.20–0.60 **Mn**, 0.20–0.60 **Si**, 0.04 **P**, 0.045 **S**; 1.00 other elements, total	**Annealed**: all **diam**, 60 (415) **TS**, 40 (275) **YS**, 35 **El**
BS 1504–240		UK	Castings	0.15–0.25 **C**, 0.50–1.00 **Mn**, 0.20–0.50 **Si**, 0.40–0.70 **Mo**, 0.050 **S**, 0.050 **P**; 0.8 max other elements, total	**Annealed or annealed and normalized**: all **diam**, (415) **TS**, (220) **YS**, 20 **El**
MIL-S-81591	1C–1020	US	Investment castings	0.15–0.25 **C**, 0.30–0.60 **Mn**, 0.20–1.00 **Si**, 0.01 **P**, 0.01 **S**	**Annealed**: all **diam**, 60 (414) **TS**, 40 (276) **YS**, 35 **El**
MIL-S-22141B	1C–1020	US	Investment castings	0.15–0.25 **C**, 0.30–0.60 **Mn**, 0.20–1.00 **Si**	**Annealed**: all **diam**, (413) **TS**, (275) **YS**, 35 (4 x D) **El**
VSM 10698	GS–18 CrMo 9 10 V 80	Switzerland	Castings	0.15–0.20 **C**, 0.80 **Mn**, 0.30–0.50 **Si**, 2.10–2.50 **Cr**, 0.90–1.10 **Mo**, 0.50 **Ni**, 0.030 **P**, 0.030 **S**	**Quenched**: all **diam**, (785) **TS**, (690) **YS**, 10 **El**
VSM 10698	GS–18 CrMo 910 V 70	Switzerland	Castings	0.15–0.20 **C**, 0.80 **Mn**, 0.30–0.50 **Si**, 2.10–2.50 **Cr**, 0.90–1.10 **Mo**, 0.50 **Ni**, 0.030 **P**, 0.030 **S**	**Quenched**: all **diam**, (690) **TS**, (590) **YS**, 13 **El**

CAST CARBON STEELS

specification number	designation	country	product forms	composition	mechanical properties (see page iv for explanation)
VSM 10698	GS–18 CrMo 910 V 60	Switzerland		0.15–0.20 **C**, 0.80 **Mn**, 0.30–0.50 **Si**, 2.10–2.50 **Cr**, 0.90–1.10 **Mo**, 0.50 **Ni**, 0.030 **P**, 0.030 **S**	**Quenched**: all **diam**, (590) **TS**, (490) **YS**, 16 **El**
DIN 17245	Grade GS–17 CrMoV 5 11	Germany	Castings	0.15–0.20 **C**, 0.50–0.80 **Mn**, 0.30–0.50 **Si**, 1.20–1.50 **Cr**, 0.90–1.10 **Mo**, 0.20–0.30 **V**, 0.040 **P**, 0.040 **S**	**Quenched and tempered**: all **diam**, (588) **TS**, (441) **YS**, 15 **El**
VSM 10698	GS–17 CrMo 55V55/1.7357	Switzerland	Castings	0.15–0.20 **C**, 0.80 **Mn**, 0.30–0.50 **Si**, 1.0–1.5 **Cr**, 0.45–0.55 **Mo**, 0.50 **Ni**, 0.030 **P**, 0.030 **S**	**Air quenched**: all **diam**, (540) **TS**, (395) **YS**, 16 **El**
VSM 10698	GS–18 CrMo 9 10V55/1.7379	Switzerland	Castings	0.15–0.20 **C**, 0.8 **Mn**, 0.30–0.50 **Si**, 2.10–2.50 **Cr**, 0.90–1.10 **Mo**, 0.50 **Ni**, 0.030 **P**, 0.030 **S**	**Quenched**: all **diam**, (540) **TS**, (395) **YS**, 18 **El**
VSM 10698	GS–17 CrMo 55V52/1.7357	Switzerland	Castings	0.15–0.20 **C**, 0.80 **Mn**, 0.30–0.50 **Si**, 1.0–1.5 **Cr**, 0.45–0.55 **Mo**, 0.50 **Ni**, 0.030 **P**, 0.030 **S**	**Quenched**: all **diam**, (510) **TS**, (345) **YS**, 18 **El**
DIN 17245	Grade GS–17 CrMo 5 5	Germany	Castings	0.15–0.20 **C**, 0.50–0.80 **Mn**, 0.30–0.50 **Si**, 1.00–1.50 **Cr**, 0.45–0.55 **Mo**, 0.040 **P**, 0.040 **S**	**Quenched and tempered**: all **diam**, (490) **TS**, (314) **YS**, 20 **El**
ASTM A 426	Grade CPH20	US	Pipe: centrifugally cast	0.15 **C**, 1.00 **Mn**, 1.50 **Si**, 11.5–14.0 **Cr**, 0.50 **Mo**, 1.00 **Ni**, 0.50 **Cu**, 0.040 **P**, 0.040 **S**, 0.10 **W**	**Normalized and tempered**: all **diam**, (621) **TS**, (448) **YS**, 18 **El**
BS 3100/1398	Grade E	UK	Sand castings	0.15 **C**, 0.70–1.0 **Cr**, 0.70–1.0 **Mo**, 0.22–0.30 **V**	**Annealed or annealed and normalized**: all **diam**, (540) **TS**, (310) **YS**, 12 **El**
BS 3100/1398	Grade D	UK	Sand castings	0.15 **C**, 0.25–0.50 **Cr**, 0.5–0.7 **Mo**, 0.22–0.30 **V**	**Annealed or annealed and normalized**: all **diam**, (510) **TS**, (310) **YS**, 17 **El**
DGS 6080		UK	Sand castings	0.15 **C**, 0.4–0.8 **Mn**, 0.4–0.6 **Mo**, 0.2–0.3 **V**	**Annealed and normalized**: all **diam**, (490) **TS**, (275) **YS**
ASTM A 352	Grade LC3	US	Castings	0.15 **C**, 0.50–0.80 **Mn**, 0.60 **Si**, 3.00–4.00 **Ni**, 0.04 **P**, 0.045 **S**	**Normalized and tempered, or quenched and tempered**: all **diam**, 70 (485) **TS**, 40 (275) **YS**, 24 **El**
ASTM A 352	Grade LC4	US	Castings	0.15 **C**, 0.50–0.80 **Mn**, 0.60 **Si**, 4.00–5.00 **Ni**, 0.04 **P**, 0.045 **S**	**Normalized and tempered, or quenched and tempered**: all **diam**, 70 (485) **TS**, 40 (275) **YS**, 24 **El**
ANSI/ASTM A 352	LC4	US	Castings: ferritic	0.15 **C**, 0.50–0.80 **Mn**, 0.60 **Si**, 4.00–5.00 **Ni**, 0.040 **P**, 0.045 **S**	**Quenched, tempered**: all **diam**, 70 (485) **TS**, 40 (275) **YS**, 24 **El**
ANSI/ASTM A 352	LC3	US	Castings: ferritic	0.15 **C**, 0.50–0.80 **Mn**, 0.60 **Si**, 3.00–4.00 **Ni**, 0.040 **P**, 0.045 **S**	**Quenched, tempered**: all **diam**, 70 (485) **TS**, 40 (275) **YS**, 24 **El**
ANSI/ASTM A 352	Grade LC4	US	Sand castings	0.15 **C**, 0.50–0.80 **Mn**, 0.60 **Si**, 4.00–5.00 **Ni**, 0.04 **P**, 0.045 **S**	**Normalized and tempered or quenched and tempered**: all **diam**, 70 (485) **TS**, 40 (275) **YS**, 24 **El**
ANSI/ASTM A 352	Grade LC3	US	Sand castings	0.15 **C**, 0.50–0.80 **Mn**, 0.60 **Si**, 3.00–4.00 **Ni**, 0.04 **P**, 0.045 **S**	**Normalized and tempered or quenched and tempered**: all **diam**, 70 (485) **TS**, 40 (275) **YS**, 24 **El**
JIS G 5152	Class 31	Japan	Castings, tube	0.15 **C**, 0.50–0.80 **Mn**, 0.60 **Si**, 3.00–4.00 **Ni**, 0.040 **P**, 0.040 **S**	**Annealed, normalized, quenched and tempered**: all **diam**, (481) **TS**, (275) **YS**, 21 **El**
NF A 32–053	FC 3–M	France	Castings	0.15 **C**, 0.80 **Mn**, 0.50 **Si**, 3.5–4.5 **Ni**, 0.040 **P**, 0.035 **S**	**As cast**: all **diam**, (450) **TS**, (230) **YS**, 18 **El**
BS 1504–503		UK	Sand castings	0.15 **C**, 3.0–4.0 **Ni**	**Annealed and normalized and tempered**: all **diam**, (450) **TS**, (265) **YS**
UNI 7317–74	G 12 Ni 14	Italy	Castings	0.15 **C**, 0.80 **Mn**, 0.60 **Si**, 3.0–4.0 **Ni**, 0.035 **P**, 0.035 **S**	**Normalized and tempered**: all **diam**, (440) **TS**, (275) **YS**, 21 **El**
ANSI/ASTM A 426	CP21	US	Pipe: centrifugally cast	0.15 **C**, 0.30–0.60 **Mn**, 0.50 **Si**, 2.65–3.35 **Cr**, 0.80–1.06 **Mo**, 0.030 **P**, 0.030 **S**	**Normalized and tempered**: all **diam**, 60 (414) **TS**, 30 (207) **YS**, 22 **El**
ANSI/ASTM A 346	CP15	US	Pipe: centrifugally cast	0.15 **C**, 0.30–0.60 **Mn**, 0.15–1.65 **Si**, 0.44–0.65 **Mo**, 0.030 **P**, 0.030 **S**	**Normalized and tempered**: all **diam**, 60 (414) **TS**, 30 (207) **YS**, 22 **El**

CAST CARBON STEELS

specification number	designation	country	product forms	composition	mechanical properties (see page iv for explanation)
ANSI/ASTM A 426	CP12	US	Pipe: centrifugally cast	0.15 **C**, 0.30–0.61 **Mn**, 0.50 **Si**, 0.80–1.25 **Cr**, 0.44–0.65 **Mo**, 0.045 **P**, 0.045 **S**	**Normalized and tempered**: all **diam**, 60 (414) **TS**, 30 (207) **YS**, 22 **El**
ANSI/ASTM A 426	CP7	US	Pipe: centrifugally cast	0.15 **C**, 0.30–0.60 **Mn**, 0.50–1.00 **Si**, 6.00–8.00 **Cr**, 0.44–0.65 **Mo**, 0.030 **P**, 0.030 **S**	**Normalized and tempered**: all **diam**, 60 (414) **TS**, 30 (207) **YS**, 22 **El**
ANSI/ASTM A 426	CP56	US	Pipe: centrifugally cast	0.15 **C**, 0.30–0.60 **Mn**, 1.00–2.00 **Si**, 4.00–6.00 **Cr**, 0.45–0.65 **Mo**, 0.030 **P**, 0.030 **S**	**Normalized and tempered**: all **diam**, 60 (414) **TS**, 30 (207) **YS**, 22 **El**
ASTM A 426	Grade CP 21	US	Pipe: centrifugally cast	0.15 **C**, 0.30–0.60 **Mn**, 0.50 **Si**, 2.65–3.35 **Cr**, 0.80–1.06 **Mo**, 0.50 **Ni**, 0.50 **Cu**, 0.030 **P**, 0.030 **S**, 0.10 **W**	**Normalized and tempered**: all **diam**, (414) **TS**, (207) **YS**, 22 **El**
ASTM A 426	Grade CP12	US	Pipe: centrifugally cast	0.15 **C**, 0.30–0.61 **Mn**, 0.50 **Si**, 0.80–1.25 **Cr**, 0.44–0.65 **Mo**, 0.50 **Ni**, 0.50 **Cu**, 0.045 **P**, 0.045 **S**, 0.10 **W**	**Normalized and tempered**: all **diam**, (414) **TS**, (207) **YS**, 22 **El**
ASTM A 426	Grade CP15	US	Pipe: centrifugally cast	0.15 **C**, 0.30–0.60 **Mn**, 0.15–1.65 **Si**, 0.44–0.65 **Mo**, 0.50 **Ni**, 0.50 **Cu**, 0.030 **P**, 0.030 **S**, 0.10 **W**	**Normalized and tempered**: all **diam**, (414) **TS**, (207) **YS**, 22 **El**
ASTM A 426	Grade CP5b	US	Pipe: centrifugally cast	0.15 **C**, 0.30–0.60 **Mn**, 1.00–2.00 **Si**, 4.0–6.0 **Cr**, 0.45–0.65 **Mo**, 0.50 **Ni**, 0.50 **Cu**, 0.030 **P**, 0.030 **S**, 0.10 **W**	**Normalized and tempered**: all **diam**, (414) **TS**, (207) **YS**, 22 **El**
ASTM A 426	Grade CP7	US	Pipe: centrifugally cast	0.15 **C**, 0.30–0.60 **Mn**, 0.50–1.00 **Si**, 6.0–8.0 **Cr**, 0.44–0.65 **Mo**, 0.50 **Ni**, 0.50 **Cu**, 0.030 **P**, 0.030 **S**, 0.10 **W**	**Normalized and tempered**: all **diam**, (414) **TS**, (207) **YS**, 22 **El**
JIS G 5202	Class 21	Japan	Pipe: centrifugally cast	0.15 **C**, 0.30–0.60 **Mn**, 0.60 **Si**, 1.00–1.50 **Cr**, 0.45–0.65 **Mo**, 0.030 **P**, 0.030 **S**	**Annealed, normalized, quenched, tempered**: all **diam**, (412) **TS**, (206) **YS**, 19 **El**
JIS G 5202	Class 32	Japan	Pipe: centrifugally cast	0.15 **C**, 0.30–0.60 **Mn**, 0.60 **Si**, 1.90–2.60 **Cr**, 0.90–1.20 **Mo**, 0.030 **P**, 0.030 **S**	**Annealed, normalized, quenched, tempered**: all **diam**, (412) **TS**, (206) **YS**, 19 **El**
BS 1504–503		UK	Castings	0.15 **C**, 0.50–0.80 **Mn**, 0.60 **Si**, 0.3 **Cr**, 3.0–4.0 **Ni**, 0.050 **S**, 0.050 **P**	**Annealed, normalized and tempered**: all **diam**, (400) **TS**, (240) **YS**, 25 **El**
IS 4491	Grade 1	India	Castings	0.15 **C**, 0.50 **Mn**, 0.60 **Si**, 0.050 **P**, 0.050 **S**; 0.80 other elements, total	**Annealed**: all **diam**, (345) **TS**, (185) **YS**, 22 **El**
BS 3100/1617	Grade A	UK	Sand castings	0.15 **C**	**Annealed or normalized**: all **diam**, (345) **TS**, (185) **YS**, 22 **El**
IS 2708	Grade 1	India	Castings	0.14–0.20 **C**, 1.20–1.70 **Mn**, 0.30–0.60 **Si**, 0.050 **P**, 0.050 **S**; 1.00 max, other elements, total	**As agreed**: all **diam**, (490) **TS**, (300) **YS**, 21 **El**
ASTM A 356	Grade 9	US	Castings	0.13–0.20 **C**, 0.50–0.90 **Mn**, 0.20–0.60 **Si**, 1.00–1.50 **Cr**, 0.90–1.20 **Mo**, 0.20–0.35 **V**, 0.035 **P**, 0.030 **S**	**Normalized and tempered**: all **diam**, 85 (585) **TS**, 60 (415) **YS**, 15 **El**
ASTM A 356	Grade 9	US	Castings	0.13–0.20 **C**, 0.50–0.90 **Mn**, 0.20–0.60 **Si**, 1.00–1.50 **Cr**, 0.90–1.20 **Mo**, 0.20–0.35 **V**, 0.035 **P**, 0.030 **S**	**Normalized or tempered**: all **diam**, 85 (585) **TS**, 60 (415) **YS**, 15 **El**
ASTM A 356	Grade 8	US	Castings	0.13–0.20 **C**, 0.50–0.90 **Mn**, 0.20–0.60 **Si**, 1.00–1.50 **Cr**, 0.90–1.20 **Mo**, 0.05–0.15 **V**, 0.035 **P**, 0.030 **S**	**Normalized and tempered**: all **diam**, 80 (550) **TS**, 50 (345) **YS**, 18 **El**
ASTM A 356	Grade 8	US	Castings	0.13–0.20 **C**, 0.50–0.90 **Mn**, 0.20–0.60 **Si**, 1.00–1.50 **Cr**, 0.90–1.20 **Mo**, 0.05–0.15 **V**, 0.035 **P**, 0.030 **S**	**Normalized or tempered**: all **diam**, 80 (550) **TS**, 50 (345) **YS**, 18 **El**
BS 2772 Part 3		UK	Sand castings	0.12–0.22 **C**, 1.30–1.70 **Mn**	**Normalized and tempered or hardened and tempered**: all **diam**, (495) **TS**, (310) **YS**
SAE Automotive J435a	Grade 0022	US	Castings	0.12–0.22 **C**, 0.50–0.90 **Mn**, 0.60 **Si**, 0.050 **P**, 0.060 **S**	
BS 3100/4241		UK	Sand castings	0.12–0.18 **C**, 0.60–1.10 **Cr**, 0.15–0.25 **Mo**, 3.00–3.75 **Ni**	**Annealed**: all **diam**, (1000) **TS**, 7 **El**

CAST CARBON STEELS

specification number	designation	country	product forms	composition	mechanical properties (see page iv for explanation)
IS 4898	Grade 3	India	Castings	0.12–0.18 **C**, 0.30–1.60 **Mn**, 0.60 **Si**, 0.60–1.10 **Cr**, 0.15–0.25 **Mo**, 3.00–3.75 **Ni**, 0.30 **Cu**, 0.040 **P**, 0.040 **S**	**Annealed**: all diam, (703) **TS**, 7 **El**
VSM 10697	GS–40/1.00416	Switzerland	Castings	0.12–0.16 **C**, 0.800 **Mn**, 0.30–0.50 **Si**, 0.40 **Cr**, 0.25 **Mo**, 0.50 **Ni**, 0.030 **P**, 0.030 **S**	**Annealed or normalized**: all **diam**, (400) **TS**, (200) **YS**, 25 **El**
VSM 10698	GS–40/10420	Switzerland	Castings	0.12–0.16 **C**, 0.80 **Mn**, 0.030–0.50 **Si**, 0.40 **Cr**, 0.25 **Mo**, 0.50 **Ni**, 0.030 **P**, 0.030 **S**	**Annealed or normalized**: all **diam**, (395) **TS**, (195) **YS**, 25 **El**
BS 3100/4242	Grade C	UK	Sand castings	0.12 **C**, 0.80 **Mn**, 3.0–4.0 **Ni**	**As required**: all **diam**, (460) **TS**, (275) **YS**, 20 **El**
IS 3038	Grade 3	India	Castings	0.11–0.19 **C**, 0.45–0.70 **Mn**, 0.20–0.50 **Si**, 0.50–0.70 **Cr**, 0.40–0.60 **Mo**, 0.20–0.35 **V**, 0.02 **Al**, 0.040 **P**, 0.045 **S**	**As agreed**: (25) **diam**, (510) **TS**, (300) **YS**, 16 **El**
AMS 5333A		US	Investment castings	0.11–0.17 **C**, 0.65–1.00 **Mn**, 0.50–1.00 **Si**, 0.35–0.65 **Cr**, 0.15–0.35 **Mo**, 0.35–0.75 **Ni**, 0.35 **Cu**, 0.04 **P**, 0.04 **S**	**Normalized**: all **diam**, 90 (621) **TS**, 65 (448) **YS**, 18 **El**
ANSI/ASTM A 426	CP2	US	Pipe: centrifugally cast	0.10–0.20 **C**, 0.30–0.61 **Mn**, 0.10–0.50 **Si**, 0.50–0.81 **Cr**, 0.44–0.65 **Mo**, 0.045 **P**, 0.045 **S**	**Normalized and tempered**: all **diam**, 60 (414) **TS**, 30 (207) **YS**, 22 **El**
ASTM A 426	Grade CP2	US	Pipe: centrifugally cast	0.10–0.20 **C**, 0.30–0.61 **Mn**, 0.10–0.50 **Si**, 0.50–0.81 **Cr**, 0.44–0.65 **Mo**, 0.50 **Ni**, 0.50 **Cu**, 0.045 **P**, 0.045 **S**, 0.10 **W**	**Normalized and tempered**: all **diam**, (414) **TS**, (207) **YS**, 22 **El**
BS HC 5		UK	Castings: aircraft quality	0.10–0.18 **C**, 0.30–0.60 **Mn**, 0.30–0.60 **Si**, 0.205 **Cr**, 0.15 **Mo**, 2.75–3.50 **Ni**, 0.30 **Cu**, 0.035 **P**, 0.035 **S**	**Hardened and tempered**: all **diam**, (700) **TS**, (350) **YS**, 13 **El**
BS 3100/4240		UK	Sand castings	0.10–0.18 **C**, 2.75–3.50 **Ni**	**Annealed or normalized**: all **diam**, (695) **TS**, 11 **El**
BS 3146: Part 1	CLA 10	UK	Investment and precision castings	0.10–0.18 **C**, 2.75–3.50 **Ni**	**Test bars–blank carburize**: all **diam**, (695) **TS**
DTD 5239		UK	Investment and precision castings	0.10–0.18 **C**, 2.75–3.50 **Ni**	**Test samples–blank carburize**: all **diam**, (685) **TS**, (345) **YS**, 13 **El**
IS 4898	Grade 2	India	Castings	0.10–0.18 **C**, 0.60–1.00 **Mn**, 0.60 **Si**, 0.25 **Cr**, 0.15 **Mo**, 0.40 **Ni**, 0.30 **Cu**, 0.050 **P**, 0.050 **S**	**Annealed or normalized**: all **diam**, (490) **TS**, 11 **El**
BS 3100/4239		UK	Sand castings	0.10–0.18 **C**	**As cast or annealed or normalized**: all **diam**, (490) **TS**, 12 **El**
BS 3146: Part 1	CLA 9	UK	Investment and precision castings	0.10–0.18 **C**	**Test bars–blank carburize**: all **diam**, (490) **TS**
IS 4898	Grade 1	India	Castings	0.10–0.18 **C**, 0.60–1.00 **Mn**, 0.60 **Si**, 0.25 **Cr**, 0.15 **Mo**, 0.40 **Ni**, 0.30 **Cu**, 0.050 **S**, 0.050 **P**	**Annealed or normalized**: all **diam**, (345) **TS**, 12 **El**
BS 1504–660		UK	Castings	0.10–0.15 **C**, 0.40–0.70 **Mn**, 0.45 **Si**, 0.30–0.50 **Cr**, 0.40–0.60 **Mo**, 0.30 **Ni**, 0.30 **Cu**, 0.030 **P**, 0.030 **S**	**Normalized and tempered**: all **diam**, (510) **TS**, (295) **YS**, 17 **El**
VSM 10698	G–X 5 CrNi 13 4 V 90	Switzerland	Castings	0.07 **C**, 0.80 **Mn**, 0.30–0.50 **Si**, 12.5–13.5 **Cr**, 0.45–0.55 **Mo**, 3.5–4.0 **Ni**, 0.030 **P**, 0.030 **S**	**Air quenched**: all **diam**, (885) **TS**, (785) **YS**, 12 **El**
VSM 10698	G–X5 CrNi 13 4 V 70/1.40313	Switzerland	Castings	0.07 **C**, 0.8 **Mn**, 0.30–0.50 **Si**, 12.5–13.5 **Cr**, 0.45–0.55 **Mo**, 3.5–4.0 **Ni**, 0.030 **P**, 0.030 **S**	**Air quenched**: all **diam**, (740) **TS**, (590) **YS**, 15 **El**
AMS 5210A		US	Castings	0.040 **C**, 0.75–1.30 **Si**, 0.12 **Cu**, 0.050 **P**, 0.050 **S**	**Annealed**: all **diam**
MIL–S–46052A	Class 260–210	US	Castings		**As agreed**: all **diam**, 260 (1793) **TS**, 210 (1448) **YS**, 6 **El**
MIL–S–46052A	Class 220–180	US	Castings		**As agreed**: all **diam**, 220 (1517) **TS**, 180 (1241) **YS**, 15 **El**
MIL–S–46052A	Class 180–150	US	Castings		**As agreed**: all **diam**, 180 (1241) **TS**, 150 (1034) **YS**, 20 **El**

CAST CARBON STEELS

specification number	designation	country	product forms	composition	mechanical properties (see page iv for explanation)
ASTM A 148	Grade 175–145	US	Castings		**Annealed, normalized, normalized and tempered, quenched and tempered**: all **diam**, 175 (1207) **TS**, 145 (1000) **YS**, 6 **El**
SAE Automotive J435a	Grade 0175	US	Castings	0.050 **P**, 0.060 **S**	**Normalized, quenched and tempered**: all **diam**, 175 (1206) **TS**, 145 (1000) **YS**, 6 **El**
ASTM A 148	Grade 175–145	US	Sand castings	0.05 **P**, 0.06 **S**	**Annealed, normalized or quenched and tempered as specified**: all **diam**, 175 (1205) **TS**, 145 (1000) **YS**, 6 **El**
ASTM A 148	Grade 175–145	US	Sand castings	0.05 **P**, 0.06 **S**	**Annealed, normalized or quenched and tempered**: all **diam**, 175 (1205) **TS**, 145 (1000) **YS**, 6 **El**
DTD 705		UK	Sand castings		**Annealed and hardened and tempered**: all **diam**, (1155) **TS**
DTD 5072		UK	Investment and precision castings		**Normalized and hardened or annealed and hardened and tempered**: all **diam**, (1155) **TS**, (910) **YS**
BS 3146: Part 1	CLA5: Grade B	UK	Investment and precision castings		**Annealed and hardened and tempered, or normalized and hardened and tempered**: all **diam**, (1155) **TS**
ASTM A 148	Grade 150–125	US	Sand castings	0.05 **P**, 0.06 **S**	**Annealed, normalized or quenched and tempered**: all **diam**, 150 (1035) **TS**, 125 (860) **YS**, 9 **El**
ASTM A 148	Grade 150–125	US	Sand castings	0.05 **P**, 0.06 **S**	**Annealed, normalized or quenched and tempered**: all **diam**, 150 (1035) **TS**, 125 (860) **YS**, 9 **El**
MIL–S–15083B	Class 150–125	US	Sand castings	0.05 **P**, 0.06 **S**	**Annealed or normalized and tempered or quenched and tempered**: all **diam**, 150 (1034) **TS**, 125 (862) **YS**, 9 **El**
ASTM A 148	Grasde 150–125	US	Castings		**Annealed, normalized, normalized and tempered, quenched and tempered**: all **diam**, 150 (1034) **TS**, 125 (862) **YS**, 9 **El**
NOM–B–353	Class 105–88	Mexico	Castings	0.060 **P**, 0.050 **S**	**Annealed, normalized, normalized and quenched, quenched and tempered**: all **diam**, (1029) **TS**, (863) **YS**, 9 **El**
NOM–B–353	Class 123–102	Mexico	Castings	0.060 **P**, 0.050 **S**	**Annealed, normalized, normalized and quenched, quenched and tempered**: all **diam**, (1025) **TS**, (1000) **YS**, 6 **El**
BS 3100/1458	Grade C	UK	Sand castings		**Hardened and tempered**: all **diam**, (1000) **TS**, (695) **YS**, 6 **El**
SAE Automotive J435a	Grade 0150	US	Castings	0.050 **P**, 0.060 **S**	**Normalized, quenched and tempered**: all **diam**, 150 (965) **TS**, 125 (862) **YS**, 9 **El**
DTD 666		UK	Sand castings		**Annealed and hardened and tempered**: all **diam**, (930) **TS**
BS 3146: Part 1	CLA5: Grade A	UK	Investment and precision castings		**Annealed and hardened and tempered, or normalized and hardened and tempered**: all **diam**, (920) **TS**
BS 3100/1458	Grade B	UK	Sand castings		**Hardened and tempered**: all **diam**, (850) **TS**, (590) **YS**, 8 **El**
DTD 5172		UK	Investment and precision castings		**Normalized and hardened and tempered, or annealed and hardened and tempered**: all **diam**, (850) **TS**, (665) **YS**

CAST CARBON STEELS

specification number	designation	country	product forms	composition	mechanical properties (see page iv for explanation)
BS 3146: Part 1	CLA 4	UK	Investment and precision castings		**Annealed and hardened and tempered**: all **diam**, (850) **TS**, (590) **YS**
IS 2644	Grade 3 CS85	India	Castings	0.050 **P**, 0.050 **S**	**As agreed**: all **diam**, (835) **TS**, (695) **YS**, 12 **El**
AAR M 201-66	Grade E	US	Castings	0.050 **P**	**Quenched and tempered**: all **diam**, 120 (827) **TS**, 100 (689) **YS**, 14 **El**
SAE Automotive J435a	Grade 0120	US	Castings	0.050 **P**, 0.060 **S**	**Normalized, quenched and tempered**: all **diam**, 120 (827) **TS**, 95 (655) **YS**, 14 **El**
MIL-S-15083B	Class 120-95	US	Sand castings	0.05 **P**, 0.06 **S**	**Annealed or normalized and tempered or quenched and tempered**: all **diam**, 120 (827) **TS**, 95 (655) **YS**, 14 **El**
ASTM A 148	Grade 120-95	US	Castings		**Annealed, normalized, normalized and tempered, quenched and tempered**: all **diam**, 120 (827) **TS**, 95 (655) **YS**, 14 **El**
ASTM A 148	Grade 120-95	US	Sand castings	0.05 **P**, 0.06 **S**	**Annealed, normalized or quenched and tempered**: all **diam**, 120 (825) **TS**, 95 (655) **YS**, 14 **El**
ASTM A 148	Grade 120-95	US	Sand castings	0.05 **P**, 0.06 **S**	**Annealed, normalized or quenched and tempered**: all **diam**, 120 (825) **TS**, 95 (655) **YS**, 14 **El**
NOM-B-353	Class 84-67	Mexico	Castings	0.060 **P**, 0.050 **S**	**Annealed normalized, normalized and quenched, quenched and tempered**: all **diam**, (824) **TS**, (657) **YS**, 14 **El**
ASTM A 148	Grade 105-85	US	Sand castings	0.05 **P**, 0.06 **S**	**Annealed, normalized or quenched and tempered**: all **diam**, 105 (725) **TS**, 85 (585) **YS**, 17 **El**
ASTM A 148	Grade 105-85	US	Sand castings	0.05 **P**, 0.06 **S**	**Annealed, normalized or quenched and tempered**: all **diam**, 105 (725) **TS**, 85 (585) **YS**, 17 **El**
ASTM 201-66	Grade D	US	Castings	0.050 **P**, 0.060 **S**	**Quenched and tempered**: all **diam**, 105 (724) **TS**, 85 (586) **YS**, 17 **El**
SAE Automotive J435a	Grade 0105	US	Castings	0.050 **P**, 0.060 **S**	**Normalized, quenched and tempered**: all **diam**, 105 (724) **TS**, 85 (586) **YS**, 17 **El**
MIL-S-15083B	Class 105-85	US	Sand castings	0.05 **P**, 0.06 **S**	**Annealed or normalized and tempered or quenched and tempered**: alloy **diam**, 105 (724) **TS**, 85 (586) **YS**, 17 **El**
ASTM A 148	Grade 105-85	US	Castings		**Annealed, normalized, normalized and tempered, quenched and tempered**: all **diam**, 105 (724) **TS**, 85 (586) **YS**, 17 **El**
IS 2644	Grade 2 CS71	India	Castings	0.050 **P**, 0.050 **S**	**As agreed**: all **diam**, (695) **TS**, (560) **YS**, 15 **El**
BS 3100/1458	Grade A	UK	Sand castings		**Hardened and tempered**: all **diam**, (695) **TS**, (500) **YS**, 11 **El**
BS 3146: Part 1	CLA 3	UK	Investment and precision castings		**Annealed and hardened and tempered**: all **diam**, (695) **TS**, (500) **YS**
IS 2644	Grade 1 CS65	India	Castings	0.050 **P**, 0.050 **S**	**As agreed**: all **diam**, (635) **TS**, (390) **YS**, 17 **El**
SAE Automotive J435a	Grade 090	US	Castings	0.050 **P**, 0.060 **S**	**Normalized and tempered, normalized, quenched and tempered**: all **diam**, 90 (621) **TS**, 60 (414) **YS**, 20 **El**
MIL-S-15083B	Class 90-60	US	Sand castings	0.05 **P**, 0.06 **S**	**Annealed or normalized and tempered or quenched and tempered**: alloy **diam**, 90 (621) **TS**, 60 (414) **YS**, 20 **El**

CAST CARBON STEELS

specification number	designation	country	product forms	composition	mechanical properties (see page iv for explanation)
ASTM A 148	Grade 90–60	US	Castings		**Annealed, normalized, normalized and tempered, quenched and tempered**: all **diam**, 90 (621) **TS**, 60 (414) **YS**, 20 **El**
ASTM A 148	Grade 90–60	US	Sand castings	0.05 **P**, 0.06 **S**	**Annealed, normalized or quenched and tempered**: all **diam**, 90 (620) **TS**, 60 (415) **YS**, 20 **El**
ASTM A 148	Grade 90–60	US	Sand castings	0.05 **P**, 0.06 **S**	**Annealed, normalized or quenched and tempered**: all **diam**, 90 (620) **TS**, 60 (415) **YS**, 20 **El**
NOM–B–353	Class 63–42	Mexico	Castings	0.060 **P**, 0.050 **S**	**Annealed, normalized, normalized and quenched, quenched and tempered**: all **diam**, (618) **TS**, (412) **YS**, 20 **El**
NBN A 22–101	AGMS 30–60	Belgium	Castings		**As agreed**: all **diam**, (600) **TS**, 14 **El**
IS 1030	Grade 30–57	India	Castings		**As agreed**: all **diam**, (570) **TS**, (300) **YS**, 15 **El**
NFA 32–051	E 30–57 M	France	Castings	0.50 **Si**, 0.040 **P**, 0.040 **S**	**Annealed, normalized or quenched and tempered**: all **diam**, (570) **TS**, (200) **YS**, 15 **El**
ISO 3755	Grade 30–57	IPO	Sand castings	0.040 **P**, 0.040 **S**	**As cast and annealed or normalized or normalized and tempered or quenched and tempered**: all **diam**, (570) **TS**, (300) **YS**, 15 **El**
SAE Automotive J435a	Grade 080	US	Castings	0.50 **P**, 0.060 **S**	**Annealed, normalized, normalized and tempered, quenched and tempered**: all **diam**, 80 (552) **TS**, 50 (345) **YS**, 22 **El**
MIL–S–15083B	Class 80–50	US	Sand castings	0.05 **P**, 0.06 **S**	**Annealed or normalized and tempered or quenched and tempered**: all **diam**, 80 (552) **TS**, 50 (345) **YS**, 22 **El**
ASTM A 148	Grade 80–40	US	Castings		**Annealed, normalized, normalized and tempered, quenched and tempered**: all **diam**, 80 (552) **TS**, 40 (276) **YS**, 18 **El**
ASTM A 148	Grade 80–50	US	Castings		**Annealed, normalized, normalized and tempered, quenched and tempered**: all **diam**, 80 (552) **TS**, 50 (345) **YS**, 22 **El**
ASTM A 148	Grade 80–40	US	Sand castings	0.05 **P**, 0.06 **S**	**Annealed, normalized or quenched and tempered**: all **diam**, 80 (550) **TS**, 40 (275) **YS**, 18 **El**
ASTM A 148	Grade 80–50	US	Sand castings	0.05 **P**, 0.06 **S**	**Annealed, normalized or quenched and tempered as specified**: all **diam**, 80 (550) **TS**, 50 (345) **YS**, 22 **El**
ASTM A 148	Grade 80–40	US	Sand castings	0.05 **P**, 0.06 **S**	**Annealed, normalized or quenched and tempered**: all **diam**, 80 (550) **TS**, 40 (275) **YS**, 18 **El**
ASTM A 148	Grade 80–50	US	Sand castings	0.05 **P**, 0.06 **S**	**Annealed, normalized or quenched and tempered**: all **diam**, 80 (550) **TS**, 50 (345) **YS**, 22 **El**
NOM–B–353	Class 56–28	Mexico	Castings	0.060 **P**, 0.050 **S**	**Annealed, normalized, normalized and quenched, quenched and tempered**: all **diam**, (549) **TS**, (274) **YS**, 18 **El**

CAST CARBON STEELS

specification number	designation	country	product forms	composition	mechanical properties (see page iv for explanation)
NOM–B–353	Class 56–35	Mexico	Castings	0.060 **P**, 0.050 **S**	**Annealed, normalized, normalized and quenched, quenched and tempered**: all **diam**, (549) **TS**, (343) **YS**, 22 **El**
IS 1030	Grade 27–54	India	Castings		**As agreed**: all **diam**, (540) **TS**, (270) **YS**, 16 **El**
IS 1030	Grade 26–52	India	Castings		**As agreed**: all **diam**, (520) **TS**, (260) **YS**, 18 **El**
NBN A 22–101	AMGS 26–52	Belgium	Castings		**As agreed**: all **diam**, (520) **TS**, 18 **El**
NF A 32–051	E 26–52–M	France	Castings	0.5 **Si**, 0.040 **P**	**Annealed, normalized or quenched and tempered**: all **diam**, (520) **TS**, (260) **YS**, 18 **El**
ISO 3755	Grade 26–52	ISO	Sand castings	0.040 **P**, 0.040 **S**	**As cast and annealed or normalized or normalized and tempered or quenched and tempered**: all **diam**, (520) **TS**, (260) **YS**, 18 **El**
ASTM 201–66	Grade B	US	Castings	.85 **Mn**, 0.050 **P**, 0.050 **S**	**Annealed, normalized**: all **diam**, 70 (483) **TS**, 38 (262) **YS**, 24 **El**
JIS G 5101	Class 4	Japan	Castings, pipe (centrifugally cast)		**Annealed, normalized, tempered**: all **diam**, (481) **TS**, (245) **YS**, 17 **El**
BS 1504–101	Grade C	UK	Castings	0.25 **Cr**, 0.15 **Mo**, 0.40 **Ni**, 0.40 **Cu**, 0.060 **S**, 0.060 **P**	**Annealed or normalized, or annealed and normalized**: all **diam**, (480) **TS**, (240) **YS**, 15 **El**
JIS G 5101	Class 3	Japan	Castings, pipe (centrifugally cast)		**Annealed, normalized, tempered**: all **diam**, (451) **TS**, (226) **YS**, 19 **El**
IS 1030	Grade 23–45	India	Castings		**As agreed**: all **diam**, (450) **TS**, (230) **YS**, 22 **El**
NBN N 22–101	AMGS 23–45	Belgium	Castings		**As agreed**: all **diam**, (450) **TS**, 22 **El**
ASTM 201–66	Grade a	US	Castings	0.85 **Mn**, 0.050 **P**, 0.050 **S**	**Unannealed, annealed, normalized**: all **diam**, 60 (414) **TS**, 30 (207) **YS**, 22 **El**
JIS G 5101	Class 2	Japan	Castings, pipe (centrifugally cast)		**Annealed, normalized, tempered**: all **diam**, (412) **TS**, (206) **YS**, 21 **El**
IS 1030	Grade 20–40	India	Castings		**As agreed**: all **diam**, (400) **TS**, (200) **YS**, 25 **El**
NBN A 22–101	AMGS 20–40	Belgium	Castings		**As agreed**: all **diam**, (400) **TS**, 25 **El**
BS 1504–101		UK	Sand castings		**Annealed or normalized or annealed and normalized**: all **diam**, (400) **TS**, (196) **YS**
BS 1504–101	Grade B	UK	Castings	0.25 **Cr**, 0.15 **Mo**, 0.40 **Ni**, 0.40 **Cu**, 0.060 **S**, 0.060 **P**	**Annealed or normalized, or annealed and normalized**: all **diam**, (385) **TS**, (195) **YS**, 20 **El**
JIS G 5101	Class 1	Japan	Castings, pipe (centrifugally cast)		**Annealed, normalized, tempered**: all **diam**, (363) **TS**, (177) **YS**, 23 **El**
BS 1504–101	Grade A	UK	Castings	0.25 **Cr**, 0.15 **Mo**, 0.40 **Ni**, 0.40 **Cu**, 0.060 **S**, 0.060 **P**	**Annealed or normalized, or annealed and normalized**: all **diam**, (360) **TS**, (180) **YS**, 20 **El**

CAST HIGH ALLOY, CORROSION RESISTANT, HEAT RESISTANT, AND ABRASION RESISTANT STEELS

specification number	designation	country	product forms	composition	mechanical properties (see page iv for explanation)
IS 4522	Grade 3	India	Castings	1.20–1.40 **C**, 1.00 **Mn**, 27.0–30.0 **Cr**, 2.00 **Si**, 0.050 **P**, 0.050 **S**	
ASTM A–128	Grade B–4	US	Castings	1.2–1.35 **C**, 11.5–14.0 **Mn**, 1.00 **Si**, 0.07 **P**	
NOM–B–351	Class B–4	Mexico	Castings	1.20–1.35 **C**, 11.5–14.0 **Mn**, 1.00 **Si**, 0.070 **P**	
ANSI/ASTM A 128	Grade B–4	US	Castings	1.2–1.35 **C**, 11.5–14.0 **Mn**, 0.07 **P**, 1.00 **S**	
IS 7520	Grade 1	India	Castings	1.2 **C**, 0.5 **Mn**, 10.00–12.00 **Si**, 0.25 **P**, 0.10 **S**	
ASTM A–128	Grade B–3	US	Castings	1.12–1.28 **C**, 11.5–14.0 **Mn**, 1.00 **Si**, 0.07 **P**	
NOM–B–351	Class B–3	Mexico	Castings	1.12–1.28 **C**, 11.5–14.0 **Mn**, 1.00 **Si**, 0.070 **P**	
ANSI/ASTM A 128	Grade B–3	US	Castings	1.12–1.28 **C**, 11.5–14.0 **Mn**, 0.07 **P**, 1.00 **S**	
ASTM A–128	Grade E–2	US	Castings	1.05–1.45 **C**, 11.5–14.0 **Mn**, 1.00 **Si**, 1.8–2.1 **Mo**, 0.07 **P**	
NOM–B–351	Class E–2	Mexico	Castings	1.05–1.45 **C**, 11.5–14.0 **Mn**, 1.00 **Si**, 1.8–2.1 **Mo**, 0.070 **P**	
ANSI/ASTM A 128	Grade E–2	US	Castings	1.05–1.45 **C**, 11.5–14.0 **Mn**, 1.8–2.1 **Mo**, 0.07 **P**, 1.00 **S**	
ASTM A–128	Grade F	US	Castings	1.05–1.35 **C**, 6.0–8.0 **Mn**, 1.00 **Si**, 0.9–1.2 **Mo**, 0.07 **P**	
ASTM A–128	Grade C	US	Castings	1.05–1.35 **C**, 11.5–14.0 **Mn**, 1.5–2.5 **Cr**, 1.00 **Si**, 0.07 **P**	
ASTM A–128	Grade A	US	Castings	1.05–1.35 **C**, 11.0 **Mn**, 1.00 **Si**, 0.07 **P**	
NOM–B–351	Class A	Mexico	Castings	1.05–1.35 **C**, 11.0 min **Mn**, 1.00 **Si**, 0.070 **P**	
ANSI/ASTM A 128	Grade F	US	Castings	1.05–1.35 **C**, 6.0–8.0 **Mn**, 0.9–1.2 **Mo**, 0.07 **P**, 1.00 **S**	
ANSI/ASTM A 128	Grade C	US	Castings	1.05–1.35 **C**, 11.5–14.0 **Mn**, 1.5–2.5 **Cr**, 0.07 **P**, 1.00 **S**	
ANSI/ASTM A 128	Grade A	US	Castings	1.05–1.35 **C**, 11.0 min **Mn**, 0.07 **P**, 1.00 **S**	
ASTM A–128	Grade B–2	US	Castings	1.05–1.2 **C**, 11.5–14.0 **Mn**, 1.00 **Si**, 0.07 **P**	
NOM–B–351	Class B–2	Mexico	Castings	1.05–1.20 **C**, 11.5–14.0 **Mn**, 1.00 **Si**, 0.070 **P**	
ANSI/ASTM A 128	Grade B–2	US	Castings	1.05–1.2 **C**, 11.5–14.0 **Mn**, 0.07 **P**, 1.00 **S**	
BS 3100/1648	Grade C	UK	Sand castings	1.0–2.0 **C**, 25.0–30.0 **Cr**, 4.0 **Ni**	
FVRDE 1025		UK	Sand castings	1.0–1.40 **C**, 11.0–14.0 **Mn**	
FVRDE 1025/A		UK	Sand castings	1.0–1.4 **C**, 11.0–14.0 **Mn**, 1.75–2.25 **Cr**	
JIS G 5131	Class 21	Japan	Castings	1.00–1.35 **C**, 11.00–14.00 **Mn**, 2.00–3.00 **Cr**, 0.80 **Si**, 0.070 **P**, 0.040 **S**, 0.40–0.70 **V**	**Water quenched**: all **diam**, (736) **TS**, (441) **YS**, 10 **El**
MIL–S–17249	Types A and B	US	Sand castings	1.00–1.35 **C**, 12.0–14.0 **Mn**, 0.75 **Cr**, 1.00 **Ni**, 0.40–1.00 **Si**, 0.50 **Mo**, 0.060 **P**	**As quenched**: all **diam**, (689) **TS**, (310) **YS**, 25 **El**
NS 1699	Sst Mn 12	Norway	Castings	1.0–1.35 **C**, 11.0–14.0 **Mn**, 1.0 **Si**, 0.08 **P**, 0.04 **S**	
NOM–B–351	Class C	Mexico	Castings	1.00–1.35 **C**, 11.5–14.0 **Mn**, 1.5–2.5 **Cr**, 1.50 **Si**, 0.070 **P**	
BS 3100/1457		UK	Sand castings	1.00–1.25 **C**, 11.00 min **Mn**	
ANSI/ASTM A 296	Grade CZ–100	US	Sand castings	1.00 **C**, 1.50 **Mn**, rem **Ni**, 2.00 **Si**, 0.030 **P**, 0.030 **S**, 1.25 **Cu**, 3.00 **Fe**	**As cast, annealed**: all **diam**, 50 (345) **TS**, 18 (125) **YS**, 10 **El**
IS 7520	Grade 2	India	Castings	1.0 **C**, 0.5 **Mn**, 14.00–16.00 **Si**, 0.25 **P**, 0.10 **S**	
BS 3100/1648	Grade B1	UK	Sand castings	1.0 **C**, 25.0–30.0 **Cr**, 4.0 **Ni**	
MIL–S–81591	IC–440C	US	Investment castings	0.95–1.20 **C**, 1.00 **Mn**, 16.0–18.0 **Cr**, 0.75 **Ni**, 1.00 **Si**, 0.35–0.75 **Mo**, 0.040 **P**, 0.030 **S**	**Quenched and tempered**

CAST HIGH ALLOY STEELS

specification number	designation	country	product forms	composition	mechanical properties (see page iv for explanation)
AMS 5352B		US	Investment castings	0.95–1.20 **C**, 1.00 **Mn**, 16.00–18.00 **Cr**, 0.75 **Ni**, 1.00 **Si**, 0.35–0.75 **Mo**, 0.040 **P**, 0.030 **S**, 0.50 **Cu**	**Annealed**: all **diam**
JIS G 5131	Class II	Japan	Castings	0.90–1.30 **C**, 11.00–14.00 **Mn**, 1.50–2.50 **Cr**, 0.80 **Si**, 0.070 **P**, 0.040 **S**	**Water quenched**: all **diam**, (736) **TS**, (392) **YS**, 20 **El**
JIS G 5131	Class 1	Japan	Castings	0.90–1.30 **C**, 11.00–14.00 **Mn**, 0.100 **P**, 0.050 **S**	
JIS G 5131	Class 3	Japan	Castings	0.90–1.20 **C**, 11.00–14.00 **Mn**, 0.30–0.80 **Si**, 0.050 **P**, 0.035 **S**	**Water quenched**: all **diam**, (736) **TS**, 35 **El**
JIS G 5131	Class 2	Japan	Castings	0.90–1.20 **C**, 11.00–14.00 **Mn**, 0.80 **Si**, 0.070 **P**, 0.040 **S**	**Water quenched**: all **diam**, (736) **TS**, 35 **El**
ASTM A–128	Grade B–1	US	Castings	0.9–1.05 **C**, 11.5–14.0 **Mn**, 1.00 **Si**, 0.07 **P**	
NOM–B–351	Class B–1	Mexico	Castings	0.90–1.05 **C**, 11.5–14.0 **Mn**, 1.00 **Si**, 0.070 **P**	
ANSI/ASTM A 128	Grade B–1	US	Castings	0.9–1.05 **C**, 11.5–14.0 **Mn**, 0.07 **P**, 1.00 **S**	
ANSI/ASTM A 567	Grade HH90	US	Sand castings	0.80–1.00 **C**, 2.00 **Mn**, 24.00–28.00 **Cr**, 11.00–14.00 **Ni**, 2.00 **Si**, 0.50 **Mo**, 0.040 **P**, 0.040 **S**; rem Fe	
IS 7520	Grade 3	India	Castings	0.8 **C**, 0.5 **Mn**, 16.00–18.00 **Si**, 0.25 **P**, 0.10 **S**	
BS 3146 Part 2	ANC 5 Grade C	UK	Investment and precision castings	0.75 **C**, 10.0–20.0 **Cr**, 55.0–65.0 **Ni**	
BS 3100/1648	Grade K	UK	Sand castings	0.75 **C**, 10.0–20.0 **Cr**, 55.0–65.0 **Ni**	
BS 3100/1648	Grade H2	UK	Sand castings	0.75 **C**, 15.0–25.0 **Cr**, 36.0–46.0 **Ni**	
BS 3100/1648	Grade H1	UK	Sand castings	0.75 **C**, 13.0–20.0 **Cr**, 30.0–40.0 **Ni**	
ASTM A–128	Grade E–1	US	Castings	0.7–1.30 **C**, 11.5–14.0 **Mn**, 1.00 **Si**, 0.9–1.20 **Mo**, 0.070 **P**	
ASTM A–128	Grade D	US	Castings	0.7–1.3 **C**, 11.5–14.0 **Mn**, 3.00–4.0 **Ni**, 1.00 **Si**, 0.07 **P**	
NOM–B–351	Class D	Mexico	Castings	0.70–1.30 **C**, 11.5–14.0 **Mn**, 3.0–4.0 **Ni**, 1.00 **Si**, 0.070 **P**	
NOM–B–351	Class E–1	Mexico	Castings	0.70–1.30 **C**, 11.5–14.0 **Mn**, 1.00 **Si**, 0.9–1.2 **Mo**, 0.070 **P**	
ANSI/ASTM A 128	Grade E–1	US	Castings	0.7–1.3 **C**, 11.5–14.0 **Mn**, 0.19–1.2 **Mo**, 0.07 **P**, 1.00 **S**	
ANSI/ASTM A 128	Grade D	US	Castings	0.7–1.3 **C**, 11.5–14.0 **Mn**, 3.0–4.0 **Ni**, 0.07 **P**, 1.00 **S**	
ANSI/ASTM A 518		US	Sand castings	14.20–14.75 **Si**, 1.50 **Mn**, 0.50 **Cr**, 0.50 **Mo**, 0.50 **Cu**, 0.70–1.10 **C**	
MIL–S–81591	IC–440A	US	Investment castings	0.60–0.75 **C**, 1.00 **Mn**, 16.0–18.0 **Cr**, 1.00 **Si**, 0.75 Mo, 0.040 **P**, 0.030 **S**	**Quenched and tempered**
BS 3146 Part 1	CLA 12: Grade C	UK	Investment, precision castings	0.55–0.65 **C**, 0.80–1.50 **Cr**, 0.20–0.40 **Mo**	
NOM–B–355	Class HD	Mexico	Castings	0.50 **C**, 1.50 **Mn**, 26.0–30.0 **Cr**, 4.0–7.0 **Ni**, 2.0 **Si**, 0.50 **Mo**, 0.04 **P**, 0.04 **S**	**As cast**: all **diam**, (517) **TS**, (241) **YS**, 8 **El**
ASTM A–297–76	Grade HD	US	Castings	0.50 **C**, 1.50 **Mn**, 26.0–30.0 **Cr**, 4.0–7.0 **Ni**, 2.00 **Si**, 0.50 **Mo**, 0.04 **P**, 0.04 **S**	**As agreed**: all **diam**, 75 (515) **TS**, 35 (240) **YS**, 8 **El**
ANSI/ASTM A 297	Grade HD	US	Sand castings	0.50 **C**, 1.50 **Mn**, 26.0–30.0 **Cr**, 4.0–7.0 **Ni**, 2.00 **Si**, 0.50 **Mo**, 0.04 **P**, 0.04 **S**	**As cast**: all **diam**, 75 (515) **TS**, 35 (240) **YS**, 8 **El**
IS 3444	Grade 5	India	Castings	0.50 **C**, 1.00 **Mn**, 26.0–30.0 **Cr**, 4.00 **Ni**, 1.00 **Si**, 0.040 **P**, 0.040 **S**	**Annealed**: all **diam**, (382) **TS**
ASTM A–297–76	Grade HC	US	Castings	0.50 **C**, 1.00 **Mn**, 26.0–30.0 **Cr**, 4.00 **Ni**, 2.00 **Si**, 0.50 **Mo**, 0.04 **P**, 0.04 **S**	**As agreed**: all **diam**, 55 (380) **TS**
ASTM A 743	Grade CC–50	US	Castings	0.50 **C**, 1.00 **Mn**, 26.0–30.0 **Cr**, 4.00 **Ni**, 1.50 **Si**, 0.04 **P**, 0.04 **S**	**Normalized, annealed**: all **diam**, (380) **TS**
ANSI/ASTM A 296	Grade CC–50	US	Sand castings	0.50 **C**, 1.00 **Mn**, 26.0–30.0 **Cr**, 4.00 **Ni**, 1.50 **Si**, 0.040 **P**, 0.040 **S**	**Annealed**: all **diam**, 55 (380) **TS**

CAST HIGH ALLOY STEELS

specification number	designation	country	product forms	composition	mechanical properties (see page iv for explanation)
ANSI/ASTM A 297	Grade HC	US	Sand castings	0.50 **C**, 1.00 **Mn**, 26.0–30.0 **Cr**, 4.00 **Ni**, 2.00 **Si**, 0.50 **Mo**, 0.04 **P**, 0.04 **S**	**As cast**: all **diam**, 55 (380) **TS**
NOM–B–354	Class CC–50	Mexico	Castings	0.50 **C**, 1.0 **Mn**, 26.0–30.0 **Cr**, 4.0 **Ni**, 1.50 **Si**, 0.040 **P**, 0.040 **S**	**Normalized**: all **diam**, (379) **TS**
NOM–B–355	Class HC	Mexico	Castings	0.50 **C**, 1.00 **Mn**, 26.0–30.0 **Cr**, 4.0 **Ni**, 2.0 **Si**, 0.50 **Mo**, 0.04 **P**, 0.04 **S**	**As cast**: all **diam**, (379) **TS**
BS 3146 Part 2	ANC 5 Grade B	UK	Investment and precision castings	0.5 **C**, 15.0–25.0 **Cr**, 36.0–46.0 **Ni**	
BS 3146 Part 2	ANC 5 Grade A	UK	Investment and precision castings	0.5 **C**, 22.0–27.0 **Cr**, 17.0–22.0 **Ni**	
BS 3100/1648	Grade G	UK	Sand castings	0.5 **C**, 17.0–23.0 **Cr**, 23.0–28.0 **Ni**	
BS 3100/1648	Grade F	UK	Sand castings	0.5 **C**, 22.0–27.0 **Cr**, 17.0–22.0 **Ni**	
BS 3100/1648	Grade E	UK	Sand castings	0.5 **C**, 22.0–27.0 **Cr**, 10.0–14.0 **Ni**	
BS 3100/1648	Grade B2	UK	Sand castings	0.5 **C**, 25.0–30.0 **Cr**, 8.0–12.0 **Ni**	
BS 3146 Part 1	CLA 12: Grades A and B	UK	Investment, precision castings	0.45–0.55 **C**, 0.80–1.20 **Cr**	**(Grade A only) Softened or annealed, normalized and tempered; annealed, quenched and tempered**: all **diam**, (695) **TS**
ANSI/ASTM A 567	Grade HI–50C	US	Sand castings	0.45–0.55 **C**, 2.00 **Mn**, 26.00–30.00 **Cr**, 14.00–18.00 **Ni**, 2.00 **Si**, 0.50 **Mo**, 0.040 **P**, 0.040 **S**, 0.75–1.25 **Nb+Ta**, 0.10–0.15 **N**; rem Fe	
ANSI/ASTM A 608	Grade HD50	US	Tube: centrifugally cast	0.45–0.55 **C**, 1.50 **Mn**, 26.0–30.0 **Cr**, 4.0–7.0 **Ni**, 0.50–2.00 **Si**, 0.50 **Mo**, 0.040 **P**, 0.040 **S**	
ASTM A 608	Grade HD50	US	Pipe: centrifugally cast	0.45–0.55 **C**, 1.5 **Mn**, 26.0–30.0 **Cr**, 4.0–7.0 **Ni**, 0.5–2.0 **Si**, 0.50 **Mo**, 0.04 **P**, 0.04 **S**	
ANSI/ASTM A 567	Grade HK–40	US	Sand castings	0.45–0.55 **C**, 2.00 **Mn**, 24.00–28.00 **Cr**, 18.00–22.00 **Ni**, 2.00 **Si**, 0.50 **Mo**, 0.040 **P**, 0.040 **S**, 0.05–0.15 **N**; rem Fe	
ANSI/ASTM A 567	Grade HT–50C	US	Sand castings	0.40–0.60 **C**, 2.00 **Mn**, 13.00–17.00 **Cr**, 33.00–37.00 **Ni**, 2.50 **Si**, 0.50 **Mo**, 0.040 **P**, 0.040 **S**, 0.75–1.25 **Nb+Ta**; rem Fe	
ANSI/ASTM A 608	Grade HX50	US	Tube: centrifugally cast	0.40–0.60 **C**, 1.50 **Mn**, 15.0–19.0 **Cr**, 64.0–68.0 **Ni**, 0.50–2.00 **Si**, 0.50 **Mo**, 0.040 **P**, 0.040 **S**	
ANSI/ASTM A 608	Grade HW50	US	Tube: centrifugally cast	0.40–0.60 **C**, 1.50 **Mn**, 10.0–14.0 **Cr**, 58.0–62.0 **Ni**, 0.50–2.00 **Si**, 0.50 **Mo**, 0.04 **P**, 0.04 **S**	
ANSI/ASTM A 608	Grade HU50	US	Tube: centrifugally cast	0.40–0.60 **C**, 1.50 **Mn**, 17.0–21.0 **Cr**, 37.0–41.0 **Ni**, 0.50–2.00 **Si**, 0.50 **Mo**, 0.040 **P**, 0.040 **S**	
ANSI/ASTM A 608	Grade HT50	US	Tube: centrifugally cast	0.40–0.60 **C**, 1.50 **Mn**, 15.0–19.0 **Cr**, 33.0–37.0 **Ni**, 0.50–2.00 **Si**, 0.50 **Mo**, 0.040 **P**, 0.040 **S**	
ASTM A 608	Grade HT50	US	Pipe: centrifugally cast	0.40–0.60 **C**, 1.5 **Mn**, 15.0–19.0 **Cr**, 33.0–37.0 **Ni**, 0.5–2.0 **Si**, 0.50 **Mo**, 0.04 **P**, 0.04 **S**	
BS 4534	Grade 8	UK	Tube: weldable, centrifugal cast	0.40–0.50 **C**, 2.0 **Mn**, 17.0–21.0 **Cr**, 33.0–37.0 **Ni**, 0.5–1.5 **Si**, 0.50 **Mo**, 0.030 **P**, 0.040 **S**	**As cast**: all **diam**, (400) **TS**, 7 **El**
JIS G 5122	Type II	Japan	Castings, pipe (centrifugally cast)	0.40 **C**, 1.00 **Mn**, 24.00–28.00 **Cr**, 4.00–6.00 **Ni**, 2.00 **Si**, 0.50 **Mo**, 0.040 **P**, 0.040 **S**	**As cast**: all **diam**, (588) **TS**
JIS G 5122	Type 3	Japan	Castings, pipe (centrifugally cast)	0.40 **C**, 1.00 **Mn**, 12.00–15.00 **Cr**, 1.00 **Ni**, 2.00 **Si**, 0.50 **Mo**, 0.040 **P**, 0.040 **S**	**Annealed**: all **diam**, (490) **TS**

CAST HIGH ALLOY STEELS

specification number	designation	country	product forms	composition	mechanical properties (see page iv for explanation)
ANSI/ASTM A 296	Grade CY–40	US	Sand castings	0.40 **C**, 1.50 **Mn**, 14.00–17.00 **Cr**, rem **Ni**, 3.00 **Si**, 0.030 **P**, 0.030 **S**, 11.00 **Fe**	**As cast, annealed**: all **diam**, 70 (485) **TS**, 28 (195) **YS**, 30 **El**
NOM–B–354	Class CY–40	Mexico	Castings	0.40 **C**, 1.5 **Mn**, 14.0–17.0 **Cr**, rem **Ni**, 3.0 **Si**, 0.030 **P**, 0.030 **S**, 11.0 **Fe**	**As agreed**: all **diam**, (483) **TS**, (193) **YS**, 30 **El**
JIS G 5122	Type 2	Japan	Castings, pipe (centrifugally cast)	0.40 **C**, 1.00 **Mn**, 25.00–28.00 **Cr**, 1.00 **Ni**, 2.00 **Si**, 0.50 **Mo**, 0.040 **P**, 0.040 **S**	**Annealed**: all **diam**, (343) **TS**
BS 3100/1648	Grade D	UK	Sand castings	0.4 **C**, 17.0–22.0 **Cr**, 6.0–10.0 **Ni**	
IS 4522	Grade 12	India	Castings	0.35–0.75 **C**, 2.00 **Mn**, 13.0–17.0 **Cr**, 33.0–37.0 **Ni**, 2.50 **Si**, 0.050 **P**, 0.050 **S**	**As cast**: all **diam**, (480) **TS**, (275) **YS**, 9 **El**
IS 4522	Grade 13	India	Castings	0.35–0.75 **C**, 2.00 **Mn**, 17.0–21.0 **Cr**, 37.0–41.0 **Ni**, 2.50 **Si**, 0.050 **P**, 0.050 **S**	**As cast**: all **diam**, (480) **TS**, (275) **YS**, 8 **El**
IS 4522	Grade 14	India	Castings	0.35–0.75 **C**, 2.00 **Mn**, 15.0–19.0 **Cr**, 64.0–68.0 **Ni**, 2.50 **Si**, 0.050 **P**, 0.050 **S**	**As cast**: all **diam**, (450) **TS**, (245) **YS**, 8 **El**
ANSI/ASTM A 297	Grade HU	US	Sand castings	0.35–0.75 **C**, 2.00 **Mn**, 17.0–21.0 **Cr**, 37.0–41.0 **Ni**, 2.50 **Si**, 0.50 **Mo**, 0.04 **P**, 0.04 **S**	**As cast**: all **diam**, 65 (450) **TS**, 4 **El**
ANSI/ASTM A 297	Grade HT	US	Sand castings	0.35–0.75 **C**, 2.00 **Mn**, 15.0–19.0 **Cr**, 33.0–37.0 **Ni**, 2.50 **Si**, 0.50 **Mo**, 0.04 **P**, 0.04 **S**	**As cast**: all **diam**, 65 (450) **TS**, 4 **El**
ASTM A 297	Grade HU	US	Castings	0.35–0.75 **C**, 2.00 **Mn**, 17.0–21.0 **Cr**, 37.0–41.0 **Ni**, 2.50 **Si**, 0.50 **Mo**, 0.040 **P**, 0.040 **S**	**As agreed**: all **diam**, 65 (450) **TS**, 4 **El**
ASTM A 297	Grade HT	US	Castings	0.35–0.75 **C**, 2.00 **Mn**, 15.0–19.0 **Cr**, 33.0–37.0 **Ni**, 2.50 **Si**, 0.50 **Mo**, 0.040 **P**, 0.040 **S**	**As agreed**: all **diam**, 65 (450) **TS**, 4 **El**
NOM–B–355	Class HT	Mexico	Castings	0.35–0.75 **C**, 2.00 **Mn**, 13.0–17.0 **Cr**, 33.0–37.0 **Ni**, 2.50 **Si**, 0.50 **Mo**, 0.040 **P**, 0.040 **S**	**Quenched and tempered**: all **diam**, (448) **TS**, 4 **El**
NOM–B–355	Class HU	Mexico	Castings	0.35–0.75 **C**, 2.00 **Mn**, 17.0–21.0 **Cr**, 37.0–41.0 **Ni**, 2.50 **Si**, 0.50 **Mo**, 0.040 **P**, 0.040 **S**	**Quenched and tempered**: all **diam**, (448) **TS**, 4 **El**
NOM–B–355	Class HP	Mexico	Castings	0.35–0.75 **C**, 2.00 **Mn**, 33.0–37.0 **Cr**, 24.0–28.0 **Ni**, 2.00 **Si**, 0.50 **Mo**, 0.040 **P**, 0.040 **S**	**As cast**: all **diam**, (434) **TS**, (234) **YS**, 4.5 **El**
ANSI/ASTM A 297	Grade HP	US	Sand castings	0.35–0.75 **C**, 2.00 **Mn**, 24.0–28.0 **Cr**, 33–37 **Ni**, 2.50 **Si**, 0.50 **Mo**, 0.04 **P**, 0.04 **S**	**As cast**: all **diam**, 62.5 (430) **TS**, 34 (235) **YS**, 4.5 **El**
ASTM A 297	Grade HP	US	Castings	0.35–0.75 **C**, 2.00 **Mn**, 24.0–28.0 **Cr**, 33.0–37.0 **Ni**, 2.50 **Si**, 0.50 **Mo**, 0.040 **P**, 0.040 **S**	**As agreed**: all **diam**, 62.5 (430) **TS**, 34 (235) **YS**, 4.5 **El**
ANSI/ASTM A 297	Grade HX	US	Sand castings	0.35–0.75 **C**, 2.00 **Mn**, 15.0–19.0 **Cr**, 64.0–68.0 **Ni**, 2.50 **Si**, 0.50 **Mo**, 0.04 **P**, 0.04 **S**	**As cast**: all **diam**, 60 (415) **TS**
ANSI/ASTM A 297	Grade HW	US	Sand castings	0.35–0.75 **C**, 2.00 **Mn**, 10.0–14.0 **Cr**, 58.0–62.0 **Ni**, 2.50 **Si**, 0.50 **Mo**, 0.04 **P**, 0.04 **S**	**As cast**: all **diam**, 60 (415) **TS**
ASTM A 297	Grade HX	US	Castings	0.35–0.75 **C**, 2.00 **Mn**, 15.0–19.0 **Cr**, 64.0–68.0 **Ni**, 2.50 **Si**, 0.50 **Mo**, 0.040 **P**, 0.040 **S**	**As agreed**: all **diam**, 60 (415) **TS**
ASTM A 297	Grade HW	US	Castings	0.35–0.75 **C**, 2.00 **Mn**, 10.0–14.0 **Cr**, 58.0–62.0 **Ni**, 2.50 **Si**, 0.50 **Mo**, 0.040 **P**, 0.040 **S**	**As agreed**: all **diam**, 60 (415) **TS**
NOM–B–355	Class HX	Mexico	Castings	0.35–0.75 **C**, 2.00 **Mn**, 15.0–19.0 **Cr**, 64.0–66.0 **Ni**, 2.50 **Si**, 0.50 **Mo**, 0.040 **P**, 0.040 **S**	**As cast**: all **diam**, (414) **TS**

CAST HIGH ALLOY STEELS

specification number	designation	country	product forms	composition	mechanical properties (see page iv for explanation)
NOM–B–355	Class HW	Mexico	Castings	0.35–0.75 **C**, 2.00 **Mn**, 10.0–14.0 **Cr**, 58.0–62.0 **Ni**, 2.50 **Si**, 0.50 **Mo**, 0.040 **P**, 0.040 **S**	**As cast**: all **diam**, (414) **TS**
JIS G 5122	Type 20	Japan	Castings, pipe (centrifugally cast)	0.35–0.75 **C**, 2.00 **Mn**, 17.00–21.00 **Cr**, 37.00–41.00 **Ni**, 2.50 **Si**, 0.50 **Mo**, 0.040 **P**, 0.040 **S**	**As cast**: all **diam**, (392) **TS**, 4 **El**
JIS G 5122	Type 15	Japan	Castings, pipe (centrifugally cast)	0.35–0.70 **C**, 2.00 **Mn**, 13.00–17.00 **Cr**, 33.00–37.00 **Ni**, 2.50 **Si**, 0.50 **Mo**, 0.040 **P**, 0.040 **S**	**As cast**: all **diam**, (441) **TS**, 4 **El**
BS 1504–330C11		UK	Castings	0.35–0.55 **C**, 2.0 **Mn**, 13.0–17.0 **Cr**, 33.0–37.0 **Ni**, 1.5 **Si**, 1.50 **Mo**, 0.040 **P**, 0.040 **S**	**As cast**: all **diam**, (450) **TS**, 3 **El**
BS 3100/4238	Grade H1C	UK	Sand castings	0.35–0.55 **C**, 13.0–17.0 **Cr**, 33.0–37.0 **Ni**	**As cast**: all **diam**, (445) **TS**, 3 **El**
BS 3100/4238	Grade H2C	UK	Sand castings	0.35–0.55 **C**, 17.0–21.0 **Cr**, 37.0–41.0 **Ni**	**As cast**: all **diam**, (445) **TS**, 3 **El**
BS 4534	Grade 9	UK	Tube: weldable, centrifugal cast	0.35–0.55 **C**, 2.0 **Mn**, 17.0–21.0 **Cr**, 33.0–37.0 **Ni**, 1.5–2.0 **Si**, 0.50 **Mo**, 0.030 **P**, 0.040 **S**	**As cast**: all **diam**, (400) **TS**, 7 **El**
JIS G 5122	Type 22	Japan	Castings, pipe (centrifugally cast)	0.35–0.45 **C**, 1.50 **Mn**, 23.00–27.00 **Cr**, 19.00–22.00 **Ni**, 1.75 **Si**, 0.50 **Mo**, 0.040 **P**, 0.040 **S**	**As cast**: all **diam**, (441) **TS**, (235) **YS**, 10 **El**
IS 7806	Grade 11	India	Castings	0.35–0.45 **C**, 1.50 **Mn**, 23.0–27.0 **Cr**, 19.0–22.0 **Ni**, 1.75 **Si**, 0.040 **P**, 0.040 **S**	**As cast**: all **diam**, (430) **TS**, (240) **YS**, 10 **El**
ASTM A–351–76	Grade HK40	US	Castings	0.35–0.45 **C**, 1.50 **Mn**, 23.0–27.0 **Cr**, 19.0–22.0 **Ni**, 1.75 **Si**, 0.040 **P**, 0.040 **S**	**As cast**: all **diam**, (425) **TS**, (240) **YS**, 10 **El**
ANSI/ASTM A 351	Grade HK40	US	Sand castings	0.35–0.45 **C**, 1.50 **Mn**, 23.0–27.0 **Cr**, 19.0–22.0 **Ni**, 1.75 **Si**, 0.040 **P**, 0.040 **S**	**As cast**: all **diam**, 62 (425) **TS**, 35 (240) **YS**, 10.0 **El**
ANSI/ASTM A 351	HK40	US	Castings	0.35–0.45 **C**, 1.50 **Mn**, 23.0–27.0 **Cr**, 19.0–22.0 **Ni**, 1.75 **Si**, 0.040 **P**, 0.040 **S**	**Solution annealed**: all **diam**, 62 (425) **TS**, 35 (240) **YS**, 10 **El**
BS 4534	Grade 6	UK	Tube: weldable, centrifugal cast	0.35–0.45 **C**, 2.0 **Mn**, 23.0–27.0 **Cr**, 18.0–22.0 **Ni**, 0.5–1.5 **Si**, 0.50 **Mo**, 0.030 **P**, 0.040 **S**	**As cast**: all **diam**, (425) **TS**, 9 **El**
ANSI/ASTM A 608	Grade HN40	US	Tube: centrifugally cast	0.35–0.45 **C**, 1.50 **Mn**, 19.0–23.0 **Cr**, 23.0–27.0 **Ni**, 0.50–2.00 **Si**, 0.50 **Mo**, 0.040 **P**, 0.040 **S**	
ANSI/ASTM A 608	Grade HL40	US	Tube: centrifugally cast	0.35–0.45 **C**, 1.50 **Mn**, 28.0–32.0 **Cr**, **Ni**, 0.50–2.00 **Si**, 0.50 **Mo**, 0.04 **P**, 0.04 **S**	
ANSI/ASTM A 608	Grade HK40	US	Tube: centrifugally cast	0.35–0.45 **C**, 1.50 **Mn**, 23.0–27.0 **Cr**, 19.0–22.0 **Ni**, 0.50–2.00 **Si**, 0.50 **Mo**, 0.04 **P**, 0.04 **S**	
ASTM A 608	Grade HK40	US	Pipe: centrifugally cast	0.35–0.45 **C**, 1.5 **Mn**, 23.0–27.0 **Cr**, 19.0–22.0 **Ni**, 0.5–2.0 **Si**, 0.50 **Mo**, 0.04 **P**, 0.04 **S**	
ASTM A 608	Grade HL40	US	Pipe: centrifugally cast	0.35–0.45 **C**, 1.5 **Mn**, 28.0–32.0 **Cr**, 18.0–22.0 **Ni**, 0.5–2.0 **Si**, 0.50 **Mo**, 0.04 **P**, 0.04 **S**	
ASTM A 608	Grade HN40	US	Pipe: centrifugally cast	0.35–0.45 **C**, 1.5 **Mn**, 19.0–23.0 **Cr**, 23.0–27.0 **Ni**, 0.5–2.0 **Si**, 0.50 **Mo**, 0.04 **P**, 0.04 **S**	
ANSI/ASTM A 567	Grade HK–40	US	Sand castings	0.35–0.45 **C**, 2.00 **Mn**, 24.00–28.00 **Cr**, 18.00–22.00 **Ni**, 2.00 **Si**, 0.50 **Mo**, 0.040 **P**, 0.040 **S**, 0.05–0.15 **N**; rem Fe	
ANSI/ASTM A 296	Grade M–35	US	Sand castings	0.35 **C**, 1.50 **Mn**, rem **Ni**, 2.00 **Si**, 26.0–33.0 **Mo**, 0.030 **P**, 0.030 **S**, 6.00 **Fe**, 0.60 **V**	**As cast, annealed**: all **diam**, 65 (450) **TS**, 30 (205) **YS**, 25 **El**

CAST HIGH ALLOY STEELS

specification number	designation	country	product forms	composition	mechanical properties (see page iv for explanation)
IS 4522	Grade 1	India	Castings	0.30–0.60 **C**, 1.00 **Mn**, 12.0–14.0 **Cr**, 2.00 **Si**, 0.050 **P**, 0.050 **S**	
IS 4522	Grade 2	India	Castings	0.30–0.60 **C**, 1.00 **Mn**, 27.0–30.0 **Cr**, 2.00 **Si**, 0.050 **P**, 0.050 **S**	
BS 1504–310C40		UK	Castings	0.30–0.50 **C**, 2.0 **Mn**, 24.0–27.0 **Cr**, 19.0–22.0 **Ni**, 1.5 **Si**, 1.50 **Mo**, 0.040 **P**, 0.040 **S**	**As cast**: all **diam**, (450) **TS**, 7 **El**
BS 3100/4238	Grade FC	UK	Sand castings	0.30–0.50 **C**, 24.0–27.0 **Cr**, 19.0–22.0 **Ni**	**As cast**: all **diam**, (445) **TS**, 7 **El**
ANSI/ASTM A 608	Grade HE 35	US	Centrifugally cast	0.30–0.40 **C**, 1.50 **Mn**, 26–30 **Cr**, 8–11 **Ni**, 0.50–2.00 **Si**, 0.50 **Mo**, 0.040 **P**, 0.040 **S**	
ANSI/ASTM A 608	Grade HI35	US	Tube: centrifugally cast	0.30–0.40 **C**, 1.50 **Mn**, 26.0–30.0 **Cr**, 14.0–18.0 **Ni**, 0.50–2.00 **Si**, 0.50 **Mo**, 0.040 **P**, 0.040 **S**	
ASTM A608–70	Grade HI35	US	Pipe: centrifugally cast	0.30–0.40 **C**, 1.5 **Mn**, 26.0–30.0 **Cr**, 14.0–18.0 **Ni**, 0.5–2.0 **Si**, 0.50 **Mo**, 0.04 **P**, 0.04 **S**	
ASTM A 608	Grade HE35	US	Pipe: centrifugally cast	0.30–0.40 **C**, 1.5 **Mn**, 26.0–30.0 **Cr**, 8.0–11.0 **Ni**, 0.5–2.0 **Si**, 0.50 **Mo**, 0.04 **P**, 0.04 **S**	
NOM–B–354	Class CE–30	Mexico	Castings	0.30 **C**, 1.50 **Mn**, 26.0–30.0 **Cr**, 8.0–11.0 **Ni**, 2.0 **Si**, 0.040 **P**, 0.040 **S**	**As agreed**: all **diam**, (552) **TS**, (276) **YS**, 10 **El**
ASTM A 743	Grade CE 30	US	Castings	0.30 **C**, 1.50 **Mn**, 26.0–30.0 **Cr**, 8.00–11.00 **Ni**, 2.00 **Si**, 0.04 **P**, 0.04 **S**	**Solution quenched**: all **diam**, (550) **TS**, (275) **YS**, 10 **El**
ANSI/ASTM A 296	Grade CE–30	US	Sand castings	0.30 **C**, 1.50 **Mn**, 26.0–30.0 **Cr**, 8.0–11.0 **Ni**, 2.00 **Si**, 0.040 **P**, 0.040 **S**	**Solution annealed**: all **diam**, 80 (550) **TS**, 40 (275) **YS**, 10 **El**
IS 3444	Grade 4	India	Castings	0.30 **C**, 1.00 **Mn**, 18.0–21.0 **Cr**, 2.00 **Ni**, 1.00 **Si**, 0.040 **P**, 0.040 **S**	**Annealed**: all **diam**, (451) **TS**, (206) **YS**
ASTM A 743	Grade CB–30	US	Castings	0.30 **C**, 1.00 **Mn**, 18.0–21.0 **Cr**, 2.00 **Ni**, 1.50 **Si**, 0.04 **P**, 0.04 **S**	**Normalized, annealed**: all **diam**, (450) **TS**, (205) **YS**
ANSI/ASTM A 296	Grade CB–30	US	Sand castings	0.30 **C**, 1.00 **Mn**, 18.0–21.0 **Cr**, 2.00 **Ni**, 1.50 **Si**, 0.040 **P**, 0.040 **S**	**Annealed**: all **diam**, 65 (450) **TS**, 30 (205) **YS**
NOM–B–354	Class CB–30	Mexico	Castings	0.30 **C**, 1.0 **Mn**, 18.0–21.0 **Cr**, 2.0 **Ni**, 1.50 **Si**, 0.040 **P**, 0.040 **S**, 0.90–1.20 **Cu**	**Normalized**: all **diam**, (448) **TS**, (207) **YS**
NF A 32–056	Z 28C 13–M	France	Castings	0.30 **C**, 1.5 **Mn**, 11.5–13.5 **Cr**, 1.2 **Si**, 0.040 **P**, 0.030 **S**	
ANSI/ASTM A 608	Grade HH33	US	Tube: centrifugally cast	0.28–0.38 **C**, 1.50 **Mn**, 24.0–26.0 **Cr**, 12.0–14.0 **Ni**, 0.50–2.00 **Si**, 0.50 **Mo**, 0.040 **P**, 0.040 **S**	
ASTM A 608	Grade HH33	US	Pipe: centrifugally cast	0.28–0.38 **C**, 1.5 **Mn**, 24.0–26.0 **Cr**, 12.0–14.0 **Ni**, 0.5–2.0 **Si**, 0.50 **Mo**, 0.04 **P**, 0.04 **S**	
AMS 5369B		US	Sand castings	0.28–0.35 **C**, 0.75–1.50 **Mn**, 18.00–21.00 **Cr**, 8.00–11.00 **Ni**, 1.00 **Si**, 1.00–1.75 **Mo**, 0.040 **P**, 0.040 **S**, 0.50 **Cu**, 0.30–0.70 **Nb+Ta**, 0.15–0.50 **Ti**, 1.00–1.75 **W**	**Solution and precipitation, heat treated**: all **diam**
NF A 32–056	Z 25 CND 25 09–M	France	Castings	0.28 **C**, 1.5 **Mn**, 23.0–27.0 **Cr**, 8.0–10.0 **Ni**, 1.2 **Si**, 1.5–2.0 **Mo**, 0.040 **P**, 0.030 **S**	**Solution annealed**: all **diam**, (600) **TS**, (300) **YS**, 6 **El**
BS 4534	Grade 5	UK	Tube, weldable, centrifugal cast	0.25–0.40 **C**, 2.0 **Mn**, 23.0–27.0 **Cr**, 11.5–14.0 **Ni**, 0.5–1.5 **Si**, 0.50 **Mo**, 0.030 **P**, 0.040 **S**	**As cast**: all **diam**, (455) **TS**, 9 **El**
ASTM A–351–76	Grade HK30	US	Castings	0.25–0.35 **C**, 1.50 **Mn**, 23.0–27.0 **Cr**, 19.0–22.0 **Ni**, 1.75 **Si**, 0.040 **P**, 0.040 **S**	**As cast**: all **diam**, (450) **TS**, (240) **YS**, 10 **El**

CAST HIGH ALLOY STEELS

specification number	designation	country	product forms	composition	mechanical properties (see page iv for explanation)
ANSI/ASTM A 351	Grade HT30	US	Sand castings	0.25–0.35 **C**, 2.00 **Mn**, 13.0–17.0 **Cr**, 33.0–37.0 **Ni**, 2.50 **Si**, 0.50 **Mo**, 0.040 **P**, 0.040 **S**	**As cast**: all **diam**, 65 (450) **TS**, 28 (195) **YS**, 15.0 **El**
ANSI/ASTM A 351	Grade HK30	US	Sand castings	0.25–0.35 **C**, 1.50 **Mn**, 23.0–27.0 **Cr**, 19.0–22.0 **Ni**, 1.75 **Si**, 0.040 **P**, 0.040 **S**	**As cast**: all **diam**, 65 (450) **TS**, 35 (240) **YS**, 10 **El**
ANSI/ASTM A 351	HK30	US	Castings	0.25–0.35 **C**, 1.50 **Mn**, 23.0–27.0 **Cr**, 19.0–22.0 **Ni**, 1.75 **Si**, 0.040 **P**, 0.040 **S**	**Solution annealed**: all **diam**, 65 (450) **TS**, 35 (240) **YS**, 10 **El**
ANSI/ASTM A 351	HT30	US	Castings	0.25–0.35 **C**, 2.00 **Mn**, 13.0–17.0 **Cr**, 33.0–37.0 **Ni**, 2.50 **Si**, 0.50 **Mo**, 0.040 **P**, 0.040 **S**	**Solution annealed**: all **diam**, 65 (450) **TS**, 28 (195) **YS**, 15 **El**
IS 7806	Grade 10	India	Castings	0.25–0.35 **C**, 1.50 **Mn**, 23.0–27.0 **Cr**, 19.0–22.0 **Ni**, 1.75 **Si**, 0.040 **P**, 0.040 **S**	**As cast**: all **diam**, (450) **TS**, (240) **YS**, 10 **El**
IS 7806	Grade 12	India	Castings	0.25–0.35 **C**, 2.00 **Mn**, 13.0–17.0 **Cr**, 33.0–37.0 **Ni**, 2.50 **Si**, 0.50 **Mo**, 0.040 **P**, 0.040 **S**	**As cast**: all **diam**, (450) **TS**, (190) **YS**, 15 **El**
ASTM A–351	Grade HT30	US	Castings	0.25–0.35 **C**, 2.00 **Mn**, 13.0–17.0 **Cr**, 33.0–37.0 **Ni**, 2.50 **Si**, 0.50 **Mo**, 0.040 **P**, 0.040 **S**	**As cast**: all **diam**, (450) **TS**, (195) **YS**, 15 **El**
JIS G 5122	Type 21	Japan	Castings, pipe (centrifugally cast)	0.25–0.35 **C**, 1.50 **Mn**, 23.00–27.00 **Cr**, 19.00–22.00 **Ni**, 1.75 **Si**, 0.50 **Mo**, 0.040 **P**, 0.040 **S**	**As cast**: all **diam**, (441) **TS**, (235) **YS**, 10 **El**
BS 4534	Grade 4	UK	Tube, weldable, centrifugal cast	0.25–0.35 **C**, 2.0 **Mn**, 18.0–21.0 **Cr**, 9.0–11.5 **Ni**, 0.5–1.5 **Si**, 0.50 **Mo**, 0.030 **P**, 0.040 **S**	**As cast**: all **diam**, (425) **TS**, 22 **El**
ASTM A 608–70	Grade HC 30	US	Pipe: centrifugally cast	0.25–0.35 **C**, 0.5–1.0 **Mn**, 26.0–30.0 **Cr**, 4.0 **Ni**, 0.5–2.0 **Si**, 0.50 **Mo**, 0.04 **P**, 0.04 **S**	
ANSI/ASTM A 608	Grade HF 30	US	Centrifugally cast	0.25–0.35 **C**, 1.50 **Mn**, 19–23 **Cr**, 9–12 **Ni**, 0.50–2.00 **Si**, 0.50 **Mo**, 0.040 **P**, 0.040 **S**	
ANSI/ASTM A 608	Grade HC 30	US	Tube: centrifugally cast	0.25–0.35 **C**, 0.5–1.0 **Mn**, 26.0–30.0 **Cr**, 4.0 **Ni**, 0.50–2.00 **Si**, 0.50 **Mo**, 0.040 **P**, 0.040 **S**	
ANSI/ASTM A 608	Grade HL30	US	Tube: centrifugally cast	0.25–0.35 **C**, 1.50 **Mn**, 28.0–32.0 **Cr**, 18.0–22.0 **Ni**, 0.50–2.00 **Si**, 0.50 **Mo**, 0.04 **P**, 0.04 **S**	
ANSI/ASTM A 608	Grade HK30	US	Tube: centrifugally cast	0.25–0.35 **C**, 1.50 **Mn**, 23.0–27.0 **Cr**, 19.0–22.0 **Ni**, 0.50–2.00 **Si**, 0.50 **Mo**, 0.040 **P**, 0.040 **S**	
ASTM A608–70	Grade HL30	US	Pipe: centrifugally cast	0.25–0.35 **C**, 1.5 **Mn**, 28.0–32.0 **Cr**, 18.0–22.0 **Ni**, 0.5–2.0 **Si**, 0.50 **Mo**, 0.04 **P**, 0.04 **S**	
ASTM A 608	Grade HF30	US	Pipe: centrifugally cast	0.25–0.35 **C**, 1.5 **Mn**, 19.0–23.0 **Cr**, 9.0–12.0 **Ni**, 0.5–2.0 **Si**, 0.50 **Mo**, 0.04 **P**, 0.04 **S**	
ASTM A 608	Grade HH30	US	Pipe: centrifugally cast	0.25–0.35 **C**, 1.5 **Mn**, 24.0–28.0 **Cr**, 11.0–14.0 **Ni**, 0.5–2.0 **Si**, 0.50 **Mo**, 0.04 **P**, 0.04 **S**	
ASTM A 608	Grade HK30	US	Pipe: centrifugally cast	0.25–0.35 **C**, 1.5 **Mn**, 23.0–27.0 **Cr**, 19.0–22.0 **Ni**, 0.5–2.0 **Si**, 0.50 **Mo**, 0.04 **P**, 0.04 **S**	
ANSI/ASTM A608	Grade HH30	US	Pipe centrifugally cast	0.25–0.35 **C**, 1.50 **Mn**, 24–28 **Cr**, 11–14 **Ni**, 0.50–2.00 **Si**, 0.50 **Mo**, 0.04 **P**, 0.04 **S**	
BS 3146 Part 2	ANC 2	UK	Investment, precision castings	0.25 **C**, 15.5–20.0 **Cr**	**Quenched and tempered**: all **diam**, (850) **TS**, (695) **YS**
IS 3444	Grade 14	India	Castings	0.25 **C**, 1.50 **Mn**, 8.0–11.0 **Cr**, 19.0–22.0 **Ni**, 2.00 **Si**, 0.040 **P**, 0.040 **S**	**Solution annealed**: all **diam**, (490) **TS**, (235) **YS**

CAST HIGH ALLOY STEELS

specification number	designation	country	product forms	composition	mechanical properties (see page iv for explanation)
ANSI/ASTM A 217	Grade WC1	US	Sand castings	0.25 **C**, 0.50–0.80 **Mn**, 0.60 **Si**, 0.45–0.65 **Mo**, 0.040 **P**, 0.045 **S**; 1.00 max, other elements, total	**Normalized and tempered**: all **diam**, 65 (450) **TS**, 35 (240) **YS**, 24 **El**
ANSI/ASTM A 426	CP1	US	Pipe: centrifugally cast	0.25 **C**, 0.30–0.80 **Mn**, 0.10–0.50 **Si**, 0.44–0.65 **Mo**, 0.045 **P**, 0.045 **S**	**Normalized, tempered**: all **diam**, 65 (448) **TS**, 35 (241) **YS**, 24 **El**
BS HC103		UK	Castings: aircraft quality	0.25 **C**, 1.0 **Mn**, 20.0–25.0 **Cr**, 10.0–13.0 **Ni**, 0.5–2.0 **Si**, 0.04 **P**, 0.040 **S**, 2.0–3.5 **W**	
MIL–S–81591	IC–310	US	Investment castings	0.25 **C**, 2.00 **Mn**, 24.0–26.0 **Cr**, 19.0–22.0 **Ni**, 1.50 **Si**, 0.040 **P**, 0.030 **S**	**Solution annealed**
AMS 5358A		US	Investment castings	0.25 **C**, 2.00 **Mn**, 17.00–19.00 **Cr**, 8.00–10.00 **Ni**, 1.00 **Si**, 0.75 **Mo**, 0.040 **P**, 0.030 **S**, 0.75 **Cu**	**Solution annealed**
BS 3100/1648	Grade	UK	Sand castings	0.25 **C**, 12.0–16.0 **Cr**	
IS 4522	Grade 10	India	Castings	0.20–0.60 **C**, 2.00 **Mn**, 28.0–32.0 **Cr**, 18.0–22.0 **Ni**, 2.50 **Si**, 0.050 **P**, 0.050 **S**	**As cast**: all **diam**, (470) **TS**, (265) **YS**, 15 **El**
ANSI/ASTM A 297	Grade HL	US	Sand castings	0.20–0.60 **C**, 2.00 **Mn**, 28.0–32.0 **Cr**, 18.0–22.0 **Ni**, 2.00 **Si**, 0.50 **Mo**, 0.04 **P**, 0.04 **S**	**As cast**: all **diam**, 65 (450) **TS**, 35 (240) **YS**, 10 **El**
ANSI/ASTM A 297	Grade HK	US	Sand castings	0.20–0.60 **C**, 2.00 **Mn**, 24.0–28.0 **Cr**, 18.0–22.0 **Ni**, 2.00 **Si**, 0.50 **Mo**, 0.04 **P**, 0.04 **S**	**As cast**: all **diam**, 65 (450) **TS**, 35 (240) **YS**, 10 **El**
ASTM A 297	Grade HL	US	Castings	0.20–0.60 **C**, 2.00 **Mn**, 28.0–32.0 **Cr**, 18.0–22.0 **Ni**, 2.00 **Si**, 0.50 **Mo**, 0.040 **P**, 0.040 **S**	**As agreed**: all **diam**, 65 (450) **TS**, 35 (240) **YS**, 10 **El**
ASTM A 297	Grade HK	US	Castings	0.20–0.60 **C**, 2.00 **Mn**, 24.0–28.0 **Cr**, 18.0–22.0 **Ni**, 2.00 **Si**, 0.50 **Mo**, 0.04 **P**, 0.04 **S**	**As agreed**: all **diam**, 65 (450) **TS**, 35 (240) **YS**, 10 **El**
NOM–B–355	Class HL	Mexico	Castings	0.20–0.60 **C**, 2.00 **Mn**, 28.0–32.0 **Cr**, 18.0–22.0 **Ni**, 2.00 **Si**, 0.50 **Mo**, 0.040 **P**, 0.040 **S**	**As cast**: all **diam**, (448) **TS**, (241) **YS**, 10 **El**
NOM–B–355	Class HK	Mexico	Castings	0.20–0.60 **C**, 2.00 **Mn**, 24.0–28.0 **Cr**, 18.0–22.0 **Ni**, 2.00 **Si**, 0.50 **Mo**, 0.04 **P**, 0.04 **S**	**As cast**: all **diam**, (448) **TS**, (241) **YS**, 10 **El**
IS 4522	Grade 6	India	Castings	0.20–0.50 **C**, 2.00 **Mn**, 26.0–30.0 **Cr**, 8.0–10.0 **Ni**, 2.00 **Si**, 0.050 **P**, 0.050 **S**	**As cast**: all **diam**, (655) **TS**, (315) **YS**, 18 **El**
IS 4522	Grade 4	India	Castings	0.20–0.50 **C**, 1.00 **Mn**, 26.0–30.0 **Cr**, 4.0–7.0 **Ni**, 2.00 **Si**, 0.050 **P**, 0.050 **S**	**As cast**: all **diam**, (590) **TS**, (390) **YS**, 14 **El**
IS 4522	Grade 5	India	Castings	0.20–0.50 **C**, 2.00 **Mn**, 18.0–20.0 **Cr**, 8.0–10.0 **Ni**, 2.00 **Si**, 0.050 **P**, 0.050 **S**	**As cast**: all **diam**, (590) **TS**, (315) **YS**, 32 **El**
IS 4522	Grade 7, type 2	India	Castings	0.20–0.50 **C**, 2.00 **Mn**, 23.0–27.0 **Cr**, 11.0–14.0 **Ni**, 2.00 **Si**, 0.050 **P**, 0.050 **S**	**As cast**: all **diam**, (590) **TS**, (275) **YS**, 13 **El**
NOM–B–355	Class HE	Mexico	Castings	0.20–0.50 **C**, 2.0 **Mn**, 26.0–30.0 **Cr**, 8.0–11.0 **Ni**, 2.0 **Si**, 0.50 **Mo**, 0.04 **P**, 0.04 **S**	**As cast**: all **diam**, (586) **TS**, (276) **YS**, 9 **El**
ASTM A 297	Grade HE	US	Castings	0.20–0.50 **C**, 2.00 **Mn**, 26.0–30.0 **Cr**, 8.0–11.0 **Ni**, 2.00 **Si**, 0.50 **Mo**, 0.04 **P**, 0.04 **S**	**As agreed**: all **diam**, 85 (585) **TS**, 40 (275) **YS**, 9 **El**
ANSI/ASTM A 297	Grade HE	US	Sand castings	0.20–0.50 **C**, 2.00 **Mn**, 26.0–30.0 **Cr**, 8.0–11.0 **Ni**, 2.00 **Si**, 0.50 **Mo**, 0.04 **P**, 0.04 **S**	**As cast**: all **diam**, 85 (585) **TS**, 40 (275) **YS**, 9 **El**
IS 4522	Grade 11	India	Castings	0.20–0.50 **C**, 2.00 **Mn**, 19.0–23.0 **Cr**, 23.0–27.0 **Ni**, 2.00 **Si**, 0.050 **P**, 0.050 **S**	**As cast**: all **diam**, (570) **TS**, (360) **YS**
IS 4522	Grade 7, type 1	India	Castings	0.20–0.50 **C**, 2.00 **Mn**, 23.0–27.0 **Cr**, 11.0–14.0 **Ni**, 2.00 **Si**, 0.050 **P**, 0.050 **S**	**As cast**: all **diam**, (550) **TS**, (345) **YS**, 22 **El**
JIS G 5122	Type 17	Japan	Castings, pipe (centrifugally cast)	0.20–0.50 **C**, 2.00 **Mn**, 26.00–30.00 **Cr**, 8.00–11.00 **Ni**, 2.00 **Si**, 0.50 **Mo**, 0.040 **P**, 0.040 **S**	**As cast**: all **diam**, (539) **TS**, (275) **YS**, 5 **El**

CAST HIGH ALLOY STEELS

specification number	designation	country	product forms	composition	mechanical properties (see page iv for explanation)
IS 4522	Grade 9	India	Castings	0.20–0.50 **C**, 2.00 **Mn**, 23.0–27.0 **Cr**, 18.0–22.0 **Ni**, 2.00 **Si**, 0.050 **P**, 0.050 **S**	**As cast**: all **diam**, (520) **TS**, (345) **YS**, 15 **El**
NOM–B–355	Class HH	Mexico	Castings	0.20–0.50 **C**, 2.00 **Mn**, 24.0–28.0 **Cr**, 11.0–14.0 **Ni**, 2.00 **Si**, 0.50 **Mo**, 0.04 **P**, 0.04 **S**	**Quenched and tempered**: all **diam**, (517) **TS**, (241) **YS**, 10 **El**
ASTM A 297	Grade HH	US	Castings	0.20–0.50 **C**, 2.00 **Mn**, 24.0–28.0 **Cr**, 11.0–14.0 **Ni**, 2.00 **Si**, 0.50 **Mo**, 0.04 **P**, 0.04 **S**	**As agreed**: all **diam**, 75 (515) **TS**, 35 (240) **YS**, 10 **El**
ANSI/ASTM A 297	Grade HH	US	Sand castings	0.20–0.50 **C**, 2.00 **Mn**, 24.0–28.0 **Cr**, 11.0–14.0 **Ni**, 2.00 **Si**, 0.50 **Mo**, 0.04 **P**, 0.04 **S**	**As cast**: all **diam**, 75 (515) **TS**, 35 (240) **YS**, 10 **El**
BS 3100/4238	Grade EC2	UK	Sand castings	0.20–0.50 **C**, 24.0–28.0 **Cr**, 11.0–14.0 **Ni**	**As cast**: all **diam**, (510) **TS**, 7 **El**
JIS G 5122	Type 13	Japan	Castings, pipe (centrifugally cast)	0.20–0.50 **C**, 2.00 **Mn**, 24.00–28.00 **Cr**, 11.00–14.00 **Ni**, 2.00 **Si**, 0.50 **Mo**, 0.040 **P**, 0.040 **S**	**As cast**: all **diam**, (490) **TS**, (235) **YS**, 10 **El**
JIS G 5122	Type 18	Japan	Castings, pipe (centrifugally cast)	0.20–0.50 **C**, 2.00 **Mn**, 26.00–30.00 **Cr**, 14.00–18.00 **Ni**, 2.00 **Si**, 0.50 **Mo**, 0.040 **P**, 0.040 **S**	**As cast**: all **diam**, (490) **TS**, (235) **YS**, 10 **El**
ASTM A 297	Grade HI	US	Castings	0.20–0.50 **C**, 2.00 **Mn**, 26.0–30.0 **Cr**, 14.0–18.0 **Ni**, 2.00 **Si**, 0.50 **Mo**, 0.04 **P**, 0.04 **S**	**As agreed**: all **diam**, 70 (485) **TS**, 35 (240) **YS**, 10 **El**
ANSI/ASTM A 297	Grade HI	US	Sand castings	0.20–0.50 **C**, 2.00 **Mn**, 26.0–30.0 **Cr**, 14.0–18.0 **Ni**, 2.00 **Si**, 0.50 **Mo**, 0.04 **P**, 0.04 **S**	**As cast**: all **diam**, 70 (485) **TS**, 35 (240) **YS**, 10 **El**
NOM–B–355	Class HI	Mexico	Castings	0.20–0.50 **C**, 2.00 **Mn**, 26.0–30.0 **Cr**, 14.0–18.0 **Ni**, 2.00 **Si**, 0.50 **Mo**, 0.04 **P**, 0.04 **S**	**As cast**: all **diam**, (483) **TS**, (241) **YS**, 10 **El**
ANSI/ASTM A 297	Grade HN	US	Sand castings	0.20–0.50 **C**, 2.00 **Mn**, 19.0–23.0 **Cr**, 23.0–27.0 **Ni**, 2.00 **Si**, 0.50 **Mo**, 0.04 **P**, 0.04 **S**	**As cast**: all **diam**, 63 (435) **TS**, 8 **El**
ASTM A 297	Grade HN	US	Castings	0.20–0.50 **C**, 2.00 **Mn**, 19.0–23.0 **Cr**, 23.0–27.0 **Ni**, 2.00 **Si**, 0.50 **Mo**, 0.040 **P**, 0.040 **S**	**As agreed**: all **diam**, 63 (435) **TS**, 8 **El**
NOM–B–355	Class HN	Mexico	Castings	0.20–0.50 **C**, 2.00 **Mn**, 19.0–23.0 **Cr**, 23.0–27.0 **Ni**, 2.00 **Si**, 0.50 **Mo**, 0.04 **P**, 0.04 **S**	**As cast**: all **diam**, (434) **TS**, 8 **El**
JIS G 5122	Type 19	Japan	Castings, pipe (centrifugally cast)	0.20–0.50 **C**, 2.00 **Mn**, 19.00–23.00 **Cr**, 23.00–27.00 **Ni**, 2.00 **Si**, 0.50 **Mo**, 0.040 **P**, 0.040 **S**	**As cast**: all **diam**, (392) **TS**, 5 **El**
BS 3100/4238	Grade EC1	UK	Sand castings	0.20–0.45 **C**, 24.0–28.0 **Cr**, 11.0–14.0 **Ni**, 0.20 **N**	**As cast**: all **diam**, (555) **TS**, 3 **El**
ASTM A 447–74	Grade II	US	Castings	0.20–0.45 **C**, 2.50 **Mn**, 23.0–28.0 **Cr**, 10.0–14.0 **Ni**, 1.75 **Si**, 0.050 **P**, 0.050 **S**, 0.20 **N**	**As cast, aged**: all **diam**, (550) **TS**, 4 **El**; **As cast**: all **diam**, (140) **TS**, 8 **El**
ASTM A 447–74	Grade I	US	Castings	0.20–0.45 **C**, 2.50 **Mn**, 23.0–28.0 **Cr**, 10.0–14.0 **Ni**, 1.75 **Si**, 0.05 **P**, 0.05 **S**, 0.20 **N**	**As cast**: all **diam**, (550) **TS**, 9 **El**
ASTM A 743	Grade CA–40	US	Castings	0.2–0.4 **C**, 1.00 **Mn**, 11.5–14.0 **Cr**, 1.0 **Ni**, 1.50 **Si**, 0.5 **Mo**, 0.04 **P**, 0.04 **S**	**Normalized and tempered, annealed**: all **diam**, (690) **TS**, (485) **YS**, 15 **El**
ANSI/ASTM A 296	Grade CA–40	US	Sand castings	0.20–0.40 **C**, 1.00 **Mn**, 11.5–14.0 **Cr**, 1.0 **Ni**, 1.50 **Si**, 0.5 **Mo**, 0.040 **P**, 0.040 **S**	**Normalized and tempered**: all **diam**, 100 (690) **TS**, 70 (485) **YS**, 15 **El**
NOM–B–354	Class CA–40	Mexico	Castings	0.20–0.40 **C**, 1.0 **Mn**, 11.5–14.0 **Cr**, 1.0 **Ni**, 1.50 **Si**, 0.5 **Mo**, 0.040 **P**, 0.040 **S**	**As agreed**: all **diam**, (689) **TS**, (483) **YS**, 15 **El**
JIS G 5122	Type 1	Japan	Castings, pipe (centrifugally cast)	0.20–0.40 **C**, 1.00 **Mn**, 12.00–15.00 **Cr**, 1.00 **Ni**, 1.50–3.00 **Si**, 0.040 **P**, 0.040 **S**	**Annealed**: all **diam**, (490) **TS**
JIS G 5122	Type 12	Japan	Castings, pipe (centrifugally cast)	0.20–0.40 **C**, 2.00 **Mn**, 18.00–23.00 **Cr**, 8.00–12.00 **Ni**, 2.00 **Si**, 0.50 **Mo**, 0.040 **P**, 0.040 **S**	**As cast**: all **diam**, (490) **TS**, (235) **YS**, 25 **El**
ASTM A 297	Grade HF	US	Castings	0.20–0.40 **C**, 2.00 **Mn**, 18.0–23.0 **Cr**, 8.0–12.0 **Ni**, 2.00 **Si**, 0.50 **Mo**, 0.04 **P**, 0.04 **S**	**As agreed**: all **diam**, 70 (485) **TS**, 35 (240) **YS**, 25 **El**

CAST HIGH ALLOY STEELS

specification number	designation	country	product forms	composition	mechanical properties (see page iv for explanation)
ANSI/ASTM A 297	Grade HF	US	Sand castings	0.20–0.40 **C**, 2.00 **Mn**, 18.0–23.0 **Cr**, 8.0–12.0 **Ni**, 2.00 **Si**, 0.50 **Mo**, 0.04 **P**, 0.04 **S**	**As cast**: all **diam**, 70 (485) **TS**, 35 (240) **YS**, 25 **El**
NOM-B-355	Class HF	Mexico	Castings	0.20–0.40 **C**, 2.0 **Mn**, 18.0–23.0 **Cr**, 8.0–12.0 **Ni**, 2.0 **Si**, 0.50 **Mo**, 0.04 **P**, 0.04 **S**	**Quenched and tempered**: all **diam**, (483) **TS**, (241) **YS**, 25 **El**
JIS G 5122	Type 16	Japan	Castings, pipe (centrifugally cast)	0.20–0.35 **C**, 2.00 **Mn**, 13.00–17.00 **Cr**, 33.00–37.00 **Ni**, 2.50 **Si**, 0.50 **Mo**, 0.040 **P**, 0.040 **S**	**As cast**: all **diam**, (441) **TS**, (196) **YS**, 15 **El**
DTD 5249		UK	Investment and precision castings	0.20–0.30 **C**, 2.9–3.5 **Cr**, 0.4–0.7 **Mo**	**Annealed and quenched and tempered**: all **diam**, (850) **TS**
BS 3146 Part 1	CLA 11	UK	Investment and precision castings	0.20–0.30 **C**, 2.90–3.50 **Cr**, 0.40–0.70 **Mo**	**Annealed and quenched and tempered**: all **diam**, (850) **TS**
IS 3444	Grade 3	India	Castings	0.20–0.30 **C**, 1.00 **Mn**, 11.5–14.0 **Cr**, 1.00 **Ni**, 1.00 **Si**, 0.50 **Mo**, 0.040 **P**, 0.040 **S**	**Quenched and tempered**: all **diam**, (696) **TS**, (470) **YS**, 15 **El**
BS 3146 Part 2	ANC 1 Grade C	UK	Investment, precision castings	0.20–0.30 **C**, 11.50–13.50 **Cr**	**Quenched and tempered**: all **diam**, (695) **TS**, (460) **YS**
DIN 17445	Grade G-X 22 CrNi 17	Germany	Castings	0.20–0.27 **C**, 1.0 **Mn**, 16.0–18.0 **Cr**, 1.0–2.0 **Ni**, 1.0 **Si**, 0.045 **P**, 0.030 **S**	**Quenched and tempered**: all **diam**, (785) **TS**, (588) **YS**, 4 **El**
DIN 17445	Grade G-X22 CrNi 17-1.4059	Germany	Sand castings	0.20–0.27 **C**, 1.0 **Mn**, 16.0–18.0 **Cr**, 1.0–2.0 **Ni**, 1.0 **Si**	**Quenched and tempered**: all **diam**, (784) **TS**, (588) **YS**, 4 **El**
DIN 17245	Grade G-X 22 CrMoV 121	Germany	Castings	0.20–0.26 **C**, 0.50–0.70 **Mn**, 11.30–12.20 **Cr**, 0.70–1.00 **Ni**, 0.20–0.40 **Si**, 1.00–1.20 **Mo**, 0.045 **P**, 0.030 **S**	**Quenched and tempered**: all **diam**, (687) **TS**, (588) **YS**, 15 **El**
DIN 17245		Germany	Castings	0.20–0.26 **C**, 0.50–0.70 **Mn**, 11.30–12.20 **Cr**, 0.70–1.00 **Ni**, 0.20–0.40 **Si**, 1.00–1.20 **Mo**, 0.045 **P**, 0.030 **S**, 0.40–0.60 **W**	**Quenched and tempered**: all **diam**, (687) **TS**, (588) **YS**, 15 **El**
BS 3100/1630	Grade B	UK	Sand castings	0.20 **C**, 11.5–13.5 **Cr**	**Quenched and tempered**: all **diam**, (695) **TS**, (470) **YS**, 11 **El**
ANSI/ASTM A 426	CP9	US	Pipe: centrifugally cast	0.20 **C**, 0.30–0.65 **Mn**, 8.00–10.00 **Cr**, 0.25–1.00 **Si**, 0.90–1.20 **Mo**, 0.030 **P**, 0.030 **S**	**Normalized, tempered**: all **diam**, 90 (621) **TS**, 60 (414) **YS**, 18 **El**
BS 1504-420C29		UK	Castings	0.20 **C**, 1.0 **Mn**, 11.5–13.5 **Cr**, 1.0 **Ni**, 1.0 **Si**, 0.040 **P**, 0.040 **S**, 0.30 **Cu**	**Hardened and tempered**: all **diam**, (620) **TS**, (450) **YS**, 13 **El**
ANSI/ASTM A 217	Grade C 12	US	Sand castings	0.20 **C**, 0.35–0.65 **Mn**, 8.00–10.00 **Cr**, 1.00 **Si**, 0.90–1.20 **Mo**, 0.040 **P**, 0.045 **S**; 1.00 max, other elements, total	**Normalized and tempered**: all **diam**, 90 (620) **TS**, 60 (415) **YS**, 18 **El**
ANSI/ASTM A 217	Grade C5	US	Sand castings	0.20 **C**, 0.40–0.70 **Mn**, 4.00–6.50 **Cr**, 0.75 **Si**, 0.45–0.65 **Mo**, 0.040 **P**, 0.045 **S**; 1.00 max, other elements, total	**Normalized and tempered**: all **diam**, 90 (620) **TS**, 60 (415) **YS**, 18 **El**
IS 3038	Grade 7	India	Castings	0.20 **C**, 0.35–0.65 **Mn**, 8.00–10.00 **Cr**, 1.00 **Si**, 0.90–1.20 **Mo**, 0.040 **P**, 0.045 **S**	**As agreed**: (25) **diam**, (620) **TS**, (420) **YS**, 15 **El**
IS 3038	Grade 6	India	Castings	0.20 **C**, 0.40–0.70 **Mn**, 4.00–6.50 **Cr**, 0.75 **Si**, 0.45–0.65 **Mo**, 0.040 **P**, 0.045 **S**	**As agreed**: (25) **diam**, (620) **TS**, (420) **YS**, 15 **El**
NOM-B-355	Class HA	Mexico	Castings	0.20 **C**, 0.35–0.65 **Mn**, 8.0–10.0 **Cr**, 1.0 **Si**, 0.90–1.20 **Mo**, 0.040 **P**, 0.040 **S**	**Quenched and tempered**: all **diam**, (617) **TS**, (411) **YS**, 18 **El**
ASTM A 451	Grade CPH20	US	Pipe: centrifugally cast	0.20 **C**, 1.50 **Mn**, 22.0–26.0 **Cr**, 12.0–15.0 **Ni**, 1.00 **Si**, 0.040 **P**, 0.040 **S**	**Solution quenched**: all **diam**, (485) **TS**, (205) **YS**, 30 **El**
ASTM A-351-76	Grade CH20	US	Castings	0.20 **C**, 1.50 **Mn**, 22.0–26.0 **Cr**, 12.0–15.0 **Ni**, 2.00 **Si**, 0.040 **P**, 0.040 **S**	**Solution treated**: all **diam**, (485) **TS**, (205) **YS**, 30 **El**
ASTM A 743	Grade CH-20	US	Castings	0.20 **C**, 1.50 **Mn**, 22.0–26.0 **Cr**, 12.0–15.0 **Ni**, 2.00 **Si**, 0.04 **P**, 0.04 **S**	**Solution quenched at 1090°C: all diam, (485) TS, (205) YS, 30 El**
ASTM A 743	Grade CF-20	US	Castings	0.20 **C**, 1.50 **Mn**, 18.0–21.0 **Cr**, 8.00–11.00 **Ni**, 2.00 **Si**, 0.04 **P**, 0.04 **S**	**Solution quenched at 1040°C: all diam, (485) TS, (205) YS, 30 El**

CAST HIGH ALLOY STEELS

specification number	designation	country	product forms	composition	mechanical properties (see page iv for explanation)
ANSI/ASTM A 296	Grade CH-20	US	Sand castings	0.20 **C**, 1.50 **Mn**, 22.0–26.0 **Cr**, 12.0–15.0 **Ni**, 2.00 **Si**, 0.040 **P**, 0.040 **S**	**Solution annealed**: all **diam**, 70 (485) **TS**, 30 (205) **YS**, 30 **El**
ANSI/ASTM A 296	Grade CF-20	US	Sand castings	0.20 **C**, 1.50 **Mn**, 18.0–21.0 **Cr**, 8.0–11.0 **Ni**, 2.00 **Si**, 0.040 **P**, 0.040 **S**	**Solution annealed**: all **diam**, 70 (485) **TS**, 30 (205) **YS**, 30 **El**
ANSI/ASTM A 217	Grade WC 6	US	Sand castings	0.20 **C**, 0.50–0.80 **Mn**, 1.00–1.50 **Cr**, 0.60 **Si**, 0.45–0.65 **Mo**, 0.040 **P**, 0.045 **S**; 1.00 max, other elements, total	**Normalized and tempered**: all **diam**, 70 (485) **TS**, 40 (275) **YS**, 20 **El**
ANSI/ASTM A 217	Grade WC5	US	Sand castings	0.20 **C**, 0.40–0.70 **Mn**, 0.50–0.90 **Cr**, 0.60–1.00 **Ni**, 0.60 **Si**, 0.90–1.20 **Mo**, 0.040 **P**, 0.045 **S**; 1.00 max, other elements, total	**Normalized and tempered**: all **diam**, 70 (485) **TS**, 40 (275) **YS**, 20 **El**
ANSI/ASTM A 217	Grade WC4	US	Sand castings	0.20 **C**, 0.50–0.80 **Mn**, 0.50–0.80 **Cr**, 0.70–1.10 **Ni**, 0.60 **Si**, 0.45–0.65 **Mo**, 0.040 **P**, 0.045 **S**; 1.00 max, other elements, total	**Normalized and tempered**: all **diam**, 70 (485) **TS**, 40 (275) **YS**, 20 **El**
ANSI/ASTM A 351	Grade CH20	US	Sand castings	0.20 **C**, 1.50 **Mn**, 22.0–26.0 **Cr**, 12.0–15.0 **Ni**, 2.00 **Si**, 0.040 **P**, 0.040 **S**	**Solution annealed**: all **diam**, 70 (485) **TS**, 30 (205) **YS**, 30 **El**
ANSI/ASTM A 351	CH20	US	Castings	0.20 **C**, 1.50 **Mn**, 22.0–26.0 **Cr**, 12.0–15.0 **Ni**, 2.00 **Si**, 0.040 **P**, 0.040 **S**	**Solution annealed**: all **diam**, 70 (485) **TS**, 30 (205) **YS**, 30 **El**
NOM-B-354	Class CF-20	Mexico	Castings	0.20 **C**, 1.50 **Mn**, 18.0–21.0 **Cr**, 8.0–11.0 **Ni**, 2.0 **Si**, 0.040 **P**, 0.040 **S**	**As agreed**: all **diam**, (483) **TS**, (207) **YS**, 30 **El**
NOM-B-354	Class CH-20	Mexico	Castings	0.20 **C**, 1.50 **Mn**, 22.0–26.0 **Cr**, 12.0–15.0 **Ni**, 2.0 **Si**, 0.040 **P**, 0.040 **S**	**As agreed**: all **diam**, (483) **TS**, (207) **YS**, 30 **El**
ANSI/ASTM A 451	CPH20	US	Pipe: centrifugally cast	0.20 **C**, 1.50 **Mn**, 22.0–26.0 **Cr**, 12.0–15.0 **Ni**, 1.00 **Si**, 0.040 **P**, 0.040 **S**	**Solution annealed**: all **diam**, 70 (483) **TS**, 30 (207) **YS**, 30 **El**
IS 7806	Grade 8	India	Castings	0.20 **C**, 1.50 **Mn**, 22.0–26.0 **Cr**, 12.0–15.0 **Ni**, 2.00 **Si**, 0.040 **P**, 0.040 **S**	**Solution annealed**: all **diam**, (480) **TS**, (210) **YS**, 29 **El**
BS 1504–245		UK	Castings	0.20 **C**, 0.50–1.0 **Mn**, 0.20–0.60 **Si**, 0.25 **Cr**, 0.45–0.65 **Mo**, 0.40 **Ni**, 0.30 **Cu**, 0.040 **P**, 0.040 **S**	**Normalized and tempered or quenched and tempered**: all **diam**, (460) **TS**, (260) **YS**, 18 **El**
ASTM A 451	Grade CPK20	US	Pipe: centrifugally cast	0.20 **C**, 1.50 **Mn**, 23.0–27.0 **Cr**, 19.0–22.0 **Ni**, 1.00 **Si**, 0.040 **P**, 0.040 **S**	**Solution quenched**: all **diam**, (450) **TS**, (195) **YS**, 30 **El**
ASTM A-351-76	Grade CK20	US	Castings	0.20 **C**, 1.50 **Mn**, 23.0–27.0 **Cr**, 19.0–22.0 **Ni**, 1.75 **Si**, 0.040 **P**, 0.040 **S**	**Solution treated**: all **diam**, (450) **TS**, (195) **YS**, 30 **El**
ASTM A 743	Grade CK-20	US	Castings	0.20 **C**, 2.00 **Mn**, 23.0–27.0 **Cr**, 19.0–22.0 **Ni**, 2.00 **Si**, 0.04 **P**, 0.04 **S**	**Solution quenched**: all **diam**, (450) **TS**, (195) **YS**, 30 **El**
ANSI/ASTM A 296	Grade CK-20	US	Sand castings	0.20 **C**, 2.00 **Mn**, 23.0–27.0 **Cr**, 19.0–22.0 **Ni**, 2.00 **Si**, 0.040 **P**, 0.040 **S**	**Solution annealed**: all **diam**, 65 (450) **TS**, 28 (195) **YS**, 30 **El**
ANSI/ASTM A 351	Grade CK20	US	Sand castings	0.20 **C**, 1.50 **Mn**, 23.0–27.0 **Cr**, 19.0–22.0 **Ni**, 1.75 **Si**, 0.040 **P**, 0.040 **S**	**Solution annealed**: all **diam**, 65 (450) **TS**, 28 (195) **YS**, 30 **El**
ANSI/ASTM A 351	CK20	US	Castings	0.20 **C**, 1.50 **Mn**, 23.0–27.0 **Cr**, 19.0–22.0 **Ni**, 1.75 **Si**, 0.040 **P**, 0.040 **S**	**Solution annealed**: all **diam**, 65 (450) **TS**, 28 (195) **YS**, 30 **El**
IS 7806	Grade 9	India	Castings	0.20 **C**, 1.50 **Mn**, 23.0–27.0 **Cr**, 19.0–22.0 **Ni**, 1.75 **Si**, 0.040 **P**, 0.040 **S**	**Solution annealed**: all **diam**, (450) **TS**, (190) **YS**, 29 **El**
NOM-B-354	Class CK-20	Mexico	Castings	0.20 **C**, 2.0 **Mn**, 23.0–27.0 **Cr**, 19.0–22.0 **Ni**, 2.0 **Si**, 0.040 **P**, 0.040 **S**	**As agreed**: all **diam**, (448) **TS**, (193) **YS**, 30 **El**
ANSI/ASTM A 451	CPK20	US	Pipe: centrifugally cast	0.20 **C**, 1.50 **Mn**, 23.0–27.0 **Cr**, 19.0–22.0 **Ni**, 1.00 **Si**, 0.040 **P**, 0.040 **S**	**Solution annealed**: all **diam**, 65 (448) **TS**, 28 (193) **YS**, 30 **El**
JIS G 5121	Type 12	Japan	Castings, pipe (centrifugally cast)	0.20 **C**, 2.00 **Mn**, 18.00–21.00 **Cr**, 8.00–11.00 **Ni**, 1.50 **Si**, 0.040 **P**, 0.040 **S**	**Solution annealed**: all **diam**, (441) **TS**, (206) **YS**, 30 **El**

CAST HIGH ALLOY STEELS

specification number	designation	country	product forms	composition	mechanical properties (see page iv for explanation)
JIS G 5121	Type 17	Japan	Castings, pipe (centrifugally cast)	0.20 **C**, 2.00 **Mn**, 22.00–26.00 **Cr**, 12.00–15.00 **Ni**, 2.00 **Si**, 0.040 **P**, 0.040 **S**	**Solution annealed**: all **diam**, (441) **TS**, (206) **YS**, 30 **El**
JIS G 5121	Type 18	Japan	Castings, pipe (centrifugally cast)	0.20 **C**, 2.00 **Mn**, 23.00–27.00 **Cr**, 19.00–22.00 **Ni**, 2.00 **Si**, 0.040 **P**, 0.040 **S**	**Solution annealed**: all **diam**, (441) **TS**, (186) **YS**, 30 **El**
DIN 17445	Grade G–X20 Cr 14–1.4027	Germany	Sand castings	0.18–0.25 **C**, 1.0 **Mn**, 12.5–14.5 **Cr**, 1.0 **Si**	**Quenched and tempered**: all **diam**, (588) **TS**, (441) **YS**, 12 **El**
DIN 17440	Grade G–X 20 Cr 14	Germany	Castings	0.18–0.25 **C**, 1.0 **Mn**, 12.5–14.5 **Cr**, 1.0 **Si**, 0.045 **P**, 0.030 **S**	**Quenched and tempered**: all **diam**, (588) **TS**, (441) **YS**, 12 **El**
ANSI/ASTM A 217	Grade WC 9	US	Sand castings	0.18 **C**, 0.40–0.70 **Mn**, 2.00–2.75 **Cr**, 0.60 **Si**, 0.90–1.20 **Mo**, 0.040 **P**, 0.045 **S**; 1.00 max, other elements, total	**Normalized and tempered**: all **diam**, 70 (485) **TS**, 40 (275) **YS**, 20 **El**
ANSI/ASTM A 426	CP 22	US	Pipe: centrifugally cast	0.18 **C**, 0.30–0.70 **Mn**, 2.00–2.75 **Cr**, 0.60 **Si**, 0.90–1.20 **Mo**, 0.030 **P**, 0.030 **S**	**Normalized, tempered**: all **diam**, 70 (483) **TS**, 40 (276) **YS**, 20 **El**
AMS 5366B		US	Investment castings	0.18 **C**, 2.00 **Mn**, 23.00–26.00 **Cr**, 19.00–22.00 **Ni**, 0.50–1.50 **Si**, 0.75 **Mo**, 0.040 **P**, 0.030 **S**, 0.75 **Cu**	
JIS G 5121	Type 2	Japan	Castings, pipe (centrifugally cast)	0.16–0.24 **C**, 1.00 **Mn**, 11.50–14.00 **Cr**, 1.00 **Ni**, 1.50 **Si**, 0.05 **Mo**, 0.040 **P**, 0.040 **S**	**Quenched and tempered**: all **diam**, (588) **TS**, (392) **YS**, 18 **El**
ASTM A 743	Grade CF–16F	US	Castings	0.16 **C**, 1.50 **Mn**, 18.0–21.0 **Cr**, 9.0–12.00 **Ni**, 2.00 **Si**, 0.04 **P**, 0.04 **S**	**Solution quenched at 1040°C: all diam, (485) TS, (205) YS, 25 El**
ANSI/ASTM A 296	Grade CF–16F	US	Sand castings	0.16 **C**, 1.50 **Mn**, 18.0–21.0 **Cr**, 9.0–12.0 **Ni**, 2.00 **Si**, 0.040 **P**, 0.040 **S**	**Solution annealed**: all **diam**, 70 (485) **TS**, 30 (205) **YS**, 25 **El**
NOM–B–354	Class CF–16F	Mexico	Castings	0.16 **C**, 1.50 **Mn**, 18.0–21.0 **Cr**, 9.0–12.0 **Ni**, 2.0 **Si**, 0.040 **P**, 0.040 **S**	**As agreed**: all **diam**, (483) **TS**, (207) **YS**, 25 **El**
AMS 5341A		US	Investment castings	0.16 **C**, 2.00 **Mn**, 18.00–21.00 **Cr**, 9.00–12.00 **Ni**, 2.00 **Si**, 0.75 **Mo**, 0.040 **P**, 0.15–0.35 **S**, 0.75 **Cu**	**Solution heat treated**: all **diam**
IS 4522	Grade 8	India	Castings	0.15–0.35 **C**, 1.50 **Mn**, 19.0–21.0 **Cr**, 13.0–15.0 **Ni**, 2.50 **Si**, 0.050 **P**, 0.050 **S**	
MIL–S–17509	Class I	US	Sand castings	0.15–0.30 **C**, 1.50 **Mn**, 17.0–20.0 **Cr**, 8.0–11.0 **Ni**, 1.50 **Si**, 0.50 **Mo**, 0.05 **P**, 0.05 **S**	**Solution annealed**: all **diam**, (482) **TS**, (206) **YS**, 30 **El**
BS 3146 Part 2	ANC 6 Grade A	UK	Investment and precision castings	0.15–0.30 **C**, 20.0–25.0 **Cr**, 10.0–15.0 **Ni**	**As cast**: all **diam**, (460) **TS**
BS 3146 Part 2	ANC 6 Grade B	UK	Investment and precision castings	0.15–0.30 **C**, 20.0–25.0 **Cr**, 10.0–15.0 **Ni**, 2.5–3.5 **W**	**As cast**: all **diam**, (460) **TS**
AMS 5361C		US	Sand and centrifugal castings	0.15–0.25 **C**, 2.00 **Mn**, 17.00–20.00 **Cr**, 12.00–15.00 **Ni**, 1.00 **Si**, 1.75–2.50 **Mo**, 0.040 **P**, 0.040 **S**, 0.75 **Cu**	**Solution heat treated**
MIL–S–81591	IC–420	US	Investment castings	0.15 **C**, 1.00 **Mn**, 12.0–14.0 **Cr**, 1.00 **Si**, 0.040 **P**, 0.030 **S**	**Quenched and tempered**: all **diam**, 180 (1241) **TS**, 150 (1034) **YS**, 2 **El**
ASTM A 487	Grade CA 15a	US	Castings	0.15 **C**, 1.00 **Mn**, 11.5–14.0 **Cr**, 1.00 **Ni**, 1.50 **Si**, 0.50 **Mo**, 0.040 **P**, 0.040 **S**	**Normalized and tempered**: all **diam**, 140 (965) **TS**, 110 (760) **YS**, 10 **El**
ANSI/ASTM A 487	CA 15a	US	Castings	0.15 **C**, 1.00 **Mn**, 11.5–14.0 **Cr**, 1.00 **Ni**, 1.50 **Si**, 0.50 **Mo**, 0.04 **P**, 0.04 **S**	**Normalized, tempered**: all **diam**, 140 (965) **TS**, 110 (760) **YS**, 10 **El**
ANSI/ASTM A 487	Class CA 15a	US	Sand castings	0.15 **C**, 1.00 **Mn**, 11.5–14.0 **Cr**, 1.00 **Ni**, 1.50 **Si**, 0.50 **Mo**, 0.04 **P**, 0.04 **S**	**Normalized and tempered**: all **diam**, 140 (965) **TS**, 110 (760) **YS**, 10 **El**
MIL–S 16993A	Grade 2	US	Castings	0.15 **C**, 1.00 **Mn**, 11.5–14.0 **Cr**, 0.65–1.0 **Ni**, 0.50 **Si**, 0.50–0.70 **Mo**, 0.05 **P**, 0.05 **S**	**Normalized and tempered**: all **diam**, (621) **TS**, (448) **YS**, 18 **El**
MIL–S 16993A	Grade 1	US	Castings	0.15 **C**, 1.00 **Mn**, 11.5–14.0 **Cr**, 1.00 **Ni**, 1.50 **Si**, 0.50 **Mo**, 0.05 **P**, 0.05 **S**	**Normalized and tempered**: all **diam**, (621) **TS**, (448) **YS**, 18 **El**

CAST HIGH ALLOY STEELS

specification number	designation	country	product forms	composition	mechanical properties (see page iv for explanation)
NOM–B–354	Class CA–15	Mexico	Castings	0.15 **C**, 1.0 **Mn**, 11.5–14.0 **Cr**, 1.0 **Ni**, 1.50 **Si**, 0.50 **Mo**, 0.040 **P**, 0.040 **S**	**As agreed**: all **diam**, (621) **TS**, (448) **YS**, 18 **El**
NOM–B–354	Class CA–15M	Mexico	Castings	0.15 **C**, 1.0 **Mn**, 11.5–14.0 **Cr**, 1.0 **Ni**, 0.65 **Si**, 0.15–1.0 **Mo**, 0.040 **P**, 0.040 **S**	**As agreed**: all **diam**, (621) **TS**, (448) **YS**, 18 **El**
ANSI/ASTM A 426	CPCA15	US	Pipe: centrifugally cast	0.15 **C**, 1.00 **Mn**, 11.5–14.0 **Cr**, 1.50 **Si**, 0.50 **Mo**, 0.040 **P**, 0.040 **S**	**Normalized, tempered**: all **diam**, 90 (621) **TS**, 65 (448) **YS**, 18 **El**
ASTM A 743	Grade CA–15M	US	Castings	0.15 **C**, 1.00 **Mn**, 11.5–14.0 **Cr**, 1.0 **Ni**, 0.65 **Si**, 0.15–1.00 **Mo**, 0.04 **P**, 0.04 **S**	**Normalized and tempered annealed**: all **diam**, (620) **TS**, (450) **YS**, 18 **El**
ASTM A 743	Grade CA–15	US	Castings	0.15 **C**, 1.00 **Mn**, 11.5–14.0 **Cr**, 1.00 **Ni**, 1.50 **Si**, 0.50 **Mo**, 0.04 **P**, 0.04 **S**	**Normalized and tempered annealed**: all **diam**, (620) **TS**, (450) **YS**, 18 **El**
ASTM A 487–76	Grade CA 15M	US	Castings	0.15 **C**, 1.00 **Mn**, 11.5–14.0 **Cr**, 1.00 **Ni**, 0.65 **Si**, 0.15–1.0 **Mo**, 0.04 **P**, 0.04 **S**, 0.50 **Cu**, 0.03 **V**, 0.10 **W**	**Normalized and tempered**: all **diam**, 90 (620) **TS**, 65 (448) **YS**, 18 **El**
ASTM A 217–75	Grade CA–15	US	Castings	0.15 **C**, 1.00 **Mn**, 11.5–14.0 **Cr**, 1.00 **Ni**, 1.50 **Si**, 0.50 **Mo**, 0.04 **P**, 0.04 **S**, 0.50 **Cu**, 0.10 **W**	**Normalized and tempered**: all **diam**, 90 (620) **TS**, 65 (450) **YS**, 18 **El**
ANSI/ASTM A 487	CA 15M	US	Castings	0.15 **C**, 1.00 **Mn**, 11.5–14.0 **Cr**, 1.0 **Ni**, 0.65 **Si**, 0.15–1.0 **Mo**, 0.040 **P**, 0.040 **S**, 0.03 **V**	**Normalized, tempered**: all **diam**, 90 (620) **TS**, 65 (450) **YS**, 18 **El**
ANSI/ASTM A 217	CA–15	US	Castings	0.15 **C**, 1.00 **Mn**, 11.5–14.0 **Cr**, 1.00 **Ni**, 1.50 **Si**, 0.50 **Mo**, 0.040 **P**, 0.040 **S**	**Normalized, tempered**: all **diam**, 90 (620) **TS**, 65 (450) **YS**, 18 **El**
MIL–S–16993 A	Class 1	US	Sand castings	0.15 **C**, 1.0 **Mn**, 11.5–14.0 **Cr**, 1.0 **Ni**, 1.5 **Si**, 0.5 **Mo**, 0.05 **P**, 0.05 **S**	**Normalized and tempered**: all **diam**, (620) **TS**, (448) **YS**, 18 **El**
MIL–S–16993 A	Class 2	US	Sand castings	0.15 **C**, 1.0 **Mn**, 11.5–14.0 **Cr**, 0.65–1.0 **Ni**, 0.50 **Si**, 0.50–0.70 **Mo**, 0.05 **P**, 0.05 **S**	**Normalized and tempered**: all **diam**, (620) **TS**, (448) **YS**, 18 **El**
ANSI/ASTM A 487	Class CA15M	US	Sand castings	0.15 **C**, 1.00 **Mn**, 11.5–14.0 **Cr**, 1.0 **Ni**, 0.65 **Si**, 0.15–1.0 **Mo**, 0.040 **P**, 0.040 **S**, 0.03 **V**	**Normalized and tempered**: all **diam**, 90 (620) **TS**, 65 (450) **YS**, 18 **El**
ANSI/ASTM A 296	Grade CA–15M	US	Sand castings	0.15 **C**, 1.00 **Mn**, 11.5–14.0 **Cr**, 1.0 **Ni**, 0.65 **Si**, 0.15–1.0 **Mo**, 0.040 **P**, 0.040 **S**	**Normalized and tempered**: all **diam**, 90 (620) **TS**, 65 (450) **YS**, 18 **El**
ANSI/ASTM A 296	Grade CA–15	US	Sand castings	0.15 **C**, 1.00 **Mn**, 11.5–14.0 **Cr**, 1.00 **Ni**, 1.50 **Si**, 0.50 **Mo**, 0.040 **P**, 0.040 **S**	**Normalized and tempered**: all **diam**, 90 (620) **TS**, 65 (450) **YS**, 18 **El**
ANSI/ASTM A 217	Grade CA–15	US	Sand castings	0.15 **C**, 1.00 **Mn**, 11.5–14.0 **Cr**, 1.00 **Ni**, 1.50 **Si**, 0.50 **Mo**, 0.040 **P**, 0.040 **S**; 1.00 max, other elements, total	**Normalized and tempered**: all **diam**, 90 (620) **TS**, 65 (450) **YS**, 18 **El**
IS 7806	Grade 1	India	Castings	0.15 **C**, 1.00 **Mn**, 11.5–14.0 **Cr**, 1.00 **Ni**, 1.50 **Si**, 0.50 **Mo**, 0.040 **P**, 0.040 **S**	**Normalized and tempered**: all **diam**, (620) **TS**, (450) **YS**, 17 **El**
IS 7806	Grade 1A	India	Castings	0.15 **C**, 1.00 **Mn**, 11.5–14.0 **Cr**, 1.00 **Ni**, 0.65 **Si**, 0.75–1.0 **Mo**, 0.040 **P**, 0.040 **S**	**Normalized and tempered**: all **diam**, (620) **TS**, (450) **YS**, 17 **El**
NF A 32–056	Z 12 C 13–M	France	Castings	0.15 **C**, 1.5 **Mn**, 11.5–13.5 **Cr**, 1.2 **Si**, 0.040 **P**, 0.030 **S**	**Quenched and tempered**: all **diam**, (600) **TS**, (400) **YS**, 14 **El**
BS 3100/1630	Grade A	UK	Sand castings	0.15 **C**, 11.5–13.5 **Cr**	**Quenched and tempered**: all **diam**, (540) **TS**, (370) **YS**, 15 **El**
BS 3146 Part 2	ANC 1 Grade A	UK	Investment, precision castings	0.15 **C**, 11.50–13.50 **Cr**	**Quenched and tempered**: all **diam**, (540) **TS**, (375) **YS**
IS 3444	Grade 1	India	Castings	0.15 **C**, 1.00 **Mn**, 11.50–14.00 **Cr**, 1.00 **Ni**, 1.50 **Si**, 0.50 **Mo**, 0.040 **P**, 0.040 **S**	**Quenched and tempered**: all **diam**, (540) **TS**, (370) **YS**, 20 **El**
JIS G 5121	Type 1	Japan	Castings, pipe (centrifugally cast)	0.15 **C**, 1.00 **Mn**, 11.50–14.00 **Cr**, 1.00 **Ni**, 1.50 **Si**, 0.05 **Mo**, 0.040 **P**, 0.040 **S**	**Quenched and tempered**: all **diam**, (539) **TS**, (343) **YS**, 20 **El**
IS 3444	Grade 1	India	Castings	0.15 **C**, 1.00 **Mn**, 11.5–14.0 **Cr**, 1.00 **Ni**, 1.50 **Si**, 0.50 **Mo**, 0.040 **P**, 0.040 **S**	**Quenched and tempered**: all **diam**, (539) **TS**, (372) **YS**, 20 **El**

CAST HIGH ALLOY STEELS

specification number	designation	country	product forms	composition	mechanical properties (see page iv for explanation)
BS 4534	Grade 7	UK	Tube: weldable, centrifugal cast	0.15 **C**, 2.0 **Mn**, 23.0–27.0 **Cr**, 19.0–23.0 **Ni**, 0.5–1.5 **Si**, 0.50 **Mo**, 0.030 **P**, 0.040 **S**	**As cast**: all **diam**, (400) **TS**, 22 **El**
BS 4534	Grade 10	UK	Tube: weldable, centrifugal cast	0.15 **C**, 2.0 **Mn**, 17.0–21.0 **Cr**, 33.0–37.0 **Ni**, 0.5–1.5 **Si**, 0.50 **Mo**, 0.030 **P**, 0.040 **S**	**As cast**: all **diam**, (370) **TS**, 22 **El**
MIL-S-81591	IC-302	US	Investment castings	0.15 **C**, 2.00 **Mn**, 17.0–19.0 **Cr**, 8.0–10.0 **Ni**, 1.00 **Si**, 0.040 **P**, 0.030 **S**	**Solution annealed**
AMS 5351C		US	Sand castings	0.15 **C**, 1.00 **Mn**, 11.50–14.00 **Cr**, 1.00 **Ni**, 1.50 **Si**, 0.50 **Mo**, 0.040 **P**, 0.040 **S**, 0.50 **Cu**	**Normalized and tempered**: all **diam**
AMS 5360 C		US	Investment castings	0.15 **C**, 2.00 **Mn**, 16.00–18.00 **Cr**, 12.00–14.00 **Ni**, 0.75 **Si**, 1.50–2.25 **Mo**, 0.040 **P**, 0.030 **S**, 0.75 **Cu**	**Solution heat treated**: all **diam**
NF A 32-056	Z 12 CN 13 02-M	France	Castings	0.14 **C**, 1.2 **Mn**, 11.5–14.0 **Cr**, 1.5–2.5 **Ni**, 0.6 **Si**, 0.040 **P**, 0.030 **S**	**Quenched and tempered**: all **diam**, (550) **TS**, (350) **YS**, 12 **El**
AMS 5372A		US	Castings	0.12–0.20 **C**, 1.00 **Mn**, 14.50–17.00 **Cr**, 1.50–2.25 **Ni**, 1.00 **Si**, 0.75 **Mo**, 0.040 **P**, 0.040 **S**, 0.75 **Cu**	**Normalized, quenched and tempered**: all **diam**, 180 (1241) **TS**, 140 (965) **YS**, 8 **El**
IS 3444	Grade 2	India	Castings	0.12–0.20 **C**, 1.00 **Mn**, 11.5–14.0 **Cr**, 1.00 **Ni**, 1.00 **Si**, 0.50 **Mo**, 0.040 **P**, 0.040 **S**	**Quenched and tempered**: all **diam**, (617) **TS**, (451) **YS**, 18 **El**
BS 1504-713		UK	Sand castings	0.12–0.20 **C**, 11.5–13.5 **Cr**	**Quenched and tempered**: all **diam**, (615) **TS**, (440) **YS**
BS 3146 Part 2	ANC 1 Grade B	UK	Investment, precision castings	0.12–0.20 **C**, 11.50–13.50 **Cr**	**Quenched and tempered**: all **diam**, (615) **TS**, (450) **YS**
BS 1504-713		UK	Castings	0.12–0.20 **C**, 1.00 **Mn**, 11.5–13.5 **Cr**, 1.00 **Ni**, 1.25 **Si**, 0.15 **Mo**, 0.050 **P**, 0.050 **S**, 0.40 **Cu**	**Hardened and tempered**: all **diam**, (550) **TS**, (400) **YS**, 18 **El**
SIS 14 23 24	SIS 23 24-12	Sweden	Castings	0.12 **C**, 2.0 **Mn**, 23.0–27.0 **Cr**, 4.5–7.0 **Ni**, 1.5 **Si**, 1.3–1.8 **Mo**	**Solution annealed**: all **diam**, (590) **TS**, (370) **YS**, 18 **El**
NOM-B-354	Class CW-12M	Mexico	Castings	0.12 **C**, 1.0 **Mn**, 15.5–20.0 **Cr**, rem **Ni**, 1.50 **Si**, 16.0–20.0 **Mo**, 0.040 **P**, 0.030 **S**, 2.50 **Co**, 7.5 **Fe**, 0.40 **V**, 5.25 **W**	**As agreed**: all **diam**, (496) **TS**, (317) **YS**, 4 **El**
ANSI/ASTM A 296	Grade N-12M	US	Sand castings	0.12 **C**, 1.00 **Mn**, 1.00 **Cr**, rem **Ni**, 1.00 **Si**, 26.0–33.0 **Mo**, 0.040 **P**, 0.030 **S**, 6.00 **Fe**, 0.60 **V**	**As cast, annealed**: all **diam**, 72 (495) **TS**, 46 (320) **YS**, 6 **El**
ANSI/ASTM A 296	Grade CW-12M	US	Sand castings	0.12 **C**, 1.00 **Mn**, 15.50–20.00 **Cr**, rem **Ni**, 1.50 **Si**, 16.00–20.00 **Mo**, 0.040 **P**, 0.030 **S**, 5.25 **W**, 0.40 **V**, 7.50 **Fe**	**As cast, annealed**: all **diam**, 72 (495) **TS**, 46 (320) **YS**, 4 **El**
ASTM A 743	Grade CG-12	US	Castings	0.12 **C**, 1.50 **Mn**, 20.0–23.0 **Cr**, 10.0–13.0 **Ni**, 2.00 **Si**, 0.04 **P**, 0.04 **S**	**Solution quenched at 1040°C: all diam, (485) TS, (195) YS, 35 El**
ANSI/ASTM A 296	Grade CG-12	US	Sand castings	0.12 **C**, 1.50 **Mn**, 20.0–23.0 **Cr**, 10.0–13.0 **Ni**, 2.00 **Si**, 0.040 **P**, 0.040 **S**	**Solution annealed**: all **diam**, 70 (485) **TS**, 28 (195) **YS**, 35 **El**
NOM-B-354	Class CG-12	Mexico	Castings	0.12 **C**, 1.50 **Mn**, 20.0–23.0 **Cr**, 10.0–13.0 **Ni**, 2.0 **Si**, 0.04 **P**, 0.04 **S**	**As agreed**: all **diam**, (483) **TS**, (193) **YS**, 35 **El**
AMS 5362E		US	Investment castings	0.12 **C**, 2.00 **Mn**, 18.00–19.50 **Cr**, 10.00–14.00 **Ni**, 1.50 **Si**, 0.75 **Mo**, 0.040 **P**, 0.030 **S**, 0.75 **Cu**, 10 x C-1.50 **Nb+Ta**	**Solution heat treated**: all **diam**, (483) **TS**, (207) **YS**, 30 (in 25.4 mm) **El**
BS 3100/1631	Grade D	UK	Sand castings	0.12 **C**, 17.0–21.0 **Cr**, 8.0 min **Ni**	**Quenched by air blast or water quenched from 1000–1100°C: all diam, (480) TS, (205) YS, 26 El**
IS 3444	Grade 13	India	Castings	0.12 **C**, 2.00 **Mn**, 16.5–18.5 **Cr**, 10.0 min **Ni**, 1.50 **Si**, 2.0–3.0 **Mo**, 0.040 **P**, 0.040 **S**, 4 x C-0.70 **Ti**	**Solution annealed**: all **diam**, (461) **TS**, (206) **YS**, 15 **El**
IS 3444	Grade 12	India	Castings	0.12 **C**, 2.00 **Mn**, 16.5–18.5 **Cr**, 10.0 min **Ni**, 1.50 **Si**, 2.0–3.0 **Mo**, 0.040 **P**, 0.040 **S**, 8 x C-1.10 **Nb**	**Solution annealed**: all **diam**, (461) **TS**, (206) **YS**, 15 **El**
IS 3444	Grade 8	India	Castings	0.12 **C**, 2.00 **Mn**, 17.0–20.0 **Cr**, 7.5 min **Ni**, 2.00 **Si**, 0.040 **P**, 0.040 **S**, 4 x C-0.70 **Ti**	**Solution annealed**: all **diam**, (461) **TS**, (206) **YS**, 21 **El**

CAST HIGH ALLOY STEELS

specification number	designation	country	product forms	composition	mechanical properties (see page iv for explanation)
IS 3444	Grade 7	India	Castings	0.12 **C**, 2.00 **Mn**, 17.0–20.0 **Cr**, 8.5 min **Ni**, 2.00 **Si**, 0.040 **P**, 0.040 **S**, 8 x C–1.10 **Nb**	**As agreed**: all **diam**, (461) **TS**, (206) **YS**, 21 **El**
IS 3444	Grade 6	India	Castings	0.12 **C**, 2.00 **Mn**, 17.0 min **Cr**, 7.0 min **Ni**, 2.00 **Si**, 0.040 **P**, 0.040 **S**	**As agreed**: all **diam**, (461) **TS**, (206) **YS**, 21 **El**
BS 1504–503LT60		UK	Castings	0.12 **C**, 0.80 **Mn**, 0.60 **Si**, 3.0–4.0 **Ni**, 0.030 **P**, 0.030 **S**	**Normalized and tempered or hardened and tempered**: all **diam**, (460) **TS**, (280) **YS**, 20 **El**
BS 1504–845	Grade Nb	UK	Sand castings	0.12 **C**, 16.5–18.5 **Cr**, 10.0 min **Ni**, 2.25–2.75 **Mo**, 8 x C–1.10 **Nb**	**Quenched**: all **diam**, (460) **TS**, (205) **YS**
DTD 5269		UK	Investment, precision castings	0.12 **C**, 17.0–20.0 **Cr**, 8.5–12.0 **Ni**	**Annealed, quenched**: all **diam**, (460) **TS**, (200) **YS**, 20 **El**
DTD 5259		UK	Investment, precision castings	0.12 **C**, 17.0–20.0 **Cr**, 7.5–12.0 **Ni**, 25.0 **Ni+Cr**	**Annealed, quenched**: all **diam**, (460) **TS**, (200) **YS**, 20 **El**
BS 3146 Part 2	ANC 4 Grade C Nb	UK	Investment, precision castings	0.12 **C**, 16.5–18.5 **Cr**, 10.0 min **Ni**, 2.25–2.75 **Mo**, 8 x C–1.10 **Nb**	**Quenched**: all **diam**, (460) **TS**, (205) **YS**
BS 3146 Part 2	ANC 4 Grade C Nb	UK	Investment and precision castings	0.12 **C**, 16.5–18.5 **Cr**, 10.0 min **Ni**, 2.25–2.75 **Mo**, 8 x C–1.10 **Nb**	**Quenched**: all **diam**, (460) **TS**, (205) **YS**
BS 1504–801		UK	Sand castings	0.12 **C**, 17.0 min **Cr**, 7.0 min **Ni**, 25.0 min **Ni+Cr**	**Quenched by air blast or water quenched from 1000–1100°C: all diam, (460) TS, (205) YS**
BS 3146 Part 2	ANC 3 Grade B Nb	UK	Investment, precision casting	0.12 **C**, 17.0–20.0 **Cr**, 8.5 min **Ni**, 8 x C–1.10 **Nb**	**Quenched by air blast or water quenched from 1000–1100°C: all diam, (460) TS, (205) YS**
BS 3146 Part 2	ANC 3 Grade A	UK	Investment, precision castings	0.12 **C**, 17.0 min **Cr**, 7.5 min **Ni**, Ni+Cr shall not be less than 25.0	**Quenched by air blast or water quenched from 1000–1100°C: all diam, (460) TS, (205) YS**
DIN 17445	Grade G–X10 CrNi 188–1,4312	Germany	Sand castings	≤0.12 **C**, 1.5 **Mn**, 17.0–19.5 **Cr**, 8.0–10.0 **Ni**, 2.0 **Si**	**Solution annealed**: all **diam**, (441) **TS**, (176) **YS**, 20 **El**
DIN 17445	Grade G–X10 CrNiMo 18 9–1.4410	Germany	Sand castings	≤0.12 **C**, 1.5 **Mn**, 17.0–19.5 **Cr**, 9.0–11.0 **Ni**, 2.0 **Si**, 2.0–2.5 **Mo**	**Solution annealed**: all **diam**, (441) **TS**, (186) **YS**, 20 min **El**
DIN 17445	Grade G–X 10 CrNi 18 8	Germany	Castings	0.12 **C**, 1.5 **Mn**, 17.0–19.5 **Cr**, 8.0–10.0 **Ni**, 2.0 **Si**, 0.045 **P**, 0.030 **S**	**Quenched**: all **diam**, (441) **TS**, (177) **YS**, 20 **El**
DIN 17440	Grade G–X 10 CrNiMo 18 9	Germany	Castings	0.12 **C**, 1.5 **Mn**, 17.0–19.5 **Cr**, 9.0–11.0 **Ni**, 2.0 **Si**, 2.0–2.5 **Mo**, 0.045 **P**, 0.030 **S**	**Quenched**: all **diam**, (441) **TS**, (186) **YS**, 20 **El**
BS 1504–801		UK	Castings	0.12 **C**, 2.00 **Mn**, 17.0 min **Cr**, 7.00 min **Ni**, 2.00 **Si**, 0.045 **P**, 0.045 **S**, 25.0 min **Ni+Cr**	**Solution annealed**: all **diam**, (415) **TS**, (185) **YS**, 20 **El**
BS 1504–821	Grade Ti	UK	Castings	0.12 **C**, 2.00 **Mn**, 17.0–20.0 **Cr**, 7.5 min **Ni**, 2.00 **Si**, 0.045 **P**, 0.045 **S**, 25.0 min **Ni+Cr**, 4 x C–0.70 **Ti**	**Solution annealed**: all **diam**, (415) **TS**, (185) **YS**, 20 **El**
BS 1504–821	Grade Nb	UK	Castings	0.12 **C**, 2.00 **Mn**, 17.0–20.0 **Cr**, 8.5 min **Ni**, 2.00 **Si**, 0.045 **P**, 0.045 **S**, 8 x C–1.10 **Nb**	**Solution annealed**: all **diam**, (415) **TS**, (185) **YS**, 20 **El**
BS 1504–845	Grade Nb	UK	Castings	0.12 **C**, 2.00 **Mn**, 16.5–18.5 **Cr**, 10.0 min **Ni**, 1.50 **Si**, 2.25–2.75 **Mo**, 0.045 **P**, 0.045 **S**, 8 x C–1.10 **Nb**	**Solution annealed**: all **diam**, (415) **TS**, (185) **YS**, 15 **El**
BS 1504–821		UK	Sand castings	0.12 **C**, 17.0–20.0 **Cr**, 7.5 min **Ni**, 4 x C–0.70 **Ti**	**Quenched**: all **diam**, (130) **TS**, (20) **YS**
BS 1504–821		UK	Sand castings	0.12 **C**, 17.0–20.0 **Cr**, 8.5 min **Ni**, 8 x C–1.10 **Nb**	**Quenched**: all **diam**, (130) **TS**, (20) **YS**
MIL–S–81591	IC–303	US	Investment castings	0.12 **C**, 2.00 **Mn**, 17.0–20.0 **Cr**, 8.0–10.0 **Ni**, 1.00 **Si**, 0.60 **Mo** 0.17 **P**, 0.15–0.35 **S**	**Solution annealed**
AMS 5365B		US	Sand castings	0.10–0.18 **C**, 2.00 **Mn**, 23.00–26.00 **Cr**, 19.00–22.00 **Ni**, 0.50–1.50 **Si**, 0.75 **Mo**, 0.040 **P**, 0.040 **S**, 0.75 **Cu**	**Solution heat treated**: all **diam**, 65 (448) **TS**, 28 (193) **YS**, 3 **El**
BS–425C11		UK	Castings	0.10 **C**, 1.00 **Mn**, 11.5–13.5 **Cr**, 3.4–4.2 **Ni**, 1.00 **Si**, 0.60 **Mo**, 0.040 **P**, 0.040 **S**	**Quenched and tempered**: all **diam**, (770) **TS**, (620) **YS**, 12 **El**

CAST HIGH ALLOY STEELS

specification number	designation	country	product forms	composition	mechanical properties (see page iv for explanation)
SIS 14 23 24	SIS 23 24–12	Sweden	Castings	0.10 **C**, 2.0 **Mn**, 24.0–27.0 **Cr**, 4.5–6.0 **Ni**, 1.0 **Si**, 1.3–1.8 **Mo**, 0.045 **P**, 0.030 **S**	**Solution annealed**: all **diam**, (590) **TS**, (370) **YS**, 18 **El**
JIS G 5121	Type II	Japan	Castings, pipe (centrifugally cast)	0.10 **C**, 1.00 **Mn**, 23.00–27.00 **Cr**, 5.00–7.00 **Ni**, 1.50 **Si**, 1.50–2.50 **Mo**, 0.040 **P**, 0.040 **S**	**Solution annealed**: all **diam**, (588) **TS**, (343) **YS**, 15 **El**
ASTM A 451	Grade CPF10MC	US	Pipe: centrifugally cast	0.10 **C**, 1.50 **Mn**, 15.0–18.0 **Cr**, 13.0–16.0 **Ni**, 1.00 **Si**, 1.75–2.25 **Mo**, 0.040 **P**, 0.040 **S**, 10 x C–1.2 **Cb**	**Solution quenched**: all **diam**, (485) **TS**, (205) **YS**, 20 **El**
ASTM A 451	Grade CPH10	US	Pipe: centrifugally cast	0.10 **C**, 1.50 **Mn**, 22.0–26.0 **Cr**, 12.0–15.0 **Ni**, 1.00 **Si**, 0.040 **P**, 0.040 **S**	**Solution quenched**: all **diam**, (485) **TS**, (205) **YS**, 30 **El**
ASTM A-351-76	Grade CH10	US	Castings	0.10 **C**, 1.50 **Mn**, 22.0–26.0 **Cr**, 12.0–15.0 **Ni**, 2.00 **Si**, 0.040 **P**, 0.040 **S**	**Solution treated**: all **diam**, (485) **TS**, (205) **YS**, 30 **El**
ASTM A-351-76	Grade CF10MC	US	Castings	0.10 **C**, 1.50 **Mn**, 15.0–18.0 **Cr**, 13.0–16.0 **Ni**, 1.50 **Si**, 1.75–2.25 **Mo**, 0.040 **P**, 0.040 **S**, 10 x C–1.20 **Cb**	**Solution annealed**: all **diam**, (485) **TS**, (205) **YS**, 20 **El**
ANSI/ASTM A 351	Grade CF10MC	US	Sand castings	0.10 **C**, 1.50 **Mn**, 15.0–18.0 **Cr**, 13.0–16.0 **Ni**, 1.50 **Si**, 1.75–2.25 **Mo**, 0.040 **P**, 0.040 **S**	**Solution annealed**: all **diam**, 70 (485) **TS**, 30 (205) **YS**, 20.0 **El**
ANSI/ASTM A 351	Grade CH10	US	Sand castings	0.10 **C**, 1.50 **Mn**, 22.0–26.0 **Cr**, 12.0–15.0 **Ni**, 2.00 **Si**, 0.040 **P**, 0.040 **S**	**Solution annealed**: all **diam**, 70 (485) **TS**, 30 (205) **YS**, 30 **El**
ANSI/ASTM A 351	CH10	US	Castings	0.10 **C**, 1.50 **Mn**, 22.0–26.0 **Cr**, 12.0–15.0 **Ni**, 2.00 **Si**, 0.040 **P**, 0.040 **S**	**Solution annealed**: all **diam**, 70 (485) **TS**, 30 (205) **YS**, 30 **El**
ANSI/ASTM A 351	CF10MC	US	Castings	0.10 **C**, 1.50 **Mn**, 15.0–18.0 **Cr**, 13.0–16.0 **Ni**, 1.50 **Si**, 1.75–2.25 **Mo**, 0.040 **P**, 0.040 **S**, 10 x C–1.20 **Nb**	**Solution annealed**: all **diam**, 70 (485) **TS**, 30 (205) **YS**, 20 **El**
ANSI/ASTM A 451	CPH10	US	Pipe: centrifugally cast	0.10 **C**, 1.50 **Mn**, 22.0–26.0 **Cr**, 12.0–15.0 **Ni**, 1.00 **Si**, 0.040 **P**, 0.040 **S**	**Solution annealed**: all **diam**, 70 (483) **TS**, 30 (207) **YS**, 30 **El**
ANSI/ASTM A 451	CPF10MC	US	Pipe: centrifugally cast	0.10 **C**, 1.50 **Mn**, 15.0–18.0 **Cr**, 13.0–16.0 **Ni**, 1.00 **Si**, 1.75–2.25 **Mo**, 0.040 **P**, 0.040 **S**, 1.35 **Nb+Ta**, 10 x C–1.2 **Nb**	**Solution annealed**: all **diam**, 70 (483) **TS**, 30 (207) **YS**, 20 **El**
IS 7806	Grade 7	India	Castings	0.10 **C**, 1.50 **Mn**, 22.0–26.0 **Cr**, 12.0–15.0 **Ni**, 2.00 **Si**, 0.040 **P**, 0.040 **S**	**Solution annealed**: all **diam**, (480) **TS**, (210) **YS**, 29 **El**
IS 7806	Grade 13	India	Castings	0.10 **C**, 1.50 **Mn**, 15.0–18.0 **Cr**, 13.0–16.0 **Ni**, 1.50 **Si**, 1.75–2.25 **Mo**, 0.040 **P**, 0.040 **S**, C x 10–1.20 **Nb**	**Solution annealed**: all **diam**, (480) **TS**, (210) **YS**, 19 **El**
NF A 32-056	Z 8 CN 25 20-M	France	Castings	0.10 **C**, 1.5 **Mn**, 23.0–27.0 **Cr**, 19.0–22.0 **Ni**, 1.2 **Si**, 0.040 **P**, 0.030 **S**, 8 x C–1.2 **Nb**	**Solution annealed**: all **diam**, (450) **TS**, (200) **YS**, 30 **El**
MIL-S-17509	Class II	US	Sand castings	0.10 **C**, 1.50 **Mn**, 17.0–20.0 **Cr**, 11.0 min **Ni**, 1.50 **Si**, 0.50 **Mo**, 0.05 **P**, 0.05 **S**, 10 x C–1.20 **Nb** or **Nb+Ta**	**Solution annealed**: all **diam**, (448) **TS**, (206) **YS**, 30 **El**
BS 4534	Grade 11	UK	Tube: weldable, centrifugal cast	0.10 **C**, 1.5 **Mn**, 19.0–22.0 **Cr**, 30.0–34.0 **Ni**, 0.3–1.0 **Si**, 0.50 **Mo**, 0.030 **P**, 0.030 **S**	**As cast**: all **diam**, (360) **TS**, 26 **El**
AMS 5363C		US	Sand and centrifugal castings	0.10 **C**, 2.00 **Mn**, 17.00–20.00 **Cr**, 9.00–12.00 **Ni**, 1.50 **Si**, 0.75 **Mo**, 0.040 **P**, 0.040 **S**, 0.75 **Cu**, 10 x C–1.35 **Nb+Ta**	**Solution heat treated**: all **diam**
SIS 14 23 02	SIS 23 02–13	Sweden	Castings	0.09–0.15 **C**, 1.5 **Mn**, 12.0–14.0 **Cr**, 1.5 **Ni**, 1.0 **Si**	**Quenched, tempered**: all **diam**, (590) **TS**, (390) **YS**, 16 **El**
SIS 14 23 02	SIS 23 02–12	Sweden	Castings	0.09–0.15 **C**, 1.5 **Mn**, 12.0–14.0 **Cr**, 1.5 **Ni**, 1.0 **Si**, 0.040 **P**, 0.035 **S**	**Annealed**: all **diam**, (490) **TS**, (290) **YS**, 18 **El**
SIS 14 23 02	SIS 23 02–12	Sweden	Castings	0.09–0.15 **C**, 1.5 **Mn**, 12.0–14.0 **Cr**, 1.5 **Ni**, 1.0 **Si**	**Annealed**: all **diam**, (400) **TS**, (290) **YS**, 18 **El**
AMS 5368A		US	Investment castings	0.08–0.15 **C**, 0.40–1.10 **Mn**, 14.50–15.50 **Cr**, 3.50–4.50 **Ni**, 0.75 **Si**, 2.00–2.60 **Mo**, 0.040 **P**, 0.030 **S**, 0.15–0.25 **Cu+N**, 0.05–0.13 **N**	**Solution annealed tempered austenite**: 0.250 (6.35) **diam**, 200 (1379) **TS**, 150 (1034) **YS**, 8 **El**

specification number	designation	country	product forms	composition	mechanical properties (see page iv for explanation)
MIL–S–81591	IC–431	US	Investment castings	0.08–0.15 **C**, 1.00 **Mn**, 15.0–17.0 **Cr**, 1.50–2.20 **Ni**, 1.00 **Si**, 0.040 **P**, 0.040 **S**, 0.03–0.12 **N**	**Quenched and tempered**: all **diam**, 170 (1172) **TS**, 130 (896) **YS**, 2 **El**
AMS 5353A		US	Investment castings	0.08–0.15 **C**, 1.00 **Mn**, 15.00–17.00 **Cr**, 1.50–2.20 **Ni**, 1.00 **Si**, 0.50 **Mo**, 0.040 **P**, 0.040 **S**, 0.50 **Cu**, 0.22 **C+N**, 0.03–0.12 **N**	**Quenched and tempered**: 0.250 (6.35) **diam**, 170 (1172) **TS**, 130 (896) **YS**, 2 **El**
AMS 5359A		US	Sand castings	0.08–0.15 **C**, 0.40–1.10 **Mn**, 14.50–15.50 **Cr**, 3.50–4.50 **Ni**, 0.75 **Si**, 2.00–2.60 **Mo**, 0.040 **P**, 0.030 **S**, 0.15–0.25 **C+N**, 0.05–0.11 **N**	**Austenite conditioned, sub-zero cooled, tempered**: all **diam**, (1138) **TS**, (965) **YS**, 8 **El**
DIN 17445	Grade G–X12 Cr 14–1,4008	Germany	Sand castings	0.08–0.15 **C**, 1.0 **Mn**, 12.0–14.0 **Cr**, 0.5–1.5 **Ni**, 1.0 **Si**	**Quenched and tempered**: all **diam**, (588) **TS**, (392) **YS**, 15 min **El**
DIN 17445	Grade G–X 12 Cr 14		Castings	0.08–0.15 **C**, 1.0 **Mn**, 12.0–14.0 **Cr**, 0.5–1.5 **Ni**, 1.0 **Si**, 0.045 **P**, 0.030 **S**	**Quenched and tempered**: all **diam**, (588) **TS**, (392) **YS**, 15 **El**
BS HC 106		UK	Castings: aircraft quality	0.08 **C**, 1.0 **Mn**, 15.0–17.5 **Cr**, 3.0–5.0 **Ni**, 1.0 **Si**, 0.040 **P**, 0.040 **S**, 2.0–3.0 **Cu**, 0.4 **Nb+Ta**	**Solution annealed and aged**: all **diam**, (1250) **TS**, (1030) **YS**, 8 **El**
MIL–S–81591	IC–17–4	US	Investment castings	0.08 **C**, 1.00 **Mn**, 15.5–17.5 **Cr**, 3.0–5.0 **Ni**, 1.00 **Si**, 0.040 **P**, 0.040 **S**, 0.45 **Cb+Ta**, 3.0–5.0 **Cu**	**Solution annealed and aged**: all **diam**, 180 (1241) **TS**, 150 (1034) **YS**, 6 **El**
DTD 5289		UK	Investment, precision castings	0.08 **C**, 18.0–20.0 **Cr**, 11.0–14.0 **Ni**, 3.0–4.0 **Mo**	**Annealed, quenched**: all **diam**, (950) **TS**, (205) **YS**, 11 **El**
NF A 32–055	Z 6 CND 13 04–M	France	Castings	0.08 **C**, 1.5 **Mn**, 11.5–13.5 **Cr**, 2.0–4.0 **Ni**, 1.20 **Si**, 0.5–1.5 **Mo**, 0.040 **P**, 0.030 **S**	**Normalized or quenched**: all **diam**, (700) **TS**, (450) **YS**, 13 **El**
NF A 32–055	Z 6 CND 13 04–M	France	Castings	0.08 **C**, 1.5 **Mn**, 11.5–13.5 **Cr**, 2.0–4.0 **Ni**, 1.20 **Si**, 0.5–1.5 **Mo**, 0.040 **P**, 0.030 **S**	**Normalized or quenched**: all **diam**, (700) **TS**, (450) **YS**, 13 **El**
NF A 32–056	Z 6 CND 13 04–M	France	Castings	0.08 **C**, 1.5 **Mn**, 11.5–13.5 **Cr**, 3.0–5.0 **Ni**, 1.2 **Si**, 0.4–1.5 **Mo**, 0.040 **P**, 0.030 **S**	**Quenched and tempered**: all **diam**, (700) **TS**, (450) **YS**, 13 **El**
NF A 32–055	Z 6 CND V 20 08–M	France	Castings	0.08 **C**, 1.5 **Mn**, 19.0–23.0 **Cr**, 7.0–9.0 **Ni**, 1.2 **Si**, 2.0–3.0 **Mo**, 0.040 **P**, 0.030 **S**, 1.0–2.0 **Cu**	**Solution annealed**: all **diam**, (600) **TS**, (320) **YS**, 15 **El**
NF A 32–056	Z 6 CNDU 20 08–M	France	Castings	0.08 **C**, 1.5 **Mn**, 19.0–23.0 **Cr**, 7.0–9.0 **Ni**, 1.2 **Si**, 2.0–3.0 **Mo**, 0.040 **P**, 0.030 **S**, 1.0–2.0 **Cu**	**Solution annealed**: all **diam**, (600) **TS**, (320) **YS**, 15 **El**
NF A 32–056	Z 6 C13 02–M	France	Castings	0.08 **C**, 1.5 **Mn**, 11.5–13.5 **Cr**, 1.0–2.5 **Ni**, 1.2 **Si**, 0.040 **P**, 0.030 **S**	**Quenched and tempered**: all **diam**, (600) **TS**, (400) **YS**, 13 **El**
ASTM A 451	Grade CPF8A	US	Pipe: centrifugally cast	0.08 **C**, 1.50 **Mn**, 18.0–21.0 **Cr**, 8.0–11.0 **Ni**, 2.00 **Si**, 0.040 **P**, 0.040 **S**	**Solution quenched**: all **diam**, (535) **TS**, (240) **YS**, 35 **El**
ASTM A 351	Grade CF8A	US	Castings	0.08 **C**, 1.50 **Mn**, 18.0–21.0 **Cr**, 8.0–11.0 **Ni**, 2.00 **Si**, 0.040 **P**, 0.040 **S**	**Solution treated**: all **diam**, (530) **TS**, (240) **YS**, 35 **El**
ANSI/ASTM A 351	Grade CF8A	US	Sand castings	0.08 **C**, 1.50 **Mn**, 18.0–21.0 **Cr**, 8.0–11.0 **Ni**, 2.00 **Si**, 0.040 **P**, 0.040 **S**	**Solution annealed**: all **diam**, 77 (530) **TS**, 35 (240) **YS**, 35 **El**
ANSI/ASTM A 351	CF8A	US	Castings	0.08 **C**, 1.50 **Mn**, 18.0–21.0 **Cr**, 8.0–11.0 **Ni**, 2.00 **Si**, 0.040 **P**, 0.040 **S**	**Solution annealed**: all **diam**, 77 (530) **TS**, 35 (240) **YS**, 35 **El**
IS 7806	Grade 3A	India	Castings	0.08 **C**, 1.50 **Mn**, 18.0–21.0 **Cr**, 8.0–11.0 **Ni**, 2.00 **Si**, 0.040 **P**, 0.040 **S**	**Solution annealed**: all **diam**, (530) **TS**, (240) **YS**, 33 **El**
ASTM 744	Grade CG–8M	US	Castings	0.08 **C**, 1.50 **Mn**, 18.0–21.0 **Cr**, 9.0–13.0 **Ni**, 1.50 **Si**, 3.0–4.0 **Mo**, 0.04 **P**, 0.04 **S**	**Solution quenched**: all **diam**, (520) **TS**, (240) **YS**, 25 **El**
ASTM A 743	Grade CG–8M	US	Castings	0.08 **C**, 1.50 **Mn**, 18.0–21.0 **Cr**, 9.0–13.0 **Ni**, 1.50 **Si**, 3.0–4.0 **Mo**, 0.04 **P**, 0.04 **S**	**Solution quenched**: all **diam**, (520) **TS**, (240) **YS**, 25 **El**
ANSI/ASTM A 296	Grade CG–8M	US	Sand castings	0.08 **C**, 1.50 **Mn**, 18.0–21.0 **Cr**, 9.0–13.0 **Ni**, 1.50 **Si**, 3.0–4.0 **Mo**, 0.040 **P**, 0.040 **S**	**Solution annealed**: all **diam**, 75 (520) **TS**, 35 (240) **YS**, 25 **El**
NOM–B–354	Class CG–8M	Mexico	Castings	0.08 **C**, 1.50 **Mn**, 18.0–21.0 **Cr**, 9.0–13.0 **Ni**, 1.50 **Si**, 3.0–4.0 **Mo**, 0.040 **P**, 0.040 **S**	**As agreed**: all **diam**, (517) **TS**, (241) **YS**, 25 **El**

CAST HIGH ALLOY STEELS

specification number	**designation**	**country**	**product forms**	**composition**	**mechanical properties** (see page iv for explanation)
BS 1504–316C71		UK	Castings	0.08 **C**, 2.0 **Mn**, 17.0–21.0 **Cr**, 8.0 min **Ni**, 1.5 **Si**, 2.0–3.0 **Mo**, 0.040 **P**, 0.040 **S**	**Annealed**: all **diam**, (510) **TS**, (260) **YS**, 26 **El**
BS 3100/1632	Grade D	UK	Sand castings	0.08 **C**, 17.0–20.0 **Cr**, 8.0 min **Ni**, 2.0–3.0 **Mo**	**Quenched**: all **diam**, (510) **TS**, (230) **YS**, 26 **El**
DTD 5279		UK	Investment, precision castings	0.08 **C**, 16.5–18.5 **Cr**, 10.0–12.0 **Ni**, 2.0–3.0 **Mo**	**Annealed, quenched**: all **diam**, (500) **TS**, (205) **YS**, 11 **El**
BS HC 105		UK	Castings: aircraft quality	0.08 **C**, 2.0 **Mn**, 17.0–20.0 **Cr**, 10.0–12.5 **Ni**, 1.5 **Si**, 2.0–3.0 **Mo**, 0.040 **P**, 0.040 **S**, 8 x C–1.0 **Nb**	**Solution annealed**: all **diam**, (500) **TS**, (210) **YS**, 20 **El**
ASTM A 451	Grade CPF8	US	Pipe: centrifugally cast	0.08 **C**, 1.50 **Mn**, 18.0–21.0 **Cr**, 8.0–11.0 **Ni**, 1.00 **Si**, 0.040 **P**, 0.040 **S**	**Solution quenched**: all **diam**, (485) **TS**, (205) **YS**, 30 **El**
ASTM A 451	Grade CPF8M	US	Pipe: centrifugally cast	0.08 **C**, 1.50 **Mn**, 18.0–21.0 **Cr**, 9.0–12.0 **Ni**, 1.00 **Si**, 2.0–3.0 **Mo**, 0.040 **P**, 0.040 **S**	**Solution quenched**: all **diam**, (485) **TS**, (205) **YS**, 30 **El**
ASTM A 451	Grade CPF8C	US	Pipe: centrifugally cast	0.08 **C**, 1.50 **Mn**, 18.0–21.0 **Cr**, 9.0–12.0 **Ni**, 1.00 **Si**, 0.040 **P**, 0.040 **S**, 8 x C–1.0 **Cb**	**Solution quenched**: all **diam**, (485) **TS**, (205) **YS**, 30 **El**
ASTM A–351–76	Grade CF8M	US	Castings	0.08 **C**, 1.50 **Mn**, 18.0–21.0 **Cr**, 9.0–12.0 **Ni**, 1.50 **Si**, 2.0–3.0 **Mo**, 0.040 **P**, 0.040 **S**	**Solution treated**: all **diam**, (485) **TS**, (205) **YS**, 30 **El**
ASTM A–351–76	Grade CF8C	US	Castings	0.08 **C**, 1.50 **Mn**, 18.0–21.0 **Cr**, 9.0–12.0 **Ni**, 2.00 **Si**, 0.040 **P**, 0.040 **S**, 8 x C–1.00 **Cb**	**Solution treated**: all **diam**, (485) **TS**, 205 **YS**, 30 **El**
ASTM 744	Grade CF–8C	US	Castings	0.08 **C**, 1.50 **Mn**, 18.0–21.0 **Cr**, 9.0–12.0 **Ni**, 2.00 **Si**, 0.04 **P**, 0.04 **S**, 8 x C–1.0 **Cb**	**Solution quenched**: all **diam**, (485) **TS**, (205) **YS**, 30 **El**
ASTM A 351	Grade CF8	US	Castings	0.08 **C**, 1.50 **Mn**, 18.0–21.0 **Cr**, 8.0–11.0 **Ni**, 2.00 **Si**, 0.040 **P**, 0.040 **S**	**Solution treated**: all **diam**, (485) **TS**, (205) **YS**, 35 **El**
ASTM 744	Grade CF–8	US	Castings	0.08 **C**, 1.50 **Mn**, 18.0–21.0 **Cr**, 8.0–11.0 **Ni**, 2.00 **Si**, 0.04 **P**, 0.04 **S**	**Solution quenched**: all **diam**, (485) **TS**, (205) **YS**, 35 **El**
ASTM 744	Grade CF–8M	US	Castings	0.08 **C**, 1.50 **Mn**, 18.0–21.0 **Cr**, 9.0–12.0 **Ni**, 2.00 **Si**, 2.0–3.0 **Mo**, 0.04 **P**, 0.04 **S**	**Solution quenched**: all **diam**, (485) **TS**, (205) **YS**, 30 **El**
ASTM A 743	Grade CF–8C	US	Castings	0.08 **C**, 1.50 **Mn**, 18.0–21.0 **Cr**, 9.0–12.0 **Ni**, 2.00 **Si**, 0.04 **P**, 0.04 **S**, 8 x C–1.0 **Cb**	**Solution quenched at 1040°C: all diam, (485) TS, (205) YS, 30 El**
ASTM A 743	Grade CF–8M	US	Castings	0.08 **C**, 1.50 **Mn**, 18.0–21.0 **Cr**, 9.0–12.0 **Ni**, 2.00 **Si**, 2.0–3.0 **Mo**, 0.040 **P**, 0.040 **S**	**Solution quenched at 1040°C: all diam, (485) TS, (205) YS, 30 El**
ASTM A 743	Grade CF–8	US	Castings	0.08 **C**, 1.50 **Mn**, 18.0–21.0 **Cr**, 8.0–11.0 **Ni**, 2.00 **Si**, 0.04 **P**, 0.04 **S**	**Solution quenched at 1040°C: all diam, (485) TS, (205) YS, 35 El**
ANSI/ASTM A 296	Grade CF–8C	US	Sand castings	0.08 **C**, 1.50 **Mn**, 18.0–21.0 **Cr**, 9.0–12.0 **Ni**, 2.00 **Si**, 0.040 **P**, 0.040 **S**	**Solution annealed**: all **diam**, 70 (485) **TS**, 30 (205) **YS**, 30 **El**
ANSI/ASTM A 296	Grade CF–8M	US	Sand castings	0.08 **C**, 1.50 **Mn**, 18.0–21.0 **Cr**, 9.0–12.0 **Ni**, 2.00 **Si**, 2.0–3.0 **Mo** ,0.04 **P**, 0.040 **S**	**Solution annealed**: all **diam**, 70 (485) **TS**, 30 (205) **YS**, 30 **El**
ANSI/ASTM A 351	Grade CF8C	US	Sand castings	0.08 **C**, 1.50 **Mn**, 18.0–21.0 **Cr**, 9.0–12.0 **Ni**, 2.00 **Si**, 0.040 **P**, 0.040 **S**	**Solution annealed**: all **diam**, 70 (485) **TS**, 30 (205) **YS**, 30 **El**
ANSI/ASTM A 351	Grade CF8M	US	Sand castings	0.08 **C**, 1.50 **Mn**, 18.0–21.0 **Cr**, 9.0–12.0 **Ni**, 1.50 **Si**, 2.0–3.0 **Mo**, 0.040 **P**, 0.040 **S**	**Solution annealed**: all **diam**, 70 (485) **TS**, 30 (205) **YS**, 30 **El**
ANSI/ASTM A 351	Grade CF8	US	Sand castings	0.08 **C**, 1.50 **Mn**, 18.0–21.0 **Cr**, 8.0–11.0 **Ni**, 2.00 **Si**, 0.040 **P**, 0.040 **S**	**Solution annealed**: all **diam**, 70 (485) **TS**, 30 (205) **YS**, 35 **El**
ANSI/ASTM A 351	CF8	US	Castings	0.08 **C**, 1.50 **Mn**, 18.0–21.0 **Cr**, 8.0–11.0 **Ni**, 2.00 **Si**, 0.040 **P**, 0.040 **S**	**Solution annealed**: all **diam**, 70 (485) **TS**, 30 (205) **YS**, 35 **El**
ANSI/ASTM A 351	CF8M	US	Castings	0.08 **C**, 1.50 **Mn**, 18.0–21.0 **Cr**, 9.0–12.0 **Ni**, 1.50 **Si**, 2.0–3.0 **Mo**, 0.040 **P**, 0.040 **S**	**Solution annealed**: all **diam**, 70 (485) **TS**, 30 (205) **YS**, 30 **El**
ANSI/ASTM A 351	CF8C	US	Castings	0.08 **C**, 1.50 **Mn**, 18.0–21.0 **Cr**, 9.0–12.0 **Ni**, 2.00 **Si**, 0.040 **P**, 0.040 **S**, 8 x C–1.00 **Nb**	**Solution annealed**: all **diam**, 70 (485) **TS**, 30 (205) **YS**, 30 **El**

CAST HIGH ALLOY STEELS

specification number	designation	country	product forms	composition	mechanical properties (see page iv for explanation)
MILITARY MIL-S-867A	Grade III	US	Castings	0.08 **C**, 1.50 **Mn**, 18.0–21.0 **Cr**, 9.0–12.0 **Ni**, 2.00 **Si**, 2.0–3.0 **Mo**, 0.05 **P**, 0.05 **S**	**Quenched**: all **diam**, (483) **TS**, (207) **YS**, 30 **El**
MILITARY MIL-S-867A	Grade II	US	Castings	0.08 **C**, 1.50 **Mn**, 18.0–21.0 **Cr**, 9.0–12.0 **Ni**, 2.00 **Si**, 0.05 **P**, 0.05 **S**, 1.1 **Cb+Ta**	**Quenched**: all **diam**, (483) **TS**, (207) **YS**, 30 **El**
MILITARY MIL-S-867A	Grade I	US	Castings	0.08 **C**, 1.50 **Mn**, 18.0–21.0 **Cr**, 8.0–11.0 **Ni**, 2.00 **Si**, 0.05 **P**, 0.05 **S**	**Quenched**: all **diam**, (483) **TS**, (193) **YS**, 35 **El**
NOM-B-354	Class CF-8M	Mexico	Castings	0.08 **C**, 1.50 **Mn**, 18.0–21.0 **Cr**, 9.0–12.0 **Ni**, 2.0 **Si**, 2.0–3.0 **Mo**, 0.040 **P**, 0.040 **S**	**As agreed**: all **diam**, (483) **TS**, (207) **YS**, 30 **El**
NOM-B-354	Class CF-8C	Mexico	Castings	0.08 **C**, 1.50 **Mn**, 18.0–21.0 **Cr**, 9.0–12.0 **Ni**, 2.0 **Si**, 0.040 **P**, 0.040 **S**, 8 x C–1.0 **Nb**, 9 x C–1.1 **Nb+Ta**	**As agreed**: all **diam**, (483) **TS**, (207) **YS**, 30 **El**
ANSI/ASTM A 451	CPF8	US	Pipe: centrifugally cast	0.08 **C**, 1.50 **Mn**, 18.0–21.0 **Cr**, 8.0–11.0 **Ni**, 1.00 **Si**, 0.040 **P**, 0.040 **S**	**Solution annealed**: all **diam**, 70 (483) **TS**, 30 (207) **YS**, 35 **El**
ANSI/ASTM A 451	CPF8C (Ta max)	US	Pipe: centrifugally cast	0.08 **C**, 1.50 **Mn**, 18.0–21.0 **Cr**, 9.0–12.0 **Ni**, 1.00 **Si**, 0.040 **P**, 0.040 **S**, 8 x C–1.0 **Nb**, 0.10 **Ta**	**Solution annealed**: all **diam**, 70 (483) **TS**, 30 (207) **YS**, 30 **El**
ANSI/ASTM A 451	CPF8C	US	Pipe: centrifugally cast	0.08 **C**, 1.50 **Mn**, 18.0–21.0 **Cr**, 9.0–12.0 **Ni**, 1.00 **Si**, 0.040 **P**, 0.040 **S**, 8 x C–1.0 **Nb**, 1.35 **Nb+Ta**	**Solution annealed**: all **diam**, 70 (483) **TS**, 30 (207) **YS**, 30 **El**
ANSI/ASTM A 451	CPF8M	US	Pipe: centrifugally cast	0.08 **C**, 1.50 **Mn**, 18.0–21.0 **Cr**, 9.0–12.0 **Ni**, 1.00 **Si**, 2.0–3.0 **Mo**, 0.040 **P**, 0.040 **S**	**Solution annealed**: all **diam**, 70 (483) **TS**, 30 (207) **YS**, 30 **El**
MIL-S-867A	Class I	US	Sand castings	0.08 **C**, 1.50 **Mn**, 18.0–21.0 **Cr**, 8.0–11.0 **Ni**, 2.00 **Si**, 0.050 **P**, 0.050 **S**	**Solution annealed**: all **diam**, 70 (483) **TS**, 28 (193) **YS**, 35 **El**
MIL-S-867A	Class II	US	Sand castings	0.08 **C**, 1.50 **Mn**, 18.0–21.0 **Cr**, 9.0–12.0 **Ni**, 2.00 **Si**, 0.050 **P**, 0.050 **S**	**Solution annealed**: all **diam**, 70 (483) **TS**, 30 (207) **YS**, 30 **El**
MIL-S-867A	Class III	US	Sand castings	0.08 **C**, 1.50 **Mn**, 18.0–21.0 **Cr**, 9.0–12.0 **Ni**, 2.00 **Si**, 2.0–3.0 **Mo**, 0.050 **P**, 0.050 **S**	**Solution annealed**: all **diam**, 70 (483) **TS**, 30 (207) **YS**, 30 **El**
AMS 5364		US	Investment castings	0.08 **C**, 2.00 **Mn**, 18.00–21.00 **Cr**, 9.00–12.00 **Ni**, 1.50 **Si**, 0.75 **Mo**, 0.040 **P**, 0.030 **S**, 0.75 **Cu**, 8 x C–1.00 **Nb+Ta**	**Solution heat treated**: 0.250 (6.35) **diam**, 70 (483) **TS**, 30 (207) **YS**, 30 **El**
BS 1504-318C17		UK	Castings	0.08 **C**, 2.0 **Mn**, 17.0–21.0 **Cr**, 10.0 min **Ni**, 1.5 **Si**, 2.0–3.0 **Mo**, 0.040 **P**, 0.040 **S**, 8 x C–1.0 **Nb**	**Annealed**: all **diam**, (480) **TS**, (240) **YS**, 18 **El**
BS 1504-317C16		UK	Castings	0.08 **C**, 2.0 **Mn**, 17.0–21.0 **Cr**, 10.0 min **Ni**, 1.5 **Si**, 3.0–4.0 **Mo**, 0.040 **P**, 0.040 **S**	**Annealed**: all **diam**, (480) **TS**, (240) **YS**, 22 **El**
BS 1504-316C16		UK	Castings	0.08 **C**, 2.0 **Mn**, 17.0–21.0 **Cr**, 10.0 min **Ni**, 1.5 **Si**, 2.0–3.0 **Mo**, 0.040 **P**, 0.040 **S**	**Annealed**: all **diam**, (480) **TS**, (240) **YS**, 26 **El**
BS 1504-315C16		UK	Castings	0.08 **C**, 2.0 **Mn**, 17.0–21.0 **Cr**, 8.0 **Ni**, 1.5 **Si**, 1.0–1.75 **Mo**, 0.040 **P**, 0.040 **S**	**Annealed**: all **diam**, (480) **TS**, (240) **YS**, 26 **El**
BS 3100/1632	Grade E	UK	Sand castings	0.08 **C**, 17.0–20.0 **Cr**, 8.0 min **Ni**, 1.0–1.75 **Mo**	**Quenched**: all **diam**, (480) **TS**, (210) **YS**, 26 **El**
BS 3100/1632	Grade B	UK	Sand castings	0.08 **C**, 17.0–20.0 **Cr**, 2.0–3.0 **Mo**, 10.0 **Ni**	**Quenched**: all **diam**, (480) **TS**, (210) **YS**, 26 **El**
BS 3100/1632	Grade A	UK	Sand castings	0.08 **C**, 18.0–20.0 **Cr**, 10.0 min **Ni**, 3.0–4.0 **Mo**	**Quenched**: all **diam**, (480) **TS**, (210) **YS**, 22 **El**
BS 3100/1631	Grade B	UK	Sand castings	0.08 **C**, 17.0–21.0 **Cr**, 8.5 min **Ni**, 8 x C min, 1.0 max **Nb**, or 5 x C min, 0.7 max **Ti**	**Quenched**: all **diam**, (480) **TS**, (205) **YS**, 22 **El**
BS 1504-304C15		UK	Castings	0.08 **C**, 2.0 **Mn**, 17.0–21.0 **Cr**, 8.0 **Ni**, 1.5 **Si**, 0.040 **P**, 0.040 **S**	**Annealed**: all **diam**, (480) **TS**, (240) **YS**, 26 **El**
BS 1504-347C17		UK	Castings	0.08 **C**, 2.0 **Mn**, 17.0–21.0 **Cr**, 8.5 min **Ni**, 1.5 **Si**, 0.040 **P**, 0.040 **S**, 8 x C–1.0 **Nb**	**Annealed**: all **diam**, (480) **TS**, (240) **YS**, 22 **El**
IS 7806	Grade 3	India	Castings	0.08 **C**, 1.50 **Mn**, 18.0–21.0 **Cr**, 8.0–11.0 **Ni**, 2.00 **Si**, 0.040 **P**, 0.040 **S**	**Solution annealed**: all **diam**, (480) **TS**, (210) **YS**, 33 **El**

CAST HIGH ALLOY STEELS

specification number	designation	country	product forms	composition	mechanical properties (see page iv for explanation)
IS 7806	Grade 5	India	Castings	0.08 **C**, 1.50 **Mn**, 18.0–21.0 **Cr**, 9.0–12.0 **Ni**, 1.50 **Si**, 2.0–3.0 **Mo**, 0.040 **P**, 0.040 **S**	**Solution annealed**: all **diam**, (480) **TS**, (210) **YS**, 29 **El**
IS 7806	Grade 5A	India	Castings	0.08 **C**, 1.50 **Mn**, 18.0–21.0 **Cr**, 9.0–12.0 **Ni**, 2.00 **Si**, 0.040 **P**, 0.040 **S**, C x 8–1.00 **Nb**	**Solution annealed**: all **diam**, (480) **TS**, (210) **YS**, 29 **El**
BS 3100/1631	Grade A	UK	Sand castings	0.08 **C**, 17.0–21.0 **Cr**, 8.0 min **Ni**	**Quenched by air blast or water quenched from 1000–1100°C: all diam, (480) TS, (205) YS, 26 El**
IS 3444	Grade 11	India	Castings	0.08 **C**, 2.00 **Mn**, 16.5–18.5 **Cr**, 10.0 min **Ni**, 1.50 **Si**, 2.0–3.0 **Mo**, 0.040 **P**, 0.040 **S**	**Solution annealed**: all **diam**, (461) **TS**, (206) **YS**, 15 **El**
IS 3444	Grade 10	India	Castings	0.08 **C**, 2.00 **Mn**, 18.0–20.0 **Cr**, 11.0–14.0 **Ni**, 1.50 **Si**, 3.0–4.0 **Mo**, 0.040 **P**, 0.040 **S**	**Solution annealed**: all **diam**, (461) **TS**, (206) **YS**, 15 **El**
IS 3444	Grade 9	India	Castings	0.08 **C**, 2.00 **Mn**, 16.5–18.5 **Cr**, 8.0 min **Ni**, 1.50 **Si**, 2.0–3.0 **Mo**, 0.040 **P**, 0.040 **S**	**Solution annealed**: all **diam**, (461) **TS**, (206) **YS**, 15 **El**
BS 3100/1632	Grade C	UK	Sand castings	0.08 **C**, 17.0–20.0 **Cr**, 10.0 min **Ni**, 2.0–3.0 **Mo**, 8 x C–1.0 **Nb**, 5 x C–0.7 **Ti**	**Quenched**: all **diam**, (460) **TS**, (210) **YS**, 18 **El**
BS 1504–846		UK	Sand castings	0.08 **C**, 18.0–20.0 **Cr**, 11.0–14.0 **Ni**, 3.0–4.0 **Mo**	**Quenched**: all **diam**, (460) **TS**, (205) **YS**
BS 1504–845	Grade B	UK	Sand castings	0.08 **C**, 16.5–18.5 **Cr**, 10.0 min **Ni**, 2.0–3.0 **Mo**	**Quenched**: all **diam**, (460) **TS**, (205) **YS**
BS 3146 Part 2	ANC 4 Grade B	UK	Investment, precision castings	0.08 **C**, 16.5–18.5 **Cr**, 10.0 min **Ni**, 2.00–3.0 **Mo**	**Quenched**: all **diam**, (460) **TS**, (205) **YS**
BS 3146 Part 2	ANC4 Grade A	UK	Investment, precision castings	0.08 **C**, 3.0–4.0 **Mn**, 18.0–20.0 **Cr**, 11.0–14.0 **Ni**	**Quenched**: all **diam**, (460) **TS**, (205) **YS**
BS 3146 Part 2	ANC 4 Grade B	UK	Investment and precision castings	0.08 **C**, 16.5–18.5 **Cr**, 10.0 min **Ni**, 2.00–3.00 **Mo**	**Quenched**: all **diam**, (460) **TS**, (205) **YS**
BS 3146 Part 2	ANC 4 Grade A	UK	Investment and precision castings	0.08 **C**, 18.0–20.0 **Cr**, 11.0–14.0 **Ni**, 3.0–4.0 **Mo**	**Quenched**: all **diam**, (460) **TS**, (205) **YS**
BS HC 104		UK	Castings: aircraft quality	0.08 **C**, 2.0 **Mn**, 17.0–21.0 **Cr**, 8.5–12.5 **Ni**, 2.0 **Si**, 0.040 **P**, 0.040 **S**, 8 x C–1.0 **Nb**	**Solution annealed**: all **diam**, (460) **TS**, (200) **YS**, 20 **El**
NF A 32–056	Z 6 CND Nb 18 12–M	France	Castings	0.08 **C**, 1.5 **Mn**, 17.0–20.0 **Cr**, 9.0–13.0 **Ni**, 1.2 **Si**, 2.0–3.0 **Mo**, 10 x C–1.2 **Nb**	**Solution annealed**: all **diam**, (450) **TS**, (200) **YS**, 35 **El**
NF A 32–056	Z 6 CN Nb 18 10–M	France	Castings	0.08 **C**, 1.5 **Mn**, 17.0–20.0 **Cr**, 8.0–11.0 **Ni**, 1.2 **Si**, 0.040 **P**, 0.030 **S**, 8 x C–1.2 **Nb**	**Solution annealed**: all **diam**, (450) **TS**, (200) **YS**, 30 **El**
ASTM A 451	Grade CPH8	US	Pipe: centrifugally cast	0.08 **C**, 1.50 **Mn**, 22.0–26.0 **Cr**, 12.0–15.0 **Ni**, 1.00 **Si**, 0.040 **P**, 0.040 **S**	**Solution quenched**: all **diam**, (450) **TS**, (195) **YS**, 30 **El**
ASTM A–351–76	Grade CH8	US	Castings	0.08 **C**, 1.50 **Mn**, 22.0–26.0 **Cr**, 12.0–15.0 **Ni**, 1.50 **Si**, 0.040 **P**, 0.040 **S**	**Solution treated**: all **diam**, (450) **TS**, (195) **YS**, 30 **El**
NF A 32–055	Z 6 CND Nb 18 12–M	France	Castings	0.08 **C**, 1.5 **Mn**, 17.0–20.0 **Cr**, 9.0–13.0 **Ni**, 1.2 **Si**, 2.0–3.0 **Mo**, 0.040 **P**, 0.030 **S**, 10 x C–1.2 **Nb**	**Solution annealed**: all **diam**, (450) **TS**, (220) **YS**, 35 **El**
NF A 32–055	Z 6 CND 18 12–M	France	Castings	0.08 **C**, 1.5 **Mn**, 17.0–20.0 **Cr**, 9.0–13.0 **Ni**, 1.2 **Si**, 2.0–3.0 **Mo**, 0.040 **P**, 0.030 **S**	**Solution annealed**: all **diam**, (450) **TS**, (200) **YS**, 35 **El**
NF A 32–055	Z 6 CN 18 18–M	France	Castings	0.08 **C**, 1.5 **Mn**, 18.0–20.0 **Cr**, 8.0–12.0 **Ni**, 1.2 **Si**, 0.040 **P**, 0.030 **S**	**Solution annealed**: all **diam**, (450) **TS**, (200) **YS**, 30 **El**
NF A 32–055	Z 6 CN Nb 18 10–M	France	Castings	0.08 **C**, 1.5 **Mn**, 17.0–20.0 **Cr**, 8.0–11.0 **Ni**, 1.2 **Si**, 0.040 **P**, 0.030 **S**, 8 x C–1.2 **Nb**	**Solution annealed**: all **diam**, (450) **TS**, (200) **YS**, 30 **El**
NF A 32–055	Z 6 NCDU 25 20 04–M	France	Castings	0.08 **C**, 1.5 **Mn**, 18.0–22.0 **Cr**, 23.0–27.0 **Ni**, 1.2 **Si**, 2.5–6.0 **Mo**, 0.040 **P**, 0.030 **S**	**Solution annealed**: all **diam**, (450) **TS**, (170) **YS**, 30 **El**
NF A 32–056	Z 6CN 18 10–M	France	Castings	0.08 **C**, 1.5 **Mn**, 17.0–20.0 **Cr**, 8.0–12.0 **Ni**, 1.2 **Si**, 0.040 **P**, 0.030 **S**	**Solution annealed**: all **diam**, (450) **TS**, (200) **YS**, 30 **El**
ANSI/ASTM A 296	Grade CF–8	US	Sand castings	0.08 **C**, 1.50 **Mn**, 18.0–21.0 **Cr**, 8.0–11.0 **Ni**, 2.00 **Si**, 0.040 **P**, 0.040 **S**	**Solution annealed**: all **diam**, 65 (450) **TS**, 28 (195) **YS**, 35 **El**

CAST HIGH ALLOY STEELS

specification number	designation	country	product forms	composition	mechanical properties (see page iv for explanation)
NF A 32–056	Z 6 NCDU 25 20 04–M	France	Castings	0.08 **C**, 1.5 **Mn**, 18.0–22.0 **Cr**, 23.0–27.0 **Ni**, 1.2 **Si**, 2.5–6.0 **Mo**, 0.040 **P**, 0.030 **S**, 1.5–3.5 **Cu**	**Solution annealed**: all diam, (450) **TS**, (170) **YS**, 30 **El**
NF A 32–056	Z 6 CND 18 12–M	France	Castings	0.08 **C**, 1.5 **Mn**, 17.0–20.0 **Cr**, 9.0–13.0 **Ni**, 1.2 **Si**, 2.0–3.0 **Mo**, 0.040 **P**, 0.030 **S**	**Solution annealed**: all diam, (450) **TS**, (200) **YS**, 35 **El**
ANSI/ASTM A 351	Grade CH8	US	Sand castings	0.08 **C**, 1.50 **Mn**, 22.0–26.0 **Cr**, 12.0–15.0 **Ni**, 2.00 **Si**, 0.040 **P**, 0.040 **S**	**Solution annealed**: all diam, 65 (450) **TS**, 28 (195) **YS**, 30 **El**
ANSI/ASTM A 351	CH8	US	Castings	0.08 **C**, 1.50 **Mn**, 22.0–26.0 **Cr**, 12.0–15.0 **Ni**, 1.50 **Si**, 0.040 **P**, 0.040 **S**	**Solution annealed**: all diam, 65 (450) **TS**, 28 (195) **YS**, 30 **El**
IS 7806	Grade 6	India	Castings	0.08 **C**, 1.50 **Mn**, 22.0–26.0 **Cr**, 12.0–15.0 **Ni**, 1.50 **Si**, 0.040 **P**, 0.040 **S**	**Solution annealed**: all diam, (450) **TS**, (190) **YS**, 29 **El**
NOM–B–354	Class CF–8	Mexico	Castings	0.08 **C**, 1.50 **Mn**, 18.0–21.0 **Cr**, 8.0–11.0 **Ni**, 2.0 **Si**, 0.040 **P**, 0.040 **S**	**As agreed**: all diam, (448) **TS**, (193) **YS**, 35 **El**
ANSI/ASTM A 451	CPH8	US	Pipe: centrifugally cast	0.08 **C**, 1.50 **Mn**, 22.0–26.0 **Cr**, 12.0–15.0 **Ni**, 1.00 **Si**, 0.040 **P**, 0.040 **S**	**Solution annealed**: all diam, 65 (448) **TS**, 28 (193) **YS**, 30 **El**
MIL–S–17509	Class III	US	Sand castings	0.08 **C**, 1.50 **Mn**, 17.0–20.0 **Cr**, 10.0 min **Ni**, 1.50 **Si**, 0.50 **Mo**, 0.05 **P**, 0.05 **S**	**Solution annealed**: all diam, (448) **TS**, (193) **YS**, 30 **El**
DIN 17445	Grade G–X7 CrNiNb 18 9–1,4552	Germany	Sand castings	0.08 **C**, 1.5 **Mn**, 17.5–20.0 **Cr**, 9.0–11.0 **Ni**, 1.5 **Si**, 8 x C **Nb**	**Solution annealed**: all diam, (441) **TS**, (176) **YS**, 6 **El**
DIN 17445	Grade G–X7 CrNiMoNb 18 10–1,4581	Germany	Sand castings	0.08 **C**, 1.5 **Mn**, 17.0–19.5 **Cr**, 10.5–12.5 **Ni**, 1.5 **Si**, 2.0–2.5 **Mo**, 8 x C **Nb**	**Solution annealed**: all diam, (441) **TS**, (186) **YS**, 20 min **El**
DIN 17440	Grade G–X7 CrNiNb 18 9	Germany	Castings	0.08 **C**, 1.5 **Mn**, 17.5–20.0 **Cr**, 9.0–11.0 **Ni**, 1.5 **Si**, 0.045 **P**, 0.030 **S**, 8 x C min **Nb**	**Quenched**: all diam, (441) **TS**, (177) **YS**, 20 **El**
DIN 17445	Grade G–X7 CrNiMoNb 18 10	Germany	Castings	0.08 **C**, 1.5 **Mn**, 17.0–19.5 **Cr**, 10.5–12.5 **Ni**, 1.5 **Si**, 2.0–2.5 **Mo**, 0.045 **P**, 0.030 **S**, 8 x C min **Nb**	**Quenched**: all diam, (441) **TS**, (186) **YS**, 20 **El**
JIS G 5121	Type 13	Japan	Castings, pipe (centrifugally cast)	0.08 **C**, 2.00 **Mn**, 18.00–21.00 **Cr**, 8.00–11.00 **Ni**, 2.00 **Si**, 0.040 **P**, 0.040 **S**	**Solution annealed**: all diam, (441) **TS**, (186) **YS**, 30 **El**
JIS G 5121	Type 14	Japan	Castings, pipe (centrifugally cast)	0.08 **C**, 2.00 **Mn**, 17.00–20.00 **Cr**, 10.00–14.00 **Ni**, 1.50 **Si**, 2.00–3.00 **Mo**, 0.040 **P**, 0.040 **S**	**Solution annealed**: all diam, (441) **TS**, (186) **YS**, 30 **El**
JIS G 5121	Type 15	Japan	Castings, pipe (centrifugally cast)	0.08 **C**, 2.00 **Mn**, 17.00–20.00 **Cr**, 10.00–14.00 **Ni**, 1.50 **Si**, 1.75–2.75 **Mo**, 0.040 **P**, 0.040 **S**, 1.00–2.50 **Cu**	**Solution annealed**: all diam, (441) **TS**, (186) **YS**, 30 **El**
JIS G 5121	Type 21	Japan	Castings, pipe (centrifugally cast)	0.08 **C**, 2.00 **Mn**, 18.00–21.00 **Cr**, 9.00–12.00 **Ni**, 2.00 **Si**, 0.040 **P**, 0.040 **S**, 10 x C–1.35 **Nb+Ta**	**Solution annealed**: all diam, (441) **TS**, (206) **YS**, 30 **El**
JIS G 5121	Type 22	Japan	Castings, pipe (centrifugally cast)	0.08 **C**, 2.00 **Mn**, 17.00–20.00 **Cr**, 10.00–14.00 **Ni**, 2.00 **Si**, 2.00–3.00 **Mo**, 0.040 **P**, 0.040 **S**, 10 x C–1.35 **Nb+Ta**	**Solution annealed**: all diam, (441) **TS**, (206) **YS**, 30 **El**
BS 1504–845	Grade B	UK	Castings	0.08 **C**, 2.00 **Mn**, 16.5–18.5 **Cr**, 10.0 min **Ni**, 1.50 **Si**, 2.00–3.00 **Mo**, 0.045 **P**, 0.045 **S**	**Solution annealed**: all diam, (415) **TS**, (185) **YS**, 15 **El**
BS 1504–846		UK	Castings	0.08 **C**, 2.00 **Mn**, 18.0–20.0 **Cr**, 11.0–14.0 **Ni**, 1.50 **Si**, 3.0–4.0 **Mo**, 0.045 **P**, 0.045 **S**	**Solution annealed**: all diam, (415) **TS**, (185) **YS**, 15 **El**
MIL–S–81591	IC–304	US	Investment castings	0.08 **C**, 2.00 **Mn**, 18.0–20.0 **Cr**, 8.0–12.0 **Ni**, 1.00 **Si**, 0.040 **P**, 0.030 **S**	**Solution annealed**
MIL–S–81591	IC–316	US	Investment castings	0.08 **C**, 2.00 **Mn**, 16.0–18.0 **Cr**, 10.0–14.0 **Ni**, 1.00 **Si**, 2.0–3.0 **Mo**, 0.040 **P**, 0.030 **S**	**Solution annealed**
MIL–S–81591	IC–321	US	Investment castings	0.08 **C**, 2.00 **Mn**, 17.0–19.0 **Cr**, 9.0–12.0 **Ni**, 1.00 **Si**, 0.040 **P**, 0.030 **S**, 5 x C min **Ti**	**Solution annealed**
MIL–S–81591	IC–347	US	Investment castings	0.08 **C**, 2.00 **Mn**, 17.0–19.5 **Cr**, 9.0–13.0 **Ni**, 1.00 **Si**, 0.040 **P**, 0.030 **S**	**Solution annealed**

specification number	designation	country	product forms	composition	mechanical properties (see page iv for explanation)
BS HC102		UK	Castings: aircraft quality	0.07 **C**, 1.0 **Mn**, 12.5–15.5 **Cr**, 3.0–6.0 **Ni**, 2.0 **Si**, 0.5–2.5 **Mo**, 0.025 **P**, 0.025 **S**, 1.0–3.5 **Cu**, 0.50 **Nb**	**Solution annealed and precipitation treated**: all **diam**, (1250) **TS**, (950) **YS**, 8 **El**
JIS G 5121	Type 23	Japan	Castings, pipe (centrifugally cast)	0.07 **C**, 1.00 **Mn**, 15.50–17.50 **Cr**, 3.00–5.00 **Ni**, 1.00 **Si**, 0.040 **P**, 0.040 **S**, 2.50–4.00 **Cu**, 0.05 **N**, 0.45 **Nb+Ta**	**Solution annealed and aged**: all **diam**, (1236) **TS**, (1030) **YS**, 6 **El**
BS HC101		UK	Castings: aircraft quality	0.07 **C**, 1.0 **Mn**, 12.5–15.5 **Cr**, 3.0–6.0 **Ni**, 2.0 **Si**, 0.5–2.5 **Mo**, 0.025 **P**, 0.025 **S**, 1.0–3.5 **Cu**, 0.5 **Nb**	**Solution annealed and precipitation treated**: all **diam**, (950) **TS**, (800) **YS**, 12 **El**
DTD 5299		UK	Investment, precision castings	0.07 **C**, 13.5–15.5 **Cr**, 4.0–6.0 **Ni**, 0.3–1.0 **Mo**, 1.0–2.5 **Cu**	**Solution annealed or precipitation hardened**: all **diam**, (950) **TS**, (775) **YS**, 11 **El**
ANSI/ASTM A 296	Grade CN-7MS	US	Sand castings	0.07 **C**, 1.00 **Mn**, 18.0–20.0 **Cr**, 22.0–25.0 **Ni**, 2.50–3.50 **Si**, 2.5–3.0 **Mo**, 0.040 **P**, 0.030 **S**, 1.5–2.0 **Cu**	**As cast or solution annealed**: all **diam**, 70 (485) **TS**, 30 (205) **YS**, 35 **El**
ASTM A 743	Grade CN-7M	US	Castings	0.07 **C**, 1.50 **Mn**, 19.0–22.0 **Cr**, 27.5–30.5 **Ni**, 1.50 **Si**, 2.0–3.0 **Mo**, 0.040 **P**, 0.040 **S**, 3.0–4.0 **Cu**	**Solution quenched**: all **diam**, (485) **TS**, (170) **YS**, 35 **El**
ASTM A 743	Grade CN-7MS	US	Castings	0.07 **C**, 1.00 **Mn**, 18.0–20.0 **Cr**, 22.0–25.0 **Ni**, 2.50–3.50 **Si**, 2.5–3.0 **Mo**, 0.04 **P**, 0.03 **S**, 1.5–2.0 **Cu**	**Solution quenched**: all **diam**, (485) **TS**, (205) **YS**, 35 **El**
ASTM 744	Grade CN-7MS	US	Castings	0.07 **C**, 1.00 **Mn**, 18.0–20.0 **Cr**, 22.0–25.0 **Ni**, 2.50–3.50 **Si**, 2.5–3.0 **Mo**, 0.04 **P**, 0.03 **S**, 1.5–2.0 **Cu**	**Solution quenched**: all **diam**, (485) **TS**, (205) **YS**, 35 **El**
DIN 17445	Grade G-X6 CrNi 189–1,4308	Germany	Sand castings	0.07 **C**, 1.5 **Mn**, 17.5–20.0 **Cr**, 9.0–11.0 **Ni**, 2.0 **Si**	**Solution annealed**: all **diam**, (441) **TS**, (176) **YS**, 20 min **El**
DIN 17445	Grade G-X6 CrNiMo 18 10–1.4408	Germany	Sand castings	0.07 **C**, 1.5 **Mn**, 17.0–19.5 **Cr**, 10.0–12.0 **Ni**, 2.0 **Si**, 2.0–2.5 **Mo**	**Solution annealed**: all **diam**, (441) **TS**, (186) **YS**, 20 min **El**
DIN 17440	Grade G-X 6 CrNi 18 9	Germany	Castings	0.07 **C**, 1.5 **Mn**, 17.5–20.0 **Cr**, 9.0–11.0 **Ni**, 2.0 **Si**, 0.045 **P**, 0.030 **S**	**Quenched**: all **diam**, (441) **TS**, (177) **YS**, 20 **El**
DIN 17440	Grade G-X6 CrNiMo 18 10	Germany	Castings	0.07 **C**, 1.5 **Mn**, 17.0–19.5 **Cr**, 10.0–12.0 **Ni**, 2.0 **Si**, 2.0–2.5 **Mo**, 0.045 **P**, 0.030 **S**	**Quenched**: all **diam**, (441) **TS**, (186) **YS**, 20 **El**
IS 3444	Grade 15	India	Castings	0.07 **C**, 1.50 **Mn**, 19.0–22.0 **Cr**, 27.5–30.5 **Ni**, 1.50 **Si**, 2.0–3.0 **Mo**, 0.040 **P**, 0.040 **S**, 3.0–4.0 **Cu**	**Solution annealed**: all **diam**, (431) **TS**, (176) **YS**
ANSI/ASTM A 296	Grade CN-7M	US	Sand castings	0.07 **C**, 1.50 **Mn**, 19.0–22.0 **Cr**, 27.5–30.5 **Ni**, 1.50 **Si**, 2.0–3.0 **Mo**, 0.040 **P**, 0.040 **S**, 3.0–4.0 **Cu**	**As cast or solution annealed**: all **diam**, 62 (430) **TS**, 25 (170) **YS**, 35 **El**
IS 7806	Grade 14	India	Castings	0.07 **C**, 1.50 **Mn**, 19.0–22.0 **Cr**, 27.5–30.5 **Ni**, 1.50 **Si**, 2.0–3.0 **Mo**, 0.040 **P**, 0.040 **S**, 3.0–4.0 **Cu**	**Solution annealed**: all **diam**, (430) **TS**, (170) **YS**, 33 **El**
IS 7806	Grade 14	India	Castings	0.07 **C**, 1.50 **Mn**, 19.0–22.0 **Cr**, 27.5–30.5 **Ni**, 1.50 **Si**, 2.0–3.0 **Mo**, 0.040 **P**, 0.040 **S**, 3.0–4.0 **Cu**	**Solution annealed**: all **diam**, (430) **TS**, (170) **YS**, 33 **El**
BS 1504–364C11		UK	Castings	0.07 **C**, 2.0 **Mn**, 20.0–24.0 **Cr**, 20.0–26.0 **Ni**, 2.5 **Si**, 3.0–6.0 **Mo**, 0.030 **P**, 0.030 **S**, 0.50 **Nb**	**Annealed**: all **diam**, (430) **TS**, (200) **YS**, 20 **El**
BS 1504–332C11		UK	Castings	0.07 **C**, 1.50 **Mn**, 19.0–22.0 **Cr**, 26.5–30.5 **Ni**, 1.50 **Si**, 2.0–3.0 **Mo**, 0.040 **P**, 0.040 **S**, 3.0–4.0 **Cu**	**Annealed**: all **diam**, (430) **TS**, (200) **YS**, 20 **El**
NOM-B-354	Class CN-7M	Mexico	Castings	0.07 **C**, 1.50 **Mn**, 19.0–22.0 **Cr**, 27.5–30.5 **Ni**, 1.50 **Si**, 2.0–3.0 **Mo**, 0.040 **P**, 0.040 **S**	**Quenched**: all **diam**, (430) **TS**, (172) **YS**, 35 **El**
ANSI/ASTM A 351	Grade CN7M	US	Sand castings	0.07 **C**, 1.50 **Mn**, 19.0–22.0 **Cr**, 27.5–30.5 **Ni**, 1.50 **Si**, 2.0–3.0 **Mo**, 0.040 **P**, 0.040 **S**, 3.0–4.0 **Cu**	**Solution annealed**: all **diam**, 62 (425) **TS**, 25 (170) **YS**, 35.0 **El**
ANSI/ASTM A 351	CN7M	US	Castings	0.07 **C**, 1.50 **Mn**, 19.0–22.0 **Cr**, 27.5–30.5 **Ni**, 1.50 **Si**, 2.0–3.0 **Mo**, 0.040 **P**, 0.040 **S**, 3.0–4.0 **Cu**	**Solution annealed**: all **diam**, 62 (425) **TS**, 25 (170) **YS**, 35 **El**
ASTM 744	Grade CN-7M	US	Castings	0.07 **C**, 1.50 **Mn**, 19.0–22.0 **Cr**, 27.5–30.5 **Ni**, 1.50 **Si**, 2.0–3.0 **Mo**, 0.04 **P**, 0.04 **S**, 3.0–4.0 **Cu**	**Solution quenched**: all **diam**, (425) **TS**, (170) **YS**, 35 **El**

CAST HIGH ALLOY STEELS

specification number	designation	country	product forms	composition	mechanical properties (see page iv for explanation)
ASTM A-351	Grade CN7M	US	Castings	0.07 **C**, 1.50 **Mn**, 19.0–22.0 **Cr**, 27.5–30.5 **Ni**, 1.50 **Si**, 2.0–3.0 **Mo**, 0.040 **P**, 0.040 **S**, 3.0–4.0 **Cu**	**Solution annealed**: all diam, (425) **TS**, (170) **YS**, 35 **El**
JIS G 5121	Type 23	Japan	Castings, pipe (centrifugally cast)	0.07 **C**, 2.00 **Mn**, 19.00–22.00 **Cr**, 27.50–30.50 **Ni**, 2.00 **Si**, 2.00–3.00 **Mo**, 0.040 **P**, 0.040 **S**, 3.00–4.00 **Cu**	**Solution annealed**: all diam, (392) **TS**, (167) **YS**, 30 **El**
NF A 32–056	Z 4 CNU 17 04–M	France	Castings	0.06 **C**, 1.5 **Mn**, 15.5–17.5 **Cr**, 3.0–5.0 **Ni**, 1.2 **Si**, 0.040 **P**, 0.030 **S**, 3.0–5.0 **Cu**	**Quenched and tempered**: all diam, (1300) **TS**
AMS 5355c		US	Investment castings	0.06 **C**, 0.70 **Mn**, 15.50–16.70 **Cr**, 3.60–4.60 **Ni**, 0.50–1.00 **Si**, 0.040 **P**, 0.030 **S**, 2.80–3.50 **Cu**, 0.050 **N**, 0.15–0.40 **Nb+Ta**	**Aged at H900**: 0.250 (6.35) **diam**, 180 (1241) **TS**, 160 (1103) **YS**, 6 **El**; **H925**: 0.250 (6.35) **diam**, 180 (1241) **TS**, 150 (1034) **YS**, 6 **El**; **H1000**: 0.250 (6.35) **diam**, 150 (1034) **TS**, 130 (896) **YS**, 8 **El**; **H1100**: 0.250 (6.35) **diam**, 130 (896) **TS**, 120 (827) **YS**, 8 **El**
AMS 5344A		US	Investment castings	0.06 **C**, 0.70 **Mn**, 15.50–16.70 **Cr**, 3.60–4.60 **Ni**, 0.50–1.00 **Si**, 0.04 **P**, 0.030 **S**, 2.80–3.50 **Cu**, 0.050 **N**, 0.15–0.40 **Nb+Ta**	**Solution annealed and aged**: 0.250 (6.35) **diam**, 180 (1241) **TS**, 160 (1103) **YS**, 4 **El**
AMS 5343A		US	Investment castings	0.06 **C**, 0.70 **Mn**, 15.50–16.70 **Cr**, 3.60–4.60 **Ni**, 0.50–1.00 **Si**, 0.025 **P**, 0.025 **S**, 2.80–3.50 **Cu**, 0.050 **N**, 0.15–0.40 **Nb+Ta**	**Solution annealed and aged**: all **diam**, 150 (1034) **TS**, 130 (896) **YS**, 4 **El**
AMS 5340A		US	Investment castings	0.06 **C**, 0.70 **Mn**, 13.50–14.25 **Cr**, 3.75–4.75 **Ni**, 0.50–1.00 **Si**, 2.00–2.50 **Mo**, 0.020 **P**, 0.025 **S**, 3.00–3.50 **Cu**, 0.050 **N**, 0.15–0.35 **Nb+Ta**	**Solution annealed and aged**: all **diam**, 150 (1034) **TS**, 130 (896) **YS**, 10 **El**
ASTM A 743	Grade CA–6N	US	Castings	0.06 **C**, 0.50 **Mn**, 10.5–12.5 **Cr**, 6.0–8.0 **Ni**, 1.00 **Si**, 0.02 **P**, 0.02 **S**	**Normalized and tempered**: all diam, (965) **TS**, (930) **YS**, 15 **El**
ANSI/ASTM A 296	Grade CA6N	US	Sand castings	0.06 **C**, 0.50 **Mn**, 10.5–12.5 **Cr**, 6.0–8.0 **Ni**, 1.00 **Si**, 0.02 **P**, 0.020 **S**	**Solution annealed and aged**: all **diam**, 140 (965) **TS**, 135 (930) **YS**, 15 **El**
AMS 5342A		US	Investment castings	0.06 **C**, 0.70 **Mn**, 15.50–16.70 **Cr**, 3.60–4.60 **Ni**, 0.50–1.00 **Si**, 0.025 **P**, 0.025 **S**, 2.80–3.50 **Cu**, 0.050 **N**, 0.15–0.40 **Nb+Ta**	**Solution annealed and aged**: all **diam**, 130 (896) **TS**, 120 (827) **YS**, 6 **El**
NF A 32–055	Z 4 CND 17 04–M	France	Castings	0.06 **C**, 1.5 **Mn**, 16.0–18.0 **Cr**, 3.0–5.0 **Ni**, 1.0 **Si**, 1.0–2.0 **Mo**, 0.040 **P**, 0.030 **S**	**Quenched**: all **diam**, (800) **TS**, (600) **YS**, 13 **El**
NF A 32–056	Z 4 CND 17 04–M	France	Castings	0.06 **C**, 1.5 **Mn**, 15.5–17.5 **Cr**, 3.0–5.0 **Ni**, 1.2 **Si**, 0.15–2.0 **Mo**, 0.040 **P**, 0.030 **S**	**Quenched and tempered**: all diam, (800) **TS**, (550) **YS**, 13 **El**
NF A 32–056	Z 4 CNVD 17 04–M	France	Castings	0.06 **C**, 1.5 **Mn**, 15.5–17.5 **Cr**, 3.0–5.0 **Ni**, 1.2 **Si**, 1.0–3.0 **Mo**, 0.040 **P**, 0.030 **S**, 2.0–4.0 **Cu**	**Quenched and tempered**: all diam, (800) **TS**, (550) **YS**, 13 **El**
ASTM A 743	Grade CA–6NM	US	Castings	0.06 **C**, 1.00 **Mn**, 11.5–14.0 **Cr**, 3.5–4.5 **Ni**, 1.00 **Si**, 0.40–1.0 **Mo**, 0.04 **P**, 0.03 **S**	**Normalized and tempered**: all diam, (760) **TS**, (550) **YS**, 15 **El**
ASTM A 487-76	Grade CA 6NM	US	Castings	0.06 **C**, 1.00 **Mn**, 11.5–14.0 **Cr**, 3.5–4.5 **Ni**, 1.00 **Si**, 0.4–1.0 **Mo**, 0.03 **P**, 0.04 **S**, 0.50 **Cu**, 0.03 **V**, 0.10 **W**	**Normalized and tempered**: all diam, 110 (760) **TS**, 80 (550) **YS**, 15 **El**
ANSI/ASTM A 487	CA6NM	US	Castings	0.06 **C**, 1.00 **Mn**, 11.5–14.0 **Cr**, 3.5–4.5 **Ni**, 1.00 **Si**, 0.4–1.0 **Mo**, 0.03 **P**, 0.04 **S**, 0.03 **V**	**Normalized, tempered**: all **diam**, 110 (760) **TS**, 80 (550) **YS**, 35 **El**
ANSI/ASTM A 487	Class CA6NM	US	Sand castings	0.06 **C**, 1.00 **Mn**, 11.5–14.0 **Cr**, 3.5–4.5 **Ni**, 1.00 **Si**, 0.4–1.0 **Mo**, 0.03 **P**, 0.04 **S**, 0.03 **V**	**Normalized and tempered**: all **diam**, 110 (760) **TS**, 80 (550) **YS**, 15 **El**
ANSI/ASTM A 296	Grade CA–6NM	US	Sand castings	0.06 **C**, 1.00 **Mn**, 11.5–14.0 **Cr**, 3.5–4.5 **Ni**, 1.00 **Si**, 0.40–1.0 **Mo**, 0.040 **P**, 0.030 **S**	**Normalized and tempered**: all **diam**, 110 (760) **TS**, 80 (550) **YS**, 15 **El**
SS 14 23 33	SS 23 33–12	Sweden	Castings	0.06 **C**, 2.0 **Mn**, 17.5–20.5 **Cr**, 8.0–11.0 **Ni**, 1.5 **Si**, 0.045 **P**, 0.030 **S**	**Solution annealed**: all **diam**, (440) **TS**, (180) **YS**, 35 **El**
SIS 14 23 66	SIS 23 66–12	Sweden	Castings	0.06 **C**, 2.0 **Mn**, 17.5–20.5 **Cr**, 13.0–16.5 **Ni**, 1.5 **Si**, 3.0–4.0 **Mo**	**Solution annealed**: all **diam**, (440) **TS**, (200) **YS**, 35 **El**
SIS 14 23 43	SIS 23 43–12	Sweden	Castings	0.06 **C**, 2.0 **Mn**, 17.0–20.0 **Cr**, 10.0–13.5 **Ni**, 1.5 **Si**, 2.5–3.2 **Mo**	**Solution annealed**: all **diam**, (440) **TS**, (200) **YS**, 35 **El**

CAST HIGH ALLOY STEELS

specification number	designation	country	product forms	composition	mechanical properties (see page iv for explanation)
SIS 14 23 33	SIS 23 33–12	Sweden	Castings	0.06 **C**, 2.0 **Mn**, 17.5–20.5 **Cr**, 8.0–11.0 **Ni**, 1.5 **Si**	**Solution annealed**: all **diam**, (440) **TS**, (180) **YS**, 35 **El**
SS 14 23 66	SS 23 66–12	Sweden	Castings	0.06 **C**, 2.0 **Mn**, 17.5–20.5 **Cr**, 13.0–16.5 **Ni**, 1.5 **Si**, 3.0–4.0 **Mo**, 0.045 **P**, 0.030 **S**	**Solution annealed**: all **diam**, (440) **TS**, (200) **YS**, 35 **El**
SS 14 23 43	SS 23 43–12	Sweden	Castings	0.06 **C**, 2.0 **Mn**, 17.0–20.0 **Cr**, 10.0–13.5 **Ni**, 1.5 **Si**, 2.5–3.2 **Mo**, 0.045 **P**, 0.030 **S**	**Solution annealed**: all **diam**, (440) **TS**, (200) **YS**, 35 **El**
SIS 14 23 33	SIS 23 33–12	Sweden	Castings	0.06 **C**, 2.0 **Mn**, 17.5–20.5 **Cr**, 8.0–11.0 **Ni**, 1.5 **Si**	
MIL–S–81591	IC–410	US	Investment castings	0.05–0.15 **C**, 1.00 **Mn**, 11.5–13.5 **Cr**, 0.50 **Ni**, 1.00 **Si**, 0.50 **Mo**, 0.040 **P**, 0.030 **S**, 0.50 **Cu**	**Quenched and tempered**: all **diam**, 95 (655) **TS**, 75 (517) **YS**, 8 **El**
MIL–S–81591	IC–304L	US	Investment castings	0.050 **C**, 1.0–2.0 **Mn**, 18.0–21.0 **Cr**, 8.0–11.0 **Ni**, 1.00 **Si**, 0.50 **Mo**, 0.040 **P**, 0.030 **S**, 0.50 **Cu**	**Solution annealed**
AMS 5370A		US	Investment castings	0.050 **C**, 1.00–2.00 **Mn**, 18.00–21.00 **Cr**, 8.00–11.00 **Ni**, 1.00 **Si**, 0.75 **Mo**, 0.040 **P**, 0.030 **S**, 0.75 **Cu**	**Solution heat treated**: all **diam**
AMS 5371A		US	Sand castings	0.050 **C**, 1.00–2.00 **Mn**, 18.00–21.00 **Cr**, 8.00–11.00 **Ni**, 0.75–1.50 **Si**, 0.75 **Mo**, 0.040 **P**, 0.040 **S**, 0.75 **Cu**	**Solution heated treated**: all **diam**
ASTM A 452–75	Grade TP 304 H	US	Pipe: centrifugally cast	0.04–0.10 **C**, 2.00 **Mn**, 18.0–20.0 **Cr**, 8.0–11.0 **Ni**, 0.75 **Si**, 0.040 **P**, 0.030 **S**	**Solution quenched**: all **diam**, (517) **TS**, (207) **YS**, 45 **El**
ASTM A 452–75	Grade TP 347 H	US	Pipe: centrifugally cast	0.04–0.10 **C**, 2.00 **Mn**, 17.0–20.0 **Cr**, 9.0–13.0 **Ni**, 0.75 **Si**, 0.040 **P**, 0.030 **S**, 8 x C–1.0 **Cb**	**Solution quenched**: all **diam**, (517) **TS**, (207) **YS**, 45 **El**
ASTM A 452–75	Grade TP 316 H	US	Pipe: centrifugally cast	0.04–0.10 **C**, 2.00 **Mn**, 16.0–18.0 **Cr**, 11.0–14.0 **Ni**, 0.75 **Si**, 2.0–3.0 **Mo**, 0.040 **P**, 0.030 **S**	**Solution quenched**: all **diam**, (517) **TS**, (207) **YS**, 45 **El**
BS 4534	Grade 1F	UK	Tube: weldable, centrifugal cast	0.04–0.09 **C**, 2.0 **Mn**, 17.0–20.0 **Cr**, 8.0 **Ni**, 1.50 **Si**, 0.040 **P**, 0.040 **S**	**As cast**: all **diam**, (425) **TS**, 26 **El**
BS 4534	Grade 2F	UK	Tube: weldable, centrifugal cast	0.04–0.09 **C**, 2.0 **Mn**, 17.0–20.0 **Cr**, 8.0 **Ni**, 1.5 **Si**, 0.040 **P**, 0.040 **S**, 8 x C–1.0 **Nb**	**As cast**: all **diam**, (425) **TS**, 22 **El**
BS 4534	Grade 3F	UK	Tube: weldable, centrifugal cast	0.04–0.09 **C**, 2.0 **Mn**, 17.0–20.0 **Cr**, 8.0 **Ni**, 1.5 **Si**, 2.0–3.0 **Mo**, 0.040 **P**, 0.040 **S**	**As cast**: all **diam**, (425) **TS**, 26 **El**
BS 4534	Grade 1	UK	Tube: weldable, centrifugal cast	0.04–0.09 **C**, 2.0 **Mn**, 17.0–19.0 **Cr**, 11.0–13.5 **Ni**, 1.0 **Si**, 0.50 **Mo**, 0.030 **P**, 0.030 **S**	**As cast**: all **diam**, (400) **TS**, 26 **El**
BS 4534	Grade 2	UK	Tube: weldable, centrifugal cast	0.04–0.09 **C**, 2.0 **Mn**, 17.0–19.0 **Cr**, 11.5–14.0 **Ni**, 1.0 **Si**, 0.50 **Mo**, 0.030 **P**, 0.030 **S**, 8 x C–1.10 **Nb**	**As cast**: all **diam**, (400) **TS**, 22 **El**
BS 4534	Grade 3	UK	Tube: weldable, centrifugal cast	0.04–0.09 **C**, 2.0 **Mn**, 16.0–18.0 **Cr**, 12.5–15.0 **Ni**, 1.0 **Si**, 2.0–2.75 **Mo**, 0.030 **P**, 0.030 **S**	**As cast**: all **diam**, (400) **TS**, 26 **El**
ASTM A–351–76	Grade CD4MCu	US	Castings	0.04 **C**, 1.00 **Mn**, 24.5–26.5 **Cr**, 4.75–6.00 **Ni**, 1.00 **Si**, 1.75–2.25 **Mo**, 0.040 **P**, 0.040 **S**, 2.75–3.25 **Cu**	**Quenched**: all **diam**, (690) **TS**, (485) **YS**, 16 **El**
ASTM 744	Grade CD–4MCu	US	Castings	0.04 **C**, 1.00 **Mn**, 24.5–26.5 **Cr**, 4.75–6.00 **Ni**, 1.00 **Si**, 1.75–2.25 **Mo**, 0.04 **P**, 0.04 **S**, 2.75–3.25 **Cu**	**Solution quenched**: all **diam**, (690) **TS**, (485) **YS**, 16 **El**
ANSI/ASTM A 296	Grade CD4MCo	US	Sand castings	0.040 **C**, 1.00 **Mn**, 24.5–26.5 **Cr**, 4.75–6.00 **Ni**, 1.00 **Si**, 1.75–2.25 **Mo**, 0.040 **P**, 0.040 **S**, 2.75–3.25 **Co**	**Solution annealed**: all **diam**, 100 (690) **TS**, 70 (485) **YS**, 16 **El**
ANSI/ASTM A 351	Grade CD4MCu	US	Sand castings	0.040 **C**, 1.00 **Mn**, 24.5–26.5 **Cr**, 4.75–6.00 **Ni**, 1.00 **Si**, 1.75–2.25 **Mo**, 0.040 **P**, 0.040 **S**, 2.75–3.25 **Cu**	**Solution annealed, tempered, quenched**: all **diam**, 100 (690) **TS**, 70 (485) **YS**, 16.0 **El**

CAST HIGH ALLOY STEELS

specification number	designation	country	product forms	composition	mechanical properties (see page iv for explanation)
ANSI/ASTM A 351	CD4MCu	US	Castings	0.04 **C**, 1.00 **Mn**, 24.5–26.5 **Cr**, 4.75–6.00 **Ni**, 1.00 **Si**, 1.75–2.25 **Mo**, 0.04 **P**, 0.04 **S**, 2.75–3.25 **Nb**	**Solution annealed**: all **diam**, 100 (690) **TS**, 70 (485) **YS**, 16 **El**
ASTM A 743	Grade CD4MCu	US	Castings	0.04 **C**, 1.00 **Mn**, 24.5–26.5 **Cr**, 4.75–6.00 **Ni**, 1.00 **Si**, 1.75–2.25 **Mo**, 0.04 **P**, 0.04 **S**, 2.75–3.25 **Cu**	**Solution quenched**: all **diam**, (689) **TS**, (483) **YS**, 16 **El**
AMS 5337		US	Investment castings	0.03 **C**, 0.10 **Mn**, 18.00–19.00 **Ni**, 0.10 **Si**, 4.50–5.50 **Mo**, 0.010 **P**, 0.010 **S**, 0.05–0.20 **Al**, 8.50–9.50 **Co**, 0.55–0.85 **Ti**	**Maraged**: all **diam**, 270 (1861) **TS**, 250 (1725) **YS**, 3 in 4D **El**
MIL–C–47041		US	Investment castings	0.030 **C**, 0.10 **Mn**, 16.00–17.50 **Ni**, 0.10 **Si**, 4.40–4.80 **Mo**, 0.01 **P**, 0.01 **S**, 0.02–0.10 **Al**, 9.50–11.00 **Co**, 0.15–0.45 **Ti**	**Solution annealed and aged**: all **diam**, 240 (1655) **TS**, 220 (1517) **YS**, 6 **El**
BS HC401		UK	Castings: aircraft quality	0.03 **C**, 0.10 **Mn**, 0.25 **Cr**, 16.0–17.5 **Ni**, 0.10 **Si**, 4.4–4.9 **Mo**, 0.010 **P**, 0.010 **S**, 0.02–0.15 **Al**, 9.5–11.0 **Co**, 0.15–0.60 **Ti**	**Maraged**: all **diam**, (1600) **TS**, (1500) **YS**, 6 **El**
ASTM A–351–76	Grade CF3MA	US	Castings	0.03 **C**, 1.50 **Mn**, 17.0–21.0 **Cr**, 9.0–13.0 **Ni**, 1.50 **Si**, 2.0–3.0 **Mo**, 0.040 **P**, 0.040 **S**	**Solution treated**: all **diam**, (550) **TS**, (255) **YS**, 30 **El**
ANSI/ASTM A 351	Grade CF3MA	US	Sand castings	0.030 **C**, 1.50 **Mn**, 17.0–21.0 **Cr**, 9.0–13.0 **Ni**, 1.50 **Si**, 2.0–3.0 **Mo**, 0.040 **P**, 0.040 **S**	**Solution annealed**: all **diam**, 80 (550) **TS**, 37 (255) **YS**, 30 **El**
ANSI/ASTM A 351	CF3MA	US	Castings	0.03 **C**, 1.50 **Mn**, 17.0–21.0 **Cr**, 9.0–13.0 **Ni**, 1.50 **Si**, 2.0–3.0 **Mo**, 0.040 **P**, 0.040 **S**	**Solution annealed**: all **diam**, 80 (550) **TS**, 37 (255) **YS**, 30 **El**
IS 7806	Grade 4A	India	Castings	0.03 **C**, 1.50 **Mn**, 17.0–21.0 **Cr**, 9.0–13.0 **Ni**, 1.50 **Si**, 2.0–3.0 **Mo**, 0.040 **P**, 0.040 **S**	**Solution annealed**: all **diam**, (550) **TS**, (260) **YS**, 29 **El**
ASTM A 451	Grade CPF3A	US	Pipe: centrifugally cast	0.03 **C**, 1.50 **Mn**, 17.0–21.0 **Cr**, 8.0–12.0 **Ni**, 2.00 **Si**, 0.040 **P**, 0.040 **S**	**Solution quenched**: all **diam**, (535) **TS**, (240) **YS**, 35 **El**
ASTM A 351	Grade CF3A	US	Castings	0.03 **C**, 1.50 **Mn**, 17.0–21.0 **Cr**, 8.0–12.0 **Ni**, 2.00 **Si**, 0.040 **P**, 0.040 **S**	**Solution treated**: all **diam**, (530) **TS**, (240) **YS**, 35 **El**
ANSI/ASTM A 351	Grade CF3A	US	Sand castings	0.030 **C**, 1.50 **Mn**, 17.0–21.0 **Cr**, 8.0–12.0 **Ni**, 2.00 **Si**, 0.040 **P**, 0.040 **S**	**Solution annealed**: all **diam**, 77 (530) **TS**, 35 (240) **YS**, 35 **El**
ANSI/ASTM A 351	CF3A	US	Castings	0.03 **C**, 1.50 **Mn**, 17.0–21.0 **Cr**, 8.0–12.0 **Ni**, 2.00 **Si**, 0.040 **P**, 0.040 **S**	**Solution annealed**: all **diam**, 77 (530) **TS**, 35 (240) **YS**, 35 **El**
IS 7806	Grade 2A	India	Castings	0.03 **C**, 1.50 **Mn**, 17.0–21.0 **Cr**, 8.0–12.0 **Ni**, 2.00 **Si**, 0.040 **P**, 0.040 **S**	**Solution annealed**: all **diam**, (530) **TS**, (240) **YS**, 33 **El**
ASTM A 451	Grade CPF3	US	Pipe: centrifugally cast	0.03 **C**, 1.50 **Mn**, 17.0–21.0 **Cr**, 8.0–12.0 **Ni**, 2.00 **Si**, 0.040 **P**, 0.040 **S**	**Solution quenched**: all **diam**, (485) **TS**, (205) **YS**, 35 **El**
ASTM A 451	Grade CPF3M	US	Pipe: centrifugally cast	0.03 **C**, 1.50 **Mn**, 17.0–21.0 **Cr**, 9.0–13.0 **Ni**, 1.50 **Si**, 2.0–3.0 **Mo**, 0.040 **P**, 0.040 **S**	**Solution quenched**: all **diam**, (485) **TS**, (205) **YS**, 30 **El**
ASTM 744	Grade CF–3	US	Castings	0.03 **C**, 1.50 **Mn**, 17.0–21.0 **Cr**, 8.0–12.0 **Ni**, 2.00 **Si**, 0.04 **P**, 0.04 **S**	**Solution quenched**: all **diam**, (485) **TS**, (205) **YS**, 35 **El**
ASTM 744	Grade CF–3M	US	Castings	0.03 **C**, 1.50 **Mn**, 17.0–21.0 **Cr**, 9.0–13.0 **Ni**, 1.50 **Si**, 2.0–3.0 **Mo**, 0.04 **P**, 0.04 **S**	**Solution quenched**: all **diam**, (485) **TS**, (205) **YS**, 30 **El**
ASTM A 351	Grade CF3	US	Castings	0.03 **C**, 1.50 **Mn**, 17.0–21.0 **Cr**, 8.0–12.0 **Ni**, 2.00 **Si**, 0.040 **P**, 0.040 **S**	**Solution treated**: all **diam**, (485) **TS**, (205) **YS**, 35 **El**
ASTM A 351	Grade CF3M	US	Castings	0.03 **C**, 1.50 **Mn**, 17.0–21.0 **Cr**, 9.0–13.0 **Ni**, 1.50 **Si**, 2.0–3.0 **Mo**, 0.040 **P**, 0.040 **S**	**Solution treated**: all **diam**, (485) **TS**, (205) **YS**, 30 **El**
ASTM A 743	Grade CF–3	US	Castings	0.03 **C**, 1.50 **Mn**, 17.0–21.0 **Cr**, 8.0–12.0 **Ni**, 2.00 **Si**, 0.04 **P**, 0.04 **S**	**As cast, solution quenched**: all **diam**, (485) **TS**, (195) **YS**, 35 **El**
ASTM A 743	Grade CF–3M	US	Castings	0.03 **C**, 1.50 **Mn**, 17.0–21.0 **Cr**, 9.0–13.0 **Ni**, 1.50 **Si**, 2.0–3.0 **Mo**, 0.04 **P**, 0.04 **S**	**As cast, solution quenched**: all **diam**, (485) **TS**, (205) **YS**, 30 **El**

CAST HIGH ALLOY STEELS

specification number	designation	country	product forms	composition	mechanical properties (see page iv for explanation)
ANSI/ASTM A 296	Grade CF–3M	US	Sand castings	0.030 **C**, 1.50 **Mn**, 17.0–21.0 **Cr**, 9.0–13.0 **Ni**, 1.50 **Si**, 2.0–3.0 **Mo**, 0.040 **P**, 0.040 **S**	**Solution annealed**: all **diam**, 70 (485) **TS**, 30 (205) **YS**, 30 **El**
ANSI/ASTM A 351	Grade CF3M	US	Sand castings	0.030 **C**, 1.50 **Mn**, 17.0–21.0 **Cr**, 9.0–13.0 **Ni**, 1.50 **Si**, 2.0–3.0 **Mo**, 0.040 **P**, 0.040 **S**	**Solution annealed**: all **diam**, 70 (485) **TS**, 30 (205) **YS**, 30 **El**
ANSI/ASTM A 351	Grade CF3	US	Sand castings	0.030 **C**, 1.50 **Mn**, 17.0–21.0 **Cr**, 8.0–12.0 **Ni**, 2.00 **Si**, 0.040 **P**, 0.040 **S**	**Solution annealed**: all **diam**, 70 (485) **TS**, 30 (205) **YS**, 35 **El**
ANSI/ASTM A 351	CF3	US	Castings	0.03 **C**, 1.50 **Mn**, 17.0–21.0 **Cr**, 8.0–12.0 **Ni**, 2.00 **Si**, 0.040 **P**, 0.040 **S**	**Solution annealed**: all **diam**, 70 (485) **TS**, 30 (205) **YS**, 35 **El**
ANSI/ASTM A 351	CF3M	US	Castings	0.03 **C**, 1.50 **Mn**, 17.0–21.0 **Cr**, 9.0–13.0 **Ni**, 1.50 **Si**, 2.0–3.0 **Mo**, 0.040 **P**, 0.040 **S**	**Solution annealed**: all **diam**, 70 (485) **TS**, 30 (205) **YS**, 30 **El**
NOM–B–354	Class CF–3M	Mexico	Castings	0.03 **C**, 1.50 **Mn**, 17.0–21.0 **Cr**, 9.0–13.0 **Ni**, 1.50 **Si**, 2.0–3.0 **Mo**, 0.040 **P**, 0.040 **S**	**Quenched or as cast**: all **diam**, (483) **TS**, (207) **YS**, 30 **El**
IS 7806	Grade 2	India	Castings	0.03 **C**, 1.50 **Mn**, 17.0–21.0 **Cr**, 8.0–12.0 **Ni**, 2.00 **Si**, 0.040 **P**, 0.040 **S**	**Solution annealed**: all **diam**, (480) **TS**, (210) **YS**, 33 **El**
IS 7806	Grade 4	India	Castings	0.03 **C**, 1.50 **Mn**, 17.0–21.0 **Cr**, 9.0–13.0 **Ni**, 1.50 **Si**, 2.0–3.0 **Mo**, 0.040 **P**, 0.040 **S**	**Solution annealed**: all **diam**, (480) **TS**, (210) **YS**, 29 **El**
ANSI/ASTM A 296	Grade CF–3	US	Sand castings	0.030 **C**, 1.50 **Mn**, 17.0–21.0 **Cr**, 8.0–12.0 **Ni**, 2.00 **Si**, 0.040 **P**, 0.040 **S**	**Solution annealed**: all **diam**, 65 (450) **TS**, 28 (195) **YS**, 35 **El**
NOM–B–354	Class CF–3	Mexico	Castings	0.03 **C**, 1.50 **Mn**, 17.0–21.0 **Cr**, 8.0–12.0 **Ni**, 2.0 **Si**, 0.040 **P**, 0.040 **S**	**Quenched or as cast**: all **diam**, (448) **TS**, (193) **YS**, 35 **El**
BS 1504–317C12		UK	Castings	0.03 **C**, 2.0 **Mn**, 17.0–21.0 **Cr**, 10.0 min **Ni**, 1.5 **Si**, 3.0–4.0 **Mo**, 0.040 **P**, 0.040 **S**	**Annealed**: all **diam**, (430) **TS**, (215) **YS**, 22 **El**
BS 1504–316C12		UK	Castings	0.03 **C**, 2.0 **Mn**, 17.0–21.0 **Cr**, 10.0 min **Ni**, 1.5 **Si**, 2.0–3.0 **Mo**, 0.040 **P**, 0.040 **S**	**Annealed**: all **diam**, (430) **TS**, (215) **YS**, 26 **El**
BS 3100/1632	Grade F	UK	Sand castings	0.030 **C**, 17.0–20.0 **Cr**, 10.0 min **Ni**, 2.0–3.0 **Mo**	**Quenched**: all **diam**, (430) **TS**, (185) **YS**, 26 **El**
BS 3100/1631	Grade C	UK	Sand castings	0.030 **C**, 17.0–21.0 **Cr**, 8.0 min **Ni**	**Quenched**: all **diam**, (430) **TS**, (185) **YS**, 26 **El**
BS 1504–304C12		UK	Castings	0.03 **C**, 2.0 **Mn**, 17.0–21.0 **Cr**, 8.0 min **Ni**, 1.5 **Si**, 0.040 **P**, 0.040 **S**	**Annealed**: all **diam**, (430) **TS**, (215) **YS**, 26 **El**
NF A 32-055	Z 2 CND 18 12–M	France	Castings	0.03 **C**, 1.5 **Mn**, 17.0–20.0 **Cr**, 9.0–13.0 **Ni**, 1.2 **Si**, 2.0–3.0 **Mo**, 0.040 **P**, 0.030 **S**	**Solution annealed**: all **diam**, (400) **TS**, (180) **YS**, 40 **El**
NF A 32–055	Z 2 CN 18 10–M	France	Castings	0.03 **C**, 1.5 **Mn**, 17.0–20.0 **Cr**, 8.0–12.0 **Ni**, 1.2 **Si**, 0.040 **P**, 0.030 **S**	**Solution annealed**: all **diam**, (400) **TS**, (180) **YS**, 35 **El**
NF A 32–056	Z 2 CN 18 10–M	France	Castings	0.03 **C**, 1.5 **Mn**, 17.0–20.0 **Cr**, 8.0–12.0 **Ni**, 1.2 **Si**, 0.040 **P**, 0.030 **S**	**Solution annealed**: all **diam**, (400) **TS**, (180) **YS**, 35 **El**
NF A 32–056	Z 2 CND 18 12–M	France	Castings	0.03 **C**, 1.5 **Mn**, 17.0–20.0 **Cr**, 9.0–13.0 **Ni**, 1.2 **Si**, 2.0–3.0 **Mo**, 0.040 **P**, 0.030 **S**	**Solution annealed**: all **diam**, (400) **TS**, (180) **YS**, 40 **El**
JIS G 5121	Type 16	Japan	Castings, pipe (centrifugally cast)	0.03 **C**, 2.00 **Mn**, 17.00–20.00 **Cr**, 12.00–16.00 **Ni**, 1.50 **Si**, 2.00–3.00 **Mo**, 0.040 **P**, 0.040 **S**	**Solution annealed**: all **diam**, (392) **TS**, (177) **YS**, 35 **El**
JIS G 5121	Type 19	Japan	Castings, pipe (centrifugally cast)	0.03 **C**, 2.00 **Mn**, 17.00–21.00 **Cr**, 8.00–12.00 **Ni**, 2.00 **Si**, 0.040 **P**, 0.040 **S**	**Solution annealed**: all **diam**, (392) **TS**, (186) **YS**, 35 **El**
JIS G 5121	Type 20	Japan	Castings, pipe (centrifugally cast)	0.03 **C**, 2.00 **Mn**, 17.00–20.00 **Cr**, 12.00–16.00 **Ni**, 2.00 **Si**, 1.75–2.75 **Mo**, 0.040 **P**, 0.040 **S**, 1.00–2.50 **Cu**	**Solution annealed**: all **diam**, (392) **TS**, (177) **YS**, 35 **El**
MIL–S–81591	IC–416	US	Investment castings	0.015 **C**, 1.25 **Mn**, 11.5–14.0 **Cr**, 0.050 **Ni**, 1.5 **Si**, 0.050 **Mo**, 0.050 **P**, 0.15–0.35 **S**, 0.50 **Cu**, 0.50 **Zr**	**Quenched and tempered**: all **diam**, 90 (621) **TS**, 65 (448) **YS**, 8 **El**

WROUGHT CARBON,
HIGH STRENGTH LOW ALLOY,
AND STRUCTURAL STEELS

WROUGHT CARBON STEELS

specification number	designation	country	product forms	composition	mechanical properties (see page iv for explanation)
BS 1429	En. 44C	UK	Wire	1.00–1.20 **C**, 0.40–0.70 **Mn**, 0.05 **P**, 0.05 **S**, 0.35 **Si**	
DIN 17222	Grade MK 101	Germany	Strip	0.98–1.05 **C**, 0.35–0.45 **Mn**, 0.035 **P**, 0.035 **S**, 0.15–0.25 **Si**	**Solution annealed**: all **diam**, (687) **TS**, (314) **YS**, 25 **El**; **Quenched and tempered**: all **diam**, (1765) **TS**, (1667) **YS**, 5 **El**
DIN 17222	MK101/1274	Germany	Strip	0.98–1.05 **C**, 0.35–0.45 **Mn**, 0.035 **P**, 0.035 **S**, 0.15–0.25 **Si**	**Softened and annealed**: all **diam**, (686) max **TS**, (314) max **YS**, 25 **El**; **Hardened and tempered**: all **diam**, (1765) **TS**, (1667) **YS**, 5 **El**
BS 970: Part 1	060A99	UK	Blooms, billets, slabs, bar, rod, forgings	0.95–1.05 **C**, 0.50–0.70 **Mn**	
NF A 35–553	XC 100	France	Strip	0.95–1.05 **C**, 0.25–0.45 **Mn**, 0.030 **P**, 0.025 **S**, 0.15–0.30 **Si**	
SIS 14 18 70	SIS 18 70–04	Sweden	Strip	0.94–1.06 **C**, 0.30–0.60 **Mn**, 0.030 **P**, 0.030 **S**, 0.10–0.35 **Si**	**Quenched**: (<0.125) **diam**, (2010) **TS**
SIS 14 18 70	SIS 18 70–02	Sweden	Strip	0.94–1.06 **C**, 0.30–0.60 **Mn**, 0.030 **P**, 0.030 **S**, 0.10–0.35 **Si**	**Annealed**: ($\leq$2) **diam**, (410) **YS**, 23 **El**
BS 970 Part 5	060A96	UK	Blooms, billets, bar, forgings	0.93–1.00 **C**, 0.50–0.70 **Mn**, 0.10–0.35 **Si**	
BS 970: Part 1	060A96	UK	Blooms, billets, slabs, bar, rod, forgings	0.93–1.00 **C**, 0.50–0.70 **Mn**	
MIL–S–46049B	AISI 1095	US	Strip	0.91–1.04 **C**, 0.30–0.50 **Mn**, 0.040 **P**, 0.050 **S**, 0.15–0.30 **Si**	
AMS 5132E		US	Bar	0.90–1.30 **C**, 0.15–0.50 **Mn**, 0.040 **P**, 0.050 **S**, 0.10–0.35 **Si**	
JIS G 4801	SUP 4	Japan	Bar, wire, rod	0.90–1.10 **C**, 0.30–0.60 **Mn**, 0.035 **P**, 0.035 **S**, 0.15–0.35 **Si**, 0.30 **Cu**	**Quenched and tempered**: all **diam**, (1128) **TS**, (883) **YS**, 7 **El**
MIL–S–8559A	1095	US	Bar	0.90–1.05 **C**, 0.30–0.50 **Mn**, 0.040 **P**, 0.050 **S**	
QQ–S–700D	SAE 1095	US	Sheet, strip	0.90–1.04 **C**, 0.30–0.50 **Mn**, 0.040 **P**, 0.050 **S**	
AISI 1095		US	Plate	0.90–1.04 **C**, 0.30–0.50 **Mn**, 0.040 **P**, 0.050 **S**	
AMS 5121E		US	Strip	0.90–1.04 **C**, 0.30–0.50 **Mn**, 0.040 **P**, 0.050 **S**, 0.10–0.30 **Si**	**Cold rolled and annealed**
AMS 5122E		US	Strip	0.90–1.04 **C**, 0.30–0.50 **Mn**, 0.040 **P**, 0.050 **S**, 0.10–0.30 **Si**	**Cold finished, hard temper**
ANSI/ASTM A 680	1095	US	Strip	0.90–1.04 **C**, 0.30–0.50 **Mn**, 0.040 **P**, 0.050 **S**, 0.15–0.30 **Si**	**Cold–rolled**
ANSI/ASTM A 684	1095	US	Strip	0.90–1.04 **C**, 0.30–0.50 **Mn**, 0.040 **P**, 0.050 **S**, 0.15–0.30 **Si**	
ANSI/ASTM A 682	1095	US	Strip	0.90–1.04 **C**, 0.30–0.50 **Mn**, 0.040 **P**, 0.050 **S**, 0.15–0.30 **Si**	
DGN–B–301	1095	Mexico	Bar	0.90–1.03 **C**, 0.30–0.50 **Mn**, 0.040 **P**, 0.050 **S**, 0.10–0.20 **Si**	**Forged or hot rolled, cold rolled and cold finished**: all **diam**, (824) **TS**, (451) **YS**, 10 **El**
ASTM A 713	Grade 1095	US	Wire	0.90–1.03 **C**, 0.30–0.50 **Mn**, 0.040 **P**, 0.050 **S**	
AISI 1095		US	Bar	0.90–1.03 **C**, 0.30–0.50 **Mn**, 0.040 **P**, 0.050 **S**	
MIL–S–11713B	3	US	Strip	0.90–1.03 **C**, 0.30–0.50 **Mn**, 0.025 **P**, 0.025 **S**, 0.15–0.25 **Si**	**Spheroidize annealed**
COPANT 330	1095	COPANT	Bar, shapes	0.90–1.03 **C**, 0.30–0.50 **Mn**, 0.040 **P**, 0.050 **S**	
COPANT 331	1095	COPANT	Bar	0.90–1.03 **C**, 0.30–0.50 **Mn**, 0.040 **P**, 0.050 **S**	
MIL–S–16974E	No. 1095	US	Bar, billets, blooms, slabs	0.90–1.03 **C**, 0.30–0.50 **Mn**, 0.040 **P**, 0.050 **S**, 0.15–0.30 **Si**	
ASTM A 108	1095	US	Bar	0.90–1.03 **C**, 0.30–0.50 **Mn**, 0.040 **P**, 0.050 **S**	
MIL–S–16788A	Class C10	US	Blooms, billets, slabs	0.90–1.03 **C**, 0.30–0.50 **Mn**, 0.040 **P**, 0.050 **S**	

specification number	designation	country	product forms	composition	mechanical properties (see page iv for explanation)
AISI 1095		US	Wire, rod	0.90–1.03 **C**, 0.30–0.50 **Mn**, 0.040 **P**, 0.050 **S**	
ASTM A 713	1095	US	Wire	0.90–1.03 **C**, 0.30–0.50 **Mn**, 0.040 **P**, 0.050 **S**	
ANSI/ASTM A 576	1095	US	Bar	0.90–1.03 **C**, 0.30–0.50 **Mn**, 0.040 **P**, 0.050 **S**	
ANSI/ASTM A 29	1095	US	Bar	0.90–1.03 **C**, 0.30–0.50 **Mn**, 0.040 **P**, 0.050 **S**	
ASTM A 689	1095	US	Bar	0.90–1.03 **C**, 0.30–0.50 **Mn**, 0.040 **P**, 0.050 **S**	
AS 1442	Grade AS 1442/K1095	australia	Bar, blooms, billets, slabs	0.90–1.03 **C**, 0.40–0.70 **Mn**, 0.050 **P**, 0.050 **S**, 0.10–0.35 **Si**	
DEF STAN 95–1/1	C1095	Canada	Bar	0.90–1.03 **C**, 0.30–0.50 **Mn**, 0.040 **P**, 0.050 **S**, 0.15–0.30 **Si**	
BS 1429	En. 44B	UK	Wire	0.90–1.00 **C**, 0.40–0.70 **Mn**, 0.05 **P**, 0.05 **S**, 0.35 **Si**	
BS 1449: Part 1	Grade 95	UK	Plate, sheet, strip	0.90–1.00 **C**, 0.30–0.60 **Mn**, 0.040 **P**, 0.040 **S**, 0.05–0.35 **Si**	
DIN 17140	Grade D95–2	Germany	Wire, rod	0.90–0.99 **C**, 0.30–0.70 **Mn**, 0.040 **P**, 0.040 **S**, 0.10–0.30 **Si**, 0.007 **N**	
JIS G 3502	SWRS 92A	Japan	Wire, rod	0.90–0.95 **C**, 0.30–0.60 **Mn**, 0.025 **P**, 0.025 **S**, 0.12–0.32 **Si**, 0.20 **Cu**	
JIS G 3502	SWRS 92B	Japan	Wire, rod	0.90–0.95 **C**, 0.60–0.90 **Mn**, 0.025 **P**, 0.025 **S**, 0.12–0.32 **Si**, 0.20 **Cu**	
AS 1595, Part 2					
NF A 35–590	1303 (Y_3 90)	France	Bar, forgings Scc 0.90 **C**, 0.40–0.60 **Mn**, 0.035 **P**, 0.035 **S**, 0.15–0.40 **Si**		
ASTM A 713	Grade 1090	US	Wire	0.85–0.98 **C**, 0.60–0.90 **Mn**, 0.040 **P**, 0.050 **S**	
AISI 1090		US	Bar	0.85–0.98 **C**, 0.60–0.90 **Mn**, 0.040 **P**, 0.050 **S**	
COPANT 331	1090	COPANT	Bar	0.85–0.98 **C**, 0.60–0.90 **Mn**, 0.040 **P**, 0.050 **S**	
AISI 1090		US	Wire, rod	0.85–0.98 **C**, 0.60–0.90 **Mn**, 0.040 **P**, 0.050 **S**	
ASTM A 713	1090	US	Wire	0.85–0.98 **C**, 0.60–0.90 **Mn**, 0.040 **P**, 0.050 **S**	
ANSI/ASTM A 576	1090	US	Bar	0.85–0.98 **C**, 0.60–0.90 **Mn**, 0.040 **P**, 0.050 **S**	
ANSI/ASTM A 29	1090	US	Bar	0.85–0.98 **C**, 0.60–0.90 **Mn**, 0.040 **P**, 0.050 **S**	
ASTM A 689	1090	US	Bar	0.85–0.98 **C**, 0.60–0.90 **Mn**, 0.040 **P**, 0.050 **S**	
NF A 35–553	XC 90	France	Strip	0.85–0.95 **C**, 0.30–0.50 **Mn**, 0.030 **P**, 0.025 **S**, 0.15–0.30 **Si**	
DGN–B–301	1090	Mexico	Bar	0.85–0.93 **C**, 0.60–0.90 **Mn**, 0.040 **P**, 0.050 **S**, 0.10–0.20 **Si**	**Forged or hot rolled, cold rolled and cold finished**: all **diam**, (843) **TS**, (461) **YS**, 10 **El**
MIL–W–8957A		US	Wire	0.85–0.90 **C**, 0.25–0.40 **Mn**, 0.025 **P**, 0.020 **S**, 0.15–0.25 **Si**, 0.08 **Cu**	**Cold drawn**: 0.042–0.043 **diam**, 364 (2510) **TS**
MIL–W–23711		US	Wire: high strength	0.85–0.90 **C**, 0.25–0.40 **Mn**, 0.025 **P**, 0.020 **S**, 0.15–0.25 **Si**, 0.08 **Cu**, 0.04 **Cr**, 0.04 **Mo**, 0.03 **Ni**	
JIS G 3502	SWRS 87A	Japan	Wire, rod	0.85–0.90 **C**, 0.30–0.60 **Mn**, 0.025 **P**, 0.025 **S**, 0.12–0.32 **Si**, 0.20 **Cu**	
JIS G 3502	SWRS 87B	Japan	Wire, rod	0.85–0.90 **C**, 0.60–0.90 **Mn**, 0.025 **P**, 0.025 **S**, 0.12–0.32 **Si**, 0.20 **Cu**	
AISI 1090		US	Plate	0.84–0.98 **C**, 0.60–0.90 **Mn**, 0.040 **P**, 0.050 **S**	

WROUGHT CARBON STEELS

specification number	designation	country	product forms	composition	mechanical properties (see page iv for explanation)
BS 970: Part 1	050A86	UK	Blooms, billets, slabs, bar, rod, forgings	0.83–0.90 **C**, 0.40–0.60 **Mn**	
BS 970: Part 1	060A86	UK	Blooms, billets, slabs, bar, rod, forgings	0.83–0.90 **C**, 0.50–0.70 **Mn**	
BS 970: Part 1	060A86	UK	Blooms, billets, slabs, bar, rod, forgings	0.83–0.90 **C**, 0.50–0.70 **Mn**	
BS 970: Part 1	080A86	UK	Blooms, billets, slabs, bar, rod, forgings	0.83–0.90 **C**, 0.70–0.90 **Mn**	
QQ–S–700D	SAE 1084	US	Sheet, strip	0.80–0.94 **C**, 0.60–0.90 **Mn**, 0.040 **P**, 0.050 **S**	
QQ–S–700D	SAE 1086	US	Sheet, strip	0.80–0.94 **C**, 0.30–0.50 **Mn**, 0.040 **P**, 0.050 **S**	
AISI 1084		US	Plate	0.80–0.94 **C**, 0.60–0.90 **Mn**, 0.040 **P**, 0.050 **S**	
AISI 1085		US	Plate	0.80–0.94 **C**, 0.70–1.00 **Mn**, 0.040 **P**, 0.050 **S**	
AISI 1086		US	Plate	0.80–0.94 **C**, 0.30–0.50 **Mn**, 0.040 **P**, 0.050 **S**	
MIL–S–46049B	AISI 1085	US	Strip	0.80–0.94 **C**, 0.70–1.00 **Mn**, 0.040 **P**, 0.050 **S**, 0.15–0.30 **Si**	
ANSI/ASTM A 680	1085	US	Strip	0.80–0.94 **C**, 0.70–1.00 **Mn**, 0.040 **P**, 0.050 **S**, 0.15–0.30 **Si**	**Cold–rolled**
ANSI/ASTM A 680	1086	US	Strip	0.80–0.94 **C**, 0.30–0.50 **Mn**, 0.040 **P**, 0.050 **S**, 0.15–0.30 **Si**	**Cold–rolled**
ANSI/ASTM A 684	1085	US	Strip	0.80–0.94 **C**, 0.70–1.00 **Mn**, 0.040 **P**, 0.050 **S**, 0.15–0.30 **Si**	
ANSI/ASTM A 684	1086	US	Strip	0.80–0.94 **C**, 0.30–0.50 **Mn**, 0.040 **P**, 0.050 **S**, 0.15–0.30 **Si**	
ANSI/ASTM A 682	1085	US	Strip	0.80–0.94 **C**, 0.70–1.00 **Mn**, 0.040 **P**, 0.050 **S**, 0.15–0.30 **Si**	
ANSI/ASTM A 682	1086	US	Strip	0.80–0.94 **C**, 0.30–0.50 **Mn**, 0.040 **P**, 0.050 **S**, 0.15–0.30 **Si**	
DGN–B–301	1085	Mexico	Bar	0.80–0.93 **C**, 0.70–1.00 **Mn**, 0.040 **P**, 0.050 **S**, 0.10–0.20 **Si**	**Forged or hot rolled, cold rolled and cold finished**: all diam, (833) **TS**, (461) **YS**, 10 **El**
DGN–B–301	1084	Mexico	Bar	0.80–0.93 **C**, 0.60–0.90 **Mn**, 0.040 **P**, 0.050 **S**, 0.10–0.20 **Si**	**Forged or hot rolled, cold rolled and cold finished**: all diam, (824) **TS**, (451) **YS**, 10 **El**
DGN–B–301	1086	Mexico	Bar	0.80–0.93 **C**, 0.30–0.50 **Mn**, 0.040 **P**, 0.050 **S**, 0.10–0.20 **Si**	**Forged or hot rolled, cold rolled and cold finished**: all diam, (775) **TS**, (422) **YS**, 10 **El**
ASTM A 713	Grade 1084	US	Wire	0.80–0.93 **C**, 0.60–0.90 **Mn**, 0.040 **P**, 0.050 **S**	
ASTM A 713	Grade 1086	US	Wire	0.80–0.93 **C**, 0.30–0.50 **Mn**, 0.040 **P**, 0.050 **S**	
AISI 1084		US	Bar	0.80–0.93 **C**, 0.60–0.90 **Mn**, 0.040 **P**, 0.050 **S**	
AS 1446	Grade AS 1446/K1084	Australia	Plate	0.80–0.93 **C**, 0.60–0.90 **Mn**, 0.050 **P**, 0.050 **S**, 0.10–0.35 **Si**	
AS 1446	Grade AS 1446/S1084	Australia	Plate	0.80–0.93 **C**, 0.60–0.90 **Mn**, 0.050 **P**, 0.050 **S**, 0.35 **Si**	
COPANT 333	1085	COPANT	Wire, rod	0.80–0.93 **C**, 0.70–1.00 **Mn**, 0.040 **P**, 0.050 **S**	
COPANT 333	1086	COPANT	Wire, rod	0.80–0.93 **C**, 0.30–0.50 **Mn**, 0.040 **P**, 0.050 **S**	
AISI 1084		US	Wire, rod	0.80–0.93 **C**, 0.60–0.90 **Mn**, 0.040 **P**, 0.050 **S**	
AISI 1086		US	Wire, rod	0.80–0.93 **C**, 0.30–0.50 **Mn**, 0.040 **P**, 0.050 **S**	
ASTM A 713	1086	US	Wire	0.80–0.93 **C**, 0.30–0.50 **Mn**, 0.040 **P**, 0.050 **S**	
ANSI/ASTM A 576	1084	US	Bar	0.80–0.93 **C**, 0.60–0.90 **Mn**, 0.040 **P**, 0.050 **S**	
ASTM A 689	1084	US	Bar	0.80–0.93 **C**, 0.60–0.90 **Mn**, 0.040 **P**, 0.050 **S**	

specification number	designation	country	product forms	composition	mechanical properties (see page iv for explanation)
ASTM A 713	1084	US	Wire	0.80–0.93 **C**, 0.60–0.90 **Mn**, 0.040 **P**, 0.050 **S**	
ANSI/ASTM A 29	1084	US	Bar	0.80–0.93 **C**, 0.60–0.90 **Mn**, 0.040 **P**, 0.050 **S**	
ANSI/ASTM A 29	1086	US	Bar	0.80–0.93 **C**, 0.30–0.50 **Mn**, 0.040 **P**, 0.050 **S**	
QQ-S-700D	SAE 1085	US	Sheet, strip	0.80–0.90 **C**, 0.70–1.00 **Mn**, 0.040 **P**, 0.050 **S**	
BS 1429	En. 42D	UK	Wire	0.80–0.90 **C**, 0.55–0.80 **Mn**, 0.05 **P**, 0.05 **S**, 0.35 **Si**	
DIN 17222	Grade M 85	Germany	Strip	0.80–0.89 **C**, 0.30–0.60 **Mn**, 0.045 **P**, 0.045 **S**, 0.10–0.25 **Si**	**Solution annealed**: all **diam**, (638) **TS**, (294) **YS**, 25 **El**; **Quenched and tempered**: all **diam**, (1177) **TS**, (1079) **YS**, 6 **El**
DIN 17222	M85/0783	Germany	Strip	0.80–0.89 **C**, 0.30–0.60 **Mn**, 0.045 **P**, 0.045 **S**, 0.10–0.25 **Si**	**Softened and annealed**: all **diam**, (637) max **TS**, (294) max **YS**, 25 **El**; **Hardened and tempered**: all **diam**, (1176) **TS**, (1079) **YS**, 6 **El**
DIN 17140	Grade D85-2	Germany	Wire, rod	0.80–0.89 **C**, 0.30–0.70 **Mn**, 0.040 **P**, 0.040 **S**, 0.10–0.30 **Si**, 0.007 **N**	
BS 970: Part 1	060A83	UK	Blooms, billets, slabs, bar, rod, forgings	0.80–0.87 **C**, 0.50–0.70 **Mn**	
BS 970: Part 1	080A83	UK	Blooms, billets, slabs, bar, rod, forgings	0.80–0.87 **C**, 0.70–0.90 **Mn**	
JIS G 3502	SWRS 82A	Japan	Wire, rod	0.80–0.85 **C**, 0.30–0.60 **Mn**, 0.025 **P**, 0.025 **S**, 0.12–0.32 **Si**, 0.20 **Cu**	
JIS G 3502	SWRS 82B	Japan	Wire, rod	0.80–0.85 **C**, 0.60–0.90 **Mn**, 0.025 **P**, 0.025 **S**, 0.12–0.32 **Si**, 0.20 **Cu**	
NF A 35-051	FM 86	France	Wire, rod	0.79–0.92 **C**, 0.60–0.90 **Mn**, 0.040 **P**, 0.040 **S**, 0.10–0.35 **Si**	
JIS G 3506	SWRH 82A	Japan	Wire, rod	0.79–0.86 **C**, 0.30–0.60 **Mn**, 0.030 **P**, 0.030 **S**, 0.15–0.35 **Si**	
JIS G 3506	SWRH 82A	Japan	Wire, rod	0.79–0.86 **C**, 0.60–0.90 **Mn**, 0.030 **P**, 0.030 **S**, 0.15–0.35 **Si**	
AS 1442	Grade AS 1442/S1082	Australia	Bar, blooms, billets, slabs	0.78–0.90 **C**, 0.60–0.90 **Mn**, 0.050 **P**, 0.050 **S**, 0.35 **Si**	
AS 1442	Grade AS 1442/K1082	Australia	Bar, blooms, billets, slabs	0.78–0.90 **C**, 0.60–0.90 **Mn**, 0.050 **P**, 0.050 **S**, 0.10–0.35 **Si**	
JIS G 3502	SWRS 80A	Japan	Wire, rod	0.78–0.83 **C**, 0.30–0.60 **Mn**, 0.025 **P**, 0.025 **S**, 0.12–0.32 **Si**, 0.20 **Cu**	
JIS G 3502	SWRS 80B	Japan	Wire, rod	0.78–0.83 **C**, 0.60–0.90 **Mn**, 0.025 **P**, 0.025 **S**, 0.12–0.32 **Si**, 0.20 **Cu**	
NF A 35-051	FM 85, grade 3	France	Wire, rod	0.76–0.93 **C**, 0.60–0.90 **Mn**, 0.040 **P**, 0.040 **S**, 0.10–0.35 **Si**	
NF A 35-051	FM 82	France	Wire, rod	0.76–0.89 **C**, 0.60–0.90 **Mn**, 0.040 **P**, 0.040 **S**, 0.10–0.35 **Si**	
IS 4454 (Part 1)	Grade 4	India	Wire	0.75–1.0 **C**, 0.8 **Mn**, 0.025 **P**, 0.025 **S**, 0.10–0.35 **Si**, 0.12 **Cu**, 0.040 **P+S**	**Cold drawn**: (0.38) **diam**, (2620) **TS**
IS 4454 (Part 1)	Grade 3	India	Wire	0.75–1.0 **C**, 0.8 **Mn**, 0.030 **P**, 0.030 **S**, 0.10–0.35 **Si**, 0.12 **Cu**, 0.050 **P+S**	**Cold drawn**: (0.38) **diam**, (2430) **TS**
JIS G 4801	SUP 3	Japan	Bar, wire, rod	0.75–0.90 **C**, 0.30–0.60 **Mn**, 0.035 **P**, 0.035 **S**, 0.15–0.35 **Si**, 0.30 **Cu**	**Quenched and tempered**: all **diam**, (1079) **TS**, (834) **YS**, 8 **El**
AMS 5110D		US	Wire	0.75–0.88 **C**, 0.60–0.90 **Mn**, 0.040 **P**, 0.050 **S**, 0.10–0.30 **Si**	**Cold drawn (wire)**: ≤0.062 (≤1.57) **diam**, 300 (2068) **TS**; **Stress relieved (spring)**: ≤0.062 (≤1.57) **diam**, 300 (2068) **TS**

WROUGHT CARBON STEELS

specification number	designation	country	product forms	composition	mechanical properties (see page iv for explanation)
DGN–B–301	1080	Mexico	Bar	0.75–0.88 **C**, 0.60–0.90 **Mn**, 0.040 **P**, 0.050 **S**, 0.10–0.20 **Si**	**Forged or hot rolled, cold rolled and/or cold finished**: all **diam**, (775) **TS**, (422) **YS**, 10 **El**
ASTM A 713	Grade 1080	US	Wire	0.75–0.88 **C**, 0.60–0.90 **Mn**, 0.040 **P**, 0.050 **S**	
AISI 1080		US	Bar	0.75–0.88 **C**, 0.60–0.90 **Mn**, 0.040 **P**, 0.050 **S**	
COPANT 330	1080	COPANT	Bar, shapes	0.75–0.88 **C**, 0.60–0.90 **Mn**, 0.040 **P**, 0.050 **S**	
COPANT 331	1080	COPANT	Bar	0.75–0.88 **C**, 0.60–0.90 **Mn**, 0.040 **P**, 0.050 **S**	
MIL–S–16974E	No. 1080	US	Bar, billets, blooms, slabs	0.75–0.88 **C**, 0.60–0.90 **Mn**, 0.040 **P**, 0.050 **S**, 0.15–0.30 **Si**	
MIL–S–16788A	Class C8	US	Blooms, billets, slabs	0.75–0.88 **C**, 0.60–0.90 **Mn**, 0.040 **P**, 0.050 **S**	
AISI 1		US	Wire, rod	0.75–0.88 **C**, 0.60–0.90 **Mn**, 0.040 **P**, 0.050 **S**	
ANSI/ASTM A 576	1080	US	Bar	0.75–0.88 **C**, 0.60–0.90 **Mn**, 0.040 **P**, 0.050 **S**	
ASTM A 689	1080	US	Bar	0.75–0.88 **C**, 0.60–0.90 **Mn**, 0.040 **P**, 0.050 **S**	
ASTM A 713	1080	US	Wire	0.75–0.88 **C**, 0.60–0.90 **Mn**, 0.040 **P**, 0.050 **S**	
ANSI/ASTM A 29	1080	US	Bar	0.75–0.88 **C**, 0.60–0.90 **Mn**, 0.040 **P**, 0.050 **S**	
BS 1449: Part 1	Grade 80	UK	Plate, sheet, strip	0.75–0.85 **C**, 0.50–0.90 **Mn**, 0.045 **P**, 0.045 **S**, 0.05–0.35 **Si**	
BS 970 Part 5	070A78	UK	Blooms, billets, bar, forgings	0.75–0.82 **C**, 0.60–0.80 **Mn**, 0.10–0.35 **Si**	
BS 970: Part 1	060A78	UK	Blooms, billets, slabs, bar, rod, forgings	0.75–0.82 **C**, 0.50–0.70 **Mn**	
BS 970: Part 1	070A78	UK	Blooms, billets, slabs, bar, rod, forgings	0.75–0.82 **C**, 0.60–0.80 **Mn**	
BS 970: Part 1	080A78	UK	Blooms, billets, slabs, bar, rod, forgings	0.75–0.82 **C**, 0.70–0.90 **Mn**	
JIS G 3502	SWRS 77A	Japan	Wire, rod	0.75–0.80 **C**, 0.30–0.60 **Mn**, 0.025 **P**, 0.025 **S**, 0.12–0.32 **Si**, 0.20 **Cu**	
JIS G 3502	SWRS 77B	Japan	Wire, rod	0.75–0.80 **C**, 0.60–0.90 **Mn**, 0.025 **P**, 0.025 **S**, 0.12–0.32 **Si**, 0.20 **Cu**	
NF A 35–590	1304($Y_3$75)	France	Bar, forgings	0.75 **C**, 0.60–0.80 **Mn**, 0.035 **P**, 0.035 **S**, 0.15–0.40 **Si**	
QQ–S–700D	SAE 1080	US	Sheet, strip	0.74–0.88 **C**, 0.60–0.90 **Mn**, 0.040 **P**, 0.050 **S**	
AISI 1080		US	Plate	0.74–0.88 **C**, 0.60–0.90 **Mn**, 0.040 **P**, 0.050 **S**	
ANSI/ASTM A 680	1080	US	Strip	0.74–0.88 **C**, 0.60–0.90 **Mn**, 0.040 **P**, 0.050 **S**, 0.15–0.30 **Si**	**Cold–rolled**
ANSI/ASTM A 684	1080	US	Strip	0.74–0.88 **C**, 0.60–0.90 **Mn**, 0.040 **P**, 0.050 **S**, 0.15–0.30 **Si**	
ANSI/ASTM A 682	1080	US	Strip	0.74–0.88 **C**, 0.60–0.90 **Mn**, 0.040 **P**, 0.050 **S**, 0.15–0.30 **Si**	
NF A 35–051	FM 80	France	Wire, rod	0.74–0.87 **C**, 0.60–0.90 **Mn**, 0.040 **P**, 0.040 **S**, 0.10–0.35 **Si**	
JIS G 3506	SWRH 77A	Japan	Wire, rod	0.74–0.81 **C**, 0.30–0.60 **Mn**, 0.030 **P**, 0.030 **S**, 0.15–0.35 **Si**	
JIS G 3506	SWRH 77B	Japan	Wire, rod	0.74–0.81 **C**, 0.60–0.90 **Mn**, 0.030 **P**, 0.030 **S**, 0.15–0.35 **Si**	
JIS G 3502	SWRS 75A	Japan	Wire, rod	0.73–0.78 **C**, 0.30–0.60 **Mn**, 0.025 **P**, 0.025 **S**, 0.12–0.32 **Si**, 0.20 **Cu**	

WROUGHT CARBON STEELS

specification number	designation	country	product forms	composition	mechanical properties (see page iv for explanation)
JIS G 3502	SWRS 75B	Japan	Wire, rod	0.73–0.78 **C**, 0.60–0.90 **Mn**, 0.025 **P**, 0.025 **S**, 0.12–0.32 **Si**, 0.20 **Cu**	
DGN–B–293		Mexico	Wire	0.72–0.93 **C**, 0.40–1.10 **Mn**, 0.040 **P**, 0.050 **S**, 0.10–0.35 **Si**	**Cold drawn**: (2.00) **diam**, (2156) **TS**, (1725) **YS**, 4 **El**
AISI 1078		US	Plate	0.72–0.86 **C**, 0.30–0.60 **Mn**, 0.040 **P**, 0.050 **S**	
ISO 683/XIV	1	ISO	Bar, rod, wire	0.72–0.85 **C**, 0.50–0.80 **Mn**, 0.050 **P**, 0.050 **S**, 0.15–0.40 **Si**	**Quenched and tempered**: all **diam**, (1180) **TS**, (880) **YS**, 6 **El**
ISO 683/XIV	2	ISO	Bar, rod, wire	0.72–0.85 **C**, 0.50–0.80 **Mn**, 0.035 **P**, 0.035 **S**, 0.15–0.40 **Si**	**Quenched and tempered**: all **diam**, (1180) **TS**, (880) **YS**, 6 **El**
NBN 253–05	C 79	Belgium	Wire	0.72–0.85 **C**, 0.50–0.80 **Mn**, 0.035 **P**, 0.035 **S**, 0.15–0.40 **Si**	**Annealed or quenched and tempered**: (≤12) **diam**, (1175) **TS**, (885) **YS**, 6 **El**
DGN–B–301	1078	Mexico	Bar	0.72–0.85 **C**, 0.30–0.60 **Mn**, 0.040 **P**, 0.050 **S**, 0.10–0.20 **Si**	**Forged or hot rolled, cold rolled and/or cold finished**: all **diam**, (686) **TS**, (382) **YS**, 12 **El**
ASTM A 713	Grade 1078	US	Wire	0.72–0.85 **C**, 0.30–0.60 **Mn**, 0.040 **P**, 0.050 **S**	
AISI 1078		US	Bar	0.72–0.85 **C**, 0.30–0.60 **Mn**, 0.040 **P**, 0.050 **S**	
AISI 1078		US	Wire, rod	0.72–0.85 **C**, 0.30–0.60 **Mn**, 0.040 **P**, 0.050 **S**	
ASTM A 713	1078	US	Wire	0.72–0.85 **C**, 0.30–0.60 **Mn**, 0.040 **P**, 0.050 **S**	
ANSI/ASTM A 576	1078	US	Bar	0.72–0.85 **C**, 0.30–0.60 **Mn**, 0.040 **P**, 0.050 **S**	
ASTM A 689	1078	US	Bar	0.72–0.85 **C**, 0.30–0.60 **Mn**, 0.040 **P**, 0.050 **S**	
ANSI/ASTM A 29	1078	US	Bar	0.72–0.85 **C**, 0.30–0.60 **Mn**, 0.040 **P**, 0.050 **S**	
NF A 35–051	FM 78	France	Wire, rod	0.72–0.83 **C**, 0.60–0.90 **Mn**, 0.040 **P**, 0.040 **S**, 0.10–0.35 **Si**	
ANSI/ASTM A 228		US	Wire: music spring	0.70–1.00 **C**, 0.20–0.60 **Mn**, 0.025 **P**, 0.030 **S**, 0.10–0.30 **Si**	**Cold drawn**: 0.004 (0.10) **diam**, 439 (3030) **TS**
ANSI/ASTM A 228		US	Wire	0.70–1.00 **C**, 0.20–0.60 **Mn**, 0.025 **P**, 0.030 **S**, 0.10–0.30 **Si**	**Hard drawn**: 0.004 (0.10) **diam**, 439 (3030) **TS**
AMS 5112G		US	Wire	0.70–1.00 **C**, 0.20–0.60 **Mn**, 0.025 **P**, 0.030 **S**, 0.10–0.30 **Si**	**Cold drawn (wire)**: 0.004 (0.10) **diam**, 439 (3027) **TS**; **Stress relieved (spring)**: 0.032 (0.81) **diam**, 327 (2255) **TS**
BS 5216 Section4	Grade 3	UK	Wire: aircraft quality	0.70–1.00 **C**, 0.25–0.75 **Mn**, 0.030 **P**, 0.030 **S**, 0.35 **Si**	**Cold drawn**: (100) **diam**, (3020) **TS**
QQ–W–470b		US	Wire	0.70–1.09 **C**, 0.20–0.60 **Mn**, 0.025 **P**, 0.03 **S**, 0.12–0.30 **Si**	**Cold drawn**: .036 **diam**, 321 (2213) **TS**
BS 2S.513		UK	Strip, spring: aircraft quality	0.70–0.90 **C**, 0.35–0.90 **Mn**, 0.040 **P**, 0.040 **S**, 0.10–0.35 **Si**	**Annealed, hardened and tempered**: all **diam**
BS S.203		UK	Wire, springs: aircraft quality	0.70–0.85 **C**, 0.65–0.80 **Mn**, 0.030 **P**, 0.030 **S**, 0.10–0.35 **Si**	**Hardened and tempered**: (0.61–1.22) **diam**, (1775) **TS**
ANSI/ASTM A 2		US	Rail: chemical composition dependent on weight	0.70–0.85 **C**, 0.60–0.90 **Mn**, 0.04 **P**, 0.10–0.40 **Si**	**As rolled**
NF A 35–051	FM 76	France	Wire,rod	0.70–0.81 **C**, 0.60–0.90 **Mn**, 0.040 **P**, 0.040 **S**, 0.10–0.35 **Si**	
DGN–B–301	1074	Mexico	Bar	0.70–0.80 **C**, 0.50–0.80 **Mn**, 0.040 **P**, 0.050 **S**, 0.10–0.20 **Si**	**Forged or hot rolled, cold rolled and cold finished**: all **diam**, (726) **TS**, (402) **YS**, 12 **El**
DIN 17222	Grade MK 75	Germany	Strip	0.70–0.80 **C**, 0.40–0.60 **Mn**, 0.035 **P**, 0.035 **S**, 0.15–0.25 **Si**	**Solution annealed**: all **diam**, (638) **TS**, (294) **YS**, 25 **El**; **Quenched and tempered**: all **diam**, (1569) **TS**, (1471) **YS**, 6 **El**
DIN 17222	Grade C 75	Germany	Strip	0.70–0.80 **C**, 0.60–0.80 **Mn**, 0.045 **P**, 0.045 **S**, 0.25–0.50 **Si**	**Solution annealed**: all **diam**, (638) **TS**, (294) **YS**, 25 **El**; **Quenched and tempered**: all **diam**, (1177) **TS**, (1079) **YS**, 6 **El**

WROUGHT CARBON STEELS

specification number	designation	country	product forms	composition	mechanical properties (see page iv for explanation)
DIN 17222	MK75/1248	Germany	Strip	0.70–0.80 **C**, 0.40–0.60 **Mn**, 0.035 **P**, 0.035 **S**, 0.15–0.25 **Si**	**Softened and annealed**: all **diam**, (637) max **TS**, (294) max **YS**, 25 **El**; **Hardened and tempered**: all **diam**, (1569) **TS**, (1471) **YS**, 6 **El**
DIN 17222	C75/0773	Germany	Strip	0.70–0.80 **C**, 0.60–0.80 **Mn**, 0.045 **P**, 0.045 **S**, 0.25–0.50 **Si**	**Softened, annealed**: all **diam**, (637) max **TS**, (294) max **YS**, 25 **El**; **Hardened, tempered**: all **diam**, (1176) **TS**, (1079) **YS**, 6 **El**
ASTM A 713	Grade 1074	US	Wire	0.70–0.80 **C**, 0.50–0.80 **Mn**, 0.040 **P**, 0.050 **S**	
ASTM A 713	Grade 1075	US	Wire	0.70–0.80 **C**, 0.40–0.70 **Mn**, 0.040 **P**, 0.050 **S**	
BS 1429	En. 42C	UK	Wire	0.70–0.80 **C**, 0.55–0.80 **Mn**, 0.05 **P**, 0.05 **S**, 0.35 **Si**	
NF A 35–553	XC 75	France	Strip	0.70–0.80 **C**, 0.40–0.70 **Mn**, 0.035 **P**, 0.035 **S**, 0.15–0.30 **Si**	
COPANT 331	1075	COPANT	Bar	0.70–0.80 **C**, 0.40–0.70 **Mn**, 0.040 **P**, 0.050 **S**	
COPANT 333	1074	COPANT	Wire, rod	0.70–0.80 **C**, 0.50–0.80 **Mn**, 0.040 **P**, 0.050 **S**	
COPANT 333	1075	COPANT	Wire, rod	0.70–0.80 **C**, 0.40–0.70 **Mn**, 0.040 **P**, 0.050 **S**	
DGN–B–301	1075	Mexico	Bar	0.70–0.80 **C**, 0.40–0.70 **Mn**, 0.040 **P**, 0.050 **S**, 0.10–0.20 **Si**	
AISI 1074		US	Wire, rod	0.70–0.80 **C**, 0.50–0.80 **Mn**, 0.040 **P**, 0.050 **S**	
AISI 1075		US	Wire, rod	0.70–0.80 **C**, 0.40–0.70 **Mn**, 0.040 **P**, 0.050 **S**	
ASTM A 713	1074	US	Wire	0.70–0.80 **C**, 0.50–0.80 **Mn**, 0.040 **P**, 0.050 **S**	
ASTM A 713	1075	US	Wire	0.70–0.80 **C**, 0.40–0.70 **Mn**, 0.040 **P**, 0.050 **S**	
ANSI/ASTM A 29	1074	US	Bar	0.70–0.80 **C**, 0.50–0.80 **Mn**, 0.040 **P**, 0.050 **S**	
ANSI/ASTM A 29	1075	US	Bar	0.70–0.80 **C**, 0.40–0.70 **Mn**, 0.040 **P**, 0.050 **S**	
DIN 17222	Grade M 75	Germany	Strip	0.70–0.79 **C**, 0.30–0.60 **Mn**, 0.045 **P**, 0.045 **S**, 0.10–0.25 **Si**	**Solution annealed**: all **diam**, (638) **TS**, (294) **YS**, 25 **El**; **Quenched and tempered**: all **diam**, (1177) **TS**, (1079) **YS**, 6 **El**
DIN 17222	M75/0763	Germany	Strip	0.70–0.79 **C**, 0.30–0.60 **Mn**, 0.045 **P**, 0.045 **S**, 0.10–0.25 **Si**	**Softened, annealed**: all **diam**, (637) max **TS**, (294) max **YS**, 25 **El**; **Hardened, tempered**: all **diam**, (1176) **TS**, (1079) **YS**, 6 **El**
DIN 17140	Grade D75–2	Germany	Wire, rod	0.70–0.79 **C**, 0.30–0.70 **Mn**, 0.040 **P**, 0.040 **S**, 0.10–0.30 **Si**, 0.007 **N**	
BS 970 Part 5	070A72	UK	Blooms, billets, bar, forgings	0.70–0.75 **C**, 0.60–0.80 **Mn**, 0.10–0.35 **Si**	
BS 970: Part 1	060A72	UK	Blooms, billets, slabs, bar, rod, forgings	0.70–0.75 **C**, 0.50–0.70 **Mn**	
BS 970: Part 1	070A72	UK	Blooms, billets, slabs, bar, rod, forgings	0.70–0.75 **C**, 0.60–0.80 **Mn**	
BS 970: Part 1	080A72	UK	Blooms, billets, slabs, bar, rod, forgings	0.70–0.75 **C**, 0.70–0.90 **Mn**	
JIS G 3502	SWRS 72A	Japan	Wire, rod	0.70–0.75 **C**, 0.30–0.60 **Mn**, 0.025 **P**, 0.025 **S**, 0.12–0.32 **Si**, 0.20 **Cu**	
JIS G 3502	SWRS 72B	Japan	Wire, rod	0.70–0.75 **C**, 0.60–0.90 **Mn**, 0.025 **P**, 0.025 **S**, 0.12–0.32 **Si**, 0.20 **Cu**	

WROUGHT CARBON STEELS

specification number	designation	country	product forms	composition	mechanical properties (see page iv for explanation)
ANSI/ASTM A 1		US	Rail: chemical composition dependent on weight	0.69–0.82 **C**, 0.70–1.00 **Mn**, 0.04 **P**, 0.05 **S**, 0.10–0.25 **Si**	**121 and over lbs/yd (60.1 and over kg/m)**: all **diam**
QQ–S–700D	SAE 1074	US	Sheet, strip	0.69–0.80 **C**, 0.50–0.80 **Mn**, 0.040 **P**, 0.050 **S**	
AISI 1074		US	Plate	0.69–0.80 **C**, 0.50–0.80 **Mn**, 0.040 **P**, 0.050 **S**	
MIL–S–46049B	AISI 1074	US	Strip	0.69–0.80 **C**, 0.50–0.80 **Mn**, 0.040 **P**, 0.050 **S**, 0.15–0.30 **Si**	
ANSI/ASTM A 680	1074	US	Strip	0.69–0.80 **C**, 0.50–0.80 **Mn**, 0.040 **P**, 0.050 **S**, 0.15–0.30 **Si**	**Cold–rolled**
ANSI/ASTM A 684	1074	US	Strip	0.69–0.80 **C**, 0.50–0.80 **Mn**, 0.040 **P**, 0.050 **S**, 0.15–0.30 **Si**	
ANSI/ASTM A 682	1074	US	Strip	0.69–0.80 **C**, 0.50–0.80 **Mn**, 0.040 **P**, 0.050 **S**, 0.15–0.30 **Si**	
JIS G 3506	SWRH 72A	Japan	Wire, rod	0.69–0.76 **C**, 0.30–0.60 **Mn**, 0.030 **P**, 0.030 **S**, 0.15–0.35 **Si**	
JIS G 3506	SWRH 72B	Japan	Wire, rod	0.69–0.76 **C**, 0.60–0.90 **Mn**, 0.030 **P**, 0.030 **S**, 0.15–0.35 **Si**	
AMS 5120H		US	Strip	0.68–0.80 **C**, 0.50–0.80 **Mn**, 0.040 **P**, 0.050 **S**, 0.10–0.30 **Si**	**Cold rolled and annealed**
DIN 17222	Grade 71 Si 7	Germany	Strip	0.68–0.75 **C**, 0.60–0.80 **Mn**, 0.035 **P**, 0.035 **S**, 1.5–1.8 **Si**	**Solution annealed**: all **diam**, (834) **TS**, (363) **YS**, 18 **El**; **Quenched and tempered**: all **diam**, (1863) **TS**, (1765) **YS**, 4 **El**
DIN 17212	Grade Cf 70	Germany	Blooms, slabs, billets, wire, bar, plate, sheet, strip, tube, forgings	0.68–0.75 **C**, 0.20–0.35 **Mn**, 0.025 **P**, 0.035 **S**, 0.15–0.35 **Si**	**Quenched and tempered**: (≤16) **diam**, (780) **TS**, (560) **YS**, 11 **El**
NF A 35–051	FM 75, grade 3	France	Wire, rod	0.67–0.81 **C**, 0.60–0.90 **Mn**, 0.040 **P**, 0.040 **S**, 0.10–0.35 **Si**	
ANSI/ASTM A 1		US	Rail: chemical composition dependent on weight	0.67–0.80 **C**, 0.70–1.00 **Mn**, 0.04 **P**, 0.05 **S**, 0.10–0.25 **Si**	**91 to 120 lbs/yd (45.2 to 59.6 kg/m)**: all **diam**
NF A 35–051	FM 72	France	Wire, rod	0.67–0.78 **C**, 0.60–0.90 **Mn**, 0.040 **P**, 0.040 **S**, 0.10–0.35 **Si**	
SIS 14 17 78	SIS 17 78–04	Sweden	Strip	0.66–0.80 **C**, 0.40–0.90 **Mn**, 0.030 **P**, 0.030 **S**, 0.15–0.40 **Si**	**Quenched**: (<0.125) **diam**, (1860) **TS**
SIS 14 17 78	SIS 17 78–11	Sweden	Strip	0.66–0.80 **C**, 0.40–0.90 **Mn**, 0.030 **P**, 0.030 **S**, 0.15–0.40 **Si**	**Cold worked**: (≤2) **diam**, (440) **YS**, 20 **El**
SIS 14 17 78	SIS 17 78–02	Sweden	Strip	0.66–0.80 **C**, 0.40–0.90 **Mn**, 0.030 **P**, 0.030 **S**, 0.15–0.40 **Si**	**Annealed**: (≤2) **diam**, (370) **YS**, 26 **El**
ANSI/ASTM A 679		US	Wire	0.65–1.00 **C**, 0.20–1.30 **Mn**, 0.040 **P**, 0.050 **S**, 0.10–0.40 **Si**	**Cold drawn**: 0.020 (0.51) **diam**, 350 (2410) **TS**
ANSI/ASTM A 679		US	Wire: spring	0.65–1.00 **C**, 0.20–1.30 **Mn**, 0.040 **P**, 0.050 **S**, 0.10–0.40 **Si**	**Hard drawn spring quality**: 0.020 (0.51) **diam**, 350 (2410) **TS**, 387 (2670) **YS**
AIR 9160/C 101	9160C391	France	Wire	0.65–0.95 **C**, 0.30–0.80 **Mn**, 0.025 **P**, 0.020 **S**, 0.10–0.35 **Si**	**Quenched and tempered**: (0.20–0.30) **diam**, (2500) **TS**
SIS 14 17 70	SIS 17 70–03	Sweden	Bar, wire	0.65–0.80 **C**, 0.50–0.80 **Mn**, 0.035 **P**, 0.035 **S**, 0.15–0.40 **Si**	**Quenched and tempered**: (2.0–2.5) **diam**, (1600) **TS**, (1350) **YS**
SIS 14 17 70	SIS 17 70–00	Sweden	Bar, strip, wire	0.65–0.80 **C**, 0.50–0.80 **Mn**, 0.035 **P**, 0.035 **S**, 0.15–0.40 **Si**	
SIS 14 17 70	SIS 17 70–02	Sweden	Bar, strip, wire	0.65–0.80 **C**, 0.50–0.80 **Mn**, 0.035 **P**, 0.035 **S**, 0.15–0.40 **Si**	
NF A 35–051	FM 70	France	Wire, rod	0.65–0.76 **C**, 0.60–0.90 **Mn**, 0.040 **P**, 0.040 **S**, 0.10–0.35 **Si**	
ASTM A 713	Grade 1572	US	Wire	0.65–0.76 **C**, 1.00–1.30 **Mn**, 0.040 **P**, 0.050 **S**	
AISI 1070		US	Plate	0.65–0.76 **C**, 0.60–0.90 **Mn**, 0.040 **P**, 0.050 **S**	
DGN–B–301	1572	Mexico	Bar	0.65–0.76 **C**, 1.00–1.30 **Mn**, 0.040 **P**, 0.050 **S**	
ANSI/ASTM A 29	1572	US	Bar	0.65–0.76 **C**, 1.00–1.30 **Mn**, 0.040 **P**, 0.050 **S**	

WROUGHT CARBON STEELS

specification number	designation	country	product forms	composition	mechanical properties (see page iv for explanation)
ASTM A 689	1572	US	Bar: spring	0.65–0.76 **C**, 1.00–1.30 **Mn**, 0.040 **P**, 0.050 **S**	
COPANT 333	1071	COPANT	Wire, rod	0.65–0.76 **C**, 0.75–1.05 **Mn**, 0.040 **P**, 0.050 **S**	
DGN–B–301	1072	Mexico	Bar	0.65–0.76 **C**, 1.00–1.30 **Mn**, 0.040 **P**, 0.050 **S**, 0.10–0.20 **Si**	
ANSI/ASTM A 680	1070	US	Strip	0.65–0.76 **C**, 0.60–0.90 **Mn**, 0.040 **P**, 0.050 **S**, 0.15–0.30 **Si**	**Cold–rolled**
ASTM A 713	1572	US	Wire	0.65–0.76 **C**, 1.00–1.30 **Mn**, 0.040 **P**, 0.050 **S**	
ANSI/ASTM A 576	1572	US	Bar	0.65–0.76 **C**, 1.00–1.30 **Mn**, 0.040 **P**, 0.050 **S**	
ANSI/ASTM A 684	1070	US	Strip	0.65–0.76 **C**, 0.60–0.90 **Mn**, 0.040 **P**, 0.050 **S**, 0.15–0.30 **Si**	
ANSI/ASTM A 682	1070	US	Strip	0.65–0.76 **C**, 0.60–0.90 **Mn**, 0.040 **P**, 0.050 **S**, 0.15–0.30 **Si**	
DGN–B–301	1070	Mexico	Bar	0.65–0.75 **C**, 0.60–0.90 **Mn**, 0.040 **P**, 0.050 **S**, 0.10–0.20 **Si**	**Forged or hot rolled, cold rolled and cold finished**: all **diam**, (706) **TS**, (382) **YS**, 12 **El**
ASTM A 713	Grade 1069	US	Wire	0.65–0.75 **C**, 0.40–0.70 **Mn**, 0.040 **P**, 0.050 **S**	
ASTM A 713	Grade 1070	US	Wire	0.65–0.75 **C**, 0.60–0.90 **Mn**, 0.040 **P**, 0.050 **S**	
AISI 1070		US	Bar	0.65–0.75 **C**, 0.60–0.90 **Mn**, 0.040 **P**, 0.050 **S**	
BS 1449: Part 1	Grade 70	UK	Plate, sheet, strip	0.65–0.75 **C**, 0.50–0.90 **Mn**, 0.045 **P**, 0.045 **S**, 0.05–0.35 **Si**	
MIL–S–11713B		US	Strip	0.65–0.75 **C**, 0.35–0.45 **Mn**, 0.025 **P**, 0.025 **S**, 0.15–0.25 **Si**	
MIL–S–11713B	2	US	Strip	0.65–0.75 **C**, 0.35–0.45 **Mn**, 0.025 **P**, 0.025 **S**, 0.15–0.25 **Si**	**Soft annealed**
MIL–S–12504D		US	Bar	0.65–0.75 **C**, 0.60–0.90 **Mn**, 0.04 **P**, 0.05 **S**, 0.15–0.30 **Si**, 0.35 **Cu**	**Annealed, cold drawn**
AS 1446	Grade AS 1446/S1070	Australia	Plate	0.65–0.75 **C**, 0.60–0.90 **Mn**, 0.050 **P**, 0.050 **S**, 0.35 **Si**	
COPANT 330	1070	COPANT	Bar, shapes	0.65–0.75 **C**, 0.60–0.90 **Mn**, 0.040 **P**, 0.050 **S**	
COPANT 331	1070	COPANT	Bar	0.65–0.75 **C**, 0.60–0.90 **Mn**, 0.040 **P**, 0.050 **S**	
COPANT 333	1069	COPANT	Wire, rod	0.65–0.75 **C**, 0.40–0.70 **Mn**, 0.040 **P**, 0.050 **S**	
COPANT 333	1070	COPANT	Wire, rod	0.65–0.75 **C**, 0.60–0.90 **Mn**, 0.040 **P**, 0.050 **S**	
COPANT 333	1072	COPANT	Wire, rod	0.65–0.75 **C**, 1.00–1.30 **Mn**, 0.040 **P**, 0.050 **S**	
DGN–B–301	1069	Mexico	Bar	0.65–0.75 **C**, 0.40–0.70 **Mn**, 0.040 **P**, 0.050 **S**, 0.10–0.20 **Si**	
AISI 1069		US	Wire, rod	0.65–0.75 **C**, 0.40–0.70 **Mn**, 0.040 **P**, 0.050 **S**	
AISI 1070		US	Wire, rod	0.65–0.75 **C**, 0.60–0.90 **Mn**, 0.040 **P**, 0.050 **S**	
ASTM A 713	1069	US	Wire	0.65–0.75 **C**, 0.40–0.70 **Mn**, 0.040 **P**, 0.050 **S**	
ASTM A 713	1070	US	Wire	0.65–0.75 **C**, 0.60–0.90 **Mn**, 0.040 **P**, 0.050 **S**	
ANSI/ASTM A 576	1070	US	Bar	0.65–0.75 **C**, 0.60–0.90 **Mn**, 0.040 **P**, 0.050 **S**	
ASTM A 689	1070	US	Bar	0.65–0.75 **C**, 0.60–0.90 **Mn**, 0.040 **P**, 0.050 **S**	
ANSI/ASTM A 29	1069	US	Bar	0.65–0.75 **C**, 0.40–0.70 **Mn**, 0.040 **P**, 0.050 **S**	
ANSI/ASTM A 29	1070	US	Bar	0.65–0.75 **C**, 0.60–0.90 **Mn**, 0.040 **P**, 0.050 **S**	
ANSI/ASTM A 29	1071	US	Bar	0.65–0.75 **C**, 0.75–1.05 **Mn**, 0.040 **P**, 0.050 **S**	
AS 1442	Grade AS 1442/S1070	Australia	Bar, blooms, billets, slabs	0.65–0.75 **C**, 0.60–0.90 **Mn**, 0.050 **P**, 0.050 **S**, 0.35 **Si**	

specification number	designation	country	product forms	composition	mechanical properties (see page iv for explanation)
AS 1442	Grade AS 1442/K1070	Australia	Bar, blooms, billets, slabs	0.65–0.75 **C**, 0.60–0.90 **Mn**, 0.050 **P**, 0.050 **S**, 0.10–0.35 **Si**	
NF A 35–553	XC 68	France	Strip	0.65–0.73 **C**, 0.40–0.70 **Mn**, 0.035 **P**, 0.035 **S**, 0.15–0.35 **Si**	
DIN 17222	Grade Ck 67	Germany	Strip	0.65–0.72 **C**, 0.60–0.80 **Mn**, 0.035 **P**, 0.035 **S**, 0.25–0.50 **Si**	**Solution annealed**: all **diam**, (638) **TS**, (294) **YS**, 25 **El**; **Quenched and tempered**: all **diam**, (1373) **TS**, (1274) **YS**, 6 **El**
DIN 17222	Grade C 67	Germany	Strip	0.65–0.72 **C**, 0.50–0.80 **Mn**, 0.045 **P**, 0.045 **S**, 0.25–0.50 **Si**	**Solution annealed**: all **diam**, (638) **TS**, (294) **YS**, 25 **El**; **Quenched and tempered**: all **diam**, (1177) **TS**, (1029) **YS**, 6 **El**
DIN 17222	CK67[3]/1231	Germany	Strip	0.65–0.72 **C**, 0.60–0.80 **Mn**, 0.035 **P**, 0.035 **S**, 0.25–0.50 **Si**	**Softened and annealed**: all **diam**, (637) max **TS**, (294) max **YS**, 25 **El**; **Hardened and tempered**: all **diam**, (1373) **TS**, (1275) **YS**, 6 **El**
DIN 17222	C67/0761	Germany	Strip	0.65–0.72 **C**, 0.60–0.80 **Mn**, 0.045 **P**, 0.045 **S**, 0.25–0.50 **Si**	**Softened, annealed**: all **diam**, (637) max **TS**, (294) max **YS**, 25 **El**; **Hardened, tempered**: all **diam**, (1176) **TS**, (1079) **YS**, 6 **El**
BS 970 Part 5	080A67	UK	Blooms, billets, bar, forgings	0.65–0.70 **C**, 0.70–0.90 **Mn**, 0.10–0.35 **Si**	
BS 970: Part 1	060A67	UK	Blooms, billets, slabs, bar, rod, forgings	0.65–0.70 **C**, 0.50–0.70 **Mn**	
BS 970: Part 1	080A67	UK	Blooms, billets, slabs, bar, rod, forgings	0.65–0.70 **C**, 0.70–0.90 **Mn**	
JIS G 3502	SWRS 67A	Japan	Wire, rod	0.65–0.70 **C**, 0.30–0.60 **Mn**, 0.025 **P**, 0.025 **S**, 0.12–0.32 **Si**, 0.20 **Cu**	
JIS G 3502	SWRS 67B	Japan	Wire, rod	0.65–0.70 **C**, 0.60–0.90 **Mn**, 0.025 **P**, 0.025 **S**, 0.12–0.32 **Si**, 0.20 **Cu**	
NF A 35–590	1305 (Y_3 65)	France	Bar, forgings	0.65 **C**, 0.60–0.80 **Mn**, 0.035 **P**, 0.035 **S**, 0.15–0.40 **Si**	
NF A 35–590	1105 (Y_1 65)	France	Bar, forgings	0.65 **C**, 0.10–0.30 **Mn**, 0.020 **P**, 0.020 **S**, 0.10–0.25 **Si**	
NF A 35–590	1165 (Y_1 xx V)	France	Bar, forgings	0.65 **C**, 0.10–0.30 **Mn**, 0.020 **P**, 0.020 **S**, 0.10–0.25 **Si**	
MIL–S–10520D	Grade 5	US	Bar, forgings	0.65 **C**, 1.00 **Mn**, .040 **P**, .050 **S**, 0.15–0.30 **Si**	**Quenched and tempered**: 1 3/4 **diam**, 76 (524) **YS**
MIL–S–10520D	Grade 7	US	Bar, forgings	0.65 **C**, 1.30 **Mn**, .040 **P**, .050 **S**, 0.15–0.30 **Si**	**Quenched and tempered**: 1 3/4 **diam**, 76 (524) **YS**
ANSI/ASTM A 1		US	Rail: chemical composition dependent on weight	0.64–0.77 **C**, 0.60–0.90 **Mn**, 0.04 **P**, 0.05 **S**, 0.10–0.25 **Si**	**81 to 90 lbs/yd (40.3 to 44.7 kg/m)**: all **diam**
JIS G 3506	SWRH 67A	Japan	Wire, rod	0.64–0.71 **C**, 0.30–0.60 **Mn**, 0.030 **P**, 0.030 **S**, 0.15–0.35 **Si**	
JIS G 3506	SWRH 67B	Japan	Wire, rod	0.64–0.71 **C**, 0.60–0.90 **Mn**, 0.030 **P**, 0.030 **S**, 0.15–0.35 **Si**	
NF A 35–051	FM 68	France	Wire, rod	0.62–0.73 **C**, 0.60–0.90 **Mn**, 0.040 **P**, 0.040 **S**, 0.10–0.35 **Si**	
NF A 33–101	AF 70,2	France	Bar, billets, blooms	0.61 **C**, 0.045 **P**, 0.045 **S**	**Normalized**: all **diam**, (690) **TS**, 15 **El**
SIS 14 17 74	SIS 17 74–06	Sweden	Wire, bar	0.60–0.95 **C**, 0.30–0.80 **Mn**, 0.035 **P**, 0.035 **S**, 0.15–0.40 **Si**	**Patented and cold worked**: (1.6–2.0) **diam**, (2150) **TS**, (1700) **YS**
SIS 14 17 74	SIS 17 74–05	Sweden	Wire, bar	0.60–0.95 **C**, 0.30–0.80 **Mn**, 0.035 **P**, 0.035 **S**, 0.15–0.40 **Si**	**Patented and cold worked**: (1.6–2.0) **diam**, (2050) **TS**, (1650) **YS**
SIS 14 17 74	SIS 17 74–04	Sweden	Wire, bar	0.60–0.95 **C**, 0.30–0.80 **Mn**, 0.035 **P**, 0.035 **S**, 0.15–0.40 **Si**	**Patented and cold worked**: (1.6–2.0) **diam**, (1750) **TS**, (1400) **YS**

specification number	designation	country	product forms	composition	mechanical properties (see page iv for explanation)
BS 2691		UK	Wire	0.60–0.90 **C**, 0.50–0.90 **Mn**, 0.050 **P**, 0.050 **S**, 0.10–0.35 **Si**	**Cold drawn, normal relaxation:** (7) **diam**, (1700) **TS**, (1480) **YS**; **Cold drawn, low relaxation:** (7) **diam**, (1700) **TS**, (1550) **YS**
IS 4454 (Part 1)	Grade 2	India	Wire	0.60–0.85 **C**, 0.8 **Mn**, 0.040 **P**, 0.040 **S**, 0.10–0.35 **Si**, 0.20 **Cu**	**Cold drawn**: (0.38) **diam**, (2040) **TS**
ANSI/ASTM A 230		US	Wire: spring	0.60–0.75 **C**, 0.60–0.90 **Mn**, 0.025 **P**, 0.030 **S**, 0.15–0.35 **Si**	**Oil tempered**: 0.062–0.092 (1.57–2.34) **diam**, 240 (1650) **TS**
ANSI/ASTM A 230		US	Wire	0.60–0.75 **C**, 0.60–0.90 **Mn**, 0.025 **P**, 0.030 **S**, 0.15–0.35 **Si**	**Quenched and tempered:** 0.062–0.092 (1.57–2.34) **diam**, 240 (1650) **TS**
AMS 5115E		US	Wire	0.60–0.75 **C**, 0.50–0.90 **Mn**, 0.025 **P**, 0.030 **S**, 0.10–0.30 **Si**	**Cold drawn, hardened, tempered (wire),Stress relieved (spring)**: 0.093–0.120 (2.36–3.05) **diam**, 210 (1448) **TS**, 45 **El**
AS 1442	Grade AS 1442/XK1068	Australia	Bar, blooms, billets, slabs	0.60–0.75 **C**, 0.60–0.90 **Mn**, 0.050 **P**, 0.050 **S**, 0.10–0.35 **Si**	
NF A 35–051	FM 66	France	Wire, rod	0.60–0.71 **C**, 0.60–0.90 **Mn**, 0.040 **P**, 0.040 **S**, 0.10–0.35 **Si**	
ASTM A 713	Grade 1566	US	Wire	0.60–0.71 **C**, 0.85–1.15 **Mn**, 0.040 **P**, 0.050 **S**	
AISI 1566		US	Bar	0.60–0.71 **C**, 0.85–1.15 **Mn**, 0.040 **P**, 0.050 **S**	
ANSI/ASTM A 29	1566	US	Bar	0.60–0.71 **C**, 0.85–1.15 **Mn**, 0.040 **P**, 0.050 **S**	
ASTM A 689	1566	US	Bar: spring	0.60–0.71 **C**, 0.85–1.15 **Mn**, 0.040 **P**, 0.050 **S**	
COPANT 333	1066	COPANT	Wire, rod	0.60–0.71 **C**, 0.85–1.15 **Mn**, 0.040 **P**, 0.050 **S**	
DGN–B–301	1066	Mexico	Bar	0.60–0.71 **C**, 0.85–1.15 **Mn**, 0.040 **P**, 0.050 **S**, 0.10–0.20 **Si**	
AISI 1566		US	Wire, rod	0.60–0.71 **C**, 0.85–1.15 **Mn**, 0.040 **P**, 0.050 **S**	
ASTM A 713	1566	US	Wire	0.60–0.71 **C**, 0.85–1.15 **Mn**, 0.040 **P**, 0.050 **S**	
ANSI/ASTM A 576	1566	US	Bar	0.60–0.71 **C**, 0.85–1.15 **Mn**, 0.040 **P**, 0.050 **S**	
IS 4454	Grade VW	India	Wire	0.60–0.70 **C**, 0.60–0.90 **Mn**, 0.025 **P**, 0.020 **S**, 0.10–0.25 **Si**, 0.06 **Cu**	**Hardened and tempered:** (1.00) **diam**, (1670) **TS**
DIN 17223/Sheet 2	Grade VD	Germany	Wire	0.60–0.70 **C**, 0.50–0.90 **Mn**, 0.030 **P**, 0.020 **S**, 0.25 **Si**, 0.06 **Cu**	**Quenched and tempered:** (1.00–1.10) **diam**, (1667) **TS**
DIN 17222	Grade 66 Si 7	Germany	Strip	0.60–0.70 **C**, 0.70–1.0 **Mn**, 0.035 **P**, 0.035 **S**, 1.5–1.8 **Si**	**Solution annealed**: all **diam**, (834) **TS**, (363) **YS**, 18 **El**; **Quenched and tempered:** all **diam**, (1765) **TS**, (1667) **YS**, 5 **El**
DGN–B–301	1065	Mexico	Bar	0.60–0.70 **C**, 0.60–0.90 **Mn**, 0.040 **P**, 0.050 **S**, 0.10–0.20 **Si**	**Forged or hot rolled, cold rolled and cold finished**: all **diam**, (686) **TS**, (382) **YS**, 12 **El**
DGN–B–301	1064	Mexico	Bar	0.60–0.70 **C**, 0.50–0.80 **Mn**, 0.040 **P**, 0.050 **S**, 0.10–0.20 **Si**	**Forged or hot rolled, cold rolled and cold finished**: all **diam**, (667) **TS**, (373) **YS**, 12 **El**
DIN 17223	FD/1.1230	Germany	Wire	0.60–0.70 **C**, 0.50–0.90 **Mn**, 0.030 **P**, 0.030 **S**, ≤0.25 **Si**, 0.12 **Cu**	**Quenched and tempered:** (1.00) **diam**, (180) **TS**
DIN 17223	VD/1.1250	Germany	Wire	0.60–0.70 **C**, 0.50–0.90 **Mn**, 0.030 **P**, 0.030 **S**, ≤0.25 **Si**, 0.12 **Cu**	**Quenched and tempered:** (1.00) **diam**, (170) **TS**
ASTM A 713	Grade 1064	US	Wire	0.60–0.70 **C**, 0.50–0.80 **Mn**, 0.040 **P**, 0.050 **S**	
ASTM A 713	Grade 1065	US	Wire	0.60–0.70 **C**, 0.60–0.90 **Mn**, 0.040 **P**, 0.050 **S**	
BS 1429	En. 42B	UK	Wire	0.60–0.70 **C**, 0.55–0.80 **Mn**, 0.05 **P**, 0.05 **S**, 0.35 **Si**	
DGN–B–301	1566	Mexico	Bar	0.60–0.70 **C**, 0.85–1.15 **Mn**, 0.040 **P**, 0.050 **S**	
COPANT 333	1064	COPANT	Wire, rod	0.60–0.70 **C**, 0.50–0.80 **Mn**, 0.040 **P**, 0.050 **S**	

WROUGHT CARBON STEELS

specification number	designation	country	product forms	composition	mechanical properties (see page iv for explanation)
COPANT 333	1065	COPANT	Wire, rod	0.60–0.70 **C**, 0.60–0.90 **Mn**, 0.040 **P**, 0.050 **S**	
AISI 1064		US	Wire, rod	0.60–0.70 **C**, 0.50–0.80 **Mn**, 0.04 **P**, 0.50 **S**	
AISI 1065		US	Wire, rod	0.60–0.70 **C**, 0.60–0.90 **Mn**, 0.040 **P**, 0.050 **S**	
ASTM A 713	1064	US	Wire	0.60–0.70 **C**, 0.50–0.80 **Mn**, 0.040 **P**, 0.050 **S**	
ASTM A 713	1065	US	Wire	0.60–0.70 **C**, 0.60–0.90 **Mn**, 0.040 **P**, 0.050 **S**	
ANSI/ASTM A 29	1064	US	Bar	0.60–0.70 **C**, 0.50–0.80 **Mn**, 0.040 **P**, 0.050 **S**	
ANSI/ASTM A 29	1065	US	Bar	0.60–0.70 **C**, 0.60–0.90 **Mn**, 0.040 **P**, 0.050 **S**	
AS 1442	Grade AS 1442/K1065	Australia	Bar, blooms, billets, slabs	0.60–0.70 **C**, 0.60–0.90 **Mn**, 0.050 **P**, 0.050 **S**, 0.10–0.35 **Si**	
AIR 9160/C25	9160C031	France	Wire, bar, forgings	0.60–0.69 **C**, 0.50–0.80 **Mn**, 0.035 **P**, 0.035 **S**, 0.10–0.40 **Si**	**Annealed**: all **diam**, (730) **TS**, (440) **YS**, 10 **El**; **Quenched and tempered**: (≤16) **diam**, (1000) **TS**, (830) **YS**, 10 **El**
DIN 17140	Grade D65–2	Germany	Wire, rod	0.60–0.69 **C**, 0.10–0.30 **Mn**, 0.040 **P**, 0.040 **S**, 0.10–0.30 **Si**, 0.007 **N**	
DIN 17222	Grade 65 Si 7	Germany	Strip	0.60–0.68 **C**, 0.70–1.0 **Mn**, 0.050 **P**, 0.050 **S**, 1.5–1.8 **Si**	**Solution annealed**: all **diam**, (834) **TS**, (363) **YS**, 18 **El**; **Quenched and tempered**: all **diam**, (1667) **TS**, (1569) **YS**, 5 **El**
BS 970: Part 1	060A62	UK	Blooms, billets, slabs, bar, rod, forgings	0.60–0.65 **C**, 0.50–0.70 **Mn**	
BS 970: Part 1	080A62	UK	Blooms, billets, slabs, bar, rod, forgings	0.60–0.65 **C**, 0.70–0.90 **Mn**	
JIS G 3502	SWRS 62A	Japan	Wire, rod	0.60–0.65 **C**, 0.30–0.60 **Mn**, 0.025 **P**, 0.025 **S**, 0.12–0.32 **Si**, 0.20 **Cu**	
JIS G 3502	SWRS 62B	Japan	Wire, rod	0.60–0.65 **C**, 0.60–0.90 **Mn**, 0.025 **P**, 0.025 **S**, 0.12–0.32 **Si**, 0.20 **Cu**	
BS 1506–162		UK	Bar	0.60 **C**, 0.60–1.00 **Mn**, 0.050 **P**, 0.050 **S**, 0.05–0.35 **Si**	**Normalized**: 4 (100) **diam**, (620) **TS**, (303) **YS**, 18 **El**; **Hardened and tempered TX**: 2 1/2 (65) **diam**
MIL–S–890	Ac	US	Forgings, bar	0.60 **C**, 0.050 **P**, 0.050 **S**	**Annealed or normalized and drawn or quenched and drawn**: all **diam**, 80 (552) **TS**, 45 (310) **YS**, 25 **El**
MIL–S–10520D	Grade 3	US	Bar, forgings	0.60 **C**, 1.00 **Mn**, .040 **P**, .050 **S**, 0.15–0.30 **Si**	**Quenched and tempered**: 1 3/4 **diam**, 76 (524) **YS**
QQ–S–700D	SAE 1065	US	Sheet, strip	0.59–0.70 **C**, 0.60–0.90 **Mn**, 0.040 **P**, 0.050 **S**	
AISI 1064		US	Plate	0.59–0.70 **C**, 0.50–0.80 **Mn**, 0.040 **P**, 0.050 **S**	
AISI 1065		US	Plate	0.59–0.70 **C**, 0.60–0.90 **Mn**, 0.040 **P**, 0.050 **S**	
MIL–S–46049B	AISI 1065	US	Strip	0.59–0.70 **C**, 0.60–0.90 **Mn**, 0.040 **P**, 0.050 **S**, 0.15–0.30 **Si**	
ANSI/ASTM A 680	1064	US	Strip	0.59–0.70 **C**, 0.50–0.80 **Mn**, 0.040 **P**, 0.050 **S**	**Cold–rolled**
ANSI/ASTM A 680	1065	US	Strip	0.59–0.70 **C**, 0.60–0.90 **Mn**, 0.040 **P**, 0.050 **S**, 0.15–0.30 **Si**	**Cold–rolled**
ANSI/ASTM A 682	1064	US	Strip	0.59–0.70 **C**, 0.50–0.80 **Mn**, 0.040 **P**, 0.050 **S**, 0.15–0.30 **Si**	
ANSI/ASTM A 682	1065	US	Strip	0.59–0.70 **C**, 0.60–0.90 **Mn**, 0.040 **P**, 0.050 **S**, 0.15–0.30 **Si**	
ANSI/ASTM A 684	1064	US	Strip	0.59–0.70 **C**, 0.50–0.80 **Mn**, 0.040 **P**, 0.050 **S**, 0.15–0.30 **Si**	

specification number	designation	country	product forms	composition	mechanical properties (see page iv for explanation)
ANSI/ASTM A 684	1065	US	Strip	0.59–0.70 **C**, 0.60–0.90 **Mn**, 0.040 **P**, 0.050 **S**, 0.15–0.30 **Si**	
JIS G 3506	SWRH 62A	Japan	Wire, rod	0.59–0.66 **C**, 0.30–0.60 **Mn**, 0.040 **P**, 0.040 **S**, 0.15–0.35 **Si**	
JIS G 3506	SWRH 62B	Japan	Wire, rod	0.59–0.66 **C**, 0.60–0.90 **Mn**, 0.040 **P**, 0.040 **S**, 0.15–0.35 **Si**	
NF A 35–051	FM 65, grade 1	France	Wire, rod	0.57–0.73 **C**, 0.60–0.90 **Mn**, 0.080 **P**, 0.055 **S**, 0.10–0.35 **Si**	
NF A 35–051	FM 65, grade 3	France	Wire, rod	0.57–0.72 **C**, 0.60–0.90 **Mn**, 0.040 **P**, 0.040 **S**, 0.10–0.35 **Si**	
NF A 35–051	FM 62	France	Wire, rod	0.57–0.68 **C**, 0.60–0.90 **Mn**, 0.040 **P**, 0.040 **S**, 0.10–0.35 **Si**	
ISO R683/1	C60	ISO	Bar, forgings	0.57–0.65 **C**, 0.60–0.90 **Mn**, 0.050 **P**, 0.050 **S**, 0.15–0.40 **Si**	**Quenched and tempered**: all **diam**, (1310) **TS**, (895) **YS**, 11 **El**; **Quenched, tempered and cold-reduced**: all **diam**, (1465) **TS**, (1175) **YS**, 7 **El**
ISO R683/1	C60e	ISO	Bar, forgings	0.57–0.65 **C**, 0.60–0.90 **Mn**, 0.035 **P**, 0.035 **S**, 0.15–0.40 **Si**	**Quenched and tempered**: all **diam**, (1310) **TS**, (895) **YS**, 11 **El**; **Quenched, tempered and cold-reduced**: all **diam**, (1465) **TS**, (1175) **YS**, 7 **El**
VSM 10648	C 60	Switzerland	Bar, sheet, plate	0.57–0.65 **C**, 0.60–0.90 **Mn**, 0.045 **P**, 0.045 **S**, 0.15–0.35 **Si**	**Cold drawn**: (≤5) **diam**, (882) **TS**, (725) **YS**, 4 **El**; **Cold drawn and normalized**: (16–100) **diam**, (686) **TS**, (382) **YS**, 14 **El**; **As rolled**: (5–16) **diam**, (833) **TS**, (568) **YS**, 11 **El**
VSM 10648	CK 60	Switzerland	Bar, sheet, plate	0.57–0.65 **C**, 0.60–0.90 **Mn**, 0.035 **P**, 0.035 **S**, 0.15–0.35 **Si**	**Cold drawn**: (≤5) **diam**, (882) **TS**, (925) **YS**, 4 **El**; **Cold drawn and normalized**: (16–100) **diam**, (686) **TS**, (382) **YS**, 14 **El**; **As rolled**: (5–16) **diam**, (833) **TS**, (568) **YS**, 11 **El**
DIN 1652	C 60 (1.0601)	Germany	Bar	0.57–0.65 **C**, 0.50–0.80 **Mn**, 0.045 **P**, 0.045 **S**, 0.15–0.35 **Si**	**Cold drawn**: all **diam**, (880) **TS**, (725) **YS**, 4 in 80 mm **El**; **Centerless turned and normalized**: all **diam**, (690) **TS**, (380) **YS**, 15 in 80 mm **El**; **Centerless turned and quenched and tempered**: all **diam**, (830) **TS**, (560) **YS**, 12 in 80 mm **El**
DIN 1652	Ck 60 (1.1221)	Germany	Bar	0.57–0.65 **C**, 0.50–0.80 **Mn**, 0.035 **P**, 0.035 **S**, 0.15–0.35 **Si**	**Cold drawn**: all **diam**, (880) **TS**, (725) **YS**, 4 in 80 mm **El**; **Centerless turned and normalized**: all **diam**, (690) **TS**, (380) **YS**, 15 in 80 mm **El**; **Centerless turned and quenched and tempered**: all **diam**, (830) **TS**, (560) **YS**, 12 in 80 mm **El**
DIN 17200	Grade C 60	Germany	Blooms, slabs, billets, wire, bar, plate, sheet, strip, tube, forgings	0.57–0.65 **C**, 0.60–0.90 **Mn**, 0.045 **P**, 0.045 **S**	**Quenched and tempered**: (≤16) **diam**, (834) **TS**, (570) **YS**, 11 **El**; **Normalized**: (>16–40) **diam**, (687) **TS**, (383) **YS**, 14 **El**
DIN 17200	Grade Ck 60	Germany	Blooms, slabs, billets, wire, bar, plate, sheet, strip, tube, forgings	0.57–0.65 **C**, 0.60–0.90 **Mn**, 0.035 **P**, 0.035 **S**, 0.15–0.35 **Si**	**Quenched and tempered**: (≤16) **diam**, (834) **TS**, (570) **YS**, 11 **El**; **Normalized**: (>16–40) **diam**, (687) **TS**, (383) **YS**, 14 **El**
ISO/R 683/111	Type C60ea	ISO	Bar, billet, rod	0.57–0.65 **C**, 0.60–0.90 **Mn**, 0.035 **P**, 0.020–0.035 **S**, 0.15–0.40 **Si**	**Quenched and tempered**: (≤16) **diam**, (833) **TS**, (568) **YS**, 11 **El**
ISO/R 683/111	Type C60eb	ISO	Bar, billet, rod	0.57–0.65 **C**, 0.60–0.90 **Mn**, 0.035 **P**, 0.030–0.050 **S**, 0.15–0.40 **Si**	**Quenched and tempered**: (≤16) **diam**, (833) **TS**, (568) **YS**, 11 **El**
ISO 683/XVIII	c60e	ISO	Bar, wire	0.57–0.65 **C**, 0.60–0.90 **Mn**, 0.035 **P**, 0.035 **S**, 0.15–0.40 **Si**	**Normalized**: all **diam**, (710) **TS**, (380) **YS**, 10 **El**

specification number	designation	country	product forms	composition	mechanical properties (see page iv for explanation)
ISO 683/XVIII	C60ea	ISO	Bar, wire	0.57–0.65 **C**, 0.60–0.90 **Mn**, 0.035 **P**, 0.020–0.035 **S**, 0.15–0.40 **Si**	**Normalized**: all **diam**, (710) **TS**, (380) **YS**, 10 **El**
ISO 683/XVIII	C60eb	ISO	Bar, wire	0.57–0.65 **C**, 0.60–0.90 **Mn**, 0.035 **P**, 0.030–0.050 **S**, 0.15–0.40 **Si**	**Normalized**: all **diam**, (710) **TS**, (380) **YS**, 10 **El**
ISO 683/XVIII	C60	ISO	Bar, wire	0.57–0.65 **C**, 0.60–0.90 **Mn**, 0.050 **P**, 0.050 **S**, 0.15–0.40 **Si**	**Normalized**: all **diam**, (710) **TS**, (380) **YS**, 10 **El**
DIN 17200	Grade Cm 60	Germany	Blooms, slabs, billets, wire, bar, plate, sheet, strip, tube, forgings	0.57–0.65 **C**, 0.60–0.90 **Mn**, 0.035 **P**, 0.020–0.035 **S**, 0.15–0.35 **Si**	**Normalized**: (>16–100) **diam**, (687) **TS**, (383) **YS**, 14 **El**; **Quenched and tempered**: (≤16) **diam**, (834) **TS**, (570) **YS**, 11 **El**
DIN 17222	CK60[3]/1221	Germany	Strip	0.57–0.65 **C**, 0.50–0.80 **Mn**, 0.035 **P**, 0.035 **S**, 0.25–0.50 **Si**	**Softened and annealed**: all **diam**, (588) max **TS**, (275) max **YS**, 30 **El**; **Hardened and tempered**: all **diam**, (1275) **TS**, (1176) **YS**, 7 **El**
DIN 17222	C60/0751	Germany	Strip	0.57–0.65 **C**, 0.50–0.80 **Mn**, 0.045 **P**, 0.045 **S**, 0.25–0.50 **Si**	**Softened and annealed**: all **diam**, (588) max **TS**, (275) max **YS**, 30 **El**; **Hardened and tempered**: all **diam**, (1176) **TS**, (1030) **YS**, 6 **El**
DIN 17222	Grade Ck 60	Germany	Strip	0.57–0.65 **C**, 0.50–0.80 **Mn**, 0.035 **P**, 0.035 **S**, 0.25–0.50 **Si**	**Solution annealed**: all **diam**, (588) **TS**, (274) **YS**, 30 **El**; **Quenched and tempered**: all **diam**, (1275) **TS**, (1177) **YS**, 7 **El**
DIN 17222	Grade C 60	Germany	Strip	0.57–0.65 **C**, 0.50–0.80 **Mn**, 0.045 **P**, 0.045 **S**, 0.25–0.50 **Si**	**Solution annealed**: all **diam**, (588) **TS**, (274) **YS**, 30 **El**; **Quenched and tempered**: all **diam**, (1177) **TS**, (1029) **YS**, 6 **El**
NF A 35-553	XC 60	France	Strip	0.57–0.65 **C**, 0.40–0.70 **Mn**, 0.035 **P**, 0.035 **S**, 0.15–0.35 **Si**	
ISO 683/XIV	6	ISO	Bar, rod, wire	0.57–0.64 **C**, 0.70–1.00 **Mn**, 0.040 **P**, 0.040 **S**, 1.70–2.20 **Si**	**Quenched and tempered**: all **diam**, (1370) **TS**, (1180) **YS**, 5 **El**
ISO 683/XIV	7	ISO	Bar, rod, wire	0.57–0.64 **C**, 0.70–1.00 **Mn**, 0.040 **P**, 0.040 **S**, 1.70–2.20 **Si**, 0.25–0.40 **Cr**	**Quenched and tempered**: all **diam**, (1370) **TS**, (1180) **YS**, 5 **El**
ISO 683/XIV	9	ISO	Bar, rod, wire	0.56–0.64 **C**, 0.70–1.00 **Mn**, 0.035 **P**, 0.035 **S**, 0.15–0.40 **Si**, 0.60–0.90 **Cr**	**Quenched and tempered**: all **diam**, (1370) **TS**, (1180) **YS**, 5 **El**
ISO 683/XIV	10	ISO	Bar, rod, wire	0.56–0.64 **C**, 0.70–1.00 **Mn**, 0.035 **P**, 0.035 **S**, 0.15–0.40 **Si**, 0.60–0.90 **Cr**, 0.0005 **B**	**Quenched and tempered**: all **diam**, (1370) **TS**, (1180) **YS**, 6 **El**
ISO 683/XIV	12	ISO	Bar, rod, wire	0.56–0.64 **C**, 0.70–1.00 **Mn**, 0.035 **P**, 0.035 **S**, 0.15–0.40 **Si**, 0.70–0.90 **Cr**, 0.25–0.35 **Mo**	**Quenched and tempered**: all **diam**, (1370) **TS**, (1180) **YS**, 6 **El**
AS 1442	Grade AS 1442/S1058	Australia	Bar, blooms, billets, slabs	0.56–0.63 **C**, 0.30–0.55 **Mn**, 0.050 **P**, 0.050 **S**, 0.35 **Si**	
AS 1442	Grade AS 1442/K1058	Australia	Bar, blooms, billets, slabs	0.56–0.63 **C**, 0.30–0.55 **Mn**, 0.050 **P**, 0.050 **S**, 0.10–0.35 **Si**	
ANSI/ASTM A 648	Grade III	US	Wire	0.55–0.88 **C**, 0.60–1.10 **Mn**, 0.040 **P**, 0.050 **S**, 0.10–0.35 **Si**	**Hard drawn**: 0.162 **diam**, (1810) **TS**
BS S.202		UK	Wire, springs: aircraft quality	0.55–0.85 **C**, 0.30–1.00 **Mn**, 0.025 **P**, 0.025 **S**, 0.10–0.35 **Si**, 0.08 **Cr**, 0.10 **Ni**	**Tempered**: (0.18–0.38) **diam**, (2470) **TS**
BS 5216 Section3	Grade 2	UK	Wire: aircraft quality	0.55–0.85 **C**, 0.30–1.00 **Mn**, 0.030 **P**, 0.030 **S**, 0.35 **Si**	**Cold drawn**: (200) **diam**, (2340) **TS**
QQ-W-428B	Type I, class II	US	Wire	0.55–0.85 **C**, 0.60–1.20 **Mn**, 0.040 **P**, 0.050 **S**, 0.10–0.35 **Si**	**Quenched and tempered**: 0.0204 **diam**, 324 (2235) **TS**
ANSI/ASTM A 229	Class II	US	Wire: spring	0.55–0.85 **C**, 0.30–1.20 **Mn**, 0.040 **P**, 0.050 **S**, 0.10–0.35 **Si**	**Oil tempered**: 0.020 (0.51) **diam**, 324 (2230) **TS**
ANSI/ASTM A 229	Class II	US	Wire	0.55–0.85 **C**, 0.30–1.20 **Mn**, 0.040 **P**, 0.050 **S**, 0.10–0.35 **Si**	**Quenched and tempered**: 0.020 (0.51) **diam**, 324 (2230) **TS**
ANSI/ASTM A 229	Class I	US	Wire: spring	0.55–0.85 **C**, 0.30–1.20 **Mn**, 0.040 **P**, 0.050 **S**, 0.10–0.35 **Si**	**Oil tempered**: 0.020 (0.51) **diam**, 293 (2020) **TS**

WROUGHT CARBON STEELS

specification number	designation	country	product forms	composition	mechanical properties (see page iv for explanation)
ANSI/ASTM A 229	Class I	US	Wire	0.55–0.85 **C**, 0.30–1.20 **Mn**, 0.040 **P**, 0.050 **S**, 0.10–0.35 **Si**	**Quenched and tempered**: 0.020 (0.51) **diam**, 293 (2020) **TS**
QQ–W–428B	Type I, class I	US	Wire	0.55–0.85 **C**, 0.60–1.20 **Mn**, 0.040 **P**, 0.050 **S**, 0.10–0.35 **Si**	**Quenched and tempered**: 0.0204 **diam**, 293 (2020) **TS**
QQ–W–428B	Type III	US	Wire	0.55–0.85 **C**, 0.60–1.20 **Mn**, 0.040 **P**, 0.050 **S**, 0.10–0.35 **Si**	
IS 4454	Grade SW	India	Wire	0.55–0.75 **C**, 0.60–0.90 **Mn**, 0.040 **P**, 0.040 **S**, 0.10–0.35 **Si**, 0.15 **Cu**	**Hardened and tempered**: (1.00) **diam**, (1760) **TS**
MIL–W–21425B	Type I	US	Wire	0.55–0.75 **C**, 0.60–1.20 **Mn**, 0.040 **P**, 0.050 **S**, 0.10–0.30 **Si**	**Quenched and tempered**: 0.050 **diam**, (1744) **TS**
BS 2803	Grade 1	UK	Wire	0.55–0.75 **C**, 0.60–0.90 **Mn**, 0.040 **P**, 0.040 **S**, 0.30 **Si**	**Oil hardened, tempered**: 0.500–0.299 **diam**, (1105) **TS**
BS 2803	Grade 11	UK	Wire	0.55–0.75 **C**, 0.60–0.90 **Mn**, 0.040 **P**, 0.040 **S**, 0.30 **Si**	**Oil hardened, tempered**: 0.500–0.299 **diam**, (1105) **TS**
BS 2803	Grade 111	UK	Wire	0.55–0.75 **C**, 0.60–0.90 **Mn**, 0.050 **P**, 0.050 **S**, 0.30 **Si**	**Oil hardened, tempered**: 0.500–0.299 **diam**, (1105) **TS**
MIL–W–21425B	Type III	US	Wire	0.55–0.75 **C**, 0.60–1.20 **Mn**, 0.040 **P**, 0.050 **S**, 0.10–0.30 **Si**	**Annealed**: 0.050 **diam**, (655) **TS**; **Annealed and drawn**: 0.050 **diam**, (689) **TS**; **Quenched and tempered**: 0.050 **diam**, (1744) **TS**
ANSI/ASTM A 1		US	Rail: chemical composition dependent on weight	0.55–0.68 **C**, 0.60–0.90 **Mn**, 0.04 **P**, 0.05 **S**, 0.10–0.25 **Si**	**60 to 80 lbs/yd (29.8 to 39.8 kg/m)**: all **diam**
AISI 1060		US	Plate	0.55–0.66 **C**, 0.60–0.90 **Mn**, 0.040 **P**, 0.050 **S**	
ANSI/ASTM A 680	1060	US	Strip	0.55–0.66 **C**, 0.60–0.90 **Mn**, 0.040 **P**, 0.050 **S**, 0.15–0.30 **Si**	**Cold–rolled**
ANSI/ASTM A 682	1060	US	Strip	0.55–0.66 **C**, 0.60–0.90 **Mn**, 0.040 **P**, 0.050 **S**, 0.15–0.30 **Si**	
ANSI/ASTM A 684	1060	US	Strip	0.55–0.66 **C**, 0.60–0.90 **Mn**, 0.040 **P**, 0.050 **S**, 0.15–0.30 **Si**	
JIS G 4801	SUP 6	Japan	Bar, wire, rod	0.55–0.65 **C**, 0.70–1.00 **Mn**, 0.035 **P**, 0.035 **S**, 1.50–1.80 **Si**, 0.30 **Cu**	**Quenched and tempered**: all **diam**, (1226) **TS**, (1079) **YS**, 9 **El**
JIS G 4801	SUP 7	Japan	Bar, wire, rod	0.55–0.65 **C**, 0.70–1.00 **Mn**, 0.035 **P**, 0.035 **S**, 1.80–2.20 **Si**, 0.30 **Cu**	**Quenched and tempered**: all **diam**, (1226) **TS**, (1079) **YS**, 9 **El**
DIN 17222	Grade 60 SiMn 5	Germany	Strip	0.55–0.65 **C**, 0.90–1.1 **Mn**, 0.050 **P**, 0.050 **S**, 1.0–1.3 **Si**	**Solution annealed**: all **diam**, (834) **TS**, (363) **YS**, 18 **El**; **Quenched and tempered**: all **diam**, (1667) **TS**, (1569) **YS**, 5 **El**
DGN–B–301	1060	Mexico	Bar	0.55–0.65 **C**, 0.60–0.90 **Mn**, 0.040 **P**, 0.050 **S**, 0.10–0.20 **Si**	**Forged or hot rolled, cold rolled and cold finished**: all **diam**, (677) **TS**, (373) **YS**, 12 **El**
ASTM A 713	Grade 1059	US	Wire	0.55–0.65 **C**, 0.50–0.80 **Mn**, 0.040 **P**, 0.050 **S**	
ASTM A 713	Grade 1060	US	Wire	0.55–0.65 **C**, 0.60–0.90 **Mn**, 0.040 **P**, 0.050 **S**	
ASTM A 713	Grade 1561	US	Wire	0.55–0.65 **C**, 0.75–1.05 **Mn**, 0.040 **P**, 0.050 **S**	
AISI 1561		US	Bar	0.55–0.65 **C**, 0.75–1.05 **Mn**, 0.040 **P**, 0.050 **S**	
AISI 1060		US	Bar	0.55–0.65 **C**, 0.60–0.90 **Mn**, 0.040 **P**, 0.050 **S**	
BS 1429	En. 45A	UK	Wire	0.55–0.65 **C**, 0.70–1.00 **Mn**, 0.05 **P**, 0.05 **S**, 1.70–2.00 **Si**	
BS 1449: Part 1	Grade 60	UK	Plate, sheet, strip	0.55–0.65 **C**, 0.50–0.90 **Mn**, 0.045 **P**, 0.045 **S**, 0.05–0.35 **Si**	
DGN–B–301	1561	Mexico	Bar	0.55–0.65 **C**, 0.75–1.05 **Mn**, 0.040 **P**, 0.050 **S**	
COPANT 330	1060	COPANT	Bar, shapes	0.55–0.65 **C**, 0.60–0.90 **Mn**, 0.040 **P**, 0.050 **S**	
COPANT 331	1060	COPANT	Bar	0.55–0.65 **C**, 0.60–0.90 **Mn**, 0.040 **P**, 0.050 **S**	
MIL–S–16974E	No. 1060	US	Bar, billets, blooms, slabs	0.55–0.65 **C**, 0.60–0.90 **Mn**, 0.040 **P**, 0.050 **S**, 0.15–0.30 **Si**	

WROUGHT CARBON STEELS

specification number	designation	country	product forms	composition	mechanical properties (see page iv for explanation)
ANSI/ASTM A 29	1561	US	Bar	0.55–0.65 **C**, 0.75–1.05 **Mn**, 0.040 **P**, 0.050 **S**	
ASTM A 689	1561	US	Bar: spring	0.55–0.65 **C**, 0.75–1.05 **Mn**, 0.040 **P**, 0.050 **S**	
MIL-S-16788A	Class C6	US	Blooms, billets, slabs	0.55–0.65 **C**, 0.60–0.90 **Mn**, 0.040 **P**, 0.050 **S**	
COPANT 333	1060	COPANT	Wire, rod	0.55–0.65 **C**, 0.60–0.90 **Mn**, 0.040 **P**, 0.050 **S**	
DGN-B-301	1059	Mexico	Bar	0.55–0.65 **C**, 0.50–0.80 **Mn**, 0.040 **P**, 0.050 **S**, 0.10–0.20 **Si**	
DGN-B-301	1061	Mexico	Bar	0.55–0.65 **C**, 0.75–1.05 **Mn**, 0.040 **P**, 0.050 **S**, 0.10–0.20 **Si**	
AISI 1059		US	Wire, rod	0.55–0.65 **C**, 0.50–0.80 **Mn**, 0.040 **P**, 0.050 **S**	
AISI 1060		US	Wire, rod	0.55–0.65 **C**, 0.60–0.90 **Mn**, 0.040 **P**, 0.050 **S**	
AISI 1561		US	Wire, rod	0.55–0.65 **C**, 0.75–1.05 **Mn**, 0.040 **P**, 0.050 **S**	
ASTM A 713	1561	US	Wire	0.55–0.65 **C**, 0.75–1.05 **Mn**, 0.040 **P**, 0.050 **S**	
ASTM A 713	1060	US	Wire	0.55–0.65 **C**, 0.60–0.90 **Mn**, 0.040 **P**, 0.050 **S**	
ANSI/ASTM A 576	1561	US	Bar	0.55–0.65 **C**, 0.55–0.65 **Mn**, 0.75–1.05 **P**, 0.040 **S**, 0.050 **Si**	
ANSI/ASTM A 576	1060	US	Bar	0.55–0.65 **C**, 0.60–0.90 **Mn**, 0.040 **P**, 0.050 **S**	
ASTM A 689	1060	US	Bar	0.55–0.65 **C**, 0.60–0.90 **Mn**, 0.040 **P**, 0.050 **S**	
ANSI/ASTM A 29	1059	US	Bar	0.55–0.65 **C**, 0.50–0.80 **Mn**, 0.040 **P**, 0.050 **S**	
ANSI/ASTM A 29	1060	US	Bar	0.55–0.65 **C**, 0.60–0.90 **Mn**, 0.040 **P**, 0.050 **S**	
AS 1442	Grade AS 1442/K1059	Australia	Bar, blooms, billets, slabs	0.55–0.65 **C**, 0.50–0.70 **Mn**, 0.050 **P**, 0.050 **S**, 0.10–0.35 **Si**	
AS 1442	Grade AS 1442/K1060	Australia	Bar, blooms, billets, slabs	0.55–0.65 **C**, 0.60–0.90 **Mn**, 0.050 **P**, 0.050 **S**, 0.10–0.35 **Si**	
NF A 35-051	FM 60	France	Wire, rod	0.55–0.63 **C**, 0.60–0.90 **Mn**, 0.040 **P**, 0.040 **S**, 0.10–0.35 **Si**	
JIS G 4051	S 58C	Japan	Bar, wire, rod	0.55–0.61 **C**, 0.60–0.90 **Mn**, 0.030 **P**, 0.035 **S**, 0.15–0.35 **Si**, 0.30 **Cu**	
BS 970: Part 1	060A57	UK	Blooms, billets, slabs, bar, rod, forgings	0.55–0.60 **C**, 0.50–0.70 **Mn**	
BS 970: Part 1	080A57	UK	Blooms, billets, slabs, bar, rod, forgings	0.55–0.60 **C**, 0.70–0.90 **Mn**	
DGN-B-302		Mexico	Bar	0.55 **C**, 0.60–0.90 **Mn**, 0.040 **P**, 0.050 **S**, 0.15–0.30 **Si**	**Hot rolled and quenched and tempered**: (<25) **diam**, (755) **TS**, (520) **YS**, 18 **El**
JIS G 3429	Class 3	Japan	Tube: seamless	0.55 **C**, 1.10 **Mn**, 0.040 **P**, 0.050 **S**	**As manufactured**: all **diam**, (657) **TS**, 18 **El**
ASTM A 291	Class 1	US	Forgings	0.55 **C**, 0.60–0.90 **Mn**, 0.040 **P**, 0.040 **S**, 0.15–0.35 **Si**	**Normalized, annealed**: ≥10 (254) **diam**, 85 (585) **TS**, 50 (345) **YS**, 22 **El**
ANSI/ASTM A 321		US	Bar	0.55 **C**, 0.60–0.90 **Mn**, 0.040 **P**, 0.050 **S**, 0.15–0.30 **Si**	**Quenched, tempered**: ≥1 (25.4) **diam**, 75 (520) **TS**, 110 (760) **YS**, 18 **El**
NF A 35-590	1306 (Y_3 55)	France	Bar, forgings	0.55 **C**, 0.60–0.80 **Mn**, 0.035 **P**, 0.035 **S**, 0.15–0.40 **Si**	
MIL-S-10520D	Grade 6	US	Bar, forgings	0.55 **C**, 1.00 **Mn**, .040 **P**, .050 **S**, 0.15–0.30 **Si**	**Quenched and tempered**: 1-3/4 **diam**, 76 (524) **YS**
ASTM A 713	1059	US	Wire	0.55 **C**, 0.50–0.80 **Mn**, 0.040 **P**, 0.050 **S**	
AISI 15B62H		US	Bar	0.54–0.67 **C**, 1.00–1.50 **Mn**, 0.040 **P**, 0.050 **S**, 0.40–0.60 **Si**, 0.0005–0.003 **B**	

WROUGHT CARBON STEELS

specification number	designation	country	product forms	composition	mechanical properties (see page iv for explanation)
AISI 15B62H		US	Wire, rod	0.54–0.67 **C**, 1.00–1.50 **Mn**, 0.040 **P**, 0.050 **S**, 0.40–0.60 **Si**	
COPANT 333	1061	COPANT	Wire, rod	0.54–0.65 **C**, 0.75–1.05 **Mn**, 0.040 **P**, 0.050 **S**	
COPANT 333	1062	COPANT	Wire, rod	0.54–0.65 **C**, 0.85–1.15 **Mn**, 0.040 **P**, 0.050 **S**	
JIS G 3506	SWRH 57A	Japan	Wire, rod	0.54–0.61 **C**, 0.30–0.60 **Mn**, 0.040 **P**, 0.040 **S**, 0.15–0.35 **Si**	
JIS G 3506	SWRH 57B	Japan	Wire, rod	0.54–0.61 **C**, 0.60–0.90 **Mn**, 0.040 **P**, 0.040 **S**, 0.15–0.35 **Si**	
NF A 35–051	FM 58	France	Wire, rod	0.52–0.63 **C**, 0.50–0.80 **Mn**, 0.040 **P**, 0.040 **S**, 0.10–0.35 **Si**	
SIS 14 20 90	SIS 20 90–05	Sweden	Bar, wire	0.52–0.60 **C**, 0.60–0.90 **Mn**, 0.035 **P**, 0.035 **S**, 1.5–2.0 **Si**, 0.3 **Cr**	**Quenched and tempered (wire)**: (2–2.5) diam, (1600) **TS**, (1350) **YS**
SIS 14 20 90	SIS 20 90–04	Sweden	Bar, forgings, wire	0.52–0.60 **C**, 0.60–0.90 **Mn**, 0.035 **P**, 0.035 **S**, 1.5–2.0 **Si** 0.3 **Cr**	**Quenched and tempered**: (≤15) **diam**, (1500) **TS**, (1300) **YS**, 6 **El**
ISO 683/XIV	5	ISO	Bar, rod, wire	0.52–0.60 **C**, 0.60–0.90 **Mn**, 0.040 **P**, 0.040 **S**, 1.50–2.00 **Si**	**Quenched and tempered**: all **diam**, (1320) **TS**, (1130) **YS**, 6 **El**
SIS 14 20 90	SIS 20 90–03	Sweden	Bar, forgings, wire	0.52–0.60 **C**, 0.60–0.90 **Mn**, 0.035 **P**, 0.035 **S**, 1.5–2.0 **Si**, 0.3 **Cr**	**Quenched and tempered**: (≤15) **diam**, (1300) **TS**, (1150) **YS**, 8 **El**
ISO R683/1	C55	ISO	Bar, forgings	0.52–0.60 **C**, 0.60–0.90 **Mn**, 0.050 **P**, 0.050 **S**, 0.15–0.40 **Si**	**Quenched and tempered**: all **diam**, (1240) **TS**, (850) **YS**, 12 **El**; **Quenched, tempered and cold-reduced**: all **diam**, (1390) **TS**, (1110) **YS**, 7 **El**
ISO R683/1	C55e	ISO	Bar, forgings	0.52–0.60 **C**, 0.60–0.90 **Mn**, 0.035 **P**, 0.035 **S**, 0.15–0.40 **Si**	**Quenched and tempered**: all **diam**, (1240) **TS**, (850) **YS**, 12 **El**; **Quenched, tempered and cold-reduced**: all **diam**, (1390) **TS**, (1110) **YS**, 7 **El**
SIS 14 20 90	SIS 20 90–06	Sweden	Bar, wire	0.52–0.60 **C**, 0.60–0.90 **Mn**, 0.035 **P**, 0.035 **S**, 1.5–2.0 **Si**, 0.3 **Cr**	**Annealed and cold worked**: all **diam**, (800) **TS**
DIN 17222	Grade 55 Si 7	Germany	Strip	0.52–0.60 **C**, 0.70–1.0 **Mn**, 0.050 **P**, 0.050 **S**, 1.5–1.8 **Si**	**Solution annealed**: all **diam**, (795) **TS**, (343) **YS**, 20 **El**; **Quenched and tempered**: all **diam**, (1569) **TS**, (1471) **YS**, 6 **El**
DIN 17200	Grade C 55	Germany	Blooms, slabs, billets, wire, bar, plate, sheet, strip, tube, forgings	0.52–0.60 **C**, 0.60–0.90 **Mn**, 0.045 **P**, 0.045 **S**, 0.15–0.35 **Si**	**Quenched and tempered**: (≤16) **diam**, (795) **TS**, (539) **YS**, 12 **El**; **Normalized**: (>16–40) **diam**, (657) **TS**, (363) **YS**, 15 **El**
DIN 17200	Grade Ck 55	Germany	Blooms, slabs, billets, wire, bar, plate, sheet, strip, tube, forgings	0.52–0.60 **C**, 0.60–0.90 **Mn**, 0.035 **P**, 0.035 **S**, 0.15–0.35 **Si**	**Quenched and tempered**: (≤16) **diam**, (795) **TS**, (539) **YS**, 12 **El**; **Normalized**: (>16–40) **diam**, (657) **TS**, (363) **YS**, 15 **El**
ISO/R 683/111	Type C55ea	ISO	Bar, billet, rod	0.52–0.60 **C**, 0.60–0.90 **Mn**, 0.035 **P**, 0.020–0.035 **S**, 0.15–0.40 **Si**	**Quenched and tempered**: (≤16) **diam**, (784) **TS**, (539) **YS**, 12 **El**
ISO/R 683/111	Type C55eb	ISO	Bar, billet, rod	0.52–0.60 **C**, 0.60–0.90 **Mn**, 0.035 **P**, 0.030–0.050 **S**, 0.15–0.40 **Si**	**Quenched and tempered**: (≤16) **diam**, (784) **TS**, (539) **YS**, 12 **El**
ISO 683/XVIII	C55e	ISO	Bar, wire	0.52–0.60 **C**, 0.60–0.90 **Mn**, 0.035 **P**, 0.035 **S**, 0.15–0.40 **Si**	**Normalized**: all **diam**, (680) **TS**, (370) **YS**, 11 **El**
ISO 683/XVIII	C55ea	ISO	Bar, wire	0.52–0.60 **C**, 0.60–0.90 **Mn**, 0.035 **P**, 0.020–0.035 **S**, 0.15–0.40 **Si**	**Normalized**: all **diam**, (680) **TS**, (370) **YS**, 11 **El**
ISO 683/XVIII	C55eb	ISO	Bar, wire	0.52–0.60 **C**, 0.60–0.90 **Mn**, 0.035 **P**, 0.030–0.050 **S**, 0.15–0.40 **Si**	**Normalized**: all **diam**, (680) **TS**, (370) **YS**, 11 **El**
ISO 683/XVIII	C55	ISO	Bar, wire	0.52–0.60 **C**, 0.60–0.90 **Mn**, 0.050 **P**, 0.050 **S**, 0.15–0.40 **Si**	**Normalized**: all **diam**, (680) **TS**, (370) **YS**, 11 **El**

WROUGHT CARBON STEELS

specification number	designation	country	product forms	composition	mechanical properties (see page iv for explanation)
DIN 17200	Grade Cm 55	Germany	Blooms, slabs, billets, wire, bar, plate, sheet, strip, tube, forgings	0.52–0.60 **C**, 0.60–0.90 **Mn**, 0.035 **P**, 0.020–0.035 **S**, 0.15–0.35 **Si**	**Normalized:** (>16–100) **diam**, (657) **TS**, (363) **YS**, 15 **El**; **Quenched and tempered:** (≤16) **diam**, (795) **TS**, (539) **YS**, 12 **El**
QQ-S-700D	SAE 1055	US	Sheet, strip	0.52–0.60 **C**, 0.60–0.90 **Mn**, 0.040 **P**, 0.050 **S**	
AISI 1055		US	Plate	0.52–0.60 **C**, 0.60–0.90 **Mn**, 0.040 **P**, 0.050 **S**	
ANSI/ASTM A 680	1055	US	Strip	0.52–0.60 **C**, 0.60–0.90 **Mn**, 0.040 **P**, 0.050 **S**, 0.15–0.30 **Si**	**Cold-rolled**
ANSI/ASTM A 682	1055	US	Strip	0.52–0.60 **C**, 0.60–0.90 **Mn**, 0.040 **P**, 0.050 **S**, 0.15–0.30 **Si**	
ANSI/ASTM A 684	1055	US	Strip	0.52–0.60 **C**, 0.60–0.90 **Mn**, 0.040 **P**, 0.050 **S**, 0.15–0.30 **Si**	
SIS 14 20 90	SIS 20 90-02	Sweden	Bar, forgings, wire	0.52–0.60 **C**, 0.60–0.90 **Mn**, 0.035 **P**, 0.035 **S**, 1.5–2.0 **Si**, 0.3 **Cr**	
SIS 14 20 90	SIS 20 90-00	Sweden	Bar, forgings, wire	0.52–0.60 **C**, 0.60–0.90 **Mn**, 0.035 **P**, 0.035 **S**, 1.5–2.0 **Si**, 0.3 **Cr**	
ISO 683/XIV	8	ISO	Bar, rod, wire	0.52–0.59 **C**, 0.70–1.00 **Mn**, 0.035 **P**, 0.035 **S**, 0.15–0.40 **Si**, 0.60–0.90 **Cr**	**Quenched and tempered:** all **diam**, (1370) **TS**, (1180) **YS**, 6 **El**
JIS G 4051	S 55C	Japan	Bar, wire, rod	0.52–0.58 **C**, 0.60–0.90 **Mn**, 0.030 **P**, 0.035 **S**, 0.15–0.35 **Si**, 0.30 **Cu**	
ANSI/ASTM A 648	Grade II		Wire	0.50–0.85 **C**, 0.60–1.10 **Mn**, 0.040 **P**, 0.050 **S**, 0.10–0.35 **Si**	**Hard drawn:** 0.162 **diam**, (1590) **TS**
DGN-B-441		Mexico	Wire	0.50–0.85 **C**, 0.50–1.10 **Mn**, 0.040 **P**, 0.050 **S**, 0.10–0.30 **Si**	**Cold drawn:** (1.25–2.25) **diam**, (1441) **TS**
IS 4454 (Part 1)	Grade 1	India	Wire	0.50–0.75 **C**, 1.0 **Mn**, 0.040 **P**, 0.050 **S**, 0.10–0.35 **Si**, 0.20 **Cu**	**Cold drawn:** (0.38) **diam**, (1700) **TS**
ANSI/ASTM A 417	Type C-sinuous	US	Wire: spring	0.50–0.75 **C**, 0.60–1.20 **Mn**, 0.040 **P**, 0.050 **S**	**Cold drawn:** 0.092 (2.34) **diam**, 235 (1620) **TS**
ANSI/ASTM A 417	Type C	US	Wire	0.50–0.75 **C**, 0.60–1.20 **Mn**, 0.040 **P**, 0.050 **S**	**Hard drawn:** 0.092 (2.34) **diam**, 235 (1620) **TS**
ANSI/ASTM A 417	Type A-zigzag, class II	US	Wire: spring	0.50–0.75 **C**, 0.60–1.20 **Mn**, 0.040 **P**, 0.050 **S**	**Cold drawn:** 0.092 (2.34) **diam**, 230 (1590) **TS**
ANSI/ASTM A 417	Type A, class II	US	Wire	0.50–0.75 **C**, 0.60–1.20 **Mn**, 0.040 **P**, 0.050 **S**	**Hard drawn:** 0.092 (2.34) **diam**, 230 (1590) **TS**
ANSI/ASTM A 417	Type B-square-formed, class II	US	Wire: spring	0.50–0.75 **C**, 0.60–1.20 **Mn**, 0.040 **P**, 0.050 **S**	**Cold drawn:** 0.092 (2.34) **diam**, 225 (1550) **TS**
ANSI/ASTM A 417	Type B, class II	US	Wire	0.50–0.75 **C**, 0.60–1.20 **Mn**, 0.040 **P**, 0.050 **S**	**Hard drawn:** 0.092 (2.34) **diam**, 225 (1550) **TS**
ANSI/ASTM A 417	Type A-zigzag, class I	US	Wire: spring	0.50–0.75 **C**, 0.60–1.20 **Mn**, 0.040 **P**, 0.050 **S**	**Cold drawn:** 0.092 (2.34) **diam**, 220 (1520) **TS**
ANSI/ASTM A 417	Type A, class I	US	Wire	0.50–0.75 **C**, 0.60–1.20 **Mn**, 0.040 **P**, 0.050 **S**	**Hard drawn:** 0.092 (2.34) **diam**, 220 (1520) **TS**
ANSI/ASTM A 417	Type B-square-formed, class I	US	Wire: spring	0.50–0.75 **C**, 0.60–1.20 **Mn**, 0.040 **P**, 0.050 **S**	**Cold drawn:** 0.092 (2.34) **diam**, 215 (1480) **TS**
ANSI/ASTM A 417	Type B, class I	US	Wire	0.50–0.75 **C**, 0.60–1.20 **Mn**, 0.040 **P**, 0.050 **S**	**Hard drawn:** 0.092 (2.34) **diam**, 215 (1480) **TS**
DGN-B-352	Grade I, no-sag	Mexico	Wire	0.50–0.75 **C**, 0.60–1.20 **Mn**, 0.040 **P**, 0.050 **S**	**As drawn:** (0.0915) **diam**, 235 **TS**
DGN-B-352	Grade II, square	Mexico	Wire	0.50–0.75 **C**, 0.60–1.20 **Mn**, 0.040 **P**, 0.050 **S**	**As drawn:** (0.0915) **diam**, 225 **TS**
DGN-B-352	Grade I, square	Mexico	Wire	0.50–0.75 **C**, 0.60–1.20 **Mn**, 0.040 **P**, 0.050 **S**	**As drawn:** (0.0915) **diam**, 215 **TS**
DGN-B-362	Grade I, zig-zag	Mexico	Wire	0.50–0.75 **C**, 0.60–1.20 **Mn**, 0.040 **P**, 0.050 **S**	**As drawn:** (0.0915) **diam**, 220 **TS**
NF A 35-051	FM 56	France	Wire, rod	0.50–0.61 **C**, 0.50–0.80 **Mn**, 0.040 **P**, 0.040 **S**, 0.10–0.35 **Si**	
BS 3 S.79		UK	Bar, billets, forgings: aircraft quality	0.50–0.60 **C**, 0.6–0.9 **Mn**, 0.040 **P**, 0.045 **S**, 0.10–0.35 **Si**	**Hardened and tempered:** all **diam**, (850) **TS**, 11 **El**
IS 5517	Grade C55Mn75	India	Bar, billet	0.50–0.60 **C**, 0.60–0.90 **Mn**, 0.10–0.35 **Si**	**Normalized, annealed or hardened and tempered:** (30) **diam**, (785) **TS**, (530) **YS**

WROUGHT CARBON STEELS

specification number	designation	country	product forms	composition	mechanical properties (see page iv for explanation)
BS 3 S.70		UK	Bar, billets, forgings: aircraft quality	0.50–0.60 **C**, 0.6–0.9 **Mn**, 0.040 **P**, 0.045 **S**, 0.10–0.35 **Si**	**Normalized**: all diam, (690) **TS**, 13 **El**
DGN–B–301	1055	Mexico	Bar	0.50–0.60 **C**, 0.60–0.90 **Mn**, 0.040 **P**, 0.050 **S**, 0.10–0.20 **Si**	**Forged or hot rolled, cold rolled and cold finished**: all diam, (647) **TS**, (353) **YS**, 12 **El**
BS 970: Part 1	070M55	UK	Blooms, billets, slabs, bar, rod, forgings	0.50–0.60 **C**, 0.50–0.90 **Mn**	**Normalized**: 2.5 diam, (620) **TS**, (315) **YS**, 12 **El**; **Hardened and tempered**: 4 **diam**, (620) **TS**, (370) **YS**, 14 **El**; **Cold drawn from normalized**: 0.50–0.625 **diam**, (705) **TS**, (550) **YS**, 7 **El**
ASTM A 713	Grade 1055	US	Wire	0.50–0.60 **C**, 0.60–0.90 **Mn**, 0.040 **P**, 0.050 **S**	
AISI 1055		US	Bar	0.50–0.60 **C**, 0.60–0.90 **Mn**, 0.040 **P**, 0.050 **S**	
BS 1429	En. 45	UK	Wire	0.50–0.60 **C**, 0.70–1.00 **Mn**, 0.05 **P**, 0.05 **S**, 1.50–2.00 **Si**	
COPANT 330	1055	COPANT	Bar, shapes	0.50–0.60 **C**, 0.60–0.90 **Mn**, 0.040 **P**, 0.050 **S**	
COPANT 331	1055	COPANT	Bar	0.50–0.60 **C**, 0.60–0.90 **Mn**, 0.040 **P**, 0.050 **S**	
COPANT 333	1055	COPANT	Wire, rod	0.50–0.60 **C**, 0.60–0.90 **Mn**, 0.040 **P**, 0.050 **S**	
AISI 1055		US	Wire, rod	0.50–0.60 **C**, 0.60–0.90 **Mn**, 0.040 **P**, 0.050 **S**	
ASTM A 713	1055	US	Wire	0.50–0.60 **C**, 0.60–0.90 **Mn**, 0.040 **P**, 0.050 **S**	
ANSI/ASTM A 576	1055	US	Bar	0.50–0.60 **C**, 0.60–0.90 **Mn**, 0.040 **P**, 0.050 **S**	
ASTM A 689	1055	US	Bar	0.50–0.60 **C**, 0.60–0.90 **Mn**, 0.040 **P**, 0.050 **S**	
ANSI/ASTM A 29	1055	US	Bar	0.50–0.60 **C**, 0.60–0.90 **Mn**, 0.040 **P**, 0.050 **S**	
AS 1443	Grade AS 1443/K1055	Australia	Bar	0.50–0.60 **C**, 0.60–0.90 **Mn**, 0.050 **P**, 0.050 **S**, 0.10–0.35 **Si**	
AS 1442	Grade AS 1442/K1055	Australia	Bar, blooms, billets, slabs	0.50–0.60 **C**, 0.60–0.90 **Mn**, 0.050 **P**, 0.050 **S**, 0.10–0.35 **Si**	
DIN 17140	Grade D55–2	Germany	Wire, rod	0.50–0.59 **C**, 0.30–0.70 **Mn**, 0.040 **P**, 0.040 **S**, 0.10–0.30 **Si**, 0.007 **N**	
ISO 683/XII	5	ISO	Bar, plate	0.50–0.57 **C**, 0.40–0.70 **Mn**, 0.035 **P**, 0.035 **S**, 0.15–0.40 **Si**	**Quenched and tempered**: (16) **diam**, (740) **TS**, (510) **YS**, 12 **El**
DIN 17212	Grade Cf 53	Germany	Blooms, slabs, billets, wire, bar, plate, sheet, strip, tube, forgings	0.50–0.57 **C**, 0.40–0.70 **Mn**, 0.025 **P**, 0.035 **S**, 0.15–0.35 **Si**	**Quenched and tempered**: ($\leq$16) **diam**, (740) **TS**, (510) **YS**, 12 **El**
DIN 17222	CK53[3]/1210	Germany	Strip	0.50–0.57 **C**, 0.40–0.70 **Mn**, 0.035 **P**, 0.035 **S**, 0.25–0.50 **Si**	**Softened and annealed**: all **diam**, (588) max **TS**, (275) max **YS**, 30 **El**; **Hardened and tempered**: all **diam**, (1176) **TS**, (1030) **YS**, 7 **El**
DIN 17222	C53/0740	Germany	Strip	0.50–0.57 **C**, 0.40–0.70 **Mn**, 0.045 **P**, 0.045 **S**, 0.25–0.50 **Si**	**Softened, annealed**: all **diam**, (588) max **TS**, (275) max **YS**, 30 **El**; **Hardened, tempered**: all **diam**, (1176) **TS**, (1030) **YS**, 6 **El**
DIN 17222	Grade Ck 53	Germany	Strip	0.50–0.57 **C**, 0.40–0.70 **Mn**, 0.035 **P**, 0.035 **S**, 0.25–0.50 **Si**	**Solution annealed**: all **diam**, (588) **TS**, (274) **YS**, 30 **El**; **Quenched and tempered**: all **diam**, (1029) **TS**, (1177) **YS**, 7 **El**
DIN 17222	Grade C 53	Germany	Strip	0.50–0.57 **C**, 0.40–0.70 **Mn**, 0.045 **P**, 0.045 **S**, 0.25–0.50 **Si**	**Solution annealed**: all **diam**, (588) **TS**, (274) **YS**, 30 **El**; **Quenched and tempered**: all **diam**, (1177) **TS**, (1029) **YS**, 6 **El**

WROUGHT CARBON STEELS

specification number	designation	country	product forms	composition	mechanical properties (see page iv for explanation)
NF A 35–553	XC 54	France	Strip	0.50–0.57 **C**, 0.40–0.70 **Mn**, 0.035 **P**, 0.035 **S**, 0.15–0.35 **Si**	
JIS G 4051	S 53C	Japan	Bar, wire, rod	0.50–0.56 **C**, 0.15–0.35 **Mn**, 0.030 **P**, 0.035 **S**, 0.15–0.35 **Si**, 0.30 **Cu**	
BS 970 Part 5	080A52	UK	Blooms, billets, bar, forgings	0.50–0.55 **C**, 0.70–0.90 **Mn**, 0.10–0.35 **Si**	
BS 970: Part 1	060A52	UK	Blooms, billets, slabs, bar, rod, forgings	0.50–0.55 **C**, 0.50–0.70 **Mn**	
BS 970: Part 1	080A52	UK	Blooms, billets, slabs, bar, rod, forgings	0.50–0.55 **C**, 0.70–0.90 **Mn**	
DIN 1652	St 70–2 (1.0633)	Germany	Bar	0.50 **C**, 0.06 **P**, 0.05 **S**	**Cold drawn**: all **diam**, (780) **TS**, (560) **YS**, 6 in 80 mm **El**; **Centerless turned and solution annealed**: all **diam**, (660) **TS**, (325) **YS**, 10 in 80 mm **El**; **Centerless turned and normalized**: all **diam**, (685) **TS**, (345) **YS**, 10 in 80 mm **El**
DIN 1623 Sheet 2	St 70–2 (1.0632.6)	Germany	Sheet	0.50 **C**, 0.060 **P**, 0.050 **S**	**Hot or cold rolled**: all **diam**, (690) **TS**, (365) **YS**, 6 in 80 mm **El**
SFS 200:E	Fe 70	Finland	Bar, plate, strip, wire, forgings	0.50 **C**, 0.050 **P**, 0.050 **S**, 0.009 **N**	**Hot worked**: (>40–100) **diam**, (686) **TS**, (343) **YS**, 10 **El**
TS 911	669.14–423/Fe 70	Turkey	Bar	0.50 **C**, 0.055 **P**, 0.055 **S**, 0.008 **N**	**Hot rolled**: all **diam**, (686) **TS**, (363) **YS**, 10 **El**
NS 13 205	St 70–2	Norway	Bar, forgings	0.50 **C**, 0.050 **P**, 0.050 **S**, 0.007 **N**	**Hot worked and normalized**: (≤16) **diam**, (686) **TS**, (363) **YS**, 10 **El**
NS 13 205	St 70–2	Norway	Bar, forgings	0.50 **C**, 0.050 **P**, 0.050 **S**, 0.007 **N**	**Hot worked and normalized**: (≤16) **diam**, (686) **TS**, (363) **YS**, 10 **El**
ASTM A 291	Class 2	US	Forgings	0.50 **C**, 0.40–0.90 **Mn**, 0.040 **P**, 0.040 **S**, 0.15–0.30 **Si**, 0.10 **V**	**Normalized, annealed**: ≥10 (254) **diam**, 95 (655) **TS**, 70 (485) **YS**, 20 **El**
MIL–S–24093	Type IV, class F	US	Forgings	0.50 **C**, 0.90 **Mn**, 0.040 **P**, 0.040 **S**, 0.10–0.30 **Si**	**Normalized and tempered or quenched and tempered**: all **diam**, 90 (621) max **TS**, 45 (310) **YS**, 22 **El**
MIL–S–24093	Type IV, class G	US	Forgings	0.50 **C**, 0.90 **Mn**, 0.040 **P**, 0.040 **S**, 0.10–0.30 **Si**	**Normalized and tempered or quenched and tempered**: all **diam**, 90 (621) max **TS**, 40 (276) **YS**, 22 **El**
NF A 33–101	AF 60,2	France	Bar, billets, blooms	0.50 **C**, 0.045 **P**, 0.045 **S**	**Normalized**: all **diam**, (590) **TS**, 19 **El**
MIL–S–20137A		US	Bar	0.50 **C**, 0.050 **P**, 0.050 **S**	**Annealed, normalized and tempered, stress relief annealed**: ≤3 **diam**, (517) **TS**, (241) **YS**, 22 **El**
MIL–S–890	B–S	US	Forgings, bar	0.50 **C**, 0.050 **P**, 0.050 **S**	**Annealed or normalized and drawn or quenched and drawn**: all **diam**, 75 (517) **TS**, 40 (276) **YS**, 22 **El**
ANSI/ASTM A 266	Class 3	US	Forgings	0.50 **C**, 0.50–0.90 **Mn**, 0.040 **P**, 0.040 **S**, 0.35 **Si**	**Normalized, tempered, or annealed, tempered**: all **diam**, 75 (515) **TS**, 37 (260) **YS**, 19 **El**
ANSI/ASTM A 266	Class 3	US	Forgings	0.50 **C**, 0.50–0.90 **Mn**, 0.040 **P**, 0.040 **S**, 0.35 **Si**	**Annealed, tempered, or normalized, tempered or quenched, tempered**: all **diam**, 75 (515) **TS**, 37 (260) **YS**, 19 **El**
ANSI/ASTM A 266	Grade 3	US	Forgings	0.50 **C**, 0.50–0.90 **Mn**, 0.040 **P**, 0.040 **S**, 0.35 **Si**	**Annealed or normalized and tempered**: all **diam**, (515) **TS**, (260) **YS**, 19 **El**
ANSI/ASTM A 288	Class 1	US	Forgings	0.50 **C**, 0.60–1.00 **Mn**, 0.025 **P**, 0.025 **S**, 0.15–0.30 **Si**	**Quenched, tempered**: all **diam**, 70 (485) **TS**, 45 (310) **YS**, 18 **El**
ANSI/ASTM A 446	Grade F	US	Sheet	0.50 **C**, 0.04 **P**, 0.04 **S**	**Hot rolled, hot dip galvanized**: all **diam**, 70 (480) **TS**, 50 (345) **YS**, 12 **El**
JIS G 3506	SWRH 52A	Japan	Wire, rod	0.49–0.56 **C**, 0.30–0.60 **Mn**, 0.040 **P**, 0.040 **S**, 0.15–0.35 **Si**	

WROUGHT CARBON STEELS

specification number	designation	country	product forms	composition	mechanical properties (see page iv for explanation)
JIS G 3506	SWRH 52B	Japan	Wire, rod	0.49–0.56 **C**, 0.60–0.90 **Mn**, 0.040 **P**, 0.040 **S**, 0.15–0.35 **Si**	
COPANT 333	1053	COPANT	Wire, rod	0.48–0.65 **C**, 0.70–1.00 **Mn**, 0.040 **P**, 0.050 **S**	
SIS 14 16 55	SIS 16 55–01	Sweden	Bar, forgings, plate, sheet, tube	0.48–0.60 **C**, 0.40–0.90 **Mn**, 0.05 **P**, 0.05 **S**	**Normalized**: all **diam**, (690) **TS**, (360) **YS**, 12 **El**
SIS 14 16 55	SIS 16 55–00	Sweden	Bar, forgings, plate, sheet, tube	0.48–0.60 **C**, 0.40–0.90 **Mn**, 0.050 **P**, 0.050 **S**	**As rolled**: all **diam**, (690) **TS**, (360) **YS**, 12 **El**
ISO 683/XIV	14	USO	Bar, rod, wire	0.48–0.56 **C**, 0.70–1.00 **Mn**, 0.035 **P**, 0.035 **S**, 0.15–0.40 **Si**, 0.90–1.20 **Cr**, 0.15–0.25 **Mo**, 0.07–0.12 **V**	**Quenched and tempered**: all **diam**, (1370) **TS**, (1180) **YS**, 6 **El**
ISO 683/XIV	13	USO	Bar, rod, wire	0.48–0.56 **C**, 0.70–1.00 **Mn**, 0.035 **P**, 0.035 **S**, 0.15–0.40 **Si**, 0.90–1.20 **Cr**, 0.15–0.25 **Mo**, 0.10–0.20 **V**	**Quenched and tempered**: all **diam**, (1370) **TS**, (1180) **YS**, 6 **El**
ISO 683/XII	4	ISO	Bar, plate	0.48–0.55 **C**, 0.60–0.90 **Mn**, 0.035 **P**, 0.035 **S**, 0.15–0.40 **Si**	**Quenched and tempered**: (16) **diam**, (740) **TS**, (510) **YS**, 13 **El**
SIS 14 16 74	SIS 16 74–05	Sweden	Bar, forgings, plate, sheet	0.48–0.55 **C**, 0.60–0.90 **Mn**, 0.035 **P**, 0.035 **S**, 0.15–0.40 **Si**	**Quenched and tempered**: all **diam**, (740) **TS**, (510) **YS**, 13 **El**
COPANT 332	1151	COPANT	Bar	0.48–0.55 **C**, 0.70–1.00 **Mn**, 0.040 **P**, 0.08–0.13 **S**	**Cold finished and annealed**: (≤15) **diam**, (725) **TS**, (590) **YS**, 10 **El**
ANSI/ASTM A 311	1151	US	Bar	0.48–0.55 **C**, 0.70–1.00 **Mn**, 0.040 **P**, 0.08–0.13 **S**	**Cold drawn, stress relieved**: ≥0.56 (14.29) **diam**, 105 (724) **TS**, 85 (586) **YS**, 10 **El**
DGN–B–296	1151	Mexico	Bar	0.48–0.55 **C**, 0.70–1.00 **Mn**, 0.040 **P**, 0.08–0.13 **S**	**Cold finished**: (<14) **diam**, (723) **TS**, (586) **YS**, 10 **El**
SIS 14 16 74	SIS 16 74–04	Sweden	Bar, forgings, plate, sheet	0.48–0.55 **C**, 0.60–0.90 **Mn**, 0.035 **P**, 0.035 **S**, 0.15–0.40 **Si**	**Quenched and tempered**: all **diam**, (700) **TS**, (440) **YS**, 15 **El**
SIS 14 16 74	SIS 16 74–03	Sweden	Bar, forgings, plate, sheet	0.48–0.55 **C**, 0.60–0.90 **Mn**, 0.035 **P**, 0.035 **S**, 0.15–0.40 **Si**	**Quenched and tempered**: all **diam**, (660) **TS**, (400) **YS**, 16 **El**
SIS 14 16 74	SIS 16 74–08	Sweden	Bar, forgings, plate, sheet	0.48–0.55 **C**, 0.60–0.90 **Mn**, 0.035 **P**, 0.035 **S**, 0.15–0.40 **Si**	**As rolled or as forged**: all **diam**, (650) **TS**, (355) **YS**, 12 **El**
SIS 14 16 74	SIS 16 74–01	Sweden	Bar, forgings, plate, sheet	0.48–0.55 **C**, 0.60–0.90 **Mn**, 0.035 **P**, 0.035 **S**, 0.15–0.40 **Si**	**Normalized**: all **diam**, (650) **TS**, (355) **YS**, 12 **El**
DGN–B–301	1050	Mexico	Bar	0.48–0.55 **C**, 0.60–0.90 **Mn**, 0.040 **P**, 0.050 **S**, 0.10–0.20 **Si**	**Forged or hot rolled, cold rolled and cold finished**: all **diam**, (618) **TS**, (343) **YS**, 15 **El**
COPANT 514	Grade 1050	COPANT	Tube: seamless	0.48–0.55 **C**, 0.60–0.90 **Mn**, 0.040 **P**, 0.050 **S**, 0.15–0.30 **Si**	**Hot finished**: (>323.9) **diam**, (550) **TS**, (345) **YS**, 10 **El**; **Annealed**: all **diam**, (470) **TS**, (265) **YS**, 18 **El**; **Normalized**: all **diam**, (540) **TS**, (345) **YS**, 12 **El**
DGN–B–203	Grade 1050	Mexico	Tube: seamless	0.48–0.55 **C**, 0.60–0.90 **Mn**, 0.040 **P**, 0.050 **S**	**Hot finished**: all **diam**, (549) **TS**, (343) **YS**, 10 **El**; **Stress relieved**: all **diam**, (568) **TS**, (480) **YS**, 6 **El**; **Tempered**: all **diam**, (470) **TS**, (265) **YS**, 18 **El**; **Normalized**: all **diam**, (539) **TS**, (343) **YS**, 12 **El**
QQ–S–637A	1151	US	Bar	0.48–0.55 **C**, 0.70–1.00 **Mn**, 0.040 **P**, 0.08–0.13 **S**, 0.15–0.35 **Pb**	
AISI 1151		US	Bar	0.48–0.55 **C**, 0.70–1.00 **Mn**, 0.040 **P**, 0.08–0.13 **S**	
AISI 1053		US	Bar	0.48–0.55 **C**, 0.70–1.00 **Mn**, 0.040 **P**, 0.050 **S**	
AISI 1050		US	Bar	0.48–0.55 **C**, 0.60–0.90 **Mn**, 0.040 **P**, 0.050 **S**	
ANSI/ASTM A 519	1050	US	Tube: seamless	0.48–0.55 **C**, 0.60–0.90 **Mn**, 0.040 **P**, 0.050 **S**	
COPANT 330	1151	COPANT	Bar, shapes	0.48–0.55 **C**, 0.70–1.00 **Mn**, 0.040 **P**, 0.08–0.13 **S**	
COPANT 331	1050	COPANT	Bar	0.48–0.55 **C**, 0.60–0.90 **Mn**, 0.040 **P**, 0.050 **S**	

specification number	designation	country	product forms	composition	mechanical properties (see page iv for explanation)
COPANT 331	1151	COPANT	Bar	0.48–0.55 **C**, 0.70–1.00 **Mn**, 0.040 **P**, 0.08–0.13 **S**	
MIL–S–16974 E	No. 1050	US	Bar, billets, blooms, slabs	0.48–0.55 **C**, 0.60–0.90 **Mn**, 0.040 **P**, 0.050 **S**, 0.15–0.30 **Si**	
ASTM A 108	1050	US	Bar	0.48–0.55 **C**, 0.60–0.90 **Mn**, 0.040 **P**, 0.050 **S**	
ASTM A 108	1151	US	Bar	0.48–0.55 **C**, 0.70–1.00 **Mn**, 0.040 **P**, 0.08–0.13 **S**	
MIL–S–16788A	Class C5	US	Blooms, billets, slabs	0.48–0.55 **C**, 0.60–0.90 **Mn**, 0.040 **P**, 0.050 **S**	
COPANT 333	1050	COPANT	Wire, rod	0.48–0.55 **C**, 0.60–0.90 **Mn**, 0.040 **P**, 0.050 **S**	
DGN–B–301	1053	Mexico	Bar	0.48–0.55 **C**, 0.70–1.00 **Mn**, 0.040 **P**, 0.050 **S**, 0.10–0.20 **Si**	
ANSI/ASTM A 576	1050	US	Bar	0.48–0.55 **C**, 0.60–0.90 **Mn**, 0.040 **P**, 0.050 **S**	
AISI 1050		US	Wire, rod	0.48–0.55 **C**, 0.60–0.90 **Mn**, 0.040 **P**, 0.050 **S**	
AISI 1053		US	Wire, rod	0.48–0.55 **C**, 0.70–1.00 **Mn**, 0.040 **P**, 0.050 **S**	
AISI 1151		US	Wire, rod	0.48–0.55 **C**, 0.70–1.00 **Mn**, 0.040 **P**, 0.08–0.13 **S**	
ANSI/ASTM A 576	1151	US	Bar	0.48–0.55 **C**, 0.48–0.55 **Mn**, 0.040 **P**, 0.08–0.13 **S**	
ANSI/ASTM A 576	1053	US	Bar	0.48–0.55 **C**, 0.70–1.00 **Mn**, 0.040 **P**, 0.050 **S**	
ASTM A 689	1050	US	Bar	0.48–0.55 **C**, 0.60–0.90 **Mn**, 0.040 **P**, 0.050 **S**	
ANSI/ASTM A 29	1151	US	Bar	0.48–0.55 **C**, 0.70–1.00 **Mn**, 0.040 **P**, 0.08–0.13 **S**	
ANSI/ASTM A 29	1050	US	Bar	0.48–0.55 **C**, 0.60–0.90 **Mn**, 0.040 **P**, 0.050 **S**	
ANSI/ASTM A 29	1053	US	Bar	0.48–0.55 **C**, 0.70–1.00 **Mn**, 0.040 **P**, 0.050 **S**	
ASTM A 689	1151	US	Bar	0.48–0.55 **C**, 0.70–1.00 **Mn**, 0.040 **P**, 0.08–0.13 **S**	
AS 1443	Grade AS 1443/S1050	Australia	Bar	0.48–0.55 **C**, 0.60–0.90 **Mn**, 0.050 **P**, 0.050 **S**, 0.35 **Si**	
AS 1443	Grade AS 1443/K1050	Australia	Bar	0.48–0.55 **C**, 0.60–0.90 **Mn**, 0.050 **P**, 0.050 **S**, 0.10–0.35 **Si**	
AS 1442	Grade AS 1442/S1050	Australia	Bar, blooms, billets, slabs	0.48–0.55 **C**, 0.60–0.90 **Mn**, 0.050 **P**, 0.050 **S**, 0.35 **Si**	
AS 1442	Grade AS 1442/K1050	Australia	Bar, blooms, billets, slabs	0.48–0.55 **C**, 0.60–0.90 **Mn**, 0.050 **P**, 0.050 **S**, 0.10–0.35 **Si**	
SIS 14 16 74	SIS 16 74–00	Sweden	Bar, forgings, plate, sheet	0.48–0.55 **C**, 0.60–0.90 **Mn**, 0.035 **P**, 0.035 **S**, 0.15–0.40 **Si**	
ASTM A 689	1053	US	Bar	0.48–0.53 **C**, 0.70–1.00 **Mn**, 0.040 **P**, 0.050 **S**	
JIS G 3507	SWRCH 48K	Japan	Wire, rod	0.48–0.51 **C**, 0.60–0.90 **Mn**, 0.030 **P**, 0.035 **S**, 0.10–0.35 **Si**	
ANSI/ASTM A 372	Class III	US	Forgings	0.48 **C**, 1.65 **Mn**, 0.04 **P**, 0.05 **S**, 0.15–0.30 **Si**	**Normalized or normalized and tempered**: all **diam**, (620) **TS**, (380) **YS**, 15 **El**
NF A 35–051	FM 55, Grade 3	France	Wire, rod	0.47–0.62 **C**, 0.50–0.80 **Mn**, 0.040 **P**, 0.040 **S**, 0.10–0.35 **Si**	
NF A 35–051	FM 52		Wire, rod	0.47–0.58 **C**, 0.50–0.80 **Mn**, 0.040 **P**, 0.040 **S**, 0.10–0.35 **Si**	
ISO 683/XIV	4	ISO	Bar, rod, wire	0.47–0.55 **C**, 0.50–0.80 **Mn**, 0.040 **P**, 0.040 **S**, 1.50–2.00 **Si**	**Quenched and tempered**: all **diam**, (1320) **TS**, (1130) **YS**, 6 **El**
DIN 17221	Grade 51 Si 7	Germany	Bar, wire, strip	0.47–0.55 **C**, 0.50–0.80 **Mn**, 0.045 **P**, 0.045 **S**, 1.5–1.8 **Si**	**Quenched and tempered**: (10) **diam**, (1320) **TS**, (1130) **YS**, 6 **El**

specification number	designation	country	product forms	composition	mechanical properties (see page iv for explanation)
ISO R683/1	C50	ISO	Bar, forgings	0.47–0.55 **C**, 0.60–0.90 **Mn**, 0.050 **P**, 0.050 **S**, 0.15–0.40 **Si**	**Quenched and tempered**: all **diam**, (1160) **TS**, (805) **YS**, 13 **El**; **Quenched, tempered and cold-reduced**: all **diam**, (1310) **TS**, (1050) **YS**, 8 **El**
ISO R683/1	C50e	ISO	Bar, forgings	0.47–0.55 **C**, 0.60–0.90 **Mn**, 0.035 **P**, 0.035 **S**, 0.15–0.40 **Si**	**Quenched and tempered**: all **diam**, (1160) **TS**, (805) **YS**, 13 **El**; **Quenched, tempered and cold-reduced**: all **diam**, (1310) **TS**, (1050) **YS**, 8 **El**
ISO/R 683/111	Type C50ea	ISO	Bar, billet, rod	0.47–0.55 **C**, 0.60–0.90 **Mn**, 0.035 **P**, 0.020–0.035 **S**, 0.15–0.40 **Si**	**Quenched and tempered**: (≤16) **diam**, (735) **TS**, (510) **YS**, 13 **El**
ISO/R 683/111	Type C50eb	ISO	Bar, billet, rod	0.47–0.55 **C**, 0.60–0.90 **Mn**, 0.035 **P**, 0.030–0.050 **S**, 0.15–0.40 **Si**	**Quenched and tempered**: (≤16) **diam**, (735) **TS**, (510) **YS**, 13 **El**
DGN–B–301	1052	Mexico	Bar	0.47–0.55 **C**, 1.20–1.50 **Mn**, 0.040 **P**, 0.050 **S**, 0.10–0.20 **Si**	**Forged or hot rolled, cold rolled and cold finished**: all **diam**, (706) **TS**, (412) **YS**, 12 **El**
ISO 683/XVIII	C50e	ISO	Bar, wire	0.47–0.55 **C**, 0.60–0.90 **Mn**, 0.035 **P**, 0.035 **S**, 0.15–0.40 **Si**	**Normalized**: all **diam**, (650) **TS**, (355) **YS**, 12 **El**
ISO 683/XVIII	C50ea	ISO	Bar, wire	0.47–0.55 **C**, 0.60–0.90 **Mn**, 0.035 **P**, 0.020–0.035 **S**, 0.15–0.40 **Si**	**Normalized**: all **diam**, (650) **TS**, (355) **YS**, 12 **El**
ISO 683/XVIII	C50eb	ISO	Bar, wire	0.47–0.55 **C**, 0.60–0.90 **Mn**, 0.035 **P**, 0.030–0.050 **S**, 0.15–0.40 **Si**	**Normalized**: all **diam**, (650) **TS**, (355) **YS**, 12 **El**
ISO 683/XVIII	C50	ISO	Bar, wire	0.47–0.55 **C**, 0.60–0.90 **Mn**, 0.050 **P**, 0.050 **S**, 0.15–0.40 **Si**	**Normalized**: all **diam**, (650) **TS**, (355) **YS**, 12 **El**
QQ–S–700D	SAE 1050	US	Sheet, strip	0.47–0.55 **C**, 0.60–0.90 **Mn**, 0.040 **P**, 0.050 **S**	
AISI 1050		US	Plate	0.47–0.55 **C**, 0.60–0.90 **Mn**, 0.040 **P**, 0.050 **S**	
AISI 1552		US	Bar	0.47–0.55 **C**, 1.20–1.50 **Mn**, 0.040 **P**, 0.050 **S**	
AMS 5085B		US	Sheet, strip, plate	0.47–0.55 **C**, 0.60–0.90 **Mn**, 0.040 **P**, 0.050 **S**, 0.10–0.35 **Si**	**Cold or hot rolled, annealed**
ANSI/ASTM A 29	1552	US	Bar	0.47–0.55 **C**, 1.20–1.50 **Mn**, 0.040 **P**, 0.050 **S**	
ASTM A 689	1552	US	Bar: spring	0.47–0.55 **C**, 1.20–1.50 **Mn**, 0.040 **P**, 0.050 **S**	
DGN–B–301	1552	Mexico	Bar	0.47–0.55 **C**, 1.20–1.50 **Mn**, 0.040 **P**, 0.050 **S**	
AISI 1552		US	Wire, rod	0.47–0.55 **C**, 1.20–1.50 **Mn**, 0.040 **P**, 0.050 **S**	
ANSI/ASTM A 680	1050	US	Strip	0.47–0.55 **C**, 0.60–0.90 **Mn**, 0.040 **P**, 0.050 **S**, 0.15–0.30 **Si**	**Cold rolled**
ANSI/ASTM A 682	1050	US	Strip	0.47–0.55 **C**, 0.60–0.90 **Mn**, 0.040 **P**, 0.050 **S**, 0.15–0.30 **Si**	
ANSI/ASTM A 576	1552	US	Bar	0.47–0.55 **C**, 1.20–1.50 **Mn**, 0.040 **P**, 0.050 **S**	
ANSI/ASTM A 684	1050	US	Strip	0.47–0.55 **C**, 0.60–0.90 **Mn**, 0.040 **P**, 0.050 **S**, 0.15–0.30 **Si**	
JIS G 3539	SWCH 50K	Japan	Wire	0.47–0.53 **C**, 0.60–0.90 **Mn**, 0.030 **P**, 0.035 **S**, 0.10–0.35 **Si**	**Annealed and cold drawn**: all **diam**, (706) **TS**, 10 **El**
JIS G 3507	SWRCH 50K	Japan	Wire, rod	0.47–0.53 **C**, 0.60–0.90 **Mn**, 0.030 **P**, 0.035 **S**, 0.10–0.35 **Si**	
JIS G 4051	S 50C	Japan	Bar, wire, rod	0.47–0.53 **C**, 0.60–0.90 **Mn**, 0.030 **P**, 0.035 **S**, 0.15–0.35 **Si**, 0.30 **Cu**	
AISI 1052		US	Plate	0.46–0.55 **C**, 1.20–1.55 **Mn**, 0.040 **P**, 0.050 **S**	
COPANT 330	1050	COPANT	Bar, shapes	0.46–0.55 **C**, 0.60–0.90 **Mn**, 0.040 **P**, 0.050 **S**	
SIS 14 19 73	SIS 19 73–04	Sweden	Bar	0.46–0.54 **C**, 0.80–1.20 **Mn**, 0.06 **P**, 0.15–0.25 **S**, 0.10–0.40 **Si**	**Cold worked**: (≤16) **diam**, (780) **TS**, (590) **YS**, 5 **El**

WROUGHT CARBON STEELS

specification number	designation	country	product forms	composition	mechanical properties (see page iv for explanation)
SIS 14 19 73	SIS 19 73–03	Sweden	Bar	0.46–0.54 **C**, 0.80–1.20 **Mn**, 0.06 **P**, 0.15–0.25 **S**, 0.10–0.40 **Si**	**Quenched and tempered:** (≤16) **diam**, (750) **TS**, (520) **YS**, 11 **El**
SIS 14 19 73	SIS 19 73–00	Sweden	Bar	0.46–0.54 **C**, 0.80–1.20 **Mn**, 0.06 **P**, 0.15–0.25 **S**, 0.10–0.40 **Si**	**As rolled:** (≤63) **diam**, (640) **TS**
DGN–B–301	1049	Mexico	Bar	0.46–0.53 **C**, 0.60–0.90 **Mn**, 0.040 **P**, 0.050 **S**, 0.10–0.20 **Si**	**Forged or hot rolled, cold rolled and cold finished:** all **diam**, (598) **TS**, (333) **YS**, 15 **El**
AISI 1049		US	Bar	0.46–0.53 **C**, 0.60–0.90 **Mn**, 0.040 **P**, 0.050 **S**	
ANSI/ASTM A 576	1049	US	Bar	0.46–0.53 **C**, 0.60–0.90 **Mn**, 0.040 **P**, 0.050 **S**	
AISI 1049		US	Wire, rod	0.46–0.53 **C**, 0.60–0.90 **Mn**, 0.040 **P**, 0.050 **S**	
ASTM A 689	1049	US	Bar	0.46–0.53 **C**, 0.60–0.90 **Mn**, 0.040 **P**, 0.050 **S**	
ANSI/ASTM A29	1049	US	Bar	0.46–0.53 **C**, 0.60–0.90 **Mn**, 0.040 **P**, 0.050 **S**	
NF A 35–553	XC 50	France	Strip	0.46–0.52 **C**, 0.50–0.80 **Mn**, 0.035 **P**, 0.035 **S**, 0.15–0.35 **Si**	
ANSI/ASTM A 227	Class II	US	Wire: spring	0.45–0.85 **C**, 0.30–1.30 **Mn**, 0.040 **P**, 0.050 **S**, 0.10–0.35 **Si**	**Cold drawn:** 0.020 (0.51) **diam**, 324 (2230) **TS**
ANSI/ASTM A 227	Class II	US	Wire	0.45–0.85 **C**, 0.30–1.30 **Mn**, 0.040 **P**, 0.050 **S**, 0.10–0.35 **Si**	**Hard drawn:** 0.020 (0.51) **diam**, 324 (2230) **TS**
ANSI/ASTM A 227	Class I	US	Wire: spring	0.45–0.85 **C**, 0.30–1.30 **Mn**, 0.040 **P**, 0.050 **S**, 0.10–0.35 **Si**	**Cold drawn:** 0.020 (0.51) **diam**, 283 (1950) **TS**
ANSI/ASTM A 227	Class I	US	Wire	0.45–0.85 **C**, 0.30–1.30 **Mn**, 0.040 **P**, 0.050 **S**, 0.10–0.35 **Si**	**Hard drawn:** 0.020 (0.51) **diam**, 283 (1950) **TS**
QQ–W–428B	Type II, class II	US	Wire	0.45–0.85 **C**, 0.60–1.30 **Mn**, 0.040 **P**, 0.050 **S**, 0.10–0.30 **Si**	**Cold drawn:** 0.0204 **diam**, 283 (1950) **TS**
QQ–W–428B	Type II, class I	US	Wire	0.45–0.85 **C**, 0.60–1.30 **Mn**, 0.040 **P**, 0.050 **S**, 0.10–0.30 **Si**	**Cold drawn:** 0.0204 **diam**, 283 (1950) **TS**
BS 5216 Section2	Grade 1	UK	Wire: aircraft quality	0.45–0.85 **C**, 0.40–1.00 **Mn**, 0.050 **P**, 0.050 **S**, 0.35 **Si**	**Cold drawn:** (200) **diam**, (1370) **TS**
IS 8056		India	Ingots, billets	0.45–0.80 **C**, 0.40–1.00 **Mn**, 0.050 **P**, 0.050 **S**, 0.15–0.35 **Si**	
MIL–W21425B	Type II	US	Wire	0.45–0.75 **C**, 0.60–1.20 **Mn**, 0.040 **P**, 0.050 **S**, 0.10–0.30 **Si**	**Cold drawn:** 0.050 **diam**, (1675) **TS**
ANSI/ASTM A 648	Grade I	US	Wire	0.45–0.75 **C**, 0.60–1.10 **Mn**, 0.040 **P**, 0.050 **S**, 0.10–0.35 **Si**	**Hard drawn:** 0.162 **diam**, (1380) **TS**
ANSI/ASTM A 407	Type A	US	Wire: spring	0.45–0.70 **C**, 0.60–1.20 **Mn**	**As drawn:** 0.048 (1.22) **diam**, 255 (1760) **TS**
ANSI/ASTM A 407	Type A	US	Wire	0.45–0.70 **C**, 0.60–1.20 **Mn**	**Hard drawn:** 0.048 (1.22) **diam**, 255 (1760) **TS**
ANSI/ASTM A 407	Type H	US	Wire: spring	0.45–0.70 **C**, 0.60–1.20 **Mn**	**As drawn:** 0.041 (1.04) **diam**, 250 (1720) **TS**
ANSI/ASTM A 407	Type H	US	Wire	0.45–0.70 **C**, 0.60–1.20 **Mn**	**Hard drawn:** 0.041 (1.04) **diam**, 250 (1720) **TS**
ANSI/ASTM A 407	Type B	US	Wire: spring	0.45–0.70 **C**, 0.60–1.20 **Mn**	**As drawn:** 0.062 (1.57) **diam**, 235 (1620) **TS**
ANSI/ASTM A 407	Type G	US	Wire: spring	0.45–0.70 **C**, 0.60–1.20 **Mn**	**As drawn:** 0.041 (1.04) **diam**, 235 (1620) **TS**
ANSI/ASTM A 407	Type G	US	Wire	0.45–0.70 **C**, 0.60–1.20 **Mn**	**Hard drawn:** 0.041 (1.04) **diam**, 235 (1620) **TS**
ANSI/ASTM A 407	Type B	US	Wire	0.45–0.70 **C**, 0.60–1.20 **Mn**	**Hard drawn:** 0.062 (1.57) **diam**, 235 (1620) **TS**
ANSI/ASTM A 407	Type F	US	Wire: spring	0.45–0.70 **C**, 0.60–1.20 **Mn**	**As drawn:** 0.080 (2.03) **diam**, 225 (1550) **TS**
ANSI/ASTM A 407	Type F	US	Wire	0.45–0.70 **C**, 0.60–1.20 **Mn**	**Hard drawn:** 0.080 (2.03) **diam**, 225 (1550) **TS**
ANSI/ASTM A 407	Type C	US	Wire: spring	0.45–0.70 **C**, 0.60–1.20 **Mn**	**As drawn:** 0.072 (1.83) **diam**, 215 (1480) **TS**
ANSI/ASTM A 407	Type D	US	Wire: spring	0.45–0.70 **C**, 0.60–1.20 **Mn**	**As drawn:** 0.048 (1.22) **diam**, 215 (1480) **TS**
ANSI/ASTM A 407	Type C	US	Wire	0.45–0.70 **C**, 0.60–1.20 **Mn**	**Hard drawn:** 0.072 (1.83) **diam**, 215 (1480) **TS**
ANSI/ASTM A 407	Type D	US	Wire	0.45–0.70 **C**, 0.60–1.20 **Mn**	**Hard drawn:** 0.048 (1.22) **diam**, 215 (1480) **TS**

WROUGHT CARBON STEELS

specification number	designation	country	product forms	composition	mechanical properties (see page iv for explanation)
ANSI/ASTM A 407	Type E	US	Wire: spring	0.45–0.70 **C**, 0.60–1.20 **Mn**	**As drawn**: 0.080 (2.03) **diam**, 200 (1380) **TS**
ANSI/ASTM A 407	Type E	US	Wire	0.45–0.70 **C**, 0.60–1.20 **Mn**	**Hard drawn**: 0.080 (2.03) **diam**, 200 (1380) **TS**
DGN-B-13	Class D	Mexico	Wire	0.45–0.60 **C**, 0.95–1.20 **Mn**, 0.040 **P**, 0.050 **S**, 0.15–0.20 **Si**	
ANSI/ASTM A 236	Grade F	US	Forgings	0.45–0.59 **C**, 0.60–0.90 **Mn**, 0.045 **P**, 0.050 **S**, 0.15 min **Si**	**Double normalized and tempered**: ≤8 **diam**, (610) **TS**, (345) **YS**, 22 **El**
ANSI/ASTM A 730	Grade F	US	Forgings	0.45–0.59 **C**, 0.60–0.90 **Mn**, 0.045 **P**, 0.050 **S**, 0.15 min **Si**	**Double normalized and tempered**: 8–12 (203–305) **diam**, 86 (595) **TS**, 48 (330) **YS**, 21 **El**
ANSI/ASTM A 236	Grade F	US	Forgings	0.45–0.59 **C**, 0.60–0.90 **Mn**, 0.045 **P**, 0.050 **S**, 0.15 min **Si**	**Double normalized and tempered**: 8–12 (203–305) **diam**, 86 (590) **TS**, 48 (330) **YS**, 21 **El**
ANSI/ASTM A 730	Grade F	US	Forgings	0.45–0.59 **C**, 0.60–0.90 **Mn**, 0.045 **P**, 0.050 **S**, 0.15 **Si**	
AISI 1551		US	Bar	0.45–0.56 **C**, 0.85–1.15 **Mn**, 0.040 **P**, 0.050 **S**	
ANSI/ASTM A 29	1551	US	Bar	0.45–0.56 **C**, 0.85–1.15 **Mn**, 0.040 **P**, 0.050 **S**	
ASTM A 689	1551	US	Bar: spring	0.45–0.56 **C**, 0.85–1.15 **Mn**, 0.040 **P**, 0.050 **S**	
COPANT 333	1051	COPANT	Wire, rod	0.45–0.56 **C**, 0.85–1.15 **Mn**, 0.040 **P**, 0.050 **S**	
DGN-B-301	1051	Mexico	Bar	0.45–0.56 **C**, 0.85–1.15 **Mn**, 0.040 **P**, 0.050 **S**, 0.10–0.20 **Si**	
DGN-B-301	1551	Mexico	Bar	0.45–0.56 **C**, 0.85–1.15 **Mn**, 0.040 **P**, 0.050 **S**	
AISI 1551		US	Wire, rod	0.45–0.56 **C**, 0.85–1.15 **Mn**, 0.040 **P**, 0.050 **S**	
ANSI/ASTM A 576	1551	US	Bar	0.45–0.56 **C**, 0.85–1.15 **Mn**, 0.040 **P**, 0.050 **S**	
IS 5517	Grade C50	India	Bar, billet	0.45–0.55 **C**, 0.60–0.90 **Mn**, 0.10–0.35 **Si**	**Normalized, annealed or hardened and tempered**: (30) **diam**, (785) **TS**, (530) **YS**
JIS G 3445	Class 17C, No. 11	Japan	Tube: seamless	0.45–0.55 **C**, 0.40–1.00 **Mn**, 0.040 **P**, 0.040 **S**, 0.40 **Si**	**As manufactured or cold finished**: all **diam**, (647) **TS**, (481) **YS**, 10 **El**
BS 970: Part 1	080M50	UK	Blooms, billets, slabs, bar, rod, forgings	0.45–0.55 **C**, 0.60–1.00 **Mn**	**Normalized**: 6 **diam**, (550) **TS**, (275) **YS**, 14 **El**; **Hardened and tempered**: 2.5 **diam**, (620) **TS**, (385) **YS**, 14 **El**; **Cold drawn from normalized**: 0.050–0.625 **diam**, (650) **TS**, (524) **YS**, 8 **El**
JIS G 3445	Class 17A, No. 11	Japan	Tube: seamless	0.45–0.55 **C**, 0.40–1.00 **Mn**, 0.040 **P**, 0.040 **S**, 0.40 **Si**	**As manufactured or cold finished**: all **diam**, (549) **TS**, (343) **YS**, 20 **El**
NF A 35-051	FM 50	France	Wire, rod	0.45–0.55 **C**, 0.50–0.80 **Mn**, 0.040 **P**, 0.040 **S**, 0.10–0.35 **Si**	
BS 1449: Part 1	Grade 50	UK	Plate, sheet, strip	0.45–0.55 **C**, 0.50–0.90 **Mn**, 0.045 **P**, 0.045 **S**, 0.05–0.35 **Si**	
JIS G 3539	SWCH 48K	Japan	Wire	0.45–0.51 **C**, 0.60–0.90 **Mn**, 0.030 **P**, 0.035 **S**, 0.10–0.35 **Si**	**Annealed and cold drawn**: all **diam**, (706) **TS**, 10 **El**
NF A 35-554	XC 48	France	Plate	0.45–0.51 **C**, 0.50–0.80 **Mn**, 0.035 **P**, 0.035 **S**, 0.10–0.40 **Si**	**Hot rolled and normalized**: (≤16) **diam**, (670) **TS**, (370) **YS**, 16 **El**
JIS G 4051	S 48C	Japan	Bar, wire, rod	0.45–0.51 **C**, 0.60–0.90 **Mn**, 0.030 **P**, 0.035 **S**, 0.15–0.35 **Si**, 0.30 **Cu**	
BS 970: Part 1	060A47	UK	Blooms, billets, slabs, bar, rod, forgings	0.45–0.50 **C**, 0.50–0.70 **Mn**	
BS 970: Part 1	080A47	UK	Blooms, billets, slabs, bar, rod, forgings	0.45–0.50 **C**, 0.70–0.90 **Mn**	
JIS G 3429	Class 2	Japan	Tube: seamless	0.45 **C**, 0.80 **Mn**, 0.040 **P**, 0.050 **S**	**As manufactured**: all **diam**, (539) **TS**, 20 **El**

WROUGHT CARBON STEELS

specification number	designation	country	product forms	composition	mechanical properties (see page iv for explanation)
MIL-S-860B	Grade A	US	Forgings: machined	0.45 **C**, 0.90 **Mn**, 0.025 **P**, 0.025 **S**, 0.15–0.35 **Si**, 0.03–0.12 **V**	**Normalized, quenched, tempered, stress relieved**: all **diam**, 75 (517) **TS**, 40 (276) **YS**, 22 **El**
ASTM A 293	Class 1	US	Forgings	0.45 **C**, 0.90 **Mn**, 0.035 **P**, 0.035 **S**, 0.15–0.35 **Si**, 0.03–0.12 **V**	**Normalized, tempered or double normalized, tempered**: all **diam**, 75 (515) **TS**, 40 (275) **YS**, 24 **El**
NFA 35-590	1307 (Y_3 45)	France	Bar, forgings	0.45 **C**, 0.60–0.80 **Mn**, 0.035 **P**, 0.035 **S**, 0.15–0.40 **Si**	
MIL-S-19434A	Class 1	US	Forgings	0.45 **C**, 0.55–0.90 **Mn**, 0.050 **P**, 0.050 min **S**, 0.15 min **Si**, 0.15 **V**	
ANSI/ASTM A 5		US	Bar	0.45 min **C**, 0.04 **P**	**As rolled**: all **diam**, (586) **TS**, 15 **El**
AISI 1548		US	Bar	0.44–0.52 **C**, 1.10–1.40 **Mn**, 0.040 **P**, 0.050 **S**	
ANSI/ASTM A 29	1548	US	Bar	0.44–0.52 **C**, 1.10–1.40 **Mn**, 0.040 **P**, 0.050 **S**	
ASTM A 689	1548	US	Bar: spring	0.44–0.52 **C**, 1.10–1.40 **Mn**, 0.040 **P**, 0.050 **S**	
DGN-B-301	1048	Mexico	Bar	0.44–0.52 **C**, 1.10–1.40 **Mn**, 0.040 **P**, 0.050 **S**, 0.10–0.20 **Si**	
DGN-B-301	1548	Mexico	Bar	0.44–0.52 **C**, 1.10–1.40 **Mn**, 0.040 **P**, 0.050 **S**	
AISI 1548		US	Wire, rod	0.44–0.52 **C**, 1.10–1.40 **Mn**, 0.040 **P**, 0.050 **S**	
ANSI/ASTM A 576	1548	US	Bar	0.44–0.52 **C**, 1.10–1.40 **Mn**, 0.040 **P**, 0.050 **S**	
JIS G 3506	SWRH 47A	Japan	Wire, rod	0.44–0.51 **C**, 0.30–0.60 **Mn**, 0.040 **P**, 0.040 **S**, 0.15–0.35 **Si**	
JIS G 3506	SWRH 47B	Japan	Wire, rod	0.44–0.51 **C**, 0.60–0.90 **Mn**, 0.040 **P**, 0.040 **S**, 0.15–0.35 **Si**	
DGN-B-301	1151	Mexico	Bar	0.43–0.55 **C**, 0.70–1.00 **Mn**, 0.040 **P**, 0.08–0.13 **S**, 0.10–0.20 **Si**	**Forged or hot rolled, cold rolled and cold finished**: all **diam**, (637) **TS**, (353) **YS**, 15 **El**
AISI 15B48H		US	Bar	0.43–0.53 **C**, 1.00–1.50 **Mn**, 0.040 **P**, 0.050 **S**, 0.15–0.30 **Si**, 0.0005–0.003 **B**	
AISI 15B48H		US	Wire, rod	0.43–0.53 **C**, 1.00–1.50 **Mn**, 0.040 **P**, 0.050 **S**, 0.15–0.30 **Si**	
AISI 1048		US	Plate	0.43–0.52 **C**, 1.05–1.40 **Mn**, 0.040 **P**, 0.050 **S**	
ASTM A 689	1547	US	Bar: spring	0.43–0.51 **C**, 1.35–1.65 **Mn**, 0.040 **P**, 0.050 **S**	
ISO 683/XIV	3	ISO	Bar, rod, wire	0.43–0.50 **C**, 0.50–0.80 **Mn**, 0.040 **P**, 0.040 **S**, 1.50–2.00 **Si**	**Quenched and tempered**: all **diam**, (1270) **TS**, (1080) **YS**, 6 **El**
SIS 14 16 72	SIS 16 72-05	Sweden	Bar, forgings, plate, sheet	0.43–0.50 **C**, 0.50–0.80 **Mn**, 0.035 **P**, 0.035 **S**, 0.15–0.40 **Si**	**Quenched and tempered**: all **diam**, (700) **TS**, (480) **YS**, 14 **El**
SIS 14 16 72	SIS 16 72-04	Sweden	Bar, forgings, plate, sheet	0.43–0.50 **C**, 0.50–0.80 **Mn**, 0.035 **P**, 0.035 **S**, 0.15–0.40 **Si**	**Quenched and tempered**: all **diam**, (660) **TS**, (410) **YS**, 16 **El**
SFS 456	CO, 45	Finland	Bar, forgings, tube	0.43–0.50 **C**, 0.50–0.80 **Mn**, 0.035 **P**, 0.035 **S**, 0.15–0.40 **Si**	**Quenched and tempered**: (60) (bar, forgings) **diam**, (650) **TS**, (410) **YS**, 16 **El**
SIS 14 16 72	SIS 16 72-03	Sweden	Bar, forgings, plate, sheet	0.43–0.50 **C**, 0.50–0.80 **Mn**, 0.035 **P**, 0.035 **S**, 0.15–0.40 **Si**	**Quenched and tempered**: all **diam**, (620) **TS**, (370) **YS**, 17 **El**
SIS 14 16 72	SIS 16 72-08	Sweden	Bar, forgings, plate, sheet	0.43–0.50 **C**, 0.50–0.80 **Mn**, 0.035 **P**, 0.035 **S**, 0.15–0.40 **Si**	**As rolled**: all **diam**, (590) **TS**, (320) **YS**, 16 **El**
SIS 14 16 72	SIS 16 72-01	Sweden	Bar, forgings, plate, sheet	0.43–0.50 **C**, 0.50–0.80 **Mn**, 0.035 **P**, 0.035 **S**, 0.15–0.40 **Si**	**As rolled**: all **diam**, (590) **TS**, (326) **YS**, 16 **El**
DGN-B-301	1046	Mexico	Bar	0.43–0.50 **C**, 0.70–1.00 **Mn**, 0.040 **P**, 0.050 **S**, 0.10–0.20 **Si**	**Forged or hot rolled, cold rolled and cold finished**: all **diam**, (588) **TS**, (325) **YS**, 15 **El**
DGN-B-301	1045	Mexico	Bar	0.43–0.50 **C**, 0.60–0.90 **Mn**, 0.040 **P**, 0.050 **S**, 0.10–0.20 **Si**	**Forged or hot rolled, cold rolled and cold finished**: all **diam**, (569) **TS**, (314) **YS**, 16 **El**

specification number	designation	country	product forms	composition	mechanical properties (see page iv for explanation)
DGN–B–203	Grade 1045	Mexico	Tube: seamless	0.43–0.50 **C**, 0.60–0.90 **Mn**, 0.040 **P**, 0.050 **S**	**Hot finished**: all **diam**, (520) **TS**, (314) **YS**, 15 **El**; **Cold finished**: all **diam**, (618) **TS**, (549) **YS**, 5 **El**; **Stress relieved**: all **diam**, (549) **TS**, (480) **YS**, 8 **El**; **Tempered**: all **diam**, (451) **TS**, (245) **YS**, 20 **El**; **Normalized**: all **diam**, (520) **TS**, (333) **YS**, 15 **El**
ANSI/ASTM A 519	1045	US	Tube: seamless	0.43–0.50 **C**, 0.60–0.90 **Mn**, 0.040 **P**, 0.050 **S**	**Hot rolled**: all **diam**, 75 (517) **TS**, 45 (310) **YS**, 15 **El**; **Cold worked**: all **diam**, 90 (621) **TS**, 80 (552) **YS**, 5 **El**; **Stress relieved**: all **diam**, 80 (552) **TS**, 70 (483) **YS**, 8 **El**; **Annealed**: all **diam**, 65 (448) **TS**, 35 (241) **YS**, 20 **El**; **Normalized**: all **diam**, 65 (517) **TS**, 48 (331) **YS**, 15 **El**
COPANT 514	Grade 1045	COPANT	Tube: seamless	0.43–0.50 **C**, 0.60–0.90 **Mn**, 0.040 **P**, 0.050 **S**, 0.15–0.30 **Si**	**Hot finished**: (>323.9) **diam**, (315) **TS**, (215) **YS**, 15 **El**; **Cold finished**: all **diam**, (410) **TS**, (345) **YS**, 5 **El**; **Annealed**: all **diam**, (275) **TS**, (175) **YS**, 30 **El**; **Normalized**: all **diam**, (390) **TS**, (315) **YS**, 30 **El**
AISI 1046		US	Bar	0.43–0.50 **C**, 0.70–1.00 **Mn**, 0.040 **P**, 0.050 **S**	
AISI 1045		US	Bar	0.43–0.50 **C**, 0.60–0.90 **Mn**, 0.040 **P**, 0.050 **S**	
AISI 1044		US	Bar	0.43–0.50 **C**, 0.30–0.60 **Mn**, 0.040 **P**, 0.050 **S**	
BS 970: Part 1	080H46	UK	Blooms, billets, slabs, bar, rod, forgings	0.43–0.50 **C**, 0.60–1.00 **Mn**	
MIL–S–46070	Grade 1045	US	Bar: cold drawn	0.43–0.50 **C**, 0.60–0.90 **Mn**, 0.040 **P**, 0.050 **S**, 0.30 **Si**	**Normalized or annealed and stress relieved**: <1.25 **diam**, 75 (517) **YS**, 15 **El**
AS 1446	Grade AS 1446/K1045	Australia	Plate	0.43–0.50 **C**, 0.60–0.90 **Mn**, 0.050 **P**, 0.050 **S**, 0.10–0.35 **Si**	
AS 1446	Grade AS 1446/S1045	Australia	Plate	0.43–0.50 **C**, 0.60–0.90 **Mn**, 0.050 **P**, 0.050 **S**, 0.35 **Si**	
COPANT 330	1045	COPANT	Bar, shapes	0.43–0.50 **C**, 0.60–0.90 **Mn**, 0.040 **P**, 0.050 **S**	
COPANT 331	1045	COPANT	Bar	0.43–0.50 **C**, 0.60–0.90 **Mn**, 0.040 **P**, 0.040 **S**	
ASTM A 108	1045	US	Bar	0.43–0.50 **C**, 0.60–0.90 **Mn**, 0.040 **P**, 0.050 **S**	
COPANT 333	1045	COPANT	Wire, rod	0.43–0.50 **C**, 0.60–0.90 **Mn**, 0.040 **P**, 0.050 **S**	
COPANT 333	1046	COPANT	Wire, rod	0.43–0.50 **C**, 0.70–1.00 **Mn**, 0.040 **P**, 0.050 **S**	
ANSI/ASTM A 575	1044	US	Bar	0.43–0.50 **C**, 0.30–0.60 **Mn**, 0.04 **P**, 0.05 **S**	
DGN–B–301	1044	Mexico	Bar	0.43–0.50 **C**, 0.30–0.60 **Mn**, 0.040 **P**, 0.050 **S**, 0.10–0.20 **Si**	
ANSI/ASTM A 576	1044	US	Bar	0.43–0.50 **C**, 0.30–0.60 **Mn**, 0.040 **P**, 0.050 **S**	
ANSI/ASTM A 576	1045	US	Bar	0.43–0.50 **C**, 0.60–0.90 **Mn**, 0.040 **P**, 0.050 **S**	
ANSI/ASTM A 576	1046	US	Bar	0.43–0.50 **C**, 0.70–1.00 **Mn**, 0.040 **P**, 0.050 **S**	
AISI 1044		US	Wire, rod	0.43–0.50 **C**, 0.30–0.60 **Mn**, 0.040 **P**, 0.050 **S**	
AISI 1045		US	Wire, rod	0.43–0.50 **C**, 0.60–0.90 **Mn**, 0.040 **P**, 0.050 **S**	
AISI 1046		US	Wire, rod	0.43–0.50 **C**, 0.70–1.00 **Mn**, 0.040 **P**, 0.050 **S**	
ASTM A 689	1046	US	Bar	0.43–0.50 **C**, 0.70–1.00 **Mn**, 0.040 **P**, 0.050 **S**	

specification number	designation	country	product forms	composition	mechanical properties (see page iv for explanation)
ASTM A 689	1045	US	Bar	0.43–0.50 **C**, 0.60–0.90 **Mn**, 0.040 **P**, 0.050 **S**	
ANSI/ASTM A 29	1044	US	Bar	0.43–0.50 **C**, 0.30–0.60 **Mn**, 0.040 **P**, 0.050 **S**	
ANSI/ASTM A 29	1045	US		0.43–0.50 **C**, 0.60–0.90 **Mn**, 0.040 **P**, 0.050 **S**	
ANSI/ASTM A 29	1046	US	Bar	0.43–0.50 **C**, 0.70–1.00 **Mn**, 0.040 **P**, 0.050 **S**	
ASTM A 689	1044	US	Bar	0.43–0.50 **C**, 0.30–0.60 **Mn**, 0.040 **P**, 0.050 **S**	
AS 1443	Grade AS 1443/S1045	Australia	Bar	0.43–0.50 **C**, 0.60–0.90 **Mn**, 0.050 **P**, 0.050 **S**, 0.35 **Si**	
AS 1443	Grade AS 1443/K1046	Australia	Bar	0.43–0.50 **C**, 0.70–1.00 **Mn**, 0.050 **P**, 0.050 **S**, 0.10–0.35 **Si**	
AS 1443	Grade AS 1443/K1045	Australia	Bar	0.43–0.50 **C**, 0.60–0.90 **Mn**, 0.050 **P**, 0.050 **S**, 0.10–0.35 **Si**	
AS 1442	Grade AS 1442/S1045	Australia	Bar, blooms, billets, slabs	0.43–0.50 **C**, 0.60–0.90 **Mn**, 0.050 **P**, 0.050 **S**, 0.35 **Si**	
AS 1442	Grade AS 1442/K1045	Australia	Bar, blooms, billets, slabs	0.43–0.50 **C**, 0.60–0.90 **Mn**, 0.050 **P**, 0.050 **S**, 0.10–0.35 **Si**	
AS 1442	Grade AS 1442/K1046	Australia	Bar, blooms, billets, slabs	0.43–0.50 **C**, 0.70–1.00 **Mn**, 0.050 **P**, 0.050 **S**, 0.10–0.35 **Si**	
SIS 14 16 72	SIS 16 72–00	Sweden	Bar, forgings, plate, sheet	0.43–0.50 **C**, 0.50–0.80 **Mn**, 0.035 **P**, 0.035 **S**, 0.15–0.40 **Si**	
ISO 683/XII	3	ISO	Bar, plate	0.43–0.49 **C**, 0.50–0.80 **Mn**, 0.035 **P**, 0.035 **S**, 0.15–0.40 **Si**	**Quenched and tempered**: (16) **diam**, (700) **TS**, (480) **YS**, 14 **El**
DIN 17212	Grade Cf 45	Germany	Blooms, slabs, billets, wire, bar, plate, sheet, strip, tube, forgings	0.43–0.49 **C**, 0.50–0.80 **Mn**, 0.025 **P**, 0.035 **S**, 0.15–0.35 **Si**	**Quenched and tempered**: (≤16) **diam**, (700) **TS**, (480) **YS**, 14 **El**
NF A 35–051	FM 48	France	Wire, rod	0.42–0.53 **C**, 0.50–0.80 **Mn**, 0.040 **P**, 0.040 **S**, 0.10–0.35 **Si**	
AISI 1045H		US	Bar	0.42–0.51 **C**, 0.50–1.00 **Mn**, 0.040 **P**, 0.050 **S**, 0.15–0.30 **Si**	
DGN–B–301	1045H	Mexico	Bar	0.42–0.51 **C**, 0.50–1.00 **Mn**, 0.040 **P**, 0.050 **S**, 0.15–0.30 **Si**	
AISI 1045H		US	Wire, rod	0.42–0.51 **C**, 0.50–1.00 **Mn**, 0.040 **P**, 0.050 **S**, 0.15–0.30 **Si**	
ISO 683/XIV	11	ISO	Bar, rod, wire	0.42–0.50 **C**, 0.50–0.80 **Mn**, 0.035 **P**, 0.035 **S**, 1.30–1.70 **Si**, 0.50–0.75 **Cr**, 0.15–0.30 **Mo**	**Quenched and tempered**: all **diam**, (1370) **TS**, (1180) **YS**, 6 **El**
ISO R683/1	C45	ISO	Bar, forgings	0.42–0.50 **C**, 0.50–0.80 **Mn**, 0.050 **P**, 0.050 **S**, 0.15–0.40 **Si**	**Quenched and tempered**: all **diam**, (1110) **TS**, (755) **YS**, 14 **El**; **Quenched, tempered and cold–reduced**: all **diam**, (1240) **TS**, (1005) **YS**, 9 **El**
ISO R683/1	C45e	ISO	Bar, forgings	0.42–0.50 **C**, 0.50–0.80 **Mn**, 0.035 **P**, 0.035 **S**, 0.15–0.40 **Si**	**Quenched and tempered**: all **diam**, (1110) **TS**, (755) **YS**, 14 **El**; **Quenched, tempered and cold–reduced**: all **diam**, (1240) **TS**, (1005) **YS**, 9 **El**
VSM 10648	C 45	Switzerland	Bar, sheet, plate	0.42–0.50 **C**, 0.50–0.80 **Mn**, 0.045 **P**, 0.045 **S**, 0.15–0.35 **Si**	**Cold drawn**: (≤5) **diam**, (784) **TS**, (647) **YS**, 4 **El**; **Cold drawn and normalized**: (16–100) **diam**, (588) **TS**, (333) **YS**, 17 **El**; **As rolled**: (5–16) **diam**, (695) **TS**, (480) **YS**, 14 **El**
VSM 10648	CK 45	Switzerland	Bar, sheet, plate	0.42–0.50 **C**, 0.50–0.80 **Mn**, 0.035 **P**, 0.035 **S**, 0.15–0.35 **Si**	**Cold drawn**: (≤5) **diam**, (784) **TS**, (647) **YS**, 4 **El**; **Cold drawn and normalized**: (16–100) **diam**, (588) **TS**, (333) **YS**, 17 **El**; **As rolled**: (5–16) **diam**, (695) **TS**, (480) **YS**, 14 **El**

specification number	designation	country	product forms	composition	mechanical properties (see page iv for explanation)
DIN 1652	C 45 (1.0503)	Germany	Bar	0.42–0.50 **C**, 0.50–0.80 **Mn**, 0.045 **P**, 0.045 **S**, 0.15–0.35 **Si**	**Cold drawn**: all **diam**, (780) **TS**, (645) **YS**, 4 in 80 mm **El**; **Centerless turned and normalized**: all **diam**, (590) **TS**, (335) **YS**, 18 in 80 mm **El**; **Centerless turned and quenched and tempered**: all **diam**, (740) **TS**, (470) **YS**, 14 in 80 mm **El**
DIN 1652	Ck 45 (1.1191)	Germany	Bar	0.42–0.50 **C**, 0.50–0.80 **Mn**, 0.035 **P**, 0.035 **S**, 0.15–0.35 **Si**	**Cold drawn**: all **diam**, (780) **TS**, (645) **YS**, 4 in 80 mm **El**; **Centerless turned and normalized**: all **diam**, (590) **TS**, (335) **YS**, 18 in 80 mm **El**; **Centerless turned and quenched and tempered**: all **diam**, (740) **TS**, (470) **YS**, 14 in 80 mm **El**
EURONORM 119-74, IV	C 45 KD	EURONORM	Wire, rod	0.42–0.50 **C**, 0.50–0.80 **Mn**, 0.035 **P**, 0.035 **S**, 0.15–0.40 **Si**	**Quenched and tempered**: (≤16) **diam**, (700) **TS**, (480) **YS**, 14 **El**
ISO/R 683/111	Type C45ea	ISO	Bar, billet, rod	0.42–0.50 **C**, 0.50–0.80 **Mn**, 0.035 **P**, 0.020–0.035 **S**, 0.15–0.40 **Si**	**Quenched and tempered**: (≤16) **diam**, (696) **TS**, (480) **YS**, 14 **El**
ISO/R 683/111	Type C45eb	ISO	Bar, billet, rod	0.42–0.50 **C**, 0.50–0.80 **Mn**, 0.035 **P**, 0.030–0.050 **S**, 0.15–0.40 **Si**	**Quenched and tempered**: (≤16) **diam**, (696) **TS**, (480) **YS**, 14 **El**
DIN 17200	Grade C 45	Germany	Blooms, slabs, billets, wire, bar, plate, sheet, strip, tube, forgings	0.42–0.50 **C**, 0.50–0.80 **Mn**, 0.045 **P**, 0.045 **S**, 0.15–0.35 **Si**	**Quenched and tempered**: (≤16) **diam**, (696) **TS**, (490) **YS**, 14 **El**; **Normalized**: (>16–40) **diam**, (588) **TS**, (334) **YS**, 17 **El**
DIN 17200	Grade Ck 45	Germany	Blooms, slabs, billets, wire, bar, plate, sheet, strip, tube, forgings	0.42–0.50 **C**, 0.50–0.80 **Mn**, 0.035 **P**, 0.035 **S**, 0.15–0.35 **Si**	**Quenched and tempered**: (≤16) **diam**, (696) **TS**, (490) **YS**, 14 **El**; **Normalized**: (>16–40) **diam**, (588) **TS**, (334) **YS**, 17 **El**
DIN 1654	Grade Cq 45	Germany	Rod	0.42–0.50 **C**, 0.50–0.80 **Mn**, 0.040 **P**, 0.040 **S**, 0.15–0.35 **Si**	**Drawn**: all **diam**, (687) **TS**
ISO/R 683/1X	Type 10	ISO	Bar, wire, rod	0.42–0.50 **C**, 0.50–0.90 **Mn**, 0.06 **P**, 0.15–0.25 **S**, 0.15–0.40 **Si**	**Quenched and tempered**: (≤16) **diam**, (647) **TS**, (451) **YS**, 11 **El**
ISO 683/XVIII	C45e	ISO	Bar, wire	0.42–0.50 **C**, 0.50–0.80 **Mn**, 0.035 **P**, 0.035 **S**, 0.15–0.40 **Si**	**Normalized**: all **diam**, (620) **TS**, (340) **YS**, 14 **El**
ISO 683/XVIII	C45ea	ISO	Bar, wire	0.42–0.50 **C**, 0.50–0.80 **Mn**, 0.035 **P**, 0.020–0.035 **S**, 0.15–0.40 **Si**	**Normalized**: all **diam**, (620) **TS**, (340) **YS**, 14 **El**
ISO 683/XVIII	C45eb	ISO	Bar, wire	0.42–0.50 **C**, 0.50–0.80 **Mn**, 0.035 **P**, 0.030–0.050 **S**, 0.15–0.40 **Si**	**Normalized**: all **diam**, (620) **TS**, (340) **YS**, 14 **El**
ISO 683/XVIII	C45	ISO	Bar, wire	0.42–0.50 **C**, 0.50–0.80 **Mn**, 0.035 **P**, 0.050 **S**, 0.15–0.40 **Si**	**Normalized**: all **diam**, (620) **TS**, (340) **YS**, 14 **El**
DIN 1651	45S20 (1.0727)	Germany	Bar	0.42–0.50 **C**, 0.50–0.90 **Mn**, 0.060 **P**, 0.15–0.25 **S**, 0.10–0.40 **Si**	**Hot rolled**: all **diam**, (590) **TS**; **Normalized**: all **diam**, (580) **TS**, (330) **YS**, 14 in 80 mm **El**; **Quenched and tempered**: all **diam**, (700) **TS**, (480) **YS**, 10 in 80 mm **El**
DIN 17200	Grade Cm 45	Germany	Blooms, slabs, billets, wire, bar, plate, sheet, strip, tube, forgings	0.42–0.50 **C**, 0.50–0.80 **Mn**, 0.035 **P**, 0.020–0.035 **S**, 0.15–0.35 **Si**	**Normalized**: (>16–100) **diam**, (588) **TS**, (334) **YS**, 17 **El**; **Quenched and tempered**: (≤16) **diam**, (696) **TS**, (490) **YS**, 14 **El**
BS 970: Part 1	Grade 080M46	UK	Blooms, billets, slabs, bar, rod, forgings	0.42–0.50 **C**, 0.60–1.00 **Mn**	**Normalized**: 2.5 **diam**, (550) **TS**, (275) **YS**, 14 **El**; **Hardened and tempered**: 4 **diam**, (550) **TS**, (330) **YS**, 16 **El**; **Cold drawn from hot rolled**: 0.50–0.625 **diam**, (620) **TS**, (500) **YS**, 7 **El**
QQ-S-700D	SAE 1045	US	Sheet, strip	0.42–0.50 **C**, 0.60–0.90 **Mn**, 0.040 **P**, 0.050 **S**	
AISI 1045		US	Plate	0.42–0.50 **C**, 0.60–0.90 **Mn**, 0.040 **P**, 0.050 **S**	

WROUGHT CARBON STEELS

specification number	designation	country	product forms	composition	mechanical properties (see page iv for explanation)
AISI 1046		US	Plate	0.42–0.50 **C**, 0.70–1.00 **Mn**, 0.040 **P**, 0.050 **S**	
ANSI/ASTM A 680	1045	US	Strip	0.42–0.50 **C**, 0.60–0.90 **Mn**, 0.040 **P**, 0.050 **S**, 0.15–0.30 **Si**	**Cold–rolled**
ANSI/ASTM A 682	1045	US	Strip	0.42–0.50 **C**, 0.60–0.90 **Mn**, 0.040 **P**, 0.050 **S**, 0.15–0.30 **Si**	
ANSI/ASTM A 684	1045	US	Strip	0.42–0.50 **C**, 0.60–0.90 **Mn**, 0.040 **P**, 0.050 **S**, 0.15–0.30 **Si**	
DGN–B–301	1146	Mexico	Bar	0.42–0.49 **C**, 0.70–1.00 **Mn**, 0.040 **P**, 0.08–0.13 **S**, 0.10–0.20 **Si**	**Forged or hot rolled, cold rolled and cold finished**: all **diam**, (588) **TS**, (324) **YS**, 15 **El**
DGN–B–301	1145	Mexico	Bar	0.42–0.49 **C**, 0.70–1.00 **Mn**, 0.040 **P**, 0.04–0.07 **S**, 0.10–0.20 **Si**	**Forged or hot rolled, cold rolled and cold finished**: all **diam**, (588) **TS**, (324) **YS**, 15 **El**
QQ–S–637A	1145	US	Bar	0.42–0.49 **C**, 0.70–1.00 **Mn**, 0.040 **P**, 0.04–0.07 **S**, 0.15–0.35 **Pb**	
QQ–S–637A	1146	US	Bar	0.42–0.49 **C**, 0.70–1.00 **Mn**, 0.040 **P**, 0.08–0.13 **S**, 0.15–0.35 **Pb**	
AISI 1146		US	Bar	0.42–0.49 **C**, 0.70–1.00 **Mn**, 0.040 **P**, 0.08–0.13 **S**	
COPANT 331	1146	COPANT	Bar	0.42–0.49 **C**, 0.70–1.00 **Mn**, 0.040 **P**, 0.08–0.13 **S**	
AISI 1146		US	Wire, rod	0.42–0.49 **C**, 0.70–1.00 **Mn**, 0.040 **P**, 0.08–0.13 **S**	
ANSI/ASTM A 576	1145	US	Bar	0.42–0.49 **C**, 0.70–1.00 **Mn**, 0.040 **P**, 0.04–0.07 **S**	
ANSI/ASTM A 576	1146	US	Bar	0.42–0.49 **C**, 0.70–1.00 **Mn**, 0.040 **P**, 0.08–0.13 **S**	
ANSI/ASTM A 29	1145	US	Bar	0.42–0.49 **C**, 0.70–1.00 **Mn**, 0.040 **P**, 0.04–0.07 **S**	
ANSI/ASTM A 29	1146	US	Bar	0.42–0.49 **C**, 0.70–1.00 **Mn**, 0.040 **P**, 0.08–0.13 **S**	
ASTM A 689	1145	US	Bar	0.42–0.49 **C**, 0.70–1.00 **Mn**, 0.040 **P**, 0.04–0.07 **S**	
ASTM A 689	1146	US	Bar	0.42–0.49 **C**, 0.70–1.00 **Mn**, 0.040 **P**, 0.08–0.13 **S**	
AS 1442	Grade AS 1442/K 1146	Australia	Bar, blooms, billets, slabs	0.42–0.49 **C**, 0.70–1.00 **Mn**, 0.050 **P**, 0.08–0.13 **S**, 0.10–0.35 **Si**	
AS 1443	Grade AS 1443/K1146	Australia	Bar	0.42–0.49 **C**, 0.70–1.00 **Mn**, 0.050 **P**, 0.08–0.13 **S**, 0.10–0.35 **Si**	
DIN 17212	Grade 45 Cr 2	Germany	Blooms, slabs, billets, wire, bar, plate, sheet, strip, tube, forgings	0.42–0.48 **C**, 0.50–0.80 **Mn**, 0.025 **P**, 0.035 **S**, 0.15–0.40 **Si**, 0.40–0.60 **Cr**	**Quenched and tempered**: (≤16) **diam**, (880) **TS**, (640) **YS**, 12 **El**
JIS 3540	SWCH 45K	Japan	Wire	0.42–0.48 **C**, 0.60–0.90 **Mn**, 0.030 **P**, 0.035 **S**, 0.10–0.35 **Si**	**Annealed and cold drawn**: all **diam**, (706) **TS**, 10 **El**
NF A 35–553	XC 45	France	Strip	0.42–0.48 **C**, 0.50–0.80 **Mn**, 0.035 **P**, 0.035 **S**, 0.10–0.35 **Si**	**Normalized**: all **diam**, (640) **TS**, (355) **YS**, 18 **El**; **Quenched and tempered**: all **diam**, (880) **TS**, (705) **YS**, 11 **El**
JIS G 3507	SWRCH 45K	Japan	Wire, rod	0.42–0.48 **C**, 0.60–0.90 **Mn**, 0.030 **P**, 0.035 **S**, 0.10–0.35 **Si**	
JIS G 4051	S 45C	Japan	Bar, wire, rod	0.42–0.48 **C**, 0.60–0.90 **Mn**, 0.030 **P**, 0.035 **S**, 0.15–0.35 **Si**, 0.30 **Cu**	
AS 1450	300	Australia	Tube: seamless or welded	0.42 **C**, 0.060 **P**, 0.060 **S**	**Hot finished, as–formed, normalized, and annealed**: all **diam**, (540) **TS**, (310) **YS**, 18 **El**
AISI 1042		US	Bar	0.40–0.70 **C**, 0.60–0.90 **Mn**, 0.040 **P**, 0.050 **S**	
JIS E 1102	Class 2: for 40 kgN rails	Japan	Plate	0.40–0.55 **C**, 0.55–1.00 **Mn**, 0.040 **P**, 0.045 **S**, 0.40 **Si**	**Quenched and tempered**: all **diam**, (686) **TS**, 12 **El**
JIS E 1102	Class 2: for 50 kg rails	Japan	Plate	0.40–0.55 **C**, 0.55–1.00 **Mn**, 0.040 **P**, 0.045 **S**, 0.40 **Si**	**Quenched and tempered**: all **diam**, (686) **TS**, 12 **El**
JIS E 1102	Class 2: for 50 kgN rails	Japan	Plate	0.40–0.55 **C**, 0.55–1.00 **Mn**, 0.040 **P**, 0.045 **S**, 0.40 **Si**	**Quenched and tempered**: all **diam**, (686) **TS**, 12 **El**

WROUGHT CARBON STEELS

specification number	designation	country	product forms	composition	mechanical properties (see page iv for explanation)
JIS E 1102	Class 2: for 60 kg rails	Japan	Plate	0.40–0.55 **C**, 0.55–1.00 **Mn**, 0.040 **P**, 0.045 **S**, 0.40 **Si**	**Quenched and tempered**: all **diam**, (686) **TS**, 12 **El**
BS 1717	CDS–107	UK	Tube	0.40–0.55 **C**, 0.3–0.9 **Mn**, 0.050 **P**, 0.050 **S**, 0.35 **Si**	**As drawn or as drawn and tempered**: all **diam**, (620) **TS**, (525) **YS**
BS 980	CDS–8	UK	Tube	0.40–0.55 **C**, 0.3–0.9 **Mn**, 0.050 **P**, 0.050 **S**, 0.35 **Si**	**Drawn or drawn and tempered**: 8 **diam**, (620) **TS**, (525) **YS**
ANSI/ASTM A 236	Grade E	US	Forgings	0.40–0.55 **C**, 0.60–0.90 **Mn**, 0.045 **P**, 0.050 **S**, 0.15 min **Si**	**Normalized and tempered**: ≤8 **diam**, (585) **TS**, (305) **YS**, 25 **El**
ANSI/ASTM A 236	Grade E	US	Forgings	0.40–0.55 **C**, 0.60–0.90 **Mn**, 0.045 **P**, 0.050 **S**, 0.15 min **Si**	**Normalized and tempered**: 8–14 (203–356) **diam**, 83 (570) **TS**, 43 (295) **YS**, 23 **El**
ANSI/ASTM A 730	Grade E	US	Forgings	0.40–0.55 **C**, 0.60–0.90 **Mn**, 0.045 **P**, 0.050 **S**, 0.15 min **Si**	**Normalized and tempered**: 8–14 (203–356) **diam**, 83 (570) **TS**, 43 (295) **YS**, 23 **El**
JIS E 1101	Class 1: for 40 kgn rails	Japan	Plate	0.40–0.55 **C**, 0.55–1.00 **Mn**, 0.040 **P**, 0.045 **S**, 0.40 **Si**	**As rolled**: all **diam**, (569) **TS**, 15 **El**
JIS E 1102	Class 1: for 50 kg rails	Japan	Plate	0.40–0.55 **C**, 0.55–1.00 **Mn**, 0.040 **P**, 0.045 **S**, 0.40 **Si**	**As rolled**: all **diam**, (569) **TS**, 15 **El**
JIS E 1102	Class 1: for 50 kgN rails	Japan	Plate	0.40–0.55 **C**, 0.55–1.00 **Mn**, 0.040 **P**, 0.045 **S**, 0.40 **Si**	**As rolled**: all **diam**, (569) **TS**, 15 **El**
ANSI/ASTM A 236	Grade D		Forgings	0.40–0.55 **C**, 0.60–0.90 **Mn**, 0.045 **P**, 0.050 **S**, 0.15 min **Si**	**Annealed, normalized or normalized and tempered**: 8–14 (203–356) **diam**, 80 (550) **TS**, 40 (275) **YS**, 21 **El**
ANSI/ASTM A 236	Grade D	US	Forgings	0.40–0.55 **C**, 0.60–0.90 **Mn**, 0.045 **P**, 0.050 **S**, 0.15 min **Si**	**Annealed, normalized, or normalized and tempered**: ≤8 **diam**, (550) **TS**, (275) **YS**, 22 **El**
ANSI/ASTM A 730	Grade D	US	Forgings	0.40–0.55 **C**, 0.60–0.90 **Mn**, 0.045 **P**, 0.050 **S**, 0.15 min **Si**	**Annealed, normalized or normalized and tempered**: 8–14 (203–356) **diam**, 80 (550) **TS**, 40 (275) **YS**, 21 **El**
ANSI/ASTM A 236	Grade C	US	Forgings	0.40–0.55 **C**, 0.60–0.90 **Mn**, 0.045 **P**, 0.050 **S**, 0.15 min **Si**	**Annealed, normalized, or normalized and tempered**: 8–14 (203–356) **diam**, 75 (515) **TS**, 37 (260) **YS**, 19 **El**
ANSI/ASTM A 236	Grade C	US	Forgings	0.40–0.55 **C**, 0.60–0.90 **Mn**, 0.045 **P**, 0.050 **S**, 0.15 min **Si**	**Annealed or normalized or normalized and tempered**: ≤8 **diam**, (515) **TS**, (260) **YS**, 20 **El**
BS 1717	CDS–107	UK	Tube	0.40–0.55 **C**, 0.3–0.9 **Mn**, 0.050 **P**, 0.050 **S**, 0.35 **Si**	**Annealed**: all **diam**, (455) **TS**, (305) **YS**; **Normalized**: all **diam**, (525) **TS**, (385) **YS**
BS 980	CDS–7	UK	Tube	0.40–0.55 **C**, 0.3–0.9 **Mn**, 0.050 **P**, 0.050 **S**, 0.35 **Si**	**Annealed or normalized**: all **diam**, (455) **TS**, (305) **YS**
ANSI/ASTM A 730	Grade C,D,E	US	Forgings	0.40–0.55 **C**, 0.60–0.90 **Mn**, 0.045 **P**, 0.050 **S**, 0.15 **Si**	
NF A 35–051	FM 46	France	Wire, rod	0.40–0.51 **C**, 0.50–0.80 **Mn**, 0.040 **P**, 0.040 **S**, 0.10–0.35 **Si**	
IS 5517	Grade C45	India	Bar, billet	0.40–0.50 **C**, 0.60–0.90 **Mn**, 0.10–0.35 **Si**	**Normalized, annealed or hardened and tempered**: (30) **diam**, (685) **TS**, (470) **YS**
ASTM A 290	Class C	US	Rings: forged or rolled	0.40–0.50 **C**, 0.60–0.90 **Mn**, 0.040 **P**, 0.040 **S**, 0.15–0.30 **Si**, 0.06 **V**	**Quenched, tempered**: all **diam**, 95 (655) **TS**, 65 (450) **YS**, 20 **El**
AS 1442	Grade AS 1442/K6	Australia	Bar	0.40–0.50 **C**, 0.50–1.00 **Mn**, 0.050 **P**, 0.050 **S**, 0.10–0.35 **Si**	**As rolled or normalized**: (≤150) **diam**, (600) **TS**, (300) **YS**, 14 **El**
AS 1442	Grade AS 1442/S6	Australia	Bar	0.40–0.50 **C**, 0.50–1.00 **Mn**, 0.050 **P**, 0.050 **S**, 0.35 **Si**	**As rolled or normalized**: (≤150) **diam**, (600) **TS**, (300) **YS**, 14 **El**
AS 1443	AS 1443/S6	Australia	Bar	0.40–0.50 **C**, 0.50–1.00 **Mn**, 0.050 **P**, 0.050 **S**, 0.35 **Si**	**As rolled or normalized**: (≤150) **diam**, (600) **TS**, (300) **YS**, 14 **El**
AS 1443	AS 1443/K6	US	Bar	0.40–0.50 **C**, 0.50–1.00 **Mn**, 0.050 **P**, 0.050 **S**, 0.10–0.35 **Si**	**As rolled or normalized**: (≤150) **diam**, (600) **TS**, (300) **YS**, 14 **El**

WROUGHT CARBON STEELS

specification number	designation	country	product forms	composition	mechanical properties (see page iv for explanation)
NF A 35–564	XC 4 2 FF	France	Bar, wire, rod	0.40–0.50 **C**, 0.030 **P**, 0.030 **S**, 0.20 **Si**, 0.20 **Cu**, 0.20 min **Al**	**Annealed:** (≤70) **diam**, (590) max **TS**
NF A 35–553	C 45	France	Strip	0.40–0.50 **C**, 0.50–0.80 **Mn**, 0.040 **P**, 0.040 **S**, 0.10–0.40 **Si**	
ASTM A 290	Class D	US	Rings: forged or rolled	0.40–0.50 **C**, 0.60–0.90 **Mn**, 0.040 **P**, 0.040 **S**, 0.15–0.30 **Si**, 0.06 **V**	**Quenched, tempered**
ANSI/ASTM A 29	M 1044	US	Bar	0.40–0.50 **C**, 0.25–0.60 **Mn**, 0.04 **P**, 0.05 **S**	
ANSI/ASTM A 575	M1044	US	Bar	0.40–0.50 **C**, 0.25–0.60 **Mn**, 0.04 **P**, 0.05 **S**	
DIN 17140	Grade D45–2	Germany	Wire, rod	0.40–0.49 **C**, 0.30–0.60 **Mn**, 0.040 **P**, 0.040 **S**, 0.10–0.30 **Si**, 0.007 **N**	
DGN–B–301	1144	Mexico	Bar	0.40–0.48 **C**, 1.35–1.65 **Mn**, 0.040 **P**, 0.24–0.33 **S**, 0.10–0.20 **Si**	**Forged or hot rolled, cold rolled and cold finished:** all **diam**, (667) **TS**, (363) **YS**, 15 **El**
AISI 1144		US	Bar	0.40–0.48 **C**, 1.35–1.65 **Mn**, 0.040 **P**, 0.24–0.33 **S**	
ANSI/ASTM A 519	1141	US	Tube: seamless	0.40–0.48 **C**, 1.35–1.65 **Mn**, 0.040 **P**, 0.24–0.33 **S**	
DGN–B–301	1042	Mexico	Bar	0.40–0.47 **C**, 0.60–0.90 **Mn**, 0.040 **P**, 0.050 **S**, 0.10–0.20 **Si**	**Forged or hot rolled, cold rolled and cold finished:** all **diam**, (549) **TS**, (304) **YS**, 16 **El**
AISI 1043		US	Bar	0.40–0.47 **C**, 0.70–1.00 **Mn**, 0.040 **P**, 0.050 **S**	
AS 1446	Grade AS 1446/K1042	Australia	Plate	0.40–0.47 **C**, 0.60–0.90 **Mn**, 0.050 **P**, 0.050 **S**, 0.10–0.35 **Si**	
AS 1446	Grade AS 1446/S1042	Australia	Plate	0.40–0.47 **C**, 0.60–0.90 **Mn**, 0.050 **P**, 0.050 **S**, 0.35 **Si**	
DGN–B–301	1043	Mexico	Bar	0.40–0.47 **C**, 0.70–1.00 **Mn**, 0.040 **P**, 0.050 **S**, 0.10–0.20 **Si** **TS**, (314) **YS**, 16 **El**	
ANSI/ASTM A 576	1042	US	Bar	0.40–0.47 **C**, 0.60–0.90 **Mn**, 0.040 **P**, 0.050 **S**	
ANSI/ASTM A 576	1043	US	Bar	0.40–0.47 **C**, 0.70–1.00 **Mn**, 0.040 **P**, 0.050 **S**	
AISI 1042		US	Wire, rod	0.40–0.47 **C**, 0.60–0.90 **Mn**, 0.040 **P**, 0.050 **S**	
AISI 1043		US	Wire, rod	0.40–0.47 **C**, 0.70–1.00 **Mn**, 0.040 **P**, 0.050 **S**	
ANSI/ASTM A 29	1042	US	Bar	0.40–0.47 **C**, 0.60–0.90 **Mn**, 0.040 **P**, 0.050 **S**	
ANSI/ASTM A 29	1043	US	Bar	0.40–0.47 **C**, 0.70–1.00 **Mn**, 0.040 **P**, 0.050 **S**	
ASTM A 689	1042	US	Bar	0.40–0.47 **C**, 0.60–0.90 **Mn**, 0.040 **P**, 0.050 **S**	
ASTM A 689	1043	US	Bar	0.40–0.47 **C**, 0.70–1.00 **Mn**, 0.040 **P**, 0.050 **S**	
AS 1443	Grade AS 1443/K1042	Australia	Bar	0.40–0.47 **C**, 0.60–0.90 **Mn**, 0.050 **P**, 0.050 **S**, 0.10–0.35 **Si**	
AS 1442	Grade AS 1442/K1042	Australia	Bar, blooms, billets, slabs	0.40–0.47 **C**, 0.60–0.90 **Mn**, 0.050 **P**, 0.050 **S**, 0.10–0.35 **Si**	
JIS G 3539	SWCH 43K	Japan	Wire	0.40–0.46 **C**, 0.60–0.90 **Mn**, 0.030 **P**, 0.035 **S**, 0.10–0.35 **Si**	**Annealed and cold drawn:** all **diam**, (667) **TS**, 11 **El**
JIS G 3507	SWRCH 43K	Japan	Wire, rod	0.40–0.46 **C**, 0.60–0.90 **Mn**, 0.030 **P**, 0.035 **S**, 0.10–0.35 **Si**	
JIS G 4051	S 43C	Japan	Bar, wire, rod	0.40–0.46 **C**, 0.60–0.90 **Mn**, 0.030 **P**, 0.035 **S**, 0.15–0.35 **Si**, 0.30 **Cu**	
BS 970: Part 1	060A42	UK	Blooms, billets, slabs, bar, rod, forgings	0.40–0.45 **C**, 0.50–0.70 **Mn**	
BS 970: Part 1	080A42	UK	Blooms, billets, slabs, bar, rod, forgings	0.40–0.45 **C**, 0.70–0.90 **Mn**	
BS 970: Part 1	212A42	UK	Blooms, billets, slabs, bar, rod, forgings	0.40–0.45 **C**, 1.0–1.3 **Mn**, 0.060 **P**, 0.12–0.20 **S**, 0.25 **Si**	

WROUGHT CARBON STEELS

specification number	designation	country	product forms	composition	mechanical properties (see page iv for explanation)
VSM 10648	St Ac 60–2	Switzerland	Bar, sheet, plate	0.40 **C**, 0.05 **P**, 0.05 **S**	**Cold drawn**: (≤5) **diam**, (784) **TS**, (666) **YS**, 5 **El**; **Cold finished**: (10–100) **diam**, (588) **TS**, (333) **YS**, 15 **El**; **Cold drawn and annealed**: (≤25) **diam**, (559) **TS**, (294) **YS**, 15 **El**; **Cold finished and normalized**: all **diam**, (588) **TS**, (314) **YS**, 15 **El**
DIN 1652	St 60–2 (1.0543)	Germany	Bar	0.40 **C**, 0.06 **P**, 0.05 **S**	**Cold drawn**: all **diam**, (690) **TS**, (490) **YS**, 6 in 80 mm **El**; **Centerless turned and solution annealed**: all **diam**, (560) **TS**, (295) **YS**, 15 in 80 mm **El**; **Centerless turned and normalized**: all **diam**, (590) **TS**, (315) **YS**, 15 in 80 mm **El**
API Spec 5AC	C–75 type 2			0.40 **C**, 1.50 **Mn**, 0.040 **P**, 0.060 **S**, 0.35 **Si**	**Quenched and tempered**: all **diam**, 95 (657) **TS**, 75 (519) **YS**
DIN 1623 Sheet 2	St 60–2 (1.0542.6)	Germany	Sheet	0.40 **C**, 0.060 **P**, 0.050 **S**	**Hot or cold rolled**: all **diam**, (590) **TS**, (335) **YS**, 10 in 80 mm **El**
SFS 200:E	Fe 60	Finland	Bar, plate, strip, wire, forgings	0.40 **C**, 0.050 **P**, 0.050 **S**, 0.009 **N**	**Hot worked**: (>40–100) **diam**, (588) **TS**, (314) **YS**, 16 **El**
TS 911	669.14–423/Fe 60	Turkey	Bar	0.40 **C**, 0.055 **P**, 0.055 **S**	**Hot rolled**: all **diam**, (588) **TS**, (333) **YS**, 15 **El**
NS 13 205	St 60–2	Norway	Bar, forgings	0.40 **C**, 0.050 **P**, 0.050 **S**, 0.007 **N**	**Hot worked and normalized**: (≤16) **diam**, (588) **TS**, (333) **YS**, 15 **El**
ASTM A 372	Class II	US	Forgings	0.40 **C**, 1.29 **Mn**, 0.04 **P**, 0.05 **S**, 0.15–0.30 **Si**	**Annealed or normalized**: all **diam**, 75 (515) **TS**, 45 (310) **YS**, 18 **El**
ANSI/ASTM A 372	Class II	US	Forgings	0.40 **C**, 1.29 **Mn**, 0.04 **P**, 0.05 **S**, 0.15–0.30 **Si**	**Normalized or normalized and tempered**: all **diam**, (515) **TS**, (310) **YS**, 18 **El**
BS 4449	Grade 460/425	UK	Bar	0.40 **C**, 0.050 **P**, 0.050 **S**	**Hot rolled**: (6–16) **diam**, (460) **TS**, 12 **El**
ANSI/ASTM A 446	Grade D	US	Sheet	0.40 **C**, 0.20 **P**, 0.04 **S**	**Hot rolled, hot dip galvanized**: all **diam**, 65 (450) **TS**, 50 (345) **YS**, 12 **El**
BS 980	ERW-3	UK	Tube	0.40 **C**, 0.6 **Mn**, 0.060 **P**, 0.060 **S**	**Welded**: 8 **diam**, (415) **TS**, (275) **YS**, 10 **El**
AISI 1049		US	Plate	0.40 **C**, 0.60–0.90 **Mn**, 0.040 **P**, 0.050 **S**	
ANSI/ASTM A 194	Grade 2	US	Bar, forgings	0.40 min **C**, 0.040 **P**, 0.050 **S**	**As forged**
AISI 1042		US	Plate	0.39–0.47 **C**, 0.60–0.90 **Mn**, 0.040 **P**, 0.050 **S**	
AISI 1043		US	Plate	0.39–0.47 **C**, 0.70–1.00 **Mn**, 0.040 **P**, 0.050 **S**	
JIS G 3506	SWRH 42A	Japan	Wire, rod	0.39–0.46 **C**, 0.30–0.60 **Mn**, 0.040 **P**, 0.040 **S**, 0.15–0.35 **Si**	
JIS G 3506	SWRH 42B	Japan	Wire, rod	0.39–0.46 **C**, 0.60–0.90 **Mn**, 0.040 **P**, 0.040 **S**, 0.15–0.35 **Si**	
NF A 33-101	AF 50, 2A	France	Bar, billets, blooms	0.39 **C**, 0.045 **P**, 0.045 **S**	**Normalized**: all **diam**, (490) **TS**, 23 **El**
SIS 14 16 50	SIS 16 50-06	Sweden	Bar	0.38–0.50 **C**, 0.40–0.90 **Mn**, 0.050 **P**, 0.050 **S**	**Cold worked**: (≤40) **diam**, (640) **TS**, (540) **YS**, 7 **El**
SIS 14 16 50	SIS 16 50-00	Sweden	Bar, forgings, plate, sheet, tube	0.38–0.50 **C**, 0.40–0.90 **Mn**, 0.050 **P**, 0.050 **S**	**As rolled**: all **diam**, (590) **TS**, (320) **YS**, 16 **El**
SIS 14 16 50	SIS 16 50-01	Sweden	Bar, forgings, plate, sheet, tube	0.38–0.50 **C**, 0.40–0.90 **Mn**, 0.050 **P**, 0.050 **S**	**Normalized**: all **diam**, (590) **TS**, (320) **YS**, 16 **El**
SIS 14 21 20	SIS 21 20-05	Sweden	Tube	0.38–0.45 **C**, 1.10–1.40 **Mn**, 0.035 **P**, 0.035 **S**, 0.15–0.40 **Si**	**Quenched and tempered**: (≤16) **diam**, (900) **TS**, (650) **YS**, 8 **El**
SIS 14 21 20	SIS 21 20-04	Sweden	Bar, forgings, tube	0.38–0.45 **C**, 1.10–1.40 **Mn**, 0.035 **P**, 0.035 **S**, 0.15–0.40 **Si**	**Quenched and tempered**: all **diam**, (800) **TS**, (550) **YS**, 12 **El**
SIS 14 21 20	SIS 21 20-03	Sweden	Bar, forgings, tube	0.38–0.45 **C**, 1.10–1.40 **Mn**, 0.035 **P**, 0.035 **S**, 0.15–0.40 **Si**	**Quenched and tempered**: all **diam**, (700) **TS**, (450) **YS**, 15 **El**

WROUGHT CARBON STEELS

specification number	designation	country	product forms	composition	mechanical properties (see page iv for explanation)
SIS 14 21 20	SIS 21 20–23	Sweden	Castings	0.38–0.45 **C**, 1.10–1.40 **Mn**, 0.035 **P**, 0.035 **S**, 0.30–0.60 **Si**	**Quenched and tempered**: (≤63) **diam**, (700) **TS**, (450) **YS**, 12 **El**
SFS 457	Co, 40 Mn 1,25	Finland	Bar, forgings, tube	0.38–0.45 **C**, 1.10–1.40 **Mn**, 0.035 **P**, 0.035 **S**, 0.15–040 **Si**	**Quenched and tempered**: (25) **diam**, (690) **TS**, (430) **YS**, 15 **El**
SIS 14 21 20	SIS 21 20–06	Sweden	Bar, forgings	0.38–0.45 **C**, 1.10–1.40 **Mn**, 0.035 **P**, 0.035 **S**, 0.15–0.40 **Si**	**Quenched and tempered**: (≤160) **diam**, (650) **TS**, (400) **YS**, 16 **El**
SIS 14 21 20	SIS 21 20–01	Sweden	Tube	0.38–0.45 **C**, 1.10–1.40 **Mn**, 0.035 **P**, 0.035 **S**, 0.15–0.40 **Si**	**Normalized**: (≤10) **diam**, (600) **TS**, (400) **YS**, 19 **El**
SIS 14 21 20	SIS 21 20–21	Sweden	Castings	0.38–0.45 **C**, 1.10–1.40 **Mn**, 0.035 **P**, 0.035 **S**, 0.30–0.60 **Si**	**Normalized**: all **diam**, (600) **TS**, (350) **YS**, 12 **El**
SFS 366	G–41 Mn5	Finland	Castings	0.38–0.45 **C**, 1.1–1.4 **Mn**, 0.035 **P**, 0.035 **S**, 0.60 **Si**	**Normalized and annealed**: all **diam**, (590) **TS**, (390) **YS**, 12 **El**; **Quenched and tempered**: (≤60) **diam**, (690) **TS**, (440) **YS**, 12 **El**
BS 970: Part 1	080H41	UK	Blooms, billets, slabs, bar, rod, forgings	0.38–0.45 **C**, 0.60–1.00 **Mn**	
SIS 14 21 20	SIS 21 20–00	Sweden	Bar, forgings, plate, sheet	0.38–0.45 **C**, 1.10–1.40 **Mn**, 0.035 **P**, 0.035 **S**, 0.15–0.40 **Si**	
SIS 14 21 20	SIS 21 20–02	Sweden	Bar, forgings, tube	0.38–0.45 **C**, 1.10–1.40 **Mn**, 0.035 **P**, 0.035 **S**, 0.15–0.40 **Si**	
DIN 17212	Grade 41 CrMo 4	Germany	Blooms, slabs, billets, wire, bar, plate, sheet, strip, tube, forgings	0.38–0.44 **C**, 0.50–0.80 **Mn**, 0.025 **P**, 0.035 **S**, 0.15–0.40 **Si**, 0.90–1.20 **Cr**, 0.15–0.30 **Mo**	**Quenched and tempered**: (≤16) **diam**, (1080) **TS**, (880) **YS**, 10 **El**
DIN 17212	Grade 42 Cr 4	Germany	Blooms, slabs, billets, wire, bar, plate, sheet, strip, tube, forgings	0.38–0.44 **C**, 0.50–0.80 **Mn**, 0.025 **P**, 0.035 **S**, 0.15–0.40 **Si**, 0.90–1.20 **Cr**	**Quenched and tempered**: (≤16) **diam**, (980) **TS**, (780) **YS**, 11 **El**
ISO 683/XII	2	ISO	Bar, plate	0.38–0.44 **C**, 0.50–0.80 **Mn**, 0.035 **P**, 0.035 **S**, 0.15–0.40 **Si**	**Quenched and tempered**: (16) **diam**, (660) **TS**, (450) **YS**, 16 **El**
BS 970: Part 1	060A40	UK	Blooms, billets, slabs, bar, rod, forgings	0.38–0.43 **C**, 0.50–0.70 **Mn**	
BS 970: Part 1	080A40	UK	Blooms, billets, slabs, bar, rod, forgings	0.38–0.43 **C**, 0.70–0.90 **Mn**	
NF A 35–051	FM 45 grade 1	France	Wire, rod	0.37–0.53 **C**, 0.50–0.80 **Mn**, 0.080 **P**, 0.055 **S**, 0.10–0.35 **Si**	
NF A 35–051	FM 45 grade 3	France	Wire, rod	0.37–0.52 **C**, 0.50–0.80 **Mn**, 0.040 **P**, 0.040 **S**, 0.10–0.35 **Si**	
NF A 35–051	FM 42	France	Wire, rod	0.37–0.48 **C**, 0.50–0.80 **Mn**, 0.040 **P**, 0.040 **S**, 0.10–0.35 **Si**	
DGN–B–301	1141	Mexico	Bar	0.37–0.45 **C**, 1.35–1.65 **Mn**, 0.040 **P**, 0.08–0.13 **S**, 0.10–0.20 **Si**	**Forged or hot rolled, cold rolled and cold finished**: all **diam**, (647) **TS**, (353) **YS**, 15 **El**
AISI 1141		US	Bar	0.37–0.45 **C**, 1.35–1.65 **Mn**, 0.040 **P**, 0.08–0.13 **S**	
ANSI/ASTM A 519	1141	US	Tube: seamless	0.37–0.45 **C**, 1.35–1.65 **Mn**, 0.040 **P**, 0.08–0.13 **S**	
AIR 9160/C 77	9160C271	France	Bar, forgings, sheet	0.37–0.44 **C**, 0.20–0.40 **Mn**, 0.015 **P**, 0.010 **S**, 0.80–1.0 **Si**, 0.40–0.60 **V**, 4.75–5.25 **Cr**, 1.20–1.40 **Mo**	**Quenched and tempered (bar, forgings)**: (≤70) **diam**, (1800) **TS**, (1500) **YS**, 7 **El**
AIR 9160/C 75	9160C261	France	Bar, forgings, sheet	0.37–0.44 **C**, 0.20–0.40 **Mn**, 0.015 **P**, 0.010 **S**, 0.80–1.0 **Si**, 0.40–0.60 **V**, 4.75–5.25 **Cr**, 1.20–1.40 **Mo**	**Quenched and tempered (bar, forgings)**: (≤70) **diam**, (1500) **TS**, (1300) **YS**, 9 **El**
ISO R683/1	C40	ISO	Bar, forgings	0.37–0.44 **C**, 0.50–0.80 **Mn**, 0.050 **P**, 0.050 **S**, 0.15–0.40 **Si**	**Quenched and tempered**: all **diam**, (1030) **TS**, (710) **YS**, 16 **El**; **Quenched, tempered and cold–reduced**: all **diam**, (1175) **TS**, (955) **YS**, 9 **El**

WROUGHT CARBON STEELS

specification number	designation	country	product forms	composition	mechanical properties (see page iv for explanation)
ISO R683/1	C40e	ISO	Bar, forgings	0.37–0.44 **C**, 0.50–0.80 **Mn**, 0.035 **P**, 0.035 **S**, 0.15–0.40 **Si**	**Quenched and tempered**: all **diam**, (1030) **TS**, (710) **YS**, 16 **El**; **Quenched, tempered and cold reduced**: all **diam**, (1175) **TS**, (955) **YS**, 9 **El**
ISO/R 683/111	Type C40ea	ISO	Bar, billet, rod	0.37–0.44 **C**, 0.50–0.80 **Mn**, 0.035 **P**, 0.020–0.035 **S**, 0.15–0.40 **Si**	**Quenched and tempered**: (≤16) **diam**, (657) **TS**, (450) **YS**, 16 **El**
ISO/R 683/111	Type C40eb	ISO	Bar, billet, rod	0.37–0.44 **C**, 0.50–0.80 **Mn**, 0.035 **P**, 0.030–0.050 **S**, 0.15–0.40 **Si**	**Quenched and tempered**: (≤16) **diam**, (657) **TS**, (450) **YS**, 16 **El**
ISO 683/XVIII	C40e	ISO	Bar, wire	0.37–0.44 **C**, 0.50–0.80 **Mn**, 0.035 **P**, 0.035 **S**, 0.15–0.40 **Si**	**Normalized**: all **diam**, (580) **TS**, (320) **YS**, 16 **El**
ISO 683/XVIII	C40ea	ISO	Bar, wire	0.37–0.44 **C**, 0.50–0.80 **Mn**, 0.035 **P**, 0.020–0.035 **S**, 0.15–0.40 **Si**	**Normalized**: all **diam**, (580) **TS**, (320) **YS**, 16 **El**
ISO 683/XVIII	C40eb	ISO	Bar, wire	0.37–0.44 **C**, 0.50–0.80 **Mn**, 0.035 **P**, 0.030–0.050 **S**, 0.15–0.40 **Si**	**Normalized**: all **diam**, (580) **TS**, (320) **YS**, 16 **El**
ISO 683/XVIII	C40	ISO	Bar, wire	0.37–0.44 **C**, 0.50–0.80 **Mn**, 0.050 **P**, 0.050 **S**, 0.15–0.40 **Si**	**Normalized**: all **diam**, (580) **TS**, (320) **YS**, 16 **El**
DGN–B–301	1140	Mexico	Bar	0.37–0.44 **C**, 0.70–1.00 **Mn**, 0.040 **P**, 0.08–0.13 **S**, 0.10–0.20 **Si**	**Forged or hot rolled, cold rolled and cold finished**: all **diam**, (549) **TS**, (304) **YS**, 16 **El**
DGN–B–301	1039	Mexico	Bar	0.37–0.44 **C**, 0.70–1.00 **Mn**, 0.040 **P**, 0.050 **S**, 0.10–0.20 **Si**	**Forged or hot rolled, cold rolled and cold finished**: all **diam**, (549) **TS**, (304) **YS**, 16 **El**
DGN–B–301	1040	Mexico	Bar	0.37–0.44 **C**, 0.60–0.90 **Mn**, 0.040 **P**, 0.050 **S**, 0.10–0.20 **Si**	**Forged or hot rolled, cold rolled and cold finished**: all **diam**, (520) **TS**, (294) **YS**, 18 **El**
QQ–S–637A	1140	US	Bar	0.37–0.44 **C**, 0.70–1.00 **Mn**, 0.040 **P**, 0.08–0.13 **S**, 0.15–0.35 **Pb**	
AISI 1140		US	Bar	0.37–0.44 **C**, 0.70–1.00 **Mn**, 0.040 **P**, 0.08–0.13 **S**	
AISI 1040		US	Bar	0.37–0.44 **C**, 0.60–0.90 **Mn**, 0.040 **P**, 0.050 **S**	
AISI 1039		US	Bar	0.37–0.44 **C**, 0.70–1.00 **Mn**, 0.040 **P**, 0.050 **S**	
ANSI/ASTM A 519	1040	US	Tube: seamless	0.37–0.44 **C**, 0.60–0.90 **Mn**, 0.040 **P**, 0.050 **S**	
MIL–S–46070	Grade 1040	US	Bar: cold drawn	0.37–0.44 **C**, 0.60–0.90 **Mn**, 0.035 **P**, 0.045 **S**, 0.30 **Si**	**Normalized or annealed and stress relieved**: <1.25 **diam**, 75 (517) **YS**, 15 **El**
DGN–B–203	Grade 1040	Mexico	Tube: seamless	0.37–0.44 **C**, 0.60–0.90 **Mn**, 0.040 **P**, 0.050 **S**	
AS 1446	Grade AS 1446/K1040	Australia	Plate	0.37–0.44 **C**, 0.60–0.90 **Mn**, 0.050 **P**, 0.050 **S**, 0.10–0.35 **Si**	
AS 1446	Grade AS 1446/S1040	Australia	Plate	0.37–0.44 **C**, 0.60–0.90 **Mn**, 0.050 **P**, 0.050 **S**, 0.35 **Si**	
COPANT 331	1040	COPANT	Bar	0.37–0.44 **C**, 0.60–0.90 **Mn**, 0.040 **P**, 0.050 **S**	
MIL–S–16974E	No. 1040	US	Bar, billets, blooms, slabs	0.37–0.44 **C**, 0.60–0.90 **Mn**, 0.040 **P**, 0.050 **S**, 0.15–0.30 **Si**	
ASTM A 108	1040	US	Bar	0.37–0.44 **C**, 0.60–0.90 **Mn**, 0.040 **P**, 0.050 **S**	
ANSI/ASTM A 545	Grade 1039	US	Wire	0.37–0.44 **C**, 0.70–1.00 **Mn**, 0.040 **P**, 0.050 **S**	
ANSI/ASTM A 546	Grade 1040	US	Wire	0.37–0.44 **C**, 0.60–0.90 **Mn**, 0.040 **P**, 0.050 **S**	
MIL–S–11310E	1040	US	Bar	0.37–0.44 **C**, 0.60–0.90 **Mn**, 0.040 **P**, 0.050 **S**, 0.20 **Si**	
MIL–S–16788A	Class C4	US	Blooms, billets, slabs	0.37–0.44 **C**, 0.60–0.90 **Mn**, 0.040 **P**, 0.050 **S**	
COPANT 333	1039	COPANT	Wire, rod	0.37–0.44 **C**, 0.70–1.00 **Mn**, 0.040 **P**, 0.050 **S**	
COPANT 333	1040	COPANT	Wire, rod	0.37–0.44 **C**, 0.60–0.90 **Mn**, 0.040 **P**, 0.050 **S**	

WROUGHT CARBON STEELS

specification number	designation	country	product forms	composition	mechanical properties (see page iv for explanation)
ANSI/ASTM A 576	1039	US	Bar	0.37–0.44 **C**, 0.70–1.00 **Mn**, 0.040 **P**, 0.050 **S**	
ANSI/ASTM A 576	1040	US	Bar	0.37–0.44 **C**, 0.60–0.90 **Mn**, 0.040 **P**, 0.050 **S**	
AISI 1039		US	Wire, rod	0.37–0.44 **C**, 0.70–1.00 **Mn**, 0.040 **P**, 0.050 **S**	
AISI 1040		US	Wire, rod	0.37–0.44 **C**, 0.60–0.90 **Mn**, 0.040 **P**, 0.050 **S**	
AISI 1140		US	Wire, rod	0.37–0.44 **C**, 0.70–1.00 **Mn**, 0.040 **P**, 0.08–0.13 **S**	
ANSI/ASTM A 576	1140	US	Bar	0.37–0.44 **C**, 0.70–1.00 **Mn**, 0.040 **P**, 0.08–0.13 **S**	
ANSI/ASTM A 29	1140	US	Bar	0.37–0.44 **C**, 0.70–1.00 **Mn**, 0.040 **P**, 0.08–0.13 **S**	
ANSI/ASTM A 29	1039	US	Bar	0.37–0.44 **C**, 0.70–1.00 **Mn**, 0.040 **P**, 0.050 **S**	
ANSI/ASTM A 29	1040	US	Bar	0.37–0.44 **C**, 0.60–0.90 **Mn**, 0.040 **P**, 0.050 **S**	
ASTM A 689	1140	US	Bar	0.37–0.44 **C**, 0.70–1.00 **Mn**, 0.040 **P**, 0.08–0.13 **S**	
ASTM A 689	1039	US	Bar	0.37–0.44 **C**, 0.70–1.00 **Mn**, 0.040 **P**, 0.050 **S**	
ASTM A 689	1040	US	Bar	0.37–0.44 **C**, 0.60–0.90 **Mn**, 0.040 **P**, 0.050 **S**	
AS 1443	Grade AS 1443/S1040	Australia	Bar	0.37–0.44 **C**, 0.60–0.90 **Mn**, 0.050 **P**, 0.050 **S**, 0.35 **Si**	
AS 1443	Grade AS 1443/K1040	Australia	Bar	0.37–0.44 **C**, 0.60–0.90 **Mn**, 0.050 **P**, 0.050 **S**, 0.10–0.35 **Si**	
AS 1443	Grade AS 1443/K1039	Australia	Bar	0.37–0.44 **C**, 0.70–1.00 **Mn**, 0.050 **P**, 0.050 **S**, 0.10–0.35 **Si**	
AS 1442	Grade AS 1442/S1040	Australia	Bar, blooms, billets, slabs	0.37–0.44 **C**, 0.60–0.90 **Mn**, 0.050 **P**, 0.050 **S**, 0.35 **Si**	
AS 1442	Grade AS 1442/K1039	Australia	Bar, blooms, billets, slabs	0.37–0.44 **C**, 0.70–1.00 **Mn**, 0.050 **P**, 0.050 **S**, 0.10–0.35 **Si**	
AS 1442	Grade AS 1442/K1040	Australia	Bar, blooms, billets, slabs	0.37–0.44 **C**, 0.60–0.90 **Mn**, 0.050 **P**, 0.050 **S**, 0.10–0.35 **Si**	
COPANT 514	Grade 1040	COPANT	Tube: seamless	0.37–0.44 **C**, 0.60–0.90 **Mn**, 0.040 **P**, 0.050 **S**, 0.20–0.35 **Si**	
JIS G 3539	SWCH 40K	Japan	Wire	0.37–0.43 **C**, 0.60–0.90 **Mn**, 0.030 **P**, 0.035 **S**, 0.10–0.35 **Si**	**Annealed or cold drawn:** all **diam**, (667) **TS**, 11 **El**
JIS G 3507	SWRCH 40K	Japan	Wire, rod	0.37–0.43 **C**, 0.60–0.90 **Mn**, 0.030 **P**, 0.035 **S**, 0.10–0.35 **Si**	
JIS G 4051	S 40C	Japan	Bar, wire, rod	0.37–0.43 **C**, 0.60–0.90 **Mn**, 0.030 **P**, 0.035 **S**, 0.15–0.35 **Si**, 0.30 **Cu**	
COPANT 330	1040	COPANT	Bar, shapes	0.37–0.40 **C**, 0.60–0.90 **Mn**, 0.040 **P**, 0.050 **S**	
AISI 1041		US	Plate	0.36–0.45 **C**, 1.30–1.65 **Mn**, 0.040 **P**, 0.050 **S**	
DIN 17200	Grade 40 Mn 4	Germany	Blooms, slabs, billets, wire, bar, plate, sheet, strip, tube, forgings	0.36–0.44 **C**, 0.80–1.10 **Mn**, 0.035 **P**, 0.035 **S**, 0.25–0.50 **Si**	**Quenched and tempered:** (≤16) **diam**, (883) **TS**, (638) **YS**, 12 **El**
BS 970: Part 1	080M40	UK	Blooms, billets, slabs, bar, rod, forgings	0.36–0.44 **C**, 0.60–1.00 **Mn**	**Normalized:** 6 **diam**, (480) **TS**, (250) **YS**, 16 **El**; **Hardened and tempered:** 2.5 **diam**, (550) **TS**, (345) **YS**, 16 **El**; **Cold drawn from hot rolled:** 0.50–0.625 **diam**, (580) **TS**, (455) **YS**, 8 **El**
AISI 1039		US	Plate	0.36–0.44 **C**, 0.70–1.00 **Mn**, 0.040 **P**, 0.050 **S**	
AISI 1040		US	Plate	0.36–0.44 **C**, 0.60–0.90 **Mn**, 0.040 **P**, 0.050 **S**	
AISI 1541		US	Bar	0.36–0.44 **C**, 1.35–1.65 **Mn**, 0.040 **P**, 0.050 **S**	
ANSI/ASTM A 519	1541	US	Tube: seamless	0.36–0.44 **C**, 1.35–1.65 **Mn**, 0.040 **P**, 0.050 **S**	

WROUGHT CARBON STEELS

specification number	designation	country	product forms	composition	mechanical properties (see page iv for explanation)
ASTM A 689	1541	US	Bar: spring	0.36–0.44 **C**, 1.35–1.65 **Mn**, 0.040 **P**, 0.050 **S**	
ANSI/ASTM A 546	Grade 1041	US	Wire	0.36–0.44 **C**, 1.35–1.65 **Mn**, 0.040 **P**, 0.050 **S**	
COPANT 333	1041	COPANT	Wire, rod	0.36–0.44 **C**, 1.35–1.65 **Mn**, 0.040 **P**, 0.050 **S**	
ANSI/ASTM A 680	1040	US	Strip	0.36–0.44 **C**, 0.60–0.90 **Mn**, 0.040 **P**, 0.050 **S**, 0.15–0.30 **Si**	**Cold–rolled**
ANSI/ASTM A 682	1040	US	Strip	0.36–0.44 **C**, 0.60–0.90 **Mn**, 0.040 **P**, 0.050 **S**, 0.15–0.30 **Si**	
ANSI/ASTM A 684	1040	US	Strip	0.36–0.44 **C**, 0.60–0.90 **Mn**, 0.040 **P**, 0.050 **S**, 0.15–0.30 **Si**	
JIS G 3507	SWRCH 41K	Japan	Wire, rod	0.36–0.44 **C**, 1.35–1.65 **Mn**, 0.030 **P**, 0.035 **S**, 0.10–0.35 **Si**	
DIN 1629, Part 4	Grade St55.4/1.0509	Germany	Tube: seamless	0.36 **C**, 0.40 **Mn**, 0.05 **P**, 0.05 **S**, 0.10–0.35 **Si**	**Annealed**: (<16) **diam**, (540) **TS**, (295) **YS**, 17 **El**
DIN 1629, Part 3	Grade St55/1.0507	Germany	Tube: seamless	0.36 **C**, 1.50 **Mn**, 0.05 **P**, 0.05 **S**, 0.55 **Si**	**Annealed**: (<16) **diam**, (540) **TS**, (295) **YS**, 17 **El**
DIN 2391 Part 2	Grade St55–1.0507	Germany	Tube	0.36 **C**, 0.05 **P**, 0.05 **S**	**Normalized**: all **diam**, (539) **TS**, (294) **YS**, 17 **El**; **Bright drawn/hard**: all **diam**, (637) **TS**, 4 **El**; **Bright drawn/soft**: all **diam**; **Annealed**: all **diam**, (490) **TS**, 18 **El**
DIN 2391 Part 2	Grade St 55.2–1.0509	Germany	Tube	0.36 **C**, 0.40 **Mn**, 0.05 **P**, 0.05 **S**, 0.10–0.35 **Si**	**Normalized**: all **diam**, (539) **TS**, (294) **YS**, 17 **El**; **Annealed**. all **diam**, (490) **TS**, 18 **El**
TS 346	Fe 55	Turkey	Pipe: seamless	0.36 **C**, 0.90 **Mn**, 0.050 **P**, 0.050 **S**, 0.35 **Si**	**As drawn**: (≤16) **diam**, (539) **TS**, (294) **YS**, 17 **El**
TS 302	Fe 55.2	Turkey	Pipe: welded or seamless	0.36 **C**, 0.050 **P**, 0.050 **S**	**As drawn or as welded**: all **diam**, (539) **TS**, (255) **YS**, 17 **El**
SFS 2148	Fe 55	Finland	Tube: seamless	0.36 **C**, 0.05 **P**, 0.05 **S**	**As drawn**: (≤16) **diam**, (539) **TS**, (274) **YS**, 17 **El**
ANSI/ASTM A 241		US	Plate	0.35–0.82 **C**, 0.050 **P**, 0.20 **Cu**	
DGN–B–269		Mexico	Shapes	0.35–0.82 **C**, 0.050 **P**, 0.20 min **Cu**	
JIS E 1102	Class 2: for 30 kg rails	Japan	Plate	0.35–0.50 **C**, 0.55–1.00 **Mn**, 0.040 **P**, 0.045 **S**, 0.40 **Si**	**Quenched and tempered**: all **diam**, (686) **TS**, 12 **El**
JIS E 1102	Class 2: for 37 kg rails	Japan	Plate	0.35–0.50 **C**, 0.55–1.00 **Mn**, 0.040 **P**, 0.045 **S**, 0.40 **Si**	**Quenched and tempered**: all **diam**, (686) **TS**, 12 **El**
JIS E 1102	Class 1: for 30 kg rails	Japan	Plate	0.35–0.50 **C**, 0.55–1.00 **Mn**, 0.040 **P**, 0.045 **S**, 0.40 **Si**	**As rolled**: all **diam**, (539) **TS**, 18 **El**
JIS E 1102	Class 1: for 37 kg rails	Japan	Plate	0.35–0.50 **C**, 0.55–1.00 **Mn**, 0.040 **P**, 0.045 **S**, 0.40 **Si**	**As rolled**: all **diam**, (539) **TS**, 18 **El**
BS 2453		UK	Wire	0.35–0.45 **C**, 0.60–1.00 **Mn**, 0.050 **P**, 0.050 **S**, 0.05–0.35 **Si**	**As drawn**: all **diam**, (1050) **TS**
BS 2S.116		UK	Bar: aircraft quality	0.35–0.45 **C**, 0.8–1.0 **Mn**, 0.040 **P**, 0.040 **S**, 0.10–0.35 **Si**	**Hardened and tempered**: all **diam**, (853) **TS**, (431) **YS**, 13 **El**
BS 2S.113		UK	Bar: aircraft quality	0.35–0.45 **C**, 0.6–0.9 **Mn**, 0.040 **P**, 0.040 **S**, 0.10–0.35 **Si**, 0.15–0.35 **Pb**	**Hardened and tempered**: all **diam**, (696) **TS**, 11 **El**
IS 5517	Grade C40	India	Bar, billet	0.35–0.45 **C**, 0.60–0.90 **Mn**, 0.10–0.35 **Si**	**Normalized, annealed or hardened and tempered**: (30) **diam**, (685) **TS**, (470) **YS**
IS 5517	Grade 40S18	India	Bar, billet	0.35–0.45 **C**, 0.80–1.20 **Mn**, 0.060 **P**, 0.14–0.22 **S**, 0.25 **Si**	**Normalized, annealed or hardened and tempered**: (30) **diam**, (685) **TS**, (470) **YS**
JIS G 3445	Class 16C, No. 11	Japan	Tube: seamless	0.35–0.45 **C**, 0.40–1.00 **Mn**, 0.040 **P**, 0.040 **S**, 0.40 **Si**	**As manufactured or cold finished**: all **diam**, (618) **TS**, (461) **YS**, 12 **El**
AS 1443	AS 1443/CD3	Australia	Bar	0.35–0.45 **C**, 0.60–0.90 **Mn**, 0.050 **P**, 0.050 **S**, 0.35 **Si**	**Cold drawn or cold rolled**: (16–38) **diam**, (610) **TS**, (480) **YS**, 19 **El**
ASTM A 290	Class A	US	Rings: forged or rolled	0.35–0.45 **C**, 0.60–0.90 **Mn**, 0.040 **P**, 0.040 **S**, 0.15–0.30 **Si**, 0.06 **V**	**Normalized, tempered**: all **diam**, 80 (550) **TS**, 45 (310) **YS**, 22 **El**

WROUGHT CARBON STEELS

specification number	designation	country	product forms	composition	mechanical properties (see page iv for explanation)
BS 2 S.93		UK	Bar, billets, forgings: aircraft quality	0.35–0.45 **C**, 0.6–0.9 **Mn**, 0.040 **P**, 0.040 **S**, 0.10–0.35 **Si**	**Normalized**: all **diam**, (540) **TS**, (310) **YS**, 15 **El**
AS 1442	Grade AS 1442/K5	Australia	Bar	0.35–0.45 **C**, 0.50–1.00 **Mn**, 0.050 **P**, 0.050 **S**, 0.10–0.35 **Si**	**As rolled or normalized**: (≤150) **diam**, (540) **TS**, (270) **YS**, 16 **El**
AS 1442	Grade AS 1442/S5	Australia	Bar	0.35–0.45 **C**, 0.50–1.00 **Mn**, 0.050 **P**, 0.050 **S**, 0.35 **Si**	**As rolled or normalized**: (≤150) **diam**, (540) **TS**, (270) **YS**, 16 **El**
AS 1443	AS 1443/S5	Australia	Bar	0.35–0.45 **C**, 0.50–1.00 **Mn**, 0.050 **P**, 0.050 **S**, 0.35 **Si**	**As rolled or normalized**: (≤150) **diam**, (540) **TS**, (270) **YS**, 16 **El**
AS 1443	AS 1443/K5	Australia	Bar	0.35–0.45 **C**, 0.50–1.00 **Mn** 0.050 **P**, 0.050 **S**, 0.10–0.35 **Si**	**As rolled or normalized**: (≤150) **diam**, (540) **TS**, (270) **YS**, 16 **El**
JIS G 3445	Class 16A, No. 11	Japan	Tube: seamless	0.35–0.45 **C**, 0.40–1.00 **Mn**, 0.040 **P**, 0.040 **S**, 0.40 **Si**	**As manufactured or cold finished**: all **diam**, (510) **TS**, (324) **YS**, 20 **El**
BS 1449: Part 1	Grade 40	UK	Plate, sheet, strip	0.35–0.45 **C**, 0.50–0.90 **Mn**, 0.045 **P**, 0.045 **S**, 0.05–0.35 **Si**	**Cold rolled**: all **diam**, (460) **TS**, (280) **YS**, 18 **El**; **Hot rolled**: all **diam**, (540) **TS**, (320) **YS**, 16 **El**
NF A 35–051	FM 40	France	Wire, rod	0.35–0.45 **C**, 0.50–0.80 **Mn**, 0.040 **P**, 0.040 **S**, 0.10–0.35 **Si**	
AISI 15B41H		US	Bar	0.35–0.45 **C**, 1.25–1.75 **Mn**, 0.040 **P**, 0.050 **S**, 0.15–0.30 **Si**, 0.0005–0.003 **B**	
AISI 1541H		US	Bar	0.35–0.45 **C**, 1.25–1.75 **Mn**, 0.040 **P**, 0.050 **S**, 0.15–0.30 **Si**	
ASTM A 290	Class B	US	Rings: forged or rolled	0.35–0.45 **C**, 0.60–0.90 **Mn**, 0.040 **P**, 0.040 **S**, 0.15–0.30 **Si**, 0.06 **V**	**Normalized, tempered**
AS 1443	Grade AS 1443/CS1040	Australia	Bar	0.35–0.45 **C**, 0.40–0.90 **Mn**, 0.060 **P**, 0.060 **S**, 0.35 **Si**	
AS 1442	Grade AS 1442/CS1040	Australia	Bar, blooms, billets, slabs	0.35–0.45 **C**, 0.40–0.90 **Mn**, 0.060 **P**, 0.060 **S**, 0.35 **Si**	
AISI 1139		US	Bar	0.35–0.43 **C**, 1.35–1.65 **Mn**, 0.040 **P**, 0.13–0.20 **S**	
DGN-B-301	1139	Mexico	Bar	0.35–0.43 **C**, 1.35–1.65 **Mn**, 0.040 **P**, 0.13–0.20 **S**, 0.10–0.20 **Si**	
DIN 17221	Grade 38 Si 7	Germany	Bar, wire, strip	0.35–0.42 **C**, 0.50–0.80 **Mn**, 0.045 **P**, 0.045 **S**, 1.5–1.8 **Si**	**Quenched and tempered**: (10) **diam**, (1180) **TS**, (1030) **YS**, 6 **El**
DGN-B-301	1038	Mexico	Bar	0.35–0.42 **C**, 0.60–0.90 **Mn**, 0.040 **P**, 0.050 **S**, 0.10–0.20 **Si**	**Forged or hot rolled, cold rolled and cold finished**: all **diam**, (523) **TS**, (284) **YS**, 18 **El**
ASTM A 544	Grade 1038	US	Wire	0.35–0.42 **C**, 0.30–0.90 **Mn**, 0.040 **P**, 0.050 **S**	
AISI 1038		US	Bar	0.35–0.42 **C**, 0.60–0.90 **Mn**, 0.040 **P**, 0.050 **S**	
COPANT 331	1038	COPANT	Bar	0.35–0.42 **C**, 0.60–0.90 **Mn**, 0.040 **P**, 0.050 **S**	
ANSI/ASTM A 546	Grade 1038	US	Wire	0.35–0.42 **C**, 0.60–0.90 **Mn**, 0.040 **P**, 0.050 **S**	
ANSI/ASTM A 545	Grade 1038	US	Wire	0.35–0.42 **C**, 0.60–0.90 **Mn**, 0.040 **P**, 0.050 **S**	
COPANT 333	1038	COPANT	Wire, rod	0.35–0.42 **C**, 0.60–0.90 **Mn**, 0.040 **P**, 0.050 **S**	
ANSI/ASTM A 576	1038	US	Bar	0.35–0.42 **C**, 0.60–0.90 **Mn**, 0.040 **P**, 0.050 **S**	
AISI 1038		US	Wire, rod	0.35–0.42 **C**, 0.60–0.90 **Mn**, 0.040 **P**, 0.050 **S**	
ANSI/ASTM A 29	1038	US	Bar	0.35–0.42 **C**, 0.60–0.90 **Mn**, 0.040 **P**, 0.050 **S**	
ASTM A 689	1038	US	Bar	0.35–0.42 **C**, 0.60–0.90 **Mn**, 0.040 **P**, 0.050 **S**	
AS 1443	Grade AS 1443/XK1038	Australia	Bar	0.35–0.42 **C**, 0.85–1.10 **Mn**, 0.050 **P**, 0.050 **S**, 0.10–0.35 **Si**	
AS 1443	Grade AS 1443/K1038	Australia	Bar	0.35–0.42 **C**, 0.60–0.90 **Mn**, 0.050 **P**, 0.050 **S**, 0.10–0.35 **Si**	

WROUGHT CARBON STEELS

specification number	designation	country	product forms	composition	mechanical properties (see page iv for explanation)
AS 1442	Grade AS 1442/K1038	Australia	Bar, blooms, billets, slabs	0.35–0.42 **C**, 0.60–0.90 **Mn**, 0.050 **P**, 0.050 **S**, 0.10–0.35 **Si**	
AS 1442	Grade AS 1442/XK 1038	Australia	Bar, blooms, billets, slabs	0.35–0.42 **C**, 0.85–1.10 **Mn**, 0.050 **P**, 0.050 **S**, 0.10–0.35 **Si**	
JIS G 3539	SWCH 38K	Japan	Wire	0.35–0.41 **C**, 0.60–0.90 **Mn**, 0.030 **P**, 0.035 **S**, 0.10–0.35 **Si**	**Annealed or cold drawn**: all **diam**, (667) **TS**, 11 **El**
JIS G 3507	SWRCH 38K	Japan	Wire, rod	0.35–0.41 **C**, 0.60–0.90 **Mn**, 0.030 **P**, 0.035 **S**, 0.10–0.35 **Si**	
JIS G 4051	S 38C	Japan	Bar, wire, rod	0.35–0.41 **C**, 0.60–0.90 **Mn**, 0.030 **P**, 0.035 **S**, 0.15–0.35 **Si**, 0.30 **Cu**	
AS G18	G18/En 15B	Austrailia	Bar, billet and bar: black, bright	0.35–0.40 **C**, 1.10–1.30 **Mn**, 0.060 **P**, 0.060 **S**, 0.05–0.35 **Si**	**Hardened, tempered**: 4 **diam**, (620) **TS**, (400) **YS**
NF A 35–554	XC 38	France	Plate	0.35–0.40 **C**, 0.50–0.80 **Mn**, 0.035 **P**, 0.035 **S**, 0.10–0.40 **Si**	**Hot rolled and normalized**: (≤16) **diam**, (580) **TS**, (325) **YS**, 20 **El**
NF A 35–553	XC 38	France	Strip	0.35–0.40 **C**, 0.50–0.80 **Mn**, 0.035 **P**, 0.035 **S**, 0.10–0.35 **Si**	**Normalized**: all **diam**, (580) **TS**, (335) **YS**, 21 **El**; **Quenched and tempered**: all **diam**, (810) **TS**, (620) **YS**, 12 **El**
AIR 9160/C23	9160C021	France	Bar, forgings	0.35–0.40 **C**, 0.50–0.80 **Mn**, 0.035 **P**, 0.035 **S**, 0.10–0.40 **Si**	**Normalized**: (≤16) **diam**, (580) **TS**, (330) **YS**, 21 **El**; **Quenched and tempered**: (≤16) **diam**, (680) **TS**, (490) **YS**, 16 **El**
NF A 35–564	XC 38 FF, 38 B 3 FF	France	Bar, wire, rod	0.35–0.40 **C**, 0.030 **P**, 0.030 **S**, 0.20 **Si**, 0.20 **Cu**, 0.20 min **Al**	**Annealed**: (≤70) **diam**, (570) max **TS**
BS 3S.105		UK	Bar: aircraft quality	0.35–0.40 **C**, 0.8–1.0 **Mn**, 0.040 **P**, 0.040 **S**, 0.15–0.35 **Si**	**Hardened and tempered**: all **diam**, 48 (331) **TS**
BS 970: Part 1	060A37	UK	Blooms, billets, slabs, bar, rod, forgings	0.35–0.40 **C**, 0.50–0.70 **Mn**	
BS 970: Part 1	080A37	UK	Blooms, billets, slabs, bar, rod, forgings	0.35–0.40 **C**, 0.70–0.90 **Mn**	
BS 970: Part 1	212A37	UK	Blooms, billets, slabs, bar, rod, forgings	0.35–0.40 **C**, 1.0–1.3 **Mn**, 0.060 max **P**, 0.12–0.20 **S**, 0.25 **Si**	
ISO 2604/1	F23Q	ISO	Forgings	0.35 **C**, 0.60–1.40 **Mn**, 0.040 **P**, 0.040 **S**, 0.10–0.40 **Si**	**Quenched and tempered**: (≤100) **diam**, (550) **TS**, (305) **YS**, 18 **El**
DNG–B–93		Mexico	Plate, sheet	0.35 **C**, 1.15 **Mn**, 0.040 **P**, 0.050 **S**, 0.30 **Si**	**As agreed**: (5–10) **diam**, (517) **TS**, (255) **YS**, 18 **El**
MIL–S–23284	Class 3	US	Forgings	0.35 **C**, 0.60–0.90 **Mn**, 0.020 **P**, 0.020 **S**, 0.35 **Si**	**Quenched and tempered and stress relieved**: all **diam**, 75 (517) **TS**, 45 (310) **YS**, 22 **El**
ANSI/ASTM A 266	Class 2	US	Forgings	0.35 **C**, 0.40–0.90 **Mn**, 0.040 **P**, 0.040 **S**, 0.15–0.35 **Si**	**Normalized, tempered, or annealed, tempered**: all **diam**, 70 (485) **TS**, 35 (240) **YS**, 20 **El**
ANSI/ASTM A 266	Class 2	US	Forgings	0.35 **C**, 0.40–0.90 **Mn**, 0.040 **P**, 0.040 **S**, 0.15–0.35 **Si**	**Annealed, tempered or normalized, tempered, or quenched, tempered**: all **diam**, 70 (485) **TS**, 35 (240) **YS**, 20 **El**
ANSI/ASTM A 515	Grade 70	US	Plate	0.35 **C**, 0.90 **Mn**, 0.035 **P**, 0.04 **S**, 0.13–0.33 **Si**	**Normalized**: 2.0–4.0 **diam**, (485) **TS**, (260) **YS**, 21 **El**
ANSI/ASTM A 266	Grade 2	US	Forgings	0.35 **C**, 0.40–0.90 **Mn**, 0.040 **P**, 0.040 **S**, 0.15–0.35 **Si**	**Annealed or normalized and tempered**: all **diam**, (485) **TS**, (240) **YS**, 20 **El**
ASTM A 695	Type B, grade 40	US	Bar	0.35 **C**, 1.10 **Mn**, 0.040 **P**, 0.050 **S**, 0.15–0.30 **Si**	**Hot rolled**: ≥3 (≥76.2) **diam**, 70 (485) **TS**, 40 (275) **YS**, 17 **El**
ANSI/ASTM A 557	Grade C2	US	Tube: electric resistance welded	0.35 **C**, 0.27–1.06 **Mn**, 0.050 **P**, 0.060 **S**	**Normalized, annealed**: all **diam**, 70 (483) **TS**, 40 (276) **YS**, 30 **El**
ANSI/ASTM A 210	Grade C	US	Tube: seamless	0.35 **C**, 0.29–1.06 **Mn**, 0.048 **P**, 0.058 **S**, 0.10 **Si**	**Hot finished, as rolled, or cold drawn, annealed**: 0.312 (7.94) **diam**, 70 (483) **TS**, 40 (276) **YS**, 30 **El**
ANSI/ASTM A 181	Grade II	US	Pipe	0.35 **C**, 0.90 **Mn**, 0.05 **P**, 0.05 **S**	**As–forged**: all **diam**, 70 (483) **TS**, 36 (248) **YS**, 18 **El**

specification number	designation	country	product forms	composition	mechanical properties (see page iv for explanation)
ANSI/ASTM A 105		US	Forgings	0.35 **C**, 0.60–1.05 **Mn**, 0.040 **P**, 0.050 **S**, 0.35 **Si**	**Annealed, or normalized, or normalized and tempered, or quenched and tempered**: all **diam**, 70 (483) **TS**, 36 (248) **YS**, 22 **El**
ANSI/ASTM A 106	Grade C	US	Pipe: seamless	0.35 **C**, 0.29–1.06 **Mn**, 0.048 **P**, 0.058 **S**, 0.10 min **Si**	**Annealed**: 0.312 (7.94) **diam**, 70 (483) **TS**, 40 (276) **YS**, 30 **El**
NOM–B–189	Grade C	Mexico	Tube: seamless	0.35 **C**, 0.29–1.06 **Mn**, 0.048 **P**, 0.058 **S**, 0.10 min **Si**	**Hot finished, cold finished and annealed, cold finished and normalized**: (12.7) **diam**, (481) **TS**, (275) **YS**, 30 **El**
JIS G 3211	Class 1	Japan	Forgings	0.35 **C**, 0.40–0.90 **Mn**, 0.030 **P**, 0.030 **S**, 0.15–0.35 **Si**, 0.06 **V**	**Quenched and tempered**: all **diam**, (481) **TS**, (245) **YS**, 20 **El**
JIS G 3212	Class 1	Japan	Forgings	0.35 **C**, 0.40–0.90 **Mn**, 0.025 **P**, 0.025 **S**, 0.15–0.35 **Si**, 0.05 **V**	**Quenched and tempered**: all **diam**, (481) **TS**, (245) **YS**, 20 **El**
BS 3602	Steel 35	UK	Pipe, tube: seamless	0.35 **C**, 0.70–1.10 **Mn**, 0.050 **P**, 0.050 **S**	**Normalized**: all **diam**, (480) **TS**, (275) **YS**, 20 **El**
BS 3602	Steel 35	UK	Pipe, tube: seamless	0.35 **C**, 0.70–1.10 **Mn**, 0.050 **P**, 0.050 **S**	**Cold drawn**: all **diam**, (480) **TS**, (275) **YS**, 20 **El**
COPANT R 208	Grade C	COPANT	Pipe: seamless	0.35 **C**, 0.29–1.06 **Mn**, 0.048 **P**, 0.058 **S**, 0.10 min **Si**	**Hot or cold finished**: ($\geq$8) **diam**, (480) **TS**, (275) **YS**, 30 **El**
COPANT R 203	Grade C	COPANT	Tube: seamless	0.35 **C**, 0.29–1.06 **Mn**, 0.048 **P**, 0.058 **S**, 0.10 min **Si**	**Hot finished, cold finished and annealed or cold finished and normalized**: ($\geq$1.58) **diam**, (480) **TS**, (275) **YS**, 30 **El**
DGN–B–178	Grade C	Mexico	Pipe: seamless	0.35 **C**, 0.29–1.06 **Mn**, 0.048 **P**, 0.058 **S**, 0.10 **Si**	**Forged and hot finished or forged, cold finished and annealed**: (8) **diam**, (480) **TS**, (275) **YS**
AS 1302	Grade 410Y	Australia	Bar	0.35 **C**, 0.050 **P**, 0.050 **S**, 0.60 **C+Mn/6**	**As rolled**: all **diam**, (470) **TS**, (410)max **YS**, 12 **El**
ISO 2604/1	F23	ISO	Forgings	0.35 **C**, 0.60–1.40 **Mn**, 0.040 **P**, 0.040 **S**, 0.10–0.40 **Si**	**Normalized, normalized and tempered, quenched and tempered**: ($\leq$63) **diam**, (460) **TS**, (255) **YS**, 18 **El**
ANSI/ASTM A 266	Class 1	US	Forgings	0.35 **C**, 0.40–0.90 **Mn**, 0.040 **P**, 0.040 **S**, 0.15–0.35 **Si**	**Normalized, tempered, or annealed, tempered**: all **diam**, 60 (415) **TS**, 30 (205) **YS**, 23 **El**
ANSI/ASTM A 266	Class 1	US	Forgings	0.35 **C**, 0.40–0.90 **Mn**, 0.040 **P**, 0.040 **S**, 0.15–0.35 **Si**	**Annealed, tempered or normalized, tempered or quenched, tempered**: all **diam**, 60 (415) **TS**, 30 (205) **YS**, 23 **El**
ANSI/ASTM A 266	Grade 1	US	Forgings	0.35 **C**, 0.40–0.90 **Mn**, 0.040 **P**, 0.040 **S**, 0.15–0.35 **Si**	**Annealed, normalized and tempered**: all **diam**, (415) **TS**, (205) **YS**, 23 **El**
ASTM A 695	Type B	US	Bar	0.35 **C**, 1.10 **Mn**, 0.040 **P**, 0.050 **S**, 0.15–0.30 **Si**	**Hot–rolled–grade 35**: $\geq$3 ($\geq$76.2) **diam**, 60 (415) **TS**, 35 (240) **YS**, 21 **El**
ANSI/ASTM A 181	Grade I	US	Pipe	0.35 **C**, 0.90 **Mn**, 0.05 **P**, 0.05 **S**	**As–forged**: all **diam**, 60 (414) **TS**, 30 (207) **YS**, 22 **El**
ANSI/ASTM A 178	Grade C	US	Tube: electric resistance welded	0.35 **C**, 0.80 **Mn**, 0.050 **P**, 0.060 **S**	**Normalized**: 0.312 (7.94) **diam**, 60 (414) **TS**, 37 (255) **YS**, 30.00 **El**
MIL–S–890	B	US	Forgings, bar	0.35 **C**, 0.050 **P**, 0.050 **S**	**Annealed or normalized and drawn or quenched and drawn**: all **diam**, 60 (414) **TS**, 30 (207) **YS**, 30 **El**
MIL–T–17188D	Class B	US	Tube: welded	0.35 **C**, 0.80 **Mn**, 0.050 **P**, 0.060 **S**	**Normalized**: all **diam**, (413) **TS**, (255) **YS**, 30 **El**
NOM–B–137	Grade C	Mexico	Tube: resistance–welded	0.35 **C**, 0.80 **Mn**, 0.050 **P**, 0.060 **S**	**Normalized**: (8.13) **diam**, (412) **TS**, (255) **YS**, 30 **El**
COPANT R 199	Grade C	COPANT	Tube	0.35 **C**, 0.80 **Mn**, 0.050 **P**, 0.060 **S**	**Normalized**: (0.89–8.13) **diam**, (410) **TS**, (255) **YS**, 30 **El**
DGN–B–106	Type 30A	Mexico	Plate	0.35 **C**, 0.30–0.80 **Mn**, 0.040 **P**, 0.050 **S**	**Hot worked**: (<8) **diam**, 55 (379) **TS**, 30 (207) **YS**, 28 **El**
DGN–B–106	Type 285B (Boiler)	Mexico	Plate	0.35 **C**, 0.80 **Mn**, 0.040 **P**, 0.20–0.35 **Cu**	**Hot worked**: (<8) **diam**, 50 (345) **TS**, 27 (186) **YS**, 29 **El**
DGN–B–106	Type 285A (Boiler)	Mexico	Plate	0.35 **C**, 0.80 **Mn**, 0.040 **P**, 0.050 **S**, 0.20–0.35 **Cu**	**Hot worked**: (<8) **diam**, 45 (310) **TS**, 24 (165) **YS**, 31 **El**

WROUGHT CARBON STEELS

specification number	designation	country	product forms	composition	mechanical properties (see page iv for explanation)
NFA 35–590	1308 (Y_3 35)	France	Bar, forgings	0.35 **C**, 0.50–0.70 **Mn**, 0.035 **P**, 0.035 **S**, 0.15–0.40 **Si**	
AISI 1038H		US	Bar	0.34–0.43 **C**, 0.50–1.00 **Mn**, 0.040 **P**, 0.050 **S**, 0.15–0.30 **Si**	
DGN–B–301	1038H	Mexico	Bar	0.34–0.43 **C**, 0.50–1.00 **Mn**, 0.040 **P**, 0.050 **S**, 0.15–0.30 **Si**	
AISI 1038H		US	Wire, rod	0.34–0.43 **C**, 0.50–1.10 **Mn**, 0.040 **P**, 0.050 **S**, 0.15–0.30 **Si**	
AISI 1038		US	Plate	0.34–0.42 **C**, 0.60–0.90 **Mn**, 0.040 **P**, 0.050 **S**	
JIS G 3506	SWRH 37	Japan	Wire, rod	0.34–0.41 **C**, 0.30–0.60 **Mn**, 0.040 **P**, 0.040 **S**, 0.15–0.35 **Si**	
AIR 9160/C 73	9160C251	France	Bar, forgings	0.34–0.40 **C**, 0.15–0.60 **Mn**, 0.015 **P**, 0.010 **S**, 0.15–0.40 **Si**, 1.60–2.0 **Cr**, 0.30–0.60 **Mo**, 3.5–4.50 **Ni**	**Quenched and tempered, annealed**: (<75) **diam**, (1760) **TS**, (1450) **YS**, 7 **El**
DIN 17212	Grade 38 Cr 4	Germany	Blooms, slabs, billets, wire, bar, plate, sheet, strip, tube, forgings	0.34–0.40 **C**, 0.60–0.90 **Mn**, 0.025 **P**, 0.035 **S**, 0.15–0.40 **Si**, 0.90–1.20 **Cr**	**Quenched and tempered**: (≤16) **diam**, (930) **TS**, (740) **YS**, 11 **El**
AS 1442	Grade AS 1442/K1138	Australia	Bar, blooms, billets, slabs	0.34–0.40 **C**, 0.70–1.00 **Mn**, 0.050 **P**, 0.08–0.13 **S**, 0.10–0.35 **Si**	
AS 1443	Grade AS 1443/K1138	Australia	Bar	0.34–0.40 **C**, 0.70–1.00 **Mn**, 0.050 **P**, 0.08–0.13 **S**, 0.10–0.35 **Si**	
BS 970: Part 1	080H36	UK	Blooms, billets, slabs, bar, rod, forgings	0.33–0.40 **C**, 0.60–1.00 **Mn**	
ISO 683/XII	1	ISO	Bar, plate	0.33–0.39 **C**, 0.50–0.80 **Mn**, 0.035 **P**, 0.035 **S**, 0.15–0.40 **Si**	**Quenched and tempered**: (16) **diam**, (620) **TS**, (420) **YS**, 17 **El**
DIN 17212	Grade Cf 35	Germany	Blooms, slabs, billets, wire, bar, plate, sheet, strip, tube, forgings	0.33–0.39 **C**, 0.50–0.80 **Mn**, 0.025 **P**, 0.035 **S**, 0.15–0.35 **Si**	**Quenched and tempered**: (≤16) **diam**, (620) **TS**, (420) **YS**, 17 **El**
BS 970: Part 1	060A35	UK	Blooms, billets, slabs, bar, rod, forgings	0.33–0.38 **C**, 0.50–0.70 **Mn**	
BS 970: Part 1	080A35	UK	Blooms, billets, slabs, bar, rod, forgings	0.33–0.38 **C**, 0.70–0.90 **Mn**	
DGN–B–243	Type I	Mexico	Plate	0.33 **C**, 0.85–1.20 **Mn**, 0.040 **P**, 0.050 **S**, 0.10 **Si**	**As rolled**: (<9.5) **diam**, (515) **TS**, (258) **YS**, 22 **El**
JIS G 3455	Class 4	Japan	Pipe: seamless	0.33 **C**, 0.30–1.00 **Mn**, 0.035 **P**, 0.035 **S**, 0.10–0.35 **Si**, 0.20 **Cu**	**As manufactured, cold finished and annealed or cold finished and normalized**: (≥8) **diam**, (481) **TS**, (275) **YS**, 25 **El**
JIS G 3456	Class 4	Japan	Pipe: seamless	0.33 **C**, 0.30–1.00 **Mn**, 0.035 **P**, 0.035 **S**, 0.10–0.35 **Si**, 0.20 **Cu**	**As manufactured or annealed**: (≥8) **diam**, (481) **TS**, (275) **YS**, 25 **El**
ANSI/ASTM A 515	Grade 65	US	Plate	0.33 **C**, 0.90 **Mn**, 0.035 **P**, 0.04 **S**, 0.13–0.33 **Si**	**Normalized**: 2.0–4.0 **diam**, (450) **TS**, (240) **YS**, 23 **El**
NF A 35–051	FM 38	France	Wire, rod	0.32–0.43 **C**, 0.50–0.80 **Mn**, 0.040 **P**, 0.040 **S**, 0.10–0.35 **Si**	
DIN 1652	C 35 (1.0501)	Germany	Bar	0.32–0.40 **C**, 0.40–0.70 **Mn**, 0.045 **P**, 0.045 **S**, 0.15–0.35 **Si**	**Cold drawn**: all **diam**, (690) **TS**, (570) **YS**, 5 in 80 mm **El**; **Centerless turned and normalized**: all **diam**, (490) **TS**, (275) **YS**, 22 in 80 mm **El**; **Centerless turned and quenched and tempered**: all **diam**, (640) **TS**, (410) **YS**, 16 in 80 mm **El**
DIN 1652	Ck 35 (1.1181)	Germany	Bar	0.32–0.40 **C**, 0.40–0.70 **Mn**, 0.035 **P**, 0.035 **S**, 0.15–0.35 **Si**	**Cold drawn**: all **diam**, (690) **TS**, (570) **YS**, 5 in 80 mm **El**; **Centerless turned and normalized**: all **diam**, (490) **TS**, (275) **YS**, 22 in 80 mm **El**; **Centerless turned and quenched and tempered**: all **diam**, (640) **TS**, (410) **YS**, 16 in 80 mm **El**

WROUGHT CARBON STEELS

specification number	designation	country	product forms	composition	mechanical properties (see page iv for explanation)
DIN 1654	Grade Cq 35	Germany	Rod	0.32–0.40 **C**, 0.40–0.70 **Mn**, 0.040 **P**, 0.040 **S**, 0.15–0.35 **Si**	**Drawn**: all **diam**, (667) **TS**
BS 970 Part 1	Grade 225M36	UK	Blooms, billets, slabs, bar, rod, forgings	0.32–0.40 **C**, 1.00–1.40 **Mn**, 0.060 **P**, 0.20–0.30 **S**, 0.25 **Si**	**Hardened and tempered**: 2.5 **diam**, (550) **TS**, (360) **YS**, 18 **El**; **Cold drawn from hot rolled**: 0.50–0.625 **diam**, (550) **TS**, (425) **YS**, 7 **El**
BS 970 Part 1	Grade 120M36	UK	Blooms, billets, slabs, bar, rod, forgings	0.32–0.40 **C**, 1.00–1.40 **Mn**	**Normalized**: 6 **diam**, (525) **TS**, (315) **YS**, 15 **El**; **Hardened and tempered**: 4 **diam**, (550) **TS**, (370) **YS**, 18 **El**; **Cold drawn from hot rolled**: 0.50–0.625 **diam**, (620) **TS**, (495) **YS**, 7 **El**
BS 970 Part 1	212M36	UK	Blooms, billets, slabs, bar, rod, forgings	0.32–0.40 **C**, 1.00–1.40 **Mn**, 0.060 **P**, 0.12–0.20 **S**, 0.25 **Si**	**Hardened and tempered**: 4 **diam**, (480) **TS**, (305) **YS**, 20 **El**; **Cold drawn from hot rolled**: 0.50–0.625 **diam**, (550) **TS**, (425) **YS**, 7 **El**
BS 970: Part 1	080M36	UK	Blooms, billets, slabs, bar, rod, forgings	0.32–0.40 **C**, 0.60–1.00 **Mn**	**Normalized**: 2.5 **diam**, (480) **TS**, (250) **YS**, 16 **El**; **Hardened and tempered**: 1.125 **diam**, (550) **TS**, (360) **YS**, 16 **El**; **Cold drawn from hot rolled**: 0.50–0.625 **diam**, (550) **TS**, (430) **YS**, 9 **El**
EURONORM 119–74, IV	C 35 B KD	EURONORM	Wire, rod	0.32–0.39 **C**, 0.50–0.80 **Mn**, 0.035 **P**, 0.035 **S**, 0.15–0.40 **Si**, 0.0005–0.0050 **B**	**Quenched and tempered**: (≤10) **diam**, (980) **TS**, (835) **YS**, 11 **El**
ISO R683/1	C35	ISO	Bar, forgings	0.32–0.39 **C**, 0.50–0.80 **Mn**, 0.050 **P**, 0.050 **S**, 0.15–0.40 **Si**	**Quenched and tempered**: all **diam**, (970) **TS**, (665) **YS**, 17 **El**; **Quenched, tempered and cold-reduced**: all **diam**, (1110) **TS**, (895) **YS**, 10 **El**
ISO 683/1	C35e	ISO	Bar, forgings	0.32–0.39 **C**, 0.50–0.80 **Mn**, 0.035 **P**, 0.035 **S**, 0.15–0.40 **Si**	**Quenched and tempered**: all **diam**, (970) **TS**, (665) **YS**, 17 **El**; **Quenched, tempered and cold-reduced**: all **diam**, (1110) **TS**, (895) **YS**, 10 **El**
VSM 10648	C 35	Switzerland	Bar, sheet, plate	0.32–0.39 **C**, 0.50–0.80 **Mn**, 0.045 **P**, 0.045 **S**, 0.15–0.35 **Si**	**Cold drawn**: (≤5) **diam**, (686) **TS**, (568) **YS**, 5 **El**; **Cold drawn and normalized**: (16–100) **diam**, (490) **TS**, (274) **YS**, 21 **El**; **As rolled**: (5–16) **diam**, (617) **TS**, (421) **YS**, 17 **El**
VSM 10648	CK 35	Switzerland	Bar, sheet, plate	0.32–0.39 **C**, 0.50–0.80 **Mn**, 0.035 **P**, 0.15–0.35 **S**	**Cold drawn**: (≤5) **diam**, (686) **TS**, (568) **YS**, 5 **El**; **Cold drawn and normalized**: (16–100) **diam**, (490) **TS**, (274) **YS**, 21 **El**; **As rolled**: (5–16) **diam**, (617) **TS**, (421) **YS**, 17 **El**
SFS 455	CO,35	Finland	Bar, forgings, tube	0.32–0.39 **C**, 0.50–0.80 **Mn**, 0.035 **P**, 0.035 **S**, 0.15–0.40 **Si**	**Quenched and tempered (bar, forgings)**: (30) **diam**, (650) **TS**, (410) **YS**, 16 **El**
SIS 14 19 57	SIS 19 57–03	Sweden	Bar	0.32–0.39 **C**, 0.80–1.20 **Mn**, 0.06 **P**, 0.15–0.25 **S**, 0.10–0.40 **Si**	**Quenched and tempered**: (≤16) **diam**, (650) **TS**, (450) **YS**, 14 **El**
SIS 14 19 57	SIS 19 57–04	Sweden	Bar	0.32–0.39 **C**, 0.80–1.20 **Mn**, 0.06 **P**, 0.15–0.25 **S**, 0.10–0.40 **Si**	**Cold worked**: (≤16) **diam**, (640) **TS**, (490) **YS**, 7 **El**
EURONORM 119–74, IV	C 35 KD	EURONORM	Wire, rod	0.32–0.39 **C**, 0.50–0.80 **Mn**, 0.035 **P**, 0.035 **S**, 0.15–0.40 **Si**	**Quenched and tempered**: (≤16) **diam**, (620) **TS**, (420) **YS**, 17 **El**
SIS 14 15 72	SIS 15 72–05	Sweden	Bar, forgings, plate, sheet, tube	0.32–0.39 **C**, 0.50–0.80 **Mn**, 0.035 **P**, 0.035 **S**, 0.15–0.40 **Si**	**Quenched and tempered**: all **diam**, (620) **TS**, (420) **YS**, 17 **El**

WROUGHT CARBON STEELS

specification number	designation	country	product forms	composition	mechanical properties (see page iv for explanation)
DIN 17200	Grade C 35	Germany	Blooms, slabs, billets, wire, bar, plate, sheet, strip, tube, forgings	0.32–0.39 **C**, 0.50–0.80 **Mn**, 0.045 **P**, 0.045 **S**, 0.15–0.35 **Si**	**Quenched and tempered**: (≤16) **diam**, (618) **TS**, (422) **YS**, 17 **El**; **Normalized**: (>16–40) **diam**, (490) **TS**, (274) **YS**, 21 **El**
DIN 17200	Grade Ck 35	Germany	Blooms, slabs, billets, wire, bar, plate, sheet, strip, tube, forgings	0.32–0.39 **C**, 0.50–0.80 **Mn**, 0.035 **P**, 0.035 **S**, 0.15–0.35 **Si**	**Quenched and tempered**: (≤16) **diam**, (618) **TS**, (422) **YS**, 17 **El**; **Normalized**: (>16–40) **diam**, (490) **TS**, (274) **YS**, 21 **El**
ISO/R 683/111	Type C35ea	ISO	Bar, billet, rod	0.32–0.39 **C**, 0.50–0.80 **Mn**, 0.035 **P**, 0.020–0.035 **S**, 0.15–0.40 **Si**	**Quenched and tempered**: (≤16) **diam**, (617) **TS**, (421) **YS**, 17 **El**
ISO/R 683/111	Type C35eb	ISO	Bar, billet, rod	0.32–0.39 **C**, 0.50–0.80 **Mn**, 0.035 **P**, 0.030–0.050 **S**, 0.15–0.40 **Si**	**Quenched and tempered**: (≤16) **diam**, (617) **TS**, (421) **YS**, 17 **El**
ISO/R 683/1X	Type 8	ISO	Bar, wire, rod	0.32–0.39 **C**, 0.90–1.20 **Mn**, 0.06 **P**, 0.15–0.25 **S**, 0.15–0.40 **Si**	**Quenched and tempered**: (≤16) **diam**, (617) **TS**, (421) **YS**, 14 **El**
DGN–B–301	1137	Mexico	Bar	0.32–0.39 **C**, 1.35–1.65 **Mn**, 0.040 **P**, 0.08–0.13 **S**, 0.10–0.20 **Si**	**Forged or hot rolled, cold rolled and cold finished**: all **diam**, (589) **TS**, (333) **YS**, 15 **El**
SIS 14 15 72	SIS 15 72–04	Sweden	Bar, forgings, plate, sheet, tube	0.32–0.39 **C**, 0.50–0.80 **Mn**, 0.035 **P**, 0.035 **S**, 0.15–0.40 **Si**	**Quenched and tempered**: all **diam**, (580) **TS**, (360) **YS**, 19 **El**
ISO/R 683/1X	Type 7	ISO	Bar, wire, rod	0.32–0.39 **C**, 0.50–0.90 **Mn**, 0.06 **P**, 0.15–0.25 **S**, 0.15–0.40 **Si**	**Quenched and tempered**: (≤16) **diam**, (570) **TS**, (392) **YS**, 14 **El**
BS 3111 Part1	Type 10	UK	Wire	0.32–0.39 **C**, 0.80–1.10 **Mn**, 0.040 **P**, 0.040 **S**, 0.15–0.35 **Si**, 0.020 **Al**, 0.0008–0.005 **B**	**Drawn and spheroidized annealed**: all **diam**, (570) max **TS**; **Drawn, spheroidized annealed and light drawn**: all **diam**, (650) max **TS**
ISO 683/XVIII	C35e	ISO	Bar, wire	0.32–0.39 **C**, 0.50–0.80 **Mn**, 0.035 **P**, 0.035 **S**, 0.15–0.40 **Si**	**Normalized**: all **diam**, (550) **TS**, (300) **YS**, 18 **El**
ISO 683/XVIII	C35ea	ISO	Bar, wire	0.32–0.39 **C**, 0.50–0.80 **Mn**, 0.035 **P**, 0.020–0.035 **S**, 0.15–0.40 **Si**	**Normalized**: all **diam**, (550) **TS**, (300) **YS**, 18 **El**
ISO 683/XVIII	C35	ISO	Bar, wire	0.32–0.39 **C**, 0.50–0.80 **Mn**, 0.050 **P**, 0.050 **S**, 0.15–0.40 **Si**	**Normalized**: all **diam**, (550) **TS**, (300) **YS**, 18 **El**
ISO 2937	Grade C 35	ISO	Tube: seamless	0.32–0.39 **C**, 0.50–0.80 **Mn**, 0.050 **P**, 0.050 **S**, 0.15–0.40 **Si**	**Hot finished**: all **diam**, (540) **TS**, (275) **YS**, 20 **El**
SIS 14 19 57	SIS 19 57–00	Sweden	Bar	0.32–0.39 **C**, 0.80–1.20 **Mn**, 0.06 **P**, 0.15–0.25 **S**, 0.10–0.40 **Si**	**As rolled**: (≤63) **diam**, (540) **TS**
SIS 14 15 72	SIS 15 72–03	Sweden	Bar, forgings, plate, sheet	0.32–0.39 **C**, 0.50–0.80 **Mn**, 0.035 **P**, 0.035 **S**, 0.15–0.40 **Si**	**Quenched and tempered**: all **diam**, (540) **TS**, (320) **YS**, 20 **El**
ISO 2938	Grade 2	ISO	Bar	0.32–0.39 **C**, 0.50–0.80 **Mn**, 0.035 **P**, 0.035 **S**, 0.15–0.40 **Si**	**Hot finished**: (≤16) **diam**, (490) **TS**, (275) **YS**, 21 **El**; **Normalized**: (≤16) **diam**, (490) **TS**, (275) **YS**, 21 **El**
DIN 1651	35S20 (1.0726)	Germany	Bar	0.32–0.39 **C**, 0.50–0.90 **Mn**, 0.060 **P**, 0.15–0.25 **S**, 0.10–0.40 **Si**	**Hot rolled**: all **diam**, (490) **TS**; **Normalized**: all **diam**, (480) **TS**, (295) **YS**, 18 in 80 mm **El**; **Quenched and tempered**: all **diam**, (620) **TS**, (420) **YS**, 13 in 80 mm **El**
SIS 14 15 72	SIS 15 72–08	sweden	Bar, forgings, plate, sheet, tube	0.32–0.39 **C**, 0.50–0.80 **Mn**, 0.035 **P**, 0.035 **S**, 0.15–0.40 **Si**	**As rolled**: all **diam**, (490) **TS**, (270) **YS**, 21 **El**
DIN 17200	Grade Cm 35	Germany	Blooms, slabs, billets, wire, bar, plate, sheet, strip, tube, forgings	0.32–0.39 **C**, 0.50–0.80 **Mn**, 0.035 **P**, 0.020–0.035 **S**, 0.15–0.35 **Si**	**Normalized**: (>16–100) **diam**, (490) **TS**, (274) **YS**, 21 **El**; **Quenched and tempered**: (≤16) **diam**, (618) **TS**, (422) **YS**, 17 **El**

specification number	designation	country	product forms	composition	mechanical properties (see page iv for explanation)
ANSI/ASTM A 519	1137	US	Tube: seamless	0.32–0.39 **C**, 1.35–1.65 **Mn**, 0.040 **P**, 0.08–0.13 **S**	**Hot rolled**: all **diam**, 70 (483) **TS**, 40 (276) **YS**, 20 **El**; **Cold worked**: all **diam**, 80 (552) **TS**, 65 (448) **YS**, 5 **El**; **Stress relieved**: all **diam**, 75 (517) **TS**, 60 (414) **YS**, 8 **El**; **Annealed**: all **diam**, 65 (448) **TS**, 35 (241) **YS**, 22 **El**; **Normalized**: all **diam**, 70 (483) **TS**, 43 (296) **YS**, 15 **El**
AISI 1137		US	Bar	0.32–0.39 **C**, 1.35–1.65 **Mn**, 0.040 **P**, 0.08–0.13 **S**	
AMS 5020A		US	Bar, forgings, tube	0.32–0.39 **C**, 1.35–1.65 **Mn**, 0.040 **P**, 0.08–0.13 **S**, 0.15–0.35 **Pb**	**Cold finished (bar, tube)**: ≤2.50 (≤63.5) **diam**; **Hot finished (bar, tube)**: >2.50 (>63.5) **diam**
AMS 5024E		US	Bar, forgings, tube	0.32–0.39 **C**, 1.35–1.65 **Mn**, 0.040 **P**, 0.08–0.13 **S**	
AS 1442	Grade AS 1442/K1137	Australia	Bar, blooms, billets, slabs	0.32–0.39 **C**, 1.35–1.65 **Mn**, 0.050 **P**, 0.08–0.13 **S**, 0.10–0.35 **Si**	
SIS 14 15 72	SIS 15 72–00	Sweden	Bar, forgings, plate, sheet, tube	0.32–0.39 **C**, 0.50–0.80 **Mn**, 0.035 **P**, 0.035 **S**, 0.15–0.40 **Si**	
JIS G 3539	SWCH 35K	Japan	Wire	0.32–0.38 **C**, 0.60–0.90 **Mn**, 0.030 **P**, 0.035 **S**, 0.10–0.35 **Si**	**Annealed and cold drawn**: all **diam**, (618) **TS**, 12 **El**
DGN–B–301	1037	Mexico	Bar	0.32–0.38 **C**, 0.70–1.00 **Mn**, 0.040 **P**, 0.050 **S**, 0.10–0.20 **Si**	**Forged or hot rolled, cold rolled and cold finished**: all **diam**, (510) **TS**, (274) **YS**, 18 **El**
DGN–B–301	1035	Mexico	Bar	0.32–0.38 **C**, 0.60–0.90 **Mn**, 0.040 **P**, 0.050 **S**, 0.10–0.20 **Si**	**Forged or hot rolled, cold rolled and cold finished**: all **diam**, (500) **TS**, (274) **YS**, 18 **El**
DGN–B–203	Grade 1035	Mexico	Tube: seamless	0.32–0.38 **C**, 0.60–0.90 **Mn**, 0.040 **P**, 0.050 **S**	**Hot finished**: all **diam**, (451) **TS**, (275) **YS**, 20 **El**; **Cold finished**: all **diam**, (588) **TS**, (520) **YS**, 5 **El**; **Stress relieved**: all **diam**, (520) **TS**, (451) **YS**, 8 **El**; **Tempered**: all **diam**, (412) **TS**, (324) **YS**, 25 **El**; **Normalized**: all **diam**, (441) **TS**, (275) **YS**, 20 **El**
COPANT 514	Grade 1035	COPANT	Tube: seamless	0.32–0.38 **C**, 0.60–0.90 **Mn**, 0.040 **P**, 0.050 **S**, 0.10–0.20 **Si**	**Hot finished**: (>323.9) **diam**, (450) **TS**, (275) **YS**, 20 **El**; **Cold finished**: all **diam**, (590) **TS**, (520) **YS**, 5 **El**; **Annealed**: all **diam**, (410) **TS**, (225) **YS**, 25 **El**; **Normalized**: all **diam**, (450) **TS**, (225) **YS**, 20 **El**
ANSI/ASTM A 519	1035	US	Tube: seamless	0.32–0.38 **C**, 0.60–0.90 **Mn**, 0.040 **P**, 0.050 **S**	**Hot rolled**: all **diam**, 65 (448) **TS**, 40 (276) **YS**, 20 **El**; **Cold worked**: all **diam**, 85 (586) **TS**, 75 (517) **YS**, 5 **El**; **Stress relieved**: all **diam**, 75 (517) **TS**, 65 (448) **YS**, 8 **El**; **Annealed**: all **diam**, 60 (414) **TS**, 33 (228) **YS**, 25 **El**; **Normalized**: all **diam**, 65 (448) **TS**, 40 (276) **YS**, 20 **El**
ASTM A 544	Grade 1035	US	Wire	0.32–0.38 **C**, 0.60–0.90 **Mn**, 0.040 **P**, 0.050 **S**	
AISI 1037		US	Bar	0.32–0.38 **C**, 0.70–1.00 **Mn**, 0.040 **P**, 0.050 **S**	
AISI 1035		US	Bar	0.32–0.38 **C**, 0.60–0.90 **Mn**, 0.040 **P**, 0.050 **S**	
MIL–S–46070	Grade 1035	US	Bar: cold drawn	0.32–0.38 **C**, 0.60–0.90 **Mn**, 0.035 **P**, 0.045 **S**, 0.30 **Si**	**Normalized or annealed and stress relieved**: <1.25 **diam**, 75 (517) **YS**, 15 **El**
AS 1446	Grade AS 1446/S1035	Australia	Plate	0.32–0.38 **C**, 0.60–0.90 **Mn**, 0.050 **P**, 0.050 **S**, 0.35 **Si**	
ASTM A 108	1035	US	Bar	0.32–0.38 **C**, 0.60–0.90 **Mn**, 0.040 **P**, 0.050 **S**	
ANSI/ASTM A 546	Grade 1035	US	Wire	0.32–0.38 **C**, 0.60–0.90 **Mn**, 0.040 **P**, 0.050 **S**	

specification number	designation	country	product forms	composition	mechanical properties (see page iv for explanation)
ANSI/ASTM A 545	Grade 1035	US	Wire	0.32–0.38 **C**, 0.60–0.90 **Mn**, 0.040 **P**, 0.050 **S**	
COPANT 333	1034	COPANT	Wire, rod	0.32–0.38 **C**, 0.50–0.80 **Mn**, 0.040 **P**, 0.050 **S**	
COPANT 333	1035	COPANT	Wire, rod	0.32–0.38 **C**, 0.60–0.90 **Mn**, 0.040 **P**, 0.050 **S**	
DGN–B–301	1034	Mexico	Bar	0.32–0.38 **C**, 0.50–0.80 **Mn**, 0.040 **P**, 0.050 **S**, 0.10–0.20 **Si**	
ANSI/ASTM A 576	1035	US	Bar	0.32–0.38 **C**, 0.60–0.90 **Mn**, 0.040 **P**, 0.050 **S**	
ANSI/ASTM A 576	1037	US	Bar	0.32–0.38 **C**, 0.70–1.00 **Mn**, 0.040 **P**, 0.050 **S**	
AISI 1035		US	Wire, rod	0.32–0.38 **C**, 0.60–0.90 **Mn**, 0.040 **P**, 0.050 **S**	
AISI 1037		US	Wire, rod	0.32–0.38 **C**, 0.70–1.00 **Mn**, 0.040 **P**, 0.050 **S**	
ANSI/ASTM A 29	1034	US	Bar	0.32–0.38 **C**, 0.50–0.80 **Mn**, 0.040 **P**, 0.050 **S**	
ANSI/ASTM A 29	1035	US	Bar	0.32–0.38 **C**, 0.60–0.90 **Mn**, 0.040 **P**, 0.050 **S**	
ANSI/ASTM A 29	1037	US	Bar	0.32–0.38 **C**, 0.70–1.00 **Mn**, 0.040 **P**, 0.050 **S**	
ASTM A 689	1035	US	Bar	0.32–0.38 **C**, 0.60–0.90 **Mn**, 0.040 **P**, 0.050 **S**	
ASTM A 689	1037	US	Bar	0.32–0.38 **C**, 0.70–1.00 **Mn**, 0.040 **P**, 0.050 **S**	
AS 1443	Grade AS 1443/S1035	Australia	Bar	0.32–0.38 **C**, 0.60–0.90 **Mn**, 0.050 **P**, 0.050 **S**, 0.35 **Si**	
AS 1443	Grade AS 1443/K1037	Australia	Bar	0.32–0.38 **C**, 0.70–1.00 **Mn**, 0.050 **P**, 0.050 **S**, 0.10–0.35 **Si**	
AS 1443	Grade AS 1443/K1035	Australia	Bar	0.32–0.38 **C**, 0.60–0.90 **Mn**, 0.050 **P**, 0.050 **S**, 0.10–0.35 **Si**	
AS 1442	Grade AS 1442/S1035	Australia	Bar, blooms, billets, slabs	0.32–0.38 **C**, 0.60–0.90 **Mn**, 0.050 **P**, 0.050 **S**, 0.35 **Si**	
AS 1442	Grade AS 1442/K1035	Australia	Bar, blooms, billets, slabs	0.32–0.38 **C**, 0.60–0.90 **Mn**, 0.050 **P**, 0.050 **S**, 0.10–0.35 **Si**	
AS 1442	Grade AS 1442/K1037	Australia	Bar, blooms, billets, slabs	0.32–0.38 **C**, 0.70–1.00 **Mn**, 0.050 **P**, 0.050 **S**, 0.10–0.35 **Si**	
JIS G 3507		Japan	Wire, rod	0.32–0.38 **C**, 0.60–0.90 **Mn**, 0.030 **P**, 0.035 **S**, 0.10–0.35 **Si**	
JIS G 4051	S 35C	Japan	Bar, wire, rod	0.32–0.38 **C**, 0.60–0.90 **Mn**, 0.030 **P**, 0.035 **S**, 0.15–0.35 **Si**, 0.30 **Cu**	
COPANT 330	1035	COPANT	Bar, shapes	0.32–0.35 **C**, 0.60–0.90 **Mn**, 0.040 **P**, 0.050 **S**	
ASTM A 696	Grade C	US	Bar	0.32 **C**, 1.04 **Mn**, 0.035 **P**, 0.045 **S**, 0.15–0.30 **Si**	**As hot-rolled, cold-finished**: 1.5 (38) **diam**, 70 (485) **TS**, 40 (275) **YS**, 18 **El**
ASTM A 696	Grade C	US	Bar	0.32 **C**, 1.04 **Mn**, 0.035 **P**, 0.045 **S**, 0.15–0.30 **Si**	**Hot-rolled or cold-rolled**: 1.5 (38) **diam**, 70 (485) **TS**, 40 (275) **YS**, 18 **El**
CSA B193	Seamless, grade X52 non–expanded	Canada	Pipe	0.32 **C**, 1.35 **Mn**, 0.04 **P**, 0.05 **S**	**Mill**: 0.250 (6.35) **diam**, 66 (455) **TS**, 52 (358) **YS**, 18 **El**
CSA B193	Seamless, grade X46 non–expanded	Canada	Pipe	0.32 **C**, 1.35 **Mn**, 0.04 **P**, 0.05 **S**	**Mill**: 0.250 (6.35) **diam**, 63 (434) **TS**, 46 (317) **YS**, 20 **El**
ASTM A 696	Grade B	US	Bar	0.32 **C**, 1.04 **Mn**, 0.035 **P**, 0.045 **S**, 0.15–0.30 **Si**	**As hot-rolled, cold-finished**: 1.5 (38) **diam**, 60 (415) **TS**, 35 (240) **YS**, 20 **El**
ASTM A 696	Grade B	US	Bar	0.32 **C**, 1.04 **Mn**, 0.035 **P**, 0.045 **S**, 0.15–0.30 **Si**	**Hot-rolled or cold-rolled**: 1.5 (38) **diam**, 60 (415) **TS**, 35 (240) **YS**, 20 **El**
JIS G 3461	Class 4	Japan	Tube: seamless or electric–resistance welded	0.32 **C**, 0.30–0.80 **Mn**, 0.035 **P**, 0.035 **S**, 0.35 **Si**, 0.20 **Cu**	**Annealed or normalized**: ($\geq$8) **diam**, (412) **TS**, (255) **YS**, 25 **El**
AISI 15B35H		US	Bar	0.31–0.39 **C**, 0.70–1.20 **Mn**, 0.040 **P**, 0.050 **S**, 0.15–0.30 **Si**, 0.0005–0.003 **B**	

WROUGHT CARBON STEELS

specification number	designation	country	product forms	composition	mechanical properties (see page iv for explanation)
DGN–B–301	15B35H	Mexico	Bar	0.31–0.39 **C**, 0.70–1.20 **Mn**, 0.040 **P**, 0.050 **S**, 0.15–0.30 **Si**, 0.0005 min **B**	
AISI 15B35H		US	Wire, rod	0.31–0.39 **C**, 0.70–1.20 **Mn**, 0.040 **P**, 0.050 **S**, 0.15–0.30 **Si**	
AMS 5082C		US	Tube	0.31–0.38 **C**, 0.60–0.90 **Mn**, 0.040 **P**, 0.050 **S**, 0.10–0.30 **Si**	**Cold finished**: ≤0.035 (≤0.89) **diam**, 90 (621) **TS**, 70 (493) **YS**, 8 **El**
QQ–S–700D	SAE 1035	US	Sheet, strip	0.31–0.38 **C**, 0.60–0.90 **Mn**, 0.040 **P**, 0.050 **S**	
AISI 1035		US	Plate	0.31–0.38 **C**, 0.60–0.90 **Mn**, 0.040 **P**, 0.050 **S**	
AISI 1037		US	Plate	0.31–0.38 **C**, 0.70–1.00 **Mn**, 0.040 **P**, 0.050 **S**	
AMS 5080F		US	Bar, forgings, tube	0.31–0.38 **C**, 0.60–0.90 **Mn**, 0.040 **P**, 0.050 **S**, 0.10–0.30 **Si**	
ANSI/ASTM A 680	1035	US	Strip	0.31–0.38 **C**, 0.60–0.90 **Mn**, 0.040 **P**, 0.050 **S**, 0.15–0.30 **Si**	**Cold–rolled**
ANSI/ASTM A 682	1035	US	Strip	0.31–0.38 **C**, 0.60–0.90 **Mn**, 0.040 **P**, 0.050 **S**, 0.15–0.30 **Si**	
ANSI/ASTM A 684	1035	US	Strip	0.31–0.38 **C**, 0.60–0.90 **Mn**, 0.040 **P**, 0.050 **S**, 0.15–0.30 **Si**	
ASTM A 414	Grade G	US	Sheet	0.31 **C**, 1.35 **Mn**, 0.035 **P**, 0.040 **S**	**Hot rolled**: 0.2299–0.1450 (5.82–3.68) **diam**, 75 (520) **TS**, 42 (290) **YS**, 16 **El**
ANSI/ASTM A 414	Grade Ct	US	Sheet	0.31 **C**, 1.35 **Mn**, 0.035 **P**, 0.040 **S**	**Hot rolled or cold rolled, annealed**: all **diam**, (520) **TS**, (290) **YS**, 16 **El**
DGN–B–275	Grade G	Mexico	Sheet	0.31 **C**, 1.35 **Mn**, 0.035 **P**, 0.040 **S**, 0.20 **Cu**	**Hot rolled**: (5–4) **diam**, (515) **TS**, (288) **YS**, 16 **El**
COPANT 37, II	AT–27	COPANT	Plate	0.31 **C**, 0.035 **P**, 0.045 **S**, 0.15–0.35 **Si**	**As rolled**: (≤25) **diam**, (490) **TS**, (270) **YS**, 21 **El**
DGN–B–106	Type 212A/B (Firebox)	Mexico	Plate	0.31 **C**, 0.90 **Mn**, 0.035 **P**, 0.04 **S**, 0.05–0.10 **Si**	**Hot worked**: (<8) **diam**, (483) **TS**, (262) **YS**, 24 **El**
DGN–B–244	Grade 55	Mexico	Plate	0.31 **C**, 0.90 **Mn**, 0.035 **P**, 0.040 **S**, 0.15–0.30 **Si**	**As rolled**: (<25.4) **diam**, (482) **TS**, (262) **YS**, 21 **El**
JIS G 3103	Class 4	Japan	Plate	0.31 **C**, 0.90 **Mn**, 0.035 **P**, 0.040 **S**, 0.15–0.30 **Si**	**Hot rolled**: (≤25) **diam**, (481) **TS**, (265) **YS**, 17 **El**
ASTM A 414	Grade F	US	Sheet	0.31 **C**, 1.20 **Mn**, 0.035 **P**, 0.040 **S**	**Hot rolled**: 02299–0.1450 (5.82–3.68) **diam**, 70 (480) **TS**, 38 (260) **YS**, 16 **El**
ANSI/ASTM A 414	Grade F	US	Sheet	0.31 **C**, 1.20 **Mn**, 0.035 **P**, 0.040 **S**	**Hot rolled or cold rolled, annealed**: all **diam**, (480) **TS**, (260) **YS**, 16 **El**
DGN–B–275	Grade F	Mexico	Sheet	0.31 **C**, 1.20 **Mn**, 0.035 **P**, 0.040 **S**, 0.20 **Cu**	**Hot rolled**: (5–4) **diam**, (480) **TS**, (261) **YS**, 16 **El**
ISO/R 630	Grade Fe 44 A	ISO	Bar, plate	0.31 **C**, 0.100 **P**, 0.075 **S**	**As rolled**: (≤16) **diam**, (470) **TS**, (274) **YS**, 23 **El**
CSA B193	Electrically welded, grade X52 Non–expanded	Canada	Pipe	0.31 **C**, 1.35 **Mn**, 0.04 **P**, 0.05 **S**	**Mill**: 0.250 (6.35) **diam**, 66 (455) **TS**, 52 (358) **YS**, 18 **El**
API Spec 5LX	Seamless, grade X52	US	Pipe	0.31 **C**, 1.35 **Mn**, 0.04 **P**, 0.05 **S**	**Non–expanded**: all **diam**, 66 (455) **TS**, 52 (359) **YS**
API Spec 5LX	Seamless, grade X52	US	Pipe	0.31 **C**, 1.35 **Mn**, 0.04 **P**, 0.05 **S**	**Non–expanded**: all **diam**, 66 (455) **TS**, 52 (359) **YS**
CSA B193	Electrically welded, grade X46 Non–expanded	Canada	Pipe	0.31 **C**, 1.35 **Mn**, 0.04 **P**, 0.05 **S**	**Mill**: 0.250 (6.35) **diam**, 63 (434) **TS**, 46 (317) **YS**, 20 **El**
API Spec 5LX	Seamless, grade X46	US	Pipe	0.31 **C**, 1.35 **Mn**, 0.04 **P**, 0.05 **S**	**Non–expanded**: all **diam**, 63 (434) **TS**, 46 (317) **YS**
API Spec 5LX	Seamless, grade X46	US	Pipe	0.31 **C**, 1.35 **Mn**, 0.04 **P**, 0.05 **S**	**Non–expanded**: all **diam**, 63 (434) **TS**, 46 (317) **YS**
TS 908	UDK 669.14.423/Fe 42	Turkey	Shapes	0.31 **C**, 0.063 **P**, 0.063 **S**	**Hot rolled**: all **diam**, (412) **TS**, (255) **YS**, 22 **El**
TS 909	UDK 629.14–423/Fe 42	Turkey	Shapes	0.31 **C**, 0.063 **P**, 0.063 **S**	**Hot rolled**: all **diam**, (412) **TS**, (255) **YS**, 20 **El**
TS 913	UDK 669.14.423/Fe 42	Turkey	Bar	0.31 **C**, 0.063 **P**, 0.063 **S**	**Hot rolled**: all **diam**, (412) **TS**, (255) **YS**, 22 **El**

specification number	designation	country	product forms	composition	mechanical properties (see page iv for explanation)
TS 912	UDK 669.14–423/Fe 42	Turkey	Shapes	0.31 **C**, 0.063 **P**, 0.063 **S**	**Hot rolled**: all **diam**, (412) **TS**, (255) **YS**, 22 **El**
ISO/R 630	Grade Fe 42 A	ISO	Bar, plate	0.31 **C**, 0.100 **P**, 0.075 **S**	**As rolled**: (≤16) **diam**, (411) **TS**, (255) **YS**, 23 **El**
DIN 17100	USt 42–1 (1.0130)	Germany	Bar, plate	0.31 **C**, 0.10 **P**, 0.063 **S**	**Normalized**: all **diam**, (410) **TS**, (255) **YS**, 22 **El**
DIN 17100	USt 42–1 (1.0130)	Germany	Strip	0.31 **C**, 0.10 **P**, 0.063 **S**	**Normalized**: all **diam**, (410) **TS**, (255) **YS**, 22 **El**; **Hot rolled**: all **diam**, (410) **TS**, (255) **YS**, 16 **El**
DIN 17100	USt 42–2 (1.0132)	Germany	Bar, plate	0.31 **C**, 0.063 **P**, 0.063 **S**	**Normalized**: all **diam**, (410) **TS**, (255) **YS**, 22 **El**
DIN 17100	USt 42–2 (1.0132)	Germany	Strip	0.31 **C**, 0.063 **P**, 0.063 **S**	**Normalized**: all **diam**, (410) **TS**, (255) **YS**, 22 **El**; **Hot rolled**: all **diam**, (410) **TS**, (255) **YS**, 16 **El**
BS 3111 PartI	Type 1	UK	Wire	0.30–0.45 **C**, 0.70–1.00 **Mn**, 0.040 **P**, 0.040 **S**, 0.10–0.35 **Si**	**Drawn and spheroidized annealed**: all **diam**, (540) max **TS**; **Drawn, spheroidized annealed and light drawn**: all **diam**, (620) max **TS**
NF A 35–051	FM 36	France	Wire, rod	0.30–0.41 **C**, 0.50–0.80 **Mn**, 0.040 **P**, 0.040 **S**, 0.10–0.35 **Si**	
AIR 9160/C 47	9160C121	France	Bar, forgings	0.30–0.40 **C**, 0.30–0.60 **Mn**, 0.025 **P**, 0.020 **S**, 0.15–0.40 **Si**, 1.60–2.00 **Cr**, 0.25–0.60 **Mo**, 3.50–4.20 **Ni**	**Annealed, quenched and tempered**: (<50) **diam**, (1760) **TS**, (1420) **YS**, 6 **El**
IS 5517	Grade C35Mn75	India	Bar, billet	0.30–0.40 **C**, 0.60–0.90 **Mn**, 0.10–0.35 **Si**	**Normalized, annealed or hardened and tempered**: (63) **diam**, (590) **TS**, (390) **YS**
BS 7S.1	Group C	UK	Bar: aircraft quality	0.30–0.40 **C**, 0.6–0.9 **Mn**, 0.040 **P**, 0.040 **S**, 0.10–0.35 **Si**, 0.15–0.35 **Pb**	**Cold drawn**: (<19) **diam**, (540) **TS**, (450) **YS**, 7 **El**
BS 1717	CDS–106	UK	Tube	0.30–0.40 **C**, 0.3–0.9 **Mn**, 0.050 **P**, 0.050 **S**, 0.35 **Si**	**As drawn or as drawn and tempered**: all **diam**, (480) **TS**, (385) **YS**
BS 1717	CDS–105	UK	Tube	0.30–0.40 **C**, 0.3–0.9 **Mn**, 0.050 **P**, 0.050 **S**, 0.35 **Si**	**Annealed**: all **diam**, (385) **TS**, (250) **YS**; **Normalized**: all **diam**, (440) **TS**, (305) **YS**
NF A 35–553	C 35	France	Strip	0.30–0.40 **C**, 0.50–0.80 **Mn**, 0.040 **P**, 0.040 **S**, 0.10–0.40 **Si**	
AISI 15B37H		US	Bar	0.30–0.39 **C**, 1.00–1.50 **Mn**, 0.040 **P**, 0.050 **S**, 0.15–0.30 **Si**, 0.0005–0.003 **B**	
DGN–B–301	15B37H	Mexico	Bar	0.30–0.39 **C**, 1.00–1.50 **Mn**, 0.040 **P**, 0.050 **S**, 0.15–0.30 **Si**, 0.0005 min **B**	
AISI 15B37H		US	Wire, rod	0.30–0.39 **C**, 1.00–1.50 **Mn**, 0.040 **P**, 0.050 **S**, 0.15–0.30 **Si**	
DIN 17140	Grade D35–2	Germany	Wire, rod	0.30–0.39 **C**, 0.30–0.60 **Mn**, 0.040 **P**, 0.040 **S**, 0.10–0.30 **Si**, 0.007 **N**	
AISI 1036		US	Plate	0.30–0.38 **C**, 1.20–1.55 **Mn**, 0.040 **P**, 0.050 **S**	
DGN–B–301	1036	Mexico	Bar	0.30–0.37 **C**, 1.20–1.50 **Mn**, 0.040 **P**, 0.050 **S**, 0.10–0.20 **Si**	**Forged or hot rolled, cold rolled and cold finished**: all **diam**, (567) **TS**, (314) **YS**, 16 **El**
ANSI/ASTM A 29	1536	US	Bar	0.30–0.37 **C**, 1.20–1.50 **Mn**, 0.040 **P**, 0.050 **S**	
ASTM A 689	1536	US	Bar: spring	0.30–0.37 **C**, 1.20–1.50 **Mn**, 0.040 **P**, 0.050 **S**	
COPANT 333	1036	COPANT	Wire, rod	0.30–0.37 **C**, 1.20–1.50 **Mn**, 0.040 **P**, 0.050 **S**	
DGN–B–301	1536	mexico	Bar	0.30–0.37 **C**, 1.20–1.50 **Mn**, 0.040 **P**, 0.050 **S**	
ANSI/ASTM A 576	1536	US	Bar	0.30–0.37 **C**, 1.20–1.50 **Mn**, 0.040 **P**, 0.050 **S**	
JIS G 3539	SWCH 33K	Japan	Wire	0.30–0.36 **C**, 0.60–0.90 **Mn**, 0.030 **P**, 0.035 **S**, 0.10–0.35 **Si**	**Annealed and cold drawn**: all **diam**, (618) **TS**, 12 **El**

WROUGHT CARBON STEELS

specification number	designation	country	product forms	composition	mechanical properties (see page iv for explanation)
COPANT 333	1033	COPANT	Wire, rod	0.30–0.36 **C**, 0.70–1.00 **Mn**, 0.040 **P**, 0.050 **S**	
JIS G 3507	SWRCH 33K	Japan	Wire, rod	0.30–0.36 **C**, 0.60–0.90 **Mn**, 0.030 **P**, 0.035 **S**, 0.10–0.35 **Si**	
JIS G 4051	S 33C	Japan	Bar, wire, rod	0.30–0.36 **C**, 0.60–0.90 **Mn**, 0.030 **P**, 0.035 **S**, 0.15–0.35 **Si**, 0.30 **Cu**	
NF A 35–553	XC 32	France	Strip	0.30–0.35 **C**, 0.50–0.80 **Mn**, 0.035 **P**, 0.035 **S**, 0.10–0.35 **Si**	**Normalized**: all **diam**, (550) **TS**, (315) **YS**, 23 **El**; **Quenched and tempered**: all **diam**, (750) **TS**, (560) **YS**, 14 **El**
NF A 35–564	XC 32 FF	France	Bar, wire, rod	0.30–0.35 **C**, 0.030 **P**, 0.030 **S**, 0.20 **Si**, 0.20 **Cu**, 0.020 min **Al**	**Annealed**: (≤70) **diam**, (540) max **TS**
BS 970: Part 1	060A32	UK	Blooms, billets, slabs, bar, rod, forgings	0.30–0.35 **C**, 0.50–0.70 **Mn**	
BS 970: Part 1	080A32	UK	Blooms, billets, slabs, bar, rod, forgings	0.30–0.35 **C**, 0.70–0.90 **Mn**	
VSM 10648	St Ac 50–2	Switzerland	Bar, sheet, plate	0.30 **C**, 0.055 **P**, 0.055 **S**	**Cold drawn**: (≤5) **diam**, (686) **TS**, (588) **YS**, 5 **El**; **Cold finished**: (10–100) **diam**, (490) **TS**, (294) **YS**, 20 **El**; **Cold drawn and annealed**: (≤25) **diam**, (461) **TS**, (255) **YS**, 20 **El**; **Cold finished and normalized**: all **diam**, (490) **TS**, (274) **YS**, 20 **El**
MIL–S–24093	Type V, class H	US	Forgings	0.30 **C**, 0.90 **Mn**, 0.040 **P**, 0.040 **S**, 0.10–0.30 **Si**, 0.25 **Cu**, 0.25 **Ni**	**Normalized and tempered or quenched and tempered**: all **diam**, 90 (621) max **TS**, 30 (207) **YS**, 30 **El**
DIN 1652	St 50 (1.0531)	Germany	Bar	0.30 **C**, 0.08 **P**, 0.05 **S**	**Cold drawn**: all **diam**, (590) **TS**, (420) **YS**, 7 in 80 mm **El**; **Centerless turned and solution annealed**: all **diam**, (460) **TS**, (255) **YS**, 20 in 80 mm **El**; **Centerless turned and normalized**: all **diam**, (490) **TS**, (275) **YS**, 20 in 80 mm **El**
DIN 1652	St 50–2 (1.0533)	Germany	Bar	0.30 **C**, 0.06 **P**, 0.05 **S**	**Cold drawn**: all **diam**, (590) **TS**, (420) **YS**, 7 in 80 mm **El**; **Centerless turned and solution annealed**: all **diam**, (460) **TS**, (255) **YS**, 20 in 80 mm **El**; **Centerless turned and normalized**: all **diam**, (490) **TS**, (275) **YS**, 20 in 80 mm **El**
ASTM A 607	Grade 70	US	Sheet, strip	0.30 **C**, 1.70 **Mn**, 0.05 **P**, 0.06 **S**, 0.005 **V**, 0.004 **Cb**, 0.015 **N**	**Hot or cold rolled**: all **diam**, 85 (590) **TS**, 70 (485) **YS**, 14 **El**
ASTM A 607	Grade 65	US	Sheet, strip	0.30 **C**, 1.55 **Mn**, 0.05 **P**, 0.06 **S**, 0.005 **V**, 0.004 **Cb**, 0.015 **N**	**Hot or cold rolled**: all **diam**, 80 (550) **TS**, 65 (450) **YS**, 16 **El**
JIS G 3445	Class 14C, No. 12	Japan	Tube: seamless or welded	0.30 **C**, 0.30–0.90 **Mn**, 0.040 **P**, 0.040 **S**, 0.35 **Si**	**As manufactured or cold finished**: (≥8) **diam**, (549) **TS**, (412) **YS**, 15 **El**
ISO 2604/1	F22Q	ISO	Forgings	0.30 **C**, 0.80–1.40 **Mn**, 0.050 **P**, 0.050 **S**, 0.10–0.40 **Si**	**Quenched and tempered**: (≤100) **diam**, (530) **TS**, 295 **YS**, 18 **El**
ASTM A 607	Grade 60	US	Sheet, strip	0.30 **C**, 1.55 **Mn**, 0.05 **P**, 0.06 **S**, 0.005 **V**, 0.004 **Cb**	**Hot or cold rolled**: all **diam**, 75 (520) **TS**, 60 (415) **YS**, 18 **El**
JIS G 3444	Class 3, No. 11	Japan	Tube: seamless or electric–resistance welded	0.30 **C**, 0.30–1.00 **Mn**, 0.040 **P**, 0.040 **S**, 0.35 **Si**	**As drawn or as welded**: all **diam**, (500) **TS**, (353) **YS**, 15 **El**
JIS G 3445	Class 14B, No. 12	Japan	Tube: seamless or welded	0.30 **C**, 0.30–0.90 **Mn**, 0.040 **P**, 0.040 **S**, 0.35 **Si**	**As manufactured or cold finished**: (≥8) **diam**, (500) **TS**, (353) **YS**, 15 **El**
SFS 200:E	Fe 50	Finland	Bar, plate, strip, wire, forgings	0.30 **C**, 0.050 **P**, 0.050 **S**, 0.009 **N**	**Hot worked**: (>40–100) **diam**, (490) **TS**, (274) **YS**, 20 **El**
TS 911	669.14–423/Fe 50	Turkey	Bar	0.30 **C**, 0.055 **P**, 0.055 **S**	**Hot rolled**: all **diam**, (490) **TS**, (294) **YS**, 20 **El**

WROUGHT CARBON STEELS

specification number	designation	country	product forms	composition	mechanical properties (see page iv for explanation)
DIN 1623 Sheet 2	St 50–2 (1.0532.6)	Germany	Sheet	0.30 **C**, 0.060 **P**, 0.050 **S**	**Hot or cold rolled**: all **diam**, (490) **TS**, (295) **YS**, 14 in 80 mm **El**
NS 13234	Grade St 50–2	Norway	Bar, forgings	0.30 **C**, 0.050 **P**, 0.050 **S**, 0.007 **N**	**Hot worked and normalized**: (≤16) **diam**, (490) **TS**, (294) **YS**, 20 **El**
JIS G 3132	Class 4	Japan	Strip	0.30 **C**, 0.30–0.90 **Mn**, 0.040 **P**, 0.040 **S**, 0.35 **Si**	**Hot rolled**: (1.0–1.6) **diam**, (490) **TS**, 15 **El**
ANSI/ASTM A 516	Grade 70	US	Plate	0.30 **C**, 0.80–1.25 **Mn**, 0.035 **P**, 0.04 **S**, 0.13–0.33 **Si**	**Normalized**: 2.0–4.0 **diam**, (485) **TS**, (260) **YS**, 21 **El**
ASTM A 350	Grade LF2	US	Forgings	0.30 **C**, 1.35 **Mn**, 0.035 **P**, 0.040 **S**, 0.15–0.30 **Si**	**Normalized or normalized, tempered**: all **diam**, 70 (483) **TS**, 36 (248) **YS**, 22 **El**
ANSI/ASTM A 556	Grade C2	US	Tube: seamless	0.30 **C**, 0.29–1.06 **Mn**, 0.048 **P**, 0.058 **S**, 0.10 min **Si**	**Annealed**: all **diam**, 70 (480) **TS**, 40 (280) **YS**, 30 **El**
ISO 2604/1	F22	ISO	Forgings	0.30 **C**, 0.80–1.40 **Mn**, 0.050 **P**, 0.050 **S**, 0.10–0.40 **Si**	**Normalized, normalized and tempered, quenched and tempered**: (≤63) **diam**, (460) **TS**, (255) **YS**, 18 **El**
ASTM A 139	Grade E	US	Pipe: electric fusion welded	0.30 **C**, 1.40 **Mn**, 0.040 **P**, 0.050 **S**	**As rolled**: ≥0.312 (≥7.9) **diam**, 66 (455) **TS**, 52 (359) **YS**, 22 **El**
API Spec 5LX	Welded, grade X52	US	Pipe	0.30 **C**, 1.35 **Mn**, 0.04 **P**, 0.05 **S**	**Non–expanded**: all **diam**, 66 (455) **TS**, 52 (359) **YS**
API Spec 5LX	Welded, grade X52	US	Pipe	0.30 **C**, 1.35 **Mn**, 0.04 **P**, 0.05 **S**	**Non expanded**: all **diam**, 66 (455) **TS**, 52 (359) **YS**
AS 1302	Grade 410C	Australia	Bar	0.30 **C**, 0.050 **P**, 0.050 **S**, 0.45 **C+Mn/6**	**As–rolled**: all **diam**, (440) **TS**, 12 **El**
API Spec 5LX	Welded, grade X46	US	Pipe	0.30 **C**, 1.35 **Mn**, 0.04 **P**, 0.05 **S**	**Non–expanded**: all **diam**, 63 (434) **TS**, 46 (317) **YS**
API Spec 5LX	Welded, grade X46	US	Pipe	0.30 **C**, 1.35 **Mn**, 0.04 **P**, 0.05 **S**	**Non expanded**: all **diam**, 63 (434) **TS**, 46 (317) **YS**
SABS 920	Type A	South Africa	Bar	0.30 **C**, 0.06 **P**, 0.06 **S**, 0.008 **N**	**Hot rolled**: (12–20) **diam**, (430) **TS**, (250) **YS**, 26 **El**
SABS 920	Type B	South Africa	Bar	0.30 **C**, 0.06 **P**, 0.06 **S**, 0.008 **N**	**Hot rolled, deformed**: (12–20) **diam**, (430) **TS**, (250) **YS**, 26 **El**
BS 4360	Grade 43A1	UK	Plate, section, bar	0.30 **C**, 0.060 **P**, 0.060 **S**	**As rolled**: (40–63) **diam**, (430) **TS**, 22 **El**
BS 4360	Grade 43A	UK	Plate, section, bar	0.30 **C**, 0.060 **P**, 0.060 **S**	**As rolled**: (40–63) **diam**, (430) **TS**, (230) **YS**, 22 **El**
BS 1717	ERW–103	UK	Tube: electric resistance butt welded	0.30 **C**, 0.6 **Mn**, 0.060 **P**, 0.060 **S**	**As welded**: all **diam**, (415) **TS**, (275) **YS**
ASTM A 372	Class I	US	Forgings	0.30 **C**, 1.00 **Mn**, 0.04 **P**, 0.05 **S**, 0.15–0.30 **Si**	**Annealed or normalized**: all **diam**, 60 (415) **TS**, 35 (240) **YS**, 20 **El**
ANSI/ASTM A 372	Class I	US	Forgings	0.30 **C**, 1.00 **Mn**, 0.04 **P**, 0.05 **S**, 0.15–0.30 **Si**	**Normalized or normalized and tempered**: all **diam**, (415) **TS**, (240) **YS**, 20 **El**
ASTM A 350	Grade LF1	US	Forgings	0.30 **C**, 0.75–1.05 **Mn**, 0.035 **P**, 0.040 **S**, 0.15–0.30 **Si**	**Normalized or normalized, tempered**: all **diam**, 60 (414) **TS**, 30 (207) **YS**, 25 **El**
ASTM A 523	Grade B	US	Pipe: seamless, electric resistance welded	0.30 **C**, 1.20 **Mn**, 0.050 **P**, 0.060 **S**	**As–rolled**: 0.312 (7.94) **diam**, 60 (414) **TS**, 35 (241) **YS**, 30 **El**
ASTM A 135	Grade B	US	Pipe: electric resistance welded	0.30 **C**, 1.20 **Mn**, 0.050 **P**, 0.060 **S**	**As rolled**: (0.312(7.94) **diam**, 60 (414) **TS**, 35 (241) **YS**, 30 **El**
ASTM A 139	Grade B	US	Pipe: electric fusion welded	0.30 **C**, 1.00 **Mn**, 0.040 **P**, 0.050 **S**	**As rolled**: 0.312 (7.94) **diam**, 60 (414) **TS**, 35 (241) **YS**, 30 **El**
ASTM A 139	Grade C	US	Pipe: electric fusion welded	0.30 **C**, 1.20 **Mn**, 0.040 **P**, 0.050 **S**	**As rolled**: ≥0.312 (≥7.9) **diam**, 60 (414) **TS**, 42 (290) **YS**, 25 **El**
ASTM A 139	Grade D	US	Pipe: electric fusion welded	0.30 **C**, 1.30 **Mn**, 0.040 **P**, 0.050 **S**	**As rolled**: ≥0.312 (≥7.9) **diam**, 60 (414) **TS**, 46 (317) **YS**, 23 **El**
ANSI/ASTM A 557	Grade B2	US	Tube: electric resistance welded	0.30 **C**, 0.27–0.93 **Mn**, 0.050 **P**, 0.060 **S**	**Normalized, annealed**: all **diam**, 60 (414) **TS**, 37 (255) **YS**, 30 **El**
ANSI/ASTM A 334	Grade 6	US	Tube: seamless, welded	0.30 **C**, 0.29–1.06 **Mn**, 0.048 **P**, 0.058 **S**, 0.10 min **Si**	**Normalized**: 0.312 (7.94) **diam**, 60 (414) **TS**, 35 (241) **YS**, 30 **El**
ANSI/ASTM A 333	Grade 6	US	Pipe: seamless, welded	0.30 **C**, 0.29–1.06 **Mn**, 0.048 **P**, 0.058 **S**, 0.10 min **Si**	**Normalized**: 0.312 (7.94) **diam**, 60 (414) **TS**, 35 (241) **YS**, 30 **El**

WROUGHT CARBON STEELS

specification number	designation	country	product forms	composition	mechanical properties (see page iv for explanation)
ANSI/ASTM A 106	Grade B	US	Pipe: seamless	0.30 **C**, 0.29–1.06 **Mn**, 0.048 **P**, 0.058 **S**, 0.10 min **Si**	**Annealed**: 0.312 (7.9) **diam**, 60 (414) **TS**, 35 (241) **YS**, 30 **El**
MIL-S-23284	Class 4	US	Forgings	0.30 **C**, 0.60–0.90 **Mn**, 0.020 **P**, 0.020 **S**, 0.35 **Si**	**Quenched and tempered and stress relieved**: all **diam**, 60 (414) **TS**, 35 (241) **YS**, 25 **El**
DGN-B-177	Type S, grade B	Mexico	Tube: seamless	0.30 **C**, 1.20 **Mn**, 0.05 **P**, 0.96 **S**	**As drawn**: (2–64) **diam**, (414) **TS**, (241) **YS**
DGN-B-177	Type E, grade B	Mexico	Tube: electric-résistant welded	0.30 **C**, 1.20 **Mn**, 0.05 **P**, 0.06 **S**	**As welded**: (2–64) **diam**, (414) **TS**, (241) **YS**
MIL-T-20157C	Type E	US	Tube, pipe: seamless	0.30 **C**, 0.29–1.06 **Mn**, 0.048 **P**, 0.045 **S**, 0.10 min **Si**	**As agreed**: all **diam**, (413) **TS**, (241) **YS**, 30 **El**
ANSI/ASTM A 53	Type S, grade B	US	Pipe: welded, seamless	0.30 **C**, 1.20 **Mn**, 0.05 **P**, 0.06 **S**	**As rolled**: all **diam**, 60 (413) **TS**, 35 (241) **YS**, 30 **El**
ANSI/ASTM A 53	Type E, grade B	US	Pipe: welded, seamless	0.30 **C**, 1.20 **Mn**, 0.05 **P**, 0.06 **S**	**As rolled**: all **diam**, 60 (413) **TS**, 35 (241) **YS**, 29.5 **El**
DGN-B-197	Grade 6	Mexico	Tube: seamless, welded	0.30 **C**, 0.29–1.06 **Mn**, 0.048 **P**, 0.058 **S**, 0.10 min **Si**	**Hot or cold finished and normalized**: (7.92) **diam**, (412) **TS**, (245) **YS**, 30 **El**
DGN-B-183	Grade B	Mexico	Pipe: electric-fusion welded	0.30 **C**, 0.30–1.00 **Mn**, 0.040 **P**, 0.050 **S**	**As welded**: (8) **diam**, (412) **TS**, (245) **YS**, 30 **El**
DGN-B-178	Grade B	Mexico	Pipe: seamless	0.30 **C**, 0.29–1.06 **Mn**, 0.048 **P**, 0.058 **S**, 0.10 **Si**	**Forged and hot finished or forged, cold finished and annealed**: (8) **diam**, (412) **TS**, (245) **YS**
JIS G 3454	Class 3	Japan	Pipe: seamless or welded	0.30 **C**, 0.30–1.00 **Mn**, 0.040 **P**, 0.040 **S**, 0.35 **Si**	**As manufactured or cold finished and annealed**: (≥8) **diam**, (412) **TS**, (245) **YS**, 25 **El**
JIS G 3455	Class 3	Japan	Pipe: seamless	0.30 **C**, 0.30–1.00 **Mn**, 0.035 **P**, 0.035 **S**, 0.10–0.35 **Si**, 0.20 **Cu**	**As manufactured, cold finished and annealed or cold finished and normalized**: (≥8) **diam**, (412) **TS**, (245) **YS**, 25 **El**
JIS G 3456	Class 3	Japan	Pipe: seamless or welded	0.30 **C**, 0.30–1.00 **Mn**, 0.035 **P**, 0.035 **S**, 0.10–0.35 **Si**, 0.20 **Cu**	**As manufactured, annealed or normalized**: (≥8) **diam**, (412) **TS**, (245) **YS**, 25 **El**
JIS G 3445	Class 14A, No. 12	Japan	Tube: seamless or welded	0.30 **C**, 0.30–0.90 **Mn**, 0.040 **P**, 0.040 **S**, 0.35 **Si**	**As manufactured or cold finished**: (≥8) **diam**, (412) **TS**, (245) **YS**, 25 **El**
ANSI/ASTM A 369	FPB	US	Pipe	0.30 **C**, 0.29–1.06 **Mn**, 0.048 **P**, 0.058 **S**, 0.10 min **Si**	**Annealed or normalized, tempered**: 0.312 (7.94) **diam**, 60 (410) **TS**, 35 (240) **YS**, 30 **El**
COPANT R 208	Grade B	COPANT	Pipe: seamless	0.30 **C**, 0.29–1.06 **Mn**, 0.048 **P**, 0.058 **S**, 0.10 min **Si**	**Hot or cold finished**: (≥8) **diam**, (410) **TS**, (245) **YS**, 30 **El**
COPANT 512	BT6	COPANT	Tube	0.30 **C**, 0.29–1.06 **Mn**, 0.048 **P**, 0.058 **S**, 0.10 min **Si**	**Normalized, normalized and tempered or quenched and tempered**: (≥8) **diam**, (410) **TS**, (240) **YS**, 30 **El**
ANSI/ASTM A 500	Grade B	US	Tube: seamless, welded	0.30 **C**, 0.05 **P**, 0.063 **S**, 0.18 **Cu**	**As-formed (round)**: 0.120 (3.05) **diam**, 58 (400) **TS**, 42 (290) **YS**, 23 **El**
ANSI/ASTM A 501		US	Tube: welded, seamless	0.30 **C**, 0.05 **P**, 0.063 **S**, 0.18 **Cu**	**As-rolled**: 0.312 (7.92) **diam**, 58 (400) **TS**, 36 (248) **YS**, 23 **El**
ANSI/ASTM A 501		US	Tube: welded or seamless	0.30 **C**, 0.05 **P**, 0.063 **S**	**Hot rolled**: all **diam**, (400) **TS**, (248) **YS**, 23 **El**
ANSI/ASTM A 500	Grade B	US	Tube: welded or seamless	0.30 **C**, 0.05 **P**, 0.063 **S**	**Cold formed**: 0.049 **diam**, (400) **TS**, (290) **YS**, 15 **El**; **As formed**: 0.049 **diam**, (400) **TS**, (317) **YS**, 15 **El**
MIL-S-23495	Class C	US	Shapes: extruded	0.30 **C**, 0.60–0.90 **Mn**, 0.04 **P**, 0.05 **S**, 0.15–0.30 **Si**	**Normalized**: ≤2 1/2 in **diam**, 58 (400) **TS**, 32 (221) **YS**, 24 **El**
DGN-B-180	Grade 1	Mexico	Pipe: seamless or welded	0.30 **C**, 0.40–1.06 **Mn**, 0.05 **P**, 0.06 **S**	**Normalized or normalized and quenched**: (≥8) **diam**, (382) **TS**, (206) **YS**, 35 **El**
DGN-B-197	Grade I	Mexico	Tube: seamless, welded	0.30 **C**, 0.40–1.06 **Mn**, 0.05 **P**, 0.06 **S**	**Hot or cold finished and normalized**: (7.92) **diam**, (382) **TS**, (206) **YS**, 35 **El**
COPANT 512	BT 1	COPANT	Tube	0.30 **C**, 0.40–1.06 **Mn**, 0.05 **P**, 0.06 **S**	**Normalized, normalized and tempered, or quenched and tempered**: (≥8) **diam**, (380) **TS**, (205) **YS**, 35 **El**

WROUGHT CARBON STEELS

specification number	designation	country	product forms	composition	mechanical properties (see page iv for explanation)
ANSI/ASTM A 334	Grade 1	US	Tube: seamless, welded	0.30 **C**, 0.40–1.06 **Mn**, 0.05 **P**, 0.06 **S**	**Normalized**: 0.312 (7.94) **diam**, 55 (379) **TS**, 30 (207) **YS**, 35 **El**
ANSI/ASTM A 333	Grade 1	US	Pipe: seamless, welded	0.30 **C**, 0.40–1.06 **Mn**, 0.05 **P**, 0.06 **S**	**Normalized**: 0.312 (7.94) **diam**, 55 (379) **TS**, 30 (207) **YS**, 35 **El**
IS 6286	Grade 2	India	Pipe	0.30 **C**, 0.29–1.06 **Mn**, 0.05 **P**, 0.05 **S**, 0.10 **Si**	**Annealed**: all **diam**, (365) **TS**, (215) **YS**
BS 980	ERW-2	UK	Tube	0.30 **C**, 0.6 **Mn**, 0.060 **P**, 0.060 **S**	**Welded**: 5 **diam**, (345) **TS**, (205) **YS**, 15 **El**
IS 6286	Grade 1	India	Pipe	0.30 **C**, 0.40–1.06 **Mn**, 0.05 **P**, 0.05 **S**	**Annealed**: all **diam**, (335) **TS**, (185) **YS**
ANSI/ASTM A 500	Grade A	US	Tube: seamless, welded	0.30 **C**, 0.05 **P**, 0.063 **S**, 0.18 **Cu**	**As–formed (round)**: 0.120 (3.05) **diam**, 45 (310) **TS**, 33 (228) **YS**, 25 **El**; **As–formed (shaped)**: 0.120 (3.05) **diam**, 45 (310) **TS**, 39 (269) **YS**, 25 **El**
ANSI/ASTM A 500	Grade A	US	Tube: welded or seamless	0.30 **C**, 0.05 **P**, 0.063 **S**	**Cold formed**: 0.049 **diam**, (310) **TS**, (228) **YS**, 20 **El**; **As formed**: 0.049 **diam**, (310) **TS**, (269) **YS**, 20 **El**
AS 1302	Grade 230S	Australia	Bar	0.30 **C**, 0.050 **P**, 0.050 **S**, 0.45 **C+Mn/6**	**As–rolled**: all **diam**, (265) **TS**, (230)max **YS**, 22 **El**
AS 1302	Grade 230R	Australia	Bar	0.30 **C**, 0.050 **P**, 0.050 **S**, 0.45 **C+Mn/6**	**As rolled**: all **diam**, (265) **TS**, (230)max **YS**, 22 **El**
ANSI/ASTM A 4		US	Bar	0.30 min **C**, 0.05 **P**	**Hot worked or cold worked and annealed**: all **diam**, (470) **TS**, 20 **El**
AISI 1033		US	Plate	0.29–0.36 **C**, 0.70–1.00 **Mn**, 0.040 **P**, 0.050 **S**	
JIS G 3506	SWRH 32	Japan	Wire, rod	0.29–0.36 **C**, 0.30–0.60 **Mn**, 0.040 **P**, 0.040 **S**, 0.15–0.35 **Si**	
AS 1450	540	Australia	Tube: seamless or welded	0.29 **C**, 0.060 **P**, 0.060 **S**	**As–drawn or stress relieved**: all **diam**, (650) **TS**, (540) **YS**
ANSI/ASTM A 612		US	Plate	0.29 **C**, 0.95–1.40 **Mn**, 0.035 **P**, 0.040 **S**, 0.13–0.33 **Si**	**Hot rolled**: ≤0.75 **diam**, 83 (570) **TS**, 50 (345) **YS**, 22 **El**
DGN–B–259	Grade A	Mexico	Plate	0.29 **C**, 0.95–1.40 **Mn**, 0.035 **P**, 0.040 **S**, 0.13–0.33 **Si**	**As rolled**: (<13) **diam**, (568) **TS**, (343) **YS**, 22 **El**
DGN–B–259	Grade B	Mexico	Plate	0.29 **C**, 0.95–1.40 **Mn**, 0.035 **P**, 0.040 **S**, 0.13–0.33 **Si**	**As rolled**: (13–19) **diam**, (556) **TS**, (343) **YS**, 22 **El**
ASTM A 607	Grade 55	US	Sheet, strip	0.29 **C**, 1.40 **Mn**, 0.05 **P**, 0.06 **S**, 0.005 **V**, 0.004 **Cb**	**Hot or cold rolled**: all **diam**, 70 (480) **TS**, 55 (380) **YS**, 20 **El**
AS 1450	380	Australia	Tube: seamless or welded	0.29 **C**, 0.060 **P**, 0.060 **S**	**As–formed**: all **diam**, (460) **TS**, (370) **YS**, 10 **El**
CSA B193	Seamless, grade X52 cold expanded	Canada	Pipe	0.29 **C**, 1.25 **Mn**, 0.04 **P**, 0.05 **S**	**Mill**: 0.250 (6.35) **diam**, 66 (455) **TS**, 52 (358) **YS**, 18 **El**
API Spec 5LX	Seamless, grade X52	US	Pipe	0.29 **C**, 1.25 **Mn**, 0.04 **P**, 0.05 **S**	**Cold–expanded**: all **diam**, 66 (455) **TS**, 52 (359) **YS**
API Spec 5LX	Seamless, grade X52	US	Pipe	0.29 **C**, 1.25 **Mn**, 0.04 **P**, 0.05 **S**	**Cold–expanded**: all **diam**, 66 (455) **TS**, 52 (359) **YS**
CSA B193	Seamless, grade X46 cold expanded	Canada	Pipe	0.29 **C**, 1.25 **Mn**, 0.04 **P**, 0.05 **S**	**Mill**: 0.250 (6.35) **diam**, 63 (434) **TS**, 46 (317) **YS**, 20 **El**
API Spec 5LX	Seamless, grade X46	US	Pipe	0.29 **C**, 1.25 **Mn**, 0.04 **P**, 0.05 **S**	**Cold–expanded**: all **diam**, 63 (434) **TS**, 46 (317) **YS**
API Spec 5LX	Seamless, grade X46	US	Pipe	0.29 **C**, 1.25 **Mn**, 0.04 **P**, 0.05 **S**	**Cold–expanded**: all **diam**, 63 (434) **TS**, 46 (317) **YS**
AS 1548–1	Grade 430	Australia	Plate	0.29 **C**, 0.55–1.30 **Mn**, 0.050 **P**, 0.050 **S**, 0.40 **Si**	**Rolled or normalized**: ≥16 **diam**, (430) **TS**, (230) **YS**, 21 **El**
AS 1750–1	Grade 430	Australia	Sections, bar	0.29 **C**, 0.55–1.30 **Mn**, 0.050 **P**, 0.050 **S**, 0.40 **Si**	**As rolled (bar)**: <25 **diam**, (430) **TS**, (230) **YS**, 21 **El**
AS 1450	250	Australia	Tube: seamless or welded	0.29 **C**, 0.060 **P**, 0.060 **S**	**Hot finished, normalized, as–formed, annealed, cold–drawn, as–drawn**: all **diam**, (420) **TS**, (250) **YS**, 22 **El**
AS 1450	250	Australia	Tube: seamless or welded	0.29 **C**, 0.060 **P**, 0.060 **S**	**Hot finished, normalized, as–formed, annealed, cold–drawn, as–drawn**: all **diam**, (420) **TS**, (250) **YS**, 22 **El**
ANSI/ASTM A 515	Grade 60	US	Plate	0.29 **C**, 0.90 **Mn**, 0.035 **P**, 0.04 **S**, 0.13–0.33 **Si**	**Normalized**: 2.0–4.0 **diam**, (415) **TS**, (220) **YS**, 25 **El**

WROUGHT CARBON STEELS

specification number	designation	country	product forms	composition	mechanical properties (see page iv for explanation)
CSA B193	Seamless, grade X42 cold expanded	Canada	Pipe	0.29 **C**, 1.25 **Mn**, 0.04 **P**, 0.05 **S**	**Mill**: 0.250 (6.35) **diam**, 60 (414) **TS**, 42 (290) **YS**, 23 **El**
CSA B193	Seamless, grade X42 non–expanded	Canada	Pipe	0.29 **C**, 1.25 **Mn**, 0.04 **P**, 0.05 **S**	**Mill**: 0.250 (6.35) **diam**, 60 (414) **TS**, 42 (290) **YS**, 23 **El**
API Spec 5LX	Seamless, grade X42	US	Pipe	0.29 **C**, 1.25 **Mn**, 0.04 **P**, 0.05 **S**	**Non–expanded**: all **diam**, 60 (414) **TS**, 42 (290) **YS**
API Spec 5LX	Seamless, grade X42	US	Pipe	0.29 **C**, 1.25 **Mn**, 0.04 **P**, 0.05 **S**	**Cold–expanded**: all **diam**, 60 (414) **TS**, 42 (290) **YS**
API Spec 5LX	Seamless, grade X42	US	Pipe	0.29 **C**, 1.25 **Mn**, 0.04 **P**, 0.05 **S**	**Non–expanded**: all **diam**, 60 (414) **TS**, 42 (290) **YS**
API Spec 5LX	Seamless, grade X42	US	Pipe	0.29 **C**, 1.25 **Mn**, 0.04 **P**, 0.05 **S**	**Cold–expanded**: all **diam**, 60 (414) **TS**, 42 (290) **YS**
ANSI/ASTM A 36		US	Plate	0.29 **C**, 0.85–1.20 **Mn**, 0.04 **P**, 0.05 **S**, 0.15–0.30 **Si**, 0.20 **Cu**	**As rolled**: >4.00 **diam**, (400) **TS**, (250) **YS**, 23 **El**
ANSI/ASTM A 36		US	Bar	0.29 **C**, 0.60–0.90 **Mn**, 0.04 **P**, 0.05 **S**, 0.20 **Cu**	**As rolled**: >4 **diam**, (400) **TS**, (250) **YS**, 23 **El**
TS 909	UDK 629.14–423/Fe 37	Turkey	Shapes	0.29 **C**, 0.063 **P**, 0.063 **S**	**Hot rolled**: all **diam**, (363) **TS**, (235) **YS**, 25 **El**
SIS 14 15 50	SIS 15 50–06	Sweden	Bar	0.28–0.40 **C**, 0.40–0.90 **Mn**, 0.050 **P**, 0.050 **S**	**Cold worked**: (≤40) **diam**, (540) **TS**, (460) **YS**, 8 **El**
SIS 14 15 50	SIS 15 50–00	Sweden	Bar, forgings, plate, sheet, tube	0.28–0.40 **C**, 0.40–0.90 **Mn**, 0.050 **P**, 0.050 **S**	**As rolled or as forged**: all **diam**, (490) **TS**, (270) **YS**, 21 **El**
ANSI/ASTM A 512	1030	US	Tube: cold–drawn buttweld	0.28–0.34 **C**, 0.60–0.90 **Mn**, 0.04 **P**, 0.05 **S**	**Stress relief annealed**: all **diam**, 80 (552) **TS**, 70 (483) **YS**, 10 **El**
DGN–B–201	Grade 1030	Mexico	Tube: butt–welded	0.28–0.34 **C**, 0.60–0.90 **Mn**, 0.040 **P**, 0.050 **S**	**Cold finished and annealed**: all **diam**, (551) **TS**, (482) **YS**, 10 **El**; **Normalized**: all **diam**, (448) **TS**, (276) **YS**, 30 **El**
DGN–B–301	1030	Mexico	Bar	0.28–0.34 **C**, 0.60–0.90 **Mn**, 0.040 **P**, 0.050 **S**, 0.10–0.20 **Si**	**Forged or hot rolled, cold rolled and cold finished**: all **diam**, (471) **TS**, (255) **YS**, 20 **El**
ASTM A 544	Grade 1030	US	Wire	0.28–0.34 **C**, 0.60–0.90 **Mn**, 0.040 **P**, 0.050 **S**	
AISI 1030		US	Bar	0.28–0.34 **C**, 0.60–0.90 **Mn**, 0.040 **P**, 0.050 **S**	
ANSI/ASTM A 519	1030	US	Tube: seamless	0.28–0.34 **C**, 0.60–0.90 **Mn**, 0.040 **P**, 0.050 **S**	
MIL–S–46070	Grade 1030	US	Bar: cold drawn	0.28–0.34 **C**, 0.60–0.90 **Mn**, 0.035 **P**, 0.045 **S**, 0.30 **Si**	**Normalized or annealed and stress relieved**: <1.25 **diam**, 75 (517) **YS**, 15 **El**
DGN–B–203	Grade 1030	Mexico	Tube: seamless	0.28–0.34 **C**, 0.60–0.90 **Mn**, 0.040 **P**, 0.050 **S**	
COPANT 330	1030	COPANT	Bar, shapes	0.28–0.34 **C**, 0.60–0.90 **Mn**, 0.040 **P**, 0.050 **S**	
COPANT 331	1030	COPANT	Bar	0.28–0.34 **C**, 0.60–0.90 **Mn**, 0.040 **P**, 0.050 **S**	
MIL–S–16974E	No. 1030	US	Bar, billets, blooms, slabs	0.28–0.34 **C**, 0.60–0.90 **Mn**, 0.040 **P**, 0.050 **S**, 0.15–0.30 **Si**	
ASTM A 108	1030	US	Bar	0.28–0.34 **C**, 0.60–0.90 **Mn**, 0.040 **P**, 0.050 **S**	
ANSI/ASTM A 546	Grade 1030	US	Wire	0.28–0.34 **C**, 0.60–0.90 **Mn**, 0.040 **P**, 0.050 **S**	
ANSI/ASTM A 545	Grade 1030	US	Wire	0.28–0.34 **C**, 0.60–0.90 **Mn**, 0.040 **P**, 0.050 **S**	
MIL–S–11310E	1030	US	Bar	0.28–0.34 **C**, 0.60–0.90 **Mn**, 0.040 **P**, 0.050 **S**, 0.20 **Si**	
MIL–S–16788A	Class C3	US	Blooms, billets, slabs	0.28–0.34 **C**, 0.60–0.90 **Mn**, 0.040 **P**, 0.050 **S**	
COPANT 333	1030	COPANT	Wire, rod	0.28–0.34 **C**, 0.60–0.90 **Mn**, 0.040 **P**, 0.050 **S**	
MIL–S–10520D	Grade 2	US	Bar, forgings	0.28–0.34 **C**, 0.60–0.90 **Mn**, .040 **P**, .050 **S**, 0.15–0.30 **Si**	**Quenched and tempered**: 1 3/4 **diam**, 76 (524) **YS**
ANSI/ASTM A 576	1030	US	Bar	0.28–0.34 **C**, 0.60–0.90 **Mn**, 0.040 **P**, 0.050 **S**	
AISI 1030		US	Wire, rod	0.28–0.34 **C**, 0.60–0.90 **Mn**, 0.040 **P**, 0.050 **S**	

WROUGHT CARBON STEELS

specification number	designation	country	product forms	composition	mechanical properties (see page iv for explanation)
ANSI/ASTM A 29	1030	US	Bar	0.28–0.34 **C**, 0.60–0.90 **Mn**, 0.040 **P**, 0.050 **S**	
ASTM A 689	1030	US	Bar	0.28–0.34 **C**, 0.60–0.90 **Mn**, 0.040 **P**, 0.050 **S**	
AS 1443	Grade AS 1443/S1030	Australia	Bar	0.28–0.34 **C**, 0.60–0.90 **Mn**, 0.050 **P**, 0.050 **S**, 0.35 **Si**	
AS 1443	Grade AS 1443/K1030	Australia	Bar	0.28–0.34 **C**, 0.60–0.90 **Mn**, 0.050 **P**, 0.050 **S**, 0.10–0.35 **Si**	
AS 1442	Grade AS 1442/S1030	Australia	Bar, blooms, billets, slabs	0.28–0.34 **C**, 0.60–0.90 **Mn**, 0.050 **P**, 0.050 **S**, 0.35 **Si**	
AS 1442	Grade AS 1442/K1030	Australia	Bar, blooms, billets, slabs	0.28–0.34 **C**, 0.60–0.90 **Mn**, 0.050 **P**, 0.050 **S**, 0.10–0.35 **Si**	
COPANT 514	Grade 1030	COPANT	Tube: seamless	0.28–0.34 **C**, 0.60–0.90 **Mn**, 0.040 **P**, 0.050 **S**, 0.20–0.35 **Si**	
ANSI/ASTM A 455	Grades I and II	US	Plate	0.28–0.33 **C**, 0.81–1.25 **Mn**, 0.040 **P**, 0.050 **S**, 0.13–0.33 **Si**	**As rolled**: ≤0.375 **diam**, (515) **TS**, (260) **YS**, 22 **El**
BS 970: Part 1	060A30	UK	Blooms, billets, slabs, bar, rod, forgings	0.28–0.33 **C**, 0.50–0.70 **Mn**	
BS 970: Part 1	080A30	UK	Blooms, billets, slabs, bar, rod, forgings	0.28–0.33 **C**, 0.70–0.90 **Mn**	
DGN–B–243	Type II	Mexico	Plate	0.28 **C**, 0.85–1.20 **Mn**, 0.040 **P**, 0.050 **S**, 0.15–0.30 **Si**	**As rolled**: (<9.5) **diam**, (515) **TS**, (258) **YS**
ANSI/ASTM A 299		US	Plate	0.28 **C**, 0.86–1.45 **Mn**, 0.035 **P**, 0.040 **S**, 0.13–0.33 **Si**	**As rolled**: all **diam**, (515) **TS**, (290) **YS**, 19 **El**
DGN–B–260		Mexico	Plate	0.28 **C**, 0.90–1.40 **Mn**, 0.035 **P**, 0.040 **S**, 0.15–0.30 **Si**	**As rolled**: (25) **diam**, (515) **TS**, (288) **YS**, 19 **El**
ANSI/ASTM A 573	Grade 70	US	Plate	0.28 **C**, 0.85–1.20 **Mn**, 0.04 **P**, 0.05 **S**, 0.15–0.30 **Si**	**Hot rolled**: >1.5 **diam**, (480) **TS**, (290) **YS**, 18 **El**
COPANT 37, II	AT–25	COPANT	Plate	0.28 **C**, 0.035 **P**, 0.045 **S**, 0.15–0.35 **Si**	**As rolled**: (≤25) **diam**, (460) **TS**, (250) **YS**, 23 **El**
CSA B193	Electrically welded, grade X52 cold expanded	Canada	Pipe	0.28 **C**, 1.25 **Mn**, 0.04 **P**, 0.05 **S**	**Mill**: 0.250 (6.35) **diam**, 66 (455) **TS**, 52 (358) **YS**, 18 **El**
API Spec 5LX	Welded, grade X52	US	Pipe	0.28 **C**, 1.25 **Mn**, 0.04 **P**, 0.05 **S**	**Cold–expanded**: all **diam**, 66 (455) **TS**, 52 (359) **YS**
API Spec 5LX	Welded, grade X52	US	Pipe	0.28 **C**, 1.25 **Mn**, 0.04 **P**, 0.05 **S**	**Cold expanded**: all **diam**, 66 (455) **TS**, 52 (359) **YS**
JIS G 3103	Class 3	Japan	Plate	0.28 **C**, 0.90 **Mn**, 0.035 **P**, 0.040 **S**, 0.15–0.30 **Si**	**Hot rolled**: (≤25) **diam**, (451) **TS**, (245) **YS**, 19 **El**
ANSI/ASTM A 516	Grade 65	US	Plate	0.28 **C**, 0.80–1.25 **Mn**, 0.035 **P**, 0.04 **S**, 0.13–0.33 **Si**	**Normalized**: 2.0–4.0 **diam**, (450) **TS**, (240) **YS**, 23 **El**
DGN–B–106	Type 212A/B	Mexico	Plate	0.28 **C**, 0.90 **Mn**, 0.040 **P**, 0.050 **S**, 0.05–0.30 **Si**	**Hot worked**: (<8) **diam**, 65 (448) **TS**, 35 (241) **YS**, 23 **El**
DGN–B–244	Grade 50	Mexico	Plate	0.28 **C**, 0.90 **Mn**, 0.035 **P**, 0.040 **S**, 0.15–0.30 **Si**	**As rolled**: (<25.4) **diam**, (448) **TS**, (241) **YS**, 23 **El**
CSA B193	Electrically welded, grade X46 cold expanded	Canada	Pipe	0.28 **C**, 1.25 **Mn**, 0.04 **P**, 0.05 **S**	**Mill**: 0.250 (6.35) **diam**, 63 (434) **TS**, 46 (317) **YS**, 20 **El**
API Spec 5LX	Welded, grade X46	US	Pipe	0.28 **C**, 1.25 **Mn**, 0.04 **P**, 0.05 **S**	**Cold–expanded**: all **diam**, 63 (434) **TS**, 46 (317) **YS**
API Spec 5LX	Welded, grade X46	US	Pipe	0.28 **C**, 1.25 **Mn**, 0.04 **P**, 0.05 **S**	**Cold expanded**: all **diam**, 63 (434) **TS**, 46 (317) **YS**
AS 1548–2	Grade 430	Australia	Plate	0.28 **C**, 0.55–1.30 **Mn**, 0.050 **P**, 0.050 **S**, 0.07–0.38 **Si**	**Rolled or normalized**: ≥16 **diam**, (430) **TS**, (240) **YS**, 21 **El**
AS 1750–2	Grade 430	Australia	Sections, bar	0.28 **C**, 0.55–1.30 **Mn**, 0.050 **P**, 0.050 **S**, 0.07–0.38 **Si**	**As rolled (bar)**: <25 **diam**, (430) **TS**, (240) **YS**, 21 **El**
ANSI/ASTM A 727		US	Forgings	0.28 **C**, 0.84–1.41 **Mn**, 0.043 **P**, 0.033 **S**, 0.13–0.32 **Si**	**Normalized, or quenched, tempered**: all **diam**, 60 (415) **TS**, 36 (250) **YS**, 22 **El**
CSA B193	Electrically welded, grade X42 cold expanded	Canada	Pipe	0.28 **C**, 1.25 **Mn**, 0.04 **P**, 0.05 **S**	**Mill**: 0.250 (6.35) **diam**, 60 (414) **TS**, 42 (290) **YS**, 23 **El**
CSA B193	Electrically welded, grade X42 Non–expanded	Canada	Pipe	0.28 **C**, 1.25 **Mn**, 0.04 **P**, 0.05 **S**	**Mill**: 0.250 (6.35) **diam**, 60 (414) **TS**, 42 (290) **YS**, 23 **El**

specification number	designation	country	product forms	composition	mechanical properties (see page iv for explanation)
SABS 719	Grade C	South Africa	Pipe: electric welded	0.28 C, 1.25 Mn, 0.04 P, 0.05 S	As welded: all diam, (414) TS, (290) YS
API Spec 5LX	Welded, grade X42	US	Pipe	0.28 C, 1.25 Mn, 0.04 P, 0.05 S	Non–expanded: all diam, 60 (414) TS, 42 (290) YS
API Spec 5LX	Welded, grade X42	US	Pipe	0.28 C, 1.25 Mn, 0.04 P, 0.05 S	Cold–expanded: all diam, 60 (414) TS, 42 (290) YS
API Spec 5LX	Welded, grade X42	US	Pipe	0.28 C, 1.25 Mn, 0.04 P, 0.05 S	Non expanded: all diam, 60 (414) TS, 42 (290) YS
API Spec 5LX	Welded, grade X42	US	Pipe	0.28 C, 1.25 Mn, 0.04 P, 0.05 S	Cold expanded: all diam, 60 (414) TS, 42 (290) YS
DIN 17100	RSt 42–1 (1.0131)	Germany	Bar, plate	0.28 C, 0.088 P, 0.055 S	Normalized: all diam, (410) TS, (255) YS, 22 El
DIN 17100	RSt 42–1 (1.0131)	Germany	Strip	0.28 C, 0.088 P, 0.055 S	Normalized: all diam, (410) TS, (255) YS, 22 El; Hot rolled: all diam, (410) TS, (255) YS, 16 El
COPANT 37, I	BM–21	COPANT	Plate	0.28 C, 0.035 P, 0.045 S	As rolled: (4.75–50) diam, (390) TS, (210) YS, 27 El
ANSI/ASTM A 285	Grade C	US	Plate	0.28 C, 0.90 Mn, 0.035 P, 0.045 S	As rolled: all diam, (380) TS, (205) YS, 27 El
DGN–B–242	Grade C	Mexico	Plate	0.28 C, 0.90 Mn, 0.035 P, 0.045 S, 0.20–0.35 Cu	As rolled: (<50) diam, (377) TS, (206) YS, 27 El
JIS G 3429	Class 1	Japan	Tube: seamless	0.28 C, 0.65 Mn, 0.040 P, 0.050 S	As manufactured: all diam, (373) TS, 30 El
NF A 35–051	FM 35 grade 1	France	Wire, rod	0.27–0.43 C, 0.50–0.80 Mn, 0.080 P, 0.055 S, 0.10–0.35 Si	
NF A 35–051	FM 35 grade 3	France	Wire, rod	0.27–0.42 C, 0.50–0.80 Mn, 0.040 P, 0.040 S, 0.10–0.35 Si	
NF A 35–051	FM 32	France	Wire, rod	0.27–0.38 C, 0.50–0.80 Mn, 0.040 P, 0.040 S, 0.10–0.35 Si	
ISO R683/1	C30	ISO	Bar, forgings	0.27–0.34 C, 0.50–0.80 Mn, 0.050 P, 0.050 S, 0.15–0.40 Si	Quenched and tempered: all diam, (915) TS, (620) YS, 18 El; Quenched, tempered and cold–reduced: all diam, (1050) TS, (835) YS, 10 El
ISO R683/1	C30e	ISO	Bar, forgings	0.27–0.34 C, 0.50–0.80 Mn, 0.035 P, 0.035 S, 0.15–0.40 Si	Quenched and tempered: all diam, (915) TS, (620) YS, 18 El; Quenched, tempered and cold–reduced: all diam, (1050) TS, (835) YS, 10 El
EURONORM 119–74, IV	C 30 B KD	EURONORM	Wire, rod	0.27–0.34 C, 0.50–0.80 Mn, 0.035 P, 0.035 S, 0.15–0.40 Si, 0.0005–0.0050 B	Quenched and tempered: (≤10) diam, (880) TS, (685) YS, 13 El
ISO/R 683/111	Type C30ea	ISO	Bar, billet, rod	0.27–0.34 C, 0.50–0.80 Mn, 0.035 P, 0.020–0.035 S, 0.15–0.40 Si	Quenched and tempered: (≤16) diam, (578) TS, (392) YS, 18 El
ISO/R 683/111	Type C30eb	ISO	Bar, billet, rod	0.27–0.34 C, 0.50–0.80 Mn, 0.035 P, 0.030–0.050 S, 0.15–0.40 Si	Quenched and tempered: (≤16) diam, (578) TS, (392) YS, 18 El
ISO 683/XVIII	C35eb	ISO	Bar, wire	0.27–0.34 C, 0.50–0.80 Mn, 0.035 P, 0.030–0.050 S, 0.15–0.40 Si	Normalized: all diam, (550) TS, (300) YS, 18 El
ISO 683/XVIII	C30e	ISO	Bar, wire	0.27–0.34 C, 0.50–0.80 Mn, 0.035 P, 0.035 S, 0.15–0.40 Si	Normalized: all diam, (510) TS, (280) YS, 20 El
ISO 683/XVIII	C30ea	ISO	Bar, wire	0.27–0.34 C, 0.50–0.80 Mn, 0.035 P, 0.020–0.035 S, 0.15–0.40 Si	Normalized: all diam, (510) TS, (280) YS, 20 El
ISO 683/XVIII	C30eb	ISO	Bar, wire	0.27–0.34 C, 0.50–0.80 Mn, 0.035 P, 0.030–0.050 S, 0.15–0.40 Si	Normalized: all diam, (510) TS, (280) YS, 20 El
ISO 683/XVIII	C30	ISO	Bar, wire	0.27–0.34 C, 0.50–0.80 Mn, 0.050 P, 0.050 S, 0.15–0.40 Si	Normalized: all diam, (510) TS, (280) YS, 20 El
QQ–S–700D	SAE 1030	US	Sheet, strip	0.27–0.34 C, 0.60–0.90 Mn, 0.040 P, 0.050 S	
AISI 1030		US	Plate	0.27–0.34 C, 0.0–0.90 Mn, 0.040 P, 0.050 S	
ANSI/ASTM A 519	1132	US	Tube: seamless	0.27–0.34 C, 1.35–1.65 Mn, 0.040 P, 0.08–0.13 S	

WROUGHT CARBON STEELS

specification number	designation	country	product forms	composition	mechanical properties (see page iv for explanation)
ANSI/ASTM A 680	1030	US	Strip	0.27–0.34 **C**, 0.60–0.90 **Mn**, 0.040 **P**, 0.050 **S**, 0.15–0.30 **Si**	**Cold–rolled**
ANSI/ASTM A 682	1030	US	Strip	0.27–0.34 **C**, 0.60–0.90 **Mn**, 0.040 **P**, 0.050 **S**, 0.15–0.30 **Si**	
ANSI/ASTM A 684	1030	US	Strip	0.27–0.34 **C**, 0.60–0.90 **Mn**, 0.040 **P**, 0.050 **S**, 0.15–0.30 **Si**	
JIS G 3539	SWCH 30K	Japan	Wire	0.27–0.33 **C**, 0.60–0.90 **Mn**, 0.030 **P**, 0.035 **S**, 0.10–0.35 **Si**	**Annealed and cold drawn**: all **diam**, (618) **TS**, 12 **El**
JIS G 3507	SWRCH 30K	Japan	Wire, rod	0.27–0.33 **C**, 0.60–0.90 **Mn**, 0.030 **P**, 0.035 **S**, 0.10–0.35 **Si**	
JIS G 4051	S 30C	Japan	Bar, wire, rod	0.27–0.33 **C**, 0.60–0.90 **Mn**, 0.030 **P**, 0.035 **S**, 0.15–0.35 **Si**, 0.30 **Cu**	
IS 961	Fe 570–HT (St58–HT)	India	Plate, bar	0.27 **C**, 0.055 **P**, 0.055 **S**	**Mill**: 6–28 **diam**, (570) **TS**, (350) **YS**, 20 **El**
NF A 36–101	A 52,2	France	Strip	0.27 **C**, 0.055 **P**, 0.055 **S**	**Hot rolled**: all **diam**, (510) **TS**, (353) **YS**, 22 **El**
DGN–B–245	Grade 55	Mexico	Plate	0.27 **C**, 0.85–1.20 **Mn**, 0.035 **P**, 0.040 **S**, 0.15–0.30 **Si**	**As rolled**: (<12.7) **diam**, (482) **TS**, (262) **YS**, 21 **El**
JIS G 3118	Class 3	Japan	Plate	0.27 **C**, 0.85–1.20 **Mn**, 0.035 **P**, 0.040 **S**, 0.15–0.30 **Si**	**Hot rolled**: (8–12.5) **diam**, (481) **TS**, (265) **YS**, 17 **El**
ISO/R 630	Grade Fe 44 B	ISO	Bar, plate	0.27 **C**, 0.075 **P**, 0.062 **S**	**As rolled**: (≤16) **diam**, (470) **TS**, (274) **YS**, 23 **El**
NF A 36–101	A 47,2	France	Strip	0.27 **C**, 0.055 **P**, 0.055 **S**	**Hot rolled**: all **diam**, (461) **TS**, (274) **YS**, 23 **El**
ASTM A 414	Grade E	US	Sheet	0.27 **C**, 1.20 **Mn**, 0.035 **P**, 0.040 **S**	**Hot rolled**: 0.2299–0.1450 (5.82–3.68) **diam**, 65 (450) **TS**, 35 (240) **YS**, 18 **El**
ANSI/ASTM A 414	Grade E	US	Sheet	0.27 **C**, 1.20 **Mn**, 0.035 **P**, 0.040 **S**	**Hot rolled or cold rolled, annealed**: all **diam**, (450) **TS**, (240) **YS**, 18 **El**
ASTM A 607	Grade 50	US	Sheet, strip	0.27 **C**, 1.40 **Mn**, 0.05 **P**, 0.06 **S**, 0.005 **V**, 0.004 **Cb**	**Hot or cold rolled**: all **diam**, 65 (450) **TS**, 50 (345) **YS**, 22 **El**
DGN–B–93	Class II, subclass II–1	Mexico	Plate, sheet	0.27 **C**, 0.80 **Mn**, 0.035 **P**, 0.040 **S**, 0.30 **Si**	**As agreed**: all **diam**, (448) **TS**, (221) **YS**, 24 **El**
ASTM A 618	Grade III	US	Tube: hot formed welded, seamless	0.27 **C**, 1.40 **Mn**, 0.05 **P**, 0.06 **S**, 0.35 **Si**, 0.01 min **V**	**As–rolled**: all **diam**, 65 (448) **TS**, 50 (345) **YS**, 20 **El**
ASTM A 714	Grade III	US	Pipe: welded, seamless	0.27 **C**, 1.40 **Mn**, 0.05 **P**, 0.06 **S**, 0.35 **Si**, 0.18 min **Cu**, 0.01 min **V**	**As rolled**: all **diam**, 65 (448) **TS**, 50 (345) **YS**, 20 **El**
ANSI/ASTM A 618	Grade III	US	Tube: welded and seamless	0.27 **C**, 1.40 **Mn**, 0.05 **P**, 0.06 **S**, 0.35 **Si**, 0.01 min **V**	**Hot formed**: all **diam**, 65 (448) **TS**, 50 (345) **YS**
DGN–B–275	Grade E	Mexico	Sheet	0.27 **C**, 1.20 **Mn**, 0.035 **P**, 0.040 **S**, 0.20 **Cu**	**Hot rolled**: (5–4) **diam**, (446) **TS**, (240) **YS**, 18 **El**
ANSI/ASTM A 500	Grade C	US	Tube: seamless, welded	0.27 **C**, 1.40 **Mn**, 0.05 **P**, 0.063 **S**, 0.18 **Cu**	**As–formed (round)**: 0.120 (3.05) **diam**, 62 (427) **TS**, 46 (317) **YS**, 21 **El**
ANSI/ASTM A 500	Grade C	US	Tube: welded or seamless	0.27 **C**, 1.40 **Mn**, 0.05 **P**, 0.063 **S**	**Cold formed**: all **diam**, (427) **TS**, (317) **YS**, 21 **El**; **As formed**: all **diam**, (427) **TS**, (345) **YS**, 21 **El**
ANSI/ASTM A 284	Grade D	US	Plate	0.27 **C**, 0.90 **Mn**, 0.04 **P**, 0.05 **S**, 0.15–0.30 **Si**	**Annealed**: all **diam**, (415) **TS**, (230) **YS**, 24 **El**
ANSI/ASTM A529		US	Plate, bar	0.27 **C**, 1.20 **Mn**, 0.04 **P**, 0.05 **S**, 0.20 min **Cu**	**As rolled**: all **diam**, 60 (414) **TS**, 42 (290) **YS**, 19 **El**
CSA B193	Seamless, grade B	Canada	Pipe	0.27 **C**, 1.15 **Mn**, 0.04 **P**, 0.05 **S**	**Mill**: 0.250 (6.35) **diam**, 60 (414) **TS**, 35 (241) **YS**, 27 **El**
ANSI/ASTM A 210	Grade A–1	US	Tube: seamless	0.27 **C**, 0.93 **Mn**, 0.048 **P**, 0.058 **S**, 0.10 **Si**	**Hot finished, as rolled, or cold drawn, annealed**: 0.312 (7.94) **diam**, 60 (414) **TS**, 37 (255) **YS**, 30 **El**
API Spec 5L	Grade B	US	Pipe: seamless	0.27 **C**, 1.15 **Mn**, 0.04 **P**, 0.05 **S**	**Mill**: all **diam**, 60 (414) **TS**, 35 (241) **YS**
DGN–B–258	Grade D	Mexico	Plate	0.27 **C**, 0.94 **Mn**, 0.04 **P**, 0.05 **S**, 0.15–0.30 **Si**	**Hot rolled**: (≤25) **diam**, (414) **TS**, (227) **YS**, 24 **El**
API Spec 5L	Grade B	US	Pipe: seamless	0.27 **C**, 1.15 **Mn**, 0.04 **P**, 0.05 **S**	**As rolled**: ≥.497 (≥12.62) **diam**, 60 (413) **TS**, 35 (241) **YS**, 30 **El**
MIL–T–16286E	Class g	US	Tube: seamless	0.27 **C**, 1.93 **Mn**, 0.048 **P**, 0.058 **S**, 0.10 min **Si**	**Normalized**: all **diam**, (413) **TS**, (255) **YS**, 30 **El**

specification number	designation	country	product forms	composition	mechanical properties (see page iv for explanation)
DGN–B–205	Grade B, type S	Mexico	Pipe: seamless	0.27 **C**, 1.15 **Mn**, 0.040 **P**, 0.050 **S**	**As drawn**: (≥8) **diam**, (412) **TS**, (245) **YS**, 30 **El**
NOM–B–189	Grade A1	Mexico	Tube: seamless	0.27 **C**, 0.93 **Mn**, 0.048 **P**, 0.058 **S**, 0.10 min **Si**	**Hot finished, cold finished and annealed, cold finished and normalized**: (12.7) **diam**, (412) **TS**, (255) **YS**, 30 **El**
DGN–B–207	Grade B2	Mexico	Tube: seamless	0.27 **C**, 0.29–0.93 **Mn**, 0.048 **P**, 0.058 **S**, 0.10 min **Si**	**Cold finished**: (≥1.14) **diam**, (412) **TS**, (255) **YS**, 30 **El**
ISO/R 630	Grade Fe 42 B	ISO	Bar, plate	0.27 **C**, 0.075 **P**, 0.062 **S**	**As rolled**: (≤16) **diam**, (411) **TS**, (255) **YS**, 23 **El**
ANSI/ASTM A 556	Grade B2	US	Tube: seamless	0.27 **C**, 0.29–0.93 **Mn**, 0.048 **P**, 0.058 **S**, 0.10 min **Si**	**Annealed**: all **diam**, 60 (410) **TS**, 37 (260) **YS**, 30 **El**
NF A 35–501	E 26 A42 grade 1	France	Sheet, plate, bar	0.27 **C**, 0.075 **P**, 0.062 **S**	**As rolled**: (3–30) **diam**, (410) **TS**, (255) **YS**, 21 **El**
NF A 35–501	E 26 A42 grade 2	France	Sheet, plate, bar	0.27 **C**, 0.062 **P**, 0.062 **S**, 0.007 N_2	**As rolled**: (3–30) **diam**, (410) **TS**, (255) **YS**, 23 **El**
COPANT R 203	Grade A–1	COPANT	Tube: seamless	0.27 **C**, 0.93 **Mn**, 0.048 **P**, 0.058 **S**, 0.10 min **Si**	**Hot finished, cold finished and annealed or cold finished and normalized**: (≥1.58) **diam**, (410) **TS**, (255) **YS**, (30) **El**
ANSI/ASTM A 36		US	Plate	0.27 **C**, 0.85–1.20 **Mn**, 0.04 **P**, 0.05 **S**, 0.15–0.30 **Si**, 0.20 **Cu**	**As rolled**: >2.50–4.0 **diam**, (400) **TS**, (250) **YS**, 23 **El**
ANSI/ASTM A 36		US	Bar	0.27 **C**, 0.60–0.90 **Mn**, 0.04 **P**, 0.05 **S**, 0.20 **Cu**	**As rolled**: >1.50–4.00 **diam**, (400) **TS**, (250) **YS**, 23 **El**
BS 4360	Grade 40A	UK	Plate, sections, bar	0.27 **C**, 0.060 **P**, 0.060 **S**	**As rolled**: (40–63) **diam**, (400) **TS**, 25 **El**
ANSI/ASTM A 29	M 1031	US	Bar	0.26–0.36 **C**, 0.25–0.60 **Mn**, 0.04 **P**, 0.05 **S**	
ANSI/ASTM A 575	M1031	US	Bar	0.26–0.36 **C**, 0.25–0.60 **Mn**, 0.04 **P**, 0.05 **S**	
BS 970: Part 1	080M30	UK	Blooms, billets, slabs, bar, rod, forgings	0.26–0.34 **C**, 0.60–1.00 **Mn**	**Normalized**: 6 **diam**, (440) **TS**, (220) **YS**, 20 **El**; **Hardened and tempered**: 2.5 **diam**, (480) **TS**, (305) **YS**, 18 **El**; **Cold drawn from hot rolled**: 0.50–0.625 **diam**, (535) **TS**, (400) **YS**, 10 **El**
MIL–S–3289A		US	Plate	0.26–0.33 **C**, 0.60–0.90 **Mn**, 0.040 **P**, 0.040 **S**, 0.10 **Si**	
MIL–S–20166B	Grade M	US	Shapes	0.26 **C**, 0.60–0.90 **Mn**, 0.035 **P**, 0.040 **S**	**Mill**: ≥0.5 **diam**, (620) max **TS**, (344) **YS**, 23 **El**
ANSI/ASTM A 381	Y 65	US	Pipe: welded	0.26 **C**, 1.40 **Mn**, 0.040 **P**, 0.050 **S**	**Normalized**: ≥0.37 (≥9.5) **diam**, 80 (552) **TS**, 65 (448) **YS**, 20 **El**
ANSI/ASTM A 572	Grade 65	US	Plate, bar, shapes	0.26 **C**, 1.35 **Mn**, 0.04 **P**, 0.05 **S**, 0.30 **Si**	**Hot rolled**: ≤.50 **diam**, (550) **TS**, (450) **YS**, 17 **El**
ANSI/ASTM A 381	Y 60	US	Pipe: welded	0.26 **C**, 1.40 **Mn**, 0.040 **P**, 0.050 **S**	**Normalized**: ≥0.37 (≥9.5) **diam**, 78 (538) **TS**, 60 (414) **YS**, 20 **El**
API Spec 5LX	Welded, grade X65	US	Pipe	0.26 **C**, 1.40 **Mn**, 0.04 **P**, 0.05 **S**, 0.02 **V**, 0.005 **Nb**	**Non or cold expanded**: all **diam**, 77 (530) **TS**, 65 (448) **YS**
API Spec 5LX	Welded, grade X65[5]	US	Pipe	0.26 **C**, 1.40 **Mn**, 0.04 **P**, 0.05 **S**, 0.02 **V**, 0.005 **Nb**	**Non or cold expanded**: all **diam**, 77 (530) **TS**, 65 (448) **YS**
ANSI/ASTM A 572	Grade 60	US	Plate, bar, shapes	0.26 **C**, 1.35 **Mn**, 0.04 **P**, 0.05 **S**, 0.30 **Si**	**Hot rolled**: 1.25 **diam**, (520) **TS**, (415) **YS**, 18 **El**
ANSI/ASTM A 381	Y 56	US	Pipe: welded	0.26 **C**, 1.40 **Mn**, 0.040 **P**, 0.050 **S**	**Normalized**: ≥0.37 (≥9.5) **diam**, 75 (517) **TS**, 56 (386) **YS**, 20 **El**
API Spec 5LX	Seamless, grade X60	US	Pipe	0.26 **C**, 1.35 **Mn**, 0.04 **P**, 0.05 **S**, 0.02 **V**, 0.005 **Nb**, 0.03 **Ti**	**Non or cold expanded**: all **diam**, 75 (517) **TS**, 60 (414) **YS**
API Spec 5LX	Welded, grade X60	US	Pipe	0.26 **C**, 1.35 **Mn**, 0.04 **P**, 0.05 **S**, 0.02 **V**, 0.005 **Nb**, 0.03 **Ti**	**Non or cold expanded**: all **diam**, 75 (517) **TS**, 60 (414) **YS**
API Spec 5LX	Seamless, grade X60[3]	US	Pipe	0.26 **C**, 1.35 **Mn**, 0.04 **P**, 0.05 **S**, 0.02 **V**, 0.005 **Nb**, 0.03 **Ti**	**Non or cold expanded**: all **diam**, 75 (517) **TS**, 60 (414) **YS**

WROUGHT CARBON STEELS

specification number	designation	country	product forms	composition	mechanical properties (see page iv for explanation)
API Spec 5LX	Welded, grade X60[3]	US	Pipe	0.26 **C**, 1.35 **Mn**, 0.04 **P**, 0.05 **S**, 0.02 **V**, 0.005 **Nb**, 0.03 **Ti**	**Non or cold expanded:** all **diam**, 75 (517) **TS**, 60 (414) **YS**
ANSI/ASTM A 381	Y 52	US	Pipe: welded	0.26 **C**, 1.40 **Mn**, 0.040 **P**, 0.050 **S**	**Normalized:** $\geq$0.37 ($\geq$9.5) **diam**, 72 (496) **TS**, 52 (359) **YS**, 20 **El**
API Spec 5Lx	Welded, grade X56	US	Pipe	0.26 **C**, 1.35 **Mn**, 0.04 **P**, 0.05 **S**, 0.02 **V**, 0.005 **Nb**, 0.03 **Ti**	**Non or cold expanded:** all **diam**, 71 (490) **TS**, 56 (386) **YS**
API Spec 5LX	Seamless, grade X56	US	Pipe	0.26 **C**, 1.35 **Mn**, 0.04 **P**, 0.05 **S**, 0.02 **V**, 0.005 **Nb**, 0.03 **Ti**	**Non or cold expanded:** all **diam**, 71 (490) **TS**, 56 (386) **YS**
API Spec 5LX	Seamless, grade X56[3]	US	Pipe	0.26 **C**, 1.35 **Mn**, 0.04 **P**, 0.05 **S**, 0.02 **V**, 0.005 **Nb**, 0.03 **Ti**	**Non or cold expanded:** all **diam**, 71 (490) **TS**, 56 (386) **YS**
API Spec 5LX	Welded, grade X56[3]	US	Pipe	0.26 **C**, 1.35 **Mn**, 0.04 **P**, 0.05 **S**, 0.02 **V**, 0.005 **Nb**, 0.03 **Ti**	**Non or cold expanded:** all **diam**, 71 (490) **TS**, 56 (386) **YS**
ASTM A 618	Grade I	US	Tube: hot formed welded, seamless structural	0.26 **C**, 1.30 **Mn**, 0.063 **S**	**As rolled:** all **diam**, 70 (483) **TS**, 50 (345) **YS**, 22 **El**
ASTM A 618	Grade II	US	Tube: hot formed welded, seamless	0.26 **C**, 1.30 **Mn**, 0.05 **P**, 0.063 **S**, 0.33 **Si**, 0.18 min **Cu**, 0.01 min **V**	**As–rolled:** all **diam**, 70 (483) **TS**, 50 (345) **YS**, 22 **El**
ASTM A 714	Grade II	US	Pipe: welded, seamless	0.26 **C**, 1.30 **Mn**, 0.05 **P**, 0.063 **S**, 0.33 **Si**, 0.18 min **Cu**, 0.01 min **V**	**As rolled:** all **diam**, 70 (483) **TS**, 50 (345) **YS**, 22 **El**
ASTM A 714	Grade I	US	Pipe: welded, seamless	0.26 **C**, 1.30 **Mn**, 0.063 **S**, 0.18 min **Cu**	**As rolled:** all **diam**, 70 (483) **TS**, 50 (345) **YS**, 22 **El**
ANSI/ASTM A 618	Grade II	US	Tube: welded, seamless	0.26 **C**, 1.30 **Mn**, 0.05 **P**, 0.063 **S**, 0.33 **Si**, 0.18 min **Cu**, 0.01 min **V**	**Hot formed:** all **diam**, 70 (483) **TS**, 50 (345) **YS**
ANSI/ASTM A 618	Grade I	US	Tube: welded, seamless	0.26 **C**, 1.30 **Mn**, 0.063 **S**	**Hot formed:** all **diam**, 70 (483) **TS**, 50 (345) **YS**
AS 1450	350	Australia	Tube: seamless or welded	0.26 **C**, 1.60 **Mn**, 0.050 **P**, 0.050 **S**	**Hot finished, normalized, as–formed, annealed, cold–drawn, as–drawn:** all **diam**, (480) **TS**, (360) **YS**, 20 **El**
ANSI/ASTM A 381	Y 50	US	Pipe: welded	0.26 **C**, 1.40 **Mn**, 0.040 **P**, 0.050 **S**	**Normalized:** $\geq$0.37 ($\geq$9.5) **diam**, 69 (476) **TS**, 50 (345) **YS**, 21 **El**
ANSI/ASTM A 381	Y 48	US	Pipe: welded	0.26 **C**, 1.40 **Mn**, 0.040 **P**, 0.050 **S**	**Normalized:** $\geq$0.37 ($\geq$9.5) **diam**, 67 (462) **TS**, 48 (331) **YS**, 21 **El**
DIN 17155	Grade H IV	Germany	Plate	0.26 **C**, 0.60 min **Mn**, 0.050 **P**, 0.050 **S**, 0.35 **Si**, 0.30 max, opt **Cr**	**Normalized:** ($\leq$16) **diam**, (461) **TS**, (284) **YS**
ANSI/ASTM A 573	Grade 65	US	Plate	0.26 **C**, 0.85–1.20 **Mn**, 0.04 **P**, 0.05 **S**, 0.15–0.30 **Si**	**Hot rolled:** >0.50–1.50 **diam**, (450) **TS**, (240) **YS**, 20 **El**
ANSI/ASTM A 606		US	Sheet, strip	0.26 **C**, 1.30 **Mn**, 0.06 **S**	**Annealed, cold rolled:** all **diam**, 65 (450) **TS**, 45 (310) **YS**, 22 **El**
ANSI/ASTM A 381	Y 46	US	Pipe: welded	0.26 **C**, 1.40 **Mn**, 0.040 **P**, 0.050 **S**	**Normalized:** $\geq$0.37 ($\geq$9.5) **diam**, 63 (434) **TS**, 46 (317) **YS**, 23 **El**
CSA B193	Electrically welded, grade B	Canada	Pipe	0.26 **C**, 1.15 **Mn**, 0.04 **P**, 0.05 **S**	**Mill:** 0.250 (6.35) **diam**, 60 (414) **TS**, 35 (241) **YS**, 27 **El**
SABS 719	Grade B	South Africa	Pipe: electric welded	0.26 **C**, 1.15 **Mn**, 0.04 **P**, 0.05 **S**	**As welded:** all **diam**, (414) **TS**, (241) **YS**
ANSI/ASTM A 381	Y 35	US	Pipe: welded	0.26 **C**, 1.40 **Mn**, 0.040 **P**, 0.050 **S**	**Normalized:** $\geq$0.37 ($\geq$9.5) **diam**, 60 (414) **TS**, 35 (241) **YS**, 26 **El**
ANSI/ASTM A 381	Y 42	US	Pipe: welded	0.26 **C**, 1.40 **Mn**, 0.040 **P**, 0.050 **S**	**Normalized:** $\geq$0.37 ($\geq$9.5) **diam**, 60 (414) **TS**, 42 (290) **YS**, 25 **El**
API Spec 5L	Grade B	US	Pipe: electric weld or submerged arc weld	0.26 **C**, 1.15 **Mn**, 0.04 **P**, 0.05 **S**	**Mill:** all **diam**, 60 (414) **TS**, 35 (241) **YS**
API Spec 5L	Grade B	US	Pipe: electric weld, submerged arc weld or gas metal arc weld	0.26 **C**, 1.15 **Mn**, 0.04 **P**, 0.05 **S**	**As rolled:** $\geq$.497 ($\geq$12.62) **diam**, 60 (413) **TS**, 35 (241) **YS**, 30 **El**
ASTM A 607	Grade 45	US	Sheet, strip	0.26 **C**, 1.40 **Mn**, 0.05 **P**, 0.06 **S**, 0.005 **V**, 0.004 **Cb**	**Hot or cold rolled:** all **diam**, 60 (410) **TS**, 45 (310) **YS**, 25 **El**

WROUGHT CARBON STEELS

specification number	designation	country	product forms	composition	mechanical properties (see page iv for explanation)
DGN–B–200		Mexico	Tube: welded or seamless	0.26 **C**, 0.040 **P**, 0.050 **S**, 0.20 min **Cu**	**As welded or as drawn**: all **diam**, (402) **TS**, (245) **YS**, 23 **El**
DGN–B–199	Grade B	Mexico	Shapes: seamless, welded	0.26 **C**, 0.040 **P**, 0.050 **S**	**Shapes**: (≥3.05) **diam**, (402) **TS**, (319) **YS**, 23 **El**
AS 1548–1	Grade 400	Australia	Plate	0.26 **C**, 0.55–1.30 **Mn**, 0.050 **P**, 0.050 **S**, 0.40 **Si**	**Rolled or normalized**: ≥16 **diam**, (400) **TS**, (215) **YS**, 23 **El**
ANSI/ASTM A 709	Grade 36	US	Plate, bar, shapes	0.26 **C**, 0.04 **P**, 0.05 **S**	**Annealed (bar, shapes)**: all **diam**, (400) **TS**, (250) **YS**, 21 **El**
COPANT 517	Grade B	COPANT	Tube	0.26 **C**, 0.04 **P**, 0.05 **S**, 0.20 min **Cu**	**As agreed**: (≥4.6) **diam**, (400) **TS**, (285) **YS**, 23 **El**
ANSI/ASTM A 36		US	Shapes	0.26 **C**, 0.04 **P**, 0.05 **S**, 0.20 **Cu**	**As rolled**: all **diam**, (400) **TS**, (250) **YS**, 21 **El**
ANSI/ASTM A 36		US	Plate	0.26 **C**, 0.80–1.20 **Mn**, 0.04 **P**, 0.05 **S**, 0.20 **Cu**	**As rolled**: >0.75–1.50 **diam**, (400) **TS**, (250) **YS**, 23 **El**
ANSI/ASTM A 36		US	Plate	0.26 **C**, 0.80–1.20 **Mn**, 0.04 **P**, 0.05 **S**, 0.15–0.30 **Si**, 0.20 **Cu**	**As rolled**: >1.50–2.50 **diam**, (400) **TS**, (250) **YS**, 23 **El**
ANSI/ASTM A 36		US	Bar	0.26 **C**, 0.04 **P**, 0.05 **S**, 0.20 **Cu**	**As rolled**: >0.75 **diam**, (400) **TS**, (250) **YS**, 23 **El**
COPANT 517	Grade A	COPANT	Tube	0.26 **C**, 0.04 **P**, 0.05 **S**, 0.20 min **Cu**	**As agreed**: (≥3) **diam**, (315) **TS**, (225) **YS**, 25 **El**
DGN–B–199	Grade A	Mexico	Shapes: seamless, welded	0.26 **C**, 0.040 **P**, 0.050 **S**, 0.20 min **Cu**	**Shapes**: (≥3.05) **diam**, (308.7) **TS**, (269.5) **YS**, 25 **El**
MIL–S–43A		US	Bar	0.25–0.40 **C**, 1.15–1.55 **Mn**, 0.040 **P**, 0.08–0.13 **S**, 0.10–0.20 **Si**	**Cold drawn and stress relieved**: ≤1.25 **diam**, 118 (814) **TS**, 75 (517) **YS**, 15 **El**
AS 1442	Grade AS 1442/K4	Australia	Bar	0.25–0.38 **C**, 0.40–1.00 **Mn**, 0.050 **P**, 0.050 **S**, 0.10–0.35 **Si**	**As rolled or normalized**: (≤150) **diam**, (500) **TS**, (250) **YS**, 20 **El**
AS 1442	Grade AS 1442/S4	Australia	Bar	0.25–0.38 **C**, 0.40–1.00 **Mn**, 0.050 **P**, 0.050 **S**, 0.35 **Si**	**As rolled or normalized**: (≤150) **diam**, (500) **TS**, (250) **YS**, 20 **El**
AS 1443	Grade 1443/S4	Australia	Bar	0.25–0.38 **C**, 0.40–1.00 **Mn**, 0.050 **P**, 0.050 **S**, 0.35 **Si**	**As rolled or normalized**: (≤150) **diam**, (500) **TS**, (250) **YS**, 20 **El**
AS 1443	AS 1443/K4	Australia	Bar	0.25–0.38 **C**, 0.40–1.00 **Mn**, 0.50 **P**, 0.50 **S**, 0.10–0.35 **Si**	**As rolled or normalized**: (≤150) **diam**, (500) **TS**, (250) **YS**, 20 **El**
IS 5517	Grade C30	India	Bar, billet	0.25–0.35 **C**, 0.60–0.90 **Mn**, 0.10–0.35 **Si**	**Normalized, annealed or hardened and tempered**: (30) **diam**, (590) **TS**, (390) **YS**
JIS G 3445	Class 15C, No. 12	Japan	Tube: seamless or welded	0.25–0.35 **C**, 0.30–1.00 **Mn**, 0.040 **P**, 0.040 **S**, 0.35 **Si**	**As manufactured or cold finished**: (≥8) **diam**, (579) **TS**, (431) **YS**, 12 **El**
BS 7S.1	Group B	UK	Bar: aircraft quality	0.25–0.35 **C**, 0.6–0.9 **Mn**, 0.040 **P**, 0.040 **S**, 0.10–0.35 **Si**, 0.15–0.35 **Pb**	**Cold drawn**: (<19) **diam**, (540) **TS**, (450) **YS**, 7 **El**
AS 1443	AS 1443/CD2	Australia	Bar	0.25–0.35 **C**, 0.30–0.90 **Mn**, 0.050 **P**, 0.050 **S**, 0.35 **Si**	**Cold drawn or cold rolled**: (16–38) **diam**, (540) **TS**, (430) **YS**, 11 **El**
BS 1449: Part 1	Grade 30	UK	Plate, sheet, strip	0.25–0.35 **C**, 0.50–0.90 **Mn**, 0.050 **P**, 0.050 **S**, 0.05–0.35 **Si**	**Hot rolled**: all **diam**, (500) **TS**, (280) **YS**, 15 **El**; **Cold rolled, annealed**: all **diam**, (430) **TS**, (250) **YS**, 20 **El**
JIS G 3445	Class 15A, No. 12	Japan	Tube: seamless or welded	0.25–0.35 **C**, 0.30–1.00 **Mn**, 0.040 **P**, 0.040 **S**, 0.35 **Si**	**As manufactured or cold finished**: (≥8) **diam**, (471) **TS**, (275) **YS**, 22 **El**
AS 1443	Grade AS 1443/CS1030	Australia	Bar	0.25–0.35 **C**, 0.30–0.90 **Mn**, 0.060 **P**, 0.060 **S**, 0.35 **Si**	
AS 1442	Grade AS 1442/CS1030	Australia	Bar, blooms, billets, slabs	0.25–0.35 **C**, 0.30–0.90 **Mn**, 0.060 **P**, 0.060 **S**, 0.35 **Si**	
AISI 1029		US	Bar	0.25–0.31 **C**, 0.60–0.90 **Mn**, 0.040 **P**, 0.050 **S**	
COPANT 333	1029	COPANT	Wire, rod	0.25–0.31 **C**, 0.60–0.90 **Mn**, 0.040 **P**, 0.050 **S**	
DGN–B–301	1029	Mexico	Bar	0.25–0.31 **C**, 0.60–0.90 **Mn**, 0.040 **P**, 0.050 **S**, 0.10–0.20 **Si**	

specification number	designation	country	product forms	composition	mechanical properties (see page iv for explanation)
ANSI/ASTM A 576	1029	US	Bar	0.25–0.31 **C**, 0.60–0.90 **Mn**, 0.040 **P**, 0.050 **S**	
AISI 1029		US	Wire, rod	0.25–0.31 **C**, 0.60–0.90 **Mn**, 0.040 **P**, 0.050 **S**	
ANSI/ASTM A 29	1029	US	Bar	0.25–0.31 **C**, 0.60–0.90 **Mn**, 0.040 **P**, 0.050 **S**	
ASTM A 689	1029	US	Bar	0.25–0.31 **C**, 0.60–0.90 **Mn**, 0.040 **P**, 0.050 **S**	
JIS G 4051	S 28C	Japan	Bar, wire, rod	0.25–0.31 **C**, 0.60–0.90 **Mn**, 0.030 **P**, 0.035 **S**, 0.15–0.35 **Si**, 0.30 **Cu**	
BS 970: Part 1	060A27	UK	Blooms, billets, slabs, bar, rod, forgings	0.25–0.30 **C**, 0.50–0.70 **Mn**	
BS 970: Part 1	080A27	UK	Blooms, billets, slabs, bar, rod, forgings	0.25–0.30 **C**, 0.70–0.90 **Mn**	
DIN 1652	St 42 (1.0140)	Germany	Bar	0.25 **C**, 0.08 **P**, 0.05 **S**	**Cold drawn**: all **diam**, (540) **TS**, (380) **YS**, 7 in 80 mm **El**; **Centerless turned and solution annealed**: all **diam**, (380) **TS**, (215) **YS**, 22 in 80 mm **El**; **Centerless turned and normalized**: all **diam**, (410) **TS**, (235) **YS**, 22 in 80 mm **El**
DIN 1652	St 42-2 (1.0181)	Germany	Bar	0.25 **C**, 0.06 **P**, 0.05 **S**	**Cold drawn**: all **diam**, (540) **TS**, (380) **YS**, 7 in 80 mm **El**; **Centerless turned and solution annealed**: all **diam**, (380) **TS**, (215) **YS**, 22 in 80 mm **El**; **Centerless turned and normalized**: all **diam**, (410) **TS**, (235) **YS**, 22 in 80 mm **El**
VSM 10648	St Ac 37-1	Switzerland	Bar, sheet, plate	0.25 **C**, 0.090 **P**, 0.063 **S**	**Cold drawn**: ($\leq$5) **diam**, (539) **TS**, (412) **YS**, 7 **El**; **Cold finished**: (10–100) **diam**, (363) **TS**, (235) **YS**, 25 **El**; **Cold drawn and annealed**: ($\leq$25) **diam**, (333) **TS**, (196) **YS**, 25 **El**; **Cold finished and normalized**: all **diam**, (363) **TS**, (216) **YS**, 25 **El**
ISO 2604/1	F17Q	ISO	Forgings	0.25 **C**, 0.90–1.70 **Mn**, 0.040 **P**, 0.040 **S**, 0.10–0.40 **Si**	**Quenched and tempered**: ($\leq$100) **diam**, (510) **TS**, (285) **YS**, 17 **El**
ISO 2604/1	F18Q	ISO	Forgings	0.25 **C**, 0.90–1.70 **Mn**, 0.040 **P**, 0.040 **S**, 0.10–0.40 **Si**, 0.015 min $\mathbf{Al}_{\mathbf{met}}$	**Quenched and tempered**: ($\leq$100) **diam**, (510) **TS**, (285) **YS**, 17 **El**
JIS G 3445	Class 13C, No. 12	Japan	Tube: seamless or welded	0.25 **C**, 0.30–0.90 **Mn**, 0.040 **P**, 0.040 **S**, 0.35 **Si**	**As manufactured or cold finished**: ($\geq$8) **diam**, (510) **TS**, (382) **YS**, 15 **El**
ISO/R 630	Grade Fe 52 B	ISO	Bar, plate	0.25 **C**, 0.065 **P**, 0.055 **S**	**As rolled**: ($\leq$30) **diam**, (490) **TS**, (343) **YS**, 22 **El**
ISO 2604/1	F17	ISO	Forgings	0.25 **C**, 0.90–1.70 **Mn**, 0.040 **P**, 0.040 **S**, 0.10–0.40 **Si**	**Normalized, normalized and tempered, quenched and tempered**: ($\leq$63) **diam**, (490) **TS**, (265) **YS**, 16 **El**
ISO 2604/1	F18	ISO	Forgings	0.25 **C**, 0.90–1.70 **Mn**, 0.040 **P**, 0.040 **S**, 0.10–0.40 **Si**, 0.015 min $\mathbf{Al}_{\mathbf{met}}$	**Normalized, normalized and tempered, quenched and tempered**: ($\leq$63) **diam**, (490) **TS**, (305) **YS**, 16 **El**
JIS G 3105	Class 2, No. 14A	Japan	Bar	0.25 **C**, 1.00–1.50 **Mn**, 0.040 **P**, 0.040 **S**, 0.15–0.40 **Si**	**Hot rolled or normalized**: all **diam**, (490) **TS**, 22 **El**
ANSI/ASTM A 572	Grade 55	US	Plate, bar, shapes	0.25 **C**, 1.35 **Mn**, 0.04 **P**, 0.05 **S**, 0.30 **Si**	**Hot rolled**: 1.50 **diam**, (485) **TS**, (380) **YS**, 20 **El**
BS 4461		UK	Bar	0.25 **C**, 0.060 **P**, 0.060 **S**	**Cold worked**: (6–16) **diam**, (460) **TS**, 12 **El**

WROUGHT CARBON STEELS

specification number	designation	country	product forms	composition	mechanical properties (see page iv for explanation)
DIN 2391 Part 2	Grade St 45–1.0408	Germany	Tube	0.25 **C**, 0.05 **P**, 0.05 **S**	**Normalized**: all **diam**, (441) **TS**, (255) **YS**, 21 **El**; **Bright drawn/hard**: all **diam**, (539) **TS**, 5 **El**; **Bright drawn/soft**: all **diam**, (470) **TS**, 10 **El**; **Annealed**: all **diam**, (314) **TS**, 28 **El**
TS 346	Fe 45	Turkey	Pipe: seamless	0.25 **C**, 0.90 **Mn**, 0.050 **P**, 0.050 **S**, 0.35 **Si**	**As drawn**: (≤16) **diam**, (441) **TS**, (255) **YS**, 21 **El**
TS 302	Fe 45.2	Turkey	Pipe: welded or seamless	0.25 **C**, 0.050 **P**, 0.050 **S**	**As drawn or as welded**: all **diam**, (441) **TS**, (226) **YS**, 21 **El**
SFS 2146	Fe 45	Finland	Tube: seamless	0.25 **C**, 0.05 **P**, 0.05 **S**, 0.30 **Cr**	**As drawn**: (≤16) **diam**, (441) **TS**, (235) **YS**, 21 **El**
JIS G 3445	Class 13B, No. 12	Japan	Tube: seamless or welded	0.25 **C**, 0.30–0.90 **Mn**, 0.040 **P**, 0.040 **S**, 0.35 **Si**	**As manufactured or cold finished**: (≥8) **diam**, (441) **TS**, (304) **YS**, 20 **El**
DIN 1629, Part 3	Grade St45/1.0408	Germany	Tube: seamless	0.25 **C**, 1.50 **Mn**, 0.05 **P**, 0.05 **S**, 0.55 **Si**	**Annealed**: (<16) **diam**, (440) **TS**, (255) **YS**, 21 **El**
BS 1502–161	Grade 28	UK	Bar	0.25 **C**, 0.55–1.20 **Mn**, 0.050 **P**, 0.050 **S**, 0.10–0.35 **Si**, 0.70 max other elements, total	**As–rolled**: ≤1 (≤25) **diam**, (432) **TS**, (247) **YS**, 45 **El**
BS 1502–151	Grade 28	UK	Bar	0.25 **C**, 0.55–1.20 **Mn**, 0.050 **P**, 0.050 **S**, 0.10 **Si**, 0.70 max other elements, total	**As–rolled**: ≤1 (≤25) **diam**, (432) **TS**, (247) **YS**, 45 **El**
BS 1501–154	Grade 28	UK	Plate	0.25 **C**, 0.40–1.20 **Mn**, 0.050 **P**, 0.050 **S**; 0.70 max other elements, total	**As supplied**: (≤9.53) **diam**, (430) **TS**, (245) **YS**, 45 **El**
BS 1501–161	Grade 28A	UK	Plate	0.25 **C**, 0.55–1.20 **Mn**, 0.050 **P**, 0.050 **S**, 0.10–0.35 **Si**; 0.70 max other elements, total	**Normalized**: (≤16) **diam**, (430) **TS**, (245) **YS**, 45 **El**
BS 1501–161	Grade 28B	UK	Plate	0.25 **C**, 0.65–1.20 **Mn**, 0.050 **P**, 0.050 **S**, 0.10–0.35 **Si**; 0.70 max other elements, total	**Normalized**: (≤16) **diam**, (430) **TS**, (245) **YS**, 45 **El**
BS 1501–151	Grade 28A	UK	Plate	0.25 **C**, 0.55 **Mn**, 0.050 **P**, 0.050 **S**, 0.35 **Si**; 0.70 max other elements, total	**Normalized**: (≤16) **diam**, (430) **TS**, (245) **YS**, 45 **El**
BS 1501–151	Grade 28B	UK	Plate	0.25 **C**, 0.65 **Mn**, 0.050 **P**, 0.050 **S**, 0.35 **Si**; 0.70 max other elements, total	**Normalized**: (≤16) **diam**, (430) **TS**, (245) **YS**, 45 **El**
BS 1449: Part 1	Grade 43/28	UK	Plate, sheet, strip	0.25 **C**, 0.90 **Mn**, 0.050 **P**, 0.050 **S**	**Hot rolled**: (≤4) **diam**, (430) **TS**, (280) **YS**, 26 **El**
BS 1449: Part 1	Grade 43/25	UK	Plate, sheet, strip	0.25 **C**, 0.90 **Mn**, 0.050 **P**, 0.050 **S**	**Hot rolled**: all **diam**, (430) **TS**, (250) **YS**, 25 **El**
IS 1914–1961 Part 4		India	Tube: seamless	0.25 **C**, 0.050 **P**, 0.050 **S**	**Annealed**: all **diam**, (420) **TS**
IS 1914–1961 Part 5		India	Tube: seamless	0.25 **C**, 0.050 **P**, 0.050 **S**	**Annealed or normalized**: all **diam**, (420) **TS**
ANSI/ASTM A 516	Grade 60	US	Plate	0.25 **C**, 0.80–1.25 **Mn**, 0.035 **P**, 0.04 **S**, 0.13–0.33 **Si**	**Normalized**: 2.0–4.0 **diam**, (415) **TS**, (220) **YS**, 25 **El**
TS 911	669.14–423/Fe 42	Turkey	Bar	0.25 **C**, 0.063 **P**, 0.063 **S**	**Hot rolled**: all **diam**, (412) **TS**, (255) **YS**, 22 **El**
NF A 36–101	A 42,1	France	Strip	0.25 **C**, 0.075 **P**, 0.062 **S**	**Hot rolled**: all **diam**, (412) **TS**, (255) **YS**, 23 **El**
NF A 36–101	A 42,2	France	Strip	0.25 **C**, 0.062 **P**, 0.062 **S**, 0.009 N_2	**Hot rolled**: all **diam**, (412) **TS**, (255) **YS**, 26 **El**
TS 416	Fe 42	Turkey	Pipe: welded	0.25 **C**, 0.08 **P**, 0.05 **S**	**As welded**: (<16) **diam**, (412) **TS**, (255) **YS**, 20 **El**
TS 416	Fe 42.2	Turkey	Pipe: welded	0.25 **C**, 0.060 **P**, 0.050 **S**	**As welded**: (<16) **diam**, (412) **TS**, (255) **YS**, 20 **El**
DGN–B–275	Grade D	Mexico	Sheet	0.25 **C**, 1.20 **Mn**, 0.035 **P**, 0.040 **S**, 0.20 **Cu**	**Hot rolled**: (5–4) **diam**, (412) **TS**, (220) **YS**, 20 **El**
JIS G 3132	Class 3	Japan	Strip	0.25 **C**, 0.30–0.90 **Mn**, 0.040 **P**, 0.040 **S**, 0.35 **Si**	**Hot rolled**: (1.0–1.6) **diam**, (412) **TS**, 20 **El**
DIN 1626, Part 2	Grade St42	Germany	Pipe: welded (commercial quality)	0.25 **C**, 0.08 **P**, 0.05 **S**	**As welded**: <16 **diam**, (410) **TS**, (255) **YS**, 20 **El**
DIN 1626, Part 3	Grade St42–2/1.0132	Germany	Pipe: welded	0.25 **C**, 1.5 **Mn**, 0.06 **P**, 0.05 **S**, 0.55 **Si**	**As welded**: (<16) **diam**, (410) **TS**, (255) **YS**, 20 **El**

WROUGHT CARBON STEELS

specification number	designation	country	product forms	composition	mechanical properties (see page iv for explanation)
NF A 33–102	AR E 26,1 (AR 42)	France	Billets, blooms, slabs	0.25 **C**, 0.075 **P**, 0.062 **S**	**Normalized**: all **diam**, (410) **TS**, (250) **YS**, 23 **El**
NF A 33–102	AR E 26,2	France	Billets, blooms, slabs	0.25 **C**, 0.075 **P**, 0.062 **S**	**Normalized**: all **diam**, (410) **TS**, (250) **YS**, 26 **El**
ASTM A 414	Grade D	US	Sheet	0.25 **C**, 1.20 **Mn**, 0.035 **P**, 0.040 **S**	**Hot rolled**: 0.2299–0.1450 (5.82–3.68) **diam**, 60 (410) **TS**, 32 (220) **YS**, 20 **El**
DIN 1626, Part 4	Grade St 42–2	Germany	Pipe: welded (specially tested)	0.25 **C**, 1.5 **Mn**, 0.06 **P**, 0.05 **S**, 0.55 **Si**	**Annealed**: (<16) **diam**, (410) **TS**, (255) **YS**, 20 **El**
ANSI/ASTM A 414	Grade D	US	Sheet	0.25 **C**, 1.20 **Mn**, 0.035 **P**, 0.040 **S**	**Hot rolled or cold rolled, annealed**: all **diam**, (410) **TS**, (220) **YS**, 20 **El**
DIN 1623 Sheet 2	USt 42–2 (1.0132.5)	Germany	Sheet	0.25 **C**, 0.060 **P**, 0.050 **S**	**Hot or cold rolled**: all **diam**, (410) **TS**, (235) **YS**, 16 in 80 mm **El**
DIN 1623 Sheet 2	RSt 42–2 (1.0132.6)	Germany	Sheet	0.25 **C**, 0.060 **P**, 0.050 **S**	**Hot or cold rolled**: all **diam**, (410) **TS**, (235) **YS**, 16 in 80 mm **El**
DIN 17100	RSt 42–2 (1.0134)	Germany	Bar, plate	0.25 **C**, 0.055 **P**, 0.055 **S**	**Normalized**: all **diam**, (410) **TS**, (255) **YS**, 22 **El**
DIN 17100	RSt 42–2 (1.0134)	Germany	Strip	0.25 **C**, 0.055 **P**, 0.055 **S**	**Normalized**: all **diam**, (410) **TS**, (255) **YS**, 22 **El**; **Hot rolled**: all **diam**, (410) **TS**, (255) **YS**, 16 **El**
DIN 17100	St 42–3 (1.0136)	Germany	Bar, plate	0.25 **C**, 0.050 **P**, 0.050 **S**	**Normalized**: all **diam**, (410) **TS**, (255) **YS**, 22 **El**
DIN 17100	St 42–3 (1.0136)	Germany	Strip	0.25 **C**, 0.050 **P**, 0.050 **S**	**Normalized**: all **diam**, (410) **TS**, (255) **YS**, 22 **El**; **Hot rolled**: all **diam**, (410) **TS**, (255) **YS**, 16 **El**
AS 1442	Grade AS 1442/K3	Australia	Bar	0.25 **C**, 1.40 **Mn**, 0.050 **P**, 0.050 **S**, 0.10–0.35 **Si**	**As rolled or normalized**: (50–170) **diam**, (410) **TS**, (230) **YS**, 22 **El**
AS 1442	Grade AS 1442/S3	Australia	Bar	0.25 **C**, 1.40 **Mn**, 0.050 **P**, 0.050 **S**, 0.35 **Si**	**As rolled or normalized**: (50–170) **diam**, (410) **TS**, (230) **YS**, 22 **El**
AS 1443	Grade AS 1443/K3	Australia	Bar	0.25 **C**, 1.40 **Mn**, 0.050 **P**, 0.050 **S**, 0.10–0.35 **Si**	**As rolled or normalized**: (50–170) **diam**, (410) **TS**, (230) **YS**, 22 **El**
AS 1443	Grade AS 1443/S3	Australia	Bar	0.25 **C**, 1.40 **Mn**, 0.050 **P**, 0.050 **S**, 0.35 **Si**	**As rolled or normalized**: (50–170) **diam**, (410) **TS**, (230) **YS**, 22 **El**
JIS G 3444	Class 2, No. 11	Japan	Tube: seamless or electric–resistance welded	0.25 **C**, 0.040 **P**, 0.040 **S**	**As drawn or as welded**: all **diam**, (402) **TS**, (235) **YS**, 23 **El**
JIS G 3350	SSC 41	Japan	Plate, strip	0.25 **C**, 0.050 **P**, 0.050 **S**	**Cold rolled**: ($\leq$5) **diam**, (402) **TS**, (245) **YS**, 21 **El**
JIS G 3353	SWH41	Japan	Strip: welded	0.25 **C**, 0.050 **P**, 0.050 **S**	**As manufactured**: ($\geq$5) **diam**, (402) **TS**, (245) **YS**, 21 **El**
JIS G 3353	SWH41L	Japan	Strip: welded	0.25 **C**, 0.050 **P**, 0.050 **S**	**As manufactured**: ($\geq$5) **diam**, (402) **TS**, (245) **YS**, 21 **El**
JIS G 3466	Class 1	Japan	Pipe	0.25 **C**, 0.040 **P**, 0.040 **S**	**As manufactured**: ($\geq$8) **diam**, (402) **TS**, (245) **YS**, 23 **El**
ASTM A 570	Grade E	US	Sheet, strip	0.25 **C**, 0.60–0.90 **Mn**, 0.04 **P**, 0.04 **S**	**Hot rolled**: $\geq$0.2299–0.0972 ($\geq$5.84–2.46) **diam**, 58 (400) **TS**, 42 (290) **YS**, 19 **El**
ANSI/ASTM A 709	Grade 36	US	Plate, bar, shapes	0.25 **C**, 0.04 **P**, 0.05 **S**	**Annealed (plate)**: $\leq$8 **diam**, (400) **TS**, (250) **YS**, 23 **El**
ANSI/ASTM A 36		US	Plate	0.25 **C**, 0.04 **P**, 0.05 **S**, 0.20 **Cu**	**As rolled**: $\leq$0.75 **diam**, (400) **TS**, (250) **YS**, 23 **El**
AS 1442	Grade AS 1442/K1	Australia	Bar	0.25 **C**, 0.40–1.00 **Mn**, 0.050 **P**, 0.050 **S**, 0.10–0.35 **Si**	**As rolled or normalized**: (50–150) **diam**, (400) **TS**, (200) **YS**, 22 **El**
AS 1443	Grade AS 1443/S1	Australia	Bar	0.25 **C**, 0.40–1.00 **Mn**, 0.050 **P**, 0.050 **S**, 0.35 **Si**	**As rolled or normalized**: 50–150 **diam**, (400) **TS**, (200) **YS**, 22 **El**
AS 1443	Grade AS 1443/K1	Australia	Bar	0.25 **C**, 0.40–1.00 **Mn**, 0.050 **P**, 0.050 **S**, 0.10–0.35 **Si**	**As rolled or normalized**: 50–150 **diam**, (400) **TS**, (200) **YS**, 22 **El**

specification number	designation	country	product forms	composition	mechanical properties (see page iv for explanation)
AS 1442	Grade AS 1442/S1	Australia	Bar	0.25 **C**, 0.40–1.00 **Mn**, 0.050 **P**, 0.050 **S** 0.35 **Si**	**As rolled or normalized:** (≤50) **diam**, (400) **TS**, (200) **YS**, 22 **El**
DGN–B–347	Grade E	Mexico	Sheet, strip	0.25 **C**, 0.60–0.90 **Mn**, 0.040 **P**, 0.040 **S**, 0.20 min **Cu**	**Hot rolled**: (0.65–1.61) **diam**, (397) **TS**, (289) **YS**, 13 **El**
JIS G 3460	Class 1	Japan	Pipe: seamless or electric–resistance welded	0.25 **C**, 1.35 **Mn**, 0.035 **P**, 0.035 **S**, 0.35 **Si**, 0.20 **Cu**	**Normalized or normalized and tempered:** (≥8) **diam**, (382) **TS**, (206) **YS**, 35 **El**
JIS G 3464	Class 1	Japan	Tube: seamless or electric–resistance welded	0.25 **C**, 1.35 **Mn**, 0.035 **P**, 0.035 **S**, 0.35 **Si**, 0.20 **Cu**	**Normalized or normalized and tempered:** (≥8) **diam**, (382) **TS**, (206) **YS**, 35 **El**
ASTM A 570	Grade D	US	Sheet, strip	0.25 **C**, 0.60–0.90 **Mn**, 0.04 **P**, 0.04 **S**	**Hot rolled:** ≥0.2299–0.0972 (≥5.84–2.46) **diam**, 55 (380) **TS**, 40 (275) **YS**, 21 **El**
ASTM A 414	Grade C	US	Sheet	0.25 **C**, 0.90 **Mn**, 0.035 **P**, 0.040 **S**	**Hot rolled**: 0.2299–0.1450 (5.82–3.68) **diam**, 55 (380) **TS**, 30 (205) **YS**, 22 **El**
AS 1594	Grade AS1594/HR280	Australia	Sheet, strip	0.25 **C**, 0.90 **Mn**, 0.040 **P**, 0.040 **S**; 0.15 grain refining elements	**Hot rolled:** ≥3 **diam**, (380) **TS**, (280) **YS**, 20 **El**
ANSI/ASTM A 570	Grade E	US	Sheet, strip	0.25 **C**, 0.60–0.90 **Mn**, 0.04 **P**, 0.04 **S**	**Hot rolled**: >0.2299–0.0972 **diam**, (380) **TS**, (290) **YS**, 19 **El**
ANSI/ASTM A 570	Grade D	US	Sheet, strip	0.25 **C**, 0.60–0.90 **Mn**, 0.04 **P**, 0.04 **S**	**Hot rolled**: 0.2299–0.0972 **diam**, (380) **TS**, (275) **YS**, 21 **El**
ANSI/ASTM A 414	Grade C	US	Sheet	0.25 **C**, 0.90 **Mn**, 0.035 **P**, 0.040 **S**	**Hot rolled or cold rolled, annealed**: all **diam**, (380) **TS**, (205) **YS**, 22 **El**
ANSI/ASTM A 446	Grade C	US	Sheet	0.25 **C**, 0.10 **P**, 0.04 **S**	**Hot rolled, hot dip galvanized**: all **diam**, 55 (380) **TS**, 40 (275) **YS**, 16 **El**
DGN–B–347	Grade D	Mexico	Sheet, strip	0.25 **C**, 0.60–0.90 **Mn**, 0.040 **P**, 0.040 **S**, 0.20 min **Cu**	**Hot rolled**: (0.65–1.61) **diam**, (377) **TS**, (274) **YS**, 15 **El**
DGN–B–275	Grade C	Mexico	Sheet	0.25 **C**, 0.90 **Mn**, 0.035 **P**, 0.040 **S**, 0.20 **Cu**	**Hot rolled**: (5–4) **diam**, (377) **TS**, (206) **YS**, 22 **El**
JIS G 3454	Class 2	Japan	Pipe: seamless or welded	0.25 **C**, 0.30–0.90 **Mn**, 0.040 **P**, 0.040 **S**, 0.35 **Si**	**As manufactured or cold finished and annealed:** (≥8) **diam**, (373) **TS**, (216) **YS**, 30 **El**
JIS G 3455	Class 2	Japan	Pipe: seamless	0.25 **C**, 0.30–0.90 **Mn**, 0.035 **P**, 0.035 **S**, 0.10–0.35 **Si**, 0.20 **Cu**	**As manufactured, cold finished and annealed or cold finished and normalized:** (≥8) **diam**, (373) **TS**, (216) **YS**, 30 **El**
JIS G 3456	Class 2	Japan	Pipe: seamless or welded	0.25 **C**, 0.30–0.90 **Mn**, 0.035 **P**, 0.035 **S**, 0.10–0.35 **Si**, 0.20 **Cu**	**As manufactured, annealed or normalized:** (≥8) **diam**, (373) **TS**, (216) **YS**, 30 **El**
JIS G 3445	Class 13A, No. 12	Japan	Tube: seamless or welded	0.25 **C**, 0.30–0.90 **Mn**, 0.040 **P**, 0.040 **S**, 0.35 **Si**	**As manufactured or cold finished:** (≥8) **diam**, (373) **TS**, (216) **YS**, 30 **El**
BS 3602	Steel 27	UK	Pipe, tube: seamless	0.25 **C**, 0.40–0.70 **Mn**, 0.050 **P**, 0.050 **S**, 0.35 **Si**	**Hot finished**: all **diam**, (370) **TS**, (220) **YS**, 25 **El**
BS 3602	Steel 27	UK	Pipe, tube: seamless	0.25 **C**, 0.40–0.70 **Mn**, 0.050 **P**, 0.050 **S**, 0.35 **Si**	**Cold drawn**: all **diam**, (370) **TS**, (220) **YS**, 25 **El**
BS 3602	Steel 27	UK	Pipe, tube: welded	0.25 **C**, 0.40–0.70 **Mn**, 0.050 **P**, 0.050 **S**, 0.35 **Si**	**Normalized**: all **diam**, (370) **TS**, (220) **YS**, 25 **El**
TS 908	UDK 669.14.423/Fe 37	Turkey	Shapes	0.25 **C**, 0.063 **P**, 0.063 **S**	**Hot rolled**: all **diam**, (363) **TS**, (235) **YS**, 25 **El**
TS913	UDK 669.14.423/Fe 37	Turkey	Bar	0.25 **C**, 0.063 **P**, 0.063 **S**	**Hot rolled**: all **diam**, (363) **TS**, (235) **YS**, 25 **El**
TS 912	UDK 669.14–423/Fe 37	Turkey	Shapes	0.25 **C**, 0.063 **P**, 0.063 **S**	**Hot rolled**: all **diam**, (363) **TS**, (235) **YS**, 25 **El**
ISO/R 630	Grade Fe 37 A	ISO	Bar, plate	0.25 **C**, 0.100 **P**, 0.075 **S**	**As rolled:** (≤16) **diam**, (362) **TS**, (235) **YS**, 26 **El**
ISO/R 630	Grade Fe 37 B	ISO	Bar, plate	0.25 **C**, 0.075 **P**, 0.062 **S**	**As rolled:** (≤16) **diam**, (362) **TS**, (235) **YS**, 26 **El**
ASTM A 570	Grade C	US	Sheet, strip	0.25 **C**, 0.25–0.60 **Mn**, 0.04 **P**, 0.04 **S**	**Hot rolled:** ≥0.2299–0.0972 (≥5.84–2.46) **diam**, 52 (360) **TS**, 33 (230) **YS**, 23 **El**
NF A 35–501	E 24 A 37 grade 1	France	Sheet, plate, bar	0.25 **C**, 0.075 **P**, 0.062 **S**	**As rolled (sheet, plate):** (3–30) **diam**, (360) **TS**, (235) **YS**, 23 **El**

WROUGHT CARBON STEELS

specification number	designation	country	product forms	composition	mechanical properties (see page iv for explanation)
NF A 35–501	E 24 A–37 grade 2	France	Sheet, plate, bar	0.25 **C**, 0.062 **P**, 0.062 **S**, 0.009 $\mathbf{N_2}$	**As rolled (sheet, plate):** (3–30) **diam**, (360) **TS**, (235) **YS**, 26 **El**
ANSI/ASTM A 570	Grade C	US	Sheet, strip	0.25 **C**, 0.25–0.60 **Mn**, 0.04 **P**, 0.04 **S**	**Hot rolled:** 0.2299–0.0972 **diam**, 52 (360) **TS**, 33 (230) **YS**, 23 **El**
DIN 17100	USt 37–1 (1.0110)	Germany	Strip	0.25 **C**, 0.090 **P**, 0.063 **S**	**Normalized:** all **diam**, (360) **TS**, (235) **YS**, 25 **El**; **Hot rolled:** all **diam**, (360) **TS**, (235) **YS**, 18 **El**
DIN 17100	USt 37–1 (1.0110)	Germany	Plate	0.25 **C**, 0.090 **P**, 0.063 **S**	**Normalized:** all **diam**, (360) **TS**, (235) **YS**, 25 **El**
DIN 17100	USt 37–1 (1.0110)	Germany	Bar	0.25 **C**, 0.090 **P**, 0.063 **S**	**Normalized:** all **diam**, (360) **TS**, (235) **YS**, 25 **El**
DGN–B–347	Grade C	Mexico	Sheet, strip	0.25 **C**, 0.25–0.60 **Mn**, 0.040 **P**, 0.040 **S**, 0.20 min **Cu**	**Hot rolled:** (0.65–1.61) **diam**, (353) **TS**, (225) **YS**, 18 **El**
DGN–B–106	Type 285B (Firebox)	Mexico	Plate	0.25 **C**, 0.80 **Mn**, 0.035 **P**, 0.040 **S**, 0.20–0.35 **Cu**	**Hot worked:** (<8) **diam**, 50 (345) **TS**, 27 (186) **YS**, 30 **El**
ASTM A 570	Grade B	US	Sheet, strip	0.25 **C**, 0.25–0.60 **Mn**, 0.04 **P**, 0.04 **S**	**Hot rolled:** ≥0.2299–0.0972 (≥5.84–2.46) **diam**, 49 (340) **TS**, 30 (205) **YS**, 25 **El**
ANSI/ASTM A 570	Grade B	US	Sheet, strip	0.25 **C**, 0.25–0.60 **Mn**, 0.04 **P**, 0.04 **S**	**Hot rolled:** 0.2299–0.0972 **diam**, 49 (340) **TS**, 30 (205) **YS**, 25 **El**
COPANT R 208	Grade A	COPANT	Pipe: seamless	0.25 **C**, 0.27–0.93 **Mn**, 0.048 **P**, 0.058 **S**, 0.10 min **Si**	**Hot or cold finished:** (≥8) **diam**, (335) **TS**, (205) **YS**, 35 **El**
DGN–B–347	Grade B	Mexico	Sheet, strip	0.25 **C**, 0.25–0.60 **Mn**, 0.040 **P**, 0.040 **S**, 0.20 min **Cu**	**Hot rolled:** (0.65–1.61) **diam**, (333) **TS**, (206) **YS**, 21 **El**
DGN–B–178	Grade A	Mexico	Pipe: seamless	0.25 **C**, 0.27–0.93 **Mn**, 0.048 **P**, 0.058 **S**, 0.10 **Si**	**Forged and hot finished or forged, cold finished and annealed:** (8) **diam**, (333) **TS**, (206) **YS**
ASTM A 523	Grade A	US	Pipe: seamless, electric resistance welded	0.25 **C**, 0.95 **Mn**, 0.050 **P**, 0.060 **S**	**As–rolled:** 0.312 (7.94) **diam**, 48 (331) **TS**, 30 (207) **YS**, 35 **El**
ASTM A 135	Grade A	US	Pipe: electric resistance welded	0.25 **C**, 0.95 **Mn**, 0.050 **P**, 0.060 **S**	**As rolled:** 0.312 (7.94) **diam**, 48 (331) **TS**, 30 (207) **YS**, 35 **El**
ANSI/ASTM A 53	Type S, grade A	US	Pipe: welded, seamless	0.25 **C**, 0.95 **Mn**, 0.05 **P**, 0.06 **S**	**As rolled:** all **diam**, 48 (331) **TS**, 30 (207) **YS**, 36 **El**
ANSI/ASTM A 53	Type E, grade A	US	Pipe: welded, seamless	0.25 **C**, 0.95 **Mn**, 0.05 **P**, 0.06 **S**	**As rolled:** all **diam**, 48 (331) **TS**, 30 (207) **YS**, 36 **El**
ANSI/ASTM A 106	Grade A	US	Pipe: seamless	0.25 **C**, 0.27–0.93 **Mn**, 0.048 **P**, 0.058 **S**, 0.10 min **Si**	**Annealed:** 0.312 (7.9) **diam**, 48 (331) **TS**, 30 (207) **YS**, 35 **El**
DGN–B–106	Type 30B	Mexico	Plate	0.25 **C**, 0.30–0.80 **Mn**, 0.035 **P**, 0.040 **S**, 0.25 **Cu**	**Hot worked:** (<8) **diam**, 48 (331) **TS**, 26 (179) **YS**, 30 **El**
MIL–T–20157C	Type A,B,C, and D	US	Tube, pipe: seamless	0.25 **C**, 0.27–0.93 **Mn**, 0.048 **P**, 0.045 **S**, 0.10 min **Si**	**As agreed:** all **diam**, (330) **TS**, (206) **YS**, 35 **El**
ANSI/ASTM A 369	FPA	US	Pipe	0.25 **C**, 0.27–0.93 **Mn**, 0.048 **P**, 0.058 **S**, 0.10 min **Si**	**Annealed or normalized, tempered:** 0.312 (7.94) **diam**, 48 (330) **TS**, 30 (210) **YS**, 35 **El**
DGN–B–177	Type S, grade A	Mexico	Tube: seamless	0.25 **C**, 0.95 **Mn**, 0.05 **P**, 0.06 **S**	**As drawn:** (2–64) **diam**, (330) **TS**, (207) **YS**
DGN–B–177	Type E, grade A	Mexico	Tube: electric-resistance welded	0.25 **C**, 0.95 **Mn**, 0.05 **P**, 0.06 **S**	**As welded:** (2–64) **diam**, (330) **TS**, (207) **YS**
ASTM A 570	Grade A	US	Sheet, strip	0.25 **C**, 0.25–0.60 **Mn**, 0.04 **P**, 0.04 **S**	**Hot rolled:** ≥0.2299–0.0972 (≥5.84–2.46) **diam**, 45 (310) **TS**, 25 (170) **YS**, 27 **El**
ANSI/ASTM A 570	Grade A	US	Sheet, strip	0.25 **C**, 0.25–0.60 **Mn**, 0.040 **P**, 0.040 **S**	**Hot rolled:** 0.2299–0.0972 **diam**, 45 (310) **TS**, 25 (170) **YS**, 27 **El**
DGN–B–347	Grade A	Mexico	Sheet, strip	0.25 **C**, 0.25–0.60 **Mn**, 0.040 **P**, 0.040 **S**, 0.20 min **Cu**	**Hot rolled:** (0.65–1.61) **diam**, (309) **TS**, (172) **YS**, 23 **El**
BS 4449	Grade 250	UK	Bar	0.25 **C**, 0.060 **P**, 0.060 **S**	**Hot rolled:** all **diam**, (250) **TS**, 22 **El**
DGN–B–247	Temper No 1	Mexico	Strip	0.25 **C**, 0.60 **Mn**, 0.04 **P**, 0.05 **S**, 0.20 min **Cu**	**Cold rolled and tempered:** (1.27) **diam**, (62) **TS**, 3 **El**
DGN–B–247	Temper No 2	Mexico	Strip	0.25 **C**, 0.60 **Mn**, 0.04 **P**, 0.05 **S**, 0.20 min **Cu**	**Cold rolled and tempered:** (1.27) **diam**, (46) **TS**, 10 **El**
DGN–B–247	Temper No 3	Japan	Strip	0.25 **C**, 0.60 **Mn**, 0.04 **P**, 0.05 **S**, 0.20 min **Cu**	**Cold rolled and tempered:** (1.27) **diam**, (39) **TS**, 20 **El**

WROUGHT CARBON STEELS

specification number	designation	country	product forms	composition	mechanical properties (see page iv for explanation)
DIN 2393 Sheet 2	Grade St 42-2-1.0132 or 1.0134	Germany	Tube	0.25 **C**, 0.05 **P**, 0.05 **S**	
DIN 2393 Sheet 2	Grade St 42-2.2-1.0132 or 1.0134	Germany	Tube	0.25 **C**, 0.05 **P**, 0.05 **S**	
BS 4482		UK	Wire	0.25 **C**, 0.060 **P**, 0.060 **S**	**Hard drawn:** ≤(12) **diam**
ASTM A 109	Tempers 1,2,3	US	Strip	0.25 **C**, 0.60 **Mn**, 0.035 **P**, 0.04 **S**	
AMS 5062C		US	Bar, forgings, tube, sheet, strip, plate	0.25 **C**, 1.00 **Mn**, 0.040 **P**, 0.050 **S**	
ASTM A 470	Class 1	US	Forgings	0.25 **C**, 0.20–0.60 **Mn**, 0.025 **P**, 0.025 **S**, 0.15–0.35 **Si**, 0.03 **V**	**Double normalized, tempered**
COPANT 511		COPANT	Pipe	0.25 **C**, 0.27–0.93 **Mn**, 0.048 **P**, 0.058 **S**	
BS 970 Part 1	216M28	UK	Blooms, billets, slabs, bar, rod, forgings	0.24–0.32 **C**, 1.10–1.50 **Mn**, 0.060 **P**, 0.12–0.20 **S**, 0.25 **Si**	**Hardened and tempered:** 2.5 **diam**, (480) **TS**, (315) **YS**, 20 **El**; **Cold drawn from hot rolled:** 0.50–0.625 **diam**, (510) **TS**, (385) **YS**, 10 **El**
BS 970: Part 1	120M28	UK	Blooms, billets, slabs, bar, rod, forgings	0.24–0.32 **C**, 1.00–1.40 **Mn**	**Normalized:** 6 **diam**, (480) **TS**, (290) **YS**, 16 **El**; **Hardened and tempered:** 4 **diam**, (550) **TS**, (370) **YS**, 16 **El**; **Cold drawn from hot rolled:** 0.50–0.625 **diam**, (580) **TS**, (455) **YS**, 8 **El**
JIS G 3506	SWRH 27	Japan	Wire, rod	0.24–0.31 **C**, 0.30–0.60 **Mn**, 0.040 **P**, 0.040 **S**, 0.15–0.35 **Si**	
DIN 17140	Grade D26-2	Germany	Wire, rod	0.24–0.29 **C**, 0.30–0.60 **Mn**, 0.040 **P**, 0.040 **S**, 0.10–0.30 **Si**, 0.007 **N**	
ANSI/ASTM A 737	Grade C	US	Plate	0.24 **C**, 1.10–1.55 **Mn**, 0.035 **P**, 0.035 **S**, 0.10–0.55 **Si**, 0.03–0.12 **V**, 0.03 **N**	**Normalized**: all **diam**, 80 (550) **TS**, 60 (415) **YS**, 23 **El**
AS 1450	430	Australia	Tube: seamless or welded	0.24 **C**, 0.060 **P**, 0.060 **S**	**As–drawn or as–drawn and stress relieved**: all **diam**, (540) **TS**, (430) **YS**
NF A 35-501	E36 A-52 grade3	France	Sheet, plate, bar	0.24 **C**, 1.60 **Mn**, 0.050 **P**, 0.050 **S**, 0.60 **Si**	**As rolled**: (3–30) **diam**, (510) **TS**, (355) **YS**, 20 **El**
NF A 35-501	E 36 A-52 grade 4	France	Sheet, plate, bar	0.24 **C**, 1.60 **Mn**, 0.045 **P**, 0.45 **S**, 0.60 **Si**	**As rolled**: (3–30) **diam**, (510) **TS**, (355) **YS**, 22 **El**
ANSI/ASTM A 537		US	Plate	0.24 **C**, 0.65–1.40 **Mn**, 0.035 **P**, 0.040 **S**, 0.13–0.55 **Si**	**Normalized**: 1.50 **diam**, (485) **TS**, (345) **YS**, 22 **El**; **quenched and tempered**: 1.50 **diam**, (550) **TS**, (415) **YS**, 22 **El**
NF A 35-501	E30 A47 grade 2	France	Sheet, plate, bar	0.24 **C**, 1.40 **Mn**, 0.055 **P**, 0.055 **S**, 0.45 **Si**	**As rolled**: (3–30) **diam**, (460) **TS**, (275) **YS**, 21 **El**
NF A 35-501	E30 A-47 grade 3	France	Sheet, plate, bar	0.24 **C**, 1.40 **Mn**, 0.050 **P**, 0.050 **S**, 0.45 **Si**	**As rolled**: (3–30) **diam**, (460) **TS**, (295) **YS**, 21 **El**
NF A 35-501	E30 A 47 grade 4	France	Sheet, plate, bar	0.24 **C**, 1.40 **Mn**, 0.045 **P**, 0.045 **S**, 0.45 **Si**	**As rolled**: (3–30) **diam**, (460) **TS**, (295) **YS**, 23 **El**
JIS G 3118	Class 2	Japan	Plate	0.24 **C**, 0.85–1.20 **Mn**, 0.035 **P**, 0.040 **S**, 0.15–0.30 **Si**	**Hot rolled**: (8–12.5) **diam**, (451) **TS**, (245) **YS**, 19 **El**
DGN-B-245	Grade 50	Mexico	Plate	0.24 **C**, 0.85–1.20 **Mn**, 0.035 **P**, 0.040 **S**, 0.15–0.30 **Si**	**As rolled**: (<12.7) **diam**, (448) **TS**, (241) **YS**, 23 **El**
NBN A 25-102	D 45	Belgium	Tube	0.24 **C**, 0.40–1.05 **Mn**, 0.045 **P**, 0.045 **S**, 0.12–0.38 **Si**	**Hot finished or cold finished and normalized**: all **diam**, (440) **TS**, (270) **YS**, 21 **El**
BS 4360	Grade 43C	UK	Hollow sections	0.24 **C**, 1.3 **Mn**, 0.060 **P**, 0.060 **S**, 0.45 **Si**	**Hot finished**: (≤16) **diam**, (430) **TS**, (255) **YS**, 22 **El**
BS 4360	Grade 43D	UK	Hollow sections	0.24 **C**, 1.3 **Mn**, 0.060 **P**, 0.060 **S**, 0.45 **Si**	**Hot finished**: (≤16) **diam**, (430) **TS**, (255) **YS** 22 **El**
COPANT 37, II	AT-23	COPANT	Plate	0.24 **C**, 0.035 **P**, 0.045 **S**, 0.15–0.35 **Si**	**As rolled**: (≤25) **diam**, (420) **TS**, (230) **YS**, 25 **El**
ANSI/ASTM A 442	Grade 60	US	Plate	0.24 **C**, 0.76–1.14 **Mn**, 0.04 **P**, 0.05 **S**, 0.13–0.33 **Si**	**As rolled**: >1.00 **diam**, (415) **TS**, (220) **YS**, 23 **El**
ANSI/ASTM A 284	Grade C	US	Plate	0.24 **C**, 0.90 **Mn**, 0.04 **P**, 0.05 **S**, 0.15–0.30 **Si**	**Annealed**: all **diam**, (415) **TS**, (205) **YS**, 25 **El**

WROUGHT CARBON STEELS

specification number	designation	country	product forms	composition	mechanical properties (see page iv for explanation)
DGN–B–106	Type 201A/B (Firebox)	Mexico	Plate	0.24 **C**, 0.80 **Mn**, 0.035 **P**, 0.04 **S**, 0.05–0.30 **Si**	**Hot worked:** (<8) **diam**, (414) **TS**, 29 **El**
DGN–B–244	Grade 45	Mexico	Plate	0.24 **C**, 0.90 **Mn**, 0.035 **P**, 0.040 **S**, 0.15–0.30 **Si**	**As rolled:** (<25.4) **diam**, (414) **TS**, (221) **YS**, 25 **El**
DGN–B–258	Grade C	Mexico	Plate	0.24 **C**, 0.90 **Mn**, 0.04 **P**, 0.05 **S**, 0.15–0.30 **Si**	**Hot rolled:** (≤25) **diam**, (414) **TS**, (207) **YS**, 25 **El**
JIS G 3103	Class 2	Japan	Plate	0.24 **C**, 0.90 **Mn**, 0.035 **P**, 0.040 **S**, 0.15–0.30 **Si**	**Hot rolled:** (≤25) **diam**, (412) **TS**, (226) **YS**, 21 **El**
BS 1501–154	Grade 26	UK	Plate	0.24 **C**, 0.40–1.20 **Mn**, 0.050 **P**, 0.050 **S**; 0.70 max other elements, total	**As supplied:** (≤9.53) **diam**, (400) **TS**, (230) **YS**, 45 **El**
MIL–S–22698A	Class C		Plate	0.24 **C**, 0.60–0.90 **Mn**, 0.040 **P**, 0.050 **S**, 0.15–0.30 **Si**	**Normalized:** ≥1–2 **diam**, 58 (400) **TS**, 32 (221) **YS**, 24 **El**
ANSI/ASTM A 515	Grade 55	US	Plate	0.24 **C**, 0.90 **Mn**, 0.035 **P**, 0.04 **S**, 0.13–0.33 **Si**	**Normalized:** 2.0–4.0 **diam**, (380) **TS**, (205) **YS**, 27 **El**
AS 1450	200	Australia	Tube: seamless or welded	0.24 **C**, 0.060 **P**, 0.060 **S**	**Hot finished, normalized, as–formed, annealed, cold drawn, as–drawn:** all **diam**, (340) **TS**, (210) **YS**, 24 **El**
ANSI/ASTM A 29	1525	US	Bar	0.23–0.29 **C**, 0.80–1.10 **Mn**, 0.040 **P**, 0.050 **S**	
ASTM A 689	1525	US	Bar: spring	0.23–0.29 **C**, 0.80–1.10 **Mn**, 0.040 **P**, 0.050 **S**	
DGN–B–301	1525	Mexico	Bar	0.23–0.29 **C**, 0.80–1.10 **Mn**, 0.040 **P**, 0.050 **S**	
ANSI/ASTM A 576	1525	US	Bar	0.23–0.29 **C**, 0.80–1.10 **Mn**, 0.040 **P**, 0.050 **S**	
BS 970: Part 1	060A25	UK	Blooms, billets, slabs, bar, rod, forgings	0.23–0.28 **C**, 0.50–0.70 **Mn**	
BS 970: Part 1	080A25	UK	Blooms, billets, slabs, bar, rod, forgings	0.23–0.28 **C**, 0.70–0.90 **Mn**	
API Spec 5LX	Welded, grade X70	US	Pipe	0.23 **C**, 1.60 **Mn**, 0.04 **P**, 0.05 **S**	**Non or cold expanded:** all **diam**, 82 (565) **TS**, 70 (483) **YS**
API Spec 5LX	Welded, grade 70[3]	US	Pipe	0.23 **C**, 1.60 **Mn**, 0.04 **P**, 0.05 **S**	**Non or cold expanded:** all **diam**, 82 (565) **TS**, 70 (483) **YS**
AS 1205	WR500/2	Australia	Bar, plate	0.23 **C**, 1.45 **Mn**, 0.050 **P**, 0.050 **S**, 0.15–0.65 **Si**, 0.17–0.48 **Cu**, 0.22–0.75 **Cr**, 0.55 **Ni**	**Hot rolled (plate):** (10) **diam**, (550) **TS**, (480) **YS**, 14 in 200 mm **El**
IS 7887		India	Wire, rod	0.23 **C**, 0.055 **P**, 0.055 **S**	**Hot rolled:** all **diam**, (540) **TS**, 23 **El**
BS 1449: Part 1	Grade 54/35	UK	Plate, sheet, strip	0.23 **C**, 1.70 **Mn**, 0.050 **P**, 0.050 **S**	**Hot rolled:** all **diam**, (540) **TS**, (350) **YS**, 18 **El**
JIS G 3444	Class 5, No. 11	Japan	Tube: seamless or electric–resistance welded	0.23 **C**, 1.50 **Mn**, 0.040 **P**, 0.040 **S**, 0.55 **Si**	**As drawn or as welded:** all **diam**, (539) **TS**, (392) **YS**, 20 **El**
AS 1205	WR400/2	Australia	Bar, plate	0.23 **C**, 1.45 **Mn**, 0.050 **P**, 0.050 **S**, 0.15–0.65 **Si**, 0.17–0.48 **Cu**, 0.22–0.75 **Cr**, 0.55 **Ni**	**Hot rolled (plate):** (≤10) **diam**, (520) **TS**, (410) **YS**, 16 in 200 mm **El**
ISO 2937	Grade TS 18	ISO	Tube: seamless	0.23 **C**, 0.80–1.50 **Mn**, 0.045 **P**, 0.045 **S**, 0.35 **Si**	**Hot finished:** all **diam**, (490) **TS**, (285) **YS**, 21 **El**
ISO/R 630	Grade Fe 52 C	ISO	Bar, plate	0.23 **C**, 0.055 **P**, 0.055 **S**	**As rolled:** (≤30) **diam**, (490) **TS**, (343) **YS**, 22 **El**
ISO/R 630	Grade Fe 52 D	ISO	Bar, plate	0.23 **C**, 0.050 **P**, 0.050 **S**	**As rolled:** (≤30) **diam**, (490) **TS**, (343) **YS**, 22 **El**
NF A 33–101	AF 50,2B	France	Bar, billets, blooms	0.23 **C**, 0.045 **P**, 0.045 **S**	**Normalized:** all **diam**, (490) **TS**, 25 **El**
ISO 2604/11	TS 18	ISO	Tube: seamless	0.23 **C**, 0.80–1.50 **Mn**, 0.045 **P**, 0.045 **S**, 0.35 **Si**	**Hot finished, normalized:** all **diam**, (490) **TS**, (285) **YS**, 21 **El**
BS 4360	Grade 50D	UK	Hollow sections	0.23 **C**, 1.5 **Mn**, 0.050 **P**, 0.050 **S**, 0.45 **Si**	**Normalized:** (≤16) **diam**, (490) **TS**, (355) **YS**, 20 **El**
BS 4360	Grade 50C	UK	Hollow sections	0.23 **C**, 1.5 **Mn**, 0.060 **P**, 0.060 **S**, 0.45 **Si**	**Hot finished:** (≤16) **diam**, (490) **TS**, (355) **YS**, 20 **El**

WROUGHT CARBON STEELS

specification number	designation	country	product forms	composition	mechanical properties (see page iv for explanation)
BS 4360	Grade 50B	UK	Hollow sections	0.23 **C**, 1.5 **Mn**, 0.060 **P**, 0.060 **S**, 0.45 **Si**	**Hot finished:** (≤16) **diam**, (490) **TS**, (355) **YS**, 20 **El**
AS 1205	WR350/2	Australia	Bar, plate	0.23 **C**, 1.45 **Mn**, 0.050 **P**, 0.050 **S**, 0.15–0.65 **Si**, 0.17–0.48 **Cu**, 0.22–0.75 **Cr**, 0.55 **Ni**	**Hot rolled (plate):** (≤10) **diam**, (480) **TS**, (340) **YS**, 15 in 200 mm **El**
ISO/R 630	Grade Fe 44 C	ISO	Bar, plate	0.23 **C**, 0.055 **P**, 0.055 **S**	**As rolled:** (≤16) **diam**, (470) **TS**, (274) **YS**, 23 **El**
ISO/R 630	Grade Fe 44 D	ISO	Bar, plate	0.23 **C**, 0.050 **P**, 0.050 **S**	**As rolled:** (≤16) **diam**, (470) **TS**, (274) **YS**, 23 **El**
AS 1835	TS 13	Australia	Tube: seamless	0.23 **C**, 0.60–1.40 **Mn**, 0.045 **P**, 0.045 **S**, 0.35 **Si**	**Annealed and normalized:** all **diam**, (460) **TS**, (265) **YS**, 21 **El**
AS 1835	TS 14	Australia	Tube: seamless	0.23 **C**, 0.80–1.40 **Mn**, 0.045 **P**, 0.045 **S**, 0.35 **Si**	**Hot finished and normalized:** all **diam**, (460) **TS**, (265) **YS**, 21 **El**
AS 1836	TW 14	Australia	Tube: welded	0.23 **C**, 0.80–1.40 **Mn**, 0.045 **P**, 0.045 **S**, 0.35 **Si**	**Normalized:** all **diam**, (460) **TS**, (265) **YS**, 21 **El**
AS 1836	TW 13	Australia	Tube: welded	0.23 **C**, 0.60–1.40 **Mn**, 0.045 **P**, 0.045 **S**, 0.35 **Si**	**Welded, hot finished, sub-critical annealed, annealed or normalized:** all **diam**, (460) **TS**, (265) **YS**, 21 **El**
ISO 2604/1	F12	ISO	Forgings	0.23 **C**, 0.60–1.40 **Mn**, 0.040 **P**, 0.040 **S**, 0.10–0.40 **Si**	**Normalized, normalized and tempered, quenched and tempered:** (≤63) **diam**, (460) **TS**, (245) **YS**, 18 **El**
ISO 2604/1	F13	ISO	Forgings	0.23 **C**, 0.60–1.40 **Mn**, 0.040 **P**, 0.040 **S**, 0.10–0.40 **Si**, 0.015 min $\mathbf{Al}_{\mathbf{met}}$	**Normalized, normalized and tempered, quenched and tempered:** (≤63) **diam**, (460) **TS**, (275) **YS**, 18 **El**
ANSI/ASTM A 709	Grade 50	US	Plate, bar, shapes	0.23 **C**, 1.35 **Mn**, 0.04 **P**, 0.05 **S**	**Annealed:** ≤2 (≤51) **diam**, (450) **TS**, (345) **YS**, 21 **El**
ANSI/ASTM A 572	Grade 50	US	Plate, bar, shapes	0.23 **C**, 1.35 **Mn**, 0.04 **P**, 0.05 **S**, 0.30 **Si**	**Hot rolled:** 2 **diam**, (450) **TS**, (345) **YS**, 21 **El**
NS 12132	NS 12132–00	Norway	Bar, rod, shapes	0.23 **C**, 0.050 **P**, 0.050 **S**, 0.007 **N**	**Hot worked:** (16) **diam**, (412) **TS**, (255) **YS**, 22 **El**
ISO/R 630	Grade Fe 42 C	ISO	Bar, plate	0.23 **C**, 0.055 **P**, 0.055 **S**	**As rolled:** (≤16) **diam**, (411) **TS**, (255) **YS**, 23 **El**
ISO/R 630	Grade Fe 42 D	ISO	Bar, plate	0.23 **C**, 0.050 **P**, 0.050 **S**	**As rolled:** (≤16) **diam**, (411) **TS**, (255) **YS**, 23 **El**
NF A 33–101	A 42,2	France	Bar, billets, blooms	0.23 **C**, 0.045 **P**, 0.045 **S**	**Normalized:** all **diam**, (410) **TS**, 26 **El**
AS 1835	TS 9	Australia	Tube: seamless	0.23 **C**, 0.40–1.20 **Mn**, 0.045 **P**, 0.045 **S**, 0.35 **Si**	**Hot finished and normalized:** all **diam**, (410) **TS**, (235) **YS**, 22 **El**
AS 1836	TW 9H	Australia	Tube: welded	0.23 **C**, 0.40–1.20 **Mn**, 0.045 **P**, 0.045 **S**, 0.35 **Si**	**Normalized:** all **diam**, (410) **TS**, (235) **YS**, 22 **El**
AS 1836	TW 9	Australia	Tube: welded	0.23 **C**, 0.40–1.20 **Mn**, 0.045 **P**, 0.045 **S**, 0.35 **Si**	**Welded, hot finished, sub-critical annealed, annealed, or normalized:** all **diam**, (410) **TS**, (235) **YS**, 22 **El**
AS 1835	TS 9H	Australia	Tube: seamless	0.23 **C**, 0.40–1.20 **Mn**, 0.045 **P**, 0.045 **S**	**Hot finished and normalized:** all **diam**, (410) **TS**, (235) **YS**, 22 **El**
JIS G 3106	Class 1A	Japan	Plate, strip, shape, bar	0.23 **C**, 2.5 x C min **Mn**, 0.040 **P**, 0.040 **S**	**Hot rolled:** (≤5) **diam**, (402) **TS**, (245) **YS**, 23 **El**
ANSI/ASTM A 573	Grade 58	US	Plate	0.23 **C**, 0.60–0.90 **Mn**, 0.04 **P**, 0.05 **S**, 0.10–0.35 **Si**	**Hot rolled:** ≥1.5 **diam**, (400) **TS**, (220) **YS**, 21 **El**
ANSI/ASTM A 131	Grade A	US	Plate, shapes, bar	0.23 **C**, 0.05 **P**, 0.05 **S**	**Normalized:** all **diam**, (400) **TS**, (235) **YS**, 24 **El**
BS 970: Part 1	070M26	UK	Blooms, billets, slabs, bar, rod, forgings	0.22–0.30 **C**, 0.50–0.90 **Mn**	**Normalized:** 2.5 **diam**, (440) **TS**, (220) **YS**, 20 **El**; **Hardened and tempered:** 1.125 **diam**, (480) **TS**, (315) **YS**, 20 **El**; **Cold drawn from hot rolled:** 0.50–0.625 **diam**, (510) **TS**, (385) **YS**, 11 **El**
MIL–S–7952A	1025	US	Sheet, strip	0.22–0.30 **C**, 0.30–0.60 **Mn**, 0.040 **P**, 0.050 **S**	**Cold rolled and annealed:** all **diam**, (379) **TS**, (248) **YS**, 22 **El**

specification number	designation	country	product forms	composition	mechanical properties (see page iv for explanation)
COPANT 331	1035	COPANT	Bar	0.22–0.30 **C**, 0.60–0.90 **Mn**, 0.040 **P**, 0.050 **S**	
ISO R683/1	C25	ISO	Bar, forgings	0.22–0.29 **C**, 0.40–0.70 **Mn**, 0.050 **P**, 0.050 **S**, 0.15–0.40 **Si**	**Quenched and tempered**: all **diam**, (850) **TS**, (570) **YS**, 19 **El**; **Quenched, tempered and cold-reduced**: all **diam**, (970) **TS**, (785) **YS**, 11 **El**
ISO R683/1	C25e	ISO	Bar, forgings	0.22–0.29 **C**, 0.40–0.70 **Mn**, 0.035 **P**, 0.035 **S**, 0.15–0.40 **Si**	**Quenched and tempered**: all **diam**, (850) **TS**, (570) **YS**, 19 **El**; **Quenched, tempered and cold-reduced**: all **diam**, (970) **TS**, (785) **YS**, 11 **El**
ISO/R 683/111	Type C25ea	ISO	Bar, billet, rod	0.22–0.29 **C**, 0.40–0.70 **Mn**, 0.035 **P**, 0.020–0.035 **S**, 0.15–0.40 **Si**	**Quenched and tempered**: ($\leq$16) **diam**, (539) **TS**, (362) **YS**, 19 **El**
ISO/R 683/111	Type C25eb	ISO	Bar, billet, rod	0.22–0.29 **C**, 0.40–0.70 **Mn**, 0.035 **P**, 0.030–0.050 **S**, 0.15–0.40 **Si**	**Quenched and tempered**: ($\leq$16) **diam**, (539) **TS**, (362) **YS**, 19 **El**
DGN–B–301	1027	Mexico	Bar	0.22–0.29 **C**, 1.20–1.50 **Mn**, 0.040 **P**, 0.050 **S**, 0.10–0.20 **Si**	**Forged or hot rolled, cold rolled and cold finished**: all **diam**, (520) **TS**, (284) **YS**, 18 **El**
JIS G 27K	SWCH 27K	Japan	Wire	0.22–0.29 **C**, 1.20–1.50 **Mn**, 0.030 **P**, 0.035 **S**, 0.10–0.35 **Si**	**Annealed or cold drawn**: all **diam**, (471) **TS**, 12 **El**
ISO 683/XVIII	C25e	ISO	Bar, wire	0.22–0.29 **C**, 0.40–0.70 **Mn**, 0.035 **P**, 0.035 **S**, 0.15–0.40 **Si**	**Normalized**: all **diam**, (470) **TS**, (260) **YS**, 22 **El**
ISO 683/XVIII	C25ea	ISO	Bar, wire	0.22–0.29 **C**, 0.40–0.70 **Mn**, 0.035 **P**, 0.020–0.035 **S**, 0.15–0.40 **Si**	**Normalized**: all **diam**, (470) **TS**, (260) **YS**, 22 **El**
ISO 683/XVIII	C25eb	ISO	Bar, wire	0.22–0.29 **C**, 0.40–0.70 **Mn**, 0.035 **P**, 0.030–0.050 **S**, 0.15–0.40 **Si**	**Normalized**: all **diam**, (470) **TS**, (260) **YS**, 22 **El**
ISO 683/XVIII	C25	ISO	Bar, wire	0.22–0.29 **C**, 0.40–0.70 **Mn**, 0.050 **P**, 0.050 **S**, 0.15–0.40 **Si**	**Normalized**: all **diam**, (470) **TS**, (260) **YS**, 22 **El**
AISI 1027		US	Plate	0.22–0.29 **C**, 1.20–1.55 **Mn**, 0.040 **P**, 0.050 **S**	
AISI 1527		US	Bar	0.22–0.29 **C**, 1.20–1.50 **Mn**, 0.040 **P**, 0.050 **S**	
AISI 1526		US	Bar	0.22–0.29 **C**, 1.10–1.40 **Mn**, 0.040 **P**, 0.050 **S**	
ANSI/ASTM A 29	1527	US	Bar	0.22–0.29 **C**, 1.20–1.50 **Mn**, 0.040 **P**, 0.050 **S**	
ANSI/ASTM A 29	1526	US	Bar	0.22–0.29 **C**, 1.10–1.40 **Mn**, 0.040 **P**, 0.050 **S**	
ASTM A 689	1526	US	Bar: spring	0.22–0.29 **C**, 1.10–1.40 **Mn**, 0.040 **P**, 0.050 **S**	
ASTM A 689	1527	US	Bar: spring	0.22–0.29 **C**, 1.20–1.50 **Mn**, 0.040 **P**, 0.050 **S**	
COPANT 333	1027	COPANT	Wire, rod	0.22–0.29 **C**, 1.20–1.50 **Mn**, 0.040 **P**, 0.050 **S**	
DGN–B–301	1526	Mexico	Bar	0.22–0.29 **C**, 1.10–1.40 **Mn**, 0.040 **P**, 0.050 **S**	
DGN–B–301	1527	Mexico	Bar	0.22–0.29 **C**, 1.20–1.50 **Mn**, 0.040 **P**, 0.050 **S**	
AISI 1526		US	Wire, rod	0.22–0.29 **C**, 1.10–1.40 **Mn**, 0.040 **P**, 0.050 **S**	
AISI 1527		US	Wire, rod	0.22–0.29 **C**, 1.20–1.50 **Mn**, 0.040 **P**, 0.050 **S**	
ANSI/ASTM A 576	1526	US	Bar	0.22–0.29 **C**, 1.10–1.40 **Mn**, 0.040 **P**, 0.050 **S**	
ANSI/ASTM A 576	1527	US	Bar	0.22–0.29 **C**, 1.20–1.50 **Mn**, 0.040 **P**, 0.050 **S**	
ANSI/ASTM A 512	1025	US	Tube: cold–drawn buttweld	0.22–0.28 **C**, 0.30–0.60 **Mn**, 0.04 **P**, 0.05 **S**	**Stress relief annealed**: all **diam**, 72 (496) **TS**, 67 (462) **YS**, 11 **El**
DGN–B–201	Grade 1025	Mexico	Tube: butt–welded	0.22–0.28 **C**, 0.30–0.60 **Mn**, 0.040 **P**, 0.050 **S**	**Cold finished and annealed**: all **diam**, (496) **TS**, (462) **YS**, 11 **El**; **Normalized**: all **diam**, (301) **TS**, (241) **YS**, 32 **El**

specification number	designation	country	product forms	composition	mechanical properties (see page iv for explanation)
JIS G 3539	SWCH 25K	Japan	Wire	0.22–0.28 **C**, 0.30–0.60 **Mn**, 0.030 **P**, 0.035 **S**, 0.10–0.35 **Si**	**Cold drawn**: (>5) **diam**, (471) **TS**, 6 **El**; **Annealed and cold drawn**: (>5) **diam**, (441) **TS**, 12 **El**
DGN-B-301	1026	Mexico	Bar	0.22–0.28 **C**, 0.60–0.90 **Mn**, 0.040 **P**, 0.050 **S**, 0.10–0.20 **Si**	**Forged or hot rolled, cold rolled and cold finished**: all **diam**, (441) **TS**, (245) **YS**, 24 **El**
DGN-B-301	1025	Mexico	Bar	0.22–0.28 **C**, 0.30–0.60 **Mn**, 0.040 **P**, 0.050 **S**, 0.10–0.20 **Si**	**Forged or hot rolled, cold rolled and cold finished**: all **diam**, (402) **TS**, (216) **YS**, 25 **El**
DGN-B-203	Grade 1025	Mexico	Tube: seamless	0.22–0.28 **C**, 0.30–0.60 **Mn**, 0.040 **P**, 0.050 **S**	**Hot finished**: all **diam**, (382) **TS**, (245) **YS**, 25 **El**; **Cold finished**: all **diam**, (520) **TS**, (451) **YS**, 5 **El**; **Stress relieved**: all **diam**, (480) **TS**, (382) **YS**, 8 **El**; **Tempered**: all **diam**, (363) **TS**, (206) **YS**, 25 **El**; **Normalized**: all **diam**, (382) **TS**, (245) **YS**, 22 **El**
COPANT 514	Grade 1025	COPANT	Tube: seamless	0.22–0.28 **C**, 0.30–0.60 **Mn**, 0.040 **P**, 0.050 **S**, 0.15–0.30 **Si**	**Hot finished**: (>323.9) **diam**, (380) **TS**, (245) **YS**, 25 **El**; **Cold finished**: all **diam**, (520) **TS**, (450) **YS**, 5 **El**; **Annealed**: all **diam**, (360) **TS**, (205) **YS**, 25 **El**; **Normalized**: all **diam**, (380) **TS**, (245) **YS**, 22 **El**
AMS 5075C		US	Tube	0.22–0.28 **C**, 0.30–0.60 **Mn**, 0.040 **P**, 0.050 **S**, 0.10–0.35 **Si**	**Cold finished**: all **diam**, 55 (379) **TS**, 36 (248) **YS**, 22 **El**
AMS 5077C		US	Tube	0.22–0.28 **C**, 0.30–0.60 **Mn**, 0.040 **P**, 0.050 **S**, 0.10–0.30 **Si**	**Normalized**: all **diam**, 55 (379) **TS**, 36 (248) **YS**, 22 **El**
ANSI/ASTM A 519	1025	US	Tube: seamless	0.22–0.28 **C**, 0.30–0.60 **Mn**, 0.040 **P**, 0.050 **S**	**Hot rolled**: all **diam**, 55 (379) **TS**, 35 (241) **YS**, 25 **El**; **Cold worked**: all **diam**, 75 (517) **TS**, 65 (448) **YS**, 5 **El**; **Stress relieved**: all **diam**, 70 (483) **TS**, 55 (379) **YS**, 8 **El**; **Annealed**: all **diam**, 55 (365) **TS**, 30 (207) **YS**, 25 **El**; **Normalized**: all **diam**, 55 (379) **TS**, 36 (248) **YS**, 22 **El**
QQ-S-700D	SAE 1025	US	Sheet, strip	0.22–0.28 **C**, 0.30–0.60 **Mn**, 0.040 **P**, 0.050 **S**	
AISI 1025		US	Plate	0.22–0.28 **C**, 0.30–0.60 **Mn**, 0.040 **P**, 0.050 **S**	
AISI 1026		US	Plate	0.22–0.28 **C**, 0.60–0.90 **Mn**, 0.040 **P**, 0.050 **S**	
AISI 1026		US	Bar	0.22–0.28 **C**, 0.60–0.90 **Mn**, 0.040 **P**, 0.050 **S**	
AISI 1025		US	Bar	0.22–0.28 **C**, 0.30–0.60 **Mn**, 0.040 **P**, 0.050 **S**	
ANSI/ASTM A 519	1026	US	Tube: seamless	0.22–0.28 **C**, 0.60–0.90 **Mn**, 0.040 **P**, 0.050 **S**	
DGN-B-203	Grade 1026	Mexico	Tube: seamless	0.22–0.28 **C**, 0.60–0.90 **Mn**, 0.040 **P**, 0.050 **S**	
COPANT 330	1025	COPANT	Bar, shapes	0.22–0.28 **C**, 0.30–0.60 **Mn**, 0.040 **P**, 0.050 **S**	
COPANT 331	1025	COPANT	Bar	0.22–0.28 **C**, 0.30–0.60 **Mn**, 0.040 **P**, 0.050 **S**	
COPANT 331	1026	COPANT	Bar	0.22–0.28 **C**, 0.60–0.90 **Mn**, 0.040 **P**, 0.050 **S**	
ASTM A 108	1025	US	Bar	0.22–0.28 **C**, 0.30–0.60 **Mn**, 0.040 **P**, 0.050 **S**	
ANSI/ASTM A 545	Grade 1026	US	Wire	0.22–0.28 **C**, 0.60–0.90 **Mn**, 0.040 **P**, 0.050 **S**	
MIL-S-11310E	1025	US	Bar	0.22–0.28 **C**, 0.30–0.60 **Mn**, 0.040 **P**, 0.050 **S**, 0.20 **Si**	
COPANT 333	1025	COPANT	Wire, rod	0.22–0.28 **C**, 0.30–0.60 **Mn**, 0.040 **P**, 0.050 **S**	
COPANT 333	1026	COPANT	Wire, rod	0.22–0.28 **C**, 0.60–0.90 **Mn**, 0.040 **P**, 0.050 **S**	

specification number	designation	country	product forms	composition	mechanical properties (see page iv for explanation)
ANSI/ASTM A 575	1025	US	Bar	0.22–0.28 **C**, 0.30–0.60 **Mn**, 0.04 **P**, 0.05 **S**	
ANSI/ASTM A 576	1026	US	Bar	0.22–0.28 **C**, 0.60–0.90 **Mn**, 0.040 **P**, 0.050 **S**	
AISI 1025		US	Wire, rod	0.22–0.28 **C**, 0.30–0.60 **Mn**, 0.040 **P**, 0.050 **S**	
AISI 1026		US	Wire, rod	0.22–0.28 **C**, 0.60–0.90 **Mn**, 0.040 **P**, 0.050 **S**	
ANSI/ASTM A 576	1025	US	Bar	0.22–0.28 **C**, 0.30–0.60 **Mn**, 0.040 **P**, 0.050 **S**	
ASTM A 689	1025	US	Bar	0.22–0.28 **C**, 0.30–0.60 **Mn**, 0.040 **P**, 0.050 **S**	
ANSI/ASTM A 29	1025	US	Bar	0.22–0.28 **C**, 0.30–0.60 **Mn**, 0.040 **P**, 0.050 **S**	
ANSI/ASTM A 29	1026	US	Bar	0.22–0.28 **C**, 0.60–0.90 **Mn**, 0.040 **P**, 0.050 **S**	
ASTM A 689	1026	US	Bar	0.22–0.28 **C**, 0.60–0.90 **Mn**, 0.040 **P**, 0.050 **S**	
AS 1443	Grade AS 1443/K1026	Australia	Bar	0.22–0.28 **C**, 0.60–0.90 **Mn**, 0.050 **P**, 0.050 **S**, 0.10–0.35 **Si**	
AS 1443	Grade AS 1443/S1025	Australia	Bar	0.22–0.28 **C**, 0.30–0.60 **Mn**, 0.050 **P**, 0.050 **S**, 0.35 **Si**	
AS 1442	Grade AS 1442/S1025	Australia	Bar, blooms, billets, slabs	0.22–0.28 **C**, 0.30–0.60 **Mn**, 0.050 **P**, 0.050 **S**, 0.35 **Si**	
AS 1442	Grade AS 1442/K1026	Australia	Bar, blooms, billets, slabs	0.22–0.28 **C**, 0.60–0.90 **Mn**, 0.050 **P**, 0.050 **S**, 0.10–0.35 **Si**	
DEF STAN 95–1/1	C1025	Canada	Bar	0.22–0.28 **C**, 0.30–0.60 **Mn**, 0.04 **P**, 0.05 **S**, 0.10–0.30 **Si**	
COPANT 514	Grade 1026	COPANT	Tube: seamless	0.22–0.28 **C**, 0.60–0.90 **Mn**, 0.040 **P**, 0.050 **S**, 0.20–0.35 **Si**	
JIS G 3507	SWRCH 25K	Japan	Wire, rod	0.22–0.28 **C**, 0.30–0.60 **Mn**, 0.030 **P**, 0.035 **S**, 0.10–0.35 **Si**	
JIS G 4051	S 25C	Japan	Bar, wire, rod	0.22–0.28 **C**, 0.30–0.60 **Mn**, 0.030 **P**, 0.035 **S**, 0.15–0.35 **Si**, 0.30 **Cu**	
JIS G 3507	SWRCH 27K	Japan	Wire, rod	0.22–0.27 **C**, 1.20–1.50 **Mn**, 0.030 **P**, 0.035 **S**, 0.10–0.35 **Si**	
ISO 4996	Grade HS490–C	ISO	Sheet: hot rolled	0.22 **C**, 1.70 **Mn**, 0.040 **P**, 0.040 **S**, 0.50 **Si**	**As rolled**: all diam, (570) **TS**, (470) **YS**, 10 **El**
ISO 4996	Grade HS490–D	ISO	Sheet: hot rolled	0.22 **C**, 1.70 **Mn**, 0.035 **P**, 0.035 **S**, 0.50 **Si**	**As rolled**: all diam, (570) **TS**, (470) **YS**, 10 **El**
ANSI/ASTM A 633	Grade E	US	Plate, bar, shapes	0.22 **C**, 1.15–1.50 **Mn**, 0.04 **P**, 0.05 **S**, 0.15–0.50 **Si**, 0.04–0.11 **V**, 0.01–0.03 **N**	**Normalized**: ≤2.5 **diam**, 80 (550) **TS**, 60 (415) **YS**, 23 **El**
DIN 1626, Part 3	Grade St52–3/1.0841	Germany	Pipe: welded	0.22 **C**, 1.5 **Mn**, 0.05 **P**, 0.05 **S**, 0.55 **Si**	**As welded**: <16 **diam**, (510) **TS**, (350) **YS**, 22 **El**
NF A 36–101	A 52,3	France	Strip	0.22 **C**, 0.050 **P**, 0.050 **S**	**Hot rolled**: all **diam**, (510) **TS**, (353) **YS**, 22 **El**
NF A 36–101	A 52,4	France	Strip	0.22 **C**, 0.045 **P**, 0.045 **S**	**Hot rolled**: all **diam**, (510) **TS**, (353) **YS**, 23 **El**
NF A 36–205	A 52,C2 and P2	France	Sheet, plate	0.22 **C**, 1.00–1.50 **Mn**, 0.04 **P**, 0.04 **S**, 0.50 **Si**, 0.25 **Cu**	**Normalized**: (3–30) **diam**, (510) **TS**, (335) **YS**, 23 **El**
NFA 36–205	A 52,CR2 and PR 2	France	Sheet, plate	0.22 **C**, 1.0–1.50 **Mn**, 0.04 **P**, 0.04 **S**, 0.50 **Si**, 0.25 **Cu**, 0.10 **V**, 0.06 **Nb**, 0.35 **Mo**	**Normalized**: (3–30) **diam**, (510) **TS**, (335) **YS**, 23 **El**
TS 416	Fe 52.3	Turkey	Pipe: welded	0.22 **C**, 1.50 **Mn**, 0.050 **P**, 0.050 **S**, 0.55 **Si**, 0.009 **N**	**As welded**: (<16) **diam**, (510) **TS**, (353) **YS**, 22 **El**
DIN 1626, Part 4	Grade St 52–3	Germany	Pipe: welded (specially tested)	0.22 **C**, 1.5 **Mn**, 0.05 **P**, 0.05 **S**, 0.55 **Si**	**Annealed**: (<16) **diam**, (510) **TS**, (350) **YS**, 22 **El**
DIN 17100	St 52–3 (1.0841)	Germany	Bar, plate	0.22 **C**, 0.050 **P**, 0.050 **S**	**Normalized**: all **diam**, (510) **TS**, (355) **YS**, 22 **El**
DIN 17100	St 52–3 (1.0841)	Germany	Strip	0.22 **C**, 0.050 **P**, 0.050 **S**	**Normalized**: all **diam**, (510) **TS**, (355) **YS**, 22 **El**; **Hot rolled**: all **diam**, (510) **TS**, (355) **YS**, 16 **El**
ANSI/ASTM A 737	Grade A	US	Plate	0.22 **C**, 0.95–1.40 **Mn**, 0.035 **P**, 0.035 **S**, 0.10–0.55 **Si**, 0.11 **V**	**Normalized**: all **diam**, 70 (485) **TS**, 50 (345) **YS**, 23 **El**

WROUGHT CARBON STEELS

specification number	designation	country	product forms	composition	mechanical properties (see page iv for explanation)
ANSI/ASTM A 737	Grade B	US	Plate	0.22 **C**, 1.10–1.55 **Mn**, 0.035 **P**, 0.035 **S**, 0.10–0.55 **Si**, 0.05 **Nb**	**Normalized**: all **diam**, 70 (485) **TS**, 50 (345) **YS**, 23 **El**
NF A 36–205	A 48, C2 and P2	France	Sheet, plate	0.22 **C**, 0.80–1.20 **Mn**, 0.04 **P**, 0.04 **S**, 0.35 **Si**, 0.25 **Cu**	**Normalized**: (3–30) **diam**, (470) **TS**, (275) **YS**, 25 **El**
NF A 36–205	A 48, CR2 and PR2	France	Sheet, plate	0.22 **C**, 1.0–1.50 **Mn**, 0.04 **P**, 0.04 **S**, 0.50 **Si**, 0.25 **Cu**	**Normalized**: (3–30) **diam**, (470) **TS**, (275) **YS**, 25 **El**
NF A 36–205	A 48, C1 and P1	France	Sheet, plate	0.22 **C**, 0.55–1.30 **Mn**, 0.05 **P**, 0.05 **S**, 0.45 **Si**	**Normalized**: (3–30) **diam**, (470) **TS**, 275 **YS**, 23 **El**
NF A 36–101	A 47,3	France	Strip	0.22 **C**, 0.050 **P**, 0.050 **S**	**Hot rolled**: all **diam**, (461) **TS**, (294) **YS**, 23 **El**
NF A 36–101	A 47,4	France	Strip	0.22 **C**, 0.045 **P**, 0.045 **S**	**Hot rolled**: all **diam**, (461) **TS**, (294) **YS**, 24 **El**
ISO 2604/III	No. TW13	ISO	Tube	0.22 **C**, 0.60–1.40 **Mn**, 0.045 **P**, 0.045 **S**, 0.35 **Si**	**As welded, annealed, normalized**: all **diam**, (460) **TS**, (265) **YS**, 21 **El**
ISO 2604/III	No. TW14	ISO	Tube	0.22 **C**, 0.80–1.40 **Mn**, 0.045 **P**, 0.045 **S**, 0.35 **Si**	**As welded, annealed, normalized**: all **diam**, (460) **TS**, (265) **YS**, 21 **El**
ISO 2604/11	TS 13	ISO	Tube: seamless	0.22 **C**, 0.60–1.40 **Mn**, 0.045 **P**, 0.045 **S**, 0.35 **Si**	**Hot finished, sub–critical annealed, annealed, normalized**: all **diam**, (460) **TS**, (265) **YS**, 21 **El**
ISO 2604/11	TS 14	ISO	Tube: seamless	0.22 **C**, 0.80–1.40 **Mn**, 0.045 **P**, 0.045 **S**, 0.35 **Si**	**Hot finished, normalized**: all **diam**, (460) **TS**, (265) **YS**, 21 **El**
ANSI/ASTM A 441		US	Plate, bar, shapes	0.22 **C**, 0.85–1.25 **Mn**, 0.04 **P**, 0.05 **S**, 0.30 **Si**, 0.20 min **Cu**, 0.20 min **V**	**As rolled (plate, bar)**: .75–1.50 **diam**, (460) **TS**, (315) **YS**, 21 **El**
DIN 2391 Part 2	Grade St 45.2–1.0418	Germany	Tube	0.22 **C**, 0.40 **Mn**, 0.05 **P**, 0.05 **S**, 0.10–0.35 **Si**	**Normalized**: all **diam**, (441) **TS**, (255) **YS**, 21 **El**; **Bright drawn/hard**: all **diam**; **Bright drawn/soft**: all **diam**, (470) **TS**, 8 **El**; **Annealed**: all **diam**, (392) **TS**, 24 **El**
DIN 17175 Part 1	St 45.8–1.0405	Germany	Tube: seamless	0.22 **C**, 0.45 min **Mn**, 0.050 **P**, 0.050 **S**, 0.10–0.35 **Si**	**Hot rolled or cold drawn, normalized or annealed**: all **diam**, (441) **TS**, (255) **YS**, 21 **El**
TS 381	UDK 621.643.2/Fe 45.8	Turkey	Pipe: seamless	0.22 **C**, 0.45 **Mn**, 0.050 **P**, 0.050 **S**, 0.10–0.35 **Si**	**As drawn**: all **diam**, (441) **TS**, (255) **YS**, 21 **El**
DIN 17135	Grade A St 45	Germany	Plate, strip, tube, bar, forgings	0.22 **C**, 0.45 min **Mn**, 0.045 **P**, 0.045 **S**, 0.35 **Si**	**Normalized**: (≤16) **diam**, (441) **TS**, (255) **YS**, 21 **El**
SS 14 14 35 E	SS 14 35–06	Sweden	Tube: welded	0.22 **C**, 0.60–1.00 **Mn**, 0.045 **P**, 0.045 **S**, 0.10–0.40 **Si**, 0.30 **Cu**, 0.25 **Cr**, 0.009 **N**	**Quenched**: all **diam**, (440) **TS**, (260) **YS**, 21 **El**
NBN 837	D 45	Belgium	Tube	0.22 **C**, 0.45–1.0 **Mn**, 0.040 **P**, 0.040 **S**, 0.15–0.35 **Si**	**Normalized or annealed**: all **diam**, (440) **TS**, (270) **YS**, 21 **El**
DIN 1629, Part 4	Grade St45.4/1.0418	Germany	Tube: seamless	0.22 **C**, 0.40 **Mn**, 0.050 **P**, 0.050 **S**, 0.10–0.35 **Si**	**Annealed**: (<16) **diam**, (440) **TS**, (255) **YS**, 21 **El**
DIN 17155	Grade H III	Germany	Plate	0.22 **C**, 0.55 min **Mn**, 0.050 **P**, 0.050 **S**, 0.35 **Si**, 0.30 max, opt **Cr**	**Normalized**: (≤16) **diam**, (432) **TS**, (274) **YS**
DIN 17100	RSt 46–2 (1.0477)	Germany	Bar, plate	0.22 **C**, 0.055 **P**, 0.055 **S**	**Normalized**: all **diam**, (430) **TS**, (285) **YS**, 22 **El**
DIN 17100	RSt 46–2 (1.0477)	Germany	Strip	0.22 **C**, 0.055 **P**, 0.055 **S**	**Normalized**: all **diam**, (430) **TS**, (285) **YS**, 22 **El**; **Hot rolled**: all **diam**, (430) **TS**, (285) **YS**, 16 **El**
DIN 17100	St 46–3 (1.0483)	Germany	Bar, plate	0.22 **C**, 0.050 **P**, 0.050 **S**	**Normalized**: all **diam**, (430) **TS**, (285) **YS**, 22 **El**
DIN 17100	St 46–3 (1.0483)	Germany	Strip	0.22 **C**, 0.050 **P**, 0.050 **S**	**Normalized**: all **diam**, (430) **TS**, (285) **YS**, 22 **El**; **Hot rolled**: all **diam**, (430) **TS**, (285) **YS**, 16 **El**
ANSI/ASTM A 572	Grade 45	US	Plate, bar, shapes	0.22 **C**, 1.35 **Mn**, 0.04 **P**, 0.05 **S**, 0.30 **Si**	**Hot rolled**: 2 **diam**, (415) **TS**, (310) **YS**, 22 **El**
DS 12011	St 428	Denmark	Rod, bar, shapes	0.22 **C**, 0.06 **P**, 0.05 **S**, 0.5 **Si**, 0.4 **Cu**, 0.3 **Cr**, 0.009 **N**	**Hot rolled**: (16) **diam**, (412) **TS**, (245) **YS**, 23 **El**

WROUGHT CARBON STEELS

specification number	designation	country	product forms	composition	mechanical properties (see page iv for explanation)
DS 12011	St 42 A	Denmark	Rod, bar, shapes	0.22 **C**, 0.08 **P**, 0.05 **S**, 0.5 **Si**, 0.4 **Cu**, 0.3 **Cr**	**Hot rolled**: (16) **diam**, (412) **TS**, (216) **YS**, 23 **El**
IS 2062		India	Bar, plate	0.22 **C**, 0.060 **P**, 0.060 **S**, 0.10 min **Si**	**Normalized**: (20–40) **diam**, (410) **TS**, (235) **YS**, 23 **El**
BS 1501–151	Grade 26A	UK	Plate	0.22 **C**, 0.50 **Mn**, 0.050 **P**, 0.050 **S**, 0.35 **Si**; 0.70 max other elements, total	**Normalized**: (≤16) **diam**, (400) **TS**, (230) **YS**, 45 **El**
BS 1501–151	Grade 26B	UK	Plate	0.22 **C**, 0.65 **Mn**, 0.050 **P**, 0.050 **S**, 0.35 **Si**; 0.70 max other elements, total	**Normalized**: (≤16) **diam**, (400) **TS**, (230) **YS**, 45 **El**
BS 1501–161	Grade 26A	UK	Plate	0.22 **C**, 0.50–1.20 **Mn**, 0.050 **P**, 0.050 **S**, 0.10–0.35 **Si**; 0.70 max other elements, total	**Normalized**: (≤16) **diam**, (400) **TS**, (230) **YS**, 45 **El**
BS 1501–161	Grade 26B	UK	Plate	0.22 **C**, 0.65–1.20 **Mn**, 0.050 **P**, 0.050 **S**, 0.10–0.35 **Si**; 0.70 max other elements, total	**Normalized**: (≤16) **diam**, (400) **TS**, (230) **YS**, 45 **El**
DGN–B–277		Mexico	Sheet, strip	0.22 **C**, 1.25 **Mn**, 0.05 **S**	**Hot rolled**: all **diam**, (400) **TS**, (343) **YS**, 22 **El**; **Annealed or normalized**: all **diam**, (451) **TS**, (314) **YS**, 22 **El**; **Cold rolled**: all **diam**, (451) **TS**, (314) **YS**, 22 **El**
ANSI/ASTM A 516	Grade 55	US	Plate	0.22 **C**, 0.56–1.25 **Mn**, 0.035 **P**, 0.04 **S**, 0.13–0.33 **Si**	**Normalized**: 2.0–4.0 **diam**, (380) **TS**, (205) **YS**, 27 **El**
ANSI/ASTM A 442	Grade 55	US	Plate	0.22 **C**, 0.76–1.14 **Mn**, 0.04 **P**, 0.05 **S**, 0.13–0.33 **Si**	**As rolled**: >1.00 **diam**, (380) **TS**, (205) **YS**, 26 **El**
NF A 36–101	A 37,1	France	Strip	0.22 **C**, 0.075 **P**, 0.062 **S**	**Hot rolled**: all **diam**, (363) **TS**, (235) **YS**, 26 **El**
NF A 36–101	A 37,2	France	Strip	0.22 **C**, 0.062 **P**, 0.062 **S**, 0.009 **N**	**Hot rolled**: all **diam**, (363) **TS**, (235) **YS**, 28 **El**
NF A 33–102	AR E24,1 (AR 37)	France	Billets, blooms, slabs	0.22 **C**, 0.075 **P**, 0.062 **S**	**Normalized**: all **diam**, (360) **TS**, (230) **YS**, 26 **El**
NF A 33–102	AR E 24,2 (AR 37)	France	Billets, blooms, slabs	0.22 **C**, 0.062 **P**, 0.062 **S**	**Normalized**: all **diam**, (360) **TS**, (230) **YS**, 28 **El**
DIN 17100	RSt 37–1 (1.0111)	Germany	Bar, plate	0.22 **C**, 0.080 **P**, 0.055 **S**	**Normalized**: all **diam**, (360) **TS**, (235) **YS**, 25 **El**
DIN 17100	RSt 37–1 (1.0111)	Germany	Strip	0.22 **C**, 0.080 **P**, 0.055 **S**	**Normalized**: all **diam**, (360) **TS**, (235) **YS**, 25 **El**; **Hot rolled**: all **diam**, (360) **TS**, (235) **YS**, 18 **El**
DIN 17100	USt 37–2 (1.0112)	Germany	Bar, plate	0.22 **C**, 0.063 **P**, 0.063 **S**	**Normalized**: all **diam**, (360) **TS**, (235) **YS**, 25 **El**
DIN 17100	USt 37–2 (1.0112)	Germany	Strip	0.22 **C**, 0.063 **P**, 0.063 **S**	**Normalized**: all **diam**, (360) **TS**, (235) **YS**, 25 **El**; **Hot rolled**: all **diam**, (360) **TS**, (235) **YS**, 18 **El**
COPANT 37, I	BM–19	COPANT	Plate	0.22 **C**, 0.35 **P**, 0.045 **S**, 0.37 **C**	**As rolled**: (4.75–50) **diam**, (350) **TS**, (190) **YS**, 28 **El**
ANSI/ASTM A 285	Grade B	US	Plate	0.22 **C**, 0.90 **Mn**, 0.035 **P**, 0.045 **S**	**As rolled**: all **diam**, (345) **TS**, (185) **YS**, 28 **El**
DGN–B–242	Grade B	Mexico	Plate	0.22 **C**, 0.90 **Mn**, 0.035 **P**, 0.045 **S**, 0.20–0.35 **Cu**	**As rolled**: (<50) **diam**, (343) **TS**, (185) **YS**, 28 **El**
DGN–B–275	Grade B	Mexico	Sheet	0.22 **C**, 0.90 **Mn**, 0.035 **P**, 0.040 **S**, 0.20 **Cu**	**Hot rolled**: (5–4) **diam**, (343) **TS**, (185) **YS**, 24 **El**
ASTM A 414	Grade B	US	Sheet	0.22 **C**, 0.90 **Mn**, 0.035 **P**, 0.040 **S**	**Hot rolled**: 0.2299–0.1450 (5.82–3.68) **diam**, 50 (340) **TS**, 27 (185) **YS**, 24 **El**
ANSI/ASTM A 414	Grade B	US	Sheet	0.22 **C**, 0.90 **Mn**, 0.035 **P**, 0.040 **S**	**Hot rolled or cold rolled, annealed**: all **diam**, (340) **TS**, (185) **YS**, 24 **El**
DGN–B–205	Grade A, type S	Mexico	Pipe: seamless	0.22 **C**, 0.90 **Mn**, 0.40 **P**, 0.050 **S**	**As drawn**: (≥8) **diam**, (333) **TS**, (206) **YS**, 35 **El**
CSA B193	Seamless, grade A	Canada	Pipe	0.22 **C**, 0.90 **Mn**, 0.040 **P**, 0.050 **S**	**Mill**: 0.250 (6.35) **diam**, 48 (331) **TS**, 30 (207) **YS**, 32 **El**
API Spec 5L	Grade A	US	Pipe: seamless	0.22 **C**, 0.90 **Mn**, 0.04 **P**, 0.05 **S**	**As rolled**: ≥.497 (≥12.62) **diam**, 48 (331) **TS**, 30 (207) **YS**, 36 **El**
NF A 35–051	FM 26 grade 3	France	Wire, rod	0.21–0.32 **C**, 0.40–0.70 **Mn**, 0.040 **P**, 0.040 **S**, 0.10–0.35 **Si**	

WROUGHT CARBON STEELS

specification number	designation	country	product forms	composition	mechanical properties (see page iv for explanation)
AISI 1526H		US	Bar	0.21–0.30 **C**, 1.00–1.50 **Mn**, 0.040 **P**, 0.050 **S**, 0.15–0.30 **Si**	
DGN–B–301	1516H	Mexico	Bar	0.21–0.30 **C**, 1.00–1.50 **Mn**, 0.040 **P**, 0.050 **S**, 0.15–0.30 **Si**	
AISI 1526H		US	Wire, rod	0.21–0.30 **C**, 1.00–1.50 **Mn**, 0.040 **P**, 0.050 **S**, 0.15–0.30 **Si**	
BS 1501–221	Grades 30A, 30B	UK	Plate	0.21 **C**, 0.90–1.50 **Mn**, 0.050 **P**, 0.050 **S**, 0.10–0.55 **Si**; 0.70 max other elements, total	**Normalized**: (≤16) **diam**, (460) **TS**, (275) **YS**, 45 **El**
BS 1501–211	Grades 30A, 30B	UK	Plate	0.21 **C**, 0.90–1.50 **Mn**, 0.050 **P**, 0.050 **S**, 0.55 **Si**; 0.70 max other elements, total	**Normalized**: (≤16) **diam**, (460) **TS**, (275) **YS**, 45 **El**
NF A 36–211	BS 3	France	Plate	0.21 **C**, 0.040 **P**, 0.040 **S**, 0.25 **Si**	**Normalized**: all **diam**, (431) **TS**, (255) **YS**, 30 **El**
BS 4360	Grade 43E	UK	Hollow sections	0.21 **C**, 1.3 **Mn**, 0.050 **P**, 0.050 **S**, 0.45 **Si**	**Normalized**: (≤16) **diam**, (430) **TS**, (270) **YS**, 22 **El**
ANSI/ASTM A 572	Grade 42	US	Plate, bar, shapes	0.21 **C**, 1.35 **Mn**, 0.04 **P**, 0.05 **S**, 0.30 **Si**	**Hot rolled**: 6 **diam**, (415) **TS**, (290) **YS**, 24 **El**
ANSI/ASTM A 524	Grade I	US	Pipe: seamless	0.21 **C**, 0.90–1.35 **Mn**, 0.048 **P**, 0.058 **S**, 0.10–0.40 **Si**	**Normalized**: ≥0.375 (≥9.5) **diam**, 60 (414) **TS**, 35 (241) **YS**, 30 **El**
DGN–B–245	Grade 45	Mexico	Plate	0.21 **C**, 0.60–0.90 **Mn**, 0.035 **P**, 0.04 **S**, 0.15–0.30 **Si**	**As rolled**: (<12.7) **diam**, (414) **TS**, (221) **YS**, 25 **El**
NF A 36–211	BS 2	France	Plate	0.21 **C**, 0.040 **P**, 0.040 **S**, 0.25 **Si**	**Normalized**: all **diam**, (412) **TS**, (265) **YS**, 32 **El**
DGN–B–206	Grade I	Mexico	Pipe: seamless	0.21 **C**, 0.90–1.35 **Mn**, 0.048 **P**, 0.058 **S**, 0.10 min **Si**	**Forged, hot finished, normalized**: (7.92–9.53) **diam**, (411.6) **TS**, (245) **YS**, 30 **El**
JIS G 3118	Class 1	Japan	Plate	0.21 **C**, 0.85–1.20 **Mn**, 0.035 **P**, 0.040 **S**, 015–0.30 **Si**	**Hot rolled**: (8–12.5) **diam**, (412) **TS**, (226) **YS**, 21 **El**
ISO 2604/III	No. TW9	ISO	Tube	0.21 **C**, 0.40–1.20 **Mn**, 0.045 **P**, 0.045 **S**, 0.35 **Si**	**As welded, annealed, normalized**: all **diam**, (410) **TS**, (235) **YS**, 22 **El**
ISO 2604/III	No. TW9H	ISO	Tube	0.21 **C**, 0.40–1.20 **Mn**, 0.045 **P**, 0.045 **S**, 0.35 **Si**	**As welded, annealed, normalized**: all **diam**, (410) **TS**, (235) **YS**, 22 **El**
ISO 2937	Grade TS 9	ISO	Tube: seamless	0.21 **C**, 0.40–1.20 **Mn**, 0.045 **P**, 0.045 **S**, 0.35 **Si**	**Hot finished**: all **diam**, (410) **TS**, (235) **YS**, 22 **El**
ISO 559	TS9/TW9	ISO	Tube: welded or seamless	0.21 **C**, 0.40–1.20 **Mn**, 0.045 **P**, 0.045 **S**, 0.35 **Si**	**As welded, hot rolled**: all **diam**, (410) **TS**, (235) **YS**, 21 **El**
BS 3601	Grade 410	UK	Pipe, tube: seamless, welded	0.21 **C**, 0.40–1.20 **Mn**, 0.050 **P**, 0.050 **S**, 0.35 **Si**	**Hot finished or as–welded**: all **diam**, (410) **TS**, (235) **YS**, 22 **El**
ISO 2604/11	TS 9		Seamless tubing	0.21 **C**, 0.40–1.20 **Mn**, 0.045 **P**, 0.045 **S**, 0.35 **Si**	**Hot finished, normalized**: all **diam**, (410) **TS**, (235) **YS**, 22 **El**
ISO 2604/11	TS 9H	ISO	Tube: seamless	0.21 **C**, 0.40–1.20 **Mn**, 0.045–0.045 **P**, 0.35 **Si**	**Hot finished, normalized**: all **diam**, (410) **TS**, (235) **YS**, 22 **El**
MIL–S–22698A	Class B	US	Plate	0.21 **C**, 0.80–1.10 **Mn**, 0.04 **P**, 0.05 **S**	**Normalized**: ≥1/2–1 **diam**, 58 (400) **TS**, 32 (221) **YS**, 24 **El**
ANSI/ASTM A 131	Grade B	US	Plate, shapes, bar	0.21 **C**, 0.80–1.10 **Mn**, 0.04 **P**, 0.04 **S**, 0.35 **Si**	**Normalized**: all **diam**, (400) **TS**, (235) **YS**, 24 **El**
ANSI/ASTM A 131	Grade D	US	Plate, shapes, bar	0.21 **C**, 0.70–1.40 **Mn**, 0.04 **P**, 0.04 **S**, 0.10–0.35 **Si**	**Normalized**: all **diam**, (400) **TS**, (235) **YS**, 24 **El**
MIL–S–23495	Class B	US	Shapes: extruded	0.21 **C**, 0.80–1.10 **Mn**, 0.04 **P**, 0.05 **S**	**As extruded**: ≤1/2 to 1 3/8 **diam**, 58 (400) **TS**, 32 (221) **YS**, 24 **El**
DGN–B–206	Grade II	Mexico	Pipe: seamless	0.21 **C**, 0.90–1.35 **Mn**, 0.048 **P**, 0.058 **S**, 0.10 min **Si**	**Forged, hot finished, normalized**: (>9.53) **diam**, (382) **TS**, (206) **YS**, 35 **El**
ANSI/ASTM A524	Grade II	US	Pipe: seamless	0.21 **C**, 0.90–1.35 **Mn**, 0.048 **P**, 0.058 **S**, 0.10–0.40 **Si**	**Normalized**: ≤0.375 (≤95) **diam**, 55 (379) **TS**, 30 (207) **YS**, 35 **El**
ISO 4995	HR 275–B	ISO	Sheet	0.21 **C**, 0.050 **P**, 0.050 **S**	**Hot rolled**: (17) **diam**, (370) **TS**, (255) **YS**
TS 908	UDK 669.14.423/Fe 34	Turkey	Shapes	0.21 **C**, 0.063 **P**, 0.063 **S**	**Hot rolled**: all **diam**, (333) **TS**, (206) **YS**, 28 **El**
TS 909	UDK 669.14–423/Fe31	Turkey	Shapes	0.21 **C**, 0.063 **P**, 0.063 **S**	**Hot rolled**: all **diam**, (333) **TS**, (206) **YS**, 28 **El**

WROUGHT CARBON STEELS

specification number	designation	country	product forms	composition	mechanical properties (see page iv for explanation)
TS 913	UDK 669.14.423/Fe 34	Turkey	Bar	0.21 **C**, 0.063 **P**, 0.063 **S**	**Hot rolled**: all **diam**, (333) **TS**, (206) **YS**, 28 **El**
TS 912	UDK 669.14–423/Fe 34	Turkey	Shapes	0.21 **C**, 0.063 **P**, 0.063 **S**	**Hot rolled**: all **diam**, (333) **TS**, (206) **YS**, 28 **El**
CSA B193	Electrically welded, grade A	Canada	Pipe	0.21 **C**, 0.90 **Mn**, 0.04 **P**, 0.05 **S**	**Mill**: 0.250 (6.35) **diam**, 48 (331) **TS**, 30 (207) **YS**, 32 **El**
API Spec 5L	Grade A	US	Pipe: seamless	0.21 **C**, 0.90 **Mn**, 0.04 **P**, 0.05 **S**	**Mill**: all **diam**, 48 (331) **TS**, 30 (207) **YS**
API Spec 5L	Grade A	US	Pipe: electric weld or submerged arc weld	0.21 **C**, 0.90 **Mn**, 0.04 **P**, 0.05 **S**	**Mill**: all **diam**, 48 (331) **TS**, 30 (207) **YS**
API Spec 5L	Grade A	US	Pipe: electric weld, submerged arc weld or gas metal arc weld	0.21 **C**, 0.90 **Mn**, 0.04 **P**, 0.05 **S**	**As rolled**: ≥.497 (≥12.62) **diam**, 48 (331) **TS**, 30 (207) **YS**, 36 **El**
DIN 17100	USt 34–1 (1.0100)	Germany	Plate	0.21 **C**, 0.10 **P**, 0.063 **S**	**Normalized**: all **diam**, (330) **TS**, (205) **YS**, 28 **El**
DIN 17100	USt 34–1 (1.0100)	Germany	Strip	0.21 **C**, 0.10 **P**, 0.063 **S**	**Normalized**: all **diam**, (330) **TS**, (205) **YS**, 28 **El**; **Hot rolled**: all **diam**, (330) **TS**, (205) **YS**, 20 **El**
DIN 17100	USt 34–1 (1.0100)	Germany	Bar	0.21 **C**, 0.10 **P**, 0.063 **S**	**Normalized**: all **diam**, (330) **TS**, (205) **YS**, 28 **El**
API Spec 5L	Grade A25, class I	US	Pipe: seamless	0.21 **C**, 0.30–0.60 **Mn**, 0.045 **P**, 0.06 **S**	**Mill**: all **diam**, 45 (310) **TS**, 25 (172) **YS**
API Spec 5L	Grade A25, class II	US	Pipe: seamless	0.21 **C**, 0.30–0.60 **Mn**, 0.045–0.080 **P**, 0.06 **S**	**Mill**: all **diam**, 45 (310) **TS**, 25 (172) **YS**
API Spec 5L	Grade A 25, class I (electric weld only)	US	Pipe: electric weld or submerged arc weld	0.21 **C**, 0.30–0.60 **Mn**, 0.045 **P**, 0.06 **S**	**Mill**: all **diam**, 45 (310) **TS**, 25 (172) **YS**
API Spec 5L	Grade A 25, class II (electric weld only)	US	Pipe: electric weld or submerged arc weld	0.21 **C**, 0.30–0.60 **Mn**, 0.045–0.080 **P**, 0.06 **S**	**Mill**: all **diam**, 45 (310) **TS**, 25 (172) **YS**
API Spec 5L	Grade A 25, class I	US	Pipe: butt weld	0.21 **C**, 0.30–0.60 **Mn**, 0.045 **P**, 0.06 **S**	**Mill**: all **diam**, 45 (310) **TS**, 25 (172) **YS**
API Spec 5L	Grade A25, class II	US	Pipe: butt weld	0.21 **C**, 0.30–0.60 **Mn**, 0.045–0.080 **P**, 0.06 **S**	**Mill**: all **diam**, 45 (310) **TS**, 25 (172) **YS**
API Spec 5L	Grade A 25, class I	US	Pipe: seamless	0.21 **C**, 0.30–0.60 **Mn**, 0.045 **P**, 0.06 **S**	**As rolled**: ≥.497 (≥12.62) **diam**, 45 (310) **TS**, 25 (172) **YS**, 38 **El**
API Spec 5L	Grade A 25, class II	US	Pipe: seamless	0.21 **C**, 0.30–0.60 **Mn**, 0.045–0.080 **P**, 0.06 **S**	**As rolled**: ≥.497 (≥12.62) **diam**, 45 (310) **TS**, 25 (172) **YS**, 38 **El**
API Spec 5L	Grade A 25, class I (electric weld only)	US	Pipe: electric weld, submerged arc weld or gas metal arc weld	0.21 **C**, 0.30–0.60 **Mn**, 0.045 **P**, 0.06 **S**	**As rolled**: ≥.497 (≥12.62) **diam**, 45 (310) **TS**, 25 (172) **YS**, 38 **El**
API Spec 5L	Grade A 25, class II (electric–weld only)	US	Pipe: electric weld, submerged arc weld or gas metal arc weld	0.21 **C**, 0.30–0.60 **Mn**, 0.045–0.080 **P**, 0.06 **S**	**As rolled**: ≥.497 (≥12.62) **diam**, 45 (310) **TS**, 25 (172) **YS**, 38 **El**
API Spec 5L	Grade A25, class I	US	Pipe: butt weld	0.21 **C**, 0.30–0.60 **Mn**, 0.045 **P**, 0.06 **S**	**As rolled**: ≥.497 (≥12.62) **diam**, 45 (310) **TS**, 25 (172) **YS**, 38 **El**
API Spec 5L	Grade A25, class II	US	Pipe: butt weld	0.21 **C**, 0.30–0.60 **Mn**, 0.045–0.080 **P**, 0.06 **S**	**As rolled**: ≥.497 (≥12.62) **diam**, 45 (310) **TS**, 25 (172) **YS**, 38 **El**
BS 980	CEW–4	UK	Tube	0.20–0.40 **C**, 0.6 **Mn**, 0.060 **P**, 0.060 **S**	**Drawn or drawn, tempered**: all **diam**, (480) **TS**, (385) **YS**
BS 980	CDS–6	UK	Tube	0.20–0.40 **C**, 0.3–0.9 **Mn**, 0.050 **P**, 0.050 **S**, 0.35 **Si**	**Drawn or drawn and tempered**: all **diam**, (480) **TS**, (385) **YS**
JIS E 1104	For 6 kg rail	Japan	Plate	0.20–0.40 **C**, 0.40–0.80 **Mn**, 0.050 **P**, 0.050 **S**, 0.40 **Si**	**As agreed**: all **diam**, (441) **TS**, 18 **El**
JIS E 1104	For 9 kg rail	Japan	Plate	0.20–0.40 **C**, 0.40–0.80 **Mn**, 0.050 **P**, 0.050 **S**, 0.40 **Si**	**As agreed**: all **diam**, (441) **TS**, 18 **El**
JIS E 1104	For 10 kg rail	Japan	Plate	0.20–0.40 **C**, 0.40–0.80 **Mn**, 0.050 **P**, 0.050 **S**, 0.40 **Si**	**As agreed**: all **diam**, (441) **TS**, 18 **El**
JIS E 1104	For 12 kg rail	Japan	Plate	0.20–0.40 **C**, 0.40–0.80 **Mn**, 0.050 **P**, 0.050 **S**, 0.40 **Si**	**As agreed**: all **diam**, (441) **TS**, 18 **El**

specification number	designation	country	product forms	composition	mechanical properties (see page iv for explanation)
JIS E 1104	For 15 kg rail	Japan	Plate	0.20–0.40 **C**, 0.40–0.80 **Mn**, 0.050 **P**, 0.050 **S**, 0.40 **Si**	**As agreed**: all **diam**, (441) **TS**, 18 **El**
JIS E 1104	For 22 kg rail	Japan	Plate	0.20–0.40 **C**, 0.40–0.80 **Mn**, 0.050 **P**, 0.050 **S**, 0.40 **Si**	**As agreed**: all **diam**, (441) **TS**, 18 **El**
BS 980	CEW–3	UK	Tube	0.20–0.40 **C**, 0.6 **Mn**, 0.060 **P**, 0.060 **S**	**Annealed or normalised**: all **diam**, (360) **TS**, (220) **YS**
BS 980	CDS–5	UK	Tube	0.20–0.40 **C**, 0.3–0.9 **Mn**, 0.050 **P**, 0.050 **S**, 0.35 **Si**	**Annealed or normalized**: all **diam**, (360) **TS**, (220) **YS**
NF A 35–051	FM 26 grade 1	France	Wire, rod	0.20–0.33 **C**, 0.40–0.70 **Mn**, 0.080 **P**, 0.055 **S**, 0.10–0.35 **Si**	
NF A 35–564	XC 25 FF, 21 B 3 FF	France	Bar, wire, rod	0.20–0.30 **C**, 0.030 **P**, 0.030 **S**, 0.20 **Si**, 0.20 **Cu**, 0.020 **Al**	**Annealed**: ($\leq$70) **diam**, (490) max **TS**
BS 1717	CEW–104	UK	Tube: cold drawn, electric resistance butt welded	0.20–0.30 **C**, 0.6 **Mn**, 0.060 **P**, 0.060 **S**	**As drawn or as drawn and tempered**: all **diam**, (440) **TS**, (360) **YS**
BS 1717	CDS–104	UK	Tube	0.20–0.30 **C**, 0.3–0.9 **Mn**, 0.050 **P**, 0.050 **S**, 0.35 **Si**	**As drawn or as drawn and tempered**: all **diam**, (440) **TS**, (360) **YS**
BS 1717	CEW–103	UK	Tube: cold drawn electric resistance butt welded	0.20–0.30 **C**, 0.6 **Mn**, 0.060 **P**, 0.060 **S**	**Annealed or normalized**: all **diam**, (330) **TS**, (195) **YS**
BS 1717	CDS–103	UK	Tube	0.20–0.30 **C**, 0.3–0.9 **Mn**, 0.050 **P**, 0.050 **S**, 0.35 **Si**	**Annealed**: all **diam**, (330) **TS**, (195) **YS**; **Normalized**: all **diam**, (385) **TS**, (250) **YS**
AS 1446	Grade AS 1446/CS1025	Australia	Plate	0.20–0.30 **C**, 0.40–0.90 **Mn**, 0.060 **P**, 0.060 **S**, 0.35 **Si**	
ANSI/ASTM A 29	M 1025	US	Bar	0.20–0.30 **C**, 0.25–0.60 **Mn**, 0.04 **P**, 0.05 **S**	
ANSI/ASTM A 575	M1025	US	Bar	0.20–0.30 **C**, 0.25–0.60 **Mn**, 0.04 **P**, 0.05 **S**	
DGN–B–301	1023	Mexico	Bar	0.20–0.25 **C**, 0.30–0.60 **Mn**, 0.040 **P**, 0.050 **S**, 0.10 **Si**	**Forged or hot rolled, cold rolled and cold finished**: all **diam**, (431) **TS**, (216) **YS**, 25 **El**
BS 1449: Part 1	Grade 22	UK	Plate, sheet, strip	0.20–0.25 **C**, 0.40–0.60 **Mn**, 0.050 **P**, 0.050 **S**	**Cold rolled, annealed**: all **diam**, (370) **TS**, (200) **YS**, 25 **El**
AISI 1023		US	Bar	0.20–0.25 **C**, 0.30–0.60 **Mn**, 0.040 **P**, 0.050 **S**	
BS 970: Part 1	040A22	UK	Blooms, billets, slabs, bar, rod, forgings	0.20–0.25 **C**, 0.30–0.50 **Mn**	
BS 970: Part 1	050A22	UK	Blooms, billets, slabs, bar, rod, forgings	0.20–0.25 **C**, 0.40–0.60 **Mn**	
BS 970: Part 1	060A22	UK	Blooms, billets, slabs, bar, rod, forgings	0.20–0.25 **C**, 0.50–0.70 **Mn**	
BS 970: Part 1	080A22	UK	Blooms, billets, slabs, bar, rod, forgings	0.20–0.25 **C**, 0.70–0.90 **Mn**	
COPANT 333	1023	COPANT	Wire, rod	0.20–0.25 **C**, 0.30–0.60 **Mn**, 0.040 **P**, 0.050 **S**	
ANSI/ASTM A 575	1023	US	Bar	0.20–0.25 **C**, 0.30–0.60 **Mn**, 0.04 **P**, 0.05 **S**	
AISI 1023		US	Wire, rod	0.20–0.25 **C**, 0.30–0.60 **Mn**, 0.040 **P**, 0.050 **S**	
ANSI/ASTM A 576	1023	US	Bar	0.20–0.25 **C**, 0.30–0.60 **Mn**, 0.040 **P**, 0.050 **S**	
ASTM A 689	1023	US	Bar	0.20–0.25 **C**, 0.30–0.60 **Mn**, 0.040 **P**, 0.050 **S**	
ANSI/ASTM A 29	1023	US	Bar	0.20–0.25 **C**, 0.30–0.60 **Mn**, 0.040 **P**, 0.050 **S**	
JIS G 3108	Type 4	Japan	Bar	0.20–0.25 **C**, 0.30–0.60 **Mn**, 0.045 **P**, 0.045 **S**	
JIS G 3505	SWRM 22	Japan	Wire, rod	0.20–0.25 **C**, 0.30–0.60 **Mn**, 0.045 **P**, 0.045 **S**	
JIS G 4051	S 22C	Japan	Bar, wire, rod	0.20–0.25 **C**, 0.30–0.60 **Mn**, 0.030 **P**, 0.035 **S**, 0.15–0.35 **Si**, 0.30 **Cu**	

WROUGHT CARBON STEELS

specification number	designation	country	product forms	composition	mechanical properties (see page iv for explanation)
ASTM A 611	Grade E	US	Sheet	0.20 **C**, 0.60 **Mn**, 0.04 **P**, 0.04 **S**	**Cold rolled**: all **diam**, 82 (570) **TS**, 80 (550) **YS**
ANSI/ASTM A 611	Grade E	US	Sheet	0.20 **C**, 0.60 **Mn**, 0.04 **P**, 0.04 **S**	**Cold rolled**: all **diam**, 82 (570) **TS**, 80 (550) **YS**
ANSI/ASTM A 446	Grade E	US	Sheet	0.20 **C**, 0.04 **P**, 0.04 **S**	**Hot rolled, hot dip galvanized**: all **diam**, 82 (570) **TS**, 80 (550) **YS**
DGN-B-348	Grade E	Mexico	Sheet	0.20 **C**, 0.60 **Mn**, 0.040 **P**, 0.040 **S**, 0.20 min **Cu**	**Cold rolled**: all **diam**, (564) **TS**, (549) **YS**
ANSI/ASTM A 678	Grade B	US	Plate	0.20 **C**, 0.70–1.35 **Mn**, 0.04 **P**, 0.05 **S**, 0.15–0.50 **Si**	**Hot rolled, quenched and tempered**: ≤0.75 **diam**, (552) **TS**, (414) **YS**, 22 **El**
ISO 4997	Grade CH550	ISO	Sheet	0.20 **C**, 1.50 **Mn**, 0.050 **P**, 0.050 **S**	**Cold rolled and annealed**: all **diam**, (550) **TS**, (550) **YS**
IS 961	Fe 540W–HT (St55–HTw)	India	Plate, bar	0.20 **C**, 0.055 **P**, 0.055 **S**	**Mill**: 6–16 **diam**, (540) **TS**, (350) **YS**, 20 **El**
JIS G 3116	Class 4	Japan	Sheet, plate, strip	0.20 **C**, 1.50 **Mn**, 0.040 **P**, 0.040 **S**, 0.55 **Si**	**Hot rolled**: (2.3–6.0) **diam**, (539) **TS**, (363) **YS**, 20 **El**
SIS 14 21 42	SIS 21 42–01	Sweden	Bar, forgings, plate, sheet	0.20 **C**, 1.08 **Mn**, 0.035 **P**, 0.035 **S**, 0.05 **Si**, 0.02 **N**	**Normalized**: all **diam**, (530) **TS**, (390) **YS**, 20 **El**
SIS 14 21 42	SIS 21 42–03	Sweden	Tube: seamless	0.20 **C**, 1.08 **Mn**, 0.035 **P**, 0.035 **S**, 0.05 **Si**, 0.02 **N**	**Normalized**: (<20) **diam**, (530) **TS**, (390) **YS**, 20 **El**
SIS 14 21 44	SIS 21 44–04	Sweden	Tube: welded	0.20 **C**, 1.8 **Mn**, 0.035 **P**, 0.035 **S**, 0.5 **Si**, 0.02 **N**	**Normalized**: (<20) **diam**, (530) **TS**, (390) **YS**, 20 **El**
SIS 14 21 44	SIS 21 44–04	Sweden	Tube: welded	0.20 **C**, 1.8 **Mn**, 0.035 **P**, 0.035 **S**, 0.5 **Si**, 0.02 **N**	**Normalized**: (<20) **diam**, (530) **TS**, (390) **YS**, 20 **El**
SIS 14 21 44	SIS 21 44–03	Sweden	Tube: seamless	0.20 **C**, 1.8 **Mn**, 0.035 **P**, 0.035 **S**, 0.5 **Si**, 0.02 **N**	**Normalized**: (<20) **diam**, (530) **TS**, (390) **YS**, 20 **El**
SIS 14 21 44	SIS 21 44–01	Sweden	Bar, forgings, plate, sheet	0.20 **C**, 1.8 **Mn**, 0.035 **P**, 0.035 **S**, 0.5 **Si**, 0.02 **N**	**Normalized**: all **diam**, (530) **TS**, (390) **YS**, 20 **El**
SIS 14 21 45	SIS 21 45–01	Sweden	Bar, forgings, plate, sheet	0.20 **C**, 1.8 **Mn**, 0.035 **P**, 0.035 **S**, 0.5 **Si**, 0.02 **N**	**Normalized**: all **diam**, (530) **TS**, (390) **YS**, 20 **El**
SIS 14 21 43	SIS 21 43–01	Sweden	Bar, forgings, plate, sheet	0.20 **C**, 1.8 **Mn**, 0.035 **P**, 0.035 **S**, 0.5 **Si**, 0.02 **N**	**Normalized**: all **diam**, (530) **TS**, (390) **YS**, 20 **El**
ISO 4996	Grade HS460–C	ISO	Sheet: hot rolled	0.20 **C**, 1.70 **Mn**, 0.040 **P**, 0.040 **S**, 0.50 **Si**	**As rolled**: all **diam**, (530) **TS**, (440) **YS**, 12 **El**
ISO 4996	Grade HS460–D	ISO	Sheet: hot rolled	0.20 **C**, 1.70 **Mn**, 0.035 **P**, 0.035 **S**, 0.50 **Si**	**As rolled**: all **diam**, (530) **TS**, (440) **YS**, 12 **El**
SFS 256	Fe 390	Finland	Sheet, strip, bar	0.20 **C**, 1.0–1.8 **Mn**, 0.035 **P**, 0.035 **S**, 0.55 **Si**, 0.02–0.20 **V**, 0.015–0.060 **Nb**, 0.02–0.20 **Ti**, 0.015–0.080 **Al**, 0.020 **N**	**Normalized**: (<60) **diam**, (520) **TS**, (390) **YS**, 20 **El**
SFS 1150	Fe 390 P	Finland	Plate, strip, bar	0.20 **C**, 1.0–1.8 **Mn**, 0.030 **P**, 0.030 **S**, 0.15–0.50 **Si**, 0.03–0.15 **V**, 0.015–0.060 **Nb**, 0.02–0.20 **Ti**, 0.015–0.080 **Al**, 0.015 **N**	**Hot rolled**: (<60) **diam**, (520) **TS**, (390) **YS**, 20 **El**
JIS G 3106	Class 4B	Japan	Plate, strip, shape, bar	0.20 **C**, 1.50 **Mn**, 0.040 **P**, 0.040 **S**, 0.55 **Si**	**Hot rolled**: (≤5) **diam**, (520) **TS**, (363) **YS**, 19 **El**
JIS G 3106	Class 4C	Japan	Plate, strip	0.20 **C**, 1.50 **Mn**, 0.040 **P**, 0.040 **S**, 0.55 **Si**	**Hot rolled**: (≤5) **diam**, (520) **TS**, (363) **YS**, 19 **El**
NS 12153	NS 12153–01	Norway	Bar, rod, shapes	0.20 **C**, 1.50 **Mn**, 0.045 **P**, 0.045 **S**, 0.55 **Si**, 0.009 **N**	**Normalized**: (16) **diam**, (510) **TS**, (353) **YS**, 22 **El**
NS 12153	NS 12153–00	Norway	Bar, rod, shapes	0.20 **C**, 1.50 **Mn**, 0.045 **P**, 0.045 **S**, 0.55 **Si**, 0.009 **N**	**Hot worked**: (16) **diam**, (510) **TS**, (353) **YS**, 22 **El**
SIS 14 21 34	SIS 21 34–04	Sweden	Tube: welded	0.20 **C**, 1.6 **Mn**, 0.035 **P**, 0.035 **S**, 0.5 **Si**, 0.02 **N**	**Normalized**: (<20) **diam**, (510) **TS**, (350) **YS**, 22 **El**
SIS 14 21 34	SIS 21 34–03	Sweden	Tube: seamless	0.20 **C**, 1.6 **Mn**, 0.035 **P**, 0.035 **S**, 0.5 **Si**, 0.02 **N**	**Normalized**: (<20) **diam**, (510) **TS**, (350) **YS**, 22 **El**
SIS 14 21 34	SIS 21 34–01	Sweden	Bar, forgings, plate, sheet	0.20 **C**, 1.6 **Mn**, 0.035 **P**, 0.035 **S**, 0.5 **Si**, 0.02 **N**	**Normalized**: all **diam**, (510) **TS**, (350) **YS**, 22 **El**
SIS 14 21 33	SIS 21 33–01	Sweden	Bar, forgings, plate, sheet	0.20 **C**, 1.6 **Mn**, 0.035 **P**, 0.035 **S**, 0.5 **Si**, 0.02 **N**	**Normalized**: all **diam**, (510) **TS**, (350) **YS**, 22 **El**
SIS 14 21 35	SIS 21 35–01	Sweden	Bar, forgings, plate, sheet	0.20 **C**, 1.6 **Mn**, 0.035 **P**, 0.035 **S**, 0.5 **Si**, 0.02 **N**	**Normalized**: all **diam**, (510) **TS**, (350) **YS**, 22 **El**
SIS 14 21 32	SIS 21 32–04	Sweden	Tube: welded	0.20 **C**, 1.6 **Mn**, 0.035 **P**, 0.035 **S**, 0.5 **Si**, 0.02 **N**	**Normalized**: (<20) **diam**, (510) **TS**, (350) **YS**, 22 **El**
SIS 14 21 32	SIS 21 32–03	Sweden	Tube: seamless	0.20 **C**, 1.6 **Mn**, 0.035 **P**, 0.035 **S**, 0.5 **Si**, 0.02 **N**	**Normalized**: (<20) **diam**, (510) **TS**, (350) **YS**, 22 **El**

WROUGHT CARBON STEELS

specification number	designation	country	product forms	composition	mechanical properties (see page iv for explanation)
SIS 14 21 32	SIS 21 32–01	Sweden	Bar, forgings, plate, sheet	0.20 **C**, 1.6 **Mn**, 0.035 **P**, 0.035 **S**, 0.5 **Si**, 0.02 **N**	**Normalized**: all **diam**, (510) **TS**, (350) **YS**, 22 **El**
NBN 629	D 52–1	Belgium	Strip	0.20 **C**, 0.90–1.50 **Mn**, 0.050 **P**, 0.050 **S**, 0.50 **Si**	**As rolled**: (3–63) **diam**, (510) **TS**, (325) **YS**, 21 **El**
NBN 629	D 52–2	Belgium	Strip	0.20 **C**, 0.90–1.50 **Mn**, 0.040 **P**, 0.040 **S**, 0.10–0.50 **Si**	**As rolled**: (3–63) **diam**, (510) **TS**, (355) **YS**, 21 **El**
NBN 630	E 52–1	Belgium	Strip	0.20 **C**, 0.90–1.50 **Mn**, 0.050 **P**, 0.050 **S**, 0.50 **Si**	**As rolled**: (3–63) **diam**, (510) **TS**, (325) **YS**, 21 **El**
NBN 630	E 52–2	Belgium	Strip	0.20 **C**, 0.90–1.50 **Mn**, 0.040 **P**, 0.040 **S**, 0.10–0.50 **Si**, 0.40 **Cr**	**As rolled**: (3–40) **diam**, (510) **TS**, (355) **YS**, 21 **El**
DIN 2391 Part 2	Grade St 52.2–1.0832	Germany	Tube	0.20 **C**, 1.5 **Mn**, 0.05 **P**, 0.05 **S**, 0.10–0.55 **Si**	**Normalized**: all **diam**, (510) **TS**, (353) **YS**, 22 **El**; **Annealed**: all **diam**, (490) **TS**, 24 **El**
AIR 9160/C27	9160C051	France	Sheet	0.20 **C**, 1.50 **Mn**, 0.040 **P**, 0.040 **S**, 0.55 **Si**	**Normalized**: (≤3) **diam**, (510) **TS**, (350) **YS**, 19 **El**
TS 346	Fe 52	Turkey	Pipe: seamless	0.20 **C**, 1.50 **Mn**, 0.050 **P**, 0.050 **S**, 0.55 **Si**	**As drawn**: (≤16) **diam**, (510) **TS**, (353) **YS**, 22 **El**
DIN 1629, Part 4	Grade St52.4/1.0832	Germany	Tube: seamless	0.20 **C**, 1.5 **Mn**, 0.05 **P**, 0.05 **S**, 0.10–0.55 **Si**	**Annealed**: (<16) **diam**, (510) **TS**, (350) **YS**, 22 **El**
DIN 1629, Part 3	Grade St52/1.0831	Germany	Tube: seamless	0.20 **C**, 1.50 **Mn**, 0.05 **P**, 0.05 **S**, 0.55 **Si**	**Annealed**: (<16) **diam**, (510) **TS**, (350) **YS**, 22 **El**
SFS 2147	Fe 52	Finland	Tube: seamless	0.20 **C**, 1.50 **Mn**, 0.05 **P**, 0.05 **S**, 0.55 **Si**	**As drawn**: (≤16) **diam**, (510) **TS**, (333) **YS**, 22 **El**
DIN 1623 Sheet 2	St 52–3 (1.0841.6)	Germany	Sheet	0.20 **C**, 0.050 **P**, 0.050 **S**	**Hot or cold rolled**: all **diam**, (510) **TS**, (355) **YS**, 16 in 80 mm **El**
DIN 17135	Grade A St 52	Germany	Plate, strip, tube, bar, forgings	0.20 **C**, 1.5 **Mn**, 0.045 **P**, 0.045 **S**, 0.55 **Si**	**Normalized**: (≤16) **diam**, (510) **TS**, (353) **YS**, 22 **El**
BS 1449: Part 1	Grade 50/35	UK	Plate, sheet, strip	0.20 **C**, 1.50 **Mn**, 0.050 **P**, 0.050 **S**	**Hot rolled**: all **diam**, (500) **TS**, (350) **YS**, 20 **El**
BS 1449: Part 1	Grade 50/45	UK	Plate, sheet, strip	0.20 **C**, 1.50 **Mn**, 0.040 **P**, 0.040 **S**	**Hot rolled**: all **diam**, (500) **TS**, (450) **YS**, 22 **El**
DIN 488	BSt 42/50 RK	Germany	Bar	0.20 **C**, 0.06 **P**, 0.05 **S**, 0.60 **Si**, 0.007 **N**	**Cold worked**: (6–28) **diam**, (500) **TS**, (420) **YS**, 10 **El**
SFS 200:E	Fe 52D	Finland	Bar, plate, strip, wire, forgings	0.20 **C**, 1.50 **Mn**, 0.045 **P**, 0.045 **S**, 0.55 **Si**, 0.009 **N**	**Hot worked and normalized**: (≤16) **diam**, (490) **TS**, (353) **YS**, 22 **El**
SFS 200:E	Fe 52C	Finland	Bar, plate, strip, wire, forgings	0.20 **C**, 1.50 **Mn**, 0.045 **P**, 0.045 **S**, 0.55 **Si**, 0.009 **N**	**Hot worked**: (≤16) **diam**, (490) **TS**, (353) **YS**, 22 **El**
DS 12011	St 50 B	Denmark	Rod, bar, shapes	0.20 **C**, 0.050 **P**, 0.050 **S**, 0.50 **Si**, 0.40 **Cu**, 0.30 **Cr**, 0.009 **N**	**Hot rolled**: (16) **diam**, (490) **TS**, (314) **YS**, 21 **El**
SS 14 21 72	SS 21 72–00	Sweden	Bar, plate, sheet	0.20 **C**, 1.0–1.6 **Mn**, 0.050 **P**, 0.050 **S**, 0.050 **Si**, 0.040 **Cu**, 0.030 **Cr**, 0.009 **N**	**As rolled**: all **diam**, (490) **TS**, (310) **YS**, 21 **El**
SS 14 21 72	SS 21 72–00	Sweden	Bar, plate, sheet	0.20 **C**, 1.0–1.6 **Mn**, 0.050 **P**, 0.050 **S**, 0.050 **Si**, 0.040 **Cu**, 0.030 **Cr**, 0.009 **N**	**As rolled**: all **diam**, (490) **TS**, (310) **YS**, 21 **El**
SS 14 21 72	SS 21 72–04	Sweden	Tube: welded	0.20 **C**, 1.0–1.6 **Mn**, 0.050 **P**, 0.050 **S**, 0.050 **Si**, 0.040 **Cu**, 0.030 **Cr**, 0.009 **N**	**Annealed**: (<5) **diam**, (490) **TS**, (330) **YS**, 21 **El**
SS 14 21 72	SS 21 72–03	Sweden	Tube: seamless	0.20 **C**, 1.0–1.6 **Mn**, 0.050 **P**, 0.050 **S**, 0.050 **Si**, 0.040 **Cu**, 0.030 **Cr**, 0.009 **N**	**As rolled or annealed**: (<5) **diam**, (490) **TS**, (330) **YS**, 21 **El**
SS 14 21 72	SS 21 72–04	Sweden	Tube: welded	0.20 **C**, 1.0–1.6 **Mn**, 0.05 **P**, 0.05 **S**, 0.05 **Si**, 0.04 **Cu**, 0.03 **Cr**, 0.009 **N**	**Annealed**: (<5) **diam**, (490) **TS**, (330) **YS**, 21 **El**
SS 14 21 72	SS 21 72–03	Sweden	Tube: seamless	0.20 **C**, 1.0–1.6 **Mn**, 0.05 **P**, 0.05 **S**, 0.05 **Si**, 0.04 **Cu**, 0.03 **Cr**, 0.009 **N**	**As rolled or annealed**: (<5) **diam**, (490) **TS**, (330) **YS**, 21 **El**
JIS G 3116	Class 3	Japan	Sheet, plate, strip	0.20 **C**, 1.50 **Mn**, 0.040 **P**, 0.040 **S**, 0.55 **Si**	**Hot rolled**: (2.3–6.0) **diam**, (490) **TS**, (324) **YS**, 22 **El**
JIS G 3106	Class 2A	Japan	Plate, strip, shape, bar	0.20 **C**, 1.50 **Mn**, 0.040 **P**, 0.040 **S**, 0.55 **Si**	**Hot rolled**: (≤5) **diam**, (490) **TS**, (324) **YS**, 22 **El**
JIS G 3106	Class 3A	Japan	Plate, strip, shape, bar	0.20 **C**, 1.50 **Mn**, 0.040 **P**, 0.040 **S**, 0.55 **Si**	**Hot rolled**: (≤5) **diam**, (490) **TS**, (363) **YS**, 19 **El**
JIS G 3106	Class 3B	Japan	Plate, strip, shape, bar	0.20 **C**, 1.50 **Mn**, 0.040 **P**, 0.040 **S**, 0.55 **Si**	**Hot rolled**: (≤5) **diam**, (490) **TS**, (363) **YS**, 19 **El**

WROUGHT CARBON STEELS

specification number	designation	country	product forms	composition	mechanical properties (see page iv for explanation)
ISO 4996	Grade HS420–C	ISO	Sheet: hot rolled	0.20 **C**, 1.70 **Mn**, 0.040 **P**, 0.040 **S**, 0.50 **Si**	**As rolled**: all **diam**, (490) **TS**, (400) **YS**, 14 **El**
ISO 4996	Grade HS420–D	ISO	Sheet: hot rolled	0.20 **C**, 1.70 **Mn**, 0.035 **P**, 0.035 **S**, 0.50 **Si**	**As rolled**: all **diam**, (490) **TS**, (400) **YS**, 14 **El**
ANSI/ASTM A 709	Grade 50W	US	Plate, bar, shapes	0.20 **C**, 1.35 **Mn**, 0.04 **P**, 0.05 **S**	**Annealed**: ≤4 (≤102) **diam**, (485) **TS**, (345) **YS**, 21 **El**
ANSI/ASTM A 588	Grade B	US	Plate, bar, shapes	0.20 **C**, 0.75–1.25 **Mn**, 0.04 **P**, 0.05 **S**, 0.15–0.30 **Si**, 0.20–0.40 **Cu**, 0.01–0.10 **V**, 0.40–0.70 **Cr**, 0.25–0.50 **Ni**	**Hot rolled (plate, bar)**: <4.0 **diam**, (485) **TS**, (345) **YS**, 21 **El**
ANSI/ASTM A 588	Grade G	US	Plate, bar, shapes	0.20 **C**, 1.20 **Mn**, 0.04 **P**, 0.05 **S**, 0.25–0.70 **Si**, 0.30–0.50 **Cu**, 0.07 **Ti**, 0.50–1.00 **Cr**, 0.10 **Mo**, 0.80 **Ni**	**Hot rolled (plate, bar)**: <4.0 **diam**, (485) **TS**, (345) **YS**, 21 **El**
ANSI/ASTM A 588	Grade H	US	Plate, bar, shapes	0.20 **C**, 1.25 **Mn**, 0.035 **P**, 0.040 **S**, 0.25–0.75 **Si**, 0.20–0.35 **Cu**, 0.02–0.10 **V**, 0.005–0.030 **Ti**, 0.10–0.25 **Cr**, 0.15 **Mo**, 0.30–0.60 **Ni**	**Hot rolled (plate, bar)**: <4.0 **diam**, (485) **TS**, (345) **YS**, 21 **El**
ANSI/ASTM A 588	Grade J	US	Plate, bar, shapes	0.20 **C**, 0.60–1.00 **Mn**, 0.04 **P**, 0.05 **S**, 0.30–0.50 **Si**, 0.30 min **Cu**, 0.03–0.05 **Ti**, 0.50–0.70 **Ni**	**Hot rolled (plate, bar)**: <4.0 **diam**, (485) **TS**, (345) **YS**, 21 **El**
ANSI/ASTM A 633	Grade C	US	Plate, bar, shapes	0.20 **C**, 1.15–1.50 **Mn**, 0.04 **P**, 0.05 **S**, 0.15–0.50 **Si**, 0.01–0.05 **Nb**	**Normalized**: ≤2.5 **diam**, 70 (480) **TS**, 50 (345) **YS**, 23 **El**
ANSI/ASTM A 633	Grade D	US	Plate, bar, shapes	0.20 **C**, 1.00–1.60 **Mn**, 0.04 **P**, 0.05 **S**, 0.15–0.50 **Si**, 0.35 **Cu**, 0.25 **Cr**, 0.08 **Mo**, 0.25 **Ni**	**Normalized**: ≤2.5 **diam**, 70 (480) **TS**, 50 (345) **YS**, 23 **El**
JIS G 3445	Class 12C, No. 12	Japan	Tube: seamless or welded	0.20 **C**, 0.25–0.60 **Mn**, 0.040 **P**, 0.040 **S**, 0.35 **Si**	**As manufactured and cold finished**: (≥8) **diam**, (471) **TS**, (353) **YS**, 20 **El**
NBN 629	D 47–1	Belgium	Strip	0.20 **C**, 0.60–1.40 **Mn**, 0.050 **P**, 0.050 **S**, 0.35 **Si**	**As rolled**: (3–63) **diam**, (460) **TS**, (275) **YS**, 22 **El**
NBN 630	E 47–1	Belgium	Strip	0.20 **C**, 0.60–1.40 **Mn**, 0.050 **P**, 0.050 **S**, 0.35 **Si**	**As rolled**: (3–63) **diam**, (460) **TS**, (275) **YS**, 22 **El**
NBN 630	E 47–2	Belgium	Strip	0.20 **C**, 0.60–1.40 **Mn**, 0.040 **P**, 0.040 **S**, 0.10–0.35 **Si**	**As rolled**: (3–40) **diam**, (460) **TS**, (295) **YS**, 22 **El**
ISO 2604/III	No. TW15	ISO	Tube	0.20 **C**, 0.80–1.40 **Mn**, 0.045 **P**, 0.045 **S**, 0.35 **Si**	**As welded, annealed, normalized**: all **diam**, (460) **TS**, (265) **YS**, 21 **El**
ISO 2604/IV	P11	ISO	Plate	0.20 **C**, 0.60–1.40 **Mn**, 0.050 **P**, 0.050 **S**, 0.40 **Si**, 0.009 **N**	**Hot rolled, normalized**: (3–16) **diam**, (460) **TS**, (285) **YS**, 22 **El**
ISO 2604/IV	P13	ISO	Plate	0.20 **C**, 0.60–1.40 **Mn**, 0.040 **P**, 0.040 **S**, 0.40 **Si**, 0.015 min Al_{met}	**Hot rolled, normalized**: (3–16) **diam**, (460) **TS**, (295) **YS**, 22 **El**
ISO 2604/IV	P15	ISO	Plate	0.20 **C**, 0.60–1.50 **Mn**, 0.040 **P**, 0.040 **S**, 0.40 **Si**, 0.015 min Al_{met}	**Hot rolled, normalized**: (3–16) **diam**, (460) **TS**, (295) **YS**, 22 **El**
BS 1501–223	Grade 30	UK	Plate	0.20 **C**, 0.90–1.50 **Mn**, 0.050 **P**, 0.050 **S**, 0.10–0.55 **Si**, 0.01–0.08 **Nb**; 0.70 max other elements, total	**Normalized**: ≤(16) **diam**, (460) **TS**, (315) **YS**, 45 **El**
BS 1501–224	Grade 30	UK	Plate	0.20 **C**, 0.90–1.50 **Mn**, 0.050 **P**, 0.050 **S**, 0.10–0.55 **Si**, 0.70 max other elements, total	**Normalized**: ≤(16) **diam**, (460) **TS**, (305) **YS**, 45 **El**
ISO 2604/11	TS 15	ISO	Tube: seamless	0.20 **C**, .80–1.40 **Mn**, 0.045 **P**, 0.045 **S**, ≤0.35 **Si**, 0.015 Al_{met}	**Hot finished, annealed, normalized**: all **diam**, (460) **TS**, (265) **YS**, 21 **El**
DIN 1652	St 37 (1.0120)	Germany	Bar	0.20 **C**, 0.08 **P**, 0.05 **S**	**Cold drawn**: all **diam**, (460) **TS**, (315) **YS**, 9 in 80 mm **El**; **Centerless turned and solution annealed**: all **diam**, (330) **TS**, (195) **YS**, 25 in 80 mm **El**; **Centerless turned and normalized**: all **diam**, (360) **TS**, (215) **YS**, 25 in 80 mm **El**

WROUGHT CARBON STEELS

specification number	designation	country	product forms	composition	mechanical properties (see page iv for explanation)
DIN 1652	St 37–2 (1.0161)	Germany	Bar	0.20 **C**, 0.06 **P**, 0.05 **S**	**Cold drawn**: all **diam**, (460) **TS**, (315) **YS**, 9 in 80 mm **El**; **Centerless turned and solution annealed**: all **diam**, (330) **TS**, (195) **YS**, 25 in 80 mm **El**; **Centerless turned and normalized**: all **diam**, (360) **TS**, (215) **YS**, 25 in 80 mm **El**
ISO 4996	Grade HS390–C	ISO	Sheet: hot rolled	0.20 **C**, 1.60 **Mn**, 0.040 **P**, 0.040 **S**, 0.50 **Si**	**As rolled**: all **diam**, (460) **TS**, (370) **YS**, 16 **El**
ISO 4996	Grade HS390–D	ISO	Sheet: hot rolled	0.20 **C**, 1.60 **Mn**, 0.035 **P**, 0.035 **S**, 0.50 **Si**	**As rolled**: all **diam**, (460) **TS**, (370) **YS**, 16 **El**
SS 14 13 12 E	SS 13 12–07	Sweden	Tube: seamless	0.20 **C**, 0.4–0.7 **Mn**, 0.06 **P**, 0.05 **S**, 0.05 **Si**, 0.009 **N**	**Cold worked**: (≤5) **diam**, (450) **TS**, (410) **YS**, 11 **El**
SS 14 13 12 E	SS 13 12–07	Sweden	Tube: seamless	0.20 **C**, 0.4–0.7 **Mn**, 0.06 **P**, 0.05 **S**, 0.25 **Si**, 0.009 **N**	**Cold worked**: (≤5) **diam**, (450) **TS**, (410) **YS**, 11 **El**
ASTM A 714	Grade V Type E, S	US	Pipe: welded, seamless	0.20 **C**, 0.35–1.06 **Mn**, 0.045 **P**, 0.050 **S**, 0.75–1.25 **Cu**, 1.60–2.24 **Ni**	**As rolled**: all **diam**, 65 (448) **TS**, 46 (317) **YS**
JIS G 3116	Class 2	Japan	Sheet, plate, strip	0.20 **C**, 1.00 **Mn**, 0.040 **P**, 0.040 **S**, 0.35 **Si**	**Hot rolled**: (2.3–6.0) **diam**, (441) **TS**, (294) **YS**, 26 **El**
SS 14 13 12 E	SS 13 12–06	Sweden	Bar	0.20 **C**, 0.4–0.7 **Mn**, 0.06 **P**, 0.05 **S**, 0.05 **Si**, 0.009 **N**	**Cold worked**: (≤50) **diam**, (440) **TS**, (370) **YS**, 11 **El**
SS 14 13 12 E	SS 13 12–06	Sweden	Bar	0.20 **C**, 0.4–0.7 **Mn**, 0.06 **P**, 0.05 **S**, 0.25 **Si**, 0.009 **N**	**Cold worked**: (≤50) **diam**, (440) **TS**, (370) **YS**, 11 **El**
SFS 200:E	Fe 44B	Finland	Bar, plate, strip, wire, forgings	0.20 **C**, 0.50 **P**, 0.050 **S**, 0.55 **Si**, 0.009 **N**	**Hot worked**: (>40–100) **diam**, (431) **TS**, (265) **YS**, 23 **El**
SIS 14 14 11 E	SIS 14 11–00	Sweden	Bar, sheet	0.20 **C**, 0.3–0.6 **Mn**, 0.08 **P**, 0.06 **S**, 0.02 **Si**	**As rolled**: all **diam**, (430) **TS**, (260) **YS**, 23 **El**
SS 14 13 12 E	SS 14 12–03	Sweden	Tube: seamless	0.20 **C**, 0.4–0.7 **Mn**, 0.06 **P**, 0.05 **S**, 0.05 **Si**	**As rolled or annealed**: (<5) **diam**, (430) **TS**, (270) **YS**, 22 **El**
SS 14 13 12 E	SS 14 12–04	Sweden	Tube: welded	0.20 **C**, 0.4–0.7 **Mn**, 0.06 **P**, 0.05 **S**, 0.05 **Si**	**Annealed**: (<5) **diam**, (430) **TS**, (270) **YS**, 22 **El**
SS 14 13 12 E	SS 14 12–00	Sweden	Bar, plate, sheet	0.20 **C**, 0.4–0.7 **Mn**, 0.06 **P**, 0.05 **S**, 0.05 **Si**	**As rolled**: all **diam**, (430) **TS**, (260) **YS**, 23 **El**
SS 14 13 12 E	SS 14 12–04	Sweden	Tube: welded	0.20 **C**, 0.4–0.7 **Mn**, 0.06 **P**, 0.05 **S**, 0.25 **Si**, 0.009 **N**	**Annealed**: (<5) **diam**, (430) **TS**, (270) **YS**, 22 **El**
SS 14 13 12 E	SS 14 12–03	Sweden	Tube: seamless	0.20 **C**, 0.4–0.7 **Mn**, 0.06 **P**, 0.05 **S**, 0.25 **Si**, 0.009 **N**	**As rolled or annealed**: (<5) **diam**, (430) **TS**, (270) **YS**, 22 **El**
SS 14 13 12 E	SS 14 12–00	Sweden	Bar, plate, sheet	0.20 **C**, 0.4–0.7 **Mn**, 0.06 **P**, 0.05 **S**, 0.25 **Si**, 0.009 **N**	**As rolled**: all **diam**, (430) **TS**, (260) **YS**, 23 **El**
BS T.62		UK	Tube: aircraft quality	0.20 **C**, 0.80 **Mn**, 0.040 **P**, 0.040 **S**, 0.10–0.35 **Si**	**Tempered and annealed**: all **diam**, (430) **TS**, (370) **YS**
SIS 14 21 22	SIS 21 22	Sweden	Sheet	0.20 **C**, 1.5 **Mn**, 0.05 **P**, 0.05 **S**	**Zinc coated**: (≤3) **diam**, (430) **TS**, (350) **YS**, 14 **El**
ISO 4996	Grade HS355–C	ISO	Sheet: hot rolled	0.20 **C**, 1.60 **Mn**, 0.040 **P**, 0.040 **S**, 0.50 **Si**	**As rolled**: all **diam**, (430) **TS**, (335) **YS**, 18 **El**
ISO 4996	Grade HS355–D	ISO	Sheet: hot rolled	0.20 **C**, 1.60 **Mn**, 0.035 **P**, 0.035 **S**, 0.50 **Si**	**As rolled**: all **diam**, (430) **TS**, (335) **YS**, 18 **El**
AS 1594	Grade AS 1594/Hr 340	Australia	Sheet, strip	0.20 **C**, 0.90 **Mn**, 0.040 **P**, 0.040 **S**	**Hot rolled**: ≥3 **diam**, (420) **TS**, (340) **YS**, 18 **El**
NF A 36–101	A 42,3	France	Strip	0.20 **C**, 0.050 **P**, 0.050 **S**	**Hot rolled**: all **diam**, (412) **TS**, (255) **YS**, 26 **El**
NF A 36–101	A 42,4	France	Strip	0.20 **C**, 0.045 **P**, 0.045 **S**	**Hot rolled**: all **diam**, (412) **TS**, (255) **YS**, 28 **El**
NBN 629	D 42–1	Belgium	Strip	0.20 **C**, 0.50–1.30 **Mn**, 0.050 **P**, 0.050 **S**, 0.35 **Si**	**As rolled**: (3–63) **diam**, (410) **TS**, (255) **YS**, 24 **El**
NBN 629	D 42–2	Belgium	Strip	0.20 **C**, 0.50–1.30 **Mn**, 0.040 **P**, 0.040 **S**, 0.10–0.35 **Si**	**As rolled**: (3–63) **diam**, (410) **TS**, (255) **YS**, 24 **El**
NBN 630	E 42–1	Belgium	Strip	0.20 **C**, 0.50–1.30 **Mn**, 0.050 **P**, 0.050 **S**, 0.35 **Si**	**As rolled**: (3–63) **diam**, (410) **TS**, (255) **YS**, 24 **El**
NBN 630	E 42–2	Belgium	Strip	0.20 **C**, 0.50–1.30 **Mn**, 0.040 **P**, 0.040 **S**, 0.10–0.35 **Si**	**As rolled**: (3–40) **diam**, (410) **TS**, (255) **YS**, 24 **El**
ISO 2604/IV	P7	ISO	Plate	0.20 **C**, 0.50–1.30 **Mn**, 0.050 **P**, 0.050 **S**, 0.35 **Si**, 0.009 **N**	**Hot rolled, normalized**: (3–16) **diam**, (410) **TS**, (235) **YS**, 24 **El**

specification number	designation	country	product forms	composition	mechanical properties (see page iv for explanation)
ISO 2604/IV	P9	ISO	Plate	0.20 **C**, 0.50–1.30 **Mn**, 0.040 **P**, 0.040 **S**, 0.35 **Si**, 0.015 min $\mathbf{Al}_{met}$	**Hot rolled, normalized:** (3–16) **diam**, (410) **TS**, (265) **YS**, 24 **El**
BS 3603	Grade 410	UK	Pipe, tube: seamless, welded	0.20 **C**, 0.60–1.20 **Mn**, 0.045 **P**, 0.045 **S**, 0.35 **Si**, 0.015 min **Al**	**Hot finished, normalized:** all **diam**, (410) **TS**, (235) **YS**, 22 **El**
NF A 33–102	AR E 26,3	France	Billets, blooms, slabs	0.20 **C**, 0.050 **P**, 0.050 **S**	**Normalized**: all **diam**, (410) **TS**, (250) **YS**, 26 **El**
NF A 36–205	A 42, C2 and P2	France	Sheet, plate	0.20 **C**, 0.60 min **Mn**, 0.04 **P**, 0.04 **S**, 0.30 **Si**, 0.25 **Cu**	**Normalized**: (3–30) **diam**, (410) **TS**, (235) **YS**, 27 **El**
NF A 35–501	E 26 A–42 grade 3	France	Sheet, plate, bar	0.20 **C**, 0.050 **P**, 0.050 **S**	**As rolled**: (3–30) **diam**, (410) **TS**, (255) **YS**, 24 **El**
NF A 35–501	E26 A–42 grade 4	France	Sheet, plate, bar	0.20 **C**, 0.045 **P**, 0.045 **S**	**As rolled**: (3–30) **diam**, (410) **TS**, (255) **YS**, 27 **El**
ISO 2604/1	F8	ISO	Forgings	0.20 **C**, 0.50–1.20 **Mn**, 0.040 **P**, 0.040 **S**, 0.10–0.40 **Si**	**Annealed, normalized, normalized and tempered, quenched and tempered:** (≤63) **diam**, (410) **TS**, (215) **YS**, 20 **El**
ISO 2604/1	F9	ISO	Forgings	0.20 **C**, 0.50–1.20 **Mn**, 0.040 **P**, 0.040 **S**, 0.10–0.40 **Si**, 0.015 min $\mathbf{Al}_{met}$	**Annealed, normalized, normalized and tempered, quenched and tempered:** (≤63) **diam**, (410) **TS**, (235) **YS**, 20 **El**
DIN 1715	Grade A St 41	Germany	Plate, strip, bar, forgings	0.20 **C**, 0.45 min **Mn**, 0.045 **P**, 0.045 **S**, 0.35 **Si**	**Normalized**: (≤16) **diam**, (402) **TS**, (255) **YS**, 22 **El**
DIN 17155	Grade H II	Germany	Plate	0.20 **C**, 0.50 min **Mn**, 0.050 **P**, 0.050 **S**, 0.35 **Si**, 0.30 max, opt **Cr**	**Normalized**: (≤16) **diam**, (402) **TS**, (255) **YS**
JIS G 3116	Class 1	Japan	Sheet, plate, strip	0.20 **C**, 0.30 min **Mn**, 0.040 **P**, 0.040 **S**	**Hot rolled**: (2.3–6.0) **diam**, (402) **TS**, (255) **YS**, 28 **El**
JIS G 3106	Class 1B	Japan	Plate, strip, shape, bar	0.20 **C**, 0.60–1.20 **Mn**, 0.040 **P**, 0.040 **S**, 0.35 **Si**	**Hot rolled**: (≤5) **diam**, (402) **TS**, (245) **YS**, 23 **El**
SIS 14 21 36	SIS 21 36–32	Sweden	Sheet	0.20 **C**, 1.50 **Mn**, 0.050 **P**, 0.050 **S**, 0.60 **Si**, 0.009 **N**	**Annealed and cold rolled:** (≤3) **diam**, (400) **TS**, (320) **YS**, 16 **El**
ISO 4997	Grade CR320–B	ISO	Sheet	0.20 **C**, 1.50 **Mn**, 0.050 **P**, 0.050 **S**	**Cold rolled and annealed:** all **diam**, (400) **TS**, (320) **YS**, 16 **El**
ISO 4997	Grade CR320–D	ISO	Sheet	0.20 **C**, 1.50 **Mn**, 0.040 **P**, 0.040 **S**	**Cold rolled and annealed:** all **diam**, (400) **TS**, (320) **YS**, 16 **El**
SIS 14 21 36	SIS 21 36	Sweden	Sheet	0.20 **C**, 1.50 **Mn**, 0.050 **P**, 0.050 **S**, 0.60 **Si**, 0.009 **N**	**As–rolled**: (≤3) **diam**, (400) **TS**, (320) **YS**, 16 **El**
SIS 14 21 21	SIS 21 21	Sweden	Sheet	0.20 **C**, 1.5 **Mn**, 0.05 **P**, 0.05 **S**	**Zinc coated**: (≤3) **diam**, (400) **TS**, (320) **YS**, 16 **El**
AS 1443	Grade AS 1443/K1	Australia	Bar	0.20 **C**, 0.40–1.00 **Mn**, 0.050 **P**, 0.050 **S**, 0.10–0.35 **Si**	**As rolled or normalized:** ≤50 **diam**, (400) **TS**, 26 **El**
AS 1443	Grade AS 1443/S1	Australia	Bar	0.20 **C**, 0.40–1.00 **Mn**, 0.050 **P**, 0.050 **S**, 0.35 **Si**	**As rolled or normalized:** ≤50 **diam**, (400) **TS**, 26 **El**
AS 1442	Grade AS 1442/S1	Australia	Bar	0.20 **C**, 0.40–1.00 **Mn**, 0.050 **P**, 0.050 **S**, 0.35 **Si**	**As rolled or normalized:** (≤50) **diam**, (400) **TS**, 26 **El**
AS 1442	Grade AS 1442/K1	Australia	Bar	0.20 **C**, 0.40–1.00 **Mn**, 0.050 **P**, 0.050 **S**, 0.10–0.35 **Si**	**As rolled or normalized:** (≤50) **diam**, (400) **TS**, 26 **El**
JIS G 3445	Class 12B, No. 12	Japan	Tube: seamless or welded	0.20 **C**, 0.25–0.60 **Mn**, 0.040 **P**, 0.040 **S**, 0.35 **Si**	**As manufactured or cold finished**: (≥8) **diam**, (392) **TS**, (275) **YS**, 25 **El**
COPANT 37, II	AT–21	COPANT	Plate	0.20 **C**, 0.035 **P**, 0.040 **S**, 0.15–0.35 **Si**	**As rolled**: (≤25) **diam**, (390) **TS**, (210) **YS**, 27 **El**
BS 1717	CEW–102	UK	Tube: cold drawn electric resistance butt welded	0.20 **C**, 0.6 **Mn**, 0.060 **P**, 0.060 **S**	**As drawn or as drawn and tempered**: all **diam**, (385) **TS**, (330) **YS**
BS 1717	CDS–102	UK	Tube	0.20 **C**, 0.050 **P**, 0.050 **S**	**As drawn or as drawn and tempered**: all **diam**, (385) **TS**, (330) **YS**
BS 980	CEW–2	UK	Tube	0.20 **C**, 0.6 **Mn**, 0.060 **P**, 0.060 **S**	**Drawn or drawn, tempered:** all **diam**, (385) **TS**, (330) **YS**
BS–980	CDS–2	UK	Tube	0.20 **C**, 0.050 **P**, 0.50 **S**	**Drawn or drawn and tempered:** all **diam**, (385) **TS**, (330) **YS**

specification number	designation	country	product forms	composition	mechanical properties (see page iv for explanation)
ANSI/ASTM A 284	Grade B	US	Plate	0.20 **C**, 0.90 **Mn**, 0.04 **P**, 0.05 **S**, 0.15–0.30 **Si**	**Annealed**: all **diam**, (380) **TS**, (190) **YS**, 27 **El**
DGN-B-93	Class I, subclass I-1	Mexico	Plate, sheet	0.20 **C**, 0.80 **Mn**, 0.035 **P**, 0.040 **S**, 0.30 **Si**	**As agreed**: (<25) **diam**, (379) **TS**, (206) **YS**, 29 **El**
DGN-B-106	Type 201A/B	Mexico	Plate	0.20 **C**, 0.80 **Mn**, 0.04 **P**, 0.05 **S**, 0.05–0.30 **Si**	**Hot worked**: (<8) **diam**, (379) **TS**, 28 **El**
DGN-B-258	Grade B	Mexico	Plate	0.20 **C**, 0.90 **Mn**, 0.04 **P**, 0.05 **S**, 0.15–0.30 **Si**	**Hot rolled**: (≤25) **diam**, (379) **TS**, (189) **YS**, 27 **El**
ASTM A 714	Grade V Type F	US	Pipe: welded, seamless	0.20 **C**, 0.35–1.06 **Mn**, 0.045 **P**, 0.050 **S**, 0.75–1.25 **Cu**, 1.60–2.24 **Ni**	**As rolled**: all **diam**, 55 (379) **TS**, 40 (276) **YS**
DGN-B-244	Grade 40	Mexico	Plate	0.20 **C**, 0.90 **Mn**, 0.035 **P**, 0.040 **S**, 0.15–0.30 **Si**	**As rolled**: (<25.4) **diam**, (377) **TS**, (207) **YS**, 27 **El**
ISO 4995	HR 275-D	ISO	Sheet	0.20 **C**, 0.040 **P**, 0.040 **S**	**Hot rolled**: (17) **diam**, (370) **TS**, (255) **YS**
BS 1449: Part 1	Grade 37/23	UK	Plate, sheet, strip	0.20 **C**, 0.80 **Mn**, 0.050 **P**, 0.050 **S**	**Hot rolled**: all **diam**, (370) **TS**, (230) **YS**, 28 **El**
SFS 200:E	Fe 37A	Finland	Bar, plate, strip, wire, forgings	0.20 **C**, 0.075 **P**, 0.050 **S**	**Hot worked**: (>40–100) **diam**, (363) **TS**, (216) **YS**, 25 **El**
DS 12011	St 37 C	Denmark	Rod, bar, shapes	0.20 **C**, 0.06 **P**, 0.05 **S**, 0.009 **N**	**Hot rolled**: (16) **diam**, (363) **TS**, (216) **YS**, 24 **El**
DS 12011	St 37 B	Denmark	Rod, bar, shapes	0.20 **C**, 0.06 **P**, 0.05 **S**, 0.009 **N**	**Hot rolled**: (16) **diam**, (363) **TS**, (215) **YS**, 24 **El**
NS 12121	NS 12121-00	Norway	Bar, rod, shapes	0.20 **C**, 0.07 **P**, 0.050 **S**	**Hot worked**: (16) **diam**, (363) **TS**, (235) **YS**, 25 **El**
TS 911	669.14-423/Fe 37	Turkey	Bar	0.20 **C**, 0.063 **P**, 0.063 **S**	**Hot rolled**: all **diam**, (363) **TS**, (235) **YS**, 25 **El**
TS 416	Fe 37	Turkey	Pipe: welded	0.20 **C**, 0.08 **P**, 0.05 **S**	**As welded**: (<16) **diam**, (363) **TS**, (235) **YS**, 23 **El**
TS 416	Fe 37.2	Turkey	Pipe: welded	0.20 **C**, 0.060 **P**, 0.050 **S**, 0.007 **N**	**As welded**: (<16) **diam**, (363) **TS**, (235) **YS**, 23 **El**
ISO/R 630	Grade Fe 37 C	ISO	Bar, plate	0.20 **C**, 0.055 **P**, 0.055 **S**	**As rolled**: (≤16) **diam**, (362) **TS**, (235) **YS**, 26 **El**
ISO/R 630	Grade Fe 37 D	ISO	Bar, plate	0.20 **C**, 0.050 **P**, 0.050 **S**	**As rolled**: (≤16) **diam**, (362) **TS**, (235) **YS**, 26 **El**
SS 14 13 13	SS 13 13-01	Sweden	Bar, plate, sheet	0.20 **C**, 0.5–0.8 **Mn**, 0.06 **P**, 0.05 **S**, 0.05 **Si**, 0.009 **N**	**Normalized**: all **diam**, (360) **TS**, (220) **YS**, 24 **El**
SS 14 13 13	SS 13 13-00	Sweden	Bar, plate	0.20 **C**, 0.5–0.8 **Mn**, 0.06 **P**, 0.05 **S**, 0.05 **Si**, 0.009 **N**	**As rolled**: all **diam**, (360) **TS**, (220) **YS**, 24 **El**
SS 14 13 13	SS 13 13-01	Sweden	Bar, plate, sheet	0.20 **C**, 0.5–0.8 **Mn**, 0.06 **P**, 0.05 **S**, 0.25 **Si**, 0.009 **N**	**Normalized**: all **diam**, (360) **TS**, (220) **YS**, 24 **El**
SS 14 13 13	SS 13 13-00	Sweden	Bar, plate	0.20 **C**, 0.5–0.8 **Mn**, 0.06 **P**, 0.05 **S**, 0.25 **Si**, 0.009 **N**	**As rolled**: (4–25) **diam**, (360) **TS**, (220) **YS**, 24 **El**
SS 14 13 12 E	SS 13 12-04	Sweden	Tube: welded	0.20 **C**, 0.4–0.7 **Mn**, 0.06 **P**, 0.05 **S**, 0.05 **Si**, 0.009 **N**	**As welded or cold worked**: (≤5) **diam**, (360) **TS**, (240) **YS**, 24 **El**
SS 14 13 12 E	SS 13 12-03	Sweden	Tube: seamless	0.20 **C**, 0.4–0.7 **Mn**, 0.06 **P**, 0.05 **S**, 0.05 **Si**, 0.009 **N**	**Hot worked**: (≤5) **diam**, (360) **TS**, (240) **YS**, 24 **El**
SS 14 13 12 E	SS 13 12-01	Sweden	Forgings	0.20 **C**, 0.4–0.7 **Mn**, 0.06 **P**, 0.05 **S**, 0.05 **Si**, 0.009 **N**	**Normalized**: (≤50) **diam**, (360) **TS**, (220) **YS**, 27 **El**
SS 14 13 12 E	SS 13 12-00	Sweden	Bar, plate, sheet	0.20 **C**, 0.4–0.7 **Mn**, 0.06 **P**, 0.05 **S**, 0.05 **Si**, 0.009 **N**	**As rolled**: all **diam**, (360) **TS**, (220) **YS**, 24 **El**
SS 14 13 12 E	SS 13 12-04	Sweden	Tube: welded	0.20 **C**, 0.4–0.7 **Mn**, 0.06 **P**, 0.05 **S**, 0.25 **Si**, 0.009 **N**	**As welded or cold worked**: (≤5) **diam**, (360) **TS**, (240) **YS**, 24 **El**
SS 14 13 12 E	SS 13 12-03	Sweden	Tube: seamless	0.20 **C**, 0.4–0.7 **Mn**, 0.06 **P**, 0.05 **S**, 0.25 **Si**, 0.009 **N**	**Hot worked**: (≤5) **diam**, (360) **TS**, (240) **YS**, 24 **El**
SS 14 13 12 E	SS 13 12-01	Sweden	Forgings	0.20 **C**, 0.4–0.7 **Mn**, 0.06 **P**, 0.05 **S**, 0.25 **Si**, 0.009 **N**	**Normalized**: (≤50) **diam**, (360) **TS**, (220) **YS**, 27 **El**
SS 14 13 12 E	SS 13 12-00	Sweden	Bar, forgings, sheet	0.20 **C**, 0.4–0.7 **Mn**, 0.06 **P**, 0.05 **S**, 0.25 **Si**, 0.009 **N**	**As rolled**: all **diam**, (360) **TS**, (220) **YS**, 24 **El**
DIN 1626, Part 2	Grade St37	Germany	Pipe: welded (commercial quality)	0.20 **C**, 0.08 **P**, 0.05 **S**	**As welded**: (<16) **diam**, (360) **TS**, (235) **YS**, 23 **El**
DIN 1626, Part 3	Grade St37-2/1.0112	Germany	Pipe: welded	0.20 **C**, 1.5 **Mn**, 0.06 **P**, 0.05 **S**, 0.55 **Si**	**As welded**: (<16) **diam**, (360) **TS**, (235) **YS**, 23 **El**

WROUGHT CARBON STEELS

specification number	designation	country	product forms	composition	mechanical properties (see page iv for explanation)
BS 1501–154	Grade 23	UK	Plate	0.20 **C**, 0.30–1.20 **Mn**, 0.050 **P**, 0.050 **S**; 0.70 max other elements, total	**As supplied**: ($\leq$9.53) **diam**, (360) **TS**, (200) **YS**, 45 **El**
NF A 36–205	A 42, C1 and P1	France	Sheet, plate	0.20 **C**, 0.45 min **Mn**, 0.05 **P**, 0.05 **S**, 0.40 **Si**	**Normalized**: (3–30) **diam**, (360) **TS**, (215) **YS**, 27 **El**
ASTM A 611	Grade D	US	Sheet	0.20 **C**, 0.90 **Mn**, 0.04 **P**, 0.04 **S**	**Cold rolled**: all **diam**, 52 (360) **TS**, 40 (275) **YS**, 20 **El**
DIN 1626, Part 4	Grade St 37–2	Germany	Pipe: welded (specially tested)	0.20 **C**, 1.5 **Mn**, 0.06 **P**, 0.05 **S**, 0.55 **Si**	**Annealed**: (<16) **diam**, (360) **TS**, (235) **YS**, 23 **El**
ANSI/ASTM A 611	Grade D	US	Sheet	0.20 **C**, 0.90 **Mn**, 0.04 **P**, 0.04 **S**	**Cold rolled**: all **diam**, 52 (360) **TS**, 40 (275) **YS**, 20 **El**
ANSI/ASTM A 446	Grade B	US	Sheet	0.20 **C**, 0.10 **P**, 0.04 **S**	**Hot rolled, hot dip galvanized**: all **diam**, 52 (360) **TS**, 37 (255) **YS**, 18 **El**
DIN 1623 Sheet 2	USt 37–2 (1.0112.5)	Germany	Sheet	0.20 **C**, 0.060 **P**, 0.050 **S**	**Hot or cold rolled**: all **diam**, (360) **TS**, (215) **YS**, 18 in 80 mm **El**
DIN 1623 Sheet 2	WUSt 37–2 (1.0112.3)	Germany	Sheet	0.20 **C**, 0.060 **P**, 0.050 **S**	**Hot or cold rolled**: all **diam**, (360) **TS**, (215) **YS**, 18 in 80 mm **El**
DIN 1623 Sheet 2	TUST 37 (1.0110.1)	Germany	Sheet	0.20 **C**, 0.080 **P**, 0.050 **S**	**Hot or cold rolled**: all **diam**, (360) **TS**, (215) **YS**, 18 in 80 mm **El**
DIN 1623 Sheet 2	RSt 37–2 (1.0112.6)	Germany	Sheet	0.20 **C**, 0.060 **P**, 0.050 **S**	**Hot or cold rolled**: all **diam**, (360) **TS**, (215) **YS**, 18 in 80 mm **El**
DGN–B–348	Grade D	Mexico	Sheet	0.20 **C**, 0.90 **Mn**, 0.040 **P**, 0.040 **S**	**Cold rolled**: all **diam**, (358) **TS**, (275) **YS**, 20 **El**
BS 1717	ERW–102	UK	Tube: electric resistance butt welded	0.20 **C**, 0.6 **Mn**, 0.060 **P**, 0.060 **S**	**As welded**: all **diam**, (345) **TS**, (205) **YS**
JIS G 3445	Class 12A, No. 12	Japan	Tube: seamless or welded	0.20 **C**, 0.25–0.60 **Mn**, 0.040 **P**, 0.040 **S**, 0.35 **Si**	**As manufactured or cold finished**: ($\geq$8) **diam**, (343) **TS**, (177) **YS**, 35 **El**
AS 1594	Grade AS1594/HR240	Australia	Sheet, strip	0.20 **C**, 0.80 **Mn**, 0.040 **P**, 0.040 **S**	**Hot rolled**: $\geq$3 **diam**, (340) **TS**, (240) **YS**, 22 **El**
JIS A 5503		Japan	Bar	0.20 **C**, 0.60 **Mn**, 0.045 **P**, 0.045 **S**, 0.30 **Si**	**Rolled**: all **diam**, (333) **TS**, 27 **El**
SABS 719	Grade A	South Africa	Pipe: electric welded	0.20 **C**, 0.90 **Mn**, 0.04 **P**, 0.05 **S**	**As welded**: all **diam**, (331) **TS**, (207) **YS**
SIS 14 14 26	SIS 14 26–32	Sweden	Sheet	0.20 **C**, 1.00 **Mn**, 0.050 **P**, 0.050 **S**, 0.40 **Si**, 0.009 **N**	**Annealed and cld rolled**: ($\leq$3) **diam**, (330) **TS**, (250) **YS**, 20 **El**
ISO 4997	Grade CR250–D	ISO	Sheet	0.20 **C**, 0.040 **P**, 0.040 **S**	**Cold rolled and annealed**: all **diam**, (330) **TS**, (250) **YS**, 20 **El**
ISO 4997	Grade CR250–B	ISO	Sheet	0.20 **C**, 0.050 **P**, 0.050 **S**	**Cold rolled and annealed**: all **diam**, (330) **TS**, (250) **YS**, 20 **El**
ASTM A 611	Grade C	US	Sheet	0.20 **C**, 0.60 **Mn**, 0.04 **P**, 0.04 **S**	**Cold rolled**: all **diam**, 48 (330) **TS**, 33 (230) **YS**, 22 **El**
ANSI/ASTM A 611	Grade C	US	Sheet	0.20 **C**, 0.60 **Mn**, 0.04 **P**, 0.04 **S**	**Cold rolled**: all **diam**, 48 (330) **TS**, 33 (230) **YS**, 22 **El**
SIS 14 14 26	SIS 14 26	Sweden	Sheet	0.20 **C**, 1.00 **Mn**, 0.050 **P**, 0.050 **S**, 0.40 **Si**, 0.009 **N**	**As–rolled**: ($\leq$3) **diam**, (330) **TS**, (250) **YS**, 20 **El**
BS 3602	Steel 23	UK	Pipe, tube: seamless	0.20 **C**, 0.40–0.70 **Mn**, 0.050 **P**, 0.050 **S**, 0.35 **Si**	**Hot finished**: all **diam**, (315) **TS**, (185) **YS**, 30 **El**
BS 3602	Steel 23	UK	Pipe, tube: seamless	0.20 **C**, 0.40–0.70 **Mn**, 0.050 **P**, 0.050 **S**, 0.35 **Si**	**Cold drawn**: all **diam**, (315) **TS**, (185) **YS**, 30 **El**
BS 3602	Steel 23	UK	Pipe, tube: welded	0.20 **C**, 0.40–0.70 **Mn**, 0.050 **P**, 0.050 **S**, 0.35 **Si**	**Normalized**: all **diam**, (315) **TS**, (185) **YS**, 30 **El**
ASTM A 611	Grade B	US	Sheet	0.20 **C**, 0.60 **Mn**, 0.04 **P**, 0.04 **S**	**Cold rolled**: all **diam**, 45 (310) **TS**, 30 (205) **YS**, 24 **El**
DGN–B–106	Type 285A (Firebox)	Mexico	Plate	0.20 **C**, 0.80 **Mn**, 0.035 **P**, 0.040 **S**, 0.20–0.35 **Cu**	**Hot worked**: (<8) **diam**, 45 (310) **TS**, 24 (165) **YS**, 32 **El**
DGN–B–348	Grade B	Mexico	Sheet	0.20 **C**, 0.60 **Mn**, 0.040 **P**, 0.040 **S**, 0.20 min **Cu**	**Cold rolled**: all **diam**, (310) **TS**, (206) **YS**, 24 **El**
ANSI/ASTM A 611	Grade B	US	Sheet	0.20 **C**, 0.60 **Mn**, 0.04 **P**, 0.04 **S**	**Cold rolled**: all **diam**, 45 (310) **TS**, 30 (205) **YS**, 24 **El**

specification number	designation	country	product forms	composition	mechanical properties (see page iv for explanation)
ANSI/ASTM A 446	Grade A	US	Sheet	0.20 **C**, 0.04 **P**, 0.04 **S**	**Hot rolled, hot dip galvanized**: all **diam**, 45 (310) **TS**, 33 (230) **YS**, 20 **El**
DGN-B-348	Grade C	Mexico	Sheet	0.20 **C**, 0.60 **Mn**, 0.040 **P**, 0.040 **S**	**Cold rolled**: all **diam**, (301) **TS**, (225) **YS**, 22 **El**
BS T.63		UK	Tube: aircraft quality	0.20 **C**, 0.80 **Mn**, 0.040 **P**, 0.040 **S**, 0.10–0.35 **Si**	**Annealed**: all **diam**, (300) **TS**, (170) **YS**
JIS G 3461	Class 1	Japan	Tube: seamless or electric–resistance welded	0.20 **C**, 0.25–0.60 **Mn**, 0.040 **P**, 0.040 **S**, 0.35 **Si**	**As manufactured or annealed**: (≥8) **diam**, (294) **TS**, 30 **El**
ASTM A 611	Grade A	US	Sheet	0.20 **C**, 0.60 **Mn**, 0.04 **P**, 0.04 **S**	**Cold rolled**: all **diam**, 42 (290) **TS**, 25 (170) **YS**, 26 **El**
ANSI/ASTM A 611	Grade A	US	Sheet	0.20 **C**, 0.60 **Mn**, 0.04 **P**, 0.04 **S**	**Cold rolled**: all **diam**, 42 (290) **TS**, 25 (170) **YS**, 26 **El**
DGN-B-348	Grade A	Mexico	Sheet	0.20 **C**, 0.60 **Mn**, 0.040 **P**, 0.040 **S**, 0.20 min **Cu**	**Cold rolled**: all **diam**, (289) **TS**, (172) **YS**, 26 **El**
BS 1449: Part 1	Grade 15	UK	Plate, sheet, strip	0.20 **C**, 0.90 **Mn**, 0.060 **P**, 0.060 **S**	**Hot rolled**: all **diam**, (280) **TS**, (170) **YS**
BS 1717	CEW-101	UK	Tube: cold drawn electric resistance butt welded	0.20 **C**, 0.6 **Mn**, 0.060 **P**, 0.060 **S**	**Annealed or normalized**: all **diam**, (275) **TS**, (150) **YS**
BS 1717	CDS-101	UK	Tube	0.20 **C**, 0.050 **P**, 0.050 **S**	**Annealed**: all **diam**, (275) **TS**, (150) **YS**; **Normalized**: all **diam**, (330) **TS**, (195) **YS**
BS 980	ERW-1	UK	Tube	0.20 **C**, 0.6 **Mn**, 0.060 **P**, 0.060 **S**	**Welded**: 3 **diam**, (275) **TS**, (150) **YS**, 20 **El**
BS 980	CEW-1	UK	Tube	0.20 **C**, 0.6 **Mn**, 0.060 **P**, 0.060 **S**	**Annealed or normalised**: all **diam**, (275) **TS**, (150) **YS**
BS 980	CDS-1	UK	Tube	0.20 **C**, 0.050 **P**, 0.050 **S**	**Annealed or normalized**: all **diam**, (275) **TS**, (150) **YS**
DS 12011	St 42 C	Denmark	Rod, bar, shapes	0.20 **C**, 0.050 **P**, 0.050 **S**, 0.50 **Si**, 0.40 **Cu**, 0.30 **Cr**, 0.009 **N**	
DIN 2391 Part 2	Grade St 521-1.0831	Germany	Tube	0.20 **C**, 1.5 **Mn**, 0.05 **P**, 0.05 **S**, 0.55 **Si**	**Normalized**: all **diam**; **Bright drawn/hard**: all **diam**, (588) **TS**, 4 **El**; **Bright drawn/soft**: all **diam**, (539) **TS**, 6 **El**; **Annealed**: all **diam**
DIN 2393 Sheet 2	Grade St 52-3 or 1.0841	Germany	Tube	0.20 **C**, 1.5 **Mn**, 0.05 **P**, 0.05 **S**, 0.55 **Si**	
DIN 2393 Sheet 2	Grade St 52-3.2-1.0841	Germany	Tube	0.20 **C**, 1.5 **Mn**, 0.05 **P**, 0.05 **S**, 0.55 **Si**	
MIL-S-24113A	Grade QT	US	Plate	0.20 **C**, 0.90–1.35 **Mn**, 0.035 **P**, 0.040 **S**, 0.15–0.45 **Si**	**Quenched and tempered**: ≤2–4 **diam**, 50 (345) **YS**, 20 **El**
MIL-S-24113A	Grade N	US	Plate	0.20 **C**, 0.90–1.35 **Mn**, 0.035 **P**, 0.040 **S**, 0.15–0.45 **Si**	**Normalized**: ≤2–4 **diam**, 42 (290) **YS**, 20 **El**
MIL-S-10520D	Grade 1	US	Bar, forgings	0.20 **C**, 0.90 **Mn**, 0.040 **P**, 0.050 **S**, 0.20 **Si**	**Quenched and tempered**: 1 3/4 **diam**, 76 (524) **YS**
AS 1442	Grade AS 1442/CS 1100	Australia	Bar, blooms, billets, slabs	0.20 **C**, 0.80–1.50 **Mn**, 0.100 **P**, 0.08–0.40 **S**, 0.35 **Si**	
ANSI/ASTM A 29	M 1023	US	Bar	0.19–0.27 **C**, 0.25–0.60 **Mn**, 0.04 **P**, 0.05 **S**	
ANSI/ASTM A 575	M 1023	US	Bar	0.19–0.27 **C**, 0.25–0.60 **Mn**, 0.04 **P**, 0.05 **S**	
EURONORM 119-74, IV	C 22 B KD	EURONORM	Wire, rod	0.19–0.25 **C**, 0.50–0.80 **Mn**, 0.035 **P**, 0.035 **S**, 0.15–0.40 **Si**, 0.0005–0.0050 **B**	**Quenched and tempered**: (≤10) **diam**, (780) **TS**, (635) **YS**, 14 **El**
DGN-B-301	1024	Mexico	Bar	0.19–0.25 **C**, 1.35–1.65 **Mn**, 0.040 **P**, 0.050 **S**, 0.10 **Si**	**Forged or hot rolled, cold rolled and cold finished**: all **diam**, (510) **TS**, (284) **YS**, 20 **El**
ASTM A 659	Grade 1023	US	Sheet, strip	0.19–0.25 **C**, 0.30–0.60 **Mn**, 0.040 **P**, 0.050 **S**	
AISI 1023		US	Plate	0.19–0.25 **C**, 0.30–0.60 **Mn**, 0.040 **P**, 0.050 **S**	
AISI 1524		US	Bar	0.19–0.25 **C**, 1.35–1.65 **Mn**, 0.040 **P**, 0.050 **S**	
ANSI/ASTM A 519	1524	US	Tube: seamless	0.19–0.25 **C**, 1.35–1.65 **Mn**, 0.040 **P**, 0.050 **S**	

WROUGHT CARBON STEELS

specification number	designation	country	product forms	composition	mechanical properties (see page iv for explanation)
COPANT 333	1024	COPANT	Wire, rod	0.19–0.25 **C**, 1.35–1.65 **Mn**, 0.040 **P**, 0.050 **S**	
DGN–B–301	1524	Mexico	Bar	0.19–0.25 **C**, 1.35–1.65 **Mn**, 0.040 **P**, 0.050 **S**, 0.10 **Si**	
ANSI/ASTM A 734	Grade B	US	Plate	0.19 **C**, 1.65 **Mn**, 0.036 **P**, 0.016 **S**, 0.37 **Si**, 0.38 **Cu**, 0.13 **V**, 0.29 **Cr**, 0.030 **N**	**Quenched and tempered**: all **diam**, 77 (530) **TS**, 65 (450) **YS**, 20 **El**
IS 3945	Grade B–N	India	Plate	0.19 **C**, 1.20 min **Mn**, 0.050 **P**, 0.50 **S**	**Mill**: (≤25) **diam**, (490) **TS**, (309) **YS**, 21 **El**
VSM 10648	St Ac 34–2	Switzerland	Bar, sheet, plate	0.19 **C**, 0.063 **P**, 0.063 **S**	**Cold drawn**: (5) **diam**, (490) **TS**, (412) **YS**, 7 **El**; **Cold finished**: (10–100) **diam**, (333) **TS**, (206) **YS**, 28 **El**; **Cold drawn and annealed**: (≤25) **diam**, (304) **TS**, (167) **YS**, 28 **El**; **Cold finished and normalized**: (all) **diam**, (333) **TS**, (186) **YS**, 28 **El**
BS 1502–221	Grade 28	UK	Bar	0.19 **C**, 0.90–1.50 **Mn**, 0.050 **P**, 0.050 **S**, 0.10–0.55 **Si**, 0.70 max other elements, total	**As–rolled**: ≤1 (≤25) **diam**, (433) **TS**, (255) **YS**, 45 **El**
BS 1502–211	Grade 28	UK	Bar	0.19 **C**, 0.90–1.50 **Mn**, 0.050 **P**, 0.050 **S**, 0.10 **Si**, 0.70 max other elements, total	**As–rolled**: ≤1 (≤25) **diam**, (433) **TS**, (255) **YS**, 45 **El**
BS 1501–221	Grades 28A, 28B	UK	Plate	0.19 **C**, 0.90–1.50 **Mn**, 0.050 **P**, 0.050 **S**, 0.10–0.55 **Si**; 0.70 max other elements, total	**Normalized**: (≤16) **diam**, (430) **TS**, (255) **YS**, 45 **El**
BS 1501–211	Grades 28A, 28B	UK	Plate	0.19 **C**, 0.90–1.50 **Mn**, 0.050 **P**, 0.050 **S**, 0.55 **Si**; 0.70 max other elements, total	**Normalized**: (≤16) **diam**, (430) **TS**, (255) **YS**, 45 **El**
AS 1450	370	Australia	Tube: seamless or welded	0.19 **C**, 0.060 **P**, 0.060 **S**	**As–drawn or as–drawn and stress relieved**: all **diam**, (430) **TS**, (370) **YS**
ISO 2604/III	No. TW10	ISO	Tube	0.19 **C**, 0.60–1.20 **Mn**, 0.045 **P**, 0.045 **S**, 0.35 **Si**	**As welded, annealed, normalized**: all **diam**, (410) **TS**, (235) **YS**, 22 **El**
AS 1835	TS 10	Australia	Tube: seamless	0.19 **C**, 0.60–1.20 **Mn**, 0.045 **P**, 0.045 **S**, 0.35 **Si**, 0.015 **Al**	**Annealed and normalized**: all **diam**, (410) **TS**, (235) **YS**, 22 **El**
AS 1836	TW·10	Australia	Tube: welded	0.19 **C**, 0.60–1.20 **Mn**, 0.045 **P**, 0.045 **S**, 0.35 **Si**, 0.015 min **Al**	**Annealed or normalized**: all **diam**, (410) **TS**, (235) **YS**, 22 **El**
ISO 2604/11	TS 10	ISO	Tube: seamless	0.19 **C**, 0.60–1.20 **Mn**, 0.045 **P**, 0.045 **S**, 0.35 **Si**, 0.015 met **Al**	**Hot finished, annealed, normalized**: all **diam**, (410) **TS**, (235) **YS**, 22 **El**
DIN 17111	Grade USt38–1	Germany	Bar, wire, rod	0.19 **C**, 0.50 **Mn**, 0.080 **P**, 0.050 **S**	**Hot rolled**: all **diam**, (373) **TS**, (227) **YS**, 25 **El**
DIN 17111	Grade USt38–2	Germany	Bar, wire, rod	0.19 **C**, 0.50 **Mn**, 0.080 **P**, 0.050 **S**, 0.007 **N**	**Hot rolled**: all **diam**, (373) **TS**, (227) **YS**, 25 **El**
DIN 17111	Grade UQSt38–2	Germany	Bar, wire, rod	0.19 **C**, 0.25–0.45 **Mn**, 0.040 **P**, 0.040 **S**, 0.007 **N**	**Hot rolled**: all **diam**, (373) **TS**, (227) **YS**, 25 **El**
NF A 33–101	AF 37,2	France	Bar, billets, blooms	0.19 **C**, 0.050 **P**, 0.050 **S**	**Normalized**: (10–100) **diam**, (360) **TS**, 30 **El**
DIN 17100	RSt 37–2 (1.0114)	Germany	Bar, plate	0.19 **C**, 0.055 **P**, 0.055 **S**	**Normalized**: all **diam**, (360) **TS**, (235) **YS**, 25 **El**
DIN 17100	RSt 37–2 (1.0114)	Germany	Strip	0.19 **C**, 0.055 **P**, 0.055 **S**	**Normalized**: all **diam**, (360) **TS**, (235) **YS**, 25 **El**; **Hot rolled**: all **diam**, (360) **TS**, (235) **YS**, 18 **El**
DIN 17100	St 37–3 (1.0116)	Germany	Bar, plate	0.19 **C**, 0.050 **P**, 0.050 **S**	**Normalized**: all **diam**, (360) **TS**, (235) **YS**, 25 **El**
DIN 17100	St 37–3 (1.0116)	Germany	Strip	0.19 **C**, 0.050 **P**, 0.050 **S**	**Normalized**: all **diam**, (360) **TS**, (235) **YS**, 25 **El**; **Hot rolled**: all **diam**, (360) **TS**, (235) **YS**, 18 **El**
DIN 17100	RSt 34–1 (1.0150)	Germany	Bar	0.19 **C**, 0.088 **P**, 0.055 **S**	**Normalized**: all **diam**, (330) **TS**, (205) **YS**, 28 **El**
DIN 17100	RSt 34–1 (1.0150)	Germany	Strip	0.19 **C**, 0.088 **P**, 0.055 **S**	**Normalized**: all **diam**, (330) **TS**, (205) **YS**, 28 **El**; **Hot rolled**: all **diam**, (330) **TS**, (205) **YS**, 20 **El**

WROUGHT CARBON STEELS

specification number	designation	country	product forms	composition	mechanical properties (see page iv for explanation)
DIN 17100	RSt 34–1 (1.0150)	Germany	Plate	0.19 **C**, 0.088 **P**, 0.055 **S**	**Normalized**: all **diam**, (330) **TS**, (205) **YS**, 28 **El**
DIN 17100	USt 34–2 (1.0102)	Germany	Bar	0.19 **C**, 0.063 **P**, 0.063 **S**	**Normalized**: all **diam**, (330) **TS**, (205) **YS**, 28 **El**
DIN 17100	USt 34–2 (1.0102)	Germany	Strip	0.19 **C**, 0.063 **P**, 0.063 **S**	**Normalized**: all **diam**, (330) **TS**, (205) **YS**, 28 **El**; **Hot rolled**: all **diam**, (330) **TS**, (205) **YS**, 20 **El**
DIN 17100	USt 34–2 (1.0102)	Germany	Plate	0.19 **C**, 0.063 **P**, 0.063 **S**	**Normalized**: all **diam**, (330) **TS**, (205) **YS**, 28 **El**
AS 1450	270	Australia	Tube: seamless or welded	0.19 **C**, 0.060 **P**, 0.060 **S**	**As–formed**: all **diam**, (320) **TS**, (260) **YS**, 15 **El**
AS 1450	170	Australia	Tube: seamless or welded	0.19 **C**, 0.060 **P**, 0.060 **S**	**Hot finished, normalized, as–formed, annealed cold drawn, as–drawn**: all **diam**, (310) **TS**, (170) **YS**, 26 **El**
AISI 1524H		US	Bar	0.18–0.26 **C**, 1.25–1.75 **Mn**, 0.040 **P**, 0.050 **S**, 0.15–0.30 **Si**	
DIN 1654	Grade Cq 22	Germany	Rod	0.18–0.25 **C**, 0.30–0.60 **Mn**, 0.040 **P**, 0.040 **S**, 0.15–0.35 **Si**	**Drawn**: all **diam**, (638) **TS**
DIN 1652	C22 (1.0402)	Germany	Bar	0.18–0.25 **C**, 0.30–0.60 **Mn**, 0.045 **P**, 0.045 **S**, 0.15–0.35 **Si**	**Cold drawn**: all **diam**, (590) **TS**, (470) **YS**, 5 in 80 mm **El**; **Centerless turned and normalized**: all **diam**, (410) **TS**, (235) **YS**, 27 in 80 mm **El**; **Centerless turned and quenched and tempered and normalized**: all **diam**, (540) **TS**, (355) **YS**, 20 in 80 mm **El**
DIN 1652	Ck 22 (1.1151)	Germany	Bar	0.18–0.25 **C**, 0.30–0.60 **Mn**, 0.035 **P**, 0.035 **S**, 0.15–0.35 **Si**	**Cold drawn**: all **diam**, (590) **TS**, (470) **YS**, 5 in 80 mm **El**; **Centerless turned and normalized**: all **diam**, (410) **TS**, (235) **YS**, 27 in 80 mm **El**; **Centerless turned and quenched and tempered**: all **diam**, (540) **TS**, (355) **YS**, 20 in 80 mm **El**
DIN 17200	Grade C 22	Germany	Blooms, slabs, billets, wire, bar, plate, sheet, strip, tube, forgings	0.18–0.25 **C**, 0.30–0.60 **Mn**, 0.045 **P**, 0.045 **S**, 0.15–0.35 **Si**	**Quenched and tempered**: (≤16) **diam**, (539) **TS**, (353) **YS**, 20 **El**; **Normalized**: (>16–40) **diam**, (412) **TS**, (235) **YS**, 27 **El**
DIN 17200	Grade Ck 22	Germany	Blooms, slabs, billets, wire, bar, plate, sheet, strip, tube, forgings	0.18–0.25 **C**, 0.30–0.60 **Mn**, 0.035 **P**, 0.035 **S**, 0.15–0.35 **Si**	**Quenched and tempered**: (≤16) **diam**, (539) **TS**, (353) **YS**, 20 **El**; **Normalized**: (>16–40) **diam**, (412) **TS**, (235) **YS**, 27 **El**
MIL–S–7952A	1020	US	Sheet, strip	0.18–0.25 **C**, 0.30–0.60 **Mn**, 0.040 **P**, 0.050 **S**	**Cold rolled and annealed**: all **diam**, (379) **TS**, (248) **YS**, 22 **El**
AISI 1024		US	Plate	0.18–0.25 **C**, 1.30–1.65 **Mn**, 0.040 **P**, 0.050 **S**	
EURONORM 119–74, IV	C 21 KD	EURONORM	Wire, rod	0.18–0.24 **C**, 0.30–0.60 **Mn**, 0.035 **P**, 0.035 **S**, 0.15–0.40 **Si**	**Quenched and tempered**: (≤16) **diam**, (500) **TS**, (325) **YS**, 20 **El**
AISI 1522		US	Bar	0.18–0.24 **C**, 1.10–1.40 **Mn**, 0.040 **P**, 0.050 **S**	
ANSI/ASTM A 29	1522	US	Bar	0.18–0.24 **C**, 1.10–1.40 **Mn**, 0.040 **P**, 0.050 **S**	
DGN–B–301	1522	Mexico	Bar	0.18–0.24 **C**, 1.10–1.40 **Mn**, 0.040 **P**, 0.050 **S**, 0.10 **Si**	
AISI 1522		US	Wire, rod	0.18–0.24 **C**, 1.10–1.40 **Mn**, 0.040 **P**, 0.050 **S**	
ANSI/ASTM A 576	1522	US	Bar	0.18–0.24 **C**, 1.10–1.40 **Mn**, 0.040 **P**, 0.050 **S**	
ASTM A 689	1522	US	Bar	0.18–0.24 **C**, 1.10–1.40 **Mn**, 0.040 **P**, 0.050 **S**	
JIS G 3539	SWCH 22A	Japan	Wire	0.18–0.23 **C**, 0.70–1.00 **Mn**, 0.030 **P**, 0.035 **S**, 0.10 **Si**, 0.02 min **Al**	**Cold drawn**: (3–4) **diam**, (686) **TS**; **Annealed and cold drawn**: (3–4) **diam**, (441) **TS**, 12 **El**

WROUGHT CARBON STEELS

specification number	designation	country	product forms	composition	mechanical properties (see page iv for explanation)
JIS G 3539	SWCH 22K	Japan	Wire	0.18–0.23 **C**, 0.70–1.00 **Mn**, 0.030 **P**, 0.035 **S**, 0.10–0.35 **Si**	**Cold drawn**: (4–5) **diam**, (569) **TS**; **Annealed and cold drawn**: (4–5) **diam**, (441) **TS**, 12 **El**
EURONORM 119–74, II	Cb 20 FF KD	EURONORM	Wire, rod	0.18–0.23 **C**, 0.30–0.60 **Mn**, 0.040 **P**, 0.040 **S**, 0.10 **Si**	**Cold rolled or cold finished**: (2–100) **diam**, (540) max **TS**
AMS 5070E		US	Bar, forgings	0.18–0.23 **C**, 0.70–1.00 **Mn**, 0.040 **P**, 0.050 **S**, 0.10–0.30 **Si**	**Cold finished**: ≤0.875 (≤22.22) **diam**, 70 (483) **TS**, 60 (414) **YS**, 18 **El**
DGN–B–301	1021	Mexico	Bar	0.18–0.23 **C**, 0.60–0.90 **Mn**, 0.040 **P**, 0.050 **S**, 0.10 **Si**	**Forged or hot rolled, cold rolled and cold finished**: all **diam**, (422) **TS**, (284) **YS**, 24 **El**
DGN–B–301	1022	Mexico	Bar	0.18–0.23 **C**, 0.70–1.00 **Mn**, 0.040 **P**, 0.050 **S**, 0.10 **Si**	**Forged or hot rolled, cold rolled and cold finished**: all **diam**, (422) **TS**, (235) **YS**, 23 **El**
JIS G 3539	SWCH 20K	Japan	Wire	0.18–0.23 **C**, 0.30–0.60 **Mn**, 0.030 **P**, 0.035 **S**, 0.10–0.35 **Si**	**Annealed and cold drawn**: all **diam**, (412) **TS**, 13 **El**
JIS G 3539	SWCH 20A	Japan	Wire	0.18–0.23 **C**, 0.30–0.60 **Mn**, 0.030 **P**, 0.035 **S**, 0.10 **Si**, 0.02 min **Al**	**Cold drawn**: (>5) **diam**, (412) **TS**, 8 **El**; **Annealed and cold drawn**: (>5) **diam**, (373) **TS**, 13 **El**
DGN–B–301	1020	Mexico	Bar	0.18–0.23 **C**, 0.30–0.60 **Mn**, 0.040 **P**, 0.050 **S**, 0.10 **Si**	**Forged or hot rolled, cold rolled and cold finished**: all **diam**, (382) **TS**, (245) **YS**, 25 **El**
ASTM A 544	Grade 1022	US	Wire	0.18–0.23 **C**, 0.70–1.00 **Mn**, 0.040 **P**, 0.050 **S**	
ASTM A 544	Grade 1020	US	Wire	0.18–0.23 **C**, 0.30–0.60 **Mn**, 0.040 **P**, 0.050 **S**	
AISI 1022		US	Bar	0.18–0.23 **C**, 0.70–1.00 **Mn**, 0.040 **P**, 0.050 **S**	
AISI 1021		US	Bar	0.18–0.23 **C**, 0.60–0.90 **Mn**, 0.040 **P**, 0.050 **S**	
AISI 1020		US	Bar	0.18–0.23 **C**, 0.30–0.60 **Mn**, 0.040 **P**, 0.050 **S**	
BS 970: Part 1	040A20	UK	Blooms, billets, slabs, bar, rod, forgings	0.18–0.23 **C**, 0.30–0.50 **Mn**	
BS 970: Part 1	050A20	UK	Blooms, billets, slabs, bar, rod, forgings	0.18–0.23 **C**, 0.40–0.60 **Mn**	
BS 970: Part 1	060A20	UK	Blooms, billets, slabs, bar, rod, forgings	0.18–0.23 **C**, 0.50–0.70 **Mn**	
BS 970: Part 1	080A20	UK	Blooms, billets, slabs, bar, rod, forgings	0.18–0.23 **C**, 0.70–0.90 **Mn**	
ANSI/ASTM A 519	1020	US	Tube: seamless	0.18–0.23 **C**, 0.30–0.60 **Mn**, 0.040 **P**, 0.050 **S**	
ANSI/ASTM A 519	1021	US	Tube: seamless	0.18–0.23 **C**, 0.60–0.90 **Mn**, 0.040 **P**, 0.050 **S**	
ANSI/ASTM A 519	1022	US	Tube: seamless	0.18–0.23 **C**, 0.70–1.00 **Mn**, 0.040 **P**, 0.050 **S**	
AS 1446	Grade AS 1446/K1022	Australia	Plate	0.18–0.23 **C**, 0.70–1.00 **Mn**, 0.050 **P**, 0.050 **S**, 0.10–0.35 **Si**	
AS 1446	Grade AS 1446/S1020	Australia	Plate	0.18–0.23 **C**, 0.30–0.60 **Mn**, 0.050 **P**, 0.050 **S**, 0.35 **Si**	
COPANT 330	1120	COPANT	Bar, shapes	0.18–0.23 **C**, 0.70–1.0 **Mn**, 0.040 **P**, 0.08–0.13 **S**	
COPANT 331	1020	COPANT	Bar	0.18–0.23 **C**, 0.30–0.60 **Mn**, 0.040 **P**, 0.050 **S**	
COPANT 331	1021	COPANT	Bar	0.18–0.23 **C**, 0.60–0.90 **Mn**, 0.040 **P**, 0.050 **S**	
COPANT 331	1022	COPANT	Bar	0.18–0.23 **C**, 0.70–1.00 **Mn**, 0.040 **P**, 0.050 **S**	
COPANT 331	1120	COPANT	Bar	0.18–0.23 **C**, 0.70–1.00 **Mn**, 0.040 **P**, 0.08–0.13 **S**	
MIL–S–16974E	No. 1022	US	Bar, billets, blooms, slabs	0.18–0.23 **C**, 0.70–1.00 **Mn**, 0.040 **P**, 0.050 **S**, 0.00–0.30 **Si**	
ASTM A 108	1022	US	Bar	0.18–0.23 **C**, 0.70–1.00 **Mn**, 0.040 **P**, 0.050 **S**	

specification number	designation	country	product forms	composition	mechanical properties (see page iv for explanation)
ASTM A 108	1020	US	Bar	0.18–0.23 **C**, 0.30–0.60 **Mn**, 0.040 **P**, 0.050 **S**	
ANSI/ASTM A 546	Grade 10B21	US	Wire	0.18–0.23 **C**, 0.80–1.10 **Mn**, 0.040 **P**, 0.050 **S**, 0.0005 min **B**	
ANSI/ASTM A 545	Grade 1022	US	Wire	0.18–0.23 **C**, 0.70–1.00 **Mn**, 0.040 **P**, 0.050 **S**	
ANSI/ASTM A 545	Grade 1021	US	Wire	0.18–0.23 **C**, 0.60–0.90 **Mn**, 0.040 **P**, 0.050 **S**	
ANSI/ASTM A 548	Grade 1021	US	Wire	0.18–0.23 **C**, 0.60–0.90 **Mn**, 0.040 **P**, 0.050 **S**	
ANSI/ASTM A 548	Grade 1022	US	Wire	0.18–0.23 **C**, 0.70–1.00 **Mn**, 0.040 **P**, 0.050 **S**	
ANSI/ASTM A548	Grade 1022 mod	US	Wire	0.18–0.23 **C**, 0.80–1.10 **Mn**, 0.040 **P**, 0.050 **S**	
MIL-S-11310E	1020	US	Bar	0.18–0.23 **C**, 0.30–0.60 **Mn**, 0.040 **P**, 0.050 **S**, 0.20 **Si**	
MIL-S-11310E	1022	US	Bar	0.18–0.23 **C**, 0.70–1.00 **Mn**, 0.040 **P**, 0.050 **S**, 0.20 **Si**	
MIL-S-16788A	Class C2	US	Blooms, billets, slabs	0.18–0.23 **C**, 0.30–0.60 **Mn**, 0.040 **P**, 0.050 **S**	
COPANT 333	1020	COPANT	Wire, rod	0.18–0.23 **C**, 0.30–0.60 **Mn**, 0.040 **P**, 0.050 **S**	
COPANT 333	1021	COPANT	Wire, rod	0.18–0.23 **C**, 0.60–0.90 **Mn**, 0.040 **P**, 0.050 **S**	
COPANT 333	1022	COPANT	Wire, rod	0.18–0.23 **C**, 0.70–1.00 **Mn**, 0.040 **P**, 0.050 **S**	
ANSI/ASTM A 575	1020	US	Bar	0.18–0.23 **C**, 0.30–0.60 **Mn**, 0.04 **P**, 0.05 **S**	
AISI 1020		US	Wire, rod	0.18–0.23 **C**, 0.30–0.60 **Mn**, 0.040 **P**, 0.050 **S**	
AISI 1021		US	Wire, rod	0.18–0.23 **C**, 0.60–0.90 **Mn**, 0.040 **P**, 0.050 **S**	
AISI 1022		US	Wire, rod	0.18–0.23 **C**, 0.70–1.00 **Mn**, 0.040 **P**, 0.050 **S**	
ANSI/ASTM A 576	1020	US	Bar	0.18–0.23 **C**, 0.30–0.60 **Mn**, 0.040 **P**, 0.050 **S**	
ANSI/ASTM A 576	1021	US	Bar	0.18–0.23 **C**, 0.60–0.90 **Mn**, 0.040 **P**, 0.050 **S**	
ANSI/ASTM A 576	1022	US	Bar	0.18–0.23 **C**, 0.70–1.00 **Mn**, 0.040 **P**, 0.050 **S**	
ASTM A 689	1020	US	Bar	0.18–0.23 **C**, 0.30–0.60 **Mn**, 0.040 **P**, 0.050 **S**	
ASTM A 689	1021	US	Bar	0.18–0.23 **C**, 0.60–0.90 **Mn**, 0.040 **P**, 0.050 **S**	
ASTM A 689	1022	US	Bar	0.18–0.23 **C**, 0.70–1.00 **Mn**, 0.040 **P**, 0.050 **S**	
ANSI/ASTM A 29	1020	US	Bar	0.18–0.23 **C**, 0.30–0.60 **Mn**, 0.040 **P**, 0.050 **S**	
ANSI/ASTM A 29	1021	US	Bar	0.18–0.23 **C**, 0.60–0.90 **Mn**, 0.040 **P**, 0.050 **S**	
ANSI/ASTM A 29	1022	US	Bar	0.18–0.23 **C**, 0.70–1.00 **Mn**, 0.040 **P**, 0.050 **S**	
AS 1443	Grade AS 1443/K1022	Australia	Bar	0.18–0.23 **C**, 0.70–1.00 **Mn**, 0.050 **P**, 0.050 **S**, 0.10–0.35 **Si**	
AS 1443	Grade AS 1443/K1020	Australia	Bar	0.18–0.23 **C**, 0.30–0.60 **Mn**, 0.050 **P**, 0.050 **S**, 0.10–0.35 **Si**	
AS 1443	Grade 1443/S1021	Australia	Bar	0.18–0.23 **C**, 0.60–0.90 **Mn**, 0.050 **P**, 0.050 **S**, 0.35 **Si**	
AS 1443	Grade AS 1443/S1020	Australia	Bar	0.18–0.23 **C**, 0.30–0.60 **Mn**, 0.050 **P**, 0.050 **S**, 0.35 **Si**	
AS 1442	Grade AS 1442/S1020	Australia	Bar, blooms, billets, slabs	0.18–0.23 **C**, 0.30–0.60 **Mn**, 0.050 **P**, 0.050 **S**, 0.35 **Si**	
AS 1442	Grade AS 1442/S1021	Australia	Bar, blooms, billets, slabs	0.18–0.23 **C**, 0.60–0.90 **Mn**, 0.050 **P**, 0.050 **S**, 0.35 **Si**	
AS 1442	Grade AS 1442/K1020	Australia	Bar, blooms, billets, slabs	0.18–0.23 **C**, 0.30–0.60 **Mn**, 0.050 **P**, 0.050 **S**, 0.10–0.35 **Si**	

WROUGHT CARBON STEELS

specification number	designation	country	product forms	composition	mechanical properties (see page iv for explanation)
AS 1442	Grade AS 1442/K1022	Australia	Bar, blooms, billets, slabs	0.18–0.23 **C**, 0.70–1.00 **Mn**, 0.050 **P**, 0.050 **S**, 0.10–0.35 **Si**	
DEF STAN 95–1/1	C1020	Canada	Bar	0.18–0.23 **C**, 0.30–0.60 **Mn**, 0.04 **P**, 0.05 **S**, 0.10–0.30 **Si**	
DEF STAN 95–1/1	CL.2.C1120	Canada	Bar	0.18–0.23 **C**, 0.60–0.90 **Mn**, 0.08–0.15 **S**	
COPANT 514	Grade TM 1021	COPANT	Tube: seamless	0.18–0.23 **C**, 0.60–0.90 **Mn**, 0.040 **P**, 0.050 **S**, 0.20–0.35 **Si**	**Hot finished:** (>323.9) **diam**, 15 **El**; **Cold finished:** all **diam**, 5 **El**; **Annealed:** all **diam**, 30 **El**; **Normalized:** all **diam**, 30 **El**
COPANT 514	Grade TM 1021	COPANT	Tube: seamless	0.18–0.23 **C**, 0.60–0.90 **Mn**, 0.040 **P**, 0.050 **S**, 0.20–0.35 **Si**	**Hot finished:** (>323.9) **diam**, 15 **El**; **Cold finished:** all **diam**, 5 **El**; **Annealed:** all **diam**, 30 **El**; **Normalized:** all **diam**, 30 **El**
COPANT 514	Grade TM 1021	COPANT	Tube: seamless	0.18–0.23 **C**, 0.60–0.90 **Mn**, 0.040 **P**, 0.050 **S**, 0.20–0.35 **Si**	**Hot finished:** (>323.9) **diam**, 15 **El**; **Cold finished:** all **diam**, 5 **El**; **Annealed:** all **diam**, 30 **El**; **Normalized:** all **diam**, 30 **El**
DIN 17140	Grade D20–2	Germany	Wire, rod	0.18–0.23 **C**, 0.30–0.60 **Mn**, 0.040 **P**, 0.040 **S**, 0.10–0.30 **Si**, 0.007 **N**	
JIS G 3507	SWRCH 20A	Japan	Wire, rod	0.18–0.23 **C**, 0.30–0.60 **Mn**, 0.030 **P**, 0.035 **S**, 0.10 **Si**, 0.02 **Al**	
JIS G 3507	SWRCH 22A	Japan	Wire, rod	0.18–0.23 **C**, 0.70–1.00 **Mn**, 0.030 **P**, 0.035 **S**, 0.10 **Si**, 0.02 **Al**	
JIS G 3507	SWRCH 20K	Japan	Wire, rod	0.18–0.23 **C**, 0.30–0.60 **Mn**, 0.030 **P**, 0.035 **S**, 0.10–0.35 **Si**	
JIS G 3507	SWRCH 22K	Japan	Wire, rod	0.18–0.23 **C**, 0.70–1.00 **Mn**, 0.030 **P**, 0.035 **S**, 0.10–0.35 **Si**	
JIS G 3505	SWRM 20	Japan	Wire, rod	0.18–0.23 **C**, 0.30–0.60 **Mn**, 0.045 **P**, 0.045 **S**	
JIS G 4051	S 20C	Japan	Bar, wire, rod	0.18–0.23 **C**, 0.30–0.60 **Mn**, 0.030 **P**, 0.035 **S**, 0.15–0.35 **Si**, 0.30 **Cu**	
JIS G 4051	S 20CK	Japan	Bar, wire, rod	0.18–0.23 **C**, 0.30–0.60 **Mn**, 0.025 **P**, 0.025 **S**, 0.15–0.35 **Si**, 0.25 **Cu**	
NF A 36–204	E 550, I	France	Plate	0.18 **C**, 1.50 **Mn**, 0.025 **P**, 0.025 **S**, 0.10–0.50 **Si**	**Normalized and tempered, quenched and tempered or aged:** (5–50) **diam**, (670) **TS**, (550) **YS**, 16 **El**
ANSI/ASTM A 656	Grade 1	US	Plate	0.18 **C**, 1.60 **Mn**, 0.040 **P**, 0.050 **S**, 0.60 **Si**, 0.05–0.15 **V**, 0.020 **Al**, 0.005–0.030 **N**	**Hot rolled:** ≤0.625 **diam**, 95 (655) **TS**, 80 (552) **YS**, 12 **El**
MIL–S–24412		US	Shapes: structural	0.18 **C**, 1.30 **Mn**, 0.035 **P**, 0.40 **S**, 0.15–0.35 **Si**, 0.02 **V**	**Mill condition:** all **diam**, 90 (621) **TS**, 45 (310) **YS**, 20 in 8 in **El**
NF A 36–204	E 500, II	France	Plate	0.18 **C**, 1.50 **Mn**, 0.025 **P**, 0.025 **S**, 0.10–0.50 **Si**	**Normalized and tempered, quenched and tempered or aged:** (5–50) **diam**, (620) **TS**, (500) **YS**, 17 **El**
MIL–S–20166B	Grade HT	US	Shapes	0.18 **C**, 1.30 **Mn**, 0.035 **P**, 0.040 **S**, 0.15–0.35 **Si**, 0.02 **V**	**Mill:** 0.5–1.5 **diam**, (620) max **TS**, (324) **YS**, 20 **El**
JIS G 3106	Class 5	Japan	Plate, strip	0.18 **C**, 1.50 **Mn**, 0.040 **P**, 0.040 **S**, 0.55 **Si**	**Hot rolled:** (6–16) **diam**, (569) **TS**, (461) **YS**, 19 **El**
JIS G 3445	Class 18C, No. 12	Japan	Tube: seamless or welded	0.18 **C**, 1.50 **Mn**, 0.040 **P**, 0.040 **S**, 0.55 **Si**	**As manufactured or cold finished:** (≥8) **diam**, (510) **TS**, (382) **YS**, 15 **El**
SFS 1150	Fe 355 P	Finland	Plate, strip, bar	0.18 **C**, 0.9–1.6 **Mn**, 0.030 **P**, 0.030 **S**, 0.15–0.50 **Si**, 0.03–0.12 **V**, 0.015–0.060 **Nb**, 0.2–0.20 **Ti**, 0.015–0.080 **Al**, 0.012 **N**	**Hot rolled:** (<60) **diam**, (490) **TS**, (355) **YS**, 22 **El**
DS 12011	St 50 D	Denmark	Rod, bar, shapes	0.18 **C**, 1.40 **Mn**, 0.040 **P**, 0.040 **S**, 0.50 **Si**, 0.30 **Cu**, 0.20 **Cr**, 0.009 **N**	**Hot rolled:** (16) **diam**, (490) **TS**, (314) **YS**, 21 **El**
DS 12011	St 50 C	Denmark	Rod, bar, shapes	0.18 **C**, 1.40 **Mn**, 0.050 **P**, 0.050 **S**, 0.50 **Si**, 0.40 **Cu**, 0.30 **Cr**, 0.009 **N**	**Hot rolled:** (16) **diam**, (490) **TS**, (314) **YS**, 21 **El**

WROUGHT CARBON STEELS

specification number	designation	country	product forms	composition	mechanical properties (see page iv for explanation)
SS 14 21 73	SS 21 73–00	Sweden	Bar, plate	0.18 **C**, 1.4 **Mn**, 0.05 **P**, 0.05 **S**, 0.05 **Si**, 0.04 **Cu**, 0.03 **Cr**, 0.009 **N**	**As rolled**: all **diam**, (490) **TS**, (310) **YS**, 21 **El**
SS 14 21 73	SS 21 73–01	Sweden	Bar, plate, sheet	0.18 **C**, 1.4 **Mn**, 0.05 **P**, 0.05 **S**, 0.05 **Si**, 0.04 **Cu**, 0.03 **Cr**, 0.009 **N**	**Normalized**: (25–40) **diam**, (490) **TS**, (300) **YS**, 21 **El**
SS 14 21 73	SS 21 73–00	Sweden	Bar, plate	0.18 **C**, 1.4 **Mn**, 0.05 **P**, 0.05 **S**, 0.05 **Si**, 0.04 **Cu**, 0.03 **Cr**, 0.009 **N**	**As rolled**: all **diam**, (490) **TS**, (310) **YS**, 21 **El**
SS 14 21 74	SS 21 74–01	Sweden	Bar, plate, sheet	0.18 **C**, 1.4 **Mn**, 0.04 **P**, 0.04 **S**, 0.35 **Si**, 0.03 **Cu**, 0.02 **Cr**, 0.009 **N**	**Normalized**: all **diam**, (490) **TS**, (310) **YS**, 21 **El**
SS 14 21 74	SS 21 74–03	Sweden	Tube: seamless	0.18 **C**, 1.4 **Mn**, 0.04 **P**, 0.04 **S**, 0.35 **Si**, 0.03 **Cu**, 0.02 **Cr**, 0.009 **N**	**Normalized**: (<5) **diam**, (490) **TS**, (310) **YS**, 21 **El**
SS 14 21 74	SS 21 74–04	Sweden	Tube: welded	0.18 **C**, 1.4 **Mn**, 0.04 **P**, 0.04 **S**, 0.35 **Si**, 0.03 **Cu**, 0.02 **Cr**, 0.009 **N**	**Normalized**: (<5) **diam**, (490) **TS**, (310) **YS**, 21 **El**
SS 14 21 74	SS 21 74–01	Sweden	Bar, plate, sheet	0.18 **C**, 1.4 **Mn**, 0.04 **P**, 0.04 **S**, 0.05 **Si**, 0.03 **Cu**, 0.02 **Cr**, 0.009 **N**	**Normalized**: all **diam**, (490) **TS**, (310) **YS**, 21 **El**
SS 14 21 74	SS 21 74–03	Sweden	Tube: seamless	0.18 **C**, 1.4 **Mn**, 0.04 **P**, 0.04 **S**, 0.05 **Si**, 0.03 **Cu**, 0.02 **Cr**, 0.009 **N**	**Normalized**: (<5) **diam**, (490) **TS**, (310) **YS**, 21 **El**
SS 14 21 74	SS 21 74–04	Sweden	Tube: welded	0.18 **C**, 1.4 **Mn**, 0.04 **P**, 0.04 **S**, 0.05 **Si**, 0.03 **Cu**, 0.02 **Cr**, 0.009 **N**	**Normalized**: (<5) **diam**, (490) **TS**, (310) **YS**, 21 **El**
JIS G 3115	Class 2	Japan	Plate	0.18 **C**, 1.50 **Mn**, 0.035 **P**, 0.040 **S**	**As rolled**: (≤16) **diam**, (490) **TS**, (314) **YS**, 16 **El**
JIS G 3106	Class 2B	Japan	Plate, strip, shape, bar	0.18 **C**, 1.50 **Mn**, 0.040 **P**, 0.040 **S**, 0.55 **Si**	**Hot rolled**: (≤5) **diam**, (490) **TS**, (324) **YS**, 22 **El**
JIS G 3106	Class 2C	Japan	Plate, strip	0.18 **C**, 1.50 **Mn**, 0.040 **P**, 0.040 **S**, 0.55 **Si**	**Hot rolled**: (≤5) **diam**, (490) **TS**, (324) **YS**, 22 **El**
JIS G 3444	Class 4, No. 11	Japan	Tube: seamless or electric–resistance welded	0.18 **C**, 1.50 **Mn**, 0.040 **P**, 0.040 **S**, 0.55 **Si**	**As drawn or as welded**: all **diam**, (490) **TS**, (314) **YS**, 23 **El**
JIS G 3445	Class 18B, No. 12	Japan	Tube: seamless or welded	0.18 **C**, 1.50 **Mn**, 0.040 **P**, 0.040 **S**, 0.040 **Si**	**As manufactured or cold finished**: (≥8) **diam**, (490) **TS**, (314) **YS**, 23 **El**
JIS G 3466	Class 2	Japan	Pipe	0.18 **C**, 1.50 **Mn**, 0.040 **P**, 0.040 **S**, 0.55 **Si**	**As manufactured**: (≥8) **diam**, (490) **TS**, (324) **YS**, 23 **El**
ANSI/ASTM A 131	Grades AH36, DH36, EH36	US	Plate, shape, bars	0.18 **C**, 0.90–1.60 **Mn**, 0.04 **P**, 0.04 **S**, 0.10–0.50 **Si**, 0.35 **Cu**, 0.10 **V**, 0.05 **Nb**, 0.065 **Al**, 0.25 **Cr**, 0.08 **Mo**, 0.40 **Ni**	**Normalized**: all **diam**, (490) **TS**, (350) **YS**, 22 **El**
ANSI/ASTM A 131	Grades AH32, DH32, EH32	US	Plate, bar, shapes	0.18 **C**, 0.90–1.60 **Mn**, 0.04 **P**, 0.04 **S**, 0.10–0.50 **Si**, 0.35 **Cu**, 0.065 **Al**, 0.25 **Cr**, 0.08 **Mo**, 0.40 **Ni**	**Normalized**: all **diam**, (470) **TS**, (315) **YS**, 22 **El**
ASTM A 714	Grade VI Type E, S	US	Pipe: welded, seamless	0.18 **C**, 0.45–1.05 **Mn**, 0.045 **P**, 0.055 **S**, 0.27–1.03 **Cu**, 0.33 **Cr**, 0.09–0.21 **Mo**, 0.35–1.15 **Ni**	**As rolled**: all **diam**, 65 (448) **TS**, 46 (317) **YS**
NBN 293	A 45 k	Belgium	Bar	0.18 **C**, 1.20 **Mn**, 0.05–0.09 **P**, 0.05–0.09 **S**, 0.35 **Si**	**As rolled**: (≥9.5) **diam**, (441) **TS**, (274) **YS**
NBN 293	A 45 m	Belgium	Bar	0.18 **C**, 1.20 **Mn**, 0.04–0.07 **P**, 0.04–0.07 **S**, 0.35 **Si**	**As rolled**: (≥9.5) **diam**, (441) **TS**, (274) **YS**
JIS G 3445	Class 18A, No. 12	Japan	Tube: seamless or welded	0.18 **C**, 1.50 **Mn**, 0.040 **P**, 0.040 **S**, 0.55 **Si**	**As manufactured or cold finished**: (≥8) **diam**, (441) **TS**, (275) **YS**, 25 **El**
DIN 17111	Grade RSt44–2	Germany	Bar, wire, rod	0.18 **C**, 0.80 **Mn**, 0.050 **P**, 0.050 **S**, 0.45 **Si**, 0.007 **N**	**Hot rolled**: all **diam**, (432) **TS**, (255) **YS**, 24 **El**
SFS 200:E	Fe 44D	Finland	Bar, plate, strip, wire, forgings	0.18 **C**, 0.45 **P**, 0.045 **S**, 0.55 **Si**, 0.009 **N**	**Hot worked and normalized**: (>40–100) **diam**, (431) **TS**, (265) **YS**, 23 **El**
SFS 200:E	Fe 44C	Finland	Bar, plate, strip, wire, forgings	0.18 **C**, 0.45 **P**, 0.045 **S**, 0.55 **Si**, 0.009 **N**	**Hot worked**: (>40–100) **diam**, (431) **TS**, (265) **YS**, 23 **El**
SS 14 14 13	SS 14 13–01	Sweden	Bar, plate, sheet	0.18 **C**, 0.8–1.4 **Mn**, 0.05 **P**, 0.05 **S**, 0.05 **Si**, 0.04 **Cu**, 0.04 **Cr**, 0.009 **N**	**Normalized (bar, plate)**: all **diam**, (430) **TS**, (250) **YS**, 23 **El**
SS 14 14 14	SS 14 14–00	Sweden	Bar	0.18 **C**, 0.8–1.4 **Mn**, 0.04 **P**, 0.04 **S**, 0.05 **Si**, 0.04 **Cu**, 0.03 **Cr**, 0.009 **N**	**As rolled**: (≤40) **diam**, (430) **TS**, (260) **YS**, 23 **El**
SS 14 14 14	SS 14 14–01	Sweden	Bar, plate, sheet	0.18 **C**, 0.8–1.4 **Mn**, 0.04 **P**, 0.04 **S**, 0.05 **Si**, 0.04 **Cu**, 0.03 **Cr**, 0.009 **N**	**Normalized**: all **diam**, (430) **TS**, (260) **YS**, 23 **El**
SS 14 14 13	SS 14 13–01	Sweden	Bar, plate, sheet	0.18 **C**, 0.8–1.4 **Mn**, 0.05 **P**, 0.05 **S**, 0.05 **Si**, 0.04 **Cu**, 0.03 **Cr**, 0.009 **N**	**Normalized**: all **diam**, (430) **TS**, (250) **YS**, 23 **El**

WROUGHT CARBON STEELS

specification number	designation	country	product forms	composition	mechanical properties (see page iv for explanation)
SS 14 14 13	SS 14 13–00	Sweden	Bar, plate	0.18 **C**, 0.8–1.4 **Mn**, 0.05 **P**, 0.05 **S**, 0.05 **Si**, 0.04 **Cu**, 0.03 **Cr**, 0.009 **N**	**As rolled**: all.**diam**, (430) **TS**, (260) **YS**, 23 **El**
SS 14 21 73	SS 21 73–01	Sweden	Bar, plate, sheet	0.18 **C**, 1.4 **Mn**, 0.05 **P**, 0.05 **S**, 0.05 **Si**, 0.04 **Cu**, 0.03 **Cr**, 0.009 **N**	**Normalized**: (25–40) **diam**, (430) **TS**, (300) **YS**, 21 **El**
SS 14 14 13	SS 14 13–00	Sweden	Bar, plate	0.18 **C**, 0.8–1.4 **Mn**, 0.05 **P**, 0.05 **S**, 0.5 **Si**, 0.4 **Cu**, 0.3 **Cr**, 0.009 **N**	**As rolled**: all **diam**, (430) **TS**, (260) **YS**, 23 **El**
ANSI/ASTM A 633	Grade A	US	Plate, bar, shapes	0.18 **C**, 1.00–1.35 **Mn**, 0.04 **P**, 0.05 **S**, 0.15–0.50 **Si**, 0.05 **Nb**	**Normalized**: $\leq$2.5 **diam**, 63 (430) **TS**, 42 (290) **YS**, 23 **El**
ANSI/ASTM A 633	Grade B	US	Plate, bar, shapes	0.18 **C**, 1.00–1.35 **Mn**, 0.04 **P**, 0.05 **S**, 0.15–0.50 **Si**, 0.10 **V**	**Normalized**: $\leq$2.5 **diam**, 63 (430) **TS**, 42 (290) **YS**, 23 **El**
DS 12011	St 42 D	Denmark	Rod, bar, shapes	0.18 **C**, 0.040 **P**, 0.040 **S**, 0.50 **Si**, 0.40 **Cu**, 0.30 **Cr**, 0.009 **N**	**Hot rolled**: (16) **diam**, (412) **TS**, (245) **YS**, 23 **El**
AIR 9160/C27	9160C041	France	Sheet	0.18 **C**, 1.50 **Mn**, 0.040 **P**, 0.040 **S**, 0.55 **Si**, 0.02 min **Al**	**Normalized**: ($\leq$3) **diam**, (410) **TS**, (250) **YS**, 23 **El**
NF A 35–075	A 42 R	France	Bar, rod	0.18 **C**, 0.060 **P**, 0.050 **S**	**As rolled**: all **diam**, (410) **TS**, (255) **YS**, 24 **El**
JIS G 3115	Class 1	Japan	Plate	0.18 **C**, 1.40 **Mn**, 0.035 **P**, 0.040 **S**, 0.15–0.35 **Si**	**As rolled**: ($\leq$16) **diam**, (402) **TS**, (235) **YS**, 17 **El**
JIS G 3106	Class 1C	Japan	Plate, strip	0.18 **C**, 0.60–1.20 **Mn**, 0.040 **P**, 0.040 **S**, 0.35 **Si**	**Hot rolled**: ($\leq$5) **diam**, (402) **TS**, (245) **YS**, 23 **El**
ANSI/ASTM A 131	Grade E	US	Plate, shapes, bar	0.18 **C**, 0.70–1.50 **Mn**, 0.04 **P**, 0.04 **S**, 0.10–0.35 **Si**	**Normalized**: all **diam**, (400) **TS**, (235) **YS**, 24 **El**
BS 980	CDS–3	UK	Tube	0.18 **C**, 0.4–0.7 **Mn**, 0.050 **P**, 0.050 **S**, 0.05–0.35 **Si**	**Drawn or drawn and tempered**: all **diam**, (385) **TS**, (330) **YS**
MIL–T–22555A	Type 1	US	Tubing: seamless	0.18 **C**, 0.30–0.60 **Mn**, 0.040 **P**, 0.050 **S**	**Annealed**: all **diam**, 55 (379) **TS**, 35 **El**
MIL–T–22555A	Type 2	US	Tubing: welded	0.18 **C**, 0.30–0.60 **Mn**, 0.040 **P**, 0.050 **S**	**Annealed**: all **diam**, 55 (379) **TS**, 35 **El**
DGN–B–245	Grade 40	Mexico	Plate	0.18 **C**, 0.60–0.90 **Mn**, 0.035 **P**, 0.040 **S**, 0.15–0.30 **Si**	**As rolled**: (<13) **diam**, (377) **TS**, (207) **YS**, 27 **El**
DIN 17111	Grade RSt38–2	Germany	Bar, wire, rod	0.18 **C**, 0.25–0.50 **Mn**, 0.050 **P**, 0.050 **S**, 0.40 **Si**, 0.007 **N**	**Hot rolled**: all **diam**, (373) **TS**, (227) **YS**, 25 **El**
DS 12011	St 37 D	Denmark	Rod, bar, shapes	0.18 **C**, 0.04 **P**, 0.04 **S**, 0.009 **N**	**Hot rolled**: (16) **diam**, (363) **TS**, (216) **YS**, 24 **El**
NS 12123	NS 12123–00	Norway	Bar, rod, shapes	0.18 **C**, 0.050 **P**, 0.050 **S**, 0.007 **N**	**Hot worked**: (16) **diam**, (363) **TS**, (235) **YS**, 25 **El**
NS 12122	NS 12122–00	Norway	Bar, rod, shapes	0.18 **C**, 0.050 **P**, 0.050 **S**, 0.007 **N**	**Hot worked**: (16) **diam**, (363) **TS**, (235) **YS**, 25 **El**
NF A 36–101	A 37,3	France	Strip	0.18 **C**, 0.050 **P**, 0.050 **S**	**Hot rolled**: all **diam**, (363) **TS**, (235) **YS**, 28 **El**
NF A 36–101	A 37,4	France	Strip	0.18 **C**, 0.045 **P**, 0.045 **S**	**Hot rolled**: all **diam**, (363) **TS**, (235) **YS**, 29 **El**
NF A 36–211	BS 1	France	Plate	0.18 **C**, 0.040 **P**, 0.040 **S**, 0.20 **Si**	**Normalized**: all **diam**, (363) **TS**, (245) **YS**, 34 **El**
BS 1501–151	Grade 23A	UK	Plate	0.18 **C**, 0.40 **Mn**, 0.050 **P**, 0.050 **S**, 0.35 **Si**; 0.07 max other elements, total	**Normalized**: ($\leq$16) **diam**, (360) **TS**, (200) **YS**, 45 **El**
BS 1501–151	Grade 23B	UK	Plate	0.18 **C**, 0.40 **Mn**, 0.050 **P**, 0.050 **S**, 0.35 **Si**; 0.70 max other elements, total	**Normalized**: ($\leq$16) **diam**, (360) **TS**, (200) **YS**, 45 **El**
BS 1501–161	Grade 23A	UK	Plate	0.18 **C**, 0.40–1.20 **Mn**, 0.050 **P**, 0.050 **S**, 0.10–0.35 **Si**; 0.70 max other elements, total	**Normalized**: ($\leq$16) **diam**, (360) **TS**, (200) **YS**, 45 **El**
BS 1501–161	Grade 23B	UK	Plate	0.18 **C**, 0.40–1.20 **Mn**, 0.050 **P**, 0.050 **S**, 0.10–0.35 **Si**; 0.70 max other elements, total	**Normalized**: ($\leq$16) **diam**, (360) **TS**, (200) **YS**, 45 **El**
NF A 35–049	A 37 Et	France	Bar, wire, rod	0.18 **C**, 0.062 **P**, 0.062 **S**	**Hot rolled (bar)**: ($\leq$30) **diam**, (360) **TS**, (235) **YS**, 28 **El**
NF A 33–102	AR E 24,3 (AR 37)	France	Billets, blooms, slabs	0.18 **C**, 0.050 **P**, 0.050 **S**	**Normalized**: all **diam**, (360) **TS**, (230) **YS**, 28 **El**
NF A 36–205	A 37,C1 and P1	France	Sheet, plate	0.18 **C**, 0.35 min **Mn**, 0.05 **P**, 0.05 **S**, 0.40 **Si**	**Normalized**: (3–30) **diam**, (360) **TS**, (215) **YS**, 28 **El**
NF A 35–501	E 24 A–37 grade 3	France	Sheet, plate, bar	0.18 **C**, 0.050 **P**, 0.050 **S**	**As rolled (sheet, plate)**: (3–30) **diam**, (360) **TS**, (235) **YS**, 24 **El**
NF A 35–501	E 24 A 37 grade 4	France	Bar, sheet, plate	0.18 **C**, 0.045 **P**, 0.045 **S**	**As rolled**: (3–30) **diam**, (360) **TS**, (235) **YS**, 28 **El**

WROUGHT CARBON STEELS

specification number	designation	country	product forms	composition	mechanical properties (see page iv for explanation)
DIN 1629, Part 3	Grade St35/1.0308	Germany	Tube: seamless	0.18 **C**, 1.50 **Mn**, 0.05 **P**, 0.05 **S**, 0.55 **Si**	**Annealed**: (<16) **diam**, (345) **TS**, (235) **YS**, 25 **El**
ANSI/ASTM A 284	Grade A	US	Plate	0.18 **C**, 0.90 **Mn**, 0.04 **P**, 0.05 **S**, 0.10–0.30 **Si**	**Annealed**: all **diam**, (345) **TS**, (170) **YS**, 28 **El**
DIN 2391 Part 2	Grade St 35–1.0308	Germany	Tube	0.18 **C**, 0.05 **P**, 0.05 **S**	**Normalized**: all **diam**, (343) **TS**, (235) **YS**, 25 **El**; **Bright drawn/hard**: all **diam**, (539) **TS**, 6 **El**; **Bright drawn/soft**: all **diam**, (372) **TS**, 10 **El**; **Annealed**: all **diam**, (314) **TS**, 28 **El**
TS 346	Fe 35	Turkey	Pipe: seamless	0.18 **C**, 0.40 **Mn**, 0.050 **P**, 0.050 **S**, 0.35 **Si**	**As drawn**: (≤16) **diam**, (343) **TS**, (235) **YS**, 25 **El**
TS 302	Fe 35.2	Turkey	Pipe: welded or seamless	0.18 **C**, 0.050 **P**, 0.050 **S**	**As drawn or as welded**: all **diam**, (343) **TS**, (196) **YS**, 25 **El**
SFS 2145	Fe 35	Finland	Tube: seamless	0.18 **C**, 0.05 **P**, 0.05 **S**	**As drawn**: (≤16) **diam**, (343) **TS**, (216) **YS**, 25 **El**
JIS G 3132	Class 2	Japan	Strip	0.18 **C**, 0.25–0.60 **Mn**, 0.040 **P**, 0.040 **S**, 0.35 **Si**	**Hot rolled**: (1.0–1.6) **diam**, (343) **TS**, 25 **El**
ISO 4995	HR235–B	ISO	Sheet	0.18 **C**, 0.050 **P**, 0.050 **S**	**Hot rolled**: (20) **diam**, (330) **TS**, (215) **YS**
ANSI/ASTM A 557	Grade A2	US	Tube: electric resistance welded	0.18 **C**, 0.27–0.63 **Mn**, 0.050 **P**, 0.060 **S**	**Normalized, annealed**: all **diam**, 47 (324) **TS**, 26 (179) **YS**, 35 **El**
DGN–B–207	Grade A2	Mexico	Tube: seamless	0.18 **C**, 0.25–0.63 **Mn**, 0.048 **P**, 0.058 **S**	**Cold finished**: (≥1.14) **diam**, (323) **TS**, (176) **YS**, 35 **El**
ANSI/ASTM A 556	Grade A2	US	Tube: seamless, cold drawn	0.18 **C**, 0.27–0.63 **Mn**, 0.048 **P**, 0.058 **S**	**Annealed**: all **diam**, 47 (320) **TS**, 26 (180) **YS**, 35 **El**
DGN–B–258	Grade A	Mexico	Plate	0.18 **C**, 0.90 **Mn**, 0.04 **P**, 0.05 **S**, 0.10–0.30 **Si**	**Hot rolled**: (≤25) **diam**, (305) **TS**, (173) **YS**, 28 **El**
BS 980	CDS–3A	UK	Tube	0.18 **C**, 0.4–0.7 **Mn**, 0.050 **P**, 0.050 **S**, 0.05–0.35 **Si**	**Annealed or normalized**: all **diam**, (275) **TS**, (150) **YS**
SFS 1255	B500	Finland	Bar	0.18 **C**, 0.06 **P**, 0.05 **S**, 0.60 **Si**, 0.08 **As**, 0.010 **N**, 0.10 **S+Mn**	**Cold finished**: (5) **diam**, (500) **YS**, 6 **El**
SFS 1256	B500P	Finland	Bar	0.18 **C**, 0.06 **P**, 0.05 **S**, 0.60 **Si**, 0.08 **As**, 0.010 **N**, 0.10 **S+Mn**	**Cold finished**: (5) **diam**, (500) **YS**, 8 **El**
DIN 2393 Sheet 2	Grade St 37–2–1.0112 or 1.0114	Germany	Tube	0.18 **C**, 0.05 **P**, 0.05 **S**	
DIN 2393 Sheet 2	Grade St 37–2.2–1.0112 or 1.0114	Germany	Tube	0.18 **C**, 0.05 **P**, 0.05 **S**	
ANSI/ASTM A 214		US	Tube: electric resistance welded	0.18 **C**, 0.27–0.63 **Mn**, 0.050 **P**, 0.060 **S**	**Normalized**
NOM–B–195		Mexico	Tube: electric resistance welded	0.18 **C**, 0.27–0.63 **Mn**, 0.050 **P**, 0.060 **S**	
NF A 35–053	FR 22	France	Wire, rod	0.17–0.28 **C**, 0.50–0.80 **Mn**, 0.040 **P**, 0.040 **S**, 0.10–0.35 **Si**	**Hot or cold drawn and annealed**: (≤30) **diam**, (600) max **TS**
AISI 1522H		US	Bar	0.17–0.25 **C**, 1.00–1.50 **Mn**, 0.040 **P**, 0.050 **S**, 0.15–0.30 **Si**	
DGN–B–301	1522H	Mexico	Bar	0.17–0.25 **C**, 1.00–1.50 **Mn**, 0.040 **P**, 0.050 **S**, 0.15–0.30 **Si**	
AISI 1522H		US	Wire, rod	0.17–0.25 **C**, 1.00–1.50 **Mn**, 0.040 **P**, 0.050 **S**, 0.15–0.30 **Si**	
QQ–S–698	1020	US	Sheet, strip	0.17–0.24 **C**, 0.30–0.60 **Mn**, 0.040 **P**, 0.050 **S**	
AISI 15B21H		US	Bar	0.17–0.24 **C**, 0.70–1.20 **Mn**, 0.040 **P**, 0.050 **S**, 0.15–0.30 **Si**, 0.0005–0.003 **B**	
ANSI/ASTM A 29	M 1020	US	Bar	0.17–0.24 **C**, 0.25–0.60 **Mn**, 0.04 **P**, 0.05 **S**	
ANSI/ASTM A 575	M 1020	US	Bar	0.17–0.24 **C**, 0.25–0.60 **Mn**, 0.04 **P**, 0.05 **S**	
AISI 15B21H		US	Wire, rod	0.17–0.24 **C**, 0.70–1.20 **Mn**, 0.040 **P**, 0.050 **S**, 0.15–0.30 **Si**	
DIN 17155	Grade 19 Mn 5	Germany	Plate	0.17–0.23 **C**, 1.00–1.30 **Mn**, 0.050 **P**, 0.050 **S**, 0.40–0.60 **Si**, 0.30 max, opt **Cr**	**Normalized**: (≤16) **diam**, (510) **TS**, (323) **YS**

WROUGHT CARBON STEELS

specification number	designation	country	product forms	composition	mechanical properties (see page iv for explanation)
BS 3111 Part1	Type 9	UK	Wire	0.17–0.23 **C**, 0.80–1.10 **Mn**, 0.040 **P**, 0.040 **S**, 0.15–0.35 **Si**, 0.020 **Al**, 0.0008–0.005 **B**	**Drawn and spheroidized annealed**: all diam, (500) max **TS**; **Drawn, spheroidized annealed, and light drawn**: all **diam**, (570) max **TS**
ISO 683/XVIII	C20e	ISO	Bar, wire	0.17–0.23 **C**, 0.30–0.60 **Mn**, 0.035 **P**, 0.035 **S**, 0.15–0.40 **Si**	**Normalized**: all **diam**, (430) **TS**, (240) **YS**, 24 **El**
ISO 683/XVIII	C20ea	ISO	Bar, wire	0.17–0.23 **C**, 0.30–0.60 **Mn**, 0.035 **P**, 0.035 **S**, 0.15–0.40 **Si**	**Normalized**: all **diam**, (430) **TS**, (240) **YS**, 24 **El**
ISO 683/XVIII	C20eb	ISO	Bar, wire	0.17–0.23 **C**, 0.30–0.60 **Mn**, 0.035 **P**, 0.030–0.050 **S**, 0.15–0.40 **Si**	**Normalized**: all **diam**, (430) **TS**, (240) **YS**, 24 **El**
ISO 683/XVIII	C20	ISO	Bar, wire	0.17–0.23 **C**, 0.30–0.60 **Mn**, 0.050 **P**, 0.050 **S**, 0.15–0.40 **Si**	**Normalized**: all **diam**, (430) **TS**, (240) **YS**, 24 **El**
ASTM A 659	Grade 1020	US	Sheet, strip	0.17–0.23 **C**, 0.30–0.60 **Mn**, 0.040 **P**, 0.050 **S**	
ASTM A 659	Grade 1021	US	Sheet, strip	0.17–0.23 **C**, 0.60–0.90 **Mn**, 0.040 **P**, 0.050 **S**	
AISI 1020		US	Plate	0.17–0.23 **C**, 0.30–0.60 **Mn**, 0.040 **P**, 0.050 **S**	
AISI 1021		US	Plate	0.17–0.23 **C**, 0.60–0.90 **Mn**, 0.040 **P**, 0.050 **S**	
AISI 1022		US	Plate	0.17–0.23 **C**, 0.70–1.00 **Mn**, 0.040 **P**, 0.050 **S**	
ANSI/ASTM A 546	Grade 10B22	US	Wire	0.17–0.23 **C**, 1.00–1.30 **Mn**, 0.040 **P**, 0.050 **S**, 0.0005 min **B**	
BS 1502–224	Grade 28	UK	Bar	0.17 **C**, 0.90–1.50 **Mn**, 0.050 **P**, 0.050 **S**, 0.10–0.55 **Si**, 0.70 max other elements, total	**As–rolled**: (≤25) diam, (433) **TS**, (285) **YS**, 45 **El**
IS 3945	Grade A–N	India	Plate	0.17 **C**, 0.80–1.50 **Mn**, 0.050 **P**, 0.050 **S**	**Mill**: (≤25) diam, (431) **TS**, (250) **YS**, 21 **El**
BS 1501–213	Grade 28	UK	Plate	0.17 **C**, 0.90–1.50 **Mn**, 0.050 **P**, 0.050 **S**, 0.55 **Si**, 0.01–0.08 **Nb**; 0.70 max other elements, total	**Normalized**: (≤16) **diam**, (430) **TS**, (300) **YS**, 45 **El**
BS 1501–223	Grade 28	UK	Plate	0.17 **C**, 0.90–1.50 **Mn**, 0.050 **P**, 0.050 **S**, 0.10–0.55 **Si**, 0.01–0.08 **Nb**; 0.70 max other elements, total	**Normalized**: ≤(16) **diam**, (430) **TS**, (300) **YS**, 45 **El**
BS 1501–224	Grade 28	UK	Plate	0.17 **C**, 0.90–1.50 **Mn**, 0.050 **P**, 0.050 **S**, 0.10–0.55 **Si**, 0.70 max other elements, total	**Normalized**: ≤(16) **diam**, (430) **TS**, (285) **YS**, 45 **El**
DIN 1652	St 34–2 (1.0151)	Germany	Bar	0.17 **C**, 0.05 **P**, 0.05 **S**	**Cold drawn**: all **diam**, (410) **TS**, (315) **YS**, 10 in 80 mm **El**; **Centerless turned and solution annealed**: all **diam**, (300) **TS**, (165) **YS**, 28 in 80 mm **El**; **Centerless turned and normalized**: all **diam**, (330) **TS**, (185) **YS**, 28 in 80 mm **El**
BS 1501–221	Grades 26A, 26B	UK	Plate	0.17 **C**, 0.90–1.50 **Mn**, 0.050 **P**, 0.050 **S**, 0.10–0.55 **Si**; 0.70 max other elements, total	**Normalized**: (≤16) **diam**, (400) **TS**, (235) **YS**, 45 **El**
BS 1501–211	Grades 26A, 26B	UK	Plate	0.17 **C**, 0.90–1.50 **Mn**, 0.050 **P**, 0.050 **S**, 0.55 **Si**; 0.70 max other elements, total	**Normalized**: (≤16) **diam**, (400) **TS**, (235) **YS**, 45 **El**
ANSI/ASTM A 662	Grade A	US	Plate	0.17 **C**, 0.85–1.40 **Mn**, 0.035 **P**, 0.040 **S**, 0.13–0.33 **Si**	**As rolled or normalized**: all **diam**, 58 (400) **TS**, 40 (275) **YS**, 23 **El**
NBN 629	D 37–1	Belgium	Strip	0.17 **C**, 0.40–1.20 **Mn**, 0.050 **P**, 0.050 **S**, 0.35 **Si**	**As rolled**: (3–63) **diam**, (365) **TS**, (235) **YS**, 26 **El**
NBN 629	D 37–2	Belgium	Strip	0.17 **C**, 0.40–1.20 **Mn**, 0.040 **P**, 0.040 **S**, 0.10–0.35 **Si**	**As rolled**: (3–63) **diam**, (365) **TS**, (235) **YS**, 26 **El**
NBN 630	E 37–2	Belgium	Strip	0.17 **C**, 0.40–1.20 **Mn**, 0.040 **P**, 0.040 **S**, 0.10–0.35 **Si**	**As rolled**: (3–40) **diam**, (365) **TS**, (235) **YS**, 26 **El**
NBN 630	E 37–1	Belgium	Strip	0.17 **C**, 0.40–1.20 **Mn**, 0.050 **P**, 0.050 **S**, 0.35 **Si**	**As rolled**: (3–63) **diam**, (365) **TS**, (235) **YS**, 26 **El**
SFS 200:E	Fe 37D	Finland	Bar, plate, strip, wire, forgings	0.17 **C**, 0.045 **P**, 0.045 **S**, 0.009 **N**	**Hot worked and normalized**: (>40–100) **diam**, (363) **TS**, (216) **YS**, 25 **El**

WROUGHT CARBON STEELS

specification number	designation	country	product forms	composition	mechanical properties (see page iv for explanation)
SFS 200:E	Fe 37C	Finland	Bar, plate, strip, wire, forgings	0.17 **C**, 0.045 **P**, 0.045 **S**, 0.009 **N**	**Hot worked**: (>40–100) **diam**, (363) **TS**, (216) **YS**, 25 **El**
SFS 200:E	Fe 37B	Finland	Bar, plate, strip, wire, forgings	0.17 **C**, 0.050 **P**, 0.050 **S**, 0.009 **N**	**Hot worked**: (>40–100) **diam**, (363) **TS**, (216) **YS**, 25 **El**
ISO 2604/III	No. TW4	ISO	Tube	0.17 **C**, 0.40–0.80 **Mn**, 0.045 **P**, 0.045 **S**, 0.35 **Si**	**As welded, annealed, normalized**: all **diam**, (360) **TS**, (215) **YS**, 24 **El**
ISO 2604/III	No. TW5	ISO	Tube	0.17 **C**, 0.40–0.80 **Mn**, 0.045 **P**, 0.045 **S**, 0.35 **Si**	**As welded, annealed, normalized**: all **diam**, (360) **TS**, (215) **YS**, 24 **El**
ISO 2604/III	No. TW6	ISO	Tube	0.17 **C**, 0.40–1.00 **Mn**, 0.045 **P**, 0.045 **S**, 0.35 **Si**	**As welded, annealed, normalized**: all **diam**, (360) **TS**, (215) **YS**, 24 **El**
ISO 2604/IV	P3R	ISO	Plate	0.17 **C**, 0.40–1.00 **Mn**, 0.050 **P**, 0.050 **S**, 0.009 **N**	**Hot rolled, normalized**: (3–16) **diam**, (360) **TS**, (205) **YS**, 26 **El**
ISO 2604/IV	P3	ISO	Plate	0.17 **C**, 0.40–1.00 **Mn**, 0.050 **P**, 0.050 **S**, 0.35 **Si**, 0.009 **N**	**Hot rolled, normalized**: (3–16) **diam**, (360) **TS**, (205) **YS**, 26 **El**
ISO 2604/IV	P5	ISO	Plate	0.17 **C**, 0.40–1.00 **Mn**, 0.040 **P**, 0.040 **S**, 0.35 **Si**, 0.015 min $\mathbf{Al}_{met}$	**Hot rolled, normalized**: (3–16) **diam**, (360) **TS**, (235) **YS**, 26 **El**
ISO 2937	Grade TS 4	ISO	Tube: seamless	0.17 **C**, 0.40–0.80 **Mn**, 0.045 **P**, 0.045 **S**, 0.35 **Si**	**Hot finished**: all **diam**, (360) **TS**, (215) **YS**, 24 **El**
ISO 559	TS4/TW4	ISO	Tube: seamless or welded	0.17 **C**, 0.40–0.80 **Mn**, 0.045 **P**, 0.35 **S**	**As welded, hot rolled**: all **diam**, (360) **TS**, (215) **YS**, 22 **El**
BS 3059 Part2	Grade 360	UK	Tube: seamless, welded	0.17 **C**, 0.40–0.80 **Mn**, 0.045 **P**, 0.045 **S**, 0.35 **Si**	**Normalized (welded)**: all **diam**, (360) **TS**, (215) **YS**, 24 **El**; **Hot finished, normalized (seamless)**: all **diam**, (360) **TS**, (215) **YS**, 24 **El**
BS 3601	Grade 360	UK	Pipe, tube: seamless, welded	0.17 **C**, 0.40–0.80 **Mn**, 0.050 **P**, 0.050 **S**, 0.35 **Si**	**Hot finished**: all **diam**, (360) **TS**, (215) **YS**, 24 **El**
NF A 36–205	A 37,C2 and P2	France	Sheet, plate	0.17 **C**, 0.40 min **Mn**, 0.04 **P**, 0.04 **S**, 0.25 **Si**, 0.25 **Cu**	**Normalized**: (3–30) **diam**, (360) **TS**, (215) **YS**, 30 **El**
AS 1836	TW4	Australia	Tube: welded	0.17 **C**, 0.40–0.80 **Mn**, 0.045 **P**, 0.045 **S**, 0.35 **Si**	**Annealed or normalized**: all **diam**, (360) **TS**, (215) **YS**, 24 **El**
AS 1835	TS 4	Australia	Tube: seamless	0.17 **C**, 0.40–0.80 **Mn**, 0.045 **P**, 0.045 **S**, 0.35 **Si**	**Annealed and normalized**: all **diam**, (360) **TS**, (215) **YS**, 24 **El**
AS 1835	TS 5	Australia	Tube: seamless	0.17 **C**, 0.40–0.80 **Mn**, 0.045 **P**, 0.045 **S**, 0.35 **Si**	**Hot finished and normalized**: all **diam**, (360) **TS**, (215) **YS**, 24 **El**
AS 1836	TW 5	Australia	Tube: welded	0.17 **C**, 0.40–0.80 **Mn**, 0.045 **P**, 0.045 **S**, 0.35 **Si**	**Normalized**: all **diam**, (360) **TS**, (215) **YS**, 24 **El**
ISO 2604/11	TS 4	ISO	Tube: seamless	0.17 **C**, 0.40–0.80 **Mn**, 0.045 **P**, 0.045 **S**, 0.35 **Si**	**Hot finished, sub–critical annealed, annealed, normalized**: all **diam**, (360) **TS**, (215) **YS**, 24 **El**
ISO 2604/11	TS 5	ISO	Tube: seamless	0.17 **C**, 0.40–0.80 **Mn**, 0.045 **P**, 0.045 **S**, 0.35 **Si**	**Hot finished, normalized**: all **diam**, (360) **TS**, (215) **YS**, 24 **El**
ISO 2604/11	TS 6	ISO	Tube: seamless	0.17 **C**, 0.40–1.00 **Mn**, 0.045 **P**, 0.045 **S**, 0.35 **Si**, 0.015 $\mathbf{Al}_{met}$	**Hot finished, annealed, normalized**: all **diam**, (360) **TS**, (215) **YS**, 24 **El**
DIN 1629, Part 4	Grade St35.4/1.0309		Tube: seamless	0.17 **C**, 0.40 **Mn**, 0.05 **P**, 0.05 **S**, 0.10–0.35 **Si**	**Annealed**: (<16) **diam**, (345) **TS**, (235) **YS**, 25 **El**
DIN 2391 Part 2	Grade St 35.2–1.0309	Germany		0.17 **C**, 0.40 **Mn**, 0.05 **P**, 0.05 **S**, 0.35 **Si**	**Normalized**: all **diam**, (343) **TS**, (235) **YS**, 25 **El**; **Bright drawn/hard**: all **diam**; **Bright drawn/soft**: all **diam**, (372) **TS**, 10 **El**; **Annealed**: all **diam**, (314) **TS**, 28 **El**
DIN 17175 Part 1	St 35.8–1.0305	Germany	Tube: seamless	0.17 **C**, 0.40 **Mn**, 0.050 **P**, 0.050 **S**, 0.35 **Si**	**Hot rolled or cold drawn, normalized or annealed**: all **diam**, (343) **TS**, (235) **YS**, 25 **El**
TS 381	UDK 621.643.2/Fe 35.8	Turkey	Pipe: seamless	0.17 **C**, 0.40 **Mn**, 0.050 **P**, 0.050 **S**, 0.35 **Si**	**As drawn**: all **diam**, (343) **TS**, (235) **YS**, 25 **El**

WROUGHT CARBON STEELS

specification number	designation	country	product forms	composition	mechanical properties (see page iv for explanation)
DIN 17135	Grade A St 35	Germany	Plate, strip, tube, bar, forgings	0.17 **C**, 0.40 min **Mn**, 0.045 **P**, 0.045 **S**, 0.35 **Si**	**Normalized**: (≤16) **diam**, (343) **TS**, (225) **YS**, 25 **El**
NBN A 25–102	D 35	Belgium	Tube	0.17 **C**, 0.36–0.84 **Mn**, 0.045 **P**, 0.045 **S**, 0.12–0.38 **Si**	**Hot finished or cold finished and normalized**: all **diam**, (340) **TS**, (240) **YS**, 25 **El**
DIN 1626, Part 3	Grade St34–2/1.0102	Germany	Pipe: welded	0.17 **C**, 1.5 **Mn**, 0.05 **P**, 0.05 **S**, 0.55 **Si**	**As welded**: (<16) **diam**, (335) **TS**, (205) **YS**, 26 **El**
DIN, 1626, Part 4	Grade St 34–2	Germany	Pipe: welded (specially tested)	0.17 **C**, 1.5 **Mn**, 0.05 **P**, 0.05 **S**, 0.55 **Si**	**Annealed**: (<16) **diam**, (335) **TS**, (205) **YS**, 26 **El**
NBN 744		Belgium	Pipe	0.17 **C**, 0.08 **P**, 0.06 **S**	**Hot rolled or cold rolled**: (20–300) **diam**, (333) **TS**, (206) **YS**, 23 **El**
TS 911	669.14–423/Fe 34	Turkey	Bar	0.17 **C**, 0.063 **P**, 0.063 **S**	**Hot rolled**: all **diam**, (333) **TS**, (206) **YS**, 28 **El**
TS 416	Fe 34.2	Turkey	Pipe: welded	0.17 **C**, 0.050 **P**, 0.050 **S**, 0.007 **N**	**As welded**: (<16) **diam**, (333) **TS**, (206) **YS**, 26 **El**
ISO 4995	HR235–D	ISO	Sheet	0.17 **C**, 0.040 **P**, 0.040 **S**	**Hot rolled**: (20) **diam**, (330) **TS**, (215) **YS**
DIN 17100	RSt 34–2 (1.0108)	Germany	Bar	0.17 **C**, 0.055 **P**, 0.055 **S**	**Normalized**: all **diam**, (330) **TS**, (205) **YS**, 28 **El**
DIN 17100	RSt 34–2 (1.0108)	Germany	Strip	0.17 **C**, 0.055 **P**, 0.055 **S**	**Normalized**: all **diam**, (330) **TS**, (205) **YS**, 28 **El**; **Hot rolled**: all **diam**, (330) **TS**, (205) **YS**, 20 **El**
DIN 17100	RSt 34–2 (1.0108)	Germany	Plate	0.17 **C**, 0.055 **P**, 0.055 **S**	**Normalized**: all **diam**, (330) **TS**, (205) **YS**, 28 **El**
NS 2501	NVR 1–1	Norway	Tube: seamless or welded	0.17 **C**, 0.050 **P**, 0.050 **S**	**Hot formed**: all **diam**, (330) **TS**, (235) **YS**, 25 **El**
COPANT 37, I	BM–17	COPANT	Plate	0.17 **C**, 0.035 **P**, 0.045 **S**, 0.32 **C**	**As rolled**: (4.75–50) **diam**, (320) **TS**, (170) **YS**, 30 **El**
ANSI/ASTM A 285	Grade A	US	Plate	0.17 **C**, 0.90 **Mn**, 0.035 **P**, 0.045 **S**	**As rolled**: all **diam**, (310) **TS**, (165) **YS**, 30 **El**
DGN–B–242	Grade A	Mexico	Plate	0.17 **C**, 0.90 **Mn**, 0.035 **P**, 0.045 **S**, 0.20–0.35 **Cu**	**As rolled**: (<50) **diam**, (309) **TS**, (165) **YS**, 30 **El**
NF A 35–590	1309 (Y_3 12)	France	Bar, forgings	0.17 **C**, 0.30–0.60 **Mn**, 0.035 **P**, 0.035 **S**, 0.15–0.40 **Si**	
SIS 14 14 50	SIS 14 50–00	Sweden	Bar	0.16–0.28 **C**, 0.40–0.90 **Mn**, 0.050 **P**, 0.050 **S**	**As rolled**: (≤63) **diam**, (430) **TS**, (250) **YS**, 24 **El**
SIS 14 14 50	SIS 14 50–01	Sweden	Forgings	0.16–0.28 **C**, 0.40–0.90 **Mn**, 0.050 **P**, 0.050 **S**	**Normalized**: (≤63) **diam**, (430) **TS**, (250) **YS**, 24 **El**
SIS 14 14 50	SIS 14 50–01	Sweden	Bar	0.16–0.28 **C**, 0.40–0.90 **Mn**, 0.050 **P**, 0.050 **S**	**Normalized**: (≤63) **diam**, (430) **TS**, (250) **YS**, 24 **El**
DIN 17115	Grade 21 Mn 4	Germany	Bar, wire, rod	0.16–0.24 **C**, 0.80–1.10 **Mn**, 0.040 **P**, 0.040 **S**, 0.10–0.25 **Si**	**Normalized**: (≤26) **diam**, (490) **TS**, (295) **YS**, 22 **El**; **Quenched and tempered**: (≤18) **diam**, (685) **TS**, (540) **YS**, 12 **El**
DIN 17115	Grade 21 Mn 4 Al	Germany	Bar, wire, rod	0.16–0.24 **C**, 0.80–1.10 **Mn**, 0.040 **P**, 0.040 **S**, 0.10–0.25 **Si**, 0.020–0.050 **Al**	**Normalized**: (≤26) **diam**, (490) **TS**, (295) **YS**, 22 **El**; **Quenched and tempered**: (≤18) **diam**, (685) **TS**, (540) **YS**, 12 **El**
BS 970: Part 1	070M20	UK	Blooms, billets, slabs, bar, rod, forgings	0.16–0.24 **C**, 0.50–0.90 **Mn**	**Normalized**: 6 **diam**, (385) **TS**, (195) **YS**, 21 **El**; **Hardened and tempered**: 0.75 **diam**, (380) **TS**, (315) **YS**, 20 **El**; **Cold drawn from hot rolled**: 0.50–0.625 **diam**, (470) **TS**, (345) **YS**, 12 **El**
ANSI/ASTM A 678	Grade A	US	Plate	0.16 **C**, 0.90–1.50 **Mn**, 0.04 **P**, 0.05 **S**, 0.15–0.50 **Si**	**Hot rolled, quenched and tempered**: ≤0.75 **diam**, (483) **TS**, (345) **YS**, 22 **El**
ANSI/ASTM A 131	Grade CS	US	Plate, shapes, bar	0.16 **C**, 1.00–1.35 **Mn**, 0.04 **P**, 0.04 **S**, 0.10–0.35 **Si**	**Normalized**: all **diam**, (400) **TS**, (235) **YS**, 24 **El**
ANSI/ASTM A 131	Grade DS	US	Plate, shapes, bar	0.16 **C**, 1.00–1.35 **Mn**, 0.04 **P**, 0.04 **S**, 0.10–0.35 **Si**	**Normalized**: all **diam**, (400) **TS**, (235) **YS**, 24 **El**
BS 1501–141		UK	Plate	0.16 **C**, 0.50 **Mn**, 0.050 **P**, 0.050 **S**; 0.70 max other elements, total	**As supplied**: (≤0.75) **diam**, (360) **TS**, 45 **El**

specification number	designation	country	product forms	composition	mechanical properties (see page iv for explanation)
NF A 35–075	A 37 R	France	Bar, rod	0.16 **C**, 0.060 **P**, 0.050 **S**	**As rolled**: all **diam**, (360) **TS**, (235) **YS**, 28 **El**
DIN 17155	Grade H I	Germany	Plate	0.16 **C**, 0.40 min **Mn**, 0.050 **P**, 0.050 **S**, 0.35 **Si**, 0.30 **Cr** max, opt	**Normalized**: (≤16) **diam**, (343) **TS**, (225) **YS**
ISO 2604/III	No. TWI	ISO	Tube	0.16 **C**, 0.30–0.70 **Mn**, 0.050 **P**, 0.050 **S**	**As welded, annealed, normalized**: all **diam**, (320) **TS**, (195) **YS**, 25 **El**
ISO 2604/III	No. TW2	ISO	Tube	0.16 **C**, 0.30–0.70 **Mn**, 0.050 **P**, 0.050 **S**	**As welded, annealed, normalized**: all **diam**, (320) **TS**, (195) **YS**, 25 **El**
ISO 2937	Grade TS 1	ISO	Tube: seamless	0.16 **C**, 0.30–0.70 **Mn**, 0.050 **P**, 0.050 **S**	**Hot finished**: all **diam**, (320) **TS**, (195) **YS**, 25 **El**
ISO 559	TS1/TW1	ISO	Tube: welded or seamless	0.16 **C**, 0.30–0.70 **Mn**, 0.050 **P**, 0.050 **S**	**As welded, hot rolled**: all **diam**, (320) **TS**, (195) **YS**, 25 **El**
BS 3059 Part1	Grade 320	UK	Tube: seamless, welded	0.16 **C**, 0.30–0.70 **Mn**, 0.050 **P**, 0.050 **S**	**Annealed, normalized**: all **diam**, (320) **TS**, (195) **YS**, 25 **El**; **Hot finished (seamless)**: all **diam**, (320) **TS**, (195) **YS**, 25 **El**
BS 3601	Grade 320	UK	Pipe, tube: seamless, welded	0.16 **C**, 0.30–0.70 **Mn**, 0.050 **P**, 0.050 **S**	**Hot finished**: all **diam**, (320) **TS**, (195) **YS**, 25 **El**
AS 1835	TS 2	Australia	Tube: seamless	0.16 **C**, 0.40–0.70 **Mn**, 0.050 **P**, 0.050 **S**	**Hot finished and normalized**: all **diam**, (320) **TS**, (195) **YS**, 25 **El**
AS 1835	TS 1	Australia	Tube: seamless	0.16 **C**, 0.30–0.70 **Mn**, 0.050 **P**, 0.050 **S**	**Annealed and normalized**: all **diam**, (320) **TS**, (195) **YS**, 25 **El**
AS 1836	TW 1	Australia	Tube: welded	0.16 **C**, 0.30–0.70 **Mn**, 0.050 **P**, 0.050 **S**	**Welded, hot finished, sub–critical annealed, annealed, or normalized**: all **diam**, (320) **TS**, (195) **YS**, 25 **El**
AS 1836	TW 2	Australia	Tube: welded	0.16 **C**, 0.30–0.70 **Mn**, 0.050 **P**, 0.050 **S**	**Normalized**: all **diam**, (320) **TS**, (195) **YS**, 25 **El**
ISO 2604/11	TS 1	ISO	Tube: seamless	0.16 **C**, 0.30–0.70 **Mn**, 0.050 **P**, 0.050 **S**	**Hot finished, sub–critical annealed, annealed, normalized**: all **diam**, (320) **TS**, (195) **YS**, 25 **El**
ISO 2604/11	TS 2	ISO	Tube: seamless	0.16 **C**, 0.40–0.70 **Mn**, 0.50 **P**, 0.050 **S**	**Hot finished, normalized**: all **diam**, (320) **TS**, (195) **YS**, 25 **El**
NF A 35–051	FM 20 grade 1	France	Wire, rod	0.15–0.27 **C**, 0.40–0.70 **Mn**, 0.080 **P**, 0.055 **S**, 0.10–0.35 **Si**	
BS 7S.1	Group A	UK	Bar: aircraft quality	0.15–0.25 **C**, 0.6–0.9 **Mn**, 0.040 **P**, 0.040 **S**, 0.10–0.35 **Si**, 0.15–0.35 **Pb**	**Cold–drawn**: (<19) **diam**, (540) **TS**, (450) **YS**, 7 **El**
ANSI/ASTM A 512	MT 1020	US	Tube: cold–drawn buttweld	0.15–0.25 **C**, 0.30–0.60 **Mn**, 0.04 **P**, 0.05 **S**	**Stress relief annealed**: all **diam**, 71 (490) **TS**, 65 (448) **YS**, 11 **El**
DGN–B–201	Grade MT1020	Mexico	Tube: butt–welded	0.15–0.25 **C**, 0.30–0.60 **Mn**, 0.040 **P**, 0.050 **S**	**Cold finished and annealed**: all **diam**, (489) **TS**, (448) **YS**, 11 **El**; **Normalized**: all **diam**, (345) **TS**, (207) **YS**, 32 **El**
AS 1443	AS 1443/CD1	Australia	Bar	0.15–0.25 **C**, 0.30–0.90 **Mn**, 0.050 **P**, 0.050 **S**, 0.35 **Si**	**Cold drawn or cold rolled**: (16–38) **diam**, (460) **TS**, (370) **YS**, 12 **El**
BS 5S.21		UK	Bar, billets, forgings: aircraft quality	0.15–0.25 **C**, 0.5–0.8 **Mn**, 0.040 **P**, 0.040 **S**, 0.10–0.35 **Si**, 0.4 **Ni**	**Normalized**: all **diam**, (382) **TS**, 20 **El**; **Cold drawn or cold rolled**: all **diam**, (431) **TS**, 12 **El**
ANSI/ASTM A 519	MT 1020	US	Tube: seamless	0.15–0.25 **C**, 0.30–0.60 **Mn**, 0.040 **P**, 0.050 **S**	**Hot rolled**: all **diam**, 50 (345) **TS**, 32 (221) **YS**, 25 **El**; **Cold worked**: all **diam**, 70 (483) **TS**, 60 (414) **YS**, 5 **El**; **Stress relieved**: all **diam**, 65 (448) **TS**, 50 (345) **YS**, 10 **El**; **Annealed**: all **diam**, 48 (331) **TS**, 28 (193) **YS**, 30 **El**; **Normalized**: all **diam**, 55 (379) **TS**, 34 (234) **YS**, 22 **El**

WROUGHT CARBON STEELS

specification number	designation	country	product forms	composition	mechanical properties (see page iv for explanation)
COPANT 514	Grade TM 1020	COPANT	Tube: seamless	0.15–0.25 **C**, 0.30–0.60 **Mn**, 0.040 **P**, 0.050 **S**, 0.10–0.20 **Si**	**Hot finished**: (>323.9) **diam**, (345) **TS**, (215) **YS**, 25 **El**; **Cold finished**: all **diam**, (480) **TS**, (410) **YS**, 5 **El**; **Annealed**: all **diam**, (335) **TS**, (195) **YS**, 30 **El**; **Normalized**: all **diam**, (380) **TS**, (235) **YS**, 22 **El**
DGN–B–203	Grade MT 1020	Mexico	Tube: seamless	0.15–0.25 **C**, 0.30–0.60 **Mn**, 0.040 **P**, 0.050 **S**	**Hot finished**: all **diam**, (343) **TS**, (216) **YS**, 25 **El**; **Cold finished**: all **diam**, (480) **TS**, (412) **YS**, 5 **El**; **Stress relieved**: all **diam**, (451) **TS**, (343) **YS**, 10 **El**; **Tempered**: all **diam**, (333) **TS**, (196) **YS**, 20 **El**; **Normalized**: all **diam**, (382) **TS**, (235) **YS**, 22 **El**
NF A 35–051	FM 20 grade 3	France	Wire, rod	0.15–0.25 **C**, 0.40–0.70 **Mn**, 0.040 **P**, 0.040 **S**, 0.10–0.35 **Si**	
ANSI/ASTM A 519	MT X1020	US	Tube: seamless	0.15–0.25 **C**, 0.70–1.00 **Mn**, 0.040 **P**, 0.050 **S**	
ANSI/ASTM A 512	MTX 1020	US	Tube: cold–drawn buttweld	0.15–0.25 **C**, 0.70–1.00 **Mn**, 0.04 **P**, 0.05 **S**	
NF A 35–553	C 20	France	Strip	0.15–0.25 **C**, 0.40–0.70 **Mn**, 0.040 **P**, 0.040 **S**, 0.10–0.40 **Si**	
DGN–B–203	Grade MT X 1020	Mexico	Tube: seamless	0.15–0.25 **C**, 0.70–1.00 **Mn**, 0.040 **P**, 0.050 **S**	
AS 1446	Grade AS 1446/CS1020	Australia	Plate	0.15–0.25 **C**, 0.30–0.90 **Mn**, 0.060 **P**, 0.060 **S**, 0.35 **Si**	
ANSI/ASTM A 236	Grade B	US	Forgings	0.15–0.25 **C**, 0.30–0.60 **Mn**, 0.045 **P**, 0.050 **S**	
DGN–B–201	Grade MTX1020	Mexico	Tube: butt–welded	0.15–0.25 **C**, 0.70–1.00 **Mn**, 0.040 **P**, 0.050 **S**	
ANSI/ASTM A 236	Grade B	US	Forgings	0.15–0.25 **C**, 0.30–0.60 **Mn**, 0.045 **P**, 0.050 **S**	
ANSI/ASTM A 730	Grade B	US	Forgings	0.15–0.25 **C**, 0.30–0.60 **Mn**, 0.045 **P**, 0.050 **S**	
AS 1443	Grade AS 1443/CS1020	Australia	Bar	0.15–0.25 **C**, 0.30–0.90 **Mn**, 0.060 **P**, 0.060 **S**, 0.35 **Si**	
AS 1442	Grade AS 1442/CS1020	Australia	Bar, blooms, billets, slabs	0.15–0.25 **C**, 0.30–0.90 **Mn**, 0.060 **P**, 0.060 **S**, 0.35 **Si**	
COPANT 514	Grade TM X 1020	COPANT	Tube: seamless	0.15–0.25 **C**, 0.60–1.00 **Mn**, 0.040 **P**, 0.050 **S**, 0.20–0.35 **Si**, 0.05 **Cr**	**Hot finished**: (>323.9) **diam**, 15 **El**; **Cold finished**: all **diam**, 5 **El**; **Annealed**: all **diam**, 30 **El**; **Normalized**: all **diam**, 30 **El**
BS 970: Part 1	150M19	UK	Blooms, billets, slabs, bar, rod, forgings	0.15–0.23 **C**, 1.30–1.70 **Mn**	**Normalized**: 6 **diam**, (480) **TS**, (290) **YS**, 18 **El**; **Hardened and tempered**: 6 **diam**, (480) **TS**, (305) **YS**, 18 **El**
BS 970: Part 1	120M19	UK	Blooms, billets, slabs, bar, rod, forgings	0.15–0.23 **C**, 1.00–1.40 **Mn**	**Normalized**: 4 **diam**, (440) **TS**, (260) **YS**, 20 **El**; **Hardened and tempered**: 4 **diam**, (480) **TS**, (315) **YS**, 18 **El**; **Cold drawn from hot rolled**: 0.50–0.625 **diam**, (535) **TS**, (400) **YS**, 11 **El**
AIR 9160/C21	9160C011	France	Bar, forgings: aircraft quality	0.15–0.22 **C**, 0.40–0.65 **Mn**, 0.035 **P**, 0.035 **S**, 0.25 **Si**	**Quenched and tempered**: (≤16) **diam**, (490) **TS**, (330) **YS**, 19 **El**; **Quenched and tempered**: (16–40) **diam**, (440) **TS**, (270) **YS**, 21 **El**; **Quenched and tempered**: (40–100) **diam**, (410) **TS**, (250) **YS**, 23 **El**; **Normalized**: all **diam**, (410) **TS**, (250) **YS**, 26 **El**

WROUGHT CARBON STEELS

specification number	designation	country	product forms	composition	mechanical properties (see page iv for explanation)
NF A 35-553	XC 18 S	France	Strip	0.15–0.22 **C**, 0.40–0.65 **Mn**, 0.035 **P**, 0.035 **S**, 0.25 **Si**	**Normalized:** all **diam**, (430) **TS**, (265) **YS**, 28 **El**; **Quenched and tempered:** all **diam**, (520) **TS**, (355) **YS**, 19 **El**
NF A 35-554	XC 18S	France	Plate	0.15–0.22 **C**, 0.40–0.65 **Mn**, 0.035 **P**, 0.035 **S**, 0.25 **Si**	**Hot rolled and normalized:** (≤16) **diam**, (410) **TS**, (255) **YS**, 26 **El**
AIR 9113/A	XC18S	France	Sheet, tube, bar, wire, rings	0.15–0.22 **C**, 0.45–0.65 **Mn**, 0.04 **P**, 0.035 **S**, 0.25 **Si**	**Normalized, annealed:** (≤1.5) **diam**, (410) **TS**, (260) **YS**, 28 **El**; **Quenched and tempered, annealed:** (≤1.5) **diam**, (540) **TS**, (350) **YS**, 17 **El**
ANSI/ASTM A 519	1518	US	Tube: seamless	0.15–0.21 **C**, 1.10–1.40 **Mn**, 0.040 **P**, 0.050 **S**	
ANSI/ASTM A 29	1518	US	Bar	0.15–0.21 **C**, 1.10–1.40 **Mn**, 0.040 **P**, 0.050 **S**	
DGN-B-301	1518	Mexico	Bar	0.15–0.21 **C**, 1.10–1.40 **Mn**, 0.040 **P**, 0.050 **S**, 0.10 **Si**	
ANSI/ASTM A 576	1518	US	Bar	0.15–0.21 **C**, 1.10–1.40 **Mn**, 0.040 **P**, 0.050 **S**	
ASTM A 689	1518	US	Bar	0.15–0.21 **C**, 1.10–1.40 **Mn**, 0.040 **P**, 0.050 **S**	
JIS G 3539	SWCH 17R	Japan	Wire	0.15–0.20 **C**, 0.30–0.60 **Mn**, 0.040 **P**, 0.040 **S**	**Cold drawn:** (≤3) **diam**, (686) **TS**; **Annealed and cold drawn:** (≤3) **diam**, (373) **TS**, 13 **El**
JIS G 3539	SWCH 17K	Japan	Wire	0.15–0.20 **C**, 0.30–0.60 **Mn**, 0.030 **P**, 0.035 **S**, 0.10–0.35 **Si**	**Cold drawn:** (4–5) **diam**, (539) **TS**; **Annealed and cold drawn:** (4–5) **diam**, (412) **TS**, 13 **El**
JIS G 3539	SWCH 18A	Japan	Wire	0.15–0.20 **C**, 0.60–0.90 **Mn**, 0.030 **P**, 0.035 **S**, 0.10 **Si**, 0.02 min **Al**	**Cold drawn:** (>4–5) **diam**, (490) **TS**; **Annealed and cold drawn:** (>4–5) **diam**, (373) **TS**, 13 **El**
ANSI/ASTM A 242		US	Shape, plate, bar	0.15–0.20 **C**, 1.00–1.35 **Mn**, 0.15–0.04 **P**, 0.05 **S**, 0.20 **Cu**	**As rolled:** 0.75 **diam**, (480) **TS**, (345) **YS**, 21 **El**
JIS G 3539	SWCH 18K	Japan	Wire	0.15–0.20 **C**, 0.60–0.90 **Mn**, 0.030 **P**, 0.035 **S**, 0.10–0.35 **Si**	**Cold drawn:** (5–30) **diam**, (441) **TS**, 7 **El**; **Annealed and cold drawn:** (5–30) **diam**, (412) **TS**, 13 **El**
JIS G 3539	SWCH 19A	Japan	Wire	0.15–0.20 **C**, 0.70–1.00 **Mn**, 0.030 **P**, 0.035 **S**, 0.10 **Si**	**Annealed and cold drawn:** all **diam**, (412) **TS**, 13 **El**
DGN-B-301	1018	Mexico	Bar	0.15–0.20 **C**, 0.60–0.90 **Mn**, 0.040 **P**, 0.050 **S**, 0.10 **Si**	**Forged or hot rolled, cold rolled and cold finished:** all **diam**, (402) **TS**, (235) **YS**, 25 **El**
DGN-B-301	1019	Mexico	Bar	0.15–0.20 **C**, 0.70–1.00 **Mn**, 0.040 **P**, 0.050 **S**, 0.10 **Si**	**Forged or hot rolled, cold rolled and cold finished:** all **diam**, (402) **TS**, (216) **YS**, 25 **El**
DGN-B-301	1017	Mexico	Bar	0.15–0.20 **C**, 0.30–0.60 **Mn**, 0.040 **P**, 0.050 **S**, 0.10 **Si**	**Forged or hot rolled, cold rolled and cold finished:** all **diam**, (363) **TS**, (225) **YS**, 26 **El**
BS 1449: Part 1	Grade 17	UK	Plate, sheet, strip	0.15–0.20 **C**, 0.40–0.60 **Mn**, 0.050 **P**, 0.050 **S**	**Cold rolled, annealed:** all **diam**, (340) **TS**, (190) **YS**, 26 **El**
ASTM A 544	Grade 1018	US	Wire	0.15–0.20 **C**, 0.60–0.90 **Mn**, 0.040 **P**, 0.050 **S**	
ASTM A 544	Grade 1117	US	Wire	0.15–0.20 **C**, 0.30–0.60 **Mn**, 0.040 **P**, 0.050 **S**	
AISI 1019		US	Bar	0.15–0.20 **C**, 0.70–1.00 **Mn**, 0.040 **P**, 0.050 **S**	
AISI 1018		US	Bar	0.15–0.20 **C**, 0.60–0.90 **Mn**, 0.040 **P**, 0.050 **S**	
AISI 1017		US	Bar	0.15–0.20 **C**, 0.30–0.60 **Mn**, 0.040 **P**, 0.050 **S**	
BS 970: Part 1	040A17	UK	Blooms, billets, slabs, bar, rod, forgings	0.15–0.20 **C**, 0.30–0.50 **Mn**	
BS 970: Part 1	050A17	UK	Blooms, billets, slabs, bar, rod, forgings	0.15–0.20 **C**, 0.40–0.60 **Mn**	

specification number	designation	country	product forms	composition	mechanical properties (see page iv for explanation)
BS 970: Part 1	060A17	UK	Blooms, billets, slabs, bar, rod, forgings	0.15–0.20 **C**, 0.50–0.70 **Mn**	
BS 970: Part 1	080A17	UK	Blooms, billets, slabs, bar, rod, forgings	0.15–0.20 **C**, 0.70–0.90 **Mn**	
AMS 5069C		US	Bar, forgings, tube	0.15–0.20 **C**, 0.60–0.90 **Mn**, 0.040 **P**, 0.050 **S**, 0.10–0.30 **Si**	
ANSI/ASTM A 519	1017	US	Tube: seamless	0.15–0.20 **C**, 0.30–0.60 **Mn**, 0.040 **P**, 0.050 **S**	
ANSI/ASTM A 519	1018	US	Tube: seamless	0.15–0.20 **C**, 0.60–0.90 **Mn**, 0.040 **P**, 0.050 **S**	
ANSI/ASTM A 519	1019	US	Tube: seamless	0.15–0.20 **C**, 0.70–1.00 **Mn**, 0.040 **P**, 0.050 **S**	
COPANT 331	1018	COPANT	Bar	0.15–0.20 **C**, 0.60–0.90 **Mn**, 0.040 **P**, 0.050 **S**	
COPANT 333	1017	COPANT	Wire, rod	0.15–0.20 **C**, 0.30–0.60 **Mn**, 0.040 **P**, 0.050 **S**	
COPANT 333	1018	COPANT	Wire, rod	0.15–0.20 **C**, 0.60–0.90 **Mn**, 0.040 **P**, 0.050 **S**	
ASTM A 108	1018	US	Bar	0.15–0.20 **C**, 0.60–0.90 **Mn**, 0.040 **P**, 0.050 **S**	
ANSI/ASTM A 545	Grade 1019	US	Wire	0.15–0.20 **C**, 0.70–1.00 **Mn**, 0.040 **P**, 0.050 **S**	
ANSI/ASTM A 545	Grade 1018	US	Wire	0.15–0.20 **C**, 0.60–0.90 **Mn**, 0.040 **P**, 0.050 **S**	
ANSI/ASTM A 548	Grade 1018	US	Wire	0.15–0.20 **C**, 0.60–0.90 **Mn**, 0.040 **P**, 0.050 **S**	
ANSI/ASTM A 548	Grade 1019	US	Wire	0.15–0.20 **C**, 0.70–1.00 **Mn**, 0.040 **P**, 0.050 **S**	
ANSI/ASTM A 548	Grade 1019 mod	US	Wire	0.15–0.20 **C**, 0.80–1.10 **Mn**, 0.040 **P**, 0.050 **S**	
ANSI/ASTM A 549	Grade 1017	US	Wire	0.15–0.20 **C**, 0.30–0.60 **Mn**, 0.040 **P**, 0.050 **S**	
ANSI/ASTM A 549	Grade 1018	US	Wire	0.15–0.20 **C**, 0.60–0.90 **Mn**, 0.040 **P**, 0.050 **S**	
MIL–S–11310E	1017	US	Bar	0.15–0.20 **C**, 0.30–0.60 **Mn**, 0.040 **P**, 0.050 **S**, 0.20 **Si**	
MIL–S–11310E	1018	US	Bar	0.15–0.20 **C**, 0.60–0.90 **Mn**, 0.040 **P**, 0.050 **S**, 0.20 **Si**	
COPANT 333	1019	COPANT	Wire, rod	0.15–0.20 **C**, 0.70–1.00 **Mn**, 0.040 **P**, 0.050 **S**	
ANSI/ASTM A 575	1017	US	Bar	0.15–0.20 **C**, 0.30–0.60 **Mn**, 0.04 **P**, 0.05 **S**	
AISI 1017		US	Wire, rod	0.15–0.20 **C**, 0.30–0.60 **Mn**, 0.040 **P**, 0.050 **S**	
AISI 1018		US	Wire, rod	0.15–0.20 **C**, 0.60–0.90 **Mn**, 0.040 **P**, 0.050 **S**	
AISI 1019		US	Wire, rod	0.15–0.20 **C**, 0.70–1.00 **Mn**, 0.040 **P**, 0.050 **S**	
ANSI/ASTM A 576	1017	US	Bar	0.15–0.20 **C**, 0.30–0.60 **Mn**, 0.040 **P**, 0.050 **S**	
ANSI/ASTM A 576	1018	US	Bar	0.15–0.20 **C**, 0.60–0.90 **Mn**, 0.040 **P**, 0.050 **S**	
ANSI/ASTM A 576	1019	US	Bar	0.15–0.20 **C**, 0.70–1.00 **Mn**, 0.040 **P**, 0.050 **S**	
ASTM A 689	1017	US	Bar	0.15–0.20 **C**, 0.30–0.60 **Mn**, 0.040 **P**, 0.050 **S**	
ASTM A 689	1018	US	Bar	0.15–0.20 **C**, 0.60–0.90 **Mn**, 0.040 **P**, 0.050 **S**	
ASTM A 689	1019	US	Bar	0.15–0.20 **C**, 0.70–1.00 **Mn**, 0.040 **P**, 0.050 **S**	
ANSI/ASTM A 29	1017	US	Bar	0.15–0.20 **C**, 0.30–0.60 **Mn**, 0.040 **P**, 0.050 **S**	
ANSI/ASTM A 29	1018	US	Bar	0.15–0.20 **C**, 0.30–0.60 **Mn**, 0.040 **P**, 0.050 **S**	
ANSI/ASTM A 29	1019	US	Bar	0.15–0.20 **C**, 0.70–1.00 **Mn**, 0.040 **P**, 0.050 **S**	

specification number	designation	country	product forms	composition	mechanical properties (see page iv for explanation)
AS 1443	Grade AS 1443/K1018	Australia	Bar	0.15–0.20 **C**, 0.60–0.90 **Mn**, 0.050 **P**, 0.050 **S**, 0.10–0.35 **Si**	
AS 1442	Grade AS 1442/K1018	Australia	Bar, blooms, billets, slabs	0.15–0.20 **C**, 0.60–0.90 **Mn**, 0.050 **P**, 0.050 **S**, 0.10–0.35 **Si**	
DEF STAN 95–1/1	C1018	Canada	Bar	0.15–0.20 **C**, 0.60–0.90 **Mn**, 0.04 **P**, 0.05 **S**, 0.10–0.30 **Si**	
JIS G 3108	Type 3	Japan	Bar	0.15–0.20 **C**, 0.30–0.60 **Mn**, 0.045 **P**, 0.045 **S**	
JIS G 3507	SWRCH 17R	Japan	Wire, rod	0.15–0.20 **C**, 0.30–0.60 **Mn**, 0.040 **P**, 0.040 **S**	
JIS G 3507	SWRCH 18A	Japan	Wire, rod	0.15–0.20 **C**, 0.60–0.90 **Mn**, 0.030 **P**, 0.035 **S**, 0.10 **Si**, 0.02 **Al**	
JIS G 3507	SWRCH 19A	Japan	Wire, rod	0.15–0.20 **C**, 0.70–1.00 **Mn**, 0.030 **P**, 0.035 **S**, 0.10 **Si**, 0.02 **Al**	
JIS G 3507	SWRCH 17K	Japan	Wire, rod	0.15–0.20 **C**, 0.30–0.60 **Mn**, 0.030 **P**, 0.035 **S**, 0.10–0.35 **Si**	
JIS G 3507	SWRCH 18K	Japan	Wire, rod	0.15–0.20 **C**, 0.60–0.90 **Mn**, 0.030 **P**, 0.035 **S**, 0.10–0.35 **Si**	
JIS G 3505	SWRM 17	Japan	Wire, rod	0.15–0.20 **C**, 0.30–0.60 **Mn**, 0.045 **P**, 0.045 **S**	
JIS G 4051	S 17C	Japan	Bar, wire, rod	0.15–0.20 **C**, 0.30–0.60 **Mn**, 0.030 **P**, 0.035 **S**, 0.15–0.35 **Si**, 0.30 **Cu**	
ANSI/ASTM A 656	Grade 2	US	Plate	0.15 **C**, 0.90 **Mn**, 0.040 **P**, 0.050 **S**, 0.10 **Si**, 0.05–0.50 **Ti**, 0.01 **Al**	**Hot rolled**: 0.625 **diam**, 95 (655) **TS**, 80 (552) **YS**, 12 **El**
ASTM A 715	Grade 80, type 1	US	Sheet, strip	0.15 **C**, 1.65 **Mn**, 0.025 **P**, 0.035 **S**, 0.10 **Si**, 0.05 min **Ti**	**Hot rolled**: 0.098 min **diam**, 90 (620) **TS**, 80 (550) **YS**, 18 **El**
ASTM A 715	Grade 80, type 2	US	Sheet, strip	0.15 **C**, 1.65 **Mn**, 0.025 **P**, 0.035 **S**, 0.60 **Si**, 0.02 min **V**, 0.005 min **N**	**Hot rolled**: 0.098 min **diam**, 90 (620) **TS**, 80 (550) **YS**, 18 **El**
ASTM A 715	Grade 80, type 3	US	Sheet, strip	0.15 **C**, 1.65 **Mn**, 0.025 **P**, 0.035 **S**, 0.60 **Si**, 0.08 **V**, 0.005 min **Nb**, 0.020 **N**	**Hot rolled**: 0.098 min **diam**, 90 (620) **TS**, 80 (550) **YS**, 18 **El**
ASTM A 715	Grade 80, type 4	US	Sheet, strip	0.15 **C**, 1.65 **Mn**, 0.025 **P**, 0.035 **S**, 0.90 **Si**, 0.005–0.06 **Nb**, 0.10 **Ti**, 0.05 min **Zr**, 0.80 **Cr**, 0.0025 **B**	**Hot rolled**: 0.098 min **diam**, 90 (620) **TS**, 80 (550) **YS**, 18 **El**
ASTM A 715	Grade 80, type 5	US	Sheet, strip	0.15 **C**, 1.65 **Mn**, 0.025 **P**, 0.035 **S**, 0.30 **Si**, 0.03 min **Nb**, 0.20 min **Mo**	**Hot rolled**: 0.098 min **diam**, 90 (620) **TS**, 80 (550) **YS**, 18 **El**
ASTM A 715	Grade 80, type 6	US	Sheet, strip	0.15 **C**, 1.65 **Mn**, 0.025 **P**, 0.035 **S**, 0.90 **Si**, 0.005–0.10 **Nb**	**Hot rolled**: 0.098 min **diam**, 90 (620) **TS**, 80 (550) **YS**, 18 **El**
ASTM A 715	Grade 80, type 7	US	Sheet, strip	0.15 **C**, 1.65 **Mn**, 0.025 **P**, 0.035 **S**, 0.60 **Si**, 0.005 min **V**, 0.005 min **Nb**, 0.020 **N**	**Hot rolled**: 0.098 min **diam**, 90 (620) **TS**, 80 (550) **YS**, 18 **El**
AS 1205	WR500/1	Australia	Bar, plate	0.15 **C**, 1.06 **Mn**, 0.055–0.16 **P**, 0.050 **S**, 0.18–0.75 **Si**, 0.12–0.48 **Cu**, 0.37–1.05 **Cr**, 0.55 **Ni**	**Hot rolled (plate)**: (10) **diam**, (550) **TS**, (480) **YS**, 14 in 200 mm **El**
ASTM A 715	Grade 70, type 1	US	Sheet, strip	0.15 **C**, 1.65 **Mn**, 0.025 **P**, 0.035 **S**, 0.10 **Si**, 0.05 min **Ti**	**Hot rolled**: 0.098 min **diam**, 80 (550) **TS**, 70 (485) **YS**, 20 **El**
ASTM A 715	Grade 70, type 2	US	Sheet, strip	0.15 **C**, 1.65 **Mn**, 0.025 **P**, 0.035 **S**, 0.60 **Si**, 0.02 min **V**, 0.005 min **N**	**Hot rolled**: 0.098 min **diam**, 80 (550) **TS**, 70 (485) **YS**, 20 **El**
ASTM A 715	Grade 70, type 3	US	Sheet, strip	0.15 **C**, 1.65 **Mn**, 0.025 **P**, 0.035 **S**, 0.60 **Si**, 0.08 **V**, 0.005 min **Nb**, 0.020 **N**	**Hot rolled**: 0.098 min **diam**, 80 (550) **TS**, 70 (485) **YS**, 20 **El**
ASTM A 715	Grade 70, type 4	US	Sheet, strip	0.15 **C**, 1.65 **Mn**, 0.025 **P**, 0.035 **S**, 0.90 **Si**, 0.005–0.06 **Nb**, 0.10 **Ti**, 0.05 min **Zr**, 0.80 **Cr**, 0.0025 **B**	**Hot rolled**: 0.098 min **diam**, 80 (550) **TS**, 70 (485) **YS**, 20 **El**
ASTM A 715	Grade 70, type 6	US	Sheet, strip	0.15 **C**, 1.65 **Mn**, 0.025 **P**, 0.035 **S**, 0.90 **Si**, 0.005–0.10 **Nb**	**Hot rolled**: 0.098 min **diam**, 80 (550) **TS**, 70 (485) **YS**, 20 **El**
ASTM A 715	Grade 70, type 7	US	Sheet, strip	0.15 **C**, 1.65 **Mn**, 0.025 **P**, 0.035 **S**, 0.60 **Si**, 0.005 min **V**, 0.005 min **Nb**, 0.020 **N**	**Hot rolled**: 0.098 min **diam**, 80 (550) **TS**, 70 (485) **YS**, 20 **El**
ISO/R 683/1X	Type 3Pb	ISO	Bar, wire, rod	0.15 **C**, 1.0–1.50 **Mn**, 0.11 **P**, 0.30–0.40 **S**, 0.05 **Si**, 0.15–0.35 **Pb**	**Cold drawn**: ($\leq$16) **diam**, (539) **TS**, (431) **YS**, 7 **El**

WROUGHT CARBON STEELS

specification number	designation	country	product forms	composition	mechanical properties (see page iv for explanation)
ISO/R 683/1X	Type 3	ISO	Bar, wire, rod	0.15 **C**, 1.0–1.50 **Mn**, 0.11 **P**, 0.30–0.40 **S**, 0.05 **Si**	**Cold drawn:** (≤16) **diam**, (539) **TS**, (431) **YS**, 7 **El**
AS 1205	WR400/1	Australia	Bar, plate	0.15 **C**, 1.06 **Mn**, 0.055–0.16 **P**, 0.050 **S**, 0.18–0.75 **Si**, 0.12–0.48 **Cu**, 0.37–1.05 **Cr**, 0.55 **Ni**	**Hot rolled (plate):** (≤10) **diam**, (520) **TS**, (410) **YS**, 15 in 200 mm **El**
SFS 605		Finland	Sheet, strip	0.15 **C**, 0.50 **Mn**	**Annealed:** (≤3) **diam**, (490) **TS**
ASTM A 715	Grade 60, type 6	US	Sheet, strip	0.15 **C**, 1.65 **Mn**, 0.025 **P**, 0.035 **S**, 0.90 **Si**, 0.005–0.10 **Nb**	**Hot rolled:** 0.098 min **diam**, 70 (485) **TS**, 60 (415) **YS**, 22 **El**
ASTM A 715	Grade 60, type 7	US	Sheet, strip	0.15 **C**, 1.65 **Mn**, 0.025 **P**, 0.035 **S**, 0.60 **Si**, 0.005 min **V**, 0.005 min **Nb**, 0.020 **N**	**Hot rolled:** 0.098 min **diam**, 70 (485) **TS**, 60 (415) **YS**, 22 **El**
ANSI/ASTM A 588	Grade C	US	Plate, bar, shapes	0.15 **C**, 0.80–1.35 **Mn**, 0.04 **P**, 0.05 **S**, 0.15–0.30 **Si**, 0.20–0.50 **Cu**, 0.01–0.10 **V**, 0.30–0.50 **Cr**, 0.20–0.50 **Ni**	**Hot rolled (plate, bar):** <4.0 **diam**, (485) **TS**, (345) **YS**, 21 **El**
ANSI/ASTM A 588	Grade E	US	Plate, bar, shapes	0.15 **C**, 1.20 **Mn**, 0.04 **P**, 0.05 **S**, 0.15–0.30 **Si**, 0.50–0.80 **Cu**, 0.05 **V**, 0.10–0.25 **Mo**, 0.75–1.25 **Ni**	**Hot rolled (plate, bar):** <4.0 **diam**, (485) **TS**, (345) **YS**, 21 **El**
AS 1205	Grade WR350/1	Australia	Bar, plate	0.15 **C**, 1.06 **Mn**, 0.055–0.16 **P**, 0.050 **S**, 0.18–0.75 **Si**, 0.12–0.48 **Cu**, 0.37–1.05 **Cr**, 0.55 **Ni**	**Hot rolled (plate):** (≤10) **diam**, (480) **TS**, (340) **YS**, 15 in 200 mm **El**
ASTM A 595	Grade C	US	Tube: tapered	0.15 **C**, 0.17–0.53 **Mn**, 0.06–0.16 **P**, 0.06 **S**, 0.19–0.81 **Si**, 0.22–0.58 **Cu**	**As fabricated:** all **diam**, 70 (480) **TS**, 60 (410) **YS**
BS 1449: Part 1	Grade 46/40	UK	Plate, sheet, strip	0.15 **C**, 1.20 **Mn**, 0.040 **P**, 0.040 **S**	**Hot rolled:** all **diam**, (460) **TS**, (400) **YS**, 22 **El**
SIS 14 14 11 E	SIS 14 11–00	Sweden	Bar, sheet	0.15 **C**, 0.5–1.1 **Mn**, 0.08 **P**, 0.06 **S**, 0.05 **Si**	**As rolled:** all **diam**, (430) **TS**, (260) **YS**, 23 **El**
SIS 14 14 11 E	SIS 14 11–00	Sweden	Bar, sheet	0.15 **C**, 0.4–1.0 **Mn**, 0.08 **P**, 0.06 **S**, 0.25 **Si**	**As rolled:** all **diam**, (430) **TS**, (260) **YS**, 23 **El**
BS 1449: Part 1	Grade 43/35	UK	Plate, sheet, strip	0.15 **C**, 1.20 **Mn**, 0.040 **P**, 0.040 **S**	**Hot rolled:** all **diam**, (430) **TS**, (350) **YS**, 25 **El**
AS 1443	AS 1443/CD5	Australia	Bar	0.15 **C**, 0.10–0.80 **Mn**, 0.04–0.090 **P**, 0.25–0.35 **S**, 0.10 **Si**	**Cold drawn or cold rolled:** (16–38) **diam**, (430) **TS**, (330) **YS**, 8 **El**
ASTM A 715	Grade 50, type 7	US	Sheet, strip	0.15 **C**, 1.65 **Mn**, 0.025 **P**, 0.035 **S**, 0.60 **Si**, 0.005 min **V**, 0.005 min **Nb**, 0.020 **N**	**Hot rolled:** 0.098 min **diam**, 60 (415) **TS**, 50 (345) **YS**, 24 **El**
ASTM A 715	Grade 50, type 6	US	Sheet, strip	0.15 **C**, 1.65 **Mn**, 0.025 **P**, 0.035 **S**, 0.90 **Si**, 0.005–0.10 **Nb**	**Hot rolled:** 0.098 min **diam**, 60 (415) **TS**, 50 (345) **YS**, 24 **El**
JIS G 3126	Type 1A	Japan	Plate	0.15 **C**, 0.70–1.50 **Mn**, 0.035 **P**, 0.035 **S**, 0.15–0.30 **Si**	**Normalized:** (6–16) **diam**, (402) **TS**, (235) **YS**, 18 **El**
JIS G 3126	Type 1B	Japan	Plate	0.15 **C**, 0.70–1.50 **Mn**, 0.035 **P**, 0.035 **S**, 0.15–0.30 **Si**	**Normalized:** (6–16) **diam**, (402) **TS**, (235) **YS**, 18 **El**
BS 1501–224	Grade 26	UK	Plate	0.15 **C**, 0.90–1.50 **Mn**, 0.050 **P**, 0.050 **S**, 0.10–0.55 **Si**, 0.70 max other elements, total	**Normalized:** ≤(16) **diam**, (400) **TS**, (265) **YS**, 45 **El**
BS 1449: Part 1	Grade 40/30	UK	Plate, sheet, strip	0.15 **C**, 1.20 **Mn**, 0.040 **P**, 0.040 **S**	**Hot rolled:** all **diam**, (400) **TS**, (300) **YS**, 28 **El**
DGN–B–301	12L14	Mexico	Bar	0.15 **C**, 0.85–1.15 **Mn**, 0.04–0.09 **P**, 0.26–0.35 **S**, 0.10–0.20 **Si**, 0.15–0.35 **Pb**	**Forged or hot rolled, cold rolled, and cold finished:** all **diam**, (392) **TS**, (235) **YS**, 22 **El**
DIN 1651	9 SMn 36 (1.0736)	Germany	Bar	0.15 **C**, 1.00–1.50 **Mn**, 0.100 **P**, 0.32–0.40 **S**, 0.05 **Si**	**Hot rolled:** all **diam**, (390) **TS**; **Normalized:** all **diam**, (380) **TS**, (235) **YS**, 23 in 80 mm **El**
DIN 1651	9 SMnPb 36 (1.0737)	Germany	Bar	0.15 **C**, 1.00–1.50 **Mn**, 0.100 **P**, 0.32–0.40 **S**, 0.05 **Si**, 0.15–0.30 **Pb**	**Hot rolled:** all **diam**, (380) **TS**; **Normalized:** all **diam**, (370) **TS**, (225) **YS**, 23 in 80 mm **El**
DGN–B–106	Type 285C (Boiler)	Mexico	Plate	0.15 **C**, 0.80 **Mn**, 0.040 **P**, 0.050 **S**, 0.20–0.35 **Cu**	**Hot worked:** (<8) **diam**, (379) **TS**, 30 (207) **YS**, 28 **El**
DS 12010	St 37	Denmark	Bar	0.15 **C**, 0.060 **P**, 0.060 **S**	**Hot rolled:** all **diam**, (363) **TS**, (196) **YS**, 25 **El**
SIS 14 13 60	SIS 13 60–10	Sweden	Sheet	0.15 **C**, 1.2 **Mn**, 0.05 **P**, 0.05 **S**	**Zinc coated:** (<3) **diam**, (360) **TS**, (280) **YS**, 18 **El**
SIS 14 13 11 E	SIS 13 11–00	Sweden	Bar, plate	0.15 **C**, 0.3–0.6 **Mn**, 0.08 **P**, 0.06 **S**, 0.02 **Si**	**As rolled:** (<40) **diam**, (360) **TS**, (220) **YS**, 24 **El**

specification number	designation	country	product forms	composition	mechanical properties (see page iv for explanation)
SIS 14 13 60	SIS 13 60	Sweden	Sheet	0.15 **C**, 1.2 **Mn**, 0.05 **P**, 0.05 **S**	**Zinc coated:** (≤3) **diam**, (360) **TS**, (280) **YS**, 18 **El**
DIN 17111	Grade U10S6	Germany	Bar, wire, rod	0.15 **C**, 0.30–0.60 **Mn**, 0.080 **P**, 0.03–0.08 **S**	**Hot rolled:** all **diam**, (343) **TS**, (226) **YS**
DIN 17111	Grade U10S10	Germany	Bar, wire, rod	0.15 **C**, 0.40–0.70 **Mn**, 0.050 **P**, 0.08–0.12 **S**	**Hot rolled:** all **diam**, (343) **TS**, (226) **YS**
NBN 837	D 35	Belgium	Tube	0.15 **C**, 0.40–0.80 **Mn**, 0.040 **P**, 0.040 **S**, 0.15–0.35 **Si**	**Normalized or annealed:** all **diam**, (340) **TS**, (240) **YS**, 25 **El**
BS 1449: Part 1	Grade 34/20	UK	Plate, sheet, strip	0.15 **C**, 0.70 **Mn**, 0.050 **P**, 0.050 **S**	**Hot or cold rolled:** all **diam**, (340) **TS**, (200) **YS**, 29 **El**
ASTM A 587		US	Pipe: electric welded	0.15 **C**, 0.27–0.63 **Mn**, 0.048 **P**, 0.058 **S**, 0.02 min **Al**	**Normalized–flanging quality:** all **diam**, 48 (331) **TS**, 30 (207) **YS**, 40 **El**
SIS 14 12 70	SIS 12 70	Sweden	Sheet	0.15 **C**, 1.0 **Mn**, 0.05 **P**, 0.05 **S**	**Zinc coated:** (≤3) **diam**, (330) **TS**, (250) **YS**, 18 **El**
BS 3059	Steel 33	UK	Tube: electric resistance welded	0.15 **C**, 0.40–0.70 **Mn**, 0.050 **P**, 0.050 **S**, 0.10–0.35 **Si**	**Normalized:** all **diam**, (325) **TS**, (185) **YS**, 25 **El**
BS 3059	Steel 33	UK	Tube: seamless	0.15 **C**, 0.40–0.70 **Mn**, 0.050 **P**, 0.050 **S**, 0.10–0.35 **Si**	**Hot finished or normalized:** all **diam**, (325) **TS**, (185) **YS**, 25 **El**
SS 14 12 32 E	SS 12 32–04	Sweden	Tube: seamless	0.15 **C**, 0.30–0.70 **Mn**, 0.050 **P**, 0.050 **S**, 0.30 **Cu**, 0.25 **Cr**, 0.009 **N**	**As rolled or quenched:** all **diam**, (320) **TS**, (200) **YS**, 25 **El**
SS 14 12 32 E	SS 12 32–06	Sweden	Tube: welded	0.15 **C**, 0.30–0.70 **Mn**, 0.050 **P**, 0.050 **S**, 0.30 **Cu**, 0.25 **Cr**, 0.009 **N**	**As rolled or quenched:** all **diam**, (320) **TS**, (200) **YS**, 25 **El**
BS 970 Part 1	220M07	UK	Blooms, billets, slabs, bar, rod, forgings	0.15 **C**, 0.90–1.30 **Mn**, 0.070 **P**, 0.20–0.30 **S**	**Hot rolled:** 4 **diam**, (315) **TS**, (195) **YS**, 22 **El**; **Cold drawn:** 0.50–0.625 **diam**, (415) **TS**, 7 **El**
BS 970 Part 1	230M07	UK	Blooms, billets, slabs, bar, rod, forgings	0.15 **C**, 0.90–1.30 **Mn**, 0.070 **P**, 0.25–0.35 **S**	**Hot rolled:** 4 **diam**, (315) **TS**, (195) **YS**, 22 **El**; **Cold drawn:** 0.50–0.625 **diam**, (415) **TS**, 7 **El**
BS 970 Part 1	240M07	UK	Blooms, billets, slabs, bar, rod, forgings	0.15 **C**, 1.10–1.50 **Mn**, 0.070 **P**, 0.30–0.60 **S**	**Hot rolled:** 2.5 **diam**, (315) **TS**, (195) **YS**, 20 **El**; **Cold drawn:** 0.50–0.625 **diam**, (400) **TS**, 7 **El**
ASTM A 539		US	Tube: electric resistance welded, coiled	0.15 **C**, 0.63 **Mn**, 0.050 **P**, 0.060 **S**	**As–welded, coiled:** 0.125 (3.18) **diam**, 45 (310) **TS**, 35 (241) **YS**, 21 **El**
ASTM A 414	Grade A	US	Sheet	0.15 **C**, 0.90 **Mn**, 0.035 **P**, 0.040 **S**	**Hot rolled:** 0.2299–0.1450 (5.82–3.68) **diam**, 45 (310) **TS**, 24 (165) **YS**, 26 **El**
ANSI/ASTM A 414	Grade A	US	Sheet	0.15 **C**, 0.90 **Mn**, 0.035 **P**, 0.040 **S**, 0.20 min **Cu**	**Hot rolled or cold rolled, annealed:** all **diam**, (310) **TS**, (165) **YS**, 26 **El**
DGN–B–275	Grade A	Mexico	Sheet	0.15 **C**, 0.90 **Mn**, 0.035 **P**, 0.040 **S**, 0.20 **Cu**	**Hot rolled:** (5–4) **diam**, (309) **TS**, (165) **YS**, 26 **El**
SIS 14 13 16	SIS 13 16–32	Sweden	Sheet	0.15 **C**, 0.70 **Mn**, 0.050 **P**, 0.050 **S**, 0.040 **Si**, 0.009 **N**	**Annealed and cold rolled:** (≤3) **diam**, (300) **TS**, (220) **YS**, 22 **El**
ISO 4997	Grade CR220–D	ISO	Sheet	0.15 **C**, 0.040 **P**, 0.040 **S**	**Cold rolled and annealed:** all **diam**, (300) **TS**, (220) **YS**, 22 **El**
ISO 4997	Grade CR220–B	ISO	Sheet	0.15 **C**, 0.050 **P**, 0.050 **S**	**Cold rolled and annealed:** all **diam**, (300) **TS**, (220) **YS**, 22 **El**
AS 1594	Grade AS1594/HR200	Australia	Sheet, strip	0.15 **C**, 0.60 **Mn**, 0.040 **P**, 0.040 **S**	**Hot rolled:** ≥3 **diam**, (300) **TS**, (200) **YS**, 24 **El**
SIS 14 13 16	SIS 13 16	Sweden	Sheet	0.15 **C**, 0.70 **Mn**, 0.050 **P**, 0.050 **S**, 0.40 **Si**, 0.009 **N**	**As–rolled:** (≤3) **diam**, (300) **TS**, (220) **YS**, 22 **El**
BS 1449: Part 1	Grade 14	UK	Plate, sheet, strip	0.15 **C**, 0.60 **Mn**, 0.050 **P**, 0.050 **S**	**Hot rolled:** all **diam**, (280) **TS**, (170) **YS**, 25 **El**
JIS G 3131	Class 1	Japan	Plate, sheet, strip	0.15 **C**, 0.60 **Mn**, 0.050 **P**, 0.050 **S**	**Hot rolled:** (<1.2) **diam**, (275) **TS**, 25 **El**
DGN–B–247	Temper No 4	Japan	Strip	0.15 **C**, 0.60 **Mn**, 0.04 **P**, 0.05 **S**	**Cold rolled and tempered:** (1.27) **diam**, (34) **TS**, 32 **El**
SIS 14 13 11 E	SIS 13 11–10	Sweden	Bar	0.15 **C**, 0.3–0.6 **Mn**, 0.08 **P**, 0.06 **S**, 0.02 **Si**	**As rolled:** (6–32) **diam**, (220) **YS**, 20 **El**

WROUGHT CARBON STEELS

specification number	designation	country	product forms	composition	mechanical properties (see page iv for explanation)
ISO 3574	CR1	ISO	Sheet	0.15 **C**, 0.60 **Mn**, 0.05 **P**, 0.05 **S**	
ISO 3573	Grade HR 1	ISO	Sheet	0.15 **C**, 0.60 **Mn**, 0.05 **P**, 0.05 **S**	
DIN 2393 Sheet 2	Grade St 34–2–1.0102 or 1.0108	Germany	Tube	0.15 **C**, 0.05 **P**, 0.05 **S**	
DIN 2393 Sheet 2	Grade St 34–2.2–1.0102 or 1.0108	Germany	Tube	0.15 **C**, 0.05 **P**, 0.05 **S**	
BS 3S.91		UK	Billets, bar, forgings: aircraft quality	0.15 **C**, 0.3–0.6 **Mn**, 0.040 **P**, 0.040 **S**, 0.10–0.35 **Si**	**Normalized**: all **diam**
NF A 36–102	Fd 02	France	Strip	0.15 **C**, 0.062 **P**, 0.062 **S**, 0.009 $\mathbf{N_2}$	
NF A 36–102	Fd Tu 3	France	Strip	0.15 **C**, 0.062 **P**, 0.062 **S**, 0.009 $\mathbf{N_2}$	
QQ–S–637A	12L14	US	Bar	0.15 **C**, 0.085–1.15 **Mn**, 0.04–0.09 **P**, 0.26–0.35 **S**, 0.15–0.85 **Pb**	
QQ–S–637A	G	US	Bar	0.15 **C**, 0.80–1.20 **Mn**, 0.04–0.09 **P**, 0.25–0.35 **S**, 0.15–0.35 **Pb**	
QQ–S–637A	H	US	Bar	0.15 **C**, 0.80–1.20 **Mn**, 0.04–0.09 **P**, 0.25–0.35 **S**, 0.15–0.35 **Pb**	
QQ–S–637A	J	US	Bar	0.15 **C**, 0.80–1.20 **Mn**, 0.04–0.09 **P**, 0.25–0.35 **S**, 0.15–0.35 **Pb**	
QQ–S–637A	K	US	Bar	0.15 **C**, 0.75–1.25 **Mn**, 0.04–0.09 **P**, 0.25–0.35 **S**, 0.15–0.35 **Pb**	
QQ–S–637A	L	US	Bar	0.15 **C**, 0.80–1.20 **Mn**, 0.04–0.09 **P**, 0.24–0.35 **S**, 0.15–0.35 **Pb**	
QQ–S–637A	M	US	Bar	0.15 **C**, 0.85–1.35 **Mn**, 0.04–0.09 **P**, 0.40 **S**, 0.15–0.35 **Pb**	
QQ–S–698	1009	US	Sheet, strip	0.15 **C**, 0.60 **Mn**, 0.040 **P**, 0.050 **S**	
ASTM A 635		US	Sheet, strip	0.15 **C**, 0.25–0.60 **Mn**, 0.035 **P**, 0.040 **S**	
ASTM A 591		US	Sheet	0.15 **C**, 0.60 **Mn**, 0.035 **P**, 0.040 **S**	
ASTM A 599		US	Sheet	0.15 **C**, 0.60 **Mn**, 0.035 **P**, 0.040 **S**, 0.20 min **Cu**; when copper steel is specified	
ASTM A 109	Tempers 4,5	US	Strip	0.15 **C**, 0.60 **Mn**, 0.035 **P**, 0.04 **S**	
ASTM A 527		US	Sheet	0.15 **C**, 0.60 **Mn**, 0.035 **P**, 0.040 **S**	
ASTM A 526		US	Sheet	0.15 **C**, 0.60 **Mn**, 0.035 **P**, 0.040 **S**	
ASTM A 463	Type 1	US	Sheet	0.15 **C**, 0.60 **Mn**, 0.035 **P**, 0.040 **S**	
AISI 1009		US	Plate	0.15 **C**, 0.60 **Mn**, 0.040 **P**, 0.050 **S**	
AISI 12L14		US	Bar	0.15 **C**, 0.85–1.15 **Mn**, 0.04–0.09 **P**, 0.26–0.35 **S**, 0.15–0.35 **Pb**	
AMS 5050G		US	Tube	0.15 **C**, 0.30–0.60 **Mn**, 0.040 **P**, 0.050 **S**	**Annealed**: ≤0.50 (≤12.7) **diam**, 32 **El**
ANSI/ASTM A 519	12L14	US	Tube: seamless	0.15 **C**, 0.85–1.15 **Mn**, 0.04–0.09 **P**, 0.26–0.35 **S**, 0.15–0.35 **Pb**	
AS 1595, Part 2	AS 1595/Temper 1	Australia	Sheet, strip	0.15 **C**, 0.60 **Mn**, 0.040 **P**, 0.040 **S**	**Cold rolled**
AS 1595, Part 2	AS 1595/Temper 2	Australia	Sheet, strip	0.15 **C**, 0.60 **Mn**, 0.040 **P**, 0.040 **S**	**Cold rolled**
AS 1595, Part 2	AS 1595/Temper 3	Australia	Sheet, strip	0.15 **C**, 0.60 **Mn**, 0.040 **P**, 0.040 **S**	**Cold rolled**
COPANT 330	12 L 14	COPANT	Bar, shapes	0.15 **C**, 0.85–1.15 **Mn**, 0.04–0.09 **P**, 0.26–0.35 **S**	
COPANT 331	12 L 14	COPANT	Bar	0.15 **C**, 0.85–1.15 **Mn**, 0.04–0.09 **P**, 0.26–0.35 **S**	
ASTM A 108	12L14	US	Bar	0.15 **C**, 0.85–1.15 **Mn**, 0.04–0.09 **P**, 0.26–0.35 **S**, 0.15–0.35 **Pb**	
ANSI/ASTM A 236	Grade A	US	Forgings	0.15 **C**, 0.30–0.60 **Mn**, 0.045 **P**, 0.050 **S**	

specification number	designation	country	product forms	composition	mechanical properties (see page iv for explanation)
ANSI/ASTM A 366		US	Sheet	0.15 **C**, 0.60 **Mn**, 0.035 **P**, 0.040 **S**	
ANSI/ASTM A 569		US	Sheet, strip	0.15 **C**, 0.60 **Mn**, 0.035 **P**, 0.040 **S**	
ISO 3575	01	ISO	Sheet: hot dipped, zinc–coated	0.15 **C**, 0.60 **Mn**, 0.05 **P**, 0.05 **S**	**As rolled**
COPANT 333	12L14	COPANT	Wire, rod	0.15 **C**, 0.80–1.20 **Mn**, 0.04–0.09 **P**, 0.25–0.35 **S**, 0.15–0.35 **Pb**	
ANSI/ASTM A 236	Grade A	US	Forgings	0.15 **C**, 0.30–0.60 **Mn**, 0.045 **P**, 0.05 **S**	
ANSI/ASTM A 730	Grade A	US	Forgings	0.15 **C**, 0.30–0.60 **Mn**, 0.045 **P**, 0.050 **S**	
DGN–B–28		Mexico	Sheet	0.15 **C**, 0.60 **Mn**, 0.035 **P**, 0.040 **S**, 0.20 **Cu**	
AISI 12214		US	Wire, rod	0.15 **C**, 0.85–1.15 **Mn**, 0.04–0.09 **P**, 0.26–0.35 **S**, 0.15–0.35 **Pb**	
ANSI/ASTM A 576	12L14	US	Bar	0.15 **C**, 0.85–1.15 **Mn**, 0.04–0.09 **P**, 0.26–0.35 **S**, 0.15–0.35 **Pb**	
ANSI/ASTM A 29	12L14	US	Bar	0.15 **C**, 0.85–1.15 **Mn**, 0.04–0.09 **P**, 0.26–0.35 **S**, 0.15–0.35 **Pb**	
ASTM A 594	Grade 1	US	Forgings	0.15 **C**, 0.50 **Mn**, 0.04 **P**, 0.04 **S**, 0.20 **Si**, 0.02 **Al**	
ASTM A 689	12L14	US	Bar	0.15 **C**, 0.85–1.15 **Mn**, 0.04–0.09 **P**, 0.26–0.35 **S**, 0.15–0.35 **Pb**	
DGN–B–247	Temper No 5	Japan	Strip	0.15 **C**, 0.60 **Mn**, 0.04 **P**, 0.05 **S**	**Cold rolled and tempered**
AS 1443	Grade AS 1443/S12L14	Australia	Bar	0.15 **C**, 0.80–1.20 **Mn**, 0.04–0.09 **P**, 0.25–0.35 **S**, 0.10 **Si**	
AS 1443	Grade AS 1443/S1214	Australia	Bar	0.15 **C**, 0.80–1.20 **Mn**, 0.04–0.09 **P**, 0.25–0.35 **S**, 0.10 **Si**	
DGN–B–248		Mexico	Sheet, strip	0.15 **C**, 0.60 **Mn**, 0.035 **P**, 0.040 **S**, 0.20 min **Cu**	
AS 1442	Grade AS 1442/S1214	Australia	Bar, blooms, billets, slabs	0.15 **C**, 0.80–1.20 **Mn**, 0.04–0.09 **P**, 0.25–0.35 **S**, 0.10 **Si**	
AS 1442	Grade AS 1442/S12L14	Australia	Bar, blooms, billets, slabs	0.15 **C**, 0.80–1.20 **Mn**, 0.04–0.09 **P**, 0.25–0.35 **S**, 0.10 **Si**	
COPANT 514	Grade 12 L 14	COPANT	Tube: seamless	0.15 **C**, 0.85–1.15 **Mn**, 0.04–0.09 **P**, 0.26–0.35 **S**, 0.15–0.35 **Pb**	
JIS G 4804	SUM 24L	Japan	Bar	0.15 **C**, 0.85–1.15 **Mn**, 0.04–0.09 **P**, 0.26–0.35 **S**, 0.10–0.35 **Pb**	
ANSI/ASTM A 194	Grade 1	US	Bar, forgings	0.15 min **C**	**As forged**
ANSI/ASTM A 67		US	Plate	0.15 min **C**, 0.05 **P**, 0.20 min **Cu**	
QQ–S–698	1018	US	Sheet, strip	0.14–0.21 **C**, 0.60–0.90 **Mn**, 0.040 **P**, 0.050 **S**	
ANSI/ASTM A 29	M 1017	US	Bar	0.14–0.21 **C**, 0.25–0.60 **Mn**, 0.04 **P**, 0.05 **S**	
ISO/R 683/1X	Type 6	ISO	Bar, wire, rod	0.14–0.20 **C**, 0.50–0.90 **Mn**, 0.06 **P**, 0.15–0.25 **S**, 0.15–0.40 **Si**	**Cold finished**: (≤16) **diam**, (539) **TS**, (412) **YS**, 7 **El**
DIN 17155	Grade 17 Mn 4	Germany	Plate	0.14–0.20 **C**, 0.90–1.20 **Mn**, 0.050 **P**, 0.050 **S**, 0.20–0.40 **Si**, 0.30 max, opt **Cr**	**Normalized**: (≤16) **diam**, (461) **TS**, (284) **YS**
DGN–B–301	1118	Mexico	Bar	0.14–0.20 **C**, 1.30–1.60 **Mn**, 0.040 **P**, 0.08–0.13 **S**, 0.10–0.20 **Si**	**Forged or hot rolled, cold rolled and cold finished**: all **diam**, (451) **TS**, (245) **YS**, 23 **El**
DGN–B–301	1119	Mexico	Bar	0.14–0.20 **C**, 1.00–1.30 **Mn**, 0.040 **P**, 0.24–0.33 **S**, 0.10–0.20 **Si**	**Forged and hot rolled, cold rolled and cold finished**: all **diam**, (422) **TS**, (235) **YS**, 23 **El**
DGN–B–301	1117	Mexico	Bar	0.14–0.20 **C**, 1.00–1.30 **Mn**, 0.040 **P**, 0.08–0.13 **S**, 0.10–0.20 **Si**	**Forged or hot rolled, cold rolled and cold finished**: all **diam**, (422) **TS**, (235) **YS**, 23 **El**

specification number	designation	country	product forms	composition	mechanical properties (see page iv for explanation)
ANSI/ASTM A 519	1118	US	Tube: seamless	0.14–0.20 **C**, 1.30–1.60 **Mn**, 0.040 **P**, 0.08–0.13 **S**	**Hot rolled**: all **diam**, 50 (345) **TS**, 35 (241) **YS**, 25 **El**; **Cold worked**: all **diam**, 75 (517) **TS**, 60 (414) **YS**, 5 **El**; **Stress relieved**: all **diam**, 70 (483) **TS**, 55 (379) **YS**, 8 **El**; **Annealed**: all **diam**, 50 (345) **TS**, 30 (207) **YS**, 25 **El**; **Normalized**: all **diam**, 55 (379) **TS**, 35 (241) **YS**, 20 **El**
QQ-S-637A	1116	US	Bar	0.14–0.20 **C**, 1.10–1.40 **Mn**, 0.040 **P**, 0.16–0.23 **S**, 0.15–0.35 **Pb**	
QQ-S-637A	1117	US	Bar	0.14–0.20 **C**, 1.00–1.30 **Mn**, 0.040 **P**, 0.08–0.13 **S**, 0.15–0.35 **Pb**	
QQ-S-637A	1119	US	Bar	0.14–0.20 **C**, 1.00–1.30 **Mn**, 0.040 **P**, 0.24–0.33 **S**, 0.15–0.35 **Pb**	
ASTM A 659	Grade 1017	US	Sheet, strip	0.14–0.20 **C**, 0.30–0.60 **Mn**, 0.040 **P**, 0.050 **S**	
ASTM A 659	Grade 1018	US	Sheet, strip	0.14–0.20 **C**, 0.60–0.90 **Mn**, 0.040 **P**, 0.050 **S**	
AISI 1017		US	Plate	0.14–0.20 **C**, 0.30–0.60 **Mn**, 0.040 **P**, 0.050 **S**	
AISI 1019		US	Plate	0.14–0.20 **C**, 0.70–1.00 **Mn**, 0.040 **P**, 0.050 **S**	
AISI 1118		US	Bar	0.14–0.20 **C**, 1.30–1.60 **Mn**, 0.040 **P**, 0.08–0.13 **S**	
AISI 1117		US	Bar	0.14–0.20 **C**, 1.00–1.30 **Mn**, 0.040 **P**, 0.08–0.13 **S**	
AMS 5022H		US	Bar, forgings, tube	0.14–0.20 **C**, 1.00–1.30 **Mn**, 0.040 **P**, 0.08–0.13 **S**	
ANSI/ASTM A 519	11L18	US	Tube: seamless	0.14–0.20 **C**, 1.30–1.60 **Mn**, 0.004 **P**, 0.08–0.13 **S**, 0.15–0.35 **Pb**	
COPANT 330	1117	COPANT	Bar, shapes	0.14–0.20 **C**, 1.0–1.3 **Mn**, 0.040 **P**, 0.08–0.13 **S**	
COPANT 330	1118	COPANT	Bar, shapes	0.14–0.20 **C**, 1.3–1.6 **Mn**, 0.040 **P**, 0.08–0.13 **S**	
COPANT 331	1117	COPANT	Bar	0.14–0.20 **C**, 1.0–1.3 **Mn**, 0.040 **P**, 0.08–0.13 **S**	
ASTM A 108	1117	US	Bar	0.14–0.20 **C**, 1.00–1.30 **Mn**, 0.040 **P**, 0.08–0.13 **S**	
COPANT 333	1117	COPANT	Wire, rod	0.14–0.20 **C**, 1.00–1.30 **Mn**, 0.040 **P**, 0.050 **S**	
DGN-B-301	1116	Mexico	Bar	0.14–0.20 **C**, 1.10–1.40 **Mn**, 0.040 **P**, 0.16–0.23 **S**, 0.10–0.20 **Si**	
AISI 1117		US	Wire, rod	0.14–0.20 **C**, 1.00–1.30 **Mn**, 0.040 **P**, 0.08–0.13 **S**	
ANSI/ASTM A 576	1116	US	Bar	0.14–0.20 **C**, 1.10–1.40 **Mn**, 0.040 **P**, 0.16–0.23 **S**	
ANSI/ASTM A 576	1117	US	Bar	0.14–0.20 **C**, 1.00–1.30 **Mn**, 0.040 **P**, 0.08–0.13 **S**	
ANSI/ASTM A 576	1119	US	Bar	0.14–0.20 **C**, 1.00–1.30 **Mn**, 0.040 **P**, 0.24–0.33 **S**	
ANSI/ASTM A 29	1116	US	Bar	0.14–0.20 **C**, 1.10–1.40 **Mn**, 0.040 **P**, 0.16–0.23 **S**	
ANSI/ASTM A 29	1117	US	Bar	0.14–0.20 **C**, 1.00–1.30 **Mn**, 0.040 **P**, 0.08–0.13 **S**	
ANSI/ASTM A 29	1119	US	Bar	0.14–0.20 **C**, 1.00–1.30 **Mn**, 0.040 **P**, 0.24–0.33 **S**	
ASTM A 689	1116	US	Bar	0.14–0.20 **C**, 1.10–1.40 **Mn**, 0.040 **P**, 0.16–0.23 **S**	
ASTM A 689	1117	US	Bar	0.14–0.20 **C**, 1.00–1.30 **Mn**, 0.040 **P**, 0.08–0.13 **S**	
ASTM A 689	1118	US	Bar	0.14–0.20 **C**, 1.30–1.60 **Mn**, 0.040 **P**, 0.08–0.13 **S**	
ASTM A 689	1119	US	Bar	0.14–0.20 **C**, 1.00–1.30 **Mn**, 0.040 **P**, 0.24–0.33 **S**	

WROUGHT CARBON STEELS

specification number	designation	country	product forms	composition	mechanical properties (see page iv for explanation)
AS 1442	Grade AS 1442/K1117	Australia	Bar, blooms, billets, slabs	0.14–0.20 **C**, 1.00–1.30 **Mn**, 0.050 **P**, 0.08–0.13 **S**, 0.10–0.35 **Si**	
AS 1443	Grade AS 1443/K1117	Australia	Bar	0.14–0.20 **C**, 1.00–1.30 **Mn**, 0.050 **P**, 0.08–0.13 **S**, 0.10–0.35 **Si**	
DEF STAN 95–1/1	CL.1.C1118	Canada	Bar	0.14–0.20 **C**, 1.30–1.60 **Mn**, 0.08–0.13 **S**	
DEF STAN 95–1/1	CL.1.C1117	Canada	Bar	0.14–0.20 **C**, 1.00–1.30 **Mn**, 0.08–0.13 **S**	
JIS G 4804	SUM 31	Japan	Bar	0.14–0.20 **C**, 1.00–1.30 **Mn**, 0.040 **P**, 0.08–0.13 **S**	
JIS G 4804	SUM 31L	Japan	Bar	0.14–0.20 **C**, 1.00–1.30 **Mn**, 0.040 **P**, 0.08–0.13 **S**, 0.10–0.35 **Pb**	
ANSI/ASTM A 575	M 1017	US	Bar	0.14–0.17 **C**, 0.25–0.60 **Mn**, 0.04 **P**, 0.05 **S**	
ISO/R 683/1X	Type 2Pb	ISO	Bar, wire, rod	0.14 **C**, 0.90–1.30 **Mn**, 0.11 **P**, 0.24–0.32 **S**, 0.05 **Si**, 0.15–0.35 **Pb**	**Cold drawn**: (≤16) **diam**, (510) **TS**, (412) **YS**, 7 **El**
ISO/R 683/1X	Type 2	ISO	Bar, wire, rod	0.14 **C**, 0.90–1.30 **Mn**, 0.11 **P**, 0.24–0.32 **S**, 0.05 **Si**	**Cold drawn**: (≤16) **diam**, (510) **TS**, (412) **YS**, 7 **El**
SIS 14 19 14	SIS 19 14–04	Sweden	Bar	0.14 **C**, 0.90–1.30 **Mn**, 0.11 **P**, 0.24–0.35 **S**, 0.05 **Si**	**Cold worked**: (≤16) **diam**, (510) **TS**, (410) **YS**, 7 **El**
SIS 14 19 12	SIS 19 12–04	Sweden	Bar	0.14 **C**, 0.90–1.30 **Mn**, 0.11 **P**, 0.24–0.35 **S**, 0.05 **Si**	**Cold worked**: (≤16) **diam**, (510) **TS**, (410) **YS**, 7 **El**
SIS 14 19 14	SIS 19 14–03	Sweden	Bar	0.14 **C**, 0.90–1.30 **Mn**, 0.11 **P**, 0.24–0.35 **S**, 0.05 **Si**	**Case hardened**: (≤16) **diam**, (490) **TS**, (290) **YS**, 15 **El**
SIS 14 19 12	SIS 19 12–03	Sweden	Bar	0.14 **C**, 0.90–1.30 **Mn**, 0.11 **P**, 0.24–0.35 **S**, 0.05 **Si**	**Case hardened**: (≤16) **diam**, (490) **TS**, (290) **YS**, 15 **El**
DIN 1651	9 SMn 28 (1.0715)	Germany	Bar	0.14 **C**, 0.90–1.30 **Mn**, 0.100 **P**, 0.24–0.32 **S**, 0.05 **Si**	**Hot rolled**: all **diam**, (390) **TS**; **Normalized**: all **diam**, (370) **TS**, (235) **YS**, 23 in 80 mm **El**
DIN 1651	9 SMnPb 28 (1.0718)	Germany	Bar	0.14 **C**, 0.90–1.30 **Mn**, 0.100 **P**, 0.24–0.32 **S**, 0.05 **Si**, 0.15–0.30 **Pb**	**Hot rolled**: all **diam**, (380) **TS**; **Normalized**: all **diam**, (370) **TS**, (225) **YS**, 23 in 80 mm **El**
SIS 14 19 14	SIS 19 14–00	Sweden	Bar	0.14 **C**, 0.90–1.30 **Mn**, 0.11 **P**, 0.24–0.35 **S**, 0.05 **Si**	**As rolled**: (≤100) **diam**, (380) **TS**
SIS 14 19 12	SIS 19 12–00	Sweden	Bar	0.14 **C**, 0.90–1.30 **Mn**, 0.11 **P**, 0.24–0.35 **S**, 0.05 **Si**	**As rolled**: (≤100) **diam**, (380) **TS**
DIN 17111	Grade USt36–1	Germany	Bar, wire, rod	0.14 **C**, 0.25–0.45 **Mn**, 0.080 **P**, 0.050 **S**	**Hot rolled**: all **diam**, (333) **TS**, (206) **YS**, 30 **El**
DIN 17111	Grade USt36–2	Germany	Bar, wire, rod	0.14 **C**, 0.25–0.50 **Mn**, 0.080 **P**, 0.050 **S**, 0.007 **N**	**Hot rolled**: all **diam**, (333) **TS**, (206) **YS**, 30 **El**
NF A 35–051	FM 8 grade 1	France	Wire, rod	0.14 **C**, 0.25–0.60 **Mn**, 0.080 **P**, 0.070 **S**	
JIS G 3539	SWCH 15K	Japan	Wire	0.13–0.8 **C**, 0.30–0.60 **Mn**, 0.030 **P**, 0.035 **S**, 0.10–0.35 **Si**	**Annealed and cold drawn**: all **diam**, (373) **TS**, 13 **El**
COPANT 330	1020	COPANT	Bar, shapes	0.13–0.23 **C**, 0.30–0.60 **Mn**, 0.040 **P**, 0.050 **S**	
COPANT 330	1022	COPANT	Bar, shapes	0.13–0.23 **C**, 0.70–1.0 **Mn**, 0.040 **P**, 0.050 **S**	
ANSI/ASTM A 512	1115	US	Tube: cold-drawn buttweld	0.13–0.20 **C**, 0.60–0.90 **Mn**, 0.04 **P**, 0.08–0.13 **S**	**Stress relief annealed**: all **diam**, 68 (469) **TS**, 62 (427) **YS**, 13 **El**
DGN–B–201	Grade 1115	Mexico	Tube: butt-welded	0.13–0.20 **C**, 0.60–0.90 **Mn**, 0.040 **P**, 0.13 **S**	**Cold finished and annealed**: all **diam**, (469) **TS**, (431) **YS**, 13 **El**
QQ–S–698	1018 modified	US	Sheet, strip	0.13–0.20 **C**, 0.60–0.90 **Mn**, 0.040 **P**, 0.050 **S**	
JIS G 3539	SWCH 16K	Japan	Wire	0.13–0.18 **C**, 0.60–0.90 **Mn**, 0.030 **P**, 0.035 **S**, 0.10–0.35 **Si**	**Cold drawn**: (3–4) **diam**, (637) **TS**; **Annealed and cold drawn**: (3–4) **diam**, (412) **TS**, 13 **El**
JIS G 3539	SWCH 15R	Japan	Wire	0.13–0.18 **C**, 0.30–0.60 **Mn**, 0.040 **P**, 0.040 **S**	**Cold drawn**: (≤3) **diam**, (588) **TS**; **Annealed and cold drawn**: (≤3) **diam**, (343) **TS**, 14 **El**
JIS G 3539	SWCH 16A	Japan	Wire	0.13–0.18 **C**, 0.60–0.90 **Mn**, 0.030 **P**, 0.035 **S**, 0.10 **Si**, 0.02 min **Al**	**Cold drawn**: (>3–4) **diam**, (588) **TS**; **Annealed and cold drawn**: (>3–4) **diam**, (373) **TS**, 13 **El**

specification number	designation	country	product forms	composition	mechanical properties (see page iv for explanation)
JIS G 3539	SWCH 15A	Japan	Wire	0.13–0.18 **C**, 0.30–0.60 **Mn**, 0.030 **P**, 0.030 **S**, 0.10 **Si**, 0.02 min **Al**	**Cold drawn:** (>4–5) **diam**, (412) **TS**; **Annealed and cold drawn:** (>4–5) **diam**, (343) **TS**, 14 **El**
DGN–B–301	1016	Mexico	Bar	0.13–0.18 **C**, 0.60–0.90 **Mn**, 0.040 **P**, 0.050 **S**, 0.10 **Si**	**Forged or hot rolled, cold rolled and cold finished:** all **diam**, (382) **TS**, (206) **YS**, 25 **El**
DGN–B–301	1015	Mexico	Bar	0.13–0.18 **C**, 0.30–0.60 **Mn**, 0.040 **P**, 0.050 **S**, 0.10 **Si**	**Forged or hot rolled, cold rolled and cold finished:** all **diam**, (343) **TS**, (186) **YS**, 28 **El**
AISI 1016		US	Bar	0.13–0.18 **C**, 0.60–0.90 **Mn**, 0.040 **P**, 0.050 **S**	
AISI 1015		US	Bar	0.13–0.18 **C**, 0.30–0.60 **Mn**, 0.040 **P**, 0.050 **S**	
BS 970: Part 1	040A15		Blooms, billets, slabs, bar, rod, forgings	0.13–0.18 **C**, 0.30–0.50 **Mn**	
BS 970: Part 1	050A15	UK	Blooms, billets, slabs, bar, rod, forgings	0.13–0.18 **C**, 0.40–0.60 **Mn**	
BS 970: Part 1	060A15	UK	Blooms, billets, slabs, bar, rod, forgings	0.13–0.18 **C**, 0.40–0.60 **Mn**	
BS 970: Part 1	080A15	UK	Blooms, billets, slabs, bar, rod, forgings	0.13–0.18 **C**, 0.70–0.90 **Mn**	
AMS 5060D		US	Bar, forgings, tube	0.13–0.18 **C**, 0.30–0.60 **Mn**, 0.040 **P**, 0.050 **S**, 0.10–0.35 **Si**	
ANSI/ASTM A 519	1015	US	Tube: seamless	0.13–0.18 **C**, 0.30–0.60 **Mn**, 0.040 **P**, 0.050 **S**	
ANSI/ASTM A 519	1016	US	Tube: seamless	0.13–0.18 **C**, 0.60–0.90 **Mn**, 0.040 **P**, 0.050 **S**	
DGN–B–13	Class C, grade C4	Mexico	Wire	0.13–0.18 **C**, 0.33–0.43 **Mn**, 0.040 **P**, 0.060 **S**	
DGN–B–13	Class C, grade C3	Mexico	Wire	0.13–0.18 **C**, 0.33–0.43 **Mn**, 0.040 **P**, 0.060 **S**	
DGN–B–13	Class C, grade C2	Mexico	Wire	0.13–0.18 **C**, 0.33–0.43 **Mn**, 0.040 **P**, 0.060 **S**	
DGN–B–13	Class C, grade C1	Mexico	Wire	0.13–0.18 **C**, 0.33–0.43 **Mn**, 0.040 **P**, 0.060 **S**	
AS 1446	Grade AS 1446/S1015	Australia	Plate	0.13–0.18 **C**, 0.30–0.60 **Mn**, 0.050 **P**, 0.050 **S**, 0.35 **Si**	
COPANT 330	1015	COPANT	Bar, shapes	0.13–0.18 **C**, 0.30–0.60 **Mn**, 0.040 **P**, 0.050 **S**	
COPANT 330	1016	COPANT	Bar, shapes	0.13–0.18 **C**, 0.60–0.90 **Mn**, 0.040 **P**, 0.050 **S**	
COPANT 330	1115	COPANT	Bar, shapes	0.13–0.18 **C**, 0.60–0.90 **Mn**, 0.040 **P**, 0.08–0.13 **S**	
COPANT 331	1015	COPANT	Bar	0.13–0.18 **C**, 0.30–0.60 **Mn**, 0.040 **P**, 0.050 **S**	
COPANT 331	1016	COPANT	Bar	0.13–0.18 **C**, 0.60–0.90 **Mn**, 0.040 **P**, 0.050 **S**	
COPANT 331	1115	COPANT	Bar	0.13–0.18 **C**, 0.60–0.90 **Mn**, 0.040 **P**, 0.08–0.13 **S**	
COPANT 333	1015	COPANT	Wire, rod	0.13–0.18 **C**, 0.30–0.60 **Mn**, 0.040 **P**, 0.050 **S**	
COPANT 333	1016	COPANT	Wire, rod	0.13–0.18 **C**, 0.60–0.90 **Mn**, 0.040 **P**, 0.050 **S**	
MIL–S–16974E	No. 1015	US	Bar, billets, blooms, slabs	0.13–0.18 **C**, 0.30–0.60 **Mn**, 0.040 **P**, 0.050 **S**, 0.00–0.30 **Si**	
ASTM A 108	1016	US	Bar	0.13–0.18 **C**, 0.60–0.90 **Mn**, 0.040 **P**, 0.050 **S**	
ASTM A 108	1015	US	Bar	0.13–0.18 **C**, 0.30–0.60 **Mn**, 0.040 **P**, 0.050 **S**	
ANSI/ASTM A 545	Grade 1016	US	Wire	0.13–0.18 **C**, 0.60–0.90 **Mn**, 0.040 **P**, 0.050 **S**	
ANSI/ASTM A 545	Grade 1015	US	Wire	0.13–0.18 **C**, 0.30–0.60 **Mn**, 0.040 **P**, 0.050 **S**	

WROUGHT CARBON STEELS

specification number	designation	country	product forms	composition	mechanical properties (see page iv for explanation)
ANSI/ASTM A 548	Grade 1016	US	Wire	0.13–0.18 **C**, 0.60–0.90 **Mn**, 0.040 **P**, 0.050 **S**	
ANSI/ASTM A 549	Grade 1015	US	Wire	0.13–0.18 **C**, 0.30–0.60 **Mn**, 0.040 **P**, 0.050 **S**	
ANSI/ASTM A 549	Grade 1016	US	Wire	0.13–0.18 **C**, 0.60–0.90 **Mn**, 0.040 **P**, 0.050 **S**	
ANSI/ASTM A 575	1015	US	Bar	0.13–0.18 **C**, 0.30–0.60 **Mn**, 0.04 **P**, 0.05 **S**	
AISI 1015		US	Wire, rod	0.13–0.18 **C**, 0.30–0.60 **Mn**, 0.040 **P**, 0.050 **S**	
AISI 1016		US	Wire, rod	0.13–0.18 **C**, 0.60–0.90 **Mn**, 0.040 **P**, 0.050 **S**	
ANSI/ASTM A 576	1015	US	Bar	0.13–0.18 **C**, 0.30–0.60 **Mn**, 0.040 **P**, 0.050 **S**	
ANSI/ASTM A 576	1016	US	Bar	0.13–0.18 **C**, 0.60–0.90 **Mn**, 0.040 **P**, 0.050 **S**	
ASTM A 689	1015	US	Bar	0.13–0.18 **C**, 0.30–0.60 **Mn**, 0.040 **P**, 0.050 **S**	
ASTM A 689	1016	US	Bar	0.13–0.18 **C**, 0.60–0.90 **Mn**, 0.040 **P**, 0.050 **S**	
ANSI/ASTM A 29	1015	US	Bar	0.13–0.18 **C**, 0.30–0.60 **Mn**, 0.040 **P**, 0.050 **S**	
ANSI/ASTM A 29	1016	US	Bar	0.13–0.18 **C**, 0.60–0.90 **Mn**, 0.040 **P**, 0.050 **S**	
AS 1443	Grade AS 1443/K1016	Australia	Bar	0.13–0.18 **C**, 0.60–0.90 **Mn**, 0.050 **P**, 0.050 **S**, 0.10–0.35 **Si**	
AS 1443	Grade AS 1443/S1016	Australia	Bar	0.13–0.18 **C**, 0.60–0.90 **Mn**, 0.050 **P**, 0.050 **S**, 0.35 **Si**	
AS 1443	Grade AS 1443/S1015	Australia	Bar	0.13–0.18 **C**, 0.30–0.60 **Mn**, 0.050 **P**, 0.050 **S**, 0.35 **Si**	
AS 1442	Grade AS 1442/S1015	Australia	Bar, blooms, billets, slabs	0.13–0.18 **C**, 0.30–0.60 **Mn**, 0.050 **P**, 0.050 **S**, 0.35 **Si**	
AS 1442	Grade AS 1442/S1016	Australia	Bar, blooms, billets, slabs	0.13–0.18 **C**, 0.60–0.90 **Mn**, 0.050 **P**, 0.050 **S**, 0.35 **Si**	
AS 1442	Grade AS 1442/K1016	Australia	Bar, blooms, billets, slabs	0.13–0.18 **C**, 0.60–0.90 **Mn**, 0.050 **P**, 0.050 **S**, 0.10–0.35 **Si**	
DEF STAN 95–1/1	CL.1.C1115	Canada	Bar	0.13–0.18 **C**, 0.60–0.80 **Mn**, 0.08–0.13 **S**	
JIS G 3507	SWRCH 15R	Japan	Wire, rod	0.13–0.18 **C**, 0.30–0.60 **Mn**, 0.040 **P**, 0.040 **S**	
JIS G 3507	SWRCH 15A	Japan	Wire, rod	0.13–0.18 **C**, 0.30–0.60 **Mn**, 0.030 **P**, 0.035 **S**, 0.10 **Si**, 0.02 **Al**	
JIS G 3507	SWRCH 16A	Japan	Wire, rod	0.13–0.18 **C**, 0.60–0.90 **Mn**, 0.030 **P**, 0.035 **S**, 0.10 **Si**, 0.02 **Al**	
JIS G 3507	SWRCH 15K	Japan	Wire, rod	0.13–0.18 **C**, 0.30–0.60 **Mn**, 0.030 **P**, 0.035 **S**, 0.10–0.35 **Si**	
JIS G 3507	SWRCH 16K	Japan	Wire, rod	0.13–0.18 **C**, 0.60–0.90 **Mn**, 0.030 **P**, 0.035 **S**, 0.10–0.35 **Si**	
JIS G 3505	SWRM 15	Japan	Wire, rod	0.13–0.18 **C**, 0.30–0.60 **Mn**, 0.045 **P**, 0.045 **S**	
JIS G 4051	S 15C	Japan	Bar, wire, rod	0.13–0.18 **C**, 0.30–0.60 **Mn**, 0.030 **P**, 0.035 **S**, 0.15–0.35 **Si**, 0.30 **Cu**	
JIS G 4051	S 15CK	Japan	Bar, wire, rod	0.13–0.18 **C**, 0.30–0.60 **Mn**, 0.025 **P**, 0.025 **S**, 0.15–0.35 **Si**, 0.25 **Cu**	
SS 14 12 32 E	SS 12 32–08	Sweden	Tube: welded	0.13 **C**, 0.30–0.70 **Mn**, 0.050 **P**, 0.050 **S**, 0.30 **Cu**, 0.25 **Cr**, 0.009 **N**	**Cold worked**: all **diam**, (400) **TS**, (360) **YS**, 25 **El**
SS 14 12 32 E	SS 12 32–08	Sweden	Tube: welded	0.13 **C**, 0.30–0.70 **Mn**, 0.050 **P**, 0.050 **S**, 0.30 **Cu**, 0.25 **Cr**, 0.009 **N**	**As rolled or quenched**: all **diam**, (400) **TS**, (360) **YS**, 12 **El**
SIS 14 12 32	SIS 12 32–08	Sweden	Tube: welded	0.13 **C**, 0.05 **P**, 0.05 **S**, 0.009 **N**	**Cold–drawn**: all **diam**, (400) **TS**, (360) **YS**, 12 **El**
ASTM A 714	Grade IV	US	Pipe: welded, seamless	0.13 **C**, 0.65 **Mn**, 0.02–0.09 **P**, 0.06 **S**, 0.22–0.48 **Cu**, 0.74–1.26 **Cr**, 0.17–0.53 **Ni**	**As rolled**: all **diam**, 58 (400) **TS**, 36 (248) **YS**

WROUGHT CARBON STEELS

specification number	designation	country	product forms	composition	mechanical properties (see page iv for explanation)
DIN 1651	9 S 20 (1.0711)	Germany	Bar	0.13 **C**, 0.60–1.20 **Mn**, 0.100 **P**, 0.18–0.25 **S**, 0.05 **Si**	**Hot rolled**: all **diam**, (363) **TS**; **Normalized**: all **diam**, (350) **TS**, (225) **YS**, 25 in 80 mm **El**
DIN 17111	Grade UQSt36–2	Germany	Bar, wire, rod	0.13 **C**, 0.25–0.45 **Mn**, 0.080 **P**, 0.050 **S**, 0.007 **N**	**Hot rolled**: all **diam**, (333) **TS**, (206) **YS**, 30 **El**
DIN 17111	Grade RSt36–2	Germany	Bar, wire, rod	0.13 **C**, 0.25–0.50 **Mn**, 0.050 **P**, 0.050 **S**, 0.007 **N**	**Hot rolled**: all **diam**, (333) **TS**, (206) **YS**, 30 **El**
SS 14 12 32 E	SS 12 32–03	Sweden	Tube: seamless	0.13 **C**, 0.30–0.70 **Mn**, 0.050 **P**, 0.050 **S**, 0.30 **Cu**, 0.25 **Cr**, 0.009 **N**	**As rolled or quenched**: all **diam**, (320) **TS**, (200) **YS**, 25 **El**
SS 14 12 32 E	SS 12 32–04	Sweden	Tube: seamless	0.13 **C**, 0.30–0.70 **Mn**, 0.050 **P**, 0.050 **S**, 0.30 **Cu**, 0.25 **Cr**, 0.009 **N**	**As rolled or quenched**: all **diam**, (320) **TS**, (200) **YS**, 25 **El**
SS 14 12 32 E	SS 12 32–05	Sweden	Tube: seamless	0.13 **C**, 0.30–0.70 **Mn**, 0.050 **P**, 0.050 **S**, 0.30 **Cu**, 0.25 **Cr**, 0.009 **N**	**As rolled or quenched**: all **diam**, (320) **TS**, (200) **YS**, 25 **El**
SS 14 12 32 E	SS 12 32–06	Sweden	Tube: welded	0.13 **C**, 0.30–0.70 **Mn**, 0.050 **P**, 0.050 **S**, 0.30 **Cu**, 0.25 **Cr**, 0.009 **N**	**Quenched**: all **diam**, (320) **TS**, (200) **YS**, 25 **El**
SIS 14 12 32	SIS 12 32–04	Sweden	Tube: welded	0.13 **C**, 0.05 **P**, 0.05 **S**, 0.009 **N**	**As–welded**: all **diam**, (310) **TS**, (180) **YS**, 25 **El**
SIS 14 12 32	SIS 12 32–03	Sweden	Tube: seamless	0.13 **C**, 0.05 **P**, 0.05 **S**, 0.009 **N**	**As–drawn**: all **diam**, (310) **TS**, (180) **YS**, 25 **El**
JIS G 3105	Class 1, No. 14A	Japan	Bar	0.13 **C**, 0.50 **Mn**, 0.040 **P**, 0.040 **S**, 0.04 **Si**	**Hot rolled**: all **diam**, (304) **TS**, 30 **El**
ISO/R 683/1X	Type 1	ISO	Bar, wire, rod	0.13 **C**, 0.60–1.20 **Mn**, 0.11 **P**, 0.18–0.25 **S**, 0.05 **Si**	**Cold drawn**: (≤16) **diam**, (490) **TS**, (392) **YS**, 8 **El**
NF A 36–102	Fd 01	France	Strip	0.13 **C**, 0.075 **P**, 0.070 **S**	
QQ–S–637A	1211	US	Bar	0.13 **C**, 0.60–0.90 **Mn**, 0.07–0.12 **P**, 0.10–0.15 **S**, 0.15–0.35 **Pb**	
QQ–S–637A	1212	US	Bar	0.13 **C**, 0.70–1.00 **Mn**, 0.07–0.12 **P**, 0.16–0.23 **S**, 0.15–0.35 **Pb**	
QQ–S–637A	1213	US	Bar	0.13 **C**, 0.70–1.00 **Mn**, 0.07–0.12 **P**, 0.24–0.33 **S**, 0.15–0.35 **Pb**	
QQ–S–637A	D	US	Bar	0.13 **C**, 0.80–1.20 **Mn**, 0.04–0.09 **P**, 0.25–0.35 **S**, 0.15–0.35 **Pb**	
QQ–S–637A	E	US	Bar	0.13 **C**, 0.80–1.20 **Mn**, 0.04–0.09 **P**, 0.25–0.35 **S**, 0.15–0.35 **Pb**, 0.03 **Te**	
QQ–S–637A	F	US	Bar	0.13 **C**, 0.85–1.35 **Mn**, 0.04–0.09 **P**, 0.40 **S**, 0.15–0.35 **Pb**	
AISI 1213		US	Bar	0.13 **C**, 0.70–1.00 **Mn**, 0.07–0.12 **P**, 0.24–0.33 **S**	
AISI 1212		US	Bar	0.13 **C**, 0.70–1.00 **Mn**, 0.07–0.12 **P**, 0.16–0.23 **S**	
AISI 1211		US	Bar	0.13 **C**, 0.60–0.90 **Mn**, 0.07–0.12 **P**, 0.10–0.15 **S**	
AMS 5010F	Type 1212	US	Bar	0.13 **C**, 0.70–1.00 **Mn**, 0.07–0.12 **P**, 0.16–0.23 **S**	
AMS 5053E		US	Tube	0.13 **C**, 0.60 **Mn**, 0.04 **P**, 0.05 **S**	**Annealed**: ≤0.50 (≤12.7) **diam**, 32 **El**
AMS 7733		US	Wire	0.13 **C**, 0.30–0.60 **Mn**, 0.04 **P**, 0.05 **S**	**Annealed**: all **diam**, 36 (248) **YS**, 15 **El**
ANSI/ASTM A 519	1213	US	Tube: seamless	0.13 **C**, 0.70–1.10 **Mn**, 0.07–0.12 **P**, 0.24–0.33 **S**	
AS 1446	Grade AS 1446/S1010	Australia	Plate	0.13 **C**, 0.30–0.60 **Mn**, 0.050 **P**, 0.050 **S**, 0.35 **Si**	
COPANT 330	1211	COPANT	Bar, shapes	0.13 **C**, 0.60–0.90 **Mn**, 0.07–0.12 **P**, 0.10–0.15 **S**	
COPANT 330	1212	COPANT	Bar, shapes	0.13 **C**, 0.70–1.00 **Mn**, 0.07–0.12 **P**, 0.16–0.23 **S**	
COPANT 330	1213	COPANT	Bar, shapes	0.13 **C**, 0.70–1.00 **Mn**, 0.07–0.12 **P**, 0.24–0.33 **S**	

specification number	designation	country	product forms	composition	mechanical properties (see page iv for explanation)
COPANT 330	B 1010	COPANT	Bar, shapes	0.13 **C**, 0.30–0.60 **Mn**, 0.07–0.12 **P**, 0.060 **S**	
COPANT 330	B 1111	COPANT	Bar, shapes	0.13 **C**, 0.60–0.90 **Mn**, 0.07–0.12 **P**, 0.10–0.15 **S**	
COPANT 330	B 1112	COPANT	Bar, shapes	0.13 **C**, 0.70–1.00 **Mn**, 0.07–0.12 **P**, 0.16–0.23 **S**	
COPANT 330	B 1113	COPANT	Bar, shapes	0.13 **C**, 0.70–1.00 **Mn**, 0.07–0.12 **P**, 0.24–0.33 **S**	
COPANT 331	B 1211	COPANT	Bar	0.13 **C**, 0.60–0.90 **Mn**, 0.07–0.12 **P**, 0.10–0.15 **S**	
COPANT 331	B 1212	COPANT	Bar	0.13 **C**, 0.70–1.00 **Mn**, 0.07–0.12 **P**, 0.16–0.23 **S**	
COPANT 331	B 1213	COPANT	Bar	0.13 **C**, 0.70–1.00 **Mn**, 0.07–0.12 **P**, 0.24–0.33 **S**	
COPANT 331	ABNT 14 L 12	COPANT	Bar	0.13 **C**, 0.80–1.10 **Mn**, 0.07–0.12 **P**, 0.30–0.40 **S**, 0.15–0.30 **Pb**	
COPANT 331	ABNT 14 L 10	COPANT	Bar	0.13 **C**, 0.70–1.00 **Mn**, 0.07–0.12 **P**, 0.20–0.30 **S**, 0.15–0.30 **Pb**	
COPANT 331	ABNT 1413	COPANT	Bar	0.13 **C**, 0.80–1.10 **Mn**, 0.07–0.12 **P**, 0.40–0.50 **S**	
COPANT 331	ABNT 14 L 13	COPANT	Bar	0.13 **C**, 0.80–1.10 **Mn**, 0.07–0.12 **P**, 0.40–0.50 **S**, 0.15–0.30 **Pb**	
COPANT 331	B 1010	COPANT	Bar	0.13 **C**, 0.30–0.60 **Mn**, 0.07–0.12 **P**, 0.060 **S**	
COPANT 331	B 1111	COPANT	Bar	0.13 **C**, 0.60–0.90 **Mn**, 0.07–0.12 **P**, 0.10–0.15 **S**	
COPANT 331	B 1112	COPANT	Bar	0.13 **C**, 0.70–1.00 **Mn**, 0.07–0.12 **P**, 0.16–0.23 **S**	
COPANT 331	B 1113	COPANT	Bar	0.13 **C**, 0.70–1.00 **Mn**, 0.07–0.12 **P**, 0.24–0.33 **S**	
ASTM A 108	1211	US	Bar	0.13 **C**, 0.60–0.90 **Mn**, 0.07–0.12 **P**, 0.10–0.15 **S**	
ASTM A 108	1212	US	Bar	0.13 **C**, 0.70–1.00 **Mn**, 0.07–0.12 **P**, 0.16–0.23 **S**	
ASTM A 108	1213	US	Bar	0.13 **C**, 0.70–1.00 **Mn**, 0.07–1.00 **P**, 0.07–0.12 **S**, 0.24–0.33 **Si**	
ANSI/ASTM A 549	Grade B1010	US	Wire	0.13 **C**, 0.30–0.60 **Mn**, 0.07–0.12 **P**, 0.060 **S**	
COPANT 333	B 1010	COPANT	Wire, rod	0.13 **C**, 0.30–0.60 **Mn**, 0.07–0.12 **P**, 0.060 **S**	
COPANT 333	1212	COPANT	Wire, rod	0.13 **C**, 0.70–1.00 **Mn**, 0.07–0.12 **P**, 0.16–0.23 **S**	
COPANT 333	1213	COPANT	Wire, rod	0.13 **C**, 0.70–1.00 **Mn**, 0.07–0.12 **P**, 0.24–0.33 **S**	
COPANT 333	B 1112	COPANT	Wire, rod	0.13 **C**, 0.70–1.00 **Mn**, 0.07–0.12 **P**, 0.16–0.23 **S**	
COPANT 333	B 1113	COPANT	Wire, rod	0.13 **C**, 0.70–1.00 **Mn**, 0.07–0.12 **P**, 0.24–0.33 **S**	
DGN–B–301	1213	Mexico	Bar	0.13 **C**, 0.70–1.00 **Mn**, 0.07–0.12 **P**, 0.24–0.33 **S**	
DGN–B–301	12L13	Mexico	Bar	0.13 **C**, 0.70–1.00 **Mn**, 0.07–0.12 **P**, 0.24–0.33 **S**, 0.10–0.20 **Si**, 0.15–0.35 **Pb**	
DGN–B–301	1211	Mexico	Bar	0.13 **C**, 0.60–0.90 **Mn**, 0.07–0.12 **P**, 0.10–0.15 **S**	
DGN–B–301	1212	Mexico	Bar	0.13 **C**, 0.70–1.00 **Mn**, 0.07–0.12 **P**, 0.16–0.23 **S**	
AISI 1211		US	Wire, rod	0.13 **C**, 0.60–0.90 **Mn**, 0.07–0.12 **P**, 0.10–0.15 **S**	
AISI 1212		US	Wire, rod	0.13 **C**, 0.70–1.00 **Mn**, 0.07–0.12 **P**, 0.16–0.23 **S**	
AISI 1213		US	Wire, rod	0.13 **C**, 0.70–1.00 **Mn**, 0.07–0.12 **P**, 0.24–0.33 **S**	

WROUGHT CARBON STEELS

specification number	designation	country	product forms	composition	mechanical properties (see page iv for explanation)
ANSI/ASTM A 576	1211	US	Bar	0.13 **C**, 0.60–0.90 **Mn**, 0.07–0.12 **P**, 0.10–0.15 **S**	
ANSI/ASTM A 576	1212	US	Bar	0.13 **C**, 0.70–1.00 **Mn**, 0.07–0.12 **P**, 0.16–0.23 **S**	
ANSI/ASTM A 576	1213	US	Bar	0.13 **C**, 0.70–1.00 **Mn**, 0.07–0.12 **P**, 0.24–0.33 **S**	
ANSI/ASTM A 29	1213	US	Bar	0.13 **C**, 0.70–1.00 **Mn**, 0.07–0.12 **P**, 0.24–0.33 **S**	
ANSI/ASTM A 29	12L13	US	Bar	0.13 **C**, 0.70–1.00 **Mn**, 0.07–0.12 **P**, 0.24–0.33 **S**, 0.15–0.35 **Pb**	
ANSI/ASTM A 29	1211	US	Bar	0.13 **C**, 0.60–0.90 **Mn**, 0.07–0.12 **P**, 0.10–0.15 **S**	
ANSI/ASTM A 29	1212	US	Bar	0.13 **C**, 0.70–1.00 **Mn**, 0.07–0.12 **P**, 0.16–0.23 **S**	
ASTM A 689	1211	US	Bar	0.13 **C**, 0.60–0.90 **Mn**, 0.07–0.12 **P**, 0.10–0.15 **S**	
ASTM A 689	1212	US	Bar	0.13 **C**, 0.70–1.00 **Mn**, 0.07–0.12 **P**, 0.16–0.23 **S**	
ASTM A 689	1213	US	Bar	0.13 **C**, 0.70–1.00 **Mn**, 0.07–0.12 **P**, 0.24–0.33 **S**	
DEF STAN 95-1/1	CL.2. B1113	Canada	Bar	0.13 **C**, 0.70–1.00 **Mn**, 0.07–0.12 **P**, 0.24–0.33 **S**	
DEF STAN 95-1/1	CL 2.C1211	Canada	Bar	0.13 **C**, 0.60–0.90 **Mn**, 0.07–0.12 **P**, 0.08–0.15 **S**	
DEF STAN 95-1/1	CL 2.C1212	Canada	Bar	0.13 **C**, 0.70–1.00 **Mn**, 0.07–0.12 **P**, 0.16–0.23 **S**	
DEF STAN 95-1/1	CL 2.C1213	Canada	Bar	0.13 **C**, 0.70–1.00 **Mn**, 0.07–0.12 **P**, 0.24–0.33 **S**	
DEF STAN 95-1/1	CL.2.B1111	Canada	Bar	0.13 **C**, 0.60–0.90 **Mn**, 0.07–0.12 **P**, 0.16–0.23 **S**	
DEF STAN 95-1/1	CL.2.B1112	Canada	Bar	0.13 **C**, 0.70–1.00 **Mn**, 0.07–0.12 **P**, 0.16–0.23 **S**	
COPANT 514	Grade 1213	COPANT	Tube: seamless	0.13 **C**, 0.70–1.10 **Mn**, 0.07–0.12 **P**, 0.24–0.33 **S**	
JIS G 4804	SUM 21	Japan	Bar	0.13 **C**, 0.70–1.00 **Mn**, 0.07–0.12 **P**, 0.16–0.23 **S**	
JIS G 4804	SUM 22	Japan	Bar	0.13 **C**, 0.70–1.00 **Mn**, 0.07–0.12 **P**, 0.24–0.33 **S**	
JIS G 4804	SUM 22L	Japan	Bar	0.13 **C**, 0.70–1.00 **Mn**, 0.07–0.12 **P**, 0.24–0.33 **S**, 0.10–0.35 **Pb**	
ASTM A 595	Grade B	US	Tube: tapered	0.12–0.29 **C**, 0.35–1.40 **Mn**, 0.05 **P**, 0.06 **S**	**As fabricated**: all **diam**, 70 (480) **TS**, 60 (410) **YS**
ANSI/ASTM A 595	Grade B	US	Tube	0.12–0.29 **C**, 1.35–1.40 **Mn**, 0.05 **P**, 0.06 **S**	**Hot rolled**: all **diam**, 70 (480) **TS**, 60 (410) **YS**
ASTM A 595	Grade A	US	Tube: tapered	0.12–0.29 **C**, 0.26–0.94 **Mn**, 0.05 **P**, 0.06 **S**	**As fabricated**: all **diam**, 65 (450) **TS**, 55 (380) **YS**
ANSI/ASTM A 595	Grade A	US	Tube	0.12–0.29 **C**, 0.26–0.94 **Mn**, 0.05 **P**, 0.06 **S**	**Hot rolled**: all **diam**, 65 (450) **TS**, 55 (380) **YS**
NF A 35-053	FR 18	France	Wire, rod	0.12–0.23 **C**, 0.40–0.70 **Mn**, 0.044 **P**, 0.044 **S**, 0.30 **Si**	**Hot or cold drawn and annealed**: ($\leq$30) **diam**, (540) may **TS**
NF A 35-051	FM 18 grade 3	France	Wire, rod	0.12–0.23 **C**, 0.40–0.70 **Mn**, 0.040 **P**, 0.040 **S**, 0.10–0.35 **Si**	
ISO 2604/11	TS 26	ISO	Tube: seamless	0.12–0.20 **C**, 0.40–0.80 **Mn**, .040 **P**, .040 **S**, 0.10–0.35 **Si**, 0.012 met **Al**, 0.25–0.35 **Mo**	**Cold finished, normalized, normalized and tempered**: all **diam**, (450) **TS**, (250) **YS**, 22 **El**
JIS G 4804	SUM 32	Japan	Bar	0.12–0.20 **C**, 0.60–1.10 **Mn**, 0.040 **P**, 0.10–0.20 **S**	
QQ-S-698	1015	US	Sheet, strip	0.12–0.19 **C**, 0.30–0.60 **Mn**, 0.040 **P**, 0.050 **S**	
ANSI/ASTM A 29	M 1015	US	Bar	0.12–0.19 **C**, 0.25–0.60 **Mn**, 0.04 **P**, 0.05 **S**	
ANSI/ASTM A 575	M 1015	US	Bar	0.12–0.19 **C**, 0.25–0.60 **Mn**, 0.04 **P**, 0.05 **S**	

WROUGHT CARBON STEELS

specification number	designation	country	product forms	composition	mechanical properties (see page iv for explanation)
SIS 14 13 70	SIS 13 70–04	Sweden	Bar, forgings	0.12–0.18 **C**, 0.50–0.90 **Mn**, 0.035 **P**, 0.020–0.035 **S**, 0.10–0.40 **Si**	**Case hardened, quenched, annealed**: (11) **diam**, (880) **TS**, (590) **YS**, 7 **El**
DIN 17210	Grade C 15	Germany	Blooms, slabs, billets, wire, bar, plate, sheet, strip, tube, forgings	0.12–0.18 **C**, 0.30–0.60 **Mn**, 0.045 **P**, 0.045 **S**, 0.15–0.35 **Si**	**Rolled or forged**: (11) **diam**, (736) **TS**, (441) **YS**, 12 **El**
DIN 17210	Grade Ck 15	Germany	Blooms, slabs, billets, wire, bar, plate, sheet, strip, tube, forgings	0.12–0.18 **C**, 0.30–0.60 **Mn**, 0.035 **P**, 0.035 **S**, 0.15–0.35 **Si**	**Rolled or forged**: (11) **diam**, (736) **TS**, (441) **YS**, 12 **El**
DIN 17210	Grade Cm 15	Germany	Blooms, slabs, billets, wire, bar, plate, sheet, strip, tube, forgings	0.12–0.18 **C**, 0.30–0.60 **Mn**, 0.035 **P**, 0.020–0.035 **S**, 0.15–0.35 **Si**	**Rolled or forged**: (11) **diam**, (736) **TS**, (441) **YS**, 12 **El**
EURONORM 119–74, III	C 15 KD	EURONORM	Wire, rod	0.12–0.18 **C**, 0.30–0.60 **Mn**, 0.035 **P**, 0.035 **S**, 0.10–0.40 **Si**	**Bright annealed**: (11) **diam**, (690) **TS**, (440) **YS**, 12 **El**
SFS 505	C15	Finland	Bar, forgings	0.12–0.18 **C**, 0.60–0.90 **Mn**, 0.035 **P**, 0.020–0.035 **S**, 0.10–0.40 **Si**	**Quenched at 780°C: (11) diam, (690) TS, (390) YS, 9 El; Quenched at 890°C: (11) diam, (880) TS, (590) YS, 7 El**
SIS 14 13 70	SIS 13 70–03	Sweden	Bar, forgings	0.12–0.18 **C**, 0.50–0.90 **Mn**, 0.035 **P**, 0.020–0.035 **S**, 0.10–0.40 **Si**	**Case hardened, quenched, annealed**: (11) **diam**, (690) **TS**, (390) **YS**, 9 **El**
SIS 14 19 26	SIS 19 26–03	Sweden	Bar	0.12–0.18 **C**, 0.80–1.20 **Mn**, 0.06 **P**, 0.15–0.25 **S**, 0.10–0.40 **Si**, 0.15–0.35 **Pb**	**Case hardened**: (≤16) **diam**, (650) **TS**, (400) **YS**, 8 **El**
SIS 14 19 22	SIS 19 22–03	Sweden	Bar	0.12–0.18 **C**, 0.80–1.20 **Mn**, 0.06 **P**, 0.10–0.40 **Si**	**Case hardened**: (≤16) **diam**, (650) **TS**, (400) **YS**, 8 **El**
ISO R 683/X1	3	ISO	Bar	0.12–0.18 **C**, 0.60–0.90 **Mn**, 0.035 **P**, 0.035 **S**, 0.15–0.40 **Si**	**Carburized hardened**: all **diam**, (638) **TS**, (392) **YS**, 10 **El**
ISO R 683/X1	3a	ISO	Bar	0.12–0.18 **C**, 0.60–0.90 **Mn**, 0.035 **P**, 0.020–0.035 **S**, 0.15–0.40 **Si**	**Carburized hardened**: all **diam**, (638) **TS**, (392) **YS**, 10 **El**
ISO R 683/X1	3b	ISO	Bar	0.12–0.18 **C**, 0.60–0.90 **Mn**, 0.035 **P**, 0.030–0.050 **S**, 0.15–0.40 **Si**	**Carburized and hardened**: all **diam**, (638) **TS**, (392) **YS**, 10 **El**
ISO R 683/X1	2	ISO	Bar	0.12–0.18 **C**, 0.30–0.60 **Mn**, 0.035 **P**, 0.035 **S**, 0.15–0.40 **Si**	**Carburized and hardened**: all **diam**, (588) **TS**, (343) **YS**, 12 **El**
ISO R 683/X1	2a	ISO	Bar	0.12–0.18 **C**, 0.30–0.60 **Mn**, 0.035 **P**, 0.020–0.035 **S**, 0.15–0.40 **Si**	**Carburized and hardened**: all **diam**, (588) **TS**, (343) **YS**, 12 **El**
ISO R 683/X1	2b	ISO	Bar	0.12–0.18 **C**, 0.30–0.60 **Mn**, 0.035 **P**, 0.030–0.050 **S**, 0.15–0.40 **Si**	**Carburized and hardened**: all **diam**, (588) **TS**, (343) **YS**, 12 **El**
DIN 1654	Grade Cq 15	Germany	Rod	0.12–0.18 **C**, 0.25–0.50 **Mn**, 0.040 **P**, 0.040 **S**, 0.15–0.35 **Si**	**Drawn**: all **diam**, (588) **TS**
BS 970 Part 3	Steel 130M15	UK	Blooms, billets, bar, forgings	0.12–0.18 **C**, 1.10–1.50 **Mn**, 0.10–0.40 **Si**	**Hardened**: 3/4 **diam**, (580) **TS**, 14 **El**
SIS 14 19 26	SIS 19 26–04	Sweden	Bar	0.12–0.18 **C**, 0.80–1.20 **Mn**, 0.06 **P**, 0.15–0.25 **S**, 0.10–0.40 **Si**	**Cold worked**: (≤16) **diam**, (550) **TS**, (420) **YS**, 7 **El**
SIS 14 19 22	SIS 1922–04	Sweden	Bar	0.12–0.18 **C**, 0.80–1.20 **Mn**, 0.06 **P**, 0.15–0.25 **S**, 0.10–0.40 **Si**	**Cold worked**: (≤16) **diam**, (550) **TS**, (420) **YS**, 7 **El**
DIN 1652	C15 (1.0401)	Germany	Bar	0.12–0.18 **C**, 0.25–0.35 **Mn**, 0.045 **P**, 0.045 **S**, 0.15–0.35 **Si**	**Cold drawn**: all **diam**, (540) **TS**, (440) **YS**, 6 in 80 mm **El**
DIN 1652	Ck 15 (1.1141)	Germany	Bar	0.12–0.18 **C**, 0.25–0.50 **Mn**, 0.035 **P**, 0.035 **S**, 0.15–0.35 **Si**	**Cold drawn**: all **diam**, (540) **TS**, (440) **YS**, 6 in 80 mm **El**
VSM 10648	C 15	Switzerland	Bar, sheet, plate	0.12–0.18 **C**, 0.30–0.60 **Mn**, 0.045 **P**, 0.045 **S**, 0.15–0.35 **Si**	**Cold drawn**: (≤5) **diam**, (539) **TS**, (441) **YS**, 6 **El**
VSM 10648		Switzerland	Bar, sheet, plate	0.12–0.18 **C**, 0.30–0.60 **Mn**, 0.035 **P**, 0.035 **S**, 0.15–0.35 **Si**	**Cold drawn**: (≤5) **diam**, (539) **TS**, (441) **YS**, 6 **El**
EURONORM 119–74, II	CB 15 FF KD	EURONORM	Wire, rod	0.12–0.18 **C**, 0.30–0.60 **Mn**, 0.040 **P**, 0.040 **S**, 0.10 **Si**	**Cold rolled or cold finished**: (2–100) **diam**, (500) max **TS**
BS 3059	Steel 45	UK	Tube: electric resistance welded or seamless	0.12–0.18 **C**, 0.90–1.20 **Mn**, 0.040 **P**, 0.035 **S**, 0.10–0.35 **Si**	**Normalized**: all **diam**, (440) **TS**, (245) **YS**, 21 **El**

WROUGHT CARBON STEELS

specification number	designation	country	product forms	composition	mechanical properties (see page iv for explanation)
BS 3059 Part2	Grade 440	UK	Tube: seamless, welded	0.12–0.18 **C**, 0.90–1.20 **Mn**, 0.040 **P**, 0.035 **S**, 0.10–0.35 **Si**	**Normalized (welded)**: all **diam**, (440) **TS**, (245) **YS**, 21 **El**; **Hot finished, normalized (seamless)**: all **diam**, (440) **TS**, (245) **YS**, 21 **El**
SIS 14 19 26	SIS 19 26–00	Sweden	Bar	0.12–0.18 **C**, 0.80–1.20 **Mn**, 0.06 **P**, 0.15–0.25 **S**, 0.10–0.40 **Si**, 0.15–0.35 **Pb**	**As rolled**: (≤63) **diam**, (440) **TS**
SIS 14 19 22	SIS 19 22–00	Sweden	Bar	0.12–0.18 **C**, 0.80–1.20 **Mn**, 0.06 **P**, 0.10–0.40 **Si**	**As rolled**: (≤63) **diam**, (440) **TS**
DIN 17115	Grade 15 Mn 3	Germany	Bar, wire, rod	0.12–0.18 **C**, 0.70–0.90 **Mn**, 0.040 **P**, 0.040 **S**, 0.10–0.20 **Si**	**Normalized**: (≤26) **diam**, (440) **TS**, (245) **YS**, 25 **El**
DIN 17115	Grade 15 Mn 3·Al	Germany	Bar, wire, rod	0.12–0.18 **C**, 0.70–0.90 **Mn**, 0.040 **P**, 0.040 **S**, 0.10–0.20 **Si**, 0.020–0.050 **Al**	**Normalized**: (≤26) **diam**, (440) **TS**, (245) **YS**, 25 **El**
BS 970 Part 3	Steel 080M15	UK	Blooms, billets, bar, forgings	0.12–0.18 **C**, 0.60–1.00 **Mn**, 0.10–0.40 **Si**	**Hardened**: 3/4 **diam**, (415) **TS**, 16 **El**
BS 970 Part 3	Steel 210M15	UK	Blooms, billets, bar, forgings	0.12–0.18 **C**, 0.90–1.30 **Mn**, 0.050 max **P**, 0.10–0.18 **S**, 0.10–0.40 **Si**	**Hardened**: 3/4 **diam**, (415) **TS**, 16 **El**
SFS 505	C15; steel 505	Finland		0.12–0.18 **C**, 0.60–0.90 **Mn**, 0.035 **P**, 0.020–0.035 **S**, 0.10–0.40 **Si**	**Hot rolled**: all **diam**, (370) **TS**, (205) **YS**, 22 **El**; **Quenched**: all **diam**, (690) **TS**, (390) **YS**, 9 **El**; **Quenched**: all **diam**, (880) **TS**, (590) **YS**, 7 **El**
SIS 14 13 70	SIS 13 70–00	Sweden	Bar, forgings, plate, sheet, strip	0.12–0.18 **C**, 0.50–0.90 **Mn**, 0.035 **P**, 0.020–0.035 **S**, 0.10–0.40 **Si**	**As rolled or as forged**: all **diam**, (360) **TS**, (210) **YS**, 22 **El**
ASTM A 659	Grade 1015	US	Sheet, strip	0.12–0.18 **C**, 0.30–0.60 **Mn**, 0.040 **P**, 0.050 **S**	
ASTM A 659	Grade 1016	US	Sheet, strip	0.12–0.18 **C**, 0.60–0.90 **Mn**, 0.040 **P**, 0.050 **S**	
AISI 1015		US	Plate	0.12–0.18 **C**, 0.30–0.60 **Mn**, 0.040 **P**, 0.050 **S**	
AISI 1016		US	Plate	0.12–0.18 **C**, 0.60–0.90 **Mn**, 0.040 **P**, 0.050 **S**	
ISO 683/XVIII	C15e	ISO	Bar, wire	0.12–0.18 **C**, 0.30–0.60 **Mn**, 0.035 **P**, 0.035 **S**, 0.15–0.40 **Si**	
ISO 683/XVIII	C15ea	ISO	Bar, wire	0.12–0.18 **C**, 0.30–0.60 **Mn**, 0.035 **P**, 0.020–0.035 **S**, 0.15–0.40 **Si**	
ISO 683/XVIII	C15eb	ISO	Bar, wire	0.12–0.18 **C**, 0.30–0.60 **Mn**, 0.035 **P**, 0.030–0.050 **S**, 0.15–0.40 **Si**	
ISO 683/XVIII	C15	ISO	Bar, wire	0.12–0.18 **C**, 0.30–0.60 **Mn**, 0.050 **P**, 0.050 **S**, 0.15–0.40 **Si**	
DIN 17140	Grade D15–2	Germany	Wire, rod	0.12–0.17 **C**, 0.30–0.60 **Mn**, 0.040 **P**, 0.040 **S**, 0.30 **Si**, 0.007 **N**	
SIS 14 12 11	SIS 12 11–34	Sweden	Wire	0.12 **C**, 0.3–0.5 **Mn**, 0.06 **P**, 0.06 **S**	**Cold worked and dry drawn**: (0.5–1.5) **diam**, (780) **TS**
SIS–14 12 11	SIS 12 11–44	Sweden	Wire	0.12 **C**, 0.3–0.5 **Mn**, 0.06 **P**, 0.06 **S**	**Cold worked and wet drawn**: (0.5–1.5) **diam**, (780) **TS**
NF A 35–053	FB 8	France	Wire, rod	0.12 **C**, 0.25–0.60 **Mn**, 0.050 **P**, 0.050 **S**, 0.011 N_2	**Hot or cold drawn**: (≤30) **diam**, (460) max **TS**
NF A 35–053	FR 8	France	Wire, rod	0.12 **C**, 0.25–0.60 **Mn**, 0.044 **P**, 0.044 **S**, 0.009 N_2	**Hot or cold drawn and annealed**: (≤30) **diam**, (450) max **TS**
MIL–S–47038A		US	Plate, sheet	0.12 **C**, 0.50–1.00 **Mn**, 0.05 **P**, 0.05 **S**, 0.15 **Si**, 0.85–1.3 **Cu**, 0.02–0.23 **Al**, 0.50–1.00 **Ni**, 0.25 **Mo**	**Hot rolled**: all **diam**, 65 (448) **TS**, 45 (310) **YS**, 22 **El**; **Precipitation hardened**: all **diam**, 92 (634) **TS**, 75 (517) **YS**, 18 **El**
ISO 3573	Grade HR 2	ISO	Sheet	0.12 **C**, 0.50 **Mn**, 0.04 **P**, 0.04 **S**	**Hot rolled**: (<3) **diam**, (430) **TS**, 26 **El**
ISO 3575	03	ISO	Sheet: hot dipped, zinc-coated	0.12 **C**, 0.50 **Mn**, 0.04 **P**, 0.04 **S**	**As agreed**: all **diam**, (430) **TS**, 24 **El**
DIN 1624	Grade St 1	Germany	Strip	0.12 **C**, 0.20–0.45 **Mn**, 0.080 **P**, 0.060 **S**, 0.03–0.20 **Si**	**Solution annealed**: all **diam**, (422) **TS**, 28 **El**; **Cold rolled**: all **diam**, (314) **TS**

WROUGHT CARBON STEELS

specification number	designation	country	product forms	composition	mechanical properties (see page iv for explanation)
ISO 3574	CR2	ISO	Sheet	0.12 **C**, 0.50 **Mn**, 0.04 **P**, 0.04 **S**	**Hot rolled, cold reduced, skin passed**: all **diam**, (370) **TS**, 31 **El**
SIS 14 13 11 E	SIS 13 11–00	Sweden	Bar, plate	0.12 **C**, 0.4–0.7 **Mn**, 0.08 **P**, 0.06 **S**, 0.05 **Si**	**As rolled**: (<40) **diam**, (360) **TS**, (220) **YS**, 24 **El**
SIS 14 13 11 E	SIS 13 11–00	Sweden	Bar, plate	0.12 **C**, 0.4–0.7 **Mn**, 0.08 **P**, 0.06 **S**, 0.25 **Si**	**As–rolled**: (<40) **diam**, (360) **TS**, (220) **YS**, 24 **El**
DS 12010	St 34	Denmark	Bar	0.12 **C**, 0.060 **P**, 0.060 **S**	**Hot rolled**: all **diam**, (332) **TS**, (186) **YS**, 30 **El**
JIS G 3445	Class 11A, No. 12	Japan	Tube: seamless or welded	0.12 **C**, 0.25–0.60 **Mn**, 0.040 **P**, 0.040 **S**, 0.35 **Si**	**As manufactured or cold finished**: ($\geq$8) **diam**, (294) **TS**, 35 **El**
SIS 14 12 11	SIS 12 11–02	Sweden	Wire	0.12 **C**, 0.3–0.5 **Mn**, 0.06 **P**, 0.06 **S**	**Cold worked and annealed**: (0.5–1.5) **diam**, (290) **TS**
BS 1449: Part 1	Grade 4	UK	Plate, sheet, strip	0.12 **C**, 0.60 **Mn**, 0.050 **P**, 0.050 **S**	**Hot rolled**: all **diam**, (280) **TS**, (170) **YS**, 25 **El**; **Cold rolled**: all **diam**, (280) **TS**, (140) **YS**
COPANT 38	EM	COPANT	Sheet	0.12 **C**, 0.20–0.60 **Mn**, 0.040 **P**, 0.040 **S**	**Hot rolled**: (1.50–3.00) **diam**, (280) **TS**, 26 **El**; **Cold rolled**: (0.30–0.50) **diam**, (270) **TS**, (280) max **YS**, 26 **El**
JIS G 3141	Class 1	Japan	Sheet, strip	0.12 **C**, 0.50 **Mn**, 0.040 **P**, 0.045 **S**	**Cold rolled**: ($\geq$0.25) **diam**, (275) **TS**, 32 **El**
SIS 14 13 11 E	SIS 13 11–10	Sweden	Bar	0.12 **C**, 0.4–0.7 **Mn**, 0.08 **P**, 0.06 **S**, 0.05 **Si**	**As rolled**: (6–32) **diam**, 220 **YS**, 20 **El**
SIS 14 13 11 E	SIS 13 11–10	Sweden	Bar	0.12 **C**, 0.4–0.7 **Mn**, 0.08 **P**, 0.06 **S**, 0.25 **Si**	**As rolled**: (6–32) **diam**, 220 **YS**, 20 **El**
NF A 36–102	Fd 12	France	Strip	0.12 **C**, 0.057 **P**, 0.057 **S**, 0.009 N_2	
NF A 36–102	Fd 2	France	Strip	0.12 **C**, 0.045 **P**, 0.045 **S**, 0.009 N_2	
NF A 36–102	Fe Tu 10	France	Strip	0.12 **C**, 0.075 **P**, 0.062 **S**, 0.013 N_2	
ASTM A 626	Type D	US	Plate	0.12 **C**, 0.06 **Mn**, 0.020 **P**, 0.050 **S**, 0.020 **Si**, 0.020 **Cu**	
ASTM A 650	Type D	US	Plate	0.12 **C**, 0.60 **Mn**, 0.020 **P**, 0.050 **S**, 0.020 **Si**, 0.20 **Cu**	
ANSI/ASTM A 657	Type D	US	Plate	0.12 **C**, 0.60 **Mn**, 0.020 **P**, 0.050 **S**, 0.020 **Si**, 0.20 **Cu**	
BS 1449: Part 1	Grade 4	UK	Plate, sheet, strip	0.12 **C**, 0.60 **Mn**, 0.050 **P**, 0.050 **S**	**Hot rolled**: all **diam**; **Cold rolled, hard tempered**: ($\leq$2) **diam**, (540) **TS**; **Cold rolled, half–hard**: ($\leq$2) **diam**, (420) **TS**; **Cold rolled, quarter–hard**: ($\leq$2) **diam**, (350) **TS**; **Cold rolled, skin passed**: ($\leq$2) **diam**, (280) **TS**; **Cold rolled, annealed**: ($\leq$2) **diam**, (280) **TS**
TS 2348	C12–1/1.0012	Turkey	Wire, rod	0.12 **C**, 0.50 **Mn**, 0.050 **P**, 0.050 **S**, 0.007 **N**	
TS 2348	C12–1/1.0012	Turkey	Wire, rod	0.12 **C**, 0.50 **Mn**, 0.050 **P**, 0.050 **S**, 0.007 **N**	
ANSI/ASTM A 625	Type D	US	Plate	0.12 **C**, 0.60 **Mn**, 0.020 **P**, 0.05 **S**, 0.020 **Si**, 0.020 **Cu**	
ISO 3575	02	ISO	Sheet: hot dipped, zinc–coated	0.12 **C**, 0.60 **Mn**, 0.04 **P**, 0.04 **S**	
SIS 14 11 52	SIS 11 52	Sweden	Sheet	0.12 **C**, 0.50 **Mn**, 0.04 **P**, 0.04 **S**	
SIS 14 11 51	SIS 11 51	Sweden	Sheet	0.12 **C**, 0.60 **Mn**, 0.040 **P**, 0.040 **S**	
SIS 14 12 11	SIS 12 11–00	Sweden	Wire	0.12 **C**, 0.3–0.5 **Mn**, 0.06 **P**, 0.06 **S**	
NF A 35–051	FM 8, Grade 3	France	Wire, rod	0.12 **C**, 0.25–0.60 **Mn**, 0.044 **P**, 0.044 **S**, 0.009 N_2	
TS 924	UDK 669.14.418/Fe–1	Turkey	Strip	0.12 **C**, 0.20–0.45 **Mn**, 0.07 **P**, 0.06 **S**, 0.03–0.20 **Si**	

specification number	designation	country	product forms	composition	mechanical properties (see page iv for explanation)
TS 924	UDK 669.14.418/Fe–0	Turkey	Strip	0.12 **C**, 0.20–0.45 **Mn**, 0.08 **P**, 0.06 **S**	
DIN 17140	Grade D12–2	Germany	Wire, rod	0.12 **C**, 0.50 **Mn**, 0.050 **P**, 0.050 **S**, 0.007 **N**	
DIN 1624	Grade St 0	Germany	Strip	0.12 **C**, 0.20–0.45 **Mn**, 0.080 **P**, 0.060 **S**	
NF A 35–051	FM 18, Grade 1	France	Wire, rod	0.11–0.24 **C**, 0.40–0.70 **Mn**, 0.080 **P**, 0.055 **S**, 0.10–0.35 **Si**	
MIL–S–866C	Class 1016	US	Bar, billets: for carburizing	0.11–0.20 **C**, 0.57–0.93 **Mn**, 0.048 **P**, 0.058 **S**, 0.40 **Cu**	
DEF STAN 95–1/1	1016	Canada	Bar	0.11–0.20 **C**, 0.57–0.93 **Mn**, 0.048 **P**, 0.058 **S**, 0.18–0.37 **Si**	
DIN 17115	RSt 41–2	Germany	Bar, wire, rod	0.11–0.17 **C**, 0.40–0.60 **Mn**, 0.040 **P**, 0.040 **S**, 0.03–0.25 **Si**	**Normalized:** (≤30) **diam**, (400) **TS**, (235) **YS**, 25 **El**
DIN 17115	Grade St 41–3	Germany	Bar, wire, rod	0.11–0.17 **C**, 0.40–0.60 **Mn**, 0.040 **P**, 0.040 **S**, 0.03–0.25 **Si**, 0.020–0.050 **Al**	**Normalized:** (≤30) **diam**, (400) **TS**, (235) **YS**, 25 **El**
COPANT 333	1013	COPANT	Wire, rod	0.11–0.16 **C**, 0.50–0.80 **Mn**, 0.040 **P**, 0.050 **S**	
ANSI/ASTM A 548	Grade 1013	US	Wire	0.11–0.16 **C**, 0.50–0.80 **Mn**, 0.040 **P**, 0.050 **S**	
DGN–B–301	1013	Mexico	Bar	0.11–0.16 **C**, 0.50–0.80 **Mn**, 0.040 **P**, 0.050 **S**, 0.10 **Si**	
AISI 1013		US	Wire, rod	0.11–0.16 **C**, 0.50–0.80 **Mn**, 0.040 **P**, 0.040 **S**	
ANSI/ASTM A 29	1013	US	Bar	0.11–0.16 **C**, 0.50–0.80 **Mn**, 0.040 **P**, 0.050 **S**	
NF A 36–102	Fd–11	France	Strip	0.11 **C**, 0.062 **P**, 0.062 **S**, 0.011 **Nb**	
NF A 36–102	Fd Tu 11	France	Strip	0.11 **C**, 0.065 **P**, 0.055 **S**	
NF A 36–102	Fd Tu 4	France	Strip	0.11 **C**, 0.044 **P**, 0.044 **S**, 0.008 **N_2**	
BS 2S.112		UK	Bar: aircraft quality	0.10–0.30 **C**, 0.7–1.3 **Mn**, 0.05 **P**, 0.10–0.18 **S**, 0.35 **Si**, 0.15–0.35 **Pb**	**Cold drawn, cold rolled, machined, ground**: all **diam**, (617) **TS**
ANSI/ASTM A 709	Grade 100	US	Plate, bar, shapes	0.10–0.21 **C**, 0.40–1.50 **Mn**, 0.035 **P**, 0.04 **S**	**Quenched and tempered:** ≤2.50 (64) **diam**, (775) **TS**, (700) **YS**, 18 **El**
ANSI/ASTM A 709	Grade 100 W	US	Plate, bar, shapes	0.10–0.21 **C**, 0.40–1.50 **Mn**, 0.035 **P**, 0.04 **S**	**Quenched and tempered:** ≤2.50 (64) **diam**, (700) **TS**, (635) **YS**, 17 **El**
ANSI/ASTM A 512	MT 1015	US	Tube: cold–drawn buttweld	0.10–0.20 **C**, 0.30–0.60 **Mn**, 0.04 **P**, 0.05 **S**	**Stress relief annealed**: all **diam**, 66 (555) **TS**, 60 (414) **YS**, 14 **El**
IS 2100	Grade 2	India	Bar, billet	0.10–0.20 **C**, 0.60–0.90 **Mn**, 0.050 **P**, 0.050 **S**	**Mill**: all **diam**, (510) **TS**, 20 **El**
ANSI/ASTM A 588	Grade D	US	Plate, bar, shapes	0.10–0.20 **C**, 0.75–1.25 **Mn**, 0.04 **P**, 0.05 **S**, 0.50–0.90 **Si**, 0.30 **Cu**, 0.04 **Nb**, 0.50–0.90 **Cr**, 0.05–0.15 **Zr**	**Hot rolled (plate, bar):** <4.00 **diam**, (485) **TS**, (345) **YS**, 21 **El**
ANSI/ASTM A 588	Grade F	US	Plate, bar, shapes	0.10–0.20 **C**, 0.50–1.00 **Mn**, 0.04 **P**, 0.05 **S**, 0.30 **Si**, 0.30–1.00 **Cu**, 0.01–0.10 **V**, 0.30 **Cr**, 0.10–0.20 **Mo**, 0.40–1.10 **Ni**	**Hot rolled (plate, bar):** <4.0 **diam**, (485) **TS**, (345) **YS**, 21 **El**
DGN–B–201	Grade MT1015	Mexico	Tube: butt–welded	0.10–0.20 **C**, 0.30–0.60 **Mn**, 0.040 **P**, 0.050 **S**	**Cold finished and annealed:** all **diam**, (455) **TS**, (413) **YS**, 14 **El**; **Normalized**: all **diam**, (296) **TS**, (172) **YS**, 34 **El**
NF A 35–564	XC 12 FF, XC 18 FF	France	Bar, wire, rod	0.10–0.20 **C**, 0.03 **P**, 0.03 **S**, 0.15 **Si**, 0.02 **Cu**, 0.02 min **Al**	**Annealed:** (≤70) **diam**, (440) max **TS**
IS 2100	Grade 1	India	Bar, billet	0.10–0.20 **C**, 0.60–0.90 **Mn**, 0.050 **P**, 0.050 **S**	**Mill**: all **diam**, (412) **TS**, 25 **El**
MIL–T–16286E	Class d	US	Tube: seamless	0.10–0.20 **C**, 0.30–0.80 **Mn**, 0.045 **P**, 0.045 **S**, 0.10–0.50 **Si** 0.44–0.65 **Mo**	**Annealed**: all **diam**, (379) **TS**, (206) **YS**, 30 **El**

WROUGHT CARBON STEELS

specification number	designation	country	product forms	composition	mechanical properties (see page iv for explanation)
COPANT 514	Grade TM 1015	COPANT	Tube: seamless	0.10–0.20 **C**, 0.30–0.60 **Mn**, 0.040 **P**, 0.050 **S**, 0.10 **Si**	**Hot finished**: (>323.9) **diam**, (335) **TS**, (245) **YS**, 15 **El**; **Cold finished**: all **diam**, (440) **TS**, (370) **YS**, 5 **El**; **Annealed**: all **diam**, (315) **TS**, (205) **YS**, 30 **El**; **Normalized**: all **diam**, (360) **TS**, (315) **YS**, 30 **El**
ANSI/ASTM A 513	MT 1015	US	Tube: electric resistance welded	0.10–0.20 **C**, 0.30–0.60 **Mn**, 0.040 **P**, 0.050 **S**	**As–welded**: all **diam**, 48 (331) **TS**, 35 (241) **YS**, 15 **El**; **Normalized**: all **diam**, 45 (310) **TS**, 30 (207) **YS**, 30 **El**; **Mandrel–drawn**: all **diam**, 65 (448) **TS**, 55 (379) **YS**, 5 **El**
COPANT R 193	BC	COPANT	Tube	0.10–0.20 **C**, 0.30–0.80 **Mn**, 0.048 **P**, 0.058 **S**, 0.25 **Si**	**Hot or cold finished**: (≥5.60) **diam**, (325) **TS**, (175) **YS**, 35 **El**
ANSI/ASTM A 161	Low–carbon steel tubes	US	Tube: seamless	0.10–0.20 **C**, 0.30–0.80 **Mn**, 0.048 **P**, 0.058 **S**, 0.25 **Si**	**Hot rolled, as rolled, cold drawn, annealed**: 0.312 (7.94) **diam**, 47 (324) **TS**, 26 (179) **YS**, 35.00 **El**
NOM–B–142		Mexico	Tube: seamless	0.10–0.20 **C**, 0.30–0.80 **Mn**, 0.048 **P**, 0.058 **S**, 0.25 **Si**	**Hot or cold finished**: (5.59) **diam**, (324) **TS**, (176) **YS**, 28 **El**
AISI 1018		US	Plate	0.1–0.20 **C**, 0.60–0.90 **Mn**, 0.040 **P**, 0.050 **S**	
ANSI/ASTM A 519	MT 1015	US	Tube: seamless	0.10–0.20 **C**, 0.30–0.60 **Mn**, 0.040 **P**, 0.050 **S**	
ANSI/ASTM A 519	MT X1015	US	Tube: seamless	0.10–0.20 **C**, 0.60–0.90 **Mn**, 0.040 **P**, 0.050 **S**	
ANSI/ASTM A 512	MTX 1015	US	Tube: cold–drawn buttweld	0.10–0.20 **C**, 0.60–0.90 **Mn**, 0.04 **P**, 0.05 **S**	
DGN–B–203	MT 1015	Mexico	Tube: seamless	0.10–0.20 **C**, 0.30–0.60 **Mn**, 0.040 **P**, 0.050 **S**	
DGN–B–203	Grade MT X 1015	Mexico	Tube: seamless	0.10–0.20 **C**, 0.60–0.90 **Mn**, 0.040 **P**, 0.050 **S**	
DGN–B–201	Grade MTX1015	Mexico	Tube: butt–welded	0.10–0.20 **C**, 0.60–0.90 **Mn**, 0.040 **P**, 0.050 **S**	
COPANT 514	Grade TMX 1015	COPANT	Tube: seamless	0.10–0.20 **C**, 0.60–0.90 **Mn**, 0.040 **P**, 0.050 **S**, 0.20–0.35 **Si**	**Hot finished**: (>323.9) **diam**, 15 **El**; **Cold finished**: all **diam**, 5 **El**; **Annealed**: all **diam**, 30 **El**; **Normalized**: all **diam**, 30 **El**
ANSI/ASTM A 588	Grade A	US	Plate, bar, shapes	0.10–0.19 **C**, 0.90–1.25 **Mn**, 0.04 **P**, 0.05 **S**, 0.15–0.30 **Si**, 0.25–0.40 **Cu**, 0.02–0.10 **V**, 0.40–0.65 **Cr**	**Hot rolled (bar, plate)**: <4.0 **diam**, (485) **TS**, (345) **YS**, 21 **El**
BS 980	CDS–4	UK	Tube	0.10–0.18 **C**, 0.6–1.0 **Mn**, 0.050 **P**, 0.070 **S**, 0.05–0.35 **Si**	**Drawn or drawn and tempered**: all **diam**, (385) **TS**, (330) **YS**
AS 1442	Grade AS 1442/XS1115	Australia	Bar, blooms, billets, slabs	0.10–0.17 **C**, 1.00–1.30 **Mn**, 0.050 **P**, 0.08–0.13 **S**, 0.35 **Si**	
AS 1443	Grade AS 1443/XS1115	Australia	Bar	0.10–0.17 **C**, 1.00–1.30 **Mn**, 0.050 **P**, 0.08–0.13 **S**, 0.35 **Si**	
AISI 1513		US	Bar	0.10–0.16 **C**, 1.10–1.40 **Mn**, 0.040 **P**, 0.050 **S**	
DGN–B–301	1513	Mexico	Bar	0.10–0.16 **C**, 1.10–1.40 **Mn**, 0.040 **P**, 0.050 **S**, 0.10 **Si**	
AISI 1513		US	Wire, rod	0.10–0.16 **C**, 1.10–1.40 **Mn**, 0.040 **P**, 0.050 **S**	
ANSI/ASTM A 576	1513	US	Bar	0.10–0.16 **C**, 1.10–1.40 **Mn**, 0.040 **P**, 0.050 **S**	
ANSI/ASTM A 29	1513	US	Bar	0.10–0.16 **C**, 1.10–1.40 **Mn**, 0.040 **P**, 0.050 **S**	
ASTM A 689	1513	US	Bar	0.10–0.16 **C**, 1.10–1.40 **Mn**, 0.040 **P**, 0.050 **S**	
BS 4S.14		UK	Bar, billets, forgings: aircraft quality	0.10–0.15 **C**, 0.4–0.7 **Mn**, 0.040 **P**, 0.040 **S**, 0.10–0.35 **Si**, 0.3 **Ni**	**Hardened and tempered**: all **diam**, 55 (539) **TS**
JIS G 3539	SWCH 12A	Japan	Wire	0.10–0.15 **C**, 0.60 **Mn**, 0.030 **P**, 0.035 **S**, 0.10 **Si**, 0.02 min **Al**	**Cold drawn**: (>3–4) **diam**, (490) **TS**; **Annealed and cold drawn**: (>3–4) **diam**, (343) **TS**, 14 **El**

WROUGHT CARBON STEELS

specification number	designation	country	product forms	composition	mechanical properties (see page iv for explanation)
JIS G 3539	SWCH 12R	Japan	Wire	0.10–0.15 **C**, 0.30–0.60 **Mn**, 0.040 **P**, 0.040 **S**	**Annealed and cold drawn:** all **diam**, (343) **TS**, 14 **El**
JIS G 3539	SWCH 12K	Japan	Wire	0.10–0.15 **C**, 0.30–0.60 **Mn**, 0.030 **P**, 0.035 **S**, 0.10–0.35 **Si**	**Annealed and cold drawn:** all **diam**, (343) **TS**, 14 **El**
DGN–B–301	1012	Mexico	Bar	0.10–0.15 **C**, 0.30–0.60 **Mn**, 0.040 **P**, 0.050 **S**, 0.10 **Si**	**Forged or hot rolled, cold rolled and cold finished:** all **diam**, (333) **TS**, (176) **YS**, 28 **El**
BS 1449: Part 1	Grade 12	UK	Plate, sheet, strip	0.10–0.15 **C**, 0.40–0.60 **Mn**, 0.050 **P**, 0.050 **S**	**Cold rolled:** all **diam**, (310) **TS**, (170) **YS**, 28 **El**
AISI 1012		US	Plate	0.10–0.15 **C**, 30.0–60.0 **Mn**, 0.040 **P**, 0.050 **S**	
AISI 1012		US	Bar	0.10–0.15 **C**, 0.30–0.60 **Mn**, 0.040 **P**, 0.050 **S**	
BS 970: Part 1	040A12	UK	Blooms, billets, slabs, bar, rod, forgings	0.10–0.15 **C**, 0.30–0.50 **Mn**	
BS 970: Part 1	050A12	UK	Blooms, billets, slabs, bar, rod, forgings	0.10–0.15 **C**, 0.40–0.60 **Mn**	
BS 970: Part 1	060A12	UK	Blooms, billets, slabs, bar, rod, forgings	0.10–0.15 **C**, 0.50–0.70 **Mn**	
ANSI/ASTM A 519	1012	US	Tube: seamless	0.10–0.15 **C**, 0.30–0.60 **Mn**, 0.040 **P**, 0.050 **S**	
AS 1446	Grade AS 1446/S1012	Australia	Plate	0.10–0.15 **C**, 0.30–0.60 **Mn**, 0.050 **P**, 0.050 **S**, 0.35 **Si**	
COPANT 333	1012	COPANT	Wire, rod	0.10–0.15 **C**, 0.30–0.60 **Mn**, 0.040 **P**, 0.050 **S**	
ANSI/ASTM A 545	Grade 1012	US	Wire	0.10–0.15 **C**, 0.30–0.60 **Mn**, 0.040 **P**, 0.050 **S**	
ANSI/ASTM A 549	Grade 1012	US	Wire	0.10–0.15 **C**, 0.30–0.60 **Mn**, 0.040 **P**, 0.050 **S**	
MIL–S–11310E	1012	US	Bar	0.10–0.15 **C**, 0.30–0.60 **Mn**, 0.040 **P**, 0.050 **S**, 0.20 **Si**	
ANSI/ASTM A 575	1012	US	Bar	0.10–0.15 **C**, 0.30–0.60 **Mn**, 0.04 **P**, 0.05 **S**	
AISI 1012		US	Wire, rod	0.10–0.15 **C**, 0.30–0.60 **Mn**, 0.040 **P**, 0.050 **S**	
ANSI/ASTM A 576	1012	US	Bar	0.10–0.15 **C**, 0.30–0.60 **Mn**, 0.040 **P**, 0.050 **S**	
ASTM A 689	1012	US	Bar	0.10–0.15 **C**, 0.30–0.60 **Mn**, 0.040 **P**, 0.050 **S**	
ANSI/ASTM A 29	1012	US	Bar	0.10–0.15 **C**, 0.30–0.60 **Mn**, 0.040 **P**, 0.050 **S**	
AS 1443	Grade AS 1443/K1012	Australia	Bar	0.10–0.15 **C**, 0.30–0.60 **Mn**, 0.050 **P**, 0.050 **S**, 0.10–0.35 **Si**	
AS 1443	Grade AS 1443/S1012	Australia	Bar	0.10–0.15 **C**, 0.30–0.60 **Mn**, 0.050 **P**, 0.050 **S**, 0.35 **Si**	
AS 1442	Grade AS 1442/S1012	Australia	Bar, blooms, billets, slabs	0.10–0.15 **C**, 0.30–0.60 **Mn**, 0.050 **P**, 0.050 **S**, 0.35 **Si**	
AS 1442	Grade AS 1442/K1012	Australia	Bar, blooms, billets, slabs	0.10–0.15 **C**, 0.30–0.60 **Mn**, 0.050 **P**, 0.050 **S**, 0.10–0.35 **Si**	
DEF STAN 95–1/1	C1012	Canada	Bar	0.10–0.15 **C**, 0.30–0.60 **Mn**, 0.04 **P**, 0.05 **S**, 0.10 **Si**	
JIS G 3108	Type 2	Japan	Bar	0.10–0.15 **C**, 0.30–0.60 **Mn**, 0.045 **P**, 0.045 **S**	
JIS G 3507	SWRCH 12R	Japan	Wire, rod	0.10–0.15 **C**, 0.30–0.60 **Mn**, 0.040 **P**, 0.040 **S**	
JIS G 3507	SWRCH 12A	Japan	Wire, rod	0.10–0.15 **C**, 0.30–0.60 **Mn**, 0.030 **P**, 0.035 **S**, 0.10 **Si**, 0.02 **Al**	
JIS G 3507	SWRCH 12K	Japan	Wire, rod	0.10–0.15 **C**, 0.30–0.60 **Mn**, 0.030 **P**, 0.035 **S**, 0.10–0.35 **Si**	
JIS G 3503	Class 2, No. 1	Japan	Wire, rod	0.10–0.15 **C**, 0.35–0.65 **Mn**, 0.020 **P**, 0.023 **S**, 0.03 **Si**, 0.20 **Cu**	
JIS G 3503	Class 2, No. 2	Japan	Wire, rod	0.10–0.15 **C**, 0.35–0.65 **Mn**, 0.030 **P**, 0.030 **S**, 0.03 **Si**, 0.30 **Cu**	
JIS G 3505	SWRM 12	Japan	Wire, rod	0.10–0.15 **C**, 0.30–0.60 **Mn**, 0.045 **P**, 0.045 **S**	

WROUGHT CARBON STEELS

specification number	designation	country	product forms	composition	mechanical properties (see page iv for explanation)
JIS G 4051	S 12C	Japan	Bar, wire, rod	0.10–0.15 **C**, 0.30–0.60 **Mn**, 0.030 **P**, 0.035 **S**, 0.15–0.35 **Si**, 0.30 **Cu**	
JIS G 3523	Class 2, No. 1	Japan	Wire	0.10–0.15 **C**, 0.35–0.65 **Mn**, 0.020 **P**, 0.023 **S**, 0.03 **Si**, 0.20 **Cu**	
JIS G 3523	Class 2, No. 2	Japan	Wire	0.10–0.15 **C**, 0.35–0.65 **Mn**, 0.030 **P**, 0.030 **S**, 0.03 **Si**, 0.30 **Cu**	
JIS G 3539	SWCH 8R	Japan	Wire	0.10 **C**, 0.60 **Mn**, 0.040 **P**, 0.040 **S**	**Cold drawn**: (≤3) **diam**, (539) **TS**; **Annealed and cold drawn**: (≤3) **diam**, (294) **TS**, 15 **El**
DIN 1614 Part 1	St W 22 (1.0332)	Germany	Sheet	0.10 **C**, 0.20–0.45 **Mn**, 0.035 **P**, 0.035 **S**	**Hot rolled**: all **diam**, (440) max **TS**, 25 in 80 mm **El**
DIN 1614 Part 1	St W 22 (1.0322)	Germany	Strip	0.10 **C**, 0.20–0.45 **Mn**, 0.035 **P**, 0.035 **S**	**Hot rolled**: all **diam**, (440) max **TS**, 25 in 80 mm **El**
NF A 35–564	XC 10 FF	France	Bar, wire, rod	0.10 **C**, 0.03 **P**, 0.03 **S**, 0.10 **Si**, 0.20 **Cu**, 0.03 min **Al**	**Annealed**: (≤70) **diam**, (410) max **TS**
ISO 3575	04	ISO	Sheet: hot dipped, zinc–coated	0.10 **C**, 0.45 **Mn**, 0.03 **P**, 0.03 **S**	**As agreed**: all **diam**, (410) **TS**, 26 **El**
SFS 606		Finland	Sheet, strip	0.10 **C**, 0.45 **Mn**	**Annealed**: (≤3) **diam**, (400) **TS**, 28 **El**
ISO 3573	Grade HR 3	ISO	Sheet	0.10 **C**, 0.45 **Mn**, 0.03 **P**, 0.03 **S**	**Hot rolled**: (<3) **diam**, (370) **TS**, 29 **El**
SFS 607		Finland	Sheet, strip	0.10 **C**, 0.45 **Mn**	**Annealed**: (≤3) **diam**, (370) **TS**, 32 **El**
ISO 3574	CR3	ISO	Sheet	0.10 **C**, 0.45 **Mn**, 0.03 **P**, 0.03 **S**	**Hot rolled, cold reduced, skin passed**: all **diam**, (350) **TS**, 35 **El**
JIS G 3539	SWCH 8A	Japan	Wire	0.10 **C**, 0.60 **Mn**, 0.030 **P**, 0.035 **S**, 0.10 **Si**, 0.02 min **Al**	**Cold drawn**: (>5) **diam**, (343) **TS**, 11 **El**; **Annealed and cold drawn**: (>5) **diam**, (294) **TS**, 15 **El**
DIN 17111	Grade U7S10	Germany	Bar, wire, rod	0.10 **C**, 0.40–0.70 **Mn**, 0.080 **P**, 0.08–0.12 **S**	**Hot rolled**: all **diam**, (314) **TS**, (206) **YS**
DGN–B–301	1008	Mexico	Bar	0.10 **C**, 0.25–0.50 **Mn**, 0.040 **P**, 0.050 **S**, 0.10 **Si**	**Forged or hot rolled, cold rolled and cold finished**: all **diam**, (304) **TS**, (167) **YS**, 30 **El**
AS 1595, Part 1	Grade CRC	Australia	Sheet	0.10 **C**, 0.50 **Mn**, 0.030 **P**, 0.035 **S**	**Cold rolled**: <3 **diam**, (300) **TS**, (200) **YS**, 35 **El**
AS 1594	Grade AS 1594/HRC	Australia	Sheet, strip	0.10 **C**, 0.50 **Mn**, 0.030 **P**, 0.035 **S**	**Hot rolled**: ≥3 **diam**, (300) **TS**, (200) **YS**, 30 **El**
TS 924	UDK 669.14.418/Fe–2	Turkey	Strip	0.10 **C**, 0.20–0.45 **Mn**, 0.06 **P**, 0.05 **S**, 0.03–0.20 **Si**	**Annealed, tempered, cold rolled**: all **diam**, (294) **TS**, 32 **El**
DIN 1624	Grade St 2	Germany	Strip	0.10 **C**, 0.20–0.45 **Mn**, 0.060 **P**, 0.050 **S**, 0.03–0.20 **Si**	**Solution annealed**: all **diam**, (294) **TS**, 32 **El**; **Cold rolled**: all **diam**, (314) **TS**, 24 **El**
BS 1449: Part 1	Grade 3	UK	Plate, strip, sheet	0.10 **C**, 0.50 **Mn**, 0.040 **P**, 0.040 **S**	**Hot rolled**: all **diam**, (290) **TS**, (170) **YS**, 28 **El**; **Cold rolled**: all **diam**, (280) **TS**, (140) **YS**, 34 **El**
COPANT 38	EP	COPANT	Sheet	0.10 **C**, 0.20–0.60 **Mn**, 0.035 **P**, 0.040 **S**	**Hot rolled**: (1.50–3.00) **diam**, (280) **TS**, (290) max **YS**, 30 **El**; **Cold rolled**: (0.30–0.50) **diam**, (270) **TS**, (270) max **YS**, 31 **El**
BS 1717	ERW–101	UK	Tube: electric resistance butt welded	0.10 **C**, 0.6 **Mn**, 0.060 **P**, 0.060 **S**	**As welded**: all **diam**, (275) **TS**, (150) **YS**
JIS G 3131	Class 2	Japan	Plate, sheet, strip	0.10 **C**, 0.50 **Mn**, 0.040 **P**, 0.040 **S**	**Hot rolled**: (<1.6) **diam**, (275) **TS**, 30 **El**
JIS G 3131	Class 3	Japan	Plate, sheet, strip	0.10 **C**, 0.50 **Mn**, 0.030 **P**, 0.035 **S**	**Hot rolled**: (<1.6) **diam**, (275) **TS**, 31 **El**
JIS G 3132	Class 1	Japan	Strip	0.10 **C**, 0.25–0.50 **Mn**, 0.040 **P**, 0.040 **S**, 0.04 **Si**	**Hot rolled**: (1.0–1.6) **diam**, (275) **TS**, 30 **El**
JIS G 3141	Class 2	Japan	Sheet, strip	0.10 **C**, 0.45 **Mn**, 0.035 **P**, 0.035 **S**	**Cold rolled**: (≥0.25) **diam**, (275) **TS**, 34 **El**
DIN 1624	Grade St 3	Germany	Strip	0.10 **C**, 0.20–0.45 **Mn**, 0.040 **P**, 0.040 **S**, 0.03–0.15 **Si**	**Solution annealed**: all **diam**, (274) **TS**, 35 **El**; **Cold rolled**: all **diam**, (314) **TS**, 26 **El**

WROUGHT CARBON STEELS

specification number	designation	country	product forms	composition	mechanical properties (see page iv for explanation)
DIN 1624	Grade St 4	Germany	Strip	0.10 **C**, 0.20–0.45 **Mn**, 0.030 **P**, 0.035 **S**, 0.03–0.10 **Si**	**Solution annealed**: all **diam**, (274) **TS**, 38 **El**; **Cold rolled**: all **diam**, (314) **TS**, 28 **El**
DIN 1623 Sheet 1	St 12 (1.0330)	Germany	Strip	0.10 **C**	**Cold rolled**: all **diam**, (270) **TS**, (280) **YS**, 28 in 80 mm **El**
DIN 1623 Sheet 1	St 13 (1.0333)	Germany	Strip	0.10 **C**	**Cold rolled**: all **diam**, (270) **TS**, (250) **YS**, 32 in 80 mm **El**
DIN 1623 Sheet 1	St 12 (1.0330)	Germany	Sheet	0.10 **C**	**Cold rolled**: all **diam**, (270) **TS**, (280) **YS**, 28 in 80 mm **El**
DIN 1623 Sheet 1	St 13 (1.0333)	Germany	Sheet	0.10 **C**	**Cold rolled**: all **diam**, (270) **TS**, (250) **YS**, 32 in 80 mm **El**
SIS 14 11 42	SIS 11 42–42	Sweden	Plate	0.10 **C**, 0.50 **Mn**, 0.04 **P**, 0.04 **S**	**Solution treated and cold rolled**: ($\leq$3) **diam**, (270) **TS**, 26 **El**
SIS 14 11 46	SIS 11 46–32	Sweden	Sheet	0.10 **C**, 0.50 **Mn**, 0.040 **P**, 0.040 **S**	**Solution treated and cold rolled**: ($\leq$3) **diam**, (270) **TS**, 33 **El**
SIS 14 11 46	SIS 11 46–42	Sweden	Sheet	0.10 **C**, 0.50 **Mn**, 0.040 **P**, 0.040 **S**	**Solution treated and cold rolled**: ($\leq$3) **diam**, (270) **TS**, 33 **El**
IS 2879		India	Wire	0.10 **C**, 0.38–0.62 **Mn**, 0.030 **P**, 0.030 **S**, 0.03 **Si**, 0.15 **Cu**	
NF A 35–051	FM 6 grade 2	France	Wire, rod	0.10 **C**, 0.25–0.50 **Mn**, 0.062 **P**, 0.050 **S**, 0.012 N_2	
NF A 35–051	FM 6 grade 3	France	Wire, rod	0.10 **C**, 0.25–0.50 **Mn**, 0.044 **P**, 0.044 **S**, 0.009 N_2	
NF A 36–102	Fd 3	France	Strip	0.10 **C**, 0.025 **P**, 0.025 **S**, 0.008 N_2	
NF A 36–102	Fd Tu 2	France	Strip	0.10 **C**, 0.075 **P**, 0.057 **S**, 0.017 N_2	
QQ–S–698	1008	US	Sheet, strip	0.10 **C**, 0.25–0.50 **Mn**, 0.040 **P**, 0.050 **S**	
ANSI/ASTM A 642		US	Sheet	0.10 **C**, 0.50 **Mn**, 0.025 **P**, 0.035 **S**	
ASTM 619	Classes I and II	US	Sheet	0.10 **C**, 0.50 **Mn**, 0.025 **P**, 0.035 **S**	
ASTM A 620	Classes I and II	US	Sheet	0.10 **C**, 0.50 **Mn**, 0.025 **P**, 0.035 **S**	
ASTM A 621		US	Sheet, strip	0.10 **C**, 0.50 **Mn**, 0.025 **P**, 0.035 **S**	
ASTM A 622		US	Sheet, strip	0.10 **C**, 0.50 **Mn**, 0.025 **P**, 0.035 **S**	
ASTM A 528		US	Sheet	0.10 **C**, 0.50 **Mn**, 0.025 **P**, 0.035 **S**	
AISI 1008		US	Plate	0.10 **C**, 0.25–0.50 **Mn**, 0.040 **P**, 0.050 **S**	
AISI 1008		US	Bar	0.10 **C**, 0.30–0.50 **Mn**, 0.040 **P**, 0.050 **S**	
AMS 5036E		US	Sheet, strip	0.10 **C**, 0.25–0.50 **Mn**, 0.04 **P**, 0.05 **S**	
ANSI/ASTM A 519	1008	US	Tube: seamless	0.10 **C**, 0.30–0.50 **Mn**, 0.040 **P**, 0.050 **S**	
AS 1595/Temper 4		Australia	Sheet, strip	0.10 **C**, 0.50 **Mn**, 0.040 **P**, 0.040 **S**	**Cold rolled**
AS 1595, Part 2	AS 1595/Temper 5	Australia	Sheet, strip	0.10 **C**, 0.50 **Mn**, 0.040 **P**, 0.040 **S**	**Cold rolled**
AS 1595, Part 2	AS 1595/Temper 6	Australia	Sheet, strip	0.10 **C**, 0.50 **Mn**, 0.040 **P**, 0.040 **S**	**Cold rolled**
TS 2348	C9–1/1.0010	Turkey	Wire, rod	0.10 **C**, 0.50 **Mn**, 0.070 **P**, 0.060 **S**	
AS 1446	Grade AS 1446/S1008	Australia	Plate	0.10 **C**, 0.25–0.50 **Mn**, 0.050 **P**, 0.050 **S**, 0.35 **Si**	
AS 1446	Grade AS 1446/C1008	Australia	Plate	0.10 **C**, 0.25–0.50 **Mn**, 0.040 **P**, 0.040 **S**	
AS 1446	Grade AS 1446/R1008	Australia	Plate	0.10 **C**, 0.25–0.50 **Mn**, 0.040 **P**, 0.050 **S**	
COPANT 330	1008	COPANT	Bar, shapes	0.10 **C**, 0.30–0.50 **Mn**, 0.040 **P**, 0.050 **S**	
COPANT 331	1008	COPANT	Bar	0.10 **C**, 0.30–0.50 **Mn**, 0.040 **P**, 0.050 **S**	
COPANT 333	1008	COPANT	Wire, rod	0.10 **C**, 0.25–0.50 **Mn**, 0.040 **P**, 0.050 **S**	
ASTM A 108	1008	US	Bar	0.10 **C**, 0.30–0.50 **Mn**, 0.040 **P**, 0.050 **S**	

WROUGHT CARBON STEELS

specification number	designation	country	product forms	composition	mechanical properties (see page iv for explanation)
ANSI/ASTM A 29	M 1008	US	Bar	0.10 **C**, 0.25–0.60 **Mn**, 0.04 **P**, 0.05 **S**	
ANSI/ASTM A 545	Grade 1008	US	Wire	0.10 **C**, 0.30–0.50 **Mn**, 0.040 **P**, 0.050 **S**	
ANSI/ASTM A 549	Grade 1008	US	Wire	0.10 **C**, 0.30–0.50 **Mn**, 0.040 **P**, 0.050 **S**	
MIL–S–11310E	1008	US	Bar	0.10 **C**, 0.30–0.50 **Mn**, 0.040 **P**, 0.050 **S**, 0.20 **Si**	
DIN 1616	Grade A U	Germany	Blackplate, tinplate	0.10 **C**, 0.20–0.45 **Mn**, 0.030 **P**, 0.035 **S**, 0.20 **Cu**	
DIN 1616	Grade A RR	Germany	Blackplate, tinplate	0.10 **C**, 0.20–0.45 **Mn**, 0.030 **P**, 0.035 **S**, 0.20 **Cu**	
DIN 1616	Grade B U	Germany	Blackplate, tinplate	0.10 **C**, 0.25–0.45 **Mn**, 0.030 **P**, 0.035 **S**, 0.20 **Cu**	
DIN 1616	Grade C U	Germany	Blackplate, tinplate	0.10 **C**, 0.25–0.45 **Mn**, 0.035 **P**, 0.040 **S**, 0.20 **Cu**	
DIN 1616	Grade D U	Germany	Blackplate, tinplate	0.10 **C**, 0.25–0.45 **Mn**, 0.06–0.14 **P**, 0.050 **S**, 0.20 **Cu**	
ANSI/ASTM A 575	1008	US	Bar	0.10 **C**, 0.30–0.50 **Mn**, 0.04 **P**, 0.05 **S**	
ANSI/ASTM A 575	M 1008	US	Bar	0.10 **C**, 0.25–0.60 **Mn**, 0.04 **P**, 0.05 **S**	
DGN–B–257		Mexico	Sheet, strip	0.10 **C**, 0.50 **Mn**, 0.025 **P**, 0.035 **S**	
DGN–B–264		Mexico	Sheet, strip	0.10 **C**, 0.50 **Mn**, 0.025 **P**, 0.035 **S**	
DGN–B–265	E.P.	Mexico	Sheet	0.10 **C**, 0.50 **Mn**, 0.040 **P**, 0.035 **S**	
DGN–B–267		Mexico	Sheet	0.10 **C**, 0.50 **Mn**, 0.025 **P**, 0.035 **S**	
DGN–B–272		Mexico	Sheet, strip	0.10 **C**, 0.50 **Mn**, 0.025 **P**, 0.035 **S**	
AISI 1008		US	Wire, rod	0.10 **C**, 0.30–0.50 **Mn**, 0.040 **P**, 0.050 **S**	
ASTM A 689	1008	US	Bar	0.10 **C**, 0.30–0.50 **Mn**, 0.040 **P**, 0.050 **S**	
ANSI/ASTM A 576	1008	US	Bar	0.10 **C**, 0.30–0.50 **Mn**, 0.040 **P**, 0.050 **S**	
ANSI/ASTM A 29	1008	US	Bar	0.10 **C**, 0.30–0.50 **Mn**, 0.040 **P**, 0.050 **S**	
ASTM A 59	Grade 2	US	Forgings	0.10 **C**, 0.60 **Mn**, 0.04 **P**, 0.04 **S**, 0.20 **Si**, 0.02 **Al**	
AS 1443	Grade AS 1443/K1008	Australia	Bar	0.10 **C**, 0.25–0.50 **Mn**, 0.050 **P**, 0.050 **S**, 0.10–0.35 **Si**	
AS 1443	Grade AS 1443/S1008	Australia	Bar	0.10 **C**, 0.25–0.50 **Mn**, 0.050 **P**, 0.050 **S**, 0.35 **Si**	
AS 1442	Grade AS 1442/R1008	Australia	Bar, blooms, billets, slabs	0.10 **C**, 0.25–0.50 **Mn**, 0.040 **P**, 0.050 **S**	
AS 1442	Grade AS 1442/S1008	Australia	Bar, blooms, billets, slabs	0.10 **C**, 0.25–0.50 **Mn**, 0.050 **P**, 0.050 **S**, 0.35 **Si**	
AS 1442	Grade AS 1442/K1008	Australia	Bar, blooms, billets, slabs	0.10 **C**, 0.25–0.50 **Mn**, 0.050 **P**, 0.050 **S**, 0.10–0.35 **Si**	
NF A 35–055	FME 8, Grade 5	France	Wire, rod	0.100 **C**, 0.40–0.60 **Mn**, 0.030 **P**, 0.030 **S**; 0.30 max, other elements, total	
NF A 35–055	FME 8, Grade 7	France	Wire, rod	0.10 **C**, 0.40–0.60 **Mn**, 0.020 **P**, 0.020 **S**; 0.30 max, other elements, total	
TS 924	UDK 669.14.418/Fe–4	Turkey	Strip	0.10 **C**, 0.20–0.45 **Mn**, 0.03 **P**, 0.035 **S**, 0.05–0.10 **Si**	
DIN 17140	Grade D9–1	Germany	Wire, rod	0.10 **C**, 0.50 **Mn**, 0.070 **P**, 0.060 **S**	
JIS G 3108	Type 1	Japan	Bar	0.10 **C**, 0.30–0.60 **Mn**, 0.045 **P**, 0.045 **S**	
JIS G 3507	SWRCH 8R	Japan	Wire, rod	0.10 **C**, 0.60 **Mn**, 0.040 **P**, 0.040 **S**	
JIS G 3507	SWRCH 8A	Japan	Wire, rod	0.10 **C**, 0.60 **Mn**, 0.030 **P**, 0.035 **S**, 0.10 **Si**, 0.02 **Al**	
JIS G 3505	SWRM 8	Japan	Wire, rod	0.10 **C**, 0.60 **Mn**, 0.045 **P**, 0.045 **S**	
BS 3111 PartI	Type 0	UK	Wire	0.09–0.25 **C**, 0.30–1.00 **Mn**, 0.050 **P**, 0.050 **S**, 0.40 **Si**	

specification number	designation	country	product forms	composition	mechanical properties (see page iv for explanation)
NF A 35–053	FR 15	France	Wire, rod	0.09–0.20 **C**, 0.40–0.70 **Mn**, 0.044 **P**, 0.044 **S**, 0.30 **Si**	**Hot or cold drawn and annealed:** (≤30) **diam**, (500) max **TS**
NF A 35–051	FM 15 grade 3	France	Wire, rod	0.09–0.20 **C**, 0.40–0.70 **Mn**, 0.040 **P**, 0.040 **S**, 0.10–0.35 **Si**	
ANSI/ASTM A 29	M 1012	US	Bar	0.09–0.16 **C**, 0.25–0.60 **Mn**, 0.04 **P**, 0.05 **S**	
ANSI/ASTM A 575	M 1012	US	Bar	0.09–0.16 **C**, 0.25–0.60 **Mn**, 0.04 **P**, 0.05 **S**	
ISO/R 683/1X	Type 5	ISO	Bar, wire, rod	0.09–0.15 **C**, 0.90–1.20 **Mn**, 0.06 **P**, 0.15–0.25 **S**, 0.15–0.40 **Si**	**Cold finished:** (≤16) **diam**, (510) **TS**, (412) **YS**, 7 **El**
DGN–B–13	Class B, grade B4	Mexico	Wire	0.09–0.12 **C**, 0.33–0.43 **Mn**, 0.040 **P**, 0.060 **S**	
DGN–B–13	Class B, grade B3	Mexico	Wire	0.09–0.12 **C**, 0.33–0.43 **Mn**, 0.040 **P**, 0.060 **S**	
DGN–B–13	Class B, grade B2	Mexico	Wire	0.09–0.12 **C**, 0.33–0.43 **Mn**, 0.040 **P**, 0.060 **S**	
DGN–B–13	Class B, grade B1	Mexico	Wire	0.09–0.12 **C**, 0.33–0.43 **Mn**, 0.040 **P**, 0.060 **S**	
DIN 17111	Grade 6P20	Germany	Bar, wire, rod	0.09 **C**, 0.20–0.45 **Mn**, 0.15–0.25 **P**, 0.050 **S**	**Hot rolled:** all **diam**, (392) **TS**, (206) **YS**
DIN 17111	Grade 6P10	Germany	Bar, wire, rod	0.09 **C**, 0.20–0.45 **Mn**, 0.08–0.15 **P**, 0.050 **S**	**Hot rolled:** all **diam**, (343) **TS**, (186) **YS**
NF A 36–102	Fd 5	France	Strip	0.09 **C**, 0.025 **P**, 0.032 **S**, 0.008 N_2	
QQ–S–637A	1215	US	Bar	0.09 **C**, 0.75–1.05 **Mn**, 0.04–0.09 **P**, 0.26–0.35 **S**, 0.15–0.35 **Pb**	
QQ–S–637A	C	US	Bar	0.09 **C**, 0.70–1.20 **Mn**, 0.07–0.12 **P**, 0.24–0.33 **S**, 0.15–0.35 **Pb**	
AISI 1215		US	Bar	0.09 **C**, 0.75–1.05 **Mn**, 0.04–0.09 **P**, 0.26–0.35 **S**	
AMS 5010F	Type 1215	US	Bar	0.09 **C**, 0.75–1.05 **Mn**, 0.04–0.09 **P**, 0.26–0.35 **S**	
ANSI/ASTM A 519	1215	US	Tube: seamless	0.09 **C**, 0.75–1.05 **Mn**, 0.04–0.09 **P**, 0.26–0.35 **S**	
COPANT 330	1215	COPANT	Bar, shapes	0.09 **C**, 0.75–1.05 **Mn**, 0.04–0.09 **P**, 0.26–0.35 **S**	
COPANT 331	1215	COPANT	Bar	0.09 **C**, 0.75–1.05 **Mn**, 0.04–0.09 **P**, 0.26–0.35 **S**	
DGN–B–301	1215	Mexico	Bar	0.09 **C**, 0.75–1.05 **Mn**, 0.04–0.09 **P**, 0.26–0.35 **S**, 0.10–0.20 **Si**	
AISI 1215		US	Wire, rod	0.09 **C**, 0.75–1.05 **Mn**, 0.04–0.09 **P**, 0.26–0.35 **S**	
ANSI/ASTM A 576	1215	US	Bar	0.09 **C**, 0.75–1.05 **Mn**, 0.04–0.09 **P**, 0.26–0.35 **S**	
ANSI/ASTM A 29	1215	US	Bar	0.09 **C**, 0.75–1.05 **Mn**, 0.04–0.09 **P**, 0.26–0.35 **S**	
ANSI/ASTM A 29	12L15	US	Bar	0.09 **C**, 0.75–1.05 **Mn**, 0.04–0.09 **P**, 0.26–0.35 **S**, 0.15–0.35 **Pb**	
ASTM A 689	1215	US	Bar	0.09 **C**, 0.75–1.05 **Mn**, 0.04–0.09 **P**, 0.26–0.35 **S**	
COPANT 514	Grade 1215	COPANT	Tube: seamless	0.09 **C**, 0.75–1.05 **Mn**, 0.04–0.09 **P**, 0.26–0.35 **S**	
JIS G 3503	Class 1, No. 1	Japan	Wire, rod	0.09 **C**, 0.35–0.65 **Mn**, 0.020 **P**, 0.023 **S**, 0.03 **Si**, 0.20 **Cu**	
JIS G 3503	Class 1, No. 2	Japan	Wire, rod	0.09 **C**, 0.35–0.65 **Mn**, 0.030 **P**, 0.030 **S**, 0.03 **Si**, 0.30 **Cu**	
JIS G 4804	SUM 23	Japan	Bar	0.09 **C**, 0.75–1.05 **Mn**, 0.04–0.09 **P**, 0.26–0.35 **S**	
JIS G 4804	SUM 23L	Japan	Bar	0.09 **C**, 0.75–1.05 **Mn**, 0.04–0.09 **P**, 0.26–0.35 **S**, 0.10–0.35 **Pb**	
JIS G 3523	Class 1, No 1	Japan	Wire	0.09 **C**, 0.35–0.65 **Mn**, 0.020 **P**, 0.023 **S**, 0.03 **Si**, 0.20 **Cu**	

WROUGHT CARBON STEELS

specification number	designation	country	product forms	composition	mechanical properties (see page iv for explanation)
JIS G 3523	Class 1, No. 2	Japan	Wire	0.09 **C**, 0.35–0.65 **Mn**, 0.030 **P**, 0.030 **S**, 0.03 **Si**, 0.30 **Cu**	
NF A 35–053	FB 15	France	Wire, rod	0.08–0.22 **C**, 0.40–0.70 **Mn**, 0.050 **P**, 0.050 **S**, 0.011 N_2	**Hot or cold**: (≤30) **diam**, (510) max **TS**
NF A 35–051	FM 15 grade 1	France	Wire, rod	0.08–0.21 **C**, 0.40–0.70 **Mn**, 0.080 **P**, 0.055 **S**, 0.35 **Si**	
AMS 5061C		US	Bar, wire	0.08–0.20 **C**, 0.40–0.80 **Mn**, 0.040 **P**, 0.050 **S**	**Cold finished**: all **diam**, 70 (483) **TS**, 10 **El**
JIS G 3455	Class 1	Japan	Pipe: seamless	0.08–0.18 **C**, 0.30–0.60 **Mn**, 0.035 **P**, 0.035 **S**, 0.10–0.35 **Si**, 0.20 **Cu**	**As manufactured, cold finished and annealed or cold finished and normalized**: (≥8) **diam**, (343) **TS**, (177) **YS**, 35 **El**
JIS G 3461	Class 3	Japan	Tube: seamless or electric–resistance welded	0.08–0.18 **C**, 0.30–0.60 **Mn**, 0.035 **P**, 0.035 **S**, 0.35 **Si**, 0.20 **Cu**	**As manufactured, annealed or normalized**: (≥8) **diam**, (343) **TS**, (177) **YS**, 35 **El**
ANSI/ASTM A 512	1110	US	Tube: cold–drawn buttweld	0.08–0.15 **C**, 0.30–0.60 **Mn**, 0.04 **P**, 0.08–0.13 **S**	**Stress relieved annealed**: all **diam**, 63 (434) **TS**, 58 (400) **YS**, 15 **El**
DGN–B–201	Grade 1110	Mexico	Tube: butt–welded	0.08–0.15 **C**, 0.30–0.60 **Mn**, 0.040 **P**, 0.130 **S**	**Cold finished and annealed**: all **diam**, (434) **TS**, (399) **YS**, 15 **El**
AS 1443	AS 1443/CD4	Australia	Bar	0.08–0.15 **C**, 1.10–1.40 **Mn**, 0.050 **P**, 0.20–0.30 **S**, 0.10 **Si**	**Cold drawn or cold rolled**: (16–38) **diam**, (430) **TS**, (330) **YS**, 12 **El**
BS 1449: Part 1	Grade 10	UK	Plate, sheet, strip	0.08–0.15 **C**, 0.60–0.90 **Mn**, 0.045 **P**, 0.045 **S**, 0.10–0.35 **Si**	
AS 1442	Grade AS 1442/XS11L12	Australia	Bar, blooms, billets, slabs	0.08–0.15 **C**, 1.10–1.40 **Mn**, 0.050 **P**, 0.20–0.30 **S**, 0.10 **Si**	
AS 1443	Grade AS 1443/XS11L12	Australia	Bar	0.08–0.15 **C**, 1.10–1.40 **Mn**, 0.050 **P**, 0.20–0.30 **S**, 0.10 **Si**	
AS 1443	Grade AS 1443/XS1112	Australia	Bar	0.08–0.15 **C**, 1.10–1.40 **Mn**, 0.050 **P**, 0.20–0.30 **S**, 0.10 **Si**	
AS 1442	Grade AS 1442/XS 1112	Australia	Bar, blooms, billets, slabs	0.08–0.15 **C**, 1.10–1.40 **Mn**, 0.050 **P**, 0.20–0.30 **S**, 0.10 **Si**	
EURONORM 119–74, II	CB 10 FU KD	EURONORM	Wire, rod	0.08–0.13 **C**, 0.30–0.60 **Mn**, 0.040 **P**, 0.040 **S**, 0.007 **N**	**Cold rolled**: (≤40) **diam**, (470) max **TS**
EURONORM 119–74, II	CB 10 FS KD	EURONORM	Wire, rod	0.08–0.13 **C**, 0.30–0.60 **Mn**, 0.040 **P**, 0.040 **S**, 0.15 **Si**, 0.007 **N**	**Cold rolled or cold finished**: (2–100) **diam**, (470) max **TS**
EURONORM 119–74, II	CB 10 FF KD	EURONORM	Wire, rod	0.08–0.13 **C**, 0.30–0.60 **Mn**, 0.040 **P**, 0.040 **S**, 0.10 **Si**	**Cold rolled or cold finished**: (2–100) **diam**, (470) max **TS**
JIS G 3539	SWCH 10R	Japan	Wire	0.08–0.13 **C**, 0.30–0.60 **Mn**, 0.040 **P**, 0.040 **S**	**Cold drawn**: (>3–4) **diam**, (441) **TS**; **Annealed and cold drawn**: (>3–4) **diam**, (294) **TS**, 15 **El**
JIS G 3539	SWCH 10K	Japan	Wire	0.08–0.13 **C**, 0.30–0.60 **Mn**, 0.030 **P**, 0.035 **S**, 0.10 **Si**	**Cold drawn**: (>5) **diam**, (363) **TS**, 10 **El**; **Annealed and cold drawn**: (>5) **diam**, (343) **TS**, 14 **El**
DGN–B–301	1108	Mexico	Bar	0.08–0.13 **C**, 0.50–0.80 **Mn**, 0.040 **P**, 0.08–0.13 **S**, 0.10–0.20 **Si**	**Forged or hot rolled, cold rolled and cold finished**: all **diam**, (343) **TS**, (186) **YS**, 30 **El**
DGN–B–301	1109	Mexico	Bar	0.08–0.13 **C**, 0.60–0.90 **Mn**, 0.040 **P**, 0.08–0.13 **S**	**Forged or hot rolled, cold rolled and/or cold finished**: all **diam**, (343) **TS**, (186) **YS**, 30 **El**
DGN–B–301	1010	Mexico	Bar	0.08–0.13 **C**, 0.30–0.60 **Mn**, 0.040 **P**, 0.050 **S**, 0.10 **Si**	**Forged or hot rolled, cold rolled and cold finished**: all **diam**, (324) **TS**, (176) **YS**, 28 **El**
JIS G 3539	SWCH 10A	Japan	Wire	0.08–0.13 **C**, 0.30–0.60 **Mn**, 0.030 **P**, 0.035 **S**, 0.10 **Si**, 0.02 min **Al**	**Annealed and cold drawn**: all **diam**, (294) **TS**, 15 **El**
QQ–S–637A	1109	US	Bar	0.08–0.13 **C**, 0.60–0.90 **Mn**, 0.040 **P**, 0.08–0.13 **S**, 0.15–0.35 **Pb**	
QQ–S–637A	1110	US	Bar	0.08–0.13 **C**, 0.30–0.60 **Mn**, 0.040 **P**, 0.08–0.13 **S**, 0.15–0.35 **Pb**	
ASTM A 544	Grade 1110 mod	US	Wire	0.08–0.13 **C**, 0.30–0.60 **Mn**, 0.040 **P**, 0.050 **S**	
ASTM A 544	Grade 1109 mod	US	Wire	0.08–0.13 **C**, 0.60–0.90 **Mn**, 0.040 **P**, 0.04–0.09 **S**	

WROUGHT CARBON STEELS

specification number	designation	country	product forms	composition	mechanical properties (see page iv for explanation)
ASTM A 544	Grade 1108 mod	US	Wire	0.08–0.13 **C**, 0.50–0.80 **Mn**, 0.040 **P**, 0.04–0.09 **S**	
ASTM A 544	Grade 1110	US	Wire	0.08–0.13 **C**, 0.30–0.60 **Mn**, 0.040 **P**, 0.08–0.13 **S**	
ASTM A 544	Grade 1109	US	Wire	0.08–0.13 **C**, 0.60–0.90 **Mn**, 0.040 **P**, 0.08–0.13 **S**	
ASTM A 544	Grade 1108	US	Wire	0.08–0.13 **C**, 0.50–0.80 **Mn**, 0.040 **P**, 0.08–0.13 **S**	
AISI 1010		US	Plate	0.08–0.13 **C**, 0.30–0.60 **Mn**, 0.040 **P**, 0.050 **S**	
AISI 1110		US	Bar	0.08–0.13 **C**, 0.30–0.60 **Mn**, 0.040 **P**, 0.08–0.13 **S**	
AISI 1010		US	Bar	0.08–0.13 **C**, 0.30–0.60 **Mn**, 0.040 **P**, 0.050 **S**	
BS 970: Part 1	040A10	UK	Blooms, billets, slabs, bar, rod, forgings	0.08–0.13 **C**, 0.30–0.50 **Mn**	
BS 970: Part 1	050A10		Blooms, billets, slabs, bar, rod, forgings	0.08–0.13 **C**, 0.40–0.60 **Mn**	
BS 970: Part 1	060A10	UK	Blooms, billets, slabs, bar, rod, forgings	0.08–0.13 **C**, 0.50–0.70 **Mn**	
AS 1446	Grade AS 1446/C1010	Australia	Plate	0.08–0.13 **C**, 0.30–0.60 **Mn**, 0.040 **P**, 0.050 **S**	
AS 1446	Grade AS 1446/R1010	Australia	Plate	0.08–0.13 **C**, 0.30–0.60 **Mn**, 0.040 **P**, 0.040 **S**	
COPANT 330	1010	COPANT	Bar, shapes	0.08–0.13 **C**, 0.30–0.60 **Mn**, 0.040 **P**, 0.050 **S**	
COPANT 330	1109	COPANT	Bar, shapes	0.08–0.13 **C**, 0.60–0.90 **Mn**, 0.040 **P**, 0.08–0.13 **S**	
COPANT 330	1110	COPANT	Bar, shapes	0.08–0.13 **C**, 0.30–0.60 **Mn**, 0.040 **P**, 0.08–0.13 **S**	
COPANT 331	1010	COPANT	Bar	0.08–0.13 **C**, 0.30–0.60 **Mn**, 0.040 **P**, 0.050 **S**	
COPANT 331	1108	COPANT	Bar	0.08–0.13 **C**, 0.50–0.80 **Mn**, 0.040 **P**, 0.050 **S**	
COPANT 331	1109	COPANT	Bar	0.08–0.13 **C**, 0.60–0.90 **Mn**, 0.040 **P**, 0.050 **S**	
COPANT 331	1110	COPANT	Bar	0.08–0.13 **C**, 0.30–0.60 **Mn**, 0.040 **P**, 0.050 **S**	
COPANT 333	1010	COPANT	Wire, rod	0.08–0.13 **C**, 0.30–0.60 **Mn**, 0.040 **P**, 0.050 **S**	
COPANT 333	1011	COPANT	Wire, rod	0.08–0.13 **C**, 0.60–0.90 **Mn**, 0.040 **P**, 0.050 **S**	
MIL–S–16974E	No. 1010	US	Bar, billets, blooms, slabs	0.08–0.13 **C**, 0.30–0.60 **Mn**, 0.040 **P**, 0.050 **S**, 0.00–0.10 **Si**	
ASTM A 108	1010	US	Bar	0.08–0.13 **C**, 0.30–0.60 **Mn**, 0.040 **P**, 0.050 **S**	
ANSI/ASTM A 545	Grade 1010	US	Wire	0.08–0.13 **C**, 0.30–0.60 **Mn**, 0.040 **P**, 0.050 **S**	
ANSI/ASTM A 549	Grade 1010	US	Wire	0.08–0.13 **C**, 0.30–0.60 **Mn**, 0.040 **P**, 0.050 **S**	
ANSI/ASTM A 549	Grade 1108	US	Wire	0.08–0.13 **C**, 0.50–0.80 **Mn**, 0.04 **P**, 0.08–0.13 **S**	
ANSI/ASTM A 549	Grade 1109	US	Wire	0.08–0.13 **C**, 0.60–0.90 **Mn**, 0.04 **P**, 0.08–0.13 **S**	
ANSI/ASTM A 549	Grade 1110	US	Wire	0.08–0.13 **C**, 0.30–0.60 **Mn**, 0.04 **P**, 0.08–0.13 **S**	
MIL–S–11310E	1010	US	Bar	0.08–0.13 **C**, 0.30–0.60 **Mn**, 0.040 **P**, 0.050 **S**, 0.20 **Si**	
MIL–S–16788A	Class C1	US	Blooms, billets, slabs	0.08–0.13 **C**, 0.30–0.60 **Mn**, 0.040 **P**, 0.050 **S**	
COPANT 333	1108	COPANT	Wire, rod	0.08–0.13 **C**, 0.50–0.80 **Mn**, 0.040 **P**, 0.08–0.13 **S**	
COPANT 333	1110	COPANT	Wire, rod	0.08–0.13 **C**, 0.30–0.60 **Mn**, 0.040 **P**, 0.050 **S**	

WROUGHT CARBON STEELS

specification number	designation	country	product forms	composition	mechanical properties (see page iv for explanation)
ANSI/ASTM A 575	1010	US	Bar	0.08–0.13 **C**, 0.30–0.60 **Mn**, 0.04 **P**, 0.05 **S**	
DGN–B–301	1011	Mexico	Bar	0.08–0.13 **C**, 0.60–0.90 **Mn**, 0.040 **P**, 0.050 **S**, 0.10 **Si**	
DGN–B–301	1110	Mexico	Bar	0.08–0.13 **C**, 0.30–0.60 **Mn**, 0.040 **P**, 0.08–0.13 **S**, 0.10–0.20 **Si**	
AISI 1010		US	Wire, rod	0.08–0.13 **C**, 0.30–0.60 **Mn**, 0.040 **P**, 0.050 **S**	
AISI 1108		US	Wire, rod	0.08–0.13 **C**, 0.50–0.80 **Mn**, 0.040 **P**, 0.08–0.13 **S**	
AISI 1110		US	Wire, rod	0.08–0.13 **C**, 0.30–0.60 **Mn**, 0.040 **P**, 0.08–0.13 **S**	
ANSI/ASTM A 576	1109	US	Bar	0.08–0.13 **C**, 0.60–0.90 **Mn**, 0.040 **P**, 0.08–0.13 **S**	
ANSI/ASTM A 576	1110	US	Bar	0.08–0.13 **C**, 0.30–0.60 **Mn**, 0.040 **P**, 0.08–0.13 **S**	
ANSI/ASTM A 576	1010	US	Bar	0.08–0.13 **C**, 0.30–0.60 **Mn**, 0.040 **P**, 0.050 **S**	
ASTM A 689	1010	US	Bar	0.08–0.13 **C**, 0.30–0.60 **Mn**, 0.040 **P**, 0.050 **S**	
ANSI/ASTM A 29	1108	US	Bar	0.08–0.13 **C**, 0.60–0.80 **Mn**, 0.040 **P**, 0.08–0.13 **S**	
ANSI/ASTM A 29	1109	US	Bar	0.08–0.13 **C**, 0.60–0.90 **Mn**, 0.040 **P**, 0.08–0.13 **S**	
ANSI/ASTM A 29	1110	US	Bar	0.08–0.13 **C**, 0.30–0.60 **Mn**, 0.040 **P**, 0.08–0.13 **S**	
ANSI/ASTM A 29	1010	US	Bar	0.08–0.13 **C**, 0.30–0.60 **Mn**, 0.040 **P**, 0.050 **S**	
ANSI/ASTM A 29	1011	US	Bar	0.08–0.13 **C**, 0.60–0.90 **Mn**, 0.040 **P**, 0.050 **S**	
ASTM A 689	1109	US	Bar	0.08–0.13 **C**, 0.60–0.90 **Mn**, 0.040 **P**, 0.08–0.13 **S**	
ASTM A 689	1110	US	Bar	0.08–0.13 **C**, 0.30–0.60 **Mn**, 0.040 **P**, 0.08–0.13 **S**	
AS 1443	Grade AS 1443/K1011	Australia	Bar	0.08–0.13 **C**, 0.60–0.90 **Mn**, 0.050 **P**, 0.050 **S**, 0.10–0.35 **Si**	
AS 1443	Grade AS 1443/K1010	Australia	Bar	0.08–0.13 **C**, 0.60–0.90 **Mn**, 0.050 **P**, 0.050 **S**, 0.10–0.35 **Si**	
AS 1443	Grade AS 1443/S1010	Australia	Bar	0.08–0.13 **C**, 0.30–0.60 **Mn**, 0.050 **P**, 0.050 **S**, 0.35 **Si**	
AS 1442	Grade AS 1442/R1010	Australia	Bar, blooms, billets, slabs	0.08–0.13 **C**, 0.30–0.60 **Mn**, 0.040 **P**, 0.050 **S**	
AS 1442	Grade AS 1442/S1010	Australia	Bar, blooms, billets, slabs	0.08–0.13 **C**, 0.30–0.60 **Mn**, 0.050 **P**, 0.050 **S**, 0.35 **Si**	
AS 1442	Grade AS 1442/K1010	Australia	Bar, blooms, billets, slabs	0.08–0.13 **C**, 0.30–0.60 **Mn**, 0.050 **P**, 0.050 **S**, 0.10–0.35 **Si**	
AS 1442	Grade AS 1442/K1011	Australia	Bar, blooms, billets, slabs	0.08–0.13 **C**, 0.60–0.90 **Mn**, 0.050 **P**, 0.050 **S**, 0.10–0.35 **Si**	
DEF STAN 95–1/1	C1010	Canada	Bar	0.08–0.13 **C**, 0.30–0.60 **Mn**, 0.04 **P**, 0.05 **S**, 0.10 **Si**	
JIS G 3507	SWRCH 10R	Japan	Wire, rod	0.08–0.13 **C**, 0.30–0.60 **Mn**, 0.040 **P**, 0.040 **S**	
JIS G 3507	SWRCH 10A	Japan	Wire, rod	0.08–0.13 **C**, 0.30–0.60 **Mn**, 0.030 **P**, 0.035 **S**, 0.10 **Si**, 0.02 **Al**	
JIS G 3507	SWRCH 10K	Japan	Wire, rod	0.08–0.13 **C**, 0.3–0.60 **Mn**, 0.030 **P**, 0.035 **S**, 0.10–0.35 **Si**	
JIS G 3505	SWRM 10	Japan	Wire, rod	0.08–0.13 **C**, 0.30–0.60 **Mn**, 0.045 **P**, 0.045 **S**	
JIS G 4051	S 10C	Japan	Bar, wire, rod	0.08–0.13 **C**, 0.30–0.60 **Mn**, 0.030 **P**, 0.035 **S**, 0.15–0.35 **Si**, 0.30 **Cu**	
JIS G 4804	SUM 11	Japan	Bar	0.08–0.13 **C**, 0.30–0.60 **Mn**, 0.040 **P**, 0.08–0.13 **S**	
JIS G 4804	SUM 12	Japan	Bar	0.08–0.13 **C**, 0.60–0.90 **Mn**, 0.040 **P**, 0.08–0.13 **S**	
SIS 14 11 11	SIS 11 11–44	Sweden	Wire	0.08 **C**, 0.25–0.50 **Mn**, 0.04 **P**, 0.04 **S**	**Cold worked and wet drawn:** (0.5–1.5) **diam**, (780) **TS**

WROUGHT CARBON STEELS

specification number	designation	country	product forms	composition	mechanical properties (see page iv for explanation)
SIS 14 11 11	SIS 11 11–34	Sweden	Wire	0.08 **C**, 0.25–0.50 **Mn**, 0.04 **P**, 0.04 **S**	**Cold worked and dry drawn:** (0.5–1.5) **diam**, (780) **TS**
NF A 36–204	E 620	France	Plate	0.08 **C**, 0.3–1.3 **Mn**, 0.030 **P**, 0.030 **S**, 0.10–0.50 **Si**	**Normalized and tempered, quenched and tempered or aged:** (5–50) **diam**, (740) **TS**, (620) **YS**, 15 **El**
NF A 36–204	E 550, I	France	Plate	0.08 **C**, 0.3–1.3 **Mn**, 0.030 **P**, 0.030 **S**, 0.10–0.50 **Si**	**Normalized and tempered, quenched and tempered or aged:** (5–50) **diam**, (670) **TS**, (550) **YS**, 16 **El**
ANSI/ASTM A 735	Class 4	US	Plate	0.08 **C**, 1.15–1.95 **Mn**, 0.04 **P**, 0.025 **S**, 0.37 **Si**, 0.18–0.37 **Cu**, 0.02–0.10 **Nb**, 0.20–0.50 **Mo**	**As rolled:** ≤.65 **diam**, (655) **TS**, (550) **YS**, 18 **El**
NF A 36–204	E 500, I	France	Plate	0.08 **C**, 0.3–1.3 **Mn**, 0.030 **P**, 0.030 **S**, 0.10–0.50 **Si**	**Normalized and tempered, quenched and tempered or aged:** (5–50) **diam**, (620) **TS**, (500) **YS**, 17 **El**
ANSI/ASTM A 735	Class 3	US	Plate	0.08 **C**, 1.15–1.95 **Mn**, 0.04 **P**, 0.025 **S**, 0.37 **Si**, 0.18–0.37 **Cu**, 0.02–0.10 **Nb**, 0.20–0.50 **Mo**	**As rolled:** ≤.65 **diam**, (620) **TS**, (515) **YS**, 18 **El**
ANSI/ASTM A 735	Class 2	US	Plate	0.08 **C**, 1.15–1.95 **Mn**, 0.04 **P**, 0.025 **S**, 0.37 **Si**, 0.18–0.37 **Cu**, 0.02–0.10 **Nb**, 0.20–0.50 **Mo**	**As rolled:** ≤.65 **diam**, (585) **TS**, (485) **YS**, 18 **El**
ANSI/ASTM A 735	Class I	US	Plate	0.08 **C**, 1.15–1.95 **Mn**, 0.04 **P**, 0.025 **S**, 0.37 **Si**, 0.18–0.37 **Cu**, 0.02–0.10 **Nb**, 0.20–0.50 **Mo**	**As rolled:** ≤0.65 **diam**, (550) **TS**, (450) **YS**, 18 **El**
SIS 14 11 60	SIS 11 60–14	Sweden	Strip	0.08 **C**, 0.35 **Mn**, 0.030 **P**, 0.040 **S**, 0.03 **Si**	**Hot–rolled, one half hard:** (≤2) **diam**, (430) **TS**, (420) **YS**, 20 **El**
NF A 35–053	FB 5	France	Wire, rod	0.08 **C**, 0.25–0.45 **Mn**, 0.050 **P**, 0.050 **S**, 0.011 N_2	**Hot or cold drawn:** (≤30) **diam**, (420) max **TS**
NF A 35–053	FR 5	France	Wire, rod	0.08 **C**, 0.25–0.45 **Mn**, 0.044 **P**, 0.044 **S**, 0.009 N_2	**Hot or cold drawn and annealed:** (≤30) **diam**, (420) max **TS**
ISO 3575	05	ISO	Sheet: hot dipped, zinc–coated	0.08 **C**, 0.45 **Mn**, 0.03 **P**, 0.03 **S**	**As agreed:** all **diam**, (410) **TS**, 29 **El**
DIN 1614 Part 1	St W 24 (1.0335)	Germany	Strip	0.08 **C**, 0.40 **Mn**, 0.025 **P**, 0.025 **S**, 0.02 **Al**	**Hot rolled:** all **diam**, (410) **TS**, 28 in 80 mm **El**
DIN 1614 Part 1	St W 24 (1.0335)	Germany	Sheet	0.08 **C**, 0.40 **Mn**, 0.025 **P**, 0.025 **S**, 0.02 **Al**	**Hot rolled:** all **diam**, (410) **TS**, 28 in 80 mm **El**
JIS G 3539	SWCH 6A	Japan	Wire	0.08 **C**, 0.60 **Mn**, 0.030 **P**, 0.035 **S**, 0.10 **Si**, 0.02 min **Al**	**Cold drawn:** (>4–5) **diam**, (392) **TS**; **Annealed and cold drawn:** (>4–5) **diam**, (294) **TS**, 15 **El**
ISO 3573	Grade HR 4	ISO	Sheet	0.08 **C**, 0.45 **Mn**, 0.03 **P**, 0.03 **S**	**Hot rolled:** (<3) **diam**, (390) **TS**, 29 **El**
DIN 1614 Part 1	St W 22 (1.0334)	Germany	Sheet	0.08 **C**, 0.20–0.40 **Mn**, 0.025 **P**, 0.025 **S**	**Hot rolled:** all **diam**, (390) **TS**, 28 in 80 mm **El**
DIN 1614 Part 1	St W 23 (1.0334)	Germany	Strip	0.08 **C**, 0.20–0.40 **Mn**, 0.025 **P**, 0.025 **S**	**Hot rolled:** all **diam**, (390) **TS**, 28 in 80 mm **El**
ISO 3574	CR4	ISO	Sheet	0.08 **C**, 0.45 **Mn**, 0.03 **P**, 0.03 **S**	**Hot rolled, cold reduced, skin passed:** all **diam**, (340) **TS**, 37 **El**
SIS 14 12 25	SIS 12 25–01	Sweden	Forgings, rod, wire	0.08 **C**, 0.4–0.6 **Mn**, 0.03 **P**, 0.03 **S**, 0.2 **Cu**, 0.1 **Cr**, 0.009 **N**	**Normalized:** (≤100) **diam**, (310) **TS**, 30 **El**
AS 1594	Grade AS 1594/HRD	Australia	Sheet, strip	0.08 **C**, 0.40 **Mn**, 0.025 **P**, 0.030 **S**	**Hot rolled:** ≥3 **diam**, (300) **TS**, (200) **YS**, 34 **El**
SIS 14 11 60	SIS 11 60–12	Sweden	Strip	0.08 **C**, 0.35 **Mn**, 0.030 **P**, 0.040 **S**, 0.03 **Si**	**Hot–rolled, annealed:** (≤2) **diam**, (300) **TS**, (280) **YS**, 27 **El**
DGN–B–301	1006	Mexico	Bar	0.08 **C**, 0.25–0.40 **Mn**, 0.040 **P**, 0.050 **S**, 0.10 **Si**	**Forged or hot rolled, cold rolled and cold finished:** all **diam**, (296) **TS**, (165) **YS**, 30 **El**
JIS G 3539	SWCH 6R	Japan	Wire	0.08 **C**, 0.60 **Mn**, 0.040 **P**, 0.040 **S**	**Annealed and cold drawn:** all **diam**, (294) **TS**, 15 **El**
BS 1449: Part 1	Grade 1	UK	Plate, sheet, strip	0.08 **C**, 0.45 **Mn**, 0.025 **P**, 0.030 **S**	**Hot rolled:** all **diam**, (290) **TS**, (170) **YS**, 34 **El**; **Cold rolled:** all **diam**, (280) **TS**, (140) **YS**, 38 **El**

WROUGHT CARBON STEELS

specification number	designation	country	product forms	composition	mechanical properties (see page iv for explanation)
BS 1449: Part 1	Grade 2	UK	Plate, sheet, strip	0.08 **C**, 0.45 **Mn**, 0.030 **P**, 0.035 **S**	**Hot rolled**: all **diam**, (290) **TS**, (170) **YS**, 34 **El**; **Cold rolled**: all **diam**, (280) **TS**, (140) **YS**, 36 **El**
SIS 14 11 11	SIS 11 11–02	Sweden	Wire	0.08 **C**, 0.25–0.50 **Mn**, 0.04 **P**, 0.04 **S**	**Cold worked and annealed**: (0.5–1.5) **diam**, (290) **TS**
COPANT 38	EEP	COPANT	Sheet	0.08 **C**, 0.20–0.50 **Mn**, 0.035 **P**, 0.040 **S**	**Hot rolled**: (1.50–3.00) **diam**, (280) **TS**, (270) max **YS**, 33 **El**; **Cold rolled**: (0.30–0.50) **diam**, (270) **TS**, (240) max **YS**, 34 **El**
SIS 14 11 60	SIS 11 60–11	Sweden	Strip	0.08 **C**, 0.35 **Mn**, 0.030 **P**, 0.040 **S**, 0.03 **Si**	**Hot–rolled, annealed**: (≤2) **diam**, (280) **TS**, (260) **YS**, 32 **El**
JIS G 3141	Class 3	Japan	Sheet, strip	0.08 **C**, 0.40 **Mn**, 0.030 **P**, 0.030 **S**	**Cold rolled**: (≥0.25) **diam**, (275) **TS**, 36 **El**
DIN 1623 Sheet 1	St 14 (1.0338)	Germany	Strip	0.08 **C**, 0.02 **Al**	**Cold rolled**: all **diam**, (270) **TS**, (220) **YS**, 36 in 80 mm **El**
DIN 1623 Sheet 1	St 14 (1.0338)	Germany	Sheet	0.08 **C**, 0.02 **Al**	**Cold rolled**: all **diam**, (270) **TS**, (220) **YS**, 36 in 80 mm **El**
SIS 14 11 47	SIS 11 47–32	Sweden	Sheet	0.08 **C**, 0.45 **Mn**, 0.030 **P**, 0.030 **S**	**Solution treated and cold rolled**: (≤3) **diam**, (270) **TS**, 37 **El**
SIS 14 11 47	SIS 11 47–42	Sweden	Sheet	0.08 **C**, 0.45 **Mn**, 0.030 **P**, 0.030 **S**	**Solution treated and cold rolled**: (≤3) **diam**, (270) **TS**, 37 **El**
NF A 35–051	FM 5 grade 2	France	Wire, rod	0.08 **C**, 0.25–0.45 **Mn**, 0.062 **P**, 0.050 **S**, 0.012 N_2	
NF A 35–051	FM 5 grade 3	France	Wire, rod	0.08 **C**, 0.25–0.45 **Mn**, 0.044 **P**, 0.044 **S**, 0.009 N_2	
NF A 36–102	Fd 4	France	Strip	0.08 **C**, 0.028 **P**, 0.033 **S**	
ASTM A 424	Type II, composition B	US	Sheet	0.08 **C**, 0.20 **Mn**, 0.015 **P**, 0.040 **S**	
ASTM A 544	Grade 1106 mod	US	Wire	0.08 **C**, 0.30–0.60 **Mn**, 0.040 **P**, 0.04–0.09 **S**	
ASTM A 544	Grade 1106	US	Wire	0.08 **C**, 0.30–0.60 **Mn**, 0.040 **P**, 0.08–0.13 **S**	
AISI 1006		US	Plate	0.08 **C**, 0.25–0.45 **Mn**, 0.040 **P**, 0.040 **S**	
BS 970: Part 1	030A04	UK	Blooms, billets, slabs, bar, rod, forgings	0.08 **C**, 0.20–0.40 **Mn**	
BS 970: Part 1	040A04	UK	Blooms, billets, slabs, bar, rod, forgings	0.08 **C**, 0.30–0.50 **Mn**	
BS 970: Part 1	050A04	UK	Blooms, billets, slabs, bar, rod, forgings	0.08 **C**, 0.40–0.60 **Mn**	
AS 1595, Part 1	Grade CRD	Australia	Sheet	0.08 **C**, 0.40 **Mn**, 0.025 **P**, 0.030 **S**	**Cold rolled**: <3 **diam**, 38 **El**
AS 1595, Part 1	Grade CRE	Australia	Sheet	0.08 **C**, 0.40 **Mn**, 0.025 **P**, 0.030 **S**	**Cold rolled**: <3 **diam**, 40 **El**
TS 2348	CF–1/1.0311	Turkey	Wire, rod	0.08 **C**, 0.45 **Mn**, 0.060 **P**, 0.050 **S**	
TS 2348	C–8–2/1.0313	Turkey	Wire, rod	0.08 **C**, 0.45 **Mn**, 0.040 **P**, 0.040 **S**, 0.007 **N**	
AS 1446	Grade AS 1446/S1006	Australia	Plate	0.08 **C**, 0.40 **Mn**, 0.050 **P**, 0.050 **S**, 0.35 **Si**	
AS 1446	Grade AS 1446/R1006	Australia	Plate	0.08 **C**, 0.25–0.40 **Mn**, 0.040 **P**, 0.050 **S**	
COPANT 330	1006	COPANT	Bar, shapes	0.08 **C**, 0.25–0.40 **Mn**, 0.040 **P**, 0.050 **S**	
COPANT 331	1006	COPANT	Bar	0.08 **C**, 0.25–0.40 **Mn**, 0.040 **P**, 0.050 **S**	
COPANT 331	B 1006	COPANT	Bar	0.08 **C**, 0.45 **Mn**, 0.07–0.12 **P**, 0.060 **S**	
COPANT 333	1006	COPANT	Wire, rod	0.08 **C**, 0.25–0.40 **Mn**, 0.040 **P**, 0.050 **S**	
ANSI/ASTM A 545	Grade 1006	US	Wire	0.08 **C**, 0.25–0.40 **Mn**, 0.040 **P**, 0.050 **S**	
MIL–S–11310E	1006	US	Bar	0.08 **C**, 0.25–0.40 **Mn**, 0.040 **P**, 0.050 **S**, 0.20 **Si**	

WROUGHT CARBON STEELS

specification number	designation	country	product forms	composition	mechanical properties (see page iv for explanation)
COPANT 333	B 1006	COPANT	Wire, rod	0.08 **C**, 0.45 **Mn**, 0.07–0.12 **P**, 0.060 **S**	
SIS 14 12 25	SIS 12 25–00	Sweden	Forgings, rod, wire	0.08 **C**, 0.4–0.6 **Mn**, 0.03 **P**, 0.03 **S**, 0.2 **Cu**, 0.1 **Cr**, 0.009 **N**	
SIS 14 11 60	SIS 11 60–02	Sweden	Strip	0.08 **C**, 0.35 **Mn**, 0.030 **P**, 0.040 **S**, 0.03 **Si**	**Annealed**: (≤2) **diam**, (250) **YS**, 38 **El**
DGN–B–265	E.E.P	Mexico	Sheet	0.08 **C**, 0.40 **Mn**, 0.040 **P**, 0.035 **S**	
AISI 1006		US	Wire, rod	0.08 **C**, 0.25–0.40 **Mn**, 0.040 **P**, 0.050 **S**	
ANSI/ASTM A 29	1006	US	Bar	0.08 **C**, 0.25–0.40 **Mn**, 0.040 **P**, 0.050 **S**	
ASTM A 594	Grade 3	US	Forgings	0.08 **C**, 0.40 **Mn**, 0.025 **P**, 0.025 **S**, 0.20 **Si**, 0.02 **Al**	
SIS 14 11 57	SIS 11 57	Sweden	Sheet	0.08 **C**, 0.45 **Mn**, 0.03 **P**, 0.03 **S**	
AS 1443	Grade AS 1443/S1006	Australia		0.08 **C**, 0.40 **Mn**, 0.050 **P**, 0.050 **S**, 0.35 **Si**	
AS 1442	Grade AS 1442/S1006	Australia	Bar, blooms, billets, slabs	0.08 **C**, 0.40 **Mn**, 0.050 **P**, 0.050 **S**, 0.35 **Si**	
SIS 14 11 11	SIS 11 11–00	Sweden	Wire	0.08 **C**, 0.25–0.50 **Mn**, 0.04 **P**, 0.04 **S**	
DIN 17140	Grade D7–1	Germany	Wire, rod	0.08 **C**, 0.45 **Mn**, 0.060 **P**, 0.050 **S**	
DIN 17140	Grade D8–2	Germany	Wire, rod	0.08 **C**, 0.45 **Mn**, 0.045 **P**, 0.045 **S**, 0.007 **N**	
JIS G 3507	SWRCH 6R	Japan	Wire, rod	0.08 **C**, 0.60 **Mn**, 0.040 **P**, 0.040 **S**	
JIS G 3507	SWRCH 6A	Japan	Wire, rod	0.08 **C**, 0.60 **Mn**, 0.030 **P**, 0.035 **S**, 0.10 **Si**, 0.02 **Al**	
JIS G 3505	SWRM 6	Japan	Wire, rod	0.08 **C**, 0.60 **Mn**, 0.045 **P**, 0.045 **S**	
SFS 608		Finland	Sheet, plate	0.075 **C**, 0.45 **Mn**, 0.020 min **Al**	**Annealed**: (≤3) **diam**, (340) **TS**, 36 **El**
ANSI/ASTM A 29	M 1010	US	Bar	0.07–0.14 **C**, 0.25–0.60 **Mn**, 0.04 **P**, 0.05 **S**	
ANSI/ASTM A 575	M 1010	US	Bar	0.07–0.14 **C**, 0.25–0.60 **Mn**, 0.04 **P**, 0.05 **S**	
DIN 17200	Grade C 10	Germany	Blooms, slabs, billets, wire, bar, plate, sheet, strip, tube, forgings	0.07–0.13 **C**, 0.30–0.60 **Mn**, 0.045 **P**, 0.045 **S**, 0.15–0.35 **Si**	**Rolled or forged**: (11) **diam**, (638) **TS**, (392) **YS**, 13 **El**
DIN 17210	Grade Ck 10	Germany	Blooms, slabs, billets, wire, bar, plate, sheet, strip, tube, forgings	0.07–0.13 **C**, 0.30–0.60 **Mn**, 0.035 **P**, 0.035 **S**, 0.15–0.35 **Si**	**Rolled or forged**: (11) **diam**, (638) **TS**, (392) **YS**, 13 **El**
SIS 14 12 65	SIS 12 65–16	Sweden	Strip	0.07–0.13 **C**, 0.25–0.45 **Mn**, 0.030 **P**, 0.040 **S**, 0.30 **Si**	**Hot-rolled, annealed**: (≤2) **diam**, (600) **TS**, (590) **YS**, 11 **El**
EURONORM 119–74, III	C 10 KD	EURONORM	Wire, rod	0.07–0.13 **C**, 0.30–0.60 **Mn**, 0.035 **P**, 0.035 **S**, 0.10–0.40 **Si**	**Bright annealed**: (11) **diam**, (590) **TS**, (390) **YS**, 13 **El**
ISO/R 683/1X	Type 4Pb	ISO	Bar, wire, rod	0.07–0.13 **C**, 0.50–0.90 **Mn**, 0.06 **P**, 0.15–0.25 **S**, 0.15–0.40 **Si**, 0.15–0.35 **Pb**	**Cold finished**: (≤16) **diam**, (490) **TS**, (392) **YS**, 8 **El**
ISO/R 683/1X	Type 4	ISO	Bar, wire, rod	0.07–0.13 **C**, 0.50–0.90 **Mn**, 0.06 **P**, 0.15–0.25 **S**, 0.15–0.40 **Si**	**Cold finished**: (≤16) **diam**, (490) **TS**, (392) **YS**, 8 **El**
VSM 10648	C 10	Switzerland	Bar, sheet, plate	0.07–0.13 **C**, 0.30–0.60 **Mn**, 0.045 **P**, 0.045 **S**, 0.15–0.35 **Si**	**Cold drawn**: (≤5) **diam**, (490) **TS**, (392) **YS**, 7 **El**
VSM 10648	CK 10	Switzerland	Bar, sheet, plate	0.07–0.13 **C**, 0.30–0.60 **Mn**, 0.035 **P**, 0.035 **S**, 0.15–0.35 **Si**	**Cold drawn**: (≤5) **diam**, (490) **TS**, (392) **YS**, 7 **El**
ISO R 683/X1	1a	ISO	Bar	0.07–0.13 **C**, 0.30–0.60 **Mn**, 0.035 **P**, 0.020–0.035 **S**, 0.15–0.40 **Si**	**Carburized and hardened**: all **diam**, (490) **TS**, (294) **YS**, 13 **El**
ISO R 683/X1	1	ISO	Bar	0.07–0.13 **C**, 0.30–0.60 **Mn**, 0.035 **P**, 0.035 **S**, 0.15–0.040 **Si**	**Carburized and hardened**: all **diam**, (490) **TS**, (294) **YS**, 13 **El**
ISO R 683/X1	1b	ISO	Bar	0.07–0.13 **C**, 0.30–0.60 **Mn**, 0.035 **P**, 0.030–0.050 **S**, 0.15–0.40 **Si**	**Carburized and hardened**: all **diam**, (490) **TS**, (294) **YS**, 13 **El**
BS 970 Part 3	Steel 045M10	UK	Blooms, billets, bar, forgings	0.07–0.13 **C**, 0.30–0.60 **Mn**, 0.10–0.40 **Si**	**Hardened**: 3/4 **diam**, (385) **TS**, 18 **El**

specification number	designation	country	product forms	composition	mechanical properties (see page iv for explanation)
SIS 14 12 65	SIS 12 65–12	Sweden	Strip	0.07–0.13 **C**, 0.25–0.45 **Mn**, 0.030 **P**, 0.040 **S**, 0.30 **Si**	**Hot–rolled, annealed:** (≤2) **diam**, (360) **TS**, (320) **YS**, 25 **El**
DIN 1651	10 S 20 (1.0721)	Germany	Bar	0.07–0.13 **C**, 0.50–0.90 **Mn**, 0.060 **P**, 0.15–0.25 **S**, 0.10–0.40 **Si**	**Hot rolled**: all **diam**, (360) **TS**; **Normalized**: all **diam**, (350) **TS**, (315) **YS**, 25 in 80 mm **El**
DIN 1651	10 SPb 20 (1.0722)	Germany	Bar	0.07–0.13 **C**, 0.50–0.90 **Mn**, 0.060 **P**, 0.15–0.25 **S**, 0.10–0.40 **Si**, 0.15–0.30 **Pb**	**Hot rolled**: all **diam**, (360) **TS**; **Normalized**: all **diam**, (350) **TS**, (205) **YS**, 25 in 80 mm **El**
SIS 14 12 65	SIS 12 65–11	Sweden	Strip	0.07–0.13 **C**, 0.25–0.45 **Mn**, 0.030 **P**, 0.040 **S**, 0.30 **Si**	**Hot–rolled, annealed:** (≤2) **diam**, (330) **TS**, (300) **YS**, 30 **El**
ISO 683/XVIII	C10e	ISO	Bar, wire	0.07–0.13 **C**, 0.30–0.60 **Mn**, 0.035 **P**, 0.035 **S**, 0.15–0.40 **Si**	
ISO 683/XVIII	C10ea	ISO	Bar, wire	0.07–0.13 **C**, 0.30–0.60 **Mn**, 0.035 **P**, 0.020–0.035 **S**, 0.15–0.40 **Si**	
ISO 683/XVIII	C10eb	ISO	Bar, wire	0.07–0.13 **C**, 0.30–0.60 **Mn**, 0.035 **P**, 0.030–0.050 **S**, 0.15–0.40 **Si**	
ISO 683/XVIII	C10	ISO	Bar, wire	0.07–0.13 **C**, 0.30–0.60 **Mn**, 0.050 **P**, 0.050 **S**, 0.15–0.40 **Si**	
SIS 14 12 65	SIS 12 65–02	Sweden	Strip	0.07–0.13 **C**, 0.25–0.45 **Mn**, 0.030 **P**, 0.040 **S**, 0.30 **Si**	**Annealed**: (≤2) **diam**, (290) **YS**, 35 **El**
JIS G 4051	S 9CK	Japan	Bar, wire, rod	0.07–0.12 **C**, 0.30–0.60 **Mn**, 0.025 **P**, 0.025 **S**, 0.15–0.35 **Si**, 0.25 **Cu**	
AISI Grade 60		US	Plate	0.07 **C**, 1.25 **Mn**, 0.015 **P**, 0.020 **S**, 0.07 **Co**	**As rolled**: all **diam**, 70 (485) **TS**, 60 (415) **YS**, 15 in 8 in **El**
AISI Grade 50		US	Plate	0.07 **C**, 1.20 **Mn**, 0.015 **P**, 0.020 **S**, 0.06 **Co**	**As rolled**: 5/16–5/8 (8–16) **diam**, 60 (415) **TS**, 50 (345) **YS**, 18 in 8 in. **El**
ANSI/ASTM A 178	Grade A	US	Tube: electric resistance welded	0.06–0.18 **C**, 0.27–0.63 **Mn**, 0.050 **P**, 0.060 **S**	**Normalized**: 0.312 (7.94) **diam**, 60 (414) **TS**, 37 (255) **YS**, 30.00 **El**
COPANT R 199	Grade A	COPANT	Tube	0.06–0.18 **C**, 0.27–0.63 **Mn**, 0.050 **P**, 0.060 **S**	**Normalized**: (0.89–8.13) **diam**, (410) **TS**, (255) **YS**, 30 **El**
ANSI/ASTM A 192		US	Tube: seamless	0.06–0.18 **C**, 0.27–0.63 **Mn**, 0.048 **P**, 0.058 **S**, 0.25 **Si**	**Hot finished, as rolled, or cold drawn, annealed**: <0.200 (<5.08) **diam**, 47 (324) **TS**, 26 (179) **YS**, 35 **El**
JIS G 3461	Class 2	Japan	Tube: seamless or electric–resistance welded	0.06–0.18 **C**, 0.25–0.60 **Mn**, 0.035 **P**, 0.035 **S**, 0.35 **Si**, 0.20 **Cu**	**As manufactured, annealed or normalized**: (≥8) **diam**, (324) **TS**, (177) **YS**, 35 **El**
ANSI/ASTM A 226		US	Tube: electric resistance welded	0.06–0.18 **C**, 0.27–0.63 **Mn**, 0.050 **P**, 0.060 **S**, 0.25 **Si**	**Normalized**
NOM–B–212		Mexico	Tube: seamless	0.06–0.18 **C**, 0.27–0.63 **Mn**, 0.048 **P**, 0.058 **S**	
NOM–B–137	Grade A	Mexico	Tube: resistance–welded	0.06–0.18 **C**, 0.27–0.63 **Mn**, 0.050 **P**, 0.060 **S**	
NOM–B–138		Mexico	Tube: resistance–welded	0.06–0.18 **C**, 0.27–0.63 **Mn**, 0.050 **P**, 0.060 **S**, 0.25 **Si**	
COPANT R 201		COPANT	Tube: seamless	0.06–0.18 **C**, 0.27–0.63 **Mn**, 0.048 **P**, 0.058 **S**	
MIL–T–16286E	Class a	US	Tube: seamless	0.06–0.18 **C**, 0.27–0.63 **Mn**, 0.048 **P**, 0.058 **S**, 0.25 **Si**	
MIL–T–17188D	Class A	US	Tube: welded	0.06–0.18 **C**, 0.27–0.63 **Mn**, 0.050 **P**, 0.060 **S**	
COPANT R 196		COPANT	Tube	0.06–0.18 **C**, 0.27–0.63 **Mn**, 0.048 **P**, 0.058 **S**	
COPANT R 200		COPANT	Tube	0.06–0.18 **C**, 0.27–0.63 **Mn**, 0.050 **P**, 0.060 **S**, 0.25 **Si**	
NOM–B–96		Mexico	Tube: seamless	0.06–0.18 **C**, 0.27–0.63 **Mn**, 0.048 **P**, 0.058 **S**, 0.25 **Si**	
DGN–B–95		Mexico	Tube: seamless	0.06–0.18 **C**, 0.27–0.63 **Mn**, 0.048 **P**, 0.058 **S**, 0.20–0.35 **Cu**	
NF A 35–053	FB 10	France	Wire, rod	0.06–0.16 **C**, 0.30–0.70 **Mn**, 0.050 **P**, 0.050 **S**, 0.011 N_2	**Hot or cold drawn**: (≤30) **diam**, (480) max **TS**

WROUGHT CARBON STEELS

specification number	designation	country	product forms	composition	mechanical properties (see page iv for explanation)
NF A 35–051	FM 10 grade 2	France	Wire, rod	0.06–0.16 **C**, 0.30–0.70 **Mn**, 0.062 **P**, 0.050 **S**, 0.012 N_2	
NF A 35–053	FR 10	France	Wire, rod	0.06–0.15 **C**, 0.30–0.70 **Mn**, 0.044 **P**, 0.044 **S**, 0.009 N_2	**Hot or cold drawn and annealed**: (≤30) **diam**, (470) **TS**
NF A 35–051	FM 10 grade 3	France	Wire, rod	0.06–0.15 **C**, 0.30–0.70 **Mn**, 0.044 **P**, 0.044 **S**, 0.009 N_2	
NF A 35–554	XC 10	France	Plate	0.06–0.14 **C**, 0.30–0.50 **Mn**, 0.035 **P**, 0.035 **S**, 0.05–0.30 **Si**	**Hot rolled and normalized**: (≤16) **diam**, (350) **TS**, (215) **YS**, 28 **El**
NF A 35–553	XC 10	France	Strip	0.06–0.14 **C**, 0.30–0.50 **Mn**, 0.035 **P**, 0.035 **S**, 0.05–0.30 **Si**	**Normalized**: all **diam**, (350) **TS**, (215) **YS**, 31 **El**; **Quenched and tempered**: all **diam**, (490) **TS**, (295) **YS**, 17 **El**
DIN 17115	Grade USt 35–2	Germany	Bar, wire, rod	0.06–0.14 **C**, 0.40–0.60 **Mn**, 0.040 **P**, 0.040 **S**, 0.007 **N**	**Normalized**: (≤40) **diam**, (345) **TS**, (215) **YS**, 30 **El**
DIN 1652	C10 (1.0301)	Germany	Bar	0.06–0.12 **C**, 0.25–0.50 **Mn**, 0.045 **P**, 0.045 **S**, 0.15–0.35 **Si**	**Cold drawn**: all **diam**, (490) **TS**, (390) **YS**, 5 in 80 mm **El**
DIN 1652	Ck 10 (1.1121)	Germany	Bar	0.06–0.12 **C**, 0.25–0.50 **Mn**, 0.035 **P**, 0.035 **S**, 0.15–0.35 **Si**	**Cold drawn**: all **diam**, (490) **TS**, (390) **YS**, 5 in 80 mm **El**
DIN 17115	Grade RSt 35–2	Germany	Bar, wire, rod	0.06–0.12 **C**, 0.40–0.60 **Mn**, 0.040 **P**, 0.040 **S**, 0.03–0.25 **Si**	**Normalized**: (≤30) **diam**, (345) **TS**, (215) **YS**, 30 **El**
DIN 17115	Grade St 35–3	Germany	Bar, wire, rod	0.06–0.12 **C**, 0.40–0.60 **Mn**, 0.040 **P**, 0.040 **S**, 0.03–0.25 **Si**, 0.020–0.050 **Al**	**Normalized**: (≤30) **diam**, (35) **TS**, (22) **YS**, 30 **El**
AS 1442	Grade AS 1442/XR 1110	Australia	Bar, blooms, billets, slabs	0.06–0.11 **C**, 0.30–0.60 **Mn**, 0.050 **P**, 0.05–0.10 **S**	
NBN A 21–221	CB 9 FU KD	Belgium	Wire	0.06–0.10 **C**, 0.25–0.60 **Mn**, 0.035 **P**, 0.035 **S**, 0.007 **N**	
NBN A 21–221	CB 9FF KD	Belgium	Wire	0.06–0.10 **C**, 0.20–0.60 **Mn**, 0.035 **P**, 0.035 **S**, 0.30 **Si**, 0.007 **N**	
AISI Grade 80		US	Sheet	0.06 **C**, 1.25 **Mn**, 0.015 **P**, 0.020 **S**, 0.10 **Co**	**Hot rolled**: ≤0.097 (≤2.46) **diam**, 90 (620) **TS**, 80 (550) **YS**, 16 **El**
ANSI/ASTM A 699	Grade 2	US	Plate, bar, shapes	0.06 **C**, 1.50–2.20 **Mn**, 0.04 **P**, 0.025 **S**, 0.35 **Si**, 0.03–0.09 **Nb**, 0.25–0.35 **Mo**	**Precipitation heat treated**: all **diam**, 90 (620) **TS**, 75 (515) **YS**, 18 **El**
ANSI/ASTM A 699	Grade I	US	Plate, bar, shapes	0.06 **C**, 1.50–2.20 **Mn**, 0.040 **P**, 0.025 **S**, 0.35 **Si**, 0.03–0.09 **Nb**, 0.25–0.35 **Mo**	**Precipitation heat treated**: all **diam**, 90 (620) **TS**, 70 (485) **YS**, 18 **El**
ANSI/ASTM A 699	Grade 4	US	Plate, bar, shapes	0.06 **C**, 1.50–2.20 **Mn**, 0.040 **P**, 0.025 **S**, 0.35 **Si**, 0.03–0.09 **Nb**, 0.25–0.35 **Mo**	**Precipitation heat treated**: all **diam**, 85 (585) **TS**, 75 (515) **YS**, 18 **El**
ANSI/ASTM A 699	Grade 3	US	Plate, bar, shapes	0.06 **C**, 1.50–2.20 **Mn**, 0.04 **P**, 0.025 **S**, 0.35 **Si**, 0.03–0.09 **Nb**, 0.25–0.35 **Mo**	**Precipitation heat treated**: all **diam**, 85 (585) **TS**, 70 (485) **YS**, 18 **El**
AISI Grade 70		US	Sheet	0.06 **C**, 1.20 **Mn**, 0.015 **P**, 0.020 **S**, 0.08 **Co**	**Hot rolled**: ≤0.097 (≤2.46) **diam**, 80 (550) **TS**, 70 (485) **YS**, 18 **El**
AISI Grade 60		US	Sheet	0.06 **C**, 0.35 **Mn**, 0.015 **P**, 0.020 **S**, 0.03 **Co**	**Hot rolled**: all **diam**, 70 (485) **TS**, 60 (415) **YS**, 21 **El**
AISI Grade 60		US	Sheet	0.06 **C**, 0.35 **Mn**, 0.020 **S**	**Galvanized**: all **diam**, 70 (485) **TS**, 60 (415) **YS**, 22 **El**
EURONORM 119–74, II	CB 4 FF KD	EURONORM	Wire, rod	0.06 **C**, 0.20–0.40 **Mn**, 0.040 **P**, 0.10 **S**	**Cold rolled or cold finished**: (2–100) **diam**, (440) max **TS**
EURONORM 119–74, II	CB 4 FU KD	EURONORM	Wire, rod	0.06 **C**, 0.20–0.40 **Mn**, 0.040 **P**, 0.040 **S**, 0.007 **N**	**Cold rolled**: (≤40) **diam**, (420) max **TS**; **Cold finished**: (≤25) **diam**, (420) max **TS**
AISI Grade 50		US	Plate	0.06 **C**, 0.34 **Mn**, 0.015 **P**, 0.020 **S**, 0.05 **Co**	**As rolled**: 5/16 (8) **diam**, 60 (415) **TS**, 50 (345) **YS**, 18 in 8 in. **El**
AISI Grade 50		US	Sheet	0.06 **C**, 0.30 **Mn**, 0.015 **P**, 0.020 **S**, 0.03 **Co**	**Hot rolled**: all **diam**, 60 (415) **TS**, 50 (345) **YS**, 25 **El**
AISI Grade 50		US	Sheet	0.06 **C**, 0.35 **Mn**, 0.020 **S**	**Cold rolled**: all **diam**, 60 (415) **TS**, 50 (345) **YS**, 24 **El**
AISI Grade 50		US	Sheet	0.06 **C**, 0.35 **Mn**, 0.020 **S**	**Galvanized**: all **diam**, 60 (415) **TS**, 50 (345) **YS**, 24 **El**
AISI Grade 40		US	Sheet	0.06 **C**, 0.35 **Mn**, 0.020 **S**	**Cold rolled**: all **diam**, 50 (345) **TS**, 40 (280) **YS**, 28 **El**

specification number	designation	country	product forms	composition	mechanical properties (see page iv for explanation)
BS 970: Part 1	015A03	UK	Blooms, billets, slabs, bar, rod, forgings	0.06 **C**, 0.30 **Mn**	
AMS 5030C		US	Wire welding	0.06 **C**, 0.25 **Mn**, 0.040 **P**, 0.040 **S**, 0.15 **Cu**	
TS 2348	C5–1/1.0312	Turkey	Wire, rod	0.06 **C**, 0.40 **Mn**, 0.050 **P**, 0.050 **S**	
TS 2348	C–6–2/1.0314	Turkey	Wire, rod	0.06 **C**, 0.40 **Mn**, 0.040 **P**, 0.040 **S**, 0.007 **N**	
COPANT 333	1005	COPANT	Wire, rod	0.06 **C**, 0.35 **Mn**, 0.040 **P**, 0.050 **S**	
MIL–S–11310E	1005	US	Bar	0.06 **C**, 0.35 **Mn**, 0.040 **P**, 0.050 **S**, 0.20 **Si**	
AISI 1005		US	Wire, rod	0.06 **C**, 0.35 **Mn**, 0.040 **P**, 0.050 **S**	
ANSI/ASTM A 29	1005	US	Bar	0.06 **C**, 0.35 **Mn**, 0.040 **P**, 0.050 **S**	
ASTM A 594	Grade 4	US	Forgings	0.06 **C**, 0.40 **Mn**, 0.015 **P**, 0.015 **S**, 0.20 **Si**, 0.015 **Al**	
DIN 17140	Grade D5–1	Germany	Wire, rod	0.06 **C**, 0.40 **Mn**, 0.050 **P**, 0.050 **S**	
DIN 17140	Grade D6–2	Germany	Wire, rod	0.06 **C**, 0.40 **Mn**, 0.040 **P**, 0.040 **S**, 0.007 **N**	
ANSI/ASTM A 512	MT 1010	US	Tube: cold-drawn buttweld	0.05–0.15 **C**, 0.30–0.60 **Mn**, 0.04 **P**, 0.05 **S**	**Stress relief annealed**: all **diam**, 63 (434) **TS**, 58 (400) **YS**, 15 **El**
DGN–B–201	Grade MT1010	Mexico	Tube: butt-welded	0.05–0.15 **C**, 0.30–0.60 **Mn**, 0.040 **P**, 0.050 **S**	**Cold finished and annealed**: all **diam**, (434) **TS**, (400) **YS**, 15 **El**; **Normalized**: all **diam**, (276) **TS**, (138) **YS**, 35 **El**
COPANT 514	Grade TM 1010	COPANT	Tube: seamless	0.05–0.15 **C**, 0.30–0.60 **Mn**, 0.040 **P**, 0.050 **S**, 0.10 **Si**	**Hot finished**: (>323.9) **diam**, (315) **TS**, (215) **YS**, 15 **El**; **Cold finished**: all **diam**, (410) **TS**, (345) **YS**, 5 **El**; **Annealed**: all **diam**, (275) **TS**, (175) **YS**, 30 **El**; **Normalized**: all **diam**, (390) **TS**, (315) **YS**, 30 **El**
ANSI/ASTM A 254		US	Tube: copper-brazed	0.05–0.15 **C**, 0.27–0.63 **Mn**, 0.050 **P**, 0.060 **S**	**As brazed**: all **diam**, 42 (290) **TS**, 25 (172) **YS**, 25 **El**
ANSI/ASTM A 519	MT 1010	US	Tube: seamless	0.05–0.15 **C**, 0.30–0.60 **Mn**, 0.040 **P**, 0.050 **S**	
DGN–B–203	Grade MT 1010	Mexico	Tube: seamless	0.05–0.15 **C**, 0.30–0.60 **Mn**, 0.040 **P**, 0.050 **S**	
EURONORM 119–74, II	CB 7 FF KD	EURONORM	Wire, rod	0.05–0.10 **C**, 0.20–0.40 **Mn**, 0.040 **P**, 0.040 **S**, 0.10 **Si**	**Cold rolled or cold finished**: (2–100) **diam**, (470) max **TS**
EURONORM 119–74, II	CB 7 FU KD	EURONORM	Wire, rod	0.05–0.10 **C**, 0.20–0.40 **Mn**, 0.040 **P**, 0.040 **S**	**Cold rolled**: (≤40) **diam**, (450) max **TS**; **Cold finished**: (≤25) **diam**, (450) max **TS**
NBN A 21–221	CB 8 FU KD	Belgium	Wire	0.05–0.10 **C**, 0.25–0.60 **Mn**, 0.040 **P**, 0.040 **S**, 0.009 **N**	
NF A35–564	XC6 FF	France	Bar, wire, rod	0.04–0.09 **C**, 0.25–0.45 **Mn**, 0.030 **P**, 0.030 **S**, 0.10 **Si**	**Normalized**: all **diam**, (310) **TS**, (185) **YS**, 35 **El**
DGN–B–13	Class A, grade A4	Mexico	Wire	0.04–0.08 **C**, 0.33–0.43 **Mn**, 0.040 **P**, 0.060 **S**	
DGN–B–13	Class A, grade A2	Mexico	Wire	0.04–0.08 **C**, 0.33–0.43 **Mn**, 0.040 **P**, 0.060 **S**	
DGN–B–13	Class A, grade A1	Mexico	Wire	0.04–0.08 **C**, 0.33–0.43 **Mn**, 0.040 **P**, 0.060 **S**	
DGN–B–13	Class A, grade A3	Mexico	Wire	0.04–0.08 **C**, 0.33–0.43 **Mn**, 0.040 **P**, 0.060 **S**	
ANSI/ASTM A 663	80	US	Bar	0.04 **C**, 0.05 **Mn**	**Hot–rolled**: all **diam**, 80 (550) **TS**, 40 (275) **YS**, 17 **El**
ANSI/ASTM A 663	75	US	Bar	0.04 **C**, 0.05 **Mn**	**Hot–rolled**: all **diam**, 75 (515) **TS**, 38 (260) **YS**, 18 **El**
ANSI/ASTM A 663	70	US	Bar	0.04 **C**, 0.05 **Mn**	**Hot–rolled**: all **diam**, 70 (485) **TS**, 35 (240) **YS**, 18 **El**
ANSI/ASTM A 663	65	US	Bar	0.04 **C**, 0.05 **Mn**	**Hot–rolled**: all **diam**, 65 (450) **TS**, 32 (225) **YS**, 20 **El**
ANSI/ASTM A 663	60	US	Bar	0.04 **C**, 0.05 **Mn**	**Hot–rolled**: all **diam**, 60 (415) **TS**, 30 (210) **YS**, 22 **El**
ANSI/ASTM A 663	55	US	Bar	0.04 **C**, 0.05 **Mn**	**Hot–rolled**: all **diam**, 55 (380) **TS**, 28 (190) **YS**, 26 **El**

WROUGHT CARBON STEELS

specification number	designation	country	product forms	composition	mechanical properties (see page iv for explanation)
ANSI/ASTM A 663	50	US	Bar	0.04 **C**, 0.05 **Mn**	**Hot–rolle**: all **diam**, 50 (345) **TS**, 25 (175) **YS**, 30 **El**
ANSI/ASTM A 663	45	US	Bar	0.04 **C**, 0.05 **Mn**	**Hot–rolled**: all **diam**, 45 (310) **TS**, 22 (155) **YS**, 33 **El**
ASTM A 424	Type II, composition A	US	Sheet	0.04 **C**, 0.12 **Mn**, 0.015 **P**, 0.040 **S**	
AIR 9160/C 79	9160C281	France	Bar, forgings, sheet	0.03 **C**, 0.10 **Mn**, 0.015 **P**, 0.010 **S**, 0.10 **Si**, 0.30–0.50 **Ti**, 0.05–0.15 **Al**, 0.003 **B**, 7.50–8.50 **Co**, 4.60–5.20 **Mo**, 17.0–19.0 **Ni**, 0.02 **Zr**	**Aged (bar, forgings)**: (≤100) **diam**, (1720) **TS**, (1600) **YS**, 6 **El**
IS 226		India	Plate, bar	0.03 **C**, 0.005 **P**, 0.005 **S**	**Mill**: (6–20) **diam**, (410) **TS**, (250) **YS**, 23 **El**
ASTM A 424	Type I	US	Sheet	0.008 **C**, 0.60 **Mn**, 0.040 **S**	
JIS G 3133	SPP	Japan	Sheet, strip	0.008 **C**, 0.50 **Mn**, 0.040 **P**, 0.040 **S**	**Cold rolled and decarburized**: (<0.60) **diam**, 36 **El**
JIS G 3522	Grade B	Japan	Wire		**Cold drawn and patented**: (0.08) **diam**, (3187) **TS**
JIS G 3522	Grade A	Japan	Wire		**Cold drawn and patented**: (0.08) **diam**, (2893) **TS**
JIS G 3521	Class C	Japan	Wire		**Cold drawn**: (0.08) **diam**, (2795) **TS**
DIN 17223/Sheet 1	Grade II	Germany	Wire	0.030 **P**, 0.030 **S**, 0.12 **Cu**	**Patented drawn**: (0.07) **diam**, (2697) **TS**
DIN 17223/Sheet 1	Grade C	Germany	Wire	0.030 **P**, 0.030 **S**, 0.12 **Cu**	**Patented drawn**: (0.07) **diam**, (2550) **TS**
NS 13 613		Norway	Wire	0.030 **P**, 0.030 **S**, 0.12 **Cu**	**As drawn**: (0.10) **diam**, (2530) **TS**
JIS G 3521	Class B	Japan	Wire		**Cold drawn**: (0.08) **diam**, (2452) **TS**
JIS C 2506	SWPE	Japan	Wire		**Patented, hard drawn, tin coated**: (0.50) **diam**, (2256) **TS**
JIS G 3521	Class A	Japan	Wire		**Cold drawn**: (0.08) **diam**, (2108) **TS**
NS 13 612		Norway	Wire	0.040 **P**, 0.040 **S**, 0.25 **Cu**	**As drawn**: (0.30) **diam**, (2060) **TS**
SIS 14 17 57	SIS 17 57–05	Sweden	Wire		**Quenched and cold worked**: (2) **diam**, (2060) **TS**, 2.5 **El**
DIN 17223/Sheet 1	Grade B	Germany	Wire	0.040 **P**, 0.040 **S**, 0.25 **Cu**	**Patented drawn**: (0.30) **diam**, (2059) **TS**
SIS 14 17 57	SIS 17 57–08	Sweden	Wire		**Quenched and cold worked**: (6.3) **diam**, (1860) **TS**, (1580) **YS**, 3.5 **El**
SIS 14 17 52	SIS 17 57–07	Sweden	Wire		**Quenched and cold worked**: (6.4) **diam**, (1820) **TS**, (1550) **YS**, 3.5 **El**
DIN 17223/Sheet 2	Grade FD	Germany	Wire	0.030 **P**, 0.030 **S**, 0.12 **Cu**	**Quenched and tempered**: (1.00–1.10) **diam**, (1765) **TS**
NS 13 611		Norway	Wire	0.040 **P**, 0.040 **S**, 0.25 **Cu**	**As drawn**: (0.30) **diam**, (1720) **TS**
DIN 17223/Sheet 1	Grade A	Germany	Wire	0.040 **P**, 0.040 **S**, 0.25 **Cu**	**Patented drawn**: (0.30) **diam**, (1716) **TS**
JIS G 3522	Grade V	Japan	Wire		**Cold drawn and patented**: (2.00) **diam**, (1716) **TS**
JIS G 3560	Class B	Japan	Wire		**Oil tempered**: (2.0) **diam**, (1716) **TS**
JIS G 3560	Class A	Japan	Wire		**Oil tempered**: (2.0) **diam**, (1618) **TS**
CSA G12	Grade 220	Canada	Wire: zinc coated		**As drawn**: all **diam**, 220 (1517) **TS**, 4 **El**
JIS G 3109	Grade D, SBPD 130/145	Japan	Bar	0.030 **P**, 0.035 **S**, 0.30 **Cu**	**Hot rolled**: all **diam**, (1422) **TS**, (1275) **YS**, 5 **El**
JIS G 3561	SWO–V	Japan	Wire		**Cold drawn and oil tempered**: (2.0) **diam**, (1422) **TS**
JIS G 3109	Grade C, SBPR 110/135	Japan	Bar	0.030 **P**, 0.035 **S**, 0.30 **Cu**	**Hot rolled**: all **diam**, (1324) **TS**, (1079) **YS**, 5 **El**
CSA G12	Grade 180	Canada	Wire: zinc coated		**As drawn**: all **diam**, 180 (1241) **TS**, 4 **El**

WROUGHT CARBON STEELS

specification number	designation	country	product forms	composition	mechanical properties (see page iv for explanation)
JIS G 3537	Grade 1	Japan	Wire		**Galvanized**: all **diam**, (1226) **TS**
JIS G 3109	Grade C, SBPR 110/125	Japan	Bar	0.030 **P**, 0.035 **S**, 0.30 **Cu**	**Hot rolled**: all **diam**, (1226) **TS**, (1079) **YS**, 5 **El**
JIS G 3109	Grade C, SBPD 110/125	Japan	Bar	0.030 **P**, 0.035 **S**, 0.30 **Cu**	**Hot rolled**: all **diam**, (1220) **TS**, (1079) **YS**, 5 **El**
JIS G 3109	Grade B, SBPR 95/120	Japan	Bar	0.030 **P**, 0.035 **S**, 0.30 **Cu**	**Hot rolled**: all **diam**, (1177) **TS**, (932) **YS**, 5 **El**
ANSI/ASTM A 521	Class AH	US	Forgings	0.90 **Mn**, 0.050 **P**, 0.050 **S**	**Normalized, quenched and tempered**: 4–7 (102–178) **diam**, 165 (1140) **TS**, 135 (930) **YS**, 12 **El**
CSA G12	Grade 160	Canada	Wire: zinc coated		**As drawn**: all **diam**, 160 (1103) **TS**, 5 **El**
JIS G 3109	Grade B, SBPD 95/110	Japan	Bar	0.030 **P**, 0.035 **S**, 0.30 **Cu**	**Hot rolled**: all **diam**, (1079) **TS**, (932) **YS**, 5 **El**
JIS G 3109	Grade B, SBPR 95/110	Japan	Bar	0.030 **P**, 0.035 **S**, 0.30 **Cu**	**Hot rolled**: all **diam**, (1079) **TS**, (932) **YS**, 5 **El**
ANSI/ASTM A 722	Grades I and II	US	Bar	0.040 **P**, 0.050 **S**	**Hot rolled**: all **diam**, (1035) **TS**
ANSI/ASTM A 722	Grades I and II	US	Bar	0.040 **P**, 0.050 **S**	**Hot rolled**: all **diam**, (1035) **TS**
SIS 14 21 37	SIS 21 37–05	Sweden	Bar		**Quenched and tempered or cold worked and artificially aged**: (26) **diam**, (1030) **TS**, (780) **YS**, 3 **El**
JIS G 3109	Grade A, SBPR 80/105	Japan	Bar	0.030 **P**, 0.035 **S**, 0.30 **Cu**	**Hot rolled**: all **diam**, (1030) **TS**, (784) **YS**, 5 **El**
API Spec 5AX	S–135	US	Pipe: welded or seamless		**Quenched and tempered or normalized and tempered**: all **diam**, 145 (1000) **TS**, 135 (930) **YS**
ANSI/ASTM A 521	Class AG	US	Forgings	0.90 **Mn**, 0.050 **P**, 0.050 **S**	**Normalized, quenched and tempered**: 4–7 (102–178) **diam**, 140 (965) **TS**, 115 (795) **YS**, 14 **El**
QQ–W–345b	Type I	US	Wire: electrical		**Mill**: 0.1040 **diam**, (955) **TS**, 1.5 **El**
JIS G 3109	Grade A, SBPR 80/95	Japan	Bar	0.030 **P**, 0.035 **S**, 0.30 **Cu**	**Hot rolled**: all **diam**, (932) **TS**, (784) **YS**, 5 **El**
JIS G 3537	Class 2	Japan	Wire		**Galvanized**: all **diam**, (883) **TS**
API Spec 5AX	P–110	US	Pipe		**Quenched and tempered or normalized and tempered**: all **diam**, 125 (860) **TS**, 110 (760) **YS**
NF A 35–552	XC 55	France	Bar		**Quenched and tempered**: ($\leq$16) **diam**, (830) **TS**, (590) **YS**, 12 **El**; **Normalized**: ($\leq$16) **diam**, (740) **TS**, (430) **YS**, 14 **El**
API Spec 5AX	P–105	US	Tube		**Quenched and tempered or normalized and tempered**: all **diam**, 120 (825) **TS**, 105 (725) **YS**
ANSI/ASTM A 521	Class AF	US	Forgings	0.90 **Mn**, 0.050 **P**, 0.050 **S**	**Normalized, quenched and tempered**: 4–7 (102–178) **diam**, 115 (795) **TS**, 95 (655) **YS**, 16 **El**
API Spec 5AX	G–105	US	Pipe: welded or seamless		**Quenched and tempered or normalized and tempered**: all **diam**, 115 (790) **TS**, 105 (725) **YS**
ANSI/ASTM A 236	Grade H	US	Forgings	0.60–0.90 **Mn**, 0.045 **P**, 0.050 **S**, 0.15 min **Si**	**Normalized, quenched and tempered**: $\leq$7 **diam**, (790) **TS**, (515) **YS**, 16 **El**
JIS G 3465	Class 13	Japan	Tube: seamless	0.040 **P**, 0.040 **S**	**Cold or hot finished**: ($\geq$8) **diam**, (785) **TS**, (520) **YS**, 15 **El**
CSA G30.16	No.'s 3, 4, 5, 6, 7, 8	Canada	Bar	0.035 **P**, 0.045 **S**	**As rolled**: all **diam**, 80 (785) **TS**, 60 (589) **YS**, 13 in 8 in **El**
CSA G30.16	No.'s 14, 16, 18	Canada	Bar	0.035 **P**, 0.045 **S**	**As rolled**: all **diam**, 80 (785) **TS**, 60 (589) **YS**, 14 **El**
CSA G30.16	No.'s 9, 10, 11, 14, 16, 18	Canada	Bar	0.035 **P**, 0.045 **S**	**As rolled**: all **diam**, 80 (785) **TS**, 60 (589) **YS**, 12 in 8 in **El**

WROUGHT CARBON STEELS

specification number	designation	country	product forms	composition	mechanical properties (see page iv for explanation)
NF A 35–552	XC 48	France	Bar		**Quenched and tempered:** (≤16) **diam**, (780) **TS**, (550) **YS**, 13 **El**; **Normalized:** (≤16) **diam**, (670) **TS**, (370) **YS**, 17 **El**
CSA G12	Grade 110	Canada	Wire: zinc coated		**As drawn:** all **diam**, 110 (758) **TS**, 5 **El**
NF A 35–552	XC 42	France	Bar		**Quenched and tempered:** (≤16) **diam**, (740) **TS**, (520) **YS**, 14 **El**; **Normalized:** (≤16) **diam**, (630) **TS**, (355) **YS**, 19 **El**
API Spec 5AX	X–95	US	Pipe: welded or seamless		**Quenched and tempered or normalized and tempered:** all **diam**, 105 (725) **TS**, 95 (655) **YS**
ANSI/ASTM A 236	Grade H	US	Forgings	0.60–0.90 **Mn**, 0.045 **P**, 0.050 **S**, 0.15 **Si**	**Normalized, quenched, tempered:** 7–10 (178–254) **diam**, 105 (725) **TS**, 65 (450) **YS**, 18 **El**
ANSI/ASTM A 730	Grade H	US	Forgings	0.60–0.90 **Mn**, 0.045 **P**, 0.050 **S**, 0.15 min **Si**	**Normalized, quenched and tempered:** 7–10 (178–254) **diam**, 105 (725) **TS**, 65 (450) **YS**, 18 **El**
IS 5433	Grade YS+56	India	Pipe	0.04 **P**, 0.06 **S**	**Hot finished or cold drawn:** all **diam**, (690) **TS**, (550) **YS**, 18 **El**
NF A 35–049	A 70 Et	France	Bar, wire	0.050 **P**, 0.050 **S**	**Hot rolled (bar):** (≤30) **diam**, (690) **TS**, (365) **YS**, 11 **El**
NF A 33–102	AR 70,2	France	Billets, blooms, slabs	0.050 **P**, 0.050 **S**	**Annealed:** all **diam**, (690) **TS**, (360) **YS**, 11 **El**
API Spec 5	N–80	US	Casing and tube		**As agreed:** all **diam**, 100 (690) **TS**, 80 (550) **YS**
API Spec 5A	E	US	Pipe: welded or seamless		**As agreed:** all **diam**, 100 (690) **TS**, 75 (515) **YS**
NF A 35–552	XC 38	France	Bar		**Quenched and tempered:** (≤16) **diam**, (690) **TS**, (490) **YS**, 16 **El**; **Normalized:** (≤16) **diam**, (580) **TS**, (335) **YS**, 21 **El**
NF A 35–501	A 70 grade 2	France	Sheet, plate, bar	0.050 **P**, 0.050 **S**	**As rolled:** (3–30) **diam**, (690) **TS**, (365) **YS**, 10 **El**
ANSI/ASTM A 521	Class AE	US	Forgings	0.90 **Mn**, 0.050 **P**, 0.050 **S**	**Normalized, quenched and tempered:** 7–10 (178–254) **diam**, 100 (690) **TS**, 75 (520) **YS**, 19 **El**
DIN 17100	St 70–2 (1.0632)	Germany	Bar, plate	0.055 **P**, 0.055 **S**	**Normalized:** all **diam**, (690) **TS**, (365) **YS**, 10 **El**
DIN 17100	St 70–2 (1.0632)	Germany	Strip	0.055 **P**, 0.055 **S**	**Normalized:** all **diam**, (690) **TS**, (365) **YS**, 10 **El**; **Hot rolled:** all **diam**, (690) **TS**, (365) **YS**, 6 **El**
QQ–W–461g	AISI 1045	US	Wire		**Hard:** 0.328–0.499 **diam**, 100 (690) **TS**; **Annealed in process:** 0.328–0.499 **diam**, 80 (550) **TS**; **Annealed:** 0.328–0.499 **diam**, 100 (690) **TS**
CSA G30.12	Grade 75	Canada	Bar	0.05 **P**	**As rolled:** 1.7–2.3 **diam**, 100 (690) **TS**, 75 (518) **YS**, 6 **El**
ASTM A615	Grade 75	US	Bar		**As–rolled:** all **diam**, 100 (689) **TS**, 75 (517) **YS**
MIL–S–13281D	B–Grade 2	US	Bar, shape, plate, sheet, strip		**Hot rolled or cold rolled, annealed or normalized:** all **diam**, (689) **TS**, (310) **YS**, 20 **El**
TS 908	UDK 669.14.423/Fe 70	Turkey	Shapes	0.055 **P**, 0.055 **S**, 0.008 **N**	**Hot rolled:** all **diam**, (686) **TS**, (363) **YS**, 10 **El**
NF A 36–101	A 70,2	France	Strip	0.050 **P**, 0.050 **S**	**Hot rolled:** all **diam**, (686) **TS**, (363) **YS**, 11 **El**
TS 909	UDK 629.14–423/Fe 70	Turkey	Shapes	0.055 **P**, 0.055 **S**, 0.008 **N**	**Hot rolled:** all **diam**, (686) **TS**, (363) **YS**, 10 **El**
TS 913	UDK 669.14.423/Fe 70	Turkey	Bar	0.055 **P**, 0.055 **S**, 0.008 **N**	**Hot rolled:** all **diam**, (686) **TS**, (363) **YS**, 10 **El**
JIS G 3537	Class 3	Japan	Wire		**Galvanized:** all **diam**, (686) **TS**

WROUGHT CARBON STEELS

specification number	designation	country	product forms	composition	mechanical properties (see page iv for explanation)
JIS G 3439	Class 4, No. 11	Japan	Tube: seamless	0.040 **P**, 0.060 **S**	**Quenched and tempered**: all **diam**, (686) **TS**, (549) **YS**, 18 **El**
JIS G 3439	Class 3, No. 11	Japan	Pipe: seamless	0.040 **P**, 0.060 **S**	**Quenched and tempered**: all **diam**, (686) **TS**, (520) **YS**, 20 **El**
JIS G 3465	Class 12	Japan	Tube: seamless	0.040 **P**, 0.040 **S**	**Cold or hot finished**: (≥8) **diam**, (686) **TS**, (441) **YS**, 16 **El**
DIN 1651	60S20 (1.0728)	Germany	Bar		**Hot rolled**: all **diam**, (670) **TS**; **Normalized**: all **diam**, (660) **TS**, (365) **YS**, 9 in 80 mm **El**; **Quenched and tempered**: all **diam**, (830) **TS**, (570) **YS**, 7 in 80 mm **El**
COPANT 755	HA 60	COPANT	Wire		**As drawn or cold rolled**: (2.6–12.5) **diam**, (660) **TS**, (600) **YS**
JIS G 3439	Class 2, No. 11	Japan	Pipe: seamless	0.040 **P**, 0.060 **S**	**As rolled**: all **diam**, (657) **TS**, (382) **YS**, 20 **El**
SABS 657	Grade CD95	South Africa	Tube	0.06 **P**, 0.06 **S**	**Cold worked**: all **diam**, (655) **TS**, (545) **YS**
API Spec 5A	K–55	US	Casing		**As agreed**: all **diam**, 95 (655) **TS**, 55 (380) **YS**
API Spec 5A	D	US	Pipe: welded or seamless		**As agreed**: all **diam**, 95 (655) **TS**, 55 (380) **YS**
COPANT R 16	A T–60	COPANT	Bar	0.050 **P**, 0.060 **S**	**Hot rolled**: (5–40) **diam**, (650) **TS**, (590) **YS**, 10 **El**
COPANT 681	P 65	COPANT	Sheet, electrical		**Hot and cold rolled**: (0.35) **diam**, (650) **TS**, (400) **YS**, 12 **El**
BS 1775	CDS 35	UK	Tube		**Cold drawn**: all **diam**, (648) **TS**, (540) **YS**
IS 3601	CDS 55	India	Tube		**Cold drawn**: all **diam**, (647) **TS**, (539) **YS**
JIS G 3117	Class 2, SRR 40	Japan	Bar		**Rerolled**: all **diam**, (637) **TS**, (392) **YS**, 12 **El**
JIS G 3465	Class 2	Japan	Tube: seamless	0.040 **P**, 0.040 **S**	**Cold or hot finished**: (≥8) **diam**, (637) **TS**, 16 **El**
ASTM A615	Grade 60	US	Bar		**As–rolled**: all **diam**, 90 (621) **TS**, 60 (414) **YS**
CSA G30.8	Grade 60, No. 6	Canada	Bar		**As rolled**: 0.750 **diam**, 90 (621) **TS**, 60 (414) **YS**, 9 in 8 in **El**
CSA G30.8	Grade 60, No. 4	Canada	Bar		**As rolled**: 0.500 **diam**, 90 (621) **TS**, 60 (414) **YS**, 9 in 8 in **El**
CSA G30.8	Grade 60, No. 5	Canada	Bar		**As rolled**: 0.625 **diam**, 90 (621) **TS**, 60 (414) **YS**, 9 in 8 in **El**
CSA G30.8	Grade 60, No. 3	Canada	Bar		**As rolled**: 0.375 **diam**, 90 (621) **TS**, 60 (414) **YS**, 9 in 8 in **El**
CSA G30.8	Grade 60, No. 7	Canada	Bar		**As rolled**: 0.875 **diam**, 90 (621) **TS**, 60 (414) **YS**, 8 in 8 in **El**
CSA G30.12	Grade 60	Canada	Bar	0.05 **P**	**As rolled**: 1.7–2.3 **diam**, 90 (621) **TS**, 60 (414) **YS**, 9 **El**
CSA G 30.8	Grade 60, No. 10	Canada	Bar		**As rolled**: 1.270 **diam**, 90 (621) **TS**, 60 (414) **YS**, 7 in 8 in **El**
CSA G30.8	Grade 60, No. 9	Canada	Bar		**As rolled**: 1.128 **diam**, 90 (621) **TS**, 60 (414) **YS**, 7 in 8 in **El**
CSA G30.8	Grade 60, No. 8	Canada	Bar		**As rolledr**: 1.000 **diam**, 90 (621) **TS**, 60 (414) **YS**, 8 in 8 in **El**
CSA G30.8	Grade 60, No. 11	Canada	Bar		**As rolled**: 1.410 **diam**, 90 (621) **TS**, 60 (414) **YS**, 7 in 8 in **El**

specification number	designation	country	product forms	composition	mechanical properties (see page iv for explanation)
NF A 35–552	XC 32	France	Bar		**Quenched and tempered:** (≤16) **diam**, (620) **TS**, (430) **YS**, 17 **El**; **Normalized:** (≤16) **diam**, (550) **TS**, (315) **YS**, 23 **El**
ANSI/ASTM A 675	90	US	Bar	0.040 **P**, 0.050 **S**	**As hot–rolled**: all **diam**, 90 (620) **TS**, 55 (380) **YS**, 14 **El**
ANSI/ASTM A 236	Grade G	US	Forgings	0.60–0.90 **Mn**, 0.045 **P**, 0.050 **S**, 0.15 min **Si**	**Quenched and tempered:** ≤4 **diam**, (620) **TS**, (380) **YS**, 20 **El**
COPANT R 15	A 63	COPANT	Bar	0.050 **P**, 0.060 **S**	**Hot rolled**: (8–40) **diam**, (620) **TS**, (370) **YS**, 15 **El**
COPANT R 14	A 63	COPANT	Bar	0.050 **P**, 0.040 **S**	**Hot rolled**: (5–40) **diam**, (620) **TS**, (370) **YS**, 15 **El**
ANSI/ASTM A 521	Class AC	US	Forgings	0.90 **Mn**, 0.050 **P**, 0.050 **S**	**Normalized and tempered**: 7–20 (178–508) **diam**, 90 (620) **TS**, 58 (400) **YS**, 21 **El**
ANSI/ASTM A 521	Class AD	US	Forgings	0.90 **Mn**, 0.050 **P**, 0.050 **S**	**Normalized, quenched and tempered**: 7–10 (178–254) **diam**, 90 (620) **TS**, 65 (450) **YS**, 20 **El**
ASTM A 695	Type D, grade 50	US	Bar	0.040 **P**, 0.050 **S**, 0.15–0.30 **Si**, 0.15–0.35 **Pb**	**Hot rolled**: ≥3 (≥76.2) **diam**, 90 (620) **TS**, 50 (345) **YS**, 14 **El**
ASTM A 695	Type C, grade 50	US	Bar	0.040 **P**, 0.08–0.13 **S**, 0.30 **Si**	**Hot rolled**: ≥3 (≥76.2) **diam**, 90 (620) **TS**, 50 (345) **YS**, 14 **El**
ASTM A 695	Type A, grade 50	US	Bar	0.040 **P**, 0.050 **S**, 0.15–0.30 **Si**	**Hot rolled**: ≥3 (≥76.2) **diam**, 90 (620) **TS**, 50 (345) **YS**, 14 **El**
COPANT 681	P 60	COPANT	Sheet, electrical		**Hot and cold rolled:** (0.35) **diam**, (600) **TS**, (370) **YS**, 15 **El**
NF A 33–102	AR 60,1	France	Billets, blooms, slabs	0.077 **P**, 0.055 **S**	**Annealed**: all **diam**, (590) **TS**, (330) **YS**, 16 **El**
NF A 33–102	AR 60,2	France	Billets, blooms, slabs	0.050 **P**, 0.050 **S**	**Annealed**: all **diam**, (590) **TS**, (330) **YS**, 16 **El**
NF A 35–501	A 60 grade 1	France	Sheet, plate, bar	0.077 **P**, 0.055 **S**	**As rolled**: (3–30) **diam**, (590) **TS**, (335) **YS**, 15 **El**
NF A 35–501	A 60 grade 2	France	Sheet, plate, bar	0.050 **P**, 0.050 **S**	**As rolled**: (3–30) **diam**, (590) **TS**, (335) **YS**, 15 **El**
COPANT R 15	A 60	COPANT	Bar	0.050 **P**, 0.060 **S**	**Hot rolled**: (8–40) **diam**, (590) **TS**, (360) **YS**, 16 **El**
DIN 17100	St 60–1 (1.0540)	Germany	Bar, plate	0.088 **P**, 0.055 **S**	**Normalized**: all **diam**, (590) **TS**, (335) **YS**, 15 **El**
DIN 17100	St 60–1 (1.0540)	Germany	Strip	0.088 **P**, 0.055 **S**	**Normalized**: all **diam**, (590) **TS**, (335) **YS**, 15 **El**; **Hot rolled**: all **diam**, (590) **TS**, (335) **YS**, 10 **El**
DIN 17100	St 60–2 (1.0542)	Germany	Bar, plate	0.055 **P**, 0.055 **S**	**Normalized**: all **diam**, (590) **TS**, (335) **YS**, 15 **El**
ANSI/ASTM A 668	Class F	US	Forgings	1.10 **Mn**, 0.050 **P**, 0.050 **S**	**Quenched, tempered, or normalized, quenched, tempered**: >4 (>102) **diam**, 90 (620) **TS**, 55 (380) **YS**, 20 **El**
DIN 17100	St 60–2 (1.0542)	Germany	Strip	0.055 **P**, 0.055 **S**	**Normalized**: all **diam**, (590) **TS**, (335) **YS**, 15 **El**; **Hot rolled**: all **diam**, (590) **TS**, (335) **YS**, 10 **El**
NF A 35–049	A 60 Et	France	Bar, wire	0.050 **P**, 0.050 **S**	**Hot rolled (bar)**: (≤30) **diam**, (590) **TS**, (335) **YS**, 16 **El**
NBN 154.13F	A 60	Belgium	Sheet		**Annealed or normalized:** all **diam**, (588) **TS**
IS 908	UDK 669.14.423/Fe 60	Turkey	Shapes	0.055 **P**, 0.055 **S**	**Hot rolled**: all **diam**, (588) **TS**, (333) **YS**, 15 **El**
NF A 35–015	Fe E 34	France	Bar, wire, rod		**Hot rolled**: (5–40) **diam**, (588) **TS**, (334) **YS**, 16 **El**
NF A 36–101	A 60,1	France	Strip	0.077 **P**, 0.055 **S**	**Hot rolled**: all **diam**, (588) **TS**, (333) **YS**, 16 **El**
NF A 36–101	A 60,2	France	Strip	0.050 **P**, 0.050 **S**	**Hot rolled**: all **diam**, (588) **TS**, (333) **YS**, 16 **El**
TS 909	UDK 629.14–423/Fe 60	Turkey	Shapes	0.055 **P**, 0.055 **S**	**Hot rolled**: all **diam**, (588) **TS**, (333) **YS**, 15 **El**

specification number	designation	country	product forms	composition	mechanical properties (see page iv for explanation)
TS 913	UDK 669.14.423/Fe 60	Turkey	Bar	0.055 **P**, 0.055 **S**	**Hot rolled**: all **diam**, (588) **TS**, (333) **YS**, 15 **El**
TS 912	UDK 669.14–423/Fe 60	Turkey	Shapes	0.055 **P**, 0.055 **S**	**Hot rolled**: all **diam**, (588) **TS**, (333) **YS**, 15 **El**
JIS G 3251	Class 6	Japan	Blooms, billets	0.035 **P**, 0.040 **S**	**Rolled, forged, hot worked**: all **diam**, (588) **TS**, (294) **YS**, 20 **El**
JIS G 3465	Class 11	Japan	Tube: seamless	0.040 **P**, 0.040 **S**	**Cold or hot finished**: (≥8) **diam**, (588) **TS**, (373) **YS**, 18 **El**
JIS G 3201	Class 6	Japan	Forgings	0.035 **P**, 0.040 **S**	**Annealed and normalized or normalized and quenched and tempered**: all **diam**, (588) **TS**, (294) **YS**, 20 **El**
ANSI/ASTM A 496		US	Wire		**As rolled**: all **diam**, (586) **TS**, (517) **YS**; **As welded**: all **diam**, (552) **TS**, (483) **YS**
ANSI/ASTM A 236	Grade G	US	Forgings	0.60–0.90 **Mn**, 0.045 **P**, 0.050 **S**, 0.15 min **Si**	**Quenched and tempered**: 4–7 (102–178) **diam**, 85 (585) **TS**, 50 (345) **YS**, 20 **El**
ANSI/ASTM A 730	Grade G	US	Forgings	0.60–0.90 **Mn**, 0.045 **P**, 0.050 **S**, 0.15 min **Si**	**Quenched and tempered**: 4–7 (178–254) **diam**, 85 (585) **TS**, 50 (345) **YS**, 20 **El**
ANSI/ASTM A 521	Class CG	US	Forgings	0.90 **Mn**, 0.050 **P**, 0.050 **S**	**Quenched and tempered or normalized, quenched and tempered**: 7–10 (178–254) **diam**, 85 (585) **TS**, 50 (345) **YS**, 19 **El**
ANSI/ASTM A 668	Class E	US	Forgings	1.10 **Mn**, 0.050 **P**, 0.050 **S**	**Double normalized, tempered**: >8 (>203) **diam**, 85 (585) **TS**, 44 (305) **YS**, 25 **El**
NBN A 24–302	BE 50	Belgium	Bar		**As agreed**: (<40) **diam**, (570) **TS**, (490) **YS**, 12 **El**
NBN A 24–303	BE 50	Belgium	Wire		**As agreed**: all **diam**, (570) **TS**, (490) **YS**
ANSI/ASTM A 521	Class CF1	US	Forgings	0.90 **Mn**, 0.050 **P**, 0.050 **S**	**Double normalized and tempered**: 8–12 (203–305) **diam**, 83 (570) **TS**, 43 (295) **YS**, 23 **El**
API Spec 5LX	Seamless, grade X70	US	Pipe		**Non or cold expanded**: all **diam**, 82 (566) **TS**, 70 (483) **YS**
API Spec 5LX	Seamless, grade X70	US	Pipe		**Non or cold expanded**: all **diam**, 82 (565) **TS**, 70 (483) **YS**
NF A 35–016	Fe E 50	France	Bar		**Hot rolled or cold finished**: (≤16) **diam**, (564) **TS**, (490) **YS**, 10 **El**
MIL–S–13281D	B–Grade 1	US	Bar, shape, plate, sheet, strip		**Hot rolled or cold rolled, annealed or normalized**: all **diam**, (552) **TS**, (276) **YS**, 25 **El**
CSA G30.8	Grade 50, No. 11	Canada	Bar		**As rolled**: 1.410 **diam**, 80 (552) **TS**, 50 (345) **YS**, 7 in 8 in **El**
CSA G30.8	Grade 50, No. 4	Canada	Bar		**As rolled**: 0.500 **diam**, 80 (552) **TS**, 50 (345) **YS**, 9 in 8 in **El**
CSA G30.8	Grade 50, No. 3	Canada	Bar		**As rolled**: 0.375 **diam**, 80 (552) **TS**, 50 (345) **YS**, 9 in 8 in **El**
CSA G30.12	Grade 50	Canada	Bar	0.05 **P**	**As rolled**: 1.7–2.3 **diam**, 80 (552) **TS**, 50 (345) **YS**, 9 **El**
CSA G30.8	Grade 50, No. 10	Canada	Bar		**As rolled**: 1.270 **diam**, 80 (552) **TS**, 50 (345) **YS**, 7 in 8 in **El**
CSA G30.8	Grade 50, No. 9	Canada	Bar		**As rolled**: 1.128 **diam**, 80 (552) **TS**, 50 (345) **YS**, 7 in 8 in **El**
CSA G30.8	Grade 50, No. 8	Canada	Bar		**As rolled**: 1.000 **diam**, 80 (552) **TS**, 50 (345) **YS**, 8 in 8 in **El**

specification number	designation	country	product forms	composition	mechanical properties (see page iv for explanation)
CSA G30.8	Grade 50, No. 6	Canada	Bar		**As rolled**: 0.750 **diam**, 80 (552) **TS**, 50 (345) **YS**, 9 in 8 in **El**
CSA G30.8	Grade 50, No. 5	Canada	Bar		**As rolled**: 0.625 **diam**, 80 (552) **TS**, 50 (345) **YS**, 9 in 8 in **El**
CSA G30.8	Grade 50, No. 7	Canada	Bar		**As rolled**: 0.875 **diam**, 80 (552) **TS**, 50 (345) **YS**, 8 in 8 in **El**
MIL-S-13281D	B-Grade 1	US	Bar, shape, plate, sheet, strip		**Hot rolled or cold rolled, annealed or normalized**: all **diam**, (552) **TS**, (276) **YS**, 25 **El**
ANSI/ASTM A 675	80	US	Bar	0.040 **P**, 0.050 **S**	**As hot-rolled**: all **diam**, 80 (550) **TS**, 40 (275) **YS**, 17 **El**
ASTM A 499		US	Bar, shapes		**Hot-rolled**: all **diam**, 80 (550) **TS**, 50 (345) **YS**, 7 **El**
COPANT R 15	A 56	COPANT	Bar	0.050 **P**, 0.060 **S**	**Hot rolled**: (8–40) **diam**, (550) **TS**, (345) **YS**, 17 **El**
COPANT R 14	A 56	COPANT	Bar	0.050 **P**, 0.040 **S**	**Hot rolled**: (5–40) **diam**, (550) **TS**, (345) **YS**, 17 **El**
ANSI/ASTM A 82		US	Wire		**As drawn**: all **diam**, (550) **TS**, (485) **YS**
ANSI/ASTM A 521	Class AA	US	Forgings	0.90 **Mn**, 0.050 **P**, 0.050 **S**	**Annealed, normalized, or normalized and tempered**: 12–20 (305–508) **diam**, 80 (550) **TS**, 50 (345) **YS**, 22 **El**
ANSI/ASTM A 521	Class AB	US	Forgings	0.90 **Mn**, 0.050 **P**, 0.050 **S**	**Normalized and tempered**: 7–20 (178–508) **diam**, 80 (550) **TS**, 55 (380) **YS**, 24 **El**
ANSI/ASTM A 521	Class CF	US	Forgings	0.90 **Mn**, 0.050 **P**, 0.050 **S**	**Normalized and tempered**: 8–12 (203–305) **diam**, 80 (550) **TS**, 40 (275) **YS**, 21 **El**
ASTM A 695	Type D, grade 45	US	Bar	0.040 **P**, 0.050 **S**, 0.15–0.30 **Si**, 0.15–0.35 **Pb**	**Hot rolled**: ≥3 (≥76.2) **diam**, 80 (550) **TS**, 45 (310) **YS**, 16 **El**
ASTM A 695	Type C, grade 45	US	Bar	0.040 **P**, 0.08–0.13 **S**, 0.30 **Si**	**Hot rolled**: ≥3 (≥76.2) **diam**, 80 (550) **TS**, 45 (310) **YS**, 16 **El**
ASTM A 695	Type A, grade 45	US	Bar	0.040 **P**, 0.050 **S**, 0.15–0.30 **Si**	**Hot rolled**: ≥3 (≥76.2) **diam**, 80 (550) **TS**, 45 (310) **YS**, 16 **El**
QQ-W-46lg	AISI 1035	US	Wire		**Hard**: 0.328–0.499 **diam**, 80 (550) **TS**; **Annealed in process**: 0.328–0.499 **diam**, 70 (480) **TS**; **Annealed**: 0.328–0.499 **diam**, 85 (585) **TS**
COPANT 755	HA 50	COPANT	Wire		**As drawn or cold rolled**: (2.6–12.5) **diam**, (550) **TS**, (500) **YS**
SABS 657	Grade 79	South Africa	Tube	0.06 **P**, 0.06 **S**	**Cold worked**: all **diam**, (545) **TS**, (345) **YS**, 15 **El**
SABS 657	Grade CD79	South Africa	Tube	0.06 **P**, 0.06 **S**	**Cold worked**: all **diam**, (545) **TS**, (435) **YS**
NBN A 24–303	BE 506	Belgium	Wire		**As agreed**: (3.5–12.0) **diam**, (540) **TS**, (490) **YS**
IS 1161	Grade YS+32	India	Tube		**Normalized**: (2.00) **diam**, (540) **TS**, (310) **YS**
NF A 35–552	XC 25	France	Bar		**Quenched and tempered**: (≤16) **diam**, (540) **TS**, (365) **YS**, 18 **El**; **Normalized**: (≤16) **diam**, (470) **TS**, (285) **YS**, 26 **El**
BS 1775	HFS 20	UK	Tube		**Hot finished**: all **diam**, (540) **TS**, (309) **YS**, 17 **El**
BS 1775	CDS 20	UK	Tube		**Cold drawn**: all **diam**, (540) **TS**, (309) **YS**, 17 **El**
BS 1775	CDS 28	UK	Tube		**Cold drawn**: all **diam**, (540) **TS**, (432) **YS**
BS 1775	CEW 28	UK	Tube		**Cold drawn, annealed, normalized, as drawn, as drawn and tempered**: all **diam**, (540) **TS**, (432) **YS**

WROUGHT CARBON STEELS

specification number	designation	country	product forms	composition	mechanical properties (see page iv for explanation)
COPANT R 16	A T–50	COPANT	Bar	0.050 **P**, 0.060 **S**	**Hot rolled**: (5–40) **diam**, (540) **TS**, (490) **YS**, 10 **El**
IS 3601	CEW 44	India	Tube		**Cold drawn**: all **diam**, (539) **TS**, (431) **YS**
IS 3601	ERW 32	India	Tube: electric resistance welded		**As welded**: all **diam**, (539) **TS**, (314) **YS**, 17 **El**
IS 3601	CDS 44	India	Tube		**Cold drawn**: all **diam**, (539) **TS**, (431) **YS**
IS 3601	CDS 32	India	Tube		**Cold drawn**: all **diam**, (539) **TS**, (314) **YS**, 17 **El**
IS 3601	HFS 32	India	Tube		**Hot finished**: all **diam**, (539) **TS**, (314) **YS**, 17 **El**
IS 3601	HFW 32	India	Tube		**Hot finished**: all **diam**, (539) **TS**, (314) **YS**, 17 **El**
JIS G 3251	Class 5	Japan	Blooms, billets	0.035 **P**, 0.040 **S**	**Rolled, forged, hot worked**: all **diam**, (539) **TS**, (275) **YS**, 23 **El**
JIS G 3465	Class 1	Japan	Tube: seamless	0.040 **P**, 0.040 **S**	**Cold or hot finished**: (≥8) **diam**, (539) **TS**, 18 **El**
JIS G 3201	Class 5	Japan	Forgings	0.035 **P**, 0.040 **S**	**Annealed and normalized or normalized and quenched and tempered**: all **diam**, (539) **TS**, (275) **YS**, 23 **El**
API Spec 5LX	Seamless, grade X65	US	Pipe		**Non or cold expanded**: all **diam**, 77 (530) **TS**, 65 (448) **YS**
API Spec 5LX	Seamless, grade X65	US	Pipe		**Non or cold expanded**: all **diam**, 77 (530) **TS**, 65 (448) **YS**
ANSI/ASTM A 521	Class CE	US	Forgings	0.90 **Mn**, 0.050 **P**, 0.050 **S**	**Annealed, normalized or normalized and tempered**: 8–12 (203–305) **diam**, 75 (520) **TS**, 37 (290) **YS**, 22 **El**
JIS G 3123	SS41B–D (hexagon)	Japan	Bar		**Cold finished**: (5.5–9) **diam**, (520) **TS**
JIS G 3439	Class 3, No. 11	Japan	Tube: seamless	0.040 **P**, 0.060 **S**	**As rolled**: all **diam**, (520) **TS**, (382) **YS**, 25 **El**
JIS G 3439	Class 1, No. 11	Japan	Pipe: seamless	0.040 **P**, 0.060 **S**	**As rolled**: all **diam**, (520) **TS**, (314) **YS**, 22 **El**
DGN–B–93	Class III, subclass III–1	Mexico	Plate, sheet	1.40 **Mn**, 0.035 **P**, 0.040 **S**, 0.30 **Si**	**As agreed**: (25–51) **diam**, (517) **TS**, (275) **YS**, 21 **El**
CSA G38		Canada	Forgings	0.40–1.00 **Mn**, 0.050 **P**, 0.050 **S**	**Annealed or normalized**: ≤8.20 **diam**, 75 (515) **TS**, 35 (260) **YS**, 19 **El**
IS 5433	Grade YS+39	India	Pipe	0.04 **P**, 0.06 **S**	**Hot finished or cold drawn**: all **diam**, (515) **TS**, (380) **YS**, 25 **El**
API Spec 5A	J–55	US	Casing and tube		**As agreed**: all **diam**, 75 (515) **TS**, 55 (380) **YS**
ANSI/ASTM A 675	75	US	Bar	0.040 **P**, 0.050 **S**	**As hot–rolled**: all **diam**, 75 (515) **TS**, 38 (260) **YS**, 18 **El**
ANSI/ASTM A 641		US	Wire		**Soft**: 0.035–0.079 (0.89–2.02) **diam**, 75 (515) max **TS**; **Medium**: 0.035–0.079 (0.89–2.02) **diam**, 70 (485) **TS**; **Hard**: 0.035–0.079 (0.89–2.02) **diam**, 90 (620) **TS**
CSA G38		Canada	Forgings	0.40–1.00 **Mn**, 0.05 **P**, 0.05 **S**	**Annealed or normalized**: ≤8 **diam**, (515) **TS**, (260) **YS**, 24 **El**
ANSI/ASTM A 668	Class D	US	Forgings	1.10 **Mn**, 0.050 **P**, 0.050 **S**	**Normalized, annealed, or normalized, tempered**: >8 (>203) **diam**, 75 (515) **TS**, 37 (260) **YS**, 24 **El**
NBN 293	A 52	Belgium	Bar		**As rolled**: (≥9.5) **diam**, (510) **TS**, (333) **YS**
NBN 154.13F	A 52	Belgium	Sheet		**Mill**: all **diam**, (510) **TS**, (353) **YS**
ISO/R 630	Grade Fe 33 O	ISO	Plate, bar		**As rolled**: (≤16) **diam**, (510) max **TS**

WROUGHT CARBON STEELS

specification number	designation	country	product forms	composition	mechanical properties (see page iv for explanation)
DIN 488	BSt 42/50 RU	Germany	Bar	0.60 **Si**	**Hot rolled**: (6–28) **diam**, (500) **TS**, (420) **YS**, 10 **El**
COPANT 681	P 50	COPANT	Sheet, electrical		**Hot and cold rolled**: (0.35) **diam**, (500) **TS**, (310) **YS**, 19 **El**
COPANT R 16	A T–46	COPANT	Bar	0.050 **P**, 0.060 **S**	**Hot rolled**: (5–40) **diam**, (495) **TS**, (450) **YS**, 11 **El**
BS 1775	HFW 23	UK	Tube		**Hot finished**: all **diam**, (494) **TS**, (355) **YS**, 19 **El**
BS 1775	HFS 23	UK	Tube		**Hot finished**: all **diam**, (494) **TS**, (355) **YS**, 19 **El**
BS 1775	CDS 23	UK	Tube		**Cold drawn**: all **diam**, (494) **TS**, (355) **YS**
BS 1775	ERW 23	UK	Tube		**As welded**: all **diam**, (494) **TS**, (355) **YS**, 19 **El**
BS 1775	CEW 23	UK	Tube		**Cold drawn, annealed, normalized, as drawn, as drawn and tempered**: all **diam**, (494) **TS**, (355) **YS**
NBN 293	A 50	Belgium	Bar		**As rolled**: ($\geq$9.5) **diam**, (490) **TS**, (265) **YS**
NBN A 24–302	BE 40	Belgium	Bar		**As agreed**: (<40) **diam**, (490) **TS**, (390) **YS**, 14 **El**
NBN 770F	Fe P 00	Belgium	Sheet		**Cold rolled**: all **diam**, (490) **TS**
NBN 770F	Fe P 10	Belgium	Sheet		**Hot rolled**: (<2) **diam**, (490) **TS**
NBN 770F	Fe P 20	Belgium	Sheet		**Hot rolled**: (<2) **diam**, (490) **TS**
NBN 154.13F	A 00	Belgium	Sheet		**Annealed or normalized**: all **diam**, (490) **TS**
NBN 154.13 F	A 50	Belgium	Sheet		**Annealed or normalized**: all **diam**, (490) **TS**
TS 908	UDK 669.14.423/Fe 50	Turkey	Shapes	0.055 **P**, 0.055 **S**	**Hot rolled**: all **diam**, (490) **TS**, (294) **YS**, 20 **El**
NF A 35–049	A 50 Et	France	Bar, wire, rod	0.050 **P**, 0.050 **S**	**Hot rolled (bar)**: ($\leq$30) **diam**, (490) **TS**, (285) **YS**, 21 **El**
NF A 33–102	AR 50,1	France	Billets, blooms, slabs	0.077 **P**, 0.055 **S**	**Annealed**: all **diam**, (490) **TS**, (290) **YS**, 21 **El**
NF A 33–102	AR 50,2	France	Billets, blooms, slabs	0.050 **P**, 0.050 **S**	**Annealed**: all **diam**, (490) **TS**, (290) **YS**, 21 **El**
NF A 36–101	A 50,1	France	Strip	0.077 **P**, 0.055 **S**	**Hot rolled**: all **diam**, (490) **TS**, (294) **YS**, 21 **El**
NF A 36–101	A 50,2	France	Strip	0.050 **P**, 0.050 **S**	**Hot rolled**: all **diam**, (490) **TS**, (294) **YS**, 21 **El**
TS 909	UDK 629.14–423/Fe 50	Turkey	Shapes	0.055 **P**, 0.055 **S**	**Hot rolled**: all **diam**, (490) **TS**, (294) **YS**, 20 **El**
TS 913	UDK 669.14.423/Fe 50	Turkey	Bar	0.055 **P**, 0.055 **S**	**Hot rolled**: all **diam**, (490) **TS**, (294) **YS**, 20 **El**
TS 912	UDK 669.14–423/Fe 50	Turkey	Shapes	0.055 **P**, 0.055 **S**	**Hot rolled**: all **diam**, (490) **TS**, (294) **YS**, 20 **El**
NF A 35–501	A 50 grade 1	France	Sheet, plate, bar	0.077 **P**, 0.055 **S**	**As rolled**: (3–30) **diam**, (490) **TS**, (295) **YS**, 19 **El**
NF A 35–501	A 50 grade 2	France	Sheet, plate, bar	0.050 **P**, 0.050 **S**	**As rolled**: (3–30) **diam**, (490) **TS**, (295) **YS**, 19 **El**
COPANT R 18	A 50–P	COPANT	Bar	0.15 **P**, 0.060 **S**	**Hot rolled**: (5–48) **diam**, (490) **TS**, (265) **YS**, 22 **El**
COPANT R 19	A 50–TP	COPANT	Bar	0.13 **P**, 0.23 **S**	**Hot rolled**: all **diam**, (490) **TS**, (265) **YS**, 20 **El**
COPANT R 15	A 50	COPANT	Bar	0.050 **P**, 0.060 **S**	**Hot rolled**: (8–40) **diam**, (490) **TS**, (315) **YS**, 20 **El**
COPANT R 14	A 50	COPANT	Bar	0.050 **P**, 0.040 **S**	**Hot rolled**: (5–40) **diam**, (490) **TS**, (315) **YS**, 20 **El**
JIS G 3251	Class 4	Japan	Blooms, billets	0.035 **P**, 0.040 **S**	**Rolled, forged, hot worked**: all **diam**, (490) **TS**, (245) **YS**, 25 **El**
DIN 17100	St 50–1 (1.0530)	Germany	Bar, plate	0.088 **P**, 0.055 **S**	**Normalized**: all **diam**, (490) **TS**, (295) **YS**, 20 **El**

specification number	designation	country	product forms	composition	mechanical properties (see page iv for explanation)
DIN 17100	St 50–1 (1.0530)	Germany	Strip	0.088 **P**, 0.055 **S**	**Normalized**: all **diam**, (490) **TS**, (295) **YS**, 20 **El**; **Hot rolled**: all **diam**, (490) **TS**, (295) **YS**, 14 **El**
DIN 17100	St 50–2 (1.0532)	Germany	Bar, plate	0.055 **P**, 0.055 **S**	**Normalized**: all **diam**, (490) **TS**, (295) **YS**, 20 **El**
DIN 17100	St 50–2 (1.0532)	Germany	Strip	0.055 **P**, 0.055 **S**	**Normalized**: all **diam**, (490) **TS**, (295) **YS**, 20 **El**; **Hot rolled**: all **diam**, (490) **TS**, (295) **YS**, 14 **El**
JIS G 3101	Class 3	Japan	Plate, strip, bar, shapes	0.050 **P**, 0.050 **S**	**Hot rolled**: ($\leq$5) **diam**, (490) **TS**, (284) **YS**, 19 **El**
JIS G 3201	Class 4	Japan	Forgings	0.035 **P**, 0.040 **S**	**Annealed and normalized or normalized and quenched and tempered**: all **diam**, (490) **TS**, (245) **YS**, 25 **El**
ANSI/ASTM A 675	70	US	Bar	0.040 **P**, 0.050 **S**	**As hot–rolled**: all **diam**, 70 (485) **TS**, 35 (240) **YS**, 18 **El**
ASTM A 695	Type D, grade 40	US	Bar	0.040 **P**, 0.050 **S**, 0.15–0.30 **Si**, 0.15–0.35 **Pb**	**Hot rolled**: $\geq$3 ($\geq$76.2) **diam**, 70 (485) **TS**, 40 (275) **YS**, 17 **El**
ASTM A 695	Type C, grade 40	US	Bar	0.040 **P**, 0.08–0.13 **S**, 0.30 **Si**	**Hot rolled**: $\geq$3 ($\geq$76.2) **diam**, 70 (485) **TS**, 40 (275) **YS**, 17 **El**
ASTM A 695	Type A, grade 40	US	Bar	0.040 **P**, 0.050 **S**, 0.15–0.30 **Si**	**Hot rolled**: $\geq$3 ($\geq$76.2) **diam**, 70 (485) **TS**, 40 (275) **YS**, 17 **El**
ASTM A615	Grade 40	US	Bar		**As–rolled**: all **diam**, 70 (483) **TS**, 40 (276) **YS**
ASTM A 672	A 516–70	US	Pipe: electric fusion welded		**Normalized, quenched, tempered**: all **diam**, 70 (483) **TS**
ASTM A 672	A 515–70	US	Pipe: electric fusion welded		**Normalized**: all **diam**, 70 (483) **TS**
ANSI/ASTM A 671	A 515 (70)	US	Pipe: electric fusion welded		**Normalized**: all **diam**, 70 (483) **TS**
ANSI/ASTM A 671	A 516 (70)	US	Pipe: electric fusion welded		**Normalized, quenched, tempered**: all **diam**, 70 (483) **TS**
CSA G30.12	Grade 40	Canada	Bar	0.05 **P**	**As rolled**: 1.7–2.3 **diam**, 70 (483) **TS**, 40 (276) **YS**, 12 **El**
CSA G30.8	Grade 40, No. 6	Canada	Bar		**As rolled**: 0.750 **diam**, 70 (483) **TS**, 40 (276) **YS**, 12 in 8 in **El**
CSA G30.8	Grade 40, No. 7	Canada	Bar		**As rolled**: 0.875 **diam**, 70 (483) **TS**, 40 (276) **YS**, 11 in 8 in **El**
CSA G 30.8	Grade 40, No. 8		Bar		**As rolled**: 1.000 **diam**, 70 (483) **TS**, 40 (276) **YS**, 10 in 8 in **El**
CSA G30.8	Grade 40, No. 9	Canada	Bar		**As rolled**: 1.128 **diam**, 70 (483) **TS**, 40 (276) **YS**, 10 in 8 in **El**
CSA G30.8	Grade 40, No. 10	Canada	Bar		**As rolled**: 1.270 **diam**, 70 (483) **TS**, 40 (276) **YS**, 10 in 8 in **El**
CSA G30.8	Grade 40, No. 11	Canada	Bar		**As rolled**: 1.410 **diam**, 70 (483) **TS**, 40 (276) **YS**, 10 in 8 in **El**
CSA G30.8	Grade 40, No.3	Canada	Bar		**As rolled**: 0.376 **diam**, 70 (483) **TS**, 40 (276) **YS**, 11 in 8 in **El**
CSA G30.8	Grade 40, No. 4	Canada	Bar		**As rolled**: 0.500 **diam**, 70 (483) **TS**, 40 (276) **YS**, 12 in 8 in **El**
CSA G30.8	Grade 40, No. 5	Canada	Bar		**As rolled**: 0.625 **diam**, 70 (483) **TS**, 40 (276) **YS**, 12 in 8 in **El**
JIS G 3111	Class 3, No. 2	Japan	Bar		**Rerolled**: all **diam**, (481) **TS**, (294) **YS**, 16 **El**
SABS 657	Grade CD70	South Africa	Tube	0.06 **P**, 0.06 **S**	**Cold worked**: all **diam**, (480) **TS**, (400) **YS**
JIS G 3112	Type 2, SD 30, No. 2	Japan	Bar	0.050 **P**, 0.050 **S**	**Hot rolled**: all **diam**, (480) **TS**, (294) **YS**, 14 **El**

WROUGHT CARBON STEELS

specification number	designation	country	product forms	composition	mechanical properties (see page iv for explanation)
JIS G 3112	Type 2, SR 30, No. 2	Japan	Bar	0.050 **P**, 0.050 **S**	**Hot rolled**: all **diam**, (480) **TS**, (294) **YS**, 16 **El**
NF A 35–016	Fe E 40	France	Bar		**Hot rolled or cold finished**: (≤20) **diam**, (475) **TS**, (412) **YS**, 14 **El**
EURONROM III	Fe P 10	EURONORM	Sheet, strip		**Hot–rolled**: ≥(3) **diam**, (470) max **TS**
NBN A 24–302	BE 35	Belgium	Bar		**As agreed**: (<40) **diam**, (470) **TS**, (345) **YS**, 18 **El**
SABS 657	Grade 68	South Africa	Tube	0.06 **P**, 0.06 **S**	**Cold worked**: all **diam**, (470) **TS**, (310) **YS**, 20 **El**
DGN–B–201	Grade 1018	Mexico	Tube: butt–welded		**Cold finished and annealed**: all **diam**, (469) **TS**, (431) **YS**, 13 **El**
BS 1775	ERW 20	UK	Tube		**As welded**: all **diam**, (463) **TS**, (309) **YS**, 20 **El**
DGN–B–201	Grade 1016	Mexico	Tube: butt–welded		**Cold finished and annealed**: all **diam**, (462) **TS**, (424) **YS**, 13 **El**
DGN–B–201	Grade MT1017	Mexico	Tube: butt–welded		**Cold finished and annealed**: all **diam**, (462) **TS**, (427) **YS**, 13 **El**
ANSI/ASTM A 521	CC 1	US	Forgings	0.90 **Mn**, 0.050 **P**, 0.050 **S**	**Annealed, normalized, or normalized and tempered**: 12–20 (305–508) **diam**, 66 (455) **TS**, 33 (230) **YS**, 22 **El**
ANSI/ASTM A 668	Class C	US	Forgings	1.10 **Mn**, 0.050 **P**, 0.050 **S**	**Annealed, or normalized, or normalized, tempered**: >12 (>203) **diam**, 66 (455) **TS**, 33 (230) **YS**, 23 **El**
DGN–B–198	Grade 3, type I	Mexico	Pipe: seamless	0.048 **P**	**As drawn**: (8–13) **diam**, (451) **TS**, (314) **YS**, 20 **El**
DGN–B–198	Grade 3, type II	Mexico	Pipe: seamless	0.050 **P**	**As drawn**: (8–13) **diam**, (451) **TS**, (314) **YS**, 20 **El**
ANSI/ASTM A 675	65	US	Bar	0.040 **P**, 0.050 **S**	**As hot–rolled**: all **diam**, 65 (450) **TS**, 32 (225) **YS**, 20 **El**
QQ–W–461g	AISI 1018 and 1020	US	Wire		**Hard**: 0.328–0.499 **diam**, 65 (450) **TS**; **Annealed in process**: 0.328–0.499 **diam**, 60 (415) **TS**; **Annealed**: 0.328–0.499 **diam**, 75 (515) **TS**
ASTM A 672	A 516–65	US	Pipe: electric fusion welded		**Normalized, quenched, tempered**: all **diam**, 65 (448) **TS**
ASTM A 672	A 515–65	US	Pipe: electric fusion welded		**Normalized**: all **diam**, 65 (448) **TS**
ANSI/ASTM A 671	A 515 (65)	US	Pipe: electric fusion welded		**Normalized**: all **diam**, 65 (448) **TS**
ANSI/ASTM A 671	A 516 (65)	US	Pipe: electric fusion welded		**Normalized, quenched, tempered**: all **diam**, 65 (448) **TS**
DGN–B–201	Grade 1011	Mexico	Tube: butt–welded		**Cold finished and annealed**: all **diam**, (448) **TS**, (406) **YS**, 13 **El**
NBN 293	A 45	Belgium	Bar		**As rolled**: (≥9.5) **diam**, (441) **TS**, (274) **YS**
JIS G 3251	Class 3	Japan	Blooms, billets	0.035 **P**, 0.040 **S**	**Rolled, forged, hot worked**: all **diam**, (441) **TS**, (226) **YS**, 27 **El**
JIS G 3113	Class 4	Japan	Plate, sheet	0.040 **P**, 0.040 **S**	**Hot rolled**: (1.6–1.9) **diam**, (441) **TS**, (304) **YS**, 29 **El**
JIS G 3201	Class 3	Japan	Forgings	0.035 **P**, 0.040 **S**	**Annealed and normalized or normalized and quenched and tempered**: all **diam**, (441) **TS**, (226) **YS**, 27 **El**
SABS 657	Grade CD63	South Africa	Tube	0.06 **P**, 0.06 **S**	**Cold worked**: all **diam**, (435) **TS**, (370) **YS**
BS 1775	CDS 24	UK	Tube		**Cold drawn**: all **diam**, (432) **TS**, (371) **YS**

WROUGHT CARBON STEELS

specification number	designation	country	product forms	composition	mechanical properties (see page iv for explanation)
BS 1775	CEW 24	UK	Tube		**Cold drawn, annealed, normalized, as drawn, as drawn and tempered**: all **diam**, (432) **TS**, (371) **YS**
NBN 770F	Fe P 11	Belgium	Sheet		**Hot rolled**: all **diam**, (431) **TS**, 25 **El**
NF A 36–102	Fd 1E	France	Strip		**Hot rolled**: all **diam**, (431) max **TS**, 33 **El**
EURONORM III	Fe P 11	EURONORM	Sheet, strip		**Hot–rolled**: ≥(3) **diam**, (430) max **TS**, 28 **El**
NF A 36–301	1 C	France	Sheet, strip		**Hot rolled and cold–finished**: (≤8) **diam**, (430) **TS**, 28 **El**
COPANT R 16	A T–40	COPANT	Bar	0.050 **P**, 0.060 **S**	**Hot rolled**: (5–40) **diam**, (430) **TS**, (390) **YS**, 12 **El**
COPANT R 15	A 44	COPANT	Bar	0.050 **P**, 0.060 **S**	**Hot rolled**: (8–40) **diam**, (430) **TS**, (275) **YS**, 22 **El**
COPANT R 14	A 44	COPANT	Bar	0.050 **P**, 0.060 **S**	**Hot rolled**: (5–40) **diam**, (430) **TS**, (275) **YS**, 22 **El**
IS 3601	HFS 25	India	Tube		**Hot finished**: all **diam**, (421) **TS**, (245) **YS**, 22 **El**
IS 3601	HFS 25	India	Tube		**Hot finished**: all **diam**, (421) **TS**, (245) **YS**, 22 **El**
IS 3601	HFS 25	India	Tube		**Hot finished**: all **diam**, (421) **TS**, (245) **YS**, 22 **El**
COPANT 688		COPANT	Wire		**As drawn**: all **diam**, (420) **TS**
BS 1775	HFW 16	UK	Tube		**Hot finished**: all **diam**, (417) **TS**, (247) **YS**, 22 **El**
BS 1775	HFS 16	UK	Tube		**Hot finished**: all **diam**, (416) **TS**, (247) **YS**, 22 **El**
BS 1775	CDS 16	UK	Tube		**Cold drawn**: all **diam**, (416) **TS**, (247) **YS**, 22 **El**
IS 5433	Grade YS+28	India	Pipe	0.04 **P**, 0.06 **S**	**Hot finished or cold drawn**: all **diam**, (415) **TS**, (275) **YS**, 32 **El**
ANSI/ASTM A 307	Grade A	US	Bar, forgings	0.06 **P**, 0.15 **S**	**As agreed**: all **diam**, 60 (415) **TS**, 18 **El**
ANSI/ASTM A 307	Grade B	US	Bar, forgings	0.04 **P**, 0.05 **S**	**As agreed**: all **diam**, 60 (415) **TS**, 18 **El**
ANSI/ASTM A 675	60	US	Bar	0.040 **P**, 0.050 **S**	**As hot–rolled**: all **diam**, 60 (415) **TS**, 30 (205) **YS**, 22 **El**
ANSI/ASTM A 283	Grade D	US	Plate	0.04 **P**, 0.05 **S**	**As rolled**: all **diam**, (415) **TS**, (230) **YS**, 23 **El**
ANSI/ASTM A 113	Grade A	US	Plate, shapes, bar	0.04 **P**, 0.05 **S**, 0.20 min **Cu**	**As rolled**: all **diam**, (415) **TS**, (230) **YS**, 24 **El**
ANSI/ASTM A 521	Class CC	US	Forgings	0.90 **Mn**, 0.050 **P**, 0.050 **S**	**Annealed, normalized or normalized and tempered**: 12 (305) **diam**, 60 (415) **TS**, 30 (205) **YS**, 25 **El**
ASTM A 695	Type D, grade 35	US	Bar	0.040 **P**, 0.050 **S**, 0.15–0.30 **Si**, 0.15–0.35 **Pb**	**Hot rolled**: ≥3 (≥76.2) **diam**, 60 (415) **TS**, 35 (240) **YS**, 21 **El**
ASTM A 695	Type C, grade 35	US	Bar	0.040 **P**, 0.08–0.13 **S**, 0.30 **Si**	**Hot rolled**: ≥ (≥76.2) **diam**, 60 (415) **TS**, 35 (240) **YS**, 21 **El**
ASTM A 695	Type A, grade 35	US	Bar	0.040 **P**, 0.050 **S**, 0.15–0.30 **Si**	**Hot rolled**: ≥3 (≥76.2) **diam**, 60 (415) **TS**, 35 (240) **YS**, 21 **El**
ANSI/ASTM A 668	Class B		Forgings	1.10 **Mn**, 0.050 **P**, 0.050 **S**	**Annealed, or normalized, or normalized, tempered**: >20 (>508) **diam**, 60 (415) **TS**, 30 (205) **YS**, 24 **El**
QQ–W–461g	AISI 1015	US	Wire		**Hard**: 0.328–0.499 **diam**, 60 (415) **TS**; **Annealed in process**: 0.328–0.499 **diam**, 55 (380) **TS**; **Annealed**: 0.328–0.499 **diam**, 70 (480) **TS**
ASTM A 672	A 516–60	US	Pipe: electric fusion welded		**Normalized, quenched, tempered**: all **diam**, 60 (414) **TS**
ASTM A 672	A 515–60	US	Pipe: electric fusion welded		**Normalized**: all **diam**, 60 (414) **TS**

WROUGHT CARBON STEELS

specification number	designation	country	product forms	composition	mechanical properties (see page iv for explanation)
ASTM A 672	A 442–60	US	Pipe: electric fusion welded		**Normalized, quenched, tempered**: all **diam**, 60 (414) **TS**
ANSI/ASTM A 671	A 442 (60)	US	Pipe: electric fusion welded		**Normalized, quenched, tempered**: all **diam**, 60 (414) **TS**
ANSI/ASTM A 671	A 515 (60)	US	Pipe: electric fusion welded		**Normalized**: all **diam**, 60 (414) **TS**
ANSI/ASTM A 671	A 516 (60)	US	Pipe: electric fusion welded		**Normalized, quenched, tempered**: all **diam**, 60 (414) **TS**
ANSI/ASTM A 589	Grade B	US	Pipe: seamless, welded	0.050 **P**, 0.060 **S**	**As–rolled**: 0.312 (7.94) **diam**, 60 (414) **TS**, 35 (241) **YS**, 30 **El**
API Spec 5A	H–40	US	Casing tube: welded or seamless		**As agreed**: all **diam**, 60 (414) **TS**, 40 (276) **YS**
MIL–S–13281D	A	US	Bar, shape, plate, sheet, strip		**Hot rolled or cold rolled, annealed or normalized**: all **diam**, (414) **TS**, (172) **YS**, 25 **El**
NBN 293	A 42	Belgium	Bar		**As rolled**: (≥9.5) **diam**, (412) **TS**, (235) **YS**
NBN 154.13 F	A 42	Belgium	Sheet		**Annealed or normalized**: all **diam**, (412) **TS**, (255) **YS**
IS 3601	CEW 38	India	Tube		**Cold drawn**: all **diam**, (412) **TS**, (373) **YS**
IS 3601	CEW 25	India	Tube		**Cold drawn**: all **diam**, (412) **TS**, (245) **YS**, 23 **El**
IS 3601	ERW 25	India	Tube: electric resistance welded		**As welded**: all **diam**, (412) **TS**, (245) **YS**, 23 **El**
IS 3601	CDS 38	India	Tube		**Cold drawn**: all **diam**, (412) **TS**, (373) **YS**
NF A 35–015	Fe E24	France	Bar, wire, rod		**Hot rolled**: (5–40) **diam**, (412) **TS**, (235) **YS**, 25 **El**
DGN–B–184	Grade B	Mexico	Pipe: electric–resistance welded	0.050 **P**, 0.060 **S**	**As welded**: (≥8) **diam**, (412) **TS**, (240) **YS**, 30 **El**
DGN–B–198	Grade 2, type I	Mexico	Pipe: seamless	0.048 **P**	**As drawn**: (8–13) **diam**, (412) **TS**, (245) **YS**, 25 **El**
DGN–B–198	Grade 2, type II	Mexico	Pipe: seamless	0.050 **P**	**As drawn**: (8–13) **diam**, (412) **TS**, (245) **YS**, 25 **El**
JIS G 3123	SS30B–D (hexagon)	Japan	Bar		**Cold finished**: (5.5–9) **diam**, (412) **TS**
JIS G 3439	Class 2, No. 11	Japan	Tube: seamless	0.040 **P**, 0.060 **S**	**As rolled**: all **diam**, (412) **TS**, (275) **YS**, 32 **El**
IS 3601	CDS 25	India	Tube		**Cold drawn**: all **diam**, (411) **TS**, (245) **YS**, 23 **El**
IS 3601	HFW 25	India	Tube		**Hot finished**: all **diam**, (411) **TS**, (245) **YS**, 23 **El**
DGN–B–281	Grade D	Mexico	Plate	0.04 **P**, 0.05 **S**, 0.20 **Cu**	**As rolled**: (19.1–101.6) **diam**, (411) **TS**, (225) **YS**, 23 **El**
EURONORM 130	Fe P 01	EURONORM	Sheet, strip		**Cold–rolled**: (<3) **diam**, (410) max **TS**, 25 **El**
IS 6631	HFS 245	India	Tube		**Hot finished**: all **diam**, (410) **TS**, (245) **YS**, 27 **El**
IS 6631	CDS 245	India	Tube		**Normalized**: all **diam**, (410) **TS**, (245) **YS**, 27 **El**
IS 1161	Grade YS+25	India	Tube		**Normalized**: (2.00) **diam**, (410) **TS**, (245) **YS**
NF A 35–552	XC 18	France	Bar		**Normalized**: (≤16) **diam**, (410) **TS**, (255) **YS**, 28 **El**; **As rolled**: (≤16) **diam**, (880) **TS**, (590) **YS**, 8 **El**
NF A 36–401	TC	France	Sheet, strip		**Cold finished**: (<3) **diam**, (410) max **TS**, 24 **El**
COPANT R 17	A 42–R	COPANT	Bar	0.040 **P**, 0.050 **S**	**Hot–rolled**: (5–48) **diam**, (410) **TS**, (215) **YS**, 25 **El**
COPANT R 18	A 42–P	COPANT	Bar	0.15 **P**, 0.060 **S**	**Hot rolled**: (5–48) **diam**, (410) **TS**, (215) **YS**, 26 **El**
COPANT R 19	A 42–TP	COPANT	Bar	0.13 **P**, 0.23 **S**	**Hot rolled**: all **diam**, (410) **TS**, (215) **YS**, 22 **El**

specification number	designation	country	product forms	composition	mechanical properties (see page iv for explanation)
JIS G 3302	SPG 2S	Japan	Sheet		**Galvanized**: (0.40–1.00) **diam**, (403) **TS**, 18 **El**
JIS G 3302	SPG 3S	Japan	Sheet		**Galvanized**: (≥0.40) **diam**, (403) **TS**, 18 **El**
NBN 770F	Fe P 01	Belgium	Sheet		**Cold rolled**: (≥0.5) **diam**, (402) **TS**, 26 **El**
NBN 770F	Fe P 21	Belgium	Sheet		**Hot rolled**: (<2) **diam**, (402) **TS**, 25 **El**
JIS G 3457	STPY 41	Japan	Pipe: electric arc welded	0.050 **P**, 0.050 **S**	**As welded**: (≥8) **diam**, (402) **TS**, (226) **YS**, 18 **El**
JIS G 3113	Class 3	Japan	Plate, sheet, strip	0.040 **P**, 0.040 **S**	**Hot rolled**: (1.6–1.9) **diam**, (402) **TS**, (255) **YS**, 31 **El**
JIS G 3108	Type B	Japan	Bar	0.045 **P**, 0.045 **S**	**Hot rolled and cold finished**: (≤25) **diam**, (402) **TS**, (235) **YS**, 20 **El**
JIS G 3104	Class 2, No. 2	Japan	Bar	0.040 **P**, 0.040 **S**	**Hot rolled**: all **diam**, (402) **TS**, 25 **El**
JIS G 3101	Class 2	Japan	Plate, strip, bar, shapes	0.050 **P**, 0.050 **S**	**Hot rolled**: (≤5) **diam**, (402) **TS**, (245) **YS**, 21 **El**
BS 1775	HLW 16	UK	Tube		**Hydraulic lapwelded**: all **diam**, (401) **TS**, (247) **YS**, 23 **El**
BS 1775	EFW 16	UK	Tube		**Electric fusion welded**: all **diam**, (401) **TS**, (247) **YS**, 23 **El**
EURONORM III	Fe P 13	EURONORM	Sheet, strip		**Hot–rolled**: ≥(3) **diam**, (400) max **TS**, 34 **El**
AISI A500	Grade B	US	Pipe		**Cold formed welded or seamless (shaped)**: all **diam**, 58 (400) **TS**, 46 (315) **YS**, 23 **El**
AISI A500	Grade B	US	Pipe		**Cold formed welded or seamless (round)**: all **diam**, 58 (400) **TS**, 42 (290) **YS**, 23 **El**
MIL–S–22698A	Class A	US	Plate	0.040 **P**, 0.050 **S**	**Hot rolled**: ≤1/2 **diam**, 58 (400) **TS**, 32 (221) **YS**, 24 **El**
MIL–S–23495	Class A	US	Shapes: extruded	0.040 **P**, 0.050 **S**	**As extruded**: ≤1/2 **diam**, 58 (400) **TS**, 32 (221) **YS**, 24 **El**
COPANT 681	P 40	COPANT	Sheet, electrical		**Hot and cold rolled**: (0.35) **diam**, (400) **TS**, (250) **YS**, 22 **El**
NBN 293	D 40 k	Belgium	Bar	0.05–0.09 **P**, 0.05–0.09 **S**	**As rolled**: (≥9.5) **diam**, (392) **TS**, (235) **YS**
NBN 293	D 40 m	Belgium	Bar	0.04–0.07 **P**, 0.04–0.07 **S**	**As rolled**: (≥9.5) **diam**, (392) **TS**, (235) **YS**
NBN 770F	Fe P 13	Belgium	Sheet		**Hot rolled**: all **diam**, (392) **TS**, 28 **El**
NF A 36–102	Fd 3E	France	Strip		**Hot rolled**: all **diam**, (392) max **TS**, (314) max **YS**, 36 **El**
JIS G 3251	Class 2	Japan	Blooms, billets	0.035 **P**, 0.040 **S**	**Rolled, forged, hot worked**: all **diam** (392) **TS**, (196) **YS**, 29 **El**
JIS G 3201	Class 2	Japan	Forgings	0.035 **P**, 0.040 **S**	**Annealed and normalized or normalized and quenched and tempered**: all **diam**, (392) **TS**, (196) **YS**, 29 **El**
EURONORM III	Fe P 12M	EURONORM	Sheet, strip		**Hot–rolled**: ≥(3) **diam**, (390) max **TS**, 32 **El**
NBN I 04–001		Belgium	Wire		**Galvanized**: (0.20–0.49) **diam**, (390) **TS**
COPANT R 15	A 40	COPANT	Bar	0.050 **P**, 0.060 **S**	**Hot rolled**: (8–40) **diam**, (390) **TS**, (245) **YS**, 24 **El**
COPANT R 14	A 40	COPANT	Bar	0.050 **P**, 0.060 **S**	**Hot rolled**: (5–40) **diam**, (390) **TS**, (245) **YS**, 24 **El**
BS 1775	ERW 16	UK	Tube		**As welded**: all **diam**, (386) **TS**, (247) **YS**, 24 **El**
BS 1775	CEW 16	UK	Tube		**Cold drawn, annealed, normalized, as drawn, as drawn and tempered**: all **diam**, (386) **TS**, (247) **YS**, 24 **El**

specification number	designation	country	product forms	composition	mechanical properties (see page iv for explanation)
IS 1161	Grade ERWYS+32	India	Tube		**Normalized:** (2.00) **diam**, (385) **TS**, (245) **YS**
SABS 657	Grade 56	South Africa	Tube	0.06 **P**, 0.06 **S**	**Cold worked:** all **diam**, (385) **TS**, (235) **YS**, 25 **El**
JIS G 3123	SS30B–D (round)	Japan	Bar		**Cold finished:** (5–20) **diam**, (382) **TS**
JIS G 3117	Class 1, SRR 24	Japan	Bar		**Rerolled:** all **diam**, (382) **TS**, (235) **YS**, 20 **El**
JIS G 3117	Class 1, SDR 24	Japan	Bar		**Rerolled:** all **diam**, (382) **TS**, (235) **YS**, 18 **El**
JIS G 3111	Class 2, No. 2	Japan	Bar		**Rerolled:** all **diam**, (382) **TS**, (235) **YS**, 20 **El**
JIS G 3112	Type 1, SD 24, No. 2	Japan	Bar	0.050 **P**, 0.050 **S**	**Hot rolled:** all **diam**, (382) **TS**, (235) **YS**, 18 **El**
JIS G 3112	Type 1, SR 24, No. 2	Japan	Bar	0.050 **P**, 0.050 **S**	**Hot rolled:** all **diam**, (382) **TS**, (235) **YS**, 20 **El**
NF A 36–301	2 C	France	Sheet, strip		**Hot rolled and cold–finished:** (≤8) **diam**, (380) **TS**, 32 **El**
ANSI/ASTM A 675	55	US	Bar	0.040 **P**, 0.050 **S**	**As hot–rolled:** all **diam**, 55 (380) **TS**, 28 (190) **YS**, 26 **El**
ANSI/ASTM A 283	Grade C	US	Plate	0.04 **P**, 0.05 **S**	**As rolled:** all **diam**, (380) **TS**, (205) **YS**, 25 **El**
ANSI/ASTM A 3		US	Bar		**As rolled:** 2.00 **diam**, (380) **TS**, 22 **El**
QQ–W–461g	AISI 1008 and 1010	US	Wire		**Hard:** 0.328–0.499 **diam**, 55 (380) **TS**; **Annealed in process:** 0.328–0.499 **diam**, 53 (365) **TS**; **Annealed:** 0.328–0.499 **diam**, 65 (450) **TS**; **Soft (zinc–coated):** >0.176 **diam**, 70 (480) **TS**; **Medium (zinc–coated):** >0.176 **diam**, 60 (415) **TS**; **Hard (zinc–coated):** >0.176 **diam**, 75 (515) **TS**
ASTM A 672	A 516–55	US	Pipe: electric fusion welded		**Normalized, quenched, tempered:** all **diam**, 55 (379) **TS**
ASTM A 672	A 515–55	US	Pipe: electric fusion welded		**Normalized:** all **diam**, 55 (379) **TS**
ASTM A 672	A 285C	US	Pipe: electric fusion welded		**Normalized:** all **diam**, 55 (379) **TS**
ASTM A 672	A 442–55	US	Pipe: electric fusion welded		**Normalized, quenched, tempered:** all **diam**, 55 (379) **TS**
ANSI/ASTM A 671	A 442 (55)	US	Pipe: electric fusion welded		**Normalized, quenched, tempered:** all **diam**, 55 (379) **TS**
ANSI/ASTM A 671	A 285 (C)	US	Pipe: electric fusion welded		**Normalized:** all **diam**, 55 (379) **TS**
DGN–B–106	Type 285C (Firebox)	Mexico	Plate	0.80 **Mn**, 0.035 **P**, 0.040 **S**, 0.20–0.35 **Cu**	**Hot worked:** (8) **diam**, 55 (379) **TS**, 30 (207) **YS**, 29 **El**
DGN–B–93	Class I, subclass I–2	Mexico	Plate, sheet	0.040 **P**, 0.050 **S**	**As agreed:** all **diam**, (379) **TS**, (206) **YS**, 27 **El**
DGN–B–281	Grade C	Mexico	Plate	0.04 **P**, 0.05 **S**, 0.20 **Cu**	**As rolled:** (19.1–101.6) **diam**, (377) **TS**, (209) **YS**, 25 **El**
JIS G 3113	Class 2	Japan	Plate, sheet, strip	0.040 **P**, 0.040 **S**	**Hot rolled:** (1.6–1.9) **diam**, (373) **TS**, (226) **YS**, 32 **El**
NBN 770F	Fe P 02	Belgium	Sheet		**Cold rolled:** (≥0.5) **diam**, (372) **TS**, 31 **El**
NBN 770F	Fe P 12	Belgium	Sheet		**Hot rolled:** all **diam**, (372) **TS**, 28 **El**
NBN 770F	Fe P 22	Belgium	Sheet		**Hot rolled:** (<2) **diam**, (372) **TS**, 30 **El**
NF A 36–102	Fd 2E	France	Strip		**Hot rolled:** all **diam**, (372) **TS**, 36 **El**
NF A 35–552	XC 12	France	Bar		**Normalized:** (≤16) **diam**, (370) **TS**, (235) **YS**, 29 **El**; **As rolled:** (≤16) **diam**, (690) **TS**, (490) **YS**, 11 **El**
NF A 36–401	E	France	Sheet, strip		**Cold finished:** (<3) **diam**, (370) **TS**, 31 **El**

WROUGHT CARBON STEELS

specification number	designation	country	product forms	composition	mechanical properties (see page iv for explanation)
NF A 36–301	3 C	France	Sheet, strip		**Hot rolled and cold–finished:** (≤8) **diam**, (370) **TS**, (290 max) **YS**, 36 **El**
DS 12011	St 37 A	Denmark	Rod, bar, shapes	0.08 **P**, 0.06 **S**	**Hot rolled**: (16) **diam**, (363) **TS**, (216) **YS**, 24 **El**
NBN 293	A 37	Belgium	Bar		**As rolled**: (≥9.5) **diam**, (363) **TS**, (216) **YS**
NBN 293	A 37 d	Belgium	Bar	0.08–0.12 **P**, 0.06–0.12 **S**	**As rolled**: (≥9.5) **diam**, (363) **TS**, (216) **YS**
NBN 293	D 37 k	Belgium	Bar	0.05–0.09 **P**, 0.05–0.09 **S**	**As rolled**: (≥9.5) **diam**, (363) **TS**, (216) **YS**
NBN 293	D 37 m	Belgium	Bar	0.04–0.07 **P**, 0.04–0.07 **S**	**As rolled**: (≥9.5) **diam**, (363) **TS**, (216) ys
NBN 770F	Fe P 23	Belgium	Sheet		**Hot rolled**: (<2) **diam**, (363) **TS**, 33 **El**
NBN 154.13 F	A 37	Belgium	Sheet		**Annealed or normalized**: all **diam**, (363) **TS**, (235) **YS**
SFS 1205	A220	Finland	Bar	0.06 **P**, 0.08 **As**, 0.010 **N**	**Hot rolled**: (6) **diam**, (360) **TS**, (220) **YS**, 18 **El**
COPANT R 17	A 37–R	COPANT	Bar	0.040 **P**, 0.050 **S**	**Hot rolled**: (5–48) **diam**, (360) **TS**, (195) **YS**, 28 **El**
COPANT R 18	A 37–P	COPANT	Bar	0.15 **P**, 0.060 **S**	**Hot rolled**: (5–48) **diam**, (360) **TS**, (195) **YS**, 28 **El**
COPANT R 19	A 37–TP	COPANT	Bar	0.13 **P**, 0.23 **S**	**Hot rolled**: all **diam**, (360) **TS**, (195) **YS**, 26 **El**
COPANT R 15	A 37	COPANT	Bar	0.050 **P**, 0.060 **S**	**Hot rolled**: (8–40) **diam**, (360) **TS**, (225) **YS**, 25 **El**
COPANT R 14	A 37	COPANT	Bar	0.050 **P**, 0.060 **S**	**Hot rolled**: (5–40) **diam**, (360) **TS**, (225) **YS**, 25 **El**
NBN 770F	Fe P 03	Belgium	Sheet		**Cold rolled**: (≥0.5) **diam**, (353) **TS**, 35 **El**
SABS 657	Grade 50	South Africa	Tube	0.06 **P**, 0.06 **S**	**Cold worked**: all **diam**, (345) **TS**, (205) **YS**, 30 **El**
ASTM A 672	A 285B	US	Pipe: electric fusion welded		**Normalized**: all **diam**, 50 (345) **TS**
ANSI/ASTM A 675	50	US	Bar	0.040 **P**, 0.050 **S**	**As hot–rolled**: all **diam**, 50 (345) **TS**, 25 (170) **YS**, 30 **El**
ANSI/ASTM A 283	Grade B	US	Plate	0.04 **P**, 0.05 **S**	**As rolled**: all **diam**, (345) **TS**, (185) **YS**, 28 **El**
CSA G12	Grade 50	Canada	Wire: zinc coated		**As drawn**: all **diam**, 50 (345) **TS**, 10 **El**
ANSI/ASTM A 113	Grade B	US	Plate, shapes, bar	0.04 **P**, 0.05 **S**, 0.20 min **Cu**	**As rolled**: all **diam**, (345) **TS**, (185) **YS**, 28 **El**
QQ–W–46lg	AISI 1006	US	Wire		**Hard**: 0.328–0.499 **diam**, 50 (345) **TS**; **Annealed in process**: 0.328–0.499 **diam**, 47 (325) **TS**; **Annealed**: 0.328–0.499 **diam**, 60 (415) max **TS**; **Soft (zinc–coated)**: >0.176 **diam**, 70 (480) max **TS**; **Medium (zinc–coated)**: >0.176 **diam**, 60 (415) **TS**; **Hard (zinc–coated)**: >0.176 **diam**, 75 (515) **TS**
NBN 770F	Fe P 04	Belgium	Sheet		**Cold rolled**: (≥0.5) **diam**, (343) **TS**, 37 **El**
NBN 770F	Fe P 24	Belgium	Sheet		**Hot rolled**: (<2) **diam**, (343) **TS**, 36 **El**
IS 3601	CDS 21	India	Tube		**Cold drawn**: all **diam**, (343) **TS**, (206) **YS**, 27 **El**
IS 3601	HFS 21	India	Tube		**Hot finished**: all **diam**, (343) **TS**, (206) **YS**, 27 **El**
DGN–B–198	Grade 1, type I	Mexico	Pipe: seamless	0.048 **P**	**As drawn**: (8–13) **diam**, (343) **TS**, (206) **YS**, 30 **El**
DGN–B–198	Grade 1, type II	Mexico	Pipe: seamless	0.050 **P**	**As drawn**: (8–13) **diam**, (343) **TS**, (206) **YS**, 30 **El**
DGN–B–281	Grade B	Mexico	Plate	0.04 **P**, 0.05 **S**, 0.20 **Cu**	**As rolled**: (19.1–101.6) **diam**, (343) **TS**, (186) **YS**, 28 **El**

WROUGHT CARBON STEELS

specification number	designation	country	product forms	composition	mechanical properties (see page iv for explanation)
NF A 35–552	XC 10	France	Bar		**Normalized:** (≤16) **diam**, (340) **TS**, (215) **YS**, 31 **El**; **As rolled:** (≤16) **diam**, (490) **TS**, (345) **YS**, 16 **El**
NF A 36–401	EC	France	Sheet, strip		**Cold finished:** (<3) **diam**, (340) **TS**, (225) max **YS**, 37 **El**
AIR 9160/C27	9160C061	France	Sheet		**Annealed:** (≤3) **diam**, (340 max) **TS**, (225 max) **YS**, 36 **El**
BS 1775	HFW 13	UK	Tube		**Hot finished:** all **diam**, (340) **TS**, (209) **YS**, 27 **El**
DIN 488	BSt 22/34 GU	Germany	Bar	0.60 **Si**	**Hot rolled:** (5–28) **diam**, (340) **TS**, (220) **YS**, 18 **El**
DIN 488	BSt 22/34 RU	Germany	Bar	0.60 **Si**	**Hot rolled:** (6–40) **diam**, (340) **TS**, (220) **YS**, 18 **El**
BS 1775	HFS 13	UK	Tube		**Hot finished:** all **diam**, (339) **TS**, (209) **YS**, 27 **El**
BS 1775	CDS 13	UK	Tube		**Cold drawn:** all **diam**, (339) **TS**, (209) **YS**, 27 **El**
NBN A 24–302	BE 22	Belgium	Bar		**As agreed:** (<40) **diam**, (335) **TS**, (215) **YS**, 24 **El**
IS 1161	Grade YS+22	India	Tube		**Normalized:** (2.00) **diam**, (335) **TS**, (210) **YS**
COPANT R 17	A 34–R	COPANT	Bar	0.040 **P**, 0.050 **S**	**Hot rolled:** (5–48) **diam**, (335) **TS**, (175) **YS**, 30 **El**
COPANT R 18	A 34–P	COPANT	Bar	0.15 **P**, 0.060 **S**	**Hot rolled:** (5–48) **diam**, (335) **TS**, (175) **YS**, 30 **El**
COPANT R 19	A 34–TP	COPANT	Bar	0.13 **P**, 0.23 **S**	**Hot rolled:** all **diam**, (335) **TS**, (175) **YS**, 28 **El**
NBN 293	A 34 K	Belgium	Bar	0.05–0.09 **P**, 0.05–0.09 **S**	**As rolled:** (≥9.5) **diam**, (333) **TS**, (196) **YS**
NBN 293	A 34 m	Belgium	Bar	0.04–0.07 **P**, 0.04–0.07 **S**	**As rolled:** (≥9.5) **diam**, (333) **TS**, (196) **YS**
NBN 154.13 F	A 34	Belgium	Sheet		**Annealed or normalized:** all **diam**, (333) **TS**, (215) **YS**
IS 3601	CEW 21	India	Tube		**Cold drawn:** all **diam**, (333) **TS**, (206) **YS**, 28 **El**
IS 3601	ERW 21	India	Tube: electric resistance welded		**As welded:** all **diam**, (333) **TS**, (206) **YS**, 28 **El**
IS 3601	HFW 21	India	Tube		**Hot finished:** all **diam**, (333) **TS**, (206) **YS**, 28 **El**
NF A 35–015	Fe E22	France	Bar, wire, rod		**Hot rolled:** (5–40) **diam**, (333) **TS**, (215) **YS**, 22 **El**
NF A 36–101	A 34,1	France	Strip	0.075 **P**, 0.062 **S**	**Hot rolled:** all **diam**, (333) **TS**, (186) **YS**, 28 **El**
NF A 36–101	A 34,2	France	Strip	0.062 **P**, 0.062 **S**, 0.009 $\mathbf{N_2}$	**Hot rolled:** all **diam**, (333) **TS**, (186) **YS**, 30 **El**
JIS G 3251	Class 1	Japan	Blooms, billets	0.035 **P**, 0.040 **S**	**Rolled, forged, hot worked:** all **diam**, (333) **TS**, (167) **YS**, 31 **El**
DGN–B–183	Grade A	Mexico	Pipe: electric–fusion welded	0.30–1.00 **Mn**, 0.040 **P**, 0.050 **S**	**As welded:** (8) **diam**, (333) **TS**, (206) **YS**, 35 **El**
JIS G 3111	Class 1, No. 2	Japan	Bar		**Rerolled:** all **diam**, (333) **TS**, 25 **El**
JIS G 3104	Class 1, No. 2	Japan	Bar	0.040 **P**, 0.040 **S**	**Hot rolled:** all **diam**, (333) **TS**, 27 **El**
JIS G 3101	Class 1	Japan	Plate, strip, bar	0.050 **P**, 0.050 **S**	**Hot rolled:** (≤5) **diam**, (333) **TS**, (206) **YS**, 26 **El**
JIS G 3201	Class 1	Japan	Forgings	0.035 **P**, 0.040 **S**	**Annealed and normalized or normalized and quenched and tempered:** all **diam**, (333) **TS**, (167) **YS**, 31 **El**
ASTM A 139	Grade A	US	Pipe: electric fusion welded	1.00 **Mn**, 0.040 **P**, 0.050 **S**	**As rolled:** 0.312 (7.94) **diam**, 48 (331) **TS**, 30 (207) **YS**, 35 **El**
ANSI/ASTM A 589	Grade A	US	Pipe: seamless, welded	0.050 **P**, 0.060 **S**	**As–rolled:** 0.312 (7.94) **diam**, 48 (331) **TS**, 30 (207) **YS**, 35 **El**
IS 6631	HFS 205	India	Pipe		**Hot finished:** all **diam**, (330) **TS**, (205) **YS**, 27 **El**

WROUGHT CARBON STEELS

specification number	designation	country	product forms	composition	mechanical properties (see page iv for explanation)
IS 6631	CDS 205	India	Tube		**Normalized**: all **diam**, (330) **TS**, (205) **YS**, 27 **El**
IS 6631	ERW 205	India	Tube		**Normalized**: all **diam**, (330) **TS**, (205) **YS**, 27 **El**
IS 6631	ERW 245	India	Tube		**Normalized**: all **diam**, (330) **TS**, (205) **YS**, 27 **El**
NF A 33–102	AR 34,1	France	Billets, blooms, slabs	0.075 **P**, 0.062 **S**	**Normalized**: all **diam**, (330) **TS**, (190) **YS**, 28 **El**
NF A 33–102	AR 34,2	France	Billets, blooms, slabs	0.062 **P**, 0.062 **S**	**Normalized**: all **diam**, (330) **TS**, (190) **YS**, 30 **El**
NF A 35–501	A 34 grade 2	France	Sheet, plate, bar	0.062 **P**, 0.062 **S**, 0.009 **N Ni**2	**As rolled**: (3–30) **diam**, (330) **TS**, (165) **YS**, 28 **El**
NF A 35–501	A 34 grade 1	France	Sheet, plate, bar	0.075 **P**, 0.062 **S**	**As rolled (sheet, plate)**: (≤30) **diam**, (330) **TS**, (165) **YS**, 26 **El**
COPANT R 209	S, Grade A	COPANT	Pipe: welded, seamless	0.048 **P**, 0.080 **S**	**As agreed**: (>8) **diam**, (330) **TS**, (205) **YS**, 35 **El**
COPANT R 209	E, Grade A	COPANT	Pipe: welded, seamless	0.050 **P**, 0.060 **S**	**As agreed**: (>8) **diam**, (330) **TS**, (205) **YS**, 35 **El**
ANSI/ASTM A 113	Grade C	US	Plate, shapes, bar	0.04 **P**, 0.05 **S**, 0.20 min **Cu**	**As rolled**: all **diam**, (330) **TS**, (180) **YS**, 29 **El**
DGN–B–184	Grade A	Mexico	Pipe: electric–resistance welded	0.050 **P**, 0.060 **S**	**As welded**: (≥8) **diam**, (328) **TS**, (206) **YS**, 35 **El**
DIN 1626, Part 2	Grade St33	Germany	Pipe: welded (commercial quality)		**As welded**: <16 **diam**, (325) **TS**, 18 **El**
ANSI/ASTM A 668	Class A	US	Forgings	1.10 **Mn**, 0.050 **P**, 0.050 **S**	**Untreated**: >20 (>508) **diam**, 47 (325) **TS**
NS 12110	NS 12110–00	Norway	Bar, rod, shapes		**Hot worked**: (<25) **diam**, (324) **TS**, (186) **YS**, 18 **El**
NF A 35–015	Fe E18	France	Bar, wire, rod		**Hot rolled**: (5–40) **diam**, (324) **TS**, (176) **YS**, 18 **El**
TS 416	Fe 33	Turkey	Pipe		**As welded**: (<16) **diam**, (324) **TS**, 18 **El**
SFS 200:E	Fe 33	Finland	Bar, plate, strip, wire, forgings		**Hot worked**: all **diam**, (323) **TS**
DS 12011	St 00	Denmark	Rod, bar, shapes		**Hot rolled**: all **diam**, (323) **TS**
NF A 36–101	A 33,2	France	Strip	0.062 **P**, 0.062 **S**	**Hot rolled**: all **diam**, (323) **TS**, (176) **YS**, 18 **El**
SIS 14 13 00	SIS 13 00–00	Sweden	Bar, plate		**As rolled**: all **diam**, (320) **TS**
UNI 4148		Italy	Tube: seamless or welded	0.05 **P**, 0.05 **S**	**As drawn or as welded**: (2.65–5.4) **diam**, (320) **TS**, 15 **El**
UNI 4149		Italy	Tube: seamless or welded	0.05 **P**, 0.05 **S**	**As drawn or as welded**: (2.65–5.4) **diam**, (320) **TS**, 15 **El**
UNI 7288	Fe 33	Italy	Tube: welded	0.05 **P**, 0.05 **S**	**As welded**: (2.3–6.3) **diam**, (320) **TS**, 15 **El**
UNI 3824		Italy	Tube: seamless	0.05 **P**, 0.05 **S**	**As drawn**: (1.8–4.05) **diam**, (320) **TS**, 15 **El**
ISO 2547	TW.0	ISO	Tube	0.06 **P**, 0.06 **S**	**As welded**: all **diam**, (320) **TS**, 15 **El**
ISO 2546 (E)	TS.0	ISO	Tube: seamless	0.06 **P**, 0.06 **S**	**Hot rolled or cold finished**: all **diam**, (320) **TS**, 15 **El**
ISO 559	TS0/TW0	ISO	Tube: welded or seamless	0.060 **P**, 0.060 **S**	**As welded, hot rolled**: all **diam**, (320) **TS**, 15 **El**
NF A 33–105	AR 33,2	France	Billets, blooms, slabs	0.062 **P**, 0.062 **S**	**Normalized**: all **diam**, (320) **TS**, (180) **YS**, 18 **El**
NF A 35–501	A 33 grade 2	France	Sheet, plate, bar	0.062 **P**, 0.062 **S**	**As rolled**: (≤30) **diam**, (320) **TS**, (175) **YS**, 18 **El**
COPANT R 209	Grade F	COPANT	Pipe: welded, seamless	0.08 **P**, 0.060 **S**	**As agreed**: (>8) **diam**, (320) **TS**, (170) **YS**, 33 **El**
DIN 17100	St 33–2 (1.0035)	Germany	Plate	0.075 **P**, 0.063 **S**	**Normalized**: all **diam**, (320) **TS**, (185) **YS**, 18 **El**
DIN 17100	St 33–2 (1.0035)	Germany	Strip	0.075 **P**, 0.063 **S**	**Normalized**: all **diam**, (320) **TS**, (185) **YS**, 18 **El**; **Hot rolled**: all **diam**, (320) **TS**, (185) **YS**, 14 **El**
DIN 17100	St 33–2 (1.0035)	Germany	Bar	0.075 **P**, 0.063 **S**	**Normalized**: all **diam**, (320) **TS**, (185) **YS**, 18 **El**

WROUGHT CARBON STEELS

specification number	designation	country	product forms	composition	mechanical properties (see page iv for explanation)
IS 1914–1961 Part 3		India	Tube: seamless		**Annealed**: all **diam**, (315) **TS**
IS 1914–1961 Part 6		India	Tube: electrical welded		**Normalized**: all **diam**, (315) **TS**
IS 1914–1961 Part 7		India	Tube: electrical welded		**Annealed or normalized**: all **diam**, (315) **TS**
IS 3601	OAW 17	India	Tube		**Cold drawn**: all **diam**, (314) **TS**, (167) **YS**, 30 **El**
IS 3601	CEW 17	India	Tube		**Cold drawn**: all **diam**, (314) **TS**, (167) **YS**, 30 **El**
IS 3601	ERW 17	India	Tube: electric resistance welded		**As welded**: all **diam**, (314) **TS**, (167) **YS**, 30 **El**
IS 3601	CDS 17	India	Tube		**Cold drawn**: all **diam**, (314) **TS**, (166) **YS**, 30 **El**
IS 3601	HFS 17	India	Tube		**Hot finished**: all **diam**, (314) **TS**, (167) **YS**, 30 **El**
IS 3601	HFW 17	India	Tube		**Hot finished**: all **diam**, (314) **TS**, (167) **YS**, 30 **El**
IS 1914–1961 Part 2		India	Tube: seamless		**Annealed or normalized**: all **diam**, (314) **TS**
JIS G 3113	Class 1	Japan	Plate, sheet, strip	0.040 **P**, 0.040 **S**	**Hot rolled**: (1.6–1.9) **diam**, (314) **TS**, (186) **YS**, 33 **El**
CSA B193	Furnace butt welded	Canada	Pipe	0.30–0.60 **Mn**, 0.045 **P**, 0.06 **S**	**Mill**: 0.125 (3.18) **diam**, 45 (310) **TS**, 25 (172) **YS**, 18 **El**
IS 280		India	Wire	0.065 **P**, 0.060 **S**	**Soft**: (1.60) **diam**, (310) **TS**; **One quarter hard**: all **diam**, (430) **TS**; **One half hard**: all **diam**, (540) **TS**; **Hard**: all **diam**, (680) **TS**
IS 1161	Grade ERWYS+25	India	Tube		**Normalized**: (2.00) **diam**, (310) **TS**, (170) **YS**
SABS 657	Grade 45	South Africa	Tube	0.06 **P**, 0.06 **S**	**Cold worked**: all **diam**, (310) **TS**, (170) **YS**, 35 **El**
ASTM A 672	A 285A	US	Pipe: electric fusion welded		**Normalized**: all **diam**, 45 (310) **TS**
ANSI/ASTM A 589	Butt welded	US	Pipe: seamless, welded	0.050 **P**, 0.060 **S**	**As-rolled**: 0.312 (7.94) **diam**, 45 (310) **TS**, 25 (172) **YS**
ANSI/ASTM A 53	Type F	US	Pipe: welded, seamless	0.08 **P**, 0.06 **S**	**As rolled**: all **diam**, 45 (310) **TS**, 25 (172) **YS**, 39 **El**
ANSI/ASTM A 675	45	US	Bar	0.040 **P**, 0.050 **S**	**As hot-rolled**: all **diam**, 45 (310) **TS**, 22 (155) **YS**, 33 **El**
ANSI/ASTM A 283	Grade A	US	Plate	0.04 **P**, 0.05 **S**	**As rolled**: all **diam**, (310) **TS**, (165) **YS**, 30 **El**
AISI A500	Grade A	US	Pipe		**Cold formed welded or seamless (shaped)**: all **diam**, 45 (310) **TS**, 39 (270) **YS**, 25 **El**
AISI A500	Grade A	US	Pipe		**Cold formed welded or seamless (round)**: all **diam**, 45 (310) **TS**, 33 (225) **YS**, 25 **El**
DGN-B-177	Type F	Mexico	Tube: butt-welded	0.08 **P**, 0.06 **S**	**As welded**: (2–64) **diam**, (310) **TS**, (173) **YS**
BS 1775	HFS 11	UK	Tube		**Hot finished**: all **diam**, (309) **TS**, (170) **YS**, 30 **El**
BS 1775	CDS 11	UK	Tube		**Cold drawn**: all **diam**, (309) **TS**, (170) **YS**, 30 **El**
BS 1775	ERW 11	UK	Tube		**As welded**: all **diam**, (309) **TS**, (170) **YS**, 30 **El**
BS 1775	CEW 11	UK	Tube		**Cold drawn, annealed, normalized, as drawn, as drawn and tempered**: all **diam**, (309) **TS**, (170) **YS**, 30 **El**
BS 1775	OAW 11	UK	Tube		**Oxy-acetylene welded**: all **diam**, (309) **TS**, (170) **YS**, 30 **El**
DGN-B-281	Grade A	Mexico	Plate	0.04 **P**, 0.05 **S**, 0.20 **Cu**	**As rolled**: (19.1–101.6) **diam**, (309) **TS**, (167) **YS**, 30 **El**
NF A 36-102	Fd O E	France	Strip		**Hot rolled**: all **diam**, (294) **TS**

WROUGHT CARBON STEELS

specification number	designation	country	product forms	composition	mechanical properties (see page iv for explanation)
JIS G 3452	SGP	Japan	Pipe	0.050 **P**, 0.050 **S**	**As manufactured or cold finished and annealed:** all **diam**, (294) **TS**, 30 **El**
JIS G 3530		Japan	Wire		**Cold drawn, annealed or normalized, galvanized:** (>7.00) **diam**, (294) **TS**
JIS G 3531		Japan	Wire		**Cold drawn, annealed or normalized, galvanized:** (>5.50–6.00) **diam**, (294) **TS**
JIS G 3108	Type A	Japan	Bar	0.045 **P**, 0.045 **S**	**Hot rolled and cold finished:** (≤25) **diam**, (294) **TS**, 26 **El**
JIS G 3444	Class 1, No. 11	Japan	Tube: seamless or electric–resistance welded	0.050 **P**, 0.050 **S**	**As drawn or as welded:** all **diam**, (294) **TS**, 30 **El**
NF A 36–301	OC	France	Sheet, strip		**Hot rolled:** (≤8) **diam**, (290) **TS**
JIS G 3314	SA1C	Japan	Sheet		**Aluminum coated:** all **diam**, (275) **TS**
JIS G 3314	SA1D	Japan	Sheet		**Aluminum coated:** (0.40–0.60) **diam**, (275) **TS**, 30 **El**
JIS G 3314	SA1E	Japan	Sheet		**Aluminum coated:** (0.40–0.60) **diam**, (275) **TS**, 34 **El**
JIS G 3314	SA2C	Japan	Sheet		**Aluminum coated:** all **diam**, (275) **TS**
EURONORM 130	Fe P 02	EURONORM	Sheet, strip		**Cold–rolled:** (<3) **diam**, (270) **TS**, 3 **El**
EURONORM 130	Fe P 04	EURONORM	Sheet, strip		**Cold–rolled:** (<3) **diam**, (270) **TS**, (225) max **YS**, 37 **El**
EURONORM 130	Fe P 03	EURONORM	Sheet, strip		**Cold–rolled:** (<3) **diam**, (270) **TS**, (225) max **YS**, 37 **El**
DIN 17223	11 1.1211	Germany	Wire	0.030 **P**, 0.030 **S**, 0.12 **Cu**	**As drawn:** (0.30) **diam**, (270) **TS**
DIN 17223	C 1.1200	Germany	Wire	0.030 **P**, 0.030 **S**, 0.12 **Cu**	**As drawn:** (0.30) **diam**, (251) **TS**
DIN 17223	B 1.0600	Germany	Wire	0.040 **P**, 0.040 **S**, 0.25 **Cu**	**As drawn:** (0.30) **diam**, (210) **TS**
DIN 17223	A 1.0500	Germany	Wire	0.040 **P**, 0.040 **S**, 0.25 **Cu**	**As drawn:** (0.30) **diam**, (175) **TS**
SFS 1212	A600H	Finland	Bar	0.06 **P**, 0.08 **As**, 0.010 **N**	**Hot rolled:** (8) **diam**, (600) **YS**, 12 **El**
SABS 920	Type C, class 1	South Africa	Bar	0.05 **P**, 0.06 **S**, 0.008 **N**	**Hot rolled, deformed:** all **diam**, (410) **YS**, 12 **El**
SABS 920	Type C, class 2	South Africa	Bar	0.05 **P**, 0.06 **S**, 0.008 **N**	**Hot rolled, deformed:** all **diam**, (450) **YS**, 10 **El**
SABS 920	Type D	South Africa	Bar	0.05 **P**, 0.06 **S**, 0.008 **N**	**Cold worked, deformed:** all **diam**, (450) **YS**, 12 **El**
TS 912	UDK 669.14–423/Fe 70	Turkey	Shapes	0.055 **P**, 0.055 **S**, 0.008 **N**	**Hot rolled:** all **diam**, (686) **TS**, (363) **YS**, 10 **El**
DS 13081		Denmark	Wire	0.06 **P**, 0.06 **S**	
ISO R 1111	T 50	ISO	Sheet: tinplate and blackplate		**Batch annealed**
ANSI/ASTM A 730	Grades G,H	US	Forgings	0.60–0.90 **Mn**, 0.045 **P**, 0.050 **S**, 0.15 **Si**	
ANSI/ASTM A 521	Class CA	US	Forgings	0.90 **Mn**, 0.050 **P**, 0.050 **S**	

WROUGHT ALLOY STEELS

specification number	designation	country	product forms	composition	mechanical properties (see page iv for explanation)
ANSI/ASTM A 231		US	Wire	0.48–0.53 **C**, 0.70–0.90 **Mn**, 0.040 **P**, 0.040 **S**, 0.20–0.35 **Si**, 0.80–1.10 **Cr**, 0.15 min **V**	**Annealed or oil tempered**: 0.020 (0.51) **diam**, 300 (2070) **TS**
AMS 6450D		US	Wire	0.48–0.53 **C**, 0.70–0.90 **Mn**, 0.025 **P**, 0.025 **S**, 0.20–0.35 **Si**, 0.80–1.10 **Cr**, 0.25 **Ni**, 0.06 **Mo**, 0.15–0.30 **V**, 0.35 **Cu**	**Cold drawn, annealed (wire), hardened, tempered (spring)**: all **diam**, 220 (1517) **TS**, 40 **El**
AMS 6448D		US	Bar, forgings, tube	0.48–0.53 **C**, 0.70–0.90 **Mn**, 0.025 **P**, 0.025 **S**, 0.20–0.35 **Si**, 0.80–1.10 **Cr**, 0.25 **Ni**, 0.06 **Mo**, 0.35 **Cu**	**Cold finished (bar)**: ≤0.500 (≤12.70) **diam**, 125 (862) max **TS**
AMS 6328F		US	Bar, forgings, tube	0.48–0.53 **C**, 0.75–1.00 **Mn**, 0.025 **P**, 0.025 **S**, 0.20–0.35 **Si**, 0.40–0.60 **Cr**, 0.40–0.70 **Ni**, 0.20–0.30 **Mo**, 0.35 **Cu**	**Cold finished (bar)**: ≤0.500 (≤12.70) **diam**, 125 (862) max **TS**
AISI 4150		US	Bar	0.48–0.53 **C**, 0.75–1.00 **Mn**, 0.035 **P**, 0.040 **S**, 0.15–0.30 **Si**, 0.80–1.10 **Cr**, 0.15–0.25 **Mo**	
AISI 5150		US	Bar	0.48–0.53 **C**, 0.70–0.90 **Mn**, 0.035 **P**, 0.040 **S**, 0.15–0.30 **Si**, 0.70–0.90 **Cr**	
AISI 6150		US	Bar	0.48–0.53 **C**, 0.70–0.90 **Mn**, 0.035 **P**, 0.040 **S**, 0.15–0.30 **Si**, 0.80–1.10 **Cr**, 0.15 **Mo**	
AISI 50B50		US	Bar	0.48–0.53 **C**, 0.75–1.00 **Mn**, 0.035 **P**, 0.040 **S**, 0.15–0.30 **Si**, 0.40–0.60 **Cr**, 0.0005–0.003 **B**	
MIL-S-8503A	AISI 6150	US	Bar	0.48–0.53 **C**, 0.70–0.90 **Mn**, 0.025 **P**, 0.025 **S**, 0.20–0.35 **Si**, 0.75–1.20 **Cr**, 0.15 min **V**	
COPANT 334	4150	COPANT	Bar	0.48–0.53 **C**, 0.75–1.00 **Mn**, 0.035 **P**, 0.040 **S**, 0.20–0.35 **Si**, 0.80–1.10 **Cr**, 0.15–0.25 **Mo**	
COPANT 334	5150	COPANT	Bar	0.48–0.53 **C**, 0.70–0.90 **Mn**, 0.035 **P**, 0.040 **S**, 0.20–0.35 **Si**, 0.70–0.90 **Cr**	
COPANT 334	6150	COPANT	Bar	0.48–0.53 **C**, 0.70–0.90 **Mn**, 0.035 **P**, 0.040 **S**, 0.20–0.35 **Si**, 0.80–1.10 **Cr**, 0.15 min **V**	
COPANT 334	8650	COPANT	Bar	0.48–0.53 **C**, 0.75–1.00 **Mn**, 0.035 **P**, 0.040 **S**, 0.20–0.35 **Si**, 0.40–0.60 **Cr**, 0.40–0.70 **Ni**, 0.15–0.25 **Mo**	
AS 1444	Grade AS 1444/4150	Australia	Bar, bloom, billet, slab	0.48–0.53 **C**, 0.75–1.00 **Mn**, 0.040 **P**, 0.040 **S**, 0.10–0.35 **Si**, 0.80–1.10 **Cr**, 0.15–0.25 **Mo**	
AS 1444	Grade AS 1444/6150	Australia	Bar, bloom, billet, slab	0.48–0.53 **C**, 0.70–0.90 **Mn**, 0.040 **P**, 0.040 **S**, 0.10–0.35 **Si**, 0.80–1.10 **Cr**, 0.15 min **V**	
DGN-B-203	Grade 4150	Mexico	Tube: seamless	0.48–0.53 **C**, 0.75–1.00 **Mn**, 0.040 **P**, 0.040 **S**, 0.20–0.35 **Si**, 0.80–1.10 **Cr**, 0.15–0.25 **Mo**	
DGN-B-203	Grade 5150	Mexico	Tube: seamless	0.48–0.53 **C**, 0.70–0.90 **Mn**, 0.040 **P**, 0.040 **S**, 0.20–0.35 **Si**, 0.70–0.90 **Cr**	
DGN-B-203	Grade 8650	Mexico	Tube: seamless	0.48–0.53 **C**, 0.75–1.00 **Mn**, 0.040 **P**, 0.040 **S**, 0.20–0.35 **Si**, 0.40–0.60 **Cr**, 0.40–0.70 **Ni**, 0.15–0.25 **Mo**	
DGN-B-203	Grade 6150	Mexico	Tube: seamless	0.48–0.53 **C**, 0.70–0.90 **Mn**, 0.040 **P**, 0.040 **S**, 0.20–0.35 **Si**, 0.80–1.10 **Cr**, 0.15 min **V**	
DGN-B-203	Grade 50B50	Mexico	Tube: seamless	0.48–0.53 **C**, 0.75–1.00 **Mn**, 0.040 **P**, 0.040 **S**, 0.20–0.35 **Si**, 0.40–0.60 **Cr**, 0.0005 min **B**	
DGN-B-203	Grade 9850	Mexico	Tube: seamless	0.48–0.53 **C**, 0.70–0.90 **Mn**, 0.040 **P**, 0.040 **S**, 0.20–0.35 **Si**, 0.70–0.90 **Cr**, 0.85–1.15 **Ni**, 0.20–0.35 **Mo**	
COPANT 514	4150	COPANT	Tube	0.48–0.53 **C**, 0.75–1.0 **Mn**, 0.040 **P**, 0.040 **S**, 0.20–0.35 **Si**, 0.80–1.10 **Cr**, 0.15–0.25 **Mo**	

WROUGHT ALLOY STEELS

specification number	designation	country	product forms	composition	mechanical properties (see page iv for explanation)
DGN–B–300	50B50	Mexico	Bar	0.48–0.53 **C**, 0.75–1.00 **Mn**, 0.035 **P**, 0.040 **S**, 0.20–0.35 **Si**, 0.40–0.60 **Cr**, 0.0005 min **B**	**Annealed**
DGN–B–300	6150	Mexico	Bar	0.48–0.53 **C**, 0.70–0.90 **Mn**, 0.035 **P**, 0.040 **S**, 0.20–0.35 **Si**, 0.80–1.10 **Cr**, 0.15 min **Mo**	**Annealed**
DGN–B–300	5150	Mexico	Bar	0.48–0.53 **C**, 0.70–0.90 **Mn**, 0.035 **P**, 0.040 **S**, 0.20–0.35 **Si**, 0.70–0.90 **Cr**	**Annealed**
DGN–B–300	4150	Mexico	Bar	0.48–0.53 **C**, 0.75–1.00 **Mn**, 0.035 **P**, 0.040 **S**, 0.20–0.35 **Si**, 0.80–1.10 **Cr**, 0.15–0.25 **Mo**	**Annealed**
ANSI/ASTM A 29	4150	US	Bar	0.48–0.53 **C**, 0.75–1.00 **Mn**, 0.035 **P**, 0.040 **S**, 0.15–0.30 **Si**, 0.80–1.10 **Cr**, 0.15–0.25 **Mo**	
ANSI/ASTM A 646	6150	US	Blooms, billets: aircraft quality	0.48–0.53 **C**, 0.70–0.90 **Mn**, 0.025 **P**, 0.025 **S**, 0.20–0.35 **Si**, 0.80–1.10 **Cr**, 0.15 min **V**	**Annealed**
ASTM A 689	50B50	US	Bar, spring	0.48–0.53 **C**, 0.75–1.00 **Mn**, 0.035 **P**, 0.040 **S**, 0.15–0.30 **Si**, 0.40–0.60 **Cr**, 0.0005 min **B**	
ASTM A 689	6150	US	Bar	0.48–0.53 **C**, 0.70–0.90 **Mn**, 0.035 **P**, 0.040 **S**, 0.15–0.30 **Si**, 0.80–1.10 **Cr**, 0.15 min **V**	
ASTM A 689	4150	US	Bar	0.48–0.53 **C**, 0.75–1.00 **Mn**, 0.035 **P**, 0.040 **S**, 0.15–0.30 **Si**, 0.80–1.10 **Cr**, 0.15–0.25 **Mo**	
ASTM A 689	5150	US	Bar	0.48–0.53 **C**, 0.70–0.90 **Mn**, 0.035 **P**, 0.040 **S**, 0.15–0.30 **Si**, 0.70–0.90 **Cr**	
ANSI/ASTM A 322	4150	US	Bar	0.48–0.53 **C**, 0.75–1.00 **Mn**, 0.035 **P**, 0.040 **S**, 0.15–0.30 **Si**, 0.80–1.10 **Cr**, 0.15–0.25 **Mo**	
ANSI/ASTM A 322	50B50	US	Bar	0.48–0.53 **C**, 0.75–1.00 **Mn**, 0.035 **P**, 0.040 **S**, 0.15–0.30 **Si**, 0.40–0.60 **Cr**, 0.0005 min **B**	
ANSI/ASTM A 322	5150	US	Bar	0.48–0.53 **C**, 0.70–0.90 **Mn**, 0.035 **P**, 0.040 **S**, 0.15–0.30 **Si**, 0.70–0.90 **Cr**	
ANSI/ASTM A 322	6150	US	Bar	0.48–0.53 **C**, 0.70–0.90 **Mn**, 0.035 **P**, 0.040 **S**, 0.15–0.30 **Si**, 0.80–1.10 **Cr**, 0.15 min **V**	
ANSI/ASTM A 29	5150	US	Bar	0.48–0.53 **C**, 0.70–0.90 **Mn**, 0.035 **P**, 0.040 **S**, 0.15–0.30 **Si**, 0.70–0.90 **Cr**	
ANSI/ASTM A 29	6150	US	Bar	0.48–0.53 **C**, 0.70–0.90 **Mn**, 0.035 **P**, 0.040 **S**, 0.15–0.30 **Si**, 0.80–1.10 **Cr**, 0.15 min **V**	
ANSI/ASTM A 29	8650	US	Bar	0.48–0.53 **C**, 0.75–1.00 **Mn**, 0.035 **P**, 0.040 **S**, 0.15–0.30 **Si**, 0.40–0.60 **Cr**, 0.40–0.70 **Ni**, 0.15–0.25 **Mo**	
AISI 6150		US	Wire, rod	0.48–0.53 **C**, 0.70–0.90 **Mn**, 0.035 **P**, 0.040 **S**, 0.15–0.30 **Si**, 0.80–1.10 **Cr**, 0.15 min **V**	
AISI 50B50		US	Wire, rod	0.48–0.53 **C**, 0.75–1.00 **Mn**, 0.035 **P**, 0.040 **S**, 0.15–0.30 **Si**, 0.40–0.60 **Cr**	
AISI 4150		US	Wire, rod	0.48–0.53 **C**, 0.75–1.00 **Mn**, 0.035 **P**, 0.040 **S**, 0.15–0.30 **Si**, 0.80–1.10 **Cr**, 0.15–0.25 **Mo**	
AISI 5150		US	Wire, rod	0.48–0.53 **C**, 0.70–0.90 **Mn**, 0.035 **P**, 0.040 **S**, 0.15–0.30 **Si**, 0.70–0.90 **Cr**	
DGN–B–301	1524H	Mexico	Bar	1.25–1.75 **C**, 1.25–1.75 **Mn**, 0.040 **P**, 0.050 **S**, 0.15–0.30 **Si**	
SABS 407	Grade 3	South Africa	Castings	1.05–1.35 **C**, 11.5–14.5 **Mn**, 1.5–2.5 **Cr**, 1.0 **Si**, 0.07 **P**	
SABS 407	Grade 2	South Africa	Castings	1.05–1.30 **C**, 11.5–14.5 **Mn**, 1.0 **Si**, 0.07 **P**	
NF A 32–071	Z 120 M 12–M	France	Castings	1.0–1.45 **C**, 11.0–14.5 **Mn**, 1.0 **Si**, 0.10 **P**, 0.06 **S**	

specification number	designation	country	product forms	composition	mechanical properties (see page iv for explanation)
SABS 407	Grade 1	South Africa	Castings	1.00–1.35 **C**, 11.0 min **Mn**, 1.0 **Si**, 0.070 **P**	
MIL–S–50783		US	Bar, billets	1.00–1.15 **C**, 1.60–1.90 **Mn**, 0.35 **P**, 0.40 **S**, 0.70–1.00 **Si**, 0.20 **Cr**, 0.25 **Ni**, 0.06 **Mo**, 0.020 **Al**, 0.35 **Cu**	
AMS 6440F		US	Bar, forgings	0.98–1.10 **C**, 0.25–0.45 **Mn**, 0.025 **P**, 0.025 **S**, 0.20–0.35 **Si**, 1.30–1.60 **Cr**, 0.25 **Ni**, 0.08 **Mo**, 0.35 **Cu**	**Cold finished**: 0.500 (12.70) max **diam**, 120 (827) max **TS**
AMS 6443C		US	Bar, forgings	0.98–1.10 **C**, 0.25–0.45 **Mn**, 0.015 **P**, 0.015 **S**, 0.20–0.35 **Si**, 0.90–1.15 **Cr**, 0.25 **Ni**, 0.06 **Mo**, 0.35 **Cu**	**Cold finished**: ≤0.500 (≤12.7) **diam**, 120 (827) **TS**
AMS 6444E		US	Bar, forgings, tube	0.98–1.10 **C**, 0.25–0.45 **Mn**, 0.015 **P**, 0.015 **S**, 0.20–0.35 **Si**, 1.30–1.60 **Cr**, 0.25 **Ni**, 0.08 **Mo**, 0.35 **Cu**	**Cold finished (bar)**: ≤0.500 (≤12.70) **diam**, 120 (827) **TS**
AMS 6446A		US	Bar, forgings	0.98–1.10 **C**, 0.25–0.45 **Mn**, 0.015 **P**, 0.015 **S**, 0.20–0.35 **Si**, 0.90–1.15 **Cr**, 0.25 **Ni**, 0.08 **Mo**, 0.35 **Cu**	**Cold finished**: ≤0.500 (≤12.7) **diam**, 120 (827) **TS**
AMS 6447B		US	Bar, forgings, tube	0.98–1.10 **C**, 0.25–0.45 **Mn**, 0.015 **P**, 0.015 **S**, 0.20–0.35 **Si**, 1.30–1.60 **Cr**, 0.25 **Ni**, 0.08 **Mo**, 0.35 **Cu**	**Cold finished (bar)**: ≤0.500 (≤12.70) **diam**, 120 (827) max **TS**
AMS 6449		US	Bar, forgings	0.98–1.10 **C**, 0.25–0.45 **Mn**, 0.025 **P**, 0.025 **S**, 0.20–0.35 **Si**, 0.90–1.15 **Cr**, 0.25 **Ni**, 0.06 **Mo**, 0.35 **Cu**	**Cold finished**: ≤0.500 (≤12.7) **diam**, 120 (827) **TS**
AISI E51100		US	Bar	0.98–1.10 **C**, 0.25–0.45 **Mn**, 0.025 **P**, 0.025 **S**, 0.15–0.30 **Si**, 0.90–1.15 **Cr**	
AISI E52100		US	Bar	0.98–1.10 **C**, 0.25–0.45 **Mn**, 0.025 **P**, 0.025 **S**, 0.15–0.30 **Si**, 1.30–1.60 **Cr**	
AMS 6441E		US	Tube	0.98–1.10 **C**, 0.25–0.45 **Mn**, 0.025 **P**, 0.025 **S**, 0.20–0.35 **Si**, 1.30–1.60 **Cr**, 0.25 **Ni**, 0.08 **Mo**, 0.35 **Cu**	
COPANT 334	52100	COPANT	Bar	0.98–1.10 **C**, 0.25–0.45 **Mn**, 0.035 **P**, 0.025 **S**, 0.20–0.35 **Si**, 1.30–1.60 **Cr**	
DGN–B–300	E 52100	Mexico	Bar	0.98–1.10 **C**, 0.25–0.45 **Mn**, 0.025 **P**, 0.025 **S**, 0.20–0.35 **Si**, 1.30–1.60 **Cr**	
DGN–B–300	E 51100	Mexico	Bar	0.98–1.10 **C**, 0.25–0.45 **Mn**, 0.025 **P**, 0.025 **S**, 0.20–0.35 **Si**, 0.90–1.15 **Cr**	
ASTM A 485	Grade 3	US	Billets, bar, tube	0.98–1.10 **C**, 0.70–0.90 **Mn**, 0.025 **P**, 0.025 **S**, 0.20–0.35 **Si**, 1.10–1.40 **Cr**, 0.25 **Ni**, 0.20–0.30 **Mo**, 0.35 **Cu**	
ASTM A 485	Grade 4	US	Billets, bar, tube	0.98–1.10 **C**, 1.05–1.35 **Mn**, 0.025 **P**, 0.025 **S**, 0.20–0.35 **Si**, 1.10–1.40 **Cr**, 0.25 **Ni**, 0.45–0.60 **Mo**, 0.35 **Cu**	
ANSI/ASTM A 646	52100	US	Blooms, billets: aircraft quality	0.98–1.10 **C**, 0.25–0.45 **Mn**, 0.025 **P**, 0.025 **S**, 0.20–0.35 **Si**, 1.30–1.60 **Cr**	**Annealed**
ASTM A 689	E51100	US	Bar	0.98–1.10 **C**, 0.25–0.45 **Mn**, 0.025 **P**, 0.025 **S**, 0.15–0.30 **Si**, 0.90–1.15 **Cr**	
ASTM A 689	E52100	US	Bar	0.98–1.10 **C**, 0.25–0.45 **Mn**, 0.025 **P**, 0.025 **S**, 0.15–0.30 **Si**, 1.30–1.60 **Cr**	
ASTM A 295	50100	US	Billets, forgings, bar, rod, coil, tube	0.98–1.10 **C**, 0.25–0.45 **Mn**, 0.025 **P**, 0.025 **S**, 0.20–0.35 **Si**, 0.40–0.60 **Cr**, 0.25 **Ni**, 0.08 **Mo**, 0.35 **Cu**	

specification number	designation	country	product forms	composition	mechanical properties (see page iv for explanation)
ASTM A 295	51100	US	Billets, forgings, bar, rod, coil, tube	0.98–1.10 **C**, 0.25–0.45 **Mn**, 0.025 **P**, 0.025 **S**, 0.20–0.35 **Si**, 0.90–1.15 **Cr**, 0.25 **Ni**, 0.08 **Mo**, 0.35 **Cu**	
ASTM A 295	52100	US	Billets, forgings, bar, rod, coil, tube	0.98–1.10 **C**, 0.25–0.45 **Mn**, 0.025 **P**, 0.025 **S**, 0.20–0.35 **Si**, 1.30–1.60 **Cr**, 0.25 **Ni**, 0.08 **Mo**, 0.35 **Cu**	
ANSI/ASTM A 322	E 51100	US	Bar	0.98–1.10 **C**, 0.25–0.45 **Mn**, 0.025 **P**, 0.025 **S**, 0.15–0.30 **Si**, 0.90–1.15 **Cr**	
ANSI/ASTM A 322	E 52100	US	Bar	0.98–1.10 **C**, 0.25–0.45 **Mn**, 0.025 **P**, 0.025 **S**, 0.15–0.30 **Si**, 1.30–1.60 **Cr**	
ANSI/ASTM A 29	E 50100	US	Bar	0.98–1.10 **C**, 0.25–0.45 **Mn**, 0.025 **P**, 0.025 **S**, 0.15–0.30 **Si**, 0.40–0.60 **Cr**	
ANSI/ASTM A 29	E 51100	US	Bar	0.98–1.10 **C**, 0.25–0.45 **Mn**, 0.025 **P**, 0.025 **S**, 0.15–0.30 **Si**, 0.90–1.15 **Cr**	
ANSI/ASTM A 29	E 52100	US	Bar	0.98–1.10 **C**, 0.25–0.45 **Mn**, 0.025 **P**, 0.025 **S**, 0.15–0.30 **Si**, 1.30–1.60 **Cr**	
AISI E 51100		US	Wire, rod	0.98–1.10 **C**, 0.25–0.45 **Mn**, 0.025 **P**, 0.025 **S**, 0.15–0.30 **Si**, 0.90–1.15 **Cr**	
AISI E 52100		US	Wire, rod	0.98–1.10 **C**, 0.25–0.45 **Mn**, 0.025 **P**, 0.025 **S**, 0.15–0.30 **Si**, 1.30–1.60 **Cr**	
DGN–B–297	E51100	Mexico	Bar	0.98–1.10 **C**, 0.25–0.45 **Mn**, 0.025 **P**, 0.025 **S**, 0.20–0.35 **Si**, 0.90–1.15 **Cr**	
DGN–B–297	E52100	Mexico	Bar	0.98–1.10 **C**, 0.25–0.45 **Mn**, 0.025 **P**, 0.025 **S**, 0.20–0.35 **Si**, 1.30–1.60 **Cr**	
AECMA prEN2224		AECMA	Bar	0.95–1.10 **C**, 0.25–0.45 **Mn**, 0.015 **P**, 0.010 **S**, 0.15–0.35 **Si**, 1.35–1.65 **Cr**, 0.40 **Ni**	**Hardened and tempered**
AECMA prEN2223		AECMA	Bar	0.95–1.10 **C**, 0.25–0.45 **Mn**, 0.015 **P**, 0.010 **S**, 0.15–0.35 **Si**, 1.35–1.65 **Cr**, 0.40 **Ni**	**Hardened and tempered**
AECMA prEN2221		AECMA	Bar	0.95–1.10 **C**, 0.25–0.45 **Mn**, 0.030 **P**, 0.020 **S**, 0.15–0.35 **Si**, 1.35–1.65 **Cr**, 0.40 **Ni**	**Hardened and tempered**
AECMA prEN2031		AECMA	Bar	0.95–1.10 **C**, 0.25–0.45 **Mn**, 0.030 **P**, 0.020 **S**, 0.15–0.35 **Si**, 1.35–1.65 **Cr**, 0.40 **Ni**	**Hardened and tempered**
NF A 35–553	100 C 6	France	Strip	0.95–1.10 **C**, 0.25–0.40 **Mn**, 0.025 **P**, 0.025 **S**, 0.10–0.35 **Si**, 1.30–1.60 **Cr**, 0.30 **Ni**	
AIR 9160/C 95	9160C361	France	Bar, forgings: bearing steel	0.95–1.10 **C**, 0.20–0.40 **Mn**, 0.030 **P**, 0.020 **S**, 0.15–0.35 **Si**, 1.35–1.60 **Cr**, 0.40 **Ni**, 0.10 **Mo**, 0.30 **V**	**Quenched and tempered**
ISO 683/XVII	1	ISO	Billets, bar, wire, tube	0.95–1.10 **C**, 0.25–0.45 **Mn**, 0.030 **P**, 0.025 **S**, 0.15–0.35 **Si**, 1.35–1.65 **Cr**	
ISO 683/XVII	2	ISO	Billets, bar, wire, tube	0.95–1.10 **C**, 0.95–1.25 **Mn**, 0.030 **P**, 0.025 **S**, 0.45–0.75 **Si**, 0.90–1.20 **Cr**	
ISO 683/XVII	3	ISO	Billets, bar, wire, tube	0.95–1.10 **C**, 0.95–1.25 **Mn**, 0.030 **P**, 0.025 **S**, 0.45–0.75 **Si**, 1.40–1.65 **Cr**	
ISO 683/XVII	4	ISO	Billets, bar, wire, tube	0.95–1.10 **C**, 0.25–0.45 **Mn**, 0.030 **P**, 0.025 **S**, 0.20–0.40 **Si**, 1.65–1.95 **Cr**, 0.20–0.40 **Mo**	
ISO 683/XVII	5	ISO	Billets, bar, wire, tube	0.95–1.10 **C**, 0.60–0.90 **Mn**, 0.030 **P**, 0.025 **S**, 0.20–0.40 **Si**, 1.65–1.95 **Cr**, 0.20–0.40 **Mo**	
BS 970 Part 2	Grade 534 A 99	UK	Blooms, billets, bar, forgings	0.95–1.10 **C**, 0.25–0.40 **Mn**, 1.20–1.60 **Cr**	

WROUGHT ALLOY STEELS

specification number	designation	country	product forms	composition	mechanical properties (see page iv for explanation)
BS 970 Part 2	Grade 535 A 99	UK	Blooms, billets, bar, forgings	0.95–1.10 **C**, 0.40–0.70 **Mn**, 1.20–1.60 **Cr**	
MIL–S–980B	Class I	US	Bar: steel, chromium alloy	0.95–1.10 **C**, 0.25–0.45 **Mn**, 0.025 **P**, 0.025 **S**, 0.20–0.35 **Si**, 1.30–1.60 **Cr**, 0.35 **Ni**, 0.08 **Mo**, 0.25 **Cu**	**Hot rolled**
DGN–B–203	E 50100	Mexico	Tube: seamless	0.95–1.10 **C**, 0.25–0.45 **Mn**, 0.025 **P**, 0.025 **S**, 0.20–0.35 **Si**, 0.40–0.60 **Cr**	
DGN–B–203	Grade E 51100	Mexico	Tube: seamless	0.95–1.10 **C**, 0.25–0.45 **Mn**, 0.025 **P**, 0.025 **S**, 0.20–0.35 **Si**, 0.90–1.15 **Cr**	
DGN–B–203	E 52100	Mexico	Tube: seamless	0.95–1.10 **C**, 0.25–0.45 **Mn**, 0.025 **P**, 0.025 **S**, 0.20–0.35 **Si**, 1.30–1.60 **Cr**	
AECMA prEN2225	FE–PL 32	AECMA	Forgings	0.95–1.10 **C**, 0.25–0.45 **Mn**, 0.015 **P**, 0.010 **S**, 0.15–0.35 **Si**, 1.35–1.65 **Cr**, 0.40 **Ni**	**Hardened and tempered**
ANSI/ASTM A 519	E 50100	US	Tube: seamless	0.95–1.10 **C**, 0.25–0.45 **Mn**, 0.025 **P**, 0.025 **S**, 0.15–0.35 **Si**, 0.40–0.60 **Cr**	
ANSI/ASTM A 519	E 51100	US	Tube: seamless	0.95–1.10 **C**, 0.25–0.45 **Mn**, 0.025 **P**, 0.025 **S**, 0.15–0.35 **Si**, 0.90–1.15 **Cr**	
ANSI/ASTM A 519	E 52100	US	Tube: seamless	0.95–1.10 **C**, 0.25–0.45 **Mn**, 0.025 **P**, 0.025 **S**, 0.15–0.35 **Si**, 1.30–1.60 **Cr**	
ANSI/ASTM A 535	52100	US	Billets, coils, bar, rod, tube	0.95–1.10 **C**, 0.25–0.45 **Mn**, 0.015 **P**, 0.015 **S**, 0.20–0.35 **Si**, 1.30–1.60 **Cr**	
ANSI/ASTM A 535	52100 Mod 3	US	Billets, coils, bar, rod, tube	0.95–1.10 **C**, 0.65–0.90 **Mn**, 0.015 **P**, 0.015 **S**, 0.20–0.35 **Si**, 1.10–1.50 **Cr**, 0.20–0.30 **Mo**	
ANSI/ASTM A 535	52100 Mod 4	US	Billets, coils, bar, rod, tube	0.95–1.10 **C**, 1.05–1.35 **Mn**, 0.015 **P**, 0.015 **S**, 0.20–0.35 **Si**, 1.10–1.50 **Cr**, 0.45–0.60 **Mo**	
SIS 14 22 58	SIS 22 58–06	Sweden	Bar, tube, wire	0.95–1.10 **C**, 0.25–0.45 **Mn**, 0.030 **P**, 0.025 **S**, 0.15–0.35 **Si**, 1.35–1.65 **Cr**	**Cold drawn**
SIS 14 22 58	SIS 22 58–02	Sweden	Bar, forgings, strip, tube, wire	0.95–1.10 **C**, 0.25–0.45 **Mn**, 0.030 **P**, 0.025 **S**, 0.15–0.35 **Si**, 1.35–1.65 **Cr**	**Soft annealed**
SIS 14 22 58	SIS 22 58–08	Sweden	Bar, tube	0.95–1.10 **C**, 0.25–0.45 **Mn**, 0.030 **P**, 0.025 **S**, 0.15–0.35 **Si**, 1.35–1.65 **Cr**	**Quenched**
SIS 14 22 58	SIS 2258–02	Sweden	Bar, forgings, strip, tube, wire	0.95–1.10 **C**, 0.25–0.45 **Mn**, 1.35–1.65 **Cr**	
SIS 14 22 58	SIS 2258–08	Sweden	Bar, tube	0.95–1.10 **C**, 0.25–0.45 **Mn**, 1.35–1.65 **Cr**	
SIS 14 22 58	SIS 2258–06	Sweden	Bar, tube, wire	0.95–1.10 **C**, 0.25–0.45 **Mn**, 1.35–1.65 **Cr**	
JIS G 4805	SUJ 1	Japan	Bar, wire	0.95–1.10 **C**, 0.50 **Mn**, 0.025 **P**, 0.025 **S**, 0.15–0.35 **Si**, 0.90–1.20 **Cr**, 0.25 **Ni**, 0.08 **Mo**, 0.25 **Cu** (bar)	
JIS G 4805	SUJ 2	Japan	Bar, wire	0.95–1.10 **C**, 0.50 **Mn**, 0.025 **P**, 0.025 **S**, 0.15–0.35 **Si**, 1.30–1.60 **Cr**, 0.25 **Ni**, 0.08 **Mo**, 0.25 **Cu** (bar)	
JIS G 4805	SUJ 3	Japan	Bar, wire	0.95–1.10 **C**, 0.90–1.15 **Mn**, 0.025 **P**, 0.025 **S**, 0.40–0.70 **Si**, 0.90–1.20 **Cr**, 0.25 **Ni**, 0.08 **Mo**, 0.25 **Cu** (bar)	
JIS G 4805	SUJ 4	Japan	Bar, wire	0.95–1.10 **C**, 0.50 **Mn**, 0.025 **P**, 0.025 **S**, 0.15–0.35 **Si**, 1.30–1.60 **Cr**, 0.25 **Ni**, 0.10–0.25 **Mo**, 0.25 **Cu** (bar)	
JIS G 4805	SUJ 5	Japan	Bar, wire	0.95–1.10 **C**, 0.90–1.15 **Mn**, 0.025 **P**, 0.025 **S**, 0.40–0.70 **Si**, 0.90–1.20 **Cr**, 0.25 **Ni**, 0.10–0.25 **Mo**, 0.25 **Cu** (bar)	

specification number	designation	country	product forms	composition	mechanical properties (see page iv for explanation)
COPANT 514	Grade E50100	COPANT	Tube: seamless	0.95–1.10 **C**, 0.25–0.45 **Mn**, 0.040 **P**, 0.050 **S**, 0.10 **Si**, 0.40–0.60 **Cr**	
COPANT 514	Grade E51100	COPANT	Tube: seamless	0.95–1.10 **C**, 0.25–0.45 **Mn**, 0.040 **P**, 0.050 **S**, 0.10 **Si**, 0.90–1.15 **Cr**	
COPANT 514	Grade E52100	COPANT	Tube: seamless	0.95–1.10 **C**, 0.25–0.45 **Mn**, 0.040 **P**, 0.050 **S**, 0.10 **Si**, 1.30–1.60 **Cr**	
AMS 6445C		US	Bar, forgings, tube	0.92–1.02 **C**, 0.95–1.25 **Mn**, 0.015 **P**, 0.015 **S**, 0.50–0.70 **Si**, 0.90–1.15 **Cr**, 0.25 **Ni**, 0.08 **Mo**, 0.35 **Cu**	**Cold finished (bar):** ≤0.500 (≤12.70) **diam**, 120 (827) max **TS**
AS G18	G18/En 31	Australia	Bar, billet	0.90–1.20 **C**, 0.30–0.75 **Mn**, 0.050 **P**, 0.050 **S**, 0.10–0.35 **Si**, 1.00–1.60 **Cr**	
AMS 6442D		US	Bar, forgings	0.9–1.10 **C**, 0.25–0.45 **Mn**, 0.025 **P**, 0.025 **S**, 0.20–0.35 **Si**, 0.40–0.60 **Cr**, 0.25 **Ni**, 0.06 **Mo**, 0.35 **Cu**	**Cold finished:** ≤0.500 (≤12.70) **diam**, 120 (827) **TS**
BS 2S.136		UK	Billets, bar, forgings, parts: aircraft quality	0.90–1.10 **C**, 0.25–0.55 **Mn**, 0.015 **P**, 0.010 **S**, 0.15–0.40 **Si**, 1.3–1.6 **Cr**, 0.4 **Ni**, 0.1 **Mo**, 0.3 **V**, 0.25 **Cu**	**Hardened and tempered:** (25) **diam**
BS 2S.135		UK	Billets, bar, forgings, parts: aircraft quality	0.90–1.10 **C**, 0.25–0.55 **Mn**, 0.030 **P**, 0.025 **S**, 0.15–0.40 **Si**, 1.3–1.6 **Cr**, 0.4 **Ni**, 0.1 **Mo**, 0.3 **V**, 0.25 **Cu**	**Hardened and tempered:** (25) **diam**
ANSI/ASTM A 535	52100 Mod 1	US	Billets, coils, bar, rod, tube	0.90–1.05 **C**, 0.95–1.25 **Mn**, 0.015 **P**, 0.015 **S**, 0.45–0.75 **Si**, 0.90–1.20 **Cr**	
MIL-S-7947A		US	Sheet, strip	0.90–1.03 **C**, 0.30–0.50 **Mn**, 0.025 **P**, 0.025 **S**, 0.15–0.30 **Si**, 0.20 **Cr**, 0.25 **Ni**, 0.06 **Mo**	
ASTM A 485	Grade 1	US	Billets, bar, tube	0.90–1.02 **C**, 0.95–1.25 **Mn**, 0.025 **P**, 0.025 **S**, 0.45–0.75 **Si**, 0.90–1.20 **Cr**, 0.25 **Ni**, 0.08 **Mo**, 0.35 **Cu**	
ANSI/ASTM A 535	52100 Mod 2	US	Billets, coils, bar, rod, tube	0.85–1.00 **C**, 1.40–1.70 **Mn**, 0.015 **P**, 0.015 **S**, 0.50–0.80 **Si**, 1.40–1.80 **Cr**	
ASTM A 485	Grade 2		Billets, bar, tube	0.85–0.97 **C**, 1.40–1.70 **Mn**, 0.025 **P**, 0.025 **S**, 0.50–0.80 **Si**, 1.40–1.75 **Cr**, 0.25 **Ni**, 0.08 **Mo**, 0.35 **Cu**	
AMS 6426B		US	Bar, forgings, tube	0.80–0.90 **C**, 0.20–0.50 **Mn**, 0.015 **P**, 0.015 **S**, 0.60–0.90 **Si**, 0.85–1.15 **Cr**, 0.15 **Ni**, 0.50–0.65 **Mo**, 0.015 **Cu**	**Hot finished and annealed (bar):** ≤0.500 (≤12.70) **diam**, 105 (724) max **TS**; **Cold finished and annealed:** ≤0.500 (≤12.70) **diam**, 125 (862) max **TS**
JIS G 3311	S85CM	Japan	Strip	0.80–0.90 **C**, 0.70–1.00 **Mn**, 0.030 **P**, 0.035 **S**, 0.15–0.30 **Si**, 0.20 **Cr**, 0.20 **Ni**, 0.30 **Cu**	
AMS 6491		US	Bar, forgings, tube	0.80–0.85 **C**, 0.15–0.35 **Mn**, 0.015 **P**, 0.008 **S**, 0.25 **Si**, 4.00–4.25 **Cr**, 0.15 **Ni**, 4.00–4.50 **Mo**, 0.90–1.10 **V**, 0.25 **Co**, 0.10 **Cu**, 0.25 **W**	**Cold finished (bar):** ≤0.500 (≤12.70) **diam**, 120 (827) max **TS**
ISO 683/XVII	31	ISO	Billets, bar, wire, tube	0.78–0.86 **C**, 0.40 **Mn**, 0.030 **P**, 0.030 **S**, 0.40 **Si**, 3.80–4.50 **Cr**, 4.70–5.20 **Mo**, 1.70–2.00 **V**, 6.00–6.70 **W**	
AMS 6490C		US	Bar, forgings, tube	0.77–0.85 **C**, 0.35 **Mn**, 0.015 **P**, 0.015 **S**, 0.25 **Si**, 3.75–4.25 **Cr**, 0.15 **Ni**, 4.00–4.50 **Mo**, 0.90–1.10 **V**, 0.25 **Co**, 0.010 **Cu**, 0.25 **W**	**Cold finished (bar):** ≤0.500 (≤12.70) **diam**, 125 (862) max **TS**
AIR 9160/C 93	9160C351	France	Bar, forgings: bearing steel	0.77–0.85 **C**, 0.35 **Mn**, 0.025 **P**, 0.015 **S**, 0.25 **Si**, 3.25–4.25 **Cr**, 0.10 **Ni**, 4.0–5.0 **Mo**, 0.90–1.10 **V**, 0.25 **Co**	**Hardened and tempered**

WROUGHT ALLOY STEELS

specification number	designation	country	product forms	composition	mechanical properties (see page iv for explanation)
ISO 683/XVII	30	ISO	Billets, bar, wire, tube	0.77–0.85 **C**, 0.35 **Mn**, 0.025 **P**, 0.020 **S**, 0.25 **Si**, 3.75–4.25 **Cr**, 4.00–4.50 **Mo**, 0.90–1.10 **V**	
AIR 9160/C 97	9160C371	France	Bar, forgings: bearing steel	0.75–0.95 **C**, 0.10–0.40 **Mn**, 0.030 **P**, 0.015 **S**, 0.10–0.40 **Si**, 4.0–5.0 **Cr**, 0.20 **Ni**, 4.5–5.50 **Mo**, 1.5–2.0 **V**, 5.5–6.50 **W**	**Hardened and tempered**
AS G18	G18/En 59	Australia	Bar, billet	0.74–0.84 **C**, 0.20–0.60 **Mn**, 0.030 **P**, 0.030 **S**, 1.75–2.25 **Si**, 19.0–20.5 **Cr**, 1.15–1.65 **Ni**	
SABS 407	Grade 4	South Africa		0.7–1.3 **C**, 11.5–14.0 **Mn**, 3.0–4.0 **Ni**, 1.0 **Si**, 0.07 **P**	
SABS 407	Grade 5	South Africa	Castings	0.7–1.3 **C**, 11.5–14.0 **Mn**, 1.0 **Si**, 0.9–1.2 **Mo**, 0.07 **P**	
MIL–S–17758A	Alloy 1	US	Bar, forgings	0.70–0.90 **C**, 13.0–15.0 **Mn**, 0.07 **P**, 0.05 **S**, 0.50–1.00 **Si**, 0.50 **Cr**, 3.0–3.5 **Ni**	**As rolled or as forged**: all **diam**, (689) **TS**, (344) **YS**, 18 **El**
MIL–S–17758A	Alloy 2	US	Bar, forgings	0.70–0.90 **C**, 13.0–15.0 **Mn**, 0.07 **P**, 0.05 **S**, 0.50–1.00 **Si**, 0.50 **Cr**, 1.75–2.25 **Ni**, 0.35–0.55 **Mo**	**As rolled or as forged**: all **diam**, (689) **TS**, (344) **YS**, 18 **El**
ISO 683/XVII	32	ISO	Billets, bar, wire, tube	0.70–0.80 **C**, 0.40 **Mn**, 0.030 **P**, 0.030 **S**, 0.40 **Si**, 3.75–4.50 **Cr**, 0.60 **Mo**, 1.00–1.25 **V**, 17.5–19.0 **W**	
JIS G 3311	S75CM	Japan	Strip	0.70–0.80 **C**, 0.60–0.90 **Mn**, 0.030 **P**, 0.035 **S**, 0.15–0.30 **Si**, 0.20 **Cr**, 0.20 **Ni**, 0.30 **Cu**	
DIN 17222	71 Si 7/5029	Germany	Strip	0.68–0.75 **C**, 0.60–0.80 **Mn**, 0.035 **P**, 0.035 **S**, 1.5–1.8 **Si**	**Softened and annealed:** all **diam**, (834) max **TS**, (363) max **YS**, 18 **El**; **Hardened and tempered:** all **diam**, (1863) **TS**, (1765) **YS**, 4 **El**
MIL–S–12504D	Mg–Mo	US	Bar	0.65–0.77 **C**, 0.75–1.05 **Mn**, 0.040 **P**, 0.040 **S**, 0.20–0.35 **Si**, 0.90–1.10 **Mo**	**Annealed, cold drawn**
JIS G 3311	S70CM	Japan	Strip	0.65–0.75 **C**, 0.60–0.90 **Mn**, 0.030 **P**, 0.035 **S**, 0.15–0.30 **Si**, 0.20 **Cr**, 0.20 **Ni**, 0.30 **Cu**	
DIN 17225	Grade 65 WMo 34 8	Germany	Bar, rod, wire	0.63–0.68 **C**, 0.30 **Mn**, 0.30 **Si**, 3.5–4.0 **Cr**, 0.80–0.90 **Mo**, 0.60–0.80 **V**	**Hot rolled (bar, rod)**: all **diam**, (1373) **TS**
DIN 17225	65 WMo 348/8239	Germany	Bar, rod	0.63–0.68 **C**, 0.3 **Mn**, 0.3 **Si**, 3.5–4.0 **Cr**, 0.80–0.90 **Mo**, 0.60–0.80 **V**, 8.0–9.0 **W**	**Hot rolled**: all **diam**, (140) **TS**
DIN 17225	Grade 67 SiCr 5	Germany	Bar, rod, wire	0.62–0.72 **C**, 0.40–0.60 **Mn**, 1.2–1.4 **Si**, 0.40–0.60 **Cr**	**Hot rolled (bar, rod)**: all **diam**, (1471) **TS**
DIN 17222	67 SiCr 5/7103	Germany	Strip	0.62–0.72 **C**, 0.40–0.60 **Mn**, 0.035 **P**, 0.035 **S**, 1.2–1.4 **Si**, 0.40–0.60 **Cr**	**Softened and annealed:** all **diam**, (834) max **TS**, (363) max **YS**, 18 **El**; **Hardened and tempered:** all **diam**, (1863) **TS**, (1765) **YS**, 4 **El**
DIN 17222	Grade 67 SiCr 5	Germany	Strip	0.62–0.72 **C**, 0.40–0.60 **Mn**, 0.035 **P**, 0.035 **S**, 1.2–1.4 **Si**, 0.40–0.60 **Cr**	**Solution annealed**: all **diam**, (834) **TS**, (363) **YS**, 18 **El**; **Quenched and tempered:** all **diam**, (1863) **TS**, (1765) **YS**, 4 **El**
DIN 17225	67 SiCr 5/7103	Germany	Bar, rod	0.62–0.72 **C**, 0.40–0.60 **Mn**, 1.2–1.4 **Si**, 0.40–0.60 **Cr**	**Hot rolled**: all **diam**, (150) **TS**
TS 2288	67 Si Cr 5	Turkey	Wire	0.62–0.72 **C**, 0.40–0.60 **Mn**, 0.035 **P**, 0.035 **S**, 1.2–1.4 **Si**, 0.40–1.60 **Cr**	
DIN 17222	66 Si 7/5028	Germany	Strip	0.60–0.70 **C**, 0.70–1.0 **Mn**, 0.035 **P**, 0.035 **S**, 1.5–1.8 **Si**	**Softened and annealed:** all **diam**, (834) max **TS**, (363) max **YS**, 18 **El**; **Hardened and tempered:** all **diam**, (1765) **TS**, (1667) **YS**, 5 **El**
TS 2288	66 Si 7	Turkey	Wire	0.60–0.70 **C**, 0.70–1.0 **Mn**, 0.035 **P**, 0.035 **S**, 1.5–1.8 **Si**	

WROUGHT ALLOY STEELS

specification number	designation	country	product forms	composition	mechanical properties (see page iv for explanation)
JIS G 3311	S65CM	Japan	Strip	0.60–0.70 **C**, 0.60–0.90 **Mn**, 0.030 **P**, 0.035 **S**, 0.15–0.30 **Si**, 0.20 **Cr**, 0.20 **Ni**, 0.30 **Cu**	
DIN 17222	65 Si7/0971	Germany	Strip	0.60–0.68 **C**, 0.70–1.0 **Mn**, 0.050 **P**, 0.050 **S**, 1.5–1.8 **Si**	**Softened and annealed**: all **diam**, (834) max **TS**, (362) max **YS**, 18 **El**; **Hardened and tempered**: all **diam**, (1667) **TS**, (1569) **YS**, 5 **El**
TS 2288	65 Si 7	Turkey	Wire	0.60–0.68 **C**, 0.70–1.0 **Mn**, 0.050 **P**, 0.050 **S**, 1.5–1.8 **Si**	
DGN–B–203	Grade 4063	Mexico	Tube: seamless	0.60–0.67 **C**, 0.75–1.00 **Mn**, 0.040 **P**, 0.040 **S**, 0.20–0.35 **Si**, 0.20–0.30 **Mo**	
COPANT 514	4063	COPANT	Tube	0.60–0.67 **C**, 0.75–1.0 **Mn**, 0.040 **P**, 0.040 **S**, 0.20–0.35 **Si**, 0.20–0.30 **Mo**	
ANSI/ASTM A 519	4063	US	Tube: seamless	0.60–0.67 **C**, 0.75–1.00 **Mn**, 0.040 **P**, 0.040 **S**, 0.15–0.35 **Si**, 0.20–0.30 **Mo**	
ANSI/ASTM A 729		US	Forgings	0.60 **C**, 1.30–1.70 **Mn**, 0.045 **P**, 0.050 **S**, 0.15 min **Si**	**Quenched and tempered**: all **diam**, 100 (690) **TS**, 65 (450) **YS**, 20 **El**
NF A 35–590	2323 (Y60 SC7)	France	Bar, forgings	0.60 **C**, 0.80 **Mn**, 0.030 **P**, 0.030 **S**, 1.70 **Si**, 0.60 **Cr**	
BS 970 Part 5	Z50A61	UK	Blooms, billets, bar, forgings	0.58–0.65 **C**, 0.70–1.00 **Mn**, 1.70–2.10 **Si**	
NF A 35–571	61 SC 7	France	Bar, wire, rod	0.57–0.64 **C**, 0.60–0.90 **Mn**, 0.035 **P**, 0.035 **S**, 1.6–2.0 **Si**, 0.20–0.45 **Cr**	**Quenched and tempered**: (≤80) **diam**, (1580) **TS**, (1430) **YS**, 6 **El**
NBN 253–05	60 SiCr 8	Belgium	Wire	0.57–0.64 **C**, 0.70–1.0 **Mn**, 0.035 **P**, 0.035 **S**, 1.70–2.20 **Si**, 0.25–0.40 **Cr**	**Annealed or quenched and tempered**: (≤30) **diam**, (1375) **TS**, (1175) **YS**, 5 **El**
NBN 253–05	60 Si 7	Belgium	Wire	0.57–0.64 **C**, 0.60–0.90 **Mn**, 0.040 **P**, 0.040 **S**, 1.50–2.0 **Si**	**Annealed or quenched and tempered**: (≤20) **diam**, (1375) **TS**, (1175) **YS**, 5 **El**
AISI 4161		US	Bar	0.56–0.64 **C**, 0.75–1.00 **Mn**, 0.035 **P**, 0.040 **S**, 0.15–0.30 **Si**, 0.70–0.90 **Cr**, 0.25–0.35 **Mo**	
AISI 5160		US	Bar	0.56–0.64 **C**, 0.75–1.00 **Mn**, 0.035 **P**, 0.040 **S**, 0.15–0.30 **Si**, 0.70–0.90 **Cr**	
AISI 9260		US	Bar	0.56–0.64 **C**, 0.75–1.00 **Mn**, 0.035 **P**, 0.040 **S**, 1.80–2.20 **Si**	
COPANT 334	5160	COPANT	Bar	0.56–0.64 **C**, 0.75–1.00 **Mn**, 0.035 **P**, 0.040 **S**, 0.20–0.35 **Si**, 0.70–0.90 **Cr**	
COPANT 334	8660	COPANT	Bar	0.56–0.64 **C**, 0.75–1.00 **Mn**, 0.035 **P**, 0.040 **S**, 0.20–0.35 **Si**, 0.40–0.60 **Cr**, 0.40–0.70 **Ni**, 0.15–0.25 **Mo**	
COPANT 334	9260	COPANT	Bar	0.56–0.64 **C**, 0.75–1.00 **Mn**, 0.035 **P**, 0.040 **S**, 1.80–2.20 **Si**	
DGN–B–300	51B60	Mexico	Bar	0.56–0.64 **C**, 0.75–1.00 **Mn**, 0.035 **P**, 0.040 **S**, 0.20–0.35 **Si**, 0.70–0.90 **Cr**, 0.0005 min **B**	**Annealed**
DGN–B–300	50B60	Mexico	Bar	0.56–0.64 **C**, 0.75–1.00 **Mn**, 0.035 **P**, 0.040 **S**, 0.20–0.35 **Si**, 0.40–0.60 **Cr**, 0.0005 min **B**	**Annealed**
DGN–B–300	9260	Mexico	Bar	0.56–0.64 **C**, 0.75–1.00 **Mn**, 0.035 **P**, 0.040 **S**, 1.80–2.20 **Si**	**Annealed**
DGN–B–300	4161	Mexico	Bar	0.56–0.64 **C**, 0.75–1.00 **Mn**, 0.035 **P**, 0.040 **S**, 0.20–0.35 **Si**, 0.70–0.90 **Cr**, 0.25–0.35 **Mo**	**Annealed**
ANSI/ASTM A 29	4161	US	Bar	0.56–0.64 **C**, 0.75–1.00 **Mn**, 0.035 **P**, 0.040 **S**, 0.15–0.30 **Si**, 0.70–0.90 **Cr**, 0.25–0.35 **Mo**	
ASTM A 689	9260	US	Bar	0.56–0.64 **C**, 0.75–1.00 **Mn**, 0.035 **P**, 0.040 **S**, 1.80–2.20 **Si**	
ASTM A 689	50B60	US	Bar	0.56–0.64 **C**, 0.75–1.00 **Mn**, 0.035 **P**, 0.040 **S**, 0.15–0.30 **Si**, 0.40–0.60 **Cr**, 0.0005 min **B**	

WROUGHT ALLOY STEELS

specification number	designation	country	product forms	composition	mechanical properties (see page iv for explanation)
ASTM A 689	51B60	US	Bar	0.56–0.64 **C**, 0.75–1.00 **Mn**, 0.035 **P**, 0.040 **S**, 0.15–0.30 **Si**, 0.70–0.90 **Cr**, 0.0005 min **B**	
ASTM A 689	5160	US	Bar	0.56–0.64 **C**, 0.75–1.00 **Mn**, 0.035 **P**, 0.040 **S**, 0.15–0.30 **Si**, 0.70–0.90 **Cr**	
ASTM A 689	4161	US	Bar	0.56–0.64 **C**, 0.75–1.00 **Mn**, 0.035 **P**, 0.040 **S**, 0.15–0.30 **Si**, 0.70–0.90 **Cr**, 0.25–0.35 **Mo**	
ANSI/ASTM A 29	9260	US	Bar	0.56–0.64 **C**, 0.75–1.00 **Mn**, 0.035 **P**, 0.040 **S**, 1.80–2.20 **Si**	
ANSI/ASTM A 322	4161	US	Bar	0.56–0.64 **C**, 0.75–1.00 **Mn**, 0.035 **P**, 0.040 **S**, 0.15–0.30 **Si**, 0.70–0.90 **Cr**, 0.25–0.35 **Mo**	
ANSI/ASTM A 322	9260	US	Bar	0.56–0.64 **C**, 0.75–1.00 **Mn**, 0.035 **P**, 0.040 **S**, 1.80–2.20 **Si**	
ANSI/ASTM A 322	50B60	US	Bar	0.56–0.64 **C**, 0.75–1.00 **Mn**, 0.035 **P**, 0.040 **S**, 0.15–0.30 **Si**, 0.40–0.60 **Cr**, 0.0005 min **B**	
ANSI/ASTM A322	51B60	US	Bar	0.56–0.64 **C**, 0.75–1.00 **Mn**, 0.035 **P**, 0.040 **S**, 0.15–0.30 **Si**, 0.70–0.90 **Cr**, 0.0005 min **B**	
ANSI/ASTM A 322	5160	US	Bar	0.56–0.64 **C**, 0.75–1.00 **Mn**, 0.035 **P**, 0.040 **S**, 0.15–0.30 **Si**, 0.70–0.90 **Cr**	
ANSI/ASTM A 29	8660	US	Bar	0.56–0.64 **C**, 0.75–1.00 **Mn**, 0.035 **P**, 0.04 **S**, 0.15–0.30 **Si**, 0.40–0.60 **Cr**, 0.40–0.70 **Ni**, 0.15–0.25 **Mo**	
AISI 50B60		US	Bar	0.56–0.64 **C**, 0.75–1.00 **Mn**, 0.035 **P**, 0.040 **S**, 0.15–0.30 **Si**, 0.40–0.60 **Cr**, 0.0005–0.0003 **B**	
AISI 51B60		US	Bar	0.56–0.64 **C**, 0.75–1.00 **Mn**, 0.035 **P**, 0.040 **S**, 0.15–0.30 **Si**, 0.70–0.90 **Cr**, 0.0005–0.003 **B**	
AISI 9260		US	Wire, rod	0.56–0.64 **C**, 0.75–1.00 **Mn**, 0.035 **P**, 0.040 **S**, 1.80–2.20 **Si**	
AISI 50B60		US	Wire, rod	0.56–0.64 **C**, 0.75–1.00 **Mn**, 0.035 **P**, 0.040 **S**, 0.15–0.30 **Si**, 0.40–0.60 **Cr**	
AISI 51B60		US	Wire, rod	0.56–0.64 **C**, 0.75–1.00 **Mn**, 0.035 **P**, 0.040 **S**, 0.15–0.30 **Si**, 0.70–0.90 **Cr**	
AISI 4161		US	Wire, rod	0.56–0.64 **C**, 0.75–1.00 **Mn**, 0.035 **P**, 0.040 **S**, 0.15–0.30 **Si**, 0.70–0.90 **Cr**, 0.25–0.35 **Mo**	
AISI 5160		US	Wire, rod	0.56–0.64 **C**, 0.75–1.00 **Mn**, 0.035 **P**, 0.040 **S**, 0.15–0.30 **Si**, 0.70–0.90 **Cr**	
DGN–B–297	4116	Mexico	Bar	0.56–0.64 **C**, 0.75–1.00 **Mn**, 0.035 **P**, 0.040 **S**, 0.20–0.35 **Si**, 0.70–0.90 **Cr**, 0.25–0.35 **Mo**	
AISI 5160		US	Sheet, strip	0.56–0.64 **C**, 0.75–1.00 **Mn**, 0.035 **P**, 0.040 **S**, 0.20–0.35 **Si**, 0.70–0.90 **Cr**	
DGN–B–297	9260	Mexico	Bar	0.56–0.64 **C**, 0.75–1.00 **Mn**, 0.035 **P**, 0.040 **S**, 1.80–2.20 **Si**	
DGN–B–297	50B60	Mexico	Bar	0.56–0.64 **C**, 0.75–1.00 **Mn**, 0.035 **P**, 0.040 **S**, 0.20–0.35 **Si**, 0.40–0.60 **Cr**	
DGN–B–297	51B60	Mexico	Bar	0.56–0.64 **C**, 0.75–1.00 **Mn**, 0.035 **P**, 0.040 **S**, 0.20–0.35 **Si**, 0.70–0.90 **Cr**	
DGN–B–297	5160	Mexico	Bar	0.56–0.64 **C**, 0.75–1.00 **Mn**, 0.035 **P**, 0.040 **S**, 0.20–0.35 **Si**, 0.70–0.90 **Cr**	
ANSI/ASTM A 29	5160	US	Bar	0.56–0.61 **C**, 0.75–1.00 **Mn**, 0.035 **P**, 0.040 **S**, 0.15–0.30 **Si**, 0.70–0.90 **Cr**	

specification number	designation	country	product forms	composition	mechanical properties (see page iv for explanation)
BS S.201		UK	Wire: aircraft quality	0.55–0.85 **C**, 0.30–1.00 **Mn**, 0.030 **P**, 0.030 **S**, 0.15–0.35 **Si**, 0.08 **Cr**, 0.10 **Ni**	**Tempered:** (0.18–0.38) **diam**, (2315) **TS**
BS 2S.131		UK	Billets, bar, forgings, parts: aircraft quality	0.55–0.70 **C**, 3.5–5.5 **Mn**, 0.035 **P**, 0.025 **S**, 0.20–0.50 **Si**, 3.0–4.0 **Cr**, 11.0–14.0 **Ni**, 0.50 **Mo**, 0.25 **V**, 1.0 **W**	**Solution annealed:** (≤150) **diam**, (620) **TS**, 40 **El**
DIN 17221	60 SiCr 7[3]) /1.0961	Germany	Springs	0.55–0.65 **C**, 0.70–1.00 **Mn**, 0.045 **P**, 0.045 **S**, 1.5–1.8 **Si**, 0.20–0.40 **Cr**	**Quenched and tempered:** all **diam**, (1320) **TS**, (1130) **YS**, 6 **El**
DIN 17221	Grade 60 SiCr 7	Germany	Bar, wire, strip	0.55–0.65 **C**, 0.70–1.00 **Mn**, 0.045 **P**, 0.045 **S**, 1.5–1.8 **Si**, 0.20–0.40 **Cr**	**Quenched and tempered:** (10) **diam**, (1320) **TS**, (1130) **YS**, 6 **El**
JIS G 4801	SUP 9A	Japan	Bar, wire, rod	0.55–0.65 **C**, 0.70–1.00 **Mn**, 0.035 **P**, 0.035 **S**, 0.15–0.35 **Si**, 0.70–1.00 **Cr**, 0.30 **Cu**	**Quenched and tempered:** all **diam**, (1226) **TS**, (1079) **YS**, 9 **El**
JIS G 4801	SUP 11A	Japan	Bar, wire, rod	0.55–0.65 **C**, 0.70–1.00 **Mn**, 0.035 **P**, 0.035 **S**, 0.15–0.35 **Si**, 0.70–1.00 **Cr**, 0.30 **Cu**	**Quenched and tempered:** all **diam**, (1226) **TS**, (1079) **YS**, 9 **El**
DIN 17222	60 SiMn5/0931	Germany	Strip	0.55–0.65 **C**, 0.90–1.10 **Mn**, 0.050 **P**, 0.050 **S**, 1.0–1.3 **Si**	**Softened and annealed:** all **diam**, (834) max **TS**, (362) max **YS**, 18 **El**; **Hardened and tempered:** all **diam**, (1667) **TS**, (1569) **YS**, 5 **El**
BS 970 Part 2	Grade 526 M 60	UK	Blooms, billets, bar, forgings	0.55–0.65 **C**, 0.50–0.80 **Mn**, 0.10–0.35 **Si**, 0.50–0.80 **Cr**	**Hardened and tempered:** 4 **diam**, (760) **TS**, (550) **YS**, 11 **El**
NF A 35–571	RH 388	France	Bar, wire, rod	0.55–0.65 **C**, 0.70–1.0 **Mn**, 0.05 **P**, 0.05 **S**, 1.5–2.0 **Si**	
TS 2288	60 Si Cr 7–1,0961	Turkey	Wire	0.55–0.65 **C**, 0.70–1.0 **Mn**, 0.045 **P**, 0.045 **S**, 1.5–1.8 **Si**, 0.20–0.40 **Cr**	
TS 2288	60 Si Mr 5	Turkey	Wire	0.55–0.65 **C**, 0.90–1.1 **Mn**, 0.050 **P**, 0.050 **S**, 1.0–1.3 **Si**	
BS 970 Part 5	527A60	UK	Blooms, billets, bar, forgings	0.55–0.65 **C**, 0.70–1.00 **Mn**, 0.10–0.35 **Si**, 0.60–0.90 **Cr**	
BS 970 Part 5	805A60	UK	Blooms, billets, bar, forgings	0.55–0.65 **C**, 0.70–1.00 **Mn**, 0.10–0.35 **Si**, 0.40–0.60 **Cr**, 0.15–0.25 **Mo**, 0.40–0.70 **V**	
BS 970 Part 5	925A60	UK	Blooms, billets, bar, forgings	0.55–0.65 **C**, 0.70–1.00 **Mn**, 1.70–2.10 **Si**, 0.20–0.40 **Cr**, 0.20–0.30 **Mo**	
BS 970 Part 5	527H60	UK	Blooms, billets, bar, forgings	0.55–0.65 **C**, 0.65–1.05 **Mn**, 0.10–0.35 **Si**, 0.55–0.95 **Cr**	
BS 970 Part 5	805H60	UK	Blooms, billets, bar, forgings	0.55–0.65 **C**, 0.65–1.05 **Mn**, 0.10–0.35 **Si**, 0.35–0.65 **Cr**, 0.35–0.75 **Ni**, 0.15–0.25 **Mo**	
AS 1444	Grade AS 1444/5160	Australia	Bar, bloom, billet, slab	0.55–0.65 **C**, 0.70–1.00 **Mn**, 0.050 **P**, 0.050 **S**, 0.10–0.35 **Si**, 0.70–0.90 **Cr**	
AS 1444	Grade AS 1444/8660	Australia	Bar, bloom, billet, slab	0.55–0.65 **C**, 0.75–1.00 **Mn**, 0.040 **P**, 0.040 **S**, 0.10–0.35 **Si**, 0.40–0.60 **Cr**, 0.40–0.70 **Ni**, 0.15–0.25 **Mo**	
AS 1444	Grade As 1444/9260	Australia	Bar, bloom, billet, slab	0.55–0.65 **C**, 0.70–1.00 **Mn**, 0.050 **P**, 0.050 **S**, 1.80–2.20 **Si**	
AS 1444	Grade AS 1444/9261	Australia	Bar, bloom, billet, slab	0.55–0.65 **C**, 0.70–1.00 **Mn**, 0.050 **P**, 0.050 **S**, 1.80–2.20 **Si**, 0.10–0.25 **Cr**	
AS 1444	Grade AS 1444/8660H	Australia	Bar, bloom, billet, slab	0.55–0.65 **C**, 0.70–1.05 **Mn**, 0.040 **P**, 0.040 **S**, 0.10–0.35 **Si**, 0.35–0.65 **Cr**, 0.35–0.75 **Ni**, 0.15–0.25 **Mo**	
AS 1444	Grade AS 1444/9260H	Australia	Bar, bloom, billet, slab	0.55–0.65 **C**, 0.65–1.10 **Mn**, 0.050 **P**, 0.050 **S**, 1.70–2.20 **Si**	
AS 1444	Grade AS 1444/9261H	Australia	Bar, bloom, billet, slab	0.55–0.65 **C**, 0.65–1.10 **Mn**, 0.050 **P**, 0.050 **S**, 1.70–2.20 **Si**, 0.05–0.35 **Cr**	
DGN–B–203	Grade 9262	Mexico	Tube: seamless	0.55–0.65 **C**, 0.75–1.00 **Mn**, 0.040 **P**, 0.040 **S**, 1.80–2.20 **Si**, 0.25–0.40 **Cr**	

specification number	designation	country	product forms	composition	mechanical properties (see page iv for explanation)
DGN-B-203	Grade 9260	Mexico	Tube: seamless	0.55-0.65 **C**, 0.70-1.00 **Mn**, 0.040 **P**, 0.040 **S**, 1.80-2.20 **Si**	
DGN-B-203	Grade 8660	Mexico	Tube: seamless	0.55-0.65 **C**, 0.75-1.00 **Mn**, 0.040 **P**, 0.040 **S**, 0.20-0.35 **Si**, 0.40-0.60 **Cr**, 0.40-0.70 **Ni**, 0.15-0.25 **Mo**	
DGN-B-203	Grade 51B60	Mexico	Tube: seamless	0.55-0.65 **C**, 0.75-1.00 **Mn**, 0.040 **P**, 0.040 **S**, 0.20-0.35 **Si**, 0.70-0.90 **Cr**, 0.0005 min **B**	
DGN-B-203	Grade 50B60	Mexico	Tube: seamless	0.55-0.65 **C**, 0.75-1.00 **Mn**, 0.040 **P**, 0.040 **S**, 0.20-0.35 **Si**, 0.40-0.60 **Cr**, 0.0005 min **B**	
DGN-B-203	Grade 5160	Mexico	Tube: seamless	0.55-0.65 **C**, 0.75-1.00 **Mn**, 0.040 **P**, 0.040 **S**, 0.20-0.35 **Si**, 0.70-0.90 **Cr**	
DGN-B-300	4161 H	Mexico	Bar	0.55-0.65 **C**, 0.65-1.10 **Mn**, 0.040 **P**, 0.035 **S**, 0.20-0.35 **Si**, 0.65-0.95 **Cr**, 0.25-0.35 **Mo**	**Annealed**
DGN-B-300	50B60 H	Mexico	Bar	0.55-0.65 **C**, 0.65-1.10 **Mn**, 0.040 **P**, 0.035 **S**, 0.20-0.35 **Si**, 0.30-0.70 **Cr**, 0.0005 min **B**	**Annealed**
DGN-B-300	51B60 H	Mexico	Bar	0.55-0.65 **C**, 0.65-1.10 **Mn**, 0.040 **P**, 0.035 **S**, 0.20-0.35 **Si**, 0.60-1.00 **Cr**, 0.0005 min **B**	**Annealed**
DGN-B-300	5160 H	Mexico	Bar	0.55-0.65 **C**, 0.65-1.10 **Mn**, 0.040 **P**, 0.035 **S**, 0.20-0.35 **Si**, 0.60-1.00 **Cr**	**Annealed**
DGN-B-300	9260 H	Mexico	Bar	0.55-0.65 **C**, 0.65-1.10 **Mn**, 0.040 **P**, 0.035 **S**, 1.70-2.20 **Si**	**Annealed**
DGN-B-300	8660 H	Mexico	Bar	0.55-0.65 **C**, 0.70-1.05 **Mn**, 0.040 **P**, 0.035 **S**, 0.20-0.35 **Si**, 0.35-0.65 **Cr**, 0.35-0.75 **Ni**, 0.15-0.25 **Mo**	
ASTM A 689	51B60	US	Bar	0.55-0.65 **C**, 0.65-1.10 **Mn**, 0.040 **P**, 0.040 **S**, 0.15-0.30 **Si**, 0.60-1.00 **Cr**, 0.0005 min **B**	
ASTM A 689	5160 H	US	Bar	0.55-0.65 **C**, 0.65-1.10 **Mn**, 0.040 **P**, 0.040 **S**, 0.15-0.30 **Si**, 0.60-1.00 **Cr**	
ASTM A 689	9260 H	US	Bar	0.55-0.65 **C**, 0.65-1.10 **Mn**, 0.040 **P**, 0.040 **S**, 1.70-2.20 **Si**	
ASTM A 689	8660 H	US	Bar	0.55-0.65 **C**, 0.70-1.05 **Mn**, 0.040 **P**, 0.040 **S**, 0.15-0.30 **Si**, 0.35-0.65 **Cr**, 0.35-0.75 **Ni**, 0.15-0.25 **Mo**	
ANSI/ASTM A 304	50B60 H	US	Bar	0.55-0.65 **C**, 0.65-1.10 **Mn**, 0.040 **P**, 0.040 **S**, 0.15-0.30 **Si**, 0.30-0.70 **Cr**, 0.0005 **B**	
ANSI/ASTM A 304	5160 H	US	Bar	0.55-0.65 **C**, 0.65-1.10 **Mn**, 0.040 **P**, 0.040 **S**, 0.15-0.30 **Si**, 0.60-1.00 **Cr**	
ANSI/ASTM A 304	51B60H	US	Bar	0.55-0.65 **C**, 0.65-1.10 **Mn**, 0.040 **P**, 0.040 **S**, 0.15-0.30 **Si**, 0.0005 min **B**	
ANSI/ASTM A 304	8660 H	US	Bar	0.55-0.65 **C**, 0.70-1.05 **Mn**, 0.040 **P**, 0.040 **S**, 0.15-0.30 **Si**, 0.35-0.65 **Cr**, 0.35-0.75 **Ni**, 0.15-0.25 **Mo**	
ANSI/ASTM A 304	9260 H	US	Bar	0.55-0.65 **C**, 0.65-1.10 **Mn**, 0.040 **P**, 0.040 **S**, 1.70-2.20 **Si**	
ANSI/ASTM A 304	4161 H	US	Bar	0.55-0.65 **C**, 0.65-1.10 **Mn**, 0.040 **P**, 0.040 **S**, 0.15-0.30 **Si**, 0.65-0.95 **Cr**, 0.25-0.35 **Mo**	
ASTM A 689	50B60 H	US	Bar	0.55-0.65 **C**, 0.65-1.10 **Mn**, 0.040 **P**, 0.040 **S**, 0.15-0.30 **Si**, 0.30-0.70 **Cr**, 0.0005 min **B**	
ASTM A 689	4161 H	US	Bar	0.55-0.65 **C**, 0.65-1.10 **Mn**, 0.040 **P**, 0.040 **S**, 0.15-0.30 **Si**, 0.65-0.95 **Cr**, 0.25-0.35 **Mo**	
AISI 5160 H		US	Wire, rod	0.55-0.65 **C**, 0.65-1.10 **Mn**, 0.15-0.30 **Si**, 0.60-1.00 **Cr**	

specification number	designation	country	product forms	composition	mechanical properties (see page iv for explanation)
AISI 9260 H		US	Wire, rod	0.55–0.65 **C**, 0.65–1.10 **Mn**, 1.70–2.20 **Si**	
AISI 50B60 H		US	Wire, rod	0.55–0.65 **C**, 0.65–1.10 **Mn**, 0.15–0.30 **Si**, 0.30–0.70 **Cr**	
AISI 51B60 H		US	Wire, rod	0.55–0.65 **C**, 0.65–1.10 **Mn**, 0.15–0.30 **Si**, 0.60–1.00 **Cr**	
AISI 4161 H		US	Wire, rod	0.55–0.65 **C**, 0.65–1.10 **Mn**, 0.15–0.30 **Si**, 0.65–0.95 **Cr**, 0.25–0.35 **Mo**	
AISI 51B60H		US	Bar	0.55–0.65 **C**, 0.65–1.10 **Mn**, 0.035 **P**, 0.040 **S**, 0.15–0.30 **Si**, 0.60–1.00 **Cr**	
AISI 50B60H		US	Bar	0.55–0.65 **C**, 0.65–1.10 **Mn**, 0.035 **P**, 0.040 **S**, 0.15–0.30 **Si**, 0.30–0.70 **Cr**	
AISI 9260H		US	Bar	0.55–0.65 **C**, 0.65–1.10 **Mn**, 0.035 **P**, 0.040 **S**, 1.70–2.20 **Si**	
AISI 8660H		US	Bar	0.55–0.65 **C**, 0.70–1.05 **Mn**, 0.035 **P**, 0.040 **S**, 0.15–0.30 **Si**, 0.35–0.65 **Cr**, 0.35–0.75 **Ni**, 0.15–0.25 **Mo**	
AISI 5160H		US	Bar	0.55–0.65 **C**, 0.65–1.00 **Mn**, 0.035 **P**, 0.040 **S**, 0.15–0.30 **Si**, 0.60–1.00 **Cr**	
AISI 4161H		US	Bar	0.55–0.65 **C**, 0.65–1.10 **Mn**, 0.035 **P**, 0.040 **S**, 0.15–0.30 **Si**, 0.65–0.95 **Cr**, 0.25–0.35 **Mo**	
ANSI/ASTM A 519	5160	US	Tube: seamless	0.55–0.65 **C**, 0.75–1.00 **Mn**, 0.040 **P**, 0.040 **S**, 0.15–0.35 **Si**, 0.70–0.90 **Cr**	
ANSI/ASTM A 519	8660	US	Tube: seamless	0.55–0.65 **C**, 0.75–1.00 **Mn**, 0.040 **P**, 0.040 **S**, 0.15–0.35 **Si**, 0.40–0.60 **Cr**, 0.40–0.70 **Ni**, 0.15–0.25 **Mo**	
ANSI/ASTM A 519	9260	US	Tube: seamless	0.55–0.65 **C**, 0.70–1.00 **Mn**, 0.040 **P**, 0.040 **S**, 1.80–2.20 **Si**	
ANSI/ASTM A 519	9262	US	Tube: seamless	0.55–0.65 **C**, 0.75–1.00 **Mn**, 0.040 **P**, 0.040 **S**, 1.80–2.20 **Si**, 0.25–0.40 **Cr**	
ANSI/ASTM A 519	50B60	US	Tube: seamless	0.55–0.65 **C**, 0.75–1.00 **Mn**, 0.040 **P**, 0.040 **S**, 0.15–0.35 **Si**, 0.40–0.60 **Cr**	
ANSI/ASTM A 519	51B60	US	Tube: seamless	0.55–0.65 **C**, 0.75–1.00 **Mn**, 0.040 **P**, 0.040 **S**, 0.15–0.35 **Si**, 0.70–0.90 **Cr**	
JIS G 3311	SUP6M	Japan	Strip	0.55–0.65 **C**, 0.70–1.00 **Mn**, 0.035 **P**, 0.035 **S**, 1.50–1.80 **Si**, 0.30 **Cu**	
COPANT 514	Grade 50B60	COPANT	Tube: seamless	0.55–0.65 **C**, 0.75–1.00 **Mn**, 0.040 **P**, 0.050 **S**, 0.10 **Si**, 0.40–0.60 **Cr**	
COPANT 514	Grade 51B60	COPANT	Tube: seamless	0.55–0.65 **C**, 0.75–1.00 **Mn**, 0.040 **P**, 0.050 **S**, 0.10 **Si**, 0.70–0.90 **Cr**	
COPANT 514	Grade 5160	COPANT	Tube: seamless	0.55–0.65 **C**, 0.75–1.00 **Mn**, 0.040 **P**, 0.050 **S**, 0.10 **Si**, 0.70–0.90 **Cr**	
COPANT 514	Grade 8660	COPANT	Tube: seamless	0.55–0.65 **C**, 0.75–1.00 **Mn**, 0.040 **P**, 0.050 **S**, 0.10 **Si**, 0.40–0.60 **Cr**, 0.40–0.70 **Ni**, 0.15–0.25 **Mo**	
COPANT 514	Grade 9262	COPANT	Tube: seamless	0.55–0.65 **C**, 0.75–1.00 **Mn**, 0.040 **P**, 0.050 **S**, 1.80–2.20 **Si**, 0.25–0.40 **Cr**	
JIS G 3311	S60CM	Japan	Strip	0.55–0.65 **C**, 0.60–0.90 **Mn**, 0.030 **P**, 0.035 **S**, 0.15–0.30 **Si**, 0.20 **Cr**, 0.20 **Ni**, 0.30 **Cu**	
DIN 17222	Grade 58 Cr V 4	Germany	Strip	0.55–0.62 **C**, 0.80–1.1 **Mn**, 0.035 **P**, 0.035 **S**, 0.15–0.35 **Si**, 0.90–1.2 **Cr**, 0.07–0.12 **V**	**Solution annealed:** all **diam**, (795) **TS**, (343) **YS**, 20 **El**; **Quenched and tempered:** all **diam**, (1863) **TS**, (1765) **YS**, 4 **El**

WROUGHT ALLOY STEELS

specification number	designation	country	product forms	composition	mechanical properties (see page iv for explanation)
DIN 17222	58 CrV4/8161	Germany	Strip	0.55–0.62 **C**, 0.80–1.1 **Mn**, 0.035 **P**, 0.035 **S**, 0.15–0.35 **Si**, 0.90–1.2 **Cr**, 0.07–0.12 **V**	**Softened and annealed:** all **diam**, (784) max **TS**, (343) max **YS**, 20 **El**; **Hardened and tempered:** all **diam**, (1863) **TS**, (1765) **YS**, 4 **El**
TS 2288	58 CrV4	Turkey	Wire	0.55–0.62 **C**, 0.80–1.10 **Mn**, 0.035 **P**, 0.035 **S**, 0.15–0.75 **Si**, 0.30–1.20 **Cr**, 0.07–0.12 **V**	
COPANT 334	58 Cr V 4	COPANT	Bar	0.55–0.62 **C**, 0.80–1.10 **Mn**, 0.035 **P**, 0.035 **S**, 0.15–0.35 **Si**, 0.90–1.20 **Cr**	
BS 970 Part 5	250A58	UK	Blooms, billets, bar, forgings	0.55–0.62 **C**, 0.70–1.00 **Mn**, 1.70–2.10 **Si**	
MIL–S–19434A	Class 6	US	Forgings	0.55 **C**, 0.60–0.90 **Mn**, 0.025 **P**, 0.025 min **S**, 0.15 min **Si**, 0.50 min **Cr**, 1.65 min **Ni**, 0.13–0.50 **Mo**, 0.15 **V**	**Quenched and tempered:** ≤10 **diam**, (1137) **TS**, (930) **YS**, 12 **El**
BS 980	CDS–15	UK	Tube	0.55 **C**, 1.0 **Mn**, 0.050 **P**, 0.050 **S**, 0.35 **Si**	**Heat treated as agreed:** all **diam**, (965) **TS**, (690) **YS**, 10 **El**
NF A 35–590	2322 (Y55 S7)	France	Bar, forgings	0.55 **C**, 0.80 **Mn**, 0.030 **P**, 0.030 **S**, 1.8 **Si**, 0.45 **Cr**	
NF A 35–590	2341 (55WC20)	France	Bar, forgings	0.55 **C**, 0.30 **Mn**, 0.030 **P**, 0.030 **S**, 1.0 **Si**, 1.0 **Cr**, 2.0 **W**	
AISI 5160		US	Plate	0.54–0.65 **C**, 0.70–1.00 **Mn**, 0.035 **P**, 0.040 **S**, 0.15–0.30 **Si**, 0.60–0.90 **Cr**	
NF A 35–571	56 SC 7	France	Bar, wire, rod	0.53–0.59 **C**, 0.60–0.90 **Mn**, 0.035 **P**, 0.035 **S**, 1.6–2.0 **Si**, 0.20–0.45 **Cr**	**Quenched and tempered:** (≤80) **diam**, (1520) **TS**, (1370) **YS**, 6 **El**
MIL–S–12504D	Mg–Cr–Mo	US	Bar	0.52–0.62 **C**, 0.75–1.05 **Mn**, 0.040 **P**, 0.040 **S**, 0.20–0.35 **Si**, 0.80–1.15 **Cr**, 0.15–0.25 **Mo**	**Annealed, cold drawn**
NBN 253–05	55 Si 7	Belgium	Wire	0.52–0.60 **C**, 0.60–0.90 **Mn**, 0.040 **P**, 0.040 **S**, 1.50–2.0 **Si**	**Annealed or quenched and tempered:** (≤12) **diam**, (1325) **TS**, (1130) **YS**, 6 **El**
DIN 17222	55 Si7/0970	Germany	Strip	0.52–0.60 **C**, 0.70–1.0 **Mn**, 0.050 **P**, 0.050 **S**, 1.5–1.8 **Si**	**Softened and annealed:** all **diam**, (784) max **TS**, (343) max **YS**, 20 **El**; **Hardened and tempered:** all **diam**, (1569) **TS**, (1471) **YS**, 6 **El**
TS 2288	55 Si 7	Turkey	Wire	0.52–0.60 **C**, 0.70–1.0 **Mn**, 0.050 **P**, 0.050 **S**, 1.5–1.8 **Si**	
NBN 253–05	55 Cr 3	Belgium	Wire	0.52–0.59 **C**, 0.70–1.0 **Mn**, 0.035 **P**, 0.035 **S**, 0.15–0.40 **Si**, 0.60–0.90 **Cr**	**Annealed or quenched and tempered:** (≤32) **diam**, (1375) **TS**, (1175) **YS**, 6 **El**
NF A 35–571	55 C 3	France	Bar, wire, rod	0.52–0.59 **C**, 0.70–1.0 **Mn**, 0.035 **P**, 0.035 **S**, 0.10–0.40 **Si**, 0.60–0.90 **Cr**	**Quenched and tempered:** (≤80) **diam**, (1370) **TS**, (1180) **YS**, 6 **El**
DIN 17221	55 Cr 3/1.7176	Germany	Springs	0.52–0.59 **C**, 0.70–1.00 **Mn**, 0.035 **P**, 0.035 **S**, 0.15–0.40 **Si**, 0.60–0.90 **Cr**	**Quenched and tempered:** all **diam**, (1370) **TS**, (1180) **YS**, 6 **El**
DIN 17221	Grade 55 Cr 3	Germany	Bar, wire, rod	0.52–0.59 **C**, 0.70–1.00 **Mn**, 0.035 **P**, 0.035 **S**, 0.15–0.40 **Si**, 0.60–0.90 **Cr**	**Quenched and tempered:** (10) **diam**, (1370) **TS**, (1180) **YS**, 6 **El**
JIS G 3311	S55CM	Japan	Strip	0.52–0.58 **C**, 0.60–0.90 **Mn**, 0.030 **P**, 0.035 **S**, 0.15–0.35 **Si**, 0.20 **Cr**, 0.20 **Ni**, 0.30 **Cu**, 0.35 **Ni+Cr**	
TS 2288	55 Cr 3–1,7176	Turkey	Wire	0.52–0.53 **C**, 0.70–1.0 **Mn**, 0.035 **P**, 0.035 **S**, 0.15–0.40 **Si**, 0.60–0.30 **Cr**	
NF A 35–553	55 S 7	France	Strip	0.51–0.60 **C**, 0.60–1.0 **Mn**, 0.040 **P**, 0.040 **S**, 1.6–2.0 **Si**, 0.45 **Cr**	
ANSI/ASTM A 401		US	Wire	0.51–0.59 **C**, 0.60–0.80 **Mn**, 0.035 **P**, 0.040 **S**, 1.20–1.60 **Si**, 0.60–0.80 **Cr**	**Cold–drawn and tempered:** 0.032 (0.81) **diam**, 300 (2070) **TS**
ANSI/ASTM A 401		US	Wire: spring	0.51–0.59 **C**, 0.60–0.80 **Mn**, 0.035 **P**, 0.040 **S**, 1.20–1.60 **Si**, 0.60–0.80 **Cr**	**Annealed, cold drawn or oil tempered:** 0.032 (0.81) **diam**, 300 (2070) **TS**

specification number	designation	country	product forms	composition	mechanical properties (see page iv for explanation)
AISI 5155		US	Bar	0.51–0.59 **C**, 0.70–0.90 **Mn**, 0.035 **P**, 0.040 **S**, 0.15–0.30 **Si**, 0.70–0.90 **Cr**	
AISI 8655		US	Bar	0.51–0.59 **C**, 0.75–1.00 **Mn**, 0.035 **P**, 0.040 **S**, 0.15–0.30 **Si**, 0.40–0.60 **Cr**, 0.40–0.70 **Ni**, 0.15–0.25 **Mo**	
COPANT 334	9255	COPANT	Bar	0.51–0.59 **C**, 0.70–0.95 **Mn**, 0.035 **P**, 0.040 **S**, 1.80–2.00 **Si**	
AS 1444	Grade AS 1444/9254	Australia	Bar, bloom, billet, slab	0.51–0.59 **C**, 0.60–0.80 **Mn**, 0.050 **P**, 0.050 **S**, 1.20–1.60 **Si**, 0.60–0.80 **Cr**	
DGN–B–300	9255	Mexico	Bar	0.51–0.59 **C**, 0.70–0.95 **Mn**, 0.035 **P**, 0.040 **S**, 1.80–2.20 **Si**	**Annealed**
DGN–B–300	8655	Mexico	Bar	0.51–0.59 **C**, 0.75–1.00 **Mn**, 0.035 **P**, 0.040 **S**, 0.20–0.35 **Si**, 0.40–0.60 **Cr**, 0.40–0.70 **Ni**, 0.15–0.25 **Mo**	**Annealed**
DGN–B–300	5155	Mexico	Bar	0.51–0.59 **C**, 0.70–0.90 **Mn**, 0.035 **P**, 0.040 **S**, 0.20–0.35 **Si**, 0.70–0.90 **Cr**	**Annealed**
ASTM A 689	9255	US	Bar	0.51–0.59 **C**, 0.70–0.95 **Mn**, 0.035 **P**, 0.040 **S**, 1.80–2.20 **Si**	
ASTM A 689	8655	US	Bar	0.51–0.59 **C**, 0.75–1.00 **Mn**, 0.035 **P**, 0.040 **S**, 0.15–0.30 **Si**, 0.40–0.60 **Cr**, 0.40–0.70 **Ni**, 0.15–0.25 **Mo**	
ASTM A 689	9254	US	Bar	0.51–0.59 **C**, 0.60–0.80 **Mn**, 0.035 **P**, 0.040 **S**, 1.20–1.60 **Si**, 0.60–0.80 **Cr**	
ASTM A 689	5155	US	Bar	0.51–0.59 **C**, 0.70–0.90 **Mn**, 0.035 **P**, 0.040 **S**, 0.15–0.30 **Si**, 0.70–0.90 **Cr**	
ANSI/ASTM A 29	9255	US	Bar	0.51–0.59 **C**, 0.70–0.95 **Mn**, 0.035 **P**, 0.040 **S**, 1.80–2.20 **Si**	
ANSI/ASTM A 29	9254	US	Bar	0.51–0.59 **C**, 0.60–0.80 **Mn**, 0.035 **P**, 0.040 **S**, 1.20–1.60 **Si**, 0.60–0.80 **Cr**	
ANSI/ASTM A 322	8655	US	Bar	0.51–0.59 **C**, 0.75–1.00 **Mn**, 0.035 **P**, 0.040 **S**, 0.15–0.30 **Si**, 0.40–0.60 **Cr**, 0.40–0.70 **Ni**, 0.15–0.25 **Mo**	
ANSI/ASTM A 322	9254	US	Bar	0.51–0.59 **C**, 0.60–0.80 **Mn**, 0.035 **P**, 0.040 **S**, 1.20–1.60 **Si**, 0.60–0.80 **Cr**	
ANSI/ASTM A 322	9254	US	Bar	0.51–0.59 **C**, 0.60–0.80 **Mn**, 0.035 **P**, 0.040 **S**, 1.20–1.60 **Si**, 0.60–0.80 **Cr**	
ANSI/ASTM A 322	9255	US	Bar	0.51–0.59 **C**, 0.70–0.95 **Mn**, 0.035 **P**, 0.040 **S**, 1.80–2.20 **Si**	
ANSI/ASTM A 322	5155	US	Bar	0.51–0.59 **C**, 0.70–0.90 **Mn**, 0.035 **P**, 0.040 **S**, 0.15–0.30 **Si**, 0.70–0.90 **Cr**	
ANSI/ASTM A 29	5155	US	Bar	0.51–0.59 **C**, 0.70–0.90 **Mn**, 0.035 **P**, 0.040 **S**, 0.15–0.30 **Si**, 0.70–0.90 **Cr**	
ANSI/ASTM A 29	8655	US	Bar	0.51–0.59 **C**, 0.75–1.00 **Mn**, 0.035 **P**, 0.040 **S**, 0.15–0.30 **Si**, 0.40–0.60 **Cr**, 0.40–0.70 **Ni**, 0.15–0.25 **Mo**	
AISI 8655		US	Wire, rod	0.51–0.59 **C**, 0.75–1.00 **Mn**, 0.035 **P**, 0.040 **S**, 0.15–0.30 **Si**, 0.40–0.60 **Cr**, 0.40–0.70 **Ni**, 0.15–0.25 **Mo**	
AISI 9254		US	Wire, rod	0.51–0.59 **C**, 0.60–0.80 **Mn**, 0.035 **P**, 0.040 **S**, 1.20–1.60 **Si**, 0.60–0.80 **Cr**	
AISI 9255		US	Wire, rod	0.51–0.59 **C**, 0.70–0.95 **Mn**, 0.035 **P**, 0.040 **S**, 1.80–2.20 **Si**	
AISI 5155		US	Wire, rod	0.51–0.59 **C**, 0.70–0.90 **Mn**, 0.035 **P**, 0.040 **S**, 0.15–0.30 **Si**, 0.70–0.90 **Cr**	

WROUGHT ALLOY STEELS

specification number	designation	country	product forms	composition	mechanical properties (see page iv for explanation)
DGN–B–297	8655	Mexico	Bar	0.51–0.59 **C**, 0.75–1.00 **Mn**, 0.035 **P**, 0.040 **S**, 0.20–0.35 **Si**, 0.40–0.60 **Cr**, 0.40–0.70 **Ni**, 0.15–0.25 **Mo**	
MIL–S–24093	Type II, class A	US	Forgings	0.51 **C**, 1.00 **Mn**, 0.040 **P**, 0.040 **S**, 0.20–0.35 **Si**, 0.80–1.10 **Cr**, 0.15–0.25 **Mo**	**Normalized and tempered or quenched and tempered:** 10 **diam**, 165 (1138) **TS**, 140 (965) **YS**, 10 **El**
MIL–S–24093	Type II class B	US	Forgings	0.51 **C**, 1.00 **Mn**, 0.040 **P**, 0.040 **S**, 0.20–0.35 **Si**, 0.80–1.10 **Cr**, 0.15–0.25 **Mo**	**Normalized and tempered or quenched and tempered:** 10 **diam**, 140 (965) **TS**, 120 (827) **YS**, 14 **El**
MIL–S–24093	Type II, class C	US	Forgings	0.51 **C**, 1.00 **Mn**, 0.040 **P**, 0.040 **S**, 0.20–0.35 **Si**, 0.80–1.10 **Cr**, 0.15–0.25 **Mo**	**Normalized and tempered or quenched and tempered:** 10 **diam**, 120 (827) **TS**, 100 (689) **YS**, 16 **El**
MIL–S–24093	Type II, class D	US	Forgings	0.51 **C**, 1.00 **Mn**, 0.040 **P**, 0.040 **S**, 0.20–0.35 **Si**, 0.80–1.10 **Cr**, 0.15–0.25 **Mo**	**Normalized and tempered or quenched and tempered:** 10 **diam**, 100 (689) **TS**, 80 (552) **YS**, 18 **El**
MIL–S–24093	Type II, class E	US	Forgings	0.51 **C**, 1.00 **Mn**, 0.040 **P**, 0.040 **S**, 0.20–0.35 **Si**, 0.80–1.10 **Cr**, 0.15–0.25 **Mo**	**Normalized and tempered or quenched and tempered:** 10 **diam**, 95 (655) **TS**, 65 (448) **YS**, 20 **El**
MIL–S–24093	Type II, class F	US	Forgings	0.51 **C**, 1.00 **Mn**, 0.040 **P**, 0.040 **S**, 0.20–0.35 **Si**, 0.80–1.10 **Cr**, 0.15–0.25 **Mo**	**Normalized and tempered or quenched and tempered:** all **diam**, 90 (621) max **TS**, 45 (310) **YS**, 22 **El**
AS G18	G18/En11	Australia	Bar, billet	0.50–0.70 **C**, 0.50–0.80 **Mn**, 0.050 **P**, 0.050 **S**, 0.10–0.35 **Si**, 0.50–0.80 **Cr**	**Hardened, tempered:** 2 1/2 **diam**, (850) **TS**, (620) **YS**, 15 **El**
JIS G 3566	SWOSC–V	Japan	Wire	0.50–0.60 **C**, 0.50–0.80 **Mn**, 0.030 **P**, 0.030 **S**, 1.20–1.30 **Si**, 0.50–0.80 **Cr**, 0.20 **Cu**	**Cold drawn and oil tempered:** (1.6) **diam**, (1961) **TS**
IS 4367	55Si2Mo[90]	India	Forgings	0.50–0.60 **C**, 0.80–1.00 **Mn**, 0.050 **P**, 0.050 **S**, 1.50–2.00 **Si**	**Hardened and tempered:** all **diam**, (1274) **TS**
JIS G 4801	SUP 9	Japan	Bar, wire, rod	0.50–0.60 **C**, 0.65–0.95 **Mn**, 0.035 **P**, 0.035 **S**, 0.15–0.35 **Si**, 0.65–0.95 **Cr**, 0.30 **Cu**	**Quenched and tempered:** all **diam**, (1226) **TS**, (1079) **YS**, 9 **El**
IS 5517	Grade 55 Cr 70	India	Bar, billet	0.50–0.60 **C**, 0.60–0.80 **Mn**, 0.10–0.35 **Si**, 0.60–0.80 **Cr**	**Normalized, annealed or hardened and tempered:** (63) **diam**, (880) **TS**, (645) **YS**
AS G18	G18/En 48A	Australia	Bar	0.50–0.60 **C**, 0.60–0.90 **Mn**, 0.050 **P**, 0.050 **S**, 1.35–1.65 **Si**, 0.55–0.85 **Cr**	
AS 1444	Grade AS 1444/5155	Australia	Bar, bloom, billet, slab	0.50–0.60 **C**, 0.70–1.00 **Mn**, 0.050 **P**, 0.050 **S**, 0.10–0.35 **Si**, 0.70–0.90 **Cr**	
AS 1444		Australia	Bar, bloom, billet, slab	0.50–0.60 **C**, 0.70–1.05 **Mn**, 0.050 **P**, 0.050 **S**, 1.60–2.20 **Si**	
AS 1444	Grade AS 1444/9245H	Australia	Bar, bloom, billet, slab	0.50–0.60 **C**, 0.50–0.80 **Mn**, 0.050 **P**, 0.050 **S**, 1.20–1.60 **Si**, 0.50–0.80 **Cr**	
DGN–B–203	Grade 5155	Mexico	Tube: seamless	0.50–0.60 **C**, 0.70–0.90 **Mn**, 0.040 **P**, 0.040 **S**, 0.20–0.35 **Si**, 0.70–0.90 **Cr**	
DGN–B–203	Grade 9255	Mexico	Tube: seamless	0.50–0.60 **C**, 0.70–0.95 **Mn**, 0.040 **P**, 0.040 **S**, 1.80–2.20 **Si**	
DGN–B–203	Grade 8655	Mexico	Tube: seamless	0.50–0.60 **C**, 0.75–1.00 **Mn**, 0.040 **P**, 0.040 **S**, 0.20–0.35 **Si**, 0.40–0.60 **Cr**, 0.40–0.70 **Ni**, 0.15–0.25 **Mo**	
DGN–B–300	5155 H	Mexico	Bar	0.50–0.60 **C**, 0.60–1.00 **Mn**, 0.040 **P**, 0.035 **S**, 0.20–0.35 **Si**, 0.60–1.00 **Cr**	**Annealed**
DGN–B–300	8655 H	Mexico	Bar	0.50–0.60 **C**, 0.70–1.05 **Mn**, 0.040 **P**, 0.035 **S**, 0.20–0.35 **Si**, 0.35–0.65 **Cr**, 0.35–0.75 **Ni**, 0.15–0.25 **Mo**	**Annealed**
ASTM A 689	5155 H	US	Bar	0.50–0.60 **C**, 0.60–1.00 **Mn**, 0.040 **P**, 0.040 **S**, 0.15–0.30 **Si**, 0.60–1.00 **Cr**	

WROUGHT ALLOY STEELS

specification number	designation	country	product forms	composition	mechanical properties (see page iv for explanation)
ASTM A 689	8655 H	US	Bar	0.50–0.60 **C**, 0.70–1.05 **Mn**, 0.040 **P**, 0.040 **S**, 0.15–0.30 **Si**, 0.35–0.65 **Cr**, 0.35–0.75 **Ni**, 0.15–0.25 **Mo**	
ANSI/ASTM A 304	5155 H	US	Bar	0.50–0.60 **C**, 0.60–1.00 **Mn**, 0.040 **P**, 0.040 **S**, 0.15–0.30 **Si**, 0.60–1.00 **Cr**	
ANSI/ASTM A 304	8655 H	US	Bar	0.50–0.60 **C**, 0.70–1.05 **Mn**, 0.040 **P**, 0.040 **S**, 0.15–0.30 **Si**, 0.35–0.65 **Cr**, 0.35–0.75 **Ni**, 0.15–0.25 **Mo**	
AISI 5155 H		US	Wire, rod	0.50–0.60 **C**, 0.60–1.00 **Mn**, 0.15–0.30 **Si**, 0.60–1.00 **Cr**	
AISI 8655 H		US	Wire, rod	0.50–0.60 **C**, 0.70–1.05 **Mn**, 0.15–0.30 **Si**, 0.35–0.65 **Cr**, 0.35–0.75 **Ni**, 0.15–0.25 **Mo**	
AISI 8655H		US	Bar	0.50–0.60 **C**, 0.70–1.05 **Mn**, 0.035 **P**, 0.040 **S**, 0.15–0.30 **Si**, 0.35–0.65 **Cr**, 0.35–0.75 **Ni**, 0.15–0.25 **Mo**	
AISI 5155H		US	Bar	0.50–0.60 **C**, 0.60–1.00 **Mn**, 0.035 **P**, 0.040 **S**, 0.15–0.30 **Si**, 0.60–1.00 **Cr**	
ANSI/ASTM A 519	5155	US	Tube: seamless	0.50–0.60 **C**, 0.70–0.90 **Mn**, 0.040 **P**, 0.040 **S**, 0.15–0.35 **Si**, 0.70–0.90 **Cr**	
ANSI/ASTM A 519	8655	US	Tube: seamless	0.50–0.60 **C**, 0.75–1.00 **Mn**, 0.040 **P**, 0.040 **S**, 0.15–0.35 **Si**, 0.40–0.60 **Cr**, 0.40–0.70 **Ni**, 0.15–0.25 **Mo**	
ANSI/ASTM A 519	9255	US	Tube: seamless	0.50–0.60 **C**, 0.70–0.95 **Mn**, 0.040 **P**, 0.040 **S**, 1.80–2.20 **Si**	
COPANT 514	Grade 5155	COPANT	Tube: seamless	0.50–0.60 **C**, 0.70–0.90 **Mn**, 0.040 **P**, 0.050 **S**, 0.10 **Si**, 0.70–0.90 **Cr**	
COPANT 514	Grade 8655	COPANT	Tube: seamless	0.50–0.60 **C**, 0.75–1.00 **Mn**, 0.040 **P**, 0.050 **S**, 0.10 **Si**, 0.40–0.60 **Cr**, 0.40–0.70 **Ni**, 0.15–0.25 **Mo**	
COPANT 514	Grade 9255	COPANT	Tube: seamless	0.50–0.60 **C**, 0.70–0.95 **Mn**, 0.040 **P**, 0.050 **S**, 1.80–2.20 **Si**	
JIS G 3311	SUP9M	Japan	Strip	0.50–0.60 **C**, 0.65–0.95 **Mn**, 0.035 **P**, 0.035 **S**, 0.15–0.35 **Si**, 0.65–0.95 **Cr**, 0.30 **Cu**	
DGN–B–297	9255	Mexico	Bar	0.50–0.51 **C**, 0.70–0.95 **Mn**, 0.035 **P**, 0.040 **S**, 1.80–2.20 **Si**	
DGN–B–297	5155	Mexico	Bar	0.50–0.51 **C**, 0.70–0.90 **Mn**, 0.035 **P**, 0.040 **S**, 0.20–0.35 **Si**, 0.70–0.90 **Cr**	
MIL–S–890	Alloy No 1	US	Forgings, bar	0.50 **C**, 0.040 **P**, 0.040 **S**; other alloying elements add as agreed.	**Annealed or normalized and drawn or quenched and drawn:** all **diam**, 170 (1172) **TS**, 140 (965) **YS**, 10 **El**
JIS G 3222	SFNCM 110S	Japan	Forgings	0.50 **C**, 0.35–1.00 **Mn**, 0.030 **P**, 0.030 **S**, 0.15–0.35 **Si**, 0.40–3.50 **Cr**, 0.40–3.50 **Ni**, 0.15–0.70 **Mo**, 0.30 **Cu**	**Quenched and tempered:** (<200) **diam**, (1079) **TS**, (883) **YS**, 11 **El**
JIS G 3222	SFNCM 110R	Japan	Forgings	0.50 **C**, 0.35–1.00 **Mn**, 0.030 **P**, 0.030 **S**, 0.15–0.35 **Si**, 0.40–3.50 **Cr**, 0.40–3.50 **Ni**, 0.15–0.70 **Mo**, 0.30 **Cu**	**Quenched and tempered:** (<100) **diam**, (1079) **TS**, (902) **YS**, 10 **El**
JIS G 3222	SFNCM 110D	Japan	Forgings	0.50 **C**, 0.35–1.00 **Mn**, 0.030 **P**, 0.030 **S**, 0.15–0.35 **Si**, 0.40–3.50 **Cr**, 0.40–3.50 **Ni**, 0.15–0.70 **Mo**, 0.30 **Cu**	**Quenched and tempered:** (<200) **diam**, (1079) **TS**, (883) **YS**, 9 **El**
JIS G 3222	SFNCM 105S	Japan	Forgings	0.50 **C**, 0.35–1.00 **Mn**, 0.030 **P**, 0.030 **S**, 0.15–0.35 **Si**, 0.40–3.50 **Cr**, 0.40–3.50 **Ni**, 0.15–0.70 **Mo**, 0.30 **Cu**	**Quenched and tempered:** (<200) **diam**, (1030) **TS**, (834) **YS**, 11 **El**
JIS G 3222	SFNCM 105R	Japan	Forgings	0.50 **C**, 0.35–1.00 **Mn**, 0.030 **P**, 0.030 **S**, 0.15–0.35 **Si**, 0.40–3.50 **Cr**, 0.40–3.50 **Ni**, 0.15–0.70 **Mo**, 0.30 **Cu**	**Quenched and tempered:** (<100) **diam**, (1030) **TS**, (853) **YS**, 11 **El**

WROUGHT ALLOY STEELS

specification number	designation	country	product forms	composition	mechanical properties (see page iv for explanation)
JIS G 3222	SFNCM 105D	Japan	Forgings	0.50 **C**, 0.35–1.00 **Mn**, 0.030 **P**, 0.030 **S**, 0.15–0.35 **Si**, 0.40–3.50 **Cr**, 0.40–3.50 **Ni**, 0.15–0.70 **Mo**, 0.30 **Cu**	**Quenched and tempered:** (<200) **diam**, (1030) **TS**, (834) **YS**, 10 **El**
MIL–S–19434A	Class 5	US	Forgings	0.50 **C**, 0.60–0.90 **Mn**, 0.025 **P**, 0.025 min **S**, 0.15 min **Si**, 0.50 min **Cr**, 1.65 min **Ni**, 0.20 min **Mo**, 0.15 **V**	**Quenched and tempered:** ≤10 **diam**, (999) **TS**, (827) **YS**, 15 **El**
JIS G 3222	SFNCM 100S	Japan	Forgings	0.50 **C**, 0.35–1.00 **Mn**, 0.030 **P**, 0.030 **S**, 0.15–0.35 **Si**, 0.40–3.50 **Cr**, 0.40–3.50 **Ni**, 0.15–0.70 **Mo**, 0.30 **Cu**	**Quenched and tempered:** (<200) **diam**, (981) **TS**, (784) **YS**, 13 **El**
JIS G 3222	SFNCM 100R	Japan	Forgings	0.50 **C**, 0.35–1.00 **Mn**, 0.030 **P**, 0.030 **S**, 0.15–0.35 **Si**, 0.40–3.50 **Cr**, 0.40–3.50 **Ni**, 0.15–0.70 **Mo**, 0.30 **Cu**	**Quenched and tempered:** (<100) **diam**, (981) **TS**, (804) **YS**, 12 **El**
JIS G 3222	SFNCM 100D	Japan	Forgings	0.50 **C**, 0.35–1.00 **Mn**, 0.030 **P**, 0.030 **S**, 0.15–0.35 **Si**, 0.40–3.50 **Cr**, 0.40–3.50 **Ni**, 0.15–0.70 **Mo**, 0.30 **Cu**	**Quenched and tempered:** (<200) **diam**, (981) **TS**, (785) **YS**, 10 **El**
JIS G 3222	SFNCM 95S	Japan	Forgings	0.50 **C**, 0.35–1.00 **Mn**, 0.030 **P**, 0.030 **S**, 0.15–0.35 **Si**, 0.40–3.50 **Cr**, 0.40–3.50 **Ni**, 0.15–0.70 **Mo**, 0.30 **Cu**	**Quenched and tempered:** (<200) **diam**, (932) **TS**, (736) **YS**, 13 **El**
JIS G 3222	SFNCM 95R	Japan	Forgings	0.50 **C**, 0.35–1.00 **Mn**, 0.030 **P**, 0.030 **S**, 0.15–0.35 **Si**, 0.40–3.50 **Cr**, 0.40–3.50 **Ni**, 0.15–0.70 **Mo**, 0.30 **Cu**	**Quenched and tempered:** (<100) **diam**, (932) **TS**, (755) **YS**, 13 **El**
JIS G 3222	SFNCM 95D	Japan	Forgings	0.50 **C**, 0.35–1.00 **Mn**, 0.030 **P**, 0.030 **S**, 0.15–0.35 **Si**, 0.40–3.50 **Cr**, 0.40–3.50 **Ni**, 0.15–0.70 **Mo**, 0.30 **Cu**	**Quenched and tempered:** (<200) **diam**, (932) **TS**, (736) **YS**, 11 **El**
JIS G 3222	SFNCM 90S	Japan	Forgings	0.50 **C**, 0.35–1.00 **Mn**, 0.030 **P**, 0.030 **S**, 0.15–0.35 **Si**, 0.40–3.50 **Cr**, 0.40–3.50 **Ni**, 0.15–0.70 **Mo**, 0.30 **Cu**	**Quenched and tempered:** (<200) **diam**, (883) **TS**, (686) **YS**, 14 **El**
JIS G 3222	SFNCM 90R	Japan	Forgings	0.50 **C**, 0.35 **Mn**, 0.030 **P**, 0.030 **S**, 0.15–0.35 **Si**, 0.40–3.50 **Cr**, 0.40–3.50 **Ni**, 0.15–0.70 **Mo**, 0.30 **Cu**	**Quenched and tempered:** (<100) **diam**, (883) **TS**, (706) **YS**, 14 **El**
JIS G 3222	SFNCM 90D	Japan	Forgings	0.50 **C**, 0.35–1.00 **Mn**, 0.030 **P**, 0.030 **S**, 0.15–0.35 **Si**, 0.40–3.50 **Cr**, 0.40–3.50 **Ni**, 0.15–0.70 **Mo**, 0.30 **Cu**	**Quenched and tempered:** (<200) **diam**, (883) **TS**, (686) **YS**, 12 **El**
MIL–S–19434A	Class 4	US	Forgings	0.50 **C**, 0.60–0.90 **Mn**, 0.025 **P**, 0.025 min **S**, 0.15 min **Si**, 0.50 min **Cr**, 1.65 min **Ni**, 0.20 min **Mo**, 0.15 **V**	**Normalized and tempered, quenched and tempered:** ≤10 **diam**, (861) **TS**, (689) **YS**, 16 **El**
JIS G 3222	SFNCM 85S	Japan	Forgings	0.50 **C**, 0.35–1.00 **Mn**, 0.030 **P**, 0.030 **S**, 0.15–0.35 **Si**, 0.40–3.50 **Cr**, 0.40–3.50 **Ni**, 0.15–0.70 **Mo**, 0.30 **Cu**	**Quenched and tempered:** (<200) **diam**, (834) **TS**, (637) **YS**, 15 **El**
JIS G 3222	SFNCM 85R	Japan	Forgings	0.50 **C**, 0.35–1.00 **Mn**, 0.030 **P**, 0.030 **S**, 0.15–0.35 **Si**, 0.40–3.50 **Cr**, 0.40–3.50 **Ni**, 0.15–0.70 **Mo**, 0.30 **Cu**	**Quenched and tempered:** (<100) **diam**, (834) **TS**, (657) **YS**, 15 **El**
JIS G 3222	SFNCM 85D	Japan	Forgings	0.50 **C**, 0.35–1.00 **Mn**, 0.030 **P**, 0.030 **S**, 0.15–0.35 **Si**, 0.40–3.50 **Cr**, 0.40–3.50 **Ni**, 0.15–0.70 **Mo**, 0.30 **Cu**	**Quenched and tempered:** (<200) **diam**, (834) **TS**, (637) **YS**, 13 **El**
MIL–S–890	Alloy No 2	US	Forgings, bar	0.50 **C**, 0.040 **P**, 0.040 **S**; other alloying elements added as agreed.	**Annealed or normalized and drawn or quenched and drawn:** all **diam**, 120 (827) **TS**, 105 (724) **YS**, 18 **El**
JIS G 3222	SFNCM 80R	Japan	Forgings	0.50 **C**, 0.35–1.00 **Mn**, 0.030 **P**, 0.030 **S**, 0.15–0.35 **Si**, 0.40–3.50 **Cr**, 0.40–3.50 **Ni**, 0.15–0.70 **Mo**, 0.30 **Cu**	**Quenched and tempered:** (<100) **diam**, (785) **TS**, (598) **YS**, 16 **El**
JIS G 3222	SFNCM 80D	Japan	Forgings	0.50 **C**, 0.35–1.00 **Mn**, 0.030 **P**, 0.030 **S**, 0.15–0.35 **Si**, 0.40–3.50 **Cr**, 0.40–3.50 **Ni**, 0.15–0.70 **Mo**, 0.30 **Cu**	**Quenched and tempered:** (<200) **diam**, (785) **TS**, (588) **YS**, 14 **El**

specification number	designation	country	product forms	composition	mechanical properties (see page iv for explanation)
JIS G 3222	SFNCM 80S	Japan	Forgings	0.50 **C**, 0.35–1.00 **Mn**, 0.030 **P**, 0.030 **S**, 0.15–0.35 **Si**, 0.40–3.50 **Cr**, 0.40–3.50 **Ni**, 0.15–0.70 **Mo**, 0.30 **Cu**	**Quenched and tempered:** (<200) **diam**, (784) **TS**, (588) **YS**, 16 **El**
BS 4T.50		UK	Tube: aircraft quality	0.50 **C**, 0.4–0.8 **Mn**, 0.040 **P**, 0.040 **S**, 0.15–0.35 **Si**, 0.8–1.2 **Cr**, 0.5 **Ni**, 0.15–0.25 **Mo**	**Hardened, normalized and tempered:** all **diam**, (770) **TS**, (700) **YS**
JIS G 3222	SFNCM 75S	Japan	Forgings	0.50 **C**, 0.35–1.00 **Mn**, 0.030 **P**, 0.030 **S**, 0.15–0.35 **Si**, 0.40–3.50 **Cr**, 0.40–3.50 **Ni**, 0.15–0.70 **Mo**, 0.30 **Cu**	**Quenched and tempered:** (<200) **diam**, (736) **TS**, (539) **YS**, 17 **El**
JIS G 3222	SFNCM 75R	Japan	Forgings	0.50 **C**, 0.35–1.00 **Mn**, 0.030 **P**, 0.030 **S**, 0.15–0.35 **Si**, 0.40–3.50 **Cr**, 0.40–3.50 **Ni**, 0.15–0.70 **Mo**, 0.30 **Cu**	**Quenched and tempered:** (<100) **diam**, (736) **TS**, (549) **YS**, 17 **El**
JIS G 3222	SFNCM 75D	Japan	Forgings	0.50 **C**, 0.35–1.00 **Mn**, 0.030 **P**, 0.030 **S**, 0.15–0.35 **Si**, 0.40–3.50 **Cr**, 0.40–3.50 **Ni**, 0.15–0.70 **Mo**, 0.30 **Cu**	**Quenched and tempered:** (<200) **diam**, (736) **TS**, (539) **YS**, 15 **El**
JIS G 3222	SFNCM 70S	Japan	Forgings	0.50 **C**, 0.35–1.00 **Mn**, 0.030 **P**, 0.030 **S**, 0.15–0.35 **Si**, 0.40–3.50 **Cr**, 0.40–3.50 **Ni**, 0.15–0.30 **Mo**, 0.30 **Cu**	**Quenched and tempered:** (<200) **diam**, (686) **TS**, (490) **YS**, 18 **El**
JIS G 3222	SFNCM 70R	Japan	Forgings	0.50 **C**, 0.35–1.00 **Mn**, 0.030 **P**, 0.030 **S**, 0.15–0.35 **Si**, 0.40–3.50 **Cr**, 0.40–3.50 **Ni**, 0.15–0.70 **Mo**, 0.30 **Cu**	**Quenched and tempered:** (<100) **diam**, (686) **TS**, (490) **YS**, 18 **El**
JIS G 3222	SFNCM 70D	Japan	Forgings	0.50 **C**, 0.35–1.00 **Mn**, 0.030 **P**, 0.030 **S**, 0.15–0.35 **Si**, 0.40–3.50 **Cr**, 0.40 **Ni**, 0.15–0.70 **Mo**, 0.30 **Cu**	**Quenched and tempered:** (<200) **diam**, (686) **TS**, (490) **YS**, 16 **El**
API Spec 5AC	C–75 Type 1	US	Casing, tube	0.50 **C**, 1.90 **Mn**, 0.040 **P**, 0.060 **S**, 0.35 **Si**, 0.15–0.40 **Mo**	**Normalized and tempered:** all **diam**, 95 (657) **TS**, 75 (519) **YS**
NF A 35–590	2332 (Y50 CV4)	France	Bar, forgings	0.50 **C**, 0.80 **Mn**, 0.030 **P**, 0.030 **S**, 0.30 **Si**, 1.0 **Cr**, 0.15 **V**	
AISI 8655		US	Plate	0.49–0.60 **C**, 0.70–1.00 **Mn**, 0.035 **P**, 0.040 **S**, 0.15–0.30 **Si**, 0.35–0.60 **Cr**, 0.40–0.70 **Ni**, 0.15–0.25 **Mo**	
AMS 6396		US	Sheet, strip, plate	0.49–0.55 **C**, 0.65–0.85 **Mn**, 0.025 **P**, 0.025 **S**, 0.20–0.35 **Si**, 0.70–0.90 **Cr**, 1.65–2.00 **Ni**, 0.20–0.30 **Mo**, 0.35 **Cu**	**Quenched and tempered:** all **diam**, 150 (1034) **TS**, 130 (896) **YS**, 8 **El**
AMS 6424		US	Bar, forgings, tube	0.49–0.55 **C**, 0.65–0.85 **Mn**, 0.025 **P**, 0.025 **S**, 0.20–0.35 **Si**, 0.70–0.90 **Cr**, 1.65–2.00 **Ni**, 0.20–0.30 **Mo**, 0.35 **Cu**	**Cold finished (bar):** ≤0.500 (≤12.70) **diam**, 135 (931) max **TS**
NBN 253–05	51 Cr Mo V 4	Belgium	Wire	0.48–0.56 **C**, 0.70–1.0 **Mn**, 0.035 **P**, 0.035 **S**, 0.15–0.40 **Si**, 0.90–1.20 **Cr**, 0.15–0.25 **Mo**, 0.07–0.12 **V**	**Annealed or quenched and tempered:** (≤60) **diam**, (1375) **TS**, (1175) **YS**, 6 **El**
DIN 17221	51CrMoV 4[4]) /1.7701	Germany	Springs	0.48–0.56 **C**, 0.70–1.10 **Mn**, 0.035 **P**, 0.035 **S**, 0.15–0.40 **Si**, 0.90–1.20 **Cr**, 0.07–0.12 **V**	**Quenched and tempered:** all **diam**, (1370) **TS**, (1180) **YS**, 6 **El**
DIN 17221	Grade 51 CrMoV4	Germany	Bar, wire, strip	0.48–0.56 **C**, 0.70–1.10 **Mn**, 0.035 **P**, 0.035 **S**, 0.15–0.40 **Si**, 0.90–1.20 **Cr**, 0.15–0.25 **Mo**, 0.07–0.12 **V**	**Quenched and tempered:** (10) **diam**, (1370) **TS**, (1180) **YS**, 6 **El**
TS 2288	51 CrMo V4–17701	Turkey	Wire	0.48–0.56 **C**, 0.70–1.10 **Mn**, 0.035 **P**, 0.035 **S**, 0.15–0.40 **Si**, 0.90–1.20 **Cr**, 0.15–0.25 **Mo**, 0.07–0.42 **V**	
AS 1443	Grade AS 1443/XK 1152	Australia	Bar	0.48–0.56 **C**, 1.35–1.65 **Mn**, 0.050 **P**, 0.24–0.33 **S**, 0.10–0.35 **Si**	
AS 1442	Grade AS 1442/XK1152	Australia	Bar, blooms, billets, slabs	0.48–0.56 **C**, 1.35–1.65 **Mn**, 0.050 **P**, 0.24–0.33 **S**, 0.10–0.35 **Si**	
SIS 14 22 30	SIS 22 30–04	Sweden	Bar, forgings, wire	0.48–0.55 **C**, 0.70–1.00 **Mn**, 0.035 **P**, 0.035 **S**, 0.15–0.40 **Si**, 0.90–1.20 **Cr**, 0.10–0.20 **V**	**Quenched and tempered:** all **diam**, (1500) **TS**, (1300) **YS**, 6 **El**
SIS 14 22 30	SIS 22 30–05	Sweden	Bar, wire	0.48–0.55 **C**, 0.70–1.00 **Mn**, 0.035 **P**, 0.035 **S**, 0.15–0.40 **Si**, 0.90–1.20 **Cr**, 0.10–0.20 **V**	**Quenched and tempered:** (4–5) **diam**, (1450) **TS**, (1250) **YS**

WROUGHT ALLOY STEELS

specification number	designation	country	product forms	composition	mechanical properties (see page iv for explanation)
NBN 253-05	50 CrV 4	Belgium	Wire	0.48–0.55 **C**, 0.70–1.0 **Mn**, 0.035 **P**, 0.035 **S**, 0.15–0.40 **Si**, 0.90–1.20 **Cr**, 0.10–0.20 **V**	**Annealed or quenched and tempered:** (≤40) **diam**, (1375) **TS**, (1175) **YS**, 6 **El**
SIS 14 22 30	SIS 22 30-03	Sweden	Bar, forgings, wire	0.48–0.55 **C**, 0.70–1.00 **Mn**, 0.035 **P**, 0.035 **S**, 0.15–0.40 **Si**, 0.90–1.20 **Cr**, 0.10–0.20 **V**	**Quenched and tempered:** (≤30) **diam**, (1300) **TS**, (1150) **YS**, 8 **El**
SIS 14 22 30	SIS 22 30-06	Sweden	Bar, wire	0.48–0.55 **C**, 0.70–1.00 **Mn**, 0.035 **P**, 0.035 **S**, 0.15–0.40 **Si**, 0.90–1.20 **Cr**, 0.10–0.20 **V**	**Annealed and cold worked:** all **diam**, (800) **TS**
MIL-S-11595D	ORD 4150	US	Bar	0.48–0.55 **C**, 0.75–1.00 **Mn**, 0.040 **P**, 0.040 **S**, 0.20–0.35 **Si**, 0.80–1.10 **Cr**, 0.15–0.25 **Mo**	
AS 1444	Grade AS 1444/5150	Australia	Bar, bloom, billet, slab	0.48–0.55 **C**, 0.70–1.00 **Mn**, 0.050 **P**, 0.050 **S**, 0.10–0.35 **Si**, 0.70–0.90 **Cr**	
SIS 14 22 30	SIS 22 30-02	Sweden	Bar, forgings, wire	0.48–0.55 **C**, 0.70–1.00 **Mn**, 0.035 **P**, 0.035 **S**, 0.15–0.40 **Si**, 0.90–1.20 **Cr**, 0.10–0.20 **V**	**Annealed**
SIS 14 22 30	SIS 22 30-00	Sweden	Bar, forgings, wire	0.48–0.55 **C**, 0.70–1.00 **Mn**, 0.035 **P**, 0.035 **S**, 0.15–0.40 **Si**, 0.90–1.20 **Cr**, 0.10–0.20 **V**	
NF A 35-571	51 S 7	France	Bar, wire, rod	0.48–0.54 **C**, 0.50–0.80 **Mn**, 0.035 **P**, 0.035 **S**, 1.6–2.0 **Si**, 0.30 **Cr**	**Quenched and tempered:** (≤80) **diam**, (1500) **TS**, (1350) **YS**, 6.5 **El**
ANSI/ASTM A 232		US	Wire	0.48–0.53 **C**, 0.70–0.90 **Mn**, 0.020 **P**, 0.035 **S**, 0.20–0.35 **Si**, 0.80–1.10 **Cr**, 0.15 **V**	**Cold drawn and tempered:** 0.020 (0.51) **diam**, 300 (2070) **TS**
ANSI/ASTM A 231		US	Wire	0.48–0.53 **C**, 0.70–0.90 **Mn**, 0.040 **P**, 0.040 **S**, 0.20–0.35 **Si**, 0.80–1.10 **Cr**, 0.15 **V**	**Cold drawn and tempered:** 0.020 (0.51) **diam**, 300 (2070) **TS**
ANSI/ASTM A 232		US	Wire	0.48–0.53 **C**, 0.70–0.90 **Mn**, 0.020 **P**, 0.035 **S**, 0.20–0.35 **Si**, 0.80–1.10 **Cr**, 0.15 min **V**	**Annealed, cold drawn or oil tempered:** 0.020 (0.51) **diam**, 300 (2070) **TS**
ANSI/ASTM A 231		US	Wire	0.48–0.53 **C**, 0.70–0.90 **Mn**, 0.040 **P**, 0.040 **S**, 0.20–0.35 **Si**, 0.80–1.10 **Cr**, 0.15 min **V**	**Annealed or oil tempered:** 0.020 (0.51) **diam**, 300 (2070) **TS**
AMS 6450D		US	Wire	0.48–0.53 **C**, 0.70–0.90 **Mn**, 0.025 **P**, 0.025 **S**, 0.20–0.35 **Si**, 0.80–1.10 **Cr**, 0.25 **Ni**, 0.06 **Mo**, 0.15–0.30 **V**, 0.35 **Cu**	**Cold drawn, annealed (wire), hardened, tempered (spring):** all **diam**, 220 (1517) **TS**, 40 **El**
AMS 6448D		US	Bar, forgings, tube	0.48–0.53 **C**, 0.70–0.90 **Mn**, 0.025 **P**, 0.025 **S**, 0.20–0.35 **Si**, 0.80–1.10 **Cr**, 0.25 **Ni**, 0.06 **Mo**, 0.35 **Cu**	**Cold finished (bar):** ≤0.500 (≤12.70) **diam**, 125 (862) max **TS**
AMS 6328F		US	Bar, forgings, tube	0.48–0.53 **C**, 0.75–1.00 **Mn**, 0.025 **P**, 0.025 **S**, 0.20–0.35 **Si**, 0.40–0.60 **Cr**, 0.40–0.70 **Ni**, 0.20–0.30 **Mo**, 0.35 **Cu**	**Cold finished (bar):** ≤0.500 (≤12.70) **diam**, 125 (862) max **TS**
AISI 4150		US	Bar	0.48–0.53 **C**, 0.75–1.00 **Mn**, 0.035 **P**, 0.040 **S**, 0.15–0.30 **Si**, 0.80–1.10 **Cr**, 0.15–0.25 **Mo**	
AISI 5150		US	Bar	0.48–0.53 **C**, 0.70–0.90 **Mn**, 0.035 **P**, 0.040 **S**, 0.15–0.30 **Si**, 0.70–0.90 **Cr**	
AISI 6150		US	Bar	0.48–0.53 **C**, 0.70–0.90 **Mn**, 0.035 **P**, 0.040 **S**, 0.15–0.30 **Si**, 0.80–1.10 **Cr**, 0.15 **Mo**	
AISI 50B50		US	Bar	0.48–0.53 **C**, 0.75–1.00 **Mn**, 0.035 **P**, 0.040 **S**, 0.15–0.30 **Si**, 0.40–0.60 **Cr**, 0.0005–0.003 **B**	
MIL-S-8503A	AISI 6150	US	Bar	0.48–0.53 **C**, 0.70–0.90 **Mn**, 0.025 **P**, 0.025 **S**, 0.20–0.35 **Si**, 0.75–1.20 **Cr**, 0.15 min **V**	
COPANT 334	4150	COPANT	Bar	0.48–0.53 **C**, 0.75–1.00 **Mn**, 0.035 **P**, 0.040 **S**, 0.20–0.35 **Si**, 0.80–1.10 **Cr**, 0.15–0.25 **Mo**	
COPANT 334	5150	COPANT	Bar	0.48–0.53 **C**, 0.70–0.90 **Mn**, 0.035 **P**, 0.040 **S**, 0.20–0.35 **Si**, 0.70–0.90 **Cr**	
COPANT 334	6150	COPANT	Bar	0.48–0.53 **C**, 0.70–0.90 **Mn**, 0.035 **P**, 0.040 **S**, 0.20–0.35 **Si**, 0.80–1.10 **Cr**, 0.15 min **V**	

specification number	designation	country	product forms	composition	mechanical properties (see page iv for explanation)
COPANT 334	8650	COPANT	Bar	0.48–0.53 **C**, 0.75–1.00 **Mn**, 0.035 **P**, 0.040 **S**, 0.20–0.35 **Si**, 0.40–0.60 **Cr**, 0.40–0.70 **Ni**, 0.15–0.25 **Mo**	
AS 1444	Grade AS 1444/4150	Australia	Bar, bloom, billet, slab	0.48–0.53 **C**, 0.75–1.00 **Mn**, 0.040 **P**, 0.040 **S**, 0.10–0.35 **Si**, 0.80–1.10 **Cr**, 0.15–0.25 **Mo**	
AS 1444	Grade AS 1444/6150	Australia	Bar, bloom, billet, slab	0.48–0.53 **C**, 0.70–0.90 **Mn**, 0.040 **P**, 0.040 **S**, 0.10–0.35 **Si**, 0.80–1.10 **Cr**, 0.15 min **V**	
DGN–B–203	Grade 4150	Mexico	Tube: seamless	0.48–0.53 **C**, 0.75–1.00 **Mn**, 0.040 **P**, 0.040 **S**, 0.20–0.35 **Si**, 0.80–1.10 **Cr**, 0.15–0.25 **Mo**	
DGN–B–203	Grade 5150	Mexico	Tube: seamless	0.48–0.53 **C**, 0.70–0.90 **Mn**, 0.040 **P**, 0.040 **S**, 0.20–0.35 **Si**, 0.70–0.90 **Cr**	
DGN–B–203	Grade 8650	Mexico	Tube: seamless	0.48–0.53 **C**, 0.75–1.00 **Mn**, 0.040 **P**, 0.040 **S**, 0.20–0.35 **Si**, 0.40–0.60 **Cr**, 0.40–0.70 **Ni**, 0.15–0.25 **Mo**	
DGN–B–203	Grade 6150	Mexico	Tube: seamless	0.48–0.53 **C**, 0.70–0.90 **Mn**, 0.040 **P**, 0.040 **S**, 0.20–0.35 **Si**, 0.80–1.10 **Cr**, 0.15 min **V**	
DGN–B–203	Grade 50B50	Mexico	Tube: seamless	0.48–0.53 **C**, 0.75–1.00 **Mn**, 0.040 **P**, 0.040 **S**, 0.20–0.35 **Si**, 0.40–0.60 **Cr**, 0.0005 min **B**	
DGN–B–203	Grade 9850	Mexico	Tube: seamless	0.48–0.53 **C**, 0.70–0.90 **Mn**, 0.040 **P**, 0.040 **S**, 0.20–0.35 **Si**, 0.70–0.90 **Cr**, 0.85–1.15 **Ni**, 0.20–0.35 **Mo**	
COPANT 514	4150	COPANT	Tube	0.48–0.53 **C**, 0.75–1.0 **Mn**, 0.040 **P**, 0.040 **S**, 0.20–0.35 **Si**, 0.80–1.10 **Cr**, 0.15–0.25 **Mo**	
DGN–B–300	50B50	Mexico	Bar	0.48–0.53 **C**, 0.75–1.00 **Mn**, 0.035 **P**, 0.040 **S**, 0.20–0.35 **Si**, 0.40–0.60 **Cr**, 0.0005 min **B**	**Annealed**
DGN–B–300	6150	Mexico	Bar	0.48–0.53 **C**, 0.70–0.90 **Mn**, 0.035 **P**, 0.040 **S**, 0.20–0.35 **Si**, 0.80–1.10 **Cr**, 0.15 min **Mo**	**Annealed**
DGN–B–300	5150	Mexico	Bar	0.48–0.53 **C**, 0.70–0.90 **Mn**, 0.035 **P**, 0.040 **S**, 0.20–0.35 **Si**, 0.70–0.90 **Cr**	**Annealed**
DGN–B–300	4150	Mexico	Bar	0.48–0.53 **C**, 0.75–1.00 **Mn**, 0.035 **P**, 0.040 **S**, 0.20–0.35 **Si**, 0.80–1.10 **Cr**, 0.15–0.25 **Mo**	**Annealed**
ANSI/ASTM A 29	4150	US	Bar	0.48–0.53 **C**, 0.75–1.00 **Mn**, 0.035 **P**, 0.040 **S**, 0.15–0.30 **Si**, 0.80–1.10 **Cr**, 0.15–0.25 **Mo**	
ANSI/ASTM A 646	6150	US	Blooms, billets: aircraft quality	0.48–0.53 **C**, 0.70–0.90 **Mn**, 0.025 **P**, 0.025 **S**, 0.20–0.35 **Si**, 0.80–1.10 **Cr**, 0.15 min **V**	**Annealed**
ASTM A 689	50B50	US	Bar, spring	0.48–0.53 **C**, 0.75–1.00 **Mn**, 0.035 **P**, 0.040 **S**, 0.15–0.30 **Si**, 0.40–0.60 **Cr**, 0.0005 min **B**	
ASTM A 689	6150	US	Bar	0.48–0.53 **C**, 0.70–0.90 **Mn**, 0.035 **P**, 0.040 **S**, 0.15–0.30 **Si**, 0.80–1.10 **Cr**, 0.15 min **V**	
ASTM A 689	4150	US	Bar	0.48–0.53 **C**, 0.75–1.00 **Mn**, 0.035 **P**, 0.040 **S**, 0.15–0.30 **Si**, 0.80–1.10 **Cr**, 0.15–0.25 **Mo**	
ASTM A 689	5150	US	Bar	0.48–0.53 **C**, 0.70–0.90 **Mn**, 0.035 **P**, 0.040 **S**, 0.15–0.30 **Si**, 0.70–0.90 **Cr**	
ANSI/ASTM A 322	4150	US	Bar	0.48–0.53 **C**, 0.75–1.00 **Mn**, 0.035 **P**, 0.040 **S**, 0.15–0.30 **Si**, 0.80–1.10 **Cr**, 0.15–0.25 **Mo**	
ANSI/ASTM A 322	50B50	US	Bar	0.48–0.53 **C**, 0.75–1.00 **Mn**, 0.035 **P**, 0.040 **S**, 0.15–0.30 **Si**, 0.40–0.60 **Cr**, 0.0005 min **B**	
ANSI/ASTM A 322	5150	US	Bar	0.48–0.53 **C**, 0.70–0.90 **Mn**, 0.035 **P**, 0.040 **S**, 0.15–0.30 **Si**, 0.70–0.90 **Cr**	

WROUGHT ALLOY STEELS

specification number	designation	country	product forms	composition	mechanical properties (see page iv for explanation)
ANSI/ASTM A 322	6150	US	Bar	0.48–0.53 **C**, 0.70–0.90 **Mn**, 0.035 **P**, 0.040 **S**, 0.15–0.30 **Si**, 0.80–1.10 **Cr**, 0.15 min **V**	
ANSI/ASTM A 29	5150	US	Bar	0.48–0.53 **C**, 0.70–0.90 **Mn**, 0.035 **P**, 0.040 **S**, 0.15–0.30 **Si**, 0.70–0.90 **Cr**	
ANSI/ASTM A 29	6150	US	Bar	0.48–0.53 **C**, 0.70–0.90 **Mn**, 0.035 **P**, 0.040 **S**, 0.15–0.30 **Si**, 0.80–1.10 **Cr**, 0.15 min **V**	
ANSI/ASTM A 29	8650	US	Bar	0.48–0.53 **C**, 0.75–1.00 **Mn**, 0.035 **P**, 0.040 **S**, 0.15–0.30 **Si**, 0.40–0.60 **Cr**, 0.40–0.70 **Ni**, 0.15–0.25 **Mo**	
AISI 6150		US	Wire, rod	0.48–0.53 **C**, 0.70–0.90 **Mn**, 0.035 **P**, 0.040 **S**, 0.15–0.30 **Si**, 0.80–1.10 **Cr**, 0.15 min **V**	
AISI 50B50		US	Wire, rod	0.48–0.53 **C**, 0.75–1.00 **Mn**, 0.035 **P**, 0.040 **S**, 0.15–0.30 **Si**, 0.40–0.60 **Cr**	
AISI 4150		US	Wire, rod	0.48–0.53 **C**, 0.75–1.00 **Mn**, 0.035 **P**, 0.040 **S**, 0.15–0.30 **Si**, 0.80–1.10 **Cr**, 0.15–0.25 **Mo**	
AISI 5150		US	Wire, rod	0.48–0.53 **C**, 0.70–0.90 **Mn**, 0.035 **P**, 0.040 **S**, 0.15–0.30 **Si**, 0.70–0.90 **Cr**	
ANSI/ASTM A 519	4150	US	Tube: seamless	0.48–0.53 **C**, 0.75–1.00 **Mn**, 0.040 **P**, 0.040 **S**, 0.15–0.35 **Si**, 0.80–1.10 **Cr**, 0.15–0.25 **Mo**	
ANSI/ASTM A 519	5150	US	Tube: seamless	0.48–0.53 **C**, 0.70–0.90 **Mn**, 0.040 **P**, 0.040 **S**, 0.15–0.35 **Si**, 0.70–0.90 **Cr**	
ANSI/ASTM A 519	6150	US	Tube: seamless	0.48–0.53 **C**, 0.70–0.90 **Mn**, 0.040 **P**, 0.040 **S**, 0.15–0.35 **Si**, 0.80–1.10 **Cr**, 0.15 min **V**	
ANSI/ASTM A 519	8650	US	Tube: seamless	0.48–0.53 **C**, 0.75–1.00 **Mn**, 0.040 **P**, 0.040 **S**, 0.15–0.35 **Si**, 0.40–0.60 **Cr**, 0.40–0.70 **Ni**, 0.15–0.25 **Mo**	
ANSI/ASTM A 519	9850	US	Tube: seamless	0.48–0.53 **C**, 0.70–0.90 **Mn**, 0.040 **P**, 0.040 **S**, 0.15–0.35 **Si**, 0.70–0.90 **Cr**, 0.85–1.15 **Ni**, 0.20–0.30 **Mo**	
ANSI/ASTM A 519	50B50	US	Tube: seamless	0.48–0.53 **C**, 0.74–1.00 **Mn**, 0.040 **P**, 0.040 **S**, 0.15–0.35 **Si**, 0.40–0.60 **Cr**	
AISI 4150		US	Sheet, strip	0.48–0.53 **C**, 0.75–1.00 **Mn**, 0.035 **P**, 0.040 **S**, 0.20–0.35 **Si**, 0.80–1.10 **Cr**, 0.15–0.25 **Mo**	
DGN-B-297	4150	Mexico	Bar	0.48–0.53 **C**, 0.75–1.00 **Mn**, 0.035 **P**, 0.040 **S**, 0.20–0.35 **Si**, 0.80–1.10 **Cr**, 0.15–0.25 **Mo**	
AISI 5150		US	Sheet, strip	0.48–0.53 **C**, 0.70–0.90 **Mn**, 0.035 **P**, 0.040 **S**, 0.20–0.35 **Si**, 0.70–0.90 **Cr**	
AISI 6150		US	Sheet, strip	0.48–0.53 **C**, 0.70–0.90 **Mn**, 0.035 **P**, 0.040 **S**, 0.20–0.35 **Si**, 0.80–1.10 **Cr**	
DGN-B-297	50B50	Mexico	Bar	0.48–0.53 **C**, 0.75–1.00 **Mn**, 0.035 **P**, 0.040 **S**, 0.20–0.35 **Si**, 0.40–0.60 **Cr**	
DGN-B-297	5150	Mexico	Bar	0.48–0.53 **C**, 0.70–0.90 **Mn**, 0.035 **P**, 0.040 **S**, 0.20–0.35 **Si**, 0.70–0.90 **Cr**	
DGN-B-297	6150	Mexico	Bar	0.48–0.53 **C**, 0.70–0.90 **Mn**, 0.035 **P**, 0.040 **S**, 0.20–0.35 **Si**, 0.80–1.10 **Cr**, 0.15 **V**	
COPANT 514	Grade 50B50	COPANT	Tube: seamless	0.48–0.53 **C**, 0.74–1.00 **Mn**, 0.040 **P**, 0.050 **S**, 0.10 **Si**, 0.40–0.60 **Cr**	
COPANT 514	Grade 5150	COPANT	Tube: seamless	0.48–0.53 **C**, 0.70–0.90 **Mn**, 0.040 **P**, 0.050 **S**, 0.10 **Si**, 0.70–0.90 **Cr**	

specification number	designation	country	product forms	composition	mechanical properties (see page iv for explanation)
COPANT 514	Grade 6150	COPANT	Tube: seamless	0.48–0.53 **C**, 0.70–0.90 **Mn**, 0.040 **P**, 0.050 **S**, 0.10 **Si**, 0.80–1.10 **Cr**, 0.15 min **V**	
COPANT 514	Grade 8650	COPANT	Tube: seamless	0.48–0.53 **C**, 0.75–1.00 **Mn**, 0.040 **P**, 0.050 **S**, 0.10 **Si**, 0.40–0.60 **Cr**, 0.40–0.70 **Ni**, 0.15–0.25 **Mo**	
COPANT 514	Grade 9850	COPANT	Tube: seamless	0.48–0.53 **C**, 0.70–0.90 **Mn**, 0.040 **P**, 0.050 **S**, 0.10 **Si**, 0.70–0.90 **Cr**, 0.85–1.15 **Ni**, 0.20–0.30 **Mo**	
TS 2288	51 Si 7–1,0903	Turkey	Wire	0.48–0.50 **C**, 0.70–1.0 **Mn**, 0.050 **P**, 0.050 **S**, 1.5–1.8 **Si**	
JIS G 3221	SFCM 100R	Japan	Forgings	0.48 **C**, 0.30–0.85 **Mn**, 0.030 **P**, 0.030 **S**, 0.15–0.35 **Si**, 0.90–1.50 **Cr**, 0.15–0.30 **Mo**, 0.03 **Cu**	**Quenched and tempered:** (<50) **diam**, (981) **TS**, (804) **YS**, 12 **El**
JIS G 3221	SFCM 100D	Japan	Forgings	0.48 **C**, 0.30–0.85 **Mn**, 0.030 **P**, 0.030 **S**, 0.15–0.35 **Si**, 0.90–1.50 **Cr**, 0.15–0.30 **Mo**, 0.03 **Cu**	**Quenched and tempered:** (<100) **diam**, (981) **TS**, (775) **YS**, 10 **El**
JIS G 3221	SFCM 95S	Japan	Forgings	0.48 **C**, 0.30–0.85 **Mn**, 0.030 **P**, 0.030 **S**, 0.15–0.35 **Si**, 0.90–1.50 **Cr**, 0.15–0.30 **Mo**	**Quenched and tempered:** (<200) **diam**, (932) **TS**, (706) **YS**, 12 **El**
JIS G 3221	SFCM 95R	Japan	Forgings	0.48 **C**, 0.30–0.85 **Mn**, 0.030 **P**, 0.030 **S**, 0.15–0.35 **Si**, 0.90–1.50 **Cr**, 0.15–0.30 **Mo**, 0.03 **Cu**	**Quenched and tempered:** (<50) **diam**, (932) **TS**, (755) **YS**, 13 **El**
JIS G 3221	SFCM 95D	Japan	Forgings	0.48 **C**, 0.30–0.85 **Mn**, 0.030 **P**, 0.030 **S**, 0.15–0.35 **Si**, 0.90–1.50 **Cr**, 0.15–0.30 **Mo**, 0.03 **Cu**	**Quenched and tempered:** (<100) **diam**, (932) **TS**, (726) **YS**, 11 **El**
JIS G 3221	SFCM 90S	Japan	Forgings	0.48 **C**, 0.30–0.85 **Mn**, 0.030 **P**, 0.030 **S**, 0.15–0.35 **Si**, 0.90–1.50 **Cr**, 0.15–0.30 **Mo**, 0.03 **Cu**	**Quenched and tempered:** (<200) **diam**, (883) **TS**, (657) **YS**, 13 **El**
JIS G 3221	SFCM 90R	Japan	Forgings	0.48 **C**, 0.30–0.85 **Mn**, 0.030 **P**, 0.030 **S**, 0.15–0.35 **Si**, 0.90–1.50 **Cr**, 0.15–0.30 **Mo**, 0.03 **Cu**	**Quenched and tempered:** (<50) **diam**, (883) **TS**, (706) **YS**, 13 **El**
JIS G 3221	SFCM 90D	Japan	Forgings	0.48 **C**, 0.30–0.85 **Mn**, 0.030 **P**, 0.030 **S**, 0.15–0.35 **Si**, 0.90–1.50 **Cr**, 0.15–0.30 **Mo**, 0.03 **Cu**	**Quenched and tempered:** (<100) **diam**, (883) **TS**, (677) **YS**, 12 **El**
JIS G 3221	SFCM 85S	Japan	Forgings	0.48 **C**, 0.30–0.85 **Mn**, 0.030 **P**, 0.030 **S**, 0.15–0.35 **Si**, 0.90–1.50 **Cr**, 0.15–0.30 **Mo**, 0.03 **Cu**	**Quenched and tempered:** (<200) **diam**, (834) **TS**, (608) **YS**, 14 **El**
JIS G 3221	SFCM 85R	Japan	Forgings	0.48 **C**, 0.30–0.85 **Mn**, 0.030 **P**, 0.030 **S**, 0.15–0.35 **Si**, 0.90–1.50 **Cr**, 0.15–0.30 **Mo**, 0.03 **Cu**	**Quenched and tempered:** (<50) **diam**, (834) **TS**, (657) **YS**, 14 **El**
JIS G 3221	SFCM 85D	Japan	Forgings	0.48 **C**, 0.30–0.85 **Mn**, 0.030 **P**, 0.030 **S**, 0.15–0.35 **Si**, 0.90–1.50 **Cr**, 0.15–0.30 **Mo**, 0.03 **Cu**	**Quenched and tempered:** (<100) **diam**, (834) **TS**, (628) **YS**, 13 **El**
JIS G 3221	SFCM 80S	Japan	Forgings	0.48 **C**, 0.30–0.85 **Mn**, 0.030 **P**, 0.030 **S**, 0.15–0.35 **Si**, 0.90–1.50 **Cr**, 0.15–0.30 **Mo**, 0.03 **Cu**	**Quenched and tempered:** (<200) **diam**, (785) **TS**, (559) **YS**, 15 **El**
JIS G 3221	SFCM 80R	Japan	Forgings	0.48 **C**, 0.30–0.85 **Mn**, 0.030 **P**, 0.030 **S**, 0.15–0.35 **Si**, 0.90–1.50 **Cr**, 0.15–0.30 **Mo**, 0.03 **Cu**	**Quenched and tempered:** (<50) **diam**, (785) **TS**, (588) **YS**, 15 **El**
JIS G 3221	SFCM 80D	Japan	Forgings	0.48 **C**, 0.30–0.85 **Mn**, 0.030 **P**, 0.030 **S**, 0.15–0.35 **Si**, 0.90–1.50 **Cr**, 0.15–0.30 **Mo**, 0.03 **Cu**	**Quenched and tempered:** (<100) **diam**, (785) **TS**, (569) **YS**, 14 **El**
JIS G 3221	SFCM 75S	Japan	Forgings	0.48 **C**, 0.30–0.85 **Mn**, 0.030 **P**, 0.030 **S**, 0.15–0.35 **Si**, 0.90–1.50 **Cr**, 0.15–0.30 **Mo**, 0.03 **Cu**	**Quenched and tempered:** (<200) **diam**, (736) **TS**, (510) **YS**, 16 **El**

WROUGHT ALLOY STEELS

specification number	designation	country	product forms	composition	mechanical properties (see page iv for explanation)
JIS G 3221	SFCM 75R	Japan	Forgings	0.48 **C**, 0.30–0.85 **Mn**, 0.030 **P**, 0.030 **S**, 0.15–0.35 **Si**, 0.90–1.50 **Cr**, 0.15–0.30 **Mo**, 0.03 **Cu**	**Quenched and tempered:** (<50) **diam**, (736) **TS**, (530) **YS**, 16 **El**
JIS G 3221	SFCM 75D	Japan	Forgings	0.48 **C**, 0.30–0.85 **Mn**, 0.030 **P**, 0.030 **S**, 0.15–0.30 **Si**, 0.90–1.50 **Cr**, 0.15–0.30 **Mo**, 0.03 **Cu**	**Quenched and tempered:** (<100) **diam**, (736) **TS**, (520) **YS**, 15 **El**
JIS G 3221	SFCM 70S	Japan	Forgings	0.48 **C**, 0.30–0.85 **Mn**, 0.030 **P**, 0.030 **S**, 0.15–0.35 **Si**, 0.90–1.50 **Cr**, 0.15–0.30 **Mo**, 0.03 **Cu**	**Quenched and tempered:** (<200) **diam**, (686) **TS**, (461) **YS**, 17 **El**
JIS G 3221	SFCM 70R	Japan	Forgings	0.48 **C**, 0.30–0.85 **Mn**, 0.030 **P**, 0.030 **S**, 0.15–0.35 **Si**, 0.90–1.50 **Cr**, 0.15–0.30 **Mo**, 0.03 **Cu**	**Quenched and tempered:** (<50) **diam**, (686) **TS**, (461) **YS**, 17 **El**
JIS G 3221	SFCM 70D	Japan	Forgings	0.48 **C**, 0.30–0.85 **Mn**, 0.030 **P**, 0.030 **S**, 0.15–0.35 **Si**, 0.90–1.50 **Cr**, 0.15–0.30 **Mo**, 0.03 **Cu**	**Quenched and tempered:** (<100) **diam**, (686) **TS**, (461) **YS**, 16 **El**
JIS G 3221	SFCM 65S	Japan	Forgings	0.48 **C**, 0.30–0.85 **Mn**, 0.030 **P**, 0.030 **S**, 0.15–0.35 **Si**, 0.90–1.50 **Cr**, 0.15–0.30 **Mo**, 0.03 **Cu**	**Quenched and tempered:** (<200) **diam**, (637) **TS**, (412) **YS**, 18 **El**
JIS G 3221	SFCM 65R	Japan	Forgings	0.48 **C**, 0.30–0.85 **Mn**, 0.030 **P**, 0.030 **S**, 0.15–0.35 **Si**, 0.90–1.50 **Cr**, 0.15–0.30 **Mo**, 0.03 **Cu**	**Quenched and tempered:** (<50) **diam**, (637) **TS**, (412) **YS**, 18 **El**
JIS G 3221	SFCM 65D	Japan	Forgings	0.48 **C**, 0.30–0.85 **Mn**, 0.030 **P**, 0.030 **S**, 0.15–0.35 **Si**, 0.90–1.50 **Cr**, 0.15–0.30 **Mo**, 0.03 **Cu**	**Quenched and tempered:** (<100) **diam**, (637) **TS**, (412) **YS**, 17 **El**
ASTM A 372	Class III	US	Forgings	0.48 **C**, 1.65 **Mn**, 0.04 **P**, 0.05 **S**, 0.15–0.30 **Si**	**Annealed or normalized:** all **diam**, 90 (620) **TS**, 55 (380) **YS**, 15 **El**
JIS G 3221	SFCM 60S	Japan	Forgings	0.48 **C**, 0.30–0.85 **Mn**, 0.030 **P**, 0.030 **S**, 0.15–0.35 **Si**, 0.90–1.50 **Cr**, 0.15–0.30 **Mo**, 0.03 **Cu**	**Quenched and tempered:** (<200) **diam**, (588) **TS**, (363) **YS**, 20 **El**
JIS G 3221	SFCM 60R	Japan	Forgings	0.48 **C**, 0.30–0.85 **Mn**, 0.030 **P**, 0.030 **S**, 0.15–0.35 **Si**, 0.90–1.50 **Cr**, 0.15–0.30 **Mo**, 0.03 **Cu**	**Quenched and tempered:** (<50) **diam**, (588) **TS**, (363) **YS**, 19 **El**
JIS G 3221	SFCM 60D	Japan	Forgings	0.48 **C**, 0.30–0.85 **Mn**, 0.030 **P**, 0.030 **S**, 0.15–0.35 **Si**, 0.90–1.50 **Cr**, 0.15–0.30 **Mo**, 0.03 **Cu**	**Quenched and tempered:** (<100) **diam**, (588) **TS**, (363) **YS**, 18 **El**
DIN 17221	50CrV4/1.8159	Germany	Springs	0.47–0.55 **C**, 0.70–1.10 **Mn**, 0.035 **P**, 0.035 **S**, 0.15–0.40 **Si**, 0.90–1.20 **Cr**, 0.10–0.20 **V**	**Quenched and tempered:** all **diam**, (1370) **TS**, (1180) **YS**, 6 **El**
DIN 17221	Grade 50 CrV 4	Germany	Bar, wire, strip	0.47–0.55 **C**, 0.70–1.10 **Mn**, 0.035 **P**, 0.035 **S**, 0.15–0.40 **Si**, 0.90–1.20 **Cr**, 0.10–0.20 **V**	**Quenched and tempered:** (10) **diam**, (1370) **TS**, (1180) **YS**, 6 **El**
DIN 17225	Grade 50 CrV4	Germany	Bar, rod, wire	0.47–0.55 **C**, 0.80–1.1 **Mn**, 0.15–0.35 **Si**, 0.90–1.2 **Cr**, 0.07–0.12 **V**	**Hot rolled (bar, rod)**: all **diam**, (1324) **TS**
NF A 35–571	50 CV 4	France	Bar, wire, rod	0.47–0.55 **C**, 0.70–1.0 **Mn**, 0.035 **P**, 0.035 **S**, 0.10–0.40 **Si**, 0.85–1.15 **Cr**, 0.10–0.20 **V**	**Quenched and tempered:** (≤80) **diam**, (1320) **TS**, (1125) **YS**, 7 **El**
DIN 17221	51 Si7/1.0903	Germany	Springs	0.47–0.55 **C**, 0.50–0.80 **Mn**, 0.045 **P**, 0.045 **S**, 1.5–1.8 **Si**	**Quenched and tempered:** all **diam**, (1320) **TS**, (1130) **YS**, 6 **El**
DIN 17200	Grade 50 CrV 4	Germany	Blooms, slabs, billets, wire, bar, plate, sheet, strip, tube, forgings	0.47–0.55 **C**, 0.70–1.10 **Mn**, 0.035 **P**, 0.035 **S**, 0.15–0.40 **Si**, 0.90–1.20 **Cr**, 0.10–0.20 **V**	**Quenched and tempered:** (≤16) **diam**, (1079) **TS**, (883) **YS**, 9 **El**
DIN 17222	Grade 50 CrV4	Germany	Strip	0.47–0.55 **C**, 0.80–1.1 **Mn**, 0.035 **P**, 0.035 **S**, 0.15–0.35 **Si**, 0.90–1.2 **Cr**, 0.07–0.12 **V**	**Solution annealed**: all **diam**, (795) **TS**, (343) **YS**, 20 **El**; **Quenched and tempered:** all **diam**, (1667) **TS**, (1569) **YS**, 5 **El**

WROUGHT ALLOY STEELS

specification number	designation	country	product forms	composition	mechanical properties (see page iv for explanation)
DIN 17222	50 CrV4/8159	Germany	Strip	0.47–0.55 **C**, 0.80–1.1 **Mn**, 0.035 **P**, 0.035 **S**, 0.15–0.35 **Si**, 0.90–1.2 **Cr**, 0.07–0.12 **V**	**Softened and annealed:** all **diam**, (784) max **TS**, (343) max **YS**, 20 **El**; **Hardened and tempered:** all **diam**, (1667) **TS**, (1569) **YS**, 5 **El**
DIN 17225	50 CrV4/8159	Germany	Bar, rod	0.47–0.55 **C**, 0.80–1.1 **Mn**, 0.15–0.35 **Si**, 0.90–1.2 **Cr**, 0.07–0.12 **V**	**Hot rolled:** all **diam**, (135) **TS**
NF A 35–553	50 CV 4	France	Strip	0.47–0.55 **C**, 0.70–1.0 **Mn**, 0.035 **P**, 0.035 **S**, 0.10–0.40 **Si**, 0.85–1.15 **Cr**, 0.10–0.20 **V**	
TS 2288	50 Cr V 4–1,8159	Turkey	Wire	0.47–0.55 **C**, 0.70–1.10 **Mn**, 0.035 **P**, 0.035 **S**, 0.15–0.40 **Si**, 0.90–1.20 **Cr**, 0.10–0.20 **V**	
MIL–S–11595D	ORD 4150 Resulperized	US	Bar	0.47–0.55 **C**, 0.70–1.00 **Mn**, 0.040 **P**, 0.05–0.09 **S**, 0.20–0.35 **Si**, 0.80–1.15 **Cr**, 0.15–0.25 **Mo**	
AS 1444	Grade AS 1444/x4150	Australia	Bar, bloom, billet, slab	0.47–0.55 **C**, 1.0–1.40 **Mn**, 0.04 **P**, 0.1 **S**, 0.10–0.40 **Si**, 0.4–0.8 **Cr**, 0.10–0.20 **Mo**	
AS 1444	Grade 1444/4150H	Australia	Bar, bloom, billet, slab	0.47–0.54 **C**, 0.65–1.10 **Mn**, 0.040 **P**, 0.040 **S**, 0.10–0.35 **Si**, 0.75–1.20 **Cr**, 0.15–0.25 **Mo**	
AS 1444	Grade AS 1444/6150H	Australia	Bar, bloom, billet, slab	0.47–0.54 **C**, 0.60–1.00 **Mn**, 0.040 **P**, 0.040 **S**, 0.10–0.35 **Si**, 0.75–1.20 **Cr**, 0.15 min **V**	
DGN–B–300	4150 H	Mexico	Bar	0.47–0.54 **C**, 0.65–1.10 **Mn**, 0.040 **P**, 0.035 **S**, 0.20–0.35 **Si**, 0.75–1.20 **Cr**, 0.15–0.25 **Mo**	**Annealed**
DGN–B–300	50B50 H	Mexico	Bar	0.47–0.54 **C**, 0.65–1.10 **Mn**, 0.040 **P**, 0.035 **S**, 0.20–0.35 **Si**, 0.30–0.70 **Cr**, 0.0005 min **B**	**Annealed**
DGN–B–300	6150 H	Mexico	Bar	0.47–0.54 **C**, 0.60–1.00 **Mn**, 0.040 **P**, 0.035 **S**, 0.20–0.35 **Si**, 0.75–1.20 **Cr**, 0.15 **V**	**Annealed**
DGN–B–300	5150 H	Mexico	Bar	0.47–0.54 **C**, 0.60–1.00 **Mn**, 0.040 **P**, 0.035 **S**, 0.20–0.35 **Si**, 0.60–1.00 **Cr**	**Annealed**
DGN–B–300	8650 H	Mexico	Bar	0.47–0.54 **C**, 0.70–1.05 **Mn**, 0.040 **P**, 0.035 **S**, 0.20–0.35 **Si**, 0.35–0.65 **Cr**, 0.35–0.75 **Ni**, 0.15–0.25 **Mo**	
ASTM A 689	4150 H	US	Bar	0.47–0.54 **C**, 0.65–1.10 **Mn**, 0.040 **P**, 0.040 **S**, 0.15–0.30 **Si**, 0.75–1.20 **Cr**, 0.15–0.25 **Mo**	
ASTM A 689	5150 H	US	Bar	0.47–0.54 **C**, 0.60–1.00 **Mn**, 0.040 **P**, 0.040 **S**, 0.15–0.30 **Si**, 0.60–1.00 **Cr**	
ASTM A 689	8650 H	US	Bar	0.47–0.54 **C**, 0.70–1.05 **Mn**, 0.040 **P**, 0.040 **S**, 0.15–0.30 **Si**, 0.35–0.65 **Cr**, 0.35–0.75 **Ni**, 0.15–0.25 **Mo**	
ASTM A 689	6150 H	US	Bar	0.47–0.54 **C**, 0.60–1.00 **Mn**, 0.040 **P**, 0.040 **S**, 0.15–0.30 **Si**, 0.75–1.00 **Cr**, 0.15 min **V**	
ANSI/ASTM A 304	50B50 H	US	Bar	0.47–0.54 **C**, 0.65–1.10 **Mn**, 0.040 **P**, 0.040 **S**, 0.15–0.30 **Si**, 0.30–0.70 **Cr**, 0.0005 **B**	
ANSI/ASTM A 304	5150 H	US	Bar	0.47–0.54 **C**, 0.60–1.00 **Mn**, 0.040 **P**, 0.040 **S**, 0.15–0.30 **Si**, 0.60–1.00 **Cr**	
ANSI/ASTM A 304	6150 H	US	Bar	0.47–0.54 **C**, 0.60–1.00 **Mn**, 0.040 **P**, 0.040 **S**, 0.15–0.30 **Si**, 0.75–1.20 **Cr**, 0.15 min **V**	
ANSI/ASTM A 304	8650 H	US	Bar	0.47–0.54 **C**, 0.70–1.05 **Mn**, 0.040 **P**, 0.040 **S**, 0.15–0.30 **Si**, 0.35–0.65 **Cr**, 0.35–0.75 **Ni**, 0.15–0.25 **Mo**	
ANSI/ASTM A 304	4150 H	US	Bar	0.47–0.54 **C**, 0.65–1.10 **Mn**, 0.040 **P**, 0.040 **S**, 0.15–0.30 **Si**, 0.75–1.20 **Cr**, 0.15–0.25 **Mo**	

specification number	designation	country	product forms	composition	mechanical properties (see page iv for explanation)
ASTM A 689	50B50 H	US	Bar	0.47–0.54 **C**, 0.65–1.10 **Mn**, 0.040 **P**, 0.040 **S**, 0.15–0.30 **Si**, 0.30–0.70 **Cr**, 0.0005 min **B**	
AISI 5150 H		US	Wire, rod	0.47–0.54 **C**, 0.60–1.00 **Mn**, 0.15–0.30 **Si**, 0.60–1.00 **Cr**	
AISI 6150 H		US	Wire, rod	0.47–0.54 **C**, 0.60–1.00 **Mn**, 0.15–0.30 **Si**, 0.75–1.20 **Cr**, 0.15 min **V**	
AISI 50B50 H		US	Wire, rod	0.47–0.54 **C**, 0.65–1.10 **Mn**, 0.15–0.30 **Si**, 0.30–0.70 **Cr**	
AISI 4150 H		US	Wire, rod	0.47–0.54 **C**, 0.65–1.10 **Mn**, 0.15–0.30 **Si**, 0.75–1.20 **Cr**, 0.15–0.25 **Mo**	
AISI 50B50H		US	Bar	0.47–0.54 **C**, 0.65–1.10 **Mn**, 0.035 **P**, 0.040 **S**, 0.15–0.30 **Si**, 0.30–0.70 **Cr**	
AISI 8650H		US	Bar	0.47–0.54 **C**, 0.70–1.05 **Mn**, 0.035 **P**, 0.040 **S**, 0.15–0.30 **Si**, 0.35–0.65 **Cr**, 0.35–0.75 **Ni**, 0.15–0.25 **Mo**	
AISI 6150H		US	Bar	0.47–0.54 **C**, 0.60–1.00 **Mn**, 0.035 **P**, 0.040 **S**, 0.15–0.30 **Si**, 0.7–1.20 **Cr**, 0.15 **V**	
AISI 5150H		US	Bar	0.47–0.54 **C**, 0.60–1.00 **Mn**, 0.035 **P**, 0.040 **S**, 0.15–0.30 **Si**, 0.60–1.00 **Cr**	
AISI 4150H		US	Bar	0.47–0.54 **C**, 0.65–1.10 **Mn**, 0.035 **P**, 0.040 **S**, 0.15–0.30 **Si**, 0.75–1.20 **Cr**, 0.15–0.25 **Mo**	
JIS G 3311	S50CM	Japan	Strip	0.47–0.53 **C**, 0.60–0.90 **Mn**, 0.030 **P**, 0.035 **S**, 0.15–0.35 **Si**, 0.20 **Cr**, 0.20 **Ni**, 0.30 **Cu**, 0.35 **Ni+Cr**	
NBN 253-05	50 Si 7	Belgium	Wire	0.47–0.50 **C**, 0.50–0.80 **Mn**, 0.040 **P**, 0.040 **S**, 1.50–2.0 **Si**	**Annealed or quenched and tempered:** (≤25) **diam**, (1325) **TS**, (1130) **YS**, 6 **El**
BS S.204		UK	Wire, springs: aircraft quality	0.46–0.54 **C**, 0.60–0.90 **Mn**, 0.025 **P**, 0.020 **S**, 0.10–0.35 **Si**, 0.80–1.10 **Cr**, 0.15–0.25 **V**	**Hardened and tempered:** all **diam**, (1392) **TS**
DIN 17200	Grade 50 CrMo 4	Germany	Blooms, slabs, billets, wire, bar, plate, sheet, strip, tube, forgings	0.46–0.54 **C**, 0.50–0.80 **Mn**, 0.035 **P**, 0.035 **S**, 0.15–0.40 **Si**, 0.90–1.20 **Cr**, 0.15–0.30 **Mo**	**Quenched and tempered:** (≤16) **diam**, (1079) **TS**, (883) **YS**, 9 **El**
BS 970 Part 5	735A50	UK	Blooms, billets, bar, forgings	0.46–0.54 **C**, 0.35–0.60 **Mn**, 0.10–0.35 **Si**, 0.80–1.10 **Cr**, 0.15 min **V**	
AISI 6150		US	Plate	0.46–0.54 **C**, 0.60–0.90 **Mn**, 0.035 **P**, 0.040 **S**, 0.15–0.30 **Si**, 0.80–1.15 **Cr**, 0.15 **V**	
DIN 17212	Grade 49 CrMo 4	Germany	Blooms, slabs, billets, wire, bar, plate, sheet, strip, tube, forgings	0.46–0.52 **C**, 0.50–0.80 **Mn**, 0.025 **P**, 0.035 **S**, 0.15–0.40 **Si**, 0.90–1.20 **Cr**, 0.15–0.30 **Mo**	
DGN-B-300	5147	Mexico	Bar	0.46–0.51 **C**, 0.70–0.95 **Mn**, 0.035 **P**, 0.040 **S**, 0.20–0.35 **Si**, 0.85–1.15 **Cr**	**Annealed**
ANSI/ASTM A 29	5147	US	Bar	0.46–0.51 **C**, 0.70–0.95 **Mn**, 0.035 **P**, 0.040 **S**, 0.15–0.30 **Si**, 0.85–1.15 **Cr**	
ASTM A 689	5147	US	Bar	0.46–0.51 **C**, 0.70–0.95 **Mn**, 0.035 **P**, 0.040 **S**, 0.15–0.30 **Si**, 0.85–1.15 **Cr**	
ANSI/ASTM A 322	5147	US	Bar	0.46–0.51 **C**, 0.70–0.95 **Mn**, 0.035 **P**, 0.040 **S**, 0.15–0.30 **Si**, 0.85–1.15 **Cr**	
AISI 5147		US	Wire, rod	0.46–0.51 **C**, 0.70–0.95 **Mn**, 0.035 **P**, 0.040 **S**, 0.15–0.30 **Si**, 0.85–1.15 **Cr**	
DGN-B-297	5147	Mexico	Bar	0.46–0.51 **C**, 0.70–0.90 **Mn**, 0.035 **P**, 0.040 **S**, 0.20–0.35 **Si**, 0.85–1.15 **Cr**	

WROUGHT ALLOY STEELS

specification number	designation	country	product forms	composition	mechanical properties (see page iv for explanation)
DGN-B-300	50B44 H	Mexico	Bar	0.46–0.49 **C**, 0.65–1.10 **Mn**, 0.040 **P**, 0.035 **S**, 0.20–0.35 **Si**, 0.30–0.70 **Cr**, 0.0005 min **B**	**Annealed**
MIL-S-24093	Type I, class A	US	Forgings	0.46 **C**, 0.85 **Mn**, 0.040 **P**, 0.040 **S**, 0.20–0.35 **Si**, 0.70–0.95 **Cr**, 1.65–2.00 **Ni**, 0.20–0.30 **Mo**	**Normalized and tempered or quenched and tempered:** 10 **diam**, 165 (1138) **TS**, 140 (965) **YS**, 10 **El**
MIL-S-24093	Type I, class B	US	Forgings	0.46 **C**, 0.85 **Mn**, 0.040 **P**, 0.040 **S**, 0.20–0.35 **Si**, 0.70–0.95 **Cr**, 1.65–2.00 **Ni**, 0.20–0.30 **Mo**	**Normalized and tempered or quenched and tempered:** 10 **diam**, 140 (965) **TS**, 120 (827) **YS**, 14 **El**
MIL-S-24093	Type I, class C	US	Forgings	0.46 **C**, 0.85 **Mn**, 0.040 **P**, 0.040 **S**, 0.20–0.35 **Si**, 0.70–0.95 **Cr**, 1.65–2.00 **Ni**, 0.20–0.30 **Mo**	**Normalized and tempered or quenched and tempered:** 10 **diam**, 120 (827) **TS**, 100 (689) **YS**, 16 **El**
MIL-S-24093	Type I, class D	US	Forgings	0.46 **C**, 0.85 **Mn**, 0.040 **P**, 0.040 **S**, 0.20–0.35 **Si**, 0.70–0.95 **Cr**, 1.65–2.00 **Ni**, 0.20–0.30 **Mo**	**Normalized and tempered or quenched and tempered:** 10 **diam**, 100 (689) **TS**, 80 (552) **YS**, 18 **El**
MIL-S-24093	Type I, class E	US	Forgings	0.46 **C**, 0.85 **Mn**, 0.040 **P**, 0.040 **S**, 0.20–0.35 **Si**, 0.70–0.95 **Cr**, 1.65–2.00 **Ni**, 0.20–0.30 **Mo**	**Normalized and tempered or quenched and tempered:** 10 **diam**, 95 (655) **TS**, 65 (448) **YS**, 20 **El**
JIS G 3565	SWOCV-V	Japan	Wire	0.45–0.55 **C**, 0.65–0.95 **Mn**, 0.030 **P**, 0.030 **S**, 0.15–0.35 **Si**, 0.80–1.10 **Cr**, 0.15–0.25 **V**, 0.20 **Cu**	**Cold drawn and oil tempered:** (2.0) **diam**, (1569) **TS**
JIS G 4801	SUP 10	Japan	Bar, wire, rod	0.45–0.55 **C**, 0.65–0.95 **Mn**, 0.035 **P**, 0.035 **S**, 0.15–0.35 **Si**, 0.80–1.10 **Cr**, 0.15–0.25 **V**, 0.30 **Cu**	**Quenched and tempered:** all **diam**, (1226) **TS**, (1079) **YS**, 10 **El**
JIS G 4311	SUH 11	Japan	Bar	0.45–0.55 **C**, 0.60 **Mn**, 0.030 **P**, 0.030 **S**, 1.00–2.00 **Si**, 7.50–9.50 **Cr**, 0.60 **Ni**	**Quenched and tempered:** (≤25) **diam**, (883) **TS**, (686) **YS**, 15 **El**
IS 4367	50Cr1V[23]	India	Forgings	0.45–0.55 **C**, 0.50–0.80 **Mn**, 0.050 **P**, 0.050 **S**, 0.10–0.35 **Si**, 0.90–1.20 **Cr**, 0.15–0.30 **V**	**Annealed**: (63) **diam**, (784) **TS**
NF A 35-571	RE 375	France	Bar, wire, rod	0.45–0.55 **C**, 0.50–0.80 **Mn**, 0.05 **P**, 0.05 **S**, 1.5–2.0 **Si**	
BS 1429	En. 47	UK	Wire	0.45–0.55 **C**, 0.50–0.80 **Mn**, 0.05 **P**, 0.05 **S**, 0.50 **Si**, 0.80–1.20 **Cr**, 0.15 min **V**	**Annealed**: all **diam**
AS G18	G18/En 47	Australia	Bar	0.45–0.55 **C**, 0.50–0.80 **Mn**, 0.050 **P**, 0.050 **S**, 0.50 **Si**, 0.80–1.20 **Cr**, 0.15 min **V**	
AS G18	G18/En 48	Australia	Bar	0.45–0.55 **C**, 0.50–0.80 **Mn**, 0.050 **P**, 0.050 **S**, 0.10–0.50 **Si**, 1.00–1.40 **Cr**	
AS 1444	Grade AS 1444/9050	Australia	Bar, bloom, billet, slab	0.45–0.55 **C**, 0.90–1.20 **Mn**, 0.050 **P**, 0.050 **S**, 0.60–0.90 **Si**	
JIS G 3311	SVP10M	Japan	Strip	0.45–0.55 **C**, 0.65–0.95 **Mn**, 0.035 **P**, 0.035 **S**, 0.15–0.35 **Si**, 0.80–1.10 **Cr**, 0.15–0.25 **V**, 0.30 **Cu**	
DGN-B-203	Grade 5147	Mexico	Tube: seamless	0.45–0.52 **C**, 0.70–0.95 **Mn**, 0.040 **P**, 0.040 **S**, 0.20–0.35 **Si**, 0.85–1.15 **Cr**	
DGN-B-300	5147 H	Mexico	Bar	0.45–0.52 **C**, 0.60–1.05 **Mn**, 0.040 **P**, 0.035 **S**, 0.20–0.35 **Si**, 0.80–1.25 **Cr**	**Annealed**
ASTM A 689	5147 H	US	Bar	0.45–0.52 **C**, 0.60–1.05 **Mn**, 0.040 **P**, 0.040 **S**, 0.15–0.30 **Si**, 0.80–1.25 **Cr**	
ANSI/ASTM A 304	5147 H	US	Bar	0.45–0.52 **C**, 0.60–1.05 **Mn**, 0.040 **P**, 0.040 **S**, 0.15–0.30 **Si**, 0.80–1.25 **Cr**	
AISI 5147 H		US	Wire, rod	0.45–0.52 **C**, 0.60–1.05 **Mn**, 0.15–0.30 **Si**, 0.80–1.25 **Cr**	
ANSI/ASTM A 519	5147	US	Tube: seamless	0.45–0.52 **C**, 0.70–0.95 **Mn**, 0.040 **P**, 0.040 **S**, 0.15–0.35 **Si**, 0.85–1.15 **Cr**	

WROUGHT ALLOY STEELS

specification number	designation	country	product forms	composition	mechanical properties (see page iv for explanation)
COPANT 514	Grade 5147	COPANT	Tube: seamless	0.45–0.52 **C**, 0.70–0.95 **Mn**, 0.040 **P**, 0.050 **S**, 0.10 **Si**, 0.85–1.10 **Cr**	
ANSI/ASTM A 579	23	US	Forgings	0.45–0.50 **C**, 0.60–0.90 **Mn**, 0.015 **P**, 0.015 **S**, 0.15–0.30 **Si**, 0.90–1.20 **Cr**, 0.40–0.70 **Ni**, 0.90–1.10 **Mo**, 0.08–0.15 **V**	**Quenched and tempered:** all **diam**, 250 (1725) **TS**, 225 (1555) **YS**, 6 **El**
AMS 6438B		US	Sheet, strip, plate	0.45–0.50 **C**, 0.60–0.90 **Mn**, 0.015 **P**, 0.015 **S**, 0.15–0.30 **Si**, 0.90–1.20 **Cr**, 0.40–0.70 **Ni**, 0.90–1.10 **Mo**, 0.08–0.15 **V**, 0.35 **Cu**	**Hardened and tempered:** all **diam**, 224 (1544) **TS**, 195 (1345) **YS**, 7 **El**
AMS 6431D		US	Bar, forgings, tube	0.45–0.50 **C**, 0.60–0.90 **Mn**, 0.010 **P**, 0.010 **S**, 0.15–0.30 **Si**, 0.90–1.20 **Cr**, 0.40–0.70 **Ni**, 0.90–1.10 **Mo**, 0.08–0.15 **V**, 0.35 **Cu**	**Hardened, quenched, stress relieved and tempered:** all **diam**, 220 (1517) **TS**, 190 (1310) **YS**, 12 **El**; **Cold finished (bar):** ≤0.500 (≤12.70) **diam**, 145 (1000) max **TS**
AISI 4047		US	Bar	0.45–0.50 **C**, 0.70–0.90 **Mn**, 0.035 **P**, 0.040 **S**, 0.15–0.30 **Si**, 0.20–0.30 **Mo**	
AISI 4147		US	Bar	0.45–0.50 **C**, 0.75–1.00 **Mn**, 0.035 **P**, 0.040 **S**, 0.15–0.30 **Si**, 0.80–1.10 **Cr**, 0.15–0.25 **Mo**	
DGN–B–203	Grade 4147	Mexico	Tube: seamless	0.45–0.50 **C**, 0.75–1.00 **Mn**, 0.040 **P**, 0.040 **S**, 0.20–0.35 **Si**, 0.80–1.10 **Cr**, 0.15–0.25 **Mo**	
DGN–B–203	Grade 4047	Mexico	Tube: seamless	0.45–0.50 **C**, 0.70–0.90 **Mn**, 0.040 **P**, 0.040 **S**, 0.20–0.35 **Si**, 0.20–0.30 **Mo**	
COPANT 514	4147	COPANT	Tube	0.45–0.50 **C**, 0.75–1.0 **Mn**, 0.040 **P**, 0.040 **S**, 0.20–0.35 **Si**, 0.80–1.10 **Cr**, 0.15–0.25 **Mo**	
COPANT 514	4047	COPANT	Tube	0.45–0.50 **C**, 0.70–0.90 **Mn**, 0.040 **P**, 0.040 **S**, 0.20–0.35 **Si**, 0.20–0.30 **Mo**	
DGN–B–300	4147	Mexico	Bar	0.45–0.50 **C**, 0.75–1.00 **Mn**, 0.035 **P**, 0.040 **S**, 0.20–0.35 **Si**, 0.80–1.10 **Cr**, 0.15–0.25 **Mo**	**Annealed**
DGN–B–300	4047	Mexico	Bar	0.45–0.50 **C**, 0.70–0.90 **Mn**, 0.035 **P**, 0.040 **S**, 0.20–0.35 **Si**, 0.20–0.30 **Mo**	**Annealed**
ANSI/ASTM A 29	4047	US	Bar	0.45–0.50 **C**, 0.70–0.90 **Mn**, 0.035 **P**, 0.040 **S**, 0.15–0.30 **Si**, 0.20–0.30 **Mo**	
ANSI/ASTM A 29	4147	US	Bar	0.45–0.50 **C**, 0.75–1.00 **Mn**, 0.035 **P**, 0.040 **S**, 0.15–0.30 **Si**, 0.80–1.10 **Cr**, 0.15–0.25 **Mo**	
ANSI/ASTM A 646	D6AC	US	Blooms, billets: aircraft quality	0.45–0.50 **C**, 0.60–0.90 **Mn**, 0.010 **P**, 0.010 **S**, 0.15–0.30 **Si**, 0.90–1.20 **Cr**, 0.40–0.70 **Ni**, 0.90–1.10 **Mo**, 0.08–0.15 **V**	**Annealed**
ASTM A 689	4047	US	Bar	0.45–0.50 **C**, 0.70–0.90 **Mn**, 0.035 **P**, 0.040 **S**, 0.15–0.30 **Si**, 0.20–0.30 **Mo**	
ASTM A 689	4147	US	Bar	0.45–0.50 **C**, 0.75–1.00 **Mn**, 0.035 **P**, 0.040 **S**, 0.15–0.30 **Si**, 0.80–1.10 **Cr**, 0.15–0.25 **Mo**	
ANSI/ASTM A 322	4047	US	Bar	0.45–0.50 **C**, 0.70–0.90 **Mn**, 0.035 **P**, 0.040 **S**, 0.15–0.30 **Si**, 0.20–0.30 **Mo**	
ANSI/ASTM A 322	4147	US	Bar	0.45–0.50 **C**, 0.75–1.00 **Mn**, 0.035 **P**, 0.040 **S**, 0.15–0.30 **Si**, 0.80–1.10 **Cr**, 0.15–0.25 **Mo**	
AISI 4047		US	Wire, rod	0.45–0.50 **C**, 0.70–0.90 **Mn**, 0.035 **P**, 0.040 **S**, 0.15–0.30 **Si**, 0.20–0.30 **Mo**	
AISI 4147		US	Wire, rod	0.45–0.50 **C**, 0.75–1.00 **Mn**, 0.035 **P**, 0.040 **S**, 0.15–0.30 **Si**, 0.80–1.10 **Cr**, 0.15–0.25 **Mo**	

specification number	designation	country	product forms	composition	mechanical properties (see page iv for explanation)
ANSI/ASTM A 519	4047	US	Tube: seamless	0.45–0.50 **C**, 0.70–0.90 **Mn**, 0.040 **P**, 0.040 **S**, 0.15–0.35 **Si**, 0.20–0.30 **Mo**	
ANSI/ASTM A 519	4147	US	Tube: seamless	0.45–0.50 **C**, 0.75–1.00 **Mn**, 0.040 **P**, 0.040 **S**, 0.15–0.35 **Si**, 0.80–1.10 **Cr**, 0.15–0.25 **Mo**	
DGN-B-297	4147	Mexico	Bar	0.45–0.50 **C**, 0.75–1.00 **Mn**, 0.035 **P**, 0.040 **S**, 0.20–0.35 **Si**, 0.80–1.10 **Cr**, 0.15–0.25 **Mo**	
DGN-B-297	4047	Mexico	Bar	0.45–0.50 **C**, 0.70–0.90 **Mn**, 0.035 **P**, 0.040 **S**, 0.20–0.35 **Si**, 0.20–0.30 **Mo**	
ANSI/ASTM A 288	Class 8	US	Forgings	0.45 **C**, 1.00 **Mn**, 0.025 **P**, 0.020 **S**, 0.15–0.35 **Si**, 0.70–1.25 **Cr**, 1.65–3.50 **Ni**, 0.20 min **Mo**, 0.07–0.12 **V**	**Quenched, tempered**: all **diam**, 165 (1140) **TS**, 150 (1035) **YS**, 12 **El**
ANSI/ASTM A 288	Class 7	US	Forgings	0.45 **C**, 1.00 **Mn**, 0.025 **P**, 0.020 **S**, 0.15–0.35 **Si**, 0.70–1.25 **Cr**, 1.65–3.50 **Ni**, 0.20 min **Mo**, 0.07–0.12 **V**	**Quenched, tempered**: all **diam**, 150 (1035) **TS**, 135 (930) **YS**, 13 **El**
ANSI/ASTM A 288	Class 6	US	Forgings	0.45 **C**, 1.00 **Mn**, 0.025 **P**, 0.020 **S**, 0.15–0.35 **Si**, 0.70–1.25 **Cr**, 1.65–3.50 **Ni**, 0.20 min **Mo**, 0.07–0.12 **V**	**Quenched, tempered**: all **diam**, 140 (965) **TS**, 125 (860) **YS**, 14 **El**
ASTM A 294	Class B7	US	Forgings	0.45 **C**, 0.60–1.00 **Mn**, 0.035 **P**, 0.035 **S**, 0.15–0.35 **Si**, 0.50–1.25 **Cr**, 1.65–3.50 **Ni**, 0.20 min **Mo**	**Normalized or quenched, tempered**: all **diam**, 140 (965) **TS**, 125 (860) **YS**, 15 **El**
ASTM A 294	Class B6	US	Forgings	0.45 **C**, 0.60–1.00 **Mn**, 0.035 **P**, 0.035 **S**, 0.15–0.35 **Si**, 0.50–1.25 **Cr**, 1.65–3.50 **Ni**, 0.20 min **Mo**	**Normalized or quenched, tempered**: all **diam**, 130 (905) **TS**, 115 (795) **YS**, 16 **El**
ANSI/ASTM A 288	Class 5	US	Forgings	0.45 **C**, 1.00 **Mn**, 0.025 **P**, 0.020 **S**, 0.15–0.35 **Si**, 0.70–1.25 **Cr**, 1.65–3.50 **Ni**, 0.20 min **Mo**, 0.07–0.12 **V**	**Quenched, tempered**: all **diam**, 130 (895) **TS**, 110 (760) **YS**, 16 **El**
ASTM A 294	Class B5	US	Forgings	0.45 **C**, 0.60–1.00 **Mn**, 0.035 **P**, 0.035 **S**, 0.15–0.35 **Si**, 0.50–1.25 **Cr**, 1.65–3.50 **Ni**, 0.20 min **Mo**	**Normalized or quenched, tempered**: all **diam**, 125 (860) **TS**, 105 (725) **YS**, 18 **El**
MIL-S-890	Alloy No 4	US	Forgings, bar	0.45 **C**, 1.00 **Mn**, 0.050 **P**, 0.050 **S**, 2.00 **Cr**, 3.75 **Ni**, 1.00 **Mo**, 0.10 **V**	**Annealed or normalized and drawn or quenched and drawn**: all **diam**, 120 (827) **TS**, 100 (690) **YS**, 15 **El**
ANSI/ASTM A 288	Class 4	US	Forgings	0.45 **C**, 1.00 **Mn**, 0.025 **P**, 0.020 **S**, 0.15–0.35 **Si**, 0.70–1.25 **Cr**, 1.65–3.50 **Ni**, 0.20 min **Mo**, 0.07–0.12 **V**	**Quenched, tempered**: all **diam**, 120 (825) **TS**, 95 (655) **YS**, 18 **El**
ASTM A 294	Class B4	US	Forgings	0.45 **C**, 0.60–1.00 **Mn**, 0.035 **P**, 0.035 **S**, 0.15–0.35 **Si**, 0.50–1.25 **Cr**, 1.65–3.50 **Ni**, 0.20 min **Mo**	**Normalized or quenched, tempered**: all **diam**, 120 (825) **TS**, 95 (655) **YS**, 18 **El**
ANSI/ASTM A 288	Class 3	US	Forgings	0.45 **C**, 0.60–1.00 **Mn**, 0.025 **P**, 0.020 **S**, 0.15–0.35 **Si**, 0.70–1.25 **Cr**, 0.15 min **Mo**	**Quenched, tempered**: all **diam**, 110 (760) **TS**, 80 (550) **YS**, 18 **El**
ASTM A 294	Class B3	US	Forgings	0.45 **C**, 0.60–1.00 **Mn**, 0.035 **P**, 0.035 **S**, 0.15–0.35 **Si**, 0.50–1.25 **Cr**, 1.65–3.50 **Ni**, 0.20 min **Mo**	**Normalized or quenched, tempered**: all **diam**, 110 (760) **TS**, 85 (585) **YS**, 19 **El**
API Spec 5AC	C-95	US	Casing, tube	0.45 **C**, 1.90 **Mn**, 0.040 **P**, 0.060 **S**, 0.35 **Si**	**Quenched and tempered**: all **diam**, 105 (725) **TS**, 95 (657) **YS**
ASTM A 291	Class 3A	US	Forgings	0.45 **C**, 0.40–0.90 **Mn**, 0.040 **P**, 0.040 **S**, 0.15–0.30 **Si**, 1.50 **Cr**, 1.00–3.00 **Ni**, 0.15 **Mo**, 0.10 **V**	**Quenched, annealed**: ≥10 (254) **diam**, 105 (725) **TS**, 80 (550) **YS**, 19 **El**
ASTM A 291	Class 3	US	Forgings	0.45 **C**, 0.40–0.90 **Mn**, 0.040 **P**, 0.040 **S**, 0.15–0.30 **Si**, 1.25 **Cr**, 0.15 min **Mo**, 0.10 **V**	**Quenched, annealed**: ≥10 (254) **diam**, 105 (725) **TS**, 80 (550) **YS**, 19 **El**
MIL-S-890	Alloy no 3	US	Forgings, bar	0.45 **C**, 0.040 **P**, 0.040 **S**; other alloying elements added as agreed.	**Annealed or normalized and drawn or quenched and drawn**: all **diam**, 105 (724) **TS**, 80 (552) **YS**, 20 **El**

WROUGHT ALLOY STEELS

specification number	designation	country	product forms	composition	mechanical properties (see page iv for explanation)
ASTM A 294	Class B2	US	Forgings	0.45 **C**, 0.60–1.00 **Mn**, 0.035 **P**, 0.035 **S**, 0.15–0.35 **Si**, 0.50–1.25 **Cr**, 1.65–3.50 **Ni**, 0.20 min **Mo**	**Normalized or quenched, tempered**: all **diam**, 100 (690) **TS**, 75 (515) **YS**, 20 **El**
MIL–S–19434A	Class 2	US	Forgings	0.45 **C**, 0.55–0.90 **Mn**, 0.050 **P**, 0.050 min **S**, 0.15 min **Si**, 1.25 **Cr**, 2.25 min **Ni**, 0.50 **Mo**, 0.15 **V**	**Normalized and tempered, quenched and tempered**: ≤10 **diam**, (655) **TS**, (482) **YS**, 20 **El**
MIL–S–890	HG	US	Forgings, bar	0.45 **C**, 0.050 **P**, 0.050 **S**; other alloying elements added as agreed	**Annealed or normalized and drawn or quenched and drawn**: all **diam**, 95 (655) **TS**, 65 (448) **YS**, 21 **El**
ANSI/ASTM A 288	Class 2	US	Forgings	0.45 **C**, 0.60–1.00 **Mn**, 0.025 **P**, 0.020 **S**, 0.15–0.35 **Si**, 0.70–1.25 **Cr**, 0.15 min **Mo**	**Quenched, tempered**: all **diam**, 90 (620) **TS**, 65 (450) **YS**, 20 **El**
ASTM A 294	Class B1	US	Forgings	0.45 **C**, 0.60–1.00 **Mn**, 0.035 **P**, 0.035 **S**, 0.15–0.35 **Si**, 0.50–1.25 **Cr**, 1.65–3.50 **Ni**, 0.20 min **Mo**	**Normalized or quenched, tempered**: all **diam**, 90 (620) **TS**, 65 (450) **YS**, 20 **El**
MIL–S–890	An	US	Forgings, bar: for propulsion shafting, rudder stocks, and pinion gears	0.45 **C**, 0.50–0.90 **Mn**, 0.050 **P**, 0.050 **S**, 0.15–0.45 **Si**, 2.75 **Ni**, 0.30–0.60 **Mo**, 0.10–0.25 **V**	**Annealed or normalized and drawn or quenched and drawn**: all **diam**, 80 (552) **TS**, 45 (310) **YS**, 25 **El**
ANSI/ASTM A 336	Grade F30	US	Forgings	0.45 **C**, 0.50–0.90 **Mn**, 0.040 **P**, 0.040 **S**, 0.15–0.45 **Si**, 0.30–0.60 **Mo**, 0.10–0.25 **V**	**Annealed or normalized and tempered**: all **diam**, (550) **TS**, (345) **YS**, 21 **El**
ASTM A 336	F30	US	Forgings	0.45 **C**, 0.50–0.90 **Mn**, 0.040 **P**, 0.040 **S**, 0.15–0.45 **Si**, 0.30–0.60 **Mo**, 0.10–0.25 **V**	**Normalized**: all **diam**, 80 (550) **TS**, 50 (345) **YS**, 21 **El**
ASTM A 336	F30	US	Forgings	0.45 **C**, 0.50–0.90 **Mn**, 0.040 **P**, 0.040 **S**, 0.15–0.45 **Si**, 0.30–0.60 **Mo**, 0.10–0.25 **V**	**Annealed or normalized, tempered**: all **diam**, 80 (550) **TS**, 50 (345) **YS**, 21 **El**
ANSI/ASTM A 469	Class 1	US	Forgings	0.45 **C**, 0.90 **Mn**, 0.025 **P**, 0.025 **S**, 0.15–0.35 **Si**, 0.03–0.12 **V**	**Quenched, tempered, stress relieved**: all **diam**, 75 (515) **TS**, 35 (240) **YS**, 20 **El**
NF A 35–590	2321 (Y45 S7)	France	Bar, forgings	0.45 **C**, 0.60 **Mn**, 0.030 **P**, 0.030 **S**, 1.8 **Si**	
NF A 35–590	2324 (Y45 SCD6)	France	Bar, forgings	0.45 **C**, 0.60 **Mn**, 0.030 **P**, 0.030 **S**, 1.5 **Si**, 0.60 **Cr**, 0.20 **Mo**	
DGN–B–300	4147 H	Mexico	Bar	0.44–0.51 **C**, 0.65–1.10 **Mn**, 0.040 **P**, 0.035 **S**, 0.20–0.35 **Si**, 0.75–1.20 **Cr**, 0.15–0.25 **Mo**	**Annealed**
DGN–B–300	4047 H	Mexico	Bar	0.44–0.51 **C**, 0.60–1.00 **Mn**, 0.040 **P**, 0.035 **S**, 0.20–0.35 **Si**, 0.20–0.35 **Mo**	**Annealed**
ASTM A 689	4147 H	US	Bar	0.44–0.51 **C**, 0.65–1.10 **Mn**, 0.040 **P**, 0.040 **S**, 0.15–0.30 **Si**, 0.75–1.20 **Cr**, 0.15–0.25 **Mo**	
ASTM A 689	4047 H	US	Bar	0.44–0.51 **C**, 0.60–1.00 **Mn**, 0.040 **P**, 0.040 **S**, 0.15–0.30 **Si**, 0.20–0.30 **Mo**	
ANSI/ASTM A 304	4147 H	US	Bar	0.44–0.51 **C**, 0.65–1.10 **Mn**, 0.040 **P**, 0.040 **S**, 0.15–0.30 **Si**, 0.75–1.20 **Cr**, 0.15–0.25 **Mo**	
ANSI/ASTM A 304	4047 H	US	Bar	0.44–0.51 **C**, 0.60–1.00 **Mn**, 0.040 **P**, 0.040 **S**, 0.15–0.30 **Si**, 0.20–0.30 **Mo**	
AISI 4047 H		US	Wire, rod	0.44–0.51 **C**, 0.60–1.00 **Mn**, 0.15–0.30 **Si**, 0.20–0.30 **Mo**	
AISI 4147 H		US		0.44–0.51 **C**, 0.65–1.10 **Mn**, 0.15–0.30 **Si**, 0.75–1.20 **Cr**, 0.15–0.25 **Mo**	
AISI 4147H		US	Bar	0.44–0.51 **C**, 0.65–1.10 **Mn**, 0.035 **P**, 0.040 **S**, 0.15–0.30 **Si**, 0.75–1.20 **Cr**, 0.15–0.25 **Mo**	
AISI 4047H		US	Bar	0.44–0.51 **C**, 0.60–1.00 **Mn**, 0.035 **P**, 0.040 **S**, 0.15–0.30 **Si**, 0.20–0.30 **Mo**	
JIS G 4103	Class 9	Japan	Bar	0.44–0.50 **C**, 0.60–0.90 **Mn**, 0.030 **P**, 0.030 **S**, 0.15–0.35 **Si**, 0.60–1.00 **Cr**, 1.60–2.00 **Ni**, 0.15–0.30 **Mo**, 0.30 **Cu**	**Rolled or forged, quenched and tempered**: (25) **diam**, (1030) **TS**, (932) **YS**, 14 **El**

WROUGHT ALLOY STEELS

specification number	designation	country	product forms	composition	mechanical properties (see page iv for explanation)
AISI 50B46		US	Bar	0.44–0.49 **C**, 0.75–1.00 **Mn**, 0.035 **P**, 0.040 **S**, 0.15–0.30 **Si**, 0.20–0.35 **Cr**, 0.0005–0.003 **B**	
DGN–B–300	50B46	Mexico	Bar	0.44–0.49 **C**, 0.75–1.00 **Mn**, 0.035 **P**, 0.040 **S**, 0.20–0.35 **Si**, 0.20–0.35 **Cr**, 0.0005 min **B**	**Annealed**
ASTM A 689	50B46	US	Bar	0.44–0.49 **C**, 0.75–1.00 **Mn**, 0.035 **P**, 0.040 **S**, 0.15–0.30 **Si**, 0.20–0.35 **Cr**, 0.0005 min **B**	
ANSI/ASTM A 322	50B46	US	Bar	0.44–0.49 **C**, 0.75–1.00 **Mn**, 0.035 **P**, 0.040 **S**, 0.15–0.30 **Si**, 0.20–0.35 **Cr**, 0.0005 min **B**	
AISI 50B46		US	Wire, rod	0.44–0.49 **C**, 0.75–1.00 **Mn**, 0.035 **P**, 0.040 **S**, 0.15–0.30 **Si**, 0.20–0.35 **Cr**	
DGN–B–297	50B46	Mexico	Bar	0.44–0.49 **C**, 0.75–1.00 **Mn**, 0.035 **P**, 0.040 **S**, 0.20–0.35 **Si**, 0.20–0.35 **Cr**, 0.0005 **B**	
COPANT 514	Grade 1144	COPANT	Tube: seamless	0.44–0.48 **C**, 1.35–1.65 **Mn**, 0.040 **P**, 0.24–0.33 **S**	
ANSI/ASTM A 29	1547	US	Bar	0.43–0.51 **C**, 1.35–1.65 **Mn**, 0.040 **P**, 0.050 **S**	
ANSI/ASTM A 576	1547	US	Bar	0.43–0.51 **C**, 1.35–1.65 **Mn**, 0.040 **P**, 0.050 **S**	
DGN–B–301	1547	Mexico	Bar	0.43–0.51 **C**, 1.35–1.65 **Mn**, 0.040 **P**, 0.050 **S**	
DGN–B–301	1047	Mexico	Bar	0.43–0.51 **C**, 1.35–1.65 **Mn**, 0.040 **P**, 0.050 **S**, 0.10–0.20 **Si**	
NBN 253–05	45 Si 7	Belgium	Wire	0.43–0.50 **C**, 0.50–0.80 **Mn**, 0.040 **P**, 0.040 **S**, 1.50–2.0 **Si**	**Annealed or quenched and tempered:** (≤25) **diam**, (1275) **TS**, (1080) **El**
DGN–B–203	Grade 5046	Mexico	Tube: seamless	0.43–0.50 **C**, 0.75–1.00 **Mn**, 0.040 **P**, 0.040 **S**, 0.20–0.35 **Si**, 0.20–0.35 **Cr**	
DGN–B–203	Grade 50B46	Mexico	Tube: seamless	0.43–0.50 **C**, 0.75–1.00 **Mn**, 0.040 **P**, 0.040 **S**, 0.20–0.35 **Si**, 0.20–0.35 **Cr**, 0.0005 min **B**	
DGN–B–300	50B46 H	Mexico	Bar	0.43–0.50 **C**, 0.65–1.10 **Mn**, 0.040 **P**, 0.035 **S**, 0.20–0.35 **Si**, 0.13–0.43 **Cr**, 0.0005 min **B**	**Annealed**
DGN–B–300	5046 H	Mexico	Bar	0.43–0.50 **C**, 0.65–1.10 **Mn**, 0.040 **P**, 0.035 **S**, 0.20–0.35 **Si**, 0.13–0.43 **Cr**	
ANSI/ASTM A 304	50B 46 H	US	Bar	0.43–0.50 **C**, 0.65–1.10 **Mn**, 0.040 **P**, 0.040 **S**, 0.15–0.30 **Si**, 0.13–0.43 **Cr**, 0.0005 **B**	
ANSI/ASTM A 304	5046 H	US	Bar	0.43–0.50 **C**, 0.65–1.10 **Mn**, 0.040 **P**, 0.040 **S**, 0.15–0.30 **Si**, 0.13–0.43 **Cr**	
ASTM A 689	50B46 H	US	Bar	0.43–0.50 **C**, 0.65–1.10 **Mn**, 0.040 **P**, 0.040 **S**, 0.15–0.30 **Si**, 0.13–0.43 **Cr**, 0.0005 min **B**	
ASTM A 689	5046 H	US	Bar	0.43–0.50 **C**, 0.65–1.10 **Mn**, 0.040 **P**, 0.040 **S**, 0.15–0.30 **Si**, 0.13–0.43 **Cr**	
AISI 50B46 H		US	Wire, rod	0.43–0.50 **C**, 0.65–1.10 **Mn**, 0.15–0.30 **Si**, 0.13–0.43 **Cr**	
AISI 50B46H		US	Bar	0.43–0.50 **C**, 0.65–1.10 **Mn**, 0.035 **P**, 0.040 **S**, 0.15–0.30 **Si**, 0.13–0.43 **Cr**	
AISI 5046H		US	Bar	0.43–0.50 **C**, 0.65–1.10 **Mn**, 0.035 **P**, 0.040 **S**, 0.15–0.30 **Si**, 0.13–0.43 **Cr**	
ANSI/ASTM A 519	5046	US	Tube: seamless	0.43–0.50 **C**, 0.75–1.00 **Mn**, 0.040 **P**, 0.040 **S**, 0.15–0.35 **Si**, 0.20–0.35 **Cr**	
ANSI/ASTM A 519	50B46	US	Tube: seamless	0.43–0.50 **C**, 0.75–1.00 **Mn**, 0.040 **P**, 0.040 **S**, 0.15–0.35 **Si**, 0.20–0.35 **Cr**	

specification number	designation	country	product forms	composition	mechanical properties (see page iv for explanation)
COPANT 514	Grade 5046	COPANT	Tube: seamless	0.43–0.50 **C**, 0.75–1.00 **Mn**, 0.040 **P**, 0.050 **S**, 0.10 **Si**, 0.20–0.35 **Cr**	
COPANT 514	Grade 50B46	COPANT	Tube: seamless	0.43–0.50 **C**, 0.75–1.00 **Mn**, 0.040 **P**, 0.050 **S**, 0.10 **Si**, 0.20–0.35 **Cr**	
AMS 6432A		US	Bar, forgings, tube	0.43–0.49 **C**, 0.60–0.90 **Mn**, 0.025 **P**, 0.025 **S**, 0.15–0.30 **Si**, 0.90–1.20 **Cr**, 0.40–0.70 **Ni**, 0.90–1.10 **Mo**, 0.08–0.15 **V**, 0.35 **Cu**	**Hardened, quenched, and tempered:** all diam, 225 (1551) **TS**, 195 (1345) **YS**, 7 **El**; **Cold finished (bar):** ≤0.500 (≤12.70) **diam**, 135 (931) max **TS**
NF A 35–571	46 S 7	France	Bar, wire, rod	0.43–0.49 **C**, 0.50–0.80 **Mn**, 0.035 **P**, 0.035 **S**, 1.60–2.0 **Si**, 0.30 **Cr**	**Quenched and tempered:** (≤80) **diam**, (1450) **TS**, (1300) **YS**, 7 **El**
JIS G 4105	Class 5	Japan	Bar	0.43–0.48 **C**, 0.60–0.85 **Mn**, 0.030 **P**, 0.030 **S**, 0.15–0.35 **Si**, 0.90–1.20 **Cr**, 0.25 **Ni**, 0.15–0.30 **Mo**, 0.30 **Cu**	**Rolled or forged, quenched and tempered:** (25) **diam**, (1030) **TS**, (883) **YS**, 12 **El**
JIS G 4104	Class 5	Japan	Bar	0.43–0.48 **C**, 0.60–0.85 **Mn**, 0.030 **P**, 0.030 **S**, 0.15–0.35 **Si**, 0.90–1.20 **Cr**, 0.25 **Ni**, 0.30 **Cu**	**Rolled or forged, quenched and tempered:** (25) **diam**, (981) **TS**, (834) **YS**, 12 **El**
JIS G 4103	Class 7	Japan	Bar	0.43–0.48 **C**, 0.70–1.00 **Mn**, 0.030 **P**, 0.030 **S**, 0.15–0.35 **Si**, 0.40–0.65 **Cr**, 0.40–0.70 **Ni**, 0.15–0.30 **Mo**, 0.30 **Cu**	**Rolled or forged, quenched and tempered:** (25) **diam**, (981) **TS**, (883) **YS**, 15 **El**
AISI 1345		US	Bar	0.43–0.48 **C**, 1.60–1.90 **Mn**, 0.035 **P**, 0.040 **S**, 0.15–0.30 **Si**	
AISI 4145		US	Bar	0.43–0.48 **C**, 0.75–1.00 **Mn**, 0.035 **P**, 0.040 **S**, 0.15–0.30 **Si**, 0.80–1.10 **Cr**, 0.15–0.25 **Mo**	
AISI 8645		US	Bar	0.43–0.48 **C**, 0.75–1.00 **Mn**, 0.035 **P**, 0.040 **S**, 0.15–0.30 **Si**, 0.40–0.60 **Cr**, 0.40–0.70 **Ni**, 0.15–0.25 **Mo**	
AISI 50B44		US	Bar	0.43–0.48 **C**, 0.75–1.00 **Mn**, 0.035 **P**, 0.040 **S**, 0.15–0.30 **Si**, 0.40–0.50 **Cr**, 0.005–0.003 **B**	
AS 1444	Grade AS 1444/5145	Australia	Bar, bloom, billet, slab	0.43–0.48 **C**, 0.70–0.90 **Mn**, 0.040 **P**, 0.040 **S**, 0.10–0.35 **Si**, 0.70–0.90 **Cr**	
AS 1444	Grade AS 1444/8645	Australia	Bar, bloom, billet, slab	0.43–0.48 **C**, 0.75–1.00 **Mn**, 0.040 **P**, 0.040 **S**, 0.10–0.35 **Si**, 0.40–0.60 **Cr**, 0.40–0.70 **Ni**, 0.15–0.25 **Mo**	
DGN–B–203	Grade 1345	Mexico	Tube: seamless	0.43–0.48 **C**, 1.60–1.90 **Mn**, 0.040 **P**, 0.040 **S**, 0.20–0.35 **Si**	
DGN–B–203	Grade 5145	Mexico	Tube: seamless	0.43–0.48 **C**, 0.70–0.90 **Mn**, 0.040 **P**, 0.040 **S**, 0.20–0.35 **Si**, 0.70–0.90 **Cr**	
DGN–B–203	Grade 8645	Mexico	Tube: seamless	0.43–0.48 **C**, 0.75–1.00 **Mn**, 0.040 **P**, 0.040 **S**, 0.20–0.35 **Si**, 0.40–0.60 **Cr**, 0.40–0.70 **Ni**, 0.15–0.25 **Mo**	
DGN–B–203	Grade 81B45	Mexico	Tube: seamless	0.43–0.48 **C**, 0.75–1.00 **Mn**, 0.040 **P**, 0.040 **S**, 0.20–0.35 **Si**, 0.35–0.55 **Cr**, 0.20–0.40 **Ni**, 0.08–0.15 **Mo**, 0.0005 min **B**	
DGN–B–203	Grade 86B45	Mexico	Tube: seamless	0.43–0.48 **C**, 0.75–1.00 **Mn**, 0.040 **P**, 0.040 **S**, 0.20–0.35 **Si**, 0.40–0.60 **Cr**, 0.40–0.70 **Ni**, 0.15–0.25 **Mo**, 0.0005 min **B**	
DGN–B–203	Grade 50B44	Mexico	Tube: seamless	0.43–0.48 **C**, 0.75–1.00 **Mn**, 0.040 **P**, 0.040 **S**, 0.20–0.35 **Si**, 0.40–0.60 **Cr**, 0.0005 min **B**	
COPANT 514	4145	COPANT	Tube	0.43–0.48 **C**, 0.75–1.0 **Mn**, 0.040 **P**, 0.040 **S**, 0.20–0.35 **Si**, 0.80–1.10 **Cr**, 0.15–0.25 **Mo**	
COPANT 514	1345	COPANT	Tube	0.43–0.48 **C**, 1.60–1.90 **Mn**, 0.040 **P**, 0.040 **S**, 0.20–0.35 **Si**	

WROUGHT ALLOY STEELS

specification number	designation	country	product forms	composition	mechanical properties (see page iv for explanation)
DGN-B-300	81B45	Mexico	Bar	0.43–0.48 **C**, 0.75–1.00 **Mn**, 0.035 **P**, 0.040 **S**, 0.20–0.35 **Si**, 0.35–0.55 **Cr**, 0.20–0.40 **Ni**, 0.08–0.15 **Mo**, 0.0005 min **B**	**Annealed**
DGN-B-300	50B44	Mexico	Bar	0.43–0.48 **C**, 0.75–1.00 **Mn**, 0.035 **P**, 0.040 **S**, 0.20–0.35 **Si**, 0.20–0.60 **Cr**, 0.0005 min **B**	**Annealed**
DGN-B-300	8645	Mexico	Bar	0.43–0.48 **C**, 0.75–1.00 **Mn**, 0.035 **P**, 0.040 **S**, 0.20–0.35 **Si**, 0.40–0.60 **Cr**, 0.40–0.70 **Ni**, 0.15–0.25 **Mo**	**Annealed**
DGN-B-300	5145	Mexico	Bar	0.43–0.48 **C**, 0.70–0.90 **Mn**, 0.035 **P**, 0.040 **S**, 0.20–0.35 **Si**, 0.70–0.90 **Cr**	**Annealed**
DGN-B-300	4145	Mexico	Bar	0.43–0.48 **C**, 0.75–1.00 **Mn**, 0.035 **P**, 0.040 **S**, 0.20–0.35 **Si**, 0.80–1.10 **Cr**, 0.15–0.25 **Mo**	**Annealed**
DGN-B-300	1345	Mexico	Bar	0.43–0.48 **C**, 1.60–1.90 **Mn**, 0.035 **P**, 0.040 **S**, 0.20–0.35 **Si**	**Annealed**
ANSI/ASTM A 29	5046	US	Bar	0.43–0.48 **C**, 0.75–1.00 **Mn**, 0.035 **P**, 0.040 **S**, 0.15–0.30 **Si**, 0.20–0.35 **Cr**	
ANSI/ASTM A 29	5145	US	Bar	0.43–0.48 **C**, 0.70–0.90 **Mn**, 0.035 **P**, 0.040 **S**, 0.15–0.30 **Si**, 0.70–0.90 **Cr**	
ANSI/ASTM A 29	1345	US	Bar	0.43–0.48 **C**, 1.60–1.90 **Mn**, 0.035 **P**, 0.040 **S**, 0.15–0.30 **Si**	
ANSI/ASTM A 29	4145	US	Bar	0.43–0.48 **C**, 0.75–1.00 **Mn**, 0.035 **P**, 0.040 **S**, 0.15–0.30 **Si**, 0.80–1.10 **Cr**, 0.15–0.25 **Mo**	
MIL-S-16974E	No 8645	US	Bar, billets, blooms, slabs	0.43–0.48 **C**, 0.75–1.00 **Mn**, 0.040 **P**, 0.040 **S**, 0.20–0.35 **Si**, 0.40–0.60 **Cr**, 0.40–0.70 **Ni**, 0.15–0.25 **Mo**	
MIL-S-16974E	No 4145	US	Bar, billets, blooms, slabs	0.43–0.48 **C**, 0.75–1.00 **Mn**, 0.040 **P**, 0.040 **S**, 0.20–0.35 **Si**, 0.80–1.10 **Cr**, 0.15–0.25 **Mo**	
MIL-S-16974E	No 6145	US	Bar, billets, blooms, slabs	0.43–0.48 **C**, 0.70–0.90 **Mn**, 0.040 **P**, 0.040 **S**, 0.20–0.35 **Si**, 0.80–1.10 **Cr**, 0.15 min **V**	
ASTM A 689	50B44	US	Bar	0.43–0.48 **C**, 0.75–1.00 **Mn**, 0.035 **P**, 0.040 **S**, 0.15–0.30 **Si**, 0.20–0.60 **Cr**, 0.0005 min **B**	
ASTM A 689	81B45	US	Bar	0.43–0.48 **C**, 0.75–1.00 **Mn**, 0.035 **P**, 0.040 **S**, 0.15–0.30 **Si**, 0.35–0.55 **Cr**, 0.20–0.40 **Ni**, 0.08–0.15 **Mo**, 0.0005 min **B**	
ASTM A 689	8645	US	Bar	0.43–0.48 **C**, 0.75–1.00 **Mn**, 0.035 **P**, 0.040 **S**, 0.15–0.30 **Si**, 0.40–0.60 **Cr**, 0.20–0.70 **Ni**, 0.15–0.25 **Mo**	
ASTM A 689	5145	US	Bar	0.43–0.48 **C**, 0.70–0.90 **Mn**, 0.035 **P**, 0.040 **S**, 0.15–0.30 **Si**, 0.70–0.90 **Cr**	
ASTM A 689	1345	US	Bar	0.43–0.48 **C**, 1.60–1.90 **Mn**, 0.035 **P**, 0.040 **S**, 0.15–0.30 **Si**	
ASTM A 689	4145	US	Bar	0.43–0.48 **C**, 0.75–1.00 **Mn**, 0.035 **P**, 0.040 **S**, 0.15–0.30 **Si**, 0.80–1.10 **Cr**, 0.15–0.25 **Mo**	
ANSI/ASTM A 322	1345	US	Bar	0.43–0.48 **C**, 1.60–1.90 **Mn**, 0.035 **P**, 0.040 **S**, 0.15–0.30 **Si**	
ANSI/ASTM A 322	4145	US	Bar	0.43–0.48 **C**, 0.75–1.00 **Mn**, 0.035 **P**, 0.040 **S**, 0.15–0.30 **Si**, 0.80–1.10 **Cr**, 0.15–0.25 **Mo**	
ANSI/ASTM A 322	8645	US	Bar	0.43–0.48 **C**, 0.75–1.00 **Mn**, 0.035 **P**, 0.040 **S**, 0.15–0.30 **Si**, 0.40–0.60 **Cr**, 0.40–0.70 **Ni**, 0.15–0.25 **Mo**	
ANSI/ASTM A 322	50B44	US	Bar	0.43–0.48 **C**, 0.75–1.00 **Mn**, 0.035 **P**, 0.040 **S**, 0.15–0.30 **Si**, 0.20–0.60 **Cr**, 0.0005 min **B**	

specification number	designation	country	product forms	composition	mechanical properties (see page iv for explanation)
ANSI/ASTM A 322	81B45	US	Bar	0.43–0.48 **C**, 0.75–1.00 **Mn**, 0.035 **P**, 0.040 **S**, 0.15–0.30 **Si**, 0.35–0.55 **Cr**, 0.20–0.40 **Ni**, 0.08–0.15 **Mo**, 0.0005 min **B**	
ANSI/ASTM A 322	5145	US	Bar	0.43–0.48 **C**, 0.70–0.90 **Mn**, 0.035 **P**, 0.040 **S**, 0.15–0.30 **Si**, 0.70–0.90 **Cr**	
ANSI/ASTM A 29	8645	US	Bar	0.43–0.48 **C**, 0.75–1.00 **Mn**, 0.035 **P**, 0.040 **S**, 0.15–0.30 **Si**, 0.40–0.60 **Cr**, 0.40–0.70 **Ni**, 0.15–0.25 **Mo**	
AISI 81B45		US	Bar	0.43–0.48 **C**, 0.75–1.00 **Mn**, 0.035 **P**, 0.040 **S**, 0.15–0.30 **Si**, 0.35–0.55 **Cr**, 0.20–0.40 **Ni**, 0.08–0.15 **Mo**, 0.0005–0.003 **B**	
AISI 8645		US	Wire, rod	0.43–0.48 **C**, 0.75–1.00 **Mn**, 0.035 **P**, 0.040 **S**, 0.15–0.30 **Si**, 0.40–0.60 **Cr**, 0.40–0.70 **Ni**, 0.15–0.25 **Mo**	
AISI 50B44		US	Wire, rod	0.43–0.48 **C**, 0.75–1.00 **Mn**, 0.035 **P**, 0.040 **S**, 0.15–0.30 **Si**, 0.40–0.60 **Cr**	
AISI 81B45		US		0.43–0.48 **C**, 0.75–1.00 **Mn**, 0.035 **P**, 0.040 **S**, 0.15–0.30 **Si**, 0.35–0.55 **Cr**, 0.20–0.40 **Ni**, 0.08–0.15 **Mo**	
AISI 1345		US	Wire, rod	0.43–0.48 **C**, 1.60–1.90 **Mn**, 0.035 **P**, 0.040 **S**, 0.15–0.30 **Si**	
AISI 4145		US	Wire, rod	0.43–0.48 **C**, 0.75–1.00 **Mn**, 0.035 **P**, 0.040 **S**, 0.15–0.30 **Si**, 0.80–1.10 **Cr**, 0.15–0.25 **Mo**	
AISI 5145		US	Wire, rod	0.43–0.48 **C**, 0.70–0.90 **Mn**, 0.035 **P**, 0.040 **S**, 0.15–0.30 **Si**, 0.70–0.90 **Cr**	
ANSI/ASTM A 519	1345	US	Tube: seamless	0.43–0.48 **C**, 1.60–1.90 **Mn**, 0.040 **P**, 0.040 **S**, 0.15–0.35 **Si**	
ANSI/ASTM A 519	4145	US	Tube: seamless	0.43–0.48 **C**, 0.75–1.00 **Mn**, 0.040 **P**, 0.040 **S**, 0.15–0.35 **Si**, 0.80–1.10 **Cr**, 0.15–0.25 **Mo**	
ANSI/ASTM A 519	5145	US	Tube: seamless	0.43–0.48 **C**, 0.70–0.90 **Mn**, 0.040 **P**, 0.040 **S**, 0.15–0.35 **Si**, 0.70–0.90 **Cr**	
ANSI/ASTM A 519	8645	US	Tube: seamless	0.43–0.48 **C**, 0.75–1.00 **Mn**, 0.040 **P**, 0.040 **S**, 0.15–0.35 **Si**, 0.40–0.60 **Cr**, 0.40–0.70 **Ni**, 0.15–0.25 **Mo**	
ANSI/ASTM A 519	50B44	US	Tube: seamless	0.43–0.48 **C**, 0.75–1.00 **Mn**, 0.040 **P**, 0.040 **S**, 0.15–0.35 **Si**, 0.40–0.60 **Cr**	
ANSI/ASTM A 519	81B45	US	Tube: seamless	0.43–0.48 **C**, 0.75–1.00 **Mn**, 0.040 **P**, 0.040 **S**, 0.15–0.35 **Si**, 0.35–0.55 **Cr**, 0.20–0.40 **Ni**, 0.08–0.15 **Mo**	
ANSI/ASTM A 519	86B45	US	Tube: seamless	0.43–0.48 **C**, 0.75–1.00 **Mn**, 0.040 **P**, 0.040 **S**, 0.15–0.35 **Si**, 0.40–0.60 **Cr**, 0.40–0.70 **Ni**, 0.15–0.25 **Mo**	
AISI 8645		US	Sheet, strip	0.43–0.48 **C**, 0.75–1.00 **Mn**, 0.035 **P**, 0.040 **S**, 0.20–0.35 **Si**, 0.40–0.60 **Cr**, 0.40–0.70 **Ni**, 0.15–0.25 **Mo**	
AISI 4145		US	Sheet, strip	0.43–0.48 **C**, 0.75–1.00 **Mn**, 0.035 **P**, 0.040 **S**, 0.20–0.35 **Si**, 0.80–1.10 **Cr**, 0.15–0.25 **Mo**	
DGN–B–297	4145	Mexico	Bar	0.43–0.48 **C**, 0.75–1.00 **Mn**, 0.035 **P**, 0.040 **S**, 0.20–0.35 **Si**, 0.80–1.10 **Cr**, 0.15–0.25 **Mo**	
AS 1442	Grade AS 1442/XK 1345	Australia	Bar, blooms, billets, slabs	0.43–0.48 **C**, 1.40–1.70 **Mn**, 0.050 **P**, 0.050 **S**, 0.10–0.35 **Si**	
AS 1443	Grade AS 1443/XK 1345	Australia	Bar	0.43–0.48 **C**, 1.40–1.70 **Mn**, 0.050 **P**, 0.050 **S**, 0.10–0.35 **Si**	
DGN–B–297	1345	Mexico	Bar	0.43–0.48 **C**, 1.60–1.90 **Mn**, 0.035 **P**, 0.040 **S**, 0.20–0.35 **Si**	

specification number	designation	country	product forms	composition	mechanical properties (see page iv for explanation)
DGN–B–297	8645	Mexico	Bar	0.43–0.48 **C**, 0.75–1.00 **Mn**, 0.035 **P**, 0.040 **S**, 0.20–0.35 **Si**, 0.40–0.60 **Cr**, 0.20–0.70 **Ni**, 0.15–0.25 **Mo**	
DGN–B–297	50B44	Mexico	Bar	0.43–0.48 **C**, 0.75–1.00 **Mn**, 0.035 **P**, 0.040 **S**, 0.20–0.35 **Si**, 0.20–0.60 **Cr**, 0.0005 **B**	
DGN–B–297	B45	Mexico	Bar	0.43–0.48 **C**, 0.75–1.00 **Mn**, 0.035 **P**, 0.040 **S**, 0.20–0.35 **Si**, 0.35–0.45 **Cr**, 0.20–0.40 **Ni**, 0.08–0.15 **Mo**	
DGN–B–297	5145	Mexico	Bar	0.43–0.48 **C**, 0.70–0.90 **Mn**, 0.035 **P**, 0.040 **S**, 0.20–0.35 **Si**, 0.70–0.90 **Cr**	
COPANT 514	Grade 50B44	COPANT	Tube: seamless	0.43–0.48 **C**, 0.75–1.00 **Mn**, 0.040 **P**, 0.050 **S**, 0.10 **Si**, 0.40–0.60 **Cr**	
COPANT 514	Grade 81B45	COPANT	Tube: seamless	0.43–0.48 **C**, 0.75–1.00 **Mn**, 0.040 **P**, 0.050 **S**, 0.10 **Si**, 0.35–0.55 **Cr**, 0.20–0.40 **Ni**, 0.08–0.15 **Mo**	
COPANT 514	Grade 86B45	COPANT	Tube: seamless	0.43–0.48 **C**, 0.75–1.00 **Mn**, 0.040 **P**, 0.050 **S**, 0.10 **Si**, 0.40–0.60 **Cr**, 0.40–0.70 **Ni**, 0.15–0.25 **Mo**	
COPANT 514	Grade 5145	COPANT	Tube: seamless	0.43–0.48 **C**, 0.70–0.90 **Mn**, 0.040 **P**, 0.050 **S**, 0.10 **Si**, 0.70–0.90 **Cr**	
COPANT 514	Grade 8645	COPANT	Tube: seamless	0.43–0.48 **C**, 0.75–1.00 **Mn**, 0.040 **P**, 0.050 **S**, 0.10 **Si**, 0.40–0.60 **Cr**, 0.40–0.70 **Ni**, 0.15–0.25 **Mo**	
DGN–B–203	Grade 4145	Mexico	Tube: seamless	0.43–0.45 **C**, 0.75–1.00 **Mn**, 0.040 **P**, 0.040 **S**, 0.20–0.35 **Si**, 0.80–1.10 **Cr**, 0.15–0.25 **Mo**	
NF A 35–571	45 SCD 6	France	Bar, wire, rod	0.42–0.50 **C**, 0.50–0.80 **Mn**, 0.035 **P**, 0.035 **S**, 1.30–1.70 **Si**, 0.50–0.75 **Cr**, 0.15–0.30 **Mo**	**Quenched and tempered:** (≤80) **diam**, (1550) **TS**, (1400) **YS**, 6 **El**
MIL–S–47036		US	Bar, forgings, tube, sheet, plate	0.42–0.50 **C**, 0.60–0.90 **Mn**, 0.015 **P**, 0.015 **S**, 0.15–0.30 **Si**, 0.90–1.20 **Cr**, 0.40–0.70 **Ni**, 0.90–1.10 **Mo**, 0.05–0.15 **V**	**Quenched and tempered:** all **diam**, 210 (1448) **TS**, 185 (1276) **YS**, 7 **El**
NBN 253–05	45 Si Cr Mo 6	Belgium	Wire	0.42–0.50 **C**, 0.50–0.80 **Mn**, 0.035 **P**, 0.035 **S**, 1.30–1.70 **Si**, 0.50–0.75 **Cr**, 0.15–0.30 **Mo**	**Annealed or quenched and tempered:** (≤45) **diam**, (1375) **TS**, (1175) **YS**, 6 **El**
BS 2S.517		UK	Sheet, strip: aircraft quality	0.42–0.50 **C**, 1.30–1.70 **Mn**, 0.040 **P**, 0.040 **S**, 0.10–0.35 **Si**	**Annealed, hardened and tempered:** (<1.6) **diam**, (1160) **TS**, (1005) **YS**, 4 **El**
BS 2S.516		UK	Sheet, strip: aircraft quality	0.42–0.50 **C**, 1.30–1.70 **Mn**, 0.040 **P**, 0.040 **S**, 0.10–0.35 **Si**	**Annealed, hardened and tempered:** (<1.6) **diam**, (930) **TS**, (770) **YS**, 6 **El**
DIN 17200	Grade 46 Cr 2	Germany	Blooms, slabs, billets, wire, bar, plate, sheet, strip, tube, forgings	0.42–0.50 **C**, 0.50–0.80 **Mn**, 0.035 **P**, 0.035 **S**, 0.15–0.40 **Si**, 0.40–0.60 **Cr**	**Quenched and tempered:** (≤16) **diam**, (883) **TS**, (638) **YS**, 12 **El**
EURONORM 119–74, IV	46 Cr 2 KD	EURONORM	Wire, rod	0.42–0.50 **C**, 0.50–0.80 **Mn**, 0.035 **P**, 0.035 **S**, 0.15–0.40 **Si**, 0.40–0.60 **Cr**	**Quenched and tempered:** (≤16) **diam**, (880) **TS**, (635) **YS**, 12 **El**
AIR 9160/C 107	9160C401	France	Bar, sheet	0.42–0.50 **C**, 0.50–0.80 **Mn**, 0.025 **P**, 0.020 **S**, 1.30–1.70 **Si**, 0.50–0.75 **Cr**, 0.15–0.30 **Mo**	**Annealed**: all **diam**, (830) **TS**; **Quenched and tempered:** all **diam**, (1600) **TS**, (1450) **YS**, 6 **El**
EURONORM 119–74, IV	46 Cr 1 KD	EURONORM	Wire, rod	0.42–0.50 **C**, 0.50–0.80 **Mn**, 0.035 **P**, 0.035 **S**, 0.15–0.40 **Si**, 0.20–0.40 **Cr**	**Quenched and tempered:** (≤16) **diam**, (800) **TS**, (550) **YS**, 13 **El**
DIN 17222	Grade C 45	Germany	Bar	0.42–0.50 **C**, 0.50–0.80 **Mn**, 0.045 **P**, 0.045 **S**, 0.15–0.35 **Si**	**Rolled, forged or drawn:** all **diam**, (588) **TS**, (353) **YS**, 18 **El**
DIN 17240	Grade Ck 45	Germany	Bar	0.42–0.50 **C**, 0.50–0.80 **Mn**, 0.035 **P**, 0.035 **S**, 0.15–0.35 **Si**	**Rolled, forged or drawn:** all **diam**, (588) **TS**, (353) **YS**, 18 **El**
NF A 35–553	45 S 7	France	Strip	0.42–0.50 **C**, 0.50–0.80 **Mn**, 0.040 **P**, 0.040 **S**, 1.60–2.0 **Si**	

specification number	designation	country	product forms	composition	mechanical properties (see page iv for explanation)
NF A 35-553	45 SCD 6	France	Strip	0.42–0.50 **C**, 0.50–0.80 **Mn**, 0.03 **P**, 0.025 **S**, 1.3–1.7 **Si**, 0.50–0.75 **Cr**, 0.15–0.30 **Mo**	
TS 2288	46 Si 7	Turkey	Wire	0.42–0.50 **C**, 0.50–0.80 **Mn**, 0.050 **P**, 0.050 **S**, 1.5–1.8 **Si**	
MIL-S-16974E	No CV-45	US	Bar, billets, blooms, slabs	0.42–0.50 **C**, 0.70–1.00 **Mn**, 0.040 **P**, 0.040 **S**, 0.20–0.40 **Si**, 0.15 min **V**	
AS 1444	Grade AS 1444/5145H	Australia	Bar, bloom, billet, slab	0.42–0.49 **C**, 0.60–1.00 **Mn**, 0.040 **P**, 0.040 **S**, 0.10–0.35 **Si**, 0.60–1.00 **Cr**	
AS 1444	Grade AS 1444/8645H	Australia	Bar, bloom, billet, slab	0.42–0.49 **C**, 0.70–1.05 **Mn**, 0.040 **P**, 0.040 **S**, 0.10–0.35 **Si**, 0.35–0.65 **Cr**, 0.35–0.75 **Ni**, 0.15–0.25 **Mo**	
DGN-B-300	1345H	Mexico	Bar	0.42–0.49 **C**, 1.45–2.05 **Mn**, 0.040 **P**, 0.035 **S**, 0.20–0.35 **Si**	**Annealed**
DGN-B-300	4145 H	Mexico	Bar	0.42–0.49 **C**, 0.65–1.10 **Mn**, 0.040 **P**, 0.035 **S**, 0.20–0.35 **Si**, 0.75–1.20 **Cr**, 0.15–0.25 **Mo**	**Annealed**
DGN-B-300	81B45 H	Mexico	Bar	0.42–0.49 **C**, 0.70–1.05 **Mn**, 0.040 **P**, 0.035 **S**, 0.20–0.35 **Si**, 0.30–0.60 **Cr**, 0.15–0.45 **Ni**, 0.08–0.15 **Mo**, 0.0005 min **B**	**Annealed**
DGN-B-300	5145 H	Mexico	Bar	0.42–0.49 **C**, 0.60–1.00 **Mn**, 0.040 **P**, 0.035 **S**, 0.20–0.35 **Si**, 0.60–1.00 **Cr**	**Annealed**
DGN-B-300	86B45 H	Mexico	Bar	0.42–0.49 **C**, 0.70–1.05 **Mn**, 0.040 **P**, 0.035 **S**, 0.20–0.35 **Si**, 0.35–0.65 **Cr**, 0.35–0.75 **Ni**, 0.15–0.25 **Mo**, 0.0005 **B**	
DGN-B-300	8645 H	Mexico	Bar	0.42–0.49 **C**, 0.70–1.05 **Mn**, 0.040 **P**, 0.035 **S**, 0.20–0.35 **Si**, 0.35–0.65 **Cr**, 0.35–0.75 **Ni**, 0.15–0.25 **Mo**	**Annealed**
ANSI/ASTM A 304	1345 H	US	Bar	0.42–0.49 **C**, 1.45–2.05 **Mn**, 0.040 **P**, 0.040 **S**, 0.15–0.30 **Si**	
ASTM A 689	4145 H	US	Bar	0.42–0.49 **C**, 0.65–1.10 **Mn**, 0.040 **P**, 0.040 **S**, 0.15–0.30 **Si**, 0.75–1.20 **Cr**, 0.15–0.25 **Mo**	
ASTM A 689	1345 H	US	Bar	0.42–0.49 **C**, 1.45–2.05 **Mn**, 0.040 **P**, 0.040 **S**, 0.15–0.30 **Si**	
ASTM A 689	5145 H	US	Bar	0.42–0.49 **C**, 0.60–1.00 **Mn**, 0.040 **P**, 0.040 **S**, 0.15–0.30 **Si**, 0.60–1.00 **Cr**	
ASTM A 689	86B45	US	Bar	0.42–0.49 **C**, 0.70–1.05 **Mn**, 0.040 **P**, 0.040 **S**, 0.15–0.30 **Si**, 0.35–0.65 **Cr**, 0.35–0.75 **Ni**, 0.15–0.25 **Mo**, 0.0005 min **B**	
ASTM A 689	8645 H	US	Bar	0.42–0.49 **C**, 0.70–1.05 **Mn**, 0.040 **P**, 0.040 **S**, 0.15–0.30 **Si**, 0.35–0.65 **Cr**, 0.35–0.75 **Ni**, 0.15–0.25 **Mo**	
ASTM A 689	81B45 H	US	Bar	0.42–0.49 **C**, 0.70–1.05 **Mn**, 0.040 **P**, 0.040 **S**, 0.15–0.30 **Si**, 0.30–0.60 **Cr**, 0.15–0.45 **Ni**, 0.08–0.15 **Mo**, 0.0005 min **B**	
ANSI/ASTM A 304	50B44 H	US	Bar	0.42–0.49 **C**, 0.65–1.10 **Mn**, 0.040 **P**, 0.040 **S**, 0.15–0.30 **Si**, 0.30–0.70 **Cr**, 0.0005 **B**	
ANSI/ASTM A 304	5145 H	US	Bar	0.42–0.49 **C**, 0.60–1.00 **Mn**, 0.040 **P**, 0.040 **S**, 0.15–0.30 **Si**, 0.60–1.00 **Cr**	
ANSI/ASTM A 304	81B45 H	US	Bar	0.42–0.49 **C**, 0.70–1.05 **Mn**, 0.040 **P**, 0.040 **S**, 0.15–0.30 **Si**, 0.30–0.60 **Cr**, 0.15–0.45 **Ni**, 0.08–0.15 **Mo**, 0.0005 min **B**	
ANSI/ASTM A 304	8645 H	US	Bar	0.42–0.49 **C**, 0.70–1.05 **Mn**, 0.040 **P**, 0.040 **S**, 0.15–0.30 **Si**, 0.35–0.65 **Cr**, 0.35–0.75 **Ni**, 0.15–0.25 **Mo**	

specification number	designation	country	product forms	composition	mechanical properties (see page iv for explanation)
ANSI/ASTM A 304	86B45 H	US	Bar	0.42–0.49 **C**, 0.70–1.05 **Mn**, 0.040 **P**, 0.040 **S**, 0.15–0.30 **Si**, 0.35–0.65 **Cr**, 0.35–0.75 **Ni**, 0.15–0.25 **Mo**, 0.0005 min **B**	
ANSI/ASTM A 304	4145 H	US	Bar	0.42–0.49 **C**, 0.65–1.10 **Mn**, 0.040 **P**, 0.040 **S**, 0.15–0.30 **Si**, 0.75–1.20 **Cr**, 0.15–0.25 **Mo**	
ASTM A 689	50B44 H	US	Bar	0.42–0.49 **C**, 0.65–1.10 **Mn**, 0.040 **P**, 0.040 **S**, 0.15–0.30 **Si**, 0.30–0.70 **Cr**, 0.0005 min **B**	
AISI 5145 H		US	Wire, rod	0.42–0.49 **C**, 0.60–1.00 **Mn**, 0.15–0.30 **Si**, 0.60–1.00 **Cr**	
AISI 8645 H		US	Wire, rod	0.42–0.49 **C**, 0.70–1.05 **Mn**, 0.15–0.30 **Si**, 0.35–0.65 **Cr**, 0.35–0.75 **Ni**, 0.15–0.25 **Mo**	
AISI 50B44 H		US	Wire, rod	0.42–0.49 **C**, 0.65–1.10 **Mn**, 0.15–0.30 **Si**, 0.30–0.70 **Cr**	
AISI 81B45 H		US	Wire, rod	0.42–0.49 **C**, 0.70–1.05 **Mn**, 0.15–0.30 **Si**, 0.30–0.60 **Cr**, 0.15–0.45 **Ni**, 0.08–0.15 **Mo**	
AISI 1345 H		US	Wire, rod	0.42–0.49 **C**, 1.45–2.05 **Mn**, 0.15–0.30 **Si**	
AISI 4145 H		US	Wire, rod	0.42–0.49 **C**, 0.65–1.10 **Mn**, 0.15–0.30 **Si**, 0.75–1.20 **Cr**, 0.15–0.25 **Mo**	
AISI 86B45H		US	Bar	0.42–0.49 **C**, 0.70–1.05 **Mn**, 0.035 **P**, 0.040 **S**, 0.15–0.30 **Si**, 0.35–0.65 **Cr**, 0.35–0.75 **Ni**, 0.15–0.25 **Mo**	
AISI 81B45H		US	Bar	0.42–0.49 **C**, 0.70–1.05 **Mn**, 0.035 **P**, 0.040 **S**, 0.15–0.30 **Si**, 0.30–0.60 **Cr**, 0.15–0.45 **Ni**, 0.08–0.15 **Mo**	
AISI 81B45H		US	Bar	0.42–0.49 **C**, 0.70–1.05 **Mn**, 0.035 **P**, 0.040 **S**, 0.15–0.30 **Si**, 0.30–0.60 **Cr**, 0.15–0.45 **Ni**, 0.08–0.15 **Mo**	
AISI 50B44H		US	Bar	0.42–0.49 **C**, 0.65–1.10 **Mn**, 0.035 **P**, 0.040 **S**, 0.15–0.30 **Si**, 0.30–0.70 **Cr**	
AISI 8645H		US	Bar	0.42–0.49 **C**, 0.70–1.05 **Mn**, 0.035 **P**, 0.040 **S**, 0.15–0.30 **Si**, 0.35–0.65 **Cr**, 0.35–0.75 **Ni**, 0.15–0.25 **Mo**	
AISI 4145H		US	Bar	0.42–0.49 **C**, 0.65–1.10 **Mn**, 0.035 **P**, 0.040 **S**, 0.15–0.30 **Si**, 0.75–1.20 **Cr**, 0.15–0.25 **Mo**	
AISI 1345H		US	Bar	0.42–0.49 **C**, 1.45–2.05 **Mn**, 0.035 **P**, 0.040 **S**, 0.15–0.30 **Si**	
JIS G 4052	SCM 5H	Japan	Bar, wire, rod	0.42–0.49 **C**, 0.55–0.90 **Mn**, 0.030 **P**, 0.030 **S**, 0.15–0.35 **Si**, 0.85–1.25 **Cr**, 0.15–0.35 **Mo**, 0.30 **Cu**	**Hot rolled, normalized, quenched**
AS 1442	Grade AS 1442/XK1145	Australia	Bar, blooms, billets, slabs	0.42–0.49 **C**, 1.35–1.65 **Mn**, 0.050 **P**, 0.12–0.20 **S**, 0.10–0.35 **Si**	
AMS 6542A		US	Bar	0.42–0.48 **C**, 0.10–0.35 **Mn**, 0.010 **P**, 0.010 **S**, 0.10 **Si**, 0.20–0.35 **Cr**, 7.00–8.50 **Ni**, 0.20–0.35 **Mo**, 0.06–0.12 **V**, 3.50–4.50 **Co**, 0.35 **Cu**	**Solution treated and aged**: all **diam**, 260 (1793) **TS**, 220 (1531) **YS**, 7 **El**
MIL–S–8949	Type D6AC	US	Bar, plate, sheet, billets	0.42–0.48 **C**, 0.60–0.90 **Mn**, 0.010 **P**, 0.010 **S**, 0.15–0.30 **Si**, 0.90–1.20 **Cr**, 0.40–0.70 **Ni**, 0.90–1.10 **Mo**, 0.07–0.15 **V**	**As agreed**: all **diam**, (1516) **TS**, (1310) **YS**, 12 in 4d **El**
AMS 6439		US	Sheet, strip, plate	0.42–0.48 **C**, 0.60–0.90 **Mn**, 0.015 **P**, 0.015 **S**, 0.15–0.30 **Si**, 0.90–1.20 **Cr**, 0.40–0.70 **Ni**, 0.90–1.10 **Mo**, 0.08–0.15 **V**, 0.35 **Cu**	**Hardened, quenched, stress relieved**: $\geq$0.250 ($\geq$6.35) **diam**, 215 (1482) **TS**, 190 (1310) **YS**, 7 **El**
ISO 683/XII	6	ISO	Bar, plate	0.42–0.48 **C**, 0.50–0.80 **Mn**, 0.035 **P**, 0.035 **S**, 0.15–0.40 **Si**, 0.40–0.60 **Cr**	**Quenched and tempered**: (16) **diam**, (880) **TS**, (640) **YS**, 12 **El**

specification number	designation	country	product forms	composition	mechanical properties (see page iv for explanation)
MIL-S-47264	Type D-6A	US	Sheet, strip, plate, billets, bar, forgings	0.42–0.48 **C**, 0.60–0.90 **Mn**, 0.020 **P**, 0.020 **S**, 0.15–0.30 **Si**, 0.90–1.20 **Cr**, 0.40–0.70 **Ni**, 0.90–1.10 **Mo**, 0.05–0.10 **V**	**Heat treated**: all **diam**, 200 (1379) **YS**, 8 **El**
MIL-S-47263	D6AC Modified	US	Sheet, strip, plate, billets, bar, forgings	0.42–0.48 **C**, 0.60–0.90 **Mn**, 0.015 **P**, 0.015 **S**, 0.015–0.30 **Si**, 0.90–1.20 **Cr**, 0.40–0.70 **Ni**, 0.90–1.10 **Mo**, 0.05–0.10 **V**	**Heat treated**: all **diam**, 200 (1379) **YS**, 8 **El**
JIS G 3311	S45CM	Japan	Strip	0.42–0.48 **C**, 0.60–0.90 **Mn**, 0.030 **P**, 0.035 **S**, 0.15–0.35 **Si**, 0.20 **Cr**, 0.20 **Ni**, 0.30 **Cu**, 0.35 **Ni+Cr**	
ANSI/ASTM A 579	83	US	Forgings	0.42–0.47 **C**, 0.10–0.35 **Mn**, 0.01 **P**, 0.01 **S**, 0.10 **Si**, 0.20–0.35 **Cr**, 7.0–8.5 **Ni**, 0.20–0.35 **Mo**, 0.06–0.12 **V**, 3.5–4.5 **Co**	**Heat treated–martensitic**: all **diam**, 280 (1930) **TS**, 250 (1725) **YS**, 4 **El**; **Heat treated–bainitic**: all **diam**, 260 (1795) **TS**, 225 (1555) **YS**, 7 **El**
NF A 35-590	2331 (Y42 CD4)	France	Bar, forgings	0.42 **C**, 0.80 **Mn**, 0.030 **P**, 0.030 **S**, 0.30 **Si**, 1.0 **Cr**, 0.2 **Mo**	
MIL-S-11595D	Chrome-Moly-Vanadium	US	Bar	0.41–0.49 **C**, 0.60–0.90 **Mn**, 0.040 **P**, 0.040 **S**, 0.20–0.35 **Si**, 0.80–1.15 **Cr**, 0.30–0.40 **Mo**, 0.20–0.30 **V**	
AISI 1345		US	Plate	0.41–0.49 **C**, 1.50–1.90 **Mn**, 0.035 **P**, 0.040 **S**, 0.15–0.30 **Si**	
AiSI 4145		US	Plate	0.41–0.49 **C**, 0.70–1.00 **Mn**, 0.035 **P**, 0.040 **S**, 0.15–0.30 **Si**, 0.80–1.15 **Cr**, 0.15–0.25 **Mo**	
NF A 35-571	45 C 4	France	Bar, wire, rod	0.41–0.48 **C**, 0.60–0.90 **Mn**, 0.035 **P**, 0.035 **S**, 0.10–0.40 **Si**, 0.85–1.15 **Cr**	**Quenched and tempered**: (≤80) **diam**, (1230) **TS**, (1080) **YS**, 7 **El**
NF A 35-553	45 C 4	France	Strip	0.41–0.48 **C**, 0.60–0.90 **Mn**, 0.035 **P**, 0.035 **S**, 0.10–0.40 **Si**, 0.85–1.15 **Cr**	
AMS 6416A		US	Bar, forgings, tube	0.41–0.46 **C**, 0.60–0.90 **Mn**, 0.015 **P**, 0.015 **S**, 1.45–1.80 **Si**, 0.70–0.95 **Cr**, 1.65–2.00 **Ni**, 0.30–0.50 **Mo**, 0.05–0.10 **V**, 0.35 **Cu**	**Normalized, hardened, quenched and tempered**: all **diam**, 280 (1931) **TS**, 230 (1586) **YS**, 7 **El**; **Cold finished (bar)**: ≤0.500 (≤12.70) **diam**, 130 (896) max **TS**
ANSI/ASTM A 579	33	US	Forgings	0.41–0.46 **C**, 0.75–1.00 **Mn**, 0.025 **P**, 0.025 **S**, 1.40–1.75 **Si**, 1.90–2.25 **Cr**, 0.45–0.60 **Mo**, 0.03–0.08 **V**	**Quenched and tempered**: all **diam**, 250 (1725) **TS**, 225 (1555) **YS**, 6 **El**
AMS 6406B		US	Sheet, strip, plate	0.41–0.46 **C**, 0.75–1.00 **Mn**, 0.015 **P**, 0.015 **S**, 1.40–1.75 **Si**, 1.90–2.25 **Cr**, 0.25 **Ni**, 0.45–0.60 **Mo**, 0.03–0.08 **V**, 0.35 **Cu**	**Cold finished (sheet and strip) hot rolled annealed (plate)**: 0.020–2.000 (0.51–50.80) **diam**, 120 (827) **TS**, 95 (655) **YS**, 15 **El**
ASTM A 289	Class A, type 6	US	Forgings	0.40–0.75 **C**, 6.00–10.00 **Mn**, 0.050 **P**, 0.040 **S**, 0.20–0.65 **Si**, 3.50–6.00 **Cr**, 6.00–10.00 **Ni**	**Solution annealed, cold worked, stress relieved**: all **diam**, 170 (1170) **TS**, 155 (1069) **YS**, 15 **El**
ASTM A 289	Class A, type 5	US	Forgings	0.40–0.75 **C**, 6.00–10.00 **Mn**, 0.050 **P**, 0.040 **S**, 0.20–0.65 **Si**, 3.50–6.00 **Cr**, 6.00–10.00 **Ni**	**Solution annealed, cold worked, stress relieved**: all **diam**, 160 (1105) **TS**, 145 (1000) **YS**, 16 **El**
ASTM A 289	Class A, type 4	US	Forgings	0.40–0.75 **C**, 6.00–10.00 **Mn**, 0.050 **P**, 0.040 **S**, 0.20–0.65 **Si**, 3.50–6.00 **Cr**, 6.00–10.00 **Ni**	**Solution annealed, cold worked, stress relieved**: all **diam**, 150 (1034) **TS**, 130 (896) **YS**, 20 **El**
ASTM A 289	Class A, type 3	US	Forgings	0.40–0.75 **C**, 6.00–10.00 **Mn**, 0.050 **P**, 0.040 **S**, 0.20–0.65 **Si**, 3.50–6.00 **Cr**, 6.00–10.00 **Ni**	**Solution annealed, cold worked, stress relieved**: all **diam**, 140 (965) **TS**, 120 (825) **YS**, 25 **El**
ASTM A 289	Class A, type 2	US	Forgings	0.40–0.75 **C**, 6.00–10.00 **Mn**, 0.050 **P**, 0.040 **S**, 0.20–0.65 **Si**, 3.50–6.00 **Cr**, 6.00–10.00 **Ni**	**Solution annealed, cold worked, stress relieved**: all **diam**, 130 (895) **TS**, 110 (760) **YS**, 25 **El**
ASTM A 289	Class A, type 9	US	Forgings	0.40–0.75 **C**, 6.00–10.00 **Mn**, 0.05 **P**, 0.045 **S**, 0.20–0.65 **Si**, 3.50–6.00 **Cr**, 6.00–10.00 **Ni**	**Solution annealed, cold worked, stress relieved**: all **diam**, 130 (895) **TS**, 90 (620) **YS**, 25 **El**
ASTM A 289	Class A, type 1	US	Forgings	0.40–0.75 **C**, 6.00–10.00 **Mn**, 0.05 **P**, 0.045 **S**, 0.20–0.65 **Si**, 3.50–6.00 **Cr**, 6.00–10.00 **Ni**	**Solution annealed, cold worked, stress relieved**: all **diam**, 125 (860) **TS**, 100 (690) **YS**, 25 **El**

WROUGHT ALLOY STEELS

specification number	designation	country	product forms	composition	mechanical properties (see page iv for explanation)
ASTM A 289	Class A, type 8	US	Forgings	0.40–0.75 **C**, 6.00–10.00 **Mn**, 0.050 **P**, 0.040 **S**, 0.20–0.65 **Si**, 3.50–6.00 **Cr**, 6.00–10.00 **Ni**	**Solution annealed, cold worked, stress relieved:** all **diam**, 120 (825) **TS**, 80 (550) **YS**, 25 **El**
ASTM A 289	Class A, type 7	US	Forgings	0.40–0.75 **C**, 6.00–10.00 **Mn**, 0.050 **P**, 0.040 **S**, 0.20–0.65 **Si**, 3.50–6.00 **Cr**, 6.00–10.00 **Ni**	**Solution annealed, cold worked, stress relieved:** all **diam**, 110 (760) **TS**, 65 (450) **YS**, 30 **El**
ASTM A 289	Class B, type 6	US	Forgings	0.40–0.60 **C**, 16.00–20.00 **Mn**, 0.08 **P**, 0.025 **S**, 0.20–0.65 **Si**, 3.50–6.00 **Cr**, 2.00 **Ni**	**Solution annealed, cold worked, stress relieved:** all **diam**, 170 (1170) **TS**, 155 (1070) **YS**, 15 **El**
ASTM A 289	Class B, type 5	US	Forgings	0.40–0.60 **C**, 16.00–20.00 **Mn**, 0.08 **P**, 0.025 **S**, 0.20–0.65 **Si**, 3.50–6.00 **Cr**, 2.00 **Ni**	**Solution annealed, cold worked, stress relieved:** all **diam**, 160 (1105) **TS**, 145 (1000) **YS**, 16 **El**
ASTM A 289	Class B, type 4	US	Forgings	0.40–0.60 **C**, 16.00–20.00 **Mn**, 0.08 **P**, 0.025 **S**, 0.20–0.65 **Si**, 3.50–6.00 **Cr**, 2.00 **Ni**	**Solution annealed, cold worked, stress relieved:** all **diam**, 150 (1035) **TS**, 130 (895) **YS**, 20 **El**
ASTM A 289	Class B, type 3	US	Forgings	0.40–0.60 **C**, 16.00–20.00 **Mn**, 0.08 **P**, 0.025 **S**, 0.20–0.65 **Si**, 3.50–6.00 **Cr**, 2.00 **Ni**	**Solution annealed, cold worked, stress relieved:** all **diam**, 140 (965) **TS**, 120 (825) **YS**, 20 **El**
ASTM A 289	Class B, type 2	US	Forgings	0.40–0.60 **C**, 16.00–20.00 **Mn**, 0.08 **P**, 0.025 **S**, 0.20–0.65 **Si**, 3.50–6.00 **Cr**, 2.00 **Ni**	**Solution annealed, cold worked, stress relieved:** all **diam**, 130 (895) **TS**, 110 (760) **YS**, 25 **El**
ASTM A 289	Class B, type 9	US	Forgings	0.40–0.60 **C**, 16.00–20.00 **Mn**, 0.08 **P**, 0.025 **S**, 0.20–0.65 **Si**, 3.50–6.00 **Cr**, 2.00 **Ni**	**Solution annealed, cold worked, stress relieved:** all **diam**, 130 (895) **TS**, 90 (620) **YS**, 25 **El**
ASTM A 289	Class B, type 1	US	Forgings	0.40–0.60 **C**, 16.00–20.00 **Mn**, 0.080 **P**, 0.025 **S**, 0.20–0.65 **Si**, 3.50–6.00 **Cr**, 2.00 **Ni**	**Solution annealed, cold worked, stress relieved:** all **diam**, 125 (860) **TS**, 100 (690) **YS**, 25 **El**
ASTM A 289	Class B, type 8	US	Forgings	0.40–0.60 **C**, 16.00–20.00 **Mn**, 0.08 **P**, 0.025 **S**, 0.20–0.65 **Si**, 3.50–6.00 **Cr**, 2.00 **Ni**	**Solution annealed, cold worked, stress relieved:** all **diam**, 120 (825) **TS**, 80 (550) **YS**, 25 **El**
ASTM A 289	Class B, type 7	US	Forgings	0.40–0.60 **C**, 16.00–20.00 **Mn**, 0.08 **P**, 0.025 **S**, 0.20–0.65 **Si**, 3.50–6.00 **Cr**, 2.00 **Ni**	**Solution annealed, cold worked, stress relieved:** all **diam**, 110 (760) **TS**, 65 (450) **YS**, 30 **El**
ANSI/ASTM A 730	Grade C	US	Forgings	0.40–0.55 **C**, 0.60–0.90 **Mn**, 0.045 **P**, 0.050 **S**, 0.15 min **Si**	**Annealed, normalized, or normalized and tempered:** 8–14 (203–356) **diam**, 75 (515) **TS**, 37 (260) **YS**, 19 **El**
AMS 6379A		US	Bar	0.40–0.53 **C**, 0.75–1.00 **Mn**, 0.040 **P**, 0.040 **S**, 0.20–0.35 **Si**, 0.80–1.10 **Cr**, 0.25 **Ni**, 0.15–0.25 **Mo**, 0.35 **Cu**, 0.035–0.060 **Te**	**Tempered:** 2.00 (50.8) max **diam**, 180 (1241) **TS**, 165 (1138) **YS**, 5 **El**
AMS 6455D		US	Sheet, strip, plate	0.40–0.53 **C**, 0.70–0.90 **Mn**, 0.025 **P**, 0.025 **S**, 0.20–0.35 **Si**, 0.80–1.10 **Cr**, 0.25 **Ni**, 0.15–0.30 **V**, 0.35 **Cu**	
DIN 17225	Grade 45 CrMoV 67	Germany	Bar, rod, wire	0.40–0.50 **C**, 0.60–0.80 **Mn**, 0.15–0.35 **Si**, 1.3–1.5 **Cr**, 0.65–0.75 **Mo**, 0.25–0.35 **V**	**Hot rolled (bar, rod):** all **diam**, (1373) **TS**
JIS G 4311	SUH 1	Japan	Bar	0.40–0.50 **C**, 0.60 **Mn**, 3.00–3.50 **Si**, 7.50–9.50 **Cr**, 0.60 **Ni**, 0.030 **P**, 0.030 **S**	**Quenched and tempered:** (≤75) **diam**, (932) **TS**, (686) **YS**, 15 **El**
AMS 6304D		US	Bar, forgings, tube	0.40–0.50 **C**, 0.40–0.70 **Mn**, 0.025 **P**, 0.025 **S**, 0.20–0.35 **Si**, 0.80–1.10 **Cr**, 0.25 **Ni**, 0.45–0.65 **Mo**, 0.25–0.35 **V**, 0.35 **Cu**	**Cold finished (bar):** ≤0.500 (≤12.70) **diam**, 125 (862) max **TS**
AMS 6305		US	Bar, forgings, tube	0.40–0.50 **C**, 0.40–0.70 **Mn**, 0.015 **P**, 0.015 **S**, 0.20–0.35 **Si**, 0.80–1.10 **Cr**, 0.25 **Ni**, 0.45–0.65 **Mo**, 0.25–0.35 **V**, 0.35 **Cu**, 0.001 **Pb**	**Cold finished:** ≤0.500 (≤12.70) **diam**, 125 (862) max **TS**
JIS G 4202	SACM 1	Japan	Bar	0.40–0.50 **C**, 0.60 **Mn**, 0.030 **P**, 0.030 **S**, 0.15–0.50 **Si**, 1.30–1.70 **Cr**, 0.25 **Ni**, 0.15–0.30 **Mo**, 0.70–1.20 **Al**, 0.30 **Cu**	**Rolled or forged, quenched and tempered:** all **diam**, (834) **TS**, (686) **YS**, 15 **El**
ANSI/ASTM A 372	Class IV	US	Forgings	0.40–0.50 **C**, 1.40–1.80 **Mn**, 0.035 **P**, 0.04 **S**, 0.15–0.35 **Si**,	**Normalized or normalized and tempered:** all **diam**, (725) **TS**, (450) **YS**, 15 **El**
ASTM A 372	Class IV	US	Forgings	0.40–0.50 **C**, 1.40–1.80 **Mn**, 0.035 **P**, 0.04 **S**, 0.15–0.35 **Si**, 0.17–0.27 **Mo**	**Annealed or normalized:** all **diam**, 105 (725) **TS**, 65 (450) **YS**, 15 **El**

WROUGHT ALLOY STEELS

specification number	designation	country	product forms	composition	mechanical properties (see page iv for explanation)
DIN 17225	45 CrMoV 67/7737	Germany	Bar, rod	0.40–0.50 **C**, 0.60–0.80 **Mn**, 0.15–0.35 **Si**, 1.3–1.5 **Cr**, 0.65–0.75 **Mo**, 0.25–0.35 **V**	**Hot rolled**: all **diam**, (140) **TS**
BS 1429	En. 50	UK	Wire	0.40–0.50 **C**, 0.50–0.70 **Mn**, 0.04 **P**, 0.04 **S**, 0.10–0.35 **Si**, 1.00–1.50 **Cr**, 0.15 min **V**	**Annealed**: all **diam**
AS G18	G18/En 52	Australia	Bar, billet	0.40–0.50 **C**, 0.30–0.60 **Mn**, 0.040 **P**, 0.040 **S**, 3.00–3.75 **Si**, 7.50–9.50 **Cr**, 0.50 **Ni**	
COPANT 332	1144	COPANT	Bar	0.40–0.48 **C**, 1.35–1.65 **Mn**, 0.040 **P**, 0.24–0.33 **S**	**Cold finished and annealed**: (≤15) **diam**, (725) **TS**, (590) **YS**, 12 **El**
ANSI/ASTM A 311	1144	US	Bar	0.40–0.48 **C**, 1.35–1.65 **Mn**, 0.040 **P**, 0.24–0.33 **S**	**Cold drawn and stress relieved**: ≤9/16 (≤14.29) **diam**, 105 (724) **TS**, 85 (586) **YS**, 12 **El**
DGN–B–296	1144	Mexico	Bar	0.40–0.48 **C**, 1.35–1.65 **Mn**, 0.040 **P**, 0.24–0.33 **S**	**Cold finished**: (<14) **diam**, (723) **TS**, (586) **YS**, 12 **El**
BS 970 Part 1	Grade 225M44	UK	Blooms, billets, slabs, bar, rod, forgings	0.40–0.48 **C**, 1.30–1.70 **Mn**, 0.060 **P**, 0.20–0.30 **S**, 0.25 **Si**	**Hardened and tempered**: 4 **diam**, (620) **TS**, (400) **YS**, 16 **El**
BS 970 Part 1	Grade 212M44	UK	Blooms, billets, slabs, bar, rod, forgings	0.40–0.48 **C**, 1.30–1.70 **Mn**, 0.060 **P**, 0.20–0.30 **S**, 0.25 **Si**	**Hardened and tempered**: 4 **diam**, (550) **TS**, (360) **YS**, 18 **El**
ASTM A 108	1144	US	Bar	0.40–0.48 **C**, 1.35–1.65 **Mn**, 0.040 **P**, 0.24–0.33 **S**	
AISI 1144		US	Wire, rod	0.40–0.48 **C**, 1.35–1.65 **Mn**, 0.040 **P**, 0.24–0.33 **S**	
ASTM A 689	1144	US	Bar	0.40–0.48 **C**, 1.35–1.65 **Mn**, 0.040 **P**, 0.24–0.33 **S**	
ANSI/ASTM A 29	1144	US	Bar	0.40–0.48 **C**, 1.35–1.65 **Mn**, 0.040 **P**, 0.24–0.33 **S**	
ANSI/ASTM A 576	1144	US	Bar	0.40–0.48 **C**, 1.35–1.65 **Mn**, 0.040 **P**, 0.24–0.33 **S**	
JIS G 4804	SUM 43	Japan	Bar	0.40–0.48 **C**, 1.35–1.65 **Mn**, 0.040 **P**, 0.24–0.33 **S**	
QQ–S–637A	1144	US	Bar	0.40–0.48 **C**, 1.35–1.65 **Mn**, 0.040 **P**, 0.24–0.33 **S**, 0.15–0.35 **Pb**	
COPANT 331	1144	COPANT	Bar	0.40–0.48 **C**, 1.35–1.65 **Mn**, 0.040 **P**, 0.24–0.33 **S**	
COPANT 330	1144	COPANT	Bar, shapes	0.40–0.48 **C**, 1.35–1.65 **Mn**, 0.040 **P**, 0.24–0.33 **S**	
AMS 6423B		US	Bar, forgings, tube	0.40–0.46 **C**, 0.75–1.00 **Mn**, 0.025 **P**, 0.025 **S**, 0.50–0.80 **Si**, 0.80–1.05 **Cr**, 0.60–0.90 **Ni**, 0.45–0.60 **Mo**, 0.01–0.06 **V**, 0.35 **Cu**	**Cold finished**: ≤0.500 (≤12.70) **diam**, 135 (931) max **TS**
JIS G 4106	SMmC 3	Japan	Bar, wire, rod	0.40–0.46 **C**, 1.35–1.65 **Mn**, 0.030 **P**, 0.030 **S**, 0.15–0.35 **Si**, 0.25 **Ni**, 0.30 **Cu**	**Hot rolled or forged, quenched and tempered**: (25) **diam**, (931) **TS**, (784) **YS**, 13 **El**
JIS G 4106	SMn 3	Japan	Bar, wire, rod	0.40–0.46 **C**, 1.35–1.65 **Mn**, 0.030 **P**, 0.030 **S**, 0.15–0.35 **Si**, 0.25 **Ni**, 0.30 **Cu**	**Hot rolled or forged, quenched and tempered**: (25) **diam**, (784) **TS**, (637) **YS**, 17 **El**
ANSI/ASTM A 646	98BV40	US	Blooms, billets: aircraft quality	0.40–0.46 **C**, 0.75–1.00 **Mn**, 0.025 **P**, 0.025 **S**, 0.50–0.80 **Si**, 0.80–1.05 **Cr**, 0.60–0.90 **Ni**, 0.45–0.60 **Mo**, 0.01–0.06 **V**, 0.0005 min **B**	**Annealed**
AMS 6419B		US	Bar, forgings,tube	0.40–0.45 **C**, 0.60–0.90 **Mn**, 0.010 **P**, 0.010 **S**, 1.45–1.80 **Si**, 0.70–0.95 **Cr**, 1.65–2.00 **Ni**, 0.30–0.50 **Mo**, 0.05–0.10 **V**, 0.35 **Cu**	**Normalized, hardened, quenched and tempered**: all **diam**, 280 (1931) **TS**, 230 (1586) **YS**, 7 **El**; **Cold finished (bar)**: ≤0.500 (≤12.70) **diam**, 130 (896) max **TS**
MIL–S–8844C	Class 3 (300M)	US	Bar, reforging stock, mechanical tube	0.40–0.45 **C**, 0.65–0.90 **Mn**, 0.010 **P**, 0.010 **S**, 1.45–1.80 **Si**, 0.70–0.95 **Cr**, 1.65–2.00 **Ni**, 0.35–0.45 **Mo**, 0.05 min **V**	**Heat treated**: <100 **diam**, (1930) **TS**, (1585) **YS**, 6 **El**

WROUGHT ALLOY STEELS

specification number	designation	country	product forms	composition	mechanical properties (see page iv for explanation)
ANSI/ASTM A 579	32	US	Forgings	0.40–0.45 **C**, 0.65–0.90 **Mn**, 0.025 **P**, 0.025 **S**, 1.45–1.80 **Si**, 0.65–0.90 **Cr**, 1.65–2.00 **Ni**, 0.30–0.45 **Mo**, 0.05 min **V**	**Quenched and tempered:** all **diam**, 250 (1725) **TS**, 225 (1555) **YS**, 6 **El**
AISI 4142		US	Bar	0.40–0.45 **C**, 0.75–1.00 **Mn**, 0.035 **P**, 0.040 **S**, 0.15–0.30 **Si**, 0.80–1.10 **Cr**, 0.15–0.25 **Mo**	
AISI 8642		US	Bar	0.40–0.45 **C**, 0.75–1.00 **Mn**, 0.035 **P**, 0.040 **S**, 0.15–0.30 **Si**, 0.40–0.60 **Cr**, 0.40–0.70 **Ni**, 0.15–0.25 **Mo**	
BS 970 Part 2	Grade 503A 42	UK	Blooms, billets, bar, forgings	0.40–0.45 **C**, 0.70–1.00 **Mn**, 0.70–1.00 **Ni**	
BS 970 Part 2	Grade 708 A 42	UK	Blooms, billets, bar, forgings	0.40–0.45 **C**, 0.70–1.00 **Mn**, 0.90–1.20 **Cr**, 0.15–0.25 **Mo**	
ASTM A 547	Grade 4142	US	Wire	0.40–0.45 **C**, 0.75–1.00 **Mn**, 0.80–1.10 **Cr**, 0.15–0.25 **Mo**	
ASTM A 547	Grade 8642	US	Wire	0.40–0.45 **C**, 0.75–1.00 **Mn**, 0.40–0.60 **Cr**, 0.40–0.70 **Ni**, 0.15–0.25 **Mo**	
AS G18	G18/En 19C	Australia	Bar, billet	0.40–0.45 **C**, 0.50–0.80 **Mn**, 0.050 **P**, 0.050 **S**, 0.10–0.35 **Si**, 0.90–1.20 **Cr**, 0.20–0.35 **Mo**	
DGN-B-203	Grade 4042	Mexico	Tube: seamless	0.40–0.45 **C**, 0.70–0.90 **Mn**, 0.040 **P**, 0.040 **S**, 0.20–0.35 **Si**, 0.20–0.30 **Mo**	
DGN-B-203	Grade 8742	Mexico	Tube: seamless	0.40–0.45 **C**, 0.75–1.00 **Mn**, 0.040 **P**, 0.040 **S**, 0.20–0.35 **Si**, 0.40–0.60 **Cr**, 0.40–0.70 **Ni**, 0.20–0.30 **Mo**	
DGN-B-203	Grade 8642	Mexico	Tube: seamless	0.40–0.45 **C**, 0.75–1.00 **Mn**, 0.040 **P**, 0.040 **S**, 0.20–0.35 **Si**, 0.40–0.60 **Cr**, 0.40–0.70 **Ni**, 0.15–0.25 **Mo**	
COPANT 514	4142	COPANT	Tube	0.40–0.45 **C**, 0.75–1.0 **Mn**, 0.040 **P**, 0.040 **S**, 0.20–0.35 **Si**, 0.80–1.10 **Cr**, 0.15–0.25 **Mo**	
COPANT 514	4042	COPANT	Tube	0.40–0.45 **C**, 0.70–0.90 **Mn**, 0.040 **P**, 0.040 **S**, 0.20–0.35 **Si**, 0.20–0.30 **Mo**	
DGN-B-300	8642	Mexico	Bar	0.40–0.45 **C**, 0.75–1.00 **Mn**, 0.035 **P**, 0.040 **S**, 0.20–0.35 **Si**, 0.40–0.60 **Cr**, 0.40–0.70 **Ni**, 0.15–0.25 **Mo**	**Annealed**
DGN-B-300	4142	Mexico	Bar	0.40–0.45 **C**, 0.75–1.00 **Mn**, 0.035 **P**, 0.040 **S**, 0.20–0.35 **Si**, 0.80–1.10 **Cr**, 0.15–0.25 **Mo**	**Annealed**
ANSI/ASTM A 29	4042	US	Bar	0.40–0.45 **C**, 0.70–0.90 **Mn**, 0.035 **P**, 0.040 **S**, 0.15–0.30 **Si**, 0.20–0.30 **Mo**	
ANSI/ASTM A 29	4142	US	Bar	0.40–0.45 **C**, 0.75–1.00 **Mn**, 0.035 **P**, 0.040 **S**, 0.15–0.30 **Si**, 0.80–1.10 **Cr**, 0.15–0.25 **Mo**	
ASTM A 689	8642	US	Bar	0.40–0.45 **C**, 0.75–1.00 **Mn**, 0.035 **P**, 0.040 **S**, 0.15–0.30 **Si**, 0.40–0.60 **Cr**, 0.40–0.70 **Ni**, 0.15–0.25 **Mo**	
ASTM A 689	4142	US	Bar	0.40–0.45 **C**, 0.75–1.00 **Mn**, 0.035 **P**, 0.040 **S**, 0.15–0.30 **Si**, 0.80–1.10 **Cr**, 0.15–0.25 **Mo**	
ANSI/ASTM A 322	4142	US	Bar	0.40–0.45 **C**, 0.75–1.00 **Mn**, 0.035 **P**, 0.040 **S**, 0.15–0.30 **Si**, 0.80–1.10 **Cr**, 0.15–0.25 **Mo**	
ANSI/ASTM A 322	8642	US	Bar	0.40–0.45 **C**, 0.75–1.00 **Mn**, 0.035 **P**, 0.040 **S**, 0.15–0.30 **Si**, 0.40–0.60 **Cr**, 0.40–0.70 **Ni**, 0.15–0.25 **Mo**	
ANSI/ASTM A 29	8642	US	Bar	0.40–0.45 **C**, 0.75–1.00 **Mn**, 0.035 **P**, 0.040 **S**, 0.15–0.30 **Si**, 0.40–0.60 **Cr**, 0.40–0.70 **Ni**, 0.15–0.25 **Mo**	

specification number	designation	country	product forms	composition	mechanical properties (see page iv for explanation)
AISI 8642		US	Wire, rod	0.40–0.45 **C**, 0.75–1.00 **Mn**, 0.035 **P**, 0.040 **S**, 0.15–0.30 **Si**, 0.40–0.60 **Cr**, 0.40–0.70 **Ni**, 0.15–0.25 **Mo**	
AISI 4142		US	Wire, rod	0.40–0.45 **C**, 0.75–1.00 **Mn**, 0.035 **P**, 0.040 **S**, 0.15–0.30 **Si**, 0.80–1.10 **Cr**, 0.15–0.25 **Mo**	
ANSI/ASTM A 519	4042	US	Tube: seamless	0.40–0.45 **C**, 0.70–0.90 **Mn**, 0.040 **P**, 0.040 **S**, 0.15–0.35 **Si**, 0.20–0.30 **Mo**	
ANSI/ASTM A 519	4142	US	Tube: seamless	0.40–0.45 **C**, 0.75–1.00 **Mn**, 0.040 **P**, 0.040 **S**, 0.15–0.35 **Si**, 0.80–1.10 **Cr**, 0.15–0.25 **Mo**	
ANSI/ASTM A 519	8642	US	Tube: seamless	0.40–0.45 **C**, 0.75–1.00 **Mn**, 0.040 **P**, 0.040 **S**, 0.15–0.35 **Si**, 0.40–0.60 **Cr**, 0.40–0.70 **Ni**, 0.15–0.25 **Mo**	
ANSI/ASTM A 519	8742	US	Tube: seamless	0.40–0.45 **C**, 0.75–1.00 **Mn**, 0.040 **P**, 0.040 **S**, 0.15–0.35 **Si**, 0.40–0.60 **Cr**, 0.40–0.70 **Ni**, 0.20–0.30 **Mo**	
AISI 4142		US	Sheet, strip	0.40–0.45 **C**, 0.75–1.00 **Mn**, 0.035 **P**, 0.040 **S**, 0.20–0.35 **Si**, 0.80–1.10 **Cr**, 0.15–0.25 **Mo**	
DGN-B-297	8642	Mexico	Bar	0.40–0.45 **C**, 0.75–1.0 **Mn**, 0.035 **P**, 0.040 **S**, 0.20–0.35 **Si**, 0.40–0.60 **Cr**, 0.40–0.70 **Ni**, 0.15–0.25 **Mo**	
DGN-B-297	4142	Mexico	Bar	0.40–0.45 **C**, 0.75–1.00 **Mn**, 0.035 **P**, 0.040 **S**, 0.20–0.35 **Si**, 0.80–1.10 **Cr**, 0.15–0.25 **Mo**	
COPANT 514	Grade 8642	COPANT	Tube: seamless	0.40–0.45 **C**, 0.75–1.00 **Mn**, 0.040 **P**, 0.050 **S**, 0.10 **Si**, 0.40–0.60 **Cr**, 0.40–0.70 **Ni**, 0.15–0.25 **Mo**	
COPANT 514	Grade 8742	COPANT	Tube: seamless	0.40–0.45 **C**, 0.75–1.00 **Mn**, 0.040 **P**, 0.050 **S**, 0.10 **Si**, 0.40–0.60 **Cr**, 0.40–0.70 **Ni**, 0.20–0.30 **Mo**	
ANSI/ASTM A 723	Grade 2, class 5	US	Forgings	0.40 **C**, 0.90 **Mn**, 0.015 **P**, 0.015 **S**, 0.35 **Si**, 0.80–2.00 **Cr**, 2.25–3.25 **Ni**, 0.30–0.50 **Mo**, 0.20 **V**	**Normalized or quenched and tempered**: all **diam**, (1310) **TS**, (1240) **YS**, **El**
ANSI/ASTM A 723	Grade 3, class 5	US	Forgings	0.40 **C**, 0.90 **Mn**, 0.015 **P**, 0.015 **S**, 0.35 **Si**, 0.80–2.00 **Cr**, 3.25–4.50 **Ni**, 0.40–0.80 **Mo**, 0.20 **V**	**Normalized or quenched and tempered**: all **diam**, (1310) **TS**, (1240) **YS**, **El**
ASTM A 723	Grade 3, class 5	US	Forgings	0.40 **C**, 0.90 **Mn**, 0.015 **P**, 0.015 **S**, 0.35 **Si**, 0.80–2.00 **Cr**, 3.25–4.50 **Ni**, 0.40–0.80 **Mo**, 0.20 **V**	**Normalized, quenched and tempered**: ≤4 (≤102) **diam**, 190 (1310) **TS**, 18 (1240) **YS**, 10 **El**
ASTM A 723	Grade 2, class 5	US	Forgings	0.40 **C**, 0.90 **Mn**, 0.015 **P**, 0.015 **S**, 0.35 **Si**, 0.80–2.00 **Cr**, 2.25–3.25 **Ni**, 0.30–0.50 **Mo**, 0.20 **V**	**Normalized, quenched and tempered**: ≤4 (≤102) **diam**, 190 (1310) **TS**, 180 (1240) **YS**, 10 **El**
ANSI/ASTM A 723	Grade 2, class 4	US	Forgings	0.40 **C**, 0.90 **Mn**, 0.015 **P**, 0.015 **S**, 0.35 **Si**, 0.80–2.00 **Cr**, 2.25–3.25 **Ni**, 0.30–0.50 **Mo**, 0.20 **V**	**Normalized or quenched and tempered**: all **diam**, (1205) **TS**, (1105) **YS**, 12 **El**
ANSI/ASTM A 723	Grade 3, class 4	US	Forgings	0.40 **C**, 0.90 **Mn**, 0.015 **P**, 0.015 **S**, 0.35 **Si**, 0.80–2.00 **Cr**, 3.25–4.50 **Ni**, 0.40–0.80 **Mo**, 0.20 **V**	**Normalized or quenched and tempered**: all **diam**, (1205) **TS**, (1105) **YS**, 12 **El**
ASTM A 723	Grade 3, class 4	US	Forgings	0.40 **C**, 0.90 **Mn**, 0.015 **P**, 0.015 **S**, 0.35 **Si**, 0.80–2.00 **Cr**, 3.25–4.50 **Ni**, 0.40–0.80 **Mo**, 0.20 **V**	**Normalized, quenched and tempered**: ≤6 (≤152) **diam**, 175 (1205) **TS**, 160 (1105) **YS**, 12 **El**
ASTM A 723	Grade 2, class 4	US	Forgings	0.40 **C**, 0.90 **Mn**, 0.015 **P**, 0.015 **S**, 0.35 **Si**, 0.80–2.00 **Cr**, 2.25–3.25 **Ni**, 0.30–0.50 **Mo**, 0.20 **V**	**Normalized, quenched and tempered**: ≤6 (≤152) **diam**, 175 (1205) **TS**, 160 (1105) **YS**, 12 **El**

WROUGHT ALLOY STEELS

specification number	designation	country	product forms	composition	mechanical properties (see page iv for explanation)
ANSI/ASTM A 723	Grade 2, class 3	US	Forgings	0.40 **C**, 0.90 **Mn**, 0.015 **P**, 0.015 **S**, 0.35 **Si**, 0.80–2.00 **Cr**, 2.25–3.25 **Ni**, 0.30–0.50 **Mo**, 0.20 **V**	**Normalized or quenched and tempered**: all **diam**, (1070) **TS**, (965) **YS**, 13 **El**
ANSI/ASTM A 723	Grade 3, class 3	US	Forgings	0.40 **C**, 0.90 **Mn**, 0.015 **P**, 0.015 **S**, 0.35 **Si**, 0.80–2.00 **Cr**, 3.25–4.50 **Ni**, 0.40–0.80 **Mo**, 0.20 **V**	**Normalized or quenched and tempered**: all **diam**, (1070) **TS**, (965) **YS**, 13 **El**
ASTM A 723	Grade 3, class 3	US	Forgings	0.40 **C**, 0.90 **Mn**, 0.015 **P**, 0.015 **S**, 0.35 **Si**, 0.80–2.00 **Cr**, 3.25–4.50 **Ni**, 0.40–0.80 **Mo**, 0.20 **V**	**Normalized, quenched and tempered**: ≤10 (≤254) **diam**, 155 (1070) **TS**, 140 (965) **YS**, 13 **El**
ASTM A 723	Grade 2, class 3	US	Forgings	0.40 **C**, 0.90 **Mn**, 0.015 **P**, 0.015 **S**, 0.35 **Si**, 0.80–2.00 **Cr**, 2.25–3.25 **Ni**, 0.30–0.50 **Mo**, 0.20 **V**	**Normalized, quenched and tempered**: ≤10 (≤254) **diam**, 155 (1070) **TS**, 140 (965) **YS**, 13 **El**
ANSI/ASTM A 723	Grade 2, class 2	US	Forgings	0.40 **C**, 0.90 **Mn**, 0.015 **P**, 0.015 **S**, 0.35 **Si**, 0.80–2.00 **Cr**, 2.25–3.25 **Ni**, 0.30–0.50 **Mo**, 0.20 **V**	**Normalized or quenched and tempered**: all **diam**, (930) **TS**, (825) **YS**, 14 **El**
ANSI/ASTM A 723	Grade 3, class 2	US	Forgings	0.40 **C**, 0.90 **Mn**, 0.015 **P**, 0.015 **S**, 0.35 **Si**, 0.80–2.00 **Cr**, 3.25–4.50 **Ni**, 0.40–0.80 **Mo**, 0.20 **V**	**Normalized or quenched and tempered**: all **diam**, (930) **TS**, (825) **YS**, 14 **El**
ASTM A 723	Grade 3, class 2	US	Forgings	0.40 **C**, 0.90 **Mn**, 0.015 **P**, 0.015 **S**, 0.35 **Si**, 0.80–2.00 **Cr**, 3.25–4.50 **Ni**, 0.40–0.80 **Mo**, 0.20 **V**	**Normalized, quenched and tempered**: all **diam**, 135 (930) **TS**, 120 (825) **YS**, 14 **El**
ASTM A 723	Grade 2, class 2	US	Forgings	0.40 **C**, 0.90 **Mn**, 0.015 **P**, 0.015 **S**, 0.35 **Si**, 0.80–2.00 **Cr**, 2.25–3.25 **Ni**, 0.30–0.50 **Mo**, 0.20 **V**	**Normalized, quenched and tempered**: all **diam**, 135 (930) **TS**, 120 (825) **YS**, 14 **El**
ANSI/ASTM A 723	Grade 2, class 1	US	Forgings	0.40 **C**, 0.90 **Mn**, 0.015 **P**, 0.015 **S**, 0.35 **Si**, 0.80–2.00 **Cr**, 2.25–3.25 **Ni**, 0.30–0.50 **Mo**, 0.20 **V**	**Normalized or quenched and tempered**: all **diam**, (795) **TS**, (690) **YS**, 16 **El**
ANSI/ASTM A 723	Grade 3, class 1	US	Forgings	0.40 **C**, 0.90 **Mn**, 0.015 **P**, 0.015 **S**, 0.35 **Si**, 0.80–2.00 **Cr**, 3.25–4.50 **Ni**, 0.40–0.80 **Mo**, 0.20 **V**	**Normalized or quenched and tempered**: all **diam**, (795) **TS**, (690) **YS**, 16 **El**
ASTM A 723	Grade 3, class 1	US	Forgings	0.40 **C**, 0.90 **Mn**, 0.015 **P**, 0.015 **S**, 0.35 **Si**, 0.80–2.00 **Cr**, 3.25–4.50 **Ni**, 0.40–0.80 **Mo**, 0.20 **V**	**Normalized, quenched and tempered**: all **diam**, 115 (795) **TS**, 100 (690) **YS**, 16 **El**
ASTM A 723	Grade 2, class 1	US	Forgings	0.40 **C**, 0.90 **Mn**, 0.015 **P**, 0.015 **S**, 0.35 **Si**, 0.80–2.00 **Cr**, 2.25–3.25 **Ni**, 0.30–0.50 **Mo**, 0.20 **V**	**Normalized, quenched and tempered**: all **diam**, 115 (795) **TS**, 100 (690) **YS**, 16 **El**
API Spec 5AC	L–80	US	Casing, tube	0.40 **C**, 1.90 **Mn**, 0.040 **P**, 0.060 **S**, 0.35 **Si**, 0.25 **Ni**, 0.35 **Cu**	**Quenched and tempered**: all **diam**, 95 (657) **TS**, 80 (549) **YS**
MIL–S–24093	Type III, class E	US	Forgings	0.40 **C**, 0.85 **Mn**, 0.040 **P**, 0.040 **S**, 0.20–0.35 **Si**, 3.75 **Ni**	**Normalized and tempered or quenched and tempered**: 10 **diam**, 95 (655) **TS**, 65 (448) **YS**, 20 **El**
MIL–S–24093	Type III, class F	US	Forgings	0.40 **C**, 0.85 **Mn**, 0.040 **P**, 0.040 **S**, 0.20–0.35 **Si**, 3.75 **Ni**	**Normalized and tempered or quenched and tempered**: all **diam**, 90 (621) max **TS**, 45 (310) **YS**, 22 **El**
NF A 35–564	42 C 2 FF, 42 C 4 FF	France	Bar, wire, rod	0.40 **C**, 0.030 **P**, 0.030 **S**, 0.30 **Si**, 0.020 **Al**	**Annealed**: (≤70) **diam**, (610) max **TS**
ANSI/ASTM A 540	B22	US	Bar, tube: seamless	0.39–0.46 **C**, 0.65–1.10 **Mn**, 0.025 **P**, 0.025 **S**, 0.15–0.35 **Si**, 0.75–1.20 **Cr**, 0.15–0.25 **Mo**	**Annealed or quenched, tempered**: 2–4 (50.8–101.6) **diam**, 115 (793) **TS**, 100 (689) **YS**, 15 **El**
BS 970 Part 2	Grade 503 H 42	UK	Blooms, billets, bar, forgings	0.39–0.46 **C**, 0.65–1.05 **Mn**, 0.10–0.35 **Si**, 0.65–1.05 **Ni**	
BS 970 Part 2	Grade 708 H 42	UK	Blooms, billets, bar, forgings	0.39–0.46 **C**, 0.65–1.05 **Mn**, 0.10–0.35 **Si**, 0.80–1.25 **Cr**, 0.15–0.25 **Mo**	
ASTM A 547	Grade 4142H	US	Wire	0.39–0.46 **C**, 0.65–1.10 **Mn**, 0.75–1.20 **Cr**, 0.15–0.25 **Mo**	
ASTM A 547	Grade 8642H	US	Wire	0.39–0.46 **C**, 0.70–1.05 **Mn**, 0.35–0.65 **Cr**, 0.35–0.75 **Ni**, 0.15–0.25 **Mo**	

WROUGHT ALLOY STEELS

specification number	designation	country	product forms	composition	mechanical properties (see page iv for explanation)
DGN–B–300	4142 H	Mexico	Bar	0.39–0.46 **C**, 0.65–1.10 **Mn**, 0.040 **P**, 0.035 **S**, 0.20–0.35 **Si**, 0.75–1.20 **Cr**, 0.15–0.25 **Mo**	**Annealed**
DGN–B–300	4042 H	Mexico	Bar	0.39–0.46 **C**, 0.60–1.00 **Mn**, 0.040 **P**, 0.035 **S**, 0.20–0.35 **Si**, 0.20–0.30 **Mo**	
DGN–B–300	8642 H	Mexico	Bar	0.39–0.46 **C**, 0.70–1.05 **Mn**, 0.040 **P**, 0.035 **S**, 0.20–0.35 **Si**, 0.35–0.65 **Cr**, 0.35–0.75 **Ni**, 0.15–0.25 **Mo**	**Annealed**
ASTM A 689	4142 H	US	Bar	0.39–0.46 **C**, 0.65–1.10 **Mn**, 0.040 **P**, 0.040 **S**, 0.15–0.30 **Si**, 0.75–1.20 **Cr**, 0.15–0.25 **Mo**	
ASTM A 689	4042 H	US	Bar	0.39–0.46 **C**, 0.60–1.00 **Mn**, 0.040 **P**, 0.040 **S**, 0.15–0.30 **Si**, 0.20–0.30 **Mo**	
ASTM A 689	8642 H	US	Bar	0.39–0.46 **C**, 0.70–1.05 **Mn**, 0.040 **P**, 0.040 **S**, 0.15–0.30 **Si**, 0.35–0.65 **Cr**, 0.35–0.75 **Ni**, 0.15–0.25 **Mo**	
ANSI/ASTM A 304	8642 H	US	Bar	0.39–0.46 **C**, 0.70–1.05 **Mn**, 0.040 **P**, 0.040 **S**, 0.15–0.30 **Si**, 0.35–0.65 **Cr**, 0.35–0.75 **Ni**, 0.15–0.25 **Mo**	
ANSI/ASTM A 304	4142 H	US	Bar	0.39–0.46 **C**, 0.65–1.10 **Mn**, 0.040 **P**, 0.040 **S**, 0.15–0.30 **Si**, 0.75–1.20 **Cr**, 0.15–0.25 **Mo**	
ANSI/ASTM A 304	4042 H	US	Bar	0.39–0.46 **C**, 0.60–1.00 **Mn**, 0.040 **P**, 0.040 **S**, 0.15–0.30 **Si**, 0.20–0.30 **Mo**	
AISI 8642 H		US	Wire, rod	0.39–0.46 **C**, 0.70–1.05 **Mn**, 0.15–0.30 **Si**, 0.35–0.65 **Cr**, 0.35–0.75 **Ni**, 0.15–0.25 **Mo**	
AISI 4142 H		US	Wire, rod	0.39–0.46 **C**, 0.65–1.10 **Mn**, 0.15–0.30 **Si**, 0.75–1.20 **Cr**, 0.15–0.25 **Mo**	
AISI 8642H		US	Bar	0.39–0.46 **C**, 0.70–1.05 **Mn**, 0.035 **P**, 0.040 **S**, 0.15–0.30 **Si**, 0.35–0.65 **Cr**, 0.35–0.75 **Ni**, 0.15–0.25 **Mo**	
AISI 4142H		US	Bar	0.39–0.46 **C**, 0.65–1.10 **Mn**, 0.035 **P**, 0.040 **S**, 0.15–0.30 **Si**, 0.75–1.20 **Cr**, 0.15–0.25 **Mo**	
AISI 4042H		US	Bar	0.39–0.46 **C**, 0.60–1.00 **Mn**, 0.035 **P**, 0.040 **S**, 0.15–0.30 **Si**, 0.20–0.30 **Mo**	
JIS G 4052	SMn 3H	Japan	Bar, wire, rod	0.39–0.46 **C**, 1.30–1.70 **Mn**, 0.030 **P**, 0.030 **S**, 0.15–0.35 **Si**, 0.30 **Cu**	**Hot rolled, normalized, quenched**
JIS G 4052	SMnC 3H	Japan	Bar, wire, rod	0.39–0.46 **C**, 1.30–1.70 **Mn**, 0.030 **P**, 0.030 **S**, 0.15–0.35 **Si**, 0.35–0.70 **Cr**, 0.30 **Cu**	**Hot rolled, normalized, quenched**
BS S.155	S155A	UK	Forging stock, billets, bar: aircraft quality	0.39–0.44 **C**, 0.60–0.90 **Mn**, 0.015 **P**, 0.015 **S**, 1.50–1.80 **Si**, 0.70–0.95 **Cr**, 1.65–2.00 **Ni**, 0.30–0.45 **Mo**, 0.05–0.10 **V**, 0.025 **P+S**	**Normalized, annealed, austenitized, quenched and tempered**: all **diam**, (1900) **TS**, (1550) **YS**, 8 **El**
BS S.155	S155C	UK	Forgings: aircraft quality	0.39–0.44 **C**, 0.60–0.90 **Mn**, 0.015 **P**, 0.015 **S**, 1.50–1.80 **Si**, 0.70–0.95 **Cr**, 1.65–2.00 **Ni**, 0.30–0.45 **Mo**, 0.05–0.10 **V**, 0.025 **P+S**	**Normalized, annealed, austenitized, quenched and tempered**: all **diam**, (1900) **TS**, (1550) **YS**, 8 **El**
BS S.155	S155B	UK	Bar: black, aircraft quality	0.39–0.44 **C**, 0.60–0.90 **Mn**, 0.015 **P**, 0.015 **S**, 1.50–1.80 **Si**, 0.70–0.95 **Cr**, 1.65–2.00 **Ni**, 0.30–0.45 **Mo**, 0.05–0.10 **V**, 0.025 **P+S**	**Normalized, annealed, austenitized, quenched and tempered**: all **diam**, (1900) **TS**, (1550) **YS**, 8 **El**
ANSI/ASTM A 193	Grade B7	US	Bar	0.38–0.48 **C**, 0.75–1.00 **Mn**, 0.04 **P**, 0.04 **S**, 0.15–0.35 **Si**, 0.80–1.10 **Cr**, 0.15–0.25 **Mo**	**Quenched and tempered or normalized and tempered:** $\geq$2.5 ($\geq$63.5) **diam**, 125 (862) **TS**, 105 (724) **YS**, 16 **El**

specification number	designation	country	product forms	composition	mechanical properties (see page iv for explanation)
ASTM A 320	L 7 AISI 4140, 4142, or 4145	US	Bar	0.38–0.48 **C**, 0.75–1.00 **Mn**, 0.040 **P**, 0.040 **S**, 0.20–0.35 **Si**, 0.80–1.10 **Cr**, 0.15–0.25 **Mo**	**Quenched, tempered:** ≥2.5 (≥63.5) **diam**, 125 (862) **TS**, 105 (724) **YS**, 16 **El**
API Spec 5AC	C–75 Type 3	US	Casing, tube	0.38–0.48 **C**, 0.75–1.00 **Mn**, 0.040 **P**, 0.040 **S**, 0.80–1.10 **Cr**, 0.15–0.25 **Mo**	**Normalized and tempered:** all **diam**, 95 (657) **TS**, 75 (519) **YS**
DIN 1654	Grade 42 CrV 6	Germany	Rod	0.38–0.46 **C**, 0.50–0.80 **Mn**, 0.035 **P**, 0.035 **S**, 0.15–0.35 **Si**, 1.4–1.7 **Cr**, 0.07–0.12 **V**	**Drawn:** all **diam**, (687) **TS**
AISI 4142		US	Plate	0.38–0.46 **C**, 0.70–1.00 **Mn**, 0.035 **P**, 0.040 **S**, 0.15–0.30 **Si**, 0.80–1.15 **Cr**, 0.15–0.25 **Mo**	
AISI 8742		US	Plate	0.38–0.46 **C**, 0.70–1.00 **Mn**, 0.035 **P**, 0.040 **S**, 0.15–0.30 **Si**, 0.35–0.60 **Cr**, 0.40–0.70 **Ni**, 0.20–0.30 **Mo**	
EURONORM 119–74, IV	42 CrMo 4 KD	EURONORM	Wire, rod	0.38–0.45 **C**, 0.50–0.80 **Mn**, 0.035 **P**, 0.035 **S**, 0.15–0.40 **Si**, 0.90–1.20 **Cr**, 0.15–0.30 **Mo**	**Quenched and tempered:** (≤16) **diam**, (1080) **TS**, (885) **YS**, 10 **El**
SIS 14 22 44	SIS 2244–06	Sweden	Bar, forgings, tube	0.38–0.45 **C**, 0.60–0.90 **Mn**, 0.035 **P**, 0.035 **S**, 0.15–0.40 **Si**, 0.90–1.20 **Cr**, 0.15–0.30 **Mo**	**Quenched and tempered:** all **diam**, (1080) **TS**, (880) **YS**, 10 **El**
ISO R 683/IV	Type 3a	ISO	Bar, billets, rod	0.38–0.45 **C**, 0.50–1.0 **Mn**, 0.035 **P**, 0.020–0.035 **S**, 0.15–0.40 **Si**, 0.90–1.20 **Cr**, 0.15–0.30 **Mo**	**Quenched and tempered:** (≤16) **diam**, (1079) **TS**, (882) **YS**, 10 **El**
ISO R 683/IV	Type 3b	ISO	Bar, billets, rod	0.38–0.45 **C**, 0.50–1.0 **Mn**, 0.035 **P**, 0.030–0.050 **S**, 0.15–0.40 **Si**, 0.90–1.20 **Cr**, 0.15–0.30 **Mo**	**Quenched and tempered:** (≤16) **diam**, (1079) **TS**, (882) **YS**, 10 **El**
DIN 17200	Grade 42 CrMoS 4	Germany	Blooms, slabs, billets, wire, bar, plate, sheet, strip, tube, forgings	0.38–0.45 **C**, 0.50–0.80 **Mn**, 0.035 **P**, 0.020–0.035 **S**, 0.15–0.40 **Si**, 0.90–1.20 **Cr**, 0.15–0.30 **Mo**	**Quenched and tempered:** (≤16) **diam**, (1079) **TS**, (883) **YS**, 10 **El**
DIN 17200	Grade 42 CrMo 4	Germany	Blooms, slabs, billets, wire, bar, plate, sheet, strip, tube, forgings	0.38–0.45 **C**, 0.50–0.80 **Mn**, 0.035 **P**, 0.035 **S**, 0.15–0.40 **Si**, 0.90–1.20 **Cr**, 0.15–0.30 **Mo**	**Quenched and tempered:** (≤16) **diam**, (1079) **TS**, (883) **YS**, 10 **El**
ISO R 683/II	Type 3	ISO	Bar, billets, rod	0.38–0.45 **C**, 0.50–1.00 **Mn**, 0.035 **P**, 0.035 **S**	**Quenched and tempered:** (≤16) **diam**, (1078) **TS**, (882) **YS**, 10 **El**
AMS 6378A		US	Bar	0.38–0.45 **C**, 0.75–1.00 **Mn**, 0.040 **P**, 0.040 **S**, 0.20–0.35 **Si**, 0.80–1.10 **Cr**, 0.25 **Ni**, 0.15–0.25 **Mo**, 0.35 **Cu**, 0.035–0.060 **Te**	**Die–drawn and tempered:** 1.50 (38.1) **diam**, 150 (1034) **TS**, 130 (896) **YS**, 5 **El**
ISO/R 683/VII	Type 3	ISO	Bar, billets, rod	0.38–0.45 **C**, 0.60–0.90 **Mn**, 0.035 **P**, 0.035 **S**, 0.15–0.40 **Si**, 0.90–1.20 **Cr**	**Quenched and tempered:** (≤16) **diam**, (980) **TS**, (784) **YS**, 11 **El**
ISO/R 683/VII	Type 3a	ISO	Bar, billets, rod	0.38–0.45 **C**, 0.60–0.90 **Mn**, 0.035 **P**, 0.020–0.035 **S**, 0.15–0.40 **Si**, 0.90–1.20 **Cr**	**Quenched and tempered:** (≤16) **diam**, (980) **TS**, (784) **YS**, 11 **El**
ISO/R 683/VII	Type 3b	ISO	Bar, billets, rod	0.38–0.45 **C**, 0.60–0.90 **Mn**, 0.035 **P**, 0.030–0.050 **S**, 0.15–0.40 **Si**, 0.90–1.20 **Cr**	**Quenched and tempered:** (≤16) **diam**, (980) **TS**, (784) **YS**, 11 **El**
EURONORM 119–74, IV	41 Cr 4 KD	EURONORM	Wire, rod	0.38–0.45 **C**, 0.50–0.80 **Mn**, 0.035 **P**, 0.035 **S**, 0.15–0.40 **Si**, 0.90–1.20 **Cr**	**Quenched and tempered:** (≤16) **diam**, (980) **TS**, (785) **YS**, 11 **El**
DIN 17200	Grade 41 Cr 4	Germany	Blooms, slabs, billets, wire, bar, plate, sheet, strip, tube, forgings	0.38–0.45 **C**, 0.50–0.80 **Mn**, 0.035 **P**, 0.035 **S**, 0.15–0.40 **Si**, 0.90–1.20 **Cr**	**Quenched and tempered:** (≤16) **diam**, (980) **TS**, (795) **YS**, 11 **El**
DIN 17200	Grade 41 CrS 4	Germany	Blooms, slabs, billets, wire, bar, plate, sheet, strip, tube, forgings	0.38–0.45 **C**, 0.50–0.80 **Mn**, 0.035 **P**, 0.020–0.035 **S**, 0.15–0.40 **Si**, 0.90–1.20 **Cr**	**Quenched and tempered:** (≤16) **diam**, (980) **TS**, (795) **YS**, 11 **El**
DIN 17211	Grade 41 CrAlMo 7	Germany	Blooms, slabs, billets, wire, bar, plate, sheet, strip, tube, forgings	0.38–0.45 **C**, 0.50–0.80 **Mn**, 0.030 **P**, 0.035 **S**, 0.20–0.50 **Si**, 1.50–1.80 **Cr**, 0.25–0.40 **Mo**, 1.50–1.80 **Al**	**Soft annealed and quenched and tempered:** (≤100) **diam**, (931) **TS**, (736) **YS**, 12 **El**

WROUGHT ALLOY STEELS

specification number	designation	country	product forms	composition	mechanical properties (see page iv for explanation)
AIR 9160/C 91	9160C341	France	Bar, forgings	0.38–0.45 **C**, 0.50–0.80 **Mn**, 0.025 **P**, 0.020 **S**, 0.10–0.40 **Si**, 1.5–1.80 **Cr**, 0.30 **Ni**, 0.20–0.40 **Mo**, 0.80–1.30 **Al**	**Quenched, tempered at 640°C and nitrided: (≤80) diam, (930) TS, (780) YS, (12) El; Quenched, tempered at 560°C and nitrided: (≤80) diam, (1080) TS, (830) YS, (10) El**
MIL–S–869C	Class A (135M)	US	Bar, billets, forgings	0.38–0.45 **C**, 0.40–0.70 **Mn**, 0.040 **P**, 0.040 **S**, 0.20–0.40 **Si**, 1.35–1.85 **Cr**, 0.30–0.45 **Mo**, 0.85–1.20 **Al**	**Quenched and tempered (bar and forgings):** ≤11/2 **diam**, 135 (930) **TS**, 100 (690) **YS**, 16 **El**
ISO 683/X	4	ISO	Bar	0.38–0.45 **C**, 0.50–0.80 **Mn**, 0.030 **P**, 0.035 **S**, 0.20–0.50 **Si**, 1.50–1.80 **Cr**, 0.25–0.40 **Mo**, 0.80–1.20 **Al**	**Nitrided:** (100) **diam**, (930) **TS**, (740) **YS**, 12 **El**
SIS 14 22 44	SIS 2244–05	Sweden	Bar, forgings	0.38–0.45 **C**, 0.60–0.90 **Mn**, 0.035 **P**, 0.035 **S**, 0.15–0.40 **Si**, 0.90–1.20 **Cr**, 0.15–0.30 **Mo**	**Quenched and tempered:** (100) **diam**, (880) **TS**, (690) **YS**, 12 **El**
MIL–S–6049A	AISI 8740	US	Bar	0.38–0.45 **C**, 0.75–1.0 **Mn**, 0.025 **P**, 0.025 **S**, 0.20–0.35 **Si**, 0.40–0.60 **Cr**, 0.40–0.70 **Ni**, 0.20–0.30 **Mo**, 0.35 **Cu**	**Quenched and tempered:** all **diam**, 125 (862) **TS**, 103 (710) **YS**, 17 **El**
SIS 14 29 40	SIS 2940–03	Sweden	Bar, forgings	0.38–0.45 **C**, 0.50–0.80 **Mn**, 0.030 **P**, 0.035 **S**, 0.20–0.50 **Si**, 1.5–1.8 **Cr**, 0.25–0.35 **Mo**, 0.90–1.20 **Al**	**Quenched and tempered:** (≤160) **diam**, (850) **TS**, (650) **YS**, 14 **El**
EURONORM 119–74, IV	41 Cr 2 KD	EURONORM	Wire, rod	0.38–0.45 **C**, 0.50–0.80 **Mn**, 0.035 **P**, 0.035 **S**, 0.15–0.40 **Si**, 0.40–0.60 **Cr**	**Quenched and tempered:** (≤16) **diam**, (830) **TS**, (590) **YS**, 13 **El**
SFS 460	Co. 42 Cr 1.1 Mo 0.20	Finland	Bar, forgings	0.38–0.45 **C**, 0.60–0.90 **Mn**, 0.035 **P**, 0.035 **S**, 0.15–0.40 **Si**, 0.90–1.20 **Cr**, 0.15–0.25 **Mo**	**Quenched and tempered:** (160) **diam**, (780) **TS**, (590) **YS**, 14 **El**
SIS 14 22 4	SIS 2244–04	Sweden	Forgings, tube	0.38–0.45 **C**, 0.60–0.90 **Mn**, 0.035 **P**, 0.035 **S**, 0.15–0.40 **Si**, 0.90–1.20 **Cr**, 0.15–0.30 **Mo**	**As rolled or as forged:** (160) **diam**, (780) **TS**, (590) **YS**, 14 **El**
DIN 1654	Grade 42 CrMo 4	Germany	Rod	0.38–0.45 **C**, 0.50–0.80 **Mn**, 0.035 **P**, 0.035 **S**, 0.15–0.35 **Si**, 0.90–1.2 **Cr**, 0.15–0.25 **Mo**	**Drawn:** all **diam**, (687) **TS**
NF A 35–553	42 CD 4	France	Strip	0.38–0.45 **C**, 0.60–0.90 **Mn**, 0.035 **P**, 0.035 **S**, 0.10–0.40 **Si**, 0.85–1.15 **Cr**, 0.15–0.30 **Mo**	
MIL–S–46047D		US	Bar, blanks	0.38–0.45 **C**, 0.75–1.00 **Mn**, 0.025 **P**, 0.020 **S**, 0.20–0.35 **Si**, 0.95–1.25 **Cr**, 0.55–0.70 **Mo**, 0.20–0.30 **V**	
SIS 14 22 44	SIS 2244–02	Sweden	Bar, forgings, tube	0.38–0.45 **C**, 0.60–0.90 **Mn**, 0.035 **P**, 0.035 **S**, 0.15–0.40 **Si**, 0.90–1.20 **Cr**, 0.15–0.30 **Mo**	
SIS 14 22 44	SIS 2244–00	Sweden	Bar, forgings, tube	0.38–0.45 **C**, 0.60–0.90 **Mn**, 0.035 **P**, 0.035 **S**, 0.15–0.40 **Si**, 0.90–1.20 **Cr**, 0.15–0.30 **Mo**	
SIS 14 29 40	SIS 9940–02	Sweden	Bar, forgings	0.38–0.45 **C**, 0.50–0.80 **Mn**, 0.030 **P**, 0.035 **S**, 0.20–0.50 **Si**, 1.5–1.8 **Cr**, 0.25–0.35 **Mo**, 0.90–1.2 **Al**	
ISO 683/XII	9	ISO	Bar, plate	0.38–0.44 **C**, 0.50–0.80 **Mn**, 0.035 **P**, 0.035 **S**, 0.15–0.40 **Si**, 0.90–1.20 **Cr**	**Quenched and tempered:** (16) **diam**, (1080) **TS**, (880) **YS**, 10 **El**
ISO 683/XII	10	ISO	Bar, plate	0.38–0.44 **C**, 0.70–1.00 **Mn**, 0.035 **P**, 0.035 **S**, 0.15–0.40 **Si**, 0.40–0.60 **Cr**, 0.40–0.70 **Ni**, 0.15–0.30 **Mo**	**Quenched and tempered:** (16) **diam**, (1030) **TS**, (830) **YS**, 10 **El**
ISO 683/XII	8	ISO	Bar, plate	0.38–0.44 **C**, 0.60–0.90 **Mn**, 0.035 **P**, 0.035 **S**, 0.15–0.40 **Si**, 0.90–1.20 **Cr**	**Quenched and tempered:** (16) **diam**, (980) **TS**, (780) **YS**, 11 **El**
DIN 1654	Grade 41 Cr 4	Germany	Rod	0.38–0.44 **C**, 0.50–0.80 **Mn**, 0.035 **P**, 0.035 **S**, 0.15–0.35 **Si**, 0.90–1.20 **Cr**	**Drawn:** all **diam**, (687) **TS**
ANSI/ASTM A 579	41	US	Forgings	0.38–0.43 **C**, 0.20–0.40 **Mn**, 0.015 **P**, 0.015 **S**, 0.80–1.00 **Si**, 4.75–5.25 **Cr**, 1.20–1.40 **Mo**, 0.40–0.60 **V**	**Air hardened:** all **diam**, 280 (1930) **TS**, 225 (1555) **YS**, 8 **El**; all **diam**, 260 (1795) **TS**, 200 (1380) **YS**, 9 **El**

specification number	designation	country	product forms	composition	mechanical properties (see page iv for explanation)
AMS 6417B		US	Bar, forgings, tube	0.38–0.43 **C**, 0.60–0.90 **Mn**, 0.010 **P**, 0.010 **S**, 1.45–1.80 **Si**, 0.70–0.95 **Cr**, 1.65–2.00 **Ni**, 0.30–0.50 **Mo**, 0.05–0.10 **V**, 0.35 **Cu**	**Normalized, hardened, quenched, and tempered:** all **diam**, 270 (1862) **TS**, 220 (1517) **YS**, 8 **El**; **Cold finished (bar):** ≤0.500 (≤12.70) **diam**, 130 (896) max **TS**
MIL–S–47262	AISI–H–11–Modified	US	Billets, bar, forgings	0.38–0.43 **C**, 0.20–0.40 **Mn**, 0.02 **P**, 0.02 **S**, 0.80–1.00 **Si**, 4.75–5.25 **Cr**, 1.20–1.40 **Mo**, 0.40–0.60 **V**	**Heat treated:** all **diam**, 260 (1793) **TS**, 220 (1517) **YS**, 8 **El**
MIL–S–8844C	Class 1 (4340)	US	Bar, reforging stock, mechanical tube	0.38–0.43 **C**, 0.65–0.90 **Mn**, 0.010 **P**, 0.010 **S**, 0.20–0.35 **Si**, 0.70–0.90 **Cr**, 1.65–2.00 **Ni**, 0.20–0.30 **Mo**	**Heat treated:** <100 **diam**, (1792) **TS**, (1496) **YS**, 6 **El**
AIR 9172	40 CDV 20	France	Bar, sheet, forgings	0.38–0.43 **C**, 0.20–0.40 **Mn**, 0.02 **P**, 0.015 **S**, 0.80–1.0 **Si**, 4.75–5.25 **Cr**, 1.20–1.40 **Mo**, 0.40–0.60 **V**	**Quenched, double tempered, annealed (bar, forgings):** all **diam**, (1765) **TS**, (1520) **YS**, 6 **El**
ANSI/ASTM A 579	22	US	Forgings	0.38–0.43 **C**, 0.60–0.90 **Mn**, 0.025 **P**, 0.025 **S**, 0.20–0.35 **Si**, 0.70–0.90 **Cr**, 1.65–2.00 **Ni**, 0.30–0.60 **Mo**, 0.05–0.10 **V**	**Quenched and tempered:** all **diam**, 190 (1310) **TS**, 180 (1240) **YS**, 10 **El**
ANSI/ASTM A 372	Class VII	US	Forgings	0.38–0.43 **C**, 0.60–0.80 **Mn**, 0.035 **P**, 0.04 **S**, 0.20–0.35 **Si**, 0.70–0.90 **Cr**, 1.65–2.00 **Ni**, 0.20–0.30 **Mo**	**Liquid quenched and tempered:** all **diam**, (1070) **TS**, (930) **YS**, 12 **El**
ASTM A 372	Class VII	US	Forgings	0.38–0.43 **C**, 0.60–0.80 **Mn**, 0.035 **P**, 0.04 **S**, 0.20–0.35 **Si**, 0.70–0.90 **Cr**, 1.65–2.00 **Ni**, 0.20–0.30 **Mo**	**Quenched, tempered:** all **diam**, 155 (1070) **TS**, 135 (930) **YS**, 12 **El**
JIS G 4105	Class 4	Japan	Bar	0.38–0.43 **C**, 0.60–0.85 **Mn**, 0.030 **P**, 0.030 **S**, 0.15–0.35 **Si**, 0.90–1.20 **Cr**, 0.25 **Ni**, 0.15–0.30 **Mo**, 0.30 **Cu**	**Rolled or forged, quenched and tempered:** (25) **diam**, (981) **TS**, (834) **YS**, 12 **El**
JIS G 4104	Class 4	Japan	Bar	0.38–0.43 **C**, 0.60–0.85 **Mn**, 0.030 **P**, 0.030 **S**, 0.15–0.35 **Si**, 0.90–1.20 **Cr**, 0.25 **Ni**, 0.30 **Cu**	**Rolled or forged, quenched and tempered:** (25) **diam**, (932) **TS**, (785) **YS**, 13 **El**
AMS 6470G		US	Bar, forgings, tube	0.38–0.43 **C**, 0.50–0.80 **Mn**, 0.025 **P**, 0.025 **S**, 0.20–0.40 **Si**, 1.40–1.80 **Cr**, 0.25 **Ni**, 0.30–0.40 **Mo**, 0.95–1.30 **Al**, 0.35 **Cu**	**Cold finished (bar):** ≤0.500 (≤12.7) **diam**, 135 (931) max **TS**
AMS 6485D		US	Bar, forgings	0.38–0.43 **C**, 0.20–0.40 **Mn**, 0.020 **P**, 0.020 **S**, 0.80–1.00 **Si**, 4.75–5.25 **Cr**, 0.25 **Ni**, 1.20–1.40 **Mo**, 0.40–0.60 **V**, 0.35 **Cu**	**Cold finished (bar):** ≤0.500 (≤12.70) **diam**, 135 (931) max **TS**; **Austenitized and tempered:** all **diam**, 260 (1793) **TS**, 215 (1482) **YS**, 8 **El**
AMS 6487E		US	Bar, forgings	0.38–0.43 **C**, 0.20–0.40 **Mn**, 0.015 **P**, 0.015 **S**, 0.80–1.00 **Si**, 4.75–5.25 **Cr**, 0.25 **Ni**, 1.20–1.40 **Mo**, 0.40–0.60 **V**, 0.35 **Cu**	**Cold finished (bar):** ≤0.500 (≤12.70) **diam**, 135 (931) max **TS**; **Austenized and tempered:** all **diam**, 260 (1793) **TS**, 215 (1482) **YS**, 8 **El**
AMS 6488A		US	Bar, forgings	0.38–0.43 **C**, 0.20–0.40 **Mn**, 0.015 **P**, 0.015 **S**, 0.80–1.00 **Si**, 4.75–5.25 **Cr**, 0.25 **Ni**, 1.20–1.40 **Mo**, 0.40–0.60 **V**, 0.35 **Cu**	**Cold finished (bar):** ≤0.500 (≤12.7) **diam**, 135 (931) max **TS**; **Austenized and tempered:** all **diam**, 260 (1793) **TS**, 215 (1482) **YS**, 8 **El**
AMS 6312C		US	Bar, forgings, tube	0.38–0.43 **C**, 0.60–0.80 **Mn**, 0.025 **P**, 0.025 **S**, 0.20–0.35 **Si**, 0.20 **Cr**, 1.65–2.00 **Ni**, 0.20–0.30 **Mo**, 0.35 **Cu**	**Cold finished (bar):** ≤0.500 (≤12.70) **diam**, 130 (896) max **TS**
AMS 6321B		US	Bar, forgings, tube	0.38–0.43 **C**, 0.75–1.00 **Mn**, 0.025 **P**, 0.025 **S**, 0.20–0.35 **Si**, 0.30–0.55 **Cr**, 0.20–0.40 **Ni**, 0.08–0.15 **Mo**, 0.35 **Cu**	**Cold finished (bar):** ≤0.500 (≤12.70) **diam**, 130 (896) max **TS**
AMS 6324D		US	Bar, forgings, tube	0.38–0.43 **C**, 0.75–1.00 **Mn**, 0.025 **P**, 0.025 **S**, 0.20–0.35 **Si**, 0.55–0.75 **Cr**, 0.55–0.85 **Ni**, 0.20–0.30 **Mo**, 0.35 **Cu**	**Cold finished:** ≤0.500 (≤12.70) **diam**, 130 (896) max **TS**
JIS G 4103	Class 6	Japan	Bar	0.38–0.43 **C**, 0.70–1.00 **Mn**, 0.030 **P**, 0.030 **S**, 0.15–0.35 **Si**, 0.40–0.65 **Cr**, 0.40–0.70 **Ni**, 0.15–0.30 **Mo**, 0.30 **Cu**	**Rolled or forged, quenched and tempered:** (25) **diam**, (883) **TS**, (785) **YS**, 17 **El**

WROUGHT ALLOY STEELS

specification number	designation	country	product forms	composition	mechanical properties (see page iv for explanation)
ASTM A 320	L 43 AISI 4340	US	Bar	0.38–0.43 **C**, 0.60–0.85 **Mn**, 0.040 **P**, 0.040 **S**, 0.20–0.35 **Si**, 0.70–0.90 **Cr**, 1.65–2.00 **Ni**, 0.20–0.30 **Mo**	**Quenched, tempered:** ≥4 (≥102) **diam**, 125 (862) **TS**, 105 (724) **YS**, 16 **El**
ASTM A 320	L 7C AISI 8740	US	Bar	0.38–0.43 **C**, 0.75–1.00 **Mn**, 0.035 **P**, 0.040 **S**, 0.20–0.35 **Si**, 0.40–0.60 **Cr**, 0.40–0.70 **Ni**, 0.20–0.30 **Mo**	**Quenched, tempered:** ≥2.5 (63.5) **diam**, 125 (862) **TS**, 105 (724) **YS**, 16 **El**
AMS 6437B		US	Sheet, strip, plate	0.38–0.43 **C**, 0.20–0.40 **Mn**, 0.020 **P**, 0.020 **S**, 0.80–1.00 **Si**, 4.75–5.25 **Cr**, 0.25 **Ni**, 1.20–1.40 **Mo**, 0.40–0.60 **V**, 0.35 **Cu**	**Hot rolled annealed**: all **diam**, 125 (862) **TS**
AMS 6415H		US	Bar, forgings, tube	0.38–0.43 **C**, 0.65–0.85 **Mn**, 0.025 **P**, 0.025 **S**, 0.20–0.35 **Si**, 0.70–0.90 **Cr**, 1.65–2.00 **Ni**, 0.20–0.30 **Mo**, 0.35 **Cu**	**Cold finished (bar):** ≤0.500 (≤12.70) **diam**, 125 (862) max **TS**
AMS 6422D		US	Bar, forgings, tube	0.38–0.43 **C**, 0.65–0.85 **Mn**, 0.025 **P**, 0.025 **S**, 0.20–0.35 **Si**, 0.70–0 **Cr**, 0.70–1.00 **Ni**, 0.15–0.25 **Mo**, 0.01–0.06 **V**, 0.0005–0.005 **B**, 0.35 **Cu**	**Cold finished (bar):** ≤0.500 (≤12.70) **diam**, 125 (862) max **TS**
AMS 6317C		US	Bar, forgings	0.38–0.43 **C**, 0.60–0.80 **Mn**, 0.025 **P**, 0.025 **S**, 0.20–0.35 **Si**, 0.20 **Cr**, 1.65–2.00 **Ni**, 0.20–0.30 **Mo**, 0.35 **Cu**	**Hardened and tempered:** ≤1.00 (≤25.40) **diam**, 125 (862) **TS**, 100 (690) **YS**, 16 **El**
AMS 6327E		US	Bar, forgings	0.38–0.43 **C**, 0.75–1.00 **Mn**, 0.025 **P**, 0.025 **S**, 0.20–0.35 **Si**, 0.40–0.60 **Cr**, 0.40–0.70 **Ni**, 0.20–0.30 **Mo**, 0.35 **Cu**	**Hardened and tempered:** ≤1.500 (≤38.10) **diam**, 125 (862) **TS**, 100 (690) **YS**, 16 **El**
AMS 6342E		US	Bar	0.38–0.43 **C**, 0.70–0.90 **Mn**, 0.025 **P**, 0.025 **S**, 0.20–0.35 **Si**, 0.70–0.90 **Cr**, 0.85–1.15 **Ni**, 0.20–0.30 **Mo**, 0.35 **Cu**	**Cold finished (bar):** ≤0.500 (≤12.70) **diam**, 125 (862) max **TS**
AMS 6382H		US	Bar, forgings, rings	0.38–0.43 **C**, 0.75–1.00 **Mn**, 0.025 **P**, 0.025 **S**, 0.20–0.35 **Si**, 0.80–1.10 **Cr**, 0.25 **Ni**, 0.15–0.25 **Mo**, 0.35 **Cu**	**Cold finished:** ≤0.500 (≤12.70) **diam**, 125 (862) **TS**
AMS 6414B		US	Bar, forgings, tube	0.38–0.43 **C**, 0.60–0.90 **Mn**, 0.015 **P**, 0.015 **S**, 0.20–0.35 **Si**, 0.70–0.90 **Cr**, 1.65–2.00 **Ni**, 0.20–0.30 **Mo**, 0.35 **Cu**	**Cold finished (bar):** ≤0.500 (≤12.70) **diam**, 125 (862) max **TS**
ANSI/ASTM A 519	4140	US	Tube: seamless	0.38–0.43 **C**, 0.75–1.00 **Mn**, 0.040 **P**, 0.040 **S**, 0.15–0.35 **Si**, 0.80–1.10 **Cr**, 0.15–0.25 **Mo**	**Hot rolled**: all **diam**, 120 (855) **TS**, 90 (621) **YS**, 15 **El**; **Stress relieved**: all **diam**, 120 (855) **TS**, 100 (689) **YS**, 10 **El**; **Annealed**: all **diam**, 80 (552) **TS**, 60 (414) **YS**, 25 **El**; **Normalized**: all **diam**, 120 (855) **TS**, 90 (621) **YS**, 20 **El**
AMS 6322G		US	Bar	0.38–0.43 **C**, 0.75–1.00 **Mn**, 0.025 **P**, 0.025 **S**, 0.20–0.35 **Si**, 0.40–0.60 **Cr**, 0.40–0.70 **Ni**, 0.20–0.30 **Mo**, 0.35 **Cu**	**Cold finished (bar):** ≤0.500 (≤12.70) **diam**, 120 (827) max **TS**
COPANT 514	Grade 4140	COPANT	Tube: seamless	0.38–0.43 **C**, 0.75–1.0 **Mn**, 0.040 **P**, 0.040 **S**, 0.20–0.35 **Si**, 0.80–1.10 **Cr**, 0.15–0.25 **Mo**	**Hot finished**: (>323.9) **diam**, (825) **TS**, (620) **YS**, 15 **El**; **Annealed**: all **diam**, (550) **TS**, (410) **YS**, 25 **El**; **Normalized**: all **diam**, (825) **TS**, (620) **YS**, 20 **El**
DGN–B–203	Grade 4140	Mexico	Tube: seamless	0.38–0.43 **C**, 0.75–1.00 **Mn**, 0.040 **P**, 0.040 **S**, 0.20–0.35 **Si**, 0.80–1.10 **Cr**, 0.15–0.25 **Mo**	**Hot finished**: all **diam**, (823) **TS**, (618) **YS**, 15 **El**; **Stress relieved**: all **diam**, (823) **TS**, (686) **YS**, 10 **El**; **Tempered**: all **diam**, (941) **TS**, (412) **YS**, 25 **El**; **Normalized**: all **diam**, (823) **TS**, (618) **YS**, 20 **El**
BS 2S.149		UK	Bar: aircraft quality	0.38–0.43 **C**, 0.65–0.85 **Mn**, 0.025 **P**, 0.020 **S**, 0.20–0.35 **Si**, 0.70–0.90 **Cr**, 1.65–2.00 **Ni**	**Annealed and cold drawn (straight)**: all **diam**, (800) **TS**; **Spheroidized and cold drawn (coil)**: all **diam**, (710) **TS**

WROUGHT ALLOY STEELS

specification number	designation	country	product forms	composition	mechanical properties (see page iv for explanation)
AMS 6472A		US	Bar, forgings	0.38–0.43 **C**, 0.50–0.80 **Mn**, 0.025 **P**, 0.025 **S**, 0.20–0.40 **Si**, 1.40–1.80 **Cr**, 0.25 **Ni**, 0.30–0.40 **Mo**, 0.95–1.30 **Al**, 0.35 **Cu**	**Quenched and tempered**: all **diam**, 112 (772) **TS**, 90 (621) **YS**, 16 **El**
MIL-S-6709A		US	Bar, rod, billets, forging stock: aircraft quality	0.38–0.43 **C**, 0.50–0.70 **Mn**, 0.025 **P**, 0.025 **S**, 0.20–0.40 **Si**, 1.40–1.80 **Cr**, 0.30–0.40 **Mo**, 0.95–1.35 **Al**	**Quenched and tempered**: all **diam**, 112 (772) **TS**, 90 (621) **YS**, 16 **El**
AMS 6325E		US	Bar, forgings	0.38–0.43 **C**, 0.75–1.00 **Mn**, 0.025 **P**, 0.025 **S**, 0.20–0.35 **Si**, 0.40–0.60 **Cr**, 0.40–0.70 **Ni**, 0.20–0.30 **Mo**, 0.35 **Cu**	**Hardened and tempered**: ≤1.75 (≤44.45) **diam**, 105 (724) **TS**, 85 (586) **YS**, 17 **El**
BS 3111 Part 1	Type 8	UK	Wire	0.38–0.43 **C**, 0.65–0.85 **Mn**, 0.040 **P**, 0.040 **S**, 0.15–0.40 **Si**, 0.70–0.90 **Cr**, 1.65–2.00 **Ni**, 0.20–0.30 **Mo**	**Drawn and spheroidized annealed**: all **diam**, (700) max **TS**; **Drawn, spheroidized annealed and light drawn**: all **diam**, (760) max **TS**
BS 3111 Part 1	Type 7	UK	Wire	0.38–0.43 **C**, 0.75–1.00 **Mn**, 0.040 **P**, 0.040 **S**, 0.15–0.40 **Si**, 0.40–0.60 **Cr**, 0.40–0.70 **Ni**, 0.20–0.30 **Mo**	**Drawn and spheroidized annealed**: all **diam**, (670) max **TS**; **Drawn, spheroidized annealed and light drawn**: all **diam**, (710) max **TS**
AISI 1340		US	Bar	0.38–0.43 **C**, 1.60–1.90 **Mn**, 0.035 **P**, 0.040 **S**, 0.15–0.30 **Si**	
AISI 4140		US	Bar	0.38–0.43 **C**, 0.75–1.00 **Mn**, 0.035 **P**, 0.040 **S**, 0.15–0.30 **Si**, 0.80–1.10 **Cr**, 0.15–0.25 **Mo**	
AISI 4340		US	Bar	0.38–0.43 **C**, 0.60–0.80 **Mn**, 0.035 **P**, 0.040 **S**, 0.15–0.30 **Si**, 0.70–0.90 **Cr**, 1.65–2.00 **Ni**, 0.20–0.30 **Mo**	
AISI E4340		US	Bar	0.38–0.43 **C**, 0.65–0.85 **Mn**, 0.025 **P**, 0.025 **S**, 0.15–0.30 **Si**, 0.70–0.90 **Cr**, 1.65–2.00 **Ni**, 0.20–0.30 **Mo**	
AISI 5140		US	Bar	0.38–0.43 **C**, 0.70–0.90 **Mn**, 0.035 **P**, 0.040 **S**, 0.15–0.30 **Si**, 0.70–0.90 **Cr**	
AISI 8640		US	Bar	0.38–0.43 **C**, 0.75–1.00 **Mn**, 0.035 **P**, 0.040 **S**, 0.15–0.30 **Si**, 0.40–0.60 **Cr**, 0.40–0.70 **Ni**, 0.15–0.25 **Mo**	
AISI 8740		US	Bar	0.38–0.43 **C**, 0.75–1.00 **Mn**, 0.035 **P**, 0.040 **S**, 0.15–0.30 **Si**, 0.40–0.60 **Cr**, 0.40–0.70 **Ni**, 0.20–0.30 **Mo**	
BS S.147		UK	Bar: aircraft quality	0.38–0.43 **C**, 0.75–1.00 **Mn**, 0.025 **P**, 0.020 **S**, 0.20–0.35 **Si**, 0.40–0.60 **Cr**, 0.40–0.70 **Ni**, 0.20–0.30 **Mo**	**Hardened and tempered**
BS 970 Part 2	Grade 530 A 40	UK	Blooms, billets, bar, forgings	0.38–0.43 **C**, 0.60–0.80 **Mn**, 0.90–1.20 **Cr**	
ASTM A 547	Grade 1340	US	Wire	0.38–0.43 **C**, 1.60–1.90 **Mn**	
ASTM A 547	Grade 4140	US	Wire	0.38–0.43 **C**, 0.75–1.00 **Mn**, 0.80–1.10 **Cr**, 0.15–0.25 **Mo**	
ASTM A 547	4340	US	Wire	0.38–0.43 **C**, 0.60–0.80 **Mn**, 0.70–0.90 **Cr**, 1.65–2.00 **Ni**, 0.20–0.30 **Mo**	
ASTM A 547	Grade 8640	US	Wire	0.38–0.43 **C**, 0.75–1.00 **Mn**, 0.40–0.60 **Cr**, 0.40–0.70 **Ni**, 0.15–0.25 **Mo**	
ASTM A 547	Grade 8740	US	Wire	0.38–0.43 **C**, 0.75–1.00 **Mn**, 0.40–0.60 **Cr**, 0.40–0.70 **Ni**, 0.20–0.30 **Mo**	
AMS 6395A		US	Sheet: strip, plate	0.38–0.43 **C**, 0.75–1.00 **Mn**, 0.025 **P**, 0.025 **S**, 0.20–0.35 **Si**, 0.80–1.10 **Cr**, 0.25 **Ni**, 0.15–0.25 **Mo**, 0.35 **Cu**	

specification number	designation	country	product forms	composition	mechanical properties (see page iv for explanation)
AMS 6323E		US	Tube	0.38–0.43 **C**, 0.75–1.00 **Mn**, 0.025 **P**, 0.025 **S**, 0.20–0.35 **Si**, 0.40–0.60 **Cr**, 0.40–0.70 **Ni**, 0.20–0.30 **Mo**, 0.35 **Cu**	
AMS 6358D		US	Sheet, strip, plate	0.38–0.43 **C**, 0.75–1.00 **Mn**, 0.025 **P**, 0.025 **S**, 0.20–0.35 **Si**, 0.40–0.60 **Cr**, 0.40–0.70 **Ni**, 0.20–0.30 **Mo**, 0.35 **Cu**	
AMS 6359C		US	Sheet, strip, plate	0.38–0.43 **C**, 0.60–0.80 **Mn**, 0.025 **P**, 0.025 **S**, 0.20–0.35 **Si**, 0.70–0.90 **Cr**, 1.65–2.00 **Ni**, 0.20–0.30 **Mo**, 0.35 **Cu**	
AMS 6381C		US	Tube	0.38–0.43 **C**, 0.75–1.00 **Mn**, 0.025 **P**, 0.025 **S**, 0.20–0.35 **Si**, 0.80–1.10 **Cr**, 0.25 **Ni**, 0.15–0.25 **Mo**, 0.35 **Cu**	
AMS 6390B		US	Tube	0.38–0.43 **C**, 0.75–1.00 **Mn**, 0.025 **P**, 0.025 **S**, 0.20–0.35 **Si**, 0.80–1.10 **Cr**, 0.25 **Ni**, 0.15–0.25 **Mo**, 0.35 **Cu**	
AS G18	G18/En 18D	Australia	Bar, billet	0.38–0.43 **C**, 0.65–0.80 **Mn**, 0.050 **P**, 0.050 **S**, 0.10–0.35 **Si**, 0.85–1.15 **Cr**	
MIL–S–5626C	AISI–4140	US	Bar, rod, billets	0.38–0.43 **C**, 0.75–1.0 **Mn**, 0.025 **P**, 0.025 **S**, 0.20–0.35 **Si**, 0.80–1.10 **Cr**, 0.25 **Ni**, 0.15–0.25 **Mo**, 0.35 **Cu**	
MIL–S–83135	4340M	US	Bar, tube	0.38–0.43 **C**, 0.65–0.90 **Mn**, 0.12 **P**, 0.12 **S**, 1.45–1.80 **Si**, 0.70–0.95 **Cr**, 1.65–2.00 **Ni**, 0.35–0.45 **Mo**, .05 min **V**	**Annealed**
COPANT 334	1340	COPANT	Bar	0.38–0.43 **C**, 1.60–1.90 **Mn**, 0.035 **P**, 0.040 **S**, 0.20–0.35 **Si**	
COPANT 334	4140	COPANT	Bar	0.38–0.43 **C**, 0.75–1.00 **Mn**, 0.035 **P**, 0.040 **S**, 0.20–0.35 **Si**, 0.80–1.10 **Cr**, 0.15–0.25 **Mo**	
COPANT 334	4340	COPANT	Bar	0.38–0.43 **C**, 0.60–0.80 **Mn**, 0.035 **P**, 0.040 **S**, 0.20–0.35 **Si**, 0.70–0.90 **Cr**, 1.65–2.00 **Ni**, 0.20–0.30 **Mo**	
COPANT 334	5140	COPANT	Bar	0.38–0.43 **C**, 0.70–0.90 **Mn**, 0.035 **P**, 0.040 **S**, 0.20–0.35 **Si**, 0.70–0.90 **Cr**	
COPANT 334	8640	COPANT	Bar	0.38–0.43 **C**, 0.75–1.00 **Mn**, 0.035 **P**, 0.040 **S**, 0.20–0.35 **Si**, 0.40–0.60 **Cr**, 0.40–0.70 **Ni**, 0.15–0.25 **Mo**	
COPANT 334	8740	COPANT	Bar	0.38–0.43 **C**, 0.75–1.00 **Mn**, 0.035 **P**, 0.040 **S**, 0.20–0.35 **Si**, 0.40–0.60 **Cr**, 0.40–0.70 **Ni**, 0.20–0.30 **Mo**	
COPANT 334	9840	COPANT	Bar	0.38–0.43 **C**, 0.70–0.90 **Mn**, 0.035 **P**, 0.040 **S**, 0.20–0.35 **Si**, 0.70–0.90 **Cr**, 0.85–1.15 **Ni**, 0.20–0.30 **Mo**	
AS 1444	Grade AS 1444/3140	Australia	Bar, bloom, billet, slab	0.38–0.43 **C**, 0.70–0.90 **Mn**, 0.040 **P**, 0.040 **S**, 0.10–0.35 **Si**, 0.55–0.75 **Cr**, 1.10–1.40 **Ni**	
AS 1444	Grade AS 1444/4140	Australia	Bar, bloom, billet, slab	0.38–0.43 **C**, 0.75–1.00 **Mn**, 0.040 **P**, 0.040 **S**, 0.10–0.35 **Si**, 0.80–1.10 **Cr**, 0.15–0.25 **Mo**	
AS 1444	Grade AS 1444/4340	Australia	Bar, bloom, billet, slab	0.38–0.43 **C**, 0.60–0.80 **Mn**, 0.040 **P**, 0.040 **S**, 0.10–0.35 **Si**, 0.70–0.90 **Cr**, 1.65–2.00 **Ni**, 0.20–0.30 **Mo**	
AS 1444	Grade AS 1444/5140	Australia	Bar, bloom, billet, slab	0.38–0.43 **C**, 0.70–0.90 **Mn**, 0.040 **P**, 0.040 **S**, 0.10–0.35 **Si**, 0.70–0.90 **Cr**	
AS 1444	Grade AS 1444/8640	Australia	Bar, bloom, billet, slab	0.38–0.43 **C**, 0.75–1.00 **Mn**, 0.040 **P**, 0.040 **S**, 0.10–0.35 **Si**, 0.40–0.60 **Cr**, 0.40–0.70 **Ni**, 0.15–0.25 **Mo**	

specification number	designation	country	product forms	composition	mechanical properties (see page iv for explanation)
AS 1444	Grade AS 1444/8740	Australia	Bar, bloom, billet, slab	0.38–0.43 **C**, 0.75–1.00 **Mn**, 0.040 **P**, 0.040 **S**, 0.10–0.35 **Si**, 0.40–0.60 **Cr**, 0.40–0.70 **Ni**, 0.20–0.30 **Mo**	
AS 1446	Grade AS 1446/XK1340	Australia	Plate	0.38–0.43 **C**, 1.40–1.70 **Mn**, 0.050 **P**, 0.050 **S**, 0.10–0.35 **Si**,	
DGN–B–203	Grade E 4340	Mexico	Tube: seamless	0.38–0.43 **C**, 0.65–0.85 **Mn**, 0.025 **P**, 0.025 **S**, 0.20–0.35 **Si**, 0.70–0.90 **Cr**, 1.65–2.00 **Ni**, 0.20–0.30 **Mo**	
DGN–B–203	Grade 4340	Mexico	Tube: seamless	0.38–0.43 **C**, 0.60–0.80 **Mn**, 0.040 **P**, 0.040 **S**, 0.20–0.35 **Si**, 0.70–0.90 **Cr**, 1.65–2.00 **Ni**, 0.20–0.30 **Mo**	
DGN–B–203	Grade 3140	Mexico	Tube: seamless	0.38–0.43 **C**, 0.70–0.90 **Mn**, 0.040 **P**, 0.040 **S**, 0.20–0.35 **Si**, 0.35–0.75 **Cr**, 1.10–1.40 **Ni**	
DGN–B–203	Grade 1340	Mexico	Tube: seamless	0.38–0.43 **C**, 1.60–1.90 **Mn**, 0.040 **P**, 0.040 **S**, 0.20–0.35 **Si**	
DGN–B–203	Grade 5140	Mexico	Tube: seamless	0.38–0.43 **C**, 0.70–0.90 **Mn**, 0.040 **P**, 0.040 **S**, 0.20–0.35 **Si**, 0.70–0.90 **Cr**	
DGN–B–203	Grade 8740	Mexico	Tube: seamless	0.38–0.43 **C**, 0.75–1.00 **Mn**, 0.040 **P**, 0.040 **S**, 0.20–0.35 **Si**, 0.40–0.60 **Cr**, 0.40–0.70 **Ni**, 0.20–0.30 **Mo**	
DGN–B–203	Grade 8640	Mexico	Tube: seamless	0.38–0.43 **C**, 0.75–1.00 **Mn**, 0.040 **P**, 0.040 **S**, 0.20–0.35 **Si**, 0.40–0.60 **Cr**, 0.40–0.70 **Ni**, 0.15–0.25 **Mo**	
DGN–B–203	Grade E 7140	Mexico	Tube: seamless	0.38–0.43 **C**, 0.50–0.70 **Mn**, 0.025 **P**, 0.025 **S**, 0.20–0.40 **Si**, 1.40–1.80 **Cr**, 0.30–0.40 **V**, 0.95–1.30 **Al**	
DGN–B–203	Grade 94B40	Mexico	Tube: seamless	0.38–0.43 **C**, 0.75–1.00 **Mn**, 0.040 **P**, 0.040 **S**, 0.20–0.35 **Si**, 0.30–0.50 **Cr**, 0.30–0.60 **Ni**, 0.08–0.15 **Mo**, 0.0005 min **B**	
DGN–B–203	Grade 9840	Mexico	Tube: seamless	0.38–0.43 **C**, 0.70–0.90 **Mn**, 0.040 **P**, 0.040 **S**, 0.20–0.35 **Si**, 0.70–0.90 **Cr**, 0.85–1.15 **Ni**, 0.20–0.30 **Mo**	
COPANT 514	E 4340	COPANT	Tube	0.38–0.43 **C**, 0.65–0.85 **Mn**, 0.025 **P**, 0.025 **S**, 0.20–0.35 **Si**, 0.70–0.90 **Cr**, 1.65–2.0 **Ni**, 0.20–0.30 **Mo**	
COPANT 514	4340	COPANT	Tube	0.38–0.43 **C**, 0.60–0.80 **Mn**, 0.040 **P**, 0.040 **S**, 0.20–0.35 **Si**, 0.70–0.90 **Cr**, 1.65–2.0 **Ni**, 0.20–0.30 **Mo**	
COPANT 514	3140	COPANT	Tube	0.38–0.43 **C**, 0.70–0.90 **Mn**, 0.040 **P**, 0.040 **S**, 0.20–0.35 **Si**, 0.55–0.75 **Cr**, 1.10–1.40 **Ni**	
COPANT 514	1340	COPANT	Tube	0.38–0.43 **C**, 1.60–1.90 **Mn**, 0.040 **P**, 0.040 **S**, 0.20–0.35 **Si**	
DGN–B–300	9840	Mexico	Bar	0.38–0.43 **C**, 0.70–0.90 **Mn**, 0.040 **P**, 0.040 **S**, 0.20–0.35 **Si**, 0.70–0.90 **Cr**, 0.85–1.15 **Ni**, 0.20–0.30 **Mo**	
DGN–B–300	8740	Mexico	Bar	0.38–0.43 **C**, 0.75–1.00 **Mn**, 0.035 **P**, 0.040 **S**, 0.20–0.35 **Si**, 0.40–0.60 **Cr**, 0.40–0.70 **Ni**, 0.20–0.30 **Mo**	**Annealed**
DGN–B–300	8640	Mexico	Bar	0.38–0.43 **C**, 0.75–1.00 **Mn**, 0.035 **P**, 0.040 **S**, 0.20–0.35 **Si**, 0.40–0.60 **Cr**, 0.40–0.70 **Ni**, 0.15–0.25 **Mo**	**Annealed**
DGN–B–300	5140	Mexico	Bar	0.38–0.43 **C**, 0.70–0.90 **Mn**, 0.035 **P**, 0.040 **S**, 0.20–0.35 **Si**, 0.70–0.90 **Cr**	**Annealed**
DGN–B–300	E 4340	Mexico	Bar	0.38–0.43 **C**, 0.65–0.85 **Mn**, 0.025 **P**, 0.025 **S**, 0.20–0.35 **Si**, 0.70–0.90 **Cr**, 1.65–2.00 **Ni**, 0.20–0.30 **Mo**	**Annealed**

WROUGHT ALLOY STEELS

specification number	designation	country	product forms	composition	mechanical properties (see page iv for explanation)
DGN–B–300	4340	Mexico	Bar	0.38–0.43 **C**, 0.60–0.80 **Mn**, 0.035 **P**, 0.040 **S**, 0.20–0.35 **Si**, 0.70–0.90 **Cr**, 1.65–2.00 **Ni**, 0.20–0.30 **Mo**	**Annealed**
DGN–B–300	4140	Mexico	Bar	0.38–0.43 **C**, 0.75–1.00 **Mn**, 0.035 **P**, 0.040 **S**, 0.20–0.35 **Si**, 0.80–1.10 **Cr**, 0.15–0.25 **Mo**	**Annealed**
DGN–B–300	1340	Mexico	Bar	0.38–0.43 **C**, 1.60–1.90 **Mn**, 0.035 **P**, 0.040 **S**, 0.20–0.35 **Si**	**Annealed**
MIL–S–47086		US	Sheet, strip, plate	0.38–0.43 **C**, 0.20–0.40 **Mn**, 0.02 **P**, 0.02 **S**, 0.80–1.00 **Si**, 4.75–5.25 **Cr**, 1.20–1.40 **Mo**, 0.40–0.60 **V**, rem **Fe**	**Cold rolled, spherodized, annealed:** all **diam**, 55 (379) **YS**, <25 **El**
ANSI/ASTM A 29	5140	US	Bar	0.38–0.43 **C**, 0.70–0.90 **Mn**, 0.035 **P**, 0.040 **S**, 0.15–0.30 **Si**, 0.70–0.90 **Cr**	
ANSI/ASTM A 29	1340	US	Bar	0.38–0.43 **C**, 1.60–1.90 **Mn**, 0.035 **P**, 0.040 **S**, 0.15–0.30 **Si**	
ANSI/ASTM A 29	4140	US	Bar	0.38–0.43 **C**, 0.75–1.00 **Mn**, 0.035 **P**, 0.040 **S**, 0.15–0.30 **Si**, 0.80–1.10 **Cr**, 0.15–0.25 **Mo**	
ANSI/ASTM A 29	4340	US	Bar	0.38–0.43 **C**, 0.60–0.80 **Mn**, 0.035 **P**, 0.040 **S**, 0.15–0.30 **Si**, 0.70–0.90 **Cr**, 1.65–2.00 **Ni**, 0.20–0.30 **Mo**	
ANSI/ASTM A 29	E 4340	US	Bar	0.38–0.43 **C**, 0.65–0.85 **Mn**, 0.025 **P**, 0.025 **S**, 0.15–0.30 **Si**, 0.70–0.90 **Cr**, 1.65–2.00 **Ni**, 0.20–0.30 **Mo**	
ANSI/ASTM A 646	4340	US	Blooms, billets: aircraft quality	0.38–0.43 **C**, 0.65–0.85 **Mn**, 0.025 **P**, 0.025 **S**, 0.20–0.35 **Si**, 0.70–0.90 **Cr**, 1.65–2.00 **Ni**, 0.20–0.30 **Mo**	**Annealed**
ANSI/ASTM A 646	300 M	US	Blooms, billets: aircraft quality	0.38–0.43 **C**, 0.65–0.90 **Mn**, 0.012 **P**, 0.012 **S**, 1.45–1.80 **Si**, 0.70–0.95 **Cr**, 1.65–2.00 **Ni**, 0.35–0.45 **Mo**, 0.05–0.10 **V**	**Annealed**
ANSI/ASTM A 646	H–11	US	Blooms, billets: aircraft quality	0.38–0.43 **C**, 0.20–0.40 **Mn**, 0.015 **P**, 0.015 **S**, 0.80–1.00 **Si**, 4.75–5.25 **Cr**, 1.20–1.40 **Mo**, 0.40–0.60 **V**	**Annealed**
ANSI/ASTM A 646	4140	US	Blooms, billets: aircraft quality	0.38–0.43 **C**, 0.75–1.00 **Mn**, 0.025 **P**, 0.025 **S**, 0.20–0.35 **Si**, 0.80–1.10 **Cr**, 0.15–0.25 **Mo**	**Annealed**
ANSI/ASTM A 646	Nit 135	US	Blooms, billets: aircraft quality	0.38–0.43 **C**, 0.50–0.70 **Mn**, 0.025 **P**, 0.025 **S**, 0.20–0.40 **Si**, 1.40–1.80 **Cr**, 0.30–0.40 **Mo**, 0.95–1.30 **Al**	
MIL–S–16974E	No 8640	US	Bar, billets, blooms, slabs	0.38–0.43 **C**, 0.75–1.00 **Mn**, 0.040 **P**, 0.040 **S**, 0.20–0.35 **Si**, 0.40–0.60 **Cr**, 0.40–0.70 **Ni**, 0.15–0.25 **Mo**	
MIL–S–16974E	No 4140	US	Bar, billets, blooms, slabs	0.38–0.43 **C**, 0.75–1.00 **Mn**, 0.040 **P**, 0.040 **S**, 0.20–0.35 **Si**, 0.80–1.10 **Cr**, 0.15–0.25 **Mo**	
MIL–S–16974E	No 4340	US	Bar, billets, blooms, slabs	0.38–0.43 **C**, 0.60–0.80 **Mn**, 0.040 **P**, 0.040 **S**, 0.20–0.35 **Si**, 0.70–0.90 **Cr**, 1.65–2.00 **Ni**, 0.20–0.30 **Mo**	
MIL–S–16974E	No 4640	US	Bar, billets, blooms, slabs	0.38–0.43 **C**, 0.60–0.80 **Mn**, 0.040 **P**, 0.040 **S**, 0.20–0.35 **Si**, 1.65–2.00 **Ni**, 0.20–0.30 **Mo**	
MIL–S–16974E	No 1340	US	Bar, billets, blooms, slabs	0.38–0.43 **C**, 1.60–1.90 **Mn**, 0.040 **P**, 0.040 **S**, 0.20–0.35 **Si**	
MIL–S–16974E	No 3140	US	Bar, billets, blooms, slabs	0.38–0.43 **C**, 0.70–0.90 **Mn**, 0.040 **P**, 0.040 **S**, 0.20–0.35 **Si**, 0.55–0.75 **Cr**, 1.10–1.40 **Ni**	
ASTM A 689	8740	US	Bar	0.38–0.43 **C**, 0.75–1.00 **Mn**, 0.035 **P**, 0.040 **S**, 0.15–0.30 **Si**, 0.40–0.60 **Cr**, 0.40–0.70 **Ni**, 0.20–0.30 **Mo**	

WROUGHT ALLOY STEELS

specification number	designation	country	product forms	composition	mechanical properties (see page iv for explanation)
ASTM A 689	8640	US	Bar	0.38–0.43 **C**, 0.75–1.00 **Mn**, 0.035 **P**, 0.040 **S**, 0.15–0.30 **Si**, 0.40–0.60 **Cr**, 0.40–0.70 **Ni**, 0.15–0.25 **Mo**	
ASTM A 689	5140	US	Bar	0.38–0.43 **C**, 0.70–0.90 **Mn**, 0.035 **P**, 0.040 **S**, 0.15–0.30 **Si**, 0.70–0.90 **Cr**	
ASTM A 689	1340	US	Bar	0.38–0.43 **C**, 1.60–1.90 **Mn**, 0.035 **P**, 0.040 **S**, 0.15–0.30 **Si**	
ASTM A 689	4140	US	Bar	0.38–0.43 **C**, 0.75–1.00 **Mn**, 0.035 **P**, 0.040 **S**, 0.15–0.30 **Si**, 0.80–1.10 **Cr**, 0.15–0.25 **Mo**	
ASTM A 689	4340	US	Bar	0.38–0.43 **C**, 0.60–0.80 **Mn**, 0.035 **P**, 0.040 **S**, 0.15–0.30 **Si**, 0.70–0.90 **Cr**, 1.65–2.00 **Ni**, 0.20–0.30 **Mo**	
ASTM A 689	E4340	US	Bar	0.38–0.43 **C**, 0.65–0.85 **Mn**, 0.025 **P**, 0.025 **S**, 0.15–0.30 **Si**, 0.70–0.90 **Cr**, 1.65–2.00 **Ni**, 0.20–0.30 **Mo**	
ANSI/ASTM A 29	8740	US	Bar	0.38–0.43 **C**, 0.75–1.00 **Mn**, 0.035 **P**, 0.040 **S**, 0.15–0.30 **Si**, 0.40–0.60 **Cr**, 0.40–0.70 **Ni**, 0.20–0.30 **Mo**	
ANSI/ASTM A 322	5140	US	Bar	0.38–0.43 **C**, 0.70–0.90 **Mn**, 0.035 **P**, 0.040 **S**, 0.15–0.30 **Si**, 0.70–0.90 **Cr**	
ANSI/ASTM A 322	1340	US	Bar	0.38–0.43 **C**, 1.60–1.90 **Mn**, 0.035 **P**, 0.040 **S**, 0.15–0.30 **Si**	
ANSI/ASTM A 322	4140	US	Bar	0.38–0.43 **C**, 0.75–1.00 **Mn**, 0.035 **P**, 0.040 **S**, 0.15–0.30 **Si**, 0.80–1.10 **Cr**, 0.15–0.25 **Mo**	
ANSI/ASTM A 322	4340	US	Bar	0.38–0.43 **C**, 0.60–0.80 **Mn**, 0.035 **P**, 0.040 **S**, 0.15–0.30 **Si**, 0.70–0.90 **Cr**, 1.65–2.00 **Ni**, 0.20–0.30 **Mo**	
ANSI/ASTM A 322	8640	US	Bar	0.38–0.43 **C**, 0.75–1.00 **Mn**, 0.035 **P**, 0.040 **S**, 0.15–0.30 **Si**, 0.40–0.60 **Cr**, 0.40–0.70 **Ni**, 0.15–0.25 **Mo**	
ANSI/ASTM A 322	8740	US	Bar	0.38–0.43 **C**, 0.75–1.00 **Mn**, 0.035 **P**, 0.040 **S**, 0.15–0.30 **Si**, 0.40–0.60 **Cr**, 0.40–0.70 **Ni**, 0.20–0.30 **Mo**	
ANSI/ASTM A 322	E 4340	US	Bar	0.38–0.43 **C**, 0.65–0.85 **Mn**, 0.025 **P**, 0.025 **S**, 0.15–0.30 **Si**, 0.70–0.90 **Cr**, 1.65–2.00 **Ni**, 0.20–0.30 **Mo**	
ANSI/ASTM A 29	8640	US	Bar	0.38–0.43 **C**, 0.75–1.00 **Mn**, 0.035 **P**, 0.040 **S**, 0.15–0.30 **Si**, 0.40–0.60 **Cr**, 0.40–0.70 **Ni**, 0.15–0.25 **Mo**	
AISI 8640		US	Wire, rod	0.38–0.43 **C**, 0.75–1.00 **Mn**, 0.035 **P**, 0.040 **S**, 0.15–0.30 **Si**, 0.40–0.60 **Cr**, 0.40–0.70 **Ni**, 0.15–0.25 **Mo**	
AISI 8740		US	Wire, rod	0.38–0.43 **C**, 0.75–1.00 **Mn**, 0.035 **P**, 0.040 **S**, 0.15–0.30 **Si**, 0.40–0.60 **Cr**, 0.40–0.70 **Ni**, 0.20–0.30 **Mo**	
AISI 1340		US	Wire, rod	0.38–0.43 **C**, 1.60–1.90 **Mn**, 0.035 **P**, 0.40 **S**, 0.15–0.30 **Si**	
AISI 4140		US	Wire, rod	0.38–0.43 **C**, 0.75–1.00 **Mn**, 0.035 **P**, 0.040 **S**, 0.15–0.30 **Si**, 0.80–1.10 **Cr**, 0.15–0.25 **Mo**	
AISI 4340		US	Wire, rod	0.38–0.43 **C**, 0.60–0.80 **Mn**, 0.035 **P**, 0.040 **S**, 0.15–0.30 **Si**, 0.70–0.90 **Cr**, 1.65–2.00 **Ni**, 0.20–0.30 **Mo**	
AISI E4340		US	Wire, rod	0.38–0.43 **C**, 0.65–0.85 **Mn**, 0.025 **P**, 0.025 **S**, 0.15–0.30 **Si**, 0.70–0.90 **Cr**, 1.65–2.00 **Ni**, 0.20–0.30 **Mo**	

WROUGHT ALLOY STEELS

specification number	designation	country	product forms	composition	mechanical properties (see page iv for explanation)
AISI 5140		US	Wire, rod	0.38–0.43 **C**, 0.70–0.90 **Mn**, 0.035 **P**, 0.040 **S**, 0.15–0.30 **Si**, 0.70–0.90 **Cr**	
ANSI/ASTM A 519	94B40	US	Tubing: seamless	0.38–0.43 **C**, 0.75–1.00 **Mn**, 0.040 **P**, 0.040 **S**, 0.15–0.35 **Si**, 0.30–0.50 **Cr**, 0.30–0.60 **Ni**, 0.08–0.15 **Mo**	
ANSI/ASTM A 519	1340	US	Tube: seamless	0.38–0.43 **C**, 1.60–1.90 **Mn**, 0.040 **P**, 0.040 **S**, 0.15–0.35 **Si**	
ANSI/ASTM A 519	3140	US	Tube: seamless	0.38–0.43 **C**, 0.70–0.90 **Mn**, 0.040 **P**, 0.040 **S**, 0.15–0.35 **Si**, 0.55–0.75 **Cr**, 1.10–1.40 **Ni**	
ANSI/ASTM A 519	4340	US	Tube: seamless	0.38–0.43 **C**, 0.60–0.80 **Mn**, 0.040 **P**, 0.040 **S**, 0.15–0.35 **Si**, 0.70–0.90 **Cr**, 1.65–2.00 **Ni**, 0.20–0.30 **Mo**	
ANSI/ASTM A 519	E 4340	US	Tube: seamless	0.38–0.43 **C**, 0.65–0.85 **Mn**, 0.025 **P**, 0.025 **S**, 0.15–0.35 **Si**, 0.70–0.90 **Cr**, 1.65–2.00 **Ni**, 0.20–0.30 **Mo**	
ANSI/ASTM A 519	5140	US	Tube: seamless	0.38–0.43 **C**, 0.70–0.90 **Mn**, 0.040 **P**, 0.040 **S**, 0.15–0.35 **Si**, 0.70–0.90 **Cr**	
ANSI/ASTM A 519	E 7140	US	Tube: seamless	0.38–0.43 **C**, 0.50–0.70 **Mn**, 0.025 **P**, 0.025 **S**, 0.15–0.40 **Si**, 1.40–1.80 **Cr**, 0.30–0.40 **V**, 0.95–1.30 **Al**	
ANSI/ASTM A 519	8640	US	Tube: seamless	0.38–0.43 **C**, 0.75–1.00 **Mn**, 0.040 **P**, 0.040 **S**, 0.15–0.35 **Si**, 0.40–0.60 **Cr**, 0.40–0.70 **Ni**, 0.15–0.25 **Mo**	
ANSI/ASTM A 519	8740	US	Tube: seamless	0.38–0.43 **C**, 0.75–1.00 **Mn**, 0.040 **P**, 0.040 **S**, 0.15–0.35 **Si**, 0.40–0.60 **Cr**, 0.40–0.70 **Ni**, 0.20–0.30 **Mo**	
ANSI/ASTM A 519	9840	US	Tube: seamless	0.38–0.43 **C**, 0.70–0.90 **Mn**, 0.040 **P**, 0.040 **S**, 0.15–0.35 **S**, 0.70–0.90 **Cr**, 0.85–1.15 **Ni**, 0.20–0.30 **Mo**	
AISI 8630		US	Sheet, strip	0.38–0.43 **C**, 0.75–1.00 **Mn**, 0.035 **P**, 0.040 **S**, 0.20–0.35 **Si**, 0.40–0.60 **Cr**, 0.40–0.70 **Ni**, 0.15–0.25 **Mo**	
AISI 5140		US	Sheet, strip	0.38–0.43 **C**, 0.70–0.90 **Mn**, 0.035 **P**, 0.040 **S**, 0.20–0.35 **Si**, 0.70–0.90 **Cr**	
AISI 4340		US	Sheet, strip	0.38–0.43 **C**, 0.60–0.80 **Mn**, 0.035 **P**, 0.040 **S**, 0.20–0.35 **Si**, 0.70–0.90 **Cr**, 1.65–2.00 **Ni**, 0.20–0.30 **Mo**	
DGN–B–297	4340	Mexico	Bar	0.38–0.43 **C**, 0.60–0.80 **Mn**, 0.035 **P**, 0.04 **S**, 0.20–0.35 **Si**, 0.70–0.90 **Cr**, 1.65–2.00 **Ni**, 0.20–0.30 **Mo**	
DGN–B–297	E 4340	Mexico	Bar	0.38–0.43 **C**, 0.65–0.85 **Mn**, 0.025 **P**, 0.025 **S**, 0.20–0.35 **Si**, 0.70–0.90 **Cr**, 1.65–2.00 **Ni**, 0.20–0.30 **Mo**	
AS 1442	Grade AS 1442/XK 1340	Australia	Bar, blooms, billets, slabs	0.38–0.43 **C**, 1.40–1.70 **Mn**, 0.050 **P**, 0.050 **S**, 0.10–0.35 **Si**	
AS 1442	Grade AS 1442/K 1340	Australia	Bar, blooms, billets, slabs	0.38–0.43 **C**, 1.60–1.90 **Mn**, 0.050 **P**, 0.050 **S**, 0.10–0.35 **Si**	
AS 1443	Grade AS 1443/K 1340	Australia	Bar	0.38–0.43 **C**, 1.60–1.90 **Mn**, 0.050 **P**, 0.050 **S**, 0.10–0.35 **Si**	
AS 1443	Grade AS 1443/XK 1340	Australia	Bar	0.38–0.43 **C**, 1.40–1.70 **Mn**, 0.050 **P**, 0.050 **S**, 0.10–0.35 **Si**	
DGN–B–297	1340	Mexico	Bar	0.38–0.43 **C**, 1.60–1.90 **Mn**, 0.035 **P**, 0.040 **S**, 0.20–0.35 **Si**	
DGN–B–297	8640	Mexico	Bar	0.38–0.43 **C**, 0.75–1.00 **Mn**, 0.035 **P**, 0.040 **S**, 0.20–0.35 **Si**, 0.40–0.60 **Cr**, 0.40–0.70 **Ni**, 0.15–0.25 **Mo**	

WROUGHT ALLOY STEELS

specification number	designation	country	product forms	composition	mechanical properties (see page iv for explanation)
DGN-B-297	8740	Mexico	Bar	0.38–0.43 **C**, 0.75–1.00 **Mn**, 0.035 **P**, 0.040 **S**, 0.20–0.35 **Si**, 0.40–0.60 **Cr**, 0.40–0.70 **Ni**, 0.20–0.30 **Mo**	
DGN-B-297	5140	Mexico	Bar	0.38–0.43 **C**, 0.70–0.90 **Mn**, 0.035 **P**, 0.040 **S**, 0.20–0.35 **Si**, 0.70–0.90 **Cr**	
DGN-B-297	4140	Mexico	Bar	0.38–0.43 **C**, 0.75–1.00 **Mn**, 0.035 **P**, 0.040 **S**, 0.20–0.35 **Si**, 0.80–1.10 **Cr**, 0.15–0.25 **Mo**	
COPANT 514	Grade 5140	COPANT	Tube: seamless	0.38–0.43 **C**, 0.70–0.90 **Mn**, 0.040 **P**, 0.050 **S**, 0.10 **Si**, 0.70–0.90 **Cr**	
COPANT 514	Grade 94B40	COPANT	Tube: seamless	0.38–0.43 **C**, 0.75–1.00 **Mn**, 0.040 **P**, 0.050 **S**, 0.10 **Si**, 0.30–0.50 **Cr**, 0.30–0.50 **Ni**, 0.08–0.15 **Mo**	
COPANT 514	Grade E7140	COPANT	Tube: seamless	0.38–0.43 **C**, 0.50–0.70 **Mn**, 0.040 **P**, 0.050 **S**, 0.10 **Si**, 1.40–1.80 **Cr**, 0.30–0.40 **V**, 0.95–1.30 **Al**	
COPANT 514	Grade 8640	COPANT	Tube: seamless	0.38–0.43 **C**, 0.75–1.00 **Mn**, 0.040 **P**, 0.050 **S**, 0.10 **Si**, 0.40–0.60 **Cr**, 0.40–0.70 **Ni**, 0.15–0.25 **Mo**	
COPANT 514	Grade 8740	COPANT	Tube: seamless	0.38–0.43 **C**, 0.75–1.00 **Mn**, 0.040 **P**, 0.050 **S**, 0.10 **Si**, 0.40–0.60 **Cr**, 0.40–0.70 **Ni**, 0.20–0.30 **Mo**	
COPANT 514	Grade 9840	COPANT	Tube: seamless	0.38–0.43 **C**, 0.70–0.90 **Mn**, 0.040 **P**, 0.040 **S**, 0.10 **Si**, 0.70–0.90 **Cr**, 0.85–1.15 **Ni**, 0.20–0.30 **Mo**	
JIS G 3311	SCM4M	Japan	Strip	0.38–0.43 **C**, 0.60–0.85 **Mn**, 0.030 **P**, 0.030 **S**, 0.15–0.35 **Si**, 0.90–1.20 **Cr**, 0.25 **Ni**, 0.15–0.30 **Mo**, 0.30 **Cu**	
DGN-B-203	Grade 50B40	Mexico	Tube: seamless	0.38–0.42 **C**, 0.75–1.00 **Mn**, 0.040 **P**, 0.040 **S**, 0.20–0.35 **Si**, 0.40–0.60 **Cr**, 0.0005 min **B**	
ANSI/ASTM A 519	50B40	US	Tube: seamless	0.38–0.42 **C**, 0.75–1.00 **Mn**, 0.040 **P**, 0.040 **S**, 0.15–0.35 **Si**, 0.40–0.60 **Cr**	
COPANT 514	Grade 50B40	COPANT	Tube: seamless	0.38–0.42 **C**, 0.75–1.00 **Mn**, 0.040 **P**, 0.050 **S**, 0.10 **Si**, 0.40–0.60 **Cr**, 0.005 **B**	
AISI 4140		US	Sheet, strip	0.38–0.4 **C**, 0.75–1.00 **Mn**, 0.035 **P**, 0.040 **S**, 0.20–0.35 **Si**, 0.80–1.10 **Cr**, 0.15–0.25 **Mo**	
JIS G 4108	Class 2, SNB 22-1	Japan	Bar	0.37–0.48 **C**, 0.61–1.14 **Mn**, 0.030 **P**, 0.030 **S**, 0.18–0.37 **Si**, 0.70–1.25 **Cr**, 0.13–0.27 **Mo**	**Hot rolled, hot forged or cold finished:** (≤38) **diam**, (1138) **TS**, (1030) **YS**, 10 **El**
JIS G 4108	Class 2, SNB 22-2	Japan	Bar	0.37–0.48 **C**, 0.61–1.14 **Mn**, 0.030 **P**, 0.030 **S**, 0.18–0.37 **Si**, 0.70–1.25 **Cr**, 0.13–0.27 **Mo**	**Hot rolled, hot forged or cold finished:** (≤78) **diam**, (1069) **TS**, (961) **YS**, 11 **El**
JIS G 4108	Class 2, SNB 22-3	Japan	Bar	0.37–0.48 **C**, 0.61–1.14 **Mn**, 0.030 **P**, 0.030 **S**, 0.18–0.37 **Si**, 0.70–1.25 **Cr**, 0.13–0.27 **Mo**	**Hot rolled, hot forged or cold finished:** (≤50) **diam**, (1000) **TS**, (892) **YS**, 12 **El**
JIS G 4108	Class 2, SNB 22-4	Japan	Bar	0.37–0.48 **C**, 0.61–1.14 **Mn**, 0.030 **P**, 0.030 **S**, 0.18–0.37 **Si**, 0.70–1.25 **Cr**, 0.13–0.27 **Mo**	**Hot rolled, hot forged or cold finished:** (≤25) **diam**, (932) **TS**, (824) **YS**, 13 **El**
JIS G 4108	Class 2, SNB 22-5	Japan	Bar	0.37–0.48 **C**, 0.61–1.14 **Mn**, 0.030 **P**, 0.030 **S**, 0.18–0.37 **Si**, 0.70–1.25 **Cr**, 0.13–0.27 **Mo**	**Hot rolled, hot forged or cold finished:** (≤50) **diam**, (824) **TS**, (716) **YS**, 15 **El**
AS G18	G18/En 54A	Australia	Bar, billet	0.37–0.47 **C**, 0.50–0.80 **Mn**, 0.045 **P**, 0.045 **S**, 1.00–2.00 **Si**, 13.0–15.0 **Cr**, 13.0–15.0 **Ni**, 0.40–0.60 **Mo**, 2.2–3.0 **W**	
COPANT 332	1141	COPANT	Bar	0.37–0.45 **C**, 1.35–1.65 **Mn**, 0.040 **P**, 0.08–0.13 **S**	**Cold finished and annealed:** (≤15) **diam**, (725) **TS**, (590) **YS**, 12 **El** 12 **El**

WROUGHT ALLOY STEELS

specification number	designation	country	product forms	composition	mechanical properties (see page iv for explanation)
ANSI/ASTM A 311	1141	US	Bar	0.37–0.45 **C**, 1.35–1.65 **Mn**, 0.040 **P**, 0.08–0.13 **S**	**Cold drawn, stress relieved:** $\leq$0.56 ($\leq$14.29) **diam**, 105 (724) **TS**, 85 (586) **YS**, 12 **El**
DGN-B-296	1141	Mexico	Bar	0.37–0.45 **C**, 1.35–1.65 **Mn**, 0.040 **P**, 0.08–0.13 **S**	**Cold finished:** (<14) **diam**, (723) **TS**, (586) **YS**, 12 **El**
ASTM A 108	1141	US	Bar	0.37–0.45 **C**, 1.35–1.65 **Mn**, 0.040 **P**, 0.08–0.13 **S**	
MIL-S-16974E	No MoV-40	US	Bar, billets, blooms, slabs	0.37–0.45 **C**, 0.60–0.90 **Mn**, 0.040 **P**, 0.040 **S**, 0.20–0.40 **Si**, 0.30–0.50 **Mo**, 0.10–0.25 **V**	
AISI 1141		US	Wire, rod	0.37–0.45 **C**, 1.35–1.65 **Mn**, 0.040 **P**, 0.08–0.13 **S**	
ASTM A 689	1141	US	Bar	0.37–0.45 **C**, 1.35–1.65 **Mn**, 0.040 **P**, 0.08–0.13 **S**	
ANSI/ASTM A 29	1141	US	Bar	0.37–0.45 **C**, 1.35–1.65 **Mn**, 0.040 **P**, 0.08–0.13 **S**	
ANSI/ASTM A 576	1141	US	Bar	0.37–0.45 **C**, 1.35–1.65 **Mn**, 0.040 **P**, 0.08–0.13 **S**	
COPANT 514	Grade 1141	COPANT	Tube: seamless	0.37–0.45 **C**, 1.35–1.65 **Mn**, 0.040 **P**, 0.08–0.13 **S**	
JIS G 4804	SUM 42	Japan	Bar	0.37–0.45 **C**, 1.35–1.65 **Mn**, 0.040 **P**, 0.08–0.13 **S**	
QQ-S-637A	1141	US	Bar	0.37–0.45 **C**, 1.35–1.65 **Mn**, 0.040 **P**, 0.08–0.13 **S**, 0.15–0.35 **Pb**	
COPANT 331	1141	COPANT	Bar	0.37–0.45 **C**, 1.35–1.65 **Mn**, 0.040 **P**, 0.08–0.13 **S**	
COPANT 330	1141	COPANT	Bar, shapes	0.37–0.45 **C**, 1.35–1.65 **Mn**, 0.040 **P**, 0.08–0.13 **S**	
ISO/R 683/VIII	Type 4	ISO	Bar, billets, rod	0.37–0.44 **C**, 0.55–0.85 **Mn**, 0.035 **P**, 0.035 **S**, 0.15–0.40 **Si**, 0.65–0.95 **Cr**, 1.60–2.00 **Ni**, 0.15–0.30 **Mo**	**Quenched and tempered:** ($\leq$16) **diam**, (1176) **TS**, (980) **YS**, 9 **El**
ISO/R 683/VIII	Type 4a	ISO	Bar, billets, rod	0.37–0.44 **C**, 0.55–0.85 **Mn**, 0.035 **P**, 0.020–0.035 **S**, 0.15–0.40 **Si**, 0.65–0.95 **Cr**, 1.60–2.00 **Ni**, 0.15–0.30 **Mo**	**Quenched and tempered:** ($\leq$16) **diam**, (1176) **TS**, (980) **YS**, 9 **El**
ISO/R 683/VIII	Type 4b	ISO	Bar, billets, rod	0.37–0.44 **C**, 0.55–0.85 **Mn**, 0.035 **P**, 0.030–0.050 **S**, 0.15–0.40 **Si**, 0.65–0.95 **Cr**, 1.60–2.00 **Ni**, 0.15–0.30 **Mo**	**Quenched and tempered:** ($\leq$16) **diam**, (1176) **TS**, (980) **YS**, 9 **El**
EURONORM 119-74, IV	40 NiCrMo 2 KD	EURONORM	Wire, rod	0.37–0.44 **C**, 0.70–1.00 **Mn**, 0.035 **P**, 0.035 **S**, 0.15–0.40 **Si**, 0.40–0.60 **Cr**, 0.40–0.70 **Ni**, 0.15–0.30 **Mo**	**Quenched and tempered:** ($\leq$16) **diam**, (1030) **TS**, (835) **YS**, 10 **El**
ISO/R 683/VII	Type 1	ISO	Bar, billets, rod	0.37–0.44 **C**, 0.70–1.00 **Mn**, 0.035 **P**, 0.035 **S**, 0.15–0.40 **Si**, 0.40–0.60 **Cr**, 0.40–0.70 **Ni**, 0.15–0.30 **Mo**	**Quenched and tempered:** ($\leq$16) **diam**, (1029) **TS**, (833) **YS**, 10 **El**
ISO/R 683/VIII	Type 1a	ISO	Bar, billets, rod	0.37–0.44 **C**, 0.70–1.00 **Mn**, 0.035 **P**, 0.020–0.035 **S**, 0.15–0.40 **Si**, 0.40–0.60 **Cr**, 0.40–0.70 **Ni**, 0.15–0.30 **Mo**	**Quenched and tempered:** ($\leq$16) **diam**, (1029) **TS**, (833) **YS**, 10 **El**
ISO/R 683/VIII	Type 1b	ISO	Bar, billets, rod	0.37–0.44 **C**, 0.70–1.00 **Mn**, 0.035 **P**, 0.030–0.050 **S**, 0.15–0.40 **Si**, 0.40–0.60 **Cr**, 0.40–0.70 **Ni**, 0.15–0.30 **Mo**	**Quenched and tempered:** ($\leq$16) **diam**, (1029) **TS**, (833) **YS**, 10 **El**
ANSI/ASTM A 540	B24	US	Bar: rolled or forged, tube: seamless, bar: bored, hollows: forged	0.37–0.44 **C**, 0.70–0.90 **Mn**, 0.025 **P**, 0.025 **S**, 0.15–0.35 **Si**, 0.70–0.95 **Cr**, 1.65–2.00 **Ni**, 0.30–0.40 **Mo**	**Annealed or quenched, tempered:** $\geq$6 (152.4) **diam**, 120 (827) **TS**, 105 (724) **YS**, 15 **El**
ANSI/ASTM A 540	B23	US	Bar, tube: seamless	0.37–0.44 **C**, 0.60–0.95 **Mn**, 0.025 **P**, 0.025 **S**, 0.15–0.35 **Si**, 0.65–0.95 **Cr**, 1.55–2.00 **Ni**, 0.20–0.30 **Mo**	**Annealed or quenched, tempered:** $\geq$6 (152.4) **diam**, 120 (827) **TS**, 105 (724) **YS**, 15 **El**
BS 970 Part 2	Grade 530 H 40	UK	Blooms, billets, bar, forgings	0.37–0.44 **C**, 0.50–0.90 **Mn**, 0.10–0.35 **Si**, 0.80–1.25 **Cr**	
ASTM A 547	Grade 1340H	US	Wire	0.37–0.44 **C**, 1.45–2.05 **Mn**	
ASTM A 547	Grade 4140H	US	Wire	0.37–0.44 **C**, 0.65–1.10 **Mn**, 0.75–1.20 **Cr**, 0.15–0.25 **Mo**	

WROUGHT ALLOY STEELS

specification number	designation	country	product forms	composition	mechanical properties (see page iv for explanation)
ASTM A 547	Grade 4340H	US	Wire	0.37–0.44 **C**, 0.55–0.90 **Mn**, 0.65–0.95 **Cr**, 1.55–2.00 **Ni**, 0.20–0.30 **Mo**	
ASTM A 547	Grade 8640H	US	Wire	0.37–0.44 **C**, 0.70–1.05 **Mn**, 0.35–0.65 **Cr**, 0.35–0.75 **Ni**, 0.15–0.25 **Mo**	
ASTM A 547	Grade 8740H	US	Wire	0.37–0.44 **C**, 0.70–1.05 **Mn**, 0.35–0.65 **Cr**, 0.35–0.75 **Ni**, 0.20–0.30 **Mo**	
AS 1444	Grade AS 1444/3140H	Australia	Bar, bloom, billet, slab	0.37–0.44 **C**, 0.60–1.00 **Mn**, 0.040 **P**, 0.040 **S**, 0.10–0.35 **Si**, 0.45–0.85 **Cr**, 1.00–1.45 **Ni**	
AS 1444	Grade 1444/4140H	Australia	Bar, bloom, billet, slab	0.37–0.44 **C**, 0.65–1.10 **Mn**, 0.040 **P**, 0.040 **S**, 0.10–0.35 **Si**, 0.75–1.20 **Cr**, 0.15–0.25 **Mo**	
AS 1444	Grade AS 1444/4340H	Australia	Bar, bloom, billet, slab	0.37–0.44 **C**, 0.55–0.90 **Mn**, 0.040 **P**, 0.040 **S**, 0.10–0.35 **Si**, 0.65–0.95 **Cr**, 1.55–2.00 **Ni**, 0.20–0.30 **Mo**	
AS 1444	Grade AS 1444/8740H	Australia	Bar, bloom, billet, slab	0.37–0.44 **C**, 0.70–1.05 **Mn**, 0.040 **P**, 0.040 **S**, 0.10–0.35 **Si**, 0.35–0.65 **Cr**, 0.35–0.75 **Ni**, 0.20–0.30 **Mo**	
DGN-B-300	1340H	Mexico	Bar	0.37–0.44 **C**, 1.45–2.05 **Mn**, 0.040 **P**, 0.20–0.35 **Si**	**Annealed**
DGN-B-300	E 4340-H	Mexico	Bar	0.37–0.44 **C**, 0.60–0.95 **Mn**, 0.040 **P**, 0.035 **S**, 0.20–0.35 **Si**, 0.65–0.95 **Cr**, 1.55–2.00 **Ni**, 0.20–0.30 **Mo**	**Annealed**
DGN-B-300	4340 H	Mexico	Bar	0.37–0.44 **C**, 0.55–0.90 **Mn**, 0.040 **P**, 0.035 **S**, 0.20–0.35 **Si**, 0.65–0.95 **Cr**, 1.55–2.00 **Ni**, 0.20–0.30 **Mo**	**Annealed**
DGN-B-300	4140 H	Mexico	Bar	0.37–0.44 **C**, 0.65–1.10 **Mn**, 0.40 **P**, 0.035 **S**, 0.20–0.35 **Si**, 0.75–1.20 **Cr**, 0.15–0.25 **Mo**	**Annealed**
DGN-B-300	50B40 H	Mexico	Bar	0.37–0.44 **C**, 0.65–1.10 **Mn**, 0.040 **P**, 0.035 **S**, 0.20–0.35 **Si**, 0.30–0.70 **Cr**, 0.0005 min **B**	
DGN-B-300	8640 H	Mexico	Bar	0.37–0.44 **C**, 0.70–1.05 **Mn**, 0.040 **P**, 0.035 **S**, 0.20–0.35 **Si**, 0.35–0.65 **Cr**, 0.35–0.75 **Ni**, 0.15–0.25 **Mo**	**Annealed**
DGN-B-300	5140 H	Mexico	Bar	0.37–0.44 **C**, 0.60–1.00 **Mn**, 0.040 **P**, 0.035 **S**, 0.20–0.35 **Si**, 0.60–1.00 **Cr**	**Annealed**
DGN-B-300	8740 H	Mexico	Bar	0.37–0.44 **C**, 0.70–1.05 **Mn**, 0.040 **P**, 0.035 **S**, 0.20–0.35 **Si**, 0.35–0.65 **Cr**, 0.35–0.75 **Ni**, 0.20–0.30 **Mo**	**Annealed**
ANSI/ASTM A 304	1340 H	US	Bar	0.37–0.44 **C**, 1.45–2.05 **Mn**, 0.040 **P**, 0.040 **S**, 0.15–0.30 **Si**	
ASTM A 689	4140 H	US	Bar	0.37–0.44 **C**, 0.65–1.10 **Mn**, 0.040 **P**, 0.040 **S**, 0.15–0.30 **Si**, 0.75–1.20 **Cr**, 0.15–0.25 **Mo**	
ASTM A 689	1340 H	US	Bar	0.37–0.44 **C**, 1.45–2.05 **Mn**, 0.040 **P**, 0.040 **S**, 0.15–0.30 **Si**	
ASTM A 689	5140 H	US	Bar	0.37–0.44 **C**, 0.60–1.00 **Mn**, 0.040 **P**, 0.040 **S**, 0.15–0.30 **Si**, 0.60–1.00 **Cr**	
ASTM A 689	8740 H	US	Bar	0.37–0.44 **C**, 0.70–1.05 **Mn**, 0.040 **P**, 0.040 **S**, 0.15–0.30 **Si**, 0.35–0.65 **Cr**, 0.35–0.75 **Ni**, 0.20–0.30 **Mo**	
ASTM A 689	8640 H	US	Bar	0.37–0.44 **C**, 0.70–1.05 **Mn**, 0.040 **P**, 0.040 **S**, 0.15–0.30 **Si**, 0.35–0.65 **Cr**, 0.35–0.75 **Ni**, 0.15–0.25 **Mo**	
ANSI/ASTM A 304	50B40 H	US	Bar	0.37–0.44 **C**, 0.65–1.10 **Mn**, 0.040 **P**, 0.040 **S**, 0.15–0.30 **Si**, 0.30–0.70 **Cr**, 0.0005 **B**	

specification number	designation	country	product forms	composition	mechanical properties (see page iv for explanation)
ANSI/ASTM A 304	5140 H	US	Bar	0.37–0.44 **C**, 0.60–1.00 **Mn**, 0.040 **P**, 0.040 **S**, 0.15–0.30 **Si**, 0.60–1.00 **Cr**	
ANSI/ASTM A 304	8640 H	US	Bar	0.37–0.44 **C**, 0.70–1.05 **Mn**, 0.040 **P**, 0.040 **S**, 0.15–0.30 **Si**, 0.35–0.65 **Cr**, 0.35–0.75 **Ni**, 0.15–0.25 **Mo**	
ANSI/ASTM A 304	8740 H	US	Bar	0.37–0.44 **C**, 0.70–1.05 **Mn**, 0.040 **P**, 0.040 **S**, 0.15–0.30 **Si**, 0.35–0.65 **Cr**, 0.35–0.75 **Ni**, 0.20–0.30 **Mo**	
ANSI/ASTM A 304	E 4340 H	US	Bar	0.37–0.44 **C**, 0.60–0.95 **Mn**, 0.025 **P**, 0.025 **S**, 0.15–0.30 **Si**, 0.65–0.95 **Cr**, 1.55–2.00 **Ni**, 0.20–0.30 **Mo**	
ANSI/ASTM A 304	4340 H	US	Bar	0.37–0.44 **C**, 0.55–0.90 **Mn**, 0.040 **P**, 0.040 **S**, 0.15–0.30 **Si**, 0.65–0.95 **Cr**, 1.55–2.00 **Ni**, 0.20–0.30 **Mo**	
ANSI/ASTM A 304	4140 H	US	Bar	0.37–0.44 **C**, 0.65–1.10 **Mn**, 0.040 **P**, 0.040 **S**, 0.15–0.30 **Si**, 0.75–1.20 **Cr**, 0.15–0.25 **Mo**	
ASTM A 689	50B40 H	US	Bar	0.37–0.44 **C**, 0.65–1.10 **Mn**, 0.040 **P**, 0.040 **S**, 0.15–0.30 **Si**, 0.30–0.70 **Cr**, 0.0005 min **B**	
ASTM A 689	E4340 H	US	Bar	0.37–0.44 **C**, 0.60–0.95 **Mn**, 0.025 **P**, 0.025 **S**, 0.15–0.30 **Si**, 0.65–0.95 **Cr**, 1.55–2.00 **Ni**, 0.20–0.30 **Mo**	
ASTM A 689	4340 H	US	Bar	0.37–0.44 **C**, 0.55–0.90 **Mn**, 0.040 **P**, 0.040 **S**, 0.15–0.30 **Si**, 0.65–0.95 **Cr**, 1.55–2.00 **Ni**, 0.20–0.30 **Mo**	
AISI E4340		US	Plate	0.37–0.44 **C**, 0.60–0.85 **Mn**, 0.025 **P**, 0.025 **S**, 0.15–0.30 **Si**, 0.65–0.90 **Cr**, 0.20–0.30 **Mo**	
AISI 5140 H		US	Wire, rod	0.37–0.44 **C**, 0.60–1.00 **Mn**, 0.15–0.30 **Si**, 0.60–1.00 **Cr**	
AISI 8640 H		US	Wire, rod	0.37–0.44 **C**, 0.70–1.05 **Mn**, 0.15–0.30 **Si**, 0.35–0.65 **Cr**, 0.35–0.75 **Ni**, 0.15–0.25 **Mo**	
AISI 8740 H		US	Wire, rod	0.37–0.44 **C**, 0.70–1.05 **Mn**, 0.15–0.30 **Si**, 0.35–0.65 **Cr**, 0.35–0.75 **Ni**, 0.20–0.30 **Mo**	
AISI 4340 H		US	Wire, rod	0.37–0.44 **C**, 0.55–0.90 **Mn**, 0.15–0.30 **Si**, 0.65–0.95 **Cr**, 1.55–2.00 **Ni**, 0.20–0.30 **Mo**	
AISI E4340 H		US	Wire, rod	0.37–0.44 **C**, 0.60–0.95 **Mn**, 0.15–0.30 **Si**, 0.65–0.95 **Cr**, 1.55–2.00 **Ni**, 0.20–0.30 **Mo**	
AISI 1340 H		US	Wire, rod	0.37–0.44 **C**, 1.45–2.05 **Mn**, 0.15–0.30 **Si**	
AISI 4140 H		US	Wire, rod	0.37–0.44 **C**, 0.65–1.10 **Mn**, 0.15–0.30 **Si**, 0.75–1.20 **Cr**, 0.15–0.25 **Mo**	
AISI 50B40H		US	Bar	0.37–0.44 **C**, 0.65–1.10 **Mn**, 0.035 **P**, 0.040 **S**, 0.15–0.30 **Si**, 0.30–0.70 **Cr**	
AISI 8740H		US	Bar	0.37–0.44 **C**, 0.70–1.05 **Mn**, 0.035 **P**, 0.040 **S**, 0.15–0.30 **Si**, 0.35–0.65 **Cr**, 0.35–0.75 **Ni**, 0.20–0.30 **Mo**	
AISI 8640H		US	Bar	0.37–0.44 **C**, 0.70–1.05 **Mn**, 0.035 **P**, 0.040 **S**, 0.15–0.30 **Si**, 0.35–0.65 **Cr**, 0.35–0.7 **Ni**, 0.15–0.25 **Mo**	
AISI 5140		US	Bar	0.37–0.44 **C**, 0.60–1.00 **Mn**, 0.035 **P**, 0.040 **S**, 0.15–0.30 **Si**, 0.60–1.00 **Cr**	
AISI E4340H		US	Bar	0.37–0.44 **C**, 0.60–0.95 **Mn**, 0.025 **P**, 0.025 **S**, 0.15–0.30 **Si**, 0.65–0.95 **Cr**, 1.55–2.00 **Ni**, 0.20–0.30 **Mo**	

WROUGHT ALLOY STEELS

specification number	designation	country	product forms	composition	mechanical properties (see page iv for explanation)
AISI 4340H		US	Bar	0.37–0.44 **C**, 0.55–0.90 **Mn**, 0.035 **P**, 0.040 **S**, 0.15–0.30 **Si**, 0.65–0.95 **Cr**, 1.55–2.00 **Ni**, 0.20–0.30 **Mo**	
AISI 4140H		US	Bar	0.37–0.44 **C**, 0.65–1.10 **Mn**, 0.035 **P**, 0.040 **S**, 0.15–0.30 **Si**, 0.75–1.20 **Cr**, 0.15–0.25 **Mo**	
AISI 1340H		US	Bar	0.37–0.44 **C**, 1.45–2.05 **Mn**, 0.035 **P**, 0.040 **S**, 0.15–0.30 **Si**	
JIS G 4052	SCr 4H	Japan	Bar, wire, rod	0.37–0.44 **C**, 0.55–0.90 **Mn**, 0.030 **P**, 0.030 **S**, 0.15–0.35 **Si**, 0.85–1.25 **Cr**, 0.30 **Cu**	**Hot rolled, normalized, quenched**
JIS G 4052	SCM 4H	Japan	Bar, wire, rod	0.37–0.44 **C**, 0.55–0.90 **Mn**, 0.030 **P**, 0.030 **S**, 0.15–0.35 **Si**, 0.85–1.25 **Cr**, 0.15–0.35 **Mo**	**Hot rolled, normalized, quenched**
ISO 683/XII	11	ISO	Bar, plate	0.37–0.43 **C**, 0.50–0.80 **Mn**, 0.035 **P**, 0.035 **S**, 0.15–0.40 **Si**, 0.60–0.90 **Cr**, 0.70–1.00 **Ni**, 0.15–0.30 **Mo**	**Quenched and tempered:** (16) **diam**, (1030) **TS**, (830) **YS**, 10 **El**
ASTM A 293	Class 6	US	Forgings	0.37 **C**, 1.00 **Mn**, 0.035 **P**, 0.035 **S**, 0.15–0.35 **Si**, 0.85–1.25 **Cr**, 0.50 **Ni**, 1.00–1.50 **Mo**, 0.20–0.30 **V**	**Normalized, tempered or double normalized, tempered:** all **diam**, 110 (760) **TS**, 85 (585) **YS**, 16 **El**
JIS G 4107	Class 2	Japan	Bar	0.36–0.50 **C**, 0.71–1.04 **Mn**, 0.045 **P**, 0.045 **S**, 0.18–0.37 **Si**, 0.75–1.15 **Cr**, 0.13–0.27 **Mo**	**Rolled or forged:** (≤63) **diam**, (863) **TS**, (726) **YS**, 16 **El**
IS 4367	40Ni3Cr^{65}Mo^{55}	India	Forgings	0.36–0.44 **C**, 0.40–0.70 **Mn**, 0.050 **P**, 0.050 **S**, 0.10–0.35 **Si**, 0.50–0.80 **Cr**, 2.25–2.75 **Ni**, 0.40–0.70 **Mo**	**Hardened and tempered:** (100) **diam**, (1519) **TS**, 8 **El**
BS 4S.99		UK	Bar, billets, forgings parts: aircraft quality	0.36–0.44 **C**, 0.45–0.7 **Mn**, 0.025 **P**, 0.020 **S**, 0.10–0.35 **Si**, 0.5–0.8 **Cr**, 2.3–2.8 **Ni**, 0.45–0.65 **Mo**	**Hardened and tempered:** all **diam**, (1230) **TS**, (1080) **YS**, 10 **El**
BS 2S.98		UK	Bar, billets, forgings: aircraft quality	0.36–0.44 **C**, 0.45–0.7 **Mn**, 0.025 **P**, 0.020 **S**, 0.10–0.35 **Si**, 0.5–0.8 **Cr**, 2.3–2.8 **Ni**, 0.45–0.65 **Mo**	**Hardened and tempered:** all **diam**, (1160) **TS**, (1005) **YS**, 10 **El**
BS S.139		UK	Bar, billets, forgings: aircraft quality	0.36–0.44 **C**, 0.45–0.7 **Mn**, 0.025 **P**, 0.020 **S**, 0.15–0.35 **Si**, 1.10–1.40 **Cr**, 1.30–1.70 **Ni**, 0.20–0.35 **Mo**	**Hardened and tempered:** all **diam**, (1080) **TS**, (860) **YS**, 10 **El**
BS 2 S.119		UK	Bar, billets, forgings: aircraft quality	0.36–0.44 **C**, 0.45–0.70 **Mn**, 0.025 **P**, 0.020 **S**, 0.15–0.35 **Si**, 1.10–1.40 **Cr**, 1.30–1.70 **Ni**, 0.20–0.35 **Mo**	**Hardened and tempered:** all **diam**, (1000) **TS**, (850) **YS**, 12 **El**
AS G18	G18/En 26	Australia	Bar, billet	0.36–0.44 **C**, 0.50–0.70 **Mn**, 0.050 **P**, 0.050 **S**, 0.10–0.35 **Si**, 0.50–0.80 **Cr**, 2.30–2.80 **Ni**, 0.40–0.70 **Mo**	**Hardened, tempered:** 6 **diam**, (930) **TS**, (740) **YS**
ANSI/ASTM A 193	Grade B16	US	Bar	0.36–0.44 **C**, 0.45–0.70 **Mn**, 0.04 **P**, 0.04 **S**, 0.15–0.35 **Si**, 0.80–1.15 **Cr**, 0.50–0.65 **Mo**, 0.25–0.35 **V**	**Quenched and tempered or normalized and tempered:** ≥2.5 (≥63.5) **diam**, 125 (862) **TS**, 105 (724) **YS**, 18 **El**
BS 3S. 95		UK	Bar, billets, forgings: aircraft quality	0.36–0.44 **C**, 0.45–0.70 **Mn**, 0.025 **P**, 0.020 **S**, 0.15–0.35 **Si**, 1.10–1.40 **Cr**, 1.30–1.70 **Ni**, 0.20–0.35 **Mo**	**Hardened and tempered:** all **diam**, (860) **TS**, (680) **YS**, 12 **El**
BS 4670	Grade 826M40	UK	Forgings	0.36–0.44 **C**, 0.45–0.70 **Mn**, 0.040 **P**, 0.040 **S**, 0.10–0.35 **Si**, 0.50–0.80 **Cr**, 2.30–2.80 **Ni**, 0.45–0.65 **Mo**	**Hardened, tempered:** (1000) **diam**, (850) **TS**, (660) **YS**, 13 **El**
BS 970 Part 2	Grade 826 M 40	UK	Blooms, billets, bar, forgings	0.36–0.44 **C**, 0.45–0.70 **Mn**, 0.10–0.35 **Si**, 0.50–0.80 **Cr**, 2.30–2.80 **Ni**, 0.45–0.65 **Mo**	**Hardened and tempered:** 10 **diam**, (830) **TS**, (665) **YS**, 12 **El**
BS 4670	Grade 818M40	UK	Forgings	0.36–0.44 **C**, 0.45–0.85 **Mn**, 0.040 **P**, 0.040 **S**, 0.10–0.35 **Si**, 1.00–1.50 **Cr**, 1.30–1.80 **Ni**, 0.20–0.40 **Mo**	**Hardened, tempered:** (1000) **diam**, (800) **TS**, (610) **YS**, 14 **El**
ANSI/ASTM A 540	B21	US	Bar, tube: seamless	0.36–0.44 **C**, 0.45–0.70 **Mn**, 0.025 **P**, 0.025 **S**, 0.15–0.35 **Si**, 0.80–1.15 **Cr**, 0.50–0.65 **Mo**, 0.25–0.35 **V**	**Annealed or quenched, tempered:** 2–6 (50.8–152.4) **diam**, 115 (793) **TS**, 10 0 (689) **YS**, 15 **El**

WROUGHT ALLOY STEELS

specification number	designation	country	product forms	composition	mechanical properties (see page iv for explanation)
BS 970 Part 2	Grade 817 M 40	UK	Blooms, billets, bar, forgings	0.36–0.44 **C**, 0.45–0.70 **Mn**, 0.10–0.35 **Si**, 1.00–1.40 **Cr**, 1.30–1.70 **Ni**, 0.20–0.35 **Mo**	**Hardened and tempered:** 10 **diam**, (760) **TS**, (580) **YS**, 13 **El**
JIS G 3539	SWCH 41K	Japan	Wire	0.36–0.44 **C**, 1.35–1.65 **Mn**, 0.030 **P**, 0.035 **S**, 0.10–0.35 **Si**	**Annealed and cold drawn:** all **diam**, (706) **TS**, 10 **El**
BS 4670	Grade 711M40	UK	Forgings	0.36–0.44 **C**, 0.60–1.00 **Mn**, 0.040 **P**, 0.040 **S**, 0.10–0.35 **Si**, 0.90–1.50 **Cr**, 0.40 **Ni**, 0.25–0.40 **Mo**	**Hardened, tempered:** (500) **diam**, (700) **TS**, (500) **YS**, 16 **El**
BS 970 Part 2	Grade 816 M 40	UK	Blooms, billets, bar, forgings	0.36–0.44 **C**, 0.45–0.70 **Mn**, 0.10–0.35 **Si**, 1.00–1.40 **Cr**, 1.30–1.70 **Ni**, 0.10–0.20 **Mo**	**Hardened and tempered:** 10 **diam**, (690) **TS**, (500) **YS**, 15 **El**
DGN–B–301	1041	Mexico	Bar	0.36–0.44 **C**, 1.35–1.65 **Mn**, 0.040 **P**, 0.050 **S**, 0.10–0.20 **Si**	**Forged or hot rolled, cold rolled and/or cold finished:** all **diam**, (637) **TS**, (353) **YS**, 15 **El**
BS 970 Part 2	Grade 530 M 40	UK	Blooms, billets, bar, forgings	0.36–0.44 **C**, 0.60–0.90 **Mn**, 0.10–0.35 **Si**, 0.90–1.20 **Cr**	**Hardened and tempered:** 4 **diam**, (620) **TS**, (470) **YS**, 17 **El**
BS 970 Part 2	Grade 640 M 40	UK	Blooms, billets, bar, forgings	0.36–0.44 **C**, 0.60–0.90 **Mn**, 0.10–0.35 **S**, 0.50–0.80 **Cr**, 1.10–1.50 **Ni**	**Hardened and tempered:** 6 **diam**, (620) **TS**, (470) **YS**, 17 **El**
BS 970 Part 2	Grade 708 M 40	UK	Blooms, billets, bar, forgings	0.36–0.44 **C**, 0.70–1.00 **Mn**, 0.10–0.35 **S**, 0.90–1.20 **Cr**, 0.15–0.25 **Mo**	**Hardened and tempered:** 6 **diam**, (620) **TS**, (470) **YS**, 17 **El**
BS 970 Part 2	Grade 709 M 40	UK	Blooms, billets, bar, forgings	0.36–0.44 **C**, 0.70–1.00 **Mn**, 0.10–0.35 **Si**, 0.90–1.20 **Cr**, 0.25–0.35 **Mo**	**Hardened and tempered:** 10 **diam**, (620) **TS**, (445) **YS**, 15 **El**
BS 970 Part 2	Grade 503 M 40	UK	Blooms, billets, bar, forgings	0.36–0.44 **C**, 0.70–1.00 **Mn**, 0.10–0.35 **Si**, 0.70–1.00 **Ni**	**Normalized:** 10 **diam**, (480) **TS**, (275) **YS**, 15 **El**; **Hardened and tempered:** 10 **diam**, (551) **TS**, (386) **YS**, 15 **El**
ANSI/ASTM A 29	1541	US	Bar	0.36–0.44 **C**, 1.35–1.65 **Mn**, 0.040 **P**, 0.050 **S**	
ANSI/ASTM A 545	Grade 1541	US	Wire	0.36–0.44 **C**, 1.35–1.65 **Mn**, 0.040 **P**, 0.050 **S**	
AISI 1340		US	Plate	0.36–0.44 **C**, 1.50–1.90 **Mn**, 0.035 **P**, 0.040 **S**, 0.15–0.30 **Si**	
AISI 4140		US	Plate	0.36–0.44 **C**, 0.70–1.00 **Mn**, 0.03 **P**, 0.040 **S**, 0.15–0.30 **Si**, 0.80–1.15 **Cr**, 0.15–0.25 **Mo**	
AISI 4340		US	Plate	0.36–0.44 **C**, 0.55–0.80 **Mn**, 0.035 **P**, 0.040 **S**, 0.15–0.30 **Si**, 0.60–0.90 **Cr**, 0.20–0.30 **Mo**	
AISI 8640		US	Plate	0.36–0.44 **C**, 0.70–1.00 **Mn**, 0.035 **P**, 0.040 **S**, 0.15–0.30 **Si**, 0.35–0.60 **Cr**, 0.40–0.70 **Ni**, 0.15–0.25 **Mo**	
AISI 1541		US	Wire, rod	0.36–0.44 **C**, 1.35–1.65 **Mn**, 0.040 **P**, 0.050 **S**	
ANSI/ASTM A 576	1541	US	Bar	0.36–0.44 **C**, 1.35–1.65 **Mn**, 0.040 **P**, 0.050 **S**	
DGN–B–301	1541	Mexico	Bar	0.36–0.44 **C**, 1.35–1.65 **Mn**, 0.040 **P**, 0.050 **S**	
COPANT 514	Grade 1041	COPANT	Tube: seamless	0.36–0.44 **C**, 1.35–1.65 **Mn**, 0.040 **P**, 0.050 **S**, 0.20–0.35 **Si**	
DGN–B–203	Grade 1041	Mexico	Tube: seamless	0.36–0.44 **C**, 1.35–1.65 **Mn**, 0.040 **P**, 0.050 **S**	
EURONORM 119–74, IV	40 NiCrMo 4 KD	EURONORM	Wire, rod	0.36–0.43 **C**, 0.50–0.80 **Mn**, 0.035 **P**, 0.035 **S**, 0.15–0.40 **Si**, 0.60–0.90 **Cr**, 0.70–1.30 **Ni**, 0.15–0.30 **Mo**	**Quenched and tempered:** (≤16) **diam**, (1030) **TS**, (835) **YS**, 10 **El**
ISO/R 683/VIII	Type 2	ISO	Bar, billets, rod	0.36–0.43 **C**, 0.50–0.80 **Mn**, 0.035 **P**, 0.035 **S**, 0.15–0.40 **Si**, 0.60–0.90 **Cr**, 0.70–1.00 **Ni**, 0.15–0.30 **Mo**	**Quenched and tempered:** (≤16) **diam**, (1029) **TS**, (833) **YS**, 10 **El**
ISO/R 683/VIII	Type 2a	ISO	Bar, billets, rod	0.36–0.43 **C**, 0.50–0.80 **Mn**, 0.035 **P**, 0.020–0.035 **S**, 0.15–0.40 **Si**, 0.60–0.90 **Cr**, 0.70–1.00 **Ni**, 0.15–0.30 **Mo**	**Quenched and tempered:** (≤16) **diam**, (1029) **TS**, (833) **YS**, 10 **El**

WROUGHT ALLOY STEELS

specification number	designation	country	product forms	composition	mechanical properties (see page iv for explanation)
ISO/R 683/VIII	Type 2b	ISO	Bar, billets, rod	0.36–0.43 **C**, 0.50–0.80 **Mn**, 0.035 **P**, 0.030–0.050 **S**, 0.15–0.40 **Si**, 0.60–0.90 **Cr**, 0.70–1.0 **Ni**, 0.15–0.30 **Mo**	**Quenched and tempered:** (≤16) **diam**, (1029) **TS**, (833) **YS**, 10 **El**
JIS G 4103	Class 8	Japan	Bar	0.36–0.43 **C**, 0.60–0.90 **Mn**, 0.030 **P**, 0.030 **S**, 0.15–0.35 **Si**, 0.60–1.00 **Cr**, 1.60–2.00 **Ni**, 0.15–0.30 **Mo**, 0.30 **Cu**	**Rolled or forged, quenched and tempered:** (25) **diam**, (981) **TS**, (883) **YS**, 16 **El**
BS 3111 Part 1	Type 6	UK	Wire	0.36–0.41 **C**, 0.45–0.70 **Mn**, 0.040 **P**, 0.040 **S**, 0.15–0.40 **Si**, 1.00–1.40 **Cr**, 1.30–1.70 **Ni**, 0.10–0.20 **Mo**	**Drawn and spheroidized annealed:** all **diam**, (670) max **TS**; **Drawn, spheroidized annealed and light drawn:** all **diam**, (710) max **TS**
BS S.148		UK	Bar: aircraft quality	0.36–0.41 **C**, 0.6–0.9 **Mn**, 0.025 **P**, 0.020 **S**, 0.15–0.35 **Si**, 0.5–0.8 **Cr**, 1.1–1.5 **Ni**	**Hardened and tempered**
JIS G 3105	Class 3, No. 14A	Japan	Bar	0.36 **C**, 1.00–1.90 **Mn**, 0.040 **P**, 0.040 **S**, 0.15–0.55 **Si**	**Quenched or tempered:** all **diam**, (686) **TS**, 17 **El**
ASTM A 291	Class 7	US	Forgings	0.35–0.50 **C**, 0.40–0.90 **Mn**, 0.040 **P**, 0.040 **S**, 0.15–0.30 **Si**, 0.60 min **Cr**, 1.65 min **Ni**, 0.20–0.60 **Mo**, 0.10 **V**	**Quenched, annealed:** ≥10 (254) **diam**, 170 (1375) **TS**, 140 (965) **YS**, 14 **El**
ASTM A 291	Class 6	US	Forgings	0.35–0.50 **C**, 0.40–0.90 **Mn**, 0.040 **P**, 0.040 **S**, 0.15–0.30 **Si**, 0.60 min **Cr**, 1.65 min **Ni**, 0.20–0.60 **Mo**, 0.10 **V**	**Quenched, annealed:** ≥10 (254) **diam**, 145 (1000) **TS**, 120 (825) **YS**, 15 **El**
ASTM A 291	Class 5	US	Forgings	0.35–0.50 **C**, 0.40–0.90 **Mn**, 0.040 **P**, 0.040 **S**, 0.15–0.30 **Si**, 0.60 min **Cr**, 1.65 min **Ni**, 0.20–0.60 **Mo**, 0.10 **V**	**Quenched, annealed:** ≥10 (254) **diam**, 140 (965) **TS**, 115 (795) **YS**, 16 **El**
ASTM A 294	Class A7	US	Forgings	0.35–0.50 **C**, 0.60–1.00 **Mn**, 0.035 **P**, 0.035 **S**, 0.15–0.35 **Si**, 0.75–1.50 **Cr**, 0.15 min **Mo**	**Normalized or quenched, tempered:** all **diam**, 140 (965) **TS**, 125 (860) **YS**, 15 **El**
ANSI/ASTM A 372	Class VIII	US	Forgings	0.35–0.50 **C**, 0.75–1.05 **Mn**, 0.035 **P**, 0.04 **S**, 0.15–0.35 **Si**, 0.80–1.15 **Cr**, 0.15–0.25 **Mo**	**Liquid quenched and tempered:** all **diam**, (930) **TS**, (760) **YS**, 15 **El**
ASTM A 372	Class VIII	US	Forgings	0.35–0.50 **C**, 0.75–1.05 **Mn**, 0.035 **P**, 0.04 **S**, 0.15–0.35 **Si**, 0.80–1.15 **Cr**, 0.15–0.25 **Mo**	**Quenched, tempered:** all **diam**, 135 (930) **TS**, 110 (760) **YS**, 15 **El**
ASTM A 294	Class A6	US	Forgings	0.35–0.50 **C**, 0.60–1.00 **Mn**, 0.035 **P**, 0.035 **S**, 0.15–0.35 **Si**, 0.75–1.50 **Cr**, 0.15 min **Mo**	**Normalized or quenched, tempered:** all **diam**, 130 (905) **TS**, 115 (795) **YS**, 16 **El**
ASTM A 294	Class A5	US	Forgings	0.35–0.50 **C**, 0.60–1.00 **Mn**, 0.035 **P**, 0.035 **S**, 0.15–0.35 **Si**, 0.75–1.50 **Cr**, 0.15 min **Mo**	**Normalized or quenched, tempered:** all **diam**, 125 (860) **TS**, 105 (725) **YS**, 18 **El**
ANSI/ASTM A 372	Class V, type E	US	Forgings	0.35–0.50 **C**, 0.75–1.05 **Mn**, 0.035 **P**, 0.04 **S**, 0.15–0.35 **Si**, 0.80–1.15 **Cr**, 0.15–0.25 **Mo**	**Liquid quenched and tempered:** all **diam**, (825) **TS**, (485) **YS**, 18 **El**
ASTM A 291	Class 4	US	Forgings	0.35–0.50 **C**, 0.40–0.90 **Mn**, 0.040 **P**, 0.040 **S**, 0.15–0.30 **Si**, 0.60 min **Cr**, 1.65 min **Ni**, 0.20–0.60 **Mo**, 0.10 **V**	**Quenched, annealed:** ≥10 (254) **diam**, 120 (825) **TS**, 95 (655) **YS**, 16 **El**
ASTM A 294	Class A4	US	Forgings	0.35–0.50 **C**, 0.60–1.00 **Mn**, 0.035 **P**, 0.035 **S**, 0.15–0.35 **Si**, 0.75–1.50 **Cr**, 0.15 min **Mo**	**Normalized or quenched, tempered:** all **diam**, 120 (825) **TS**, 95 (655) **YS**, 18 **El**
ASTM A 372	Class V, Type E	US	Forgings	0.35–0.50 **C**, 0.75–1.05 **Mn**, 0.035 **P**, 0.04 **S**, 0.15–0.35 **Si**, 0.80–1.15 **Cr**, 0.15–0.25 **Mo**	**Quenched, tempered:** all **diam**, 120 (825) **TS**, 70 (485) **YS**, 18 **El**
ASTM A 294	Class A3	US	Forgings	0.35–0.50 **C**, 0.60–1.00 **Mn**, 0.035 **P**, 0.035 **S**, 0.15–0.35 **Si**, 0.75–1.50 **Cr**, 0.15 min **Mo**	**Normalized or quenched, tempered:** all **diam**, 110 (760) **TS**, 85 (585) **YS**, 19 **El**
ASTM A 294	Class A2	US	Forgings	0.35–0.50 **C**, 0.60–1.00 **Mn**, 0.035 **P**, 0.035 **S**, 0.15–0.35 **Si**, 0.75–1.50 **Cr**, 0.15 min **Mo**	**Normalized or quenched, tempered:** all **diam**, 100 (690) **TS**, 75 (515) **YS**, 20 **El**
ASTM A 294	Class A1	US	Forgings	0.35–0.50 **C**, 0.60–1.00 **Mn**, 0.035 **P**, 0.035 **S**, 0.15–0.35 **Si**, 0.75–1.50 **Cr**, 0.15 min **Mo**	**Normalized or quenched, tempered:** all **diam**, 90 (620) **TS**, 65 (450) **YS**, 20 **El**
AS G18	G18/En 54	Australia	Bar, billet	0.35–0.50 **C**, 1.50 **Mn**, 0.045 **P**, 0.045 **S**, 1.00–2.50 **Si**, 12.0–16.0 **Cr**, 10.0 min **Ni**, 2.00–4.00 **W**	

WROUGHT ALLOY STEELS

specification number	designation	country	product forms	composition	mechanical properties (see page iv for explanation)
BS 970 Part 2	Grade 897 M 39	UK	Blooms, billets, bar, forgings	0.35–0.49 **C**, 0.45–0.70 **Mn**, 0.025 **P**, 0.025 **S**, 0.10–0.35 **Si**, 3.00–3.50 **Cr**, 0.80–1.10 **Mo**, 0.15–0.25 **V**	**Hardened and tempered:** 2.50 **diam**, (1175) **TS**, (1035) **YS**, 8 **El**
JIS G 4108	Class 3, SNB 23–1	Japan	Bar	0.35–0.46 **C**, 0.56–0.99 **Mn**, 0.030 **P**, 0.030 **S**, 0.18–0.37 **Si**, 0.60–1.00 **Cr**, 1.50–2.05 **Ni**, 0.18–0.32 **Mo**	**Hot rolled, hot forged or cold finished:** (≤75) **diam**, (1138) **TS**, (1030) **YS**, 10 **El**
JIS G 4108	Class 4, SNB 24–1	Japan	Bar	0.35–0.46 **C**, 0.66–0.94 **Mn**, 0.030 **P**, 0.030 **S**, 0.18–0.37 **Si**, 0.65–1.00 **Cr**, 1.60–2.05 **Ni**, 0.28–0.42 **Mo**	**Hot rolled, hot forged or cold finished:** (≤150) **diam**, (1138) **TS**, (1030) **YS**, 10 **El**
JIS G 4108	Class 3, SNB 23–2	Japan	Bar	0.35–0.46 **C**, 0.56–0.99 **Mn**, 0.030 **P**, 0.030 **S**, 0.18–0.37 **Si**, 0.60–1.00 **Cr**, 1.50–2.05 **Ni**, 0.18–0.32 **Mo**	**Hot rolled, hot forged or cold finished:** (≤75) **diam**, (1069) **TS**, (961) **YS**, 11 **El**
JIS G 4108	Class 4, SNB 24–2	Japan	Bar	0.35–0.46 **C**, 0.66–0.94 **Mn**, 0.030 **P**, 0.030 **S**, 0.18–0.37 **Si**, 0.65–1.00 **Cr**, 1.60–2.05 **Ni**, 0.28–0.42 **Mo**	**Hot rolled, hot forged or cold finished:** (≤175) **diam**, (1069) **TS**, (961) **YS**, 11 **El**
JIS G 4108	Class 3, SNB 23–3	Japan	Bar	0.35–0.46 **C**, 0.56–0.99 **Mn**, 0.030 **P**, 0.030 **S**, 0.18–0.37 **Si**, 0.60–1.00 **Cr**, 1.50–2.05 **Ni**, 0.18–0.32 **Mo**	**Hot rolled, hot forged or cold finished:** (≤75) **diam**, (1000) **TS**, (892) **YS**, 12 **El**
JIS G 4108	Class 4, SNB 24–3	Japan	Bar	0.35–0.46 **C**, 0.66–0.94 **Mn**, 0.030 **P**, 0.030 **S**, 0.18–0.37 **Si**, 0.65–1.00 **Cr**, 1.60–2.05 **Ni**, 0.28–0.42 **Mo**	**Hot rolled, hot forged or cold finished:** (≤75) **diam**, (1000) **TS**, (892) **YS**, 12 **El**
JIS G 4108	Class 3, SNB 23–4	Japan	Bar	0.35–0.46 **C**, 0.56–0.99 **Mn**, 0.030 **P**, 0.030 **S**, 0.18–0.37 **Si**, 0.60–1.00 **Cr**, 1.50–2.05 **Ni**, 0.18–0.32 **Mo**	**Hot rolled, hot forged or cold finished:** (≤75) **diam**, (932) **TS**, (824) **YS**, 13 **El**
JIS G 4108	Class 4, SNB 24–4	Japan	Bar	0.35–0.46 **C**, 0.66–0.94 **Mn**, 0.030 **P**, 0.030 **S**, 0.18–0.37 **Si**, 0.65–1.00 **Cr**, 1.60–2.05 **Ni**, 0.28–0.42 **Mo**	**Hot rolled, hot forged or cold finished:** (≤75) **diam**, (932) **TS**, (824) **YS**, 13 **El**
JIS G 4108	Class 3, SNB 23–5	Japan	Bar	0.35–0.46 **C**, 0.56–0.99 **Mn**, 0.030 **P**, 0.030 **S**, 0.18–0.37 **Si**, 0.60–1.00 **Cr**, 1.50–2.05 **Ni**, 0.18–0.32 **Mo**	**Hot rolled, hot forged or cold finished:** (≤150) **diam**, (824) **TS**, (716) **YS**, 15 **El**
JIS G 4108	Class 4, SNB 24–5	Japan	Bar	0.35–0.46 **C**, 0.66–0.94 **Mn**, 0.030 **P**, 0.030 **S**, 0.18–0.37 **Si**, 0.65–1.00 **Cr**, 1.60–2.05 **Ni**, 0.28–0.42 **Mo**	**Hot rolled, hot forged or cold finished:** (≤150) **diam**, (824) **TS**, (716) **YS**, 15 **El**
IS 5517	Grade 40NiCr1Mo15	India	Bar, billet	0.35–0.45 **C**, 0.40–0.70 **Mn**, 0.10–0.35 **Si**, 0.90–1.30 **Cr**, 1.20–1.60 **Ni**, 0.10–0.20 **Mo**	**Normalized, annealed or hardened and tempered:** (30) **diam**, (1,08) **TS**, (860) **YS**
ASTM A 290	Class K	US	Rings: forged or rolled	0.35–0.45 **C**, 0.60–0.90 **Mn**, 0.040 **P**, 0.040 **S**, 0.20–0.35 **Si**, 0.60–0.90 **Cr**, 1.65–2.00 **Ni**, 0.20–0.50 **Mo**, 0.10 **V**	**Quenched, tempered:** all **diam**, 170 (1175) **TS**, 145 (1000) **YS**, 10 **El**
ASTM A 290	Class I	US	Rings: forged or rolled	0.35–0.45 **C**, 0.60–0.90 **Mn**, 0.040 **P**, 0.040 **S**, 0.20–0.35 **Si**, 0.60–0.90 **Cr**, 1.65–2.00 **Ni**, 0.20–0.50 **Mo**, 0.10 **V**	**Quenched, tempered:** all **diam**, 145 (1000) **TS**, 120 (825) **YS**, 14 **El**
IS 5517	Grade 40Cr1Mo28	India	Bar, billet	0.35–0.45 **C**, 0.50–0.80 **Mn**, 0.10–0.35 **Si**, 0.90–1.20 **Cr**, 0.20–0.35 **Mo**	**Normalized, annealed or hardened and tempered:** (30) **diam**, (980) **TS**, (785) **YS**
IS 4367	40Ni2Cr1Mo[28]	India	Forgings	0.35–0.45 **C**, 0.40–0.70 **Mn**, 0.050 **P**, 0.050 **S**, 0.10–0.35 **Si**, 0.90–1.30 **Cr**, 1.25–1.75 **Ni**, 0.20–0.35 **Mo**	**Hardened and tempered:** (100) **diam**, (980) **TS**, 13 **El**
JIS G 4311	SUH 3	Japan	Bar	0.35–0.45 **C**, 0.60 **Mn**, 1.80–2.50 **Si**, 10.00–12.00 **Cr**, 0.60 **Ni**, 0.70–1.30 **Mo**, 0.030 **P**, 0.030 **S**	**Quenched and tempered:** (≤25) **diam**, (932) **TS**, (686) **YS**, 15 **El**
IS 5517	Grade 40Cr1	India	Bar, billet	0.35–0.45 **C**, 0.60–0.90 **Mn**, 0.10–0.35 **Si**, 0.90–1.20 **Cr**	**Normalized, annealed or hardened and tempered:** (30) **diam**, (880) **TS**, (685) **YS**
IS 5517	Grade 40Cr2AlIMo18	India	Bar, billet	0.35–0.45 **C**, 0.40–0.70 **Mn**, 0.10–0.45 **Si**, 1.50–1.80 **Cr**, 0.30 **Ni**, 0.10–0.25 **Mo**, 0.90–1.30 **Al**	**Normalized, annealed or hardened and tempered:** (63) **diam**, (880) **TS**, (685) **YS**

specification number	designation	country	product forms	composition	mechanical properties (see page iv for explanation)
IS 5517	Grade 40Ni3	India	Bar, billet	0.35–0.45 **C**, 0.50–0.80 **Mn**, 0.10–0.35 **Si**, 0.30 **Cr**, 3.20–3.60 **Ni**	**Normalized, annealed or hardened and tempered:** (63) **diam**, (880) **TS**, (685) **YS**
ASTM A 290	Class G	US	Rings: forged or rolled	0.35–0.45 **C**, 0.60–0.90 **Mn**, 0.040 **P**, 0.040 **S**, 0.20–0.35 **Si**, 0.60–0.90 **Cr**, 1.65–2.00 **Ni**, 0.20–0.50 **Mo**, 0.10 **V**	**Quenched, tempered:** all **diam**, 125 (860) **TS**, 100 (690) **YS**, 15 **El**
B S 2S.117		UK	Bar, billets, forgings: aircraft quality	0.35–0.45 **C**, 0.6–0.9 **Mn**, 0.040 **P**, 0.040 **S**, 0.10–0.35 **Si**, 0.9–1.2 **Cr**	**Hardened and tempered:** all **diam**, (850) **TS**, (680) **YS**, 13 **El**
AS G18	G18/En 20B	Australia	Bar, billet	0.35–0.45 **C**, 0.40–0.70 **Mn**, 0.050 **P**, 0.050 **S**, 0.10–0.35 **Si**, 1.00–1.50 **Cr**, 0.50–0.90 **Mo**	**Hardened, tempered:** 2 1/2 **diam**, (850) **TS**, (680) **YS**
IS 4367	40Cr1Mo[28]	India	Forgings	0.35–0.45 **C**, 0.50–0.80 **Mn**, 0.050 **P**, 0.050 **S**, 0.10–0.35 **Si**, 0.90–1.20 **Cr**, 0.20–0.35 **Mo**	**Hardened and tempered:** (100) **diam**, (784) **TS**, 16 **El**
AS G18	G18/En 24	Australia	Bar, billet	0.35–0.45 **C**, 0.45–0.70 **Mn**, 0.050 **P**, 0.050 **S**, 0.10–0.35 **Si**, 0.90–1.40 **Cr**, 1.30–1.80 **Ni**, 0.20–0.35 **Mo**	**Hardened, tempered:** 6 **diam**, (770) **TS**, (585) **YS**
BS 1506–621	Grade B	UK	Bar	0.35–0.45 **C**, 0.40–0.70 **Mn**, 0.050 **P**, 0.050 **S**, 0.10–0.35 **Si**, 1.00–1.50 **Cr**, 0.40 **Ni**, 0.50–0.90 **Mo**	**Hardened and tempered T:** 4 **diam**, (760) **TS**, (635) **YS**, 18 **El**; **Hardened and tempered U:** 2.5 **diam**, (825) **TS**, (660) **YS**, 17 **El**; **Hardened and tempered V:** 1.125 **diam**, (895) **TS**, (715) **YS**, 16 **El**
MIL–S–19434A	Class 3	US	Forgings	0.35–0.45 **C**, 0.70–1.05 **Mn**, 0.050 **P**, 0.050 min **S**, 0.15 min **Si**, 0.75–1.15 **Cr**, 0.13–0.27 **Mo**, 0.15 **V**	**Normalized and tempered, quenched and tempered:** ≤10 **diam**, (758) **TS**, (551) **YS**, 19 **El**
ASTM A 290	Class E	US	Rings: forged or rolled	0.35–0.45 **C**, 0.70–1.00 **Mn**, 0.040 **P**, 0.040 **S**, 0.20–0.35 **Si**, 0.80–1.15 **Cr**, 0.15–0.25 **Mo**, 0.06 **V**	**Quenched, tempered:** all **diam**, 105 (725) **TS**, 75 (515) **YS**, 20 **El**
AS G18	G18/En 41B	Australia	Bar, billet	0.35–0.45 **C**, 0.65 **Mn**, 0.050 **P**, 0.050 **S**, 0.10–0.45 **Si**, 1.40–1.80 **Cr**, 0.40 **Ni**, 0.10–0.25 **Mo**, 0.90–1.30 **Al**	**Hardened, tempered:** 6 **diam**, (690) **TS**, (525) **YS**
AS G18	G18/En 19	Australia	Bar, billet	0.35–0.45 **C**, 0.50–0.80 **Mn**, 0.050 **P**, 0.050 **S**, 0.10–0.35 **Si**, 0.90–1.50 **Cr**, 0.20–0.40 **Mo**	**Hardened, tempered:** 6 **diam**, (690) **TS**, (525) **YS**
AS G18	G18/En 19A	Australia	Bar, billet	0.35–0.45 **C**, 0.50–0.80 **Mn**, 0.050 **P**, 0.050 **S**, 0.10–0.35 **Si**, 0.90–1.20 **Cr**, 0.20–0.35 **Mo**	**Hardened, tempered:** 6 **diam**, (690) **TS**, (525) **YS**
AS G18	G18/En 18	Australia	Bar, billet	0.35–0.45 **C**, 0.60–0.95 **Mn**, 0.050 **P**, 0.050 **S**, 0.10–0.35 **Si**, 0.85–1.15 **Cr**	**Hardened, tempered:** 4 **diam**, (690) **TS**, (525) **YS**
IS 4367	40Cr1	India	Forgings	0.35–0.45 **C**, 0.60–0.90 **Mn**, 0.050 **P**, 0.050 **S**, 0.10–0.35 **Si**, 0.90–1.20 **Cr**	**Hardened and tempered:** (100) **diam**, (686) **TS**, 18 **El**
IS 5517	Grade 40Mn2S12	India	Bar, billet	0.35–0.45 **C**, 1.30–1.70 **Mn**, 0.060 **P**, 0.08–0.15 **S**, 0.25 **Si**	**Normalized, annealed or hardened and tempered:** (60) **diam**, (685) **TS**, (490) **YS**
BS 1506–621	Grade A	UK	Bar	0.35–0.45 **C**, 0.50–0.80 **Mn**, 0.050 **P**, 0.050 **S**, 0.10–0.35 **Si**, 0.90–1.20 **Cr**, 0.20–0.35 **Mo**	**Hardened and tempered R:** 6 **diam**, (620) **TS**, (470) **YS**, 22 **El**; **Hardened and tempered T:** 2.5 **diam**, (760) **TS**, (635) **YS**, 18 **El**; **Hardened and tempered V:** 1.125 **diam**, (825) **TS**, (660) **YS**, 17 **El**
BS 3111 Part 1	Type 3	UK	Wire	0.35–0.45 **C**, 0.70–0.90 **Mn**, 0.040 **P**, 0.040 **S**, 0.15–0.40 **Si**, 0.90–1.20 **Cr**	**Drawn and spheroidized annealed:** all **diam**, (610) max **TS**; **Drawn, spheroidized annealed and light drawn:** all **diam**, (680) max **TS**
ASTM A 290	Class J	US	Rings: forged or rolled	0.35–0.45 **C**, 0.60–0.90 **Mn**, 0.040 **P**, 0.040 **S**, 0.20–0.35 **Si**, 0.60–0.90 **Cr**, 1.65–2.00 **Ni**, 0.20–0.50 **Mo**, 0.10 **V**	**Quenched, tempered**

WROUGHT ALLOY STEELS

specification number	designation	country	product forms	composition	mechanical properties (see page iv for explanation)
ASTM A 290	Class L	US	Rings: forged or rolled	0.35–0.45 C, 0.60–0.90 Mn, 0.040 P, 0.040 S, 0.20–0.35 Si, 0.60–0.90 Cr, 1.65–2.00 Ni, 0.20–0.50 Mo, 0.10 V	Quenched, tempered
ASTM A 290	Class H	US	Rings: forged or rolled	0.35–0.45 C, 0.60–0.90 Mn, 0.040 P, 0.040 S, 0.20–0.35 Si, 0.60–0.90 Cr, 1.65–2.00 Ni, 0.20–0.50 Mo, 0.10 V	Quenched, tempered
ASTM A 290	Class F	US	Rings: forged or rolled	0.35–0.45 C, 0.70–1.00 Mn, 0.040 P, 0.040 S, 0.20–0.35 Si, 0.80–1.15 Cr, 0.15–0.25 Mo, 0.06 V	Quenched, tempered
DEF STAN 10–13/2	Grade K115	UK	Forgings	0.35–0.45 C, 0.25–0.55 Mn, 0.012 P, 0.012 S, 0.60–0.85 Si, 1.30–1.80 Cr, 1.60–2.10 Ni, 0.80–1.10 Mo, 0.15–0.35 V	Hardened and tempered: (≤90) diam, (1150) YS, 8 El
DEF STAN 10–13/2	Grade K120	UK	Forgings	0.35–0.45 C, 0.25–0.55 Mn, 0.012 P, 0.012 S, 0.60–0.85 Si, 1.30–1.80 Cr, 1.60–2.10 Ni, 0.80–1.10 Mo, 0.15–0.35 V	Hardened and tempered: (≤80) diam, (1200) YS, 8 El
DEF STAN 10–13/2	Grade K125	UK	Forgings	0.35–0.45 C, 0.25–0.55 Mn, 0.012 P, 0.012 S, 0.60–0.85 Si, 1.30–1.80 Cr, 1.60–2.10 Ni, 0.80–1.10 Mo, 0.15–0.35 V	Hardened and tempered: (≤70) diam, (1250) YS, 8 El
DEF STAN 10–13/2	Grade K 130	UK	Forgings	0.35–0.45 C, 0.25–0.55 Mn, 0.012 P, 0.012 S, 0.60–0.85 Si, 1.30–1.80 Cr, 1.60–2.10 Ni, 0.80–1.10 Mo, 0.15–0.35 V	Hardened and tempered: (≤60) diam, (1300) YS, 7 El
DEF STAN 10–13/2	Grade K 135	UK	Forgings	0.35–0.45 C, 0.25–0.55 Mn, 0.012 P, 0.012 S, 0.60–0.85 Si, 1.30–1.80 Cr, 1.60–2.10 Ni, 0.80–1.10 Mo, 0.15–0.35 V	Hardened and tempered: (≤50) diam, (1350) YS, 7 El
DEF STAN 10–13/2	Grade K 140	UK	Forgings	0.35–0.45 C, 0.25–0.55 Mn, 0.012 P, 0.012 S, 0.60–0.85 Si, 1.30–1.80 Cr, 1.60–2.10 Ni, 0.80–1.10 Mo, 0.15–0.35 V	Hardened and tempered: (≤40) diam, (1400) YS, 7 El
DEF STAN 10–13/2	Grade L115	UK	Forgings	0.35–0.45 C, 0.35–0.70 Mn, 0.012 P, 0.012 S, 0.10–0.35 Si, 2.50–3.50 Cr, 0.40 Ni, 0.70–1.20 Mo, 0.10–0.30 V	Hardened and tempered: (≤40) diam, (1150) YS, 8 El
AISI 15B41H		US	Wire, rod	0.35–0.45 C, 1.25–1.75 Mn, 0.040 P, 0.050 S, 0.15–0.30 Si	
DGN–B–301	1541H	Mexico	Bar	0.35–0.45 C, 1.25–1.75 Mn, 0.040 P, 0.050 S, 0.15–0.30 Si	
BS S.138		UK	Bar, billets, forgings: aircraft quality	0.35–0.43 C, 0.45–0.7 Mn, 0.015 P, 0.010 S, 0.10–0.35 Si, 3.0–3.5 Cr, 0.4 Ni, 0.80–1.10 Mo, 0.15–0.25 V, 0.40 Cu, 0.030	
					Hardened and tempered: all diam, (1540) TS, (1205) YS, 8 El
BS S.134		UK	Bar, billets, forgings: aircraft quality	0.35–0.43 C, 0.45–0.7 Mn, 0.025 P, 0.020 S, 0.10–0.35 Si, 3.0–3.5 Cr, 0.4 Ni, 0.80–1.10 Mo, 0.15–0.25 V	Hardened and tempered: 1 1/8 diam, (1540) TS, (1216) YS, 8 El
BS 3S.132		UK	Billets, bar, forgings, parts: aircraft quality	0.35–0.43 C, 0.40–0.70 Mn, 0.020 P, 0.020 S, 0.10–0.35 Si, 3.0–3.5 Cr, 0.30 Ni, 0.80–1.10 Mo, 0.15–0.25 V, 0.030	
					Hardened and tempered: (≤70) diam, (1320) TS, (1130) YS, 8 El
AIR 9160/C 49	9160C131	France	Bar	0.35–0.43 C, 0.40–0.70 Mn, 0.020 P, 0.020 S, 0.10–0.35 Si, 0.30 Ni, 0.80–1.10 Mo, 0.15–0.25 V, 0.03 W	Annealed, quenched and tempered: (<50) diam, (1250) TS, (1050) YS, 10 El
AMS 6471A		US	Bar, forging, tube	0.35–0.43 C, 0.50–0.80 Mn, 0.015 P, 0.015 S, 0.20–0.40 Si, 1.40–1.80 Cr, 0.25 Ni, 0.30–0.40 Mo, 0.95–1.30 Al, 0.35 Cu	Cold finished (bar): ≤0.500 (≤12.70) diam, 135 (931) max TS

WROUGHT ALLOY STEELS

specification number	designation	country	product forms	composition	mechanical properties (see page iv for explanation)
BS 4670	897M39	UK	Forgings	0.35–0.43 **C**, 0.45–0.70 **Mn**, 0.035 **P**, 0.035 **S**, 0.10–0.35 **Si**, 3.00–3.50 **Cr**, 0.40 **Ni**, 0.80–1.10 **Mo**, 0.15–0.25 **V**	**Hardened tempered**: (1000)* **diam**, (850) **TS**, (660) **YS**, 13 **El**
BS 3111 Part 1	Type 5	UK	Wire	0.35–0.43 **C**, 0.70–0.90 **Mn**, 0.040 **P**, 0.040 **S**, 0.15–0.40 **Si**, 0.90–1.10 **Cr**, 0.15–0.25 **Mo**	**Drawn and spheroidized annealed**: all **diam**, (670) max **TS**; **Drawn, spheroidized annealed and light drawn**: all **diam**, (710) max **TS**
BS 970 Part 2	Grade 905 M 39	UK	Blooms, billets, bar, forgings	0.35–0.43 **C**, 0.40–0.65 **Mn**, 0.025 **P**, 0.025 **S**, 0.10–0.45 **Si**, 1.40–1.80 **Cr**, 0.15–0.25 **Mo**, 0.90–1.30 **Al**	**Hardened and tempered**: 6 **diam**, (625) **TS**, (470) **YS**, 17 **El**
BS 970 Part 2	Grade 945 A 40	UK	Blooms, billets, bar, forgings	0.35–0.43 **C**, 1.20–1.60 **Mn**, 0.40–0.60 **Cr**, 0.60–0.90 **Ni**, 0.15–0.25 **Mo**	
AISI 1139		US	Wire, rod	0.35–0.43 **C**, 1.35–1.65 **Mn**, 0.040 **P**, 0.13–0.20 **S**	
ASTM A 689	1139	US	Bar	0.35–0.43 **C**, 1.35–1.65 **Mn**, 0.040 **P**, 0.13–0.20 **S**	
ANSI/ASTM A 29	1139	US	Bar	0.35–0.43 **C**, 1.35–1.65 **Mn**, 0.040 **P**, 0.13–0.20 **S**	
ANSI/ASTM A 576	1139	US	Bar	0.35–0.43 **C**, 1.35–1.65 **Mn**, 0.040 **P**, 0.13–0.20 **S**	
QQ-S-637A	1139	US	Bar	0.35–0.43 **C**, 1.35–1.65 **Mn**, 0.040 **P**, 0.13–0.20 **S**, 0.15–0.35 **Pb**	
DIN 17211	Grade 39 CrMoV 139	Germany	Blooms, slabs, billets, wire, bar, plate, sheet, strip, tube, forgings	0.35–0.42 **C**, 0.40–0.70 **Mn**, 0.030 **P**, 0.035 **S**, 0.15–0.40 **Si**, 3.00–3.50 **Cr**, 0.80–1.10 **Mo**, 0.15–0.25 **V**	**Soft annealed and quenched and tempered**: (≤70) **diam**, (1275) **TS**, (1079) **YS**, 8 **El**
ISO 683/X	2	ISO	Bar	0.35–0.42 **C**, 0.40–0.70 **Mn**, 0.030 **P**, 0.035 **S**, 0.15–0.40 **Si**, 3.00–3.50 **Cr**, 0.80–1.10 **Mo**, 0.15–0.25 **V**	**Nitrided**: (70) **diam**, (1270) **TS**, (1080) **YS**, 8 **El**
DIN 17221	38 Si 7/1.0970	Germany	Springs	0.35–0.42 **C**, 0.50–0.80 **Mn**, 0.045 **P**, 0.045 **S**, 1.5–1.8 **Si**	**Quenched and tempered**: all **diam**, (1180) **TS**, (1030) **YS**, 6 **El**
SIS 14 22 42	SIS 22 42–03	Sweden	Bar, forgings, wire	0.35–0.42 **C**, 0.30–0.60 **Mn**, 0.80–1.20 **Si**, 5.0–5.5 **Cr**, 1.20–1.60 **Mo**, 0.85–1.15 **V**	**Quenched**: (≤75) **diam**, (130) **TS**, (110) **YS**, 8 **El**
TS 2288	38 Si 6	Turkey	Wire	0.35–0.42 **C**, 0.50–0.80 **Mn**, 0.050 **P**, 0.050 **S**, 1.4–1.6 **Si**	
TS 2288	38 Si 7–1,0970	Turkey	Wire	0.35–0.42 **C**, 0.50–0.80 **Mn**, 0.045 **P**, 0.045 **S**, 1.5–1.8 **Si**	
SIS 14 22 42	SIS 22 42–02	Sweden	Bar, forgings, wire	0.35–0.42 **C**, 0.30–0.60 **Mn**, 0.80–1.20 **Si**, 5.0–5.5 **Cr**, 1.20–1.60 **Mo**, 0.85–1.15 **V**	**Annealed**
JIS G 4106	SMn 2	Japan	Bar, wire, rod	0.35–0.41 **C**, 1.20–1.50 **Mn**, 0.030 **P**, 0.030 **S**, 0.15–0.35 **Si**, 0.25 **Ni**, 0.30 **Cu**	**Hot rolled or forged, quenched and tempered**: (25) **diam**, (735) **TS**, (588) **YS**, 18 **El**
AM 6300A		US	Bar, forgings	0.35–0.40 **C**, 0.70–0.90 **Mn**, 0.040 **P**, 0.040 **S**, 0.20–0.3 **Si**, 0.20 **Cr**, 0.2 **Ni**, 0.20–0.30 **Mo**, 0.35 **Cu**	**Cold finished (bar)**: ≤0.500 (≤12.70) **diam**, 130 (896) max **TS**
AMS 6412G		US	Bar, forgings	0.35–0.40 **C**, 0.65–0.85 **Mn**, 0.025 **P**, 0.025 **S**, 0.20–0.35 **Si**, 0.70–0.90 **Cr**, 1.65–2.00 **Ni**, 0.20–0.30 **Mo**, 0.35 **Cu**	**Cold finished (bar)**: ≤0.500 (≤12.70) **diam**, 130 (896) max **TS**
ASTM A 320	L 7B AISI 4137	US	Bar	0.35–0.40 **C**, 0.70–0.90 **Mn**, 0.035 **P**, 0.040 **S**, 0.20–0.35 **Si**, 0.80–1.10 **Cr**, 0.15–0.25 **Mo**	**Quenched, tempered**: ≥2.5 (≥63.5) **diam**, 125 (862) **TS**, 105 (724) **YS**, 16 **El**
ASTM A 320	L 7A AISI 4037	US	Bar	0.35–0.40 **C**, 0.70–0.90 **Mn**, 0.035 **P**, 0.040 **S**, 0.20–0.35 **Si**, 0.20–0.30 **Mo**	**Quenched, tempered**: ≥2.5 (63.5) **diam**, 125 (862) **TS**, 105 (724) **YS**, 16 **El**
BS 3111 Part 1	Type 2	UK	Wire	0.35–0.40 **C**, 0.70–0.90 **Mn**, 0.040 **P**, 0.040 **S**, 0.15–0.40 **Si**, 0.20–0.30 **Mo**	**Drawn and sphoroidized annealed**: all **diam**, (570) max **TS**; **Drawn, spheroidized annealed and light drawn**: all **diam**, (670) max **TS**

WROUGHT ALLOY STEELS

specification number	designation	country	product forms	composition	mechanical properties (see page iv for explanation)
DGN–B–203	Grade 4137	Mexico	Tube: seamless	0.35–0.40 **C**, 0.70–0.90 **Mn**, 0.040 **P**, 0.040 **S**, 0.20–0.35 **Si**, 0.80–1.10 **Cr**, 0.15–0.25 **Mo**	**Hot finished**: all diam, (480) **TS**, (275) **YS**, 20 **El**; **Cold finished**: all **diam**, (549) **TS**, (451) **YS**, 5 **El**; **Stress relieved**: all **diam**, (520) **TS**, (412) **YS**, 8 **El**; **Tempered**: all **diam**, (451) **TS**, (245) **YS**, 22 **El**; **Normalized**: all **diam**, (480) **TS**, (294) **YS**, 15 **El**
AISI 4037		US	Bar	0.35–0.40 **C**, 0.70–0.90 **Mn**, 0.035 **P**, 0.040 **S**, 0.15–0.30 **Si**, 0.20–0.30 **Mo**	
AISI 4137		US	Bar	0.35–0.40 **C**, 0.70–0.90 **Mn**, 0.035 **P**, 0.040 **S**, 0.15–0.30 **Si**, 0.80–1.10 **Cr**, 0.15–0.25 **Mo**	
AISI 8637		US	Bar	0.35–0.40 **C**, 0.75–1.00 **Mn**, 0.035 **P**, 0.040 **S**, 0.15–0.30 **Si**, 0.40–0.60 **Cr**, 0.40–0.70 **Ni**, 0.15–0.25 **Mo**	
NF A 35–553	38 C 4	France	Strip	0.35–0.40 **C**, 0.60–0.90 **Mn**, 0.035 **P**, 0.035 **S**, 0.10–0.40 **Si**, 0.85–1.15 **Cr**	
BS 970 Part 2	Grade 503 A 37	UK	Blooms, billets, bar, forgings	0.35–0.40 **C**, 0.70–1.00 **Mn**, 0.70–1.00 **Ni**	
BS 970 Part 2	Grade 605 A 37	UK	Blooms, billets, bar, forgings	0.35–0.40 **C**, 1.30–1.70 **Mn**, 0.22–0.32 **Mo**	
BS 970 Part 2	Grade 708 A 37	UK	Blooms, billets, bar, forgings	0.35–0.40 **C**, 0.70–1.00 **Mn**, 0.90–1.20 **Cr**, 0.15–0.25 **Mo**	
BS 3S.102		UK	Bar: aircraft quality	0.35–0.40 **C**, 0.8–1.0 **Mn**, 0.040 **P**, 0.040 **S**, 0.15–0.35 **Si**, 0.20–0.35 **Mo**	**Hardened and tempered**: all **diam**
ASTM A 547	Grade 4037	US	Wire	0.35–0.40 **C**, 0.70–0.90 **Mn**, 0.20–0.30 **Mo**	
ASTM A 547	Grade 4137	US	Wire	0.35–0.40 **C**, 0.70–0.90 **Mn**, 0.80–1.10 **Cr**, 0.15–0.25 **Mo**	
ASTM A 547	Grade 8637	US	Wire	0.35–0.40 **C**, 0.75–1.00 **Mn**, 0.40–0.60 **Cr**, 0.40–0.70 **Ni**, 0.15–0.25 **Mo**	
AMS 6421A		US	Bar, forgings, tube	0.35–0.40 **C**, 0.65–0.85 **Mn**, 0.025 **P**, 0.025 **S**, 0.20–0.35 **Si**, 0.70–0.90 **Cr**, 0.70–1.00 **Ni**, 0.15–0.25 **Mo**, 0.0005–0.005 **B**, 0.35 **Cu**	
AMS 6413E		US	Tube	0.35–0.40 **C**, 0.65–0.85 **Mn**, 0.025 **P**, 0.025 **S**, 0.20–0.35 **Si**, 0.70–0.90 **Cr**, 1.65–2.00 **Ni**, 0.20–0.30 **Mo**, 0.35 **Cu**	
AS G18	G18/En 19B	Australia	Bar, billet	0.35–0.40 **C**, 0.50–0.80 **Mn**, 0.050 **P**, 0.050 **S**, 0.10–0.35 **Si**, 0.90–1.20 **Cr**, 0.20–0.35 **Mo**	
AS G18	G18/En 16C	Australia	Bar, billet	0.35–0.40 **C**, 1.30–1.80 **Mn**, 0.050 **P**, 0.050 **S**, 0.10–0.35 **Si**, 0.20–0.35 **Mo**	
COPANT 334	4037	COPANT	Bar	0.35–0.40 **C**, 0.70–0.90 **Mn**, 0.035 **P**, 0.040 **S**, 0.20–0.35 **Si**, 0.20–0.30 **Mo**	
COPANT 334	8637	COPANT	Bar	0.35–0.40 **C**, 0.75–1.00 **Mn**, 0.035 **P**, 0.040 **S**, 0.20–0.35 **Si**, 0.40–0.60 **Cr**, 0.40–0.73 **Ni**, 0.15–0.25 **Mo**	
AS 1444	Grade AS 1444/4037	Australia	Bar, bloom, billet, slab	0.35–0.40 **C**, 0.70–0.90 **Mn**, 0.040 **P**, 0.040 **S**, 0.10–0.35 **Si**, 0.20–0.30 **Mo**	
DGN–B–203	E 4337	Mexico	Tube: seamless	0.35–0.40 **C**, 0.65–0.85 **Mn**, 0.025 **P**, 0.025 **S**, 0.20–0.35 **Si**, 0.70–0.90 **Cr**, 1.65–2.00 **Ni**, 0.20–0.30 **Mo**	
DGN–B–203	Grade 4337	Mexico	Tube: seamless	0.35–0.40 **C**, 0.60–0.80 **Mn**, 0.040 **P**, 0.040 **S**, 0.20–0.35 **Si**, 0.70–0.90 **Cr**, 1.65–2.00 **Ni**, 0.20–0.30 **Mo**	

WROUGHT ALLOY STEELS

specification number	designation	country	product forms	composition	mechanical properties (see page iv for explanation)
DGN–B–203	Grade 4037	Mexico	Tube: seamless	0.35–0.40 **C**, 0.70–0.90 **Mn**, 0.040 **P**, 0.040 **S**, 0.20–0.35 **Si**, 0.20–0.30 **Mo**	
DGN–B–203	Grade 8637	Mexico	Tube: seamless	0.35–0.40 **C**, 0.75–1.00 **Mn**, 0.040 **P**, 0.040 **S**, 0.20–0.35 **Si**, 0.40–0.60 **Cr**, 0.40–0.70 **Ni**, 0.15–0.25 **Mo**	
COPANT 514	E 4337	COPANT	Tube	0.35–0.40 **C**, 0.65–0.85 **Mn**, 0.025 **P**, 0.025 **S**, 0.20–0.35 **Si**, 0.70–0.90 **Cr**, 1.65–2.0 **Ni**, 0.20–0.30 **Mo**	
COPANT 514	4337	COPANT	Tube	0.35–0.40 **C**, 0.60–0.80 **Mn**, 0.040 **P**, 0.040 **S**, 0.20–0.35 **Si**, 0.70–0.90 **Cr**, 1.65–2.0 **Ni**, 0.20–0.30 **Mo**	
COPANT 514	4137	COPANT	Tube	0.35–0.40 **C**, 0.70–0.90 **Mn**, 0.040 **P**, 0.040 **S**, 0.20–0.35 **Si**, 0.80–1.10 **Cr**, 0.15–0.25 **Mo**	
COPANT 514	4037	COPANT	Tube	0.35–0.40 **C**, 0.70–0.90 **Mn**, 0.040 **P**, 0.040 **S**, 0.20–0.35 **Si**, 0.20–0.30 **Mo**	
DGN–B–300	8637	Mexico	Bar	0.35–0.40 **C**, 0.75–1.00 **Mn**, 0.035 **P**, 0.040 **S**, 0.20–0.35 **Si**, 0.40–0.60 **Cr**, 0.40–0.70 **Ni**, 0.15–0.25 **Mo**	**Annealed**
DGN–B–300	4137	Mexico	Bar	0.35–0.40 **C**, 0.70–0.90 **Mn**, 0.035 **P**, 0.040 **S**, 0.20–0.35 **Si**, 0.80–1.10 **Cr**, 0.15–0.25 **Mo**	**Annealed**
DGN–B–300	4037	Mexico	Bar	0.35–0.40 **C**, 0.70–0.90 **Mn**, 0.035 **P**, 0.040 **S**, 0.20–0.35 **Si**, 0.20–0.30 **Mo**	**Annealed**
ANSI/ASTM A 29	4037	US	Bar	0.35–0.40 **C**, 0.70–0.90 **Mn**, 0.035 **P**, 0.040 **S**, 0.15–0.30 **Si**, 0.20–0.30 **Mo**	
ANSI/ASTM A 29	4137	US	Bar	0.35–0.40 **C**, 0.70–0.90 **Mn**, 0.035 **P**, 0.040 **S**, 0.15–0.30 **Si**, 0.80–1.10 **Cr**, 0.15–0.25 **Mo**	
ASTM A 689	8637	US	Bar	0.35–0.40 **C**, 0.75–1.00 **Mn**, 0.035 **P**, 0.040 **S**, 0.15–0.30 **Si**, 0.40–0.60 **Cr**, 0.40–0.70 **Ni**, 0.15–0.25 **Mo**	
ASTM A 689	4037	US	Bar	0.35–0.40 **C**, 0.70–0.90 **Mn**, 0.035 **P**, 0.040 **S**, 0.15–0.30 **Si**, 0.20–0.30 **Mo**	
ASTM A 689	4137	US	Bar	0.35–0.40 **C**, 0.70–0.90 **Mn**, 0.035 **P**, 0.040 **S**, 0.15–0.30 **Si**, 0.80–1.10 **Cr**, 0.15–0.25 **Mo**	
ANSI/ASTM A 322	4037	US	Bar	0.35–0.40 **C**, 0.70–0.90 **Mn**, 0.035 **P**, 0.040 **S**, 0.15–0.30 **Si**, 0.20–0.30 **Mo**	
ANSI/ASTM A 322	4137	US	Bar	0.35–0.40 **C**, 0.70–0.90 **Mn**, 0.035 **P**, 0.040 **S**, 0.15–0.30 **Si**, 0.80–1.10 **Cr**, 0.15–0.25 **Mo**	
ANSI/ASTM A 322	8637	US	Bar	0.35–0.40 **C**, 0.75–1.00 **Mn**, 0.035 **P**, 0.040 **S**, 0.15–0.30 **Si**, 0.40–0.60 **Cr**, 0.40–0.70 **Ni**, 0.15–0.25 **Mo**	
ANSI/ASTM A 29	8637	US	Bar	0.35–0.40 **C**, 0.75–1.00 **Mn**, 0.035 **P**, 0.040 **S**, 0.15–0.30 **Si**, 0.40–0.60 **Cr**, 0.40–0.70 **Ni**, 0.15–0.25 **Mo**	
AISI 8637		US	Wire, rod	0.35–0.40 **C**, 0.75–1.00 **Mn**, 0.035 **P**, 0.040 **S**, 0.15–0.30 **Si**, 0.40–0.60 **Cr**, 0.40–0.70 **Ni**, 0.15–0.25 **Mo**	
AISI 4037		US	Wire, rod	0.35–0.40 **C**, 0.70–0.90 **Mn**, 0.035 **P**, 0.040 **S**, 0.15–0.30 **Si**, 0.20–0.30 **Mo**	
AISI 4137		US	Wire, rod	0.35–0.40 **C**, 0.70–0.90 **Mn**, 0.035 **P**, 0.040 **S**, 0.15–0.30 **Si**, 0.80–1.10 **Cr**, 0.15–0.25 **Mo**	

WROUGHT ALLOY STEELS

specification number	designation	country	product forms	composition	mechanical properties (see page iv for explanation)
ANSI/ASTM A 519	4037	US	Tube: seamless	0.35–0.40 **C**, 0.70–0.90 **Mn**, 0.040 **P**, 0.040 **S**, 0.15–0.35 **Si**, 0.20–0.30 **Mo**	
ANSI/ASTM A 519	4137	US	Tube: seamless	0.35–0.40 **C**, 0.70–0.90 **Mn**, 0.040 **P**, 0.040 **S**, 0.15–0.35 **Si**, 0.80–1.10 **Cr**, 0.15–0.25 **Mo**	
ANSI/ASTM A 519	4337	US	Tube: seamless	0.35–0.40 **C**, 0.60–0.80 **Mn**, 0.040 **P**, 0.040 **S**, 0.15–0.35 **Si**, 0.70–0.90 **Cr**, 1.65–2.00 **Ni**, 0.20–0.30 **Mo**	
ANSI/ASTM A 519	E 4337	US	Tube: seamless	0.35–0.40 **C**, 0.65–0.85 **Mn**, 0.025 **P**, 0.025 **S**, 0.15–0.35 **Si**, 0.70–0.90 **Cr**, 1.65–2.00 **Ni**, 0.20–0.30 **Mo**	
ANSI/ASTM A 519	8637	US	Tube: seamless	0.35–0.40 **C**, 0.75–1.00 **Mn**, 0.040 **P**, 0.040 **S**, 0.15–0.35 **Si**, 0.40–0.60 **Cr**, 0.40–0.70 **Ni**, 0.10–0.25 **Mo**	
DGN-B-297	4037	Mexico	Bar	0.35–0.40 **C**, 0.70–0.90 **Mn**, 0.035 **P**, 0.040 **S**, 0.20–0.35 **Si**, 0.20–0.30 **Mo**	
DGN-B-297	8637	Mexico	Bar	0.35–0.40 **C**, 0.75–1.00 **Mn**, 0.035 **P**, 0.040 **S**, 0.20–0.35 **Si**, 0.40–0.60 **Cr**, 0.40–0.70 **Ni**, 0.15–0.25 **Mo**	
DGN-B-297	4137	Mexico	Bar	0.35–0.40 **C**, 0.70–0.90 **Mn**, 0.035 **P**, 0.040 **S**, 0.20–0.35 **Si**, 0.80–1.10 **Cr**, 0.15–0.25 **Mo**	
COPANT 514	Grade 8637	COPANT	Tube: seamless	0.35–0.40 **C**, 0.75–1.00 **Mn**, 0.040 **P**, 0.050 **S**, 0.10 **Si**, 0.40–0.60 **Cr**, 0.40–0.70 **Ni**, 0.15–0.25 **Mo**	
AS G18	G18/En 18C	Australia	Bar, billet	0.35–0.38 **C**, 0.65–0.80 **Mn**, 0.050 **P**, 0.050 **S**, 0.10–0.35 **Si**, 0.85–1.15 **Cr**	
ANSI/ASTM A 723	Grade 1, class 5	US	Forgings	0.35 **C**, 0.90 **Mn**, 0.015 **P**, 0.015 **S**, 0.35 **Si**, 0.80–2.00 **Cr**, 1.50–2.25 **Ni**, 0.20–0.40 **Mo**, 0.20 **V**	**Normalized or quenched and tempered**: all **diam**, (1310) **TS**, (1240) **YS**, 10 **El**
ASTM A 723	Grade 1, class 5	US	Forgings	0.35 **C**, 0.90 **Mn**, 0.015 **P**, 0.015 **S**, 0.35 **Si**, 0.80–2.00 **Cr**, 1.50–2.25 **Ni**, 0.20–0.40 **Mo**, 0.20 **V**	**Normalized, quenched and tempered**: ≤4 (≤102) **diam**, 190 (1310) **TS**, 180 (1240) **YS**, 10 **El**
ANSI/ASTM A 723	Grade 1, class 4	US	Forgings	0.35 **C**, 0.90 **Mn**, 0.015 **P**, 0.015 **S**, 0.35 **Si**, 0.80–2.00 **Cr**, 1.50–2.25 **Ni**, 0.20–0.40 **Mo**, 0.20 **V**	**Normalized or quenched and tempered**: all **diam**, (1205) **TS**, (1105) **YS**, 12 **El**
ASTM A 723	Grade 1, class 4	US	Forgings	0.35 **C**, 0.90 **Mn**, 0.015 **P**, 0.015 **S**, 0.35 **Si**, 0.80–2.00 **Cr**, 1.50–2.25 **Ni**, 0.20–0.40 **Mo**, 0.20 **V**	**Normalized, quenched and tempered**: ≤6 (≤152) **diam**, 175 (1205) **TS**, 160 (1105) **YS**, 12 **El**
ANSI/ASTM A 723	Grade 1, class 3	US	Forgings	0.35 **C**, 0.90 **Mn**, 0.015 **P**, 0.015 **S**, 0.35 **Si**, 0.80–2.00 **Cr**, 1.50–2.25 **Ni**, 0.20–0.40 **Mo**, 0.20 **V**	**Normalized or quenched and tempered**: all **diam**, (1070) **TS**, (965) **YS**, 13 **El**
ASTM A 723	Grade 1, class 3	US	Forgings	0.35 **C**, 0.90 **Mn**, 0.015 **P**, 0.015 **S**, 0.35 **Si**, 0.80–2.00 **Cr**, 1.50–2.25 **Ni**, 0.20–0.40 **Mo**, 0.20 **V**	**Normalized, quenched and tempered**: ≤10 (≤254) **diam**, 155 (1070) **TS**, 140 (965) **YS**, 13 **El**
ASTM A 294	Class C7	US	Forgings	0.35 **C**, 0.60–0.90 **Mn**, 0.035 **P**, 0.035 **S**, 0.15–0.35 **Si**, 0.70 **Cr**, 1.50–3.50 **Ni**, 0.20 min **Mo**, 0.03–0.12 **V**	**Normalized or quenched, tempered**: all **diam**, 140 (965) **TS**, 125 (860) **YS**, 15 **El**
ANSI/ASTM A 723	Grade 1, class 2	US	Forgings	0.35 **C**, 0.90 **Mn**, 0.015 **P**, 0.015 **S**, 0.35 **Si**, 0.80–2.00 **Cr**, 1.50–2.25 **Ni**, 0.20–0.40 **Mo**, 0.20 **V**	**Normalized or quenched and tempered**: all **diam**, (930) **TS**, (825) **YS**, 14 **El**
ASTM A 723	Grade 1, class 2	US	Forgings	0.35 **C**, 0.90 **Mn**, 0.015 **P**, 0.015 **S**, 0.35 **Si**, 0.80–2.00 **Cr**, 1.50–2.25 **Ni**, 0.20–0.40 **Mo**, 0.20 **V**	**Normalized, quenched and tempered**: all **diam**, 135 (930) **TS**, 120 (825) **YS**, 14 **El**

specification number	designation	country	product forms	composition	mechanical properties (see page iv for explanation)
ASTM A 294	Class C6	US	Forgings	0.35 **C**, 0.60–0.90 **Mn**, 0.035 **P**, 0.035 **S**, 0.15–0.35 **Si**, 0.70 **Cr**, 1.50–3.50 **Ni**, 0.20 min **Mo**, 0.03–0.12 **V**	**Normalized or quenched, tempered**: all **diam**, 130 (905) **TS**, 115 (795) **YS**, 16 **El**
ASTM A 294	Class C5	US	Forgings	0.35 **C**, 0.60–0.90 **Mn**, 0.035 **P**, 0.035 **S**, 0.15–0.35 **Si**, 0.70 **Cr**, 1.50–3.50 **Ni**, 0.20 min **Mo**, 0.03–0.12 **V**	**Normalized or quenched, tempered**: all **diam**, 125 (860) **TS**, 105 (725) **YS**, 18 **El**
ASTM A 293	Class 5	US	Forgings	0.35 **C**, 0.70 **Mn**, 0.035 **P**, 0.035 **S**, 0.15–0.35 **Si**, 1.25 **Cr**, 2.50 min **Ni**, 0.25 min **Mo**, 0.03 min **V**	**Normalized, tempered or double normalized, tempered**: all **diam**, 120 (825) **TS**, 95 (655) **YS**, 17 **El**
ASTM A 294	Class C4	US	Forgings	0.35 **C**, 0.60–0.90 **Mn**, 0.035 **P**, 0.035 **S**, 0.15–0.35 **Si**, 0.70 **Cr**, 1.50–3.50 **Ni**, 0.20 min **Mo**, 0.03–0.12 **V**	**Normalized or quenched, tempered**: all **diam**, 120 (825) **TS**, 95 (655) **YS**, 18 **El**
ANSI/ASTM A 723	Grade 1,class 1	US	Forgings	0.35 **C**, 0.90 **Mn**, 0.015 **P**, 0.015 **S**, 0.35 **Si**, 0.80–2.00 **Cr**, 1.50–2.25 **Ni**, 0.20–0.40 **Mo**, 0.20 **V**	**Normalized or quenched and tempered**: all **diam**, (795) **TS**, (690) **YS**, 16 **El**
ASTM A 723	Grade 1, class 1	US	Forgings	0.35 **C**, 0.90 **Mn**, 0.015 **P**, 0.015 **S**, 0.35 **Si**, 0.80–2.00 **Cr**, 1.50–2.25 **Ni**, 0.20–0.40 **Mo**, 0.20 **V**	**Normalized, quenched and tempered**: all **diam**, 115 (795) **TS**, 100 (690) **YS**, 16 **El**
ASTM A 294	Class C3	US	Forgings	0.35 **C**, 0.60–0.90 **Mn**, 0.035 **P**, 0.035 **S**, 0.15–0.35 **Si**, 0.70 **Cr**, 1.50–3.50 **Ni**, 0.20 min **Mo**, 0.03–0.12 **V**	**Normalized or quenched, tempered**: all **diam**, 110 (760) **TS**, 85 (585) **YS**, 19 **El**
ASTM A 293	Class 4	US	Forgings	0.35 **C**, 0.70 **Mn**, 0.035 **P**, 0.035 **S**, 0.15–0.35 **Si**, 0.75 **Cr**, 2.50 min **Ni**, 0.25 min **Mo**, 0.03–0.12 **V**	**Normalized, tempered or double normalized, tempered**: all **diam**, 105 (725) **TS**, 80 (550) **YS**, 18 **El**
ANSI/ASTM A 336	Grade F32	US	Forgings	0.35 **C**, 0.50–0.90 **Mn**, 0.040 **P**, 0.040 **S**, 0.15–0.45 **Si**, 3.00–3.60 **Cr**, 0.50–1.00 **Ni**, 0.30–0.50 **Mo**, 0.05–0.15 **V**	**Annealed or normalized and tempered**: all **diam**, (690) **TS**, (415) **YS**, 18 **El**
ASTM A 336	F32	US	Forgings	0.35 **C**, 0.50–0.90 **Mn**, 0.040 **P**, 0.040 **S**, 0.15–0.45 **Si**, 3.00–3.60 **Cr**, 0.50–1.00 **Ni**, 0.30–0.50 **Mo**, 0.05–0.15 **V**	**Normalized**: all **diam**, 100 (690) **TS**, 60 (415) **YS**, 18 **El**
ASTM A 294	Class C2	US	Forgings	0.35 **C**, 0.60–0.90 **Mn**, 0.035 **P**, 0.035 **S**, 0.15–0.35 **Si**, 0.70 **Cr**, 1.50–3.50 **Ni**, 0.20 min **Mo**, 0.03–0.12 **V**	**Normalized or quenched, tempered**: all **diam**, 100 (690) **TS**, 75 (515) **YS**, 20 **El**
ASTM A 336	F32	US	Forgings	0.35 **C**, 0.50–0.90 **Mn**, 0.040 **P**, 0.040 **S**, 0.15–0.45 **Si**, 3.00–3.60 **Cr**, 0.50–1.00 **Ni**, 0.30–0.50 **Mo**, 0.05–0.15 **V**	**Annealed or normalized, tempered**: all **diam**, 100 (690) **TS**, 60 (415) **YS**, 18 **El**
ANSI/ASTM A 336	Grade F31	US	Forgings	0.35 **C**, 0.50–0.90 **Mn**, 0.040 **P**, 0.040 **S**, 0.10–0.40 **Si**, 2.25–3.00 **Ni**, 0.20–0.50 **Mo**, 0.15 **V**	**Annealed or normalized and tempered**: all **diam**, (655) **TS**, (485) **YS**, 18 **El**
ASTM A 336	F31	US	Forgings	0.35 **C**, 0.50–0.90 **Mn**, 0.040 **P**, 0.040 **S**, 0.10–0.40 **Si**, 2.25–3.00 **Ni**, 0.20–0.50 **Mo**, 0.15 **V**	**Normalized**: all **diam**, 95 (655) **TS**, 70 (485) **YS**, 18 **El**
ASTM A 336	F31	US	Forgings	0.35 **C**, 0.50–0.90 **Mn**, 0.040 **P**, 0.040 **S**, 0.10–0.40 **Si**, 2.25–3.00 **Ni**, 0.20–0.50 **Mo**, 0.15 **V**	**Annealed or normalized, tempered**: all **diam**, 95 (655) **TS**, 70 (485) **YS**, 18 **El**
ASTM A 294	Class C1	US	Forgings	0.35 **C**, 0.60–0.90 **Mn**, 0.035 **P**, 0.035 **S**, 0.15–0.35 **Si**, 0.70 **Cr**, 1.50–3.50 **Ni**, 0.20 min **Mo**, 0.03–0.12 **V**	**Normalized or quenched, tempered**: all **diam**, 90 (620) **TS**, 65 (450) **YS**, 20 **El**
ANSI/ASTM A 508	Grade 1	US	Forgings	0.35 **C**, 0.40–1.05 **Mn**, 0.025 **P**, 0.025 **S**, 0.15–0.40 **Si**, 0.25 **Cr**, 0.40 **Ni**, 0.10 **Mo**, 0.05 **V**	**Quenched and tempered**: all **diam**, (485) **TS**, (240) **YS**, 20 **El**
ANSI/ASTM A 541	Class 1	US	Forgings	0.35 **C**, 0.40–0.90 **Mn**, 0.050 **P**, 0.050 **S**, 0.15–0.35 **Si**, 0.25 **Cr**, 0.40 **Ni**, 0.10 **Mo**, 0.05 **V**	**Quenched and tempered**: all **diam**, 70 (480) **TS**, 35 (240) **YS**, 20 **El**
ANSI/ASTM A 541	Grade 1	US	Forgings	0.35 **C**, 0.40–0.90 **Mn**, 0.050 **P**, 0.050 **S**, 0.15–0.35 **Si**, 0.25 **Cr**, 0.40 **Ni**, 0.10 **Mo**, 0.05 **V**	**Quenched and tempered**: all **diam**, (480) **TS**, (240) **YS**, 20 **El**

WROUGHT ALLOY STEELS

specification number	designation	country	product forms	composition	mechanical properties (see page iv for explanation)
AISI 1541H		US	Wire, rod	0.35 **C**, 1.25–1.75 **Mn**, 0.040 **P**, 0.050 **S**, 0.15–0.30 **Si**	
JIS G 4108	Class 1, SNB 21-1	Japan	Bar	0.34–0.46 **C**, 0.42–0.73 **Mn**, 0.030 **P**, 0.030 **S**, 0.18–0.37 **Si**, 0.75–1.20 **Cr**, 0.47–0.68 **Mo**, 0.22–0.38 **V**	**Hot rolled, hot forged or cold finished:** (≤100) **diam**, (1138) **TS**, (1030) **YS**, 10 **El**
JIS G 4108	Class 1, SNB 21-2	Japan	Bar	0.34–0.46 **C**, 0.42–0.73 **Mn**, 0.030 **P**, 0.030 **S**, 0.18–0.37 **Si**, 0.75–1.20 **Cr**, 0.47–0.68 **Mo**, 0.22–0.38 **V**	**Hot rolled, hot forged or cold finished:** (≤100) **diam**, (1069) **TS**, (961) **YS**, 11 **El**
JIS G 4108	Class 1, SNB 21-3	Japan	Bar	0.34–0.46 **C**, 0.42–0.73 **Mn**, 0.030 **P**, 0.030 **S**, 0.18–0.37 **Si**, 0.75–1.20 **Cr**, 0.47–0.68 **Mo**, 0.22–0.38 **V**	**Hot rolled, hot forged or cold finished:** (≤75) **diam**, (1000) **TS**, (892) **YS**, 12 **El**
JIS G 4108	Class 1, SNB 21-4	Japan	Bar	0.34–0.46 **C**, 0.42–0.73 **Mn**, 0.030 **P**, 0.030 **S**, 0.18–0.37 **Si**, 0.75–1.20 **Cr**, 0.47–0.68 **Mo**, 0.22–0.38 **V**	**Hot rolled, hot forged or cold finished:** (≤75) **diam**, (932) **TS**, (824) **YS**, 13 **El**
JIS G 4107	Class 3	Japan	Bar	0.34–0.46 **C**, 0.42–0.73 **Mn**, 0.045 **P**, 0.045 **S**, 0.18–0.37 **Si**, 0.75–1.20 **Cr**, 0.47–0.68 **Mo**, 0.22–0.38 **V**	**Rolled or forged:** (≤63) **diam**, (863) **TS**, (726) **YS**, 18 **El**
JIS G 4108	Class 1, SNB 21-5	Japan	Bar	0.34–0.46 **C**, 0.42–0.73 **Mn**, 0.030 **P**, 0.030 **S**, 0.18–0.37 **Si**, 0.75–1.20 **Cr**, 0.47–0.68 **Mo**, 0.22–0.38 **V**	**Hot rolled, hot forged or cold finished:** (≤50) **diam**, (824) **TS**, (716) **YS**, 15 **El**
BS 2S.146		UK	Bar, billets, forgings, parts: aircraft quality	0.34–0.42 **C**, 0.15–0.60 **Mn**, 0.015 **P**, 0.010 **S**, 0.15–0.35 **Si**, 1.6–2.0 **Cr**, 3.5–4.5 **Ni**, 0.40–0.60 **Mo**	**Hardened and tempered:** all **diam**, (1760) **TS**, (1420) **YS**, 8 **El**
BS 970 Part 2	Grade 945 M 38	UK	Blooms, billets, bar, forgings	0.34–0.42 **C**, 1.20–1.60 **Mn**, 0.10–0.35 **Si**, 0.40–0.60 **Cr**, 0.60–0.90 **Ni**, 0.15–0.25 **Mo**	**Hardened and tempered:** 10 **diam**, (625) **TS**, (445) **YS**, 15 **El**
BS 970 Part 2	Grade 608 M 38	UK	Blooms, billets, bar, forgings	0.34–0.42 **C**, 1.30–1.70 **Mn**, 0.10–0.35 **S**, 0.40–0.55 **Mo**	**Hardened and tempered:** 10 **diam**, (620) **TS**, (445) **YS**, 15 **El**
ISO/R 683/VII	Type 2	ISO	Bar, billets, rod	0.34–0.41 **C**, 0.60–0.90 **Mn**, 0.035 **P**, 0.035 **S**, 0.15–0.40 **Si**, 0.90–1.20 **Cr**	**Quenched and tempered:** (≤16) **diam**, (931) **TS**, (735) **YS**, 11 **El**
ISO/R 683/VII	Type 2a	ISO	Bar, billets, rod	0.34–0.41 **C**, 0.60–0.90 **Mn**, 0.035 **P**, 0.020–0.035 **S**, 0.15–0.40 **Si**, 0.90–1.20 **Cr**	**Quenched and tempered:** (≤16) **diam**, (931) **TS**, (735) **YS**, 11 **El**
ISO/R 683/VII	Type 2b	ISO	Bar, billets, rod	0.34–0.41 **C**, 0.60–0.90 **Mn**, 0.035 **P**, 0.035–0.050 **S**, 0.15–0.40 **Si**, 0.90–1.20 **Cr**	**Quenched and tempered:** (≤16) **diam**, (931) **TS**, (735) **YS**, 11 **El**
DIN 17200	Grade 37 Cr 4	Germany	Blooms, slabs, billets, wire, bar, plate, sheet, strip, tube, forgings	0.34–0.41 **C**, 0.60–0.90 **Mn**, 0.035 **P**, 0.035 **S**, 0.15–0.40 **Si**, 0.90–1.20 **Cr**	**Quenched and tempered:** (≤16) **diam**, (931) **TS**, (736) **YS**, 11 **El**
DIN 17200	Grade 37 CrS 4	Germany	Blooms, slabs, billets, wire, bar, plate, sheet, strip, tube, forgings	0.34–0.41 **C**, 0.60–0.90 **Mn**, 0.035 **P**, 0.020–0.035 **S**, 0.15–0.40 **Si**, 0.90–1.20 **Cr**	**Quenched and tempered:** (≤16) **diam**, (931) **TS**, (736) **YS**, 11 **El**
EURONORM 119-74, IV	37 Cr 4 KD	EURONORM	Wire, rod	0.34–0.41 **C**, 0.60–0.90 **Mn**, 0.035 **P**, 0.035 **S**, 0.15–0.40 **Si**, 0.90–1.20 **Cr**	**Quenched and tempered:** (≤16) **diam**, (930) **TS**, (735) **YS**, 11 **El**
DIN 17200	Grade 38 Cr 2	Germany	Blooms, slabs, billets, wire, bar, plate, sheet, strip, tube, forgings	0.34–0.41 **C**, 0.50–0.80 **Mn**, 0.035 **P**, 0.035 **S**, 0.15–0.40 **Si**, 0.40–0.60 **Cr**	**Quenched and tempered:** (≤16) **diam**, (795) **TS**, (539) **YS**, 14 **El**
EURONORM 119-74, IV	38 Cr 2 KD	EURONORM	Wire, rod	0.34–0.41 **C**, 0.50–0.80 **Mn**, 0.035 **P**, 0.035 **S**, 0.15–0.40 **Si**, 0.40–0.60 **Cr**	**Quenched and tempered:** (≤16) **diam**, (780) **TS**, (540) **YS**, 14 **El**
EURONROM 119-74, IV	38 Cr 1 KD	EURONORM	Wire, rod	0.34–0.41 **C**, 0.50–0.80 **Mn**, 0.035 **P**, 0.035 **S**, 0.15–0.40 **Si**, 0.20–0.40 **Cr**	**Quenched and tempered:** (≤16) **diam**, (690) **TS**, (470) **YS**, 15 **El**
BS 970 Part 2	Grade 503 H 37	UK	Blooms, billets, bar, forgings	0.34–0.41 **C**, 0.65–1.05 **Mn**, 0.10–0.35 **Si**, 0.65–1.05 **Ni**	
BS 970 Part 2	Grade 605 H 37	UK	Blooms, billets, bar, forgings	0.34–0.41 **C**, 1.25–1.75 **Mn**, 0.10–0.35 **Si**, 0.22–0.32 **Mo**	
BS 970 Part 2	Grade 608 H 37	UK	Blooms, billets, bar, forgings	0.34–0.41 **C**, 1.25–1.75 **Mn**, 0.10–0.35 **Si**, 0.40–0.55 **Mo**	

specification number	designation	country	product forms	composition	mechanical properties (see page iv for explanation)
BS 970 Part 2	Grade 708 H 37	UK	Blooms, billets, bar, forgings	0.34–0.41 **C**, 0.65–1.05 **Mn**, 0.10–0.35 **Si**, 0.80–1.25 **Cr**, 0.15–0.25 **Mo**	
ASTM A 547	Grade 4037H	US	Wire	0.34–0.41 **C**, 0.60–1.00 **Mn**, 0.20–0.30 **Mo**	
ASTM A 547	Grade 4137H	US	Wire	0.34–0.41 **C**, 0.60–1.00 **Mn**, 0.75–1.20 **Cr**, 0.15–0.25 **Mo**	
ASTM A 547	Grade 8637H	US	Wire	0.34–0.41 **C**, 0.70–1.05 **Mn**, 0.35–0.65 **Cr**, 0.35–0.75 **Ni**, 0.15–0.25 **Mo**	
DGN–B–300	4037 H	Mexico	Bar	0.34–0.41 **C**, 0.60–1.00 **Mn**, 0.040 **P**, 0.035 **S**, 0.20–0.35 **Si**, 0.20–0.30 **Mo**	**Annealed**
DGN–B–300	4137 H	Mexico	Bar	0.34–0.41 **C**, 0.60–1.00 **Mn**, 0.040 **P**, 0.035 **S**, 0.20–0.35 **Si**, 0.75–1.20 **Cr**, 0.15–0.25 **Mo**	**Annealed**
DGN–B–300	8637 H	Mexico	Bar	0.34–0.41 **C**, 0.70–1.05 **Mn**, 0.040 **P**, 0.035 **S**, 0.20–0.35 **Si**, 0.35–0.65 **Cr**, 0.35–0.75 **Ni**, 0.15–0.25 **Mo**	**Annealed**
ASTM A 689	4137 H	US	Bar	0.34–0.41 **C**, 0.60–1.00 **Mn**, 0.040 **P**, 0.040 **S**, 0.15–0.30 **Si**, 0.75–1.20 **Cr**, 0.15–0.25 **Mo**	
ASTM A 689	4037 H	US	Bar	0.34–0.41 **C**, 0.60–1.00 **Mn**, 0.040 **P**, 0.040 **S**, 0.15–0.30 **Si**, 0.20–0.30 **Mo**	
ASTM A 689	8637 H	US	Bar	0.34–0.41 **C**, 0.70–1.05 **Mn**, 0.040 **P**, 0.040 **S**, 0.15–0.30 **Si**, 0.35–0.65 **Cr**, 0.35–0.75 **Ni**, 0.15–0.25 **Mo**	
ANSI/ASTM A 304	8637 H	US	Bar	0.34–0.41 **C**, 0.70–1.05 **Mn**, 0.040 **P**, 0.040 **S**, 0.15–0.30 **Si**, 0.35–0.65 **Cr**, 0.35–0.75 **Ni**, 0.15–0.25 **Mo**	
ANSI/ASTM A 304	4037 H	US	Bar	0.34–0.41 **C**, 0.60–1.00 **Mn**, 0.040 **P**, 0.040 **S**, 0.15–0.30 **Si**, 0.20–0.30 **Mo**	
ANSI/ASTM A 304	4137 H	US	Bar	0.34–0.41 **C**, 0.60–1.00 **Mn**, 0.040 **P**, 0.040 **S**, 0.15–0.30 **Si**, 0.75–1.20 **Cr**, 0.15–0.25 **Mo**	
AISI 8637 H		US	Wire, rod	0.34–0.41 **C**, 0.70–1.05 **Mn**, 0.15–0.30 **Si**, 0.35–0.65 **Cr**, 0.35–0.75 **Ni**, 0.15–0.25 **Mo**	
AISI 4037 H		US	Wire, rod	0.34–0.41 **C**, 0.60–1.00 **Mn**, 0.15–0.30 **Si**, 0.20–0.30 **Mo**	
AISI 4137 H		US	Wire, rod	0.34–0.41 **C**, 0.60–1.00 **Mn**, 0.15–0.30 **Si**, 0.75–1.20 **Cr**, 0.15–0.25 **Mo**	
AISI 8637H		US	Bar	0.34–0.41 **C**, 0.70–1.05 **Mn**, 0.035 **P**, 0.040 **S**, 0.15–0.30 **Si**, 0.35–0.65 **Cr**, 0.35–0.75 **Ni**, 0.15–0.65 **Mo**	
AISI 4137H		US	Bar	0.34–0.41 **C**, 0.60–1.00 **Mn**, 0.035 **P**, 0.040 **S**, 0.15–0.30 **Si**, 0.75–1.20 **Cr**, 0.15–0.25 **Mo**	
AISI 4037H		US	Bar	0.34–0.41 **C**, 0.60–1.00 **Mn**, 0.035 **P**, 0.040 **S**, 0.15–0.30 **Si**, 0.20–0.30 **Mo**	
JIS G 4052	SMn 2H	Japan	Bar, wire, rod	0.34–0.41 **C**, 1.15–1.55 **Mn**, 0.030 **P**, 0.030 **S**, 0.15–0.35 **Si**, 0.30 **Cu**	**Hot rolled, normalized, quenched**
EURONORM 119–74, IV	38 CrB 1 KD	EURONORM	Wire, rod	0.34–0.40 **C**, 0.50–0.80 **Mn**, 0.035 **P**, 0.035 **S**, 0.15–0.40 **Si**, 0.20–0.40 **Cr**, 0.0005–0.0050 **B**	**Quenched and tempered:** (≤10) **diam**, (1080) **TS**, (980) **YS**, 10 **El**
ISO 683/XII	7	ISO	Bar, plate	0.34–0.40 **C**, 0.60–0.90 **Mn**, 0.035 **P**, 0.035 **S**, 0.15–0.40 **Si**, 0.90–1.20 **Cr**	**Quenched and tempered:** (16) **diam**, (930) **TS**, (740) **YS**, 11 **El**
AMS 5028		US	Wire	0.34–0.40 **C**, 0.60–0.90 **Mn**, 0.008 **P**, 0.008 **S**, 0.15–0.30 **Si**, 0.90–1.20 **Cr**, 0.40–0.70 **Ni**, 0.90–1.10 **Mo**, 0.05–0.10 **V**, 0.35 **Cu**, 0.0010 **H**, 0.0050 **N**, 0.0025 **O**	

specification number	designation	country	product forms	composition	mechanical properties (see page iv for explanation)
BS 970 Part 2	Grade 530 A 36	UK	Blooms, billets, bar, forgings	0.34–0.39 **C**, 0.60–0.80 **Mn**, 0.90–1.20 **Cr**	
COPANT 334	37 Mn Si 5	COPANT	Bar	0.33–0.51 **C**, 1.10–1.40 **Mn**, 0.035 **P**, 0.035 **S**, 1.10–1.40 **Si**	
BS 3111 Part 1	Type 4	UK	Wire	0.33–0.41 **C**, 0.60–0.90 **Mn**, 0.040 **P**, 0.040 **S**, 0.15–0.40 **Si**, 0.50–0.80 **Cr**, 1.10–1.50 **Ni**	**Drawn and spheroidized annealed**: all diam, (610) max **TS**; **Drawn, spheroidized annealed and light drawn**: all diam, (680) max **TS**
ISO/R 683/V	Type 2b	ISO	Bar, billet, rod	0.33–0.40 **C**, 1.30–1.65 **Mn**, 0.035 **P**, 0.030–0.050 **S**, 0.15–0.40 **Si**	**Quenched and tempered:** (≤16) **diam**, (833) **TS**, (637) **YS**, 12 **El**
ISO/R 683/V	Type 2a	ISO	Bar, billet, rod	0.33–0.40 **C**, 1.30–1.65 **Mn**, 0.035 **P**, 0.020–0.035 **S**, 0.15–0.40 **Si**	**Quenched and tempered:** (≤16) **diam**, (833) **TS**, (637) **YS**, 12 **El**
ISO/R 683/V	Type 2	ISO	Bar, billet, rod	0.33–0.40 **C**, 1.30–1.65 **Mn**, 0.035 **P**, 0.035 **S**, 0.15–0.40 **Si**	**Quenched and tempered:** (≤16) **diam**, (833) **TS**, (637) **YS**, 12 **El**
IS 4367	37Si2Mn[90]	India	Forgings	0.33–0.40 **C**, 0.80–1.00 **Mn**, 0.050 **P**, 0.050 **S**, 1.50–2.00 **Si**	**Hardened and tempered:** (100) **diam**, (784) **TS**
BS 970: Part 2	Grade 530 H 36	UK	Blooms, billets, bar, forgings	0.33–0.40 **C**, 0.50–0.90 **Mn**, 0.10–0.35 **Si**, 0.80–1.25 **Cr**	
AISI 4137		US	Plate	0.33–0.40 **C**, 0.65–0.95 **Mn**, 0.035 **P**, 0.040 **S**, 0.15–0.30 **Si**, 0.80–1.15 **Cr**, 0.15–0.25 **Mo**	
AISI 8637		US	Plate	0.33–0.40 **C**, 0.70–1.00 **Mn**, 0.035 **P**, 0.040 **S**, 0.15–0.30 **Si**, 0.35–0.60 **Cr**, 0.40–0.70 **Ni**, 0.15–0.25 **Mo**	
AMS 6429B		US	Bar, forgings, tube, rings	0.33–0.38 **C**, 0.60–0.90 **Mn**, 0.010 **P**, 0.010 **S**, 0.40–0.60 **Si**, 0.6–0.90 **Cr**, 1.65–2.00 **Ni**, 0.30–0.40 **Mo**, 0.17–0.23 **V**, 0.35 **Cu**	**Hardened, quenched, and tempered:** all **diam**, 240 (1655) **TS**, 210 (1448) **YS**, 10 **El**; **Annealed and cold finished:** ≤0.500 (≤12.70) **diam**, 130 (896) max **TS**
AMS 6435B		US	Sheet, strip, plate	0.33–0.38 **C**, 0.60–0.90 **Mn**, 0.010 **P**, 0.010 **S**, 0.40–0.60 **Si**, 0.65–0.90 **Cr**, 1.65–2.00 **Ni**, 0.30–0.40 **Mo**, 0.17–0.23 **V**, 0.35 **Cu**	**Hardened, quenched and tempered:** ≤0.070 (≤1.78) **diam**, 240 (1655) **TS**, 210 (1448) **YS**, 5 **El**
AMS 5029A		US	Wire	0.33–0.38 **C**, 0.60–0.90 **Mn**, 0.008 **P**, 0.008 **S**, 0.25 **Si**, 0.65–0.90 **Cr**, 1.65–2.00 **Ni**, 0.30–0.40 **Mo**, 0.17–0.23 **V**, 0.0010 **H**, 0.0050 **N**, 0.0025 **O**	**Cold drawn (weld properties):** 0.250 (6.35) **diam**, 234 (1614) **TS**, 3 **El**
AMS 6433B		US	Sheet, strip, plate	0.33–0.38 **C**, 0.60–0.90 **Mn**, 0.015 **P**, 0.015 **S**, 0.40–0.60 **Si**, 0.65–0.90 **Cr**, 1.65–2.00 **Ni**, 0.30–0.40 **Mo**, 0.17–0.23 **V**, 0.35 **Cu**	**Austenitized, quenched and tempered:** all **diam**, 205 (1413) **TS**, 190 (1310) **YS**, 5 **El**
JIS G 4105	Class 3	Japan	Bar	0.33–0.38 **C**, 0.60–0.85 **Mn**, 0.030 **P**, 0.030 **S**, 0.15–0.35 **Si**, 0.90–1.20 **Cr**, 0.25 **Ni**, 0.15–0.30 **Mo**, 0.30 **Cu**	**Rolled or forged, quenched and tempered:** (25) **diam**, (932) **TS**, (785) **YS**, 15 **El**
AMS 6330C		US	Bar, forgings, tube	0.33–0.38 **C**, 0.60–0.80 **Mn**, 0.025 **P**, 0.025 **S**, 0.20–0.35 **Si**, 0.55–0.75 **Cr**, 1.10–1.40 **Ni**, 0.06 **Mo**, 0.35 **Cu**	**Cold finished (bar):** ≤0.500 (≤12.70) **diam**, 130 (896) max **TS**
JIS G 4104	Class 3	Japan	Bar	0.33–0.38 **C**, 0.60–0.85 **Mn**, 0.030 **P**, 0.030 **S**, 0.15–0.35 **Si**, 0.90–1.20 **Cr**, 0.25 **Ni**, 0.30 **Cu**	**Rolled or forged, quenched and tempered:** (25) **diam**, (883) **TS**, (736) **YS**, 15 **El**
AMS 6352C		US	Sheet: strip, plate	0.33–0.38 **C**, 0.70–0.90 **Mn**, 0.025 **P**, 0.025 **S**, 0.20–0.35 **Si**, 0.80–1.10 **Cr**, 0.25 **Ni**, 0.15–0.25 **Mo**, 0.35 **Cu**	**Quenched and tempered:** all **diam**, 125 (862) **TS**
AMS 6357E		US	Sheet, strip, plate	0.33–0.38 **C**, 0.75–1.00 **Mn**, 0.025 **P**, 0.025 **S**, 0.15–0.35 **Si**, 0.40–0.60 **Cr**, 0.40–0.70 **Ni**, 0.20–0.30 **Mo**, 0.35 **Cu**	**Austenitized and quenched:** ≤0.499 (≤12.67) **diam**, 125 (862) **TS**
AMS 6320G		US	Bar, forgings, rings	0.33–0.38 **C**, 0.75–1.00 **Mn**, 0.025 **P**, 0.025 **S**, 0.20–0.35 **Si**, 0.40–0.60 **Cr**, 0.40–0.70 **Ni**, 0.20–0.30 **Mo**, 0.35 **Cu**	**Cold finished (bar):** ≤0.500 (≤12.70) **diam**, 120 (827) max **TS**

WROUGHT ALLOY STEELS

specification number	designation	country	product forms	composition	mechanical properties (see page iv for explanation)
AMS 6535E		US	Tube	0.33–0.38 **C**, 0.75–1.00 **Mn**, 0.025 **P**, 0.025 **S**, 0.20–0.35 **Si**, 0.40–0.60 **Cr**, 0.40–0.70 **Ni**, 0.20–0.30 **Mo**, 0.35 **Cu**	**Cold finished, normalized and tempered**: ≤0.188 (≤4.70) **diam**, 100 (690) **TS**, 85 (586) **YS**, 8 **El**
AMS 6365F		US	Tube	0.33–0.38 **C**, 0.70–0.90 **Mn**, 0.025 **P**, 0.025 **S**, 0.20–0.35 **Si**, 0.80–1.10 **Cr**, 0.25 **Ni**, 0.15–0.25 **Mo**, 0.35 **Cu**	**Cold finished, normalized and tempered**: ≤0.188 (≤4.78) **diam**, 100 (690) **TS**, 85 (586) **YS**, 8 **El**
AS G18	G18/En 111A	Australia	Bar, billet	0.33–0.38 **C**, 0.60–0.90 **Mn**, 0.050 **P**, 0.050 **S**, 0.10–0.35 **Si**, 0.45–0.75 **Cr**, 1.00–1.50 **Ni**	**Hardened, tempered**: 6 **diam**, (690) **TS**, (525) **YS**
MIL–T–6733	AISI 8735	US	Tube: seamless, aircraft quality	0.33–0.38 **C**, 0.75–1.00 **Mn**, 0.040 **P**, 0.040 **S**, 0.20–0.35 **Si**, 0.40–0.60 **Cr**, 0.40–0.70 **Ni**, 0.20–0.30 **Mo**	**Annealed**: all **diam**, 100 (690) **TS**; **Normalized**: ≤0.188 **diam**, 100 (690) **TS**, 85 (586) **YS**, 12 **El**; **Quenched and tempered**: all **diam**, 125 (862) **TS**, 100 (690) **YS**, 12 **El**; **Quenched and tempered**: all **diam**, 150 (1034) **TS**, 135 (930) **YS**, 10 **El**; **Quenched and tempered**: all **diam**, 180 (1241) **TS**, 165 (1138) **YS**, 8 **El**
MIL–S–18733A		US	Plate, sheet, strip: aircraft quality	0.33–0.38 **C**, 0.70–0.90 **Mn**, 0.025 **P**, 0.025 **S**, 0.20–0.35 **Si**, 0.80–1.10 **Cr**, 0.25 **Ni**, 0.15–0.25 **Mo**; rem **Fe**	**Annealed**: all **diam**, 90 (621) **TS**; **Normalized**: <0.063 **diam**, 95 (655) **TS**, 75 (517) **YS**, 10 **El**
AISI 1335		US	Bar	0.33–0.38 **C**, 1.60–1.90 **Mn**, 0.035 **P**, 0.040 **S**, 0.15–0.30 **Si**	
AISI 5135		US	Bar	0.33–0.38 **C**, 0.60–0.80 **Mn**, 0.035 **P**, 0.040 **S**, 0.15–0.30 **Si**, 0.80–1.05 **Cr**	
MIL–W–21425B		US	Bar, plate, sheet, strip	0.33–0.38 **C**, 0.60–0.90 **Mn**, 0.010 **P**, 0.010 **S**, 0.40–0.60 **Si**, 0.65–0.90 **Cr**, 1.65–2.00 **Ni**, 0.30–0.40 **Mo**, 0.17–0.23 **V**	**Annealed**; **Spheroidize annealed**
BS 970 Part 2	Grade 640 A 35	UK	Blooms, billets, bar, forgings	0.33–0.38 **C**, 0.60–0.90 **Mn**, 0.50–0.80 **Cr**, 1.10–1.50 **Ni**	
ASTM A 547	Grade 1335	US	Wire	0.33–0.38 **C**, 1.60–1.90 **Mn**	
ASTM A 547	Grade 4135	US	Wire	0.33–0.38 **C**, 0.70–0.90 **Mn**, 0.80–1.10 **Cr**, 0.15–0.25 **Mo**	
AMS 6434B		US	Sheet, strip, plate	0.33–0.38 **C**, 0.60–0.80 **Mn**, 0.025 **P**, 0.025 **S**, 0.20–0.35 **Si**, 0.65–0.90 **Cr**, 1.65–2.00 **Ni**, 0.30–0.40 **Mo**, 0.17–0.23 **V**, 0.35 **Cu**	
AMS 6282E		US	Tube	0.33–0.38 **C**, 0.75–1.00 **Mn**, 0.025 **P**, 0.025 **S**, 0.20–0.35 **Si**, 0.40–0.60 **Cr**, 0.40–0.70 **Ni**, 0.20–0.30 **Mo**, 0.35 **Cu**	
AMS 6372E		US	Tube	0.33–0.38 **C**, 0.70–0.90 **Mn**, 0.025 **P**, 0.025 **S**, 0.20–0.35 **Si**, 0.80–1.10 **Cr**, 0.25 **Ni**, 0.15–0.25 **Mo**, 0.35 **Cu**	
MIL–S–81081A		US	Sheet: hot or cold rolled	0.33–0.38 **C**, 0.60–0.90 **Mn**, 0.015 **P**, 0.015 **S**, 0.40–0.60 **Si**, 0.65–0.90 **Cr**, 1.65–2.00 **Ni**, 0.30–0.40 **Mo**, 0.17–0.23 **V**	**Hot or cold finished, annealed**
MIL–S–81054A		US	Bar, forgings	0.33–0.38 **C**, 0.60–0.85 **Mn**, 0.025 **P**, 0.025 **S**, 0.40–0.60 **Si**, 0.65–0.90 **Cr**, 1.65–2.00 **Ni**, 0.30–0.40 **Mo**, 0.17–0.23 **V**	**Normalized, tempered**
COPANT 334	3135	COPANT	Bar	0.33–0.38 **C**, 0.60–0.80 **Mn**, 0.035 **P**, 0.040 **S**, 0.20–0.35 **Si**, 0.55–0.75 **Cr**, 1.10–1.40 **Ni**	
COPANT 334	4135	COPANT	Bar	0.33–0.38 **C**, 0.70–0.90 **Mn**, 0.035 **P**, 0.040 **S**, 0.20–0.35 **Si**, 0.80–1.10 **Cr**, 0.15–0.25 **Mo**	
COPANT 334	5135	COPANT	Bar	0.33–0.38 **C**, 0.60–0.80 **Mn**, 0.035 **P**, 0.040 **S**, 0.20–0.35 **Si**, 0.80–1.05 **Cr**	

WROUGHT ALLOY STEELS

specification number	designation	country	product forms	composition	mechanical properties (see page iv for explanation)
DGN–B–203	Grade 4135	Mexico	Tube: seamless	0.33–0.38 **C**, 0.70–0.90 **Mn**, 0.040 **P**, 0.040 **S**, 0.20–0.35 **Si**, 0.80–1.10 **Cr**, 0.15–0.25 **Mo**	
DGN–B–203	Grade 1335	Mexico	Tube: seamless	0.33–0.38 **C**, 1.60–1.90 **Mn**, 0.040 **P**, 0.040 **S**, 0.20–0.35 **Si**	
DGN–B–203	Grade 5135	Mexico	Tube: seamless	0.33–0.38 **C**, 0.60–0.80 **Mn**, 0.040 **P**, 0.040 **S**, 0.20–0.35 **Si**, 0.80–1.05 **Cr**	
DGN–B–203	Grade 8735	Mexico	Tube: seamless	0.33–0.38 **C**, 0.75–1.00 **Mn**, 0.040 **P**, 0.040 **S**, 0.20–0.35 **Si**, 0.40–0.60 **Cr**, 0.40–0.70 **Ni**, 0.20–0.30 **Mo**	
COPANT 514	4135	COPANT	Tube	0.33–0.38 **C**, 0.70–0.90 **Mn**, 0.040 **P**, 0.040 **S**, 0.20–0.35 **Si**, 0.80–1.10 **Cr**, 0.15–0.25 **Mo**	
COPANT 514	1335	COPANT	Tube	0.33–0.38 **C**, 1.60–1.90 **Mn**, 0.040 **P**, 0.040 **S**, 0.20–0.35 **Si**	
DGN–B–300	5135	Mexico	Bar	0.33–0.38 **C**, 0.60–0.80 **Mn**, 0.035 **P**, 0.040 **S**, 0.20–0.35 **Si**, 0.80–1.05 **Cr**	**Annealed**
DGN–B–300	1335	Mexico	Bar	0.33–0.38 **C**, 1.60–1.90 **Mn**, 0.035 **P**, 0.040 **S**, 0.20–0.35 **Si**	**Annealed**
ANSI/ASTM A 29	5135	US	Bar	0.33–0.38 **C**, 0.60–0.80 **Mn**, 0.035 **P**, 0.040 **S**, 0.15–0.30 **Si**, 0.80–1.05 **Cr**	
ANSI/ASTM A 29	4135	US	Bar	0.33–0.38 **C**, 0.70–0.90 **Mn**, 0.035 **P**, 0.040 **S**, 0.15–0.30 **Si**, 0.80–1.10 **Cr**, 0.15–0.25 **Mo**	
ANSI/ASTM A 646	4335 Mod	US	Blooms, billets: aircraft quality	0.33–0.38 **C**, 0.60–0.90 **Mn**, 0.025 **P**, 0.025 **S**, 0.40–0.60 **Si**, 0.65–0.90 **Cr**, 1.65–2.00 **Ni**, 0.30–0.40 **Mo**, 0.17–0.23 **V**	**Annealed**
MIL–S–16974E	No 8635	US	Bar, billets, blooms, slabs	0.33–0.38 **C**, 0.75–1.00 **Mn**, 0.040 **P**, 0.040 **S**, 0.20–0.35 **Si**, 0.40–0.60 **Cr**, 0.40–0.70 **Ni**, 0.15–0.25 **Mo**	
MIL–S–16974E	No 4135	US	Bar, billets, blooms, slabs	0.33–0.38 **C**, 0.70–0.90 **Mn**, 0.040 **P**, 0.040 **S**, 0.20–0.35 **Si**, 0.80–1.10 **Cr**, 0.15–0.25 **Mo**	
MIL–S–16974E	No 1335	US	Bar, billets, blooms, slabs	0.33–0.38 **C**, 1.60–1.90 **Mn**, 0.040 **P**, 0.040 **S**, 0.20–0.35 **Si**	
ASTM A 689	5135	US	Bar	0.33–0.38 **C**, 0.60–0.80 **Mn**, 0.035 **P**, 0.040 **S**, 0.15–0.30 **Si**, 0.80–1.05 **Cr**	
ASTM A 689	1335	US	Bar	0.33–0.38 **C**, 1.60–1.90 **Mn**, 0.035 **P**, 0.040 **S**, 0.15–0.30 **Si**	
ANSI/ASTM A 322	5135	US	Bar	0.33–0.38 **C**, 0.60–0.80 **Mn**, 0.035 **P**, 0.040 **S**, 0.15–0.30 **Si**, 0.80–1.05 **Cr**	
ANSI/ASTM A 322	1335	US	Bar	0.33–0.38 **C**, 1.60–1.90 **Mn**, 0.035 **P**, 0.040 **S**, 0.15–0.30 **Si**	
ANSI/ASTM A 29	1335	US	Bar	0.33–0.38 **C**, 1.60–1.90 **Mn**, 0.035 **P**, 0.040 **S**, 0.15–0.30 **Si**	
AISI 1335		US	Wire, rod	0.33–0.38 **C**, 1.60–1.90 **Mn**, 0.035 **P**, 0.040 **S**, 0.15–0.30 **Si**	
AISI 5135		US	Wire, rod	0.33–0.38 **C**, 0.60–0.80 **Mn**, 0.035 **P**, 0.040 **S**, 0.15–0.30 **Si**, 0.80–1.05 **Cr**	
ANSI/ASTM A 519	1335	US	Tube: seamless	0.33–0.38 **C**, 1.60–1.90 **Mn**, 0.040 **P**, 0.040 **S**, 0.15–0.35 **Si**	
ANSI/ASTM A 519	4135	US	Tube: seamless	0.33–0.38 **C**, 0.70–0.90 **Mn**, 0.040 **P**, 0.040 **S**, 0.15–0.35 **Si**, 0.80–1.10 **Cr**, 0.15–0.25 **Mo**	
ANSI/ASTM A 519	5135	US	Tube: seamless	0.33–0.38 **C**, 0.60–0.80 **Mn**, 0.040 **P**, 0.040 **S**, 0.15–0.35 **Si**, 0.80–1.05 **Cr**	
ANSI/ASTM A 519	8735	US	Tube: seamless	0.33–0.38 **C**, 0.75–1.00 **Mn**, 0.040 **P**, 0.040 **S**, 0.15–0.35 **Si**, 0.40–0.60 **Cr**, 0.40–0.70 **Ni**, 0.20–0.30 **Mo**	

WROUGHT ALLOY STEELS

specification number	designation	country	product forms	composition	mechanical properties (see page iv for explanation)
AS 1442	Grade AS 1442/XK 1335	Australia	Bar, blooms, billets, slabs	0.33–0.38 **C**, 1.40–1.70 **Mn**, 0.050 **P**, 0.050 **S**, 0.10–0.35 **Si**	
AS 1443	Grade AS 1443/XK 1335	Australia	Bar	0.33–0.38 **C**, 1.40–1.70 **Mn**, 0.050 **P**, 0.050 **S**, 0.10–0.35 **Si**	
DGN–B–297	1335	Mexico	Bar	0.33–0.38 **C**, 1.60–1.90 **Mn**, 0.035 **P**, 0.040 **S**, 0.20–0.35 **Si**	
DGN–B–297	5135	Mexico	Bar	0.33–0.38 **C**, 0.60–0.90 **Mn**, 0.035 **P**, 0.040 **S**, 0.20–0.35 **Si**, 0.80–1.05 **Cr**	
COPANT 514	Grade 8735	COPANT	Tube: seamless	0.33–0.38 **C**, 0.75–0.90 **Mn**, 0.040 **P**, 0.050 **S**, 0.10 **Si**, 0.40–0.60 **Cr**, 0.40–0.70 **Ni**, 0.20–0.30 **Mo**	
JIS G 3311	SCM3M	Japan	Strip	0.33–0.38 **C**, 0.60–0.85 **Mn**, 0.030 **P**, 0.030 **S**, 0.15–0.35 **Si**, 0.90–1.20 **Cr**, 0.25 **Ni**, 0.15–0.30 **Mo**, 0.30 **Cu**	
BS 3111 Part 1	Type 2/2	UK	Wire	0.32–0.45 **C**, 0.80–1.00 **Mn**, 0.040 **P**, 0.040 **S**, 0.16–0.40 **Si**, 0.25–0.35 **Mo**	**Drawn and spheroidized annealed**: all **diam**, (590) max **TS**; **Drawn, spheroidized annealed, and light drawn**: all **diam**, (700) max **TS**
IS 5517	Grade 37Mn2	India	Bar, billet	0.32–0.42 **C**, 1.30–1.70 **Mn**, 0.10–0.35 **Si**	**Normalized, annealed or hardened and tempered**: (15) **diam**, (880) **TS**, (685) **YS**
IS 4367	37Mn2	India	Forgings	0.32–0.42 **C**, 1.30–1.70 **Mn**, 0.050 **P**, 0.050 **S**, 0.10–0.35 **Si**	**Hardened and tempered**: (100) **diam**, (686) **TS**, 18 **El**
DIN 17200	Grade 36 CrNiMo 4	Germany	Blooms, slabs, billets, wire, bar, plate, sheet, strip, tube, forgings	0.32–0.40 **C**, 0.50–0.80 **Mn**, 0.035 **P**, 0.035 **S**, 0.15–0.40 **Si**, 2.80–3.30 **Cr**, 0.90–1.20 **Ni**, 0.15–0.30 **Mo**	**Quenched and tempered**: (≤16) **diam**, (1079) **TS**, (883) **YS**, 10 **El**
JIS G 4102	Class 3	Japan	Bar	0.32–0.40 **C**, 0.35–0.65 **Mn**, 0.030 **P**, 0.030 **S**, 0.15–0.35 **Si**, 0.60–1.00 **Cr**, 3.00–3.50 **Ni**, 0.30 **Cu**	**Rolled or forged, quenched and tempered**: (25) **diam**, (932) **TS**, (785) **YS**, 15 **El**
BS 2S.114		UK	Bar, billets, forgings: aircraft quality	0.32–0.40 **C**, 1.3–1.7 **Mn**, 0.040 **P**, 0.045 **S**, 0.10–0.35 **Si**, 0.22–0.32 **Mo**	**Hardened and tempered**: all **diam**, (850) **TS**, (665) **YS**, 13 **El**
JIS G 4102	Class 1	Japan	Bar	0.32–0.40 **C**, 0.50–0.80 **Mn**, 0.030 **P**, 0.030 **S**, 0.15–0.35 **Si**, 0.50–0.90 **Cr**, 1.00–1.50 **Ni**, 0.30 **Cu**	**Rolled or forged, quenched and tempered**: (25) **diam**, (736) **TS**, (588) **YS**, 22 **El**
BS 970 Part 2	Grade 605 M 36	UK	Blooms, billets, bar, forgings	0.32–0.40 **C**, 1.30–1.70 **Mn**, 0.10–0.35 **Si**, 0.22–0.32 **Mo**	**Hardened and tempered**: 10 **diam**, (620) **TS**, (445) **YS**, 15 **El**
BS 970 Part 2	Grade 606 M 36	UK	Blooms, billets, bar, forgings	0.32–0.40 **C**, 1.30–1.70 **Mn**, 0.040 **P**, 0.15–0.25 **S**, 0.25 **Si**, 0.22–0.32 **Mo**	**Hardened and tempered**: 4 **diam**, (620) **TS**, (470) **YS**, 15 **El**
BS 970 Part 1	150M36	UK	Blooms, billets, slabs, bar, rod, forgings	0.32–0.40 **C**, 1.30–1.70 **Mn**	**Normalized**: 6 **diam**, (550) **TS**, (345) **YS**, 14 **El**; **Hardened and tempered**: 6 **diam**, (550) **TS**, (360) **YS**, 18 **El**
DIN 17240	Grade C 35	Germany	Bar	0.32–0.40 **C**, 0.40–0.70 **Mn**, 0.045 **P**, 0.045 **S**, 0.15–0.35 **Si**, 0.50 **Cr**	**Rolled, forged or drawn**: all **diam**, (490) **TS**, (274) **YS**, 22 **El**
DIN 17240	Grade Ck 35	Germany	Bar	0.32–0.40 **C**, 0.40–0.70 **Mn**, 0.035 **P**, 0.035 **S**, 0.15–0.35 **Si**, 0.50 **Cr**	**Rolled, forged or drawn**: all **diam**, (490) **TS**, (274) **YS**, 22 **El**
BS 970 Part 1	Grade 216M36	UK	Blooms, billets, slabs, bar, rod, forgings	0.32–0.40 **C**, 1.30–1.70 **Mn**, 0.060 **P**, 0.12–0.20 **S**, 0.25 **Si**	**Hardened and tempered**: 4 **diam**, (480) **TS**, (305) **YS**, 20 **El**; **Cold drawn from hot rolled**: 0.50–0.625 **diam**, (580) **TS**, (455) **YS**, 7 **El**
JIS G 3311	SNC3M	Japan	Strip	0.32–0.40 **C**, 0.35–0.65 **Mn**, 0.030 **P**, 0.030 **S**, 0.15–0.35 **Si**, 0.60–1.00 **Cr**, 3.00–3.50 **Ni**, 0.30 **Cu**	
SIS 14 25 41	SIS 2541–06	Sweden	Bar, forgings	0.32–0.39 **C**, 0.50–0.80 **Mn**, 0.035 **P**, 0.035 **S**, 0.15–0.40 **Si**, 1.20–1.60 **Cr**, 1.20–1.60 **Ni**, 0.15–0.25 **Mo**	**Quenched**: (≤40) **diam**, (1500) **TS**, (1200) **YS**, 7 **El**

specification number	designation	country	product forms	composition	mechanical properties (see page iv for explanation)
EURONORM 119–74, IV	35 CrNiMo 6 KD	EURONORM	Wire, rod	0.32–0.39 **C**, 0.50–0.80 **Mn**, 0.035 **P**, 0.035 **S**, 0.15–0.40 **Si**, 1.30–1.70 **Cr**, 1.30–1.70 **Ni**, 0.15–0.30 **Mo**	**Quenched and tempered:** (≤16) **diam**, (1180) **TS**, (980) **YS**, 9 **El**
ISO/R 683/VIII	Type 3	ISO	Bar, billets, rod	0.32–0.39 **C**, 0.50–0.80 **Mn**, 0.035 **P**, 0.035 **S**, 0.15–0.40 **Si**, 1.30–1.70 **Cr**, 1.30–1.70 **Ni**, 0.15–0.30 **Mo**	**Quenched and tempered:** (≤16) **diam**, (1176) **TS**, (980) **YS**, 9 **El**
ISO/R 683/VIII	Type 3a	ISO	Bar, billets, rod	0.32–0.39 **C**, 0.50–0.80 **Mn**, 0.035 **P**, 0.020–0.035 **S**, 0.15–0.40 **Si**, 1.30–1.70 **Cr**, 1.30–1.70 **Ni**, 0.15–0.30 **Mo**	**Quenched and tempered:** (≤16) **diam**, (1176) **TS**, (980) **YS**, 9 **El**
ISO/R 683/VIII	Type 3b	ISO	Bar, billets, rod	0.32–0.39 **C**, 0.50–0.80 **Mn**, 0.035 **P**, 0.030–0.050 **S**, 0.15–0.40 **Si**, 1.30–1.70 **Cr**, 1.30–1.70 **Ni**, 0.15–0.30 **Mo**	**Quenched and tempered:** (≤16) **diam**, (1176) **TS**, (980) **YS**, 9 **El**
SIS 14 25 41	SIS 2541–04	Sweden	Bar, forgings	0.32–0.39 **C**, 0.50–0.80 **Mn**, 0.035 **P**, 0.035 **S**, 0.15–0.40 **Si**, 1.20–1.60 **Cr**, 1.20–1.60 **Ni**, 0.15–0.25 **Mo**	**Quenched and tempered:** (≤40) **diam**, (1100) **TS**, (900) **YS**, 10 **El**
JIS G 3441	Class 3, STKS 3E	Japan	Tube	0.32–0.39 **C**, 0.40–0.85 **Mn**, 0.030 **P**, 0.030 **S**, 0.15–0.35 **Si**, 0.40–0.65 **Cr**, 0.15–0.25 **Mo**	**Quenched and tempered:** all **diam**, (1030) **TS**, (931) **YS**, 10 **El**
JIS G 3441	Class 4, STKS 4E	Japan	Tube	0.32–0.39 **C**, 0.70–1.00 **Mn**, 0.030 **P**, 0.030 **S**, 0.15–0.35 **Si**, 0.40–0.65 **Cr**, 0.40–0.70 **Ni**, 0.20–0.30 **Mo**	**Quenched and tempered:** all **diam**, (1030) **TS**, (931) **YS**, 10 **El**
SIS 14 25 41	SIS 2541–05	Sweden	Bar, forgings	0.32–0.39 **C**, 0.50–0.80 **Mn**, 0.035 **P**, 0.035 **S**, 0.15–0.40 **Si**, 1.20–1.60 **Cr**, 1.20–1.60 **Ni**, 0.15–0.25 **Mo**	**Quenched and tempered:** (≤100) **diam**, (1000) **TS**, (800) **YS**, 11 **El**
SIS 14 25 41	SIS 2541–03	Sweden	Bar, forgings	0.32–0.39 **C**, 0.50–0.80 **Mn**, 0.035 **P**, 0.035 **S**, 0.15–0.40 **Si**, 1.20–1.60 **Cr**, 1.20–1.60 **Ni**, 0.15–0.25 **Mo**	**Quenched and tempered:** (≤250) **diam**, (900) **TS**, (700) **YS**, 12 **El**
JIS G 3441	Class 3, STKS 3D	Japan	Tube	0.32–0.39 **C**, 0.40–0.85 **Mn**, 0.030 **P**, 0.030 **S**, 0.15–0.35 **Si**, 0.80–1.20 **Cr**, 0.15–0.25 **Mo**	**Quenched and tempered:** all **diam**, (863) **TS**, (686) **YS**, 12 **El**
JIS G 3441	Class 4, STKS 4D	Japan	Tube	0.32–0.39 **C**, 0.70–1.00 **Mn**, 0.030 **P**, 0.030 **S**, 0.15–0.35 **Si**, 0.40–0.65 **Cr**, 0.40–0.70 **Ni**, 0.20–0.30 **Mo**	**Quenched and tempered:** all **diam**, (863) **TS**, (686) **YS**, 12 **El**
SIS 14 25 41	SIS 2541–08	Sweden	Bar, forgings	0.32–0.39 **C**, 0.50–0.80 **Mn**, 0.035 **P**, 0.035 **S**, 0.15–0.0 **Si**, 1.20–1.60 **Cr**, 1.20–1.60 **Ni**, 0.15–0.25 **Mo**	**Quenched and tempered:** (≤250) **diam**, (800) **TS**, (600) **YS**, 13 **El**
SFS 461	Co. 35 Cr 1.4 Mo 0.2 Ni 1.4	Finland	Bar, forgings	0.32–0.39 **C**, 0.50–0.80 **Mn**, 0.035 **P**, 0.035 **S**, 0.15–0.40 **Si**, 1.20–1.60 **Cr**, 1.20–1.60 **Ni**, 0.15–0.25 **Mo**	**Quenched and tempered:** (220) **diam**, (780) **TS**, (590) **YS**, 13 **El**
ISO/R 683/IX	Type 9	ISO	Bar, wire, rod, steel	0.32–0.39 **C**, 1.30–1.65 **Mn**, 0.06 **P**, 0.15–0.25 **S**, 0.15–0.25 **Si**	**Quenched and tempered:** (≤16) **diam**, (735) **TS**, (510) **YS**, 12 **El**
MIL–T–6735A	AISI 4135	US	Tube: seamless, aircraft quality	0.32–0.39 **C**, 0.70–0.90 **Mn**, 0.025 **P**, 0.025 **S**, 0.20–0.35 **Si**, 0.80–1.10 **Cr**, 0.15–0.25 **Mo**	**Annealed:** all **diam**, 100 (690) **TS**; **Normalized:** ≤0.187 **diam**, 100 (690) **TS**, 85 (586) **YS**, 12 **El**; **Quenched and tempered:** all **diam**, 125 (862) **TS**, 100 (690) **YS**, 12 **El**; **Quenched and tempered:** all **diam**, 150 (1034) **TS**, 135 (930) **YS**, 10 **El**; **Quenched and tempered:** all **diam**, 180 (1241) **TS**, 165 (1138) **YS**, 8 **El**; **Quenched and tempered:** all **diam**, 200 (1379) **TS**, 165 (1138) **YS**, 7 **El**
ANSI/ASTM A 311	1137	US	Bar	0.32–0.39 **C**, 1.35–1.65 **Mn**, 0.040 **P**, 0.08–0.13 **S**	**Cold drawn, stress relieved:** ≤0.56 (14.29) **diam**, 100 (690) **TS**, 80 (552) **YS**, 15 **El**
DGN–B–296	1137	Mexico	Bar	0.32–0.39 **C**, 1.35–1.65 **Mn**, 0.040 **P**, 0.08–0.13 **S**	**Cold finished:** (14) **diam**, (689) **TS**, (551) **YS**, 15 **El**

WROUGHT ALLOY STEELS

specification number	designation	country	product forms	composition	mechanical properties (see page iv for explanation)
JIS G 3441	Class 3, STKS 3A	Japan	Tube	0.32–0.39 **C**, 0.40–0.85 **Mn**, 0.030 **P**, 0.030 **S**, 0.15–0.35 **Si**, 0.80–1.20 **Cr**, 0.15–0.25 **Mo**	**Annealed**: all **diam**, (686) **TS**
JIS G 3441	Class 4, STKS 4A	Japan	Tube	0.32–0.39 **C**, 0.70–1.00 **Mn**, 0.030 **P**, 0.030 **S**, 0.15–0.35 **Si**, 0.40–0.65 **Cr**, 0.40–0.70 **Ni**, 0.20–0.30 **Mo**	**Annealed**: all **diam**, (686) **TS**
COPANT 332	1137	COPANT	Bar	0.32–0.39 **C**, 1.35–1.65 **Mn**, 0.040 **P**, 0.08–0.13 **S**	**Cold finished and annealed**: (≤15) **diam**, (685) **TS**, (550) **YS**, 15 **El**
JIS G 3441	Class 3, STKS 3C	Japan	Tube	0.32–0.39 **C**, 0.40–0.85 **Mn**, 0.030 **P**, 0.030 **S**, 0.15–0.35 **Si**, 0.80–1.20 **Cr**, 0.15–0.25 **Mo**	**Cold finished**: all **diam**, (657) **TS**, (549) **YS**, 10 **El**
JIS G 3441	Class 4, STKS 4C	Japan	Tube	0.32–0.39 **C**, 0.70–1.00 **Mn**, 0.030 **P**, 0.030 **S**, 0.15–0.35 **Si**, 0.40–0.65 **Cr**, 0.40–0.70 **Ni**, 0.20–0.30 **Mo**	**Cold finished**: all **diam**, (657) **TS**, (549) **YS**, 10 **El**
JIS G 3441	Class 3, STKS 3B	Japan	Tube	0.32–0.39 **C**, 0.40–0.85 **Mn**, 0.030 **P**, 0.030 **S**, 0.15–0.35 **Si**, 0.80–1.20 **Cr**, 0.15–0.25 **Mo**	**Normalized or normalized and tempered**: all **diam**, (549) **TS**, (392) **YS**, 12 **El**
JIS G 3441	Class 4, STKS 4B	Japan	Tube	0.32–0.39 **C**, 0.70–1.00 **Mn**, 0.030 **P**, 0.030 **S**, 0.15–0.35 **Si**, 0.40–0.65 **Cr**, 0.40–0.70 **Ni**, 0.20–0.30 **Mo**	**Normalized or normalized and tempered**: all **diam**, (549) **TS**, (392) **YS**, 12 **El**
COPANT 514	Grade 1137	COPANT	Tube: seamless	0.32–0.39 **C**, 1.35–1.65 **Mn**, 0.040 **P**, 0.08–0.13 **S**	**Hot finished**: (>323.9) **diam**, (480) **TS**, (275) **YS**, 20 **El**; **Cold finished**: all **diam**, (550) **TS**, (450) **YS**, 5 **El**; **Annealed**: all **diam**, (450) **TS**, (245) **YS**, 22 **El**; **Normalized**: all **diam**, (345) **TS**, (295) **YS**, 15 **El**
ASTM A 108	1137	US	Bar	0.32–0.39 **C**, 1.35–1.65 **Mn**, 0.040 **P**, 0.08–0.13 **S**	
AISI 1335		US	Plate	0.32–0.39 **C**, 1.50–1.90 **Mn**, 0.035 **P**, 0.040 **S**, 0.15–0.30 **Si**	
AISI 4135		US	Plate	0.32–0.39 **C**, 0.65–0.95 **Mn**, 0.035 **P**, 0.040 **S**, 0.15–0.30 **Si**, 0.80–1.15 **Cr**, 0.15–0.25 **Mo**	
SIS 14 25 41	SIS 2541-02	Sweden	Bar	0.32–0.39 **C**, 0.50–0.80 **Mn**, 0.035 **P**, 0.035 **S**, 0.15–0.40 **Si**, 1.20–1.60 **Cr**, 1.20–1.60 **Ni**, 0.15–0.25 **Mo**	
ASTM A 689	1137	US	Bar	0.32–0.39 **C**, 1.35–1.65 **Mn**, 0.040 **P**, 0.08–0.13 **S**	
ANSI/ASTM A 29	1137	US	Bar	0.32–0.39 **C**, 1.35–1.65 **Mn**, 0.040 **P**, 0.08–0.13 **S**	
ANSI/ASTM A 576	1137	US	Bar	0.32–0.39 **C**, 1.35–1.65 **Mn**, 0.040 **P**, 0.08–0.13 **S**	
JIS G 4052	SCM 3H	Japan	Bar, wire, rod	0.32–0.39 **C**, 0.55–0.90 **Mn**, 0.030 **P**, 0.030 **S**, 0.15–0.35 **Si**, 0.85–1.25 **Cr**, 0.15–0.35 **Mo**, 0.30 **Cu**	**Hot rolled, normalized, quenched**
AS 1443	Grade AS 1443/K 1137	Australia	Bar	0.32–0.39 **C**, 1.35–1.65 **Mn**, 0.050 **P**, 0.08–0.13 **S**, 0.10–0.35 **Si**	
JIS G 4804	SUM 41	Japan	Bar	0.32–0.39 **C**, 1.35–1.65 **Mn**, 0.040 **P**, 0.08–0.13 **S**	
QQ-S-637A	1137	US	Bar	0.32–0.39 **C**, 1.35–1.65 **Mn**, 0.040 **P**, 0.08–0.13 **S**, 0.15–0.35 **Pb**	
COPANT 331	1137	COPANT	Bar	0.32–0.39 **C**, 1.35–1.65 **Mn**, 0.040 **P**, 0.08–0.13 **S**	
COPANT 330	1137	COPANT	Bar, shapes	0.32–0.39 **C**, 1.35–1.65 **Mn**, 0.040 **P**, 0.08–0.13 **S**	
AMS 6430B		US	Bar	0.32–0.38 **C**, 0.60–0.90 **Mn**, 0.015 **P**, 0.015 **S**, 0.40–0.60 **Si**, 0.65–0.90 **Cr**, 1.65–2.00 **Ni**, 0.30–0.40 **Mo**, 0.17–0.23 **V**, 0.35 **Cu**	**Hardened, quenched and tempered**: all **diam**, 205 (1413) **TS**, 190 (1310) **YS**, 10 **El**; **Cold finished (bar)**: ≤0.500 (≤12.70) **diam**, 140 (965) max **TS**

WROUGHT ALLOY STEELS

specification number	designation	country	product forms	composition	mechanical properties (see page iv for explanation)
AMS 6428B		US	Bar, forgings, tube	0.32–0.38 **C**, 0.60–0.80 **Mn**, 0.025 **P**, 0.025 **S**, 0.20–0.35 **Si**, 0.65–0.90 **Cr**, 1.65–2.00 **Ni**, 0.30–0.40 **Mo**, 0.17–0.25 **V**, 0.35 **Cu**	**Cold finished (bar):** ≤0.500 (≤12.70) **diam**, 135 (931) max **TS**
BS 970 Part 2	Grade 640 H 35	UK	Blooms, billets, bar, forgings	0.32–0.38 **C**, 0.55–0.95 **Mn**, 0.10–0.35 **Si**, 0.45–0.85 **Cr**, 1.00–1.50 **Ni**	
ASTM A 547	Grade 1335H	US	Wire	0.32–0.38 **C**, 1.45–2.05 **Mn**	
ASTM A 547	Grade 4135H	US	Wire	0.32–0.38 **C**, 0.60–1.00 **Mn**, 0.75–1.20 **Cr**, 0.15–0.25 **Mo**	
DGN–B–300	1335H	Mexico	Bar	0.32–0.38 **C**, 1.45–2.05 **Mn**, 0.040 **P**, 0.035 **S**, 0.20–0.35 **Si**	**Annealed**
DGN–B–300	4135–H	Mexico	Bar	0.32–0.38 **C**, 0.60–1.00 **Mn**, 0.040 **P**, 0.035 **S**, 0.20–0.35 **Si**, 0.75–1.20 **Cr**, 0.15–0.25 **Mo**	
DGN–B–300	5135 H	Mexico	Bar	0.32–0.38 **C**, 0.50–0.90 **Mn**, 0.040 **P**, 0.035 **S**, 0.20–0.35 **Si**, 0.70–1.15 **Cr**	**Annealed**
ANSI/ASTM A 304	1335 H	US	Bar	0.32–0.38 **C**, 1.45–2.05 **Mn**, 0.040 **P**, 0.040 **S**, 0.15–0.30 **Si**	
ASTM A 689	4135 H	US	Bar	0.32–0.38 **C**, 0.60–1.00 **Mn**, 0.040 **P**, 0.040 **S**, 0.15–0.30 **Si**, 0.75–1.20 **Cr**, 0.15–0.25 **Mo**	
ASTM A 689	1335 H	US	Bar	0.32–0.38 **C**, 1.45–2.05 **Mn**, 0.040 **P**, 0.040 **S**, 0.15–0.30 **Si**	
ASTM A 689	5135 H	US	Bar	0.32–0.38 **C**, 0.50–0.90 **Mn**, 0.040 **P**, 0.040 **S**, 0.15–0.30 **Si**, 0.70–1.15 **Cr**	
ANSI/ASTM A 304	4135 H	US	Bar	0.32–0.38 **C**, 0.60–1.00 **Mn**, 0.040 **P**, 0.040 **S**, 0.15–0.30 **Si**, 0.75–1.20 **Cr**, 0.15–0.25 **Mo**	
ANSI/ASTM A 304	5135 H	US	Bar	0.32–0.38 **C**, 0.50–0.90 **Mn**, 0.040 **P**, 0.040 **S**, 0.15–0.30 **Si**, 0.70–1.15 **Cr**	
AISI 5135 H		US	Wire, rod	0.32–0.38 **C**, 0.50–0.90 **Mn**, 0.15–0.30 **Si**, 0.70–1.15 **Cr**	
AISI 1335 H		US	Wire, rod	0.32–0.38 **C**, 1.45–2.05 **Mn**, 0.15–0.30 **Si**	
AISI 5135H		US	Bar	0.32–0.38 **C**, 0.50–0.90 **Mn**, 0.035 **P**, 0.040 **S**, 0.15–0.30 **Si**, 0.70–1.15 **Cr**	
AISI 4135H		US	Bar	0.32–0.38 **C**, 0.60–1.00 **Mn**, 0.035 **P**, 0.040 **S**, 0.15–0.30 **Si**, 0.75–1.20 **Cr**, 0.15–0.25 **Mo**	
AISI 1335H		US	Bar	0.32–0.38 **C**, 1.45–2.05 **Mn**, 0.035 **P**, 0.040 **S**, 0.15–0.30 **Si**	
JIS G 4052	SCr 3H	Japan	Bar, wire, rod	0.32–0.38 **C**, 0.55–0.90 **Mn**, 0.030 **P**, 0.030 **S**, 0.15–0.35 **Si**, 0.85–1.25 **Cr**, 0.30 **Cr**	**Hot rolled, normalized, quenched**
JIS G 3311	S35CM	Japan	Strip	0.32–0.38 **C**, 0.60–0.90 **Mn**, 0.030 **P**, 0.035 **S**, 0.15–0.35 **Si**, 0.20 **Cr**, 0.20 **Ni**, 0.30 **Cu**, 0.35 **Ni**+**Cr**	
JIS G 3112	Type 5, SD 50, No. 2	Japan	Bar	0.32 **C**, 1.80 **Mn**, 0.050 **P**, 0.050 **S**, 0.60 **C** + **Mn**/6	**Hot rolled:** all **diam**, (618) **TS**, (490) **YS**, 12 **El**
MIL–s–24286		US	Plate	0.32 **C**, 1.00 **Mn**, 0.25 **P**, 0.25 **S**, 0.75 **Si**, 0.40 **Cr**, 0.70 **Ni**, 0.15 **Mo**	
MIL–S–13812B		US	Plate	0.32 **C**, 1.00 **Mn**, 0.04 **P**, 0.04 **S**, 0.60–1.00 **Si**, 1.25 **Cr**, 0.50 **Ni**, 0.20 **Mo**	**Hot rolled, heat treated**
AISI 1137		US	Wire, rod	0.32–0.30 **C**, 1.35–1.65 **Mn**, 0.040 **P**, 0.08–0.13 **S**	
ANSI/ASTM A 372	Class V, type B	US	Forgings	0.31–0.39 **C**, 0.70–1.00 **Mn**, 0.035 **P**, 0.04 **S**, 0.15–0.35 **Si**, 0.80–1.15 **Cr**, 0.15–0.25 **Mo**	**Liquid quenched and tempered:** all **diam**, (825) **TS**, (485) **YS**, 18 **El**
ANSI/ASTM A 372	Class V, type D	US	Forgings	0.31–0.39 **C**, 0.75–1.05 **Mn**, 0.035 **P**, 0.04 **S**, 0.15–0.35 **Si**, 0.40–0.65 **Cr**, 0.40–0.70 **Ni**, 0.15–0.25 **Mo**	**Liquid quenched and tempered:** all **diam**, (825) **TS**, (485) **YS**, 18 **El**

WROUGHT ALLOY STEELS

specification number	designation	country	product forms	composition	mechanical properties (see page iv for explanation)
ASTM A 372	Class V, type B	US	Forgings	0.31–0.39 **C**, 0.70–1.00 **Mn**, 0.035 **P**, 0.04 **S**, 0.15–0.35 **Si**, 0.80–1.15 **Cr**, 0.15–0.25 **Mo**	**Quenched, tempered**: all **diam**, 120 (825) **TS**, 70 (485) **YS**, 18 **El**
ASTM A 372	Class V, type D	US	Forgings	0.31–0.39 **C**, 0.75–1.05 **Mn**, 0.035 **P**, 0.04 **S**, 0.15–0.35 **Si**, 0.40–0.65 **Cr**, 0.40–0.70 **Ni**, 0.15–0.25 **Mo**	**Quenched, tempered**: all **diam**, 120 (825) **TS**, 70 (485) **YS**, 18 **El**
ANSI/ASTM A 579	21	US	Forgings	0.31–0.38 **C**, 0.60–0.90 **Mn**, 0.025 **P**, 0.025 **S**, 0.20–0.35 **Si**, 0.65–0.90 **Cr**, 1.65–2.00 **Ni**, 0.30–0.60 **Mo**, 0.17–0.23 **V**	**Quenched and tempered**: all **diam**, 190 (1310) **TS**, 180 (1240) **YS**, 10 **El**
ANSI/ASTM A 469	Class 5	US	Forgings	0.31 **C**, 0.70 **Mn**, 0.015 **P**, 0.018 **S**, 0.15–0.30 **Si**, 0.50 **Cr**, 3.00 min **Ni**, 0.20–0.70 **Mo**, 0.05–0.15 **V**	**Quenched, tempered, stress relieved**: all **diam**, 110 (760) **TS**, 90 (620) **YS**, 15 **El**
BS 980	CDS–14	UK	Tube	0.30–0.45 **C**, 0.3–0.7 **Mn**, 0.050 **P**, 0.050 **S**, 0.35 **Si**, 2.75–3.5 **Ni**	**Drawn**: 8 **diam**, (620) **TS**, (525) **YS**
IS 5517	Grade 35Mn2Mo28	India	Bar, billet	0.30–0.40 **C**, 1.30–1.80 **Mn**, 0.10–0.35 **Si**, 0.20–0.35 **Mo**	**Normalized, annealed or hardened and tempered**: (30) **diam**, (980) **TS**, (785) **YS**
IS 5517	Grade 32Mn2Mo45	India	Bar, billet	0.30–0.40 **C**, 1.30–1.80 **Mn**, 0.10–0.35 **Si**, 0.35–0.55 **Mo**	**Normalized, annealed or hardened and tempered**: (63) **diam**, (980) **TS**, (785) **YS**
IS 5517	Grade 35NilCr60	India	Bar, billet	0.30–0.40 **C**, 0.60–0.90 **Mn**, 0.10–0.35 **Si**, 0.45–0.75 **Cr**, 1.00–1.50 **Ni**	**Normalized, annealed or hardened and tempered**: (63) **diam**, (880) **TS**, (685) **YS**
MIL–S–869C	Class D (135G)	US	Bar, billets, forgings	0.30–0.40 **C**, 0.40–0.70 **Mn**, 0.040 **P**, 0.040 **S**, 0.20–0.40 **Si**, 0.90–1.40 **Cr**, 0.15–0.25 **Mo**, 0.85–1.20 **Al**	**Quenched and tempered**: ≤11/2 **diam**, 125 (862) **TS**, 100 (690) **YS**, 18 **El**
IS 4367	35Mn2Mo[28]	India	Forgings	0.30–0.40 **C**, 1.30–1.80 **Mn**, 0.050 **P**, 0.050 **S**, 0.10–0.35 **Si**, 0.20–0.35 **Mo**	**Hardened and tempered**: (100) **diam**, (784) **TS**, 16 **El**
IS 4367	35Ni1Cr[60]	India	Forgings	0.30–0.40 **C**, 0.60–0.90 **Mn**, 0.050 **P**, 0.050 **S**, 0.10–0.35 **Si**, 0.45–0.75 **Cr**, 1.00–1.50 **Ni**	**Hardened and tempered**: (100) **diam**, (784) **TS**, 16 **El**
MIL–S–869C	Class B (EZ)	US	Bar, billets, forgings	0.30–0.40 **C**, 0.50–1.10 **Mn**, 0.040 **P**, 0.060 **S**, 0.20–0.40 **Si**, 1.00–1.50 **Cr**, 0.15–0.25 **Mo**, 0.85–1.20 **Al**, 0.15–0.25 **Se**	**Quenched and tempered**: ≤11/2 **diam**, 106 (730) **TS**, 76 (524) **YS**, 20 **El**
AS G18	G18/En16	Australia	Bar, billet	0.30–0.40 **C**, 1.30–1.80 **Mn**, 0.050 **P**, 0.050 **S**, 0.10–0.35 **Si**, 0.20–0.35 **Mo**	**Hardened, tempered**: 6 **diam**, (690) **TS**, (525) **YS**
AS G18	G18/En 111	Australia	Bar, billet	0.30–0.40 **C**, 0.60–0.90 **Mn**, 0.050 **P**, 0.050 **S**, 0.10–0.35 **Si**, 0.45–0.75 **Cr**, 1.00–1.50 **Ni**	**Hardened, tempered**: 6 **diam**, (690) **TS**, (525) **YS**
AS G18	G18/En 16D	Australia	Bar, billet	0.30–0.40 **C**, 1.30–1.80 **Mn**, 0.050 **P**, 0.050 **S**, 0.10–0.35 **Si**, 0.20–0.35 **Mo**	**Hardened, tempered**: 6 **diam**, (690) **TS**, (525) **YS**
AS G18	G18/En 15A	Australia	Bar, billet	0.30–0.40 **C**, 1.30–1.70 **Mn**, 0.060 **P**, 0.060 **S**, 0.05–0.35 **Si**	**Hardened, tempered**: 4 **diam**, (620) **TS**, (430) **YS**
AS G18	G18/En 15	Australia	Bar, billet	0.30–0.40 **C**, 1.30–1.70 **Mn**, 0.050 **P**, 0.050 **S**, 0.10–0.35 **Si**	**Hardened, tempered**: 6 **diam**, (620) **TS**, (430) **YS**
NF A 35–564	30 CD 4 FF, 35 CD 4 FF	France	Bar, wire, rod	0.30–0.40 **C**, 0.030 **P**, 0.030 **S**, 0.30 **Si**	**Annealed**: (≤70) **diam**, (610) max **TS**
NF A 35–564	38 CB 1 FF, 38 C 2 FF, 32 C 4 FF, 38 C 4 FF	France	Bar, wire, rod	0.30–0.40 **C**, 0.030 **P**, 0.030 **S**, 0.30 **Si**, 0.020 **Al**	**Annealed**: (≤70) **diam**, (590) max **TS**
DIN 17200	Grade 34 CrNiMo 6	Germany	Blooms, slabs, billets, wire, bar, plate, sheet, strip, tube, forgings	0.30–0.38 **C**, 0.40–0.70 **Mn**, 0.035 **P**, 0.035 **S**, 0.15–0.40 **Si**, 1.40–1.70 **Cr**, 1.40–1.70 **Ni**, 0.15–0.30 **Mo**	**Quenched and tempered**: (≤16) **diam**, (1177) **TS**, (980) **YS**, 9 **El**
ISO/R 683/VIII	Type 6	ISO	Bar, billets, rod	0.30–0.37 **C**, 0.30–0.60 **Mn**, 0.035 **P**, 0.035 **S**, 0.15–0.40 **Si**, 1.60–2.00 **Cr**, 3.70–4.20 **Ni**, 0.25–0.45 **Mo**	**Quenched and tempered**: (≤16) **diam**, (1225) **TS**, (1029) **YS**, 9 **El**
ISO/R 683/VIII	Type 6a	ISO	Bar, billets, rod	0.30–0.37 **C**, 0.30–0.60 **Mn**, 0.035 **P**, 0.020–0.035 **S**, 0.15–0.40 **Si**, 1.60–2.00 **Cr**, 3.70–4.20 **Ni**, 0.25–0.45 **Mo**	**Quenched and tempered**: (≤16) **diam**, (1225) **TS**, (1029) **YS**, 9 **El**

WROUGHT ALLOY STEELS

specification number	designation	country	product forms	composition	mechanical properties (see page iv for explanation)
ISO/R 683/VIII	Type 6b	ISO	Bar, billets, rod	0.30–0.37 **C**, 0.30–0.60 **Mn**, 0.035 **P**, 0.030–0.050 **S**, 0.15–0.40 **Si**, 1.60–2.00 **Cr**, 3.70–4.20 **Ni**, 0.25–0.45 **Mo**	**Quenched and tempered:** (≤16) **diam**, (1225) **TS**, (1029) **YS**, 9 **El**
AIR 9160/C 43	9160C101	France	Bar, forgings	0.30–0.37 **C**, 0.50–0.80 **Mn**, 0.025 **P**, 0.020 **S**, 0.15–0.40 **Si**, 0.90–1.20 **Cr**, 0.40 **Ni**, 0.15–0.30 **Mo**	**Annealed, quenched and tempered:** (<25) **diam**, (1080) **TS**, (930) **YS**, 10 **El**
SIS 14 22 34	SIS 2234–07	Sweden	Bar, forgings	0.30–0.37 **C**, 0.50–0.80 **Mn**, 0.035 **P**, 0.035 **S**, 0.15–0.40 **Si**, 0.90–1.20 **Cr**, 0.15–0.30 **Mo**	**Quenched and tempered:** (<25) **diam**, (1080) **TS**, (880) **YS**, 10 **El**
AIR 9160/C 45	9160C111	France	Bar, forgings	0.30–0.37 **C**, 0.60–0.90 **Mn**, 0.025 **P**, 0.020 **S**, 0.10–0.40 **Si**, 0.80–1.10 **Cr**, 1.20–1.60 **Ni**	**Annealed, quenched and tempered:** (<16) **diam**, (1030) **TS**, (880) **YS**, 12 **El**
ISO R 683/II	Type 2	ISO	Bar, billets, rod	0.30–0.37 **C**, 0.50–0.80 **Mn**, 0.035 **P**, 0.035 **S**, 0.15–0.40 **Si**, 0.90–1.20 **Cr**, 0.15–0.30 **Mo**	**Quenched and tempered:** (≤16) **diam**, (980) **TS**, (785) **YS**, 11 **El**
ISO R 683/IV	Type 2a	ISO	Bar, billets, rod	0.30–0.37 **C**, 0.50–0.80 **Mn**, 0.035 **P**, 0.020–0.035 **P**, 0.020–0.035 **S**, 0.15–0.40 **Si**, 0.90–1.20 **Cr**, 0.15–0.30 **Mo**	**Quenched and tempered:** (≤16) **diam**, (980) **TS**, (792) **YS**, 11 **El**
ISO R 683/IV	Type 2b	ISO	Bar, billets, rod	0.30–0.37 **C**, 0.50–0.80 **Mn**, 0.035 **P**, 0.030–0.050 **S**, 0.15–0.40 **Si**, 0.90–1.20 **Cr**, 0.15–0.30 **Mo**	**Quenched and tempered:** (≤16) **diam**, (980) **TS**, (792) **YS**, 11 **El**
EURONORM 119–74, IV	34 CrMo 4 KD	EURONORM	Wire, rod	0.30–0.37 **C**, 0.50–0.80 **Mn**, 0.035 **P**, 0.035 **S**, 0.15–0.40 **Si**, 0.90–1.20 **Cr**, 0.15–0.30 **Mo**	**Quenched and tempered:** (≤16) **diam**, (980) **TS**, (785) **YS**, 11 **El**
SIS 14 22 34	SIS 2234–06	Sweden	Bar, forgings	0.30–0.37 **C**, 0.50–0.80 **Mn**, 0.035 **P**, 0.035 **S**, 0.15–0.40 **Si**, 0.90–1.20 **Cr**, 0.15–0.30 **Mo**	**Quenched and tempered:** (<25) **diam**, (980) **TS**, (780) **YS**, 11 **El**
DIN 17200	Grade 34 CrMoS 4	Germany	Blooms, slabs, billets, wire, bar, plate, sheet, strip, tube, forgings	0.30–0.37 **C**, 0.50–0.80 **Mn**, 0.035 **P**, 0.020–0.035 **S**, 0.15–0.40 **Si**, 0.90–1.20 **Cr**, 0.15–0.30 **Mo**	**Quenched and tempered:** (≤16) **diam**, (980) **TS**, (795) **YS**, 11 **El**
DIN 17200	Grade 34 CrMo 4	Germany	Blooms, slabs, billets, wire, bar, plate, sheet, strip, tube, forgings	0.30–0.37 **C**, 0.50–0.80 **Mn**, 0.035 **P**, 0.035 **S**, 0.15–0.40 **Si**, 0.90–1.20 **Cr**, 0.15–0.30 **Mo**	**Quenched and tempered:** (≤16) **diam**, (980) **TS**, (795) **YS**, 11 **El**
DIN 17200	Grade 34 Cr 4	Germany	Blooms, slabs, billets, wire, bar, plate, sheet, strip, tube, forgings	0.30–0.37 **C**, 0.60–0.90 **Mn**, 0.035 **P**, 0.035 **S**, 0.15–0.40 **Si**, 0.90–1.20 **Cr**	**Quenched and tempered:** (≤16) **diam**, (883) **TS**, (687) **YS**, 12 **El**
DIN 17200	Grade 34 CrS 4	Germany	Blooms, slabs, billets, wire, bar, plate, sheet, strip, tube, forgings	0.30–0.37 **C**, 0.60–0.90 **Mn**, 0.035 **P**, 0.020–0.035 **S**, 0.15–0.40 **Si**, 0.90–1.20 **Cr**	**Quenched and tempered:** (≤16) **diam**, (883) **TS**, (687) **YS**, 12 **El**
ISO/R 683/VII	Type 1	ISO	Bar, billets, rod	0.30–0.37 **C**, 0.60–0.90 **Mn**, 0.035 **P**, 0.035 **S**, 0.15–0.40 **Si**, 0.90–1.20 **Cr**	**Quenched and tempered:** (≤16) **diam**, (882) **TS**, (686) **YS**, 12 **El**
ISO/R 683/VII	Type 1a	ISO	Bar, billets, rod	0.30–0.37 **C**, 0.60–0.90 **Mn**, 0.035 **P**, 0.020–0.035 **S**, 0.15–0.40 **Si**, 0.90–1.20 **Cr**	**Quenched and tempered:** (≤16) **diam**, (882) **TS**, (686) **YS**, 12 **El**
ISO/R 683/VII	Type 1b	ISO	Bar, billets, rod	0.30–0.37 **C**, 0.60–0.90 **Mn**, 0.035 **P**, 0.030–0.050 **S**, 0.15–0.40 **Si**, 0.90–1.20 **Cr**	**Quenched and tempered:** (≤16) **diam**, (882) **TS**, (686) **YS**, 12 **El**
EURONORM 119–74, IV	34 Cr 4 KD	EURONORM	Wire, rod	0.30–0.37 **C**, 0.60–0.90 **Mn**, 0.035 **P**, 0.035 **S**, 0.15–0.40 **Si**, 0.90–1.20 **Cr**	**Quenched and tempered:** (≤16) **diam**, (880) **TS**, (685) **YS**, 12 **El**
SIS 14 22 34	SIS 2234–05	Sweden	Bar, forgings	0.30–0.37 **C**, 0.50–0.80 **Mn**, 0.035 **P**, 0.035 **S**, 0.15–0.40 **Si**, 0.90–1.20 **Cr**, 0.15–0.30 **Mo**	**Quenched and tempered:** (<40) **diam**, (880) **TS**, (690) **YS**, 12 **El**
DIN 17211	Grade 34 CrAlMo 5	Germany	Blooms, slabs, billets, wire, bar, plate, sheet, strip, tube, forgings	0.30–0.37 **C**, 0.50–0.80 **Mn**, 0.030 **P**, 0.035 **S**, 0.20–0.50 **Si**, 1.00–1.30 **Cr**, 0.15–0.25 **Mo**, 0.80–1.20 **Al**	**Soft annealed and quenched and tempered:** (≤70) **diam**, (795) **TS**, (588) **YS**, 14 **El**
DIN 17211	Grade 34 CrAlNi 7	Germany	Blooms, slabs, billets, wire, bar, plate, sheet, strip, tube, forgings	0.30–0.37 **C**, 0.40–0.70 **Mn**, 0.030 **P**, 0.035 **S**, 0.15–0.40 **Si**, 1.50–1.80 **Cr**, 0.85–1.15 **Ni**, 0.15–0.25 **Mo**, 0.80–1.20 **Al**	**Soft annealed and quenched and tempered:** (70–250) **diam**, (795) **TS**, (588) **YS**, 13 **El**
ISO 683/X	3	ISO	Bar	0.30–0.37 **C**, 0.50–0.80 **Mn**, 0.030 **P**, 0.035 **S**, 0.20–0.50 **Si**, 1.00–1.30 **Cr**, 0.15–0.25 **Mo**, 0.80–1.20 **Al**	**Nitrided:** (70) **diam**, (780) **TS**, (590) **YS**, 14 **El**

WROUGHT ALLOY STEELS

specification number	designation	country	product forms	composition	mechanical properties (see page iv for explanation)
SIS 14 22 34	SIS 2234–04	Sweden	Bar, forgings	0.30–0.37 **C**, 0.50–0.80 **Mn**, 0.035 **P**, 0.035 **S**, 0.15–0.40 **Si**, 0.90–1.20 **Cr**, 0.15–0.30 **Mo**	**Quenched and tempered:** (<100) **diam**, (780) **TS**, (590) **YS**, 14 **El**
SIS 14 22 34	SIS 2234–03	Sweden	Bar, forgings	0.30–0.37 **C**, 0.50–0.80 **Mn**, 0.035 **P**, 0.035 **S**, 0.15–0.40 **Si**, 0.90–1.20 **Cr**, 0.15–0.30 **Mo**	**Quenched and tempered:** (<250) **diam**, (690) **TS**, (490) **YS**, 15 **El**
DIN 1654	Grade 34 Cr 4	Germany	Rod	0.30–0.37 **C**, 0.50–0.80 **Mn**, 0.035 **P**, 0.035 **S**, 0.15–0.35 **Si**, 0.90–1.2 **Cr**	**Drawn:** all **diam**, (687) **TS**
SFS 459	Co. 35 Cr 1.1 Mo 0.20	Finland	Bar, forgings	0.30–0.37 **C**, 0.50–0.80 **Mn**, 0.035 **P**, 0.035 **S**, 0.15–0.40 **Si**, 0.90–1.20 **Cr**, 0.15–0.25 **Mo**	**Quenched and tempered:** (180) **diam**, (650) **TS**, (460) **YS**, 15 **El**
DIN 17211	Grade 34 CrAlS 5	Germany	Blooms, slabs, billets, wire, bar, plate, sheet, strip, tube, forgings	0.30–0.37 **C**, 0.60–0.90 **Mn**, 0.100 **P**, 0.07–0.11 **S**, 0.15–0.40 **Si**, 1.00–1.30 **Cr**, 0.80–1.20 **Al**	**Soft annealed and quenched and tempered:** (≤60) **diam**, (638) **TS**, (441) **YS**, 12 **El**
NF A 35–553	35 CD 4	France	Strip	0.30–0.37 **C**, 0.60–0.90 **Mn**, 0.035 **P**, 0.035 **S**, 0.10–0.40 **Si**, 0.85–1.15 **Cr**, 0.15–0.30 **Mo**	
NF A 35–553	35 NC 15	France	Strip	0.30–0.37 **C**, 0.35–0.60 **Mn**, 0.035 **P**, 0.035 **S**, 0.10–0.40 **Si**, 1.50–1.90 **Cr**, 3.5–4.0 **Ni**	
SIS 14 22 34	SIS 2234–00	Sweden	Bar, forgings	0.30–0.37 **C**, 0.50–0.80 **Mn**, 0.035 **P**, 0.035 **S**, 0.15–0.40 **Si**, 0.90–1.20 **Cr**, 0.15–0.30 **Mo**	
SIS 14 22 34	SIS 2234–02	Sweden	Bar, forgings	0.30–0.37 **C**, 0.50–0.80 **Mn**, 0.035 **P**, 0.035 **S**, 0.15–0.40 **Si**, 0.90–1.20 **Cr**, 0.15–0.30 **Mo**	
JIS G 4106	SMn 1	Japan	Bar, wire, rod	0.30–0.36 **C**, 1.20–1.50 **Mn**, 0.030 **P**, 0.030 **S**, 0.15–0.35 **Si**, 0.25 **Ni**, 0.30 **Cu**	**Hot rolled or forged, quenched and tempered:** (25) **diam**, (686) **TS**, (539) **YS**, 20 **El**
NBN A 21–221	C 32 B KD	Belgium	Wire	0.30–0.35 **C**, 0.40–0.60 **Mn**, 0.035 **P**, 0.035 **S**, 0.15–0.40 **Si**, 0.2–0.4 **Cr**, 0.001–0.005 **B**	**Quenched and tempered:** (≤10) **diam**, (830) **TS**, (785) **YS**, 14 **El**
AISI 5132		US	Bar	0.30–0.35 **C**, 0.60–0.80 **Mn**, 0.035 **P**, 0.040 **S**, 0.15–0.35 **Si**, 0.75–1.00 **Cr**	
NF A 35–553	32 C 4	France	Strip	0.30–0.35 **C**, 0.60–0.90 **Mn**, 0.035 **P**, 0.035 **S**, 0.10–0.40 **Si**, 0.85–1.15 **Cr**	
BS 970 Part 2	Grade 530 A 32	UK	Blooms, billets, bar, forgings	0.30–0.35 **C**, 0.60–0.80 **Mn**, 0.90–1.20 **Cr**	
BS 970 Part 2	Grade 605 A 32	UK	Blooms, billets, bar, forgings	0.30–0.35 **C**, 1.30–1.70 **Mn**, 0.22–0.32 **Mo**	
AMS 6356B		US	Sheet, strip, plate	0.30–0.35 **C**, 0.40–0.60 **Mn**, 0.025 **P**, 0.025 **S**, 0.15–0.50 **Si**, 0.80–1.10 **Cr**, 0.25 **Ni**, 0.15–0.25 **Mo**, 0.35 **Cu**	
AS G18	G18/En 16B	Australia	Bar, billet	0.30–0.35 **C**, 1.30–1.80 **Mn**, 0.050 **P**, 0.050 **S**, 0.10–0.35 **Si**, 0.20–0.35 **Mo**	
AS 1444	Grade AS 1444/5132	Australia	Bar, bloom, billet, slab	0.30–0.35 **C**, 0.60–0.80 **Mn**, 0.040 **P**, 0.040 **S**, 0.10–0.35 **Si**, 0.75–1.00 **Cr**	
DGN–B–203	Grade 5132	Mexico	Tube: seamless	0.30–0.35 **C**, 0.60–0.80 **Mn**, 0.040 **P**, 0.040 **S**, 0.20–0.35 **Si**, 0.75–1.00 **Cr**	
DGN–B–300	5132	Mexico	Bar	0.30–0.35 **C**, 0.60–0.80 **Mn**, 0.035 **P**, 0.040 **S**, 0.20–0.35 **Si**, 0.75–1.00 **Cr**	**Annealed**
ANSI/ASTM A 29	5132	US	Bar	0.30–0.35 **C**, 0.60–0.80 **Mn**, 0.035 **P**, 0.040 **S**, 0.15–0.30 **Si**, 0.75–1.00 **Cr**	
ANSI/ASTM A 29	4032	US	Bar	0.30–0.35 **C**, 0.70–0.90 **Mn**, 0.035 **P**, 0.040 **S**, 0.15–0.30 **Si**, 0.20–0.30 **Mo**	
ASTM A 689	5132	US	Bar	0.30–0.35 **C**, 0.60–0.80 **Mn**, 0.035 **P**, 0.040 **S**, 0.15–0.30 **Si**, 0.75–1.00 **Cr**	
ANSI/ASTM A 322	5132	US	Bar	0.30–0.35 **C**, 0.60–0.80 **Mn**, 0.035 **P**, 0.040 **S**, 0.15–0.30 **Si**, 0.75–1.00 **Cr**	

WROUGHT ALLOY STEELS

specification number	designation	country	product forms	composition	mechanical properties (see page iv for explanation)
AISI 5132		US	Wire, rod	0.30–0.35 **C**, 0.60–0.80 **Mn**, 0.035 **P**, 0.040 **S**, 0.15–0.30 **Si**, 0.75–1.00 **Cr**	
ANSI/ASTM A 519	5132	US	Tube: seamless	0.30–0.35 **C**, 0.60–0.80 **Mn**, 0.040 **P**, 0.040 **S**, 0.15–0.35 **Si**, 0.75–1.00 **Cr**	
DGN–B–297	5132	Mexico	Bar	0.30–0.35 **C**, 0.60–0.90 **Mn**, 0.035 **P**, 0.040 **S**, 0.20–0.35 **Si**, 0.75–1.00 **Cr**	
COPANT 514	Grade 5132	COPANT	Tube: seamless	0.30–0.35 **C**, 0.60–0.90 **Mn**, 0.040 **P**, 0.040 **S**, 0.10 **Si**, 0.75–1.00 **Cr**	
COPANT 514	Grade 513	COPANT	Tube: seamless	0.30–0.35 **C**, 0.60–0.90 **Mn**, 0.040 **P**, 0.040 **S**, 0.10 **Si**, 0.80–1.05 **Cr**	
ISO 2604/1	F36	ISO	Forgings	0.30 **C**, 0.30–0.80 **Mn**, 0.040 **P**, 0.040 **S**, 0.15–0.40 **Si**, 2.75–3.50 **Cr**, 0.45–0.65 **Mo**	**Normalized and tempered, quenched and tempered:** all **diam**, (740) **TS**, (560) **YS**, 14 **El**
ASTM A 293	Class 3	US	Forgings	0.30 **C**, 0.70 **Mn**, 0.035 **P**, 0.035 **S**, 0.15–0.35 **Si**, 0.75 **Cr**, 2.00 min **Ni**, 0.25 min **Mo**, 0.03–0.12 **V**	**Normalized, tempered or double normalized, tempered:** all **diam**, 95 (655) **TS**, 70 (480) **YS**, 20 **El**
BS 1506–625		UK	Bar	0.30 **C**, 0.30–0.70 **Mn**, 0.040 **P**, 0.040 **S**, 0.50 **Si**, 4.00–6.00 **Cr**, 0.45–0.65 **Mo**	**Normalized**: all **diam**, (620) **TS**, (524) **YS**, 19 **El**; **Hardened and tempered**: all **diam**
NF A 35–564	38 MB 5 FF	France	Bar, wire, rod	0.30 **C**, 0.030 **P**, 0.030 **S**, 0.30 **Si**, 0.020 **Al**	**Annealed**: (≤70) **diam**, (590) max **TS**
ANSI/ASTM A 706		US	Bar	0.30 **C**, 1.50 **Mn**; Si, Cu, Ni, Cr, Ti, Zr optional	**Hot rolled**: 0.375 **diam**, (550) **TS**, (415) **YS**, 14 **El**
ASTM A 293	Class 2	US	Forgings	0.30 **C**, 0.70 **Mn**, 0.035 **P**, 0.035 **S**, 0.15–0.35 **Si**, 0.75 **Cr**, 2.00 min **Ni**, 0.25 min **Mo**, 0.03–0.12 **V**	**Normalized, tempered or double normalized, tempered:** all **diam**, 80 (550) **TS**, 55 (380) **YS**, 22 **El**
CSA G30.16	No. 20	Canada	Bar	0.30 **C**, 1.60 **Mn**, 0.50 **Si**, 0.035 **P**, 0.045 **S**	**As rolled**: (19.5) **diam**, (550) **TS**, (400) **YS**, 13 in 200 mm **El**
CSA G30.16	No. 15	Canada	Bar	0.30 **C**, 1.60 **Mn**, 0.50 **Si**, 0.035 **P**, 0.045 **S**	**As rolled**: (16.0) **diam**, (550) **TS**, (400) **YS**, 13 in 200 in **El**
CSA G30.16	No. 10	Canada	Bar	0.30 **C**, 1.60 **Mn**, 0.50 **Si**, 0.035 **P**, 0.045 **S**	**As rolled**: (11.3) **diam**, (550) **TS**, (400) **YS**, 13 in 200 mm **El**
CSA G30.16	No. 30	Canada	Bar	0.30 **C**, 1.60 **Mn**, 0.50 **Si**, 0.035 **P**, 0.045 **S**	**As rolled**: (29.9) **diam**, (550) **TS**, (400) **YS**, 12 in 200 mm **El**
CSA G30.16	No. 35	Canada	Bar	0.30 **C**, 1.60 **Mn**, 0.50 **Si**, 0.035 **P**, 0.045 **S**	**As rolled**: (35.7) **diam**, (550) **TS**, (400) **YS**, 12 in 200 mm **El**
CSA G30.16	No. 45	Canada	Bar	0.30 **C**, 1.60 **Mn**, 0.50 **Si**, 0.035 **P**, 0.045 **S**	**As rolled**: (43.7) **diam**, (550) **TS**, (400) **YS**, 12 in 200 mm **El**
CSA G30.16	No. 55	Canada	Bar	0.30 **C**, 1.60 **Mn**, 0.50 **Si**, 0.035 **P**, 0.045 **S**	**As rolled**: (56.4) **diam**, (550) **TS**, (400) **YS**, 12 in 200 mm **El**
CSA G30.16	No. 25	Canada	Bar	0.30 **C**, 1.60 **Mn**, 0.50 **Si**, 0.035 **P**, 0.045 **S**	**As rolled**: (25.2) **diam**, (550) **TS**, (400) **YS**, 13 in 200 mm **El**
JIS G 3101	Class 4	Japan	Plate, strip, bar, shapes	0.30 **C**, 1.60 **Mn**, 0.040 **P**, 0.040 **S**	**Hot rolled**: (≤5) **diam**, (539) **TS**, (402) **YS**, 16 **El**
ANSI/ASTM A 508	Grade 1a	US	Forgings	0.30 **C**, 0.70–1.35 **Mn**, 0.025 **P**, 0.025 **S**, 0.15–0.35 **Si**, 0.25 **Cr**, 0.40 **Ni**, 0.10 **Mo**, 0.05 **V**	**Quenched and tempered**: all **diam**, (485) **TS**, (240) **YS**, 20 **El**
ASTM A 350	LF5	US	Forgings	0.30 **C**, 1.35 **Mn**, 0.035 **P**, 0.040 **S**, 0.20–0.35 **Si**, 1.0–2.0 **Ni**	**Normalized or normalized, tempered**: all **diam**, 70 (483) **TS**, 37 (259) **YS**, 22 **El**
MIL–S–872A	Class b	US	Bar, billets, forgings	0.30 **C**, 0.80 **Mn**, 0.040 **P**, 0.040 **S**, 0.15–0.40 **Si**, 0.25 **Cr**, 0.25 **Ni**, 0.40–0.60 **Mo**, 0.35 **Cu**	**Normalized and tempered**: ≤10 **diam**, 70 (483) **TS**, 45 (310) **YS**, 25 **El**
MIL–T–16343C	Type I	US	Tube: seamless	0.30 **C**, 0.90 **Mn**, 0.045 **P**, 0.060 **S**, 0.30 **Si**, 0.50 **Ni**, 0.30 **Cr**+**Mo**, 0.35 **Cu**	**As rolled**: all **diam**, (413) **TS**, (227) **YS**, 20 **El**
DGN–B–180	Grade 6	Mexico	Pipe: seamless or welded	0.30 **C**, 0.29–1.06 **Mn**, 0.048 **P**, 0.058 **S**, 0.10 min **Si**	**Normalized or normalized and quenched**: (≥8) **diam**, (412) **TS**, (245) **YS**, 30 **El**
MIL–T–16343 C	Types II,III	US	Tube: welded	0.30 **C**, 0.90 **Mn**, 0.045 **P**, 0.060 **S**, 0.30 **Si**, 0.50 **Ni**, 0.30 **Cr**+**Mo**, 0.35 **Cu**	**As welded**: all **diam**, (344) **TS**, (227) **YS**, 20 **El**

WROUGHT ALLOY STEELS

specification number	designation	country	product forms	composition	mechanical properties (see page iv for explanation)
MIL–S–13823B		US	Shapes, bar, flats, special section	0.30 **C**, 1.00 **Mn**, 0.04 **P**, 0.04 **S**, 0.60–1.00 **Si**, 1.25 **Cr**, 0.20 **Mo**, 0.10 **V**	**Hot formed and heat treated**
AIR 9160/C 89	9160C331	France	Bar, forgings	0.29–0.36 **C**, 0.40–0.70 **Mn**, 0.025 **P**, 0.020 **S**, 0.10–0.40 **Si**, 2.80–3.30 **Cr**, 0.30 **Ni**, 0.70–1.20 **Mo**, 0.15–0.35 **V**	**Quenched, tempered at 640°C and nitrided: (≤80) diam, (950) TS, (800) YS, 14 El; Quenched, tempered at 620°C and nitrided: (≤80) diam, (1080) TS, (880) YS, 12 El; Quenched and tempered at 570°C not nitrided: (≤80) diam, (1200) TS, (1000) YS, 10 El**
JIS G 4052	SMn 1H	Japan	Bar, wire, rod	0.29–0.36 **C**, 1.15–1.55 **Mn**, 0.030 **P**, 0.030 **S**, 0.30 **Cu**	**Hot rolled, normalized, quenched**
BS 970 Part 2	Grade 530 H 32	UK	Blooms, billets, bar, forgings	0.29–0.35 **C**, 0.50–0.90 **Mn**, 0.10–0.35 **Si**, 0.80–1.25 **Cr**	
BS 970 Part 2	Grade 605 H 32	UK	Blooms, billets, bar, forgings	0.29–0.35 **C**, 1.25–1.75 **Mn**, 0.10–0.35 **Si**, 0.22–0.32 **Mo**	
AS 1444	Grade AS 1444/5132H	Australia	Bar, bloom, billet, slab	0.29–0.35 **C**, 0.50–0.90 **Mn**, 0.040 **P**, 0.040 **S**, 0.10–0.35 **Si**, 0.65–1.10 **Cr**	
DGN–B–300	4032H	Mexico	Bar	0.29–0.35 **C**, 0.60–1.00 **Mn**, 0.040 **P**, 0.035 **S**, 0.20–0.35 **Si**, 0.20–0.30 **Mo**	
DGN–B–300	5132 H	Mexico	Bar	0.29–0.35 **C**, 0.50–0.90 **Mn**, 0.040 **P**, 0.035 **S**, 0.20–0.35 **Si**, 0.65–1.10 **Cr**	**Annealed**
ASTM A 689	4032 H	US	Bar	0.29–0.35 **C**, 0.60–1.00 **Mn**, 0.040 **P**, 0.040 **S**, 0.15–0.30 **Si**, 0.20–0.30 **Mo**	
ASTM A 689	5132 H	US	Bar	0.29–0.35 **C**, 0.50–0.90 **Mn**, 0.040 **P**, 0.040 **S**, 0.15–0.30 **Si**, 0.65–1.10 **Cr**	
ANSI/ASTM A 304	5132 H	US	Bar	0.29–0.35 **C**, 0.50–0.90 **Mn**, 0.040 **P**, 0.040 **S**, 0.15–0.30 **Si**, 0.65–1.10 **Cr**	
ANSI/ASTM A 304	4032 H	US	Bar	0.29–0.35 **C**, 0.60–1.00 **Mn**, 0.040 **P**, 0.040 **S**, 0.15–0.30 **Si**, 0.20–0.30 **Mo**	
AISI 5132 H		US	Wire, rod	0.29–0.35 **C**, 0.50–0.90 **Mn**, 0.15–0.30 **Si**, 0.65–1.10 **Cr**	
AISI 5132H		US	Bar	0.29–0.35 **C**, 0.50–0.90 **Mn**, 0.035 **P**, 0.040 **S**, 0.15–0.30 **Si**, 0.65–1.10 **Cr**	
AISI 4032H		US	Bar	0.29–0.35 **C**, 0.60–1.00 **Mn**, 0.035 **P**, 0.040 **S**, 0.15–0.30 **Si**, 0.20–0.30 **Mo**	
AMS 6524A		US	Sheet, strip, plate	0.29–0.34 **C**, 0.10–0.35 **Mn**, 0.01 **P**, 0.01 **S**, 0.20 **Si**, 0.90–1.10 **Cr**, 7.00–8.00 **Ni**, 0.90–1.10 **Mo**, 0.06–0.12 **V**, 4.25–4.75 **Co**, 0.35 **Cu**	**Normalized, hardened and quenched**: <0.250 (<6.35) **diam**, 220 (1517) **TS**, 185 (1276) **YS**, 6 **El**
AMS 6526A		US	Bar, forgings, tube, rings	0.29–0.34 **C**, 0.10–0.35 **Mn**, 0.010 **P**, 0.010 **S**, 0.20 **Si**, 0.90–1.10 **Cr**, 7.00–8.00 **Ni**, 0.90–1.10 **Mo**, 0.06–0.12 **V**, 4.25–4.75 **Co**, 0.3 **Cu**	**Annealed and cold finished (bar)**: ≤0.500 (≤12.70) **diam**, 165 (1138) max **TS**; **Normalized, hardened, and tempered**: all **diam**, 220 (1517) **TS**, 190 (1310) **YS**, 10 **El**
ANSI/ASTM A 646	HP 9–4–30	US	Blooms, billets: aircraft quality	0.29–0.34 **C**, 0.10–0.35 **Mn**, 0.010 **P**, 0.010 **S**, 0.10 **Si**, 0.90–1.10 **Cr**, 7.0–8.0 **Ni**, 0.90–1.10 **Mo**, 0.06–0.12 **V**, 4.25–4.75 **Co**	**Annealed**
ANSI/ASTM A 541	Class 2	US	Forgings	0.29 **C**, 0.50–0.90 **Mn**, 0.030 **P**, 0.040 **S**, 0.15–0.35 **Si**, 0.25–0.45 **Cr**, 0.50–1.00 **Ni**, 0.55–0.70 **Mo**, 0.05 **V**	**Quenched and tempered**: all **diam**, 90 (620) **TS**, 65 (450) **YS**, 16 el
JIS G 3112	Type 4, SD 40, No. 2	Japan	Bar	0.29 **C**, 1.80 **Mn**, 0.050 **P**, 0.050 **S**, 0.55 **C** + **Mn**/6	**Hot rolled**: all **diam**, (559) **TS**, (392) **YS**, 16 **El**
BS 4670	976M33	UK	Forgings	0.28–0.38 **C**, 0.20–0.60 **Mn**, 0.035 **P**, 0.035 **S**, 0.10–0.35 **Si**, 0.90–1.70 **Cr**, 2.90–3.60 **Ni**, 0.45–0.65 **Mo**, 0.08–0.15 **V**	**Hardened, tempered**: (1000) **diam**, (850) **TS**, (710) **YS**, 13 **El**

specification number	designation	country	product forms	composition	mechanical properties (see page iv for explanation)
SIS 14 25 34	SIS 2534–01	Sweden	Bar, forgings	0.28–0.35 **C**, 0.40–0.70 **Mn**, 0.035 **P**, 0.035 **S**, 0.15–0.40 **Si**, 0.90–1.20 **Cr**, 3.0–3.5 **Ni**, 0.20–0.30 **Mo**	**Quenched:** (≤100) **diam**, (1500) **TS**, (1200) **YS**, 7 **El**
SIS 14 22 40	SIS 2240–08	Sweden	Bar, forgings	0.28–0.35 **C**, 0.40–0.70 **Mn**, 0.035 **P**, 0.035 **S**, 0.15–0.40 **Si**, 2.80–3.30 **Cr**, 0.30 **Ni**, 0.40–0.60 **Mo**	**Quenched:** (≤100) **diam**, (1500) **TS**, (1200) **YS**, 7 **El**
SIS 14 22 40	SIS 2240–08	Sweden	Bar, forgings	0.28–0.35 **C**, 0.40–0.70 **Mn**, 0.035 **P**, 0.035 **S**, 0.15–0.40 **Si**, 2.80–3.30 **Cr**, 0.30 **Ni**, 0.40–0.60 **Mo**	**Quenched:** all **diam**, (1500) **TS**, (1200) **YS**, 7 **El**
DIN 17200	Grade 32 CrMo 12	Germany	Blooms, slabs, billets, wire, bar, plate, sheet, strip, tube, forgings	0.28–0.35 **C**, 0.40–0.70 **Mn**, 0.035 **P**, 0.035 **S**, 0.15–0.40 **Si**, 2.80–3.30 **Cr**, 0.30 **Ni**, 0.30–0.50 **Mo**	**Quenched and tempered:** (≤16) **diam**, (1226) **TS**, (1029) **YS**, 9 **El**
SIS 14 22 40	SIS 2240–06	Sweden	Bar, forgings	0.28–0.35 **C**, 0.40–0.70 **Mn**, 0.035 **P**, 0.035 **S**, 0.15–0.40 **Si**, 2.80–3.30 **Cr**, 0.30 **Ni**, 0.40–0.60 **Mo**	**Quenched and tempered:** (≤100) **diam**, (1100) **TS**, (900) **YS**, 10 **El**
SIS 14 22 40	SIS 2240–06	Sweden	Bar, forgings	0.28–0.35 **C**, 0.40–0.70 **Mn**, 0.035 **P**, 0.035 **S**, 0.15–0.40 **Si**, 2.80–3.30 **Cr**, 0.30 **Ni**, 0.40–0.60 **Mo**	**Quenched and tempered:** all **diam**, (1100) **TS**, (900) **YS**, 10 **El**
ISO 683/X	1	ISO	Bar	0.28–0.35 **C**, 0.40–0.70 **Mn**, 0.030 **P**, 0.035 **S**, 0.15–0.40 **Si**, 2.80–3.30 **Cr**, 0.30 **Ni**, 0.30–0.50 **Mo**	**Nitrided:** (16) **diam**, (1080) **TS**, (880) **YS**, 10 **El**
ISO/R 683/VI	Grade 1	ISO	Bar, billets, rod	0.28–0.35 **C**, 0.40–0.70 **Mn**, 0.035 **P**, 0.035 **S**, 0.15–0.40 **Si**, 2.80–3.30 **Cr**, 0.30 **Ni**, 0.30–0.50 **Mo**	**Quenched and tempered:** (≤16) **diam**, (1079) **TS**, (882) **YS**, 10 **El**
DIN 17211	Grade 31 CrMo 12	Germany	Blooms, slabs, billets, wire, bar, plate, sheet, strip, tube, forgings	0.28–0.35 **C**, 0.40–0.70 **Mn**, 0.030 **P**, 0.035 **S**, 0.15–0.40 **Si**, 2.80–3.30 **Cr**, 0.30 **Ni**, 0.30–0.50 **Mo**	**Soft annealed and quenched and tempered:** (≤16) **diam**, (1079) **TS**, (883) **YS**, 10 **El**
SIS 14 22 40	SIS 2240–05	Sweden	Bar	0.28–0.35 **C**, 0.40–0.70 **Mn**, 0.035 **P**, 0.035 **S**, 015–0.40 **Si**, 2.80–3.30 **Cr**, 0.30 **Ni**, 0.40–0.60 **Mo**	**Quenched and tempered:** (≤150) **diam**, (1000) **TS**, (800) **YS**, 11 **El**
SIS 14 22 40	SIS 22 40–05	Sweden	Bar, forgings	0.28–0.35 **C**, 0.40–0.70 **Mn**, 0.035 **P**, 0.035 **S**, 0.15–0.40 **Si**, 2.80–3.30 **Cr**, 0.30 **Ni**, 0.40–0.60 **Mo**	**Quenched and tempered:** all **diam**, (1000) **TS**, (800) **YS**, 11 **El**
AIR 9160/C 87	9160C321	France	Bar, forgings	0.28–0.35 **C**, 0.40–0.70 **Mn**, 0.025 **P**, 0.020 **S**, 0.10–0.40 **Si**, 2.8–3.30 **Cr**, 0.30 **Ni**, 0.30–0.50 **Mo**	**Quenched, tempered at 625°C and nitrided: (≤80) diam, (930) TS, (780) YS, 14 El; Quenched, tempered at 580°C and nitrided: (≤80) diam, (1080) TS, (880) YS, 11 El**
SIS 14 25 34	SIS 2534–03	Sweden	Bar, forgings	0.28–0.35 **C**, 0.40–0.70 **Mn**, 0.035 **P**, 0.035 **S**, 0.15–0.40 **Si**, 0.90–1.20 **Cr**, 3.0–3.5 **Ni**, 0.20–0.30 **Mo**	**Quenched and tempered:** (≤250) **diam**, (900) **TS**, (700) **YS**, 15 **El**
SIS 14 22 40	SIS 2240–04	Sweden	Bar, forgings	0.28–0.35 **C**, 0.40–0.70 **Mn**, 0.035 **P**, 0.035 **S**, 0.15–0.40 **Si**, 2.80–3.30 **Cr**, 0.30 **Ni**, 0.40–0.60 **Mo**	**Quenched and hardened:** (≤300) **diam**, (900) **TS**, (700) **YS**, 12 **El**
SIS 14 22 40	SIS 2240–04	Sweden	Bar, forgings	0.28–0.35 **C**, 0.40–0.70 **Mn**, 0.035 **P**, 0.035 **S**, 0.15–0.40 **Si**, 2.80–3.30 **Cr**, 0.30 **Ni**, 0.40–0.60 **Mo**	**Quenched and tempered:** all **diam**, (900) **TS**, (700) **YS**, 12 **El**
COPANT 334	4130	COPANT	Bar	0.28–0.35 **C**, 0.40–0.60 **Mn**, 0.035 **P**, 0.040 **S**, 0.20–0.35 **Si**, 0.80–1.10 **Cr**, 0.15–0.25 **Mo**	
SIS 14 25 34	SIS 2534–02	Sweden	Bar, forgings	0.28–0.35 **C**, 0.40–0.70 **Mn**, 0.035 **P**, 0.035 **S**, 0.15–0.40 **Si**, 0.90–1.20 **Cr**, 3.0–3.5 **Ni**, 0.20–0.30 **Mo**	
SIS 14 22 40	SIS 2240–02	Sweden	Bar, forgings	0.28–0.35 **C**, 0.40–0.70 **Mn**, 0.035 **P**, 0.035 **S**, 0.15–0.40 **Si**, 2.80–3.30 **Cr**, 0.30 **Ni**, 0.40–0.60 **Mo**	

WROUGHT ALLOY STEELS

specification number	designation	country	product forms	composition	mechanical properties (see page iv for explanation)
SIS 14 22 40	SIS 2240-02	Sweden	Bar, forgings	0.28–0.35 **C**, 0.40–0.70 **Mn**, 0.035 **P**, 0.035 **S**, 0.15–0.40 **Si**, 2.80–3.30 **Cr**, 0.30 **Ni**, 0.40–0.60 **Mo**	
ANSI/ASTM A 579	82	US	Forgings	0.28–0.34 **C**, 0.10–0.35 **Mn**, 0.01 **P**, 0.01 **S**, 0.10 **Si**, 0.90–1.10 **Cr**, 7.0–8.5 **Ni**, 0.90–1.10 **Mo**, 0.06–0.12 **V**, 4.0–5.0 **Co**	**Heat treated**: all diam, 210 (1450) **TS**, 200 (1380) **YS**, 10 **El**
AMS 6411B		US	Bar, forgings, tube	0.28–0.33 **C**, 0.65–1.00 **Mn**, 0.015 **P**, 0.015 **S**, 0.15–0.35 **Si**, 0.75–1.00 **Cr**, 1.65–2.00 **Ni**, 0.35–0.50 **Mo**, 0.05–0.10 **V**, 0.35 **Cu**	**Normalized, hardened, quenched and tempered:** all **diam**, 220 (1517) **TS**, 185 (1276) **YS**, 10 **El**; **Cold finished (bar)**: ≤0.500 (≤12.70) **diam**, 130 (896) max **TS**
MIL-S-8699A	4330	US	Bar, forging stock	0.28–0.33 **C**, 0.80–1.00 **Mn**, 0.025 **P**, 0.025 **S**, 0.20–0.35 **Si**, 0.75–0.95 **Cr**, 1.65–2.00 **Ni**, 0.35–0.50 **Mo**, 0.05–0.10 **V**; rem Fe	**Hardened and tempered:** all **diam**, (1516) **TS**, (1310) **YS**, 10 **El**
MIL-S-8699A	AISI 433	US	Bar, forging stock	0.28–0.33 **C**, 0.80–1.00 **Mn**, 0.025 **P**, 0.025 **S**, 0.20–0.35 **Si**, 0.75–0.95 **Cr**, 1.65–2.00 **Ni**, 0.35–0.50 **Mo**, 0.05–0.10 **V**; rem **Fe**	**Hardened and tempered:** all **diam**, (1516) **TS**, (1310) **YS**, 10 **El**
AMS 6362A		US	Tube	0.28–0.33 **C**, 0.40–0.60 **Mn**, 0.025 **P**, 0.025 **S**, 0.20–0.35 **Si**, 0.80–1.10 **Cr**, 0.25 **Ni**, 0.15–0.25 **Mo**, 0.35 **Cu**	**Quenched and tempered:** all **diam**, 150 (1034) **TS**, 135 (931) **YS**, 10 **El**
AMS 6427E		US	Bar, forgings, tube	0.28–0.33 **C**, 0.75–1.00 **Mn**, 0.025 **P**, 0.025 **S**, 0.20–0.35 **Si**, 0.75–1.00 **Cr**, 1.65–2.00 **Ni**, 0.35–0.50 **Mo**, 0.05–0.10 **V**, 0.35 **Cu**	**Cold finished (bar)**: ≤0.500 (≤12.70) **diam**, 130 (896) **TS**
AMS 6351B		US	Sheet, strip, plate	0.28–0.33 **C**, 0.40–0.60 **Mn**, 0.025 **P**, 0.025 **S**, 0.20–0.35 **Si**, 0.80–1.10 **Cr**, 0.25 **Ni**, 0.15–0.25 **Mo**, 0.35 **Cu**	**Hardened and tempered:** ≤0.375–0.500 (≤9.52–12.70) **diam**, 125 (862) **TS**
AMS 6350E		US	Sheet, strip, plate	0.28–0.33 **C**, 0.40–0.60 **Mn**, 0.025 **P**, 0.025 **S**, 0.20–0.35 **Si**, 0.80–1.10 **Cr**, 0.25 **Ni**, 0.15–0.25 **Mo**, 0.35 **Cu**	**Hardened and tempered:** ≤0.249 (≤6.31) **diam**, 125 (862) **TS**
AMS 6280F		US	Bar, forgings, rings	0.28–0.33 **C**, 0.70–0.90 **Mn**, 0.025 **P**, 0.025 **S**, 0.20–0.35 **Si**, 0.40–0.60 **Cr**, 0.40–0.70 **Ni**, 0.15–0.25 **Mo**, 0.35 **Cu**	**Cold finished (bar)**: ≤0.500 (≤12.70) **diam**, 125 (862) max **TS**
AMS 6302C		US	Bar, forgings, tube	0.28–0.33 **C**, 0.45–0.65 **Mn**, 0.025 **P**, 0.025 **S**, 0.55–0.75 **Si**, 1.00–1.50 **Cr**, 0.25 **Ni**, 0.40–0.60 **Mo**, 0.20–0.30 **V**, 0.35 **Cu**	**Cold finished (bar)**: ≤0.500 (≤12.70) **diam**, 125 (862) max **TS**
AMS 6361A		US	Tube	0.28–0.33 **C**, 0.40–0.60 **Mn**, 0.025 **P**, 0.025 **S**, 0.20–0.35 **Si**, 0.80–1.10 **Cr**, 0.25 **Ni**, 0.15–0.25 **Mo**, 0.35 **Cu**	**Quenched and tempered:** all **diam**, 125 (862) **TS**, 100 (690) **YS**, 12 **El**
MIL-S-6050A	AISI-8630	US	Bar, reforging stock: aircraft quality	0.28–0.33 **C**, 0.70–0.90 **Mn**, 0.025 **P**, 0.025 **S**, 0.20–0.35 **Si**, 0.40–0.60 **Cr**, 0.40–0.70 **Ni**, 0.15–0.25 **Mo**, 0.35 **Cu**	**Quenched and tempered:** all **diam**, 125 (862) **TS**, 100 (690) **YS**, 17 **El**
MIL-S-6758A	AISI 4130	US	Bar: aircraft quality	0.28–0.33 **C**, 0.40–0.60 **Mn**, 0.025 **P**, 0.025 **S**, 0.20–0.35 **Si**, 0.80–1.10 **Cr**, 0.25 **Ni**, 0.15–0.25 **Mo**	**Hardened and tempered:** all **diam**, 125 (862) **TS**, 100 (690) **YS**, 17 **El**
JIS G 4104	Class 2	Japan	Bar	0.28–0.33 **C**, 0.60–0.85 **Mn**, 0.030 **P**, 0.030 **S**, 0.15–0.35 **Si**, 0.90–1.20 **Cr**, 0.25 **Ni**, 0.15–0.30 **Mo**, 0.30 **Cu**	**Rolled or forged, quenched and tempered:** (25) **diam**, (834) **TS**, (686) **YS**, 18 **El**
AMS 6370H		US	Bar, forgings, rings	0.28–0.33 **C**, 0.40–0.60 **Mn**, 0.025 **P**, 0.025 **S**, 0.15–0.35 **Si**, 0.80–1.10 **Cr**, 0.25 **Ni**, 0.15–0.25 **Mo**, 0.35 **Cu**	**Cold finished (bar)**: ≤0.500 (≤12.70) **diam**, 120 (827) max **TS**
JIS G 4104	Class 2	Japan	Bar	0.28–0.33 **C**, 0.60–0.85 **Mn**, 0.030 **P**, 0.030 **S**, 0.15–0.35 **Si**, 0.90–1.20 **Cr**, 0.25 **Ni**, 0.30 **Cu**	**Rolled or forged, quenched and tempered:** (25) **diam**, (785) **TS**, (637) **YS**, 18 **El**

specification number	designation	country	product forms	composition	mechanical properties (see page iv for explanation)
AMS 6530F		US	Tube	0.28–0.33 **C**, 0.70–0.90 **Mn**, 0.025 **P**, 0.025 **S**, 0.20–0.35 **Si**, 0.40–0.60 **Cr**, 0.40–0.70 **Ni**, 0.15–0.25 **Mo**, 0.35 **Cu**	**Cold finished, normalized and tempered:** ≤0.188 (≤4.78) **diam**, 95 (655) **TS**, 75 (517) **YS**, 10 **El**
AMS 6550F		US	Tube	0.28–0.33 **C**, 0.70–0.90 **Mn**, 0.025 **P**, 0.025 **S**, 0.20–0.35 **Si**, 0.40–0.60 **Cr**, 0.40–0.70 **Ni**, 0.15–0.25 **Mo**, 0.35 **Cu**	**Cold finished, normalized and tempered:** ≤0.188 (≤4.78) **diam**, 95 (655) **TS**, 75 (517) **YS**, 10 **El**
AMS 6360G		US	Tube	0.28–0.33 **C**, 0.40–0.60 **Mn**, 0.025 **P**, 0.025 **S**, 0.20–0.35 **Si**, 0.80–1.10 **Cr**, 0.25 **Ni**, 0.15–0.25 **Mo**, 0.35 **Cu**	**Cold finished, normalized and tempered:** ≤0.188 (≤4.78) **diam**, 95 (655) **TS**, 75 (517) **YS**, 10 **El**
ANSI/ASTM A 519	4130	US	Tube: seamless	0.28–0.33 **C**, 0.40–0.60 **Mn**, 0.040 **P**, 0.040 **S**, 0.15–0.35 **Si**, 0.80–1.10 **Cr**, 0.15–0.25 **Mo**	**Hot rolled**: all **diam**, 90 (621) **TS**, 70 (483) **YS**, 20 **El**; **Stress relieved**: all **diam**, 105 (724) **TS**, 85 (586) **YS**, 10 **El**; **Annealed**: all **diam**, 75 (517) **TS**, 55 (379) **YS**, 30 **El**; **Normalized**: all **diam**, 90 (621) **TS**, 60 (414) **YS**, 20 **El**
COPANT 514	Grade 4130	COPANT	Tube: seamless	0.28–0.33 **C**, 0.40–0.60 **Mn**, 0.040 **P**, 0.040 **S**, 0.20–0.35 **Si**, 0.80–1.10 **Cr**, 0.15–0.25 **Mo**	**Hot finished**: (>323.9) **diam**, (620) **TS**, (480) **YS**, 20 **El**; **Annealed**: all **diam**, (520) **TS**, (380) **YS**, 30 **El**; **Normalized**: all **diam**, (620) **TS**, (410) **YS**, 20 **El**
MIL-S-18729C		US	Plate, sheet, strip: aircraft quality	0.28–0.33 **C**, 0.40–0.60 **Mn**, 0.025 **P**, 0.025 **S**, 0.20–0.35 **Si**, 0.80–1.10 **Cr**, 0.25 **Ni**, 0.15–0.25 **Mo**	**Annealed**: all **diam**, (586) **TS**; **Modified annealed**: all **diam**, (655) **TS**; **Normalized**: ≤0.062 **diam**, (655) **TS**, (517) **YS**, 8 **El**
AMS 6461E		US	Wire	0.28–0.33 **C**, 0.60–0.90 **Mn**, 0.008 **P**, 0.008 **S**, 0.20–0.35 **Si**, 0.80–1.10 **Cr**, 0.25 **Ni**, 0.06 **Mo**, 0.15–0.25 **V**, 0.35 **Cu**, 0.0025 **H**, 0.005 **N**, 0.0025 **O**, 0.012 **P+S**	**Cold drawn (weld properties):** 0.250 (6.35) **diam**, 162 **TS**, 5 **El**
AISI 1330		US	Bar	0.28–0.33 **C**, 1.60–1.90 **Mn**, 0.035 **P**, 0.040 **S**, 0.15–0.30 **Si**	
AISI 4130		US	Bar	0.28–0.33 **C**, 0.40–0.60 **Mn**, 0.035 **P**, 0.040 **S**, 0.15–0.30 **Si**, 0.80–1.10 **Cr**, 0.15–0.25 **Mo**	
AISI 5130		US	Bar	0.28–0.33 **C**, 0.70–0.90 **Mn**, 0.035 **P**, 0.040 **S**, 0.15–0.30 **Si**, 0.80–1.10 **Cr**	
AISI 8630		US	Bar	0.28–0.33 **C**, 0.70–0.90 **Mn**, 0.035 **P**, 0.040 **S**, 0.15–0.30 **Si**, 0.40–0.60 **Cr**, 0.40–0.70 **Ni**, 0.15–0.25 **Mo**	
BS 970 Part 2	Grade 530 A 30	UK	Blooms, billets, bar, forgings	0.28–0.33 **C**, 0.60–0.80 **Mn**, 0.90–1.20 **Cr**	
AMS 6458D		US	Wire	0.28–0.33 **C**, 0.45–0.65 **Mn**, 0.008 **P**, 0.008 **S**, 0.55–0.75 **Si**, 1.15–1.35 **Cr**, 0.25 **Ni**, 0.40–0.60 **Mo**, 0.20–0.40 **V**, 0.35 **Cu**, 0.0025 **H**, 0.005 **N**, 0.0025 **O**	
AMS 6462D		US	Wire	0.28–0.33 **C**, 0.70–0.90 **Mn**, 0.025 **P**, 0.025 **S**, 0.20–0.35 **Si**, 0.80–1.10 **Cr**, 0.25 **Ni**, 0.06 **Mo**, 0.15–0.25 **V**, 0.35 **Cu**	
AMS 6458D		US	Wire	0.28–0.33 **C**, 0.45–0.65 **Mn**, 0.008 **P**, 0.008 **S**, 0.55–0.75 **Si**, 1.15–1.35 **Cr**, 0.25 **Ni**, 0.40–0.60 **Mo**, 0.20–0.40 **V**, 0.35 **Cu**, 0.0025 **H**, 0.005 **N**, 0.0025 **O**	
AMS 6281E		US	Tube	0.28–0.33 **C**, 0.70–0.90 **Mn**, 0.025 **P**, 0.025 **S**, 0.20–0.35 **Si**, 0.40–0.60 **Cr**, 0.40–0.70 **Ni**, 0.15–0.25 **Mo**, 0.35 **Cu**	
AMS 6355H		US	Sheet, strip, plate	0.28–0.33 **C**, 0.70–0.90 **Mn**, 0.025 **P**, 0.025 **S**, 0.20–0.35 **Si**, 0.40–0.60 **Cr**, 0.40–0.70 **Ni**, 0.15–0.25 **Mo**, 0.35 **Cu**	

specification number	designation	country	product forms	composition	mechanical properties (see page iv for explanation)
AMS 6371E		US	Tube	0.28–0.33 **C**, 0.40–0.60 **Mn**, 0.025 **P**, 0.025 **S**, 0.20–0.35 **Si**, 0.80–1.10 **Cr**, 0.25 **Ni**, 0.15–0.25 **Mo**, 0.35 **Cu**	
MIL–S–46128A		US	Bar: cold finished	0.28–0.33 **C**, 0.75–1.00 **Mn**, 0.025 **P**, 0.025 **S**, 0.15–0.30 **Si**, 0.70–0.95 **Cr**, 1.65–2.00 **Ni**, 0.35–0.50 **Mo**, 0.05–0.10 **V**	
COPANT 334	1330	COPANT	Bar	0.28–0.33 **C**, 1.60–1.90 **Mn**, 0.035 **P**, 0.040 **S**, 0.20–0.35 **Si**	
COPANT 334	5130	COPANT	Bar	0.28–0.33 **C**, 0.70–0.90 **Mn**, 0.035 **P**, 0.040 **S**, 0.20–0.35 **Si**, 0.80–1.10 **Cr**	
COPANT 334	8630	COPANT	Bar	0.28–0.33 **C**, 0.70–0.90 **Mn**, 0.035 **P**, 0.040 **S**, 0.20–0.35 **Si**, 0.40–0.60 **Cr**, 0.40–0.70 **Ni**, 0.15–0.25 **Mo**	
AS 1444	Grade AS 1444/4130	Australia	Bar, bloom, billet, slab	0.28–0.33 **C**, 0.40–0.60 **Mn**, 0.040 **P**, 0.040 **S**, 0.10–0.35 **Si**, 0.80–1.10 **Cr**, 0.15–0.25 **Mo**	
DGN–B–203	Grade 1330	Mexico	Tube: seamless	0.28–0.33 **C**, 1.60–1.90 **Mn**, 0.040 **P**, 0.040 **S**, 0.20–0.35 **Si**	
DGN–B–203	Grade 5130	Mexico	Tube: seamless	0.28–0.33 **C**, 0.70–0.90 **Mn**, 0.040 **P**, 0.040 **S**, 0.20–0.35 **Si**, 0.80–1.10 **Cr**	
DGN–B–203	Grade 8630	Mexico	Tube: seamless	0.28–0.33 **C**, 0.70–0.90 **Mn**, 0.040 **P**, 0.040 **S**, 0.20–0.35 **Si**, 0.40–0.60 **Cr**, 0.40–0.70 **Ni**, 0.15–0.25 **Mo**	
DGN–B–203	Grade 94B30	Mexico	Tube: seamless	0.28–0.33 **C**, 0.75–1.00 **Mn**, 0.040 **P**, 0.040 **S**, 0.20–0.35 **Si**, 0.30–0.50 **Cr**, 0.30–0.60 **Ni**, 0.08–0.15 **Mo**, 0.0005 min **B**	
COPANT 514	1330	COPANT	Tube	0.28–0.33 **C**, 1.60–1.90 **Mn**, 0.040 **P**, 0.040 **S**, 0.20–0.35 **Si**	
DGN–B–300	94B30	Mexico	Bar	0.28–0.33 **C**, 0.75–1.00 **Mn**, 0.035 **P**, 0.040 **S**, 0.20–0.35 **Si**, 0.30–0.50 **Cr**, 0.30–0.60 **Ni**, 0.08–0.15 **Mo**	**Annealed**
DGN–B–300	94B30	Mexico	Bar	0.28–0.33 **C**, 0.75–1.00 **Mn**, 0.035 **P**, 0.040 **S**, 0.20–0.35 **Si**, 0.30–0.50 **Cr**, 0.30–0.60 **Ni**, 0.08–0.15 **Mo**	**Annealed**
DGN–B–300	8630	Mexico		0.28–0.33 **C**, 0.70–0.90 **Mn**, 0.035 **P**, 0.040 **S**, 0.20–0.35 **Si**, 0.40–0.60 **Cr**, 0.40–0.70 **Ni**, 0.15–0.25 **Mo**	**Annealed**
DGN–B–300	5130	Mexico	Bar	0.28–0.33 **C**, 0.70–0.90 **Mn**, 0.035 **P**, 0.040 **S**, 0.20–0.35 **Si**, 0.80–1.10 **Cr**	**Annealed**
DGN–B–300	1330	Mexico	Bar	0.28–0.33 **C**, 1.60–1.90 **Mn**, 0.035 **P**, 0.040 **S**, 0.20–0.35 **Si**	**Annealed**
DGN–B–300	4130	Mexico	Bar	0.28–0.33 **C**, 0.40–0.60 **Mn**, 0.035 **P**, 0.040 **S**, 0.20–0.35 **Si**, 0.80–1.10 **Cr**, 0.15–0.25 **Mo**	
ANSI/ASTM A 29	5130	US	Bar	0.28–0.33 **C**, 0.70–0.90 **Mn**, 0.035 **P**, 0.040 **S**, 0.15–0.30 **Si**, 0.80–1.10 **Cr**	
ANSI/ASTM A 29	4130	US	Bar	0.28–0.33 **C**, 0.40–0.60 **Mn**, 0.035 **P**, 0.040 **S**, 0.15–0.30 **Si**, 0.80–1.10 **Cr**, 0.15–0.25 **Mo**	
ANSI/ASTM A 646	4330 Mod	US	Blooms, billets: aircraft quality	0.28–0.33 **C**, 0.75–1.00 **Mn**, 0.025 **P**, 0.025 **S**, 0.20–0.35 **Si**, 0.70–0.95 **Cr**, 1.65–2.00 **Ni**, 0.35–0.50 **Mo**, 0.05–0.10 **V**	**Annealed**
ANSI/ASTM A 646	4130	US	Blooms, billets: aircraft quality	0.28–0.33 **C**, 0.40–0.60 **Mn**, 0.025 **P**, 0.025 **S**, 0.20–0.35 **Si**, 0.80–1.10 **Cr**, 0.15–0.25 **Mo**	**Annealed**
MIL–S–16974E	No 8630	US	Bar, billets, blooms, slabs	0.28–0.33 **C**, 0.70–0.90 **Mn**, 0.040 **P**, 0.040 **S**, 0.20–0.35 **Si**, 0.40–0.60 **Cr**, 0.40–0.70 **Ni**, 0.15–0.25 **Mo**	

specification number	designation	country	product forms	composition	mechanical properties (see page iv for explanation)
MIL–S–16974E	No 3130	US	Bar, billets, blooms, slabs	0.28–0.33 **C**, 0.60–0.80 **Mn**, 0.040 **P**, 0.040 **S**, 0.20–0.35 **Si**, 0.55–0.75 **Cr**, 1.10–1.40 **Ni**	
MIL–S–16974E	No 4130	US	Bar, billets, blooms, slabs	0.28–0.33 **C**, 0.40–0.60 **Mn**, 0.040 **P**, 0.040 **S**, 0.20–0.35 **Si**, 0.80–1.10 **Cr**, 0.15–0.25 **Mo**	
MIL–S–16974E	No 1330	US	Bar, billets, blooms, slabs	0.28–0.33 **C**, 1.60–1.90 **Mn**, 0.040 **P**, 0.040 **S**, 0.20–0.35 **Si**	
ASTM A 689	94B30	US	Bar	0.28–0.33 **C**, 0.75–1.00 **Mn**, 0.035 **P**, 0.040 **S**, 0.15–0.30 **Si**, 0.30–0.50 **Cr**, 0.30–0.60 **Ni**, 0.08–0.15 **Mo**, 0.0005 min **B**	
ASTM A 689	8630	US	Bar	0.28–0.33 **C**, 0.70–0.90 **Mn**, 0.035 **P**, 0.040 **S**, 0.15–0.30 **Si**, 0.40–0.60 **Cr**, 0.40–0.70 **Ni**, 0.15–0.25 **Mo**	
ASTM A 689	5130	US	Bar	0.28–0.33 **C**, 0.70–0.90 **Mn**, 0.035 **P**, 0.040 **S**, 0.15–0.30 **Si**, 0.80–1.10 **Cr**	
ASTM A 689	1330	US	Bar	0.28–0.33 **C**, 1.60–1.90 **Mn**, 0.035 **P**, 0.040 **S**, 0.15–0.30 **Si**	
ASTM A 689	4130	US	Bar	0.28–0.33 **C**, 0.40–0.60 **Mn**, 0.035 **P**, 0.040 **S**, 0.15–0.30 **Si**, 0.80–1.10 **Cr**, 0.15–0.25 **Mo**	
ANSI/ASTM A 322	8630	US	Bar	0.28–0.33 **C**, 0.70–0.90 **Mn**, 0.035 **P**, 0.040 **S**, 0.15–0.30 **Si**, 0.40–0.60 **Cr**, 0.40–0.70 **Ni**, 0.15–0.25 **Mo**	
ANSI/ASTM A 322	5130	US	Bar	0.28–0.33 **C**, 0.70–0.90 **Mn**, 0.035 **P**, 0.040 **S**, 0.15–0.30 **Si**, 0.80–1.10 **Cr**	
ANSI/ASTM A 322	4130	US	Bar	0.28–0.33 **C**, 0.40–0.60 **Mn**, 0.035 **P**, 0.040 **S**, 0.15–0.30 **Si**, 0.80–1.10 **Cr**, 0.15–0.25 **Mo**	
ANSI/ASTM A 322	1330	US	Bar	0.28–0.33 **C**, 1.60–1.90 **Mn**, 0.035 **P**, 0.040 **S**, 0.15–0.30 **Si**	
ANSI/ASTM A 322	94B30	US	Bar	0.28–0.33 **C**, 0.75–1.00 **Mn**, 0.035 **P**, 0.040 **S**, 0.15–0.30 **Si**, 0.30–0.50 **Cr**, 0.30–0.60 **Ni**, 0.08–0.15 **Mo**	
ANSI/ASTM A 29	1330	US	Bar	0.28–0.33 **C**, 1.60–1.90 **Mn**, 0.035 **P**, 0.040 **S**, 0.15–0.30 **Si**	
ANSI/ASTM A 29	8630	US	Bar	0.28–0.33 **C**, 0.70–0.90 **Mn**, 0.035 **P**, 0.040 **S**, 0.15–0.30 **Si**, 0.40–0.60 **Cr**, 0.40–0.70 **Ni**, 0.15–0.25 **Mo**	
AISI 94B30		US	Bar	0.28–0.33 **C**, 0.75–1.00 **Mn**, 0.035 **P**, 0.040 **S**, 0.15–0.30 **Si**, 0.30–0.50 **Cr**, 0.30–0.60 **Ni**, 0.08–0.15 **Mo**, 0.0005–0.003 **B**	
AISI 8630		US	Wire, rod	0.28–0.33 **C**, 0.70–0.90 **Mn**, 0.035 **P**, 0.040 **S**, 0.15–0.30 **Si**, 0.40–0.60 **Cr**, 0.40–0.70 **Ni**, 0.15–0.25 **Mo**	
AISI 94B30		US	Wire, rod	0.28–0.33 **C**, 0.75–1.00 **Mn**, 0.035 **P**, 0.040 **S**, 0.15–0.30 **Si**, 0.30–0.50 **Cr**, 0.30–0.60 **Ni**, 0.08–0.15 **Mo**	
AISI 1330		US	Wire, rod	0.28–0.33 **C**, 1.60–1.90 **Mn**, 0.035 **P**, 0.040 **S**, 0.15–0.30 **Si**	
AISI 4130		US	Wire, rod	0.28–0.33 **C**, 0.40–0.60 **Mn**, 0.035 **P**, 0.040 **S**, 0.15–0.30 **Si**, 0.80–1.10 **Cr**, 0.15–0.25 **Mo**	
AISI 5130		US	Wire, rod	0.28–0.33 **C**, 0.70–0.90 **Mn**, 0.035 **P**, 0.040 **S**, 0.15–0.30 **Si**, 0.80–1.10 **Cr**	
ANSI/ASTM A 519	1330	US	Tube: seamless	0.28–0.33 **C**, 1.60–1.90 **Mn**, 0.040 **P**, 0.040 **S**, 0.15–0.35 **Si**	
ANSI/ASTM A 519	5130	US	Tube: seamless	0.28–0.33 **C**, 0.70–0.90 **Mn**, 0.040 **P**, 0.040 **S**, 0.15–0.35 **Si**, 0.80–1.10 **Cr**	

specification number	designation	country	product forms	composition	mechanical properties (see page iv for explanation)
ANSI/ASTM A 519	8630	US	Tube: seamless	0.28–0.33 **C**, 0.70–0.90 **Mn**, 0.040 **P**, 0.040 **S**, 0.15–0.35 **Si**, 0.40–0.70 **Cr**, 0.40–0.60 **Ni**, 0.15–0.25 **Mo**	
ANSI/ASTM A 519	94B30	US	Tube: seamless	0.28–0.33 **C**, 0.75–0.100 **Mn**, 0.040 **P**, 0.040 **S**, 0.15–0.35 **Si**, 0.30–0.50 **Cr**, 0.30–0.60 **Ni**, 0.08–0.15 **Mo**	
AISI 8630		US	Sheet, strip	0.28–0.33 **C**, 0.70–0.90 **Mn**, 0.035 **P**, 0.040 **S**, 0.20–0.35 **Si**, 0.40–0.60 **Cr**, 0.40–0.70 **Ni**, 0.15–0.25 **Mo**	
AISI 4130		US	Sheet, strip	0.28–0.33 **C**, 0.40–0.60 **Mn**, 0.035 **P**, 0.040 **S**, 0.20–0.35 **Si**, 0.80–1.10 **Cr**, 0.15–0.25 **Mo**	
AS 1442	Grade AS 1442/XK 1330	Australia	Bar, blooms, billets, slabs	0.28–0.33 **C**, 1.40–1.70 **Mn**, 0.050 **P**, 0.050 **S**, 0.10–0.35 **Si**	
AS 1443	Grade AS 1443/XK 1330	Australia	Bar	0.28–0.33 **C**, 1.40–1.70 **Mn**, 0.050 **P**, 0.050 **S**, 0.10–0.35 **Si**	
DGN–B–297	1330	Mexico	Bar	0.28–0.33 **C**, 1.60–1.90 **Mn**, 0.035 **P**, 0.040 **S**, 0.20–0.35 **Si**	
DGN–B–297	94B30	Mexico	Bar	0.28–0.33 **C**, 0.75–1.00 **Mn**, 0.035 **P**, 0.040 **S**, 0.20–0.35 **Si**, 0.30–0.50 **Cr**, 0.30–0.60 **Ni**, 0.08–0.15 **Mo**	
DGN–B–297	5130	Mexico	Bar	0.28–0.33 **C**, 0.70–0.90 **Mn**, 0.035 **P**, 0.040 **S**, 0.20–0.35 **Si**, 0.80–1.10 **Cr**	
DGN–B–297	8630	Mexico	Bar	0.28–0.33 **C**, 0.70–0.90 **Mn**, 0.035 **P**, 0.040 **S**, 0.20–0.35 **Si**, 0.40–0.60 **Cr**, 0.40–0.70 **Ni**, 0.15–0.25 **Mo**	
DGN–B–297	4130	Mexico	Bar	0.28–0.33 **C**, 0.40–0.60 **Mn**, 0.035 **P**, 0.040 **S**, 0.20–0.35 **Si**, 0.80–1.10 **Cr**, 0.15–0.25 **Mo**	
COPANT 514	Grade 5130	COPANT	Tube: seamless	0.28–0.33 **C**, 0.70–0.90 **Mn**, 0.040 **P**, 0.050 **S**, 0.10 **Si**, 0.80–1.10 **Cr**	
COPANT 514	Grade 94B30	COPANT	Tube: seamless	0.28–0.33 **C**, 0.75–1.00 **Mn**, 0.040 **P**, 0.40 **S**, 0.10 **Si**, 0.30–0.50 **Cr**, 0.30–0.60 **Ni**, 0.08–0.15 **Mo**	
COPANT 514	Grade 8630	COPANT	Tube: seamless	0.28–0.33 **C**, 0.70–0.90 **Mn**, 0.040 **P**, 0.050 **S**, 0.10 **Si**, 0.40–0.60 **Cr**, 0.40–0.70 **Ni**, 0.15–0.25 **Mo**	
JIS G 3311	SCM2M	Japan	Strip	0.28–0.33 **C**, 0.60–0.85 **Mn**, 0.030 **P**, 0.030 **S**, 0.15–0.35 **Si**, 0.90–1.20 **Cr**, 0.25 **Ni**, 0.15–0.30 **Mo**, 0.30 **Cu**	
ANSI/ASTM A 471	Class 9	US	Forgings	0.28 **C**, 0.70 **Mn**, 0.015 **P**, 0.015 **S**, 0.15–0.35 **Si**, 0.75–2.00 **Cr**, 2.00–4.00 **Ni**, 0.20–0.70 **Mo**, 0.05 **V**	**Quenched and tempered**: all **diam**, 170 (1170) **TS**, 155 (1070) **YS**, 12 **El**
ANSI/ASTM A 471	Class 8	US	Forgings	0.28 **C**, 0.70 **Mn**, 0.015 **P**, 0.015 **S**, 0.15–0.35 **Si**, 0.75–2.00 **Cr**, 2.00–4.00 **Ni**, 0.20–0.70 **Mo**, 0.05 min **V**	**Quenched and tempered**: all **diam**, 160 (1105) **TS**, 145 (1000) **YS**, 13 **El**
ANSI/ASTM A 471	Class 7	US	Forgings	0.28 **C**, 0.70 **Mn**, 0.015 **P**, 0.015 **S**, 0.15–0.35 **Si**, 0.75–2.00 **Cr**, 2.00–4.00 **Ni**, 0.20–0.70 **Mo**, 0.05 min **V**	**Quenched and tempered**: all **diam**, 150 (1035) **TS**, 135 (930) **YS**, 14 **El**
ANSI/ASTM A 471	Class 6	US	Forgings	0.28 **C**, 0.70 **Mn**, 0.015 **P**, 0.015 **S**, 0.15–0.35 **Si**, 0.75–2.00 **Cr**, 2.00–4.00 **Ni**, 0.20–0.70 **Mo**, 0.05 min **V**	**Quenched and tempered**: all **diam**, 140 (965) **TS**, 125 (860) **YS**, 15 **El**
ANSI/ASTM A 471	Class 5	US	Forgings	0.28 **C**, 0.70 **Mn**, 0.015 **P**, 0.015 **S**, 0.15–0.35 **Si**, 0.75–2.00 **Cr**, 2.00–4.00 **Ni**, 0.20–0.70 **Mo**, 0.05 min **V**	**Quenched and tempered**: all **diam**, 130 (900) **TS**, 115 (790) **YS**, 16 **El**
ANSI/ASTM A 471	Class 4	US	Forgings	0.28 **C**, 0.70 **Mn**, 0.015 **P**, 0.015 **S**, 0.15–0.35 **Si**, 0.75–2.00 **Cr**, 2.00–4.00 **Ni**, 0.20–0.70 **Mo**, 0.05 min **V**	**Quenched and tempered**: all **diam**, 120 (830) **TS**, 105 (725) **YS**, 17 **El**

WROUGHT ALLOY STEELS

specification number	designation	country	product forms	composition	mechanical properties (see page iv for explanation)
MIL-S-860B	Grade E	US	Forgings	0.28 **C**, 0.20–0.60 **Mn**, 0.015 **P**, 0.018 **S**, 0.15–0.30 **Si**, 1.25–2.00 **Cr**, 3.25–4.00 **Ni**, 0.30–0.60 **Mo**, 0.05–0.15 **V**	**Normalized, quenched, tempered, stress relieved:** all **diam**, 120 (827) **TS**, 95 (655) **YS**, 18 **El**
ANSI/ASTM A 469	Class 8	US	Forgings	0.28 **C**, 0.60 **Mn**, 0.015 **P**, 0.018 **S**, 0.15–0.30 **Si**, 1.25–2.00 **Cr**, 3.25–4.00 **Ni**, 0.30–0.60 **Mo**, 0.05–0.15 **V**	**Quenched, tempered, stress relieved:** all **diam**, 120 (825) **TS**, 100 (690) **YS**, 16 **El**
ANSI/ASTM A 469	Class 7	US	Forgings	0.28 **C**, 0.60 **Mn**, 0.015 **P**, 0.018 **S**, 0.15–0.30 **Si**, 1.25–2.00 **Cr**, 3.25–4.00 **Ni**, 0.30–0.60 **Mo**, 0.05–0.15 **V**	**Quenched, tempered, stress relieved:** all **diam**, 110 (760) **TS**, 90 (620) **YS**, 17 **El**
ANSI/ASTM A 471	Class 3	US	Forgings	0.28 **C**, 0.70 **Mn**, 0.015 **P**, 0.015 **S**, 0.15–0.35 **Si**, 0.75–2.00 **Cr**, 2.00–4.00 **Ni**, 0.20–0.70 **Mo**, 0.05 min **V**	**Quenched and tempered:** all **diam**, 110 (760) **TS**, 95 (655) **YS**, 18 **El**
ASTM A 470	Class 6	US	Forging	0.28 **C**, 0.20–0.60 **Mn**, 0.015 **P**, 0.018 **S**, 0.15–0.30 **Si**, 1.25–2.00 **Cr**, 3.25–4.00 **Ni**, 0.25–0.60 **Mo**, 0.05–0.15 **V**	**Normalized, quenched, tempered:** all **diam**, 105 (725) **TS**, 85 (585) **YS**, 18 **El**
ASTM A 470	Class 4	US	Forging	0.28 **C**, 0.20–0.60 **Mn**, 0.015 **P**, 0.018 **S**, 0.15–0.30 **Si**, 0.75 **Cr**, 2.50 min **Ni**, 0.25 min **Mo**, 0.03 min **V**	**Double normalized, tempered:** all **diam**, 105 (725) **TS**, 85 (585) **YS**, 17 **El**
ANSI/ASTM A 471	Class 2	US	Forgings	0.28 **C**, 0.70 **Mn**, 0.015 **P**, 0.015 **S**, 0.15–0.35 **Si**, 0.75–2.00 **Cr**, 2.00–4.00 **Ni**, 0.20–0.70 **Mo**, 0.05 min **V**	**Quenched and tempered:** all **diam**, 105 (725) **TS**, 85 (585) **YS**, 19 **El**
MIL-S-860B	Grade D	US	Forgings	0.28 **C**, 0.20–0.60 **Mn**, 0.015 **P**, 0.018 **S**, 0.15–0.30 **Si**, 1.25–0.30 **Si**, 1.25–2.00 **Cr**, 3.25–4.00 **Ni**, 0.30–0.60 **Mo**, 0.05–0.15 **V**	**Normalized, quenched, tempered, stress relieved:** all **diam**, 105 (724) **TS**, 85 (586) **YS**, 18 **El**
ANSI/ASTM A 469	Class 6	US	Forgings	0.28 **C**, 0.60 **Mn**, 0.015 **P**, 0.018 **S**, 0.15–0.30 **Si**, 1.25–2.00 **Cr**, 3.25–4.00 **Ni**, 0.30–0.60 **Mo**, 0.05–0.15 **V**	**Quenched, tempered, stress relieved:** all **diam**, 100 (690) **TS**, 80 (550) **YS**, 18 **El**
ANSI/ASTM A 471	Class 1	US		0.28 **C**, 0.70 **Mn**, 0.015 **P**, 0.015 **S**, 0.15–0.35 **Si**, 0.75–2.00 **Cr**, 2.00–4.00 **Ni**, 0.20–0.70 **Mo**, 0.05 min **V**	**Quenched and tempered:** all **diam**, 100 (690) **TS**, 75 (520) **YS**, 20 **El**
MIL-S-23284	Class 1	US	Forgings	0.28 **C**, 0.15–0.45 **Mn**, 0.020 **P**, 0.020 **S**, 0.35 **Si**, 0.50 **Cr**, 2.75–3.50 **Ni**, 0.25–0.60 **Mo**, 0.08 **V**	**Quenched and tempered and stress relieved:** all **diam**, 95 (655) **TS**, 75 (517) **YS**, 20 **El**
MIL-S-860B	Grade C	US	Forgings	0.28 **C**, 0.20–0.60 **Mn**, 0.015 **P**, 0.018 **S**, 0.15–0.30 **Si**, 0.75 **Cr**, 2.50 min **Ni**, 0.25 min **Mo**, 0.03 min **V**	**Normalized, quenched, tempered, stress relieved:** all **diam**, 90 (621) **TS**, 70 (483) **YS**, 20 **El**
ASTM A 470	Class 5	US	Forging	0.28 **C**, 0.20–0.60 **Mn**, 0.015 **P**, 0.018 **S**, 0.15–0.30 **Si**, 1.25–2.00 **Cr**, 3.25–4.00 **Ni**, 0.25–0.60 **Mo**, 0.05–0.15 **V**	**Normalized, quenched, tempered:** all **diam**, 90 (620) **TS**, 70 (483) **YS**, 20 **El**
ASTM A 470	Class 3	US	Forging	0.28 **C**, 0.20–0.60 **Mn**, 0.015 **P**, 0.018 **S**, 0.15–0.30 **Si**, 0.75 **Cr**, 2.50 min **Ni**, 0.25 min **Mo**, 0.03 min **V**	**Double normalized, tempered:** all **diam**, 90 (620) **TS**, 70 (483) **YS**, 20 **El**
JIS G 3213	Class 12 B	Japan	Forgings	0.28 **C**, 0.60–0.90 **Mn**, 0.035 **P**, 0.035 **S**, 0.15–0.35 **Si**, 0.44–0.65 **Mo**	**Annealed or normalized and tempered:** all **diam**, (481) **TS**, (275) **YS**, 25 **El**
ANSI/ASTM A 440		US	Plate, bar, shapes	0.28 **C**, 1.10–1.60 **Mn**, 0.04 **P**, 0.05 **S**, 0.30 **Si**, 0.20 min **Cu**	**As rolled (plate, bar):** 0.75–1.50 **diam**, (460) **TS**, (315) **YS**, 21 **El**
ASTM A 470	Class 7	US	Forgings	0.28 **C**, 0.20–0.60 **Mn**, 0.015 **P**, 0.018 **S**, 0.15–0.30 **Si**, 1.25–2.00 **Cr**, 3.25–4.00 **Ni**, 0.25–0.60 **Mo**, 0.05–0.15 **V**	**Normalized, quenched, tempered**
SIS 14 21 68	SIS 2168-00	Sweden	Bar	0.28 **C**, 1.6 **Mn**, 0.060 **P**, 0.060 **S**, 0.60 **Si**	**As rolled:** (6) **diam**, (590) **YS**, 12 **El**
SFS 1211	A400Hs	Finland	Bar	0.28 **C**, 1.6 **Mn**, 0.06 **P**, 0.05 **S**, 0.15–0.55 **Si**, 0.08 **As**, 0.010 **N**	**Hot rolled:** (6) **diam**, (400) **YS**, 15 **El**

WROUGHT ALLOY STEELS

specification number	designation	country	product forms	composition	mechanical properties (see page iv for explanation)
DEF STAN 10–13/2	Grade F60	UK	Forgings	0.27–0.42 **C**, 0.45–0.70 **Mn**, 0.015 **P**, 0.015 **S**, 0.10–0.35 **Si**, 0.90–1.40 **Cr**, 1.30–1.80 **Ni**, 0.20–0.35 **Mo**, 0.05 **V**	**Hardened and tempered:** (≤110) **diam**, (600) **YS**, 11 **El**
DEF STAN 10–13/2	Grade F55	UK	Forgings	0.27–0.42 **C**, 0.45–0.70 **Mn**, 0.015 **P**, 0.015 **S**, 0.10–0.35 **Si**, 0.90–1.40 **Cr**, 1.30–1.80 **Ni**, 0.20–0.35 **Mo**, 0.05 **V**	**Hardened and tempered:** ≤(125) **diam**, (550) **YS**, 11 **El**
DEF STAN 10–13/2	Grade F65	UK	Forgings	0.27–0.42 **C**, 0.45–0.70 **Mn**, 0.015 **P**, 0.015 **S**, 0.10–0.35 **Si**, 0.90–1.40 **Cr**, 1.30–1.80 **Ni**, 0.20–0.35 **Mo**, 0.05 **V**	**Hardened and tempered:** (≤90) **diam**, (650) **YS**, 11 **El**
DEF STAN 10–13/2	Grade F70	UK	Forgings	0.27–0.42 **C**, 0.45–0.70 **Mn**, 0.015 **P**, 0.015 **S**, 0.10–0.35 **Si**, 0.90–1.40 **Cr**, 1.30–1.80 **Ni**, 0.20–0.35 **Mo**, 0.05 **V**	**Hardened and tempered:** (≤70) **diam**, 700 **YS**, 11 **El**
DEF STAN 10–13/2	Grade F75	UK	Forgings	0.27–0.42 **C**, 0.45–0.70 **Mn**, 0.015 **P**, 0.015 **S**, 0.10–0.35 **Si**, 0.90–1.40 **Cr**, 1.30–1.80 **Ni**, 0.20–0.35 **Mo**, 0.05 **V**	**Hardened and tempered:** (≤50) **diam**, (750) **YS**, 10 **El**
DEF STAN 10–13/2	Grade J100	UK	Forgings	0.27–0.40 **C**, 0.20–0.70 **Mn**, 0.012 **P**, 0.012 **S**, 0.10–0.35 **Si**, 0.70–1.20 **Cr**, 3.00–3.60 **Ni**, 0.50–0.80 **Mo**, 0.10–0.30 **V**	**Hardened and tempered:** (≤150) **diam**, (1000) **YS**, 9 **El**
DEF STAN 10–13/2	Grade J105	UK	Forgings	0.27–0.40 **C**, 0.20–0.70 **Mn**, 0.012 **P**, 0.012 **S**, 0.10–0.35 **Si**, 0.70–1.20 **Cr**, 3.00–3.60 **Ni**, 0.50–0.80 **Mo**, 0.10–0.30 **V**	**Hardened and tempered:** (≤150) **diam**, (1050) **YS**, 9 **El**
DEF STAN 10–13/2	Grade J110	UK	Forgings	0.27–0.40 **C**, 0.20–0.70 **Mn**, 0.012 **P**, 0.012 **S**, 0.10–0.35 **Si**, 0.70–1.20 **Cr**, 3.00–3.60 **Ni**, 0.50–0.80 **Mo**, 0.10–0.30 **V**	**Hardened and tempered:** (≤140) **diam**, (1100) **YS**, 8 **El**
DEF STAN 10–13/2	Grade J115	UK	Forgings	0.27–0.40 **C**, 0.20–0.70 **Mn**, 0.012 **P**, 0.012 **S**, 0.10–0.35 **Si**, 0.70–1.20 **Cr**, 3.00–3.60 **Ni**, 0.50–0.80 **Mo**, 0.10–0.30 **V**	**Hardened and tempered:** (≤130) **diam**, (1150) **YS**, 8 **El**
DEF STAN 10–13/2	Grade J120	UK	Forgings	0.27–0.40 **C**, 0.20–0.70 **Mn**, 0.012 **P**, 0.012 **S**, 0.10–0.35 **Si**, 0.70–1.20 **Cr**, 3.00–3.60 **Ni**, 0.50–0.80 **Mo**, 0.10–0.30 **V**	**Hardened and tempered:** (≤115) **diam**, (1200) **YS**, 8 **El**
DEF STAN 10–13/2	Grade J125	UK	Forgings	0.27–0.40 **C**, 0.20–0.70 **Mn**, 0.012 **P**, 0.012 **S**, 0.10–0.35 **Si**, 0.70–1.20 **Cr**, 3.00–3.60 **Ni**, 0.50–0.80 **Mo**, 0.10–0.30 **V**	**Hardened and tempered:** (≤100) **diam**, (1250) **YS**, 8 **El**
JIS G 4105	Class 1	Japan	Bar	0.27–0.37 **C**, 0.30–0.60 **Mn**, 0.030 **P**, 0.030 **S**, 0.15–0.35 **Si**, 1.00–1.50 **Cr**, 0.25 **Ni**, 0.15–0.30 **Mo**, 0.30 **Cu**	**Rolled or forged, quenched and tempered:** (25) **diam**, (883) **TS**, (736) **YS**, 16 **El**
ANSI/ASTM A 471	Class 10	US	Forgings	0.27–0.37 **C**, 0.70–1.00 **Mn**, 0.015 **P**, 0.015 **S**, 0.20 min **Si**, 0.85–1.25 **Cr**, 0.50 **Ni**, 1.00–1.50 **Mo**, 0.20–0.30 **V**	**Quenched and tempered:** all **diam**, 105 (725) **TS**, 85 (585) **YS**, 15 **El**
JIS G 3311	SCM1M	Japan	Strip	0.27–0.37 **C**, 0.30–0.60 **Mn**, 0.030 **P**, 0.030 **S**, 0.15–0.35 **Si**, 1.00–1.50 **Cr**, 0.25 **Ni**, 0.15–0.30 **Mo**, 0.30 **Cu**	
BS 2 S.120		UK	Bar, billets, forgings: aircraft quality	0.27–0.35 **C**, 0.45–0.7 **Mn**, 0.025 **P**, 0.020 **S**, 0.15–0.35 **Si**, 0.5–0.8 **Cr**, 2.3–2.8 **Ni**, 0.45–0.65 **Mo**	**Hardened and tempered:** all **diam**, (1540) **TS**, (1125) **YS**, 8 **El**
BS S.153	S153B	UK	Bar: black, aircraft quality	0.27–0.35 **C**, 0.45–0.70 **Mn**, 0.025 **P**, 0.020 **S**, 0.15–0.35 **Si**, 0.50–0.80 **Cr**, 2.3–2.8 **Ni**, 0.45–0.65 **Mo**	**Annealed, hardened and tempered:** all **diam**, (1230) **TS**, (1030) **YS**, 9 **El**
BS S.153	S153D	UK	Bar: bright, aircraft quality	0.27–0.35 **C**, 0.45–0.70 **Mn**, 0.025 **P**, 0.020 **S**, 0.15–0.35 **Si**, 0.50–0.80 **Cr**, 2.3–2.8 **Ni**, 0.45–0.65 **Mo**	**Annealed, hardened and tempered:** all **diam**, (1230) **TS**, (1030) **YS**, 9 **El**
BS S.153	S153A	UK	Forging stock, billets, bar: aircraft quality	0.27–0.35 **C**, 0.45–0.70 **Mn**, 0.025 **P**, 0.020 **S**, 0.15–0.35 **Si**, 0.50–0.80 **Cr**, 2.3–2.8 **Ni**, 0.45–0.65 **Mo**	**Annealed, hardened and tempered:** all **diam**, (1230) **TS**, (1030) **YS**, 9 **El**

WROUGHT ALLOY STEELS

specification number	designation	country	product forms	composition	mechanical properties (see page iv for explanation)
BS S.153	S153C	UK	Forgings: aircraft quality	0.27–0.35 **C**, 0.45–0.70 **Mn**, 0.025 **P**, 0.020 **S**, 0.15–0.35 **Si**, 0.50–0.80 **Cr**, 2.3–2.8 **Ni**, 0.45–0.65 **Mo**	**Annealed, hardened and tempered**: all **diam**, (1230) **TS**, (1030) **YS**, 9 **El**
BS 2S.140		UK	Billets, bar, forgings, parts: aircraft quality	0.27–0.35 **C**, 0.45–0.70 **Mn**, 0.025 **P**, 0.020 **S**, 0.15–0.35 **Si**, 0.50–0.80 **Cr**, 2.3–2.8 **Ni**, 0.45–0.65 **Mo**	**Hardened and tempered**: (≤150) **diam**, (1080) **TS**, (1280) **YS**, 10 **El**
BS 2S. 97		UK	Bar, billets, forgings: aircraft quality	0.27–0.35 **C**, 0.45–0.7 **Mn**, 0.025 **P**, 0.020 **S**, 0.15–0.35 **Si**, 0.50–0.80 **Cr**, 2.3–2.8 **Ni**, 0.45–0.65 **Mo**	**Hardened and tempered**: all **diam**, (1000) **TS**, (850) **YS**, 12 **El**
BS S.154	S154B	UK	Bar: black, aircraft quality	0.27–0.35 **C**, 0.45–0.70 **Mn**, 0.025 **P**, 0.020 **S**, 0.15–0.35 **Si**, 0.50–0.80 **Cr**, 2.3–2.8 **Ni**, 0.45–0.65 **Mo**	**Annealed, hardened and tempered**: all **diam**, (880) **TS**, (690) **YS**, 12 **El**
BS S.154	S154D	UK	Bar: bright, aircraft quality	0.27–0.35 **C**, 0.45–0.70 **Mn**, 0.025 **P**, 0.020 **S**, 0.15–0.35 **Si**, 0.50–0.80 **Cr**, 2.3–2.8 **Ni**, 0.45–0.65 **Mo**	**Annealed, hardened and tempered**: all **diam**, (880) **TS**, (690) **YS**, 12 **El**
BS S.154	S154A	UK	Forging stock, billets, bar: aircraft quality	0.27–0.35 **C**, 0.45–0.70 **Mn**, 0.025 **P**, 0.020 **S**, 0.15–0.35 **Si**, 0.50–0.80 **Cr**, 2.3–2.8 **Ni**, 0.45–0.65 **Mo**	**Annealed, hardened and tempered**: all **diam**, (880) **TS**, (690) **YS**, 12 **El**
BS S.154	S154C	UK	Forgings: aircraft quality	0.27–0.35 **C**, 0.45–0.70 **Mn**, 0.025 **P**, 0.020 **S**, 0.15–0.35 **Si**, 0.50–0.80 **Cr**, 2.3–2.8 **Ni**, 0.45–0.65 **Mo**	**Annealed, hardened and tempered**: all **diam**, (880) **TS**, (690) **YS**, 12 **El**
AS G18	G18/En 25	Australia	Bar, billet	0.27–0.35 **C**, 0.50–0.70 **Mn**, 0.050 **P**, 0.050 **S**, 0.10–0.35 **Si**, 0.50–0.80 **Cr**, 2.30–2.80 **Ni**, 0.40–0.70 **Mo**	**Hardened, tempered**: 6 **diam**, (850) **TS**, (680) **YS**
JIS G 4102	Class 2	Japan	Bar	0.27–0.35 **C**, 0.35–0.65 **Mn**, 0.030 **P**, 0.030 **S**, 0.15–0.35 **Si**, 0.60–1.00 **Cr**, 2.50–3.00 **Ni**, 0.30 **Cu**	**Rolled or forged, quenched and tempered**: (25) **diam**, (834) **TS**, (686) **YS**, 18 **El**
JIS G 4103	Class 1	Japan	Bar	0.27–0.35 **C**, 0.60–0.90 **Mn**, 0.030 **P**, 0.030 **S**, 0.15–0.35 **Si**, 0.60–1.00 **Cr**, 1.60–2.00 **Ni**, 0.15–0.30 **Mo**, 0.30 **Cu**	**Rolled or forged, quenched and tempered**: (25) **diam**, (834) **TS**, (686) **YS**, 20 **El**
BS 4670	Grade 826M31	UK	Forgings	0.27–0.35 **C**, 0.45–0.70 **Mn**, 0.040 **P**, 0.040 **S**, 0.10–0.35 **Si**, 0.50–0.80 **Cr**, 2.30–2.80 **Ni**, 0.45–0.65 **Mo**	**Hardened, tempered**: (1000) **diam**, (800) **TS**, (610) **YS**, 14 **El**
BS 970 Part 2	Grade 826 M 31	UK	Blooms, billets, bar, forgings	0.27–0.35 **C**, 0.45–0.70 **Mn**, 0.10–0.35 **Si**, 0.50–0.80 **Cr**, 2.30–2.80 **Ni**, 0.45–0.65 **Mo**	**Hardened and tempered**: 10 **diam**, (760) **TS**, (580) **YS**, 13 **El**
BS 970 Part 2	Grade 830 M 31	UK	Blooms, billets, bar, forgings	0.27–0.35 **C**, 0.45–0.70 **Mn**, 0.10–0.35 **Si**, 0.90–1.20 **Cr**, 2.75–3.25 **Ni**, 0.25–0.35 **Mo**	**Hardened and tempered**: 10 **diam**, (760) **TS**, (580) **YS**, 13 **El**
BS 970 Part 2	Grade 653 M 31	UK	Blooms, billets, bar, forgings	0.27–0.35 **C**, 0.45–0.70 **Mn**, 0.10–0.35 **S**, 0.90–1.20 **Cr**, 2.75–3.25 **Ni**	**Hardened and tempered**: 6 **diam**, (690) **TS**, (525) **YS**, 15 **El**
BS 970 Part 2	Grade 905 M 31	UK	Blooms, billets, bar, forgings	0.27–0.35 **C**, 0.40–0.65 **Mn**, 0.025 **P**, 0.025 **S**, 0.10–0.45 **Si**, 1.40–1.80 **Cr**, 0.15–0.25 **Mo**, 0.90–1.30 **Al**	**Hardened and tempered**: 4 **diam**, (625) **TS**, (470) **YS**, 17 **El**
JIS G 3311	SNC2M	Japan	Strip	0.27–0.35 **C**, 0.35–0.65 **Mn**, 0.030 **P**, 0.030 **S**, 0.15–0.35 **Si**, 0.60–1.00 **Cr**, 2.50–3.00 **Ni**, 0.30 **Cu**	
EURONORM 119–74, IV	30 NiCrMo 2 KD	EURONORM	Wire, rod	0.27–0.34 **C**, 0.70–1.00 **Mn**, 0.035 **P**, 0.035 **S**, 0.15–0.40 **Si**, 0.40–0.60 **Cr**, 0.40–0.70 **Ni**, 0.15–0.30 **Mo**	**Quenched and tempered**: (≤16) **diam**, (930) **TS**, (735) **YS**, 11 **El**
DGN–B–301	1132	Mexico	Bar	0.27–0.34 **C**, 1.35–1.65 **Mn**, 0.040 **P**, 0.08–0.13 **S**, 0.10–0.20 **Si**,	**Forged and hot rolled, cold rolled and cold finished**: all **diam**, (608) **TS**, (314) **YS**, 16 **El**
MIL–S–16974E	No MnV–30	US	Bar, billets, blooms, slabs	0.27–0.34 **C**, 1.40–1.80 **Mn**, 0.040 **P**, 0.040 **S**, 0.20–0.35 **Si**, 0.00–0.25 **Cr**, 0.00–0.25 **Ni**, 0.15–0.25 **V**	

WROUGHT ALLOY STEELS

specification number	designation	country	product forms	composition	mechanical properties (see page iv for explanation)
MIL–S–16974E	No MoV–30	US	Bar, billets, blooms, slabs	0.27–0.34 **C**, 0.60–0.90 **Mn**, 0.040 **P**, 0.040 **S**, 0.20–0.40 **Si**, 0.30–0.50 **Mo**, 0.10–0.25 **V**	
AISI 4130		US	Plate	0.27–0.34 **C**, 0.35–0.60 **Mn**, 0.035 **P**, 0.040 **S**, 0.15–0.30 **Si**, 0.80–1.15 **Cr**, 0.15–0.25 **Mo**	
AISI 8630		US	Plate	0.27–0.34 **C**, 0.60–0.90 **Mn**, 0.035 **P**, 0.040 **S**, 0.15–0.30 **Si**, 0.35–0.60 **Cr**, 0.40–0.70 **Ni**, 0.15–0.25 **Mo**	
AISI 8630		US	Plate	0.27–0.34 **C**, 0.60–0.90 **Mn**, 0.035 **P**, 0.040 **S**, 0.15–0.30 **Si**, 0.35–0.60 **Cr**, 0.40–0.70 **Ni**, 0.15–0.25 **Mo**	
AISI 1330		US	Plate	0.27–0.34 **C**, 1.50–1.90 **Mn**, 0.035 **P**, 0.040 **S**, 0.65–0.30 **Si**	
ASTM A 689	1132	US	Bar	0.27–0.34 **C**, 1.35–1.65 **Mn**, 0.040 **P**, 0.08–0.13 **S**	
ANSI/ASTM A 29	1132	US	Bar	0.27–0.34 **C**, 1.35–1.65 **Mn**, 0.040 **P**, 0.08–0.13 **S**	
ANSI/ASTM A 576	1132	US	Bar	0.27–0.34 **C**, 1.35–1.65 **Mn**, 0.040 **P**, 0.08–0.13 **S**	
JIS G 4052	SCr 2H	Japan	Bar, wire, rod	0.27–0.34 **C**, 0.55–0.90 **Mn**, 0.030 **P**, 0.030 **S**, 0.15–0.35 **Si**, 0.85–1.25 **Cr**, 0.30 **Cu**	**Hot rolled, normalized, quenched**
COPANT 514	Grade 1132	COPANT	Tube: seamless	0.27–0.34 **C**, 1.35–1.65 **Mn**, 0.040 **P**, 0.08–0.13 **S**	
QQ–S–637A	1132	US	Bar	0.27–0.34 **C**, 1.35–1.65 **Mn**, 0.040 **P**, 0.08–0.13 **S**, 0.15–0.35 **Pb**	
ANSI/ASTM A 579	13	US	Forgings	0.27–0.33 **C**, 0.40–0.60 **Mn**, 0.025 **P**, 0.025 **S**, 0.20–0.35 **Si**, 0.80–1.10 **Cr**, 0.15–0.25 **Mo**, 0.05–0.10 **V**	**Quenched and tempered**: all **diam**, 190 (1310) **TS**, 180 (1240) **YS**, 10 **El**
AMS 6385C		US	Sheet, strip, plate	0.27–0.33 **C**, 0.45–0.65 **Mn**, 0.025 **P**, 0.025 **S**, 0.55–0.75 **Si**, 1.00–1.50 **Cr**, 0.25 **Ni**, 0.40–0.60 **Mo**, 0.20–0.30 **V**, 0.35 **Cu**	**Normalized and tempered**: ≤0.050 (≤1.27) **diam**, 135 (931) **TS**, 115 (793) **YS**, 8 **El**
MIL–T–15119A	Grade A 4130	US	Tube: seamless	0.27–0.33 **C**, 0.40–0.60 **Mn**, 0.025 **P**, 0.025 **S**, 0.20–0.35 **Si**, 0.80–1.10 **Cr**, 0.15–0.25 **Mo**	**Cold drawn, heat treated**: all **diam**, 110 (758) **TS**, 85 (586) **YS**, 12 **El**
MIL–T–15119A	Grade B 8630	US	Tube: seamless	0.27–0.33 **C**, 0.70–0.90 **Mn**, 0.025 **P**, 0.025 **S**, 0.20–0.35 **Si**, 0.40–0.60 **Cr**, 0.40–0.70 **Ni**, 0.15–0.25 **Mo**	**Cold drawn, heat treated**: all **diam**, 110 (758) **TS**, 85 (586) **YS**, 12 **El**
MIL–T–6734	AISI 8630	US	Tube: welded, aircraft quality	0.27–0.33 **C**, 0.70–0.90 **Mn**, 0.040 **P**, 0.040 **S**, 0.20–0.35 **Si**, 0.40–0.60 **Cr**, 0.40–0.70 **Ni**, 0.15–0.25 **Mo**	**Annealed**: all **diam**, 95 (655) **TS**; **Normalized**: ≤0.035 **diam**, 95 (655) **TS**, 75 (517) **YS**, 10 **El**; **Quenched and tempered**: all **diam**, 125 (862) **TS**, 100 (690) **YS**, 12 **El**; **Quenched and tempered**: all **diam**, 150 (1034) **TS**, 135 (930) **YS**, 10 **El**; **Quenched and tempered**: all **diam**, 180 (1241) **TS**, 165 (1138) **YS**, 8 **El**
MIL–T–6732	AISI 8630	US	Tube: seamless, aircraft quality	0.27–0.33 **C**, 0.70–0.90 **Mn**, 0.040 **P**, 0.040 **S**, 0.20–0.35 **Si**, 0.40–0.60 **Cr**, 0.40–0.70 **Ni**, 0.15–0.25 **Mo**	**Annealed**: all **diam**, 95 (655) **TS**; **Normalized**: ≤0.035 **diam**, 95 (655) **TS**, 75 (517) **YS**, 10 **El**; **Quenched and tempered**: all **diam**, 125 (862) **TS**, 100 (690) **YS**, 12 **El**; **Quenched and tempered**: all **diam**, 150 (1034) **TS**, 135 (930) **YS**, 10 **El**; **Quenched and tempered**: all **diam**, 180 (1241) **TS**, 165 (1138) **YS**, 8 **El**

WROUGHT ALLOY STEELS

specification number	designation	country	product forms	composition	mechanical properties (see page iv for explanation)
MIL–T–6736B	AISI 4130	US	Tube: seamless or welded, aircraft quality	0.27–0.33 **C**, 0.40–0.60 **Mn**, 0.025 **P**, 0.025 **S**, 0.20–0.35 **Si**, 0.80–1.10 **Cr**, 0.15–0.25 **Mo**	**Annealed**: all **diam**, 95 (655) **TS**; **Normalized**: ≤0.035 **diam**, 95 (655) **TS**, 75 (517) **YS**, 10 **El**; **Quenched and tempered**: all **diam**, 125 (862) **TS**, 100 (690) **YS**, 12 **El**; **Quenched and tempered**: all **diam**, 150 (1034) **TS**, 135 (930) **YS**, 10 **El**; **Quenched and tempered**: all **diam**, 180 (1241) **TS**, 165 (1138) **YS**, 8 **El**
BS 970 Part 2	Grade 530 H 30	UK	Blooms, billets, bar, forgings	0.27–0.33 **C**, 0.50–0.90 **Mn**, 0.10–0.35 **Si**, 0.80–1.25 **Cr**	
AS 1444	Grade AS 1444/4130H	Australia	Bar, bloom, billet, slab	0.27–0.33 **C**, 0.30–0.70 **Mn**, 0.040 **P**, 0.040 **S**, 0.10–0.35 **Si**, 0.75–1.20 **Cr**, 0.15–0.25 **Mo**	
AS 1444	Grade 1444/86B30H	Australia	Bar, bloom, billet, slab	0.27–0.33 **C**, 0.60–0.95 **Mn**, 0.040 **P**, 0.040 **S**, 0.10–0.35 **Si**, 0.35–0.65 **Cr**, 0.35–0.75 **Ni**, 0.15–0.25 **Mo**	
DGN–B–300	1330H	Mexico	Bar	0.27–0.33 **C**, 1.45–2.05 **Mn**, 0.040 **P**, 0.035 **S**, 0.20–0.35 **Si**	**Annealed**
DGN–B–300	4130 H	Mexico	Bar	0.27–0.33 **C**, 0.30–0.70 **Mn**, 0.040 **P**, 0.035 **S**, 0.20–0.35 **Si**, 0.75–1.20 **Cr**, 0.15–0.25 **Mo**	**Annealed**
DGN–B–300	5130 H	Mexico	Bar	0.27–0.33 **C**, 0.60–1.10 **Mn**, 0.040 **P**, 0.035 **S**, 0.20–0.35 **Si**, 0.75–1.20 **Cr**	**Annealed**
DGN–B–300	86B30 H	Mexico	Bar	0.27–0.33 **C**, 0.60–0.95 **Mn**, 0.20–0.35 **Si**, 0.35–0.65 **Cr**, 0.35–0.75 **Ni**, 0.15–0.25 **Mo**, 0.0005 min **B**	
DGN–B–300	8630 H	Mexico	Bar	0.27–0.33 **C**, 0.60–0.95 **Mn**, 0.040 **P**, 0.035 **S**, 0.20–0.35 **Si**, 0.35–0.65 **Cr**, 0.35–0.75 **Ni**, 0.15–0.25 **Mo**	**Annealed**
ASTM A 689	4130 H	US	Bar	0.27–0.33 **C**, 0.30–0.70 **Mn**, 0.040 **P**, 0.040 **S**, 0.15–0.30 **Si**, 0.75–1.20 **Cr**, 0.15–0.25 **Mo**	
ASTM A 689	1330 H	US	Bar	0.27–0.33 **C**, 1.45–2.05 **Mn**, 0.040 **P**, 0.040 **S**, 0.15–0.30 **Si**	
ASTM A 689	5130 H	US	Bar	0.27–0.33 **C**, 0.60–1.10 **Mn**, 0.040 **P**, 0.040 **S**, 0.15–0.30 **Si**, 0.75–1.20 **Cr**	
ASTM A 689	94B30 H	US	Bar	0.27–0.33 **C**, 0.70–1.05 **Mn**, 0.040 **P**, 0.040 **S**, 0.15–0.30 **Si**, 0.25–0.55 **Cr**, 0.25–0.65 **Ni**, 0.08–0.15 **Mo**, 0.0005 min **B**	
ASTM A 689	8630 H	US	Bar	0.27–0.33 **C**, 0.60–0.95 **Mn**, 0.040 **P**, 0.040 **S**, 0.15–0.30 **Si**, 0.35–0.65 **Cr**, 0.35–0.75 **Ni**, 0.15–0.25 **Mo**	
ANSI/ASTM A 304	5130 H	US	Bar	0.27–0.33 **C**, 0.60–1.10 **Mn**, 0.040 **P**, 0.040 **S**, 0.15–0.30 **Si**, 0.75–1.20 **Cr**	
ANSI/ASTM A 304	94B30 H	US	Bar	0.27–0.33 **C**, 0.70–1.05 **Mn**, 0.040 **P**, 0.040 **S**, 0.15–0.30 **Si**, 0.25–0.55 **Cr**, 0.25–0.65 **Ni**, 0.08–0.15 **Mo**, 0.0005 min **B**	
ANSI/ASTM A 304	8630 H	US	Bar	0.27–0.33 **C**, 0.60–0.95 **Mn**, 0.040 **P**, 0.040 **S**, 0.15–0.30 **Si**, 0.35–0.65 **Cr**, 0.35–0.75 **Ni**, 0.15–0.25 **Mo**	
ANSI/ASTM A 304	1330 H	US	Bar	0.27–0.33 **C**, 1.45–2.05 **Mn**, 0.040 **P**, 0.040 **S**, 0.15–0.30 **Si**	
ANSI/ASTM A 304	4130 H	US	Bar	0.27–0.33 **C**, 0.30–0.70 **Mn**, 0.040 **P**, 0.040 **S**, 0.15–0.30 **Si**, 0.75–1.20 **Cr**, 0.15–0.25 **Mo**	
AISI 5130 H		US	Wire, rod	0.27–0.33 **C**, 0.60–1.00 **Mn**, 0.15–0.30 **Si**, 0.75–1.20 **Cr**	
AISI 8630 H		US	Wire, rod	0.27–0.33 **C**, 0.60–0.95 **Mn**, 0.15–0.30 **Si**, 0.35–0.65 **Cr**, 0.35–0.75 **Ni**, 0.15–0.25 **Mo**	

specification number	designation	country	product forms	composition	mechanical properties (see page iv for explanation)
AISI 86B30 H		US	Wire, rod	0.27–0.33 **C**, 0.60–0.95 **Mn**, 0.15–0.30 **Si**, 0.35–0.65 **Cr**, 0.35–0.75 **Ni**, 0.15–0.25 **Mo**	
AISI 94B30 H		US	Wire, rod	0.27–0.33 **C**, 0.70–1.05 **Mn**, 0.15–0.30 **Si**, 0.25–0.55 **Cr**, 0.25–0.65 **Ni**, 0.08–0.15 **Mo**	
AISI 1330 H		US	Wire, rod	0.27–0.33 **C**, 1.45–2.05 **Mn**, 0.15–0.30 **Si**	
AISI 4130H		US	Wire, rod	0.27–0.33 **C**, 0.30–0.70 **Mn**, 0.15–0.30 **Si**, 0.75–1.20 **Cr**, 0.15–0.25 **Mo**	
AISI 94B30		US	Bar	0.27–0.33 **C**, 0.70–1.05 **Mn**, 0.035 **P**, 0.040 **S**, 0.15–0.30 **Si**, 0.25–0.55 **Cr**, 0.25–0.65 **Ni**, 0.08–0.15 **Mo**	
AISI 86B30H		US	Bar	0.27–0.33 **C**, 0.60–0.95 **Mn**, 0.035 **P**, 0.040 **S**, 0.15–0.30 **Si**, 0.35–0.65 **Cr**, 0.35–0.75 **Ni**, 0.15–0.25 **Mo**	
AISI 8630H		US	Bar	0.27–0.33 **C**, 0.60–0.95 **Mn**, 0.035 **P**, 0.040 **S**, 0.15–0.30 **Si**, 0.35–0.65 **Cr**, 0.35–0.75 **Ni**, 0.15–0.25 **Mo**	
AISI 5130H		US	Bar	0.27–0.33 **C**, 0.60–1.00 **Mn**, 0.035 **P**, 0.040 **S**, 0.15–0.30 **Si**, 0.75–1.20 **Cr**	
AISI 4130H		US	Bar	0.27–0.33 **C**, 0.60–1.00 **Mn**, 0.035 **P**, 0.040 **S**, 0.15–0.30 **Si**, 0.75–1.20 **Cr**, 0.15–0.25 **Mo**	
AISI 1330H		US	Bar	0.27–0.33 **C**, 1.45–2.05 **Mn**, 0.035 **P**, 0.040 **S**, 0.15–0.30 **Si**	
JIS G 3311	S30CM	Japan	Strip	0.27–0.33 **C**, 0.60–0.90 **Mn**, 0.030 **P**, 0.035 **S**, 0.15–0.35 **Si**, 0.20 **Cr**, 0.20 **Ni**, 0.30 **Cu**, 0.35 **Ni+Cr**	
ANSI/ASTM A 469	Class 4	US	Forgings	0.27 **C**, 0.70 **Mn**, 0.015 **P**, 0.018 **S**, 0.15–0.30 **Si**, 0.50 **Cr**, 3.00 min **Ni**, 0.20–0.60 **Mo**, 0.03 min **V**	**Quenched, tempered, stress relieved**: all **diam**, 100 (690) **TS**, 80 (550) **YS**, 17 **El**
ANSI/ASTM A 508	Grade 22	US	Forgings	0.27 **C**, 0.50–1.00 **Mn**, 0.025 **P**, 0.025 **S**, 0.15–0.40 **Si**, 0.25–0.45 **Cr**, 0.50–1.00 **Ni**, 0.55–0.70 **Mo**, 0.05 **V**	**Quenched and tempered**: all **diam**, (620) **TS**, (450) **YS**, 16 **El**
ANSI/ASTM A 541	Grade 2A	US	Forgings	0.27 **C**, 0.50–0.90 **Mn**, 0.035 **P**, 0.040 **S**, 0.15–0.35 **Si**, 0.25–0.45 **Cr**, 0.50–1.00 **Ni**, 0.55–0.70 **Mo**, 0.05 **V**	**Quenched and tempered**: all **diam**, (620) **TS**, (450) **YS**, 16 **El**
ANSI/ASTM A 469	Class 3	US	Forgings	0.27 **C**, 0.60 **Mn**, 0.015 **P**, 0.018 **S**, 0.15–0.30 **Si**, 0.50 **Cr**, 2.50 min **Ni**, 0.20–0.50 **Mo**, 0.03 min **V**	**Quenched, tempered, stress relieved**: all **diam**, 90 (620) **TS**, 70 (485) **YS**, 20 **El**
ANSI/ASTM A 508	Class 2a	US	Forgings	0.27 **C**, 0.50–1.00 **Mn**, 0.025 **P**, 0.025 **S**, 0.15–0.40 **Si**, 0.25–0.45 **Cr**, 0.50–1.00 **Ni**, 0.55–0.70 **Mo**, 0.05 **V**	**Quenched and tempered**: all **diam**, 90 (620) **TS**, 65 (450) **YS**, 16 **El**
ANSI/ASTM A 508	Grade 2	US	Forgings	0.27 **C**, 0.50–1.00 **Mn**, 0.025 **P**, 0.025 **S**, 0.15–0.40 **Si**, 0.25–0.45 **Cr**, 0.50–1.00 **Ni**, 0.55–0.70 **Mo**, 0.05 **V**	**Quenched and tempered**: all **diam**, (550) **TS**, (345) **YS**, 18 **El**
ANSI/ASTM A 541	Grade 2	US	Forgings	0.27 **C**, 0.50–0.90 **Mn**, 0.035 **P**, 0.040 **S**, 0.15–0.35 **Si**, 0.25–0.45 **Cr**, 0.50–1.00 **Ni**, 0.55–0.70 **Mo**, 0.05 **V**	**Quenched and tempered**: all **diam**, (550) **TS**, (340) **YS**, 18 **El**
ANSI/ASTM A 508	Class 2	US	Forgings	0.27 **C**, 0.50–1.00 **Mn**, 0.025 **P**, 0.025 **S**, 0.15–0.40 **Si**, 0.25–0.45 **Cr**, 0.50–1.00 **Ni**, 0.55–0.70 **Mo**, 0.05 **V**	**Quenched and tempered**: all **diam**, 80 (550) **TS**, 50 (345) **YS**, 18 **El**
JIS G 3211	Class 2	Japan	Forgings	0.27 **C**, 0.50–0.80 **Mn**, 0.030 **P**, 0.030 **S**, 0.15–0.35 **Si**, 0.25–0.45 **Cr**, 0.50–0.90 **Ni**, 0.55–0.70 **Mo**, 0.06 **V**	**Quenched and tempered**: all **diam**, (549) **TS**, (343) **YS**, 18 **El**

WROUGHT ALLOY STEELS

specification number	designation	country	product forms	composition	mechanical properties (see page iv for explanation)
JIS G 3212	Class 2	Japan	Forgings	0.27 **C**, 0.40–0.90 **Mn**, 0.025 **P**, 0.025 **S**, 0.15–0.35 **Si**, 0.25–0.45 **Cr**, 0.50–0.90 **Ni**, 0.05 **V**	**Quenched and tempered: all diam**, (549) **TS**, (343) **YS**, 18 **El**
BS 4360	Grade 50A	UK	Plate, section, bar	0.27 **C**, 1.70 **Mn**, 0.060 **P**, 0.060 **S**	**As rolled:** (40–63) **diam**, (490) **TS**, 20 **El**
JIS G 3112	Type 3, Sd 35, No.2	Japan	Bar	0.27 **C**, 1.60 **Mn**, 0.050 **P**, 0.050 **S**, 0.50 **C** + **Mn**/6	**Hot rolled: all diam**, (490) **TS**, (343) **YS**, 18 **El**
JIS G 4052	SNC 2H	Japan	Bar, wire, rod	0.26–0.35 **C**, 0.30–0.70 **Mn**, 0.030 **P**, 0.030 **S**, 0.15–0.35 **Si**, 0.55–1.05 **Cr**, 2.45–3.00 **Ni**, 0.30 **Cu**	**Hot rolled, normalized, quenched**
BS 4S. 28		UK	Bar, billets, forgings: aircraft quality	0.26–0.34 **C**, 0.45–0.7 **Mn**, 0.025 **P**, 0.020 **S**, 0.10–0.35 **Si**, 1.1–1.4 **Cr**, 3.9–4.3 **Ni**, 0.20–0.35 **Mo**	**Hardened and tempered: all diam**, (1540) **TS**, (1125) **YS**, 8 **El**
AS G18	G18/En 30B	Australia	Bar, billet	0.26–0.34 **C**, 0.40–0.60 **Mn**, 0.050 **P**, 0.050 **S**, 0.10–0.35 **Si**, 1.10–1.40 **Cr**, 3.90–4.30 **Ni**, 0.20–0.40 **Mo**	**Hardened, tempered: all diam**, (1540) **TS**, (1310) **YS**
BS 970 Part 2	Grade 835 M 30	UK	Blooms, billets, bar, forgings	0.26–0.34 **C**, 0.45–0.70 **Mn**, 0.025 **P**, 0.025 **S**, 0.10–0.35 **Si**, 1.10–1.40 **Cr**, 3.90–4.30 **Ni**, 0.20–0.35 **Mo**	**Hardened and tempered:** 6 **diam**, (1380) **TS**, (1105) **YS**, 7 **El**
DIN 17200	Grade 30 CrMoV 9	Germany	Blooms, slabs, billets, wire, bar, plate, sheet, strip, tube, forgings	0.26–0.34 **C**, 0.40–0.70 **Mn**, 0.035 **P**, 0.035 **S**, 0.15–0.40 **Si**, 2.30–2.70 **Cr**, 0.15–0.25 **Mo**, 0.10–0.20 **V**	**Quenched and tempered:** (≤16) **diam**, (1226) **TS**, (1029) **YS**, 9 **El**
ANSI/ASTM A 372	Class V, type A	US	Forgings	0.26–0.34 **C**, 0.40–0.70 **Mn**, 0.035 **P**, 0.04 **S**, 0.15–0.35 **Si**, 0.80–1.15 **Cr**, 0.15–0.25 **Mo**	**Liquid quenched and tempered: all diam**, (825) **TS**, (485) **YS**, 18 **El**
ANSI/ASTM A 372	Class V, type C	US	Forgings	0.26–0.34 **C**, 0.70–1.00 **Mn**, 0.035 **P**, 0.04 **S**, 0.15–0.35 **Si**, 0.40–0.65 **Cr**, 0.40–0.70 **Ni**, 0.15–0.25 **Mo**	**Liquid quenched and tempered: all diam**, (825) **TS**, (485) **YS**, 18 **El**
ASTM A 372	Class V, type A	US	Forgings	0.26–0.34 **C**, 0.40–0.70 **Mn**, 0.035 **P**, 0.04 **S**, 0.15–0.35 **Si**, 0.80–1.15 **Cr**, 0.15–0.25 **Mo**	**Quenched, tempered: all diam**, 120 (825) **TS**, 70 (485) **YS**, 18 **El**
ASTM A 372	Class V, type C	US	Forgings	0.26–0.34 **C**, 0.70–1.00 **Mn**, 0.035 **P**, 0.04 **S**, 0.15–0.35 **Si**, 0.40–0.65 **Cr**, 0.40–0.70 **Ni**, 0.15–0.25 **Mo**	**Quenched, tempered: all diam**, 120 (825) **TS**, 70 (485) **YS**, 18 **El**
BS 970 Part 2	Grade 823 M 30	UK	Blooms, billets, bar, forgings	0.26–0.34 **C**, 0.35–0.60 **Mn**, 0.10–0.35 **Si**, 1.80–2.20 **Cr**, 1.80–2.20 **Ni**, 0.30–0.50 **Mo**	**Hardened and tempered:** 10 **diam**, (760) **TS**, (580) **YS**, 13 **El**
BS 970 Part 2	Grade 605 M 30	UK	Blooms, billets, bar, forgings	0.26–0.34 **C**, 1.30–1.70 **Mn**, 0.10–0.35 **Si**, 0.22–0.32 **Mo**	**Hardened and tempered:** 6 **diam**, (625) **TS**, (470) **YS**, 17 **El**
EURONORM 119–74, IV	30 CrNiMo 8 KD	EURONORM	Wire, rod	0.26–0.33 **C**, 0.30–0.60 **Mn**, 0.035 **P**, 0.035 **S**, 0.15–0.40 **Si**, 1.80–2.20 **Cr**, 1.80–2.20 **Ni**, 0.30–0.50 **Mo**	**Quenched and tempered:** (≤16) **diam**, (1230) **TS**, (1030) **YS**, 9 **El**
DIN 17200	Grade 30 CrNiMo 8	Germany	Blooms, slabs, billets, wire, bar, plate, sheet, strip, tube, forgings	0.26–0.33 **C**, 0.70–1.10 **Mn**, 0.035 **P**, 0.035 **S**, 0.15–0.40 **Si**, 1.80–2.20 **Cr**, 1.80–2.20 **Ni**, 0.30–0.50 **Mo**	**Quenched and tempered:** (≤16) **diam**, (1226) **TS**, (1029) **YS**, 9 **El**
ISO/R 683/VIII	Type 5	ISO	Bar, billets, rod	0.26–0.33 **C**, 0.30–0.60 **Mn**, 0.035 **P**, 0.035 **S**, 0.15–0.40 **Si**, 1.80–2.20 **Cr**, 1.80–2.20 **Ni**, 0.30–0.50 **Mo**	**Quenched and tempered:** (≤16) **diam**, (1225) **TS**, (1029) **YS**, 9 **El**
ISO/R 683/VIII	Type 5a	ISO	Bar, billets, rod	0.26–0.33 **C**, 0.30–0.60 **Mn**, 0.035 **P**, 0.020–0.035 **S**, 0.15–0.40 **Si**, 1.80–2.20 **Cr**, 1.80–2.20 **Ni**, 0.30–0.50 **Mo**	**Quenched and tempered:** (≤16) **diam**, (1225) **TS**, (1029) **YS**, 9 **El**
ISO/R 683/VIII	Type 5b	ISO	Bar, billets, rod	0.26–0.33 **C**, 0.30–0.60 **Mn**, 0.035 **P**, 0.030–0.050 **S**, 0.15–0.40 **Si**, 1.80–2.20 **Cr**, 1.80–2.20 **Ni**, 0.30–0.50 **Mo**	**Quenched and tempered:** (≤16) **diam**, (1225) **TS**, (1029) **YS**, 9 **El**
AIR 9160/C 41	9160C091	France	Bar, forgings	0.26–0.33 **C**, 0.20–0.60 **Mn**, 0.025 **P**, 0.020 **S**, 0.10–0.40 **Si**, 1.20–1.50 **Cr**, 3.30–4.30 **Ni**, 0.30–0.60 **Mo**	**Annealed, quenched and tempered:** (<40) **diam**, (1080) **TS**, (880) **YS**, 10 **El**
JIS G 3441	Class 1, STKS 1E	Japan	Tube	0.26–0.33 **C**, 0.40–0.85 **Mn**, 0.030 **P**, 0.030 **S**, 0.15–0.35 **Si**, 0.80–1.20 **Cr**, 0.15–0.25 **Mo**	**Quenched and tempered: all diam**, (1030) **TS**, (932) **YS**, 10 **El**

WROUGHT ALLOY STEELS

specification number	designation	country	product forms	composition	mechanical properties (see page iv for explanation)
JIS G 3441	Class 2, STKS 2E	Japan	Tube	0.26–0.33 **C**, 0.60–0.90 **Mn**, 0.030 **P**, 0.030 **S**, 0.15–0.35 **Si**, 0.40–0.65 **Cr**, 0.40–0.65 **Ni**, 0.15–0.25 **Mo**	**Quenched and tempered:** all **diam**, (1030) **TS**, (932) **YS**, 10 **El**
JIS G 3441	Class 1, STKS 1D	Japan	Tube	0.26–0.33 **C**, 0.40–0.85 **Mn**, 0.030 **P**, 0.030 **S**, 0.15–0.35 **Si**, 0.80–1.20 **Cr**, 0.15–0.25 **Mo**	**Quenched and tempered:** all **diam**, (863) **TS**, (686) **YS**, 12 **El**
JIS G 3441	Class 2, STKS 2D	Japan	Tube	0.26–0.33 **C**, 0.60–0.90 **Mn**, 0.030 **P**, 0.030 **S**, 0.15–0.35 **Si**, 0.40–0.65 **Cr**, 0.40–0.70 **Ni**, 0.15–0.25 **Mo**	**Quenched and tempered:** all **diam**, (863) **TS**, (686) **YS**, 12 **El**
JIS G 3441	Class 1, STKS 1A	Japan	Tube	0.26–0.33 **C**, 0.40–0.85 **Mn**, 0.030 **P**, 0.030 **S**, 0.15–0.35 **Si**, 0.80–1.20 **Cr**, 0.15–0.25 **Mo**	**Annealed:** all **diam**, (657) **TS**
JIS G 3441	Class 2, STKS 2A	Japan	Tube	0.26–0.33 **C**, 0.60–0.90 **Mn**, 0.030 **P**, 0.030 **S**, 0.15–0.35 **Si**, 0.40–0.65 **Cr**, 0.40–0.70 **Ni**, 0.15–0.25 **Mo**	**Annealed:** all **diam**, (657) **TS**
JIS G 3441	Class 1, STKS 1C	Japan	Tube	0.26–0.33 **C**, 0.40–0.85 **Mn**, 0.030 **P**, 0.030 **S**, 0.15–0.35 **Si**, 0.80–1.20 **Cr**, 0.15–0.25 **Mo**	**Cold finished:** all **diam**, (618) **TS**, (490) **YS**, 10 **El**
JIS G 3441	Class 2, STKS 2C	Japan	Tube	0.26–0.33 **C**, 0.60–0.90 **Mn**, 0.030 **P**, 0.030 **S**, 0.15–0.35 **Si**, 0.40–0.65 **Cr**, 0.40–0.70 **Ni**, 0.15–0.25 **Mo**	**Cold finished:** all **diam**, (618) **TS**, (490) **YS**, 10 **El**
JIS G 3441	Class 1, STKS 1B	Japan	Tube	0.26–0.33 **C**, 0.40–0.85 **Mn**, 0.030 **P**, 0.030 **S**, 0.15–0.35 **Si**, 0.80–1.20 **Cr**, 0.15–0.25 **Mo**	**Normalized or normalized and tempered:** all **diam**, (549) **TS**, (392) **YS**, 12 **El**
JIS G 3441	Class 2, STKS 2B	Japan	Tube	0.26–0.33 **C**, 0.60–0.90 **Mn**, 0.030 **P**, 0.030 **S**, 0.15–0.35 **Si**, 0.40–0.65 **Cr**, 0.40–0.70 **Ni**, 0.15–0.25 **Mo**	**Normalized or normalized and tempered:** all **diam**, (549) **TS**, (392) **YS**, 12 **El**
BS 1717	CDS–109	UK	Tube	0.26 **C**, 1.2–1.75 **Mn**, 0.050 **P**, 0.050 **S**, 0.35 **Si**, 0.15–0.25 **Mo**	**As drawn:** all **diam**, (620) **TS**, (550) **YS**
BS 1717	CDS–110	UK	Tube	0.26 **C**, 0.4–0.8 **Mn**, 0.050 **P**, 0.050 **S**, 0.35 **Si**, 0.8–1.2 **Cr**, 0.15–0.30 **Mo**	**As drawn:** all **diam**, (620) **TS**, (550) **YS**
BS 980	CDS–11	UK	Tube	0.26 **C**, 1.2–1.7 **Mn**, 0.050 **P**, 0.050 **S**, 0.35 **Si**, 0.15–0.25 **Mo**	**Drawn and tempered:** 8 **diam**, (620) **TS**, (525) **YS**
BS 980	CDS–12	UK	Tube	0.26 **C**, 0.4–0.8 **Mn**, 0.050 **P**, 0.050 **S**, 0.35 **Si**, 0.8–1.2 **Cr**, 0.15–0.30 **Mo**	**Drawn and tempered:** 8 **diam**, (620) **TS**, (525) **YS**
IS 4367	21CrlMo[28]	India	Forgings	0.26 **C**, 0.50–0.80 **Mn**, 0.050 **P**, 0.050 **S**, 0.10–0.35 **Si**, 0.90–1.20 **Cr**, 0.20–0.35 **Mo**	**Annealed:** (100) **diam**, (588) **TS**
MIL–S–23284	Class 2	US	Forgings	0.26 **C**, 0.15–0.45 **Mn**, 0.020 **P**, 0.020 **S**, 0.35 **Si**, 0.50 **Cr**, 2.75–3.25 **Ni**, 0.25–0.60 **Mo**, 0.05 **V**	**Quenched and tempered and stress relieved:** all **diam**, 80 (552) **TS**, 55 (379) **YS**, 22 **El**
BS 4360	Grade 55E	UK	Plate, section, bar	0.26 **C**, 1.70 **Mn**, 0.050 **P**, 0.050 **S**, 0.65 **Si**	**Normalized:** (25–40) **diam**, (550) **TS**, (415) **YS**, 19 **El**
BS 4360	Grade 55C	UK	Plate, section, bar	0.26 **C**, 1.70 **Mn**, 0.050 **P**, 0.050 **S**, 0.65 **Si**	**As rolled:** (25–40) **diam**, (550) **TS**, (415) **YS**, 19 **El**
BS 980	CDS–10	UK	Tube	0.26 **C**, 1.2–1.7 **Mn**, 0.050 **P**, 0.050 **S**, 0.35 **Si**	**Drawn or drawn and tempered:** 6 **diam**, (550) **TS**, (415) **YS**
AS 1548–6	Grade 490	Australia	Plate	0.26 **C**, 0.85–1.70 **Mn**, 0.050 **P**, 0.050 **S**, 0.07–0.60 **Si**	**As–rolled or normalized:** ≤16 **diam**, (490) **TS**, (280) **YS**, 19 **El**
AS 1750–6	Grade 490	Australia	Section, bar	0.26 **C**, 0.85–1.70 **Mn**, 0.050 **P**, 0.050 **S**, 0.07–0.60 **Si**	**As rolled (bar):** ≤25 **diam**, (490) **TS**, (280) **YS**, 19 **El**
AS 1750–6	Grade 490	Australia	Sections, bar	0.26 **C**, 0.85–1.70 **Mn**, 0.050 **P**, 0.050 **S**, 0.07–0.60 **Si**	**As rolled (bar):** <25 **diam**, (490) **TS**, (280) **YS**, 19 **El**
BS 4360	Grade 43B	UK	Plate, section, bar	0.26 **C**, 1.60 **Mn**, 0.060 **P**, 0.060 **S**	**As rolled:** (40–63) **diam**, (430) **TS**, (230) **YS**, 22 **El**
BS 980	CDS–9	UK	Tube	0.26 **C**, 1.2–1.7 **Mn**, 0.050 **P**, 0.050 **S**, 0.35 **Si**	**Annealed:** all **diam**, (415) **TS**, (250) **YS**
BS 980	CDS–13	UK	Tube	0.25–0.45 **C**, 0.5–1.0 **Mn**, 0.050 **P**, 0.050 **S**, 0.35 **Si**, 0.8–1.2 **Cr**, 0.15–0.30 **Mo**	**Drawn:** 8 **diam**, (620) **TS**, (525) **YS**

WROUGHT ALLOY STEELS

specification number	designation	country	product forms	composition	mechanical properties (see page iv for explanation)
DEF STAN 10–13/2	Grade H 65	UK	Forgings	0.25–0.45 **C**, 0.20–0.70 **Mn**, 0.015 **P**, 0.015 **S**, 0.10–0.35 **Si**, 0.70–1.20 **Cr**, 2.70–3.30 **Ni**, 0.40–0.70 **Mo**	**Hardened and tempered:** (≤200) **diam**, (650) **YS**, 11 **El**
DEF STAN 10–13/2	Grade H70	UK	Forgings	0.25–0.45 **C**, 0.20–0.70 **Mn**, 0.015 **P**, 0.015 **S**, 0.10–0.35 **Si**, 0.70–1.20 **Cr**, 2.70–3.30 **Ni**, 0.40–0.70 **Mo**	**Hardened and tempered:** (≤180) **diam**, (700) **YS**, 11 **El**
DEF STAN 10–13/2	Grade H75	UK	Forgings	0.25–0.45 **C**, 0.20–0.70 **Mn**, 0.015 **P**, 0.015 **S**, 0.10–0.35 **Si**, 0.70–1.20 **Cr**, 2.70–3.30 **Ni**, 0.40–0.70 **Mo**	**Hardened and tempered:** (≤170) **diam**, (750) **YS**, 10 **El**
DEF STAN 10–13/2	Grade H80	UK	Forgings	0.25–0.45 **C**, 0.20–0.70 **Mn**, 0.015 **P**, 0.015 **S**, 0.10–0.35 **Si**, 0.70–1.20 **Cr**, 2.70–3.30 **Ni**, 0.40–0.70 **Mo**	**Hardened and tempered:** (≤160) **diam**, (800) **YS**, 10 **El**
DEF STAN 10–13/2	Grade H85	UK	Forgings	0.25–0.45 **C**, 0.20–0.70 **Mn**, 0.015 **P**, 0.015 **S**, 0.10–0.35 **Si**, 0.70–1.20 **Cr**, 2.70–3.30 **Ni**, 0.40–0.70 **Mo**	**Hardened and tempered:** (≤150) **diam**, (850) **YS**, 10 **El**
DEF STAN 10–13/2	Grade H90	UK	Forgings	0.25–0.45 **C**, 0.20–0.70 **Mn**, 0.015 **P**, 0.015 **S**, 0.10–0.35 **Si**, 0.70–1.20 **Cr**, 2.70–3.30 **Ni**, 0.40–0.70 **Mo**	**Hardened and tempered:** (≤140) **diam**, (900) **YS**, 9 **El**
DEF STAN 10–13/2	Grade H95	UK	Forgings	0.25–0.45 **C**, 0.20–0.70 **Mn**, 0.015 **P**, 0.015 **S**, 0.10–0.35 **Si**, 0.70–1.20 **Cr**, 2.70–3.30 **Ni**, 0.40–0.70 **Mo**	**Hardened and tempered:** (≤130) **diam**, (950) **YS**, 9 **El**
DEF STAN 10–13/2	Grade H100	UK	Forgings	0.25–0.45 **C**, 0.20–0.70 **Mn**, 0.015 **P**, 0.015 **S**, 0.10–0.35 **Si**, 0.70–1.20 **Cr**, 2.70–3.30 **Ni**, 0.40–0.70 **Mo**	**Hardened and tempered:** (≤115) **diam**, (1000) **YS**, 9 **El**
DEF STAN 10–13/2	Grade H105	UK	Forgings	0.25–0.45 **C**, 0.20–0.70 **Mn**, 0.015 **P**, 0.015 **S**, 0.10–0.35 **Si**, 0.70–1.20 **Cr**, 2.70–3.30 **Ni**, 0.40–0.70 **Mo**	**Hardened and tempered:** (≤100) **diam**, (1050) **YS**, 9 **El**
MIL–S–21946A		US	Bar, forgings, plate, sheet, strip, shapes	0.25–0.40 **C**, 10.5–12.5 **Mn**, 0.045 **P**, 0.05–0.15 **S**, 0.75 **Si**, 1.0 **Cr**, 7.0–8.5 **Ni**, 18.5 min **Mn+Ni**	**Hot rolled; bar and forgings:** all **diam**, (551) **TS**, (172) **YS**, 35 **El**
BS 1506–240		UK	Bar	0.25–0.40 **C**, 0.40–0.90 **Mn**, 0.050 **P**, 0.050 **S**, 0.10–0.35 **Si**, 0.40 min **Mo**	**Hardened and tempered Q:** 2.5 **diam**, (550) **TS**, (345) **YS**, 22 **El**
DIN 17225	Grade 30 WCrV 17 9	Germany	Bar, rod, wire	0.25–0.35 **C**, 0.20–0.40 **Mn**, 0.15–0.35 **Si**, 2.2–2.5 **Cr**, 0.50–0.70 **V**, 4.0–4.5 **W**	**Hot rolled (bar, rod):** all **diam**, (1373) **TS**
JIS G 4103	Class 5	Japan	Bar	0.25–0.35 **C**, 0.35–0.60 **Mn**, 0.030 **P**, 0.030 **S**, 0.15–0.35 **Si**, 2.50–3.50 **Cr**, 2.50–3.50 **Ni**, 0.50–0.70 **Mo**, 0.30 **Cu**	**Rolled or forged, quenched and tempered:** (25) **diam**, (1079) **TS**, (883) **YS**, 15 **El**
MIL–S–860B	Grade F	US	Forgings	0.25–0.35 **C**, 1.00 **Mn**, 0.015 **P**, 0.018 **S**, 0.15–0.35 **Si**, 0.90–1.50 **Cr**, 0.75 **Ni**, 1.00–1.50 **Mo**, 0.20–0.30 **V**	**Normalized, quenched, tempered, stress relieved:** all **diam**, 115 (793) **TS**, 85 (586) **YS**, 17 **El**
ASTM A 470	Class 8	US	Forgings	0.25–0.35 **C**, 1.00 **Mn**, 0.015 **P**, 0.018 **S**, 0.15–0.35 **Si**, 0.90–1.50 **Cr**, 0.75 **Ni**, 1.00–1.50 **Mo**, 0.20–0.30 **V**	**Double normalized, tempered:** all **diam**, 105 (725) **TS**, 85 (585) **YS**, 17 **El**
AS G18	G18/En 41A	Australia	Bar, billet	0.25–0.35 **C**, 0.65 **Mn**, 0.050 **P**, 0.050 **S**, 0.10–0.45 **Si**, 1.40–1.80 **Cr**, 0.40 **Ni**, 0.10–0.25 **Mo**, 0.90–1.30 **Al**	**Hardened, tempered:** 6 **diam**, (690) **TS**, (525) **YS**
AS G18	G18/En 29B	Australia	Bar, billet	0.25–0.35 **C**, 0.65 **Mn**, 0.050 **P**, 0.050 **S**, 0.10–0.35 **Si**, 2.50–3.50 **Cr**, 0.40 **Ni**, 0.30–0.70 **Mo**	**Hardened, tempered:** 6 **diam**, (690) **TS**, (525) **YS**
DIN 17225	30 WCrV 179/5467	Germany	Bar, rod	0.25–0.35 **C**, 0.20–0.40 **Mn**, 0.15–0.35 **Si**, 2.2–2.5 **Cr**, 0.50–0.70 **V**, 4.0–4.5 **W**	**Hot rolled:** all **diam**, (140) **TS**
BS 4670	Grade 722M29	UK	Forgings	0.25–0.33 **C**, 0.45–0.70 **Mn**, 0.035 **P**, 0.035 **S**, 0.10–0.35 **Si**, 3.00–3.50 **Cr**, 0.40 **Ni**, 0.45–0.65 **Mo**	**Hardened, tempered:** (1000) **diam**, (650) **TS**, (470) **YS**, 17 **El**

WROUGHT ALLOY STEELS

specification number	designation	country	product forms	composition	mechanical properties (see page iv for explanation)
DIN 17200	Grade 28 Mn 6	Germany	Blooms, slabs, billets, wire, bar, plate, sheet, strip, tube, forgings	0.25–0.32 **C**, 1.30–1.65 **Mn**, 0.035 **P**, 0.035 **S**	**Quenched and tempered:** (≤16) **diam**, (795) **TS**, (588) **YS**, 13 **El**
ISO/R 683/V	Type 1b	ISO	Bar, billet, rod	0.25–0.32 **C**, 1.30–1.65 **Mn**, 0.035 **P**, 0.030–0.050 **S**, 0.15–0.40 **Si**	**Quenched and tempered:** (≤16) **diam**, (784) **TS**, (588) **YS**, 13 **El**
ISO/R 683/V	Type 1a	ISO	Bar, billet, rod	0.25–0.32 **C**, 1.30–1.65 **Mn**, 0.035 **P**, 0.020–0.035 **S**, 0.15–0.40 **Si**	**Quenched and tempered:** (≤16) **diam**, (784) **TS**, (588) **YS**, 13 **El**
ISO/R 683/V	Type 1	ISO	Bar, billet, rod	0.25–0.32 **C**, 1.30–1.65 **Mn**, 0.035 **P**, 0.035 **S**, 0.15–0.40 **Si**	**Quenched and tempered:** (≤16) **diam**, (784) **TS**, (588) **YS**, 13 **El**
AMS 6303B		US	Bar, forgings	0.25–0.30 **C**, 0.60–0.90 **Mn**, 0.025 **P**, 0.025 **S**, 0.55–0.75 **Si**, 1.00–1.50 **Cr**, 0.50 **Ni**, 0.40–0.60 **Mo**, 0.75–0.95 **V**, 0.50 **Cu**	**Cold finished (bar):** ≤0.500 (≤12.70) **diam**, 125 (862) max **TS**
AISI 4027		US	Bar	0.25–0.30 **C**, 0.70–0.90 **Mn**, 0.035 **P**, 0.040 **S**, 0.15–0.30 **Si**, 0.20–0.30 **Mo**	
AISI 4028		US	Bar	0.25–0.30 **C**, 0.70–0.90 **Mn**, 0.035 **P**, 0.035–0.050 **S**, 0.15–0.30 **Si**, 0.20–0.30 **Mo**	
AISI 8627		US	Bar	0.25–0.30 **C**, 0.70–0.90 **Mn**, 0.035 **P**, 0.040 **S**, 0.15–0.30 **Si**, 0.40–0.60 **Cr**, 0.40–0.70 **Ni**, 0.15–0.25 **Mo**	
AS G18	G18/En 16A	Australia	Bar, billet	0.25–0.30 **C**, 1.30–1.80 **Mn**, 0.050 **P**, 0.050 **S**, 0.10–0.35 **Si**, 0.20–0.35 **Mo**	
COPANT 334	4027	COPANT	Bar	0.25–0.30 **C**, 0.70–0.90 **Mn**, 0.035 **P**, 0.040 **S**, 0.20–0.35 **Si**, 0.20–0.30 **Mo**	
COPANT 334	28 Cr 4	COPANT	Bar	0.25–0.30 **C**, 0.50–0.80 **Mn**, 0.035 **P**, 0.035 **S**, 0.15–0.35 **Si**, 0.90–1.10 **Cr**	
DGN-B-203	Grade 4028	Mexico	Tube: seamless	0.25–0.30 **C**, 0.70–0.90 **Mn**, 0.040 **P**, 0.035–0.050 **S**, 0.20–0.35 **Si**, 0.20–0.30 **Mo**	
DGN-B-203	Grade 4027	Mexico	Tube: seamless	0.25–0.30 **C**, 0.70–0.90 **Mn**, 0.040 **P**, 0.040 **S**, 0.20–0.35 **Si**, 0.20–0.30 **Mo**	
DGN-B-203	Grade 8627	Mexico	Tube: seamless	0.25–0.30 **C**, 0.70–0.90 **Mn**, 0.040 **P**, 0.040 **S**, 0.20–0.35 **Si**, 0.40–0.60 **Cr**, 0.40–0.70 **Ni**, 0.15–0.25 **Mo**	
COPANT 514	4028	COPANT	Tube	0.25–0.30 **C**, 0.70–0.90 **Mn**, 0.040 **P**, 0.035–0.050 **S**, 0.20–0.35 **Si**, 0.20–0.30 **Mo**	
COPANT 514	4027	COPANT	Tube	0.25–0.30 **C**, 0.70–0.90 **Mn**, 0.040 **P**, 0.040 **S**, 0.20–0.35 **Si**, 0.20–0.30 **Mo**	
DGN-B-300	8627	Mexico	Bar	0.25–0.30 **C**, 0.70–0.90 **Mn**, 0.035 **P**, 0.040 **S**, 0.20–0.35 **Si**, 0.40–0.60 **Cr**, 0.40–0.70 **Ni**, 0.15–0.25 **Mo**	**Annealed**
DGN-B-300	4027	Mexico	Bar	0.25–0.30 **C**, 0.70–0.90 **Mn**, 0.035 **P**, 0.040 **S**, 0.20–0.35 **Si**, 0.20–0.30 **Mo**	**Annealed**
DGN-B-300	4028	Mexico	Bar	0.25–0.30 **C**, 0.70–0.90 **Mn**, 0.035 **P**, 0.035–0.050 **S**, 0.20–0.35 **Si**, 0.20–0.30 **Mo**	**Annealed**
ANSI/ASTM A 29	4027	US	Bar	0.25–0.30 **C**, 0.70–0.90 **Mn**, 0.035 **P**, 0.040 **S**, 0.15–0.30 **Si**, 0.20–0.30 **Mo**	
ANSI/ASTM A 29	4028	US	Bar	0.25–0.30 **C**, 0.70–0.90 **Mn**, 0.035 **P**, 0.035–0.050 **S**, 0.15–0.30 **Si**, 0.20–0.30 **Mo**	
ASTM A 689	8627	US	Bar	0.25–0.30 **C**, 0.70–0.90 **Mn**, 0.035 **P**, 0.040 **S**, 0.15–0.30 **Si**, 0.40–0.60 **Cr**, 0.40–0.70 **Ni**, 0.15–0.25 **Mo**	

WROUGHT ALLOY STEELS

specification number	designation	country	product forms	composition	mechanical properties (see page iv for explanation)
ASTM A 689	4027	US	Bar	0.25–0.30 **C**, 0.70–0.90 **Mn**, 0.035 **P**, 0.040 **S**, 0.15–0.30 **Si**, 0.20–0.30 **Mo**	
ASTM A 689	4028	US	Bar	0.25–0.30 **C**, 0.70–0.90 **Mn**, 0.035 **P**, 0.035–0.050 **S**, 0.15–0.30 **Si**, 0.20–0.30 **Mo**	
ANSI/ASTM A 322	8627	US	Bar	0.25–0.30 **C**, 0.70–0.90 **Mn**, 0.035 **P**, 0.040 **S**, 0.15–0.30 **Si**, 0.40–0.60 **Cr**, 0.40–0.70 **Ni**, 0.15–0.25 **Mo**	
ANSI/ASTM A 322	4027	US	Bar	0.25–0.30 **C**, 0.70–0.90 **Mn**, 0.035 **P**, 0.040 **S**, 0.15–0.30 **Si**, 0.20–0.30 **Mo**	
ANSI/ASTM A 322	4028	US	Bar	0.25–0.30 **C**, 0.70–0.90 **Mn**, 0.035 **P**, 0.035–0.050 **S**, 0.15–0.30 **Si**, 0.20–0.30 **Mo**	
ANSI/ASTM A 29	8627	US	Bar	0.25–0.30 **C**, 0.70–0.90 **Mn**, 0.035 **P**, 0.040 **S**, 0.15–0.30 **Si**, 0.40–0.60 **Cr**, 0.40–0.70 **Ni**, 0.15–0.25 **Mo**	
AISI 8627		US	Wire, rod	0.25–0.30 **C**, 0.70–0.90 **Mn**, 0.035 **P**, 0.040 **S**, 0.15–0.30 **Si**, 0.40–0.60 **Cr**, 0.40–0.70 **Ni**, 0.15–0.25 **Mo**	
AISI 4027		US	Wire, rod	0.25–0.30 **C**, 0.70–0.90 **Mn**, 0.035 **P**, 0.040 **S**, 0.15–0.30 **Si**, 0.20–0.30 **Mo**	
AISI 4028				0.25–0.30 **C**, 0.70–0.90 **Mn**, 0.035 **P**, 0.035–0.050 **S**, 0.15–0.30 **Si**, 0.20–0.30 **Mo**	
ANSI/ASTM A 519	4027	US	Tube: seamless	0.25–0.30 **C**, 0.70–0.90 **Mn**, 0.040 **P**, 0.040 **S**, 0.15–0.35 **Si**, 0.20–0.30 **Mo**	
ANSI/ASTM A 519	4028	US	Tube: seamless	0.25–0.30 **C**, 0.70–0.90 **Mn**, 0.040 **P**, 0.035–0.050 **S**, 0.15–0.35 **Si**, 0.20–0.30 **Mo**	
ANSI/ASTM A 519	8627	US	Tube: seamless	0.25–0.30 **C**, 0.70–0.90 **Mn**, 0.040 **P**, 0.040 **S**, 0.15–0.35 **Si**, 0.40–0.60 **Cr**, 0.40–0.70 **Ni**, 0.15–0.25 **Mo**	
DGN-B-297	4027	Mexico	Bar	0.25–0.30 **C**, 0.70–0.90 **Mn**, 0.035 **P**, 0.040 **S**, 0.20–0.35 **Si**, 0.20–0.30 **Mo**	
DGN-B-297	4028	Mexico	Bar	0.25–0.30 **C**, 0.70–0.90 **Mn**, 0.035 **P**, 0.035–0.050 **S**, 0.20–0.35 **Si**, 0.20–0.30 **Mo**	
DGN-B-297	8627	Mexico	Bar	0.25–0.30 **C**, 0.70–0.90 **Mn**, 0.035 **P**, 0.040 **S**, 0.20–0.35 **Si**, 0.40–0.60 **Cr**, 0.40–0.70 **Ni**, 0.15–0.25 **Mo**	
COPANT 514	Grade 8627	COPANT	Tube: seamless	0.25–0.30 **C**, 0.70–0.90 **Mn**, 0.040 **P**, 0.050 **S**, 0.10 **Si**, 0.40–0.60 **Cr**, 0.40–0.70 **Ni**, 0.15–0.25 **Mo**	
ANSI/ASTM A 225	Grade C	US	Plate	0.25 **C**, 1.60 **Mn**, 0.04 **P**, 0.04 **S**, 0.13–0.32 **Si**, 0.37–0.73 **Ni**, 0.11–0.20 **V**	**As rolled or normalized or stress relieved**: all diam, (725) **TS**, (485) **YS**, 20 **El**
ANSI/ASTM A 533	Grade C, class 3	US	Plate	0.25 **C**, 1.10–1.55 **Mn**, 0.035 **P**, 0.040 **S**, 0.13–0.32 **Si**, 0.67–1.03 **Ni**, 0.41–0.64 **Mo**	**Quenched and tempered**: all **diam**, (690) **TS**, (570) **YS**, 16 **El**
ANSI/ASTM A 533	Grade D,class 3	US	Plate	0.25 **C**, 1.10–1.55 **Mn**, 0.035 **P**, 0.040 **S**, 0.13–0.32 **Si**, 0.17–0.43 **Ni**, 0.41–0.64 **Mo**	**Quenched and tempered**: all **diam**, (690) **TS**, (570) **YS**, 16 **El**
ANSI/ASTM A 533	Grade A,class 3	US	Plate	0.25 **C**, 1.10–1.55 **Mn**, 0.035 **P**, 0.040 **S**, 0.13–0.32 **Si**, 0.41–0.64 **Mo**	**Quenched and tempered**: all **diam**, (690) **TS**, (570) **YS**, 16 **El**
ANSI/ASTM A 533	Grade B,class 3	US	Plate	0.25 **C**, 1.10–1.55 **Mn**, 0.035 **P**, 0.040 **S**, 0.13–0.32 **Si**, 0.37–0.73 **Ni**, 0.41–0.64 **Mo**	**Quenched and tempered**: all **diam**, (690) **TS**, (570) **YS**, 16 **El**
ANSI/ASTM A 533	Grade D,class 2	US	Plate	0.25 **C**, 1.10–1.55 **Mn**, 0.035 **P**, 0.040 **S**, 0.13–0.32 **Si**, 0.17–0.43 **Ni**, 0.41–0.64 **Mo**	**Quenched and tempered**: all **diam**, (620) **TS**, (485) **YS**, 16 **El**

specification number	designation	country	product forms	composition	mechanical properties (see page iv for explanation)
ANSI/ASTM A 533	Grade A,class 2	US	Plate	0.25 **C**, 1.10–1.55 **Mn**, 0.035 **P**, 0.040 **S**, 0.13–0.32 **Si**, 0.41–0.64 **Mo**	**Quenched and tempered**: all **diam**, (620) **TS**, (485) **YS**, 16 **El**
ANSI/ASTM A 533	Grade B,class 2	US	Plate	0.25 **C**, 1.10–1.55 **Mn**, 0.035 **P**, 0.040 **S**, 0.13–0.32 **Si**, 0.37–0.73 **Ni**, 0.41–0.64 **Mo**	**Quenched and tempered**: all **diam**, (620) **TS**, (485) **YS**, 16 **El**
JIS G 3120	Class 1B	Japan	Plate	0.25 **C**, 1.15–1.50 **Mn**, 0.035 **P**, 0.040 **S**, 0.15–0.30 **Si**, 0.45–0.60 **Mo**	**Quenched and tempered**: (≤20) **diam**, (618) **TS**, (481) **YS**, 16 **El**
JIS G 3120	Class 2B	Japan	Plate	0.25 **C**, 1.15–1.50 **Mn**, 0.035 **P**, 0.040 **S**, 0.15–0.30 **Si**, 0.40–0.70 **Ni**, 0.45–0.60 **Mo**	**Quenched and tempered**: (≤20) **diam**. (618) **TS**, (481) **YS**, 16 **El**
JIS G 3120	Class 3B	Japan	Plate	0.25 **C**, 1.15–1.50 **Mn**, 0.035 **P**, 0.040 **S**, 0.15–0.30 **Si**, 0.70–1.00 **Ni**, 0.45–0.60 **Mo**	**Quenched and tempered**: (≤20) **diam**, (618) **TS**, (481) **YS**, 16 **El**
ANSI/ASTM A 202	Grade B	US	Plate	0.25 **C**, 1.00–1.45 **Mn**, 0.04 **P**, 0.04 **S**, 0.54–0.96 **Si**, 0.31–0.64 **Cr**	**As rolled**: all **diam**, (585) **TS**, (325) **YS**, 18 **El**
DGN–B–368	Grade B	Mexico	Plate	0.25 **C**, 1.05–1.40 **Mn**, 0.035 **P**, 0.04 **S**, 0.60–0.90 **Si**, 0.35–0.60 **Cr**	**As rolled**: (51) **diam**, (583) **TS**, (323) **YS**, 18 **El**
ISO 4998	Grade 550	ISO	Sheet: zinc–coated	0.25 **C**, 1.70 **Mn**, 0.05 **P**, 0.05 **S**	**Hot rolled or cold reduced**: all **diam**, (560) **TS**, (550) **YS**
MIL–S–860B	Grade B	US	Forgings	0.25 **C**, 0.20–0.60 **Mn**, 0.015 **P**, 0.018 **S**, 0.15–0.30 **Si**, 0.75 **Cr**, 2.50 min **Ni**, 0.25 min **Mo**, 0.03 min **V**	**Normalized, quenched, tempered, stress relieved**: all **diam**, 80 (552) **TS**, 55 (379) **YS**, 22 **El**
ANSI/ASTM A 336	Grade F 5a	US	Forgings	0.25 **C**, 0.60 **Mn**, 0.040 **P**, 0.030 **S**, 0.50 **Si**, 4.0–6.0 **Cr**, 0.50 **Ni**, 0.45–0.65 **Mo**	**Annealed or normalized and tempered**: all **diam**, (550) **TS**, (345) **YS**, 19 **El**
ASTM A 336	F5a	US	Forgings	0.25 **C**, 0.60 **Mn**, 0.040 **P**, 0.030 **S**, 0.50 **Si**, 4.0–6.0 **Cr**, 0.50 **Ni**, 0.45–0.65 **Mo**	**Normalized**: all **diam**, 80 (550) **TS**, 50 (345) **YS**, 19 **El**
ANSI/ASTM A 533	Grade D,class 1	US	Plate	0.25 **C**, 1.10–1.55 **Mn**, 0.035 **P**, 0.040 **S**, 0.13–0.32 **Si**, 0.17–0.43 **Ni**, 0.41–0.64 **Mo**	**Quenched and tempered**: all **diam**, (550) **TS**, (345) **YS**, 18 **El**
ANSI/ASTM A 533	Grade A,class 1	US	Plate	0.25 **C**, 1.10–1.55 **Mn**, 0.035 **P**, 0.040 **S**, 0.13–0.32 **Si**, 0.41–0.64 **Mo**	**Quenched and tempered**: all **diam**, (550) **TS**, (345) **YS**, 18 **El**
ANSI/ASTM A 533	Grade B,class 1	US	Plate	0.25 **C**, 1.10–1.55 **Mn**, 0.035 **P**, 0.040 **S**, 0.13–0.32 **Si**, 0.37–0.73 **Ni**, 0.41–0.64 **Mo**	**Quenched and tempered**: all **diam**, (550) **TS**, (345) **YS**, 18 **El**
ANSI/ASTM A 533	Grade C,class 1	US	Plate	0.25 **C**, 1.10–1.55 **Mn**, 0.035 **P**, 0.040 **S**, 0.13–0.32 **Si**, 0.67–1.03 **Ni**, 0.41–0.64 **Mo**	**Quenched and tempered**: all **diam**, (550) **TS**, (345) **YS**, 18 **El**
ANSI/ASTM A 533	Grade C,class 2	US	Plate	0.25 **C**, 1.10–1.55 **Mn**, 0.035 **P**, 0.040 **S**, 0.13–0.32 **Si**, 0.67–1.03 **Ni**, 0.41–0.64 **Mo**	**Quenched and tempered**: all **diam**, (550) **TS**, (345) **YS**, 16 **El**
ASTM A 470	Class 2	US	Forging	0.25 **C**, 0.20–0.60 **Mn**, 0.015 **P**, 0.018 **S**, 0.15–0.30 **Si**, 0.75 **Cr**, 2.50 min **Ni**, 0.25 min **Mo**, 0.03 min **V**	**Double normalized, tempered**: all **diam**, 80 (550) **TS**, 55 (380) **YS**, 22 **El**
ANSI/ASTM A 469	Class 2	US	Forgings	0.25 **C**, 0.60 **Mn**, 0.015 **P**, 0.018 **S**, 0.15–0.30 **Si**, 0.50 **Cr**, 2.50 min **Ni**, 0.20–0.50 **Mo**, 0.03 min **V**	**Quenched, tempered, stress relieved**: all **diam**, 80 (550) **TS**, 55 (380) **YS**, 20 **El**
ASTM A 336	F5a	US	Forgings	0.25 **C**, 0.60 **Mn**, 0.040 **P**, 0.030 **S**, 0.50 **Si**, 4.0–6.0 **Cr**, 0.50 **Ni**, 0.45–0.65 **Mo**	**Annealed or normalized, tempered**: all **diam**, 80 (550) **TS**, 50 (345) **YS**, 19 **El**
JIS G 3120	Class 1A	Japan	Plate	0.25 **C**, 1.15–1.50 **Mn**, 0.035 **P**, 0.040 **S**, 0.15–0.30 **Si**, 0.45–0.60 **Mo**	**Quenched and tempered**: (≤20) **diam**, (549) **TS**, (343) **YS**, 18 **El**
JIS G 3120	Class 2A	Japan	Plate	0.25 **C**, 1.15–1.50 **Mn**, 0.035 **P**, 0.040 **S**, 0.15–0.30 **Si**, 0.40–0.70 **Ni**, 0.45–0.60 **Mo**	**Quenched and tempered**: (≤20) **diam**, (549) **TS**, (343) **YS**, 18 **El**
JIS G 3120	Class 3A	Japan	Plate	0.25 **C**, 1.15–1.50 **Mn**, 0.035 **P**, 0.040 **S**, 0.15–0.30 **Si**, 0.70–1.00 **Ni**, 0.45–0.60 **Mo**	**Quenched and tempered**: (≤20) **diam**, (549) **TS**, (343) **YS**, 18 **El**
AS 1548–5	Grade 490	Australia	Plate	0.25 **C**, 0.85–1.70 **Mn**, 0.050 **P**, 0.050 **S**, 0.07–0.60 **Si**, 0.005–0.09 **Nb**	**Normalized**: 3–16 **diam**, (490) **TS**, (325) **YS**, 20 **El**
ISO 4998	Grade 320	ISO	Sheet: zinc–coated	0.25 **C**, 1.70 **Mn**, 0.05 **P**, 0.05 **S**	**Hot rolled or cold reduced**: all **diam**, (430) **TS**, (320) **YS**, 16 **El**

WROUGHT ALLOY STEELS

specification number	designation	country	product forms	composition	mechanical properties (see page iv for explanation)
BS 4360	Grade 40B	UK	Plate, sections, bar	0.25 **C**, 1.60 **Mn**, 0.060 **P**, 0.060 **S**	**As rolled**: (40–63) **diam**, (400) **TS**, (220) **YS**, 25 **El**
ISO 4998	Grade 280	ISO	Sheet: zinc–coated	0.25 **C**, 1.70 **Mn**, 0.05 **P**, 0.05 **S**	**Hot rolled or cold reduced**: all **diam**, (390) **TS**, (280) **YS**, 18 **El**
ISO 4998	Grade 250	ISO	Sheet: zinc–coated	0.25 **C**, 1.70 **Mn**, 0.05 **P**, 0.05 **S**	**Hot rolled or cold reduced**: all **diam**, (350) **TS**, (250) **YS**, 18 **El**
ISO 4998	Grade 220	ISO	Sheet: zinc–coated	0.25 **C**, 1.70 **Mn**, 0.05 **P**, 0.05 **S**	**Hot rolled or cold reduced**: all **diam**, (320) **TS**, (220) **YS**, 20 **El**
AS 1548–5	Grade 490 R	Australia	Plate	0.25 **C**, 0.85–1.70 **Mn**, 0.050 **P**, 0.050 **S**, 0.07–0.60 **Si**, 0.005–0.09 **Nb**	
BS 970 Part 1	150M28	UK	Blooms, billets, slabs, bar, rod, forgings	0.24–0.32 **C**, 1.30–1.70 **Mn**	**Normalized**: 6 **diam**, (525) **TS**, (315) **YS**, 16 **El**; **Hardened and tempered**: 6 **diam**, (550) **TS**, (360) **YS**, 16 **El**
AISI 8627		US	Plate	0.24–0.31 **C**, 0.60–0.90 **Mn**, 0.035 **P**, 0.040 **S**, 0.15–0.30 **Si**, 0.35–0.60 **Cr**, 0.40–0.70 **Ni**, 0.15–0.25 **Mo**	
ANSI/ASTM A 579	81	US	Forgings	0.24–0.30 **C**, 0.10–0.35 **Mn**, 0.01 **P**, 0.01 **S**, 0.10 **Si**, 0.35–0.60 **Cr**, 7.0–9.0 **Ni**, 0.35–0.60 **Mo**, 0.06–0.12 **V**, 3.5–4.5 **Co**	**Heat treated**: all **diam**, 190 (1310) **TS**, 180 (1240) **YS**, 13 **El**
AMS 6546A		US	Sheet, strip, plate	0.24–0.30 **C**, 0.10–0.35 **Mn**, 0.010 **P**, 0.010 **S**, 0.10 **Si**, 0.35–0.60 **Cr**, 7.00–9.00 **Ni**, 0.35–0.60 **Mo**, 0.06–0.12 **V**, 3.50–4.50 **Co**, 0.35 **Cu**	**Normalized, hardened and tempered**: ≥0.250–0.375 (0.020–0.060) **diam**, 185 (1276) **TS**, 175 (1207) **YS**, 5 min **El**
AMS 6540B		US	Bar, forgings, tube, rings	0.24–0.30 **C**, 0.10–0.35 **Mn**, 0.010 **P**, 0.010 **S**, 0.35 **Si**, 0.35–0.60 **Cr**, 7.00–9.00 **Ni**, 0.35–0.60 **Mo**, 0.06–0.12 **V**, 3.50–4.50 **Co**, 0.35 **Cu**	**Annealed and cold finished (bar)**: ≤0.500 (≤12.70) **diam**, 180 (1241) max **TS**; **Normalized, hardened, and tempered**: all **diam**, 185 (1276) **TS**, 175 (1207) **YS**, 13 **El**
DIN 17115	Grade 27 MnSi 5	Germany	Bar, wire, rod	0.24–0.30 **C**, 1.10–1.60 **Mn**, 0.040 **P**, 0.040 **S**, 0.30–0.55 **Si**, 0.020–0.050 **Al**	**Quenched and tempered**: (≤25) **diam**, (980) **TS**, (785) **YS**, 8 **El**
DGN–B–300	4028H	Mexico	Bar	0.24–0.30 **C**, 0.60–1.00 **Mn**, 0.040 **P**, 0.035–0.050 **S**, 0.20–0.35 **Si**, 0.20–0.30 **Mo**	**Annealed**
DGN–B–300	4027H	Mexico	Bar	0.24–0.30 **C**, 0.60–1.00 **Mn**, 0.040 **P**, 0.035 **S**, 0.20–0.35 **Si**, 0.20–0.30 **Mo**	**Annealed**
DGN–B–300	8627 H	Mexico	Bar	0.24–0.30 **C**, 0.60–0.95 **Mn**, 0.040 **P**, 0.035 **S**, 0.20–0.35 **Si**, 0.35–0.65 **Cr**, 0.35–0.75 **Ni**, 0.15–0.25 **Mo**	**Annealed**
ANSI/ASTM A 304	4027 H	US	Bar	0.24–0.30 **C**, 0.60–1.00 **Mn**, 0.040 **P**, 0.040 **S**, 0.15–0.30 **Si**, 0.20–0.30 **Mo**	
ANSI/ASTM A 304	4028 H	US	Bar	0.24–0.30 **C**, 0.60–1.00 **Mn**, 0.040 **P**, 0.035–0.050 **S**, 0.15–0.30 **Si**, 0.20–0.30 **Mo**	
ASTM A 689	4028 H	US	Bar	0.24–0.30 **C**, 0.60–1.00 **Mn**, 0.040 **P**, 0.035–0.050 **S**, 0.15–0.30 **Si**, 0.20–0.30 **Mo**	
ASTM A 689	4027 H	US	Bar	0.24–0.30 **C**, 0.60–1.00 **Mn**, 0.040 **P**, 0.040 **S**, 0.15–0.30 **Si**, 0.20–0.30 **Mo**	
ASTM A 689	8627 H	US	Bar	0.24–0.30 **C**, 0.60–0.95 **Mn**, 0.040 **P**, 0.040 **S**, 0.15–0.30 **Si**, 0.35–0.65 **Cr**, 0.35–0.75 **Ni**, 0.15–0.25 **Mo**	
ANSI/ASTM A 304	8627 H	US	Bar	0.24–0.30 **C**, 0.60–0.95 **Mn**, 0.040 **P**, 0.040 **S**, 0.15–0.30 **Si**, 0.35–0.65 **Cr**, 0.35–0.75 **Ni**, 0.15–0.25 **Mo**	

specification number	designation	country	product forms	composition	mechanical properties (see page iv for explanation)
AISI 8627 H		US	Wire, rod	0.24–0.30 **C**, 0.60–0.95 **Mn**, 0.15–0.30 **Si**, 0.35–0.65 **Cr**, 0.35–0.75 **Ni**, 0.15–0.25 **Mo**	
AISI 4027 H		US	Wire, rod	0.24–0.30 **C**, 0.60–1.00 **Mn**, 0.15–0.30 **Si**, 0.20–0.30 **Mo**	
AISI 4028 H		US	Wire, rod	0.24–0.30 **C**, 0.60–1.00 **Mn**, 0.15–0.30 **Si**, 0.20–0.30 **Mo**	
AISI 8627H		US	Bar	0.24–0.30 **C**, 0.60–0.95 **Mn**, 0.035 **P**, 0.040 **S**, 0.15–0.30 **Si**, 0.35–0.65 **Cr**, 0.35–0.75 **Ni**, 0.15–0.25 **Mo**	
AISI 4028H		US	Bar	0.24–0.30 **C**, 0.60–1.00 **Mn**, 0.035 **P**, 0.035–0.050 **S**, 0.15–0.30 **Si**, 0.20–0.30 **Mo**	
AISI 4027H		US	Bar	0.24–0.30 **C**, 0.60–1.00 **Mn**, 0.035 **P**, 0.040 **S**, 0.15–0.30 **Si**, 0.20–0.30 **Mo**	
AISI 4626		US	Bar	0.24–0.29 **C**, 0.45–0.65 **Mn**, 0.035 **P**, 0.040 **S**, 0.15–0.30 **Si**, 0.70–1.00 **Ni**, 0.15–0.25 **Mo**	
DGN–B–203	Grade 4427	Mexico	Tube: seamless	0.24–0.29 **C**, 0.70–0.90 **Mn**, 0.040 **P**, 0.040 **S**, 0.20–0.35 **Si**, 0.35–0.45 **Mo**	
COPANT 514	4427	COPANT	Tube	0.24–0.29 **C**, 0.70–0.90 **Mn**, 0.040 **P**, 0.040 **S**, 0.20–0.35 **Si**, 0.35–0.45 **Mo**	
DGN–B–300	4626	Mexico	Bar	0.24–0.29 **C**, 0.45–0.65 **Mn**, 0.035 **P**, 0.040 **S**, 0.20–0.35 **Si**, 0.70–1.00 **Ni**, 0.15–0.25 **Mo**	**Annealed**
ANSI/ASTM A 29	4427	US	Bar	0.24–0.29 **C**, 0.70–0.90 **Mn**, 0.035 **P**, 0.040 **S**, 0.15–0.30 **Si**, 0.35–0.45 **Mo**	
ANSI/ASTM A 29	4626	US	Bar	0.24–0.29 **C**, 0.45–0.65 **Mn**, 0.035 **P**, 0.040 **S**, 0.15–0.30 **Si**, 0.70–1.00 **Ni**, 0.15–0.25 **Mo**	
ASTM A 689	4626	US	Bar	0.24–0.29 **C**, 0.45–0.65 **Mn**, 0.035 **P**, 0.040 **S**, 0.15–0.30 **Si**, 0.70–1.00 **Ni**, 0.15–0.25 **Mo**	
ANSI/ASTM A 322	4626	US	Bar	0.24–0.29 **C**, 0.45–0.65 **Mn**, 0.035 **P**, 0.040 **S**, 0.15–0.30 **Si**, 0.70–1.00 **Ni**, 0.15–0.25 **Mo**	
AISI 4626		US	Wire, rod	0.24–0.29 **C**, 0.45–0.65 **Mn**, 0.035 **P**, 0.040 **S**, 0.15–0.30 **Si**, 0.70–1.00 **Ni**, 0.15–0.25 **Mo**	
ANSI/ASTM A 519	4427	US	Tube: seamless	0.24–0.29 **C**, 0.70–0.90 **Mn**, 0.040 **P**, 0.040 **S**, 0.15–0.35 **Si**, 0.35–0.45 **Mo**	
DGN–B–297	4226	Mexico	Bar	0.24–0.29 **C**, 0.45–0.65 **Mn**, 0.035 **P**, 0.040 **S**, 0.20–0.35 **Si**, 0.70–1.00 **Ni**, 0.15–0.25 **Mo**	
MIL–S–22664A	Hy 100	US	Shapes	0.24 **C**, 0.10–0.40 **Mn**, 0.025 **P**, 0.025 **S**, 0.15–0.35 **Si**, 1.35–1.85 **Cr**, 2.75–3.50 **Ni**, 0.30–0.60 **Mo**	**Quenched and tempered**: all **diam**, 120 (827) **TS**, 100 (689) **YS**, 18 **El**
ANSI/ASTM A 738		US	Plate	0.24 **C**, 1.60 **Mn**, 0.035 **P**, 0.040 **S**, 0.13–0.55 **Si**	**Quenched and tempered**: >2.50 **diam**, (515) **TS**, (310) **YS**, 20 **El**
BS 4360	Grade 50C	UK	Plate, section, bar	0.24 **C**, 1.60 **Mn**, 0.060 **P**, 0.060 **S**, 0.55 **Si**	**Normalized**: (40–63) **diam**, (490) **TS**, (340) **YS**, 20 **El**
BS 4360	Grade 50B	UK	Plate, section, bar	0.24 **C**, 1.60 **Mn**, 0.060 **P**, 0.060 **S**, 0.55 **Si**	**Normalized**: (40–63) **diam**, (490) **TS**, (340) **YS**, 20 **El**
SIS 14 21 65	SIS 2165–00	Sweden	Bar	0.24 **C**, 1.60 **Mn**, 0.060 **P**, 0.050 **S**, 0.60 **Si**	**As rolled**: (6) **diam**, (390) **YS**, 15 **El**
DGN–B–203	Grade 4130	Mexico	Tube: seamless	0.23–0.33 **C**, 0.40–0.60 **Mn**, 0.040 **P**, 0.040 **S**, 0.20–0.35 **Si**, 0.80–1.10 **Cr**, 0.15–0.25 **Mo**	**Hot finished**: all **diam**, (618) **TS**, (480) **YS**, 20 **El**; **Stress relieved**: all **diam**, (725) **TS**, (588) **YS**, 10 **El**; **Tempered**: all **diam**, (520) **TS**, (451) **YS**, 30 **El**; **Normalized**: all **diam**, (618) **TS**, (412) **YS**, 20 **El**

WROUGHT ALLOY STEELS

specification number	designation	country	product forms	composition	mechanical properties (see page iv for explanation)
DEF STAN 10–13/2	Grade G55	UK	Forgings	0.23–0.33 **C**, 0.45–0.70 **Mn**, 0.015 **P**, 0.015 **S**, 0.10–0.35 **Si**, 0.70–1.20 **Cr**, 2.30–2.90 **Ni**, 0.30–0.60 **Mo**	**Hardened and tempered:** (≤200) **diam**, (550) **YS**, 11 **El**
DEF STAN 10–13/2	Grade G60	UK	Forgings	0.23–0.33 **C**, 0.45–0.70 **Mn**, 0.015 **P**, 0.015 **S**, 0.10–0.35 **Si**, 0.70–1.20 **Cr**, 2.30–2.90 **Ni**, 0.30–0.60 **Mo**	**Hardened and tempered:** (≤190) **diam**, (600) **YS**, 11 **El**
DEF STAN 10–13/2	Grade G65	UK	Forgings	0.23–0.33 **C**, 0.45–0.70 **Mn**, 0.015 **P**, 0.015 **S**, 0.10–0.35 **Si**, 0.70–1.20 **Cr**, 2.30–2.90 **Ni**, 0.30–0.60 **Mo**	**Hardened and tempered:** (≤180) **diam**, (650) **YS**, 11 **El**
DEF STAN 10–13/2	Grade G70	UK	Forgings	0.23–0.33 **C**, 0.45–0.70 **Mn**, 0.015 **P**, 0.015 **S**, 0.10–0.35 **Si**, 0.70–1.20 **Cr**, 2.30–2.90 **Ni**, 0.30–0.60 **Mo**	**Hardened and tempered:** (≤165) **diam**, (700) **YS**, 11 **El**
DEF STAN 10–13/2	Grade G75	UK	Forgings	0.23–0.33 **C**, 0.45–0.70 **Mn**, 0.015 **P**, 0.015 **S**, 0.10–0.35 **Si**, 0.70–1.20 **Cr**, 2.30–2.90 **Ni**, 0.30–0.60 **Mo**	**Hardened and tempered:** (≤150) **diam**, (750) **YS**, 10 **El**
DIN 17210	Grade 25 MoCr 4	Germany	Blooms, slabs, billets, wire, plate, sheet, strip, tube, forgings	0.23–0.29 **C**, 0.60–0.90 **Mn**, 0.035 **P**, 0.035 **S**, 0.15–0.40 **Si**, 0.40–0.60 **Cr**, 0.40–0.50 **Mo**	**Rolled or forged:** (11) **diam**, (1079) **TS**, (736) **YS**, 7 **El**
DIN 17210	Grade 25 MoCrS 4	Germany	Blooms, slabs, billets, wire, plate, sheet, strip, tube, forgings	0.23–0.29 **C**, 0.60–0.90 **Mn**, 0.035 **P**, 0.020–0.035 **S**, 0.15–0.40 **Si**, 0.40–0.60 **Cr**, 0.40–0.50 **Mo**	**Rolled or forged:** (11) **diam**, (1077) **TS**, (736) **YS**, 7 **El**
AISI 4626 H		US	Wire, rod	0.23–0.29 **C**, 0.40–0.70 **Mn**, 0.15–0.30 **Si**, 0.65–1.05 **Ni**, 0.15–0.25 **Mo**	
AISI 4626H		US	Bar	0.23–0.29 **C**, 0.40–0.70 **Mn**, 0.035 **P**, 0.040 **S**, 0.15–0.30 **Si**, 0.65–1.05 **Ni**, 0.15–0.25 **Mo**	
MIL–S–7108A(ASG)		US	Bar, forging stock	0.23–0.28 **C**, 1.20–1.50 **Mn**, 0.040 **P**, 0.040 **S**, 1.30–1.70 **Si**, 0.40 **Cr**, 1.65–2.00 **Ni**, 0.35–0.45 **Mo**	**Hardened and tempered:** all **diam**, (1516) **TS**, (1310) **YS**, 10 **El**
ANSI/ASTM A 579	31	US	Forgings	0.23–0.28 **C**, 1.20–1.50 **Mn**, 0.025 **P**, 0.025 **S**, 1.30–1.70 **Si**, 0.20–0.40 **Cr**, 1.65–2.00 **Ni**, 0.35–0.45 **Mo**	**Quenched and tempered:** all **diam**, 190 (1310) **TS**, 180 (1240) **YS**, 10 **El**
ANSI/ASTM A 579	11	US	Forgings	0.23–0.28 **C**, 0.20 **Mn**, 0.01 **P**, 0.01 **S**, 0.10 **Si**, 1.40–1.65 **Cr**, 2.75–3.25 **Ni**, 0.8–1.0 **Mo**, 0.03–0.07 **Nb**	**Quenched and tempered:** all **diam**, 175 (1210) **TS**, 160 (1105) **YS**, 12 **El**
AMS 6418 E		US	Bar, forgings, rings, tube	0.23–0.28 **C**, 1.20–1.50 **Mn**, 0.025 **P**, 0.025 **S**, 1.30–1.70 **Si**, 0.20–0.40 **Cr**, 1.65–2.00 **Ni**, 0.35–0.45 **Mo**, 0.35 **Cu**	**Cold finished (bar):** ≤0.500 (≤12.70) **diam**, 140 (965) max **TS**
AS G18	G18/En 35B	Australia	Bar, billet	0.23–0.28 **C**, 0.30–0.60 **Mn**, 0.050 **P**, 0.050 **S**, 0.10–0.35 **Si**, 1.50–2.00 **Ni**, 0.20–0.30 **Mo**	**Blank carburized, hardened:** all **diam**, (850) **TS**
AISI 8625		US	Bar	0.23–0.28 **C**, 0.70–0.90 **Mn**, 0.035 **P**, 0.040 **S**, 0.15–0.30 **Si**, 0.40–0.60 **Cr**, 0.40–0.70 **Ni**, 0.15–0.25 **Mo**	
DGN–B–203	Grade 8625	Mexico	Tube: seamless	0.23–0.28 **C**, 0.70–0.90 **Mn**, 0.040 **P**, 0.040 **S**, 0.20–0.35 **Si**, 0.40–0.60 **Cr**, 0.40–0.70 **Ni**, 0.15–0.25 **Mo**	
DGN–B–300	8625	Mexico	Bar	0.23–0.28 **C**, 0.70–0.90 **Mn**, 0.035 **P**, 0.040 **S**, 0.20–0.35 **Si**, 0.40–0.60 **Cr**, 0.40–0.70 **Ni**, 0.15–0.25 **Mo**	**Annealed**
MIL–S–16974E	No 8625	US	Bar, billets, blooms, slabs	0.23–0.28 **C**, 0.70–0.90 **Mn**, 0.040 **P**, 0.040 **S**, 0.20–0.35 **Si**, 0.40–0.60 **Cr**, 0.40–0.70 **Ni**, 0.15–0.25 **Mo**	
MIL–S–16974E	No TS8625	US	Bar, billets, blooms, slabs	0.23–0.28 **C**, 0.70–0.90 **Mn**, 0.040 **P**, 0.040 **S**, 0.20–0.35 **Si**, 0.55–0.75 **Cr**, 0.30–0.60 **Ni**, 0.08–0.15 **Mo**	

specification number	designation	country	product forms	composition	mechanical properties (see page iv for explanation)
ASTM A 689	8625	US	Bar	0.23–0.28 **C**, 0.70–0.90 **Mn**, 0.035 **P**, 0.040 **S**, 0.15–0.30 **Si**, 0.40–0.70 **Cr**, 0.40–0.60 **Ni**, 0.15–0.25 **Mo**	
ANSI/ASTM A 322	8625	US	Bar	0.23–0.28 **C**, 0.70–0.90 **Mn**, 0.035 **P**, 0.040 **S**, 0.15–0.30 **Si**, 0.40–0.60 **Cr**, 0.40–0.70 **Ni**, 0.15–0.25 **Mo**	
ANSI/ASTM A 29	8625	US	Bar	0.23–0.28 **C**, 0.70–0.90 **Mn**, 0.035 **P**, 0.040 **S**, 0.15–0.30 **Si**, 0.40–0.60 **Cr**, 0.40–0.70 **Ni**, 0.15–0.25 **Mo**	
AISI 8625		US	Wire, rod	0.23–0.28 **C**, 0.70–0.90 **Mn**, 0.035 **P**, 0.040 **S**, 0.15–0.30 **Si**, 0.40–0.60 **Cr**, 0.40–0.70 **Ni**, 0.15–0.25 **Mo**	
ANSI/ASTM A 519	8625	US	Tube: seamless	0.23–0.28 **C**, 0.70–0.90 **Mn**, 0.040 **P**, 0.040 **S**, 0.15–0.35 **Si**, 0.40–0.60 **Cr**, 0.40–0.70 **Ni**, 0.15–0.25 **Mo**	
AS 1442	Grade AS 1442/XK 1325	Australia	Bar, blooms, billets, slabs	0.23–0.28 **C**, 1.40–1.70 **Mn**, 0.050 **P**, 0.050 **S**, 0.10–0.35 **Si**	
AS 1443	Grade AS 1443/XK 1325	Australia	Bar	0.23–0.28 **C**, 1.40–1.70 **Mn**, 0.050 **P**, 0.050 **S**, 0.10–0.35 **Si**	
DGN–B–297	8625	Mexico	Bar	0.23–0.28 **C**, 0.70–0.90 **Mn**, 0.035 **P**, 0.040 **S**, 0.20–0.35 **Si**, 0.40–0.60 **Cr**, 0.40–0.70 **Ni**, 0.15–0.25 **Mo**	
COPANT 514	Grade 8625	COPANT	Tube: seamless	0.23–0.28 **C**, 0.70–0.90 **Mn**, 0.040 **P**, 0.050 **S**, 0.10 **Si**, 0.40–0.60 **Cr**, 0.40–0.70 **Ni**, 0.15–0.25 **Mo**	
ANSI/ASTM A 543	Grade A, class 2	US	Plate	0.23 **C**, 0.40 **Mn**, 0.035 **P**, 0.040 **S**, 0.18–0.37 **Si**, 1.44–2.06 **Cr**, 2.53–3.32 **Ni**, 0.41–0.64 **Mo**, 0.03 **V**	**Quenched and tempered:** all **diam**, (795) **TS**, (690) **YS**, 14 **El**
ANSI/ASTM A 543	Grade B, class 2	US	Plate	0.23 **C**, 0.40 **Mn**, 0.020 **P**, 0.020 **S**, 0.18–0.37 **Si**, 1.44–2.06 **Cr**, 2.53–3.32 **Ni**, 0.41–0.64 **Mo**, 0.03 **V**	**Quenched and tempered:** all **diam**, (795) **TS**, (690) **YS**, 14 **El**
ANSI/ASTM A 508	Grade 4a	US	Forgings	0.23 **C**, 0.20–0.40 **Mn**, 0.020 **P**, 0.020 **S**, 0.15–0.40 **Si**, 1.50–2.00 **Cr**, 2.75–3.90 **Ni**, 0.40–0.60 **Mo**, 0.03 **V**	**Quenched and tempered:** all **diam**, (795) **TS**, (690) **YS**, 16 **El**
ANSI/ASTM A 508	Grade 5a	US	Forgings	0.23 **C**, 0.20–0.40 **Mn**, 0.020 **P**, 0.020 **S**, 0.30 **Si**, 1.50–2.00 **Cr**, 2.75–3.90 **Ni**, 0.40–0.60 **Mo**, 0.08 **V**	**Quenched and tempered:** all **diam**, (795) **TS**, (690) **YS**, 16 **El**
ANSI/ASTM A 508	Class 4a	US	Forgings	0.23 **C**, 0.20–0.40 **Mn**, 0.020 **P**, 0.020 **S**, 0.15–0.40 **Si**, 1.50–2.00 **Cr**, 2.75–3.90 **Ni**, 0.40–0.60 **Mo**, 0.03 **V**	**Quenched and tempered:** all **diam**, 115 (795) **TS**, 100 (690) **YS**, 16 **El**
ANSI/ASTM A 508	Class 5a	US	Forgings	0.23 **C**, 0.20–0.40 **Mn**, 0.020 **P**, 0.020 **S**, 0.30 **Si**, 1.50–2.00 **Cr**, 2.75–3.90 **Ni**, 0.40–0.60 **Mo**, 0.08 **V**	**Quenched and tempered:** all **diam**, 115 (795) **TS**, 100 (690) **YS**, 16 **El**
ANSI/ASTM A 541	Grade 7A	US	Forgings	0.23 **C**, 0.20–0.40 **Mn**, 0.035 **P**, 0.040 **S**, 0.30 **Si**, 1.25–2.00 **Cr**, 2.75–3.90 **Ni**, 0.40–0.60 **Mo**, 0.03 **V**	**Quenched and tempered:** all **diam**, (790) **TS**, (690) **YS**, 16 **El**
ANSI/ASTM A 541	Grade 8A	US	Forgings	0.23 **C**, 0.20–0.40 **Mn**, 0.035 **P**, 0.040 **S**, 0.30 **Si**, 1.25–2.00 **Cr**, 2.75–3.90 **Ni**, 0.40–0.60 **Mo**, 0.08 **V**	**Quenched and tempered:** all **diam**, (790) **TS**, (690) **YS**, 16 **El**
ISO 2604/1	F40	ISO	Forgings	0.23 **C**, 0.30–1.00 **Mn**, 0.040 **P**, 0.040 **S**, 0.15–0.40 **Si**, 11.0–12.5 **Cr**, 0.30–1.0 **Ni**, 0.70–1.20 **Mo**, 0.20–0.35 **V**	**Quenched and tempered:** all **diam**, (780) **TS**, (540) **YS**, 14 **El**
ANSI/ASTM A 543	Grade A, class 1	US	Plate	0.23 **C**, 0.40 **Mn**, 0.035 **P**, 0.040 **S**, 0.18–0.37 **Si**, 1.44–2.06 **Cr**, 2.53–3.32 **Ni**, 0.41–0.64 **Mo**, 0.03 **V**	**Quenched and tempered:** all **diam**, (725) **TS**, (585) **YS**, 14 **El**

WROUGHT ALLOY STEELS

specification number	designation	country	product forms	composition	mechanical properties (see page iv for explanation)
ANSI/ASTM A 543	Grade B, class 1	US	Plate	0.23 **C**, 0.40 **Mn**, 0.020 **P**, 0.020 **S**, 0.18–0.37 **Si**, 1.44–2.06 **Cr**, 2.53–3.32 **Ni**, 0.41–0.64 **Mo**, 0.03 **V**	**Quenched and tempered:** all **diam**, (725) **TS**, (585) **YS**, 14 **El**
ANSI/ASTM A 508	Grade 4	US	Forgings	0.23 **C**, 0.20–0.40 **Mn**, 0.020 **P**, 0.020 **S**, 0.15–0.40 **Si**, 1.50–2.00 **Cr**, 2.79–3.90 **Ni**, 0.40–0.60 **Mo**, 0.03 **V**	**Quenched and tempered:** all **diam**, (725) **TS**, (585) **YS**, 18 **El**
ANSI/ASTM A 508	Grade 5	US	Forgings	0.23 **C**, 0.20–0.40 **Mn**, 0.020 **P**, 0.020 **S**, 0.30 **Si**, 1.50–2.00 **Cr**, 2.75–3.90 **Ni**, 0.40–0.60 **Mo**, 0.08 **V**	**Quenched and tempered:** all **diam**, (725) **TS**, (585) **YS**, 18 **El**
ANSI/ASTM A 508	Class 4	US	Forgings	0.23 **C**, 0.20–0.40 **Mn**, 0.020 **P**, 0.020 **S**, 0.15–0.40 **Si**, 1.50–2.00 **Cr**, 2.75–3.90 **Ni**, 0.40–0.60 **Mo**, 0.03 **V**	**Quenched and tempered:** all **diam**, 105 (725) **TS**, 85 (585) **YS**, 18 **El**
ANSI/ASTM A 508	Class 5	US	Forgings	0.23 **C**, 0.20–0.40 **Mn**, 0.020 **P**, 0.020 **S**, 0.30 **Si**, 1.50–2.00 **Cr**, 2.75–3.90 **Ni**, 0.40–0.60 **Mo**, 0.08 **V**	**Quenched and tempered:** all **diam**, 105 (725) **TS**, 85 (585) **YS**, 18 **El**
ANSI/ASTM A 541	Grade 7	US	Forgings	0.23 **C**, 0.20–0.40 **Mn**, 0.035 **P**, 0.040 **S**, 0.30 **Si**, 1.25–2.00 **Cr**, 2.75–3.90 **Ni**, 0.40–0.60 **Mo**, 0.03 **V**	**Quenched and tempered:** all **diam**, (720) **TS**, (590) **YS**, 18 **El**
ANSI/ASTM A 541	Grade 8	US	Forgings	0.23 **C**, 0.20–0.40 **Mn**, 0.035 **P**, 0.040 **S**, 0.30 **Si**, 1.25–2.00 **Cr**, 2.75–3.90 **Ni**, 0.40–0.60 **Mo**, 0.08 **V**	**Quenched and tempered:** all **diam**, (720) **TS**, (590) **YS**, 18 **El**
ANSI/ASTM A 543	Grade A, class 3	US	Plate	0.23 **C**, 0.40 **Mn**, 0.035 **P**, 0.040 **S**, 0.18–0.37 **Si**, 1.44–2.06 **Cr**, 2.53–3.32 **Ni**, 0.41–0.64 **Mo**, 0.03 **V**	**Quenched and tempered:** all **diam**, (620) **TS**, (485) **YS**, 16 **El**
ANSI/ASTM A 543	Grade B, class 3	US	Plate	0.23 **C**, 0.40 **Mn**, 0.020 **P**, 0.020 **S**, 0.18–0.37 **Si**, 1.44–2.06 **Cr**, 2.53–3.32 **Ni**, 0.41–0.64 **Mo**, 0.03 **V**	**Quenched and tempered:** all **diam**, (620) **TS**, (485) **YS**, 16 **El**
ANSI/ASTM A 508	Grade 4b	US	Forgings	0.23 **C**, 0.20–0.40 **Mn**, 0.020 **P**, 0.020 **S**, 0.15–0.40 **Si**, 1.50–2.00 **Cr**, 2.75–3.90 **Ni**, 0.40–0.60 **Mo**, 0.03 **V**	**Quenched and tempered:** all **diam**, (620) **TS**, (485) **YS**, 20 **El**
ANSI/ASTM A 541	Grade 7B	US	Forgings	0.23 **C**, 0.20–0.40 **Mn**, 0.035 **P**, 0.040 **S**, 0.30 **Si**, 1.25–2.00 **Cr**, 2.75–3.90 **Ni**, 0.40–0.60 **Mo**, 0.03 **V**	**Quenched and tempered:** all **diam**, (620) **TS**, (480) **YS**, 20 **El**
ANSI/ASTM A 508	Class 4b	US	Forgings	0.23 **C**, 0.20–0.40 **Mn**, 0.020 **P**, 0.020 **S**, 0.15–0.40 **Si**, 1.50–2.00 **Cr**, 2.75–3.90 **Ni**, 0.40–0.60 **Mo**, 0.03 **V**	**Quenched and tempered:** all **diam**, 90 (620) **TS**, 70 (485) **YS**, 20 **El**
ANSI/ASTM A 572	Grade 65	US	Plate, bar, shapes	0.23 **C**, 1.65 **Mn**, 0.04 **P**, 0.05 **S**, 0.30 **Si**	**Hot rolled:** 0.50–1.25 **diam**, (550) **TS**, (450) **YS**, 17 **El**
ANSI/ASTM A 204	Grade C	US	Plate	0.23 **C**, 0.90 **Mn**, 0.04 **P**, 0.04 **S**, 0.13–0.32 **Si**, 0.41–0.64 **Mo**	**As rolled or normalized:** all **diam**, (515) **TS**, (295) **YS**, 20 **El**
BS 1501–221	Grades 32 A, 32 B	UK	Plate	0.23 **C**, 0.90–1.60 **Mn**, 0.050 **P**, 0.050 **S**, 0.10–0.55 **Si**; 0.70 max other elements, total	**Normalized:** (≤16) **diam**, (490) **TS**, (290) **YS**, 45 **El**
BS 1501–211	Grades 32 A, 32 B	UK	Plate	0.23 **C**, 0.90–1.60 **Mn**, 0.050 **P**, 0.050 **S**, 0.55 **Si**; 0.70 max other elements, total	**Normalized:** (≤16) **diam**, (490) **TS**, (290) **YS**, 45 **El**
AS 1548–7	Grade 430	Australia	Plate	0.23 **C**, 0.80–1.60 **Mn**, 0.050 **P**, 0.050 **S**, 0.07–0.60 **Si**	**Normalized:** ≤16 **diam**, (430) **TS**, (275) **YS**, 21 **El**
AS 1750–7	Grade 430	Australia	Bar	0.23 **C**, 0.80–1.60 **Mn**, 0.050 **P**, 0.050 **S**, 0.07–0.60 **Si**	**As rolled or normalized:** ≤25 **diam**, (430) **TS**, (275) **YS**, 21 **El**
IS 5517	Grade 27Mn2	India	Bar, billet	0.22–0.32 **C**, 1.30–1.70 **Mn**, 0.10–0.35 **Si**	**Normalized, annealed or hardened and tempered:** (30) **diam**, (685) **TS**, (490) **YS**
BS S.535		UK	Sheet, strip: aircraft quality	0.22–0.29 **C**, 0.50–0.80 **Mn**, 0.020 **P**, 0.015 **S**, 0.15–0.35 **Si**, 0.90 1.20 **Cr**, 0.30 **Ni**, 0.15–0.25 **Mo**	**Hardened and tempered:** all **diam**, (1160) **TS**, (1005) **YS**, 4 in (<1.5) **El**
BS 2T.60		UK	Tube: aircraft quality	0.22–0.29 **C**, 0.5–0.8 **Mn**, 0.020 **P**, 0.015 **S**, 0.15–0.35 **Si**, 0.9–1.2 **Cr**, 0.30 **Ni**, 0.15–0.25 **Mo**	**Hardened and tempered:** all **diam**, (1150) **TS**, (1050) **YS**, 6 **El**

specification number	designation	country	product forms	composition	mechanical properties (see page iv for explanation)
SIS 14 22 25	SIS 2225–07	Sweden	Bar, tube	0.22–0.29 **C**, 0.50–0.80 **Mn**, 0.025 **P**, 0.020 **S**, 0.15–0.40 **Si**, 0.90–1.20 **Cr**, 0.30 **Ni**, 0.15–0.25 **Mo**	**Quenched and tempered:** (–12) **diam**, (1080) **TS**, (880) **YS**, 8 **El**
AECMA prEN2205		AECMA	Bar	0.22–0.29 **C**, 0.50–0.80 **Mn**, 0.020 **P**, 0.015 **S**, 0.15–0.35 **Si**, 0.90–1.20 **Cr**, 0.30 **Ni**, 0.15–0.25 **Mo**	**Quenched and tempered:** all **diam**, (900) **TS**, (700) **YS**, 12 **El**
AECMA prEN2211		AECMA	Tube: seamless	0.22–0.29 **C**, 0.50–0.80 **Mn**, 0.020 **P**, 0.015 **S**, 0.15–0.35 **Si**, 0.90–1.20 **Cr**, 0.30 **Ni**, 0.15–0.25 **Mo**	**Quenched and tempered:** all **diam**, (900) **TS**, (700) **YS**, 10 **El**
BS 2S.142		UK	Billets, bar, forgings, parts: aircraft quality	0.22–0.29 **C**, 0.50–0.80 **Mn**, 0.020 **P**, 0.015 **S**, 0.15–0.35 **Si**, 0.9–1.2 **Cr**, 0.30 **Ni**, 0.15–0.25 **Mo**	**Hardened and tempered:** (≤40) **diam**, (900) **TS**, (700) **YS**, 12 **El**
AECMA prEN2207	FE–PL 43 S	AECMA	Forgings	0.22–0.29 **C**, 0.50–0.80 **Mn**, 0.020 **P**, 0.015 **S**, 0.15–0.35 **Si**, 0.90–1.20 **Cr**, 0.30 **Ni**, 0.15–0.25 **Mo**	**Hardened and tempered:** all **diam**, (900) **TS**, (700) **YS**, 12 **El**
DIN 17200	Grade 25 CrMo 4	Germany	Blooms, slabs, billets, wire, bar, plate, sheet, strip, tube, forgings	0.22–0.29 **C**, 0.50–0.80 **Mn**, 0.035 **P**, 0.035 **S**, 0.15–0.40 **Si**, 0.90–1.20 **Cr**, 0.15–0.30 **Mo**	**Quenched and tempered:** (≤16) **diam**, (883) **TS**, (687) **YS**, 12 **El**
ISO R 683/II	Type 1	ISO	Bar, billets, rod	0.22–0.29 **C**, 0.50–0.80 **Mn**, 0.035 **P**, 0.035 **S**	**Quenched and tempered:** (≤16) **diam**, (882) **TS**, (686) **YS**, 12 **El**
AIR 9160/C 35	9160C081	France	Bar, forgings	0.22–0.29 **C**, 0.50–0.80 **Mn**, 0.020 **P**, 0.015 **S**, 0.10–0.25 **Si**, 0.90–1.20 **Cr**, 0.30 **Ni**, 0.15–0.25 **Mo**	**Annealed, quenched and tempered:** (<16) **diam**, (880) **TS**, (740) **YS**, 12 **El**
EURONORM 119–74, IV	25 Cr Mo 4 KD	EURONORM	Wire, rod	0.22–0.29 **C**, 0.50–0.80 **Mn**, 0.035 **P**, 0.035 **S**, 0.15–0.40 **Si**, 0.90–1.20 **Cr**, 0.15–0.30 **Mo**	**Quenched and tempered:** (≤16) **diam**, (880) **TS**, (685) **YS**, 12 **El**
BS T.65		UK	Tube: aircraft quality	0.22–0.29 **C**, 0.5–0.8 **Mn**, 0.020 **P**, 0.015 **S**, 0.15–0.35 **Si**, 0.9–1.2 **Cr**, 0.30 **Ni**, 0.15–0.25 **Mo**	**Hardened and tempered:** all **diam**, (880) **TS**, (700) **YS**, 10 **El**
SIS 14 22 25	SIS 2225–05	Sweden	Bar, forgings, plate, sheet, tube	0.22–0.29 **C**, 0.50–0.80 **Mn**, 0.025 **P**, 0.020 **S**, 0.15–0.40 **Si**, 0.90–1.20 **Cr**, 0.30 **Ni**, 0.15–0.25 **Mo**	**Quenched and tempered (plate, sheet, tube):** all **diam**, (880) **TS**, (690) **YS**, 10 **El**
BS S.534		UK	Sheet, strip: aircraft quality	0.22–0.29 **C**, 0.50–0.80 **Mn**, 0.020 **P**, 0.015 **S**, 0.15–0.35 **Si**, 0.90–1.20 **Cr**, 0.30 **Ni**, 0.15–0.25 **Mo**	**Hardened and tempered:** all **diam**, (860) **TS**, (695) **YS**, 8 in (<1.5) **El**
SIS 14 22 25	SIS 2225–04	Sweden	Bar, forgings, tube	0.22–0.29 **C**, 0.50–0.80 **Mn**, 0.025 **P**, 0.020 **S**, 0.15–0.40 **Si**, 0.90–1.20 **Cr**, 0.30 **Ni**, 0.15–0.25 **Mo**	**Quenched and tempered:** all **diam**, (780) **TS**, (590) **YS**, 15 **El**
BS S.158		UK	Bar: aircraft quality	0.22–0.29 **C**, 0.50–0.80 **Mn**, 0.020 **P**, 0.015 **S**, 0.15–0.35 **Si**, 0.9–1.2 **Cr**, 0.30 **Ni**, 0.15–0.25 **Mo**	**Hardened and tempered:** all **diam**, (750) max **TS**
BS 2T.53		UK	Tube: aircraft quality	0.22–0.29 **C**, 0.5–0.8 **Mn**, 0.020 **P**, 0.015 **S**, 0.15–0.35 **Si**, 0.9–1.2 **Cr**, 0.30 **Ni**, 0.15–0.25 **Mo**	**Hardened, normalized, and tempered:** all **diam**, (700) **TS**, (620) **YS**
SIS 14 22 25	SIS 2225–03	Sweden	Bar, forgings	0.22–0.29 **C**, 0.50–0.80 **Mn**, 0.025 **P**, 0.020 **S**, 0.15–0.40 **Si**, 0.90–1.20 **Cr**, 0.30 **Ni**, 0.15–0.25 **Mo**	**Quenched and tempered:** (100) **diam**, (690) **TS**, (490) **YS**, 17 **El**
AECMA prEN2212		AECMA	Plate, sheet, strip	0.22–0.29 **C**, 0.50–0.80 **Mn**, 0.020 **P**, 0.015 **S**, 0.15–0.35 **Si**, 0.90–1.20 **Cr**, 0.30 **Ni**, 0.15–0.25 **Mo**	**Normalized and tempered:** (0.5–3) **diam**, (670) **TS**, (500) max **YS**, 13 **El**
NF A 35–554	25 CD 4 S	France	Plate	0.22–0.29 **C**, 0.50–0.80 **Mn**, 0.030 **P**, 0.025 **S**, 0.10–0.25 **Si**, 0.85–1.15 **Cr**, 0.15–0.30 **Mo**	**Hot rolled, normalized:** (≤16) **diam**, (670) **TS**, (470) **YS**, 13 **El**
AIR 9160/C 37	9160C083	France	Sheet	0.22–0.29 **C**, 0.50–0.80 **Mn**, 0.020 **P**, 0.015 **S**, 0.10–0.25 **Si**, 0.90–1.20 **Cr**, 0.30 **Ni**, 0.15–0.25 **Mo**	**Normalized:** (0.5–12) **diam**, (670) **TS**, (490) **YS**, 13 **El**; **Quenched and tempered:** (0.5–20) **diam**, (880) **TS**, (690) **YS**, 10 **El**

WROUGHT ALLOY STEELS

specification number	designation	country	product forms	composition	mechanical properties (see page iv for explanation)
AIR 9160/C 39	9160C083	France	Tube: seamless	0.22–0.29 **C**, 0.50–0.80 **Mn**, 0.020 **P**, 0.015 **S**, 0.10–0.25 **Si**, 0.90–1.20 **Cr**, 0.30 **Ni**, 0.15–0.25 **Mo**	**Normalized, cold finished, tempered**: (0.5–5) **diam**, (660) **TS**, (490) **YS**, 13 **El**; **Normalized and tempered**: (0.5–3.5) **diam**, (660) **TS**, (490) **YS**, 15 **El**; **Quenched and tempered**: (2–12) **diam**, (880) **TS**, (690) **YS**, 10 **El**
SIS 14 22 25	SIS 2225–01	Sweden	Forgings, plate, sheet, tube	0.22–0.29 **C**, 0.50–0.80 **Mn**, 0.025 **P**, 0.020 **S**, 0.15–0.40 **Si**, 0.90–1.20 **Cr**, 0.30 **Ni**, 0.15–0.25 **Mo**	**Normalized (plate, sheet, tube)**: all **diam**, (660) **TS**, (490) **YS**, 13 **El**
AECMA prEN2206		AECMA	Bar	0.22–0.29 **C**, 0.50–0.80 **Mn**, 0.020 **P**, 0.015 **S**, 0.15–0.35 **Si**, 0.90–1.20 **Cr**, 0.30 **Ni**, 0.15–0.25 **Mo**	**Quenched and tempered**: (≤150) **diam**, (650) **TS**, (480) **YS**, 15 **El**
AECMA prEN2210		AECMA	Tube: seamless	0.22–0.29 **C**, 0.50–0.80 **Mn**, 0.020 **P**, 0.015 **S**, 0.15–0.35 **Si**, 0.90–1.20 **Cr**, 0.30 **Ni**, 0.15–0.25 **Mo**	**Normalized and tempered**: all **diam**, (650) **TS**, (500) **YS**, 15 **El**
AECMA prEN2247		AECMA	Tube: seamless	0.22–0.29 **C**, 0.50–0.80 **Mn**, 0.020 **P**, 0.015 **S**, 0.15–0.35 **Si**, 0.90–1.20 **Cr**, 0.30 **Ni**, 0.15–0.25 **Mo**	**Normalized, drawn and tempered**: all **diam**, (650) **TS**, (520) **YS**, 13 **El**
SFS 458	Co. 25 Cr 1.1 Mo 0.20	Finland	Bar, forgings, tube	0.22–0.29 **C**, 0.50–0.80 **Mn**, 0.035 **P**, 0.035 **S**, 0.15–0.40 **Si**, 0.90–1.20 **Cr**, 0.30 **Ni**, 0.15–0.25 **Mo**	**Quenched and tempered (bar, forgings)**: (120) **diam**, (650) **TS**, (460) **YS**, 17 **El**
AECMA prEN2208	FE–PL 43 S	AECMA	Forgings	0.22–0.29 **C**, 0.50–0.80 **Mn**, 0.020 **P**, 0.015 **S**, 0.15–0.35 **Si**, 0.90–1.20 **Cr**, 0.30 **Ni**, 0.15–0.25 **Mo**	**Hardened and tempered**: ≤150 **diam**, (650) **TS**, (480) **YS**, 15 **El**
SIS 14 22 25	SIS 2225–06	Sweden	Bar, forgings	0.22–0.29 **C**, 0.50–0.80 **Mn**, 0.025 **P**, 0.020 **S**, 0.15–0.40 **Si**, 0.90–1.20 **Cr**, 0.30 **Ni**, 0.15–0.25 **Mo**	**Quenched and tempered**: (100–160) **diam**, (640) **TS**, (410) **YS**, 16 **El**
NF A 35–553	25 CD 4	France	Strip	0.22–0.29 **C**, 0.60–0.90 **Mn**, 0.035 **P**, 0.035 **S**, 0.10–0.40 **Si**, 0.85–1.15 **Cr**, 0.15–0.30 **Mo**	
AISI 8625		US	Plate	0.22–0.29 **C**, 0.60–0.90 **Mn**, 0.035 **P**, 0.040 **S**, 0.15–0.30 **Si**, 0.35–0.60 **Cr**, 0.40–0.70 **Ni**, 0.15–0.25 **Mo**	
SIS 14 22 25	SIS 2225–02	Sweden	Bar, forgings, plate, sheet, tube	0.22–0.29 **C**, 0.50–0.80 **Mn**, 0.025 **P**, 0.020 **S**, 0.15–0.40 **Si**, 0.90–1.20 **Cr**, 0.30 **Ni**, 0.15–0.25 **Mo**	
SIS 14 22 25	SIS 2225–00	Sweden	Bar, forgings, plate, sheet	0.22–0.29 **C**, 0.50–0.80 **Mn**, 0.025 **P**, 0.020 **S**, 0.15–0.40 **Si** 0.90–1.20 **Cr**, 0.30 **Ni**, 0.15–0.25 **Mo**	
BS 970 Part 3	Grade 805 M 25	UK	Blooms, billets, bar, forgings	0.22–0.28 **C**, 0.60–0.95 **Mn**, 0.10–0.35 **Si**, 0.35–0.65 **Cr**, 0.35–0.75 **Ni**, 0.15–0.25 **Mo**	**Hardened**: 0.75 **diam**, (900) **TS**, 9 **El**
BS 970 Part 3	Grade 805 H 25	UK	Blooms, billets, bar, forgings	0.22–0.28 **C**, 0.60–0.95 **Mn**, 0.10–0.35 **Si**, 0.35–0.65 **Cr**, 0.35–0.75 **Ni**, 0.15–0.25 **Mo**	
DGN–B–300	8625 H	Mexico	Bar	0.22–0.28 **C**, 0.60–0.95 **Mn**, 0.040 **P**, 0.035 **S**, 0.20–0.35 **Si**, 0.35–0.65 **Cr**, 0.35–0.75 **Ni**, 0.15–0.25 **Mo**	**Annealed**
ASTM A 689	8625 H	US	Bar	0.22–0.28 **C**, 0.60–0.95 **Mn**, 0.040 **P**, 0.040 **S**, 0.15–0.30 **Si**, 0.35–0.65 **Cr**, 0.35–0.75 **Ni**, 0.15–0.25 **Mo**	
ANSI/ASTM A 304	8625 H	US	Bar	0.22–0.28 **C**, 0.60–0.95 **Mn**, 0.040 **P**, 0.040 **S**, 0.15–0.30 **Si**, 0.35–0.65 **Cr**, 0.35–0.75 **Ni**, 0.15–0.25 **Mo**	
AISI 8625 H		US	Wire, rod	0.22–0.28 **C**, 0.60–0.95 **Mn**, 0.15–0.30 **Si**, 0.35–0.65 **Cr**, 0.35–0.75 **Ni**, 0.15–0.25 **Mo**	

WROUGHT ALLOY STEELS

specification number	designation	country	product forms	composition	mechanical properties (see page iv for explanation)
AISI 8625H		US	Bar	0.22–0.28 **C**, 0.60–0.95 **Mn**, 0.035 **P**, 0.040 **S**, 0.15–0.30 **Si**, 0.35–0.65 **Cr**, 0.35–0.75 **Ni**, 0.15–0.25 **Mo**	
BS 970 Part 3	Grade 665 A 24	UK	Blooms, billets, bar, forgings	0.22–0.27 **C**, 0.45–0.65 **Mn**, 0.25 **Cr**, 1.60–2.00 **Ni**, 0.20–0.30 **Mo**	
BS 970 Part 3	Grade 805 A 24	UK	Blooms, billets, bar, forgings	0.22–0.27 **C**, 0.70–0.90 **Mn**, 0.40–0.60 **Cr**, 0.40–0.70 **Ni**, 0.15–0.25 **Mo**	
MIL–S–22664A	Hy 80	US	Shapes	0.22 **C**, 0.10–0.40 **Mn**, 0.025 **P**, 0.025 **S**, 0.15–0.35 **Si**, 1.35–1.85 **Cr**, 2.50–3.25 **Ni**, 0.30–0.60 **Mo**	**Quenched and tempered**: all **diam**, 95 (655) **TS**, 80 (552) **YS**, 20 **El**
ANSI/ASTM A 678	Grade C	US	Plate	0.22 **C**, 1.00–1.60 **Mn**, 0.040 **P**, 0.050 **S**, 0.20–0.50 **Si**	**Hot rolled, quenched and tempered**: ≤0.75 **diam**, 95 (655) **TS**, 75 (517) **YS**, 19 **El**
SS 14 14 34 E	SS 14 34–06	Sweden	Tube: seamless	0.22 **C**, 0.60–1.00 **Mn**, 0.045 **P**, 0.045 **S**, 0.10–0.40 **Si**, 0.25 **Cr**, 0.30 **Cu**, 0.009 **N**	**Quenched**: all **diam**, (640) **TS**, (260) **YS**, 21 **El**
ANSI/ASTM A 724	Grade A	US	Plate	0.22 **C**, 0.95–1.65 **Mn**, 0.035 **P**, 0.040 **S**, 0.60 **Si**	**Quenched and tempered**: all **diam**, 90 (620) **TS**, 70 (485) **YS**, 19 **El**
ISO 2604/1	F35	ISO	Forgings	0.22 **C**, 0.30–0.80 **Mn**, 0.040 **P**, 0.040 **S**, 0.15–0.40 **Si**, 2.75–3.50 **Cr**, 0.45–0.65 **Mo**	**Normalized and tempered, quenched and tempered**: all **diam**, (590) **TS**, (430) **YS**, 15 **El**
NF A 36–201	E 420, II	France	Sheet, plate	0.22 **C**, 1.60 **Mn**, 0.035 **P**, 0.035 **S**, 0.55 **Si**, 0.80 **Cr**, 0.80 **Ni**, 0.80 **Mo**, 0.80 **Cu**	**Normalized or normalized and tempered**: (5–16) **diam**, (550) **TS**, (420) **YS**, 19 **El**
NF A 36–206	18 MD 4.05	France	Plate	0.22 **C**, 0.90–1.50 **Mn**, 0.035 **P**, 0.035 **S**, 0.10–0.40 **Si**, 0.30 **Cr**, 0.50 **Ni**, 0.35–0.60 **Mo**, 0.04 **V**, 0.25 **Cu**	**Normalized and tempered**: (3.0–30.0) **diam**, (510) **TS**, (345) **YS**, 21 **El**
NF A 36–205	A 52, C1 and P1	France	Sheet, plate	0.22 **C**, 0.90–1.60 **Mn**, 0.05 **P**, 0.05 **S**, 0.60 **Si**	**Normalized**: (3–30) **diam**, (510) **TS**, (335) **YS**, 22 **El**
NF A 36–205	A 52, CR1 and PR1	France	Sheet, plate	0.22 **C**, 0.90–1.60 **Mn**, 0.05 **P**, 0.05 **S**, 0.60 **Si**, 0.35 **Mo**, 0.10 **V**, 0.05 **Nb**	**Normalized**: (3–30) **diam**, (510) **TS**, (335) **YS**, 22 **El**
BS 1501–224	Grade 32	UK	Plate	0.22 **C**, 0.90–1.60 **Mn**, 0.050 **P**, 0.050 **S**, 0.10–0.55 **Si**, 0.70 max other elements, total	**Normalized**: ≤(16) **diam**, (490) **TS**, (325) **YS**, 45 **El**
BS 1501–223	Grade 32	UK	Plate	0.22 **C**, 0.90–1.60 **Mn**, 0.050 **P**, 0.050 **S**, 0.10–0.55 **Si**, 0.01–0.08 **Mo**, 0.70 max other elements, total	**Normalized**: ≤(16) **diam**, (490) **TS**, (340) **YS**, 45 **El**
BS 1501–213	Grade 32	UK	Plate	0.22 **C**, 0.90–1.60 **Mn**, 0.050 **P**, 0.050 **S**, 0.55 **Si**, 0.01–0.08 **Ni**; 0.70 max other elements, total	**Normalized**: (≤16) **diam**, (490) **TS**, (340) **YS**, 45 **El**
SS 14 21 01 E	SS 21 01–15	Sweden	Tube: seamless	0.22 **C**, 0.80–1.50 **Mn**, 0.045 **P**, 0.045 **S**, 0.10–0.50 **Si**, 0.25 **Cr**, 0.30 **Cu**, 0.009 **N**	**As rolled or quenched**: all **diam**, (490) **TS**, (310) **YS**, 21 **El**
SS 14 21 01 E	SS 21 01–05	Sweden	Tube: seamless	0.22 **C**, 0.80–1.50 **Mn**, 0.045 **P**, 0.045 **S**, 0.10–0.50 **Si**, 0.25 **Cr**, 0.30 **Cu**, 0.009 **N**	**As rolled or quenched**: all **diam**, (490) **TS**, (310) **YS**, 21 **El**
SS 14 21 01 E	SS 21 01–06	Sweden	Tube: welded	0.22 **C**, 0.80–1.50 **Mn**, 0.045 **P**, 0.045 **S**, 0.10–0.50 **Si**, 0.25 **Cr**, 0.30 **Cu**, 0.009 **N**	**Quenched**: all **diam**, (490) **TS**, (310) **YS**, 21 **El**
BS 4360	Grade 50D	UK	Plate, section, bar	0.22 **C**, 1.60 **Mn**, 0.050 **P**, 0.050 **S**, 0.10–0.55 **Si**	**Normalized**: (40–63) **diam**, (490) **TS**, (340) **YS**, 20 **El**
BS 4360	Grade 50D1	UK	Plate, section, bar	0.22 **C**, 1.60 **Mn**, 0.050 **P**, 0.050 **S**, 0.10–0.55 **Si**	**Normalized**: (40–63) **diam**, (490) **TS**, 20 **El**
NF A 36–205	A 48, CR1 and PR1	France	Sheet, plate	0.22 **C**, 0.55–1.60 **Mn**, 0.05 **P**, 0.05 **S**, 0.60 **Si**	**Normalized**: (3–30) **diam**, (470) **TS**, (275) **YS**, 23 **El**
ANSI/ASTM A 662	Grade B	US	Plate	0.22 **C**, 0.80–1.55 **Mn**, 0.035 **P**, 0.040 **S**, 0.13–0.33 **Si**	**As rolled or normalized**: all **diam**, 65 (450) **TS**, 40 (275) **YS**, 23 **El**
ISO 4995	HR 355–B	ISO	Sheet	0.22 **C**, 1.60 **Mn**, 0.050 **P**, 0.050 **S**, 0.55 **Si**	**Hot rolled**: (15) **diam**, (450) **TS**, (335) **YS**
MIL–S–872A	Class a	US	Bar, billets, forgings	0.22 **C**, 0.80 **Mn**, 0.040 **P**, 0.040 **S**, 0.15–0.40 **Si**, 0.25 **Cr**, 0.25 **Ni**, 0.40–0.60 **Mo**, 0.35 **Cu**	**Normalized and tempered**: ≤10 **diam**, 65 (448) **TS**, 35 (241) **YS**, 25 **El**

WROUGHT ALLOY STEELS

specification number	designation	country	product forms	composition	mechanical properties (see page iv for explanation)
SS 14 14 34E	SS 14 34–05	Sweden	Tube: seamless	0.22 **C**, 0.60–1.00 **Mn**, 0.045 **P**, 0.045 **S**, 0.10–0.40 **Si**, 0.25 **Cr**, 0.30 **Cu**, 0.009 **N**	**As rolled or quenched:** all **diam**, (440) **TS**, (260) **YS**, 21 **El**
BS 4360	Grade 43C	UK	Plate, section, bar	0.22 **C**, 1.6 **Mn**, 0.060 **P**, 0.060 **S**	**As rolled:** (40–63) **diam**, (430) **TS**, (235) **YS**, 22 **El**
BS 4360	Grade 40C	UK	Plate, sections, bar	0.22 **C**, 1.60 **Mn**, 0.060 **P**, 0.060 **S**	**As rolled:** (40–63) **diam**, (400) **TS**, (220) **YS**, 25 **El**
SFS 1206	A220S	Finland	Bar	0.22 **C**, 1.8 **Mn**, 0.06 **P**, 0.05 **S**, 0.55 **Si**, 0.08 **As**, 0.010 **N**	**Hot rolled:** (6) **diam**, (360) **TS**, (220) **YS**, 20 **El**
SS 14 14 35 E	SS 14 35–05	Sweden	Tube: seamless	0.22 **C**, 0.60–1.00 **Mn**, 0.045 **P**, 0.045 **S**, 0.10–0.40 **Si**, 0.25 **Cr**, 0.30 **Cu**, 0.009 **N**	
AIR 9113/A	25CD4S	France	Forgings, sheet, tube, bar	0.21–0.28 **C**, 0.4–0.8 **Mn**, 0.03 **P**, 0.025 **S**, 0.25 **Si**, 0.8–1.20 **Cr**, 0.30 **Ni**, 0.15–0.30 **Mo**	**Normalized, annealed:** (≤1.5) **diam**, (670) **TS**, (490) **YS**, 13 **El**; **Quenched and tempered:** (≤1.5) **diam**, (880) **TS**, (740) **YS**, 10 **El**
DIN 17115	Grade 24 MnNiCrMo 6 2	Germany	Bar, wire, rod	0.21–0.27 **C**, 1.40–1.70 **Mn**, 0.025 **P**, 0.025 **S**, 0.15–0.35 **Si**, 0.20–0.40 **Cr**, 0.40–0.70 **Ni**, 0.20–0.30 **Mo**, 0.020–0.050 **Al**	**Quenched and tempered:** (≤25) **diam**, (1080) **TS**, (885) **YS**, 10 **El**
AMS 6475D		US	Bar, forgings, tube	0.21–0.26 **C**, 0.50–0.70 **Mn**, 0.025 **P**, 0.025 **S**, 0.20–0.40 **Si**, 1.00–1.25 **Cr**, 3.25–3.75 **Ni**, 0.20–0.30 **Mo**, 1.10–1.40 **Al**, 0.35 **Cu**	**Cold finished (bar):** ≤0.500 (≤12.70) **diam**, 125 (862) max **TS**; **Precipitation heat treatment:** all **diam**, 165 (1138) **TS**, 120 (827) **YS**, 13 **El**
ANSI/ASTM A 203	Grade B	US	Plate	0.21–0.25 **C**, 0.70 **Mn**, 0.04 **P**, 0.04 **S**, 0.13–0.32 **Si**, 2.03–2.57 **Ni**	**Normalized:** 2 **diam**, (485) **TS**, (275) **YS**, 21 **El**
NBN A 25–102	20 Mn Mo 45	Belgium	Tube	0.21 **C**, 1.24 **Mn**, 0.039 **P**, 0.039 **S**, 0.38 **Si**, 0.55 **Cr**, 0.59 **Mo**, 0.63 **Nb**	**Hot or cold finished or normalized or annealed:** all **diam**, (540) **TS**, (390) **YS**, 21 **El**
ANSI/ASTM	Grade 2, class II	US	Plate	0.21 **C**, 0.51–0.84 **Mn**, 0.035 **P**, 0.040 **S**, 0.13–0.32 **Si**, 0.46–0.85 **Cr**, 0.40–0.65 **Mo**	**Annealed or normalized and tempered:** all **diam**, (485) **TS**, (310) **YS**, 22 **El**
JIS G 3213	Class 13 B	Japan	Forgings	0.21 **C**, 0.30–0.80 **Mn**, 0.035 **P**, 0.035 **S**, 0.10–0.60 **Si**, 0.50–0.81 **Cr**, 0.44–0.65 **Mo**	**Annealed or normalized and tempered:** all **diam**, (481) **TS**, (275) **YS**, 20 **El**
JIS G 4109	Class 1	Japan	Plate	0.21 **C**, 0.51–0.84 **Mn**, 0.035 **P**, 0.040 **S**, 0.13–0.32 **Si**, 0.46–0.85 **Cr**, 0.40–0.65 **Mo**	**Hot rolled and annealed:** (8–20) **diam**, (382) **TS**, (226) **YS**, 18 **El**; **Hot rolled, normalized, tempered:** (≤20) **diam**, (481) **TS**, (314) **YS**, 18 **El**
ANSI/ASTM A 387	Grade 2, class I	US	Plate	0.21 **C**, 0.51–0.84 **Mn**, 0.035 **P**, 0.040 **S**, 0.13–0.32 **Si**, 0.46–0.85 **Cr**, 0.40–0.65 **Mo**	**Annealed or normalized and tempered:** all **diam**, (380) **TS**, (230) **YS**, 22 **El**
BS 980	CDS–17	UK	Tube	0.20–0.35 **C**, 0.3–0.7 **Mn**, 0.050 **P**, 0.050 **S**, 0.35 **Si**, 1.0–1.5 **Cr**, 3.5–4.5 **Ni**	**Hardened, tempered:** all **diam**, (1170) **TS**, (1035) **YS**, 5 **El**
BS 5T.2		UK	Tube: aircraft quality	0.20–0.30 **C**, 0.50–0.80 **Mn**, 0.040 **P**, 0.040 **S**, 0.15–0.35 **Si**, 0.5–1.5 **Cr**, 3.0–5.0 **Ni**, 0.25 **Mo**	**Hardened and tempered:** all **diam**, (1300) **TS**, (1200) **YS**, 4 **El**
BS 2T.57		UK	Tube: aircraft quality	0.20–0.30 **C**, 0.50–0.80 **Mn**, 0.040 **P**, 0.040 **S**, 0.15–0.35 **Si**, 0.5–1.5 **Cr**, 3.0–5.0 **Ni**, 0.25 **Mo**	**Hardened and tempered:** all **diam**, (1150) **TS**, (1050) **YS**, 4 **El**
IS 4367	25Cr3Mo[55]	India	Forgings	0.20–0.30 **C**, 0.40–0.70 **Mn**, 0.050 **P**, 0.050 **S**, 0.10–0.35 **Si**, 2.90–3.40 **Cr**, 0.30 **Ni**, 0.45–0.65 **Mo**	**Hardened and tempered:** (100) **diam**, (1078) **TS**, 12 **El**
BS 980	CDS–16	UK	Tube	0.20–0.30 **C**, 0.3–0.7 **Mn**, 0.050 **P**, 0.050 **S**, 0.35 **Si**, 1.0–1.5 **Cr**, 3.5–4.5 **Ni**, 0.20 opt. **Mo**	**Hardened, tempered:** all **diam**, (1035) **TS**, (895) **YS**, 7 **El**
JIS G 4103	Class 2	Japan	Bar	0.20–0.30 **C**, 0.35–0.60 **Mn**, 0.030 **P**, 0.030 **S**, 0.15–0.35 **Si**, 1.00–1.50 **Cr**, 3.00–3.50 **Ni**, 0.15–0.30 **Mo**, 0.30 **Cu**	**Rolled or forged, quenched and tempered:** (25) **diam**, (932) **TS**, (834) **YS**, 18 **El**
AS G18	G18/En 20A	Australia	Bar, billet	0.20–0.30 **C**, 0.40–0.70 **Mn**, 0.050 **P**, 0.050 **S**, 0.10–0.35 **Si**, 0.50–1.00 **Cr**, 0.50–0.80 **Mo**	**Hardened, tempered:** 2 1/2 **diam**, (850) **TS**, (680) **YS**

WROUGHT ALLOY STEELS

specification number	designation	country	product forms	composition	mechanical properties (see page iv for explanation)
AS G18	G18/En 40B	Australia	Bar, billet	0.20–0.30 **C**, 0.40–0.65 **Mn**, 0.050 **P**, 0.050 **S**, 0.10–0.35 **Si**, 2.90–3.50 **Cr**, 0.40 **Ni**, 0.40–0.70 **Mo**	**Hardened, tempered**: 6 **diam**, (690) **TS**, (525) **YS**
NF A 35–564	20 MC 5 FF	France	Bar, wire, rod	0.20–0.30 **C**, 0.030 **P**, 0.030 **S**, 0.30 **Si**, 0.02 min **Al**	**Annealed**: (≤70) **diam**, (590) max **TS**
NF A 35–564	20 NC 6 FF, 19 NCB 6 FF	France	Bar, wire, rod	0.20–0.30 **C**, 0.030 **P**, 0.030 **S**, 0.30 **Si**, 0.020 **Al**	**Annealed**: (≤70) **diam**, (590) max **TS**
AS G18	G18/En 14B	Australia	Bar, billet	0.20–0.30 **C**, 1.30–1.70 **Mn**, 0.060 **P**, 0.060 **S**, 0.10–0.35 **Si**, 0.40 **Ni**	**Normalized**: 6 **diam**, (590) **TS**, (355) **YS**, 17 **El**; **Hardened, tempered**: 4 **diam**, (620) **TS**, (430) **YS**; **Cold drawn**: 2 **diam**, (690) **TS**
AS 1443	AS 1443/K10	Australia	Bar	0.20–0.30 **C**, 1.30–1.70 **Mn**, 0.050 **P**, 0.050 **S**, 0.10–0.35 **Si**	**As rolled or normalized**: (≤150) **diam**, (580) **TS**, (330) **YS**, 16 **El**
AS 1442	Grade AS 1442/K10	Australia	Bar	0.20–0.30 **C**, 1.30–1.70 **Mn**, 0.050 **P**, 0.050 **S**, 0.10–0.35 **Si**	**As rolled or normalized**: (≤150) **diam**, (580) **TS**, (330) **YS**, 16 **El**
NF A 35–564	25 CD 4 FF	France	Bar, wire, rod	0.20–0.30 **C**, 0.030 **P**, 0.030 **S**, 0.30 **Si**, 0.020 **Al**	**Annealed**: (≤70) **diam**, (570) max **TS**
NF A 35–564	20 MB 5 FF	France	Bar, wire, rod	0.20–0.30 **C**, 0.030 **P**, 0.030 **S**, 0.30 **Si**, 0.020 **Al**	**Annealed**: (≤70) **diam**, (560) max **TS**
NF A 35–564	20 NCD 2 FF, 19 NCDB 2 FF	France	Bar, wire, rod	0.20–0.30 **C**, 0.030 **P**, 0.030 **S**, 0.30 **Si**, 0.020 **Al**	**Annealed**: (≤70) **diam**, (560) max **TS**
ANSI/ASTM A 336	Grade F1	US	Forgings	0.20–0.30 **C**, 0.60–0.80 **Mn**, 0.040 **P**, 0.040 **S**, 0.20–0.35 **Si**, 0.40–0.60 **Mo**	**Annealed or normalized and tempered**: all **diam**, (485) **TS**, (275) **YS**, 20 **El**
ASTM A 336	F1	US	Forgings	0.20–0.30 **C**, 0.60–0.80 **Mn**, 0.040 **P**, 0.040 **S**, 0.20–0.35 **Si**, 0.40–0.60 **Mo**	**Normalized**: all **diam**, 70 (485) **TS**, 40 (275) **YS**, 20 **El**
ASTM A 336	F1	US	Forgings	0.20–0.30 **C**, 0.60–0.80 **Mn**, 0.040 **P**, 0.040 **S**, 0.20–0.35 **Si**, 0.40–0.60 **Mo**	**Annealed or normalized, tempered**: all **diam**, 70 (485) **TS**, 40 (275) **YS**, 20 **El**
BS 4S.106		UK	Billets, bar, forgings, parts: aircraft quality	0.20–0.28 **C**, 0.40–0.70 **Mn**, 0.020 **P**, 0.020 **S**, 0.10–0.35 **Si**, 3.0–3.5 **Cr**, 0.30 **Ni**, 0.50–0.70 **Mo**, 0.030	**Solution annealed**: (≤150) **diam**, (930) **TS**, (740) **YS**, 13 **El**
AS G18	G18/En 35	Australia	Bar, billet	0.20–0.28 **C**, 0.30–0.60 **Mn**, 0.050 **P**, 0.050 **S**, 0.10–0.35 **Si**, 1.50–2.00 **Ni**, 0.20–0.30 **Mo**	**Blank carburized, hardened**: all **diam**, (850) **TS**
BS 970 Part 2	Grade 722 M 24	UK	Blooms, billets, bar, forgings	0.20–0.28 **C**, 0.45–0.70 **Mn**, 0.025 **P**, 0.025 **S**, 0.10–0.35 **Si**, 3.00–3.50 **Cr**, 0.45–0.65 **Mo**	**Hardened and tempered**: 10 **diam**, (760) **TS**, (580) **YS**, 13 **El**
DIN 17240	Grade 24 CrMo V 55	Germany	Bar	0.20–0.28 **C**, 0.30–0.60 **Mn**, 0.035 **P**, 0.035 **S**, 0.15–0.35 **Si**, 1.2–1.5 **Cr**, 0.60 **Ni**, 0.50–0.60 **Mo**, 0.15–0.25 **V**	**Rolled, forged or drawn**: all **diam**, (687) **TS**, (539) **YS**, 17 **El**
ISO 2604/1	F31	ISO	Forgings	0.20–0.28 **C**, 0.50–0.80 **Mn**, 0.040 **P**, 0.040 **S**, 0.15–0.40 **Si**, 0.90–1.20 **Cr**, 0.20–0.35 **Mo**, 0.020 $\mathbf{Al_{met}}$	**Quenched and tempered**: all **diam**, (640) **TS**, (410) **YS**, 15 **El**
DIN 17240	Grade 24 CrMo 5	Germany	Bar	0.20–0.28 **C**, 0.50–0.80 **Mn**, 0.035 **P**, 0.035 **S**, 0.15–0.35 **Si**, 0.90–1.2 **Cr**, 0.60 **Ni**, 0.20–0.30 **Mo**	**Rolled, forged or drawn**: all **diam**, (588) **TS**, (310) **YS**, 18 **El**
MIL–S–869C	Class C(N)	US	Bar, billets, forgings	0.20–0.27 **C**, 0.40–0.70 **Mn**, 0.040 **P**, 0.040 **S**, 0.20–0.40 **Si**, 0.95–1.35 **Cr**, 3.25–3.75 **Ni**, 0.20–0.30 **Mo**, 0.85–1.20 **Al**	**Quenched and tempered (bar and forgings)**: ≤3 **diam**, 125 (862) **TS**, 105 (724) **YS**, 19 **El**
DIN 17115	Grade 23 MnNiCrMo 5 2	Germany	Bar, wire, rod	0.20–0.26 **C**, 1.10–1.40 **Mn**, 0.025 **P**, 0.025 **S**, 0.15–0.35 **Si**, 0.40–0.60 **Cr**, 0.40–0.70 **Ni**, 0.20–0.30 **Mo**, 0.020–0.050 **Al**	**Quenched and tempered**: (≤25) **diam**, (1080) **TS**, (885) **YS**, 10 **El**
DIN 17115	Grade 23 MnNiCrMo 6 4	Germany	Bar, wire, rod	0.20–0.26 **C**, 1.40–1.70 **Mn**, 0.020 **P**, 0.020 **S**, 0.15–0.35 **Si**, 0.20–0.40 **Cr**, 0.90–1.10 **Ni**, 0.40–0.55 **Mo**, 0.020–0.050 **Al**	**Quenched and tempered**: (≤25) **diam**, (1080) **TS**, (885) **YS**, 10 **El**

WROUGHT ALLOY STEELS

specification number	designation	country	product forms	composition	mechanical properties (see page iv for explanation)
BS 970 Part 3	Grade 665 M 23	UK	Blooms, billets, bar, forgings	0.20–0.26 **C**, 0.35–0.75 **Mn**, 0.10–0.35 **Si**, 1.50–2.00 **Ni**, 0.20–0.30 **Mo**	**Hardened**: 0.75 **diam**, (830) **TS**, 10 **El**
BS 970 Part 3	Grade 665 H 23	UK	Blooms, billets, bar, forgings	0.20–0.26 **C**, 0.35–0.75 **Mn**, 0.10–0.35 **Si**, 1.50–2.00 **Ni**, 0.20–0.30 **Mo**	
JIS G 4105	Class 24	Japan	Bar	0.20–0.25 **C**, 0.60–0.85 **Mn**, 0.030 **P**, 0.030 **S**, 0.15–0.35 **Si**, 0.90–1.20 **Cr**, 0.25 **Ni**, 0.35–0.45 **Mo**, 0.30 **Cu**	**Rolled or forged, quenched and tempered**: (25) **diam**, (1030) **TS**, 12 **El**
ANSI/ASTM A 437	B4B	US	Bar	0.20–0.25 **C**, 0.50–1.00 **Mn**, 0.025 **P**, 0.025 **S**, 0.15–0.35 **Si**, 11.00–12.50 **Cr**, 0.50–1.00 **Ni**, 0.90–1.25 **Mo**, 0.20–0.30 **V**, 0.05 **Al**	
JIS G 4311	SUH 616	Japan	Bar	0.20–0.25 **C**, 0.50–1.00 **Mn**, 0.50 **Si**, 11.00–13.00 **Cr**, 0.50–1.00 **Ni**, 0.75–1.25 **Mo**, 0.75–1.25 **W**, 0.20–0.30 **V**, 0.040 **P**, 0.030 **S**	**Quenched and tempered**: (≤75) **diam**, (883) **TS**, (735) **YS**, 10 **El**
AS G18	G18/En 35A	Australia	Bar, billet	0.20–0.25 **C**, 0.30–0.60 **Mn**, 0.050 **P**, 0.050 **S**, 0.10–0.35 **Si**, 1.50–2.00 **Ni**, 0.20–0.30 **Mo**	**Blank carburized, hardened**: all **diam**, (850) **TS**
ANSI/ASTM A 437	B4C	US	Bar	0.20–0.25 **C**, 0.50–1.00 **Mn**, 0.025 **P**, 0.025 **S**, 0.15–0.35 **Si**, 11.00–12.50 **Cr**, 0.50–1.00 **Ni**, 0.90–1.25 **Mo**, 0.20–0.30 **V**, 0.05 **Al**, 0.04	
AISI 4023		US	Bar	0.20–0.25 **C**, 0.70–0.90 **Mn**, 0.035 **P**, 0.040 **S**, 0.15–0.30 **Si**, 0.20–0.30 **Mo**	
AISI 4024		US	Bar	0.20–0.25 **C**, 0.70–0.90 **Mn**, 0.035 **P**, 0.035–0.050 **S**, 0.15–0.30 **Si**, 0.20–0.30 **Mo**	
AISI 8622		US	Bar	0.20–0.25 **C**, 0.70–0.90 **Mn**, 0.030 **P**, 0.040 **S**, 0.15–0.30 **Si**, 0.40–0.60 **Cr**, 0.40–0.70 **Ni**, 0.15–0.25 **Mo**	
AISI 8822		US	Bar	0.20–0.25 **C**, 0.75–1.00 **Mn**, 0.035 **P**, 0.040 **S**, 0.15–0.30 **Si**, 0.40–0.60 **Cr**, 0.40–0.70 **Ni**, 0.30–0.40 **Mo**	
BS 970 Part 3	Grade 665 A 22	UK	Blooms, billets, bar, forgings	0.20–0.25 **C**, 0.45–0.65 **Mn**, 0.25 **Cr**, 1.60–2.00 **Ni**, 0.20–0.30 **Mo**	
BS 970 Part 3	Grade 805 A 22	UK	Blooms, billets, bar, forgings	0.20–0.25 **C**, 0.70–0.90 **Mn**, 0.40–0.60 **Cr**, 0.40–0.70 **Ni**, 0.15–0.25 **Mo**	
AMS 6436A		US	Sheet	0.20–0.25 **C**, 0.60–0.90 **Mn**, 0.025 **P**, 0.025 **S**, 0.55–0.75 **Si**, 1.00–1.50 **Cr**, 0.25 **Ni**, 0.40–0.60 **Mo**, 0.75–0.95 **V**, 0.35 **Cu**	
COPANT 334	8822	COPANT	Bar	0.20–0.25 **C**, 0.75–1.00 **Mn**, 0.035 **P**, 0.040 **S**, 0.20–0.35 **Si**, 0.40–0.60 **Cr**, 0.40–0.70 **Ni**, 0.30–0.40 **Mo**	
COPANT 334	23 Cr 4	COPANT	Bar	0.20–0.25 **C**, 0.50–0.80 **Mn**, 0.035 **P**, 0.035 **S**, 0.15–0.35 **Si**, 0.80–1.10 **Cr**	
DGN–B–203	Grade 4422	Mexico	Tube: seamless	0.20–0.25 **C**, 0.70–0.90 **Mn**, 0.040 **P**, 0.040 **S**, 0.20–0.35 **Si**, 0.35–0.45 **Mo**	
DGN–B–203	Grade 4024	Mexico	Tube: seamless	0.20–0.25 **C**, 0.70–0.90 **Mn**, 0.040 **P**, 0.050 **S**, 0.20–0.35 **Si**, 0.20–0.30 **Mo**	
DGN–B–203	Grade 4023	Mexico	Tube: seamless	0.20–0.25 **C**, 0.70–0.90 **Mn**, 0.040 **P**, 0.040 **S**, 0.20–0.35 **Si**, 0.20–0.30 **Mo**	
DGN–B–203	Grade 8822	Mexico	Tube: seamless	0.20–0.25 **C**, 0.75–1.00 **Mn**, 0.040 **P**, 0.040 **S**, 0.20–0.35 **Si**, 0.40–0.60 **Cr**, 0.40–0.70 **Ni**, 0.30–0.40 **Mo**	

specification number	designation	country	product forms	composition	mechanical properties (see page iv for explanation)
DGN–B–203	Grade 8622	Mexico	Tube: seamless	0.20–0.25 **C**, 0.70–0.90 **Mn**, 0.040 **P**, 0.040 **S**, 0.20–0.35 **Si**, 0.40–0.60 **Cr**, 0.40–0.70 **Ni**, 0.15–0.25 **Mo**	
COPANT 514	4422	COPANT	Tube	0.20–0.25 **C**, 0.70–0.90 **Mn**, 0.040 **P**, 0.040 **S**, 0.20–0.35 **Si**, 0.35–0.45 **Mo**	
COPANT 514	4024	COPANT	Tube	0.20–0.25 **C**, 0.70–0.90 **Mn**, 0.040 **P**, 0.050 **S**, 0.20–0.35 **Si**, 0.20–0.30 **Mo**	
COPANT 514	4023	COPANT	Tube	0.20–0.25 **C**, 0.70–0.90 **Mn**, 0.040 **P**, 0.040–0.055 **S**, 0.20–0.35 **Si**, 0.20–0.30 **Mo**	
DGN–B–300	8822	Mexico	Bar	0.20–0.25 **C**, 0.75–1.00 **Mn**, 0.035 **P**, 0.040 **S**, 0.20–0.35 **Si**, 0.40–0.60 **Cr**, 0.40–0.70 **Ni**, 0.30–0.40 **Mo**	**Annealed**
DGN–B–300	8622	Mexico	Bar	0.20–0.25 **C**, 0.70–0.90 **Mn**, 0.35 **P**, 0.040 **S**, 0.20–0.35 **Si**, 0.40–0.60 **Cr**, 0.40–0.70 **Ni**, 0.15–0.25 **Mo**	**Annealed**
DGN–B–300	4023	Mexico	Bar	0.20–0.25 **C**, 0.70–0.90 **Mn**, 0.035 **P**, 0.040 **S**, 0.20–0.35 **Si**, 0.20–0.30 **Mo**	**Annealed**
DGN–B–300	4024	Mexico	Bar	0.20–0.25 **C**, 0.70–0.90 **Mn**, 0.035 **P**, 0.035–0.050 **S**, 0.20–0.35 **Si**, 0.20–0.30 **Mo**	**Annealed**
MIL–S–16974E	No 1023W	US	Bar, billets, blooms, slab	0.20–0.25 **C**, 0.30–0.60 **Mn**, 0.040 **P**, 0.050 **S**, 0.15–0.30 **Si**, 0.15 **Cr**, 0.25 **Ni**, 0.06 **Mo**	
ANSI/ASTM A 29	4422	US	Bar	0.20–0.25 **C**, 0.70–0.90 **Mn**, 0.035 **P**, 0.040 **S**, 0.15–0.30 **Si**, 0.35–0.45 **Mo**	
ANSI/ASTM A 29	4023	US	Bar	0.20–0.25 **C**, 0.70–0.90 **Mn**, 0.035 **P**, 0.040 **S**, 0.15–0.30 **Si**, 0.20–0.30 **Mo**	
ANSI/ASTM A 29	4024	US	Bar	0.20–0.25 **C**, 0.70–0.90 **Mn**, 0.035 **P**, 0.035–0.050 **S**, 0.15–0.30 **Si**, 0.20–0.30 **Mo**	
ASTM A 689	8822	US	Bar	0.20–0.25 **C**, 0.75–1.00 **Mn**, 0.035 **P**, 0.040 **S**, 0.15–0.30 **Si**, 0.40–0.60 **Cr**, 0.40–0.70 **Ni**, 0.30–0.40 **Mo**	
ASTM A 689	8622	US	Bar	0.20–0.25 **C**, 0.70–0.90 **Mn**, 0.035 **P**, 0.040 **S**, 0.15–0.30 **Si**, 0.40–0.70 **Cr**, 0.40–0.60 **Ni**, 0.15–0.25 **Mo**	
ASTM A 689	4023	US	Bar	0.20–0.25 **C**, 0.70–0.90 **Mn**, 0.035 **P**, 0.040 **S**, 0.15–0.30 **Si**, 0.20–0.30 **Mo**	
ASTM A 689	4024	US	Bar	0.20–0.25 **C**, 0.70–0.90 **Mn**, 0.035 **P**, 0.035–0.050 **S**, 0.15–0.30 **Si**, 0.20–0.30 **Mo**	
ANSI/ASTM A 29	8822	US	Bar	0.20–0.25 **C**, 0.75–1.00 **Mn**, 0.035 **P**, 0.040 **S**, 0.15–0.30 **Si**, 0.40–0.60 **Cr**, 0.40–0.70 **Ni**, 0.30–0.40 **Mo**	
ANSI/ASTM A 322	4023	US	Bar	0.20–0.25 **C**, 0.70–0.90 **Mn**, 0.035 **P**, 0.040 **S**, 0.15–0.30 **Si**, 0.20–0.30 **Mo**	
ANSI/ASTM A 322	4024	US	Bar	0.20–0.25 **C**, 0.70–0.90 **Mn**, 0.035 **P**, 0.035–0.050 **S**, 0.15–0.30 **Si**, 0.20–0.30 **Mo**	
ANSI/ASTM A 322	8822	US	Bar	0.20–0.25 **C**, 0.75–1.00 **Mn**, 0.035 **P**, 0.040 **S**, 0.15–0.30 **Si**, 0.40–0.60 **Cr**, 0.40–0.70 **Ni**, 0.30–0.40 **Mo**	
ANSI/ASTM A 322	8622	US	Bar	0.20–0.25 **C**, 0.70–0.90 **Mn**, 0.035 **P**, 0.040 **S**, 0.15–0.30 **Si**, 0.40–0.60 **Cr**, 0.40–0.70 **Ni**, 0.15–0.25 **Mo**	

specification number	designation	country	product forms	composition	mechanical properties (see page iv for explanation)
ANSI/ASTM A 29	8622	US	Bar	0.20–0.25 **C**, 0.70–0.90 **Mn**, 0.035 **P**, 0.040 **S**, 0.15–0.30 **Si**, 0.40–0.60 **Cr**, 0.40–0.70 **Ni**, 0.15–0.25 **Mo**	
AISI 8622		US	Wire, rod	0.20–0.25 **C**, 0.70–0.90 **Mn**, 0.035 **P**, 0.040 **S**, 0.15–0.30 **Si**, 0.40–0.60 **Cr**, 0.40–0.70 **Ni**, 0.15–0.25 **Mo**	
AISI 8822		US	Wire, rod	0.20–0.25 **C**, 0.75–1.00 **Mn**, 0.035 **P**, 0.040 **S**, 0.15–0.30 **Si**, 0.40–0.60 **Cr**, 0.40–0.70 **Ni**, 0.30–0.40 **Mo**	
AISI 4023		US	Wire, rod	0.20–0.25 **C**, 0.70–0.90 **Mn**, 0.035 **P**, 0.040 **S**, 0.15–0.30 **Si**, 0.20–0.30 **Mo**	
AISI 4024		US	Wire, rod	0.20–0.25 **C**, 0.70–0.90 **Mn**, 0.035 **P**, 0.035–0.050 **S**, 0.15–0.30 **Si**, 0.20–0.30 **Mo**	
ANSI/ASTM A 519	4023	US	Tube: seamless	0.20–0.25 **C**, 0.70–0.90 **Mn**, 0.040 **P**, 0.040–0.035 **S**, 0.15–0.35 **Si**, 0.20–0.30 **Mo**	
ANSI/ASTM A 519	4024	US	Tube: seamless	0.20–0.25 **C**, 0.70–0.90 **Mn**, 0.040 **P**, 0.050 **S**, 0.15–0.35 **Si**, 0.20–0.30 **Mo**	
ANSI/ASTM A 519	4422	US	Tube: seamless	0.20–0.25 **C**, 0.70–0.90 **Mn**, 0.040 **P**, 0.040 **S**, 0.15–0.35 **Si**, 0.35–0.45 **Mo**	
ANSI/ASTM A 519	8622	US	Tube: seamless	0.20–0.25 **C**, 0.70–0.90 **Mn**, 0.040 **P**, 0.040 **S**, 0.15–0.35 **Si**, 0.40–0.60 **Cr**, 0.40–0.70 **Ni**, 0.15–0.25 **Mo**	
ANSI/ASTM A 519	8822	US	Tube: seamless	0.20–0.25 **C**, 0.75–1.00 **Mn**, 0.040 **P**, 0.040 **S**, 0.15–0.35 **Si**, 0.40–0.60 **Cr**, 0.40–0.70 **Ni**, 0.30–0.40 **Mo**	
ASTM A 534	4023	US	Bar, wire, tube, rods, billets	0.20–0.25 **C**, 0.70–0.90 **Mn**, 0.035 **P**, 0.040 **S**, 0.20–0.35 **Si**, 0.20–0.30 **Mo**	**As–rolled or normalized and tempered**
DGN–B–297	4023	Mexico	Bar	0.20–0.25 **C**, 0.70–0.90 **Mn**, 0.035 **P**, 0.040 **S**, 0.20–0.35 **Si**, 0.20–0.30 **Mo**	
DGN–B–297	4024	Mexico	Bar	0.20–0.25 **C**, 0.70–0.90 **Mn**, 0.035 **P**, 0.035–0.050 **S**, 0.20–0.35 **Si**, 0.20–0.30 **Mo**	
DGN–B–297	8822	Mexico	Bar	0.20–0.25 **C**, 0.75–1.00 **Mn**, 0.035 **P**, 0.040 **S**, 0.20–0.35 **Si**, 0.40–0.60 **Cr**, 0.40–0.70 **Ni**, 0.30–0.40 **Mo**	
DGN–B–297	8622	Mexico	Bar	0.20–0.25 **C**, 0.70–0.90 **Mn**, 0.035 **P**, 0.040 **S**, 0.20–0.35 **Si**, 0.40–0.60 **Cr**, 0.40–0.70 **Ni**, 0.15–0.25 **Mo**	
COPANT 514	Grade 8622	COPANT	Tube: seamless	0.20–0.25 **C**, 0.70–0.90 **Mn**, 0.040 **P**, 0.050 **S**, 0.10 **Si**, 0.40–0.60 **Cr**, 0.40–0.60 **Ni**, 0.15–0.25 **Mo**	
COPANT 514	Grade 8822	COPANT	Tube: seamless	0.20–0.25 **C**, 0.75–1.00 **Mn**, 0.040 **P**, 0.050 **S**, 0.10 **Si**, 0.40–0.60 **Cr**, 0.40–0.70 **Ni**, 0.30–0.40 **Mo**	
AS G18	G18/En 354	Australia	Bar, billet	0.20 **C**, 0.50–1.00 **Mn**, 0.050 **P**, 0.050 **S**, 0.35 **Si**, 0.75–1.25 **Cr**, 1.50–2.00 **Ni**, 0.10–0.20 **Mo**	**Blank carburized, hardened: all diam**, (1310) **TS**
AS G18	G18/En 355	Australia	Bar, billet	0.20 **C**, 0.40–0.70 **Mn**, 0.050 **P**, 0.050 **S**, 0.35 **Si**, 1.40–1.70 **Cr**, 1.80–2.20 **Ni**, 0.15–0.25 **Mo**	**Blank carburized, hardened: all diam**, (1160) **TS**
ANSI/ASTM A 579	12a	US	Forgings	0.20 **C**, 0.60–0.90 **Mn**, 0.015 **P**, 0.015 **S**, 0.20–0.35 **Si**, 0.40–0.70 **Cr**, 4.75–5.25 **Ni**, 0.30–0.65 **Mo**, 0.05–0.10 **V**	**Quenched and tempered: all diam**, 150 (1045) **TS**, 140 (965) **YS**, 13 **El**
AS G18	G18/En 352	Australia	Bar, billet	0.20 **C**, 0.50–1.00 **Mn**, 0.050 **P**, 0.050 **S**, 0.35 **Si**, 0.60–1.00 **Cr**, 0.85–1.25 **Ni**, 0.10 **Mo**	**Blank carburized, hardened: all diam**, (850) **TS**

WROUGHT ALLOY STEELS

specification number	designation	country	product forms	composition	mechanical properties (see page iv for explanation)
NF A 36–201	E 460,I	France	Sheet, plate	0.20 **C**, 1.70 **Mn**, 0.035 **P**, 0.035 **S**, 0.50 **Si**, 0.02–0.15 **V**, 0.015–0.06 **Nb**	**Normalized or normalized and tempered**: (5–16) **diam**, (590) **TS**, (460) **YS**, 17 **El**
SIS 14 21 08	SIS 21 08–03	Sweden	Forgings, wire, rod	0.20 **C**, 0.9–1.6 **Mn**, 0.04 **P**, 0.04 **S**, 0.5 **Si**, 0.1 **Cr**, 0.2 **Cu**, 0.009 **N**	**Quenched, tempered**: (≤40) **diam**, (590) **TS**, 18 **El**
NF A 35–564	16 MC 5 FF	France	Bar, wire, rod	0.20 **C**, 0.030 **P**, 0.030 **S**, 0.20 **Si**, 0.02 min **Al**	**Annealed**: (≤70) **diam**, (560) max **TS**
NF A 35–564	10 NC 6 FF, 16 NC 6 FF	France	Bar, wire, rod	0.20 **C**, 0.030 **P**, 0.030 **S**, 0.20 **Si**, 0.020 **Al**	**Annealed**: (≤70) **diam**, (560) max **TS**
NF A 36–201	E 420,I	France	Sheet, plate	0.20 **C**, 1.60 **Mn**, 0.035 **P**, 0.035 **S**, 0.50 **Si**, 0.02–0.12 **V**, 0.015–0.06 **Nb**	**Normalized or normalized and tempered**: (5–16) **diam**, (550) **TS**, (420) **YS**, 19 **El**
NF A 35–564	18 CD 4 FF	France	Bar, wire, rod	0.20 **C**, 0.030 **P**, 0.030 **S**, 0.20 **Si**, 0.020 **Al**	**Annealed**: (≤70) **diam**, (550) max **TS**
ANSI/ASTM A 302	Grade B	US	Plate	0.20 **C**, 1.10–1.55 **Mn**, 0.035 **P**, 0.040 **S**, 0.13–0.32 **Si**, 0.41–0.64 **Mo**	**As rolled or normalized**: all **diam**, (550) **TS**, (345) **YS**, 18 **El**
ANSI/ASTM A 302	Grade C	US	Plate	0.20 **C**, 1.10–1.55 **Mn**, 0.035 **P**, 0.040 **S**, 0.13–0.32 **Si**, 0.37–0.73 **Ni**, 0.41–0.64 **Mo**	**As rolled or normalized**: all **diam**, (550) **TS**, (345) **YS**, 20 **El**
ANSI/ASTM A 302	Grade D	US	Plate	0.20 **C**, 1.10–1.55 **Mn**, 0.035 **P**, 0.040 **S**, 0.13–0.32 **Si**, 0.67–1.03 **Ni**, 0.41–0.64 **Mo**	**As rolled or normalized**: all **diam**, (550) **TS**, (345) **YS**, 20 **El**
JIS G 3119	Class 1B, No. 1A	Japan	Plate	0.20 **C**, 1.15–1.50 **Mn**, 0.035 **P**, 0.040 **S**, 0.15–0.30 **Si**, 0.45–0.60 **Mo**	**Hot rolled**: (8–20) **diam**, (549) **TS**, (343) **YS**, 15 **El**
JIS G 3119	Class 2, No. 1A	Japan	Plate	0.20 **C**, 1.15–1.50 **Mn**, 0.035 **P**, 0.040 **S**, 0.15–0.30 **Si**, 0.40–0.70 **Ni**, 0.45–0.60 **Mo**	**Hot rolled**: (8–20) **diam**, (549) **TS**, (343) **YS**, 17 **El**
JIS G 3119	Class 3, No. 1A	Japan	Plate	0.20 **C**, 1.15–1.50 **Mn**, 0.035 **P**, 0.040 **S**, 0.15–0.30 **Si**, 0.70–1.00 **Ni**, 0.45–0.60 **Mo**	**Hot rolled**: (8–20) **diam**, (549) **TS**, (343) **YS**, 17 **El**
ISO 2604/1	F32Q	ISO	Forgings	0.20 **C**, 0.40–0.70 **Mn**, 0.040 **P**, 0.040 **S**, 0.15–0.40 **Si**, 0.85–1.15 **Cr**, 0.45–0.65 **Mo**, 0.020 $\mathbf{Al_{met}}$	**Quenched and tempered**: all **diam**, (540) **TS**, (375) **YS**, 15 **El**
NF A 36–201	E 375, I	France	Sheet, plate	0.20 **C**, 1.50 **Mn**, 0.035 **P**, 0.035 **S**, 0.50 **Si**, 0.015–0.06 **Nb**	**Normalized or normalized and tempered**: (5–16) **diam**, (530) **TS**, (375) **YS**, 21 **El**
SIS 14 21 17	SIS 2117–01	Sweden	Bar, forgings, plate, sheet	0.20 **C**, 1.8 **Mn**, 0.035 **P**, 0.035 **S**, 0.05 **Si**, 0.02 **N**	**Normalized**: all **diam**, (530) **TS**, (490) **YS**, 20 **El**
SIS 14 21 16	SIS 2116–01	Sweden	Bar, forgings, plate, sheet	0.20 **C**, 1.8 **Mn**, 0.035 **P**, 0.035 **S**, 0.05 **Si**, 0.02 **N**	**Normalized**: all **diam**, (530) **TS**, (390) **YS**, 20 **El**
SFS 256	Fe 390	Finland	Structurals	0.20 **C**, 1.00–1.80 **Mn**, 0.035 **P**, 0.035 **S**, 0.55 **Si**, 0.02–0.20 **V**	**Normalized**: (<60) **diam**, (520) **TS**, (390) **YS**, 20 **El**
JIS G 3119	Class 1A, No. 1A	Japan	Plate	0.20 **C**, 0.95–1.30 **Mn**, 0.035 **P**, 0.040 **S**, 0.15–0.30 **Si**, 0.45–0.60 **Mo**	**Hot rolled**: (8–20) **diam**, (520) **TS**, (314) **YS**, 15 **El**
JIS G 3115	Class 3	Japan	Plate	0.20 **C**, 1.60 **Mn**, 0.035 **P**, 0.040 **S**, 0.15–0.55 **Si**	**As rolled**: (≤16) **diam**, (520) **TS**, (353) **YS**, 14 **El**
ANSI/ASTM A 225	Grade B	US	Plate	0.20 **C**, 1.45 **Mn**, 0.04 **P**, 0.04 **S**, 0.13–0.32 **Si**, 0.07–0.16 **V**	**As rolled or normalized or stress relieved**: all **diam**, (515) **TS**, (295) **YS**, 20 **El**
ANSI/ASTM A 302	Grade A	US	Plate	0.20 **C**, 0.90–1.35 **Mn**, 0.035 **P**, 0.040 **S**, 0.13–0.32 **Si**, 0.41–0.64 **Mo**	**As rolled or normalized**: all **diam**, (515) **TS**, (310) **YS**, 19 **El**
NF A 36–206	15 MDV 4.05	France	Plate	0.20 **C**, 0.90–1.50 **Mn**, 0.035 **P**, 0.035 **S**, 0.10–0.40 **Si**, 0.30 **Cr**, 0.50 **Ni**, 0.35–0.60 **Mo**, 0.04–0.10 **V**, 0.25 **Cu**	**Normalized and tempered**: (3.0–30.0) **diam**, (510) **TS**, (345) **YS**, 21 **El**
SIS 14 21 06	SIS 2106–01	Sweden	Bar, forgings, plate, sheet	0.20 **C**, 1.6 **Mn**, 0.035 **P**, 0.035 **S**, 0.05 **Si**, 0.02 **N**	**Normalized**: all **diam**, (510) **TS**, (350) **YS**, 22 **El**
SIS 14 21 07	SIS 2107–01	Sweden	Bar, forgings, plate, sheet	0.20 **C**, 1.6 **Mn**, 0.035 **P**, 0.035 **S**, 0.05 **Si**, 0.02 **N**	**Normalized**: all **diam**, (510) **TS**, (350) **YS**, 22 **El**
NF A 36–208	1.5 Ni (15N6) 355	France	Plate	0.20 **C**, 0.80–1.50 **Mn**, 0.030 **P**, 0.025 **S**, 0.40 **Si**, 1.30–1.70 **Ni**, 0.05 **V**, 0.015 min **Al**	**Normalized, normalized and tempered or quenched and tempered**: (3–30) **diam**, (490) **TS**, (355) **YS**, 22 **El**

WROUGHT ALLOY STEELS

specification number	designation	country	product forms	composition	mechanical properties (see page iv for explanation)
ISO 2604/1	F44	ISO	Forgings	0.20 **C**, 0.80 **Mn**, 0.040 **P**, 0.040 **S**, 0.15–0.40 **Si**, 3.25–3.75 **Ni**, 0.015 min Al_{met}	**Normalized and tempered, quenched and tempered:** all **diam**, (490) **TS**, (275) **YS**, 16 **El**
SIS 14 21 08	SIS 21 08–01	Sweden	Forgings, rod, wire	0.20 **C**, 0.9–1.6 **Mn**, 0.04 **P**, 0.04 **S**, 0.5 **Si**, 0.1 **Cr**, 0.2 **Cu**, 0.009 **N**	**Normalized:** (≤100) **diam**, (490) **TS**, 22 **El**
SS 14 21 01 E	SS 2101–00	Sweden	Bar	0.20 **C**, 0.80–1.60 **Mn**, 0.050 **P**, 0.050 **S**, 0.10–0.50 **Si**, 0.25 **Cr**, 0.30 **Cu**, 0.009 **N**	**As rolled:** (<16) **diam**, (490) **TS**, (310) **YS**, 21 **El**
SS 14 2101 E	SS 2101–01	Sweden	Plate, sheet, bar	0.20 **C**, 0.80–1.60 **Mn**, 0.050 **P**, 0.050 **S**, 0.10–0.50 **Si**, 0.25 **Cr**, 0.30 **Cu**, 0.009 **N**	**Normalized:** all **diam**, (490) **TS**, (310) **YS**, 21 **El**
ISO 2938	Grade 1	ISO	Bar	0.20 **C**, 1.6 **Mn**, 0.045 **P**, 0.045 **S**, 0.50 **Si**	**Hot finished:** (≤16) **diam**, (490) **TS**, (335) **YS**, 21 **El**; **Normalized:** (≤16) **diam**, (490) **TS**, (345) **YS**, 21 **El**
ISO 2604/IV	P16	ISO	Plate	0.20 **C**, 0.90–1.60 **Mn**, 0.050 **P**, 0.050 **S**, 0.10–0.50 **Si**, 0.009 **N**	**Hot rolled, normalized:** (3–16) **diam**, (490) **TS**, (305) **YS**, 21 **El**
ISO 2604/IV	P18	ISO	Plate	0.20 **C**, 0.90–1.60 **Mn**, 0.040 **P**, 0.040 **S**, 0.10–0.50 **Si**, 0.015 min met **Al**	**Hot rolled, normalized:** (3–16) **diam**, (490) **TS**, (315) **YS**, 21 **El**
ANSI/ASTM A 203	Grade E	US	Plate	0.20 **C**, 0.70 **Mn**, 0.04 **P**, 0.04 **S**, 0.13–0.32 **Si**, 3.18–3.82 **Ni**	**Normalized:** <2 **diam**, (485) **TS**, (275) **YS**, 21 **El**
ANSI/ASTM A 204	Grade B	US	Plate	0.20 **C**, 0.90 **Mn**, 0.04 **P**, 0.04 **S**, 0.13–0.32 **Si**, 0.41–0.64 **Mo**	**As rolled or normalized:** all **diam**, (485) **TS**, (275) **YS**, 21 **El**
ASTM A 350	LF3	US	Forgings	0.20 **C**, 0.90 **Mn**, 0.035 **P**, 0.040 **S**, 0.20–0.35 **Si**, 3.25–3.75 **Ni**	**Normalized or normalized, tempered:** all **diam**, 70 (483) **TS**, 37 (259) **YS**, 22 **El**
JIS G 3103	Class 6	Japan	Plate	0.20 **C**, 0.90 **Mn**, 0.035 **P**, 0.040 **S**, 0.15–0.30 **Si**, 0.45–0.60 **Mo**	**Hot rolled:** (≤25) **diam**, (481) **TS**, (275) **YS**, 17 **El**
NF A 36-208	1.5 Ni (15N6) 285	France	Plate	0.20 **C**, 0.30–0.70 **Mn**, 0.030 **P**, 0.025 **S**, 0.40 **Si**, 1.30–1.70 **Ni**, 0.05 **V**, 0.015 min **Al**	**Normalized, normalized and tempered or quenched and tempered:** (3–30) **diam**, (470) **TS**, (285) **YS**, 23 **El**
NF A 36–206	15 CD 4.05	France	Plate	0.20 **C**, 0.40–0.85 **Mn**, 0.035 **P**, 0.035 **S**, 0.10–0.40 **Si**, 0.75–1.25 **Cr**, 0.30 **Ni**, 0.40–0.60 **Mo**, 0.04 **V**, 0.25 **Cu**	**Normalized and tempered:** (3–30) **diam**, (470) **TS**, (295) **YS**, 23 **El**
BS 1501–213	Grade 30	UK	Plate	0.20 **C**, 0.90–1.60 **Mn**, 0.050 **P**, 0.050 **S**, 0.55 **Si**, 0.01–0.08 **Nb**, 0.70 max other elements, total	**Normalized:** (≤16) **diam**, (460) **TS**, (315) **YS**, 45 **El**
NF A 36–206	15 CD 2.05	France	Plate	0.20 **C**, 0.45–0.95 **Mn**, 0.035 **P**, 0.035 **S**, 0.10–0.35 **Si**, 0.35–0.65 **Cr**, 0.30 **Ni**, 0.40–0.60 **Mo**, 0.04 **V**, 0.25 **Cu**	**Normalized and tempered:** (3–30) **diam**, (450) **TS**, (275) **YS**, 25 **El**
NBN 629	16 Mo 5	Belgium	Strip	0.20 **C**, 0.50–0.90 **Mn**, 0.040 **P**, 0.040 **S**, 0.15–0.35 **Si**, 0.45–0.65 **Mo**	**Temper pass:** (3–40) **diam**, (450) **TS**, (285) **YS**, 23 **El**
ISO 4995	HR 355–D	ISO	Sheet	0.20 **C**, 1.60 **Mn**, 0.040 **P**, 0.040 **S**, 0.55 **Si**	**Hot rolled:** (15) **diam**, (450) **TS**, (335) **YS**
COPANT 512	BT9	COPANT	Tube	0.20 **C**, 0.40–1.06 **Mn**, 0.045 **P**, 0.050 **S**, 1.60–2.24 **Ni**, 0.75–1.25 **Cu**	**Normalized, normalized and tempered or quenched and tempered:** (≥8) **diam**, (435) **TS**, (315) **YS**, 25 **El**
ASTM A 350	LF9	US	Forgings	0.20 **C**, 0.40–1.06 **Mn**, 0.035 **P**, 0.040 **S**, 0.20–0.35 **Si**, 1.60–2.24 **Ni**, 0.75–1.25 **Cu**	**Normalized or normalized, tempered:** all **diam**, 63 (434) **TS**, 46 (317) **YS**, 25 **El**
ANSI/ASTM A 334	Grade 9	US	Tube: seamless, welded	0.20 **C**, 0.40–1.06 **Mn**, 0.045 **P**, 0.050 **S**, 1.60–2.24 **Ni**, 0.75–1.25 **Cu**	**Normalized:** 0.312 (7.94) **diam**, 63 (434) **TS**, 46 (317) **YS**, 28 **El**
ANSI/ASTM A 333	Grade 9	US	Pipe: seamless, welded	0.20 **C**, 0.40–1.06 **Mn**, 0.045 **P**, 0.050 **S**, 1.60–2.24 **Ni**, 0.75–1.25 **Cu**	**Normalized:** 0.312 (7.94) **diam**, 63 (434) **TS**, 46 (317) **YS**, 28 **El**
DGN–B–197	Grade 9	Mexico	Tube: seamless, welded	0.20 **C**, 0.40–1.06 **Mn**, 0.045 **P**, 0.050 **S**, 1.60–2.24 **Ni**, 0.75–1.25 **Cu**	**Hot or cold finished and normalized:** (7.92) **diam**, (431) **TS**, (314) **YS**, 35 **El**

WROUGHT ALLOY STEELS

specification number	designation	country	product forms	composition	mechanical properties (see page iv for explanation)
NF A 36–206	15 D 3	France	Plate	0.20 **C**, 0.45–0.85 **Mn**, 0.040 **P**, 0.035 **S**, 0.10–0.35 **Si**, 0.30 **Cr**, 0.30 **Ni**, 0.25–0.40 **Mo**, 0.04 **V**, 0.25 **Cu**	**Normalized and tempered:** (3.0–30.0) **diam**, (430) **TS**, (265) **YS**, 25 **El**
NBN 629	16 Mo 3	Belgium	Strip	0.20 **C**, 0.50–0.90 **Mn**, 0.040 **P**, 0.040 **S**, 0.15–0.35 **Si**, 0.25–0.35 **Mo**	**Temper pass:** (3–40) **diam**, (430) **TS**, (275) **YS**, 24 **El**
SIS 14 14 30 E	SIS 14 30–00	Sweden	Bar, plate, sheet	0.20 **C**, 0.50–1.10 **Mn**, 0.050 **P**, 0.050 **S**, 0.40 **Si**, 0.25 **Cr**, 0.30 **Cu**, 0.009 **N**	**As rolled:** (<40) **diam**, (430) **TS**, (260) **YS**, 24 **El**
SIS 14 14 30 E	SIS 14 30–01	Sweden	Bar, plate, sheet	0.20 **C**, 0.40–1.00 **Mn**, 0.05 **P**, 0.050 **S**, 0.40 **Si**, 0.25 **Cr**, 0.30 **Cu**, 0.009 **N**	**Normalized:** all **diam**, (430) **TS**, (260) **YS**, 24 **El**
SIS 14 14 30 E	SIS 14 30–00	Sweden	Bar	0.20 **C**, 0.40–1.00 **Mn**, 0.050 **P**, 0.050 **S**, 0.40 **Si**, 0.25 **Cr**, 0.30 **Cu**, 0.009 **N**	**As rolled:** (<40) **diam**, (430) **TS**, (260) **YS**, 24 **El**
ISO 2604/1	F32	ISO	Forgings	0.20 **C**, 0.40–0.70 **Mn**, 0.040 **P**, 0.040 **S**, 0.15–0.40 **Si**, 0.85–1.15 **Cr**, 0.45–0.65 **Mo**, 0.020 $\mathbf{Al}_{met}$	**Normalized and tempered, quenched and tempered:** all **diam**, (410) **TS**, (255) **YS**, 18 **El**
JIS G 3114	Class 1A	Japan	Plate, shape	0.20 **C**, 1.40 **Mn**, 0.040 **P**, 0.040 **S**, 0.35 **Si**, 0.20–0.65 **Cr**, 0.20–0.60 **Cu**	**Hot rolled:** (≤16) **diam**, (402) **TS**, (245) **YS**, 18 **El**
JIS G 3114	Class 1B	Japan	Plate, shape	0.20 **C**, 1.40 **Mn**, 0.040 **P**, 0.040 **S**, 0.35 **Si**, 0.20–0.65 **Cr**, 0.20–0.60 **Cu**	**Hot rolled:** (≤16) **diam**, (402) **TS**, (245) **YS**, 18 **El**
JIS G 3114	Class 1C	Japan	Plate	0.20 **C**, 1.40 **Mn**, 0.040 **P**, 0.040 **S**, 0.35 **Si**, 0.20–0.65 **Cr**, 0.20–0.60 **Cu**	**Hot rolled:** (≤16) **diam**, (402) **TS**, (245) **YS**, 18 **El**
BS 980	CDS–18	UK	Tube	0.20 **C**, 1.0 **Mn**, 0.050 **P**, 0.050 **S**, 1.0 **Si**, 12.0–14.0 **Cr**, 1.0 **Ni**	**Annealed:** all **diam**, (385) **TS**, (250) **YS**
MIL–S–21952B	HY–100	US	Bar: for ships	0.20 **C**, 0.10–0.40 **Mn**, 0.025 **P**, 0.025 **S**, 0.15–0.35 **Si**, 1.00–1.80 **Cr**, 2.00–3.25 **Ni**, 0.20–0.60 **Mo**	**Quenched and tempered, austenitized:** all **diam**, (689) **YS**, 18 **El**
MIL–S–22958A	Grade HY–100	US	Shapes: structural	0.20 **C**, 0.10–0.40 **Mn**, 0.025 **P**, 0.025 **S**, 0.15–0.35 **Si**, 1.00–1.80 **Cr**, 2.25–3.50 **Ni**, 0.20–0.60 **Mo**, 0.03 **V**, 0.25 **Cu**, 0.02 **Ti**	**Hot rolled, quenched and drawn:** <5/8 **diam**, 100 (690) **YS**, 18 **El**
MIL–S–23009A	Hy 100	US	Forgings	0.20 **C**, 0.10–0.40 **Mn**, 0.025 **P**, 0.025 **S**, 0.15–0.35 **Si**, 1.00–1.80 **Cr**, 2.25–3.50 **Ni**, 0.20–0.60 **Mo**	**Quenched and tempered:** all **diam**, 80 (552) **YS**, 20 **El**
SIS 14 21 08	SIS 21 08–02	Sweden	Rod, wire	0.20 **C**, 0.9–1.6 **Mn**, 0.04 **P**, 0.04 **S**, 0.5 **Si**, 0.1 **Cr**, 0.1 **Cr**, 0.2 **Cu**, 0.009 **N**	**Soft annealed**
SIS 14 21 08	SIS 21 08–00	Sweden	Forgings, rod, wire	0.20 **C**, 0.9–1.6 **Mn**, 0.04 **P**, 0.04 **S**, 0.5 **Si**, 0.1 **Cr**, 0.2 **Cu**, 0.009 **N**	
BS 970 Part 3	Grade 805 M 22	UK	Blooms, billets, bar, forgings	0.19–0.25 **C**, 0.60–0.95 **Mn**, 0.10–0.35 **Si**, 0.35–0.65 **Cr**, 0.35–0.75 **Ni**, 0.15–0.25 **Mo**	**Hardened:** 0.75 **diam**, (830) **TS**, 10 **El**
JIS G 3539	SWCH 24K	Japan	Wire	0.19–0.25 **C**, 1.35–1.65 **Mn**, 0.030 **P**, 0.035 **S**, 0.10–0.35 **Si**	**Annealed and cold drawn:** all **diam**, (471) **TS**, 12 **El**
BS 970 Part 3	Grade 805 H 22	UK	Blooms, billets, bar, forgings	0.19–0.25 **C**, 0.60–0.95 **Mn**, 0.10–0.35 **Si**, 0.35–0.65 **Cr**, 0.35–0.75 **Ni**, 0.15–0.25 **Mo**	
AS 1444	Grade AS 1444/4622H	Australia	Bar, bloom, billet, slab	0.19–0.25 **C**, 0.60–1.00 **Mn**, 0.040 **P**, 0.040 **S**, 0.10–0.35 **Si**, 1.55–2.00 **Ni**, 0.20–0.30 **Mo**	
AS 1444	Grade AS 1444/8622H	Australia	Bar, bloom, billet, slab	0.19–0.25 **C**, 0.60–0.95 **Mn**, 0.040 **P**, 0.040 **S**, 0.10–0.35 **Si**, 0.35–0.65 **Cr**, 0.35–0.75 **Ni**, 0.15–0.25 **Mo**	
DGN–B–300	8622 H	Mexico	Bar	0.19–0.25 **C**, 0.60–0.95 **Mn**, 0.040 **P**, 0.035 **S**, 0.20–0.35 **Si**, 0.35–0.65 **Cr**, 0.35–0.75 **Ni**, 0.15–0.25 **Mo**	**Annealed**
DGN–B–300	8822 H	Mexico	Bar	0.19–0.25 **C**, 0.70–1.05 **Mn**, 0.040 **P**, 0.035 **S**, 0.20–0.35 **Si**, 0.35–0.65 **Cr**, 0.35–0.75 **Ni**, 0.30–0.40 **Mo**	**Annealed**

specification number	designation	country	product forms	composition	mechanical properties (see page iv for explanation)
ANSI/ASTM A 29	1524	US	Bar	0.19–0.25 **C**, 1.35–1.65 **Mn**, 0.040 **P**, 0.050 **S**	
ANSI/ASTM A 545	Grade 1524	US	Wire	0.19–0.25 **C**, 1.35–1.65 **Mn**, 0.040 **P**, 0.050 **S**	
ASTM	8622 H	US	Bar	0.19–0.25 **C**, 0.60–0.95 **Mn**, 0.040 **P**, 0.040 **S**, 0.15–0.30 **Si**, 0.35–0.65 **Cr**, 0.35–0.75 **Ni**, 0.15–0.25 **Mo**	
ANSI/ASTM A 304	8622 H	US	Bar	0.19–0.25 **C**, 0.60–0.95 **Mn**, 0.040 **P**, 0.040 **S**, 0.15–0.30 **Si**, 0.35–0.65 **Cr**, 0.35–0.75 **Ni**, 0.15–0.25 **Mo**	
ANSI/ASTM A 304	8822 H	US	Bar	0.19–0.25 **C**, 0.70–1.05 **Mn**, 0.040 **P**, 0.040 **S**, 0.15–0.30 **Si**, 0.35–0.65 **Cr**, 0.35–0.75 **Ni**, 0.30–0.40 **Mo**	
AISI 8622		US	Plate	0.19–0.25 **C**, 0.60–0.90 **Mn**, 0.035 **P**, 0.040 **S**, 0.15–0.30 **Si**, 0.35–0.60 **Cr**, 0.40–0.70 **Ni**, 0.15–0.25 **Mo**	
AISI 8622 H		US	Wire, rod	0.19–0.25 **C**, 0.60–0.95 **Mn**, 0.15–0.30 **Si**, 0.35–0.65 **Cr**, 0.35–0.75 **Ni**, 0.15–0.25 **Mo**	
AISI 8822 H		US	Wire, rod	0.19–0.25 **C**, 0.70–1.05 **Mn**, 0.15–0.30 **Si**, 0.35–0.65 **Cr**, 0.35–0.75 **Ni**, 0.30–0.40 **Mo**	
AISI 8822H		US	Bar	0.19–0.25 **C**, 0.70–1.05 **Mn**, 0.035 **P**, 0.040 **S**, 0.15–0.30 **Si**, 0.35–0.65 **Cr**, 0.35–0.75 **Ni**, 0.30–0.40 **Mo**	
AISI 8622H		US	Bar	0.19–0.25 **C**, 0.60–0.95 **Mn**, 0.035 **P**, 0.040 **S**, 0.15–0.30 **Si**, 0.3–0.65 **Cr**, 0.35–0.75 **Ni**, 0.15–0.25 **Mo**	
AISI 1524		US	Wire, rod	0.19–0.25 **C**, 1.35–1.65 **Mn**, 0.040 **P**, 0.050 **S**	
ASTM A 689	1524	US	Bar	0.19–0.25 **C**, 1.35–1.65 **Mn**, 0.040 **P**, 0.050 **S**	
ANSI/ASTM A 576	1524	US	Bar	0.19–0.25 **C**, 1.35–1.65 **Mn**, 0.040 **P**, 0.050 **S**	
ANSI/ASTM A 576	1524	US	Bar	0.19–0.25 **C**, 1.35–1.65 **Mn**, 0.040 **P**, 0.050 **S**	
JIS G 4052	SCM 24H	Japan	Bar, wire, rod	0.19–0.25 **C**, 0.55–0.90 **Mn**, 0.030 **P**, 0.030 **S**, 0.15–0.35 **Si**, 0.85–1.25 **Cr**, 0.35–0.45 **Mo**, 0.30 **Cu**	**Hot rolled, normalized, quenched**
JIS G 3507	SWRCH 24K	Japan	Wire, rod	0.19–0.25 **C**, 1.35–1.65 **Mn**, 0.030 **P**, 0.035 **S**, 0.10–0.35 **Si**	
JIS G 3114	Class 3	Japan	Plate	0.19 **C**, 1.40 **Mn**, 0.040 **P**, 0.040 **S**, 0.75 **Si**, 0.30–1.20 **Cr**, 0.20–0.70 **Cu**	**Hot rolled:** (≤16) **diam**, (569) **TS**, (461) **YS**, 19 **El**
JIS G 3114	Class 2A	Japan	Plate, shape	0.19 **C**, 1.40 **Mn**, 0.040 **P**, 0.040 **S**, 0.75 **Si**, 0.30–1.20 **Cr**, 0.20–0.70 **Cu**	**Hot rolled:** (≤16) **diam**, (490) **TS**, (363) **YS**, 15 **El**
JIS G 3114	Class 2B	Japan	Plate, shape	0.19 **C**, 1.40 **Mn**, 0.040 **P**, 0.040 **S**, 0.75 **Si**, 0.30–1.20 **Cr**, 0.20–0.70 **Cu**	**Hot rolled:** (≤16) **diam**, (490) **TS**, (363) **YS**, 15 **El**
JIS G 3114	Class 2C	Japan	Plate	0.19 **C**, 1.40 **Mn**, 0.040 **P**, 0.040 **S**, 0.75 **Si**, 0.30–1.20 **Cr**, 0.20–0.70 **Cu**	**Hot rolled:** (≤16) **diam**, (490) **TS**, (363) **YS**, 15 **El**
DGN–B–197	Grade 3	Mexico	Tube: seamless, welded	0.19 **C**, 0.31–0.64 **Mn**, 0.05 **P**, 0.05 **S**, 0.18–0.37 **Si**, 3.18–3.82 **Ni**	**Hot or cold finished and normalized:** (7.92) **diam**, (470) **TS**, (245) **YS**, 30 **El**
DGN–B–180	Grade 7	Mexico	Pipe	0.19 **C**, 0.90 **Mn**, 0.04 **P**, 0.05 **S**, 0.13–0.32 **Si**, 2.03–2.57 **Ni**	**Normalized or normalized and quenched:** (≥8) **diam**, (451) **TS**, (245) **YS**, 30 **El**
DGN–B–180	Grade 3	Mexico	Pipe: seamless or welded	0.19 **C**, 0.31–0.64 **Mn**, 0.05 **P**, 0.05 **S**, 0.18–0.37 **Si**, 3.18–3.82 **Ni**	**Normalized or normalized and quenched:** (≥8) **diam**, (451) **TS**, (245) **YS**, 30 **El**
DGN–B–197	Grade 7	Mexico	Tube: seamless, welded	0.19 **C**, 0.90 **Mn**, 0.04 **P**, 0.05 **S**, 0.13–0.32 **Si**, 2.03–2.57 **Ni**	**Hot or cold finished and normalized:** (7.92) **diam**, (451) **TS**, (245) **YS**, 30 **El**

WROUGHT ALLOY STEELS

specification number	designation	country	product forms	composition	mechanical properties (see page iv for explanation)
ANSI/ASTM A 334	Grade 7	US	Tube: seamless, welded	0.19 **C**, 0.90 **Mn**, 0.04 **P**, 0.05 **S**, 0.13–0.32 **Si**, 2.03–2.57 **Ni**	**Normalized**: 0.312 (7.94) **diam**, 65 (448) **TS**, 35 (241) **YS**, 30 **El**
ANSI/ASTM A 334	Grade 3	US	Tube: seamless, welded	0.19 **C**, 0.31–0.64 **Mn**, 0.05 **P**, 0.05 **S**, 0.18–0.37 **Si**, 3.18–3.82 **Ni**	**Normalized**: 0.312 (7.94) **diam**, 65 (448) **TS**, 35 (241) **YS**, 30 **El**
ANSI/ASTM A 333	Grade 7	US	Pipe: seamless, welded	0.19 **C**, 0.90 **Mn**, 0.04 **P**, 0.05 **S**, 0.13–0.32 **Si**, 2.03–2.57 **Ni**	**Normalized**: 0.312 (7.94) **diam**, 65 (448) **TS**, 35 (241) **YS**, 30 **El**
ANSI/ASTM A 333	Grade 3	US	Pipe: seamless, welded	0.19 **C**, 0.31–0.64 **Mn**, 0.05 **P**, 0.05 **S**, 0.18–0.37 **Si**, 3.18–3.82 **Ni**	**Normalized**: 0.312 (7.94) **diam**, 65 (448) **TS**, 35 (241) **YS**, 30 **El**
COPANT 512	BT7	COPANT	Tube	0.19 **C**, 0.90 **Mn**, 0.04 **P**, 0.05 **S**, 0.13–0.32 **Si**, 2.03–2.57 **Ni**	**Normalized, normalized and tempered or quenched and tempered**: (≥8) **diam**, (445) **TS**, (240) **YS**, 30 **El**
COPANT 512	BT3	COPANT	Tube	0.19 **C**, 0.31–0.64 **Mn**, 0.05 **P**, 0.05 **S**, 0.18–0.37 **Si**, 3.18–3.82 **Ni**	**Normalized, normalized and tempered or quenched and tempered**: (≥8) **diam**, (445) **TS**, (240) **YS**, 30 **El**
BS 4360	Grade 43E	UK	Plate, section, bar	0.19 **C**, 1.60 **Mn**, 0.050 **P**, 0.050 **S**, 0.10–0.55 **Si**	**Normalized**: (40–63) **diam**, (430) **TS**, (255) **YS**, 22 **El**
BS 4360	Grade 43D	UK	Plate, section, bar	0.19 **C**, 1.60 **Mn**, 0.050 **P**, 0.050 **S**	**Normalized**: (40–63) **diam**, (430) **TS**, (255) **YS**, 22 **El**
BS 4360	Grade 40D	UK	Plate, sections, bar	0.19 **C**, 1.60 **Mn**, 0.060 **P**, 0.060 **S**	**Normalized**: (40–63) **diam**, (400) **TS**, (240) **YS**, 25 **El**
BS 4360	Grade 40E	UK	Plate, section, bar	0.19 **C**, 1.60 **Mn**, 0.050 **P**, 0.050 **S**, 0.10–0.55 **Si**	**Normalized**: (40–63) **diam**, (400) **TS**, (240) **YS**, 25 **El**
IS 6286	Grade 3	India	Pipe	0.19 **C**, 0.90 **Mn**, 0.04 **P**, 0.05 **S**, 0.13–0.32 **Si**, 2.03–2.57 **Ni**	**Annealed**: all **diam**, (395) **TS**, (215) **YS**
AS G18	G18/En 55	Australia	Bar, billet	0.18–0.45 **C**, 1.00 **Mn**, 0.045 **P**, 0.045 **S**, 1.00–2.50 **Si**, 17.0 min **Cr**, 6.00–12.0 **Ni**, 2.00–4.00 **W**	
BS 2S. 92		UK	Bar, billets, forgings: aircraft quality	0.18–0.26 **C**, 1.3–1.7 **Mn**, 0.040 **P**, 0.045 **S**, 0.10–0.35 **Si**, 0.25 **Cr**, 0.40 **Ni**, 0.10 **Mo**	**Hardened and tempered**: all **diam**, (620) **TS**, (495) **YS**, 15 **El**
AISI 1524H		US	Wire, rod	0.18–0.26 **C**, 1.25–1.75 **Mn**, 0.040 **P**, 0.050 **S**, 0.15–0.30 **Si**	
ISO 2604/1	F29	ISO	Forgings	0.18–0.25 **C**, 0.50–0.80 **Mn**, 0.040 **P**, 0.040 **S**, 0.15–0.40 **Si**, 0.45–0.65 **Mo**, 0.012 $\mathbf{Al}_{\mathbf{met}}$	**Normalized and tempered, quenched and tempered**: all **diam**, (450) **TS**, (275) **YS**, 16 **El**
ISO 2604/1	F27	ISO	Forgings	0.18–0.25 **C**, 0.50–0.80 **Mn**, 0.040 **P**, 0.040 **S**, 0.15–0.40 **Si**, 0.25–0.35 **Mo**, 0.012 $\mathbf{Al}_{\mathbf{met}}$	**Normalized and tempered, quenched and tempered**: all **diam**, (440) **TS**, (250) **YS**, 17 **El**
ASTM A 689	8822 H	US	Bar	0.18–0.25 **C**, 0.70–1.05 **Mn**, 0.040 **P**, 0.040 **S**, 0.15–0.30 **Si**, 0.35–0.65 **Cr**, 0.35–0.75 **Ni**, 0.30–0.40 **Mo**	
DIN 17115	Grade 21 MnSi 5	Germany	Bar, wire, rod	0.18–0.24 **C**, 1.10–1.60 **Mn**, 0.040 **P**, 0.040 **S**, 0.30–0.55 **Si**, 0.020–0.050 **Al**	**Quenched and tempered**: (≤16) **diam**, (980) **TS**, (785) **YS**, 8 **El**
SIS 14 25 12	SIS 25 12–03	Sweden	Bar, forgings	0.18–0.23 **C**, 0.70–1.10 **Mn**, 0.035 **P**, 0.030–0.050 **S**, 0.15–0.40 **Si**, 0.60–1.00 **Cr**, 0.80–1.20 **Ni**, 0.10 **Mo**	**Case hardened, quenched, annealed**: (11) **diam**, (1080) **TS**, (740) **YS**, 8 **El**
JIS G 4105	Class 22	Japan	Bar	0.18–0.23 **C**, 0.60–0.85 **Mn**, 0.030 **P**, 0.030 **S**, 0.15–0.35 **Si**, 0.90–1.20 **Cr**, 0.25 **Ni**, 0.15–0.30 **Mo**, 0.30 **Cu**	**Rolled or forged, quenched and tempered**: (25) **diam**, (932) **TS**, 14 **El**
AMS 6274H		US	Bar, forgings, tube	0.18–0.23 **C**, 0.75–1.00 **Mn**, 0.025 **P**, 0.025 **S**, 0.20–0.35 **Si**, 0.40–0.60 **Cr**, 0.40–0.70 **Ni**, 0.15–0.25 **Mo**, 0.35 **Cu**	**Cold finished (bar)**: ≤0.500 (≤12.70) **diam**, 130 (896) max **TS**
AMS 6276D		US	Bar, forgings, tube	0.18–0.23 **C**, 0.70–1.00 **Mn**, 0.015 **P**, 0.015 **S**, 0.20–0.35 **Si**, 0.40–0.60 **Cr**, 0.40–0.70 **Ni**, 0.15–0.25 **Mo**, 0.35 **Cu**	**Cold finished (bar)**: ≤0.500 (≤12.70) **diam**, 125 (862) max **TS**
AMS 6277B		US	Bar, forgings, tube	0.18–0.23 **C**, 0.70–1.00 **Mn**, 0.015 **P**, 0.15 **S**, 0.20–0.35 **Si**, 0.40–0.60 **Cr**, 0.40–0.70 **Ni**, 0.15–0.25 **Mo**, 0.35 **Cu**	**Cold finished (bar)**: ≤0.500 (≤12.70) **diam**, 125 (862) max **TS**

WROUGHT ALLOY STEELS

specification number	designation	country	product forms	composition	mechanical properties (see page iv for explanation)
AS G18	G18/En 362	Australia	Bar, billet	0.18–0.23 **C**, 0.70–1.00 **Mn**, 0.050 **P**, 0.050 **S**, 0.35 **Si**, 0.55–0.80 **Cr**, 0.40–0.70 **Ni**, 0.08–0.15 **Mo**	**Blank carburized, hardened**: all **diam**, (850) **TS**
JIS G 4104	Class 22	Japan	Bar	0.18–0.23 **C**, 0.60–0.85 **Mn**, 0.030 **P**, 0.030 **S**, 0.15–0.35 **Si**, 0.90–1.20 **Cr**, 0.25 **Ni**, 0.30 **Cu**	**Rolled or forged, quenched and tempered**: (25) **diam**, (834) **TS**, 14 **El**
NBN A 21–221	C 20 B KD	Belgium	Wire	0.18–0.23 **C**, 0.70–1.30 **Mn**, 0.035 **P**, 0.035 **S**, 0.15–0.40 **Si**, 0.2–0.4 **Cr**, 0.001–0.005 **B**	**Quenched and tempered**: (≤10) **diam**, (780) **TS**, (735) **YS**, 14 **El**
DGN–B–203	Grade 4118	Mexico	Tube: seamless	0.18–0.23 **C**, 0.70–0.90 **Mn**, 0.040 **P**, 0.040 **S**, 0.20–0.35 **Si**, 0.40–0.60 **Cr**, 0.08–0.15 **Mo**	**Hot finished**: all **diam**, (343) **TS**, (245) **YS**, 25 **El**; **Cold finished**: all **diam**, (520) **TS**, (412) **YS**, 5 **El**; **Stress relieved**: all **diam**, (539) **TS**, (480) **YS**, 8 **El**; **Tempered**: all **diam**, (343) **TS**, (206) **YS**, 25 **El**; **Normalized**: all **diam**, (382) **TS**, (245) **YS**, 20 **El**
AISI 4118		US	Bar	0.18–0.23 **C**, 0.70–0.90 **Mn**, 0.035 **P**, 0.040 **S**, 0.15–0.30 **Si**, 0.40–0.60 **Cr**, 0.08–0.15 **Mo**	
AISI 4820		US	Bar	0.18–0.23 **C**, 0.50–0.70 **Mn**, 0.035 **P**, 0.040 **S**, 0.15–0.30 **Si**, 3.25–3.75 **Ni**, 0.20–0.30 **Mo**	
AISI 8620		US	Bar	0.18–0.23 **C**, 0.70–0.90 **Mn**, 0.035 **P**, 0.040 **S**, 0.15–0.30 **Si**, 0.40–0.60 **Cr**, 0.40–0.70 **Ni**	
AISI 8720		US	Bar	0.18–0.23 **C**, 0.70–0.90 **Mn**, 0.035 **P**, 0.040 **S**, 0.15–0.30 **Si**, 0.40–0.60 **Cr**, 0.40–0.70 **Ni**, 0.20–0.30 **Mo**	
NF A 35–553	20 NCD 2	France	Strip	0.18–0.23 **C**, 0.70–0.90 **Mn**, 0.035 **P**, 0.035 **S**, 0.10–0.40 **Si**, 0.40–0.60 **Cr**, 0.40–0.70 **Ni**, 0.15–0.30 **Mo**	
BS 970 Part 3	Grade 805 A 20	UK	Blooms, billets, bar, forgings	0.18–0.23 **C**, 0.70–0.90 **Mn**, 0.40–0.60 **Cr**, 0.40–0.70 **Ni**, 0.15–0.25 **Mo**	
COPANT 334	8720	COPANT	Bar	0.18–0.23 **C**, 0.70–0.90 **Mn**, 0.035 **P**, 0.040 **S**, 0.20–0.35 **Si**, 0.40–0.60 **Cr**, 0.40–0.70 **Ni**, 0.20–0.30 **Mo**	
MIL–S–8690B	8620	US	Bar	0.18–0.23 **C**, 0.70–1.00 **Mn**, 0.025 **P**, 0.025 **S**, 0.20–0.35 **Si**, 0.40–0.60 **Cr**, 0.40–0.70 **Ni**, 0.15–0.25 **Mo**, 0.35 **Cu**	
AS 1444	Grade AS 1444/8620	Australia	Bar, bloom, billet, slab	0.18–0.23 **C**, 0.70–0.90 **Mn**, 0.040 **P**, 0.040 **S**, 0.10–0.35 **Si**, 0.40–0.60 **Cr**, 0.40–0.70 **Ni**, 0.15–0.25 **Mo**	
AS 1446	Grade AS 1446/XK1320	Australia	Plate	0.18–0.23 **C**, 1.40–1.70 **Mn**, 0.050 **P**, 0.050 **S**, 0.10–0.35 **Si**	
DGN–B–203	Grade 4820	Mexico	Tube: seamless	0.18–0.23 **C**, 0.50–0.70 **Mn**, 0.040 **P**, 0.040 **S**, 0.20–0.35 **Si**, 3.25–3.75 **Ni**, 0.20–0.30 **Mo**	
DGN–B–203	Grade 4621	Mexico	Tube: seamless	0.18–0.23 **C**, 0.70–0.90 **Mn**, 0.040 **P**, 0.040 **S**, 0.20–0.35 **Si**, 1.65–2.00 **Ni**, 0.20–0.30 **Mo**	
DGN–B–203	Grade 4520	Mexico	Tube: seamless	0.18–0.23 **C**, 0.45–0.65 **Mn**, 0.040 **P**, 0.040 **S**, 0.20–0.35 **Si**, 0.45–0.65 **Mo**	
DGN–B–203	Grade 8720	Mexico	Tube: seamless	0.18–0.23 **C**, 0.70–0.90 **Mn**, 0.040 **P**, 0.040 **S**, 0.20–0.35 **Si**, 0.40–0.60 **Cr**, 0.40–0.70 **Ni**, 0.20–0.30 **Mo**	
DGN–B–203	Grade 8620	Mexico	Tube: seamless	0.18–0.23 **C**, 0.70–0.90 **Mn**, 0.040 **P**, 0.040 **S**, 0.20–0.35 **Si**, 0.40–0.60 **Cr**, 0.40–0.70 **Ni**, 0.15–0.25 **Mo**	
COPANT 514	4621	COPANT	Tube	0.18–0.23 **C**, 0.70–0.90 **Mn**, 0.040 **P**, 0.040 **S**, 0.20–0.35 **Si**, 1.65–2.0 **Ni**, 0.20–0.30 **Mo**	

specification number	designation	country	product forms	composition	mechanical properties (see page iv for explanation)
COPANT 514	4520	COPANT	Tube	0.18–0.23 **C**, 0.45–0.65 **Mn**, 0.040 **P**, 0.040 **S**, 0.20–0.35 **Si**, 0.45–0.60 **Mo**	
COPANT 514	4118	COPANT	Tube	0.18–0.23 **C**, 0.70–0.90 **Mn**, 0.040 **P**, 0.040 **S**, 0.20–0.35 **Si**, 0.40–0.60 **Cr**, 0.08–0.15 **Mo**	
DGN–B–300	8720	Mexico	Bar	0.18–0.23 **C**, 0.70–0.90 **Mn**, 0.035 **P**, 0.040 **S**, 0.20–0.35 **Si**, 0.40–0.60 **Cr**, 0.40–0.70 **Ni**, 0.20–0.30 **Mo**	**Annealed**
DGN–B–300	8620	Mexico	Bar	0.18–0.23 **C**, 0.70–0.90 **Mn**, 0.035 **P**, 0.040 **S**, 0.20–0.35 **Si**, 0.40–0.60 **Cr**, 0.40–0.70 **Ni**, 0.15–0.25 **Mo**	**Annealed**
DGN–B–300	4820	Mexico	Bar	0.18–0.23 **C**, 0.50–0.70 **Mn**, 0.035 **P**, 0.040 **S**, 0.20–0.35 **Si**, 3.25–3.75 **Ni**, 0.20–0.30 **Mo**	**Annealed**
DGN–B–300	4621	Mexico	Bar	0.18–0.23 **C**, 0.70–0.90 **Mn**, 0.035 **P**, 0.040 **S**, 0.20–0.35 **Si**, 1.65–2.00 **Ni**, 0.20–0.30 **Mo**	**Annealed**
DGN–B–300	4419	Mexico	Bar	0.18–0.23 **C**, 0.45–0.65 **Mn**, 0.035 **P**, 0.040 **S**, 0.20–0.35 **Si**, 0.45–0.60 **Mo**	**Annealed**
ANSI/ASTM A 29	4621	US	Bar	0.18–0.23 **C**, 0.70–0.90 **Mn**, 0.035 **P**, 0.040 **S**, 0.15–0.30 **Si**, 1.65–2.00 **Ni**, 0.20–0.30 **Mo**	
ANSI/ASTM A 29	4820	US	Bar	0.18–0.23 **C**, 0.50–0.70 **Mn**, 0.035 **P**, 0.040 **S**, 0.15–0.30 **Si**, 3.25–3.75 **Ni**, 0.20–0.30 **Mo**	
ANSI/ASTM A 29	4118	US	Bar	0.18–0.23 **C**, 0.70–0.90 **Mn**, 0.035 **P**, 0.040 **S**, 0.15–0.30 **Si**, 0.40–0.60 **Cr**, 0.08–0.15 **Mo**	
ANSI/ASTM A 29	4419	US	Bar	0.18–0.23 **C**, 0.45–0.65 **Mn**, 0.035 **P**, 0.040 **S**, 0.15–0.30 **Si**, 0.45–0.60 **Mo**	
ANSI/ASTM A 646	8620	US	Blooms, billets: aircraft quality	0.18–0.23 **C**, 0.70–0.90 **Mn**, 0.025 **P**, 0.025 **S**, 0.20–0.35 **Si**, 0.40–0.60 **Cr**, 0.40–0.70 **Ni**, 0.15–0.25 **Mo**	**Annealed**
MIL–S–16974E	No 8620	US	Bar, billets, blooms, slabs	0.18–0.23 **C**, 0.70–0.90 **Mn**, 0.040 **P**, 0.040 **S**, 0.20–0.35 **Si**, 0.40–0.60 **Cr**, 0.40–0.70 **Ni**, 0.15–0.25 **Mo**	
MIL–S–16974E	No TS8620	US	Bar, billets, blooms, slabs	0.18–0.23 **C**, 0.70–0.90 **Mn**, 0.040 **P**, 0.040 **S**, 0.20–0.35 **Si**, 0.55–0.75 **Cr**, 0.30–0.60 **Ni**, 0.08–0.15 **Mo**	
MIL–S–16974E	No 1320	US	Bar, billets, blooms, slabs	0.18–0.23 **C**, 1.60–1.90 **Mn**, 0.040 **P**, 0.040 **S**, 0.20–0.35 **Si**	
ASTM A 689	8720	US	Bar	0.18–0.23 **C**, 0.70–0.90 **Mn**, 0.035 **P**, 0.040 **S**, 0.15–0.30 **Si**, 0.40–0.60 **Cr**, 0.40–0.70 **Ni**, 0.20–0.30 **Mo**	
ASTM A 689	8620	US	Bar	0.18–0.23 **C**, 0.70–0.90 **Mn**, 0.035 **P**, 0.040 **S**, 0.15–0.30 **Si**, 0.40–0.60 **Cr**, 0.40–0.70 **Ni**, 0.15–0.25 **Mo**	
ASTM A 689	4820	US	Bar	0.18–0.23 **C**, 0.50–0.70 **Mn**, 0.035 **P**, 0.040 **S**, 0.15–0.30 **Si**, 3.25–3.75 **Ni**, 0.20–0.30 **Mo**	
ASTM A 689	4118	US	Bar	0.18–0.23 **C**, 0.70–0.90 **Mn**, 0.035 **P**, 0.040 **S**, 0.15–0.30 **Si**, 0.40–0.60 **Cr**, 0.08–0.15 **Mo**	
ASTM A 689	4419	US	Bar	0.18–0.23 **C**, 0.45–0.65 **Mn**, 0.035 **P**, 0.040 **S**, 0.15–0.30 **Si**, 0.45–0.60 **Mo**	
ASTM A 689	4621	US	Bar	0.18–0.23 **C**, 0.70–0.90 **Mn**, 0.035 **P**, 0.040 **S**, 0.15–0.30 **Si**, 1.65–2.00 **Ni**, 0.20–0.30 **Mo**	
ANSI/ASTM A 322	4621	US	Bar	0.18–0.23 **C**, 0.70–0.90 **Mn**, 0.035 **P**, 0.040 **S**, 0.15–0.30 **Si**, 1.65–2.00 **Ni**, 0.20–0.30 **Mo**	

WROUGHT ALLOY STEELS

specification number	designation	country	product forms	composition	mechanical properties (see page iv for explanation)
ANSI/ASTM A 322	4820	US	Bar	0.18–0.23 **C**, 0.50–0.70 **Mn**, 0.035 **P**, 0.040 **S**, 0.15–0.30 **Si**, 3.25–3.75 **Ni**, 0.20–0.30 **Mo**	
ANSI/ASTM A 322	4118	US	Bar	0.18–0.23 **C**, 0.70–0.90 **Mn**, 0.035 **P**, 0.040 **S**, 0.15–0.30 **Si**, 0.40–0.60 **Cr**, 0.08–0.15 **Mo**	
ANSI/ASTM A 322	4419	US	Bar	0.18–0.23 **C**, 0.45–0.65 **Mn**, 0.035 **P**, 0.040 **S**, 0.15–0.30 **Si**, 0.45–0.60 **Mo**	
ANSI/ASTM A 322	8720	US	Bar	0.18–0.23 **C**, 0.70–0.90 **Mn**, 0.035 **P**, 0.040 **S**, 0.15–0.30 **Si**, 0.40–0.60 **Cr**, 0.40–0.70 **Ni**, 0.20–0.30 **Mo**	
ANSI/ASTM A 322	8620	US	Bar	0.18–0.23 **C**, 0.70–0.90 **Mn**, 0.035 **P**, 0.040 **S**, 0.15–0.30 **Si**, 0.40–0.60 **Cr**, 0.40–0.70 **Ni**, 0.15–0.25 **Mo**	
ANSI/ASTM A 29	8620	US	Bar	0.18–0.23 **C**, 0.70–0.90 **Mn**, 0.035 **P**, 0.040 **S**, 0.15–0.30 **Si**, 0.40–0.60 **Cr**, 0.40–0.70 **Ni**, 0.15–0.25 **Mo**	
ANSI/ASTM A 29	8720	US	Bar	0.18–0.23 **C**, 0.70–0.90 **Mn**, 0.035 **P**, 0.040 **S**, 0.15–0.30 **Si**, 0.40–0.60 **Cr**, 0.40–0.70 **Ni**, 0.20–0.30 **Mo**	
AISI 8620		US	Wire, rod	0.18–0.23 **C**, 0.70–0.90 **Mn**, 0.035 **P**, 0.040 **S**, 0.15–0.30 **Si**, 0.40–0.60 **Cr**, 0.40–0.70 **Ni**, 0.15–0.25 **Mo**	
AISI 8720		US	Wire, rod	0.18–0.23 **C**, 0.70–0.90 **Mn**, 0.035 **P** 0.040 **S**, 0.15–0.30 **Si**, 0.40–0.60 **Cr**, 0.40–0.70 **Ni**, 0.20–0.30 **Mo**	
AISI 4118		US	Wire, rod	0.18–0.23 **C**, 0.70–0.90 **Mn**, 0.035 **P**, 0.040 **S**, 0.15–0.30 **Si**, 0.40–0.60 **Cr**, 0.08–0.15 **Mo**	
AISI 4419		US	Wire, rod	0.18–0.23 **C**, 0.45–0.65 **Mn**, 0.035 **P**, 0.040 **S**, 0.15–0.30 **Si**, 0.45–0.60 **Mo**	
AISI 4621		US	Wire, rod	0.18–0.23 **C**, 0.70–0.90 **Mn**, 0.035 **P**, 0.040 **S**, 0.15–0.30 **Si**, 1.65–2.00 **Ni**, 0.20–0.30 **Mo**	
AISI 4820		US	Wire, rod	0.18–0.23 **C**, 0.50–0.70 **Mn**, 0.035 **P**, 0.040 **S**, 0.15–0.30 **Si**, 3.25–3.75 **Ni**, 0.20–0.30 **Mo**	
ANSI/ASTM A 519	4118	US	Tube: seamless	0.18–0.23 **C**, 0.70–0.90 **Mn**, 0.040 **P**, 0.040 **S**, 0.15–0.35 **Si**, 0.40–0.60 **Cr**, 0.08–0.15 **Mo**	
ANSI/ASTM A 519	4520	US	Tube: seamless	0.18–0.23 **C**, 0.45–0.65 **Mn**, 0.040 **P**, 0.040 **S**, 0.15–0.35 **Si**, 0.45–0.60 **Mo**	
ANSI/ASTM A 519	4621	US	Tube: seamless	0.18–0.23 **C**, 0.70–0.90 **Mn**, 0.040 **P**, 0.040 **S**, 0.15–0.35 **Si**, 1.65–2.00 **Ni**, 0.20–0.30 **Mo**	
ANSI/ASTM A 519	4820	US	Tube: seamless	0.18–0.23 **C**, 0.50–0.70 **Mn**, 0.040 **P**, 0.040 **S**, 0.15–0.35 **Si**, 3.25–3.75 **Ni**, 0.20–0.30 **Mo**	
ANSI/ASTM A 519	8620	US	Tube: seamless	0.18–0.23 **C**, 0.70–0.90 **Mn**, 0.040 **P**, 0.040 **S**, 0.15–0.35 **Si**, 0.40–0.60 **Cr**, 0.40–0.70 **Ni**, 0.15–0.25 **Mo**	
ANSI/ASTM A 519	8720	US	Tube: seamless	0.18–0.23 **C**, 0.70–0.90 **Mn**, 0.040 **P**, 0.040 **S**, 0.15–0.35 **Si**, 0.40–0.60 **Cr**, 0.40–0.70 **Ni**, 0.20–0.30 **Mo**	
DGN–B–297	4419	Mexico	Bar	0.18–0.23 **C**, 0.45–0.65 **Mn**, 0.035 **P**, 0.040 **S**, 0.20–0.35 **Si**, 0.45–0.60 **Mo**	
ANSI/ASTM A 535	4820	US	Billets, coils, bar, rod, tube	0.18–0.23 **C**, 0.50–0.70 **Mn**, 0.015 **P**, 0.015 **S**, 0.20–0.35 **Si**, 3.25–3.75 **Ni**, 0.20–0.30 **Mo**	

WROUGHT ALLOY STEELS

specification number	designation	country	product forms	composition	mechanical properties (see page iv for explanation)
ANSI/ASTM A 535	8620	US	Billets, coils, bar, rod, tube	0.18–0.23 **C**, 0.70–0.90 **Mn**, 0.015 **P**, 0.015 **S**, 0.20–0.35 **Si**, 0.40–0.60 **Cr**, 0.40–0.70 **Ni**, 0.15–0.25 **Mo**	
ASTM A 534	4118	US	Bar, wire, tube, rods, billets	0.18–0.23 **C**, 0.70–0.90 **Mn**, 0.035 **P**, 0.040 **S**, 0.20–0.35 **Si**, 0.40–0.60 **Cr**, 0.08–0.15 **Mo**	**As-rolled or normalized and tempered**
ASTM A 534	8620	US	Bar, wire, tube, rods, billets	0.18–0.23 **C**, 0.70–0.90 **Mn**, 0.035 **P**, 0.040 **S**, 0.20–0.35 **Si**, 0.40–0.60 **Cr**, 0.40–0.70 **Ni**, 0.15–0.25 **Mo**	**As-rolled or normalized and tempered**
SIS 14 25 12	SIS 25 12–02	Sweden	Bar, forgings	0.18–0.23 **C**, 0.70–1.10 **Mn**, 0.035 **P**, 0.030–0.050 **S**, 0.15–0.40 **Si**, 0.60–1.00 **Cr**, 0.80–1.20 **Ni**, 0.10 **Mo**	**Annealed**
SIS 14 25 12	SIS 25 12–00	Sweden	Bar, forgings	0.18–0.23 **C**, 0.70–1.10 **Mn**, 0.035 **P**, 0.030–0.050 **S**, 0.15–0.40 **Si**, 0.60–1.00 **Cr**, 0.80–1.20 **Ni**, 0.10 **Mo**	**As rolled or as forged**
AS 1442	Grade AS 1442/XK 1320	Australia	Bar, blooms, billets, slabs	0.18–0.23 **C**, 1.40–1.70 **Mn**, 0.050 **P**, 0.050 **S**, 0.10–0.35 **Si**	
AS 1443	Grade AS 1443/XK 1320	Australia	Bar	0.18–0.23 **C**, 1.40–1.70 **Mn**, 0.050 **P**, 0.050 **S**, 0.10–0.35 **Si**	
DGN–B–297	4621	Mexico	Bar	0.18–0.23 **C**, 0.70–0.90 **Mn**, 0.035 **P**, 0.040 **S**, 0.20–0.35 **Si**, 1.65–2.00 **Ni**, 0.20–0.30 **Mo**	
DGN–B–297	4820	Mexico	Bar	0.18–0.23 **C**, 0.50–0.70 **Mn**, 0.035 **P**, 0.040 **S**, 0.20–0.35 **Si**, 3.25–3.75 **Ni**, 0.20–0.30 **Mo**	
DGN–B–297	8620	Mexico	Bar	0.18–0.23 **C**, 0.70–0.90 **Mn**, 0.035 **P**, 0.040 **S**, 0.20–0.35 **Si**, 0.40–0.60 **Cr**, 0.40–0.70 **Ni**, 0.15–0.25 **Mo**	
DGN–B–297	4118	Mexico	Bar	0.18–0.23 **C**, 0.70–0.90 **Mn**, 0.035 **P**, 0.040 **S**, 0.20–0.35 **Si**, 0.40–0.60 **Cr**, 0.08–0.15 **Mo**	
COPANT 514	Grade 4820	COPANT	Tube: seamless	0.18–0.23 **C**, 0.50–0.70 **Mn**, 0.040 **P**, 0.050 **S**, 0.10 **Si**, 3.25–3.75 **Ni**, 0.20–0.30 **Mo**	
COPANT 514	Grade 8620	COPANT	Tube: seamless	0.18–0.23 **C**, 0.70–0.90 **Mn**, 0.040 **P**, 0.050 **S**, 0.10 **Si**, 0.40–0.60 **Cr**, 0.40–0.70 **Ni**, 0.15–0.25 **Mo**	
COPANT 514	Grade 8720	COPANT	Tube: seamless	0.18–0.23 **C**, 0.70–0.90 **Mn**, 0.040 **P**, 0.050 **S**, 0.10 **Si**, 0.40–0.60 **Cr**, 0.40–0.70 **Ni**, 0.20–0.30 **Mo**	
NF A 36–201	E 375,III	France	Sheet, plate	0.18–0.20 **C**, 1.50 **Mn**, 0.03 **P**, 0.03 **S**, 0.50 **Si**, 0.80 **Cr**, 0.80 **Ni**, 0.80 **Mo**, 0.80 **Cu**	**Normalized or normalized and tempered:** (5–16) **diam**, (530) **TS**, (375) **YS**, 21 **El**
NF A 36–204	E 690	France	Plate	0.18 **C**, 1.60 **Mn**, 0.030 **P**, 0.030 **S**, 0.10–0.50 **Si**	**Normalized and tempered, quenched and tempered or aged:** (5–50) **diam**, (790) **TS**, (690) **YS**, 14 **El**
NF A 36–204	E 620, II	France	Plate	0.18 **C**, 1.60 **Mn**, 0.025 **P**, 0.025 **S**, 0.10–0.50 **Si**	**Normalized and tempered, quenched and tempered or aged:** (5–50) **diam**, (740) **TS**, (620) **YS**, 15 **El**
ANSI/ASTM A 372	Class VI	US	Forgings	0.18 **C**, 0.10–0.40 **Mn**, 0.025 **P**, 0.025 **S**, 0.15–0.35 **Si**, 1.00–1.80 **Cr**, 2.00–3.25 **Ni**, 0.20–0.60 **Mo**	**Liquid quenched and tempered:** all **diam**, (690) **TS**, (550) **YS**, 20 **El**
ASTM A 372	Class VI	US	Forgings	0.18 **C**, 0.10–0.40 **Mn**, 0.025 **P**, 0.025 **S**, 0.15–0.35 **Si**, 1.00–1.80 **Cr**, 2.00–3.25 **Ni**, 0.20–0.60 **Mo**	**Quenched, tempered:** all **diam**, 100 (690) **TS**, 80 (550) **YS**, 20 **El**
JIS G 3115	Class 5	Japan	Plate	0.18 **C**, 1.60 **Mn**, 0.035 **P**, 0.040 **S**, 0.15–0.75 **Si**, 0.45 **C** + Mn/6 + Si/24 + Ni/40 + Cr/5 + Mo/4 + V/14	**Quenched and tempered:** (≤16) **diam**, (608) **TS**, (490) **YS**, 18 **El**
NF A 36–201	E 460,II	France	Sheet, plate	0.18 **C**, 1.70 **Mn**, 0.035 **P**, 0.035 **S**, 0.40 **Si**, 0.70 **Cr**, 0.2–0.7 **Ni**, 0.70 **Mo**, 0.70 **Cu**	**Normalized or normalized and tempered:** (5–16) **diam**, (590) **TS**, (460) **YS**, 17 **El**

WROUGHT ALLOY STEELS

specification number	designation	country	product forms	composition	mechanical properties (see page iv for explanation)
JIS G 3115	Class 4	Japan	Plate	0.18 **C**, 1.60 **Mn**, 0.035 **P**, 0.040 **S**, 0.15–0.75 **Si**, 0.44 **C+Mn/6+Si/24+Ni/40+Cr/5+Mo/4+V/14**	**Quenched and tempered:** (≤16) **diam**, (569) **TS**, (451) **YS**, 19 **El**
ANSI/ASTM A 541	Class 4	US	Forgings	0.18 **C**, 1.30 **Mn**, 0.035 **P**, 0.040 **S**, 0.15–0.25 **Si**, 0.15 **Cr**, 05 **Ni**, 0.05 **Mo**, 0.02–0.12 **V**	**Quenched and tempered:** all **diam**, 80 (550) **TS**, 50 (340) **YS**, 18 **El**
ANSI/ASTM A 541	Grade 4	US	Forgings	0.18 **C**, 1.30 **Mn**, 0.035 **P**, 0.040 **S**, 0.15–0.35 **Si**, 0.15 **Cr**, 0.25 **Ni**, 0.05 **Mo**, 0.02–0.12 **V**	**Quenched and tempered:** all **diam**, (550) **TS**, (340) **YS**, 18 **El**
NF A 36-201	A 375 II	France	Sheet, plate	0.18 **C**, 1.50 **Mn**, 0.035 **P**, 0.035 **S**, 0.50 **Si**, 0.2–0.10 **V**, 0.015–0.06 **Nb**	**Normalized or normalized and tempered:** (5–16) **diam**, (530) **TS**, (375) **YS**, 21 **El**
NF A 36-201	E 355, I	France	Sheet, plate	0.18 **C**, 1.50 **Mn**, 0.035 **P**, 0.035 **S**, 0.50 **Si**, 0.015–0.06 **Nb**	**Normalized or normalized and tempered:** (5–16) **diam**, (510) **TS**, (355) **YS**, 22 **El**
NBN 629	14 Mn Mo V 55	Belgium	Strip	0.18 **C**, 0.90–1.40 **Mn**, 0.035 **P**, 0.035 **S**, 0.15–0.35 **Si**, 0.30 **Cr**, 0.40–0.60 **Mo**, 0.04–0.08 **V**	**Temper pass:** (3–40) **diam**, (510) **TS**, (345) **YS**, 21 **El**
NF A 36-208	0.5 Ni (10 N2) 355	France	Plate	0.18 **C**, 0.85–1.65 **Mn**, 0.035 **P**, 0.030 **S**, 0.40 **Si**, 0.30–0.80 **Ni**, 0.8 **V**, 0.015 min **Al**, 0.06 **Nb**, 0.10 **Nb+V**	**Normalized:** (3–30) **diam**, (490) **TS**, (355) **YS**, 22 **El**
ISO 2604/IV	P41	ISO	Plate	0.18 **C**, 0.80 **Mn**, 0.035 **P**, 0.035 **S**, 0.15–0.35 **Si**, 1.30–1.70 **Ni**	**Hot rolled, normalized, normalized and tempered, quenched and tempered:** (3–30) **diam**, (490) **TS**, (275) **YS**, 22 **El**
ISO 2604/IV	P42	ISO	Plate	0.18 **C**, 1.50 **Mn**, 0.035 **P**, 0.035 **S**, 0.15–0.35 **Si**, 1.30–1.70 **Ni**	**Hot rolled, normalized:** (3–30) **diam**, (490) **TS**, (345) **YS**, 22 **El**
NBN 630	18 Ni 2	Belgium	Strip	0.18 **C**, 1.50 **Mn**, 0.030 **P**, 0.030 **S**, 0.10–0.35 **Si**, 0.4–0.7 **Ni**	**Quenched and tempered or normalized:** (3–100) **diam**, (490) **TS**, (355) **YS**, 21 **El**
NBN 630	18 Ni 6	Belgium	Strip	0.18 **C**, 1.50 **Mn**, 0.030 **P**, 0.030 **S**, 0.15–0.35 **Si**, 1.3–1.7 **Ni**	**Quenched and tempered or normalized:** (3–100) **diam**, (490) **TS**, (355) **YS**, 21 **El**
EURONORM 129	FeE 355 Ni 6	EURONORM	Plate, strip	0.18 **C**, 0.80–1.50 **Mn**, 0.025 **P**, 0.020 **S**, 0.35 **Si**, 0.25 **Cr**, 1.30–1.70 **Ni**, 0.10 **Mo**, 0.05 **V**, 0.015_{met} or 0.020 tot. (min) **Al**, 0.35 **Cu**	**Normalized, or normalized and tempered, or quenched and tempered:** ≤(35) **diam**, (490) **TS**, (355) **YS**, 22 **El**
SFS 255	Fe 355	Finland	Shapes: structural	0.18 **C**, 0.90–1.60 **Mn**, 0.035 **P**, 0.035 **S**, 0.55 **Si**, 0.02–0.15 **V**	**Normalized:** (<60) **diam**, (490) **TS**, (355) **YS**, 22 **El**
JIS G 3126	Type 3	Japan	Plate	0.18 **C**, 0.80–1.60 **Mn**, 0.035 **P**, 0.035 **S**, 0.15–0.55 **Si**	**Quenched and tempered:** (6–16) **diam**, (490) **TS**, (363) **YS**, 20 **El**
ANSI/ASTM A 225	Grade A	US	Plate	0.18 **C**, 1.45 **Mn**, 0.04 **P**, 0.04 **S**, 0.13–0.32 **Si**, 0.07–0.16 **V**	**As rolled or normalized or stress relieved:** all **diam**, (485) **TS**, (275) **YS**, 21 **El**
NBN 629	13 Mo Cr V 6	Belgium	Strip	0.18 **C**, 0.40–0.80 **Mn**, 0.035 **P**, 0.035 **S**, 0.15–0.35 **Si**, 0.30–0.60 **Cr**, 0.50–0.70 **Mo**, 0.25–0.35 **V**	**Temper pass:** (3–40) **diam**, (470) **TS**, (325) **YS**, 20 **El**
EURONORM 129	FeE 285 Ni 6	EURONORM	Plate, strip	0.18 **C**, 0.30–0.70 **Mn**, 0.025 **P**, 0.020 **S**, 0.35 **Si**, 0.25 **Cr**, 1.30–1.70 **Ni**, 0.10 **Mo**, 0.05 **V**, 0.015_{met} or 0.020 tot. (min) **Al**, 0.35 **Cu**	**Normalized, or normalized and tempered, or quenched and tempered:** ≤(35) **diam**, (470) **TS**, (285) **YS**, 22 **El**
ISO 2604/IV	P44	ISO	Plate	0.18 **C**, 0.80 **Mn**, 0.035 **P**, 0.035 **S**, 0.15–0.35 **Si**, 3.25–3.75 **Ni**	**Hot rolled, normalized and tempered, quenched and tempered:** (3–30) **diam**, (460) **TS**, (345) **YS**, 22 **El**
JIS G 3103	Class 5	Japan	Plate	0.18 **C**, 0.90 **Mn**, 0.035 **P**, 0.040 **S**, 0.15–0.30 **Si**, 0.45–0.60 **Mo**	**Hot rolled:** (≤25) **diam**, (451) **TS**, (255) **YS**, 19 **El**
JIS G 3460	Class 2	Japan	Pipe: seamless or electric resistance welded	0.18 **C**, 0.30–0.60 **Mn**, 0.030 **P**, 0.030 **S**, 0.10–0.3 **Si**, 3.20–3.80 **Ni**	**Normalized or normalized and tempered:** (≥8) **diam**, (451) **TS**, (245) **YS**, 30 **El**
JIS G 3464	Class 2	Japan	Tube: seamless or electric resistance welded	0.18 **C**, 0.30–0.60 **Mn**, 0.030 **P**, 0.030 **S**, 0.10–0.35 **Si**, 3.20–3.80 **Ni**	**Normalized or normalized and tempered:** (≥8) **diam**, (451) **TS**, (245) **YS**, 30 **El**

WROUGHT ALLOY STEELS

specification number	designation	country	product forms	composition	mechanical properties (see page iv for explanation)
ANSI/ASTM A 204	Grade A	US	Plate	0.18 **C**, 0.90 **Mn**, 0.04 **P**, 0.04 **S**, 0.15–0.30 **Si**, 0.41–0.64 **Mo**	**As rolled or normalized:** all **diam**, (450) **TS**, (255) **YS**, 23 **El**
NBN 629	14 Cr Mo 45	Belgium	Strip	0.18 **C**, 0.40–0.80 **Mn**, 0.035 **P**, 0.035 **S**, 0.15–0.35 **Si**, 0.80–1.15 **Cr**, 0.40–0.60 **Mo**	**Temper pass:** (3–40) **diam**, (440) **TS**, (295) **YS**, 22 **El**
ISO 2604/1	F37	ISO	Forgings	0.18 **C**, 0.30–0.80 **Mn**, 0.040 **P**, 0.040 **S**, 0.15–0.40 **Si**, 4.00–6.00 **Cr**, 0.45–0.65 **Mo**, 0.020 $\mathbf{Al_{met}}$	**Annealed:** all **diam**, (410) **TS**, (205) **YS**, 18 **El**; **Normalized and tempered, quenched and tempered:** all **diam**, (640) **TS**, (420) **YS**, 14 **El**
MIL-S-21952B	HY-80	US	Bar: for ships	0.18 **C**, 0.10–0.40 **Mn**, 0.025 **P**, 0.025 **S**, 0.15–0.35 **Si**, 1.00–1.80 **Cr**, 2.00–3.25 **Ni**, 0.20–0.60 **Mo**	**Quenched and tempered, austenitized:** all **diam**, (551) **YS**, 20 **El**
MIL-S-22958 A	Grade HY-80	US	Shapes, structural	0.18 **C**, 0.10–0.40 **Mn**, 0.025 **P**, 0.025 **S**, 0.15–0.35 **Si**, 1.00–1.80 **Cr**, 2.00–3.25 **Ni**, 0.20–0.60 **Mo**, 0.03 **V**, 0.25 **Cu**, 0.02 **Ti**	**Hot rolled, quenched and drawn:** <5/8 **diam**, 80 (552) **YS**, 19 **El**
MIL-S-23009A	Hy 80	US	Forgings	0.18 **C**, 0.10–0.40 **Mn**, 0.025 **P**, 0.025 **S**, 0.15–0.35 **Si**, 1.00–1.80 **Cr**, 2.00–3.25 **Ni**, 0.20–0.60 **Mo**	**Quenched and tempered:** all **diam**, 80 (552) **YS**, 20 **El**
NBN 837	10 Cr Mo 910	Belgium	Tube	0.18–0.15 **C**, 0.40–0.60 **Mn**, 0.040 **P**, 0.040 **S**, 0.15–0.50 **Si**, 2.0–2.50 **Cr**, 0.90–1.10 **Mo**	**Normalized or annealed:** all **diam**, (440) **TS**, (260) **YS**, 20 **El**
ASTM A 692		US	Tube: seamless	0.17–0.26 **C**, 0.46–0.94 **Mn**, 0.045 **P**, 0.045 **S**, 0.18–0.37 **Si**, 0.42–0.68 **Mo**	**Annealed:** 0.312 (7.94) **diam**, 64 (441) **TS**, 42 (290) **YS**, 20 **El**
BS 2S.514		UK	Sheet, strip: aircraft quality	0.17–0.25 **C**, 1.30–1.70 **Mn**, 0.040 **P**, 0.040 **S**, 0.10–0.35 **Si**, 0.25 **Cr**, 0.40 **Ni**, 0.10 **Mo**	**Hardened and tempered:** (<1.6) **diam**, (770) **TS**, (620) **YS**, 8 **El**
BS 4T.45		UK	Tube: aircraft quality	0.17–0.25 **C**, 1.30–1.70 **Mn**, 0.040 **P**, 0.040 **S**, 0.10–0.35 **Si**, 0.25 **Cr**, 0.40 **Ni**, 0.10 **Mo**	**Hardened and tempered:** all **diam**, (700) **TS**, (620) **YS**
DIN 17240	Grade 21 CrMo V 5 11	Germany	Bar	0.17–0.25 **C**, 0.30–0.50 **Mn**, 0.035 **P**, 0.035 **S**, 0.30–0.60 **Si**, 1.2–1.5 **Cr**, 0.60 **Ni**, 1.0–1.2 **Mo**, 0.25–0.35 **V**	**Rolled, forged or drawn:** all **diam**, (687) **TS**, (539) **YS**, 17 **El**
BS T.64		UK	Tube: aircraft quality	0.17–0.25 **C**, 1.3–1.7 **Mn**, 0.040 **P**, 0.040 **S**, 0.10–0.35 **Si**, 0.25 **Cr**, 0.40 **Ni**, 0.10 **Mo**	**Hardened and tempered:** all **diam**, (550) **TS**, (460) **YS**
BS 2S.515		UK	Sheet, strip: aircraft quality	0.17–0.25 **C**, 1.30–1.70 **Mn**, 0.040 **P**, 0.040 **S**, 0.10–0.35 **Si**, 0.25 **Cr**, 0.40 **Ni**, 0.10 **Mo**	**Annealed:** (<1.6) **diam**, (460) **TS**, 14 **El**
BS 2S.510		UK	Sheet, strip: aircraft quality	0.17–0.25 **C**, 0.40–0.80 **Mn**, 0.040 **P**, 0.040 **S**, 0.10–0.35 **Si**, 0.25 **Cr**, 0.30 **Ni**, 0.10 **Mo**	**Annealed:** (<1.6) **diam**, (430) **TS**, (255) **YS**, 18 **El**
AISI 8620		US	Plate	0.17–0.25 **C**, 0.60–0.90 **Mn**, 0.035 **P**, 0.040 **S**, 0.15–0.30 **Si**, 0.35–0.60 **Cr**, 0.40–0.70 **Ni**, 0.15–0.25 **Mo**	
AS 1444	Grade AS 1444/X1320H	Australia	Bar, bloom, billet, slab	0.17–0.24 **C**, 1.30–1.80 **Mn**, 0.040 **P**, 0.040 **S**, 0.10–0.35 **Si**	
AMS 6523A		US	Sheet, strip, plate	0.17–0.23 **C**, 0.20–0.40 **Mn**, 0.010 **P**, 0.010 **S**, 0.20 **Si**, 0.65–0.85 **Cr**, 8.50–9.50 **Ni**, 0.90–1.10 **Mo**, 0.06–0.12 **V**, 4.25–4.75 **Co**, 0.35 **Cu**	**Normalized, hardened quenched and tempered:** ≤0.249 (≤0.632) **diam**, 190 (1310) **TS**, 175 (1200) **YS**, 5 **El**
AMS 6525		US	Bar, forgings, tube, rings	0.17–0.23 **C**, 0.20–0.40 **Mn**, 0.010 **P**, 0.010 **S**, 0.20 **Si**, 0.65–0.85 **Cr**, 8.50–9.50 **Ni**, 0.90–1.10 **Mo**, 0.06–0.12 **V**, 4.25–4.75 **Co**, 0.35 **Cu**	**Annealed and aged (bar):** ≤0.500 (≤12.70) **diam**, 180 (1241) **TS**; **Normalized, hardened, and tempered:** all **diam**, 190 (1310) **TS**, 180 (1241) **YS**, 12 **El**
SFS 509	20 Ni Cr Mo 5	Finland	Bar, forgings	0.17–0.23 **C**, 0.70–1.10 **Mn**, 0.035 **P**, 0.050 **S**, 0.15–0.40 **Si**, 0.80–1.20 **Cr**, 1.00–1.40 **Ni**, 0.08–0.16 **Mo**	**Quenched:** (11) **diam**, (1230) **TS**, (830) **YS**, 7 **El**

WROUGHT ALLOY STEELS

specification number	designation	country	product forms	composition	mechanical properties (see page iv for explanation)
SIS 14 25 23	SIS 25 23–03	Sweden	Bar, forgings	0.17–0.23 **C**, 0.70–1.10 **Mn**, 0.035 **P**, 0.030–0.050 **S**, 0.15–0.40 **Si**, 0.80–1.20 **Cr**, 1.00–1.40 **Ni**, 0.08–0.16 **Mo**	**Case hardened, quenched, annealed:** (11) **diam**, (1230) **TS**, (830) **YS**, 7 **El**
EURONORM 119–74, III	20 NiCrMo 2 KD	EURONORM	Wire, rod	0.17–0.23 **C**, 0.60–0.90 **Mn**, 0.035 **P**, 0.035 **S**, 0.15–0.40 **Si**, 0.35–0.65 **Cr**, 0.40–0.70 **Ni**, 0.15–0.25 **Mo**	**Bright annealed:** (11) **diam**, (1030) **TS**, (785) **YS**, 7 **El**
DIN 17115	Grade 20 NiCrMo 2	Germany	Bar, wire, rod	0.17–0.23 **C**, 0.60–0.90 **Mn**, 0.025 **P**, 0.025 **S**, 0.10–0.25 **Si**, 0.35–0.65 **Cr**, 0.40–0.70 **Ni**, 0.15–0.25 **Mo**, 0.020–0.050 **Al**	**Quenched and tempered:** (≤18) **diam**, (1030) **TS**, (835) **YS**, 10 **El**
JIS G 4105	Class 23	Japan	Bar	0.17–0.23 **C**, 0.70–1.00 **Mn**, 0.030 **P**, 0.030 **S**, 0.15–0.35 **Si**, 0.90–1.20 **Cr**, 0.25 **Ni**, 0.15–0.30 **Mo**, 0.30 **Cu**	**Rolled or forged, quenched or tempered:** (25) **diam**, (981) **TS**, 14 **El**
JIS G 4103	Class 23		Bar	0.17–0.23 **C**, 0.40–0.70 **Mn**, 0.030 **P**, 0.030 **S**, 0.15–0.35 **Si**, 0.40–0.65 **Cr**, 1.60–2.00 **Ni**, 0.15–0.35 **Mo**, 0.30 **Cu**	**Rolled or forged, quenched and tempered:** (25) **diam**, (980.7) **TS**, 15 **El**
SFS 506	21 Ni Cr Mo 2	Finland	Bar, forgings	0.17–0.23 **C**, 0.60–0.90 **Mn**, 0.035 **P**, 0.050 **S**, 0.15–0.40 **Si**, 0.35–0.65 **Cr**, 0.35–0.75 **Ni**, 0.15–0.25 **Mo**	**Quenched:** (11) **diam**, (980) **TS**, (640) **YS**, 8 **El**
ISO R 683/XI	12	ISO	Bar	0.17–0.23 **C**, 0.60–0.90 **Mn**, 0.035 **P**, 0.035 **S**, 0.15–0.40 **Si**, 0.35–0.65 **Cr**, 0.40–0.70 **Ni**, 0.15–0.24 **Mo**	**Carburized and hardened:** all **diam**, (980) **TS**, (638) **YS**, 8 **El**
ISO R 683/XI	12a	ISO	Bar	0.17–0.23 **C**, 0.60–0.90 **Mn**, 0.035 **P**, 0.020–0.035 **S**, 0.15–0.40 **Si**, 0.35–0.65 **Cr**, 0.40–0.70 **Ni**, 0.15–0.24 **Mo**	**Carburized and hardened:** all **diam**, (980) **TS**, (638) **YS**, 8 **El**
SIS 14 25 06	SIS 25 06–03	Sweden	Bar, forgings	0.17–0.23 **C**, 0.60–0.95 **Mn**, 0.035 **P**, 0.030–0.050 **S**, 0.15–0.40 **Si**, 0.35–0.65 **Cr**, 0.35–0.75 **Ni**, 0.15–0.25 **Mo**	**Case hardened, quenched, annealed:** (11) **diam**, (980) **TS**, (640) **YS**, 8 **El**
ISO R 683/XI	8	ISO	Bar	0.17–0.23 **C**, 0.60–0.90 **Mn**, 0.035 **P**, 0.035 **S**, 0.15–0.40 **Si**, 0.30–0.50 **Cr**, 0.40–0.50 **Mo**	**Carburized and hardened:** all **diam**, (932) **TS**, (638) **YS**, 9 **El**
ISO R 683/XI	8a	ISO	Bar	0.17–0.23 **C**, 0.60–0.90 **Mn**, 0.035 **P**, 0.020–0.035 **S**, 0.15–0.40 **Si**, 0.30–0.50 **Cr**, 0.40–0.50 **Mo**	**Carburized and hardened:** all **diam**, (932) **TS**, (638) **YS**, 9 **El**
EURONORM 119–74, III	20 MoCr 4 KD	EURONORM	Wire, rod	0.17–0.23 **C**, 0.60–0.90 **Mn**, 0.035 **P**, 0.035 **S**, 0.15–0.40 **Si**, 0.30–0.50 **Cr**, 0.40–0.50 **Mo**	**Bright annealed:** (11) **diam**, (930) **TS**, (685) **YS**, 9 **El**
ISO R 683/XI	6	ISO	Bar	0.17–0.23 **C**, 0.40–0.70 **Mn**, 0.035 **P**, 0.035 **S**, 0.15–0.40 **Si**, 1.60–2.00 **Ni**, 0.20–0.30 **Mo**	**Carburized and hardened:** all **diam**, (883) **TS**, (588) **YS**, 9 **El**
ISO R 683/XI	6a	ISO	Bar	0.17–0.23 **C**, 0.40–0.70 **Mn**, 0.035 **P**, 0.020–0.035 **S**, 0.15–0.40 **Si**, 1.60–2.00 **Ni**, 0.20–0.30 **Mo**	**Carburized and hardened:** all **diam**, (883) **TS**, (588) **YS**, 9 **El**
AMS 6299B		US	Bar, forgings, tube	0.17–0.23 **C**, 0.40–0.70 **Mn**, 0.025 **P**, 0.025 **S**, 0.20–0.35 **Si**, 0.35–0.65 **Cr**, 1.55–2.00 **Ni**, 0.20–0.30 **Mo**, 0.35 **Cu**	**Cold finished (bar):** ≤0.500 (≤12.70) **diam**, 125 (862) max **TS**
JIS G 4106	SMnC 21	Japan	Bar, wire, rod	0.17–0.23 **C**, 1.20–1.50 **Mn**, 0.030 **P**, 0.030 **S**, 0.15–0.35 **Si**, 0.35–0.70 **Cr**, 0.25 **Ni**, 0.30 **Cu**	**Hot rolled or forged, quenched and tempered:** (25) **diam**, (835) **TS**, 13 **El**
ISO R 683/XI	4	ISO	Bar	0.17–0.23 **C**, 0.60–0.90 **Mn**, 0.035 **P**, 0.035 **S**, 0.15–0.40 **Si**, 0.70–1.00 **Cr**	**Carburized and hardened:** all **diam**, (834) **TS**, (539) **YS**, 10 **El**
ISO R 683/XI	4a	ISO	Bar	0.17–0.23 **C**, 0.60–0.90 **Mn**, 0.035 **P**, 0.020–0.035 **S**, 0.15–0.40 **Si**, 0.70–1.00 **Cr**	**Carburized and hardened:** all **diam**, (834) **TS**, (539) **YS**, 10 **El**
JIS G 4103	Class 21	Japan	Bar	0.17–0.23 **C**, 0.60–0.90 **Mn**, 0.030 **P**, 0.030 **S**, 0.15–0.35 **Si**, 0.40–0.65 **Cr**, 0.40–0.70 **Ni**, 0.15–0.30 **Mo**, 0.30 **Cu**	**Rolled or forged, quenched and tempered:** (25) **diam**, (834) **TS**, 17 **El**
BS 970 Part 3	Grade 665 M 20	UK	Blooms, billets, bar, forgings	0.17–0.23 **C**, 0.35–0.75 **Mn**, 0.10–0.35 **Si**, 1.50–2.00 **Ni**, 0.20–0.30 **Mo**	**Hardened:** 0.75 **diam**, (760) **TS**, 11 **El**

WROUGHT ALLOY STEELS

specification number	designation	country	product forms	composition	mechanical properties (see page iv for explanation)
BS 970 Part 3	Grade 805 M 20	UK	Blooms, billets, bar, forgings	0.17–0.23 **C**, 0.60–0.95 **Mn**, 0.10–0.35 **Si**, 0.35–0.65 **Cr**, 0.35–0.75 **Ni**, 0.15–0.25 **Mo**	**Hardened**: 0.75 **diam**, (760) **TS**, 11 **El**
BS 970 Part 3	Grade 527 M 20	UK	Blooms, billets, bar, forgings	0.17–0.23 **C**, 0.60–0.90 **Mn**, 0.10–0.35 **Si**, 0.60–0.90 **Cr**	**Hardened**: 0.75 **diam**, (690) **TS**, 12 **El**
ISO 2604/II	TS 40	ISO	Tube: seamless	0.17–0.23 **C**, 1.00 **Mn**, 0.030 **P**, 0.030 **S**, 0.50 **Si**, 10.00–12.50 **Cr**, 0.30–0.80 **Ni**, 0.80–1.20 **Mo**, 0.25–0.35 **V**, 0.25–0.35 **V**	**Cold finished, normalized and tempered**: all **diam**, (690) **TS**, (435) **YS**, 15 **El**
JIS G 4106	SMn 21	Japan	Bar, wire, rod	0.17–0.23 **C**, 1.20–1.50 **Mn**, 0.030 **P**, 0.030 **S**, 0.15–0.35 **Si**, 0.25 **Ni**, 0.30 **Cu**	**Hot rolled or forged, quenched and tempered**: (25) **diam**, (686) **TS**, 14 **El**
ANSI/ASTM A 203	Grade A	US	Plate	0.17–0.23 **C**, 0.70 **Mn**, 0.04 **P**, 0.04 **S**, 0.13–0.32 **Si**, 2.03–2.57 **Ni**	**Normalized**: <2 **diam**, (450) **TS**, (255) **YS**, 23 **El**
ISO 683/XVII	11	ISO	Billets, bar, wire, tube	0.17–0.23 **C**, 0.40–0.70 **Mn**, 0.035 **P**, 0.035 **S**, 0.15–0.40 **Si**, 1.60–2.00 **Ni**, 0.20–0.30 **Mo**	
ISO 683/XVII	12	ISO	Billets, bar, wire, tube	0.17–0.23 **C**, 0.60–0.90 **Mn**, 0.035 **P**, 0.035 **S**, 0.15–0.40 **Si**, 0.35–0.65 **Cr**, 0.40–0.70 **Ni**, 0.15–0.25 **Mo**	
ISO 683/XVII	13	ISO	Billets, bar, wire, tube	0.17–0.23 **C**, 0.40–0.70 **Mn**, 0.035 **P**, 0.035 **S**, 0.15–0.40 **Si**, 0.35–0.65 **Cr**, 0.90–1.20 **Ni**, 0.15–0.25 **Mo**	
ISO 683/XVII	14	ISO	Billets, bar, wire, tube	0.17–0.23 **C**, 0.40–0.70 **Mn**, 0.035 **P**, 0.035 **S**, 0.15–0.40 **Si**, 0.35–0.65 **Cr**, 1.60–2.00 **Ni**, 0.20–0.30 **Mo**	
BS 970 Part 3	Grade 665 H 20	UK	Blooms, billets, bar, forgings	0.17–0.23 **C**, 0.35–0.75 **Mn**, 0.10–0.35 **Si**, 1.50–2.00 **Ni**, 0.20–0.30 **Mo**	
BS 970 Part 3	Grade 805 H 20	UK	Blooms, billets, bar, forgings	0.17–0.23 **C**, 0.60–0.95 **Mn**, 0.10–0.35 **Si**, 0.35–0.65 **Cr**, 0.35–0.75 **Ni**, 0.15–0.25 **Mo**	
NBN A 21–221	C 20 KD	Belgium	Wire	0.17–0.23 **C**, 0.70–1.0 **Mn**, 0.040 **P**, 0.050 **S**, 0.10–0.40 **Si**	
SFS 506	21 NiCrMo2: steel 506	Finland	Bar, forgings	0.17–0.23 **C**, 0.60–0.95 **Mn**, 0.035 **P**, 0.050 **S**, 0.15–0.40 **Si**, 0.35–0.65 **Cr**, 0.35–0.75 **Ni**, 0.15–0.25 **Mo**	
SFS 509	20 NiCrMo5: steel 509	Finland	Bar, forgings	0.17–0.23 **C**, 0.70–1.10 **Mn**, 0.035 **P**, 0.050 **S**, 0.15–0.40 **Si**, 0.80–1.20 **Cr**, 1.00–1.40 **Ni**, 0.08–0.16 **Mo**	
AS 1444	Grade AS 1444/4620H	Australia	Bar, bloom, billet, slab	0.17–0.23 **C**, 0.35–0.75 **Mn**, 0.040 **P**, 0.040 **S**, 0.10–0.35 **Si**, 1.55–2.00 **Ni**, 0.20–0.30 **Mo**	
AS 1444	Grade AS 1444/5120H	Australia	Bar, bloom, billet, slab	0.17–0.23 **C**, 0.60–1.00 **Mn**, 0.040 **P**, 0.040 **S**, 0.10–0.35 **Si**, 0.60–1.00 **Cr**	
AS 1444	Grade AS 1444/8620H	Australia	Bar, bloom, billet, slab	0.17–0.23 **C**, 0.60–0.95 **Mn**, 0.040 **P**, 0.040 **S**, 0.10–0.35 **Si**, 0.35–0.65 **Cr**, 0.35–0.75 **Ni**, 0.15–0.25 **Mo**	
DGN–B–300	4720 H	Mexico	Bar	0.17–0.23 **C**, 0.45–0.75 **Mn**, 0.040 **P**, 0.035 **S**, 0.20–0.35 **Si**, 0.30–0.60 **Cr**, 0.85–1.25 **Ni**, 0.15–0.25 **Mo**	**Annealed**
DGN–B–300	4621 H		Bar	0.17–0.23 **C**, 0.60–1.00 **Mn**, 0.040 **P**, 0.035 **S**, 0.20–0.35 **Si**, 1.55–2.00 **Ni**, 0.20–0.30 **Mo**	**Annealed**
DGN–B–300	4620 H	Mexico	Bar	0.17–0.23 **C**, 0.35–0.75 **Mn**, 0.040 **P**, 0.035 **S**, 0.20–0.35 **Si**, 1.55–2.00 **Ni**, 0.20–0.30 **Mo**	**Annealed**
DGN–B–300	4419 H	Mexico	Bar	0.17–0.23 **C**, 0.35–0.75 **Mn**, 0.040 **P**, 0.035 **S**, 0.20–0.35 **Si**, 0.45–0.60 **Mo**	**Annealed**
DGN–B–300	4320 H	Mexico	Bar	0.17–0.23 **C**, 0.40–0.70 **Mn**, 0.040 **P**, 0.035 **S**, 0.20–0.35 **Si**, 0.35–0.65 **Cr**, 1.55–2.00 **Ni**, 0.20–0.30 **Mo**	**Annealed**

WROUGHT ALLOY STEELS

specification number	designation	country	product forms	composition	mechanical properties (see page iv for explanation)
DGN–B–300	4118 H	Mexico	Bar	0.17–0.23 **C**, 0.60–1.00 **Mn**, 0.040 **P**, 0.035 **S**, 0.20–0.35 **Si**, 0.30–0.70 **Cr**, 0.08–0.15 **Mo**	**Annealed**
DGN–B–300	5120 H	Mexico	Bar	0.17–0.23 **C**, 0.60–1.00 **Mn**, 0.040 **P**, 0.035 **S**, 0.20–0.35 **Si**, 0.60–1.00 **Cr**	**Annealed**
DGN–B–300	4820 H	Mexico	Bar	0.17–0.23 **C**, 0.40–0.80 **Mn**, 0.040 **P**, 0.035 **S**, 0.20–0.35 **Si**, 3.20–3.80 **Ni**, 0.20–0.30 **Mo**	**Annealed**
DGN–B–300	8620 H	Mexico	Bar	0.17–0.23 **C**, 0.60–0.95 **Mn**, 0.040 **P**, 0.035 **S**, 0.20–0.35 **Si**, 0.35–0.65 **Cr**, 0.35–0.75 **Ni**, 0.15–0.25 **Mo**	**Annealed**
DGN–B–300	8720 H	Mexico	Bar	0.17–0.23 **C**, 0.60–0.95 **Mn**, 0.040 **P**, 0.035 **S**, 0.20–0.35 **Si**, 0.35–0.65 **Cr**, 0.35–0.75 **Ni**, 0.20–0.30 **Mo**	**Annealed**
ASTM A 689	4118 H	US	Bar	0.17–0.23 **C**, 0.60–1.00 **Mn**, 0.040 **P**, 0.040 **S**, 0.15–0.30 **Si**, 0.30–0.70 **Cr**, 0.08–0.15 **Mo**	
ASTM A 689	5120 H	US	Bar	0.17–0.23 **C**, 0.60–1.00 **Mn**, 0.040 **P**, 0.040 **S**, 0.15–0.30 **Si**, 0.60–1.00 **Cr**	
ASTM A 689	8720 H	US	Bar	0.17–0.23 **C**, 0.60–0.95 **Mn**, 0.040 **P**, 0.040 **S**, 0.15–0.30 **Si**, 0.35–0.65 **Cr**, 0.35–0.75 **Ni**, 0.20–0.30 **Mo**	
ASTM A 689	8620 H	US	Bar	0.17–0.23 **C**, 0.60–0.95 **Mn**, 0.040 **P**, 0.040 **S**, 0.15–0.30 **Si**, 0.35–0.65 **Cr**, 0.35–0.75 **Ni**, 0.15–0.25 **Mo**	
ANSI/ASTM A 304	5120 H	US	Bar	0.17–0.23 **C**, 0.60–1.00 **Mn**, 0.040 **P**, 0.040 **S**, 0.15–0.30 **Si**, 0.60–1.00 **Cr**	
ANSI/ASTM A 304	4720 H	US	Bar	0.17–0.23 **C**, 0.45–0.75 **Mn**, 0.040 **P**, 0.040 **S**, 0.15–0.30 **Si**, 0.30–0.60 **Cr**, 0.85–1.25 **Ni**, 0.15–0.25 **Mo**	
ANSI/ASTM A 304	4820 H	US	Bar	0.17–0.23 **C**, 0.40–0.80 **Mn**, 0.040 **P**, 0.040 **S**, 0.15–0.30 **Si**, 3.20–3.80 **Ni**, 0.20–0.30 **Mo**	
ANSI/ASTM A 646	HP 9–4–20	US	Blooms, billets: aircraft quality	0.17–0.23 **C**, 0.20–0.40 **Mn**, 0.010 **P**, 0.010 **S**, 0.10 **Si**, 0.65–0.85 **Cr**, 8.5–9.5 **Ni**, 0.90–1.10 **Mo**, 0.06–0.12 **V**, 4.25–4.75 **Co**	**Annealed**
ANSI/ASTM A 304	8620 H	US	Bar	0.17–0.23 **C**, 0.60–0.95 **Mn**, 0.040 **P**, 0.040 **S**, 0.15–0.30 **Si**, 0.35–0.65 **Cr**, 0.35–0.75 **Ni**, 0.15–0.25 **Mo**	
ANSI/ASTM A 304	8720 H	US	Bar	0.17–0.23 **C**, 0.60–0.95 **Mn**, 0.040 **P**, 0.040 **S**, 0.15–0.30 **Si**, 0.35–0.5 **Cr**, 0.35–0.75 **Ni**, 0.20–0.30 **Mo**	
ANSI/ASTM A 304	4320 H	US	Bar	0.17–0.23 **C**, 0.40–0.70 **Mn**, 0.040 **P**, 0.040 **S**, 0.15–0.30 **Si**, 0.35–0.65 **Cr**, 1.55–2.00 **Ni**, 0.20–0.30 **Mo**	
ANSI/ASTM A 304	4419 H	US	Bar	0.17–0.23 **C**, 0.35–0.75 **Mn**, 0.040 **P**, 0.040 **S**, 0.15–0.30 **Si**, 0.45–0.60 **Mo**	
ANSI/ASTM A 304	4118 H	US	Bar	0.17–0.23 **C**, 0.60–1.00 **Mn**, 0.040 **P**, 0.040 **S**, 0.15–0.30 **Si**, 0.30–0.70 **Cr**, 0.08–0.15 **Mo**	
ANSI/ASTM A 304	4620 H	US	Bar	0.17–0.23 **C**, 0.35–0.75 **Mn**, 0.040 **P**, 0.040 **S**, 0.15–0.30 **Si**, 1.55–2.00 **Ni**, 0.20–0.30 **Mo**	
ANSI/ASTM A 304	4621 H	US	Bar	0.17–0.23 **C**, 0.60–1.00 **Mn**, 0.040 **P**, 0.040 **S**, 0.15–0.30 **Si**, 1.55–2.00 **Ni**, 0.20–0.30 **Mo**	
ASTM A 689	4820 H	US	Bar	0.17–0.23 **C**, 0.40–0.80 **Mn**, 0.040 **P**, 0.040 **S**, 0.15–0.30 **Si**, 3.20–3.80 **Ni**, 0.20–0.30 **Mo**	

WROUGHT ALLOY STEELS

specification number	designation	country	product forms	composition	mechanical properties (see page iv for explanation)
ASTM A 689	4720 H	US	Bar	0.17–0.23 **C**, 0.45–0.75 **Mn**, 0.040 **P**, 0.040 **S**, 0.15–0.30 **Si**, 0.30–0.60 **Cr**, 0.85–1.25 **Ni**, 0.15–0.25 **Mo**	
ASTM A 689	4621 H	US	Bar	0.17–0.23 **C**, 0.60–1.00 **Mn**, 0.040 **P**, 0.040 **S**, 0.15–0.30 **Si**, 1.55–2.00 **Ni**, 0.20–0.30 **Mo**	
ASTM A 689	4620 H	US	Bar	0.17–0.23 **C**, 0.35–0.75 **Mn**, 0.040 **P**, 0.040 **S**, 0.15–0.30 **Si**, 1.55–2.00 **Ni**, 0.20–0.30 **Mo**	
ASTM A 689	4419 H	US	Bar	0.17–0.23 **C**, 0.35–0.75 **Mn**, 0.040 **P**, 0.040 **S**, 0.15–0.30 **Si**, 0.45–0.60 **Mo**	
ASTM A 689	4320 H	US	Bar	0.17–0.23 **C**, 0.40–0.70 **Mn**, 0.040 **P**, 0.040 **S**, 0.15–0.30 **Si**, 0.35–0.65 **Cr**, 1.55–2.00 **Ni**, 0.20–0.30 **Mo**	
AISI 4118		US	Plate	0.17–0.23 **C**, 0.60–0.90 **Mn**, 0.035 **P**, 0.040 **S**, 0.15–0.30 **Si**, 0.40–0.65 **Cr**, 0.08–0.15 **Mo**	
AISI 4720 H		US	Wire, rod	0.17–0.23 **C**, 0.45–0.75 **Mn**, 0.15–0.30 **Si**, 0.30–0.60 **Cr**, 0.85–1.25 **Ni**, 0.15–0.25 **Mo**	
AISI 4820 H		US	Wire, rod	0.17–0.23 **C**, 0.40–0.80 **Mn**, 0.15–0.30 **Si**, 3.20–3.80 **Ni**, 0.20–0.30 **Mo**	
AISI 5120 H		US	Wire, rod	0.17–0.23 **C**, 0.60–1.00 **Mn**, 0.15–0.30 **Si**, 0.60–1.00 **Cr**	
AISI 8620 H		US	Wire, rod	0.17–0.23 **C**, 0.60–0.95 **Mn**, 0.15–0.30 **Si**, 0.35–0.65 **Cr**, 0.35–0.75 **Ni**, 0.15–0.25 **Mo**	
AISI 8720 H		US	Wire, rod	0.17–0.23 **C**, 0.60–0.95 **Mn**, 0.15–0.30 **Si**, 0.35–0.65 **Cr**, 0.35–0.75 **Ni**, 0.20–0.30 **Mo**	
AISI 4419 H		US	Wire, rod	0.17–0.23 **C**, 0.35–0.75 **Mn**, 0.15–0.30 **Si**, 0.45–0.60 **Mo**	
AISI 4620 H		US	Wire, rod	0.17–0.23 **C**, 0.35–0.75 **Mn**, 0.15–0.30 **Si**, 1.55–2.00 **Ni**, 0.20–0.30 **Mo**	
AISI 4621 H		US	Wire, rod	0.17–0.23 **C**, 0.60–1.00 **Mn**, 0.15–0.30 **Si**, 1.55–2.00 **Ni**, 0.20–0.30 **Mo**	
AISI 4118 H		US	Wire, rod	0.17–0.23 **C**, 0.60–1.00 **Mn**, 0.15–0.30 **Si**, 0.30–0.70 **Cr**, 0.08–0.15 **Mo**	
AISI 4320 H		US	Wire, rod	0.17–0.23 **C**, 0.40–0.70 **Mn**, 0.15–0.30 **Si**, 0.35–0.65 **Cr**, 1.55–2.00 **Ni**, 0.20–0.30 **Mo**	
AISI 8720H		US	Bar	0.17–0.23 **C**, 0.60–0.95 **Mn**, 0.035 **P**, 0.040 **S**, 0.15–0.30 **Si**, 0.35–0.65 **Cr**, 0.35–0.75 **Ni**, 0.20–0.30 **Mo**	
AISI 8620H		US	Bar	0.17–0.23 **C**, 0.60–0.95 **Mn**, 0.035 **P**, 0.040 **S**, 0.15–0.30 **Si**, 0.35–0.65 **Cr**, 0.35–0.75 **Ni**, 0.15–0.25 **Mo**	
AISI 5120H		US	Bar	0.17–0.23 **C**, 0.60–1.00 **Mn**, 0.035 **P**, 0.040 **S**, 0.15–0.30 **Si**, 0.60–1.00 **Cr**	
AISI 4820H		US	Bar	0.17–0.23 **C**, 0.40–0.80 **Mn**, 0.035 **P**, 0.040 **S**, 0.15–0.30 **Si**, 3.20–3.80 **Ni**, 0.20–0.30 **Mo**	
AISI 4720H		US	Bar	0.17–0.23 **C**, 0.45–0.75 **Mn**, 0.035 **P**, 0.040 **S**, 0.15–0.30 **Si**, 0.30–0.60 **Cr**, 0.85–1.25 **Ni**, 0.15–0.25 **Mo**	
AISI 4620H		US	Bar	0.17–0.23 **C**, 0.35–0.75 **Mn**, 0.035 **P**, 0.040 **S**, 0.15–0.30 **Si**, 1.55–2.00 **Ni**, 0.20–0.30 **Mo**	
AISI 4320H		US	Bar	0.17–0.23 **C**, 0.40–0.70 **Mn**, 0.035 **P**, 0.040 **S**, 0.15–0.30 **Si**, 0.35–0.65 **Cr**, 1.55–2.00 **Ni**, 0.20–0.30 **Mo**	

WROUGHT ALLOY STEELS

specification number	designation	country	product forms	composition	mechanical properties (see page iv for explanation)
AISI 4118H		US	Bar	0.17–0.23 **C**, 0.60–1.00 **Mn**, 0.035 **P**, 0.040 **S**, 0.15–0.30 **Si**, 0.30–0.70 **Cr**, 0.08–0.15 **Mo**	
SIS 14 25 23	SIS 25 23–02	Sweden	Bar, forgings	0.17–0.23 **C**, 0.70–1.10 **Mn**, 0.035 **P**, 0.030–0.050 **S**, 0.15–0.40 **Si**, 0.80–1.20 **Cr**, 1.00–1.40 **Ni**, 0.08–0.16 **Mo**	**As rolled or as forged**
SIS 14 25 06	SIS 25–06–00	Sweden	Bar, forgings	0.17–0.23 **C**, 0.60–0.95 **Mn**, 0.035 **P**, 0.030–0.050 **S**, 0.15–0.40 **Si**, 0.35–0.65 **Cr**, 0.35–0.75 **Ni**, 0.15–0.25 **Mo**	**As rolled or as forged**
JIS G 4052	SCr 22H	Japan	Bar, wire, rod	0.17–0.23 **C**, 0.55–0.90 **Mn**, 0.030 **P**, 0.030 **S**, 0.15–0.55 **Si**, 0.85–1.25 **Cr**, 0.30 **Cu**	**Hot rolled, normalized, quenched**
JIS G 4052	SCM 22H	Japan	Bar, wire, rod	0.17–0.23 **C**, 0.55–0.90 **Mn**, 0.030 **P**, 0.030 **S**, 0.15–0.35 **Si**, 0.85–1.25 **Cr**, 0.15–0.35 **Mo**, 0.30 **Cu**	**Hot rolled, normalized, quenched**
JIS G 4052	SNCM 21H	Japan	Bar, wire, rod	0.17–0.23 **C**, 0.60–0.95 **Mn**, 0.030 **P**, 0.030 **S**, 0.15–0.35 **Si**, 0.35–0.65 **Cr**, 0.35–0.75 **Ni**, 0.15–0.30 **Mo**, 0.30 **Cu**	**Hot rolled, normalized, quenched**
JIS G 4052	SNCM 23H	Japan	Bar, wire, rod	0.17–0.23 **C**, 0.40–0.70 **Mn**, 0.030 **P**, 0.030 **S**, 0.15–0.35 **Si**, 0.35–0.65 **Cr**, 1.55–2.00 **Ni**, 0.15–0.30 **Mo**, 0.30 **Cu**	**Hot rolled, normalized, quenched**
SIS 14 25 06	SIS 25 06–08	Sweden	Bar, forgings	0.17–0.23 **C**, 0.60–0.95 **Mn**, 0.035 **P**, 0.030–0.050 **S**, 0.35–0.65 **Cr**, 0.35–0.75 **Ni**, 0.15–0.25 **Mo**	**As rolled or as forged**
JIS G 3311	SNCM21M	Japan	Strip	0.17–0.23 **C**, 0.60–0.90 **Mn**, 0.030 **P**, 0.030 **S**, 0.15–0.35 **Si**, 0.40–0.65 **Cr**, 0.40–0.70 **Ni**, 0.15–0.30 **Mo**, 0.30 **Cu**	
SFS 510	20 Mn Cr 5	Finland	Bar, forgings	0.17–0.22 **C**, 1.10–1.40 **Mn**, 0.035 **P**, 0.050 **S**, 0.15–0.40 **Si**, 1.00–1.30 **Cr**	**Quenched:** (11) **diam**, (1080) **TS**, (740) **YS**, 7 **El**
DIN 17210	Grade 20 MnCr 5	Germany	Blooms, slabs, billets, wire, bar, plate, sheet, strip, tube, forgings	0.17–0.22 **C**, 1.10–1.40 **Mn**, 0.035 **P**, 0.035 **S**, 0.15–0.40 **Si**, 1.00–1.30 **Cr**	**Rolled or forged:** (11) **diam**, (1079) **TS**, (736) **YS**, 7 **El**
DIN 17210	Grade 20 MnCrS 5	Germany	Blooms, slabs, billets, wire, plate, sheet, strip, tube, forgings	0.17–0.22 **C**, 1.10–1.40 **Mn**, 0.035 **P**, 0.035 **S**, 0.15–0.40 **Si**, 1.00–1.30 **Cr**	**Rolled or forged:** (11) **diam**, (1079) **TS**, (736) **YS**, 7 **El**
IS 4367	20MnCrl	India	Forgings	0.17–0.22 **C**, 1.00–1.45 **Mn**, 0.050 **P**, 0.050 **S**, 0.10–0.35 **Si**, 1.00–1.30 **Cr**	**Refined and quenched:** (60) **diam**, (980) **TS**, 8 **El**
AMS 6294D		US	Bar, forgings	0.17–0.22 **C**, 0.45–0.65 **Mn**, 0.025 **P**, 0.025 **S**, 0.20–0.35 **Si**, 0.20 **Cr**, 1.65–2.00 **Ni**, 0.20–0.30 **Mo**, 0.35 **Cu**	**Cold finished:** ≤0.500 (≤12.700) **diam**, 130 (896) max **TS**
DIN 17210	Grade 20 MoCr 4	Germany	Blooms, slabs, billets, wire, bar, plate, sheet, strip, tube, forgings	0.17–0.22 **C**, 0.60–0.90 **Mn**, 0.035 **P**, 0.035 **S**, 0.15–0.40 **Si**, 0.30–0.50 **Cr**, 0.40–0.50 **Mo**	**Rolled or forged:** (11) **diam**, (883) **TS**, (638) **YS**, 9 **El**
DIN 17210	Grade 20 MoCrS 4	Germany	Blooms, slabs, billets, wire, plate, sheet, strip, tube, forgings	0.17–0.22 **C**, 0.60–0.90 **Mn**, 0.035 **P**, 0.020–0.035 **S**, 0.15–0.40 **Si**, 0.30–0.50 **Cr**, 0.40–0.50 **Mo**	**Rolled or forged:** (11) **diam**, (883) **TS**, (638) **YS**, 9 **El**
AISI 4620		US	Bar	0.17–0.22 **C**, 0.45–0.65 **Mn**, 0.035 **P**, 0.040 **S**, 0.15–0.30 **Si**, 1.65–2.00 **Ni**, 0.20–0.30 **Mo**	
AISI 4720		US	Bar	0.17–0.22 **C**, 0.50–0.70 **Mn**, 0.035 **P**, 0.040 **S**, 0.15–0.30 **Si**, 0.35–0.55 **Cr**, 0.90–1.20 **Ni**, 0.15–0.25 **Mo**	
AISI 5120		US	Bar	0.17–0.22 **C**, 0.70–0.90 **Mn**, 0.035 **P**, 0.040 **S**, 0.15–0.30 **Si**, 0.70–0.90 **Cr**	
BS 970 Part 3	Grade 527 A 19	UK	Blooms, billets, bar, forgings	0.17–0.22 **C**, 0.70–0.90 **Mn**, 0.70–0.90 **Cr**	

WROUGHT ALLOY STEELS

specification number	designation	country	product forms	composition	mechanical properties (see page iv for explanation)
BS 970 Part 3	Grade 665 A 19	UK	Blooms, billets, bar, forgings	0.17–0.22 **C**, 0.45–0.65 **Mn**, 0.25 **Cr**, 1.60–2.00 **Ni**, 0.20–0.30 **Mo**	
COPANT 334	3120	COPANT	Bar	0.17–0.22 **C**, 0.60–0.80 **Mn**, 0.035 **P**, 0.040 **S**, 0.20–0.35 **Si**, 0.55–0.75 **Cr**, 1.10–1.40 **Ni**	
COPANT 334	4320	COPANT	Bar	0.17–0.22 **C**, 0.45–0.65 **Mn**, 0.035 **P**, 0.040 **S**, 0.20–0.35 **Si**, 0.40–0.60 **Cr**, 1.65–2.00 **Ni**, 0.20–0.30 **Mo**	
COPANT 334	4620	COPANT	Bar	0.17–0.22 **C**, 0.45–0.65 **Mn**, 0.035 **P**, 0.040 **S**, 0.20–0.35 **Si**, 1.65–2.00 **Ni**, 0.20–0.30 **Mo**	
COPANT 334	5120	COPANT	Bar	0.17–0.22 **C**, 0.70–0.90 **Mn**, 0.035 **P**, 0.040 **S**, 0.20–0.35 **Si**, 0.70–0.90 **Cr**	
COPANT 334	20 Mn Cr 5	COPANT	Bar	0.17–0.22 **C**, 1.10–1.40 **Mn**, 0.035 **P**, 0.035 **S**, 0.15–0.35 **Si**, 1.00–1.30 **Cr**	
SFS 510	20 MnCr5: steel 510	Finland	Bar, forgings	0.17–0.22 **C**, 1.10–1.40 **Mn**, 0.035 **P**, 0.050 **S**, 0.15–0.40 **Si**, 1.00–1.30 **Cr**	
AS 1444	Grade AS 1444/4620	Australia	Bar, bloom, billet, slab	0.17–0.22 **C**, 0.45–0.65 **Mn**, 0.040 **P**, 0.040 **S**, 0.10–0.35 **Si**, 1.65–2.00 **Ni**, 0.20–0.30 **Mo**	
DGN–B–203	Grade 4720	Mexico	Tube: seamless	0.17–0.22 **C**, 0.50–0.70 **Mn**, 0.040 **P**, 0.040 **S**, 0.20–0.35 **Si**, 0.35–0.55 **Cr**, 0.90–1.20 **Ni**, 0.15–0.25 **Mo**	
DGN–B–203	Grade 4620	Mexico	Tube: seamless	0.17–0.22 **C**, 0.45–0.65 **Mn**, 0.040 **P**, 0.040 **S**, 0.20–0.35 **Si**, 1.65–2.00 **Ni**, 0.20–0.30 **Mo**	
DGN–B–203	Grade 5120	Mexico	Tube: seamless	0.17–0.22 **C**, 0.70–0.90 **Mn**, 0.040 **P**, 0.040 **S**, 0.20–0.35 **Si**, 0.70–0.90 **Cr**	
DGN–B–203	Grade 6120	Mexico	Tube: seamless	0.17–0.22 **C**, 0.70–0.90 **Mn**, 0.040 **P**, 0.040 **S**, 0.20–0.35 **Si**, 0.70–0.90 **Cr**, 0.10 min **V**	
COPANT 514	4720	COPANT	Tube	0.17–0.22 **C**, 0.50–0.70 **Mn**, 0.040 **P**, 0.040 **S**, 0.20–0.35 **Si**, 0.35–0.55 **Cr**, 0.90–1.20 **Ni**, 0.15–0.25 **Mo**	
COPANT 514	4620	COPANT	Tube	0.17–0.22 **C**, 0.45–0.65 **Mn**, 0.040 **P**, 0.040 **S**, 0.20–0.35 **Si**, 1.65–2.0 **Ni**, 0.20–0.30 **Mo**	
COPANT 514	4150	COPANT	Tube	0.17–0.22 **C**, 0.45–0.65 **Mn**, 0.040 **P**, 0.040 **S**, 0.20–0.35 **Si**, 0.40–0.60 **Cr**, 1.65–2.0 **Ni**, 0.20–0.30 **Mo**	
DGN–B–300	5120	Mexico	Bar	0.17–0.22 **C**, 0.70–0.90 **Mn**, 0.035 **P**, 0.040 **S**, 0.20–0.35 **Si**, 0.70–0.90 **Cr**	**Annealed**
DGN–B–300	4720	Mexico	Bar	0.17–0.22 **C**, 0.50–0.70 **Mn**, 0.035 **P**, 0.040 **S**, 0.20–0.35 **Si**, 0.35–0.55 **Cr**, 0.90–1.20 **Ni**, 0.15–0.25 **Mo**	**Annealed**
DGN–B–300	4620	Mexico	Bar	0.17–0.22 **C**, 0.45–0.65 **Mn**, 0.035 **P**, 0.040 **S**, 0.20–0.35 **Si**, 1.65–2.00 **Ni**, 0.20–0.30 **Mo**	**Annealed**
DGN–B–300	4320	Mexico	Bar	0.17–0.22 **C**, 0.45–0.65 **Mn**, 0.035 **P**, 0.040 **S**, 0.20–0.35 **Si**, 0.40–0.60 **Cr**, 1.65–2.00 **Ni**, 0.20–0.30 **Mo**	**Annealed**
ANSI/ASTM A 29	4620	US	Bar	0.17–0.22 **C**, 0.45–0.65 **Mn**, 0.035 **P**, 0.040 **S**, 0.15–0.30 **Si**, 1.65–2.00 **Ni**, 0.20–0.30 **Mo**	
ANSI/ASTM A 29	4720	US	Bar	0.17–0.22 **C**, 0.50–0.70 **Mn**, 0.035 **P**, 0.040 **S**, 0.15–0.30 **Si**, 0.35–0.55 **Cr**, 0.90–1.20 **Ni**, 0.15–0.25 **Mo**	
ANSI/ASTM A 29	5120	US	Bar	0.17–0.22 **C**, 0.70–0.90 **Mn**, 0.035 **P**, 0.040 **S**, 0.15–0.30 **Si**, 0.70–0.90 **Cr**	

WROUGHT ALLOY STEELS

specification number	designation	country	product forms	composition	mechanical properties (see page iv for explanation)
ANSI/ASTM A 29	4320	US	Bar	0.17–0.22 **C**, 0.45–0.65 **Mn**, 0.035 **P**, 0.040 **S**, 0.15–0.30 **Si**, 0.40–0.60 **Cr**, 1.65–2.00 **Ni**, 0.20–0.30 **Mo**	
ANSI/ASTM A 646	4620	US	Blooms, billets: aircraft quality	0.17–0.22 **C**, 0.45–0.65 **Mn**, 0.025 **P**, 0.025 **S**, 0.20–0.35 **Si**, 1.65–2.00 **Ni**, 0.20–0.30 **Mo**	**Annealed**
ASTM A 689	5120	US	Bar	0.17–0.22 **C**, 0.70–0.90 **Mn**, 0.035 **P**, 0.040 **S**, 0.15–0.30 **Si**, 0.70–0.90 **Cr**	
ASTM A 689	4320	US	Bar: spring	0.17–0.22 **C**, 0.45–0.65 **Mn**, 0.035 **P**, 0.040 **S**, 0.15–0.30 **Si**, 0.40–0.60 **Cr**, 1.65–2.00 **Ni**, 0.20–0.30 **Mo**	
ASTM A 689	4620	US	Bar	0.17–0.22 **C**, 0.45–0.65 **Mn**, 0.035 **P**, 0.040 **S**, 0.15–0.30 **Si**, 1.65–2.00 **Ni**, 0.20–0.30 **Mo**	
ASTM A 689	4720	US	Bar	0.17–0.22 **C**, 0.50–0.70 **Mn**, 0.035 **P**, 0.040 **S**, 0.15–0.30 **Si**, 0.35–0.55 **Cr**, 0.90–1.20 **Ni**, 0.15–0.25 **Mo**	
ANSI/ASTM A 322	4620	US	Bar	0.17–0.22 **C**, 0.45–0.65 **Mn**, 0.035 **P**, 0.040 **S**, 0.15–0.30 **Si**, 1.65–2.00 **Ni**, 0.20–0.30 **Mo**	
ANSI/ASTM A 322	4720	US	Bar	0.17–0.22 **C**, 0.50–0.70 **Mn**, 0.035 **P**, 0.040 **S**, 0.15–0.30 **Si**, 0.35–0.55 **Cr**, 0.90–1.20 **Ni**, 0.15–0.25 **Mo**	
ANSI/ASTM A 322	5120	US	Bar	0.17–0.22 **C**, 0.70–0.90 **Mn**, 0.035 **P**, 0.040 **S**, 0.15–0.30 **Si**, 0.70–0.90 **Cr**	
ANSI/ASTM A 322	4320	US	Bar	0.17–0.22 **C**, 0.45–0.65 **Mn**, 0.035 **P**, 0.040 **S**, 0.15–0.30 **Si**, 0.40–0.60 **Cr**, 1.65–2.00 **Ni**, 0.20–0.30 **Mo**	
AISI 4320		US	Wire, rod	0.17–0.22 **C**, 0.45–0.65 **Mn**, 0.035 **P**, 0.040 **S**, 0.15–0.30 **Si**, 0.40–0.60 **Cr**, 1.65–2.00 **Ni**, 0.20–0.30 **Mo**	
AISI 4620		US	Wire, rod	0.17–0.22 **C**, 0.45–0.65 **Mn**, 0.035 **P**, 0.040 **S**, 0.15–0.30 **Si**, 1.65–2.00 **Ni**, 0.20–0.30 **Mo**	
AISI 4720		US	Wire, rod	0.17–0.22 **C**, 0.50–0.70 **Mn**, 0.035 **P**, 0.040 **S**, 0.15–0.30 **Si**, 0.35–0.55 **Cr**, 0.90–1.20 **Ni**, 0.15–0.25 **Mo**	
AISI 5120		US	Wire, rod	0.17–0.22 **C**, 0.70–0.90 **Mn**, 0.035 **P**, 0.040 **S**, 0.15–0.30 **Si**, 0.70–0.90 **Cr**	
ANSI/ASTM A 519	4320	US	Tube: seamless	0.17–0.22 **C**, 0.45–0.65 **Mn**, 0.040 **P**, 0.040 **S**, 0.15–0.35 **Si**, 0.40–0.60 **Cr**, 1.65–2.00 **Ni**, 0.20–0.30 **Mo**	
ANSI/ASTM A 519	4620	US	Tube: seamless	0.17–0.22 **C**, 0.45–0.65 **Mn**, 0.040 **P**, 0.040 **S**, 0.15–0.35 **Si**, 1.65–2.00 **Ni**, 0.20–0.30 **Mo**	
ANSI/ASTM A 519	4720	US	Tube: seamless	0.17–0.22 **C**, 0.50–0.70 **Mn**, 0.040 **P**, 0.040 **S**, 0.15–0.35 **Si**, 0.35–0.55 **Cr**, 0.90–1.20 **Ni**, 0.15–0.25 **Mo**	
ANSI/ASTM A 519	5120	US	Tube: seamless	0.17–0.22 **C**, 0.70–0.90 **Mn**, 0.040 **P**, 0.040 **S**, 0.15–0.35 **Si**, 0.70–0.90 **Cr**	
ANSI/ASTM A 519	6120	US	Tube: seamless	0.17–0.22 **C**, 0.70–0.90 **Mn**, 0.040 **P**, 0.040 **S**, 0.15–0.35 **Si**, 0.70–0.90 **Cr**, 0.10 min **V**	
DGN-B-297	4320	Mexico	Bar	0.17–0.22 **C**, 0.45–0.65 **Mn**, 0.035 **P**, 0.040 **S**, 0.20–0.35 **Si**, 0.40–0.60 **Cr**, 1.65–2.00 **Ni**, 0.20–0.30 **Mo**	
ANSI/ASTM A 535	4320	US	Billets, coils, bar, rod, tube	0.17–0.22 **C**, 0.45–0.65 **Mn**, 0.015 **P**, 0.015 **S**, 0.20–0.35 **Si**, 0.40–0.60 **Cr**, 1.65–2.00 **Ni**, 0.20–0.30 **Mo**	

WROUGHT ALLOY STEELS

specification number	designation	country	product forms	composition	mechanical properties (see page iv for explanation)
ANSI/ASTM A 535	4620	US	Billets, coils, bar, rod, tube	0.17–0.22 **C**, 0.45–0.65 **Mn**, 0.015 **P**, 0.015 **S**, 0.20–0.35 **Si**, 1.65–2.00 **Ni**, 0.20–0.30 **Mo**	
ANSI/ASTM A 535	4720	US	Billets, coils, bar, rod, tube	0.17–0.22 **C**, 0.50–0.70 **Mn**, 0.015 **P**, 0.015 **S**, 0.20–0.35 **Si**, 0.35–0.55 **Cr**, 0.90–1.20 **Ni**, 0.15–0.25 **Mo**	
ASTM A 534	5120	US	Bar, wire, tube, rods, billets	0.17–0.22 **C**, 0.70–0.90 **Mn**, 0.035 **P**, 0.040 **S**, 0.20–0.35 **Si**, 0.70–0.90 **Cr**	**As–rolled or normalized and tempered**
ASTM A 534	4720	US	Bar, wire, tube, rods, billets	0.17–0.22 **C**, 0.70–0.90 **Mn**, 0.035 **P**, 0.040 **S**, 0.20–0.35 **Si**, 0.35–0.55 **Cr**, 0.90–1.20 **Ni**, 0.15–0.25 **Mo**	**As–rolled or normalized and tempered**
ASTM A 534	4620	US	Bar, wire, tube, rods, billets	0.17–0.22 **C**, 0.45–0.65 **Mn**, 0.035 **P**, 0.040 **S**, 0.20–0.35 **Si**, 1.65–2.00 **Ni**, 0.20–0.30 **Mo**	**As–rolled or normalized and tempered**
ASTM A 534	4320	US	Bar, wire, tube, rods, billets	0.17–0.22 **C**, 0.45–0.65 **Mn**, 0.035 **P**, 0.040 **S**, 0.20–0.35 **Si**, 0.40–0.60 **Cr**, 1.65–2.00 **Ni**, 0.20–0.30 **Mo**	**As–rolled or normalized and tempered**
DGN–B–297	4620	Mexico	Bar	0.17–0.22 **C**, 0.45–0.65 **Mn**, 0.035 **P**, 0.040 **S**, 0.20–0.35 **Si**, 1.65–2.00 **Ni**, 0.20–0.30 **Mo**	
DGN–B–297	4720	Mexico	Bar	0.17–0.22 **C**, 0.50–0.70 **Mn**, 0.035 **P**, 0.040 **S**, 0.20–0.35 **Si**, 0.35–0.55 **Cr**, 0.90–1.20 **Ni**, 0.15–0.25 **Mo**	
COPANT 514	Grade 5120	COPANT	Tube: seamless	0.17–0.22 **C**, 0.70–0.90 **Mn**, 0.040 **P**, 0.050 **S**, 0.10 **Si**, 0.70–0.90 **Cr**	
DGN–B–203	Grade 4320	Mexico	Tube: seamless	0.17–0.20 **C**, 0.45–0.65 **Mn**, 0.040 **P**, 0.040 **S**, 0.20–0.35 **Si**, 0.40–0.60 **Cr**, 1.65–2.00 **Ni**, 0.20–0.30 **Mo**	
DGN–B–297	5120	Mexico	Bar	0.17–0.20 **C**, 0.70–0.90 **Mn**, 0.035 **P**, 0.040 **S**, 0.20–0.35 **Si**, 0.70–0.90 **Cr**	
COPANT 514	Grade 6120	COPANT	Tube: seamless	0.17–0.20 **C**, 0.70–0.90 **Mn**, 0.040 **P**, 0.050 **S**, 0.10 **Si**, 0.70–0.90 **Cr**, 0.10 min **V**	
ANSI/ASTM A 202	Grade A	US	Plate	0.17 **C**, 1.00–1.45 **Mn**, 0.04 **P**, 0.04 **S**, 0.54–0.96 **Si**, 0.31–0.64 **Cr**	**As rolled**: all **diam**, (515) **TS**, (310) **YS**, 19 **El**
ANSI/ASTM A 387	Grade 11,class II	US	Plate	0.17 **C**, 0.36–0.69 **Mn**, 0.035 **P**, 0.040 **S**, 0.44–0.86 **Si**, 0.94–1.56 **Cr**, 0.40–0.70 **Mo**	**Annealed or normalized and tempered**: all **diam**, (515) **TS**, (310) **YS**, 22 **El**
DGN–B–368	Grade A	Mexico	Plate	0.17 **C**, 1.05–1.40 **Mn**, 0.035 **P**, 0.05 **S**, 0.60–0.90 **Si**, 0.35–0.60 **Cu**	**As rolled**: (51) **diam**, (515) **TS**, (309) **YS**, 19 **El**
NF A 36–206	10 CD 9.10	France	Plate	0.17 **C**, 0.40–0.85 **Mn**, 0.035 **P**, 0.035 **S**, 0.10–0.40 **Si**, 1.95–2.55 **Cr**, 0.30 **Ni**, 0.90–1.15 **Mo**, 0.04 **V**, 0.25 **Cu**	**Normalized and tempered**: (3–30) **diam**, (510) **TS**, (295) **YS**, 22 **El**
NF A 36–208	3.5 Ni (12N14) 355	France	Plate	0.17 **C**, 0.30–0.80 **Mn**, 0.030 **P**, 0.025 **S**, 0.40 **Si**, 3.25–3.75 **Ni**, 0.05 **V**, 0.015 min **Al**	**Normalized, normalized and tempered or quenched and tempered**: (3–30) **diam**, (490) **TS**, (355) **YS**, 22 **El**
JIS G 3127	Class 3B	Japan	Plate	0.17 **C**, 0.70 **Mn**, 0.025 **P**, 0.025 **S**, 0.15–0.30 **Si**, 3.25–3.75 **Ni**	**Hot rolled and normalized**: (6–16) **diam**, (481) **TS**, (275) **YS**, 22 **El**
NF A 36–208	3.5 Ni (12 N14) 285	France	Plate	0.17 **C**, 0.30–0.80 **Mn**, 0.030 **P**, 0.025 **S**, 0.40 **Si**, 3.25–3.75 **Ni**, 0.05 **V**, 0.015 min **Al**	**Normalized, normalized and tempered or quenched and tempered**: (3–30) **diam**, (460) **TS**, (285) **YS**, 23 **El**
JIS G 3127	Class 2	Japan	Plate	0.17 **C**, 0.70 **Mn**, 0.025 **P**, 0.025 **S**, 0.15–0.30 **Si**, 2.10–2.50 **Ni**	**Hot rolled and normalized**: (6–16) **diam**, (451) **TS**, (255) **YS**, 24 **El**
ANSI/ASTM A 203	Grade D	US	Plate	0.17 **C**, 0.70 **Mn**, 0.04 **P**, 0.04 **S**, 0.13–0.32 **Si**, 3.18–3.82 **Ni**	**Normalized**: <2 **diam**, (450) **TS**, (255) **YS**, 23 **El**
ANSI/ASTM A 387	Grade 11,class I	US	Plate	0.17 **C**, 0.36–0.69 **Mn**, 0.035 **P**, 0.040 **S**, 0.44–0.86 **Si**, 0.94–1.56 **Cr**, 0.40–0.70 **Mo**	**Annealed or normalized and tempered**: all **diam**, (415) **TS**, (240) **YS**, 22 **El**

WROUGHT ALLOY STEELS

specification number	designation	country	product forms	composition	mechanical properties (see page iv for explanation)
JIS G 4109	Class 3	Japan	Plate	0.17 **C**, 0.36–0.69 **Mn**, 0.035 **P**, 0.040 **S**, 0.44–0.86 **Si**, 0.94–1.56 **Cr**, 0.40–0.70 **Mo**	**Hot rolled and annealed:** (8–20) **diam**, (412) **TS**, (235) **YS**, 19 **El**; **Hot rolled, normalized, tempered:** (≤20) **diam**, (520) **TS**, (314) **YS**, 18 **El**
JIS G 4109	Class 2	Japan	Plate	0.17 **C**, 0.36–0.69 **Mn**, 0.035 **P**, 0.040 **S**, 0.13–0.32 **Si**, 0.74–1.21 **Cr**, 0.40–0.65 **Mo**	**Hot rolled and annealed:** (8–20) **diam**, (382) **TS**, (226) **YS**, 19 **El**; **Hot rolled, normalized, tempered:** (≤20) **diam**, (451) **TS**, (275) **YS**, 19 **El**
ANSI/ASTM A 387	Grade 12,class I	US	Plate	0.17 **C**, 0.36–0.69 **Mn**, 0.035 **P**, 0.040 **S**, 0.13–0.32 **Si**, 0.74–1.21 **Cr**, 0.40–0.65 **Mo**	**Annealed or normalized and tempered:** all **diam**, (380) **TS**, (230) **YS**, 22 **El**
SS 14 13 30E	SS 13 30–16	Sweden	Tube, welded	0.17 **C**, 0.40–0.80 **Mn**, 0.045 **P**, 0.045 **S**, 0.15–0.40 **Si**, 0.25 **Cr**, 0.30 **Cu**, 0.009 **N**	**Quenched:** all **diam**, (360) **TS**, (220) **YS**, 25 **El**
SS 14 13 30 E	SS 13 30–06	Sweden	Tube: welded	0.17 **C**, 0.40–0.80 **Mn**, 0.045 **P**, 0.045 **S**, 0.15–0.40 **Si**, 0.25 **Cr**, 0.30 **Cu**, 0.009 **N**	**Quenched:** all **diam**, (360) **TS**, (220) **YS**, 25 **El**
SS 14 13 30 E	SS 13 30–05	Sweden	Tube: seamless	0.17 **C**, 0.40–0.80 **Mn**, 0.045 **P**, 0.045 **S**, 0.15–0.40 **Si**, 0.25 **Cr**, 0.30 **Cu**, 0.009 **N**	**As rolled or quenched:** all **diam**, (360) **TS**, (220) **YS**, 25 **El**
SS 14 13 30 E	SS 13 30–01	Sweden	Bar, plate, sheet	0.17 **C**, 0.40–1.00 **Mn**, 0.050 **P**, 0.050 **S**, 0.40 **Si**, 0.25 **Cr**, 0.30 **Cu**, 0.009 **N**	**Normalized:** all **diam**, (360) **TS**, (220) **YS**, 26 **El**
SS 14 13 30 E	SS 13 30–00	Sweden	Bar	0.17 **C**, 0.40–1.00 **Mn**, 0.045 **P**, 0.045 **S**, 0.15–0.40 **Si**, 0.25 **Cr**, 0.30 **Cu**, 0.009 **N**	**As rolled:** (<40) **diam**, (360) **TS**, (220) **YS**, 26 **El**
ANSI/ASTM A 387	Grade 12,class II	US	Plate	0.17 **C**, 0.36–0.69 **Mn**, 0.035 **P**, 0.040 **S**, 0.13–0.32 **Si**, 0.74–1.21 **Cr**, 0.40–0.65 **Mo**	**Annealed or normalized and tempered:** all **diam**, 22 **El**
SS 14 13 30 E	SS 13 30–15	Sweden	Tube: seamless	0.17 **C**, 0.40–0.80 **Mn**, 0.045 **P**, 0.045 **S**, 0.15–0.40 **Si**, 0.25 **Cr**, 0.30 **Cu**, 0.009 **N**	
IS 4922	St 71	India	Tube	0.16–0.24 **C**, 1.3–1.70 **Mn**, 0.050 **P**, 0.050 **S**, 0.10–0.35 **Si**, 0.30 **Ni**	**Softened, drawn, tempered or hardened, tempered:** all **diam**, (696) **TS**, (617) **YS**
NBN A 25-102	X 20 Cr Mo V 121	Belgium	Tube	0.16–0.24 **C**, 0.27–0.84 **Mn**, 0.033 **P**, 0.033 **S**, 0.07–0.55 **Si**, 10.85–12.65 **Cr**, 0.27–0.83 **Ni**, 0.76–1.25 **Mo**, 0.22–0.38 **V**	**Hot or cold finished or normalized or annealed:** all **diam**, (690) **TS**, (490) **YS**, 17 **El**
IS 5517	Grade 20Mn2	India	Bar, billet	0.16–0.24 **C**, 1.30–1.70 **Mn**, 0.10–0.35 **Si**	**Normalized, annealed or hardened and tempered:** (15) **diam**, (685) **TS**, (490) **YS**
IS 4367	20Mn2	India	Forgings	0.16–0.24 **C**, 1.30–1.70 **Mn**, 0.050 **P**, 0.050 **S**, 0.10–0.35 **Si**	**Hardened and tempered:** (63) **diam**, (588) **TS**, 18 **El**
IS 4922	St 55	India	Tube	0.16–0.24 **C**, 1.3–1.70 **Mn**, 0.050 **P**, 0.050 **S**, 0.10–0.35 **Si**, 0.30 **Ni**	**Softened, drawn, tempered hardened, tempered:** all **diam**, (539) **TS**, (461) **YS**
IS 2041	Type 2 steel 20Mn 2	India	Plate	0.16–0.24 **C**, 1.30–1.70 **Mn**, 0.050 **P**, 0.050 **S**, 0.10 **Si**, 0.25 **Cr**, 0.30 **Ni**, 0.15 **Mo**, 0.40 **Cu**	**Normalized:** (63–100) **diam**, (510) **TS**, (294) **YS**, 20 **El**
NBN A 25–102	19 Mn 5	Belgium	Tube	0.16–0.24 **C**, 0.96–1.35 **Mn**, 0.055 **P**, 0.055 **S**, 0.37–0.65 **Si**, 0.30 **Cr**	**Hot or cold finished and normalized:** (17–59) **diam**, (510) **TS**, (310) **YS** 19 **El**
ANSI/ASTM A 605		US	Plate	0.16–0.23 **C**, 0.20–0.40 **Mn**, 0.010 **P**, 0.010 **S**, 0.12 **Si**, 0.61–0.89 **Cr**, 8.40–9.60 **Ni**, 0.86–1.14 **Mo**, 0.04–0.14 **V**, 4.15–5.10 **Co**	**Quenched and tempered:** ≥4.00 **diam**, (1310) **TS**, (1210) **YS**, 14 **El**
JIS G 4052	SMn 21H	Japan	Bar, wire, rod	0.16–0.23 **C**, 1.15–1.55 **Mn**, 0.030 **P**, 0.030 **S**, 0.15–0.35 **Si**, 0.30 **Cu**	**Hot rolled, normalized, quenched**
JIS G 4052	SMnC 21H	Japan	Bar, wire, rod	0.16–0.23 **C**, 1.15–1.55 **Mn**, 0.030 **P**, 0.030 **S**, 0.15–0.35 **Si**, 0.35–0.70 **Cr**, 0.30 **Cu**	**Hot rolled, normalized, quenched**
AISI 4620		US	Plate	0.16–0.22 **C**, 0.40–0.65 **Mn**, 0.035 **P**, 0.040 **S**, 0.15–0.30 **Si**, 1.65–2.00 **Ni**, 0.20–0.30 **Mo**	

WROUGHT ALLOY STEELS

specification number	designation	country	product forms	composition	mechanical properties (see page iv for explanation)
AISI 6118		US	Bar	0.16–0.21 **C**, 0.50–0.70 **Mn**, 0.035 **P**, 0.040 **S**, 0.15–0.30 **Si**, 0.50–0.70 **Cr**, 0.10–0.15 **Mo**	
DGN-B-203	Grade 4718	Mexico	Tube: seamless	0.16–0.21 **C**, 0.70–0.90 **Mn**, 0.040 **P**, 0.040 **S**, 0.20–0.35 **Si**, 0.35–0.55 **Cr**, 0.90–1.20 **Ni**, 0.30–0.40 **Mo**	
DGN-B-203	Grade 6118	Mexico	Tube: seamless	0.16–0.21 **C**, 0.50–0.70 **Mn**, 0.040 **P**, 0.040 **S**, 0.20–0.35 **Si**, 0.50–0.70 **Cr**, 0.10–0.15 **V**	
COPANT 514	4718	COPANT	Tube	0.16–0.21 **C**, 0.70–0.90 **Mn**, 0.040 **P**, 0.040 **S**, 0.20–0.35 **Si**, 0.35–0.55 **Cr**, 0.90–1.20 **Ni**, 0.30–0.40 **Mo**	
DGN-B-300	6118	Mexico	Bar	0.16–0.21 **C**, 0.50–0.70 **Mn**, 0.035 **P**, 0.040 **S**, 0.20–0.35 **Si**, 0.50–0.70 **Cr**, 0.10–0.15 **Mo**	**Annealed**
DGN-B-300	4718	Mexico	Bar	0.16–0.21 **C**, 0.70–0.90 **Mn**, 0.035 **P**, 0.040 **S**, 0.20–0.35 **Si**, 0.35–0.55 **Cr**, 0.90–1.20 **Ni**, 0.30–0.40 **Mo**	**Annealed**
ANSI/ASTM A 29	4718	US	Bar	0.16–0.21 **C**, 0.70–0.90 **Mn**, 0.035 **P**, 0.040 **S**, 0.15–0.30 **Si**, 0.35–0.55 **Cr**, 0.90–1.20 **Ni**, 0.30–0.40 **Mo**	
ASTM A 689	6118	US	Bar	0.16–0.21 **C**, 0.50–0.70 **Mn**, 0.035 **P**, 0.040 **S**, 0.15–0.30 **Si**, 0.50–0.70 **Cr**, 0.10–0.15 **Mo**	
ASTM A 689	4718	US	Bar	0.16–0.21 **C**, 0.70–0.90 **Mn**, 0.035 **P**, 0.040 **S**, 0.15–0.30 **Si**, 0.35–0.55 **Cr**, 0.90–1.20 **Ni**, 0.30–0.40 **Mo**	
ANSI/ASTM A 322	4718	US	Bar	0.16–0.21 **C**, 0.70–0.90 **Mn**, 0.035 **P**, 0.040 **S**, 0.15–0.30 **Si**, 0.35–0.55 **Cr**, 0.90–1.20 **Ni**, 0.30–0.40 **Mo**	
ANSI/ASTM A 322	6118	US	Bar	0.16–0.21 **C**, 0.50–0.70 **Mn**, 0.035 **P**, 0.040 **S**, 0.15–0.30 **Si**, 0.50–0.70 **Cr**, 0.10–0.15 **V**	
ANSI/ASTM A 29	6118	US	Bar	0.16–0.21 **C**, 0.50–0.70 **Mn**, 0.035 **P**, 0.040 **S**, 0.15–0.30 **Si**, 0.50–0.70 **Cr**, 0.10–0.15 **V**	
AISI 4718		US	Wire, rod	0.16–0.21 **C**, 0.70–0.90 **Mn**, 0.035 **P**, 0.040 **S**, 0.15–0.30 **Si**, 0.35–0.55 **Cr**, 0.90–1.20 **Ni**, 0.30–0.40 **Mo**	
AISI 6118		US	Wire, rod	0.16–0.21 **C**, 0.50–0.70 **Mn**, 0.035 **P**, 0.040 **S**, 0.15–0.30 **Si**, 0.50–0.70 **Cr**, 0.10–0.15 **V**	
ANSI/ASTM A 519	4718	US	Tube: seamless	0.16–0.21 **C**, 0.70–0.90 **Mn**, 0.040 **P**, 0.040 **S**, 0.15–0.35 **Si**, 0.35–0.55 **Cr**, 0.90–1.20 **Ni**, 0.30–0.40 **Mo**	
ANSI/ASTM A 519	6118	US	Tube: seamless	0.16–0.21 **C**, 0.50–0.70 **Mn**, 0.040 **P**, 0.040 **S**, 0.15–0.35 **Si**, 0.50–0.70 **Cr**, 0.10–0.15 **V**	
DGN-B-297	4718	Mexico	Bar	0.16–0.21 **C**, 0.70–0.90 **Mn**, 0.035 **P**, 0.040 **S**, 0.20–0.35 **Si**, 0.35–0.55 **Cr**, 0.90–1.20 **Ni**, 0.30–0.40 **Mo**	
DGN-B-297	6118	Mexico	Bar	0.16–0.21 **C**, 0.50–0.70 **Mn**, 0.035 **P**, 0.040 **S**, 0.20–0.35 **Si**, 0.50–0.70 **Cr**, 0.10–0.15 **V**	
COPANT 514	Grade 6118	COPANT	Tube: seamless	0.16–0.21 **C**, 0.50–0.70 **Mn**, 0.040 **P**, 0.050 **S**, 0.10 **Si**, 0.50–0.70 **Cr**, 0.10–0.15 **V**	
NF A 36-201	E 355, II	France	Sheet, plate	0.16–0.18 **C**, 1.50 **Mn**, 0.035 **P**, 0.035 **S**, 0.50 **Si**	**Normalized or normalized and tempered:** (5–16) **diam**, (510) **TS**, (355) **YS**, 22 **El**
NF A 36-201	E 355, III	France	Sheet, plate	0.16 **C**, 1.50 **Mn**, 0.03 **P**, 0.03 **S**, 0.50 **Si**, 0.80 **Cr**, 0.80 **Ni**, 0.80 **Mo**, 0.80 **Cu**	**Normalized or normalized and tempered:** (5–16) **diam**, (510) **TS**, (355) **YS**, 22 **El**

specification number	designation	country	product forms	composition	mechanical properties (see page iv for explanation)
EURONORM 129	FeE 355 Ni 2	EURONORM	Plate, strip	0.16 **C**, 0.85–1.65 **Mn**, 0.030 **P**, 0.025 **S**, 0.35 **Si**, 0.25 **Cr**, 0.30–0.80 **Ni**, 0.10 **Mo**, 0.08 **V**, 0.015_{met} or 0.020 tot. (min) **Al**, 0.35 **Cu**, 0.06 **Nb**	**Normalized:** ≤(35) **diam**, (490) **TS**, (355) **YS**, 22 **El**
SIS 14 21 03 E	SIS 2103–01	Sweden	Bar, plate, sheet	0.16 **C**, 0.90–1.60 **Mn**, 0.040 **P**, 0.040 **S**, 0.10–0.50 **Si**, 0.25 **Cr**, 0.30 **Cu**, 0.009 **N**	**Normalized:** all **diam**, (490) **TS**, (310) **YS**, 21 **El**
BS 980	CDS–19	UK	Tube	0.16 **C**, 2.0 **Mn**, 0.050 **P**, 0.050 **S**, 0.20 min **Si**, 17.5 min **Cr**, 7.5 min **Ni**	**Annealed descaled:** all **diam**, (480) **TS**, (205) **YS**
JIS G 3126	Type 2A	Japan	Plate	0.16 **C**, 0.80–1.60 **Mn**, 0.035 **P**, 0.035 **S**, 0.15–0.55 **Si**	**Normalized:** (6–16) **diam**, (441) **TS**, (324) **YS**, 22 **El**
JIS G 3126	Type 2B	Japan	Plate	0.16 **C**, 0.80–1.60 **Mn**, 0.035 **P**, 0.035 **S**, 0.15–0.55 **Si**	**Quenched and tempered:** (6–16) **diam**, (441) **TS**, (324) **YS**, 22 **El**
SIS 14 14 32 E	SIS 14 32–01	Sweden	Bar, plate, sheet	0.16 **C**, 0.8–1.4 **Mn**, 0.040 **P**, 0.040 **S**, 0.15–0.40 **Si**, 0.25 **Cr**, 0.30 **Cu**, 0.009 **N**	**Normalized:** all **diam**, (430) **TS**, (260) **YS**, 24 **El**
NF A 36–208	0.5 Ni (10 N2) 285	France	Plate	0.16 **C**, 0.70–1.50 **Mn**, 0.035 **P**, 0.030 **S**, 0.40 **Si**, 0.30–0.80 **Ni**, 0.08 **V**, 0.015 min **Al**, 0.06 **Nb**, 0.10 **Nb+V**	**Normalized:** (3–30) **diam**, (420) **TS**, (285) **YS**, 25 **El**
AS G18	G18/En 29A	Australia	Bar, billet	0.15–0.25 **C**, 0.65 **Mn**, 0.050 **P**, 0.050 **S**, 0.10–0.35 **Si**, 2.50–3.50 **Cr**, 0.40 **Ni**, 0.30–0.70 **Mo**	**Hardened, tempered:** 6 **diam**, (690) **TS**, (525) **YS**
ANSI/ASTM A 541	Class 3	US	Forgings	0.15–0.25 **C**, 1.20–1.50 **Mn**, 0.035 **P**, 0.040 **S**, 0.15–0.35 **Si**, 0.25 **Cr**, 0.40–1.00 **Ni**, 0.45–0.60 **Mo**, 0.05 **V**	**Quenched and tempered:** all **diam**, 80 (550) **TS**, 50 (340) **YS**, 18 **El**
ANSI/ASTM A 508	Grade 3	US	Forgings	0.15–0.25 **C**, 1.20–1.50 **Mn**, 0.025 **P**, 0.025 **S**, 0.15–0.40 **Si**, 0.25 **Cr**, 0.40–1.00 **Ni**, 0.45–0.60 **Mo**, 0.05 **V**	**Quenched and tempered:** all **diam**, (550) **TS**, (345) **YS**, 18 **El**
ANSI/ASTM A 541	Grade 3	US	Forgings	0.15–0.25 **C**, 1.20–1.50 **Mn**, 0.035 **P**, 0.040 **S**, 0.15–0.35 **Si**, 0.25 **Cr**, 0.40–1.00 **Ni**, 0.45–0.60 **Mo**, 0.05 **V**	**Quenched and tempered:** all **diam**, (550) **TS**, (340) **YS**, 18 **El**
ANSI/ASTM A 508	Class 3	US	Forgings	0.15–0.25 **C**, 1.20–1.50 **Mn**, 0.025 **P**, 0.025 **S**, 0.15–0.40 **Si**, 0.25 **Cr**, 0.40–1.00 **Ni**, 0.45–0.60 **Mo**, 0.05 **V**	**Quenched and tempered:** all **diam**, 80 (550) **TS**, 50 (345) **YS**, 18 **El**
JIS G 3211	Class 3	Japan	Forgings	0.15–0.25 **C**, 1.20–1.50 **Mn**, 0.030 **P**, 0.030 **S**, 0.15–0.35 **Si**, 0.40–0.80 **Ni**, 0.45–0.60 **Mo**, 0.06 **V**	**Quenched and tempered:** all **diam**, (549) **TS**, (343) **YS**, 18 **El**
JIS G 3212	Class 3	Japan	Forgings	0.15–0.25 **C**, 1.20–1.50 **Mn**, 0.025 **P**, 0.025 **S**, 0.15–0.35 **Si**, 0.40–0.80 **Ni**, 0.45–0.60 **Mo**, 0.05 **V**	**Quenched and tempered:** all **diam**, (549) **TS**, (343) **YS**, 18 **El**
AS 1443	AS 1443/K9	Australia	Bar	0.15–0.25 **C**, 1.30–1.70 **Mn**, 0.050 **P**, 0.050 **S**, 0.10–0.35 **Si**	**As rolled or normalized:** (≤150) **diam**, (540) **TS**, (300) **YS**, 18 **El**
AS 1442	Grade AS 1442/K9	Australia	Bar	0.15–0.25 **C**, 1.30–1.70 **Mn**, 0.050 **P**, 0.050 **S**, 0.10–0.35 **Si**	**As rolled or normalized:** (≤150) **diam**, (540) **TS**, (300) **YS**, 18 **El**
IS 2041	Type 1 steel 20Mo55	India	Plate	0.15–0.25 **C**, 0.40–0.70 **Mn**, 0.050 **P**, 0.050 **S**, 0.10–0.35 **Si**, 0.25 **Cr**, 0.30 **Ni**, 0.45–0.65 **Mo**, 0.40 **Cu**	**Normalized:** all **diam**, (470) **TS**, (274) **YS**, 20 **El**
COPANT 513	T17	COPANT	Tube	0.15–0.25 **C**, 0.30–0.61 **Mn**, 0.045 **P**, 0.045 **S**, 0.15–0.35 **Si**, 0.80–1.25 **Cr**, 0.15 min **V**	**Normalized and tempered, cold finished and tempered:** (>8) **diam**, (430) **TS**, (205) **YS**, 30 **El**
ANSI/ASTM A 213	Grade T17	US	Tube: seamless	0.15–0.25 **C**, 0.30–0.61 **Mn**, 0.045 **P**, 0.045 **S**, 0.15–0.35 **Si**, 0.80–1.25 **Cr**, 0.15 min **V**	**Annealed:** 0.312 (7.94) **diam**, 60 (414) **TS**, 30 (207) **YS**, 30 **El**
ANSI/ASTM A 209	Grade T1a	US	Tube: seamless	0.15–0.25 **C**, 0.30–0.80 **Mn**, 0.045 **P**, 0.045 **S**, 0.10–0.50 **Si**, 0.44–0.65 **Mo**	**Annealed:** 0.312 (7.94) **diam**, 60 (414) **TS**, 32 (221) **YS**, 30 **El**

WROUGHT ALLOY STEELS

specification number	designation	country	product forms	composition	mechanical properties (see page iv for explanation)
NOM–B–193	Grade T 1a	Mexico	Tube: seamless	0.15–0.25 **C**, 0.30–0.80 **Mn**, 0.045 **P**, 0.045 **S**, 0.10–0.50 **Si**, 0.44–0.65 **Mo**	**Hot or cold finished:** (0.89–12.7) **diam**, (414) **TS**, (221) **YS**, 30 **El**
ANSI/ASTM A 250	Grade T 1a	US	Tube: electric, resistance, welded	0.15–0.25 **C**, 0.30–0.80 **Mn**, 0.045 **P**, 0.045 **S**, 0.10–0.50 **Si**, 0.44–0.65 **Mo**	**Normalized:** 0.312 (7.94) **diam**, 60 (414) **TS**, 32 (221) **YS**, 30 **El**
NOM–B–194	T 17	Mexico	Tube: seamless	0.15–0.25 **C**, 0.30–0.61 **Mn**, 0.045 **P**, 0.045 **S**, 0.15–0.35 **Si**, 0.80–1.25 **Cr**, 0.15 **V**	**Annealed or normalized and quenched:** (0.38–12.7) **diam**, (414) **TS**, (207) **YS**
DGN–B–219	Grade T1a	Mexico	Tube: electric resistance welded	0.15–0.25 **C**, 0.30–0.80 **Mn**, 0.045 **P**, 0.045 **S**, 0.10–0.50 **Si**, 0.44–0.65 **Mo**	**As welded:** (7.92) **diam**, (412) **TS**, (216) **YS**, 30 **El**
JIS G 3462	Class 13	Japan	Tube: seamless	0.15–0.25 **C**, 0.30–0.80 **Mn**, 0.035 **P**, 0.035 **S**, 0.10–0.50 **Si**, 0.45–0.65 **Mo**	**Full annealed or annealed, normalized and tempered:** (≥8) **diam**, (412) **TS**, (206) **YS**, 30 **El**
COPANT R 204	Grade T–1a	COPANT	Tube: seamless	0.15–0.25 **C**, 0.30–0.80 **Mn**, 0.045 **P**, 0.045 **S**, 0.10–0.50 **Si**, 0.44–0.65 **Mo**	**Hot or cold finished:** (>8) **diam**, (410) **TS**, (220) **YS**, 30 **El**
ANSI/ASTM A 730	Grade B	US	Forgings	0.15–0.25 **C**, 0.30–0.60 **Mn**, 0.045 **P**, 0.050 **S**	
BS 4670:1971	Grade 785M19	UK	Forgings	0.15–0.23 **C**, 1.40–1.80 **Mn**, 0.040 **P**, 0.040 **S**, 0.10–0.35 **Si**, 0.40 **Cr**, 0.40–0.70 **Ni**, 0.15–0.35 **Mo**	**Hardened and tempered:** (500) **diam**, (600) **TS**, (440) **YS**, 18 **El**
BS 970: Part 2	Grade 785 M 19	UK	Blooms, billets, bar, forgings	0.15–0.23 **C**, 1.40–1.80 **Mn**, 0.10–0.35 **Si**, 0.40–0.70 **Ni**, 0.15–0.35 **Mo**	**Hardened and tempered:** 10 **diam**, (555) **TS**, (400) **YS**, 16 **El**
NF A 35–553	18 CD 4	France	Strip	0.15–0.22 **C**, 0.60–0.90 **Mn**, 0.035 **P**, 0.035 **S**, 0.10–0.40 **Si**, 0.85–1.15 **Cr**, 0.15–0.30 **Mo**	
COPANT 334	18 CD 4	COPANT	Bar	0.15–0.22 **C**, 0.60–0.80 **Mn**, 0.040 **P**, 0.035 **S**, 0.35 **Si**, 0.85–1.15 **Cr**, 0.20–0.30 **Mo**	
EURONORM 119–74, III	18 CrMo 4 KD	EURONORM	Wire, rod	0.15–0.21 **C**, 0.60–0.90 **Mn**, 0.035 **P**, 0.035 **S**, 0.15–0.40 **Si**, 0.85–1.15 **Cr**, 0.15–0.25 **Mo**	**Bright annealed:** (11) **diam**, (1080) **TS**, (835) **YS**, 8 **El**
ISO R 683/XI	7	ISO	Bar	0.15–0.21 **C**, 0.60–0.90 **Mn**, 0.035 **P**, 0.035 **S**, 0.15–0.40 **Si**, 0.85–1.15 **Cr**, 0.15–0.25 **Mo**	**Carburized and hardened:** all **diam**, (1029) **TS**, (686) **YS**, 8 **El**
ISO R 683/XI	7a	ISO	Bar	0.15–0.21 **C**, 0.60–0.90 **Mn**, 0.035 **P**, 0.020–0.035 **S**, 0.15–0.40 **Si**, 0.85–1.15 **Cr**, 0.15–0.25 **Mo**	**Carburized and hardened:** all **diam**, (1029) **TS**, (686) **YS**, 8 **El**
ANSI/ASTM A 514	Grade A	US	Plate	0.15–0.21 **C**, 0.80–1.10 **Mn**, 0.035 **P**, 0.04 **S**, 0.40–0.80 **Si**, 0.50–0.80 **Cr**, 0.18–0.28 **Mo**, 0.0025 **B**, 0.05–0.15 **Zr**	**Quenched and tempered:** ≥0.75–2.50 **diam**, (760) **TS**, (690) **YS**, 18 **El**
ANSI/ASTM A 514	Grade G	US	Plate	0.15–0.21 **C**, 0.80–1.10 **Mn**, 0.035 **P**, 0.04 **S**, 0.50–0.90 **Si**, 0.50–0.90 **Cr**, 0.40–0.60 **Mo**, 0.0025 **B**, 0.05–0.15 **Zr**	**Quenched and tempered:** ≥0.75–2.50 **diam**, (760) **TS**, (690) **YS**, 18 **El**
ANSI/ASTM A 514	Grade N	US	Plate	0.15–0.21 **C**, 0.80–1.10 **Mn**, 0.035 **P**, 0.04 **S**, 0.40–0.90 **Si**, 0.50–0.80 **Cr**, 0.25 **Mo**, 0.0005–0.0025 **B**, 0.05–0.15 **Zr**	**Quenched and tempered:** ≥0.75 **diam**, (760) **TS**, (690) **YS**, 18 **El**
AMS 6386B	Type 1	US	Sheet, plate	0.15–0.21 **C**, 0.80–1.10 **Mn**, 0.035 **P**, 0.040 **S**, 0.40–0.80 **Si**, 0.50–0.80 **Cr**, 0.18–0.28 **Mo**, 0.0005–0.005 **B**, 0.05–0.15 **Zr**	**Hardened, tempered:** 1.250 (31.75) **diam**, 110 (758) **TS**, 100 (690) **YS**, 18 **El**
AMS 6386B	Type 6	US	Sheet, plate	0.15–0.21 **C**, 0.80–1.10 **Mn**, 0.035 **P**, 0.040 **S**, 0.50–0.90 **Si**, 0.50–0.90 **Cr**, 0.40–0.60 **Mo**, 0.0005–0.005 **B**, 0.05–0.15 **Zr**	**Hardened, tempered:** 1.250–2.000 (31.75–50.80) **diam**, 110 (758) **TS**, 100 (690) **YS**, 18 **El**
ANSI/ASTM A 739	Grade B 11	US	Bar	0.15–0.21 **C**, 0.40–0.65 **Mn**, 0.035 **P**, 0.040 **S**, 0.50–0.80 **Si**, 1.00–1.50 **Cr**, 0.45–0.65 **Mo**	**Hot–rolled, normalized and tempered:** all **diam**, 70 (483) **TS**, 45 (310) **YS**, 18 **El**
DGN–B–300	4718 H	Mexico	Bar	0.15–0.21 **C**, 0.60–0.95 **Mn**, 0.040 **P**, 0.035 **S**, 0.20–0.35 **Si**, 0.30–0.60 **Cr**, 0.85–1.25 **Ni**, 0.30–0.40 **Mo**	**Annealed**

WROUGHT ALLOY STEELS

specification number	designation	country	product forms	composition	mechanical properties (see page iv for explanation)
DGN–B–300	6118 H	Mexico	Bar	0.15–0.21 **C**, 0.40–0.80 **Mn**, 0.040 **P**, 0.035 **S**, 0.20–0.35 **Si**, 0.40–0.80 **Cr**, 0.10–0.15 **V**	**Annealed**
ANSI/ASTM A 304	4718 H	US	Bar	0.15–0.21 **C**, 0.60–0.95 **Mn**, 0.040 **P**, 0.040 **S**, 0.15–0.30 **Si**, 0.30–0.60 **Cr**, 0.85–1.25 **Ni**, 0.30–0.40 **Mo**	
ASTM A 689	6118 H	US	Bar	0.15–0.21 **C**, 0.40–0.80 **Mn**, 0.040 **P**, 0.040 **S**, 0.15–0.30 **Si**, 0.40–0.80 **Cr**, 0.10–0.15 **V**	
ANSI/ASTM A 304	6118 H	US	Bar	0.15–0.21 **C**, 0.40–0.80 **Mn**, 0.040 **P**, 0.040 **S**, 0.15–0.30 **Si**, 0.40–0.80 **Cr**, 0.10–0.15 **V**	
ASTM A 689	4718 H	US	Bar	0.15–0.21 **C**, 0.60–0.95 **Mn**, 0.040 **P**, 0.040 **S**, 0.15–0.30 **Si**, 0.30–0.60 **Cr**, 0.85–1.25 **Ni**, 0.30–0.40 **Mo**	
AISI 8617		US	Plate	0.15–0.21 **C**, 0.60–0.90 **Mn**, 0.035 **P**, 0.040 **S**, 0.15–0.30 **Si**, 0.35–0.60 **Cr**, 0.40–0.70 **Ni**, 0.15–0.25 **Mo**	
AISI 4617		US	Plate	0.15–0.21 **C**, 0.40–0.65 **Mn**, 0.035 **P**, 0.040 **S**, 0.15–0.30 **Si**, 1.60–2.00 **Ni**, 0.20–0.30 **Mo**	
AISI 4718 H		US	Wire, rod	0.15–0.21 **C**, 0.60–0.95 **Mn**, 0.15–0.30 **Si**, 0.30–0.60 **Cr**, 0.85–1.25 **Ni**, 0.30–0.40 **Mo**	
AISI 6118 H		US	Wire, rod	0.15–0.21 **C**, 0.40–0.80 **Mn**, 0.15–0.30 **Si**, 0.40–0.80 **Cr**, 0.10–0.15 **V**	
AISI 6118H		US	Bar	0.15–0.21 **C**, 0.40–0.80 **Mn**, 0.035 **P**, 0.040 **S**, 0.15–0.30 **Si**, 0.40–0.80 **Cr**, 0.10–0.15 **V**	
DIN 17210	Grade 18 CrNi 8	Germany	Blooms, slabs, billets, wire, plate, sheet, strip, tube, forgings	0.15–0.20 **C**, 0.40–0.60 **Mn**, 0.035 **P**, 0.035 **S**, 0.15–0.40 **Si**, 1.80–2.10 **Cr**, 1.80–2.10 **Ni**	**Rolled or forged:** (11) **diam**, (1226) **TS**, (834) **YS**, 7 **El**
AMS 6272F		US	Bar, forgings, tube	0.15–0.20 **C**, 0.70–1.00 **Mn**, 0.025 **P**, 0.025 **S**, 0.20–0.35 **Si**, 0.40–0.60 **Cr**, 0.40–0.70 **Ni**, 0.15–0.25 **Mo**, 0.35 **Cu**	**Cold finished (bar):** ≤0.500 (≤12.70) **diam**, 130 (896) max **TS**
AMS 6275C		US	Bar, forgings, tubes	0.15–0.20 **C**, 0.75–1.00 **Mn**, 0.025 **P**, 0.025 **S**, 0.20–0.35 **Si**, 0.30–0.50 **Cr**, 0.30–0.60 **Ni**, 0.08–0.15 **Mo**, 0.35 **Cu**	**Cold finished (bar):** ≤0.500 (≤12.70) **diam**, 130 (896) max **TS**
AMS 6292D		US	Bar, forgings	0.15–0.20 **C**, 0.45–0.65 **Mn**, 0.025 **P**, 0.025 **S**, 0.20–0.35 **Si**, 0.20 **Cr**, 1.65–2.00 **Ni**, 0.20–0.30 **Mo**, 0.35 **Cu**	**Cold finished (bar):** ≤0.500 (≤12.70) **diam**, 125 (862) max **TS**
JIS G 4311	SUH 600	Japan	Bar	0.15–0.20 **C**, 0.50–1.00 **Mn**, 0.50 **Si**, 10.00–13.00 **Cr**, 0.60 **Ni**, 0.30–0.90 **Mo**, 0.75–1.25 **W**, 0.10–0.40 **V**, 0.05–0.10 **N**, 0.20–0.60 **Nb+Ta**, 0.040 **P**, 0.030 **S**	**Quenched and tempered:** (≤75) **diam**, (834) **TS**, (686) **YS**, 15 **El**
NBN A 21–221	C 17 B KD	Belgium	Wire	0.15–0.20 **C**, 0.70–1.30 **Mn**, 0.035 **P**, 0.035 **S**, 0.15–0.40 **Si**, 0.1–0.4 **Cr**, 0.001–0.005 **B**	**Quenched and tempered:** (≤10) **diam**, (780) **TS**, (640) **YS**, 15 **El**
AISI 4817		US	Bar	0.15–0.20 **C**, 0.40–0.60 **Mn**, 0.035 **P**, 0.040 **S**, 0.15–0.30 **Si**, 3.25–3.75 **Ni**, 0.20–0.30 **Mo**	
AISI 5117		US	Bar	0.15–0.20 **C**, 0.70–0.90 **Mn**, 0.035 **P**, 0.040 **S**, 0.15–0.30 **Si**, 0.70–0.90 **Cr**	
AISI 8617		US	Bar	0.15–0.20 **C**, 0.70–0.90 **Mn**, 0.035 **P**, 0.040 **S**, 0.15–0.30 **Si**, 0.40–0.60 **Cr**, 0.40–0.70 **Ni**, 0.15–0.25 **Mo**	
BS 970 Part 3	Grade 665 A 17	UK	Blooms, billets, bar, forgings	0.15–0.20 **C**, 0.45–0.65 **Mn**, 0.25 **Cr**, 1.60–2.00 **Ni**, 0.20–0.30 **Mo**	
BS 970 Part 3	Grade 805 A 17	UK	Blooms, billets, bar, forgings	0.15–0.20 **C**, 0.70–0.90 **Mn**, 0.40–0.60 **Cr**, 0.40–0.70 **Ni**, 0.15–0.25 **Mo**	

WROUGHT ALLOY STEELS

specification number	designation	country	product forms	composition	mechanical properties (see page iv for explanation)
BS 970 Part 3	Grade 822 A 17	UK	Blooms, billets, bar, forgings	0.15–0.20 **C**, 0.50–0.70 **Mn**, 1.40–1.70 **Cr**, 1.80–2.20 **Ni**, 0.15–0.25 **Mo**	
AMS 6242C		US	Bar	0.15–0.20 **C**, 0.35–0.65 **Mn**, 0.040 **P**, 0.20–0.35 **S**, 0.20–0.35 **Si**, 4.75–5.25 **Ni**	
COPANT 334	4817	COPANT	Bar	0.15–0.20 **C**, 0.40–0.60 **Mn**, 0.035 **P**, 0.040 **S**, 0.20–0.35 **Si**, 3.25–3.75 **Ni**, 0.20–0.30 **Mo**	
COPANT 334	8617	COPANT	Bar	0.15–0.20 **C**, 0.70–0.90 **Mn**, 0.035 **P**, 0.040 **S**, 0.20–0.35 **Si**, 0.40–0.60 **Cr**, 0.40–0.70 **Ni**, 0.15–0.25 **Mo**	
DGN–B–203	Grade 4817	Mexico	Tube: seamless	0.15–0.20 **C**, 0.40–0.60 **Mn**, 0.040 **P**, 0.040 **S**, 0.20–0.35 **Si**, 3.25–3.75 **Ni**, 0.20–0.30 **Mo**	
DGN–B–203	Grade 4617	Mexico	Tube: seamless	0.15–0.20 **C**, 0.45–0.65 **Mn**, 0.040 **P**, 0.040 **S**, 0.20–0.65 **Si**, 1.65–2.00 **Ni**, 0.20–0.30 **Mo**	
DGN–B–203	Grade 8617	Mexico	Tube: seamless	0.15–0.20 **C**, 0.70–0.90 **Mn**, 0.040 **P**, 0.040 **S**, 0.20–0.35 **Si**, 0.40–0.60 **Cr**, 0.40–0.70 **Ni**, 0.15–0.25 **Mo**	
DGN–B–203	Grade 94B17	Mexico	Tube: seamless	0.15–0.20 **C**, 0.75–1.00 **Mn**, 0.040 **P**, 0.040 **S**, 0.20–0.35 **Si**, 0.30–0.50 **Cr**, 0.30–0.60 **Ni**, 0.08–0.15 **Mo**, 0.0005 min **B**	
COPANT 514	4617	COPANT	Tube	0.15–0.20 **C**, 0.45–0.65 **Mn**, 0.040 **P**, 0.040 **S**, 0.20–0.35 **Si**, 1.65–2.0 **Ni**, 0.20–0.30 **Mo**	
DGN–B–300	94B17	Mexico	Bar	0.15–0.20 **C**, 0.75–1.00 **Mn**, 0.035 **P**, 0.040 **S**, 0.20–0.35 **Si**, 0.30–0.50 **Cr**, 0.30–0.60 **Ni**, 0.08–0.15 **Mo**, 0.0005 min **B**	**Annealed**
DGN–B–300	8617	Mexico	Bar	0.15–0.20 **C**, 0.70–0.90 **Mn**, 0.035 **P**, 0.040 **S**, 0.20–0.35 **Si**, 0.40–0.60 **Cr**, 0.40–0.70 **Ni**, 0.15–0.25 **Mo**	**Annealed**
DGN–B–300	4817	Mexico	Bar	0.15–0.20 **C**, 0.40–0.60 **Mn**, 0.035 **P**, 0.040 **S**, 0.20–0.35 **Si**, 3.25–3.75 **Ni**, 0.20–0.30 **Mo**	**Annealed**
ANSI/ASTM A 29	4817	US	Bar	0.15–0.20 **C**, 0.40–0.60 **Mn**, 0.035 **P**, 0.040 **S**, 0.15–0.30 **Si**, 3.25–3.75 **Ni**, 0.20–0.30 **Mo**	
ASTM A 689	94B17	US	Bar	0.15–0.20 **C**, 0.75–1.00 **Mn**, 0.035 **P**, 0.040 **S**, 0.15–0.30 **Si**, 0.30–0.50 **Cr**, 0.30–0.60 **Ni**, 0.08–0.15 **Mo**, 0.0005 min **B**	
ASTM A 689	8617	US	Bar	0.15–0.20 **C**, 0.70–0.90 **Mn**, 0.035 **P**, 0.040 **S**, 0.15–0.30 **Si**, 0.40–0.60 **Cr**, 0.40–0.70 **Ni**, 0.15–0.25 **Mo**	
ASTM A 689	4817	US	Bar	0.15–0.20 **C**, 0.40–0.60 **Mn**, 0.035 **P**, 0.040 **S**, 0.15–0.30 **Si**, 3.25–3.75 **Ni**, 0.20–0.30 **Mo**	
ANSI/ASTM A 322	4817	US	Bar	0.15–0.20 **C**, 0.40–0.60 **Mn**, 0.035 **P**, 0.040 **S**, 0.15–0.30 **Si**, 3.25–3.75 **Ni**, 0.20–0.30 **Mo**	
ANSI/ASTM A 322	94B17	US	Bar	0.15–0.20 **C**, 0.75–1.00 **Mn**, 0.035 **P**, 0.040 **S**, 0.15–0.30 **Si**, 0.30–0.50 **Cr**, 0.30–0.60 **Ni**, 0.08–0.15 **Mo**	
ANSI/ASTM A 322	8617	US	Bar	0.15–0.20 **C**, 0.70–0.90 **Mn**, 0.035 **P**, 0.040 **S**, 0.15–0.30 **Si**, 0.40–0.60 **Cr**, 0.40–0.70 **Ni**, 0.15–0.25 **Mo**	
ANSI/ASTM A 29	8617	US	Bar	0.15–0.20 **C**, 0.70–0.90 **Mn**, 0.035 **P**, 0.040 **S**, 0.15–0.30 **Si**, 0.40–0.60 **Cr**, 0.40–0.70 **Ni**, 0.15–0.25 **Mo**	

WROUGHT ALLOY STEELS

specification number	designation	country	product forms	composition	mechanical properties (see page iv for explanation)
AISI 94B17		US	Bar	0.15–0.20 **C**, 0.75–1.00 **Mn**, 0.035 **P**, 0.040 **S**, 0.15–0.30 **Si**, 0.30–0.50 **Cr**, 0.30–0.60 **Ni**, 0.08–0.15 **Mo**, 0.0005–0.003 **B**	
AISI 8617		US	Wire, rod	0.15–0.20 **C**, 0.70–0.90 **Mn**, 0.035 **P**, 0.040 **S**, 0.15–0.30 **Si**, 0.40–0.60 **Cr**, 0.40–0.70 **Ni**, 0.15–0.25 **Mo**	
AISI 94B17		US	Wire, rod	0.15–0.20 **C**, 0.75–1.00 **Mn**, 0.035 **P**, 0.040 **S**, 0.15–0.30 **Si**, 0.30–0.50 **Cr**, 0.30–0.60 **Ni**, 0.08–0.15 **Mo**	
AISI 4817		US	Wire, rod	0.15–0.20 **C**, 0.40–0.60 **Mn**, 0.035 **P**, 0.040 **S**, 0.15–0.30 **Si**, 3.25–3.75 **Ni**, 0.20–0.30 **Mo**	
ANSI/ASTM A 519	4617	US	Tube: seamless	0.15–0.20 **C**, 0.45–0.65 **Mn**, 0.040 **P**, 0.040 **S**, 0.15–0.35 **Si**, 1.65–2.00 **Ni**, 0.20–0.30 **Mo**	
ANSI/ASTM A 519	4817	US	Tube: seamless	0.15–0.20 **C**, 0.40–0.60 **Mn**, 0.040 **P**, 0.040 **S**, 0.15–0.35 **Si**, 3.25–3.75 **Ni**, 0.20–0.30 **Mo**	
ANSI/ASTM A 519	8617	US	Tube: seamless	0.15–0.20 **C**, 0.70–0.90 **Mn**, 0.040 **P**, 0.040 **S**, 0.15–0.35 **Si**, 0.40–0.60 **Cr**, 0.40–0.70 **Ni**, 0.15–0.25 **Mo**	
ANSI/ASTM A 519	94B17	US	Tube: seamless	0.15–0.20 **C**, 0.75–1.00 **Mn**, 0.040 **P**, 0.040 **S**, 0.15–0.35 **Si**, 0.30–0.50 **Cr**, 0.30–0.60 **Ni**, 0.08–0.15 **Mo**	
AISI 8617		US	Sheet, strip	0.15–0.20 **C**, 0.70–0.90 **Mn**, 0.035 **P**, 0.040 **S**, 0.20–0.35 **Si**, 0.40–0.60 **Cr**, 0.40–0.70 **Ni**, 0.15–0.25 **Mo**	
AISI 8617		US	Sheet, strip	0.15–0.20 **C**, 0.70–0.90 **Mn**, 0.035 **P**, 0.040 **S**, 0.20–0.35 **Si**, 0.40–0.60 **Cr**, 0.40–0.70 **Ni**, 0.15–0.25 **Mo**	
DGN–B–297	94B17	Mexico	Bar	0.15–0.20 **C**, 0.75–1.00 **Mn**, 0.035 **P**, 0.040 **S**, 0.20–0.35 **Si**, 0.30–0.50 **Cr**, 0.30–0.60 **Ni**, 0.08–0.15 **Mo**	
DGN–B–297	4817	Mexico	Bar	0.15–0.20 **C**, 0.40–0.60 **Mn**, 0.035 **P**, 0.040 **S**, 0.20–0.35 **Si**, 3.25–3.75 **Ni**, 0.20–0.30 **Mo**	
DGN–B–297	8617	Mexico	Bar	0.15–0.20 **C**, 0.70–0.90 **Mn**, 0.035 **P**, 0.040 **S**, 0.20–0.35 **Si**, 0.40–0.60 **Cr**, 0.40–0.70 **Ni**, 0.15–0.25 **Mo**	
COPANT 514	Grade 4817	COPANT	Tube: seamless	0.15–0.20 **C**, 0.40–0.60 **Mn**, 0.040 **P**, 0.050 **S**, 0.10 **Si**, 3.25–3.75 **Ni**, 0.20–0.30 **Mo**	
COPANT 514	Grade 94B17	COPANT	Tube: seamless	0.15–0.20 **C**, 0.75–1.00 **Mn**, 0.040 **P**, 0.050 **S**, 0.10 **Si**, 0.30–0.50 **Cr**, 0.30–0.60 **Ni**, 0.08–0.15 **Mo**	
COPANT 514	Grade 8617	COPANT	Tube: seamless	0.15–0.20 **C**, 0.70–0.90 **Mn**, 0.040 **P**, 0.050 **S**, 0.10 **Si**, 0.40–0.60 **Cr**, 0.40–0.70 **Ni**, 0.15–0.25 **Mo**	
AS G18	G18/En 36A	Australia	Bar, billet	0.15 **C**, 0.30–0.60 **Mn**, 0.050 **P**, 0.050 **S**, 0.10–0.35 **Si**, 0.60–1.10 **Cr**, 3.00–3.75 **Ni**	**Blank carburized, hardened:** all **diam**, (850) **TS**
ANSI/ASTM A 542	Class 2	US	Plate	0.15 **C**, 0.27–0.63 **Mn**, 0.035 **P**, 0.035 **S**, 0.50 **Si**, 1.88–2.62 **Cr**, 0.85–1.15 **Mo**	**Quenched and tempered:** all **diam**, (795) **TS**, (690) **YS**, 13 **El**
ANSI/ASTM A 541	Grade 6A	US	Forgings	0.15 **C**, 0.30–0.60 **Mn**, 0.035 **P**, 0.040 **S**, 0.50 **Si**, 2.00–2.50 **Cr**, 0.50 **Ni**, 0.90–1.10 **Mo**, 0.05 **V**	**Quenched and tempered:** all **diam**, (790) **TS**, (690) **YS**, 15 **El**
ANSI/ASTM A 542	Class 1	US	Plate	0.15 **C**, 0.27–0.63 **Mn**, 0.035 **P**, 0.035 **S**, 0.50 **Si**, 1.88–2.62 **Cr**, 0.85–1.15 **Mo**	**Quenched and tempered:** all **diam**, (725) **TS**, (585) **YS**, 14 **El**
ANSI/ASTM A 541	Grade 6	US	Forgings	0.15 **C**, 0.30–0.60 **Mn**, 0.035 **P**, 0.040 **S**, 0.50 **Si**, 2.00–2.50 **Cr**, 0.50 **Ni**, 0.90–1.10 **Mo**, 0.05 **V**	**Quenched and tempered:** all **diam**, (720) **TS**, (590) **YS**, 16 **El**

specification number	designation	country	product forms	composition	mechanical properties (see page iv for explanation)
ANSI/ASTM A 645		US	Plate	0.15 **C**, 0.26–0.64 **Mn**, 0.035 **P**, 0.035 **S**, 0.18–0.37 **Si**, 4.65–5.35 **Ni**, 0.17–0.38 **Mo**, 0.01–0.16 **Al**, 0.025 **N**	**Quenched and tempered:** all **diam**, (655) **TS**, 450 **YS**, 20 **El**
ANSI/ASTM A 542	Class 3	US	Plate	0.15 **C**, 0.27–0.63 **Mn**, 0.035 **P**, 0.035 **S**, 0.50 **Si**, 1.88–2.62 **Cr**, 0.85–1.15 **Mo**	**Quenched and tempered:** all **diam**, (655) **TS**, (515) **YS**, 20 **El**
ANSI/ASTM A 473	501 A	US	Forgings	0.15 **C**, 0.30–0.60 **Mn**, 0.030 **P**, 0.030 **S**, 0.50–1.00 **Si**, 6.00–8.00 **Cr**, 0.45–0.65 **Mo**	**Tempered**: all **diam**, 90 (620) **TS**, 65 (450) **YS**, 20 **El**; **Annealed**: all **diam**, 60 (414) **TS**, 30 (205) **YS**, 20 **El**
SIS 14 22 03 E	SIS 2203–05	Sweden	Tube: seamless	0.15 **C**, 0.30–0.60 **Mn**, 0.030 **P**, 0.030 **S**, 0.50–0.80 **Si**, 8.00–10.00 **Cr**, 0.90–1.10 **Mo**, 0.020 **Al**, 0.25 **Cu**	**Normalized and annealed:** all **diam**, (590) **TS**, (390) **YS**, 18 **El**
JIS G 3213	Class 26 B	Japan	Forgings	0.15 **C**, 0.30–0.60 **Mn**, 0.030 **P**, 0.030 **S**, 0.50–1.00 **Si**, 8.00–10.00 **Cr**, 0.90–1.10 **Mo**	**Annealed or normalized and tempered:** all **diam**, (588) **TS**, (382) **YS**, 20 **El**
ANSI/ASTM A 542	Class 4	US	Plate	0.15 **C**, 0.27–0.63 **Mn**, 0.035 **P**, 0.035 **S**, 0.50 **Si**, 1.88–2.62 **Cr**, 0.85–1.15 **Mo**	**Quenched and tempered:** all **diam**, (585) **TS**, (415) **YS**, 20 **El**
ISO 2604/1	F34Q	ISO	Forgings	0.15 **C**, 0.40–0.70 **Mn**, 0.040 **P**, 0.040 **S**, 0.15–0.40 **Si**, 2.00–2.50 **Cr**, 0.90–1.20 **Mo**, 0.020 $\mathbf{Al}_{met}$	**Quenched and tempered:** all **diam**, (540) **TS**, (335) **YS**, 15 **El**
JIS G 3127	Class 3C	Japan	Plate	0.15 **C**, 0.70 **Mn**, 0.025 **P**, 0.025 **S**, 0.15–0.30 **Si**, 3.25–3.75 **Ni**	**Hot rolled and quenched and tempered:** (6–16) **diam**, (539) **TS**, (441) **YS**, 21 **El**
MIL–S–16598B		US	Bar	0.15 **C**, 0.50 **Mn**, 0.35 **Si**, 35.0–36.5 **Ni**, 0.15–0.25 **Se**	**Hot rolled or centerless ground:** all **diam**, (517) **TS**, (310) **YS**, 30 **El**
ANSI/ASTM A 336	Grade F 21	US	Forgings	0.15 **C**, 0.30–0.60 **Mn**, 0.030 **P**, 0.030 **S**, 0.50 **Si**, 2.65–3.25 **Cr**, 0.80–1.06 **Mo**	**Annealed or normalized and tempered:** all **diam**, (515) **TS**, (310) **YS**, 18 **El**
ANSI/ASTM A 336	Grade F22	US	Forgings	0.15 **C**, 0.30–0.60 **Mn**, 0.030 **P**, 0.030 **S**, 0.50 **Si**, 2.00–2.50 **Cr**, 0.90–1.10 **Mo**	**Annealed or normalized and tempered:** all **diam**, (515) **TS**, (310) **YS**, 18 **El**
ASTM A 336	F22	US	Forgings	0.15 **C**, 0.30–0.60 **Mn**, 0.030 **P**, 0.030 **S**, 0.50 **Si**, 2.00–2.50 **Cr**, 0.90–1.10 **Mo**	**Normalized:** all **diam**, 75 (515) **TS**, 45 (310) **YS**, 18 **El**
ASTM A 336	F21	US	Forgings	0.15 **C**, 0.30–0.60 **Mn**, 0.030 **P**, 0.030 **S**, 0.50 **Si**, 2.65–3.25 **Cr**, 0.80–1.06 **Mo**	**Normalized:** all **diam**, 75 (515) **TS**, 45 (310) **YS**, 18 **El**
ANSI/ASTM A 387	Grade 5, class II	US	Plate	0.15 **C**, 0.27–0.63 **Mn**, 0.040 **P**, 0.030 **S**, 0.55 **Si**, 3.90–6.10 **Cr**, 0.40–0.70 **Mo**	**Annealed or normalized and tempered:** all **diam**, (515) **TS**, (310) **YS**, 18 **El**
ANSI/ASTM A 387	Grade 7,class II	US	Plate	0.15 **C**, 0.25–0.65 **Mn**, 0.030 **P**, 0.030 **S**, 1.05 **Si**, 5.90–8.10 **Cr**, 0.40–0.70 **Mo**	**Annealed or normalized and tempered:** all **diam**, (515) **TS**, (310) **YS**, 18 **El**
ANSI/ASTM A 387	Grade 9,class II	US	Plate	0.15 **C**, 0.25–0.65 **Mn**, 0.030 **P**, 0.030 **S**, 1.05 **Si**, 7.90–10.10 **Cr**, 0.85–1.15 **Mo**	**Annealed or normalized and tempered:** all **diam**, (515) **TS**, (310) **YS**, 18 **El**
ANSI/ASTM A 387	Grade 21,class II	US	Plate	0.15 **C**, 0.27–0.63 **Mn**, 0.035 **P**, 0.035 **S**, 0.050 **Si**, 2.63–3.37 **Cr**, 0.85–1.15 **Mo**	**Annealed or normalized and tempered:** all **diam**, (515) **TS**, (310) **YS**, 18 **El**
ANSI/ASTM A 387	Grade 22,class II	US	Plate	0.15 **C**, 0.27–0.63 **Mn**, 0.035 **P**, 0.035 **S**, 0.50 **Si**, 1.88–2.62 **Cr**, 0.85–1.15 **Mo**	**Annealed or normalized and tempered:** all **diam**, (515) **TS**, (310) **YS**, 18 **El**
ASTM A 336	F21	US	Forgings	0.15 **C**, 0.30–0.60 **Mn**, 0.030 **P**, 0.030 **S**, 0.50 **Si**, 2.65–3.25 **Cr**, 0.80–1.06 **Mo**	**Annealed or normalized, tempered:** all **diam**, 75 (515) **TS**, 45 (310) **YS**, 18 **El**
ASTM A 336	F22	US	Forgings	0.15 **C**, 0.30–0.60 **Mn**, 0.030 **P**, 0.030 **S**, 0.50 **Si**, 2.00–2.50 **Cr**, 0.90–1.10 **Mo**	**Annealed or normalized, tempered:** all **diam**, 75 (515) **TS**, 45 (310) **YS**, 18 **El**
IS 4367	10Cr2Mo1	India	Forgings	0.15 **C**, 0.40–0.70 **Mn**, 0.050 **P**, 0.050 **S**, 0.50 **Si**, 2.00–2.50 **Cr**, 0.30 **Ni**, 0.90–1.10 **Mo**	**Normalized and tempered:** all **diam**, (490) **TS**, 20 **El**
NBN A 25–102	14 Mo V 63	Belgium	Tube	0.15 **C**, 0.53 **Mn**, 0.044 **P**, 0.044 **S**, 0.32 **Si**, 0.55 **Cr**, 0.59 **Mo**, 0.30 **V**	**Hot or cold finished or normalized or annealed:** all **diam**, (490) **TS**, (360) **YS**, 20 **El**

WROUGHT ALLOY STEELS

specification number	designation	country	product forms	composition	mechanical properties (see page iv for explanation)
EURONORM 129	FeE 355 Ni 14	EURONORM	Plate, strip	0.15 **C**, 0.30–0.80 **Mn**, 0.025 **P**, 0.020 **S**, 0.35 **Si**, 0.25 **Cr**, 3.25–3.75 **Ni**, 0.10 **Mo**, 0.05 **V**, 0.015_{met} or 0.020 tot. (min) **Al**, 0.35 **Cu**	**Normalized, or normalized and tempered, or quenched and tempered**: ≤(35) **diam**, (490) **TS**, (355) **YS**, 22 **El**
ISO 2604/1	F34	ISO	Forgings	0.15 **C**, 0.40–0.70 **Mn**, 0.040 **P**, 0.040 **S**, 0.15–0.40 **Si**, 2.00–2.50 **Cr**, 0.90–1.20 **Mo**, 0.020 met **Al**	**Normalized and tempered, quenched and tempered**: all **diam**, (490) **TS**, (275) **YS**, 18 **El**
MIL–S–18410	Class b	US	Bar, billets, forgings	0.15 **C**, 0.30–0.60 **Mn**, 0.040 **P**, 0.040 **S**, 0.50 **Si**, 2.00–2.50 **Cr**, 0.90–1.10 **Mo**	**Normalized and drawn or liquid quenched and drawn**: all **diam**, 70 (483) **TS**, 40 (276) **YS**, 20 **El**
JIS G 3213	Class 24 B	Japan	Forgings	0.15 **C**, 0.30–0.60 **Mn**, 0.030 **P**, 0.030 **S**, 0.50 **Si**, 2.00–2.50 **Cr**, 0.87–1.13 **Mo**	**Annealed or normalized and tempered**: all **diam**, (481) **TS**, (275) **YS**, 20 **El**
ANSI/ASTM A 595	Grade C	US	Tube	0.15 **C**, 0.17–0.53 **Mn**, 0.06–0.16 **P**, 0.06 **S**, 0.19–0.81 **Si**, 0.24–1.31 **Cr**, 0.68 **Ni**, 0.22–0.58 **Cu**	**Hot rolled**: all **diam**, 70 (480) **TS**, 60 (410) **YS**
BS 3059 Part 2	Grade 629	UK	Tube	0.15 **C**, 0.30–0.60 **Mn**, 0.030 **P**, 0.030 **S**, 0.25–1.00 **Si**, 8.00–10.00 **Cr**, 0.90–1.10 **Mo**, 0.020 **Al**	**Annealed**: all **diam**, (470) **TS**, (185) **YS**, 20 **El**; **Normalized and tempered**: all **diam**, (590) **TS**, (400) **YS**, 18 **El**
NBN 629	12 Cr Mo 9 10	Belgium	Strip	0.15 **C**, 0.40–0.80 **Mn**, 0.035 **P**, 0.035 **S**, 0.15–0.50 **Si**, 2.0–2.5 **Cr**, 0.90–1.10 **Mo**	**Temper pass**: (3–40) **diam**, (470) **TS**, (295) **YS**, 22 **El**
JIS G 3127	Class 3A	Japan	Plate	0.15 **C**, 0.70 **Mn**, 0.025 **P**, 0.025 **S**, 0.15–0.30 **Si**, 3.25–3.75 **Ni**	**Hot rolled and normalized**: (6–16) **diam**, (451) **TS**, (255) **YS**, 24 **El**
ISO 2604/IV	P43	ISO	Plate	0.15 **C**, 0.80 **Mn**, 0.035 **P**, 0.035 **S**, 0.15–0.35 **Si**, 3.25–3.75 **Ni**	**Hot rolled, normalized, normalized and tempered**: (3–30) **diam**, (450) **TS**, (275) **YS**, 23 **El**
BS 1501–503		UK	Plate	0.15 **C**, 0.30–0.80 **Mn**, 0.025 **P**, 0.030 **S**, 0.10–0.35 **Si**, 0.30 **Cr**, 3.25–3.75 **Ni**, 0.10 **Mo**, 0.020 min **Al**, 0.30 **Cu**	**Normalized or quenched & tempered**: (<37) **diam**, (450) **TS**, (260) **YS**, 20 **El**
EURONORM 129	Fe E 285 Ni 14	EURONORM	Plate, strip	0.15 **C**, 0.30–0.80 **Mn**, 0.025 **P**, 0.020 **S**, 0.35 **Si**, 0.25 **Cr**, 3.25–3.75 **Ni**, 0.10 **Mo**, 0.05 **V**, 0.015_{met} or 0.020 tot. (min) **Al**, 0.35 **Cu**	**Normalized, or normalized and tempered, or quenched and tempered**: ≤(35) **diam**, (450) **TS**, (285) **YS**, 23 **El**
DIN 17175 Part 1	10 CrMo 910-1.7380	Germany	Tube: seamless	≤0.15 **C**, 0.40–0.60 **Mn**, 0.040 **P**, 0.040 **S**, 0.15–0.50 **Si**, 2.0–2.5 **Cr**, 0.9–1.1 **Mo**	**Hot rolled or cold drawn, normalized or annealed**: (441) **TS**, (265) **YS**, 20 **El**
TS 381	UDK 621.643.2/10CrMo 910	Turkey	Pipe: seamless	0.15 **C**, 0.40–0.60 **Mn**, 0.040 **P**, 0.040 **S**, 0.15–0.50 **Si**, 2.0–2.5 **Cr**, 0.90–1.10 **Mo**	**As drawn**: all **diam**, (441) **TS**, (265) **YS**, 20 **El**
BS 3603	Grade 503	UK	Pipe, tube: seamless	0.15 **C**, 0.30–0.80 **Mn**, 0.025 **P**, 0.020 **S**, 0.15–0.35 **Si**, 3.25–3.75 **Ni**	**Normalized, normalized and tempered**: all **diam**, (440) **TS**, (245) **YS**, 16 **El**
ISO 2604/11	TS 43	ISO	Tube: seamless	0.15 **C**, 0.30–0.80 **Mn**, 0.040 **P**, 0.040 **S**, 0.15–0.35 **Si**, 3.25–3.75 **Ni**	**Cold finished, normalized**: all **diam**, (440) **TS**, (245) **YS**, 16 **El**; **Cold finished, normalized and tempered**: all **diam**, (440) **TS**, (245) **YS**, 16 **El**
COPANT 513	T22	COPANT	Tube	0.15 **C**, 0.30–0.60 **Mn**, 0.030 **P**, 0.030 **S**, 0.50 **Si**, 1.90–2.60 **Cr**, 0.87–1.13 **Mo**	**Normalized and tempered, cold finished and tempered**: (>8) **diam**, (430) **TS**, (205) **YS**, 30 **El**
COPANT 513	T21	COPANT	Tube	0.15 **C**, 0.30–0.60 **Mn**, 0.030 **P**, 0.030 **S**, 0.50 **Si**, 2.65–3.35 **Cr**, 0.80–1.06 **Mo**	**Normalized and tempered, cold finished and tempered**: (>8) **diam**, (430) **TS**, (205) **YS**, 30 **El**
ANSI/ASTM A 336	Grade F 21a	US	Forgings	0.15 **C**, 0.30–0.60 **Mn**, 0.030 **P**, 0.030 **S**, 0.50 **Si**, 2.65–3.25 **Cr**, 0.80–1.06 **Mo**	**Annealed or normalized and tempered**: all **diam**, (415) **TS**, (205) **YS**, 20 **El**
ANSI/ASTM A 336	Grade F22a	US	Forgings	0.15 **C**, 0.30–0.60 **Mn**, 0.030 **P**, 0.030 **S**, 0.50 **Si**, 2.00–2.50 **Cr**, 0.90–1.10 **Mo**	**Annealed or normalized and tempered**: all **diam**, (415) **TS**, (205) **YS**, 20 **El**

WROUGHT ALLOY STEELS

specification number	designation	country	product forms	composition	mechanical properties (see page iv for explanation)
ANSI/ASTM A 336	Grade F5	US	Forgings	0.15 **C**, 0.30–0.60 **Mn**, 0.030 **P**, 0.030 **S**, 0.50 **Si**, 4.0–6.0 **Cr**, 0.50 **Ni**, 0.45–0.65 **Mo**	**Annealed or normalized and tempered**: all **diam**, (415) **TS**, (250) **YS**, 19 **El**
ASTM A 336	F5	US	Forgings	0.15 **C**, 0.30–0.60 **Mn**, 0.030 **P**, 0.030 **S**, 0.50 **Si**, 4.0–6.0 **Cr**, 0.50 **Ni**, 0.45–0.65 **Mo**	**Normalized**: all **diam**, 60 (415) **TS**, 36 (250) **YS**, 19 **El**
ASTM A 336	F22a	US	Forgings	0.15 **C**, 0.30–0.60 **Mn**, 0.030 **P**, 0.030 **S**, 0.50 **Si**, 2.00–2.50 **Cr**, 0.90–1.10 **Mo**	**Normalized**: all **diam**, 60 (415) **TS**, 30 (205) **YS**, 20 **El**
ASTM A 336	F21a	US	Forgings	0.15 **C**, 0.30–0.60 **Mn**, 0.030 **P**, 0.030 **S**, 0.50 **Si**, 2.65–3.25 **Cr**, 0.80–1.06 **Mo**	**Normalized**: all **diam**, 60 (415) **TS**, 30 (205) **YS**, 20 **El**
ANSI/ASTM A 387	Grade 5,class I	US	Plate	0.15 **C**, 0.27–0.63 **Mn**, 0.040 **P**, 0.030 **S**, 0.55 **Si**, 3.90–6.10 **Cr**, 0.40–0.70 **Mo**	**Annealed or normalized and tempered**: all **diam**, (415) **TS**, (205) **YS**, 18 **El**
ANSI/ASTM A 387	Grade 7,class I	US	Plate	0.15 **C**, 0.25–0.65 **Mn**, 0.030 **P**, 0.030 **S**, 1.05 **Si**, 5.90–8.10 **Cr**, 0.40–0.70 **Mo**	**Annealed or normalized and tempered**: all **diam**, (415) **TS**, (205) **YS**, 18 **El**
ANSI/ASTM A 387	Grade 9,class I	US	Plate	0.15 **C**, 0.25–0.65 **Mn**, 0.030 **P**, 0.030 **S**, 1.05 **Si**, 7.90–10.10 **Cr**, 0.85–1.15 **Mo**	**Annealed or normalized and tempered**: all **diam**, (415) **TS**, (205) **YS**, 18 **El**
ANSI/ASTM A 387	Grade 21,class I	US	Plate	0.15 **C**, 0.27–0.63 **Mn**, 0.035 **P**, 0.035 **S**, 0.50 **Si**, 2.63–3.37 **Cr**, 0.85–1.15 **Mo**	**Annealed or normalized and tempered**: all **diam**, (415) **TS**, (205) **YS**, 18 **El**
ANSI/ASTM A 387	Grade 22,class I	US	Plate	0.15 **C**, 0.27–0.63 **Mn**, 0.035 **P**, 0.035 **S**, 0.50 **Si**, 1.88–2.62 **Cr**, 0.85–1.15 **Mo**	**Annealed or normalized and tempered**: all **diam**, (415) **TS**, (205) **YS**, 18 **El**
ASTM A 336	F21a	US	Forgings	0.15 **C**, 0.30–0.60 **Mn**, 0.030 **P**, 0.030 **S**, 0.50 **Si**, 2.65–3.25 **Cr**, 0.80–1.06 **Mo**	**Annealed or normalized, tempered**: all **diam**, 60 (415) **TS**, 30 (205) **YS**, 20 **El**
ASTM A 336	F22a	US	Forgings	0.15 **C**, 0.30–0.60 **Mn**, 0.030 **P**, 0.030 **S**, 0.50 **Si**, 2.00–2.50 **Cr**, 0.90–1.10 **Mo**	**Annealed or normalized, tempered**: all **diam**, 60 (415) **TS**, 30 (205) **YS**, 20 **El**
ASTM A 336	F5	US	Forgings	0.15 **C**, 0.30–0.60 **Mn**, 0.030 **P**, 0.030 **S**, 0.50 **Si**, 4.0–6.0 **Cr**, 0.50 **Ni**, 0.45–0.65 **Mo**	**Annealed or normalized, tempered**: all **diam**, 60 (415) **TS**, 36 (250) **YS**, 19 **El**
BS 3604	CD 660	UK	Pipe: seamless	0.15 **C**, 0.40–0.70 **Mn**, 0.040 **P**, 0.040 **S**, 0.10–0.35 **Si**, 0.25–0.50 **Cr**, 0.50–0.70 **Mo**, 0.22–0.28 **V**	**Normalized, tempered**: 0.71 **diam**, (414) **TS**, (262) **YS**, 26 **El**
BS 3604	HF 660	UK	Pipe: seamless	0.15 **C**, 0.40–0.70 **Mn**, 0.040 **P**, 0.040 **S**, 0.10–0.35 **Si**, 0.25–0.50 **Cr**, 0.50–0.70 **Mo**, 0.22–0.28 **V**	**Normalized, tempered**: 0.71 **diam**, (414) **TS**, (262) **YS**, 26 **El**
ANSI/ASTM A 213	Grade T11	US	Tube: seamless	0.15 **C**, 0.30–0.60 **Mn**, 0.030 **P**, 0.030 **S**, 0.50–1.0 **Si**, 1.00–1.50 **Cr**, 0.44–0.65 **Mo**	**Annealed**: 0.312 (7.94) **diam**, 60 (414) **TS**, 30 (207) **YS**, 30 **El**
ANSI/ASTM A 213	Grade T12	US	Tube: seamless	0.15 **C**, 0.30–0.61 **Mn**, 0.045 **P**, 0.045 **S**, 0.50 **Si**, 0.80–1.25 **Cr**, 0.44–0.65 **Mo**	**Annealed**: 0.312 (7.94) **diam**, 60 (414) **TS**, 30 (207) **YS**, 30 **El**
ANSI/ASTM A 213	Grade T21	US	Tube: seamless	0.15 **C**, 0.30–0.60 **Mn**, 0.030 **P**, 0.030 **S**, 0.50 **Si**, 2.65–3.35 **Cr**, 0.80–1.06 **Mo**	**Annealed**: 0.312 (7.94) **diam**, 60 (414) **TS**, 30 (207) **YS**, 30 **El**
ANSI/ASTM A 213	Grade T22	US	Tube: seamless	0.15 **C**, 0.30–0.60 **Mn**, 0.030 **P**, 0.030 **S**, 0.50 **Si**, 1.90–2.60 **Cr**, 0.87–1.13 **Mo**	**Annealed**: 0.312 (7.94) **diam**, 60 (414) **TS**, 30 (207) **YS**, 30 **El**
ANSI/ASTM A 200	Grade T22	US	Tube: seamless	0.15 **C**, 0.30–0.60 **Mn**, 0.030 **P**, 0.030 **S**, 0.50 **Si**, 1.90–2.60 **Cr**, 0.87–1.13 **Mo**	**Annealed**: 0.312 (7.94) **diam**, 60 (414) **TS**, 25 (172) **YS**, 30 **El**
ANSI/ASTM A 200	Grade T5	US	Tube: seamless	0.15 **C**, 0.30–0.60 **Mn**, 0.030 **P**, 0.030 **S**, 0.50 **Si**, 4.00–6.00 **Cr**, 0.45–0.65 **Mo**	**Annealed**: 0.312 (7.94) **diam**, 60 (414) **TS**, 25 (172) **YS**, 30 **El**
ANSI/ASTM A 200	Grade T7	US	Tube: seamless	0.15 **C**, 0.30–0.60 **Mn**, 0.030 **P**, 0.030 **S**, 0.50–1.00 **Si**, 6.00–8.00 **Cr**, 0.45–0.65 **Mo**	**Annealed**: 0.312 (7.94) **diam**, 60 (414) **TS**, 25 (172) **YS**, 30 **El**
ANSI/ASTM A 200	Grade T9	US	Tube: seamless	0.15 **C**, 0.30–0.60 **Mn**, 0.030 **P**, 0.030 **S**, 0.25–1.00 **Si**, 8.00–10.00 **Cr**, 0.90–1.10 **Mo**	**Annealed**: 0.312 (7.94) **diam**, 60 (414) **TS**, 25 (172) **YS**, 30 **El**
ANSI/ASTM A 200	Grade T11	US	Tube: seamless	0.15 **C**, 0.30–0.60 **Mn**, 0.030 **P**, 0.030 **S**, 0.50–1.00 **Si**, 1.00–1.50 **Cr**, 0.44–0.65 **Mo**	**Annealed**: 0.312 (7.94) **diam**, 60 (414) **TS**, 25 (172) **YS**, 30 **El**

WROUGHT ALLOY STEELS

specification number	designation	country	product forms	composition	mechanical properties (see page iv for explanation)
ANSI/ASTM A 200	Grade T21	US	Tube: seamless	0.15 **C**, 0.30–0.60 **Mn**, 0.030 **P**, 0.030 **S**, 0.50 **Si**, 2.65–3.35 **Cr**, 0.80–1.06 **Mo**	**Annealed**: 0.312 (7.94) **diam**, 60 (414) **TS**, 25 (172) **YS**, 30 **El**
ANSI/ASTM A 200	Grade T4	US	Tube: seamless	0.15 **C**, 0.30–0.60 **Mn**, 0.030 **P**, 0.030 **S**, 0.50–1.00 **Si**, 2.15–2.85 **Cr**, 0.44–0.65 **Mo**	**Annealed**: 0.312 (7.94) **diam**, 60 (414) **TS**, 25 (172) **YS**, 30 **El**
ANSI/ASTM A 200	Grade T3b	US	Tube: seamless	0.15 **C**, 0.30–0.60 **Mn**, 0.030 **P**, 0.030 **S**, 0.50 **Si**, 1.65–2.35 **Cr**, 0.44–0.65 **Mo**	**Annealed**: 0.312 (7.94) **diam**, 60 (414) **TS**, 25 (172) **YS**, 30 **El**
ANSI/ASTM A 199	Grade T22	US	Tube: seamless	0.15 **C**, 0.30–0.60 **Mn**, 0.030 **P**, 0.030 **S**, 0.50 **Si**, 1.90–2.60 **Cr**, 0.87–1.13 **Mo**	**Annealed**: 0.312 (7.94) **diam**, 60 (414) **TS**, 25 (172) **YS**, 30 **El**
ANSI/ASTM A 199	Grade T21	US	Tube: seamless	0.15 **C**, 0.30–0.60 **Mn**, 0.030 **P**, 0.030 **S**, 0.50 **Si**, 2.65–3.35 **Cr**, 0.80–1.06 **Mo**	**Annealed**: 0.312 (7.94) **diam**, 60 (414) **TS**, 25 (172) **YS**, 30 **El**
ANSI/ASTM A 199	Grade T11	US	Tube: seamless	0.15 **C**, 0.30–0.60 **Mn**, 0.030 **P**, 0.030 **S**, 0.50–1.00 **Si**, 1.00–1.50 **Cr**, 0.44–0.65 **Mo**	**Annealed**: 0.312 (7.94) **diam**, 60 (414) **TS**, 25 (172) **YS**, 30 **El**
ANSI/ASTM A 199	Grade T9	US	Tube: seamless	0.15 **C**, 0.30–0.60 **Mn**, 0.030 **P**, 0.030 **S**, 0.25–1.00 **Si**, 8.00–10.00 **Cr**, 0.90–1.10 **Mo**	**Annealed**: 0.312 (7.94) **diam**, 60 (414) **TS**, 25 (172) **YS**, 30 **El**
ANSI/ASTM A 199	Grade T7	US	Tube: seamless	0.15 **C**, 0.30–060 **Mn**, 0.030 **P**, 0.030 **S**, 0.50–1.00 **Si**, 6.00–8.00 **Cr**, 0.45–0.65 **Mo**	**Annealed**: 0.312 (7.94) **diam**, 60 (414) **TS**, 25 (172) **YS**, 30 **El**
ANSI/ASTM A 199	Grade T5	US	Tube: seamless	0.15 **C**, 0.30–0.60 **Mn**, 0.030 **P**, 0.030 **S**, 0.50 **Si**, 4.00–6.00 **Cr**, 0.45–0.65 **Mo**	**Annealed**: 0.312 (7.94) **diam**, 60 (414) **TS**, 25 (172) **YS**, 30 **El**
ANSI/ASTM A 199	Grade T4	US	Tube: seamless	0.15 **C**, 0.30–0.60 **Mn**, 0.030 **P**, 0.030 **S**, 0.50–1.00 **Si**, 2.15–2.85 **Cr**, 0.44–0.65 **Mo**	**Annealed**: 0.312 (7.94) **diam**, 60 (414) **TS**, 25 (172) **YS**, 30 **El**
ANSI/ASTM A 199	Grade T3b	US	Tube: seamless	0.15 **C**, 0.30–0.60 **Mn**, 0.030 **P**, 0.030 **S**, 0.50 **Si**, 1.65–2.35 **Cr**, 0.44–0.65 **Mo**	**Annealed**: 0.312 (7.94) **diam**, 60 (414) **TS**, 25 (172) **YS**, 30 **El**
NOM–B–194	Grade T 12	Mexico	Tube: seamless	0.15 **C**, 0.30–0.61 **Mn**, 0.045 **P**, 0.045 **S**, 0.50 **Si**, 0.80–1.25 **Cr**, 0.44–0.65 **Mo**	**Hot or cold finished and annealed**: (0.38–12.7) **diam**, (414) **TS**, (207) **YS**
ANSI/ASTM A 473	501 B	US	Forgings	0.15 **C**, 0.30–0.60 **Mn**, 0.030 **P**, 0.030 **S**, 0.50–1.00 **Si**, 8.00–10.00 **Cr**, 0.90–1.10 **Mo**	**Annealed**: all **diam**, 60 (414) **TS**, 30 (205) **YS**, 20 **El**; **Tempered**: all **diam**, 100 (690) **TS**, 70 (485) **YS**, 20 **El**
ANSI/ASTM A 423	Grade 1	US	Tube: seamless, welded	0.15 **C**, 0.55 **Mn**, 0.06–0.16 **P**, 0.060 **S**, 0.10 min **Si**, 0.24–1.31 **Cr**, 0.20–0.70 **Ni**, 0.20–0.60 **Cu**	**Normalized**: 0.31 (7.9) **diam**, 60 (414) **TS**, 37 (255) **YS**, 25 **El**
ANSI/ASTM A 423	Grade 2	US	Tube: seamless, welded	0.15 **C**, 0.50–1.00 **Mn**, 0.04 **P**, 0.05 **S**, 0.40–1.10 **Ni**, 0.10 min **Mo**, 0.30–1.00 **Cu**	**Normalized**: 0.31 (7.9) **diam**, 60 (414) **TS**, 37 (255) **YS**, 25 **El**
ANSI/ASTM A 405	P24	US	Pipe: seamless	0.15 **C**, 0.30–0.60 **Mn**, 0.030 **P**, 0.030 **S**, 0.10–0.35 **Si**, 0.80–1.25 **Cr**, 0.87–1.13 **Mo**, 0.15–0.25 **V**	**Annealed**: 0.312 (7.94) **diam**, 60 (414) **TS**, 30 (207) **YS**, 30 **El**; **Normalized and tempered**: 0.312 (7.94) **diam**, 80 (552) **TS**, 50 (345) **YS**, 25 **El**
ANSI/ASTM A 335	P5	US	Pipe: seamless	0.15 **C**, 0.30–0.60 **Mn**, 0.030 **P**, 0.030 **S**, 0.50 **Si**, 4.00–6.00 **Cr**, 0.45–0.65 **Mo**	**Normalized or annealed**: 0.312 (7.94) **diam**, 60 (414) **TS**, 30 (207) **YS**, 30 **El**
ANSI/ASTM A 335	P5b	US	Pipe: seamless	0.15 **C**, 0.30–0.60 **Mn**, 0.030 **P**, 0.030 **S**, 1.00–2.00 **Si**, 4.00–6.00 **Cr**, 0.45–0.65 **Mo**	**Normalized or annealed**: 0.312 (7.94) **diam**, 60 (414) **TS**, 30 (207) **YS**, 30 **El**
ANSI/ASTM A 335	P7	US	Pipe: seamless	0.15 **C**, 0.30–0.60 **Mn**, 0.030 **P**, 0.030 **S**, 0.50–1.00 **Si**, 6.00–8.00 **Cr**, 0.45–0.65 **Mo**	**Normalized or annealed**: 0.312 (7.94) **diam**, 60 (414) **TS**, 30 (207) **YS**, 30 **El**
ANSI/ASTM A 335	P9	US	Pipe: seamless	0.15 **C**, 0.30–0.60 **Mn**, 0.030 **P**, 0.030 **S**, 0.25–1.00 **Si**, 8.00–10.00 **Cr**, 0.90–1.10 **Mo**	**Normalized or annealed**: 0.312 (7.94) **diam**, 60 (414) **TS**, 30 (207) **YS**, 30 **El**
ANSI/ASTM A 335	P11	US	Pipe: seamless	0.15 **C**, 0.30–0.60 **Mn**, 0.030 **P**, 0.030 **S**, 0.50–1.00 **Si**, 1.00–1.50 **Cr**, 0.44–0.65 **Mo**	**Normalized or annealed**: 0.312 (7.94) **diam**, 60 (414) **TS**, 30 (207) **YS**, 30 **El**
ANSI/ASTM A 335	P12	US	Pipe: seamless	0.15 **C**, 0.30–0.61 **Mn**, 0.045 **P**, 0.045 **S**, 0.50 **Si**, 0.80–1.25 **Cr**, 0.44–0.65 **Mo**	**Normalized or annealed**: 0.312 (7.94) **diam**, 60 (414) **TS**, 30 (207) **YS**, 30 **El**
ANSI/ASTM A 335	P15	US	Pipe: seamless	0.15 **C**, 0.30–0.60 **Mn**, 0.030 **P**, 0.030 **S**, 1.15–1.65 **Si**, 0.44–0.65 **Mo**	**Normalized or annealed**: 0.312 (7.94) **diam**, 60 (414) **TS**, 30 (207) **YS**, 30 **El**

specification number	designation	country	product forms	composition	mechanical properties (see page iv for explanation)
ANSI/ASTM A 335	P21	US	Pipe: seamless	0.15 **C**, 0.30–0.60 **Mn**, 0.030 **P**, 0.030 **S**, 0.50 **Si**, 2.65–3.35 **Cr**, 0.80–1.06 **Mo**	**Normalized or annealed**: 0.312 (7.94) **diam**, 60 (414) **TS**, 30 (207) **YS**, 30 **El**
ANSI/ASTM A 335	P22	US	Pipe: seamless	0.15 **C**, 0.30–0.60 **Mn**, 0.030 **P**, 0.030 **S**, 0.50 **Si**, 1.90–2.60 **Cr**, 0.87–1.13 **Mo**	**Normalized or annealed**: 0.312 (7.94) **diam**, 60 (414) **TS**, 30 (207) **YS**, 30 **El**
ANSI/ASTM A 213	Grade T 3b	US	Tube: seamless	0.15 **C**, 0.30–0.60 **Mn**, 0.030 **P**, 0.030 **S**, 0.50 **Si**, 1.65–2.35 **Cr**, 0.44–0.65 **Mo**	**Annealed**: 0.312 (7.94) **diam**, 60 (414) **TS**, 30 (207) **YS**, 30 **El**
ANSI/ASTM A 213	Grade T5	US	Tube: seamless	0.15 **C**, 0.30–0.60 **Mn**, 0.03 **P**, 0.03 **S**, 0.50 **Si**, 4.00–6.00 **Cr**, 0.45–0.65 **Mo**	**Annealed**: 0.312 (7.94) **diam**, 60 (414) **TS**, 30 (207) **YS**, 30 **El**
ANSI/ASTM A 213	Grade T5b	US	Tube: seamless	0.15 **C**, 0.30–0.60 **Mn**, 0.03 **P**, 0.03 **S**, 1.00–2.00 **Si**, 4.00–6.00 **Cr**, 0.45–0.65 **Mo**	**Annealed**: 0.312 (7.94) **diam**, 60 (414) **TS**, 30 (207) **YS**, 30 **El**
ANSI/ASTM A 213	Grade T7	US	Tube: seamless	0.15 **C**, 0.30–0.60 **Mn**, 0.03 **P**, 0.03 **S**, 0.50–1.00 **Si**, 6.00–8.00 **Cr**, 0.45–0.65 **Mo**	**Annealed**: 0.312 (7.94) **diam**, 60 (414) **TS**, 30 (207) **YS**, 30 **El**
ANSI/ASTM A 213	Grade T9	US	Tube: seamless	0.15 **C**, 0.30–0.60 **Mn**, 0.03 **P**, 0.03 **S**, 0.25–1.00 **Si**, 8.00–10.00 **Cr**, 0.90–1.10 **Mo**	**Annealed**: 0.312 (7.94) **diam**, 60 (414) **TS**, 30 (207) **YS**, 30 **El**
NOM–B–194	T 36	Mexico	Tube: seamless	0.15 **C**, 0.30–0.60 **Mn**, 0.030 **P**, 0.030 **S**, 0.50 **Si**, 1.65–2.35 **Cr**, 0.44–0.65 **Mo**	**Annealed or normalized and quenched**: (0.38–12.7) **diam**, (414) **TS**, (207) **YS**
NOM–B–194	T 5	Mexico	Tube: seamless	0.15 **C**, 0.30–0.60 **Mn**, 0.03 **P**, 0.03 **S**, 0.50 **Si**, 4.0–6.0 **Cr**, 0.45–0.65 **Mo**	**Annealed or normalized and quenched**: (0.38–12.7) **diam**, (414) **TS**, (207) **YS**
NOM–B–194	T 56	Mexico	Tube: seamless	0.15 **C**, 0.30–0.60 **Mn**, 0.03 **P**, 0.03 **S**, 1.0–2.0 **Si**, 4.0–6.0 **Cr**, 0.45–0.65 **Mo**	**Annealed or normalized and quenched**: (0.38–12.7) **diam**, (414) **TS**, (207) **YS**
NOM–B–194	T 7	Mexico	Tube: seamless	0.15 **C**, 0.30–0.60 **Mn**, 0.03 **P**, 0.03 **S**, 0.50–1.0 **Si**, 6.0–8.0 **Cr**, 0.45–0.65 **Mo**	**Annealed or normalized and quenched**: (0.38–12.7) **diam**, (414) **TS**, (207) **YS**
NOM–B–194	T 9	Mexico	Tube: seamless	0.15 **C**, 0.30–0.60 **Mn**, 0.03 **P**, 0.03 **S**, 0.25–1.0 **Si**, 8.0–10.0 **Cr**, 0.90–1.10 **Mo**	**Annealed or normalized and quenched**: (0.38–12.7) **diam**, (414) **TS**, (207) **YS**
NOM–B–194	T 21	Mexico	Tube: seamless	0.15 **C**, 0.30–0.60 **Mn**, 0.03 **P**, 0.03 **S**, 0.50 **Si**, 2.65–3.35 **Cr**, 0.80–1.06 **Mo**	**Annealed or normalized and quenched**: (0.38–12.7) **diam**, (414) **TS**, (207) **YS**
NOM–B–194	T 11	Mexico	Tube: seamless	0.15 **C**, 0.30–0.60 **Mn**, 0.03 **P**, 0.03 **S**, 0.50–1.0 **Si**, 1.0–1.5 **Cr**, 0.44–0.65 **Mo**	**Annealed and normalized and quenched**: (0.38–12.7) **diam**, (414) **TS**, (207) **YS**
NOM–B–194	T 22	Mexico	Tube: seamless	0.15 **C**, 0.30–0.60 **Mn**, 0.03 **P**, 0.03 **S**, 0.50 **Si**, 1.90–2.60 **Cr**, 0.87–1.13 **Mo**	**Annealed or normalized and quenched**: (0.38–12.7) **diam**, (414) **TS**, (207) **YS**
MIL–T–18165B	Class 1	US	Tube, pipe: seamless	0.15 **C**, 0.30–0.60 **Mn**, 0.030 **P**, 0.030 **S**, 0.50–1.00 **Si**, 1.00–1.50 **Cr**, 0.44–0.65 **Mo**	**Annealed, normalized and tempered**: ≥0.312 **diam**, (413) **TS**, (206) **YS**, 30 **El**
MIL–T–18165B	Class 2	US	Tube, pipe: seamless	0.15 **C**, 0.30–0.60 **Mn**, 0.030 **P**, 0.030 **S**, 0.50 **Si**, 1.90–2.60 **Cr**, 0.87–1.13 **Mo**	**Annealed, normalized and tempered**: ≥0.312 **diam**, (413) **TS**, (206) **YS**, 30 **El**
MIL–T–16286E	Class E	US	Tube: seamless	0.15 **C**, 0.30–0.60 **Mn**, 0.030 **P**, 0.030 **S**, 0.50 **Si**, 1.90–2.60 **Cr**, 0.87–1.13 **Mo**	**Fully annealed**: all **diam**, (413) **TS**, (206) **YS**, 30 **El**
DGN–B–191	Grade T 22	Mexico	Tube: seamless	0.15 **C**, 0.30–0.60 **Mn**, 0.030 **P**, 0.030 **S**, 0.50 **Si**, 1.90–2.60 **Cr**, 0.87–1.13 **Mo**	**Cold finished and annealed**: (≥8) **diam**, (412) **TS**, (176) **YS**, 30 **El**
DGN–B–191	Grade T 21	Mexico	Tube: seamless	0.15 **C**, 0.30–0.60 **Mn**, 0.030 **P**, 0.030 **S**, 0.50 **Si**, 2.65–3.35 **Cr**, 0.80–1.06 **Mo**	**Cold finished and annealed**: (≥8) **diam**, (412) **TS**, (176) **YS**, 30 **El**
DGN–B–191	Grade T 11	Mexico	Tube: seamless	0.15 **C**, 0.30–0.60 **Mn**, 0.030 **P**, 0.030 **S**, 0.50–1.00 **Si**, 1.00–1.50 **Cr**, 0.44–0.65 **Mo**	**Cold finished and annealed**: (≥8) **diam**, (412) **TS**, (176) **YS**, 30 **El**
DGN–B–191	Grade T 9	Mexico	Tube: seamless	0.15 **C**, 0.30–0.60 **Mn**, 0.030 **P**, 0.030 **S**, 0.25–1.00 **Si**, 8.00–10.00 **Cr**, 0.90–1.10 **Mo**	**Cold finished and annealed**: (≥8) **diam**, (412) **TS**, (176) **YS**, 30 **El**
DGN–B–191	Grade T 7	Mexico	Tube: seamless	0.15 **C**, 0.30–0.60 **Mn**, 0.030 **P**, 0.030 **S**, 0.50–1.00 **Si**, 6.00–8.00 **Cr**, 0.45–0.65 **Mo**	**Cold finished and annealed**: (≥8) **diam**, (412) **TS**, (176) **YS**, 30 **El**
DGN–B–191	Grade T 5	Mexico	Tube: seamless	0.15 **C**, 0.30–0.60 **Mn**, 0.030 **P**, 0.030 **S**, 0.50 **Si**, 4.00–6.00 **Cr**, 0.45–0.65 **Mo**	**Cold finished and annealed**: (≥8) **diam**, (412) **TS**, (176) **YS**, 30 **El**

WROUGHT ALLOY STEELS

specification number	designation	country	product forms	composition	mechanical properties (see page iv for explanation)
DGN–B–191	Grade T 4	Mexico	Tube: seamless	0.15 **C**, 0.30–0.60 **Mn**, 0.030 **P**, 0.030 **S**, 0.50–1.00 **Si**, 2.15–2.85 **Cr**, 0.44–0.65 **Mo**	**Cold finished and annealed:** (≥8) **diam**, (412) **TS**, (176) **YS**, 30 **El**
DGN–B–191	Grade T 3b	Mexico	Tube: seamless	0.15 **C**, 0.30–0.60 **Mn**, 0.030 **P**, 0.030 **S**, 0.50 **Si**, 1.65–2.35 **Cr**, 0.44–0.65 **Mo**	**Cold finished and annealed:** (≥8) **diam**, (412) **TS**, (176) **YS**, 30 **El**
NOM–B–192	Grade T 22	Mexico	Tube: seamless	0.15 **C**, 0.30–0.60 **Mn**, 0.030 **P**, 0.030 **S**, 0.50 **Si**, 1.90–2.60 **Cr**, 0.87–1.13 **Mo**	**Hot or cold finished:** (≥16) **diam**, (412) **TS**, (172) **YS**, 30 **El**
NOM–B–192	Grade T 21	Mexico	Tube: seamless	0.15 **C**, 0.30–0.60 **Mn**, 0.030 **P**, 0.030 **S**, 0.50 **Si**, 2.65–3.35 **Cr**, 0.80–1.06 **Mo**	**Hot or cold finished:** (≥16) **diam**, (412) **TS**, (172) **YS**, 30 **El**
NOM–B–192	Grade T 11	Mexico	Tube: seamless	0.15 **C**, 0.30–0.60 **Mn**, 0.030 **P**, 0.030 **S**, 0.50–1.00 **Si**, 1.00–1.50 **Cr**, 0.44–0.65 **Mo**	**Hot or cold finished:** (≥16) **diam**, (412) **TS**, (172) **YS**, 30 **El**
NOM–B–192	Grade T 9	Mexico	Tube: seamless	0.15 **C**, 0.30–0.60 **Mn**, 0.030 **P**, 0.030 **S**, 0.25–1.00 **Si**, 8.00–10.00 **Cr**, 0.90–1.10 **Mo**	**Hot or cold finished:** (≥16) **diam**, (412) **TS**, (172) **YS**, 30 **El**
NOM–B–192	Grade T 7	Mexico	Tube: seamless	0.15 **C**, 0.30–0.60 **Mn**, 0.030 **P**, 0.030 **S**, 0.50–1.00 **Si**, 6.00–8.00 **Cr**, 0.45–0.65 **Mo**	**Hot or cold finished:** (≥16) **diam**, (412) **TS**, (172) **YS**, 30 **El**
NOM–B–192	Grade T 5	Mexico	Tube: seamless	0.15 **C**, 0.30–0.60 **Mn**, 0.030 **P**, 0.030 **S**, 0.50 **Si**, 4.00–6.00 **Cr**, 0.45–0.65 **Mo**	**Hot or cold finished:** (≥16) **diam**, (412) **TS**, (172) **YS**, 30 **El**
DGN–B–217	Grade I	Mexico	Tube: seamless and welded	0.15 **C**, 0.55 **Mn**, 0.06–0.16 **P**, 0.060 **S**, 0.10 min **Si**, 0.24–1.31 **Cr**, 0.20–0.70 **Ni**, 0.20–0.60 **Cu**	**Hot or cold finished and normalized:** (0.89–12.7) **diam**, (412) **TS**, (255) **YS**, 25 **El**
DGN–B–217	Grade II	Mexico	Tube: seamless, welded	0.15 **C**, 0.50–1.00 **Mn**, 0.040 **P**, 0.050 **S**, 0.40–1.10 **Ni**, 0.10 min **Mo**, 0.30–1.00 **Cu**	**Hot or cold finished:** (0.89–12.7) **diam**, (412) **TS**, (255) **YS**, 25 **El**
NOM–B–192	Grade T 4	Mexico	Tube: seamless	0.15 **C**, 0.30–0.60 **Mn**, 0.030 **P**, 0.030 **S**, 0.50–1.00 **Si**, 2.15–2.85 **Cr**, 0.44–0.65 **Mo**	**Hot or cold finished:** (≥15.5) **diam**, (412) **TS**, (172) **YS**, 30 **El**
NOM–B–192	Grade T 3b	Mexico	Tube: seamless	0.15 **C**, 0.30–0.60 **Mn**, 0.030 **P**, 0.030 **S**, 0.50 **Si**, 1.65–2.35 **Cr**, 0.44–0.65 **Mo**	**Hot or cold finished:** (≥15.5) **diam**, (412) **TS**, (172) **YS**, 30 **El**
DGN–B–181	Grade P–22	Mexico	Tube: seamless	0.15 **C**, 0.30–0.60 **Mn**, 0.030 **P**, 0.030 **S**, 0.50 **Si**, 1.90–2.60 **Cr**, 0.87–1.13 **Mo**	**Annealed or normalized and quenched:** (8–60) **diam**, (412) **TS**, (206) **YS**, 30 **El**
DGN–B–181	Grade P–5	Mexico	Tube: seamless	0.15 **C**, 0.30–0.60 **Mn**, 0.030 **P**, 0.030 **S**, 0.50 **Si**, 4.0–6.0 **Cr**, 0.45–0.65 **Mo**	**Annealed or normalized and quenched:** (8–60) **diam**, (412) **TS**, (206) **YS**, 30 **El**
DGN–B–181	Grade P–56	Mexico	Tube: seamless	0.15 **C**, 0.30–0.60 **Mn**, 0.030 **P**, 0.030 **S**, 1.00–2.00 **Si**, 4.00–6.00 **Cr**, 0.45–0.65 **Mo**	**Annealed or normalized and quenched:** (8–60) **diam**, (412) **TS**, (206) **YS**, 30 **El**
DGN–B–181	Grade P–7	Mexico	Tube: seamless	0.15 **C**, 0.30–0.60 **Mn**, 0.030 **P**, 0.030 **S**, 0.50–1.00 **Si**, 6.00–8.00 **Cr**, 0.44–0.65 **Mo**	**Annealed or normalized and quenched:** (8–60) **diam**, (412) **TS**, (206) **YS**, 30 **El**
DGN–B–181	Grade P–9	Mexico	Tube: seamless	0.15 **C**, 0.30–0.60 **Mn**, 0.030 **P**, 0.030 **S**, 0.25–1.00 **Si**, 8.00–10.00 **Cr**, 0.90–1.10 **Mo**	**Annealed or normalized and quenched:** (8–60) **diam**, (412) **TS**, (206) **YS**, 30 **El**
DGN–B–181	Grade P–11	Mexico	Tube: seamless	0.15 **C**, 0.30–0.60 **Mn**, 0.030 **P**, 0.030 **S**, 0.50–1.00 **Si**, 1.00–1.50 **Cr**, 0.44–0.65 **Mo**	**Annealed or normalized and quenched:** (8–60) **diam**, (412) **TS**, (206) **YS**, 30 **El**
DGN–B–181	Grade P–2	Mexico	Tube: seamless	0.15 **C**, 0.30–0.61 **Mn**, 0.045 **P**, 0.045 **S**, 0.50 **Si**, 0.80–1.25 **Cr**, 0.44–0.65 **Mo**	**Hot or cold finished:** (8–60) **diam**, (412) **TS**, (206) **YS**, 30 **El**
DGN–B–181	Grade P–15	Mexico	Tube: seamless	0.15 **C**, 0.30–0.60 **Mn**, 0.030 **P**, 0.030 **S**, 1.15–1.65 **Si**, 0.44–0.65 **Mo**	**Annealed or normalized and quenched:** (8–60) **diam**, (412) **TS**, (206) **YS**, 30 **El**
DGN–B–181	Grade P–21	Mexico	Tube: seamless	0.15 **C**, 0.30–0.60 **Mn**, 0.030 **P**, 0.030 **S**, 0.50 **Si**, 2.65–3.35 **Cr**, 0.80–1.06 **Mo**	**Annealed or normalized and quenched:** (8–60) **diam**, (412) **TS**, (206) **YS**, 30 **El**
JIS G 3458	Class 22	Japan	Pipe: seamless	0.15 **C**, 0.30–0.60 **Mn**, 0.035 **P**, 0.035 **S**, 0.50 **Si**, 0.80–1.25 **Cr**, 0.45–0.65 **Mo**	**Annealed:** (≥8) **diam**, (412) **TS**, (206) **YS**, 30 **El**
JIS G 3458	Class 23	Japan	Pipe: seamless	0.15 **C**, 0.30–0.60 **Mn**, 0.030 **P**, 0.030 **S**, 0.50–1.00 **Si**, 1.00–1.50 **Cr**, 1.00–1.50 **Mo**	**Full annealed or normalized and tempered:** (≥8) **diam**, (412) **TS**, (206) **YS**, 30 **El**

WROUGHT ALLOY STEELS

specification number	designation	country	product forms	composition	mechanical properties (see page iv for explanation)
JIS G 3458	Class 24	Japan	Pipe: seamless	0.15 **C**, 0.30–0.60 **Mn**, 0.030 **P**, 0.030 **S**, 0.50 **Si**, 1.90–2.60 **Cr**, 0.87–1.13 **Mo**	**Full annealed or normalized and tempered**: (≥8) **diam**, (412) **TS**, (206) **YS**, 30 **El**
JIS G 3458	Class 25	Japan	Pipe: seamless	0.15 **C**, 0.30–0.60 **Mn**, 0.030 **P**, 0.030 **S**, 0.50 **Si**, 4.00–6.00 **Cr**, 0.45–0.65 **Mo**	**Full annealed or normalized and tempered**: (≥8) **diam**, (412) **TS**, (206) **YS**, 30 **El**
JIS G 3458	Class 26	Japan	Pipe: seamless	0.15 **C**, 0.30–0.60 **Mn**, 0.030 **P**, 0.030 **S**, 0.25–1.00 **Si**, 8.00–10.00 **Cr**, 0.90–1.10 **Mo**	**Full annealed or normalized and tempered**: (≥8) **diam**, (412) **TS**, (206) **YS**, 30 **El**
JIS G 3213	Class 22 A	Japan	Forgings	0.15 **C**, 0.30–0.61 **Mn**, 0.035 **P**, 0.035 **S**, 0.50 **Si**, 0.80–1.25 **Cr**, 0.44–0.65 **Mo**	**Annealed or normalized and tempered**: all **diam**, (412) **TS**, (206) **YS**, 22 **El**
JIS G 3213	Class 23 A	Japan	Forgings	0.15 **C**, 0.30–0.60 **Mn**, 0.030 **P**, 0.030 **S**, 0.50–1.00 **Si**, 1.00–1.50 **Cr**, 0.44–0.65 **Mo**	**Annealed or normalized and tempered**: all **diam**, (412) **TS**, (206) **YS**, 22 **El**
JIS G 3213	Class 24 A	Japan	Forgings	0.15 **C**, 0.30–0.60 **Mn**, 0.030 **P**, 0.030 **S**, 0.50 **Si**, 1.90–2.60 **Cr**, 0.87–1.13 **Mo**	**Annealed or normalized and tempered**: all **diam**, (412) **TS**, (206) **YS**, 22 **El**
JIS G 3213	Class 26 A	Japan	Forgings	0.15 **C**, 0.30–0.60 **Mn**, 0.030 **P**, 0.030 **S**, 0.25–1.00 **Si**, 8.00–10.00 **Cr**, 0.90–1.10 **Mo**	**Annealed or normalized and tempered**: all **diam**, (412) **TS**, (206) **YS**, 22 **El**
JIS G 3462	Class 22	Japan	Tube: seamless	0.15 **C**, 0.30–0.60 **Mn**, 0.035 **P**, 0.035 **S**, 0.50 **Si**, 0.80–1.25 **Cr**, 0.45–0.65 **Mo**	**Full annealed or annealed, normalized and tempered**: (≥8) **diam**, (412) **TS**, (206) **YS**, 30 **El**
JIS G 3462	Class 23	Japan	Tube: seamless	0.15 **C**, 0.30–0.60 **Mn**, 0.030 **P**, 0.030 **S**, 0.50–1.00 **Si**, 1.00–1.50 **Cr**, 0.45–0.65 **Mo**	**Full annealed or normalized and tempered**: (≥8) **diam**, (412) **TS**, (206) **YS**, 30 **El**
JIS G 3462	Class 24	Japan	Tube: seamless	0.15 **C**, 0.30–0.60 **Mn**, 0.030 **P**, 0.030 **S**, 0.50 **Si**, 1.90–2.60 **Cr**, 0.87–1.13 **Mo**	**Full annealed or normalized and tempered**: (≥8) **diam**, (412) **TS**, (206) **YS**, 30 **El**
JIS G 3462	Class 25	Japan	Tube: seamless	0.15 **C**, 0.30–0.60 **Mn**, 0.030 **P**, 0.030 **S**, 0.50 **Si**, 4.00–6.00 **Cr**, 0.45–0.65 **Mo**	**Full annealed or normalized and tempered**: (≥8) **diam**, (412) **TS**, (206) **YS**, 30 **El**
JIS G 3462	Class 26	Japan	Tube: seamless	0.15 **C**, 0.30–0.60 **Mn**, 0.030 **P**, 0.030 **S**, 0.25–1.00 **Si**, 8.00–10.00 **Cr**, 0.90–1.10 **Mo**	**Full annealed or normalized and tempered**: (≥8) **diam**, (412) **TS**, (206) **YS**, 30 **El**
JIS G 4109	Class 4	Japan	Plate	0.15 **C**, 0.27–0.63 **Mn**, 0.035 **P**, 0.035 **S**, 0.50 **Si**, 1.88–2.62 **Cr**, 0.85–1.15 **Mo**	**Hot rolled and annealed**: (≤20) **diam**, (412) **TS**, (206) **YS**, 18 **El**; **Hot rolled, normalized, tempered**: (≤20) **diam**, (520) **TS**, (314) **YS**, 18 **El**
JIS G 4109	Class 5	Japan	Plate	0.15 **C**, 0.27–0.63 **Mn**, 0.035 **P**, 0.035 **S**, 0.50 **Si**, 2.63–3.37 **Cr**, 0.85–1.15 **Mo**	**Hot rolled and annealed**: (≤20) **diam**, (412) **TS**, (206) **YS**, 18 **El**; **Hot rolled, normalized, tempered**: (≤20) **diam**, (520) **TS**, (314) **YS**, 18 **El**
JIS G 4109	Class 6	Japan	Plate	0.15 **C**, 0.27–0.63 **Mn**, 0.035 **P**, 0.030 **S**, 0.55 **Si**, 4.00–6.00 **Cr**, 0.40–0.70 **Mo**	**Hot rolled and annealed**: (≤20) **diam**, (412) **TS**, (206) **YS**, 18 **El**; **Hot rolled, normalized, tempered**: (≤20) **diam**, (520) **TS**, (314) **YS**, 18 **El**
IS 6630	10Cr2Mo1	India	Pipe	0.15 **C**, 0.40–0.70 **Mn**, 0.040 **P**, 0.040 **S**, 0.50 **Si**, 2.00–2.50 **Cr**, 0.90–1.20 **Mo**	**Annealed**: all **diam**, (410) **TS**, (135) **YS**, 20 **El**; **Normalized, tempered**: all **diam**, (490) **TS**, (275) **YS**, 16 **El**
IS 6630	10Cr5Mo[55]	India	Pipe	0.15 **C**, 0.40–0.70 **Mn**, 0.030 **P**, 0.030 **S**, 0.50 **Si**, 4.0–6.0 **Cr**, 0.45–0.65 **Mo**	**Annealed**: all **diam**, (410) **TS**, (205) **YS**, 20 **El**
ISO 2604/II	TS 37	ISO	Tube: seamless	0.15 **C**, 0.30–0.60 **Mn**, 0.030 **P**, 0.030 **S**, 0.50 **Si**, 4.00–6.00 **Cr**, 0.45–0.65 **Mo**, 0.02 $\mathbf{Al}_{met}$	**Cold finished, annealed**: all **diam**, (410) **TS**, (205) **YS**, 20 **El**
ISO 2604/II	TS 38	ISO	Tube: seamless	0.15 **C**, 0.30–0.60 **Mn**, 0.030 **P**, 0.030 **S**, 0.25–1.00 **Si**, 8.00–10.00 **Cr**, 0.90–1.10 **Mo**, 0.25–0.35 **V**, 0.02 $\mathbf{Al}_{met}$	**Cold finished, annealed**: all **diam**, (410) **TS**, (135) **YS**, 20 **El**; **Cold finished, normalized and tempered**: all **diam**, (590) **TS**, (390) **YS**, 18 **El**
COPANT R 194	T22	COPANT	Tube	0.15 **C**, 0.30–0.60 **Mn**, 0.030 **P**, 0.030 **S**, 0.50 **Si**, 1.90–2.60 **Cr**, 0.87–1.13 **Mo**	**Hot or cold finished**: (≥5.6) **diam**, (410) **TS**, (170) **YS**, 30 **El**

specification number	designation	country	product forms	composition	mechanical properties (see page iv for explanation)
COPANT R 194	T21	COPANT	Tube	0.15 **C**, 0.30–0.60 **Mn**, 0.030 **P**, 0.030 **S**, 0.50 **Si**, 2.65–3.35 **Cr**, 0.80–1.06 **Mo**	**Hot or cold finished:** (≥5.6) **diam**, (410) **TS**, (170) **YS**, 30 **El**
COPANT R 194	T11	COPANT	Tube	0.15 **C**, 0.30–0.60 **Mn**, 0.030 **P**, 0.030 **S**, 0.50–1.00 **Si**, 1.00–1.50 **Cr**, 0.44–0.65 **Mo**	**Hot or cold finished:** (≥5.6) **diam**, (410) **TS**, (170) **YS**, 30 **El**
COPANT R 194	T9	COPANT	Tube	0.15 **C**, 0.30–0.60 **Mn**, 0.030 **P**, 0.030 **S**, 0.25–1.00 **Si**, 8.00–10.00 **Cr**, 0.90–1.10 **Mo**	**Hot or cold finished:** (≥5.6) **diam**, (410) **TS**, (170) **YS**, 30 **El**
COPANT R 194	T7	COPANT	Tube	0.15 **C**, 0.30–0.60 **Mn**, 0.030 **P**, 0.030 **S**, 0.50–1.0 **Si**, 6.0–8.0 **Cr**, 0.45–0.65 **Mo**	**Hot or cold finished:** (≥5.6) **diam**, (410) **TS**, (170) **YS**, 30 **El**
COPANT R 194	T5	COPANT	Tube	0.15 **C**, 0.30–0.60 **Mn**, 0.030 **P**, 0.030 **S**, 0.50 **Si**, 4.0–6.0 **Cr**, 0.45–0.65 **Mo**	**Hot or cold finished:** (≥5.6) **diam**, (410) **TS**, (170) **YS**, 30 **El**
COPANT R 194	T4	COPANT	Tube	0.15 **C**, 0.30–0.60 **Mn**, 0.030 **P**, 0.030 **S**, 0.50–1.0 **Si**, 2.15–2.85 **Cr**, 0.44–0.65 **Mo**	**Hot or cold finished:** (≥5.6) **diam**, (410) **TS**, (170) **YS**, 30 **El**
COPANT R 194	T 3b	COPANT	Tube	0.15 **C**, 0.30–0.60 **Mn**, 0.030 **P**, 0.030 **S**, 0.50 **Si**, 1.65–2.35 **Cr**, 0.44–0.65 **Mo**	**Hot or cold finished:** (≥5.6) **diam**, (410) **TS**, (170) **YS**, 30 **El**
COPANT 513	T5b	COPANT	Tube	0.15 **C**, 0.30–0.60 **Mn**, 0.030 **P**, 0.030 **S**, 1.0–2.0 **Si**, 4.00–6.00 **Cr**, 0.45–0.65 **Mo**	**Normalized and tempered, cold finished and tempered:** (>8) **diam**, (410) **TS**, (205) **YS**, 30 **El**
COPANT 513	T7	COPANT	Tube	0.15 **C**, 0.30–0.60 **Mn**, 0.030 **P**, 0.030 **S**, 0.50–1.00 **Si**, 6.00–8.00 **Cr**, 0.45–0.65 **Mo**	**Normalized and tempered, cold finished and tempered:** (>8) **diam**, (410) **TS**, (205) **YS**, 30 **El**
COPANT 513	T9	COPANT	Tube	0.15 **C**, 0.30–0.60 **Mn**, 0.030 **P**, 0.030 **S**, 0.25–1.00 **Si**, 8.00–10.00 **Cr**, 0.90–1.10 **Mo**	**Normalized and tempered, cold finished and tempered:** (>8) **diam**, (410) **TS**, (205) **YS**, 30 **El**
COPANT 513	T11	COPANT	Tube	0.15 **C**, 0.30–0.60 **Mn**, 0.030 **P**, 0.030 **S**, 0.50–1.00 **Si**, 1.00–1.50 **Cr**, 0.44–0.65 **Mo**	**Normalized and tempered, cold finished and tempered:** (>8) **diam**, (410) **TS**, (205) **YS**, 30 **El**
COPANT 513	T12	COPANT	Tube	0.15 **C**, 0.30–0.61 **Mn**, 0.045 **P**, 0.045 **S**, 0.50 **Si**, 0.80–1.25 **Cr**, 0.44–0.65 **Mo**	**Hot or cold finished and annealed:** (>8) **diam**, (410) **TS**, (205) **YS**, 30 **El**
COPANT 513	T5	COPANT	Tube	0.15 **C**, 0.30–0.60 **Mn**, 0.030 **P**, 0.030 **S**, 0.50 **Si**, 4.00–6.00 **Cr**, 0.45–0.65 **Mo**	**Normalized and tempered, cold finished and tempered:** (>8) **diam**, (410) **TS**, (205) **YS**, 30 **El**
COPANT 513	T3b	COPANT	Tube	0.15 **C**, 0.30–0.60 **Mn**, 0.030 **P**, 0.030 **S**, 0.50 **Si**, 1.65–2.35 **Cr**, 0.44–0.65 **Mo**	**Normalized and tempered, cold finished and tempered:** (>8) **diam**, (410) **TS**, (205) **YS**, 30 **El**
COPANT 509	P21	COPANT	Pipe	0.15 **C**, 0.30–0.60 **Mn**, 0.030 **P**, 0.030 **S**, 0.50 **Si**, 2.65–3.35 **Cr**, 0.80–1.06 **Mo**	**Hot or cold finished:** (≥8) **diam**, (410) **TS**, (205) **YS**, 30 **El**
COPANT 509	P15	COPANT	Pipe	0.15 **C**, 0.30–0.60 **Mn**, 0.030 **P**, 0.030 **S**, 1.15–1.65 **Si**, 0.44–0.65 **Mo**	**Hot or cold finished:** (≥8) **diam**, (410) **TS**, (205) **YS**, 30 **El**
COPANT 509	P22	COPANT	Pipe	0.15 **C**, 0.30–0.60 **Mn**, 0.030 **P**, 0.030 **S**, 0.50 **Si**, 1.90–2.60 **Cr**, 0.87–1.13 **Mo**	**Hot or cold finished:** (≥8) **diam**, (410) **TS**, (205) **YS**, 30 **El**
COPANT 509	P12	COPANT	Pipe	0.15 **C**, 0.30–0.61 **Mn**, 0.045 **P**, 0.045 **S**, 0.30 **Si**, 0.80–1.25 **Cr**, 0.44–0.65 **Mo**	**Hot or cold finished:** (≥8) **diam**, (410) **TS**, (205) **YS**, 30 **El**
COPANT 509	P11	COPANT	Pipe	0.15 **C**, 0.30–0.60 **Mn**, 0.030 **P**, 0.030 **S**, 0.50–1.00 **Si**, 1.00–1.50 **Cr**, 0.44–0.65 **Mo**	**Hot or cold finished:** (≥8) **diam**, (410) **TS**, (205) **YS**, 30 **El**
COPANT 509	P9	COPANT	Pipe	0.15 **C**, 0.30–0.60 **Mn**, 0.030 **P**, 0.030 **S**, 0.25–1.00 **Si**, 8.00–10.00 **Cr**, 0.50–1.10 **Mo**	**Cold finished and annealed:** (≥8) **diam**, (410) **TS**, (205) **YS**, 30 **El**
COPANT 509	P7	COPANT	Pipe	0.15 **C**, 0.30–0.60 **Mn**, 0.030 **P**, 0.030 **S**, 0.50–1.00 **Si**, 6.00–8.00 **Cr**, 0.44–0.85 **Mo**	**Hot or cold finished:** (≥8) **diam**, (410) **TS**, (205) **YS**, 30 **El**
COPANT 509	P56	COPANT	Pipe	0.15 **C**, 0.30–0.60 **Mn**, 0.030 **P**, 0.030 **S**, 1.00–2.00 **Si**, 4.00–6.00 **Cr**, 0.45–0.65 **Mo**	**Hot or cold finished:** (≥8) **diam**, (410) **TS**, (205) **YS**, 30 **El**

WROUGHT ALLOY STEELS

specification number	designation	country	product forms	composition	mechanical properties (see page iv for explanation)
COPANT 509	P5	COPANT	Pipe	0.15 **C**, 0.30–0.60 **Mn**, 0.030 **P**, 0.030 **S**, 0.50 **Si**, 4.00–6.00 **Cr**, 0.45–0.65 **Mo**	**Hot or cold finished and annealed or normalized and tempered**: (≥8) **diam**, (410) **TS**, (205) **YS**, 30 **El**
ANSI/ASTM A 369	FP3b	US	Pipe	0.15 **C**, 0.30–0.60 **Mn**, 0.030 **P**, 0.030 **S**, 0.50 **Si**, 1.65–2.35 **Cr**, 0.44–0.65 **Mo**	**Annealed or normalized, tempered**: 0.312 (7.94) **diam**, 60 (410) **TS**, 30 (210) **YS**, 30 **El**
ANSI/ASTM A 369	FP5	US	Pipe	0.15 **C**, 0.30–0.60 **Mn**, 0.030 **P**, 0.030 **S**, 0.50 **Si**, 4.00–6.00 **Cr**, 0.45–0.65 **Mo**	**Annealed or normalized, tempered**: 0.312 (7.94) **diam**, 60 (410) **TS**, 30 (210) **YS**, 30 **El**
ANSI/ASTM A 369	FP7	US	Pipe	0.15 **C**, 0.30–0.60 **Mn**, 0.030 **P**, 0.030 **S**, 0.50–1.00 **Si**, 6.00–8.00 **Cr**, 0.44–0.65 **Mo**	**Annealed or normalized, tempered**: 0.312 (7.94) **diam**, 60 (410) **TS**, 30 (210) **YS**, 30 **El**
ANSI/ASTM A 369	FP9	US	Pipe	0.15 **C**, 0.30–0.60 **Mn**, 0.030 **P**, 0.030 **S**, 0.50–1.00 **Si**, 8.00–10.00 **Cr**, 0.90–1.10 **Mo**	**Annealed, or normalized, tempered**: 0.312 (7.94) **diam**, 60 (410) **TS**, 30 (210) **YS**, 30 **El**
ANSI/ASTM A 369	FP11	US	Pipe	0.15 **C**, 0.30–0.60 **Mn**, 0.030 **P**, 0.030 **S**, 0.50–1.00 **Si**, 1.00–1.50 **Cr**, 0.44–0.65 **Mo**	**Annealed, or normalized, tempered**: 0.312 (7.94) **diam**, 60 (410) **TS**, 30 (210) **YS**, 30 **El**
ANSI/ASTM A 369	FP12	US	Pipe	0.15 **C**, 0.30–0.61 **Mn**, 0.045 **P**, 0.045 **S**, 0.50 **Si**, 0.80–1.25 **Cr**, 0.44–0.65 **Mo**	**Annealed or normalized, tempered**: 0.312 (7.94) **diam**, 60 (410) **TS**, 30 (210) **YS**, 30 **El**
ANSI/ASTM A 369	FP21	US	Pipe	0.15 **C**, 0.30–0.60 **Mn**, 0.030 **P**, 0.030 **S**, 0.50 **Si**, 2.65–3.35 **Cr**, 0.80–1.06 **Mo**	**Annealed or normalized, tempered**: 0.312 (7.94) **diam**, 60 (410) **TS**, 30 (210) **YS**, 30 **El**
ANSI/ASTM A 369	FP22	US	Pipe	0.15 **C**, 0.30–0.60 **Mn**, 0.030 **P**, 0.030 **S**, 0.50 **Si**, 1.90–2.60 **Cr**, 0.87–1.13 **Mo**	**Annealed or normalized, tempered**: 0.312 (7.94) **diam**, 60 (410) **TS**, 30 (210) **YS**, 30 **El**
BS 1501–503		UK	Bar	0.15 **C**, 0.30–0.60 **Mn**, 0.040 **P**, 0.040 **S**, 0.10–0.35 **Si**, 0.3 **Cr**, 3.25–3.75 **Ni**	**Normalized**: 4 **diam**, (400) **TS**, (225) **YS**
BS 1501–620	Grade B	UK	Bar	0.15 **C**, 0.40–0.70 **Mn**, 0.050 **P**, 0.050 **S**, 0.10–0.30 **Si**, 0.70–1.00 **Cr**, 0.40 **Ni**, 0.45–0.65 **Mo**, 0.40 **Cu**	**Normalized**: all **diam**, (400) **TS**, (205) **YS**
BS 3604	HF 621	UK	Pipe: seamless	0.15 **C**, 0.30–0.60 **Mn**, 0.040 **P**, 0.040 **S**, 0.50–1.00 **Si**, 1.00–1.50 **Cr**, 0.45–0.65 **Mo**	**Normalized, rolled, or hot drawn**: 0.71 **diam**, (372) **TS**, (207) **YS**, 29 **El**
BS 3604	CD 621	UK	Pipe: seamless	0.15 **C**, 0.30–0.60 **Mn**, 0.040 **P**, 0.040 **S**, 0.50–1.00 **Si**, 1.00–1.50 **Cr**, 0.45–0.65 **Mo**	**Normalized**: 0.71 **diam**, (372) **TS**, (207) **YS**, 29 **El**
BS 3604	CD 625	UK	Pipe: seamless	0.15 **C**, 0.40–0.70 **Mn**, 0.040 **P**, 0.040 **S**, 0.50 **Si**, 4.00–6.00 **Cr**, 0.45–0.65 **Mo**	**Cold drawn**: 0.71 **diam**, (372) **TS**, (186) **YS**, 29 **El**
BS 3604	HF 625	UK	Pipe: seamless	0.15 **C**, 0.40–0.70 **Mn**, 0.040 **P**, 0.040 **S**, 0.50 **Si**, 4.00–6.00 **Cr**, 0.45–0.65 **Mo**	**Hot finished**: 0.71 **diam**, (372) **TS**, (186) **YS**, 29 **El**
BS 3604	CD 620	UK	Pipe: seamless	0.15 **C**, 0.40–0.70 **Mn**, 0.050 **P**, 0.050 **S**, 0.10–0.35 **Si**, 0.70–1.10 **Cr**, 0.45–0.65 **Mo**	**Normalized**: 0.71 **diam**, (372) **TS**, (207) **YS**, 29 **El**
BS 1501–625		UK	Bar	0.15 **C**, 0.30–0.70 **Mn**, 0.045 **P**, 0.045 **S**, 0.50 **Si**, 4.00–6.00 **Cr**, 0.40 **Ni**, 0.45–0.65 **Mo**, 0.40 **Cu**	**Annealed**: all **diam**, (370) **TS**, (195) **YS**
BS 1501–620	Grade A	UK	Bar	0.15 **C**, 0.40–0.70 **Mn**, 0.050 **P**, 0.050 **S**, 0.10–0.30 **Si**, 0.45–0.75 **Cr**, 0.40 **Ni**, 0.45–0.65 **Mo**, 0.40 **Cu**	**Normalized**: all **diam**, (360) **TS**, (205) **YS**
NF A 36–208	0.5 Ni (10 N2) 245	France	Plate	0.15 **C**, 0.70–1.50 **Mn**, 0.035 **P**, 0.030 **S**, 0.40 **Si**, 0.30–0.80 **Ni**, 0.08 **V**, 0.015 min **Al**, 0.06 **Nb**, 0.10 **Nb+V**	
ANSI/ASTM A 730	Grade A	US	Forgings	0.15 **C**, 0.30–0.60 **Mn**, 0.045 **P**, 0.050 **S**	
JIS G 3213	Class 25	Japan	Forgings	0.15 **C**, 0.30–0.60 **Mn**, 0.030 **P**, 0.030 **S**, 0.50 **Si**, 4.00–6.00 **Cr**, 0.44–0.65 **Mo**	
BS 970 Part 3	Grade 815 M 17	UK	Blooms, billets, bar, forgings	0.14–0.20 **C**, 0.60–0.90 **Mn**, 0.10–0.35 **Si**, 0.80–1.20 **Cr**, 1.20–1.70 **Ni**, 0.10–0.20 **Mo**	**Hardened**: 0.75 **diam**, (1380) **TS**, 8 **El**
BS 970 Part 3	Grade 822 M 17	UK	Blooms, billets, bar, forgings	0.14–0.20 **C**, 0.40–0.70 **Mn**, 0.10–0.35 **Si**, 1.30–1.70 **Cr**, 1.75–2.25 **Ni**, 0.15–0.25 **Mo**	**Hardened**: 0.75 **diam**, (1175) **TS**, 8 **El**

WROUGHT ALLOY STEELS

specification number	designation	country	product forms	composition	mechanical properties (see page iv for explanation)
ISO R 683/XI	13	ISO	Bar	0.14–0.20 **C**, 0.60–0.90 **Mn**, 0.035 **P**, 0.035 **S**, 0.15–0.40 **Si**, 0.80–1.1 **Cr**, 1.2–1.6 **Ni**, 0.15–0.25 **Mo**	**Carburized and hardened:** all **diam**, (1079) **TS**, (736) **YS**, 8 **El**
ISO R 683/XI	13a	ISO	Bar	0.14–0.20 **C**, 0.60–0.90 **Mn**, 0.035 **P**, 0.020–0.035 **S**, 0.15–0.40 **Si**, 0.80–1.1 **Cr**, 1.2–1.6 **Ni**, 0.15–0.25 **Mo**	**Carburized and hardened:** all **diam**, (1079) **TS**, (736) **YS**, 8 **El**
BS 970 Part 3	Grade 820 M 17	UK	Blooms, billets, bar, forgings	0.14–0.20 **C**, 0.60–0.90 **Mn**, 0.10–0.35 **Si**, 0.80–1.20 **Cr**, 1.50–2.00 **Ni**, 0.10–0.20 **Mo**	**Hardened**: 0.75 **diam**, (1035) **TS**, 8 **El**
AMS 6264E		US	Bar, forgings, tube	0.14–0.20 **C**, 0.40–0.70 **Mn**, 0.025 **P**, 0.025 **S**, 0.20–0.35 **Si**, 1.00–1.40 **Cr**, 3.00–3.50 **Ni**, 0.08–0.15 **Mo**, 0.35 **Cu**	**Cold finished (bar)**: ≤0.500 (≤12.70) **diam**, 125 (862) max **TS**
BS 970 Part 3	Grade 637 M 17	UK	Blooms, billets, bar, forgings	0.14–0.20 **C**, 0.60–0.90 **Mn**, 0.10–0.35 **Si**, 0.60–1.00 **Cr**, 0.85–1.25 **Ni**	**Hardened**: 0.75 **diam**, (830) **TS**, 10 **El**
BS 970 Part 3	Grade 665 M 17	UK	Blooms, billets, bar, forgings	0.14–0.20 **C**, 0.35–0.75 **Mn**, 0.10–0.35 **Si**, 1.50–2.00 **Ni**, 0.20–0.30 **Mo**	**Hardened**: 0.75 **diam**, (690) **TS**, 12 **El**
BS 970 Part 3	Grade 805 M 17	UK	Blooms, billets, bar, forgings	0.14–0.20 **C**, 0.60–0.95 **Mn**, 0.10–0.35 **Si**, 0.35–0.65 **Cr**, 0.35–0.75 **Ni**, 0.15–0.25 **Mo**	**Hardened**: 0.75 **diam**, (690) **TS**, 12 **El**
AS G18	G18/En 34	Australia	Bar, billet	0.14–0.20 **C**, 0.30–0.60 **Mn**, 0.050 **P**, 0.050 **S**, 0.10–0.35 **Si**, 1.50–2.00 **Ni**, 0.20–0.30 **Mo**	**Blank carburized, hardened:** all **diam**, (690) **TS**
COPANT 514	Grade 1118	COPANT	Tube: seamless	0.14–0.20 **C**, 1.30–1.60 **Mn**, 0.040 **P**, 0.08–0.13 **S**	**Hot finished**: (>323.9) **diam**, (345) **TS**, (245) **YS**, 25 **El**; **Cold finished**: all **diam**, (520) **TS**, (410) **YS**, 5 **El**; **Annealed**: all **diam**, (345) **TS**, (205) **YS**, 25 **El**; **Normalized**: all **diam**, (380) **TS**, (245) **YS**, 20 **El**
ISO 683/XVII	15	ISO	Billets, bar, wire, tube	0.14–0.20 **C**, 0.60–0.90 **Mn**, 0.035 **P**, 0.035 **S**, 0.15–0.40 **Si**, 0.80–1.10 **Cr**, 1.20–1.60 **Ni**, 0.15–0.25 **Mo**	
ISO 683/XVII	16	ISO	Billets, bar, wire, tube	0.14–0.20 **C**, 0.40–0.70 **Mn**, 0.035 **P**, 0.035 **S**, 0.15–0.40 **Si**, 1.30–1.60 **Cr**, 3.25–3.75 **Ni**, 0.15–0.25 **Mo**	
BS 970 Part 3	Grade 637 H 17	UK	Blooms, billets, bar, forgings	0.14–0.20 **C**, 0.60–0.90 **Mn**, 0.10–0.35 **Si**, 0.60–1.00 **Cr**, 0.85–1.25 **Ni**	
BS 970 Part 3	Grade 665 H 17	UK	Blooms, billets, bar, forgings	0.14–0.20 **C**, 0.35–0.75 **Mn**, 0.10–0.35 **Si**, 1.50–2.00 **Ni**, 0.20–0.30 **Mo**	
BS 970 Part 3	Grade 805 H 17	UK	Blooms, billets, bar, forgings	0.14–0.20 **C**, 0.60–0.95 **Mn**, 0.10–0.35 **Si**, 0.35–0.65 **Cr**, 0.35–0.75 **Ni**, 0.15–0.25 **Mo**	
BS 970 Part 3	Grade 815 H 17	UK	Blooms, billets, bar, forgings	0.14–0.20 **C**, 0.60–0.90 **Mn**, 0.10–0.35 **Si**, 0.80–1.20 **Cr**, 1.20–1.70 **Ni**, 0.10–0.20 **Mo**	
BS 970 Part 3	Grade 820 H 17	UK	Blooms, billets, bar, forgings	0.14–0.20 **C**, 0.60–0.90 **Mn**, 0.10–0.35 **Si**, 0.80–1.20 **Cr**, 1.50–2.00 **Ni**, 0.10–0.20 **Mo**	
BS 970 Part 3	Grade 822 H 17	UK	Blooms, billets, bar, forgings	0.14–0.20 **C**, 0.40–0.70 **Mn**, 0.10–0.35 **Si**, 1.30–1.70 **Cr**, 1.75–2.25 **Ni**, 0.15–0.25 **Mo**	
NBN A 21–221	C 17 KD	Belgium	Wire	0.14–0.20 **C**, 0.60–0.90 **Mn**, 0.040 **P**, 0.050 **S**, 0.10–0.40 **Si**	
AS 1444	Grade AS 1444/8617H	Australia	Bar, bloom, billet, slab	0.14–0.20 **C**, 0.60–0.95 **Mn**, 0.040 **P**, 0.040 **S**, 0.10–0.35 **Si**, 0.35–0.65 **Cr**, 0.35–0.75 **Ni**, 0.15–0.25 **Mo**	
AS 1444	Grade AS 1444/94B17H	Australia	Bar, bloom, billet, slab	0.14–0.20 **C**, 0.70–1.05 **Mn**, 0.040 **P**, 0.040 **S**, 0.10–0.35 **Si**, 0.25–0.55 **Cr**, 0.25–0.65 **Ni**, 0.08–0.15 **Mo**	
DGN–B–300	4817 H	Mexico	Bar	0.14–0.20 **C**, 0.30–0.70 **Mn**, 0.040 **P**, 0.035 **S**, 0.20–0.35 **Si**, 3.20–3.80 **Ni**, 0.20–0.30 **Mo**	**Annealed**

WROUGHT ALLOY STEELS

specification number	designation	country	product forms	composition	mechanical properties (see page iv for explanation)
DGN–B–300	8617 H	Mexico	Bar	0.14–0.20 **C**, 0.60–0.95 **Mn**, 0.040 **P**, 0.035 **S**, 0.20–0.35 **Si**, 0.35–0.65 **Cr**, 0.35–0.75 **Ni**, 0.15–0.25 **Mo**	**Annealed**
DGN–B–300	94B17 H	Mexico	Bar	0.14–0.20 **C**, 0.70–1.05 **Mn**, 0.040 **P**, 0.035 **S**, 0.20–0.35 **Si**, 0.25–0.55 **Cr**, 0.25–0.65 **Ni**, 0.08–0.15 **Mo**, 0.0005 min **B**	**Annealed**
ASTM A 108	1118	US	Bar	0.14–0.20 **C**, 1.30–1.60 **Mn**, 0.040 **P**, 0.08–0.13 **S**	
ASTM A 689	94B17 H	US	Bar	0.14–0.20 **C**, 0.70–1.05 **Mn**, 0.040 **P**, 0.040 **S**, 0.15–0.30 **Si**, 0.25–0.55 **Cr**, 0.25–0.65 **Ni**, 0.08–0.15 **Mo**, 0.0005 min **B**	
ASTM A 689	8617 H	US	Bar	0.14–0.20 **C**, 0.60–0.95 **Mn**, 0.040 **P**, 0.040 **S**, 0.15–0.30 **Si**, 0.35–0.65 **Cr**, 0.35–0.75 **Ni**, 0.15–0.25 **Mo**	
ANSI/ASTM A 304	8617 H	US	Bar	0.14–0.20 **C**, 0.60–0.95 **Mn**, 0.040 **P**, 0.040 **S**, 0.15–0.30 **Si**, 0.35–0.65 **Cr**, 0.35–0.75 **Ni**, 0.15–0.25 **Mo**	
ANSI/ASTM A 304	94B17 H	US	Bar	0.14–0.20 **C**, 0.70–1.05 **Mn**, 0.040 **P**, 0.040 **S**, 0.15–0.30 **Si**, 0.25–0.55 **Cr**, 0.25–0.65 **Ni**, 0.08–0.15 **Mo**, 0.0005 min **B**	
ANSI/ASTM A 304	4817 H	US	Bar	0.14–0.20 **C**, 0.30–0.70 **Mn**, 0.040 **P**, 0.040 **S**, 0.15–0.30 **Si**, 3.20–3.80 **Ni**, 0.20–0.30 **Mo**	
ASTM A 689	4817 H	US	Bar	0.14–0.20 **C**, 0.30–0.70 **Mn**, 0.040 **P**, 0.040 **S**, 0.15–0.30 **Si**, 3.20–3.80 **Ni**, 0.20–0.30 **Mo**	
AISI 4817 H		US	Wire, rod	0.14–0.20 **C**, 0.30–0.70 **Mn**, 0.15–0.30 **Si**, 3.20–3.80 **Ni**, 0.20–0.30 **Mo**	
AISI 8617 H		US	Wire, rod	0.14–0.20 **C**, 0.60–0.95 **Mn**, 0.15–0.30 **Si**, 0.35–0.65 **Cr**, 0.35–0.75 **Ni**, 0.15–0.25 **Mo**	
AISI 94B17 H		US	Wire, rod	0.14–0.20 **C**, 0.70–1.05 **Mn**, 0.15–0.30 **Si**, 0.25–0.55 **Cr**, 0.25–0.65 **Ni**, 0.08–0.15 **Mo**	
AISI 94B17H		US	Bar	0.14–0.20 **C**, 0.70–1.05 **Mn**, 0.035 **P**, 0.040 **S**, 0.15–0.30 **Si**, 0.25–0.55 **Cr**, 0.25–0.65 **Ni**, 0.08–0.15 **Mo**	
AISI 8617H		US	Bar	0.14–0.20 **C**, 0.60–0.95 **Mn**, 0.035 **P**, 0.040 **S**, 0.15–0.30 **Si**, 0.35–0.65 **Cr**, 0.35–0.75 **Ni**, 0.15–0.25 **Mo**	
AISI 4817H		US	Bar	0.14–0.20 **C**, 0.30–0.70 **Mn**, 0.035 **P**, 0.040 **S**, 0.15–0.30 **Si**, 3.20–3.80 **Ni**, 0.20–0.30 **Mo**	
AISI 1118		US	Wire, rod	0.14–0.20 **C**, 1.30–1.60 **Mn**, 0.040 **P**, 0.08–0.13 **S**	
ANSI/ASTM A 29	1118	US	Bar	0.14–0.20 **C**, 1.30–1.60 **Mn**, 0.040 **P**, 0.08–0.13 **S**	
ANSI/ASTM A 576	1118	US	Bar	0.14–0.20 **C**, 1.30–1.60 **Mn**, 0.040 **P**, 0.08–0.13 **S**	
COPANT 514	Grade 11 L 18	COPANT	Tube: seamless	0.14–0.20 **C**, 1.30–1.60 **Mn**, 0.040 **P**, 0.08–0.13 **S**, 0.20–0.35 **Si**, 0.15–0.35 **Pb**	
QQ–S–637A	1118	US	Bar	0.14–0.20 **C**, 1.30–1.60 **Mn**, 0.040 **P**, 0.08–0.13 **S**, 0.15–0.35 **Pb**	
COPANT 331	1118	COPANT	Bar	0.14–0.20 **C**, 1.3–1.6 **Mn**, 0.040 **P**, 0.08–0.13 **S**	
SFS 511	17 Cr Ni Mo 6	Finland	Bar, forgings	0.14–0.19 **C**, 0.40–0.60 **Mn**, 0.035 **P**, 0.050 **S**, 0.15–0.40 **Si**, 1.50–1.80 **Cr**, 1.40–1.70 **Ni**, 0.25–0.35 **Mo**	**Quenched**: (11) **diam**, (1180) **TS**, (830) **YS**, 7 **El**

WROUGHT ALLOY STEELS

specification number	designation	country	product forms	composition	mechanical properties (see page iv for explanation)
DIN 17210	Grade 17 CrNiMo 6	Germany	Blooms, slabs, billets, wire, plate, sheet, strip, tube, forgings	0.14–0.19 **C**, 0.40–0.60 **Mn**, 0.035 **P**, 0.035 **S**, 0.15–0.40 **Si**, 1.50–1.80 **Cr**, 1.40–1.70 **Ni**, 0.25–0.35 **Mo**	**Rolled or forged:** (11) **diam**, (1177) **TS**, (834) **YS**, 7 **El**
DIN 17210	Grade 16 MnCr 5	Germany	Blooms, slabs, billets, wire, bar, plate, sheet, strip, tube, forgings	0.14–0.19 **C**, 1.00–1.30 **Mn**, 0.035 **P**, 0.15–0.40 **S**, 0.15–0.40 **Si**, 0.80–1.10 **Cr**	**Rolled or forged:** (11) **diam**, (883) **TS**, (638) **YS**, 9 **El**
DIN 17210	Grade 16 MnCrS 5	Germany	Blooms, slabs, billets, wire, bar, plate, sheet, strip, tube, forgings	0.14–0.19 **C**, 1.00–1.30 **Mn**, 0.035 **P**, 0.020–0.035 **S**, 0.15–0.40 **Si**, 0.80–1.10 **Cr**	**Rolled or forged:** (11) **diam**, (883) **TS**, (638) **YS**, 9 **El**
IS 4367	17Mn1Cr[95]	India	Forgings	0.14–0.19 **C**, 1.00–1.30 **Mn**, 0.050 **P**, 0.050 **S**, 0.10–0.35 **Si**, 0.80–1.10 **Cr**	**Refined and quenched:** all **diam**, (784) **TS**, 10 **El**
BS 970 Part 3	Grade 637 A 16	UK	Blooms, billets, bar, forgings	0.14–0.19 **C**, 0.70–0.90 **Mn**, 0.70–1.00 **Cr**, 0.90–1.00 **Ni**, 0.10 **Mo**	
BS 970 Part 3	Grade 815 A 16	UK	Blooms, billets, bar, forgings	0.14–0.19 **C**, 0.70–0.90 **Mn**, 0.90–1.20 **Cr**, 1.20–1.60 **Ni**, 0.10–0.20 **Mo**	
BS 970 Part 3	Grade 820 A 16	UK	Blooms, billets, bar, forgings	0.14–0.19 **C**, 0.70–0.90 **Mn**, 0.90–1.20 **Cr**, 1.60–2.00 **Ni**, 0.10–0.20 **Mo**	
MIL-S-83030A	II	US	Bar, billets	0.14–0.19 **C**, 0.45–0.60 **Mn**, 0.015 **P**, 0.015 **S**, 0.20–0.35 **Si**, 1.25–1.75 **Cr**, 3.25–4.00 **Ni**, 0.35 **Cu**; rem **Fe**	**As rolled, annealed**
COPANT 334	16 Mn Cr 5	COPANT	Bar	0.14–0.19 **C**, 1.00–1.30 **Mn**, 0.035 **P**, 0.035 **S**, 0.15–0.35 **Si**, 0.80–1.10 **Cr**	
MIL-S-7393C	Composition II	US	Bar, billets	0.14–0.19 **C**, 0.45–0.60 **Mn**, 0.025 **P**, 0.025 **S**, 0.20–0.35 **Si**, 1.25–1.75 **Cr**, 3.25–4.00 **Ni**, 0.35 **Cu**; rem Fe	
SFS 511	17NiCrMo6: steel 511	Finland	Bar, forgings	0.14–0.19 **C**, 0.40–0.60 **Mn**, 0.035 **P**, 0.050 **S**, 0.15–0.40 **Si**, 1.50–1.80 **Cr**, 1.40–1.70 **Ni**, 0.25–0.35 **Mo**	
BS 5S.82		UK	Billets, bar, forgings, parts: aircraft quality	0.14–0.18 **C**, 0.25–0.55 **Mn**, 0.025 **P**, 0.020 **S**, 0.15–0.40 **Si**, 1.0–1.4 **Cr**, 3.8–4.3 **Ni**, 0.20–0.30 **Mo**	**Normalized, softened:** (20) **diam**, (1320) **TS**, (1030) **YS**, 8 **El**
BS S.156	S156B	UK	Bar: black, aircraft quality	0.14–0.18 **C**, 0.25–0.55 **Mn**, 0.015 **P**, 0.012 **S**, 0.10–0.35 **Si**, 1.0–1.4 **Cr**, 3.8–4.3 **Ni**, 0.20–0.30 **Mo**	**Normalized, annealed, carburized, hardened and tempered:** all **diam**, (1320) **TS**, (1030) **YS**, 11 **El**
BS S.156	S156D	UK	Bar: bright, aircraft quality	0.14–0.18 **C**, 0.25–0.55 **Mn**, 0.015 **P**, 0.012 **S**, 0.10–0.35 **Si**, 1.0–1.4 **Cr**, 3.8–4.3 **Ni**, 0.20–0.30 **Mo**	**Normalized, annealed, carburized, hardened, and tempered:** all **diam**, (1320) **TS**, (1030) **YS**, 11 **El**
BS S.156	S156A	UK	Forging stock, billets, bar: aircraft quality	0.14–0.18 **C**, 0.25–0.55 **Mn**, 0.015 **P**, 0.012 **S**, 0.10–0.35 **Si**, 1.0–1.4 **Cr**, 3.8–4.3 **Ni**, 0.20–0.30 **Mo**	**Normalized, annealed, carburized, hardened, and tempered:** all **diam**, (1320) **TS**, (1030) **YS**, 11 **El**
BS S.156	S156C	UK	Forgings: aircraft quality	0.14–0.18 **C**, 0.25–0.55 **Mn**, 0.015 **P**, 0.012 **S**, 0.10–0.35 **Si**, 1.0–1.4 **Cr**, 3.8–4.3 **Ni**, 0.20–0.30 **Mo**	**Normalized, annealed, carburized, hardened, and tempered:** all **diam**, (1320) **TS**, (1030) **YS**, 11 **El**
AIR 9160/C 85	9160C311	France	Bar, forgings	0.14–0.18 **C**, 0.35–0.45 **Mn**, 0.025 **P**, 0.020 **S**, 0.10–0.30 **Si**, 1.0–1.30 **Cr**, 4.0–4.50 **Ni**, 0.15–0.35 **Mo**	**Normalized and tempered:** ($\leq$16) **diam**, (1310) **TS**, (1030) **YS**, 8 **El**
AMS 6468		US	Wire	0.14–0.17 **C**, 0.40–0.55 **Mn**, 0.008 **P**, 0.008 **S**, 0.15–0.25 **Si**, 0.90–1.05 **Cr**, 9.75–10.25 **Ni**, 0.40–0.50 **Mo**, 0.06–0.10 **V**, 3.50–4.00 **Co**, 0.10 **Cu**, 0.0010 **H**, 0.0080 **N**, 0.0050 **O**	
NF A 36-208	5 Ni (Z10N05) 390	France	Plate	0.14 **C**, 0.30–0.80 **Mn**, 0.030 **P**, 0.025 **S**, 0.40 **Si**, 3.75–4.25 **Ni**, 0.05 **V**, 0.015 min **Al**	**Normalized, normalized and tempered or quenched and tempered:** (3–30) **diam**, (540) **TS**, (390) **YS**, 23 **El**

WROUGHT ALLOY STEELS

specification number	designation	country	product forms	composition	mechanical properties (see page iv for explanation)
ANSI/ASTM A 734	Grade A	US	Plate	0.14 **C**, 0.41–0.79 **Mn**, 0.036 **P**, 0.016 **S**, 0.37 **Si**, 0.84–1.26 **Cr**, 0.85–1.25 **Ni**, 0.22–0.43 **Mo**	**Quenched and tempered:** all **diam**, 77 (530) **TS**, 65 (450) **YS**, 20 **El**
EURONORM 129	FeE 285 Ni 2	EURONORM	Plate, strip	0.14 **C**, 0.70–1.50 **Mn**, 0.030 **P**, 0.025 **S**, 0.35 **Si**, 0.25 **Cr**, 0.30–0.80 **Ni**, 0.10 **Mo**, 0.08 **V**, 0.015_{met} or 0.020 tot. (min) **Al**, 0.35 **Cu**, 0.06 **Nb**	**Normalized:** (≤35) **diam**, (410) **TS**, (285) **YS**, 24 **El**
ANSI/ASTM A 209	Grade T1b	US	Tube: seamless	0.14 **C**, 0.30–0.80 **Mn**, 0.045 **P**, 0.045 **S**, 0.10–0.50 **Si**, 0.44–0.65 **Mo**	**Annealed:** 0.312 (7.94) **diam**, 53 (365) **TS**, 28 (193) **YS**, 30 **El**
NOM–B–193	Grade T 16	Mexico	Tube: seamless	0.14 **C**, 0.30–0.80 **Mn**, 0.045 **P**, 0.045 **S**, 0.10–0.50 **Si**, 0.44–0.65 **Mo**	**Hot or cold finished:** (0.89–12.7) **diam**, (365) **TS**, (193) **YS**, 30 **El**
ANSI/ASTM A 250	Grade T 1b	US	Tube: electric, resistance, welded	0.14 **C**, 0.30–0.80 **Mn**, 0.045 **P**, 0.045 **S**, 0.10–0.50 **Si**, 0.44–0.65 **Mo**	**Normalized:** 0.312 (7.94) **diam**, 53 (365) **TS**, 28 (193) **YS**, 30 **El**
COPANT R 204	Grade T–16	COPANT	Tube: seamless	0.14 **C**, 0.30–0.80 **Mn**, 0.045 **P**, 0.045 **S**, 0.10–0.50 **Si**, 0.44–0.65 **Mo**	**Hot or cold finished:** (>8) **diam**, (360) **TS**, (190) **YS**, 30 **El**
NF A 35–056	FG 12 MS 6.4	France	Wire, rod	0.14 **C**, 1.30–1.60 **Mn**, 0.030 **P**, 0.030 **S**, 0.90–1.20 **Si**, 0.15 **Cr**, 0.15 **Ni**, 0.12 **Cu**	
NF A 35–056	FG 12 MS 7.4	France	Wire, rod	0.14 **C**, 1.50–1.80 **Mn**, 0.030 **P**, 0.030 **S**, 0.90–1.20 **Si**, 0.15 **Cr**, 0.15 **Ni**, 0.12 **Cu**	
NF A 35–056	FG 12 MSD 6	France	Wire, rod	0.14 **C**, 1.70–2.10 **Mn**, 0.030 **P**, 0.030 **S**, 0.50–0.80 **Si**, 0.15 **Cr**, 0.15 **Ni**, 0.40–0.60 **Mo**, 0.12 **Cu**	
NF A 35–056	FG 12 MS 6	France	Wire, rod	0.14 **C**, 1.30–1.60 **Mn**, 0.030 **P**, 0.030 **S**, 0.70–1.0 **Si**, 0.15 **Cr**, 0.15 **Ni**, 0.12 **Cu**	
ANSI/ASTM A 592	Grade A	US	Forgings	0.13–0.23 **C**, 0.75–1.15 **Mn**, 0.035 **P**, 0.040 **S**, 0.35–0.86 **Si**, 0.46–0.84 **Cr**, 0.15–0.31 **Mo**, 0.0025 **B**, 0.04–0.16 **Zr**	**Quenched and tempered:** all **diam**, (795) **TS**, (690) **YS**, 18 **El**
ANSI/ASTM A 517	Grade A	US	Plate	0.13–0.23 **C**, 0.75–1.15 **Mn**, 0.035 **P**, 0.040 **S**, 0.34–0.86 **Si**, 0.46–0.84 **Cr**, 0.15–0.31 **Mo**, 0.0025 **B**, 0.04–0.16 **Zr**	**Quenched and tempered:** all **diam**, (795) **TS**, (690) **YS**, 16 **El**
ANSI/ASTM A 517	Grade B	US	Plate	0.13–0.23 **C**, 0.65–1.05 **Mn**, 0.035 **P**, 0.040 **S**, 0.18–0.37 **Si**, 0.36–0.69 **Cr**, 0.12–0.28 **Mo**, 0.02–0.09 **V**, 0.0005–0.005 **B**, 0.01–0.04 **Ti**	**Quenched and tempered:** all **diam**, (795) **TS**, (690) **YS**, 16 **El**
ANSI/ASTM A 517	Grade G	US	Plate	0.13–0.23 **C**, 0.75–1.15 **Mn**, 0.035 **P**, 0.040 **S**, 0.44–0.96 **Si**, 0.46–0.94 **Cr**, 0.36–0.64 **Mo**, 0.0025 **B**, 0.04–0.16 **Zr**	**Quenched and tempered:** all **diam**, (795) **TS**, (690) **YS**, 16 **El**
DGN–B–297	8720	Mexico	Bar	0.13–0.23 **C**, 0.70–0.90 **Mn**, 0.035 **P**, 0.040 **S**, 0.20–0.35 **Si**, 0.40–0.60 **Cr**, 0.40–0.70 **Ni**, 0.20–0.30 **Mo**	
NBN A 25–102	17 Mn 4	Belgium	Tube	0.13–0.21 **C**, 0.86–1.25 **Mn**, 0.055 **P**, 0.055 **S**, 0.17–0.43 **Si**, 0.35 **Cr**	**Hot or cold finished and normalized:** (17–59) **diam**, (460) **TS**, (270) **YS**, 23 **El**
JIS G 4103	Class 26	Japan	Bar	0.13–0.20 **C**, 0.80–1.20 **Mn**, 0.030 **P**, 0.030 **S**, 0.15–0.35 **Si**, 1.40–1.80 **Cr**, 2.80–3.20 **Ni**, 0.40–0.60 **Mo**, 0.30 **Cu**	**Rolled or forged, quenched and tempered:** (25) **diam**, (1177) **TS**, 12 **El**
ANSI/ASTM A 514	Grade D	US	Plate	0.13–0.20 **C**, 0.40–0.70 **Mn**, 0.035 **P**, 0.04 **S**, 0.20–0.35 **Si**, 0.85–1.20 **Cr**, 0.15–0.25 **Mo**, 0.0015–0.005 **B**, 0.20–0.40 **Cu**, 0.04–0.10 **Ti**	**Quenched and tempered:** ≥0.75–2.50 **diam**, (760) **TS**, (690) **YS**, 18 **El**
ANSI/ASTM A 514	Grade L	US	Plate	0.13–0.20 **C**, 0.40–0.70 **Mn**, 0.035 **P**, 0.04 **S**, 0.20–0.35 **Si**, 1.15–1.65 **Cr**, 0.25–0.40 **Mo**, 0.0015–0.005 **B**, 0.20–0.40 **Cu**, 0.04–0.10 **Ti**	**Quenched and tempered:** ≥.75–2.50 **diam**, (760) **TS**, (690) **YS**, 18 **El**

WROUGHT ALLOY STEELS

specification number	designation	country	product forms	composition	mechanical properties (see page iv for explanation)
AMS 6386B	Type 4	US	Sheet, plate	0.13–0.20 **C**, 0.40–0.70 **Mn**, 0.035 **P**, 0.040 **S**, 0.20–0.35 **Si**, 0.85–1.20 **Cr**, 0.15–0.25 **Mo**, 0.0005–0.005 **B**, 0.20–0.40 **Cu**, 0.04–0.10 **Ti+V**	**Hardened, tempered**: 1.250 (31.75) **diam**, 110 (758) **TS**, 100 (690) **YS**, 18 **El**
AMS 6386B	Type 8	US	Sheet, plate	0.13–0.20 **C**, 0.40–0.70 **Mn**, 0.035 **P**, 0.040 **S**, 0.20–0.35 **Si**, 1.15–1.65 **Cr**, 0.25–0.40 **Mo**, 0.0005–0.005 **B**, 0.20–0.40 **Cu**, 0.04–0.10 **Ti+V**	**Hardened, tempered and descaled**: 1.250–2.000 (31.75–50.80) **diam**, 110 (758) **TS**, 100 (690) **YS**, 18 **El**
ISO R 683/XI	5	ISO	Bar	0.13–0.19 **C**, 1.0–1.30 **Mn**, 0.035 **P**, 0.035 **S**, 0.15–0.40 **Si**, 0.80–1.10 **Cr**	**Carburized and hardened**: all **diam**, (932) **TS**, (638) **YS**, 9 **El**
ISO R 683/XI	5a	ISO	Bar	0.13–0.19 **C**, 1.0–1.30 **Mn**, 0.035 **P**, 0.020–0.035 **S**, 0.15–0.40 **Si**, 0.80–1.10 **Cr**	**Carburized and hardened**: all **diam**, (932) **TS**, (638) **YS**, 9 **El**
EURONORM 119–74, III	16 MnCr 5 KD	EURONORM	Wire, rod	0.13–0.19 **C**, 1.0–1.30 **Mn**, 0.035 **P**, 0.035 **S**, 0.15–0.40 **Si**, 0.80–1.10 **Cr**	**Bright annealed**: (11) **diam**, (930) **TS**, (685) **YS**, 9 **El**
ISO 683/XVII	10	ISO	Billets, bar, wire, tube	0.13–0.19 **C**, 1.00–1.30 **Mn**, 0.035 **P**, 0.035 **S**, 0.15–0.40 **Si**, 0.80–1.10 **Cr**	
SIS 14 25 11	SIS 25 11-03	Sweden	Bar, forgings	0.13–0.18 **C**, 0.70–1.10 **Mn**, 0.035 **P**, 0.030–0.050 **S**, 0.15–0.40 **Si**, 0.60–1.00 **Cr**, 0.80–1.20 **Ni**, 0.10 **Mo**	**Case hardened, quenched, annealed**: (11) **diam**, (980) **TS**, (640) **YS**, 8 **El**
JIS G 4105	Class 21	Japan	Bar	0.13–0.18 **C**, 0.60–0.85 **Mn**, 0.030 **P**, 0.030 **S**, 0.15–0.35 **Si**, 0.90–1.20 **Cr**, 0.25 **Ni**, 0.15–0.30 **Mo**, 0.30 **Cu**	**Rolled or forged, quenched and tempered**: (25) **diam**, (834) **TS**, 16 **El**
JIS G 4104	Class 21	Japan	Bar	0.13–0.18 **C**, 0.60–0.85 **Mn**, 0.030 **P**, 0.030 **S**, 0.15–0.35 **Si**, 0.90–1.20 **Cr**, 0.25 **Ni**, 0.30 **Cu**	**Rolled or forged, quenched and tempered**: (25) **diam**, (785) **TS**, 15 **El**
BS 1501–622	Grade 45	UK	Plate	0.13–0.18 **C**, 0.40–0.80 **Mn**, 0.040 **P**, 0.040 **S**, 0.20–0.50 **Si**, 2.00–2.50 **Cr**, 0.30 **Ni**, 0.90–1.20 **Mo**, 0.30 **Cu**, 0.03	**Normalized**: (51) **diam**, (690) **TS**, (555) **YS**, 15 **El**
AISI 4615		US	Bar	0.13–0.18 **C**, 0.45–0.65 **Mn**, 0.035 **P**, 0.040 **S**, 0.15–0.30 **Si**, 1.65–2.00 **Ni**, 0.20–0.30 **Mo**	
AISI 4815		US	Bar	0.13–0.18 **C**, 0.40–0.60 **Mn**, 0.035 **P**, 0.040 **S**, 0.15–0.30 **Si**, 3.25–3.75 **Ni**, 0.20–0.30 **Mo**	
AISI 8615		US	Bar	0.13–0.18 **C**, 0.70–0.90 **Mn**, 0.035 **P**, 0.040 **S**, 0.15–0.30 **Si**, 0.40–0.60 **Cr**, 0.40–0.70 **Ni**, 0.15–0.25 **Mo**	
BS 970 Part 3	Grade 659 A 15	UK	Blooms, billets, bar, forgings	0.13–0.18 **C**, 0.30–0.50 **Mn**, 1.00–1.30 **Cr**, 3.90–4.30 **Ni**	
BS 970 Part 3	Grade 805 A 15	UK	Blooms, billets, bar, forgings	0.13–0.18 **C**, 0.70–0.90 **Mn**, 0.40–0.70 **Cr**, 0.40–0.70 **Ni**, 0.15–0.25 **Mo**	
COPANT 334	3115	COPANT	Bar	0.13–0.18 **C**, 0.40–0.60 **Mn**, 0.035 **P**, 0.040 **S**, 0.20–0.35 **Si**, 0.55–0.75 **Cr**, 1.10–1.40 **Ni**	
COPANT 334	5115	COPANT	Bar	0.13–0.18 **C**, 0.70–0.90 **Mn**, 0.035 **P**, 0.040 **S**, 0.20–0.35 **Si**, 0.70–0.90 **Cr**	
COPANT 334	8615	COPANT	Bar	0.13–0.18 **C**, 0.70–0.90 **Mn**, 0.035 **P**, 0.040 **S**, 0.20–0.35 **Si**, 0.40–0.60 **Cr**, 0.40–0.70 **Ni**, 0.15–0.25 **Mo**	
COPANT 334	9315	COPANT	Bar	0.13–0.18 **C**, 0.45–0.65 **Mn**, 0.025 **P**, 0.025 **S**, 0.20–0.35 **Si**, 1.00–1.40 **Cr**, 3.00–3.50 **Ni**, 0.08–0.15 **Mo**	
AS 1444	Grade AS 1444/4615	Australia		0.13–0.18 **C**, 0.45–0.65 **Mn**, 0.040 **P**, 0.040 **S**, 0.10–0.35 **Si**, 1.65–2.00 **Ni**, 0.20–0.30 **Mo**	

WROUGHT ALLOY STEELS

specification number	designation	country	product forms	composition	mechanical properties (see page iv for explanation)
DGN-B-203	Grade 5115	Mexico	Tube: seamless	0.13–0.18 **C**, 0.70–0.90 **Mn**, 0.040 **P**, 0.040 **S**, 0.20–0.35 **Si**, 0.70–0.90 **Cr**	
DGN-B-203	Grade 4815	Mexico	Tube: seamless	0.13–0.18 **C**, 0.40–0.60 **Mn**, 0.040 **P**, 0.040 **S**, 0.20–0.35 **Si**, 3.25–3.75 **Ni**, 0.20–0.30 **Mo**	
DGN-B-203	Grade 4615	Mexico	Tube: seamless	0.13–0.18 **C**, 0.45–0.65 **Mn**, 0.040 **P**, 0.040 **S**, 0.20–0.35 **Si**, 1.65–2.00 **Ni**, 0.20–0.30 **Mo**	
DGN-B-203	Grade 8615	Mexico	Tube: seamless	0.13–0.18 **C**, 0.70–0.90 **Mn**, 0.040 **P**, 0.040 **S**, 0.20–0.35 **Si**, 0.40–0.60 **Cr**, 0.40–0.70 **Ni**, 0.15–0.25 **Mo**	
DGN-B-203	Grade 8115	Mexico	Tube: seamless	0.13–0.18 **C**, 0.70–0.90 **Mn**, 0.040 **P**, 0.040 **S**, 0.25–0.35 **Si**, 0.30–0.50 **Cr**, 0.20–0.40 **Ni**, 0.08–0.15 **Mo**	
DGN-B-203	Grade 94B15	Mexico	Tube: seamless	0.13–0.18 **C**, 0.75–1.00 **Mn**, 0.040 **P**, 0.040 **S**, 0.20–0.35 **Si**, 0.30–0.60 **Cr**, 0.30–0.60 **Ni**, 0.08–0.15 **Mo**, 0.0005 min **B**	
COPANT 514	4615	COPANT	Tube	0.13–0.18 **C**, 0.45–0.65 **Mn**, 0.040 **P**, 0.040 **S**, 0.20–0.35 **Si**, 1.65–2.0 **Ni**, 0.20–0.30 **Mo**	
DGN-B-300	8615	Mexico	Bar	0.13–0.18 **C**, 0.70–0.90 **Mn**, 0.035 **P**, 0.040 **S**, 0.20–0.35 **Si**, 0.40–0.60 **Cr**, 0.40–0.70 **Ni**, 0.15–0.25 **Mo**	**Annealed**
DGN-B-300	4815	Mexico	Bar	0.13–0.18 **C**, 0.40–0.60 **Mn**, 0.035 **P**, 0.040 **S**, 0.20–0.35 **Si**, 3.25–3.75 **Ni**, 0.20–0.30 **Mo**	**Annealed**
DGN-B-300	4615	Mexico	Bar	0.13–0.18 **C**, 0.45–0.65 **Mn**, 0.035 **P**, 0.040 **S**, 0.20–0.35 **Si**, 1.65–2.00 **Ni**, 0.20–0.30 **Mo**	**Annealed**
ANSI/ASTM A 29	4615	US	Bar	0.13–0.18 **C**, 0.45–0.65 **Mn**, 0.035 **P**, 0.040 **S**, 0.15–0.30 **Si**, 1.65–2.00 **Ni**, 0.20–0.30 **Mo**	
ANSI/ASTM A 29	4815	US	Bar	0.13–0.18 **C**, 0.40–0.60 **Mn**, 0.035 **P**, 0.040 **S**, 0.15–0.30 **Si**, 3.25–3.75 **Ni**, 0.20–0.30 **Mo**	
ANSI/ASTM A 29	5115	US	Bar	0.13–0.18 **C**, 0.70–0.90 **Mn**, 0.035 **P**, 0.040 **S**, 0.15–0.30 **Si**, 0.70–0.90 **Cr**	
MIL-S-16974E	No 8615	US	Bar, billets, blooms, slabs	0.13–0.18 **C**, 0.70–0.90 **Mn**, 0.040 **P**, 0.040 **S**, 0.20–0.35 **Si**, 0.40–0.60 **Cr**, 0.40–0.70 **Ni**, 0.15–0.25 **Mo**	
MIL-S-16974E	No TS8615	US	Bar, billets, blooms, slabs	0.13–0.18 **C**, 0.70–0.90 **Mn**, 0.040 **P**, 0.040 **S**, 0.20–0.35 **Si**, 0.55–0.75 **Cr**, 0.30–0.60 **Ni**, 0.08–0.15 **Mo**	
ASTM A 689	8615	US	Bar	0.13–0.18 **C**, 0.70–0.90 **Mn**, 0.035 **P**, 0.040 **S**, 0.15–0.30 **Si**, 0.40–0.60 **Cr**, 0.40–0.70 **Ni**, 0.15–0.25 **Mo**	
ASTM A 689	4815	US	Bar	0.13–0.18 **C**, 0.40–0.60 **Mn**, 0.035 **P**, 0.040 **S**, 0.15–0.30 **Si**, 3.25–3.75 **Ni**, 0.20–0.30 **Mo**	
ASTM A 689	4615	US	Bar	0.13–0.18 **C**, 0.45–0.65 **Mn**, 0.035 **P**, 0.040 **S**, 0.15–0.30 **Si**, 1.65–2.00 **Ni**, 0.20–0.30 **Mo**	
ANSI/ASTM A 322	4815	US	Bar	0.13–0.18 **C**, 0.40–0.60 **Mn**, 0.035 **P**, 0.040 **S**, 0.15–0.30 **Si**, 3.25–3.75 **Ni**, 0.20–0.30 **Mo**	
ANSI/ASTM A 322	4615	US	Bar	0.13–0.18 **C**, 0.45–0.65 **Mn**, 0.035 **P**, 0.040 **S**, 0.15–0.30 **Si**, 1.65–2.00 **Ni**, 0.20–0.30 **Mo**	
ANSI/ASTM	8615	US	Bar	0.13–0.18 **C**, 0.70–0.90 **Mn**, 0.035 **P**, 0.040 **S**, 0.15–0.30 **Si**, 0.40–0.60 **Cr**, 0.40–0.70 **Ni**, 0.15–0.25 **Mo**	

WROUGHT ALLOY STEELS

specification number	designation	country	product forms	composition	mechanical properties (see page iv for explanation)
ANSI/ASTM A 29	8115	US	Bar	0.13–0.18 **C**, 0.70–0.90 **Mn**, 0.035 **P**, 0.040 **S**, 0.15–0.30 **Si**, 0.30–0.50 **Cr**, 0.20–0.40 **Ni**, 0.08–0.15 **Mo**	
ANSI/ASTM A 29	8615	US	Bar	0.13–0.18 **C**, 0.70–0.90 **Mn**, 0.035 **P**, 0.040 **S**, 0.15–0.30 **Si**, 0.40–0.60 **Cr**, 0.40–0.70 **Ni**, 0.15–0.25 **Mo**	
AISI 8615		US	Wire, rod	0.13–0.18 **C**, 0.70–0.90 **Mn**, 0.035 **P**, 0.040 **S**, 0.15–0.30 **Si**, 0.40–0.60 **Cr**, 0.40–0.70 **Ni**, 0.15–0.25 **Mo**	
AISI 4615		US	Wire, rod	0.13–0.18 **C**, 0.45–0.65 **Mn**, 0.035 **P**, 0.040 **S**, 0.15–0.30 **Si**, 1.65–2.00 **Ni**, 0.20–0.30 **Mo**	
AISI 4815		US	Wire, rod	0.13–0.18 **C**, 0.40–0.60 **Mn**, 0.035 **P**, 0.040 **S**, 0.15–0.30 **Si**, 3.25–3.75 **Ni**, 0.20–0.30 **Mo**	
ANSI/ASTM A 519	4615	US	Tube: seamless	0.13–0.18 **C**, 0.45–0.65 **Mn**, 0.040 **P**, 0.040 **S**, 0.15–0.35 **Si**, 1.65–2.00 **Ni**, 0.20–0.30 **Mo**	
ANSI/ASTM A 519	4815	US	Tube: seamless	0.13–0.18 **C**, 0.40–0.60 **Mn**, 0.040 **P**, 0.040 **S**, 0.15–0.35 **Si**, 3.25–3.75 **Ni**, 0.20–0.30 **Mo**	
ANSI/ASTM A 519	5115	US	Tube: seamless	0.13–0.18 **C**, 0.70–0.90 **Mn**, 0.040 **P**, 0.040 **S**, 0.15–0.35 **Si**, 0.70–0.90 **Cr**	
ANSI/ASTM A 519	8115	US	Tube: seamless	0.13–0.18 **C**, 0.70–0.90 **Mn**, 0.040 **P**, 0.040 **S**, 0.15–0.35 **Si**, 0.30–0.50 **Cr**, 0.20–0.40 **Ni**, 0.08–0.15 **Mo**	
ANSI/ASTM A 519	8615	US	Tube: seamless	0.13–0.18 **C**, 0.70–0.90 **Mn**, 0.040 **P**, 0.040 **S**, 0.15–0.35 **Si**, 0.40–0.60 **Cr**, 0.40–0.70 **Ni**, 0.15–0.25 **Mo**	
ANSI/ASTM A 519	94B15	US	Tube: seamless	0.13–0.18 **C**, 0.75–1.00 **Mn**, 0.040 **P**, 0.040 **S**, 0.15–0.35 **Si**, 0.30–0.50 **Cr**, 0.30–0.60 **Ni**, 0.08–0.15 **Mo**	
SIS 14 25 11	SIS 25 11–08	Sweden	Bar, forgings	0.13–0.18 **C**, 0.70–1.10 **Mn**, 0.035 **P**, 0.030–0.050 **S**, 0.15–0.40 **Si**, 0.60–1.00 **Cr**, 0.80–1.20 **Ni**, 0.10 **Mo**	**As rolled or as forged**
SIS 14 25 11	SIS 25 11–00	Sweden	Bar, forgings	0.13–0.18 **C**, 0.70–1.10 **Mn**, 0.035 **P**, 0.030–0.050 **S**, 0.15–0.40 **Si**, 0.60–1.00 **Cr**, 0.80–1.20 **Ni**, 0.10 **Mo**	**As rolled or as forged**
AISI 8615		US	Sheet, strip	0.13–0.18 **C**, 0.70–0.90 **Mn**, 0.035 **P**, 0.040 **S**, 0.20–0.35 **Si**, 0.40–0.60 **Cr**, 0.40–0.70 **Ni**, 0.15–0.25 **Mo**	
DGN–B–297	4615	Mexico	Bar	0.13–0.18 **C**, 0.45–0.65 **Mn**, 0.035 **P**, 0.040 **S**, 0.20–0.35 **Si**, 1.65–2.00 **Ni**, 0.20–0.30 **Mo**	
DGN–B–297	4815	Mexico	Bar	0.13–0.18 **C**, 0.40–0.60 **Mn**, 0.035 **P**, 0.040 **S**, 0.20–0.35 **Si**, 3.25–3.75 **Ni**, 0.20–0.30 **Mo**	
DGN–B–297	8615	Mexico	Bar	0.13–0.18 **C**, 0.70–0.90 **Mn**, 0.035 **P**, 0.040 **S**, 0.20–0.35 **Si**, 0.40–0.60 **Cr**, 0.40–0.70 **Ni**, 0.15–0.25 **Mo**	
COPANT 514	Grade 5115	COPANT	Tube: seamless	0.13–0.18 **C**, 0.70–0.90 **Mn**, 0.040 **P**, 0.050 **S**, 0.10 **Si**, 0.70–0.90 **Cr**	
COPANT 514	Grade 94B15	COPANT	Tube: seamless	0.13–0.18 **C**, 0.75–1.00 **Mn**, 0.040 **P**, 0.050 **S**, 0.10 **Si**, 0.30–0.50 **Cr**, 0.30–0.60 **Ni**, 0.08–0.15 **Mo**	
COPANT 514	Grade 8115	COPANT	Tube: seamless	0.13–0.18 **C**, 0.70–0.90 **Mn**, 0.040 **P**, 0.050 **S**, 0.10 **Si**, 0.30–0.50 **Cr**, 0.20–0.40 **Ni**, 0.08–0.15 **Mo**	

WROUGHT ALLOY STEELS

specification number	designation	country	product forms	composition	mechanical properties (see page iv for explanation)
COPANT 514	Grade 8615	COPANT	Tube: seamless	0.13–0.18 **C**, 0.70–0.90 **Mn**, 0.040 **P**, 0.050 **S**, 0.10 **Si**, 0.40–0.60 **Cr**, 0.40–0.70 **Ni**, 0.15–0.25 **Mo**	
COPANT 514	Grade 4815	COPANT	Tube: seamless	0.13–0.18 **C**, 0.40–0.60 **Mn**, 0.040 **P**, 0.040 **S**, 0.10 **Si**, 3.25–3.75 **Ni**, 0.20–0.30 **Mo**	
JIS G 3311	SCM21M	Japan	Strip	0.13–0.18 **C**, 0.60–0.85 **Mn**, 0.030 **P**, 0.030 **S**, 0.15–0.35 **Si**, 0.90–1.20 **Cr**, 0.25 **Ni**, 0.15–0.30 **Mo**, 0.30 **Cu**	
AS G18	G18/En 361	Australia	Bar, billet	0.13–0.17 **C**, 0.70–1.00 **Mn**, 0.050 **P**, 0.050 **S**, 0.35 **Si**, 0.55–0.80 **Cr**, 0.40–0.70 **Ni**, 0.08–0.15 **Mo**	**Blank carburized, hardened:** all **diam**, (690) **TS**
ANSI/ASTM A 353		US	Plate	0.13 **C**, 0.90 **Mn**, 0.035 **P**, 0.040 **S**, 0.13–0.32 **Si**, 8.40–9.60 **Ni**	**Double normalized and tempered:** all **diam**, (690) **TS**, (515) **YS**, 20 **El**
ANSI/ASTM A 553	Grade I	US	Plate	0.13 **C**, 0.90 **Mn**, 0.035 **P**, 0.040 **S**, 0.13–0.32 **Si**, 8.40–9.60 **Ni**	**Quenched and tempered:** all **diam**, (690) **TS**, (585) **YS**, 20 **El**
ANSI/ASTM A 553	Grade II	US	Plate	0.13 **C**, 0.90 **Mn**, 0.035 **P**, 0.040 **S**, 0.13–0.32 **Si**, 7.40–8.60 **Ni**	**Quenched and tempered:** all **diam**, (690) **TS**, (585) **YS**, 20 **El**
ISO 2604/II	TS 45	ISO	Tube: seamless	0.13 **C**, 0.30–0.80 **Mn**, 0.040 **P**, 0.040 **S**, 0.15–0.30 **Si**, 8.50–9.50 **Ni**	**Cold finished, quenched and tempered, normalized and normalized and tempered:** all **diam**, (690) **TS**, (510) **YS**, 15 **El**
COPANT 512	BT8	COPANT	Tube	0.13 **C**, 0.90 **Mn**, 0.045 **P**, 0.045 **S**, 0.13–0.32 **Si**, 8.40–9.60 **Ni**	**Normalized, normalized and tempered or quenched and tempered:** (≥8) **diam**, (690) **TS**, (520) **YS**, 22 **El**
ISO 2604/1	F45	ISO	Forgings	0.13 **C**, 0.80 **Mn**, 0.040 **P**, 0.040 **S**, 0.15–0.40 **Si**, 8.50–10.00 **Ni**, 0.015 min met **Al**	**Normalized and quenched and tempered, quenched and tempered:** all **diam**, (690) **TS**, (490) **YS**, 15 **El**
ANSI/ASTM A 334	Grade 8	US	Tube: seamless, welded	0.13 **C**, 0.90 **Mn**, 0.045 **P**, 0.045 **S**, 0.13–0.32 **Si**, 8.40–9.60 **Ni**	**Normalized:** 0.312 (7.94) **diam**, 100 (689) **TS**, 75 (517) **YS**, 22 **El**
ANSI/ASTM A 333	Grade 8	US	Pipe: seamless, welded	0.13 **C**, 0.90 **Mn**, 0.045 **P**, 0.045 **S**, 0.13–0.32 **Si**, 8.40–9.60 **Ni**	**Normalized, tempered:** 0.312 (7.94) **diam**, 100 (689) **TS**, 75 (517) **YS**, 22 **El**
DGN–B–180	Grade 8	Mexico	Pipe	0.13 **C**, 0.90 **Mn**, 0.045 **P**, 0.045 **S**, 0.13–0.32 **Si**, 8.40–9.60 **Ni**	**Quenched and tempered or double normalized and quenched:** (≥8) **diam**, (686) **TS**, (519) **YS**, 22 **El**
DGN–B–197	Grade 8	Mexico	Tube: seamless, welded	0.13 **C**, 0.90 **Mn**, 0.045 **P**, 0.045 **S**, 0.13–0.32 **Si**, 8.40–9.60 **Ni**	**Quenched and tempered or double normalized and quenched:** (7.92) **diam**, (686) **TS**, (519) **YS**, 22 **El**
EURONORM 129	FeE 245 Ni 2	EURONORM	Plate, strip	0.13 **C**, 0.70–1.50 **Mn**, 0.030 **P**, 0.025 **S**, 0.35 **Si**, 0.25 **Cr**, 0.30–0.80 **Ni**, 0.10 **Mo**, 0.08 **V**, 0.015_{met} or 0.020 tot. (min) **Al**, 0.35 **Cu**, 0.06 **Nb**	**Normalized:** ≤(35) **diam**, (360) **TS**, (245) **YS**, 24 **El**
NF A 35–056	FG 10 MS 5	France	Wire, rod	0.13 **C**, 1.00–1.30 **Mn**, 0.030 **P**, 0.030 **S**, 0.50–0.80 **Si**, 0.15 **Cr**, 0.15 **Ni**, 0.12 **Cu**	
ANSI/ASTM A 514	Grade B	US	Plate	0.12–0.21 **C**, 0.70–1.00 **Mn**, 0.035 **P**, 0.04 **S**, 0.20–0.35 **Si**, 0.40–0.65 **Cr**, 0.15–0.25 **Mo**, 0.03–0.08 **V**, 0.0005–0.005 **B**, 0.01–0.03 **Ti**	**Quenched and tempered:** ≥0.75–2.50 **diam**, (760) **TS**, (690) **YS**, 18 **El**
ANSI/ASTM A 514	Grade H	US	Plate	0.12–0.21 **C**, 0.95–1.30 **Mn**, 0.035 **P**, 0.04 **S**, 0.20–0.35 **Si**, 0.40–0.65 **Cr**, 0.30–0.70 **Ni**, 0.20–0.30 **Mo**, 0.03–0.08 **V**, 0.0005–0.005 **B**	**Quenched and tempered:** ≥0.75–2.50 **diam**, (760) **TS**, (690) **YS**, 18 **El**
ANSI/ASTM A 514	Grade J	US	Plate	0.12–0.21 **C**, 0.45–0.70 **Mn**, 0.035 **P**, 0.04 **S**, 0.20–0.35 **Si**, 0.50–0.65 **Mo**, 0.001–0.005 **B**	**Quenched and tempered:** ≥0.75–2.50 **diam**, (760) **TS**, (690) **YS**, 18 **El**

WROUGHT ALLOY STEELS

specification number	designation	country	product forms	composition	mechanical properties (see page iv for explanation)
ANSI/ASTM A 514	Grade M	US	Plate	0.12–0.21 **C**, 0.45–0.70 **Mn**, 0.035 **P**, 0.04 **S**, 0.20–0.35 **Si**, 1.20–1.50 **Ni**, 0.45–0.60 **Mo**, 0.001–0.005 **B**	**Quenched and tempered:** ≥0.75–2.50 **diam**, (760) **TS**, (690) **YS**, 18 **El**
AMS 6386B	Type 2	US	Sheet, plate	0.12–0.21 **C**, 0.70–1.00 **Mn**, 0.035 **P**, 0.040 **S**, 0.20–0.35 **Si**, 0.40–0.65 **Cr**, 0.15–0.25 **Mo**, 0.03–0.08 **V**, 0.0005–0.005 **B**, 0.01–0.03 **Ti**	**Hardened, tempered and descaled:** 1.250 (31.75) **diam**, 110 (758) **TS**, 100 (690) **YS**, 18 **El**
AMS 6386B	Type 5	US	Sheet, plate	0.12–0.21 **C**, 0.45–0.70 **Mn**, 0.035 **P**, 0.040 **S**, 0.20–0.35 **Si**, 0.50–0.65 **Mo**, 0.0005–0.005 **B**	**Hardened tempered:** 1.250 (31.75) **diam**, 110 (758) **TS**, 100 (690) **YS**, 18 **El**
AMS 6386B	Type 7	US	Sheet, plate	0.12–0.21 **C**, 0.95–1.30 **Mn**, 0.035 **P**, 0.040 **S**, 0.20–0.35 **Si**, 0.40–0.65 **Cr**, 0.30–0.70 **Ni**, 0.20–0.30 **Mo**, 0.03–0.08 **V**, 0.0005–0.005 **B**	**Hardened, tempered:** 1.250–2.000 (3.75–50.80) **diam**, 110 (758) **TS**, 100 (690) **YS**, 18 **El**
AMS 6386B	Type 10	US	Sheet, plate	0.12–0.21 **C**, 0.45–0.70 **Mn**, 0.035 **P**, 0.040 **S**, 0.20–0.35 **Si**, 1.20–1.50 **Ni**, 0.45–0.60 **Mo**, 0.0005–0.005 **B**	**Hardened, tempered and descaled:** ≥1.250–2.000 (≥31.75–50.80) **diam**, 110 (758) **TS**, 100 (690) **YS**, 18 **El**
ANSI/ASTM A 514	Grade P	US	Plate	0.12–0.21 **C**, 0.45–0.70 **Mn**, 0.035 **P**, 0.04 **S**, 0.20–0.35 **Si**, 0.85–1.20 **Cr**, 1.20–1.50 **Ni**, 0.45–0.60 **Mo**, 0.001–0.005 **B**	**Quenched and tempered:** ≥2.50–4.0 **diam**, (690) **TS**, (620) **YS**, 17 **El**
IS 4367	16NiCr2Mo[20]	India	Forgings	0.12–0.20 **C**, 0.40–0.70 **Mn**, 0.050 **P**, 0.050 **S**, 0.10–0.35 **Si**, 1.40–1.70 **Cr**, 1.80–2.20 **Ni**, 0.15–0.25 **Mo**	**Refined and quenched:** all **diam**, (1323) **TS**, 9 **El**
AMS 6386B	Type 11	US	Sheet, plate	0.12–0.20 **C**, 0.40–0.70 **Mn**, 0.035 **P**, 0.040 **S**, 0.20–0.35 **Si**, 1.40–2.00 **Cr**, 0.40–0.60 **Mo**, 0.0005–0.005 **B**, 0.20–0.40 **Cu**, 0.04–0.10 **Ti+V**	**Hardened, tempered:** >2.000–4.000 (>50.80–101.60) **diam**, 110 (758) **TS**, 100 (690) **YS**, 18 **El**
ANSI/ASTM A 514	Grade E	US	Plate	0.12–0.20 **C**, 0.40–0.70 **Mn**, 0.035 **P**, 0.04 **S**, 0.20–0.35 **Si**, 1.40–2.00 **Cr**, 0.40–0.60 **Mo**, 0.0015–0.005 **B**, 0.20–0.40 **Cu**, 0.04–0.10 **Ti**	**Quenched and tempered:** ≥2.50–4.0 **diam**, (690) **TS**, (620) **YS**, 7 **El**
ISO 2604/IV	P30	ISO	Plate	0.12–0.20 **C**, 0.90–1.40 **Mn**, 0.040 **P**, 0.040 **S**, 0.15–0.35 **Si**, 0.30 **Cr**, 0.40–0.60 **Mo**, 0.012 $\mathbf{Al}_{met}$	**Hot rolled, normalized, tempered:** (3–16) **diam**, (510) **TS**, (355) **YS**, 21 **El**
ISO 2604/111	No TW26	ISO	Tube: welded	0.12–0.20 **C**, 0.40–0.80 **Mn**, 0.040 **P**, 0.040 **S**, 0.10–0.35 **Si**	**Normalized, normalized and tempered:** all **diam**, (450) **TS**, (250) **YS**, 22 **El**
ISO 2604/IV	P28	ISO	Plate	0.12–0.20 **C**, 0.50–0.80 **Mn**, 0.035 **P**, 0.035 **S**, 0.15–0.35 **Si**, 0.30 **Cr**, 0.40–0.60 **Mo**, 0.012 $\mathbf{Al}_{met}$	**Hot rolled, normalized, tempered:** (3–16) **diam**, (450) **TS**, (285) **YS**, 23 **El**
BS 3059 Part 2	Grade 243	UK	Tube	0.12–0.20 **C**, 0.40–0.80 **Mn**, 0.040 **P**, 0.040 **S**, 0.10–0.35 **Si**, 0.25–0.35 **Mo**, 0.012 **Al**	**Normalized:** all **diam**, (450) **TS**, (250) **YS**, 22 **El**
ISO 2604/1	F28	ISO	Forgings	0.12–0.20 **C**, 0.50–0.80 **Mn**, 0.040 **P**, 0.040 **S**, 0.15–0.40 **Si**, 0.45–0.65 **Mo**, 0.012 $\mathbf{Al}_{met}$	**Normalized and tempered, quenched and tempered:** all **diam**, (450) **TS**, (275) **YS**, 16 **El**
DIN 17175 Part 1	15 Mo3–1.5415	Germany	Tube: seamless	0.12–0.20 **C**, 0.50–0.80 **Mn**, 0.040 **P**, 0.040 **S**, 0.15–0.35 **Si**, 0.25–0.35 **Mo**	**Hot rolled or cold drawn, normalized or annealed:** all **diam**, (441) **TS**, (284) **YS**, 22 **El**
TS 381	UDK 621.643.2/15 Mo 3	Turkey	Pipe: seamless	0.12–0.20 **C**, 0.50–0.80 **Mn**, 0.040 **P**, 0.040 **S**, 0.15–0.35 **Si**, 0.25–0.35 **Mo**	**As drawn:** all **diam**, (441) **TS**, (284) **YS**, 22 **El**
IS 6630	16Mo[30]	India	Pipe	0.12–0.20 **C**, 0.40–0.80 **Mn**, 0.040 **P**, 0.040 **S**, 0.10–0.35 **Si**, 0.25–0.35 **Mo**	**Normalized, or normalized and tempered:** all **diam**, (440) **TS**, (275) **YS**, 22 **El**
ISO 2604/IV	P26	ISO	Plate	0.12–0.20 **C**, 0.50–0.80 **Mn**, 0.030 **P**, 0.040 **S**, 0.15–0.35 **Si**, 0.30 **Cr**, 0.25–0.35 **Mo**, 0.012 $\mathbf{Al}_{met}$	**Hot rolled, normalized, tempered:** (3–16) **diam**, (440) **TS**, (260) **YS**, 24 **El**
NBN 837	15 Mo 3	Belgium	Tube	0.12–0.20 **C**, 0.50–0.80 **Mn**, 0.040 **P**, 0.040 **S**, 0.15–0.35 **Si**, 0.25–0.35 **Mo**	**Normalized or annealed:** all **diam**, (440) **TS**, (280) **YS**, 22 **El**

WROUGHT ALLOY STEELS

specification number	designation	country	product forms	composition	mechanical properties (see page iv for explanation)
ISO 2604/1	F26	ISO	Forgings	0.12–0.20 **C**, 0.50–0.80 **Mn**, 0.040 **P**, 0.040 **S**, 0.15–0.40 **Si**, 0.25–0.35 **Mo**, 0.012 $\mathbf{Al_{met}}$	**Normalized and tempered, quenched and tempered:** all **diam**, (440) **TS**, (250) **YS**, 17 **El**
SIS 14 29 12 E	SIS 2912–05	Sweden	Tube: seamless	0.12–0.20 **C**, 0.50–0.80 **Mn**, 0.030 **P**, 0.040 **S**, 0.15–0.35 **Si**, 0.30 **Cr**, 0.25–0.35 **Mo**, 0.020 $\mathbf{Al_{met}}$ 0.30 **Cu**	**Normalized**: all **diam**, (440) **TS**, (280) **YS**, 22 **El**
DIN 17155	Grade 15 Mo 3	Germany	Plate	0.12–0.20 **C**, 0.50–0.70 **Mn**, 0.040 **P**, 0.040 **S**, 0.15–0.35 **Si**, 0.25–0.35 **Mo**	**Normalized**: (≤16) **diam**, (432) **TS**, (274) **YS**
SIS 14 29 12 E	SIS 2912–01	Sweden	Bar, plate, sheet	0.12–0.20 **C**, 0.50–0.80 **Mn**, 0.030 **P**, 0.040 **S**, 0.15–0.35 **Si**, 0.30 **Cr**, 0.25–0.35 **Mo**, 0.012 $\mathbf{Al_{met}}$ 0.30 **Cu**	**Normalized**: all **diam**, (430) **TS**, (270) **YS**, 24 **El**
MIL–S–16216H	HY–100	US	Plate	0.12–0.20 **C**, 0.10–0.40 **Mn**, 0.025 **P**, 0.025 **S**, 0.15–0.35 **Si**, 1.00–1.80 **Cr**, 2.25–3.50 **Ni**, 0.20–0.60 **Mo**, 0.03 **V**, 0.25 **Cu**, 0.02 **Ti**	**Hot rolled, quenched and tempered:** <0.75 **diam**, (689) **YS**, 17 **El**
IS 4367	15Ni4Cr1	India	Forgings	0.12–0.18 **C**, 0.40–0.70 **Mn**, 0.050 **P**, 0.050 **S**, 0.10–0.35 **Si**, 1.00–1.40 **Cr**, 3.80–4.30 **Ni**	**Refined and quenched:** all **diam**, (1323) **TS**, 9 **El**
AS G18	G18/En 39B	Australia	Bar, billet	0.12–0.18 **C**, 0.50 **Mn**, 0.050 **P**, 0.050 **S**, 0.10–0.35 **Si**, 1.00–1.40 **Cr**, 3.80–4.50 **Ni**, 0.15–0.35 **Mo**	**Blank carburized, hardened:** all **diam**, (1310) **TS**
ISO R 683/XI	15	ISO	Bar	0.12–0.18 **C**, 0.25–0.55 **Mn**, 0.035 **P**, 0.035 **S**, 0.15–0.40 **Si**, 1.1–1.4 **Cr**, 3.8–4.3 **Ni**, 0.20–0.30 **Mo**	**Carburized and hardened:** all **diam**, (1275) **TS**, (883) **YS**, 7 **El**
ISO R 683/XI	15a	ISO	Bar	0.12–0.18 **C**, 0.25–0.55 **Mn**, 0.035 **P**, 0.020–0.035 **S**, 0.15–0.40 **Si**, 1.1–1.4 **Cr**, 3.8–4.3 **Ni**, 0.20–0.30 **Mo**	**Carburized and hardened:** all **diam**, (1275) **TS**, (883) **YS**, 7 **El**
BS 970 Part 3	Grade 659 M 15	UK	Blooms, billets, bar, forgings	0.12–0.18 **C**, 0.25–0.50 **Mn**, 0.10–0.35 **Si**, 1.00–1.40 **Cr**, 3.90–4.30 **Ni**	**Hardened**: 0.75 **diam**, (1175) **TS**, 8 **El**
BS 970 Part 3	Grade 835 M 15	UK	Blooms, billets, bar, forgings	0.12–0.18 **C**, 0.25–0.50 **Mn**, 0.10–0.35 **Si**, 1.00–1.40 **Cr**, 3.90–4.30 **Ni**, 0.15–0.30 **Mo**	**Hardened**: 0.75 **diam**, (1175) **TS**, 8 **El**
AECMA prEN2214		AECMA	Bar	0.12–0.18 **C**, 0.80–1.10 **Mn**, 0.020 **P**, 0.015 **S**, 0.20 **Si**, 1.25–1.50 **Cr**, 0.80–1.00 **Mo**, 0.20–0.30 **V**	**Quenched and tempered:** all **diam**, (1080) **TS**, (930) **YS**, 10 **El**
AECMA prEN2220		AECMA	Tube: seamless	0.12–0.18 **C**, 0.80–1.10 **Mn**, 0.020 **P**, 0.015 **S**, 0.20 **Si**, 1.25–1.50 **Cr**, 0.80–1.00 **Mo**, 0.20–0.30 **V**	**Quenched and tempered:** all **diam**, (1080) **TS**, (930) **YS**, 10 **El**
AECMA prEN2252	FE–PL 52 S	AECMA	Forgings	0.12–0.18 **C**, 0.80–1.00 **Mn**, 0.020 **P**, 0.015 **S**, 0.20 **Si**, 1.25–1.50 **Cr**, 0.80–1.00 **Mo**, 0.20–0.30 **V**	**Hardened and tempered:** all **diam**, (1080) **TS**, (930) **YS**, 10 **El**
JIS G 4103	Class 25	Japan	Bar	0.12–0.18 **C**, 0.30–0.60 **Mn**, 0.030 **P**, 0.030 **S**, 0.15–0.35 **Si**, 0.70–1.00 **Cr**, 4.00–4.50 **Ni**, 0.15–0.30 **Mo**, 0.30 **Cu**	**Rolled or forged, quenched and tempered:** (25) **diam**, (1079) **TS**, 12 **El**
IS 4367	15Ni2Cr1Mo[15]	India	Forgings	0.12–0.18 **C**, 0.60–1.00 **Mn**, 0.050 **P**, 0.050 **S**, 0.10–0.35 **Si**, 0.75–1.25 **Cr**, 1.50–2.00 **Ni**, 0.10–0.20 **Mo**	**Refined and quenched:** all **diam**, (1078) **TS**, 9 **El**
AECMA prEN2216		AECMA	Sheet	0.12–0.18 **C**, 0.80–1.10 **Mn**, 0.020 **P**, 0.015 **S**, 0.20 **Si**, 1.25–1.50 **Cr**, 0.20–0.30 **V**	**Quenched and tempered:** all **diam**, (1050) **TS**, (900) **YS**, 10 **El**
AECMA prEN2219		AECMA	Tube: seamless	0.12–0.18 **C**, 0.80–1.10 **Mn**, 0.020 **P**, 0.015 **S**, 0.20 **Si**, 1.25–1.50 **Cr**, 0.80–1.00 **Mo**, 0.20–0.30 **V**	**Quenched and tempered:** all **diam**, (1030) **TS**, (880) **YS**, 10 **El**
AECMA prEN2215		AECMA	Sheet	0.12–0.18 **C**, 0.80–1.10 **Mn**, 0.020 **P**, 0.015 **S**, 0.20 **Si**, 1.25–1.50 **Cr**, 0.80–1.00 **Mo**, 0.20–0.30 **V**	**Quenched and tempered:** all **diam**, (980) **TS**, (780) **YS**, 10 **El**

WROUGHT ALLOY STEELS

specification number	designation	country	product forms	composition	mechanical properties (see page iv for explanation)
AECMA prEN2213		AECMA	Bar	0.12–0.18 **C**, 0.80–1.10 **Mn**, 0.020 **P**, 0.015 **S**, 0.20 **Si**, 1.25–1.50 **Cr**, 0.80–1.00 **Mo**, 0.20–0.30 **V**	**Quenched and tempered:** all **diam**, (980) **TS**, (780) **YS**, 12 **El**
AECMA prEN2218		AECMA	Tube: seamless	0.12–0.18 **C**, 0.80–1.10 **Mn**, 0.020 **P**, 0.015 **S**, 0.20 **Si**, 1.25–1.50 **Cr**, 0.80–1.00 **Mo**, 0.20–0.30 **V**	**Quenched and tempered:** all **diam**, (980) **TS**, (780) **YS**, 10 **El**
NF A 35–554	15 CDV 6	France	Plate	0.12–0.18 **C**, 0.80–1.10 **Mn**, 0.020 **P**, 0.015 **S**, 0.20 **Si**, 1.25–1.50 **Cr**, 0.80–1.10 **Mo**, 0.20–0.30 **V**	**Air quenched and tempered:** (≤6) **diam**, (980) **TS**, (780) **YS**, 10 **El**; **Oil quenched and tempered:** (≤16) **diam**, (1080) **TS**, (930) **YS**, 10 **El**
AIR 9160/C 29	9160C071	France	Bar, forgings	0.12–0.18 **C**, 0.80–1.10 **Mn**, 0.020 **P**, 0.015 **S**, 0.20 **Si**, 1.25–1.50 **Cr**, 0.80–1.0 **Mo**, 0.20–0.30 **V**	**Annealed, quenched and tempered:** (<16) **diam**, (980) **TS**, (780) **YS**, 12 **El**
AIR 9160/C 31	9160C072	France	Sheet	0.12–0.18 **C**, 0.80–1.10 **Mn**, 0.020 **P**, 0.015 **S**, 0.20 **Si**, 1.25–1.50 **Cr**, 0.80–1.0 **Mo**, 0.20–0.30 **V**	**Annealed, quenched and tempered:** (<2) **diam**, (980) **TS**, (780) **YS**, 10 **El**
AIR 9160/C 33	9160C073	France	Tube, seamless	0.12–0.18 **C**, 0.80–1.10 **Mn**, 0.020 **P**, 0.015 **S**, 0.20 **Si**, 1.25–1.50 **Cr**, 0.80–1.0 **Mo**, 0.20–0.30 **V**	**Annealed, quenched and tempered:** (<4) **diam**, (980) **TS**, (780) **YS**, 10 **El**
IS 4367	15NiCr1Mo[12]	India	Forgings	0.12–0.18 **C**, 0.60–1.00 **Mn**, 0.050 **P**, 0.050 **S**, 0.10–0.35 **Si**, 0.75–1.25 **Cr**, 1.00–1.50 **Ni**, 0.08–0.15 **Mo**	**Refined and quenched:** all **diam**, (980) **TS**, 9 **El**
ISO R 683/XI	9	ISO	Bar	0.12–0.18 **C**, 0.60–0.90 **Mn**, 0.035 **P**, 0.035 **S**, 0.15–0.40 **Si**, 0.80–1.10 **Cr**, 1.3–1.7 **Ni**	**Carburized and hardened:** all **diam**, (980) **TS**, (638) **YS**, 8 **El**
ISO R 683/XI	9a	ISO	Bar	0.12–0.18 **C**, 0.60–0.90 **Mn**, 0.035 **P**, 0.020–0.035 **S**, 0.15–0.40 **Si**, 0.80–1.10 **Cr**, 1.3–1.7 **Ni**	**Carburized hardened:** all **diam**, (980) **TS**, (638) **YS**, 8 **El**
JIS G 4103	Class 22	Japan	Bar	0.12–0.18 **C**, 0.40–0.70 **Mn**, 0.030 **P**, 0.030 **S**, 0.15–0.35 **Si**, 0.40–0.65 **Cr**, 1.60–2.00 **Ni**, 0.15–0.30 **Mo**, 0.30 **Cu**	**Rolled or forged, quenched and tempered:** (25) **diam**, (883) **TS**, 16 **El**
AS G18	G18/En 36B	Australia	Bar, billet	0.12–0.18 **C**, 0.30–0.60 **Mn**, 0.050 **P**, 0.050 **S**, 0.10–0.35 **Si**, 0.60–1.10 **Cr**, 3.00–3.75 **Ni**	**Blank carburized, hardened:** all **diam**, (850) **TS**
DIN 17210	Grade 15 Cr 3	Germany	Blooms, slabs, billets, wire, bar, plate, sheet, strip, tube, forgings	0.12–0.18 **C**, 0.40–0.60 **Mn**, 0.035 **P**, 0.035 **S**, 0.15–0.40 **Si**, 0.40–0.70 **Cr**	**Rolled or forged:** (11) **diam**, (795) **TS**, (510) **YS**, 10 **El**
JIS G 4102	Class 21	Japan	Bar	0.12–0.18 **C**, 0.35–0.65 **Mn**, 0.030 **P**, 0.030 **S**, 0.15–0.35 **Si**, 0.20–0.50 **Cr**, 2.00–2.50 **Ni**, 0.30 **Cu**	**Rolled or forged, quenched and tempered:** (25) **diam**, (785) **TS**, 17 **El**
EURONORM 119–74, III	15 Cr 2 KD	EURONORM	Wire, rod	0.12–0.18 **C**, 0.40–0.60 **Mn**, 0.035 **P**, 0.035 **S**, 0.15–0.40 **Si**, 0.40–0.70 **Cr**	**Bright annealed:** (11) **diam**, (780) **TS**, (510) **YS**, 10 **El**
BS S.133		UK	Bar, billets, forgings: aircraft quality	0.12–0.18 **C**, 0.6–0.9 **Mn**, 0.025 **P**, 0.020 **S**, 0.10–0.35 **Si**, 0.4–0.8 **Cr**, 0.7–1.1 **Ni**	**Hardened and tempered:** all **diam**, (775) **TS**, 12 **El**
AECMA prEN2251		AECMA	Tube: seamless	0.12–0.18 **C**, 0.80–1.00 **Mn**, 0.020 **P**, 0.015 **S**, 0.20 **Si**, 1.25–1.50 **Cr**, 0.80–1.00 **Mo**, 0.20–0.30 **V**	**Quenched and tempered:** all **diam**, (700) **TS**, (550) **YS**, 12 **El**
BS 970 Part 3	Grade 635 M 15	UK	Blooms, billets, bar, forgings	0.12–0.18 **C**, 0.60–0.90 **Mn**, 0.10–0.35 **Si**	**Hardened:** 0.75 **diam**, (690) **TS**, 12 **El**
IS 4367	15Cr[65]	India	Forgings	0.12–0.18 **C**, 0.40–0.60 **Mn**, 0.050 **P**, 0.050 **S**, 0.10–0.35 **Si**, 0.50–0.80 **Cr**	**Refined and quenched:** all **diam**, (588) **TS**, 13 **El**
BS 970 Part 3	Steel 214M15	UK	Blooms, billets, bar, forgings	0.12–0.18 **C**, 1.20–1.60 **Mn**, 0.050 max **P**, 0.10–0.18 **S**, 0.10–0.40 **Si**	**Hardened:** 3/4 **diam**, (580) **TS**, 12 **El**
BS 970 Part 3	Grade 523 M 15	UK	Blooms, billets, bar, forgings	0.12–0.18 **C**, 0.30–0.60 **Mn**, 0.10–0.35 **Si**, 0.30 0.60 **Cr**	**Hardened:** 0.75 **diam**, (555) **TS**, 13 **El**
ANSI/ASTM A 739	Grade B 22	US	Bar	0.12–0.18 **C**, 0.30–0.60 **Mn**, 0.035 **P**, 0.040 **S**, 0.50 **Si**, 2.00–2.50 **Cr**, 0.90–1.10 **Mo**	**Hot-rolled, normalized and tempered:** all **diam**, 75 (517) **TS**, 45 (310) **YS**, 18 **El**

specification number	designation	country	product forms	composition	mechanical properties (see page iv for explanation)
BS 1501–620	Grade 31	UK	Plate	0.12–0.18 **C**, 0.40–0.70 **Mn**, 0.040 **P**, 0.040 **S**, 0.10–0.40 **Si**, 0.70–1.20 **Cr**, 0.30 **Ni**, 0.45–0.65 **Mo**, 0.30 **Cu**, 0.03	**Normalized:** (76) **diam**, (450) **TS**, (315) **YS**, 16 **El**
JIS G 4102	Class 22	Japan	Bar	0.12–0.18 **C**, 0.35–0.65 **Mn**, 0.030 **P**, 0.030 **S**, 0.15–0.35 **Si**, 0.70–1.00 **Cr**, 3.00–3.50 **Ni**, 0.30 **Cu**	**Rolled or forged, quenched and tempered:** (25) **diam**, (98) **TS**, 12 **El**
NF A 35–553	16 NC 6	France	Strip	0.12–0.18 **C**, 0.60–0.90 **Mn**, 0.035 **P**, 0.035 **S**, 0.10–0.40 **Si**, 0.85–1.15 **Cr**, 1.20–1.60 **Ni**	
BS 970 Part 3	Grade 635 H 15	UK	Blooms, billets, bar, forgings	0.12–0.18 **C**, 0.60–0.90 **Mn**, 0.10–0.35 **Si**, 0.40–0.80 **Cr**, 0.70–1.10 **Ni**	
BS 970 Part 3	Grade 659 H 15	UK	Blooms, billets, bar, forgings	0.12–0.18 **C**, 0.25–0.50 **Mn**, 0.10–0.35 **Si**, 1.00–1.40 **Cr**, 3.90–4.30 **Ni**	
BS 970 Part 3	Grade 835 H 15	UK	Blooms, billets, bar, forgings	0.12–0.18 **C**, 0.25–0.50 **Mn**, 0.10–0.35 **Si**, 1.00–1.40 **Cr**, 3.90–4.30 **Ni**, 0.15–0.30 **Mo**	
BS 970 Part 3	Grade 835 A 15	UK	Blooms, billets, bar, forgings	0.12–0.18 **C**, 0.30–0.50 **Mn**, 1.00–1.30 **Cr**, 3.90–4.30 **Ni**, 0.15–0.25 **Mo**	
MIL–S–16216H	HY–80	US	Plate	0.12–0.18 **C**, 0.10–0.40 **Mn**, 0.025 **P**, 0.025 **S**, 0.15–0.35 **Si**, 1.00–1.80 **Cr**, 2.00–3.25 **Ni**, 0.20–0.60 **Mo**, 0.03 **V**, 0.25 **Cu**, 0.02 **Ti**	**Hot rolled, quenched and tempered:** <0.75 **diam**, (551) **YS**, 19 **El**
AS 1444	Grade AS 1444/4615H	Australia	Bar, bloom, billet, slab	0.12–0.18 **C**, 0.45–0.65 **Mn**, 0.040 **P**, 0.040 **S**, 0.10–0.35 **Si**, 1.55–2.00 **Ni**, 0.20–0.30 **Mo**	
AECMA prEN2252	FE–PL 52 S	AECMA	Forgings	0.12–0.18 **C**, 0.80–1.00 **Mn**, 0.020 **P**, 0.015 **S**, 0.20 **Si**, 1.25–1.50 1.35–1.65 **Cr**, 0.40 **Ni**	**Hardened and tempered**
DGN–B–300	4815 H	Mexico	Bar	0.12–0.18 **C**, 0.30–0.70 **Mn**, 0.040 **P**, 0.035 **S**, 0.20–0.35 **Si**, 3.20–3.80 **Ni**, 0.20–0.30 **Mo**	**Annealed**
DGN–B–300	98B15 H	Mexico	Bar	0.12–0.18 **C**, 0.70–1.05 **Mn**, 0.040 **P**, 0.035 **S**, 0.20–0.35 **Si**, 0.25–0.55 **Cr**, 0.25–0.65 **Ni**, 0.08–0.15 **Mo**, 0.0005 **B**	
ASTM A 689	94B15 H	US	Bar	0.12–0.18 **C**, 0.70–1.05 **Mn**, 0.040 **P**, 0.040 **S**, 0.15–0.30 **Si**, 0.25–0.55 **Cr**, 0.25–0.65 **Ni**, 0.08–0.15 **Mo**, 0.0005 min **B**	
ANSI/ASTM A 304	4815 H	US	Bar	0.12–0.18 **C**, 0.30–0.70 **Mn**, 0.040 **P**, 0.040 **S**, 0.15–0.30 **Si**, 3.20–3.80 **Ni**, 0.20–0.30 **Mo**	
ANSI/ASTM A 304	94B15 H	US	Bar	0.12–0.18 **C**, 0.70–1.05 **Mn**, 0.040 **P**, 0.040 **S**, 0.15–0.30 **Si**, 0.25–0.55 **Cr**, 0.25–0.65 **Ni**, 0.08–0.15 **Mo**, 0.0005 min **B**	
ASTM A 689	4815 H	US	Bar	0.12–0.18 **C**, 0.30–0.70 **Mn**, 0.040 **P**, 0.040 **S**, 0.15–0.30 **Si**, 3.20–3.80 **Ni**, 0.20–0.30 **Mo**	
AISI 8615		US	Plate	0.12–0.18 **C**, 0.60–0.90 **Mn**, 0.035 **P**, 0.040 **S**, 0.15–0.30 **Si**, 0.35–0.60 **Cr**, 0.40–0.70 **Ni**, 0.15–0.25 **Mo**	
AISI 4615		US	Plate	0.12–0.18 **C**, 0.40–0.65 **Mn**, 0.035 **P**, 0.040 **S**, 0.15–0.30 **Si**, 1.65–2.00 **Ni**, 0.20–0.30 **Mo**	
AISI 4815 H		US	Wire, rod	0.12–0.18 **C**, 0.30–0.70 **Mn**, 0.15–0.30 **Si**, 3.20–3.80 **Ni**, 0.20–0.30 **Mo**	
AISI 94B15H		US	Bar	0.12–0.18 **C**, 0.70–1.05 **Mn**, 0.035 **P**, 0.040 **S**, 0.15–0.30 **Si**, 0.25–0.55 **Cr**, 0.25–0.65 **Ni**, 0.08–0.15 **Mo**	

WROUGHT ALLOY STEELS

specification number	designation	country	product forms	composition	mechanical properties (see page iv for explanation)
AISI 4815H		US	Bar	0.12–0.18 **C**, 0.30–0.70 **Mn**, 0.035 **P**, 0.040 **S**, 0.15–0.30 **Si**, 3.20–3.80 **Ni**, 0.20–0.30 **Mo**	
AS 1442	Grade AS1442/XK 1315	Australia	Bar, blooms, billets, slabs	0.12–0.18 **C**, 1.40–1.70 **Mn**, 0.050 **P**, 0.050 **S**, 0.10–0.35 **Si**	
AS 1443	Grade AS 1443/XK 1315	Australia	Bar	0.12–0.18 **C**, 1.40–1.70 **Mn**, 0.050 **P**, 0.050 **S**, 0.10–0.35 **Si**	
JIS G 4052	SCr 21H	Japan	Bar, wire, rod	0.12–0.18 **C**, 0.55–0.90 **Mn**, 0.030 **P**, 0.030 **S**, 0.15–0.35 **Si**, 0.85–1.25 **Cr**, 0.30 **Cu**	**Hot rolled, normalized, quenched**
JIS G 4052	SCM 21H	Japan	Bar, wire, rod	0.12–0.18 **C**, 0.55–0.90 **Mn**, 0.030 **P**, 0.030 **S**, 0.15–0.35 **Si**, 0.85–1.25 **Cr**, 0.15–0.35 **Mo**, 0.30 **Cu**	**Hot rolled, normalized, quenched**
JIS G 3311	SNC21M	Japan	Strip	0.12–0.18 **C**, 0.35–0.65 **Mn**, 0.030 **P**, 0.030 **S**, 0.15–0.35 **Si**, 0.20–0.50 **Cr**, 2.00–2.50 **Ni**, 0.30 **Cu**	
JIS G 3311	SNCM22M	Japan	Strip	0.12–0.18 **C**, 0.40–0.70 **Mn**, 0.030 **P**, 0.030 **S**, 0.15–0.35 **Si**, 0.40–0.65 **Cr**, 1.60–2.00 **Ni**, 0.15–0.30 **Mo**, 0.30 **Cu**	
AIR 9160/C 83	9160C301	France	Bar, forgings	0.12–0.17 **C**, 0.30–0.60 **Mn**, 0.025 **P**, 0.020 **S**, 0.15–0.40 **Si**, 0.80–1.10 **Cr**, 3.0–3.50 **Ni**, 0.20–0.30 **Mo**	**Quenched and tempered:** ($\leq$16) **diam**, (1180) **TS**, (980) **YS**, 8 **El**
BS S.157	S157B	UK	Bar: black, aircraft quality	0.12–0.17 **C**, 0.30–0.60 **Mn**, 0.025 **P**, 0.020 **S**, 0.15–0.40 **Si**, 0.80–1.10 **Cr**, 3.0–3.5 **Ni**, 0.20–0.30 **Mo**	**Annealed, carburized, hardened and tempered:** all **diam**, (1180) **TS**, (930) **YS**, 8 **El**
BS S.157	S157D	UK	Bar: bright, aircraft quality	0.12–0.17 **C**, 0.30–0.60 **Mn**, 0.025 **P**, 0.020 **S**, 0.15–0.40 **Si**, 0.80–1.10 **Cr**, 3.0–3.5 **Ni**, 0.20–0.30 **Mo**	**Annealed, carburized, hardened and tempered:** all **diam**, (1180) **TS**, (930) **YS**, 8 **El**
BS S.157	S157A	UK	Forging stock, billets, bar: aircraft quality	0.12–0.17 **C**, 0.30–0.60 **Mn**, 0.025 **P**, 0.020 **S**, 0.15–0.40 **Si**, 0.80–1.10 **Cr**, 3.0–3.5 **Ni**, 0.20–0.30 **Mo**	**Annealed, carburized, hardened and tempered:** all **diam**, (1180) **TS**, (930) **YS**, 8 **El**
BS S.157	S157C	UK	Forgings: aircraft quality	0.12–0.17 **C**, 0.30–0.60 **Mn**, 0.025 **P**, 0.020 **S**, 0.15–0.40 **Si**, 0.8–1.1 **Cr**, 3.0–3.5 **Ni**, 0.20–0.30 **Mo**	**Annealed, carburized, hardened and tempered:** all **diam**, (1180) **TS**, (930) **YS**, 8 **El**
DIN 17210	Grade 15 CrNi 6	Germany	Blooms, slabs, billets, wire, plate, sheet, strip, tube, forgings	0.12–0.17 **C**, 0.40–0.60 **Mn**, 0.035 **P**, 0.035 **S**, 0.15–0.40 **Si**, 1.40–1.70 **Cr**, 1.40–1.70 **Ni**	**Rolled or forged:** (11) **diam**, (961) **TS**, (687) **YS**, 8 **El**
BS 1501–282		UK	Plate	0.12–0.17 **C**, 0.90–1.30 **Mn**, 0.040 **P**, 0.040 **S**, 0.40 **Si**, 0.30–0.70 **Cr**, 1.40–1.60 **Ni**, 0.30–0.40 **Mo**, 0.08–0.12 **V**, 0.30 **Cu**	**Normalized:** (76) **diam**, (570) **TS**, (415) **YS**, 18 **El**
BS 970 Part 3	Grade 523 A 14	UK	Blooms, billets, bar, forgings	0.12–0.17 **C**, 0.30–0.50 **Mn**, 0.30–0.50 **Cr**	
BS 970 Part 3	Grade 635 A 14	UK	Blooms, billets, bar, forgings	0.12–0.17 **C**, 0.70–0.90 **Mn**, 0.50–0.75 **Cr**, 0.70–1.00 **Ni**, 0.10 **Mo**	
DGN–B–203	Grade 5015	Mexico	Tube: seamless	0.12–0.17 **C**, 0.30–0.50 **Mn**, 0.040 **P**, 0.040 **S**, 0.20–0.35 **Si**, 0.30–0.50 **Ni**	
DGN–B–300	5015	Mexico	Bar	0.12–0.17 **C**, 0.30–0.50 **Mn**, 0.035 **P**, 0.040 **S**, 0.20–0.35 **Si**, 0.30–0.50 **Cr**	**Annealed**
ANSI/ASTM A 29	5015	US	Bar	0.12–0.17 **C**, 0.30–0.50 **Mn**, 0.035 **P**, 0.040 **S**, 0.15–0.30 **Si**, 0.30–0.50 **Cr**	
ASTM A 689	5015	US	Bar	0.12–0.17 **C**, 0.30–0.50 **Mn**, 0.035 **P**, 0.040 **S**, 0.15–0.30 **Si**, 0.30–0.50 **Cr**	
ANSI/ASTM A 322	5015	US	Bar	0.12–0.17 **C**, 0.30–0.50 **Mn**, 0.035 **P**, 0.040 **S**, 0.15–0.30 **Si**, 0.30–0.50 **Cr**	

WROUGHT ALLOY STEELS

specification number	designation	country	product forms	composition	mechanical properties (see page iv for explanation)
AISI 5015		US	Wire, rod	0.12–0.17 **C**, 0.30–0.50 **Mn**, 0.035 **P**, 0.040 **S**, 0.15–0.30 **Si**, 0.30–0.50 **Cr**	
ANSI/ASTM A 519	5015	US	Tube: seamless	0.12–0.17 **C**, 0.30–0.50 **Mn**, 0.040 **P**, 0.040 **S**, 0.15–0.35 **Si**, 0.30–0.50 **Cr**	
DGN–B–297	5015	Mexico	Bar	0.12–0.17 **C**, 0.30–0.50 **Mn**, 0.035 **P**, 0.040 **S**, 0.20–0.35 **Si**, 0.30–0.50 **Cr**	
COPANT 514	Grade 5015	COPANT	Tube: seamless	0.12–0.17 **C**, 0.30–0.50 **Mn**, 0.040 **P**, 0.050 **S**, 0.10 **Si**, 0.30–0.50 **Cr**	
ANSI/ASTM A 579	12	US	Forgings	0.12 **C**, 0.60–0.90 **Mn**, 0.010 **P**, 0.010 **S**, 0.20–0.35 **Si**, 0.40–0.70 **Cr**, 4.75–5.25 **Ni**, 0.30–0.65 **Mo**, 0.05–0.10 **V**	**Quenched and tempered:** all **diam**, 150 (1045) **TS**, 140 (965) **YS**, 13 **El**
NF A 36–208	9 Ni (Z8N09) 585	France	Plate	0.12 **C**, 0.30–0.80 **Mn**, 0.030 **P**, 0.025 **S**, 0.40 **Si**, 8.5–10.0 **Ni**, 0.05 **V**, 0.015 min **Al**	**Normalized, normalized and tempered or quenched and tempered:** (3–30) **diam**, (690) **TS**, (585) **YS**, 18 **El**
JIS G 3127	Class 9A	Japan	Plate	0.12 **C**, 0.90 **Mn**, 0.025 **P**, 0.025 **S**, 0.15–0.30 **Si**, 8.50–9.50 **Ni**	**Hot rolled, double normalized, tempered:** (6–16) **diam**, (686) **TS**, (520) **YS**, 21 **El**
JIS G 3127	Class 9B	Japan	Plate	0.12 **C**, 0.90 **Mn**, 0.025 **P**, 0.025 **S**, 0.15–0.30 **Si**, 8.50–9.50 **Ni**	**Hot rolled and quenched and tempered:** (6–16) **diam**, (686) **TS**, (588) **YS**, 21 **El**
NF A 36–208	9 Ni (Z8N09) 490	France	Plate	0.12 **C**, 0.30–0.80 **Mn**, 0.030 **P**, 0.025 **S**, 0.40 **Si**, 8.5–10.0 **Ni**, 0.05 **V**, 0.015 min **Al**	**Normalized, normalized and tempered or quenched and tempered:** (3–30) **diam**, (640) **TS**, (490) **YS**, 18 **El**
NF A 36–203	E 490 D	France	Sheet, plate	0.12 **C**, 1.70 **Mn**, 0.030 **P**, 0.030 **S**, 0.50 **Si**, 0.01–0.08 **V**, 0.01–0.10 **Al**, 0.01–0.08 **Nb**, 0.01–0.12 **Ti**	**Hot rolled:** (1.5–10.0) **diam**, (540) **TS**, (490) **YS**, 18 **El**
NBN 630	12 Ni 14	Belgium	Strip	0.12 **C**, 1.0 **Mn**, 0.030 **P**, 0.030 **S**, 0.15–0.35 **Si**, 3.25–3.75 **Ni**	**Quenched and tempered or normalized:** (3–100) **diam**, (540) **TS**, (275) **YS**, 21 **El**
NBN 630	12 Ni 20	Belgium	Strip	0.12 **C**, 1.0 **Mn**, 0.030 **P**, 0.030 **S**, 0.15–0.35 **Si**, 4.75–5.25 **Ni**	**Quenched and tempered or normalized:** (3–100) **diam**, (540) **TS**, (390) **YS**, 21 **El**
EURONORM 129	FeE 390 Ni 20	EURONORM	Plate, strip	0.12 **C**, 0.30–0.80 **Mn**, 0.025 **P**, 0.020 **S**, 0.35 **Si**, 0.25 **Cr**, 4.75–5.25 **Ni**, 0.10 **Mo**, 0.05 **V**, 0.015_{met} or 0.020 tot. (min) **Al**, 0.35 **Cu**	**Normalized, or normalized and tempered, or quenched and tempered:** ≤(35) **diam**, (540) **TS**, (390) **YS**, 23 **El**
NF A 36–203	E 445 D	France	Sheet, plate	0.12 **C**, 1.60 **Mn**, 0.030 **P**, 0.030 **S**, 0.50 **Si**, 0.01–0.08 **V**, 0.01–0.10 **Al**, 0.01–0.08 **Nb**, 0.01–0.12 **Ti**	**Hot rolled:** (1.5–10.0) **diam**, (500) **TS**, (445) **YS**, 20 **El**
NF A 36–203	E 430 D	France	Sheet, plate	0.12 **C**, 1.60 **Mn**, 0.030 **P**, 0.030 **S**, 0.50 **Si**, 0.01–0.08 **V**, 0.01–0.10 **Al**, 0.01–0.08 **Nb**, 0.01–0.12 **Ti**	**Cold rolled:** (0.5–3.0) **diam**, (490) **TS**, (430) **YS**
JIS G 3125	Class 1	Japan	Plate, sheet, strip, shape	0.12 **C**, 0.20–0.50 **Mn**, 0.070–0.150 **P**, 0.040 **S**, 0.25–0.75 **Si**, 0.30–1.25 **Cr**, 0.65 **Ni**, 0.25–0.60 **Cu**	**Hot rolled:** (≤6.0) **diam**, (481) **TS**, (343) **YS**, 22 **El**
JIS G 3125	Class 2	Japan	Plate, sheet, strip	0.12 **C**, 0.20–0.50 **Mn**, 0.070–0.150 **P**, 0.040 **S**, 0.25–0.75 **Si**, 0.30–1.25 **Cr**, 0.65 **Ni**, 0.25–0.60 **Cu**	**Cold rolled:** (0.6–2.3) **diam**, (451) **TS**, (314) **YS**, 26 **El**
NF A 36–203	E 390D	France	Sheet, plate	0.12 **C**, 1.50 **Mn**, 0.030 **P**, 0.030 **S**, 0.50 **Si**, 0.01–0.08 **V**, 0.01–0.08 **Al**, 0.01–0.06 **Nb**, 0.02–0.10 **Ti**	**Cold rolled:** (0.5–3.0) **diam**, (450) **TS**, (390) **YS**, 23 **El**; **Hot rolled:** (1.5–10.0) **diam**, (450) **TS**, (390) **YS**, 23 **El**
IS 4367	$07Cr^{90}Mo^{55}$	India	Forgings	0.12 **C**, 0.40–0.70 **Mn**, 0.050 **P**, 0.050 **S**, 0.10–0.60 **Si**, 0.70–1.10 **Cr**, 0.30 **Ni**, 0.45–0.65 **Mo**	**Normalized and tempered:** all **diam**, (441) **TS**
NOM–B–194	Grade T 5c	Mexico	Tube: seamless	0.12 **C**, 0.30–0.60 **Mn**, 0.030 **P**, 0.030 **S**, 0.50 **Si**, 4.0–6.0 **Cr**, 0.45–0.65 **Mo**	**Quenched:** (0.38–12.7) **diam**, (414) **TS**, (207) **YS**

WROUGHT ALLOY STEELS

specification number	designation	country	product forms	composition	mechanical properties (see page iv for explanation)
ANSI/ASTM A 335	P5c	US	Pipe: seamless	0.12 **C**, 0.30–0.60 **Mn**, 0.030 **P**, 0.030 **S**, 0.50 **Si**, 4.00–6.00 **Cr**, 0.45–0.65 **Mo**, 4 x C–0.70 **Ti**	**Normalized, or annealed**: 0.312 (7.94) **diam**, 60 (414) **TS**, 30 (207) **YS**, 30 **El**
ANSI/ASTM A 333	Grade 4	US	Pipe: seamless, welded	0.12 **C**, 0.50–1.05 **Mn**, 0.04 **P**, 0.04 **S**, 0.08–0.37 **Si**, 0.44–1.01 **Cr**, 0.47–0.98 **Ni**, 0.04–0.30 **Al**, 0.40–0.75 **Cu**	**Normalized**: 0.312 (7.94) **diam**, 60 (414) **TS**, 35 (241) **YS**, 30 **El**
ANSI/ASTM A 213	Grade T5c	US	Tube: seamless	0.12 **C**, 0.30–0.60 **Mn**, 0.03 **P**, 0.03 **S**, 0.50 **Si**, 4.00–6.00 **Cr**, 0.45–0.65 **Mo**	**Annealed**: 0.312 (7.94) **diam**, 60 (414) **TS**, 30 (207) **YS**, 30 **El**
DGN–B–180	Grade 4	Mexico	Pipe: seamless	0.12 **C**, 0.50–1.65 **Mn**, 0.040 **P**, 0.040 **S**, 0.08–0.37 **Si**, 0.44–1.01 **Cr**, 0.47–0.98 **Ni**	**Normalized or normalized and quenched**: (≥8) **diam**, (412) **TS**, (245) **YS**, 30 **El**
DGN–B–181	Grade P–5c	Mexico	Tube: seamless	0.12 **C**, 0.30–0.60 **Mn**, 0.030 **P**, 0.030 **S**, 0.50 **Si**, 4.00–6.00 **Cr**, 0.45–0.65 **Mo**, 8–10 x C **Cb**, or 4 x C–0.70 **Ti**	**Annealed or normalized and quenched**: (8–60) **diam**, (412) **TS**, (206) **YS**, 30 **El**
NF A 36–203	E 335 D	France	Sheet, plate	0.12 **C**, 1.50 **Mn**, 0.030 **P**, 0.030 **S**, 0.50 **Si**, 0.01–0.08 **V**, 0.01–0.08 **Al**, 0.01–0.06 **Nb**, 0.01–0.10 **Ti**	**Cold rolled**: (0.5–3.0) **diam**, (410) **TS**, (335) **YS**, 26 **El**; **Hot rolled**: (1.5–10.0) **diam**, (410) **TS**, (335) **YS**, 26 **El**
COPANT 513	T5C	COPANT	Tube	0.12 **C**, 0.30–0.60 **Mn**, 0.030 **P**, 0.030 **S**, 0.50 **Si**, 4.00–6.00 **Cr**, 0.45–0.65 **Mo**, 5 x C–0.70 **Ti**	**Normalized**: (>8) **diam**, (410) **TS**, (205) **YS**, 30 **El**
COPANT 509	P5c	COPANT	Pipe	0.12 **C**, 0.30–0.60 **Mn**, 0.030 **P**, 0.030 **S**, 0.50 **Si**, 4.00–6.00 **Cr**, 0.45–0.65 **Mo**, 8–10 x C **Cb**, 4 x C–0.70 **Ti**	**Normalized**: (≥8) **diam**, (410) **TS**, (205) **YS**, 30 **El**
ANSI/ASTM A 562		US	Plate	0.12 **C**, 1.20 **Mn**, 0.04 **P**, 0.05 **S**, 0.15–0.50 **Si**, 4 x C min **V**, 0.15 **Cu**	**Normalized**: all **diam**, (380) **TS**, (205) **YS**, 20 **El**
NF A 36–203	E 275 D	France	Sheet, plate	0.12 **C**, 1.30 **Mn**, 0.030 **P**, 0.030 **S**, 0.50 **Si**, 0.01–0.08 **Al**, 0.01–0.06 **Nb**, 0.01–0.10 **Ti**	**Cold rolled**: (0.5–3.0) **diam**, (370) **TS**, (275) **YS**, 30 **El**; **Hot rolled**: (1.5–10.0) **diam**, (370) **TS**, (275) **YS**, 30 **El**
IS 6286	Grade 4	India	Pipe	0.12 **C**, 0.50–1.05 **Mn**, 0.04 **P**, 0.04 **S**, 0.08–0.37 **Si**, 0.44–1.01 **Cr**, 0.47–0.98 **Ni**, 0.04–0.30 **Al**, 0.40–0.75 **Cu**	**Annealed**: all **diam**, (365) **TS**, (215) **YS**
NF A 35–056	FG 10 M 5 A Ti 5	France	Wire, rod	0.12 **C**, 1.10–1.40 **Mn**, 0.030 **P**, 0.030 **S**, 0.50–0.80 **Si**, 0.15 **Cr**, 0.15 **Ni**, 0.05–0.20 **Al**, 0.12 **Cu**, 0.05–0.20 **Ti**	
MIL–S–24371A		US	Plate	0.12 **C**, 0.60–0.90 **Mn**, 0.010 **P**, 0.010 **S**, 0.15–0.35 **Si**, 0.40–0.70 **Cr**, 4.75–5.25 **Ni**, 0.30–0.65 **Mo**, 0.05–0.10 **V**	**Quenched and tempered**: all **diam**, 130 (896) **YS**, 14 **El**
MIL–S–24512		US	Forgings	0.12 **C**, 0.60–0.90 **Mn**, 0.010 **P**, 0.010 **S**, 0.20–0.35 **Si**, 0.40–0.70 **Cr**, 4.75–5.25 **Ni**, 0.30–0.65 **Mo**, 0.05–0.10 **V**	**Quenched and tempered**: all **diam**, 130 (896) **YS**, 15 **El**
NF A 35–056	FG 10 MS 4	France	Wire, rod	0.12 **C**, 0.80–1.10 **Mn**, 0.030 **P**, 0.030 **S**, 0.40–0.70 **Si**, 0.15 **Cr**, 0.15 **Ni**, 0.12 **Cu**	
ANSI/ASTM A 517	Grade D	US	Plate	0.11–0.22 **C**, 0.36–0.74 **Mn**, 0.035 **P**, 0.040 **S**, 0.18–0.37 **Si**, 0.79–1.26 **Cr**, 0.12–0.28 **Mo**, 0.0015–0.005 **B**, 0.17–0.43 **Cu**, 0.03–0.11 **Ti**	**Quenched and tempered**: all **diam**, (795) **TS**, (690) **YS**, 16 **El**
ANSI/ASTM A 517	Grade L	US	Plate	0.11–0.22 **C**, 0.36–0.74 **Mn**, 0.035 **P**, 0.040 **S**, 0.18–0.37 **Si**, 1.09–1.71 **Cr**, 0.22–0.43 **Mo**, 0.0015–0.005 **B**, 0.17–0.43 **Cu**, 0.03–0.11 **Ti**	**Quenched and tempered**: all **diam**, (795) **TS**, (690) **YS**, 16 **El**
NBN A 25–102	15 Mo 3	Belgium	Tube	0.11–0.21 **C**, 0.47–0.84 **Mn**, 0.044 **P**, 0.044 **S**, 0.12–0.38 **Si**, 0.22–0.39 **Mo**	**Hot or cold finished and normalized**: all **diam**, (440) **TS**, (280) **YS**, 22 **El**
AMS 5602A		US	Bar, forgings	0.11–0.20 **C**, 1.00 **Mn**, 0.040 **P**, 0.030 **S**, 1.00 **Si**, 4.00–6.00 **Cr**, 0.40–0.60 **Mo**	
MIL–S–866C	Class 3115	US	Bar, billets: for carburizing	0.11–0.20 **C**, 0.37–0.63 **Mn**, 0.045 **P**, 0.045 **S**, 0.18–0.37 **Si**, 0.52–0.78 **Cr**, 1.05–1.45 **Ni**, 0.40 **Cu**	

WROUGHT ALLOY STEELS

specification number	designation	country	product forms	composition	mechanical properties (see page iv for explanation)
MIL-S-866C	Class 4615	US	Bar, billet: for carburizing	0.11–0.20 **C**, 0.42–0.68 **Mn**, 0.045 **P**, 0.045 **S**, 0.18–0.37 **Si**, 1.60–2.05 **Ni**, 0.18–0.32 **Mo**, 0.40 **Cu**	
MIL-S-866C	Class 8615	US	Bar, billets: for carburizing	0.11–0.20 **C**, 0.67–0.93 **Mn**, 0.045 **P**, 0.045 **S**, 0.18–0.37 **Si**, 0.37–0.63 **Cr**, 0.37–0.73 **Ni**, 0.13–0.27 **Mo**, 0.40 **Cu**	
MIL-S-866C	Class TS 8615	US	Bar, billets: for carburizing	0.11–0.20 **C**, 0.67–0.93 **Mn**, 0.045 **P**, 0.045 **S**, 0.18–0.37 **Si**, 0.52–0.78 **Cr**, 0.27–0.63 **Ni**, 0.06–0.17 **Mo**, 0.40 **Cu**	
JIS G 4052	SNC 21H	Japan	Bar, wire, rod	0.11–0.18 **C**, 0.30–0.70 **Mn**, 0.030 **P**, 0.030 **S**, 0.15–0.35 **Si**, 0.20–0.55 **Cr**, 1.95–2.50 **Ni**, 0.30 **Cu**	**Hot rolled, normalized, quenched**
JIS G 4052	SNC 22H	Japan	Bar, wire, rod	0.11–0.18 **C**, 0.30–0.70 **Mn**, 0.030 **P**, 0.030 **S**, 0.15–0.35 **Si**, 0.65–1.05 **Cr**, 2.95–3.50 **Ni**	**Hot rolled, normalized, quenched**
ISO R 683/XI	14	ISO	Bar	0.11–0.17 **C**, 0.30–0.60 **Mn**, 0.035 **P**, 0.035 **S**, 0.15–0.40 **Si**, 0.80–1.1 **Cr**, 3.0–3.5 **Ni**, 0.20–0.30 **Mo**	**Carburized and hardened:** all **diam**, (1128) **TS**, (785) **YS**, 8 **El**
ISO R 683/XI	14a	ISO	Bar	0.11–0.17 **C**, 0.30–0.60 **Mn**, 0.035 **P**, 0.020–0.035 **S**, 0.15–0.035 **Si**, 0.80–1.1 **Cr**, 3.0–3.5 **Ni**, 0.20–0.30 **Mo**	**Carburized and hardened:** all **diam**, (1128) **TS**, (785) **YS**, 8 **El**
ISO R 683/XI	10	ISO	Bar	0.11–0.17 **C**, 0.35–0.65 **Mn**, 0.035 **P**, 0.035 **S**, 0.15–0.40 **Si**, 1.4–1.7 **Cr**, 1.3–1.7 **Mo**	**Carburized and hardened:** all **diam**, (1029) **TS**, (687) **YS**, 8 **El**
ISO R 683/XI	10a	ISO	Bar	0.11–0.17 **C**, 0.35–0.65 **Mn**, 0.035 **P**, 0.020–0.035 **S**, 0.15–0.40 **Si**, 1.4–1.7 **Cr**, 1.3–1.7 **Ni**	**Carburized and hardened:** all **diam**, (1029) **TS**, (687) **YS**, 8 **El**
AMS 6270J		US	Bar, forgings, tube	0.11–0.17 **C**, 0.70–1.00 **Mn**, 0.025 **P**, 0.025 **S**, 0.20–0.35 **Si**, 0.40–0.60 **Cr**, 0.40–0.60 **Ni**, 0.15–0.25 **Mo**, 0.35 **Cu**	**Cold finished (bar):** ≤0.500 (≤12.70) **diam**, 130 (896) max **TS**
AMS 6263E		US	Bar, forgings, tube	0.11–0.17 **C**, 0.40–0.70 **Mn**, 0.025 **P**, 0.025 **S**, 0.20–0.35 **Si**, 1.00–1.40 **Cr**, 3.00–3.50 **Ni**, 0.08–0.15 **Mo**, 0.35 **Cu**	**Cold finished (bar):** ≤0.500 (≤12.70) **diam**, 125 (862) max **TS**
AMS 6290D		US	Bar, forgings	0.11–0.17 **C**, 0.45–0.65 **Mn**, 0.025 **P**, 0.025 **S**, 0.20–0.35 **Si**, 0.20 **Cr**, 1.65–2.00 **Ni**, 0.20–0.30 **Mo**, 0.35 **Cu**	**Cold finished (bar):** ≤0.500 (≤12.70) **diam**, 125 (862) max **TS**
BS 1501-271		UK	Plate	0.11–0.17 **C**, 1.00–1.50 **Mn**, 0.040 **P**, 0.040 **S**, 0.40 **Si**, 0.40–0.70 **Cr**, 0.70 **Ni**, 0.20–0.28 **Mo**, 0.04–0.12 **V**, 0.30 **Cu**	**Normalized:** (>76) **diam**, (560) **TS**, (415) **YS**, 16 **El**
NF A 35-553	14 NC 11	France	Strip	0.11–0.17 **C**, 0.35–0.60 **Mn**, 0.035 **P**, 0.035 **S**, 0.10–0.40 **Si**, 0.60–0.90 **Cr**, 2.5–3.0 **Ni**	
NBN 837	12 Cr Mo WV 4524	Belgium	Tube	0.11–0.15 **C**, 0.30–0.60 **Mn**, 0.030 **P**, 0.030 **S**, 0.50 **Si**, 1.0–1.20 **Cr**, 0.45–0.65 **Mo**, 0.35–0.45 **V**, 0.45–0.65 **W**	**Normalized or annealed:** all **diam**, (640) max **TS**, (390) **YS**, 18 **El**
DGN-B-83	501	Mexico	Bar	0.11 **C**, 1.0 **Mn**, 0.040 **P**, 0.030 **S**, 1.0 **Si**, 4.0–6.0 **Cr**, 0.40–0.65 **Mo**	**Hot or cold rolled:** all **diam**, (480) **TS**, (206) **YS**, 28 **El**
ANSI/ASTM A 517	Grade H	US	Plate	0.10–0.23 **C**, 0.90–1.35 **Mn**, 0.035 **P**, 0.040 **S**, 0.18–0.37 **Si**, 0.36–0.69 **Cr**, 0.27–0.73 **Ni**, 0.17–0.33 **Mo**, 0.02–0.09 **V**, 0.005 **B**, min	**Quenched and tempered:** all **diam**, (795) **TS**, (690) **YS**, 16 **El**
ANSI/ASTM A 517	Grade J	US	Plate	0.10–0.23 **C**, 0.41–0.74 **Mn**, 0.035 **P**, 0.040 **S**, 0.18–0.37 **Si**, 0.46–0.69 **Mo**, 0.001–0.005 **B**	**Quenched and tempered:** all **diam**, (795) **TS**, (690) **YS**, 16 **El**
ANSI/ASTM A 517	Grade M	US	Plate	0.10–0.23 **C**, 0.41–0.74 **Mn**, 0.035 **P**, 0.040 **S**, 0.18–0.37 **Si**, 1.15–1.55 **Ni**, 0.41–0.64 **Mo**, 0.001–0.005 **B**	**Quenched and tempered:** all **diam**, (795) **TS**, (690) **YS**, 16 **El**

specification number	designation	country	product forms	composition	mechanical properties (see page iv for explanation)
ANSI/ASTM A 517	Grade P	US	Plate	0.10–0.23 **C**, 0.41–0.74 **Mn**, 0.035 **P**, 0.040 **S**, 0.18–0.37 **Si**, 0.79–1.26 **Cr**, 1.15–1.55 **Ni**, 0.41–0.64 **Mo**, 0.001–0.005 **B**	**Quenched and tempered:** all **diam**, (795) **TS**, (690) **YS**, 16 **El**
ANSI/ASTM A 592	Grade E	US	Forgings	0.10–0.22 **C**, 0.37–0.74 **Mn**, 0.035 **P**, 0.040 **S**, 0.18–0.37 **Si**, 1.34–2.06 **Cr**, 0.36–0.64 **Mo**, 0.0015–0.005 **B**, 0.17–0.43 **Cu**, 0.03–0.11 **Ti**	**Quenched and tempered:** all **diam**, (795) **TS**, (690) **YS**, 18 **El**
ANSI/ASTM A 517	Grade E	US	Plate	0.10–0.22 **C**, 0.36–0.74 **Mn**, 0.035 **P**, 0.040 **S**, 0.18–0.37 **Si**, 1.34–2.06 **Cr**, 0.36–0.64 **Mo**, 0.0015–0.005 **B**, 0.17–0.43 **Cu**, 0.03–0.11 **Ti**	**Quenched and tempered:** all **diam**, (795) **TS**, (690) **YS**, 16 **El**
ANSI/ASTM A 514	Grade C	US	Plate	0.10–0.20 **C**, 1.10–1.50 **Mn**, 0.035 **P**, 0.04 **S**, 0.15–0.30 **Si**, 0.20–0.30 **Mo**, 0.001–0.005 **B**	**Quenched and tempered:** ≥0.75–2.50 **diam**, (760) **TS**, (690) **YS**, 18 **El**
ANSI/ASTM A 514	Grade K	US	Plate	0.10–0.20 **C**, 1.10–1.50 **Mn**, 0.035 **P**, 0.04 **S**, 0.15–0.30 **Si**, 0.45–0.55 **Mo**, 0.001–0.005 **B**	**Quenched and tempered:** ≥0.75–2.50 **diam**, (760) **TS**, (690) **YS**, 18 **El**
AMS 6386B	Type 3	US	Sheet, plate	0.10–0.20 **C**, 1.10–1.50 **Mn**, 0.035 **P**, 0.040 **S**, 0.15–0.30 **Si**, 0.20–0.30 **Mo**, 0.0005–0.005 **B**	**Hardened, tempered and descaled:** 1.250 (31.75) **diam**, 110 (758) **TS**, 100 (690) **YS**, 18 **El**
AMS 6386B	Type 9	US	Sheet, plate	0.10–0.20 **C**, 1.10–1.50 **Mn**, 0.035 **P**, 0.040 **S**, 0.15–0.30 **Si**, 0.45–0.55 **Mo**, 0.0005–0.005 **B**	**Hardened, tempered and descaled:** 1.250–2.000 (31.75–50.80) **diam**, 110 (758) **TS**, 100 (690) **YS**, 18 **El**
AMS 6386B	Type 12	US	Sheet, plate	0.10–0.20 **C**, 0.60–1.00 **Mn**, 0.035 **P**, 0.040 **S**, 0.15–0.35 **Si**, 0.40–0.65 **Cr**, 0.70–1.00 **Ni**, 0.40–0.60 **Mo**, 0.03–0.08 **V**, 0.0005–0.005 **B**, 0.15–0.50 **Cu**	**Hardened, tempered and descaled:** >2.000–4.000 (>50.80–101.60) **diam**, 110 (758) **TS**, 100 (690) **YS**, 18 **El**
ANSI/ASTM A 514	Grade F	US	Plate	0.10–0.20 **C**, 0.60–1.00 **Mn**, 0.035 **P**, 0.04 **S**, 0.15–0.35 **Si**, 0.40–0.65 **Cr**, 0.70–1.00 **Ni**, 0.40–0.60 **Mo**, 0.03–0.08 **V**, 0.0005–0.006 **B**, 0.15–0.50 **Cu**	**Quenched and tempered:** ≥2.5–4.0 **diam**, (690) **TS**, (620) **YS**, 17 **El**
AS G18	G18/En 40A	Australia	Bar, billet	0.10–0.20 **C**, 0.40–0.65 **Mn**, 0.050 **P**, 0.050 **S**, 0.10–0.35 **Si**, 2.90–3.50 **Cr**, 0.40 **Ni**, 0.40–0.70 **Mo**	**Hardened, tempered:** 6 **diam**, (690) **TS**, (525) **YS**
ANSI/ASTM A 541	Grade 5	US	Forgings	0.10–0.20 **C**, 0.30–0.80 **Mn**, 0.035 **P**, 0.040 **S**, 0.50–1.00 **Si**, 1.00–1.50 **Cr**, 0.50 **Ni**, 0.45–0.65 **Mo**, 0.05 **V**	**Quenched and tempered:** all **diam**, (550) **TS**, (340) **YS**, 18 **El**
AMS 5502A		US	Sheet, strip	0.10–0.20 **C**, 1.00 **Mn**, 0.040 **P**, 0.030 **S**, 1.00 **Si**, 4.00–6.00 **Cr**, 0.40–0.60 **Mo**	**Cold or hot rolled:** ≤0.050 **diam**, 75 (517) **TS**, 20 **El**; **Annealed and tempered:** ≤0.050 **diam**, 170 (1172) **TS**, 140 **YS**, 10 **El**
ANSI/ASTM A 336	Grade F12	US	Forgings	0.10–0.20 **C**, 0.30–0.80 **Mn**, 0.040 **P**, 0.040 **S**, 0.10–0.60 **Si**, 0.80–1.10 **Cr**, 0.45–0.65 **Mo**	**Annealed or normalized and tempered:** all **diam**, (485) **TS**, (275) **YS**, 18 **El**
ASTM A 336	F12	US	Forgings	0.10–0.20 **C**, 0.30–0.80 **Mn**, 0.040 **P**, 0.040 **S**, 0.10–0.60 **Si**, 0.80–1.10 **Cr**, 0.45–0.65 **Mo**	**Normalized:** all **diam**, 70 (485) **TS**, 40 (275) **YS**, 18 **El**
ASTM A 336	F12	US	Forgings	0.10–0.20 **C**, 0.30–0.80 **Mn**, 0.040 **P**, 0.040 **S**, 0.10–0.60 **Si**, 0.80–1.10 **Cr**, 0.45–0.65 **Mo**	**Annealed or normalized, tempered:** all **diam**, 70 (485) **TS**, 40 (275) **YS**, 18 **El**
JIS G 3213	Class 22 B	Japan	Forgings	0.10–0.20 **C**, 0.30–0.80 **Mn**, 0.035 **P**, 0.035 **S**, 0.10–0.60 **Si**, 0.80–1.25 **Cr**, 0.44–0.65 **Mo**	**Annealed or normalized and quenched:** all **diam**, (481) **TS**, (206) **YS**, 22 **El**
JIS G 3213	Class 23 B	Japan	Forgings	0.10–0.20 **C**, 0.30–0.80 **Mn**, 0.030 **P**, 0.030 **S**, 0.50–1.00 **Si**, 1.00–1.50 **Cr**, 0.44–0.65 **Mo**	**Annealed or normalized and tempered:** all **diam**, (481) **TS**, (275) **YS**, 20 **El**
IS 6630	$15Cr^{90}Mo^{55}$	India	Pipe	0.10–0.20 **C**, 0.40–0.70 **Mn**, 0.040 **P**, 0.040 **S**, 0.10–0.35 **Si**, 0.70–1.10 **Cr**, 0.45–0.65 **Mo**	**Normalized and tempered:** all **diam**, (440) **TS**, 275 **YS**, 22 **El**
ANSI/ASTM A 213	Grade T2	US	Tube: seamless	0.10–0.20 **C**, 0.30–0.61 **Mn**, 0.045 **P**, 0.045 **S**, 0.10–0.30 **Si**, 0.50–0.81 **Cr**, 0.44–0.65 **Mo**	**Annealed:** 0.312 (7.94) **diam**, 60 (414) **TS**, 30 (207) **YS**, 30 **El**
NOM–B–194	Grade T 2	Mexico	Tube: seamless	0.10–0.20 **C**, 0.30–0.61 **Mn**, 0.045 **P**, 0.045 **S**, 0.10–0.30 **Si**, 0.50–0.81 **Cr**, 0.44–0.65 **Mo**	**Hot or cold finished and annealed:** (0.38–12.7) **diam**, (414) **TS**, (207) **YS**

WROUGHT ALLOY STEELS

specification number	designation	country	product forms	composition	mechanical properties (see page iv for explanation)
MIL–T–0020155B		US	Tube, pipe: seamless	0.10–0.20 **C**, 0.30–0.80 **Mn**, 0.045 **P**, 0.045 **S**, 0.10–0.50 **Si**, 0.44–0.65 **Mo**	**As agreed**: all **diam**, (413) **TS**, (241) **YS**, 30 **El**
JIS G 3462	Class 20	Japan	Tube: seamless	0.10–0.20 **C**, 0.30–0.60 **Mn**, 0.035 **P**, 0.035 **S**, 0.10–0.50 **Si**, 0.50–0.80 **Cr**, 0.40–0.65 **Mo**	**Full annealed or annealed, normalized and tempered:** (≥8) **diam**, (412) **TS**, (206) **YS**, 30 **El**
COPANT 513	T2	COPANT	Tube	0.10–0.20 **C**, 0.30–0.61 **Mn**, 0.045 **P**, 0.045 **S**, 0.10–0.30 **Si**, 0.50–0.81 **Cr**, 0.44–0.65 **Mo**	**Hot or cold finished and annealed**: (>8) **diam**, (410) **TS**, (205) **YS**, 30 **El**
DGN–B–219	Grade T1	Mexico	Tube: electric resistance welded	0.10–0.20 **C**, 0.30–0.80 **Mn**, 0.045 **P**, 0.041 **S**, 0.10–0.50 **Si**, 0.44–0.65 **Mo**	**As welded**: (≥7.92) **diam**, (382) **TS**, (206) **YS**, 30 **El**
DGN–B–181	Grade P–1	Mexico	Pipe: seamless	0.10–0.20 **C**, 0.30–0.80 **Mn**, 0.045 **P**, 0.045 **S**, 0.10–0.50 **Si**, 0.44–0.65 **Mo**	**Hot or cold finished:** (8–60) **diam**, (382) **TS**, (206) **YS**, 30 **El**
DGN–B–181	Grade P–2	Mexico	Tube: seamless	0.10–0.20 **C**, 0.30–0.61 **Mn**, 0.045 **P**, 0.045 **S**, 0.10–0.50 **Si**, 0.50–0.81 **Cr**, 0.44–0.65 **Mo**	**Hot or cold finished:** (8–60) **diam**, (382) **TS**, (206) **YS**, 30 **El**
JIS G 3458	Class 12	Japan	Pipe: seamless	0.10–0.20 **C**, 0.30–0.80 **Mn**, 0.035 **P**, 0.035 **S**, 0.10–0.50 **Si**, 0.45–0.65 **Mo**	**Annealed:** (≥8) **diam**, (382) **TS**, (206) **YS**, 30 **El**
JIS G 3213	Class 12 A	Japan	Forgings	0.10–0.20 **C**, 0.30–0.80 **Mn**, 0.035 **P**, 0.035 **S**, 0.10–0.50 **Si**, 0.44–0.65 **Mo**	**Annealed or normalized and tempered**: all **diam**, (382) **TS**, (206) **YS**, 22 **El**
JIS G 3213	Class 13 A	Japan	Forgings	0.10–0.20 **C**, 0.30–0.61 **Mn**, 0.035 **P**, 0.035 **S**, 0.10–0.30 **Si**, 0.50–0.81 **Cr**, 0.44–0.65 **Mo**	**Annealed or normalized and tempered**: all **diam**, (382) **TS**, (206) **YS**, 22 **El**
JIS G 3462	Class 12	Japan	Tube: seamless	0.10–0.20 **C**, 0.30–0.80 **Mn**, 0.035 **P**, 0.035 **S**, 0.10–0.50 **Si**, 0.45–0.65 **Mo**	**Full annealed or annealed, normalized and tempered:** (≥8) **diam**, (382) **TS**, (206) **YS**, 30 **El**
COPANT R 204	Grade T–1	COPANT	Tube: seamless	0.10–0.20 **C**, 0.30–0.80 **Mn**, 0.045 **P**, 0.045 **S**, 0.10–0.50 **Si**, 0.44–0.65 **Mo**	**Hot or cold finished:** (>8) **diam**, (380) **TS**, (205) **YS**, 30 **El**
COPANT R 193	T1	COPANT	Tube	0.10–0.20 **C**, 0.30–0.80 **Mn**, 0.045 **P**, 0.045 **S**, 0.10–0.50 **Si**, 0.44–0.65 **Mo**	**Hot or cold finished:** (≥5.60) **diam**, (380) **TS**, (205) **YS**, 30 **El**
COPANT 509	P2	COPANT	Pipe	0.10–0.20 **C**, 0.30–0.61 **Mn**, 0.045 **P**, 0.045 **S**, 0.10–0.30 **Si**, 0.50–0.81 **Cr**, 0.44–0.65 **Mo**	**Hot or cold finished:** (≥8) **diam**, (380) **TS**, (205) **YS**, 30 **El**
COPANT 509	P1	COPANT	Pipe	0.10–0.20 **C**, 0.30–0.80 **Mn**, 0.045 **P**, 0.045 **S**, 0.10–0.50 **Si**, 0.44–0.65 **Mo**	**Hot or cold finished:** (≥8) **diam**, (380) **TS**, (205) **YS**, 30 **El**
ANSI/ASTM A 369	FP1	US	Pipe	0.10–0.20 **C**, 0.30–0.80 **Mn**, 0.045 **P**, 0.045 **S**, 0.10–0.50 **Si**, 0.44–0.65 **Mo**	**Annealed or normalized, tempered:** 0.312 (7.94) **diam**, 55 (380) **TS**, 30 (210) **YS**, 30 **El**
ANSI/ASTM A 369	FP2	US	Pipe	0.10–0.20 **C**, 0.30–0.61 **Mn**, 0.045 **P**, 0.045 **S**, 0.10–0.30 **Si**, 0.50–0.81 **Cr**, 0.44–0.65 **Mo**	**Annealed or normalized, tempered:** 0.312 (7.94) **diam**, 55 (380) **TS**, 30 (210) **YS**, 30 **El**
ANSI/ASTM A 209	Grade T1	US	Tube: seamless	0.10–0.20 **C**, 0.30–0.80 **Mn**, 0.045 **P**, 0.045 **S**, 0.10–0.50 **Si**, 0.44–0.65 **Mo**	**Annealed:** 0.312 (7.94) **diam**, 55 (379) **TS**, 30 (207) **YS**, 30 **El**
NOM–B–193	Grade T 1	Mexico	Tube: seamless	0.10–0.20 **C**, 0.30–0.80 **Mn**, 0.045 **P**, 0.045 **S**, 0.10–0.50 **Si**, 0.44–0.65 **Mo**	**Hot or cold finished:** (0.89–12.7) **diam**, (379) **TS**, (207) **YS**, 30 **El**
NOM–B–142	Grade Ti	Mexico	Tube: seamless	0.10–0.20 **C**, 0.30–0.80 **Mn**, 0.045 **P**, 0.045 **S**, 0.10–0.50 **Si**, 0.44–0.65 **Mo**	**Hot or cold finished:** (5.59) **diam**, (379) **TS**, (207) **YS**, 22 **El**
ANSI/ASTM A 161	Grade T1	US	Tube: seamless	0.10–0.20 **C**, 0.30–0.80 **Mn**, 0.045 max **P**, 0.045 max **S**, 0.10–0.50 **Si**, 0.44–0.65 **Mo**	**Hot rolled, as rolled, cold drawn, annealed:** 0.312 (7.94) **diam**, 55 (379) **TS**, 30 (207) **YS**, 30 **El**
ANSI/ASTM A 335	P1	US	Pipe: seamless	0.10–0.20 **C**, 0.30–0.80 **Mn**, 0.045 **P**, 0.045 **S**, 0.10–0.50 **Si**, 0.44–0.65 **Mo**	**Normalized or annealed:** 0.312 (7.94) **diam**, 55 (379) **TS**, 30 (207) **YS**, 30 **El**
ANSI/ASTM A 335	P2	US	Pipe: seamless	0.10–0.20 **C**, 0.30–0.61 **Mn**, 0.045 **P**, 0.045 **S**, 0.10–0.30 **Si**, 0.50–0.81 **Cr**, 0.44–0.65 **Mo**	**Normalized or annealed:** 0.312 (7.94) **diam**, 55 (379) **TS**, 30 (207) **YS**, 30 **El**
ANSI/ASTM A 250	Grade T1	US	Tube: electric, resistance, welded	0.10–0.20 **C**, 0.30–0.80 **Mn**, 0.045 **P**, 0.045 **S**, 0.10–0.50 **Si**, 0.44–0.65 **Mo**	**Normalized:** 0.312 (7.94) **diam**, 55 (379) **TS**, 30 (207) **YS**, 30 **El**

specification number	designation	country	product forms	composition	mechanical properties (see page iv for explanation)
BS 1501–240		UK	Bar	0.10–0.20 **C**, 0.45–0.80 **Mn**, 0.050 **P**, 0.050 **S**, 0.10–0.35 **Si**, 0.25 **Cr**, 0.40 **Ni**, 0.40–0.70 **Mo**, 0.40 **Cu**	**Normalized**: all **diam**, (370) **TS**, (195) **YS**
MIL–S–18410	Class a	US	Bar, billets, forgings	0.10–0.20 **C**, 0.30–0.80 **Mn**, 0.040 **P**, 0.040 **S**, 0.50–1.00 **Si**, 1.00–1.50 **Cr**, 0.45–0.65 **Mo**	**Annealed**
AS 1443	AS 1443/K8	Australia	Bar	0.10–0.18 **C**, 1.30–1.70 **Mn**, 0.050 **P**, 0.050 **S**, 0.10–0.35 **Si**	**As rolled or normalized**: (≤150) **diam**, (480) **TS**, (270) **YS**, 22 **El**
AS 1442	Grade AS 1442/K8	Australia	Bar	0.10–0.18 **C**, 1.30–1.70 **Mn**, 0.050 **P**, 0.050 **S**, 0.10–0.35 **Si**	**As rolled or normalized**: (≤150) **diam**, (480) **TS**, (270) **YS**, 22 **El**
ISO 2604/IV	P32	ISO	Plate	0.10–0.18 **C**, 0.40–0.80 **Mn**, 0.040 **P**, 0.040 **S**, 0.15–0.35 **Si**, 0.70–1.30 **Cr**, 0.40–0.60 **Mo**, 0.020 Al_{met}	**Hot rolled, normalized and tempered**: (3–16) **diam**, (470) **TS**, (305) **YS**, 20 **El**
IS 6630	$14Cr^{45}Mo^{60}V^{27}$	India	Pipe	0.10–0.18 **C**, 0.40–0.70 **Mn**, 0.040 **P**, 0.040 **S**, 0.10–0.35 **Si**, 0.30–0.60 **Cr**, 0.50–0.70 **Mo**, 0.22–0.32 **V**	**Normalized and tempered**: all **diam**, (460) **TS**, (270) **YS**, 15 **El**
AS 1835	TS 33	Australia	Tube: seamless	0.10–0.18 **C**, 0.40–0.70 **Mn**, 0.040 **P**, 0.040 **S**, 0.10–0.35 **Si**, 0.30–0.60 **Cr**, 0.50–0.70 **Mo**, 0.22–0.32 **V**, 0.02 **Al**	**Normalized and tempered**: all **diam**, (460) **TS**, (275) **YS**, 15 **El**
ISO 2604/II	TS 33	ISO	Tube: seamless	0.10–0.18 **C**, 0.40–0.70 **Mn**, 0.040 **P**, 0.040 **S**, 0.10–0.35 **Si**, 0.30–0.60 **Cr**, 0.50–0.70 **Mo**, 0.22–0.32 **V**, 0.02 met **Al**	**Cold finished, normalized and tempered**: all **diam**, (460) **TS**, (275) **YS**, 15 **El**
ISO 2604/1	F33	ISO	Forgings	0.10–0.18 **C**, 0.40–0.70 **Mn**, 0.040 **P**, 0.040 **S**, 0.15–0.40 **Si**, 0.30–0.60 **Cr**, 0.50–0.70 **Mo**, 0.22–0.35 **V**, 0.020 Al_{met}	**Normalized and tempered, quenched and tempered**: all **diam**, (460) **TS**, (275) **YS**, 16 **El**
DIN 17175 Part 1	13CrMo 44–1.7335	Germany	Tube: seamless	0.10–0.18 **C**, 0.40–0.70 **Mn**, 0.040 **P**, 0.040 **S**, 0.15–0.35 **Si**, 0.7–1.0 **Cr**, 0.40–0.50 **Mo**	**Hot rolled or cold drawn, normalized or annealed**: all **diam**, (441) **TS**, (294) **YS**, 22 **El**
TS 381	UDK 621.643.2/15Cr Mo 44	Turkey	Pipe: seamless	0.10–0.18 **C**, 0.40–0.70 **Mn**, 0.040 **P**, 0.040 **S**, 0.15–0.50 **Si**, 0.40–0.50 **Mo**	**As drawn**: all **diam**, (441) **TS**, (294) **YS**, 22 **El**
ISO 2604/111	No TW32	ISO	Tube: welded	0.10–0.18 **C**, 0.40–0.70 **Mn**, 0.040 **P**, 0.040 **S**, 0.10–0.35 **Si**	**Normalized, normalized and tempered**: all **diam**, (440) **TS**, (275) **YS**, 22 **El**
AS 1835	TS 32	Australia	Tube: seamless	0.10–0.18 **C**, 0.40–0.70 **Mn**, 0.040 **P**, 0.040 **S**, 0.10–0.35 **Si**, 0.70–1.10 **Cr**, 0.45–0.65 **Mo**, 0.020 **Al**	**Normalized and tempered**: all **diam**, (440) **TS**, (275) **YS**, 22 **El**
AS 1836	TW 32	Australia	Tube: welded	0.10–0.18 **C**, 0.40–0.70 **Mn**, 0.040 **P**, 0.040 **S**, 0.10–0.35 **Si**, 0.70–1.10 **Cr**, 0.45–0.65 **Mo**	**Normalized and tempered**: all **diam**, (440) **TS**, (275) **YS**, 22 **El**
NBN 837	13 Cr Mo 44	Belgium	Tube	0.10–0.18 **C**, 0.40–0.70 **Mn**, 0.040 **P**, 0.040 **S**, 0.15–0.35 **Si**, 0.7–1.0 **Cr**, 0.40–0.50 **Mo**	**Normalized or annealed**: all **diam**, (440) **TS**, (290) **YS**, 22 **El**
ISO 2604/II	TS 32	ISO	Tube: seamless	0.10–0.18 **C**, 0.40–0.70 **Mn**, 0.040 **P**, 0.040 **S**, 0.10–0.35 **Si**, 0.70–1.10 **Cr**, 0.45–0.65 **Mo**, 0.02 Al_{met}	**Cold finished, normalized and tempered**: all **diam**, (440) **TS**, (275) **YS**, 22 **El**
SIS 14 22 16 E	SIS 2216–04	Sweden	Bar, forgings, plate, sheet	0.10–0.18 **C**, 0.40–0.80 **Mn**, 0.040 **P**, 0.040 **S**, 0.15–0.35 **Si**, 0.70–1.30 **Cr**, 0.40–0.60 **Mo**, 0.020 **Al**, 0.25 **Cu**	**Normalized and annealed**: all **diam**, (440) **TS**, (300) **YS**, 20 **El**
SIS 14 2216 E	SIS 2216–05	Sweden	Tube: seamless	0.10–0.18 **C**, 0.40–0.70 **Mn**, 0.050 **P**, 0.040 **S**, 0.15–0.35 **Si**, 0.70–1.10 **Cr**, 0.45–0.65 **Mo**, 0.020 **Al**, 0.25 **Cu**	**Normalized and annealed**: all **diam**, (440) **TS**, (280) **YS**, 22 **El**
DIN 17155	Grade 13 CrMo 44	Germany	Plate	0.10–0.18 **C**, 0.40–0.70 **Mn**, 0.040 **P**, 0.040 **S**, 0.15–0.35 **Si**, 0.70–1.00 **Cr**, 0.40–0.50 **Mo**	**Quenched and tempered**: (≤16) **diam**, (432) **TS**, (304) **YS**
BS 1501–260		UK	Plate	0.10–0.17 **C**, 0.40–0.80 **Mn**, 0.040 **P**, 0.040 **S**, 0.10–0.40 **Si**, 0.25 **Cr**, 0.30 **Ni**, 0.40–0.60 **Mo**, 0.001–0.005 **B**	**Normalized**: (>51) **diam**, (560) **TS**, (450) **YS**, 16 **El**

WROUGHT ALLOY STEELS

specification number	designation	country	product forms	composition	mechanical properties (see page iv for explanation)
AMS 6354A		US	Sheet, strip, plate	0.10–0.17 **C**, 0.50–0.80 **Mn**, 0.025 **P**, 0.035 **S**, 0.60–0.90 **Si**, 0.50–0.75 **Cr**, 0.25 **Ni**, 0.15–0.25 **Mo**, 0.35 **Cu**, 0.05–0.10 **Zr**	**Hot or cold rolled and annealed:** $\leq$0.5 ($\leq$12.7) **diam**, 70 (483) **TS**, 50 (345) **YS**, 22 **El**
AMS 6460B		US	Wire	0.10–0.17 **C**, 0.50–0.80 **Mn**, 0.040 **P**, 0.040 **S**, 0.60–0.90 **Si**, 0.50–0.75 **Cr**, 0.25 **Ni**, 0.15–0.25 **Mo**, 0.35 **Cu**, 0.05–0.15 **Zr**	
ISO R 683/XI	11	ISO	Bar	0.10–0.16 **C**, 0.35–0.65 **Mn**, 0.035 **P**, 0.035 **S**, 0.15–0.40 **Si**, 0.60–0.90 **Cr**, 2.75–3.25 **Ni**	**Carburized and hardened:** all **diam**, (980) **TS**, (638) **YS**, 8 **El**
ISO R 683/XI	11a	ISO	Bar	0.10–0.16 **C**, 0.35–0.65 **Mn**, 0.035 **P**, 0.020–0.035 **S**, 0.15–0.40 **Si**, 0.60–0.90 **Cr**, 2.75–3.25 **Ni**	**Carburized and hardened:** all **diam**, (980) **TS**, (638) **YS**, 8 **El**
BS 970 Part 3	Grade 832 M 13	UK	Blooms, billets, bar, forgings	0.10–0.16 **C**, 0.35–0.60 **Mn**, 0.10–0.35 **Si**, 0.70–1.00 **Si**, 0.70–1.00 **Cr**, 3.00–3.75 **Ni**, 0.10–0.25 **Mo**	**Hardened:** 0.75 **diam**, (970) **TS**, 8 **El**
AIR 9160/C 81	9160C291	France	Bar, forgings	0.10–0.16 **C**, 0.35–0.65 **Mn**, 0.025 **P**, 0.020 **S**, 0.15–0.40 **Si**, 0.60–0.90 **Cr**, 2.75–3.25 **Ni**	**Quenched and tempered:** ($\leq$16) **diam**, (930) **TS**, (730) **YS**, 11 **El**
BS 970 Part 3	Grade 655 M 13	UK	Blooms, billets, bar, forgings	0.10–0.16 **C**, 0.35–0.60 **Mn**, 0.10–0.35 **Si**, 0.70–1.00 **Cr**, 3.00–3.75 **Ni**	**Hardened:** 0.75 **diam**, (900) **TS**, 9 **El**
AIR 9113/A	15CDV6	France	Sheet, tube, bar, forgings	0.10–0.16 **C**, 0.8–1.1 **Mn**, 0.030 **P**, 0.030 **S**, 0.20 **Si**, 1.25–1.50 **Cr**, 0.5 **Ni**, 0.8–1.0 **Mo**	**Annealed:** all **diam**, (640) max **TS**, 22 **El**; **Quenched and tempered:** ($\leq$6) **diam**, (980) **TS**, (750) **YS**, 12 **El**; **Quenched and tempered:** all **diam**, (1030) **TS**, (930) **YS**, 10 **El**
NBN A 25–102	12 Cr Mo W V 4524	Belgium	Tube	0.10–0.16 **C**, 0.27–0.63 **Mn**, 0.033 **P**, 0.033 **S**, 0.55 **Si**, 0.95–1.25 **Cr**, 0.41–0.69 **Mo**, 0.32–0.48 **V**, 0.42–0.68 **W**	**Hot or cold finished or normalized or annealed:** all **diam**, (640) **TS**, (390) **YS**, 18 **El**
BS 970 Part 3	Grade 655 h 13	UK	Blooms, billets, bar, forgings	0.10–0.16 **C**, 0.35–0.60 **Mn**, 0.10–0.35 **Si**, 0.70–1.00 **Cr**, 3.00–3.75 **Ni**	
BS 970 Part 3	Grade 832 H 13	UK	Blooms, billets, bar, forgings	0.10–0.16 **C**, 0.35–0.60 **Mn**, 0.10–0.35 **S**, 0.70–1.00 **Cr**, 3.00–3.75 **Ni**, 0.10–0.25 **Mo**	
IS 4367	13Ni3Cr80	India	Forgings	0.10–0.15 **C**, 0.40–0.70 **Mn**, 0.050 **P**, 0.050 **S**, 0.10–0.35 **Si**, 0.60–1.00 **Cr**, 3.00–3.50 **Ni**	**Refined and quenched:** all **diam**, (833) **TS**, 12 **El**
BS 5S.15		UK	Bar, billets, forgings: aircraft quality	0.10–0.15 **C**, 0.35–0.6 **Mn**, 0.025 **P**, 0.020 **S**, 0.10–0.35 **Si**, 0.30 **Cr**, 2.75–3.25 **Ni**	**Hardened and tempered:** all **diam**, (774) **TS**, 12 **El**
AS G18	G18/En 33	Australia	Bar, billet	0.10–0.15 **C**, 0.30–0.60 **Mn**, 0.050 **P**, 0.050 **S**, 0.10–0.35 **Si**, 0.30 **Cr**, 2.75–3.50 **Ni**	**Hardened:** all **diam**, (690) **TS**
BS 1501–622	Grade 31	UK	Plate	0.10–0.15 **C**, 0.40–0.80 **Mn**, 0.040 **P**, 0.040 **S**, 0.20–0.50 **Si**, 2.00–2.50 **Cr**, 0.30 **Ni**, 0.90–1.20 **Mo**, 0.30 **Cu**, 0.03	**Normalized:** (51) **diam**, (480) **TS**, (280) **YS**, 16 **El**
BS 3059 Part 2	Grade 620	UK	Tube	0.10–0.15 **C**, 0.40–0.70 **Mn**, 0.040 **P**, 0.040 **S**, 0.10–0.35 **Si**, 0.70–1.10 **Cr**, 0.45–0.65 **Mo**, 0.020 **Al**	**Normalized:** all **diam**, (460) **TS**, (180) **YS**, 22 **El**
BS 3059	Steel 620	UK	Tube: seamless	0.10–0.15 **C**, 0.40–0.70 **Mn**, 0.040 max **P**, 0.040 max **S**, 0.10–0.35 **Si**, 0.70–1.10 **Cr**, 0.30 **Ni**, 0.45–0.65 **Mo**, 0.25 **Cu**, 0.03	**Normalized or normalized and tempered:** all **diam**, (440) **TS**, (235) **YS**, 17 **El**

WROUGHT ALLOY STEELS

specification number	designation	country	product forms	composition	mechanical properties (see page iv for explanation)
BS 3059	Steel 620	UK	Tube: electric resistance welded	0.10–0.15 C, 0.40–0.70 Mn, 0.040 P, 0.040 S, 0.10–0.35 Si, 0.70–1.10 Cr, 0.30 Ni, 0.45–0.65 Mo, 0.25 Cu, 0.03	**Normalized:** all diam, (440) TS, (235) YS, 17 El
BS 970 Part 3	Grade 655 A 12	UK	Blooms, billets, bar, forgings	0.10–0.15 C, 0.40–0.60 Mn, 0.75–1.00 Cr, 3.00–3.50 Ni	
ASTM A 534	Krupp	US	Bar, wire, tube, rods, billets	0.10–0.15 C, 0.45–0.65 Mn, 0.20–0.35 Si, 1.40–1.75 Cr, 3.25–3.75 Ni	**As–rolled or normalized and tempered**
AMS 6544		US	Plate	0.10–0.14 C, 0.05–0.25 Mn, 0.010 P, 0.006 S, 0.10 Si, 1.80–2.20 Cr, 9.50–10.50 Ni, 0.90–1.10 Mo, 0.025 Al, 7.50–8.50 Co, 0.0075 N, 0.025 O, 0.015 Ti	**Hot rolled or hot finished solution heat treated and aged:** 0.375–2.000 (9.52–50.80) diam, 190 (1310) TS, 180 (1241) YS, 14 El
AMS 6543		US	Bar, forgings, billets	0.10–0.14 C, 0.05–0.25 Mn, 0.010 P, 0.006 S, 0.10 Si, 1.80–2.20 Cr, 9.50–10.50 Ni, 0.90–1.10 Mo, 0.025 Al, 7.50–8.50 Co, 0.0075 N, 0.0025 O, 0.015 Ti	**Solution heat treated and aged:** ≥0.500–2.000 (≥12.70–50.80) diam, 190 (1310) TS, 180 (1241) YS, 12 El
AMS 6465		US	Wire	0.10–0.14 C, 0.07–0.17 Mn, 0.006 P, 0.006 S, 0.15–0.25 Si, 1.80–2.20 Cr, 9.50–10.50 Ni, 0.90–1.10 Mo, 0.04–0.09 V, 0.01–0.03 Al, 7.50–8.50 Co, 0.0003 H, 0.005 N, 0.0025 O, 0.02 Ti	**Cold drawn, stress relieved (weld properties):** 0.375 (9.52) diam, 15 El
ISO 2604/IV	P45	ISO	Plate	0.10 C, 0.80 Mn, 0.035 P, 0.035 S, 0.15–0.35 Si, 8.50–10.0 Ni	**Hot rolled, normalized, normalized and tempered, quenched and tempered:** (3–30) diam, (690) TS, (495) YS, 19 El
BS 1501–509		UK	Plate	0.10 C, 0.30–0.80 Mn, 0.025 P, 0.030 S, 0.10–0.30 Si, 0.30 Cr, 8.75–9.75 Ni, 0.20 Mo, 0.020 Al, 0.30 Cu	**Double normalized and tempered or quenched and tempered:** (<51) diam, (690) TS, (525) YS, 18 El
BS 1501–510		UK	Plate	0.10 C, 0.30–0.80 Mn, 0.025 P, 0.030 S, 0.10–0.30 Si, 0.30 Cr, 8.75–9.75 Ni, 0.20 Mo, 0.020 Al, 0.30 Cu	**Quenched and tempered:** (<51) diam, (690) TS, (590) YS, 18 El
BS 3603	Grade 509	UK	Pipe, tube: seamless	0.10 C, 0.30–0.80 Mn, 0.025 P, 0.020 S, 0.15–0.30 Si, 8.50–9.50 Ni	**Quenched and tempered and normalized and tempered:** all diam, (690) TS, (510) YS, 15 El
EURONORM 129	FeE 585 Ni 36	EURONORM	Plate, strip	0.10 C, 0.30–0.80 Mn, 0.025 P, 0.020 S, 0.35 Si, 0.25 Cr, 8.50–10.0 Ni, 0.10 Mo, 0.05 V, 0.015_{met} or 0.020 tot. (min) Al, 0.35 Cu	**Normalized, or normalized and tempered, or quenched and tempered:** ≤(35) diam, (690) TS, (585) YS, 18 El
EURONORM 129	FeE 490 Ni 36	EURONORM	Plate, strip	0.10 C, 0.30–0.80 Mn, 0.025 P, 0.020 S, 0.35 Si, 0.25 Cr, 8.50–10.0 Ni, 0.10 Mo, 0.05 V, 0.015_{met} or 0.020 tot. (min) Al, 0.35 Cu	**Normalized, or normalized and tempered, or quenched and tempered:** ≤(35) diam, (640) TS, (490) YS, 18 El
NBN 630	10 Ni 36	Belgium	Strip	0.10 C, 0.80 Mn, 0.035 P, 0.035 S, 0.15–0.35 Si, 8.0–10.0 Ni	**Quenched and tempered or normalized:** (3–100) diam, (590) TS, (490) YS, 17 El
ANSI/ASTM A 658		US	Plate	0.10 C, 0.50 Mn, 0.025 P, 0.025 S, 0.35 Si, 0.50 Cr, 35.0–37.00 Ni, 0.50 Mo, 0.50 Co	**Hot rolled, annealed:** all diam, (448) TS, (241) YS, 30 El
DGN–B–83	502	Mexico	Bar	0.10 C, 1.0 Mn, 0.040 P, 0.030 S, 1.00 Si, 4.0–6.0 Cr, 0.40–0.65 Mo	**Hot or cold rolled:** all diam, (441) TS, (176) YS, 30 El
ANSI/ASTM A 473	502	US	Forgings	0.10 C, 1.00 Mn, 0.040 P, 0.030 S, 1.00 Si, 4.00–6.00 Cr, 0.40–0.65 Mo	**Annealed:** all diam, 60 (414) TS, 30 (205) YS, 20 El
BS 2 S.511		UK	Sheet, strip: aircraft quality	0.10 C, 0.50 Mn, 0.040 P, 0.040 S, 0.20 Si, 0.15 Cr, 0.20 Ni, 0.05 Mo	**Annealed:** (<1.6) diam, (280) TS, 26 El
AMS 6466B		US	Wire	0.10 C, 0.60 Mn, 0.03 P, 0.03 S, 0.25–0.60 Si, 4.50–6.00 Cr, 0.60 Ni, 0.45–0.65 Mo, 0.35 Cu	

WROUGHT ALLOY STEELS

specification number	designation	country	product forms	composition	mechanical properties (see page iv for explanation)
NF A 35–590	2881 (Y10 NC 6)	France	Bar, forgings	0.10 **C**, 0.70 **Mn**, 0.030 **P**, 0.030 **S**, 0.30 **Si**, 1.0 **Cr**, 1.5 **Ni**	
NF A 35–590	2882 (10NC 12)	France	Bar, forgings	0.10 **C**, 0.40 **Mn**, 0.030 **P**, 0.030 **S**, 0.30 **Si**, 0.80 **Cr**, 3.0 **Ni**	
ANSI/ASTM A 314	502	US	Bar, forgings, billets	0.10 **C**, 1.00 **Mn**, 0.040 **P**, 0.030 **S**, 1.00 **Si**, 4.00–6.00 **Cr**, 0.40–0.65 **Mo**	
ANSI/ASTM A 193	Grade B5	US	Bar	0.10 min **C**, 1.00 **Mn**, 0.040 **P**, 0.030 **S**, 1.00 **Si**, 4.00–6.00 **Cr**, 0.40–0.65 **Mo**	**Quenched and tempered or normalized and tempered**: $\geq$4 ($\geq$101.6) **diam**, 100 (689) **TS**, 80 (552) **YS**, 16 **El**
ANSI/ASTM A 473	501	US	Forgings	0.10 min **C**, 1.00 **Mn**, 0.040 **P**, 0.030 **S**, 1.00 **Si**, 4.00–6.00 **Cr**, 0.40–0.65 **Mo**	**Tempered**: all **diam**, 90 (620) **TS**, 65 (450) **YS**, 20 **El**; **Annealed**: all **diam**, 60 (414) **TS**, 30 (205) **YS**, 20 **El**
ANSI/ASTM A 314	501	US	Bar, forgings, billets	0.10 min **C**, 1.00 **Mn**, 0.040 **P**, 0.030 **S**, 1.00 **Si**, 4.00–6.00 **Cr**, 0.40–0.65 **Mo**	
NBN A 25–102	13 Cr Mo 44	Belgium	Tube	0.09–0.19 **C**, 0.37–0.73 **Mn**, 0.044 **P**, 0.044 **S**, 0.12–0.38 **Si**, 0.65–1.05 **Cr**, 0.36–0.54 **Mo**	**Hot or cold finished or normalized or annealed**: all **diam**, (440) **TS**, (290) **YS**, 22 **El**
BS 1501–281		UK	Plate	0.09–0.15 **C**, 0.90–1.30 **Mn**, 0.040 **P**, 0.040 **S**, 0.40 **Si**, 0.40–0.70 **Cr**, 0.70–1.00 **Ni**, 0.20–0.28 **Mo**, 0.04–0.12 **V**, 0.10 **Nb**, 0.30 **Cu**, 0.015 **N**	**Normalized**: (>76) **diam**, (560) **TS**, (415) **YS**, 16 **El**
BS 1501–621		UK	Plate	0.09–0.15 **C**, 0.40–0.70 **Mn**, 0.040 **P**, 0.040 **S**, 0.15–0.35 **Si**, 1.00–1.50 **Cr**, 0.30 **Ni**, 0.45–0.65 **Mo**, 0.30 **Cu**,	**Normalized**: (76) **diam**, (450) **TS**, (315) **YS**, 16 **El**
BS 1501–620	Grade 27	UK	Plate	0.09–0.15 **C**, 0.40–0.70 **Mn**, 0.040 **P**, 0.040 **S**, 0.10–0.40 **Si**, 0.70–1.20 **Cr**, 0.30 **Ni**, 0.45–0.65 **Mo**, 0.30 **Cu**,	**Normalized**: (76) **diam**, (420) **TS**, (285) **YS**, 19 **El**
COPANT 334	12 NC 3	COPANT	Bar	0.09–0.15 **C**, 0.30–0.60 **Mn**, 0.035 **P**, 0.035 **S**, 0.35 **Si**, 0.40–0.70 **Cr**, 0.50–0.80 **Ni**	
DGN–B–203	Grade 4012	Mexico	Tube: seamless	0.09–0.14 **C**, 0.75–1.00 **Mn**, 0.040 **P**, 0.040 **S**, 0.20–0.35 **Si**, 0.15–0.25 **Mo**	
COPANT 514	4012	COPANT	Tube	0.09–0.14 **C**, 0.75–1.0 **Mn**, 0.040 **P**, 0.040 **S**, 0.20–0.35 **Si**, 0.15–0.25 **Mo**	
DGN–B–300	4012	Mexico	Bar	0.09–0.14 **C**, 0.75–1.00 **Mn**, 0.035 **P**, 0.040 **S**, 0.20–0.35 **Si**, 0.15–0.25 **Mo**	**Annealed**
ANSI/ASTM A 29	4012	US	Bar	0.09–0.14 **C**, 0.75–1.00 **Mn**, 0.035 **P**, 0.040 **S**, 0.15–0.30 **Si**, 0.15–0.25 **Mo**	
ASTM A 689	4012	US	Bar	0.09–0.14 **C**, 0.75–1.00 **Mn**, 0.035 **P**, 0.040 **S**, 0.15–0.30 **Si**, 0.15–0.25 **Mo**	
ANSI/ASTM A 322	4012	US	Bar	0.09–0.14 **C**, 0.75–1.00 **Mn**, 0.035 **P**, 0.040 **S**, 0.15–0.30 **Si**, 0.15–0.25 **Mo**	
AISI 4012		US	Wire, rod	0.09–0.14 **C**, 0.75–1.00 **Mn**, 0.035 **P**, 0.040 **S**, 0.15–0.30 **Si**, 0.15–0.25 **Mo**	
ANSI/ASTM A 519	4012	US	Tube: seamless	0.09–0.14 **C**, 0.75–1.00 **Mn**, 0.040 **P**, 0.040 **S**, 0.15–0.35 **Si**, 0.15–0.25 **Mo**	
DGN–B–297	4012	Mexico	Bar	0.09–0.14 **C**, 0.75–1.00 **Mn**, 0.035 **P**, 0.040 **S**, 0.20–0.35 **Si**, 0.15–0.25 **Mo**	
JIS G 4107	Class 1	Japan	Bar	0.09 **C**, 1.03 **Mn**, 0.045 **P**, 0.035 **S**, 1.05 **Si**, 3.90–6.10 **Cr**, 0.35–0.70 **Mo**	**Rolled or forged**: ($\leq$100) **diam**, (686) **TS**, (549) **YS**, 16 **El**

WROUGHT ALLOY STEELS

specification number	designation	country	product forms	composition	mechanical properties (see page iv for explanation)
ANSI/ASTM A 736	Class 2	US	Plate	0.09 C, 0.36–0.74 Mn, 0.025 P, 0.025 S, 0.35 Si, 0.56–0.94 Cr, 0.67–1.03 Ni, 0.12–0.28 Mo, 0.95–1.35 Cu, 0.02 Nb	**Normalized or quenched and precipitation hardened:** all diam, (585) TS, (515) YS, 20 El
ANSI/ASTM A 736	Class 1	US	Plate	0.09 C, 0.36–0.74 Mn, 0.025 P, 0.025 S, 0.35 Si, 0.56–0.94 Cr, 0.67–1.03 Ni, 0.12–0.28 Mo, 0.95–1.35 Cu, 0.02 Nb	**Normalized or quenched and precipitation hardened:** all diam, (495) TS, (450) YS, 20 El
ANSI/ASTM A 592	Grade F	US	Forgings	0.08–0.22 C, 0.55–1.05 Mn, 0.035 P, 0.040 S, 0.13–0.37 Si, 0.36–0.79 Cr, 0.67–1.03 Ni, 0.36–0.64 Mo, 0.02–0.09 V, 0.002–0.006 B, 0.12–0.53 Cu	**Quenched and tempered:** all diam, (795) TS, (690) YS, 18 El
ANSI/ASTM A 517	Grade C	US	Plate	0.08–0.22 C, 1.05–1.55 Mn, 0.035 P, 0.040 S, 0.13–0.32 Si, 0.17–0.33 Mo, 0.001–0.005 B	**Quenched and tempered:** all diam, (795) TS, (690) YS, 16 El
ANSI/ASTM A 517	Grade F	US	Plate	0.08–0.22 C, 0.55–1.05 Mn, 0.035 P, 0.040 S, 0.13–0.37 Si, 0.36–0.69 Cr, 0.67–1.03 Ni, 0.36–0.64 Mo, 0.02–0.09 V, 0.005–0.006 B, 0.12–0.53 Cu	**Quenched and tempered:** all diam, (795) TS, (690) YS, 16 El
ANSI/ASTM A 517	Grade K	US	Plate	0.08–0.22 C, 1.05–1.55 Mn, 0.035 P, 0.040 S, 0.13–0.32 Si, 0.42–0.58 Mo, 0.001–0.005 B	**Quenched and tempered:** all diam, (795) TS, (690) YS, 16 El
ISO 2604/IV	P34	ISO	Plate	0.08–0.18 C, 0.40–0.80 Mn, 0.040 P, 0.040 S, 0.15–0.50 Si, 2.00–2.50 Cr, 0.90–1.10 Mo, 0.020 Al_{met}	**Hot rolled, normalized and tempered:** (3–16) diam, (480) TS, (275) YS, 18 El
ISO 2604/IV	P33	ISO	Plate	0.08–0.18 C, 0.40–0.70 Mn, 0.040 P, 0.040 S, 0.15–0.35 Si, 0.30–0.60 Cr, 0.50–0.70 Mo, 0.22–0.35 V, 0.020 Al_{met}	**Hot rolled, normalized and tempered:** (3–16) diam, (460) TS, (285) YS, 19 El
BS S.150		UK	Billets, bar, forgings, parts: aircraft quality	0.08–0.16 C, 0.3–1.2 Mn, 0.030 P, 0.025 S, 0.15–0.60 Si, 9.8–11.2 Cr, 0.6–1.2 Ni, 0.4–0.8 Mo, 0.10–0.25 V, 0.030–0.075 N, 0.15–0.45 Nb	**Hardened, tempered:** all diam, (930) TS, (780) YS, 10 El
BS 3059	Steel 622/50	UK	Tube: seamless	0.08–0.15 C, 0.40–0.70 Mn, 0.040 max P, 0.040 max S, 0.50 max Si, 2.00–2.50 Cr, 0.30 Ni, 0.90–1.20 Mo, 0.25 Cu, 0.03	**Normalized and tempered:** all diam, (490) TS, (265) YS, 16 El
SIS 14 22 18 E	SIS 2218–05	Sweden	Bar, forgings, plate, sheet	0.08–0.15 C, 0.40–0.70 Mn, 0.040 P, 0.040 S, 0.15–0.50 Si, 2.00–2.50 Cr, 0.90–1.10 Mo, 0.020 Al_{met} 0.25 Cu	**Normalized and annealed:** all diam, (490) TS, (280) YS, 16 El
SIS 14 22 18 E	SIS 2218–04	Sweden	Bar, forgings, plate, sheet	0.08–0.15 C, 0.40–0.70 Mn, 0.040 P, 0.040 S, 0.15–0.50 Si, 2.00–2.50 Cr, 0.90–1.10 Mo, 0.020 Al_{met} 0.25 Cu	**Normalized and annealed:** all diam, (480) TS, (270) YS, 18 El
BS 3059 Part 2	Grade 622	UK	Tube	0.08–0.15 C, 0.40–0.70 Mn, 0.040 P, 0.040 S, 0.50 Si, 2.00–2.50 Cr, 0.90–1.20 Mo, 0.020 Al	**Annealed:** all diam, (440) TS, (175) YS, 20 El; **Normalized and tempered:** all diam, (490) TS, (275) YS, 20 El
AS 1835	TS 34	Australia	Tube: seamless	0.08–0.15 C, 0.40–0.70 Mn, 0.040 P, 0.040 S, 0.50 Si, 2.00–2.50 Cr, 0.90–1.20 Mo, 0.020 Al	**Annealed:** all diam, (440) TS, (175) YS, 20 El; **Normalized and tempered:** all diam, (490) TS, (275) YS, 16 El
NBN 837	X 12 Cr Mo 5	Belgium	Tube	0.08–0.15 C, 0.30–0.60 Mn, 0.030 P, 0.030 S, 0.50 Si, 4.0–6.0 Cr, 0.45–0.65 Mo	**Normalized or annealed:** all diam, (440) TS, (220) YS, 21 El
NBN 837	X 12 Cr Mo 91	Belgium	Tube	0.08–0.15 C, 0.30–0.60 Mn, 0.030 P, 0.030 S, 0.25–1.0 Si, 8.0–10.0 Cr, 0.90–1.10 Mo	**Normalized or annealed:** all diam, (440) TS, (250) YS, 21 El
BS 3059	Steel 622/42	UK	Tube: seamless	0.08–0.15 C, 0.40–0.70 Mn, 0.040 P, 0.040 S, 0.50 Si, 2.00–2.50 Cr, 0.30 Ni, 0.90–1.20 Mo, 0.25 Cu, 0.03	**Annealed:** all diam, (410) TS, (235) YS, 20 El

WROUGHT ALLOY STEELS

specification number	designation	country	product forms	composition	mechanical properties (see page iv for explanation)
ISO 2604/II	TS 34	ISO	Tube: seamless	0.08–0.15 **C**, 0.40–0.70 **Mn**, .040 **P**, .040 **S**, 0.50 **Si**, 2.00–2.50 **Cr**, 0.90–1.20 **Mo**, 0.02 **Al**	**Cold finished, annealed**: all **diam**, (410) **TS**, (135) **YS**, 20 **El**; **Cold finished, normalized and tempered**: all **diam**, (490) **TS**, (275) **YS**, 16 **El**
BS 3604	CD 622	UK	Pipe: seamless	0.08–0.15 **C**, 0.40–0.70 **Mn**, 0.040 **P**, 0.040 **S**, 0.50 **Si**, 2.00–2.50 **Cr**, 0.90–1.20 **Mo**	**Annealed**: 0.71 **diam**, (372) **TS**, (206) **YS**, 29 **El**; **Normalized, tempered**: 0.71 **diam**, (427) **TS**, (234) **YS**, 25 **El**
BS 3604	HF 622	UK	Pipe: seamless	0.08–0.15 **C**, 0.40–0.70 **Mn**, 0.040 **P**, 0.040 **S**, 0.50 **Si**, 2.00–2.50 **Cr**, 0.90–1.20 **Mo**	**Annealed**: 0.71 **diam**, (372) **TS**, (206) **YS**, 29 **El**; **Normalized, tempered**: 0.71 **diam**, (427) **TS**, (234) **YS**, 25 **El**
AMS 6266D		US	Bar, forgings, tube	0.08–0.13 **C**, 0.75–1.00 **Mn**, 0.025 **P**, 0.025 **S**, 0.20–0.40 **Si**, 0.40–0.60 **Cr**, 1.65–2.00 **Ni**, 0.20–0.30 **Mo**, 0.03–0.08 **V**, 0.35 **Cu**	**Cold finished (bar)**: ≤0.500 (≤12.70) **diam**, 125 (862) max **TS**
MIL–S–83030A	I	US	Bar, billets	0.08–0.13 **C**, 0.45–0.60 **Mn**, 0.015 **P**, 0.015 **S**, 0.20–0.35 **Si**, 1.25–1.75 **Cr**, 3.25–3.75 **Ni**, 0.35 **Cu**; rem **Fe**	**As rolled, annealed**
COPANT 334	3310	COPANT	Bar	0.08–0.13 **C**, 0.45–0.60 **Mn**, 0.035 **P**, 0.040 **S**, 0.20–0.35 **Si**, 1.40–1.75 **Cr**, 3.25–3.75 **Ni**	
COPANT 334	9310	COPANT	Bar	0.08–0.13 **C**, 0.45–0.65 **Mn**, 0.025 **P**, 0.025 **S**, 0.20–0.35 **Si**, 1.00–1.40 **Cr**, 3.00–3.50 **Ni**, 0.08–0.15 **Mo**	
MIL–S–7393C	Composition I	US	Bar, billets	0.08–0.13 **C**, 0.45–0.60 **Mn**, 0.025 **P**, 0.025 **S**, 0.20–0.35 **Si**, 1.25–1.75 **Cr**, 3.25–3.75 **Ni**, 0.35 **Cu**; rem **Fe**	
DGN–B–203	Grade E3310	Mexico	Tube: seamless	0.08–0.13 **C**, 0.45–0.60 **Mn**, 0.025 **P**, 0.025 **S**, 0.20–0.35 **Si**, 1.40–1.75 **Cr**, 3.25–3.75 **Ni**	
DGN–B–203	Grade E 9310	Mexico	Tube: seamless	0.08–0.13 **C**, 0.45–0.65 **Mn**, 0.025 **P**, 0.025 **S**, 0.20–0.35 **Si**, 1.00–1.40 **Cr**, 3.00–3.50 **Ni**, 0.08–0.15 **Mo**	
COPANT 514	E 3310	COPANT	Tube	0.08–0.13 **C**, 0.45–0.60 **Mn**, 0.025 **P**, 0.025 **S**, 0.20–0.35 **Si**, 1.40–1.75 **Cr**, 3.25–3.75 **Ni**	
ANSI/ASTM A 646	3310	US	Blooms, billets: aircraft quality	0.08–0.13 **C**, 0.45–0.60 **Mn**, 0.025 **P**, 0.025 **S**, 0.20–0.35 **Si**, 1.40–1.75 **Cr**, 3.25–3.75 **Ni**	**Annealed**
ANSI/ASTM A 646	9310	US	Blooms, billets: aircraft quality	0.08–0.13 **C**, 0.45–0.65 **Mn**, 0.025 **P**, 0.025 **S**, 0.20–0.35 **Si**, 1.00–1.40 **Cr**, 3.00–3.50 **Ni**, 0.08–0.15 **Mo**	**Annealed**
ANSI/ASTM A 29	E9310	US	Bar	0.08–0.13 **C**, 0.45–0.65 **Mn**, 0.025 **P**, 0.025 **S**, 0.15–0.30 **Si**, 1.00–1.40 **Cr**, 3.00–3.50 **Ni**, 0.08–0.15 **Mo**	
ANSI/ASTM A 519	E3310	US	Tube: seamless	0.08–0.13 **C**, 0.45–0.60 **Mn**, 0.025 **P**, 0.025 **S**, 0.15–0.35 **Si**, 1.40–1.75 **Cr**, 3.25–3.75 **Ni**	
ANSI/ASTM A 519	E 9310	US	Tube: seamless	0.08–0.13 **C**, 0.45–0.65 **Mn**, 0.025 **P**, 0.025 **S**, 0.15–0.35 **Si**, 1.00–1.40 **Cr**, 3.00–3.50 **Ni**, 0.08–0.15 **Mo**	
ANSI/ASTM A 535	9310	US	Billets, coils, bar, rod, tube	0.08–0.13 **C**, 0.45–0.65 **Mn**, 0.015 **P**, 0.015 **S**, 0.20–0.35 **Si**, 1.00–1.40 **Cr**, 3.00–3.50 **Ni**, 0.08–0.15 **Mo**	
ASTM A 534	E–9310	US	Bar, wire, tube, rods, billets	0.08–0.13 **C**, 0.45–0.65 **Mn**, 0.025 **P**, 0.025 **S**, 0.20–0.35 **Si**, 1.00–1.40 **Cr**, 3.00–3.50 **Ni**, 0.08–0.15 **Mo**	**As–rolled or normalized and tempered**
ASTM A 534	E–3310	US	Bar, wire, tube, rods, billets	0.08–0.13 **C**, 0.45–0.60 **Mn**, 0.025 **P**, 0.025 **S**, 0.20–0.35 **Si**, 1.40–1.75 **Cr**, 3.25–3.75 **Ni**	**As–rolled or normalized and tempered**

WROUGHT ALLOY STEELS

specification number	designation	country	product forms	composition	mechanical properties (see page iv for explanation)
ANSI/ASTM A 535	3310	US	Billets, coils, bar, rod, tube	0.08–0.13 **C**, 0.45–0.60 **Mn**, 0.015 **P**, 0.015 **S**, 0.20–0.35 **Si**, 1.40–1.75 **Cr**, 3.25–3.75 **Ni**	
COPANT 514	Grade E9310	COPANT	Tube: seamless	0.08–0.13 **C**, 0.45–0.65 **Mn**, 0.025 **P**, 0.025 **S**, 0.10 **Si**, 1.00–1.40 **Cr**, 3.00–3.50 **Ni**, 0.08–0.15 **Mo**	
NBN 837	X 10 Cr Mo V Nb 92	Belgium	Tube	0.08–0.12 **C**, 0.90–1.20 **Mn**, 0.030 **P**, 0.030 **S**, 0.20–0.40 **Si**, 9.0–10.0 **Cr**, 1.80–2.20 **Mo**, 0.25–0.45 **V**, 0.40–0.60 **Nb**	**Normalized or annealed:** all **diam**, (590) **TS**, (390) **YS**, 18 **El**
ISO 2604/II	TS 39	ISO	Tube: seamless	0.08 **C**, 1.00 **Mn**, 0.040 **P**, 0.030 **S**, 1.00 **Si**, 11.5–14.0 **Cr**, 0.50 **Ni**	**Cold finished, annealed:** all **diam**, (440) **TS**, (245) **YS**, 20 **El**; **Cold finished, quenched and tempered**: all **diam**, (590) **TS**, (390) **YS**, 18 **El**
JIS G 4312	SUH 409	Japan	Sheet, plate	0.08 **C**, 1.00 **Mn**, 1.00 **Si**, 10.50–11.75 **Cr**, 0.60 **Ni**, 0.040 **P**, 0.030 **S**, 6 x C–0.75 **Ti**	**Annealed**: all **diam**, (363) **TS**, (177) **YS**, 22 **El**
NBN A 25–102	10 Cr Mo 910	Belgium	Tube	0.07–0.16 **C**, 0.37–0.63 **Mn**, 0.044 **P**, 0.044 **S**, 0.12–0.55 **Si**, 1.95–2.60 **Cr**, 0.86–1.15 **Mo**	**Hot or cold finished or normalized or annealed:** all **diam**, (440) **TS**, (260) **YS**, 20 **El**
NBN A 25–102	X 12 Cr Mo 5	Belgium	Tube	0.07–0.16 **C**, 0.27–0.63 **Mn**, 0.033 **P**, 0.033 **S**, 0.55 **Si**, 3.90–6.10 **Cr**, 0.41–0.69 **Mo**	**Hot and cold finished and normalized:** all **diam**, (440) **TS**, (220) **YS**, 21 **El**
NBN A 25–102	X 12 Cr Mo 91	Belgium	Tube	0.07–0.16 **C**, 0.27–0.63 **Mn**, 0.033 **P**, 0.033 **S**, 0.22–1.05 **Si**, 7.90–10.01 **Cr**, 0.86–1.15 **Mo**	**Hot and cold finished and normalized:** all **diam**, (440) **TS**, (250) **YS**, 21 **El**
NF A 35–056	FS 12 M8	France	Wire, rod	0.07–0.14 **C**, 1.80–2.20 **Mn**, 0.030 **P**, 0.030 **S**, 0.10 **Si**, 0.15 **Cr**, 0.15 **Ni**, 0.12 **Cu**	
NF A 35–056	FS 12 MD 8	France	Wire, rod	0.07–0.14 **C**, 1.80–2.20 **Mn**, 0.030 **P**, 0.030 **S**, 0.10 **Si**, 0.15 **Cr**, 0.15 **Ni**, 0.45–0.60 **Mo**, 0.12 **Cu**	
NF A 35–056	FS 12 M 6	France	Wire, rod	0.07–0.14 **C**, 1.40–1.70 **Mn**, 0.030 **P**, 0.030 **S**, 0.10 **Si**, 0.15 **Cr**, 0.15 **Ni**, 0.12 **Cu**	
NF A 35–056	FS 12 MD 4	France	Wire, rod	0.07–0.14 **C**, 0.90–1.20 **Mn**, 0.030 **P**, 0.030 **S**, 0.10 **Si**, 0.15 **Cr**, 0.15 **Ni**, 0.45–0.60 **Mo**, 0.12 **Cu**	
NF A 35–056	FS 12 M4	France	Wire, rod	0.07–0.14 **C**, 0.90–1.20 **Mn**, 0.030 **P**, 0.030 **S**, 0.10 **Si**, 0.15 **Cr**, 0.15 **Ni**, 0.12 **Cu**	
AMS 6250G		US	Bar, forgings, tube	0.07–0.13 **C**, 0.40–0.70 **Mn**, 0.025 **P**, 0.025 **S**, 0.20–0.35 **Si**, 1.25–1.75 **Cr**, 3.25–3.75 **Ni**, 0.06 **Mo**, 0.35 **Cu**	**Cold finished (bar):** ≤0.500 (≤12.70) **diam**, 125 (862) max **TS**
AMS 6260H		US	Bar, forgings, tube	0.07–0.13 **C**, 0.40–0.70 **Mn**, 0.025 **P**, 0.025 **S**, 0.20–0.35 **Si**, 1.00–1.40 **Cr**, 3.00–3.50 **Ni**, 0.08–0.15 **Mo**, 0.35 **Cu**	**Cold finished (bar):** ≤0.500 (≤12.70) **diam**, 125 (862) max **TS**
AMS 6265D		US	Bar, forgings, tube	0.07–0.13 **C**, 0.40–0.70 **Mn**, 0.015 **P**, 0.015 **S**, 0.20–0.35 **Si**, 1.00–1.40 **Cr**, 3.00–3.50 **Ni**, 0.08–0.15 **Mo**, 0.35 **Cu**	**Cold finished (bar):** ≤0.500 (≤12.70) **diam**, 125 (862) max **TS**
AMS 6267B		US	Bar, forgings, tube	0.07–0.13 **C**, 0.40–0.70 **Mn**, 0.015 **P**, 0.015 **S**, 0.20–0.35 **Si**, 1.00–1.40 **Cr**, 3.00–3.50 **Ni**, 0.08–0.15 **Mo**, 0.35 **Cu**	**Cold finished (bar):** ≤0.500 (≤12.70) **diam**, 125 (862) max **TS**
MIL–S–83030A	III	US	Bar, billets	0.07–0.13 **C**, 0.40–0.70 **Mn**, 0.015 **P**, 0.015 **S**, 0.20–0.35 **Si**, 1.00–1.40 **Cr**, 3.00–3.50 **Ni**, 0.80–0.15 **Mo**, 0.35 **Cu**; rem **Fe**	**As rolled, annealed**
MIL–S–7393C	Composition III	US	Bar, billets	0.07–0.13 **C**, 0.40–0.70 **Mn**, 0.025 **P**, 0.025 **S**, 0.20–0.35 **Si**, 1.00–1.40 **Cr**, 3.00–3.50 **Ni**, 0.08–0.15 **Mo**, 0.35 **Cu**; rem Fe	
DGN–B–300	9310 H	Mexico	Bar	0.07–0.13 **C**, 0.40–0.70 **Mn**, 0.040 **P**, 0.035 **S**, 0.20–0.35 **Si**, 1.00–1.45 **Cr**, 2.95–3.55 **Ni**, 0.08–0.15 **Mo**	

WROUGHT ALLOY STEELS

specification number	designation	country	product forms	composition	mechanical properties (see page iv for explanation)
ASTM A 689	9310 H	US	Bar	0.07–0.13 **C**, 0.40–0.70 **Mn**, 0.025 **P**, 0.025 **S**, 0.15–0.30 **Si**, 1.00–1.45 **Cr**, 2.95–3.55 **Ni**, 0.08–0.15 **Mo**	
ANSI/ASTM A 304	9310 H	US	Bar	0.07–0.13 **C**, 0.40–0.70 **Mn**, 0.025 **P**, 0.025 **S**, 0.15–0.30 **Si**, 1.00–1.45 **Cr**, 2.95–3.55 **Ni**, 0.08–0.15 **Mo**	
AISI 9310H		US	Bar	0.07–0.13 **C**, 0.40–0.70 **Mn**, 0.03 **P**, 0.040 **S**, 0.15–0.30 **Si**, 1.00–1.45 **Cr**, 2.95–3.55 **Ni**, 0.08–0.15 **Mo**	
NF A 35–553	10 NC 6	France	Strip	0.07–0.12 **C**, 0.60–0.90 **Mn**, 0.035 **P**, 0.035 **S**, 0.10–0.40 **Si**, 0.80–1.10 **Cr**, 1.20–1.60 **Ni**	
ANSI/ASTM A 710	Grade A, class 1	US	Plate, shapes, bar	0.07 **C**, 0.40–0.70 **Mn**, 0.025 **P**, 0.025 **S**, 0.35 **Si**, 0.60–0.90 **Cr**, 0.70–1.00 **Ni**, 0.15–0.25 **Mo**, 1.00–1.30 **Cu**, 0.02 **Nb**	**Precipitation heat treated:** ≥.50–.75 **diam**, (585) **TS**, (515) **YS**, 20 **El**
ANSI/ASTM A 710	Grade A, class 3	US	Plate, shapes, bar	0.07 **C**, 0.40–0.70 **Mn**, 0.025 **P**, 0.025 **S**, 0.35 **Si**, 0.60–0.90 **Cr**, 0.70–1.00 **Ni**, 0.15–0.25 **Mo**, 1.00–1.30 **Cu**, 0.02 **Nb**	**Precipitation heat treated:** ≥.50–.75 **diam**, (585) **TS**, (515) **YS**, 20 **El**
ANSI/ASTM A 710	Grade A, class 2	US	Plate, shapes, bar	0.07 **C**, 0.40–0.70 **Mn**, 0.025 **P**, 0.025 **S**, 0.35 **Si**, 0.60–0.90 **Cr**, 0.70–1.00 **Ni**, 0.15–0.25 **Mo**, 1.00–1.30 **Cu**, 0.02 **Nb**	**Precipitation heat treated:** ≥.50–.75 **diam**, (495) **TS**, (450) **YS**, 20 **El**
NF A 35–056	FS 12	France	Wire, rod	0.06–0.13 **C**, 0.40–0.60 **Mn**, 0.030 **P**, 0.030 **S**, 0.10 **Si**, 0.15 **Cr**, 0.15 **Ni**, 0.12 **Cu**	
BS S.152	S152B	UK	Bar: black, aircraft quality	0.06–0.11 **C**, 0.6–1.1 **Mn**, 0.028 **P**, 0.020 **S**, 0.10–0.70 **Si**, 9.8–11.2 **Cr**, 0.20–0.80 **Ni**, 0.5–1.0 **Mo**, 0.10–0.35 **V**, 0.004–0.012 **B**, 5.0–7.0 **Co**, 0.010–0.035 **N**, 0.20–0.45 **Nb**	**Annealed, hardened, tempered and retempered:** all **diam**, (1000) **TS**, (880) **YS**, 12 **El**
BS S.152	S152D	UK	Bar: bright, aircraft quality	0.06–0.11 **C**, 0.6–1.1 **Mn**, 0.028 **P**, 0.020 **S**, 0.10–0.70 **Si**, 9.8–11.2 **Cr**, 0.20–0.80 **Ni**, 0.5–1.0 **Mo**, 0.10–0.35 **V**, 0.004–0.012 **B**, 5.0–7.0 **Co**, 0.010–0.035 **N**, 0.20–0.45 **Nb**	**Annealed, hardened, tempered and retempered:** all **diam**, (1000) **TS**, (880) **YS**, 12 **El**
BS S.152	S152A	UK	Forging stock, billets, bar: aircraft quality	0.06–0.11 **C**, 0.6–1.1 **Mn**, 0.028 **P**, 0.020 **S**, 0.10–0.70 **Si**, 9.8–11.2 **Cr**, 0.20–0.80 **Ni**, 0.5–1.0 **Mo**, 0.10–0.35 **V**, 0.004–0.012 **B**, 5.0–7.0 **Co**, 0.010–0.035 **N**, 0.20–0.45 **Nb**	**Annealed, hardened, tempered and retempered:** all **diam**, (1000) **TS**, (880) **YS**, 12 **El**
BS S.152	S152C	UK	Forgings: aircraft quality	0.06–0.11 **C**, 0.6–1.1 **Mn**, 0.028 **P**, 0.020 **S**, 0.10–0.70 **Si**, 9.8–11.2 **Cr**, 0.20–0.80 **Ni**, 0.5–1.0 **Mo**, 0.10–0.35 **V**, 0.004–0.012 **B**, 5.0–7.0 **Co**, 0.010–0.035 **N**, 0.20–0.45 **Nb**	**Annealed, hardened, tempered and retempered:** all **diam**, (1000) **TS**, (880) **YS**, 12 **El**
ASTM A 699	Class 1	US	Bar, plate, shapes	0.06 **C**, 1.20–1.90 **Mn**, 0.04 **P**, 0.025 **S**, 0.35 **Si**, 0.25–0.35 **Mo**, 0.03–0.09 **Nb**	**As rolled:** ≤0.625 (≤16) **diam**, 90 (620) **TS**, 70 (485) **YS**, 18 **El**
ASTM A 699	Class 2	US	Bar, plate, shapes	0.06 **C**, 1.20–1.90 **Mn**, 0.04 **P**, 0.025 **S**, 0.35 **Si**, 0.25–0.35 **Mo**, 0.03–0.09 **Nb**	**Precipitation hardened:** ≤0.625 (≤16) **diam**, 90 (620) **TS**, 75 (515) **YS**, 18 **El**
ANSI/ASTM A 710	Grade B	US	Plate, shapes, bar	0.06 **C**, 0.40–0.65 **Mn**, 0.025 **P**, 0.025 **S**, 0.20–0.35 **Si**, 1.20–1.50 **Ni**, 1.00–1.30 **Cu**, 0.02 **Nb**	**Precipitation heat treated:** ≥0.50–0.75 **diam**, (605) **TS**, (515) **YS**, 18 **El**
ASTM A 699	Class 3	US	Plate	0.06 **C**, 1.20–1.90 **Mn**, 0.04 **P**, 0.025 **S**, 0.35 **Si**, 0.25–0.35 **Mo**, 0.03–0.09 **Nb**	**As rolled:** ≤0.625 (≤16) **diam**, 85 (585) **TS**, 70 (485) **YS**, 18 **El**
ASTM A 699	Class 4	US	Plate	0.06 **C**, 1.20–1.90 **Mn**, 0.04 **P**, 0.025 **S**, 0.35 **Si**, 0.25–0.35 **Mo**, 0.03–0.09 **Nb**	**Precipitation hardened:** ≤0.625 (≤16) **diam**, 85 (585) **TS**, 75 (515) **YS**, 18 **El**
NF A 35–056	FS 10	France	Wire, rod	0.05–0.12 **C**, 0.40–0.60 **Mn**, 0.030 **P**, 0.030 **S**, 0.15 **Cr**, 0.15 **Ni**, 0.12 **Cu**	

WROUGHT ALLOY STEELS

specification number	designation	country	product forms	composition	mechanical properties (see page iv for explanation)
NF A 35–056	FS 10	France	Wire, rod	0.05–0.12 **C**, 0.40–0.60 **Mn**, 0.030 **P**, 0.030 **S**, 0.15 **Cr**, 0.15 **Ni**, 0.12 **Cu**	
MIL–S–468508	Grade 300 A	US	Bar, plate, sheet, strip, forgings	0.03 **C**, 0.10 **Mn**, 0.010 **P**, 0.010 **S**, 0.10 **Si**, 18.0–19.0 **Ni**, 4.6–5.2 **Mo**, 0.05–0.15 **Al**, 8.5–9.5 **Co**, 0.5–0.8 **Ti**, rem **Fe**	**Maraged (bar, plate, forgings)**: all **diam**, 287 (1979) **TS**, 5 **El**
AMS 6521		US	Sheet, strip, plate	0.03 **C**, 0.10 **Mn**, 0.010 **P**, 0.010 **S**, 0.10 **Si**, 18.00–19.00 **Ni**, 4.60–5.20 **Mo**, 0.05–0.15 **Al**, 0.50–0.80 **Ti**	**Solution heat treated**: 70.065–0.090 **diam**, 280 (1931) **TS**, 270 (1868) **YS**, 2.5 **El**
MIL–S–47139	Type II, classes I and II	US	Bar, plate, sheet, strip, forgings	0.03 **C**, 0.10 **Mn**, 0.01 **P**, 0.01 **S**, 0.10 **Si**, 18.0–19.0 **Ni**, 4.6–5.2 **Mo**, 0.05–0.15 **Al**, 0.003 **B**, 0.05 **Ca**, 8.5–9.5 **Co**, 0.5–0.8 **Ti**, 0.02 **Zr**	**Maraged (bar, plate, forgings)**: all **diam**, 280 (1931) **TS**, 270 (1862) **YS**, 5 **El**
ANSI/ASTM A 538	Grade C	US	Plate	0.03 **C**, 0.10 **Mn**, 0.010 **P**, 0.010 **S**, 0.10 **Si**, 18.00–19.00 **Ni**, 4.60–5.20 **Mo**, 0.05–0.15 **Al**, 0.003 **B**, 0.05 **Ca**, 7.00–8.50 **Co**, 0.55–0.80 **Ti**, 0.02 **Zr**	**Maraged**: all **diam**, (1930) **TS**, (1900) **YS**, 6 **El**
ANSI/ASTM A 579	73	US	Forgings	0.03 **C**, 0.10 **Mn**, 0.01 **P**, 0.01 **S**, 0.10 **Si**, 18.0–19.0 **Ni**, 4.6–5.2 **Mo**, 0.05–0.15 **Al**, 0.003 **B**, 0.06 **Ca**, 8.5–9.5 **Co**, 0.50–0.80 **Ti**, 0.02 **Zr**	**Maraged**: all **diam**, 280 (1930) **TS**, 275 (1800) **YS**, 9 **El**
ANSI/ASTM A 579	72	US	Forgings	0.03 **C**, 0.10 **Mn**, 0.01 **P**, 0.01 **S**, 0.10 **Si**, 17.0–19.0 **Ni**, 4.6–5.2 **Mo**, 0.05–0.15 **Al**, 0.003 **B**, 0.06 **C**, 7.0–8.5 **Co**, 0.30–0.50 **Ti**, 0.02 **Zr**	**Maraged**: all **diam**, 255 (1760) **TS**, 250 (1725) **YS**, 10 **El**
AMS 6520		US	Sheet, strip, plate	0.03 **C**, 0.10 **Mn**, 0.010 **P**, 0.010 **S**, 0.10 **Si**, 17.00–19.00 **Ni**, 4.60–5.20 **Mo**, 0.05–0.15 **Al**, 7.00–8.50 **Co**, 0.30–0.50 **Ti**	**Solution heat treated, aged**: 0.065–0.090 **diam**, 255 (1758) **TS**, 245 (1689) **YS**, 2.5 **El**
MIL–S–47139	Type I, classes I and II	US	Bar, plate, sheet, strip, forgings	0.03 **C**, 0.10 **Mn**, 0.010 **P**, 0.010 **S**, 0.10 **Si**, 17.0–19.0 **Ni**, 4.6–5.2 **Mo**, 0.05–0.15 **Al**, 0.003 **B**, 0.05 **Ca**, 7.0–8.5 **Co**, 0.3–0.5 **Ti**, 0.02 **Zr**	**Maraged (bar, plate, forgings)**: all **diam**, 240 (1655) **TS**, 230 (1586) **YS**, 6 **El**
ANSI/ASTM A 538	Grade B	US	Plate	0.03 **C**, 0.10 **Mn**, 0.010 **P**, 0.010 **S**, 0.10 **Si**, 17.00–19.00 **Ni**, 4.60–5.10 **Mo**, 0.05–0.15 **Al**, 0.003 **B**, 0.05 **Ca**, 7.00–8.50 **Co**, 0.30–0.50 **Ti**, 0.02 **Zr**	**Maraged**: all **diam**, (1650) **TS**, (1580) **YS**, 6 **El**
ANSI/ASTM A 538	Grade A	US	Plate	0.03 **C**, 0.10 **Mn**, 0.010 **P**, 0.010 **S**, 0.10 **Si**, 17.00–19.00 **Ni**, 4.00–4.50 **Mo**, 0.05–0.15 **Al**, 0.003 **B**, 0.05 **Ca**, 7.0–8.5 **Co**, 0.10–0.25 **Ti**, 0.02 **Zr**	**Maraged**: all **diam**, (1450) **TS**, (1380) **YS**, 8 **El**
ANSI/ASTM A 579	71	US	Forgings	0.03 **C**, 0.10 **Mn**, 0.01 **P**, 0.01 **S**, 0.10 **Si**, 17.0–19.0 **Ni**, 3.0–3.5 **Mo**, 0.05–0.15 **Al**, 0.003 **B**, 0.06 **C**, 8.0–9.0 **Co**, 0.15–0.25 **Ti**, 0.02 **Zr**	**Maraged**: all **diam**, 210 (1450) **TS**, 200 (1380) **YS**, 12 **El**
ANSI/ASTM A 579	75	US	Forgings	0.03 **C**, 0.10 **Mn**, 0.01 **P**, 0.01 **S**, 0.12 **Si**, 4.75–5.25 **Cr**, 11.5–12.5 **Ni**, 2.75–3.25 **Mo**, 0.35–0.50 **Al**, 0.10–0.25 **Ti**	**Maraged**: all **diam**, 190 (1310) **TS**, 180 (1240) **YS**, 14 **El**
ANSI/ASTM A 590		US	Plate	0.03 **C**, 0.10 **Mn**, 0.010 **P**, 0.010 **S**, 0.10 **Si**, 4.50–5.50 **Cr**, 11.50–12.50 **Ni**, 2.75–3.25 **Mo**, 0.40 **Al**, 0.20–0.35 **Ti**	**Maraged**: all **diam**, (1300) **TS**, (1240) **YS**, 14 **El**
ANSI/ASTM A 579	74	US	Forgings	0.03 **C**, 0.10 **Mn**, 0.01 **P**, 0.01 **S**, 0.12 **Si**, 4.75–5.25 **Cr**, 11.5–12.5 **Ni**, 2.75–3.25 **Mo**, 0.25–0.40 **Al**, 0.05–0.15 **Ti**	**Maraged**: all **diam**, 170 (1175) **TS**, 160 (1105) **YS**, 15 **El**
ANSI/ASTM A 669		US	Tube: seamless	0.030 **C**, 1.20–2.00 **Mn**, 0.030 **P**, 0.030 **S**, 1.40–2.00 **Si**, 18.0–19.0 **Cr**, 4.25–5.25 **Ni**, 2.50–3.00 **Mo**	**Solution annealed**: all **diam**, 92 (630) **TS**, 64 (440) **YS**, 30 **El**
MIL–S–468508	Grade 250	US	Bar, plate, sheet, strip, forgings	0.03 **C**, 0.10 **Mn**, 0.010 **P**, 0.010 **S**, 0.10 **Si**, 17.9–19.0 **Ni**, 4.6–5.2 **Mo**, 0.05–0.15 **Al**, 7.0–8.5 **Co**, 0.3–0.5 **Ti**, rem **Fe**	**Maraged (bar, plate, forgings)**: all **diam**, 240 (1655) **YS**, 6 **El**
MIL–S–468508	Grade 200	US	Bar, plate, sheet, strip, forgings	0.03 **C**, 0.10 **Mn**, 0.010 **P**, 0.010 **S**, 0.10 **Si**, 17.0–19.0 **Ni**, 3.0–3.5 **Mo**, 0.05–0.15 **Al**, 8.0–9.0 **Co**, 0.15–0.25 **Ti**, rem **Fe**	**Maraged (bar, plate, forgings)**: all **diam**, 200 (1379) **YS**, 8 **El**

WROUGHT ALLOY STEELS

specification number	designation	country	product forms	composition	mechanical properties (see page iv for explanation)
MIL-S-468508	Grade 300	US	Bar, plate, sheet, strip, forgings	0.03 **C**, 0.10 **Mn**, 0.010 **P**, 0.010 **S**, 0.10 **Si**, 18.0–19.0 **Ni**, 4.6–5.2 **Mo**, 0.05–0.15 **Al**, 8.5–9.5 **Co**, 0.5–0.8 **Ti**, rem **Fe**	**Maraged (bar, plate, forgings)**: all **diam**, 280 (1931) **YS**, 5 **El**
ANSI/ASTM A 646	Marage 200	US	Blooms, billets: aircraft quality	0.03 **C**, 0.10 **Mn**, 0.010 **P**, 0.010 **S**, 0.10 **Si**, 17.0–19.0 **Ni**, 3.0–3.50 **Mo**, 0.05–0.15 **Al**, 8.0–9.0 **Co**, 0.10 **Ti**	**Annealed**
ANSI/ASTM A 646	Marage 250	US	Blooms, billets: aircraft quality	0.03 **C**, 0.10 **Mn**, 0.010 **P**, 0.010 **S**, 0.10 **Si**, 17.0–19.0 **Ni**, 4.6–5.2 **Mo**, 0.05–0.15 **Al**, 7.0–8.5 **Co**, 0.30–0.50 **Ti**; B, Zr, Ca added	**Annealed**
ANSI/ASTM A 646	Marage 300	US	Blooms, billets: aircraft quality	0.03 **C**, 0.10 **Mn**, 0.010 **P**, 0.010 **S**, 0.10 **Si**, 18.0–19.0 **Ni**, 4.7–5.2 **Mo**, 0.05 **Al**, 8.5–9.5 **Co**, 0.50–0.80 **Ti**	**Annealed**
MIL-S-3090B	Grade 2	US	Billets	0.02 **C**, 0.40 **Mn**, 0.020 **P**, 0.025 **S**, 0.25 **Si**, 0.25 **Cr**, 0.40 **Ni**, 0.025 **Al**, 0.15; **other elements, total**	
MIL-S-3090B	Grade 1	US	Billets	0.02 **C**, 0.40 **Mn**, 0.010 **P**, 0.010 **S**, 0.25 **Si**, 0.25 **Cr**, 0.40 **Ni**, 0.025 **Al**, 0.15; **other elements, total**	
AMS 6463		US	Wire	0.010 **C**, 0.10 **Mn**, 0.010 **P**, 0.010 **S**, 0.10 **Si**, 18.00–19.00 **Ni**, 4.50–6.00 **Mo**, 0.05–0.15 **Al**, 8.00–9.00 **Co**, 0.0025 **H**, 0.005 **N**, 0.0025 **O**, 0.65–0.80 **Ti**	**Solution heat treated, maraged (weld properties)**: 0.250 (6.35) **diam**, 280 (1931) **TS**, 270 (1862) **YS**, 3 **El**
ANSI/ASTM A 240	Grade XM 27	US	Plate, sheet, strip	0.010 **C**, 0.40 **Mn**, 0.40 **Si**, 25.00–27.50 **Cr**, 0.50 **Ni**, 0.75–1.50 **Mo**, 0.20 **Cu**, 0.015 **N**, 0.50 **Ni + Cu**, 0.020 **P**, 0.020 **S**	**Annealed**: all **diam**, (450) **TS**, (275) **YS**, 22 **El**
NF A 35-552	35 NCD 16	France	Bar		**Quenched and tempered**: (≤16) **diam**, (1230) **TS**, (1030) **YS**, 9 **El**
NF A 35-552	30 CND 8	France	Bar		**Quenched and tempered**: (≤16) **diam**, (1230) **TS**, (1030) **YS**, 10 **El**
NF A 35-552	20 MC 5	France	Bar		**Quenched and tempered**: (≤16) **diam**, (1230) **TS**, (980) **YS**, 8 **El**
ANSI/ASTM A 668	Class N	US	Forgings	0.040 **P**, 0.040 **S**	**Normalized, quenched, tempered**: ≥4 (102) **diam**, 170 (1175) **TS**, 140 (965) **YS**, 13 **El**
NF A 35-552	18 CD 4	France	Bar		**Quenched and tempered**: (≤16) **diam**, (1130) **TS**, (880) **YS**, 8 **El**
NF A 35-552	50 CV 4	France	Bar		**Quenched and tempered**: (≤16) **diam**, (1130) **TS**, (930) **YS**, 8 **El**
NF A 35-552	20 NCD 2	France	Bar		**Quenched and tempered**: (≤16) **diam**, (1130) **TS**, (930) **YS**, 8 **El**
NF A 35-552	18 NCD 6	France	Bar		**Quenched and tempered**: (≤16) **diam**, (1130) **TS**, (880) **YS**, 8 **El**
NF A 35-552	60 SC 7	France	Bar		**Quenched and tempered**: (≤16) **diam**, (1130) **TS**, (930) **YS**, 8 **El**
NF A 35-552	42 CD 4	France	Bar		**Quenched and tempered**: (≤16) **diam**, (1080) **TS**, (930) **YS**, 10 **El**
NF A 35-552	30 CD 12	France	Bar		**Quenched and tempered**: (≤16) **diam**, (1080) **TS**, (880) **YS**, 10 **El**
NF A 35-552	16 NC 6	France	Bar		**Quenched and tempered**: (≤16) **diam**, (1080) **TS**, (835) **YS**, 9 **El**
NF A 35-552	14 NC 11	France	Bar		**Quenched and tempered**: (≤16) **diam**, (1080) **TS**, (880) **YS**, 8 **El**

WROUGHT ALLOY STEELS

specification number	designation	country	product forms	composition	mechanical properties (see page iv for explanation)
NF A 35–552	35 NCD 6	France	Bar		**Quenched and tempered:** (≤16) **diam**, (1080) **TS**, (880) **YS**, 10 **El**
NF A 35–552	16 MC 5	France	Bar		**Quenched and tempered:** (≤16) **diam**, (1080) **TS**, (835) **YS**, 10 **El**
NF A 35–552	55 S 7	France	Bar		**Quenched and tempered:** (≤16) **diam**, (1080) **TS**, (880) **YS**, 9 **El**
NF A 35–552	45 SCD 6	France	Bar		**Quenched and tempered:** (≤16) **diam**, (1080) **TS**, (930) **YS**, 9 **El**
ANSI/ASTM A 434	Class BD	US	Bar		**Hot–rolled, quenched, tempered:** ≥1.5 (38.1) **diam**, 155 (1070) **TS**, 130 (900) **YS**, 14 **El**
DGN–B–298	Type BD	Mexico	Bar		**Hot or cold rolled and quenched and tempered:** (>38.1) **diam**, (1068) **TS**, (892) **YS**, 14 **El**
NF A 35–552	40 NCD 3	France	Bar		**Quenched and tempered:** (≤16) **diam**, (1030) **TS**, (835) **YS**, 10 **El**
COPANT 336	Type BD	COPANT	Bar		**Hot rolled:** (<50) **diam**, (1030) **TS**, (835) **YS**, 14 **El**; **Quenched and tempered:** (<50) **diam**, (910) **TS**, (715) **YS**, 14 **El**
ANSI/ASTM A 668	Class M	US	Forgings	0.040 **P**, 0.040 **S**	**Normalized, quenched, tempered:** ≥4 (102) **diam**, 145 (1000) **TS**, 120 (825) **YS**, 15 **El**
BS 4486 1969		UK	Bar		**Hot rolled:** 7/8 (20) **diam**, 143 (986) **TS**, 121 (834) **YS**, 6 **El**
NF A 35–552	42 C 4	France	Bar		**Quenched and tempered:** (≤16) **diam**, (980) **TS**, (785) **YS**, 10 **El**
NF A 35–552	35 CD 4	France	Bar		**Quenched and tempered:** (≤16) **diam**, (980) **TS**, (835) **YS**, 11 **El**
NF A 35–552	35 NC 6	France	Bar		**Quenched and tempered:** (≤16) **diam**, (980) **TS**, (785) **YS**, 11 **El**
NF A 35–552	40 CAD 6.12	France	Bar		**Quenched and tempered:** (≤16) **diam**, (980) **TS**, (785) **YS**, 10 **El**
NF A 35–552	45 S 7	France	Bar		**Quenched and tempered:** (≤16) **diam**, (980) **TS**, (785) **YS**, 11 **El**
MIL–S–13281D	C		Bar, shape, plate, sheet, strip		**Hot rolled or cold rolled, annealed or normalized:** all **diam**, (965) **TS**, (483) **YS**, 18 **El**
NF A 35–552	38 C 4	France	Bar		**Quenched and tempered:** (≤16) **diam**, (930) **TS**, (735) **YS**, 11 **El**
NF A 35–552	30 CD 4	France	Bar		**Quenched and tempered:** (≤16) **diam**, (930) **TS**, (785) **YS**, 12 **El**
ANSI/ASTM A 434	Class BC	US	Bar		**Hot rolled or cold finished, quenched, tempered:** ≥1.5 (38.1) **diam**, 130 (900) **TS**, 110 (760) **YS**, 16 **El**
DGN–B–298	Type BC	Mexico	Bar		**Hot or cold rolled and quenched and tempered:** (>38) **diam**, (892) **TS**, (755) **YS**, 16 **El**
NF A 35–552	42 C 2	France	Bar		**Quenched and tempered:** (≤16) **diam**, (880) **TS**, (685) **YS**, 12 **El**
NF A 35–552	32 C 4	France	Bar		**Quenched and tempered:** (≤16) **diam**, (880) **TS**, (685) **YS**, 12 **El**

WROUGHT ALLOY STEELS

specification number	designation	country	product forms	composition	mechanical properties (see page iv for explanation)
NF A 35-552	25 CD 4	France	Bar		**Quenched and tempered**: (≤16) **diam**, (880) **TS**, (735) **YS**, 12 **El**
NF A 35-552	30 NC 11	France	Bar		**Quenched and tempered**: (≤16) **diam**, (880) **TS**, (685) **YS**, 12 **El**
NF A 35-552	30 CAD 6.12	France	Bar		**Quenched and tempered**: (≤16) **diam**, (880) **TS**, (685) **YS**, 12 **El**
ANSI/ASTM A 238	Grade F	US	Forgings	0.045 **P**, 0.050 **S**	**Normalized, quenched and tempered**: ≤4 **diam**, (860) **TS**, (725) **YS**, 16 **El**
ANSI/ASTM A 730	Grade N	US	Forgings	0.045 **P**, 0.050 **S**	**Normalized, quenched and tempered**: all **diam**, 125 (860) **TS**, 105 (725) **YS**, 16 **El**
ANSI/ASTM A 668	Class L	US	Forgings	0.040 **P**, 0.040 **S**	**Normalized, quenched, tempered**: ≥4 (102) **diam**, 125 (860) **TS**, 105 (725) **YS**, 16 **El**
COPANT 336	Type BC	COPANT	Bar		**Hot rolled or cold finished**: (<50) **diam**, (835) **TS**, (735) **YS**, 16 **El**; **Quenched and tempered**: (120-180) **diam**, (735) **TS**, (590) **YS**, 16 **El**
NF A 35-552	20 NC 6	France	Bar		**Quenched and tempered**: (≤16) **diam**, (830) **TS**, (685) **YS**, 12 **El**; **As rolled**: (≤16) **diam**, (1230) **TS**, (980) **YS**, 14 **El**
NF A 35-552	38 C 2	France	Bar		**Quenched and tempered**: (≤16) **diam**, (830) **TS**, (635) **YS**, 13 **El**
NF A 35-552	35 M 5	France	Bar		**Quenched and tempered**: (≤16) **diam**, (830) **TS**, (635) **YS**, 12 **El**
ANSI/ASTM A 730	Grade N	US	Forgings	0.045 **P**, 0.050 **S**	**Normalized, quenched and tempered**: 4-7 (102-178) **diam**, 115 (795) **TS**, 95 (655) **YS**, 16 **El**
ANSI/ASTM A 671	A 517(P)	US	Pipe: electric, fusion, welded		**Quenched, tempered**: all **diam**, 113 (779) **TS**
ANSI/ASTM A 671	A 517(M)	US	Pipe: electric, fusion, welded		**Quenched, tempered**: all **diam**, 112 (772) **TS**
ANSI/ASTM A 671	A 517(L)	US	Pipe: electric, fusion, welded		**Quenched, tempered**: all **diam**, 111 (765) **TS**
BS 1506-661		UK	Bar		**Normalized and tempered**: all **diam**, (760) **TS**, (550) **YS**, 16 **El**
ANSI/ASTM A 434	Class BB	US	Bar		**Hot rolled or cold finished, quenched, tempered**: ≥1.5 (38.1) **diam**, 110 (760) **TS**, 90 (620) **YS**, 20 **El**
ANSI/ASTM A 238	Grade F	US	Forgings		**Normalized, quenched, tempered**: 7-10 (178-254) **diam**, 110 (760) **TS**, 85 (585) **YS**, 16 **El**
ANSI/ASTM A 671	A 517(K)	US	Pipe: electric, fusion, welded		**Quenched, tempered**: all **diam**, 110 (758) **TS**
DGN-B-298	Type BB	Mexico	Bar		**Hot or cold rolled and quenched and tempered**: (>38.1) **diam**, (755) **TS**, (617) **YS**, 20 **El**
ANSI/ASTM A 671	A 517(J)	US	Pipe: electric, fusion, welded		**Quenched, tempered**: all **diam**, 109 (752) **TS**
ANSI/ASTM A 671	A 517(H)	US	Pipe: electric, fusion, welded		**Quenched, tempered**: all **diam**, 108 (745) **TS**
ANSI/ASTM A 671	A 517(G)	US	Pipe: electric, fusion, welded		**Quenched, tempered**: all **diam**, 107 (738) **TS**
COPANT 336	Type BB	COPANT	Bar		**Hot rolled or cold finished**: (<50) **diam**, (735) **TS**, (590) **YS**, 20 **El**; **Quenched and tempered**: (120-180) **diam**, (640) **TS**, (490) **YS**, 20 **El**

WROUGHT ALLOY STEELS

specification number	designation	country	product forms	composition	mechanical properties (see page iv for explanation)
ANSI/ASTM A 671	A 517(F)	US	Pipe: electric, fusion, welded		**Quenched, tempered**: all **diam**, 106 (731) **TS**
ANSI/ASTM A 238	Grade E	US	Forgings	0.045 **P**, 0.050 **S**	**Normalized, quenched and tempered**: ≤7 **diam**, (725) **TS**, (550) **YS**, 20 **El**
ANSI/ASTM A 730	Grade M	US	Forgings	0.045 **P**, 0.050 **S**	**Normalized, quenched and tempered**: all **diam**, 105 (725) **TS**, 80 (550) **YS**, 20 **El**
ANSI/ASTM A 668	Class K	US	Forgings	0.040 **P**, 0.040 **S**	**Normalized, quenched, tempered**: ≥7 (178) **diam**, 105 (725) **TS**, 80 (550) **YS**, 20 **El**
ANSI/ASTM A 671	A 517(E)	US	Pipe: electric, fusion, welded		**Quenched, tempered**: all **diam**, 105 (724) **TS**
ANSI/ASTM A 671	A 517(D)	US	Pipe: electric, fusion, welded		**Quenched, tempered**: all **diam**, 104 (717) **TS**
ANSI/ASTM A 671	A 517(C)	US	Pipe: electric, fusion, welded		**Quenched, tempered**: all **diam**, 103 (710) **TS**
ANSI/ASTM A 671	A 517(B)	US	Pipe: electric, fusion, welded		**Quenched, tempered**: all **diam**, 102 (703) **TS**
ANSI/ASTM A 671	A 517(A)	US	Pipe: electric, fusion, welded		**Quenched, tempered**: all **diam**, 101 (696) **TS**
ANSI/ASTM A 238	Grade E	US	Forgings		**Normalized, quenched, tempered**: 7–10 (178–254) **diam**, 100 (690) **TS**, 75 (515) **YS**, 19 **El**
ANSI/ASTM A 730	Grade M	US	Forgings	0.045 **P**, 0.050 **S**	**Normalized, quenched and tempered**: 7–10 (178–254) **diam**, 100 (690) **TS**, 75 (515) **YS**, 19 **El**
ASTM A 672	A533–C13	US	Pipe: electric fusion welded		**Quenched, tempered**: all **diam**, 100 (689) **TS**
ANSI/ASTM A 671	A 353	US	Pipe: electric, fusion, welded		**Normalized, tempered**: all **diam**, 99 (683) **TS**
ANSI/ASTM A 671	A 553(I)	US	Pipe: electric, fusion, welded		**Normalized, tempered**: all **diam**, 99 (683) **TS**
ANSI/ASTM A 671	A 553(II)	US	Pipe: electric, fusion, welded		**Normalized, tempered**: all **diam**, 98 (676) **TS**
ANSI/ASTM A 238	Grade C	US	Forgings	0.045 **P**, 0.050 **S**	**Normalized and tempered**: ≤5 **diam**, (655) **TS**, (495) **YS**, 23 **El**
ANSI/ASTM A 238	Grade D	US	Forgings	0.045 **P**, 0.050 **S**	**Normalized, quenched and tempered**: ≤7 **diam**, (655) **TS**, (485) **YS**, 23 **El**
ANSI/ASTM A 730	Grade K	US	Forgings	0.045 **P**, 0.050 **S**	**Normalized and tempered**: all **diam**, 95 (655) **TS**, 72 (495) **YS**, 23 **El**
ANSI/ASTM A 730	Grade L	US	Forgings	0.045 **P**, 0.050 **S**	**Normalized, quenched and tempered**: all **diam**, 95 (655) **TS**, 70 (485) **YS**, 23 **El**
ANSI/ASTM A 668	Class J	US	Forgings	0.040 **P**, 0.040 **S**	**Normalized, tempered, or normalized, quenched, tempered**: ≥7 (178) **diam**, 95 (655) **TS**, 70 (485) **YS**, 20 **El**
ANSI/ASTM A 238	Grade C	US	Forgings		**Normalized, tempered**: 5–9 (127–229) **diam**, 95 (655) **TS**, 70 (485) **YS**, 22 **El**
ANSI/ASTM A 730	Grade K	US	Forgings	0.045 **P**, 0.050 **S**	**Normalized and tempered**: 5–9 (127–229) **diam**, 95 (655) **TS**, 70 (485) **YS**, 22 **El**
JIS C 2555	Class P 65	Japan	Sheet		**As agreed**: all **diam**, (637) **TS**, (392) **YS**, 12 **El**
ASTM A 672	A533–C12	US	Pipe: electric fusion welded		**Quenched, tempered**: all **diam**, 90 (621) **TS**
ANSI/ASTM A 238	Grade B	US	Forgings	0.45 **P**, 0.050 **S**	**Normalized and tempered**: ≤5 **diam**, (620) **TS**, (415) **YS**, 24 **El**
ANSI/ASTM A 730	Grade J	US	Forgings	0.045 **P**, 0.050 **S**	**Normalized and tempered**: all **diam**, 90 (620) **TS**, 60 (415) **YS**, 24 **El**
ANSI/ASTM A 668	Class H	US	Forgings	0.040 **P**, 0.040 **S**	**Normalized, tempered**: ≥7 (178) **diam**, 90 (620) **TS**, 60 (415) **YS**, 22 **El**

WROUGHT ALLOY STEELS

specification number	designation	country	product forms	composition	mechanical properties (see page iv for explanation)
ANSI/ASTM A 238	Grade B	US	Forgings		**Normalized, tempered**: 5–9 (127–229) **diam**, 90 (620) **TS**, 60 (415) **YS**, 22 **El**
ANSI/ASTM A 238	Grade D	US	Forgings		**Normalized, quenched, tempered**: 7–10 (178–254) **diam**, 90 (620) **TS**, 65 (450) **YS**, 20 **El**
ANSI/ASTM A 730	Grade J	US	Forgings	0.045 **P**, 0.050 **S**	**Normalized and tempered**: 5–9 (127–229) **diam**, 90 (620) **TS**, 60 (415) **YS**, 22 **El**
ANSI/ASTM A 730	Grade L	US	Forgings	0.045 **P**, 0.050 **S**	**Normalized, quenched and tempered**: 7–10 (178–254) **diam**, 90 (620) **TS**, 65 (450) **YS**, 20 **El**
NF A 35–552	20 M 5	France	Bar		**Quenched and tempered**: ($\leq$16) **diam**, (590) **TS**, (440) **YS**, 19 **El**
JIS C 2555	Class P 60	Japan	Sheet		**As agreed**: all **diam**, (588) **TS**, (363) **YS**, 15 **El**
ASTM A 672	A 202B	US	Pipe: electric fusion welded		**As–welded**: all **diam**, 85 (586) **TS**
MIL–S–18728C		US	Plate, sheet, strip		**Annealed**: all **diam**, 85 (581) **TS**; **Modified annealed**: <0.062 **diam**, 95 (655) **TS**, 75 (517) **YS**, 10 **El**; **Normalized**: <0.062 **diam**, 95 (655) **TS**, 75 (517) **YS**, 8 **El**
ASTM A 672	A 537B	US	Pipe: electric fusion welded		**Quenched, tempered**: all **diam**, 80 (552) **TS**
ASTM A 672	A533–C11	US	Pipe: electric fusion welded		**Quenched, tempered**: all **diam**, 80 (552) **TS**
ASTM A 672	A 302–B, C, or D	US	Pipe: electric fusion welded		**Normalized, tempered**: all **diam**, 80 (552) **TS**
ANSI/ASTM A 671	A 537(II)	US	Pipe: electric, fusion, welded		**Quenched, tempered**: all **diam**, 80 (552) **TS**
ANSI/ASTM A 238	Grade A	US	Forgings	0.045 **P**, 0.050 **S**	**Normalized and tempered**: $\leq$8 **diam**, (550) **TS**, (380) **YS**, 28 **El**
ANSI/ASTM A 730	Grade I	US	Forgings	0.045 **P**, 0.050 **S**	**Normalized and tempered**: all **diam**, 80 (550) **TS**, 55 (380) **YS**, 28 **El**
ANSI/ASTM A 668	Class G	US	Forgings	0.040 **P**, 0.040 **S**	**Annealed, or normalized, or normalized, tempered**: $\geq$12 (305) **diam**, 80 (550) **TS**, 50 (345) **YS**, 24 **El**
ANSI/ASTM A 238	Grade A	US	Forgings		**Normalized, tempered**: 8–20 (203–508) **diam**, 80 (550) **TS**, 55 (380) **YS**, 28 **El**
ANSI/ASTM A 730	Grade 1	US	Forgings	0.045 **P**, 0.050 **S**	**Normalized and tempered**: 8–20 (203–508) **diam**, 80 (550) **TS**, 55 (380) **YS**, 28 **El**
ASTM A 672	A 299	US	Pipe: electric fusion welded		**Normalized**: all **diam**, 75 (517) **TS**
ASTM A 672	A 225B	US	Pipe: electric fusion welded		**As–welded**: all **diam**, 75 (517) **TS**
ASTM A 672	A 204C	US	Pipe: electric fusion welded		**As–welded**: all **diam**, 75 (517) **TS**
ASTM A 672	A 202A	US	Pipe: electric fusion welded		**As–welded**: all **diam**, 75 (517) **TS**
ASTM A 672	A 302–A	US	Pipe: electric fusion welded		**Normalized, tempered**: all **diam**, 75 (517) **TS**
ANSI/ASTM A 671	A 299	US	Pipe: electric, fusion, welded		**Normalized**: all **diam**, 75 (517) **TS**
JIS G 3123	SS41B–D (Round)	Japan	Bar		**Cold finished**: (5–20) **diam**, (500) **TS**
ANSI/ASTM A 671	A 203(E)	US	Pipe: electric, fusion, welded		**Normalized**: all **diam**, 71 (490) **TS**
JIS C 2555	Class P 50	Japan	Sheet		**As agreed**: all **diam**, (490) **TS**, (304) **YS**, 19 **El**
ASTM A 672	A 537A		Pipe: electric fusion welded		**Normalized**: all **diam**, 70 (483) **TS**

WROUGHT ALLOY STEELS

specification number	designation	country	product forms	composition	mechanical properties (see page iv for explanation)
ASTM A 672	A 225A	US	Pipe: electric fusion welded		**As-welded**: all **diam**, 70 (483) **TS**
ASTM A 672	A 204B	US	Pipe: electric fusion welded		**As-welded**: all **diam**, 70 (483) **TS**
ANSI/ASTM A 671	A 203(B)	US	Pipe: electric, fusion, welded		**Normalized**: all **diam**, 70 (483) **TS**
ANSI/ASTM A 671	A 537(I)	US	Pipe: electric, fusion, welded		**Normalized**: all **diam**, 70 (483) **TS**
ANSI/ASTM A 671	A 203(D)	US	Pipe: electric, fusion, welded		**Normalized**: all **diam**, 66 (455) **TS**
ASTM A 672	A 204A	US	Pipe: electric fusion welded		**As-welded**: all **diam**, 65 (448) **TS**
ANSI/ASTM A 671	A 203(A)	US	Pipe: electric, fusion, welded		**Normalized**: all **diam**, 65 (448) **TS**
JIS C 2555	Class P 40	Japan	Sheet		**As agreed**: all **diam**, (392) **TS**, (245) **YS**, 22 **El**
JIS C 2552	Class S 18	Japan	Strip		**Cold rolled**: all **diam**, (382) **TS**, 20 **El**
JIS C 2552	Class S 20	Japan	Strip		**Cold rolled**: all **diam**, (363) **TS**, 22 **El**
ASTM A618	Grade I	US	Pipe		**Hot formed welded or seamless**: all **diam**, 50 (345) **TS**, 70 (480) **YS**
ASTM A618	Grade II	US	Pipe		**Hot formed welded or seamless**: all **diam**, 50 (345) **TS**, 70 (480) **YS**
ASTM A618	Grade III	US	Pipe		**Hot formed welded or seamless**: all **diam**, 50 (345) **TS**, 65 (445) **YS**
JIS C 2552	Class S 23	Japan	Strip		**Cold rolled**: all **diam**, (343) **TS**, 26 **El**
AISI 4028		US	Wire, rod		

WROUGHT TOOL STEELS

WROUGHT TOOL STEELS

specification number	designation	country	product forms	composition	mechanical properties (see page iv for explanation)
AISI type D7		US	Bar	2.35 **C**, 12.00 **Cr**, 1.00 **Mo**, 4.00 **V**	
NF A 35-590	2237 (Z 230 CVD 12.04)	France	Bar, forgings	2.3 **C**, 0.3 **Mn**, 12 **Cr**, 1.0 **Mo**, 4.0 **V**, 0.030 **P**, 0.030 **S**, 0.30 **Si**	
AISI type D3		US	Bar	2.25 **C**, 12.00 **Cr**	
AISI type D4		US	Bar	2.25 **C**, 12.00 **Cr**, 1.00 **Mo**	
AISI type A7		US	Bar	2.25 **C**, 5.25 **Cr**, 1.00 **Mo**, 1.00 **W**, 4.75 **V**	
COPANT 337	D3	COPANT	Bar, forgings	2.25 **C**, 12.00 **Cr**, 0.030 **P**, 0.030 **S**	
COPANT 337	D6	COPANT	Bar, forgings	2.25 **C**, 12.00 **Cr**, 1.00 **W**, 0.030 **P**, 0.030 **S**, 1.00 **Si**	
DGN-B-82	D 7	Mexico	Bar	2.20–2.50 **C**, 0.30–0.50 **Mn**, 12.00–13.00 **Cr**, 0.80–1.10 **Mo**, 3.75–4.25 **V**, 0.30–0.50 **Si**	
DGN-B-82	A 7	Mexico	Bar	2.15–2.50 **C**, 0.30–0.80 **Mn**, 5.00–5.50 **Cr**, 0.80–1.30 **Mo**, 0.95–1.30 **W**, 3.75–5.00 **V**, 0.30–0.80 **Si**	
ANSI/ASTM A 681	D7	US	Bar, plate, sheet, strip, rod, wire, forgings	2.15–2.50 **C**, 0.60 **Mn**, 11.50–13.50 **Cr**, 0.70–1.20 **Mo**, 3.80–4.40 **V**, 0.030 **P**, 0.030 **S**, 0.60 **Si**	**Annealed**
DGN-B-82	D 4	Mexico	Bar	2.10–2.30 **C**, 0.20–0.40 **Mn**, 11.50–12.50 **Cr**, 0.70–0.90 **Mo**, 0.20–0.80 **V**, 0.10–0.40 **Si**	
DGN-B-82	D 3	Mexico	Bar	2.10–2.30 **C**, 0.20–0.40 **Mn**, 11.50–12.50 **Cr**, 0.50 **Ni**, 0.20–1.00 **V**, 0.10–0.40 **Si**	
SFS 900	SFS 909	Finland	Bar, forgings	2.10 **C**, 0.75 **Mn**, 13.00 **Cr**, 1.30 **W**, 0.30 **Si**	
ANSI/ASTM A 681	D4	US	Bar, plate, sheet, strip, rod, wire, forgings	2.05–2.40 **C**, 0.60 **Mn**, 11.00–13.00 **Cr**, 0.70–1.20 **Mo**, 1.00 **V**, 0.030 **P**, 0.030 **S**, 0.60 **Si**	**Annealed**
ANSI/ASTM A 681	A7	US	Bar, plate, sheet, strip, rod, wire, forgings	2.00–2.85 **C**, 0.80 **Mn**, 5.00–5.75 **Cr**, 0.90–1.40 **Mo**, 0.50–1.50 **W**, 3.90–5.15 **V**, 0.030 **P**, 0.030 **S**, 0.50 **Si**	**Annealed**
ASTM A 685	Type D3	US	Rectangular bar: finish, machined	2.00–2.35 **C**, 0.60 **Mn**, 11.00–13.50 **Cr**, 1.00 **W**, 1.00 **V**, 0.030 **P**, 0.030 **S**, 0.60 **Si**	
ANSI/ASTM A 681	D3	US	Bar, plate, sheet, strip, rod, wire, forgings	2.00–2.35 **C**, 0.60 **Mn**, 11.00–13.50 **Cr**, 1.00 **W**, 1.00 **V**, 0.030 **P**, 0.030 **S**, 0.60 **Si**	**Annealed**
IS 3749	T215Cr12	India	Bar, rings, shapes	2.00–2.30 **C**, 0.25–0.50 **Mn**, 11.0–13.0 **Cr**, 0.80 **Mo**, 0.80 **V**, 0.035 **P**, 0.035 **S**, 0.10–0.35 **Si**	**Annealed**
IS: 4367	T215Cr12	India	Forgings	2.00–2.30 **C**, 0.25–0.50 **Mn**, 11.0–13.0 **Cr**, 0.80 **Mo**, 0.80 **V**, 0.10–0.35 **Si**	**Annealed**
NF A 35-590	2234 (Z 200 CD 12)	France	Bar, forgings	2.0 **C**, 0.3 **Mn**, 12.0 **Cr**, 0.8 **Mo**, 0.2 **V**, 0.030 **P**, 0.030 **S**, 0.3 **Si**	
NF A 35-590	2233 (Z200 C 12)	France	Bar, forgings	2.0 **C**, 0.30 **Mn**, 12.0 **Cr**, 0.030 **P**, 0.030 **S**, 0.30 **Si**	
BS 4659	BD 3	UK	Bar, section, coil, rod, sheet, strip, forgings	1.90–2.30 **C**, 0.60 **Mn**, 12.0–13.0 **Cr**, 0.50 **V**, 0.60 **Si**	
NS 13882	NS 13882-02	Norway	Bar, forgings	1.90–2.20 **C**, 0.60–0.90 **Mn**, 12.0–13.5 **Cr**, 1.00–1.50 **W**, 0.030 **P**, 0.020 **S**, 0.20–0.40 **Si**	**Annealed**
SFS 909		Finland	Bar, forgings	1.90–2.20 **C**, 0.60–0.90 **Mn**, 12.0–13.5 **Cr**, 1.00–1.50 **W**, 0.030 **P**, 0.020 **S**, 0.20–0.40 **Si**	
SIS 14 23 12	SIS 23 12-02	Sweden	Bar, forgings	1.90–2.20 **C**, 0.60–0.90 **Mn**, 12.0–13.5 **Cr**, 1.00–1.50 **W**, 0.030 **P**, 0.020 **S**, 0.20–0.40 **Si**	
JIS G 4404	SKD 1	Japan	Bar, forgings	1.80–2.40 **C**, 0.60 **Mn**, 12.00–15.00 **Cr**, 0.50 **Ni**, 0.30 **V**, 0.25 **Cu**, 0.030 **P**, 0.030 **S**, 0.40 **Si**	**Annealed; Annealed and quenched and tempered**

WROUGHT TOOL STEELS

specification number	designation	country	product forms	composition	mechanical properties (see page iv for explanation)
JIS G 4404	SKD 2	Japan	Bar, forgings	1.80–2.20 **C**, 0.60 **Mn**, 12.00–15.00 **Cr**, 0.50 **Ni**, 2.50–3.50 **W**, 0.25 **Cu**, 0.030 **P**, 0.030 **S**, 0.40 **Si**	**Annealed**; **Annealed and quenched and tempered**
NF A 35–590	2236 (Z 180 CKD 12.03)	France	Bar, forgings	1.80 **C**, 0.3 **Mn**, 12 **Cr**, 0.8 **Mo**, 0.5 **V**, 3.0 **Co**, 0.030 **P**, 0.030 **S**, 0.3 **Si**	
NF A 35–590	4375 (Z 175 KWDCV 10–07–05–05–04)	France	Bar, forgings	1.75 **C**, 0.3 **Mn**, 4.0 **Cr**, 5.0 **Mo**, 6.5 **W**, 5.0 **V**, 10.0 **Co**, 0.030 **P**, 0.030 **S**, 0.30 **Si**	
NF A 35–590	4175 (Z 165 WKCV 12–10–05–04)	France	Bar, forgings	1.65 **C**, 0.3 **Mn**, 4.0 **Cr**, 1.0 **Mo**, 12.0 **W**, 5.0 **V**, 10.0 **Co**, 0.030 **P**, 0.030 **S**, 0.30 **Si**	
BS 4659	BD 2A	UK	Bar, section, coil, rod, sheet, strip, forgings	1.60–1.90 **C**, 0.60 **Mn**, 12.0–13.0 **Cr**, 0.70–0.90 **Mo**, 0.25–1.00 **V**, 0.60 **Si**	
AISI type T15		US	Bar	1.60 **C**, 4.00 **Cr**, 12.00 **W**, 5.00 **V**, 5.00 **Co**	
NF A 35–590	2235 (Z 160 CDV 12)	France	Bar, forgings	1.6 **C**, 0.3 **Mn**, 12 **Cr**, 0.8 **Mo**, 0.4 **V**, 0.030 **P**, 0.030 **S**, 0.3 **Si**	
IS 3749	T160Cr12	India	Bar, rings, shapes	1.50–1.70 **C**, 0.25–0.50 **Mn**, 11.0–13.0 **Cr**, 0.80 **Mo**, 0.80 **V**, 0.035 **P**, 0.035 **S**, 0.10–0.35 **Si**	**Annealed**
COPANT 337	T15	COPANT	Bar, forgings	1.50–1.60 **C**, 0.20–0.40 **Mn**, 3.75–5.00 **Cr**, 1.00 **Mo**, 12.00–13.00 **W**, 4.50–5.25 **V**, 4.75–5.25 **Co**, 0.030 **P**, 0.030 **S**, 0.20–0.40 **Si**	
DGN–B–82	T 15	Mexico	Bar	1.50–1.60 **C**, 0.10–0.40 **Mn**, 4.50–4.75 **Cr**, 0.50 **Mo**, 12.50–13.50 **W**, 4.50–4.75 **V**, 4.75–5.25 **Co**, 0.10–0.40 **Si**	
DGN–B–82	M 15	Mexico	Bar	1.50–1.60 **C**, 0.10–0.40 **Mn**, 4.00–4.75 **Cr**, 3.00–5.00 **Mo**, 6.25–6.75 **W**, 4.75–5.25 **V**, 4.75–5.25 **Co**, 0.10–0.40 **Si**	
ANSI/ASTM A 600	T15	US	Bar, forgings, plate, sheet, strip	1.50–1.60 **C**, 0.15–0.40 **Mn**, 3.75–5.00 **Cr**, 1.00 **Mo**, 11.75–13.00 **W**, 4.50–5.25 **V**, 4.75–5.25 **Co**, 0.03 **P**, 0.03 **S**, 0.15–0.40 **Si**	**Annealed**
AISI type D2		US	Bar	1.50 **C**, 12.00 **Cr**, 1.00 **Mo**, 1.00 **V**	
AISI type D5		US	Bar	1.50 **C**, 12.00 **Cr**, 1.00 **Mo**, 3.00 **Co**	
NF A 35–590	4171 (Z 150 WKCV 12–05–05–04)	France	Bar, forgings	1.5 **C**, 0.3 **Mn**, 4.0 **Cr**, 0.5 **Mo**, 12.0 **W**, 5.0 **V**, 5.0 **Co**, 0.030 **P**, 0.030 **S**, 0.30 **Si**	
NF A 35–590	4373 (Z 150 WDKCV 07–05–05–05–04)	France	Bar, forgings	1.5 **C**, 0.3 **Mn**, 4.0 **Cr**, 5.0 **Mo**, 6.5 **W**, 5.0 **V**, 5.0 **Co**, 0.030 **P**, 0.030 **S**, 0.30 **Si**	
SIS 14 23 10	SIS 23 10–02	Sweden	Bar, forgings	1.45–1.65 **C**, 0.30–0.60 **Mn**, 11.0–13.0 **Cr**, 0.70–0.90 **Mo**, 0.70–1.00 **V**, 0.030 **P**, 0.020 **S**, 0.20–0.40 **Si**	
BS 4659	BM 15	UK	Bar, section, coil, rod, sheet, strip, forgings	1.45–1.60 **C**, 0.40 **Mn**, 4.5–5.0 **Cr**, 2.75–3.25 **Mo**, 6.25–7.0 **W**, 4.75–5.25 **V**, 4.5–5.5 **Co**, 0.40 **Si**	
JIS G 4403	SKH 10	Japan	Bar, forgings	1.45–1.60 **C**, 0.40 **Mn**, 3.80–4.50 **Cr**, 0.25 **Ni**, 11.50–13.50 **W**, 4.20–5.20 **V**, 4.20–5.20 **Co**, 0.25 **Cu**, 0.030 **P**, 0.030 **S**, 0.40 **Si**	**Annealed**; **Quenched and tempered**
AISI type 06		US	Bar	1.45 **C**, 0.80 **Mn**, 0.25 **Mo**, 1.00 **Si**	
COPANT 337	D2	COPANT	Bar, forgings	1.40–1.60 **C**, 0.20–0.60 **Mn**, 11.00–13.00 **Cr**, 0.70–1.20 **Mo**, 1.00 **Co**, 0.030 **P**, 0.030 **S**, 0.20–0.60 **Si**	
BS 4659	BT 15	UK	Bar, section, coil, rod, sheet, strip, forgings	1.40–1.60 **C**, 0.40 **Mn**, 4.25–5.0 **Cr**, 1.0 **Mo**, 12.0–13.0 **W**, 4.75–5.25 **V**, 4.5–5.5 **Co**, 0.40 **Si**	
BS 4659	BD 2	UK	Bar, section, coil, rod, sheet, strip, forgings	1.40–1.60 **C**, 0.60 **Mn**, 11.5–12.5 **Cr**, 0.70–1.20 **Mo**, 0.25–1.00 **V**, 0.60 **Si**	

specification number	designation	country	product forms	composition	mechanical properties (see page iv for explanation)
JIS G 4404	SKD 11	Japan	Bar, forgings	1.40–1.60 **C**, 0.60 **Mn**, 11.00–13.00 **Cr**, 0.50 **Ni**, 0.80–1.20 **Mo**, 0.20–0.50 **V**, 0.25 **Cu**, 0.030 **P**, 0.030 **S**, 0.40 **Si**	**Annealed; Annealed and quenched and tempered**
ASTM A 685	Type D2	US	Rectangular bar: finish, machined	1.40–1.60 **C**, 0.60 **Mn**, 11.00–13.00 **Cr**, 0.70–1.20 **Mo**, 1.10 **V**, 1.00 **Co**, 0.030 **P**, 0.030 **S**, 0.60 **Si**	
DGN–B–82	D 2	Mexico	Bar	1.40–1.60 **C**, 0.20–0.40 **Mn**, 11.50–12.50 **Cr**, 0.70–0.90 **Mo**, 0.20–1.00 **V**, 0.10–0.40 **Si**	
ANSI/ASTM A 681	D2	US	Bar, plate, sheet, strip, rod, wire, forgings	1.40–1.60 **C**, 0.60 **Mn**, 11.00–13.00 **Cr**, 0.70–1.20 **Mo**, 1.10 **V**, 1.00 **Co**, 0.030 **P**, 0.030 **S**, 0.60 **Si**	**Annealed**
ANSI/ASTM A 681	D5	US	Bar, plate, sheet, strip, rod, wire, forgings	1.40–1.60 **C**, 0.60 **Mn**, 11.00–13.00 **Cr**, 0.70–1.20 **Mo**, 1.00 **V**, 2.50–3.50 **Co**, 0.030 **P**, 0.030 **S**, 0.60 **Si**	**Annealed**
NF A 35–590	2121 (140 SMD 4)	France	Bar, forgings	1.4 **C**, 1.0 **Mn**, 0.3 **Mo**, 0.030 **P**, 0.030 **S**, 1.0 **Si**	
NF A 35–590	2132 (140 C 3)	France	Bar, forgings	1.4 **C**, 0.3 **Mn**, 0.75 **Cr**, 0.15 **V**, 0.030 **P**, 0.030 **S**, 0.3 **Si**	
DGN–B–82	D 5	Mexico	Bar	1.35–1.60 **C**, 0.20–0.40 **Mn**, 12.00–13.00 **Cr**, 0.15–0.50 **Ni**, 0.80–1.15 **Mo**, 0.40–0.60 **V**, 0.70–3.50 **Co**, 0.40–0.60 **Si**	
AISI type A10		US	Bar	1.35 **C**, 1.80 **Mn**, 1.80 **Ni**, 1.50 **Mo**, 1.25 **Si**	
NF A 35–590	1230 (Y_2 xxC)	France	Bar, forgings	1.35 **C**, 0.10–0.40 **Mn**, 0.025 **P**, 0.025 **S**, 0.10–0.30 **Si**	
NF A 35–590	1200 (Y_2 135)	France	Bar, forgings	1.35 **C**, 0.10–0.40 **Mn**, 0.025 **P**, 0.025 **S**, 0.10–0.30 **Si**	
COPANT 337	O6	COPANT	Bar, forgings	1.30–1.55 **C**, 0.40–1.00 **Mn**, 0.30 **Cr**, 0.20–0.30 **Mo**, 0.030 **P**, 0.030 **S**, 0.75–1.25 **Si**	
IS 3749	T140W4Cr50	India	Bar, rings, shapes	1.30–1.50 **C**, 0.25–0.50 **Mn**, 0.30–0.70 **Cr**, 3.50–4.20 **W**, 0.035 **P**, 0.035 **S**, 0.10–0.35 **Si**	**Annealed**
JIS G 4401	Class 1	Japan	Bar, forgings	1.30–1.50 **C**, 0.50 **Mn**, 0.20 **Cr**, 0.25 **Ni**, 0.25 **Cu**, 0.030 **P**, 0.030 **S**, 0.35 **Si**	**Annealed; Annealed and quenched and tempered**
JIS G 4404	SKS 8	Japan	Bar, forgings	1.30–1.50 **C**, 0.50 **Mn**, 0.20–0.50 **Cr**, 0.25 **Ni**, 0.25 **Cu**, 0.030 **P**, 0.030 **S**, 0.35 **Si**	**Annealed; Annealed and quenched and tempered**
JIS G 4404	SKS 1	Japan	Bar, forgings	1.30–1.40 **C**, 0.50 **Mn**, 0.50–1.00 **Cr**, 0.25 **Ni**, 4.00–5.00 **W**, 0.20 **V**, 0.25 **Cu**, 0.030 **P**, 0.030 **S**, 0.35 **Si**	**Annealed; Annealed and quenched and tempered**
AISI type M4		US	Bar	1.30 **C**, 4.00 **Cr**, 4.50 **Mo**, 5.50 **W**, 4.00 **V**	
NF A 35–590	4161 (Z 130 WCV 12–04–04)	France	Bar, forgings	1.3 **C**, 0.3 **Mn**, 4.0 **Cr**, 0.5 **Mo**, 12.0 **W**, 3.5 **V**, 0.030 **P**, 0.030 **S**, 0.30 **Si**	
NF A 35–590	4361 (Z 130 WDCV 06–05–04–04)	France	Bar, forgings	1.30 **C**, 0.3 **Mn**, 4.0 **Cr**, 4.5 **Mo**, 5.5 **W**, 4.0 **V**, 0.030 **P**, 0.030 **S**, 0.30 **Si**	
ASTM A 685	Type 06	US	Bar: finish, machined	1.25–1.55 **C**, 0.30–1.10 **Mn**, 0.30 **Cr**, 0.20–0.30 **Mo**, 0.030 **P**, 0.030 **S**, 0.55–1.50 **Si**	
ANSI/ASTM A 681	O6	US	Bar, plate, sheet, strip, rod, wire, forgings	1.25–1.55 **C**, 0.30–1.10 **Mn**, 0.30 **Cr**, 0.20–0.30 **Mo**, 0.030 **P**, 0.030 **S**, 0.55–1.50 **Si**	**Annealed**
ANSI/ASTM A 681	A10	US	Bar, plate, sheet, strip, rod, wire, forgings	1.25–1.50 **C**, 1.60–2.10 **Mn**, 0.030 **Cr**, 1.55–2.05 **Ni**, 1.25–1.75 **Mo**, 0.030 **P**, 0.030 **S**, 1.00–1.50 **Si**	**Annealed**
IS 3749	T133	India	Bar, rings, shapes	1.25–1.40 **C**, 0.20–0.35 **Mn**, 0.035 **P**, 0.035 **S**, 0.10–0.35 **Si**	**Annealed**

WROUGHT TOOL STEELS

specification number	designation	country	product forms	composition	mechanical properties (see page iv for explanation)
IS 3749	T133Cr45	India	Bar, rings, shapes	1.25–1.40 **C**, 0.20–0.35 **Mn**, 0.30–0.60 **Cr**, 0.30 **V**, 0.035 **P**, 0.035 **S**, 0.10–0.35 **Si**	**Annealed**
IS 4367	T133	India	Forgings	1.25–1.40 **C**, 0.20–0.35 **Mn**, 0.10–0.30 **Si**	**Annealed**
COPANT 337	M4	COPANT	Bar, forgings	1.25–1.40 **C**, 0.15–0.40 **Mn**, 3.75–4.75 **Cr**, 4.25–5.50 **Mo**, 5.25–6.50 **W**, 3.75–4.50 **V**, 0.030 **P**, 0.030 **S**, 0.20–0.45 **Si**	
BS 4659	BM 4	UK	Bar, section, coil, rod, sheet, strip, forgings	1.25–1.40 **C**, 0.40 **Mn**, 3.75–4.5 **Cr**, 4.25–5.0 **Mo**, 5.75–6.5 **W**, 3.75–4.25 **V**, 0.60 **Co**, 0.40 **Si**	
BS 4659	BT 42	UK	Bar, section, coil, rod, sheet, strip, forgings	1.25–1.40 **C**, 0.40 **Mn**, 3.75–4.5 **Cr**, 2.75–3.5 **Mo**, 8.5–9.5 **W**, 2.75–3.25 **V**, 9.0–10.0 **Co**, 0.40 **Si**	
JIS G 4403	SKH 54	Japan	Bar, forgings	1.25–1.40 **C**, 0.40 **Mn**, 3.80–4.50 **Cr**, 0.25 **Ni**, 4.50–5.50 **Mo**, 5.30–6.50 **W**, 3.90–4.50 **V**, 0.25 **Cu**, 0.030 **P**, 0.030 **S**, 0.40 **Si**	**Annealed; Quenched and tempered**
DGN–B–82	F 3	Mexico	Bar	1.25–1.40 **C**, 0.10–0.40 **Mn**, 0.50–1.00 **Cr**, 3.50–4.00 **W**, 0.10–0.40 **Si**	
DGN–B–82	F 2	Mexico	Bar	1.25–1.40 **C**, 0.10–0.40 **Mn**, 0.20–0.40 **Cr**, 0.20–0.40 **Mo**, 3.25–4.00 **W**, 0.10–0.50 **Si**	
ANSI/ASTM A 600	M4	US	Bar, forgings, plate, sheet, strip	1.25–1.40 **C**, 0.15–0.40 **Mn**, 3.75–4.75 **Cr**, 4.25–5.50 **Mo**, 5.25–6.50 **W**, 3.75–4.50 **V**, 0.03 **P**, 0.03 **S**, 0.20–0.45 **Si**	**Annealed**
DGN–B–82	M 4	Mexico	Bar	1.25–1.30 **C**, 0.10–0.40 **Mn**, 4.25–4.50 **Cr**, 4.50–4.75 **Mo**, 5.50–6.00 **W**, 3.75–4.25 **V**, 0.10–0.40 **Si**	
AISI type M46		US	Bar	1.25 **C**, 4.00 **Cr**, 8.25 **Mo**, 2.00 **W**, 3.20 **V**, 8.25 **Co**	
AISI type A3		US	Bar	1.25 **C**, 5.00 **Cr**, 1.00 **Mo**, 1.00 **V**	
ANSI/ASTM A 600	M46	US	Bar, forgings, plate, sheet, strip	1.22–1.30 **C**, 0.20–0.40 **Mn**, 3.70–4.20 **Cr**, 8.00–8.50 **Mo**, 1.90–2.20 **W**, 3.00–3.30 **V**, 7.80–8.80 **Co**, 0.03 **P**, 0.03 **S**, 0.40–0.65 **Si**	**Annealed**
DGN–B–82	T 9	Mexico	Bar	1.22–1.28 **C**, 0.10–0.40 **Mn**, 3.75–4.25 **Cr**, 0.75 **Mo**, 18.00–18.50 **W**, 3.75–4.25 **V**, 0.10–0.40 **Si**	
ANSI/ASTM A 681	F2	US	Bar, plate, sheet, strip, rod, wire, forgings	1.20–1.40 **C**, 0.50 **Mn**, 0.20–0.40 **Cr**, 3.00–4.50 **W**, 0.030 **P**, 0.030 **S**, 0.50 **Si**	**Annealed**
COPANT 337	R1	COPANT	Bar, forgings	1.20–1.35 **C**, 0.40 **Mn**, 3.75–5.00 **Cr**, 3.30–4.00 **Mo**, 9.75–11.25 **W**, 3.00–3.50 **V**, 10.00–11.25 **Co**, 0.030 **P**, 0.030 **S**, 0.45 **Si**	
SFS 918		Finland	Bar, forgings	1.20–1.35 **C**, 0.20–0.40 **Mn**, 3.8–4.5 **Cr**, 3.3–3.8 **Mo**, 9.0–10.5 **W**, 3.0–3.5 **V**, 9.5–11.0 **Co**, 0.030 **P**, 0.030 **S**, 0.15–0.40 **Si**	
JIS G 3311	SKS11M	Japan	Strip	1.20–1.30 **C**, 0.50 **Mn**, 0.20–0.50 **Cr**, 0.25 **Ni**, 3.00–4.00 **W**, 0.10–0.30 **V**, 0.25 **Cu**, 0.030 **P**, 0.030 **S**, 0.35 **Si**	
JIS G 4404	SKS 11	Japan	Bar, forgings	1.20–1.30 **C**, 0.50 **Mn**, 0.20–0.50 **Cr**, 0.25 **Ni**, 3.00–4.00 **W**, 0.10–0.30 **V**, 0.25 **Cu**, 0.030 **P**, 0.030 **S**, 0.35 **Si**	**Annealed; Annealed and quenched and tempered**
DGN–B–82	A 3	Mexico	Bar	1.20–1.30 **C**, 0.40–0.60 **Mn**, 5.00–5.50 **Cr**, 1.05–1.25 **Mo**, 0.90–1.10 **V**, 0.10–0.40 **Si**	

WROUGHT TOOL STEELS

specification number	designation	country	product forms	composition	mechanical properties (see page iv for explanation)
ANSI/ASTM A 681	A3	US	Bar, plate, sheet, strip, rod, wire, forgings	1.20–1.30 **C**, 0.40–0.60 **Mn**, 4.75–5.50 **Cr**, 0.90–1.40 **Mo**, 0.80–1.40 **V**, 0.030 **P**, 0.030 **S**, 0.50 **Si**	**Annealed**
SFS 900	SFS 918	Finland	Bar, forgings	1.20 **C**, 0.30 **Mn**, 4.00 **Cr**, 3.50 **Mo**, 9.50 **W**, 3.20 **V**, 10.00 **Co**, 0.30 **Si**	
AISI type M43		US	Bar	1.20 **C**, 3.75 **Cr**, 8.00 **Mo**, 2.75 **W**, 1.60 **V**, 8.25 **Co**	
AISI type 07		US	Bar	1.20 **C**, 0.75 **Cr**, 1.75 **W**	
AISI type M3	Class 2	US	Bar	1.20 **C**, 4.00 **Cr**, 5.00 **Mo**, 6.00 **W**, 3.00 **V**	
NF A 35-590	1161 (Y_1 xxV)	France	Bar, forgings	1.20 **C**, 0.10–0.30 **Mn**, 0.020 **P**, 0.020 **S**, 0.10–0.25 **Si**	
NF A 35-590	1231 (Y_2 xxC)	France	Bar, forgings	1.20 **C**, 0.10–0.40 **Mn**, 0.025 **P**, 0.025 **S**, 0.10–0.30 **Si**	
NF A 35-590	1101 (Y_1 120)	France	Bar, forgings	1.20 **C**, 0.10–0.30 **Mn**, 0.020 **P**, 0.020 **S**, 0.10–0.25 **Si**	
NF A 35-590	1201 (Y_2 120)	France	Bar, forgings	1.20 **C**, 0.10–0.40 **Mn**, 0.025 **P**, 0.025 **S**, 0.10–0.30 **Si**	
COPANT 337	M3, type 2	COPANT	Bar, forgings	1.15–2.25 **C**, 0.15–0.40 **Mn**, 3.75–4.50 **Cr**, 4.75–6.50 **Mo**, 5.00–6.75 **W**, 2.75–3.25 **V**, 0.030 **P**, 0.030 **S**, 0.20–0.45 **Si**	
COPANT 337	M43	COPANT	Bar, forgings	1.15–2.25 **C**, 0.20–0.40 **Mn**, 3.50–4.25 **Cr**, 7.50–8.50 **Mo**, 2.25–3.00 **W**, 1.50–1.75 **V**, 7.75–8.75 **Co**, 0.030 **P**, 0.030 **S**, 0.15–0.50 **Si**	
BS 4656	BF 1	UK	Bar, section, coil, rod, sheet, strip, forgings	1.15–1.35 **C**, 0.40 **Mn**, 0.25–0.50 **Cr**, 1.3–1.6 **W**, 0.30 **V**, 0.40 **Si**	
IS: 4367	T123W14Co5CrV4	India	Forgings	1.15–1.30 **C**, 0.20–0.40 **Mn**, 4.00–4.50 **Cr**, 0.60 **Mo**, 13.0–14.5 **W**, 3.70–4.20 **V**, 4.75–5.25 **Co**, 0.10–0.35 **Si**	**Annealed**
JIS G 4403	SKH 57	Japan	Bar, forgings	1.15–1.30 **C**, 0.40 **Mn**, 3.80–4.50 **Cr**, 0.25 **Ni**, 3.00–4.00 **Mo**, 9.00–11.00 **W**, 3.00–3.70 **V**, 9.00–11.00 **Co**, 0.25 **Cu**, 0.030 **P**, 0.030 **S**, 0.40 **Si**	**Annealed; Quenched and tempered**
ANSI/ASTM A 600	M3 Class 2	US	Bar, forgings, plate, sheet, strip	1.15–1.25 **C**, 0.15–0.40 **Mn**, 3.75–4.50 **Cr**, 4.75–6.50 **Mo**, 5.00–6.75 **W**, 2.75–3.25 **V**, 0.03 **P**, 0.03 **S**, 0.20–0.45 **Si**	**Annealed**
ANSI/ASTM A 600	M43	US	Bar, forgings, plate, sheet, strip	1.15–1.25 **C**, 0.20–0.40 **Mn**, 3.50–4.25 **Cr**, 7.50–8.50 **Mo**, 2.25–3.00 **W**, 1.50–1.75 **V**, 7.75–8.75 **Co**, 0.03 **P**, 0.03 **S**, 0.15–0.65 **Si**	**Annealed**
AISI type M44		US	Bar	1.15 **C**, 4.25 **Cr**, 6.25 **Mo**, 5.25 **W**, 2.00 **V**, 12.00 **Co**	
COPANT 337	O7	COPANT	Bar, forgings	1.10–1.30 **C**, 0.50 **Mn**, 0.60–0.85 **Cr**, 0.30 **Mo**, 1.25–1.90 **W**, 0.30 **V**, 0.030 **P**, 0.030 **S**, 0.50 **Si**	
BS 4656	BW 1C	UK	Bar, section, coil, rod, sheet, strip, forgings	1.1–1.3 **C**, 0.35 **Mn**, 0.15 **Cr**, 0.20 **Ni**, 0.10 **Mo**, 0.30 **Si**	
JIS G 311	SK2M	Japan	Strip	1.10–1.30 **C**, 0.50 **Mn**, 0.20 **Cr**, 0.25 **Ni**, 0.30 **Cu**, 0.030 **P**, 0.030 **S**, 0.35 **Si**	
JIS G 4401	Class 2	Japan	Bar, forgings	1.10–1.30 **C**, 0.50 **Mn**, 0.20 **Cr**, 0.25 **Ni**, 0.25 **Cu**, 0.030 **P**, 0.030 **S**, 0.35 **Si**	**Annealed; Annealed and quenched and tempered**
DGN-B-82	O 7	Mexico	Bar	1.10–1.30 **C**, 0.10–0.40 **Mn**, 0.40–0.75 **Cr**, 0.20–0.30 **Mo**, 1.40–1.80 **W**, 0.15–0.30 **V**, 0.10–0.40 **Si**	

specification number	designation	country	product forms	composition	mechanical properties (see page iv for explanation)
ANSI/ASTM A 681	O7	US	Bar, plate, sheet, strip, rod, wire, forgings	1.10–1.30 **C**, 1.00 **Mn**, 0.35–0.85 **Cr**, 0.30 **Mo**, 1.00–2.00 **W**, 0.40 **V**, 0.030 **P**, 0.030 **S**, 0.60 **Si**	**Annealed**
IS 3749	T118	India	Bar, rings, shapes	1.10–1.25 **C**, 0.20–0.35 **Mn**, 0.035 **P**, 0.035 **S**, 0.10–0.35 **Si**	**Annealed**
IS 3749	T118Cr45	India	Bar, rings, shapes	1.10–1.25 **C**, 0.20–0.35 **Mn**, 0.30–0.60 **Cr**, 0.30 **V**, 0.035 **P**, 0.035 **S**, 0.10–0.35 **Si**	**Annealed**
IS 4367	$T118Cr^{45}$	India	Forgings	1.10–1.25 **C**, 0.20–0.35 **Mn**, 0.30–0.60 **Cr**, 0.30 **V**, 0.10–0.30 **Si**	**Annealed**
JIS G 4403	SKH 53	Japan	Bar, forgings	1.10–1.25 **C**, 0.40 **Mn**, 3.80–4.50 **Cr**, 0.25 **Ni**, 4.80–6.20 **Mo**, 5.50–6.70 **W**, 2.80–3.30 **V**	**Annealed; Quenched and tempered**
DGN–B–82	F 1	Mexico	Bar	1.10–1.25 **C**, 0.10–0.40 **Mn**, 1.10–1.50 **W**, 0.10–0.40 **Si**	
JIS G 3311	SKS7M	Japan	Strip	1.10–1.20 **C**, 0.50 **Mn**, 0.20–0.50 **Cr**, 0.25 **Ni**, 2.00–2.50 **W**, 0.20 **V**, 0.25 **Cu**, 0.030 **P**, 0.030 **S**, 0.35 **Si**	
JIS G 4404	SKS 7	Japan	Bar, forgings	1.10–1.20 **C**, 0.50 **Mn**, 0.20–0.50 **Cr**, 0.25 **Ni**, 2.00–2.50 **W**, 0.20 **V**, 0.25 **Cu**, 0.030 **P**, 0.030 **S**, 0.35 **Si**	**Annealed; Annealed and quenched and tempered**
DGN–B–82	M 3, Class 2	Mexico	Bar	1.10–1.20 **C**, 0.10–0.40 **Mn**, 4.00–4.25 **Cr**, 5.00–6.25 **Mo**, 5.60–6.25 **W**, 3.00–3.30 **V**, 0.10–0.40 **Si**	
ANSI/ASTM A 600	M44	US	Bar, forgings, plate, sheet, strip	1.10–1.20 **C**, 0.20–0.40 **Mn**, 4.00–4.75 **Cr**, 6.00–7.00 **Mo**, 5.00–5.75 **W**, 1.85–2.20 **V**, 11.00–12.25 **Co**, 0.03 **P**, 0.03 **S**, 0.30–0.55 **Si**	**Annealed**
AISI type M47		US	Bar	1.10 **C**, 3.75 **Cr**, 9.50 **Mo**, 1.50 **W**, 1.25 **V**, 5.00 **Co**	
AISI type 05		US	Bar	1.10 **C**, 0.50 **Cr**	
AISI type L2		US	Bar	1.10 **C**, 1.00 **Cr**, 0.20 **V**	
AISI type M41		US	Bar	1.10 **C**, 4.25 **Cr**, 3.75 **Mo**, 6.75 **W**, 2.00 **V**, 5.00 **Co**	
AISI type M42		US	Bar	1.10 **C**, 3.75 **Cr**, 9.50 **Mo**, 1.50 **W**, 1.15 **V**, 8.00 **Co**, 0.55 **Si**	
NF A 35–590	2142 (110 WC 20)	France	Bar, forgings	1.1 **C**, 0.3 **Mn**, 0.75 **Cr**, 2.0 **W**, 0.030 **P**, 0.030 **S**, 0.3 **Si**	
ANSI/ASTM A 600	M41	US	Bar, forgings, plate, sheet, strip	1.05–1.15 **C**, 0.20–0.60 **Mn**, 3.75–4.50 **Cr**, 3.25–4.25 **Mo**, 6.25–7.00 **W**, 1.75–2.25 **V**, 4.75–5.75 **Co**, 0.03 **P**, 0.03 **S**, 0.15–0.50 **Si**	**Annealed**
ANSI/ASTM A 600	M42	US	Bar, forgings, plate, sheet, strip	1.05–1.15 **C**, 0.15–0.40 **Mn**, 3.50–4.25 **Cr**, 9.00–10.00 **Mo**, 1.15–1.85 **W**, 0.95–1.35 **V**, 7.75–8.75 **Co**, 0.03 **P**, 0.03 **S**, 0.15–0.65 **Si**	**Annealed**
ANSI/ASTM A 600	M47	US	Bar, forgings, plate, sheet, strip	1.05–1.15 **C**, 0.15–0.40 **Mn**, 3.50–4.00 **Cr**, 9.25–10.00 **Mo**, 1.30–1.80 **W**, 1.15–1.35 **V**, 4.75–5.25 **Co**, 0.03 **P**, 0.03 **S**, 0.20–0.45 **Si**	**Annealed**
AISI type M3	Class 1	US	Bar	1.05 **C**, 4.00 **Cr**, 5.00 **Mo**, 6.00 **W**, 2.40 **V**	
NF A 35–590	1162 (Y_7 xxV)	France	Bar, forgings	1.05 **C**, 0.10–0.30 **Mn**, 0.020 **P**, 0.020 **S**, 0.10–0.25 **Si**	
NF A 35–590	1232 (Y_2 xxC)	France	Bar, forgings	1.05 **C**, 0.10–0.40 **Mn**, 0.025 **P**, 0.025 **S**, 0.10–0.30 **Si**	
NF A 35–590	1102 (Y_7 105)	France	Bar, forgings	1.05 **C**, 0.10–0.30 **Mn**, 0.020 **P**, 0.020 **S**, 0.10–0.25 **Si**	
NF A 35–590	1202 (Y_2 105)	France	Bar, forgings	1.05 **C**, 0.10–0.40 **Mn**, 0.025 **P**, 0.025 **S**, 0.10–0.30 **Si**	

WROUGHT TOOL STEELS

specification number	designation	country	product forms	composition	mechanical properties (see page iv for explanation)
IS 3749	T110W2Cr1	India	Bar, rings, shapes	1.00–1.20 **C**, 0.25–0.50 **Mn**, 0.90–1.30 **Cr**, 1.25–1.75 **W**, 0.035 **P**, 0.035 **S**, 0.10–0.35 **Si**	**Annealed**
IS: 4367	T110W2Cr1	India	Forgings	1.00–1.20 **C**, 0.90–1.30 **Mn**, 0.90–1.30 **Cr**, 1.25–1.75 **W**, 0.10–0.35 **Si**	**Annealed**
COPANT 337	M3, type 1	COPANT	Bar, forgings	1.0–1.10 **C**, 0.15–0.40 **Mn**, 3.75–4.50 **Cr**, 4.75–6.50 **Mo**, 5.0–6.75 **W**, 2.25–2.75 **V**, 0.030 **P**, 0.030 **S**, 0.20–0.45 **Si**	
BS 4659	BM 42	UK	Bar, section, coil, rod, sheet, strip, forgings	1.00–1.10 **C**, 0.40 **Mn**, 3.5–4.25 **Cr**, 9.0–10.0 **Mo**, 1.0–2.0 **W**, 1.0–1.3 **V**, 7.5–8.5 **Co**, 0.40 **Si**	
JIS G 3311	SK3M	Japan	Strip	1.00–1.10 **C**, 0.50 **Mn**, 0.20 **Cr**, 0.25 **Ni**, 0.30 **Cu**, 0.030 **P**, 0.030 **S**, 0.35 **Si**	
JIS G 3311	SKS2M	Japan	Strip	1.00–1.10 **C**, 0.80 **Mn**, 0.50–1.00 **Cr**, 0.25 **Ni**, 1.00–1.50 **W**, 0.20 **V**, 0.25 **Cu**, 0.030 **P**, 0.030 **S**, 0.35 **Si**	
JIS G 4401	Class 3	Japan	Bar, forgings	1.00–1.10 **C**, 0.50 **Mn**, 0.20 **Cr**, 0.25 **Ni**, 0.25 **Cu**, 0.030 **P**, 0.030 **S**, 0.35 **Si**	**Annealed; Annealed and quenched and tempered**
JIS G 4403	SKH 52	Japan	Bar, forgings	1.00–1.10 **C**, 0.40 **Mn**, 3.80–4.50 **Cr**, 0.25 **Ni**, 4.80–6.20 **Mo**, 5.50–6.70 **W**, 2.30–2.80 **V**, 0.25 **Cu**, 0.030 **P**, 0.030 **S**, 0.40 **Si**	**Annealed; Quenched and tempered**
JIS G 4404	SKS 2	Japan	Bar, forgings	1.00–1.10 **C**, 0.80 **Mn**, 0.50–1.00 **Cr**, 0.25 **Ni**, 1.00–1.50 **W**, 0.20 **V**, 0.25 **Cu**, 0.030 **P**, 0.030 **S**, 0.35 **Si**	**Annealed; Annealed and quenched and tempered**
JIS G 4404	SKS 21	Japan	Bar, forgings	1.00–1.10 **C**, 0.50 **Mn**, 0.20–0.50 **Cr**, 0.25 **Ni**, 0.50–1.00 **W**, 0.10–0.25 **V**, 0.25 **Cu**, 0.030 **P**, 0.030 **S**, 0.35 **Si**	**Annealed; Annealed and quenched and tempered**
JIS G 4404	SKS 43	Japan	Bar, forgings	1.00–1.10 **C**, 0.30 **Mn**, 0.20 **Cr**, 0.10–0.25 **V**, 0.25 **Cu**, 0.030 **P**, 0.030 **S**, 0.25 **Si**	**Annealed; Annealed and quenched and tempered**
JIS G 4404	SKS 93	Japan	Bar, forgings	1.00–1.10 **C**, 0.80–1.10 **Mn**, 0.20–0.60 **Cr**, 0.25 **Cu**, 0.030 **P**, 0.030 **S**, 0.50 **Si**	**Annealed; Annealed and quenched and tempered**
DGN–B–82	M 3 Class 1	Mexico	Bar	1.0–1.10 **C**, 0.10–0.40 **Mn**, 4.00–4.25 **Cr**, 5.70–6.25 **Mo**, 6.00–6.25 **W**, 2.40–2.55 **V**, 0.10–0.40 **Si**	
ANSI/ASTM A 600	M3 Class 1	US	Bar, forgings, plate, sheet, strip	1.00–1.10 **C**, 0.15–0.40 **Mn**, 3.75–4.50 **Cr**, 4.75–6.50 **Mo**, 5.00–6.75 **W**, 2.25–2.75 **V**, 0.03 **P**, 0.03 **S**, 0.20–0.45 **Si**	**Annealed**
SFS 900	SFS 906	Finland	Bar, forgings	1.00 **C**, 0.30 **Mn**, 0.20 **Si**	
SFS 900	SFS 908	Finland	Bar, forgings	1.00 **C**, 0.60 **Mn**, 5.20 **Cr**, 1.10 **Mo**, 0.20 **V**, 0.20 **Si**	
AISI type A2		US	Bar	1.00 **C**, 5.00 **Cr**, 1.00 **Mo**	
AISI type A4		US	Bar	1.00 **C**, 2.00 **Mn**, 1.00 **Cr**, 1.00 **Mo**	
AISI type M7		US	Bar	1.00 **C**, 4.00 **Cr**, 8.75 **Mo**, 1.75 **W**, 2.00 **V**	
AISI type M10		US	Bar	1.00 **C**, 4.00 **Cr**, 8.00 **Mo**, 2.00 **V**	
NF A 35–590	2131 (100 C3)	France	Bar, forgings	1.0 **C**, 0.3 **Mn**, 0.75 **Cr**, 0.15 **V**, 0.030 **P**, 0.030 **S**, 0.3 **Si**	
NF A 35–590	2133 (Y 100 C 6)	France	Bar, forgings	1.0 **C**, 0.3 **Mn**, 1.5 **Cr**, 0.15 **V**, 0.030 **P**, 0.030 **S**, 0.3 **Si**	
NF A 35–590	2141 (100 WC 10)	France	Bar, forgings	1.0 **C**, 0.3 **Mn**, 0.5 **Cr**, 1.0 **W**, 0.2 **V**, 0.030 **P**, 0.030 **S**, 0.3 **Si**	
NF A 35–590	2231 (Z 100 CDV 5)	France	Bar, forgings	1.0 **C**, 0.3 **Mn**, 5.0 **Cr**, 1.0 **Mo**, 0.3 **V**, 0.030 **P**, 0.030 **S**, 0.3 **Si**	
COPANT 337	M7	COPANT	Bar, forgings	0.98–1.05 **C**, 0.15–0.40 **Mn**, 3.50–4.00 **Cr**, 8.40–9.10 **Mo**, 1.40–2.10 **W**, 1.75–2.25 **V**, 0.030 **P**, 0.030 **S**, 0.20–0.50 **Si**	

WROUGHT TOOL STEELS

specification number	designation	country	product forms	composition	mechanical properties (see page iv for explanation)
ANSI/ASTM A 600	M7	US	Bar, forgings, plate, sheet, strip	0.97–1.05 **C**, 0.15–0.40 **Mn**, 3.50–4.00 **Cr**, 8.20–9.20 **Mo**, 1.40–2.10 **W**, 1.75–2.25 **V**, 0.03 **P**, 0.03 **S**, 0.20–0.55 **Si**	**Annealed**
DGN–B–82	M 7	Mexico	Bar	0.97–1.03 **C**, 0.10–0.40 **Mn**, 3.75–4.00 **Cr**, 8.50–8.75 **Mo**, 1.50–1.75 **W**, 1.90–2.10 **V**, 0.10–0.40 **Si**	
SIS 14 27 82	SIS 27 82–02	Sweden	Bar, forgings, wire	0.96–1.04 **C**, 0.20–0.40 **Mn**, 3.5–4.5 **Cr**, 8.2–9.2 **Mo**, 1.5–2.0 **W**, 1.9–2.2 **V**, 0.030 **P**, 0.030 **S**, 0.15–0.40 **Si**	
ANSI/ASTM A 681	F1	US	Bar, plate, sheet, strip, rod, wire, forgings	0.95–1.25 **C**, 0.50 **Mn**, 1.00–1.75 **W**, 0.030 **P**, 0.030 **S**, 0.50 **Si**	**Annealed**
IS 3749	T103	India	Bar, rings, shapes	0.95–1.10 **C**, 0.20–0.35 **Mn**, 0.035 **P**, 0.035 **S**, 0.10–0.35 **Si**	**Annealed**
IS 3749	T103V23	India	Bar, rings, shapes	0.95–1.10 **C**, 0.20–0.35 **Mn**, 0.15–0.30 **V**, 0.035 **P**, 0.035 **S**, 0.10–0.35 **Si**	**Annealed**
IS 4367	T103V[23]	India	Forgings	0.95–1.10 **C**, 0.20–0.35 **Mn**, 0.15–0.30 **V**, 0.10–0.30 **Si**	**Annealed**
COPANT 337	L7	COPANT	Bar, forgings	0.95–1.10 **C**, 0.25–0.50 **Mn**, 1.10–1.75 **Cr**, 0.30–0.50 **Mo**, 0.030 **P**, 0.030 **S**, 0.15–0.40 **Si**	
SFS 906		Finland	Bar, forgings	0.95–1.10 **C**, 0.20–0.40 **Mn**, 0.030 **P**, 0.020 **S**, 0.10–0.30 **Si**	
BS 4656	BW 1B	UK	Bar, section, coil, rod, sheet, strip, forgings	0.95–1.1 **C**, 0.35 **Mn**, 0.15 **Cr**, 0.20 **Ni**, 0.10 **Mo**, 0.30 **Si**	
BS 4656	BW 2	UK	Bar, section, coil, rod, sheet, strip, forgings	0.95–1.1 **C**, 0.35 **Mn**, 0.15 **Cr**, 0.20 **Ni**, 0.10 **Mo**, 0.15–0.35 **V**, 0.30 **Si**	
SIS 14 18 80	SIS 18 80–02	Sweden	Bar, forgings	0.95–1.10 **C**, 0.20–0.40 **Mn**, 0.030 **P**, 0.020 **S**, 0.10–0.30 **Si**	
DGN–B–82	L 3	Mexico	Bar	0.95–1.10 **C**, 0.25–0.80 **Mn**, 1.30–1.70 **Cr**, 0.10–0.30 **V**, 0.50 **Si**	
ANSI/ASTM A 681	L3	US	Bar, plate, sheet, strip, rod, wire, forgings	0.95–1.10 **C**, 0.25–0.80 **Mn**, 1.30–1.70 **Cr**, 0.10–0.30 **V**, 0.030 **P**, 0.030 **S**, 0.50 **Si**	**Annealed**
NS 13860	NS 13860–02	Norway	Bar, forgings	0.95–1.05 **C**, 0.45–0.75 **Mn**, 5.0–5.5 **Cr**, 1.00–1.20 **Mo**, 0.15–0.25 **V**, 0.030 **P**, 0.020 **S**, 0.15–0.30 **Si**	**Annealed**
COPANT 337	M2, high C	COPANT	Bar, forgings	0.95–1.05 **C**, 0.15–0.40 **Mn**, 3.75–4.50 **Cr**, 4.50–5.50 **Mo**, 5.50–6.75 **W**, 1.75–2.20 **V**, 0.030 **P**, 0.030 **S**, 0.20–0.45 **Si**	
COPANT 337	M10, high C	COPANT	Bar, forgings	0.95–1.05 **C**, 0.15–0.40 **Mn**, 3.75–4.50 **Cr**, 7.75–8.50 **Mo**, 1.80–2.20 **V**, 0.030 **P**, 0.030	
COPANT 337	L3	COPANT	Bar, forgings	0.95–1.05 **C**, 0.30–0.60 **Mn**, 1.30–1.70 **Cr**, 0.10–0.30 **V**, 0.030 **P**, 0.030 **S**, 0.15–0.40 **Si**	
SFS 908		Finland	Bar, forgings	0.95–1.05 **C**, 0.45–0.75 **Mn**, 5.0–5.5 **Cr**, 1.00–1.20 **Mo**, 0.15–0.25 **V**, 0.030 **P**, 0.020 **S**, 0.15–0.30 **Si**	
BS 4656	BA 2	UK	Bar, section, coil, rod, sheet, strip, forgings	0.95–1.05 **C**, 0.30–0.70 **Mn**, 4.75–5.25 **Cr**, 0.90–1.1 **Mo**, 0.15–0.40 **V**, 0.40 **Si**	
BS 4656	BL 3	UK	Bar, section, coil, rod, sheet, strip, forgings	0.95–1.05 **C**, 0.40 **Mn**, 1.3–1.5 **Cr**, 0.10–0.30 **V**, 0.40 **Si**	
JIS G 4404	SKS 31	Japan	Bar, forgings	0.95–1.05 **C**, 0.90–1.20 **Mn**, 0.80–1.20 **Cr**, 0.25 **Ni**, 1.00–1.50 **W**, 0.25 **Cu**, 0.030 **P**, 0.030 **S**, 0.35 **Si**	**Annealed; Annealed and quenched and tempered**
JIS G 4404	SKD 12	Japan	Bar, forgings	0.95–1.05 **C**, 0.60–0.90 **Mn**, 4.50–5.50 **Cr**, 0.50 **Ni**, 0.80–1.20 **Mo**, 0.20–0.50 **V**, 0.25 **Cu**, 0.030 **P**, 0.030 **S**, 0.40 **Si**	**Annealed; Annealed and quenched and tempered**

WROUGHT TOOL STEELS

specification number	designation	country	product forms	composition	mechanical properties (see page iv for explanation)
SIS 14 22 60	SIS 22 60–02	Sweden	Bar, forgings	0.95–1.05 **C**, 0.45–0.75 **Mn**, 5.0–5.5 **Cr**, 1.00–1.20 **Mo**, 0.15–0.25 **V**, 0.030 **P**, 0.020 **S**, 0.15–0.30 **Si**	
ASTM A 685	Type A2	US	Rectangular bar: finish, machined	0.95–1.05 **C**, 1.00 **Mn**, 4.75–5.50 **Cr**, 0.90–1.40 **Mo**, 0.15–0.50 **V**, 0.030 **P**, 0.030 **S**, 0.50 **Si**	
ASTM A 685	Type A4	US	Rectangular bar: finish, machined	0.95–1.05 **C**, 1.80–2.20 **Mn**, 0.90–2.20 **Cr**, 0.90–1.40 **Mo**, 0.030 **P**, 0.030 **S**, 0.50 **Si**	
DGN–B–82	A 5	Mexico	Bar	0.95–1.05 **C**, 2.75–3.25 **Mn**, 0.80–1.20 **Cr**, 0.80–1.20 **Mo**, 0.10–0.40 **Si**	
DGN–B–82	A 4	Mexico	Bar	0.95–1.05 **C**, 1.75–2.25 **Mn**, 0.80–1.20 **Cr**, 0.80–1.20 **Mo**, 0.10–0.40 **Si**	
DGN–B–82	A 2	Mexico	Bar	0.95–1.05 **C**, 0.40–0.85 **Mn**, 4.75–5.25 **Cr**, 0.90–1.15 **Mo**, 0.15–0.50 **V**, 0.10–0.40 **Si**	
ANSI/ASTM A 600	M2 high C	US	Bar, forgings, plate, sheet, strip	0.95–1.05 **C**, 0.15–0.40 **Mn**, 3.75–4.50 **Cr**, 4.50–5.50 **Mo**, 5.50–6.75 **W**, 1.75–2.20 **V**, 0.03 **P**, 0.03 **S**, 0.20–0.45 **Si**	**Annealed**
ANSI/ASTM A 600	M10 high C	US	Bar, forgings, plate, sheet, strip	0.95–1.05 **C**, 0.10–0.40 **Mn**, 3.75–4.50 **Cr**, 7.75–8.50 **Mo**, 1.80–2.20 **V**, 0.03 **P**, 0.03 **S**, 0.20–0.45 **Si**	**Annealed**
ANSI/ASTM A 681	A2	US	Bar, plate, sheet, strip, rod, wire, forgings	0.95–1.05 **C**, 1.00 **Mn**, 4.75–5.50 **Cr**, 0.90–1.40 **Mo**, 0.15–0.50 **V**, 0.030 **P**, 0.030 **S**, 0.50 **Si**	**Annealed**
ANSI/ASTM A 681	A4	US	Bar, plate, sheet, strip, rod, wire, forgings	0.95–1.05 **C**, 1.80–2.20 **Mn**, 0.90–2.20 **Cr**, 0.90–1.40 **Mo**, 0.030 **P**, 0.030 **S**, 0.50 **Si**	**Annealed**
ANSI/ASTM A 681	A5	US	Bar, plate, sheet, strip, rod, wire, forgings	0.95–1.05 **C**, 2.80–3.20 **Mn**, 0.90–1.20 **Cr**, 0.90–1.40 **Mo**, 0.030 **P**, 0.030 **S**, 0.50 **Si**	**Annealed**
SFS 900	SFS 907	Finland	Bar, forgings	0.93 **C**, 1.20 **Mn**, 0.50 **Cr**, 0.50 **W**, 0.10 **V**, 0.30 **Si**	
DGN–B–82	L 7	Mexico	Bar	0.90–1.25 **C**, 0.30–0.70 **Mn**, 1.10–1.50 **Cr**, 0.30–0.50 **Mo**, 0.10–0.40 **Si**	
IS 3749	T105Cr1	India	Bar, rings, shapes	0.90–1.20 **C**, 0.20–0.40 **Mn**, 1.00–1.60 **Cr**, 0.035 **P**, 0.035 **S**, 0.10–0.35 **Si**	**Annealed**
IS 3749	T105Cr1Mn60	India	Bar, rings, shapes	0.90–1.20 **C**, 0.40–0.80 **Mn**, 1.00–1.60 **Cr**, 0.035 **P**, 0.035 **S**, 0.10–0.35 **Si**	**Annealed**
IS 3749	T105W2Cr60V25	India	Bar, rings, shapes	0.90–1.20 **C**, 0.25–0.50 **Mn**, 0.40–0.80 **Cr**, 0.25 max **Mo**, 1.25–1.75 **W**, 0.20–0.30 **V**, 0.035 **P**, 0.035 **S**, 0.10–0.35 **Si**	**Annealed**
IS 4367	T105Cri	India	Forgings	0.90–1.20 **C**, 0.20–0.40 **Mn**, 1.00–1.60 **Cr**, 0.10–0.35 **Si**	**Annealed**
DGN–B–82	O 1	Mexico	Bar	0.90–1.10 **C**, 1.10–1.40 **Mn**, 0.40–0.60 **Cr**, 0.40–0.60 **W**, 0.15–0.30 **V**, 0.10–0.40 **Si**	
DGN–B–82	L 1	Mexico	Bar	0.90–1.10 **C**, 0.10–0.40 **Mn**, 1.20–1.60 **Cr**, 0.10–0.40 **Si**	
DGN–B–82	D 1	Mexico	Bar	0.90–1.10 **C**, 0.20–0.40 **Mn**, 11.50–12.50 **Cr**, 0.70–0.90 **Mo**, 0.30–0.80 **V**, 0.10–0.40 **Si**	
COPANT 337	A2	COPANT	Bar, forgings	0.90–1.05 **C**, 0.30–0.90 **Mn**, 4.75–5.50 **Cr**, 0.90–1.50 **Mo**, 0.15–0.50 **V**, 0.030 **P**, 0.030 **S**, 0.15–0.40 **Si**	
SIS 14 20 92	SIS 20 92–02	Sweden	Bar, forgings	0.90–1.05 **C**, 0.60–0.90 **Mn**, 0.90–1.15 **Cr**, 0.030 **P**, 0.020 **S**, 1.35–1.65 **Si**	
JIS G 3311	SK4M	Japan	Strip	0.90–1.00 **C**, 0.50 **Mn**, 0.20 **Cr**, 0.25 **Ni**, 0.30 **Cu**, 0.030 **P**, 0.030 **S**, 0.35 **Si**	

specification number	designation	country	product forms	composition	mechanical properties (see page iv for explanation)
JIS G 4401	Class 4	Japan	Bar, forgings	0.90–1.00 **C**, 0.50 **Mn**, 0.20 **Cr**, 0.25 **Ni**, 0.25 **Cu**, 0.030 **P**, 0.030 **S**, 0.35 **Si**	**Annealed; Annealed and quenched and tempered**
JIS G 4404	SKS 3	Japan	Bar, forgings	0.90–1.00 **C**, 0.90–1.20 **Mn**, 0.50–1.00 **Cr**, 0.25 **Ni**, 0.50–1.00 **W**, 0.25 **Cu**, 0.030 **P**, 0.030 **S**, 0.35 **Si**	**Annealed; Annealed and quenched and tempered**
JIS G 4404	SKS 94	Japan	Bar, forgings	0.90–1.00 **C**, 0.80–1.10 **Mn**, 0.20–0.60 **Cr**, 0.25 **Ni**, 0.25 **Cu**, 0.030 **P**, 0.030 **S**, 0.50 **Si**	**Annealed; Annealed and quenched and tempered**
DGN–B–82	O 2	Mexico	Bar	0.90–1.0 **C**, 1.50–1.80 **Mn**, 0.15–0.30 **Cr**, 0.20–0.40 **Mo**, 0.10–0.25 **V**, 0.10–0.40 **Si**	
AISI type 01		US	Bar	0.90 **C**, 1.00 **Mn**, 0.50 **Cr**, 0.50 **W**	
AISI type 02		US	Bar	0.90 **C**, 1.60 **Mn**	
AISI type M33		US	Bar	0.90 **C**, 4.00 **Cr**, 9.50 **Mo**, 1.50 **W**, 1.15 **V**, 8.00 **Co**	
AISI type M34		US	Bar	0.90 **C**, 4.00 **Cr**, 8.00 **Mo**, 2.00 **W**, 2.00 **V**, 8.00 **Co**	
NF A 35–590	2211 (90 MV 8)	France	Bar, forgings	0.90 **C**, 2.0 **Mn**, 0.20 **V**, 0.030 **P**, 0.030 **S**, 0.30 **Si**	
NF A 35–590	1163 (Y_7 xxV)	France	Bar, forgings	0.90 **C**, 0.10–0.30 **Mn**, 0.020 **P**, 0.020 **S**, 0.10–0.25 **Si**	
NF A 35–590	1233 (Y_2 xxC)	France	Bar, forgings	0.90 **C**, 0.10–0.40 **Mn**, 0.025 **P**, 0.025 **S**, 0.10–0.30 **Si**	
NF A 35–590	2212 (90 MCW 5)	France	Bar, forgings	0.90 **C**, 1.25 **Mn**, 0.5 **Cr**, 0.5 **W**, 0.030 **P**, 0.030 **S**, 0.030 **Si**	
NF A 35–590	1103 (Y_7 90)	France	Bar, forgings	0.90 **C**, 0.10–0.30 **Mn**, 0.020 **P**, 0.020 **S**, 0.10–0.25 **Si**	
NF A 35–590	1203 (Y_2 90)	France	Bar, forgings	0.90 **C**, 0.10–0.40 **Mn**, 0.025 **P**, 0.025 **S**, 0.10–0.30 **Si**	
SFS 900	SFS 917	Finland	Bar, forgings	0.88 **C**, 0.30 **Mn**, 4.00 **Cr**, 5.00 **Mo**, 6.50 **W**, 1.90 **V**, 5.00 **Co**, 0.30 **Si**	
DGN–B–82	M 34	Mexico	Bar	0.87–0.93 **C**, 0.10–0.40 **Mn**, 3.50–4.00 **Cr**, 8.45–8.95 **Mo**, 1.30–1.80 **W**, 1.85–2.25 **V**, 8.00–8.50 **Co**, 0.10–0.40 **Si**	
SFS 900	SFS 916	Finland	Bar, forgings	0.86 **C**, 0.30 **Mn**, 4.00 **Cr**, 5.00 **Mo**, 6.50 **W**, 1.90 **V**, 0.30 **Si**	
JIS G 4410	SKC 11	Japan	Rod	0.85–1.10 **C**, 0.50 **Mn**, 0.80–1.50 **Cr**, 0.40 **Mo**, 0.25 **V**, 0.25 **Cu**, 0.030 **P**, 0.030 **S**, 0.15–0.35 **Si**	**Quenched and tempered**
COPANT 337	O1	COPANT	Bar, forgings	0.85–1.05 **C**, 1.00–1.40 **Mn**, 0.40–0.60 **Cr**, 0.40–0.60 **W**, 0.030 **P**, 0.030 **S**, 0.15–0.40 **Si**	
COPANT 337	O2	COPANT	Bar, forgings	0.85–1.05 **C**, 1.40–1.80 **Mn**, 0.35 **Cr**, 0.030 **P**, 0.030 **S**, 0.15–0.40 **Si**	
AISI type M2		US	Bar	0.85–1.00 **C**, 4.00 **Cr**, 5.00 **Mo**, 6.00 **W**, 2.00 **V**	
NS 13840	NS 13840–02	Norway	Bar, forgings	0.85–1.00 **C**, 1.10–1.30 **Mn**, 0.40–0.60 **Cr**, 0.40–0.60 **W**, 0.05–0.15 **V**, 0.030 **P**, 0.030 **S**, 0.20–0.40 **Si**	**Annealed**
SFS 907		Finland	Bar, forgings	0.85–1.00 **C**, 1.10–1.30 **Mn**, 0.40–0.60 **Cr**, 0.40–0.60 **W**, 0.05–0.15 **V**, 0.030 **P**, 0.020 **S**, 0.20–0.40 **Si**	
BS 4656	BO 1	UK	Bar, section, coil, rod, sheet, strip, forgings	0.85–1.0 **C**, 1.1–1.35 **Mn**, 0.40–0.60 **Cr**, 0.40–0.60 **W**, 0.25 **V**, 0.40 **Si**	
ASTM A 685	Type 01	US	Rectangular bar: finish, machined	0.85–1.00 **C**, 1.00–1.40 **Mn**, 0.40–0.60 **Cr**, 0.40–0.60 **W**, 0.30 **V**, 0.030 **P**, 0.030 **S**, 0.50 **Si**	
SIS 14 21 40	SIS 21 40–02	Sweden	Bar, forgings	0.85–1.00 **C**, 1.10–1.30 **Mn**, 0.40–0.60 **Cr**, 0.40–0.60 **W**, 0.05–0.15 **V**, 0.030 **P**, 0.020 **S**, 0.20–0.40 **Si**	

WROUGHT TOOL STEELS

specification number	designation	country	product forms	composition	mechanical properties (see page iv for explanation)
ANSI/ASTM A 681	O1	US	Bar, plate, sheet, strip, rod, wire, forgings	0.85–1.00 **C**, 1.00–1.40 **Mn**, 0.40–0.60 **Cr**, 0.40–0.60 **W**, 0.30 **V**	**Annealed**
IS 3749	T90	India	Bar, rings, shapes	0.85–0.95 **C**, 0.20–0.35 **Mn**, 0.035 **P**, 0.035 **S**, 0.10–0.35 **Si**	**Annealed**
IS 3749	T90V23	India	Bar, rings, shapes	0.85–0.95 **C**, 0.20–0.35 **Mn**, 0.15–0.30 **V**, 0.035 **P**, 0.035 **S**, 0.10–0.35 **Si**	**Annealed**
IS 3749	T90Mn2W50Cr45	India	Bar, rings, shapes	0.85–0.95 **C**, 1.25–1.75 **Mn**, 0.30–0.60 **Cr**, 0.40–0.60 **W**, 0.25 **V**, 0.035 **P**, 0.035 **S**, 0.10–0.35 **Si**	**Annealed**
IS 4367	$T90Mn2W^{50}Cr^{45}$	India	Forgings	0.85–0.95 **C**, 1.25–1.75 **Mn**, 0.30–0.60 **Cr**, 0.40–0.60 **W**, 0.25 **V**, 0.10–0.35 **Si**	**Annealed**
BS 4659	BM 34	UK	Bar, section, coil, rod, sheet, strip, forgings	0.85–0.95 **C**, 0.40 **Mn**, 3.75–4.5 **Cr**, 8.0–9.0 **Mo**, 1.7–2.2 **W**, 1.75–2.05 **V**, 7.75–8.75 **Co**, 0.40 **Si**	
BS 4656	BO 2	UK	Bar, section, coil, rod, sheet, strip, forgings	0.85–0.95 **C**, 1.5–1.8 **Mn**, 0.25 **V**, 0.40 **Si**	
BS 4656	BW 1A	UK	Bar, section, coil, rod, sheet, strip, forgings	0.85–0.95 **C**, 0.35 **Mn**, 0.15 **Cr**, 0.20 **Ni**, 0.10 **Mo**, 0.30 **Si**	
ASTM A 685	Type 02	US	Bar: finish, machined	0.85–0.95 **C**, 1.40–1.80 **Mn**, 0.35 **Cr**, 0.30 **Mo**, 0.30 **V**, 0.030 **P**, 0.030 **S**, 0.50 **Si**	
DGN–B–82	M 33	Mexico	Bar	0.85–0.95 **C**, 0.10–0.40 **Mn**, 3.50–4.00 **Cr**, 9.25–9.75 **Mo**, 1.30–1.70 **W**, 1.00–1.30 **V**, 7.75–8.25 **Co**, 0.10–0.40 **Si**	
ANSI/ASTM A 681	O2	US	Bar, plate, sheet, strip, rod, wire, forgings	0.85–0.95 **C**, 1.40–1.80 **Mn**, 0.35 **Cr**, 0.30 **Mo**, 0.30 **V**, 0.030 **P**, 0.030 **S**, 0.50 **Si**	**Annealed**
ANSI/ASTM A 600	M33	US	Bar, forgings, plate, sheet, strip	0.85–0.92 **C**, 0.15–0.40 **Mn**, 3.50–4.00 **Cr**, 9.00–10.00 **Mo**, 1.30–2.10 **W**, 1.00–1.35 **V**, 7.75–8.75 **Co**, 0.03 **P**, 0.03 **S**, 0.15–0.50 **Si**	**Annealed**
ANSI/ASTM A 600	M34	US	Bar, forgings, plate, sheet, strip	0.85–0.92 **C**, 0.15–0.40 **Mn**, 3.50–4.00 **Cr**, 7.75–9.20 **Mo**, 1.40–2.10 **W**, 1.90–2.30 **V**, 7.75–8.75 **Co**, 0.03 **P**, 0.03 **S**, 0.20–0.45 **Si**	**Annealed**
DGN–B–82	M 10	Mexico	Bar	0.85–0.90 **C**, 0.10–0.40 **Mn**, 4.00–4.25 **Cr**, 8.00–8.50 **Mo**, 1.90–2.10 **V**, 0.10–0.40 **Si**	
AISI type M1		US	Bar	0.85 **C**, 4.00 **Cr**, 8.50 **Mo**, 1.50 **W**, 1.00 **V**	
NF A 35–590	4203 (Z 85 WCV 18–04–02)	France	Bar, forgings	0.85 **C**, 0.3 **Mn**, 4.0 **Cr**, 0.5 **Mo**, 18.0 **W**, 2.0 **V**, 0.030 **P**, 0.030 **S**, 0.30 **Si**	
NF A 35–590	4301 (Z85 WDCV 06–05–04–02)	France	Bar, forgings	0.85 **C**, 0.3 **Mn**, 4.0 **Cr**, 5.0 **Mo**, 6.0 **W**, 2.0 **V**, 0.030 **P**, 0.030 **S**, 0.30 **Si**	
NF A 35–590	4371 (Z 85 WDKCV 06–05–05–04–01)	France	Bar, forgings	0.85 **C**, 0.3 **Mn**, 4.0 **Cr**, 5.0 **Mo**, 6.0 **W**, 2.0 **V**, 5.0 **Co**, 0.030 **P**, 0.030 **S**, 0.30 **Si**	
COPANT 337	M10, intermediate C	COPANT	Bar, forgings	0.84–0.94 **C**, 0.15–0.40 **Mn**, 3.75–4.50 **Cr**, 7.75–8.50 **Mo**, 1.80–2.20 **V**, 0.030 **P**, 0.030 **S**, 0.20–0.45 **Si**	
ANSI/ASTM A 600	M10 regular C	US	Bar, forgings, plate, sheet, strip	0.84–0.94 **C**, 0.10–0.40 **Mn**, 3.75–4.50 **Cr**, 7.75–8.50 **Mo**, 1.80–2.20 **V**, 0.03 **P**, 0.03 **S**, 0.20–0.45 **Si**	**Annealed**
SFS 917		Finland	Bar, wire, forgings	0.84–0.92 **C**, 0.20–0.40 **Mn**, 3.5–4.5 **Cr**, 4.5–5.5 **Mo**, 6.0–7.0 **W**, 1.7–2.1 **V**, 4.5–5.5 **Co**, 0.030 **P**, 0.030 **S**, 0.15–0.40 **Si**	

WROUGHT TOOL STEELS

specification number	designation	country	product forms	composition	mechanical properties (see page iv for explanation)
SIS 14 27 23	SIS 27 23–02	Sweden	Bar, forgings, wire	0.84–0.92 **C**, 0.20–0.40 **Mn**, 3.5–4.5 **Cr**, 4.5–5.5 **Mo**, 6.0–7.0 **W**, 1.7–2.1 **V**, 4.5–5.5 **Co**, 0.030 **P**, 0.030 **S**, 0.15–0.40 **Si**	
SIS 14 27 24	SIS 27 24–02	Sweden	Bar, forgings, wire	0.84–0.92 **C**, 0.20–0.40 **Mn**, 3.5–4.5 **Cr**, 2.8–3.6 **Mo**, 6.0–7.0 **W**, 1.8–2.2 **V**, 0.030 **P**, 0.030 **S**, 0.15–0.40 **Si**	
SFS 916		Finland	Strip, bar, wire, forgings	0.82–0.90 **C**, 0.20–0.40 **Mn**, 3.5–4.5 **Cr**, 4.5–5.5 **Mo**, 6.0–7.0 **W**, 1.7–2.1 **V**, 0.030 **P**, 0.030 **S**, 0.15–0.40 **Si**	
DGN–B–82	W 5	Mexico	Bar	0.80–1.20 **C**, 0.10–0.40 **Mn**, 0.30–0.50 **Cr**, 0.10–0.40 **Si**	
DGN–B–82	W 4	Mexico	Bar	0.80–1.20 **C**, 0.10–0.40 **Mn**, 0.15–0.30 **Cr**, 0.10–0.40 **Si**	
IS 3749	T85	India	Bar, rings, shapes	0.80–0.90 **C**, 0.50–0.80 **Mn**, 0.035 **P**, 0.035 **S**, 0.10–0.35 **Si**	**Annealed**
IS 4367	T85	India	Forgings	0.80–0.90 **C**, 0.50–0.80 **Mn**, 0.10–0.35 **Si**	**Annealed**
COPANT 337	M36	COPANT	Bar, forgings	0.80–0.90 **C**, 0.15–0.40 **Mn**, 3.75–4.50 **Cr**, 4.50–5.50 **Mo**, 5.50–6.50 **W**, 1.75–2.25 **V**, 7.75–8.75 **Co**, 0.030 **P**, 0.030 **S**, 0.20–0.45 **Si**	
BS 4659	BM 2	UK	Bar, section, coil, rod, sheet, strip, forgings	0.80–0.90 **C**, 0.40 **Mn**, 3.75–4.5 **Cr**, 4.75–5.5 **Mo**, 6.0–6.75 **W**, 1.75–2.05 **V**, 0.60 **Co**, 0.40 **Si**	
JIS G 3311	SK5M	Japan	Strip	0.80–0.90 **C**, 0.50 **Mn**, 0.20 **Cr**, 0.25 **Ni**, 0.30 **Cu**, 0.030 **P**, 0.030 **S**, 0.35 **Si**	
JIS G 4401	Class 5	Japan	Bar, forging	0.80–0.90 **C**, 0.50 **Mn**, 0.20 **Cr**, 0.25 **Ni**, 0.25 **Cu**, 0.030 **P**, 0.030 **S**, 0.35 **Si**	**Annealed; Annealed and quenched and tempered**
JIS G 4403	SKH 9	Japan	Bar, forgings	0.80–0.90 **C**, 0.40 **Mn**, 3.80–4.50 **Cr**, 0.25 **Ni**, 4.50–5.50 **Mo**, 5.50–6.70 **W**, 1.60–2.20 **V**, 0.25 **Cu**, 0.030 **P**, 0.030 **S**, 0.40 **Si**	**Annealed; Quenched and tempered**
JIS G 4403	SKH 55	Japan	Bar, forgings	0.80–0.90 **C**, 0.40 **Mn**, 3.80–4.50 **Cr**, 0.25 **Ni**, 4.80–6.20 **Mo**, 5.50–6.70 **W**, 1.70–2.30 **V**, 4.50–5.50 **Co**, 0.25 **Cu**, 0.030 **P**, 0.030 **S**, 0.40 **Si**	**Annealed; Quenched and tempered**
JIS G 4403	SKH 56	Japan	Bar, forgings	0.80–0.90 **C**, 0.40 **Mn**, 3.80–4.50 **Cr**, 0.25 **Ni**, 4.80–6.20 **Mo**, 5.50–6.70 **W**, 1.70–2.30 **V**, 7.00–9.00 **Co**, 0.25 **Cu**, 0.030 **P**, 0.030 **S**, 0.40 **Si**	**Annealed; Quenched and tempered**
JIS G 4404	SKS 44	Japan	Bar, forgings	0.80–0.90 **C**, 0.30 **Mn**, 0.20 **Cr**, 0.10–0.25 **V**, 0.25 **Cu**, 0.030 **P**, 0.030 **S**, 0.25 **Si**	**Annealed; Annealed and quenched and tempered**
JIS G 4404	SKS 95	Japan	Bar, forgings	0.80–0.90 **C**, 0.80–1.10 **Mn**, 0.20–0.60 **Cr**, 0.25 **Ni**, 0.25 **Cu**, 0.030 **P**, 0.030 **S**, 0.50 **Si**	**Annealed; Annealed and quenched and tempered**
SIS 14 27 22	SIS 27 22–02	Sweden	Bar, forgings, strip, wire	0.80–0.90 **C**, 0.20–0.40 **Mn**, 3.5–4.5 **Cr**,4.5–5.5 **Mo**, 6.0–7.0 **W**, 1.7–2.1 **V**, 0.030 **P**, 0.030 **S**, 0.15–0.40 **Si**	
DGN–B–82	M 36	Mexico	Bar	0.80–0.90 **C**, 0.10–0.40 **Mn**, 3.75–4.25 **Cr**, 4.25–5.25 **Mo**, 5.50–6.00 **W**, 1.65–2.00 **V**, 7.75–9.00 **Co**, 0.10–0.40 **Si**	
ANSI/ASTM A 600	T2	US	Bar, forgings, plate, sheet, strip	0.80–0.90 **C**, 0.20–0.40 **Mn**, 3.75–4.50 **Cr**, 1.00 **Mo**, 17.50–19.00 **W**, 1.80–2.40 **V**, 0.03 **P**, 0.03 **S**, 0.20–0.40 **Si**	**Annealed**
ANSI/ASTM A 600	M36	US	Bar, forgings, plate, sheet, strip	0.80–0.90 **C**, 0.15–0.40 **Mn**, 3.75–4.50 **Cr**, 4.50–5.50 **Mo**, 5.50–6.50 **W**, 1.75–2.25 **V**, 7.75–8.75 **Co**, 0.03 **P**, 0.03 **S**, 0.20–0.45 **Si**	**Annealed**

WROUGHT TOOL STEELS

specification number	designation	country	product forms	composition	mechanical properties (see page iv for explanation)
DGN–B–82	T 2	Mexico	Bar	0.80–0.85 **C**, 0.10–0.40 **Mn**, 4.00–4.25 **Cr**, 0.50–0.75 **Mo**, 18.00–18.50 **W**, 2.00–2.15 **V**, 0.10–0.40 **Si**	
DGN–B–82	M 30	Mexico	Bar	0.80–0.85 **C**, 0.10–0.40 **Mn**, 3.75–4.25 **Cr**, 8.25–8.50 **Mo**, 1.50–1.80 **W**, 1.10–1.40 **V**, 4.75–5.25 **Co**, 0.10–0.40 **Si**	
DGN–B–82	M 35	Mexico	Bar	0.80–0.85 **C**, 0.10–0.40 **Mn**, 3.90–4.40 **Cr**, 4.75–5.25 **Mo**, 6.15–6.65 **W**, 1.75–2.15 **V**, 4.75–5.25 **Co**, 0.10–0.40 **Si**	
DGN–B–82	M 2	Mexico	Bar	0.80–0.85 **C**, 0.10–0.40 **Mn**, 4.00–4.25 **Cr**, 4.75–5.25 **Mo**, 6.00–6.50 **W**, 1.70–2.10 **V**, 0.10–0.40 **Si**	
AISI type T2		US	Bar	0.80 **C**, 4.00 **Cr**, 18.00 **W**, 2.00 **V**	
AISI type T5		US	Bar	0.80 **C**, 4.00 **Cr**, 18.00 **W**, 2.00 **V**, 8.00 **Co**	
AISI type T6		US	Bar	0.80 **C**, 4.50 **Cr**, 20.00 **W**, 1.50 **V**, 12.00 **Co**	
AISI type M6		US	Bar	0.80 **C**, 4.00 **Cr**, 5.00 **Mo**, 4.00 **W**, 1.50 **V**, 12.00 **Co**	
AISI type M30		US	Bar	0.80 **C**, 4.00 **Cr**, 8.00 **Mo**, 2.00 **W**, 1.25 **V**, 5.00 **Co**	
AISI type M36		US	Bar	0.80 **C**, 4.00 **Cr**, 5.00 **Mo**, 6.00 **W**, 8.00 **Co**	
NF A 35–590	4151 (Z 80 WCDV 12.04–02–02)	France	Bar, forgings	0.8 **C**, 0.3 **Mn**, 4.0 **Cr**, 2.0 **Mo**, 12.0 **W**, 2.0 **V**, 0.030 **P**, 0.030 **S**, 0.30 **Si**	
NF A 35–590	4201 (Z 80 WCV 18–04–01)	France	Bar, forgings	0.8 **C**, 0.3 **Mn**, 4.0 **Cr**, 0.5 **Mo**, 18.0 **W**, 1.0 **V**, 0.030 **P**, 0.030 **S**, 0.30 **Si**	
NF A 35–590	4271 (Z 80 WKCV 18–05–04–01)	France	Bar, forgings	0.8 **C**, 0.3 **Mn**, 4.0 **Cr**, 1.0 **Mo**, 18.0 **W**, 1.0 **V**, 5.0 **Co**, 0.030 **P**, 0.030 **S**, 0.30 **Si**	
NF A 35–590	4275 (Z 80 WKCV 18–10–04–02)	France	Bar, forgings	0.80 **C**, 0.3 **Mn**, 4.0 **Cr**, 1.0 **Mo**, 18.0 **W**, 1.6 **V**, 10.0 **Co**, 0.030 **P**, 0.030 **S**, 0.30 **Si**	
COPANT 337	M2, intermediate C	COPANT	Bar, forgings	0.78–0.88 **C**, 0.15–0.40 **Mn**, 3.75–4.50 **Cr**, 4.50–5.50 **Mo**, 5.50–6.75 **W**, 1.75–2.20 **V**, 0.030 **P**, 0.030 **S**, 0.20–0.45 **Si**	
ANSI/ASTM A 600	M1	US	Bar, forgings, plate, sheet, strip	0.78–0.88 **C**, 0.15–0.40 **Mn**, 3.50–4.00 **Cr**, 8.20–9.20 **Mo**, 1.40–2.10 **W**, 1.00–1.35 **V**, 0.03 **P**, 0.03 **S**, 0.20–0.50 **Si**	**Annealed**
ANSI/ASTM A 600	M2 regular C	US	Bar, forgings, plate, sheet, strip	0.78–0.88 **C**, 0.15–0.40 **Mn**, 3.75–4.50 **Cr**, 4.50–5.50 **Mo**, 5.50–6.75 **W**, 1.75–2.20 **V**, 0.03 **P**, 0.03 **S**, 0.20–0.45 **Si**	**Annealed**
DGN–B–82	M 1	Mexico	Bar	0.78–0.85 **C**, 0.10–0.40 **Mn**, 3.75–4.00 **Cr**, 8.00–9.00 **Mo**, 1.50–1.65 **W**, 1.00–1.25 **V**, 0.10–0.40 **Si**	
COPANT 337	M1	COPANT	Bar, forgings	0.78–0.84 **C**, 0.15–0.40 **Mn**, 3.50–4.00 **Cr**, 8.20–9.20 **Mo**, 1.40–2.10 **W**, 1.00–1.30 **V**, 0.030 **P**, 0.20–0.45 **Si**, 0.030 **S**	
COPANT 337	M1	COPANT	Bar, forgings	0.78–0.84 **C**, 0.15–0.40 **Mn**, 3.50–4.00 **Cr**, 8.20–9.20 **Mo**, 1.40–2.10 **W**, 1.00–1.30 **V**, 0.030 **P**, 0.030 **S**, 0.20–0.45 **Si**	
DGN–B–82	T 5	Mexico	Bar	0.77–0.85 **C**, 0.10–0.40 **Mn**, 4.00–4.50 **Cr**, 0.65–1.00 **Mo**, 18.50–19.00 **W**, 1.85–2.00 **V**, 7.60–9.00 **Co**	
IS 3749	T 80Mn65	India	Bar, rings, shapes	0.75–0.85 **C**, 0.50–0.80 **Mn**, 0.035 **P**, 0.035 **S**, 0.10–0.35 **Si**	**Annealed**
IS 3749	T80	India	Bar, rings, shapes	0.75–0.85 **C**, 0.20–0.35 **Mn**, 0.035 **P**, 0.035 **S**, 0.10–0.35 **Si**	**Annealed**

WROUGHT TOOL STEELS

specification number	designation	country	product forms	composition	mechanical properties (see page iv for explanation)
IS 3749	T80V23	India	Bar, rings, shapes	0.75–0.85 **C**, 0.20–0.35 **Mn**, 0.15–0.30 **V**, 0.035 **P**, 0.035 **S**, 0.10–0.35 **Si**	**Annealed**
COPANT 337	T5	COPANT	Bar, forgings	0.75–0.85 **C**, 0.20–0.40 **Mn**, 3.75–5.00 **Cr**, 0.50–1.25 **Mo**, 17.50–19.00 **W**, 1.80–2.40 **V**, 7.00–9.50 **Co**, 0.030 **P**, 0.030 **S**, 0.20–0.40 **Si**	
COPANT 337	T8	COPANT	Bar, forgings	0.75–0.85 **C**, 0.20–0.40 **Mn**, 3.75–5.00 **Cr**, 0.40–1.00 **Mo**, 13.25–14.75 **W**, 1.80–2.40 **V**, 4.25–4.75 **Co**, 0.030 **P**, 0.030 **S**, 0.20–0.40 **Si**	
BS 4659	BM 1	UK	Bar, section, coil, rod, sheet, strip, forgings	0.75–0.85 **C**, 0.40 **Mn**, 3.75–4.5 **Cr**, 8.0–9.0 **Mo**, 1.0–2.0 **W**, 1.0–1.25 **V**, 0.60 **Co**, 0.40 **Si**	
BS 4659	BT 2	UK	Bar, section, coil, rod, sheet, strip, forgings	0.75–0.85 **C**, 0.40 **Mn**, 3.75–4.5 **Cr**, 0.7 **Mo**, 17.5–18.5 **W**, 1.75–2.05 **V**, 0.60 **Co**, 0.40 **Si**	
BS 4659	BT 5	UK	Bar, section, coil, rod, sheet, strip, forgings	0.75–0.85 **C**, 0.40 **Mn**, 3.75–4.5 **Cr**, 1.0 **Mo**, 18.5–19.5 **W**, 1.75–2.05 **V**, 9.0–10.0 **Co**, 0.40 **Si**	
BS 4659	BT 6	UK	Bar, section, coil, rod, sheet, strip, forgings	0.75–0.85 **C**, 0.4 **Mn**, 3.75–4.5 **Cr**, 1.0 **Mo**, 20.0–21.0 **W**, 1.25–1.75 **V**, 11.25–12.25 **Co**, 0.40 **Si**	
BS 4659	BT 20	UK	Bar, section, coil, rod, sheet, strip, forgings	0.75–0.85 **C**, 0.40 **Mn**, 4.25–5.0 **Cr**, 1.0 **Mo**, 21.0–22.5 **W**, 1.4–1.6 **V**, 0.60 **Co**, 0.40 **Si**	
JIS G 3311	SKS5M	Japan	Strip	0.75–0.85 **C**, 0.50 **Mn**, 0.50 **Cr**, 0.70–1.30 **Ni**, 0.25 **Cu**, 0.030 **P**, 0.030 **S**, 0.35 **Si**	
JIS G 3311	SKS51M	Japan	Strip	0.75–0.85 **C**, 0.50 **Mn**, 0.50 **Cr**, 1.30–2.00 **Ni**, 0.25 **Cu**, 0.030 **P**, 0.030 **S**, 0.35 **Si**	
JIS G 4404	SKS 5	Japan	Bar, forgings	0.75–0.85 **C**, 0.50 **Mn**, 0.20–0.50 **Cr**, 0.70–1.30 **Ni**, 0.25 **Cu**, 0.030 **P**, 0.030 **S**	**Annealed; Annealed and quenched and tempered**
JIS G 4404	SKS 51	Japan	Bar, forgings	0.75–0.85 **C**, 0.50 **Mn**, 0.20–0.50 **Cr**, 1.30–2.00 **Ni**, 0.25 **Cu**, 0.030 **P**, 0.030 **S**, 0.35 **Si**	**Annealed; Annealed and quenched and tempered**
JIS G 4404	SKS 42	Japan	Bar, forgings	0.75–0.85 **C**, 0.50 **Mn**, 0.25–0.50 **Cr**, 1.50–2.50 **W**, 0.15–0.30 **V**, 0.25 **Cu**, 0.030 **P**, 0.030 **S**, 0.30 **Si**	**Annealed; Annealed and quenched and tempered**
DGN–B–82	T 6	Mexico	Bar	0.75–0.85 **C**, 0.10–0.40 **Mn**, 4.00–4.50 **Cr**, 0.60–0.80 **Mo**, 18.75–20.50 **W**, 1.60–2.00 **V**, 11.50–12.25 **Co**, 0.10–0.40 **Si**	
ANSI/ASTM A 600	T5	US	Bar, forgings, plate, sheet, strip	0.75–0.85 **C**, 0.20–0.40 **Mn**, 3.75–5.00 **Cr**, 0.50–1.25 **Mo**, 17.50–19.00 **W**, 1.80–2.40 **V**, 7.00–9.50 **Co**, 0.03 **P**, 0.03 **S**, 0.20–0.40 **Si**	**Annealed**
ANSI/ASTM A 600	T6	US	Bar, forgings, plate, sheet, strip	0.75–0.85 **C**, 0.20–0.40 **Mn**, 4.00–4.75 **Cr**, 0.40–1.00 **Mo**, 18.50–21.00 **W**, 1.50–2.10 **V**, 11.00–13.00 **Co**, 0.03 **P**, 0.03 **S**, 0.20–0.40 **Si**	**Annealed**
ANSI/ASTM A 600	T8	US	Bar, forgings, plate, sheet, strip	0.75–0.85 **C**, 0.20–0.40 **Mn**, 3.75–4.50 **Cr**, 0.40–1.00 **Mo**, 13.25–14.75 **W**, 1.80–2.40 **V**, 4.25–5.75 **Co**, 0.03 **P**, 0.03 **S**, 0.20–0.40 **Si**	**Annealed**
ANSI/ASTM A 600	M6	US	Bar, forging, plate, sheet, strip	0.75–0.85 **C**, 0.15–0.40 **Mn**, 3.75–4.50 **Cr**, 4.50–5.50 **Mo**, 3.75–4.75 **W**, 1.30–1.70 **V**, 11.00–13.00 **Co**, 0.03 **P**, 0.03 **S**, 0.20–0.45 **Si**	**Annealed**
ANSI/ASTM A 600	M30	US	Bar, forgings, plate, sheet, strip	0.75–0.85 **C**, 0.15–0.40 **Mn**, 3.50–4.25 **Cr**, 7.75–9.00 **Mo**, 1.30–2.30 **W**, 1.00–1.40 **V**, 4.50–5.50 **Co**, 0.03 **P**, 0.03 **S**, 0.20–0.45 **Si**	**Annealed**

WROUGHT TOOL STEELS

specification number	designation	country	product forms	composition	mechanical properties (see page iv for explanation)
DGN–B–82	T 8	Mexico	Bar	0.75–0.80 **C**, 0.10–0.40 **Mn**, 3.75–4.25 **Cr**, 0.75 **Mo**, 13.75–14.0 **W**, 2.00–2.25 **V**, 5.00–5.25 **Co**, 0.10–0.40 **Si**	
DGN–B–82	M 6	Mexico	Bar	0.75–0.80 **C**, 0.10–0.40 **Mn**, 3.75–4.25 **Cr**, 4.75–5.25 **Mo**, 3.75–4.25 **W**, 1.25–1.55 **V**, 11.50–12.50 **Co**, 0.10–0.40 **Si**	
AISI type T4		US	Bar	0.75 **C**, 4.00 **Cr**, 18.00 **W**, 1.00 **V**, 5.00 **Co**	
AISI type T8		US	Bar	0.75 **C**, 4.00 **Cr**, 14.00 **W**, 2.00 **V**, 5.00 **Co**	
AISI type T1		US	Bar	0.75 **C**, 4.00 **Cr**, 18.00 **W**, 1.00 **V**	
NF A 35–590	1164 (Y_7 xxV)	France	Bar, forgings	0.75 **C**, 0.10–0.30 **Mn**, 0.020 **P**, 0.020 **S**, 0.10–0.25 **Si**	
NF A 35–590	1234 (Y_2 xxC)	France	Bar, forgings	0.75 **C**, 0.10–0.40 **Mn**, 0.025 **P**, 0.025 **S**, 0.10–0.30 **Si**	
NF A 35–590	1104 (Y_7 75)	France	Bar, forgings	0.75 **C**, 0.10–0.30 **Mn**, 0.020 **P**, 0.020 **S**, 0.10–0.25 **Si**	
NF A 35–590	1204 (Y_2 75)	France	Bar, forgings	0.75 **C**, 0.10–0.40 **Mn**, 0.025 **P**, 0.025 **S**, 0.10–0.30 **Si**	
JIS G 4410	SKC 3	Japan	Rod	0.70–0.85 **C**, 0.50 **Mn**, 0.20 **Cr**, 0.25 **Ni**, 0.25 **V**, 0.25 **Cu**, 0.030 **P**, 0.030 **S**, 0.15–0.35 **Si**, 0.25 **Ti**	**Quenched and tempered**
JIS G 4403	SKH 2	Japan	Bar, forgings	0.70–0.85 **C**, 0.40 **Mn**, 3.80–4.50 **Cr**, 0.25 **Ni**, 17.00–19.00 **W**, 0.80–1.20 **V**, 0.25 **Cu**, 0.030 **P**, 0.030 **S**, 0.40 **Si**	**Annealed; Quenched and tempered**
JIS G 4403	SKH 3	Japan	Bar, forgings	0.70–0.85 **C**, 0.40 **Mn**, 3.80–4.50 **Cr**, 0.25 **Ni**, 17.00–19.00 **W**, 0.80–1.20 **V**, 4.50–5.50 **Co**, 0.25 **Cu**, 0.030 **P**, 0.030 **S**, 0.40 **Si**	**Annealed; Quenched and tempered**
JIS G 4403	SKH 4 A	Japan	Bar, forgings	0.70–0.85 **C**, 0.40 **Mn**, 3.80–4.50 **Cr**, 0.25 **Ni**, 17.00–19.00 **W**, 1.00–1.50 **V**, 9.00–11.00 **Co**, 0.25 **Cu**, 0.030 **P**, 0.030 **S**, 0.40 **Si**	**Annealed; Quenched and tempered**
JIS G 4403	SKH 4 B	Japan	Bar, forgings	0.70–0.85 **C**, 0.40 **Mn**, 3.80–4.50 **Cr**, 0.25 **Ni**, 18.00–20.00 **W**, 1.00–1.50 **V**, 14.00–16.00 **Co**, 0.25 **Cu**, 0.030 **P**, 0.030 **S**, 0.40 **Si**	**Annealed; Quenched and tempered**
IS 3749	T75	India	Bar, rings, shapes	0.70–0.80 **C**, 0.50–0.80 **Mn**, 0.035 **P**, 0.035 **S**, 0.10–0.35 **Si**	**Annealed**
IS 4367	T75	India	Forgings	0.70–0.80 **C**, 0.50–0.80 **Mn**, 0.10–0.35 **Si**	**Annealed**
IS: 4367	T75W18Co10Cr4V2 Mo[75]	India	Forgings	0.70–0.80 **C**, 0.20–0.40 **Mn**, 4.00–4.50 **Cr**, 0.50–1.00 **Mo**, 17.5–19.0 **W**, 1.50–2.00 **V**, 9.00–10.00 **Co**, 0.10–0.35 **Si**	**Annealed**
BS 4659	BT 1	UK	Bar, section, coil, rod, sheet, strip, forgings	0.70–0.80 **C**, 0.40 **Mn**, 3.75–4.5 **Cr**, 0.7 **Mo**, 17.5–18.5 **W**, 1.0–1.25 **V**, 0.60 **Co**, 0.40 **Si**	
BS 4659	BT 4	UK	Bar, section, coil, rod, sheet, strip, forgings	0.70–0.80 **C**, 0.40 **Mn**, 3.75–4.5 **Cr**, 1.0 **Mo**, 17.5–18.5 **W**, 1.0–1.25 **V**, 4.5–5.5 **Co**, 0.40 **Si**	
JIS G 3311	SK6M	Japan	Strip	0.70–0.80 **C**, 0.50 **Mn**, 0.20 **Cr**, 0.25 **Ni**, 0.30 **Cu**, 0.030 **P**, 0.030 **S**, 0.35 **Si**	
JIS G 4404	SKT 6	Japan	Bar, forgings	0.70–0.80 **C**, 0.60–1.00 **Mn**, 0.80–1.10 **Cr**, 2.50–3.00 **Ni**, 0.30–0.50 **Mo**, 0.20 **V**, 0.25 **Cu**, 0.030 **P**, 0.030 **S**, 0.35 **Si**	**Annealed**
JIS G 4401	Class 6	Japan	Bar, forgings	0.70–0.80 **C**, 0.50 **Mn**, 0.20 **Cr**, 0.25 **Ni**, 0.25 **Cu**, 0.030 **P**, 0.030 **S**, 0.35 **Si**	**Annealed; Annealed and quenched and tempered**

WROUGHT TOOL STEELS

specification number	designation	country	product forms	composition	mechanical properties (see page iv for explanation)
ANSI/ASTM A 600	T4	US	Bar, forgings, plate, sheet, strip	0.70–0.80 **C**, 0.10–0.40 **Mn**, 3.75–4.50 **Cr**, 0.40–1.00 **Mo**, 17.50–19.00 **W**, 0.80–1.20 **V**, 4.25–5.75 **Co**, 0.03 **P**, 0.03 **S**, 0.20–0.40 **Si**	**Annealed**
DGN–B–82	T 4	Mexico	Bar	0.70–0.75 **C**, 0.10–0.40 **Mn**, 4.00–4.50 **Cr**, 0.60–0.80 **Mo**, 18.00–19.00 **W**, 1.00–1.25 **V**, 4.75–5.25 **Co**, 0.10–0.40 **Si**	
DGN–B–82	T 7	Mexico	Bar	0.70–0.75 **C**, 0.10–0.40 **Mn**, 4.50–5.00 **Cr**, 13.50–14.50 **W**, 1.50–1.80 **V**, 0.10–0.40 **Si**	
DGN–B–82	T 1	Mexico	Bar	0.70–0.75 **C**, 0.10–0.40 **Mn**, 4.00–4.10 **Cr**, 0.70 **Mo**, 18.00–18.25 **W**, 1.00–1.20 **V**, 0.10–0.40 **Si**	
AISI type A6		US	Bar	0.70 **C**, 2.00 **Mn**, 1.00 **Cr**, 1.25 **Mo**	
AISI type L6		US	Bar	0.70 **C**, 0.75 **Cr**, 1.50 **Ni**, 0.25 **Mo**	
DGN–B–82	L 2	Mexico	Bar	0.65–1.10 **C**, 0.10–0.60 **Mn**, 0.75–1.50 **Cr**, 0.15–0.30 **V**, 0.10–0.40 **Si**	
COPANT 337	T1	COPANT	Bar, forgings	0.65–0.80 **C**, 0.20–0.40 **Mn**, 3.75–4.50 **Cr**, 17.25–18.75 **W**, 0.90–1.30 **V**, 0.030 **P**, 0.030 **S**, 0.20–0.40 **Si**	
DGN–B–82	L 6	Mexico	Bar	0.65–0.80 **C**, 0.40–0.75 **Mn**, 0.75–1.20 **Cr**, 1.25–2.20 **Ni**, 0.20–0.40 **Mo**, 0.15 **V**, 0.10–0.40 **Si**	
ANSI/ASTM A 600	T 1	US	Bar, forgings, plate, sheet, strip	0.65–0.80 **C**, 0.10–0.40 **Mn**, 3.75–4.50 **Cr**, 17.25–18.75 **W**, 0.90–1.30 **V**, 0.03 **P**, 0.03 **S**, 0.20–0.40 **Si**	**Annealed**
IS 3749	T 70Mn65	India	Bar, rings, shapes	0.65–0.75 **C**, 0.50–0.80 **Mn**, 0.035 **P**, 0.035 **S**, 0.10–0.35 **Si**	**Annealed**
IS 3749	T70	India	Bar, rings, shapes	0.65–0.75 **C**, 0.20–0.35 **Mn**, 0.035 **P**, 0.035 **S**, 0.10–0.35 **Si**	**Annealed**
IS: 4367	T70W18Cr4V1	India	Forgings	0.65–0.75 **C**, 0.20–0.40 **Mn**, 4.00–4.50 **Cr**, 0.60 **Mo**, 17.5–19.0 **W**, 1.00–1.50 **V**, 0.10–0.35 **Si**	**Annealed**
COPANT 337	A6	COPANT	Bar, forgings	0.65–0.75 **C**, 1.80–2.50 **Mn**, 0.90–1.20 **Cr**, 0.90–1.40 **Mo**, 0.030 **P**, 0.030 **S**, 0.15–0.40 **Si**	
BS 4656	BA 6	UK	Bar, section, coil, rod, sheet, strip, forgings	0.65–0.75 **C**, 1.8–2.1 **Mn**, 0.85–1.15 **Cr**, 1.2–1.6 **Mo**, 0.40 **Si**	
ASTM A 685	Type A6	US	Rectangular bar: finish, machined	0.65–0.75 **C**, 1.80–2.50 **Mn**, 0.90–1.20 **Cr**, 0.90–1.40 **Mo**, 0.030 **P**, 0.030 **S**, 0.50 **Si**	
DGN–B–82	A 6	Mexico	Bar	0.65–0.75 **C**, 1.75–2.25 **Mn**, 0.80–1.20 **Cr**, 1.20–1.50 **Mo**, 0.10–0.40 **Si**	
ANSI/ASTM A 681	A6	US	Bar, plate, sheet, strip, rod, wire, forgings	0.65–0.75 **C**, 1.80–2.50 **Mn**, 0.90–1.20 **Cr**, 0.90–1.40 **Mo**, 0.030 **P**, 0.030 **S**, 0.50 **Si**	**Annealed**
ANSI/ASTM A 681	L6	US	Bar, plate, sheet, strip, rod, wire, forgings	0.65–0.75 **C**, 0.25–0.80 **Mn**, 0.60–1.20 **Cr**, 1.25–2.00 **Ni**, 0.50 **Mo**, 0.030 **P**, 0.030 **S**, 0.50 **Si**	**Annealed**
NF A 35–590	3548 (Z 65 WDCV 6.05)	France	Bar, forgings	0.65 **C**, 0.3 **Mn**, 4.0 **Cr**, 5.0 **Mo**, 6.0 **W**, 2.0 **V**, 0.030 **P**, 0.030 **S**, 0.30 **Si**	
DGN–B–82	H 42	Mexico	Bar	0.63–0.68 **C**, 0.10–0.40 **Mn**, 4.00–4.50 **Cr**, 4.75–5.25 **Mo**, 6.15–6.65 **W**, 1.75–2.05 **V**, 0.10–0.40 **Si**	
AISI type W1		US	Bar	0.60–1.40 **C**	
AISI type W2		US	Bar	0.60–1.40 **C**	

WROUGHT TOOL STEELS

specification number	designation	country	product forms	composition	mechanical properties (see page iv for explanation)
COPANT 337	W1	COPANT	Bar, forgings	0.60–1.40 **C**, 0.15–0.40 **Mn**, 0.15 **Cr**, 0.030 **P**, 0.030 **S**, 0.10–0.35 **Si**	
COPANT 337	W2	COPANT	Bar, forgings	0.60–1.40 **C**, 0.15–0.40 **Mn**, 0.15 **Cr**, 0.15–0.35 **V**, 0.030 **P**, 0.030 **S**, 0.10–0.35 **Si**	
DGN–B–82	W 2	Mexico	Bar	0.60–1.40 **C**, 0.10–0.40 **Mn**, 0.15–0.25 **V**, 0.10–0.40 **Si**	
DGN–B–82	W 1	Mexico	Bar	0.60–1.40 **C**, 0.10–0.40 **Mn**, 0.10–0.40 **Si**	
ANSI/ASTM A 681	H41	US	Bar, plate, sheet, strip, rod, wire, forgings	0.60–0.75 **C**, 0.15–0.40 **Mn**, 3.50–4.00 **Cr**, 8.20–9.20 **Mo**, 1.40–2.10 **W**, 1.00–1.30 **V**, 0.030 **P**, 0.030 **S**, 0.20–0.45 **Si**	**Annealed**
IS 3749	T65	India	Bar, rings, shapes	0.60–0.70 **C**, 0.50–0.80 **Mn**, 0.035 **P**, 0.035 **S**, 0.10–0.35 **Si**	**Annealed**
BS 4659	BT 21	UK	Bar, section, coil, rod, sheet, strip, forgings	0.60–0.70 **C**, 0.40 **Mn**, 3.5–4.25 **Cr**, 0.7 **Mo**, 13.5–14.5 **W**, 0.40–0.60 **V**, 0.60 **Co**, 0.40 **Si**	
JIS G 3311	SK7M	Japan	Strip	0.60–0.70 **C**, 0.50 **Mn**, 0.20 **Cr**, 0.25 **Ni**, 0.20 **V**, 0.30 **Cu**, 0.030 **P**, 0.030 **S**, 0.35 **Si**	
JIS G 4401	Class 7	Japan	Bar, forgings	0.60–0.70 **C**, 0.50 **Mn**, 0.20 **Cr**, 0.25 **Ni**, 0.25 **Cu**, 0.030 **P**, 0.030 **S**, 0.35 **Si**	**Annealed; Annealed and quenched and tempered**
AISI type H42		US	Bar	0.60 **C**, 4.00 **Cr**, 5.00 **Mo**, 6.00 **W**, 2.00 **V**	
NF A 35–590	3547 (Z 60 WCV 18)	France	Bar, forgings	0.60 **C**, 0.2 **Mn**, 4.25 **Cr**, 18 **W**, 1.0 **V**, 0.030 **P**, 0.030 **S**, 0.30 **Si**	
ANSI/ASTM A 681	H42	US	Bar, plate, sheet, strip, rod, wire, forgings	0.55–0.70 **C**, 0.15–0.40 **Mn**, 3.75–4.50 **Cr**, 4.50–5.50 **Mo**, 5.50–6.75 **W**, 1.75–2.20 **V**, 0.030 **P**, 0.030 **S**, 0.20–0.45 **Si**	**Annealed**
IS 3749	T60	India	Bar, rings, shapes	0.55–0.65 **C**, 0.50–0.80 **Mn**, 0.035 **P**, 0.035 **S**, 0.10–0.35 **Si**	**Annealed**
IS 3749	T60Ni1	India	Bar, rings, shapes	0.55–0.65 **C**, 0.50–0.80 **Mn**, 0.30 max **Cr**, 1.00–1.50 **Ni**, 0.035 **P**, 0.035 **S**, 0.10–0.35 **Si**	**Annealed**
DGN–B–82	H 43	Mexico	Bar	0.55–0.65 **C**, 0.10–0.40 **Mn**, 3.50–4.25 **Cr**, 8.00–8.50 **Mo**, 1.75–2.05 **V**, 0.10–0.40 **Si**	
DGN–B–82	H 41	Mexico	Bar	0.55–0.65 **C**, 0.10–0.40 **Mn**, 3.50–4.00 **Cr**, 8.45–8.95 **Mo**, 1.55–1.85 **W**, 0.85–1.15 **V**, 0.10–0.40 **Si**	
AISI type A8		US	Bar	0.55 **C**, 5.00 **Cr**, 1.25 **Mo**, 1.25 **W**	
AISI type S5		US	Bar	0.55 **C**, 0.80 **Mn**, 0.40 **Mo**, 2.00 **Si**	
NF A 35–590	3381 (55 NCDV 7)	France	Bar, forgings	0.55 **C**, 0.6 **Mn**, 0.8 **Cr**, 1.75 **Ni**, 0.3 **Mo**, 0.2 **V**, 0.030 **P**, 0.030 **S**, 0.30 **Si**	
SIS 14 25 50	SIS 25 50–02	Sweden	Bar, forgings	0.52–0.60 **C**, 0.30–0.50 **Mn**, 0.90–1.10 **Cr**, 2.8–3.2 **Ni**, 0.25–0.35 **Mo**, 0.030 **P**, 0.020 **S**, 0.20–0.40 **Si**	
DGN–B–82	H 26	Mexico	Bar	0.50–0.65 **C**, 0.10–0.40 **Mn**, 3.75–4.25 **Cr**, 17.50–18.50 **W**, 0.85–1.15 **V**, 0.10–0.40 **Si**	
ANSI/ASTM A 681	H43	US	Bar, plate, sheet, strip, rod, wire, forgings	0.50–0.65 **C**, 0.15–0.40 **Mn**, 3.75–4.50 **Cr**, 7.75–8.50 **Mo**, 1.80–2.20 **V**, 0.030 **P**, 0.030 **S**, 0.20–0.45 **Si**	**Annealed**
ANSI/ASTM A 681	S4	US	Bar, plate, sheet, strip, rod, wire, forgings	0.50–0.65 **C**, 0.60–0.95 **Mn**, 0.35 **Cr**, 0.35 **V**, 0.030 **P**, 0.030 **S**, 1.75–2.25 **Si**	**Annealed**
ANSI/ASTM A 681	S5	US	Bar, plate, sheet, strip, rod, wire, forgings	0.50–0.65 **C**, 0.60–1.00 **Mn**, 0.35 **Cr**, 0.20–1.35 **Mo**, 0.35 **V**, 0.030 **P**, 0.030 **S**, 1.75–2.25 **Si**	**Annealed**
IS 3749	T55	India	Bar, rings, shapes	0.50–0.60 **C**, 0.60–0.90 **Mn**, 0.035 **P**, 0.035 **S**, 0.10–0.35 **Si**	**Annealed**

specification number	designation	country	product forms	composition	mechanical properties (see page iv for explanation)
IS 3749	T55Ni2Cr65Mo30	India	Bar, rings, shapes	0.50–0.60 **C**, 0.50–0.80 **Mn**, 0.50–0.80 **Cr**, 1.25–1.75 **Ni**, 0.25–0.35 **Mo**, 0.035 **P**, 0.035 **S**, 0.10–0.35 **Si**	**Annealed**
IS 3749	T55Cr70	India	Bar, rings, shapes	0.50–0.60 **C**, 0.60–0.80 **Mn**, 0.60–0.80 **Cr**, 0.035 **P**, 0.035 **S**, 0.10–0.35 **Si**	**Annealed**
IS 3749	T55Cr70V15	India	Bar, rings, shapes	0.50–0.60 **C**, 0.60–0.80 **Mn**, 0.60–0.80 **Cr**, 0.10–0.20 **V**, 0.035 **P**, 0.035 **S**, 0.10–0.35 **Si**	**Annealed**
IS 3749	T55Si2Mn90	India	Bar, rings, shapes	0.50–0.60 **C**, 0.80–1.00 **Mn**, 0.035 **P**, 0.035 **S**, 1.50–2.00 **Si**	**Annealed**
IS 3749	T55Si2Mn90Mo33	India	Bar, rings, shapes	0.50–0.60 **C**, 0.80–1.00 **Mn**, 0.25–0.40 **Mo**, 0.12–0.20 **V**, 0.035 **P**, 0.035 **S**, 1.50–2.00 **Si**	**Annealed**
IS 4367	T55Cr^{20}V^{15}	India	Forgings	0.50–0.60 **C**, 0.60–0.80 **Mn**, 0.60–0.80 **Cr**, 0.10–0.20 **V**, 0.10–0.35 **Si**	**Annealed**
IS 4367	T55Si2Mn^{90}	India	Forgings	0.50–0.60 **C**, 0.80–1.00 **Mn**, 1.50–2.00 **Si**	**Annealed**
IS 4367	T55Ni2Cr^{65}Mo^{30}	India	Forgings	0.50–0.60 **C**, 0.50–0.90 **Mn**, 0.50–0.80 **Cr**, 1.25–1.75 **Ni**, 0.25–0.35 **Mo**, 0.10–0.35 **Si**	**Annealed**
COPANT 337	C1	COPANT	Bar, forgings	0.50–0.60 **C**, 0.70–1.00 **Mn**, 0.80–1.10 **Cr**, 0.40–0.60 **Mo**, 0.10 min **V**, 0.030 **P**, 0.030 **S**, 0.15–0.40 **Si**	
COPANT 337	C2	COPANT	Bar, forgings	0.50–0.60 **C**, 0.60–0.70 **Mn**, 0.80–1.10 **Cr**, 1.60–2.10 **Ni**, 0.60–0.90 **Mo**, 0.10 min **V**, 0.030 **P**, 0.030 **S**, 0.15–0.40 **Si**	
COPANT 337	S5	COPANT	Bar, forgings	0.50–0.60 **C**, 0.60–1.00 **Mn**, 0.35 **Cr**, 0.30–0.60 **Mo**, 0.35 **V**, 0.030 **P**, 0.030 **S**, 1.75–2.25 **Si**	
BS 4656	BS 5	UK	Bar, section, coil, rod, sheet, strip, forgings	0.50–0.60 **C**, 0.60–0.80 **Mn**, 0.30–0.60 **Mo**, 0.10–0.30 **V**, 1.6–2.1 **Si**	
BS 4659	BH 26	UK	Bar, section, coil, rod, sheet, strip, forgings	0.50–0.60 **C**, 0.40 **Mn**, 3.75–4.5 **Cr**, 0.60 **Mo**, 17.5–18.5 **W**, 1.0–1.5 **V**, 0.60 **Co**, 0.40 **Si**	
IS 3748	T55W14Cr3V45	India	Bar, blanks, rings, shapes	0.50–0.60 **C**, 0.20–0.40 **Mn**, 2.80–3.30 **Cr**, 13.0–15.0 **W**, 0.30–0.60 **V**, 0.10–0.35 **Si**	**Annealed**
JIS G 4404	SKT 2	Japan	Bar, forgings	0.50–0.60 **C**, 0.80–1.20 **Mn**, 0.80–1.20 **Cr**, 0.25 **Ni**, 0.20 **V**, 0.25 **Cu**, 0.030 **P**, 0.030 **S**, 0.35 **Si**	**Annealed**
JIS G 4404	SKT 3	Japan	Bar, forging	0.50–0.60 **C**, 0.60–1.00 **Mn**, 0.90–1.20 **Cr**, 0.25–0.60 **Ni**, 0.30–0.50 **Mo**, 0.20 **V**, 0.25 **Cu**, 0.030 **P**, 0.030 **S**, 0.35 **Si**	**Annealed**
JIS 4404	SKT 4	Japan	Bar, forgings	0.50–0.60 **C**, 0.60–1.00 **Mn**, 0.70–1.00 **Cr**, 1.30–2.00 **Ni**, 0.20–0.50 **Mo**, 0.20 **V**, 0.25 **Cu**, 0.030 **P**, 0.030 **S**, 0.35 **Si**	**Annealed**
JIS G 4404	SKT 5	Japan	Bar, forgings	0.50–0.60 **C**, 0.60–1.00 **Mn**, 1.00–1.50 **Cr**, 0.20–0.50 **Mo**, 0.10–0.30 **V**, 0.25 **Cu**, 0.030 **P**, 0.030 **S**, 0.35 **Si**	**Annealed**
DGN–B–82	S 5	Mexico	Bar	0.50–0.60 **C**, 0.75–1.00 **Mn**, 0.15–0.40 **Cr**, 0.20–0.50 **Mo**, 0.15–0.30 **V**, 1.75–2.25 **Si**	
DGN–B–82	S 4	Mexico	Bar	0.50–0.60 **C**, 0.75–1.00 **Mn**, 0.15–0.30 **Cr**, 0.15–0.30 **V**, 1.75–2.25 **Si**	
DGN–B–82	S 2	Mexico	Bar	0.50–0.60 **C**, 0.40–0.60 **Mn**, 0.40–0.60 **Mo**, 0.15–0.30 **V**, 0.70–1.20 **Si**	
DGN–B–82	H 16	Mexico	Bar	0.50–0.60 **C**, 0.50–0.70 **Mn**, 7.00–7.50 **Cr**, 7.00–7.50 **W**, 0.80–1.00 **Si**	

WROUGHT TOOL STEELS

specification number	designation	country	product forms	composition	mechanical properties (see page iv for explanation)
ANSI/ASTM A 681	A8	US	Bar, plate, sheet, strip, rod, wire, forgings	0.50–0.60 **C**, 0.50 **Mn**, 4.75–5.50 **Cr**, 1.15–1.65 **Mo**, 1.00–1.50 **W**, 0.030 **P**, 0.030 **S**, 0.75–1.10 **Si**	**Annealed**
AISI type H26		US	Bar	0.50 **C**, 4.00 **Cr**, 18.00 **W**, 1.00 **V**	
AISI type A9		US	Bar	0.50 **C**, 5.00 **Cr**, 1.50 **Ni**, 1.40 **Mo**, 1.00 **V**	
AISI type S1		US	Bar	0.50 **C**, 1.50 **Cr**, 2.50 **W**	
AISI type S2		US	Bar	0.50 **C**, 0.50 **Mo**, 1.00 **Si**	
AISI type S7		US	Bar	0.50 **C**, 3.25 **Cr**, 1.40 **Mo**	
SFS 900	SFS 910	Finland	Bar, forgings	0.49 **C**, 0.30 **Mn**, 1.20 **Cr**, 0.25 **Mo**, 2.30 **W**, 0.15 **V**, 0.90 **Si**	
ANSI/ASTM A 681	L2	US	Bar, plate, sheet, strip, rod, wire, forgings	0.45–1.00 **C**, 0.10–0.90 **Mn**, 0.70–1.20 **Cr**, 0.25 **Mo**, 0.10–0.30 **V**, 0.030 **P**, 0.030 **S**, 0.50 **Si**	**Annealed**
IS 3749	T50	India	Bar, rings, shapes	0.45–0.55 **C**, 0.60–0.90 **Mn**, 0.035 **P**, 0.035 **S**	**Annealed**
IS 3749	T50Cr1V23	India	Bar, rings, shapes	0.45–0.55 **C**, 0.50–0.80 **Mn**, 0.90–1.20 **Cr**, 0.15–0.30 **V**, 0.035 **P**, 0.035 **S**, 0.10–0.35 **Si**	**Annealed**
IS 3749	T50W2Cr1V18	India	Bar, rings, shapes	0.45–0.55 **C**, 0.20–0.40 **Mn**, 1.00–1.50 **Cr**, 1.75–2.25 **W**, 0.10–0.25 **V**, 0.035 **P**, 0.035 **S**, 0.50–1.00 **Si**	**Annealed**
IS: 4367	T50W2CriV[18]	India	Forgings	0.45–0.55 **C**, 0.20–0.40 **Mn**, 1.00–1.50 **Cr**, 1.75–2.25 **W**, 0.10–0.25 **V**, 0.50–1.00 **Si**	**Annealed**
COPANT 337	H26	COPANT	Bar, forgings	0.45–0.55 **C**, 0.15–0.40 **Mn**, 3.75–4.50 **Cr**, 1.00 **Mo**, 17.25–19.00 **W**, 0.75–1.25 **V**, 0.030 **P**, 0.030 **S**, 0.20–0.50 **Si**	
COPANT 337	S7	COPANT	Bar, forgings	0.45–0.55 **C**, 0.15–0.40 **Mn**, 1.25–1.75 **Cr**, 0.60 **Mo**, 2.00–3.00 **W**, 0.15–0.30 **V**, 0.030 **P**, 0.030 **S**, 0.15–1.20 **Si**	
COPANT 337	S7	COPANT	Bar, forgings	0.45–0.55 **C**, 0.60–0.80 **Mn**, 2.75–3.50 **Cr**, 1.30–1.80 **Mo**, 0.15–0.30 **V**, 0.030 **P**, 0.030 **S**, 0.20–0.40 **Si**	
COPANT 337	L10	COPANT	Bar, forgings	0.45–0.55 **C**, 0.30–0.60 **Mn**, 0.80–1.10 **Cr**, 3.25–4.00 **Ni**, 0.30–0.50 **Mo**, 0.030 **P**, 0.030 **S**, 0.15–0.40 **Si**	
BS 4656	BS 1	UK	Bar, section, coil, rod, sheet, strip, forgings	0.45–0.55 **C**, 0.30–0.70 **Mn**, 1.2–1.7 **Cr**, 2.0–2.5 **W**, 0.10–0.30 **V**, 0.70–1.0 **Si**	
BS 4656	BS 2	UK	Bar, section, coil, rod, sheet, strip, forgings	0.45–0.55 **C**, 0.30–0.50 **Mn**, 0.30–0.60 **Mo**, 0.10–0.30 **V**, 0.90–1.2 **Si**	
JIS G 4404	SKS 4	Japan	Bar, forgings	0.45–0.55 **C**, 0.50 **Mn**, 0.50–1.00 **Cr**, 0.50–1.00 **W**, 0.25 **Cu**, 0.030 **P**, 0.030 **S**, 0.35 **Si**	**Annealed; Annealed and quenched and tempered**
ASTM A 685	Type S7	US	Bar: finish, machined	0.45–0.55 **C**, 0.20–0.80 **Mn**, 3.00–3.50 **Cr**, 1.30–1.80 **Mo**, 0.20–0.30 **V**, 0.030 **P**, 0.030 **S**, 0.20–1.00 **Si**	
DGN–B–82	O 6	Mexico	Bar	0.45–0.55 **C**, 0.35–1.00 **Mn**, 0.20 **Cr**, 0.15–0.30 **Mo**, 0.80–1.20 **Si**.	
DGN–B–82	A 10	Mexico	Bar	0.45–0.55 **C**, 1.65–2.05 **Mn**, 1.65–2.05 **Ni**, 1.35–1.65 **Mo**, 1.05–1.35 **Si**	
DGN–B–82	A 9	Mexico	Bar	0.45–0.55 **C**, 0.30–0.50 **Mn**, 5.00–5.50 **Cr**, 1.35–1.65 **Ni**, 1.35–1.65 **Mo**, 0.85–1.15 **V**, 0.90–1.10 **Si**	
DGN–B–82	A 8	Mexico	Bar	0.45–0.55 **C**, 0.10–0.40 **Mn**, 5.00–5.50 **Cr**, 1.25–1.75 **Mo**, 1.10–1.40 **W**, 0.20–0.50 **V**, 0.90–1.10 **Si**	

WROUGHT TOOL STEELS

specification number	designation	country	product forms	composition	mechanical properties (see page iv for explanation)
DGN–B–82	S 7	Mexico	Bar	0.45–0.55 **C**, 0.60–0.80 **Mn**, 3.00–3.50 **Cr**, 1.20–1.60 **Mo**, 0.10–0.40 **Si**	
DGN–B–82	H 24	Mexico	Bar	0.45–0.55 **C**, 0.10–0.40 **Mn**, 2.75–3.50 **Cr**, 14.00–15.50 **W**, 0.40–0.70 **V**, 0.10–0.40 **Si**	
ANSI/ASTM A 681	H26	US	Bar, plate, sheet, strip, rod, wire, forgings	0.45–0.55 **C**, 0.15–0.40 **Mn**, 3.75–4.50 **Cr**, 17.25–19.00 **W**, 0.75–1.25 **V**, 0.030 **P**, 0.030 **S**, 0.15–0.40 **Si**	**Annealed**
ANSI/ASTM A 681	A9	US	Bar, plate, sheet, strip, rod, wire, forgings	0.45–0.55 **C**, 0.50 **Mn**, 4.75–5.50 **Cr**, 1.25–1.75 **Ni**, 1.30–1.80 **Mo**, 0.80–1.40 **V**, 0.030 **P**, 0.030 **S**, 0.95–1.15 **Si**	**Annealed**
ANSI/ASTM A 681	S7	US	Bar, plate, sheet, strip, rod, wire, forgings	0.45–0.55 **C**, 0.20–0.80 **Mn**, 3.00–3.50 **Cr**, 1.30–1.80 **Mo**, 0.20–0.30 **V**, 0.030 **P**, 0.030 **S**, 0.20–1.00 **Si**	**Annealed**
AISI type H24		US	Bar	0.45 **C**, 3.00 **Cr**, 15.00 **W**, 0.50 **V**	
AISI type S6		US	Bar	0.45 **C**, 1.40 **Mn**, 1.50 **Cr**, 0.40 **Mo**, 2.25 **Si**	
NF A 35–590	3331 (45 CDV 6)	France	Bar, forgings	0.45 **C**, 0.3 **Mn**, 1.5 **Cr**, 0.8 **Mo**, 0.25 **V**, 0.030 **P**, 0.030 **S**, 0.3 **Si**	
SFS 910		Finland	Bar, forgings	0.44–0.53 **C**, 0.20–0.40 **Mn**, 1.0–1.3 **Cr**, 0.20–0.30 **Mo**, 2.0–2.5 **W**, 0.10–0.20 **V**, 0.030 **P**, 0.020 **S**, 0.70–1.10 **Si**	
SIS 14 27 10	SIS 27 10–02	Sweden	Bar, forgings	0.44–0.53 **C**, 0.20–0.40 **Mn**, 1.0–1.3 **Cr**, 0.20–0.30 **Mo**, 2.0–2.5 **W**, 0.10–0.20 **V**, 0.030 **P**, 0.020 **S**, 0.70–1.10 **Si**	
COPANT 337	H24	COPANT	Bar, forgings	0.42–0.55 **C**, 0.15–0.40 **Mn**, 2.50–3.50 **Cr**, 1.00 **Mo**, 14.00–16.00 **W**, 0.40–0.60 **V**, 0.030 **P**, 0.030 **S**, 0.15–0.40 **Si**	
ANSI/ASTM A 681	H24	US	Bar, plate, sheet, strip, rod, wire, forgings	0.42–0.53 **C**, 0.15–0.40 **Mn**, 2.50–3.50 **Cr**, 14.00–16.00 **W**, 0.40–0.60 **V**, 0.030 **P**, 0.030 **S**, 0.15–0.40 **Si**	**Annealed**
COPANT 337	S2	COPANT	Bar, forgings	0.40–0.55 **C**, 0.30–0.50 **Mn**, 0.30–0.60 **Mo**, 0.50 **V**, 0.030 **P**, 0.030 **S**, 0.90–1.20 **Si**	
ANSI/ASTM A 681	S1	US	Bar, plate, sheet, strip, rod, wire, forgings	0.40–0.55 **C**, 0.10–0.40 **Mn**, 1.00–1.80 **Cr**, 0.50 **Mo**, 1.50–3.00 **W**, 0.15–0.30 **V**, 0.030 **P**, 0.030 **S**, 0.15–1.20 **Si**	**Annealed**
ANSI/ASTM A 681	S2	US	Bar, plate, sheet, strip, rod, wire, forgings	0.40–0.55 **C**, 0.30–0.50 **Mn**, 0.30–0.60 **Mo**, 0.50 **V**, 0.030 **P**, 0.030 **S**, 0.90–1.20 **Si**	**Annealed**
IS 3749	T45Cr1Si95	India	Bar, rings, shapes	0.40–0.50 **C**, 0.55–0.75 **Mn**, 1.20–1.60 **Cr**, 0.035 **P**, 0.035 **S**, 0.80–1.10 **Si**	**Annealed**
DGN–B–82	S 6	Mexico	Bar	0.40–0.50 **C**, 1.00–1.50 **Mn**, 1.00–1.50 **Cr**, 0.30–0.50 **Mo**, 0.20–0.40 **V**, 2.00–2.50 **Si**	
DGN–B–82	S 1	Mexico	Bar	0.40–0.50 **C**, 0.10–0.40 **Mn**, 1.15–1.65 **Cr**, 2.00–2.50 **W**, 0.15–0.30 **V**, 0.10–0.40 **Si**	
ANSI/ASTM A 681	S6	US	Bar, plate, sheet, strip, rod, wire, forgings	0.40–0.50 **C**, 1.20–1.50 **Mn**, 1.20–1.50 **Cr**, 0.30–0.50 **Mo**, 0.20–0.40 **V**, 0.030 **P**, 0.030 **S**, 2.00–2.50 **Si**	**Annealed**
AISI type H10		US	Bar	0.40 **C**, 3.25 **Cr**, 2.50 **Mo**, 0.40 **Co**	
AISI type H19		US	Bar	0.40 **C**, 4.25 **Cr**, 4.25 **W**, 2.00 **V**, 4.25 **Co**	
AISI type H14		US	Bar	0.40 **C**, 5.00 **Cr**, 5.00 **W**	
NF A 35–590	3541 (Z 40 WCV 5)	France	Bar, forgings	0.40 **C**, 0.3 **Mn**, 4.0 **Cr**, 0.5 **Mo**, 5.0 **W**, 0.5 **V**, 0.030 **P**, 0.030 **S**, 0.30 **Si**	
DGN–B–82	H 22	Mexico	Bar	0.38–0.48 **C**, 0.10–0.40 **Mn**, 2.00–3.50 **Cr**, 10.50–12.00 **W**, 0.30–0.45 **V**, 0.10–0.40 **Si**	

WROUGHT TOOL STEELS

specification number	designation	country	product forms	composition	mechanical properties (see page iv for explanation)
NF A 35–590	3431 (Z 38 CDV 5)	France	Bar, forgings	0.38 **C**, 0.3 **Mn**, 5.0 **Cr**, 1.25 **Mo**, 0.5 **V**, 0.030 **P**, 0.030 **S**, 1.0 **Si**	
NF A 35–590	3432 (Z 38 CDWV 5)	France	Bar, forgings	0.38 **C**, 0.3 **Mn**, 5.0 **Cr**, 1.25 **Mo**, 1.25 **W**, 0.5 **V**, 0.030 **P**, 0.030 **S**, 1.0 **Si**	
SFS 900	SFS 913	Finland	Bar, forgings	0.37 **C**, 0.40 **Mn**, 5.00 **Cr**, 1.10 **Mo**, 0.45 **V**, 1.05 **Si**	
IS 3749	T40Ni3Cr65Mo55	India	Bar, rings, shapes	0.36–0.44 **C**, 0.40–0.70 **Mn**, 0.50–0.80 **Cr**, 2.25–2.75 **Ni**, 0.40–0.70 **Mo**, 0.035 **P**, 0.035 **S**, 0.10–0.35 **Si**	**Annealed**
IS 3749	T40Ni3	India	Bar, rings, shapes	0.35–0.45 **C**, 0.50–0.80 **Mn**, 0.30 **Cr**, 3.20–3.60 **Ni**, 0.035 **P**, 0.035 **S**, 0.10–0.35 **Si**	**Annealed**
IS 3749	T40Ni2Cr1Mo28	India	Bar, rings, shapes	0.35–0.45 **C**, 0.40–0.70 **Mn**, 0.90–1.30 **Cr**, 1.25–1.75 **Ni**, 0.20–0.35 **Mo**, 0.035 **P**, 0.035 **S**, 0.10–0.35 **Si**	**Annealed**
IS 3749	T40W2Cr1V18	India	Bar, rings, shapes	0.35–0.45 **C**, 0.20–0.40 **Mn**, 1.00–1.50 **Cr**, 1.75–2.25 **W**, 0.10–0.25 **V**, 0.035 **P**, 0.035 **S**, 0.50–1.00 **Si**	**Annealed**
IS 4367	T40Ni2Cr1Mo[28]	India	Forgings	0.35–0.45 **C**, 0.40–0.70 **Mn**, 0.90–1.30 **Cr**, 1.25–1.75 **Ni**, 0.20–0.35 **Mo**, 0.10–0.35 **Si**	**Annealed**
COPANT 337	H10	COPANT	Bar, forgings	0.35–0.45 **C**, 0.25–0.60 **Mn**, 3.00–3.75 **Cr**, 2.00–3.00 **Mo**, 0.75 **V**, 0.030 **P**, 0.030 **S**, 0.80–1.20 **Si**	
COPANT 337	H13	COPANT	Bar, forgings	0.35–0.45 **C**, 0.20–0.50 **Mn**, 4.75–5.50 **Cr**, 1.10–1.75 **Mo**, 0.80–1.20 **V**	
BS 4659	BH 19	UK	Bar, section, coil, rod, sheet, strip, forgings	0.35–0.45 **C**, 0.40 **Mn**, 4.0–4.5 **Cr**, 0.45 **Mo**, 2.0–2.4 **V**, 4.0–4.5 **Co**, 0.40 **Si**	
JIS G 4404	SKS 41	Japan	Bar, forgings	0.35–0.45 **C**, 0.50 **Mn**, 1.00–1.50 **Cr**, 2.50–3.50 **W**, 0.25 **Cu**, 0.030 **P**, 0.030 **S**, 0.35 **Si**	**Annealed; Annealed and quenched and tempered**
DGN–B–82	H 19	Mexico	Bar	0.35–0.45 **C**, 0.10–0.40 **Mn**, 4.00–4.50 **Cr**, 0.40–0.50 **Mo**, 4.00–4.50 **W**, 2.00–2.40 **V**, 4.00–4.50 **Co**, 0.10–0.40 **Si**	
DGN–B–82	H 13	Mexico	Bar	0.35–0.45 **C**, 0.20–0.50 **Mn**, 5.00–5.50 **Cr**, 1.20–1.50 **Mo**, 0.85–1.15 **V**, 0.90–1.10 **Si**	
DGN–B–82	H 11	Mexico	Bar	0.35–0.45 **C**, 0.10–0.40 **Mn**, 5.00–5.50 **Cr**, 1.20–1.50 **Mo**, 0.30–0.50 **V**, 0.90–1.10 **Si**	
DGN–B–82	H 10	Mexico	Bar	0.35–0.45 **C**, 0.40–0.70 **Mn**, 3.00–3.50 **Cr**, 2.25–2.75 **Mo**, 0.25–0.40 **V**, 0.80–1.20 **Si**	
ANSI/ASTM A 681	H10	US	Bar, plate, sheet, strip, rod, wire, forgings	0.35–0.45 **C**, 0.25–0.70 **Mn**, 3.00–3.75 **Cr**, 2.00–3.00 **Mo**, 0.25–0.75 **V**, 0.030 **P**, 0.030 **S**, 0.80–1.20 **Si**	**Annealed**
ANSI/ASTM A 681	H14	US	Bar, plate, sheet, strip, rod, wire, forgings	0.35–0.45 **C**, 0.20–0.50 **Mn**, 4.75–5.50 **Cr**, 4.00–5.25 **W**, 0.030 **P**, 0.030 **S**, 0.80–1.20 **Si**	**Annealed**
SIS 14 22 42	SIS 22 42–03	Sweden	Bar, forgings, wire	0.35–0.42 **C**, 0.30–0.60 **Mn**, 5.0–5.5 **Cr**, 1.20–1.60 **Mo**, 0.85–1.15 **V**, 0.030 **P**, 0.020 **S**, 0.80–1.20 **Si**	**Quenched and tempered:** (<75) **diam**, (130) **TS**, (110) **YS**, 8 **El**
SIS 14 22 42	SIS 22 42–02	Sweden	Bar, forgings, wire	0.35–0.42 **C**, 0.30–0.60 **Mn**, 5.0–5.5 **Cr**, 1.20–1.60 **Mo**, 0.85–1.15 **V**, 0.030 **P**, 0.020 **S**, 0.80–1.20 **Si**	
AISI type H11		US	Bar	0.35 **C**, 5.00 **Cr**, 1.50 **Mo**, 0.40 **Co**	
AISI type H13		US	Bar	0.35 **C**, 5.00 **Cr**, 1.50 **Mo**, 1.00 **V**	
AISI type H21		US	Bar	0.35 **C**, 3.50 **Cr**, 9.00 **W**, 0.50 **V**	
AISI type H22		US	Bar	0.35 **C**, 2.00 **Cr**, 11.00 **W**, 0.40 **V**	
AISI type P20		US	Bar	0.35 **C**, 1.70 **Cr**, 0.40 **Mo**	

WROUGHT TOOL STEELS

specification number	designation	country	product forms	composition	mechanical properties (see page iv for explanation)
AISI type H12		US	Bar	0.35 **C**, 5.00 **Cr**, 1.50 **Mo**, 1.50 **W**, 0.40 **V**	
NF A 35–590	3382 (Y35 NCD 16)	France	Bar, forgings	0.35 **C**, 0.4 **Mn**, 1.8 **Cr**, 4.0 **Ni**, 0.4 **Mo**, 0.1 **V**, 0.030 **P**, 0.030 **S**, 0.30 **Si**	
COPANT 337	H11	COPANT	Bar, forgings	0.33–0.43 **C**, 0.20–0.50 **Mn**, 4.75–5.50 **Cr**, 1.10–1.75 **Mo**, 0.30–0.60 **V**, 0.030 **P**, 0.030 **S**, 0.80–1.20 **Si**	
JIS G 4410	SKC 24	Japan	Bar, forgings	0.33–0.43 **C**, 0.50 **Mn**, 0.30–0.70 **Cr**, 2.50–3.50 **Ni**, 0.15–0.40 **Mo**, 0.25 **Cu**, 0.030 **P**, 0.030 **S**, 0.15–0.35 **Si**	**Quenched and tempered**
ANSI/ASTM A 681	H11	US	Bar, plate, sheet, strip, rod, wire, forgings	0.33–0.43 **C**, 0.20–0.50 **Mn**, 4.75–5.50 **Cr**, 1.10–1.60 **Mo**, 0.30–0.60 **V**, 0.030 **P**, 0.030 **S**, 0.80–1.20 **Si**	**Annealed**
ANSI/ASTM A 681	H13	US	Bar, plate, sheet, strip, rod, wire, forgings	0.32–0.45 **C**, 0.20–0.50 **Mn**, 4.75–5.50 **Cr**, 1.10–1.75 **Mo**, 0.80–1.20 **V**, 0.030 **P**, 0.030 **S**, 0.80–1.20 **Si**	**Annealed**
ANSI/ASTM A 681	H19	US	Bar, plate, sheet, strip, rod, wire, forgings	0.32–0.45 **C**, 0.20–0.50 **Mn**, 4.00–4.75 **Cr**, 0.30–0.55 **Mo**, 3.75–4.50 **W**, 1.75–2.20 **V**, 4.00–4.50 **Co**, 0.030 **P**, 0.030 **S**, 0.20–0.50 **Si**	**Annealed**
SFS 913		Finland	Bar, forgings	0.32–0.42 **C**, 0.3–0.5 **Mn**, 4.5–5.5 **Cr**, 0.80–1.40 **Mo**, 0.30–0.60 **V**, 0.030 **P**, 0.020 **S**, 0.90–1.20 **Si**	
BS 4659	BH 11	UK	Bar, section, coil, rod, sheet, strip, forgings	0.32–0.42 **C**, 0.40 **Mn**, 4.75–5.25 **Cr**, 1.25–1.75 **Mo**, 0.30–0.50 **V**, 0.85–1.15 **Si**	
BS 4659	BH 13	UK	Bar, section, coil, rod, sheet, strip, forgings	0.32–0.42 **C**, 0.40 **Mn**, 4.75–5.25 **Cr**, 1.25–1.75 **Mo**, 0.90–1.10 **V**, 0.85–1.15 **Si**	
JIS G 4404	SKD 6	Japan	Bar, forgings	0.32–0.42 **C**, 0.50 **Mn**, 4.50–5.50 **Cr**, 0.25 **Ni**, 1.00–1.50 **Mo**, 0.30–0.50 **V**, 0.25 **Cu**, 0.030 **P**, 0.030 **S**, 0.80–1.20 **Si**	**Annealed; Annealed and quenched and tempered**
JIS G 4404	SKD 61	Japan	Bar, forgings	0.32–0.42 **C**, 0.50 **Mn**, 4.50–5.50 **Cr**, 0.25 **Ni**, 1.00–1.50 **Mo**, 0.80–1.20 **V**, 0.25 **Cu**, 0.030 **P**, 0.030 **S**, 0.80–1.20 **Si**	**Annealed; Annealed and quenched and tempered**
JIS G 4404	SKD 62	Japan	Bar, forgings	0.32–0.42 **C**, 0.50 **Mn**, 4.50–5.50 **Cr**, 0.25 **Ni**, 1.00–1.50 **Mo**, 1.00–1.50 **W**, 0.20–0.60 **V**, 0.25 **Cu**, 0.030 **P**, 0.030 **S**, 0.80–1.20 **Si**	**Annealed; Annealed and quenched and tempered**
NF A 35–590	3383 (32 NDC 18.12)	France	Bar, forgings	0.32 **C**, 0.3 **Mn**, 0.5 **Cr**, 4.5 **Ni**, 1.2 **Mo**, 0.030 **P**, 0.030 **S**, 0.30 **Si**	
IS: 4367	T35Cr5MoV1	India	Forgings	0.30–0.40 **C**, 0.25–0.50 **Mn**, 4.75–5.25 **Cr**, 1.20–1.60 **Mo**, 1.00–1.20 **V**, 0.80–1.20 **Si**	**Annealed**
COPANT 337	H12	COPANT	Bar, forgings	0.30–0.40 **C**, 0.20–0.50 **Mn**, 4.75–5.50 **Cr**, 1.25–1.75 **Mo**, 1.00–1.70 **W**, 0.50 **V**, 0.030 **P**, 0.030 **S**, 0.80–1.20 **Si**	
COPANT 337	P20	COPANT	Bar, forgings	0.30–0.40 **C**, 0.60–0.90 **Mn**, 1.50–1.90 **Cr**, 0.30–0.50 **Mo**, 0.30 **V**, 0.030 **P**, 0.030 **S**, 0.50–0.80 **Si**	
BS 4659	BH 10	UK	Bar, section, coil, rod, sheet, strip, forgings	0.30–0.40 **C**, 0.40 **Mn**, 2.8–3.2 **Cr**, 2.65–2.95 **Mo**, 0.30–0.50 **V**, 1.10 **Si**	
BS 4659	BH 10A	UK	Bar, section, coil, rod, sheet, strip, forgings	0.30–0.40 **C**, 0.40 **Mn**, 2.8–3.2 **Cr**, 2.65–2.95 **Mo**, 0.30–1.10 **V**, 2.8–3.2 **Co**, 1.10 **Si**	
BS 4659	BH 12	UK	Bar, section, coil, rod, sheet, strip, forgings	0.30–0.40 **C**, 0.40 **Mn**, 4.75–5.25 **Cr**, 1.25–1.75 **Mo**, 1.25–1.75 **W**, 0.50 **V**, 0.85–1.15 **Si**	

WROUGHT TOOL STEELS

specification number	designation	country	product forms	composition	mechanical properties (see page iv for explanation)
IS 3748	T35Cr5Mo1V30	India	Bar, blanks, rings, shapes	0.30–0.40 **C**, 0.25–0.50 **Mn**, 4.75–5.25 **Cr**, 1.20–1.60 **Mo**, 0.20–0.40 **V**, 0.80–1.20 **Si**	**Annealed**
IS 3748	T35Cr5MoV1	India	Bar, blanks, rings, shapes	0.30–0.40 **C**, 0.25–0.50 **Mn**, 4.75–5.25 **Cr**, 1.20–1.60 **Mo**, 1.00–1.20 **V**, 0.80–1.20 **Si**	**Annealed**
IS 3748	T35Cr5MoW1V30	India	Bar, blanks, rings, shapes	0.30–0.40 **C**, 0.25–0.50 **Mn**, 4.75–5.25 **Cr**, 1.20–1.60 **Mo**, 1.20–1.60 **W**, 0.20–0.40 **V**, 0.80–1.20 **Si**	**Annealed**
DGN–B–82	H 14	Mexico	Bar	0.30–0.40 **C**, 0.10–0.40 **Mn**, 5.00–5.50 **Cr**, 0.20–0.30 **Mo**, 4.25–5.00 **W**, 0.20–0.30 **V**, 0.50 **Co**, 0.90–1.15 **Si**	
DGN–B–82	H 12	Mexico	Bar	0.30–0.40 **C**, 0.10–0.40 **Mn**, 5.00–5.50 **Cr**, 1.25–1.75 **Mo**, 1.00–1.55 **W**, 0.20–0.50 **V**, 0.90–1.10 **Si**	
ANSI/ASTM A 681	H12	US	Bar, plate, sheet, strip, rod, wire, forgings	0.30–0.40 **C**, 0.20–0.50 **Mn**, 4.75–5.50 **Cr**, 1.25–1.75 **Mo**, 1.00–1.70 **W**, 0.50 **V**, 0.030 **P**, 0.030 **S**, 0.80–1.20 **Si**	**Annealed**
ANSI/ASTM A 681	H22	US	Bar, plate, sheet, strip, rod, wire, forgings	0.30–0.40 **C**, 0.15–0.40 **Mn**, 1.75–3.75 **Cr**, 10.00–11.75 **W**, 0.25–0.50 **V**, 0.030 **P**, 0.030 **S**, 0.15–0.40 **Si**	**Annealed**
DGN–B–82	P 20	Mexico	Bar	0.30–0.35 **C**, 0.65–0.90 **Mn**, 0.70–0.90 **Cr**, 0.20–0.45 **Mo**, 0.40–0.60 **Si**	
AISI type H23		US	Bar	0.30 **C**, 12.00 **Cr**, 12.00 **W**, 1.00 **V**	
NF A 35–590	3451 (30 DCV 28)	France	Bar, forgings	0.30 **C**, 0.3 **Mn**, 2.8 **Cr**, 2.8 **Mo**, 0.5 **V**, 0.030 **P**, 0.030 **S**, 0.30 **Si**	
NF A 35–590	3452 (30 DCKV 28)	France	Bar, forgings	0.30 **C**, 0.3 **Mn**, 2.8 **Cr**, 2.8 **Mo**, 0.5 **V**, 2.5 **Co**, 0.030 **P**, 0.030 **S**, 0.30 **Si**	
NF A 35–590	3543 (Z 30 W CV 9)	France	Bar, forgings	0.30 **C**, 0.30 **Mn**, 3.0 **Cr**, 9.0 **W**, 0.4 **V**, 0.030 **P**, 0.030 **S**, 0.30 **Si**	
ANSI/ASTM A 681	P20	US	Bar, plate, sheet, strip, rod, wire, forgings	0.28–0.40 **C**, 0.60–1.00 **Mn**, 1.40–2.00 **Cr**, 0.30–0.55 **Mo**	
IS 3749	T31Ni3Cr65Mo55	India	Bar, rings, shapes	0.27–0.35 **C**, 0.40–0.70 **Mn**, 0.50–0.80 **Cr**, 2.25–2.75 **Ni**, 0.40–0.70 **Mo**, 0.035 **P**, 0.035 **S**, 0.10–0.35 **Si**	**Annealed**
COPANT 337	H21	COPANT	Bar, forgings	0.26–0.36 **C**, 0.15–0.40 **Mn**, 2.40–3.75 **Cr**, 0.60 **Mo**, 8.75–10.00 **W**, 0.20–0.60 **V**, 0.030 **P**, 0.030 **S**, 0.20–0.50 **Si**	
ANSI/ASTM A 681	H21	US	Bar, plate, sheet, strip, rod, wire, forgings	0.26–0.36 **C**, 0.15–0.40 **Mn**, 3.00–3.75 **Cr**, 8.50–10.00 **W**, 0.30–0.60 **V**, 0.030 **P**, 0.030 **S**, 0.15–0.50 **Si**	**Annealed**
IS 3749	T30Ni4Cr1	India	Bar, rings, shapes	0.26–0.34 **C**, 0.40–0.70 **Mn**, 1.10–1.40 **Cr**, 3.90–4.30 **Ni**, 0.035 **P**, 0.035 **S**, 0.10–0.35 **Si**	**Annealed**
IS: 4367	T33W9Cr3V[38]	India	Forgings	0.25–0.40 **C**, 0.20–0.40 **Mn**, 2.80–3.30 **Cr**, 8.00–10.00 **W**, 0.25–0.50 **V**, 0.10–0.35 **Si**	**Annealed**
IS 3748	T33W9Cr3V38	India	Bar, blanks, rings, shapes	0.25–0.40 **C**, 0.20–0.40 **Mn**, 2.80–3.30 **Cr**, 8.00–10.00 **W**, 0.25–0.50 **V**, 0.035 **P**, 0.035 **S**, 0.10–0.35 **Si**	**Annealed**
BS 4659	BH 21	UK	Bar, section, coil, rod, sheet, strip, forgings	0.25–0.35 **C**, 0.40 **Mn**, 2.25–3.25 **Cr**, 0.60 **Mo**, 8.5–10.0 **W**, 0.40 **V**, 0.40 **Si**	
JIS G 4404	SKD 4	Japan	Bar, forgings	0.25–0.35 **C**, 0.60 **Mn**, 2.00–3.00 **Cr**, 0.25 **Ni**, 5.00–6.00 **W**, 0.30–0.50 **V**, 0.25 **Cu**, 0.030 **P**, 0.030 **S**, 0.40 **Si**	**Annealed; Annealed and quenched and tempered**
JIS G 4404	SKD 5	Japan	Bar, forgings	0.25–0.35 **C**, 0.60 **Mn**, 2.00–3.00 **Cr**, 0.25 **Ni**, 9.00–10.00 **W**, 0.30–0.50 **V**, 0.25 **Cu**, 0.030 **P**, 0.030 **S**, 0.40 **Si**	**Annealed; Annealed and quenched and tempered**

specification number	designation	country	product forms	composition	mechanical properties (see page iv for explanation)
DGN-B-82	H 21	Mexico	Bar	0.25–0.35 **C**, 0.10–0.40 **Mn**, 3.00–3.50 **Cr**, 9.00–10.0 **W**, 0.25–0.60 **V**, 0.10–0.40 **Si**	
DGN-B-82	H 20	Mexico	Bar	0.25–0.35 **C**, 0.10–0.40 **Mn**, 1.80–2.20 **Cr**, 9.00–10.0 **W**, 0.40–0.60 **V**, 0.10–0.40 **Si**	
DGN-B-82	H 23	Mexico	Bar	0.25–0.35 **C**, 0.10–0.40 **Mn**, 11.50–12.50 **Cr**, 11.50–12.50 **W**, 0.90–1.10 **V**, 0.40–0.60 **Si**	
ANSI/ASTM A 681	H23	US	Bar, plate, sheet, strip, rod, wire, forgings	0.25–0.35 **C**, 0.15–0.40 **Mn**, 11.00–12.75 **Cr**, 11.00–12.75 **W**, 0.75–1.25 **V**, 0.030 **P**, 0.030 **S**, 0.15–0.60 **Si**	**Annealed**
AISI type H25		US	Bar	0.25 **C**, 4.00 **Cr**, 15.00 **W**, 0.50 **V**	
ANSI/ASTM A 681	H25	US	Bar, plate, sheet, strip, rod, wire, forgings	0.22–0.32 **C**, 0.15–0.40 **Mn**, 3.75–4.50 **Cr**, 14.00–16.00 **W**, 0.40–0.60 **V**, 0.030 **P**, 0.030 **S**, 0.15–0.40 **Si**	**Annealed**
JIS G 4403	SKH 5	Japan	Bar, forgings	0.20–0.40 **C**, 0.40 **Mn**, 3.80–4.50 **Cr**, 0.25 **Ni**, 17.00–22.00 **W**, 1.00–1.50 **V**, 16.00–17.00 **Co**, 0.25 **Cu**, 0.030 **P**, 0.030 **S**, 0.40 **Si**	**Annealed; Quenched and tempered**
BS 4659	BH 21A	UK	Bar, section, coil, rod, sheet, strip, forgings	0.20–0.30 **C**, 0.40 **Mn**, 2.25–3.25 **Cr**, 2.0–2.5 **Ni**, 0.60 **Mo**, 8.5–10.0 **W**, 0.50 **V**, 0.40 **Si**	
DGN-B-82	H 25	Mexico	Bar	0.20–0.30 **C**, 0.10–0.40 **Mn**, 3.50–4.00 **Cr**, 14.00–15.00 **W**, 0.40–0.60 **V**, 0.10–0.40 **Si**	
AISI type P21		US	Bar	0.20 **C**, 4.00 **Ni**, 1.20 **Al**	
COPANT 337	C3	COPANT	Bar, forgings	0.20 **C**, 0.70 **Mn**, 3.00 **Ni**, 3.35 **Mo**, 0.030 **P**, 0.030 **S**, 0.25 **Si**	
NF A 35-590	3455 (20 DN 32.12)	France	Bar, forgings	0.20 **C**, 0.5 **Mn**, 3.0 **Ni**, 3.2 **Mo**, 0.030 **P**, 0.030 **S**, 0.30 **Si**	
NF A 35-590	3545 (Z 25 WCKD V9)	France	Bar, forgings	0.20 **C**, 0.3 **Mn**, 2.5 **Cr**, 1.0 **Mo**, 8.5 **W**, 0.4 **V**, 2.0 **Co**, 0.030 **P**, 0.030 **S**, 0.60 **Si**	
ANSI/ASTM A 681	P21	US	Bar, plate, sheet, strip, rod, wire, forgings	0.18–0.22 **C**, 0.20–0.40 **Mn**, 0.20–0.30 **Cr**, 0.90–4.25 **Ni**, 0.15–0.25 **V**, 1.05–1.25 **Al**, 0.030 **P**, 0.030 **S**, 0.20–0.40 **Si**	
DGN-B-82	P 21	Mexico	Bar	0.15–0.25 **C**, 0.10–0.40 **Mn**, 0.20–0.30 **Cr**, 3.90–4.30 **Ni**, 0.15–0.30 **V**, 1.00–1.40 **Al**, 0.10–0.40 **Si**	
JIS G 4410	SKC 31	Japan	Bar, forgings	0.12–0.25 **C**, 0.60–1.20 **Mn**, 1.20–1.80 **Cr**, 2.80–3.20 **Ni**, 0.40–0.70 **Mo**, 0.25 **Cu**, 0.030 **P**, 0.030 **S**, 0.15–0.35 **Si**	**Quenched and tempered**
IS: 4367	T16NiCr2Mo[20]	India	Forgings	0.12–0.20 **C**, 0.40–0.70 **Mn**, 1.40–1.70 **Cr**, 1.80–2.20 **Ni**, 0.15–0.25 **Mo**, 0.10–0.35 **Si**	**Annealed**
IS: 4367	T15Cr[65]	India	Forgings	0.12–0.18 **C**, 0.40–0.60 **Mn**, 0.50–0.80 **Cr**, 0.10–0.35 **Si**	**Annealed**
IS: 4367	T15NiCr1Mo[12]	India	Forgings	0.12–0.18 **C**, 0.60–1.00 **Mn**, 0.75–1.25 **Cr**, 1.00–1.50 **Ni**, 0.08–0.15 **Mo**, 0.10–0.35 **Si**	**Annealed**
DGN-B-82	P 6	Mexico	Bar	0.12 **C**, 0.40–0.60 **Mn**, 1.25–1.75 **Cr**, 3.25–4.00 **Ni**, 0.10–0.40 **Si**	
ANSI/ASTM A 689	P4	US	Bar, plate, sheet, strip, rod, wire, forgings	0.12 **C**, 0.20–0.60 **Mn**, 4.00–5.25 **Cr**, 0.40–1.00 **Mo**, 0.030 **P**, 0.030 **S**, 0.10–0.40 **Si**	**Annealed**
AISI type P3		US	Bar	0.10 **C**, 0.60 **Cr**, 1.25 **Ni**	
AISI type P5		US	Bar	0.10 **C**, 2.25 **Cr**	
AISI type P6		US	Bar	0.10 **C**, 1.50 **Cr**, 3.50 **Ni**	
COPANT 337	P4	COPANT	Bar, forgings	0.10 **C**, 0.20–0.50 **Mn**, 4.25–5.00 **Cr**, 0.40–0.75 **Mo**, 0.30 **V**, 0.030 **P**, 0.030 **S**, 0.15–0.30 **Si**	

WROUGHT TOOL STEELS

specification number	designation	country	product forms	composition	mechanical properties (see page iv for explanation)
DGN-B-82	P 5	Mexico	Bar	0.10 **C**, 0.30–0.50 **Mn**, 2.00–2.60 **Cr**, 0.10–0.40 **Si**	
DGN-B-82	P 4	Mexico	Bar	0.10 **C**, 0.10–0.40 **Mn**, 3.90–5.00 **Cr**, 0.35–0.55 **Mo**, 0.10–0.40 **Si**	
DGN-B-82	P 3	Mexico	Bar	0.10 **C**, 0.40–0.60 **Mn**, 0.50–0.70 **Cr**, 1.10–1.40 **Ni**, 0.10–0.40 **Si**	
DGN-B-82	P 2	Mexico	Bar	0.10 **C**, 0.30–0.70 **Mn**, 1.00–1.40 **Cr**, 0.45–0.65 **Ni**, 0.20–0.30 **Mo**, 0.10–0.40 **Si**	
DGN-B-82	P 1	Mexico	Bar	0.10 **C**, 0.10–0.30 **Mn**, 0.10 **V**, 0.10–0.40 **Si**	
ANSI/ASTM A 681	P2	US	Bar, plate, sheet, strip, rod, wire, forgings	0.10 **C**, 0.10–0.40 **Mn**, 0.75–1.25 **Cr**, 0.10–0.50 **Ni**, 0.15–0.40 **Mo**, 0.030 **P**, 0.030 **S**, 0.10–0.40 **Si**	**Annealed**
ANSI/ASTM A 681	P3	US	Bar, plate, sheet, strip, rod, wire, forgings	0.10 **C**, 0.20–0.60 **Mn**, 0.40–0.75 **Cr**, 1.00–1.50 **Ni**, 0.030 **P**, 0.030 **S**, 0.40 **Si**	**Annealed**
ANSI/ASTM A 681	P5	US	Bar, plate, sheet, strip, rod, wire, forgings	0.10 **C**, 0.20–0.60 **Mn**, 2.00–2.50 **Cr**, 0.35 **Ni**, 0.030 **P**, 0.030 **S**, 0.40 **Si**	**Annealed**
NF A 35-590	2831 (Z 8 CDV 5)	France	Bar, forgings	0.08 **C**, 0.3 **Mn**, 5.0 **Cr**, 1.0 **Mo**, 0.3 **V**, 0.030 **P**, 0.030 **S**, 0.2 **Si**	
AISI type P2		US	Bar	0.07 **C**, 2.00 **Cr**, 0.50 **Ni**, 0.20 **Mo**	
AISI type P4		US	Bar	0.07 **C**, 5.00 **Cr**, 0.75 **Mo**	
ANSI/ASTM A 681	P6	US	Bar, plate, sheet, strip, rod, wire, forgings	0.05–0.15 **C**, 0.35–0.70 **Mn**, 1.25–1.75 **Cr**, 3.25–3.75 **Ni**, 0.030 **P**, 0.030 **S**, 0.10–0.40 **Si**	**Annealed**

WROUGHT STAINLESS, HEAT RESISTANT, AND CORROSION RESISTANT STEELS

WROUGHT STAINLESS STEELS

specification number	designation	country	product forms	composition	mechanical properties (see page iv for explanation)
AMS 5749		US	Bar, forging, tube, wire	1.10–1.20 **C**, 0.30–0.60 **Mn**, 0.20–0.40 **Si**, 14.00–15.00 **Cr**, 0.40 **Ni**, 3.75–4.25 **Mo**, 1.10–1.30 **W**, 0.35 **Cu**, 1.10–1.30 **V**, 0.015 **P**, 0.010 **S**	**Cold finished, annealed (wire)**: all **diam**, 130 (896) max **TS**
AISI 440C		US	Bar, wire	0.95–1.25 **C**, 1.00 **Mn**, 1.00 **Si**, 16.00–18.00 **Cr**, 0.75 **Mo**, 0.040 **P**, 0.030 **S**	**Annealed (bar)**: all **diam**, 110 (758) max **TS**, 65 (448) max **YS**, 14 **El**; **Annealed and cold finished (bar)**: 1 (25.40) **diam**, 125 (862) max **TS**, 100 (689) max **YS**, 7 **El**
ANSI/ASTM A 580	Grade 440 C	US	Wire	0.95–1.20 **C**, 1.00 **Mn**, 1.00 **Si**, 16.00–18.00 **Cr**, 0.75 **Mo**, 0.040 **P**, 0.030 **S**	**Annealed**: all **diam**, 140 (970) max **TS**
AMS 5632D	Type I	US	Bar, forgings, wire	0.95–1.20 **C**, 1.25 **Mn**, 1.00 **Si**, 16.00–18.00 **Cr**, 0.75 **Ni**, 0.40–0.60 **Mo**, 0.50 **Cu**, 0.08 **N**, 0.040 **P**, 0.10–0.35 **S**, 0.05	**Annealed and cold finished wire**: all **diam**, 140 (965) max **TS**
AMS 5632D	Type II	US	Bar, forgings, wire	0.95–1.20 **C**, 1.25 **Mn**, 1.00 **Si**, 16.00–18.00 **Cr**, 0.75 **Ni**, 0.40–0.60 **Mo**, 0.50 **Cu**, 0.08 **Ni**, 0.040 **P**, 0.030 **S**, 0.05	**Annealed and cold finished wire**: all **diam**, 140 (965) max **TS**
DGN–B–83	440 C	Mexico	Bar	0.95–1.20 **C**, 1.0 **Mn**, 1.0 **Si**, 16.0–18.0 **Cr**, 0.75 **Mo**, 0.040 **P**, 0.030 **S**	**Hot or cold rolled**: all **diam**, (735) **TS**, (451) **YS**, 14 **El**
ANSI/ASTM A 493	Type 440C	US	Bar, wire	0.95–1.20 **C**, 1.00 **Mn**, 1.00 **Si**, 16.00–18.00 **Cr**, 0.75 **Mo**, 0.040 **P**, 0.030 **S**	**Lightly drafted (wire)**: ≥0.156 (≥3.96) **diam**, 100 (690) **TS**; **Annealed (wire)**: ≥0.156 (≥3.96) **diam**, 90 (620) **TS**
ASTM A 582	440F	US	Bar	0.95–1.20 **C**, 1.25 **Mn**, 1.00 **Si**, 16.00–18.00 **Cr**, 0.50 **Ni**, 0.60 **Mo**, 0.60 **Cu**, 0.06 **P**, 0.15 min **S**	
ASTM A 582	440FSe	US	Bar	0.95–1.20 **C**, 1.25 **Mn**, 1.00 **Si**, 16.00–18.00 **Cr**, 0.50 **Ni**, 0.60 **Mo**, 0.60 **Cu**, 0.06 **P**, 0.06 **S**, 0.15 min **Se**	
ANSI/ASTM A 473	440C	US	Forgings	0.95–1.20 **C**, 1.00 **Mn**, 1.00 **Si**, 16.00–18.00 **Cr**, 0.75 **Mo**, 0.040 **P**, 0.030 **S**	**Annealed**
ANSI/ASTM A 314	440C	US	Bar, forgings, billets	0.95–1.20 **C**, 1.00 **Mn**, 1.00 **Si**, 16.00–18.00 **Cr**, 0.75 **Mo**, 0.040 **P**, 0.030 **S**	
ANSI/ASTM A 276	440C	US	Bar, shapes	0.95–1.20 **C**, 1.00 **Mn**, 1.00 **Si**, 16.00–18.00 **Cr**, 0.75 **Mo**, 0.040 **P**, 0.030 **S**	**Annealed**
MIL–S–862B	Class 440C	US	Bar, billets	0.95–1.2 **C**, 1.0 **Mn**, 1.0 **Si**, 16.0–18.0 **Cr**, 0.75 **Mo**, 0.040 **P**, 0.030 **S**	
MIL–S–862B	Class 440F	US	Bar, billets	0.95–1.2 **C**, 1.25 **Mn**, 1.0 **Si**, 16.0–18.0 **Cr**, 0.75 **Mo**, 0.060 **P**, 0.050 **S**	
MIL–S–862B	Class 440F Se	US	Bar, billets	0.95–1.2 **C**, 1.25 **Mn**, 1.0 **Si**, 16.0–18.0 **Cr**, 0.75 **Mo**, 0.060 **P**, 0.050 **S**, 0.15 min **Se**	
ISO 683/XII	A–1b	ISO	Bar, sheet, plate	0.95–1.20 **C**, 1.0 **Mn**, 1.0 **Si**, 16.0–18.0 **Cr**, 0.50 **Ni**, 0.75 **Mo**, 0.040 **P**, 0.030 **S**	
AMS 5618		US	Bar, forgings	0.95–1.20 **C**, 1.00 **Mn**, 1.00 **Si**, 16.00–18.00 **Cr**, 0.75 **Ni**, 0.40–0.60 **Mo**, 0.025 **P**, 0.015 **S**	
AMS 5630D		US	Bar, forgings	0.95–1.20 **C**, 1.00 **Mn**, 1.00 **Si**, 16.00–18.00 **Cr**, 0.75 **Ni**, 0.40–0.65 **Mo**, 0.50 **Cu**, 0.040 **P**, 0.030 **S**	
ISO 683/XVII	21	ISO	Billets, bar, wire, tube, ring	0.95–1.20 **C**, 1.00 **Mn**, 1.00 **Si**, 16.0–18.0 **Cr**, 0.50 **Ni**, 0.35–0.75 **Mo**, 0.040 **P**, 0.030 **S**	
JIS G 4303	SUS 440C	Japan	Bar	0.95–1.20 **C**, 1.00 **Mn**, 1.00 **Si**, 16.00–18.00 **Cr**, 0.60 **Ni**, 0.75 **Mo**	**Quenched and tempered**

specification number	designation	country	product forms	composition	mechanical properties (see page iv for explanation)
JIS G 4303	SUS 440F	Japan	Bar	0.95–1.20 **C**, 1.25 **Mn**, 1.00 **Si**, 16.00–18.00 **Cr**, 0.60 **Ni**, 0.75 **Mo**, 0.060 **P**, 0.15 **S**	**Quenched and tempered**
JIS G 4308	SUS 440 C	Japan	Wire, rod	0.95–1.20 **C**, 1.00 **Mn**, 1.00 **Si**, 16.00–18.00 **Cr**, 0.60 **Ni**, 0.75 **Mo**, 0.040 **P**, 0.030 **S**	
CSA G110.3	Type 440C	Canada	Bar, billets	0.95–1.20 **C**, 1.00 **Mn**, 1.00 **Si**, 16.00–18.00 **Cr**, 0.75 **Mo**, 0.040 **P**, 0.030 **S**	
AECMA prEN2226	FE–PM 43	AECMA	Forgings	0.95–1.10 **C**, 1.00 **Mn**, 1.00 **Si**, 16.0–18.0 **Cr**, 0.50 **Ni**, 0.35–0.75 **Mo**, 0.030 **P**, 0.020 **S**	**Hardened and tempered**
AECMA prEN2227	FE–PM 44	AECMA	Forgings	0.95–1.10 **C**, 1.00 **Mn**, 1.00 **Si**, 16.0–18.0 **Cr**, 0.50 **Ni**, 0.35–0.75 **Mo**, 0.025 **P**, 0.015 **S**	**Hardened and tempered**
AECMA prEn2030		AECMA	Bar	0.95–1.10 **C**, 1.00 **Mn**, 1.00 **Si**, 16.0–18.0 **Cr**, 0.50 **Ni**, 0.35–0.75 **Mo**, 0.030 **P**, 0.020 **S**	**Hardened and tempered**
AECMA prEn2159		AECMA	Bar	0.95–1.10 **C**, 1.00 **Mn**, 1.00 **Si**, 16.00–18.00 **Cr**, 0.50 **Ni**, 0.35–0.75 **Mo**, 0.025 **P**, 0.015 **S**	**Hardened and tempered**: all **diam**
AIR 9160	9160C381	France	Bar, forgings: bearing steel	0.95–1.10 **C**, 1.0 **Mn**, 0.030 **P**, 0.020 **S**, 1.0 **Si**, 16.0–18.0 **Cr**, 0.75 **Ni**, 0.35–0.75 **Mo**	**Hardened and tempered**
NF A 35–575	Z 100 CD 17	France	Wire, rod	0.90–1.20 **C**, 1.0 **Mn**, 1.0 **Si**, 16.0–18.0 **Cr**, 0.35–0.75 **Mo**, 0.040 **P**, 0.030 **S**	**Quenched and tempered**: all **diam**, (880) max **TS**
IS 6529	105Cr18Mo[50]	India	Blooms, billets, slabs	0.90–1.20 **C**, 1.0 **Mn**, 1.0 **Si**, 16.0–19.0 **Cr**, 0.50 **Ni**, 0.75 **Mo**, 0.040 **P**, 0.030 **S**	**Annealed or solution annealed**
IS 6603	105Cr18Mo50	India	Bar	0.90–1.20 **C**, 1.00 **Mn**, 1.00 **Si**, 16.0–19.0 **Cr**, 0.50 **Ni**, 0.75 **Mo**, 0.040 **P**, 0.030 **S**	**Annealed**; **Quenched and tempered**
IS 6911	105Cr18Mo[50]	India	Plate, sheet, strip	0.90–1.20 **C**, 1.0 **Mn**, 1.0 **Si**, 16.0–19.0 **Cr**, 0.50 **Ni**, 0.75 **Mo**, 0.030 **S**, 0.040 **P**	**Annealed**
ISO 683/XV	3	ISO	Bar: hot rolled	0.80–0.90 **C**, 1.5 **Mn**, 1.0 **Si**, 16.5–18.5 **Cr**, 2.0–2.5 **Mo**, 0.30–0.60 **V**, 0.040 **P**, 0.030 **S**	**Quenched and tempered**: all **diam**, (1080) **TS**, (835) **YS**, 12 **El**
MIL–S–6721B	Cb (348)	US	Plate, sheet, strip	0.8 **C**, 2.0 **Mn**, 1.0 **Si**, 17.0–19.0 **Cr**, 9.0–13.0 **Ni**, 1.5 **Mo**, 0.5 **Cu**, 0.2 **Co**, 0.1 **Nb+Ta**, 0.040 **P**, 0.030 **S**; 0.5 other elements, total; rem Fe	**Solution annealed**: all **diam**, 100 (690) **TS**, 40 **El**
ANSI/ASTM A 580	Grade 440B	US	Wire	0.75–0.95 **C**, 1.00 **Mn**, 1.00 **Si**, 16.00–18.00 **Cr**, 0.75 **Mo**, 0.040 **P**, 0.030 **S**	**Annealed**: all **diam**, 140 (970) max **TS**
AISI 440B		US	Bar, wire	0.75–0.95 **C**, 1.00 **Mn**, 1.00 **Si**, 16.00–18.00 **Cr**, 0.75 **Mo**, 0.040 **P**, 0.030 **S**	**Annealed (bar)**: all **diam**, 107 (738) max **TS**, 62 (427) max **YS**, 18 **El**; **Annealed and cold finished (bar)**: 1 (25.40) **diam**, 120 (827) max **TS**, 95 (655) max **YS**, 9 **El**
DGN–B–83	440 B	Mexico	Bar	0.75–0.95 **C**, 1.0 **Mn**, 1.0 **Si**, 16.0–18.0 **Cr**, 0.75 **Mo**, 0.040 **P**, 0.030 **S**	**Hot or cold rolled**: all **diam**, (735) **TS**, (431) **YS**, 18 **El**
ANSI/ASTM A 473	440B	US	Forgings	0.75–0.95 **C**, 1.00 **Mn**, 1.00 **Si**, 16.00–18.00 **Cr**, 0.75 **Mo**, 0.040 **P**, 0.030 **S**	**Annealed**
ANSI/ASTM A 314	440B	US	Bar, forgings, billets	0.75–0.95 **C**, 1.00 **Mn**, 1.00 **Si**, 16.00–18.00 **Cr**, 0.75 **Mo**, 0.040 **P**, 0.030 **S**	
ANSI/ASTM A 276	440B	US	Bar, shapes	0.75–0.95 **C**, 1.00 **Mn**, 1.00 **Si**, 16.00–18.00 **Cr**, 0.75 **Mo**, 0.040 **P**, 0.030 **S**	**Annealed**
MIL–S–862B	Class 440B	US	Bar, billets	0.75–0.95 **C**, 1.0 **Mn**, 1.0 **Si**, 16.0–18.0 **Cr**, 0.75 **Mo**, 0.040 **P**, 0.030 **S**	
JIS G 4303	SUS 440B	Japan	Bar	0.75–0.95 **C**, 1.00 **Mn**, 1.00 **Si**, 16.00–18.00 **Cr**, 0.60 **Ni**, 0.75 **Mo**, 0.040 **P**, 0.030 **S**	**Quenched and tempered**

WROUGHT STAINLESS STEELS

specification number	designation	country	product forms	composition	mechanical properties (see page iv for explanation)
CSA G110.3	Type 440B	Canada	Bar, billets	0.75–0.95 **C**, 1.00 **Mn**, 1.00 **Si**, 16.00–18.00 **Cr**, 0.75 **Mo**, 0.040 **P**, 0.030 **S**	
ISO 683/XV	4	ISO	Bar: hot rolled	0.75–0.85 **C**, 0.80 **Mn**, 1.75–2.50 **Si**, 19.0–21.0 **Cr**, 1.0–1.7 **Ni**, 0.040 **P**, 0.030 **S**	**Quenched and tempered:** all **diam**, (930) **TS**, (735) **YS**, 10 **El**
JIS G 4311	SUH 4	Japan	Bar	0.75–0.85 **C**, 0.20–0.60 **Mn**, 1.75–2.25 **Si**, 19.00–20.50 **Cr**, 1.15–1.65 **Ni**, 0.030 **P**, 0.030 **S**	**Quenched and tempered:** (≤75) **diam**, (883) **TS**, (686) **YS**
BS 970 Part 4	Grade 44365	UK	Blooms, billets, bars, forgings, rod	0.75–0.85 **C**, 0.30–0.75 **Mn**, 1.75–2.25 **Si**, 19.0–21.0 **Cr**, 1.20–1.70 **Ni**, 0.040 **P**, 0.030 **S**	**Hardened, tempered, and retempered**
BS 25145	S145A	UK	Forging stock, billet and bar: aircraft quality	0.7 **C**, 1.00 **Mn**, 0.60 **Si**, 13.2–14.7 **Cr**, 5.0–5.8 **Ni**, 1.20–2.00 **Mo**, 1.20–2.00 **Cu**, 0.10–0.40 **Nb**, 0.035 **P**, 0.025 **S**	**Annealed**: all **diam**, (1270) **TS**, (1030) **YS**, 10 **El**
BS 25145	S145C	UK	Forgings: aircraft quality	0.7 **C**, 1.00 **Mn**, 0.60 **Si**, 13.2–14.7 **Cr**, 5.0–5.8 **Ni**, 1.20–2.00 **Mo**, 1.20–2.00 **Cu**	**Solution treated**: all **diam**, (1270) **TS**, (1030) **YS**, 10 **El**
ISO 683/XV	10	ISO	Bar	0.65–0.75 **C**, 5.5–7.0 **Mn**, 0.45–0.85 **Si**, 20.0–22.0 **Cr**, 1.4–1.9 **Ni**, 0.18–0.28 **N**, 0.050 **P**, 0.025–0.065 **S**	**Solution treated and precipitation hardened:** all **diam**, (1030) **TS**, (540) **YS**, 20 **El**
ANSI/ASTM A 580	Grade 440 A	US	Wire	0.60–0.75 **C**, 1.00 **Mn**, 1.00 **Si**, 16.00–18.00 **Cr**, 0.75 **Mo**, 0.040 **P**, 0.030 **S**	**Annealed**: all **diam**, 140 (970) max **TS**
DGN–B–83	440 A	Mexico	Bar	0.60–0.75 **C**, 1.0 **Mn**, 1.0 **Si**, 16.0–18.0 **Cr**, 0.75 **Mo**, 0.040 **P**, 0.030 **S**	**Hot or cold rolled**: all **diam**, (726) **TS**, (412) **YS**, 20 **El**
AISI 440 A		US	Strip, bar, wire	0.60–0.75 **C**, 1.00 **Mn**, 1.00 **Si**, 16.00–18.00 **Cr**, 0.75 **Mo**, 0.040 **P**, 0.030 **S**	**Annealed (strip)**: all **diam**, 100 (689) max **TS**, 60 (414) max **YS**, 20 **El**
DGN–B–171	Grade MT 440A	Mexico	Tube: seamless	0.60–0.75 **C**, 1.00 **Mn**, 1.00 **Si**, 16.0–18.0 **Cr**, 0.75 **Mo**, 0.040 **P**, 0.030 **S**	**Hot or cold finished and annealed:** (≥7.92) **diam**, (657) **TS**, (382) **YS**, 15 **El**
ANSI/ASTM A 511	MT 440A	US	Tube: seamless	0.60–0.75 **C**, 1.00 **Mn**, 1.00 **Si**, 16.0–18.0 **Cr**, 0.75 **Mo**, 0.040 **P**, 0.030 **S**	**Annealed**: 0.31 (7.9) **diam**, 95 (655) **TS**, 55 (379) **YS**, 15 **El**
JIS G 4307	SUS 440A	Japan	Strip	0.60–0.75 **C**, 1.00 **Mn**, 1.00 **Si**, 16.00–18.00 **Cr**, 0.6 **Ni**, 0.75 **Mo**, 0.040 **P**, 0.030 **S**	**Cold rolled, annealed, quenched and tempered:** all **diam**, (588) **TS**, (245) **YS**, 15 **El**
JIS G 4305	SUS 440A	Japan	Sheet, plate	0.60–0.75 **C**, 1.00 **Mn**, 1.00 **Si**, 16.00–18.00 **Cr**, 0.60 **Ni**, 0.75 **Mo**, 0.040 **P**, 0.030 **S**	**Cold rolled and annealed:** all **diam**, (588) **TS**, (245) **YS**, 15 **El**
JIS G 4306	SUS 440A	Japan	Strip	0.60–0.75 **C**, 1.00 **Mn**, 1.00 **Si**, 16.00–18.00 **Cr**, 0.60 **Ni**, 0.75 **Mo**, 0.040 **P**, 0.030 **S**	**Hot rolled and annealed:** all **diam**, (588) **TS**, (245) **YS**, 15 **El**
ANSI/ASTM A 473	440A	US	Forgings	0.60–0.75 **C**, 1.00 **Mn**, 1.00 **Si**, 16.00–18.00 **Cr**, 0.75 **Mo**, 0.040 **P**, 0.030 **S**	**Annealed**
ANSI/ASTM A 314	440A	US	Bar, forgings, billets	0.60–0.75 **C**, 1.00 **Mn**, 1.00 **Si**, 16.00–18.00 **Cr**, 0.75 **Mo**, 0.040 **P**, 0.030 **S**	
ANSI/ASTM A 276	440A	US	Bar, shapes	0.60–0.75 **C**, 1.00 **Mn**, 1.00 **Si**, 16.00–18.00 **Cr**, 0.75 **Mo**, 0.040 **P**, 0.030 **S**	**Annealed**
MIL–S–862B	Class 440A	US	Bar, billets	0.6–0.75 **C**, 1.0 **Mn**, 1.0 **Si**, 16.0–18.0 **Cr**, 0.75 **Mo**, 0.040 **P**, 0.030 **S**	
AMS 5631		US	Bar, forgings	0.60–0.75 **C**, 1.00 **Mn**, 1.00 **Si**, 16.00–18.00 **Cr**, 0.75 **Ni**, 0.75 **Mo**, 0.040 **P**, 0.030 **S**	
JIS G 4303	SUS 440A	Japan	Bar	0.60–0.75 **C**, 1.00 **Mn**, 1.00 **Si**, 16.00–18.00 **Cr**, 0,60 **Ni**, 0.75 **Mo**, 0.040 **P**, 0.030 **S**	**Quenched and tempered**
CSA G110.3	Type 440A	Canada	Bar, billets	0.60–0.75 **C**, 1.00 **Mn**, 1.00 **Si**, 16.00–18.00 **Cr**, 0.75 **Mo**, 0.040 **P**, 0.030 **S**	
ISO 683/XV	8	ISO	Bar	0.48–0.58 **C**, 8.0–10.0 **Mn**, 0.25 **Si**, 20.0–23.0 **Cr**, 3.25–4.5 **Ni**, 0.38–0.55 **N**, 0.050 **P**, 0.035 **S**	**Solution treated and precipitation hardened:** all **diam**, (1030) **TS**, (640) **YS**, 8 **El**

WROUGHT STAINLESS STEELS

specification number	designation	country	product forms	composition	mechanical properties (see page iv for explanation)
ISO 683/XV	9	ISO	Bar	0.48–0.58 **C**, 8.0–10.0 **Mn**, 0.25 **Si**, 20.0–23.0 **Cr**, 3.25–4.5 **Ni**, 0.38–0.55 **N**, 0.050 **P**, 0.035–0.090 **S**	**Solution treated and precipition hardened**: all **diam**, (1030) **TS**, (640) **YS**, 8 **El**
JIS G 4311	SUH 35	Japan	Bar	0.48–0.58 **C**, 8.00–10.00 **Mn**, 0.35 **Si**, 20.00–22.00 **Cr**, 3.25–4.50 **Ni**, 0.35–0.50 **N**, 0.040 **P**, 0.030 **S**	**Solution annealed and aged**: (≤25) **diam**, (883) **TS**, (686) **YS**, 8 **El**
JIS G 4311	SUH 36	Japan	Bar	0.48–0.58 **C**, 8.00–10.00 **Mn**, 0.35 **Si**, 20.00–22.00 **Cr**, 3.25–4.50 **Ni**, 0.35–0.50 **N**, 0.040 **P**, 0.040–0.090 **S**	**Solution annealed and aged**: (≤25) **diam**, (883) **TS**, (686) **YS**, 8 **El**
BS 970 Part 4	Grade 352S54	UK	Bar, rod	0.48–0.58 **C**, 8.0–10.0 **Mn**, 0.45 **Si**, 20.0–22.0 **Cr**, 3.25–4.50 **Ni**, 0.90 min **C+N**, 0.38–0.50 **N**, 2.00–3.00 **Nb**, 0.040 **P**, 0.035–0.080 **S**	**Solution treated, quenched, precipitation hardened**
BS 970 Part 4	Grade 352S52	UK	Bar, rod	0.48–0.58 **C**, 8.0–10.0 **Mn**, 0.45 **Si**, 20.0–22.0 **Cr**, 3.25–4.50 **Ni**, 0.90 min **C+N**, 0.38–0.50 **N**, 2.00–3.00 **Nb**, 0.040 **P**, 0.035 **S**	**Solution treated, quenched, precipitation hardened**
BS 970 Part 4	Grade 349S54	UK	Bar, rod	0.48–0.58 **C**, 8.0–10.0 **Mn**, 0.25 **Si**, 20.0–22.0 **Cr**, 3.25–4.50 **Ni**, 0.90 min **C+N**, 0.38–0.50 **N**, 0.040 **P**, 0.035–0.080 **S**	**Solution treated, quenched, precipitation hardened**
BS 970 Part 4	Grade 349S52	UK	Bar, rod	0.48–0.58 **C**, 8.0–10.0 **Mn**, 0.25 **Si**, 20.0–22.0 **Cr**, 3.25–4.50 **Ni**, 0.90 min **C+N**, 0.38–0.50 **N**, 0.040 **P**, 0.035 **S**	**Solution treated, quenched, precipitation hardened**
ISO 683/XII	6a	ISO	Bar, sheet, plate	0.42–0.50 **C**, 1.0 **Mn**, 1.0 **Si**, 12.5–14.5 **Cr**, 1.0 **Ni**, 0.040 **P**, 0.030 **S**	
ISO 683/XVII	20	ISO	Billets, bar, wire, tube, ring	0.42–0.50 **C**, 1.00 **Mn**, 1.00 **Si**, 12.5–14.5 **Cr**, 1.00 **Ni**, 0.040 **P**, 0.030 **S**	
DIN 17440	Grade X 45 CrMoV 15	Germany	Sheet, strip, bar, wire, tube, forgings	0.42–0.48 **C**, 1.0 **Mn**, 1.0 **Si**, 13.8–15.0 **Cr**, 0.45–0.60 **Mo**, 0.045 **P**, 0.030 **S**	**Annealed**: (≤5) **diam**, (900) max **TS**
ISO 683/XV	1	ISO	Bar	0.40–0.50 **C**, 0.80 **Mn**, 2.75–3.75 **Si**, 7.5–9.5 **Cr**, 0.50 **Ni**, 0.040 **P**, 0.030 **S**	**Quenched and tempered**: all **diam**, (930) **TS**, (685) **YS**, 16 **El**
ISO 683/XV	6	ISO	Bar	0.40–0.50 **C**, 0.80–1.5 **Mn**, 2.0–3.0 **Si**, 17.0–20.0 **Cr**, 8.0–10.0 **Ni**, 0.80–1.20 **W**, 0.045 **P**, 0.030 **S**	**Solution treated**: all **diam**, (885) **TS**, (440) **YS**, 30 **El**
DIN 17440	Grade X 40 Cr 13	Germany	Sheet, strip, bar, wire, tube, forgings	0.40–0.50 **C**, 1.0 **Mn**, 1.0 **Si**, 12.0–14.0 **Cr**, 0.045 **P**, 0.030 **S**	**Annealed**: (≤5) **diam**, (800) max **TS**
AMS 5561	Class I, II, III	US	Tube	0.40 **C**, 00–10.00 **Mn**, 1.00 **Si**, 19.00–21.50 **Cr**, 5.50–7.50 **Ni**, 0.75 **Mo**, 0.50 **Cu**, 0.15–0.40 **N**, 0.030 **P**, 0.030 **S**	**Cold finished**: all **diam**, 142 (979) **TS**, 120 (827) **YS**, 20 **El**
BS 2S.111		UK	Billets, bar and forgings: aircraft quality	0.37–0.47 **C**, 0.5–1.0 **Mn**, 1.0–2.0 **Si**, 13.0–15.0 **Cr**, 13.0–15.0 **Ni**, 0.4–0.6 **Mo**, 2.2–3.0 **W**, 0.035 **P**, 0.025 **S**	**Annealed or quenched**
BS 970 Part 4	Grade 331S42	UK	Bar, rod	0.37–0.47 **C**, 0.50–1.00 **Mn**, 1.00–2.00 **Si**, 13.0–15.0 **Cr**, 13.0–15.0 **Ni**, 0.40–0.70 **Mo**, 2.20–3.00 **W**, 0.040 **P**, 0.030 **S**	
IS 6529	40Cr13	India	Blooms, billets, slabs	0.36–0.45 **C**, 1.0 **Mn**, 1.0 **Si**, 12.5–14.5 **Cr**, 1.0 **Ni**, 0.040 **P**, 0.030 **S**	**Annealed or solution annealed**
ISO 683/XII	6	ISO	Bar, sheet, plate	0.36–0.45 **C**, 1.0 **Mn**, 1.0 **Si**, 12.5–14.5 **Cr**, 1.0 **Ni**, 0.040 **P**, 0.030 **S**	
IS 6603	40Cr13	India	Bar	0.36–0.45 **C**, 1.00 **Mn**, 1.00 **Si**, 12.5–14.5 **Cr**, 1.00 **Ni**, 0.040 **P**, 0.030 **S**	**Annealed**; **Quenched and tempered**
IS 6911	40Cr13	India	Plate, sheet, strip	0.36–0.45 **C**, 1.0 **Mn**, 1.0 **Si**, 12.5–14.5 **Cr**, 1.0 **Ni**, 0.030 **S**, 0.040 **P**	**Annealed**

WROUGHT STAINLESS STEELS

specification number	designation	country	product forms	composition	mechanical properties (see page iv for explanation)
ISO 683/XV	5	ISO	Bar	0.35–0.50 **C**, 1.0 **Mn**, 2.0 **Si**, 12.0–15.0 **Cr**, 12.0–15.0 **Ni**, 2.0–3.0 **W**, 0.045 **P**, 0.030 **S**	**Solution treated**: all **diam**, (785) **TS**, (345) **YS**, 35 **El**
BS 970 Part 4	Grade 331S40	UK	Bar, rod	0.35–0.50 **C**, 0.50–1.00 **Mn**, 1.00–2.00 **Si**, 12.0–15.0 **Cr**, 12.0–15.0 **Ni**, 2.00–3.00 **W**, 0.040 **P**, 0.030 **S**	
ISO 683/XV	2	ISO	Bar: hot rolled	0.35–0.45 **C**, 0.80 **Mn**, 1.8–3.0 **Si**, 9.5–11.5 **Cr**, 0.70–1.3 **Mo**, 0.040 **P**, 0.030 **S**	**Quenched and tempered**: all **diam**, (930) **TS**, (735) **YS**, 15 **El**
JIS G 4311	SUH 31	Japan	Bar	0.35–0.45 **C**, 0.60 **Mn**, 1.50–2.50 **Si**, 14.00–16.00 **Cr**, 13.00–15.00 **Ni**, 2.00–3.00 **W**, 0.040 **P**, 0.030 **S**	**Solution annealed**: (≤25) **diam**, (735) **TS**, (314) **YS**, 30 **El**
NF A 35–575	Z 40 C 14	France	Wire, rod	0.35–0.45 **C**, 1.0 **Mn**, 1.0 **Si**, 12.5–14.5 **Cr**	**Quenched and tempered**: all **diam**, (730) max **TS**
AMS 5506C		US	Strip, sheet, plate	0.30–0.40 **C**, 1.00 **Mn**, 1.00 **Si**, 12.00–14.00 **Cr**, 0.50 **Ni**, 0.50 **Mo**, 0.50 **Cu**, 0.15 **Al**, 0.040 **P**, 0.030 **S**, 0.05	**Annealed**: <0.030 (<0.76) **diam**, 100 (690) **TS**, 12 **El**
QQ–S–766C	Class 420	US	Strip, sheet, plate	0.30–0.40 **C**, 1.00 **Mn**, 1.00 **Si**, 12.00–14.00 **Cr**, 0.50 **Mo**, 0.040 **P**, 0.030 **S**	**Annealed**: ≤0.015 **diam**, 100 (690) max **TS**, 12 **El**
ASTM A 582	420F	US	Bar	0.30–0.40 **C**, 1.25 **Mn**, 1.00 **Si**, 12.00–14.00 **Cr**, 0.50 **Ni**, 0.60 **Cu**, 0.06 **P**, 0.15 min **S**	
AMS 5620C	Type I	US	Bar, forgings	0.30–0.40 **C**, 1.25 **Mn**, 1.00 **Si**, 12.00–14.00 **Cr**, 0.50 **Ni**, 0.60 **Mo** or **Zr**, 0.060 **P**, 0.030 **S**, 0.18–0.35 **Se**	
AMS 5620C	Type II	US	Bar, forgings	0.30–0.40 **C**, 1.25 **Mn**, 1.00 **Si**, 12.00–14.00 **Cr**, 0.50 **Ni**, 0.60 **Mo** or **Zr**, 0.060 **P**, 0.15–0.35 **S**	
AMS 5621A		US	Bar, forgings	0.30–0.40 **C**, 1.00 **Mn**, 1.00 **Si**, 12.00–14.00 **Cr**, 0.50 **Ni**, 0.50 **Mo**, 0.50 **Cu**, 0.040 **P**, 0.030 **S**	
DGN–B–207	Grade C2	Mexico	Tube: seamless	0.30 **C**, 0.29–1.06 **Mn**, 0.10 min **Si**, 0.048 **P**, 0.058 **S**	**Cold finished**: all **diam**, (480) **TS**, (274) **YS**, 30 **El**
SIS 14 15 50	SIS 15 50–01	Sweden	Bar, forgings, plate, sheet, tube	0.28–0.40 **C**, 0.40–0.90 **Mn**, 0.05 **P**, 0.05 **S**	**Normalized**: all **diam**, (490) **TS**, (270) **YS**, 21 **El**
BS 970 Part 4	Grade 420S45	UK	Blooms, billets, bar, forgings	0.28–0.36 **C**, 1.00 **Mn**, 0.80 **Si**, 12.0–14.0 **Cr**, 1.00 **Ni**, 0.040 **P**, 0.030 **S**	**Hardened and tempered**: ≤6 **diam**, (690) **TS**, (525) **YS**, 15 **El**
BS 1449 Part 2	Grade 420S45	UK	Plate, sheet, strip	0.28–0.36 **C**, 1.00 **Mn**, 0.80 **Si**, 12.0–14.0 **Cr**, 1.00 **Ni**, 0.040 **P**, 0.030 **S**	**Hardened and tempered**
SIS 14 23 04	SIS 23 04–08	Sweden	Strip	0.28–0.35 **C**, 1.0 **Mn**, 1.0 **Si**, 12.5–14.5 **Cr**, 1.0 **Ni**	**Quenched**: (<3) **diam**, (1470) **TS**, (1080) **YS**
SIS 14 23 04	SIS 23 04–08	Sweden	Strip	0.28–0.35 **C**, 1.0 **Mn**, 1.0 **Si**, 12.5–14.5 **Cr**, 1.0 **Ni**, 0.040 **P**, 0.030 **S**	**Quenched**: (<3) **diam**, (1470) **TS**, (1080) **YS**
ANSI/ASTM A 458	Grade 651	US	Bar	0.28–0.35 **C**, 0.75–1.50 **Mn**, 0.30–0.80 **Si**, 18.00–20.00 **Cr**, 8.00–11.00 **Ni**, 1.00–1.75 **Mo**, 1.00–1.75 **W**, 0.50 **Cu**, 0.25–0.60 **Nb+Ta**, 0.040 **P**, 0.030 **S**, 0.10–0.35 **Ti**	**Hot worked or hot, cold worked**: ≥1 (≥25.4) **diam**, 120 (827) **TS**, 90 (621) **YS**, 18.0 **El**; **Hot worked or cold worked, stress relieved**: ≥1 (≥25.4) **diam**, 95 (655) **TS**, 45 (310) **YS**, 20.0 **El**
ANSI/ASTM A 457	Grade 651	US	Plate, sheet, strip	0.28–0.35 **C**, 0.75–1.50 **Mn**, 0.30–0.80 **Si**, 18.00–20.00 **Cr**, 1.00–1.75 **Mo**, 1.00–1.75 **W**, 0.50 **Cu**, 0.25–0.60 **Nb+Ta**, 0.040 **P**, 0.030 **S**, 0.10–0.35 **Ti**	**Stress relieved, annealed**: 0.040 (1.02) **diam**, 120 (827) **TS**, 80 (552) **YS**, 12 **El**
AMS 5538B		US	Strip, sheet, plate	0.28–0.35 **C**, 0.075–1.50 **Mn**, 0.30–0.80 **Si**, 18.00–21.00 **Cr**, 8.00–11.00 **Ni**, 1.25–2.00 **Mo**, 1.00–1.75 **W**, 0.50 **Cu**, 0.40 **P**, 0.030 **S**, 0.40–0.75 **Ti**	**Solution treated**: all **diam**, 95 (827) **TS**, 45 (310) **YS**, 30 **El**
SIS 14 23 04	SIS 23 04–02	Sweden	Bar, forgings, strip, wire	0.28–0.35 **C**, 1.0 **Mn**, 1.0 **Si**, 12.5–14.5 **Cr**, 1.0 **Ni**	**Annealed (strip)**: all **diam**, (780) max **TS**

WROUGHT STAINLESS STEELS

specification number	designation	country	product forms	composition	mechanical properties (see page iv for explanation)
SIS 14 23 04	SIS 23 04–02	Sweden	Bar, forgings, plate, sheet, strip, wire	0.28–0.35 **C**, 1.0 **Mn**, 1.0 **Si**, 12.5–14.5 **Cr**, 1.0 **Ni**, 0.040 **P**, 0.030 **S**	**Annealed (plate)**: all **diam**, (780) max **TS**
ANSI/ASTM A 477	Grade 651	US	Forgings, billets	0.28–0.35 **C**, 0.75–1.50 **Mn**, 0.30–0.80 **Si**, 18.00–20.00 **Cr**, 8.00–11.00 **Ni**, 1.00–1.75 **Mo**, 1.00–1.75 **W**, 0.50 **Cu**, 0.25–0.60 **Nb+Ta**, 0.040 **P**, 0.030 **S**, 0.10–0.35 **Ti**	**Hot–cold worked 1500–1200 °F (815–650 °C): all diam, 100 (690) TS, 60 (415) YS, 10 El; all diam, 95 (655) TS, 45 (310) YS, 20 El**
ASTM A 453	Grade 651, class A	US	Bar	0.28–0.35 **C**, 0.75–1.50 **Mn**, 0.30–0.80 **Si**, 18.00–21.00 **Cr**, 8.00–11.00 **Ni**, 1.00–1.75 **Mo**, 1.00–1.75 **W**, 0.50 **Cu**, 0.25–0.60 **Nb**, 0.040 **P**, 0.030 **S**, 0.10–0.35 **Ti**	**Solution treated and aged**: all **diam**, 100 (689) **TS**, 70 (483) **YS**, 18 **El**
AMS 5526E		US	Strip, sheet, plate	0.28–0.35 **C**, 0.75–1.50 **Mn**, 0.30–0.80 **Si**, 18.00–21.00 **Cr**, 8.00–11.00 **Ni**, 1.00–1.75 **Mo**, 1.00–1.75 **W**, 0.50 **Cu**, 0.25–0.60 **Nb+Ta**, 0.040 **P**, 0.030 **S**	**Solution treated**: all **diam**, 95 (655) **TS**, 45 (310) **YS**, 30 **El**
ANSI/ASTM A 565	619	US	Bar, forgings	0.27–0.32 **C**, 0.95–1.35 **Mn**, 0.50 **Si**, 11.00–12.00 **Cr**, 0.50 **Ni**, 2.50–3.00 **Mo**, 0.20–0.30 **V**, 0.025 **P**, 0.025 **S**	**Quenched, tempered**: all **diam**, 140 (965) **TS**, 110 (760) **YS**, 8 **El**
JIS G 4303	SUS 420J2	Japan	Bar	0.26–0.40 **C**, 1.00 **Mn**, 1.00 **Si**, 12.00–14.00 **Cr**, 0.60 **Ni**, 0.040 **P**, 0.030 **S**	**Quenched and tempered**: (≤75) **diam**, (735) **TS**, (539) **YS**, 12 **El**
JIS G 4303	SUS 420F	Japan	Bar	0.26–0.40 **C**, 1.25 **Mn**, 1.00 **Si**, 12.00–14.00 **Cr**, 0.60 **Ni**, 0.60 **Mo**, 0.060 **P**, 0.15 **S**	**Quenched and tempered**: (≤75) **diam**, (735) **TS**, (539) **YS**, 12 **El**
JIS G 4307	SUS 420J2	Japan	Strip	0.26–0.40 **C**, 1.00 **Mn**, 1.00 **Si**, 12.00–14.00 **Cr**, 0.6 **Ni**, 0.75 **Mo**, 0.040 **P**, 0.030 **S**	**Cold rolled, annealed, quenched and tempered**: all **diam**, (539) **TS**, (226) **YS**, 18 **El**
JIS 4305	SUS 420J2	Japan	Sheet, plate	0.26–0.40 **C**, 1.00 **Mn**, 1.00 **Si**, 12.00–14.00 **Cr**, 0.60 **Ni**, 0.040 **P**, 0.030 **S**	**Cold rolled and annealed**: all **diam**, (539) **TS**, (226) **YS**, 18 **El**
JIS G 4306	SUS 420J2	Japan	Strip	0.26–0.40 **C**, 1.00 **Mn**, 1.00 **Si**, 12.00–14.00 **Cr**, 0.60 **Ni**, 0.040 **P**, 0.030 **S**	**Hot rolled and annealed**: all **diam**, (539) **TS**, (226) **YS**, 18 **El**
JIS G 4308	SUS 420 J2	Japan	Wire, rod	0.26–0.40 **C**, 1.00 **Mn**, 1.00 **Si**, 12.00–14.00 **Cr**, 0.60 **Ni**, 0.040 **P**, 0.030 **S**	
JIS G 4313	SUS 420 J2–CSP	Japan	Strip	0.26–0.40 **C**, 1.00 **Mn**, 1.00 **Si**, 12.00–14.00 **Cr**, 0.60 **Ni**, 0.040 **P**, 0.030 **S**	**Annealed**
ISO 683/XII	5	ISO	Bar, sheet, plate	0.26–0.35 **C**, 1.0 **Mn**, 1.0 **Si**, 12.0–14.0 **Cr**, 1.0 **Ni**, 0.040 **P**, 0.030 **S**	**Quenched and tempered**: all **diam**, (780) **TS**, (590) **YS**, 11 **El**
IS 6603	30Cr13	India	Bar	0.26–0.35 **C**, 1.00 **Mn**, 1.00 **Si**, 12.0–14.0 **Cr**, 1.00 **Ni**, 0.040 **P**, 0.030 **S**	**Annealed (martensitic)**: (≥5–100) **diam**, (780) **TS**, (590) **YS**, 11 **El**; **Annealed (cutlery); Quenched and tempered**
IS 6911	30Cr13	India	Plate, sheet, strip	0.26–0.35 **C**, 1.0 **Mn**, 1.0 **Si**, 12.0–14.0 **Cr**, 1.0 **Ni**, 0.030 **S**, 0.040 **P**	**Annealed**: all **diam**, (780) **TS**, (590) **YS**, 11 **El**
IS 6529	30Cr13	India	Blooms, billets, slabs	0.26–0.35 **C**, 1.0 **Mn**, 1.0 **Si**, 12.0–14.0 **Cr**, 1.0 **Ni**, 0.040 **P**, 0.030 **S**	**Annealed or solution annealed**
IS 6911	30Cr13	India	Plate, sheet, strip	0.26–0.35 **C**, 1.0 **Mn**, 1.0 **Si**, 12.0–14.0 **Cr**, 1.0 **Ni**, 0.030 **S**, 0.040 **P**	**Annealed**
MIL–S–17759B	Composition II	US	Bar, billets, forgings, wire	0.26–0.33 **C**, 3.00–4.00 **Mn**, 1.00 **Si**, 17.0–19.0 **Cr**, 8.0–10.0 **Ni**, 0.18–0.33 **P**, 0.035 **S**	**Solution annealed and doubled aged**: all **diam**, (827) **TS**, (620) **YS**, 15 **El**
AMS 5027A		US	Wire	0.26–0.32 **C**, 0.60–0.90 **Mn**, 0.10–0.30 **Si**, 0.90–1.20 **Cr**, 0.40–0.70 **Ni**, 0.90–1.10 **Mo**, 0.35 **Cu**, 0.05–0.10 **V**, 0.0010 **H**, 0.0050 **N**, 0.0025 **O**, 0.010 **P**, 0.010 **S**	

WROUGHT STAINLESS STEELS

specification number	designation	country	product forms	composition	mechanical properties (see page iv for explanation)
JIS G 4311	SUH 38	Japan	Bar	0.25–0.35 **C**, 1.20 **Mn**, 1.00 **Si**, 19.00–21.00 **Cr**, 10.00–12.00 **Ni**, 1.80–2.50 **Mo**, 0.01–0.010 **B**, 0.18–0.25 **P**, 0.030 **S**	**Solution annealed and aged:** (≤25) **diam**, (883) **TS**, (490) **YS**, 20 **El**
AS G18	G18/En 56D	Australia	Bar, billet, bar: black, bright	0.25–0.35 **C**, 1.00 **Mn**, 1.00 **Si**, 12.0–14.0 **Cr**, 1.00 **Ni**, 0.045 **P**, 0.045 **S**	**Hardened, tempered**: 6 **diam**, (540) **TS**, (385) **YS**
NF A 35–572	Z 30 C 13	France	Bar, sections	0.25–0.34 **C**, 1.0 **Mn**, 1.0 **Si**, 12.0–14.0 **Cr**, 0.04 **P**, 0.03 **S**	**Quenched and tempered:** (≤25) **diam**, (830) **TS**, (635) **YS**, 11 **El**
NF A 35–575	Z 30 C 13	France	Wire, rod	0.25–0.34 **C**, 1.0 **Mn**, 1.0 **Si**, 12.0–14.0 **Cr**, 0.040 **P**, 0.030 **S**	**Quenched and tempered:** all **diam**, (780) max **TS**
NF A 35–577	Z 30 C 13 (DF)	France	Bar, wire, rod	0.25–0.34 **C**, 1.0 **Mn**, 1.0 **Si**, 12.0–14.0 **Cr**, 1.0 **Ni**, 0.040 **P**, 0.030 **S**	**Annealed**: (6) **diam**, (690) max **TS**
NF A 35–583	Z 30 C 14	France	Wire, rod	0.25–0.34 **C**, 1.0 **Mn**, 0.75 **Si**, 12–15 **Cr**, 0.50 **Ni**, 0.50 **Mo**, 0.030 **P**, 0.020 **S**	
AIR 9160	9160C181	France	Bar, forgings	0.25–0.32 **C**, 1.0 **Mn**, 0.80 **Si**, 12.0–14.0 **Cr**, 1.0 **Ni**, 0.035 **P**, 0.025 **S**	**Quenched and tempered:** (<110) **diam**, (880) **TS**, (690) **YS**, 10 **El**
AS G18	G18/En 57	Australia	Bar, billet, bar: black, bright	0.25 **C**, 1.00 **Mn**, 0.10–1.00 **Si**, 15.5–20.0 **Cr**, 1.00–3.00 **Ni**, 0.045 **P**, 0.045 **S**	**Hardened, tempered**: 6 **diam**, (850) **TS**, (680) **YS**
AISI 314		US	Bar, sheet, plate	0.25 **C**, 2.00 **Mn**, 1.50–3.00 **Si**, 23.00–26.00 **Cr**, 19.00–22.00 **Ni**, 0.045 **P**, 0.030 **S**	**Annealed (bar)**: all **diam**, 100 (689) max **TS**, 50 (345) max **YS**, 45 **El**
AISI 310		US	Sheet, strip, plate, bar, wire	0.25 **C**, 2.00 **Mn**, 1.50 **Si**, 24.00–26.00 **Cr**, 19.00–22.00 **Ni**, 0.045 **P**, 0.030 **S**	**Annealed (sheet)**: all **diam**, 95 (655) max **TS**, 45 (310) max **YS**, 45 **El**
ANSI/ASTM A 580	Grade 310	US	Wire	0.25 **C**, 2.00 **Mn**, 1.50 **Si**, 24.00–26.00 **Cr**, 19.00–22.00 **Ni**, 0.045 **P**, 0.030 **S**	**Cold finished**: all **diam**, 90 (620) **TS**, 45 (310) **YS**, 35 **El**; **Annealed**: all **diam**, 75 (520) **TS**, 30 (210) **YS**, 35 **El**
ANSI/ASTM A 580	Grade 314	US	Wire	0.25 **C**, 2.00 **Mn**, 1.50–3.00 **Si**, 23.00–26.00 **Cr**, 19.00–22.00 **Ni**, 0.045 **P**, 0.030 **S**	**Cold finished**: all **diam**, 90 (620) **TS**, 45 (310) **YS**, 35 **El**; **Annealed**: all **diam**, 75 (520) **TS**, 30 (210) **YS**, 35 **El**
JIS G 4311	SUH 310	Japan	Bar	0.25 **C**, 2.00 **Mn**, 1.50 **Si**, 24.00–26.00 **Cr**, 19.00–22.00 **Ni**, 0.040 **P**, 0.030 **S**	**Solution annealed:** (≤180) **diam**, (588) **TS**, (206) **YS**, 40 **El**
JIS G 4312	SUH 310	Japan	Sheet, plate	0.25 **C**, 2.00 **Mn**, 1.50 **Si**, 24.00–26.00 **Cr**, 19.00–22.00 **Ni**, 0.040 **P**, 0.030 **S**	**Solution annealed**: all **diam**, (588) **TS**, (206) **YS**, 35 **El**
AS 1449	Grade AS 1449/310	Australia	Sheet, strip, plate	0.25 **C**, 2.00 **Mn**, 1.50 **Si**, 24.00–26.00 **Cr**, 19.00–22.00 **Ni**, 0.045 **P**, 0.030 **S**	**Annealed**: (≤1.2) **diam**, (520) **TS**, (205) **YS**, 40 **El**
CSA G110.6	Type 310	Canada	Plate, sheet, strip	0.25 **C**, 2.00 **Mn**, 1.50 **Si**, 24.00–26.00 **Cr**, 19.00–22.00 **Ni**, 0.045 **P**, 0.030 **S**	**Hot rolled and annealed or hot rolled, quenched and tempered:** all **diam**, 75 (517) **TS**, 30 (207) **YS**, 40 **El**
QQ–S–766C	Class 310	US	Strip, sheet, plate	0.25 **C**, 2.00 **Mn**, 1.50 **Si**, 24.00–26.00 **Cr**, 19.00–22.00 **Ni**, 0.045 **P**, 0.030 **S**	**Annealed**: all **diam**, 75 (517) **TS**, 30 (207) **YS**, 40 **El**
ANSI/ASTM A 473	310	US	Forgings	0.25 **C**, 2.00 **Mn**, 1.50 **Si**, 24.00–26.00 **Cr**, 19.00–22.00 **Ni**, 0.045 **P**, 0.030 **S**	**Solution annealed**: all **diam**, 75 (515) **TS**, 30 (205) **YS**, 40 **El**
ANSI/ASTM A 473	314	US	Forgings	0.25 **C**, 2.00 **Mn**, 1.50–3.00 **Si**, 23.00–26.00 **Cr**, 19.00–22.00 **Ni**, 0.045 **P**, 0.030 **S**	**Solution annealed**: all **diam**, 75 (515) **TS**, 30 (205) **YS**, 40 **El**
ANSI/ASTM A 276	314	US	Bar, shapes	0.25 **C**, 2.00 **Mn**, 1.50–3.00 **Si**, 23.00–26.00 **Cr**, 19.00–22.00 **Ni**, 0.045 **P**, 0.030 **S**	**Annealed**: all **diam**, 75 (515) **TS**, 30 (205) **YS**, 40 **El**
ANSI/ASTM A 276	310	US	Bar, shapes	0.25 **C**, 2.00 **Mn**, 1.50 **Si**, 24.00–26.00 **Cr**, 19.00–22.00 **Ni**, 0.045 **P**, 0.030 **S**	**Annealed**: all **diam**, 75 (515) **TS**, 30 (205) **YS**, 40 **El**
ASTM A 167	Type 310	US	Plate, sheet, strip	0.25 **C**, 2.00 **Mn**, 1.50 **Si**, 24.00–26.00 **Cr**, 19.00–22.00 **Ni**, 0.045 **P**, 0.030 **S**	**Solution annealed**: all **diam**, 75 (515) **TS**, 30 (205) **YS**, 40 **El**
DGN–B–83	314	Mexico	Bar	0.25 **C**, 2.0 **Mn**, 1.5–3.0 **Si**, 23.0–26.0 **Cr**, 19.0–22.0 **Ni**, 0.045 **P**, 0.030 **S**	**Hot or cold rolled**: all **diam**, (510) **TS**, (206) **YS**, 40 **El**

WROUGHT STAINLESS STEELS

specification number	designation	country	product forms	composition	mechanical properties (see page iv for explanation)
DGN–B–83	310	Mexico	Bar	0.25 **C**, 2.0 **Mn**, 1.50 **Si**, 24.0–26.0 **Cr**, 19.0–22.0 **Ni**, 0.045 **P**, 0.030 **S**	**Hot or cold rolled**: all **diam**, (510) **TS**, (206) **YS**, 40 **El**
ANSI/ASTM A 314	310	US	Bar, forgings, billets	0.25 **C**, 2.00 **Mn**, 1.50 **Si**, 24.00–26.00 **Cr**, 19.00–22.00 **Ni**, 0.045 **P**, 0.030 **S**	
ANSI/ASTM A 314	314	US	Bar, forgings, billets	0.25 **C**, 2.00 **Mn**, 1.50–3.00 **Si**, 23.00–26.00 **Cr**, 19.00–22.00 **Ni**, 0.045 **P**, 0.030 **S**	
AS 1444	Grade AS 1444/310	Australia	Bar, bloom, billet, slab	0.25 **C**, 2.00 **Mn**, 1.50 **Si**, 24.00–26.00 **Cr**, 19.00–22.00 **Ni**, 0.045 **P**, 0.040 **S**	
SIS 14 23 22	SIS 23 22–02	Sweden	Bar, forgings, plate, sheet, tube	0.25 **C**, 1.5 **Mn**, 1.5 **Si**, 24.0–28.0 **Cr**, 0.040 **P**, 0.030 **S**	
MIL–S–862B	Class 310	US	Bar, billets	0.25 **C**, 2.0 **Mn**, 1.5 **Si**, 24.0–26.0 **Cr**, 10.0–22.0 **Ni**, 0.045 **P**, 0.030 **S**	
CSA G110.3	Type 310	Canada	Bar, billets	0.25 **C**, 2.00 **Mn**, 1.50 **Si**, 24.00–26.00 **Cr**, 19.00–22.00 **Ni**, 0.045 **P**, 0.030 **S**	
CSA G110.3	Type 314	Canada	Bar, billets	0.25 **C**, 2.00 **Mn**, 1.50–3.00 **Si**, 23.00–26.00 **Cr**, 19.00–22.00 **Ni**, 0.045 **P**, 0.030 **S**	
SIS 14 23 22	SIS 23 22–02	Sweden	Bar, forgings, plate, sheet, tube	0.25 **C**, 1.5 **Mn**, 1.5 **Si**, 24.0–28.0 **Cr**, 0.040 **P**, 0.030 **S**	**Annealed (plate)**
ASTM A 582	420FSe	US	Bar	0.20–0.40 **C**, 1.25 **Mn**, 1.00 **Si**, 12.00–14.00 **Cr**, 0.50 **Ni**, 0.60 **Mo**, 0.60 **Cu**, 0.06 **P**, 0.06 **S**, 0.15 **Se**	
BS 970 Part 4	Grade 420S.37	UK	Blooms, billets, bar, forgings	0.20–0.28 **C**, 1.00 **Mn**, 0.80 **Si**, 12.0–14.0 **Cr**, 1.00 **Ni**, 0.040 **P**, 0.030 **S**	**Hardened and tempered**: ≤6 **diam**, (690) **TS**, (525) **YS**, 15 **El**
BS 970 Part 4	Grade 416S37	UK	Blooms, billets, bar, forgings	0.20–0.28 **C**, 1.50 **Mn**, 1.00 **Si**, 12.0–14.0 **Cr**, 1.00 **Ni**, 0.60 **Mo**, 0.040 **P**, 0.15–0.30 **S**	**Hardened and tempered**: ≤6 **diam**, (690) **TS**, (525) **YS**, 11 **El**
SIS 14 23 17	SIS 23 17–03	Sweden	Bar, forgings, wire	0.20–0.26 **C**, 0.30–0.80 **Mn**, 0.10–0.50 **Si**, 11.0–12.5 **Cr**, 0.30–0.80 **Ni**, 1.0–1.4 **Mo**, 0.25–0.35 **V**, 0.030–0.060 **N**, 0.035 **P**, 0.035 **S**	**Quenched and tempered**: (≤200) **diam**, (780) **TS**, (640) **YS**, 16 **El**
ANSI/ASTM A 579	52	US	Forgings	0.20–0.25 **C**, 0.50–1.00 **Mn**, 0.20–0.60 **Si**, 11.0–13.5 **Cr**, 0.75–1.25 **Ni**, 0.75–1.25 **Mo**, 0.75–1.25 **W**, 0.20–0.30 **V**, 0.05 **Al**, 0.25 **Co**, 0.025 **P**, 0.025 **S**, 0.04	
AISI 422		US	Bar	0.20–0.25 **C**, 1.00 **Mn**, 0.75 **Si**, 11.00–13.00 **Cr**, 0.50–1.00 **Ni**, 0.75–1.25 **Mo**, 0.75–1.25 **W**, 0.15–0.30 **V**	**Quenched and tempered**: 1–3 (25.4–76.2) **diam**, 145 (1000) max **TS**, 125 (862) max **YS**, 18 **El**
ANSI/ASTM A 565	616	US	Bar, forgings	0.20–0.25 **C**, 0.50–1.00 **Mn**, 0.50 **Si**, 11.00–12.50 **Cr**, 0.50–1.00 **Ni**, 0.90–1.25 **Mo**, 0.90–1.25 **W**, 0.20–0.30 **V**	**Quenched, tempered**: all **diam**, 140 (965) **TS**, 110 (760) **YS**, 13 **El**
AM 5655A		US	Bar, forgings, wire	0.20–0.25 **C**, 1.00 **Mn**, 0.20–0.60 **Si**, 11.00–13.50 **Cr**, 0.50–1.00 **Ni**, 0.75–1.25 **Mo**, 0.75–1.25 **W**, 0.50 **Cu**, 0.17–0.30 **V**, 0.040 **P**, 0.030 **S**	**Hardened, tempered, aged**: all **diam**, 140 (965) **TS**, 115 (793) **YS**, 13 **El**
ANSI/ASTM A 579	53	US	Forgings	0.20 **C**, 1.00 **Mn**, 1.00 **Si**, 15.0–17.0 **Cr**, 1.25–2.50 **Ni**, 0.025 **P**, 0.025 **S**	**Quenched and tempered**: all **diam**, 175 (1210) **TS**, 140 (965) **YS**, 12 **El**
ANSI/ASTM A 580	Grade 431	US	Wire	0.20 **C**, 1.00 **Mn**, 1.00 **Si**, 15.00–17.00 **Cr**, 1.25–2.50 **Ni**, 0.040 **P**, 0.030 **S**	**Annealed**: all **diam**, 140 (970) max **TS**
DGN–B–83	431	Mexico	Bar	0.20 **C**, 1.0 **Mn**, 1.0 **Si**, 15.0–17.0 **Cr**, 1.25–2.5 **Ni**, 0.040 **P**, 0.030 **S**	**Hot or cold rolled**: all **diam**, (863) **TS**, (657) **YS**, 20 **El**
AISI 431		US	Bar, wire	0.20 **C**, 1.00 **Mn**, 1.00 **Si**, 15.00–17.00 **Cr**, 1.25–2.50 **Ni**, 0.040 **P**, 0.030 **S**	**Annealed (bar)**: all **diam**, 125 (862) max **TS**, 95 (655) max **YS**, 20 **El**; **Annealed and cold finished (bar)**: 1 (25.40) **diam**, 130 (896) max **TS**, 110 (758) max **YS**, 15 **El**

WROUGHT STAINLESS STEELS

specification number	designation	country	product forms	composition	mechanical properties (see page iv for explanation)
ANSI/ASTM A 473	431	US	Forgings	0.20 **C**, 1.00 **Mn**, 1.00 **Si**, 15.00–17.00 **Cr**, 1.25–2.50 **Ni**, 0.040 **P**, 0.030 **S**	**Tempered**: all **diam**, 115 (795) **TS**, 90 (620) **YS**, 15 **El**; **Quenched, tempered**: all **diam**, 175 (1210) **TS**, 135 (930) **YS**, 13 **El**
JIS G 4303	SUS 431	Japan	Bar	0.20 **C**, 1.00 **Mn**, 1.00 **Si**, 15.00–17.00 **Cr**, 1.25–2.50 **Ni**, 0.040 **P**, 0.030 **S**	**Quenched and tempered**: (≤75) **diam**, (785) **TS**, (588) **YS**, 15 **El**
DGN-B-171	Grade MT 431	Mexico	Tube: seamless	0.20 **C**, 1.00 **Mn**, 1.00 **Si**, 15.0–17.0 **Cr**, 1.25–2.50 **Ni**, 0.040 **P**, 0.030 **S**	**Hot or cold finished and annealed**: (≥7.92) **diam**, (725) **TS**, (617) **YS**, 20 **El**
ANSI/ASTM A 511	MT 431	US	Tube: seamless	0.20 **C**, 1.00 **Mn**, 1.00 **Si**, 15.0–17.0 **Cr**, 1.25–2.50 **Ni**, 0.040 **P**, 0.030 **S**	**Annealed**: 0.31 (7.9) **diam**, 105 (724) **TS**, 90 (621) **YS**, 20 **El**
ANSI/ASTM A 493	Type 431	US	Bar, wire	0.20 **C**, 1.00 **Mn**, 1.00 **Si**, 15.00–17.00 **Cr**, 1.25–2.50 **Ni**, 0.040 **P**, 0.030 **S**	**Lightly drafted (wire)**: ≥0.156 (≥3.96) **diam**, 100 (690) **TS**; **Annealed (wire)**: ≥0.156 (≥3.96) **diam**, 90 (620) **TS**
AISI 309		US	Sheet, strip, plate, bar, wire	0.20 **C**, 2.00 **Mn**, 1.00 **Si**, 22.00–24.00 **Cr**, 12.00–15.00 **Ni**, 0.045 **P**, 0.030 **S**	**Annealed (sheet)**: all **diam**, 90 (621) max **TS**, 45 (310) max **YS**, 45 **El**
ANSI/ASTM A 580	Grade 309	US	Wire	0.20 **C**, 2.00 **Mn**, 1.00 **Si**, 22.00–24.00 **Cr**, 12.00–15.00 **Ni**, 0.045 **P**, 0.030 **S**	**Cold finished**: all **diam**, 90 (620) **TS**, 45 (310) **YS**, 35 **El**; **Annealed**: all **diam**, 75 (520) **TS**, 30 (210) **YS**, 35 **El**
JIS G 4312	SUH 309	Japan	Sheet, plate	0.20 **C**, 2.00 **Mn**, 1.00 **Si**, 22.00–24.00 **Cr**, 12.00–15.00 **Ni**, 0.040 **P**, 0.030 **S**	**Solution annealed**: all **diam**, (559) **TS**, (206) **YS**, 40 **El**
JIS G 4311	SUH 309	Japan	Bar	0.20 **C**, 2.00 **Mn**, 1.00 **Si**, 22.00–24.00 **Cr**, 12.00–15.00 **Ni**, 0.040 **P**, 0.030 **S**	**Solution annealed**: (≤180) **diam**, (559) **TS**, (206) **YS**, 45 **El**
AISI 442		US	Bar	0.20 **C**, 1.00 **Mn**, 1.00 **Si**, 18.00–23.00 **Cr**, 0.040 **P**, 0.030 **S**	**Annealed**: 2 (50.80) **diam**, 80 (552) max **TS**, 45 (310) max **YS**, 20 **El**
AISI 446		US	Sheet, strip, plate, bar, wire	0.20 **C**, 1.50 **Mn**, 1.00 **Si**, 23.00–27.00 **Cr**, 0.040 **P**, 0.030 **S**	**Annealed (sheet)**: all **diam**, 80 (552) max **TS**, 50 (345) max **YS**, 20 **El**
DGN-B-83	442	Mexico	Bar	0.20 **C**, 1.0 **Mn**, 1.0 **Si**, 18.0–23.0 **Cr**, 0.040 **P**, 0.030 **S**	**Hot or cold rolled**: all **diam**, (549) **TS**, (314) **YS**, 20 **El**
DGN-B-171	Grade MT 329	Mexico	Tube: seamless	0.20 **C**, 1.00 **Mn**, 0.75 **Si**, 23.0–28.0 **Cr**, 2.50–5.00 **Ni**, 1.0–2.0 **Mo**, 0.040 **P**, 0.030 **S**	**Hot or cold finished and annealed**: (≥7.92) **diam**, (519) **TS**, (314) **YS**, 10 **El**
CSA 110.5	Type 442	Canada	Sheet	0.20 **C**, 1.00 **Mn**, 1.00 **Si**, 18.00–23.00 **Cr**, 0.60 **Ni**	**Hot rolled, annealed, quenched and tempered**: all **diam**, 75 (517) **TS**, 40 (276) **YS**, 20 **El**
CSA G110.5	Type 446	Canada	Sheet	0.20 **C**, 1.50 **Mn**, 1.00 **Si**, 23.00–27.00 **Cr**, 0.60 **Ni**, 0.25 **N**, 0.040 **P**, 0.030 **S**	**Hot rolled, annealed, quenched and tempered**: all **diam**, 75 (517) **TS**, 40 (276) **YS**, 20 **El**
MIL-S-17996	Class 1	US	Sheet, bar, forgings, plate, strip, shapes	0.20 **C**, 5.0–7.0 **Mn**, 1.00 **Si**, 16.0–18.5 **Cr**, 3.5–5.5 **Ni**, 0.25 **N**, 0.05 **P**, 0.03 **S**	**Annealed (bar and forgings)**: all **diam**, (517) **TS**, (151) **YS**, 35 **El**
ANSI/ASTM A 511	MT 329	US	Tube: seamless	0.20 **C**, 1.00 **Mn**, 0.75 **Si**, 23.0–28.0 **Cr**, 2.50–5.00 **Ni**, 1.0–2.0 **Mo**, 0.040 **P**, 0.030 **S**	**Annealed**: 0.31 (7.9) **diam**, 75 (517) **TS**, 45 (310) **YS**, 10 **El**
CSA G110.5	Type 446	Canada	Strip	0.20 **C**, 1.50 **Mn**, 1.00 **Si**, 23.00–27.00 **Cr**, 0.60 **Ni**, 0.25 **N**, 0.040 **P**, 0.030 **S**	**Cold rolled and annealed**: all **diam**, 75 (517) **TS**, 40 (276) **YS**, 20 **El**
CSA G110.5	Type 442	Canada	Strip	0.20 **C**, 1.00 **Mn**, 1.00 **Si**, 18.00–23.00 **Cr**, 0.60 **Ni**, 0.040 **P**, 0.030 **S**	**Cold rolled and annealed**: all **diam**, 75 (517) **TS**, 40 (276) **YS**, 20 **El**
CSA G110.6	Type 309	Canada	Plate, sheet, strip	0.20 **C**, 2.00 **Mn**, 1.00 **Si**, 22.00–24.00 **Cr**, 12.00–15.00 **Ni**, 0.045 **P**, 0.030 **S**	**Hot rolled and annealed or hot rolled, quenched and tempered**: all **diam**, 75 (517) **TS**, 30 (207) **YS**, 40 **El**
QQ-S-766C	Class 446	US	Strip, sheet, plate	0.20 **C**, 1.50 **Mn**, 1.00 **Si**, 23.00–27.00 **Cr**, 0.25 **N**, 0.040 **P**, 0.030 **S**	**Annealed**: ≤0.015 **diam**, 75 (517) **TS**, 40 (276) **YS**, 16 **El**
QQ-S-766C	Class 309	US	Strip, sheet, plate	0.20 **C**, 2.00 **Mn**, 1.00 **Si**, 22.00–24.00 **Cr**, 12.00–15.00 **Ni**, 0.045 **P**, 0.030 **S**	**Annealed**: all **diam**, 75 (517) **TS**, 30 (207) **YS**, 40 **El**
ANSI/ASTM A 473	309	US	Forgings	0.20 **C**, 2.00 **Mn**, 1.00 **Si**, 22.00–24.00 **Cr**, 12.00–15.00 **Ni**, 0.045 **P**, 0.030 **S**	**Solution annealed**: all **diam**, 75 (515) **TS**, 30 (205) **YS**, 40 **El**

WROUGHT STAINLESS STEELS

specification number	designation	country	product forms	composition	mechanical properties (see page iv for explanation)
ANSI/ASTM A 276	309	US	Bar, shapes	0.20 **C**, 2.00 **Mn**, 1.00 **Si**, 22.00–24.00 **Cr**, 12.00–15.00 **Ni**, 0.045 **P**, 0.030 **S**	**Annealed**: all **diam**, 75 (515) **TS**, 30 (205) **YS**, 40 **El**
ASTM A 176	Type 446	US	Plate, sheet, strip	0.20 **C**, 1.50 **Mn**, 1.00 **Si**, 23.00–27.00 **Cr**, 0.60 **Ni**, 0.25 **N**, 0.040 **P**, 0.030 **S**	**Annealed**: all **diam**, 75 (515) **TS**, 40 (275) **YS**, 20 **El**
ASTM A 176	Type 442	US	Plate, sheet, strip	0.20 **C**, 1.00 **Mn**, 1.00 **Si**, 18.00–23.00 **Cr**, 0.60 **Ni**, 0.040 **P**, 0.040 **S**	**Annealed**: all **diam**, 75 (515) **TS**, 40 (275) **YS**, 20 **El**
ASTM A 67	Type 309	US	Plate, sheet, strip	0.20 **C**, 2.00 **Mn**, 1.00 **Si**, 22.00–24.00 **Cr**, 12.00–15.00 **Ni**, 0.045 **P**, 0.030 **S**	**Solution annealed**: all **diam**, 75 (515) **TS**, 30 (205) **YS**, 40 **El**
DGN–B–83	309	Mexico	Bar	0.20 **C**, 2.0 **Mn**, 1.0 **Si**, 22.0–24.0 **Cr**, 12.0–15.0 **Ni**, 0.045 **P**, 0.030 **S**	**Hot or cold rolled**: all **diam**, (510) **TS**, (206) **YS**, 40 **El**
DGN–B–216	Grade TP329	Mexico	Tube: seamless, welded	0.20 **C**, 1.00 **Mn**, 0.75 **Si**, 23.0–28.0 **Cr**, 2.50–5.00 **Ni**, 1.0–2.0 **Mo**, 0.040 **P**, 0.030 **S**	**As drawn or as welded**: (7.93) **diam**, (510) **TS**, (304) **YS**, 10 **El**
JIS G 4311	SUH 446	Japan	Bar	0.20 **C**, 1.50 **Mn**, 1.00 **Si**, 20.00–22.50 **Cr**, 0.60 **Ni**, 0.25 **N**, 0.040 **P**, 0.030 **S**	**Annealed**: all **diam**, (510) **TS**, (275) **YS**, 20 **El**
JIS G 4312	SUH 446	Japan	Sheet, plate	0.20 **C**, 1.50 **Mn**, 1.00 **Si**, 23.00–27.00 **Cr**, 0.60 **Ni**, 0.25 **N**, 0.040 **P**, 0.030 **S**	**Annealed**: all **diam**, (510) **TS**, (275) **YS**, 20 **El**
ANSI/ASTM A 473	446	US	Forgings	0.20 **C**, 1.50 **Mn**, 1.00 **Si**, 23.00–27.00 **Cr**, 0.75 **Ni**, 0.25 **N**, 0.040 **P**, 0.030 **S**	**Annealed**: all **diam**, 70 (485) **TS**, 40 (275) **YS**, 20 **El**
ANSI/ASTM A 511	MT 443	US	Tube: seamless	0.20 **C**, 1.00 **Mn**, 1.00 **Si**, 18.0–23.0 **Cr**, 0.50 **Ni**, 0.90–1.25 **Cu**, 0.040 **P**, 0.030 **S**	**Annealed**: 0.31 (7.9) **diam**, 70 (483) **TS**, 40 (276) **YS**, 20 **El**
ANSI/ASTM A 511	MT 446	US	Tube: seamless	0.20 **C**, 1.50 **Mn**, 1.00 **Si**, 23.0–30.0 **Cr**, 0.50 **Ni**, 0.25 **N**, 0.040 **P**, 0.030 **S**	**Annealed**: 0.31 (7.9) **diam**, 70 (483) **TS**, 40 (276) **YS**, 18 **El**
ANSI/ASTM A 268	TP 443	US	Tube: seamless, welded	0.20 **C**, 1.00 **Mn**, 0.75 **Si**, 18.0–23.0 **Cr**, 0.50 **Ni**, 0.90–1.25 **Cu**, 0.040 **P**, 0.030 **S**	**Annealed**: 0.312 (7.94) **diam**, 70 (483) **TS**, 40 (276) **YS**, 20 **El**
ANSI/ASTM A 268	TP 446	US	Tube: seamless, welded	0.20 **C**, 1.50 **Mn**, 0.75 **Si**, 23.0–30.0 **Cr**, 0.50 **Ni**, 0.10–0.25 **N**, 0.040 **P**, 0.030 **S**	**Annealed**: 0.312 (7.94) **diam**, 70 (483) **TS**, 40 (276) **YS**, 18 **El**
DGN–B–171	MT 443	Mexico	Tube: seamless	0.20 **C**, 1.00 **Mn**, 1.00 **Si**, 18.0–23.0 **Cr**, 0.50 **Ni**, 0.90–1.25 **Cu**, 0.040 **P**, 0.030 **S**	**Hot or cold finished and annealed**: (≥7.92) **diam**, (480) **TS**, (274) **YS**, 20 **El**
DGN–B–171	Grade MT 446	Mexico	Tube: seamless	0.20 **C**, 1.50 **Mn**, 1.00 **Si**, 23.0–30.0 **Cr**, 0.50 **Ni**, 0.25 N_2, 0.040 **P**, 0.030 **S**	**Hot or cold finished and annealed**: (7.92) **diam**, (480) **TS**, (274) **YS**, 18 **El**
DGN–B–83	446	Mexico	Bar	0.20 **C**, 1.5 **Mn**, 1.0 **Si**, 23.0–27.0 **Cr**, 0.25 **N**, 0.040 **P**, 0.030 **S**	**Hot or cold rolled**: all **diam**, (480) **TS**, (274) **YS**, 28 **El**
DGN–B–216	Grade TP443	Mexico	Tube: seamless, welded	0.20 **C**, 1.00 **Mn**, 0.75 **Si**, 18.0–23.0 **Cr**, 0.50 **Ni**, 0.90–1.25 **Cu**	**As drawn or as welded**: (7.93) **diam**, (480) **TS**, (274) **YS**, 20 **El**
DGN–B–216	Grade TP446	Mexico	Tube: seamless, welded	0.20 **C**, 1.50 **Mn**, 0.75 **Si**, 23.0–30.0 **Cr**, 0.50 **Ni**, 0.10–0.25 **N** 0.040 **P**, 0.030 **S**	**As drawn or as welded**: (7.93) **diam**, (480) **TS**, (274) **YS**, 18 **El**
ANSI/ASTM A 276	446	US	Bar, shapes	0.20 **C**, 1.50 **Mn**, 1.00 **Si**, 23.00–27.00 **Cr**, 0.25 **N**, 0.040 **P**, 0.030 **S**	**Annealed**: all **diam**, 70 (480) **TS**, 40 (275) **YS**, 20 **El**
ANSI/ASTM A 580	Grade 446	US	Wire	0.20 **C**, 1.50 **Mn**, 1.00 **Si**, 23.00–27.00 **Cr**, 0.25 **N**, 0.040 **P**, 0.030 **S**	**Annealed**: all **diam**, 70 (480) **TS**, 40 (280) **YS**, 20 **El**
ANSI/ASTM A 314	431	US	Bar, forgings, billets	0.20 **C**, 1.00 **Mn**, 1.00 **Si**, 15.00–17.00 **Cr**, 1.25–2.50 **Ni**, 0.040 **P**, 0.030 **S**	
ANSI/ASTM A 314	446	US	Bar, forgings, billets	0.20 **C**, 1.50 **Mn**, 1.00 **Si**, 23.00–27.00 **Cr**, 0.25 **N**, 0.040 **P**, 0.030 **S**	
ANSI/ASTM A 314	309	US	Bar, forgings, billets	0.20 **C**, 2.00 **Mn**, 1.00 **Si**, 22.00–24.00 **Cr**, 12.00–15.00 **Ni**	
AS 1444	Grade AS 1444/431	Australia	Bar, bloom, billet, slab	0.20 **C**, 1.00 **Mn**, 1.00 **Si**, 15.00–17.00 **Cr**, 1.25–2.50 **Ni**, 0.040 **P**, 0.040 **S**, 0.60 **Zr** or **Mo**	

WROUGHT STAINLESS STEELS

specification number	designation	country	product forms	composition	mechanical properties (see page iv for explanation)
ANSI/ASTM A 276	431	US	Bar, shapes	0.20 **C**, 1.00 **Mn**, 1.00 **Si**, 15.00–17.00 **Cr**, 1.25–2.50 **Ni**, 0.040 **P**, 0.030 **S**	**Annealed**
MIL-S-862B	Class 309	US	Bar, billets	0.20 **C**, 2.0 **Mn**, 1.0 **Si**, 22.0–24.0 **Cr**, 12.0–15.0 **Ni**, 0.045 **P**, 0.03 **S**	
MIL-S-862B	Class 431	US	Bar, billets	0.20 **C**, 1.0 **Mn**, 1.0 **Si**, 15.0–17.0 **Cr**, 1.25–2.5 **Ni**, 0.040 **P**, 0.030 **S**	
MIL-S-862B	Class 446	US	Bar, billets	0.2 **C**, 1.5 **Mn**, 1.0 **Si**, 23.0–27.0 **Cr**, 0.25 **N**, 0.040 **P**, 0.030 **S**	
NF A 35-583	Z 15 CNM 19.8	France	Wire, rod	0.20 **C**, 5.5–8.0 **Mn**, 1.50 **Si**, 17.0–20.0 **Cr**, 7.5–9.5 **Ni**, 0.030 **P**, 0.020 **S**	
CSA G110.3	Type 309	Canada	Bar, billets	0.20 **C**, 2.00 **Mn**, 1.00 **Si**, 22.00–24.00 **Cr**, 12.00–15.00 **Ni**, 0.045 **P**, 0.030 **S**	
CSA G110.3	Type 431	Canada	Bar, billets	0.20 **C**, 1.00 **Mn**, 1.00 **Si**, 15.00–17.00 **Cr**, 1.25–2.50 **Ni**, 0.040 **P**, 0.030 **S**	
CSA G110.3	Type 446	Canada	Bar, billets	0.20 **C**, 1.50 **Mn**, 1.00 **Si**, 23.00–27.00 **Cr**, 0.25 **N**, 0.040 **P**, 0.030 **S**	
SIS 14 23 03	SIS 23 03-08	Sweden	Strip	0.18–0.25 **C**, 1.0 **Mn**, 1.0 **Si**, 12.0–14.0 **Cr**, 1.0 **Ni**	**Quenched**: (<3) **diam**, (1470) **TS**, (1080) **YS**
SIS 14 23 03	SIS 23 03-08	Sweden	Strip	0.18–0.25 **C**, 1.0 **Mn**, 1.0 **Si**, 12.0–14.0 **Cr**, 1.0 **Ni**, 0.040 **P**, 0.030 **S**	**Quenched and tempered**: (<3) **diam**, (1470) **TS**, (1080) **YS**
SIS 14 23 03	SIS 23 03-04	Sweden	Bar, forgings, plate, sheet, strip, wire	0.18–0.25 **C**, 1.0 **Mn**, 1.0 **Si**, 12.0–14.0 **Cr**, 1.0 **Ni**, 0.040 **P**, 0.030 **S**	**Quenched and tempered (except plate, wire)**: all **diam**, (880) **TS**, (690) **YS**, 14 **El**
SIS 14 23 03	SIS 23 03-02	Sweden	Bar, forgings, strip, wire	0.18–0.25 **C**, 1.0 **Mn**, 1.0 **Si**, 12.0–14.0 **Cr**, 1.0 **Ni**	**Annealed (bar, forgings, strip)**: all **diam**, (740) max **TS**
SIS 14 23 03	SIS 23 03-02	Sweden	Bar, forgings, plate, sheet, strip, wire	0.18–0.25 **C**, 1.0 **Mn**, 1.0 **Si**, 12.0–14.0 **Cr**, 1.0 **Ni**, 0.040 **P**, 0.030 **S**	**Annealed (bar, forgings, strip)**: all **diam**, (740) max **TS**
BS 3S.62		UK	Bar, billets, forgings: aircraft quality	0.18–0.25 **C**, 1.0 **Mn**, 0.8 **Si**, 12.0–14.0 **Cr**, 1.0 **Ni**, 0.030 **P**, 0.025 **S**	**Hardened and tempered**: all **diam**, (690) **TS**, (525) **YS**, 15 **El**
SIS 14 23 03	SIS 23 03-03	Sweden	Bar, forgings, sheet, strip, wire	0.18–0.25 **C**, 1.0 **Mn**, 1.0 **Si**, 12.0–14.0 **Cr**, 1.0 **Ni**, 0.040 **P**, 0.030 **S**	**Quenched and tempered (except wire)**: all **diam**, (690) **TS**, (490) **YS**, 16 **El**
AS G18	G18/En 56CM	Australia	Bar, billet, bar: black, bright	0.18–0.25 **C**, 1.50 **Mn**, 1.00 **Si**, 12.0–14.0 **Cr**, 1.00 **Ni**, 0.60 **Mo**, 0.045 **P**, 0.35 **Pb**, 0.75 **S**, 0.60 **Se**, 0.60 **Zr**	**Hardened, tempered**: 6 **diam**, (540) **TS**
AS G18	G18/En 56C	Australia	Bar, billet, bar: black, bright	0.18–0.25 **C**, 1.00 **Mn**, 1.00 **Si**, 12.0–14.0 **Cr**, 1.00 **Ni**, 0.045 **P**, 0.045 **S**	**Hardened, tempered**: 6 **diam**, (540) **TS**, (385) **YS**
MIL-S-861A	Class 422	US	Bar	0.18–0.23 **C**, 1.00 **Mn**, 1.00 **Si**, 12.0–14.0 **Cr**, 0.50–1.00 **Ni**, 0.75–1.25 **Mo**, 0.75–1.25 **W**, 0.20–0.50 **V**, 0.03 **P**, 0.04 **S**	**Quenched and tempered**: <8 1/4 **diam**, 120 (827) **TS**, 85 (586) **YS**, 17 **El**
AMS 5652C		US	Bar, forgings, tube, wire, rings	0.18 **C**, 1.00–2.00 **Mn**, 1.50–2.30 **Si**, 23.00–25.00 **Cr**, 19.00–22.00 **Ni**, 0.75 **Mo**, 0.50 **Cu**, 0.040 **P**, 0.030 **S**	**Solution heat treated, cold finished (wire)**: all **diam**, 125 (862) max **TS**
ANSI/ASTM A 479	XM-30	US	Bar, shapes	0.18 **C**, 1.00 **Mn**, 1.00 **Si**, 11.50–13.50 **Cr**, 0.05–0.30 **Nb**, 0.040 **P**, 0.030 **S**	**Annealed**: all **diam**, 70 (485) **TS**, 40 (275) **YS**, 13 **El**; **Quenched, tempered**: all **diam**, 125 (865) **TS**, 100 (690) **YS**, 13 **El**
ANSI/ASTM A 479	Grade XM30	US	Bar, shapes	0.18 **C**, 1.00 **Mn**, 1.00 **Si**, 11.50–13.50 **Cr**, 0.05–0.30 **Cb**, 0.040 **P**, 0.030 **S**	**Annealed**: all **diam**, (485) **TS**, (275) **YS**, 13 **El**; **Quenched and tempered**: all **diam**, (865) **TS**, (690) **YS**, 13 **El**
ANSI/ASTM A 276	XM-30	US	Bar, shapes	0.18 **C**, 1.00 **Mn**, 1.00 **Si**, 11.50–13.50 **Cr**, 0.05–0.30 **Nb**, 0.040 **P**, 0.030 **S**	**Annealed**: all **diam**, 70 (480) **TS**, 40 (275) **YS**, 13 **El**; **Intermediate temper**: all **diam**, 125 (860) **TS**, 100 (690) **YS**, 13 **El**

specification number	designation	country	product forms	composition	mechanical properties (see page iv for explanation)
SIS 14 23 21	SIS 23 21–03	Sweden	Bar, forgings	0.17–0.25 **C**, 1.0 **Mn**, 1.0 **Si**, 16.0–18.0 **Cr**, 1.25–2.5 **Ni**, 0.040 **P**, 0.030 **S**	**Quenched and tempered:** (<200) **diam**, (890) **TS**, (640) **YS**
ISO 683/XII	9b	ISO	Bar, sheet, plate	0.17–0.25 **C**, 1.0 **Mn**, 1.0 **Si**, 16.0–18.0 **Cr**, 1.5–2.5 **Ni**, 0.040 **P**, 0.030 **S**	**Quenched and tempered:** all **diam**, (880) **TS**, (690) **YS**, 9 **El**
SIS 14 23 21	SIS 23 21–02	Sweden	Bar, forgings	0.17–0.25 **C**, 1.0 **Mn**, 1.0 **Si**, 16.0–18.0 **Cr**, 1.25–2.5 **Ni**, 0.040 **P**, 0.030 **S**	**Annealed**
BS 3059 Part 2	Grade 762	UK	Tube	0.17–0.23 **C**, 1.00 **Mn**, 0.50 **Si**, 10.00–12.50 **Cr**, 0.3–0.8 **Ni**, 0.80–1.20 **Mo**, 0.70 **W**, 0.25–0.35 **V**, 0.030 **P**, 0.030 **S**	**Normalized and tempered:** all **diam**, (720) **TS**, (470) **YS**, 15 **El**
DIN 17440	Grade X 20 Cr 13	Germany	Sheet, strip, bar, wire, tube, forgings	0.17–0.22 **C**, 1.0 **Mn**, 1.0 **Si**, 12.0–14.0 **Cr**, 0.045 **P**, 0.030 **S**	**Annealed:** (≤5) **diam**, (750) max **TS**; **Tempered:** (≤15) **diam**, (650) **TS**, (450) **YS**, 18 **El**
ISO 683/XII	4	ISO	Bar, sheet, plate	0.16–0.25 **C**, 1.0 **Mn**, 1.0 **Si**, 12.0–14.0 **Cr**, 1.0 **Ni**, 0.040 **P**, 0.030 **S**	**Quenched and tempered:** all **diam**, (690) **TS**, (490) **YS**, 14 **El**
IS 6603	20Cr13	India	Bar	0.16–0.25 **C**, 1.0 **Mn**, 1.0 **Si**, 12.0–14.0 **Cr**, 1.0 **Ni**, 0.040 **P**, 0.030 **S**	**Annealed (martensitic):** (5–100) **diam**, (690) **TS**, (490) **YS**, 14 **El**
IS 6911	20Cr13	India	Plate, sheet, strip	0.16–0.25 **C**, 1.0 **Mn**, 1.0 **Si**, 12.0–14.0 **Cr**, 1.0 **Ni**, 0.030 **S**, 0.040 **P**	**Annealed:** all **diam**, (690) **TS**, (490) **YS**, 14 **El**
JIS G 4303	SUS 420J1	Japan	Bar	0.16–0.25 **C**, 1.00 **Mn**, 1.00 **Si**, 12.00–14.00 **Cr**, 0.60 **Ni**, 0.040 **P**, 0.030 **S**	**Quenched and tempered:** (≤75) **diam**, (637) **TS**, (441) **YS**, 20 **El**
IS 6529	20Cr13	India	Blooms, billets, slabs	0.16–0.25 **C**, 1.0 **Mn**, 1.0 **Si**, 12.0–14.0 **Cr**, 1.0 **Ni**, 0.040 **P**, 0.030 **S**	**Annealed or solution annealed**
JIS G 4308	SVS 420J1	Japan	Wire, rod	0.16–0.25 **C**, 1.00 **Mn**, 1.00 **Si**, 12.00–14.00 **Cr**, 0.60 **Ni**, 0.040 **P**, 0.030 **S**	
AS G18	G18/En 58D	Australia	Bar, billets	0.16 **C**, 2.00 **Mn**, 0.20 min **Si**, 11.0–14.0 **Cr**, 11.0–14.0 **Ni**, 0.045 **P**, 0.045 **S**	**Solution annealed or quenched:** (6) **diam**, (540) **TS**, (185) **YS**
AS G18	G18/En 58A	Australia	Bar, billets	0.16 **C**, 2.00 **Mn**, 0.20 min **Si**, 17.0–20.0 **Cr**, 7.0–10.0 **Ni**, 0.045 **P**, 0.045 **S**	**Solution annealed or quenched:** (6) **diam**, (540) **TS**, (185) **YS**
BS 980	CDS–20	UK	Tube: seamless	0.16 **C**, 2.0 **Mn**, 0.20 **Si**, 17.5 min **Cr**, 7.5 min **Ni**, 10 x C **Nb** or 5 x C **Ti** 0.050 **P**, 0.050 **S**	**Annealed:** all **diam**, (480) **TS**, (205) **YS**
BS 1506–801	Grade A	UK	Bar	0.16 **C**, 2.00 **Mn**, 0.20 min **Si**, 17.0–20.0 **Cr**, 7.0–10.0 **Ni**, 25.0 **Ni+Cr**, 0.045 **S**, 0.045 **P**	**Solution annealed:** all **diam**, (480) **TS**, (185) **YS**, 30 **El**; **Cold drawn:** 0.75 **diam**, (770) **TS**, (620) **YS**, 12 **El**
BS 1506–801	Grade AM	UK	Bar	0.16 **C**, 2.00 **Mn**, 0.20 min **Si**, 17.0–20.0 **Cr**, 7.0–10.0 **Ni**, 25.0 min **Ni+Cr**, 0.20–0.40 **S**, 0.045 **P**	**Solution annealed:** all **diam**, (480) **TS**, (185) **YS**, 30 **El**; **Cold drawn:** 0.75 **diam**, (770) **TS**, (620) **YS**, 12 **El**
ISO 683/XV	7	ISO	Bar	0.15–0.25 **C**, 1.0–1.5 **Mn**, 0.70–1.0 **Si**, 20.0–22.0 **Cr**, 10.5–12.5 **Ni**, 0.15–0.20 **N**, 0.045 **P**, 0.030 **S**	**Solution treated and precipitation hardened:** all **diam**, (835) **TS**, (440) **YS**, 25 **El**
JIS G 4311	SUH 37	Japan	Bar	0.15–0.25 **C**, 1.00–1.60 **Mn**, 1.00 **Si**, 20.50–22.50 **Cr**, 10.00–12.00 **Ni**, 0.15–0.30 **N**, 0.040 **P**, 0.030 **S**	**Solution annealed and aged:** (≤25) **diam**, (785) **TS**, (392) **YS**, 35 **El**
JIS G 4311	SUH 21	Japan	Bar	0.10 **C**, 1.00 **Mn**, 1.50 **Si**, 17.00–21.00 **Cr**, 0.60 **Ni**, 2.00–4.00 **Al**, 0.040 **P**, 0.030 **S**	**Annealed:** all **diam**, (441) **TS**, (245) **YS**, 15 **El**
BS 2S.124		UK	Bar, billets, forgings: aircraft quality	0.15–0.25 **C**, 1.5 **Mn**, 1.0 **Si**, 12.0–14.0 **Cr**, 1.0 **Ni**, 0.6 **Mo**, 1.0 **Mo+Zr**, 0.045 **P**, 0.15–0.40 **S**, 0.6 **Zr**	**Hardened and tempered:** all **diam**, (690) **TS**, (450) **YS**, 11 **El**
BS 970 Part 4	Grade 381S34	UK	Bar, rod	0.15–0.25 **C**, 1.50 **Mn**, 0.75–1.25 **Si**, 20.0–22.0 **Cr**, 10.5–12.5 **Ni**, 0.15–0.30 **N**, 0.040 **P**, 0.030 **S**	**Solution treated**
NF A 35–575	Z 20 C 13	France	Wire, rod	0.15–0.24 **C**, 1.0 **Mn**, 1.0 **Si**, 12.0–14.0 **Cr**, 0.040 **P**, 0.030 **S**	**Quenched and tempered:** all **diam**, (730) max **TS**

WROUGHT STAINLESS STEELS

specification number	designation	country	product forms	composition	mechanical properties (see page iv for explanation)
NF A 35-572	Z 20 C 13	France	Sheet, strip, plate, bar, sections	0.15–0.24 **C**, 1.0 **Mn**, 1.0 **Si**, 12.0–14.0 **Cr**, 0.04 **P**, 0.03 **S**	**Quenched and tempered:** (5–25) **diam**, (730) **TS**, (540) **YS**, 14 **El**
DIN 17440	Grade X 22 CrNi 17	Germany	Sheet, strip, bar, wire, tube, forgings	0.15–0.23 **C**, 1.0 **Mn**, 1.0 **Si**, 16.0–18.0 **Cr**, 1.5–2.5 **Ni**, 0.045 **P**, 0.030 **S**	**Annealed:** (≤5) **diam**, (950) max **TS**; **Tempered:** (≤15) **diam**, (800) **TS**, (600) **YS**, 14 **El**
AMS 5508B		US	Strip, sheet, plate	0.15–0.20 **C**, 0.50 **Mn**, 0.50 **Si**, 12.00–14.00 **Cr**, 1.80–2.20 **Ni**, 0.50 **Mo**, 2.50–3.50 **W**, 0.50 **Cu**, 0.15 **Al**, 0.040 **P**, 0.030 **S**, 0.05	**Annealed:** all **diam**, 150 (1034) max **TS**, 10 **El**
ANSI/ASTM A 565	615	US	Bar, forgings	0.15–0.20 **C**, 0.50 **Mn**, 0.50 **Si**, 12.00–14.00 **Cr**, 1.80–2.20 **Ni**, 0.50 **Mo**, 2.50–3.50 **W**, 0.040 **P**, 0.030 **S**	**Quenched, tempered:** all **diam**, 140 (965) **TS**, 110 (760) **YS**, 15 **El**
DGN-B-150	Type AE/330	Mexico	Wire	0.15–0.20 **C**, 1.0–2.5 **Mn**, 0.60–0.90 **Si**, 17.0–19.0 **Cr**, 35.0–38.0 **Ni**, 0.25 **Cu**, 0.07 N_2, 0.030 **P**, 0.030 **S**	
AMS 5688F		US	Wire	0.15 **C**, 2.00 **Mn**, 1.00 **Si**, 17.00–19.00 **Cr**, 8.00–10.00 **Ni**, 0.75 **Mo**, 0.75 **Cu**, 0.040 **P**, 0.030 **S**	**Spring temper cold drawn, or rolled (round coil):** ≥0.009 (≥0.23) **diam**, 325 (2241) **TS**
ANSI/ASTM A 313	302	US	Wire	0.15 **C**, 2.00 **Mn**, 1.00 **Si**, 17.00–19.00 **Cr**, 8.00–10.00 **Ni**, 0.10 **N**, 0.045 **P**, 0.030 **S**	**Cold drawn:** ≥0.009 (≥0.23) **diam**, 325 (2240) **TS**
ANSI/ASTM A 313	XM-28	US	Wire	0.15 **C**, 11.00–14.00 **Mn**, 1.00 **Si**, 16.50–19.00 **Cr**, 0.50–2.50 **Ni**, 0.20–0.45 **N**, 0.060 **P**, 0.030 **S**	**Cold drawn:** ≥0.009 (0.23) **diam**, 325 (2240) **TS**
ASTM A 313	Type XM-28	US	Wire	0.15 **C**, 11.00–14.00 **Mn**, 1.00 **Si**, 16.50–19.00 **Cr**, 0.50–2.50 **Ni**, 0.20–0.45 **N**, 0.060 **P**, 0.030 **S**	**Cold drawn:** >0.009 (0.23) **diam**, 325 (2240) **TS**
ASTM A 313	Type 302	US	Wire	0.15 **C**, 2.00 **Mn**, 1.00 **Si**, 17.00–19.00 **Cr**, 8.00–10.00 **Ni**, 0.10 **N**, 0.045 **P**, 0.030 **S**	**Cold drawn:** >0.009 (>0.23) **diam**, 325 (2240) **TS**
AIR 9160	9160C411	France	Wire, strip	0.15 **C**, 2.0 **Mn**, 0.025 **Si**, 17.0–20.0 **Cr**, 8.0–11.0 **Ni**, 1.0 **P**, 0.035 **S**	**Solution annealed (wire):** (0.20–0.30) **diam**, (2050) **TS**
ANSI/ASTM A 492	Type 302	US	Wire	0.15 **C**, 2.00 **Mn**, 1.00 **Si**, 17.00–19.00 **Cr**, 8.00–10.00 **Ni**, 0.10 **N**, 0.045 **P**, 0.030 **S**	**Cold drawn:** 0.091–0.100 (2.30–2.54) **diam**, 235 (1620) **TS**
AMS 5519G		US	Strip, sheet	0.15 **C**, 2.00 **Mn**, 1.00 **Si**, 17.00 min **Cr**, 7.00 min **Ni**, 0.75 **Mo**, 0.75 **Cu**, 0.040 **P**, 0.030 **S**	**Solution treated:** ≤0.015 (≤0.38) **diam**, 185 (1276) **TS**, 140 (965) **YS**, 8 **El**
ANSI/ASTM A 579	51	US	Forgings	0.15 **C**, 1.00 **Mn**, 1.00 **Si**, 11.5–13.5 **Cr**, 0.75 **Ni**, 0.50 **Mo**, 0.50 **Cu**, 0.05 **Al**, 0.025 **P**, 0.025 **S**, 0.05	**Quenched and tempered:** all **diam**, 175 (1210) **TS**, 140 (965) **YS**, 12 **El**
DIN 17225	Grade X 12 CrNi 17 7	Germany	Bar, rod, wire	0.15 **C**, 2.0 **Mn**, 1.0 **Si**, 16.0–18.0 **Cr**, 7.0–8.0 **Ni**	**Cold rolled (bar, rod):** all **diam**, (1177) **TS**
ANSI/ASTM A 666	302, grade D	US	Sheet, strip, plate, bar	0.15 **C**, 2.00 **Mn**, 1.00 **Si**, 17.00–19.00 **Cr**, 8.00–10.00 **Ni**, 0.045 **P**, 0.030 **S**	**Annealed (plate, sheet, strip):** >0.030 (>0.76) **diam**, 150 (1035) **TS**, 110 (760) **YS**, 10 **El**
ANSI/ASTM A 666	301, grade D	US	Sheet, strip, plate, bar	0.15 **C**, 2.00 **Mn**, 1.00 **Si**, 16.00–18.00 **Cr**, 6.00–8.00 **Ni**, 0.045 **P**, 0.030 **S**	**Annealed:** >0.030 (>0.76) **diam**, 150 (1035) **TS**, 110 (760) **YS**, 18 **El**
ANSI/ASTM A 666	202, grade D	US	Sheet, strip, plate, bar	0.15 **C**, 7.50–10.00 **Mn**, 1.00 **Si**, 17.00–19.00 **Cr**, 4.00–6.00 **Ni**, 0.25 **N**, 0.060 **P**, 0.030 **S**	**Bright annealed (sheet, strip, plate):** >0.030 (>0.76) **diam**, 150 (1035) **TS**, 110 (760) **YS**, 10 **El**
ANSI/ASTM A 666	201, grade D	US	Sheet, strip, plate, bar	0.15 **C**, 5.50–7.50 **Mn**, 1.00 **Si**, 16.00–18.00 **Cr**, 3.50–5.50 **Ni**, 0.25 **N**, 0.060 **P**, 0.030 **S**	**Bright annealed (plate, sheet, strip):** >0.030 (>0.76) **diam**, 150 (1035) **TS**, 110 (760) **YS**, 10 **El**
ANSI/ASTM A 666	Type 302, grade B	US	Sheet, strip, plate, bar	0.15 **C**, 2.00 **Mn**, 1.00 **Si**, 17.00–19.00 **Cr**, 8.00–10.00 **Ni**, 0.045 **P**, 0.030 **S**	**Cold rolled (plate, sheet, strip):** ≤0.015 (≤0.38) **diam**, 150 (1035) **TS**, 110 (760) **YS**, 9 **El**

WROUGHT STAINLESS STEELS

specification number	designation	country	product forms	composition	mechanical properties (see page iv for explanation)
ANSI/ASTM A 666	Type 301, grade D	US	Sheet, strip, plate, bar	0.15 **C**, 2.00 **Mn**, 1.00 **Si**, 16.00–18.00 **Cr**, 6.00–8.00 **Ni**, 0.045 **P**, 0.030 **S**	**Cold rolled (plate, sheet, strip)**: ≤0.015 (≤0.38) **diam**, 150 (1035) **TS**, 110 (760) **YS**, 15 **El**
ANSI/ASTM A 666	Type 201, grade D	US	Sheet, strip, plate, bar	0.15 **C**, 5.50–7.50 **Mn**, 1.00 **Si**, 16.00–18.00 **Cr**, 3.50–5.50 **Ni**, 0.25 **N**, 0.060 **P**, 0.030 **S**	**Bright annealed (plate, sheet, strip)**: 0.015 **diam**, (1035) **TS**, (760) **YS**, 9 **El**
ANSI/ASTM A 666	Type 202, grade D	US	Sheet, strip, plate, bar	0.15 **C**, 7.50–10.00 **Mn**, 1.00 **Si**, 17.00–19.00 **Cr**, 4.00–6.00 **Ni**, 0.060 **P**, 0.030 **S**	**Bright annealed (plate, sheet, strip)**: 0.015 **diam**, (1035) **TS**, (760) **YS**, 9 **El**
ANSI/ASTM A 666	Type 301, grade D	US	Sheet, strip, plate, bar	0.15 **C**, 2.00 **Mn**, 1.00 **Si**, 16.00–18.00 **Cr**, 6.00–8.00 **Ni**, 0.045 **P**, 0.030 **S**	**Annealed (plate, sheet, strip)**: 0.015 **diam**, (1035) **TS**, (760) **YS**, 15 **El**
ANSI/ASTM A 666	Type 302, grade D	US	Sheet, strip, plate, bar	0.15 **C**, 2.00 **Mn**, 1.00 **Si**, 17.00–19.00 **Cr**, 8.00–10.00 **Ni**, 0.045 **P**, 0.030 **S**	**Annealed (plate, sheet, strip)**: 0.015 **diam**, (1035) **TS**, (760) **YS**, 9 **El**
ANSI/ASTM A 666	Type 201, grade D	US	Sheet, strip, plate, bar	0.15 **C**, 5.50–7.50 **Mn**, 1.00 **Si**, 16.00–18.00 **Cr**, 3.50–5.50 **Ni**, 0.060 **P**, 0.060 **S**, 0.25 **W**	**Cold rolled (plate, sheet, strip)**: ≤0.015 (≤0.38) **diam**, 150 (1035) **TS**, 110 (760) **YS**, 9 **El**
ANSI/ASTM A 666	Type 202, grade D	US	Sheet, strip, plate, bar	0.15 **C**, 7.50–10.00 **Mn**, 1.00 **Si**, 17.00–19.00 **Cr**, 4.00–6.00 **Ni**, 0.25 **N**, 0.060 **P**, 0.060 **S**	**Cold rolled (plate, sheet, strip)**: ≤0.015 (≤0.38) **diam**, 150 (1035) **TS**, 110 (760) **YS**, 9 **El**
AMS 5518E		US	Strip, sheet	0.15 **C**, 2.00 **Mn**, 1.00 **Si**, 17.00 min **Cr**, 7.00 min **Ni**, 0.75 **Mo**, 0.75 **Cu**, 0.040 **P**, 0.030 **S**	**Solution treated**: ≤0.015 (≤0.38) **diam**, 150 (1034) **TS**, 110 (758) **YS**, 15 **El**
ANSI/ASTM A 580	Grade 414	US	Wire	0.15 **C**, 1.00 **Mn**, 1.00 **Si**, 11.50–13.50 **Cr**, 1.25–2.50 **Ni**, 0.040 **P**, 0.030 **S**	**Annealed**: all **diam**, 150 (1030) max **TS**
ANSI/ASTM A 478	Type 302	US	Wire	0.15 **C**, 2.00 **Mn**, 1.00 **Si**, 17.00–19.00 **Cr**, 8.00–10.00 **Ni**, 0.10 **N**, 0.045 **P**, 0.030 **S**	**Annealed**: 0.002–0.005 (0.05–0.13) **diam**, 145 (1000) **TS**, 30 **El**; **Cold drawn**: 0.030–0.125 (0.76–3.18) **diam**, 120 (830) **TS**, 15 **El**
BS S.205		UK	Wire: aircraft quality	0.15 **C**, 0.50–2.0 **Mn**, 0.20–1.0 **Si**, 17.0–19.0 **Cr**, 7.5–9.0 **Ni**, 0.035 **P**, 0.025 **S**	**Tempered**: 0.315–0.394 **diam**, (1000) **TS**
JIS G 4313	SUS 301–CSP	Japan	Strip	0.15 **C**, 2.00 **Mn**, 1.00 **Si**, 16.00–18.00 **Cr**, 6.00–8.00 **Ni**, 0.040 **P**, 0.030 **S**	**One half hard**: (≥0.30) **diam**, (932) **TS**, (510) **YS**, 10 **El**; **Three quarters hard**: (≥0.30) **diam**, (1128) **TS**, (745) **YS**, 5 **El**; **Full hard**: (≥0.30) **diam**, (1324) **TS**, (1030) **YS**; **Extra hard**: (≥0.30) **diam**, (1569) **TS**, (1275) **YS**
AMS 5637B		US	Bar, wire	0.15 **C**, 2.00 **Mn**, 1.00 **Si**, 17.00–19.00 **Cr**, 7.00–9.00 **Ni**, 0.75 **Mo**, 0.75 **Cu**, 0.040 **P**, 0.030 **S**	**Solution heat treated**: all **diam**, 125 (862) **TS**, 100 (690) **YS**, 17 **El**
AMS 5517F		US	Strip, sheet	0.15 **C**, 2.00 **Mn**, 1.00 **Si**, 17.00 min **Cr**, 7.00 min **Ni**, 0.75 **Mo**, 0.75 **Cu**, 0.040 **P**, 0.030 **S**	**Solution treated**: all **diam**, 125 (862) **TS**, 75 (517) **YS**, 25 **El**
ANSI/ASTM A 666	302, grade C	US	Sheet, strip, plate, bar	0.15 **C**, 2.00 **Mn**, 1.00 **Si**, 17.00–19.00 **Cr**, 8.00–10.00 **Ni**, 0.045 **P**, 0.030 **S**	**Annealed (sheet, strip, plate)**: >0.030 (>0.76) **diam**, 125 (860) **TS**, 75 (515) **YS**, 12 **El**
ANSI/ASTM A 666	301, grade C	US	Sheet, strip, plate, bar	0.15 **C**, 2.00 **Mn**, 1.00 **Si**, 16.00–18.00 **Cr**, 6.00–8.00 **Ni**, 0.045 **P**, 0.030 **S**	**Annealed (plate, sheet, strip)**: >0.030 (>0.76) **diam**, 125 (860) **TS**, 75 (515) **YS**, 25 **El**
ANSI/ASTM A 666	202, grade C	US	Sheet, strip, plate, bar	0.15 **C**, 7.50–10.00 **Mn**, 1.00 **Si**, 17.00–19.00 **Cr**, 4.00–6.00 **Ni**, 0.25 **N**, 0.060 **P**, 0.030 **S**	**Bright annealed (plate, sheet, strip)**: ≤0.030(≤0.76) **diam**, 125 (860) **TS**, 75 (515) **YS**, 12 **El**
ANSI/ASTM A 666	201, grade C	US	Sheet, strip, plate, bar	0.15 **C**, 5.50–7.50 **Mn**, 1.00 **Si**, 16.00–18.00 **Cr**, 3.50–5.50 **Ni**, 0.25 **N**, 0.060 **P**, 0.030 **S**	**Bright annealed (plate, sheet, strip)**: >0.030 (>0.76) **diam**, 125 (860) **TS**, 75 (515) **YS**, 20 **El**
ANSI/ASTM A 666	Type 302, grade C	US	Sheet, strip, plate, bar	0.15 **C**, 2.00 **Mn**, 1.00 **Si**, 17.00–19.00 **Cr**, 8.00–10.00 **Ni**, 0.045 **P**, 0.030 **S**	**Cold rolled (plate, sheet, strip)**: ≤0.015 (≤0.38) **diam**, 125 (860) **TS**, 75 (515) **YS**, 10 **El**
ANSI/ASTM A 666	Type 301, grade C	US	Sheet, strip, plate, bar	0.15 **C**, 2.00 **Mn**, 1.00 **Si**, 16.00–18.00 **Cr**, 6.00–8.00 **Ni**, 0.045 **P**, 0.030 **S**	**Cold rolled (plate, sheet, strip)**: ≤0.015 (≤0.38) **diam**, 125 (860) **TS**, 75 (515) **YS**, 25 **El**
IS 6528	10Cr17Ni7	India	Wire	0.15 **C**, 2.0 **Mn**, 1.0 **Si**, 16.0–18.0 **Cr**, 6.0–8.0 **Ni**, 0.045 **P**, 0.030 **S**	**Cold worked**: all **diam**, (860) **TS**, (690) **YS**, 12 **El**

WROUGHT STAINLESS STEELS

specification number	designation	country	product forms	composition	mechanical properties (see page iv for explanation)
IS 6528	10Cr17Mo6Ni4	India	Wire	0.15 **C**, 5.5–7.5 **Mn**, 1.0 **Si**, 16.0–18.0 **Cr**, 3.5–5.5 **Ni**, 0.060 **P**, 0.030 **S**	**Cold worked**: all diam, (860) **TS**, (690) **YS**, 12 **El**
ANSI/ASTM A 666	Type 201, grade C	US	Sheet, strip, plate, bar	0.15 **C**, 5.50–7.50 **Mn**, 1.00 **Si**, 16.00–18.00 **Cr**, 3.50–5.50 **Ni**, 0.25 **N**, 0.060 **P**, 0.030 **S**	**Bright annealed (plate, sheet, strip)**: 0.015 **diam**, (860) **TS**, (515) **YS**, 20 **El**
ANSI/ASTM A 666	Type 202, grade C	US	Sheet, strip, plate, bar	0.15 **C**, 7.50–10.00 **Mn**, 1.00 **Si**, 17.00–19.00 **Cr**, 4.00–6.00 **Ni**, 0.25 **N**, 0.060 **P**, 0.030 **S**	**Bright annealed (plate, sheet, strip)**: 0.015 **diam**, (860) **TS**, (515) **YS**, 12 **El**
ANSI/ASTM A 666	Type 301, grade C	US	Sheet, strip, plate, bar	0.15 **C**, 2.00 **Mn**, 1.00 **Si**, 16.00–18.00 **Cr**, 6.00–8.00 **Ni**, 0.045 **P**, 0.030 **S**	**Annealed (plate, sheet, strip)**: 0.015 **diam**, (860) **TS**, (515) **YS**, 25 **El**
ANSI/ASTM A 666	Type 302, grade C	US	Sheet, strip, plate, bar	0.15 **C**, 2.00 **Mn**, 1.00 **Si**, 17.00–19.00 **Cr**, 8.00–10.00 **Ni**, 0.045 **P**, 0.030 **S**	**Annealed (plate, sheet, strip)**: 0.015 **diam**, (860) **TS**, (515) **YS**, 10 **El**
ANSI/ASTM A666	Type 201, grade C	US	Sheet, strip, plate, bar	0.15 **C**, 5.50–7.50 **Mn**, 1.00 **Si**, 16.00–18.00 **Cr**, 3.50–5.50 **Ni**, 0.060 **P**, 0.060 **S**, 0.25 **W**	**Cold rolled (plate, sheet, strip)**: ≤0.015 (≤0.38) **diam**, 125 (860) **TS**, 75 (515) **YS**, 20 **El**
ANSI/ASTM A 666	Type 202, grade C	US	Sheet, strip, plate, bar	0.15 **C**, 7.50–10.00 **Mn**, 1.00 **Si**, 17.00–19.00 **Cr**, 4.00–6.00 **Ni**, 0.25 **N**, 0.060 **P**, 0.030 **S**	**Cold rolled (plate, sheet, strip)**: ≤0.015 (≤0.38) **diam**, 125 (860) **TS**, 75 (515) **YS**, 12 **El**
IS 6911	10Cr17Ni7	India	Plate, sheet, strip	0.15 **C**, 2.0 **Mn**, 1.0 **Si**, 16.0–18.0 **Cr**, 6.0–8.0 **Ni**, 0.030 **S**, 0.045 **P**	**Cold rolled**: (0.5–0.8) **diam**, (830) **TS**, (490) **YS**, 25 **El**
IS 6911	10Cr17Mn6Ni4N[20]	India	Plate, sheet, strip	0.15 **C**, 5.5–7.5 **Mn**, 1.0 **Si**, 16.0–18.0 **Cr**, 3.5–5.5 **Ni**, 0.030 **S**, 0.060 **P**	**Cold rolled**: (0.5–0.8) **diam**, (830) **TS**, (490) **YS**, 20 **El**
MIL–S–17759B	Composition I	US	Bar, billets, forgings, wire	0.15 **C**, 1.00 **Mn**, 1.00 **Si**, 16.0–18.0 **Cr**, 9.5–12.0 **Ni**, 0.20–0.40 **P**, 0.040 **S**	**Solution annealed and aged for 24 h**: all **diam**, (827) **TS**, (551) **YS**, 18 **El**
AISI 414		US	Sheet, strip, plate, bar, wire	0.15 **C**, 1.00 **Mn**, 1.00 **Si**, 11.50–13.50 **Cr**, 1.25–2.50 **Ni**, 0.040 **P**, 0.030 **S**	**Annealed (sheet strip)**: all **diam**, 120 (827) max **TS**, 105 (724) max **YS**, 15 **El**
DGN–B–83	414	Mexico	Bar	0.15 **C**, 1.0 **Mn**, 1.0 **Si**, 11.5–13.5 **Cr**, 1.25–2.5 **Ni**, 0.040 **P**, 0.030 **S**	**Hot or cold rolled**: all **diam**, (794) **TS**, (617) **YS**, 20 **El**
ANSI/ASTM A 276	414	US	Bar, shapes	0.15 **C**, 1.00 **Mn**, 1.00 **Si**, 11.50–13.50 **Cr**, 1.25–2.50 **Ni**, 0.040 **P**, 0.030 **S**	**Intermediate temper**: all **diam**, 115 (790) **TS**, 90 (620) **YS**, 15 **El**
AISI 301		US	Sheet, strip	0.15 **C**, 2.00 **Mn**, 1.00 **Si**, 16.00–18.00 **Cr**, 6.00–8.00 **Ni**, 0.045 **P**, 0.030 **S**	**Annealed**: all **diam**, 110 (758) max **TS**, 40 (276) max **YS**, 60 **El**; **Quarter hard**: all **diam**, 125 (862) **TS**, 75 (517) **YS**, 25 **El**; **Half hard**: all **diam**, 150 (1034) **TS**, 110 (758) **YS**, 18 **El**; **Three quarters hard**: all **diam**, 175 (1207) **TS**, 135 (862) **YS**, 12 **El**; **Full hard**: all **diam**, 185 (16) **TS**, 140 (965) **YS**, 9 **El**
ANSI/ASTM A 193	Grade B6	US	Bar	0.15 **C**, 1.00 **Mn**, 1.00 **Si**, 11.50–13.50 **Cr**, 0.040 **P**, 0.03 **S**	**Solution annealed**: ≤4 (≤101.6) **diam**, 110 (758) **TS**, 85 (586) **YS**, 15 **El**
ANSI/ASTM A 276	XM–19	US	Bar, shapes	0.15 **C**, 4.00–6.00 **Mn**, 1.00 **Si**, 20.50–23.50 **Cr**, 11.50–13.50 **Ni**, 1.50–3.00 **Mo**, 0.10–0.30 **V**, 0.20–0.40 **N**, 0.10–0.30 **Nb**, 0.040 **P**, 0.030 **S**	**Annealed**: all **diam**, 100 (690) **TS**, 55 (380) **YS**, 35 **El**
MIL–S–861A	Class 403	US	Bar	0.15 **C**, 1.00 **Mn**, 0.50 **Si**, 11.5–13.0 **Cr**, 0.040 **P**, 0.030 **S**	**Quenched and tempered**: <8 1/4 **diam**, 100 (690) **TS**, 70 (483) **YS**, 20 **El**
AMS 5591E		US	Tube	0.15 **C**, 1.00 **Mn**, 1.00 **Si**, 11.50–13.50 **Cr**, 0.75 **Ni**, 0.60 **Mo**, 0.50 **Cu**, 0.05 **Al**, 0.08 **N**, 0.040 **P**, 0.030 **S**, 0.05	**Annealed**: all **diam**, 100 (690) max **TS**, 25 **El**
AMS 5636B		US	Bar, wire	0.15 **C**, 2.00 **Mn**, 1.00 **Si**, 17.00–19.00 **Cr**, 7.00–10.00 **Ni**, 0.75 **Mo**, 0.75 **Cu**, 0.040 **P**, 0.030 **S**	**Solution treated**: all **diam**, 100 (690) **TS**; 60 (414) **YS**, 32 **El**
ANSI/ASTM A 580	Grade XM–28	US	Wire	0.15 **C**, 11.00–14.00 **Mn**, 1.00 **Si**, 16.50–19.00 **Cr**, 0.50–2.50 **Ni**, 0.20–0.45 **N**, 0.040 **P**, 0.030 **S**	**Annealed**: all **diam**, 100 (690) **TS**, 55 (380) **YS**, 30 **El**

WROUGHT STAINLESS STEELS

specification number	designation	country	product forms	composition	mechanical properties (see page iv for explanation)
ANSI/ASTM A 511	MT 414	US	Tube: seamless	0.15 **C**, 1.00 **Mn**, 1.00 **Si**, 11.5–13.5 **Cr**, 1.25–2.50 **Ni**, 0.040 **P**, .030 **S**	**Annealed**: 0.31 (7.9) **diam**, 100 (689) **TS**, 65 (448) **YS**, 15 **El**
DGN–B–171	Grade MT 414	Mexico	Tube: seamless	0.15 **C**, 1.00 **Mn**, 1.00 **Si**, 15.0–17.0 **Cr**, 1.25–2.50 **Ni**, 0.040 **P**, 0.030 **S**	**Hot or cold finished and annealed**: ($\geq$7.92) **diam**, (686) **TS**, (451) **YS**, 15 **El**
AS 1449	Grade AS 1449/201	Australia	Sheet, strip, plate	0.15 **C**, 5.50–7.50 **Mn**, 1.00 **Si**, 16.00–18.00 **Cr**, 3.50–5.50 **Ni**, 0.25 **N**, 0.060 **P**, 0.030 **S**	**Annealed**: ($\leq$1.2) **diam**, (660) **TS**, (300) **YS**, 40 **El**
ANSI/ASTM A 666	201, grade B	US	Sheet, strip, plate, bar	0.15 **C**, 5.50–7.50 **Mn**, 1.00 **Si**, 16.00–18.00 **Cr**, 3.50–5.50 **Ni**, 0.25 **N**, 0.060 **P**, 0.030 **S**	**Bright annealed (plate, sheet, strip)**: >0.030 (>0.76) **diam**, 95 (655) **TS**, 45 (310) **YS**, 40 **El**
MIL–S–860B	Grade G	US	Forgings, machined	0.15 **C**, 1.00 **Mn**, 0.50 **Si**, 11.5–13.0 **Cr**, 0.50 **Ni**, 0.50 **Mo**, 0.015 **P**, 0.018 **S**	**Normalized, quenched and tempered,**: all **diam**, 95 (655) **TS**, 70 (483) **YS**, 18 **El**
ANSI/ASTM A 666	Type 201, grade B	US	Sheet, strip, plate, bar	0.15 **C**, 5.50–7.50 **Mn**, 1.00 **Si**, 16.00–18.00 **Cr**, 3.50–5.50 **Ni**, 0.25 **N**, 0.060 **P**, 0.030 **S**	**Bright annealed (plate, sheet, strip)**: $\geq$0.015 **diam**, (655) **TS**, (275) **YS**, 40 **El**
AISI 201		US	Sheet, strip	0.15 **C**, 5.50–7.50 **Mn**, 1.00 **Si**, 16.00–18.00 **Cr**, 3.50–5.50 **Ni**, 0.25 **N**, 0.060 **P**, 0.030 **S**	**Annealed**: all **diam**, 95 (655) max **TS**, 45 (310) max **YS**, 40 **El**; **1/4 hard**: all **diam**, 125 (862) **TS**, 75 (517) **YS**, 20 **El**; **1/2 hard**: all **diam**, 150 (1034) **TS**, 110 (578) **YS**, 9 **El**; **3/4 hard**: all **diam**, 175 (1207) **TS**, 135 (931) **YS**, 3 **El**; **Full hard**: all **diam**, 185 (1276) **TS**, 140 (965) **YS**, 3 **El**
AISI 302B		US	Sheet, strip, plate, bar	0.15 **C**, 2.00 **Mn**, 2.00–3.00 **Si**, 17.00–19.00 **Cr**, 8.00–10.00 **Ni**, 0.045 **P**, 0.030 **S**	**Annealed (sheet)**: all **diam**, 95 (655) max **TS**, 40 (276) max **YS**, 55 **El**
AISI 420		US	Strip, bar, wire	0.15 **C**, 1.00 **Mn**, 1.00 **Si**, 12.00–14.00 **Cr**, 0.040 **P**, 0.030 **S**	**Annealed (strip)**: all **diam**, 95 (655) max **TS**, 50 (345) max **YS**, 20 **El**
ANSI/ASTM A 412	Type 201	US	Plate, sheet, strip	0.15 **C**, 5.50–7.50 **Mn**, 1.00 **Si**, 16.00–18.00 **Cr**, 3.50–5.50 **Ni**, 0.060 **P**, 0.030 **S**, 0.25 **N**	**Annealed**: 0.015 (0.38) **diam**, 95 (655) **TS**, 45 (310) **YS**, 40 **El**; **1/4 hard**: 0.015 (0.38) **diam**, 125 (860) **TS**, 75 (515) **YS**, 20 **El**; **1/2 hard**: 0.015 (0.38) **diam**, 150 (1025) **TS**, 110 (760) **YS**, 9 **El**; **3/4 hard**: 0.015 (0.38) **diam**, 175 (1205) **TS**, 135 (930) **YS**, 3 **El**; **Full hard**: 0.015 (0.38) **diam**, 185 (1275) **TS**, 140 (965) **YS**, 3 **El**
ANSI/ASTM A 666	Type 201, grade B	US	Sheet, strip, plate, bar	0.15 **C**, 5.50–7.50 **Mn**, 1.00 **Si**, 16.00–18.00 **Cr**, 3.50–5.50 **Ni**, 0.060 **P**, 0.030 **S**, 0.25 **N**	**Cold rolled (plate, sheet, strip)**: $\leq$0.015 ($\leq$0.38) **diam**, 95 (655) **TS**, 45 (310) **YS**, 40 **El**
ISO 683/XII	A–2	ISO	Bar, sheet, plate	0.15 **C**, 5.5–7.5 **Mn**, 1.0 **Si**, 16.0–18.0 **Cr**, 3.5–5.5 **Ni**, 0.05–0.25 **N**, 0.060 **P**, 0.030 **S**	**Solution treated**: all **diam**, (640) **TS**, (300) **YS**, 40 **El**
ISO/683/XII	A–3	ISO	Bar, sheet, plate	0.15 **C**, 7.5–10.5 **Mn**, 1.0 **Si**, 17.0–19.0 **Cr**, 4.0–6.0 **Ni**, 0.05–0.25 **N**, 0.060 **P**, 0.030 **S**	**Solution treated**: all **diam**, (640) **TS**, (300) **YS**, 40 **El**
IS 6603	10Cr17Mn6Ni4	India	Bar	0.15 **C**, 5.5–7.5 **Mn**, 1.0 **Si**, 16.0–18.0 **Cr**, 3.5–5.5 **Ni**, 0.05–0.25 **N**, 0.060 **P**, 0.030 **S**	**Softened**: (5–100) **diam**, (640) **TS**, (300) **YS**, 40 **El**; **Cold rolled**: (0.5–2.3) **diam**, (830) **TS**, (490) **YS**, 25 **El**
IS 6911	10Cr17Mn6Ni4N[20]	India	Plate, sheet, strip	0.15 **C**, 5.5–7.5 **Mn**, 1.0 **Si**, 16.0–18.0 **Cr**, 3.5–5.5 **Ni**, 0.030 **S**, 0.060 **P**	**Softened**: (0.5–3) **diam**, (640) **TS**, (300) **YS**, 38 **El**
JIS G 4305	SUS 201	Japan	Sheet, plate	0.15 **C**, 5.50–7.50 **Mn**, 1.00 **Si**, 16.00–18.00 **Cr**, 3.50–5.50 **Ni**, 0.25 **N**, 0.060 **P**, 0.030 **S**	**Cold rolled and solution annealed**: all **diam**, (637) **TS**, (245) **YS**, 40 **El**
JIS G 4306	SUS 201	Japan	Strip	0.15 **C**, 5.50–7.50 **Mn**, 1.00 **Si**, 16.00–18.00 **Cr**, 3.50–5.50 **Ni**, 0.25 **N**, 0.060 **P**, 0.030 **S**	**Hot rolled and solution annealed**: all **diam**, (637) **TS**, (245) **YS**, 40 **El**
JIS G 4307	SUS 201	Japan	Strip	0.15 **C**, 5.50–7.50 **Mn**, 1.00 **Si**, 16.00–18.00 **Cr**, 3.50–5.50 **Ni**, 0.25 **N**, 0.060 **P**, 0.030 **S**	**Cold rolled and solution annealed**: all **diam**, (637) **TS**, (245) **YS**, 40 **El**
AISI 202		US	Sheet, strip	0.15 **C**, 7.50–10.00 **Mn**, 1.00 **Si**, 17.00–19.00 **Cr**, 4.00–6.00 **Ni**, 0.25 **N**, 0.060 **P**, 0.030 **S**	**Annealed**: all **diam**, 90 (621) max **TS**, 45 (310) max **YS**, 40 **El**; **Quarter hard**: all **diam**, 125 (862) **TS**, 75 (517) **YS**, 12 **El**

WROUGHT STAINLESS STEELS

specification number	designation	country	product forms	composition	mechanical properties (see page iv for explanation)
AISI 302		US	Plate, sheet, strip, bar, wire	0.15 **C**, 2.00 **Mn**, 1.00 **Si**, 17.00–19.00 **Cr**, 8.00–10.00 **Ni**, 0.045 **P**, 0.030 **S**	**Annealed (plate)**: all **diam**, 90 (621) max **TS**, 35 (241) max **YS**, 60 **El**
AISI 303		US	Bar, wire	0.15 **C**, 2.00 **Mn**, 1.00 **Si**, 17.00–19.00 **Cr**, 8.00–10.00 **Ni**, 0.60 **Mo**, 0.20 **P**, 0.15 min **S**	**Annealed**: all **diam**, 90 (621) max **TS**, 35 (241) max **YS**, 50 **El**; **Annealed and cold drawn**: 1 (25.40) **diam**, 100 (689) max **TS**, 60 (414) max **YS**, 40 **El**; **Cold drawn, high tensile**: 7/8 (22.22) **diam**, 125 (862) max **TS**, 95 (655) **YS**, 20 **El**
AISI 303Se		US	Bar, wire	0.15 **C**, 2.00 **Mn**, 1.00 **Si**, 17.00–19.00 **Cr**, 8.00–10.00 **Ni**	**Annealed (bar)**: all **diam**, 90 (621) max **TS**, 35 (241) max **YS**, 50 **El**; **Annealed and cold drawn (bar)**: 1 (25.40) **diam**, 100 (689) max **TS**, 60 (414) max **YS**, 40 **El**; **Cold drawn, high tensile (bar)**: 7/8 (22.22) **diam**, 125 (862) max **TS**, 95 (655) max **YS**, 20 **El**
ANSI/ASTM A 666	301, grade B	US	Sheet, strip, plate, bar	0.15 **C**, 2.00 **Mn**, 1.00 **Si**, 16.00–18.00 **Cr**, 6.00–8.00 **Ni**, 0.045 **P**, 0.030 **S**	**Annealed**: >0.030 (>0.76) **diam**, 90 (620) **TS**, 45 (310) **YS**, 40 **El**
ANSI/ASTM A 666	202, grade B	US	Sheet, strip, plate, bar	0.15 **C**, 7.50–10.00 **Mn**, 1.00 **Si**, 17.00–19.00 **Cr**, 4.00–6.00 **Ni**, 0.25 **N**, 0.060 **P**, 0.030 **S**	**Bright annealed (plate, sheet, strip)**: >0.030 (>0.76) **diam**, 90 (620) **TS**, 45 (310) **YS**, 40 **El**
ANSI/ASTM A 666	Type 301, grade B	US	Sheet, strip, plate, bar	0.15 **C**, 2.00 **Mn**, 1.00 **Si**, 16.00–18.00 **Cr**, 6.00–8.00 **Ni**, 0.045 **P**, 0.030 **S**	**Cold rolled (plate, sheet, strip)**: ≤0.015 (≤0.38) **diam**, 90 (620) **TS**, 45 (310) **YS**, 40 **El**
IS 6528	10Cr17Ni7	India	Wire	0.15 **C**, 2.0 **Mn**, 1.0 **Si**, 16.0–18.0 **Cr**, 6.0–8.0 **Ni**, 0.045 **P**, 0.030 **S**	**Annealed or solution annealed**: all **diam**, (620) **TS**, (310) **YS**, 35 **El**
IS 6528	10Cr17Mo6Ni4	India	Wire	0.15 **C**, 5.5–7.5 **Mn**, 1.0 **Si**, 16.0–18.0 **Cr**, 3.5–5.5 **Ni**, 0.060 **P**, 0.030 **S**	**Annealed or solution annealed**: all **diam**, (620) **TS**, (310) **YS**, 35 **El**
MIL–S–17996	Class 2	US	Sheet, bar, forgings, plate, strip, shapes	0.15 **C**, 13.0–18.5 **Mn**, 1.00 **Si**, 14.0–18.0 **Cr**, 1.0 **Ni**, 0.05 **P**, 0.03 **S**	**Annealed**: all **diam**, (620) **TS**, (275) **YS**, 40 **El**
ANSI/ASTM A 666	Type 202, grade B	US	Sheet, strip, plate, bar	0.15 **C**, 7.50–10.00 **Mn**, 1.00 **Si**, 17.00–19.00 **Cr**, 4.00–6.00 **Ni**, 0.25 **N**, 0.060 **P**, 0.030 **S**	**Bright annealed (plate, sheet, strip)**: ≥0.015 **diam**, (620) **TS**, (310) **YS**, 40 **El**
ANSI/ASTM A 666	Type 301, grade B	US	Sheet, strip, plate, bar	0.15 **C**, 2.00 **Mn**, 1.00 **Si**, 16.00–18.00 **Cr**, 6.00–8.00 **Ni**, 0.045 **P**, 0.030 **S**	**Annealed (plate, sheet, strip)**: 0.015 **diam**, (620) **TS**, (310) **YS**, 40 **El**
ANSI/ASTM A 580	Grade 302B	US	Wire	0.15 **C**, 2.00 **Mn**, 2.00–3.00 **Si**, 17.00–19.00 **Cr**, 8.00–10.00 **Ni**, 0.045 **P**, 0.030 **S**	**Cold finished**: all **diam**, 90 (620) **TS**, 45 (310) **YS**, 35 **El**; **Annealed**: all **diam**, 75 (520) **TS**, 30 (210) **YS**, 35 **El**
ANSI/ASTM A 580	Type 302	US	Wire	0.15 **C**, 2.00 **Mn**, 1.00 **Si**, 17.00–19.00 **Cr**, 8.00–10.00 **Ni**, 0.045 **P**, 0.030 **S**, 0.10 **N**	**Cold finished A**: all **diam**, 90 (620) **TS**, 45 (310) **YS**, 35 **El**; **Annealed**: all **diam**, 75 (520) **TS**, 30 (210) **YS**, 35 **El**; **Cold finished B**: all **diam**, 125 (860) **TS**, 100 (690) **YS**, 12 **El**
BS 3014	Grade 2	UK	Tube	0.15 **C**, 0.50–2.00 **Mn**, 0.20–1.00 **Si**, 17.5–19.5 **Cr**, 7.5–9.5 **Ni**, 0.040 **P**, 0.040 **S**	**As welded**: ≤1 **diam**, (620) **TS**, (310) **YS**, 30 **El**; **Cold drawn**: ≤1 **diam**, (690) **TS**, (465) **YS**, 15 **El**; **Annealed**: ≤1 **diam**, (540) **TS**, (195) **YS**, 45 **El**
ANSI/ASTM A 412	Type 202	US	Plate, sheet, strip	0.15 **C**, 7.50–10.00 **Mn**, 1.00 **Si**, 17.00–19.00 **Cr**, 4.00–6.00 **Ni**, 0.060 **P**, 0.030 **S**, 0.25 **N**	**Annealed**: 0.015 (0.38) **diam**, 90 (620) **TS**, 45 (310) **YS**, 40 **El**; **1/4 hard**: 0.015 (0.38) **diam**, 125 (860) **TS**, 75 (515) **YS**, 12 **El**
ANSI/ASTM A666	Type 202, grade B	US	Sheet, strip, plate, bar	0.15 **C**, 7.50–10.00 **Mn**, 1.00 **Si**, 17.00–19.00 **Cr**, 4.00–6.00 **Ni**, 0.25 **N**, 0.060 **P**, 0.030 **S**	**Cold rolled (plate, sheet, strip)**: ≤0.015 (≤0.38) **diam**, 90 (620) **TS**, 45 (310) **YS**, 40 **El**
DGN–B–83	303 Se	Mexico	Bar	0.15 **C**, 2.0 **Mn**, 1.0 **Si**, 18.0–20.0 **Cr**, 8.0–12.0 **Ni**, 0.045 **P**, 0.030 **S**, 0.15 min **Se**	**Hot or cold rolled**: all **diam**, (618) **TS**, (225) **YS**, 50 **El**
DGN–B–83	303	Mexico	Bar	0.15 **C**, 2.0 **Mn**, 1.0 **Si**, 17.0–19.0 **Cr**, 8.0–10.0 **Ni**, 0.60 **Mo**, 0.20 **P**, 0.15 min **S**	**Hot or cold rolled**: all **diam**, (618) **TS**, (225) **YS**, 50 **El**

WROUGHT STAINLESS STEELS

specification number	designation	country	product forms	composition	mechanical properties (see page iv for explanation)
ASTM A 177	Type 301	US	Sheet, strip	0.15 **C**, 2.00 **Mn**, 1.00 **Si**, 16.00–18.00 **Cr**, 6.00–8.00 **Ni**, 0.045 **P**, 0.030 **S**	**Cold rolled, 1/4 hard**: >0.015 (>0.38) **diam**, 125 (605) **TS**, 75 (365) **YS**, 25 **El**; **Cold rolled, 1/2 hard**: >0.015 (>0.38) **diam**, 150 (725) **TS**, 110 (530) **YS** 18 **El**; **Cold rolled, 3/4 hard**: >0.015 (>0.38) **diam**, 175 (850) **TS**, 135 (655) **YS**, 12 **El**; **Cold rolled, full hard**: >0.015 (>0.38) **diam**, 185 (895) **TS**, 140 (675) **YS**, 9 **El**
ASTM A 581	Type 303	US	Wire	0.15 **C**, 2.00 **Mn**, 1.00 **Si**, 17.00–19.00 **Cr**, 8.00–10.00 **Ni**, 0.60 **Mo**, 0.20 **P**, 0.15 min **S**	**Annealed**: 0.5 **diam**, 85 (590) **TS**; **Cold worked**: 0.5 **diam**, 115 (790) **TS**
ASTM A 581	Type 303 Se	US	Wire	0.15 **C**, 2.00 **Mn**, 1.00 **Si**, 17.00–19.00 **Cr**, 8.00–10.00 **Ni**, 0.20 **P**, 0.06 **S**, 0.15 min **Se**	**Annealed**: 0.5 **diam**, 85 (590) **TS**; **Cold worked**: 0.5 **diam**, 115 (790) **TS**
ASTM A 581	Type 416	US	Wire	0.15 **C**, 1.25 **Mn**, 1.00 **Si**, 12.00–14.00 **Cr**, 0.60 **Mo**, 0.06 **P**, 0.15 min **S**	**Annealed**: 0.5 **diam**, 85 (590) **TS**; **Intermediate temper**: 0.5 **diam**, 115 (790) **TS**; **Hard temper**: 0.5 **diam**, 140 (1000) **TS**
ASTM A 581	Type 416Se	US	Wire	0.15 **C**, 1.25 **Mn**, 1.00 **Si**, 12.00–14.00 **Cr**, 0.06 **P**, 0.06 **S**, 0.15 min **Se**	**Annealed**: 0.5 **diam**, 85 (590) **TS**; **Intermediate temper**: 0.5 **diam**, 115 (790) **TS**; **Hard temper**: 0.5 **diam**, 140 (1000) **TS**
ASTM A 581	Type XM–2	US	Wire	0.15 **C**, 2.00 **Mn**, 1.00 **Si**, 17.00–19.00 **Cr**, 8.00–10.00 **Ni**, 0.40–0.60 **Mo**, 0.60–1.00 **Al**, 0.05 **P**, 0.11–0.16 **S**	**Annealed**: 0.5 **diam**, 85 (590) **TS**; **Cold worked**: 0.5 **diam**, 115 (790) **TS**
ASTM A 581	Type XM–3	US	Wire	0.15 **C**, 2.00 **Mn**, 1.00 **Si**, 17.00–19.00 **Cr**, 8.00–10.00 **Ni**, 0.60 **Mo**, 0.04 **P**, 0.12–0.30 **Pb**, 0.12–0.25 **S**	**Annealed**: 0.5 **diam**, 85 (590) **TS**; **Cold worked**: 0.5 **diam**, 115 (790) **TS**
ASTM A 581	Type XM–5	US	Wire	0.15 **C**, 2.50–4.50 **Mn**, 1.00 **Si**, 17.00–19.00 **Cr**, 7.00–10.00 **Ni**, 0.60 **Mo**, 0.20 **P**, 0.25 min **S**	**Annealed**: 0.5 **diam**, 85 (590) **TS**; **Cold worked**: 0.5 **diam**, 115 (790) **TS**
ASTM A 581	Type XM–6	US	Wire	0.15 **C**, 1.50–2.50 **Mn**, 1.00 **Si**, 12.00–14.00 **Cr**, 0.60 **Mo**, 0.06 **P**, 0.15 min **S**	**Annealed**: 0.5 **diam**, 85 (590) **TS**; **Intermediate temper**: 0.5 **diam**, 115 (790) **TS**; **Hard temper**: 0.5 **diam**, 140 (1000) **TS**
IS 6603	10Cr17Ni7	India	Bar	0.15 **C**, 2.0 **Mn**, 1.0 **Si**, 16.0–18.0 **Cr**, 6.0–8.0 **Ni**, 0.045 **P**, 0.030 **S**	**Softened**: (0.5–3) **diam**, (590) **TS**, 220 **YS**, 38 **El**; **Cold drawn**: (45) **diam**, (830) **TS**, (490) **YS**, 20 **El**; **Cold rolled**: (0.5–3.3) **diam**, (830) **TS**, (490) **YS**, 25 **El**
IS 6911	10Cr17Ni7	India	Plate, sheet, strip	0.15 **C**, 2.0 **Mn**, 1.0 **Si**, 16.0–18.0 **Cr**, 6.0–8.0 **Ni**, 0.030 **S**, 0.045 **P**	**Softened**: (0.50–3) **diam**, (590) **TS**, (220) **YS**, 38 **El**
JIS G 4303	SUS 403	Japan	Bar	0.15 **C**, 1.00 **Mn**, 0.50 **Si**, 11.50–13.00 **Cr**, 0.60 **Ni**, 0.040 **P**, 0.030 **S**	**Quenched and tempered**: (≤75) **diam**, (588) **TS**, (392) **YS**, 25 **El**
JIS G 4304	SUS 202	Japan	Sheet, plate	0.15 **C**, 7.50–10.00 **Mn**, 1.00 **Si**, 17.00–19.00 **Cr**, 4.00–6.00 **Ni**, 0.25 **N**, 0.060 **P**, 0.030 **S**	**Hot rolled and solution annealed**: all **diam**, (588) **TS**, (245) **YS**, 40 **El**
JIS G 4306	SUS 202	Japan	Strip	0.15 **C**, 7.50–10.00 **Mn**, 1.00 **Si**, 17.00–19.00 **Cr**, 4.00–6.00 **Ni**, 0.25 **N**, 0.060 **P**, 0.030 **S**	**Hot rolled and solution annealed**: all **diam**, (588) **TS**, (245) **YS**, 40 **El**
JIS G 4307	SUS 202	Japan	Strip	0.15 **C**, 7.50–10.00 **Mn**, 1.00 **Si**, 17.00–19.00 **Cr**, 4.00–6.00 **Ni**, 0.25 **N**, 0.060 **P**, 0.030 **S**	**Cold rolled and solution annealed**: all **diam**, (588) **TS**, (206) **YS**, 40 **El**
JIS G 3446	SUS 410 TKB	Japan	Tube: seamless or welded	0.15 **C**, 1.00 **Mn**, 1.00 **Si**, 11.50–13.50 **Cr**, 0.60 **Ni**, 0.040 **P**, 0.030 **S**	**Quenched and tempered**: (≥8) **diam**, (588) **TS**, (392) **YS**, 12 **El**

WROUGHT STAINLESS STEELS

specification number	designation	country	product forms	composition	mechanical properties (see page iv for explanation)
AMS 5640L	Type I	US	Bar, forgings, wire	0.15 C, 2.00 Mn, 1.00 Si, 17.00–19.00 Cr, 8.00–10.00 Ni, 0.75 Mo, 0.75 Cu, 0.15 P, 0.15–0.40 S	**Solution heat treated, cold finished (wire)**: all diam, 85 (586) TS
AMS 5640L	Type II	US	Bar, forgings, wire	0.15 C, 2.00 Mn, 1.00 Si, 17.00–19.00 Cr, 8.00–10.00 Ni, 0.75 Mo, 0.75 Cu, 0.12–0.17 P, 0.04 S, 0.15–0.40 Se	**Solution heat treated, cold finished (wire)**: all diam, 85 (586) TS
AMS 5640L	Type III	US	Bar, forgings, wire	0.15 C, 2.50–4.50 Mn, 1.00 Si, 17.00–19.00 Cr, 7.00–10.00 Ni, 0.75 Mo, 0.75 Cu, 0.20 P, 0.15–0.40 S	**Solution heat treated, cold finished (wire)**: all diam, 85 (586) TS
ANSI/ASTM A 666	302, grade B	US	Sheet, strip, plate, bar	0.15 C, 2.00 Mn, 1.00 Si, 17.00–19.00 Cr, 8.00–10.00 Ni, 0.045 P, 0.030 S	**Annealed (sheet, strip, plate)**: >0.030 (>0.76) diam, 85 (585) TS, 45 (310) YS, 40 El
ANSI/ASTM A 666	Type 302, grade B	US	Sheet, strip, plate, bar	0.15 C, 2.00 Mn, 1.00 Si, 17.00–19.00 Cr, 8.00–10.00 Ni, 0.045 P, 0.030 S	**Cold rolled (plate, sheet, strip)**: ≤0.015 (≤0.38) diam, 85 (585) TS, 45 (310) YS, 40 El
ANSI/ASTM A 493	Type 302	US	Bar, wire	0.15 C, 2.00 Mn, 1.00 Si, 17.00–19.00 Cr, 8.00–10.00 Ni, 0.10 N, 0.045 P, 0.030 S	**Lightly drafted (wire)**: ≥0.156 (≥3.96) diam, 85 (585) TS; **Annealed (wire)**: ≥0.156 (≥3.96) diam, 80 (550) TS
ANSI/ASTM A 666	Type 302, grade B	US	Sheet, strip, plate, bar	0.15 C, 2.00 Mn, 1.00 Si, 17.00–19.00 Cr, 8.00–10.00 Ni, 0.045 P, 0.030 S	**Annealed (plate, sheet, strip)**: 0.015 diam, (585) TS, (310) YS, 40 El
JIS G 4311	SUH 330	Japan	Bar	0.15 C, 2.00 Mn, 1.50 Si, 14.00–17.00 Cr, 33.00–37.00 Ni, 0.040 P, 0.030 S	**Solution annealed**: (≤180) diam, (559) TS, (206) YS, 40 El
JIS G 4312	SUH 330	Japan	Sheet, plate	0.15 C, 2.00 Mn, 1.50 Si, 14.00–17.00 Cr, 33.00–37.00 Ni, 0.040 P, 0.030 S	**Solution annealed**: all diam, (559) TS, (206) YS, 35 El
AS G18	G18/En 58B	Australia	Bar, billets	0.15 C, 2.00 Mn, 0.20 min Si, 17.0–20.0 Cr, 7.0–10.0 Ni, 0.045 P, 0.045 S, 4 x C min Ti	**Solution annealed or quenched**: (6) diam, (540) TS, (185) YS
AS G18	G18/En 58C	Australia	Bar, billets	0.15 C, 2.00 Mn, 0.20 min Si, 17.0–20.0 Cr, 9.0–12.0 Ni, 0.045 P, 0.045 S, 4 x C min Ti	**Solution annealed or quenched**: (6) diam, (540) TS, (185) YS
BS 1449 Part 2	Grade 309S24	UK	Plate, sheet, strip	0.15 C, 0.50–2.00 Mn, 0.20–1.00 Si, 22.0–25.0 Cr, 13.0–16.0 Ni, 0.045 P, 0.030 S	**Solution annealed**: (≥3.0) (sheet and strip) diam, (540) TS, (215) YS, 40 El
BS 1449 Part 2	Grade 310S24	UK	Plate, sheet, strip	0.15 C, 0.50–2.00 Mn, 0.20–1.00 Si, 23.0–26.0 Cr, 19.0–22.0 Ni, 0.045 P, 0.030 S	**Solution annealed**: (≥3.0) (sheet and strip) diam, (540) TS, (215) YS, 40 El
BS 1449 Part 2	Grade 312S24	UK	Plate, sheet, strip	0.15 C, 0.50–2.00 Mn, 0.20–1.00 Si, 23.0–26.0 Cr, 16.0–19.0 Ni, 0.045 P, 0.030 S	**Solution annealed**: (≥3.0) (sheet and strip) diam, (540) TS, (215) YS, 40 El
BS 1449 Part 2	Grade 301S21	UK	Sheet, strip	0.15 C, 0.50–2.00 Mn, 0.20–1.00 Si, 16.0–18.0 Cr, 6.0–8.0 Ni, 0.045 P, 0.030 S	**Solution annealed**: (0.50–1.0) diam, (540) TS, (215) YS, 30 El; **Quarter hard**: (0.50–1.0) diam, (850) TS, (510) YS, 25 El; **Half hard**: (0.50–1.0) diam, (1000) TS, (725) YS, 10 El; **Three-quarters hard**: (0.50–1.0) diam, (1160) TS, (900) YS, 5 El; **Hard**: (0.50–1.0) diam, (1240) TS, (925) YS, 4 El
BS 970 Part 4	Grade 310S24	UK	Blooms, billets, bar, forgings	0.15 C, 0.50–2.00 Mn, 0.20–1.00 Si, 23.0–26.0 Cr, 19.0–22.0 Ni, 0.045 P, 0.030 S	**Annealed**: all diam, (540) TS, 40 El
BS S.125		UK	Bar, billets, forgings, aircraft quality	0.15 C, 0.5–2.0 Mn, 0.20–1.0 Si, 22.0–25.0 Cr, 13.0–16.0 Ni, 0.035 P, 0.025 S, 4 x C min Ti	**Annealed or quenched**: all diam, (540) TS, (215) YS, 28 El
BS S.126		UK	Bar, billets, forgings: aircraft quality	0.15 C, 0.5–2.0 Mn, 0.20–1.0 Si, 22.0–25.0 Cr, 13.0–16.0 Ni, 8xC min Nb, 0.035 P, 0.025 S	**Annealed or quenched**: all diam, (540) TS, (215) YS, 28 El
BS S.127		UK	Bar, billets, forgings: aircraft quality	0.15 C, 0.5–2.0 Mn, 0.20–1.0 Si, 23.0–26.0 Cr, 16.0–19.0 Ni, 0.035 P, 0.025 S, 4 x C min Ti	**Annealed or quenched**: all diam, (540) TS, (215) YS, 28 El
BS S.128		UK	Bar, billets, forgings: aircraft quality	0.15 C, 0.5–2.0 Mn, 0.20–1.0 Si, 23.0–26.0 Cr, 16.0–19.0 Ni, 8 x C min Nb, 0.035 P, 0.025 S	**Annealed or quenched**: all diam, (540) TS, (215) YS, 28 El

WROUGHT STAINLESS STEELS

specification number	designation	country	product forms	composition	mechanical properties (see page iv for explanation)
JIS G 4303	SUS 410	Japan	Bar	0.15 **C**, 1.00 **Mn**, 1.00 **Si**, 11.50–13.50 **Cr**, 0.60 **Ni**	**Quenched and tempered:** (≤75) **diam**, (539) **TS**, (343) **YS**, 25 **El**
JIS G 4303	SUS 416	Japan	Bar	0.15 **C**, 1.25 **Mn**, 1.00 **Si**, 12.00–14.00 **Cr**, 0.60 **Ni**, 0.60 **Mo**, 0.060 **P**, 0.15 **S**	**Quenched and tempered:** (≤75) **diam**, (539) **TS**, (343) **YS**, 25 **El**
COPANT 513	TP 310	COPANT	Tube	0.15 **C**, 2.00 **Mn**, 0.75 **Si**, 24.0–26.0 **Cr**, 19.00–22.00 **Ni**, 0.040 **P**, 0.030 **S**	**Hot or cold finished:** (>8) **diam**, (520) **TS**, (205) **YS**, 35 **El**
AS 1449	Grade AS 1449/301	Australia	Sheet, strip, plate	0.15 **C**, 2.00 **Mn**, 1.00 **Si**, 16.00–18.00 **Cr**, 6.00–8.00 **Ni**, 0.045 **P**, 0.030 **S**	**Annealed:** (≤1.2) **diam**, (520) **TS**, (205) **YS**, 40 **El**
AS 1449	Grade AS 1449/302	Australia	Sheet, strip, plate	0.15 **C**, 2.00 **Mn**, 1.00 **Si**, 17.00–19.00 **Cr**, 8.00–10.00 **Ni**, 0.045 **P**, 0.030 **S**	**Annealed:** (≤1.2) **diam**, (520) **TS**, (205) **YS**, 40 **El**
AS 1449	Grade AS 1449/420	Australia	Sheet, strip, plate	0.15 **C**, 1.00 **Mn**, 1.00 **Si**, 12.00–14.00 **Cr**, 0.040 **P**, 0.030 **S**	**Annealed:** (≤1.2) **diam**, (520) **TS**, 12 **El**
JIS G 3459	SUS 309 STP	Japan	Pipe: seamless or welded	0.15 **C**, 2.00 **Mn**, 1.00 **Si**, 22.00–24.00 **Cr**, 12.00–15.00 **Ni**, 0.040 **P**, 0.030 **S**	**Solution annealed:** (≥8) **diam**, (520) **TS**, (206) **YS**, 35 **El**
JIS G 3459	SUS 310 STP	Japan	Pipe: seamless or welded	0.15 **C**, 2.00 **Mn**, 1.50 **Si**, 24.00–26.00 **Cr**, 19.00–22.00 **Ni**, 0.040 **P**, 0.030 **S**	**Solution annealed:** (≥8) **diam**, (520) **TS**, (206) **YS**, 35 **El**
JIS G 3463	SUS 309 STB	Japan	Tube: seamless or welded	0.15 **C**, 2.00 **Mn**, 1.00 **Si**, 22.00–24.00 **Cr**, 12.00–15.00 **Ni**, 0.040 **P**, 0.030 **S**	**Solution annealed:** (≥8) **diam**, (520) **TS**, (206) **YS**, 35 **El**
JIS G 3463	SUS 310 STB	Japan	Tube: seamless or welded	0.15 **C**, 2.00 **Mn**, 1.50 **Si**, 24.00–26.00 **Cr**, 19.00–22.00 **Ni**, 0.040 **P**, 0.030 **S**	**Solution annealed:** (≥8) **diam**, (520) **TS**, (206) **YS**, 35 **El**
JIS G 4303	SUS 201	Japan	Bar	0.15 **C**, 5.50–7.50 **Mn**, 1.00 **Si**, 16.00–18.00 **Cr**, 3.50–5.50 **Ni**, 0.25 **N**, 0.060 **P**, 0.030 **S**	**Solution annealed:** (≤180) **diam**, (520) **TS**, (275) **YS**, 40 **El**
JIS G 4303	SUS 202	Japan	Bar	0.15 **C**, 7.50–10.00 **Mn**, 1.00 **Si**, 17.00–19.00 **Cr**, 4.00–6.00 **Ni**, 0.25 **N**, 0.060 **P**, 0.030 **S**	**Solution annealed:** (≤180) **diam**, (520) **TS**, (275) **YS**, 40 **El**
JIS G 4303	SUS 301	Japan	Bar	0.15 **C**, 2.00 **Mn**, 1.00 **Si**, 16.00–18.00 **Cr**, 0.040 **P**, 0.030 **S**	**Solution annealed:** (≤180) **diam**, (520) **TS**, (206) **YS**, 40 **El**
JIS G 4303	SUS 302	Japan	Bar, forgings	0.15 **C**, 2.00 **Mn**, 1.00 **Si**, 17.00–19.00 **Cr**, 0.040 **P**, 0.030 **S**	**Solution annealed:** (≤180) **diam**, (520) **TS**, (206) **YS**, 40 **El**
JIS G 4303	SUS 303	Japan	Bar	0.15 **C**, 2.00 **Mn**, 1.00 **Si**, 17.00–19.00 **Cr**, 8.00–10.00 **Ni**, 0.60 **Mo**, 0.20 **P**, 0.15 **S**	**Solution annealed:** (≤180) **diam**, (520) **TS**, (206) **YS**, 40 **El**
JIS G 4303	SUS 303Se	Japan	Bar	0.15 **C**, 2.00 **Mn**, 1.00 **Si**, 17.00–19.00 **Cr**, 8.00–10.00 **Ni**, 0.20 **P**, 0.060 **S**, 0.15 **Se**	**Solution annealed:** (≤180) **diam**, (520) **TS**, (206) **YS**, 40 **El**
JIS G 4304	SUS 302	Japan	Sheet, plate	0.15 **C**, 2.00 **Mn**, 1.00 **Si**, 17.00–19.00 **Cr**, 8.00–10.00 **Ni**, 0.040 **P**, 0.030 **S**	**Hot rolled and solution annealed:** all **diam**, (520) **TS**, (206) **YS**, 40 **El**
JIS G 4305	SUS 302	Japan	Sheet, plate	0.15 **C**, 2.00 **Mn**, 1.00 **Si**, 17.00–19.00 **Cr**, 8.00–10.00 **Ni**, 0.040 **P**, 0.030 **S**	**Cold rolled and solution annealed:** all **diam**, (520) **TS**, (206) **YS**, 40 **El**
JIS G 4306	SUS 301	Japan	Strip	0.15 **C**, 2.00 **Mn**, 1.00 **Si**, 16.00–18.00 **Cr**, 6.00–8.00 **Ni**, 0.040 **P**, 0.030 **S**	**Hot rolled and solution annealed:** all **diam**, (520) **TS**, (206) **YS**, 40 **El**
JIS G 4306	SUS 302	Japan	Strip	0.15 **C**, 2.00 **Mn**, 1.00 **Si**, 17.00–19.00 **Cr**, 8.00–10.00 **Ni**, 0.040 **P**, 0.030 **S**	**Hot rolled and solution annealed:** all **diam**, (520) **TS**, (206) **YS**, 40 **El**
JIS G 4307	SUS 301	Japan	Strip	0.15 **C**, 2.00 **Mn**, 1.00 **Si**, 16.00–18.00 **Cr**, 6.00–8.00 **Ni**, 0.040 **P**, 0.030 **S**	**Cold rolled and solution annealed:** all **diam**, (520) **TS**, (206) **YS**, 40 **El**
JIS G 4307	SUS 302	Japan	Strip	0.15 **C**, 2.00 **Mn**, 1.00 **Si**, 17.00–19.00 **Cr**, 8.00–10.00 **Ni**, 0.040 **P**, 0.030 **S**	**Cold rolled and solution annealed:** all **diam**, (520) **TS**, (206) **YS**, 40 **El**
JIS G 3214	SUS F 310	Japan	Forgings	0.15 **C**, 2.00 **Mn**, 1.00 **Si**, 24.00–26.00 **Cr**, 19.00–22.00 **Ni**, 0.040 **P**, 0.030 **S**	**Solution annealed:** (≤130) **diam**, (520) **TS**, (206) **YS**, 35 **El**

WROUGHT STAINLESS STEELS

specification number	designation	country	product forms	composition	mechanical properties (see page iv for explanation)
JIS G 4305	SUS 301	Japan	Sheet, plate	0.15 **C**, 2.00 **Mn**, 1.00 **Si**, 16.00–18.00 **Cr**, 6.00–8.00 **Ni**, 0.040 **P**, 0.030 **S**	**Cold rolled and solution annealed**: all **diam**, (520) **TS**, (206) **YS**, 40 **El**; **One quarter hard**: (0.4) **diam**, (863) **TS**, (510) **YS**, 25 **El**; **One half hard**: (0.4) **diam**, (1030) **TS**, (755) **YS**, 9 **El**; **Three quarters hard**: (0.4) **diam**, (1206) **TS**, (932) **YS**, 3 **El**; **Full hard**: (0.4) **diam**, (1275) **TS**, (961) **YS**, 3 **El**
DGN–B–171	Grade MT 310	Mexico	Tube: seamless	0.15 **C**, 2.00 **Mn**, 1.00 **Si**, 24.0–26.0 **Cr**, 19.0–22.0 **Ni**, 0.040 **P**, 0.030 **S**	**Hot or cold finished and annealed**: (≥7.92) **diam**, (519) **TS**, (206) **YS**, 35 **El**
DGN–B–218	Grade TP309	Mexico	Tube: welded	0.15 **C**, 2.00 **Mn**, 0.75 **Si**, 22.0–24.0 **Cr**, 12.0–15.0 **Ni**, 0.040 **P**, 0.030 **S**	**Cold finished and quenched or tempered**: (≥7.92) **diam**, (519) **TS**, (206) **YS**, 35 **El**
DGN–B–218	Grade TP310	Mexico	Tube: welded	0.15 **C**, 2.00 **Mn**, 0.75 **Si**, 24.0–26.0 **Cr**, 19.0–22.0 **Ni**, 0.040 **P**, 0.030 **S**	**Cold finished and quenched or tempered**: (≥7.92) **diam**, (519) **TS**, (206) **YS**, 35 **El**
DGN–B–171	Grade MT303Se	Mexico	Tube: seamless	0.15 **C**, 2.00 **Mn**, 1.00 **Si**, 17.0–19.0 **Cr**, 8.0–11.0 **Ni**, 0.040 **P**, 0.030 **S**, 0.12–0.20 **Se**	**Hot or cold finished**: (≥7.92) **diam**, (519) **TS**, (206) **YS**, 35 **El**
DGN–B–171	Grade MT309	Mexico	Tube: seamless	0.15 **C**, 2.00 **Mn**, 1.00 **Si**, 22.0–24.0 **Cr**, 12.0–15.0 **Ni**, 0.040 **P**, 0.030 **S**	**Hot or cold finished and annealed**: (≥7.92) **diam**, (519) **TS**, (206) **YS**, 35 **El**
DGN–B–185	Grade TP309	Mexico	Pipe: seamless, welded	0.15 **C**, 2.00 **Mn**, 0.75 **Si**, 22.0–24.0 **Cr**, 12.0–15.0 **Ni**, 0.040 **P**, 0.030 **S**	**Quenched or tempered**: (≥8) **diam**, (519) **TS**, (206) **YS**, 35 **El**
DGN–B–185	Grade TP310	Mexico	Pipe: seamless, welded	0.15 **C**, 2.00 **Mn**, 0.75 **Si**, 24.0–26.0 **Cr**, 19.0–22.0 **Ni**, 0.040 **P**, 0.030 **S**	**Quenched or tempered**: (≥8) **diam**, (519) **TS**, (206) **YS**, 35 **El**
NOM–B–194	Grade TP 310	Mexico	Tube: seamless	0.15 **C**, 2.00 **Mn**, 0.75 **Si**, 24.0–26.0 **Cr**, 19.00–22.0 **Ni**, 0.040 **P**, 0.030 **S**	**Quenched**: (0.38–12.7) **diam**, (517) **TS**, (207) **YS**
CSA G110.9	Type 302	Canada	Plate	0.15 **C**, 2.00 **Mn**, 1.00 **Si**, 17.00–19.00 **Cr**, 8.00–10.00 **Ni**, 0.045 **P**, 0.030 **S**	**Hot rolled, annealed, quenched and tempered**: all **diam**, 75 (517) **TS**, 30 (207) **YS**, 40 **El**
ANSI/ASTM A 511	MT 309	US	Tube: seamless	0.15 **C**, 2.00 **Mn**, 1.00 **Si**, 22.0–24.0 **Cr**, 12.0–15.0 **Ni**, 0.040 **P**, 0.030 **S**	**Solution annealed**: 0.31 (7.9) **diam**, 75 (517) **TS**, 30 (207) **YS** 35 **El**
ANSI/ASTM A 511	MT 310	US	Tube: seamless	0.15 **C**, 2.00 **Mn**, 1.00 **Si**, 24.0–26.0 **Cr**, 19.0–22.0 **Ni**, 0.040 **P**, 0.030 **S**	**Solution annealed**: 0.31 (7.9) **diam**, 75 (517) **TS**, 30 (207) **YS**, 35 **El**
ANSI/ASTM A 409	TP 309	US	Pipe: welded	0.15 **C**, 2.00 **Mn**, 0.75 **Si**, 22.0–24.0 **Cr**, 12.0–15.0 **Ni**, 0.040 **P**, 0.030 **S**	**Solution annealed**: all **diam**, 75 (517) **TS**, 30 (207) **YS**, 30 **El**
ANSI/ASTM A 409	TP 310	US	Pipe: welded	0.15 **C**, 2.00 **Mn**, 0.75 **Si**, 24.0–26.0 **Cr**, 19.0–22.0 **Ni**, 0.040 **P**, 0.030 **S**	**Solution annealed**: all **diam**, 75 (517) **TS**, 30 (207) **YS**, 30 **El**
ANSI/ASTM A 312	TP 309	US	Pipe: seamless or welded	0.15 **C**, 2.00 **Mn**, 0.75 **S**, 22.0–24.0 **Cr**, 12.0–15.0 **Ni**, 0.040 **P**, 0.030 **S**	**Solution annealed**: 0.31 (7.94) **diam**, 75 (517) **TS**, 30 (207) **YS**, 35 **El**
ANSI/ASTM A 312	TP 310	US	Pipe: seamless or welded	0.15 **C**, 2.00 **Mn**, 0.75 **Si**, 24.0–26.0 **Cr**, 19.0–22.0 **Ni**, 0.040 **P**, 0.030 **S**	**Solution annealed**: 0.31 (7.94) **diam**, 75 (517) **TS**, 30 (207) **YS**, 35 **El**
CSA G110.9	Type 302	Canada	Sheet	0.15 **C**, 2.00 **Mn**, 1.00 **Si**, 17.00–19.00 **Cr**, 8.00–10.00 **Ni**, 0.045 **P**, 0.030 **S**	**Hot or cold rolled and annealed**: all **diam**, 75 (517) **TS**, 30 (207) **YS**, 40 **El**
CSA G110.9	Type 302	Canada	Strip	0.15 **C**, 2.00 **Mn**, 1.00 **Si**, 17.00–19.00 **Cr**, 8.00–10.00 **Ni**, 0.045 **P**, 0.030 **S**	**Cold rolled and annealed**: all **diam**, 75 (517) **TS**, 30 (207) **YS**, 40 **El**
ASTM A 320	B8F AISI 303	US	Bar	0.15 **C**, 2.00 **Mn**, 1.00 **Si**, 17.00–19.00 **Cr**, 8.00–10.00 **Ni**, 0.60 **Mo**, 0.20 **P**, 0.15–0.35 **S**, 0.60 **Zr**	**Solution treated**: all **diam**, 75 (517) **TS**, 30 (207) **YS**, 35 **El**; **Solution treated, strain hardened**: (19.0–25.4) 0.75–1.0 **diam**, 115 (793) **TS**, 80 (552) **YS**, 15 **El**
ASTM A 320	B8F AISI 303 Se	US	Bar	0.15 **C**, 2.00 **Mn**, 1.00 **Si**, 17.00–19.00 **Cr**, 8.00–10.00 **Ni**, 0.20 **P**, 0.06 **S**, 0.15–0.35 **Se**	**Solution treated**: all **diam**, 75 (517) **TS**, 30 (207) **YS**, 35 **El**; **Solution treated, strain hardened**: (19.0–25.4) 0.75–1.0 **diam**, 115 (793) **TS**, 80 (552) **YS**, 15 **El**

WROUGHT STAINLESS STEELS

specification number	designation	country	product forms	composition	mechanical properties (see page iv for explanation)
CSA G110.6	Type 302B	Canada	Plate, sheet, strip	0.15 **C**, 2.00 **Mn**, 2.00–3.00 **Si**, 17.00–19.00 **Cr**, 8.00–10.00 **Ni**, 0.045 **P**, 0.030 **S**	**Hot rolled and annealed or hot rolled, quenched and tempered:** all **diam**, 75 (517) **TS**, 30 (207) **YS**, 40 **El**
CSA G110.6	Type 302	Canada	Plate, sheet, strip	0.15 **C**, 2.00 **Mn**, 1.00 **Si**, 17.00–19.00 **Cr**, 8.00–10.00 **Ni**, 0.045 **P**, 0.030 **S**	**Hot rolled and annealed or hot rolled, quenched and tempered:** all **diam**, 75 (517) **TS**, 30 (207) **YS**, 40 **El**
CSA G110.6	Type 301	Canada	Plate, sheet, strip	0.15 **C**, 2.00 **Mn**, 1.00 **Si**, 16.00–18.00 **Cr**, 6.00–8.00 **Ni**	**Hot rolled and annealed or hot rolled, quenched and tempered:** all **diam**, 75 (517) **TS**, 30 (207) **YS**, 40 **El**
CSA G110.6	Type 202	Canada	Plate, sheet, strip	0.15 **C**, 7.50–10.00 **Mn**, 1.00 **Si**, 17.00–19.00 **Cr**, 4.00–6.00 **Ni**, 0.25 **N**, 0.060 **P**, 0.030 **S**	**Hot rolled and annealed or hot rolled, quenched and tempered:** all **diam**, 75 (517) **TS**, 30 (207) **YS**, 40 **El**
CSA G110.6	Type 201	Canada	Plate, sheet, strip	0.15 **C**, 5.50–7.50 **Mn**, 1.00 **Si**, 16.00–18.00 **Cr**, 3.50–5.50 **Ni**, 0.25 **N**, 0.060 **P**, 0.030 **S**	**Hot rolled and annealed or hot rolled, quenched and tempered:** all **diam**, 75 (517) **TS**, 30 (207) **YS**, 40 **El**
AMS 5635A		US	Bar, forgings, wire	0.15 **C**, 2.00 **Mn**, 1.00 **Si**, 17.00–19.00 **Cr**, 8.00–10.00 **Ni**, 0.75 **Mo**, 0.75 **Cu**, 0.040 **P**, 0.12–0.30 **Pb**, 0.12–0.30 **S**	**Hot finished (bar)**: all **diam**, 75 (517) **TS**, 30 (207) **YS**, 40 **El**; **Cold finished (bar,wire)**: ≤0.500 (≤12.70) **diam**, 90 (621) **TS**, 45 (310) **YS**, 35 **El**
AMS 5516H		US	Strip, sheet, plate	0.15 **C**, 2.00 **Mn**, 1.00 **Si**, 17.00–19.00 **Cr**, 8.00–10.00 **Ni**, 0.75 **Mo**, 0.75 **Cu**, 0.040 **P**, 0.030 **S**	**Solution treated:** ≥0.002–0.003 (≥0.05–0.08) **diam**, 75 (517) **TS**, 36 (248) **YS**, 30 **El**
AISI 416		US	Bar, wire	0.15 **C**, 1.25 **Mn**, 1.00 **Si**, 12.00–14.00 **Cr**, 0.60 **Mo**	**Annealed (bar)**: all **diam**, 75 (517) max **TS**, 40 (276) max **YS**, 30 **El**; **Tempered (bar)**: all **diam**, 110 (758) max **TS**, 85 (586) max **YS**, 18 **El**; **Tempered and cold finished (bar)**: all **diam**, 100 (689) max **TS**, 85 (586) max **YS**, 13 **El**
AISI 416 Se		US	Bar, wire	0.15 **C**, 1.25 **Mn**, 1.00 **Si**, 12.00–14.00 **Cr**, 0.060 **P**, 0.060 **S**, 0.15 min **Se**	**Annealed (bar)**: all **diam**, 75 (517) max **TS**, 40 (276) max **YS**, 30 **El**; **Tempered (bar)**: all **diam**, 110 (758) max **TS**, 85 (586) max **YS**, 18 **El**; **Tempered and cold finished (bar)**: 1 (25.40) **diam**, 100 (689) max **TS**, 85 (586) max **YS**, 13 **El**
ANSI/ASTM A 511	MT 303Se	US	Tube: seamless	0.15 **C**, 2.00 **Mn**, 1.00 **Si**, 17.0–19.0 **Cr**, 8.0–11.0 **Ni**, 0.040 **P**, 0.040 **S**, 0.12–0.2 **Se**	**Solution annealed**: 0.31 (7.9) **diam**, 75 (517) **TS**, 30 (207) **YS**, 35 **El**
QQ-S-766C	Class 202	US	Strip, sheet, plate	0.15 **C**, 7.50–10.00 **Mn**, 1.00 **Si**, 17.00–19.00 **Cr**, 4.00–6.00 **Ni**, 0.25 **N**, 0.060 **P**, 0.035 **S**	**Annealed**: all **diam**, 75 (517) **TS**, 40 (276) **YS**, 40 **El**; **1/4 hard**: all **diam**, 125 (862) **TS**, 75 (517) **YS**, 12 **El**; **1/2 hard**: ≤0.015 **diam**, 150 (1034) **TS**, 110 (758) **YS**, 15 **El**
QQ-S-766C	302	US	Strip, sheet, plate	0.15 **C**, 2.00 **Mn**, 1.00 **Si**, 17.00 **Cr**, 8.00 **Ni**, 0.045 **P**, 0.035 **S**	**Annealed**: ≤0.015 **diam**, 75 (517) **TS**, 30 (207) **YS**, 40 **El**; **1/4 hard**: all **diam**, 125 (862) **TS**, 75 (517) **YS**, 25 **El**; **1/2 hard**: ≤0.015 **diam**, 150 (1034) **TS**, 110 (758) **YS**, 15 **El**
QQ-S-766C	Class 201	US	Strip, sheet, plate	0.15 **C**, 5.50–7.50 **Mn**, 1.00 **Si**, 16.00–18.00 **Cr**, 3.50–5.50 **Ni**, 0.25 **N**, 0.060 **P**, 0.035 **S**	**Annealed**: all **diam**, 75 (517) **TS**, 40 (276) **YS**, 40 **El**; **Quarter hard**: all **diam**, 125 (862) **TS**, 75 (517) **YS**, 20 **El**; **Half hard**: ≤0.015 **diam**, 150 (1034) **TS**, 110 (758) **YS**, 15 **El**; **Three quarters hard**: ≤0.015 **diam**, 175 (1207) **TS**, 135 (931) **YS**, 3 **El**; **Full hard**: ≤0.015 **diam**, 185 (1206) **TS**, 140 (965) **YS**, 3 **El**

WROUGHT STAINLESS STEELS

specification number	designation	country	product forms	composition	mechanical properties (see page iv for explanation)
QQ–S–766C	Class 301	US	Strip, sheet, plate	0.15 **C**, 2.00 **Mn**, 1.00 **Si**, 16.00 **Cr**, 6.00 **Ni**, 0.045 **P**, 0.035 **S**	**Annealed**: ≤0.015 **diam**, 75 (517) **TS**, 30 (207) **YS**, 40 **El**; **1/4 hard**: all **diam**, 125 (862) **TS**, 75 (517) **YS**, 25 **El**; **1/2 hard**: ≤0.015 **diam**, 150 (1034) **TS**, 110 (758) **YS**, 15 **El**; **3/4 hard**: ≤0.015 **diam**, 175 (1207) **TS**, 135 (931) **YS**, 10 **El**; **Full hard**: ≤0.015 **diam**, 185 (1276) **TS**, 140 (965) **YS**, 8 **El**
ANSI/ASTM A 213	TP 310	US	Tube: seamless	0.15 **C**, 2.00 **Mn**, 0.75 **Si**, 24.0–26.0 **Cr**, 19.0–22.0 **Ni**, 0.040 **P**, 0.030 **S**	**Solution annealed**: 0.312 (7.94) **diam**, 75 (517) **TS**, 30 (207) **YS**, 35 **El**
ANSI/ASTM A 632	TP 310	US	Tube: seamless or welded	0.15 **C**, 2.00 **Mn**, 0.75 **Si**, 24.0–26.0 **Cr**, 19.0–22.0 **Ni**, 0.040 **P**, 0.030 **S**	**Solution annealed**: 0.005–0.065 (0.13–1.65) **diam**, 75 (517) **TS**, 30 (207) **YS**, 35 **El**
ANSI/ASTM A 554	MT–301	US	Tube: welded	0.15 **C**, 2.00 **Mn**, 1.00 **Si**, 16.0–18.0 **Cr**, 6.0–8.0 **Ni**, 0.040 **P**, 0.030 **S**	**Round annealed**: 0.312 (7.94) **diam**, 75 (517) **TS**, 30 (207) **YS**, 35 **El**
ANSI/ASTM A 554	MT–302	US	Tube: welded	0.15 **C**, 2.00 **Mn**, 1.00 **Si**, 17.0–19.0 **Cr**, 8.0–10.0 **Ni**, 0.040 **P**, 0.030 **S**	**Round annealed**: 0.312 (7.94) **diam**, 75 (517) **TS**, 30 (207) **YS**, 35 **El**
ANSI/ASTM A 554	MT–309	US	Tube: welded	0.15 **C**, 2.00 **Mn**, 1.00 **Si**, 22.0–24.0 **Cr**, 12.0–15.0 **Ni**, 0.040 **P**, 0.030 **S**	**Round annealed**: 0.312 (7.94) **diam**, 75 (517) **TS**, 30 (207) **YS**, 35 **El**
ANSI/ASTM A 554	MT–310	US	Tube: welded	0.15 **C**, 2.00 **Mn**, 1.00 **Si**, 24.0–26.0 **Cr**, 19.0–22.0 **Ni**, 0.040 **P**, 0.030 **S**	**Round annealed**: 0.312 (7.94) **diam**, 75 (517) **TS**, 30 (207) **YS**, 35 **El**
ANSI/ASTM A 554	MT–330	US	Tube: welded	0.15 **C**, 2.00 **Mn**, 1.00 **Si**, 14.0–16.0 **Cr**, 33.0–36.0 **Ni**, 0.040 **P**, 0.030 **S**	**Round annealed**: 0.312 (7.94) **diam**, 75 (517) **TS**, 30 (207) **YS**, 35 **El**
ANSI/ASTM A 473	302B	US	Forgings	0.15 **C**, 2.00 **Mn**, 2.00–3.00 **Si**, 17.00–19.00 **Cr**, 8.00–10.00 **Ni**, 0.045 **P**, 0.030 **S**	**Solution annealed**: all **diam**, 75 (515) **TS**, 30 (205) **YS**, 40 **El**
ANSI/ASTM A 473	303	US	Forgings	0.15 **C**, 2.00 **Mn**, 1.00 **Si**, 17.00–19.00 **Cr**, 8.00–10.00 **Ni**, 0.60 **Mo**, 0.20 **P**, 0.15 min **S**	**Solution annealed**: all **diam**, 75 (515) **TS**, 30 (205) **YS**, 40 **El**
ANSI/ASTM A 473	303 Se	US	Forgings	0.15 **C**, 2.00 **Mn**, 1.00 **Si**, 17.00–19.00 **Cr**, 8.00–10.00 **Ni**, 0.20 **P**, 0.06 **S**, 0.15 min **Se**	**Solution annealed**: all **diam**, 75 (515) **TS**, 30 (205) **YS**, 40 **El**
ANSI/ASTM A 666	302, grade A	US	Sheet, strip, plate, bar	0.15 **C**, 2.00 **Mn**, 1.00 **Si**, 17.00–19.00 **Cr**, 8.00–10.00 **Ni**, 0.045 **P**, 0.030 **S**	**Annealed (plate, sheet, strip)**: >0.030 (>0.76) **diam**, 75 (515) **TS**, 30 (205) **YS**, 40 **El**
ANSI/ASTM A 666	301, grade A	US	Sheet, strip, plate, bar	0.15 **C**, 2.00 **Mn**, 1.00 **Si**, 16.00–18.00 **Cr**, 6.00–8.00 **Ni**, 0.045 **P**, 0.030 **S**	**Annealed (plate, sheet, strip)**: >0.030 (>0.76) **diam**, 75 (515) **TS**, 30 (205) **YS**, 40 **El**
ANSI/ASTM A 479	302	US	Bar, shapes	0.15 **C**, 2.00 **Mn**, 1.00 **Si**, 17.00–19.00 **Cr**, 8.00–10.00 **Ni**, 0.10 **N**, 0.045 **P**, 0.030 **S**	**Solution annealed**: all **diam**, 75 (515) **TS**, 30 (205) **YS**, 30 **El**
ANSI/ASTM A 473	302	US	Forgings	0.15 **C**, 2.00 **Mn**, 1.00 **Si**, 17.00–19.0 **Cr**, 8.00–10.00 **Ni**, 0.10 **N**, 0.045 **P**, 0.030 **S**	**Solution annealed**: all **diam**, 75 (515) **TS**, 30 (205) **YS**, 40 **El**
ANSI/ASTM A 666	Type 302, grade A	US	Sheet, strip, plate, bar	0.15 **C**, 2.00 **Mn**, 1.00 **Si**, 17.00–19.00 **Cr**, 8.00–10.00 **Ni**, 0.045 **P**, 0.030 **S**	**Cold rolled (plate, sheet, strip)**: ≤0.015 (≤0.38) **diam**, 75 (515) **TS**, 30 (205) **YS**, 40 **El**
ANSI/ASTM A 666	Type 301, grade A	US	Sheet, strip, plate, bar	0.15 **C**, 2.00 **Mn**, 1.00 **Si**, 16.00–18.00 **Cr**, 6.00–8.00 **Ni**, 0.045 **P**, 0.030 **S**	**Cold rolled (plate, sheet, strip)**: 0.015 (0.38) **diam**, 75 (515) **TS**, 30 (205) **YS**, 40 **El**
ANSI/ASTM A 276	202	US	Bar, shapes	0.15 **C**, 7.50–10.00 **Mn**, 1.00 **Si**, 17.00–19.00 **Cr**, 4.00–6.00 **Ni**, 0.25 **N**, 0.060 **P**, 0.030 **S**	**Annealed**: all **diam**, 75 (515) **TS**, 40 (275) **YS**, 40 **El**; **Cold worked–high tensile**: ≥0.75 (≥19.05) **diam**, 125 (860) **TS**, 100 (690) **YS**, 12 **El**
ANSI/ASTM A 276	201	US	Bar, shapes	0.15 **C**, 5.50–7.50 **Mn**, 1.00 **Si**, 16.00–18.00 **Cr**, 3.50–5.60 **Ni**, 0.25 **N**, 0.060 **P**, 0.030 **S**	**Annealed**: all **diam**, 75 (515) **TS**, 40 (275) **YS**, 40 **El**
ASTM A 336	F25	US	Forgings	0.15 **C**, 2.00 **Mn**, 1.00 **Si**, 24.00–26.00 **Cr**, 19.00–22.00 **Ni**	**Solution annealed**: all **diam**, 75 (515) **TS**, 30 (205) **YS**, 30 **El**
ASTM A 240	Type 302	US	Plate, sheet, strip	0.15 **C**, 2.00 **Mn**, 1.00 **Si**, 17.00–19.00 **Cr**, 8.00–10.00 **Ni**, 0.10 **N**, 0.045 **P**, 0.030 **S**	**Solution annealed, hot rolled or cold rolled**: all **diam**, 75 (515) **TS**, 30 (205) **YS**, 40 **El**

WROUGHT STAINLESS STEELS

specification number	designation	country	product forms	composition	mechanical properties (see page iv for explanation)
ASTM A 167	Type 301	US	Plate, sheet, strip	0.15 **C**, 2.00 **Mn**, 1.00 **Si**, 16.00–18.00 **Cr**, 6.00–8.00 **Ni**, 0.045 **P**, 0.030 **S**	**Solution annealed**: all **diam**, 75 (515) **TS**, 30 (205) **YS**, 40 **El**
ASTM A 167	Type 302	US	Plate, sheet, strip	0.15 **C**, 2.00 **Mn**, 1.00 **Si**, 17.00–19.00 **Cr**, 8.00–10.00 **Ni**, 0.045 **P**, 0.030 **S**	**Solution annealed**: all **diam**, 75 (515) **TS**, 30 (205) **YS**, 40 **El**
ASTM A 167	Type 302B	US	Plate, sheet, strip	0.15 **C**, 2.00 **Mn**, 2.00–3.00 **Si**, 17.00–19.00 **Cr**, 8.00–10.00 **Ni**, 0.045 **P**, 0.030 **S**	**Solution annealed**: all **diam**, 75 (515) **TS**, 30 (205) **YS**, 40 **El**
ASTM A 336	F25	US	Forgings	0.15 **C**, 2.00 **Mn**, 1.00 **Si**, 24.00–26.00 **Cr**, 19.00–22.00 **Ni**, 0.040 **P**, 0.030 **S**	**Solution annealed**: all **diam**, 75 (515) **TS**, 30 (205) **YS**, 30 **El**
ANSI/ASTM A 666	Type 301, grade A	US	Sheet, strip, plate, bar	0.15 **C**, 2.00 **Mn**, 1.00 **Si**, 16.00–18.00 **Cr**, 6.00–8.00 **Ni**, 0.045 **P**, 0.030 **S**	**Annealed (plate, sheet, strip)**: ≥0.015 **diam**, (515) **TS**, (205) **YS**, 40 **El**
ANSI/ASTM A 666	Type 302, grade A	US	Sheet, strip, plate, bar	0.15 **C**, 2.00 **Mn**, 1.00 **Si**, 17.00–19.00 **Cr**, 8.00–10.00 **Ni**, 0.045 **P**, 0.030 **S**	**Annealed (plate, sheet, strip, bar)**: ≥0.015 **diam**, (515) **TS**, (205) **YS**, 40 **El**
ANSI/ASTM A 479	Grade 302	US	Bar, shapes	0.15 **C**, 2.00 **Mn**, 1.00 **Si**, 17.00–19.00 **Cr**, 8.00–10.00 **Ni**, 0.10 **N**, 0.045 **P**, 0.030 **S**	**Solution annealed**: all **diam**, (515) **TS**, (205) **YS**, 30 **El**
ANSI/ASTM A 336	Grade F25	US	Forgings	0.15 **C**, 2.00 **Mn**, 1.00 **Si**, 24.00–26.00 **Cr**, 19.00–22.00 **Ni**, 0.040 **P**, 0.030 **S**	**Solution annealed**: all **diam**, (515) **TS**, (205) **YS**, 30 **El**
ANSI/ASTM A 240	Grade 302	US	Plate, sheet, strip	0.15 **C**, 2.00 **Mn**, 1.00 **Si**, 17.00–19.00 **Cr**, 8.00–10.00 **Ni**, 0.10 **N**, 0.045 **P**, 0.030 **S**	**Solution annealed**: all **diam**, (515) **TS**, (205) **YS**, 40 **El**
ANSI/ASTM A 249	TP 309	US	Tube: welded	0.15 **C**, 2.00 **Mn**, 0.75 **Si**, 22.0–24.0 **Cr**, 12.0–15.0 **Ni**, 0.040 **P**, 0.030 **S**	**Solution annealed**: 0.312 (7.94) **diam**, 75 (515) **TS**, 30 (205) **YS**, 35 **El**
ANSI/ASTM A 249	TP 310	US	Tube: welded	0.15 **C**, 2.00 **Mn**, 0.75 **Si**, 24.0–26.0 **Cr**, 19.0–22.0 **Ni**, 0.040 **P**, 0.030 **S**	**Solution annealed**: 0.312 (7.94) **diam**, 75 (515) **TS**, 30 (205) **YS**, 35 **El**
DGN–B–83	302	Mexico	Bar	0.15 **C**, 2.0 **Mn**, 1.0 **Si**, 17.0–19.0 **Cr**, 8.0–10.0 **Ni**, 0.045 **P**, 0.030 **S**	**Hot or cold rolled**: all **diam**, (510) **TS**, (206) **YS**, 40 **El**
DGN–B–83	302B	Mexico	Bar	0.15 **C**, 2.0 **Mn**, 2.0–3.0 **Si**, 17.0–19.0 **Cr**, 8.0–10.0 **Ni**, 0.045 **P**, 0.030 **S**	**Hot or cold rolled**: all **diam**, (510) **TS**, (206) **YS**, 40 **El**
DGN–B–83	416	Mexico	Bar	0.15 **C**, 1.25 **Mn**, 1.0 **Si**, 12.0–14.0 **Cr**, 0.60 **Mo**, 0.060 **P**, 0.15 min **S**	**Hot or cold rolled**: all **diam**, (510) **TS**, (274) **YS**, 30 **El**
DGN–B–83	416 Se	Mexico	Bar	0.15 **C**, 1.25 **Mn**, 1.0 **Si**, 12.0–14.0 **Cr**, 0.060 **P**, 0.060 **S**, 0.15 min **Se**	**Hot or cold rolled**: all **diam**, (510) **TS**, (274) **YS**, 30 **El**
ISO 2604/II	TS 68	ISO	Tube: seamless	0.15 **C**, 2.00 **Mn**, 0.75 **Si**, 24.00–26.00 **Cr**, 19.00–22.00 **Ni**, 0.045 **P**, 0.030 **S**	**Cold finished, quenched**: all **diam**, (510) **TS**, (205) **YS**, 30 **El**
DIN 17440	Grade X 12 CrNiS 18 8	Germany	Sheet, strip, bar, wire, tube, forgings	0.15 **C**, 2.0 **Mn**, 1.0 **Si**, 17.0–19.0 **Cr**, 8.0–10.0 **Ni**, 0.040 **P**, 0.15–0.35 **S**	**Quenched**: (≤60) **diam**, (500) **TS**, (215) **YS**, 50 **El**
ISO 2604/1	F68	ISO	Forgings	0.15 **C**, 2.00 **Mn**, 1.50 **Si**, 24.00–26.00 **Cr**, 19.00–23.00 **Ni**, 0.045 **P**, 0.030 **S**	**Quenched**: all **diam**, (490) **TS**, (205) **YS**, 30 **El**
ANSI/ASTM A 479	403	US	Bar, shapes	0.15 **C**, 1.00 **Mn**, 1.00 **Si**, 11.50–13.50 **Cr**, 0.040 **P**, 0.030 **S**	**Annealed**: all **diam**, 70 (485) **TS**, 40 (275) **YS**, 20 **El**; **Annealed, tempered–1**: all **diam**, 70 (485) **TS**, 40 (275) **YS**, 20 **El**; **Annealed, tempered–2**: all **diam**, 110 (760) **TS**, 85 (585) **YS**, 15 **El**; **Annealed, tempered–3**: all **diam**, 130 (900) **TS**, 100 (690) **YS**, 12 **El**

WROUGHT STAINLESS STEELS

specification number	designation	country	product forms	composition	mechanical properties (see page iv for explanation)
ANSI/ASTM A 479	410	US	Bar, shapes	0.15 **C**, 1.00 **Mn**, 1.00 **Si**, 11.50–13.50 **Cr**, 0.040 **P**, 0.030 **S**	**Annealed**: all **diam**, 70 (485) **TS**, 40 (275) **YS**, 20 **El**; **Annealed, tempered–1**: all **diam**, 70 (485) **TS**, 40 (275) **YS**, 20 **El**; **Annealed, tempered–2**: all **diam**, 110 (760) **TS**, 85 (585) **YS**, 15 **El**; **Annealed, tempered–3**: all **diam**, 130 (900) **TS**, 100 (690) **YS**, 12 **El**
ANSI/ASTM A 473	403	US	Forgings	0.15 **C**, 1.00 **Mn**, 0.50 **Si**, 11.50–13.00 **Cr**, 0.040 **P**, 0.030 **S**	**Annealed**: all **diam**, 70 (485) **TS**, 40 (275) **YS**, 20 **El**
ANSI/ASTM A 473	410	US	Forgings	0.15 **C**, 1.00 **Mn**, 1.00 **Si**, 11.50–13.50 **Cr**, 0.75 **Ni**, 0.040 **P**, 0.030 **S**	**Annealed**: all **diam**, 70 (485) **TS**, 40 (275) **YS**, 20 **El**
ANSI/ASTM A 473	416	US	Forgings	0.15 **C**, 1.25 **Mn**, 1.00 **Si**, 12.00–14.00 **Cr**, 0.60 **Mo**, 0.06 **P**, 0.15 min **S**	**Annealed**: all **diam**, 70 (485) **TS**, 40 (275) **YS**, 20 **El**
ANSI/ASTM A 473	416Se	US	Forgings	0.15 **C**, 1.25 **Mn**, 1.00 **Si**, 12.00–14.00 **Cr**, 0.03 **P**, 0.06 **S**, 0.15 min **Se**	**Annealed**: all **diam**, 70 (485) **TS**, 40 (275) **YS**, 20 **El**
ASTM A 176	Type 403	US	Plate, sheet, strip	0.15 **C**, 1.00 **Mn**, 0.50 **Si**, 11.50–13.00 **Cr**, 0.60 **Ni**, 0.040 **P**, 0.030 **S**	**Annealed**: all **diam**, 70 (485) **TS**, 30 (205) **YS**, 25 **El**
ANSI/ASTM A 493	Type 410	US	Bar, wire	0.15 **C**, 1.00 **Mn**, 1.00 **Si**, 11.50–13.50 **Cr**, 0.040 **P**, 0.030 **S**	**Lightly drafted (wire)**: $\geq$0.156 ($\geq$3.96) **diam**, 70 (485) **TS**; **Annealed (wire)**: $\geq$0.156 ($\geq$3.96) **diam**, 65 (450) **TS**
ANSI/ASTM A 479	Grade 403	US	Bar, shapes	0.15 **C**, 1.00 **Mn**, 0.50 **Si**, 11.50–13.00 **Cr**, 0.040 **P**, 0.030 **S**	**Annealed 1**: all **diam**, (485) **TS**, (275) **YS**, 20 **El**; **Annealed 2**: all **diam**, (760) **TS**, (585) **YS**, 15 **El**; **Annealed 3**: all **diam**, (900) **TS**, (690) **YS**, 12 **El**
ANSI/ASTM A 479	Grade 410	US	Bar, shapes	0.15 **C**, 1.00 **Mn**, 1.00 **Si**, 11.50–13.50 **Cr**, 0.040 **P**, 0.030 **S**	**Annealed 1**: all **diam**, (485) **TS**, (275) **YS**, 20 **El**; **Annealed 2**: all **diam**, (760) **TS**, (585) **YS**, 15 **El**; **Annealed 3**: all **diam**, (900) **TS**, (690) **YS**, 12 **El**
CSA G110.5	Type 403	Canada	Plate	0.15 **C**, 1.00 **Mn**, 0.50 **Si**, 11.50–13.00 **Cr**, 0.60 **Ni**, 0.040 **P**, 0.030 **S**	**Hot rolled, annealed, quenched and tempered**: $\leq$0.050 **diam**, 70 (483) **TS**, 30 (207) **YS**, 20 **El**
CSA G110.5	Type 403	Canada	Strip	0.15 **C**, 1.00 **Mn**, 0.50 **Si**, 11.50–13.00 **Cr**, 0.60 **Ni**, 0.040 **P**, 0.030 **S**	**Cold rolled and annealed**: $\leq$0.050 **diam**, 70 (483) **TS**, 30 (207) **YS**, 20 **El**
CSA G110.5	Type 403	Canada	Sheet	0.15 **C**, 1.00 **Mn**, 0.50 **Si**, 11.50–13.00 **Cr**, 0.60 **Ni**, 0.040 **P**, 0.030 **S**	**Hot or cold rolled and annealed**: $\leq$0.050 **diam**, 70 (483) **TS**, 30 (207) **YS**, 20 **El**
AISI 403		US	Sheet, strip, bar, wire	0.15 **C**, 1.00 **Mn**, 0.50 **Si**, 11.50–13.00 **Cr**, 0.040 **P**, 0.00 **S**	**Annealed (sheet)**: all **diam**, 70 (483) max **TS**, 45 (310) max **YS**, 25 **El**
AISI 410		US	Sheet, strip, plate, bar, wire	0.15 **C**, 1.00 **Mn**, 1.00 **Si**, 11.50–13.50 **Cr**, 0.040 **P**, 0.030 **S**	**Annealed (sheet)**: all **diam**, 70 (483) max **TS**, 45 (310) max **YS**, 25 **El**
QQ-S-766C	Class 410	US	Strip, sheet, plate	0.15 **C**, 1.00 **Mn**, 1.00 **Si**, 11.50–13.50 **Cr**, 0.60 **Mo**, 0.040 **P**, 0.30 **S**	**Annealed**: all **diam**, 70 (483) **TS**, 35 (241) **YS**, 20 **El**
DGN-B-83	403	Mexico	Bar	0.15 **C**, 1.0 **Mn**, 0.50 **Si**, 11.5–13.0 **Cr**, 0.040 **P**, 0.030 **S**	**Hot or cold rolled**: all **diam**, (480) **TS**, (274) **YS**, 20 **El**
DGN-B-83	410	Mexico	Bar	0.15 **C**, 1.0 **Mn**, 1.0 **Si**, 11.5–13.5 **Cr**, 0.040 **P**, 0.030 **S**	**Hot or cold rolled**: all **diam**, (480) **TS**, (274) **YS**, 20 **El**
ANSI/ASTM A 276	410	US	Bar, shapes	0.15 **C**, 1.00 **Mn**, 1.00 **Si**, 11.50–13.50 **Cr**, 0.040 **P**, 0.030 **S**	**Annealed**: all **diam**, 70 (480) **TS**, 40 (275) **YS**, 20 **El**; **Intermediate temper**: all **diam**, 100 (690) **TS**, 80 (550) **YS**, 15 **El**; **Hard temper**: all **diam**, 120 (830) **TS**, 90 (620) **YS**, 12 **El**
ANSI/ASTM A 276	403	US	Bar, shapes	0.15 **C**, 1.00 **Mn**, 0.50 **Si**, 11.50–13.00 **Cr**, 0.040 **P**, 0.030 **S**	**Annealed**: all **diam**, 70 (480) **TS**, 40 (275) **YS**, 20 **El**; **Intermediate temper**: all **diam**, 100 (690) **TS**, 80 (550) **YS**, 15 **El**; **Hard temper**: all **diam**, 120 (830) **TS**, 90 (620) **YS**, 12 **El**

WROUGHT STAINLESS STEELS

specification number	designation	country	product forms	composition	mechanical properties (see page iv for explanation)
ANSI/ASTM A 580	Grade 403	US	Wire	0.15 **C**, 1.00 **Mn**, 0.50 **Si**, 11.50–13.00 **Cr**, 0.040 **P**, 0.030 **S**	**Annealed**: all **diam**, 70 (480) **TS**, 40 (280) **YS**, 20 **El**; **Cold finished T**: all **diam**, 100 (690) **TS**, 80 (550) **YS**, 12 **El**; **Cold finished H**: all **diam**, 120 (830) **TS**, 90 (620) **YS**, 12 **El**
ANSI/ASTM A 580	Grade 410	US	Wire	0.15 **C**, 1.00 **Mn**, 1.00 **Si**, 11.50–13.50 **Cr**, 0.040 **P**, 0.030 **S**	**Annealed**: all **diam**, 70 (480) **TS**, 40 (280) **YS**, 20 **El**; **Cold finished T**: all **diam**, 100 (690) **TS**, 80 (550) **YS**, 12 **El**; **Cold finished H**: all **diam**, 120 (830) **TS**, 90 (620) **YS**, 12 **El**
AS 1449	Grade AS 1449/410	Australia	Sheet, strip, plate	0.15 **C**, 1.00 **Mn**, 1.00 **Si**, 11.50–13.50 **Cr**, 0.040 **P**, 0.030 **S**	**Annealed**: (≤1.2) **diam**, (450) **TS**, (205) **YS**, 20 **El**
ASTM A 240	Type 410	US	Plate, sheet, strip	0.15 **C**, 1.00 **Mn**, 1.00 **Si**, 11.50–13.50 **Cr**, 0.75 **Ni**, 0.040 **P**, 0.030 **S**	**Hot rolled or cold rolled, annealed**: all **diam**, 65 (450) **TS**, 30 (205) **YS**, 20 **El**
ASTM A 176	Type 410	US	Plate, sheet, strip	0.15 **C**, 1.00 **Mn**, 1.00 **Si**, 11.50–13.50 **Cr**, 0.75 **Ni**, 0.040 **P**, 0.030 **S**	**Annealed**: all **diam**, 65 (450) **TS**, 30 (205) **YS**, 22 **El**
ANSI/ASTM A 240	Grade 410	US	Plate, sheet, strip	0.15 **C**, 1.00 **Mn**, 1.00 **Si**, 11.50–13.50 **Cr**, 0.75 **Ni**, 0.040 **P**, 0.030 **S**	**Annealed**: all **diam**, (450) **TS**, (205) **YS**, 20 **El**
CSA G110.5	Type 410	Canada	Sheet	0.15 **C**, 1.00 **Mn**, 1.00 **Si**, 11.50–13.50 **Cr**, 0.75 **Ni**, 0.040 **P**, 0.035 **S**	**Hot rolled, annealed, quenched and tempered**: all **diam**, 65 (448) **TS**, 30 (207) **YS**, 20 **El**
CSA G110.9	Type 410	Canada	Plate	0.15 **C**, 1.00 **Mn**, 1.00 **Si**, 11.50–13.50 **Cr**, 0.75 **Ni**, 0.040 **P**, 0.030 **S**	**Hot rolled, annealed, quenched and tempered**: all **diam**, 65 (448) **TS**, 30 (207) **YS**, 20 **El**
CSA G110.5	Type 410	Canada	Strip	0.15 **C**, 1.00 **Mn**, 1.00 **Si**, 11.50–13.50 **Cr**, 0.75 **Ni**, 0.040 **P**, 0.030 **S**	**Cold rolled and annealed**: ≤0.050 **diam**, 65 (448) **TS**, 30 (207) **YS**, 20 **El**
CSA G110.9	Type 410	Canada	Strip	0.15 **C**, 1.00 **Mn**, 1.00 **Si**, 11.50–13.50 **Cr**, 0.75 **Ni**, 0.040 **P**, 0.030 **S**	**Cold rolled and annealed**: all **diam**, 65 (448) **TS**, 30 (207) **YS**, 20 **El**
CSA G110.9	Type 410	Canada	Sheet	0.15 **C**, 1.00 **Mn**, 1.00 **Si**, 11.50–13.50 **Cr**, 0.75 **Ni**, 0.040 **P**, 0.030 **S**	**Hot or cold rolled and annealed**: all **diam**, 65 (448) **TS**, 30 (207) **YS**, 20 **El**
JIS G 4304	SUS 403	Japan	Sheet, plate	0.15 **C**, 1.00 **Mn**, 0.50 **Si**, 11.50–13.00 **Cr**, 0.6 **Ni**, 0.040 **P**, 0.030 **S**	**Hot rolled and annealed**: all **diam**, (441) **TS**, (206) **YS**, 20 **El**
JIS G 4304	SUS 410	Japan	Sheet, plate	0.15 **C**, 1.00 **Mn**, 1.00 **Si**, 11.50–13.50 **Cr**, 0.6 **Ni**, 0.040 **P**, 0.030 **S**	**Hot rolled and annealed**: all **diam**, (441) **TS**, (206) **YS**, 20 **El**
JIS G 4307	SUS 410	Japan	Strip	0.15 **C**, 1.00 **Mn**, 1.00 **Si**, 11.50–13.50 **Cr**, 0.6 **Ni**, 0.040 **P**, 0.030 **S**	**Cold rolled, annealed, quenched and tempered**: all **diam**, (441) **TS**, (206) **YS**, 20 **El**
JIS G 4305	SUS 403	Japan	Sheet, plate	0.15 **C**, 1.00 **Mn**, 0.50 **Si**, 11.50–13.00 **Cr**, 0.60 **Ni**, 0.040 **P**, 0.030 **S**	**Cold rolled and annealed**: all **diam**, (441) **TS**, (206) **YS**, 20 **El**
JIS G 4305	SUS 410	Japan	Sheet, plate	0.15 **C**, 1.00 **Mn**, 1.00 **Si**, 11.50–13.50 **Cr**, 0.60 **Ni**, 0.040 **P**, 0.030 **S**	**Cold rolled and annealed**: all **diam**, (441) **TS**, (206) **YS**, 20 **El**
JIS G 4306	SUS 410	Japan	Strip	0.15 **C**, 1.00 **Mn**, 1.00 **Si**, 11.50–13.50 **Cr**, 0.60 **Ni**, 0.040 **P**, 0.030 **S**	**Hot rolled and annealed**: all **diam**, (441) **TS**, (206) **YS**, 20 **El**
ISO 683/XII	14	ISO	Bar, sheet, plate	0.15 **C**, 2.0 **Mn**, 1.0 **Si**, 16.0–18.0 **Cr**, 6.0–8.0 **Ni**, 0.045 **P**, 0.030 **S**	**Solution treated**: all **diam**, (440) **TS**, (220) **YS**, 40 **El**
ANSI/ASTM A 511	MT 403	US	Tube: seamless	0.15 **C**, 1.00 **Mn**, 0.50 **Si**, 11.5–13.0 **Cr**, 0.50 **Ni**, 0.60 **Mo**, 0.040 **P**, 0.030 **S**	**Annealed**: 0.31 (7.9) **diam**, 60 (414) **TS**, 30 (207) **YS**, 20 **El**
ANSI/ASTM A 511	MT 410	US	Tube: seamless	0.15 **C**, 1.00 **Mn**, 1.00 **Si**, 11.5–13.5 **Cr**, 0.50 **Ni**, 0.040 **P**, 0.030 **S**	**Annealed**: 0.31 (7.9) **diam**, 60 (414) **TS**, 30 (207) **YS**, 20 **El**
ANSI/ASTM A 511	MT 416Se	US	Tube: seamless	0.15 **C**, 1.25 **Mn**, 1.00 **Si**, 12.0–14.0 **Cr**, 0.50 **Ni**, 0.060 **P**, 0.060 **S**, 0.12–0.20 **Se**	**Annealed**: 0.31 (7.9) **diam**, 60 (414) **TS**, 35 (241) **YS**, 20 **El**
ANSI/ASTM A 268	TP 410	US	Tube: seamless, welded	0.15 **C**, 1.00 **Mn**, 0.75 **Si**, 11.5–13.5 **Cr**, 0.50 **Ni**, 0.040 **P**, 0.030 **S**	**Annealed**: 0.312 (7.94) **diam**, 60 (414) **TS**, 30 (207) **YS**, 20 **El**

specification number	designation	country	product forms	composition	mechanical properties (see page iv for explanation)
DGN–B–171	Grade MT 403	Mexico	Tube: seamless	0.15 **C**, 1.00 **Mn**, 0.50 **Si**, 11.5–13.0 **Cr**, 0.35–0.60 **Ni**, 0.60 **Mo**, 0.040 **P**, 0.030 **S**	**Hot or cold finished and annealed:** (≥7.92) **diam**, (412) **TS**, (206) **YS**, 20 **El**
DGN–B–171	Grade MT 410	Mexico	Tube: seamless	0.15 **C**, 1.00 **Mn**, 1.00 **Si**, 11.5–13.5 **Cr**, 0.50 **Ni**, 0.040 **P**, 0.030 **S**	**Hot or cold finished and annealed:** (≥7.92) **diam**, (412) **TS**, (206) **YS**, 20 **El**
DGN–B–171	Grade MT 416 Se	Mexico	Tube: seamless	0.15 **C**, 1.25 **Mn**, 1.00 **Si**, 12.0–14.0 **Cr**, 0.50 **Ni**, 0.060 **P**, 0.060 **S**, 0.12–0.20 **Se**	**Hot or cold finished and annealed:** (≥7.92) **diam**, (412) **TS**, (245) **YS**, 20 **El**
DGN–B–216	Grade TP410	Mexico	Tube: seamless, welded	0.15 **C**, 1.00 **Mn**, 0.75 **Si**, 11.5–13.5 **Cr**, 0.50 **Ni**, 0.040 **P**, 0.030 **S**	**As drawn or as welded:** (≥7.93) **diam**, (412) **TS**, (206) **YS**, 20 **El**
JIS G 3463	SUS 410 TB	Japan	Tube: seamless or welded	0.15 **C**, 1.00 **Mn**, 1.00 **Si**, 11.50–13.50 **Cr**, 0.040 **P**, 0.030 **S**	**Annealed:** (≥8) **diam**, (412) **TS**, (206) **YS**, 20 **El**
JIS G 3446	SUS 410 TKA	Japan	Tube: seamless or welded	0.15 **C**, 1.00 **Mn**, 1.00 **Si**, 11.50–13.50 **Cr**, 0.60 **Ni**, 0.040 **P**, 0.030 **S**	**Normalized or normalized and tempered:** (≥8) **diam**, (412) **TS**, (206) **YS**, 20 **El**
ANSI/ASTM A 473	202	US	Forgings	0.15 **C**, 7.50–10.00 **Mn**, 1.00 **Si**, 17.00–19.00 **Cr**, 4.00–6.00 **Ni**, 0.25 **N**, 0.060 **P**, 0.030 **S**	**Solution annealed**: all **diam**, 45 (310) **TS**, 90 (620) **YS**, 40 **El**
DIN 17 225	X12CrNi177/4310	Germany	Wire	≤0.15 **C**, ≤2.0 **Mn**, ≤1.0 **Si**, 16.0–18.0 **Cr**, 7.0–8.0 **Ni**	**Cold drawn**: all **diam**, (120) **TS**
ASTM A 582	XM–2	US	Bar	0.15 **C**, 2.00 **Mn**, 1.00 **Si**, 17.00–19.00 **Cr**, 8.00–10.00 **Ni**, 0.40–0.60 **Mo**, 0.60–1.00 **Al**, 0.05 **P**, 0.11–0.16 **S**	
ASTM A 582	XM–3	US	Bar	0.15 **C**, 2.00 **Mn**, 1.00 **Si**, 17.00–19.00 **Cr**, 8.00–10.00 **Ni**, 0.60 **Mo**, 0.04 **P**, 0.12–0.30 **Pb**, 0.12–0.25 **S**	
ASTM A 582	XM–5	US	Bar	0.15 **C**, 2.50–4.50 **Mn**, 1.00 **Si**, 17.00–19.00 **Cr**, 7.00–10.00 **Ni**, 0.60 **Mo**, 0.20 **P**, 0.25 min **S**	
ASTM A 582	XM–6	US	Bar	0.15 **C**, 1.50–2.50 **Mn**, 1.00 **Si**, 12.00–14.00 **Cr**, 0.60 **Mo**	
ASTM A 582	416 Se	US	Bar	0.15 **C**, 1.25 **Mn**, 1.00 **Si**, 12.00–14.00 **Cr**, 0.06 **P**, 0.06 **S**, 0.15 min **Se**	
ASTM A 582	303	US	Bar	0.15 **C**, 2.00 **Mn**, 1.00 **Si**, 17.00–19.00 **Cr**, 8.00–10.00 **Ni**, 0.60 **Mo**, 0.20 **P**, 0.15 min **S**	
ASTM A 582	303Se	US	Bar	0.15 **C**, 2.00 **Mn**, 1.00 **Si**, 17.00–19.00 **Cr**, 8.00–10.00 **Ni**, 0.20 **P**, 0.06 **S**, 0.15 min **Se**	
ASTM A 582	416	US	Bar	0.15 **C**, 1.25 **Mn**, 1.00 **Si**, 12.00–14.00 **Cr**, 0.60 **Mo**	
ANSI/ASTM A 473	414	US	Forgings	0.15 **C**, 1.00 **Mn**, 1.00 **Si**, 11.50–13.50 **Cr**, 1.25–2.50 **Ni**, 0.040 **P**, 0.030 **S**	**Annealed**; **Tempered**: all **diam**, 115 (795) **TS**, 90 (620) **YS**, 15 **El**; **Quenched, tempered**: all **diam**, 125 (860) **TS**, 100 (690) **YS**, 15 **El**
ANSI/ASTM A 314	202	US	Bar, forgings, billets	0.15 **C**, 7.50–10.00 **Mn**, 1.00 **Si**, 17.00–19.00 **Cr**, 4.00–6.00 **Ni**, 0.25 **N**, 0.060 **P**, 0.030 **S**	
ANSI/ASTM A 314	302	US	Bar, forgings, billets	0.15 **C**, 2.00 **Mn**, 1.00 **Si**, 17.00–19.00 **Cr**, 8.00–10.00 **Ni**, 0.10 **N**, 0.045 **P**, 0.030 **S**	
ANSI/ASTM A 314	302B	US	Bar, forgings, billets	0.15 **C**, 2.00 **Mn**, 2.00–3.00 **Si**, 17.00–19.00 **Cr**, 8.00–10.00 **Ni**, 0.045 **P**, 0.030 **S**	
ANSI/ASTM A 314	303	US	Bar, forgings, billets	0.15 **C**, 2.00 **Mn**, 1.00 **Si**, 17.00–19.00 **Cr**, 8.00–10.00 **Ni**, 0.60 **Mo**, 0.20 **P**, 0.15 min **S**	
ANSI/ASTM A 314	303Se	US	Bar, forgings, billets	0.15 **C**, 2.00 **Mn**, 1.00 **Si**, 17.00–19.00 **Cr**, 8.00–10.00 **Ni**, 0.20 **P**, 0.06 **S**, 0.15 min **Se**	
ANSI/ASTM A 314	403	US	Bar, forgings, billets	0.15 **C**, 1.00 **Mn**, 0.50 **Si**, 11.50–13.00 **Cr**, 0.040 **P**, 0.030 **S**	
ANSI/ASTM A 314	410	US	Bar, forgings, billets	0.15 **C**, 1.00 **Mn**, 1.00 **Si**, 11.50–13.50 **Cr**, 0.040 **P**, 0.030 **S**	

WROUGHT STAINLESS STEELS

specification number	designation	country	product forms	composition	mechanical properties (see page iv for explanation)
ANSI/ASTM A 314	414	US	Bar, forgings, billets	0.15 **C**, 1.00 **Mn**, 1.00 **Si**, 11.50–13.50 **Cr**, 1.25–2.50 **Ni**, 0.040 **P**, 0.030 **S**	
ANSI/ASTM A 314	416	US	Bar, forgings, billets	0.15 **C**, 1.25 **Mn**, 1.00 **Si**, 12.00–14.00 **Cr**, 0.60 **Mo**, 0.06 **P**, 0.15 min **S**	
ANSI/ASTM A 314	416Se	US	Bar, forgings, billets	0.15 **C**, 1.25 **Mn**, 1.00 **Si**, 12.00–14.00 **Cr**, 0.06 **P**, 0.06 **S**, 0.15 min **Se**	
AS 1444	Grade AS 1444/302	Australia	Bar, bloom, billet, slab	0.15 **C**, 2.00 **Mn**, 1.00 **Si**, 17.0–19.0 **Cr**, 8.00–10.00 **Ni**, 0.045 **P**, 0.040 **S**, 0.60 **Zr** or mo	
AS 1444	Grade AS 1444/303	Australia	Bar,bloom, billet, slab	0.15 **C**, 2.00 **Mn**, 1.00 **Si**, 17.00–19.00 **Cr**, 8.00–10.00 **Ni**, 0.20 **P**, 0.15 min **S**, 0.60 **Zr** or mo	
AS 1444	Grade AS 1444/416	Australia	Bar, bloom, billet, slab	0.15 **C**, 1.25 **Mn**, 1.00 **Si**, 12.00–14.00 **Cr**, 0.06 **P**, 0.15 min **S**, 0.60 **Zr** or mo	
AS 1444	Grade AS 1444/410	Australia	Bar, bloom, billet, slab	0.15 **C**, 1.00 **Mn**, 1.00 **Si**, 11.50–13.50 **Cr**, 0.040 **P**, 0.040 **S**, 0.60 **Zr** or mo	
ANSI/ASTM A 276	420	US	Bar, shapes	0.15 **C**, 1.00 **Mn**, 1.00 **Si**, 12.00–14.00 **Cr**, 0.040 **P**, 0.030 **S**	**Annealed**
MIL–S–861A	Class 410	US	Bar	0.15 **C**, 1.00 **Mn**, 1.00 **Si**, 11.5–13.5 **Cr**, 0.040 **P**, 0.030 **S**	**Annealed**
MIL–S–862B	Class 403	US	Bar, forgings	0.15 **C**, 1.0 **Mn**, 0.50 **Si**, 11.5–13.0 **Cr**, 0.040 **P**, 0.030 **S**	
MIL–S–862B	Class 410	US	Bar, billets	0.15 **C**, 1.0 **Mn**, 1.0 **Si**, 11.5–13.5 **Cr**, 0.040 **P**, 0.030 **S**	
MIL–S–862B	Class 414	US	Bar, billets	0.15 **C**, 1.0 **Mn**, 1.0 **Si**, 11.5–13.5 **Cr**, 1.25–2.5 **Ni**, 0.040 **P**, 0.030 **S**	
MIL–S–862B	Class 416	US	Bar, billets	0.15 **C**, 1.25 **Mn**, 1.0 **Si**, 12.0–14.0 **Cr**, 0.6 **Mo**, 0.06 **P**, 0.15 **S**, 0.6 **Zr**	
MIL–S–862B	Class 416Se	US	Bar, billets	0.15 **C**, 1.25 **Mn**, 1.0 **Si**, 12.0–14.0 **Cr**, 0.06 **P**, 0.06 **S**, 0.15 min **Se**	
MIL–S–862B	Class 420	US	Bar, billets	0.15 **C**, 1.0 **Mn**, 1.0 **Si**, 12.0–14.0 **Cr**, 0.040 **P**, 0.030 **S**	
MIL–S–862B	Class 302	US	Bar, billets	0.15 **C**, 2.00 **Mn**, 1.00 **Si**, 17.0–19.0 **Cr**, 8.0–10.0 **Ni**, 0.045 **P**, 0.30 **S**	
MIL–S–862B	Class 303	US	Bar, billets	0.15 **C**, 2.0 **Mn**, 1.0 **Si**, 17.0–19.0 **Cr**, 8.0–10.0 **Ni**, 0.6 **Mo**, 0.20 **P**, 0.15 **S**, 0.60 **Zr**	
MIL–S–862B	Class 303Se	US	Bar, billets	0.15 **C**, 2.0 **Mn**, 1.0 **Si**, 17.0–19.0 **Cr**, 8.0–10.0 **Ni**, 0.20 **P**, 0.06 **S**, 0.15 min **Se**	
IS 6529	10Cr17Ni7	India	Blooms, billets, slabs	0.15 **C**, 2.0 **Mn**, 1.0 **Si**, 16.0–18.0 **Cr**, 6.0–8.0 **Ni**, 0.045 **P**, 0.030 **S**	**Annealed, or solution annealed**
IS 6529	10Cr17Mn6Ni4	India	Blooms, billets, slabs	0.15 **C**, 5.5–7.5 **Mn**, 1.0 **Si**, 16.0–18.0 **Cr**, 3.5–5.5 **Ni**, 0.045 **P**, 0.030 **S**	**Annealed, or solution annealed**
AMS 5694C		US	Wire	0.15 **C**, 1.25–2.50 **Mn**, 0.25–0.60 **Si**, 26.0–28.0 **Cr**, 20.50–22.50 **Ni**, 0.75 **Mo**, 0.50 **Cu**	
AMS 5776A		US	Welding wire	0.15 **C**, 1.00 **Mn**, 1.00 **Si**, 11.50–13.50 **Cr**, 0.75 **Ni**, 0.50 **Mo**, 0.50 **Cu**, 0.05 **Al**, 0.08 **N**, 0.025 **P**, 0.015 **S**, 0.030 **P**+**S**, 0.05	
AMS 5610J		US	Bar, forgings	0.15 **C**, 1.25 **Mn**, 1.00 **Si**, 11.50–13.50 **Cr**, 0.75 **Ni**, 0.50 **Cu**, 0.60 **Mo** or **Zr**, 0.060 **P**, 0.030 **S**, 0.18–0.35 **Se**	
AMS 5638		US	Bar, forgings	0.15 **C**, 2.00 **Mn**, 1.00 **Si**, 17.00–19.00 **Cr**, 8.50–10.50 **Ni**, 0.40–0.60 **Mo**, 0.50 **Cu**, 0.60–1.00 **Al**, 0.40 **P**, 0.11–0.16 **S**	

WROUGHT STAINLESS STEELS

specification number	designation	country	product forms	composition	mechanical properties (see page iv for explanation)
AMS 5500A		US	Sheet	0.15 **C**, 2.00 **Mn**, 1.00 **Si**, 17.00–19.00 **Cr**, 8.00–10.00 **Ni**, 0.50 **Mo**, 0.50 **Cu**, 0.040 **P**, 0.030 **S**	
AMS 5600A		US	Sheet	0.15 **C**, 2.00 **Mn**, 1.00 **Si**, 17.00–19.00 **Cr**, 8.00–10.00 **Ni**, 0.50 **Mo**, 0.50 **Cu**, 0.040 **P**, 0.030 **S**	
IS 6527	10Cr17Ni7	India	Wire, rod	0.15 **C**, 2.0 **Mn**, 1.0 **Si**, 16.0–18.0 **Cr**, 6.0–8.0 **Ni**, 0.030 **S**, 0.045 **P**	**Annealed**
IS 6527	10Cr17Mn6Ni4	India	Wire, rod	0.15 **C**, 5.5–7.5 **Mn**, 1.0 **Si**, 16.0–18.0 **Cr**, 3.5–5.5 **Ni**, 0.030 **S**, 0.060 **P**	**Annealed**
NF A 36–209	Z 12 CN 25–20	France	Plate	0.15 **C**, 2.0 **Mn**, 1.0 **Si**, 23.0–26.0 **Cr**, 18.0–21.0 **Ni**, 0.040 **P**, 0.030 **S**	
JIS G 4308	SUS 302	Japan	Wire, rod	0.15 **C**, 2.00 **Mn**, 1.00 **Si**, 17.00–19.00 **Cr**, 8.00–10.00 **Ni**, 0.040 **P**, 0.030 **S**	
JIS G 4308	SUS 303	Japan	Wire, rod	0.15 **C**, 2.00 **Mn**, 1.00 **Si**, 17.00–19.00 **Cr**, 8.00–10.00 **Ni**, 0.60 **Mo**, 0.20 **P**, 0.15 **S**	
JIS G 4308	SUS 410	Japan	Wire, rod	0.15 **C**, 1.00 **Mn**, 1.00 **Si**, 11.50–13.50 **Cr**, 0.60 **Ni**, 0.040 **P**, 0.030 **S**	
JIS G 4308	SUS 416	Japan	Wire, rod	0.15 **C**, 1.25 **Mn**, 1.00 **Si**, 12.00–14.00 **Cr**, 0.60 **Ni**, 0.60 **Mo**, 0.060 **P**, 0.15 **S**	
JIS G 4305	SUS 202	Japan	Sheet, plate	0.15 **C**, 7.50–10.00 **Mn**, 1.00 **Si**, 4.00–6.00 **Ni**, 0.25 **N**, 0.060 **P**, 0.030 **S**	**Cold rolled and solution annealed**: all **diam**, (588) **TS**, (245) **YS**, 40 **El**
JIS G 4316	SUS Y 310	Japan	Wire, rod	0.15 **C**, 1.00–2.50 **Mn**, 0.60 **Si**, 25.00–28.00 **Cr**, 20.00–22.50 **Ni**, 0.030 **P**, 0.030 **S**	
DEF STAN 95–1/1	Class 303	Canada	Bar	0.15 **C**, 2.00 **Mn**, 1.00 **Si**, 17.0–19.0 **Cr**, 8.0–10.0 **Ni**, 0.20 **P**, 0.06 **S**, 0.15 **Se**	
CSA G110.3	Type 202	Canada	Bar, billets	0.15 **C**, 7.50–10.00 **Mn**, 1.00 **Si**, 17.00–19.00 **Cr**, 4.00–6.00 **Ni**, 0.25 **N**, 0.060 **P**, 0.030 **S**	
CSA G110.3	Type 302	Canada	Bar, billets	0.15 **C**, 2.00 **Mn**, 1.00 **Si**, 17.00–19.00 **Cr**, 8.00–10.00 **Ni**, 0.045 **P**, 0.030 **S**	
CSA G110.3	Type 302B	Canada	Bar, billets	0.15 **C**, 2.00 **Mn**, 2.00–3.00 **Si**, 17.00–19.00 **Cr**, 8.00–10.00 **Ni**, 0.045 **P**, 0.030 **S**	
CSA G110.3	Type 303	Canada	Bar, billets	0.15 **C**, 2.00 **Mn**, 1.00 **Si**, 17.00–19.00 **Cr**, 8.00–10.00 **Ni**, 0.60 **Mo**, 0.20 **P**, 0.15 min **S**	
CSA G110.3	Type 303Se	Canada	Bar, billets	0.15 **C**, 2.00 **Mn**, 1.00 **Si**, 17.00–19.00 **Cr**, 8.00–10.00 **Ni**, 0.20 **P**, 0.06 **S**, 0.15 **Se**	
CSA G110.3	Type 403	Canada	Bar, billets	0.15 **C**, 1.00 **Mn**, 0.50 **Si**, 11.50–13.00 **Cr**, 0.040 **P**, 0.030 **S**	
CSA G110.3	Type 410	Canada	Bar, billets	0.15 **C**, 1.00 **Mn**, 1.00 **Si**, 11.50–13.50 **Cr**, 0.040 **P**, 0.030 **S**	
CSA G110.3	Type 414	Canada	Bar, billets	0.15 **C**, 1.00 **Mn**, 1.00 **Si**, 11.50–13.50 **Cr**, 1.25–2.50 **Ni**, 0.040 **P**, 0.030 **S**	
CSA G110.3	Type 416	Canada	Bar, billets	0.15 **C**, 1.25 **Mn**, 1.00 **Si**, 12.00–14.00 **Cr**, 0.60 **Mo**, 0.06 **P**, 0.15 min **S**	
CSA G110.3	Type 416Se	Canada	Bar, billets	0.15 **C**, 1.25 **Mn**, 1.00 **Si**, 12.00–14.00 **Cr**, 0.06 **P**, 0.06 **S**, 0.15 min **Se**	
ANSI/ASTM A 580	Grade 420	US	Wire	0.15 min **C**, 1.00 **Mn**, 1.00 **Si**, 12.00–14.00 **Cr**, 0.040 **P**, 0.030 **S**	**Annealed**: all **diam**, 125 (860) max **TS**
DGN–B–83	420	Mexico	Bar	0.15 min **C**, 1.0 **Mn**, 1.0 **Si**, 12.0–14.0 **Cr**, 0.040 **P**, 0.030 **S**	**Hot or cold rolled**: all **diam**, (657) **TS**, (343) **YS**, 25 **El**

WROUGHT STAINLESS STEELS

specification number	designation	country	product forms	composition	mechanical properties (see page iv for explanation)
DGN-B-83	420F	Mexico	Bar	0.15 min **C**, 1.25 **Mn**, 1.0 **Si**, 12.0–14.0 **Cr**, 0.60 **Mo**, 0.060 **P**, 0.15 min **S**	**Hot or cold rolled**: all **diam**, (657) **TS**, (382) **YS**, 22 **El**
AISI 420F		US	Bar, wire	0.15 min **C**, 1.25 **Mn**, 1.00 **Si**, 12.00–14.00 **Cr**, 0.60 **Mo**, 0.060 **P**, 0.15 min **S**	**Annealed (bar)**: all **diam**, 95 (655) max **TS**, 55 (379) max **YS**, 22 **El**; **Annealed and cold finished (bar)**: 1.0 (25.40) **diam**, 110 (758) max **TS**, 100 (689) max **YS**, 14 **El**
ANSI/ASTM A 473	420	US	Forgings	0.15 min **C**, 1.00 **Mn**, 1.00 **Si**, 12.00–14.00 **Cr**, 0.040 **P**, 0.030 **S**	**Annealed**
ANSI/ASTM A 314	420	US	Bar, forgings, billets	0.15 min **C**, 1.00 **Mn**, 1.00 **Si**, 12.00–14.00 **Cr**, 0.040 **P**, 0.030 **S**	
AS 1444	Grade AS 1444/420	Australia	Bar, bloom, billet, slab	0.15 min **C**, 1.00 **Mn**, 1.00 **Si**, 12.00–14.00 **Cr**, 0.040 **P**, 0.040 **S**, 0.60 **Zr** or mo	
CSA G110.3	Type 420	Canada	Bar, billets	0.15 min **C**, 1.00 **Mn**, 1.00 **Si**, 12.00–14.00 **Cr**, 0.040 **P**, 0.030 **S**	
BS 970 Part 4	Grade 420S.29	UK	Blooms, billets, bar, forgings	0.14–0.20 **C**, 1.00 **Mn**, 0.80 **Si**, 11.5–13.5 **Cr**, 1.00 **Ni**, 0.040 **P**, 0.030 **S**	**Hardened and tempered**: $\leq$6 **diam**, (690) **TS**, (525) **YS**, 15 **El**
BS 970 Part 4	Grade 416S29	UK	Blooms, billets, bars, forgings	0.14–0.20 **C**, 1.50 **Mn**, 1.00 **Si**, 11.5–13.5 **Cr**, 1.00 **Ni**, 0.60 **Mo**, 0.040 **P**, 0.15–0.30 **S**	**Hardened and tempered**: $\leq$6 **diam**, (690) **TS**, (525) **YS**, 11 **El**
MIL-S-18732D		US	Bar, wire, tube: special quality	0.13–0.17 **C**, 0.30–0.80 **Mn**, 0.20–0.60 **Si**, 15.50–16.50 **Cr**, 2.00–3.00 **Ni**, 0.25 **Mo**, 0.10 **N**, 0.040 **P**, 0.030 **S**: rem Fe	**Quenched, tempered and retempered**: all **diam**, 200 (1379) **TS**, 150 (1034) **YS**, 10 **El**
MIL-S-8967		US	Bar, wire, forgings, tube	0.13–0.17 **C**, 0.30–0.80 **Mn**, 0.20–0.60 **Si**, 15.50–16.50 **Cr**, 2.00–3.00 **Ni**, 0.25 **Mo**, 0.10 **N**, 0.025 **P**, 0.025 **S**	**Annealed or heat treated**
AISI 205		US	Plate	0.12–0.25 **C**, 14.00–15.50 **Mn**, 0.50 **Si**, 16.50–18.00 **Cr**, 1.00–1.75 **Ni**, 0.32–0.40 **N**, 0.030 **P**, 0.030 **S**	**Annealed**: all **diam**, 120.5 (831) max **TS**, 69 max **YS**, 58 **El**
BS 5S.80		UK	Billets, bar, forgings and parts: aircraft quality	0.12–0.20 **C**, 1.0 **Mn**, 1.0 **Si**, 15.0–18.0 **Cr**, 2.0–3.0 **Ni**, 0.030 **P**, 0.025 **S**	**Hardened, tempered and retempered**: ($\leq$100) **diam**, (880) **TS**, (690) **YS**, 12 **El**
BS 2S137		UK	Bar: aircraft quality	0.12–0.20 **C**, 1.5 **Mn**, 1.0 **Si**, 15.0–18.0 **Cr**, 2.0–3.0 **Ni**, 0.6 **Mo**, **Mo**, 0.030 **P**, 0.15–0.30 **S**	**Hardened, tempered and retempered**: ($\leq$70) **diam**, (880) **TS**, (690) **YS**, 11 **El**
AIR 9160	9160C171	France	Bar, forgings	0.12–0.20 **C**, 1.0 **Mn**, 1.0 **Si**, 15.0–18.0 **Cr**, 2.0–3.0 **Ni**, 0.035 **P**, 0.025 **S**	**Quenched and tempered at 600–625 °C: (<100) diam, (880) TS, (690) YS, 12 El; Quenched and tempered at 300–380 °C: all diam, (1350) TS, (1050) YS, 10 El**
BS 970 Part 4	Grade 431S29	UK	Blooms, billets, bar, forgings	0.12–0.20 **C**, 1.00 **Mn**, 0.80 **Si**, 15.0–18.0 **Cr**, 2.00–3.00 **Ni**, 0.040 **P**, 0.030 **S**	**Hardened and tempered**: $\leq$6 **diam**, (850) **TS**, (680) **YS**, 11 **El**
BS 970 Part 4	Grade 441S29	UK	Blooms, billets, bar, forgings	0.12–0.20 **C**, 1.50 **Mn**, 1.00 **Si**, 15.0–18.0 **Cr**, 2.00–3.00 **Ni**, 0.60 **Mo**, 0.040 **P**, 0.15–0.30 **S**	**Hardened and tempered**: $\leq$2.5 **diam**, (850) **TS**, (680) **YS**, 8 **El**
BS 970 Part 4	Grade 441S49	UK	Blooms, billets, bar, forgings	0.12–0.20 **C**, 1.50 **Mn**, 1.00 **Si**, 15.0–18.0 **Cr**, 2.00–3.00 **Ni**, 0.60 **Mo**, 0.040 **P**, 0.060 **S**, 0.15–0.30 **Se**	**Hardened and tempered**: $\leq$2.5 **diam**, (850) **TS**, (680) **YS**, 8 **El**
AS G18	G18/En 56B	Australia	Bar, billet, bar: black, bright	0.12–0.18 **C**, 1.00 **Mn**, 1.00 **Si**, 12.0–14.0 **Cr**, 1.00 **Ni**, 0.045 **P**, 0.045 **S**	**Hardened, tempered**: 6 **diam**, (540) **TS**, (385) **YS**
AS G18	G18/En 56BM	Australia	Bar, billet, bar: black, bright	0.12–0.18 **C**, 1.50 **Mn**, 1.00 **Si**, 12.0–14.0 **Cr**, 1.00 **Ni**, 0.60 **Mo**, 0.045 **P**, 0.35 **Pb**, 0.75 **S**, 0.60 **Se**, 0.60 **Zr**	**Hardened, tempered**: 6 **diam**, (540) **TS**
DIN 17440	Grade X 15 Cr 13	Germany	Sheet, strip, bar, wire, tube, forgings	0.12–0.17 **C**, 1.0 **Mn**, 1.0 **Si**, 12.0–14.0 **Cr**, 0.045 **P**, 0.030 **S**	**Annealed**: ($\leq$5) **diam**, (750) max **TS**; **Tempered**: ($\leq$15) **diam**, (650) **TS**, (450) **YS**, 18 **El**

WROUGHT STAINLESS STEELS

specification number	designation	country	product forms	composition	mechanical properties (see page iv for explanation)
AMS 5628D		US	Bar, forgings, tube	0.12–0.17 **C**, 0.30–0.80 **Mn**, 0.20–0.60 **Si**, 15.50–17.00 **Cr**, 2.00–3.00 **Ni**, 0.50 **Mo**, 0.50 **Cu**, 0.10 **N**, 0.040 **P**, 0.030 **S**	
AMS 5612B		US	Bar, forgings, tube, rings	0.12–0.15 **C**, 0.60 **Mn**, 0.50 **Si**, 11.50–12.50 **Cr**, 0.75 **Ni**, 0.20 **Mo**, 0.50 **Cu**, 0.05 **Al**, 0.08 **N**, 0.025 **P**, 0.025 **S**, 0.05	**Annealed and aged:** all **diam**, 180 (1241) **TS**, 147 (1014) **YS**, 10 **El**
DIN 17224	Grade X 12 CrNi 17 7	Germany	Wire, strip	0.12 **C**, 2.0 **Mn**, 1.0 **Si**, 16.0–18.0 **Cr**, 7.0–9.0 **Ni**, 0.045 **P**, 0.030 **S**	**Cold drawn (wire):** (≤0.2) **diam**, (2157) **TS**; **Cold drawn and tempered (wire):** (≤0.2) **diam**, (2304) **TS**
SIS 14 23 31	SIS 23 31–06	Sweden	Wire	0.12 **C**, 2.0 **Mn**, 1.0 **Si**, 17.0–19.0 **Cr**, 7.0–9.5 **Ni**, 0.045 **P**, 0.030 **S**	**Cold drawn:** (<0.10) **diam**, (2110) **TS**, (1810) **YS**
ANSI/ASTM A 313	305	US	Wire	0.12 **C**, 2.00 **Mn**, 1.00 **Si**, 17.00–19.00 **Cr**, 10.50–13.00 **Ni**, 0.045 **P**, 0.030 **S**	**Cold drawn:** ≥0.009 (≥0.23) **diam**, 245 (1690) **TS**
ASTM A 313	Type 305	US	Wire	0.12 **C**, 2.00 **Mn**, 1.00 **Si**, 17.00–19.00 **Cr**, 10.50–13.00 **Ni**, 0.045 **P**, 0.030 **S**	**Cold drawn:** >0.009 (>0.23) **diam**, 245 (1690) **TS**
SIS 14 23 31	SIS 23 31–19	Sweden	Strip	0.12 **C**, 2.0 **Mn**, 1.0 **Si**, 17.0–19.0 **Cr**, 7.0–9.5 **Ni**	**Cold worked:** (1.4) **diam**, (1570) **TS**, (1320) **YS**
SIS 14 23 31	SIS 23 31–19	Sweden	Strip	0.12 **C**, 2.0 **Mn**, 1.0 **Si**, 17.0–19.0 **Cr**, 7.0–9.5 **Ni**, 0.045 **P**, 0.030 **S**	**Cold worked:** (<1.4) **diam**, (1570) **TS**, (1320) **YS**
ANSI/ASTM A 492	Type 305	US	Wire	0.12 **C**, 2.00 **Mn**, 1.00 **Si**, 17.00–19.00 **Cr**, 10.50–13.00 **Ni**, 0.045 **P**, 0.030 **S**	**Cold drawn:** 0.091–0.100 (2.30–2.54) **diam**, 205 (1410) **TS**
SIS 14 23 31	SIS 23 31–18	Sweden	Strip	0.12 **C**, 2.0 **Mn**, 1.0 **Si**, 17.0–19.0 **Cr**, 7.0–9.5 **Ni**	**Cold worked:** (<1.5) **diam**, (1370) **TS**, (1230) **YS**
SIS 14 23 31	SIS 23 31–18	Sweden	Strip	0.12 **C**, 2.0 **Mn**, 1.0 **Si**, 17.0–19.0 **Cr**, 7.0–9.5 **Ni**, 0.045 **P**, 0.030 **S**	**Cold worked:** (<1.5) **diam**, (1370) **TS**, (1230) **YS**
SIS 14 23 31	SIS 23 31–06	Sweden	Wire	0.12 **C**, 2.0 **Mn**, 1.0 **Si**, 17.0–19.0 **Cr**, 7.0–9.5 **Ni**	**Cold drawn:** (<8) **diam**, (1270) **TS**, (980) **YS**
SIS 14 23 31	SIS 23–31–17	Sweden	Strip	0.12 **C**, 2.0 **Mn**, 1.0 **Si**, 17.0–19.0 **Cr**, 7.0–9.5 **Ni**	**Cold worked:** (<2.0) **diam**, (1230) **TS**, (1130) **YS**
SIS 14 23 31	SIS 23 31–17	Sweden	Strip	0.12 **C**, 2.0 **Mn**, 1.0 **Si**, 17.0–19.0 **Cr**, 7.0–9.5 **Ni**, 0.045 **P**, 0.030 **S**	**Cold worked:** (<2.0) **diam**, (1230) **TS**, (1130) **YS**
SIS 14 23 31	SIS 23 31–16	Sweden	Strip	0.12 **C**, 2.0 **Mn**, 1.0 **Si**, 17.0–19.0 **Cr**, 7.0–9.5 **Ni**	**Cold worked:** (<2.0) **diam**, (1080) **TS**, (980) **YS**
SIS 14 23 31	SIS 23 31–16	Sweden	Strip	0.12 **C**, 2.0 **Mn**, 1.0 **Si**, 17.0–19.0 **Cr**, 7.0–9.5 **Ni**, 0.045 **P**, 0.030 **S**	**Cold worked:** (<2.0) **diam**, (1080) **TS**, (980) **YS**
ANSI/ASTM A 478	Type 305	US	Wire	0.12 **C**, 2.00 **Mn**, 1.00 **Si**, 17.00–19.00 **Cr**, 10.50–13.00 **Ni**, 0.045 **P**, 0.030 **S**	**Annealed:** 0.002–0.005 (0.05–0.13) **diam**, 145 (1000) **TS**, 30 **El**; **Cold drawn:** 0.030–0.125 (0.76–3.18) **diam**, 120 (830) **TS**, 15 **El**
ANSI/ASTM A 580	Grade XM–31	US	Wire	0.12 **C**, 14.00–16.00 **Mn**, 0.30–1.00 **Si**, 17.00–18.50 **Cr**, 1.00 **Ni**, 0.35 **N**, 0.045 **P**, 0.030 **S**	**Cold finished A:** all **diam**, 130 (900) **TS**, 85 (590) **YS**, 24 **El**; **Annealed:** all **diam**, 100 (690) **TS**, 50 (340) **YS**, 40 **El**; **Cold finished B:** all **diam**, 220 (1520) **TS**, 190 (1310) **YS**, 5 **El**
SIS 14 23 31	SIS 23 31–14	Sweden	Strip	0.12 **C**, 2.0 **Mn**, 1.0 **Si**, 17.0–19.0 **Cr**, 7.0–9.5 **Ni**	**Cold worked:** (<2.0) **diam**, (890) **TS**, (590) **YS**
SIS 14 23 31	SIS 23 31–14	Sweden	Strip	0.12 **C**, 2.0 **Mn**, 1.0 **Si**, 17.0–19.0 **Cr**, 7.0–9.5 **Ni**, 0.045 **P**, 0.030 **S**	**Cold worked:** (<2.0) **diam**, (890) **TS**, (590) **YS**
AMS 5738A		US	Bar, wire	0.12 **C**, 0.020–2.00 **Mn**, 1.00 **Si**, 17.00–19.00 **Cr**, 8.00–10.00 **Ni**, 0.75 **Mo**, 0.75 **Cu**, 0.17 **P**, 0.10 **S**, 0.35 **Se**	**Solution treated, cold worked (bar):** ≤0.750(≤19.05) **diam**, 125 (862) **TS**, 100 (690) **YS**, 12 **El**
IS 6528	08Cr18Ni9	India	Wire	0.12 **C**, 2.0 **Mn**, 1.0 **Si**, 17.0–19.0 **Cr**, 8.0–10.0 **Ni**, 0.045 **P**, 0.030 **S**	**Cold worked:** all **diam**, (860) **TS**, (690) **YS**, 12 **El**

WROUGHT STAINLESS STEELS

specification number	designation	country	product forms	composition	mechanical properties (see page iv for explanation)
ASTM A 240	Type XM31	US	Plate, sheet, strip	0.12 **C**, 14.00–16.00 **Mn**, 0.30–1.00 **Si**, 17.00–18.50 **Cr**, 1.00 **Ni**, 0.35 **N**, 0.045 **P**, 0.030 **S**	**Solution annealed, hot rolled or cold rolled (sheet)**: all **diam**, 125 (860) **TS**, 70 (485) **YS**, 40 **El**
ANSI/ASTM A 240	Grade XM 31	US	Sheet	0.12 **C**, 14.00–16.00 **Mn**, 0.30–1.00 **Si**, 17.00–18.50 **Cr**, 1.00 **Ni**, 0.35 min **N**, 0.045 **P**, 0.030 **S**	**Solution annealed**: all **diam**, (860) **TS**, (485) **YS**, 40 **El**
IS 6911	07Cr18Ni9	India	Plate, sheet, strip	0.12 **C**, 2.0 **Mn**, 1.0 **Si**, 17.0–19.0 **Cr**, 8.0–10.0 **Ni**, 0.030 **S**, 0.045 **P**	**Cold rolled**: (0.5–0.8) **diam**, (830) **TS**, (490) **YS**, 12 **El**
ANSI/ASTM A 412	Type XM–14	US	Plate, sheet, strip	0.12 **C**, 14.00–16.00 **Mn**, 1.00 **Si**, 17.00–19.00 **Cr**, 5.00–6.00 **Ni**, 0.35–0.50 **N**, 0.060 **P**, 0.030 **S**	**Annealed**: 0.015 (0.38) **diam**, 105 (725) **TS**, 55 (380) **YS**, 40 **El**
ANSI/ASTM A 240	Grade XM 31	US	Strip	0.12 **C**, 14.00–16.00 **Mn**, 0.30–1.00 **Si**, 17.00–18.50 **Cr**, 1.00 **Ni**, 0.35 min **N**, 0.045 **P**, 0.030 **S**	**Solution annealed**: all **diam**, (725) **TS**, (380) **YS**, 40 **El**
AMS 5514C		US	Strip, sheet, plate	0.12 **C**, 2.00 **Mn**, 1.00 **Si**, 17.00–19.00 **Cr**, 10.00–13.00 **Ni**, 0.75 **Mo**, 0.75 **Cu**, 0.040 **P**, 0.030 **S**	**Solution treated**: <0.025 (<0.64) **diam**, 100 (690) max **TS**, 45 **El**
SIS 14 23 31	SIS 23 31–12	Sweden	Strip	0.12 **C**, 2.0 **Mn**, 1.0 **Si**, 17.0–19.0 **Cr**, 7.0–9.5 **Ni**	**Cold worked**: (<20) **diam**, (690) **TS**, (290) **YS**
SIS 14 23 31	SIS 23 31–12	Sweden	Strip	0.12 **C**, 2.0 **Mn**, 1.0 **Si**, 17.0–19.0 **Cr**, 7.0–9.5 **Ni**, 0.045 **P**, 0.030 **S**	**Cold worked**: (<2.0) **diam**, (690) **TS**, (290) **YS**
MIL–S–7720A	302	US	Bar, wire, forging stock	0.12 **C**, 2.0 **Mn**, 1.0 **Si**, 17.0–19.0 **Cr**, 8.0–10.0 **Ni**, 0.50 **Cu**, 0.04 **P**, 0.03 **S**	**Annealed**: all **diam**, (689) **TS**, 35 **El**
NF A 35–575	Z 10 CN 18.09	France	Wire, rod	0.12 **C**, 2.0 **Mn**, 1.0 **Si**, 17.0–19.0 **Cr**, 7.5–9.5 **Ni**, 0.040 **P**, 0.030 **S**	**Stress hardened 0%**: all **diam**, (640) **TS**; **Stress hardened 40%**: all **diam**, (1180) **TS**; **Stress hardened 60%**: all **diam**, (1520) **TS**; **Stress hardened 80%**: all **diam**, (1860) **TS**
IS 6528	08Cr18Ni9	India	Wire	0.12 **C**, 2.0 **Mn**, 1.0 **Si**, 17.0–19.0 **Cr**, 8.0–10.0 **Ni**, 0.045 **P**, 0.030 **S**	**Annealed or solution annealed**: all **diam**, (620) **TS**, (310) **YS**, 35 **El**
ANSI/ASTM A 580	Grade 305	US	Wire	0.12 **C**, 2.00 **Mn**, 1.00 **Si**, 17.00–19.00 **Cr**, 10.50–13.00 **Ni**, 0.045 **P**, 0.030 **S**	**Cold finished**: all **diam**, 90 (620) **TS**, 45 (310) **YS**, 35 **El**; **Annealed**: all **diam**, 75 (520) **TS**, 30 (210) **YS**, 35 **El**
SIS 14 23 31	SIS 23 31–11	Sweden	Strip	0.12 **C**, 2.0 **Mn**, 1.0 **Si**, 17.0–19.0 **Cr**, 7.0–9.5 **Ni**	**Cold worked**: (<2.5) **diam**, (620) **TS**, (260) **YS**
SIS 14 23 31	SIS 23 31–11	Sweden	Strip	0.12 **C**, 2.0 **Mn**, 1.0 **Si**, 17.0–19.0 **Cr**, 7.0–9.5 **Ni**, 0.045 **P**, 0.030 **S**	**Cold worked**: (<2.5) **diam**, (620) **TS**, (260) **YS**
ASTM A 581	Type 430F	US	Wire	0.12 **C**, 1.25 **Mn**, 1.00 **Si**, 16.00–18.00 **Cr**, 0.60 **Mo**, 0.06 **P**, 0.15 min **S**	**Annealed**: 0.5 **diam**, 85 (590) **TS**
ASTM A 581	Type 430FSe	US	Wire	0.12 **C**, 1.25 **Mn**, 1.00 **Si**, 16.00–18.00 **Cr**, 0.06 **P**, 0.6 **S**, 0.15 min **Se**	**Annealed**: 0.5 **diam**, 85 (590) **TS**
SIS 14 23 24	SIS 23 24–02	Sweden	Bar, forgings, plate, sheet, tube, wire	0.12 **C**, 2.0 **Mn**, 1.5 **Si**, 23.0–27.0 **Cr**, 4.5–7.0 **Ni**, 1.3–1.8 **Mo**, 0.045 **P**, 0.030 **S**	**Solution annealed (except wire)**: all **diam**, (590) **TS**, (440) **YS**, 20 **El**
AISI 305		US	Sheet, strip, plate, wire	0.12 **C**, 2.00 **Mn**, 1.00 **Si**, 17.00–19.00 **Cr**, 10.50–13.00 **Ni**, 0.045 **P**, 0.030 **S**	**Annealed (sheet)**: all **diam**, 85 (586) max **TS**, 38 (262) max **YS**, 50 **El**
ASTM A 336	F6	US	Forgings	0.12 **C**, 1.00 **Mn**, 1.00 **Si**, 11.5–13.5 **Cr**, 0.50 **Ni**, 0.040 **P**, 0.030 **S**	**Solution annealed**: all **diam**, 85 (585) **TS**, 55 (380) **YS**, 18 **El**
ASTM A 336	F6	US	Forgings	0.12 **C**, 1.00 **Mn**, 1.00 **Si**, 11.5–13.5 **Cr**, 0.50 **Ni**, 0.040 **P**, 0.030 **S**	**Annealed**: all **diam**, 85 (585) **TS**, 55 (380) **YS**, 18 **El**
ANSI/ASTM A 336	Grade F6	US	Forgings	0.12 **C**, 1.00 **Mn**, 1.00 **Si**, 11.5–13.5 **Cr**, 0.50 **Ni**, 0.040 **P**, 0.030 **S**	**Annealed or normalized and tempered**: all **diam**, (585) **TS**, (380) **YS**, 18 **El**

WROUGHT STAINLESS STEELS

specification number	designation	country	product forms	composition	mechanical properties (see page iv for explanation)
NF A 35–573	Z 10 CN 18.09	France	Sheet, strip, plate	0.12 **C**, 2.0 **Mn**, 1.0 **Si**, 17.0–19.0 **Cr**, 7.5–9.5 **Ni**, 0.040 **P**, 0.030 **S**	**Cold rolled:** (≤5) **diam**, (560) **TS**, (295) **YS**, 45 **El**; **Hot rolled:** (≤20) **diam**, (560) **TS**, (285) **YS**, 43 **El**
AISI 430F		US	Bar, wire	0.12 **C**, 1.25 **Mn**, 1.00 **Si**, 16.00–18.00 **Cr**, 0.60 **Mo**, 0.060 **P**, 0.15 min **S**	**Annealed (bar)**: all **diam**, 80 (552) max **TS**, 55 (379) max **YS**, 25 **El**; **Annealed and cold finished (bar):** 1 (25.40) **diam**, 90 (621) max **TS**, 80 (552) max **YS**, 15 **El**
AISI 430FSe		US	Bar	0.12 **C**, 1.25 **Mn**, 1.00 **Si**, 16.00–18.00 **Cr**, 0.060 **P**, 0.060 **S**, 0.15 min **Se**	**Annealed**: all **diam**, 80 (552) max **TS**, 55 (379) max **YS**, 25 **El**; **Annealed and cold finished**: 1 (25.40) **diam**, 90 (621) max **TS**, 80 (552) max **YS**, 15 **El**
BS T.71		UK	Tube: aircraft quality	0.12 **C**, 0.5–2.0 **Mn**, 0.2–1.0 **Si**, 23.0–26.0 **Cr**, 16.0–19.0 **Ni**, 0.035 **P**, 0.025 **S**, 5 x C–0.9 **Ti**	**Annealed**: all **diam**, (550) **TS**, (210) **YS**, 30 **El**
BS T.70		UK	Tube: aircraft quality	0.12 **C**, 0.5–2.0 **Mn**, 0.2–1.0 **Si**, 23.0–26.0 **Cr**, 16.0–19.0 **Ni**, 10 x C–1.4 **Nb**, 0.035 **P**, 0.025 **S**	**Annealed**: all **diam**, (550) **TS**, (210) **YS**, 30 **El**
ANSI/ASTM A 493	Type 305	US	Bar, wire	0.12 **C**, 2.00 **Mn**, 1.00 **Si**, 17.00–19.00 **Cr**, 10.50–13.00 **Ni**, 0.045 **P**, 0.030 **S**	**Lightly drafted (wire)**: ≥0.156 (≥3.96) **diam**, 80 (550) **TS**; **Annealed (wire)**: ≥0.156 (≥3.96) **diam**, 75 (520) **TS**
DGN–B–83	430F	Mexico	Bar	0.12 **C**, 1.25 **Mn**, 1.0 **Si**, 16.0–18.0 **Cr**, 0.60 **Mo**, 0.060 **P**, 0.15 min **S**	**Hot or cold rolled**: all **diam**, (549) **TS**, (372) **YS**, 25 **El**
DGN–B–83	430 FSe	Mexico	Bar	0.12 **C**, 1.25 **Mn**, 1.0 **Si**, 16.0–18.0 **Cr**, 0.060 **P**, 0.060 **S**, 0.15 min **Se**	**Hot or cold rolled**: all **diam**, (549) **TS**, (372) **YS**, 25 **El**
AS G18	G18/En 56A	Australia	Bar, billet, bar: black, bright	0.12 **C**, 1.00 **Mn**, 1.00 **Si**, 12.0–14.0 **Cr**, 1.00 **Ni**, 0.045 **P**, 0.045 **S**	**Hardened, tempered**: 6 **diam**, (540) **TS**, (385) **YS**
AS G18	G18/En 56AM	Australia	Bar, billet, bar: black, bright	0.12 **C**, 1.50 **Mn**, 1.00 **Si**, 12.0–14.0 **Cr**, 1.00 **Ni**, 0.60 **Mo**, 0.045 **P**, 0.35 **Pb**, 0.75 **S**, 0.60 **Se**, 0.60 **Zr**	**Hardened, tempered**: 6 **diam**, (540) **TS**
BS S.531		UK	Sheet, strip: aircraft quality	0.12 **C**, 0.5–2.0 **Mn**, 0.2–1.0 **Si**, 23.0–26.0 **Cr**, 16.0–19.0 **Ni**, 10 x C–1.4 **Nb**, 0.035 **P**, 0.025 **S**	**Annealed and quenched**: (<1.5) **diam**, (540) **TS**, (210) **YS**, 22 **El**
BS S.530		UK	Sheet, strip: aircraft quality	0.12 **C**, 0.5–2.0 **Mn**, 0.2–1.0 **Si**, 23.0–26.0 **Cr**, 16.0–19.0 **Ni**, 0.035 **P**, 0.025 **S**, 5 x C–0.9 **Ti**	**Annealed and quenched**: (<1.5) **diam**, (540) **TS**, (210) **YS**, 22 **El**
BS S.529		UK	Sheet, strip: aircraft quality	0.12 **C**, 0.5–2.0 **Mn**, 0.2–1.0 **Si**, 22.0–25.0 **Cr**, 13.0–16.0 **Ni**, 10 x C–1.4 **Nb**, 0.035 **P**, 0.025 **S**	**Annealed and quenched**: (<1.5) **diam**, (540) **TS**, (210) **YS**, 22 **El**
BS S.528		UK	Sheet, strip: aircraft quality	0.12 **C**, 0.5–2.0 **Mn**, 0.2–1.0 **Si**, 22.0–25.0 **Cr**, 13.0–16.0 **Ni**, 0.035 **P**, 0.025 **S**, 5 x C–0.9 **Ti**	**Annealed and quenched**: (<1.5) **diam**, (540) **TS**, (210) **YS**, 22 **El**
AS G18	G18/En 58H	Australia	Bar, billets	0.12 **C**, 2.00 **Mn**, 0.20 min **Si**, 17.0–20.0 **Cr**, 8.0–12.0 **Ni**, 1.50–2.50 **Mo**, 0.045 **P**, 0.045 **S**	**Solution annealed or quenched**: (6) **diam**, (540) **TS**, (185) **YS**,
AS G18	G18/En 58J	Australia	Bar, billets	0.12 **C**, 2.00 **Mn**, 0.20 min **Si**, 17.0–20.0 **Cr**, 8.0–12.0 **Ni**, 2.50–3.50 **Mo**, 0.045 **P**, 0.045 **S**	**Solution annealed or quenched**: (6) **diam**, (540) **TS**, (185) **YS**
BS 1449 Part 2	Grade 302S25	UK	Sheet, strip	0.12 **C**, 0.50–2.00 **Mn**, 0.20–1.00 **Si**, 17.0–19.0 **Cr**, 8.0–11.0 **Ni**, 0.045 **P**, 0.030 **S**	**Solution annealed**: (0.50–1.6) **diam**, (540) **TS**, (215) **YS**, 30 **El**
BS 3S.61		UK	Bar, billets, forgings: aircraft quality	0.12 **C**, 1.0 **Mn**, 0.8 **Si**, 11.5–13.5 **Cr**, 1.0 **Ni**, 0.030 **P**, 0.025 **S**	**Hardened and tempered**: all **diam**, (540) **TS**, (355) **YS**, 20 **El**
AISI 434		US	Sheet, strip, wire	0.12 **C**, 1.00 **Mn**, 1.00 **Si**, 16.00–18.00 **Cr**, 0.75–1.25 **Mo**, 0.040 **P**, 0.030 **S**	**Annealed (sheet)**: all **diam**, 77 (531) max **TS**, 53 (365) **YS**, 23 **El**
AISI 436		US	Sheet, strip	0.12 **C**, 1.00 **Mn**, 1.00 **Si**, 16.00–18.00 **Cr**, 0.75–1.25 **Mo**, 5 x C–0.70 **Cb+Ta**, 0.040 **P**, 0.030 **S**	**Annealed**: all **diam**, 77 (531) max **TS**, 53 (365) max **YS**, 23 **El**
BS 1506–713	Grade A,R	UK	Bar	0.12 **C**, 1.00 **Mn**, 1.00 **Si**, 11.5–13.5 **Cr**, 1.00 **Ni**, 0.045 **S**, 0.045 **P**	**Hardened in oil or air and tempered A**: all **diam**, (525) **TS**, (345) **YS**, 25 **El**; **Hardened in oil or air and tempered R**: all **diam**, (620) **TS**, (480) **YS**, 17 **El**

WROUGHT STAINLESS STEELS

specification number	designation	country	product forms	composition	mechanical properties (see page iv for explanation)
DGN–B–218	Grade TP305	Mexico	Tube: welded	0.12 **C**, 2.00 **Mn**, 1.00 **Si**, 17.0–19.0 **Cr**, 10.0–13.0 **Ni**, 0.045 **P**, 0.030 **S**	**Cold finished and quenched or tempered:** (≥7.92) **diam**, (519) **TS**, (206) **YS**, 35 **El**
DGN–B–171	Grade MT305	Mexico	Tube: seamless	0.12 **C**, 2.00 **Mn**, 1.00 **Si**, 17.0–19.0 **Cr**, 10.0–13.0 **Ni**, 0.040 **P**, 0.030 **S**	**Hot or cold finished and annealed:** (≥7.92) **diam**, (519) **TS**, (206) **YS**, 35 **El**
ANSI/ASTM A 511	MT 305	US	Tube: seamless	0.12 **C**, 2.00 **Mn**, 1.00 **Si**, 17.0–19.0 **Cr**, 10.0–13.0 **Ni**, 0.040 **P**, 0.030 **S**	**Solution annealed:** 0.31 (7.9) **diam**, 75 (517) **TS**, 30 (207) **YS**, 35 **El**
AMS 5641B		US	Bar, forgings, wire	0.12 **C**, 2.00 **Mn**, 0.70 **Si**, 17.00–20.00 **Cr**, 8.00–12.00 **Ni**, 0.75 **Mo**, 0.75 **Cu**, 0.11–0.17 **P**, 0.040 **S**, 0.15–0.30 **Se**	**Solution heat treated, cold finished (bar, wire):** 2.75 (69.85) **diam**, 75 (517) **TS**, 35 **El**
AISI 430		US	Sheet, strip, wire, plate, bar	0.12 **C**, 1.00 **Mn**, 1.00 **Si**, 16.00–18.00 **Cr**, 0.040 **P**, 0.030 **S**	**Annealed (sheet): all diam**, 75 (517) max **TS**, 50 (345) max **YS**, 25 **El**
ANSI/ASTM A 554	MT–305	US	Tube: welded	0.12 **C**, 2.00 **Mn**, 1.00 **Si**, 17.0–19.0 **Cr**, 10.0–13.0 **Ni**, 0.040 **P**, 0.030 **S**	**Round annealed:** 0.312 (7.94) **diam**, 75 (517) **TS**, 30 (207) **YS**, 35 **El**
ANSI/ASTM A 473	305	US	Forgings	0.12 **C**, 2.00 **Mn**, 1.00 **Si**, 17.00–19.00 **Cr**, 10.50–13.00 **Ni**, 0.045 **P**, 0.030 **S**	**Solution annealed:** all **diam**, 75 (515) **TS**, 30 (205) **YS**, 40 **El**
ANSI/ASTM A 276	305	US	Bar, shapes	0.12 **C**, 2.00 **Mn**, 1.00 **Si**, 17.00–19.00 **Cr**, 10.50–13.00 **Ni**, 0.045 **P**, 0.030 **S**	**Annealed:** all **diam**, 75 (515) **TS**, 30 (205) **YS**, 40 **El**
ASTM A 240	Type 305	US	Plate, sheet, strip	0.12 **C**, 2.00 **Mn**, 1.00 **Si**, 17.00–19.00 **Cr**, 10.50–13.00 **Ni**, 0.045 **P**, 0.030 **S**	**Solution annealed, hot rolled or cold rolled:** all **diam**, 75 (515) **TS**, 30 (205) **YS**, 40 **El**
ANSI/ASTM A 240	Grade 305	US	Plate, sheet, strip	0.12 **C**, 2.00 **Mn**, 1.00 **Si**, 17.00–19.00 **Cr**, 10.50–13.00 **Ni**, 0.045 **P**, 0.030 **S**	**Solution annealed:** all **diam**, (515) **TS**, (205) **YS**, 40 **El**
ANSI/ASTM A 249	TP 305	US	Tube: welded	0.12 **C**, 2.00 **Mn**, 1.00 **Si**, 17.0–19.0 **Cr**, 10.0–13.0 **Ni**, 0.045 **P**, 0.030 **S**	**Solution annealed:** 0.312 (7.94) **diam**, 75 (515) **TS**, 30 (205) **YS**, 35 **El**
DGN–B–83	305	Mexico	Bar	0.12 **C**, 2.0 **Mn**, 1.0 **Si**, 17.0–19.0 **Cr**, 10.5–13.0 **Ni**, 0.045 **P**, 0.030 **S**	**Hot or cold rolled:** all **diam**, (510) **TS**, (206) **YS**, 40 **El**
BS 970 Part 4	Grade 302S25	UK	Blooms, billets, bar, forgings	0.12 **C**, 0.50–2.00 **Mn**, 0.20–1.00 **Si**, 17.0–19.0 **Cr**, 8.00–11.00 **Ni**, 0.045 **P**, 0.030 **S**	**Annealed:** all **diam**, (510) **TS**, (210) **YS**, 40 **El**
BS 970 Part 4	Grade 321S20	UK	Blooms, billets, bar, forgings	0.12 **C**, 0.50–2.00 **Mn**, 0.20–1.00 **Si**, 17.0–19.0 **Cr**, 8.00–11.0 **Ni**, 0.045 **P**, 0.030 **S**, 5 x C–0.90 **Ti**	**Annealed:** all **diam**, (510) **TS**, (210) **YS**, 40 **El**
BS 970 Part 4	Grade 326S36	UK	Blooms, billets, bar, forgings	0.12 **C**, 1.00–2.00 **Mn**, 0.20–1.00 **Si**, 16.5–18.5 **Cr**, 10.0–13.0 **Ni**, 2.25–3.0 **Mo**, 0.045 **P**, 0.060 **S**, 0.15–0.30 **Se**	**Annealed:** all **diam**, (510) **TS**, 40 **El**
BS 970 Part 4	Grade 325S21	UK	Blooms, billets, bar, forgings	0.12 **C**, 1.00–2.00 **Mn**, 0.20–1.00 **Si**, 17.0–19.0 **Cr**, 8.0–11.0 **Ni**, 0.045 **P**, 0.15–0.30 **S**, 5 x C–0.90 **Ti**	**Annealed:** all **diam**, (510) **TS**, 40 **El**
BS 970 Part 4	Grade 303S41	UK	Blooms, billets, bar, forgings	0.12 **C**, 1.00–2.00 **Mn**, 0.20–1.00 **Si**, 17.0–19.0 **Cr**, 8.0–11.0 **Ni**, 0.045 **P**, 0.060 **S**, 0.15–0.30 **Se**	**Annealed:** all **diam**, (510) **TS**, 40 **El**
BS 970 Part 4	Grade 303S21	UK	Blooms, billets, bar, forgings	0.12 **C**, 1.00–2.00 **Mn**, 0.20–1.00 **Si**, 17.0–19.0 **Cr**, 8.0–11.0 **Ni**, 0.045 **P**, 0.15–0.30 **S**	**Annealed:** all **diam**, (510) **TS**, 40 **El**
AIR 9424	Z 10 CNT 18	France	Tube: seamless	0.12 **C**, 2.0 **Mn**, 1.0 **Si**, 17.0–20.0 **Cr**, 9.0–13.0 **Ni**, 0.045 **P**, 0.03 **S**, 5 x C **Ti**	**Quenched:** (<4) **diam**, (500) **TS**, (210) **YS**, 40 **El**
ISO 683/XII	12	ISO	Bar, sheet, plate	0.12 **C**, 2.0 **Mn**, 1.0 **Si**, 17.0–19.0 **Cr**, 8.0–10.0 **Ni**, 0.045 **P**, 0.030 **S**	**Solution treated:** all **diam**, (490) **TS**, (210) **YS**, 40 **El**
ISO 683/XII	17	ISO	Bar, sheet, plate	0.12 **C**, 2.0 **Mn**, 1.0 **Si**, 17.0–19.0 **Cr**, 8.0–10.0 **Ni**, 0.60 **Mo**, 0.20 **P**, 0.15–0.35 **S**	**Solution treated:** all **diam**, (490) **TS**, (210) **YS**, 35 **El**
AISI 429		US	Bar, forgings, plate	0.12 **C**, 1.00 **Mn**, 1.00 **Si**, 14.00–16.00 **Cr**, 0.040 **P**, 0.030 **S**	**Annealed (bar):** all **diam**, 71 (490) **TS**, 40 (276) max **YS**, 30 **El**

WROUGHT STAINLESS STEELS

specification number	designation	country	product forms	composition	mechanical properties (see page iv for explanation)
IS 6603	07Cr18Ni9	India	Bar	0.12 **C**, 2.0 **Mn**, 1.0 **Si**, 17.0–19.0 **Cr**, 8.0–10.0 **Ni**, 0.045 **P**, 0.030 **S**	**Softened**: (5–100) **diam**, (490) **TS**, (210) **YS**, 40 **El**; **Cold drawn (austentic):** (45) **diam**, (830) **TS**, (490) **YS**, 20 **El**; **Cold rolled (austenitic):** (0.5–2.8) **diam**, (830) **TS**, (490) **YS**, 12 **El**
IS 6911	07Cr18Ni9	India	Plate, sheet, strip	0.12 **C**, 2.0 **Mn**, 1.0 **Si**, 17.0–19.0 **Cr**, 8.0–10.0 **Ni**, 0.030 **S**, 0.045 **P**	**Softened**: (0.5–3) **diam**, (490) **TS**, (210) **YS**, 38 **El**
AIR 9160	9160C201	France	Bar, sheet, tube	0.12 **C**, 2.0 **Mn**, 1.0 **Si**, 17.0–19.0 **Cr**, 10.0–13.0 **Ni**, 0.035 **P**, 0.025 **S**, 5 x C–0.80 **Ti**	**Solution annealed**: (<50) **diam**, (490) **TS**, (220) **YS**, 40 **El**; **Cold rolled**: (<30) **diam**, (800) **TS**, (700) **YS**, 10 **El**; **Solution annealed (bar)**: (<50) **diam**, (490) **TS**, (210) **YS**, 37 **El**
AIR 9113	Z10CNT18	France	Bar, wire, tube, sheet	0.12 **C**, 2.0 **Mn**, 1.0 **Si**, 17.0–20.0 **Cr**, 9.0–13.0 **Ni**, 0.045 **P**, 0.03 **S**, 5 x C min **Ti**	**Quenched and tempered**: all **diam**, (490) **TS**, (200) **YS**, 42 **El**; **Partial anneal**: all **diam**, (830) **TS**, (690) **YS**, 14 **El**
NF A 35–572	Z 10 CN 18–09	France	Bar, sections	0.12 **C**, 2.0 **Mn**, 1.0 **Si**, 17.0–19.0 **Cr**, 7.5–9.5 **Ni**, 0.040 **P**, 0.030 **S**	**Austenitized**: (≤25) **diam**, (490) **TS**, (215) **YS**, 45 **El**
SIS 14 23 31	SIS 23 31–02	Sweden	Bar, forgings, sheet, strip, wire	0.12 **C**, 2.0 **Mn**, 1.0 **Si**, 17.0–19.0 **Cr**, 7.0–9.5 **Ni**, 0.045 **P**, 0.030 **S**	**Solution annealed (except wire)**: all **diam**, (490) **TS**, (210) **YS**, 45 **El**
SIS 14 23 46	SIS 23 46 02	Sweden	Bar, tube, wire	0.12 **C**, 2.0 **Mn**, 1.0 **Si**, 17.0–19.0 **Cr**, 8.0–10.0 **Ni**, 0.60 **Mo**, 0.060 **P**, 0.15–0.35 **S**	**Solution annealed (bar, tube)**: all **diam**, (490) **TS**, (210) **YS**, 35 **El**
SIS 14 23 46	SIS 23 46–02	Sweden	Bar	0.12 **C**, 2.0 **Mn**, 1.0 **Si**, 17.0–19.0 **Cr**, 8.0–10.0 **Ni**, 0.60 **Mo**, 0.060 **P**, 0.15–0.35 **S**	**Solution annealed**: (<100) **diam**, (490) **TS**, (210) **YS**, 35 **El**
ANSI/ASTM A 479	430	US	Bar, shapes	0.12 **C**, 1.00 **Mn**, 1.00 **Si**, 16.00–18.00 **Cr**, 0.040 **P**, 0.030 **S**	**Annealed**: all **diam**, 70 (485) **TS**, 40 (275) **YS**, 20 **El**
ANSI/ASTM A 473	430	US	Forgings	0.12 **C**, 1.00 **Mn**, 1.00 **Si**, 16.00–18.00 **Cr**, 0.75 **Ni**, 0.040 **P**, 0.030 **S**	**Annealed**: all **diam**, 70 (485) **TS**, 35 (240) **YS**, 20 **El**
ANSI/ASTM A 473	430F	US	Forgings	0.12 **C**, 1.25 **Mn**, 1.00 **Si**, 16.00–18.00 **Cr**, 0.75 **Ni**, 0.60 **Mo**, 0.06 **P**, 0.15 min **S**	**Annealed**: all **diam**, 70 (485) **TS**, 40 (275) **YS**, 20 **El**
ANSI/ASTM A 473	430FSe	US	Forgings	0.12 **C**, 1.25 **Mn**, 1.00 **Si**, 16.00–18.00 **Cr**, 0.75 **Ni**, 0.06 **P**, **S**, 0.15 min **Se**	**Annealed**: all **diam**, 70 (485) **TS**, 40 (275) **YS**, 20 **El**
ASTM A 167	Type 305	US	Plate, sheet, strip	0.12 **C**, 2.00 **Mn**, 1.00 **Si**, 17.00–19.00 **Cr**, 10.50–13.00 **Ni**, 0.045 **P**, 0.030 **S**	**Solution annealed**: all **diam**, 70 (485) **TS**, 25 (170) **YS**, 40 **El**
ANSI/ASTM A 493	Type 430	US	Bar, wire	0.12 **C**, 1.00 **Mn**, 1.00 **Si**, 16.00–18.00 **Cr**, 0.040 **P**, 0.030 **S**	**Lightly drafted (wire)**: ≥0.156 (≥3.96) **diam**, 70 (485) **TS**; **Annealed (wire)**: ≥0.156 (≥3.96) **diam**, 65 (450) **TS**
ANSI/ASTM A 493	Type 429	US	Bar, wire	0.12 **C**, 1.00 **Mn**, 1.00 **Si**, 14.00–16.00 **Cr**, 0.040 **P**, 0.030 **S**	**Lightly drafted (wire)**: ≥0.156 (≥3.96) **diam**, 70 (485) **TS**; **Annealed (wire)**: ≥0.156 (≥3.96) **diam**, 65 (450) **TS**
ANSI/ASTM A 479	Grade 430	US	Bar, shapes	0.12 **C**, 1.00 **Mn**, 1.00 **Si**, 16.00–18.00 **Cr**, 0.040 **P**, 0.030 **S**	**Annealed**: all **diam**, (485) **TS**, (275) **YS**, 20 **El**
CSA G110.9	Type 305	Canada	Plate	0.12 **C**, 2.00 **Mn**, 1.00 **Si**, 17.00–19.00 **Cr**, 10.00–13.00 **Ni**, 0.045 **P**, 0.030 **S**	**Hot rolled, annealed, quenched and tempered**: all **diam**, 70 (483) **TS**, 25 (172) **YS**, 40 **El**
CSA G110.9	Type 305	Canada	Sheet	0.12 **C**, 2.00 **Mn**, 1.00 **Si**, 17.00–19.00 **Cr**, 10.00–13.00 **Ni**, 0.045 **P**, 0.030 **S**,	**Hot or cold rolled and annealed**: all **diam**, 70 (483) **TS**, 25 (172) **YS**, 40 **El**
CSA G110.9	Type 305	Canada	Strip	0.12 **C**, 2.00 **Mn**, 1.00 **Si**, 17.00–19.00 **Cr**, 10.00–13.00 **Ni**, 0.045 **P**, 0.030 **S**	**Cold rolled and annealed**: all **diam**, 70 (483) **TS**, 25 (172) **YS**, 40 **El**
CSA G110.6	Type 305	Canada	Plate, sheet, strip	0.12 **C**, 2.00 **Mn**, 1.00 **Si**, 17.00–19.00 **Cr**, 10.00–13.00 **Ni**, 0.045 **P**, 0.030 **S**	**Hot rolled and annealed or hot rolled, quenched and tempered**: all **diam**, 70 (483) **TS**, 25 (172) **YS**, 40 **El**

WROUGHT STAINLESS STEELS

specification number	designation	country	product forms	composition	mechanical properties (see page iv for explanation)
QQ-S-766C	Class 305	US	Strip, sheet, plate	0.12 **C**, 2.00 **Mn**, 1.00 **Si**, 17.00 **Cr**, 10.00 **Ni**, 0.045 **P**, 0.035 **S**	**Annealed**: all **diam**, 70 (483) **TS**, 40 **El**
QQ-S-766C	Class 430	US	Strip, sheet, plate	0.12 **C**, 1.00 **Mn**, 1.00 **Si**, 14.00–18.00 **Cr**, 0.040 **P**, 0.030 **S**	**Annealed**: all **diam**, 70 (483) **TS**, 35 (241) **YS**, 20 **El**
JIS G 4303	SUS 305	Japan	Bar	0.12 **C**, 2.00 **Mn**, 1.00 **Si**, 17.00–19.00 **Cr**, 10.50–13.00 **Ni**, 0.040 **P**, 0.030 **S**	**Solution annealed**: (≤180) **diam**, (481) **TS**, (177) **YS**, 40 **El**
JIS G 4304	SUS 305	Japan	Sheet, plate	0.12 **C**, 2.00 **Mn**, 1.00 **Si**, 17.00–19.00 **Cr**, 10.50–13.00 **Ni**, 0.040 **P**, 0.030 **S**	**Hot rolled and solution annealed**: all **diam**, (481) **TS**, (177) **YS**, 40 **El**
JIS G 4305	SUS 305	Japan	Sheet, plate	0.12 **C**, 2.00 **Mn**, 1.00 **Si**, 17.00–19.00 **Cr**, 10.50–13.00 **Ni**, 0.040 **P**, 0.030 **S**	**Cold rolled and solution annealed**: all **diam**, (481) **TS**, (177) **YS**, 40 **El**
JIS G 4306	SUS 305	Japan	Strip	0.12 **C**, 2.00 **Mn**, 1.00 **Si**, 17.00–19.00 **Cr**, 10.50–13.00 **Ni**, 0.040 **P**, 0.030 **S**	**Hot rolled and solution annealed**: all **diam**, (481) **TS**, (177) **YS**, 40 **El**
JIS G 4307	SUS 305	Japan	Strip	0.12 **C**, 2.00 **Mn**, 1.00 **Si**, 17.00–19.00 **Cr**, 10.50–13.00 **Ni**, 0.040 **P**, 0.030 **S**	**Cold rolled and solution annealed**: all **diam**, (481) **TS**, (177) **YS**, 40 **El**
DGN-B-83	429	Mexico	Bar	0.12 **C**, 1.0 **Mn**, 1.0 **Si**, 14.0–16.0 **Cr**, 0.040 **P**, 0.030 **S**	**Hot or cold rolled**: all **diam**, (480) **TS**, (247) **YS**, 20 **El**
DGN-B-83	430	Mexico	Bar	0.12 **C**, 1.0 **Mn**, 1.0 **Si**, 16.0–18.0 **Cr**, 0.040 **P**, 0.030 **S**	**Hot or cold rolled**: all **diam**, (480) **TS**, (247) **YS**, 20 **El**
ANSI/ASTM A 276	430	US	Bar, shapes	0.12 **C**, 1.00 **Mn**, 1.00 **Si**, 16.00–18.00 **Cr**, 0.040 **P**, 0.030 **S**	**Annealed**: all **diam**, 70 (480) **TS**, 40 (275) **YS**, 20 **El**
ANSI/ASTM A 276	429	US	Bar, shapes	0.12 **C**, 1.00 **Mn**, 1.00 **Si**, 14.00–16.00 **Cr**, 0.040 **P**, 0.030 **S**	**Annealed**: all **diam**, 70 (480) **TS**, 40 (275) **YS**, 20 **El**
ISO 2604/II	TS 69	ISO	Tube: seamless	0.12 **C**, 1.50 **Mn**, 1.00 **Si**, 19.00–23.00 **Cr**, 30.00–35.00 **Ni**, 0.15–0.60 **Al**, 0.045 **P**, 0.030 **S**, 0.15–0.60 **Ti**	**Cold finished, quenched**: all **diam**, (480) **TS**, (165) **YS**, 25 **El**
BS 1506-821	Grade Ti	UK	Bar	0.12 **C**, 0.50–2.00 **Mn**, 0.20–1.00 **Si**, 17.0–20.0 **Cr**, 7.5 min **Ni**, 25.0 min **Ni+Cr**, 4 x C–0.70 **Ti**, 0.045 **S**, 0.045 **P**	**Solution annealed**: all **diam**, (480) **TS**, (185) **YS**, 30 **El**; **Cold drawn**: 0.75 **diam**, (770) **TS**, (620) **YS**, 12 **El**
BS 1506-821	Grade TiM	UK	Bar	0.12 **C**, 0.50–2.00 **Mn**, 0.20–1.00 **Si**, 17.0–20.0 **Cr**, 7.5 min **Ni**, 0.5 **Mo**, 25.0 min **Ni+Cr**, 4 x C–0.70 **Ti**, 0.5 **Zr**, 0.40 **S**, 0.045 **P**	**Solution annealed**: all **diam**, (480) **TS**, (185) **YS**, 30 **El**; **Cold drawn**: 0.75 **diam**, (770) **TS**, (620) **YS**, 12 **El**
BS 1501-821	Grade Ti	UK	Bar	0.12 **C**, 0.50–2.00 **Mn**, 0.20–1.00 **Si**, 17.0–20.0 **Cr**, 7.5 min **Ni**, 25.0 **Ni+Cr**, 4 x C–0.70 **Ti**, 0.045 **S**, 0.045 **P**	**Annealed**: all **diam**, (480) **TS**, (435) **YS**
ANSI/ASTM A 580	Grade 430	US	Wire	0.12 **C**, 1.00 **Mn**, 1.00 **Si**, 16.00–18.00 **Cr**, 0.040 **P**, 0.030 **S**	**Annealed**: all **diam**, 70 (480) **TS**, 40 (280) **YS**, 20 **El**
JIS G 4303	SUS 429	Japan	Bar	0.12 **C**, 1.00 **Mn**, 1.00 **Si**, 14.00–16.00 **Cr**, 0.60 **Ni**, 0.040 **P**, 0.030 **S**	**Annealed**: (≤75) **diam**, (451) **TS**, (206) **YS**, 22 **El**
JIS G 4303	SUS 430	Japan	Bar	0.12 **C**, 1.00 **Mn**, 0.75 **Si**, 16.00–18.00 **Cr**, 0.60 **Ni**, 0.040 **P**, 0.030 **S**	**Annealed**: (≤75) **diam**, (451) **TS**, (206) **YS**, 22 **El**
JIS G 4303	SUS 430F	Japan	Bar	0.12 **C**, 1.25 **Mn**, 1.00 **Si**, 16.00–18.00 **Cr**, 0.60 **Ni**, 0.60 **Mo**, 0.060 **P**, 0.15 **S**	**Annealed**: (≤75) **diam**, (451) **TS**, (206) **YS**, 22 **El**
JIS G 4303	SUS 434	Japan	Bar	0.12 **C**, 1.00 **Mn**, 1.00 **Si**, 16.00–18.00 **Cr**, 0.60 **Ni**, 0.75–1.25 **Mo**, 0.040 **P**, 0.030 **S**	**Annealed**: (≤75) **diam**, (451) **TS**, (206) **YS**, 22 **El**
JIS G 4304	SUS 429	Japan	Sheet, plate	0.12 **C**, 1.00 **Mn**, 1.00 **Si**, 14.00–16.00 **Cr**, 0.6 **Ni**, 0.040 **P**, 0.030 **S**	**Hot rolled and annealed**: all **diam**, (451) **TS**, (206) **YS**, 22 **El**
JIS G 4304	SUS 430	Japan	Sheet, plate	0.12 **C**, 1.00 **Mn**, 0.75 **Si**, 16.00–18.00 **Cr**, 0.6 **Ni**, 0.040 **P**, 0.030 **S**	**Hot rolled and annealed**: all **diam**, (451) **TS**, (206) **YS**, 22 **El**
JIS G 4304	SUS 434	Japan	Sheet, plate	0.12 **C**, 1.00 **Mn**, 1.00 **Si**, 16.00–18.00 **Cr**, 0.6 **Ni**, 0.75–1.25 **Mo**, 0.040 **P**, 0.030 **S**	**Hot rolled and annealed**: all **diam**, (451) **TS**, (206) **YS**, 22 **El**
JIS G 4307	SUS 430	Japan	Strip	0.12 **C**, 1.00 **Mn**, 0.75 **Si**, 16.00–18.00 **Cr**, 0.6 **Ni**, 0.040 **P**, 0.030 **S**	**Cold rolled and solution annealed**: all **diam**, (451) **TS**, (206) **YS**, 22 **El**

WROUGHT STAINLESS STEELS

specification number	designation	country	product forms	composition	mechanical properties (see page iv for explanation)
JIS G 4307	SUS 434	Japan	Strip	0.12 **C**, 1.00 **Mn**, 1.00 **Si**, 16.00–18.00 **Cr**, 0.6 **Ni**, 0.75–1.25 **Mo**, 0.040 **P**, 0.030 **S**	**Cold rolled and solution annealed:** all **diam**, (451) **TS**, (206) **YS**, 22 **El**
JIS G 4305	SUS 429	Japan	Sheet, plate	0.12 **C**, 1.00 **Mn**, 1.00 **Si**, 14.00–16.00 **Cr**, 0.60 **Ni**, 0.040 **P**, 0.030 **S**	**Cold rolled and annealed:** all **diam**, (451) **TS**, (206) **YS**, 22 **El**
JIS G 4305	SUS 430	Japan	Sheet, plate	0.12 **C**, 1.00 **Mn**, 0.75 **Si**, 16.00–18.00 **Cr**, 0.60 **Ni**, 0.040 **P**, 0.030 **S**	**Cold rolled and annealed:** all **diam**, (451) **TS**, (206) **YS**, 22 **El**
JIS G 4305	SUS 434	Japan	Sheet, plate	0.12 **C**, 1.00 **Mn**, 1.00 **Si**, 16.00–18.00 **Cr**, 0.60 **Ni**, 0.75–1.25 **Mo**, 0.040 **P**, 0.030 **S**	**Cold rolled and annealed:** all **diam**, (451) **TS**, (206) **YS**, 22 **El**
JIS G 4306	SUS 430	Japan	Strip	0.12 **C**, 1.00 **Mn**, 0.75 **Si**, 16.00–18.00 **Cr**, 0.60 **Ni**, 0.040 **P**, 0.030 **S**	**Hot rolled and annealed:** all **diam**, (451) **TS**, (206) **YS**, 22 **El**
JIS G 4306	SUS 434	Japan	Strip	0.12 **C**, 1.00 **Mn**, 1.00 **Si**, 16.00–18.00 **Cr**, 0.60 **Ni**, 0.75–1.25 **Mo**, 0.040 **P**, 0.030 **S**	**Hot rolled and annealed:** all **diam**, (451) **TS**, (206) **YS**, 22 **El**
ANSI/ASTM A 473	429	US	Forgings	0.12 **C**, 1.00 **Mn**, 1.00 **Si**, 14.00–16.00 **Cr**, 0.75 **Ni**, 0.040 **P**, 0.030 **S**	**Annealed:** all **diam**, 65 (450) **TS**, 35 (240) **YS**, 23 **El**
AS 1449	Grade AS 1449/430	Australia	Sheet, strip, plate	0.12 **C**, 1.00 **Mn**, 16.00–18.00 **Cr**, 0.040 **P**, 0.030 **S**	**Annealed:** (≤1.2) **diam**, (450) **TS**, (205) **YS**, 20 **El**
ASTM A 240	Type 430	US	Plate, sheet, strip	0.12 **C**, 1.00 **Mn**, 1.00 **Si**, 16.00–18.00 **Cr**, 0.75 **Ni**, 0.040 **P**, 0.030 **S**	**Hot rolled or cold rolled, annealed:** all **diam**, 65 (450) **TS**, 30 (205) **YS**, 22 **El**
ASTM A 240	Type 429	US	Plate, sheet, strip	0.12 **C**, 1.00 **Mn**, 1.00 **Si**, 14.00–16.00 **Cr**, 0.75 **Ni**, 0.040 **P**, 0.030 **S**	**Hot rolled or cold rolled, annealed:** all **diam**, 65 (450) **TS**, 30 (205) **YS**, 22 **El**
ASTM A 176	Type 430	US	Plate, sheet, strip	0.12 **C**, 1.00 **Mn**, 1.00 **Si**, 16.00–18.00 **Cr**, 0.75 **Ni**, 0.040 **P**, 0.030 **S**	**Annealed:** all **diam**, 65 (450) **TS**, 30 (205) **YS**, 22 **El**
ASTM A 176	Type 429	US	Plate, sheet, strip	0.12 **C**, 1.00 **Mn**, 1.00 **Si**, 14.00–16.00 **Cr**, 0.75 **Ni**, 0.040 **P**, 0.030 **S**	**Annealed:** all **diam**, 65 (450) **TS**, 30 (205) **YS**, 22 **El**
ANSI/ASTM A 240	Grade 429	US	Plate, sheet, strip	0.12 **C**, 1.00 **Mn**, 1.00 **Si**, 14.00–16.00 **Cr**, 0.75 **Ni**, 0.040 **P**, 0.030 **S**	**Annealed:** all **diam**, (450) **TS**, (205) **YS**, 22 **El**
ANSI/ASTM A 240	Grade 430	US	Plate, sheet, strip	0.12 **C**, 1.00 **Mn**, 1.00 **Si**, 16.00–18.00 **Cr**, 0.75 **Ni**, 0.040 **P**, 0.030 **S**	**Annealed:** all **diam**, (450) **TS**, (205) **YS**, 22 **El**
CSA G110.9	Type 430A	Canada	Plate	0.12 **C**, 1.00 **Mn**, 1.00 **Si**, 14.00–16.00 **Cr**, 0.75 **Ni**, 0.040 **P**, 0.030 **S**	**Hot rolled, annealed, quenched and tempered:** ≤0.050 **diam**, 65 (448) **TS**, 30 (207) **YS**, 20 **El**
CSA G110.5	Type 430	Canada	Sheet	0.12 **C**, 1.00 **Mn**, 1.00 **Si**, 14.00–18.00 **Cr**, 0.75 **Ni**, 0.040 **P**, 0.030 **S**	**Hot rolled, annealed, quenched and tempered:** all **diam**, 65 (448) **TS**, 30 (207) **YS**, 20 **El**
CSA G110.9	Type 430A	Canada	Plate	0.12 **C**, 1.00 **Mn**, 1.00 **Si**, 14.00–16.00 **Cr**, 0.75 **Ni**, 0.040 **P**, 0.030 **S**	**Hot rolled, annealed, quenched and tempered:** ≤0.050 **diam**, 65 (448) **TS**, 30 (207) **YS**, 20 **El**
CSA G110.9	Type 430B	Canada	Sheet	0.12 **C**, 1.00 **Mn**, 1.00 **Si**, 16.00–18.00 **Cr**, 0.75 **Ni**, 0.040 **P**, 0.030 **S**,	**Hot or cold rolled and annealed:** ≤ 0.050 **diam**, 65 (448) **TS**, 30 (207) **YS**, 20 **El**
CSA G110.9	Type 430A	Canada	Sheet	0.12 **C**, 1.00 **Mn**, 1.00 **Si**, 14.00–16.00 **Cr**, 0.75 **Ni**, 0.040 **P**, 0.030 **S**	**Hot or cold rolled and annealed:** ≤0.050 **diam**, 65 (448) **TS**, 30 (207) **YS**, 20 **El**
CSA G110.5	Type 430	Canada	Strip	0.12 **C**, 1.00 **Mn**, 1.00 **Si**, 14.00–18.00 **Cr**, 0.75 **Ni**, 0.040 **P**, 0.030 **S**	**Cold rolled and annealed:** ≤0.050 **diam**, 65 (448) **TS**, 30 (207) **YS**, 20 **El**
CSA G110.9	Type 430B	Canada	Strip	0.12 **C**, 1.00 **Mn**, 1.00 **Si**, 16.00–18.00 **Cr**, 0.75 **Ni**, 0.040 **P**, 0.030 **S**	**Cold rolled and annealed:** ≤0.050 **diam**, 65 (448) **TS**, 30 (207) **YS**, 20 **El**
CSA G110.9	Type 430A	Canada	Strip	0.12 **C**, 1.00 **Mn**, 1.00 **Si**, 14.00–16.00 **Cr**, 0.75 **Ni**, 0.040 **P**, 0.030 **S**	**Cold rolled and annealed:** ≤0.050 **diam**, 65 (448) **TS**, 30 (207) **YS**, 20 **El**
ISO 683/XII	8a	ISO	Bar, sheet, plate	0.12 **C**, 1.5 **Mn**, 1.0 **Si**, 16.0–18.0 **Cr**, 0.50 **Ni**, 0.60 **Mo**, 0.060 **P**, 0.15–0.35 **S**	**Annealed:** all **diam**, (440) **TS**, (250) **YS**, 15 **El**
ISO 683/XII	9b	ISO	Bar, sheet, plate	0.12 **C**, 1.5 **Mn**, 1.0 **Si**, 16.0–18.0 **Cr**, 0.50 **Ni**, 0.60 **Mo**, 0.060 **P**, 0.15–0.35 **S**, 5 x C–0.80 **Ti**	**Annealed:** all **diam**, (440) **TS**, (250) **YS**, 18 **El**

WROUGHT STAINLESS STEELS

specification number	designation	country	product forms	composition	mechanical properties (see page iv for explanation)
ISO 2604/IV	P69	ISO	Plate	0.12 **C**, 2.00 **Mn**, 1.00 **Si**, 19.0–23.0 **Cr**, 30.0–35.0 **Ni**, 0.15–0.60 **Al**, 0.045 **P**, 0.030 **S**, 0.15–0.50 **Ti**	**Hot rolled, quenched:** (3–40) **diam**, (430) **TS**, (165) **YS**, 25 **El**
ANSI/ASTM A 511	MT 429	US	Tube: seamless	0.12 **C**, 1.00 **Mn**, 1.00 **Si**, 14.0–16.0 **Cr**, 0.50 **Ni**, 0.040 **P**, 0.030 **S**	**Annealed:** 0.31 (7.9) **diam**, 60 (414) **TS**, 35 (241) **YS**, 20 **El**
ANSI/ASTM A 511	MT 430	US	Tube: seamless	0.12 **C**, 1.00 **Mn**, 1.00 **Si**, 16.0–18.0 **Cr**, 0.50 **Ni**, 0.040 **P**, 0.030 **S**	**Annealed:** 0.31 (7.9) **diam**, 60 (414) **TS**, 35 (241) **YS**, 20 **El**
ANSI/ASTM A 268	TP 429	US	Tube: seamless, welded	0.12 **C**, 1.00 **Mn**, 0.75 **Si**, 14.0–16.0 **Cr**, 0.50 **Ni**, 0.040 **P**, 0.030 **S**	**Annealed:** 0.312 (7.94) **diam**, 60 (414) **TS**, 35 (241) **YS**, 20 **El**
ANSI/ASTM A 268	TP 430	US	Tube: seamless, welded	0.12 **C**, 1.00 **Mn**, 0.75 **Si**, 16.0–18.0 **Cr**, 0.50 **Ni**, 0.040 **P**, 0.030 **S**	**Annealed:** 0.312 (7.94) **diam**, 60 (414) **TS**, 35 (241) **YS**, 20 **El**
ASTM A 651	TP 430	US	Tube: welded or seamless	0.12 **C**, 1.00 **Mn**, 0.75 **Si**, 16.00–18.00 **Cr**, 0.50 **Ni**, 0.040 **P**, 0.030 **S**	**As welded or as drawn:** all **diam**, 60 (414) **TS**, 30 (207) **YS**
ASTM A 651	TP 434	US	Tube: seamless or welded	0.12 **C**, 1.00 **Mn**, 1.00 **Si**, 16.00–18.00 **Cr**, 0.75–1.25 **Mo**, 0.040 **P**, 0.030 **S**	**As welded or drawn:** all **diam**, 60 (414) **TS**, 30 (207) **YS**
ANSI/ASTM A 554	MT–429	US	Tube: welded	0.12 **C**, 1.00 **Mn**, 1.00 **Si**, 14.0–16.0 **Cr**, 0.50 **Ni**, 0.040 **P**, 0.030 **S**	**Round annealed:** 0.312 (7.94) **diam**, 60 (414) **TS**, 35 (241) **YS**, 20 **El**
ANSI/ASTM A 554	MT–430	US	Tube: welded	0.12 **C**, 1.00 **Mn**, 1.00 **Si**, 16.0–18.0 **Cr**, 0.50 **Ni**, 0.040 **P**, 0.030 **S**	**Round annealed:** 0.312 (7.94) **diam**, 60 (414) **TS**, 35 (241) **YS**, 20 **El**
DGN–B–171	Grade MT 430	Mexico	Tube: seamless	0.12 **C**, 1.00 **Mn**, 1.00 **Si**, 14.0–18.0 **Cr**, 0.50 **Ni**, 0.040 **P**, 0.030 **S**	**Hot or cold finished and annealed:** (≥7.92) **diam**, (412) **TS**, (245) **YS**, 20 **El**
DGN–B–216	Grade TP430	Mexico	Tube: seamless, welded	0.12 **C**, 1.00 **Mn**, 0.75 **Si**, 14.0–18.0 **Cr**, 0.50 **Ni**, 0.040 **P**, 0.030 **S**	**As drawn or as welded:** (≥7.93) **diam**, (412) **TS**, (206) **YS**, 20 **El**
JIS G 3446	SUS 430 TK	Japan	Tube: seamless or welded	0.12 **C**, 1.00 **Mn**, 0.75 **Si**, 16.00–18.00 **Cr**, 0.60 **Ni**, 0.040 **P**, 0.030 **S**	**Annealed:** (≥8) **diam**, (412) **TS**, (245) **YS**, 20 **El**
JIS G 3463	SUS 430 TB	Japan	Tube: seamless or welded	0.12 **C**, 1.00 **Mn**, 0.75 **Si**, 16.00–18.00 **Cr**, 0.040 **P**, 0.030 **S**	**Annealed:** (≥8) **diam**, (412) **TS**, (245) **YS**, 20 **El**
DIN 17224	X12CrNi177/1.4310	Germany	Wire, strip	0.12 **C**, 2.0 **Mn**, 1.0 **Si**, 16.0–18.0 **Cr**, 7.0–9.0 **Ni**, 0.045 **P**, 0.030 **S**	**Hard drawn (wire):** (<0.2) **diam**, (220) **TS**; **Tempered or quench–age hardened:** (<0.2) **diam**, (235) **TS**
CSA G110.9	Type 430B	Canada	Plate	0.12 **C**, 1.00 **Mn**, 1.00 **Si**, 16.00–18.00 **Cr**, 0.75 **Ni**, 0.040 **P**, 0.030 **S**	**Hot rolled, annealed, quenched and tempered:** ≤0.050 **diam**, 65 (448) (207) **TS**, 30 **YS**, 25 **El**
AS G18	G18/En 60	Australia	Bar, billet, bar: black, bright	0.12 **C**, 1.00 **Mn**, 1.00 **Si**, 16.0–18.0 **Cr**, 0.50 **Ni**, 0.045 **P**, 0.045 **S**	
AS G18	G18/En 61	Australia	Bar, billet, bar: black, bright	0.12 **C**, 1.00 **Mn**, 1.00 **Si**, 20.0–22.0 **Cr**, 0.50 **Ni**, 0.045 **P**, 0.045 **S**	
ASTM A 582	430F	US	Bar	0.12 **C**, 1.25 **Mn**, 1.00 **Si**, 16.00–18.00 **Cr**, 0.60 **Mo**, 0.06 **P**, 0.15 min **S**	
ASTM A 582	430FSe	US	Bar	0.12 **C**, 1.25 **Mn**, 1.00 **Si**, 16.00–18.00 **Cr**, 0.06 **P**, 0.06 **S**, 0.15 min **Se**	
ANSI/ASTM A 314	430FSe	US	Bar, forgings, billets	0.12 **C**, 1.25 **Mn**, 1.00 **Si**, 14.00–18.00 **Cr**, 0.06 **P**, 0.06 **S**, 0.15 min **Se**	
ANSI/ASTM A 314	305	US	Bar, forgings, billets	0.12 **C**, 2.00 **Mn**, 1.00 **Si**, 17.00–19.00 **Cr**, 10.50–13.00 **Ni**, 0.045 **P**, 0.030 **S**	
ANSI/ASTM A 314	429	US	Bar, forgings, billets	0.12 **C**, 1.00 **Mn**, 1.00 **Si**, 14.00–16.00 **Cr**, 0.040 **P**, 0.030 **S**	
ANSI/ASTM A 314	430	US	Bar, forgings, billets	0.12 **C**, 1.00 **Mn**, 1.00 **Si**, 16.00–18.00 **Cr**, 0.040 **P**, 0.030 **S**	
ANSI/ASTM A 314	430F	US	Bar, forgings, billets	0.12 **C**, 1.25 **Mn**, 1.00 **Si**, 14.00–18.00 **Cr**, 0.60 **Mo**, 0.06 **P**, 0.15 min **S**	

WROUGHT STAINLESS STEELS

specification number	designation	country	product forms	composition	mechanical properties (see page iv for explanation)
DGN–B–150	Type AE–410	Mexico	Wire	0.12 **C**, 0.60 **Mn**, 0.50 **Si**, 11.5–13.5 **Cr**, 0.60 **Ni**, 0.60 **Mo**, 0.07 N_2, 0.030 **P**, 0.030 **S**	
AS 1444	Grade AS 1444/430F	Australia	Bar, bloom, billet, slab	0.12 **C**, 1.25 **Mn**, 1.00 **Si**, 14.00–18.00 **Cr**, 0.06 **P**, 0.15 min **S**, 0.60 **Zr** or mo	
AS 1444	Grade AS 1444/430	Australia	Bar, bloom, billet, slab	0.12 **C**, 1.00 **Mn**, 1.00 **Si**, 14.00–18.00 **Cr**, 0.040 **P**, 0.040 **S**, 0.60 **Zr** or mo	
DGN–B–150	Type AE–309	Mexico	Wire	0.12 **C**, 1.0–2.5 **Mn**, 0.25–0.60 **Si**, 23.0–25.0 **Cr**, 12.0–14.0 **Ni**, 0.25 **Cu**, 0.07 N_2, 0.030 **P**, 0.030 **S**	
MIL–S–862B	Class 430	US	Bar, billets	0.12 **C**, 1.0 **Mn**, 1.0 **Si**, 14.0–18.0 **Cr**, 0.040 **P**, 0.030 **S**	
MIL–S–862B	Class 430F	US	Bar, billets	0.12 **C**, 1.25 **Mn**, 1.0 **Si**, 14.0–18.0 **Cr**, 0.6 **Mo**, 0.06 **P**, 0.06 **S**, 0.60 **Zr**	
MIL–S–862B	Class 430F Se	US	Bar, billets	0.12 **C**, 1.25 **Mn**, 1.0 **Si**, 14.0–18.0 **Cr**, 0.06 **P**, 0.06 **S**, 0.15 min **Se**	
IS 6529	07Cr18Ni9	India	Blooms, billets, slabs	0.12 **C**, 2.0 **Mn**, 1.0 **Si**, 17.0–19.0 **Cr**, 8.0–10.0 **Ni**, 0.045 **P**, 0.030 **S**	**Annealed, or solution annealed**
AMS 5627B		US	Bar, forgings, tube, rings	0.12 **C**, 1.00 **Mn**, 1.00 **Si**, 16.00–18.00 **Cr**, 0.75 **Ni**, 0.50 **Mo**, 0.50 **Cu**, 0.40 **P**, 0.030 **S**	
AMS 5522D		US	Strip, sheet, plate	0.12 **C**, 1.00–2.00 **Mn**, 1.70–2.30 **Si**, 23.00–25.00 **Cr**, 19.00–22.00 **Ni**, 0.75 **Mo**, 0.50 **Cu**, 0.040 **P**, 0.030 **S**	
IS 6527	07Cr18Ni9	India	Wire, rod	0.12 **C**, 2.0 **Mn**, 1.0 **Si**, 17.0–19.0 **Cr**, 8.0–10.0 **Ni**, 0.030 **S**, 0.045 **P**	**Annealed**
BS 1506–713	Grade AX	UK	Bar	0.12 **C**, 1.00 **Mn**, 1.00 **Si**, 11.50–13.50 **Cr**, 1.00 **Ni**, 0.045 **P**, 0.045 **S**	**Hardened and tempered AX 1200°F (650°C) to 1380°F (750°C)**
BS 1506–713	Grade BX	UK	Bar	0.12 **C**, 1.00 **Mn**, 1.00 **Si**, 11.5–13.50 **Cr**, 1.00 **Ni**, 0.045 **P**, 0.045 **S**	**Hardened and tempered BX 550°C (1020°F) min**
BS 1506–713	Grade TX	UK	Bar	0.12 **C**, 1.00 **Mn**, 1.00 **Si**, 11.5–13.50 **Cr**, 1.00 **Ni**, 0.045 **P**, 0.045 **S**	**Hardened and tempered TX 500°C (930°F) min**
BS 1506–713	Grade WX	UK	Bar	0.12 **C**, 1.00 **Mn**, 1.00 **Si**, 11.5–13.50 **Cr**, 1.00 **Ni**, 0.045 **P**, 0.045 **S**	**Hardened and tempered WX 200°C (390°F) to 500°C (930°F)**
NF A 36–209	Z 10 CN 18–09	France	Plate	0.12 **C**, 2.0 **Mn**, 1.0 **Si**, 17.0–19.0 **Cr**, 8.0–10.0 **Ni**, 0.040 **P**, 0.030 **S**	
JIS G 4308	SUS 305	Japan	Wire, rod	0.12 **C**, 2.00 **Mn**, 1.00 **Si**, 17.00–19.00 **Cr**, 10.50–13.00 **Ni**, 0.040 **P**, 0.030 **S**	
JIS G 4308	SUS 430	Japan	Wire, rod	0.12 **C**, 1.00 **Mn**, 0.75 **Si**, 16.00–18.00 **Cr**, 0.60 **Ni**, 0.040 **P**, 0.030 **S**	
JIS G 4308	SUS 430 F	Japan	Wire, rod	0.12 **C**, 1.25 **Mn**, 1.00 **Si**, 16.00–18.00 **Cr**, 0.60 **Ni**, 0.60 **Mo**, 0.060 **P**, 0.15 **S**	
JIS G 4316	SUS Y 309	Japan	Wire, rod	0.12 **C**, 1.00–2.50 **Mn**, 0.60 **Si**, 23.00–25.00 **Cr**, 12.00–14.00 **Ni**, 0.030 **P**, 0.030 **S**	
JIS G 4316	SUS Y 309 Mo	Japan	Wire, rod	0.12 **C**, 1.00–2.50 **Mn**, 0.60 **Si**, 23.00–25.00 **Cr**, 12.00–14.00 **Ni**, 2.00–3.00 **Mo**, 0.030 **P**, 0.030 **S**	
JIS G 4316	SUS Y 410	Japan	Wire, rod	0.12 **C**, 0.60 **Mn**, 0.50 **Si**, 11.50–13.50 **Cr**, 0.60 **Ni**, 0.60 **Mo**, 0.030 **P**, 0.030 **S**	
CSA G110.3	Type 305	Canada	Bar, billets	0.12 **C**, 2.00 **Mn**, 1.00 **Si**, 17.00–19.00 **Cr**, 10.00–13.00 **Ni**, 0.045 **P**, 0.030 **S**	
CSA G110.3	Type 430	Canada	Bar, billets	0.12 **C**, 1.00 **Mn**, 1.00 **Si**, 14.00–18.00 **Cr**, 0.040 **P**, 0.030 **S**	

WROUGHT STAINLESS STEELS

specification number	designation	country	product forms	composition	mechanical properties (see page iv for explanation)
CSA G110.3	Type 430F	Canada	Bar, billets	0.12 **C**, 1.25 **Mn**, 1.00 **Si**, 14.00–18.00 **Cr**, 0.60 **Mo**, 0.06 **P**, 0.15 min **S**	
CSA G110.3	Type 430F Se	Canada	Bar, billets	0.12 **C**, 1.25 **Mn**, 1.00 **Si**, 14.00–18.00 **Cr**, 0.06 **P**, 1.00 **S**, 0.15 min **Se**	
NF A 35–590	3636 (Z12 NCS 37.18)	France	Bar, forgings	0.12 **C**, 1.50 **Mn**, 2.0 **Si**, 18.0 **Cr**, 37.0 **Ni**, 0.030 **P**, 0.030 **S**	
NF A 35–572	Z 15 CN 16.02	France	Bar, sections	0.10–0.20 **C**, 1.0 **Mn**, 1.0 **Si**, 15.0–17.0 **Cr**, 1.5–3.0 **Ni**, 0.04 **P**, 0.03 **S**	**Quenched and tempered**: (≤25) **diam**, (880) **TS**, (685) **YS**, 12 **El**
ISO 683/XII	9	ISO	Bar, sheet, plate	0.10–0.20 **C**, 1.0 **Mn**, 1.0 **Si**, 15.0–18.0 **Cr**, 1.5–3.0 **Ni**, 0.040 **P**, 0.030 **S**	**Quenched and tempered**: all **diam**, (830) **TS**, (640) **YS**, 10 **El**
IS 6603	15Cr16Ni2	India	Bar	0.10–0.20 **C**, 1.0 **Mn**, 1.0 **Si**, 15.0–18.0 **Cr**, 1.5–3.0 **Ni**, 0.040 **P**, 0.030 **S**	**Annealed**: (5–100) **diam**, (830) **TS**, (640) **YS**, 10 **El**
IS 6911	15Cr16Ni2	India	Plate, sheet, strip	0.10–0.20 **C**, 1.0 **Mn**, 1.0 **Si**, 15.0–18.0 **Cr**, 1.5–3.0 **Ni**, 0.030 **S**, 0.040 **P**	**Annealed**: all **diam**, (830) **TS**, (640) **YS**, 10 **El**
ASTM A 336	F10	US	Forgings	0.10–0.20 **C**, 0.50–0.80 **Mn**, 1.00–1.40 **Si**, 7.00–9.00 **Cr**, 19.00–22.00 **Ni**	**Solution annealed**: all **diam**, 80 (550) **TS**, 30 (205) **YS**, 25 **El**
ASTM A 336	F10	US	Forgings	0.10–0.20 **C**, 0.50–0.80 **Mn**, 1.00–1.40 **Si**, 7.00–9.00 **Cr**, 19.00–22.00 **Ni**, 0.030 **P**, 0.030 **S**	**Solution annealed**: all **diam**, 80 (550) **TS**, 30 (205) **YS**, 25 **El**
ANSI/ASTM A 336	Grade F10	US	Forgings	0.10–0.20 **C**, 0.50–0.80 **Mn**, 1.00–1.40 **Si**, 7.00–9.00 **Cr**, 19.00–22.00 **Ni**, 0.030 **P**, 0.030 **S**	**Solution annealed**: all **diam**, (550) **TS**, (205) **YS**, 25 **El**
IS 6529	15Cr16Ni2	India	Blooms, billets, slabs	0.10–0.20 **C**, 1.0 **Mn**, 1.0 **Si**, 15.0–18.0 **Cr**, 1.5–3.0 **Ni**, 0.040 **P**, 0.030 **S**	**Annealed or solution annealed**
SIS 14 23 83	SIS 23 83–03	Sweden	Bar, wire	0.10–0.17 **C**, 1.5 **Mn**, 1.0 **Si**, 16.0–18.0 **Cr**, 0.5 **Ni**, 0.60 **Mo**, 0.060 **P**, 0.15–0.35 **S**	**Quenched and tempered**: all **diam**, (640) **TS**, (440) **YS**, 12 **El**
DIN 17440	Grade X 12 CrMoS 17	Germany	Sheet, strip, bar, wire, tube, forgings	0.10–0.17 **C**, 1.5 **Mn**, 1.0 **Si**, 15.5–17.5 **Cr**, 0.2–0.3 **Mo**, 0.040 **P**, 0.15–0.35 **S**	**Annealed**: (≤5) **diam**, (550) **TS**, (300) **YS**, 20 **El**; **Tempered**: (≤15) **diam**, (700) **TS**, (450) **YS**, 12 **El**
SIS 14 23 83	SIS 23 83–02	Sweden	Bar, wire	0.10–0.17 **C**, 1.5 **Mn**, 1.0 **Si**, 16.0–18.0 **Cr**, 0.5 **Ni**, 0.60 **Mo**, 0.060 **P**, 0.15–0.35 **S**	**Annealed**: all **diam**, (490) **TS**, (250) **YS**, 18 **El**
MIL–W–8958		US	Wire	0.10–0.15 **C**, 0.50–1.25 **Mn**, 0.50 **Si**, 15.00–16.00 **Cr**, 4.00–5.00 **Ni**, 2.50–3.25 **Mo**, 0.17–0.28 **C+N**, 0.07–0.13 **N**, 0.040 **P**, 0.030 **S**	**Cold drawn**: 0.040–0.045 **diam**, 380 (2620) **TS**
ASTM A 693	Type 634	US	Plate, sheet, strip	0.10–0.15 **C**, 0.50–1.25 **Mn**, 0.50 **Si**, 15.00–16.00 **Cr**, 4.00–5.00 **Ni**, 2.50–3.25 **Mo**, 0.040 **P**, 0.030 **S**	**Precipitation hardened**: all **diam**, 190 (1310) **TS**, 165 (1140) **YS**, 10 **El**
MIL–S–8840B	AM 355	US	Sheet, strip	0.10–0.15 **C**, 0.50–1.25 **Mn**, 0.50 **Si**, 15.00–16.00 **Cr**, 4.00–5.00 **Ni**, 2.50–3.25 **Mo**, 0.07–0.13 **N**, 0.040 **P**, 0.030 **S**	**Reheat treated to SCT 1000**: >0.020–0.1875 **diam**, (1172) **TS**, (1034) **YS**, 8 **El**
ISO 683/XVI	6	ISO	Forgings, bar, plate, sheet, strip, wire	0.10–0.15 **C**, 0.50–1.25 **Mn**, 0.50 **Si**, 15.0–16.0 **Cr**, 4.00–5.00 **Ni**, 2.50–3.25 **Mo**, 0.070–0.13 **N**, 0.040 **P**, 0.030 **S**	**Precipitation hardened (bar, forgings, wire, rod)**: all **diam**, (1170) **TS**, (1070) **YS**, 11 **El**
ANSI/ASTM A 579	64	US	Forgings	0.10–0.15 **C**, 0.50–1.25 **Mn**, 0.50 **Si**, 15.0–16.0 **Cr**, 4.0–5.0 **Ni**, 2.50–3.25 **Mo**, 0.07–0.13 **N**, 0.025 **P**, 0.025 **S**	**Precipitation hardened**: all **diam**, 165 (1140) **TS**, 140 (965) **YS**, 12 **El**
AMS 5547C		US	Strip, sheet	0.10–0.15 **C**, 0.50–1.25 **Mn**, 0.50 **Si**, 15.00–16.00 **Cr**, 4.00–5.00 **Ni**, 2.50–3.25 **Mo**, 0.07–0.13 **N**, 0.040 **P**, 0.030 **S**	**Solution treated**: all **diam**, 165 (1138) **TS**, 140 (965) **YS**, 10 **El**
AMS 5549C		US	Plate	0.10–0.15 **C**, 0.50–1.25 **Mn**, 0.50 **Si**, 15.00–16.00 **Cr**, 4.00–5.00 **Ni**, 2.50–3.25 **Mo**, 0.07–0.13 **N**, 0.040 **P**, 0.030 **S**	**Solution treated**: all **diam**, 165 (1138) **TS**, 140 (965) **YS**, 12 **El**

WROUGHT STAINLESS STEELS

specification number	designation	country	product forms	composition	mechanical properties (see page iv for explanation)
AIR 9160	9160C151	France	Bar, sheet, tube, forgings	0.10–0.15 **C**, 0.30–0.60 **Mn**, 0.80 **Si**, 11.5–13.0 **Cr**, 0.30–0.80 **Ni**, 0.035 **P**, 0.025 **S**	**Quenched and tempered (bar)**: (≤70) **diam**, (590) **TS**, (410) **YS**, 160 **El**
ASTM A 705	634	US	Forgings	0.10–0.15 **C**, 0.50–1.25 **Mn**, 0.50 **Si**, 15.00–16.00 **Cr**, 4.00–5.00 **Ni**, 2.50–3.25 **Mo**, 0.07–0.13 **N**, 0.040 **P**, 0.030 **S**	**Solution annealed**
AMS 5780		US	Wire	0.10–0.15 **C**, 0.50–1.25 **Mn**, 0.50 max **Si**, 15.00–16.00 **Cr**, 4.00–5.00 **Ni**, 2.50–3.25 **Mo**, 0.07–0.13 **N**, 0.040 **P**, 0.030 **S**	
AMS 5613L		US	Bar, forgings, tube, rings	0.10–0.15 **C**, 1.00 **Mn**, 1.00 **Si**, 11.50–13.50 **Cr**, 0.75 **Ni**, 0.50 **Mo**, 0.50 **Cu**, 0.05 **Al**, 0.08 **N**, 0.040 **P**, 0.030 **S**, 0.05	
ANSI/ASTM A 564	634	US	Bar, shapes	0.10–0.15 **C**, 0.50–1.25 **Mn**, 0.50 **Si**, 15.00–16.00 **Cr**, 4.00–5.00 **Ni**, 2.50–3.25 **Mo**, 0.07–0.13 **N**, 0.040 **P**, 0.030 **S**	**Solution annealed**
AIR 9160	9160C141	France	Bar, forgings	0.10 **C**, 1.50 **Mn**, 1.0 **Si**, 15.0–17.0 **Cr**, 3.50–5.0 **Ni**, 0.80–1.50 **Mo**, 0.035 **P**, 0.025 **S**	**Annealed, solution treated and tempered**: all **diam**, (900) **TS**, (700) **YS**, 16 **El**; **Solution treated and tempered**: all **diam**, (1100) **TS**, (900) **YS**, 14 **El**
AISI 329		US	Strip, bar	0.10 **C**, 2.00 **Mn**, 1.00 **Si**, 25.00–30.00 **Cr**, 3.00–6.00 **Ni**, 1.00–2.00 **Mo**, 0.040 **P**, 0.030 **S**	**Annealed**: all **diam**, 105 (724) max **TS**, 80 (552) max **YS**, 25 **El**
NF A 35-577	Z 8 CN 18.12 (DF)	France	Bar, wire, rod	0.10 **C**, 2.0 **Mn**, 1.0 **Si**, 17.0–19.0 **Cr**, 11.0–13.0 **Ni**, 0.040 **P**, 0.030 **S**	**Solution annealed**: (6) **diam**, (620) max **TS**
NF A 35-575	Z 8 CD 17.01	France	Wire, rod	0.10 **C**, 1.0 **Mn**, 1.0 **Si**, 16.0–18.0 **Cr**, 0.50 **Ni**, 0.9–1.3 **Mo**, 0.040 **P**, 0.030 **S**	**Stress hardened 0%**: all **diam**, (590) **TS**; **Stress hardened 40%**: all **diam**, (780) **TS**; **Stress hardened 60%**: all **diam**, (880) **TS**
NF A 35-577	Z 8 C 17	France	Bar, wire, rod	0.10 **C**, 1.0 **Mn**, 1.0 **Si**, 16.0–18.0 **Cr**, 0.5 **Ni**, 0.040 **P**, 0.030 **S**	**Annealed**: (6) **diam**, (560) max **TS**
NF A 35-575	Z 8 CN 18.12	France	Wire, rod	0.10 **C**, 2.0 **Mn**, 1.0 **Si**, 17.0–19.0 **Cr**, 11.0–13.0 **Ni**, 0.040 **P**, 0.030 **S**	**Stress hardened 0%**: all **diam**, (540) **TS**; **Stress hardened 40%**: all **diam**, (1030) **TS**; **Stress hardened 60%**: all **diam**, (1220) **TS**; **Stress hardened 80%**: all **diam**, (1470) **TS**; **Austenitized**: all **diam**, (490) **TS**, (180) **YS**, 50 **El**
NF A 35-575	Z 8 C 17	France	Wire, rod	0.10 **C**, 1.0 **Mn**, 1.0 **Si**, 16.0–18.0 **Cr**, 0.50 **Ni**, 0.040 **P**, 0.030 **S**	**Stress hardened 0%**: all **diam**, (540) **TS**; **Stress hardened 40%**: all **diam**, (730) **TS**; **Stress hardened 60%**: all **diam**, (830) **TS**; **Stress hardened 80%**: all **diam**, (1030) **TS**
DIN 17440	Grade X 10 CrNiTi 18 9	Germany	Sheet, strip, bar, wire, tube, forgings	0.10 **C**, 2.0 **Mn**, 1.0 **Si**, 17.0–19.0 **Cr**, 9.0–11.5 **Ni**, 0.045 **P**, 0.030 **S**, 5 x C min **Ti**	**Quenched**: (≤20) **diam**, (500) **TS**, (205) **YS**, 40 **El**
DIN 17440	Grade X 10 CrNiNb 18 9	Germany	Sheet, strip, bar, wire, tube, forgings	0.10 **C**, 2.0 **Mn**, 1.0 **Si**, 17.0–19.0 **Cr**, 9.0–11.5 **Ni**, 8 x C min **Nb**, 0.045 **P**, 0.030 **S**	**Quenched**: (≤60) **diam**, (500) **TS**, (205) **YS**, 40 **El**
DIN 17440	Grade X 10 CrNiMoTi 18 10	Germany	Sheet, strip, bar, wire, tube, forgings	0.10 **C**, 2.0 **Mn**, 1.0 **Si**, 16.5–18.5 **Cr**, 10.5–13.5 **Ni**, 2.0–2.5 **Mo**, 0.045 **P**, 0.030 **S**, 5 x C min **Ti**	**Quenched**: (≤20) **diam**, (500) **TS**, (225) **YS**, 40 **El**
DIN 17440	Grade X10 CrNiMoNb 18 10	Germany	Sheet, strip, bar, wire, tube, forgings	0.10 **C**, 2.0 **Mn**, 1.0 **Si**, 16.5–18.5 **Cr**, 10.5–13.5 **Ni**, 2.0–2.5 **Mo**, 8 x C min **Nb**, 0.045 **P**, 0.030 **S**	**Quenched**: (≤60) **diam**, (500) **TS**, (225) **YS**, 40 **El**
ISO 683/XII	13	ISO	Bar, sheet, plate	0.10 **C**, 2.0 **Mn**, 1.0 **Si**, 17.0–19.0 **Cr**, 11.0–13.0 **Ni**, 0.045 **P**, 0.030 **S**	**Solution treated**: all **diam**, (490) **TS**, (180) **YS**, 40 **El**

WROUGHT STAINLESS STEELS

specification number	designation	country	product forms	composition	mechanical properties (see page iv for explanation)
EURONORM 119–74, V	X 8 CrNi 18 12 KD	EURONORM	Wire, rod	0.10 **C**, 2.0 **Mn**, 1.0 **Si**, 17.0–19.0 **Cr**, 11.0–13.0 **Ni**, 0.045 **P**, 0.030 **S**	**Solution annealed:** (15–63) **diam**, (490) **TS**, (175) **YS**, 40 **El**
ISO 2604/IV	P52	ISO	Plate	0.10 **C**, 2.00 **Mn**, 1.00 **Si**, 17.0–19.0 **Cr**, 10.0–12.0 **Ni**, 0.50 **Mo**, 8 x C–1.0 **Nb**, 0.045 **P**, 0.030 **S**	**Hot rolled, quenched:** (3–16) **diam**, (490) **TS**, (205) **YS**, 35 **El**
ISO 2604/IV	P55	ISO	Plate	0.10 **C**, 2.00 **Mn**, 1.00 **Si**, 17.0–19.0 **Cr**, 10.0–12.0 **Ni**, 0.50 **Mo**, 0.045 **P**, 0.030 **S**, 5 x C–0.80 **Ti**	**Hot rolled, quenched:** (3–16) **diam**, (490) **TS**, (195) **YS**, 35 **El**
NF A 35–572	Z 8 CD 17–01	France	Sheet, strip, plate, bar, sections	0.10 **C**, 1.0 **Mn**, 1.0 **Si**, 16.0–18.0 **Cr**, 0.50 **Ni**, 0.9–1.3 **Mo**, 0.04 **P**, 0.03 **S**	**Austenitized (bars, sections):** (≤25) **diam**, (490) **TS**, (275) **YS**, 18 **El**
ANSI/ASTM A 493	Type XM–7	US	Bar, wire	0.10 **C**, 2.00 **Mn**, 1.00 **Si**, 17.00–19.00 **Cr**, 8.00–10.00 **Ni**, 3.00–4.00 **Cu**, 0.045 **P**, 0.030	**Lightly drafted, annealed (wire):** ≥0.156 (≥3.96) **diam**, 70 (485) **TS**
CSA G110.5	Type 434	Canada	Sheet	0.10 **C**, 1.00 **Mn**, 1.00 **Si**, 16.00–20.00 **Cr**, 0.60 **Ni**, 0.75–1.25 **Mo**, 0.040 **P**, 0.030 **S**	**Hot rolled, annealed, quenched and tempered:** all **diam**, 70 (483) **TS**, 30 (207) **YS**, 20 **El**
AISI 502		US	Sheet, strip, plate, bar, wire	0.10 **C**, 1.00 **Mn**, 1.00 **Si**, 4.00–6.00 **Cr**, 0.40–0.65 **Mo**	**Annealed (sheet):** all **diam**, 70 (483) max **TS**, 30 **El**
IS 6528	05Cr17	India	Wire	0.10 **C**, 1.0 **Mn**, 1.0 **Si**, 16.0–18.0 **Cr**, 0.50 **Ni**, 0.040 **P**, 0.030 **S**	**Annealed or solution annealed:** all **diam**, (480) **TS**, (270) **YS**, 16 **El**
BS 1449 Part 2	Grade 305S19	UK	Sheet, strip	0.10 **C**, 0.50–2.00 **Mn**, 0.20–1.00 **Si**, 17.0–19.0 **Cr**, 11.0–13.0 **Ni**, 0.045 **P**, 0.030 **S**	**Solution annealed:** (≥3.0) **diam**, (460) **TS**, (170) **YS**, 40 **El**
DIN 17440	Grade X 8 Cr 17	Germany	Sheet, strip, bar, wire, tube, forgings	0.10 **C**, 1.0 **Mn**, 1.0 **Si**, 15.5–17.5 **Cr**, 0.045 **P**, 0.030 **S**	**Annealed:** (≤5) **diam**, (450) **TS**, (270) **YS**, 20 **El**
DIN 17440	Grade X 8 CrTi 17	Germany	Sheet, strip, bar, wire, tube, forgings	0.10 **C**, 1.0 **Mn**, 1.0 **Si**, 16.0–18.0 **Cr**, 0.045 **P**, 0.030 **S**, 7 x C min **Ti**	**Annealed:** (≤5) **diam**, (450) **TS**, (270) **YS**, 20 **El**
DIN 17440	Grade X 8 CrNb 17	Germany	Sheet, strip, bar, wire, tube, forgings	0.10 **C**, 1.0 **Mn**, 1.0 **Si**, 16.0–18.0 **Cr**, 12 x C min **Nb**, 0.045 **P**, 0.030 **S**	**Annealed:** (≤5) **diam**, (450) **TS**, (270) **YS**, 20 **El**
JIS G 4312	SUH 21	Japan	Sheet, plate	0.10 **C**, 1.00 **Mn**, 1.50 **Si**, 17.00–21.00 **Cr**, 0.60 **Ni**, 2.00–4.00 **Al**, 0.040 **P**, 0.030 **S**	**Annealed:** all **diam**, (441) **TS**, (245) **YS**, 15 **El**
ISO 683/XII	8	ISO	Bar, sheet, plate	0.10 **C**, 1.0 **Mn**, 1.0 **Si**, 16.0–18.0 **Cr**, 0.50 **Ni**, 0.040 **P**, 0.030 **S**	**Annealed:** all **diam**, (440) **TS**, (250) **YS**, 18 **El**
ISO 683/XII	9c	ISO	Bar, sheet, plate	0.10 **C**, 1.0 **Mn**, 1.0 **Si**, 16.0–18.0 **Cr**, 0.90–1.30 **Mo**, 0.040 **P**, 0.030 **S**	**Annealed:** all **diam**, (440) **TS**, (250) **YS**, 18 **El**
EURONORM 119–74,V	X 8 Cr 17 KD	EURONORM	Wire, rod	0.10 **C**, 1.0 **Mn**, 1.0 **Si**, 16.0–18.0 **Cr**, 0.50 **Ni**, 0.040 **P**, 0.030 **S**	**Annealed:** (1.5–15) **diam**, (440) **TS**, (245) **YS**, 18 **El**
IS 6603	05Cr17	India	Bar	0.10 **C**, 1.0 **Mn**, 1.0 **Si**, 16.0–18.0 **Cr**, 0.50 **Ni**, 0.040 **P**, 0.030 **S**	**Annealed:** (5–25) **diam**, (440) **TS**, (250) **YS**, 16 **El**
IS 6911	05Cr17	India	Plate, sheet, strip	0.10 **C**, 1.0 **Mn**, 1.0 **Si**, 16.0–18.0 **Cr**, 0.50 **Ni**, 0.030 **S**, 0.040 **P**	**Annealed:** (0.5–3.0) **diam**, (440) **TS**, (250) **YS**, 17 **El**
NF A 35–572	Z 8 C 17	France	Sheet, strip, plate, bar, sections	0.10 **C**, 1.0 **Mn**, 1.0 **Si**, 16.0–18.0 **Cr**, 0.50 **Ni**, 0.04 **P**, 0.03 **S**	**Annealed:** (5–25) **diam**, (440) **TS**, (245) **YS**, 18 **El**
SIS 14 23 20	SIS 23 20–02	Sweden	Bar, forgings, plate, sheet, strip, tube, wire	0.10 **C**, 1.0 **Mn**, 1.0 **Si**, 16.0–18.0 **Cr**, 0.50 **Ni**, 0.040 **P**, 0.030 **S**	**Annealed (except strip, wire):** all **diam**, (440) **TS**, (250) **YS**, 18 **El**
BS 1449 Part 2	Grade 442S19	UK	Sheet, strip	0.10 **C**, 1.00 **Mn**, 0.80 **Si**, 18.0–22.0 **Cr**, 0.50 **Ni**, 0.040 **P**, 0.030 **S**	**Solution annealed:** (≥3.0) **diam**, (430) **TS**, (245) **YS**, 22 **El**
BS 1449 Part 2	Grade 430S15	UK	Plate, sheet, strip	0.10 **C**, 1.00 **Mn**, 0.80 **Si**, 16.0–18.0 **Cr**, 0.50 **Ni**, 0.040 **P**, 0.030 **S**	**Solution annealed:** (≥3.0) (sheet and strip) **diam**, (430) **TS**, (245) **YS**, 22 **El**
BS 1449 Part 2	Grade 434S19	UK	Sheet, strip	0.10 **C**, 1.00 **Mn**, 0.80 **Si**, 16.0–18.0 **Cr**, 0.50 **Ni**, 0.90–1.30 **Mo**, 0.040 **P**, 0.030 **S**	**Solution annealed:** (≥3.0) **diam**, (430) **TS**, (245) **YS**, 22 **El**

WROUGHT STAINLESS STEELS

specification number	designation	country	product forms	composition	mechanical properties (see page iv for explanation)
BS 970 Part 4	Grade 430S.15	UK	Blooms, billets, bar, forgings	0.10 **C**, 1.00 **Mn**, 0.80 **Si**, 16.0–18.0 **Cr**, 0.50 **Ni**, 0.040 **P**, 0.030 **S**	**Annealed:** ≤2.5 **diam**, (430) **TS**, (280) **YS**, 20 **El**
ANSI/ASTM A 268	TP 430 Ti	US	Tube: seamless, welded	0.10 **C**, 1.00 **Mn**, 1.00 **Si**, 16.00–19.50 **Cr**, 0.75 **Ni**, 0.040 **P**, 0.030 **S**, 12 x C–0.75 **Ti**	**Annealed:** 0.312 (7.94) **diam**, 60 (414) **TS**, 35 (241) **YS**, 20 **El**
ASTM A 651	TP 430 Ti	US	Tube: seamless or welded	0.10 **C**, 1.00 **Mn**, 1.00 **Si**, 16.00–19.50 **Cr**, 0.75 **Ni**, 0.040 **P**, 0.030 **S**, 5 x C–0.75 **Ti**	**As welded or as drawn:** all **diam**, 60 (414) **TS**, 30 (207) **YS**
ANSI/ASTM A 554	MT–430–Ti	US	Tube: welded	0.10 **C**, 1.00 **Mn**, 1.00 **Si**, 16.0–19.5 **Cr**, 0.075 **Ni**, 0.040 **P**, 0.030 **S**, 5 x C–0.75 **Ti**	**Round annealed:** 0.312 (7.94) **diam**, 60 (414) **TS**, 30 (207) **YS**, 20 **El**
AMS 7724		US	Wire: iron base	0.10 **C**, 1.00–2.00 **Mn**, 1.00 **Si**, 20.00–22.50 **Cr**, 19.00–21.00 **Ni**, 2.50–3.50 **Mo**, 2.00–3.00 **W**, 18.50–21.00 **Co**, 0.75–1.25 **Nb+Ta**, 0.10–0.20 **N**, 0.040 **P**, 0.030 **S**; rem Fe	**As sintered:** all **diam**, (250) **TS**, (135) **YS**, 10 **El**
DGN–B–150	Type AE–430	Mexico	Wire	0.10 **C**, 0.60 **Mn**, 0.50 **Si**, 15.5–17.0 **Cr**, 0.60 **Ni**, 0.60 **Mo**, 0.07 N_2, 0.030 **P**, 0.030 **S**	
MIL–S–862B	Class 322	US	Bar, forgings	0.10 **C**, 1.0 **Mn**, 1.5 **Si**, 16.0–18.0 **Cr**, 6.0–8.0 **Ni**, 0.50 **Al**, 0.045 **P**, 0.030 **S**, 1.5 **Ti**	
IS 6529	05Cr17	India	Blooms, billets, slabs	0.10 **C**, 1.0 **Mn**, 1.0 **Si**, 16.0–18.0 **Cr**, 0.50 **Ni**, 0.040 **P**, 0.030 **S**	**Annealed or solution annealed**
IS 6527	05Cr17	India	Wire, rod	0.10 **C**, 1.0 **Mn**, 1.0 **Si**, 16.0–18.0 **Cr**, 0.50 **Ni**, 0.030 **S**, 0.040 **P**	**Annealed**
NF A 36–209	Z 8 CN 18–12	France	Plate	0.10 **C**, 2.0 **Mn**, 1.0 **Si**, 17.0–19.0 **Cr**, 11.0–13.0 **Ni**, 0.040 **P**, 0.030 **S**	
NF A 36–209	Z 8 CNDT 17–12	France	Plate	0.10 **C**, 2.0 **Mn**, 1.0 **Si**, 16.0–18.0 **Cr**, 11.0–13.0 **Ni**, 2.0–2.5 **Mo**, 0.040 **P**, 0.030 **S**, 5 x C–0.60 **Ti** or 10 x C–1.0 **Nb+Ta**	
NF A 35–583	Z 8 C 17	France	Wire, rod	0.10 **C**, 1.0 **Mn**, 0.75 **Si**, 15.5–18.0 **Cr**, 0.50 **Ni**, 0.50 **Mo**, 0.030 **P**, 0.020 **S**	
SIS 14 23 40	SIS 24 40–02	Sweden	Wire	0.10 **C**, 2.0 **Mn**, 1.0 **Si**, 16.5–18.0 **Cr**, 8.0–10.0 **Ni**, 1.3–1.8 **Mo**, 0.045 **P**, 0.030 **S**	
SIS 14 23 40	SIS 23 40–04	Sweden	Bar, wire	0.10 **C**, 2.0 **Mn**, 1.0 **Si**, 16.5–18.0 **Cr**, 8.0–10.0 **Ni**, 1.3–1.8 **Mo**, 0.045 **P**, 0.030 **S**	**Cold worked:** all **diam**, (780) **YS**, 10 **El**
JIS G 4316	SUS Y 430	Japan	Wire, rod	0.10 **C**, 0.60 **Mn**, 0.50 **Si**, 15.50–17.00 **Cr**, 0.60 **Ni**, 0.030 **P**, 0.030 **S**	
CSA G110.3	Type 502	Canada	Bar, billets	0.10 **C**, 1.00 **Mn**, 1.00 **Si**, 4.00–6.00 **Cr**, 0.40–0.65 **Mo**, 0.040 **P**, 0.030 **S**	
AISI 501		US	Bar, plate	0.10 min **C**, 1.00 **Mn**, 1.00 **Si**, 4.00–6.00 **Cr**, 0.40–0.65 **Mo**	**Annealed (bar):** all **diam**, 70 (483) max **TS**, 30 (207) max **YS**, 28 **El**; **Oil quenched from 1650°F (898°C) and tempered at: 1000°F (538°C) (bar): all diam, 175 (1207) max TS, 135 (931) max YS, 15 El; 1100°F (593°C) (bar): all diam, 140 (965) max TS, 110 (758) max YS, 18 El; 1200°F (649°C) (bar): all diam, 115 (793) max TS, 90 (621) max YS, 20 El**
CSA G110.3	Type 501	Canada	Bar, billets	0.10 min **C**, 1.00 **Mn**, 1.00 **Si**, 4.00–6.00 **Cr**, 0.40–0.65 **Mo**, 0.040 **P**, 0.030 **S**	
IS 6528	12Cr13	India	Wire	0.09–0.15 **C**, 1.0 **Mn**, 1.0 **Si**, 11.5–14.0 **Cr**, 1.0 **Ni**, 0.040 **P**, 0.030 **S**	**Intermediate temper:** all **diam**, (690) **TS**, (550) **YS**, 12 **El**

WROUGHT STAINLESS STEELS

specification number	designation	country	product forms	composition	mechanical properties (see page iv for explanation)
ISO 683/XII	3	ISO	Bar, sheet, plate	0.09–0.15 **C**, 1.0 **Mn**, 1.0 **Si**, 11.5–14.0 **Cr**, 1.0 **Ni**, 0.040 **P**, 0.030 **S**	**Quenched and tempered**: all **diam**, (590) **TS**, (410) **YS**, 16 **El**
EURONORM 119–74, V	X 12 Cr 13 KD	EURONORM	Wire, rod	0.09–0.15 **C**, 1.0 **Mn**, 1.0 **Si**, 11.5–14.0 **Cr**, 0.50 **Ni**, 0.040 **P**, 0.030 **S**	**Annealed**: (1.5–63) **diam**, (590) **TS**, (410) **YS**, 16 **El**
IS 6603	12Cr13	India	Bar	0.09–0.15 **C**, 1.0 **Mn**, 1.0 **Si**, 11.5–14.5 **Cr**, 1.0 **Ni**, 0.040 **P**, 0.030 **S**	**Annealed (martensitic)**: (5–100) **diam**, (590) **TS**, (410) **YS**, 16 **El**
IS 6911	12Cr13	India	Plate, sheet, strip	0.09–0.15 **C**, 1.0 **Mn**, 1.0 **Si**, 11.5–14.5 **Cr**, 1.0 **Ni**, 0.030 **S**, 0.040 **P**	**Annealed**: all **diam**, (590) **TS**, (410) **YS**, 16 **El**
SIS 14 23 02	SIS 23 02–03	Sweden	Bar, forgings, plate, sheet, strip, wire	0.09–0.15 **C**, 1.0 **Mn**, 1.0 **Si**, 12.0–14.0 **Cr**, 1.0 **Ni**, 0.040 **P**, 0.030 **S**	**Quenched and tempered (except wire)**: all **diam**, (590) **TS**, (410) **YS**, 16 **El**
BS 970 Part 4	Grade 410S.21	UK	Blooms, billets, bar, forgings	0.09–0.15 **C**, 1.00 **Mn**, 0.80 **Si**, 11.5–13.5 **Cr**, 1.00 **Ni**, 0.040 **P**, 0.030 **S**	**Hardened and tempered**: ≤6 **diam**, (540) **TS**, (370) **YS**, 20 **El**
BS 970 Part 4	Grade 416S21	UK	Blooms, billets, bar, forgings	0.09–0.15 **C**, 1.50 **Mn**, 1.00 **Si**, 11.5–13.5 **Cr**, 1.00 **Ni**, 0.60 **Mo**, 0.040 **P**, 0.15–0.30 **S**	**Hardened and tempered**: ≤6 **diam**, (540) **TS**, (370) **YS**, 15 **El**
BS 970 Part 4	Grade 416S41	UK	Blooms, billets, bar, forgings	0.09–0.15 **C**, 1.50 **Mn**, 1.00 **Si**, 11.5–13.5 **Cr**, 1.00 **Ni**, 0.60 **Mo**, 0.040 **P**, 0.060 **S**, 0.15–0.30 **Se**	**Hardened and tempered**: ≤6 **diam**, (540) **TS**, (370) **YS**, 15 **El**
IS 6528	12Cr13	India	Wire	0.09–0.15 **C**, 1.0 **Mn**, 1.0 **Si**, 11.5–14.0 **Cr**, 1.0 **Ni**, 0.040 **P**, 0.030 **S**	**Annealed or solution annealed**: all **diam**, (480) **TS**, (270) **YS**, 16 **El**
SIS 14 23 02	SIS 23 02–02	Sweden	Bar, forgings, plate, sheet, strip, wire	0.09–0.15 **C**, 1.0 **Mn**, 1.0 **Si**, 12.0–14.0 **Cr**, 1.0 **Ni**, 0.040 **P**, 0.030 **S**	**Annealed (wire)**: all **diam**, (440) **TS**, (250) **YS**, 20 **El**
IS 6529	12Cr13	India	Blooms, billets, slabs	0.09–0.15 **C**, 1.0 **Mn**, 1.0 **Si**, 11.5–14.0 **Cr**, 1.0 **Ni**, 0.040 **P**, 0.030 **S**	**Annealed or solution annealed**
IS 6527	12Cr13	India	Wire, rod	0.09–0.15 **C**, 1.0 **Mn**, 1.0 **Si**, 11.5–14.0 **Cr**, 1.0 **Ni**, 0.030 **S**, 0.040 **P**	**Annealed**
ANSI/ASTM A 313	631	US	Wire	0.09 **C**, 1.00 **Mn**, 1.00 **Si**, 16.00–18.00 **Cr**, 6.50–7.75 **Ni**, 0.75–1.50 **Al**, 0.040 **P**, 0.030 **S**	**Cold drawn, aged 900°F: 0.010–0.015 (0.25–0.38) diam, 335 (2310) TS**
ASTM A 313	Type 631	US	Wire	0.09 **C**, 1.00 **Mn**, 1.00 **Si**, 16.00–18.00 **Cr**, 6.50–7.75 **Ni**, 0.75–1.50 **Al**, 0.040 **P**, 0.030 **S**	**Cold drawn**: 0.010–>0.015 (0.25–>0.38) **diam**, 295 (2035) **TS**; **Aged**: 0.010–>0.015 (0.25–>0.38) **diam**, 335 (2310) **TS**
DIN 17224	Grade X 7 CrNiAl 17 7	Germany	Wire, strip	0.09 **C**, 1.0 **Mn**, 1.0 **Si**, 16.0–18.0 **Cr**, 6.5–7.75 **Ni**, 0.75–1.50 **Al**	**Cold drawn (wire)**: (≤0.2) **diam**, (1962) **TS**; **Cold drawn and tempered (wire)**: (≤0.2) **diam**, (2255) **TS**; **Quenched (wire)**: (≤0.2) **diam**, (785) **TS**
AMS 5673C		US	Wire	0.09 **C**, 1.00 **Mn**, 1.00 **Si**, 16.00 18.00 **Cr**, 6.50–7.75 **Ni**, 0.75 **Mo**, 0.50 **Cu**, 0.75–1.50 **Al**, 0.040 **P**, 0.030 **S**	**As cold–drawn**: 0.016–0.020 (0.41–0.51) **diam**, 275 (1896) **TS**; **Precipitation–hardened**: 0.016–0.020 (0.41–0.51) **diam**, 335 (2310) **TS**
AMS 5529B		US	Strip, sheet	0.09 **C**, 1.00 **Mn**, 1.00 **Si**, 16.00–18.00 **Cr**, 6.50–7.75 **Ni**, 0.75–1.50 **Al**	**Solution treated and aged**: all **diam**, 240 (1655) **TS**, 230 (1586) **YS**, 1 **El**
ANSI/ASTM A 579	63	US	Forgings	0.09 **C**, 1.00 **Mn**, 0.50 **Si**, 14.0–15.25 **Cr**, 6.5–7.75 **Ni**, 2.0–2.75 **Mo**, 0.75–1.25 **Al**, 0.025 **P**, 0.025 **S**	**Precipitation hardened**: all **diam**, 225 (1555) **TS**, 200 (1380) **YS**, 5 **El**
ISO 683/XVI	3	ISO	Forgings, bar, plate, sheet, strip, wire	0.09 **C**, 1.00 **Mn**, 1.00 **Si**, 14.0–16.0 **Cr**, 6.50–7.75 **Ni**, 2.00–3.00 **Mo**, 0.75–1.50 **Al**, 0.040 **P**, 0.030 **S**	**Precipition hardened (bar, forgings, wire, rod)**: all **diam**, (1380) **TS**, (1090) **YS**, 6 **El**
ISO 683/XVI	2	ISO	Forgings, bar, plate, sheet, strip, wire	0.09 **C**, 1.00 **Mn**, 1.00 **Si**, 16.0–18.0 **Cr**, 6.50–7.75 **Ni**, 0.50 **Cu**, 0.75–1.50 **Al**, 0.040 **P**, 0.030 **S**	**Precipitation hardened (bar, forgings, wire, rod)**: all **diam**, (1270) **TS**, (1030) **YS**, 6 **El**
AMS 5568A		US	Tube	0.09 **C**, 1.00 **Mn**, 1.00 **Si**, 16.00–18.00 **Cr**, 6.50–7.75 **Ni**, 0.75–1.50 **Al**, 0.040 **P**, 0.030 **S**	**Solution treated and aged**: all **diam**, 180 (1241) **TS**, 150 (1034) **YS**, 6 **El**

WROUGHT STAINLESS STEELS

specification number	designation	country	product forms	composition	mechanical properties (see page iv for explanation)
AMS 5528D		US	Strip, plate, sheet	0.09 **C**, 1.00 **Mn**, 1.00 **Si**, 16.00–18.00 **Cr**, 6.50–7.75 **Ni**, 0.75–1.50 **Al**, 0.040 **P**, 0.030 **S**	**Solution treated:** ≥0.005–0.010 (≥0.13–0.25) **diam**, 180 (1241) **TS**, 150 (1034) **YS**, 4 **El**
ANSI/ASTM A 579	62	US	Forgings	0.09 **C**, 1.00 **Mn**, 1.00 **Si**, 16.0–18.0 **Cr**, 6.5–7.75 **Ni**, 0.75–1.50 **Al**, 0.025 **P**, 0.025 **S**	**Precipitation hardened:** all **diam**, 180 (1240) **TS**, 160 (1105) **YS**, 6 **El**
AIR 9160	9160C211	France	Bar, sheet	0.09 **C**, 1.0 **Mn**, 1.0 **Si**, 14.0–16.0 **Cr**, 6.5–7.75 **Ni**, 2.0–3.0 **Mo**, 0.75–1.50 **Al**, 0.035 **P**, 0.025 **S**	**Solution annealed and stabilized (sheet):** (<3) **diam**, (1220) **TS**, (1100) **YS**, 6 **El**
AISI S17700		US	Sheet, plate, bar	0.09 **C**, 1.00 **Mn**, 0.040 **Si**, 16.00–18.00 **Cr**, 6.50–7.75 **Ni**, 0.75–1.50 **Al**, 0.040 **P**, 0.040 **S**	**Solution treated (sheet):** all **diam**, 160 (1103) max **TS**, 145 (1000) max **YS**, 5 **El**; **Solution treated plus 900°F (482°C), 1h, air cool (sheet): all diam, 210 (1517) max TS, 200 (1379) max YS, 7 El; Solution treated plus 1150°F (620°C), 4h, air cool (sheet): all diam, 160 (1103) max TS, 150 (1034) max YS, 11 El**
ASTM A 693	Type 631	US	Plate, sheet, strip	0.09 **C**, 1.00 **Mn**, 1.00 **Si**, 16.00–18.00 **Cr**, 6.50–7.75 **Ni**, 0.75–1.50 **Al**, 0.040 **P**, 0.030 **S**	**Solution annealed**: 0.010 (0.25) max **diam**, 150 (1035) max **TS**, 65 (450) m ax **YS**; **Precipitation hardened:** 0.0015–0.0049 (0.038–0.124) **diam**, 180 (1240) **TS**, 150 (1035) **YS**, 3 **El**
ASTM A 693	Type 632	US	Plate, sheet, strip	0.09 **C**, 1.00 **Mn**, 1.00 **Si**, 14.00–16.00 **Cr**, 6.50–7.75 **Ni**, 2.00–3.00 **Mo**, 0.75–1.50 **Al**, 0.040 **P**, 0.030 **S**	**Solution annealed**: 0.0015–4.0 (0.038–102) **diam**, 150 (1035) max **TS**, 65 (450) max **YS**, 25 **El**; **Precipitation hardened:** 0.0015–0.0049 (0.038–0.124) **diam**, 190 (1310) **TS**, 170 (1170) **YS**, 2 **El**
MIL–S–8955	PH 15–7 Mo	US	Plate, sheet, strip	0.09 **C**, 1.0 **Mn**, 1.00 **Si**, 14.0–16.0 **Cr**, 6.50–7.75 **Ni**, 2.00–3.00 **Mo**, 0.75–1.50 **Al**, 0.04 **P**, 0.03 **S**; rem Fe	**Cold rolled, solution annealed:** all **diam**, (1034) max **TS**, (448) max **YS**, 25 **El**
MIL–S–25043C		US	Plate, sheet, strip	0.09 **C**, 1.00 **Mn**, 1.00 **Si**, 16.00–18.00 **Cr**, 6.50–7.75 **Ni**, 0.75–1.50 **Al**, 0.040 **P**, 0.030 **S**: rem Fe	**Annealed**: all **diam**, 150 (1034) **TS**, 65 (448) **YS**, 20 **El**
QQ–S–766C	Class 323	US	Strip, sheet, plate	0.09 **C**, 1.00 **Mn**, 1.00 **Si**, 16.00–18.00 **Cr**, 6.50–7.75 **Ni**, 0.75–1.50 **Al**, 0.045 **P**, 0.030 **S**	**Annealed, quenched and tempered**: all **diam**, 150 (1034) **TS**, 55 (379) **YS**, 20 **El**
JIS G 4304	SUS 631	Japan	Sheet, plate	0.09 **C**, 1.00 **Mn**, 1.00 **Si**, 16.00–18.00 **Cr**, 6.50–7.75 **Ni**, 0.75–1.50 **Al**, 0.040 **P**, 0.030 **S**	**Hot rolled and solution annealed**: all **diam**, (1030) **TS**, (382) **YS**, 20 **El**; **Hot rolled and aged:** (≤3.0) **diam**, (1138) **TS**, (961) **YS**, 3 **El**
JIS G 4307	SUS 631	Japan	Strip	0.09 **C**, 1.00 **Mn**, 1.00 **Si**, 16.00–18.00 **Cr**, 6.50–7.75 **Ni**, 0.75–1.50 **Al**, 0.040 **P**, 0.030 **S**	**Cold rolled and solution annealed**: all **diam**, (1030) **TS**, (382) **YS**, 20 **El**; **Cold rolled and aged:** (≤3) **diam**, (1138) **TS**, (961) **YS**, 35 **El**
JIS G 4305	SUS 631	Japan	Sheet, plate	0.09 **C**, 1.00 **Mn**, 1.00 **Si**, 16.00–18.00 **Cr**, 6.50–7.75 **Ni**, 0.75–1.50 **Al**, 0.040 **P**, 0.030 **S**	**Cold rolled and solution annealed**: all **diam**, (1030) **TS**, (382) **YS**, 20 **El**; **Cold rolled and aged:** (≤3.0) **diam**, (1138) **TS**, (961) **YS**, 3 **El**
JIS G 4306	SUS 631	Japan	Strip	0.09 **C**, 1.00 **Mn**, 1.00 **Si**, 16.00–18.00 **Cr**, 6.50–7.75 **Ni**, 0.75–1.50 **Al**, 0.040 **P**, 0.030 **S**	**Hot rolled and solution annealed**: all **diam**, (1030) **TS**, (382) **YS**, 20 **El**; **Hot rolled and aged:** (≤3.0) **diam**, (1138) **TS**, (961) **YS**, 3 **El**
JIS G 4303	SUS 631	Japan	Bar	0.09 **C**, 1.00 **Mn**, 1.00 **Si**, 16.00–18.00 **Cr**, 6.50–7.75 **Ni**, 0.75–1.50 **Al**, 0.040 **P**, 0.030 **S**	**Solution annealed**: (≤75) **diam**, (1030) **TS**, (382) **YS**, 20 **El**; **Solution annealed and aged:** (≤75) **diam**, (1138) **TS**, (961) **YS**, 5 **El**

WROUGHT STAINLESS STEELS

specification number	designation	country	product forms	composition	mechanical properties (see page iv for explanation)
JIS G 4313	SUS 631–CSP	Japan	Strip	0.09 **C**, 1.00 **Mn**, 1.00 **Si**, 12.00–14.00 **Cr**, 0.60 **Ni**, 0.040 **P**, 0.030 **S**	**Annealed:** (≥0.30) **diam**, (1030) **TS**, 20 **El**; **One half hard:** (≥0.30) **diam**, (1079) **TS**, 5 **El**; **Three quarters hard:** (≥0.30) **diam**, (1177) **TS**; **Full hard:** (≥0.30) **diam**, (1422) **TS**; **Aged:** (≥0.30) **diam**, (1138) **TS**, (961) **YS**
BS 1449 Part 2	Grade 410S21	UK	Plate, sheet, strip	0.09 **C**, 1.00 **Mn**, 0.80 **Si**, 11.5–13.5 **Cr**, 1.00 **Ni**, 0.040 **P**, 0.030 **S**	**Hardened and tempered:** (≥3.0) **diam**, (550) **TS**, (340) **YS**, 20 **El**
BS 1449 Part 2	Grade 409S17	UK	Plate, sheet, strip	0.09 **C**, 1.00 **Mn**, 0.80 **Si**, 10.5–12.5 **Cr**, 0.70 **Ni**, 0.040 **P**, 0.030 **S**, 5 x C–0.70 **Ti**	**Solution annealed:** (≥3.0) **diam**, (420) **TS**, (230) **YS**, 22 **El**
DIN 17224	X7CrNiAl177/1.4568	Germany	Wire, strip	0.09 **C**, 1.0 **Mn**, 1.0 **Si**, 16.0–18.0 **Cr**, 6.5–7.75 **Ni**, 0.7–1.50 **Al**, 0.045 **P**, 0.030 **S**	**Hard drawn (wire):** (<0.2) **diam**, (200) **TS**; **Tempered or quench–age hardened:** (<0.2) **diam**, (230) **TS**; **Quenched:** (<0.2) **diam**, (80) **TS**
ASTM A 705	632	US	Forgings	0.09 **C**, 1.00 **Mn**, 1.00 **Si**, 14.00–16.00 **Cr**, 6.50–7.7 **Ni**, 2.00–3.00 **Mo**, 0.75–1.50 **Al**, 0.040 **P**, 0.030 **S**	**Solution annealed**
ASTM A 705	631	US	Forgings	0.09 **C**, 1.00 **Mn**, 1.00 **Si**, 16.00–18.00 **Cr**, 6.50–7.75 **Ni**, 0.75–1.50 **Al**, 0.040 **P**, 0.030 **S**	**Solution annealed:** ≥0.5 (≥12.70) **diam**
MIL–W–46078B	17–7PH	US	Wire, spring	0.09 **C**, 1.00 **Mn**, 1.00 **Si**, 16.00–18.00 **Cr**, 6.50–7.75 **Ni**, 0.75–1.50 **Al**, 0.040 **P**, 0.030 **S**	
JIS G 4308	SUS 631J1	Japan	Wire, rod	0.09 **C**, 1.00 **Mn**, 1.00 **Si**, 16.00–18.00 **Cr**, 7.00–8.50 **Ni**, 0.040 **P**, 0.030 **S**	
ANSI/ASTM A 564	631	US	Bar, shapes	0.09 **C**, 1.00 **Mn**, 1.00 **Si**, 16.00–18.00 **Cr**, 6.50–7.75 **Ni**, 0.75–1.50 **Al**, 0.040 **P**, 0.030 **S**	**Solution annealed**
ANSI/ASTM A 564	632	US	Bar, shapes	0.09 **C**, 1.00 **Mn**, 1.00 **Si**, 14.00–16.00 **Cr**, 6.50–7.75 **Ni**, 2.00–3.00 **Mo**, 0.75–1.50 **Al**, 0.040 **P**, 0.030 **S**	**Solution annealed**
DGN–B–171	Grade MT302	Mexico	Tube: seamless	0.08–0.20 **C**, 2.00 **Mn**, 1.00 **Si**, 17.0–19.0 **Cr**, 8.0–10.0 **Ni**, 0.040 **P**, 0.030 **S**	**Hot or cold finished and annealed:** (≥7.92) **diam**, (519) **TS**, (206) **YS**, 35 **El**
ANSI/ASTM A 511	MT 302	US	Tube: seamless	0.08–0.20 **C**, 2.00 **Mn**, 1.00 **Si**, 17.0–19.0 **Cr**, 8.0–10.0 **Ni**, 0.040 **P**, 0.030 **S**	**Solution annealed:** 0.31 (7.9) **diam**, 75 (517) **TS**, 30 (207) **YS**, 35 **El**
JIS G 4303	SUS 410J1	Japan	Bar	0.08–0.18 **C**, 1.00 **Mn**, 0.60 **Si**, 11.50–14.00 **Cr**, 0.60 **Ni**, 0.30–0.60 **Mo**, 0.040 **P**, 0.030 **S**	**Quenched and tempered:** (≤75) **diam**, (686) **TS**, (490) **YS**, 20 **El**
ISO 683/XV	12	ISO	Bar	0.08–0.16 **C**, 1.0–2.0 **Mn**, 1.0 **Si**, 20.0–22.5 **Cr**, 19.0–21.0 **Ni**, 2.5–3.5 **Mo**, 2.0–3.0 **W**, 18.5–21.5 **Co**, 0.75–1.25 **Nb**, 0.045 **P**, 0.030 **S**	**Solution treated and precipitation hardened:** all **diam**, (885) **TS**, (390) **YS**, 25 **El**
JIS G 4311	SUH 661	Japan	Bar	0.08–0.16 **C**, 1.00–2.00 **Mn**, 1.00 **Si**, 20.00–22.50 **Cr**, 0.60 **Ni**, 2.50–3.50 **Mo**, 2.00–3.00 **W**, 18.50–21.00 **Co**, 0.10–0.20 **N**, 0.75–1.25 **Nb+Ta**, 0.040 **P**, 0.030 **S**	**Solution annealed:** (≤180) **diam**, (686) **TS**, (314) **YS**, 35 **El**; **Solution annealed and aged:** (≤75) **diam**, (755) **TS**, (343) **YS**, 30 **El**
AIR 9160	9160C241	France	Bar	0.08–0.15 **C**, 0.70–1.30 **Mn**, 0.50 **Si**, 15.0–16.0 **Cr**, 4.0–5.0 **Ni**, 2.5–3.25 **Mo**, 0.20 **Cu**, 0.05–0.15 N_2, 0.035 **P**, 0.025 **S**	**Solution annealed and stabilized at 540°C: all diam, (1150) TS, (1000) YS, 13 El; Solution annealed and stabilized at 400°C: all diam, (1400) TS, (1150) YS, 7 El**
AIR 9160	9160C161	France	Bar, forgings, sheet	0.08–0.15 **C**, 0.50–0.90 **Mn**, 0.35 **Si**, 11.0–12.5 **Cr**, 2.0–3.0 **Ni**, 1.50–2.0 **Mo**, 0.25–0.40 **V**, 0.020–0.040 **N**, 0.035 **P**, 0.025 **S**	**Quenched and tempered bar, forgings:** (<40) **diam**, (1080) **TS**, (890) **YS**, 8 **El**

WROUGHT STAINLESS STEELS

specification number	designation	country	product forms	composition	mechanical properties (see page iv for explanation)
ANSI/ASTM A 565	XM-32	US	Bar, forgings	0.08–0.15 **C**, 0.50–0.90 **Mn**, 0.35 **Si**, 11.00–12.50 **Cr**, 2.00–3.00 **Ni**, 1.50–2.00 **Mo**, 0.25–0.40 **V**, 0.01–0.05 **N**, 0.025 **P**, 0.025 **S**	**Quenched, tempered**: all **diam**, 145 (1000) **TS**, 115 (795) **YS**, 15 **El**
AMS 5515F		US	Strip, sheet, plate	0.08–0.15 **C**, 2.00 **Mn**, 1.00 **Si**, 17.00–19.00 **Cr**, 7.00–10.00 **Ni**, 0.75 **Mo**, 0.75 **Cu**, 0.040 **P**, 0.030 **S**	**Solution treated**: ≤0.025 (≤0.64) **diam**, 120 (827) max **TS**, 50 **El**
NF A 35-575	Z 12 CN 17.07	France	Wire, rod	0.08–0.15 **C**, 2.0 **Mn**, 1.0 **Si**, 16.0–18.0 **Cr**, 6.0–8.0 **Ni**, 0.040 **P**, 0.030 **S**	**Stress hardened 0%**: all **diam**, (690) **TS**; **Stress hardened 40%**: all **diam**, (1320) **TS**; **Stress hardened 60%**: all **diam**, (1760) **TS**; **Stress hardened 80%**: all **diam**, (2060) **TS**
NF A 35-575	Z 12 C 13	France	Wire, rod	0.08–0.15 **C**, 1.0 **Mn**, 1.0 **Si**, 11.5–13.5 **Cr**, 0.040 **P**, 0.030 **S**	**Quenched and tempered**: all **diam**, (690) max **TS**
ISO 683/XII	7	ISO	Bar, sheet, plate	0.08–0.15 **C**, 1.5 **Mn**, 1.0 **Si**, 12.0–14.0 **Cr**, 1.0 **Ni**, 0.60 **Mo**, 0.060 **P**, 0.15–0.35 **S**	**Quenched and tempered**: all **diam**, (640) **TS**, (440) **YS**, 12 **El**
NF A 35-572	Z 12 C 13	France	Sheet, strip, plate, bar, sections	0.08–0.15 **C**, 1.0 **Mn**, 1.0 **Si**, 11.5–13.5 **Cr**, 0.04 **P**, 0.03 **S**	**Quenched and tempered**: (5–25) **diam**, (640) **TS**, (440) **YS**, 16 **El**
NF A 35-573	Z 12 CN 17.07	France	Sheet, strip, plate	0.08–0.15 **C**, 2.0 **Mn**, 1.0 **Si**, 16.0–18.0 **Cr**, 6.0–8.0 **Ni**, 0.040 **P**, 0.030 **S**	**Cold rolled**: (≤5) **diam**, (610) **TS**, (305) **YS**, 45 **El**; **Hot rolled**: (≤20) **diam**, (610) **TS**, (295) **YS**, 43 **El**
NF A 35-577	Z 12 C 13 (DF)	France	Bar, wire, rod	0.08–0.15 **C**, 1.0 **Mn**, 1.0 **Si**, 11.5–13.5 **Cr**, 0.5 **Ni**, 0.040 **P**, 0.030 **S**	**Annealed**: (6) **diam**, (590) max **TS**
NF A 35-573	Z 12 CN 18.07	France	Sheet, strip, plate	0.08–0.15 **C**, 2.0 **Mn**, 2.0 **Si**, 17.0–19.0 **Cr**, 6.5–8.5 **Ni**, 0.5 **Cu**, 0.040 **P**, 0.030 **S**	**Austenitized**: all **diam**, (590) **TS**, (245) **YS**, 45 **El**; **Stress hardened**: (≤20) **diam**, (740) **TS**, (490) **YS**, 30 **El**
NF A 35-572	Z 12 CN 17-07	France	Bar, sections	0.08–0.15 **C**, 2.0 **Mn**, 1.0 **Si**, 16.0–18.0 **Cr**, 6.0–8.0 **Ni**, 0.04 **P**, 0.03 **S**	**Austenitized**: (≤25) **diam**, (590) **TS**, (245) **YS**, 40 **El**
SIS 14 23 80	SIS 23 80-03	Sweden	Bar, wire	0.08–0.15 **C**, 1.5 **Mn**, 1.0 **Si**, 12.0–14.0 **Cr**, 1.0 **Ni**, 0.60 **Mo**, 0.060 **P**, 0.15–0.35 **S**	**Quenched and tempered**: all **diam**, (590) **TS**, (410) **YS**, 12 **El**
SIS 14 23 80	SIS 23 80-02	Sweden	Bar, wire	0.08–0.15 **C**, 1.5 **Mn**, 1.0 **Si**, 12.0–14.0 **Cr**, 1.0 **Ni**, 0.60 **Mo**, 0.060 **P**, 0.15–0.35 **S**	**Annealed**: all **diam**, (440) **TS**, (250) **YS**, 14 **El**
DGN-B-150	Type AE-310	Mexico	Wire	0.08–0.15 **C**, 1.0–2.5 **Mn**, 0.25–0.60 **Si**, 25.0–28.0 **Cr**, 20.0–22.5 **Ni**, 0.25 **Cu**, 0.07 N_2, 0.030 **P**, 0.030 **S**	
DGN-B-150	Type AE-312	Mexico	Wire	0.08–0.15 **C**, 1.0–2.5 **Mn**, 0.25–0.60 **Si**, 28.0–32.0 **Cr**, 8.0–10.5 **Ni**, 0.25 **Cu**, 0.07 N_2, 0.030 **P**, 0.030 **S**	
AMS 5615C		US	Bar, forgings	0.08–0.15 **C**, 1.00 **Mn**, 1.00 **Si**, 11.50–13.50 **Cr**, 1.25–2.50 **Ni**, 0.60 **Mo**, 0.50 **Cu**, 0.040 **P**, 0.030 **S**	
NF A 36-209	Z 12 CN 17-08	France	Plate	0.08–0.15 **C**, 2.0 **Mn**, 1.0 **Si**, 16.0–18.0 **Cr**, 6.5–8.5 **Ni**, 0.040 **P**, 0.030 **S**	
NF A 35-583	Z 12 CN 25.20	France	Wire, rod	0.08–0.15 **C**, 1.0–2.5 **Mn**, 0.6 **Si**, 24.5–27.5 **Cr**, 19.0–22.0 **Ni**, 0.030 **P**, 0.020 **S**	
BS S.141		UK	Bar, billets, forgings: aircraft quality	0.08–0.14 **C**, 1.0 **Mn**, 0.8 **Si**, 12.0–14.0 **Cr**, 1.0 **Ni**, 0.030 **P**, 0.025 **S**	**Hardened and tempered**: all **diam**, (590) **TS**, (415) **YS**, 20 **El**
BS S.538		UK	Sheet, strip: aircraft quality	0.08–0.13 **C**, 0.5–0.9 **Mn**, 0.35 **Si**, 11.0–12.5 **Cr**, 2.0–3.0 **Ni**, 1.5–2.0 **Mo**, 0.25–0.40 **V**, 0.020–0.040 **N**, 0.030 **P**, 0.025 **S**	**Annealed, hardened and tempered**: (≥1.6) **diam**, (930) **TS**, (760) **YS**, 9 **El**
BS S.151		UK	Billets, bar, forgings, parts: aircraft quality	0.08–0.13 **C**, 0.5–0.9 **Mn**, 0.35 **Si**, 11.0–12.5 **Cr**, 2.0–3.0 **Ni**, 1.5–2.0 **Mo**, 0.25–0.40 **V**, 0.020–0.040 **N**, 0.030 **P**, 0.025 **S**	**Hardened, tempered**: all **diam**, (930) **TS**, (760) **YS**, 14 **El**

WROUGHT STAINLESS STEELS

specification number	designation	country	product forms	composition	mechanical properties (see page iv for explanation)
ISO 683/XVI	5	ISO	Forgings, bar, plate, sheet, strip, wire	0.08–0.12 **C**, 0.50–1.25 **Mn**, 0.50 **Si**, 16.0–17.0 **Cr**, 4.00–5.00 **Ni**, 2.50–3.25 **Mo**, 0.07–0.13 **N**, 0.040 **P**, 0.030 **S**	**Precipitation hardened (bar, forgings, wire, rod)**: all **diam**, (1140) **TS**, (1030) **YS**
DIN 17440	Grade X 10 Cr 13	Germany	Sheet, strip, bar, wire, tube, forgings	0.08–0.12 **C**, 1.0 **Mn**, 1.0 **Si**, 12.0–14.0 **Cr**, 0.045 **P**, 0.030 **S**	**Annealed**: (≤5) **diam**, (550) **TS**, (300) **YS**, 20 **El**; **Tempered**: (≤15) **diam**, (600) **TS**, (450) **YS**, 18 **El**
AMS 5774A		US	Welding wire	0.08–0.12 **C**, 0.50–1.25 **Mn**, 0.50 **Si**, 16.00–17.00 **Cr**, 4.00–5.00 **Ni**, 2.50–3.25 **Mo**, 0.07–0.13 **N**, 0.040 **P**, 0.030 **S**	
NF A 35-583	Z 10 C 14	France	Wire, rod	0.08–0.12 **C**, 1.0 **Mn**, 0.75 **Si**, 12–15 **Cr**, 0.50 **Ni**, 0.50 **Mo**, 0.030 **P**, 0.020 **S**	
ANSI/ASTM A 313	304	US	Wire	0.08 **C**, 2.00 **Mn**, 1.00 **Si**, 18.00–20.00 **Cr**, 8.00–10.50 **Ni**, 0.10 **N**, 0.045 **P**, 0.030 **S**	**Cold drawn**: ≥0.009 (≥0.23) **diam**, 325 (2240) **TS**
ASTM A 313	Type 304	US	Wire	0.08 **C**, 2.00 **Mn**, 1.00 **Si**, 18.00–20.00 **Cr**, 8.00–10.50 **Ni**, 0.10 **N**, 0.045 **P**, 0.030 **S**	**Cold drawn**: >0.009 (>0.23) **diam**, 325 (2240) **TS**
ANSI/ASTM A 313	316	US	Wire	0.08 **C**, 2.00 **Mn**, 1.00 **Si**, 16.00–18.00 **Cr**, 10.00–14.00 **Ni**, 2.00–3.00 **Mo**, 0.045 **P**, 0.030 **S**	**Cold drawn**: ≥0.009 (≥0.23) **diam**, 245 (1690) **TS**
ANSI/ASTM A 313	321	US	Wire	0.08 **C**, 2.00 **Mn**, 1.00 **Si**, 17.00–19.00 **Cr**, 9.00–12.00 **Ni**, 0.045 **P**, 0.030 **S**, 5 x C min **Ti**	**Cold drawn**: ≥0.009 (≥0.23) **diam**, 245 (1690) **TS**
ANSI/ASTM A 313	347	US	Wire	0.08 **C**, 2.00 **Mn**, 1.00 **Si**, 17.00–19.00 **Cr**, 9.00–13.00 **Ni**, 10 x C min **Nb+Ta**, 0.045 **P**, 0.030 **S**	**Cold drawn**: ≥0.009 (≥0.23) **diam**, 245 (1690) **TS**
ASTM A 313	Type 347	US	Wire	0.08 **C**, 2.00 **Mn**, 1.00 **Si**, 17.00–19.00 **Cr**, 9.00–13.00 **Ni**, 10 x C min **Cb+Ta**, 0.045 **P**, 0.030 **S**	**Cold drawn**: 0.009 (0.23) **diam**, 245 (1690) **TS**
ASTM A 313	Type 321	US	Wire	0.08 **C**, 2.00 **Mn**, 1.00 **Si**, 17.00–19.00 **Cr**, 9.00–12.00 **Ni**, 0.045 **P**, 0.030 **S**, 5 x C min **Ti**	**Cold drawn**: >0.009 (>0.23) **diam**, 245 (1690) **TS**
ASTM A 313	Type 316	US	Wire	0.08 **C**, 2.00 **Mn**, 1.00 **Si**, 16.00–18.00 **Cr**, 10.00–14.00 **Ni**, 2.00–3.00 **Mo**, 0.10 **N**, 0.045 **P**, 0.030 **S**	**Cold drawn**: >0.009 (>0.23) **diam**, 245 (1690) **TS**
ANSI/ASTM A 492	Type XM-17	US	Wire	0.08 **C**, 7.50–9.00 **Mn**, 1.00 **Si**, 17.50–22.00 **Cr**, 5.00–7.00 **Ni**, 2.00–3.00 **Mo**, 0.25–0.50 **N**, 0.045 **P**, 0.030 **S**	**Cold drawn**: 0.091–0.100 (2.30–2.54) **diam**, 235 (1620) **TS**
ANSI/ASTM A 492	Type 304	US	Wire	0.08 **C**, 2.00 **Mn**, 1.00 **Si**, 18.00–20.00 **Cr**, 8.00–10.50 **Ni**, 0.10 **N**, 0.045 **P**, 0.030 **S**	**Cold drawn**: 0.091–0.100 (2.30–2.54) **diam**, 235 (1620) **TS**
ANSI/ASTM A 492	Type 316	US	Wire	0.08 **C**, 2.00 **Mn**, 1.00 **Si**, 16.00–18.00 **Cr**, 10.00–14.00 **Ni**, 2.00–3.00 **Mo**, 0.10 **N**, 0.045 **P**, 0.030 **S**	**Cold drawn**: 0.091–0.100 (2.30–2.54) **diam**, 205 (1410) **TS**
ISO 683/XVI	7	ISO	Forgings, bar, plate, sheet, strip, wire	0.08 **C**, 1.00 **Mn**, 1.00 **Si**, 16.0–17.5 **Cr**, 6.00–7.75 **Ni**, 0.40 **Al**, 0.040 **P**, 0.030 **S**, 0.40–1.20 **Ti**	**Precipitation hardened (bar, forgings, wire, rod)**: all **diam**, (1310) **TS**, (1180) **YS**, 10 **El**
ASTM A 453	Grade 665, class A	US	Bar	0.08 **C**, 1.25–2.00 **Mn**, 0.10–0.80 **Si**, 12.00–15.00 **Cr**, 24.00–28.00 **Ni**, 1.25–2.25 **Mo**, 0.25 **Cu**, 0.25 **Al**, 0.01–0.07 **B**, 0.040 **P**, 0.030 **S**, 2.70–3.30 **Ti**	**Solution treated and aged**: all **diam**, 170 (1172) **TS**, 120 (827) **YS**, 12 **El**
SIS 14 25 70	SIS 25 70-08	Sweden	Bar, forgings, wire	0.08 **C**, 2.0 **Mn**, 1.0 **Si**, 13.5–16.0 **Cr**, 24.0–27.0 **Ni**, 1.0–1.5 **Mo**, 0.10–0.50 **V**, 0.35 **Al**, 0.003–0.010 **B**, 0.025 **P**, 0.025 **S**, 1.9–2.3 **Ti**	**Solution treated, cold worked, artificially aged**: (≤12) **diam**, (1100) **TS**, (1000) **YS**, 8 **El**
SIS 14 25 70	SIS 25 70-08	Sweden	Bar, forgings, wire	0.08 **C**, 2.0 **Mn**, 1.0 **Si**, 13.5–16.0 **Cr**, 24.0–27.0 **Ni**, 1.0–1.5 **Mo**, 0.10–0.50 **V**	**Solution treated, cold worked and artificially aged**: (<12) **diam**, (1100) **TS**, (1000) **YS**, 8 **El**
AECMA prEn2232		AECMA	Tube: seamless	0.08 **C**, 2.00 **Mn**, 1.00 **Si**, 17.00–20.00 **Cr**, 8.00–12.00 **Ni**, 0.040 **P**, 0.030 **S**	**Annealed**: all **diam**, (1050) **TS**, (750) **YS**, 7 **El**

WROUGHT STAINLESS STEELS

specification number	designation	country	product forms	composition	mechanical properties (see page iv for explanation)
ANSI/ASTM A 666	316, grade D	US	Sheet, strip, plate, bar	0.08 **C**, 2.00 **Mn**, 1.00 **Si**, 16.00–18.00 **Cr**, 10.00–14.00 **Ni**, 2.00–3.00 **Mo**, 0.045 **P**, 0.030 **S**	**Annealed (plate, sheet, strip):** 0.030 (0.76) **diam**, 150 (1035) **TS**, 110 (760) **YS**, 7 **El**
ANSI/ASTM A 666	304, grade D	US	Sheet, strip, plate, bar	0.08 **C**, 2.00 **Mn**, 1.00 **Si**, 18.00–20.00 **Cr**, 8.00–10.50 **Ni**, 0.045 **P**, 0.030 **S**	**Annealed (plate, sheet, strip):** >0.030 (>0.76) **diam**, 150 (1035) **TS**, 110 (760) **YS**, 7 **El**
ANSI/ASTM A 666	Type 316, grade D	US	Sheet, strip, plate, bar	0.08 **C**, 2.00 **Mn**, 1.00 **Si**, 16.00–18.00 **Cr**, 10.00–14.00 **Ni**, 2.00–3.00 **Mo**, 0.045 **P**, 0.030 **S**	**Cold rolled (plate, sheet, strip):** ≤0.015 (≤0.38) **diam**, 150 (1035) **TS**, 110 (760) **YS**, 6 **El**
ANSI/ASTM A 666	Type 304, grade A	US	Sheet, strip, plate, bar	0.08 **C**, 2.00 **Mn**, 1.00 **Si**, 18.00–20.00 **Cr**, 8.00–10.50 **Ni**, 0.045 **P**, 0.030 **S**	**Cold rolled (plate, sheet, strip):** ≤0.015 (≤0.38) **diam**, 150 (1035) **TS**, 110 (760) **YS**, 6 **El**
ANSI/ASTM A 666	Type 304, grade D	US	Sheet, strip, plate, bar	0.08 **C**, 2.00 **Mn**, 1.00 **Si**, 18.00–20.00 **Cr**, 8.00–10.50 **Ni**, 0.045 **P**, 0.030 **S**	**Annealed (plate, sheet, strip):** 0.015 **diam**, (1035) **TS**, (760) **YS**, 6 **El**
ANSI/ASTM A 666	Type 316, grade D	US	Sheet, strip, plate, bar	0.08 **C**, 2.00 **Mn**, 1.00 **Si**, 16.00–18.00 **Cr**, 10.00–14.00 **Ni**, 2.00–3.00 **Mo**, 0.045 **P**, 0.030 **S**	**Annealed (plate, sheet, strip):** 0.015 **diam**, (1035) **TS**, (760) **YS**, 6 **El**
MIL–T–5695D	Type II	US	Tube: welded	0.08 **C**, 2.0 **Mn**, 0.75 **Si**, 18.0–20.0 **Cr**, 8.0–11.0 **Ni**, 0.70 **Mo**, 0.70 **Cu**	**Cold drawn, 1/2 H:** all **diam**, 150 (1034) **TS**, 110 (759) **YS**, 7 **El**
ANSI/ASTM A 478	Type 317	US	Wire	0.08 **C**, 2.00 **Mn**, 1.00 **Si**, 18.00–20.00 **Cr**, 11.00–15.00 **Ni**, 3.00–4.00 **Mo**, 0.10 **N**, 0.045 **P**, 0.030 **S**	**Annealed**: 0.002–0.005 (0.05–0.13) **diam**, 145 (1000) **TS**, 30 **El**; **Cold drawn**: 0.030–0.125 (0.76–3.18) **diam**, 120 (830) **TS**, 15 **El**
ANSI/ASTM A 478	Type 316	US	Wire	0.08 **C**, 2.00 **Mn**, 1.00 **Si**, 16.00–18.00 **Cr**, 10.00–14.00 **Ni**, 2.00–3.00 **Mo**, 0.10 **N**, 0.045 **P**, 0.030 **S**	**Annealed**: 0.002–0.005 (0.05–0.13) **diam**, 145 (1000) **TS**, 30 **El**; **Cold drawn**: 0.030–0.125 (0.76–3.18) **diam**, 120 (830) **TS**, 15 **El**
ANSI/ASTM A 478	Type 304	US	Wire	0.08 **C**, 2.00 **Mn**, 1.00 **Si**, 18.00–20.00 **Cr**, 8.00–10.50 **Ni**, 0.10 **N**, 0.045 **P**, 0.030 **S**	**Annealed**: 0.002–0.005 (0.05–0.13) **diam**, 145 (1000) **TS**, 30 **El**; **Cold drawn**: 0.030–0.125 (0.76–3.18) **diam**, 120 (830) **TS**, 15 **El**
AIR 9160	9160C231	France	Bar	0.08 **C**, 1.0–2.0 **Mn**, 0.40–1.0 **Si**, 13.5–16.0 **Cr**, 24.0–27.0 **Ni**, 1.0–1.50 **Mo**, 0.10–0.50 **V**, 0.35 **Al**, 0.001–0.010 **B**, 0.030 **P**, 0.015 **S**, 1.90–2.30 **Ti**	**Solution treated and tempered:** all **diam**, (960) **TS**, (660) **YS**, 10 **El**
JIS G 4311	SUH 660	Japan	Bar	0.08 **C**, 2.00 **Mn**, 1.00 **Si**, 13.50–16.00 **Cr**, 24.00–27.00 **Ni**, 1.00–1.50 **Mo**, 0.10–0.50 **V**, 0.35 **Al**, 0.001–0.010 **B**, 0.040 **P**, 0.030 **S**, 1.90–2.35 **Ti**	**Solution annealed and aged:** (≤180) **diam**, (902) **TS**, (588) **YS**, 18 **El**
AECMA prEn2120		AECMA	Bar	0.08 **C**, 2.00 **Mn**, 1.00 **Si**, 17.0–20.0 **Cr**, 8.0–11.0 **Ni**, 0.040 **P**, 0.030 **S**	**Annealed and cold finished:** (0.25–0.5) **diam**, (900) **TS**
SIS 14 25 70	SIS 25 70–04	Sweden	Bar, forgings, sheet, wire	0.08 **C**, 2.0 **Mn**, 1.0 **Si**, 13.5–16.0 **Cr**, 24.0–27.0 **Ni**, 1.0–1.5 **Mo**, 0.10–0.50 **V**, 0.35 **Al**, 0.003–0.010 **B**, 0.025 **P**, 0.025 **S**, 1.9–2.3 **Ti**	**Solution treated and artificially aged**: all **diam**, (900) **TS**, (600) **YS**, 15 **El**
SIS 14 25 70	SIS 25 70–04	Sweden	Bar, forgings, plate, wire	0.08 **C**, 2.0 **Mn**, 1.0 **Si**, 13.5–16.0 **Cr**, 24.0–27.0 **Ni**, 1.0–1.5 **Mo**, 0.10–0.50 **V**, 0.35 **Al**, 0.003–0.010 **B**, 1.9–2.3 **Ti**	**Solution annealed and artificially aged:** all **diam**, (900) **TS**, (600) **YS**, 15 **El**
ASTM A 453	Grade 660 class A, B	US	Bar	0.08 **C**, 2.00 **Mn**, 1.00 **Si**, 13.50–16.00 **Cr**, 24.00–27.00 **Ni**, 1.00–1.50 **Mo**, 0.10–0.50 **V**, 0.35 **Al**, 0.0010–0.010 **B**, 0.040 **P**, 0.030 **S**, 1.90–2.35 **Ti**	**Solution treated and aged:** all **diam**, 130 (896) **TS**, 85 (586) **YS**, 15 **El**
ASTM A 453	Grade 662, class A	US	Bar	0.08 **C**, 0.40–1.00 **Mn**, 0.40–1.00 **Si**, 12.00–15.00 **Cr**, 24.00–28.00 **Ni**, 2.00–3.50 **Mo**, 0.50 **Cu**, 0.35 **Al**, 0.0010–0.010 **B**, 0.040 **P**, 0.030 **S**, 1.80–2.10 **Ti**	**Solution treated and aged:** all **diam**, 130 (896) **TS**, 85 (586) **YS**, 15 **El**
AMS 5674A		US	Wire	0.08 **C**, 2.00 **Mn**, 1.00 **Si**, 17.00–19.00 **Cr**, 9.00–12.00 **Ni**, 0.75 **Mo**, 0.50 **Cu**, 10 x C–1.10 **Nb+Ta**, 0.040 **P**, 0.030 **S**	**Solution heat treated (coil):** ≥0.020 ≥(0.508) **diam**, 125 max (862) max **TS**

WROUGHT STAINLESS STEELS

specification number	designation	country	product forms	composition	mechanical properties (see page iv for explanation)
AMS 5689A		US	Wire	0.08 **C**, 2.00 **Mn**, 1.00 **Si**, 17.00–19.00 **Cr**, 8.00–11.00 **Ni**, 0.75 **Mo**, 0.50 **Cu**, 0.040 **P**, 0.030 **S**, 6 x C–0.70 **Ti**	**Solution heat treated (coil)**: 0.010–0.020 (0.254–0.508) **diam**, (862) 125 max **TS**
AMS 5639D		US	Bar, forgings, tube, rings	0.08 **C**, 2.00 **Mn**, 1.00 **Si**, 18.00–20.00 **Cr**, 8.00–12.00 **Ni**, 0.75 **Mo**, 0.75 **Cu**, 0.040 **P**, 0.030 **S**	**Solution heat treated (wire)**: all **diam**, 125 (862) max **TS**
AMS 5642G	Type I	US	Bar, forgings, wire	0.08 **C**, 2.00 **Mn**, 1.00 **Si**, 17.00–19.00 **Cr**, 9.00–12.00 **Ni**, 0.75 **Mo**, 10 x C–1.10 **Nb+Ti**, 0.040 **P**, 0.18–0.35 **S**	**Solution heat treated, cold finished (wire)**: all **diam**, 125 (862) max **TS**
AMS 5642G	Type II	US	Bar, forgings, wire	0.08 **C**, 2.00 **Mn**, 1.00 **Si**, 17.00–19.00 **Cr**, 9.00–12.00 **Ni**, 0.75 **Mo**, 0.75 **Cu**, 10 x C–1.10 **Nb+Ta**, 0.11–0.17 **P**, 0.030 **S**, 0.15–0.35 **Se**	**Solution heat treated, cold finished (wire)**: all **diam**, 125 (862) max **TS**
AMS 5648E		US	Bar, forgings, tube, rings, wire	0.08 **C**, 1.25–2.00 **Mn**, 1.00 **Si**, 16.00–18.00 **Cr**, 10.00–14.00 **Ni**, 2.00–3.00 **Mo**, 0.75 **Cu**, 0.040 **P**, 0.030 **S**	**Solution heat treated, cold finished (wire)**: all **diam**, 125 (862) **TS**
AMS 5649B		US	Bar, forgings, wire	0.08 **C**, 1.00–2.00 **Mn**, 1.00 **Si**, 17.00–19.00 **Cr**, 12.00–14.00 **Ni**, 1.75–2.50 **Mo**, 0.50 **Cu**, 0.20 **P**, 0.10–0.20 **S**	**Solution heat treated, cold finished**: all **diam**, 125 (862) max **TS**
AMS 5650B		US	Bar, forgings, tube, rings, wire	0.08 **C**, 2.00 **Mn**, 1.00 **Si**, 22.00–24.00 **Cr**, 12.00–15.00 **Ni**, 0.75 **Mo**, 0.50 **Cu**, 0.040 **P**, 0.030 **S**	**Solution heat treated, cold finished (wire)**: all **diam**, 125 (862) max **TS**
AMS 5651E		US	Bar, forgings, tube, rings, wire	0.08 **C**, 2.00 **Mn**, 0.30–0.80 **Si**, 24.00–26.00 **Cr**, 19.00–22.00 **Ni**, 0.75 **Mo**, 0.50 **Cu**, 0.040 **P**, 0.030 **S**	**Solution heat treated, cold finished (wire)**: all **diam**, 125 (862) max **TS**
ANSI/ASTM A 193	Grade B8T	US	Bar	0.08 **C**, 2.00 **Mn**, 1.00 **Si**, 17.00–19.00 **Cr**, 9.00–12.00 **Ni**, 0.045 **P**, 0.030 **S**, 5 x C min **Ti**	**Solution annealed**: ≤0.75 (≤19.05) **diam**, 125 (862) **TS**, 100 (689) **YS**, 12 **El**
ANSI/ASTM A 193	Grade B8P	US	Bar	0.08 **C**, 2.00 **Mn**, 1.00 **Si**, 17.00–19.00 **Cr**, 10.50–13.00 **Ni**, 0.045 **P**, 0.030 **S**	**Solution annealed**: ≤0.75 (≤19.05) **diam**, 125 (862) **TS**, 100 (689) **YS**, 12 **El**
ANSI/ASTM A 193	Grade B8C	US	Bar	0.08 **C**, 2.00 **Mn**, 1.00 **Si**, 17.00–19.00 **Cr**, 9.00–13.00 **Ni**, 10 x C mi n **Nb+Ta**, 0.045 **P**, 0.030 **S**	**Solution annealed**: ≤0.75 (≤19.05) **diam**, 125 (862) **TS**, 100 (689) **YS**, 12 **El**
ANSI/ASTM A 666	316, grade C	US	Sheet, strip, plate, bar	0.08 **C**, 2.00 **Mn**, 1.00 **Si**, 16.00–18.00 **Cr**, 10.00–14.00 **Ni**, 2.00–3.00 **Mo**, 0.045 **P**, 0.030 **S**	**Annealed (plate, sheet, strip)**: >0.030 (>0.76) **diam**, 125 (860) **TS**, 75 (515) **YS**, 10 **El**
ANSI/ASTM A 666	304, grade C	US	Sheet, strip, plate, bar	0.08 **C**, 2.00 **Mn**, 1.00 **Si**, 18.00–20.00 **Cr**, 8.00–10.50 **Ni**, 0.045 **P**, 0.030 **S**	**Annealed (plate, sheet, strip)**: >0.030 (>0.76) **diam**, 125 (860) **TS**, 75 (515) **YS**, 12 **El**
ANSI/ASTM A 666	Type 316, grade C	US	Sheet, strip, plate, bar	0.08 **C**, 2.00 **Mn**, 1.00 **Si**, 16.00–18.00 **Cr**, 10.00–14.00 **Ni**, 2.00–3.00 **Mo**, 0.045 **P**, 0.030 **S**	**Cold rolled (plate, strip, sheet)**: ≤0.015 (≤0.38) **diam**, 125 (860) **TS**, 75 (515) **YS**, 10 **El**
ANSI/ASTM A 666	Type 304, grade C	US	Sheet, strip, plate, bar	0.08 **C**, 2.00 **Mn**, 1.00 **Si**, 18.00–20.00 **Cr**, 8.00–10.50 **Ni**, 0.045 **P**, 0.030 **S**	**Cold rolled (plate, sheet, strip)**: ≤0.015 (≤0.38) **diam**, 125 (860) **TS**, 75 (515) **YS**, 10 **El**
IS 6528	04Cr18Ni10	India	Wire	0.08 **C**, 2.0 **Mn**, 1.0 **Si**, 17.0–20.0 **Cr**, 8.0–12.0 **Ni**, 0.045 **P**, 0.030 **S**	**Cold worked**: all **diam**, (860) **TS**, (690) **YS**, 12 **El**
IS 6528	04Cr17Ni12Mo2	India	Wire	0.08 **C**, 2.0 **Mn**, 1.0 **Si**, 16.0–18.5 **Cr**, 10.0–14.0 **Ni**, 2.0–3.0 **Mo**, 0.045 **P**, 0.030 **S**	**Cold worked**: all **diam**, (860) **TS**, (690) **YS**, 12 **El**
ANSI/ASTM A 666	Type 304, grade C	US	Sheet, strip, plate, bar	0.08 **C**, 2.00 **Mn**, 1.00 **Si**, 18.00–20.00 **Cr**, 8.00–10.50 **Ni**, 0.045 **P**, 0.030 **S**	**Annealed (plate, sheet, strip)**: 0.015 **diam**, (860) **TS**, (515) **YS**, 10 **El**
ANSI/ASTM A 666	Type 316, grade C	US	Sheet, strip, plate, bar	0.08 **C**, 2.00 **Mn**, 1.00 **Si**, 16.00–18.00 **Cr**, 10.00–14.00 **Ni**, 2.00–3.00 **Mo**, 0.045 **P**, 0.030 **S**	**Annealed (plate, sheet, strip)**: 0.015 **diam**, (860) **TS**, (515) **YS**, 10 **El**
AECMA prEn2231		AECMA	Tube: seamless	0.08 **C**, 2.00 **Mn**, 1.00 **Si**, 17.00–20.00 **Cr**, 8.00–12.00 **Ni**, 0.040 **P**, 0.030 **S**	**Annealed**: all **diam**, (850) **TS**, (520) **YS**, 15 **El**
IS 6911	04Cr18Ni10	India	Plate, sheet, strip	0.08 **C**, 2.0 **Mn**, 1.0 **Si**, 17.0–20.0 **Cr**, 8.0–12.0 **Ni**, 0.030 **S**, 0.045 **P**	**Cold rolled**: (0.5–0.8) **diam**, (830) **TS**, (490) **YS**, 12 **El**

specification number	designation	country	product forms	composition	mechanical properties (see page iv for explanation)
MIL-T-5695D	Type I	US	Tube: seamless	0.08 **C**, 2.0 **Mn**, 0.75 **Si**, 18.0–20.0 **Cr**, 8.0–11.0 **Ni**, 0.70 **Mo**, 0.70 **Cu**, 0.040 **P**, 0.030 **S**; rem Fe	**Cold drawn, 1/4 H:** ≤5/16 **diam**, 120 (827) **TS**, 75 (517) **YS**, 12 **El**
AMS 5570J		US	Tube	0.08 **C**, 2.00 **Mn**, 0.40–1.00 **Si**, 17.00–20.00 **Cr**, 9.00–13.00 **Ni**, 0.75 **Mo**, 0.50 **Cu**, 0.040 **P**, 0.030 **S**, 6 x C–0.70 **Ti**	**Solution treated:** ≤0.016 (≤0.41) **diam**, 120 (827) **TS**, 33 **El**
AMS 5571D		US	Tube	0.08 **C**, 2.00 **Mn**, 0.50–1.00 **Si**, 17.00–19.00 **Cr**, 9.00–13.00 **Ni**, 0.75 **Mo**, 0.50 **Cu**, 10 x C–1.10 **Nb+Ta**, 0.040 **P**, 0.030 **S**	**Solution treated:** ≤0.016 (≤0.41) **diam**, 120 (827) **TS**, 33 **El**
AMS 5575H		US	Tube	0.08 **C**, 2.00 **Mn**, 1.00 **Si**, 17.00–19.00 **Cr**, 9.00–12.00 **Ni**, 0.75 **Mo**, 0.50 **Cu**, 10 x C–1.10 **Nb+Ta**, 0.040 **P**, 0.030 **S**	**Solution treated:** ≤0.016 (≤0.41) **diam**, 120 (827) **TS**, 33 **El**
AMS 5576E		US	Tube	0.08 **C**, 2.00 **Mn**, 1.00 **Si**, 17.00–19.00 **Cr**, 9.00–13.00 **Ni**, 0.75 **Mo**, 0.50 **Cu**, 0.040 **P**, 0.030 **S**, 6 x C–0.70 **Ti**	**Solution treated:** ≤0.016 (≤0.41) **diam**, 120 (827) **TS**, 33 **El**
ANSI/ASTM A 564	635	US	Bar, shapes	0.08 **C**, 1.00 **Mn**, 1.00 **Si**, 16.00–17.50 **Cr**, 6.00–7.50 **Ni**, 0.40 **Al**, 0.040 **P**, 0.030 **S**, 0.40–1.20 **Ti**	**Solution annealed**: all **diam**, 120 (827) **TS**, 75 (517) **YS**, 10 **El**
ASTM A 705	635	US	Forgings	0.08 **C**, 1.00 **Mn**, 1.00 **Si**, 16.00–17.50 **Cr**, 6.00–7.50 **Ni**, 0.40 **Al**, 0.040 **P**, 0.030 **S**, 0.40–1.20 **Ti**	**Solution annealed**: all **diam**, 120 (825) **TS**, 75 (515) **YS**, 10 **El**
ASTM A 693	Type 635	US	Plate, sheet, strip	0.08 **C**, 1.00 **Mn**, 1.00 **Si**, 16.00–17.50 **Cr**, 6.00–7.50 **Ni**, 0.40–1.20 **Ti**, 0.040 **P**, 0.030 **S**	**Solution annealed**: 0.030 (0.76) **diam**, 120 (825) max **TS**, 75 (515) max **YS**, 3 **El**; **Precipitation hardened**: 0.030 (0.76) **diam**, 190 (1310) **TS**, 170 (1170) **YS**, 3 **El**
BS T.69		UK	Tube: aircraft quality	0.08 **C**, 0.5–2.0 **Mn**, 0.2–1.0 **Si**, 17.0–19.0 **Cr**, 9.0–11.0 **Ni**, 0.035 **P**, 0.025 **S**, 5 x C–0.70 **Ti**	**Cold drawn and tempered:** all **diam**, (800) **TS**, (700) **YS**
BS T.68		UK	Tube: aircraft quality	0.08 **C**, 0.5–2.0 **Mn**, 0.2–1.0 **Si**, 17.0–19.0 **Cr**, 9.0–12.0 **Ni**, 10 x C–1.0 **Nb**, 0.035 **P**, 0.025 **S**	**Cold drawn and tempered:** all **diam**, (800) **TS**, (700) **YS**
AMS 5560F		US	Tube	0.08 **C**, 2.00 **Mn**, 1.00 **Si**, 18.00–20.00 **Cr**, 8.00–12.00 **Ni**, 0.75 **Mo**, 0.75 **Cu**, 0.040 **P**, 0.030 **S**	**Solution treated:** ≤0.016 (≤0.41) **diam**, 115 (793) **TS**, 35 **El**
AMS 5565F		US	Tube	0.08 **C**, 2.00 **Mn**, 1.00 **Si**, 18.00–20.00 **Cr**, 8.00–11.00 **Ni**, 0.75 **Mo**, 0.75 **Cu**, 0.040 **P**, 0.030 **S**	**Solution treated:** ≤0.016 (≤0.41) **diam**, 115 (793) max **TS**, 35 **El**
AMS 5567B	Type I, II	US	Tube	0.08 **C**, 2.00 **Mn**, 0.75 **Si**, 18.00–20.00 **Cr**, 8.00–12.00 **Ni**, 0.75 **Mo**, 0.75 **Cu**, 0.040 **P**, 0.030 **S**	**Solution treated:** ≤0.016 (≤0.41) **diam**, 115 (793) **TS**, 30 (207) **YS**, 35 **El**
AMS 5573F		US	Tube	0.08 **C**, 1.25–2.00 **Mn**, 1.00 **Si**, 16.00–18.00 **Cr**, 10.00–14.00 **Ni**, 2.00–3.00 **Mo**, 0.75 **Cu**, 0.040 **P**, 0.030 **S**	**Solution treated:** ≤0.016 (≤0.41) **diam**, 115 (793) max **TS**, 35 **El**
AMS 5512F		US	Strip, sheet, plate	0.08 **C**, 2.00 **Mn**, 0.50–1.00 **Si**, 17.00–19.00 **Cr**, 9.00–12.00 **Ni**, 0.75 **Mo**, 0.50 **Cu**, 10 x C–1.10 **Nb+Ta**, 0.040 **P**, 0.030 **S**	**Solution treated:** >0.002–0.003 (>0.051–0.076) **diam**, 115 (793) max **TS**, 20 **El**
AISI 308		US	Wire	0.08 **C**, 2.00 **Mn**, 1.00 **Si**, 19.00–21.00 **Cr**, 10.00–12.00 **Ni**, 0.045 **P**, 0.030 **S**	**Soft temper**: 0.062 (1.57) **diam**, 115 (793) **TS**, 80 (552) **YS**, 40 **El**
BS S.525		UK	Sheet, strip: aircraft quality	0.08 **C**, 0.5–2.0 **Mn**, 0.2–1.0 **Si**, 17.0–19.0 **Cr**, 9.0–11.0 **Ni**, 10 x C–1.0 **Nb**, 0.035 **P**, 0.025 **S**	**Cold-rolled, cold-rolled and tempered**: all **diam**, (790) **TS**, (635) **YS**, 11 in less than 1.5mm **El**
BS S.524		UK	Sheet, strip: aircraft quality	0.08 **C**, 0.5–2.0 **Mn**, 0.2–1.0 **Si**, 17.0–19.0 **Cr**, 9.0–11.0 **Ni**, 0.035 **P**, 0.025 **S**, 5 x C–0.70 **Ti**	**Cold-rolled, cold-rolled and tempered**: all **diam**, (790) **TS**, (635) **YS**, 11 in <1.5 mm **El**

WROUGHT STAINLESS STEELS

specification number	designation	country	product forms	composition	mechanical properties (see page iv for explanation)
JIS G 4313	SUS 304–CSP	Japan	Strip	0.08 **C**, 2.00 **Mn**, 1.00 **Si**, 18.00–20.00 **Cr**, 8.00–10.50 **Ni**, 0.040 **P**, 0.030 **S**	**One half hard**: (≥0.30) **diam**, (785) **TS**, (471) **YS**, 6 **El**; **Three quarters hard**: (≥0.30) **diam**, (932) **TS**, (667) **YS**, 3 **El**; **Full hard**: (≥0.30) **diam**, (1128) **TS**, (883) **YS**
MIL–S–7720A	316	US	Bar, wire, forging stock	0.08 **C**, 2.0 **Mn**, 1.0 **Si**, 16.0–18.0 **Cr**, 10.0–14.0 **Ni**, 1.75–3.00 **Mo**, 0.50 **Cu**, 0.04 **P**, 0.03 **S**	**Cold finished**: ≤0.75 **diam**, (758) **TS**, (655) **YS**, 15 **El**
AMS 5686C		US	Wire	0.08 **C**, 2.00 **Mn**, 1.00 **Si**, 17.00–19.00 **Cr**, 10.00–13.00 **Ni**, 0.75 **Mo**, 0.75 **Cu**, 0.040 **P**, 0.030 **S**	**Solution heat treated**: all **diam**, (758) max **TS**
AMS 5510L		US	Strip, sheet, plate	0.08 **C**, 2.00 **Mn**, 0.40–1.00 **Si**, 17.00–19.00 **Cr**, 9.00–12.00 **Ni**, 0.75 **Mo**, 0.50 **Cu**, 0.040 **P**, 0.030 **S**, 6 x C–0.70 **Ti**	**Solution treated**: ≥0.002–0.003 (>0.051–0.076) **diam**, 110 (758) max **TS** 20 **El**
AECMA prEn2230		AECMA	Tube: seamless	0.08 **C**, 2.00 **Mn**, 1.00 **Si**, 17.00–20.00 **Cr**, 8.00–12.00 **Ni**, 0.040 **P**, 0.030 **S**	**Annealed**: all **diam**, (730) **TS**, (520) **YS**, 20 **El**
JIS G 3446	SUS 304 TKB	Japan	Tube: seamless or welded	0.08 **C**, 2.00 **Mn**, 1.00 **Si**, 18.00–20.00 **Cr**, 8.00–11.00 **Ni**, 0.040 **P**, 0.030 **S**	**Solution annealed, cold worked, annealed**: (≥8) **diam**, (726) **TS**, (520) **YS**, 20 **El**
JIS G 3446	SUS 316 TKB	Japan	Tube: seamless or welded	0.08 **C**, 2.00 **Mn**, 1.00 **Si**, 16.00–18.00 **Cr**, 10.00–14.00 **Ni**, 2.00–3.00 **Mo**, 0.040 **P**, 0.030 **S**	**Solution annealed, cold worked, annealed**: (≥8) **diam**, (726) **TS**, (520) **YS**, 20 **El**
JIS G 3446	SUS 321 TKB	Japan	Tube: seamless or welded	0.08 **C**, 2.00 **Mn**, 1.00 **Si**, 17.00–19.00 **Cr**, 9.00–13.00 **Ni**, 0.040 **P**, 0.030 **S**, 5 x C min **Ti**	**Solution annealed, cold worked, annealed**: (≥8) **diam**, (726) **TS**, (520) **YS**, 20 **El**
JIS G 3446	SUS 347 TKB	Japan	Tube: seamless or welded	0.08 **C**, 2.00 **Mn**, 1.00 **Si**, 17.00–19.00 **Cr**, 9.00–13.00 **Ni**, 10 x C min **Nb+Ta**, 0.040 **P**, 0.030 **S**	**Solution annealed, cold worked, annealed**: (≥8) **diam**, (726) **TS**, (520) **YS**, 20 **El**
JIS G 4312	SUH 660	Japan	Sheet, plate	0.08 **C**, 2.00 **Mn**, 1.00 **Si**, 13.50–16.00 **Cr**, 24.00–27.00 **Ni**, 1.00–1.50 **Mo**, 0.10–0.50 **V**, 0.30 **Al**, 0.001–0.010 **B**, 0.040 **P**, 0.030 **S**, 1.90–2.35 **Ti**	**Solution annealed**: all **diam**, (726) **TS**, 25 **El**; **Solution annealed and aged**: all **diam**, (902) **TS**, (588) **YS**, 15 **El**
AMS 5572C		US	Tube	0.08 **C**, 2.00 **Mn**, 0.75 **Si**, 24.00–26.00 **Cr**, 19.00–22.00 **Ni**, 0.75 **Mo**, 0.50 **Cu**, 0.040 **P**, 0.030 **S**	**Solution treated**: ≤0.312 (≤7.92) **diam**, 105 (724 max) **TS**, 40 **El**
AMS 5577C		US	Tube	0.08 **C**, 2.00 **Mn**, 0.75 **Si**, 24.00–26.00 **Cr**, 19.00–22.00 **Ni**, 0.75 **Mo**, 0.50 **Cu**, 0.040 **P**, 0.030 **S**	**Solution treated**: ≤0.311 (≤7.91) **diam**, 105 (724) **TS**, 40 **El**
MIL–T–6737B	Type 347	US	Tube: welded	0.08 **C**, 2.00 **Mn**, 1.00 **Si**, 17.0–20.0 **Cr**, 9.0–13.0 **Ni**, 0.70 **Cu**, 10 x C min **Nb**, 0.040 **P**, 0.030 **S**	**Solution annealed**: all **diam**, (723) **TS**, 35 **El**
MIL–T–6737B	Type 321	US	Tube: welded	0.08 **C**, 2.00 **Mn**, 1.00 **Si**, 17.0–20.0 **Cr**, 9.0–13.0 **Ni**, 0.70 **Cu**, 0.040 **P**, 0.030 **S**, 0.75 **Ti**	**Solution annealed**: all **diam**, (723) **TS**, 35 **El**
MIL–T–8606C	Type 347	US	Tube: seamless, welded	0.08 **C**, 2.00 **Mn**, 1.00 **Si**, 17.0–20.0 **Cr**, 9.0–13.0 **Ni**, 0.70 **Cu**, 10 x C–1.10 **Nb**, 0.040 **P**, 0.030 **S**; rem Fe	**Solution annealed**: all **diam**, (723) max **TS**, 35 **El**
MIL–T–8606C	Type 321	US	Tube: seamless, welded	0.08 **C**, 2.00 **Mn**, 1.00 **Si**, 17.0–20.0 **Cr**, 9.0–13.0 **Ni**, 0.70 **Cu**, 0.040 **P**, 0.030 **S**, 5 x C–0.75 **Ti**; rem Fe	**Solution annealed**: all **diam**, (723) max **TS**, 35 **El**
ANSI/ASTM A 479	XM–29	US	Bar, shapes	0.08 **C**, 11.50–14.50 **Mn**, 1.00 **Si**, 17.00–19.00 **Cr**, 2.25–3.75 **Ni**, 0.20–0.40 **N**, 0.060 **P**, 0.030 **S**,	**Solution annealed**: all **diam**, 100 (690) **TS**, 55 (380) **YS**, 50 **El**
MIL–S–6721B	Ti (321)	US	Plate, sheet, strip	0.08 **C**, 2.0 **Mn**, 1.0 **Si**, 17.0–19.0 **Cr**, 8.0–11.0 **Ni**, 1.5 **Mo**, 0.5 **Cu**, 0.040 **P**, 0.030 **S**, 6 x C–0.75 **Ti** 0.5 other elements, total; rem Fe	**Solution annealed**: all **diam**, 100 (690) **TS**, 40 **El**

specification number	designation	country	product forms	composition	mechanical properties (see page iv for explanation)
MIL-S-6721B	Cb-Ta (347)	US	Plate, sheet, strip	0.08 **C**, 2.0 **Mn**, 1.0 **Si**, 17.0-19.0 **Cr**, 9.0-13.0 **Ni**, 1.5 **Mo**, 0.5 **Cu**, 0.5 **Nb**, 10 x C-1.25 **Nb+Ta**, 0.040 **P**, 0.030 **S**; 0.5 other elements, total; rem Fe.	**Solution annealed**: all diam, 100 (690) **TS**, 40 **El**
ASTM A 240	Type XM17	US	Plate, sheet, strip	0.08 **C**, 7.50-9.00 **Mn**, 1.00 **Si**, 17.50-22.00 **Cr**, 5.00-7.00 **Ni**, 2.00-3.00 **Mo**, 0.25-0.50 **N**, 0.045 **P**, 0.030 **S**	**Solution annealed, hot rolled or cold rolled (sheet, strip)**: all **diam**, 100 (690) **TS**, 60 (415) **YS**, 40 **El**
ASTM A 240	Type XM29	US	Plate, sheet, strip	0.08 **C**, 11.50-14.50 **Mn**, 1.00 **Si**, 17.00-19.00 **Cr**, 2.25-3.75 **Ni**, 0.20-0.40 **N**, 0.060 **P**, 0.030 **S**	**Solution annealed, hot rolled or cold rolled (sheet, strip)**: all **diam**, 100 (690) **TS**, 60 (415) **YS**, 40 **El**
ANSI/ASTM A 412	Type XM-29	US	Plate, sheet, strip	0.08 **C**, 11.50-14.50 **Mn**, 1.00 **Si**, 17.00-19.00 **Cr**, 2.25-3.75 **Ni**, 0.20-0.40 **N**, 0.060 **P**, 0.030 **S**	**Annealed (sheet, strip)**: 0.015 (0.38) **diam**, 100 (690) **TS**, 60 (415) **YS**, 40 **El**
ANSI/ASTM A 479	Grade XM 29	US	Bar, shapes	0.08 **C**, 11.50-14.50 **Mn**, 1.00 **Si**, 17.00-19.00 **Cr**, 2.25-3.75 **Ni**, 0.20-0.40 **N**, 0.060 **P**, 0.030 **S**	**Solution annealed**: all **diam**, (690) **TS**, (380) **YS**, 30 **El**
ANSI/ASTM A 240	Grade XM 17	US	Sheet, strip	0.08 **C**, 7.50-9.00 **Mn**, 1.00 **Si**, 17.50-22.00 **Cr**, 5.00-7.00 **Ni**, 2.00-3.00 **Mo**, 0.25-0.50 **N**, 0.045 **P**, 0.030 **S**	**Solution annealed**: all **diam**, (690) **TS**, (415) **YS**, 40 **El**
ANSI/ASTM A 240	Grade XM 29	US	Sheet, strip	0.08 **C**, 11.50-14.50 **Mn**, 1.00 **Si**, 17.00-19.00 **Cr**, 2.25-3.75 **Ni**, 0.20-0.40 **N**, 0.060 **P**, 0.030 **S**	**Solution annealed**: all **diam**, (690) **TS**, (415) **YS**, 40 **El**
AMS 5574A		US	Tube	0.08 **C**, 2.00 **Mn**, 1.00 **Si**, 22.00-24.00 **Cr**, 12.00-15.00 **Ni**, 0.75 **Mo**, 0. **Cu**, 0.040 **P**, 0.030 **S**	**Solution treated**: all **diam**, 100 (690) **TS**, 40 **El**
AMS 5654B		US	Bar, forgings, tube, rings, wire	0.08 **C**, 2.00 **Mn**, 1.00 **Si**, 17.00-19.00 **Cr**, 9.00-13.00 **Ni**, 0.75 **Mo**, 0.50 **Cu**, 10 x C-1.10 **Nb+Ta**, 0.020 **P**, 0.020 **S**	**Solution heat treated, cold finished (wire)**: all **diam**, 100 (690) max **TS**
AMS 5513C		US	Strip, sheet, plate	0.08 **C**, 2.00 **Mn**, 1.00 **Si**, 18.00-20.00 **Cr**, 8.00-11.00 **Ni**, 0.75 **Mo**, 0.75 **Cu**, 0.040 **P**, 0.030 **S**	**Solution treated**: all **diam**, 100 (690) max **TS**, 40 **El**
AMS 5521D		US	Sheet, strip, plate	0.08 **C**, 2.00 **Mn**, 0.75 **Si**, 24.00-26.00 **Cr**, 19.00-22.00 **Ni**, 0.75 **Mo**, 0.50 **Cu**, 0.040 **P**, 0.030 **S**	**Cold rolled and solution treated**: all **diam**, 100 (690) max **TS**, 40 **El**
AMS 5523B		US	Strip, sheet, plate	0.08 **C**, 2.00 **Mn**, 1.00 **Si**, 22.00-24.00 **Cr**, 12.00-15.00 **Ni**, 0.75 **Mo**, 0.50 **Cu**, 0.040 **P**, 0.030 **S**	**Solution treated**: all **diam**, 100 (690) max **TS**, 40 **El**
AMS 5524E		US	Strip, sheet, plate	0.08 **C**, 2.00 **Mn**, 1.00 **Si**, 16.00-18.00 **Cr**, 10.00-14.00 **Ni**, 2.00-3.00 **Mo**, 0.75 **Cu**, 0.040 **P**, 0.030 **S**	**Solution treated**: ≤0.025 (≤0.64) **diam**, 100 (690) max **TS**, 40 **El**
AMS 5727B		US	Forgings	0.08 **C**, 2.00 **Mn**, 1.00 **Si**, 15.00 **Cr**, 24.00-27.00 **Ni**, 5.50-7.00 **Mo**, 0.50 **Cu**, 0.10-0.20 **N**, 0.030 **P**, 0.030 **S**	**Stress relieved**: all **diam**, (690) **TS**, (550) **YS**, 10 **El**
ANSI/ASTM A 412	Type XM-10	US	Plate, sheet, strip	0.08 **C**, 8.00-10.00 **Mn**, 1.00 **Si**, 19.00-21.50 **Cr**, 5.50-7.50 **Ni**, 0.060 **P**, 0.030 **S**, 0.15-0.40 **N**	**Annealed**: 0.015 (0.38) **diam**, 100 (690) **TS**, 60 (415) **YS**, 40 **El**; **10% cold rolled**: 0.015 (0.38) **diam**, 130 (895) **TS**, 115 (795) **YS**, 15 **El**; **Annealed (plate)**: all **diam**, 90 (620) **TS**, 50 (345) **YS**
ANSI/ASTM A 580	Grade XM-29	US	Wire	0.08 **C**, 11.50-14.50 **Mn**, 1.00 **Si**, 17.00-19.00 **Cr**, 2.25-3.75 **Ni**, 0.20-0.40 **N**, 0.060 **P**, 0.030 **P**	**Annealed**: all **diam**, 100 (690) **TS**, 55 (380) **YS**, 30 **El**
ANSI/ASTM A 249	TP XM-29	US	Tube: welded	0.08 **C**, 11.50-14.50 **Mn**, 1.00 **Si**, 17.00-19.00 **Cr**, 2.25-3.75 **Ni**, 0.20-0.40 **N**, 0.040 **P**, 0.030 **S**	**Solution annealed**: 0.312 (7.94) **diam**, 100 (690) **TS**, 55 (380) **YS**, 35 **El**
MIL-T-8506A	Type 304	US	Tube: seamless, welded	0.08 **C**, 2.00 **Mn**, 1.00 **Si**, 18.00-20.00 **Cr**, 8.00-12.00 **Ni**, 0.50 **Mo**, 0.50 **Cu**, 0.03 **P**, 0.030 **S**	**Solution annealed**: >0.010 **diam**, (689) **TS**, 35 **El**
MIL-T-8808A	347	US	Tube:seamless, welded	0.08 **C**, 2.00 **Mn**, 1.00 **Si**, 17.0-20.0 **Cr**, 9.00-13.00 **Ni**, 0.50 **Mo**, 0.50 **Cu**, 1.10 **Nb**, 0.040 **P**, 0.030 **S**	**Solution annealed**: >3% of OD **diam**, (689) max **TS**, (206) **YS**, 35 **El**

WROUGHT STAINLESS STEELS

specification number	designation	country	product forms	composition	mechanical properties (see page iv for explanation)
MIL–T–8808A	321	US	Tube: seamless, welded	0.08 **C**, 2.00 **Mn**, 1.00 **Si**, 17.0–20.0 **Cr**, 9.0–12.0 **Ni**, 0.50 **Mo**, 0.50 **Cu**, 0.040 **P**, 0.030 **S**, 0.75 **Ti**	**Solution annealed**: >3% of OD **diam**, (689) max **TS**, (206) **YS**, 35 **El**
AMS 5566F	Type I, II	US	Tube	0.08 **C**, 2.00 **Mn**, 0.75 **Si**, 18.00–20.00 **Cr**, 8.00–12.00 **Ni**, 0.75 **Mo**, 0.75 **Cu**, 0.040 **P**, 0.030 **S**	**Cold finished**: all **diam**, 95 (655) **TS**
AISI 310S		US	Sheet, strip, plate, bar, wire	0.08 **C**, 2.00 **Mn**, 1.50 **Si**, 24.00–26.00 **Cr**, 19.00–22.00 **Ni**, 0.045 **P**, 0.030 **S**	**Annealed (sheet)**: all **diam**, 95 (655) max **TS**, 45 (310) max **YS**, 45 **El**
AISI 347		US	Sheet, strip, plate	0.08 **C**, 2.00 **Mn**, 1.00 **Si**, 17.00–19.00 **Cr**, 9.00–13.00 **Ni**, 10 x C min **Cb+Ta**, 0.20 **Co**, 0.04 **P**, 0.030 **S**	**Annealed**: all **diam**, 95 (655) max **TS**, 40 (276) max **YS**, 45 **El**
ANSI/ASTM A 193	Grade B8M	US	Bar	0.08 **C**, 2.00 **Mn**, 1.00 **Si**, 16.00–18.00 **Cr**, 10.00–14.00 **Ni**, 2.00–3.00 **Mo**, 0.045 **P**, 0.030 **S**	**Solution annealed**: (25.4–31.6) 1.0–1.25 **diam**, 95 (655) **TS**, 65 (448) **YS**, 25 **El**
SIS 14 25 70	SIS 25 70–03	Sweden	Bar, forgings, sheet, wire	0.08 **C**, 2.0 **Mn**, 1.0 **Si**, 13.5–16.0 **Cr**, 24.0–27.0 **Ni**, 1.0–1.5 **Mo**, 0.10–0.50 **V**, 0.35 **Al**, 0.003–0.010 **B**, 0.025 **P**, 0.025 **S**, 1.9–2.3 **Ti**	**Solution annealed**: (≤100) **diam**, (650) **TS**, (250) **YS**, 45 **El**
SIS 14 25 70	SIS 25 70–03	Sweden	Bar, forgings, plate, wire	0.08 **C**, 2.0 **Mn**, 1.0 **Si**, 13.5–16.0 **Cr**, 24.0–27.0 **Ni**, 1.0–1.5 **Mo**, 0.10–0.50 **V**, 0.35 **Al**, 0.003–0.010 **B**, 1.9–2.3 **Ti**	**Solution annealed**: all **diam**, (650) **TS**, (250) **YS**, 45 **El**
NF A 35–575	Z 6 CNDT 17.12	France	Wire, rod	0.08 **C**, 2.0 **Mn**, 1.0 **Si**, 16.0–18.0 **Cr**, 10.5–13.0 **Ni**, 2.0–2.5 **Mo**, 0.040 **P**, 0.030 **S**, 5 x C–0.6 **Ti**	**Stress hardened 0%**: all **diam**, (640) **TS**; **Stress hardened 40%**: all **diam**, (1130) **TS**; **Stress hardened 60%**: all **diam**, (1370) **TS**; **Stress hardened 80%**: all **diam**, (1620) **TS**
AISI 304N		US	Sheet, bar	0.08 **C**, 2.00 **Mn**, 1.00 **Si**, 18.00–20.00 **Cr**, 8.00–10.50 **Ni**, 0.10–0.16 **N**, 0.045 **P**, 0.030 **S**	**Annealed (sheet)**: all **diam**, 90 (621) max **TS**, 48 (331) max **YS**, 50 **El**
AISI 309S		US	Sheet, strip, plate, bar, wire	0.08 **C**, 2.00 **Mn**, 1.00 **Si**, 22.00–24.00 **Cr**, 12.00–15.00 **Ni**, 0.045 **P**, 0.030 **S**	**Annealed (sheet)**: all **diam**, 90 (621) max **TS**, 45 (310) max **YS**, 45 **El**
AISI 316N		US	Sheet, bar	0.08 **C**, 2.00 **Mn**, 1.00 **Si**, 16.00–18.00 **Cr**, 10.00–14.00 **Ni**, 2.00–3.00 **Mo**, 0.10–0.16 **N**, 0.045 **P**, 0.030 **S**	**Annealed (sheet)**: all **diam**, 90 (621) max **TS**, 48 (331) max **YS**, 48 **El**
AISI 317		US	Sheet, strip, plate, bar	0.08 **C**, 2.00 **Mn**, 1.00 **Si**, 18.00–20.00 **Cr**, 11.00–15.00 **Ni**, 3.00–4.00 **Mo**, 0.045 **P**, 0.030 **S**	**Annealed (sheet)**: all **diam**, 90 (621) max **TS**, 40 (276) max **YS**, 45 **El**
AISI 321		US	Sheet, strip, plate, bar, wire	0.08 **C**, 2.00 **Mn**, 1.00 **Si**, 17.00–19.00 **Cr**, 9.00–12.00 **Ni**, 0.045 **P**, 0.030 **S**	**Annealed (Sheet)**: all **diam**, 90 (621) max **TS**, 35 (241) max **YS**, 45 **El**
ANSI/ASTM A 473	XM–10	US	Forgings	0.08 **C**, 8.00–10.00 **Mn**, 1.00 **Si**, 19.00–21.50 **Cr**, 5.50–7.50 **Ni**, 0.15–0.40 **N**, 0.060 **P**, 0.030 **S**	**Solution annealed**: all **diam**, 90 (620) **TS**, 50 (345) **YS**, 45 **El**
ANSI/ASTM A 479	XM–17	US	Bar, shapes	0.08 **C**, 7.50–9.00 **Mn**, 1.00 **Si**, 17.50–22.00 **Cr**, 5.00–7.00 **Ni**, 2.00–3.00 **Mo**, 0.25–0.50 **N**, 0.045 **P**, 0.030 **S**	**Solution annealed**: all **diam**, 90 (620) **TS**, 50 (345) **YS**, 40 **El**
ANSI/ASTM A 276	XM–21	US	Bar, shapes	0.08 **C**, 2.00 **Mn**, 1.00 **Si**, 18.00–20.00 **Cr**, 8.00–10.50 **Ni**, 0.16–0.30 **N**, 0.045 **P**, 0.030 **S**	**Annealed**: all **diam**, 90 (620) **TS**, 50 (345) **YS**, 30 **El**; **Cold worked–high tensile**: ≥1 (≥25.40) **diam**, 145 (1000) **TS**, 125 (860) **YS**, 15 **El**
IS 6528	04Cr18Ni10	India	Wire	0.08 **C**, 2.0 **Mn**, 1.0 **Si**, 17.0–20.0 **Cr**, 8.0–12.0 **Ni**, 0.045 **P**, 0.030 **S**	**Annealed or solution annealed**: all **diam**, (620) **TS**, (310) **YS**, 35 **El**
IS 6528	04Cr17Ni12Mo2	India	Wire	0.08 **C**, 2.0 **Mn**, 1.0 **Si**, 16.0–18.5 **Cr**, 10.0–14.0 **Ni**, 2.0–3.0 **Mo**, 0.045 **P**, 0.030 **S**	**Annealed or solution annealed**: all **diam**, (620) **TS**, (310) **YS**, 35 **El**
ANSI/ASTM A 312	TP XM–10	US	Pipe: seamless or welded	0.08 **C**, 8.00–10.00 **Mn**, 1.00 **Si**, 19.00–21.50 **Cr**, 5.50–7.50 **Ni**, 0.15–0.40 **N**, 0.040 **P**, 0.030 **S**	**Solution annealed**: 0.31 (7.94) **diam**, 90 (620) **TS**, 50 (345) **YS**, 35 **El**

WROUGHT STAINLESS STEELS

specification number	designation	country	product forms	composition	mechanical properties (see page iv for explanation)
ASTM A 240	Type XM21	US	Plate, sheet, strip	0.08 **C**, 2.00 **Mn**, 1.00 **Si**, 18.00–20.00 **Cr**, 8.00–10.50 **Ni**, 0.16–0.30 **N**, 0.045 **P**, 0.030 **S**	**Solution annealed, hot rolled or cold rolled (sheet, strip):** all **diam**, 90 (620) **TS**, 50 (345) **YS**, 30 **El**
ANSI/ASTM A 479	Grade XM 17	US	Bar, shapes	0.08 **C**, 7.50–9.00 **Mn**, 1.00 **Si**, 17.50–22.00 **Cr**, 5.00–7.00 **Ni**, 2.00–3.00 **Mo**, 0.25–0.50 **N**, 0.045 **P**, 0.030 **S**	**Solution annealed**: all **diam**, (620) **TS**, (345) **YS**, 40 **El**
ANSI/ASTM A 240	Grade XM 21	US	Sheet, strip	0.08 **C**, 2.00 **Mn**, 1.00 **Si**, 18.00–20.00 **Cr**, 8.00–10.50 **Ni**, 0.16–0.30 **N**, 0.045 **P**, 0.030 **S**	**Solution annealed**: all **diam**, (620) **TS**, (345) **YS**, 30 **El**
ANSI/ASTM A 240	Grade XM 17	US	Plate	0.08 **C**, 7.50–9.00 **Mn**, 1.00 **Si**, 17.50–22.00 **Cr**, 5.00–7.00 **Ni**, 2.00–3.00 **Mo**, 0.25–0.50 **N**, 0.045 **P**, 0.030 **S**	**Solution annealed**: all **diam**, (620) **TS**, (345) **YS**, 40 **El**
ANSI/ASTM A 580	Grade 304	US	Wire	0.08 **C**, 2.00 **Mn**, 1.00 **Si**, 18.00–20.00 **Cr**, 8.00–10.50 **Ni**, 0.045 **P**, 0.030 **S**, 0.10 **N**	**Cold finished A**: all **diam**, 90 (620) **TS**, 45 (310) **YS**, 35 **El**; **Annealed**: all **diam**, 75 (520) **TS**, 30 (210) **YS**, 35 **El**; **Cold finished B**: all **diam**, 125 (860) **TS**, 100 (690) **YS**, 12 **El**
ANSI/ASTM A 580	Grade 308	US	Wire	0.08 **C**, 2.00 **Mn**, 1.00 **Si**, 19.00–21.00 **Cr**, 10.00–12.00 **Ni**, 0.045 **P**, 0.030 **S**	**Cold finished**: all **diam**, 90 (620) **TS**, 45 (310) **YS**, 35 **El**; **Annealed**: all **diam**, 75 (520) **TS**, 30 (210) **YS**, 35 **El**
ANSI/ASTM A 580	Grade 309S	US	Wire	0.08 **C**, 2.00 **Mn**, 1.00 **Si**, 22.00–24.00 **Cr**, 12.00–15.00 **Ni**, 0.045 **P**, 0.030 **S**	**Cold finished**: all **diam**, 90 (620) **TS**, 45 (310) **YS**, 35 **El**; **Annealed**: all **diam**, 75 (520) **TS**, 30 (210) **YS**, 35 **El**
ANSI/ASTM A 580	Grade 310S	US	Wire	0.08 **C**, 2.00 **Mn**, 1.50 **Si**, 24.00–26.00 **Cr**, 19.00–22.00 **Ni**, 0.045 **P**, 0.030 **S**	**Cold finished**: all **diam**, 90 (620) **TS**, 45 (310) **YS**, 35 **El**; **Annealed**: all **diam**, 75 (520) **TS**, 30 (210) **YS**, 35 **El**
ANSI/ASTM A 580	Grade 316	US	Wire	0.08 **C**, 2.00 **Mn**, 1.00 **Si**, 16.00–18.00 **Cr**, 10.00–14.00 **Ni**, 2.00–3.00 **Mo**, 0.045 **P**, 0.030 **S**, 0.10 **N**	**Cold finished A**: all **diam**, 90 (620) **TS**, 45 (310) **YS**, 35 **El**; **Annealed**: all **diam**, 75 (520) **TS**, 30 (210) **YS**, 35 **El**; **Cold finished B**: all **diam**, 125 (860) **TS**, 100 (690) **YS**, 12 **El**
ANSI/ASTM A 580	Grade 317	US	Wire	0.08 **C**, 2.00 **Mn**, 1.00 **Si**, 18.00–20.00 **Cr**, 11.00–15.00 **Ni**, 3.00–4.00 **Mo**, 0.045 **P**, 0.030 **S**, 0.10 **N**	**Cold finished A**: all **diam**, 90 (620) **TS**, 45 (310) **YS**, 35 **El**; **Annealed**: all **diam**, 75 (520) **TS**, 30 (210) **YS**, 35 **El**; **Cold finished B**: all **diam**, 125 (860) **TS**, 100 (690) **YS**, 12 **El**
ANSI/ASTM A 580	Grade 321	US	Wire	0.08 **C**, 2.00 **Mn**, 1.00 **Si**, 17.00–19.00 **Cr**, 9.00–12.00 **Ni**, 0.045 **P**, 0.030 **S**, 5 x C min **Ti**	**Cold finished**: all **diam**, 90 (620) **TS**, 45 (310) **YS**, 35 **El**; **Annealed**: all **diam**, 75 (520) **TS**, 30 (210) **YS**, 35 **El**
ANSI/ASTM A 580	Grade 347	US	Wire	0.08 **C**, 2.00 **Mn**, 1.00 **Si**, 17.00–19.00 **Cr**, 9.00–13.00 **Ni**, 0.045 **P**, 0.030 **S**, 10 x C min **Cb+Ta**	**Cold finished**: all **diam**, 90 (620) **TS**, 45 (310) **YS**, 35 **El**; **Annealed**: all **diam**, 75 (520) **TS**, 30 (210) **YS**, 35 **El**
ANSI/ASTM A 580	Grade 348	US	Wire	0.08 **C**, 2.00 **Mn**, 1.00 **Si**, 17.00–19.00 **Cr**, 9.00–13.00 **Ni**, 0.045 **P**, 0.030 **S**, 10 x C min **Cb+Ta**, 0.10 **Ta**, 0.20 **Co**	**Cold finished**: all **diam**, 90 (620) **TS**, 45 (310) **YS**, 35 **El**; **Annealed**: all **diam**, 75 (520) **TS**, 30 (210) **YS**, 35 **El**
AMS 5697A		US	Wire	0.08 **C**, 2.00 **Mn**, 1.00 **Si**, 18.00–20.00 **Cr**, 8.00–11.00 **Ni**, 0.75 **Mo**, 0.75 **Cu**, 0.040 **P**, 0.030 **S**	**Solution treated**: all **diam**, (620) **TS**, 35 **El**
BS 3014	Grade 1	UK	Tube	0.08 **C**, 0.50–2.00 **Mn**, 0.20–1.00 **Si**, 17.5–19.5 **Cr**, 8.0–10.0 **Ni**, 0.040 **P**, 0.040 **S**	**As welded**: ≤1 **diam**, (620) **TS**, (310) **YS**, 30 **El**; **Cold drawn**: ≤1 **diam**, (690) **TS**, (465) **YS**, 15 **El**; **Annealed**: ≤1 **diam**, (540) **TS**, (195) **YS**, 45 **El**
BS 3014	Grade 5	UK	Tube	0.08 **C**, 0.50–2.00 **Mn**, 0.20–1.00 **Si**, 17.0–20.0 **Cr**, 9.0–13.0 **Ni**, 10 x C–1.0 **Nb**, 0.040 **P**, 0.040 **S**	**As welded**: ≤1 **diam**, (620) **TS**, (310) **YS**, 30 **El**; **Cold drawn**: ≤1 **diam**, (690) **TS**, (465) **YS**, 15 **El**; **Annealed**: ≤1 **diam**, (540) **TS**, (195) **YS**, 45 **El**

specification number	designation	country	product forms	composition	mechanical properties (see page iv for explanation)
BS 3014	Grade 6	UK	Tube	0.08 **C**, 0.50–2.00 **Mn**, 0.20–1.00 **Si**, 16.5–18.5 **Cr**, 10.0–12.0 **Ni**, 2.5–3.0 **Mo**, 0.040 **P**, 0.040 **S**	**As welded:** ≤1 **diam**, (620) **TS**, (310) **YS**, 30 **El**; **Cold drawn:** ≤1 **diam**, (690) **TS**, (465) **YS**, 15 **El**; **Annealed:** ≤1 **diam**, (540) **TS**, (195) **YS**, 45 **El**
NF A 35–577	Z 6 CND 17.11 (DF)	France	Bar, wire, rod	0.08 **C**, 2.0 **Mn**, 1.0 **Si**, 16.0–18.0 **Cr**, 10.0–12.0 **Ni**, 2–2.5 **Mo**, 0.040 **P**, 0.030 **S**	**Solution annealed**: (6) **diam**, (620) max **TS**
ANSI/ASTM A 580	Grade XM–10	US	Wire	0.08 **C**, 8.00–10.00 **Mn**, 1.00 **Si**, 19.00–21.50 **Cr**, 5.50–7.50 **Ni**, 0.15–0.40 **N**, 0.060 **P**, 0.030 **S**	**Annealed**: all **diam**, 90 (620) **TS**, 50 (340) **YS**, 45 **El**
ASTM A 581	Type XM–1	US	Wire	0.08 **C**, 5.00–6.00 **Mn**, 1.00 **Si**, 16.00–18.00 **Cr**, 5.00–6.50 **Ni**, 0.50 **Mo**, 1.75–2.25 **Cu**, 0.04 **P**, 0.18–0.35 **S**	**Annealed**: 0.5 **diam**, 85 (590) **TS**; **Cold worked**: 0.5 **diam**, 115 (790) **TS**
ASTM A 581	Type XM–34	US	Wire	0.08 **C**, 1.25–2.50 **Mn**, 1.00 **Si**, 17.50–19.50 **Cr**, 1.50–2.50 **Mo**, 0.04 **P**, 0.15 min **S**	**Annealed**: 0.5 **diam**, 85 (590) **TS**
NF A 35–577	Z 6 C 13 (DF)	France	Bar, wire, rod	0.08 **C**, 1.0 **Mn**, 1.0 **Si**, 11.5–13.5 **Cr**, 0.5 **Ni**, 0.040 **P**, 0.030 **S**	**Annealed**: (≥6) **diam**, (590) max **TS**
NF A 35–575	Z 6 CNT 18.10	France	Wire, rod	0.08 **C**, 2.0 **Mn**, 1.0 **Si**, 17.0–19.0 **Cr**, 9.0–11.0 **Ni**, 0.040 **P**, 0.030 **S**, 5 x C–0.6 **Ti**	**Stress hardened 0%**: all **diam**, (590) **TS**; **Stress hardened 40%**: all **diam**, (1030) **TS**; **Stress hardened 60%**: all **diam**, (1220) **TS**; **Stress hardened 80%**: all **diam**, (1470) **TS**
JIS G 3459	SUS 329 JITP	Japan	Pipe: seamless or welded	0.08 **C**, 1.50 **Mn**, 1.00 **Si**, 23.00–28.00 **Cr**, 3.00–6.00 **Ni**, 1.00–3.00 **Mo**, 0.040 **P**, 0.030 **S**	**Solution annealed**: (≥8) **diam**, (588) **TS**, (392) **YS**, 18 **El**
JIS G 3463	SUS 329JITB	Japan	Tube: seamless or welded	0.08 **C**, 1.50 **Mn**, 1.00 **Si**, 23.00–28.00 **Cr**, 3.00–6.00 **Ni**, 1.00–3.00 **Mo**, 0.040 **P**, 0.030 **S**	**Solution annealed**: (≥8) **diam**, (588) **TS**, (392) **YS**, 18 **El**
JIS G 4303	SUS 329J1	Japan	Bar	0.08 **C**, 1.50 **Mn**, 1.00 **Si**, 23.00–28.00 **Cr**, 3.00–6.00 **Ni**, 1.00–3.00 **Mo**, 0.040 **P**, 0.030 **S**	**Solution annealed**: (≤75) **diam**, (588) **TS**, (392) **YS**, 18 **El**
JIS G 4304	SUS 329J1	Japan	Sheet, plate	0.08 **C**, 1.50 **Mn**, 1.00 **Si**, 23.00–28.00 **Cr**, 3.00–6.00 **Ni**, 1.00–3.00 **Mo**, 0.040 **P**, 0.030 **S**	**Hot rolled and solution annealed**: all **diam**, (588) **TS**, (392) **YS**, 18 **El**
JIS G 4307	SUS 329J1	Japan	Strip	0.08 **C**, 1.50 **Mn**, 1.00 **Si**, 23.00–28.00 **Cr**, 3.00–6.00 **Ni**, 1.00–3.00 **Mo**, 0.040 **P**, 0.030 **S**	**Cold rolled and solution annealed**: all **diam**, (588) **TS**, (392) **YS**, 18 **El**
JIS G 4305	SUS 329J1	Japan	Sheet, plate	0.08 **C**, 1.50 **Mn**, 1.00 **Si**, 23.00–28.00 **Cr**, 3.00–6.00 **Ni**, 1.00–3.00 **Mo**, 0.040 **P**, 0.030 **S**	**Cold rolled and solution annealed**: all **diam**, (588) **TS**, (392) **YS**, 18 **El**
JIS G 4306	SUS 329J1	Japan	Strip	0.08 **C**, 1.50 **Mn**, 1.00 **Si**, 23.00–28.00 **Cr**, 3.00–6.00 **Ni**, 1.00–3.00 **Mo**, 0.040 **P**, 0.030 **S**	**Hot rolled and solution annealed**: all **diam**, (588) **TS**, (392) **YS**, 18 **El**
AMS 5645J		US	Bar, forgings, tube, rings, wire	0.08 **C**, 2.00 **Mn**, 1.00 **Si**, 17.00–19.00 **Cr**, 8.00–12.00 **Ni**, 0.75 **Mo**, 0.50 **Cu**, 6 x C–0.70 **Nb+Ti**, 0.40 **P**, 0.030 **S**	**Solution heat treated and cold finished (wire)**: all **diam**, 85 (586) **TS**
AMS 5646G		US	Bar, forgings, tube, rings, wire	0.08 **C**, 2.00 **Mn**, 1.00 **Si**, 17.00–19.00 **Cr**, 9.00–12.00 **Ni**, 0.75 **Mo**, 0.50 **Cu**, 10 x C 1.10 **Nb+Ta**, 0.040 **P**, 0.030 **S**	**Solution heat treated, cold finished (wire)**: all **diam**, 85 (586) **TS**
AMS 5762		US	Bar, forgings, wire	0.08 **C**, 5.00–6.50 **Mn**, 0.20–0.70 **Si**, 16.00–18.00 **Cr**, 5.00–6.50 **Ni**, 0.50 **Mo**, 1.75–2.25 **Cu**, 0.04 **P**, 0.18–0.35 **S**	**Solution heat treated**: all **diam**, 85 (586) **TS**
AISI 316F		US	Sheet, bar	0.08 **C**, 2.00 **Mn**, 1.00 **Si**, 16.00–18.00 **Cr**, 10.00–14.00 **Ni**, 1.75–2.50 **Mo**, 0.20 **P**, 0.10 min **S**	**Annealed (sheet)**: all **diam**, 85 (586) max **TS**, 38 (262) max **YS**, 60 **El**
ANSI/ASTM A 666	316, grade B	US	Sheet, strip, plate, bar	0.08 **C**, 2.00 **Mn**, 1.00 **Si**, 16.00–18.00 **Cr**, 10.00–14.00 **Ni**, 2.00–3.00 **Mo**, 0.045 **P**, 0.030 **S**	**Annealed (plate, sheet, strip)**: >0.030 (>0.76) **diam**, 85 (585) **TS**, 45 (310) **YS**, 35 **El**
ANSI/ASTM A 666	Type 316, grade B	US	Sheet, strip, plate, bar	0.08 **C**, 2.00 **Mn**, 1.00 **Si**, 16.00–18.00 **Cr**, 10.00–14.00 **Ni**, 2.00–3.00 **Mo**, 0.045 **P**, 0.030 **S**	**Cold rolled (plate, sheet, strip)**: ≤0.015 (≤0.38) **diam**, 85 (585) **TS**, 45 (310) **YS**, 35 **El**

WROUGHT STAINLESS STEELS

specification number	designation	country	product forms	composition	mechanical properties (see page iv for explanation)
ANSI/ASTM A 493	Type 347	US	Bar, wire	0.08 **C**, 2.00 **Mn**, 1.00 **Si**, 17.00–19.00 **Cr**, 9.00–13.00 **Ni**, 0.045 **P**, 0.030 **S**, 10 x C–1.10 **Nb+Ta**	**Lightly drafted (wire):** ≥0.156 (≥3.96) **diam**, 85 (585) **TS**; **Annealed (wire):** ≥0.156 (≥3.96) **diam**, 80 (550) **TS**
ANSI/ASTM A 493	Type 321	US	Bar, wire	0.08 **C**, 2.00 **Mn**, 1.00 **Si**, 17.00–19.00 **Cr**, 9.00–12.00 **Ni**, 0.045 **P**, 0.030 **S**, 5 x C–0.70 **Ti**	**Lightly drafted (wire):** ≥0.156 (≥3.96) **diam**, 85 (585) **TS**; **Annealed (wire):** ≥0.156 (≥3.96) **diam**, 80 (550) **TS**
ANSI/ASTM A 666	Type 316, grade B	US	Sheet, strip, plate, bar	0.08 **C**, 2.00 **Mn**, 1.00 **Si**, 16.00–18.00 **Cr**, 10.00–14.00 **Ni**, 2.00–3.00 **Mo**, 0.045 **P**, 0.030 **S**	**Annealed (plate, sheet, strip):** 0.015 **diam**, (585) **TS**, (310) **YS**, 35 **El**
ANSI/ASTM A 479	Grade 316	US	Bar, shapes	0.08 **C**, 2.00 **Mn**, 1.00 **Si**, 16.00–18.00 **Cr**, 10.00–14.00 **Ni**, 2.00–3.00 **Mo**, 0.10 **N**, 0.045 **P**, 0.030 **S**	**Strain hardened**: all **diam**, (585) **TS**, (450) **YS**, 30 **El**
ANSI/ASTM A 240	Grade XM 21	US	Plate	0.08 **C**, 2.00 **Mn**, 1.00 **Si**, 18.00–20.00 **Cr**, 8.00–10.50 **Ni**, 0.16–0.30 **N**, 0.045 **P**, 0.030 **S**	**Solution annealed**: all **diam**, (585) **TS**, (275) **YS**, 30 **El**
AISI 304		US	Sheet, strip, plate, bar, wire	0.08 **C**, 2.00 **Mn**, 1.00 **Si**, 18.00–20.00 **Cr**, 8.00–10.50 **Ni**, 0.045 **P**, 0.030 **S**	**Annealed**: all **diam**, 84 (579) max **TS**, 42 (290) max **YS**, 55 **El**
AISI 316		US	Sheet, strip, plate, bar, wire	0.08 **C**, 2.00 **Mn**, 1.00 **Si**, 16.00–18.00 **Cr**, 10.00–14.00 **Ni**, 0.045 **P**, 0.030 **S**	**Annealed (sheet)**: all **diam**, 84 (579) max **TS**, 42 (290) max **YS**, 50 **El**
NF A 35–577	Z 6 NC 18.16 (DF)	France	Bar, wire, rod	0.08 **C**, 2.0 **Mn**, 1.0 **Si**, 15.0–17.0 **Cr**, 17.0–19.0 **Ni**, 0.040 **P**, 0.030 **S**	**Solution annealed**: (6) **diam**, (570) max **TS**
NOM–B–194	Grade TP 316N	Mexico	Tube: seamless	0.08 **C**, 2.00 **Mn**, 0.75 **Si**, 16.0–18.0 **Cr**, 11.00–14.0 **Ni**, 2.00–3.0 **Mo**, 0.10–0.16 $\mathbf{N_2}$ **P**, 0.030 **S**	**Quenched**: (0.38–12.7) **diam**, (552) **TS**, (241) **YS**
NOM–B–194	Grade TP 304N	Mexico	Tube: seamless	0.08 **C**, 2.00 **Mn**, 0.75 **Si**, 18.0–20.0 **Cr**, 8.00–11.0 **Ni**, 0.10–0.16 $\mathbf{N_2}$ **P**, 0.030 **S**	**Quenched**: (0.38–12.7) **diam**, (552) **TS**, (241) **YS**
ANSI/ASTM A 312	TP 304N	US	Pipe: seamless or welded	0.08 **C**, 2.00 **Mn**, 0.75 **Si**, 18.0–20.0 **Cr**, 8.00–11.0 **Ni**, 0.10–0.16 **N**, 0.040 **P**, 0.030 **S**	**Solution annealed**: 0.31 (7.94) **diam**, 80 (552) **TS**, 35 (241) **YS**, 35 **El**
ANSI/ASTM A 312	TP 316N	US	Pipe: seamless or welded	0.08 **C**, 2.00 **Mn**, 0.75 **Si**, 16.0–18.0 **Cr**, 11.0–14.0 **Ni**, 2.00–3.00 **Mo**, 0.10–0.16 **N**, 0.040 **P**, 0.030 **S**	**Solution annealed**: 0.31 (7.94) **diam**, 80 (552) **TS**, 35 (241) **YS**, 35 **El**
AISI 330		US	Sheet, strip, plate, bar	0.08 **C**, 2.00 **Mn**, 0.75–1.50 **Si**, 17.00–20.00 **Cr**, 34.00–37.00 **Ni**, 0.040 **P**, 0.000 **S**	**Annealed**: all **diam**, 80 (552) max **TS**, 38 (262) max **YS**, 40 **El**
ANSI/ASTM A 666	304, grade B	US	Sheet, strip, plate, bar	0.08 **C**, 2.00 **Mn**, 1.00 **Si**, 18.00–20.00 **Cr**, 8.00–10.50 **Ni**, 0.045 **P**, 0.030 **S**	**Annealed (plate, sheet, strip):** >0.030 (>0.76) **diam**, 80 (550) **TS**, 45 (310) **YS**, 35 **El**
ANSI/ASTM A 479	304N	US	Bar, shapes	0.08 **C**, 2.00 **Mn**, 1.00 **Si**, 18.00–20.00 **Cr**, 8.00–12.00 **Ni**, 0.10–0.16 **N**, 0.045 **P**, 0.030 **S**	**Solution annealed**: all **diam**, 80 (550) **TS**, 35 (240) **YS**, 30 **El**
ANSI/ASTM A 479	316N	US	Bar, shapes	0.08 **C**, 2.00 **Mn**, 1.00 **Si**, 16.00–18.00 **Cr**, 10.00–14.00 **Ni**, 2.00–3.00 **Mo**, 0.10–0.16 **Ni**, 0.045 **P**, 0.030 **S**	**Solution annealed**: all **diam**, 80 (550) **TS**, 35 (240) **YS**, 30 **El**
ANSI/ASTM A 666	Type 304, grade B	US	Sheet, strip, plate, bar	0.08 **C**, 2.00 **Mn**, 1.00 **Si**, 18.00–20.00 **Cr**, 8.00–10.50 **Ni**, 0.045 **P**, 0.030 **S**	**Cold rolled (plate, sheet, strip):** ≤0.015 (≤0.38) **diam**, 80 (550) **TS**, 45 (310) **YS**, 35 **El**
ANSI/ASTM A 276	316N	US	Bar, shapes	0.08 **C**, 2.00 **Mn**, 1.00 **Si**, 16.00–18.00 **Cr**, 10.00–14.00 **Ni**, 2.00–3.00 **Mo**, 0.10–0.16 **N**, 0.045 **P**, 0.030 **S**	**Annealed**: all **diam**, 80 (550) **TS**, 35 (240) **YS**, 30 **El**
ANSI/ASTM A 276	304N	US	Bar, shapes	0.08 **C**, 2.00 **Mn**, 1.00 **Si**, 18.00–20.00 **Cr**, 8.00–10.50 **Ni**, 0.10–0.16 **N**, 0.045 **P**, 0.030 **S**	**Annealed**: all **diam**, 80 (550) **TS**, 35 (240) **YS**, 30 **El**
BS T.67		UK	Tube: aircraft quality	0.08 **C**, 0.5–2.0 **Mn**, 0.2–1.0 **Si**, 17.0–19.0 **Cr**, 9.0–12.0 **Ni**, 0.035 **P**, 0.025 **S**, 5 x C–0.70 **Ti**	**Annealed**: all **diam**, (550) **TS**, (210) **YS**
BS T.66		UK	Tube: aircraft quality	0.08 **C**, 0.5–2.0 **Mn**, 0.2–1.0 **Si**, 17.0–19.0 **Cr**, 9.0–12.0 **Ni**, 10 x C–1.0 **Nb**, 0.035 **P**, 0.025 **S**	**Annealed**: all **diam**, (550) **TS**, (210) **YS**

WROUGHT STAINLESS STEELS

specification number	designation	country	product forms	composition	mechanical properties (see page iv for explanation)
BS T72–T73	T72	UK	Tube: aircraft quality	0.08 **C**, 0.5–2.0 **Mn**, 0.2–1.0 **Si**, 17.0–19.0 **Cr**, 9.0–12.0 **Ni**, 0.50 **Cu**, 10 x C–1.0 **Nb**, 0.035 **P**, 0.025 **S**	**Solution annealed**: (≤0.7) **diam**, (550) **TS**, (210) **YS**, 40 **El**
BS T72–T73	T73	UK	Tube: aircraft quality	0.08 **C**, 0.5–2.0 **Mn**, 0.2–1.0 **Si**, 17.0–19.0 **Cr**, 9.0–12.0 **Ni**, 0.50 **Cu**, 0.035 **P**, 0.025 **S**, 5 x C–0.50 **Ti**	**Solution annealed**: (≤0.7) **diam**, (550) **TS**, (210) **YS**, 40 **El**
ANSI/ASTM A 376	TP 304N	US	Pipe: seamless	0.08 **C**, 2.00 **Mn**, 0.75 **Si**, 18.0–20.0 **Cr**, 8.00–11.0 **Ni**, 0.10–0.16 **N**, 0.040 **P**, 0.030 **S**	**Solution annealed**: 0.312 (7.94) **diam**, 80 (550) **TS**, 35 (240) **YS**, 35 **El**
ANSI/ASTM A 376	TP 316N	US	Pipe: seamless	0.08 **C**, 2.00 **Mn**, 0.75 **Si**, 16.0–18.0 **Cr**, 11.0–14.0 **Ni**, 2.00–3.00 **Mo**, 0.10–0.16 **N**, 0.040 **P**, 0.030 **S**	**Solution annealed**: 0.312 (7.94) **diam**, 80 (550) **TS**, 35 (240) **YS**, 35 **El**
ASTM A 240	Type 316N	US	Plate, sheet, strip	0.08 **C**, 2.00 **Mn**, 1.00 **Si**, 16.00–18.00 **Cr**, 10.00–14.00 **Ni**, 2.00–3.00 **Mo**, 0.10–0.16 **N**, 0.045 **P**, 0.030 **S**	**Solution annealed, hot rolled or cold rolled**: all **diam**, 80 (550) **TS**, 35 (240) **YS**, 30 **El**
ASTM A 240	Type 304N	US	Plate, sheet, strip	0.08 **C**, 2.00 **Mn**, 1.00 **Si**, 18.00–20.00 **Cr**, 8.00–10.50 **Ni**, 0.10–0.16 **N**, 0.045 **P**, 0.030 **S**	**Solution annealed, hot rolled or cold rolled**: all **diam**, 80 (550) **TS**, 35 (240) **YS**, 30 **El**
ANSI/ASTM A 493	Type 316	US	Bar, wire	0.08 **C**, 2.00 **Mn**, 1.00 **Si**, 16.00–18.00 **Cr**, 10.00–14.00 **Ni**, 2.00–3.00 **Mo**, 0.10 **N**, 0.045 **P**, 0.030 **S**	**Lightly drafted (wire)**: ≥0.156 (≥3.96) **diam**, 80 (550) **TS**; **Annealed (wire)**: ≥0.156 (≥3.96) **diam**, 75 (520) **TS**
ANSI/ASTM A 493	Type 304	US	Bar, wire	0.08 **C**, 2.00 **Mn**, 1.00 **Si**, 18.00–20.00 **Cr**, 8.00–10.50 **Ni**, 0.10 **N**, 0.045 **P**, 0.030 **S**	**Lightly drafted (wire)**: ≥0.156 (≥3.96) **diam**, 80 (550) **TS**; **Annealed (wire)**: ≥0.156 (≥3.96) **diam**, 75 (520) **TS**
ANSI/ASTM A 666	Type 304, grade B	US	Sheet, strip, plate, bar	0.08 **C**, 2.00 **Mn**, 1.00 **Si**, 18.00–20.00 **Cr**, 8.00–10.50 **Ni**, 0.045 **P**, 0.030 **S**	**Annealed (plate, sheet, strip)**: 0.015 **diam**, (550) **TS**, (310) **YS**, 35 **El**
ANSI/ASTM A 479	Grade 304N	US	Bar, shapes	0.08 **C**, 2.00 **Mn**, 1.00 **Si**, 18.00–20.00 **Cr**, 8.00–12.00 **Ni**, 0.10–0.16 **N**, 0.045 **P**, 0.030 **S**	**Solution annealed**: all **diam**, (550) **TS**, (240) **YS**, 30 **El**
ANSI/ASTM A 479	Grade 316N	US	Bar, shapes	0.08 **C**, 2.00 **Mn**, 1.00 **Si**, 16.00–18.00 **Cr**, 10.00–14.00 **Ni**, 2.00–3.00 **Mo**, 0.10–0.16 **N**, 0.045 **P**, 0.030 **S**	**Solution annealed**: all **diam**, (550) **TS**, (240) **YS**, 30 **El**
ANSI/ASTM A 240	Grade 304N	US	Plate, sheet, strip	0.08 **C**, 2.00 **Mn**, 1.00 **Si**, 18.00–20.00 **Cr**, 8.00–10.50 **Ni**, 0.10–0.16 **N**, 0.045 **P**, 0.030 **S**	**Solution annealed**: all **diam**, (550) **TS**, (240) **YS**, 30 **El**
ANSI/ASTM A 240	Grade 316N	US	Plate, sheet, strip	0.08 **C**, 2.00 **Mn**, 1.00 **Si**, 16.00–18.00 **Cr**, 10.00–14.00 **Ni**, 2.00–3.00 **Mo**, 0.10–0.16 **N**, 0.045 **P**, 0.030 **S**	**Solution annealed**: all **diam**, (550) **TS**, (240) **YS**, 30 **El**
ANSI/ASTM A 249	TP 304N	US	Tube: welded	0.08 **C**, 2.00 **Mn**, 0.75 **Si**, 18.0–20.0 **Cr**, 8.00–11.0 **Ni**, 0.10–0.16 **N**, 0.040 **P**, 0.030 **S**	**Solution annealed**: 0.312 (7.94) **diam**, 80 (550) **TS**, 35 (240) **YS**, 35 **El**
ANSI/ASTM A 249	TP 316N	US	Tube: welded	0.08 **C**, 2.00 **Mn**, 0.75 **Si**, 16.0–18.0 **Cr**, 11.0–14.0 **Ni**, 2.00–3.00 **Mo**, 0.10–0.16 **N**, 0.040 **P**, 0.030 **S**	**Solution annealed**: 0.312 (7.94) **diam**, 80 (550) **TS**, 35 (240) **YS**, 35 **El**
SS 14 23 38	SS 23 38–29	Sweden	Plate, sheet, strip	0.08 **C**, 2.0 **Mn**, 1.0 **Si**, 17.0–19.0 **Cr**, 9.0–12.0 **Ni**, 10 x C–1.0 **Nb**+1/2 **Ta**, 0.045 **P**, 0.030 **S**	**Cold finished**: all **diam**, (550) **TS**, (350) **YS**, 30 **El**
SS 14 23 50	SS 23 50–29	Sweden	Plate, sheet, strip	0.08 **C**, 2.0 **Mn**, 1.0 **Si**, 16.0–18.5 **Cr**, 10.5–14.0 **Ni**, 2.0–2.5 **Mo**, 5 x C–0.80 **Ti**, 0.045 **P**, 0.030 **S**	**Cold finished**: (<30) **diam**, (550) **TS**, (350) **YS**, 30 **El**
SS 14 23 37	SS 23 37–29	Sweden	Plate, sheet, strip	0.08 **C**, 2.0 **Mn**, 1.0 **Si**, 17.0–19.0 **Cr**, 9.0–12.0 **Ni**, 0.045 **P**, 0.030 **S**, 0.80 **Ti**	**Cold finished**: all **diam**, (550) **TS**, (350) **YS**, 40 **El**
NF A 35–573	Z 6 CNDNb 17.12	France	Plate, sheet, strip	0.08 **C**, 2.0 **Mn**, 1.0 **Si**, 16.0–18.0 **Cr**, 10.5–13.0 **Ni**, 2.0–2.5 **Mo**, 0.040 **P**, 0.030 **S**	**Cold rolled**: (≤5) **diam**, (540) **TS**, (275) **YS**, 40 **El**; **Hot rolled**: (≤20) **diam**, (540) **TS**, (265) **YS**, 38 **El**
NF A 35–573	Z 6 CNDT 17.12	France	Sheet, strip, plate	0.08 **C**, 2.0 **Mn**, 1.0 **Si**, 16.0–18.0 **Cr**, 10.5–13.0 **Ni**, 2.0–2.5 **Mo**, 0.040 **P**, 0.030 **S**	**Cold rolled**: (≤5) **diam**, (540) **TS**, (275) **YS**, 40 **El**; **Hot rolled**: (≤20) **diam**, (540) **TS**, (265) **YS**, 38 **El**

WROUGHT STAINLESS STEELS

specification number	designation	country	product forms	composition	mechanical properties (see page iv for explanation)
AS G18	G18/En 58E	Australia	Bar, billets	0.08 **C**, 2.00 **Mn**, 0.20 min **Si**, 17.5–20.0 **Cr**, 8.0–12.0 **Ni**, 0.045 **P**, 0.045 **S**, 4 x C min **Ti**	**Solution annealed or quenched:** (6) **diam**, (540) **TS**, (185) **YS**,
BS 1449 Part 2	Grade 320S17	UK	Plate, sheet, strip	0.08 **C**, 0.50–2.00 **Mn**, 0.20–1.00 **Si**, 16.5–18.5 **Cr**, 11.0–14.0 **Ni**, 2.25–3.00 **Mo**, 0.045 **P**, 0.030 **S**, 4 x C–0.60 **Ti**	**Solution annealed:** (≥3.0) **diam**, (540) **TS**, (210) **YS**, 40 **El**
BS 2S.129		UK	Billets, bar, forgings and parts: aircraft quality	0.08 **C**, 0.5–2.0 **Mn**, 0.20–1.0 **Si**, 17.0–19.0 **Cr**, 8.0–11.0 **Ni**, 0.7 **Mo**, 0.035 **P**, 0.025 **S**, 0.8 **Ti**	**Solution annealed:** all **diam**, (540) **TS**, (210) **YS**, 35 **El**
BS 2S130		UK	Bar, billets, forgings and parts: aircraft quality	0.08 **C**, 0.5–2.0 **Mn**, 0.20–1.0 **Si**, 17.0–19.0 **Cr**, 8.0–11.0 **Ni**, 1.0 **Mo**, 10 x C–1.1 **Nb**, 0.035 **P**, 0.025 **S**	**Solution annealed:** all **diam**, (540) **TS**, (210) **YS**, 35 **El**
BS S.526		UK	Sheet, strip: aircraft quality	0.08 **C**, 0.5–2.0 **Mn**, 0.2–1.0 **Si**, 17.0–19.0 **Cr**, 9.0–11.0 **Ni**, 0.035 **P**, 0.025 **S**, 5 x C–0.70 **Ti**	**Solution annealed:** all **diam**, (540) **TS**, (210) **YS**, 30 in <1.5 mm **El**
BS S.527		UK	Sheet, strip: aircraft quality	0.08 **C**, 0.5–2.0 **Mn**, 0.2–1.0 **Si**, 17.0–19.0 **Cr**, 9.0–11.0 **Ni**, 10 x C–1.0 **Nb**, 0.035 **P**, 0.025 **S**	**Solution annealed:** all **diam**, (540) **TS**, (210) **YS**, 30 in 1.5 mm **El**
NF A 35–577	Z 6 CNU 18.10 (DF)	France	Bar, wire, rod	0.08 **C**, 2.0 **Mn**, 1.0 **Si**, 16.5–18.5 **Cr**, 8.5–10.5 **Ni**, 3–4 **Cu**, 0.040 **P**, 0.030 **S**	**Solution annealed:** (6) **diam**, (540) max **TS**
NF A 35–573	Z 6 CNNb 18.10	France	Sheet, strip, plate	0.08 **C**, 2.0 **Mn**, 1.0 **Si**, 17.0–19.0 **Cr**, 9.0–11.0 **Ni**, 10xC–1.0 **Nb+Ta**, 0.040 **P**, 0.030 **S**	**Cold rolled:** (≤5) **diam**, (530) **TS**, (265) **YS**, 40 **El**; **Hot rolled:** (≤20) **diam**, (530) **TS**, (255) **YS**, 38 **El**
NF A 35–573	Z 6 CNT 18 10	France	Sheet, strip, plate	0.08 **C**, 2.0 **Mn**, 1.0 **Si**, 17.0–19.0 **Cr**, 9.0–11.0 **Ni**, 0.040 **P**, 0.030 **S**	**Cold rolled:** (≤5) **diam**, (530) **TS**, (265) **YS**, 40 **El**; **Hot rolled:** (≤20) **diam**, (530) **TS**, (255) **YS**, 38 **El**
COPANT 513	TP 304	COPANT	Tube	0.08 **C**, 2.00 **Mn**, 0.75 **Si**, 18.0–20.0 **Cr**, 8.00–11.00 **Ni**, 0.040 **P**, 0.030 **S**	**Hot or cold finished:** (>8) **diam**, (520) **TS**, (205) **YS**, 35 **El**
COPANT 513	TP 348	COPANT	Tube	0.08 **C**, 2.00 **Mn**, 1.00 **Si**, 17.0–20.0 **Cr**, 9.00–13.00 **Ni**, 10 x C–1.0 **Cb+Ta**, 0.040 **P**, 0.030 **S**, 0.10 **Ta**	**Hot or cold finished:** (>8) **diam**, (520) **TS**, (205) **YS**, 35 **El**
COPANT 513	TP 347	COPANT	Tube	0.08 **C**, 2.00 **Mn**, 1.00 **Si**, 17.0–20.0 **Cr**, 9.00–13.00 **Ni**, 10 x C–1.0 **Cb+Ta**, 0.030 **P**, 0.030 **S**	**Hot or cold finished:** (>8) **diam**, (520) **TS**, (205) **YS**, 35 **El**
COPANT 513	TP 321	COPANT	Tube	0.08 **C**, 2.00 **Mn**, 0.75 **Si**, 17.0–20.0 **Cr**, 9.00–13.00 **Ni**, 0.030 **P**, 0.030 **S**, 5 x C–0.60 **Ti**	**Hot or cold finished:** (>8) **diam**, (520) **TS**, (205) **YS**, 35 **El**
COPANT 513	TP 316	COPANT	Tube	0.08 **C**, 2.00 **Mn**, 0.75 **Si**, 16.0–18.0 **Cr**, 11.00–14.00 **Ni**, 2.00–3.00 **Mo**, 0.030 **P**, 0.030 **S**	**Hot or cold finished:** (>8) **diam**, (520) **TS**, (205) **YS**, 35 **El**
ANSI/ASTM A 376	TP 304	US	Pipe: seamless	0.08 **C**, 2.00 **Mn**, 0.75 **Si**, 18.0–20.0 **Cr**, 8.00–11.0 **Ni**, 0.040 **P**, 0.030 **S**	**Solution annealed:** 0.312 (7.94) **diam**, 75 (520) **TS**, 30 (210) **YS**, 35 **El**
ANSI/ASTM A 376	TP 316	US	Pipe: seamless	0.08 **C**, 2.00 **Mn**, 0.75 **Si**, 16.0–18.0 **Cr**, 11.0–14.0 **Ni**, 2.00–3.00 **Mo**, 0.040 **P**, 0.030 **S**	**Solution annealed:** 0.312 (7.94) **diam**, 75 (520) **TS**, 30 (210) **YS**, 35 **El**
ANSI/ASTM A 376	TP 321	US	Pipe: seamless	0.08 **C**, 2.00 **Mn**, 0.75 **Si**, 17.0–20.0 **Cr**, 9.00–13.0 **Ni**, 0.040 **P**, 0.030 **S**, 5 x C–0.60 **Ti**	**Solution annealed:** 0.312 (7.94) **diam**, 75 (520) **TS**, 30 (210) **YS**, 35 **El**
ANSI/ASTM A 376	TP 347	US	Pipe: seamless	0.08 **C**, 2.00 **Mn**, 0.75 **Si**, 17.0–20.0 **Cr**, 9.00–13.0 **Ni**, 10 x C–1.00 **Nb+Ta**, 0.040 **P**, 0.030 **S**	**Solution annealed:** 0.312 (7.94) **diam**, 75 (520) **TS**, 30 (210) **YS**, 35 **El**
ANSI/ASTM A 376	TP 348	US	Pipe: seamless	0.08 **C**, 2.00 **Mn**, 0.75 **Si**, 17.0–20.0 **Cr**, 9.00–13.0 **Ni**, 10 x C–1.00 **Nb+Ta**, 0.040 **P**, 0.030 **S**, 0.10 **Ta**	**Solution annealed:** 0.312 (7.94) **diam**, 75 (520) **TS**, 30 (210) **YS**, 35 **El**
AS 1449	Grade AS 1449/316	Australia	Sheet, strip, plate	0.08 **C**, 2.00 **Mn**, 16.00–18.00 **Cr**, 10.00–14.00 **Ni**, 2.00–3.00 **Mo**, 0.045 **P**, 0.030 **S**	**Annealed:** (≤1.2) **diam**, (520) **TS**, (205) **YS**, 40 **El**
AS 1449	Grade AS 1449/304	Australia	Sheet, strip, plate	0.08 **C**, 2.00 **Mn**, 1.00 **Si**, 18.00–20.00 **Cr**, 8.00–10.50 **Ni**, 0.045 **P**, 0.030 **S**	**Annealed:** (≤1.2) **diam**, (520) **TS**, (205) **YS**, 40 **El**

WROUGHT STAINLESS STEELS

specification number	designation	country	product forms	composition	mechanical properties (see page iv for explanation)
AS 1449	Grade AS 1449/316Ti	Australia	Sheet, strip, plate	0.08 **C**, 2.00 **Mn**, 1.00 **Si**, 16.00–18.00 **Cr**, 10.00–14.00 **Ni**, 2.00–3.00 **Mo**, 0.045 **P**, 4 x C min **Ti**	**Annealed**: (≤1.2) **diam**, (520) **TS**, (205) **YS**, 40 **El**
AS 1449	Grade AS 1449/317	Australia	Sheet, strip, plate	0.08 **C**, 2.00 **Mn**, 1.00 **Si**, 18.00–20.00 **Cr**, 11.00–15.00 **Ni**, 3.00–4.00 **Mo**, 0.045 **P**, 0.030 **S**	**Annealed**: (≤1.2) **diam**, (520) **TS**, (205) **YS**, 40 **El**
AS 1449	Grade AS 1449/321	Australia	Sheet, strip, plate	0.08 **C**, 2.00 **Mn**, 1.00 **Si**, 17.00–19.00 **Cr**, 9.00–12.00 **Ni**, 5 x C min **Ti**	**Annealed**: (≤1.2) **diam**, (520) **TS**, (205) **YS**, 48 **El**
JIS G 3446	SUS 304 TKA	Japan	Tube: seamless or welded	0.08 **C**, 2.00 **Mn**, 1.00 **Si**, 18.00–20.00 **Cr**, 8.00–11.00 **Ni**, 0.040 **P**, 0.030 **S**	**Solution annealed**: (≥8) **diam**, (520) **TS**, (206) **YS**, 35 **El**
JIS G 3446	SUS 316 TKA	Japan	Tube: seamless or welded	0.08 **C**, 2.00 **Mn**, 1.00 **Si**, 16.00–18.00 **Cr**, 10.00–14.00 **Ni**, 2.00–3.00 **Mo**, 0.040 **P**, 0.030 **S**	**Solution annealed**: (≥8) **diam**, (520) **TS**, (206) **YS**, 35 **El**
JIS G 3446	SUS 321 TKA	Japan	Tube: seamless or welded	0.08 **C**, 2.00 **Mn**, 1.00 **Si**, 17.00–19.00 **Cr**, 9.00–13.00 **Ni**, 0.040 **P**, 0.030 **S**, 5 x C min **Ti**	**Solution annealed**: (≥8) **diam**, (520) **TS**, (206) **YS**, 35 **El**
JIS G 3446	SUS 347 TKA	Japan	Tube: seamless or welded	0.08 **C**, 2.00 **Mn**, 1.00 **Si**, 17.00–19.00 **Cr**, 9.00–13.00 **Ni**, 10 x C min **Nb+Ta**, 0.040 **P**, 0.030 **S**	**Solution annealed**: (≥8) **diam**, (520) **TS**, (206) **YS**, 35 **El**
JIS G 3447	SUS 304 TBS	Japan	Tube: seamless or welded	0.08 **C**, 2.00 **Mn**, 1.00 **Si**, 18.00–20.00 **Cr**, 8.00–11.00 **Ni**, 0.040 **P**, 0.030 **S**	**Solution annealed**: all **diam**, (520) **TS**, 35 **El**
JIS G 3447	SUS 316 TBS	Japan	Tube: seamless or welded	0.08 **C**, 2.00 **Mn**, 1.00 **Si**, 16.00–18.00 **Cr**, 10.00–14.00 **Ni**, 2.00–3.00 **Mo**, 0.040 **P**, 0.030 **S**	**Solution annealed**: all **diam**, (520) **TS**, 35 **El**
JIS G 3459	SUS 304 TP	Japan	Pipe: seamless or welded	0.08 **C**, 2.00 **Mn**, 1.00 **Si**, 18.00–20.00 **Cr**, 8.00–11.00 **Ni**, 0.040 **P**, 0.030 **S**	**Solution annealed**: (≥8) **diam**, (520) **TS**, (206) **YS**, 35 **El**
JIS G 3459	SUS 321 TP	Japan	Pipe: seamless or welded	0.08 **C**, 2.00 **Mn**, 1.00 **Si**, 17.00–19.00 **Cr**, 9.00–13.00 **Ni**, 0.040 **P**, 0.030 **S**, 5 x C min **Ti**	**Solution annealed**: (≥8) **diam**, (520) **TS**, (206) **YS**, 35 **El**
JIS G 3459	SUS 316 TP	Japan	Pipe: seamless or welded	0.08 **C**, 2.00 **Mn**, 1.00 **Si**, 16.00–18.00 **Cr**, 10.00–14.00 **Ni**, 2.00–3.00 **Mo**, 0.040 **P**, 0.030 **S**	**Solution annealed**: (≤8) **diam**, (520) **TS**, (206) **YS**, 35 **El**
JIS G 3459	SUS 347 TP	Japan	Pipe: seamless or welded	0.08 **C**, 2.00 **Mn**, 1.00 **Si**, 17.00–19.00 **Cr**, 9.00–13.00 **Ni**, 10 x C min **Nb+Ta**, 0.040 **P**, 0.030 **S**	**Solution annealed**: (≥8) **diam**, (520) **TS**, (206) **YS**, 35 **El**
JIS G 3463	SUS 304 TB	Japan	Tube: seamless or welded	0.08 **C**, 2.00 **Mn**, 1.00 **Si**, 18.00–20.00 **Cr**, 8.00–11.00 **Ni**, 0.040 **P**, 0.030 **S**	**Solution annealed**: (≥8) **diam**, (520) **TS**, (206) **YS**, 35 **El**
JIS G 3463	SUS 321 TB	Japan	Tube: seamless or welded	0.08 **C**, 2.00 **Mn**, 1.00 **Si**, 17.00–19.00 **Cr**, 9.00–13.00 **Ni**, 0.040 **P**, 0.030 **S**, 5 x C min **Ti**	**Solution annealed**: (≥8) **diam**, (520) **TS**, (206) **YS**, 35 **El**
JIS G 3463	SUS 316 TB	Japan	Tube: seamless or welded	0.08 **C**, 2.00 **Mn**, 1.00 **Si**, 16.00–18.00 **Cr**, 10.00–14.00 **Ni**, 2.00–3.00 **Mo**, 0.040 **P**, 0.030 **S**	**Solution annealed**: (≥8) **diam**, (520) **TS**, (206) **YS**, 35 **El**
JIS G 3463	SUS 347 TB	Japan	Tube: seamless or welded	0.08 **C**, 2.00 **Mn**, 1.00 **Si**, 17.00–19.00 **Cr**, 9.00–13.00 **Ni**, 10 x C min **Nb+Ta**, 0.040 **P**, 0.030 **S**	**Solution annealed**: (≥8) **diam**, (520) **TS**, (206) **YS**, 35 **El**
JIS G 4303	SUS 304	Japan	Bar	0.08 **C**, 2.00 **Mn**, 1.00 **Si**, 18.00–20.00 **Cr**, 8.00–10.50 **Ni**, 0.040 **P**, 0.030 **S**	**Solution annealed**: (≤180) **diam**, (520) **TS**, (206) **YS**, 40 **El**
JIS G 4303	SUS 308	Japan	Bar	0.08 **C**, 2.00 **Mn**, 1.00 **Si**, 19.00–21.00 **Cr**, 10.00–12.00 **Ni**, 0.040 **P**, 0.030 **S**	**Solution annealed**: (≤180) **diam**, (520) **TS**, (206) **YS**, 40 **El**
JIS G 4303	SUS 309S	Japan	Bar	0.08 **C**, 2.00 **Mn**, 1.00 **Si**, 22.00–24.00 **Cr**, 12.00–15.00 **Ni**, 0.040 **P**, 0.030 **S**	**Solution annealed**: (≤180) **diam**, (520) **TS**, (206) **YS**, 40 **El**
JIS G 4303	SUS 310S	Japan	Bar	0.08 **C**, 2.00 **Mn**, 1.50 **Si**, 24.00–26.00 **Cr**, 19.00–22.00 **Ni**, 0.040 **P**, 0.030 **S**	**Solution annealed**: (≤180) **diam**, (520) **TS**, (206) **YS**, 40 **El**
JIS G 4303	SUS 316	Japan	Bar	0.08 **C**, 2.00 **Mn**, 1.00 **Si**, 16.00–18.00 **Cr**, 10.00–14.00 **Ni**, 2.00–3.00 **Mo**, 0.040 **P**, 0.030 **S**	**Solution annealed**: (≤180) **diam**, (520) **TS**, (206) **YS**, 40 **El**

WROUGHT STAINLESS STEELS

specification number	designation	country	product forms	composition	mechanical properties (see page iv for explanation)
JIS G 4303	SUS 316 J1	Japan	Bar	0.08 **C**, 2.00 **Mn**, 1.00 **Si**, 17.00–19.00 **Cr**, 10.00–14.00 **Ni**, 1.20–2.75 **Mo**, 1.00–2.50 **Cu**, 0.040 **P**, 0.030 **S**	**Solution annealed:** (≤180) **diam**, (520) **TS**, (206) **YS**, 40 **El**
JIS G 4303	SUS 317	Japan	Bar	0.08 **C**, 2.00 **Mn**, 1.00 **Si**, 18.00–20.00 **Cr**, 11.00–15.00 **Ni**, 3.00–4.00 **Mo**, 0.040 **P**, 0.030 **S**	**Solution annealed:** (≤180) **diam**, (520) **TS**, (206) **YS**, 40 **El**
JIS G 4303	SUS 321	Japan	Bar	0.08 **C**, 2.00 **Mn**, 1.00 **Si**, 17.00–19.00 **Cr**, 9.00–13.00 **Ni**, 0.040 **P**, 0.030 **S**, 5 x C min **Ti**	**Solution annealed:** (≤180) **diam**, (520) **TS**, (206) **YS**, 40 **El**
JIS G 4303	SUS 347	Japan	Bar	0.08 **C**, 2.00 **Mn**, 1.00 **Si**, 17.00–19.00 **Cr**, 9.00–13.00 **Ni**, 10 x C min **Nb+Ta**, 0.040 **P**, 0.030 **S**	**Solution annealed:** (≤180) **diam**, (520) **TS**, (206) **YS**, 40 **El**
JIS G 4303	SUS XM15J1	Japan	Bar	0.08 **C**, 2.00 **Mn**, 3.00–5.00 **Si**, 15.00–20.00 **Cr**, 11.50–15.00 **Ni**, 0.040 **P**, 0.030 **S**	**Solution annealed:** (≤180) **diam**, (520) **TS**, (206) **YS**, 40 **El**
JIS G 4304	SUS 304	Japan	Sheet, plate	0.08 **C**, 2.00 **Mn**, 1.00 **Si**, 18.00–20.00 **Cr**, 8.00–10.50 **Ni**, 0.040 **P**, 0.030 **S**	**Hot rolled and solution annealed:** all **diam**, (520) **TS**, (206) **YS**, 40 **El**
JIS G 4304	SUS 309S	Japan	Sheet, plate	0.08 **C**, 2.00 **Mn**, 1.00 **Si**, 22.00–24.00 **Cr**, 12.00–15.00 **Ni**, 0.040 **P**, 0.030 **S**	**Hot rolled and solution annealed:** all **diam**, (520) **TS**, (206) **YS**, 40 **El**
JIS G 4304	SUS 310S	Japan	Sheet, plate	0.08 **C**, 2.00 **Mn**, 1.50 **Si**, 24.00–26.00 **Cr**, 19.00–22.00 **Ni**, 0.040 **P**, 0.030 **S**	**Hot rolled and solution annealed:** all **diam**, (520) **TS**, (206) **YS**, 40 **El**
JIS G 4304	SUS 316	Japan	Sheet, plate	0.08 **C**, 2.00 **Mn**, 1.00 **Si**, 16.00–18.00 **Cr**, 10.00–14.00 **Ni**, 2.00–3.00 **Mo**, 0.040 **P**, 0.030 **S**	**Hot rolled and solution annealed:** all **diam**, (520) **TS**, (206) **YS**, 40 **El**
JIS G 4304	SUS 316J1	Japan	Sheet, plate	0.08 **C**, 2.00 **Mn**, 1.00 **Si**, 17.00–19.00 **Cr**, 10.00–14.00 **Ni**, 1.20–2.75 **Mo**, 1.00–2.50 **Cu**, 0.040 **P**, 0.030 **S**	**Hot rolled and solution annealed:** all **diam**, (520) **TS**, (206) **YS**, 40 **El**
JIS G 4304	SUS 317	Japan	Sheet, plate	0.08 **C**, 2.00 **Mn**, 1.00 **Si**, 18.00–20.00 **Cr**, 11.00–15.00 **Ni**, 3.00–4.00 **Mo**, 0.040 **P**, 0.030 **S**	**Hot rolled and solution annealed:** all **diam**, (520) **TS**, (206) **YS**, 40 **El**
JIS G 4304	SUS 321	Japan	Sheet, plate	0.08 **C**, 2.00 **Mn**, 1.00 **Si**, 17.00–19.00 **Cr**, 9.00–13.00 **Ni**, 0.040 **P**, 0.030 **S**, 5 x C min **Ti**	**Hot rolled and solution annealed:** all **diam**, (520) **TS**, (206) **YS**, 40 **El**
JIS G 4304	SUS 347	Japan	Sheet, plate	0.08 **C**, 2.00 **Mn**, 1.00 **Si**, 17.00–19.00 **Cr**, 9.00–13.00 **Ni**, 10 x C min **Nb+Ta**, 0.040 **P**, 0.030 **S**	**Hot rolled and solution annealed:** all **diam**, (520) **TS**, (206) **YS**, 40 **El**
JIS G 4304	SUS XM15J1	Japan	Sheet, plate	0.08 **C**, 2.00 **Mn**, 3.00–5.00 **Si**, 15.00–20.00 **Cr**, 11.50–15.00 **Ni**, 0.040 **P**, 0.030 **S**	**Hot rolled and solution treated:** all **diam**, (520) **TS**, (206) **YS**, 40 **El**
JIS G 4307	SUS 347	Japan	Strip	0.08 **C**, 2.00 **Mn**, 3.00–5.00 **Si**, 17.00–19.00 **Cr**, 9.00–13.00 **Ni**, 10 x C min **Nb+Ta**, 0.040 **P**, 0.030 **S**	**Cold rolled and solution annealed:** all **diam**, (520) **TS**, (206) **YS**, 40 **El**
JIS G 4307	SUS XM15J1	Japan	Strip	0.08 **C**, 2.00 **Mn**, 3.00–5.00 **Si**, 15.00–20.00 **Cr**, 11.50–15.00 **Ni**, 0.040 **P**, 0.030 **S**	**Cold rolled and annealed:** all **diam**, (520) **TS**, (206) **YS**, 40 **El**
JIS G 4305	SUS 304	Japan	Sheet, plate	0.08 **C**, 2.00 **Mn**, 1.00 **Si**, 18.00–20.00 **Cr**, 8.00–10.50 **Ni**, 0.040 **P**, 0.030 **S**	**Cold rolled and solution annealed:** all **diam**, (520) **TS**, (206) **YS**, 40 **El**
JIS G 4305	SUS 309S	Japan	Sheet, plate	0.08 **C**, 2.00 **Mn**, 1.00 **Si**, 22.00–24.00 **Cr**, 12.00–15.00 **Ni**, 0.040 **P**, 0.030 **S**	**Cold rolled and solution annealed:** all **diam**, (520) **TS**, (206) **YS**, 40 **El**
JIS G 4305	SUS 310S	Japan	Sheet, plate	0.08 **C**, 2.00 **Mn**, 1.50 **Si**, 24.00–26.00 **Cr**, 19.00–22.00 **Ni**, 0.040 **P**, 0.030 **S**	**Cold rolled and solution annealed:** all **diam**, (520) **TS**, (206) **YS**, 40 **El**
JIS G 4305	SUS 316	Japan	Sheet, plate	0.08 **C**, 2.00 **Mn**, 1.00 **Si**, 16.00–18.00 **Cr**, 10.00–14.00 **Ni**, 2.00–3.00 **Mo**, 0.040 **P**, 0.030 **S**	**Cold rolled and solution annealed:** all **diam**, (520) **TS**, (206) **YS**, 40 **El**
JIS G 4305	SUS 316J1	Japan	Sheet, plate	0.08 **C**, 2.00 **Mn**, 1.00 **Si**, 17.00–19.00 **Cr**, 10.00–14.00 **Ni**, 1.20–2.75 **Mo**, 1.00–2.50 **Cu**, 0.040 **P**, 0.030 **S**	**Cold rolled and solution annealed:** all **diam**, (520) **TS**, (206) **YS**, 40 **El**
JIS G 4305	SUS 317	Japan	Sheet, plate	0.08 **C**, 2.00 **Mn**, 1.00 **Si**, 18.00–20.00 **Cr**, 11.00–15.00 **Ni**, 3.00–4.00 **Mo**, 0.040 **P**, 0.030 **S**	**Cold rolled and solution annealed:** all **diam**, (520) **TS**, (206) **YS**, 40 **El**

WROUGHT STAINLESS STEELS

specification number	designation	country	product forms	composition	mechanical properties (see page iv for explanation)
JIS G 4305	SUS 321	Japan	Sheet, plate	0.08 **C**, 2.00 **Mn**, 1.00 **Si**, 17.00–19.00 **Cr**, 9.00–13.00 **Ni**, 0.040 **P**, 0.030 **S**, 5 x C min **Ti**	**Cold rolled and solution annealed:** all **diam**, (520) **TS**, (206) **YS**, 40 **El**
JIS G 4305	SUS 347	Japan	Sheet, plate	0.08 **C**, 2.00 **Mn**, 1.00 **Si**, 17.00–19.00 **Cr**, 9.00–13.00 **Ni**, 10 x C min **Nb+Ta**, 0.040 **P**, 0.030 **S**	**Cold rolled and solution annealed:** all **diam**, (520) **TS**, (206) **YS**, 40 **El**
JIS G4305	SUS XM15J1	Japan	Sheet, plate	0.08 **C**, 2.00 **Mn**, 3.00–5.00 **Si**, 15.00–20.00 **Cr**, 11.50–15.00 **Ni**, 0.040 **P**, 0.030 **S**	**Cold rolled and solution annealed:** all **diam**, (520) **TS**, (206) **YS**, 40 **El**
JIS G 4306	SUS 304	Japan	Strip	0.08 **C**, 2.00 **Mn**, 1.00 **Si**, 18.00–20.00 **Cr**, 8.00–10.50 **Ni**, 0.040 **P**, 0.030 **S**	**Hot rolled and solution annealed:** all **diam**, (520) **TS**, (206) **YS**, 40 **El**
JIS G 4306	SUS 309S	Japan	Strip	0.08 **C**, 2.00 **Mn**, 1.00 **Si**, 22.00–24.00 **Cr**, 12.00–15.00 **Ni**, 0.040 **P**, 0.030 **S**	**Hot rolled and solution annealed:** all **diam**, (520) **TS**, (206) **YS**, 40 **El**
JIS G 4306	SUS 310S	Japan	Strip	0.08 **C**, 2.00 **Mn**, 1.50 **Si**, 24.00–26.00 **Cr**, 19.00–22.00 **Ni**, 0.040 **P**, 0.030 **S**	**Hot rolled and solution annealed:** all **diam**, (520) **TS**, (206) **YS**, 40 **El**
JIS G 4306	SUS 316	Japan	Strip	0.08 **C**, 2.00 **Mn**, 1.00 **Si**, 16.00–18.00 **Cr**, 10.00–14.00 **Ni**, 2.00–3.00 **Mo**, 0.040 **P**, 0.030 **S**	**Hot rolled and solution annealed:** all **diam**, (520) **TS**, (206) **YS**, 40 **El**
JIS G 4306	SUS 321	Japan	Strip	0.08 **C**, 2.00 **Mn**, 1.00 **Si**, 17.00–19.00 **Cr**, 9.00–13.00 **Ni**, 0.040 **P**, 0.030 **S**, 5 x C min **Ti**	**Hot rolled and solution annealed:** all **diam**, (520) **TS**, (206) **YS**, 40 **El**
JIS G 4306	SUS 347	Japan	Strip	0.08 **C**, 2.00 **Mn**, 1.00 **Si**, 17.00–19.00 **Cr**, 9.00–13.00 **Ni**, 10 x C min **Nb+Ta**, 0.040 **P**, 0.030 **S**	**Hot rolled and solution annealed:** all **diam**, (520) **TS**, (206) **YS**, 40 **El**
JIS G 4306	SUS XM15J1	Japan	Strip	0.08 **C**, 2.00 **Mn**, 3.00–5.00 **Si**, 15.00–20.00 **Cr**, 11.50–15.00 **Ni**, 0.040 **P**, 0.030 **S**	**Hot rolled and solution annealed:** all **diam**, (520) **TS**, (206) **YS**, 40 **El**
JIS G 4307	SUS 304	Japan	Strip	0.08 **C**, 2.00 **Mn**, 1.00 **Si**, 18.00–20.00 **Cr**, 8.00–10.50 **Ni**, 0.040 **P**, 0.030 **S**	**Cold rolled and solution annealed:** all **diam**, (520) **TS**, (206) **YS**, 40 **El**
JIS G 4307	SUS 309S	Japan	Strip	0.08 **C**, 2.00 **Mn**, 1.00 **Si**, 22.00–24.00 **Cr**, 12.00–15.00 **Ni**, 0.040 **P**, 0.030 **S**	**Cold rolled and solution annealed:** all **diam**, (520) **TS**, (206) **YS**, 40 **El**
JIS G 4307	SUS 310S	Japan	Strip	0.08 **C**, 2.00 **Mn**, 1.50 **Si**, 24.00–26.00 **Cr**, 19.00–22.00 **Ni**, 0.040 **P**, 0.030 **S**	**Cold rolled and solution annealed:** all **diam**, (520) **TS**, (206) **YS**, 40 **El**
JIS G 4307	SUS 316	Japan	Strip	0.08 **C**, 2.00 **Mn**, 1.00 **Si**, 16.00–18.00 **Cr**, 10.00–14.00 **Ni**, 2.00–3.00 **Mo**, 0.040 **P**, 0.030 **S**	**Cold rolled and solution annealed:** all **diam**, (520) **TS**, (206) **YS**, 40 **El**
JIS G 4307	SUS 321	Japan	Strip	0.08 **C**, 2.00 **Mn**, 1.00 **Si**, 17.00–19.00 **Cr**, 9.00–13.00 **Ni**, 0.040 **P**, 0.030 **S**, 5 x C min **Ti**	**Cold rolled and solution annealed:** all **diam**, (520) **TS**, (206) **YS**, 40 **El**
JIS G 3214	SUS F 304	Japan	Forgings	0.08 **C**, 2.00 **Mn**, 1.00 **Si**, 18.00–20.00 **Cr**, 8.00–11.00 **Ni**, 0.040 **P**, 0.030 **S**	**Solution annealed:** (≤130) **diam**, (520) **TS**, (206) **YS**, 45 **El**
JIS G 3214	SUS F 316	Japan	Forgings	0.08 **C**, 2.00 **Mn**, 1.00 **Si**, 16.00–18.00 **Cr**, 10.00–14.00 **Ni**, 2.00–3.00 **Mo**, 0.040 **P**, 0.030 **S**	**Solution annealed:** (≤130) **diam**, (520) **TS**, (206) **YS**, 45 **El**
JIS G 3214	SUS F 321	Japan	Forgings	0.08 **C**, 2.00 **Mn**, 1.00 **Si**, 17.00–20.00 **Cr**, 9.00–13.00 **Ni**, 0.040 **P**, 0.030 **S**, 5 x C min **Ti**	**Solution annealed:** (≤130) **diam**, (520) **TS**, (206) **YS**, 45 **El**
JIS G 3214	SUS F 347	Japan	Forgings	0.08 **C**, 2.00 **Mn**, 1.00 **Si**, 17.00–20.00 **Cr**, 9.00–13.00 **Ni**, 10 x C min **Nb+Ta**, 0.040 **P**, 0.030 **S**	**Solution annealed:** all **diam**, (520) **TS**, (206) **YS**, 45 **El**
DGN–B–185	Grade TP304	Mexico	Pipe: seamless	0.08 **C**, 2.00 **Mn**, 0.75 **Si**, 18.0–20.0 **Cr**, 8.00–11.00 **Ni**, 0.040 **P**, 0.030 **S**	**Quenched or tempered:** (≥8) **diam**, (520) **TS**, (206) **YS**, 35 **El**
DGN–B–171	Grade MT 310S	Mexico	Tube: seamless	0.08 **C**, 2.00 **Mn**, 1.00 **Si**, 24.0–26.0 **Cr**, 19.0–22.0 **Ni**, 0.040 **P**, 0.030 **S**	**Hot or cold finished and annealed:** (≥7.92) **diam**, (519) **TS**, (206) **YS**, 35 **El**
DGN–B–171	Grade MT 316	Mexico	Tube: seamless	0.08 **C**, 2.00 **Mn**, 1.00 **Si**, 16.0–18.0 **Cr**, 11.0–14.0 **Ni**, 2.0–3.0 **Mo**, 0.040 **P**, 0.030 **S**	**Hot or cold finished and annealed:** (≥7.92) **diam**, (519) **TS**, (206) **YS**, 35 **El**
DGN–B–171	Grade MT 317	Mexico	Tube: seamless	0.08 **C**, 2.00 **Mn**, 1.00 **Si**, 18.0–20.0 **Cr**, 11.0–14.0 **Ni**, 3.0–4.0 **Mo**, 0.040 **P**, 0.030 **S**	**Hot or cold finished and annealed:** (≥7.92) **diam**, (519) **TS**, (206) **YS**, 35 **El**

specification number	designation	country	product forms	composition	mechanical properties (see page iv for explanation)
DGN–B–171	Grade MT 321	Mexico	Tube: seamless	0.08 **C**, 2.00 **Mn**, 1.00 **Si**, 17.0–20.0 **Cr**, 9.0–13.0 **Ni**, 0.040 **P**, 0.030 **S**, 5 x C–0.60 **Ti**	**Hot or cold finished and annealed:** (≥7.92) **diam**, (519) **TS**, (206) **YS**, 35 **El**
DGN–B–171	Grade MT 347	Mexico	Tube: seamless	0.08 **C**, 2.00 **Mn**, 1.00 **Si**, 17.0–20.0 **Cr**, 9.0–13.0 **Ni**, 10 x C–1.0 **Cb+Ta**, 0.040 **P**, 0.030 **S**	**Hot or cold finished and annealed:** (≥7.92) **diam**, (519) **TS**, (206) **YS**, 35 **El**
DGN–B–218	Grade TP304	Mexico	Tube: welded	0.08 **C**, 2.00 **Mn**, 0.75 **Si**, 18.0–20.0 **Cr**, 8.0–11.0 **Ni**, 0.040 **P**, 0.030 **S**	**Cold finished and quenched or tempered:** (≥7.92) **diam**, (519) **TS**, (206) **YS**, 35 **El**
DGN–B–218	Grade TP316	Mexico	Tube: welded	0.08 **C**, 2.00 **Mn**, 0.75 **Si**, 16.0–18.0 **Cr**, 11.0–14.0 **Ni**, 2.00–3.00 **Mo**, 0.040 **P**, 0.030 **S**	**Cold finished and quenched or tempered:** (≥7.92) **diam**, (519) **TS**, (206) **YS**, 35 **El**
DGN–B–218	Grade TP317	Mexico	Tube: welded	0.08 **C**, 2.00 **Mn**, 0.75 **Si**, 18.0–20.0 **Cr**, 11.0–14.0 **Ni**, 3.00–4.00 **Mo**, 0.040 **P**, 0.030 **S**	**Cold finished and quenched or tempered:** (≥7.92) **diam**, (519) **TS**, (206) **YS**, 35 **El**
DGN–B–218	Grade TP321	Mexico	Tube: welded	0.08 **C**, 2.00 **Mn**, 0.75 **Si**, 17.0–20.0 **Cr**, 9.0–13.0 **Ni**, 0.040 **P**, 0.030 **S**, 5 x C–0.60 **Ti**	**Cold finished and quenched or tempered:** (≥7.92) **diam**, (519) **TS**, (206) **YS**, 35 **El**
DGN–B–218	Grade TP347	Mexico	Tube: welded	0.08 **C**, 2.00 **Mn**, 0.75 **Si**, 17.0–20.0 **Cr**, 9.0–13.0 **Ni**, 10 x C–1.0 **Cb+Ta**, 0.040 **P**, 0.030 **S**	**Cold finished and quenched or tempered:** (≥7.92) **diam**, (519) **TS**, (206) **YS**, 35 **El**
DGN–B–218	Grade TP348	Mexico	Tube: welded	0.08 **C**, 2.00 **Mn**, 0.75 **Si**, 17.0–20.0 **Cr**, 9.0–13.0 **Ni**, 10 x C–1.0 **Cb+Ta**, 0.040 **P**, 0.030 **S**, 0.10 **Ta**	**Cold finished and quenched or tempered:** (≥7.92) **diam**, (519) **TS**, (206) **YS**, 35 **El**
DGN–B–196	Grade TP 347	Mexico	Tube: seamless	0.08 **C**, 2.00 **Mn**, 0.75 **Si**, 17.0–20.0 **Cr**, 9.0–13.0 **Ni**, 10 x C–1.0 **Cb+Ta**, 0.040 **P**, 0.030 **S**	**Hot or cold finished:** (8) **diam**, (519) **TS**, (206) **YS**, 35 **El**
DGN–B–196	Grade TP 321	Mexico	Tube: seamless	0.08 **C**, 2.00 **Mn**, 0.75 **Si**, 17.0–20.0 **Cr**, 9.0–13.0 **Ni**, 0.040 **P**, 0.030 **S**	**Hot or cold finished:** (8) **diam**, (519) **TS**, (206) **YS**, 35 **El**
DGN–B–196	Grade TP 304	Mexico	Tube: seamless	0.08 **C**, 2.00 **Mn**, 0.75 **Si**, 18.0–20.0 **Cr**, 8.0 **Ni**, 0.040 **P**, 0.75 **Si**	**Hot or cold finished:** (7.92) **diam**, (519) **TS**, (206) **YS**, 35 **El**
DGN–B–171	Grade MT304	Mexico	Tube: seamless	0.08 **C**, 2.00 **Mn**, 1.00 **Si**, 18.0–20.0 **Cr**, 8.0–13.0 **Ni**, 0.040 **P**, 0.030 **S**	**Hot or cold finished and annealed:** (≥7.92) **diam**, (519) **TS**, (206) **YS**, 35 **El**
DGN–B–171	Grade MT309S	Mexico	Tube: seamless	0.08 **C**, 2.00 **Mn**, 1.00 **Si**, 22.0–24.0 **Cr**, 12.0–15.0 **Ni**, 0.040 **P**, 0.030 **S**	**Hot or cold finished and annealed:** (≥7.92) **diam**, (519) **TS**, (206) **YS**, 35 **El**
DGN–B–186	Grade TP 348	Mexico	Pipe: seamless	0.08 **C**, 2.00 **Mn**, 0.75 **Si**, 17.0–20.0 **Cr**, 9.0–13.0 **Ni**, 8xC–1.00 **Cb+Ta**, 0.030 **P**, 0.030 **S**, 0.10 **Ta**	**Hot or cold finished and quenched or tempered:** (8) **diam**, (519) **TS**, (206) **YS**, 35 **El**
DGN–B–186	Grade TP347	Mexico	Pipe: seamless	0.08 **C**, 2.00 **Mn**, 0.75 **Si**, 17.0–20.0 **Cr**, 9.0–13.0 **Ni**, 0.030 **P**, 0.030 **S**	**Hot or cold finished:** (8) **diam**, (519) **TS**, (206) **YS**, 35 **El**
DGN–B–186	Grade TP316	Mexico	Pipe: seamless	0.08 **C**, 2.00 **Mn**, 0.75 **Si**, 16.0–18.0 **Cr**, 11.0–14.0 **Ni**, 2.00–3.00 **Mo**, 0.030 **P**, 0.030 **S**	**Hot or cold finished and quenched or tempered:** (8) **diam**, (519) **TS**, (206) **YS**, 35 **El**
DGN–B–186	Grade TP321	Mexico	Pipe: seamless	0.08 **C**, 2.00 **Mn**, 0.75 **Si**, 17.0–20.0 **Cr**, 9.0–13.0 **Ni**, 0.030 **P**, 0.030 **S**, 5 x C–0.60 **Ti**	**Hot or cold finished and quenched or tempered:** (8) **diam**, (519) **TS**, (206) **YS**, 35 **El**
DGN–B–185	Grade TP316	Mexico	Pipe: seamless, welded	0.08 **C**, 2.00 **Mn**, 0.75 **Si**, 16.0–18.0 **Cr**, 11.0–14.0 **Ni**, 2.0–3.0 **Mo**, 0.040 **P**, 0.030 **S**	**Quenched or tempered:** (≥8) **diam**, (519) **TS**, (206) **YS**, 35 **El**
DGN–B–185	Grade TP317	Mexico	Pipe: seamless, welded	0.08 **C**, 2.00 **Mn**, 0.75 **Si**, 18.0–20.0 **Cr**, 11.0–14.0 **Ni**, 3.0–4.0 **Mo**, 0.040 **P**, 0.030 **S**	**Quenched or tempered:** (≥8) **diam**, (519) **TS**, (206) **YS**, 35 **El**
DGN–B–185	Grade TP321	Mexico	Pipe: seamless, welded	0.08 **C**, 2.00 **Mn**, 0.75 **Si**, 17.0–20.0 **Cr**, 9.0–13.0 **Ni**, 0.040 **P**, 0.030 **S**, 5 x C–0.60 **Ti**	**Quenched and tempered:** (≥8) **diam**, (519) **TS**, (206) **YS**, 35 **El**
DGN–B–185	Grade TP347	Mexico	Pipe: seamless, welded	0.08 **C**, 2.00 **Mn**, 0.75 **Si**, 17.0–20.0 **Cr**, 9.0–13.0 **Ni**, 0.040 **P**, 0.030 **S**	**Quenched and tempered:** (≥8) **diam**, (519) **TS**, (206) **YS**, 35 **El**
DGN–B–185	Grade TP348	Mexico	Pipe: seamless, welded	0.08 **C**, 2.00 **Mn**, 0.75 **Si**, 17.0–20.0 **Cr**, 9.0–13.0 **Ni**, 10 x C–1.00 **Cb+Ta**, 0.040 **P**, 0.030 **S**, 0.10 **Ta**	**Quenched or tempered:** (≥8) **diam**, (519) **TS**, (206) **YS**, 35 **El**

WROUGHT STAINLESS STEELS

specification number	designation	country	product forms	composition	mechanical properties (see page iv for explanation)
NOM–B–194	Grade TP 321	Mexico	Tube: seamless	0.08 **C**, 2.00 **Mn**, 0.75 **Si**, 17.0–20.0 **Cr**, 9.00–13.0 **Ni**, 0.040 **P**, 0.030 **S**, 5 x C–0.60 **Ti**	**Quenched**: (0.38–12.7) **diam**, (517) **TS**, (207) **YS**
NOM–B–194	Grade TP 347	Mexico	Tube: seamless	0.08 **C**, 2.00 **Mn**, 0.75 **Si**, 17.0–20.0 **Cr**, 9.00–13.0 **Ni**, 0.040 **P**, 0.030 **S**, 10 x C–1 **Cb+Ta**	**Quenched**: (0.38–12.7) **diam**, (517) **TS**, (207) **YS**
NOM–B–194	Grade TP 348	Mexico	Tube: seamless	0.08 **C**, 2.00 **Mn**, 0.75 **Si**, 17.0–20.0 **Cr**, 9.00–13.0 **Ni**, 10 x C–1 **Cb+Ta**, 0.040 **P**, 0.030 **S**, 0.10 **Ta**	**Quenched**: (0.38–12.7) **diam**, (517) **TS**, (207) **YS**
NOM–B–194	Grade XM–15	Mexico	Tube: seamless	0.08 **C**, 2.00 **Mn**, 1.5–2.5 **Si**, 17.0–19.0 **Cr**, 17.50–18.50 **Ni**, 0.040 **P**, 0.030 **S**	**Quenched**: (0.38–12.7) **diam**, (517) **TS**, (207) **YS**
CSA G110.9	Type 317	Canada	Plate	0.08 **C**, 2.00 **Mn**, 1.00 **Si**, 18.00–20.00 **Cr**, 11.00–15.00 **Ni**, 3.00–4.00 **Mo**, 0.045 **P**, 0.030 **S**	**Hot rolled, annealed, quenched and tempered**: all **diam**, 75 (517) **TS**, 30 (207) **YS**, 35 **El**
CSA G110.9	Type 309S	Canada	Plate	0.08 **C**, 2.00 **Mn**, 1.00 **Si**, 22.00–24.00 **Cr**, 12.00–15.00 **Ni**, 0.045 **P**, 0.030 **S**	**Hot rolled, annealed, quenched and tempered**: all **diam**, 75(517) **TS**, 30 (207) **YS**, 40 **El**
CSA G110.9	Type 304	Canada	Plate	0.08 **C**, 2.00 **Mn**, 1.00 **Si**, 18.00–20.00 **Cr**, 8.00–12.00 **Ni**, 0.045 **P**, 0.030 **S**	**Hot rolled, annealed, quenched and tempered**: all **diam**, 75 (517) **TS**, 30 (207) **YS**, 40 **El**
CSA G110.9	Type 321	Canada	Plate	0.08 **C**, 2.00 **Mn**, 1.00 **Si**, 17.00–19.00 **Cr**, 9.00–12.00 **Ni**, 0.045 **P**, 0.030 **S**, 5 x C–0.70 **Ti**	**Hot rolled, annealed, quenched and tempered**: all **diam**, 75 (517) **TS**, 30 (207) **YS**, 40 **El**
CSA G110.9	Type 316	Canada	Plate	0.08 **C**, 2.00 **Mn**, 1.00 **Si**, 16.00–18.00 **Cr**, 10.00–14.00 **Ni**, 2.00–3.00 **Mo**, 0.045 **P**, 0.030 **S**	**Hot rolled, annealed, quenched and tempered**: all **diam**, 75 (517) **TS**, 30 (207) **YS**, 40 **El**
CSA G110.9	Type 310S	Canada	Plate	0.08 **C**, 2.00 **Mn**, 1.50 **Si**, 24.00–26.00 **Cr**, 19.00–22.00 **Ni**, 0.045 **P**, 0.030 **S**	**Hot rolled, annealed, quenched and tempered**: all **diam**, 75 (517) **TS**, 30 (207) **YS**, 40 **El**
CSA G110.9	Type 348	Canada	Plate	0.08 **C**, 2.00 **Mn**, 1.00 **Si**, 17.00–19.00 **Cr**, 9.00–13.00 **Ni**, 10 x C–1.10 **Cb+Ta**, 0.20 **Co**, 0.045 **P**, 0.030 **S**, 0.10 **Ta**	**Hot rolled, annealed, quenched and tempered**: all **diam**, 75 (517) **TS**, 30 (207) **YS**, 40 **El**
CSA G110.9	Type 347	Canada	Plate	0.08 **C**, 2.00 **Mn**, 1.00 **Si**, 17.00–19.00 **Cr**, 9.00–13.00 **Ni**, 10 x C–1.10 **Cb+Ta**, 0.045 **P**, 0.030 **S**	**Hot rolled, annealed, quenched and tempered**: all **diam**, 75 (517) **TS**, 30 (207) **YS**, 40 **El**
MIL–P–1144D	Grade 347	US	Pipe: seamless, welded	0.08 **C**, 2.0 **Mn**, 0.75 **Si**, 17.0–20.0 **Cr**, 9.0–13.0 **Ni**, 10 x C–1.00 **Nb+Ta**, 0.040 **P**, 0.030 **S**	**Solution annealed**: all **diam**, 75 (517) **TS**, 30 (207) **YS**, 35 **El**
ANSI/ASTM A 511	MT 309S	US	Tube: seamless	0.08 **C**, 2.00 **Mn**, 1.00 **Si**, 22.0–24.0 **Cr**, 12.0–15.0 **Ni**, 0.040 **P**, 0.030 **S**	**Solution annealed**: 0.31 (7.9) **diam**, 75 (517) **TS**, 30 (207) **YS**, 35 **El**
ANSI/ASTM A 511	MT 310S	US	Tube: seamless	0.08 **C**, 2.00 **Mn**, 1.00 **Si**, 24.0–26.0 **Cr**, 19.0–22.0 **Ni**, 0.040 **P**, 0.030 **S**	**Solution annealed**: 0.31 (7.9) **diam**, 75 (517) **TS**, 30 (207) **YS**, 35 **El**
ANSI/ASTM A 511	MT 316	US	Tube: seamless	0.08 **C**, 2.00 **Mn**, 1.00 **Si**, 16.0–18.0 **Cr**, 11.0–14.0 **Ni**, 2.0–3.0 **Mo**, 0.040 **P**, 0.030 **S**	**Solution annealed**: 0.31 (7.9) **diam**, 75 (517) **TS**, 30 (207) **YS**, 35 **El**
ANSI/ASTM A 511	MT 317	US	Tube: seamless	0.08 **C**, 2.00 **Mn**, 1.00 **Si**, 18.0–20.0 **Cr**, 11.0–14.0 **Ni**, 3.0–4.0 **Mo**, 0.040 **P**, 0.030 **S**	**Solution annealed**: 0.31 (7.9) **diam**, 75 (517) **TS**, 30 (207) **YS**, 35 **El**
ANSI/ASTM A 511	MT 321	US	Tube: seamless	0.08 **C**, 2.00 **Mn**, 1.00 **Si**, 17.0–20.0 **Cr**, 9.0–13.0 **Ni**, 0.040 **P**, 0.030 **S**, 5 x C–0.60 **Ti**	**Solution annealed**: 0.31 (7.9) **diam**, 75 (517) **TS**, 30 (207) **YS**, 35 **El**
ANSI/ASTM A 511	MT 347	US	Tube: seamless	0.08 **C**, 2.00 **Mn**, 1.00 **Si**, 17.0–20.0 **Cr**, 9.0–13.0 **Ni**, 10 x C–1.00 **Nb+Ta**	**Solution annealed**: 0.31 (7.9) **diam**, 75 (517) **TS**, 30 (207) **YS**, 35 **El**
ANSI/ASTM A 409	TP 304	US	Pipe: welded	0.08 **C**, 2.00 **Mn**, 0.75 **Si**, 18.0–20.0 **Cr**, 8.00–11.0 **Ni**, 0.040 **P**, 0.030 **S**	**Solution annealed**: all **diam**, 75 (517) **TS**, 30 (207) **YS**, 30 **El**
ANSI/ASTM A 409	TP 316	US	Pipe: welded	0.08 **C**, 2.00 **Mn**, 0.75 **Si**, 16.0–18.0 **Cr**, 11.0–14.0 **Ni**, 2.00–3.00 **Mo**, 0.040 **P**, 0.030 **S**	**Solution annealed**: all **diam**, 75 (517) **TS**, 30 (207) **YS**, 30 **El**
ANSI/ASTM A 409	TP 317	US	Pipe: welded	0.08 **C**, 2.00 **Mn**, 0.75 **Si**, 18.0–20.0 **Cr**, 11.0–14.0 **Ni**, 3.00–4.00 **Mo**, 0.040 **P**, 0.030 **S**	**Solution annealed**: all **diam**, 75 (517) **TS**, 30 (207) **YS**, 30 **El**
ANSI/ASTM A 409	TP 321	US	Pipe: welded	0.08 **C**, 2.00 **Mn**, 0.75 **Si**, 17.0–20.0 **Cr**, 9.00–13.0 **Ni**, 0.040 **P**, 0.030 **S**, 5 x C–0.70 **Ti**	**Solution annealed**: all **diam**, 75 (517) **TS**, 30 (207) **YS**, 30 **El**

WROUGHT STAINLESS STEELS

specification number	designation	country	product forms	composition	mechanical properties (see page iv for explanation)
ANSI/ASTM A 409	TP 347	US	Pipe: welded	0.08 **C**, 2.00 **Mn**, 0.75 **Si**, 17.0–20.0 **Cr**, 9.00–13.0 **Ni**, 10 x C–1.0 **Nb+Ta**, 0.040 **P**, 0.030 **S**	**Solution annealed**: all **diam**, 75 (517) **TS**, 30 (207) **YS**, 30 **El**
ANSI/ASTM A 409	TP 348	US	Pipe: welded	0.08 **C**, 2.00 **Mn**, 10 x C–1.0 **Nb+Ta**, 0.040 **P**, 0.030 **S**, 0.10 **Ta**	**Solution annealed**: all **diam**, 75 (517) **TS**, 30 (207) **YS**, 30 **El**
ANSI/ASTM A 312	TP 304	US	Pipe: seamless or welded	0.08 **C**, 2.00 **Mn**, 0.75 **Si**, 18.0–20.0 **Cr**, 8.00–11.0 **Ni**, 0.040 **P**, 0.030 **S**	**Solution annealed**: 0.31 (7.94) **diam**, 75 (517) **TS**, 30 (207) **YS**, 35 **El**
ANSI/ASTM A 312	TP 316	US	Pipe: seamless or welded	0.08 **C**, 2.00 **Mn**, 0.75 **Si**, 16.0–18.0 **Cr**, 11.0–14.0 **Ni**, 2.00–3.00 **Mo**, 0.040 **P**, 0.030 **S**	**Solution annealed**: 0.31 (7.94) **diam**, 75 (517) **TS**, 30 (207) **YS**, 35 **El**
ANSI/ASTM A 312	TP 317	US	Pipe: seamless or welded	0.08 **C**, 2.00 **Mn**, 0.75 **Si**, 18.0–20.0 **Cr**, 11.0–14.0 **Ni**, 3.00–4.00 **Mo**, 0.040 **P**, 0.030 **S**	**Solution annealed**: 0.31 (7.94) **diam**, 75 (517) **TS**, 30 (207) **YS**, 35 **El**
ANSI/ASTM A 312	TP 321	US	Pipe: seamless or welded	0.08 **C**, 2.00 **Mn**, 0.75 **Si**, 17.0–20.0 **Cr**, 9.00–13.00 **Ni**, 0.040 **P**, 0.030 **S**, 5 x C–0.70 **Ti**	**Solution annealed**: 0.31 (7.94) **diam**, 75 (517) **TS**, 30 (207) **YS**, 35 **El**
ANSI/ASTM A 312	TP 347	US	Pipe: seamless or welded	0.08 **C**, 2.00 **Mn**, 0.75 **Si**, 17.0–20.0 **Cr**, 9.00–13.0 **Ni**, 10 x C–1.00 **Nb+Ta**, 0.040 **P**, 0.030 **S**	**Solution annealed**: 0.31 (7.94) **diam**, 75 (517) **TS**, 30 (207) **YS**, 35 **El**
ANSI/ASTM A 312	TP 348	US	Pipe: seamless or welded	0.08 **C**, 2.00 **Mn**, 0.75 **Si**, 17.0–20.0 **Cr**, 9.00–13.0 **Ni**, 10 x C–1.00 **Nb+Ta**, 0.040 **P**, 0.030 **S**, 0.10 **Ta**	**Solution annealed**: 0.31 (7.94) **diam**, 75 (517) **TS**, 30 (207) **YS**, 35 **El**
ANSI/ASTM A 312	TP XM–15	US	Pipe: seamless or welded	0.08 **C**, 2.00 **Mn**, 1.50–2.50 **Si**, 17.0–19.0 **Cr**, 17.50–18.50 **Ni**, 0.030 **P**, 0.030 **S**	**Solution annealed**: 0.31 (7.94) **diam**, 75 (517) **TS**, 30 (207) **YS**, 35 **El**
ANSI/ASTM A 271	TP 304	US	Tube: seamless	0.08 **C**, 2.00 **Mn**, 0.75 **Si**, 18.0–20.0 **Cr**, 8.0–11.0 **Ni**, 0.040 **P**, 0.030 **S**	**Solution annealed**: 0.31 (7.94) **diam**, 75 (517) **TS**, 30 (207) **YS**, 35 **El**
ANSI/ASTM A 271	TP 321	US	Tube: seamless	0.08 **C**, 2.00 **Mn**, 0.75 **Si**, 17.0–20.0 **Cr**, 9.00–13.0 **Ni**, 0.040 **P**, 0.030 **S**, 5 x C–0.60 **Ti**	**Solution annealed**: 0.31 (7.94) **diam**, 75 (517) **TS**, 30 (207) **YS**, 35 **El**
ANSI/ASTM A 271	TP 347	US	Tube: seamless	0.08 **C**, 2.00 **Mn**, 0.75 **Si**, 17.0–20.0 **Cr**, 9.00–13.0 **Ni**, 0.040 **P**, 0.030 **S**, 10 x C–1.0 **Ta+Nb**	**Solution annealed**: 0.31 (7.94) **diam**, 75 (517) **TS**, 30 (207) **YS**, 35 **El**
MIL–T–16286E	Class c TP–321	US	Tube: seamless	0.08 **C**, 2.00 **Mn**, 0.75 **Si**, 17.0–20.0 **Cr**, 9.0–13.0 **Ni**, 0.040 **P**, 0.030 **S**, 5 x C–0.60 **Ti**	**Solution annealed and tempered**: all **diam**, (517) **TS**, (206) **YS**, 35 **El**
MIL–T–16286E	Class c TP–347	US	Tube: seamless	0.08 **C**, 2.00 **Mn**, 0.75 **Si**, 17.0–20.0 **Cr**, 9.0–13.0 **Ni**, 8 x C–1.00 **Nb+Ta**, 0.040 **P**, 0.030 **S**	**Solution annealed and tempered**: all **diam**, (517) **TS**, (206) **YS**, 35 **El**
MIL–T–8504A	Type 304	US	Tube: seamless, welded	0.08 **C**, 2.00 **Mn**, 1.00 **Si**, 18.0–20.0 **Cr**, 8.00–12.00 **Ni**, 0.50 **Mo**, 0.50 **Cu**, 0.03 **P**, 0.030 **S**	**Solution annealed**: all **diam**, (517) **TS**, (206) **YS**, 40 **El**
CSA G 110.9	Type 321	Canada	Sheet	0.08 **C**, 2.00 **Mn**, 1.00 **Si**, 17.00–19.00 **Cr**, 9.00–12.00 **Ni**, 0.045 **P**, 0.030 **S**, 5 x C–0.70 **Ti**	**Hot or cold rolled and annealed**: all **diam**, 75 (517) **TS**, 30 (207) **YS**, 40 **El**
CSA G 110.9	Type 317	Canada	Sheet	0.08 **C**, 2.00 **Mn**, 1.00 **Si**, 18.00–20.00 **Cr**, 11.00–15.00 **Ni**, 3.00–4.00 **Mo**, 0.045 **P**, 0.030 **S**	**Hot or cold rolled and annealed**: all **diam**, 75 (517) **TS**, 30 (207) **YS**, 35 **El**
CSA G110.9	Type 316	Canada	Sheet	0.08 **C**, 2.00 **Mn**, 1.00 **Si**, 16.00–18.00 **Cr**, 10.00–14.00 **Ni**, 2.00–3.00 **Mo**, 0.045 **P**, 0.030 **S**	**Hot or cold rolled and annealed**: all **diam**, 75 (517) **TS**, 30 (207) **YS**, 40 **El**
CSA G 110.9	Type 310S	Canada	Sheet	0.08 **C**, 2.00 **Mn**, 1.50 **Si**, 24.00–26.00 **Cr**, 19.00–22.00 **Ni**, 0.045 **P**, 0.030 **S**	**Hot or cold rolled and annealed**: all **diam**, 75 (517) **TS**, 30 (207) **YS**, 40 **El**
CSA G110.9	Type 309S	Canada	Sheet	0.08 **C**, 2.00 **Mn**, 1.00 **Si**, 22.00–24.00 **Cr**, 12.00–15.00 **Ni**, 0.045 **P**, 0.030 **S**	**Hot or cold rolled and annealed**: all **diam**, 75 (517) **TS**, 30 (207) **YS**, 40 **El**
CSA G110.9	Type 304	Canada	Sheet	0.08 **C**, 2.00 **Mn**, 1.00 **Si**, 18.00–20.00 **Cr**, 8.00–12.00 **Ni**, 0.045 **P**, 0.030 **S**	**Hot or cold rolled and annealed**: all **diam**, 75 (517) **TS**, 30 (207) **YS**, 40 **El**
CSA G110.9	Type 317	Canada	Strip	0.08 **C**, 2.00 **Mn**, 1.00 **Si**, 18.00–20.00 **Cr**, 11.00–15.00 **Ni**, 3.00–4.00 **Mo**, 0.045 **P**, 0.030 **S**	**Cold rolled and annealed**: all **diam**, 75 (517) **TS**, 30 (207) **YS**, 35 **El**
CSA G110.9	Type 321	Canada	Strip	0.08 **C**, 2.00 **Mn**, 1.00 **Si**, 17.00–19.00 **Cr**, 9.00–12.00 **Ni**, 0.045 **P**, 0.030 **S**, 5 x C–0.70 **Ti**	**Cold rolled and annealed**: all **diam**, 75 (517) **TS**, 30 (207) **YS**, 40 **El**

WROUGHT STAINLESS STEELS

specification number	designation	country	product forms	composition	mechanical properties (see page iv for explanation)
CSA G110.9	Type 347	Canada	Strip	0.08 **C**, 2.00 **Mn**, 1.00 **Si**, 17.00–19.00 **Cr**, 9.00–13.00 **Ni**, 10 x C–1.10 **Cb+Ta**, 0.045 **P**, 0.030 **S**	**Cold rolled and annealed**: all **diam**, 75 (517) **TS**, 30 (207) **YS**, 40 **El**
CSA G110.9	Type 348	Canada	Strip	0.08 **C**, 2.00 **Mn**, 1.00 **Si**, 17.00–19.00 **Cr**, 9.00–13.00 **Ni** 10 x C–1.10 **Cb+Ta**, 0.20 **Co**, 0.045 **P**, 0.030 **S**, 0.10 **Ta**	**Cold rolled and annealed**: all **diam**, 75 (517) **TS**, 30 (207) **YS**, 40 **El**
CSA G110.9	Type 309S	Canada	Strip	0.08 **C**, 2.00 **Mn**, 1.00 **Si**, 22.00–24.00 **Cr**, 12.00–15.00 **Ni**, 0.045 **P**, 0.030 **S**	**Cold rolled and annealed**: all **diam**, 75 (517) **TS**, 30 (207) **YS**, 40 **El**
CSA G110.9	Type 310S	Canada	Strip	0.08 **C**, 2.00 **Mn**, 1.50 **Si**, 24.00–26.00 **Cr**, 19.00–22.00 **Ni**, 0.045 **P**, 0.30 **S**	**Cold rolled and annealed**: all **diam**, 75 (517) **TS**, 30 (207) **YS**, 40 **El**
CSA G110.9	Type 316	Canada	Strip	0.08 **C**, 2.00 **Mn**, 1.00 **Si**, 16.00–18.00 **Cr**, 10.00–14.00 **Ni**, 2.00–3.00 **Mo**, 0.045 **P**, 0.030 **S**	**Cold rolled and annealed**: all **diam**, 75 (517) **TS**, 30 (207) **YS**, 40 **El**
CSA G110.9	Type 304	Canada	Strip	0.08 **C**, 2.00 **Mn**, 1.00 **Si**, 18.00–20.00 **Cr**, 8.00–12.00 **Ni**, 0.045 **P**, 0.030 **S**	**Cold rolled and annealed**: all **diam**, 75 (517) **TS**, 30 (207) **YS**, 40 **El**
MIL–P–1144D	Grade 304	US	Pipe: seamless, welded	0.08 **C**, 2.0 **Mn**, 0.75 **Si**, 18.0–20.0 **Cr**, 8.0–11.0 **Ni**, 0.040 **P**, 0.030 **S**	**Solution annealed**: all **diam**, 75 (517) **TS**, 30 (207) **YS**, 35 **El**
MIL–P–1144D	Grade 304	US	Pipe: seamless, welded	0.08 **C**, 2.0 **Mn**, 0.75 **Si**, 18.0–20.0 **Cr**, 8.0–11.0 **Ni**, 0.040 **P**, 0.030 **S**	**Solution annealed**: all **diam**, 75 (517) **TS**, 30 (207) **YS**, 35 **El**
MIL–P–1144D	Grade 316	US	Pipe: seamless, welded	0.08 **C**, 2.0 **Mn**, 0.75 **Si**, 16.0–18.0 **Cr**, 11.0–14.0 **Ni**, 2.0–3.0 **Mo**, 0.040 **P**, 0.030 **S**	**Solution annealed**: all **diam**, 75 (517) **TS**, 30 (207) **YS**, 35 **El**
MIL–P–1144D	Grade 321	US	Pipe: seamless, welded	0.08 **C**, 2.0 **Mn**, 0.75 **Si**, 17.0–20.0 **Cr**, 9.0–13.0 **Ni**, 0.040 **P**, 0.030 **S**, 5 x C–0.60 **Ti**	**Solution annealed**: all **diam**, 75 (517) **TS**, 30 (207) **YS**, 35 **El**
ASTM A 688	TP 316	US	Tube: welded	0.08 **C**, 2.00 **Mn**, 0.75 **Si**, 16.00–18.00 **Cr**, 11.00–14.00 **Ni**, 2.00–3.00 **Mo**, 0.040 **P**, 0.030 **S**	**Solution annealed**: all **diam**, 75 (517) **TS**, 30 (207) **YS**, 35 **El**
ASTM A 651	TP 316	US	Tube: welded or seamless	0.08 **C**, 2.00 **Mn**, 0.75 **Si**, 16.00–18.00 **Cr**, 11.00–14.00 **Ni**, 2.00–3.00 **Mo**, 0.040 **P**, 0.030 **S**	**As welded or as drawn**: all **diam**, 75 (517) **TS**, 30 (207) **YS**
ASTM A 320	B8 AISI 304	US	Bar	0.08 **C**, 2.00 **Mn**, 1.00 **Si**, 18.00–20.00 **Cr**, 8.00–12.00 **Ni**, 0.045 **P**, 0.030 **S**	**Solution treated**: all **diam**, 75 (517) **TS**, 30 (207) **YS**, 35 **El**; **Solution treated, strain hardened**: (19.0–25.4) 0.75–1.0 **diam**, 115 (793) **TS**, 80 (552) **YS**, 15 **El**
ASTM A 320	B8C AISI 347	US	Bar	0.08 **C**, 2.00 **Mn**, 1.00 **Si**, 17.00–19.00 **Cr**, 9.00–13.00 **Ni**, 10 x C min **Nb+Ta**, 0.045 **P**, 0.030 **S**	**Solution treated**: all **diam**, 75 (517) **TS**, 30 (207) **YS**, 35 **El**; **Solution treated, strain hardened**: (19.0–25.4) 0.75–1.0 **diam**, 115 (793) **TS**, 80 (552) **YS**, 15 **El**
ASTM A 320	B8T AISI 321	US	Bar	0.08 **C**, 2.00 **Mn**, 1.00 **Si**, 17.00–19.00 **Cr**, 9.00–12.00 **Ni**, 0.045 **P**, 0.030 **S**, 5 x C min **Ti**	**Solution treated**: all **diam**, 75 (517) **TS**, 30 (207) **YS**, 35 **El**; **Solution treated, strain hardened**: (19.0–25.4) 0.75–1.0 **diam**, 115 (793) **TS**, 80 (552) **YS**, 15 **El**
ASTM A 320	B8M AISI 316	US	Bar	0.08 **C**, 2.00 **Mn**, 1.00 **Si**, 16.00–18.00 **Cr**, 10.00–14.00 **Ni**, 2.00–3.00 **Mo**, 0.045 **P**, 0.030 **S**	**Solution treated**: all **diam**, 75 (517) **TS**, 30 (207) **YS**, 35 **El**; **Solution treated, strain hardened**: (19.0–25.4) 0.75–1.0 **diam**, 115 (793) **TS**, 80 (552) **YS**, 15 **El**
ASTM A 688	TP 304	US	Tube: welded	0.08 **C**, 2.00 **Mn**, 0.75 **Si**, 18.00–20.00 **Cr**, 8.00–11.00 **Ni**, 0.040 **P**, 0.030 **S**	**Solution annealed**: all **diam**, 75 (517) **TS**, 30 (207) **YS**, 35 **El**
CSA G110.6	Type 316	Canada	Plate, sheet, strip	0.08 **C**, 2.00 **Mn**, 1.00 **Si**, 16.00–18.00 **Cr**, 10.00–14.00 **Ni**, 2.00–3.00 **Mo**, 0.045 **P**, 0.030 **S**	**Hot rolled and annealed or hot rolled, quenched and tempered**: all **diam**, 75 (517) **TS**, 30 (207) **YS**, 40 **El**
CSA G110.6	Type 310S	Canada	Plate, sheet, strip	0.08 **C**, 2.00 **Mn**, 1.50 **Si**, 24.00–26.00 **Cr**, 19.00–22.00 **Ni**, 0.045 **P**, 0.030 **S**	**Hot rolled and annealed or hot rolled, quenched and tempered**: all **diam**, 75 (517) **TS**, 30 (207) **YS**, 40 **El**

WROUGHT STAINLESS STEELS

specification number	designation	country	product forms	composition	mechanical properties (see page iv for explanation)
CSA G110.6	Type 309S	Canada	Plate, sheet, strip	0.08 **C**, 2.00 **Mn**, 1.00 **Si**, 22.00–24.00 **Cr**, 12.00–15.00 **Ni**, 0.045 **P**, 0.030 **S**	**Hot rolled and annealed or hot rolled, quenched and tempered:** all **diam**, 75 (517) **TS**, 30 (207) **YS**, 40 **El**
CSA G110.6	Type 308	Canada	Plate, sheet, strip	0.08 **C**, 2.00 **Mn**, 1.00 **Si**, 19.00–21.00 **Cr**, 10.00–12.00 **Ni**, 0.045 **P**, 0.030 **S**	**Hot rolled and annealed or hot rolled, quenched and tempered:** all **diam**, 75 (517) **TS**, 30 (207) **YS**, 40 **El**
CSA G110.6	Type 304	Canada	Plate, sheet, strip	0.08 **C**, 2.00 **Mn**, 1.00 **Si**, 18.00–20.00 **Cr**, 8.00–12.00 **Ni**, 0.045 **P**, 0.030 **S**	**Hot rolled and annealed or hot rolled, quenched and tempered:** all **diam**, 75 (517) **TS**, 30 (207) **YS**, 40 **El**
CSA G110.6	Type 317	Canada	Plate, sheet, strip	0.08 **C**, 2.00 **Mn**, 1.00 **Si**, 18.00–20.00 **Cr**, 11.00–15.00 **Ni**, 3.00–4.00 **Mo**, 0.045 **P**, 0.030 **S**	**Hot rolled and annealed or hot rolled, quenched and tempered:** all **diam**, 75 (517) **TS**, 30 (207) **YS**, 40 **El**
CSA G110.6	Type 321	Canada	Plate, sheet, strip	0.08 **C**, 2.00 **Mn**, 1.00 **Si**, 17.00–19.00 **Cr**, 9.00–12.00 **Ni**, 0.045 **P**, 0.030 **S**, 5 x C min **Ti**	**Hot rolled and annealed or hot rolled, quenched and tempered:** all **diam**, 75 (517) **TS**, 30 (207) **YS**, 40 **El**
CSA G110.6	Type 347	Canada	Plate, sheet, strip	0.08 **C**, 2.00 **Mn**, 1.00 **Si**, 17.00–19.00 **Cr**, 9.00–13.00 **Ni**, 10 x C–1.10 **Cb+Ta**, 0.045 **P**, 0.030 **S**	**Hot rolled and annealed or hot rolled, quenched and tempered:** all **diam**, 75 (517) **TS**, 30 (207) **YS**, 40 **El**
CSA G110.6	Type 348	Canada	Plate, sheet, strip	0.08 **C**, 2.00 **Mn**, 1.00 **Si**, 17.00–19.00 **Cr**, 9.00–13.00 **Ni**, 10 x C–1.10 **Cb+Ta**, 0.20 **Co**, 0.045 **P**, 0.030 **S**, 0.10 **Ta**	**Hot rolled and annealed or hot rolled, quenched and tempered:** all **diam**, 75 (517) **TS**, 30 (207) **YS**, 40 **El**
CSA G110.9	Type 347	Canada	Sheet	0.08 **C**, 2.00 **Mn**, 1.00 **Si**, 17.00–19.00 **Cr**, 9.00–13.00 **Ni**, 10 x C–1.10 **Cb+Ta**, 0.045 **P**, 0.030 **S**	**Hot or cold rolled and annealed:** all **diam**, 75 (517) **TS**, 30 (207) **YS**, 40 **El**
CSA G110.9	Type 348	Canada	Sheet	0.08 **C**, 2.00 **Mn**, 1.00 **Si**, 17.00–19.00 **Cr**, 9.00–13.00 **Ni**, 10 x C–1.10 **Cb+Ta**, 0.20 **Co**, 0.045 **P**, 0.030 **S**	**Hot or cold rolled and annealed:** all **diam**, 75 (517) **TS**, 30 (207) **YS**, 40 **El**
AMS 5556D	Type I, II	US	Tube	0.08 **C**, 2.00 **Mn**, 0.50–1.00 **Si**, 17.00–19.00 **Cr**, 9.00–13.00 **Ni**, 0.75 **Mo**, 0.50 **Cu**, 10 x C–1.10 **Nb+Ta**, 0.040 **P**, 0.030 **S**	**Solution treated:** $\leq$0.016 ($\leq$0.41) **diam**, 75 (517) **TS**, 30 (207) **YS** , 33 **El**
AMS 5557E	Type I, II	US	Tube	0.08 **C**, 2.00 **Mn**, 0.40–1.00 **Si**, 17.00–20.00 **Cr**, 8.00–13.00 **Ni**, 0.75 **Mo**, 0.50 **Cu**, 0.040 **P**, 0.030 **S**, 6 x C–0.70 **Ti**	**Solution treated:** $\leq$0.016 ($\leq$0.41) **diam**, 75 (517) **TS**, 30 (207) **YS** , 33 **El**
AMS 5559C		US	Tube	0.08 **C**, 2.00 **Mn**, 0.40–1.00 **Si**, 17.00–19.00 **Cr**, 9.00–12.00 **Ni**, 0.75 **Mo**, 0.50 **Cu**, 0.040 **P**, 0.030 **S**	**Descaled and passivated:** all **diam**, 75 (517) **TS**, 35 (241) **YS**, 40 **El**
AISI 384		US	Wire	0.08 **C**, 2.00 **Mn**, 1.00 **Si**, 15.00–17.00 **Cr**, 17.00–19.00 **Ni**, 0.045 **P**, 0.030 **S**	**Annealed at 1900°F: 0.500 (12.70) diam, 75 (517) TS, 35 (241) YS, 55 El; Lightly drafted, as for cold heading wire: 0.200 (5.08) diam, 78 (538) TS, 45 (310) YS**
ANSI/ASTM A 511	MT 304	US	Tube: seamless	0.08 **C**, 2.00 **Mn**, 1.00 **Si**, 18.0–20.0 **Cr**, 8.0–11.0 **Ni**, 0.040 **P**, 0.030 **S**	**Solution annealed:** 0.31 (7.9) **diam**, 75 (517) **TS**, 30 (207) **YS**, 35 **El**
QQ–S–766C	Class 348	US	Strip, sheet, plate	0.08 **C**, 2.00 **Mn**, 1.00 **Si**, 17.00 **Cr**, 9.00–13.00 **Ni**, 0.20 **Co**, 0.045 **P**, 0.030 **S**, 0.10 **Ta**	**Annealed:** all **diam**, 75 (517) **TS**, 30 (207) **YS**, 40 **El**
QQ–S–766C	Class 316	US	Strip, sheet, plate	0.08 **C**, 2.00 **Mn**, 1.00 **Si**, 16.00 **Cr**, 10.00–14.00 **Ni**, 2.00–3.00 **Mo**, 0.045 **P**, 0.030 **S**	**Annealed:** all **diam**, 75 (517) **TS**, 30 (207) **YS**, 40 **El**; **1/4 hard:** all **diam**, 125 (862) **TS**, 90 (621) **YS**, 10 **El**
QQ–S–766C	Class 304	US	Strip, sheet, plate	0.08 **C**, 2.00 **Mn**, 1.00 **Si**, 18.00 **Cr**, 8.00 **Ni**, 0.045 **P**, 0.035 **S**	**Annealed:** all **diam**, 75 (517) **TS**, 30 (207) **YS**, 40 **El**
QQ–S–766C	Class 347	US	Strip, sheet, plate	0.08 **C**, 2.00 **Mn**, 1.00 **Si**, 17.00 **Cr**, 9.00–13.00 **Ni**, 0.045 **P**, 0.030 **S**	**Annealed:** all **diam**, 75 (517) **TS**, 30 (207) **YS**, 40 **El**
QQ–S–766C	Class 321	US	Strip, sheet, plate	0.08 **C**, 2.00 **Mn**, 1.00 **Si**, 17.00 **Cr**, 9.00–12.00 **Ni**, 0.045 **P**, 0.030 **S**	**Annealed:** all **diam**, 75 (517) **TS**, 30 (207) **YS**, 40 **El**

WROUGHT STAINLESS STEELS

specification number	designation	country	product forms	composition	mechanical properties (see page iv for explanation)
ANSI/ASTM A 213	TP 304	US	Tube: seamless	0.08 **C**, 2.00 **Mn**, 0.75 **Si**, 18.0–20.0 **Cr**, 8.00–11.00 **Ni**, 0.040 **P**, 0.030 **S**	**Solution annealed:** 0.312 (7.94) **diam**, 75 (517) **TS**, 30 (207) **YS**, 35 **El**
ANSI/ASTM A 213	TP 304N	US	Tube: seamless	0.08 **C**, 2.00 **Mn**, 0.75 **Si**, 18.0–20.0 **Cr**, 8.00–11.0 **Ni**, 0.10–0.16 **N**, 0.040 **P**, 0.030 **S**	**Solution annealed:** 0.312 (7.94) **diam**, 75 (517) **TS**, 30 (207) **YS**, 35 **El**
ANSI/ASTM A 213	TP 316	US	Tube: seamless	0.08 **C**, 2.00 **Mn**, 0.75 **Si**, 16.0–18.0 **Cr**, 11.0–14.0 **Ni**, 2.00–3.00 **Mo**, 0.040 **P**, 0.030 **S**	**Solution annealed:** 0.312 (7.94) **diam**, 75 (517) **TS**, 30 (207) **YS**, 35 **El**
ANSI/ASTM A 213	TP 316N	US	Tube: seamless	0.08 **C**, 2.00 **Mn**, 0.75 **Si**, 16.0–18.0 **Cr**, 11.0–14.0 **Ni**, 2.00–3.00 **Mo**, 0.10–0.16 **N**, 0.040 **P**, 0.030 **S**	**Solution annealed:** 0.312 (7.94) **diam**, 75 (517) **TS**, 30 (207) **YS**, 35 **El**
ANSI/ASTM A 213	TP 321	US	Tube: seamless	0.08 **C**, 2.00 **Mn**, 0.75 **Si**, 17.0–20.0 **Cr**, 9.00–13.0 **Ni**, 0.040 **P**, 0.030 **S**, 5 x C–0.60 **Ti**	**Solution annealed:** 0.312 (7.94) **diam**, 75 (517) **TS**, 30 (207) **YS**, 35 **El**
ANSI/ASTM A 213	TP 347	US	Tube: seamless	0.08 **C**, 2.00 **Mn**, 0.75 **Si**, 17.0–20.0 **Cr**, 9.00–13.0 **Ni**, 0.040 **P**, 0.030 **S**, 10 x C–1.00 **Ta+Nb**	**Solution annealed:** 0.312 (7.94) **diam**, 75 (517) **TS**, 30 (207) **YS**, 35 **El**
ANSI/ASTM A 213	TP 348	US	Tube: seamless	0.08 **C**, 2.00 **Mn**, 0.75 **Si**, 17.0–20.0 **Cr**, 9.00–13.0 **Ni**, 0.040 **P**, 0.030 **S**, 0.10 **Ti**, 10 x C–1.00 **Ta+Nb**	**Solution annealed:** 0.312 (7.94) **diam**, 75 (517) **TS**, 30 (207) **YS**, 35 **El**
ANSI/ASTM A 213	XM–15	US	Tube: seamless	0.08 **C**, 2.00 **Mn**, 1.50–2.50 **Si**, 17.00–19.00 **Cr**, 17.50–18.50 **Ni**, 0.030 **P**, 0.030 **S**	**solution annealed:** 0.312 (7.94) **diam**, 75 (517) **TS**, 30 (207) **YS**, 35 **El**
ANSI/ASTM A 193	Grade B8	US	Bar	0.08 **C**, 2.00 **Mn**, 1.00 **Si**, 18.00–20.00 **Cr**, 8.00–12.00 **Ni**, 0.045 **P**, 0.030 **S**	**Solution annealed:** all **diam**, 75 (517) **TS**, 30 (207) **YS**, 30 **El**
ANSI/ASTM A 632	TP 304	US	Tube: seamless or welded	0.08 **C**, 2.00 **Mn**, 0.75 **Si**, 18.0–20.0 **Cr**, 8.0–11.0 **Ni**, 0.040 **P**, 0.030 **S**	**Solution annealed:** 0.005–0.065 (0.13–1.65) **diam**, 75 (517) **TS**, 30 (207) **YS**, 35 **El**
ANSI/ASTM A 632	TP 316	US	Tube: seamless or welded	0.08 **C**, 2.00 **Mn**, 0.75 **Si**, 16.0–18.0 **Cr**, 11.0–14.0 **Ni**, 2.00–3.00 **Mo**, 0.040 **P**, 0.030 **S**	**Solution annealed:** 0.005–0.065 (0.13–1.65) **diam**, 75 (517) **TS**, 30 (207) **YS**, 35 **El**
ANSI/ASTM A 632	TP 317	US	Tube: seamless or welded	0.08 **C**, 2.00 **Mn**, 0.75 **Si**, 18.0–20.0 **Cr**, 11.0–14.0 **Ni**, 3.00–4.00 **Mo**, 0.040 **P**, 0.030 **S**	**Solution annealed:** 0.005–0.065 (0.13–1.65) **diam**, 75 (517) **TS**, 30 (207) **YS**, 35 **El**
ANSI/ASTM A 632	TP 321	US	Tube: seamless or welded	0.08 **C**, 2.00 **Mn**, 0.75 **Si**, 17.0–20.0 **Cr**, 9.0–13.0 **Ni**, 0.040 **P**, 0.030 **S**, 5 x C–0.60 **Ti**	**Solution annealed:** 0.005–0.065 (0.13–1.65) **diam**, 75 (517) **TS**, 30 (207) **YS**, 35 **El**
ANSI/ASTM A 632	TP 347	US	Tube: seamless or welded	0.08 **C**, 2.00 **Mn**, 0.75 **Si**, 17.0–20.0 **Cr**, 9.0–13.0 **Ni**, 10 x C–1.0 **Nb+Ta**, 0.040 **P**, 0.030 **S**	**Solution annealed:** 0.005–0.065 (0.13–1.65) **diam**, 75 (517) **TS**, 30 (207) **YS**, 35 **El**
ANSI/ASTM A 632	TP 348	US	Tube: seamless or welded	0.08 **C**, 2.00 **Mn**, 0.75 **Si**, 17.0–20.0 **Cr**, 9.0–13.0 **Ni**, 10 x C–1.0 **Nb+Ta**, 0.040 **P**, 0.030 **S**, 0.10 **Ta**	**Solution annealed:** 0.005–0.065 (0.13–1.65) **diam**, 75 (517) **TS**, 30 (207) **YS**, 35 **El**
ANSI/ASTM A 554	MT–304	US	Tube: welded	0.08 **C**, 2.00 **Mn**, 1.00 **Si**, 18.0–20.0 **Cr**, 8.0–11.0 **Ni**, 0.040 **P**, 0.030 **S**	**Round annealed:** 0.312 (7.94) **diam**, 75 (517) **TS**, 30 (207) **YS**, 35 **El**
ANSI/ASTM A 554	MT–309S	US	Tube: welded	0.08 **C**, 2.00 **Mn**, 1.00 **Si**, 22.0–24.0 **Cr**, 12.0–15.0 **Ni**, 0.040 **P**, 0.030 **S**	**Round annealed:** 0.312 (7.94) **diam**, 75 (517) **TS**, 30 (207) **YS**, 35 **El**
ANSI/ASTM A 554	MT–309S–Cb	US	Tube: welded	0.08 **C**, 2.00 **Mn**, 1.00 **Si**, 22.0–24.0 **Cr**, 12.0–15.0 **Ni**, 10 x C–1.00 **Nb+Ta**, 0.040 **P**, 0.030 **S**	**Round annealed:** 0.312 (7.94) **diam**, 75 (517) **TS**, 30 (207) **YS**, 35 **El**
ANSI/ASTM A 554	MT–310S	US	Tube: welded	0.08 **C**, 2.00 **Mn**, 1.00 **Si**, 24.0–26.0 **Cr**, 19.0–22.0 **Ni**, 0.040 **P**, 0.030 **S**	**Round annealed:** 0.312 (7.94) **diam**, 75 (517) **TS**, 30 (207) **YS**, 35 **El**
ANSI/ASTM A 554	MT–316	US	Tube: welded	0.08 **C**, 2.00 **Mn**, 1.00 **Si**, 16.0–18.0 **Cr**, 11.0–14.0 **Ni**, 2.0–3.0 **Mo**, 0.040 **P**, 0.030 **S**	**Round annealed:** 0.312 (7.94) **diam**, 75 (517) **TS**, 30 (207) **YS**, 35 **El**
ANSI/ASTM A 554	MT–317	US	Tube: welded	0.08 **C**, 2.00 **Mn**, 1.00 **Si**, 18.0–20.0 **Cr**, 11.0–14.0 **Ni**, 3.0–4.0 **Mo**, 0.040 **P**, 0.030 **S**	**Round annealed:** 0.312 (7.94) **diam**, 75 (517) **TS**, 30 (207) **YS**, 35 **El**
ANSI/ASTM A 554	MT–321	US	Tube: welded	0.08 **C**, 2.00 **Mn**, 1.00 **Si**, 17.0–20.0 **Cr**, 9.0–13.0 **Ni**, 0.040 **P**, 0.030 **S**, 5 x C–0.60 **Ti**	**Round annealed:** 0.312 (7.94) **diam**, 75 (517) **TS**, 30 (207) **YS**, 35 **El**
ANSI/ASTM A 554	MT–347	US	Tube: welded	0.08 **C**, 2.00 **Mn**, 1.00 **Si**, 17.0–20.0 **Cr**, 9.0–13.0 **Ni**, 10 x C–1.00 **Nb+Ta**, 0.040 **P**, 0.030 **S**	**Round annealed:** 0.312 (7.94) **diam**, 75 (517) **TS**, 30 (207) **YS**, 35 **El**

WROUGHT STAINLESS STEELS

specification number	designation	country	product forms	composition	mechanical properties (see page iv for explanation)
ANSI/ASTM A 479	321	US	Bar, shapes	0.08 **C**, 2.00 **Mn**, 1.00 **Si**, 17.00–19.00 **Cr**, 9.00–12.00 **Ni**, 0.045 **P**, 0.030 **S**, 5 x C min **Ti**	**Solution annealed**: all **diam**, 75 (515) **TS**, 30 (205) **YS**, 30 **El**
ANSI/ASTM A 479	347	US	Bar, shapes	0.08 **C**, 2.00 **Mn**, 1.00 **Si**, 17.00–19.00 **Cr**, 9.00–13.00 **Ni**, 10 x C min **Nb+Ta**, 0.045 **P**, 0.030 **S**	**Solution annealed**: all **diam**, 75 (515) **TS**, 30 (205) **YS**, 30 **El**
ANSI/ASTM A 479	348	US	Bar, shapes	0.08 **C**, 2.00 **Mn**, 1.00 **Si**, 17.00–19.00 **Cr**, 9.00–13.00 **Ni**, 0.20 **Co**, 10 x C min **Nb+Ta**, 0.045 **P**, 0.030 **S**, 0.01 **Ta**	**Solution annealed**: all **diam**, 75 (515) **TS**, 30 (205) **YS**, 30 **El**
ANSI/ASTM A 473	304	US	Forgings	0.08 **C**, 2.00 **Mn**, 1.00 **Si**, 18.00–20.00 **Cr**, 8.00–10.50 **Ni**, 0.10 **N**, 0.045 **P**, 0.030 **S**	**Solution annealed**: ≥5 (≥127) **diam**, 75 (515) **TS**, 30 (205) **YS**, 40 **El**
ANSI/ASTM A 473	308	US	Forgings	0.08 **C**, 2.00 **Mn**, 1.00 **Si**, 19.00–21.00 **Cr**, 10.00–12.00 **Ni**, 0.045 **P**, 0.030 **S**	**Solution annealed**: all **diam**, 75 (515) **TS**, 30 (205) **YS**, 40 **El**
ANSI/ASTM A 666	316, grade A	US	Sheet, strip, plate, bar	0.08 **C**, 2.00 **Mn**, 1.00 **Si**, 16.00–18.00 **Cr**, 10.00–14.00 **Ni**, 2.00–3.00 **Mo**, 0.045 **P**, 0.030 **S**	**Annealed (plate, sheet, strip)**: 0.030 (0.76) **diam**, 75 (515) **TS**, 30 (205) **YS**, 40 **El**
ANSI/ASTM A 666	304, grade A	US	Sheet, strip, plate, bar	0.08 **C**, 2.00 **Mn**, 1.00 **Si**, 18.00–20.00 **Cr**, 8.00–10.50 **Ni**, 0.045 **P**, 0.030 **S**	**Annealed (plate, sheet, strip)**: >0.030 (>0.76) **diam**, 75 (515) **TS**, 30 (205) **YS**, 40 **El**
ANSI/ASTM A 473	309S	US	Forgings	0.08 **C**, 2.00 **Mn**, 1.00 **Si**, 22.00–24.00 **Cr**, 12.00–15.00 **Ni**, 0.045 **P**, 0.030 **S**	**Solution annealed**: all **diam**, 75 (515) **TS**, 30 (205) **YS**, 40 **El**
ANSI/ASTM A 473	310S	US	Forgings	0.08 **C**, 2.00 **Mn**, 1.50 **Si**, 24.00–26.00 **Cr**, 19.00–22.00 **Ni**, 0.045 **P**, 0.030 **S**	**Solution annealed**: all **diam**, 75 (515) **TS**, 30 (205) **YS**, 40 **El**
ANSI/ASTM A 473	316	US	Forgings	0.08 **C**, 2.00 **Mn**, 1.00 **Si**, 16.00–18.00 **Cr**, 10.00–14.00 **Ni**, 2.00–3.00 **Mo**, 0.10 **N**, 0.045 **P**, 0.030 **S**	**Solution annealed**: ≥5 (127) **diam**, 75 (515) **TS**, 30 (205) **YS**, 40 **El**
ANSI/ASTM A 473	317	US	Forgings	0.08 **C**, 2.00 **Mn**, 1.00 **Si**, 18.00–20.00 **Cr**, 11.00–15.00 **Ni**, 3.00–4.00 **Mo**, 0.10 **N**, 0.045 **P**, 0.030 **S**	**Solution annealed**: all **diam**, 75 (515) **TS**, 30 (205) **YS**, 40 **El**
ANSI/ASTM A 473	321	US	Forgings	0.08 **C**, 2.00 **Mn**, 1.00 **Si**, 17.00–19.00 **Cr**, 9.00–12.00 **Ni**, 0.045 **P**, 0.030 **S**, 5 x C min **Ti**	**Solution annealed**: all **diam**, 75 (515) **TS**, 30 (205) **YS**, 40 **El**
ANSI/ASTM A 473	347	US	Forgings	0.08 **C**, 2.00 **Mn**, 10 x C min **Nb+Ta**, 0.045 **P**, 0.030 **S**	**Solution annealed**: all **diam**, 75 (515) **TS**, 30 (205) **YS**, 40 **El**
ANSI/ASTM A 473	348	US	Forgings	0.08 **C**, 2.00 **Mn**, 0.20 **Co**, 10 x C min **Nb+Ta**, 0.045 **P**, 0.030 **S**, 0.10 **Ta**	**Solution annealed**: all **diam**, 75 (515) **TS**, 30 (205) **YS**, 40 **El**
ANSI/ASTM A 479	ER308	US	Bar,shapes	0.08 **C**, 1.00–2.50 **Mn**, 0.25–0.60 **Si**, 19.50–22.00 **Cr**, 9.00–11.00 **Ni**, 0.030 **P**, 0.030 **S**	**Solution annealed**: all **diam**, 75 (515) **TS**, 30 (205) **YS**, 30 **El**
ANSI/ASTM A 479	310S	US	Bar, shapes	0.08 **C**, 2.00 **Mn**, 1.50 **Si**, 24.00–26.00 **Cr**, 19.00–22.00 **Ni**, 0.045 **P**, 0.030 **S**	**Solution annealed**: all **diam**, 75 (515) **TS**, 30 (205) **YS**, 30 **El**
ANSI/ASTM A 479	316	US	Bar, shapes	0.08 **C**, 2.00 **Mn**, 1.00 **Si**, 16.00–18.00 **Cr**, 10.00–14.00 **Ni**, 2.00–3.00 **Mo**, 0.10 **N**, 0.045 **P**, 0.030 **S**	**Solution annealed**: all **diam**, 75 (515) **TS**, 30 (205) **YS**, 30 **El**; **Solution annealed, strain hardened**: all **diam**, 85 (585) **TS**, 65 (450) **YS**, 30 **El**
ANSI/ASTM A 479	304	US	Bar, shapes	0.08 **C**, 2.00 **Mn**, 1.00 **Si**, 18.00–20.00 **Cr**, 8.00–10.50 **Ni**, 0.10 **N**, 0.045 **P**, 0.030 **S**	**Solution annealed**: all **diam**, 75 (515) **TS**, 30 (205) **YS**, 30 **El**
ANSI/ASTM A666	Type 316, grade A	US	Sheet, strip, plate, bar	0.08 **C**, 2.00 **Mn**, 1.00 **Si**, 16.00–18.00 **Cr**, 10.00–14.00 **Ni**, 2.00–3.00 **Mo**, 0.045 **P**, 0.030 **S**	**Cold rolled (plate, sheet, strip)**: ≤0.015 (≤0.38) **diam**, 75 (515) **TS**, 30 (205) **YS**, 40 **El**
ANSI/ASTM A 666	Type 304, grade A	US	Sheet, strip, plate, bar	0.08 **C**, 2.00 **Mn**, 1.00 **Si**, 18.00–20.00 **Cr**, 8.00–10.50 **Ni**, 0.045 **P**, 0.030 **S**	**Cold rolled (plate, sheet, strip)**: ≤0.015 (≤0.38) **diam**, 75 (515) **TS**, 30 (205) **YS**, 40 **El**
ANSI/ASTM A 276	348	US	Bar, shapes	0.08 **C**, 2.00 **Mn**, 1.00 **Si**, 17.00–19.00 **Cr**, 9.00–13.00 **Ni**, 0.20 **Co**, 10 x C min **Nb- Ta**, 0.045 **P**, 0.030 **S**, 0.10 **Ta**	**Annealed**: all **diam**, 75 (515) **TS**, 30 (205) **YS**, 40 **El**
ANSI/ASTM A 276	347	US	Bar, shapes	0.08 **C**, 2.00 **Mn**, 1.00 **Si**, 17.00–19.00 **Cr**, 9.00–13.00 **Ni**, 10 x C min **Nb- Ta**, 0.045 **P**, 0.030 **S**	**Annealed**: all **diam**, 75 (515) **TS**, 30 (205) **YS**, 40 **El**

WROUGHT STAINLESS STEELS

specification number	designation	country	product forms	composition	mechanical properties (see page iv for explanation)
ANSI/ASTM A 276	321	US	Bar, shapes	0.08 **C**, 2.00 **Mn**, 1.00 **Si**, 17.00–19.00 **Cr**, 9.00–12.00 **Ni**, 0.045 **P**, 0.030 **S**, 5 x C min **Ti**	**Annealed**: all **diam**, 75 (515) **TS**, 30 (205) **YS**, 40 **El**
ANSI/ASTM A 276	317	US	Bar, shapes	0.08 **C**, 2.00 **Mn**, 1.00 **Si**, 18.00–20.00 **Cr**, 11.00–15.00 **Ni**, 3.00–4.00 **Mo**, 0.10 **N**, 0.045 **P**, 0.030 **S**	**Annealed**: all **diam**, 75 (515) **TS**, 30 (205) **YS**, 40 **El**
ANSI/ASTM A 276	316	US	Bar, shapes	0.08 **C**, 2.00 **Mn**, 1.00 **Si**, 16.00–18.00 **Cr**, 10.00–14.00 **Ni**, 2.00–3.00 **Mo**, 0.10 **N**, 0.045 **P**, 0.030 **S**	**Annealed**: all **diam**, 75 (515) **TS**, 30 (205) **YS**, 40 **El**; **Cold worked–high tensile**: ≥0.75 (≥19.05) **diam**, 125 (860) **TS**, 100 (690) **YS**, 12 **El**
ANSI/ASTM A 276	309S	US	Bar, shapes	0.08 **C**, 2.00 **Mn**, 1.00 **Si**, 22.00–24.00 **Cr**, 12.00–15.00 **Ni**, 0.045 **P**, 0.030 **S**	**Annealed**: all **diam**, 75 (515) **TS**, 30 (205) **YS**, 40 **El**
ANSI/ASTM A 276	308	US	Bar, shapes	0.08 **C**, 2.00 **Mn**, 1.00 **Si**, 19.00–21.00 **Cr**, 10.00–12.00 **Ni**, 0.045 **P**, 0.030 **S**	**Annealed**: all **diam**, 75 (515) **TS**, 30 (205) **YS**, 40 **El**
COPANT R 195	TP 347	COPANT	Tube	0.08 **C**, 2.00 **Mn**, 0.75 **Si**, 17.0–20.0 **Cr**, 9.0–13.0 **Ni**, 10 x C–1.0 **Cb+Ta**, 0.040 **P**, 0.030 **S**	**Hot or cold finished**: (≥5.65) **diam**, (515) **TS**, (205) **YS**, 35 **El**
COPANT R 195	TP 321	COPANT	Tube	0.08 **C**, 2.00 **Mn**, 0.75 **Si**, 17.0–20.0 **Cr**, 9.0–13.0 **Ni**, 0.040 **P**, 0.030 **S**, 5 x C–0.60 **Ti**	**Hot or cold finished**: (≥5.65) **diam**, (515) **TS**, (205) **YS**, 35 **El**
COPANT R 195	TP 304	COPANT	Tube	0.08 **C**, 2.00 **Mn**, 0.75 **Si**, 18.0–20.0 **Cr**, 8.0–11.0 **Ni**, 0.040 **P**, 0.030 **S**	**Hot or cold finished**: (≥5.60) **diam**, (515) **TS**, (205) **YS**, 35 **El**
ASTM A 240	Type XM15	US	Plate, sheet, strip	0.08 **C**, 2.00 **Mn**, 1.50–2.50 **Si**, 17.00–19.00 **Cr**, 17.50–18.50 **Ni**, 0.030 **P**, 0.030 **S**	**Solution annealed, hot rolled or cold rolled**: all **diam**, 75 (515) **TS**, 30 (205) **YS**, 40 **El**
ASTM A 240	Type 348	US	Plate, sheet, strip	0.08 **C**, 2.00 **Mn**, 1.00 **Si**, 17.00–19.00 **Cr**, 9.00–13.00 **Ni**, 10 x C–1.10 **Cb+Ta**, 0.20 **Co**, 0.045 **P**, 0.030 **S**, 0.10 **Ta**	**Solution annealed, hot rolled or cold rolled**: all **diam**, 75 (515) **TS**, 30 (205) **YS**, 40 **El**
ASTM A 240	Type 347	US	Plate, sheet, strip	0.08 **C**, 2.00 **Mn**, 1.00 **Si**, 17.00–19.00 **Cr**, 9.00–13.00 **Ni**, 10 x C–1.10 **Cb+Ta**, 0.045 **P**, 0.030 **S**	**Solution annealed, hot rolled or cold rolled**: all **diam**, 75 (515) **TS**, 30 (205) **YS**, 40 **El**
ASTM A 240	Type 321	US	Plate, sheet, strip	0.08 **C**, 2.00 **Mn**, 1.00 **Si**, 17.00–19.00 **Cr**, 9.00–12.00 **Ni**, 0.045 **P**, 0.030 **S**, 5 x C–0.70 **Ti**	**Solution annealed, hot rolled or cold rolled**: all **diam**, 75 (515) **TS**, 30 (205) **YS**, 40 **El**
ASTM A 240	Type 317	US	Plate, sheet, strip	0.08 **C**, 2.00 **Mn**, 1.00 **Si**, 18.00–20.00 **Cr**, 11.00–15.00 **Ni**, 3.00–4.00 **Mo**, 0.10 **N**, 0.045 **P**, 0.030 **S**	**Solution annealed, hot rolled or cold rolled**: all **diam**, 75 (515) **TS**, 30 (205) **YS**, 35 **El**
ASTM A 240	Type 316	US	Plate, sheet, strip	0.08 **C**, 2.00 **Mn**, 1.00 **Si**, 16.00–18.00 **Cr**, 10.00–14.00 **Ni**, 2.00–3.00 **Mo**, 0.10 **N**, 0.045 **P**, 0.030 **S**	**Solution annealed, hot rolled or cold rolled**: all **diam**, 75 (515) **TS**, 30 (205) **YS**, 40 **El**
ASTM A 240	Type 310S	US	Plate, sheet, strip	0.08 **C**, 2.00 **Mn**, 1.50 **Si**, 24.00–26.00 **Cr**, 19.00–22.00 **Ni**, 0.045 **P**, 0.030 **S**	**Solution annealed, hot rolled or cold rolled**: all **diam**, 75 (515) **TS**, 30 (205) **YS**, 40 **El**
ASTM A 240	Type 309S	US	Plate, sheet, strip	0.08 **C**, 2.00 **Mn**, 1.00 **Si**, 22.00–24.00 **Cr**, 12.00–15.00 **Ni**, 0.045 **P**, 0.030 **S**	**Solution annealed, hot rolled or cold rolled**: all **diam**, 75 (515) **TS**, 30 (205) **YS**, 40 **El**
ASTM A 240	Type 304	US	Plate, sheet, strip	0.08 **C**, 2.00 **Mn**, 1.00 **Si**, 18.00–20.00 **Cr**, 8.00–10.50 **Ni**, 0.10 **N**, 0.045 **P**, 0.030 **S**	**Solution annealed, hot rolled or cold rolled**: all **diam**, 75 (515) **TS**, 30 (205) **YS**, 40 **El**
ASTM A 167	Type XM–15	US	Plate, sheet, strip	0.08 **C**, 2.00 **Mn**, 1.50–2.50 **Si**, 17.00–19.00 **Cr**, 17.50–18.50 **Ni**, 0.030 **P**, 0.030 **S**	**Solution annealed**: all **diam**, 75 (515) **TS**, 30 (205) **YS**, 40 **El**
ASTM A 167	Type 304	US	Plate, sheet, strip	0.08 **C**, 2.00 **Mn**, 1.00 **Si**, 18.00–20.00 **Cr**, 8.00–10.50 **Ni**, 0.045 **P**, 0.030 **S**	**Solution annealed**: all **diam**, 75 (515) **TS**, 30 (205) **YS**, 40 **El**
ASTM A 167	Type 308	US	Plate, sheet, strip	0.08 **C**, 2.00 **Mn**, 1.00 **Si**, 19.00–21.00 **Cr**, 10.00–12.00 **Ni**, 0.045 **P**, 0.030 **S**	**Solution annealed**: all **diam**, 75 (515) **TS**, 30 (205) **YS**, 40 **El**
ASTM A 167	Type 309S	US	Plate, sheet, strip	0.08 **C**, 2.00 **Mn**, 1.00 **Si**, 22.00–24.00 **Cr**, 12.00–15.00 **Ni**, 0.045 **P**, 0.030 **S**	**Solution annealed**: all **diam**, 75 (515) **TS**, 30 (205) **YS**, 40 **El**
ASTM A 167	Type 310S	US	Plate, sheet, strip	0.08 **C**, 2.00 **Mn**, 1.50 **Si**, 24.00–26.00 **Cr**, 19.00–22.00 **Ni**, 0.045 **P**, 0.030 **S**	**Solution annealed**: all **diam**, 75 (515) **TS**, 30 (205) **YS**, 40 **El**

WROUGHT STAINLESS STEELS

specification number	designation	country	product forms	composition	mechanical properties (see page iv for explanation)
ASTM A 167	Type 316	US	Plate, sheet, strip	0.08 **C**, 2.00 **Mn**, 1.00 **Si**, 16.00–18.00 **Cr**, 10.00–14.00 **Ni**, 2.00–3.00 **Mo**, 0.045 **P**, 0.030 **S**	**Solution annealed**: all diam, 75 (515) **TS**, 30 (205) **YS**, 40 **El**
ASTM A 167	Type 317	US	Plate, sheet, strip	0.08 **C**, 2.00 **Mn**, 1.00 **Si**, 18.00–20.00 **Cr**, 11.00–15.00 **Ni**, 3.00–4.00 **Mo**, 0.045 **P**, 0.030 **S**	**Solution annealed**: all diam, 75 (515) **TS**, 30 (205) **YS**, 35 **El**
ASTM A 167	Type 321	US	Plate, sheet, strip	0.08 **C**, 2.00 **Mn**, 1.00 **Si**, 17.00–19.00 **Cr**, 9.00–12.00 **Ni**, 0.045 **P**, 0.030 **S**, 5 x C **Ti**	**Solution annealed**: all diam, 75 (515) **TS**, 30 (205) **YS**, 40 **El**
ASTM A 167	Type 347	US	Plate, sheet, strip	0.08 **C**, 2.00 **Mn**, 1.00 **Si**, 17.00–19.00 **Cr**, 9.00–13.00 **Ni**, 10 x C–1.10 **Cb+Ta**, 0.045 **P**, 0.030 **S**	**Solution annealed**: all diam, 75 (515) **TS**, 30 (205) **YS**, 40 **El**
ASTM A 167	Type 348	US	Plate, sheet, strip	0.08 **C**, 2.00 **Mn**, 1.00 **Si**, 17.00–19.00 **Cr**, 9.00–13.00 **Ni**, 10 x C–1.10 **Cb+Ta**, 0.20 **Co**, 0.045 **P**, 0.030 **S**, 0.10 **Ta**	**Solution annealed**: all diam, 75 (515) **TS**, 30 (205) **YS**, 40 **El**
ANSI/ASTM A 666	Type 304, grade A	US	Sheet, strip, plate, bar	0.08 **C**, 2.00 **Mn**, 1.00 **Si**, 18.00–20.00 **Cr**, 8.00–10.50 **Ni**, 0.045 **P**, 0.030 **S**	**Annealed (plate, sheet, strip, bar)**: ≥0.015 **diam**, (515) **TS**, (205) **YS**, 40 **El**
ANSI/ASTM A 666	Type 316, grade A	US	Sheet, strip, plate, bar	0.08 **C**, 2.00 **Mn**, 1.00 **Si**, 16.00–18.00 **Cr**, 10.00–14.00 **Ni**, 2.00–3.00 **Mo**, 0.045 **P**, 0.030 **S**	**Annealed (plate, sheet, strip, bar)**: ≥0.015 **diam**, (515) **TS**, (205) **YS**, 40 **El**
ANSI/ASTM A 479	Grade 304	US	Bar, shapes	0.08 **C**, 2.00 **Mn**, 1.00 **Si**, 18.00–20.00 **Cr**, 8.00–10.50 **Ni**, 0.10 **N**, 0.045 **P**, 0.030 **S**	**Solution annealed**: all **diam**, (515) **TS**, (205) **YS**, 30 **El**
ANSI/ASTM A 479	Grade ER308	US	Bar, shapes	0.08 **C**, 1.00–2.50 **Mn**, 0.25–0.60 **Si**, 19.50–22.00 **Cr**, 9.00–11.00 **Ni**, 0.030 **P**, 0.030 **S**	**Solution annealed**: all **diam**, (515) **TS**, (205) **YS**, 30 **El**
ANSI/ASTM A 479	Grade 310S	US	Bar, shapes	0.08 **C**, 2.00 **Mn**, 1.50 **Si**, 24.00–26.00 **Cr**, 19.00–22.00 **Ni**, 0.045 **P**, 0.030 **S**	**Solution annealed**: all **diam**, (515) **TS**, (205) **YS**, 30 **El**
ANSI/ASTM A 479	Grade 316	US	Bar, shapes	0.08 **C**, 2.00 **Mn**, 1.00 **Si**, 16.00–18.00 **Cr**, 10.00–14.00 **Ni**, 2.00–3.00 **Mo**, 0.10 **N**, 0.045 **P**, 0.030 **S**	**Solution annealed**: all **diam**, (515) **TS**, (205) **YS**, 30 **El**
ANSI/ASTM A 240	Grade 304	US	Plate, sheet, strip	0.08 **C**, 2.00 **Mn**, 1.00 **Si**, 18.00–20.00 **Cr**, 8.00–10.50 **Ni**, 0.10 **N**, 0.045 **P**, 0.030 **S**	**Solution annealed**: all **diam**, (515) **TS**, (205) **YS**, 40 **El**
ANSI/ASTM A 240	Grade 309S	US	Plate, sheet, strip	0.08 **C**, 2.00 **Mn**, 1.00 **Si**, 22.00–24.00 **Cr**, 12.00–15.00 **Ni**, 0.045 **P**, 0.030 **S**	**Solution annealed**: all **diam**, (515) **TS**, (205) **YS**, 40 **El**
ANSI/ASTM A 240	Grade 310S	US	Plate, sheet, strip	0.08 **C**, 2.00 **Mn**, 1.50 **Si**, 24.00–26.00 **Cr**, 19.00–22.00 **Ni**, 0.045 **P**, 0.030 **S**	**Solution annealed**: all **diam**, (515) **TS**, (205) **YS**, 40 **El**
ANSI/ASTM A 240	Grade 316	US	Plate, sheet, strip	0.08 **C**, 2.00 **Mn**, 1.00 **Si**, 16.00–18.00 **Cr**, 10.00–14.00 **Ni**, 2.00–3.00 **Mo**, 0.045 **P**, 0.030 **S**	**Solution annealed**: all **diam**, (515) **TS**, (205) **YS**, 40 **El**
ANSI/ASTM A 240	Grade 317	US	Plate, sheet, strip	0.08 **C**, 2.00 **Mn**, 1.00 **Si**, 18.00–20.00 **Cr**, 11.00–15.00 **Ni**, 3.00–4.00 **Mo**, 0.10 **N**, 0.045 **P**, 0.030 **S**	**Solution annealed**: all **diam**, (515) **TS**, (205) **YS**, 35 **El**
ANSI/ASTM A 240	Grade XM 15	US	Plate, sheet, strip	0.08 **C**, 2.00 **Mn**, 1.50–2.50 **Si**, 17.00–19.00 **Cr**, 17.50–18.50 **Ni**, 0.030 **P**, 0.030 **S**	**Solution annealed**: all **diam**, (515) **TS**, (205) **YS**, 40 **El**
ANSI/ASTM A 240	Grade 348	US	Plate, sheet, strip	0.08 **C**, 2.00 **Mn**, 1.00 **Si**, 17.00–19.00 **Cr**, 9.00–13.00 **Ni**, 8 x C–1.10 **Cb+Ta**, 0.20 **Co**, 0.045 **P**, 0.030 **S**, 0.10 **Ta**	**Solution annealed**: all **diam**, (515) **TS**, (205) **YS**, 40 **El**
ANSI/ASTM A 240	Grade 347	US	Plate, sheet, strip	0.08 **C**, 2.00 **Mn**, 1.00 **Si**, 17.00–19.00 **Cr**, 9.00–13.00 **Ni**, 10 x C–1.10 **Cb+Ta**, 0.045 **P**, 0.030 **S**	**Solution annealed**: all **diam**, (515) **TS**, (205) **YS**, 40 **El**
ANSI/ASTM A 240	Grade 321	US	Plate, sheet, strip	0.08 **C**, 2.00 **Mn**, 1.00 **Si**, 17.00–19.00 **Cr**, 9.00–12.00 **Ni**, 0.045 **P**, 0.030 **S**, 5 x C–0.70 **Ti**	**Solution annealed**: all **diam**, (515) **TS**, (205) **YS**, 40 **El**
ANSI/ASTM A 479	Grade 348	US	Bar, shapes	0.08 **C**, 2.00 **Mn**, 1.00 **Si**, 17.00–19.00 **Cr**, 9.00–13.00 **Ni**, 10 x C min **Cb+Ta**, 0.20 **Co**, 0.045 **P**, 0.030 **S**, 0.01 **Ta**	**Solution annealed**: all **diam**, (515) **TS**, (205) **YS**, 30 **El**

specification number	designation	country	product forms	composition	mechanical properties (see page iv for explanation)
ANSI/ASTM A 479	Grade 347	US	Bar, shapes	0.08 **C**, 2.00 **Mn**, 1.00 **Si**, 17.00–19.00 **Cr**, 9.00–13.00 **Ni**, 10 x C min **Cb+Ta**, 0.045 **P**, 0.030 **S**	**Solution annealed**: all **diam**, (515) **TS**, (205) **YS**, 30 **El**
ANSI/ASTM A 479	Grade 321	US	Bar, shapes	0.08 **C**, 2.00 **Mn**, 1.00 **Si**, 17.00–19.00 **Cr**, 9.00–12.00 **Ni**, 0.045 **P**, 0.030 **S**, 5 x C min **Ti**	**Solution annealed**: all **diam**, (515) **TS**, (205) **YS**, 30 **El**
ANSI/ASTM A 249	TP 304	US	Tube: welded	0.08 **C**, 2.00 **Mn**, 0.75 **Si**, 18.0–20.0 **Cr**, 8.00–11.0 **Ni**, 0.040 **P**, 0.030 **S**	**Solution annealed**: 0.312 (7.94) **diam**, 75 (515) **TS**, 30 (205) **YS**, 35 **El**
ANSI/ASTM A 249	TP 316	US	Tube: welded	0.08 **C**, 2.00 **Mn**, 0.75 **Si**, 16.0–18.0 **Cr**, 11.0–14.0 **Ni**, 2.00–3.00 **Mo**, 0.040 **P**, 0.030 **S**	**Solution annealed**: 0.312 (7.94) **diam**, 75 (515) **TS**, 30 (205) **YS**, 35 **El**
ANSI/ASTM A 249	TP 317	US	Tube: welded	0.08 **C**, 2.00 **Mn**, 0.75 **Si**, 18.0–20.0 **Cr**, 11.0–14.0 **Ni**, 3.00–4.00 **Mo**, 0.040 **P**, 0.030 **S**	**Solution annealed**: 0.312 (7.94) **diam**, 75 (515) **TS**, 30 (205) **YS**, 35 **El**
ANSI/ASTM A 249	TP 321	US	Tube: welded	0.08 **C**, 2.00 **Mn**, 0.75 **Si**, 17.0–20.0 **Cr**, 9.00–13.00 **Ni**, 0.040 **P**, 0.030 **S**, 5 x C–0.70 **Ti**	**Solution annealed**: 0.312 (7.94) **diam**, 75 (515) **TS**, 30 (205) **YS**, 35 **El**
ANSI/ASTM A 249	TP 347	US	Tube: welded	0.08 **C**, 2.00 **Mn**, 0.75 **Si**, 17.0–20.0 **Cr**, 9.00–13.0 **Ni**, 10 x C–1.0 **Nb+Ta**, 0.040 **P**, 0.030 **S**	**Solution annealed**: 0.312 (7.94) **diam**, 75 (515) **TS**, 30 (205) **YS**, 35 **El**
ANSI/ASTM A 249	TP 348	US	Tube: welded	0.08 **C**, 2.00 **Mn**, 0.75 **Si**, 17.0–20.0 **Cr**, 9.00–13.0 **Ni**, 0.040 **P**, 0.030 **S**, 0.10 **Ta**, 10 x C–1.0 **Ta+Nb**	**Solution annealed**: 0.312 (7.94) **diam**, 75 (515) **TS**, 30 (205) **YS**, 35 **El**
ANSI/ASTM A 249	TP XM–15	US	Tube: welded austenitic	0.08 **C**, 2.00 **Mn**, 1.50–2.50 **Si**, 17.00–19.00 **Cr**, 17.50–18.50 **Ni**, 0.030 **P**, 0.030 **S**	**Solution annealed**: 0.312 (7.94) **diam**, 75 (515) **TS**, 30 (205) **YS**, 35 **El**
DGN–B–83	317	Mexico	Bar	0.08 **C**, 2.0 **Mn**, 1.0 **Si**, 18.20 **Cr**, 11.0–15.0 **Ni**, 3.0–4.0 **Mo**, 0.045 **P**, 0.030 **S**	**Hot or cold rolled**: all **diam**, (510) **TS**, (206) **YS**, 40 **El**
DGN–B–83	321	Mexico	Bar	0.08 **C**, 2.0 **Mn**, 1.0 **Si**, 17.0–19.0 **Cr**, 9.0–12.0 **Ni**, 0.045 **P**, 0.030 **S**, 5 x C min **Ti**	**Hot or cold rolled**: all **diam**, (510) **TS**, (206) **YS**, 40 **El**
DGN–B–83	316	Mexico	Bar	0.08 **C**, 2.0 **Mn**, 1.0 **Si**, 16.0–18.0 **Cr**, 10.0–14.0 **Ni**, 2.0–3.0 **Mo**, 0.045 **P**, 0.030 **S**	**Hot or cold rolled**: all **diam**, (510) **TS**, (206) **YS**, 40 **El**
DGN–B–83	310 S	Mexico	Bar	0.08 **C**, 2.0 **Mn**, 1.50 **Si**, 24.0–26.0 **Cr**, 19.0–22.0 **Ni**, 0.045 **P**, 0.030 **S**	**Hot or cold rolled**: all **diam**, (510) **TS**, (206) **YS**, 40 **El**
DGN–B–83	309S	Mexico	Bar	0.08 **C**, 2.0 **Mn**, 1.0 **Si**, 22.0–24.0 **Cr**, 12.0–15.0 **Ni**, 0.045 **P**, 0.030 **S**	**Hot or cold rolled**: all **diam**, (510) **TS**, (206) **YS**, 40 **El**
DGN–B–83	304	Mexico	Bar	0.08 **C**, 2.0 **Mn**, 1.0 **Si**, 18.0–20.0 **Cr**, 8.0–12.0 **Ni**, 0.045 **P**, 0.030 **S**	**Hot or cold rolled**: all **diam**, (510) **TS**, (206) **YS**, 40 **El**
DGN–B–83	308	Mexico	Bar	0.08 **C**, 2.0 **Mn**, 1.0 **Si**, 19.0–21.0 **Cr**, 10.0–12.0 **Ni**, 0.045 **P**, 0.030 **S**	**Hot or cold rolled**: all **diam**, (510) **TS**, (206) **YS**, 40 **El**
DGN–B–83	347	Mexico	Bar	0.08 **C**, 2.0 **Mn**, 1.0 **Si**, 17.0–19.0 **Cr**, 9.0–12.0 **Ni**, 10 x C min **Cb+Ta**, 0.045 **P**, 0.030 **S**	**Hot or cold rolled**: all **diam**, (510) **TS**, (206) **YS**
DGN–B–83	348	Mexico	Bar	0.08 **C**, 2.0 **Mn**, 1.0 **Si**, 17.0–19.0 **Cr**, 9.0–13.0 **Ni**, 10 x C min **Cb+Ta**, 0.20 **Co**, 0.045 **P**, 0.030 **S**, 0.10 **Ta**	**Hot or cold rolled**: all **diam**, (510) **TS**, (206) **YS**, 40 **El**
IS: 6913	Grade D	India	Tube	0.08 **C**, 2.0 **Mn**, 1.0 **Si**, 16.0–18.5 **Cr**, 10.5–14.0 **Ni**, 2.0–3.0 **Mo**, 0.045 **P**, 0.030 **S**	**Solution annealed**: all **diam**, (510) **TS**, 30 **El**
ISO 2604/II	TS 50	ISO	Tube: seamless	0.08 **C**, 2.00 **Mn**, 1.00 **Si**, 17.00–19.00 **Cr**, 9.00–13.00 **Ni**, 10 x C–1.00 **Nb**, 0.045 **P**, 0.030 **S**	**Cold finished, quenched**: all **diam**, (510) **TS**, (205) **YS**, 30 **El**
ISO 2604/II	TS 53	ISO	Tube: seamless	0.08 **C**, 2.00 **Mn**, 1.00 **Si**, 17.00–19.00 **Cr**, 9.00–13.00 **Ni**, 0.045 **P**, 0.030 **S**, 5 x C–0.80 **Ti**	**Cold finished, quenched**: all **diam**, (510) **TS**, (195) **YS**, 30 **El**
BS 3605 Section4	Grade 347S17	UK	Pipe: welded	0.08 **C**, 0.50–2.00 **Mn**, 0.20–1.00 **Si**, 17.0–19.0 **Cr**, 9.0–12.0 **Ni**, 10 x c–1.00 **Nb**, 0.040 **P**, 0.030 **S**	**Solution annealed**: all **diam**, (510) **TS**, (245) **YS**, 35 **El**

specification number	designation	country	product forms	composition	mechanical properties (see page iv for explanation)
BS 3605 Section 4	Grade 321S22	UK	Pipe: welded	0.08 **C**, 0.50–2.00 **Mn**, 0.20–1.00 **Si**, 17.0–19.0 **Cr**, 9.0–12.0 **Ni**, 0.040 **P**, 0.030 **S**, 5 x c–0.60 **Ti**	**Solution annealed**: all **diam**, (510) **TS**, (235) **YS**, 35 **El**
BS 3605 Section 3	Grade 347S18	UK	Pipe: seamless	0.08 **C**, 0.50–2.00 **Mn**, 0.20–1.00 **Si**, 17.0–19.0 **Cr**, 10.0–13.0 **Ni**, 10 x C–20 x C or 1.00 **Nb**, 0.040 **P**, 0.030 **S**	**Solution annealed**: all **diam**, (510) **TS**, (245) **YS**, 35 **El**
BS 3605 Section 3	Grade 321S18	UK	Pipe: seamless	0.08 **C**, 0.50–2.00 **Mn**, 0.20–1.00 **Si**, 17.0–19.0 **Cr**, 10.0–13.0 **Ni**, 0.040 **P**, 0.030 **S**, 5 x C–0.60 **Ti**	**Solution annealed**: all **diam**, (510) **TS**, (235) **YS**, 35 **El**
BS 1449 Part 2	Grade 347S17	UK	Plate, sheet, strip	0.08 **C**, 0.50–2.00 **Mn**, 0.20–1.00 **Si**, 17.0–19.0 **Cr**, 9.0–12.0 **Ni**, 10C–1.00 **Nb**, 0.045 **P**, 0.030 **S**	**Solution annealed**: (≥3.0) **diam**, (510) **TS**, (210) **YS**, 40 **El**
BS 1449 Part 2	Grade 321S12	UK	Plate, sheet, strip	0.08 **C**, 0.50–2.00 **Mn**, 0.20–1.00 **Si**, 17.0–19.0 **Cr**, 9.0–12.0 **Ni**, 0.045 **P**, 0.030 **S**, 5 x C–0.70 **Ti**	**Solution annealed**: (≥3.0) **diam**, (510) **TS**, (210) **YS**, 40 **El**
BS 1449 Part 2	Grade 302S17	UK	Sheet, strip	0.08 **C**, 0.50–2.00 **Mn**, 0.20–1.00 **Si**, 17.0–19.0 **Cr**, 8.0–11.0 **Ni**, 0.045 **P**, 0.030 **S**	**Solution annealed**: (0.50–1.6) **diam**, (510) **TS**, (210) **YS**, 30 **El**
BS 4127 Part 2		UK	Tube	0.08 **C**, 0.50–2.00 **Mn**, 0.20–1.0 **Si**, 17.0–19.0 **Cr**, 8.0–11.0 **Ni**, 0.045 **P**, 0.03 **S**	**Mill**: all **diam**, (510) **TS**, 30 **El**
BS 970 Part 4	Grade 347S17	UK	Blooms, billets, bar, forgings	0.08 **C**, 0.50–2.00 **Mn**, 0.20–1.00 **Si**, 17.0–19.0 **Cr**, 9.0–12.0 **Ni**, 10 x C–1.00 **Nb**, 0.045 **P**, 0.030 **S**	**Annealed**: all **diam**, (510) **TS**, (210) **YS**, 40 **El**
BS 3605 Section 2	Grade 321S18	UK	Pipe: seamless	0.08 **C**, 0.50–2.00 **Mn**, 0.20–1.00 **Si**, 17.0–19.0 **Cr**, 10.0–13.0 **Ni**, 0.040 **P**, 0.030 **S**, 5C–0.60 **Ti**	**Solution annealed**: all **diam**, (510) **TS**, (235) **YS**, 35 **El**
BS 3605 Section 2	Grade 347S18	UK	Pipe: seamless	0.08 **C**, 0.50–2.00 **Mn**, 0.20–1.00 **Si**, 17.0–19.0 **Cr**, 10.0–13.0 **Ni**, 10 x C–20 x C or 1.00 **Nb**, 0.040 **P**, 0.030 **S**	**Solution annealed**: all **diam**, (510) **TS**, (245) **YS**, 35 **El**
BS 3605 Section 5	Grade 347S17	UK	Pipe: welded	0.08 **C**, 0.50–2.00 **Mn**, 0.20–1.00 **Si**, 17.0–19.0 **Cr**, 9.0–12.0 **Ni**, 10 x C–1.00 **Nb**, 0.040 **P**, 0.030 **S**	**Solution annealed**: all **diam**, (510) **TS**, (245) **YS**, 35 **El**
BS 3605 Section 5	Grade 321S22	UK	Pipe: welded	0.08 **C**, 0.50–2.00 **Mn**, 0.20–1.00 **Si**, 17.0–19.0 **Cr**, 9.0–12.0 **Ni**, 0.040 **P**, 0.030 **S**, 5 x C–0.60 **Ti**	**Solution annealed**: all **diam**, (510) **TS**, (235) **YS**, 35 **El**
NF A 35–572	Z 6 CNDT 17–12	France	Bar, sections	0.08 **C**, 2.0 **Mn**, 1.0 **Si**, 16.0–18.0 **Cr**, 10.5–13.0 **Ni**, 2.0–2.5 **Mo**, 0.040 **P**, 0.030 **S**, 5 x C–0.60 **Ti**	**Austenitized**: (≤25) **diam**, (510) **TS**, (215) **YS**, 40 **El**
NF A 35–572	Z 6 CNDNb 17–12	France	Bar, sections	0.08 **C**, 2.0 **Mn**, 1.0 **Si**, 16.0–18.0 **Cr**, 10.5–13.0 **Ni**, 2.0–2.5 **Mo**, 10 x C–1.0 **Nb+Ta**, 0.040 **P**, 0.030 **S**	**Austenitized**: (≤25) **diam**, (510) **TS**, (215) **YS**, 40 **El**
NF A 35–572	Z 6 CNDT 17.13	France	Bar, sections	0.08 **C**, 2.0 **Mn**, 1.0 **Si**, 16.0–18.0 **Cr**, 11.5–13.5 **Ni**, 2.5–3.0 **Mo**, 0.040 **P**, 0.030 **S**, 5 x C–0.6 **Ti**	**Austenitized**: (≤25) **diam**, (510) **TS**, (215) **YS**, 40 **El**
NF A 35–572	Z 6 CNDNb 17.13	France	Bar, sections	0.08 **C**, 2.0 **Mn**, 1.0 **Si**, 16.0–18.0 **Cr**, 11.5–13.5 **Ni**, 2.5–3.0 **Mo**, 10 x C–1.0 **Nb+Ta**, 0.040 **P**, 0.030 **S**	**Austenitized**: (≤25) **diam**, (510) **TS**, (215) **YS**, 40 **El**
SS 14 23 38	SS 23 38–23	Sweden	Tube: welded	0.08 **C**, 2.0 **Mn**, 1.0 **Si**, 17.0–19.0 **Cr**, 9.0–13.0 **Ni**, 10 x C–1.0 **Nb**+1/2 **Ta**, 0.045 **P**, 0.030 **S**	**Solution annealed**: all **diam**, (510) **TS**, (220) **YS**, 40 **El**
SS 14 23 38	SS 23 38–24	Sweden	Tube: seamless	0.08 **C**, 2.0 **Mn**, 1.0 **Si**, 17.0–19.0 **Cr**, 9.0–13.0 **Ni**, 10 x C–1.0 **Nb**+1/2 **Ta**, 0.045 **P**, 0.030 **S**	**Solution annealed**: (<10) **diam**, (510) **TS**, (220) **YS**, 40 **El**
SS 14 23 38	SS 23 38–25	Sweden	Tube: welded	0.08 **C**, 2.0 **Mn**, 1.0 **Si**, 17.0–19.0 **Cr**, 9.0–13.0 **Ni**, 10 x C–1.0 **Nb**+1/2 **Ta**, 0.045 **P**, 0.030 **S**	**Solution annealed**: all **diam**, (510) **TS**, (220) **YS**, 40 **El**

WROUGHT STAINLESS STEELS

specification number	designation	country	product forms	composition	mechanical properties (see page iv for explanation)
SS 14 23 50	SS 23 50–22	Sweden	Tube: seamless	0.08 **C**, 2.0 **Mn**, 1.0 **Si**, 16.0–18.5 **Cr**, 10.5–14.0 **Ni**, 2.0–2.5 **Mo**, 5 x C–0.80 **Ti**, 0.045 **P**, 0.030 **S**	**Solution annealed**: (<10) **diam**, (510) **TS**, (220) **YS**, 40 **El**
SS 14 23 50	SS 23 50–23	Sweden	Tube: welded	0.08 **C**, 2.0 **Mn**, 1.0 **Si**, 16.0–18.5 **Cr**, 10.5–14.0 **Ni**, 2.0–2.5 **Mo**, 5 x C–0.80 **Ti**, 0.045 **P**, 0.030 **S**	**Solution annealed**: all **diam**, (510) **TS**, (220) **YS**, 40 **El**
SS 14 23 50	SS 23 50–24	Sweden	Tube: seamless	0.08 **C**, 2.0 **Mn**, 1.0 **Si**, 16.0–18.5 **Cr**, 10.5–14.0 **Ni**, 2.0–2.5 **Mo**, 5 x C–0.80 **Ti**, 0.045 **P**, 0.030 **S**	**Solution annealed**: (<10) **diam**, (510) **TS**, (220) **YS**, 40 **El**
SS 14 23 50	SS 23 50–25	Sweden	Tube: welded	0.08 **C**, 2.0 **Mn**, 1.0 **Si**, 16.0–18.5 **Cr**, 10.5–14.0 **Ni**, 2.0–2.5 **Mo**, 5 x C–0.80 **Ti**, 0.045 **P**, 0.030 **S**	**Solution annealed**: all **diam**, (510) **TS**, (220) **YS**, 40 **El**
SS 14 23 37	SS 23 37–25	Sweden	Tube: welded	0.08 **C**, 2.0 **Mn**, 1.0 **Si**, 17.0–19.0 **Cr**, 9.0–13.0 **Ni**, 0.045 **P**, 0.030 **S**, 0.80 **Ti**	**Solution annealed**: all **diam**, (510) **TS**, (210) **YS**, 40 **El**
SS 14 23 37	SS 23 37–24	Sweden	Tube: seamless	0.08 **C**, 2.0 **Mn**, 1.0 **Si**, 17.0–19.0 **Cr**, 9.0–13.0 **Ni**, 0.045 **P**, 0.030 **S**, 0.80 **Ti**	**Solution annealed**: (<10) **diam**, (510) **TS**, (210) **YS**, 40 **El**
SS 14 23 37	SS 23 37–23	Sweden	Tube: welded	0.08 **C**, 2.0 **Mn**, 1.0 **Si**, 17.0–19.0 **Cr**, 9.0–13.0 **Ni**, 0.045 **P**, 0.030 **S**, 0.80 **Ti**	**Solution annealed**: all **diam**, (510) **TS**, (210) **YS**, 40 **El**
SS 14 23 37	SS 23 37–22	Sweden	Tube: seamless	0.08 **C**, 2.0 **Mn**, 1.0 **Si**, 17.0–19.0 **Cr**, 9.0–13.0 **Ni**, 0.045 **P**, 0.030 **S**, 0.80 **Ti**	**Solution annealed**: (<10) **diam**, (510) **TS**, (290) **YS**, 40 **El**
SS 14 23 38	SS 23 38–22	Sweden	Tube: seamless	0.08 **C**, 2.0 **Mn**, 1.0 **Si**, 17.0–19.0 **Cr**, 9.0–13.0 **Ni**, 10 x C–1.0 **Nb**+1/2 **Ta**, 0.045 **P**, 0.030 **S**	**Solution annealed**: (<10) **diam**, (510) **TS**, (220) **YS**, 40 **El**
AISI S30430		US	Wire	0.08 **C**, 2.00 **Mn**, 1.00 **Si**, 17.00–19.00 **Cr**, 8.00–10.00 **Ni**, 3.00–4.00 **Cu**, 0.045 **P**, 0.030 **S**	**Annealed**: 0.1–1.0 (2.54–25.4) **diam**, 73 (503) **TS**, 31 (214) **YS**, 70 **El**; **Soft temper**: 0.1–1.0 (2.54–25.4) **diam**, 81 (558) **TS**, 55 (379) **YS**
AECMA prEn2228		AECMA	Sheet	0.08 **C**, 2.00 **Mn**, 1.00 **Si**, 17.0–20.0 **Cr**, 8.0–11.0 **Ni**, 0.040 **P**, 0.030 **S**	**Annealed**: all **diam**, (500) **TS**, (190) **YS**, 35 **El**
AECMA prEn2231		AECMA	Tube: seamless	0.08 **C**, 2.00 **Mn**, 1.00 **Si**, 17.00–20.00 **Cr**, 8.00–12.00 **Ni**, 0.040 **P**, 0.030 **S**	**Annealed**: all **diam**, (500) **TS**, (190) **YS**, 35 **El**
NF A 35–572	Z 6 CNT 18.10	France	Bar, sections	0.08 **C**, 2.0 **Mn**, 1.0 **Si**, 17.0–19.0 **Cr**, 9.0–11.0 **Ni**, 0.040 **P**, 0.030 **S**, 5 x C–0.6 **Ti**	**Austenitized**: (≤25) **diam**, (500) **TS**, (205) **YS**, 40 **El**
NF A 35–572	Z 6 CNNb 18–10	France	Bar, sections	0.08 **C**, 2.0 **Mn**, 1.0 **Si**, 17.0–19.0 **Cr**, 9.0–11.0 **Ni**, 10 x C–1.0 **Nb**+**Ta**, 0.040 **P**, 0.030 **S**	**Austenitized**: (≤25) **diam**, (500) **TS**, (205) **YS**, 40 **El**
IS:6913	Grade B	India	Tube	0.08 **C**, 2.0 **Mn**, 1.0 **Si**, 17.0–20.0 **Cr**, 9.0–13.0 **Ni**	**Solution annealed**: all **diam**, (490) **TS**, 30 **El**
ISO 2604/1	F66	ISO	Forgings	0.08 **C**, 2.00 **Mn**, 1.00 **Si**, 16.50–18.50 **Cr**, 11.00–14.00 **Ni**, 2.00–3.00 **Mo**, 0.045 **P**, 0.030 **S**, 5 x C–0.80 **Ti**	**Quenched**: all **diam**, (490) **TS**, (205) **YS**, 30 **El**
ISO 2604/1	F53	ISO	Forgings	0.08 **C**, 2.00 **Mn**, 1.00 **Si**, 17.00–19.00 **Cr**, 9.00–13.00 **Ni**, 0.045 **P**, 0.030 **S**, 5 x C–0.80 **Ti**	**Quenched**: all **diam**, (490) **TS**, (195) **YS**, 30 **El**
ISO 2604/1	F55	ISO	Forgings	0.08 **C**, 2.00 **Mn**, 1.00 **Si**, 17.00–19.00 **Cr**, 9.00–13.00 **Ni**, 0.50 **Mo**, 0.045 **P**, 0.030 **S**, 5 x C–0.80 **Ti**	**Quenched**: all **diam**, (490) **TS**, (195) **YS**, 30 **El**
ISO 2604/1	F52	ISO	Forgings	0.08 **C**, 2.00 **Mn**, 1.00 **Si**, 17.00–19.00 **Cr**, 9.00–13.00 **Ni**, 0.50 **Mo**, 10 x C–1.00 **Nb**, 0.045 **P**, 0.030 **S**	**Quenched**: all **diam**, (490) **TS**, (205) **YS**, 30 **El**
ISO 2604/1	F50	ISO	Forgings	0.08 **C**, 2.00 **Mn**, 1.00 **Si**, 17.00–19.00 **Cr**, 9.00–13.00 **Ni**, 10 x C–1.00 **Nb**, 0.045 **P**, 0.030 **S**	**Quenched**: all **diam**, (490) **TS**, (205) **YS**, 30 **El**
ISO 683/XII	16	ISO	Bar, sheet, plate	0.08 **C**, 2.0 **Mn**, 1.0 **Si**, 17.0–19.0 **Cr**, 9.0–12.0 **Ni**, 5 x C–1.0 **Nb**, 0.045 **P**, 0.030 **S**	**Solution treated**: all **diam**, (490) **TS**, (210) **YS**, 35 **El**

specification number	designation	country	product forms	composition	mechanical properties (see page iv for explanation)
ISO 683/XII	15	ISO	Bar, sheet, plate	0.08 **C**, 2.0 **Mn**, 1.0 **Si**, 17.0–19.0 **Cr**, 9.0–12.0 **Ni**, 0.045 **P**, 0.030 **S**, 5 x C–0.80 **Ti**	**Solution treated**: all **diam**, (490) **TS**, 210 **YS**, 35 **El**
ISO 683/XII	21	ISO	Bar, sheet, plate	0.08 **C**, 2.0 **Mn**, 1.0 **Si**, 16.0–18.5 **Cr**, 10.5–14.0 **Ni**, 2.0–2.5 **Mo**, 0.045 **P**, 0.030 **S**, 5 x C–0.80 **Ti**	**Solution treated**: all **diam**, (490) **TS**, (220) **YS**, 35 **El**
ISO 683/XII	23	ISO	Bar, sheet, plate	0.08 **C**, 2.0 **Mn**, 1.0 **Si**, 16.0–18.5 **Cr**, 10.5–14.0 **Ni**, 2.0–2.5 **Mo**, 10 x C–1.0 **Nb**, 0.045 **P**, 0.030 **S**	**Solution treated**: all **diam**, (490) **TS**, (220) **YS**, 35 **El**
ISO 683/XII	21a	ISO	Bar, sheet, plate	0.08 **C**, 2.0 **Mn**, 1.0 **Si**, 16.0–18.5 **Cr**, 11.0–14.5 **Ni**, 2.5–3.0 **Mo**, 0.045 **P**, 0.030 **S**, 5 x C–0.80 **Ti**	**Solution treated**: all **diam**, (490) **TS**, (220) **YS**, 35 **El**
ISO 683/XII	23a	ISO	Bar, sheet, plate	0.08 **C**, 2.0 **Mn**, 1.0 **Si**, 16.0–18.5 **Cr**, 11.0–14.5 **Ni**, 2.5–3.0 **Mo**, 10 x C–1.0 **Nb**, 0.045 **P**, 0.030 **S**	**Solution treated**: all **diam**, (490) **TS**, (220) **YS**, 35 **El**
EURONORM 119–74, V	X 6 CrNiMo 17 12 2 KD	EURONORM	Wire, rod	0.08 **C**, 2.0 **Mn**, 1.0 **Si**, 16.0–18.5 **Cr**, 10.5–13.5 **Ni**, 2.0–2.5 **Mo**, 0.045 **P**, 0.030 **S**	**Solution annealed**: (16–63) **diam**, (490) **TS**, (205) **YS**, 40 **El**
ISO 2604/IV	P50	ISO	Plate	0.08 **C**, 2.00 **Mn**, 1.00 **Si**, 17.0–19.0 **Cr**, 9.0–12.0 **Ni**, 10 x C–1.0 **Nb**, 0.045 **P**, 0.030 **S**	**Hot rolled, quenched**: (3–40) **diam**, (490) **TS**, (205) **YS**, 40 **El**
ISO 2604/IV	P53	ISO	Plate	0.08 **C**, 2.00 **Mn**, 1.00 **Si**, 17.0–19.0 **Cr**, 9.0–12.0 **Ni**, 0.045 **P**, 0.030 **S**, 5 x C–0.80 **Ti**	**Hot rolled, quenched**: (3–40) **diam**, (490) **TS**, (195) **YS**, 40 **El**
IS 6603	04Cr18Ni10	India	Bar	0.08 **C**, 2.0 **Mn**, 1.0 **Si**, 17.0–20.0 **Cr**, 8.0–12.0 **Ni**, 0.045 **P**, 0.030 **S**	**Softened**: (5–100) **diam**, (490) **TS**, (200) **YS**, 40 **El**; **Cold drawn (austenitic)**: (45) **diam**, (830) **TS**, (490) **YS**, 20 **El**; **Cold rolled (austenitic)**: (0.5–2.8) **diam**, (830) **TS**, (490) **YS**, 12 **El**
IS 6603	04Cr17Ni12Mo2Ti20	India	Bar	0.080 **C**, 2.0 **Mn**, 1.0 **Si**, 16.0–18.5 **Cr**, 10.5–14.0 **Ni**, 2.0–3.0 **Mo**, 0.045 **P**, 0.030 **S**, 5C–0.8 **Ti**	**Softened**: (5–100) **diam**, (490) **TS**, 220 **YS**, 35 **El**
IS 6603	04Cr17Ni12Mo2	India	Bar	0.08 **C**, 2.0 **Mn**, 1.0 **Si**, 16.0–18.5 **Cr**, 10.0–14.0 **Ni**, 2.0–3.0 **Mo**, 0.045 **P**, 0.030 **S**	**Softened**: (5–100) **diam**, (490) **TS**, (210) **YS**, 40 **El**
IS 6603	04Cr18Ni10Ti20	India	Bar	0.08 **C**, 2.0 **Mn**, 1.0 **Si**, 17.0–19.0 **Cr**, 9.0–12.0 **Ni**, 0.045 **P**, 0.030 **S**, 5C–0.80 **Ti**	**Softened**: (5–100) **diam**, (490) **TS**, (210) **YS**, 35 **El**
IS 6911	04Cr18Ni10	India	Plate, sheet, strip	0.08 **C**, 2.0 **Mn**, 1.0 **Si**, 17.0–20.0 **Cr**, 8.0–12.0 **Ni**, 0.030 **S**, 0.045 **P**	**Softened**: (0.5–3) **diam**, (490) **TS**, (200) **YS**, 38 **El**
IS 6911	04Cr18Ni10Ti[20]	India	Plate, sheet, strip	0.08 **C**, 2.0 **Mn**, 1.0 **Si**, 17.0–19.0 **Cr**, 9.0–12.0 **Ni**, 0.030 **S**, 0.045 **P**, 5C–0.80 **Ti**	**Softened**: (0.50–3) **diam**, (490) **TS**, (210) **YS** 33 **El**
IS 6911	04Cr18Ni10Nb[40]	India	Plate, sheet, strip	0.08 **C**, 2.0 **Mn**, 1.0 **Si**, 17.0–19.0 **Cr**, 9.0–12.0 **Ni**, 10C–1.0 **Nb**, 0.030 **S**, 0.045 **P**	**Softened**: (0.5–3) **diam**, (490) **TS**, (210) **YS**, 33 **El**
IS 6911	04Cr17Ni12Mo2	India	Plate, sheet, strip	0.08 **C**, 2.0 **Mn**, 1.0 **Si**, 16.0–18.5 **Cr**, 10.0–14.0 **Ni**, 2.0–3.0 **Mo**, 0.030 **S**, 0.045 **P**	**Softened**: (0.5–3) **diam**, (490) **TS**, (210) **YS**, 38 **El**
IS 6911	04Cr17Ni12Mo2Ti[20]	India	Plate, sheet, strip	0.080 **C**, 2.0 **Mn**, 1.0 **Si**, 16.0–18.0 **Cr**, 10.5–14.0 **Ni**, 2.0–3.0 **Mo**, 0.030 **S**, 0.045 **P**, 5C–0.8 **Ti**	**Softened**: (0.5–3) **diam**, (490) **TS**, (220) **YS**, 33 **El**
BS 970 Part 4	Grade 321S12	UK	Blooms, billets, bar, forgings	0.08 **C**, 0.50–1.00 **Mn**, 0.20–1.00 **Si**, 17.0–19.0 **Cr**, 9.00–12.00 **Ni**, 0.045 **P**, 0.030 **S**, 5 x C–0.70 **Ti**	**Annealed**: all **diam**, (490) **TS**, (195) **YS**, 40 **El**
BS 970 Part 4	Grade 320S17	UK	Blooms, billets, bar, forgings	0.08 **C**, 0.50–2.00 **Mn**, 0.20–1.00 **Si**, 16.5–18.5 **Cr**, 11.0–14.0 **Ni**, 2.25–3.0 **Mo**, 0.045 **P**, 0.030 **S**, 4 x C–0.60 **Ti**	**Annealed**: all **diam**, (490) **TS**, 40 **El**
NF A 36–209	Z 6 CNT 18–11	France	Plate	0.080 **C**, 2.0 **Mn**, 1.0 **Si**, 17.0–19.0 **Cr**, 10.0–12.0 **Ni**, 0.040 **P**, 0.030 **S**, 5xC–0.6 **Ti**	**Hot rolled**: (<3) **diam**, (490) **TS**, (215) **YS**, 35 **El**; **Cold rolled**: (<3) **diam**, (490) **TS**, (215) **YS**, 35 **El**

specification number	designation	country	product forms	composition	mechanical properties (see page iv for explanation)
NF A 35–575	Z 6 NC 18.16	France	Wire, rod	0.08 **C**, 2.0 **Mn**, 1.0 **Si**, 15.0–17.0 **Cr**, 17.0–19.0 **Ni**, 0.040 **P**, 0.030 **S**	**Stress hardened 0%**: all **diam**, (490) **TS**; **Stress hardened 40%**: all **diam**, (880) **TS**; **Stress hardened 60%**: all **diam**, (1080) **TS**; **Stress hardened 80%**: all **diam**, (1320) **TS**; **Austenitized**: all **diam**, (440) **TS**, (180) **YS**, 45 **El**
NF A 35–575	Z 6 CNU 18.10	France	Wire, rod	0.08 **C**, 2.0 **Mn**, 1.0 **Si**, 16.5–18.5 **Cr**, 8.5–10.5 **Ni**, 3.0–4.0 **Cu**, 0.040 **P**, 0.030 **S**	**Stress hardened 0%**: all **diam**, (490) **TS**; **Stress hardened 40%**: all **diam**, (880) **TS**; **Stress hardened 60%**: all **diam**, (1080) **TS**; **Stress hardened 80%**: all **diam**, (1320) **TS**; **Austenitized**: all **diam**, (470) **TS**, (200) **YS**, 45 **El**
SS 14 23 38	SS 23 38–26	Sweden	Tube: welded	0.08 **C**, 2.0 **Mn**, 1.0 **Si**, 17.0–19.0 **Cr**, 9.0–13.0 **Ni**, 10 x C–1.0 **Nb**+1/2 **Ta**, 0.045 **P**, 0.030 **S**	**Solution annealed**: (<30) **diam**, (490) **TS**, (220) **YS**, 40 **El**
SS 14 23 38	SS 23 38–27	Sweden	Bar, forgings, plate, sheet, strip	0.08 **C**, 2.0 **Mn**, 1.0 **Si**, 17.0–19.0 **Cr**, 9.0–12.0 **Ni**, 10 x C–1.0 **Nb**+1/2 **Ta**, 0.045 **P**, 0.030 **S**	**Solution annealed**: all **diam**, (490) **TS**, (220) **YS**, 40 **El**
SS 14 23 50	SS 23 50–02	Sweden	Bar, forgings, plate, sheet, strip, tube	0.08 **C**, 2.0 **Mn**, 1.0 **Si**, 16.0–18.5 **Cr**, 10.5–14.0 **Ni**, 2.0–2.5 **Mo**, 5 x C–0.80 **Ti**, 0.045 **P**, 0.030 **S**	**Solution annealed**: all **diam**, (490) **TS**, (220) **YS**, 40 **El**
SS 14 23 50	SS 23 50–26	Sweden	Tube: welded	0.08 **C**, 2.0 **Mn**, 1.0 **Si**, 16.0–18.5 **Cr**, 10.5–14.0 **Ni**, 2.0–2.5 **Mo**, 5 x C–0.80 **Ti**, 0.045 **P**, 0.030 **S**	**Solution annealed**: (<30) **diam**, (490) **TS**, (220) **YS**, 40 **El**
SS 14 23 50	SS 23 50–27	Sweden	Bar, forgings	0.08 **C**, 2.0 **Mn**, 1.0 **Si**, 16.0–18.5 **Cr**, 10.5–14.0 **Ni**, 2.0–2.5 **Mo**, 5 x C–0.80 **Ti**, 0.045 **P**, 0.030 **S**	**Solution annealed**: (<50) **diam**, (490) **TS**, (220) **YS**, 40 **El**
SS 14 23 50	SS 23 50–28	Sweden	Plate, sheet, strip	0.08 **C**, 2.0 **Mn**, 1.0 **Si**, 16.0–18.5 **Cr**, 10.5–14.0 **Ni**, 2.0–2.5 **Mo**, 5 x C–0.80 **Ti**, 0.045 **P**, 0.030 **S**	**Solution annealed**: (<5) **diam**, (490) **TS**, (220) **YS**, 40 **El**
SIS 14 23 25	SIS 23 25–02	Sweden	Bar, wire	0.08 **C**, 1.0 **Mn**, 1.0 **Si**, 16.0–19.0 **Cr**, 0.50 **Ni**, 1.3–2.0 **Mo**, 0.040 **P**, 0.030 **S**	**Annealed**: all **diam**, (490) **TS**, (330) **YS**, 25 **El**
SS 14 23 37	SS 23 37–28	Sweden	Plate, sheet, strip	0.08 **C**, 2.0 **Mn**, 1.0 **Si**, 17.0–19.0 **Cr**, 9.0–12.0 **Ni**, 0.045 **P**, 0.030 **S**, 0.80 **Ti**	**Solution annealed**: all **diam**, (490) **TS**, (210) **YS**, 40 **El**
SS 14 23 37	SS 23 37–27	Sweden	Bar, forgings	0.08 **C**, 2.0 **Mn**, 1.0 **Si**, 17.0–19.0 **Cr**, 9.0–12.0 **Ni**, 0.045 **P**, 0.030 **S**, 0.80 **Ti**	**Solution annealed**: (<50) **diam**, (490) **TS**, (210) **YS**, 40 **El**
SS 14 23 37	SS 23 37–26	Sweden	Tube: welded	0.08 **C**, 2.0 **Mn**, 1.0 **Si**, 17.0–19.0 **Cr**, 9.0–13.0 **Ni**, 0.045 **P**, 0.030 **S**, 0.80 **Ti**	**Solution annealed**: (<30) **diam**, (490) **TS**, (210) **YS**, 40 **El**
SS 14 23 37	SS 23 37–02	Sweden	Bar, forgings, plate, sheet, strip, tube	0.08 **C**, 2.0 **Mn**, 1.0 **Si**, 17.0–19.0 **Cr**, 9.0–12.0 **Ni**, 0.045 **P**, 0.030 **S**, 0.80 **Ti**	**Solution annealed**: all **diam**, (490) **TS**, (210) **YS**, 40 **El**
SS 14 23 38	SS 23 38–02	Sweden	Bar, forgings, plate, sheet, strip, tube	0.08 **C**, 2.0 **Mn**, 1.0 **Si**, 17.0–19.0 **Cr**, 9.0–12.0 **Ni**, 10 x C–1.0 **Nb**+1/2 **Ta**, 0.045 **P**, 0.030 **S**	**Solution annealed**: all **diam**, (490) **TS**, (220) **YS**, 40 **El**
ASTM A 336	F8	US	Forgings	0.08 **C**, 2.00 **Mn**, 1.00 **Si**, 18.00–20.00 **Cr**, 8.00–11.00 **Ni**, 0.040 **P**, 0.030 **S**	**Solution annealed**: all **diam**, 70 (485) **TS**, 30 (205) **YS**, 30 **El**
ASTM A 336	F8m	US	Forgings	0.08 **C**, 2.00 **Mn**, 1.00 **Si**, 16.00–18.00 **Cr**, 10.00–14.00 **Ni**, 2.00–3.00 **Mo**, 0.040 **P**, 0.030 **S**	**Solution annealed**: all **diam**, 70 (485) **TS**, 30 (205) **YS**, 30 **El**
ASTM A 336	F8c	US	Forgings	0.08 **C**, 2.00 **Mn**, 0.85 **Si**, 17.00–19.00 **Cr**, 9.00–12.00 **Ni**, 10 x C–1.00 **Nb**, 0.040 **P**, 0.030 **S**	**Solution annealed**: all **diam**, 70 (485) **TS**, 30 (205) **YS**, 30 **El**
ASTM A 336	F8t	US	Forgings	0.08 **C**, 2.50 **Mn**, 0.85 **Si**, 17.00 min **Cr**, 9.00 min **Ni**, 0.035 **P**, 0.030 **S**, 5 x C–0.60 **Ti**	**Solution annealed**: all **diam**, 70 (485) **TS**, 30 (205) **YS**, 30 **El**

WROUGHT STAINLESS STEELS

specification number	designation	country	product forms	composition	mechanical properties (see page iv for explanation)
ASTM A 336	F8	US	Forgings	0.08 **C**, 2.00 **Mn**, 1.00 **Si**, 18.00–20.00 **Cr**, 8.00–11.00 **Ni**, 0.040 **P**, 0.030 **S**	**Solution annealed**: all **diam**, 70 (485) **TS**, 30 (205) **YS**, 30 **El**
ASTM A 336	F8m	US	Forgings	0.08 **C**, 2.00 **Mn**, 1.00 **Si**, 16.00–18.00 **Cr**, 10.00–14.00 **Ni**, 2.00–3.00 **Mo**, 0.040 **P**, 0.030 **S**	**Solution annealed**: all **diam**, 70 (485) **TS**, 30 (205) **YS**, 30 **El**
ASTM A 336	F8c	US	Forgings	0.08 **C**, 2.00 **Mn**, 0.85 **Si**, 17.00–19.00 **Cr**, 9.00–12.00 **Ni**, 10 x C–1.00 **Nb**, 0.040 **P**, 0.030 **S**	**Solution annealed**: all **diam**, 70 (485) **TS**, 30 (205) **YS**, 30 **El**
ASTM A 336	F8t	US	Forgings	0.08 **C**, 2.50 **Mn**, 0.85 **Si**, 17.00 min **Cr**, 9.00 min **Ni**, 0.035 **P**, 0.030 **S**, 5 x C–0.60 **Ti**	**Solution annealed**: all **diam**, 70 (485) **TS**, 30 (205) **YS**, 30 **El**
ANSI/ASTM A 493	Type 385	US	Bar, wire	0.08 **C**, 2.00 **Mn**, 1.00 **Si**, 15.00–17.00 **Cr**, 17.00–19.00 **Ni**, 0.045 **P**, 0.030 **S**	**Lightly drafted (wire)**: ≥0.156 (≥3.96) **diam**, 70 (485) **TS**; **Annealed (wire)**: ≥0.156 (≥3.96) **diam**, 65 (450) **TS**
ANSI/ASTM A 493	Type 384	US	Bar, wire	0.08 **C**, 2.00 **Mn**, 1.00 **Si**, 15.00–17.00 **Cr**, 17.00–19.00 **Ni**, 0.045 **P**, 0.030 **S**	**Lightly drafted (wire)**: ≥0.156 (≥3.96) **diam**, 70 (485) **TS**; **Annealed (wire)**: ≥0.156 (≥3.96) **diam**, 65 (450) **TS**
ANSI/ASTM A 336	Grade F8	US	Forgings	0.08 **C**, 2.00 **Mn**, 1.00 **Si**, 18.00–20.00 **Cr**, 8.00–11.00 **Ni**, 0.040 **P**, 0.030 **S**	**Solution annealed**: all **diam**, (485) **TS**, (205) **YS**, 30 **El**
ANSI/ASTM A336	Grade F8M	US	Forgings	0.08 **C**, 2.00 **Mn**, 1.00 **Si**, 16.00–18.00 **Cr**, 10.00–14.00 **Ni**, 2.00–3.00 **Mo**, 0.040 **P**, 0.030 **S**	**Solution annealed**: all **diam**, (485) **TS**, (205) **YS**, 30 **El**
ANSI/ASTM A 336	Grade F8C	US	Forgings	0.08 **C**, 2.00 **Mn**, 0.85 **Si**, 17.00–19.00 **Cr**, 9.00–12.00 **Ni**, 0.040 **P**, 0.030 **S**	**Solution annealed**: all **diam**, (485) **TS**, (205) **YS**, 30 **El**
ANSI/ASTM A 336	Grade F8T	US	Forgings	0.08 **C**, 2.50 **Mn**, 0.85 **Si**, 17.00 min **Cr**, 9.00 min **Ni**, 0.035 **P**, 0.030 **S**	**Solution annealed**: all **diam**, (485) **TS**, (205) **YS**, 30 **El**
JIS G 4303	SUS 305J1	Japan	Bar	0.08 **C**, 2.00 **Mn**, 1.00 **Si**, 16.50–19.00 **Cr**, 11.00–13.50 **Ni**, 0.040 **P**, 0.030 **S**	**Solution annealed**: (≤180) **diam**, (481) **TS**, (177) **YS**, 40 **El**
JIS G 4303	SUS 384	Japan	Bar	0.08 **C**, 2.00 **Mn**, 1.00 **Si**, 15.00–17.00 **Cr**, 17.00–19.00 **Ni**, 0.040 **P**, 0.030 **S**	**Solution annealed**: (≤180) **diam**, (481) **TS**, (177) **YS**, 40 **El**
JIS G 4303	SUS 385	Japan	Bar	0.08 **C**, 2.00 **Mn**, 1.00 **Si**, 11.50–13.50 **Cr**, 14.00–16.00 **Ni**, 0.040 **P**, 0.030 **S**	**Solution annealed**: (≤180) **diam**, (481) **TS**, (177) **YS**, 40 **El**
JIS G 4303	SUS XM7	Japan	Bar	0.08 **C**, 2.00 **Mn**, 1.00 **Si**, 17.00–19.00 **Cr**, 8.50–10.50 **Ni**, 3.00–4.00 **Cu**, 0.040 **P**, 0.030 **S**	**Solution annealed**: (≤18) **diam**, (481) **TS**, (177) **YS**, 40 **El**
DGN-B-83	405	Mexico	Bar	0.08 **C**, 1.0 **Mn**, 1.0 **Si**, 11.5–14.5 **Cr**, 0.10–0.30 **Al**, 0.040 **P**, 0.030 **S**	**Hot or cold rolled**: all **diam**, (480) **TS**, (247) **YS**, 30 **El**
IS 6528	04Cr13	India	Wire	0.08 **C**, 1.0 **Mn**, 1.0 **Si**, 11.5–14.5 **Cr**, 0.040 **P**, 0.030 **S**	**Annealed or solution annealed**: all **diam**, (480) **TS**, (270) **YS**, 16 **El**
BS 1506–801	Grade B	UK	Bar	0.08 **C**, 2.00 **Mn**, 0.20 min **Si**, 17.5–20.0 **Cr**, 8.0–11.0 **Ni**, 0.045 **S**, 0.045 **P**	**Solution annealed**: all **diam**, (480) **TS**, (185) **YS**, 30 **El**; **Cold drawn**: 0.75 **diam**, (770) **TS**, (620) **YS**, 12 **El**
BS 1506–821	Grade Nb	UK	Bar	0.08 **C**, 0.05–2.00 **Mn**, 0.20–1.00 **Si**, 17.0–20.0 **Cr**, 9.0 min **Ni**, 10 x C–1.00 **Nb**, 0.045 **S**, 0.045 **P**	**Solution annealed**: all **diam**, (480) **TS**, (185) **YS**, 30 **El**; **Cold drawn**: 0.75 **diam**, (770) **TS**, (620) **YS**, 12 **El**
BS 1506–845		UK	Bar	0.08 **C**, 2.0 **Mn**, 0.20–1.0 **Si**, 16.0–18.0 **Cr**, 10.0 min **Ni**, 2.5–3.0 **Mo**, 0.050 **S**, 0.050 **P**	**Solution annealed**: all **diam**, (480) **TS**, (185) **YS**, 30 **El**; **Cold drawn**: 0.75 **diam**, (770) **TS**, (620) **YS**, 12 **El**
BS 1501–801	Grade B	UK	Bar	0.08 **C**, 2.00 **Mn**, 0.20 min **Si**, 17.5–20.0 **Cr**, 8.0–11.0 **Ni**, 0.045 **S**, 0.045 **P**	**Annealed**: all **diam**, (480) **TS**, (185) **YS**
BS 1501–821	Grade Nb	UK	Bar	0.08 **C**, 0.50–2.00 **Mn**, 0.20–1.00 **Si**, 17.0–20.0 **Cr**, 9.0 min **Ni**, 10 x C–1.00 **Nb**, 0.045 **S**, 0.045 **P**	**Annealed**: all **diam**, (480) **TS**, (435) **YS**
BS 1501–845	Grade B	UK	Bar	0.08 **C**, 2.00 **Mn**, 0.20–1.00 **Si**, 16.5–18.5 **Cr**, 10.0 min **Ni**, 2.25–3.00 **Mo**, 0.045 **S**, 0.045 **P**	**Annealed**: all **diam**, (480) **TS**, (185) **YS**

WROUGHT STAINLESS STEELS

specification number	designation	country	product forms	composition	mechanical properties (see page iv for explanation)
BS 1501–845	Grade Ti	UK	Bar	0.08 **C**, 2.00 **Mn**, 0.20–0.60 **Si**, 16.5–18.5 **Cr**, 10.0 min **Ni**, 2.25–3.00 **Mo**, 4 x C–0.50 **Ti**, 0.045 **S**, 0.045 **P**	**Annealed**: all **diam**, (480) **TS**, (185) **YS**
BS 1501–846		UK	Bar	0.08 **C**, 2.00 **Mn**, 0.20–1.00 **Si**, 18.0–20.0 **Cr**, 11.0–14.0 **Ni**, 3.0–4.0 **Mo**, 0.045 **S**, 0.045 **P**	**Annealed**: all **diam**, (480) **TS**, (185) **YS**
ANSI/ASTM A 580	Grade 405	US	Wire	0.08 **C**, 1.00 **Mn**, 1.00 **Si**, 11.50–14.50 **Cr**, 0.10–0.30 **Al**, 0.040 **P**, 0.030 **S**	**Annealed**: all **diam**, 70 (480) **TS**, 40 (280) **YS**, 20 **El**
DGN–B–186	Grade TP304	Mexico	Pipe: seamless	0.08 **C**, 2.00 **Mn**, 0.75 **Si**, 18.0–20.0 **Cr**, 8.0–11.0 **Ni**, 0.030 **P**, 0.030 **S**	**Hot or cold finished and quenched or tempered**: (8) **diam**, (480) **TS**, (206) **YS**, 35 **El**
EURONORM 119–74, V	X 6 CrNiCu 18 10 4 KD	EURONORM	Wire, rod	0.08 **C**, 2.0 **Mn**, 1.0 **Si**, 16.0–18.5 **Cr**, 8.5–10.5 **Ni**, 3.0–4.0 **Cu**, 0.045 **P**, 0.030 **S**	**Solution annealed**: (15–63) **diam**, (470) **TS**, (195) **YS**, 45 **El**
ANSI/ASTM A 473	410S	US	Forgings	0.08 **C**, 1.00 **Mn**, 1.00 **Si**, 11.50–13.50 **Cr**, 0.75 **Ni**, 0.040 **P**, 0.030 **S**	**Annealed**: all **diam**, 65 (450) **TS**, 35 (240) **YS**, 22 **El**
DIN 17440	Grade X 7 Cr 13	Germany	Sheet, strip, bar, wire, tube, forgings	0.08 **C**, 1.0 **Mn**, 1.0 **Si**, 12.0–14.0 **Cr**, 0.045 **P**, 0.030 **S**	**Annealed**: (≤5) **diam**, (450) **TS**, (250) **YS**, 20 **El**; **Tempered**: (≤15) **diam**, (550) **TS**, (400) **YS**, 18 **El**
DIN 17440	Grade X 7 CrAl 13	Germany	Sheet, strip, bar, wire, tube, forgings	0.08 **C**, 1.0 **Mn**, 1.0 **Si**, 12.0–14.0 **Cr**, 0.10–0.30 **Al**, 0.045 **P**, 0.030 **S**	**Annealed**: (≤5) **diam**, (450) **TS**, (250) **YS**, 20 **El**; **Tempered**: (≤15) **diam**, (550) **TS**, (400) **YS**, 18 **El**
AISI 405		US	Plate, sheet, bar, wire	0.08 **C**, 1.00 **Mn**, 1.00 **Si**, 11.50–14.50 **Cr**, 0.10–0.30 **Al**, 0.040 **P**, 0.030 **S**	**Annealed (plate)**: all **diam**, 65 (448) max **TS**, 40 (276) max **YS**, 30 **El**
AISI 409		US	Sheet, strip, plate, bar	0.08 **C**, 1.00 **Mn**, 1.00 **Si**, 10.50–11.75 **Cr**, 0.045 **P**, 0.045 **S**	**Annealed (sheet)**: all **diam**, 65 (448) max **TS**, 35 (241) max **YS**, 25 **El**
ISO 683/XII	1	ISO	Bar, sheet, plate	0.08 **C**, 1.0 **Mn**, 1.0 **Si**, 11.5–14.0 **Cr**, 0.50 **Ni**, 0.10–0.30 **Al**, 0.040 **P**, 0.030 **S**	**Annealed**: all **diam**, (440) **TS**, (250) **YS**, 20 **El**
EURONORM 119–74, V	X6 NiCr 18 16 KD	EURONORM	Wire, rod	0.08 **C**, 2.0 **Mn**, 1.0 **Si**, 15.0–17.0 **Cr**, 17.0–19.0 **Ni**, 0.045 **P**, 0.030 **S**	**Solution annealed**: (15–63) **diam**, (440) **TS**, (175) **YS**, 45 **El**
IS 6603	04Cr13	India	Bar	0.08 **C**, 1.0 **Mn**, 1.0 **Si**, 11.5–14.5 **Cr**, 0.10–0.30 **Al**, 0.040 **P**, 0.030 **S**	**Annealed**: (5–25) **diam**, (440) **TS**, (250) **YS**, 20 **El**
IS 6911	04Cr13	India	Plate, sheet, strip	0.08 **C**, 1.0 **Mn**, 1.0 **Si**, 11.5–14.5 **Cr**, 0.030 **S**, 0.040 **P**	**Annealed**: (0.5–3) **diam**, (440) **TS**, (250) **YS**, 18 **El**
SIS 14 23 01	SIS 23 01–23	Sweden	Tube: welded	0.08 **C**, 1.0 **Mn**, 1.0 **Si**, 12.0–14.0 **Cr**, 0.50 **Ni**, 0.040 **P**, 0.030 **S**	**Annealed**: all **diam**, (440) **TS**, (250) **YS**, 20 **El**
SIS 14 23 01	SIS 23 01–22	Sweden	Tube: seamless	0.08 **C**, 1.0 **Mn**, 1.0 **Si**, 12.0–14.0 **Cr**, 0.50 **Ni**, 0.040 **P**, 0.030 **S**	**Annealed**: all **diam**, (440) **TS**, (250) **YS**, 20 **El**
SIS 14 23 01	SIS 23 01–02	Sweden	Bar, forgings, plate, strip, tube, wire	0.08 **C**, 1.0 **Mn**, 1.0 **Si**, 12.0–14.0 **Cr**, 0.50 **Ni**, 0.040 **P**, 0.030 **S**	**Annealed (except wire)**: all **diam**, (440) **TS**, (250) **YS**, 20 **El**
AS 1449	Grade AS 1449/409	Australia	Sheet, strip, plate	0.08 **C**, 1.00 **Mn**, 1.00 **Si**, 10.50–11.75 **Cr**, 0.045 **P**, 0.045 **S**, 6 x C–0.75 **Ti**	**Annealed**: (≤1.2) **diam**, (420) **TS**, (205) **YS**, 20 **El**
AS 1449	Grade AS 1449/410S	Australia	Sheet, strip, plate	0.08 **C**, 1.00 **Mn**, 1.00 **Si**, 11.50–13.50 **Cr**, 0.040 **P**, 0.030 **S**	**Annealed**: (≤1.2) **diam**, (420) **TS**, (205) **YS**, 20 **El**
BS 1449 Part 2	Grade 403S17	UK	Plate, sheet, strip	0.08 **C**, 1.00 **Mn**, 0.80 **Si**, 12.0–14.0 **Cr**, 0.50 **Ni**, 0.040 **P**, 0.030 **S**	**Solution annealed**: (≥3.0) **diam**, (420) **TS**, (245) **YS**, 22 **El**
BS 1449 Part 2	Grade 405S17	UK	Plate, sheet, strip	0.08 **C**, 1.00 **Mn**, 0.80 **Si**, 12.0–14.0 **Cr**, 0.50 **Ni**, 0.10–0.30 **Al**, 0.040 **P**, 0.030 **S**	**Solution annealed**: (≥3.0) **diam**, (420) **TS**, (245) **YS**, 22 **El**
BS 970 Part 4	Grade 403S17	UK	Blooms, billets, bar, forgings	0.08 **C**, 1.00 **Mn**, 0.80 **Si**, 12.0–14.0 **Cr**, 0.50 **Ni**, 0.040 **P**, 0.030 **S**	**Annealed**: all **diam**, (420) **TS**, (280) **YS**, 20 **El**
NF A 35–572	Z 6 C 13	France	Sheet, strip, plate, bar, sections	0.08 **C**, 1.0 **Mn**, 1.0 **Si**, 11.5–13.5 **Cr**, 0.04 **P**, 0.03 **S**	**Annealed**: (5–25) **diam**, (420) **TS**, (225) **YS**, 20 **El**

WROUGHT STAINLESS STEELS

specification number	designation	country	product forms	composition	mechanical properties (see page iv for explanation)
NF A 35–572	Z 6 CA 13	France	Sheet, strip, plate, bar, sections	0.08 **C**, 1.0 **Mn**, 1.0 **Si**, 11.5–13.5 **Cr**, 0.10–0.30 **Al**, 0.04 **P**, 0.03 **S**	**Annealed**: (5–25) **diam**, (420) **TS**, (225) **YS**, 20 **El**
ASTM A 240	Type 410S	US	Plate, sheet, strip	0.08 **C**, 1.00 **Mn**, 1.00 **Si**, 11.50–13.50 **Cr**, 0.60 **Ni**, 0.040 **P**, 0.030 **S**	**Hot rolled or cold rolled, annealed**: all **diam**, 60 (415) **TS**, 30 (205) **YS**, 22 **El**
ASTM A 240	Type 405	US	Plate, sheet, strip	0.08 **C**, 1.00 **Mn**, 1.00 **Si**, 11.50–14.50 **Cr**, 0.60 **Ni**, 0.10–0.30 **Al**, 0.040 **P**, 0.030 **S**	**Hot rolled or cold rolled, annealed**: all **diam**, 60 (415) **TS**, 25 (170) **YS**, 20 **El**
ASTM A 176	Type 410S	US	Plate, sheet, strip	0.08 **C**, 1.00 **Mn**, 1.00 **Si**, 11.50–13.50 **Cr**, 0.60 **Ni**, 0.040 **P**, 0.030 **S**	**Annealed**: all **diam**, 60 (415) **TS**, 30 (205) **YS**, 22 **El**
ASTM A 176	Type 409	US	Plate, sheet, strip	0.08 **C**, 1.00 **Mn**, 1.00 **Si**, 10.50–11.75 **Cr**, 0.50 **Ni**, 0.045 **P**, 0.045 **S**, 6 x C–0.75 **Ti**	**Annealed**: all **diam**, 60 (415) **TS**, 30 (205) **YS**, 22 **El**
ASTM A 176	Type 405	US	Plate, sheet, strip	0.08 **C**, 1.00 **Mn**, 1.00 **Si**, 11.50–14.50 **Cr**, 0.60 **Ni**, 0.10–0.30 **Al**, 0.040 **P**, 0.030 **S**	**Annealed**: all **diam**, 60 (415) **TS**, 25 (170) **YS**, 20 **El**
ANSI/ASTM A 479	Grade 405	US	Bar, shapes	0.08 **C**, 1.00 **Mn**, 1.00 **Si**, 11.50–14.50 **Cr**, 0.60 **Ni**, 0.10–0.30 **Al**, 0.040 **P**, 0.030 **S**	**Annealed**: all **diam**, (415) **TS**, (170) **YS**, 20 **El**
ANSI/ASTM A 240	Grade 405	US	Plate, sheet, strip	0.08 **C**, 1.00 **Mn**, 1.00 **Si**, 11.50–14.50 **Cr**, 0.60 **Ni**, 0.10–0.30 **Al**, 0.040 **P**, 0.030 **S**	**Annealed**: all **diam**, (415) **TS**, (170) **YS**, 20 **El**
ANSI/ASTM A 240	Grade 410S	US	Plate, sheet, strip	0.08 **C**, 1.00 **Mn**, 1.00 **Si**, 11.50–13.50 **Cr**, 0.60 **Ni**, 0.040 **P**, 0.030 **S**	**Annealed**: all **diam**, (415) **TS**, (205) **YS**, 22 **El**
ANSI/ASTM A 473	405	US	Forgings	0.08 **C**, 1.00 **Mn**, 1.00 **Si**, 11.50–14.50 **Cr**, 0.60 **Ni**, 0.10–0.30 **Al**, 0.040 **P**, 0.030 **S**	**Annealed**: all **diam**, 60 (414) **TS**, 30 (205) **YS**, 20 **El**
CSA G110.9	Type 405	Canada	Plate	0.08 **C**, 1.00 **Mn**, 1.00 **Si**, 11.50–14.50 **Cr**, 0.60 **Ni**, 0.10–0.30 **Al**, 0.040 **P**, 0.030 **S**	**Hot rolled, annealed, quenched and tempered**: all **diam**, 60 (414) **TS**, 25 (173) **YS**, 20 **El**
CSA G110.5	Type 405	Canada	Plate	0.08 **C**, 1.00 **Mn**, 1.00 **Si**, 11.50–14.50 **Cr**, 0.60 **Ni**, 0.10–0.30 **Al**, 0.040 **P**, 0.030 **S**	**Hot rolled, annealed, quenched and tempered**: all **diam**, 60 (414) **TS**, 25 (173) **YS**, 20 **El**
CSA G110.5	Type 410S	Canada	Sheet	0.08 **C**, 1.00 **Mn**, 1.00 **Si**, 11.50–13.50 **Cr**, 0.60 **Ni**, 0.040 **P**, 0.030 **S**	**Hot rolled, annealed, quenched and tempered**: all **diam**, 60 (414) **TS**, 30 (207) **YS**, 20 **El**
ANSI/ASTM A 511	MT 405	US	Tube: seamless	0.08 **C**, 1.00 **Mn**, 1.00 **Si**, 11.5–14.5 **Cr**, 0.50 **Ni**, 0.10–0.30 **Al**, 0.040 **P**, 0.030 **S**	**Annealed**: 0.31 (7.9) **diam**, 60 (414) **TS**, 30 (207) **YS**, 20 **El**
ANSI/ASTM A 268	TP 405	US	Tube: seamless, welded	0.08 **C**, 1.00 **Mn**, 0.75 **Si**, 11.5–13.5 **Cr**, 0.50 **Ni**, 0.10–0.30 **Al**, 0.040 **P**, 0.030 **S**	**Annealed**: (7.94) 0.312 **diam**, 60 (414) **TS**, 30 (207) **YS**, 20 **El**
ANSI/ASTM A 268	TP 409	US	Tube: seamless, welded	0.08 **C**, 1.00 **Mn**, 1.00 **Si**, 10.50–11.75 **Cr**, 0.50 **Ni**, 0.045 **P**, 0.045 **P**, 0.045 **S**, 6 x C min, 0.75 **Ti**	**Annealed**: 0.312 (7.94) **diam**, 60 (414) **TS**, 30 (207) **YS**, 20 **El**
CSA G110.9	Type 410S	Canada	Sheet	0.08 **C**, 1.00 **Mn**, 1.00 **Si**, 11.50–13.50 **Cr**, 0.60 **Ni**, 0.045 **P**, 0.030 **S**	**Hot or cold rolled and annealed**: ≤0.050 **diam**, 60 (414) **TS**, 30 (207) **YS**, 20 **El**
CSA G110.5	Type 410S	Canada	Strip	0.08 **C**, 1.00 **Mn**, 1.00 **Si**, 11.50–13.50 **Cr**, 0.60 **Ni**, 0.040 **P**, 0.030 **S**	**Cold rolled and annealed**: ≤0.050 **diam**, 60 (414) **TS**, 30 (207) **YS**, 20 **El**
CSA G110.5	Type 405	Canada	Strip	0.08 **C**, 1.00 **Mn**, 1.00 **Si**, 11.50–14.50 **Cr**, 0.60 **Ni**, 0.10–0.30 **Al**, 0.040 **P**, 0.030 **S**	**Cold rolled and annealed**: all **diam**, 60 (414) **TS**, 25 (172) **YS**, 20 **El**
CSA G110.9	Type 405	Canada	Strip	0.08 **C**, 1.00 **Mn**, 1.00 **Si**, 11.50–14.50 **Cr**, 0.60 **Ni** 0.10–0.30 **Al**, 0.040 **P**, 0.030 **S**	**Cold rolled and annealed**: all **diam**, 60 (414) **TS**, 25 (172) **YS**, 20 **El**
CSA G110.9	Type 410S	Canada	Strip	0.08 **C**, 1.00 **Mn**, 1.00 **Si**, 11.50–13.50 **Cr**, 0.60 **Ni**, 0.040 **P**, 0.030 **S**	**Cold rolled and annealed**: ≤0.050 **diam**, 60 (414) **TS**, 30 (207) **YS**, 20 **El**
ASTM A 651	TP 409	US	Tube: seamless or welded	0.08 **C**, 1.00 **Mn**, 1.00 **Si**, 10.50–11.75 **Cr**, 0.50 **Ni**, 0.045 **P**, 0.045 **S**, 6 x C–0.75 **Ti**	**As welded or as drawn**: all **diam**, 60 (414) **TS**, 30 (207) **YS**
CSA G110.9	Type 405	Canada	Sheet	0.08 **C**, 1.00 **Mn**, 1.00 **Si**, 11.50–14.50 **Cr**, 0.60 **Ni**, 0.10–0.30 **Al**, 0.040 **P**, 0.030 **S**	**Hot or cold rolled and annealed**: all **diam**, 60 (414) **TS**, 25 (172) **YS**, 20 **El**

specification number	designation	country	product forms	composition	mechanical properties (see page iv for explanation)
CSA G110.5	Type 405	Canada	Sheet	0.08 **C**, 1.00 **Mn**, 1.00 **Si**, 11.50–14.50 **Cr**, 0.60 **Ni**, 0.10–0.30 **Al**, 0.040 **P**, 0.030 **S**	**Hot or cold rolled and annealed**: all **diam**, 60 (414) **TS**, 25 (172) **YS**, 20 **El**
DGN–B–171	Grade MT 405	Mexico	Tube: seamless	0.08 **C**, 1.00 **Mn**, 1.00 **Si**, 11.5–14.5 **Cr**, 0.50 **Ni**, 0.10–0.30 **Al**, 0.040 **P**, 0.030 **S**	**Hot or cold finished and annealed**: (≥7.92) **diam**, (412) **TS**, (206) **YS**, 20 **El**
DGN–B–216	Grade TP405	Mexico	Tube: seamless, welded	0.08 **C**, 1.00 **Mn**, 0.75 **Si**, 11.5–13.5 **Cr**, 0.50 **Ni**, 0.10–0.30 **Al**, 0.040 **P**, 0.030 **S**	**As drawn or as welded**: (≥7.93) **diam**, (412) **TS**, (206) **YS**, 20 **El**
JIS G 4303	SUS 405	Japan	Bar	0.08 **C**, 1.00 **Mn**, 1.00 **Si**, 11.50–14.50 **Cr**, 0.60 **Ni**, 0.10–0.30 **Al**, 0.040 **P**, 0.030 **S**	**Annealed**: (≤75) **diam**, (412) **TS**, (177) **YS**, 20 **El**
JIS G 4304	SUS 405	Japan	Sheet, plate	0.08 **C**, 1.00 **Mn**, 1.00 **Si**, 11.50–14.50 **Cr**, 0.6 **Ni**, 0.10–0.30 **Al**, 0.040 **P**, 0.030 **S**	**Hot rolled and annealed**: all **diam**, (412) **TS**, (177) **YS**, 20 **El**
JIS G 4307	SUS 405	Japan	Strip	0.08 **C**, 1.00 **Mn**, 1.00 **Si**, 11.50–14.50 **Cr**, 0.6 **Ni**, 0.10–0.30 **Al**, 0.040 **P**, 0.030 **S**	**Cold rolled and solution annealed**: all **diam**, (412) **TS**, (177) **YS**, 20 **El**
JIS G 4307	SUS 410S	Japan	Strip	0.08 **C**, 1.00 **Mn**, 1.00 **Si**, 11.50–13.50 **Cr**, 0.6 **Ni**, 0.040 **P**, 0.030 **S**	**Cold rolled, annealed, quenched and tempered**: all **diam**, (412) **TS**, (206) **YS**, 20 **El**
JIS G 4305	SUS 405	Japan	Sheet, plate	0.08 **C**, 1.00 **Mn**, 1.00 **Si**, 11.50–14.50 **Cr**, 0.60 **Ni**, 0.10–0.30 **Al**, 0.040 **P**, 0.030 **S**	**Cold rolled and annealed**: all **diam**, (412) **TS**, (177) **YS**, 20 **El**
JIS G 4305	SUS 410S	Japan	Sheet, plate	0.08 **C**, 1.00 **Mn**, 1.00 **Si**, 11.50–13.50 **Cr**, 0.60 **Ni**, 0.040 **P**, 0.030 **S**	**Cold rolled and annealed**: all **diam**, (412) **TS**, (206) **YS**, 20 **El**
JIS G 4306	SUS 405	Japan	Strip	0.08 **C**, 1.00 **Mn**, 1.00 **Si**, 11.50–14.50 **Cr**, 0.60 **Ni**, 0.10–0.30 **Al**, 0.040 **P**, 0.030 **S**	**Hot rolled and annealed**: all **diam**, (412) **TS**, (177) **YS**, 20 **El**
JIS G 4306	SUS 410S	Japan	Strip	0.08 **C**, 1.00 **Mn**, 1.00 **Si**, 11.50–13.50 **Cr**, 0.60 **Ni**, 0.040 **P**, 0.030 **S**	**Hot rolled and annealed**: all **diam**, (412) **TS**, (206) **YS**, 20 **El**
AS 1449	Grade AS 1449/405	Australia	Sheet, strip, plate	0.08 **C**, 1.00 **Mn**, 1.00 **Si**, 11.50–14.50 **Cr**, 0.10–0.30 **Al**, 0.040 **P**, 0.030 **S**	**Annealed**: (≤1.2) **diam**, (410) **TS**, (170) **YS**, 20 **El**
ISO 683/XII	2	ISO	Bar, sheet, plate	0.08 **C**, 1.0 **Mn**, 1.0 **Si**, 11.5–14.0 **Cr**, 0.50 **Ni**, 0.10–0.30 **Al**, 0.040 **P**, 0.030 **S**	**Annealed**: all **diam**, (410) **TS**, (250) **YS**, 20 **El**
JIS G 4311	SUH 409	Japan	Bar	0.08 **C**, 1.00 **Mn**, 1.00 **Si**, 7.50–9.50 **Cr**, 0.60 **Ni**, 0.030 **P**, 0.030 **S**, 6 x C–0.75 **Ti**	**Annealed**: all **diam**, (363) **TS**, (177) **YS**, 22 **El**
CSA G110.9	Type 410S	Canada	Plate	0.08 **C**, 1.00 **Mn**, 1.00 **Si**, 11.50–13.50 **Cr**, 0.60 **Ni**, 0.040 **P**, 0.030 **S**	**Hot rolled, annealed, quenched and tempered**: ≤0.050 **diam**, 60 (414) (207) **TS**, 30 **YS**, 20 **El**
ANSI/ASTM A 268	TP 329	US	Tube: seamless, welded	0.08 **C**, 1.00 **Mn**, 0.75 **Si**, 23.0–.0 **Cr**, .50–5.00 **Ni**, 1.0–2.0 **Mo**, 0.040 **P**, 0.030 **S**	**Annealed**: 0.312 (7.94) **diam**, 90 (21) **TS**, 70 (483) **YS**, 20 **El**
ASTM A 582	XM–34	US	Bar	0.08 **C**, 1.25–2.50 **Mn**, 1.00 **Si**, 17.50–19.50 **Cr**, 1.50–2.50 **Mo**, 0.04 **P**, 0.15 min **S**	
ASTM A 582	XM–1	US	Bar	0.08 **C**, 5.00–6.50 **Mn**, 1.00 **Si**, 16.00–18.00 **Cr**, 5.00–6.50 **Ni**, 0.50 **Mo**, 1.75–2.25 **Cu**, 0.04 **P**, 0.18–0.35 **S**	
ANSI/ASTM A 314	XM–10	US	Bar, forgings, billets	0.08 **C**, 8.00–10.00 **Mn**, 1.00 **Si**, 19.00–21.50 **Cr**, 5.50–7.50 **Ni**, 0.15–0.40 **N**, 0.060 **P**, 0.030 **S**	
ANSI/ASTM A 314	304	US	Bar, forgings, billets	0.08 **C**, 2.00 **Mn**, 1.00 **Si**, 18.00–20.00 **Cr**, 8.00–10.50 **Ni**, 0.10 **N**, 0.045 **P**, 0.030 **S**	
ANSI/ASTM A 314	308	US	Bar, forgings, billets	0.08 **C**, 2.00 **Mn**, 1.00 **Si**, 19.00–21.00 **Cr**, 10.00–12.00 **Ni**, 0.045 **P**, 0.030 **S**	
ANSI/ASTM A 314	309S	US	Bar, forgings, billets	0.08 **C**, 2.00 **Mn**, 1.00 **Si**, 22.00–24.00 **Cr**, 12.00–15.00 **Ni**, 0.045 **P**, 0.030 **S**	
ANSI/ASTM A 314	310S	US	Bar, forgings, billets	0.08 **C**, 2.00 **Mn**, 1.50 **Si**, 24.00–26.00 **Cr**, 19.00–22.00 **Ni**, 0.045 **P**, 0.030 **S**	

WROUGHT STAINLESS STEELS

specification number	designation	country	product forms	composition	mechanical properties (see page iv for explanation)
ANSI/ASTM A 314	316	US	Bar, forgings, billets	0.08 **C**, 2.00 **Mn**, 1.00 **Si**, 16.00–18.00 **Cr**, 10.00–14.00 **Ni**, 2.00–3.00 **Mo**, 0.10 **N**, 0.045 **P**, 0.030 **S**	
ANSI/ASTM A 314	317	US	Bar, forgings, billets	0.08 **C**, 2.00 **Mn**, 1.00 **Si**, 18.00–20.00 **Cr**, 11.00–15.00 **Ni**, 3.00–4.00 **Mo**, 0.10 **N**, 0.045 **P**, 0.030 **S**	
ANSI/ASTM A 314	321	US	Bar, forgings, billets	0.08 **C**, 2.00 **Mn**, 1.00 **Si**, 17.00–19.00 **Cr**, 9.00–12.00 **Ni**, 0.045 **P**, 0.030 **S**, 5 x C min **Ti**	
ANSI/ASTM A 314	347	US	Bar, forgings, billets	0.08 **C**, 2.00 **Mn**, 1.00 **Si**, 17.00–19.00 **Cr**, 9.00–13.00 **Ni**, 10 x C **Nb+Ta**, 0.045 **P**, 0.030 **S**	
ANSI/ASTM A 314	348	US	Bar, forgings, billets	0.08 **C**, 2.00 **Mn**, 1.00 **Si**, 17.00–19.00 **Cr**, 9.00–13.00 **Ni**, 10 x C **Nb+Ta**, 0.045 **P**, 0.030 **S**, 0.10 **Ta**	
ANSI/ASTM A 314	405	US	Bar, forgings, billets	0.08 **C**, 1.00 **Mn**, 1.00 **Si**, 11.50–14.50 **Cr**, 0.10–0.30 **Al**, 0.040 **P**, 0.030 **S**	
AS 1444	Grade 1444/304	Australia	Bar, bloom, billet, slab	0.08 **C**, 2.00 **Mn**, 1.00 **Si**, 18.00–20.00 **Cr**, 8.00–12.00 **Ni**, 0.045 **P**, 0.040 **S**	
AS 1444	Grade AS 1444/316	Australia	Bar, bloom, billet, slab	0.08 **C**, 2.00 **Mn**, 1.00 **Si**, 16.00–18.00 **Cr**, 10.00–14.00 **Ni**, 2.00–3.00 **Mo**, 0.045 **P**, 0.040 **S**	
AS 1444	Grade AS 1444/317	Australia	Bar, bloom, billet, slab	0.08 **C**, 2.00 **Mn**, 1.00 **Si**, 18.00–20.00 **Cr**, 11.00–15.00 **Ni**, 3.00–4.00 **Mo**, 0.045 **P**, 0.040 **S**	
AS 1444	Grade AS 1444/321	Australia	Bar, bloom, billet, slab	0.08 **C**, 2.00 **Mn**, 1.00 **Si**, 17.00–19.00 **Cr**, 9.00–12.00 **Ni**, 0.045 **P**, 0.040 **S**, 5 x C min **Ti**	
DGN–B–150	Type AE–347	Mexico	Wire	0.08 **C**, 1.0–2.5 **Mn**, 0.25–0.60 **Si**, 19.0–21.5 **Cr**, 9.0–11.0 **Ni**, 0.03 **Cu**, 0.85–1.10 **Cb**, 0.07 $\mathbf{N_2}$, 0.030 **P**, 0.030 **S**	
DGN–B–176		Mexico	Pipe: welded, seamless	0.08 **C**, 2.00 **Mn**, 0.75 **Si**, 18.0–20.0 **Cr**, 8.0–11.0 **Ni**, 0.040 **P**, 0.030 **S**	
ANSI/ASTM A 276	405	US	Bar, shapes	0.08 **C**, 1.00 **Mn**, 1.00 **Si**, 11.50–14.50 **Cr**, 0.10–0.30 **Al**, 0.040 **P**, 0.030 **S**	**Annealed**
DGN–B–150	Type AE–308	Mexico	Wire	0.08 **C**, 1.0–2.5 **Mn**, 0.25–0.60 **Si**, 19.5–22.0 **Cr**, 9.0–11.0 **Ni**, 0.25 **Cu**, 0.07 $\mathbf{N_2}$, 0.030 **P**, 0.030 **S**	
DGN–B–150	Type AE–316	Mexico	Wire	0.08 **C**, 1.0–2.5 **Mn**, 0.25–0.60 **Si**, 18.0–20.0 **Cr**, 11.0–14.0 **Ni**, 2.0–3.0 **Mo**, 0.25 **Cu**, 0.07 $\mathbf{N_2}$, 0.030 **P**, 0.030 **S**	
MIL–S–861A	Class 405	US	Bar	0.08 **C**, 1.00 **Mn**, 1.00 **Si**, 11.5–13.5 **Cr**, 0.10–0.30 **Al**, 0.040 **P**, 0.040 **S**	**Annealed**
MIL–S–862B	Class 316	US	Bar, billets	0.08 **C**, 2.0 **Mn**, 1.0 **Si**, 16.0–18.0 **Cr**, 10.0–14.0 **Ni**, 2.0–3.0 **Mo**, 0.045 **P**, 0.030 **S**	
MIL–S–862B	Class 317	US	Bar, billets	0.08 **C**, 2.0 **Mn**, 1.0 **Si**, 18.0–20.0 **Cr**, 11.0–15.0 **Ni**, 3.0–4.0 **Mo**, 0.045 **P**, 0.030 **S**	
MIL–S–862B	Class 321	US	Bar, billets	0.08 **C**, 2.0 **Mn**, 1.0 **Si**, 17.0–19.0 **Cr**, 9.0–12.0 **Ni**, 0.045 **P**, 0.030 **S**, 5 x C **Ti**	
MIL–S–862B	Class 347	US	Bar, billets	0.08 **C**, 2.0 **Mn**, 1.0 **Si**, 17.0–19.0 **Cr**, 9.0–13.0 **Ni**, 10 x C **Nb+Ta**, 0.045 **P**, 0.030 **S**	
MIL–S–862B	Class 405	US	Bar, billets	0.08 **C**, 1.0 **Mn**, 1.0 **Si**, 11.5–14.5 **Cr**, 0.10–0.30 **Al**, 0.040 **P**, 0.030 **S**	
MIL–S–862B	Class 304	US	Bar, billets	0.08 **C**, 2.0 **Mn**, 1.0 **Si**, 18.0–20.0 **Cr**, 8.0–12.0 **Ni**, 0.045 **P**, 0.030 **S**	

specification number	designation	country	product forms	composition	mechanical properties (see page iv for explanation)
MIL-T-8973	321	US	Tube	0.08 **C**, 2.00 **Mn**, 1.00 **Si**, 17.0–20.0 **Cr**, 9.0–12.0 **Ni**, 0.50 **Mo**, 0.50 **Cu**, 0.040 **P**, 0.030 **S**, 0.75 **Ti**	**Cold drawn**: all **diam**, 75 (517) **YS**, 20 **El**
MIL-T-8973	347	US	Tube	0.08 **C**, 2.00 **Mn**, 1.00 **Si**, 17.0–20.0 **Cr**, 9.0–13.0 **Ni**, 0.50 **Mo**, 0.50 **Cu**, 1.10 **Nb**, 0.040 **P**, 0.030 **S**	**Cold drawn**: all **diam**, 75 (517) **YS**, 20 **El**
IS 6529	04Cr13	India	Blooms, billets, slabs	0.08 **C**, 1.0 **Mn**, 1.0 **Si**, 11.5–14.5 **Cr**, 0.040 **P**, 0.030 **S**	**Annealed or solution annealed**
IS 6529	04Cr18Ni10	India	Blooms, billets, slabs	0.08 **C**, 2.0 **Mn**, 1.0 **Si**, 17.0–20.0 **Cr**, 8.0–12.0 **Ni**, 0.045 **P**, 0.030 **S**	**Annealed, or solution annealed**
IS 6529	04Cr18Ni10Ti[20]	India	Blooms, billets, slabs	0.08 **C**, 2.0 **Mn**, 1.0 **Si**, 17.0–19.0 **Cr**, 9.0–12.0 **Ni**, 0.045 **P**, 0.030 **S**, 5C–0.80 **Ti**	**Annealed, or solution annealed**
IS 6529	04Cr18Ni10Nb[40]	India	Blooms, billets, slabs	0.08 **C**, 2.0 **Mn**, 1.0 **Si**, 17.0–19.0 **Cr**, 9.0–12.0 **Ni**, 10C–1.0 **Nb**, 0.045 **P**, 0.030 **S**	**Annealed, or solution annealed**
IS 6529	04Cr17Ni12Mo2	India	Blooms, billets, slabs	0.08 **C**, 2.0 **Mn**, 1.0 **Si**, 16.0–18.5 **Cr**, 10.0–14.0 **Ni**, 2.0–3.0 **Mo**, 0.045 **P**, 0.030 **S**	**Annealed, or solution annealed**
IS 6529	04Cr17Ni12Mo2Ti[20]	India	Blooms, billets, slabs	0.080 **C**, 2.0 **Mn**, 1.0 **Si**, 16.0–18.5 **Cr**, 10.5–14.0 **Ni**, 2.0–3.0 **Mo**, 0.045 **P**, 0.030 **S**, 5C–0.8 **Ti**	**Annealed, or solution annealed**
ANSI/ASTM A 269	TP 304	US	Tube: seamless, welded	0.08 **C**, 2.00 **Mn**, 0.75 **Si**, 18.0–20.0 **Cr**, 8.00–11.0 **Ni**, 0.040 **P**, 0.030 **S**	
ANSI/ASTM A 269	TP 316	US	Tube: seamless or welded	0.08 **C**, 2.00 **Mn**, 0.75 **Si**, 16.0–18.0 **Cr**, 11.0–14.0 **Ni**, 2.0–3.0 **Mo**, 0.040 **P**, 0.030 **S**	
ANSI/ASTM A 269	TP 317	US	Tube: seamless or welded	0.08 **C**, 2.00 **Mn**, 0.75 **Si**, 18.0–20.0 **Cr**, 11.0–14.0 **Ni**, 3.0–4.0 **Mo**, 0.040 **P**, 0.030 **S**	
ANSI/ASTM A 269	TP 321	US	Tube: seamless or welded	0.08 **C**, 2.00 **Mn**, 0.75 **Si**, 17.0–20.0 **Cr**, 9.00–13.0 **Ni**, 0.040 **P**, 0.030 **S**, 5 x C–0.70 **Ti**	
ANSI/ASTM A 269	TP 347	US	Tube: seamless or welded	0.08 **C**, 2.00 **Mn**, 0.75 **Si**, 17.0–20.0 **Cr**, 9.00–13.0 **Ni**, 0.040 **P**, 0.030 **S**, 10 x C–1.0 **Ta+Nb**	
ANSI/ASTM A 269	TP 348	US	Tube: seamless or welded	0.08 **C**, 2.00 **Mn**, 0.75 **Si**, 17.0–20.0 **Cr**, 9.00–13.0 **Ni**, 0.040 **P**, 0.030 **S**, 0.10 **Ta**, 10 x C–1.0 **Ta+Nb**	
ANSI/ASTM A 269	TP XM-10	US	Tube: seamless or welded	0.08 **C**, 8.00–10.00 **Mn**, 1.00 **Si**, 19.00–21.50 **Cr**, 5.50–7.50 **Ni**, 0.15–0.40 **N**, 0.060 **P**, 0.030 **S**	
ANSI/ASTM A 269	TP XM-15	US	Tube: seamless or welded	0.08 **C**, 2.00 **Mn**, 1.50–2.50 **Si**, 17.0–19.0 **Cr**, 17.50–18.50 **Ni**, 0.030 **P**, 0.030 **S**	
ANSI/ASTM A 270	Type 304	US	Tube: seamless or welded	0.08 **C**, 2.00 **Mn**, 0.75 **Si**, 18.0–20.0 **Cr**, 8.00–11.0 **Ni**, 0.040 **P**, 0.030 **S**	
MIL-S-27419	347	US	Billets	0.08 **C**, 2.00 **Mn**, 1.00 **Si**, 17.0–20.0 **Cr**, 9.0–13.0 **Ni**, 0.70 **Cu**, 1.10 **Nb**, 0.025 **P**, 0.025 **S**	
MIL-S-27419	321	US	Billets	0.08 **C**, 2.00 **Mn**, 1.00 **Si**, 17.0–20.0 **Cr**, 9.0–13.0 **Ni**, 0.70 **Cu**, 0.025 **P**, 0.025 **S**, 0.75 **Ti**	
ASTM A 651	TP 304	US	Tube: seamless or welded	0.08 **C**, 2.00 **Mn**, 0.75 **Si**, 18.00–20.00 **Cr**, 8.00–11.00 **Ni**, 0.040 **P**, 0.030 **S**	
AMS 5690G		US	Wire	0.08 **C**, 2.00 **Mn**, 1.00 **Si**, 16.00–18.00 **Cr**, 10.00–14.00 **Ni**, 2.00–3.00 **Mo**, 0.75 **Cu**, 0.040 **P**, 0.030 **S**	
AMS 5650B		US	Tube	0.08 **C**, 2.00 **Mn**, 1.00 **Si**, 22.00–24.00 **Cr**, 12.00–15.00 **Ni**, 0.75 **Mo**, 0.50 **Cu**, 0.040 **P**, 0.030 **S**	

WROUGHT STAINLESS STEELS

specification number	designation	country	product forms	composition	mechanical properties (see page iv for explanation)
AMS 5651E		US	Tube	0.08 **C**, 2.00 **Mn**, 0.30–0.80 **Si**, 24.00–26.00 **Cr**, 19.00–22.00 **Ni**, 0.75 **Mo**, 0.50 **Cu**, 0.040 **P**, 0.030 **S**	
AMS 5804B		US	Wire	0.08 **C**, 2.00 **Mn**, 1.00 **Si**, 13.50–16.00 **Cr**, 24.00–27.00 **Ni**, 1.00–1.50 **Mo**, 0.10–0.50 **V**, 0.35 **S**, 0.0030–0.010 **B**, 0.020 **P**, 0.015 **S**, 2.00–2.45 **Ti**	
IS 6527	04Cr13	India	Wire, rod	0.08 **C**, 1.0 **Mn**, 1.0 **Si**, 11.5–14.5 **Cr**, 0.030 **S**, 0.040 **P**	**Annealed**
IS 6527	04Cr18Ni10	India	Wire, rod	0.08 **C**, 2.0 **Mn**, 1.0 **Si**, 17.0–20.0 **Cr**, 8.0–12.0 **Ni**, 0.030 **S**, 0.045 **P**	**Annealed**
IS 6527	04Cr17Ni12M02	India	Wire, rod	0.08 **C**, 2.0 **Mn**, 1.0 **Si**, 16.0–18.5 **Cr**, 10.0–14.0 **Ni**, 2.0–3.0 **Mo**, 0.030 **S**, 0.045 **P**	**Annealed**
NF A 35–583	Z 6 CNNb 20.10	France	Wire, rod	0.08 **C**, 1.0–2.5 **Mn**, 0.6 **Si**, 18.0–21.0 **Cr**, 8.5–11.0 **Ni**, 10 x C–1.00 **Nb**, 0.030 **P**, 0.020 **S**	
NF A 35–583	Z 6 CNDNb 19.13	France	Wire, rod	0.08 **C**, 1.0–2.5 **Mn**, 0.6 **Si**, 17.0–20.0 **Cr**, 11.0–14.0 **Ni**, 2.5–3.0 **Mo**, 8 x C–1.0 **Nb**, 0.030 **P**, 0.020 **S**	
JIS G 4303	SUS 410S	Japan	Bar	0.08 **C**, 1.00 **Mn**, 1.00 **Si**, 11.50–13.50 **Cr**, 0.60 **Ni**, 0.040 **P**, 0.030 **S**	**Annealed**
JIS G 4308	SUS 30 Se	Japan	Wire, rod	0.08 **C**, 2.00 **Mn**, 1.00 **Si**, 17.00–19.00 **Cr**, 8.00–10.00 **Ni**, 0.20 **P**, 0.060 **S**, 0.15 **Se**	
JIS G 4308	SUS 304	Japan	Wire, rod	0.08 **C**, 2.00 **Mn**, 1.00 **Si**, 18.00–20.00 **Cr**, 8.00–10.50 **Ni**, 0.040 **P**, 0.030 **S**	
JIS G 4308	SUS 305 J1	Japan	Wire, rod	0.08 **C**, 2.00 **Mn**, 1.00 **Si**, 16.50–19.00 **Cr**, 11.00–13.50 **Ni**, 0.040 **P**, 0.030 **S**	
JIS G 4308	SUS 309 S	Japan	Wire, rod	0.08 **C**, 2.00 **Mn**, 1.00 **Si**, 22.00–24.00 **Cr**, 12.00–15.00 **Ni**, 0.040 **P**, 0.030 **S**	
JIS G 4308	SUS 310 S	Japan	Wire, rod	0.08 **C**, 2.00 **Mn**, 1.50 **Si**, 24.00–26.00 **Cr**, 19.00–22.00 **Ni**, 0.040 **P**, 0.030 **S**	
JIS G 4308	SUS 310 S	Japan	Wire, rod	0.08 **C**, 2.00 **Mn**, 1.50 **Si**, 24.00–26.00 **Cr**, 19.00–22.00 **Ni**, 0.040 **P**, 0.030 **S**	
JIS G 4308	SUS 316	Japan	Wire, rod	0.08 **C**, 2.00 **Mn**, 1.00 **Si**, 16.00–18.00 **Cr**, 10.00–14.00 **Ni**, 2.00–3.00 **Mo**, 0.040 **P**, 0.030 **S**	
JIS G 4308	SUS 321	Japan	Wire, rod	0.08 **C**, 2.00 **Mn**, 1.00 **Si**, 17.00–19.00 **Cr**, 9.00–13.00 **Ni**, 0.040 **P**, 0.030 **S**, 5 x C min **Ti**	
JIS G 4308	SUS 347	Japan	Wire, rod	0.08 **C**, 2.00 **Mn**, 1.00 **Si**, 17.00–19.00 **Cr**, 9.00–13.00 **Ni**, 10 x C min **Nb+Ta**, 0.040 **P**, 0.030 **S**	
JIS G 4308	SUS 384	Japan	Wire, rod	0.08 **C**, 2.00 **Mn**, 1.00 **Si**, 15.00–17.00 **Cr**, 17.00–19.00 **Ni**, 0.040 **P**, 0.030 **S**	
JIS G 4308	SUS 385	Japan	Wire, rod	0.08 **C**, 2.00 **Mn**, 1.00 **Si**, 11.50–13.50 **Cr**, 14.00–16.00 **Ni**, 0.040 **P**, 0.030 **S**	
JIS G 4308	SUS XM7	Japan	Wire, rod	0.08 **C**, 2.00 **Mn**, 1.00 **Si**, 17.00–19.00 **Cr**, 8.50–10.50 **Ni**, 3.00–4.00 **Cu**, 0.040 **P**, 0.030 **S**	
JIS G 4316	SUS Y 308	Japan	Wire, rod	0.08 **C**, 1.00–2.50 **Mn**, 0.60 **Si**, 19.50–22.00 **Cr**, 9.00–11.00 **Ni**, 0.030 **P**, 0.030 **S**	
JIS G 4316	SUS Y 310 S	Japan	Wire, rod	0.08 **C**, 1.00–2.50 **Mn**, 0.60 **Si**, 25.00–28.00 **Cr**, 20.00–22.50 **Ni**, 0.030 **P**, 0.030 **S**	
JIS G 4316	SUS Y 316	Japan	Wire, rod	0.08 **C**, 1.00–2.50 **Mn**, 0.60 **Si**, 18.00–20.00 **Cr**, 11.00–14.00 **Ni**, 2.00–3.00 **Mo**, 0.030 **P**, 0.030 **S**	

WROUGHT STAINLESS STEELS

specification number	designation	country	product forms	composition	mechanical properties (see page iv for explanation)
JIS G 4316	SUS Y 317	Japan	Wire, rod	0.08 **C**, 1.00–2.50 **Mn**, 0.60 **Si**, 18.50–20.50 **Cr**, 13.00–15.00 **Ni**, 3.00–4.00 **Mo**, 0.030 **P**, 0.030 **S**	
JIS G 4316	SUS Y 321	Japan	Wire, rod	0.08 **C**, 1.00–2.50 **Mn**, 0.60 **Si**, 18.50–20.50 **Cr**, 9.00–10.50 **Ni**, 0.030 **P**, 0.030 **S**, 9 x C–1.00 **Ti**	
JIS G 4316	SUS Y 347	Japan	Wire, rod	0.08 **C**, 1.00–2.50 **Mn**, 0.60 **Si**, 19.00–21.50 **Cr**, 9.00–11.00 **Ni**, 10 x C–1.00 **Nb+Ta**, 0.030 **P**, 0.030 **S**	
DEF STAN 95–1/1	Class 304	Canada	Bar	0.08 **C**, 2.00 **Mn**, 1.00 **Si**, 18.0–20.0 **Cr**, 8.0–12.0 **Ni**, 0.045 **P**, 0.030 **S**	
CSA G110.3	Type 304	Canada	Bar, billets	0.08 **C**, 2.00 **Mn**, 1.00 **Si**, 18.00–20.00 **Cr**, 8.00–12.00 **Ni**, 0.045 **P**, 0.030 **S**	
CSA G110.3	Type 308	Canada	Bar, billets	0.08 **C**, 2.00 **Mn**, 1.00 **Si**, 19.00–21.00 **Cr**, 10.00–12.00 **Ni**, 0.045 **P**, 0.030 **S**	
CSA G110.3	Type 309S	Canada	Bar, billets	0.08 **C**, 2.00 **Mn**, 1.00 **Si**, 22.00–24.00 **Cr**, 12.00–15.00 **Ni**, 0.045 **P**, 0.030 **S**	
CSA G110.3	Type 310S	Canada	Bar, billets	0.08 **C**, 2.00 **Mn**, 1.50 **Si**, 24.00–26.00 **Cr**, 19.00–22.00 **Ni**, 0.045 **P**, 0.030 **S**	
CSA G110.3	Type 316	Canada	Bar, billets	0.08 **C**, 2.00 **Mn**, 1.00 **Si**, 16.00–18.00 **Cr**, 10.00–14.00 **Ni**, 2.00–3.00 **Mo**, 0.045 **P**, 0.030 **S**	
CSA G110.3	Type 317	Canada	Bar, billets	0.08 **C**, 2.00 **Mn**, 1.00 **Si**, 18.00–20.00 **Cr**, 11.00–15.00 **Ni**, 3.00–4.00 **Mo**, 0.045 **P**, 0.030 **S**	
CSA G110.3	Type 321	Canada	Bar, billets	0.08 **C**, 2.00 **Mn**, 1.00 **Si**, 17.00–19.00 **Cr**, 9.00–12.00 **Ni**, 0.045 **P**, 0.030 **S**, 5 x C min **Ti**	
CSA G110.3	Type 347	Canada	Bar, billets	0.08 **C**, 2.00 **Mn**, 1.00 **Si**, 17.00–19.00 **Cr**, 9.00–13.00 **Ni**, 10 x C **Nb+Ta**, 0.045 **P**, 0.030 **S**	
CSA G110.3	Type 348	Canada	Bar, billets	0.08 **C**, 2.00 **Mn**, 1.00 **Si**, 17.00–19.00 **Cr**, 9.00–13.00 **Ni**, 0.25 **Co**, 10 x C **Nb+Ta**, 0.045 **P**, 0.030 **S**	
CSA G110.3	Type 405	Canada	Bar, billets	0.08 **C**, 1.00 **Mn**, 1.00 **Si**, 11.50–14.50 **Cr**, 0.10–0.30 **Al**, 0.040 **P**, 0.030 **S**	
SIS 14 23 61	SS 23 61–02	Sweden	Forgings, plate, sheet, strip, tube, wire	0.08 **C**, 2.0 **Mn**, 1.5 **Si**, 24.0–26.0 **Cr**, 19.0–22.0 **Ni**, 0.045 **P**, 0.030 **S**	
DGN–B–229	Grade TP 304	Mexico	Tube: seamless or welded	0.08 **C**, 2.00 **Mn**, 0.75 **Si**, 18.0–20.0 **Cr**, 8.0–11.0 **Ni**, 0.040 **P**, 0.030 **S**	
DGN–B–229	Grade TP 316	Mexico	Tube: seamless or welded	0.08 **C**, 2.00 **Mn**, 0.75 **Si**, 16.0–18.0 **Cr**, 11.0–14.0 **Ni**, 2.0–3.0 **Mo**, 0.040 **P**, 0.030 **S**	
DGN–B–229	Grade TP 317	Mexico	Tube: seamless or welded	0.08 **C**, 2.00 **Mn**, 0.75 **Si**, 18.0–20.0 **Cr**, 11.0–14.0 **Ni**, 3.00–4.00 **Mo**, 0.040 **P**, 0.030 **S**	
DGN–B–229	Grade TP 321	Mexico	Tube: seamless or welded	0.08 **C**, 2.00 **Mn**, 0.75 **Si**, 17.0–20.0 **Cr**, 9.0–13.0 **Ni**, 0.040 **P**, 0.030 **S**, 5 x C–0.60 **Ti**	
DGN–B–229	Grade TP 347	Mexico	Tube: seamless or welded	0.08 **C**, 2.00 **Mn**, 0.75 **Si**, 17.0–20.0 **Cr**, 9.0–13.0 **Ni**, 10 x C–1.0 **Cb+Ta**, 0.040 **P**, 0.030 **S**	
DGN–B–229	Grade TP 348	Mexico	Tube: seamless or welded	0.08 **C**, 2.00 **Mn**, 0.75 **Si**, 17.0–20.0 **Cr**, 9.0–13.0 **Ni**, 10 x C–1.0 **Cb+Ta**, 0.040 **P**, 0.030 **S**, 0.10 **Ta**	
SIS 14 23 61	SIS 23 61–02	Sweden	Bar, forgings, plate, sheet, strip, wire	0.08 **C**, 2.0 **Mn**, 1.5 **Si**, 24.0–26.0 **Cr**, 19.0–22.0 **Ni**, 0.045 **P**, 0.030 **S**	
SIS 14 23 61	SIS 23 61–02	Sweden	Tube	0.08 **C**, 2.0 **Mn**, 1.5 **Si**, 23.0–26.0 **Cr**, 19.0–22.0 **Ni**, 0.045 **P**, 0.030 **S**	

WROUGHT STAINLESS STEELS

specification number	designation	country	product forms	composition	mechanical properties (see page iv for explanation)
MIL–S–8840B	AM 350	US	Sheet, strip	0.07–0.11 **C**, 0.50–1.25 **Mn**, 0.50 **Si**, 16.00–17.00 **Cr**, 4.00–5.00 **Ni**, 2.50–3.25 **Mo**, 0.07–0.13 **N**, 0.040 **P**, 0.030 **S**	**Heat treated to SCT 850**: >0.020–0.1875 **diam**, (1275) **TS**, (1103) **YS**, 8 **El**
AMS 5745A		US	Bar, forgings	0.07–0.11 **C**, 0.50–1.25 **Mn**, 0.50 **Si**, 16.00–17.00 **Cr**, 4.00–5.00 **Ni**, 2.50–3.25 **Mo**, 0.07–0.13 **N**, 0.040 **P**, 0.030 **S**	**Solution heat treated, sub–zero cooled, austenite conditioned, sub–zero cooling, tempered**: all **diam**, 165 (1138) **TS**, 140 (965) **YS**, 10 **El**
DIN 17224	Grade X 5 CrNiMo 18 10	Germany	Wire, strip	0.07 **C**, 2.0 **Mn**, 1.0 **Si**, 16.5–18.5 **Cr**, 10.5–13.5 **Ni**, 2.0–2.5 **Mo**	**Cold drawn (wire)**: (≤0.2) **diam**, (1618) **TS**; **Cold drawn and tempered (wire)**: (≤0.2) **diam**, (1716) **TS**
ANSI/ASTM A 579	61	US	Forgings	0.07 **C**, 1.00 **Mn**, 1.00 **Si**, 16.0–18.0 **Cr**, 6.5–7.75 **Ni**, 0.75–1.50 **Al**, 0.025 **P**, 0.025 **S**	**Precipitation hardened**: all **diam**, 200 (1380) **TS**, 180 (1240) **YS**, 8 **El**
JIS G 4303	SUS 630	Japan	Bar	0.07 **C**, 1.25 **Mn**, 1.00 **Si**, 15.50–17.50 **Cr**, 3.00–5.00 **Ni**, 3.00–5.00 **Cu**, 0.15–0.45 **Nb+Ta**, 0.040 **P**, 0.030 **S**	**Solution annealed and aged**: (≤75) **diam**, (1314) **TS**, (1177) **YS**, 10 **El**
ASTM A 693	Type XM–12	US	Plate, sheet, strip	0.07 **C**, 1.00 **Mn**, 1.00 **Si**, 14.00–15.50 **Cr**, 3.50–5.50 **Ni**, 2.50–4.50 **Cu**, 0.040 **P**, 0.030 **S**	**Precipitation hardened**: 0.1874 (4.761) **diam**, 190 (1310) **TS**, 170 (1170) **YS**, 5 **El**
ISO 683/XVI	1	ISO	Forgings, bar, plate, sheet, strip, wire, rod	0.07 **C**, 1.00 **Mn**, 1.00 **Si**, 15.5–17.5 **Cr**, 3.00–5.00 **Ni**, 3.00–5.00 **Cu**, 0.15–0.45 **Nb+Ta**, 0.040 **P**, 0.030 **S**	**Precipitation hardened (bar, forgings, wire, rod)**: all **diam**, (1310) **TS**, (1170) **YS**, 10 **El**
ISO 683/XVI	4	ISO	Forgings, bar, plate, sheet, strip, wire	0.07 **C**, 1.00 **Mn**, 1.00 **Si**, 14.0–15.5 **Cr**, 3.50–5.50 **Ni**, 2.50–4.50 **Cu**, 5 x C–0.45 **Nb+Ta**, 0.040 **P**, 0.030 **S**	**Precipitation hardened (bar, forgings, wire, rod)**: all **diam**, (1310) **TS**, (1170) **YS**, 10 **El**
AMS 5659C		US	Bar, forgings, rings, wire	0.07 **C**, 1.00 **Mn**, 1.00 **Si**, 14.00–15.50 **Cr**, 3.50–5.50 **Ni**, 0.50 **Mo**, 2.50–4.50 **Cu**, 5 x C–0.45 **Nb+Ta**, 0.30 **P**, 0.015 **S**	**H 900 (bar, forgings, rings)**: all **diam**, 190 (1310) **TS**, 170 (1172) **YS**, 10 **El**; **H 925**: all **diam**, 170 (1172) **TS**, 155 (1069) **YS**, 10 **El**; **H 1025**: all **diam**, 155 (1069) **TS**, 145 (1000) **YS**, 12 **El**; **H 1075**: all **diam**, 145 (1000) **TS**, 125 (862) **YS**, 13 **El**; **H 1100**: all **diam**, 140 (965) **TS**, 115 (793) **YS**, 14 **El**; **H 1150**: all **diam**, 135 (931) **TS**, 105 (724) **YS**, 16 **El**
AMS 5604 A		US	Strip, sheet, plate	0.07 **C**, 1.00 **Mn**, 1.00 **Si**, 15.50–17.50 **Cr**, 3.00–5.00 **Ni**, 3.00–5.00 **Cu**, 0.15–0.45 **Nb**, 0.040 **P**, 0.030 **S**	**Cold rolled, solution treated and aged (sheet, strip)**: ≥0.015–0.1875 (≥0.38–4.762) **diam**, 185 (1276) **TS**, 160 (1103) **YS**, 3 **El**
BS 2S145	S145B	UK	Bar: black, aircraft quality	0.07 **C**, 1.00 **Mn**, 0.60 **Si**, 13.2–14.7 **Cr**, 5.0–5.8 **Ni**, 1.20–2.00 **Mo**, 1.20–2.00 **Cu**, 0.10–0.40 **Nb**, 0.035 **P**, 0.025 **S**	**Solution treated**: all **diam**, (1270) **TS**, (1030) **YS**, 10 **El**
BS 2S.145	S145D	UK	Bar: bright, aircraft quality	0.07 **C**, 1.00 **Mn**, 0.60 **Si**, 13.2–14.7 **Cr**, 5.0–5.8 **Ni**, 1.20–2.00 **Mo**, 1.20–2.00 **Cu**, 0.10–0.40 **Nb**, 0.035 **P**, 0.025 **S**	**Solution treated**: all **diam**, (1270) **TS**, (1030) **YS**, 10 **El**
ASTM A 693	Type 630	US	Plate, sheet, strip	0.07 **C**, 1.00 **Mn**, 1.00 **Si**, 15.50–17.50 **Cr**, 3.00–5.00 **Ni**, 3.00–5.00 **Cu**, 0.040 **P**, 0.030 **S**	**Solution annealed**: 0.015–4.0 (0.38–102) **diam**, 185 (1255) max **TS**, 160 (1105) max **YS**, 3 **El**; **Precipitation hardened**: 0.1874 (4.761) max **diam**, 190 (1310) **TS**, 170 (1170) **YS**, 5 **El**
ISO 683/XVI	9	ISO	Forgings, bar, plate, sheet, strip, wire	0.07 **C**, 1.00 **Mn**, 0.60 **Si**, 13.2–14.7 **Cr**, 5.00–5.80 **Ni**, 1.20–2.00 **Mo**, 1.20–2.00 **Cu**, 0.20–0.70 **Nb+Ta**, 0.040 **P**, 0.030 **S**	**Precipitation hardened (bar, forging, wire, rod)**: all **diam**, (1130) **TS**, (1030) **YS**, 12 **El**
BS 25144	S144B	UK	Bar: black, aircraft quality	0.07 **C**, 1.00 **Mn**, 0.60 **Si**, 13.2–14.7 **Cr**, 5.0–5.8 **Ni**, 1.20–2.00 **Mo**, 1.20–2.00 **Cu**, 0.10–0.40 **Nb**, 0.035 **P**, 0.025 **S**	**Hardened**: all **diam**, (1130) **TS**, (1030) **YS**, 12 **El**
BS 2S.144	S144D	UK	Bar: bright, aircraft quality	0.07 **C**, 1.00 **Mn**, 0.60 **Si**, 13.2–14.7 **Cr**, 5.0–5.8 **Ni**, 1.20–2.00 **Mo**, 1.20–2.00 **Cu**	**Hardened**: all **diam**, (1130) **TS**, (1030) **YS**, 12 **El**

WROUGHT STAINLESS STEELS

specification number	designation	country	product forms	composition	mechanical properties (see page iv for explanation)
BS 2S.144	S144E	UK	Bar: aircraft quality	0.07 **C**, 1.00 **Mn**, 0.60 **Si**, 13.2–14.7 **Cr**, 5.0–5.8 **Ni**, 1.20–2.00 **Mo**, 1.20–2.00 **Cu**, 0.10–0.40 **Nb**, 0.035 **P**, 0.025 **S**	**Hardened and cold drawn or cold rolled**: all **diam**, (1130) **TS**, (1030) **YS**, 12 **El**
BS 2S.144	S144A	UK	Forging stock, billet and bar: aircraft quality	0.07 **C**, 1.00 **Mn**, 0.60 **Si**, 13.2–14.7 **Cr**, 5.0–5.8 **Ni**, 1.20–2.00 **Mo**, 1.20–2.00 **Cu**, 0.10–0.40 **Nb**, 0.035 **P**, 0.025 **S**	**Softened**: all **diam**, (1130) **TS**, (1030) **YS**, 12 **El**
BS 2S.144	S144C	UK	Forgings: aircraft quality	0.07 **C**, 1.00 **Mn**, 0.60 **Si**, 13.2–14.7 **Cr**, 5.0–5.8 **Ni**, 1.20–2.00 **Mo**, 1.20–2.00 **Cu**, 0.10–0.40 **Nb**, 0.035 **P**, 0.025 **S**	**Hardened**: all **diam**, (1130) **TS**, (1030) **YS**, 12 **El**
AISI S15500		US	Sheet, strip, plate, bar	0.07 **C**, 1.00 **Mn**, 1.00 **Si**, 14.00–15.00 **Cr**, 3.50–5.50 **Ni**, 2.50–4.50 **Cu**, 0.15–0.45 **Cb+Ta**, 0.04 **P**, 0.03 **S**	**Solution treated**: all **diam**, 160 (1103) max **TS**, 145 (1000) max **YS**, 15 **El**; **Solution treated, plus 900°F (482°C), 1h, air cool: all diam, 200 (1379) max TS, 185 (1276) max YS, 14 El; Solution treated, plus 1150°F (620°C), 4h, air cool: all diam, 145 (1000) max TS, 125 (862) max YS, 19 El**
AISI S17400		US	Bar, sheet, plate	0.07 **C**, 1.00 **Mn**, 1.00 **Si**, 15.50–17.50 **Cr**, 3.00–5.00 **Ni**, 3.00–5.00 **Cu**, 0.15–0.45 **Cb+Ta**, 0.040 **P**, 0.030 **S**	**Solution treated**: all **diam**, 160 (1103) max **TS**, 145 (1000) max **YS**, 15 **El**; **Solution treated plus 900°F (482°C), 1h, air cool: all diam, 200 (1379) max TS, 185 (1276) max YS, 14 El; Solution treated plus 1150°F (620°C), 4h, air cool: all diam, 145 (1379) max TS, 125 (862) max YS, 19 El**
AMS 5862A		US	Strip, sheet, plate	0.07 **C**, 1.00 **Mn**, 1.00 **Si**, 14.00–15.50 **Cr**, 3.50–5.50 **Ni**, 2.50–4.50 **Cu**, 5 x C–0.45 **Nb+Ta**, 0.030 **P**, 0.015 **S**	**Solution treated and aged**: 0.015–0.1875 (0.38–4.762) **diam**, 155 (1069) **TS**, 145 (1000) **YS**, 5 **El**
BS 2S.143		UK	Billets, bar, forgings and parts: aircraft quality	0.07 **C**, 1.00 **Mn**, 0.60 **Si**, 13.2–14.7 **Cr**, 5.0–5.8 **Ni**, 1.20–2.00 **Mo**, 1.20–2.00 **Cu**, 0.10–0.40 **Nb**, 0.035 **P**, 0.025 **S**	**Solution annealed and precipitation treated**: all **diam**, (930) **TS**, (780) **YS**, 15 **El**
AIR 9160	9160C221	France	Bar	0.07 **C**, 1.0 **Mn**, 1.0 **Si**, 13.5–15.5 **Cr**, 3.0–5.0 **Ni**, 1.0–1.60 **Mo**, 0.035 **P**, 0.025 **S**	**Quenched and tempered**: (<40) **diam**, (930) **TS**, (690) **YS**, 12 **El**
BS 1449 Part 2	Grade 284S16	UK	Plate, sheet, strip	0.07 **C**, 7.00–10.00 **Mn**, 1.00 **Si**, 16.5–18.5 **Cr**, 4.00–6.50 **Ni**, 0.15–0.25 **N**, 0.060 **P**, 0.030 **S**	**Solution annealed**: (≥3.0) (sheet, strip) **diam**, (630) **TS**, (300) **YS**, 40 **El**
NF A 35–577	Z 6 CN 18.09 (DF)	France	Bar, wire, rod	0.07 **C**, 2.0 **Mn**, 1.0 **Si**, 17.0–19.0 **Cr**, 8.0–10.0 **Ni**, 0.040 **P**, 0.030 **S**	**Solution annealed**: (6) **diam**, (620) max **TS**
NF A 35–575	Z 6 CND 17.11	France	Wire, rod	0.07 **C**, 2.0 **Mn**, 1.0 **Si**, 16.0–18.0 **Cr**, 10.0–12.5 **Ni**, 2.0–2.5 **Mo**, 0.040 **P**, 0.030 **S**	**Stress hardened 0%**: all **diam**, (590) **TS**; **Stress hardened 40%**: all **diam**, (1030) **TS**; **Stress hardened 60%**: all **diam**, (1270) **TS**; **Stress hardened 80%**: all **diam**, (1520) **TS**
NF A 35–575	Z 6 CN 18.09	France	Wire, rod	0.07 **C**, 2.0 **Mn**, 1.0 **Si**, 17.0–19.0 **Cr**, 8.0–10.0 **Ni**, 0.040 **P**, 0.030 **S**	**Stress hardened 0%**: all **diam**, (590) **TS**; **Stress hardened 40%**: all **diam**, (1130) **TS**; **Stress hardened 60%**: all **diam**, (1320) **TS**; **Stress hardened 80%**: all **diam**, (1670) **TS**
BS 1449 Part 2	Grade 316S16	UK	Plate, sheet, strip	0.07 **C**, 0.50–2.00 **Mn**, 0.20–1.00 **Si**, 16.5–18.5 **Cr**, 10.0–13.0 **Ni**, 2.25–3.00 **Mo**, 0.045 **P**, 0.030 **S**	**Solution annealed**: (≥3.0) (sheet and strip) **diam**, (540) **TS**, (210) **YS**, 40 **El**
BS 1449 Part 2	Grade 315S16	UK	Sheet, strip	0.07 **C**, 0.50–2.00 **Mn**, 0.20–1.00 **Si**, 16.5–18.5 **Cr**, 9.0–11.0 **Ni**, 1.25–1.75 **Mo**, 0.045 **P**, 0.030 **S**	**Solution annealed**: (0.5–1.6) **diam**, (540) **TS**, (210) **YS**, 30 **El**

WROUGHT STAINLESS STEELS

specification number	designation	country	product forms	composition	mechanical properties (see page iv for explanation)
NF A 35–573	Z 6 CND 17.11	France	Sheet, strip, plate	0.07 **C**, 2.0 **Mn**, 1.0 **Si**, 16.0–18.0 **Cr**, 10.0–12.5 **Ni**, 2.0–2.5 **Mo**, 0.040 **P**, 0.030 **S**	**Cold rolled:** (≤5) **diam**, (530) **TS**, (265) **YS**, 45 **El**; **Hot rolled:** (≤20) **diam**, (530) **TS**, (255) **YS**, 43 **El**
ISO 2604/II	TS 60	ISO	Tube: seamless	0.07 **C**, 2.00 **Mn**, 1.00 **Si**, 16.00–18.50 **Cr**, 11.00–14.00 **Ni**, 2.00–2.50 **Mo**, 0.045 **P**, 0.030 **S**	**Cold finished, quenched:** all **diam**, (510) **TS**, (205) **YS**, 30 **El**
ISO 2604/II	TS 61	ISO	Tube: seamless	0.07 **C**, 2.00 **Mn**, 1.00 **Si**, 16.00–18.50 **Cr**, 11.00–14.50 **Ni**, 2.50–3.00 **Mo**, 0.045 **P**, 0.030 **S**	**Cold finished, quenched:** all **diam**, (510) **TS**, (205) **YS**, 30 **El**
BS 3605 Section 4	Grade 316S26	UK	Pipe: welded	0.07 **C**, 0.50–2.00 **Mn**, 0.20–1.00 **Si**, 16.0–18.5 **Cr**, 10.0–13.0 **Ni**, 2.0–3.0 **Mo**, 0.040 **P**, 0.030 **S**	**Solution annealed**: all **diam**, (510) **TS**, (245) **YS**, 35 **El**
BS 3605 Section 3	Grade 316S18	UK	Pipe: seamless	0.07 **C**, 0.50–2.00 **Mn**, 0.20–1.00 **Si**, 16.0–18.5 **Cr**, 11.0–14.0 **Ni**, 2.0–3.0 **Mo**, 0.040 **P**, 0.030 **S**	**Solution annealed**: all **diam**, (510) **TS**, (245) **YS**, 35 **El**
BS 3605 Section 2	Grade 316S18	UK	Pipe: seamless	0.07 **C**, 0.50–2.00 **Mn**, 0.20–1.00 **Si**, 16.0–18.5 **Cr**, 11.0–14.0 **Ni**, 2.0–3.0 **Mo**, 0.040 **P**, 0.030 **S**	**Solution annealed**: all **diam**, (510) **TS**, (245) **YS**, 35 **El**
BS 3605 Section 5	Grade 316S26	UK	Pipe: welded	0.07 **C**, 0.50–2.00 **Mn**, 0.20–1.00 **Si**, 16.0–18.5 **Cr**, 10.0–13.0 **Ni**, 2.0–3.0 **Mo**, 0.040 **P**, 0.030 **S**	**Solution annealed**: all **diam**, (510) **TS**, (245) **YS**, 35 **El**
NF A 36–209	Z 6 CN 18–09	France	Plate	0.070 **C**, 2.0 **Mn**, 1.0 **Si**, 17.0–19.0 **Cr**, 8.0–10.0 **Ni**, 0.040 **P**, 0.030 **S**	**Hot rolled**: (<3) **diam**, (510) **TS**, (205) **YS**, 40 **El**; **Cold rolled**: (<3) **diam**, (510) **TS**, (205) **YS**, 40 **El**
NF A 35–572	Z 6 CND 17–11	France	Bar, sections	0.07 **C**, 2.0 **Mn**, 1.0 **Si**, 16.0–18.0 **Cr**, 10.0–12.5 **Ni**, 2.0–2.5 **Mo**, 0.040 **P**, 0.030 **S**	**Austenitized**: (≤25) **diam**, (500) **TS**, (205) **YS**, 45 **El**
NF A 35–572	Z 6 CND 17.12	France	Bar, sections	0.07 **C**, 2.0 **Mn**, 1.0 **Si**, 16.0–18.0 **Cr**, 11.0–13.0 **Ni**, 2.5–3.0 **Mo**, 0.040 **P**, 0.030 **S**	**Austenitized**: (≤25) **diam**, (500) **TS**, (205) **YS**, 45 **El**
DIN 17440	Grade X 5 CrNi 18 9	Germany	Sheet, strip, bar, wire, tube, forgings	0.07 **C**, 2.0 **Mn**, 1.0 **Si**, 17.0–20.0 **Cr**, 8.5–10.0 **Ni**, 0.045 **P**, 0.030 **S**	**Quenched**: (≤60) **diam**, (500) **TS**, (185) **YS**, 50 **El**
DIN 17440	Grade X 5 CrNi 19 11	Germany	Sheet, strip, bar, wire, tube, forgings	0.07 **C**, 2.0 **Mn**, 1.0 **Si**, 17.0–20.0 **Cr**, 10.5–12.0 **Ni**, 0.045 **P**, 0.030 **S**	**Quenched**: (≤60) **diam**, (500) **TS**, (185) **YS**, 50 **El**
DIN 17440	Grade X 5 CrNiMo 18 10	Germany	Sheet, strip, bar, wire, tube, forgings	0.07 **C**, 2.0 **Mn**, 1.0 **Si**, 16.5–18.5 **Cr**, 10.5–13.5 **Ni**, 2.0–2.5 **Mo**, 0.045 **P**, 0.030 **S**	**Quenched**: (≤60) **diam**, (500) **TS**, (205) **YS**, 45 **El**
DIN 17440	Grade X 5 CrNiMo 18 12	Germany	Sheet, strip, bar, wire, tube, forgings	0.07 **C**, 2.0 **Mn**, 1.0 **Si**, 16.5–18.5 **Cr**, 11.5–14.0 **Ni**, 2.5–3.0 **Mo**, 0.045 **P**, 0.030 **S**	**Quenched**: (≤60) **diam**, (500) **TS**, (205) **YS**, 45 **El**
ISO 2604/1	F62	ISO	Forgings	0.07 **C**, 2.00 **Mn**, 1.00 **Si**, 16.00–18.00 **Cr**, 10.00–14.00 **Ni**, 2.00–3.00 **Mo**, 0.045 **P**, 0.030 **S**	**Quenched**: all **diam**, (490) **TS**, (205) **YS**, 30 **El**
ISO 2604/1	F49	ISO	Forgings	0.07 **C**, 2.00 **Mn**, 1.00 **Si**, 17.00–19.00 **Cr**, 8.00–12.00 **Ni**, 0.50 **Mo**, 0.045 **P**, 0.030 **S**	**Quenched**: all **diam**, (490) **TS**, (195) **YS**, 30 **El**
ISO 2604/1	F47	ISO	Forgings	0.07 **C**, 2.00 **Mn**, 1.00 **Si**, 17.00–19.00 **Cr**, 8.00–12.00 **Ni**, 0.045 **P**, 0.030 **S**	**Quenched**: all **diam**, (490) **TS**, (195) **YS**, 30 **El**
ISO 683/XII	11	ISO	Bar, sheet, plate	0.07 **C**, 2.0 **Mn**, 1.0 **Si**, 17.0–19.0 **Cr**, 8.0–11.0 **Ni**, 0.045 **P**, 0.030 **S**	**Solution treated**: all **diam**, (490) **TS**, (200) **YS**, 40 **El**
ISO 683/XII	20	ISO	Bar, sheet, plate	0.07 **C**, 2.0 **Mn**, 1.0 **Si**, 16.0–18.5 **Cr**, 10.5–14.0 **Ni**, 2.0–2.5 **Mo**, 0.045 **P**, 0.030 **S**	**Solution treated**: all **diam**, (490) **TS**, (210) **YS**, 40 **El**
ISO 683/XII	20a	ISO	Bar, sheet, plate	0.07 **C**, 2.0 **Mn**, 1.0 **Si**, 16.0–18.5 **Cr**, 11.0–14.5 **Ni**, 2.5–3.0 **Mo**, 0.045 **P**, 0.030 **S**	**Solution treated**: all **diam**, (490) **TS**, (210) **YS**, 40 **El**
ISO 683/XII	25	ISO	Bar, sheet, plate	0.07 **C**, 2.0 **Mn**, 1.0 **Si**, 17.5–19.5 **Cr**, 13.0–16.0 **Ni**, 3.0–4.0 **Mo**, 0.045 **P**, 0.030 **S**	**Solution treated**: all **diam**, (490) **TS**, (210) **YS**, 35 **El**
ISO 2604/II	TS 47	ISO	Tube: seamless	0.07 **C**, 2.00 **Mn**, 1.00 **Si**, 17.00–19.00 **Cr**, 8.00–12.00 **Ni**, 0.045 **P**, 0.030 **S**	**Cold finished, quenched:** all **diam**, (490) **TS**, (195) **YS**, 30 **El**

WROUGHT STAINLESS STEELS

specification number	designation	country	product forms	composition	mechanical properties (see page iv for explanation)
EURONORM 119–74, V	X 6 CrNi 18 10 KD	EURONORM	Wire, rod	0.07 **C**, 2.0 **Mn**, 1.0 **Si**, 17.0–19.0 **Cr**, 8.0–11.0 **Ni**, 0.045 **P**, 0.030 **S**	**Solution annealed**: (15–63) **diam**, (490) **TS**, (195) **YS**, 40 **El**
ISO 2604/IV	P47	ISO	Plate	0.07 **C**, 2.00 **Mn**, 1.00 **Si**, 17.0–19.0 **Cr**, 8.0–11.0 **Ni**, 0.045 **P**, 0.030 **S**	**Hot rolled, quenched**: (3–30) **diam**, (490) **TS**, (195) **YS**, 50 **El**
ISO 2604/IV	P49	ISO	Plate	0.07 **C**, 2.00 **Mn**, 1.00 **Si**, 17.0–19.0 **Cr**, 9.0–11.5 **Ni**, 0.50 **Mo**, 0.045 **P**, 0.030 **S**	**Hot rolled, quenched**: (3–16) **diam**, (490) **TS**, (185) **YS**, 45 **El**
ISO 2604/IV	P60	ISO	Plate	0.07 **C**, 2.00 **Mn**, 1.00 **Si**, 16.0–18.5 **Cr**, 10.5–14.0 **Ni**, 2.0–2.5 **Mo**, 0.045 **P**, 0.030 **S**	**Hot rolled, quenched**: (3–40) **diam**, (490) **TS**, (205) **YS**, 45 **El**
ISO 2604/IV	P61	ISO	Plate	0.07 **C**, 2.00 **Mn**, 1.00 **Si**, 16.0–18.5 **Cr**, 11.0–14.5 **Ni**, 2.5–3.0 **Mo**, 0.045 **P**, 0.030 **S**	**Hot rolled, quenched**: (3–40) **diam**, (490) **TS**, (205) **YS**, 45 **El**
NF A 35–572	Z 6 CN 18–09	France	Bar, sections	0.07 **C**, 2.0 **Mn**, 1.0 **Si**, 17.0–19.0 **Cr**, 8.0–10.0 **Ni**, 0.04 **P**, 0.03 **S**	**Austenitized**: (≤25) **diam**, (490) **TS**, (195) **YS**, 45 **El**
SIS 14 23 32	SIS 23 32–02	Sweden	Plate, sheet, strip	0.07 **C**, 2.0 **Mn**, 1.0 **Si**, 17.0–19.0 **Cr**, 8.0–11.0 **Ni**, 0.045 **P**, 0.030 **S**	**Solution annealed**: all **diam**, (490) **TS**, (210) **YS**, 45 **El**
ANSI/ASTM A 479	XM–8	US	Bar, shapes	0.07 **C**, 1.00 **Mn**, 1.00 **Si**, 17.00–19.00 **Cr**, 0.50 **Ni**, 0.15 **Al**, 0.040 **P**, 0.030 **S**, 12 x C min **Ti**	**Annealed**: all **diam**, 70 (485) **TS**, 40 (275) **YS**, 20 **El**
ANSI/ASTM A 479	Grade XM8	US	Bar, shapes	0.07 **C**, 1.00 **Mn**, 1.00 **Si**, 17.00–19.00 **Cr**, 0.50 **Ni**, 0.15 **Al**, 0.040 **P**, 0.030 **S**, 12 x C min **Ti**	**Annealed**: all **diam**, (485) **TS**, (275) **YS**, 20 **El**
BS 970 Part 4	Grade 315S16	UK	Blooms, billets, bar, forgings	0.07 **C**, 0.50–2.00 **Mn**, 0.20–1.00 **Si**, 16.5–18.5 **Cr**, 9.0–11.0 **Ni**, 1.25–1.75 **Mo**, 0.045 **P**, 0.030 **S**	**Annealed**: all **diam**, (460) **TS**
BS 970 Part 4	Grade 316S13	UK	Blooms, billets, bar, forgings	0.07 **C**, 0.50–2.00 **Mn**, 0.20–1.00 **Si**, 16.5–18.5 **Cr**, 10.0–13.0 **Ni**, 2.25–3.0 **Mo**, 0.045 **P**, 0.030 **S**	**Annealed**: all **diam**, (460) **TS**, 40 **El**
ASTM A 240	Type XM8	US	Plate, sheet, strip	0.07 **C**, 1.00 **Mn**, 1.00 **Si**, 17.00–19.00 **Cr**, 0.50 **Ni**, 0.15 **Al**,	**Hot rolled or cold rolled, annealed**: all **diam**, 65 (450) **TS**, 30 (205) **YS**, 22 **El**
ANSI/ASTM A 240	Grade XM 8	US	Plate, sheet, strip	0.07 **C**, 1.00 **Mn**, 1.00 **Si**, 17.00–19.00 **Cr**, 0.50 **Ni**, 0.15 **Al**, 0.04 **P**, 0.03 **S**, 12 x C–1.10 **Ti**	**Annealed**: all **diam**, (450) **TS**, (205) **YS**, 22 **El**
DIN 17440	Grade X 6 CrMo 17	Germany	Sheet, strip, bar, wire, tube, forgings	0.07 **C**, 1.0 **Mn**, 1.0 **Si**, 16.0–18.0 **Cr**, 0.9–1.2 **Mo**, 0.045 **P**, 0.030 **S**	**Annealed**: (≤5) **diam**, (450) **TS**, (270) **YS**, 20 **El**
ANSI/ASTM A 268	TP XM–8	US	Tube: seamless, welded	0.07 **C**, 1.00 **Mn**, 1.00 **Si**, 17.00–19.00 **Cr**, 0.50 **Ni**, 0.15 **Al**, 0.040 **P**, 0.030 **S**, 12 x C min, 1.10 **Ti**	**Annealed**: 0.312 (7.94) **diam**, 60 (414) **TS**, 30 (207) **YS**, 20 **El**
ASTM A 651	TP XM8	US	Tube: seamless or welded	0.07 **C**, 1.00 **Mn**, 1.00 **Si**, 17.00–19.00 **Cr**, 0.50 **Ni**, 0.15 **Al**, 0.040 **P**, 0.030 **S**, 12 x C–1.10 **Ti**	**As welded or as drawn**: all **diam**, 60 (414) **TS**, 30 (207) **YS**
ASTM A 705	XM–12	US	Forgings	0.07 **C**, 1.00 **Mn**, 1.00 **Si**, 14.00–15.50 **Cr**, 3.50–5.50 **Ni**, 2.50–4.50 **Cu**, 0.15–0.45 **Nb+Ta**, 0.040 **P**, 0.030 **S**	**Solution annealed**: <0.5 (<12.70) **diam**
ASTM A 705	630	US	Forgings	0.07 **C**, 1.00 **Mn**, 1.00 **Si**, 15.50–17.50 **Cr**, 3.00–5.00 **Ni**, 3.00–5.00 **Cu**, 0.15–0.45 **Nb+Ta**, 0.040 **P**, 0.030 **S**	**Solution annealed**: <0.5 (≥12.70) **diam**
MIL–S–862B	Class 324	US	Bar, billets	0.07 **C**, 1.0 **Mn**, 1.0 **Si**, 15.5–17.5 **Cr**, 3.0–5.0 **Ni**, 3.0–5.0 **Cu**, 0.15–0.40 **Nb+Ta**, 0.045 **P**, 0.030 **S**	
MIL–P–47183		US	Plate: hot rolled, heat treated	0.07 **C**, 1.00 **Mn**, 1.00 **Si**, 15.50–17.50 **Cr**, 3.00–5.00 **Ni**, 3.00–5.00 **Cu**, 0.040 **P**, 0.030 **S**; rem Fe	
AMS 5680D		US	Wire	0.07 **C**, 2.00 **Mn**, 0.50–1.00 **Si**, 17.00–20.00 **Cr**, 9.00–13.00 **Ni**, 0.75 **Mo**, 0.50 **Cu**, 12 x C **Nb+Ta**, 0.040 **P**, 0.030 **S**	

WROUGHT STAINLESS STEELS

specification number	designation	country	product forms	composition	mechanical properties (see page iv for explanation)
BS 4106		UK	Wire	0.07 **C**, 0.50–2.00 **Mn**, 0.20–1.00 **Si**, 16.5–18.5 **Cr**, 10.0–13.0 **Ni**, 2.25–3.00 **Mo**, 0.040 **P**, 0.035 **S**	
ANSI/ASTM A 564	630	US	Bar, shapes	0.07 **C**, 1.00 **Mn**, 1.00 **Si**, 15.50–17.50 **Cr**, 3.00–5.00 **Ni**, 3.00–5.00 **Cu**, 0.15–0.45 **Nb+Ta**, 0.040 **P**, 0.030 **S**	**Solution annealed**
ANSI/ASTM A 564	XM–12	US	Bar, shapes	0.07 **C**, 1.00 **Mn**, 1.00 **Si**, 14.00–15.50 **Cr**, 3.50–5.50 **Ni**, 2.50–4.50 **Cu**, 0.15–0.45 **Nb+Ta**, 0.040 **P**, 0.030 **S**	**Solution annealed**
BS 3059 Part 2	Grade 1250	UK	Tube	0.06–0.15 **C**, 5.50–7.00 **Mn**, 0.20–1.00 **Si**, 14.0–16.0 **Cr**, 9.0–11.0 **Ni**, 0.80–1.20 **Mo**, 0.15–0.40 **V**, 0.003–0.009 **B**, 0.75–1.25 **Nb**, 0.040 **P**, 0.030 **S**	**Solution treated**: all diam, (540) **TS**, (270) **YS**, 30 **El**
NF A 35–583	Z 10 CN 24.13	France	Wire, rod	0.06–0.12 **C**, 1.0–2.5 **Mn**, 0.6 **Si**, 22.0–25.0 **Cr**, 12.0–14.0 **Ni**, 0.030 **P**, 0.020 **S**	
AMS 5861		US	Sheet, strip, plate	0.06 **C**, 4.00–6.00 **Mn**, 1.00 **Si**, 20.50–23.50 **Cr**, 11.50–13.50 **Ni**, 1.50–3.00 **Mo**, 0.10–0.30 **V**, 0.02 **Al**, 0.20–0.40 **N**, 0.10–0.30 **Nb**, 0.040 **P**, 0.030 **S**, 0.02 **Ti**, 0.02 **Zr**	**Annealed**: <0.1875 (<4.762) **diam**, 120 (827) **TS**, 75 (517) **YS**, 30 **El**
ASTM A 240	Type XM19	US	Plate, sheet, strip	0.06 **C**, 4.00–6.00 **Mn**, 1.00 **Si**, 20.50–23.50 **Cr**, 11.50–13.50 **Ni**, 1.50–3.00 **Mo**, 0.10–0.30 **V**, 0.10–0.30 **Cb**, 0.20–0.40 **N**, 0.040 **P**, 0.030 **S**	**Solution annealed, hot rolled or cold rolled (sheet, strip)**: all **diam**, 120 (825) **TS**, 75 (515) **YS**, 30 **El**
ANSI/ASTM A 412	Type XM–19	US	Plate, sheet, strip	0.06 **C**, 4.00–6.00 **Mn**, 1.00 **Si**, 20.50–23.50 **Cr**, 11.50–13.50 **Ni**, 1.50–3.00 **Mo**, 0.10–0.30 **V**, 0.10–0.30 **Cb**, 0.20–0.40 **N**, 0.040 **P**, 0.030 **S**	**Annealed (sheet, strip)**: 0.015 (0.38) **diam**, 120 (825) **TS**, 75 (515) **YS**, 30 **El**
ANSI/ASTM A 240	Grade XM 19	US	Sheet, strip	0.06 **C**, 4.00–6.00 **Mn**, 1.00 **Si**, 20.50–23.50 **Cr**, 11.50–13.50 **Ni**, 1.50–3.00 **Mo**, 0.10–0.30 **V**, 0.10–0.30 **Cb**, 0.040 **P**, 0.030 **S**	**Solution annealed**: all **diam**, (825) **TS**, (515) **YS**, 30 **El**
ANSI/ASTM A 479	XM–19	US	Bar, shapes	0.06 **C**, 4.00–6.00 **Mn**, 1.00 **Si**, 20.50–23.50 **Cr**, 11.50–13.50 **Ni**, 1.50–3.00 **Mo**, 0.10–0.300 **V**, 0.20–0.40 **N**, 0.10–0.30 **Nb**, 0.040 **P**, 0.030 **S**	**Solution annealed**: all **diam**, 110 (760) **TS**, 55 (415) **YS**, 35 **El**
ANSI/ASTM A 479	Grade XM 19	US	Bar, shapes	0.06 **C**, 4.00–6.00 **Mn**, 1.00 **Si**, 20.50–23.50 **Cr**, 11.50–13.50 **Ni**, 1.50–3.00 **Mo**, 0.10–0.300 **V**, 0.10–0.30 **Cb**, 0.20–0.40 **N**, 0.040 **P**, 0.030 **S**	**Solution annealed**: all **diam**, (760) **TS**, (415) **YS**, 35 **El**
ANSI/ASTM A 240	Grade XM 19	US	Plate	0.06 **C**, 4.00–6.00 **Mn**, 1.00 **Si**, 20.50–23.50 **Cr**, 11.50–13.50 **Ni**, 1.50–3.00 **Mo**, 0.10–0.30 **V**, 0.10–0.30 **Cb**, 0.040 **P**, 0.030 **S**	**Solution annealed**: all **diam**, (690) **TS**, (380) **YS**, 35 **El**
AMS 5764A		US	Bar, forgings, extrusions, rings, wire	0.06 **C**, 4.00–6.00 **Mn**, 1.00 **Si**, 20.50–23.50 **Cr**, 11.50–13.50 **Ni**, 1.50–3.00 **Mo**, 0.10–0.30 **V**, 0.02 **Al**, 0.20–0.40 **N**, 0.10–0.30 **Nb**, 0.040 **P**, 0.030 **S**, 0.02 **Ti**, 0.02 **Zr**	**Solution treated**: all **diam**, 100 (690) **TS**, 55 (379) **YS**, 35 **El**
ANSI/ASTM A 580	Grade XM–19	US	Wire	0.06 **C**, 4.00–6.00 **Mn**, 1.00 **Si**, 20.50–23.50 **Cr**, 11.50–13.50 **Ni**, 1.50–3.00 **Mo**, 0.10–0.30 **V**, 0.10–0.30 **Cb**, 0.20–0.40 **N**, 0.040 **P**, 0.030 **S**	**Annealed**: all **diam**, 100 (690) **TS**, 55 (380) **YS**, 35 **El**
ANSI/ASTM A 249	TP XM–19	US	Tube: welded	0.06 **C**, 4.00–6.00 **Mn**, 1.00 **Si**, 20.50–23.50 **Cr**, 11.50–13.50 **Ni**, 1.50–3.00 **Mo**, 0.10–0.30 **V**, 0.10–0.30 **Nb+Ta**, 0.20–0.40 **N**, 0.040 **P**, 0.030 **S**	**Solution annealed**: 0.312 (7.94) **diam**, 100 (690) **TS**, 55 (380) **YS**, 35 **El**
ANSI/ASTM A 312	TP XM–29	US	Pipe: seamless or welded	0.060 **C**, 11.50–14.50 **Mn**, 1.00 **Si**, 17.0–19.0 **Cr**, 2.25–3.75 **Ni**, 0.20–0.40 **N**, 0.060 **P**, 0.030 **S**	**Solution annealed**: 0.31 (7.94) **diam**, 100 (689) **TS**, 55 (379) **YS**, 35 **El**
ASTM A 688	TP XM–29	US	Tube: welded	0.060 **C**, 11.50–14.50 **Mn**, 1.00 **Si**, 17.00–19.00 **Cr**, 2.25–3.75 **Ni**, 0.20–0.40 **N**, 0.060 **P**, 0.030 **S**	**Solution annealed**: all **diam**, 100 (689) **TS**, 55 (379) **YS**, 35 **El**

WROUGHT STAINLESS STEELS

specification number	designation	country	product forms	composition	mechanical properties (see page iv for explanation)
ANSI/ASTM A 276	XM–26	US	Bar, shapes	0.06 **C**, 1.00 **Mn**, 1.00 **Si**, 25.00–27.00 **Cr**, 6.00–7.00 **Ni**, 0.040 **P**, 0.030 **S**, 0.25 **Ti**	**Annealed**: all **diam**, 90 (620) **TS**, 65 (450) **YS**, 20 **El**
BS 1449 Part 2	Grade 317S16	UK	Plate, sheet, strip	0.06 **C**, 0.50–2.00 **Mn**, 0.20–1.00 **Si**, 17.5–19.5 **Cr**, 12.0–15.0 **Ni**, 3.00–4.00 **Mo**, 0.045 **P**, 0.030 **S**	**Solution annealed**: (≥3.0) (sheet and strip) **diam**, (540) **TS**, (210) **YS**, 35 **El**
BS 1449 Part 2	Grade 304S16	UK	Sheet, strip	0.06 **C**, 0.50–2.00 **Mn**, 0.20–1.00 **Si**, 17.5–19.0 **Cr**, 9.0–11.0 **Ni**, 0.045 **P**, 0.030 **S**	**Solution annealed**: (≥3.0) **diam**, (510) **TS**, (210) **YS**, 40 **El**
BS 1449 Part 2	Grade 304S15	UK	Plate, sheet, strip	0.06 **C**, 0.50–2.00 **Mn**, 0.20–1.00 **Si**, 17.5–19.0 **Cr**, 8.00–11.0 **Ni**, 0.045 **P**, 0.030 **S**	**Solution annealed**: (≥3.0) (sheet and strip) **diam**, (510) **TS**, (210) **YS**, 40 **El**
BS 3605 Section 4	Grade 304S25	UK	Pipe: welded	0.06 **C**, 0.50–2.00 **Mn**, 0.20–1.00 **Si**, 17.0–19.0 **Cr**, 8.0–11.0 **Ni**, 0.040 **P**, 0.030 **S**	**Solution annealed**: all **diam**, (490) **TS**, (235) **YS**, 35 **El**
BS 3605 Section 3	Grade 304S18	UK	Pipe: seamless	0.06 **C**, 0.50–2.00 **Mn**, 0.20–1.00 **Si**, 17.0–19.0 **Cr**, 9.0–12.0 **Ni**, 0.040 **P**, 0.030 **S**	**Solution annealed**: all **diam**, (490) **TS**, (235) **YS**, 35 **El**
BS 3605 section 2	Grade 304S18	UK	Pipe: seamless	0.06 **C**, 0.50–2.00 **Mn**, 0.20–1.00 **Si**, 17.0–19.0 **Cr**, 9.0–12.0 **Ni**, 0.040 **P**, 0.030 **S**	**Solution annealed**: all **diam**, (490) **TS**, (235) **YS**, 35 **El**
BS 3605 Section 5	Grade 304S25	UK	Pipe: welded	0.06 **C**, 0.50–2.00 **Mn**, 0.20–1.00 **Si**, 17.0–19.0 **Cr**, 8.0–11.0 **Ni**, 0.040 **P**, 0.030 **S**	**Solution annealed**: all **diam**, (490) **TS**, (235) **YS**, 35 **El**
ASTM A 240	Type XM33	US	Plate, sheet, strip	0.06 **C**, 0.75 **Mn**, 0.75 **Si**, 25.00–27.00 **Cr**, 0.50 **Ni**, 0.75–1.50 **Mo**, 0.20 **Cu**, 0.04 **N**, 0.040 **P**, 0.020 **S**, 0.20–1.00 **Ti**, 7 x (C+N) min **Ti**	**Hot rolled or cold rolled, annealed**: all **diam**, 68 (470) **TS**, 45 (310) **YS**, 20 **El**
ASTM A 176	Type XM33	US	Plate, sheet, strip	0.06 **C**, 0.75 **Mn**, 0.75 **Si**, 25.0–27.0 **Cr**, 0.50 **Ni**, 0.20 **Cu**, 0.04 **N**, 0.75–1.50 **Mo**, 0.040 **P**, 0.020 **S**, 0.20–1.00 and 7 x (c+n) min **Ti**	**Annealed**: all **diam**, 68 (470) **TS**, 45 (310) **YS**, 20 **El**
ANSI/ASTM A 240	Grade XM 33	US	Plate, sheet, strip	0.06 **C**, 0.75 **Mn**, 0.75 **Si**, 25.00–27.00 **Cr**, 0.50 **Ni**, 0.75–1.50 **Mo**, 0.20 **Cu**, 0.04 **N**, 0.040 **P**, 0.020 **S**, 0.60–1.00 and 7 x (c+n) **Ti**	**Annealed**: all **diam**, (470) **TS**, (310) **YS**, 20 **El**
ANSI/ASTM A 268	TP XM–33	US	Tube: seamless, welded	0.06 **C**, 0.75 **Mn**, 0.75 **Si**, 25.0–27.0 **Cr**, 0.50 **Ni**, 0.75–1.50 **Mo**, 0.20 **Cu**, 0.040 **N**, 0.040 **P**, 0.020 **S**, 0.20–1.00 with 7 x (C+N) min **Ti**	**Annealed**: 0.312 (7.94) **diam**, 68 (469) **TS**, 45 (310) **YS**, 20 **El**
BS 970 Part 4	Grade 304S15	UK	Blooms, billets, bar, forgings	0.06 **C**, 0.50–2.00 **Mn**, 0.20–1.00 **Si**, 17.5–19.0 **Cr**, 8.0–11.0 **Ni**, 0.045 **P**, 0.030 **S**	**Annealed**: ≤2.5 **diam**, (460) **TS**, (170) **YS**, 40 **El**
BS 970 Part 4	Grade 317S16	UK	Blooms, billets, bar, forgings	0.06 **C**, 0.50–2.00 **Mn**, 0.20–1.00 **Si**, 17.5–19.5 **Cr**, 12.0–15.0 **Ni**, 3.0–4.0 **Mo**, 0.045 **P**, 0.030 **S**	**Annealed**: all **diam**, (460) **TS**, 40 **El**
ANSI/ASTM A 731	TP XM–33	US	Pipe: seamless or welded	0.06 **C**, 0.75 **Mn**, 0.75 **Si**, 25.0–27.0 **Cr**, 0.50 **Ni**, 0.75–1.50 **Mo**, 0.20 **Cu**, 0.040 **N**, 0.04 **P**, 0.02 **S**, 0.20–1.00 **Ti**, 7 x (c+n) min **Ti**	**Annealed**: all **diam**, 65 (450) **TS**, 40 (275) **YS**, 20 **El**
ANSI/ASTM A 269	TP XM–19	US	Tube: seamless or welded	0.060 **C**, 4.00–6.00 **Mn**, 1.00 **Si**, 20.50–23.50 **Cr**, 11.50–13.50 **Ni**, 1.50–3.00 **Mo**, 0.10–0.30 **V**, 0.10–0.30 **Nb+Ta**, 0.20–0.40 **N**, 0.040 **P**, 0.030 **S**	
ANSI/ASTM A 269	TP XM–29	US	Tube: seamless or welded	0.060 **C**, 11.50–14.50 **Mn**, 1.00 **Si**, 17.0–19.0 **Cr**, 2.25–3.75 **Ni**, 0.20–0.40 **N**, 0.060 **P**, 0.030 **S**	
ANSI/ASTM A 376	16–8–2H	US	Pipe: seamless	0.05–0.10 **C**, 2.00 **Mn**, 0.75 **Si**, 14.5–16.5 **Cr**, 7.50–9.50 **Ni**, 1.5–2.0 **Mo**, 0.040 **P**, 0.030 **S**	**Solution annealed**: 0.312 (7.94) **diam**, 75 (520) **TS**, 30 (210) **YS**, 35 **El**
DGN–B–186	Grade 16–8–2H	Mexico	Pipe: seamless	0.05–0.10 **C**, 2.00 **Mn**, 0.75 **Si**, 14.5–16.5 **Cr**, 7.3–9.0 **Ni**, 1.5–2.0 **Mo**, 0.030 **P**, 0.030 **S**	**Hot or cold finished and quenched or tempered**: (8) **diam**, (519) **TS**, (206) **YS**, 35 **El**

WROUGHT STAINLESS STEELS

specification number	designation	country	product forms	composition	mechanical properties (see page iv for explanation)
ANSI/ASTM A 430	FP 16–8–2H	US	Pipe	0.05–0.10 **C**, 2.00 **Mn**, 0.75 **Si**, 14.5–16.5 **Cr**, 7.50–9.50 **Ni**, 1.5–2.0 **Mo**, 0.040 **P**, 0.030 **S**	**Solution annealed: all diam**, 70 (483) **TS**, 30 (207) **YS**, 45 **El**
ANSI/ASTM A 313	XM–16	US	Wire	0.05 **C**, 0.50 **Mn**, 0.50 **Si**, 11.00–12.50 **Cr**, 7.50–9.50 **Ni**, 1.50–2.50 **Cu**, 0.50 **Mo**, 0.10–0.50 **Nb+Ta**, 0.040 **P**, 0.030 **S**, 0.80–1.40 **Ti**	**Cold drawn, aged:** 0.010–0.040 (0.25–1.02) **diam**, 320 (2205) **TS**
SS 14 23 43	SS 23 43–04	Sweden	Wire	0.05 **C**, 2.0 **Mn**, 1.0 **Si**, 16.0–18.5 **Cr**, 10.5–14.0 **Ni**, 2.5–3.0 **Mo**, 0.045 **P**, 0.030 **S**	**Cold drawn:** (<0.10) **diam**, (1910) **TS**, (1670) **YS**
ASTM A 313	Type XM–16	US	Wire	0.05 **C**, 0.05 **Mn**, 0.50 **Si**, 11.00–12.50 **Cr**, 7.50–9.50 **Ni**, 0.50 **Mo**, 1.50–2.50 **Cu**, 0.040 **P**, 0.030 **S**, 0.80–1.40 **Ti**	**Cold drawn:** 0.010–>0.040 (0.25–>1.02) **diam**, 245 (1690) **TS**; **Aged:** 0.010–>0.040 (0.25–>1.02) **diam**, 320 (2205) **TS**
AMS 5672		US	Wire	0.05 **C**, 0.50 **Mn**, 0.50 **Si**, 11.00–12.50 **Cr**, 7.50–9.50 **Ni**, 0.50 **Mo**, 1.50–2.50 **Cu**, 0.10–0.50 **Nb+Ta**, 0.025 **P**, 0.025 **S**, 0,80–1.40 **Ti**	**Spring temper, cold drawn:** (0.251≥1.00) 0.010≥0.040 **diam**, 245 (1689) **TS**; **Precipitation heat treated:** (0.25≥1.00) 0.010≥0.040 **diam**, (2137) 310 **TS**
AMS 5601B		US	Strip, sheet	0.05 **C**, 1.00 **Mn**, 1.00 **Si**, 13.75–15.00 **Cr**, 7.75–8.75 **Ni**, 2.00–3.00 **Mo**, 0.75–1.50 **Al**, 0.015 **P**, 0.010 **S**	**Solution treated and aged:** ≥0.005–0.010 (≥0.013–0.25) **diam**, 220 (1517) **TS**, 190 (1310) **YS**, 2 **El**
ASTM A 693	Type XM–13	US	Plate, sheet, strip	0.05 **C**, 0.20 **Mn**, 0.10 **Si**, 12.25–13.25 **Cr**, 7.50–8.50 **Ni**, 2.00–2.50 **Mo**, 0.90–1.35 **Al**, 0.010 **P**, 0.008 **S**	**Precipitation hardened:** 0.019 (0.50) **diam**, 220 (1515) **TS**, 205 (1410) **YS**, 6 **El**
MIL–S–46123A	Level II	US	Bar, wire, forgings	0.05 **C**, 0.05 **Mn**, 0.30 **Si**, 14.00–15.00 **Cr**, 6.00–7.00 **Ni**	**Annealed and aged: all diam**, 180 (1241) **TS**, 175 (1207) **YS**, 10 **El**
AMS 5739A		US	Bar, forgings, rings, wire	0.05 **C**, 0.50 **Mn**, 0.30 **Si**, 14.00–15.00 **Cr**, 6.00–7.00 **Ni**, 0.03 **P**, 0.03 **S**, 0.55–0.90 **Ti**	**Solution heat treated, maraged at 900°F + 25: all diam, 180 (1241) TS, 175 (1207) YS, 10 El**
AMS 5763		US	Bar, forgings, tube, rings, wire	0.05 **C**, 1.00 **Mn**, 1.00 **Si**, 14.00–16.00 **Cr**, 6.00–7.00 **Ni**, 0.50–1.00 **Mo**, 1.25–1.75 **Cu**, 8 x C min **Nb+Ta**, 0.030 **P**, 0.030 **S**	**Precipitation heat treated:** all **diam**, 180 (1241) **TS**, 170 (1172) **YS**, 10 **El**
AMS 5773		US	Bar, forgings, tube, rings, wire	0.05 **C**, 1.00 **Mn**, 1.00 **Si**, 14.00–16.00 **Cr**, 6.00–7.00 **Ni**, 0.50–1.00 **Mo**, 1.25–1.75 **Cu**, 8 x C min **Nb+Ta**, 0.015 **P**, 0.015 **S**	**H 900 (bar, forgings, tube, rings)**: all **diam**, 180 (1241) **TS**, 170 (1172) **YS**, 10 **El**; **H 950 (bar, forgings, tube, rings)**: all **diam**, 170 (1172) **TS**, 160 (1103) **YS**, 10 **El**; **H 1000**: all **diam**, 160 (1103) **TS**, 150 (1034) **YS**, 12 **El**; **H 1050**: all **diam**, 145 (1000) **TS**, 135 (931) **YS**, 12 **El**; **H 1100**: all **diam**, 130 (896) **TS**, 105 (724) **YS**, 16 **El**; **H 1150**: all **diam**, 125 (862) **TS**, 75 (517) **YS**, 18 **El**
SIS 14 23 43	SIS 23 43–04	Sweden	Wire	0.05 **C**, 2.0 **Mn**, 1.0 **Si**, 16.0–18.5 **Cr**, 10.5–14.0 **Ni**, 2.5–3.0 **Mo**	**Cold drawn:** (<8) **diam**, (1230) **TS**, (880) **YS**
AMS 5860		US	Sheet, strip, plate	0.05 **C**, 0.50 **Mn**, 0.50 **Si**, 11.00–12.50 **Cr**, 7.50–9.50 **Ni**, 0.50 **Mo**, 1.50–2.50 **Cu**, 0.10–0.50 **Nb+Ta**, 0.025 **P**, 0.025 **S**	**Solution heat treated:** all **diam**, 175 (1207) **TS**, 160 (1103) **YS**, 3 **El**; **Precipitation heat treatment:** >0.020–0.062 (>0.510–1.575) **diam**, 225 (1551) **TS**, 210 (1448) **YS**, 3 **El**
ASTM A 693	Type XM–16	US	Plate, sheet, strip	0.05 **C**, 0.50 **Mn**, 0.50 **Si**, 11.00–12.50 **Cr**, 7.50–9.50 **Ni**, 0.50 **Mo**, 1.50–2.50 **Cu**, 0.040 **P**, 0.030 **S**, 0.80–1.40 **Ti**	**Solution annealed:** 0.010 (0.25) **diam**, 175 (1205) max **TS**, 160 (1105) max 3 **El**; **Precipitation hardened:** 0.021–0.062 (0.52–1.57) **diam**, 222 (1525) **TS**, 205 (1410) 3 **El**
ASTM A 693	Type XM–25	US	Plate, sheet, strip	0.05 **C**, 1.00 **Mn**, 1.00 **Si**, 14.00–16.00 **Cr**, 5.00–7.00 **Ni**, 0.50–1.00 **Mo**, 1.25–1.75 **Cu**, 0.030 **P**, 0.030 **S**	**Solution annealed:** 0.010 (0.25) **diam**, 165 (1205) max **TS**, 150 (1035) max 4 **El**; **Precipitation hardened:** 0.020 (0.51) **diam**, 180 (1240) **TS**, 170 (1170) **YS**, 3 **El**

specification number	designation	country	product forms	composition	mechanical properties (see page iv for explanation)
AISI S13800		US	Bar, plate	0.05 **C**, 0.10 **Mn**, 0.10 **Si**, 12.25–13.25 **Cr**, 7.50–8.50 **Ni**, 2.00–2.50 **Mo**	**Solution treated**: all **diam**, 160 (1103) max **TS**, 120 (827) max **YS**, 17 **El**; **Solution treated plus 950°F (510°C), 4h, air cool: all diam, 225 (1151) max TS, 210 (1448) max YS, 12 El; Solution treated plus 1150°F (620°C), 4h, air cool: all diam, 145 (1000) max TS, 105 (724) max YS, 20 El**
MIL–S–46123A	Level I	US	Bar, wire, forgings	0.05 **C**, 0.05 **Mn**, 0.30 **Si**, 14.00–15.00 **Cr**, 6.00–7.00 **Ni**, 0.03 **P**, 0.03 **S**, 0.55 **Ti**	**Annealed and aged**: all **diam**, 155 (1069) **TS**, 145 (1000) **YS**, 12 **El**
AMS 5603B		US	Strip, sheet	0.05 **C**, 0.10 **Mn**, 0.10 **Si**, 14.75–15.50 **Cr**, 8.00–8.75 **Ni**, 2.00–2.50 **Mo**, 0.90–1.35 **Al**, 0.01 **N**, 0.010 **P**, 0.008 **S**	**Solution treated and aged**: ≥0.005 (≥0.13) **diam**, 150 (1034) **TS**, 65 (448) **YS**, 20 **El**
ANSI/ASTM A 564	XM–25	US	Bar, shapes	0.05 **C**, 1.00 **Mn**, 1.00 **Si**, 14.00–16.00 **Cr**, 5.00–7.00 **Ni**, 0.50–1.00 **Mo**, 1.25–1.75 **Cu**, 8 x C min **Nb**, 0.030 **P**, 0.030 **S**	**Solution annealed**: ≥0.5 (13) **diam**, 125 (862) **TS**, 95 (655) **YS**, 10 **El**
ASTM A 705	XM–25	US	Forgings	0.05 **C**, 1.00 **Mn**, 1.00 **Si**, 14.00–16.00 **Cr**, 5.00–7.00 **Ni**, 0.50–1.00 **Mo**, 1.25–1.75 **Cu**, 8 x C min **Nb**, 0.030 **P**, 0.030 **S**	**Solution annealed**: ≥0.5 (≥12.7) **diam**, 125 (860) **TS**, 95 (655) **YS**, 10 **El**
SS 14 23 74	SS 23 74–29	Sweden	Plate, sheet, strip	0.05 **C**, 2.0 **Mn**, 1.0 **Si**, 16.0–18.5 **Cr**, 9.0–12.5 **Ni**, 2.5–3.0 **Mo**, 0.15–0.22 **N**, 0.045 **P**, 0.030 **S**	**Cold finished**: all **diam**, (600) **TS**, (400) **YS**, 30 **El**
SS 14 23 70	SS 23 70–29	Sweden	Plate, sheet, strip	0.05 **C**, 2.0 **Mn**, 1.0 **Si**, 17.0–19.0 **Cr**, 7.0–10.0 **Ni**, 0.15–0.22 **N**, 0.045 **P**, 0.030 **S**	**Cold finished**: all **diam**, (600) **TS**, (400) **YS**, 30 **El**
SS 14 23 70	SS 23 70–02	Sweden	Bar, forgings, plate, sheet: strip	0.05 **C**, 2.0 **Mn**, 1.0 **Si**, 17.0–19.0 **Cr**, 7.0–10.0 **Ni**, 0.15–0.22 **N**, 0.045 **P**, 0.030 **S**	**Solution annealed**: all **diam**, (590) **TS**, (290) **YS**, 40 **El**
SS 14 23 70	SS 23 70–27	Sweden	Bar, forgings	0.05 **C**, 2.0 **Mn**, 1.0 **Si**, 17.0–19.0 **Cr**, 7.0–10.0 **Ni**, 0.15–0.22 **N**, 0.045 **P**, 0.030 **S**	**Solution annealed**: (<50) **diam**, (590) **TS**, (290) **YS**, 40 **El**
SS 14 23 70	SS 23 70–28	Sweden	Plate, sheet, strip	0.05 **C**, 2.0 **Mn**, 1.0 **Si**, 17.0–19.0 **Cr**, 7.0–10.0 **Ni**, 0.15–0.22 **N**, 0.045 **P**, 0.030 **S**	**Solution annealed**: all **diam**, (590) **TS**, (290) **YS**, 40 **El**
SS 14 23 74	SS 23 74–02	Sweden	Bar, forgings, plate, sheet, strip	0.05 **C**, 2.0 **Mn**, 1.0 **Si**, 16.0–18.5 **Cr**, 9.0–12.5 **Ni**, 2.5–3.0 **Mo**, 0.15–0.22 **N**, 0.045 **P**, 0.030 **S**	**Solution annealed**: all **diam**, (590) **TS**, (310) **YS**, 40 **El**
SS 14 23 74	SS 23 74–27	Sweden	Bar, forgings	0.05 **C**, 2.0 **Mn**, 1.0 **Si**, 16.0–18.5 **Cr**, 9.0–12.5 **Ni**, 2.5–3.0 **Mo**, 0.15–0.22 **N**, 0.045 **P**, 0.030 **S**	**Solution annealed**: (<50) **diam**, (590) **TS**, (310) **YS**, 40 **El**
SS 14 23 74	SS 23 74–28	Sweden	Plate, sheet, strip	0.05 **C**, 2.0 **Mn**, 1.0 **Si**, 16.0–18.5 **Cr**, 9.0–12.5 **Ni**, 2.5–3.0 **Mo**, 0.15–0.22 **N**, 0.045 **P**, 0.030 **S**	**Solution annealed**: all **diam**, (590) **TS**, (310) **YS**, 40 **El**
SS 14 23 33	SS 23 33–29	Sweden	Plate, sheet, strip	0.05 **C**, 2.0 **Mn**, 1.0 **Si**, 17.0–19.0 **Cr**, 8.0–11.0 **Ni**, 0.045 **P**, 0.030 **S**	**Cold rolled**: all **diam**, (550) **TS**, (350) **YS**, 35 **El**
SS 14 23 47	SS 23 47–29	Sweden	Plate, sheet, strip	0.05 **C**, 2.0 **Mn**, 1.0 **Si**, 16.0–18.5 **Cr**, 10.5–14.0 **Ni**, 2.0–2.5 **Mo**, 0.045 **P**, 0.030 **S**	**Cold finished**: all **diam**, (550) **TS**, (350) **YS**, 35 **El**
SS 14 23 66	SS 23 66–29	Sweden	Plate, sheet, strip	0.05 **C**, 2.0 **Mn**, 1.0 **Si**, 17.5–19.5 **Cr**, 13.0–16.0 **Ni**, 3.0–4.0 **Mo**, 0.045 **P**, 0.030 **S**	**Cold finished**: all **diam**, (550) **TS**, (350) **YS**, 30 **El**
SS 14 23 43	SS 23 43–29	Sweden	Plate, sheet, strip	0.05 **C**, 2.0 **Mn**, 1.0 **Si**, 16.0–18.5 **Cr**, 10.5–14.0 **Ni**, 2.5–3.0 **Mo**, 0.045 **P**, 0.030 **S**	**Cold finished**: all **diam**, (550) **TS**, (350) **YS**, 35 **El**
SS 14 23 47	SS 23 47–25	Sweden	Tube: welded	0.05 **C**, 2.0 **Mn**, 1.0 **Si**, 16.0–18.5 **Cr**, 10.5–14.0 **Ni**, 2.0–2.5 **Mo**, 0.045 **P**, 0.030 **S**	**Solution annealed**: all **diam**, (490) **TS**, (220) **YS**, 45 **El**
SS 14 23 47	SS 23 47–26	Sweden	Tube: welded	0.05 **C**, 2.0 **Mn**, 1.0 **Si**, 16.0–18.5 **Cr**, 10.5–14.0 **Ni**, 2.0–2.5 **Mo**, 0.045 **P**, 0.030 **S**	**Solution annealed**: (<30) **diam**, (490) **TS**, (220) **YS**, 45 **El**

WROUGHT STAINLESS STEELS

specification number	designation	country	product forms	composition	mechanical properties (see page iv for explanation)
SS 14 23 47	SS 23 47–27	Sweden	Bar, forgings	0.05 **C**, 2.0 **Mn**, 1.0 **Si**, 16.0–18.5 **Cr**, 10.5–14.0 **Ni**, 2.0–2.5 **Mo**, 0.045 **P**, 0.030 **S**	**Solution annealed**: (<50) **diam**, (490) **TS**, (220) **YS**, 45 **El**
SS 14 23 47	SS 23 47–28	Sweden	Plate, sheet, strip	0.05 **C**, 2.0 **Mn**, 1.0 **Si**, 16.0–18.5 **Cr**, 10.5–14.0 **Ni**, 2.0–2.5 **Mo**, 0.045 **P**, 0.030 **S**	**Solution annealed**: all **diam**, (490) **TS**, (220) **YS**, 45 **El**
SS 14 23 43	SS 23 43–02	Sweden	Bar, forgings, plate, sheet, strip, tube, wire	0.05 **C**, 2.0 **Mn**, 1.0 **Si**, 16.0–18.5 **Cr**, 10.5–14.0 **Ni**, 2.5–3.0 **Mo**, 0.045 **P**, 0.030 **S**	**Solution annealed**: all **diam**, (490) **TS**, (220) **YS**, 45 **El**
SS 14 23 66	SS 23 66–27	Sweden	Bar, forgings	0.05 **C**, 2.0 **Mn**, 1.0 **Si**, 17.5–19.5 **Cr**, 13.0–16.0 **Ni**, 3.0–4.0 **Mo**, 0.045 **P**, 0.030 **S**	**Solution annealed**: (<50) **diam**, (490) **TS**, (230) **YS**, 40 **El**
SS 14 23 66	SS 23 66–28	Sweden	Plate, sheet, strip	0.05 **C**, 2.0 **Mn**, 1.0 **Si**, 17.5–19.5 **Cr**, 13.0–16.0 **Ni**, 3.0–4.0 **Mo**, 0.045 **P**, 0.030 **S**	**Solution annealed**: all **diam**, (490) **TS**, (230) **YS**, 40 **El**
SS 14 23 66	SS 23 66–02	Sweden	Bar, forgings, plate, sheet, strip	0.05 **C**, 2.0 **Mn**, 1.0 **Si**, 17.5–19.5 **Cr**, 13.0–16.0 **Ni**, 3.0–4.0 **Mo**, 0.045 **P**, 0.030 **S**	**Solution annealed**: all **diam**, (490) **TS**, (230) **YS**, 40 **El**
SS 14 23 33	SS 23 33–02	Sweden	Bar, forgings, plate, sheet, strip, tube, wire	0.05 **C**, 2.0 **Mn**, 1.0 **Si**, 17.0–19.0 **Cr**, 8.0–11.0 **Ni**, 0.045 **P**, 0.030 **S**	**Solution treated (except strip, wire)**: all **diam**, (490) **TS**, (210) **YS**, 45 **El**
SS 14 23 33	SS 23 33–25	Sweden	Tube: welded	0.05 **C**, 2.0 **Mn**, 1.0 **Si**, 17.0–19.0 **Cr**, 8.0–11.0 **Ni**, 0.045 **P**, 0.030 **S**	**Solution annealed**: all **diam**, (490) **TS**, (190) **YS**, 45 **El**
SS 14 23 33	SS 23 33–24	Sweden	Tube: seamless	0.05 **C**, 2.0 **Mn**, 1.0 **Si**, 17.0–19.0 **Cr**, 8.0–11.0 **Ni**, 0.045 **P**, 0.030 **S**	**Solution annealed**: (<10) **diam**, (490) **TS**, (210) **YS**, 45 **El**
SS 14 23 33	SS 23 33–23	Sweden	Tube: welded	0.05 **C**, 2.0 **Mn**, 1.0 **Si**, 17.0–19.0 **Cr**, 8.0–11.0 **Ni**, 0.045 **P**, 0.030 **S**	**Solution annealed**: all **diam**, (490) **TS**, (210) **YS**, 45 **El**
SS 14 23 33	SS 23 33–22	Sweden	Tube: seamless	0.05 **C**, 2.0 **Mn**, 1.0 **Si**, 17.0–19.0 **Cr**, 8.0–11.0 **Ni**, 0.045 **P**, 0.030 **S**	**Solution annealed**: (<10) **diam**, (490) **TS**, (210) **YS**, 45 **El**
SS 14 23 33	SS 23 33–28	Sweden	Plate, sheet, strip	0.05 **C**, 2.0 **Mn**, 1.0 **Si**, 17.0–19.0 **Cr**, 8.0–11.0 **Ni**, 0.045 **P**, 0.030 **S**	**Solution annealed**: all **diam**, (490) **TS**, (210) **YS**, 45 **El**
SS 14 23 33	SS 23 33–27	Sweden	Bar, forgings	0.05 **C**, 2.0 **Mn**, 1.0 **Si**, 17.0–19.0 **Cr**, 8.0–11.0 **Ni**, 0.045 **P**, 0.030 **S**	**Solution annealed**: (<50) **diam**, (490) **TS**, (210) **YS**, 45 **El**
SS 14 23 33	SS 23 33–26	Sweden	Tube: welded	0.05 **C**, 2.0 **Mn**, 1.0 **Si**, 17.0–19.0 **Cr**, 8.0–11.0 **Ni**, 0.045 **P**, 0.030 **S**	**Solution annealed**: (<30) **diam**, (490) **TS**, (210) **YS**, 45 **El**
SS 14 23 43	SS 23 43–22	Sweden	Tube: seamless	0.05 **C**, 2.0 **Mn**, 1.0 **Si**, 16.0–18.5 **Cr**, 10.5–14.0 **Ni**, 2.5–3.0 **Mo**, 0.045 **P**, 0.030 **S**	**Solution annealed**: (<10) **diam**, (490) **TS**, (220) **YS**, 45 **El**
SS 14 23 43	SS 23 43–23	Sweden	Tube: welded	0.05 **C**, 2.0 **Mn**, 1.0 **Si**, 16.0–18.5 **Cr**, 10.5–14.0 **Ni**, 2.5–3.0 **Mo**, 0.045 **P**, 0.030 **S**	**Solution annealed**: all **diam**, (490) **TS**, (220) **YS**, 45 **El**
SS 14 23 43	SS 23 43–24	Sweden	Tube: seamless	0.05 **C**, 2.0 **Mn**, 1.0 **Si**, 16.0–18.5 **Cr**, 10.5–14.0 **Ni**, 2.5–3.0 **Mo**, 0.045 **P**, 0.030 **S**	**Solution annealed**: (<10) **diam**, (490) **TS**, (220) **YS**, 45 **El**
SS 14 23 43	SS 23 43–25	Sweden	Tube: welded	0.05 **C**, 2.0 **Mn**, 1.0 **Si**, 16.0–18.5 **Cr**, 10.5–14.0 **Ni**, 2.5–3.0 **Mo**, 0.045 **P**, 0.030 **S**	**Solution annealed**: all **diam**, (490) **TS**, (220) **YS**, 45 **El**
SS 14 23 43	SS 23 43–26	Sweden	Tube: welded	0.05 **C**, 2.0 **Mn**, 1.0 **Si**, 16.0–18.5 **Cr**, 10.5–14.0 **Ni**, 2.5–3.0 **Mo**, 0.045 **P**, 0.030 **S**	**Solution annealed**: (<30) **diam**, (490) **TS**, (220) **YS**, 45 **El**
SS 14 23 43	SS 23 43–27	Sweden	Bar, forgings	0.05 **C**, 2.0 **Mn**, 1.0 **Si**, 16.0–18.5 **Cr**, 10.5–14.0 **Ni**, 2.5–3.0 **Mo**, 0.045 **P**, 0.030 **S**	**Solution annealed**: (<50) **diam**, (490) **TS**, (220) **YS**, 45 **El**
SS 14 23 43	SS 23 43–28	Sweden	Plate, sheet, strip	0.05 **C**, 2.0 **Mn**, 1.0 **Si**, 16.0–18.5 **Cr**, 10.5–14.0 **Ni**, 2.5–3.0 **Mo**, 0.045 **P**, 0.030 **S**	**Solution annealed**: (5–30) **diam**, (490) **TS**, (220) **YS**, 45 **El**
SS 14 23 47	SS 23 47–02	Sweden	Bar, forgings, plate, sheet, strip, tube	0.05 **C**, 2.0 **Mn**, 1.0 **Si**, 16.0–18.5 **Cr**, 10.5–14.0 **Ni**, 2.0–2.5 **Mo**, 0.045 **P**, 0.030 **S**	**Solution annealed**: (<50) **diam**, (490) **TS**, (220) **YS**, 45 **El**
SS 14 23 47	SS 23 47–22	Sweden	Tube: seamless	0.05 **C**, 2.0 **Mn**, 1.0 **Si**, 16.0–18.5 **Cr**, 10.5–14.0 **Ni**, 2.0–2.5 **Mo**, 0.045 **P**, 0.030 **S**	**Solution annealed**: (<10) **diam**, (490) **TS**, (220) **YS**, 45 **El**
SS 14 23 47	SS 23 47–23	Sweden	Tube: welded	0.05 **C**, 2.0 **Mn**, 1.0 **Si**, 16.0–18.5 **Cr**, 10.5–14.0 **Ni**, 2.0–2.5 **Mo**, 0.045 **P**, 0.030 **S**	**Solution annealed**: all **diam**, (490) **TS**, (220) **YS**, 45 **El**

specification number	designation	country	product forms	composition	mechanical properties (see page iv for explanation)
SS 14 23 47	SS 23 47–24	Sweden	Tube: seamless	0.05 **C**, 2.0 **Mn**, 1.0 **Si**, 16.0–18.5 **Cr**, 10.5–14.0 **Ni**, 2.0–2.5 **Mo**, 0.045 **P**, 0.030 **S**	**Solution annealed**: (<10) **diam**, (490) **TS**, (220) **YS**, 45 **El**
ASTM A 693	Type XM–9	US	Plate, sheet, strip	0.05 **C**, 0.50 **Mn**, 0.30 **Si**, 14.00–14.50 **Cr**, 6.25–7.00 **Ni**, 0.030 **Mo**, 0.10 **Al**, 0.030 **P**, 0.030 **S**, 0.60–0.90 **Ti**	**Solution heat treated**: >0.010 (>0.25) **diam**, 150 (10.35) max **TS**, 125 (860) max **YS**, 4 **El**; **Hardened or precipitation heat treated**: >0.010 (>0.25) **diam**, 180 (1240) **TS**, 160 (1105) **YS**, 3 **El**
ASTM A 705	XM–13	US	Forgings	0.05 **C**, 0.20 **Mn**, 0.10 **Si**, 12.25–13.25 **Cr**, 7.50–8.50 **Ni**, 2.00–2.50 **Mo**, 0.90–1.35 **Al**, 0.01 **N**, 0.010 **P**, 0.008 **S**	**Solution annealed**: <0.5 (<12.70) **diam**
ASTM A 705	XM–16	US	Forgings	0.05 **C**, 0.50 **Mn**, 0.50 **Si**, 11.00–12.50 **Cr**, 7.50–9.50 **Ni**, 0.50 **Mo**, 1.50–2.50 **Cu**, 0.10–0.50 **Nb+Ta**, 0.040 **P**, 0.030 **S**, 0.80–1.40 **Ti**	
ASTM A 705	XM–9	US	Forgings	0.05 **C**, 0.50 **Mn**, 0.30 **Si**, 14.00–14.50 **Cr**, 6.25–7.00 **Ni**, 0.30 **Mo**, 0.10 **Al**, 0.030 **P**, 0.030 **S**, 0.60–0.90 **Ti**	
AMS 5863		US	Strip	0.05 **C**, 1.00 **Mn**, 1.00 **Si**, 14.00–16.00 **Cr**, 6.00–7.00 **Ni**, 0.50–1.00 **Mo**, 1.25–1.75 **Cu**, 8 x C–1.00 **Nb+Ta**, 0.030 **P**, 0.030 **S**	
NF A 35–583	Z 3 C 14	France	Wire, rod	0.05 **C**, 1.0 **Mn**, 0.75 **Si**, 12–15 **Cr**, 0.50 **Ni**, 0.50 **Mo**, 0.030 **P**, 0.020 **S**	
ANSI/ASTM A 564	XM–9	US	Bar, shapes	0.05 **C**, 0.50 **Mn**, 0.30 **Si**, 14.00–14.50 **Cr**, 6.25–7.00 **Ni**, 0.30 **Mo**, 0.10 **Al**, 0.030 **P**, 0.030 **S**, 0.60–0.90 **Ti**	
ANSI/ASTM A 564	XM–13	US	Bar, shapes	0.05 **C**, 0.20 **Mn**, 0.10 **Si**, 12.25–13.25 **Cr**, 7.50–8.50 **Ni**, 2.00–2.50 **Mo**, 0.01 **N**, 0.010 **P**, 0.008 **S**	**Solution annealed**: >0.5 (>12.70) **diam**
ANSI/ASTM A 564	XM–16	US	Bar, shapes	0.05 **C**, 0.50 **Mn**, 0.50 **Si**, 11.00–12.50 **Cr**, 7.50–9.50 **Ni**, 0.50 **Mo**, 1.50–2.50 **Cu**, 0.10–0.50 **Nb+Ta**, 0.040 **P**, 0.030 **S**, 0.80–1.40 **Ti**	**Solution annealed**
ANSI/ASTM A 249	TP 321H	US	Tube: welded	0.04–1.0 **C**, 2.00 **Mn**, 0.75 **Si**, 17.0–20.0 **Cr**, 9.00–13.0 **Ni**, 0.040 **P**, 0.030 **S**, 4 x C–0.60 **Ti**	**Solution annealed**: 0.312 (7.94) **diam**, 75 (515) **TS**, 30 (205) **YS**, 35 **El**
ANSI/ASTM A 430	FP 304N	US	Pipe	0.04–0.10 **C**, 2.00 **Mn**, 0.75 **Si**, 18.0–20.0 **Cr**, 8.00–11.0 **Ni**, 0.10–0.16 **N**, 0.040 **P**, 0.030 **S**	**Solution annealed**: all **diam**, 75 (550) **TS**, 35 (240) **YS**, 45 **El**
ANSI/ASTM A 430	FP 316N	US	Pipe	0.04–0.10 **C**, 2.00 **Mn**, 0.75 **Si**, 16.0–18.0 **Cr**, 11.0–14.0 **Ni**, 2.00–3.00 **Mo**, 0.10–0.16 **N**, 0.040 **P**, 0.030 **S**	**Solution annealed**: all **diam**, 75 (550) **TS**, 35 (240) **YS**, 45 **El**
ISO 2604/IV	P67	ISO	Plate	0.04–0.10 **C**, 1.50 **Mn**, 0.20–0.60 **Si**, 15.5–17.5 **Cr**, 15.5–17.5 **Ni**, 1.6–2.0 **Mo**, 10 x C–1.20 **Nb**, 0.045 **P**, 0.030 **S**	**Hot rolled, quenched**: (3–40) **diam**, (530) **TS**, (215) **YS**, 35 **El**
COPANT 513	TP 304H	COPANT	Tube	0.04–0.10 **C**, 2.00 **Mn**, 0.75 **Si**, 18.0–20.0 **Cr**, 8.00–11.00 **Ni**, 0.040 **P**, 0.030 **S**	**Solution annealed and quenched**: (>8) **diam**, (520) **TS**, (205) **YS**, 35 **El**
COPANT 513	TP 348H	COPANT	Tube	0.04–0.10 **C**, 2.00 **Mn**, 1.00 **Si**, 17.0–20.0 **Cr**, 9.00–13.00 **Ni**, 8 x C–1.0 **Cb+Ta**, 0.040 **P**, 0.030 **S**, 0.10 **Ta**	**Solution annealed and quenched**: (>8) **diam**, (520) **TS**, (205) **YS**, 35 **El**
COPANT 513	TP 347H	COPANT	Tube	0.04–0.10 **C**, 2.00 **Mn**, 1.00 **Si**, 17.0–20.0 **Cr**, 9.00–13.00 **Ni**, 8 x C–1.0 **Cb+Ta**, 0.030 **P**, 0.030 **S**	**Solution annealed and quenched**: (>8) **diam**, (520) **TS**, (205) **YS**, 35 **El**
COPANT 513	TP 321H	COPANT	Tube	0.04–0.10 **C**, 2.00 **Mn**, 0.75 **Si**, 17.0–20.0 **Cr**, 9.00–13.00 **Ni**, 0.030 **P**, 0.030 **S**, 4 x C–0.60 **Ti**	**Solution annealed and quenched**: (>8) **diam**, (520) **TS**, (205) **YS**, 35 **El**
COPANT 513	TP 316H	COPANT	Tube	0.04–0.10 **C**, 2.00 **Mn**, 0.75 **Si**, 16.0–18.0 **Cr**, 11.00–14.00 **Ni**, 2.00–3.00 **Mo**, 0.030 **P**, 0.030 **S**	**Solution annealed and quenched**: (>8) **diam**, (520) **TS**, (205) **YS**, 35 **El**

WROUGHT STAINLESS STEELS

specification number	designation	country	product forms	composition	mechanical properties (see page iv for explanation)
ANSI/ASTM A 376	TP 304H	US	Pipe: seamless	0.04–0.10 **C**, 2.00 **Mn**, 0.75 **Si**, 18.0–20.0 **Cr**, 8.00–11.0 **Ni**, 0.040 **P**, 0.030 **S**	**Solution annealed**: 0.312 (7.94) **diam**, 75 (520) **TS**, 30 (210) **YS**, 35 **El**
ANSI/ASTM A 376	TP 316H	US	Pipe: seamless	0.04–0.10 **C**, 2.00 **Mn**, 0.75 **Si**, 16.0–18.0 **Cr**, 11.0–14.0 **Ni**, 2.00–3.00 **Mo**, 0.040 **P**, 0.030 **S**	**Solution annealed**: 0.312 (7.94) **diam**, 75 (520) **TS**, 30 (210) **YS**, 35 **El**
ANSI/ASTM A 376	TP 321H	US	Pipe: seamless	0.04–0.10 **C**, 2.00 **Mn**, 0.75 **Si**, 17.0–20.0 **Cr**, 9.00–13.0 **Ni**, 0.040 **P**, 0.030 **S**, 4 x C–0.60 **Ti**	**Solution annealed**: 0.312 (7.94) **diam**, 75 (520) **TS**, 30 (210) **YS**, 35 **El**
ANSI/ASTM A 376	TP 347H	US	Pipe: seamless	0.04–0.10 **C**, 2.00 **Mn**, 0.75 **Si**, 17.0–20.0 **Cr**, 9.00–13.0 **Ni**, 8 x C–1.00 **Nb+Ta**, 0.040 **P**, 0.030 **S**	**Solution annealed**: 0.312 (7.94) **diam**, 75 (520) **TS**, 30 (210) **YS**, 35 **El**
JIS G 3459	SUS 304 HTP	Japan	Pipe: seamless or welded	0.04–0.10 **C**, 2.00 **Mn**, 0.75 **Si**, 18.00–20.00 **Cr**, 8.00–11.00 **Ni**, 0.040 **P**, 0.030 **S**	**Solution annealed**: (≥8) **diam**, (520) **TS**, (206) **YS**, 35 **El**
JIS G 3459	SUS 321 HTP	Japan	Pipe: seamless or welded	0.04–0.10 **C**, 2.00 **Mn**, 0.75 **Si**, 17.00–20.00 **Cr**, 9.00–13.00 **Ni**, 0.030 **P**, 0.030 **S**, 4 x C–0.60 **Ti**	**Solution annealed**: (≥8) **diam**, (520) **TS**, (206) **YS**, 35 **El**
JIS G 3459	SUS 316 HTP	Japan	Pipe: seamless or welded	0.04–0.10 **C**, 2.00 **Mn**, 0.75 **Si**, 16.00–18.00 **Cr**, 11.00–14.00 **Ni**, 2.00–3.00 **Mo**, 0.030 **P**, 0.030 **S**	**Solution annealed**: (≥8) **diam**, (520) **TS**, (206) **YS**, 35 **El**
JIS G 3459	SUS 347 HTP	Japan	Pipe: seamless or welded	0.04–0.10 **C**, 2.00 **Mn**, 1.00 **Si**, 17.00–20.00 **Cr**, 9.00–13.00 **Ni**, 8xC–1.00 **Nb+Ta**, 0.030 **P**, 0.030 **S**	**Solution annealed**: (≥8) **diam**, (520) **TS**, (206) **YS**, 35 **El**
JIS G 3463	SUS 304 HTB	Japan	Tube: seamless or welded	0.04–0.10 **C**, 2.00 **Mn**, 0.75 **Si**, 18.00–20.00 **Cr**, 8.00–11.00 **Ni**, 0.040 **P**, 0.030 **S**	**Solution annealed**: (≥8) **diam**, (520) **TS**, (206) **YS**, 35 **El**
JIS G 3463	SUS 321 HTB	Japan	Tube: seamless or welded	0.04–0.10 **C**, 2.00 **Mn**, 0.75 **Si**, 17.00–20.00 **Cr**, 9.00–13.00 **Ni**, 0.030 **P**, 0.030 **S**, 4 x C–0.60 **Ti**	**Solution annealed**: (≥8) **diam**, (520) **TS**, (206) **YS**, 35 **El**
JIS G 3463	SUS 316 HTB	Japan	Tube: seamless or welded	0.04–0.10 **C**, 2.00 **Mn**, 0.75 **Si**, 16.00–18.00 **Cr**, 11.00–14.00 **Ni**, 2.00–3.00 **Mo**, 0.030 **P**, 0.030 **S**	**Solution annealed**: (≥8) **diam**, (520) **TS**, (206) **YS**, 35 **El**
JIS G 3463	SUS 347 HTB	Japan	Tube: seamless or welded	0.04–0.10 **C**, 2.00 **Mn**, 1.00 **Si**, 17.00–20.00 **Cr**, 9.00–13.00 **Ni**, 8xC–1.00 **Nb+Ta**, 0.030 **P**, 0.030 **S**	**Solution annealed**: (≥8) **diam**, (520) **TS**, (206) **YS**, 35 **El**
JIS G 3214	SUS F 304 H	Japan	Forgings	0.04–0.10 **C**, 2.00 **Mn**, 1.00 **Si**, 18.00–20.00 **Cr**, 8.00–11.00 **Ni**, 0.040 **P**, 0.030 **S**	**Solution annealed**: (≤130) **diam**, (520) **TS**, (206) **YS**, 45 **El**
JIS G 3214	SUS F 316 H	Japan	Forgings	0.04–0.10 **C**, 2.00 **Mn**, 1.00 **Si**, 16.00–18.00 **Cr**, 11.00–14.00 **Ni**, 2.00–3.00 **Mo**, 0.040 **P**, 0.030 **S**	**Solution annealed**: (≤130) **diam**, (520) **TS**, (206) **YS**, 45 **El**
JIS G 3214	SUS F 321 H	Japan	Forgings	0.04–0.10 **C**, 2.00 **Mn**, 1.00 **Si**, 17.00–20.00 **Cr**, 9.00–13.00 **Ni**, 0.030 **P**, 0.030 **S**, 4 x C–0.60 **Ti**	**Solution annealed**: (≤130) **diam**, (520) **TS**, (206) **YS**, 45 **El**
JIS G 3214	SUS F 347 H	Japan	Forgings	0.04–0.10 **C**, 2.00 **Mn**, 1.00 **Si**, 17.00–20.00 **Cr**, 9.00–13.00 **Ni**, 8 x C–1.00 **Nb+Ta**, 0.030 **P**, 0.030 **S**	**Solution annealed**: (≤130) **diam**, (520) **TS**, (206) **YS**, 45 **El**
DGN–B–218	Grade TP304H	Mexico	Tube: welded	0.04–0.10 **C**, 2.00 **Mn**, 0.75 **Si**, 18.0–20.0 **Cr**, 8.0–11.0 **Ni**, 0.040 **P**, 0.030 **S**	**Cold finished and solution annealed**: (≥7.92) **diam**, (519) **TS**, (206) **YS**, 35 **El**
DGN–B–218	Grade TP316H	Mexico	Tube: welded	0.04–0.10 **C**, 2.00 **Mn**, 0.75 **Si**, 16.0–18.0 **Cr**, 11.0–14.0 **Ni**, 2.00–3.00 **Mo**, 0.040 **P**, 0.030 **S**	**Cold finished and solution annealed**: (≥7.92) **diam**, (519) **TS**, (206) **YS**, 35 **El**
DGN–B–218	Grade TP321H	Mexico	Tube: welded	0.04–0.10 **C**, 2.00 **Mn**, 0.75 **Si**, 17.0–20.0 **Cr**, 9.0–13.0 **Ni**, 0.030 **P**, 0.030 **S**, 4 x C–0.60 **Ti**	**Cold finished and solution annealed**: (≥7.92) **diam**, (519) **TS**, (206) **YS**, 35 **El**
DGN–B–218	Grade TP347H	Mexico	Tube: welded	0.04–0.10 **C**, 2.00 **Mn**, 0.75 **Si**, 17.0–20.0 **Cr**, 9.0–13.0 **Ni**, 8 x C–1.0 **Cb+Ta**, 0.040 **P**, 0.030 **S**	**Cold finished and solution annealed**: (≥7.92) **diam**, (519) **TS**, (206) **YS**, 35 **El**
DGN–B–218	Grade TP348H	Mexico	Tube: welded	0.04–0.10 **C**, 2.00 **Mn**, 0.75 **Si**, 17.0–20.0 **Cr**, 9.0–13.0 **Ni**, 8 x C–1.0 **Cb+Ta**, 0.040 **P**, 0.030 **S**, 0.10 **Ta**	**Cold finished and solution annealed**: (≥7.92) **diam**, (519) **TS**, (206) **YS**, 35 **El**
DGN–B–196	Grade TP 347H	Mexico	Tube: seamless	0.04–0.10 **C**, 2.00 **Mn**, 0.75 **Si**, 17.0–20.0 **Cr**, 9.0–13.0 **Ni**, 8 x C–1.0 **Cb+Ta**, 0.040 **P**, 0.030 **S**	**Hot or cold finished**: (8) **diam**, (519) **TS**, (206) **YS**, 35 **El**
DGN–B–196	Grade TP 321H	Mexico	Tube: seamless	0.04–0.10 **C**, 2.00 **Mn**, 0.75 **Si**, 17.0–20.0 **Cr**, 9.0–13.0 **Ni**, 0.040 **P**, 0.030 **S**, 4 x C–0.60 **Ti**	**Hot or cold finished**: (8) **diam**, (519) **TS**, (206) **YS**, 35 **El**

specification number	designation	country	product forms	composition	mechanical properties (see page iv for explanation)
DGN–B–196	Grade TP 304H	Mexico	Tube: seamless	0.04–0.10 **C**, 2.00 **Mn**, 0.75 **Si**, 18.0–20.0 **Cr**, 8.0–11.0 **Ni**, 0.040 **P**, 0.030 **S**	**Hot or cold finished**: (8) **diam**, (519) **TS**, (206) **YS**, 35 **El**
DGN–B–186	Grade TP347H	Mexico	Pipe: seamless	0.04–0.10 **C**, 2.00 **Mn**, 0.75 **Si**, 17.0–20.0 **Cr**, 9.0–13.0 **Ni**, 10 x C–1.00 **Cb+Ta**, 0.030 **P**, 0.030 **S**	**Hot or cold finished and solution treated**: (8) **diam**, (519) **TS**, (206) **YS**, 35 **El**
DGN–B–186	Grade TP321H	Mexico	Pipe: seamless	0.04–0.10 **C**, 2.00 **Mn**, 0.75 **Si**, 17.0–20.0 **Cr**, 9.0–13.0 **Ni**, 0.030 **P**, 0.030 **S**, 4 x C–0.60 **Ti**	**Hot or cold finished and quenched or tempered**: (8) **diam**, (519) **TS**, (206) **YS**, 35 **El**
DGN–B–186	Grade TP304H	Mexico	Pipe: seamless	0.04–0.10 **C**, 2.00 **Mn**, 0.75 **Si**, 18.0–20.0 **Cr**, 8.0–11.0 **Ni**, 0.030 **P**, 0.030 **S**	**Hot or cold finished and solution treated**: (8) **diam**, (519) **TS**, (206) **YS**, 35 **El**
DGN–B–186	Grade TP316H	Mexico	Pipe: seamless	0.04–0.10 **C**, 2.00 **Mn**, 0.75 **Si**, 16.0–18.0 **Cr**, 11.0–14.0 **Ni**, 2.00–3.00 **Mo**, 0.030 **P**, 0.030 **S**	**Hot or cold finished and solution treated**: (8) **diam**, (519) **TS**, (206) **YS**, 35 **El**
DGN–B–185	Grade TP304H	Mexico	Pipe: seamless, welded	0.04–0.10 **C**, 2.00 **Mn**, 0.75 **Si**, 18.0–20.0 **Cr**, 8.00–11.00 **Ni**, 0.040 **P**, 0.030 **S**	**Hot rolled and solution annealed**: (≥8) **diam**, (519) **TS**, (206) **YS**, 35 **El**
DGN–B–185	Grade TP316H	Mexico	Pipe: seamless, welded	0.04–0.10 **C**, 2.00 **Mn**, 0.75 **Si**, 16.0–18.0 **Cr**, 11.0–14.0 **Ni**, 2.0–3.0 **Mo**, 0.040 **P**, 0.030 **S**	**Hot rolled and solution annealed**: (≥8) **diam**, (519) **TS**, (206) **YS**, 35 **El**
DGN–B–185	Grade TP321H	Mexico	Pipe: seamless, welded	0.04–0.10 **C**, 2.00 **Mn**, 0.75 **Si**, 17.0–20.0 **Cr**, 9.0–13.0 **Ni**, 0.040 **P**, 0.030 **S**, 4 x C–0.60 **Ti**	**Hot rolled and solution annealed**: (≥8) **diam**, (519) **TS**, (206) **YS**, 35 **El**
DGN–B–185	Grade TP347H	Mexico	Pipe: seamless, welded	0.04–0.10 **C**, 2.00 **Mn**, 0.75 **Si**, 17.0–20.0 **Cr**, 9.0–13.0 **Ni**, 8 x C–1.00 **Cb+Ta**, 0.040 **P**, 0.030 **S**	**Hot rolled or solution annealed**: (≥8) **diam**, (519) **TS**, (206) **YS**, 35 **El**
DGN–B–185	Grade TP348H	Mexico	Pipe: seamless, welded	0.04–0.10 **C**, 2.00 **Mn**, 0.75 **Si**, 17.0–20.0 **Cr**, 9.0–13.0 **Ni**, 8 x C–1.00 **Cb+Ta**, 0.040 **P**, 0.030 **S**, 0.10 **Ta**	**Hot rolled and solution annealed**: (≥8) **diam**, (519) **TS**, (206) **YS**, 35 **El**
NOM–B–194	Grade TP 321H	Mexico	Tube: seamless	0.04–0.10 **C**, 2.00 **Mn**, 0.75 **Si**, 17.0–20.0 **Cr**, 9.00–13.0 **Ni**, 0.040 **P**, 0.030 **S**, 4 x C–0.60 **Ti**	**Hot or cold finished and solution annealed**: (0.38–12.7) **diam**, (517) **TS**, (207) **YS**
NOM–B–194	Grade TP 347H	Mexico	Tube: seamless	0.04–0.10 **C**, 2.00 **Mn**, 0.75 **Si**, 17.0–20.0 **Cr**, 9.00–13.0 **Ni**, 0.040 **P**, 0.030 **S**	**Hot or cold finished and solution annealed**: (0.38–12.7) **diam**, (517) **TS**, (207) **YS**
NOM–B–194	Grade TP 348H	Mexico	Tube: seamless	0.04–0.10 **C**, 2.00 **Mn**, 0.75 **Si**, 17.0–20.0 **Cr**, 9.00–13.0 **Ni**, 8 x C–1 **Cb+Ta**, 0.040 **P**, 0.030 **S**, 0.10 **Ta**	**Hot or cold finished and solution annealed**: (0.38–12.7) **diam**, (517) **TS**, (207) **YS**
NOM–B–194	Grade TP 316H	Mexico	Tube: seamless	0.040–0.10 **C**, 2.00 **Mn**, 0.75 **Si**, 16.0–18.0 **Cr**, 11.00–14.0 **Ni**, 2.00–3.0 **Mo**, 0.040 **P**, 0.030 **S**	**Hot or cold finished and solution annealed**: (0.38–12.7) **diam**, (517) **TS**, (207) **YS**
NOM–B–194	Grade TP 304H	Mexico	Tube: seamless	0.04–0.10 **C**, 2.00 **Mn**, 0.75 **Si**, 18.0–20.0 **Cr**, 8.00–11.0 **Ni**, 0.040 **P**, 0.030 **S**	**Hot or cold finished and solution annealed**: (0.38–12.7) **diam**, (517) **TS**, (207) **YS**
ANSI/ASTM A 452	TP 304H	US	Pipe:cold-wrought (centrifugally cast)	0.04–0.10 **C**, 2.00 **Mn**, 0.75 **Si**, 18.0–20.0 **Cr**, 8.00–11.0 **Ni**, 0.040 **P**, 0.030 **S**	**Solution annealed**: 8 (203) OD **diam**, 75 (517) **TS**, 30 (217) **YS**, 45 **El**
ANSI/ASTM A 452	TP 347H	US	Pipe: cold-wrought (centrifugally cast)	0.04–0.10 **C**, 2.00 **Mn**, 0.75 **Si**, 17.0–20.0 **Cr**, 9.00–13.0 **Ni**, 8 x C–1.00 **Nb+Ta**, 0.040 **P**, 0.030 **S**	**Solution annealed**: 8 (203) OD **diam**, 75 (517) **TS**, 30 (207) **YS**, 45 **El**
ANSI/ASTM A 452	TP 316H	US	Pipe: cold-wrought (centrifugally cast)	0.04–0.10 **C**, 2.00 **Mn**, 0.75 **Si**, 16.0–18.0 **Cr**, 11.0–14.0 **Ni**, 2.00–3.00 **Mo**, 0.040 **P**, 0.030 **S**	**Solution annealed**: 8 (203) OD **diam**, 75 (517) **TS**, 30 (207) **YS**, 45 **El**
ANSI/ASTM A 312	TP 304H	US	Pipe: seamless or welded	0.04–0.10 **C**, 2.00 **Mn**, 0.75 **Si**, 18.0–20.0 **Cr**, 8.00–11.00 **Ni**, 0.040 **P**, 0.030 **S**	**Solution annealed**: 0.31 (7.94) **diam**, 75 (517) **TS**, 30 (207) **YS**, 35 **El**
ANSI/ASTM A 312	TP 316H	US	Pipe: seamless or welded	0.04–0.10 **C**, 2.00 **Mn**, 0.75 **Si**, 16.0–18.0 **Cr**, 11.0–14.0 **Ni**, 2.00–3.00 **Mo**, 0.040 **P**, 0.030 **S**	**Solution annealed**: 0.31 (7.94) **diam**, 75 (517) **TS**, 30 (207) **YS**, 35 **El**
ANSI/ASTM A 312	TP 321H	US	Pipe: seamless or welded	0.04–0.10 **C**, 2.00 **Mn**, 0.75 **Si**, 17.0–20.0 **Cr**, 9.00–13.0 **Ni**, 0.040 **P**, 0.030 **S**, 4 x C–0.60 **Ti**	**Solution annealed**: 0.31 (7.94) **diam**, 75 (517) **TS**, 30 (207) **YS**, 35 **El**
ANSI/ASTM A 312	TP 347H	US	Pipe: seamless or welded	0.04–0.10 **C**, 2.00 **Mn**, 0.75 **Si**, 17.0–20.0 **Cr**, 9.00–13.0 **Ni**, 8 x C–1.0 **Nb+Ta**, 0.040 **P**, 0.030 **S**	**Solution annealed**: 0.31 (7.94) **diam**, 75 (517) **TS**, 30 (207) **YS**, 35 **El**

WROUGHT STAINLESS STEELS

specification number	designation	country	product forms	composition	mechanical properties (see page iv for explanation)
ANSI/ASTM A 312	TP 348H	US	Pipe: seamless or welded	0.04–0.10 **C**, 2.00 **Mn**, 0.75 **Si**, 17.0–20.0 **Cr**, 9.00–13.0 **Ni**, 8 x C–1.0 **Nb+Ta**, 0.040 **P**, 0.030 **S**, 0.10 **Ta**	**Solution annealed**: 0.31 (7.94) **diam**, 75 (517) **TS**, 30 (207) **YS**, 35 **El**
ANSI/ASTM A 271	TP 304H	US	Tube: seamless	0.04–0.10 **C**, 2.00 **Mn**, 0.75 **Si**, 18.0–20.0 **Cr**, 8.00–11.0 **Ni**, 0.040 **P**, 0.030 **S**	**Solution annealed**: 0.31 (7.94) **diam**, 75 (517) **TS**, 30 (207) **YS**, 35 **El**
ANSI/ASTM A 271	TP 321H	US	Tube: seamless	0.04–0.10 **C**, 2.00 **Mn**, 0.75 **Si**, 17.0–20.0 **Cr**, 9.00–13.0 **Ni**, 0.040 **P**, 0.030 **S**, 4 x C–0.60 **Ti**	**Solution annealed**: 0.31 (7.94) **diam**, 75 (517) **TS**, 30 (207) **YS**, 35 **El**
ANSI/ASTM A 271	TP 347H	US	Tube: seamless	0.04–0.10 **C**, 2.00 **Mn**, 0.75 **Si**, 17.0–20.0 **Cr**, 9.00–13.0 **Ni**, 0.040 **P**, 0.030 **S**, 8 x C–1.0 **Ta+Nb**	**Solution annealed**: 0.31 (7.94) **diam**, 75 (517) **TS**, 30 (207) **YS**, 35 **El**
ANSI/ASTM A 213	TP 304H	US	Tube: seamless	0.04–0.10 **C**, 2.00 **Mn**, 0.75 **Si**, 18.0–20.0 **Cr**, 8.00–11.0 **Ni**, 0.040 **P**, 0.030 **S**	**Solution annealed**: 0.312 (7.94) **diam**, 75 (517) **TS**, 30 (207) **YS**, 35 **El**
ANSI/ASTM A 213	TP 316H	US	Tube: seamless	0.04–0.10 **C**, 2.00 **Mn**, 0.75 **Si**, 16.0–18.0 **Cr**, 11.0–14.0 **Ni**, 2.00–3.00 **Mo**, 0.040 **P**, 0.030 **S**	**Solution annealed**: 0.312 (7.94) **diam**, 75 (517) **TS**, 30 (207) **YS**, 35 **El**
ANSI/ASTM A 213	TP 321H	US	Tube: seamless	0.04–0.10 **C**, 2.00 **Mn**, 0.75 **Si**, 17.0–20.0 **Cr**, 9.00–13.0 **Ni**, 0.040 **P**, 0.030 **S**, 4 x C–0.60 **Ti**	**Solution annealed**: 0.312 (7.94) **diam**, 75 (517) **TS**, 30 (207) **YS**, 35 **El**
ANSI/ASTM A 213	TP 347H	US	Tube: seamless	0.04–0.10 **C**, 2.00 **Mn**, 0.75 **Si**, 17.0–20.0 **Cr**, 9.00–13.0 **Ni**, 0.040 **P**, 0.030 **S**, 8 x C–1.0 **Ta+Nb**	**Solution annealed**: 0.312 (7.94) **diam**, 75 (517) **TS**, 30 (207) **YS**, 35 **El**
ANSI/ASTM A 213	TP 348H	US	Tube: seamless	0.04–0.10 **C**, 2.00 **Mn**, 0.75 **Si**, 17.0–20.0 **Cr**, 9.00–13.0 **Ni**, 0.040 **P**, 0.030 **S**, 0.10 **Ta**, 8 x C–1.0 **Ta+Nb**	**Solution annealed**: 0.312 (7.94) **diam**, 75 (517) **TS**, 30 (207) **YS**, 35 **El**
ANSI/ASTM A 479	321H	US	Bar, shapes	0.04–0.10 **C**, 2.00 **Mn**, 1.00 **Si**, 17.00–19.00 **Cr**, 9.00–12.00 **Ni**, 0.040 **P**, 0.030 **S**, 4 x C–0.70 **Ti**	**Solution annealed**: all **diam**, 75 (515) **TS**, 30 (205) **YS**, 30 **El**
ANSI/ASTM A 479	347H	US	Bar, shapes	0.04–0.10 **C**, 2.00 **Mn**, 1.00 **Si**, 17.00–19.00 **Cr**, 9.00–13.00 **Ni**, 8 x C–1.00 **Nb**, 0.040 **P**, 0.030 **S**	**Solution annealed**: all **diam**, 75 (515) **TS**, 30 (205) **YS**, 30 **El**
ANSI/ASTM A 479	348H	US	Bar, shapes	0.04–0.10 **C**, 2.00 **Mn**, 1.00 **Si**, 17.00–19.00 **Cr**, 0.20 **Co**, 8 x C–1.00 **Nb**, 0.040 **P**, 0.030 **S**	**Solution annealed**: all **diam**, 75 (515) **TS**, 30 (205) **YS**, 30 **El**
ANSI/ASTM A 479	304H	US	Bar, shapes	0.04–0.10 **C**, 2.00 **Mn**, 1.00 **Si**, 18.00–20.00 **Cr**, 8.00–10.50 **Ni**, 0.040 **P**, 0.030 **S**	**Solution annealed**: all **diam**, 75 (515) **TS**, 30 (205) **YS**, 30 **El**
ANSI/ASTM A 479	316H	US	Bar, shapes	0.04–0.10 **C**, 2.00 **Mn**, 1.00 **Si**, 16.00–18.00 **Cr**, 10.00–14.00 **Ni**, 2.00–3.00 **Mo**, 0.040 **P**, 0.030 **S**	**Solution annealed**: all **diam**, 75 (515) **TS**, 30 (205) **YS**, 30 **El**
COPANT R 195	TP 321H	COPANT	Tube	0.04–0.10 **C**, 2.00 **Mn**, 0.75 **Si**, 17.0–20.0 **Cr**, 9.0–13.0 **Ni**, 0.040 **P**, 0.030 **S**, 4 x C–0.60 **Ti**	**Hot or cold finished**: (≥5.65) **diam**, (515) **TS**, (205) **YS**, 35 **El**
COPANT R 195	TP 304H	COPANT	Tube	0.04–0.10 **C**, 2.00 **Mn**, 0.75 **Si**, 18.0–20.0 **Cr**, 8.0–11.0 **Ni**, 0.040 **P**, 0.030 **S**	**Hot or cold finished**: (≥5.65) **diam**, (515) **TS**, (205) **YS**, 35 **El**
COPANT R 195	TP 347H	COPANT	Tube	0.04–0.10 **C**, 2.00 **Mn**, 0.75 **Si**, 17.0–19.0 **Cr**, 9.0–13.0 **Ni**, 8 x C–1.0 **Cb+Ta**, 0.040 **P**, 0.030 **S**	**Hot or cold finished**: (≥5.65) **diam**, (515) **TS**, (205) **YS**, 35 **El**
ASTM A 240	Type 348H	US	Plate, sheet, strip	0.04–0.10 **C**, 2.00 **Mn**, 1.00 **Si**, 17.00–19.00 **Cr**, 9.00–13.00 **Ni**, 8 x C–1.00 **Cb+Ta**, 0.20 **Co**, 0.045 **P**, 0.030 **S**, 0.10 **Ta**	**Solution annealed, hot rolled or cold rolled**: all **diam**, 75 (515) **TS**, 30 (205) **YS**, 40 **El**
ASTM A 240	Type 347H	US	Plate, sheet, strip	0.04–0.10 **C**, 2.00 **Mn**, 1.00 **Si**, 17.00–19.00 **Cr**, 9.00–13.00 **Ni**, 8 x C–1.00 **Cb+Ta**, 0.045 **P**, 0.030 **S**	**Solution annealed, hot rolled or cold rolled**: all **diam**, 75 (515) **TS**, 30 (205) **YS**, 40 **El**
ASTM A 240	Type 321H	US	Plate, sheet, strip	0.04–0.10 **C**, 2.00 **Mn**, 1.00 **Si**, 17.00–19.00 **Cr**, 9.00–12.00 **Ni**, 0.045 **P**, 0.030 **S**, 4 x C–0.70 **Ti**	**Solution annealed, hot rolled or cold rolled**: all **diam**, 75 (515) **TS**, 30 (205) **YS**, 40 **El**
ASTM A 240	Type 316H	US	Plate, sheet, strip	0.04–0.10 **C**, 2.00 **Mn**, 1.00 **Si**, 16.00–18.00 **Cr**, 10.00–14.00 **Ni**, 2.00–3.00 **Mo**, 0.045 **P**, 0.030 **S**	**Solution annealed, hot rolled or cold rolled**: all **diam**, 75 (515) **TS**, 30 (205) **YS**, 40 **El**
ASTM A 240	Type 304H	US	Plate, sheet, strip	0.04–0.10 **C**, 2.00 **Mn**, 1.00 **Si**, 18.00–20.00 **Cr**, 8.00–10.50 **Ni**, 0.045 **P**, 0.030 **S**	**Solution annealed, hot rolled or cold rolled**: all **diam**, 75 (515) **TS**, 30 (205) **YS**, 40 **El**

specification number	designation	country	product forms	composition	mechanical properties (see page iv for explanation)
ANSI/ASTM A 479	Grade 304H	US	Bar, shapes	0.04–0.10 **C**, 2.00 **Mn**, 1.00 **Si**, 18.00–20.00 **Cr**, 8.00–10.50 **Ni**, 0.040 **P**, 0.030 **S**	**Solution annealed**: all **diam**, (515) **TS**, (205) **YS**, 30 **El**
ANSI/ASTM A 479	Grade 316H	US	Bar, shapes	0.04–0.10 **C**, 2.00 **Mn**, 1.00 **Si**, 16.00–18.00 **Cr**, 10.00–14.00 **Ni**, 2.00–3.00 **Mo**, 0.040 **P**, 0.030 **S**	**Solution annealed**: all **diam**, (515) **TS**, (205) **YS**, 30 **El**
ANSI/ASTM A 240	Grade 304H	US	Plate, sheet, strip	0.04–0.10 **C**, 2.00 **Mn**, 1.00 **Si**, 18.00–20.00 **Cr**, 8.00–10.50 **Ni**, 0.045 **P**, 0.030 **S**	**Solution annealed**: all **diam**, (515) **TS**, (205) **YS**, 40 **El**
ANSI/ASTM A 240	Grade 316H	US	Plate, sheet, strip	0.04–0.10 **C**, 2.00 **Mn**, 1.00 **Si**, 16.00–18.00 **Cr**, 10.00–14.00 **Ni**, 2.00–3.00 **Mo**, 0.045 **P**, 0.030 **S**	**Solution annealed**: all **diam**, (515) **TS**, (205) **YS**, 40 **El**
ANSI/ASTM A 240	Grade 348H	US	Plate, sheet, strip	0.04–0.10 **C**, 2.00 **Mn**, 1.00 **Si**, 17.00–19.00 **Cr**, 9.00–13.00 **Ni**, 8 x C–1.00 **Cb+Ta**, 0.20 **Co**, 0.045 **P**, 0.030 **S**, 0.10 **Ta**	**Solution annealed**: all **diam**, (515) **TS**, (205) **YS**, 40 **El**
ANSI/ASTM A 240	Grade 347H	US	Plate, sheet, strip	0.04–0.10 **C**, 2.00 **Mn**, 1.00 **Si**, 17.00–19.00 **Cr**, 9.00–13.00 **Ni**, 8 x C–1.00 **Cb+Ta**, 0.045 **P**, 0.030 **S**	**Solution annealed**: all **diam**, (515) **TS**, (205) **YS**, 40 **El**
ANSI/ASTM A 240	Grade 321H	US	Plate, sheet, strip	0.04–0.10 **C**, 2.00 **Mn**, 1.00 **Si**, 17.00–19.00 **Cr**, 9.00–12.00 **Ni**, 0.045 **P**, 0.030 **S**, 4 x C–0.70 **Ti**	**Solution annealed**: all **diam**, (515) **TS**, (205) **YS**, 40 **El**
ANSI/ASTM A 479	Grade 321H	US	Bar, shapes	0.04–0.10 **C**, 2.00 **Mn**, 1.00 **Si**, 17.00–19.00 **Cr**, 9.00–12.00 **Ni**, 0.040 **P**, 0.030 **S**, 4 x C–0.70 **Ti**	**Solution annealed**: all **diam**, (515) **TS**, (205) **YS**, 30 **El**
ANSI/ASTM A 479	Grade 348H	US	Bar, shapes	0.04–0.10 **C**, 2.00 **Mn**, 1.00 **Si**, 17.00–19.00 **Cr**, 8 x C–1.00 **Cb**, 0.20 **Co**, 0.040 **P**, 0.030 **S**	**Solution annealed**: all **diam**, (515) **TS**, (205) **YS**, 30 **El**
ANSI/ASTM A 479	Grade 347H	US	Bar, shapes	0.04–0.10 **C**, 2.00 **Mn**, 1.00 **Si**, 17.00–19.00 **Cr**, 9.00–13.00 **Ni**, 8 x C–1.00 **Cb**, 0.040 **P**, 0.030 **S**	**Solution annealed**: all **diam**, (515) **TS**, (205) **YS**, 30 **El**
ANSI/ASTM A 249	TP 304H	US	Tube: welded	0.04–0.10 **C**, 2.00 **Mn**, 0.75 **Si**, 18.0–20.0 **Cr**, 8.00–11.0 **Ni**, 0.040 **P**, 0.030 **S**	**Solution annealed**: 0.312 (7.94) **diam**, 75 (515) **TS**, 30 (205) **YS**, 35 **El**
ANSI/ASTM A 249	TP 316H	US	Tube: welded	0.04–0.10 **C**, 2.00 **Mn**, 0.75 **Si**, 16.0–18.0 **Cr**, 11.0–14.0 **Ni**, 2.00–3.00 **Mo**, 0.040 **P**, 0.030 **S**	**Solution annealed**: 0.312 (7.94) **diam**, 75 (515) **TS**, 30 (205) **YS**, 35 **El**
ANSI/ASTM A 249	TP 347H	US	Tube: welded	0.04–0.10 **C**, 2.00 **Mn**, 0.75 **Si**, 17.0–20.0 **Cr**, 9.00–13.0 **Ni**, 0.040 **P**, 0.030 **S**, 8 x C–1.0 **Ta+Nb**	**Solution annealed**: 0.312 (7.94) **diam**, 75 (515) **TS**, 30 (205) **YS**, 35 **El**
ANSI/ASTM A 249	TP 348H	US	Tube: welded	0.04–0.10 **C**, 2.00 **Mn**, 0.75 **Si**, 17.0–20.0 **Cr**, 9.00–13.00 **Ni**, 0.040 **P**, 0.030 **S**, 0.10 **Ta**, 8 x C–1.0 **Ta+Nb**	**Solution annealed**: 0.312 (7.94) **diam**, 75 (515) **TS**, 30 (205) **YS**, 35 **El**
ISO 2604/1	F54B	ISO	Forgings	0.04–0.10 **C**, 2.00 **Mn**, 1.00 **Si**, 17.00–19.00 **Cr**, 9.00–13.00 **Ni**, 0.045 **P**, 0.030 **S**, 5 x C–0.80 **Ti**	**Quenched**: all **diam**, (510) **TS**, (195) **YS**, 30 **El**
ISO 2604/II	TS 56	ISO	Tube: seamless	0.04–0.10 **C**, 2.00 **Mn**, 0.20–0.80 **Si**, 16.00–20.00 **Cr**, 11.00–14.00 **Ni**, 10 x C–1.4 **Nb**, 0.045 **P**, 0.030 **S**	**Cold finished, quenched**: all **diam**, (510) **TS**, (205) **YS**, 30 **El**
ISO 2604/1	F56	ISO	Forgings	0.04–0.10 **C**, 2.00 **Mn**, 1.00 **Si**, 15.00–17.00 **Cr**, 12.00–14.00 **Ni**, 10 x C–1.20 **Nb**, 0.045 **P**, 0.030 **S**	**Quenched**: all **diam**, (490) **TS**, (205) **YS**, 30 **El**
ISO 2604/1	F54A	ISO	Forgings	0.04–0.10 **C**, 2.00 **Mn**, 1.00 **Si**, 17.00–19.00 **Cr**, 9.00–13.00 **Ni**, 0.045 **P**, 0.030 **S**, 5 x C–0.80 **Ti**	**Quenched**: all **diam**, (490) **TS**, (155) **YS**, 30 **El**
ISO 2604/1	F51	ISO	Forgings	0.04–0.10 **C**, 2.00 **Mn**, 1.00 **Si**, 17.00–19.00 **Cr**, 9.00–13.00 **Ni**, 10 x C–1.00 **Nb**, 0.045 **P**, 0.030 **S**	**Quenched**: all **diam**, (490) **TS**, (205) **YS**, 30 **El**
ISO 2604/II	TS 54	ISO	Tube: seamless	0.04–0.10 **C**, 2.00 **Mn**, 0.20–0.80 **Si**, 17.00–20.00 **Cr**, 9.00–13.00 **Ni**, 0.045 **P**, 0.030 **S**, 4 x C–0.60 **Ti**	**Quenched at 1070°C: all diam, (490) TS, (155) YS, 30 El; Quenched at 950°C: all diam, (510) TS, (195) YS, 30 El**
ISO 2604/IV	P56	ISO	Plate	0.04–0.10 **C**, 1.50 **Mn**, 0.30–0.60 **Si**, 15.0–17.0 **Cr**, 12.0–14.0 **Ni**, 10 x C–1.20 **Nb**, 0.045 **P**, 0.030 **S**	**Hot rolled, quenched**: (3–40) **diam**, (490) **TS**, (205) **YS**, 35 **El**
ANSI/ASTM A 430	FP 304	US	Pipe	0.04–0.10 **C**, 2.00 **Mn**, 0.75 **Si**, 18.0–20.0 **Cr**, 8.00–11.0 **Ni**, 0.040 **P**, 0.030 **S**	**Solution annealed**: all **diam**, 70 (483) **TS**, 30 (207) **YS**, 45 **El**

WROUGHT STAINLESS STEELS

specification number	designation	country	product forms	composition	mechanical properties (see page iv for explanation)
ANSI/ASTM A 430	FP 304H	US	Pipe	0.04–0.10 **C**, 2.00 **Mn**, 0.75 **Si**, 18.0–20.0 **Cr**, 8.00–11.0 **Ni**, 0.040 **P**, 0.030 **S**	**Solution annealed**: all **diam**, 70 (483) **TS**, 30 (207) **YS**, 45 **El**
ANSI/ASTM A 430	FP 316	US	Pipe	0.04–0.10 **C**, 2.00 **Mn**, 0.75 **Si**, 16.0–18.0 **Cr**, 11.0–14.0 **Ni**, 2.00–3.00 **Mo**, 0.040 **P**, 0.030 **S**	**Solution annealed**: all **diam**, 70 (483) **TS**, 30 (207) **YS**, 45 **El**
ANSI/ASTM A 430	FP 316H	US	Pipe	0.04–0.10 **C**, 2.00 **Mn**, 0.75 **Si**, 16.0–18.0 **Cr**, 11.0–14.0 **Ni**, 2.00–3.00 **Mo**, 0.040 **P**, 0.030 **S**	**Solution annealed**: all **diam**, 70 (483) **TS**, 30 (207) **YS**, 45 **El**
ANSI/ASTM A 430	FP 321	US	Pipe	0.04–0.10 **C**, 2.00 **Mn**, 0.75 **Si**, 17.0–20.0 **Cr**, 9.00–13.0 **Ni**, 0.040 **P**, 0.030 **S**, 4 x C–0.60 **Ti**	**Solution annealed**: all **diam**, 70 (483) **TS**, 30 (207) **YS**, 45 **El**
ANSI/ASTM A 430	FP 321H	US	Pipe	0.04–0.10 **C**, 2.00 **Mn**, 0.75 **Si**, 17.0–20.0 **Cr**, 9.00–13.0 **Ni**, 0.040 **P**, 0.030 **S**, 4 x C–0.60 **Ti**	**Solution annealed**: all **diam**, 70 (483) **TS**, 30 (207) **YS**, 45 **El**
ANSI/ASTM A 430	FP 347	US	Pipe	0.04–0.10 **C**, 2.00 **Mn**, 0.75 **Si**, 17.0–13.0 **Cr**, 9.00–13.0 **Ni**, 8 x C–1.00 **Nb**, 0.040 **P**, 0.030 **S**	**Solution annealed**: all **diam**, 70 (483) **TS**, 30 (207) **YS**, 45 **El**
ANSI/ASTM A 430	FP 347H	US	Pipe	0.04–0.10 **C**, 2.00 **Mn**, 0.75 **Si**, 17.0–20.0 **Cr**, 9.00–13.0 **Ni**, 8 x C–1.00 **Nb**, 0.040 **P**, 0.030 **S**	**Solution annealed**: all **diam**, 70 (483) **TS**, 30 (207) **YS**, 45 **El**
BS 3605 Section 3	Grade 321S59(1010)	UK	Pipe: seamless	0.04–0.09 **C**, 0.50–2.00 **Mn**, 0.20–1.00 **Si**, 17.0–19.0 **Cr**, 10.0–13.0 **Ni**, 0.040 **P**, 0.030 **S**, 5 x C–0.60 **Ti**	**Solution annealed (1010)**: all **diam**, (510) **TS**, (235) **YS**, 35 **El**
BS 3605 Section 3	Grade 347S59	UK	Pipe: seamless	0.04–0.09 **C**, 0.50–2.00 **Mn**, 0.20–1.00 **Si**, 17.0–19.0 **Cr**, 11.0–14.0 **Ni**, 10 x C–20 x C or 1.00 **Nb**, 0.040 **P**, 0.030 **S**	**Solution annealed**: all **diam**, (510) **TS**, (245) **YS**, 35 **El**
BS 3605 Section 3	Grade 316S59	UK	Pipe: seamless	0.04–0.09 **C**, 0.50–2.00 **Mn**, 0.20–1.00 **Si**, 16.0–18.0 **Cr**, 12.0–14.0 **Ni**, 2.0–2.75 **Mo**, 0.001–0.006 **B**, 0.040 **P**, 0.030 **S**	**Solution annealed**: all **diam**, (510) **TS**, (245) **YS**, 35 **El**
BS 3059	Steel 855	UK	Tube: seamless	0.04–0.09 **C**, 1.00–2.00 **Mn**, 0.25–0.75 **Si**, 16.0–17.5 **Cr**, 12.0–14.0 **Ni**, 2.00–2.75 **Mo**, 0.001–0.006 **B**, 0.040 **P**, 0.030 **S**	**Solution heat treated**: all **diam**, (510) **TS**, (185) **YS**, 30 **El**
BS 3059	Steel 832 Nb	UK	Tube: seamless	0.04–0.09 **C**, 0.50–2.00 **Mn**, 0.20–0.80 **Si**, 17.0–19.0 **Cr**, 11.0–13.0 **Ni**, 10 x C–1.10 **Nb**, 0.040 **P**, 0.030 **S**	**Solution heat treated**: all **diam**, (510) **TS**, (205) **YS**, 30 **El**
BS 3059	Steel 832 Ti	UK	Tube: seamless	0.04–0.09 **C**, 0.50–2.00 **Mn**, 0.20–0.80 **Si**, 17.0–20.0 **Cr**, 9.0–13.0 **Ni**, 0.040 **P**, 0.030 **S**, 4 x C min **Ti**	**Solution heat treated**: all **diam**, (510) **TS**, (165) **YS**, 30 **El**
BS 3059 Part 2	Grade 347S59	UK	Tube	0.04–0.09 **C**, 0.50–2.00 **Mn**, 0.20–1.00 **Si**, 17.0–19.0 **Cr**, 9.0–13.0 **Ni**, 8 x C–1.00 **Nb**, 0.040 **P**, 0.030 **S**	**Solution treated**: all **diam**, (510) **TS**, (245) **YS**, 30 **El**
BS 3059 Part 2	Grade 321S59 (1010)	UK	Tube	0.04–0.09 **C**, 0.50–2.00 **Mn**, 0.20–1.00 **Si**, 17.0–19.0 **Cr**, 9.0–13.0 **Ni**, 0.040 **P**, 0.030 **S**, 4 x C–0.60 **Ti**	**Solution treated**: all **diam**, (510) **TS**, (235) **YS**, 30 **El**
BS 3059 Part 2	Grade 316S59	UK	Tube	0.04–0.09 **C**, 0.50–2.00 **Mn**, 0.20–1.00 **Si**, 16.0–18.0 **Cr**, 11.0–14.0 **Ni**, 2.00–2.75 **Mo**, 0.040 **P**, 0.030 **S**	**Solution treated**: all **diam**, (510) **TS**, (245) **YS**, 30 **El**
ISO 2604/1	F64	ISO	Forgings	0.04–0.09 **C**, 2.00 **Mn**, 1.00 **Si**, 16.00–17.50 **Cr**, 10.00–14.00 **Ni**, 2.00–3.00 **Mo**, 0.045 **P**, 0.030 **S**	**Quenched**: all **diam**, (490) **TS**, (205) **YS**, 30 **El**
ISO 2604/1	F48	ISO	Forgings	0.04–0.09 **C**, 2.00 **Mn**, 1.00 **Si**, 17.00–19.00 **Cr**, 8.00–12.00 **Ni**, 0.045 **P**, 0.030 **S**	**Quenched**: all **diam**, (490) **TS**, (195) **YS**, 30 **El**
ISO 2604/II	TS 48	ISO	Tube: seamless	0.04–0.09 **C**, 2.00 **Mn**, 0.75 **Si**, 17.00–20.00 **Cr**, 8.00–12.00 **Ni**, 0.045 **P**, 0.030 **S**	**Cold finished, quenched**: all **diam**, (490) **TS**, (195) **YS**, 30 **El**
BS 3605 Section 3	Grade 304S59	UK	Pipe: seamless	0.04–0.09 **C**, 0.50–2.00 **Mn**, 0.20–1.00 **Si**, 17.0–19.0 **Cr**, 9.0–12.0 **Ni**, 0.040 **P**, 0.030 **S**	**Solution annealed**: all **diam**, (490) **TS**, (235) **YS**, 35 **El**
BS 3059 Part 2	Grade 321S59 (1105)	UK	Tube	0.04–0.09 **C**, 0.50–2.00 **Mn**, 0.20–1.00 **Si**, 17.0–19.0 **Cr**, 9.0–13.0 **Ni**, 0.040 **P**, 0.030 **S**, 4 x C–0.60 **Ti**	**Solution treated**: all **diam**, (490) **TS**, (195) **YS**, 30 **El**

WROUGHT STAINLESS STEELS

specification number	designation	country	product forms	composition	mechanical properties (see page iv for explanation)
BS 3059 Part 2	Grade 304S59	UK	Tube	0.04–0.09 **C**, 0.50–2.00 **Mn**, 0.20–1.00 **Si**, 17.0–19.0 **Cr**, 9.0–12.0 **Ni**, 0.040 **P**, 0.030 **S**	**Solution treated**: all **diam**, (490) **TS**, (235) **YS**, 30 **El**
BS 3604 Section 3	Grade 321559(1105)	UK	Pipe: seamless	0.04–0.09 **C**, 0.50–2.00 **Mn**, 0.20–1.00 **Si**, 17.0–19.0 **Cr**, 10.0–13.0 **Ni**, 0.040 **P**, 0.030 **S**, 5 x C – 0.60 **Ti**	**Solution annealed**: all **diam**, (490) **TS**, (195) **YS**, 35 **El**
ISO 683/XVI	8	ISO	Forgings, bar, plate, sheet, strip, wire	0.04–0.07 **C**, 0.80–1.80 **Mn**, 0.60 **Si**, 15.0–16.0 **Cr**, 5.00–5.80 **Ni**, 1.20–2.00 **Mo**, 1.40–2.10 **Cu**, 0.040 **P**, 0.030 **S**, 0.05–0.15 **Ti**	**Precipitation hardened (bar, forgings, wire, rod)**: all **diam**, (1180) **TS**, (980) **YS**, 6 **El**
BS S.533		UK	Sheet, strip: aircraft quality	0.04–0.07 **C**, 0.80–1.80 **Mn**, 0.60 **Si**, 15.3–16.0 **Cr**, 5.0–5.8 **Ni**, 1.20–2.00 **Mo**, 1.40–2.10 **Cu**, 0.035 **P**, 0.025 **S**, 0.05–0.15 **Ti**	**Solution annealed and precipitation heat treated**: (<1.5) **diam**, (1176) **TS**, (990) **YS**, 9 **El**
BS S.532		UK	Sheet,strip: aircraft quality	0.04–0.07 **C**, 0.80–1.80 **Mn**, 0.60 **Si**, 15.3–16.0 **Cr**, 5.0–5.8 **Ni**, 1.20–2.00 **Mo**, 1.40–2.10 **Cu**, 0.035 **P**, 0.025 **S**, 0.5–0.15 **Ti**	**Solution annealed and precipitation heat treated**: (≤1.5) **diam**, (985) **TS**, (805) **YS**, 12 **El**
ANSI/ASTM A 412	Type XM–11	US	Plate, sheet, strip	0.04 **C**, 8.00–10.00 **Mn**, 1.00 **Si**, 19.00–21.50 **Cr**, 5.50–7.50 **Ni**, 0.15–0.40 **N**, 0.060 **P**, 0.030 **S**	**Annealed (sheet, strip)**: 0.015 (0.38) **diam**, 100 (690) **TS**, 60 (415) **YS**, 40 **El**; **10% cold rolled**: 0.015 (0.38) **diam**, 130 (895) **TS**, 115 (795) **YS**, 15 **El**
AMS 5562		US	Tube	0.04 **C**, 8.00–10.00 **Mn**, 1.00 **Si**, 19.00–21.50 **Cr**, 5.50–7.50 **Ni**, 0.75 **Mo**, 0.50 **Cu**, 0.15–0.40 **N**, 0.060 **P**, 0.030 **S**	**Solution treated**: all **diam**, 100 (690) **TS**, 60 (414) **YS**, 45 **El**
AMS 5595B		US	Strip, sheet, plate	0.04 **C**, 8.00–10.00 **Mn**, 1.00 **Si**, 19.00–21.50 **Cr**, 5.50–7.50 **Ni**, 0.15–0.40 **N**, 0.060 **P**, 0.030 **S**	**Solution treated**: ≤0.1875 (≤4.762) **diam**, 100 (690) **TS**, 60 (414) **YS**, 40 **El**
AMS 5656A		US	Bar, forgings, rings, wire	0.04 **C**, 8.00–10.00 **Mn**, 1.00 **Si**, 19.00–21.50 **Cr**, 5.50–7.50 **Ni**, 0.060 **P**, 0.030 **S**	**Solution treated and descaled**: all **diam**, 90 (621) **TS**, 50 (345) **YS**, 40 **El**
ANSI/ASTM A 473	XM–11	US	Forgings	0.04 **C**, 8.00–10.00 **Mn**, 1.00 **Si**, 19.00–21.50 **Cr**, 5.50–7.50 **Ni**, 0.15–0.40 **N**, 0.060 **P**, 0.030 **S**	**Solution annealed**: all **diam**, 90 (620) **TS**, 50 (345) **YS**, 45 **El**
ANSI/ASTM A 312	TP XM–11	US	Pipe: seamless or welded	0.04 **C**, 8.00–10.00 **Mn**, 1.00 **Si**, 19.00–21.50 **Cr**, 5.50–7.50 **Ni**, 0.15–0.40 **N**, 0.040 **P**, 0.030 **S**	**Solution annealed**: 0.31 (7.94) **diam**, 90 (620) **TS**, 50 (345) **YS**, 35 **El**
ANSI/ASTM A 580	Grade XM–11	US	Wire	0.04 **C**, 8.00–10.00 **Mn**, 1.00 **Si**, 19.00–21.00 **Cr**, 5.50–7.50 **Ni**, 0.15–0.40 **N**, 0.060 **P**, 0.030 **S**	**Annealed**: all **diam**, 90 (620) **TS**, 50 (340) **YS**, 45 **El**
ANSI/ASTM A 632	TP 304L	US	Tube: seamless or welded	0.040 **C**, 2.00 **Mn**, 0.75 **Si**, 18.0–20.0 **Cr**, 8.0–13.0 **Ni**, 0.040 **P**, 0.030 **S**	**Solution annealed**: 0.005–0.065 (0.13–1.65) **diam**, 75 (517) **TS**, 30 (207) **YS**, 35 **El**
ANSI/ASTM A 632	TP 316L	US	Tube: seamless or welded	0.040 **C**, 2.00 **Mn**, 0.75 **Si**, 16.0–18.0 **Cr**, 10.0–15.0 **Ni**, 2.00–3.00 **Mo**, 0.040 **P**, 0.030 **S**	**Solution annealed**: 0.005–0.065 (0.13–1.65) **diam**, 75 (517) **TS**, 30 (207) **YS**, 35 **El**
ISO 2604/II	TS 63	ISO	Tube: seamless	0.04 **C**, 1.00–2.00 **Mn**, 0.75 **Si**, 16.00–18.00 **Cr**, 12.00–14.00 **Ni**, 2.00–2.75 **Mo**, 0.045 **P**, 0.030 **S**	**Cold finished, quenched**: all **diam**, (510) **TS**, (205) **YS**, 30 **El**
ISO 2604/II	TS 67	ISO	Tube: seamless	0.04 **C**, 1.00–1.50 **Mn**, 0.30–0.60 **Si**, 15.50–17.50 **Cr**, 15.50–17.50 **Ni**, 1.60–2.00 **Mo**, 10 x C–10 x C+0.4 **Nb**, 0.045 **P**, 0.030 **S**	**Cold finished, quenched**: all **diam**, (510) **TS**, (215) **YS**, 30 **El**
AIR 9113	Z3CN18	France	Bar, wire, tube, sheet	0.04 **C**, 2.0 **Mn**, 1.0 **Si**, 17.0–20.0 **Cr**, 9.0–12.0 **Ni**, 0.045 **P**, 0.03 **S**	**Quenched and tempered**: all **diam**, (440) **TS**, (170) **YS**, 47 **El**; **Partial anneal**: all **diam**, (690) **TS**, (490) **YS**, 23 **El**
ANSI/ASTM A 314	XM–11	US	Bar, forgings, billets	0.04 **C**, 8.00–10.00 **Mn**, 1.00 **Si**, 19.00–21.50 **Cr**, 5.50–7.50 **Ni**, 0.15–0.40 **N**, 0.060 **P**, 0.030 **S**	
ANSI/ASTM A 269	TP XM–11	US	Tube: seamless or welded	0.04 **C**, 8.00–10.00 **Mn**, 1.00 **Si**, 19.00–21.50 **Cr**, 5.50–7.50 **Ni**, 0.15–0.40 **N**, 0.060 **P**, 0.030 **S**	
DGN–B–171	Grade MT 316L	Mexico	Tube: seamless	0.035 **C**, 2.00 **Mn**, 1.00 **Si**, 16.0–18.0 **Cr**, 10.0–15.0 **Ni**, 2.0–3.0 **Mo**, 0.040 **P**, 0.030 **S**	**Hot or cold finished and annealed**: (≥7.92) **diam**, (519) **TS**, (206) **YS**, 35 **El**

WROUGHT STAINLESS STEELS

specification number	designation	country	product forms	composition	mechanical properties (see page iv for explanation)
DGN–B–171	Grade MT304L	Mexico	Tube: seamless	0.035 **C**, 2.00 **Mn**, 1.00 **Si**, 18.0–20.0 **Cr**, 8.0–13.0 **Ni**, 0.040 **P**, 0.030 **S**	**Hot or cold finished and annealed:** (≥7.92) **diam**, (519) **TS**, (206) **YS**, 35 **El**
ANSI/ASTM A 511	MT 316L	US	Tube: seamless	0.035 **C**, 2.00 **Mn**, 1.00 **Si**, 16.0–18.0 **Cr**, 10.0–15.0 **Ni**, 2.0–3.0 **Mo**, 0.040 **P**, 0.030 **S**	**Solution annealed:** 0.31 (7.9) **diam**, 75 (517) **TS**, 30 (207) **YS**, 35 **El**
ANSI/ASTM A 511	MT 304L	US	Tube: seamless	0.035 **C**, 2.00 **Mn**, 1.00 **Si**, 18.0–20.0 **Cr**, 8.0–13.0 **Ni**, 0.040 **P**, 0.030 **S**	**Solution annealed:** 0.31 (7.9) **diam**, 75 (517) **TS**, 30 (207) **YS**, 35 **El**
ANSI/ASTM A213	TP 304L	US	Tube: seamless	0.035 **C**, 2.00 **Mn**, 0.75 **Si**, 18.0–20.0 **Cr**, 8.00–13.0 **Ni**, 0.040 **P**, 0.030 **S**	**Solution annealed:** 0.312 (7.94) **diam**, 75 (517) **TS**, 30 (207) **YS**, 35 **El**
ANSI/ASTM A 213	TP 316L	US	Tube: seamless	0.035 **C**, 2.00 **Mn**, 0.75 **Si**, 16.0–18.0 **Cr**, 10.0–15.0 **Ni**, 2.00–3.00 **Mo**, 0.040 **P**, 0.030 **S**	**Solution annealed:** 0.312 (7.94) **diam**, 75 (517) **TS**, 30 (207) **YS**, 35 **El**
ANSI/ASTM A 249	TP 304L	US	Tube: welded	0.035 **C**, 2.00 **Mn**, 0.75 **Si**, 18.0–20.0 **Cr**, 8.00–13.0 **Ni**, 0.040 **P**, 0.030 **S**	**Solution annealed:** 0.312 (7.94) **diam**, 70 (485) **TS**, 25 (170) **YS**, 35 **El**
ANSI/ASTM A 249	TP 316L	US	Tube: welded	0.035 **C**, 2.00 **Mn**, 0.75 **Si**, 16.0–18.0 **Cr**, 10.0–15.0 **Ni**, 2.00–3.00 **Mo**, 0.040 **P**, 0.030 **S**	**Solution annealed:** 0.312 (7.94) **diam**, 70 (485) **TS**, 25 (170) **YS**, 35 **El**
NOM–B–194	Grade TP 304L	Mexico	Tube: seamless	0.035 **C**, 2.00 **Mn**, 0.75 **Si**, 18.0–20.0 **Cr**, 8.00–13.0 **Ni**, 0.040 **P**, 0.030 **S**	**Quenched:** (1.12–12.7) **diam**, (483) **TS**, (172) **YS**
NOM–B–194	Grade TP 316L	Mexico	Tube: seamless	0.035 **C**, 2.00 **Mn**, 0.75 **Si**, 16.0–18.0 **Cr**, 10.00–15.0 **Ni**, 2.00–3.0 **Mo**, 0.040 **P**, 0.030 **S**	**Quenched:** (1.12–12.7) **diam**, (483) **TS**, (172) **YS**
ANSI/ASTM A 312	TP 304L	US	Pipe: seamless or welded	0.035 **C**, 2.00 **Mn**, 0.75 **Si**, 18.0–20.0 **Cr**, 8.00–13.0 **Ni**, 0.040 **P**, 0.030 **S**	**Solution annealed:** 0.31 (7.94) **diam**, 70 (483) **TS**, 25 (172) **YS**, 35 **El**
ANSI/ASTM A 312	TP 316L	US	Pipe: seamless or welded	0.035 **C**, 2.00 **Mn**, 0.75 **Si**, 16.0–18.0 **Cr**, 10.0–15.0 **Ni**, 2.00–3.00 **Mo**, 0.040 **P**, 0.030 **S**	**Solution annealed:** 0.31 (7.94) **diam**, 70 (483) **TS**, 25 (172) **YS**, 35 **El**
MIL–P–1144D	Grade 304L	US	Pipe: seamless, welded	0.035 **C**, 2.0 **Mn**, 0.75 **Si**, 18.0–20.0 **Cr**, 8.0–13.0 **Ni**, 0.040 **P**, 0.030 **S**	**Solution annealed:** all **diam**, 70 (483) **TS**, 25 (173) **YS**, 35 **El**
MIL–P–1144D	Grade 316L	US	Pipe: seamless, welded	0.035 **C**, 2.0 **Mn**, 0.75 **Si**, 16.0–18.0 **Cr**, 10.0–15.0 **Ni**, 2.0–3.0 **Mo**, 0.040 **P**, 0.030 **S**	**Solution annealed:** all **diam**, 70 (483) **TS**, 25 (173) **YS**, 35 **El**
ASTM A 688	TP 304L	US	Tube: welded	0.035 **C**, 2.00 **Mn**, 0.75 **Si**, 18.00–20.00 **Cr**, 8.00–13.00 **Ni**, 0.040 **P**, 0.030 **S**	**Solution annealed:** all **diam**, 70 (483) **TS**, 25 (172) **YS**, 35 **El**
ASTM A 688	TP 316L	US	Tube: welded	0.035 **C**, 2.00 **Mn**, 0.75 **Si**, 16.00–18.00 **Cr**, 10.0–15.0 **Ni**, 2.00–3.00 **Mo**, 0.040 **P**, 0.030 **S**	**Solution annealed:** all **diam**, 70 (483) **TS**, 25 (172) **YS**, 35 **El**
ANSI/ASTM A 554	MT–304L	US	Tube: welded	0.035 **C**, 2.00 **Mn**, 1.00 **Si**, 18.0–20.0 **Cr**, 8.0–13.0 **Ni**, 0.040 **P**, 0.030 **S**	**Round annealed:** 0.312 (7.94) **diam**, 70 (483) **TS**, 25 (172) **YS**, 35 **El**
ANSI/ASTM A 554	MT–316L	US	Tube: welded	0.035 **C**, 2.00 **Mn**, 1.00 **Si**, 16.0–18.0 **Cr**, 10.0–15.0 **Ni**, 2.0–3.0 **Mo**, 0.040 **P**, 0.030 **S**	**Round annealed:** 0.312 (7.94) **diam**, 70 (483) **TS**, 25 (172) **YS**, 35 **El**
DGN–B–218	Grade TP304L	Mexico	Tube: welded	0.035 **C**, 2.00 **Mn**, 0.75 **Si**, 18.0–20.0 **Cr**, 8.0–13.0 **Ni**, 0.040 **P**, 0.030 **S**	**Cold finished and quenched or tempered:** (≥7.92) **diam**, (480) **TS**, (176) **YS**, 35 **El**
DGN–B–218	Grade TP316L	Mexico	Tube: welded	0.035 **C**, 2.00 **Mn**, 0.75 **Si**, 16.0–18.0 **Cr**, 10.0–15.0 **Ni**, 2.00–3.00 **Mo**, 0.040 **P**, 0.030 **S**	**Cold finished and quenched or tempered:** (≥7.92) **diam**, (480) **TS**, (176) **YS**, 35 **El**
COPANT 513	TP 304L	COPANT	Tube	0.035 **C**, 2.00 **Mn**, 0.75 **Si**, 18.0–20.0 **Cr**, 8.00–11.00 **Ni**, 0.040 **P**, 0.030 **S**	**Hot or cold finished:** (>8) **diam**, (480) **TS**, (175) **YS**, 35 **El**
COPANT 513	TP 316L	COPANT	Tube	0.035 **C**, 2.00 **Mn**, 0.75 **Si**, 16.0–18.0 **Cr**, 10.00–15.00 **Ni**, 2.00–3.00 **Mo**	**Hot or cold finished:** (>8) **diam**, (480) **TS**, (175) **YS**, 35 **El**
DGN–B–185	Grade TP304L	Mexico	Pipe: seamless, welded	0.035 **C**, 2.00 **Mn**, 0.75 **Si**, 18.0–20.0 **Cr**, 8.00–13.00 **Ni**, 0.040 **P**, 0.030 **S**	**Quenched or tempered:** (≥8) **diam**, (480) **TS**, (176) **YS**, 35 **El**
DGN–B–185	Grade TP316L	Mexico	Pipe: seamless, welded	0.035 **C**, 2.00 **Mn**, 0.75 **Si**, 16.0–18.0 **Cr**, 10.0–15.0 **Ni**, 2.0–3.0 **Mo**, 0.040 **P**, 0.030 **S**	**Quenched and tempered:** (≥8) **diam**, (480) **TS**, (176) **YS**, 35 **El**
AIR 9424	Z 3 CN 18	France	Tube: seamless	0.035 **C**, 2.0 **Mn**, 1.0 **Si**, 17.0–20.0 **Cr**, 9.0–12.0 **Ni**, 0.045 **P**, 0.030 **S**	**Quenched:** (<4) **diam**, (440) **TS**, (170) **YS**, 47 **El**

specification number	designation	country	product forms	composition	mechanical properties (see page iv for explanation)
ANSI/ASTM A 269	TP 304L	US	Tube: seamless, welded	0.035 **C**, 2.00 **Mn**, 0.75 **Si**, 18.0–20.0 **Cr**, 8.00–13.0 **Ni**, 0.040 **P**, 0.030 **S**	
ANSI/ASTM A 269	TP 316L	US	Tube: seamless or welded	0.035 **C**, 2.00 **Mn**, 0.75 **Si**, 16.0–18.0 **Cr**, 10.0–15.0 **Ni**, 2.0–3.0 **Mo**, 0.040 **P**, 0.030 **S**	
DGN–B–229	Grade TP 304L	Mexico	Tube: seamless or welded	0.035 **C**, 2.00 **Mn**, 0.75 **Si**, 18.0–20.0 **Cr**, 8.0–13.0 **Ni**, 0.040 **P**, 0.030 **S**	
DGN–B–229	Grade TP 316L	Mexico	Tube: seamless or welded	0.035 **C**, 2.00 **Mn**, 0.75 **Si**, 16.0–18.0 **Cr**, 10.0–15.0 **Ni**, 2.0–3.0 **Mo**, 0.040 **P**, 0.030 **S**	
ISO 2604/IV	P48	ISO	Plate	0.03–0.07 **C**, 2.00 **Mn**, 1.00 **Si**, 17.0–19.0 **Cr**, 8.0–11.0 **Ni**, 0.045 **P**, 0.030 **S**	**Hot rolled, quenched**: (3–40) **diam**, (490) **TS**, (195) **YS**, 50 **El**
ISO 2604/IV	P63	ISO	Plate	0.03–0.07 **C**, 2.00 **Mn**, 1.00 **Si**, 16.0–18.5 **Cr**, 10.5–14.0 **Ni**, 2.0–2.5 **Mo**, 0.045 **P**, 0.030 **S**	**Hot rolled, quenched**: (3–40) **diam**, (490) **TS**, (205) **YS**, 40 **El**
ANSI/ASTM A 492	Type XM–18	US	Wire	0.03 **C**, 7.50–9.00 **Mn**, 1.00 **Si**, 17.50–22.00 **Cr**, 5.00–7.00 **Ni**, 2.00–3.00 **Mo**, 0.25–0.50 **N**, 0.045 **P**, 0.030 **S**	**Cold drawn**: 0.091–0.100 (2.30–2.54) **diam**, 235 (1620) **TS**
AMS 5617C	Grade 1	US	Bar, forgings	0.03 **C**, 0.50 **Mn**, 0.50 **Si**, 11.00–12.50 **Cr**, 7.50–9.50 **Ni**, 0.50 **Mo**, 1.50–2.50 **Cu**, 0.015 **N**, 0.50 **Nb+Ta**, 0.015 **P**, 0.015 **S**, 0.90–1.40 **Ti**	**Precipitation hardened (bar)**: ≤4.000 (≤101.60) **diam**, 225 (1551) **TS**, 210 (1448) **YS**, 10 **El**
ANSI/ASTM A 478	Type 316L	US	Wire	0.03 **C**, 2.00 **Mn**, 1.00 **Si**, 16.00–18.00 **Cr**, 10.00–14.00 **Ni**, 2.00–3.00 **Mo**, 0.10 **N**, 0.045 **P**, 0.030 **S**	**Annealed**: 0.002–0.005 (0.05–0.13) **diam**, 145 (1000) **TS**, 30 **El**; **Cold drawn**: 0.030–0.125 (0.76–3.18) **diam**, 120 (830) **TS**, 15 **El**
ANSI/ASTM A 478	Type 304L	US	Wire	0.03 **C**, 2.00 **Mn**, 1.00 **Si**, 18.00–20.00 **Cr**, 8.00–12.00 **Ni**, 0.10 **N**, 0.045 **P**, 0.030 **S**	**Annealed**: 0.002–0.005 (0.05–0.13) **diam**, 145 (1000) **TS**, 30 **El**; **Cold drawn**: 0.030–0.125 (0.76–3.18) **diam**, 120 (830) **TS**, 15 **El**
AMS 5507C		US	Strip, sheet, plate	0.030 **C**, 2.00 **Mn**, 1.00 **Si**, 16.00–18.00 **Cr**, 10.00–14.00 **Ni**, 2.00–3.00 **Mo**, 0.75 **Cu**, 0.040 **P**, 0.030 **S**	**Solution treated**: ≤0.025 (≤0.64) **diam**, 100 (960) max **TS**, 40 **El**
AMS 5647D		US	Bar, forgings, tube, rings, wire	0.030 **C**, 2.00 **Mn**, 1.00 **Si**, 18.00–20.00 **Cr**, 8.00–11.00 **Ni**, 0.75 **Mo**, 0.75 **Cu**, 0.040 **P**, 0.030 **S**	**Solution heat treated, cold finished (wire)**: all **diam**, 125 (862) max **TS**
AMS 5653A		US	Bar, forgings, tube, rings, wire	0.030 **C**, 1.25–2.00 **Mn**, 1.00 **Si**, 16.00–18.00 **Cr**, 10.00–14.00 **Ni**, 2.00–3.00 **Mo**, 0.75 **Cu**, 0.040 **P**, 0.030 **S**	**Solution heat treated, cold finished (wire)**: all **diam**, 125 (862) max **TS**
MIL–T–8606C	Type 304L	US	Tube: seamless, welded	0.03 **C**, 2.00 **Mn**, 1.00 **Si**, 18.0–20.0 **Cr**, 8.0–11.0 **Ni**, 0.50 **Mo**, 0.50 **Cu**, 0.040 **P**, 0.030 **S**, rem Fe	**Solution annealed**: all **diam**, (723) max **TS**, 35 **El**
ASTM A 240	Type XM18	US	Plate, sheet, strip	0.03 **C**, 7.50–9.00 **Mn**, 1.00 **Si**, 17.50–22.00 **Cr**, 5.00–7.00 **Ni**, 2.00–3.00 **Mo**, 0.25–0.50 **N**, 0.045 **P**, 0.030 **S**	**Solution annealed, hot rolled or cold rolled (sheet, strip)**: all **diam**, 100 (690) **TS**, 60 (415) **YS**, 40 **El**
ANSI/ASTM A 240	Grade XM 18	US	Sheet, strip	0.03 **C**, 7.50–9.00 **Mn**, 1.00 **Si**, 17.50–22.00 **Cr**, 5.00–7.00 **Ni**, 2.00–3.00 **Mo**, 0.25–0.50 **N**, 0.045 **P**, 0.030 **S**	**Solution annealed**: all **diam**, (690) **TS**, (415) **YS**, 40 **El**
AMS 5507B		US	Strip, sheet, plate	0.030 **C**, 2.00 **Mn**, 1.00 **Si**, 16.00–18.00 **Cr**, 10.00–14.00 **Ni**, 2.00–3.00 **Mo**, 0.75 **Cu**, 0.040 **P**, 0.030 **S**	**Solution treated**: ≤0.025 (≤0.64) **diam**, 100 (690) max **TS**, 40 **El**
AMS 5511D		US	Strip, sheet, plate	.030 **C**, 2.00 **Mn**, 1.00 **Si**, 18.00–20.00 **Cr**, 8.00–11.00 **Ni**, 0.75 **Mo**, 0.75 **Cu**, 0.040 **P**, 0.030 **S**	**Solution treated**: all **diam**, 100 (690) max **TS**, 40 **El**
ANSI/ASTM A 479	XM–18	US	Bar, shapes	0.03 **C**, 7.50–9.00 **Mn**, 1.00 **Si**, 17.50–22.00 **Cr**, 5.00–7.00 **Ni**, 2.00–3.00 **Mo**, 0.25–0.50 **N**, 0.045 **P**, 0.030 **S**	**Solution annealed**: all **diam**, 90 (620) **TS**, 50 (345) **YS**, 40 **El**

specification number	designation	country	product forms	composition	mechanical properties (see page iv for explanation)
IS 6528	02Cr18Ni11	India	Wire	0.030 **C**, 2.0 **Mn**, 1.0 **Si**, 17.0–20.0 **Cr**, 9.0–13.0 **Ni**, 0.045 **P**, 0.030 **S**	**Annealed or solution annealed**: all **diam**, (620) **TS**, (310) **YS**, 35 **El**
IS 6528	02Cr17Ni12Mo2	India	Wire	0.030 **C**, 2.0 **Mn**, 1.0 **Si**, 16.0–18.5 **Cr**, 10.5–14.0 **Ni**, 2.0–3.0 **Mo**, 0.045 **P**, 0.030 **S**	**Annealed or solution annealed**: all **diam**, (620) **TS**, (310) **YS**, 35 **El**
ANSI/ASTM A 479	Grade XM 18	US	Bar, shapes	0.03 **C**, 7.50–9.00 **Mn**, 1.00 **Si**, 17.50–22.00 **Cr**, 5.00–7.00 **Ni**, 2.00–3.00 **Mo**, 0.25–0.50 **N**, 0.045 **P**, 0.030 **S**	**Solution annealed**: all **diam**, (620) **TS**, (345) **YS**, 40 **El**
ANSI/ASTM A 240	Grade XM 18	US	Plate	0.03 **C**, 7.50–9.00 **Mn**, 1.00 **Si**, 17.50–22.00 **Cr**, 5.00–7.00 **Ni**, 2.00–3.00 **Mo**, 0.25–0.50 **N**, 0.045 **P**, 0.030 **S**	**Solution annealed**: all **diam**, (620) **TS**, (345) **YS**, 40 **El**
ANSI/ASTM A 580	Grade 304L	US	Wire	0.03 **C**, 2.00 **Mn**, 1.00 **Si**, 18.00–20.00 **Cr**, 8.00–12.00 **Ni**, 0.045 **P**, 0.030 **S**, 0.10 **N**	**Cold finished**: all **diam**, 90 (620) **TS**, 45 (310) **YS**, 35 **El**; **Annealed**: all **diam**, 70 (480) **TS**, 25 (170) **YS**, 35 **El**
ANSI/ASTM A 580	Grade 316L	US	Wire	0.03 **C**, 2.00 **Mn**, 1.00 **Si**, 16.00–18.00 **Cr**, 10.00–14.00 **Ni**, 2.00–3.00 **Mo**, 0.045 **P**, 0.030 **S**, 0.10 **N**	**Cold finished**: all **diam**, 90 (620) **TS**, 45 (310) **YS**, 35 **El**; **Annealed**: all **diam**, 70 (480) **TS**, 25 (170) **YS**, 35 **El**
EURONORM 119–74, V	X2 CrNiMoN 18 13 3 KD	EURONORM	Wire, rod	0.03 **C**, 2.0 **Mn**, 1.0 **Si**, 16.5–18.5 **Cr**, 12.0–14.5 **Ni**, 2.5–3.0 **Mo**, 0.14–0.22 **N**, 0.045 **P**, 0.030 **S**	**Solution annealed**: (15–63) **diam**, (600) **TS**, (300) **YS**, 35 **El**
DIN 17440	Grade X 2 CrNiMoN 18 12	Germany	Sheet, strip, bar, wire, tube, forgings	0.03 **C**, 2.0 **Mn**, 1.0 **Si**, 16.5–18.5 **Cr**, 10.5–13.5 **Ni**, 2.0–2.5 **Mo**, 0.12–0.20 **N**, 0.045 **P**, 0.030 **S**	**Quenched**: (≤60) **diam**, (600) **TS**, (280) **YS**, 40 **El**
DIN 17440	Grade X 2 CrNiMoN 18 13	Germany	Sheet, strip, bar, wire, tube, forgings	0.03 **C**, 2.0 **Mn**, 1.0 **Si**, 16.5–18.5 **Cr**, 12.0–14.5 **Ni**, 2.5–3.0 **Mo**, 0.14–0.22 **N**, 0.045 **P**, 0.030 **S**	**Quenched**: (≤60) **diam**, (600) **TS**, (300) **YS**, 40 **El**
SS 14 23 71	SS 23 71–29	Sweden	Plate, sheet, strip	0.030 **C**, 2.0 **Mn**, 1.0 **Si**, 17.0–19.0 **Cr**, 8.0–11.0 **Ni**, 0.15–0.22 **N**, 0.045 **P**, 0.030 **S**	**Cold finished**: all **diam**, (600) **TS**, (400) **YS**, 30 **El**
SS 14 23 75	SS 23 75–29	Sweden	Plate, sheet, strip	0.030 **C**, 2.0 **Mn**, 1.0 **Si**, 16.0–18.5 **Cr**, 9.5–13.0 **Ni**, 2.5–3.0 **Mo**, 0.15–0.22 **N**, 0.045 **P**, 0.030 **S**	**Solution annealed**: all **diam**, (600) **TS**, (400) **YS**, 30 **El**
AISI 317L		US	Sheet, plate, tube	0.030 **C**, 2.00 **Mn**, 1.00 **Si**, 18.00–20.00 **Cr**, 11.00–15.00 **Ni**, 3.00–4.00 **Mo**, 0.045 **P**, 0.030 **S**	**Annealed (sheet)**: all **diam**, 86 (593) max **TS**, 38 (262) max **YS**, 55 **El**; **Annealed (plate)**: all **diam**, 85 (586) max **TS**, 35 (241) max **YS**, 55 **El**; **Annealed (tube)**: all **diam**, 86 (593) max **TS**, 50 (345) max **YS**, 55 **El**
NF A 35–577	Z 2 CN 18.10 (DF)	France	Bar, wire, rod	0.03 **C**, 2.0 **Mn**, 1.0 **Si**, 17.0–19.0 **Cr**, 9.0–11.0 **Ni**, 0.040 **P**, 0.030 **S**	**Solution annealed**: (6) **diam**, (590) max **TS**
NF A 35–577	Z 2 CND 17.12 (DF)	France	Bar, wire, rod	0.03 **C**, 2.0 **Mn**, 1.0 **Si**, 16.0–18.0 **Cr**, 11.0–13.0 **Ni**, 2–2.5 **Mo**, 0.040 **P**, 0.030 **S**	**Solution annealed**: (6) **diam**, (590) max **TS**
NF A 35–577	Z 2 CND 17.13 (DF)	France	Bar, wire, rod	0.03 **C**, 2.0 **Mn**, 1.0 **Si**, 16.0–18.0 **Cr**, 12.0–14.0 **Ni**, 2.5–3.0 **Mo**, 0.040 **P**, 0.030 **S**	**Solution annealed**: (6) **diam**, (590) max **TS**
NF A 35–575	Z 2 CN 18.09	France	Wire, rod	0.03 **C**, 2.0 **Mn**, 1.0 **Si**, 17.0–19.0 **Cr**, 8.0–10.0 **Ni**, 0.040 **P**, 0.030 **S**	**Stress hardened 0%**: all **diam**, (590) **TS**; **Stress hardened 40%**: all **diam**, (1130) **TS**; **Stress hardened 60%**: all **diam**, (1320) **TS**; **Stress hardened 80%**: all **diam**, (1670) **TS**; **Austenitized**: all **diam**, (440) **TS**, (180) **YS**, 45 **El**
SS 14 23 75	SS 23 75–02	Sweden	Bar, forgings, plate, sheet, strip, tube	0.030 **C**, 2.0 **Mn**, 1.0 **Si**, 16.0–18.0 **Cr**, 9.5–13.0 **Ni**, 2.5–3.0 **Mo**, 0.15–0.22 **N**, 0.045 **P**, 0.030 **S**	**Solution annealed**: all **diam**, (590) **TS**, (290) **YS**, 40 **El**

specification number	designation	country	product forms	composition	mechanical properties (see page iv for explanation)
SS 14 23 75	SS 23 75–22	Sweden	Tube: seamless	0.030 **C**, 2.0 **Mn**, 1.0 **Si**, 16.0–18.5 **Cr**, 9.5–13.0 **Ni**, 2.5–3.0 **Mo**, 0.15–0.22 **N**, 0.045 **P**, 0.030 **S**	**Solution annealed**: (<10) **diam**, (590) **TS**, (290) **YS**, 40 **El**
SS 14 23 75	SS 23 75–23	Sweden	Tube: welded	0.030 **C**, 2.0 **Mn**, 1.0 **Si**, 16.0–18.5 **Cr**, 9.5–13.0 **Ni**, 2.5–3.0 **Mo**, 0.15–0.22 **N**, 0.045 **P**, 0.030 **S**	**Solution annealed**: all **diam**, (590) **TS**, (290) **YS**, 40 **El**
SS 14 23 75	SS 23 75–24	Sweden	Tube: seamless	0.030 **C**, 2.0 **Mn**, 1.0 **Si**, 16.0–18.5 **Cr**, 9.5–13.0 **Ni**, 2.5–3.0 **Mo**, 0.15–0.22 **N**, 0.045 **P**, 0.030 **S**	**Solution annealed**: (<10) **diam**, (590) **TS**, (290) **YS**, 40 **El**
SS 14 23 75	SS 23 75–25	Sweden	Tube: welded	0.030 **C**, 2.0 **Mn**, 1.0 **Si**, 16.0–18.5 **Cr**, 9.5–13.0 **Ni**, 2.5–3.0 **Mo**, 0.15–0.22 **N**, 0.045 **P**, 0.030 **S**	**Solution annealed**: all **diam**, (590) **TS**, (290) **YS**, 40 **El**
SS 14 23 75	SS 23 75–26	Sweden	Tube: welded	0.030 **C**, 2.0 **Mn**, 1.0 **Si**, 16.0–18.5 **Cr**, 9.5–13.0 **Ni**, 2.5–3.0 **Mo**, 0.15–0.22 **N**, 0.045 **P**, 0.030 **S**	**Solution annealed**: (<30) **diam**, (590) **TS**, (270) **YS**, 40 **El**
SS 14 23 75	SS 23 75–27	Sweden	Bar, forgings	0.030 **C**, 2.0 **Mn**, 1.0 **Si**, 16.0–18.5 **Cr**, 9.5–13.0 **Ni**, 2.5–3.0 **Mo**, 0.15–0.22 **N**, 0.045 **P**, 0.030 **S**	**Solution annealed**: (<50) **diam**, (590) **TS**, (290) **YS**, 40 **El**
SS 14 23 75	SS 23 75–28	Sweden	Plate, sheet, strip	0.030 **C**, 2.0 **Mn**, 1.0 **Si**, 16.0–18.5 **Cr**, 9.5–13.0 **Ni**, 2.5–3.0 **Mo**, 0.15–0.22 **N**, 0.045 **P**, 0.030 **S**	**Solution annealed**: all **diam**, (590) **TS**, (290) **YS**, 40 **El**
AISI 304L		US	Sheet, strip, plate, bar	0.030 **C**, 2.00 **Mn**, 1.00 **Si**, 18.00–20.00 **Cr**, 8.00–12.00 **Ni**, 0.045 **P**, 0.030 **S**	**Annealed (sheet)**: all **diam**, 81 (558) max **TS**, 39 (269) max **YS**, 55 **El**
AISI 316L		US	Sheet, strip, plate, bar	0.030 **C**, 2.00 **Mn**, 1.00 **Si**, 16.00–18.00 **Cr**, 10.00–14.00 **Ni**, 2.00–3.00 **Mo**, 0.045 **P**, 0.030 **S**	**Annealed (sheet)**: all **diam**, 81 (558) max **TS**, 42 (290) max **YS**, 50 **El**
EURONORM 119–74, V	X2 CrNiN 18 10 KD	EURONORM	Wire, rod	0.03 **C**, 2.0 **Mn**, 1.0 **Si**, 17.0–19.0 **Cr**, 9.0–11.5 **Ni**, 0.12–0.20 **N**, 0.045 **P**, 0.030 **S**	**Solution annealed**: (15–63) **diam**, (550) **TS**, (270) **YS**, 35 **El**
DIN 17440	Grade X 2 CrNiN 18 10	Germany	Sheet, strip, bar, wire, tube, forgings	0.03 **C**, 2.0 **Mn**, 1.0 **Si**, 17.0–19.0 **Cr**, 9.0–11.5 **Ni**, 0.12–0.20 **N**, 0.045 **P**, 0.030 **S**	**Quenched**: (≤60) **diam**, (550) **TS**, (270) **YS**, 40 **El**
SS 14 23 52	SS 23 52–29	Sweden	Plate, sheet, strip	0.030 **C**, 2.0 **Mn**, 1.0 **Si**, 17.0–19.0 **Cr**, 9.0–12.0 **Ni**, 0.045 **P**, 0.030 **S**	**Cold finished**: all **diam**, (550) **TS**, (350) **YS**, 35 **El**
SS 14 23 53	SS 23 53–29	Sweden	Sheet	0.030 **C**, 2.0 **Mn**, 1.0 **Si**, 16.0–18.5 **Cr**, 11.5–14.5 **Ni**, 2.5–3.0 **Mo**, 0.045 **P**, 0.030 **S**	**Cold finished**: (<5) **diam**, (550) **TS**, (350) **YS**, 35 **El**
SS 14 23 67	SS 23 67–29	Sweden	Plate, sheet, strip	0.030 **C**, 2.0 **Mn**, 1.0 **Si**, 17.5–19.5 **Cr**, 14.0–17.0 **Ni**, 3.0–4.0 **Mo**, 0.045 **P**, 0.030 **S**	**Cold finished**: (<30) **diam**, (550) **TS**, (350) **YS**, 30 **El**
SS 14 23 48	SS 23 48–29	Sweden	Plate, sheet, strip	0.030 **C**, 2.0 **Mn**, 1.0 **Si**, 16.0–18.5 **Cr**, 11.0–14.0 **Ni**, 2.0–2.5 **Mo**, 0.045 **P**, 0.030 **S**	**Cold finished**: (<5) **diam**, (550) **TS**, (350) **YS**, 35 **El**
NF A 35–575	Z 2 CND 17.13	France	Wire, rod	0.030 **C**, 2.0 **Mn**, 1.0 **Si**, 16.0–18.0 **Cr**, 11.5–13.5 **Ni**, 2.5–3.0 **Mo**, 0.040 **P**, 0.030 **S**	**Stress hardened 0%**: all **diam**, (540) **TS**; **Stress hardened 40%**: all **diam**, (980) **TS**; **Stress hardened 60%**: all **diam**, (1220) **TS**; **Stress hardened 80%**: all **diam**, (1470) **TS**
NF A 35–575	Z 2 CND 17.12	France	Wire, rod	0.030 **C**, 2.0 **Mn**, 1.0 **Si**, 16.0–18.0 **Cr**, 10.5–13.0 **Ni**, 2.0–2.5 **Mo**, 0.040 **P**, 0.030 **S**	**Stress hardened 0%**: all **diam**, (540) **TS**; **Stress hardened 40%**: all **diam**, (980) **TS**; **Stress hardened 60%**: all **diam**, (1220) **TS**; **Stress hardened 80%**: all **diam**, (1470) **TS**

specification number	designation	country	product forms	composition	mechanical properties (see page iv for explanation)
NF A 35-575	Z 2 CN 18.10	France	Wire, rod	0.030 **C**, 2.0 **Mn**, 1.0 **Si**, 17.0–19.0 **Cr**, 9.0–11.0 **Ni**, 0.040 **P**, 0.030 **S**	**Stress hardened 0%**: all **diam**, (540) **TS**; **Stress hardened 40%**: all **diam**, (1080) **TS**; **Stress hardened 60%**: all **diam**, (1270) **TS**; **Stress hardened 80%**: all **diam**, (1620) **TS**
SS 14 23 71	SS 23 71-02	Sweden	Bar, forgings, plate, sheet, strip, tube	0.030 **C**, 2.0 **Mn**, 1.0 **Si**, 17.0–19.0 **Cr**, 8.0–11.0 **Ni**, 0.15–0.22 **N**, 0.045 **P**, 0.030 **S**	**Solution annealed**: all **diam**, (540) **TS**, (270) **YS**, 40 **El**
SS 14 23 71	SS 23 71-22	Sweden	Tube: seamless	0.030 **C**, 2.0 **Mn**, 1.0 **Si**, 17.0–19.0 **Cr**, 8.0–11.0 **Ni**, 0.15–0.22 **N**, 0.045 **P**, 0.030 **S**	**Solution annealed**: (<10) **diam**, (540) **TS**, (270) **YS**, 40 **El**
SS 14 23 71	SS 23 71-23	Sweden	Tube: welded	0.030 **C**, 2.0 **Mn**, 1.0 **Si**, 17.0–19.0 **Cr**, 8.0–11.0 **Ni**, 0.15–0.22 **N**, 0.045 **P**, 0.030 **S**	**Solution annealed**: all **diam**, (540) **TS**, (270) **YS**, 40 **El**
SS 14 23 71	SS 23 71-24	Sweden	Tube: seamless	0.030 **C**, 2.0 **Mn**, 1.0 **Si**, 17.0–19.0 **Cr**, 8.0–11.0 **Ni**, 0.15–0.22 **N**, 0.045 **P**, 0.030 **S**	**Solution annealed**: (<10) **diam**, (540) **TS**, (270) **YS**, (40) **El**
SS 14 23 71	SS 23 71-25	Sweden	Tube: welded	0.030 **C**, 2.0 **Mn**, 1.0 **Si**, 17.0–19.0 **Cr**, 8.0–11.0 **Ni**, 0.15–0.22 **N**, 0.045 **P**, 0.030 **S**	**Solution annealed**: all **diam**, (540) **TS**, (270) **YS**, 40 **El**
SS 14 23 71	SS 23 71-26	Sweden	Tube: welded	0.030 **C**, 2.0 **Mn**, 1.0 **Si**, 17.0–19.0 **Cr**, 8.0–11.0 **Ni**, 0.15–0.22 **N**, 0.045 **P**, 0.030 **S**	**Solution annealed**: (<30) **diam**, (540) **TS**, (270) **YS**, 40 **El**
SS 14 23 71	SS 23 71-27	Sweden	Bar, forgings, plate, sheet, strip	0.030 **C**, 2.0 **Mn**, 1.0 **Si**, 17.0–19.0 **Cr**, 8.0–11.0 **Ni**, 0.15–0.22 **N**, 0.045 **P**, 0.030 **S**	**Solution annealed**: all **diam**, (540) **TS**, (270) **YS**, 40 **El**
NF A 35-573	Z 2 CND 19.15	France	Sheet, strip, plate	0.030 **C**, 2.0 **Mn**, 1.0 **Si**, 17.5–19.5 **Cr**, 14.0–16.0 **Ni**, 3.0–4.0 **Mo**, 0.040 **P**, 0.030 **S**	**Cold rolled**: (≤5) **diam**, (520) **TS**, (265) **YS**, 40 **El**; **Hot rolled**: (≤20) **diam**, (520) **TS**, (245) **YS**, 38 **El**
CSA G110.9	Type 317L	Canada	Plate	0.03 **C**, 2.00 **Mn**, 1.00 **Si**, 18.00–20.00 **Cr**, 11.00–15.00 **Ni**, 3.00–4.00 **Mo**, 0.045 **P**, 0.030 **S**	**Hot rolled, annealed, quenched and tempered**: all **diam**, 75 (517) **TS**, 30 (207) **YS**, 35 **El**
CSA G 110.9	Type 317L	Canada	Sheet	0.03 **C**, 2.00 **Mn**, 1.00 **Si**, 18.00–20.00 **Cr**, 11.00–15.00 **Ni**, 3.00–4.00 **Mo**, 0.045 **P**, 0.030 **S**	**Hot or cold rolled and annealed**: all **diam**, 75 (517) **TS**, 30 (207) **YS**, 35 **El**
CSA G110.9	Type 317L	Canada	Strip	0.03 **C**, 2.00 **Mn**, 1.00 **Si**, 18.00–20.00 **Cr**, 11.00–15.00 **Ni**, 3.00–4.00 **Mo**, 0.045 **P**, 0.030 **S**	**Cold rolled and annealed**: all **diam**, 75 (517) **TS**, 30 (207) **YS**, 35 **El**
CSA G110.6	Type 317L	Canada	Plate, sheet, strip	0.03 **C**, 2.00 **Mn**, 1.00 **Si**, 18.00–20.00 **Cr**, 11.00–15.00 **Ni**, 3.00–4.00 **Mo**, 0.045 **P**, 0.030 **S**	**Hot rolled and annealed or hot rolled, quenched and tempered**: all **diam**, 75 (517) **TS**, 30 (207) **YS**, 35 **El**
ASTM A 240	Type 317L	US	Plate, sheet, strip	0.030 **C**, 2.00 **Mn**, 1.00 **Si**, 18.00–20.00 **Cr**, 11.00–15.00 **Ni**, 3.00–4.00 **Mo**, 0.10 **N**, 0.045 **P**, 0.030 **S**	**Solution annealed, hot rolled or cold rolled**: all **diam**, 75 (515) **TS**, 30 (205) **YS**, 35 **El**
ASTM A 167	Type 317L	US	Plate, sheet, strip	0.03 **C**, 2.00 **Mn**, 1.00 **Si**, 18.00–20.00 **Cr**, 11.00–15.00 **Ni**, 3.00–4.00 **Mo**, 0.045 **P**, 0.030 **S**	**Solution annealed**: all **diam**, 75 (515) **TS**, 30 (205) **YS**, 35 **El**
ANSI/ASTM A 240	Grade 317L	US	Plate, sheet, strip	0.030 **C**, 2.00 **Mn**, 1.00 **Si**, 18.00–20.00 **Cr**, 11.00–15.00 **Ni**, 3.00–4.00 **Mo**, 0.10 **N**, 0.045 **P**, 0.030 **S**	**Solution annealed**: all **diam**, (515) **TS**, (205) **YS**, 35 **El**
DGN-B-83	308 L	Mexico	Bar	0.03 **C**, 2.0 **Mn**, 1.0 **Si**, 19.0–21.0 **Cr**, 10.0–12.0 **Ni**, 0.045 **P**, 0.030 **S**	**Hot or cold rolled**: all **diam**, (510) **TS**, (206) **YS**, 40 **El**
NF A 35-573	Z 2 CND 17.13	France	Sheet, strip, plate	0.030 **C**, 2.00 **Mn**, 1.00 **Si**, 16.0–18.0 **Cr**, 11.5–13.5 **Ni**, 2.5–3.0 **Mo**, 0.040 **P**, 0.030 **S**	**Cold rolled**: (≤5) **diam**, (500) **TS**, (255) **YS**, 45 **El**; **Hot rolled**: (≤20) **diam**, (500) **TS**, (245) **YS**, 43 **El**
NF A 35-573	Z 2 CND 17.12	France	Sheet, strip, plate	0.03 **C**, 2.0 **Mn**, 1.0 **Si**, 16.0–18.0 **Cr**, 10.5–13.0 **Ni**, 2.0–2.5 **Mo**, 0.040 **P**, 0.030 **S**	**Cold rolled**: (≤5) **diam**, (500) **TS**, (255) **YS**, 45 **El**; **Hot rolled**: (≤20) **diam**, (500) **TS**, (245) **YS**, 43 **El**
BS T.75		UK	Tube: aircraft quality	0.030 **C**, 0.5–2.0 **Mn**, 0.2–1.0 **Si**, 16.5–18.5 **Cr**, 11.0–14.0 **Ni**, 2.25–3.0 **Mo**, 0.035 **P**, 0.025 **S**	**Solution annealed**: (<0.7) **diam**, (500) **TS**, (190) **YS**, 40 **El**
BS T.74		UK	Tube: aircraft quality	0.030 **C**, 0.5–2.0 **Mn**, 0.2–1.0 **Si**, 17.5–19.0 **Cr**, 9.0–12.0 **Ni**, 0.035 **P**, 0.025 **S**	**Solution annealed**: (<0.7) **diam**, (500) **TS**, (190) **YS**, 40 **El**

WROUGHT STAINLESS STEELS

specification number	designation	country	product forms	composition	mechanical properties (see page iv for explanation)
DIN 17440	Grade X 2 CrNiMo 18 16	Germany	Sheet, strip, bar, wire, tube, forgings	0.03 **C**, 2.0 **Mn**, 1.0 **Si**, 17.0–19.0 **Cr**, 15.0–17.0 **Ni**, 3.0–4.0 **Mo**, 0.045 **P**, 0.030 **S**	**Quenched**: (≤60) **diam**, (500) **TS**, (195) **YS**, 45 **El**
NF A 35–573	Z 2 CN 18.10	France	Sheet, strip, plate	0.03 **C**, 2.0 **Mn**, 1.0 **Si**, 17.0–19.0 **Cr**, 9.0–11.0 **Ni**, 0.040 **P**, 0.030 **S**	**Cold rolled**: (≤5) **diam**, (490) **TS**, (245) **YS**, 45 **El**; **Hot rolled**: (≤20) **diam**, (490) **TS**, (235) **YS**, 43 **El**
IS:6913	Grade C	India	Tube	0.03 **C**, 2.0 **Mn**, 1.0 **Si**, 16.0–18.5 **Cr**, 10.5–14.0 **Ni**, 2.0–3.0 **Mo**, 0.045 **P**, 0.030 **S**	**Solution annealed**: all **diam**, (490) **TS**, 30 **El**
IS:6913	Grade A	India	Tube	0.030 **C**, 2.0 **Mn**, 1.0 **Si**, 17.0–20.0 **Cr**, 9.0–13.0 **Ni**, 0.045 **P**, 0.030 **S**	**Solution annealed**: all **diam**, (490) **TS**, 30 **El**
ISO 683/XII	24	ISO	Bar, sheet, plate	0.030 **C**, 2.0 **Mn**, 1.0 **Si**, 17.5–19.5 **Cr**, 14.0–17.0 **Ni**, 3.0–4.0 **Mo**, 0.045 **P**, 0.030 **S**	**Solution treated**: all **diam**, (490) **TS**, (200) **YS**, 35 **El**
ISO 2604/II	TS 46	ISO	Tube: seamless	0.03 **C**, 2.00 **Mn**, 1.00 **Si**, 17.00–19.00 **Cr**, 9.00–13.00 **Ni**, 0.045 **P**, 0.030 **S**	**Cold finished, quenched**: all **diam**, (490) **TS**, (175) **YS**, 30 **El**
ISO 2604/II	TS 57	ISO	Tube: seamless	0.03 **C**, 2.00 **Mn**, 1.00 **Si**, 16.00–18.50 **Cr**, 11.00–14.00 **Ni**, 2.00–2.50 **Mo**, 0.045 **P**, 0.030 **S**	**Cold finished, quenched**: all **diam**, (490) **TS**, (185) **YS**, 30 **El**
ISO 2604/II	TS 58	ISO	Tube: seamless	0.03 **C**, 2.00 **Mn**, 1.00 **Si**, 16.00–18.50 **Cr**, 11.50–14.50 **Ni**, 2.50–3.00 **Mo**, 0.045 **P**, 0.030 **S**	**Cold finished, quenched**: all **diam**, (490) **TS**, (185) **YS**, 30 **El**
BS 3605 Section 4	Grade 316S22	UK	Pipe: welded	0.03 **C**, 0.50–2.00 **Mn**, 0.20–1.00 **Si**, 16.0–18.5 **Cr**, 11.0–14.0 **Ni**, 2.0–3.0 **Mo**, 0.040 **P**, 0.030 **S**	**Solution annealed**: all **diam**, (490) **TS**, (215) **YS**, 35 **El**
BS 3605 Section 4	304S22	UK	Pipe: welded	0.03 **C**, 0.50–2.00 **Mn**, 0.20–1.00 **Si**, 17.0–19.0 **Cr**, 0.040 **P**, 0.030 **S**	**Solution annealed**: all **diam**, (490) **TS**, (205) **YS**, 35 **El**
BS 3605 Section 3	Grade 316S14	UK	Pipe: seamless	0.03 **C**, 0.50–2.00 **Mn**, 0.20–1.00 **Si**, 16.0–18.5 **Cr**, 12.0–15.0 **Ni**, 2.0–3.0 **Mo**, 0.040 **P**, 0.030 **S**	**Solution annealed**: all **diam**, (490) **TS**, (215) **YS**, 35 **El**
BS 3605 Section 3	304S14	UK	Pipe: seamless	0.03 **C**, 0.50–2.00 **Mn**, 0.20–1.00 **Si**, 17.0–19.0 **Cr**, 10.0–13.0 **Ni**, 0.040 **P**, 0.030 **S**	**Solution annealed**: all **diam**, (490) **TS**, (205) **YS**, 35 **El**
BS 1449 Part 2	Grade 316S12	UK	Plate, sheet, strip	0.03 **C**, 0.50–2.00 **Mn**, 0.20–1.00 **Si**, 16.5–18.5 **Cr**, 11.0–14.0 **Ni**, 2.25–3.0 **Mo**, 0.045 **P**, 0.030 **S**	**Solution annealed**: (≥3.0) (sheet and strip) **diam**, (490) **TS**, (195) **YS**, 40 **El**
BS 1449 Part 2	Grade 317S12	UK	Plate, sheet, strip	0.03 **C**, 0.50–2.00 **Mn**, 0.20–1.00 **Si**, 17.5–19.5 **Cr**, 14.0–17.0 **Ni**, 3.00–4.00 **Mo**, 0.045 **P**, 0.030 **S**	**Solution annealed**: (≥3.0) (sheet and strip) **diam**, (490) **TS**, (195) **YS**, 35 **El**
BS 1449 Part 2	Grade 304S12	UK	Plate, sheet, strip	0.03 **C**, 0.50–2.00 **Mn**, 0.20–1.00 **Si**, 17.5–19.0 **Cr**, 9.0–12.0 **Ni**, 0.045 **P**, 0.030 **S**	**Solution annealed**: (≥3.0) (sheet and strip) **diam**, (490) **TS**, (195) **YS**, 40 **El**
BS S.537		UK	Sheet, strip: aircraft quality	0.030 **C**, 0.5–2.0 **Mn**, 0.2–1.0 **Si**, 16.5–18.5 **Cr**, 11.0–14.0 **Ni**, 2.25–3.0 **Mo**, 0.035 **P**, 0.025 **S**	**Solution annealed or quenched**: all **diam**, (490) **TS**, (195) **YS**, 30 in less than 1.5 mm **El**
BS 3605 Section 2	304S14	UK	Pipe: seamless	0.03 **C**, 0.50–2.00 **Mn**, 0.20–1.00 **Si**, 17.0–19.0 **Cr**, 10.0–13.0 **Ni**, 0.040 **P**, 0.030 **S**	**Solution annealed**: all **diam**, (490) **TS**, (205) **YS**, 35 **El**
BS 3605 Section 2	Grade 316S14	UK	Pipe: seamless	0.03 **C**, 0.50–2.00 **Mn**, 0.20–1.00 **Si**, 16.0–18.5 **Cr**, 12.0–15.0 **Ni**, 2.0–3.0 **Mo**, 0.040 **P**, 0.030 **S**	**Solution annealed**: all **diam**, (490) **TS**, (215) **YS**, 35 **El**
BS 3605 Section 5	Grade 316S22	UK	Pipe: welded	0.03 **C**, 0.50–2.00 **Mn**, 0.20–1.00 **Si**, 16.0–18.5 **Cr**, 11.0–14.0 **Ni**, 2.0–3.0 **Mo**, 0.040 **P**, 0.030 **S**	**Solution annealed**: all **diam**, (490) **TS**, (215) **YS**, 35 **El**
BS 3605 Section 5	304S22	UK	Pipe: welded	0.03 **C**, 0.50–2.00 **Mn**, 0.20–1.00 **Si**, 17.0–19.0 **Cr**, 9.0–12.0 **Ni**, 0.040 **P**, 0.030 **S**	**Solution annealed**: all **diam**, (490) **TS**, (205) **YS**, 35 **El**
BS S.536		UK	Sheet, strip: aircraft quality	0.030 **C**, 0.5–2.0 **Mn**, 0.2–1.0 **Si**, 17.5–19.0 **Cr**, 9.0–12.0 **Ni**, 0.035 **P**, 0.025 **S**	**Solution annealed and quenched**: all **diam**, (490) **TS**, (195) **YS**, 30 in 1.5 mm **El**
NF A 35–572	Z 2 CND 19–15	France	Bar, section	0.03 **C**, 2.0 **Mn**, 1.0 **Si**, 17.5–19.5 **Cr**, 14.0–16.0 **Ni**, 3.0–4.0 **Mo**, 0.040 **P**, 0.030 **S**	**Austenitized**: (≤25) **diam**, (490) **TS**, (205) **YS**, 40 **El**

specification number	designation	country	product forms	composition	mechanical properties (see page iv for explanation)
SS 14 23 48	SS 23 48–02	Sweden	Bar, forgings, plate, sheet	0.030 **C**, 2.0 **Mn**, 1.0 **Si**, 16.0–18.5 **Cr**, 11.0–14.0 **Ni**, 2.0–2.5 **Mo**, 0.045 **P**, 0.030 **S**	**Solution annealed**: all **diam**, (490) **TS**, (210) **YS**, 45 **El**
SS 14 23 48	SS 23 48–22	Sweden	Tube: seamless	0.030 **C**, 2.0 **Mn**, 1.0 **Si**, 16.0–18.5 **Cr**, 11.0–14.0 **Ni**, 2.0–2.5 **Mo**, 0.045 **P**, 0.030 **S**	**Solution annealed**: (<10) **diam**, (490) **TS**, (210) **YS**, 45 **El**
SS 14 23 48	SS 23 48–23	Sweden	Tube: welded	0.030 **C**, 2.0 **Mn**, 1.0 **Si**, 16.0–18.5 **Cr**, 11.0–14.0 **Ni**, 2.0–2.5 **Mo**, 0.045 **P**, 0.030 **S**	**Solution annealed**: all **diam**, (490) **TS**, (210) **YS**, 45 **El**
SS 14 23 48	SS 23 48–24	Sweden	Tube: seamless	0.030 **C**, 2.0 **Mn**, 1.0 **Si**, 16.0–18.5 **Cr**, 11.0–14.0 **Ni**, 2.0–2.5 **Mo**, 0.045 **P**, 0.030 **S**	**Solution annealed**: (<10) **diam**, (490) **TS**, (210) **YS**, 45 **El**
SS 14 23 48	SS 23 48–25	Sweden	Tube: welded	0.030 **C**, 2.0 **Mn**, 1.0 **Si**, 16.0–18.5 **Cr**, 11.0–14.0 **Ni**, 2.0–2.5 **Mo**, 0.045 **P**, 0.030 **S**	**Solution annealed**: all **diam**, (490) **TS**, (210) **YS**, 45 **El**
SS 14 23 48	SS 23 48–26	Sweden	Tube: welded	0.030 **C**, 2.0 **Mn**, 1.0 **Si**, 16.0–18.5 **Cr**, 11.0–14.0 **Ni**, 2.0–2.5 **Mo**, 0.045 **P**, 0.030 **S**	**Solution annealed**: (<30) **diam**, (490) **TS**, (210) **YS**, 45 **El**
SS 14 23 48	SS 23 48–27	Sweden	Bar, forgings	0.030 **C**, 2.0 **Mn**, 1.0 **Si**, 16.0–18.5 **Cr**, 11.0–14.0 **Ni**, 2.0–2.5 **Mo**, 0.045 **P**, 0.030 **S**	**Solution annealed**: (<50) **diam**, (490) **TS**, (210) **YS**, 45 **El**
SS 14 23 52	SS 23 52–22	Sweden	Tube: seamless	0.030 **C**, 2.0 **Mn**, 1.0 **Si**, 17.0–19.0 **Cr**, 9.0–12.0 **Ni**, 0.045 **P**, 0.030 **S**	**Solution annealed**: (<10) **diam**, (490) **TS**, (190) **YS**, 45 **El**
SS 14 23 52	SS 23 52–23	Sweden		0.030 **C**, 2.0 **Mn**, 1.0 **Si**, 17.0–19.0 **Cr**, 9.0–12.0 **Ni**, 0.045 **P**, 0.030 **S**	**Solution annealed**: all **diam**, (490) **TS**, (190) **YS**, 45 **El**
SS 14 23 52	SS 23 52–24	Sweden	Tube: seamless	0.030 **C**, 2.0 **Mn**, 1.0 **Si**, 17.0–19.0 **Cr**, 9.0–12.0 **Ni**, 0.045 **P**, 0.030 **S**	**Solution annealed**: (<10) **diam**, (490) **TS**, (190) **YS**, 45 **El**
SS 14 23 52	SS 23 52–25	Sweden	Tube: welded	0.030 **C**, 2.0 **Mn**, 1.0 **Si**, 17.0–19.0 **Cr**, 9.0–12.0 **Ni**, 0.045 **P**, 0.030 **S**	**Solution annealed**: all **diam**, (490) **TS**, (190) **YS**, 45 **El**
SS 14 23 53	SS 23 53–02	Sweden	Bar, forgings, plate, sheet, strip, tube	0.030 **C**, 2.0 **Mn**, 1.0 **Si**, 16.0–18.5 **Cr**, 11.5–14.5 **Ni**, 2.5–3.0 **Mo**, 0.045 **P**, 0.030 **S**	**Solution annealed**: all **diam**, (490) **TS**, (210) **YS**, 45 **El**
SS 14 23 53	SS 23 53–22	Sweden	Tube: seamless	0.030 **C**, 2.0 **Mn**, 1.0 **Si**, 16.0–18.5 **Cr**, 11.5–14.5 **Ni**, 2.5–3.0 **Mo**, 0.045 **P**, 0.030 **S**	**Solution annealed**: (<10) **diam**, (490) **TS**, (210) **YS**, 45 **El**
SS 14 23 53	SS 23 53–23	Sweden	Tube: welded	0.030 **C**, 2.0 **Mn**, 1.0 **Si**, 16.0–18.5 **Cr**, 11.5–14.5 **Ni**, 2.5–3.0 **Mo**, 0.045 **P**, 0.030 **S**	**Solution annealed**: all **diam**, (490) **TS**, (210) **YS**, 45 **El**
SS 14 23 53	SS 23 53–24	Sweden	Tube: seamless	0.030 **C**, 2.0 **Mn**, 1.0 **Si**, 16.0–18.5 **Cr**, 11.5–14.5 **Ni**, 2.5–3.0 **Mo**, 0.045 **P**, 0.030 **S**	**Solution annealed**: (<10) **diam**, (490) **TS**, (210) **YS**, 45 **El**
SS 14 23 53	SS 23 53–25	Sweden	Tube: welded	0.030 **C**, 2.0 **Mn**, 1.0 **Si**, 16.0–18.5 **Cr**, 11.5–14.5 **Ni**, 2.5–3.0 **Mo**, 0.045 **P**, 0.030 **S**	**Solution annealed**: all **diam**, (490) **TS**, (210) **YS**, 45 **El**
SS 14 23 53	SS 23 53–26	Sweden	Tube: welded	0.030 **C**, 2.0 **Mn**, 1.0 **Si**, 16.0–18.5 **Cr**, 11.5–14.5 **Ni**, 2.5–3.0 **Mo**, 0.045 **P**, 0.030 **S**	**Solution annealed**: (<30) **diam**, (490) **TS**, (210) **YS**, 45 **El**
SS 14 23 53	SS 23 53–27	Sweden	Bar, forgings	0.030 **C**, 2.0 **Mn**, 1.0 **Si**, 16.0–18.5 **Cr**, 11.5–14.5 **Ni**, 2.5–3.0 **Mo**, 0.045 **P**, 0.030 **S**	**Solution annealed**: (<50) **diam**, (490) **TS**, (210) **YS**, 45 **El**
SS 14 23 53	SS 23 53–28	Sweden	Plate, sheet, strip	0.030 **C**, 2.0 **Mn**, 1.0 **Si**, 16.0–18.5 **Cr**, 11.5–14.5 **Ni**, 2.5–3.0 **Mo**, 0.045 **P**, 0.030 **S**	**Solution annealed**: all **diam**, (490) **TS**, (210) **YS**, 45 **El**
SS 14 23 67	SS 23 67–02	Sweden	Bar, forgings, sheet, strip, tube	0.030 **C**, 2.0 **Mn**, 1.0 **Si**, 17.5–19.5 **Cr**, 14.0–17.0 **Ni**, 3.0–4.0 **Mo**, 0.045 **P**, 0.030 **S**	**Solution annealed**: all **diam**, (490) **TS**, (220) **YS**, 40 **El**
SS 14 23 67	SS 23 67–22	Sweden	Tube, welded	0.030 **C**, 2.0 **Mn**, 1.0 **Si**, 17.5–19.5 **Cr**, 14.0–17.0 **Ni**, 3.0–4.0 **Mo**, 0.045 **P**, 0.030 **S**	**Solution annealed**: (<10) **diam**, (490) **TS**, (220) **YS**, 40 **El**
SS 14 23 67	SS 23 67–23	Sweden	Tube, welded	0.030 **C**, 2.0 **Mn**, 1.0 **Si**, 17.5–19.5 **Cr**, 14.0–17.0 **Ni**, 3.0–4.0 **Mo**, 0.045 **P**, 0.030 **S**	**Solution annealed**: all **diam**, (490) **TS**, (220) **YS**, 40 **El**
SS 14 23 67	SS 23 67–24	Sweden	Tube: seamless	0.030 **C**, 2.0 **Mn**, 1.0 **Si**, 17.5–19.5 **Cr**, 14.0–17.0 **Ni**, 3.0–4.0 **Mo**, 0.045 **P**, 0.030 **S**	**Solution annealed**: (<10) **diam**, (490) **TS**, (220) **YS**, 40 **El**
SS 14 23 67	SS 23 67–25	Sweden	Tube, welded	0.030 **C**, 2.0 **Mn**, 1.0 **Si**, 17.5–19.5 **Cr**, 14.0–17.0 **Ni**, 3.0–4.0 **Mo**, 0.045 **P**, 0.030 **S**	**Solution annealed**: all **diam**, (490) **TS**, (220) **YS**, 40 **El**

specification number	designation	country	product forms	composition	mechanical properties (see page iv for explanation)
SS 14 23 67	SS 23 67–26	Sweden	Tube: welded	0.030 **C**, 2.0 **Mn**, 1.0 **Si**, 17.5–19.5 **Cr**, 14.0–17.0 **Ni**, 3.0–4.0 **Mo**, 0.045 **P**, 0.030 **S**	**Solution annealed**: (<30) **diam**, (490) **TS**, (200) **YS**, 40 **El**
SS 14 23 67	SS 23 67–27	Sweden	Bar, forgings	0.030 **C**, 2.0 **Mn**, 1.0 **Si**, 17.5–19.5 **Cr**, 14.0–17.0 **Ni**, 3.0–4.0 **Mo**, 0.045 **P**, 0.030 **S**	**Solution annealed**: (<50) **diam**, (490) **TS**, (220) **YS**, 40 **El**
SS 14 23 67	SS 23 67–28	Sweden	Plate, sheet, strip	0.030 **C**, 2.0 **Mn**, 1.0 **Si**, 17.5–19.5 **Cr**, 14.0–17.0 **Ni**, 3.0–4.0 **Mo**, 0.045 **P**, 0.030 **S**	**Solution annealed**: all **diam**, (490) **TS**, (220) **YS**, 40 **El**
SS 14 23 48	SS 23 48–28	Sweden	Plate, sheet, strip	0.030 **C**, 2.0 **Mn**, 1.0 **Si**, 16.0–18.5 **Cr**, 11.0–14.0 **Ni**, 2.0–2.5 **Mo**, 0.045 **P**, 0.030 **S**	**Solution annealed**: (<5) **diam**, (490) **TS**, (210) **YS**, 45 **El**
ANSI/ASTM A 479	316L	US	Bar, shapes	0.030 **C**, 2.00 **Mn**, 1.00 **Si**, 16.00–18.00 **Cr**, 10.00–14.00 **Ni**, 2.00–3.00 **Mo**, 0.10 **N**, 0.045 **P**, 0.030 **S**	**Solution annealed**: all **diam**, 70 (485) **TS**, 25 (170) **YS**, 30 **El**
ANSI/ASTM A 479	304L	US	Bar, shapes	0.030 **C**, 2.00 **Mn**, 1.00 **Si**, 18.00–20.00 **Cr**, 8.00–12.00 **Ni**, 0.10 **N**, 0.045 **P**, 0.030 **S**	**Solution annealed**: all **diam**, 70 (485) **TS**, 25 (170) **YS**, 30 **El**
ASTM A 240	Type 316L	US	Plate, sheet, strip	0.030 **C**, 2.00 **Mn**, 1.00 **Si**, 16.00–18.00 **Cr**, 10.00–14.00 **Ni**, 2.00–3.00 **Mo**, 0.10 **N**, 0.045 **P**, 0.030 **S**	**Solution annealed, hot rolled or cold rolled**: all **diam**, 70 (485) **TS**, 25 (170) **YS**, 40 **El**
ASTM A 240	Type 304L	US	Plate, sheet, strip	0.030 **C**, 2.00 **Mn**, 1.00 **Si**, 18.00–20.00 **Cr**, 8.00–12.00 **Ni**, 0.10 **N**, 0.045 **P**, 0.030 **S**	**Solution annealed, hot rolled or cold rolled**: all **diam**, 70 (485) **TS**, 25 (170) **YS**, 40 **El**
ASTM A 167	Type 304L	US	Plate, sheet, strip	0.030 **C**, 2.00 **Mn**, 1.00 **Si**, 18.00–20.00 **Cr**, 8.00–12.00 **Ni**, 0.045 **P**, 0.030 **S**	**Solution annealed**: all **diam**, 70 (485) **TS**, 25 (170) **YS**, 40 **El**
ASTM A 167	Type 316L	US	Plate, sheet, strip	0.030 **C**, 2.00 **Mn**, 1.00 **Si**, 16.00–18.00 **Cr**, 10.00–14.00 **Ni**, 2.00–3.00 **Mo**, 0.045 **P**, 0.030 **S**	**Solution annealed**: all **diam**, 70 (485) **TS**, 25 (170) **YS**, 40 **El**
ANSI/ASTM A 479	Grade 304L	US	Bar, shapes	0.030 **C**, 2.00 **Mn**, 1.00 **Si**, 18.00–20.00 **Cr**, 8.00–12.00 **Ni**, 0.10 **N**, 0.045 **P**, 0.030 **S**	**Solution annealed**: all **diam**, (485) **TS**, (170) **YS**, 30 **El**
ANSI/ASTM A 479	Grade 316L	US	Bar, shapes	0.030 **C**, 2.00 **Mn**, 1.00 **Si**, 16.00–18.00 **Cr**, 10.00–14.00 **Ni**, 2.00–3.00 **Mo**, 0.10 **N**, 0.045 **P**, 0.030 **S**	**Solution annealed**: all **diam**, (485) **TS**, (170) **YS**, 30 **El**
ANSI/ASTM A 240	Grade 304L	US	Plate, sheet, strip	0.030 **C**, 2.00 **Mn**, 1.00 **Si**, 18.00–20.00 **Cr**, 8.00–12.00 **Ni**, 0.10 **N**, 0.045 **P**, 0.030 **S**	**Solution annealed**: all **diam**, (485) **TS**, (170) **YS**, 40 **El**
ANSI/ASTM A 240	Grade 316L	US	Plate, sheet, strip	0.030 **C**, 2.00 **Mn**, 1.00 **Si**, 16.00–18.00 **Cr**, 10.00–14.00 **Ni**, 2.00–3.00 **Mo**, 0.045 **P**, 0.030 **S**	**Solution annealed**: all **diam**, (485) **TS**, (170) **YS**, 40 **El**
DGN–B–83	316 L	Mexico	Bar	0.03 **C**, 2.0 **Mn**, 1.0 **Si**, 16.0–18.0 **Cr**, 10.0–14.0 **Ni**, 2.0–3.0 **Mo**, 0.045 **P**, 0.030 **S**	**Hot or cold rolled**: all **diam**, (483) **TS**, (172) **YS**, 40 **El**
DGN–B–83	304 L	Mexico	Bar	0.03 **C**, 2.0 **Mn**, 1.0 **Si**, 18.0–20.0 **Cr**, 8.0–12.0 **Ni**, 0.045 **P**, 0.030 **S**	**Hot or cold rolled**: all **diam**, (483) **TS**, (172) **YS**, 40 **El**
CSA G110.9	Type 304L	Canada	Plate	0.03 **C**, 2.00 **Mn**, 1.00 **Si**, 18.00–20.00 **Cr**, 8.00–12.00 **Ni**, 0.045 **P**, 0.030 **S**	**Hot rolled, annealed, quenched and tempered**: all **diam**, 70 (483) **TS**, 25 (172) **YS**, 40 **El**
CSA G110.9	Type 316L	Canada	Plate	0.03 **C**, 2.00 **Mn**, 1.00 **Si**, 16.00–18.00 **Cr**, 10.00–14.00 **Ni**, 2.00–3.00 **Mo**, 0.045 **P**, 0.030 **S**	**Hot rolled, annealed, quenched and tempered**: all **diam**, 70 (483) **TS**, 25 (172) **YS**, 40 **El**
CSA G 110.9	Type 316L	Canada	Sheet	0.03 **C**, 2.00 **Mn**, 1.00 **Si**, 16.00–18.00 **Cr**, 10.00–14.00 **Ni**, 2.00–3.00 **Mo**, 0.045 **P**, 0.030 **S**	**Hot or cold rolled and annealed**: all **diam**, 70 (483) **TS**, 25 (172) **YS**, 40 **El**
CSA G110.9	Type 304L	Canada	Sheet	0.03 **C**, 2.00 **Mn**, 1.00 **Si**, 18.00–20.00 **Cr**, 8.00–12.00 **Ni**, 0.045 **P**, 0.030 **S**	**Hot or cold rolled and annealed**: all **diam**, 70 (483) **TS**, 25 (172) **YS**, 40 **El**
CSA G110.9	Type 316L	Canada	Strip	0.03 **C**, 2.00 **Mn**, 1.00 **Si**, 16.00–18.00 **Cr**, 10.00–14.00 **Ni**, 2.00–3.00 **Mo**, 0.045 **P**, 0.030 **S**	**Cold rolled and annealed**: all **diam**, 70 (483) **TS**, 25 (172) **YS**, 40 **El**
CSA G110.9	Type 304L	Canada	Strip	0.03 **C**, 2.00 **Mn**, 1.00 **Si**, 18.00–20.00 **Cr**, 8.00–12.00 **Ni**, 0.045 **P**, 0.030 **S**	**Cold rolled and annealed**: all **diam**, 70 (483) **TS**, 25 (172) **YS**, 40 **El**
CSA G110.6	Type 316L	Canada	Plate, sheet, strip	0.03 **C**, 2.00 **Mn**, 16.00–18.00 **Cr**, 10.00–14.00 **Ni**, 2.00–3.00 **Mo**, 0.045 **P**, 0.030 **S**	**Hot rolled and annealed or hot rolled, quenched and tempered**: all **diam**, 70 (483) **TS**, 25 (172) **YS**, 40 **El**

specification number	designation	country	product forms	composition	mechanical properties (see page iv for explanation)
CSA G110.6	Type 304L	Canada	Plate, sheet, strip	0.03 **C**, 2.00 **Mn**, 1.00 **Si**, 18.00–20.00 **Cr**, 8.00–12.00 **Ni**, 0.045 **P**, 0.030 **S**	**Hot rolled and annealed or hot rolled, quenched and tempered**: all **diam**, 70 (483) **TS**, 25 (172) **YS**, 40 **El**
QQ–S–766C	Class 304L	US	Strip, sheet, plate	0.03 **C**, 2.00 **Mn**, 1.00 **Si**, 18.00 **Cr**, 8.00 **Ni**, 0.045 **P**, 0.035 **S**	**Annealed**: all **diam**, 70 (483) **TS**, 40 **El**
QQ–S–766C	Class 316L	US	Strip, sheet, plate	0.03 **C**, 2.00 **Mn**, 1.00 **Si**, 16.00 **Cr**, 10.00–14.00 **Ni**, 2.00–3.00 **Mo**, 0.045 **P**, 0.030 **S**	**Annealed**: all **diam**, 70 (483) **TS**, 40 (276) **El**
JIS G 3447	SUS 304L TBS	Japan	Tube: seamless or welded	0.030 **C**, 2.00 **Mn**, 1.00 **Si**, 18.00–20.00 **Cr**, 9.00–13.00 **Ni**, 0.040 **P**, 0.030 **S**	**Solution annealed**: all **diam**, (481) **TS**, 35 **El**
JIS G 3447	SUS 316L TBS	Japan	Tube: seamless or welded	0.030 **C**, 2.00 **Mn**, 1.00 **Si**, 16.00–18.00 **Cr**, 12.00–16.00 **Ni**, 2.00–3.00 **Mo**	**Solution annealed**: all **diam**, (481) **TS**, 35 **El**
JIS G 3459	SUS 304 LTP	Japan	Pipe: seamless or welded	0.030 **C**, 2.00 **Mn**, 1.00 **Si**, 18.00–20.00 **Cr**, 9.00–13.00 **Ni**, 0.040 **P**, 0.030 **S**	**Solution annealed**: (≥8) **diam**, (481) **TS**, (177) **YS**, 35 **El**
JIS G 3459	SUS 316 LTP	Japan	Pipe: seamless or welded	0.030 **C**, 2.00 **Mn**, 1.00 **Si**, 16.00–18.00 **Cr**, 12.00–16.00 **Ni**, 2.00–3.00 **Mo**, 0.040 **P**, 0.030 **S**	**Solution annealed**: (≥8) **diam**, (481) **TS**, (177) **YS**, 35 **El**
JIS G 3463	SUS 304 LTB	Japan	Tube: seamless or welded	0.030 **C**, 2.00 **Mn**, 1.00 **Si**, 18.00–20.00 **Cr**, 9.00–13.00 **Ni**, 0.040 **P**, 0.030 **S**	**Solution annealed**: (≥8) **diam**, (481) **TS**, (177) **YS**, 35 **El**
JIS G 3463	SUS 316 LTB	Japan	Tube: seamless or welded	0.030 **C**, 2.00 **Mn**, 1.00 **Si**, 16.00–18.00 **Cr**, 12.00–16.00 **Ni**, 2.00–3.00 **Mo**, 0.040 **P**, 0.030 **S**	**Solution annealed**: (≥8) **diam**, (481) **TS**, (177) **YS**, 35 **El**
JIS G 4303	SUS 304L	Japan	Bar	0.030 **C**, 2.00 **Mn**, 1.00 **Si**, 18.00–20.00 **Cr**, 9.00–13.00 **Ni**, 0.040 **P**, 0.030 **S**	**Solution annealed**: (≤180) **diam**, (481) **TS**, (177) **YS**, 40 **El**
JIS G 4303	SUS 316L	Japan	Bar	0.030 **C**, 2.00 **Mn**, 1.00 **Si**, 16.00–18.00 **Cr**, 12.00–15.00 **Ni**, 2.00–3.00 **Mo**, 0.040 **P**, 0.030 **S**	**Solution annealed**: (≤180) **diam**, (481) **TS**, (177) **YS**, 40 **El**
JIS G 4303	SUS 316 JIL	Japan	Bar	0.030 **C**, 2.00 **Mn**, 1.00 **Si**, 17.00–19.00 **Cr**, 12.00–16.00 **Ni**, 1.20–2.75 **Mo**, 1.00–2.50 **Cu**, 0.040 **P**, 0.030 **S**	**Solution annealed**: (≤180) **diam**, (481) **TS**, (177) **YS**, 40 **El**
JIS G 4303	SUS 317L	Japan	Bar	0.030 **C**, 2.00 **Mn**, 1.00 **Si**, 18.00–20.00 **Cr**, 11.00–15.00 **Ni**, 3.00–4.00 **Mo**, 0.040 **P**, 0.030 **S**	**Solution annealed**: (≤180) **diam**, (481) **TS**, (177) **YS**, 40 **El**
JIS G 4304	SUS 304L	Japan	Sheet, plate	0.030 **C**, 2.00 **Mn**, 1.00 **Si**, 18.00–20.00 **Cr**, 9.00–13.00 **Ni**, 0.040 **P**, 0.030 **S**	**Hot rolled and solution annealed**: all **diam**, (481) **TS**, (177) **YS**, 40 **El**
JIS G 4304	SUS 316L	Japan	Sheet, plate	0.030 **C**, 2.00 **Mn**, 1.00 **Si**, 16.00–18.00 **Cr**, 12.00–15.00 **Ni**, 2.00–3.00 **Mo**, 0.040 **P**, 0.030 **S**	**Hot rolled and solution annealed**: all **diam**, (481) **TS**, (177) **YS**, 40 **El**
JIS G 4304	SUS 316JIL	Japan	Sheet, plate	0.030 **C**, 2.00 **Mn**, 1.00 **Si**, 17.00–19.00 **Cr**, 12.00–16.00 **Ni**, 1.20–2.75 **Mo**, 1.00–2.50 **Cu**, 0.040 **P**, 0.030 **S**	**Hot rolled and solution annealed**: all **diam**, (481) **TS**, (177) **YS**, 40 **El**
JIS G 4304	SUS 317L	Japan	Sheet, plate	0.030 **C**, 2.00 **Mn**, 1.00 **Si**, 18.00–20.00 **Cr**, 11.00–15.00 **Ni**, 3.00–4.00 **Mo**, 0.040 **P**, 0.030 **S**	**Hot rolled and solution annealed**: all **diam**, (481) **TS**, (177) **YS**, 40 **El**
JIS G 4305	SUS 304L	Japan	Sheet, plate	0.030 **C**, 2.00 **Mn**, 1.00 **Si**, 18.00–20.00 **Cr**, 9.00–13.00 **Ni**, 0.040 **P**, 0.030 **S**	**Cold rolled and solution annealed**: all **diam**, (481) **TS**, (177) **YS**, 40 **El**
JIS G 4305	SUS 316L	Japan	Sheet, plate	0.030 **C**, 2.00 **Mn**, 1.00 **Si**, 16.00–18.00 **Cr**, 12.00–15.00 **Ni**, 2.00–3.00 **Mo**, 0.040 **P**, 0.030 **S**	**Cold rolled and solution annealed**: all **diam**, (481) **TS**, (177) **YS**, 40 **El**
JIS G 4305	SUS 316L	Japan	Sheet, plate	0.030 **C**, 2.00 **Mn**, 1.00 **Si**, 16.00–18.00 **Cr**, 12.00–15.00 **Ni**, 2.00–3.00 **Mo**, 0.040 **P**, 0.030 **S**	**Cold rolled and solution annealed**: all **diam**, (481) **TS**, (177) **YS**, 40 **El**
JIS G 4305	SUS 316J1L	Japan	Sheet, plate	0.030 **C**, 2.00 **Mn**, 1.00 **Si**, 17.00–19.00 **Cr**, 12.00–16.00 **Ni**, 1.20–2.75 **Mo**, 1.00–2.50 **Cu**, 0.040 **P**, 0.030 **S**	**Coid rolled and solution annealed**: all **diam**, (481) **TS**, (177) **YS**, 40 **El**
JIS G 4305	SUS 317L	Japan	Sheet, plate	0.030 **C**, 2.00 **Mn**, 1.00 **Si**, 18.00–20.00 **Cr**, 11.00–15.00 **Ni**, 3.00–4.00 **Mo**, 0.040 **P**, 0.030 **S**	**Cold rolled and solution annealed**: all **diam**, (481) **TS**, (177) **YS**, 40 **El**

WROUGHT STAINLESS STEELS

specification number	designation	country	product forms	composition	mechanical properties (see page iv for explanation)
JIS G 4306	SUS 304L	Japan	Strip	0.030 **C**, 2.00 **Mn**, 1.00 **Si**, 18.00–20.00 **Cr**, 9.00–13.00 **Ni**, 0.040 **P**, 0.030 **S**	**Hot rolled and solution annealed**: all **diam**, (481) **TS**, (177) **YS**, 40 **El**
JIS G 4306	SUS 316L	Japan	Strip	0.030 **C**, 2.00 **Mn**, 1.00 **Si**, 16.00–18.00 **Cr**, 12.00–15.00 **Ni**, 2.00–3.00 **Mo**, 0.040 **P**, 0.030 **S**	**Hot rolled and solution annealed**: all **diam**, (481) **TS**, (177) **YS**, 40 **El**
JIS G 4307	SUS 304L	Japan	Strip	0.030 **C**, 2.00 **Mn**, 1.00 **Si**, 18.00–20.00 **Cr**, 9.00–13.00 **Ni**, 0.040 **P**, 0.030 **S**	**Cold rolled and solution annealed**: all **diam**, (481) **TS**, (177) **YS**, 40 **El**
JIS G 4307	SUS 316L	Japan	Strip	0.030 **C**, 2.00 **Mn**, 1.00 **Si**, 16.00–18.00 **Cr**, 12.00–15.00 **Ni**, 2.00–3.00 **Mo**, 0.040 **P**, 0.030 **S**	**Cold rolled and solution annealed**: all **diam**, (481) **TS**, (177) **YS**, 40 **El**
ANSI/ASTM A 276	316L	US	Bar, shapes	0.03 **C**, 2.00 **Mn**, 1.00 **Si**, 16.00–18.00 **Cr**, 10.00–14.00 **Ni**, 2.00–3.00 **Mo**, 0.10 **N**, 0.045 **P**, 0.030 **S**	**Annealed**: all **diam**, 70 (480) **TS**, 25 (170) **YS**, 40 **El**
ANSI/ASTM A 276	304L	US	Bar, shapes	0.03 **C**, 2.00 **Mn**, 1.00 **Si**, 18.00–20.00 **Cr**, 8.00–12.00 **Ni**, 0.10 **N**, 0.045 **P**, 0.030 **S**	**Annealed**: all **diam**, 70 (480) **TS**, 25 (170) **YS**, 40 **El**
AS 1449	Grade AS 1449/316L	Australia	Sheet, strip, plate	0.030 **C**, 2.00 **Mn**, 1.00 **Si**, 16.00–18.00 **Cr**, 10.00–14.00 **Ni**, 2.00–3.00 **Mo**, 0.045 **P**, 0.030 **S**	**Annealed**: (≤1.2) **diam**, (480) **TS**, (170) **YS**, 40 **El**
AS 1449	Grade AS 1449/304L	Australia	Sheet, strip, plate	0.030 **C**, 2.00 **Mn**, 1.00 **Si**, 18.00–20.00 **Cr**, 8.00–12.00 **Ni**, 0.045 **P**, 0.030 **S**	**Annealed**: (≤1.2) **diam**, (480) **TS**, (170) **YS**, 40 **El**
NF A 35–572	Z 2 CND 17–12	France	Bar, sections	0.03 **C**, 2.0 **Mn**, 1.0 **Si**, 16.0–18.0 **Cr**, 10.5–13.0 **Ni**, 2.0–2.5 **Mo**, 0.040 **P**, 0.030 **S**	**Austenitized**: (≤25) **diam**, (480) **TS**, (195) **YS**, 45 **El**
NF A 35–572	Z 2 CND 17.13	France	Bar, sections	0.030 **C**, 2.0 **Mn**, 1.0 **Si**, 16.0–18.0 **Cr**, 11.5–13.5 **Ni**, 2.5–3.0 **Mo**, 0.040 **P**, 0.030 **S**	**Austenitized**: (≤25) **diam**, (480) **TS**, (195) **YS**, 45 **El**
NF A 35–572	Z 2 CN 18–10	France	Bar, sections	0.03 **C**, 2.0 **Mn**, 1.0 **Si**, 17.0–19.0 **Cr**, 9.0–11.0 **Ni**, 0.040 **P**, 0.030 **S**	**Austenitized**: (≤25) **diam**, (470) **TS**, (185) **YS**, 45 **El**
BS 970 Part 4	Grade 304S12	UK	Blooms, billets, bar, forgings	0.03 **C**, 0.50–2.00 **Mn**, 0.20–1.00 **Si**, 17.5–19.0 **Cr**, 9.0–12.0 **Ni**, 0.045 **P**, 0.030 **S**	**Annealed**: all **diam**, (460) **TS**, (170) **YS**, 40 **El**
BS 970 Part 4	Grade 316S12	UK	Blooms, billets, bar, forgings	0.03 **C**, 0.50–2.00 **Mn**, 0.20–1.00 **Si**, 16.5–18.5 **Cr**, 11.0–14.0 **Ni**, 2.25–3.0 **Mo**, 0.045 **P**, 0.030 **S**	**Annealed**: all **diam**, (460) **TS**, 40 **El**
BS 970 Part 4	Grade 317S12	UK	Blooms, billets, bar, forgings	0.03 **C**, 0.50–2.00 **Mn**, 0.20–1.00 **Si**, 17.5–19.5 **Cr**, 14.0–17.0 **Ni**, 3.0–4.0 **Mo**, 0.045 **P**, 0.030 **S**	**Annealed**: all **diam**, (460) **TS**, 40 **El**
NF A 36–209	Z 2 CN 18–10	France	Plate	0.030 **C**, 2.0 **Mn**, 1.0 **Si**, 17.0–19.0 **Cr**, 9.0–11.0 **Ni**, 0.040 **P**, 0.030 **S**	**Hot rolled**: (<3) **diam**, (460) **TS**, (185) **YS**, 40 **El**; **Cold rolled**: (<3) **diam**, (460) **TS**, (185) **YS**, 40 **El**
SS 14 23 52	SS 23 52–02	Sweden	Bar, forgings, plate, sheet, strip, tube	0.030 **C**, 2.0 **Mn**, 1.0 **Si**, 17.0–19.0 **Cr**, 9.0–12.0 **Ni**, 0.045 **P**, 0.030 **S**	**Solution annealed**: all **diam**, (460) **TS**, (190) **YS**, 45 **El**
SS 14 23 52	SS 23 52–26	Sweden	Tube: welded	0.030 **C**, 2.0 **Mn**, 1.0 **Si**, 17.0–19.0 **Cr**, 9.0–12.0 **Ni**, 0.045 **P**, 0.030 **S**	**Solution annealed**: (<30) **diam**, (460) **TS**, (190) **YS**, 45 **El**
SS 14 23 52	SS 23 52–27	Sweden	Bar, forgings, plate, sheet, strip	0.030 **C**, 2.0 **Mn**, 1.0 **Si**, 17.0–19.0 **Cr**, 9.0–12.0 **Ni**, 0.045 **P**, 0.030 **S**	**Solution annealed**: all **diam**, (460) **TS**, (190) **YS**, 45 **El**
BS 1506–801	Grade C	UK	Bar	0.03 **C**, 0.50–2.00 **Mn**, 0.20–1.00 **Si**, 17.5–20.0 **Cr**, 10.0 min **Ni**, 0.045 **S**, 0.045 **P**	**Solution annealed**: all **diam**, (455) **TS**, (180) **YS**, 30 **El**; **Cold drawn**: 0.75 **diam**, (770) **TS**, (620) **YS**, 12 **El**
BS 1501–801	Grade C	UK	Bar	0.03 **C**, 0.50–2.00 **Mn**, 0.20–1.00 **Si**, 17.5–20.0 **Cr**, 10.0 min **Ni**, 0.045 **S**, 0.045 **P**	**Annealed**: all **diam**, (455) **TS**, (180) **YS**
JIS G 3214	SUS F 304 L	Japan	Forgings	0.030 **C**, 2.00 **Mn**, 1.00 **Si**, 18.00–20.00 **Cr**, 9.00–13.00 **Ni**, 0.040 **P**, 0.030 **S**	**Solution annealed**: all **diam**, (451) **TS**, (177) **YS**, 30 **El**
JIS G 3214	SUS F 316 L	Japan	Forgings	0.030 **C**, 2.00 **Mn**, 1.00 **Si**, 16.00–18.00 **Cr**, 12.00–15.00 **Ni**, 2.00–3.00 **Mo**, 0.040 **P**, 0.030 **S**	**Solution annealed**: all **diam**, (451) **TS**, (177) **YS**, 30 **El**

WROUGHT STAINLESS STEELS

specification number	designation	country	product forms	composition	mechanical properties (see page iv for explanation)
ANSI/ASTM A 473	304L	US	Forgings	0.03 **C**, 2.00 **Mn**, 1.00 **Si**, 18.00–20.00 **Cr**, 8.00–12.00 **Ni**, 0.10 **N**, 0.045 **P**, 0.030 **S**	**Solution annealed**: all **diam**, 65 (450) **TS**, 25 (170) **YS**, 40 **El**
ANSI/ASTM A 473	316L	US	Forgings	0.03 **C**, 2.00 **Mn**, 1.00 **Si**, 16.00–18.00 **Cr**, 10.00–14.00 **Ni**, 2.00–3.00 **Mo**, 0.10 **N**, 0.045 **P**, 0.030 **S**	**Solution annealed**: all **diam**, 65 (450) **TS**, 25 (170) **YS**, 40 **El**
DIN 17440	Grade X 2 CrNi 18 9	Germany	Sheet, strip, bar, wire, tube, forgings	0.03 **C**, 2.0 **Mn**, 1.0 **Si**, 17.0–20.0 **Cr**, 10.0–12.5 **Ni**, 0.045 **P**, 0.030 **S**	**Quenched**: (≤60) **diam**, (450) **TS**, (175) **YS**, 50 **El**
DIN 17440	Grade X 2 CrNiMo 18 10	Germany	Sheet, strip, bar, wire, tube, forgings	0.03 **C**, 2.0 **Mn**, 1.0 **Si**, 16.5–18.5 **Cr**, 11.0–14.0 **Ni**, 2.0–2.5 **Mo**, 0.045 **P**, 0.030 **S**	**Quenched**: (≤60) **diam**, (450) **TS**, (195) **YS**, 45 **El**
DIN 17440	Grade X 2 CrNiMo 18 12	Germany	Sheet, strip, bar, wire, tube, forgings	0.03 **C**, 2.0 **Mn**, 1.0 **Si**, 16.5–18.5 **Cr**, 12.5–15.0 **Ni**, 2.5–3.0 **Mo**, 0.045 **P**, 0.030 **S**	**Quenched**: (≤60) **diam**, (450) **TS**, (195) **YS**, 45 **El**
ISO 2604/1	F59	ISO	Forgings	0.03 **C**, 2.00 **Mn**, 1.00 **Si**, 16.00–18.00 **Cr**, 11.00–15.00 **Ni**, 2.00–3.00 **Mo**, 0.045 **P**, 0.030 **S**	**Quenched**: all **diam**, (440) **TS**, (185) **YS**, 30 **El**
ISO 2604/1	F46	ISO	Forgings	0.03 **C**, 2.00 **Mn**, 1.00 **Si**, 17.0–19.0 **Cr**, 8.00–12.00 **Ni**, 0.045 **P**, 0.030 **S**	**Quenched**: all **diam**, (440) **TS**, (175) **YS**, 30 **El**
ISO 683/XII	10	ISO	Bar, sheet, plate	0.030 **C**, 2.0 **Mn**, 1.0 **Si**, 17.0–19.0 **Cr**, 9.0–12.0 **Ni**, 0.045 **P**, 0.030 **S**	**Solution treated**: all **diam**, (440) **TS**, 180 **YS**, 40 **El**
ISO 683/XII	19	ISO	Bar, sheet, plate	0.030 **C**, 2.0 **Mn**, 1.0 **Si**, 16.0–18.5 **Cr**, 11.0–14.0 **Ni**, 2.0–2.5 **Mo**, 0.045 **P**, 0.030 **S**	**Solution treated**: all **diam**, (440) **TS**, (200) **YS**, 40 **El**
ISO 683/XII	19a	ISO	Bar, sheet, plate	0.030 **C**, 2.0 **Mn**, 1.0 **Si**, 16.0–18.5 **Cr**, 11.5–14.5 **Ni**, 2.5–3.0 **Mo**, 0.045 **P**, 0.030 **S**	**Solution treated**: all **diam**, (440) **TS**, (200) **YS**, 40 **El**
EURONORM 119–74, V	X 3 Cr Ni 18 10 KD	EURONORM	Wire, rod	0.030 **C**, 2.0 **Mn**, 1.0 **Si**, 17.0–19.0 **Cr**, 9.0–12.0 **Ni**, 0.045 **P**, 0.030 **S**	**Solution annealed**: (15–63) **diam**, (440) **TS**, (175) **YS**, 40 **El**
EURONORM 119–74, V	X3 CrNiMo 17 12 2 KD	EURONORM	Wire, rod	0.03 **C**, 2.0 **Mn**, 1.0 **Si**, 16.0–18.5 **Cr**, 10.5–13.5 **Ni**, 2.0–2.5 **Mo**, 0.045 **P**, 0.030 **S**	**Solution annealed**: (15–63) **diam**, (440) **TS**, (195) **YS**, 40 **El**
ISO 2604/IV	P46	ISO	Plate	0.03 **C**, 2.00 **Mn**, 1.00 **Si**, 17.0–19.0 **Cr**, 9.0–12.0 **Ni**, 0.045 **P**, 0.030 **S**	**Hot rolled, quenched**: (3–30) **diam**, (440) **TS**, (175) **YS**, 50 **El**
ISO 2604/IV	P57	ISO	Plate	0.03 **C**, 2.00 **Mn**, 1.00 **Si**, 16.0–18.5 **Cr**, 11.0–14.0 **Ni**, 2.0–2.5 **Mo**, 0.045 **P**, 0.030 **S**	**Hot rolled, quenched**: (3–40) **diam**, (440) **TS**, (185) **YS**, 45 **El**
ISO 2604/IV	P58	ISO	Plate	0.03 **C**, 2.00 **Mn**, 1.00 **Si**, 16.0–18.5 **Cr**, 11.5–14.5 **Ni**, 2.5–3.0 **Mo**, 0.045 **P**, 0.030 **S**	**Hot rolled, quenched**: (3–40) **diam**, (440) **TS**, (185) **YS**, 45 **El**
IS 6603	02Cr17Ni12Mo2	India	Bar	0.030 **C**, 2.0 **Mn**, 1.0 **Si**, 16.0–18.5 **Cr**, 10.5–14.0 **Ni**, 2.0–3.0 **Mo**, 0.045 **P**, 0.030 **S**	**Softened**: (5–100) **diam**, (440) **TS**, (200) **YS**, 40 **El**
IS 6603	02Cr18Ni11	India	Bar	0.030 **C**, 2.0 **Mn**, 1.0 **Si**, 17.0–20.0 **Cr**, 9.0–13.0 **Ni**, 0.045 **P**, 0.030 **S**	**Softened**: (5–100) **diam**, (440) **TS**, (180) **YS**, 40 **El**
IS 6911	02Cr18Ni11	India	Plate, sheet, strip	0.030 **C**, 2.0 **Mn**, 1.0 **Si**, 17.0–20.0 **Cr**, 9.0–13.0 **Ni**, 0.030 **S**, 0.045 **P**	**Softened**: (0.5–3) **diam**, (440) **TS**, (180) **YS**, 38 **El**
IS 6911	02Cr17Ni12Mo2	India	Plate, sheet, strip	0.030 **C**, 2.0 **Mn**, 1.0 **Si**, 16.0–18.5 **Cr**, 10.5–14.0 **Ni**, 2.0–3.0 **Mo**, 0.030 **S**, 0.045 **P**	**Softened**: (0.5–3) **diam**, (440) **TS**, (200) **YS**, 38 **El**
AIR 9160	9160C191	France	Bar, shapes, wire, tube, sheet	0.030 **C**, 2.0 **Mn**, 1.0 **Si**, 17.0–19.0 **Cr**, 9.0–11.0 **Ni**, 0.035 **P**, 0.025 **S**	**Solution annealed (bar)**: (<50) **diam**, (440) **TS**, (180) **YS**, 45 **El**
ANSI/ASTM A 314	304L	US	Bar, forgings, billets	0.03 **C**, 2.00 **Mn**, 1.00 **Si**, 18.00–20.00 **Cr**, 8.00–12.00 **Ni**, 0.10 **N**, 0.045 **P**, 0.030 **S**	
ANSI/ASTM A 314	316L	US	Bar, forgings, billets	0.03 **C**, 2.00 **Mn**, 1.00 **Si**, 16.00–18.00 **Cr**, 10.00–14.00 **Ni**, 2.00–3.00 **Mo**, 0.10 **N**, 0.045 **P**, 0.030 **S**	
AS 1444	Grade AS 1444/304L	Australia	Bar, bloom, billet, slab	0.030 **C**, 2.00 **Mn**, 1.00 **Si**, 18.00–20.00 **Cr**, 8.00–12.00 **Ni**, 0.045 **P**, 0.040 **S**	

specification number	designation	country	product forms	composition	mechanical properties (see page iv for explanation)
AS 1444	Grade AS 1444/316L	Australia	Bar, bloom, billet, slab	0.030 **C**, 2.00 **Mn**, 1.00 **Si**, 16.00–18.00 **Cr**, 10.00–14.00 **Ni**, 2.00–3.00 **Mo**, 0.045 **P**, 0.040 **S**	
AS 1444	Grade AS 1444/317L	Australia	Bar, bloom, billet, slab	0.030 **C**, 2.00 **Mn**, 1.00 **Si**, 18.00–20.00 **Cr**, 11.00–15.00 **Ni**, 3.00–4.00 **Mo**, 0.045 **P**, 0.040 **S**	
DGN–B–150	Type AE–308 EBC	Mexico	Wire	0.03 **C**, 1.0–2.5 **Mn**, 0.25–0.60 **Si**, 19.5–22.0 **Cr**, 9.0–11.0 **Ni**, 0.25 **Cu**, 0.07 N_2, 0.030 **P**, 0.030 **S**	
DGN–B–150	Type AE–316 EBC	Mexico	Wire	0.03 **C**, 1.0–2.5 **Mn**, 0.25–0.60 **Si**, 18.0–20.0 **Cr**, 11.0–14.0 **Ni**, 2.0–3.0 **Mo**, 0.25 **Cu**, 0.07 N_2, 0.030 **P**, 0.030 **S**	
MIL–S–862B	Class 304L	US	Bar, billets	0.03 **C**, 2.0 **Mn**, 1.0 **Si**, 18.0–20.0 **Cr**, 8.0–12.0 **Ni**, 0.045 **P**, 0.030 **S**	
MIL–S–862B	Class 316L	US	Bar, billets	0.03 **C**, 2.0 **Mn**, 1.0 **Si**, 16.0–18.0 **Cr**, 10.0–14.0 **Ni**, 2.0–3.0 **Mo**, 0.045 **P**, 0.030 **S**	
MIL–T–8973	304L	US	Tube	0.03 **C**, 2.00 **Mn**, 1.00 **Si**, 18.0–20.0 **Cr**, 8.0–11.0 **Ni**, 0.50 **Mo**, 0.50 **Cu**, 0.040 **P**, 0.030 **S**	**Cold drawn**: all **diam**, 75 (517) **YS**, 20 **El**
MIL–T–8973	316L	US	Tube	0.03 **C**, 2.00 **Mn**, 1.00 **Si**, 16.0–18.0 **Cr**, 10.0–14.0 **Ni**, 2.00–3.00 **Mo**, 0.50 **Cu**, 0.040 **P**, 0.030 **S**	**Cold drawn**: all **diam**, 75 (517) **YS**, 20 **El**
IS 6529	02Cr18Ni11	India	Blooms, billets, slabs	0.030 **C**, 2.0 **Mn**, 1.0 **Si**, 17.0–20.0 **Cr**, 9.0–13.0 **Ni**, 0.045 **P**, 0.030 **S**	**Annealed, or solution annealed**
IS 6529	02Cr17Ni12Mo2	India	Blooms, billets, slabs	0.030 **C**, 2.0 **Mn**, 1.0 **Si**, 16.0–18.5 **Cr**, 10.5–14.0 **Ni**, 2.0–3.0 **Mo**, 0.045 **P**, 0.030 **S**	**Annealed, or solution annealed**
MIL–S–27419	304L	US	Billets	0.03 **C**, 2.00 **Mn**, 1.00 **Si**, 18.0–20.0 **Cr**, 8.0–11.0 **Ni**, 0.50 **Mo**, 0.50 **Cu**, 0.025 **P**, 0.025 **S**	
IS 6527	02Cr18Ni11	India	Wire, rod	0.030 **C**, 2.0 **Mn**, 1.0 **Si**, 17.0–20.0 **Cr**, 9.0–13.0 **Ni**, 0.030 **S**, 0.045 **P**	**Annealed**
IS 6527	02Cr17Ni12M02	India	Wire, rod	0.030 **C**, 2.0 **Mn**, 1.0 **Si**, 16.0–18.5 **Cr**, 10.5–14.0 **Ni**, 2.0–3.0 **Mo**, 0.030 **S**, 0.045 **P**	**Annealed**
NF A 36–209	Z 2 CND 17–12	France	Plate	0.030 **C**, 2.0 **Mn**, 1.0 **Si**, 16.0–18.0 **Cr**, 11.0–13.0 **Ni**, 2.0–2.5 **Mo**, 0.040 **P**, 0.030 **S**	
NF A 35–583	Z 2 CN 20.10	France	Wire, rod	0.03 **C**, 1.0–2.5 **Mn**, 0.6 **Si**, 18.5–21.5 **Cr**, 9.0–11.5 **Ni**, 0.030 **P**, 0.020 **S**	
NF A 35–583	Z 2 CNS 20.10	France	Wire, rod	0.03 **C**, 1.0–2.5 **Mn**, 0.6–1.1 **Si**, 18.5–21.5 **Cr**, 9.0–11.5 **Ni**, 0.03 **P**, 0.02 **S**	
NF A 35–583	Z 2 CND 19.13	France	Wire, rod	0.03 **C**, 1.0–2.5 **Mn**, 0.6 **Si**, 17.0–20.0 **Cr**, 12.0–14.5 **Ni**, 2.5–3.0 **Mo**, 0.030 **P**, 0.020 **S**	
NF A 35–583	Z 2 CNDS 19.13	France	Wire, rod	0.03 **C**, 1.0–2.5 **Mn**, 0.6–1.1 **Si**, 17.0–20.0 **Cr**, 11.5–14.0 **Ni**, 2.5–3.0 **Mo**, 0.030 **P**, 0.020 **S**	
NF A 35–583	Z 2 CND 20.10	France	Wire, rod	0.03 **C**, 1.0–2.5 **Mn**, 0.6 **Si**, 19.0–22.0 **Cr**, 9.0–11.5 **Ni**, 2.5–3.2 **Mo**, 0.030 **P**, 0.020 **S**	
NF A 35–583	Z 2 CN 24.13	France	Wire, rod	0.03 **C**, 1.0–2.5 **Mn**, 0.6 **Si**, 22.0–25.0 **Cr**, 11.5–14.0 **Ni**, 0.030 **P**, 0.020 **S**	
NF A 35–583	Z 2 CNM 25.20	France	Wire, rod	0.03 **C**, 6–8 **Mn**, 0.6 **Si**, 24.5–27.5 **Cr**, 19.0–22.0 **Ni**, 0.030 **P**, 0.020 **S**	
JIS G 4308	SUS 304 L	Japan	Wire, rod	0.030 **C**, 2.00 **Mn**, 1.00 **Si**, 18.00–20.00 **Cr**, 9.00–13.00 **Ni**, 0.040 **P**, 0.030 **S**	

WROUGHT STAINLESS STEELS

specification number	designation	country	product forms	composition	mechanical properties (see page iv for explanation)
JIS G 4308	SUS 316L	Japan	Wire, rod	0.030 **C**, 2.00 **Mn**, 1.00 **Si**, 16.00–18.00 **Cr**, 12.00–15.00 **Ni**, 2.00–3.00 **Mo**	
JIS G 4316	SUS Y 308 L	Japan	Wire, rod	0.030 **C**, 1.00–2.50 **Mn**, 0.60 **Si**, 19.50–22.00 **Cr**, 9.00–11.00 **Ni**, 0.030 **P**, 0.030 **S**	
JIS G 4316	SUS Y 316 L	Japan	Wire, rod	0.030 **C**, 1.00–2.50 **Mn**, 0.60 **Si**, 18.00–20.00 **Cr**, 11.00–14.00 **Ni**, 2.00–3.00 **Mo**, 0.030 **P**, 0.030 **S**	
JIS G 4316	SUS Y 316 JIL	Japan	Wire, rod	0.030 **C**, 1.00–2.50 **Mn**, 0.60 **Si**, 18.00–20.00 **Cr**, 11.00–14.00 **Ni**, 2.00–3.00 **Mo**, 1.00–2.50 **Cu**	
CSA G110.3	Type 304L	Canada	Bar, billets	0.03 **C**, 2.00 **Mn**, 1.00 **Si**, 18.00–20.00 **Cr**, 8.00–12.00 **Ni**, 0.045 **P**, 0.030 **S**	
CSA G110.3	Type 316L	Canada	Bar, billets	0.03 **C**, 2.00 **Mn**, 1.00 **Si**, 16.00–18.00 **Cr**, 10.00–14.00 **Ni**, 2.00–3.00 **Mo**, 0.045 **P**, 0.030 **S**	
SS 14 23 26	SS 23 26–28	Sweden	Sheet, strip	0.025 **C**, 0.5 **Mn**, 1.0 **Si**, 17.0–19.0 **Cr**, 0.50 **Ni**, 2.0–2.5 **Mo**, 0.025 **N**, 0.040 **P**, 0.020 **S**, 0.20–0.80 **Ti+C+N**	**Annealed:** (≤2.3) **diam**, (440) **TS**, (340) **YS**, 25 **El**
SS 14 23 26	SS 23 26–26	Sweden	Tube: welded	0.025 **C**, 0.5 **Mn**, 1.0 **Si**, 17.0–19.0 **Cr**, 0.50 **Ni**, 2.0–2.5 **Mo**, 0.025 **N**, 0.040 **P**, 0.020 **S**, 0.20–0.80 **Ti+C+N**	**Annealed:** (≤2.3) **diam**, (440) **TS**, (340) **YS**, 25 **El**
SS 14 23 26	SS 23 26–23	Sweden	Tube: welded	0.025 **C**, 0.5 **Mn**, 1.0 **Si**, 17.0–19.0 **Cr**, 0.50 **Ni**, 2.0–2.5 **Mo**, 0.025 **N**, 0.040 **P**, 0.020 **S**, 0.20–0.80 **Ti+C+N**	**Annealed:** (≤2.3) **diam**, (440) **TS**, (340) **YS**, 25 **El**
SS 14 23 26	SS 23 26–22	Sweden	Tube: seamless	0.025 **C**, 0.5 **Mn**, 1.0 **Si**, 17.0–19.0 **Cr**, 0.50 **Ni**, 2.0–2.5 **Mo**, 0.025 **N**, 0.040 **P**, 0.020 **S**, 0.20–0.80 **Ti+C+N**	**Annealed:** (≤2.3) **diam**, (440) **TS**, (340) **YS**, 25 **El**
SS 14 23 26	SS 23 26–02	Sweden	Plate, sheet, strip, tube, wire	0.025 **C**, 0.5 **Mn**, 1.0 **Si**, 17.0–19.0 **Cr**, 0.50 **Ni**, 2.0–2.5 **Mo**, 0.025 **N**, 0.040 **P**, 0.020 **S**, 0.20–0.80 **Ti+C+N**	**Annealed:** all **diam**, (440) **TS**, (340) **YS**, 25 **El**
NF A 35–583	Z 1 CN 20.10	France	Wire, rod	0.02 **C**, 1.0–2.5 **Mn**, 0.6 **Si**, 18.5–21.5 **Cr**, 9.0–11.5 **Ni**, 0.030 **P**, 0.020 **S**	
AMS 5617C	Grade 2	US	Bar, forgings	0.010 **C**, 0.50 **Mn**, 0.20 **Si**, 11.00–12.50 **Cr**, 7.50–9.50 **Ni**, 0.50 **Mo**, 1.50–2.50 **Cu**, 0.010 **N**, 0.50 **Nb+Ta**, 0.010 **P**, 0.010 **S**, 1.00–1.35 **Ti**	**Precipitation hardened (bar):** ≤4.000 (≤101.60) **diam**, 225 (1551) **TS**, 210 (1448) **YS**, 10 **El**
ANSI/ASTM A 493	Type XM–27	US	Bar, wire	0.010 **C**, 0.40 **Mn**, 0.40 **Si**, 25.00–27.5 **Cr**, 0.50 **Ni**, 0.75–1.50 **Mo** , 0.2 **Cu**, 0.020 **P**, 0.020 **S**, 0.0150 **N**, 0.5 **Ni+Cu**	**Lightly drafted (wire):** ≥0.156 (≥3.96) **diam**, 75 (520) **TS**; **Annealed (wire):** ≥0.156 (≥3.96) **diam**, 60 (415) **TS**
ANSI/ASTM A 479	XM–27	US	Bar, shapes	0.010 **C**, 0.40 **Mn**, 0.40 **Si**, 25.00–27.50 **Cr**, 0.50 **Ni**, 0.75–1.50 **Mo**, 0.20 **Cu**, 0.015 **N**, 0.02 **P**, 0.02 **S**	**Annealed:** all **diam**, 65 (450) **TS**, 40 (275) **YS**
ANSI/ASTM A 276	XM–27	US	Bar, shapes	0.010 **C**, 0.40 **Mn**, 0.40 **Si**, 25.00–27.50 **Cr**, 0.50 **Ni**, 0.75–1.50 **Mo**, 0.20 **Cu**, 0.015 **N**, 0.50 **Ni+Cu**, 0.020 **P**, 0.020 **S**	**Annealed:** all **diam**, 65 (450) **TS**, 40 (275) **YS**, 16 **El**
ANSI/ASTM A 268	TP XM–27	US	Tube: seamless, welded	0.01 **C**, 0.40 **Mn**, 0.40 **Si**, 25.0–27.5 **Cr**, 0.5 **Ni**, 0.75–1.50 **Mo**, 0.2 **Cu**, 0.015 **N**, 0.02 **P**, 0.02 **S**	**Annealed:** 0.312 (7.94) **diam**, 65 (450) **TS**, 40 (275) **YS**, 20 **El**
ASTM A 240	Type XM27	US	Plate, sheet, strip	0.010 **C**, 0.40 **Mn**, 0.40 **Si**, 25.00–27.50 **Cr**, 0.50 **Ni**, 0.75 **Mo**, 0.20 **Cu**, 0.015 **N**, 0.50 **Ni+Cu**, 0.020 **P**, 0.020 **S**	**Hot rolled or cold rolled, annealed:** all **diam**, 65 (450) **TS**, 40 (275) **YS**, 22 **El**
ASTM A 176	Type XM27	US	Plate, sheet, strip	0.010 **C**, 0.40 **Mn**, 0.40 **Si**, 25.00–27.50 **Cr**, 0.50 **Ni**, 0.75–1.50 **Mo**, 0.20 **Cu**, 0.015 **N**, 0.50 **Ni+Cu**, 0.020 **P**, 0.020 **S**	**Annealed:** all **diam**, 65 (450) **TS**, 40 (275) **YS**, 22 **El**
ANSI/ASTM A 479	Grade XM27	US	Bar, shapes	0.010 **C**, 0.40 **Mn**, 0.40 **Si**, 25.00–27.00 **Cr**, 0.50 **Ni**, 0.75–1.50 **Mo**, 0.20 **Cu**, 0.015 **N**, 0.02 **P**, 0.02 **S**	**Annealed:** all **diam**, (450) **TS**, (275) **YS**

specification number	designation	country	product forms	composition	mechanical properties (see page iv for explanation)
ANSI/ASTM A 731	TP XM–27	US	Pipe: seamless or welded	0.01 **C**, 0.40 **Mn**, 0.40 **Si**, 25.0–27.5 **Cr**, 0.50 **Ni**, 0.75–1.50 **Mo**, 0.20 **Cu**, 0.015 **N**, 0.02 **P**, 0.02 **S**	**Annealed**: all **diam**, 65 (450) **TS**, 40 (275) **YS**, 20 **El**
ANSI/ASTM A 314	XM–27	US	Bar, forgings, billets	0.010 **C**, 0.40 **Mn**, 0.40 **Si**, 25.00–27.50 **Cr**, 0.50 **Ni**, 0.75–1.50 **Mo**, 0.015 **N**, 0.50 **Ni+Cu**, 0.020 **P**, 0.020 **S**	
JIS G 3535		Japan	Wire		**As drawn**: (≤0.28) **diam**, (1961) **TS**
JIS C 2507	NMWE	Japan	Wire		**Solution annealed hand drawn, tin coated**: (1.00) **diam**, (1765) **TS**
ASTM A 693	Type 633	US	Plate, sheet, strip		**Solution annealed**: 0.001–0.0015 (0.03–0.038) **diam**, 200 (1380) max **TS**, 90 (620) max **YS**, 8 **El**; **Precipitation hardened**: 0.0005–0.0015 (0.022–0.038) **diam**, 185 (1275) **TS**, 150 (1035) **YS**, 2 **El**
AMS 5643K		US	Bar, forgings, tube, rings, wire	0.0 **C**, 1.00 **Mn**, 1.00 **Si**, 15.00–17.50 **Cr**, 3.00–5.00 **Ni**, 0.50 **Mo**, 3.00–5.00 **Cu**, 5 x C–0.45 **Nb+Ta**, 0.040 **P**, 0.030 **S**	**H 900**: all **diam**, 190 (1310) **TS**, 170 (1172) **YS**, 10 **El**; **H 925**: all **diam**, 170 (1172) **TS**, 155 (1069) **YS**, 10 **El**; **H 1025**: all **diam**, 155 (1069) **TS**, 145 (1000) **YS**, 12 **El**; **H 1075**: all **diam**, 145 (1000) **TS**, 125 (862) **YS**, 13 **El**; **H 1100**: all **diam**, 140 (965) **TS**, 115 (793) **YS**, 14 **El**; **H 1150**: all **diam**, 135 (931) **TS**, 105 (724) **YS**, 16 **El**
JIS G 4309	SUS 304, 1/2 hard	Japan	Wire		**Solution annealed and heavy drawn**: (0.80–1.60) **diam**, (1128) **TS**
JIS G 4309	SUS 316, 1/2 hard	Japan	Wire		**Solution annealed and heavy drawn**: (0.80–1.60) **diam**, (1128) **TS**
JIS G 4309	SUS 303, Soft No. 2	Japan	Wire		**Solution annealed**: (0.80–1.60) **diam**, (785) **TS**
JIS G 4309	SUS 303 Se, Soft No. 2	Japan	Wire		**Solution annealed**: (0.80–1.60) **diam**, (785) **TS**
JIS G 4309	SUS 304, Soft No.2	Japan	Wire		**Solution annealed**: (0.80–1.60) **diam**, (785) **TS**
JIS G 4309	Class 316, Soft No. 2	Japan	Wire		**Solution annealed**: (0.80–1.60) **diam**, (785) **TS**
JIS G 4309	SUS 430, Soft No. 2	Japan	Wire		**Annealed and light drawn**: (0.80–1.60) **diam**, (785) **TS**
JIS G 4309	SUS 430F, Soft No. 2	Japan	Wire		**Annealed and light drawn**: (0.80–1.60) **diam**, (785) **TS**
JIS G 4309	SUS 410, Soft No. 2	Japan	Wire		**Annealed and light drawn**: (0.80–1.60) **diam**, (785) **TS**
JIS G 4309	SUS 416, Soft No. 2	Japan	Wire		**Annealed and light drawn**: (0.80–1.60) **diam**, (785) **TS**
JIS G 4309	SUS 420J1, Soft No. 2	Japan	Wire		**Annealed and light drawn**: (0.80–1.60) **diam**, (785) **TS**
JIS G 4309	SUS 420J2, Soft No. 2	Japan	Wire		**Annealed and light drawn**: (0.80–1.60) **diam**, (785) **TS**
JIS G 4309	SUS 440C, Soft No. 2	Japan	Wire		**Annealed and light drawn**: (0.80–1.60) **diam**, (785) **TS**
NF A 35–575	Z 12 CF 13	France	Wire, rod		**Quenched and tempered**: all **diam**, (690) max **TS**
JIS G 4309	SUS 303, Soft No. 1	Japan	Wire		**Cold drawn and solution annealed**: (0.030–0.050) **diam**, (686) **TS**
JIS G 4309	SUS 303 Se, Soft No. 1	Japan	Wire		**Cold drawn and solution annealed**: (0.030–0.050) **diam**, (686) **TS**
JIS G 4309	SUS 304, Soft No. 1	Japan	Wire		**Cold drawn and solution annealed**: (0.030–0.050) **diam**, (686) **TS**, 10 **El**

WROUGHT STAINLESS STEELS

specification number	designation	country	product forms	composition	mechanical properties (see page iv for explanation)
JIS G 4309	SUS 304L, Soft No. 1	Japan	Wire		**Cold drawn and solution annealed**: (0.030–0.050) **diam**, (686) **TS**, 10 **El**
JIS G 4309	SUS 305, Soft No. 1	Japan	Wire		**Cold drawn and solution annealed**: (0.030–0.050) **diam**, (686) **TS**, 10 **El**
JIS G 4309	SUS 305J1,Soft No. 1	Japan	Wire		**Cold drawn and solution annealed**: (0.030–0.050) **diam**, (686) **TS**, 10 **El**
JIS G 4309	SUS 309S, Soft No. 1	Japan	Wire		**Cold drawn and solution annealed**: (0.030–0.050) **diam**, (686) **TS**, 10 **El**
JIS G 4309	SUS 310S, Soft No. 1	Japan	Wire		**Cold drawn and solution annealed**: (0.030–0.050) **diam**, (686) **TS**, 10 **El**
JIS G 4309	SUS 316, Soft No. 1	Japan	Wire		**Cold drawn and solution annealed**: (0.030–0.050) **diam**, (686) **TS**, 10 **El**
JIS G 4309	SUS 316L, Soft No. 1	Japan	Wire		**Cold drawn and solution annealed**: (0.030–0.050) **diam**, (686) **TS**, 10 **El**
JIS G 4309	SUS 321, Soft No. 1	Japan	Wire		**Cold drawn and solution annealed**: (0.030–0.050) **diam**, (686) **TS**, 10 **El**
NF A 35–575	Z 10 CNF 18.09	France	Wire, rod		**Stress hardened 0%**: all **diam**, (640) **TS**; **Stress hardened 40%**: all **diam**, (1180) **TS**; **Stress hardened 60%**: all **diam**, (1520) **TS**
JIS G 4309	SUS 347, Soft No. 1	Japan	Wire		**Cold drawn and solution annealed**: (0.030–0.050) **diam**, (637) **TS**, 10 **El**
QQ–W–423B	Grade 310	US	Wire		**Annealed**: all **diam**, (620) **TS**
NF A 35–575	Z 10 CF 17	France	Wire, rod		**Stress hardened 0%**: all **diam**, (560) **TS**; **Stress hardened 40%**: all **diam**, (750) **TS**; **Stress hardened 60%**: all **diam**, (850) **TS**
JIS G 4315	SUS 304, Class B	Japan	Wire		**Cold drawn and solution annealed**: all **diam**, (559) **TS**, 25 **El**
QQ–W–423B	Grade 347 A and B	US	Wire		**Annealed**: all **diam**, (550) **TS**; **Spring temper**: >.009 **diam**, (1690) **TS**
QQ–W–423B	Grade 321 A and B	US	Wire		**Annealed**: all **diam**, (550) **TS**; **Spring temper**: >.009 **diam**, (1690) **TS**
QQ–W–423B	Grade 316 A and B	US	Wire		**Annealed**: all **diam**, (550) **TS**; **Spring temper**: >.009 **diam**, (1690) **TS**
QQ–W–423B	Grade 305 A and B	US	Wire		**Annealed**: all **diam**, (550) **TS**; **Spring temper**: >.009 **diam**, (1690) **TS**
QQ–W–423B	Grade 304 A and B	US	Wire		**Annealed**: all **diam**, (550) **TS**; **Spring temper**: >.009 **diam**, (2240) **TS**
QQ–W–423B	Grade 302 A and B	US	Wire		**Annealed**: all **diam**, (550) **TS**; **Spring tempered**: >.009 **diam**, (2240) **TS**
JIS G 4315	SUS 304, Class A	Japan	Wire		**Cold drawn and solution annealed**: all **diam**, (539) **TS**, 40 **El**
NF A 35–573	Z 6 CN 18.09	France	Sheet, strip, plate		**Cold rolled**: ($\leq$5) **diam**, (520) **TS**, (255) **YS**, 45 **El**; **Hot rolled**: ($\leq$20) **diam**, (520) **TS**, (245) **YS**, 43 **El**
ANSI/ASTM A 276	310S	US	Bar, shapes	2.00 **Mn**, 1.50 **Si**, 24.00–26.00 **Cr**, 19.00–22.00 **Ni**, 0.045 **P**, 0.030 **S**	**Annealed**: all **diam**, 75 (515) **TS**, 30 (205) **YS**, 40 **El**
JIS G 4315	SUS 305, Class B	Japan	Wire		**Cold drawn and solution annealed**: all **diam**, (510) **TS**, 25 **El**

specification number	designation	country	product forms	composition	mechanical properties (see page iv for explanation)
JIS G 4315	SUS 305 J1, Class A	Japan	Wire		**Cold drawn and solution annealed**: all **diam**, (510) **TS**, 25 **El**
JIS G 4315	SUS 305 J1, Class B	Japan	Wire		**Cold drawn and solution annealed**: all **diam**, (510) **TS**, 25 **El**
JIS G 4315	SUS 305, Class A	Japan	Wire		**Cold drawn and solution annealed**: all **diam**, (490) **TS**, 40 **El**
QQ-W-423B	Grade 430	US	Wire		**Annealed**: all **diam**, (480) **TS**
JIS G 4315	SUS 384, Class B	Japan	Wire		**Cold drawn and solution annealed**: all **diam**, (461) **TS**, 25 **El**
JIS G 4315	SUS 385, Class B	Japan	Wire		**Cold drawn and solution annealed**: all **diam**, (461) **TS**, 25 **El**
JIS G 4315	SUS XM7, Class B	Japan	Wire		**Cold drawn and solution annealed**: all **diam**, (461) **TS**, 10 **El**
JIS G 4315	SUS 430, Class B	Japan	Wire		**Annealed and light drawn**: all **diam**, (461) **TS**, 10 **El**
JIS G 4315	SUS 410, Class B	Japan	Wire		**Annealed and light drawn**: all **diam**, (461) **TS**, 10 **El**
JIS G 4315	SUS 384, Class A	Japan	Wire		**Cold drawn and solution annealed**: all **diam**, (441) **TS**, 40 **El**
JIS G 4315	SUS 385, Class A	Japan	Wire		**Cold drawn and solution annealed**: all **diam**, (441) **TS**, 40 **El**
JIS G 4315	SUS XM7, Class A	Japan	Wire		**Cold drawn and solution annealed**: all **diam**, (441) **TS**, 40 **El**
ANSI/ASTM A 479	405	US	Bar, shapes	0.08 **C**, 1.00 **Mn**, 1.00 **Si**, 11.50–14.50 **Cr**, 0.60 **Ni**, 0.10–0.30 **Al**, 0.040 **P**, 0.030 **S**	**Annealed**: all **diam**, 60 (415) **TS**, 25 (170) **YS**, 20 **El**
DIN 17224	X5CrNiMo1810/1.4401	Germany	Wire, strip	0.7 **C**, 2.0 **Mn**, 1.0 **Si**, 16.5–18.5 **Cr**, 10.5–13.5 **Ni**, 2.0–2.5 **Mo**, 0.045 **P**, 0.030 **S**	**Hard drawn (wire)**: (<0.2) **diam**, (165) **TS**; **Tempered or quench-age hardened**: (<0.2) **diam**, (175) **TS**
ASTM A 693	Type XM-24	US	Plate, sheet, strip		**Solution annealed**: 0.0015–4.00 (0.038–101.6) **diam**, 150 (1035) max 65 (450) max **YS**, 20 **El**; **Precipitation hardened**: 0.005–0.0099 (0.22–0.251) **diam**, 220 (1515) **TS**, 190 (1310) **YS**, 2 **El**

INDEX

INDEX

INDEX

specification number page

INDEX

INDEX

specification number **page**

specification number **page**

specification number **page**

INDEX

INDEX

INDEX

INDEX

INDEX

specification number page

INDEX

specification number page

specification number page

specification number page

INDEX

specification number page

ISMEO SERIE ORIENTALE ROMA VOL. 25

ACT-FIELD SCHOOL PROJECT REPORTS AND MEMOIRS
ARCHIVAL STUDIES, 2

TOPONYMY OF THE SWĀT VALLEY
LINGUISTIC ARCHAEOLOGY

MATTEO DE CHIARA

PRESENTATION BY

ADRIANO V. ROSSI

WITH A NOTE BY

LUCA M. OLIVIERI

ISMEO – ASSOCIAZIONE INTERNAZIONALE DI STUDI SUL MEDITERRANEO E L'ORIENTE
ITALIAN ARCHAEOLOGICAL MISSION IN PAKISTAN

CREDITS

The publication of the research was funded by a contribution from

ISMEO – ASSOCIAZIONE INTERNAZIONALE DI STUDI SUL MEDITERRANEO E L'ORIENTE

PROGETTO MIUR "STUDI E RICERCHE SULLE CULTURE DELL'ASIA E DELL'AFRICA: TRADIZIONE E CONTINUITÀ, RIVITALIZZAZIONE E DIVULGAZIONE"

INALCO – INSTITUT NATIONAL DE LANGUES ET CIVILISATIONS ORIENTALES

CeRMI UMR 8041 – CENTRE DE RECHERCHE SUR LE MONDE IRANIEN – CNRS

2020
Published by:
Afzaal Ahmad
Sang-e-Meel Publications

954.9122 De Chiara, Matteo
Toponymy of the Swat Valley /
Matteo De Chiara. – Lahore: Sang-e-Meel Publications, 2020.
354 pp.
1. Geography - History.
I. Title

ISBN-10: 969-35-3298-8
ISBN-13: 978-969-35-3298-2

Sang-e-Meel Publications
25 Shahrah-e-Pakistan (Lower Mall), Lahore 54000, Pakistan
Ph. +92-423-722-0100 / +92-423-7228143
http://www.sangemeel.com email: smp@sangemeel.com

Cover: The lower Swāt valley (Photo by L.M. OLIVIERI)

ACT-FIELD SCHOOL PROJECT REPORTS AND MEMOIRS

PUBLICATION PLAN
(to date)

VOLUME I (2013[1]), (2014[2])*

Construction Activities in Swat District (2011-2013)
Khyber-Pakhtunkhwa – Pakistan

THE NEW SWAT ARCHAEOLOGICAL MUSEUM.
ARCHITECTURAL STUDY AND MASTERPLAN
Ivano Marati and Candida Vassallo

VOLUME II (2014[1])

Excavations and Conservation Activities
in Swat District (2011-2013) Khyber-Pakhtunkhwa – Pakistan. 1

THE LAST PHASES OF THE URBAN SITE OF
BIR-KOT-GHWANDAI (BARIKOT).
THE BUDDHIST SITES OF GUMBAT AND AMLUK-DARA (BARIKOT)
Luca M. Olivieri and others

VOLUME III (2016)

Excavations and Conservation Activities
in Swat District (2011-2013) Khyber-Pakhtunkhwa – Pakistan. 2

EXCAVATIONS AT THE PROTOHISTORIC
GRAVEYARDS OF GOGDARA AND UDEGRAM
Edited by Massimo Vidale, Roberto Micheli and Luca M. Olivieri

VOLUME IV (in preparation)◊

Excavations and Conservation Activities
in Swat District (2011-2013) Khyber-Pakhtunkhwa – Pakistan. 3

RESTORATION AND CONSERVATION ACTIVITIES
AT SAIDU SHARIF I AND JAHANABAD
Edited by Luca M. Olivieri

VOLUME V (2015)

Excavations and Conservation Activities
in Swat District (2011-2013) Khyber-Pakhtunkhwa – Pakistan. 4

THE GHAZNAVID MOSQUE AND THE ISLAMIC SETTLEMENT
AT MT. RAJA GIRA, UDEGRAM
Alessandra Bagnera

VOLUME VI. 1 (forthcoming)°

TERRACOTTA FIGURINES FROM THE EXCAVATIONS IN THE HISTORIC SETTLEMENT
AT BĪR-KOṬ-GHWAṆḌAI (BARIKOT) SWAT, PAKISTAN (1977-2019)
ANIMAL FIGURINES
Gennaro Alterio

VOLUME VI.2 (forthcoming)°

TERRACOTTA FIGURINES FROM THE EXCAVATIONS IN THE HISTORIC SETTLEMENT
AT BĪR-KOṬ-GHWAṆḌAI (BARIKOT) SWAT, PAKISTAN (1977-2019)
HUMAN FIGURINES
Giuseppina Esposito

SPECIAL VOLUME, 1 (2014[1]), (2015[2])*

BUDDHIST ARCHITECTURE IN THE SWAT VALLEY, PAKISTAN.
STUPAS, VIHARAS, A DWELLING UNIT
Domenico Faccenna and Piero Spagnesi

SPECIAL VOLUME, 2.1-2 (2020)

CERAMICS FROM THE EXCAVATIONS IN THE HISTORIC SETTLEMENT
AT BĪR-KOṬ-GHWAṆḌAI (BARIKOT) SWAT, PAKISTAN (1984-1992)
Pierfrancesco Callieri and Luca M. Olivieri

SPECIAL VOLUME, 2.3 (in preparation)

CERAMICS FROM THE EXCAVATIONS IN THE HISTORIC SETTLEMENT AT BĪR-KOṬ-GHWAṆḌAI
(BARIKOT) SWAT, PAKISTAN (1998-2017). THE EARLY-HISTORIC PHASES
Elisa Iori

* * *

SERIES MINOR, 1 (2014[1]), (2017[2])◊

DIGGING UP.
FIELDWORK GUIDELINES FOR ARCHAEOLOGY STUDENTS
Luca M. Olivieri

SERIES MINOR, 2 (2015)

TALKING STONES.
PAINTED ROCK SHELTERS OF THE SWAT VALLEY
Luca M. Olivieri

SERIES MINOR, 3 (in preparation)

ON SWAT.
BIBLIOGRAPHIC REPERTORY FOR ARCHAEOLOGY STUDENTS
Edited by Aatif Iqbal and Rafiullah Khan

SERIES MINOR, 4 (2016)

LIVING AND ARCHAEOLOGICAL LANDSCAPES OF SWAT
A GUIDE TO THE VALLEYS OF KANDAK AND KOTAH
A FIELD COMPANION TO TALKING STONES
Carla Biagioli, Matteo De Chiara, Efrem Ferrari, Aftab ur-Rehman Rana and Shafiq Ahmad Khan

* * *

ARCHIVAL STUDIES, 1 (2015)

SIR AUREL STEIN AND THE 'LORDS OF THE MARCHES'
NEW ARCHIVAL MATERIALS
Luca M. Olivieri

ARCHIVAL STUDIES, 2 (2020)

TOPONYMY OF THE SWAT VALLEY
LINGUISTIC ARCHAEOLOGY
Matteo De Chiara

N.B.: Superscript numerals indicate the year of the edition: the first editions was printed by Sang-e-Meel Publications (Lahore). The second digital edition is published by BraDyPus.Books (Bologna)* and by Sang-e-Meel Publications (Lahore)◊. ° = Online publication (ebook) by Sang-e-Meel Publications (Lahore).

TABLE OF CONTENTS

PRESENTATION

By Adriano V. ROSSI, President, ISMEO

Giuseppe TUCCI, in his book *La via dello Swat* (Roma 1978[2], pp. 24-31), describes his first feelings when he arrived for the first time to Saidu Sharif. Over 60 years later, the researchers working on the steps of Giuseppe Tucci have still the same feelings. This year the Mission of the IsMEO (now ISMEO-Ca' Foscari) in Pakistan – sponsored, like the other ISMEO Missions in Asia and Africa, by the Italian Ministry of Foreign Affairs and International Cooperation – completes its 65th year of continuous archaeological activity. The Mission's fieldwork and archaeological campaigns in Swāt (from Butkara I and II, Udegram, Loebanr, Katelai to Saidu Sharif, Barikot etc.), are reflected in countless contributions on the art and archaeology of Gandhāra, the prehistory, palaeobotany, etc., published in the volumes of "Reports and Memoirs", and, more recently, also in this Series with the historic Pakistani publishing house Sang-e Meel.

Over the past decade, the Mission, thanks to the tireless enthusiasm of its director Luca Maria OLIVIERI, has completed the study of the areas around Bir-kot-ghwandai, where hundreds of new archaeological sites have been identified, almost all Buddhist, including dozens of new painted shelters, which confirm the importance of the area for the knowledge of rock art of Swāt. Thanks to the studies on Buddhist rock art, an ample corpus of sculptures has been surveyed and interpreted, which not only return a previously unknown image of late-ancient Buddhism in the region, but have paved the way for similar research in adjacent areas, from Baltistan to Ladakh, today conducted by international research groups. An important project of the Mission, connected to these materials, was conducted together with the University of Padua, and regarded the restoration of the Buddhist rock sculptures of Jahanabad damaged by the Taliban during the uprising of 2007-2009.

The ISMEO (now ISMEO-Ca' Foscari) Mission is internationally known for the role it played in the study of Gandharan art and archeology, of the settlement and of the funerary archeology from proto-history to the Islamic era. A recent development of its activities is the study of genomics and bio-archeology in collaboration with the Harvard Medical School and the Max Planck Institute. Swāt, with its data on the human genome, is among the areas of the ancient world best studied from the point of view of DNA. An exceptional article on this topic was published in *Science* in September 2019.

I would like also to point out here that the main excavation site of the Mission, the archaeological site of Barikot, has recently seen a strong financial intervention from the Government of the Khyber-Pakhtunkhwa, to which we must all be grateful. The Government has acquired for the community the land where the ancient city stood, as a heritage for future generations.

As Matteo DE CHIARA emphasizes, the present book deals with an aspect of Swāt until now quite neglected: toponymy. Indeed, notwithstanding the abundance of publications on the archaeology of the Swāt Valley (see the references cited in this book, and OLIVIERI 2006a for the previous bibliography), much work still remains to be done in this specific field, and many others related to the main archaeological research.

The main goal of this work is to offer new materials on the linguistic and ethnic situation of Swāt from a diachronic point of view. Therefore, the book does not provide a full synchronic description of all toponyms: it tries to provide instead a general presentation of every item,

its geographical position, previous mentions, a summary description, and an abridged etymological analysis of the items, to the extent that it can be proposed within the framework of today's knowledge.
Swāt toponyms have always attracted the attention of travelers and scholars, and have been treated in many sources since the 17th century, starting from the descriptions contained in KHUSHAL KHAN KHAṬṬAK's *Swāt nāma*. Several archaeological surveys were used in this book, especially for the maps attached in the appendix (STEIN 1929 and 1930, TUCCI 1958, OLIVIERI ET AL. 2006, FILIGENZI 2015 and OLIVIERI 2015a). All the above-mentioned archaeological and historical works show a strong interest in the etymology (sometimes folk etymology) of toponyms, thus confirming the importance of this approach. The Author even consulted HAKIMZAY's *Daγa zmunǧ kəlay day* (1997), a small neglected volume on Swāt toponymy, which nevertheless contains many useful and interesting remarks.
All toponyms have been originally collected from the maps of the Pakistani Government (printed in the period from 1950 to 1984), later verified on the 1977 maps as produced by the Soviet Geographical Services and on those produced by the US army, which were consulted and used to integrate the cartographic base, and lastly, with data retrieved from Google maps and Google Earth. Confirmation, correction and additional data have been checked with Pashto speakers and residents of the Valley, by virtue of the long association of the Author with the Pashto speaking inhabitants of the region (I would like to remind here that the first variety of Pashto learned and spoken by the Author has been the Pashto variety of Swāt).
It is another reason for my great satisfaction that this work was conducted in collaboration with CNRS and INALCO, a great institution with which, since more than thirty years, L'Orientale University of Naples and IsMEO/ISMEO collaborate closely, especially for Indo-Iranian and Central Asian languages, literatures and cultures.
In conclusion, I hope I have managed to give at least an idea, on behalf of ISMEO – an international association that today unites over 300 scholars from all over the world in the same project of a scientific network conceived almost a century ago by Giuseppe Tucci, which reveals itself more and more valid every day – of what the presence of Italian research, in a context of great political sensitivity but also of great cultural significance, begun to enhance in a pioneering way over 60 years ago, and which today, with the efforts of researchers and institutions of numerous countries – among whom certainly not secondary those of the *new Pakistan* – has perhaps finally managed to bring back the attention of world culture.

FOREWORD

Swāt valley represents a paradise for scholars dealing with archaeology, history, anthropology, linguistics... The chronological stratification of civilizations, languages and cultures offers the possibility of developing endless research projects.
The present work deals with an aspect of Swāt until now quite neglected: toponymy. Indeed, notwithstanding the abundance of publications on the archaeology of the Swāt valley (cf. OLIVIERI 2006, 2009b, 2014 and 2018 for a general bibliographical survey), much work still remains to be done in this specific field. The task has been rendered particularly irksome due to the difficulties of free circulation in the region, especially after the beginning of the war in 2007. Nowadays a fully stabilised situation has re-opened the region to research and to economic development.
The main goal of this work is to offer new materials on the linguistic and ethnic situation of Swāt from a diachronic point of view. Therefore, I do not intend to provide a full synchronic description of all toponyms, even if sometimes more materials were available (cf. for instance in the case of Barikot), but I try to provide a general presentation of every item, its position, previous mentions, a summary description, and an etymological analysis (see conclusions). A more detailed survey will surely bring interesting surprises and remarks, as suggested by the micro-toponymy of the limited areas of the Kandak and nearby valleys (see Appendix).

All toponyms were originally collected from the maps of the Pakistani Government from 1950 and 1984, on whose margins we read: "Surveyed 1926-27; this map planimetry is based on ground survey of 1926-27; ground verified for main detail during 1983-84, whereas metric contours have been photogrammetrically surveyed using aerial photography of 1953-54".
All data were later verified with the 1977 maps of the Soviet Union and on those of the US army, which were consulted and used to integrate the cartographic base, and lastly, with Google maps and Google Earth, before being confirmed, corrected and improved with Pashto speakers and residents *in loco*.
Swāt toponyms have a long life and have been treated in many sources since the 19th century and even before (cf. for instance the descriptions contained in KHUSHAL KHAN KHAṬṬAK's *Swāt nāma*: RAVERTY 1862: 278-281 and SULTAN-I-ROME 2014). All English gazetteers from the 19th and of the beginning of the 20th century were also carefully compared (RAVERTY 1862[1] and 1888, BELLEW 1864, and so on[2]). Many toponyms appear also in the Swāt folk tales by INAYAT-UR-RAHMAN (1968 and 1984), such as Bāmākhela, Langar, Nāgwa, Dārmai, Bālākoṭ,

---

1 This work contains many useful and interesting data on Swāt. At the beginning, major RAVERTY states:

> In August, 1858, I sent an intelligent man, a native of Kandahár, who had been for many years in my service, and who spoke and understood the Pushto language well, for the purpose of obtaining a scarce work in the Pushto language 'the history of the Yúsufzí tribe, and their conquests in Suwát and other districts near Pesháwar, by Shaykh malí, Yúsufzí,' a copy of which, I was informed, was in the possession of the chiefs of Tárṛnah, one of the divisions of Suwát. That valley, although so close to Pesháwar, is almost a *terra incognita* to us. [...] The person I sent had on previous occasions collected information for me, on such matters, and was acquainted with the chief points on which inquiry should be made; but I also furnished him with a number of questions, the replies to which have been embodied in the following pages, and will account for the rambling style in which, I fear, it has been written.

2 Among others, see also CUNNINGHAM 1871: 81-83 and FOUCHER 1901.

Guligrām, Gogdara, Dangrām, Jāmbil, Gāškoṛ, Ušo, Torwāl, Kānǰu, etc. We must not forget the numerous archaeological surveys, which were used also to draw the maps in the appendix (in particular, Stein 1929 and 1930, Tucci 1958, Olivieri et al. 2006, Filigenzi 2015 and Olivieri 2015a). All the above-mentioned archaeological and historical works show a strong interest in the etymology of all toponyms, thus confirming the importance of this approach. I consulted also Hakimzay's Pashto book (1997), a small neglected volume on Swāt toponymy, which nevertheless contains many useful and interesting remarks.
For the entries in the Gazetteer I tried to keep the names of places appearing on the Pakistani maps, but in a normalized form. Here are some considerations, which guided me in the choice of the criteria for the quotation form of place names (see also Pons 2019):

1) If one remains bound to the Pashto writing, then one should provide a form without dash and with upper case: Malam Jabba (= <mlm jbh>).

2) However, the dash seems fundamental in order to point out that the toponym is the same: Malam-Jabba.

3) On the other hand, to use both parts of the toponym, for instance Malamjabba, Amlukdara, Allahdanddheri, does not seem a good idea, as it would render reading and identification difficult.

4) In conclusion, the adopted criterion has been to quote toponyms with dash and second element in small letters: Malam-jabba.

5) Some compound toponyms are without blank spaces and without dash, for instance Loebanr ('big garden'), in order to keep the parallel with the Pashto where the two terms are united (<lwybnr>).

In the Gazetteer, the alphabetic order of the entries is the Latin one.
After the main entry, I added the Pashto script, for which I consulted all available administrative sources, gazetteers, internet and maps, and, when this was not available, I supplemented with my own script. All these names were checked by Muhammad Ali Dinakhel, who also provided useful comments on pronunciation and variants of some toponyms; I thank him warmly for his help.
Place names are followed, in brackets, by the transcription of the Pashto according to the phonological system of Pashto and to the criteria already established by Septfonds (1994: 43) and the ALA (Atlas Linguistique de l'Afghanistan: see Kieffer 1974 and De Chiara/Septfonds 2019: 13-14, 98):

	bilabials	**dentals**	**retroflexed**	**velars**	**uvulars**
occlusives	p b	t d	ṭ ḍ	k g	*q*
affricates		c j č ǰ			
fricatives	*f*	s | z	x̌ ǧ	x γ	*h*
nasals	m	n	ṇ		
liquids		l r	ṛ		
semi-vowels	w	y			

Tab. 1. Pashto phonological system: consonants.

frontal	central	posterior
i		u
e		o
	ə	
	a ā	

Tab. 2. Pashto phonological system: vowels.

ا	a	ذ	z	ف	f
آ	ā	ر	r	ق	q
ب	b	ړ	ṛ	ک	k
پ	p	ز	z	ګ	g
ت	t	ژ	ž	ل	l
ټ	ṭ	ږ	ğ	م	m
ث	s	س	s	ن	n
ج	ǰ	ش	š	ڼ	ṇ
چ	č	ښ	x̌	و	w
ځ	j	ص	s	ه	h
څ	c	ض	z	ی	ay
ح	h	ط	t	ي	i
خ	x	ظ	z	ې	e
د	d	ع	ʿ	ۍ	áy
ډ	ḍ	غ	γ	ئ	əy

Tab. 3. Transcription of Pashto script.

Pashto transcriptions and meanings of Pashto words are based on ASLANOV 1966 (Pashto-Russian), TASHRIHI 1979 (Pashto-Pashto), DARYĀB 1994 (Pashto-Pashto), AKBAR 2015 (Pashto-French), RAVERTY 1860 (Pashto-English), BELLEW 1867 (Pashto-English) and PASHTOON 2009 (English translation of ASLANOV 1966). When necessary, other monolingual and bilingual dictionaries have also been consulted. RAVERTY's and BELLEW's dictionaries were particularly useful in that, even if over 150 years old, they reproduce the dialect of the Yusufzai area under observation.

I have tried to etymologize all toponyms, but many etyma remain unknown or doubtful. As will be shown in the introduction, the toponyms can be attributed to different linguistic strata: Pashto, Indo-Aryan, Dardic and Kafiri, Arabic, Chinese. Other linguistic origins can also not be excluded, as an Austroasiatic substrate (see WITZEL 1999a), even if they have not yet been identified. Accordingly, many smaller and bigger dictionaries and grammars have been consulted to assist the etymological analysis. In particular:

Indo-Aryan: KEWA and EWAia, MACDONELL 1929, MASICA 1991, MONIER-WILLIAMS 1899, PLATTS 1884, T- (TURNER 1966);

Dardic and Kafiri: AFTAB 2015, BAART 1999, BAART/SAGAR 2004, BARTH/MORGENSTIERNE 1958, BASHIR 2005, BUDDRUSS 1960 and 1967, FUSSMAN 1972, GRIERSON 1929,

IIFL III and IV, MORGENSTIERNE 1930a, 1940, 1941, 1942a, 1945, 1950, 1954, TRAIL/COOPER 1999;

Iranian: ANDREEV/PEŠČEREVA 1957, BARTHOLOMAE 1904, CHEUNG 2007, DKS, ÈDEL'MAN 1986, EP, ÈSIJ, ÈSKJ, EVP, EVShG, GRJUNBERG/ÈDEL'MAN 1987, HALLBERG 1992, HÜBSCHMANN 1895, IESOJ, IIFL I and II, ILEB, MONCHI-ZADEH 1990, NEVP, MORGENSTIERNE 1932, 1942, SGS, SOKOLOVA 1960, STEBLIN-KAMENSKIJ 1999, STEINGASS 1963[5];

Dravidian: DED;

Turkish and Mongolian: DÖRFER 1963-1975 and 1967.

Regarding the comparison with the Austroasiatic languages, unfortunately we do not have many works available. Apart from the general manuals, see KUIPER 1948, 1950, 1955 and 1991; WITZEL 1999a and 1999b.[3]

At the end of the volume I put two indexes: one of the toponyms according to their typology (1. streams, 2. lakes, 3. peaks, 4. passes, 5. pastures and 6. villages), the other according to their Tehsil of belonging (1. Barikot, 2. Babuzai, 3. Kabal, 4. Charbagh, 5. Khwazakhela, 6. Maṭṭa, 7. Bahrain).

To draw all the maps I used the programs QGIS and Adobe Illustrator, and I am grateful to Emmanuel GIRAUDET for his help in all phases of the work. I would like also to thank Alex P. REALL for his editing of the English.

I am deeply indebted to Luca Maria OLIVIERI, director of the Archaeological Mission in Swāt (ISMEO-University "Ca' Foscari" of Venice), and owe him huge gratitude for all his materials, suggestions, encouragement, and for having been the person who launched me into this work and who brought me to Swāt: without his unconditional help and friendship this study would not exist.

I warmly thank also all my friends in Swāt,[4] who never ceased helping me in loco and at a distance, providing me with abundant information and support: *tāso ta ḍera manana* and *xwdāy de mu māl ši*!

I benefited also from the support of the Italian Archaeological Mission to Swāt, of the ISMEO of Rome (my thanks to its president, Adriano Valerio ROSSI, also for his careful reading of the text and useful suggestions), of the Inalco of Paris and of the research unit CeRMI of the CNRS.

This study is dedicated to Giuseppe TUCCI, beyond any doubt the most important Italian orientalist of the 20th century, and to the Italian Archaeological Mission founded by him in 1956. I hope with this work to contribute to the improvement of our knowledge of this region and to the innovative methodological model, based on a multidisciplinary approach, which is being tested and undertaken in Swāt under Luca's guidance.

---

3 On the classification of the Austroasiatic languages, see SIDWELL 2009 and JENNY/SIDWELL 2014. See also PINNOW 1963 and 1966.

4 It would be impossible to list everybody. I will at least mention some of them here: SHAFIQ, ALI, AKHTAR MUNIR (TOTA), YUSUF, IKRAM, ABDUL QAYUM, ZUBAIR, etc.

INTRODUCTION

LOCATION

Swāt is a District[5] located in the northern part of Pakistan. The former name of the province where Swāt is situated was, after 1901, North-West Frontier Province (NWFP), as it represented the western frontier of the British Rāj. In April 2010, however, the province's name was changed to Khyber Pukhtunkhwa (KPK) by the Pakistani Senate.

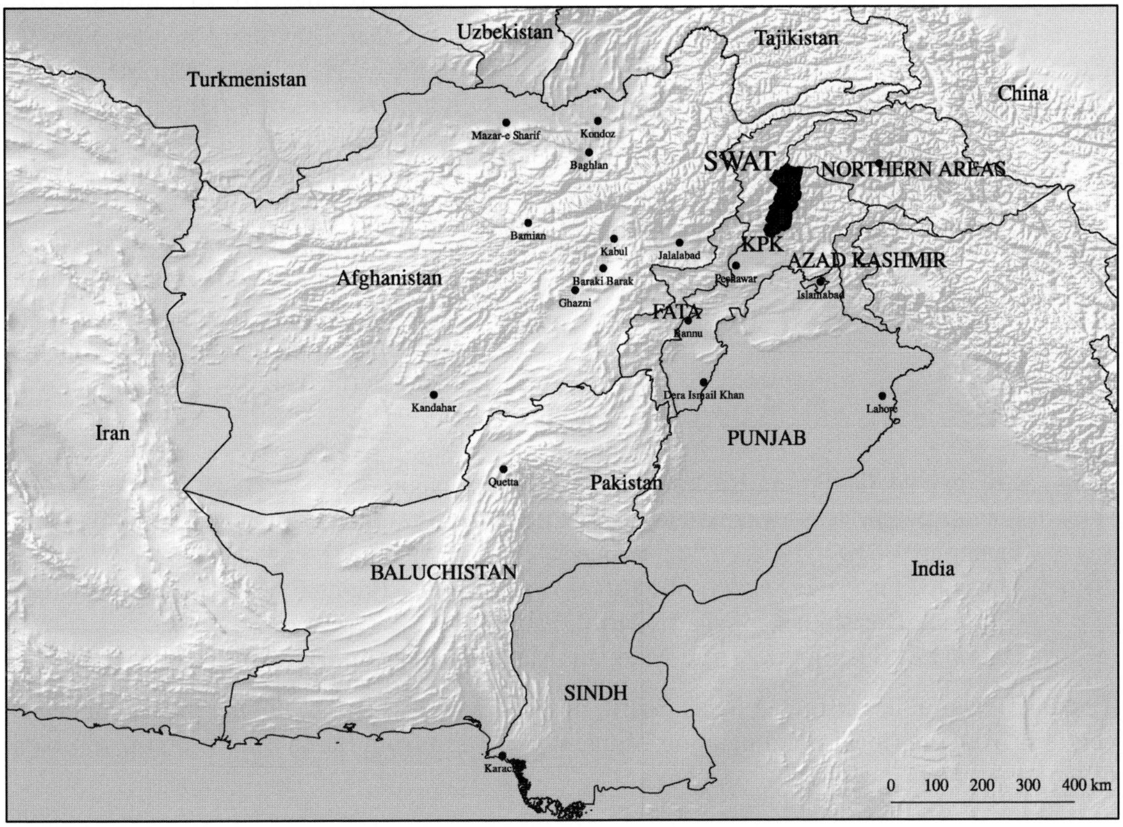

Fig. 1. Location of Swāt in Pakistan and in the KPK.

From an administrative point of view, Swāt adjoins the districts of Malakand[6] in the south-west, Buner in the south-east, Lower and Upper Dir in the west, Shangla and Kohistan in the east, Chitral and Ghilgit in the north-west and north-east respectively.

[5] According to the Khyber Pakhtunkhwa Local Government Act of 2013, p. 4, "'district' means a revenue district notified under the West Pakistan Land Revenue Act, 1967 (W.P. Act No. XVII of 1967)".

[6] "In 1970, following the abolition of the princely states, the agency became the Malakand Division, which was divided into districts, one of which was the Malakand Protected Area, known as Malakand District. In the year

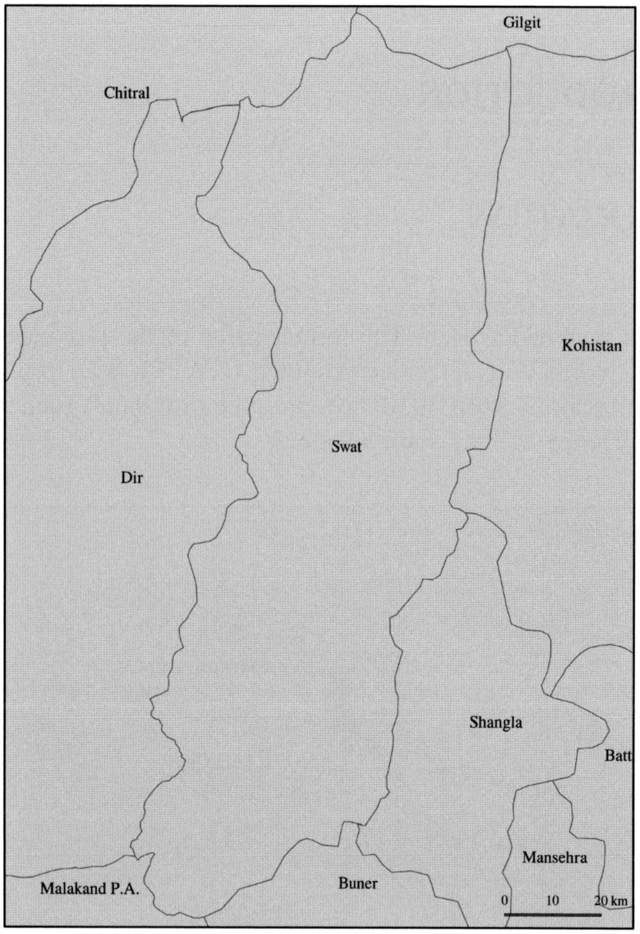

Fig. 2. Frontiers of Swāt.

According to the National Disaster Management Authority of Pakistan, Swāt has 7 Tehsils,[7] which are, starting from the south: Barikot, Babuzai, Kabal, Charbagh, Khwazakhela, Maṭṭa and Bahrain. Each tehsil is further divided into Councils[8] (= 64 Councils):

– Barikot has 4 Councils: Barikot, Ghaligay, Kota, Shamozi.
– Babuzai 16: Islampur, Kokarai, Tindodag, Udigram, Dangram Sangota, Qambar, Manglawar, Aka Maruf Bami Khel, Amankot Faizabad, Gulkada, Banr, Malakanan Landakass, Saidu Sharif, Malukabad, Rahimabad, Rang Muhallah.
– Kabal 12: Koz Abakhel Kabal, Bar Abakhel Kabal, Hazara, Totano Bandai, Kanjo, Bara Bandai, Koza Bandai, Kalakalay, Dewlai, Qalagay, Shah Derai, Tal.
– Charbagh 4: Taligram, Kashora, Charbagh, Gulibagh.
– Khwazakhela 7: Khwazakhela, Jano Chamtail, Shalpeen, Kotanai, Shin, Miandam, Fatehpur.
– Maṭṭa 13: Pir Kalay, Arkot, Showar, Gowalari, Beha, Bartana, Maṭṭa Kharari, Baydara, Chuprial, Dorishkhela, Ashari, Darmi, Sakhra.
– Bahrain 8: Bashigram, Tirat, Madyan, Mankial, Bahrain, Balakot, Kalam, Utrur.

The chief town of the district is Saidu Sharif, in the Tehsil of Babuzai, but the main commercial centre is Mingora (local pronunciation Mingawǝra), 2 km from Saidu Sharif, on the left bank of the Swāt river.

2000 the Malakand Division was abolished. Despite the constitutional changes since 1970, the expression Malakand Agency is still used, sometimes of the entire area of the former Agency, but more often of Malakand District. Before 1970 the area was a Tribal Area known as the Malakand Protected Area, part of the Malakand Agency. In 1970 it became Malakand District, a Provincially Administered Tribal Area, until 2000 part of Malakand Division" (*ibid.*).

7 "'Tehsil' means a Tehsil notified under the West Pakistan Land Revenue Act, 1967 (W.P. Act No. XVII of 1967)" (*ibid.*, p. 8).

8 "'Local council' means a District Council, Tehsil Council, Town Council, Village Council or, as the case may be, Neighbourhood Council" (*ibid.*, p. 5), where "'Neighbourhood' means a mohallah, a group of streets, lanes or roads, in areas with urban characteristics, designated as Neighbourhood by Government" (*ibid.*, p. 7).

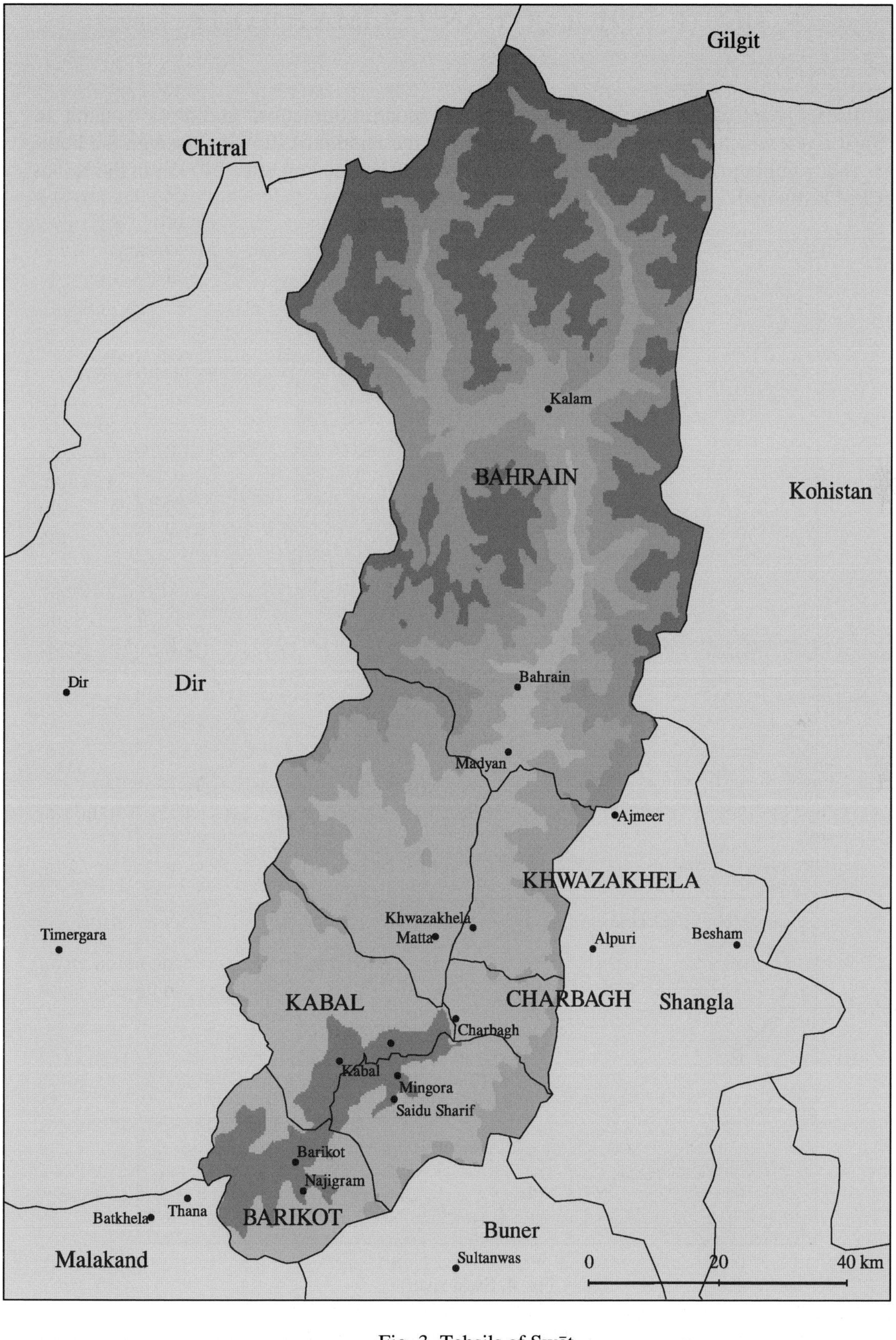

Fig. 3. Tehsils of Swāt.

GEOMORPHOLOGY AND CLIMATOLOGY

Swāt district is spread over an area of about 5,000 square kilometres,[9] and owes its name to the Swāt river, which originates in the mountains of the Hindukuš, flowing through the homonym valley until the confluence with the Panjkora river and ending after 240 km in the Kabul river and lastly in the Indus, near Nowshera.

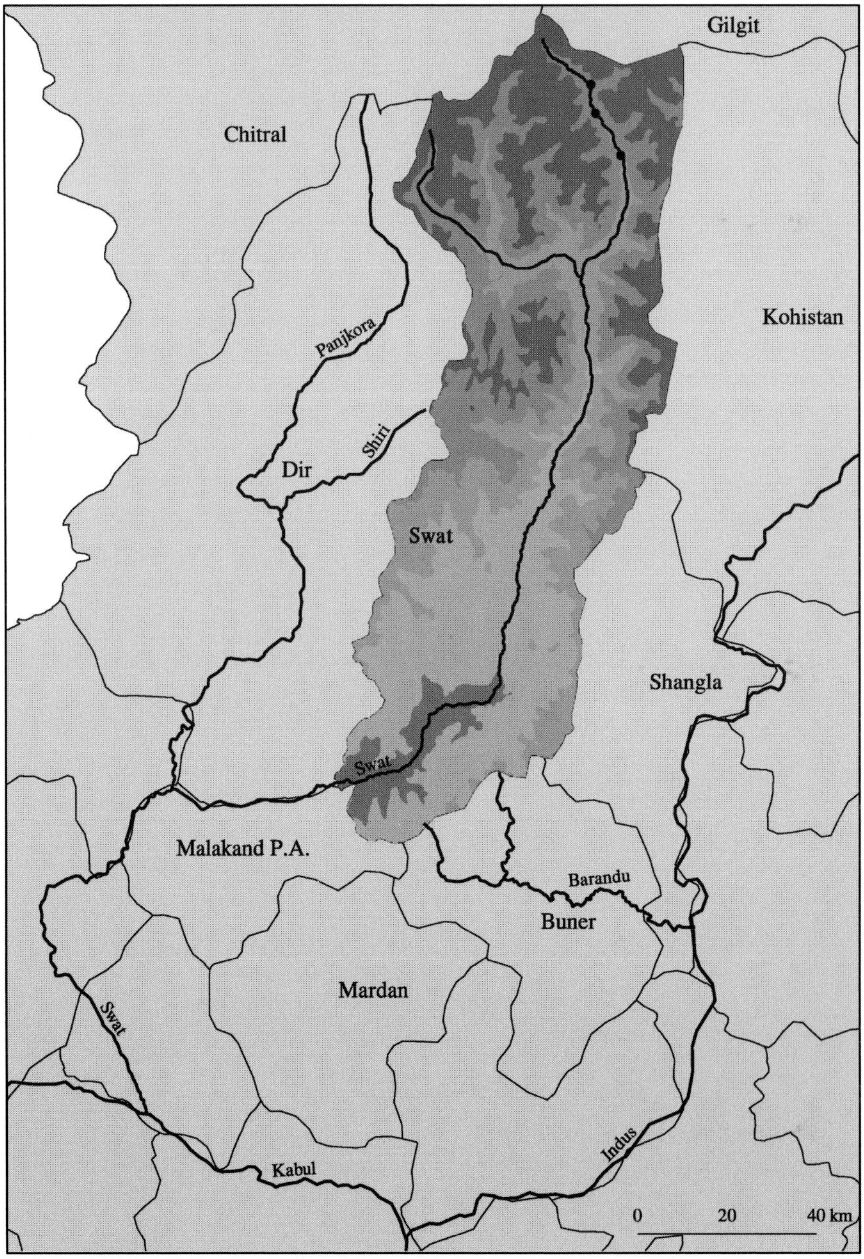

Fig. 4. Swāt river.

9 SULTAN-I-ROME (2008: 16), providing also historic information on the extension of Swāt State and District, speaks of 3,756 sq. miles (= 10,000 km^2); OLIVIERI (2009a: 14) speaks of 2,000 sq. km.

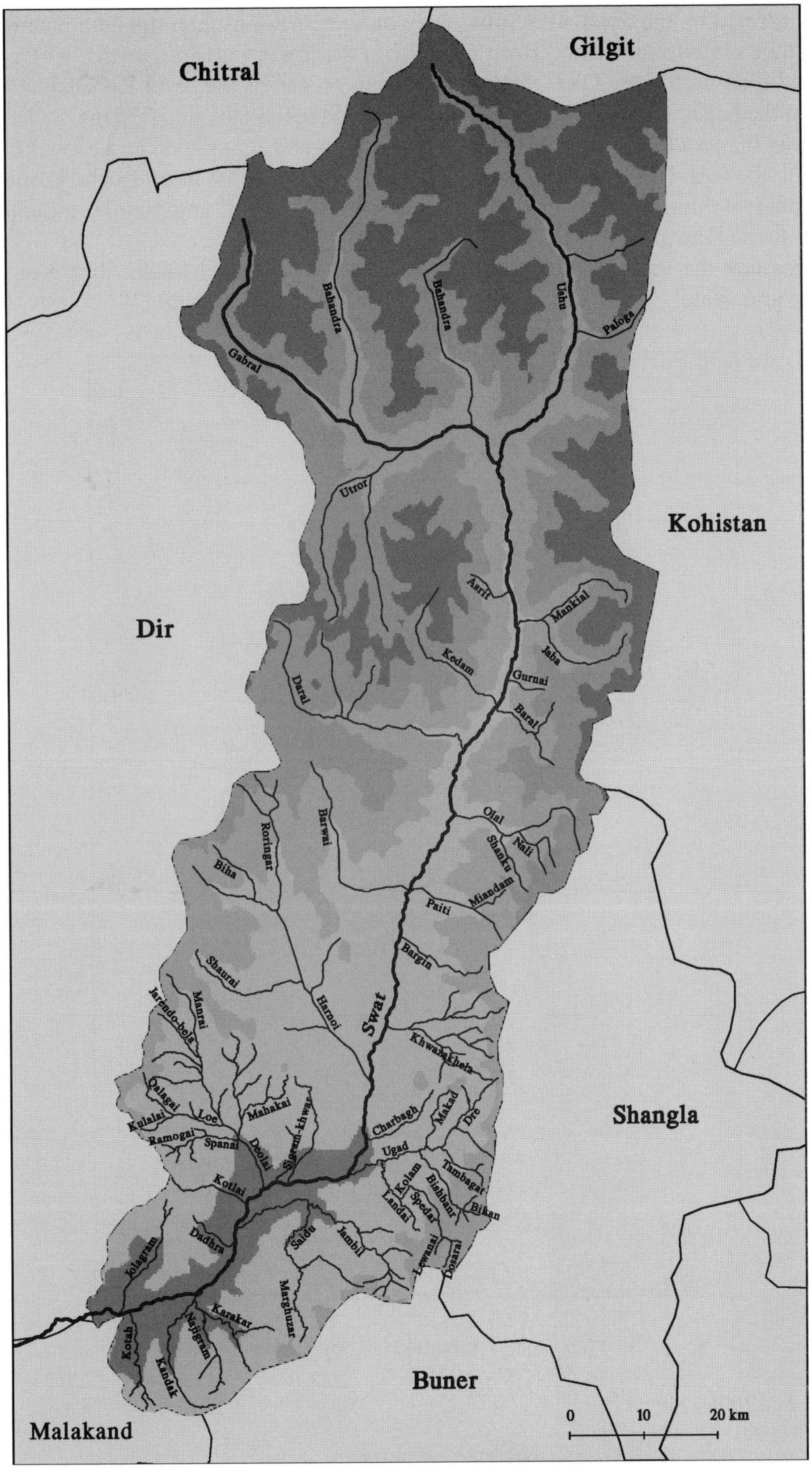

Fig. 5. Swāt river and its tributaries.

The valley created by the Swāt river (obviously more spread out than the administrative unit), has an average altitude increasing from 600 msl in the lower part (*kuz swāt*), where the plain is larger and more fertile, to 3,000 msl in the narrow gorges of the Swāt Kohistan.[10] The main peaks are in the north: the Falak-sar (6,257 m) and the Mankial-tsukai (5,725 m).[11]
The valley is bordered "to the south by the Ilam range and its extension westward, as far as Hazarnao; to the west by the Utman Khel hills and Bajawar; to the north by the Larram mountains with their western and eastern prolongations, the Kamrani and Munjai mountains; and to the east by the Ghwarband peak".[12]
Many passes link the valley to the adjoining regions: Malakand, Morah, Shah Kot, Karakar, Churat, Jawarai, Kalel, Kotkay, Jarugu Sar, Qadar, Manjey and Katgala.[13]

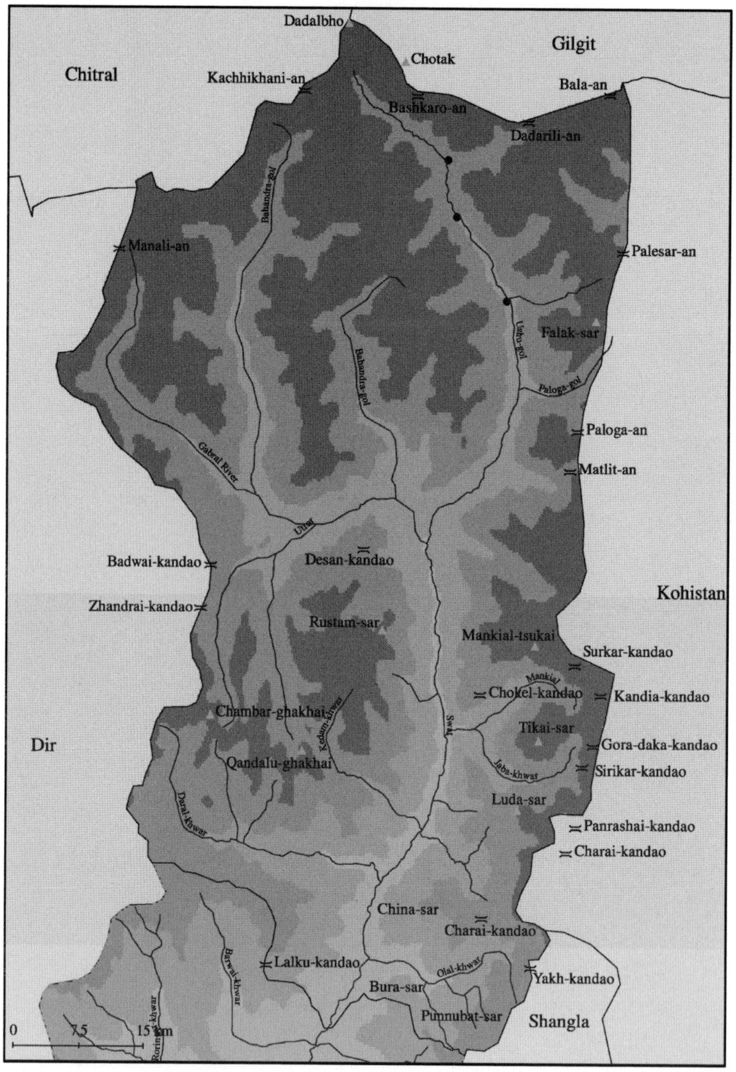

Fig. 6. Some passes and mountains of Swāt, Tehsil of Bahrain.

[10] See Sultan-i-Rome 2008: 14 ff.

[11] See, among others, Olivieri 2009a: 14.

[12] Sultan-i-Rome 2008: 16-17. See also Bellew 1864: 37-38.

[13] Sultan-i-Rome 2008: 17. Interestingly, some of these names have been identified with some places in Palestine, as for instance Morah with Moriah: according to these authors, this gives a further demonstration of the fact that the Pashtun would be one of the ten lost tribes of Israel, the Ban-i Israel: see Raverty 1862.

The climate is temperate: not very cold in winter, not very hot in summer.[14] As a consequence, the region is verdant. In the past, the entire valley was covered by great forests, as witnessed by Greek, Chinese and other travellers. This accounts for one of the names of Swāt: Uḍḍiyāna, the "garden" in Sanskrit, Tibetan Orgyan (this name, however, could also mean "the country of the Uḍi/Urdi/Aurddi", see *infra*). Nowadays the country has suffered massive deforestation (see SULTAN-I-ROME 2016).

TEHSILS

Barikot

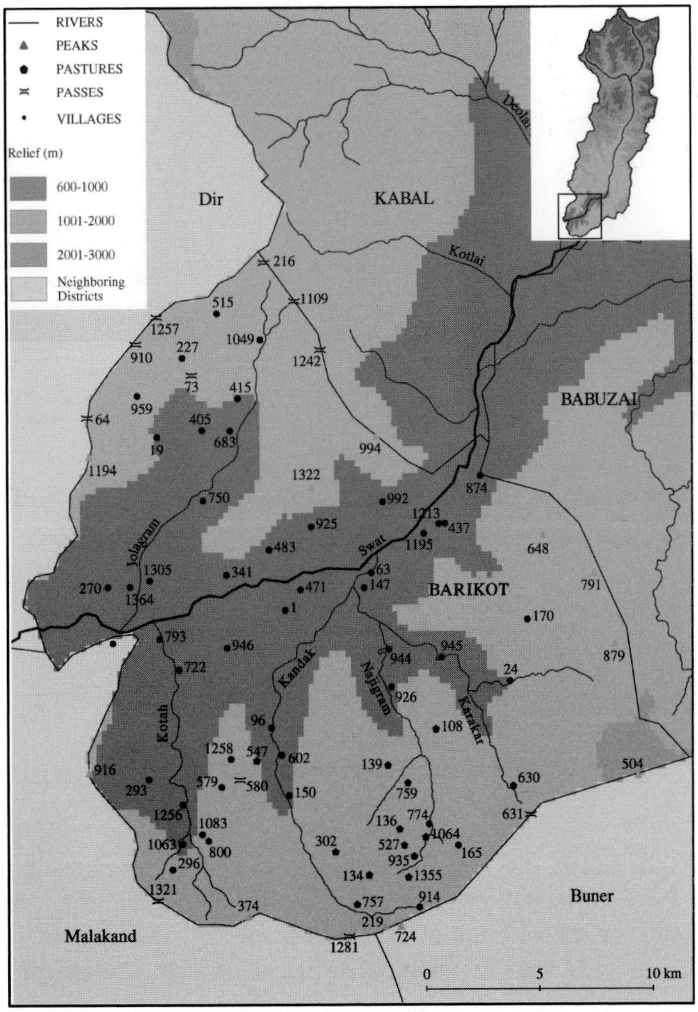

Fig. 7. Tehsil of Barikot.

[14] More information about climate, fauna and flora, and so on, can be found in BELLEW 1864; MCMAHON/RAMSAY 1981^2 [1901]: 3-5; SULTAN-I-ROME 2008: 18-19. SULTAN-I-ROME (2016) proposes a long analysis of the "Land and forest Governance in Swat": see also BARTH 1956a, speaking about "Ecologic Relationships of Ethnic Groups in Swat, North Pakistan".

Barikot is the southernmost Tehsil of Swāt. Its largest city is the town of Barikot, which is located at a distance of 20 km away from Mingora. Its average elevation ranges from 600 meters to the 2,811 meters of Mount Ilam. The mountains (11 peaks are named) are not very high and mainly divide Barikot from Babuzai. The plain is fertile and has many inhabitants. 45 villages are named in the Gazetteer, but all the Tehsil is densely populated. Most of the pasturageland (14 pastures are named) is located in the southern regions, near the boundary with Buner. The passes (11) lead to Dir to the north, and to Malakand.
Many streams flow into the Swāt river from both sides: the Kotah Khwar, the Kandak Khwar, the Jolagram Khwar, the Najigram Khwar and the Karakar Khwar. It can be observed that many stream names are derived from village names, these latter being mainly of Indo-Aryan origin.

Babuzai

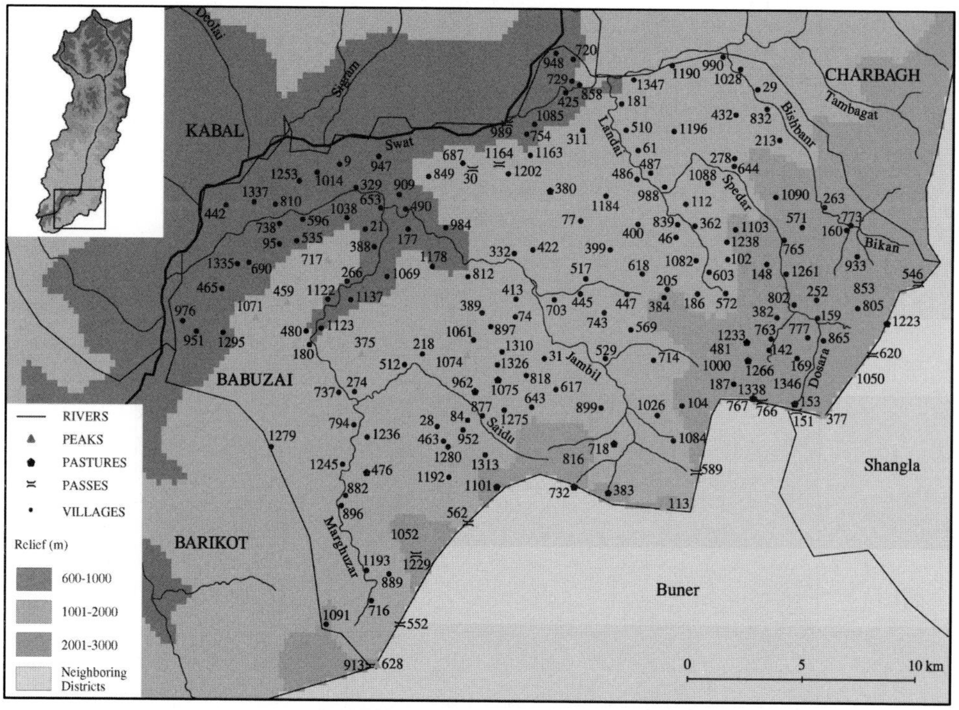

Fig. 8. Tehsil of Babuzai.

Proceeding towards the north, the Tehsil of Babuzai is even more densely inhabited: we find 151 village names. Located in Babuzai are Saidu Sharif, the capital of Swāt, and Mingora, the main market town and the most populous centre in Swāt.
The majority of passes (12) lead to Shangla in the south-east section of the Tehsil, and to Buner in the south.
The rivers, all tributaries of the left side of the Swāt river, for the most part have recent names: the Saidu Khwar, the Dosar Khwar, the Landai Khwar and the Lewanai Khwar. However, some of the stream names are of Indo-Aryan origin, such as Jambil Khwar and Spedar Khwar (see conclusions to this chapter).
In the Gazetteer are named also 16 peaks and 13 pastures.

Kabal

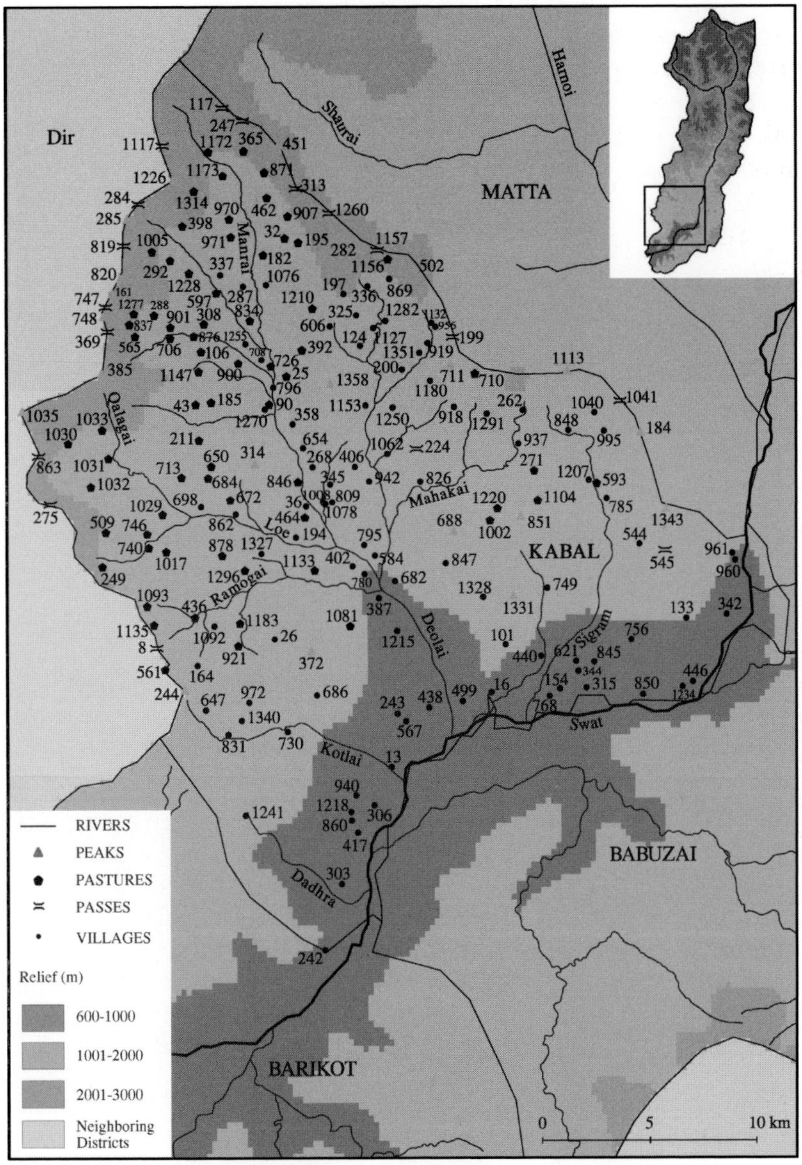

Fig. 9. Tehsil of Kabal.

The Tehsil of Kabal rises from the plain of Swāt to the slopes bordering Dir, where the majority of passes are located (17 passes are mentioned in the Gazetteer). The plain is densely inhabited (98 village names) and full of pastures (70 pasture names).
All streams are tributaries of the Swāt river on its right side and the main stream is the Deolai Khwar, flowing into the Swāt river near Aligram and Hazara.
The mountains (21 peaks are named) are not very high in comparison with Swāt Kohistan, but Ningulai, the last village of the Tehsil of Kabal in the north, is probably the last village before the elevation begins to grow.
The main town is Kabal, in the lower part of the Tehsil, between the Kotlai and the Deolai Khwar.

Charbagh

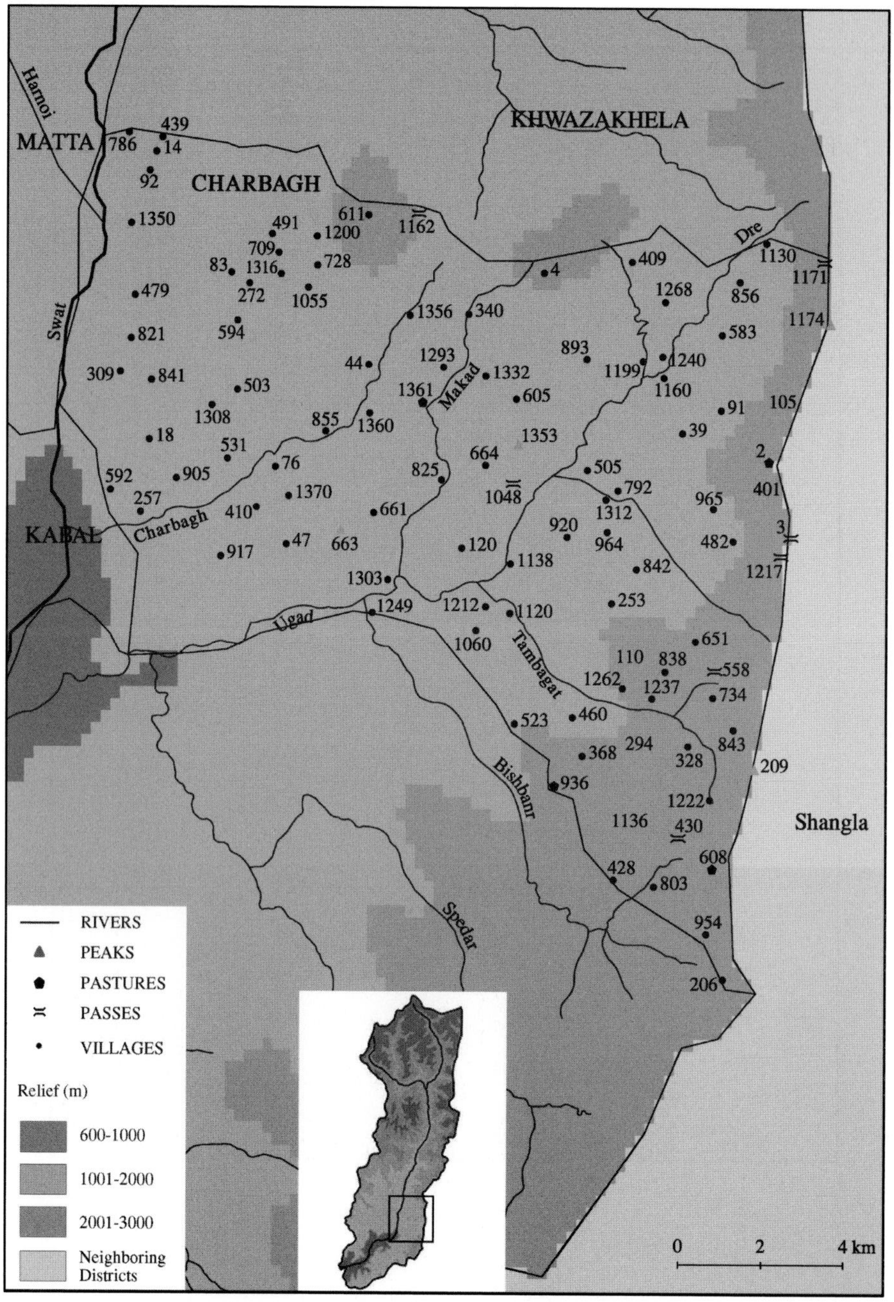

Fig. 10. Tehsil of Charbagh.

The Tehsil of Charbagh is the smallest of all the Tehsils of Swāt. Located to the north of Babuzai, it is characterised by a nearly complete absence of pastures (only 4). Instead, it is densely inhabited (85 villages) and the only mountains (9) are at the frontier with Shangla (7 passes are also mentioned in the Gazetteer). Not many streams irrigate this Tehsil. Its main town is Charbagh, located at the end of the plain of the Swāt river, where the ground begins to rise.

Khwazakhela

North of Charbagh, there is the Tehsil of Khwazakhela, taking its name from the main town, located in the low part of the Tehsil, on the Khwazakhela Khwar. Densely inhabited too (135 villages), the few pastures (10) and higher mountains (10) are located towards the boundary with Shangla (7 passes are also named). In its northern part, it reaches the height of 2,000-3,000 msl. Streams begin to be rare.

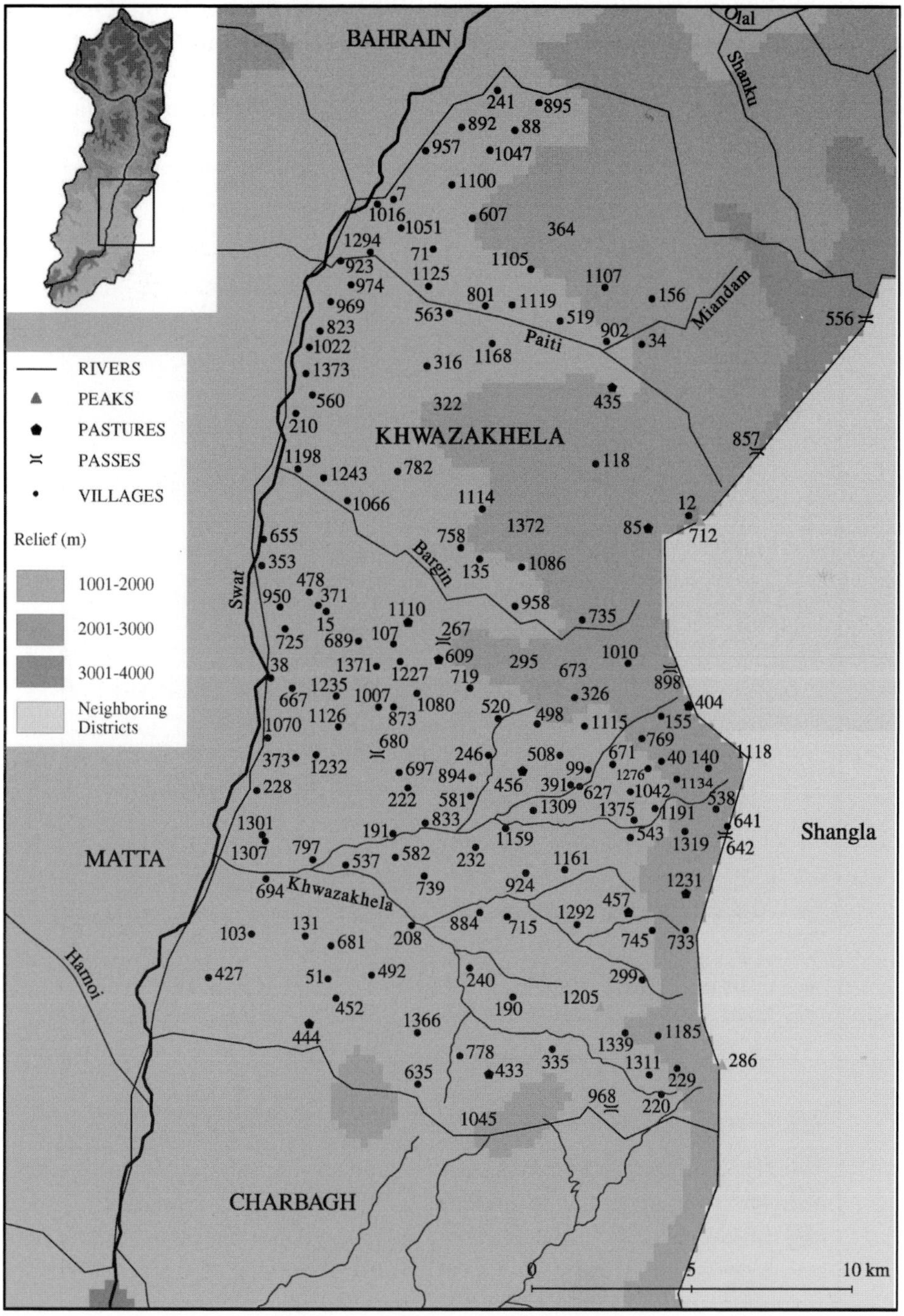

Fig. 11. Tehsil of Khwazakhela.

Maṭṭa

The Tehsil of Maṭṭa derives its name from the town of Maṭṭa, in the southern part, at the confluence between the Harnoi Khwar and the Swāt river. As a general rule, the main towns of all Tehsils are located in the valley of the Swāt river, as these are the more fertile regions, as well as the most densely inhabited and the more reachable by road.
Dar Banda is the only pasture in the northern region, at the boundary with the Tehsil of Bahrain, but in total 20 are the pastures listed in the Gazetteer.
Quite densely inhabited (250 villages), the passes (7) lead to the bordering District of Dir. In the upper part, it reaches 3,000 msl. (10 peaks are also mentioned in the Gazetteer). Located in Maṭṭa are the springs of the Harnoi Khwar.
Previously, this Tehsil was divided in two sub-Tehsils: Maṭṭa Sebujni and Maṭṭa Khararai.

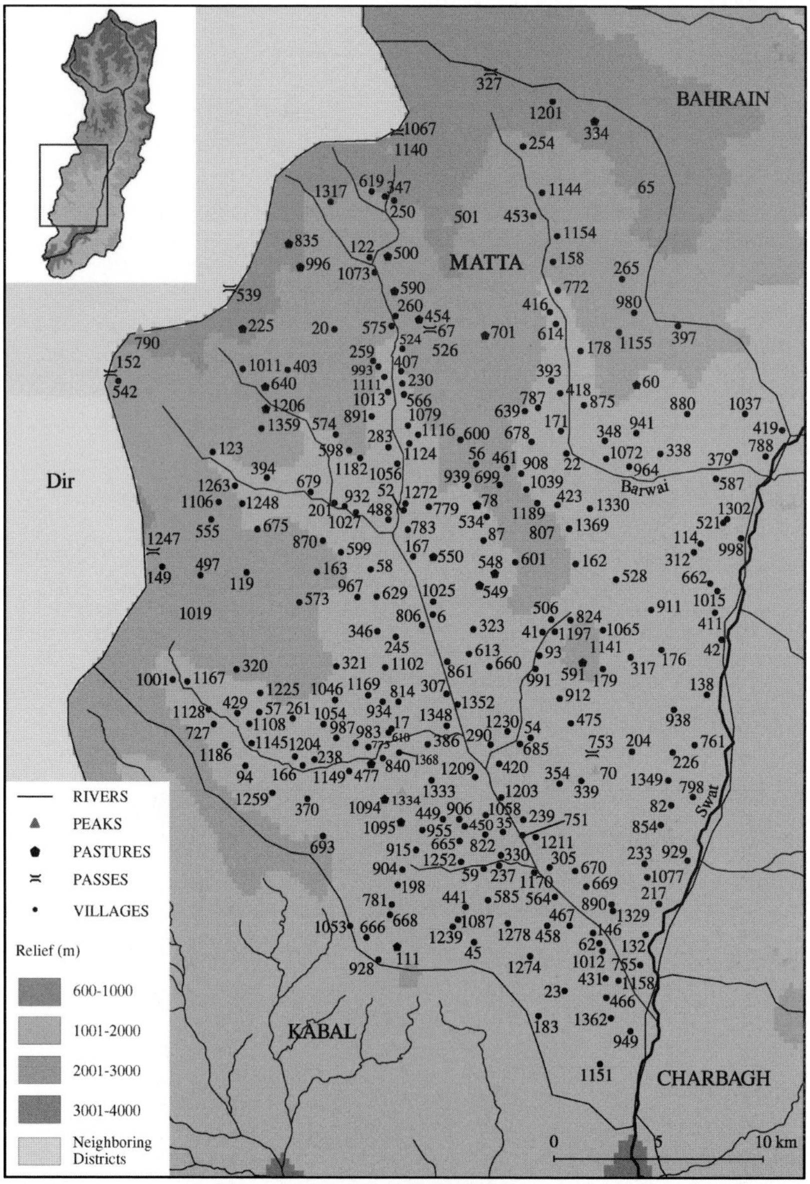

Fig. 12. Tehsil of Maṭṭa.

Bahrain

The Tehsil of Bahrain is the biggest one. It is located north of Maṭṭa and Khwazakhela. Its main town is Bahrain, the old Baranial, in the southern part, in the valley of the Swāt river at the confluence with the Daral Khwar. It is densely inhabited (232 villages) in the tight valley of the Swāt river, but less so in the mountainous regions at the boundaries with Dir, to the west, Kohistan, to the east, and Gilgit and Chitral, to the north.

Formerly, Kalam represented a different administrative unit, however nowadays Kalam and Bahrain are merged in a unique Tehsil. Indeed, the Tehsil of Bahrain has for a long time been independent from the rest of Swāt and remains quite isolated. The last remnants of the Dardic populations originating in the valley live here. The main town in the Tehsil of Kalam is Kalam and is located at the confluence of the Gabral river and the Ushu Gol. As the average elevation is very high, only few villages exist: Kalam, Gabral, Ushu, Utrot and Kas amongst others. Three lakes are also named in the Gazetteer.

Few pastures exist in this Tehsil (18), but many passes (21) link it with Shangla, Kohistan, Dir, Chitral and Gilgit. The two highest mountains of Swāt, the Mankial Tsukai and the Falak Sar, are both located in this Tehsil. 11 peaks in total are mentioned in the Gazetteer.

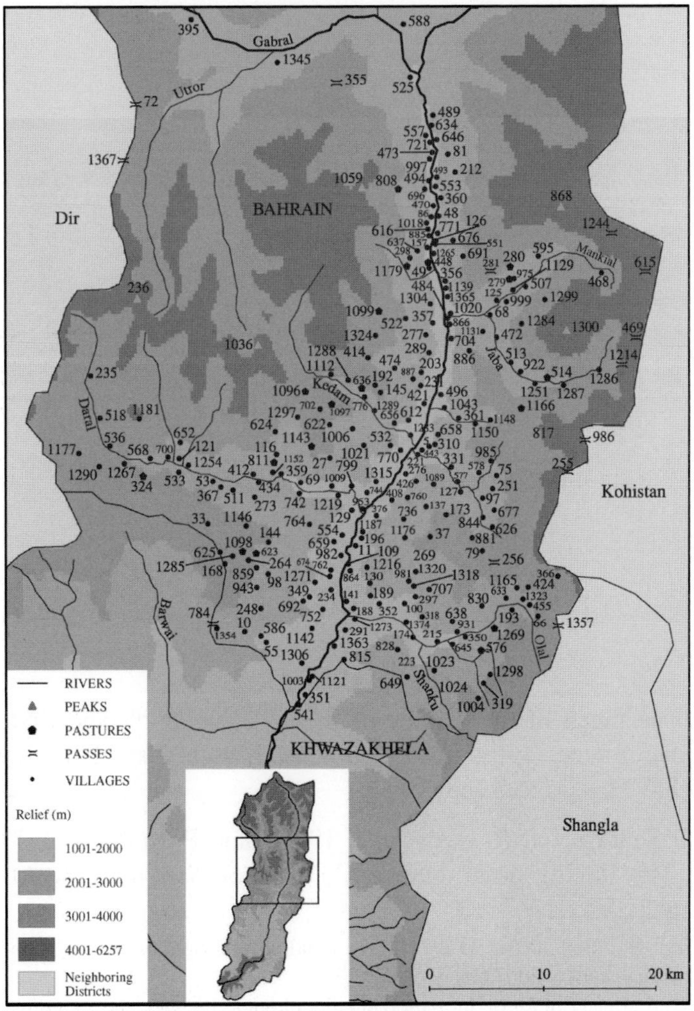

Fig. 13. Lower part of the Tehsil of Bahrain.

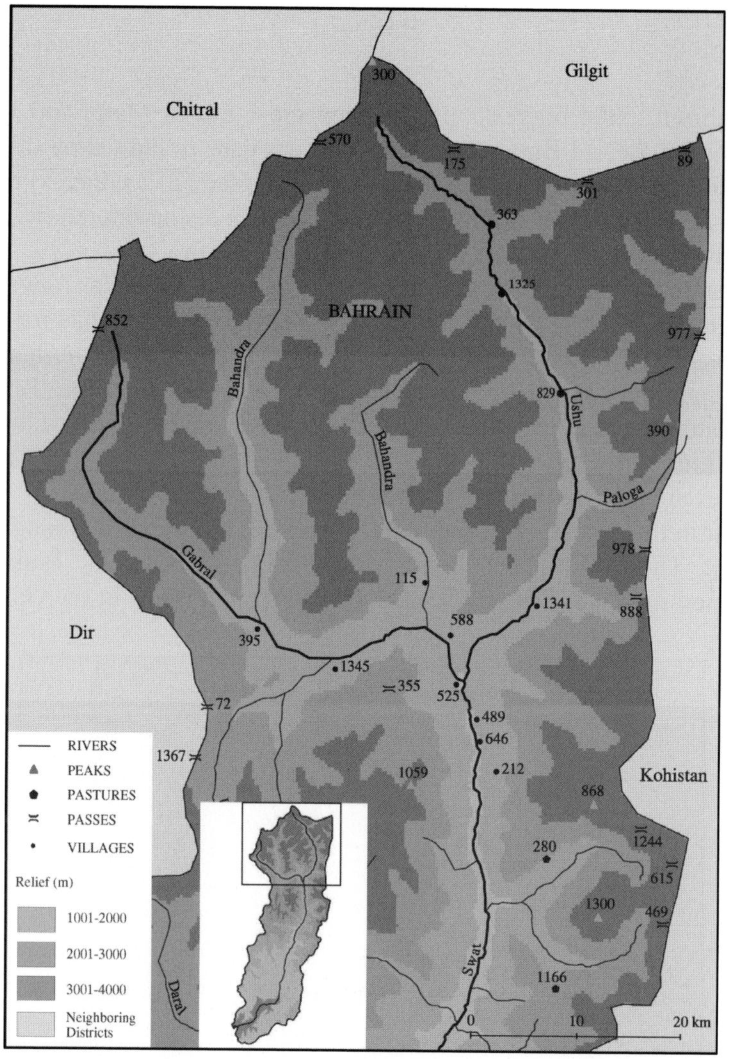

Fig. 14. Upper part of the Tehsil of Bahrain (Kalam).

HISTORY[15]

Toponymy can tell us much of the history of the Swāt valley.[16] The first historical sources quote this region in reference to its name, coinciding with that of its main river. For this, many etymologies have been proposed:[17]

- *suvāstu* Sanskrit (cf. Ṛg-veda VIII, 19, 37 and PĀṆINI IV, 2, 77: see AGRAWALA 1953: 34) 'having good dwelling', = Greek *Soastḗnē* (ARRIAN, *Indica* IV, 11

[15] On the prehistory, see OLIVIERI 2009a: 33-36 and the detailed bibliography in ID. 2006. For further historical details, see KHAN 1963, HAROON 2007 and SIDDIQUE 2014.

[16] Hans KRAHE remarked already in 1949, in a short methodological booklet, the importance of the toponyms as historical sources ("Ortsnamen als Geschichtsquelle").

[17] See SULTAN-I-ROME 2008: 13-14.

Σόαστος, see also STRABO VII, I *Suastus*) = Iranian *hu-asp*? = Chinese (XUANZANG) *Su-po-fa-su-to* (< *subhavastu*).[18] According to TUCCI (1997: 47 n. 58a), "[t]he IA, having mainly wooden or mud houses (see BURROW in BASHAM 1975, p. 25 of Swāt) must have been greatly impressed by the stone-houses of Swāt; therefore the traditional interpretation of Suvāstu: 'The place of fine dwellings' may appear, in the light of the recent excavations, equally adequate";
- < *sveta* 'white', referring to the clearness of the waters of Swāt river;
- < *aswad* (Arabic) 'black', referring to the fertility of the land in the valley as it appeared to the eyes of the Arabic invaders;
- < *saut* (Arabic) 'echo', for the echo of mountains;
- < *su* (Syriac) 'sun' + *at* 'hearth': 'the land attributed to the sun'.

The Sanskrit etymology, *Suvāstu*, is the most probable, and would be apparently confirmed by one of the successive names of Swāt, Uḍḍiyāna, the "garden" in Sanskrit.[19] In this case, then, Indo-Aryan origin. Indeed, from the archaeological studies it emerges that the Indo-Aryans were the first inhabitants of this region, successively attacked, invaded, populated and visited by the Greeks of Alexander the Great, the Tibetans, the Chinese, and so on.[20]
After the Vedas and Pāṇini, the first mentions of Swāt are by the Greek historians, in particular Arrian. In 327 BC Alexander the Great crossed the Panjkora river and reached Swāt in order to attack the town of Massaga, the capital of this region, nowadays recognizable as modern Mingora (cf. *Gazetteer*). This name can possibly be compared to the Masakavati river in Pāṇini.

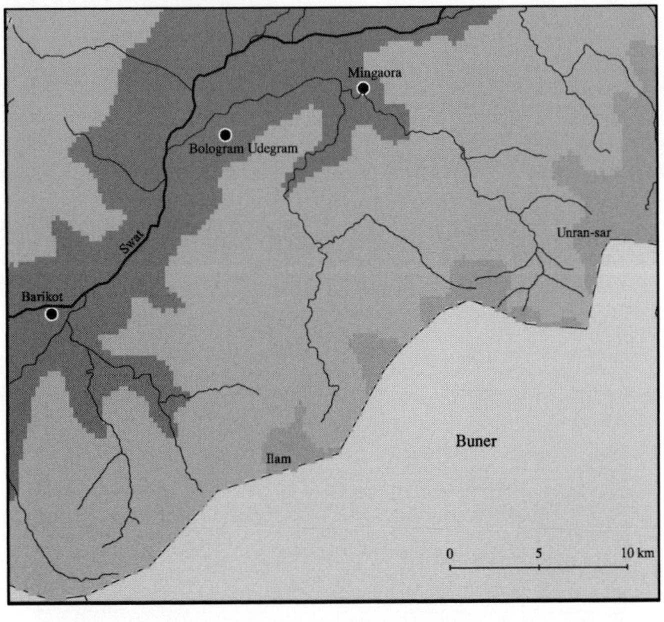

Fig. 15. Greek towns and mountains in Swāt.

[18] See TUCCI 1977: 39.

[19] This name, however, is related by TUCCI (1977: 39) with the people of the Urdi, Aurddi, Uḍi, etc.: "The Tibetan name Orgyan is so explained by Buddhagupta, a Tibetan pilgrim who went to Swāt in the 16th century: 'The name Orgyan is derived from Uḍḍiyāna on account of the similarity [in pronunciation of *ḍ* and *ṛ*]' [note 45 "Is there any relation between Urdi, Aurddāyanī and uddäi, ura 'above, up'? Morgenstierne 1956, III, 3, p. 63 [= IIFL]"]". For a detailed analysis of the name Uḍḍiyāna, see LÉVY 1915: 104-112.

[20] Nowadays we have a lot of literature on this topic. Among others: TUCCI 1963b and the articles collected in the volume of 1997; SULTAN-I-ROME 2008; OLIVIERI 2009a.

Among the towns mentioned by the Greek historians, we find also *Ora*, the modern Udegram, and *Bazira*, the modern Barikot. We find also mentions of Mount Aornos (linguistically identifiable with the Unran Sar, but probably Mount Ilam), where the inhabitants of Bazira found shelter (see fig. 15).[21]

Soon after Alexander the Great left Swāt, the Indian Maurya dynasty imposed Buddhism on the region, in particular with its main king, Aśoka.

Fig. 16. Rock sculpture with Bodhisattva in Arabkhan-china (FILIGENZI 2015: fig. 36).

Fig. 17. The back side of the Shrine of Gumbat/ Balo Kale (photo of the author).

Fig. 18. Stūpa of Abbasaheb-china (photo of the author).

[21] There exists a large bibliography on the passage of Alexander the Great in these regions: apart the well-known researches of STEIN and TUCCI, see, among others, OLIVIERI 1996, 2015c and COLORU/OLIVIERI 2019 and bibliography.

In 403 AD, Fa-hsien, followed in 519 by Sung Yun, two Chinese pilgrims, attested that Buddhism was very important across the entire region. However, in 630 Xuanzang already related the decadence of this religion, even if Swāt was probably the starting point of the conversion of Tibet to the dharma (Padmasambhava was probably a native of Swāt: see OLIVIERI 2016).

Between the 5th and the 8th centuries, even if we do not have any historical source, Swāt was probably involved in the wars between Chinese and Tibetans, before the arrival of the Kushanas. For the successive epochs we possess only Arabic sources, for the dynasties of the Turki Shahis and of the Hindu Shahis, between the 8th and the 11th centuries. The situation definitely changed with Mahmud-e Ghaznavi in the 11th century and the progressive Islamization of the valley.

Nowadays Swāt valley is principally inhabited by Pashtuns Yusufzais. The penetration of the Pashtuns into the valley was probably progressive, starting from the 15th century, but little by little they came to dominate the local populations (beyond doubt Dards) and since the half of the 16th century they ruled over the entire region. The first consequence was a war with the Moghuls, in particular Babur and Akbar, this latter principally due to his religious differences with Bayazid Ansari or Pir-i Roshan ('the Master of the Light'), founder of the Roshaniyya.[22] However, the preaching of the defender of orthodox Islam, Sayyid Ali Shah Tarmezi, called Pir Baba (his zyārat is located in Buner, south of Swāt, near mount Ilam, and is still today a pilgrimage destination), and of his main pupil, Abdur Rashid, said Akhund Darwaza, brought the Yusufzais back to orthodoxy.

At the beginning of the 19th century, Sayyid Ahmed Shah Brelwi, a Wahabite who longed for the creation of an Islamic state, found protection with Sayyid Akbar Shah, a descendant of Pir Baba, of Hanafite faith. This latter, however, left him soon after and the consequences of this were the prelude to the battle of Ambela[23] and to the two battles of Malakand against the British in the second half of the 19th century. The songs of these battles were recorded and published by J. DARMESTETER in his *Chants populaires des Afghans* (Paris 1888-1890). A minor consequence at the time but capital for the history of Swāt was the accession to power of Abdul Ghafur, known as Akhund of Swāt or Saidu Baba, nowadays still venerated in Saidu Sharif. He was the founder of the dynasty of the Mianguls.

Between the end of the 19th and the beginning of the 20th century many revolts against British rule took place, led by the Lewanai Faqir, 'the crazy beggar', until the establishment of the "Yusufzai State of Swāt", lasting from 1917 to 1969, by the Miangul dynasty.

In 1969, the last Wali of Swāt renounced the kingdom and established the accession of Swāt district into Pakistan.[24] This free choice granted many privileges to the region, which was the first in the area to have a public healthcare system, public schools, the Aurangzeb College, and so on.

ECONOMY[25]

Major RAVERTY, at the end of the 19th century, provides a detailed historical analysis of the former administrative and economic system introduced into Swāt by Shaikh Mali, as well as of the division of the valley into the different units:

---

22 See SULTAN-I-ROME 2008: 24-25, OLIVIERI 2009a: 61 ff., and DE CHIARA forthcoming a.

23 See HOPKINS 2013: 41-42.

24 See BARTH 1985.

25 For all information on economy, demography, urbanisation, etc., see INAM-UR-RAHIM/VIARO 2002.

Shaikh Malí first divided Suwát for convenience sake into two nominal parts, lying on either side of the river. To that portion lying between the right bank and the mountains bordering it on the north-west, and comprising the eight minor dara'hs already referred to, opening into it, he gave the name of *lánw-dah*, the plural form of the Pus'hto adjective *lúnd*, signifying "moist," "damp," etc., from its enjoying a greater portion of moisture than the other, for, where the river separates into several branches [...] is part of this moist tract, hence its name. To the other portion of Suwát, lying between the left bank and the mountains on the south-east, and containing the other seventeen minor dara'hs, he gave the name of *wuchah*, signifying "dry," "arid," etc. [...] The bounds of the *lánw-dah* half of the valley were fixed by the Shaikh from B'ṛangolaey, the boundary village of Lower Suwát, nearly facing Tútakán, on the opposite bank of the river, as far up as Lanḍaey, the lowest village to the north, just opposite Pí'á, a tract extending in length about sixty miles. The *wuchah* portion extended from the village of Tútakán, in Lower Suwat, to Pí'á, the boundary village of Upper Suwát, a distance of sixty-three miles.[26]

Until the mid-1950s, the economic system used in Swāt by the Yusufzais was that of *wesh*, also named by RAVERTY in the preceding quotation. According to ATAYEE (1979: 104-106, n. 361),

Wesh means distribution. [...] Wesh is a very old custom, coming into existence when nomadic life gave way to settle agricultural life. We know from history that the ancient nomads fostered the WESH system from the very beginning of settled agricultural life up to the dawn of state institute. In the 15th century A.D. Sheikh Malli brought the WESH system into a new code of law which he called Dafter 'code' (literally meaning office). From then on the ten year cyclic WESH system came into being. [...] This cyclic distribution of land was in force quite recently in the ten year cyclic WESH system land, owned in common, was redistributed and no one had a permanent plot of his own. The last WESH effected was in 1956 A.D: (1335 A.H.). [...] When objective conditions favourable to the development and consolidation of private property developed, the WESH system weakened up. Despite this and despite the long struggle led by the opponents of Sheikh Malli, the Yousifzai tribes keep the WESH among themselves secretly without the knowledge of central government.

MCMAHON and RAMSAY provide a complete description of the *wesh* system (cf. also s.v. *serai* in the glossary of geonyms):

On the occupation of this country by the Pathans all lands were divided between the sub-divisions of each tribe. The portion, *daftar*, of each main sub-division was called a *tappa*. Each *tappa* was sub-divided between the various sub-sections (*khel*) of the tribal sub-division, and the *daftar* of each *khel* was then again sub-divided into shares (called *bakhra* or *brakha*) among the individual members of the *khel*. Any person possessing a share, however small, in a *daftar* is called a *daftari*. Such is the importance attaching to the status of *daftari*, that a man who by alienating or losing his ancestral share of land ceases to be a *daftari* is no longer entitled to be called a 'Pathan', but becomes a 'Fakir', without a voice in village or tribal councils. In order as far as possible to make the shares of each *daftari* equal in value, the lands of a *khel* were classed according to the nature of the soil and facilities of irrigation into *vands* (or *wands*), each bearing some distinctive local name. A *daftari*'s share, calculated by some recognized unit of measurement (known by different names in each locality, such as *pacha*, *rupiya*, *paisa*, *tora*, *ghwaye*, *nimakai*, *tirao*, *pao*, &c.) was not of necessity a compact piece of land, but was often composed of plots, distant from each other, in several *wands*. Each *khel* proceeded to build villages, sometimes only one, sometimes several on its share of land.[27]

---

[26] RAVERTY 1888: 206.

[27] MCMAHON/RAMSAY 1916: 17 and 1981^2: 42, as quoted by SULTAN-I-ROME 2016: 45-46.

This economic system, on one hand very "democratic" and egalitarian, permitted the periodic shift of the different kind of fields: the more fertile in the plain (*xkata/kuẓa*), the less fertile in the mountains (*porta/bara*), and those adjoining the Swāt river frequently subjected to floods. But on the other hand, it had catastrophic consequences on the environment: indeed, every family cared about its own short-term interest without thinking about the common interest of the tribe as a whole. For this reason, we find only a few orchards and very often these are of spontaneous origin. This is also reflected by the toponymy: indeed, we find a great number of places linked to orchards and presenting the term °*baṇ* 'forest' or other tree and bush names.
Swāt valley was once covered with forests, as studied in detail by SULTAN-I-ROME 2016. Nowadays massive deforestation has changed the environment of lower Swāt and made the densely populated region vulnerable to heavy rain and flooding of the Swāt river in the rainy season.

Fig. 19. The lower Swāt valley (photo L.M. OLIVIERI).

Fig. 20. Mingora (source web)

Fig. 21. Bahrain (source web)

Regarding the composition of these forests, we read in SULTAN-I-ROME (2016: 131-133):

> The sources available show that the forests of Indus Kohistan, Shangla (Shanglapar), and Buner areas of Swat State comprised: (1) Mixed silver fir, spruce, kail and broadleaved forests; (2) Pure kail forests; (3) Deodar (*cedrus deodara*); (4) Pure chir forests; and (5) Scrub forests. Of these: type (1) trees were situated in Alpurai, Kanra, and Besham and to some extent in the upper parts of Chakisar, Puran, Martung, Daggar, and Chagharzai *tahsil*s; type (2) were situated in the lower Indus Kohistan and to a small degree in Chagharzai, Gadizai, Salarzai, and Daggar *tahsil*s of Buner; type (3) was admixed with the forests mentioned in types (1) and (2) and found at places in Kanra West, Alpurai, Upal, and Shang blocks; type (4) occupied major part of the then later Buner Forest Range while in lower Indus Kohistan they were found in the lower parts of Chakisar, Besham, Martung, and Puran *tahsil*s; and type (5) were found in the lower hills in the later Buner Forest Range and some in Puran, Martung, Chakisar, and Besham *tahsils*.
>
> The forests of proper Swat Valley comprised the following types: (1) Scrub forests; (2) Chir (*pinus roxburghii*) forests; (3) Deodar (*cedrus deodara*) forests; (4) Blue pine (*pinus wallichiana*) forests; (5) Silver fir (*abies pindrow* and *abies webbiana*) and spruce (*piecea smithiana*) forests; and (6) Oak forests. Of these: type (1) forests were situated between 2,500' to 3,500' elevations in the valley; type (2) forests were confined to Barikot, Marghuzar, Qalagay, and Manarai areas; scattered groups of type (3) forests were found in Qalagay, Marghuzar, Piya, and Tirat areas; of the type (4) forests kail was found throughout Swat and small groups of deodar were found in the Marghuzar and Piya forests, and a number of chir trees were also found in Marghuzar, Jambil, Manarai and Shawar forests; type (5) covered very extensive areas above the kail forests in Swat Proper, and groups of high level kail were also noticeable in the upper reaches in Miandam; and type (6) forests comprised holly oak (*quercus dilatata*), *banj* oak (*quercus ilex*), white oak (*quercus incana*) and brown oak (*quercus semicarpifolia*); of these holly oak was found scattered in kail forests, white oak was found in Barikot, Marghuzar, Manarai, and Shawar regions, a few patches of *banj* oak were growing in places like Shah Dherai, etc. and brown oak was found in pure patches in the forests of Roringar, Lalku, and Miandam regions.[28]

[28] See also FAQIR MUHAMMAD KHAN, n.p.: 12-15 and QADEER KHAN, n.p.: 14-20, quoted by SULTAN-I-ROME, *ibid.*

ETHNOGRAPHY

In 1910 the General Staff Army Headquarters published a "Dictionary of the Pathan Tribes on the North-West Frontier of India", providing us with a very analytical list of all tribes, clans, divisions, sub-divisions, sections and minor fractions living in this area,[29] with all numerical statistics at the time.

The complete list is as follows: Aba Khel, Abazai, Adinzai, Aka Khel, Aka Maruf, Akozai, Ali Khel, Allahi Khel, Amaddi Khel, Arab Khel, Asha Khel, Ashlors, As Khel, Azi Khel, Baba Khel, Babu Khel, Babuzai, Bahram-ka-Khel, Baezai, Bali Khel, Bami Khel, Bao Khel, Barat Khel, Barkhan Khel, Bar Sulizai, Bazi Khel, Busa Khel, Chandan Khel, Daori Khel, Dodal, Durdani Khel, Fateh Khel, Fazil Khel, Garwis, Ghaibi Khel, Gujars, Hasan Khel, Ibrahim Khel, Idal Khel, Ismail Khel, Juggi Khel, Jula Khel, Kachu Khel, Kari Khel, Karim Khel, Kata Khel, Kemal Khel, Khadakzai, Khadish Khel, Khanda Khel, Khan Khel, Khwaja Khel, Khwazozai, Kuz Sulizai, Lunda Khel, Macha Khel, Maddi Khel, Mali Khel, Malik Khel, Mama Khel, Mardan Khel, Marjan Khel, Maturizai, Mir Hasan Khel, Mira Khel, Mirwas Khel, Mudah Khel, Mulla Khel, Muradu Khel, Musa Khel, Nazr Ali Khel, Nekpi/Nikbi Khel, Nur Muhammad Khel, Padshah Khel, Painda Khel, Panjgol, Panjmiral, Pira Khel, Ranizai Bar, Ranizai Sam, Richbin Khel, Samel/Ismail Khel, Sebujni, Shaba Khel, Shamizai, Shamozai, Sherga Khel, Sin/Sen Khel, Suleman Khel, Sultan-ka-Khel, Swatis, Umar Khel, Umarzai, Umbara Khel, Umr Khel, Usmani Khel, Utmanzai, Waro Usman Khel, Ya/Aya Khel, Yakub Khel, Yusafzai, Zaman Kha Khel, Zerdast Khel.

According to this census, the tribes living in Swāt were Yusufzai Pashtuns[30] (Akozai[31]), the Garwis[32] and the Gujars.[33]

The term "Swati" may indicate "that portion of the Akozai clan of Yusufzais which inhabits Swat"[34] and the first inhabitants of the Swāt valley, expelled by the Yusufzais.[35] Nowa-

---

[29] General Staff Army Headquarters 1910: 5.

[30] "A great group of Pathan tribes which include those of the Black Mountain, the Bunerwals, the Yusafzai Swatis, the people of Dir and the Panjkora valley and the inhabitants of the Ysafzai plain in British territory. They all claim descent from one Mandai, his son Yusaf, and grandson Mandan. From Yusaf's four sons, Isa, Musa, Mail, and Ako are descended, respectively, the Isazais, Iliaszais, Malizais and Akozais: Ako was also the progenitor of the Ranizais. The Utmanzais are descended from Mandan" (General Staff Army Headquarters 1910: 55). The Yusufzais would be the descendants of Yusuf and lastly of Kharshbun (or Krishyun), son of Sarbanr, son of the mythic Qais *alias* Abdurrashid (see CAROE 1958: 11-14).

[31] "A large clan of Yusafzais, inhabiting both banks of the Swat river, sometimes known as Upper and Lower Swatis" (General Staff Army Headquarters 1910: 11). According to MCMAHON/RAMSAY 1981[2] [1901]: 130, this clan was in turn divided into Ranizai (Sultan Kha Khel, Usmani Khel, Bahram Kha Khel, Utmanzai, Khwaza Khel, Ali Khel: lower Swāt, left bank); Baezai (Kuz Sulizai – Aba Khel, Musa Khel –, Babuzai – Aba Khel, Maruf Khel, Barat Khel, Bami Khel, Aba Khel –, Bar Sulizai – Azzi Khel, Jinki Khel, Maturizai –: upper Swāt, left bank); Khadakzai and Abazai (lower Swāt, right bank); Khwazazai (Shamizai, Sibat Khel e Juna Khel – Sebujni –, Nikbi Khel: upper Swāt, right bank; Adinzai – Utmanzai, Babu Khel –: lower Swāt, right bank; and Malizai: Dir).

[32] "A non-Pathan tribe inhabiting the head of the Swat valley. They are probably allied to the Kohistanis" (General Staff Army Headquarters 1910: 22).

[33] "A stalwart Mussalman pastoral tribe, probably of the same origin as the Jats, scattered in large numbers amongst the Pathan tribes, to whom they are subject, from the Black Mountain to the Kunar river. They own separate villages in or near the lower hills, and till the soil, for which they pay rent. In summer they migrate with their flocks to the mountains. Gujars are also numerous in north-western India and Kashmir. They speak the language of their winter homes, but have a few words peculiar to themselves. They are probably the descendants of the original inhabitants of the country, or at least represent some earlier wave of invasion than that of the Pathans" (*ibid.*: 22).

[34] *Ibid.*: 51.

[35] "The original inhabitants of Swat, sometimes called Dehgans, and, according to some authorities, of Indian origin. Driven out of Swat and Buner by the Akozai Yusafzais at the end of the fifteenth century, they emi-

days the situation has not changed very much but all minorities tend to be assimilated by the Pashtuns.

An historical detailed description of the ethnic composition of lower Swāt can be found in RAVERTY 1888: 207-208, also providing information about the names of the Tehsils:

> The Ákhúnd, Darwezah, whose grandfather left his native country of Nangrahár, or Nek-Anhár, and accompanied the Yúsufzís in their migration eastwards, as their Peshwá or spiritual guide, and received his share in the distribution made by Shaikh Malí, refers to the distribution in the following words: "The Malik, Shaikh Malí, made a census of the whole *ulús* of Yúsuf and Mandaṛ, male and female, great and small, with the object of dividing Suwát and its lands equally among the Yúsufzís. The Akozí and 'Ísází divisions were found to contain just 6,000 persons, and the Malízí and Ilyászí proved to be much the same in point of numbers, a total of just 12,000. The Yúsufzís and Mandaṛs were of about the same strength, namely, about 12,000 each. The Nangraháris, Lamghánís, and Kábulís, who had accompanied the Yúsufzís and Mandaṛs from the west, were not included in the census, neither were the inhabitants of those parts whom the Afgháns found there [...].
>
> Since the period in question vast changes have taken place. For a long time past the Dara'h of Suwát has become the almost exclusive portion of the Akozí Yúsufzís which sub-tribe is again subdivided into several khels or sections, of whom the Khwádozís and Bá'ízís are the most numerous. The *wuchah* division is in the possession of the Rárnízís and Bá'ízís, and the *lánw-dah* is held by the Khwádozís. These two clans, the Khwádozís and the Bá'ízís, are again subdivided into smaller sections. From Tútakán to Tárnah dwell the Rárnízís, who also hold a few villages under the low hills south of the mountain range of which the Malah-khanḍ forms a portion, such as Tsaná-koṭ, or, as sometimes called, Sháh-koṭ, and Dargaey. The chief town of the Rárnízís is Allah-ḍanḍ, which is the residence of the chief. From the town of Tárnah to the village of Maní-hár or Mán-yár, to the north, are the Tsolízís [...] From Maní-hár or Mán-yár northwards as far as Chhár-Bágh, are the Bábúzis; and from thence still farther northwards, are the Matúṛízís [...] From thence to Khonah the whole of the Khází Khel, a numerous clan, are located, and from Khonah as far north as Pí'á, the most northerly village of the Yúsufzí Afgháns in Upper Suwát, are the Jánakís, or Jának Khel. [...]
>
> Crossing over into the *lánw-dah*, we find the different clans or sections of the Khwádozí, and two other divisions of the Akozí Yúsufzís, located as follows, from south to north: From B'ṛangolaey to Rámoṛah are the S'hádakzí or K'hádakzí and Abází Akozís, who dwell together. From Rámoṛah to Úchh or Úchhúnah, or Úchhún, the two villages of Úchh, as far as Súe-galí are the Shamúzís. From Súe-galí to Ním-galí are the Nikbí Khel [...] From Nímgalí to Lanḍaey the Ṣábit and Chúní (now known as Ṣabchúní) are located, who hold a few small villages, and the remainder, to the south, are the Shámízís.

grated eastwards, under the leadership of the Saiyid Jalal Baba, a son of the famous Pir Baba of Buner. Crossing the Indus, they settled in Tikri, Allai, Deshi, Nandihar, Pakli, Konsh, Bogarmang, Agror, Balakot, and Garhi Habibulla, north of Hazara, of which their descendants are the present inhabitants" (*ibid.*). See also SULTAN-I-ROME 2013: 15: "The Swatis are those Pukhtuns who had occupied and inhabited the Swat Valley for centuries, prior to their expulsion and the subsequent occupation of Swat by the Yusufzai in the sixteenth century. However, it is noteworthy that in a recent study Muhammad Akhtar has questioned the ethnicity of these Swatis as Pukhtuns. He is of the opinion that these Swatis were Gabris by religion and Tajak by origin".

LANGUAGES

In addition to Yusufzai Pashto, other residual languages are spoken by a few peoples in the north of the valley. In particular, two Dardic languages: *baškarīk*,[36] spoken, according to Fussman (1972, I: 27), "dans trois villages près des sources du Swāt (région de Kalām)", and *tōrwālī*, "parlé dans quelques villages de la haute vallée de Swāt, dans une zone limitée au N[ord] par l'aire B[aškarīk], au Sud par l'aire [Pashto]".[37]
According to the same G. Fussman, *dameli* (*dâmia-bâṣa*) and *gawar-bati* (*narisati*) are also native of Swāt, but afterwards the Damelis and the Gawars "en auraient été expulsés vers le milieu du XVe siècle par les Pathans" (FUSSMAN 1972, I: 23).

Pashto is an eastern Iranian language belonging to the Indo-Iranian branch of the Indo-European family. The *yusufzəy pəxto* (YP) dialect spoken in the valley is a "hard" dialect of the "zone A".[38] It is one of the most eastern dialects in the Pashto-speaking area, and it is much affected by contact with the Indo-Aryan languages, in particular Urdu, the national language of Pakistan.

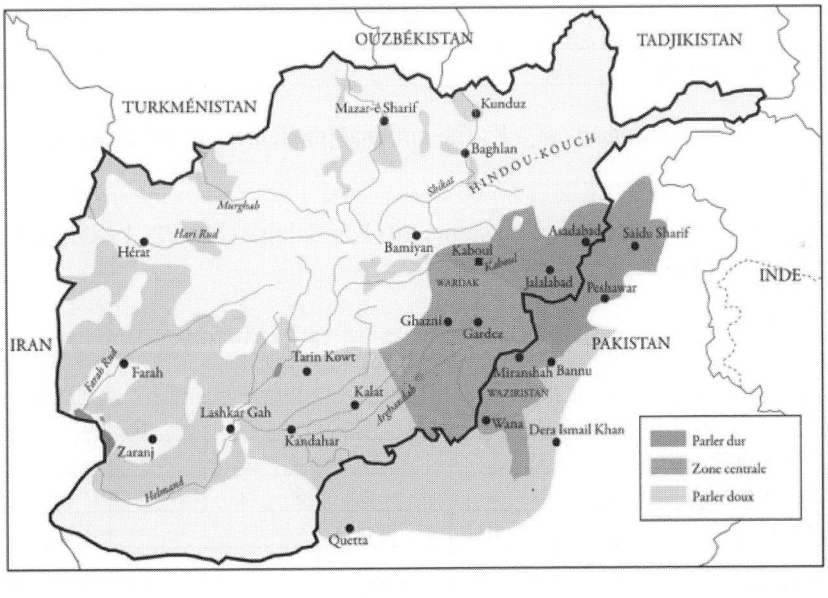

Fig. 22. Pashto-speaking area and dialects (SEPTFONDS/KABIR 2013: 6).

[36] *Diri*, according to LEECH, *Gārwī* or *Gāwrī*, according to the *LSI*, *Garhwī*, according to the *Imperial Gazetteer of India* 1908: 32; *Kohistana* according to BARTH 1956b; *Kalami Kohistani* according to RENSCH 1992. On this language, see BAART 1999 and BAART/SAGAR 2004.

[37] FUSSMAN 1972, I: 27. See also BIDDULPH 1971: 69-71.

[38] See KIEFFER 1975: 5, explaining the existence of three zones in the Pashto area: "hard" dialects (A), "soft" dialects (C) and a group of geographically intermediary dialects, or "manjanəy" (B). See also SEPTFONDS 2006 for a definitive statement of the question.

REMARKS ON THE YUSUFZAI DIALECT OF SWĀT

Phonologic system[39]

Consonants

As compared with the Manjanəy and “soft” dialects, the phonologic system of YP is very simplified. In particular, phonemes x̌, ǧ, c, j and ž merge with other phonemes: x̌ > x; ǧ > g; c > s; j > z; ž > ǰ (even if this latter change is not systematic).[40] See the following table:

YP		(bilabial)	(dental)	(retroflex)	(palatal)	(velar)	(pharyngeal)
obstruent	(Occlusive)	p b	t d	ṭ ḍ		k g	
	(Affricate)				č ǰ		
	(Fricative)		s z		š (ž)	x γ	(h)
sonant	(Nasal)	m	n	ṇ			
	(Liquid)		l				
			r	ṛ			
	(Semi-vowel)	w			y		

Tab. 4. Consonants of YP. The optional phonemes are in brackets.

In comparison with the consonantal systems of Kandahari (PENZL 1955: see table 5) and Jadrāni (SEPTFONDS 1994: see table 6):[41]

Kandahari		(bilabial)	(dental)	(retroflex)	(palatal)	(velar)	(uvular)	(pharyngeal)
obstruent	(Occlusive)	p b	t d	ṭ ḍ		k g	q	’
	(Affricate)		**c j**		č ǰ			
	(Fricative)	f	s z	**ṣ ẓ**	š ž	x γ		h
sonant	(Nasal)	m	n	ṇ				
	(Liquid)		l					
			r	ṛ				
	(Semi-vowel)	w			y			

Tab. 5. In this system we can observe the “elegant” phonemes **f**, **q**, **h**, **’**, rarely appearing in other dialects.

39 See HALLBERG 1992 and GRIERSON 1921: 31-39, in particular pp. 35-39. On page 35, he points out (the author of the 1898 survey is Sir Harold A. DEANE, at the time a politician in Malakand: see OLIVIERI 2015) that “*ts* and *dz* are pronounced *ś* and *ż*, respectively. Also that the short ^{a} is rarely used; a full *a* being used instead. In other respects the dialect is much the same as that of the Yūsufzais”.

40 See also HALLBERG 1992: 11.

41 The Pashto dialects of the Hazara district can also be compared in this concern: see MORGENSTIERNE/LLOYD-JAMES 1928.

Jadrāni		(bilabial)	(dental)	(retroflex)	(palatal)	(velar)
obstruent	(Occlusive)	p b	t d	ṭ ḍ		k g
	(Affricate)		**c j**		č ǰ	
	(Fricative)		s z	**x̌ ǧ**	š ž	x γ
sonant	(Nasal)	m	n	ṇ		
	(Liquid)		l			
			r	ṛ		
	(Semi-vowel)	w			y	

Tab. 6. Jadrani consonantal system.

Remarks:

c > *s* in every position, initial, internal or final: *sok* instead of *cok* 'who', *sə́nga* instead of *cə́nga* 'how', *ski* instead of *cəṣí* 'he drinks', *pási* instead of *pā́ci* 'he gets up', *xars* instead of *xarc* 'expenses'. Consequently, *s* in Swāt is represented in the Pashto script by ث (*s*), س (*s*), ص (*s*), څ (*c*).[42]

j > *z*: *zal* instead of *jal* 'time', *zan* instead of *jān* 'self', *zəmá* instead of *jəmā́* 'my', *zmə́ka* instead of *jmə́ka* 'hearth', *xatiz* instead of *xatij* 'east'. However, after another consonant *j* tends to be conserved: *nmunj* 'pray'. *z* in Swāt is represented in Pashto script by ذ (*z*), ز (*z*), ض (*z*), ظ (*z*), ځ (*j*).

ž > *ǰ* in the majority of cases: *ǰaṛí* instead of *žāṛí* 'he/she cries', *ǰə́ba* instead of *žə́ba* 'tongue', *ǰránda* instead of *žránda* 'mill; padlock', *roǰá* instead of *rožá* 'Ramadan'. In some cases also *ž* > *z*: *zər* instead of *žər* 'quick', *nizdé* instead of *nə́žde* 'near'.

š is kept: *šəltālú* 'peach', *məšə́r* 'elder', *təš* 'void'.

h tends to be dropped but sometimes it is pronounced, as in *naha* 'nine' instead of *na(a)*.

x represents خ (x) and ښ (x̌): *xə* 'good, well' (*x̌ə*), *xáwra* 'hearth' (*x̌ā́wra*), *maxám* 'evening' (*māx̌ā́m*), *axtár* 'feast', *ux* 'camel' (*ux̌*), *məx* 'face', *xax* 'buried' (*xax̌*).

g represents گ (g) and ږ (ǧ): *gíra* 'beard' (*ǧíra*), *gáṭa* 'rock', *ǰagəṛá* 'battle with firearms' (vs. *šer/šar* 'battle with bladed weapons'), *agə́y* 'egg' (*hagə́y*), *γwag* 'ear' (*γwaǧ*), *partúk* 'trousers' (*partúg*).[43]

Consonantal groups tend to be simplified, with the loss of the last consonant, mainly at the end of the word and syllable: *wax* instead of *waxt* 'time', *sax* instead of *saxt* 'hard, difficult'; *alə́m* instead of *axlə́m* 'I buy, take', *pínlas* instead of *pínjlas* 'fifteen'.

There is progressive assimilation: *ṭik tɛ* instead of *ṭik day* 'ok'; *səngálle* instead of *cə́nga hāl day* 'how are you?', or *sə́nga čelle* instead of *cə́nga če hāl day* 'how are you?', *bač-či* instead of *bač-ši* 'he escapes'.

w before a vowel tends to be almost not pronounced, with consequent reinforcement of the vowel, or to become *y*: *wi* > *yi* > *i* [i:] 'it/he/she is', *wu* > *u* [u:] 'it/he was', *wa* > *a* [a:] 'she was'. But cf. *wadə́*, *rawán*, etc.

Normally, the variant with *y* is preferred to that with *w*: *yeredə́l* instead of *weredə́l* 'to fear', etc.

[42] In Arabic, all these letters represent different phonemes, which in STD Pashto already do not exist.

[43] Non-systematic devoicing of the final.

Vowels

i						u
	e		ə[44]		o	
		(ɛ)				
			a			

Tab. 7. Vowels of YP.

Remarks:

ɛ represents the diphthongs *ay* and *āy* in STD. However, the opposition between *e* and *ɛ* is very weak, sometimes impossible to be detected: cf. *raγɛ* vs. *raγe*, for instance.

ā (ˡ) is not pronounced as in Afghan ([ɑ]), but rather following the Indian norm, as [a:]: the opposition between *a* and *ā* is then quantitative instead of qualitative. In the initial position, the opposition is neutralized: [asm′a:n] 'sky' (*āsmān*).

-*ə́y* (in final and stressed position only) is the only diphthong kept: *agə́y* 'egg' (*hagə́y*), *kursə́y* 'chair' (*kwərsə́y*).

ə_e > i: *kilɛ* instead of *kəlɛ* 'village', *nízde* instead of *nə́ẓ̌de* 'near', *ništá* 'there is not' < **nə šte* < *nə šta*.

o_i > u: *stóre* 'star', pl. *stúri*.

e_i > i: *kigi* 'he becomes' (*keği*).

ã : *a* + *ṛ* is sometimes nasalised: *špāṛas* 'sixteen'.

(h)am 'also' also has the variants *hum* and *həm*.

Lexicon

The YP has many loanwords from Urdu and English. For instance, when one wants the public bus to be stopped, one says: *ustaz, dəlta brek wāla* 'master, stop here' (litt. 'make a pause'), with *brek* ← English *break*.

Numbers

yau '1', *dwa* '2', *dre* '3', *salor* '4', *pinzə* '5', *špag* '6', *wə* '7', *atə* '8', *naha* '9', *las* '10', *yaúlas* '11', *dwolas* '12', *dyarlas* '13', *salorlas* '14', *pinlas* '15', *špāṛas* '16', *wəlas* '17', *atəlas* '18', *nolas* '19', *šəl* '20', *yauwiš* '21', *dwiš* '22', *deriš* '23', *saleriš* '24', *pinǰiš* '25', *špagiš* '26', *owiš* '27', *atiš* '28', etc.

---

44 ʌ in HALLBERG 1992.

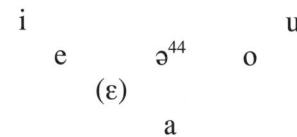

LINGUISTIC FEATURES OF SWĀT TOPONYMS

According to what is stated above, the toponyms and geonyms are pronounced differently from STD Pashto, as for instance:

- *serɛ* instead of *ceray*
- *γāxɛ* instead of *γāx̌ay*, *naxtar* instead of *nax̌tar*
- *megɛ* instead of *meǧay*
- *inzar tangɛ* instead of *injər tangay*
- simplification of the final consonantal groups, as in Akhun Kalat < Akhund.

From the morphological point of view, we find the typical genitival construction of Pashto, *də* N(obl.) + Name, dropping the preposition *də*. Consequently, the *-o* found in many toponyms is the termination of the oblique plural: Kontaro Banda instead of *də kawntaro bānda*, where *kawntaro* is the oblique plural of *kawntar*; Saiyidano Nawe Kalai for *də sayidāno nəway kəlay*; Asharo Paiza instead of *də ašāṛo paiza*.
In the same manner, sometimes the ending *-e* can be the oblique singular of the feminine declension ending in *-a*, and the ending *-i* can represent the oblique singular of the masculine declension in *-ay*:

- Jobe Kandao for *də ǰobe kanḍaw*, from *ǰoba*
- Ghakhe Banda instead of *də γāx̌i bānda*, from *γāx̌ay*
- Ghwai Banda instead of *də γwayi bānda*, from *γwayay*.

Plurals are also used, in particular *-una* for the inanimate masculine and *-e* for the feminine in *-a*:

- Arkhuna, from *arāx*
- Kasuna, from *kas*
- Shnai, *šne* adjective fem. pl. from *šin*

Many suffixes are employed:

- *-i*: Shini
- *-(a/o)lay*: Balalai, Chankolai
- *-(y)āṇ*: Bandanr
- *-(u/o)ṛay*: Churarai
- *-ak*: Dakorak
- *-un*: Dandun Qala
- *-al*: Daral Khwar
- *-yāl*: Dardial
- *-gay*: Jabagai
- *-yār*: Kadiar
- *-kay*: Karandukai
- *-mār*: Kudimar
- *-ti*: Mirati Kandao
- *-man*: Pirman Derai
- *-eṭ*: Ramet
- *-oṭay*: Ramotai Loe Sar
- *-ter*: Samter
- *-in*: Tut Banrin

Past participles can also be found in the toponyms, as in Naredalai, possibly from *naṛedəl*.

The majority of toponyms are formed by compound words, as for instance:

- Amlukbanr 'wood of sloes'
- Bishgram 'resting village'
- Manzghundai Banda 'pasture of the hill in the middle'
- Waliabad 'town of the Wali'

CONCLUSIONS

Toponyms show very interesting characteristics, in particular the presence of linguistic features not belonging to Pashto. We must recall here that, at the time of the "Yusufzai State of Swāt", the ruler of Swāt "Pashtunised" many village names (see KHAN 1963); for instance: Baranial became Bahrain, Paitəy > Fatehpur, Kateləy > Amankoṭ, Taxtaban > Kulader, Manglaor [Čəlgut] > Gharibābād, Islampur > Sālāmpur, Chuṛrai > Madyan, Chindakhwara > Kabal, etc.

Notwithstanding this reform, non-Pashto names still exist nowadays. "The importance of a human settlement may be attested not only by the occupation continuity, but often by the fortunes of its toponym. Few cities in South Asia show both features Pataliputra-Patna and Purushapura-Peshawar, for example. On the other hand, legendary cities of the past, like Pushkalavati, were already deserted and their names forgotten in ancient times. Long-lasting toponyms sometimes survive in nowadays undescriptive modern settlements" (IORI/ OLIVIERI forthcoming). In many cases, very ancient toponyms still survive for modern designations.

In the case of Geonyms, i.e. the generic names of place (see *infra*), we find names of non-Pashto origin, in the majority of cases Indo-Aryan. For instance, there are two names for 'stream' in toponyms: Pashto *xwaṛ* and Dardic *gol* (see DE CHIARA 2019), the latter only in three cases, all in the Tehsil of Bahrain (Kalam).

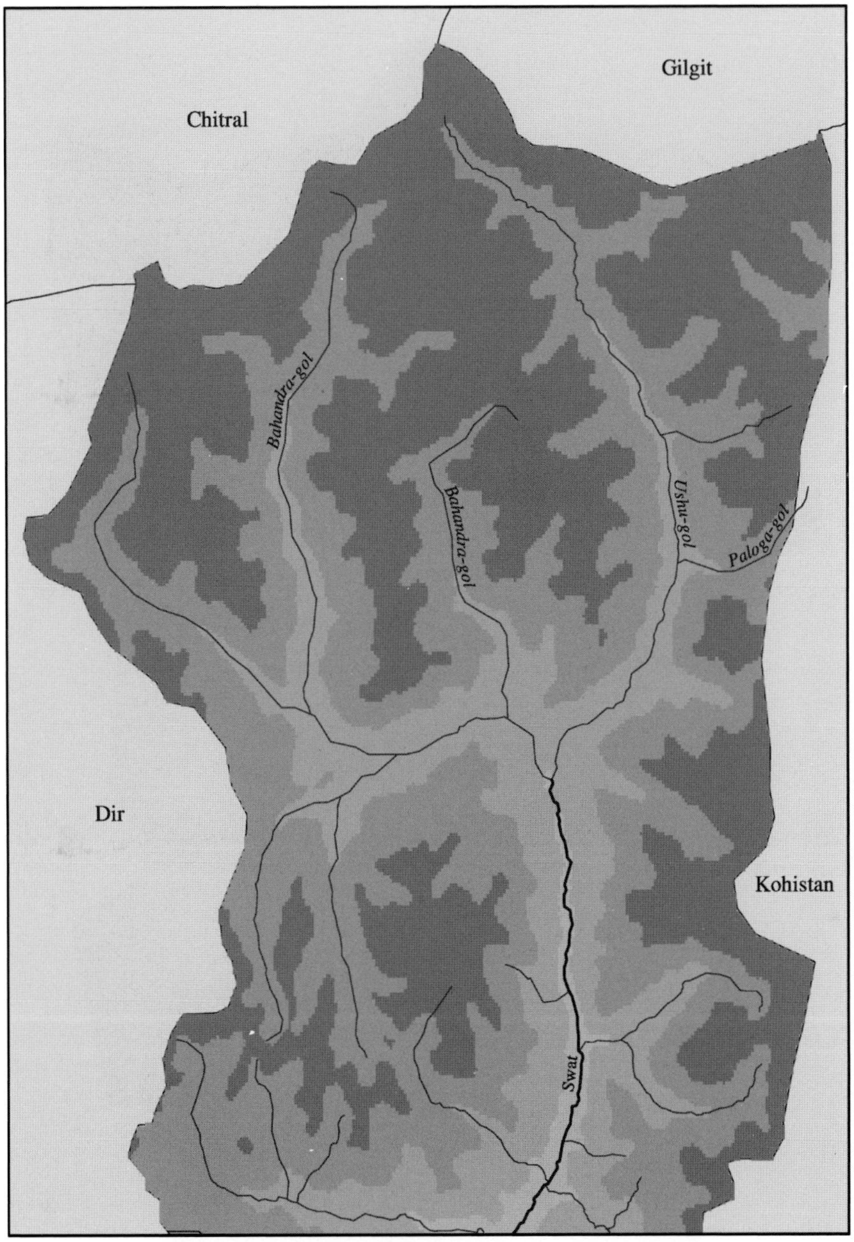

Fig. 23. Geonyms with *gol*.

For the names of "mountain" and "pass" we find four main designations:

- Pashto *γar* 'mountain'
- Pashto *sar* 'top, topmost part, apex, summit'
- Pashto *cuka* 'top, apex, sharp peak (of a mountain), pinnacle, crown, mountain top', probably already a loanword from Dardic
- Dardic *an* 'high mountain slopes'.

For the latter case too the unique attestations are in the north, in particular in the Tehsil of Bahrain (Kalam).

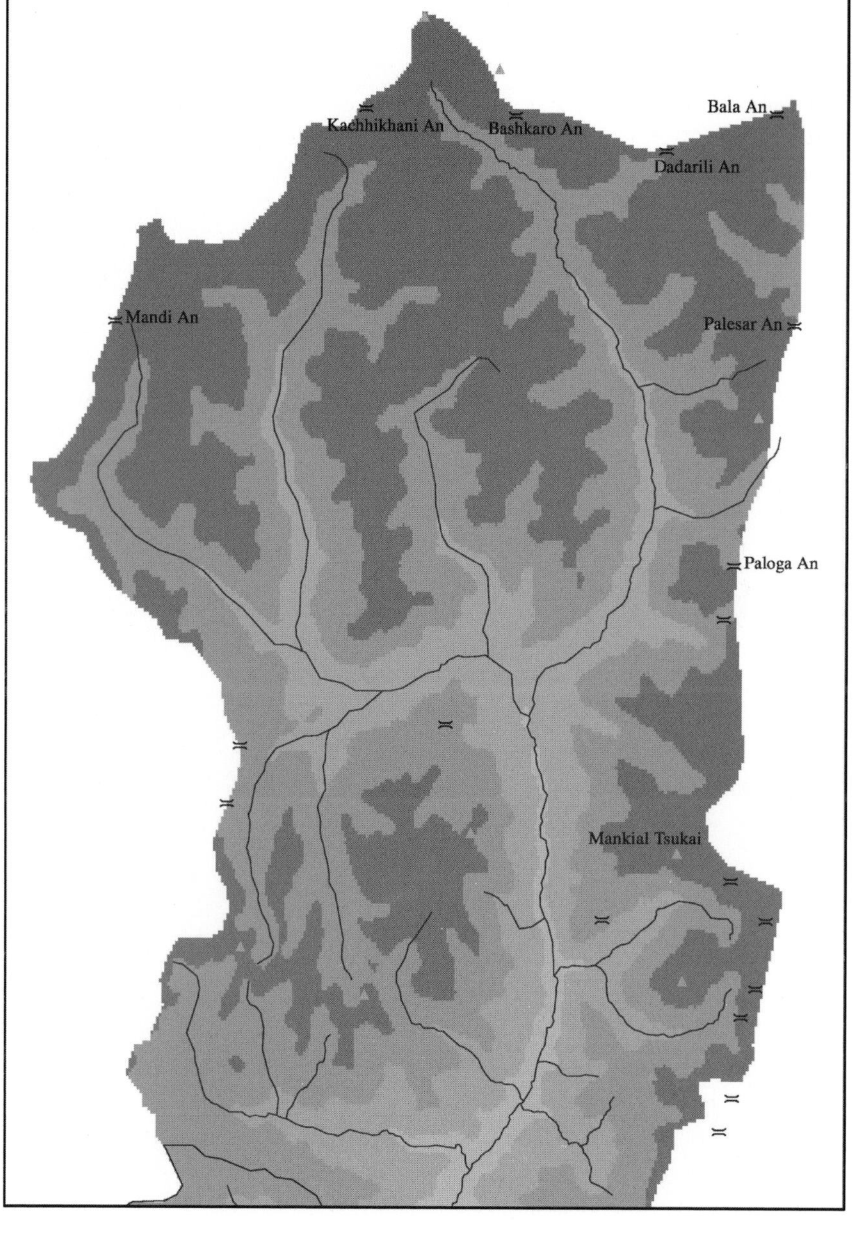

Fig. 24. Geonyms with *an* and *tsuka(i)*.

Lastly, for the name of 'village' we find two main designations: Pashto *kəlay* and Dardic *(°)grām*. In this case, however, the names presenting the Dardic suffix are located in the southern part of the valley, along the course of the Swāt river and of its two main tributaries, the Harnoi-khwar and the Bishigram-khwar. This same °*grām* is very common also in the regions bordering Swāt: Dir, Buner, Shangla and so on.
From this we can derive at least three consequences:

1) The centres around the Swāt river date back to ancient times and were sufficiently famous for their name to be maintained during the time.

2) Contrariwise, the villages in the north of the valley were accessible only with difficulty and were considerably less populated. It is probable that the construction materials of

the houses and buildings were temporary, so no material trace and onomastic attestation is expected to be found.

3) In Torwali the word °*grām* shows the regular derivation *gām*, whilst in Dameli and Khowari the form coincides with *grām*. This would prove FUSSMAN's proposal (see *supra*) that the speakers of these languages were natives of Swāt who would have been expelled from this region by the Pashtuns in the 15th century.

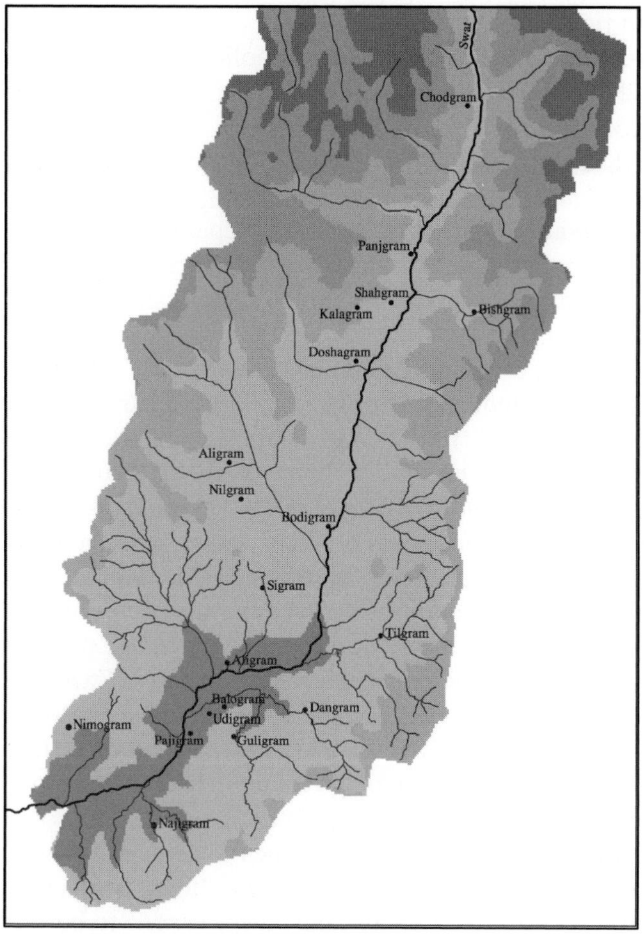

Fig. 25. Geonyms with °*grām*.

We cannot always establish the correct etymology of the toponyms: on the contrary, many cases still remain unexplained but it is not difficult to identify a generic linguistic origin, even if a detailed analysis is not possible.

Hydronyms (see map 5)

The hydronyms are in general the most conservative toponyms, reflecting more ancient linguistic strata. This is also confirmed in Swāt, where we find many names of Indian origin. These are located principally in the northern part of the valley, in the Tehsils of Kalam and Bahrain, but are present also in the rest of the valley.

Here are some examples of hydronyms of Indian etymology (see also De Chiara 2019: 69-72 for details):

- **Asrit-khwar**: < IA: Sanskrit *ā-sru-*, present *ā-sravati* 'to flow near or towards; to flow, stream'; cf. also many Sanskrit river names in *-sarit* 'river'
- **Bahandra-gol**: Probably linked to Pashto *bahedəl* 'to flow', ← IA: cf. Sanskrit *vahana-* 'carrying', 'flowing of water', 'ship', Lhd. *vauhaṇ* 'mountain torrent', Panǰ. *vahiṇ, vaihaṇ* 'flowing of a stream', *vahṇ, ba°* 'flowing, surface of a roughly ploughed field'
- **Dadhra-khwar:** cf. T6882 **dhōdda-* 'hollow, swollen': N. *dhodro, dhotro* 'hollow'; and T5577 **ḍhaḍḍhara-* 'hollow': Pkt. *ḍhaḍḍhara-* 'old'; Si. *ḍhaḍharu* 'hollow in tree trunk; belly of a vessel'
- **Gabral**: Kal. *gha* 'small valley, vale or ravine where a stream or streambed flows' + **ghala-* 'stream'?
- **Kandak-khwar**: Cf. the river name in Nepal Gaṇḍakī, cf. Skt. *gaṇḍakī* 'N. of a river in the northern part of India' (Mahabhārata), ← Muṇḍa **gaṇḍak'* 'river'
- **Kulalai-khwar**: T3352 *kulyā-* 'small river, canal, ditch': Pkt. *kullā-* 'stream, channel'
- **Nali-darra**: IA: cf. Dam. *nalī*, etc. (T6943: *nadī́* 'river' RV: Pa. *nadī-* 'river', Pkt. *ṇaī-*, Si. *nāī* 'mountain torrent'; Lhd. *naī* 'natural watercourse, flood from the hills'; Panj. *naī̃, nai* 'river'. With early nasalization **nandī-*: Ash. *nẽdī, nēdī́*, Wg. *nādī́*, Kt. *nanī́*, Dm. *nalī* < **nanī* (NTS xii 126), Paš. lauṛ. *nandī́*, ar. *nádī*, Niṅg. *nandī́*, Shum. *nā́dī*, Woṭ. *nyed*, Gaw. *nẽ́ndi*, Bshk. *nʌndə*, Tor. *ned*, Sv. *nẽelī*)
- **Olal-khwar**: Tor. *olāl* 'stream of Chail valley' and the verb Tor. *uluṭu-* 'to roll'. Cf. T2377 *ullāla* '*springing up or out': M. *ulāḷ, ullāḷ, ulhāḷ* m. 'a spring'; T2373 *ullalati* 'jumps out': Pkt. *ullalaï* 'jumps up, wobbles'
- **Paloga-gol**: Cf. Kal. *palargá N.* The summer village of Palarga in upper Rumbur Valley. Cf. also Kal. *paḷáik V.* To flee, run away. *Etym:* pálāyatē 'flees' T7955: *pálāyatē* 'flees'. Caus. **palāpayati*; 1. Pa. *palāyati, palēti* 'runs away'; NiDoc. *palayiti* absol. 'having fled'; Pkt. *palāyaï, palaï* 'flees', *paḍāiavva-*; Dm. *paléim* 'I flee', Tir. imper. *palẽ́*, Woṭ. *pal-*, Kal. 1st sg. pres. *palā́am*; P. *palāuṇā* 'to run away'
- **Shaurai-khwar**: cf. T12269 *śaṭati* 'goes', **śāṭayati* 'drives': Paš.lauṛ. *šāṛ-*, gul. *šāṛ-*, dar. weg. *šāṛ-*, *šaṛ-*, kuṛ. *šoṛ-*, ar. *šuṛ-* 'to go away, wander, flow'; Paš.lauṛ. *šāṛai-* 'to carry off, lead away', dar. weg. *ṣarāi-* 'to herd (cattle)'
- **Ugad-khwar**: Cf. Tor. *ugan* 'watery', but also Torwali *ughu* 'ugly, deformed' (?)
- **Ushu-gol**: Cf. Kalasha *oš* 'cold, ice, snow', < Sanskrit *avaśyā-* 'dew'.

However, many stream names are derived directly from the name of the main village through which they flow, regardless of whether the village has an Indo-Aryan or a Pashto name:

- **Barwai Khwar**
- **Bishbanr Khwar**
- **Dosara Khwar**
- **Jaba Khwar**
- **Jolagram Khwar**
- **Khwazakhela Khwar**
- **Mahakai Khwar**
- **Najigram Khwar**
- **Qalagai Khwar**
- **Saidu Khwar**

- **Sigram Khwar**
- **Tambagat Khwar**

In one case, the Jolagram Khwar, the name of the stream is based on an Indian toponym which no longer exists. We can conclude, then, that the hydronym was quite ancient and that the same type of nomenclature was used in the valley during the different historical periods and cultures. Indeed, only a few names are of certain Pashto origin. Among these are:

- **Bargin Khwar**: Pšt. *bārgā́h* 'palace, mansion' (referred to the village)? Cf. Prs. *bārgin* 'cistern, sink, stagnant, fetid, or putrid water' (STEINGASS)
- **Landai Khwar**: Pšt. 'lower stream'
- **Lewanai Khwar**: Pšt. 'crazy stream'
- **Loe Khwar**: Pšt. 'great (*loy*) stream'
- **Manrai Khwar**: Pšt. 'stream of the apples (*maṇá*)'?
- **Ramogai Khwar**: Pšt. *rama* 'herd, flock' + sf. *-gay*? 'Place of the herd'?
- **Roringar Khwar**: Cf. Pšt. *roró* 'gradually, slowly'? Or cf. Roria. Or, maybe better, T10772 *ruta-* 'made to resound': Khow. *ruru korik* 'to make a noise with the feet, (the sky) to thunder'
- **Spanai Khwar**: Pšt. *spaṇkay* 'spark'?
- **Spedar Khwar**: Cf. Pšt. (Prs.) *saped* 'white poplar'? Cf. also Spedar Banda, Pšt. 'pasture of the white poplar (*sapedā́r, spedā́r*)' (?)

See fig. 26 for a general view of the different etymologies.

Oronyms

The names of mountains are the most difficult to be analysed. Cf. for instance the name of mount Ilam, which is considered of Chinese origin (cf. *infra* Gazetteer). In many cases the ancient name has been replaced by a local descriptive name: for example Mārāno Sar, 'the mountain of the serpents', and Jogyāno Sar, 'the mountain of the Yogis' (the local name of Mount Ilam).

Pastures, Passes and Villages

The names of pastures and passes are not very ancient, often being just local designations or having been replaced at the time of the Yusufzai State of Swāt.
For the names of villages, in some cases we have ancient forms, such as the names with °*grām*, mentioned above.
In many cases we find names linked to woods and trees:

- **°Banr (*baṇ*)** 'forest'
- **Amlukbanr (*amlukbaṇ*)** 'forest of the sloes'
- **Asharbanr (*ašārbaṇ*)** 'forest of the silver firs'
- **Ghuzbanr (*γuzbaṇ*)** 'forest of the walnuts'
- **Gujarbanr (*gujarbaṇ*)** 'forest of the Gujars'
- **Loebanr (*loybaṇ*)** 'big forest'
- **Mabanr (*mābaṇ*)** 'garden of the moon'
- **Surbanr (*surbaṇ*)** 'red forest'
- **Tut banrin (*tut baṇin*)** 'densely wooded by mulberries'
- **Achro Banda (*ačro bānda*)** 'pasture of the silver firs'

- **Ranjro Sar (*ranǰro sar*)** 'mountain of the deodars'
- **Nakhtar (*naxtar*)** 'Himalayan pine'
- **Talgo Nakhtar** 'id.'
- **Shaurai Khwar (*šawray xwaṛ*)** 'river of the small sissoo'?
- **Banj Banda (*banǰ bānda*)** 'pasture of the quercus ilex'
- **Tarkana (*tarkāna*)** 'maple'
- **Baret (*baret*)** 'bird cherry'

To explain this we must refer to the *wesh* system: as stated by STEIN (1929: 52),

> the total absence of gardens and fruit-trees in this fertile and well-watered valley was striking. It was a sad illustration, seen also elsewhere in Swat, of the effects of the surviving Pathan custom of *wesh*, which requires that all land held by a tribal sub-section shall change hands among the different families that compose it at short intervals, usually of four or five years. Such a custom, while significant enough of the democratic spirit prevailing among Pathan tribes, is evidently not calculated to encourage the planting of trees or gardens by those whose tenure of the land would end in a few years.

This explains why tree names are so important in Swāt toponymy.

In conclusion, a study of this kind can open new perspectives and offers many possibilities. A more in-depth investigation, valley by valley, could also enhance our knowledge: cf., such as, for instance, the Appendix, based on the pioneering study done by L.M. OLIVIERI and M. VIDALE (2006) on the archaeology in the valleys of the Kandak and other streams in the same area. A strong influence of Gujar toponymy appears: this influence is obviously more recent compared with other toponyms, but this gives us new information on the ethnic changes in the valley.
The innovative research contained in this volume is a first contribution to the domain of toponymy and therefore will inevitably contain many wrong analyses and inaccuracies; I hope that this will not affect its usefulness. Many of the collected toponyms can also be found in the nearby districts, such as Buner and Dir;[45] a larger comparison will certainly allow a better understanding of the historical and geographical backgrounds, and of the patterns of place naming and therefore of the etymologies of the toponyms. Two paths should then be followed in future research in this domain: a micro-toponymy collection, devoted to local names and traditions; and a macro-toponymy collection, outlining more general comparisons and historical influences. Some of the substrate influences in all these regions still remain unknown or understudied, like for instance a possible Muṇḍa presence, which could be revealed by some toponyms with peculiar patterns of composition, such as doubling of syllables (cf. Karakar) or specific prefixes and suffixes (cf. Karamar) (see KUIPER's and WITZEL's researches *infra*).[46]
All these aspects deserve further investigation and my hope is that this work will lead to new interest and energy, and will be considered not a conclusive result, but an open and collaborative starting point.

[45] The name of Dir is another example of unknown etymology, which could go back to the Greek or earlier age: cf. for instance *Dyrta*, nevertheless identified by EGGERMONT 1984 with Daggar or some other place in Buner.

[46] Another instance of Muṇḍa presence could be the name of the Tehsil of Munda in Lower Dir, with its centre Munda-qālā. However, more research is needed.

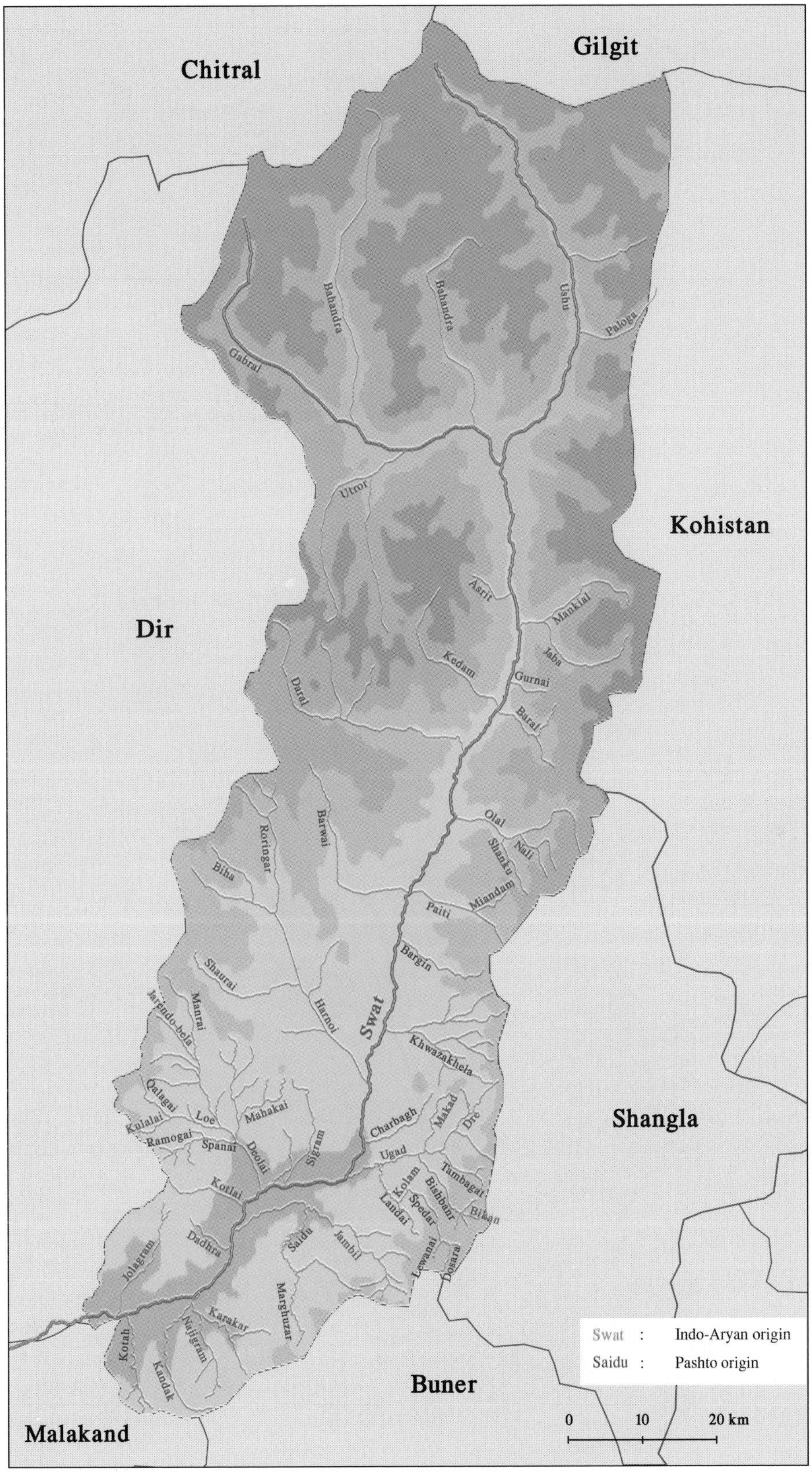

Fig. 26. Rivers etymologies.

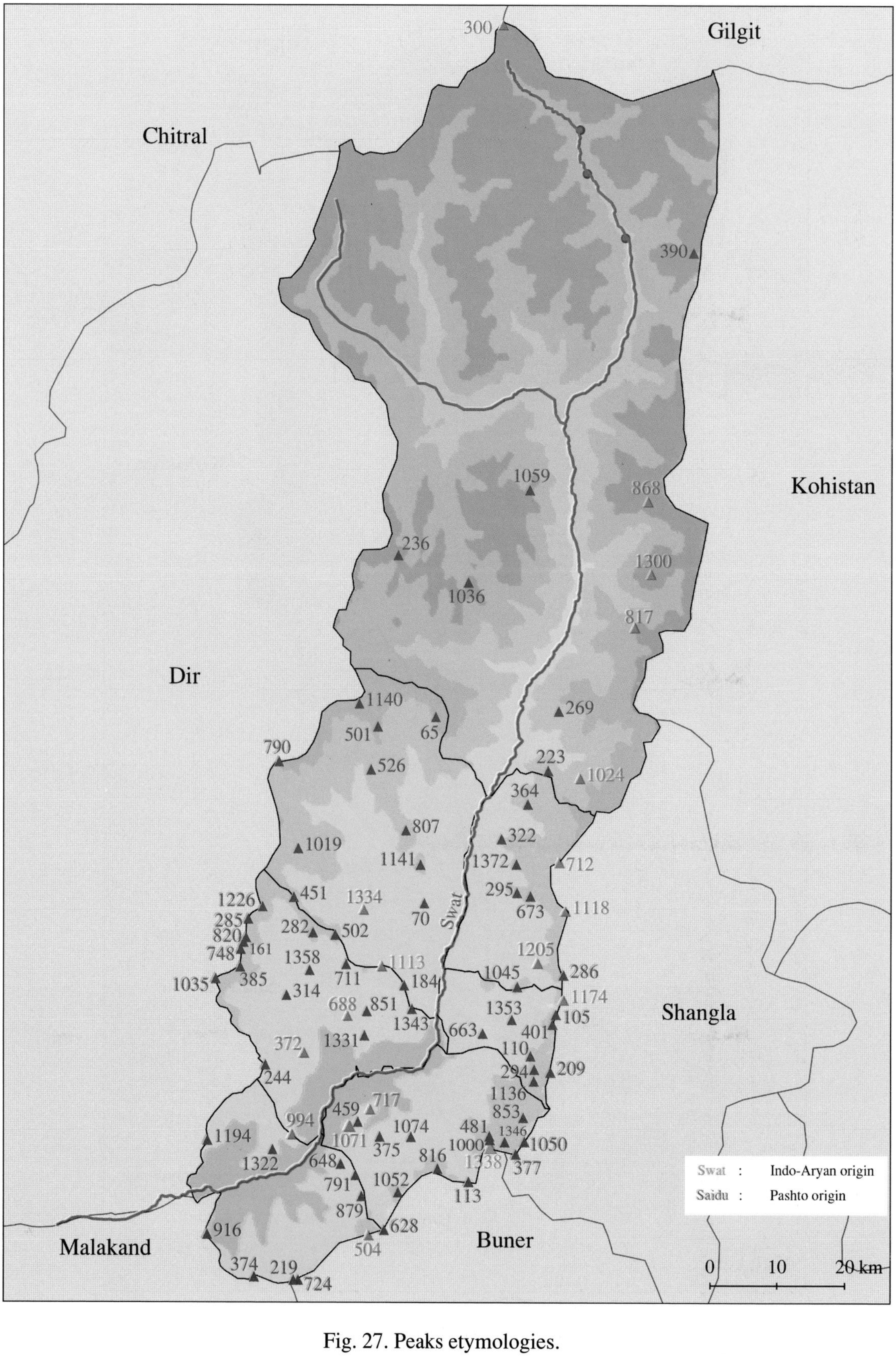

Fig. 27. Peaks etymologies.

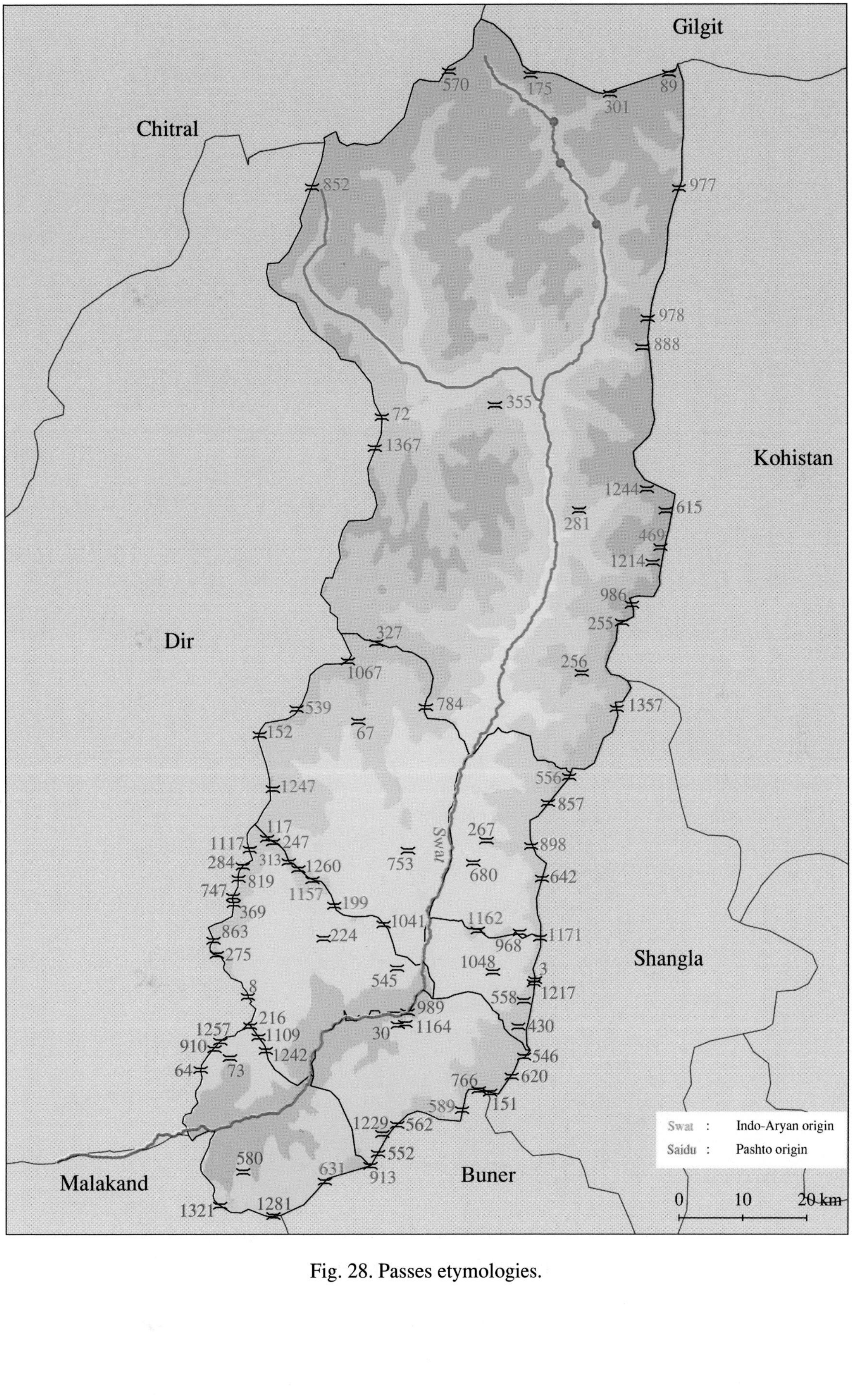

Fig. 28. Passes etymologies.

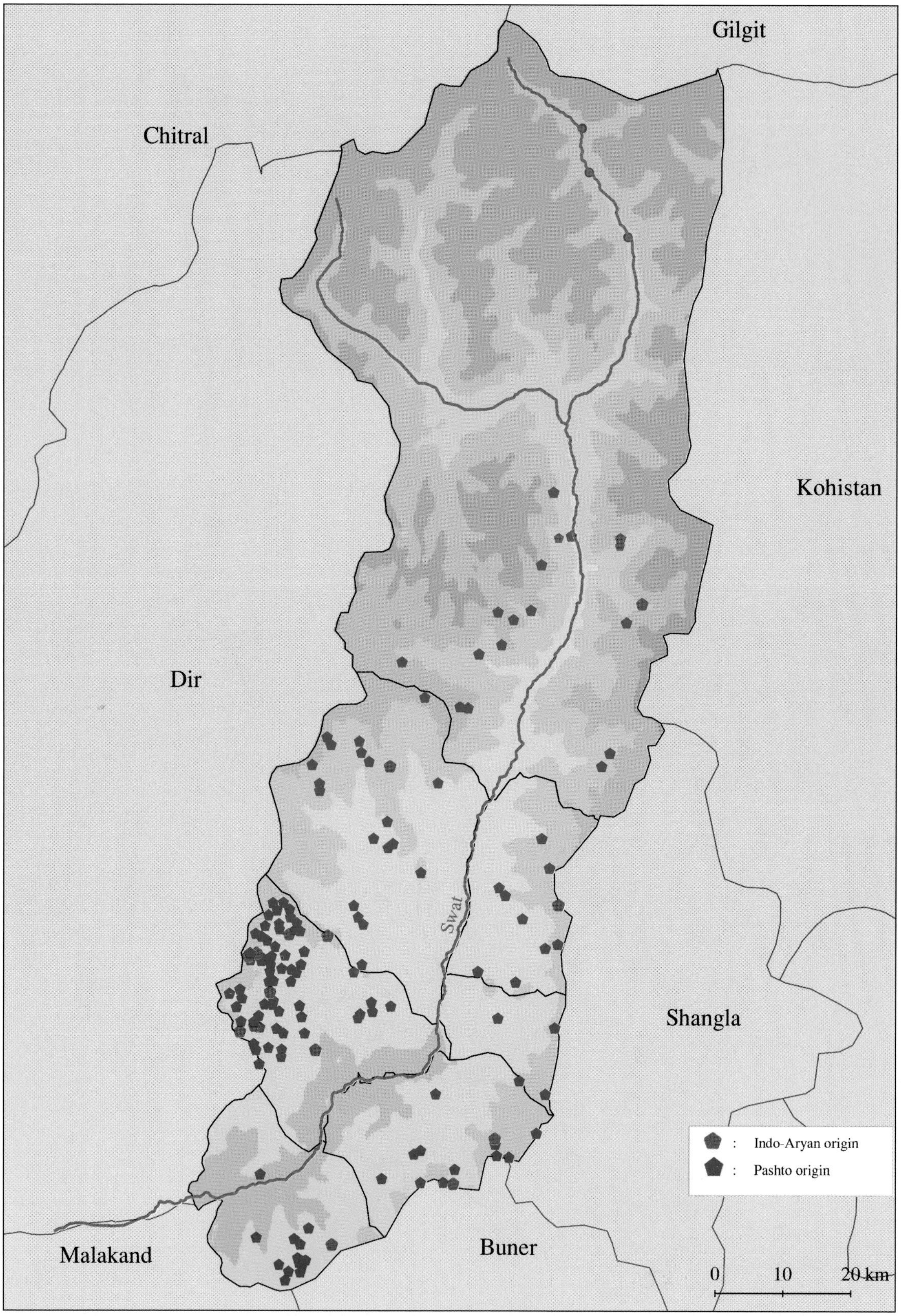

Fig. 29. Pastures etymologies.

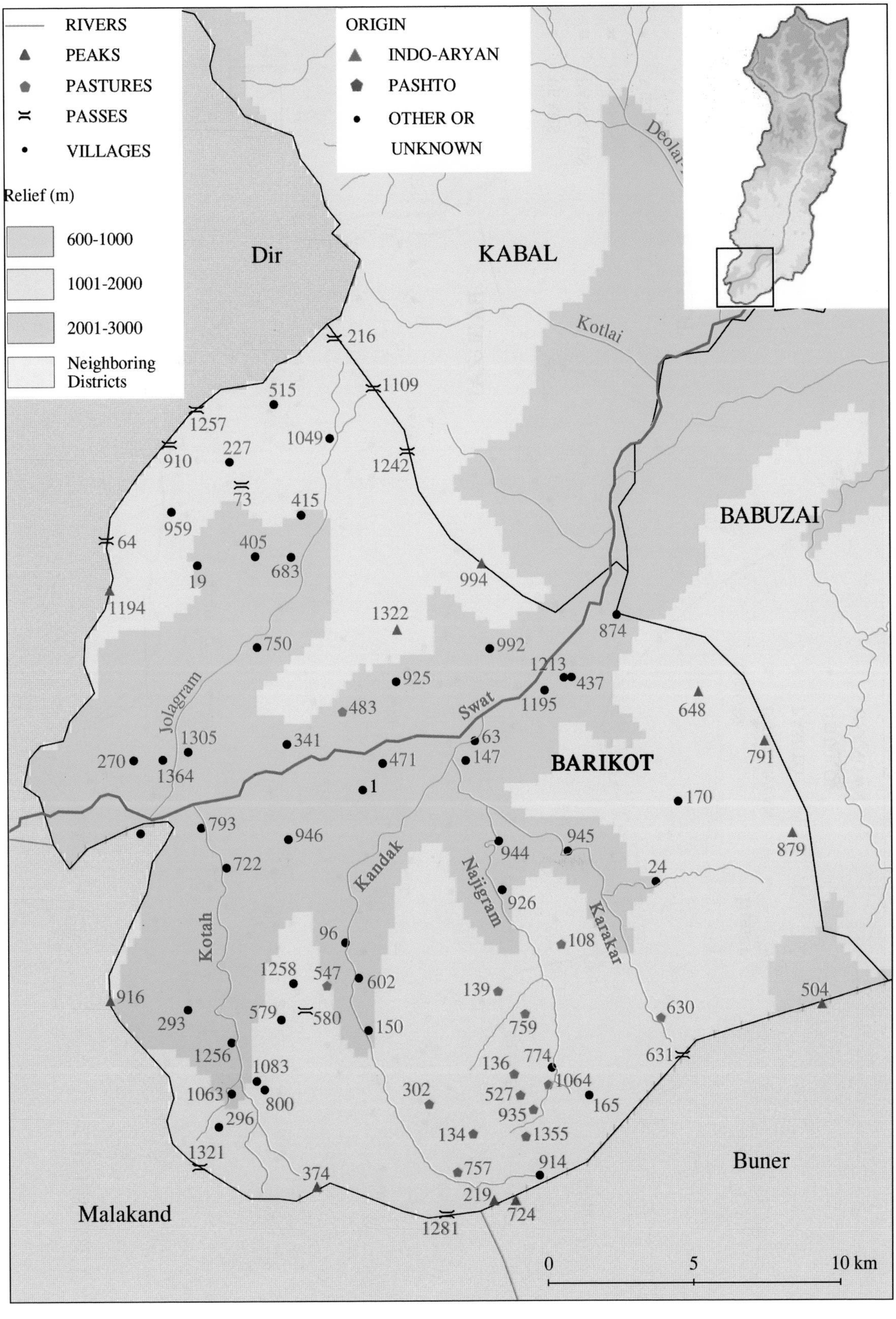

Fig. 30. Etymologies of the toponyms in the Tehsil of Barikot.

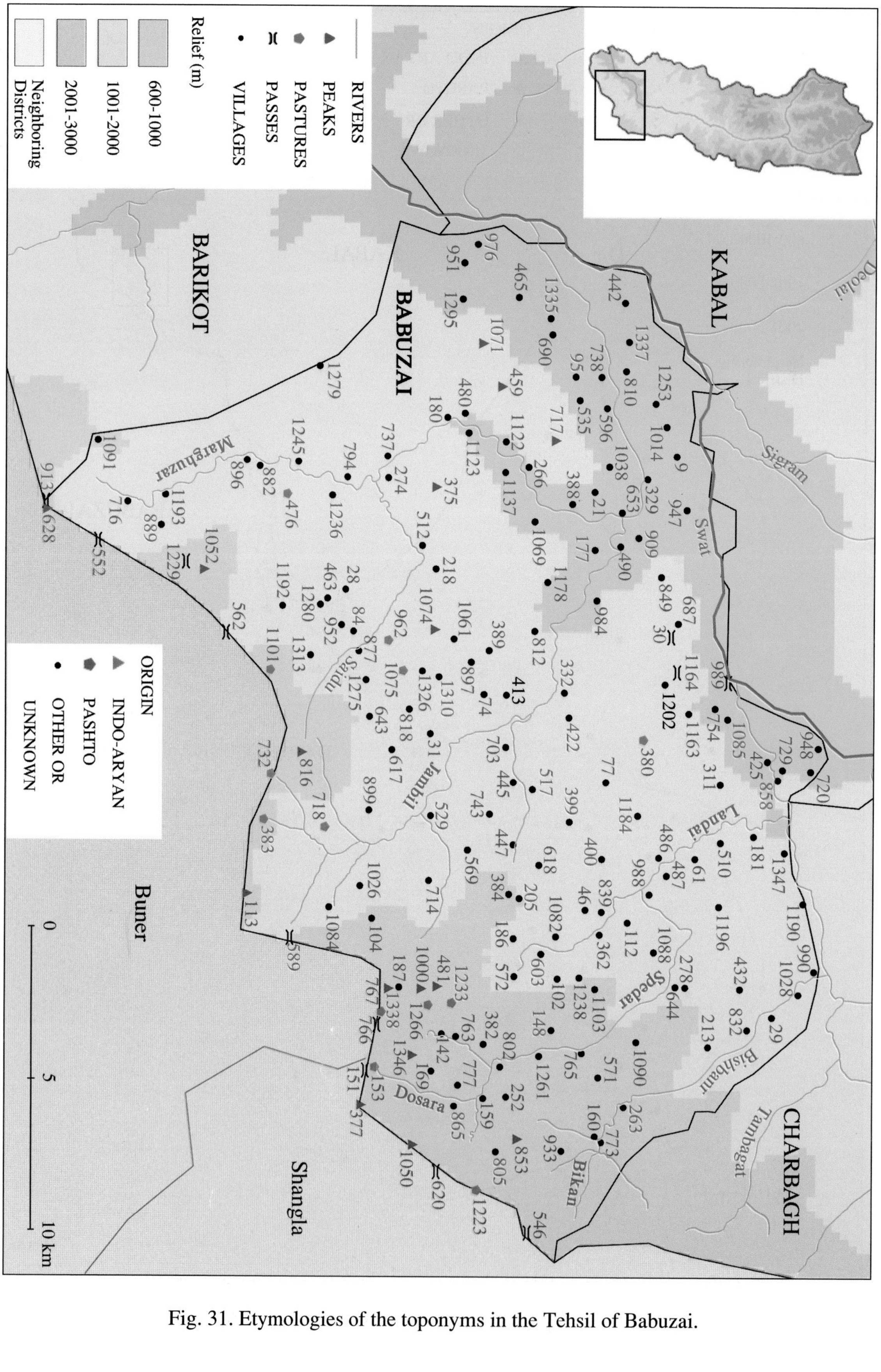

Fig. 31. Etymologies of the toponyms in the Tehsil of Babuzai.

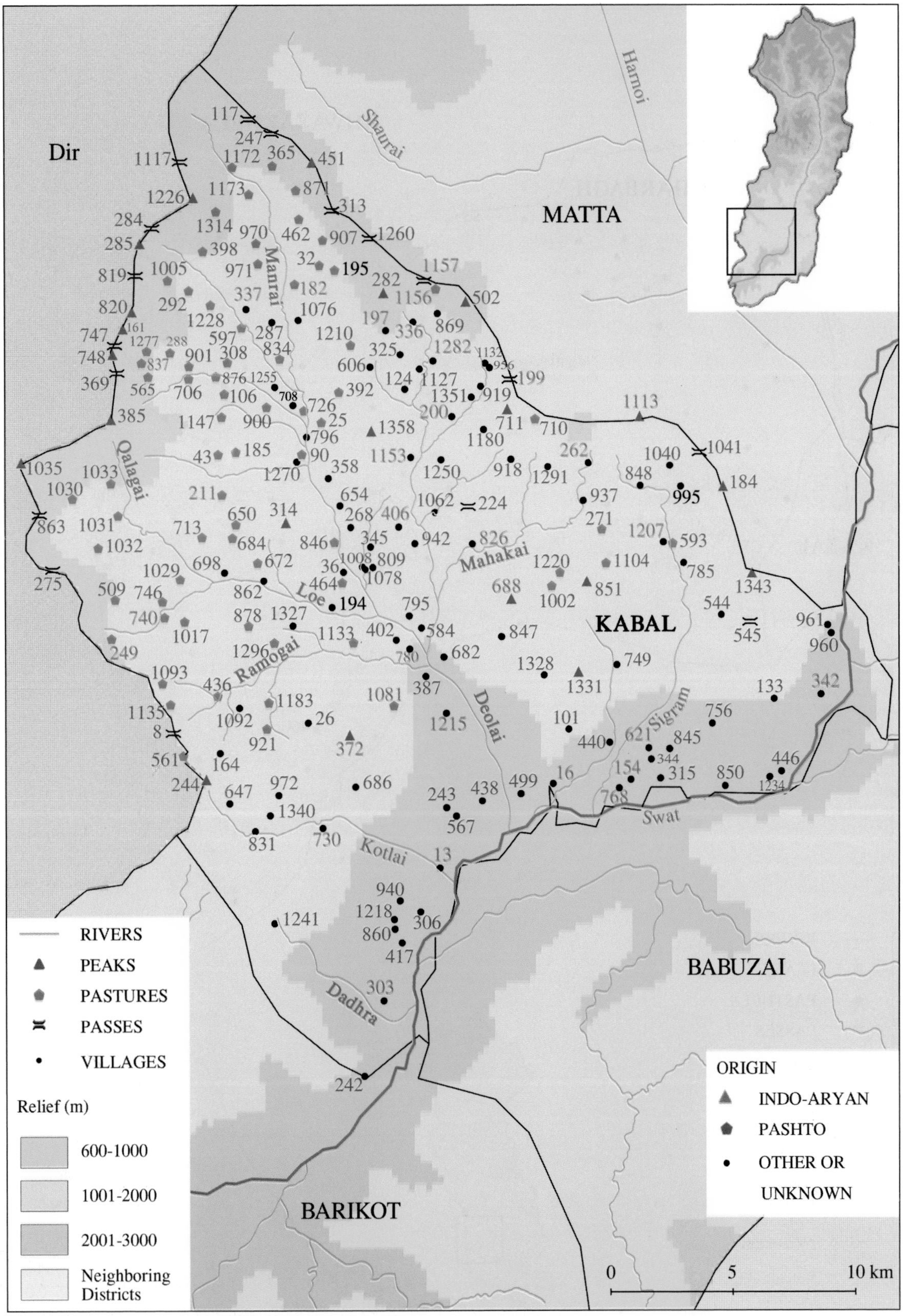

Fig. 32. Etymologies of the toponyms in the Tehsil of Kabal.

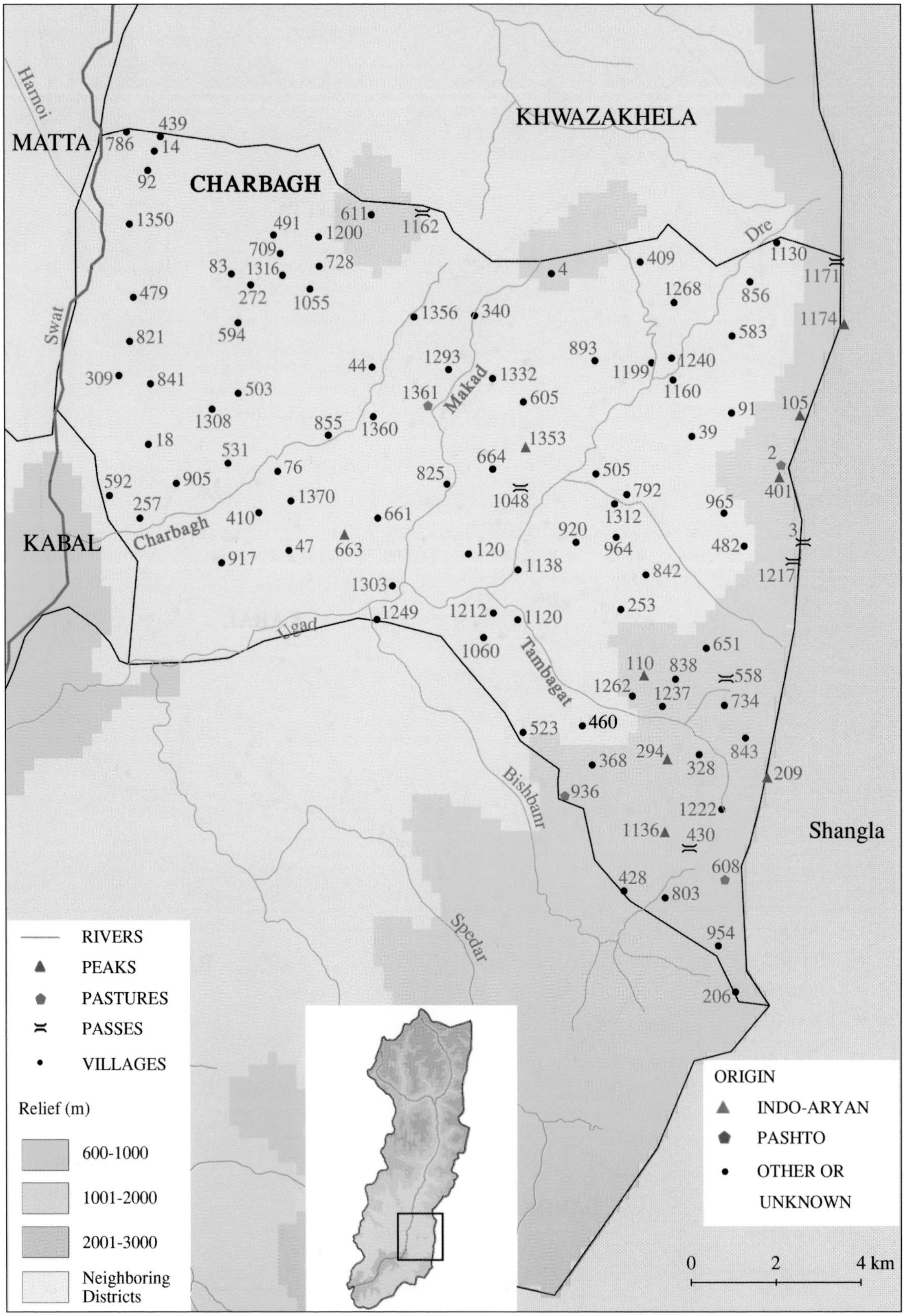

Fig. 33. Etymologies of the toponyms in the Tehsil of Charbagh.

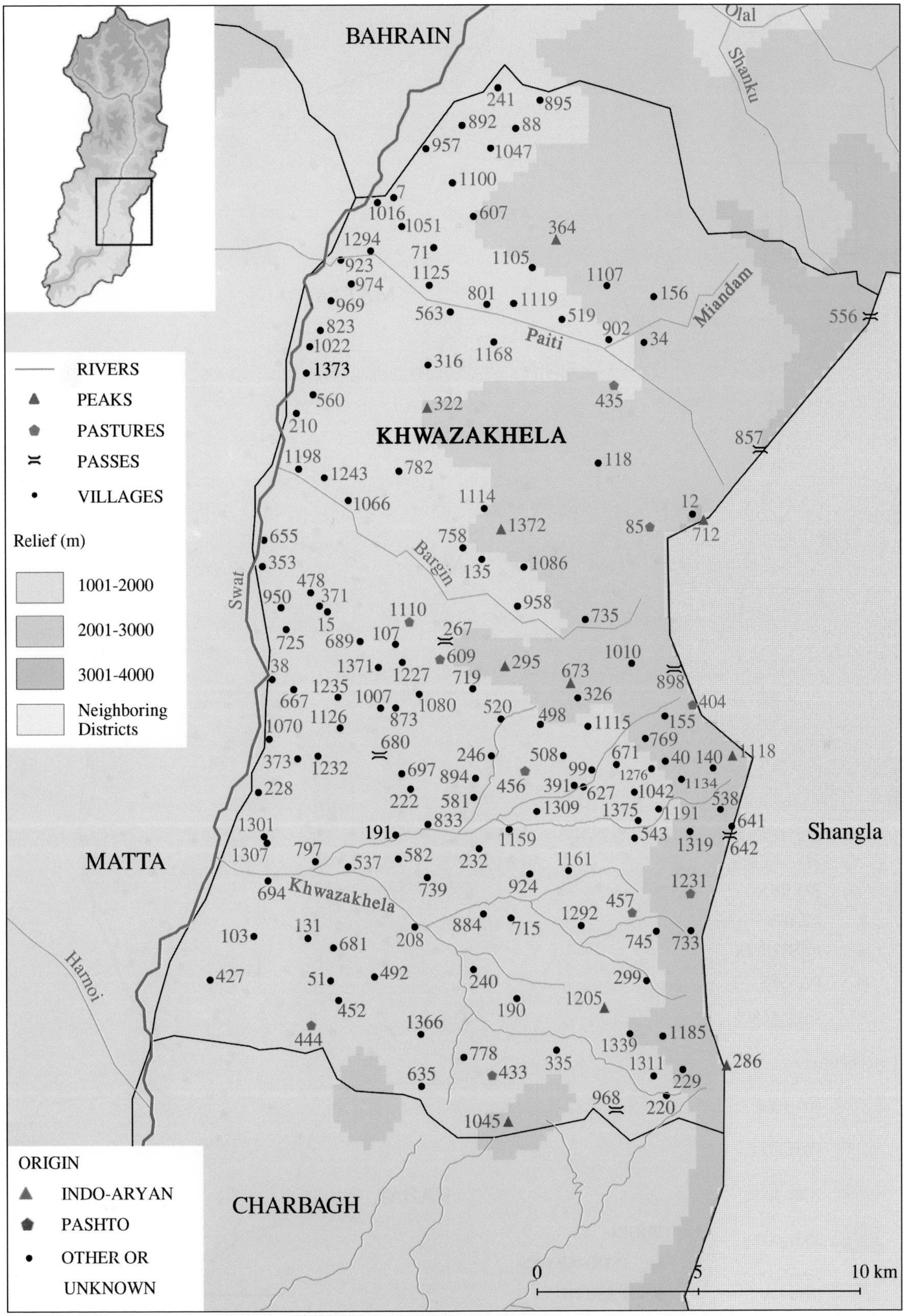

Fig. 34. Etymologies of the toponyms in the Tehsil of Khwazakhela.

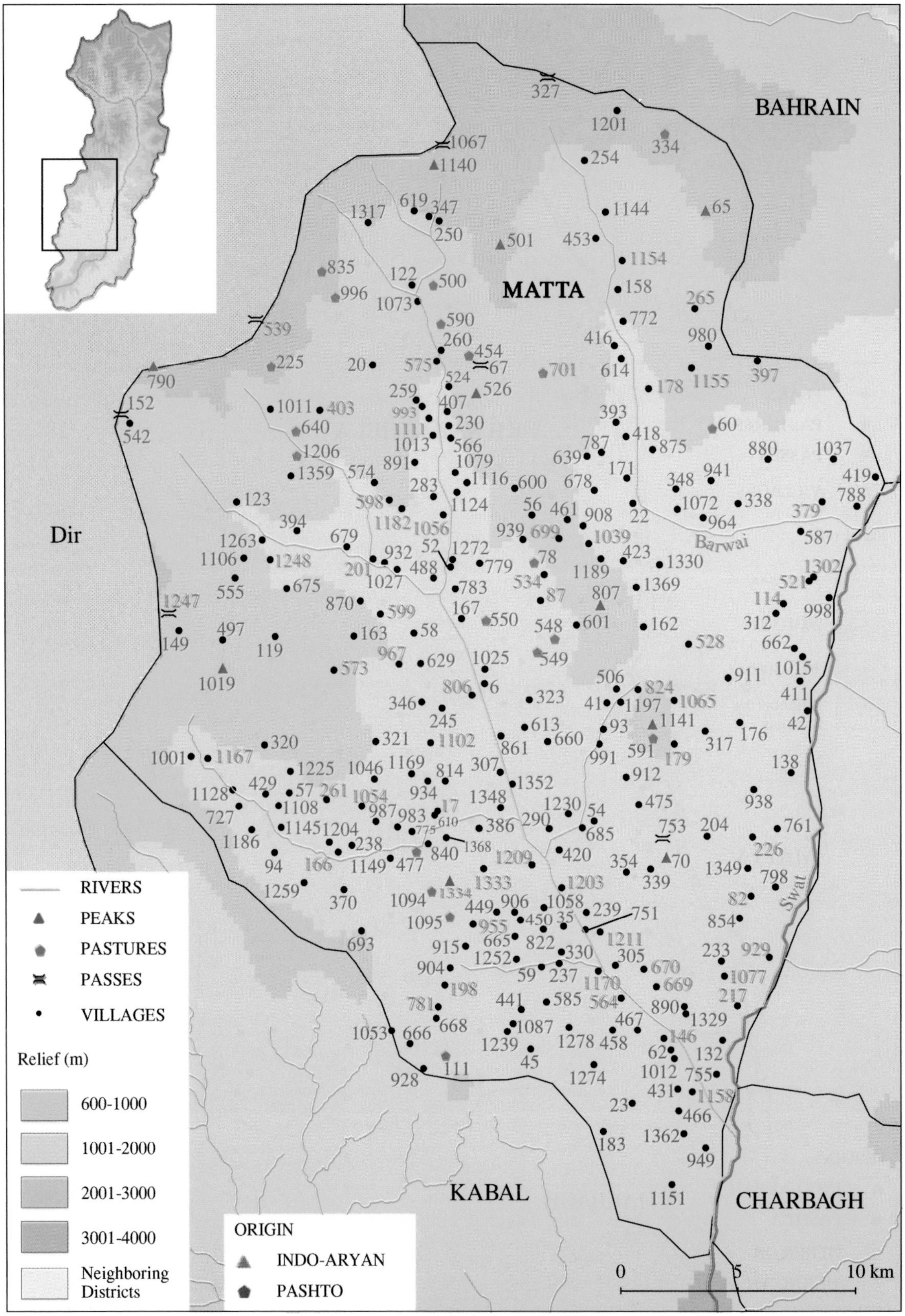

Fig. 35. Etymologies of the toponyms in the Tehsil of Maṭṭa.

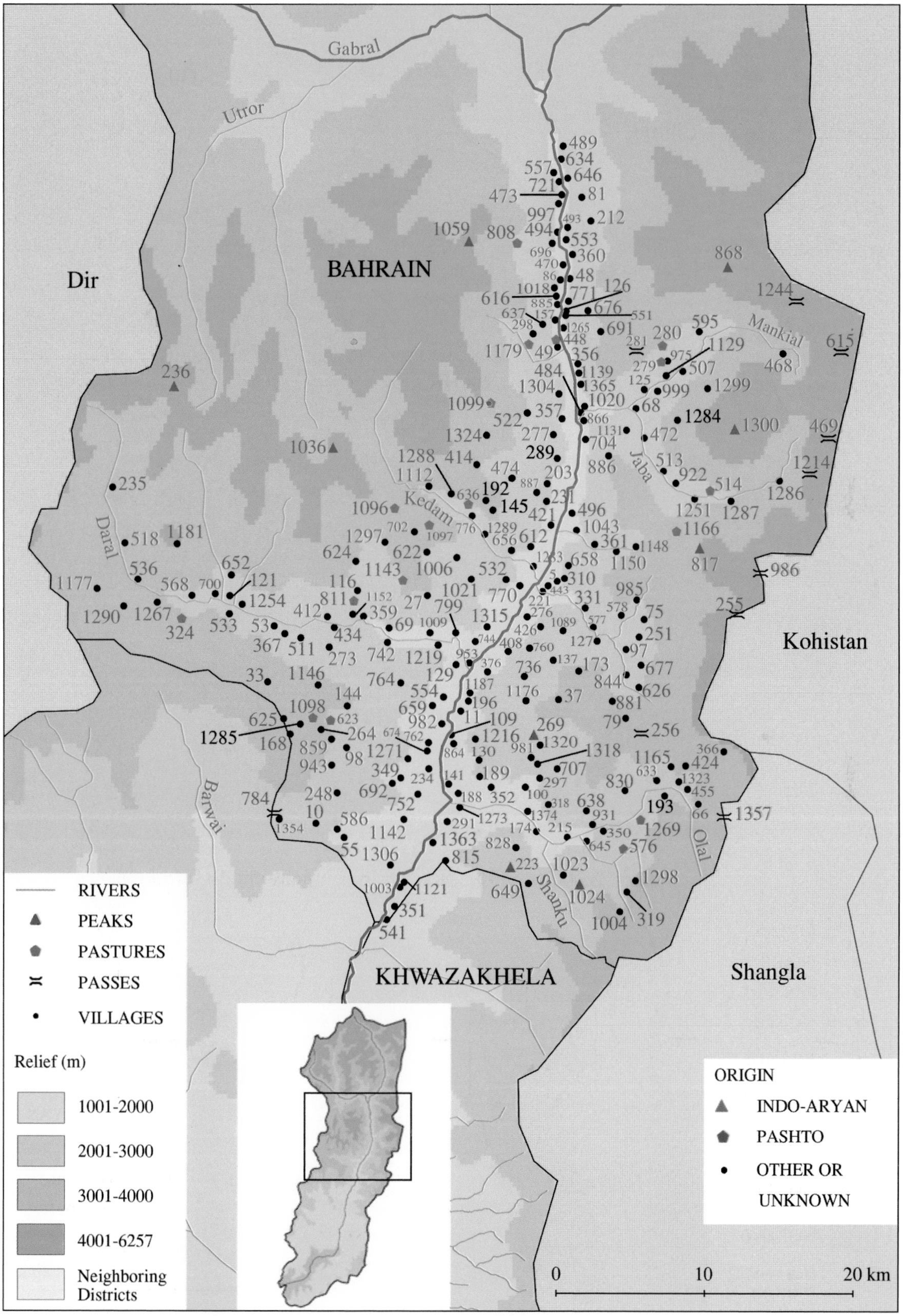

Fig. 36. Etymologies of the toponyms in the lower part of the Tehsil of Bahrain.

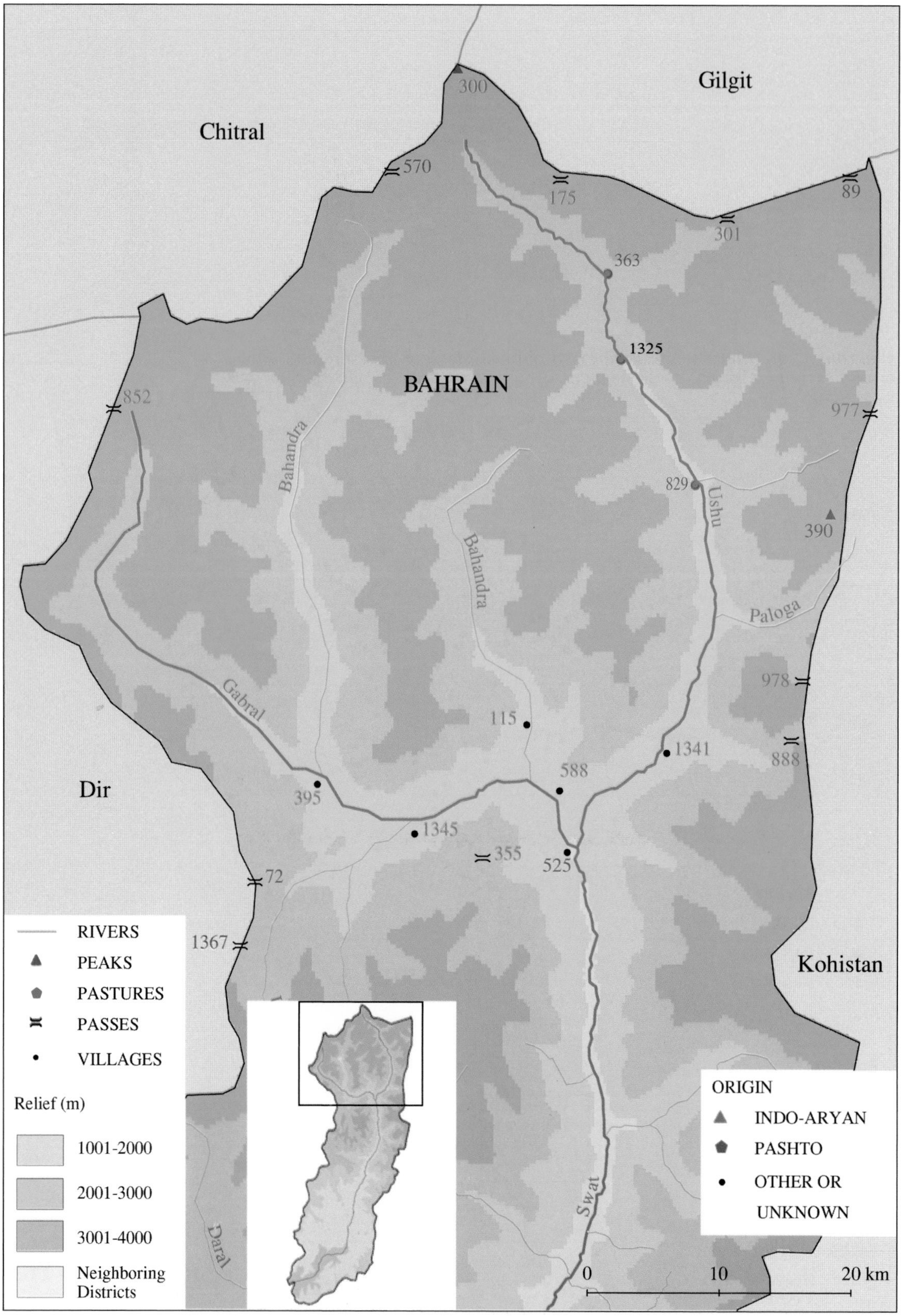

Fig. 37. Etymologies of the toponyms in the upper part of the Tehsil of Bahrain (Kalam).

TOPONYMICAL ATLAS OF THE SWĀT VALLEY

GLOSSARY OF GEONYMS

AN (***ă̄n***, **ان**) 'high mountain slopes'. — Khow. *an* (BASHIR 2005); cf. Kal. *ān* 'mountain pass, boundary' (← Khow., TRAIL/COOPER 1999).

BANDA (***bānḍá***, **بانده**) 'pen for cattle (summer pasturing); fence behind which cattle are driven; small village; camp of nomads, cattle herders; settlements; body, torso; *used in geographical place names*: Guǰarobānḍa (an inhabited locality)'. See SULTAN-I-ROME 2016: 535: 'hamlet; remote pasture in the hills with a few residential houses'. — Pšt. ← IA. (BELLEW); cf. Bal. *bhándá* 'a pen for sheep' ← Si. *bháṇo, bhánḍo*; see T9436: Lhd. *bhāṇ, bhāṇā* 'cattle-shed', Si. *bhāṇo* 'cattle-fold'; T9442 and *bhán* and *bhánḍá*. Cf. also Tor. *bān* 'summer pasture'.

BAR (***bar***, **بر**) 'top; upper'. — Pšt. < Ir. **upari*? (EVP 15, NEVP 15: "< Av. *upairi*, not necessarily borr. from Prs.").

BELA (***bela***, **بیله**) 'village, town, city'? — Cf. Ambela in Buner, for instance, but also Bal. Las Bela [*Baluchistan District Gazetteer Series*, vol. VIII - *Las Bela*, ALLAHABAD 1907: 208: "To the ancients it was known as Armáel, Armábel, or Armábil", and ELLIOTT 1867: 364-365: "I am disposed to consider that Armá-bel is the ancient and correct reading; and that its name is partly preserved in, while its position corresponds with, the modern Bela, the capital of the province of Las. [...] What adds much to the probability of this identification is, that Bela is mentioned in the native histories, not simply as Bela, but as Kárá-Bela; showing that it has been usual to prefix another name, which is now dropped in ordinary converse"] and many other toponyms. According to ASSADORIAN (2017: 52), "Many old place names with toponymical formants were found in this region: *-bēl/-wīl* (< *wēl* < OIr. **waiti-*): *Ardabīl* (< **Arta-waiti-*, Arm. *Artawēt*), *Andabīl*, *Šūrābīl* the name of a lake in Ardabīl), and *Lavandvīl* (near Āstārā)". But we can quote also the town of *Erbil*, the ancient Greek Ἄρβηλα, Old Persian *Arbairā*, Akkadian *arba'ū ilū*, Sumerian *Urbilum, Urbelum, Urbillum*. Beyond the meanings, if we could connect Sumerian *bil/bel* with the form *bela*, we would have here a proof of a large ancient continuum over a very spread area. See DE CHIARA 2019: 68-69. However, according to IKRAM, p.c., *bela* means 'branch of river'.

CHAM (***čam***, **چم**) 'part, branch (of a tribe), clan; quartier, district'. — Pšt. < Ir. **kămi-* (MORGENSTIERNE 1942a: 263); see also ROSSI 1998: 390; for semantic parallels cf. Skt. *grāma-*, MPrs. *grāmag* 'Reichtum, Besitz', Prth. *gr'mg*, Sogd. budd. *γr'm'k* 'riches', Oss. I. *æryom* 'Bündel, Gepäck, Bürde, Ladung', Bal. *grām* 'Bürde' (EWAia I 507-508); Ur. *cā̃dam* 'name of a clan of *Rājpūts*' and *camāyan* 'name of a clan of the *Gūjar* tribe in Panipat Bargar' (PLATTS 1884: 419, 441)?

CHINA (***činá***, **چینه**) 'spring, source'. — Pšt. < Ir. **kanyā-* (MORGENSTIERNE 1942a: 263; see also SKJÆRVØ 1989: 401; NEVP 20; WITCZAK 2006: 116-117); cf. Av. *xan-* 'spring' (NEVP 20), Av. *xąniia-, xaiiana-* 'zum Brunnen gehörig'; Khot. *khāha-* (DKS 74), Sogd. budd. *γ'γh*, man. *x'x* (GMS §395); MPrs. *x'n*, Prth. *x'n* 'spring' (ELFENBEIN 1989: 354); Kurd. *kānī*, Wanji *kayn* 'spring' (NEVP 20; ÈSKJ I: 513-514), Bal. *kāni* 'small spring of water', Brah. *kāni (k'āni)* (EILERS 1964: 211 n. 94; ILEB-A181; ELFENBEIN 1989: 354), Wa. *kək* 'spring' < **kāka-* (STEBLIN-KAMENSKIJ 1999: 220-221), Yγn. *xok* (GMS §395), Mnj. *xū̃γa, xū̃ga*, Yd. *xū̃γo* (IIFL II 266), Orm. *xākə* (MORGENSTIERNE 1932a: 34), Xu. Roš. *xāy, xāyak* 'creek, pool', Oro. *xay* 'canal, brook, reservoir' < ***hwayā*

(EVShG 99), ← Prs. *xā*, *xānī* (ANDREEV/ PEŠČEREVA 1957: 360); Skt. *khan-* (NEVP 20), but only *khá-*[3] 'cavity, hollow', *khaná* 'digging, rooting up', derived from *khan-* 'to dig' (MONIER-WILLIAMS 334, 336), *kha* '(hole), spring, well' (MACDONELL 1929: 80), *kha-* 'opening' (unklar) (EWAia I 442), *khā-* 'spring' (KEWA I 307; EWAia I 451).

DERAI (*ḍeráy*, ډېرى) 'hill, hillock' /// but cf. also *derá* 'dwelling, shelter; residence; stopping place camp, temporary quarters; hut'. — Pšt. ← IA. (BELLEW, DARMESTETER 1888-1890: § 8, COLETTI 1980: 37: Hi. *ḍherī*, Lhd. *ḍher* 'much, many', *ḍherī* 'hillock').

DOP (*ḍop*, ډوپ) 'hill, hillock' (?). — Dard. **ḍop* 'hill': cf. T5580 **ḍhappa-* 'lump', in particular n. 11 **ḍhubba-*, in M. *ḍhubā* 'little hill': in this regard, we could consider here a Dard. **ḍ(h)up* derived of this root with the meaning of 'hill, hillock, lump'. For a parallel on the semantic core, see ROSSI 2002. [Other possibility: Tor. *ḍap* 'piebald', possibly linked to the root Skt. **dhuppā-* (T6825): Si. *dhupa* 'heat of sun', Lhd. *dhupp*, *dhup*; Gaw. *adup* 'absence of sunshine'?]

GARAI (*gaṛáy*, ګړى) 'small fortress, fort, castle' /// 'bottom of a valley or gully'. — Pšt. ← IA. (RAVERTY, BELLEW, DARMESTETER 1888-1890: §8, LORIMER 1915: Hind. *gaṛhī* 'forteresse'). For the latter cf. Ur. *gaṛhā* (Hi.) 'a hole, hollow, cavity, pit' (PLATTS 909).

GHAKHAI (*γā̂x̌ay*, غاښى) 'crest (of mountain); mountain pass'. — Pšt., derivative of Pšt. *γāx̌* 'tooth' < Ir. **gaštra-*, *gaz-* 'to bite'? See EP. 333, MORGENSTIERNE 1926: 34, EVP 28, IIFL II 524, EMMERICK 1970: 68, ÈDEL'MAN 1986: 145, GRJUNBERG/ ÈDEL'MAN 1987: 32-33, MONCHI-ZADEH 1990: 65, STEBLIN-KAMENSKIJ 1999: 187, NEVP 33, ÈSIJ III 92, CHEUNG 2007.

GHAR (*γar*, غر) 'mountain'. — Pšt. < Ir. **gar-*, cf. Av. *gairi-*, Khot. *gara-*, *ggari-*, Khwar. *γryck*, etc. See EP. 37; EVP 26; IIFL II 212; EVSHG 110; DKS 80; ÈDEL'MAN 1986: 145; GRJUNBERG/ÈDEL'MAN 1987: 32; EWAIA I 487; STEBLIN-KAMENSKIJ 1999: 187; NEVP 32.

GOL (*gol*, ګول) 'side valley having a stream with water'. — Khow. origin. See BASHIR 2005, MORGENSTIERNE 1930b: 442; FUSSMAN 1972, II: 314-316: "**Ghala-* est bien attesté dans les langues dardes et kafires, le plus souvent au sens de vallée (A., W., Kt., Pr., Dm., Shum., G.B., Kal., Kho., B.), parfois aus sens de ruisseau (Tir. *g'alə*, P 16 *ghal*, P 13 *gālä*), plus rarement au sens de rivière (P 7 ALA *gāla*, P Q-š ALA *gal*, P 27 Leech *gal*)" (p. 315). See also TUCCI 1977: 17.

KAMAR (*kamár*, كمر) 'precipice, slope; steep cliff, vertical mountainside'. — Pšt. ← Prs. *kamar* 'altitudo, collis, tumulus, saxum' (HÜBSCHMANN 867; see also ÈSIJ IV: 191: Pšt. ← Taǰ. Prs. Dari) See EILERS 1954: 371 ff. ("*Kamar* 'Kreuz, Rücken' (Gürtelgegend) → 'Berg; Terrasse, Steilhang' ~ *sar* 'Haupf, Kopf' → 'Gipfel', auch 'Vorgebirge'") and BARTH/MORGENSTIERNE 1958: 125 (*kámer* 'rock/cliff'). Cf. Prs. *kamar* 'the middle of anything, waist; the middle of a mountain, etc.' (STEINGASS) and Prs. *kemer* 'Höhe, Berg' (HORN 867), Phl. *kamāl* 'head (*daevic*)' (MACKENZIE 1970: 48).

KANDAO (*kanḍáw*, كنډو) '(mountain) pass; excavation, hollow'. — Pšt. ← IA? See BARTH/ MORGENSTIERNE 1958: 125 (*kandów* 'pass'). Cf. Pšt. *kandəl* 'to dig', Prs. *kandan*? In this case, strange evolution *d* > *ḍ*. Instead, cf. T3792 *khaṇḍá*: "As 'hill, mountain pass' (< '*rock' < 'piece' or < '*pass' < 'gap' [...])"; cf. Gaw. *khaṇḍa* 'hill pasture'; Bašk. *khan* 'hill', Tor. *khān*, (GRIERSON) *khaṇḍ*, Mai. *khān*, Chil. Gau. *kān*, Phal. *khā̃ṇ*; Sh. koh. *khũṇ* (s. MORGENSTIERNE 1940: 240); cf. also Par. *khandī* 'mountain peak' ← IA (IIFL I: 265). Pšt. *-aw/-ow* < ?

KHWAR (*xwaṛ* خوړ) 'ravine, gully, hollow; wadi, dry river valley, streambed that is dry most of the year (except in the event of heavy rains)'. — Pšt. < **hwṛda-*. See EP. 348, comparing Bal. *kaur*; EVP 99 ("The comparison with *kaur* is phonetically imposs. Nor is a connexion with Ar. Prs. *xaur* 'valley, low ground' prob."); NEVP 97 ("but cf. Prs. *xul*, Soi *hole*, Kandulai *wulä*, Sivandi *fäle* 'hole, hollow' (< **hwṛda-*)?"). According to ROSSI (p.c.), connexion with Ar.-Prs. cannot be hastily discarded. See also TUCCI 1977: 41-42 n. 52: "The expression of Curtius *currenti amne praeruptis ripis* indicates what today is called a *khwaṛ*, an impetuous torrent, which runs violently in spring, or in the rainy season: it digs in the cretaceous soil deep ravines, difficult to cross; it usually dries up in the hot months".

KILI (*kə́lay*, کلی) 'village'. "KALAY: A cluster of houses of a KHEL is called KALAY. Sometimes different KHELS may live in the same KALAY. Such KHELS have a common blood relation" (ATAYEE 1979: 41, n. 136). — Pšt. < Ir. **kata-ka-*? See DARMESTETER 1888-1890: §14; cf. Av. *kata-* 'house', MPrs. man. *kdg*, Prs. *kad* 'house', Oss. D *kæt* 'stable' < **kata-* or **kaθa-*, IESOJ IV, 590 (EP. 341; MORGENSTIERNE 1925: 65; EVP 32; GRJUNBERG/ÈDEL'MAN 1987: 35; SKJÆRVØ 1989: 398; NEVP 39).

KUZ (*kuz*, کوز) 'down, downward; lower'. — Pšt. < Ir. **kubza-*. See EVP 35; SGS 17; Khot. *kūysa-* 'courbé'; Sogd. budd. *kwz(z)* (MACKENZIE 1970: 94, 367), Khwar. *'kz* 'gobin', *kzyk* 'bosse' (TREMBLAY 2005: 179); Prs. *kūz* < *kuž* < **kubžá-* (HÜBSCHMANN 1895: 89), Orm. *nikiz-* 'to sow' < **niš-kūzaya-* (MORGENSTIERNE 1932a: 24); Skt. *kubja-* 'crooked, humpbacked'; Arm. **kuz* > *kzut'iwn* 'gibbosité' (HÜBSCHMANN 1897: 269); "**bž* semble sporadiquement en iranien s'être dépalatalisé en **bz*: wan. *wowuz* 'mite', [...]" (TREMBLAY 2005: 179).

LOE (*loy*, لوی) 'big'. — Pšt. < Ir. **dahă-ka-*? See TOMASCHEK 1880: 816; EVP 36, "etym. unknown"; SKJÆRVØ 1989: 398; STEBLIN-KAMENSKIJ 1999: 227; NEVP 47; CHEUNG 2005: 129 ("This word is possibly a regional borrowing, cf. Wa. *lap*, Sar. *lɛwr* 'id.'. For similar words see STEBLIN-KAMENSKIJ 1999: 227"), Išk. *lip*, Šγ. Roš. Xu. Bart. Oro. Yzg. *lap* 'much', Sar. *lɛwr, lawr* 'big' < ? (EVShG 42), Wa. *lup* 'big', Tal. *lap* 'much' (STEBLIN-KAMENSKIJ 1999: 227), Kho. *lott* 'big', Paš., Gaw., Wot. *lau, lou* 'much' < **bahura-*? (T9193), Bašg. *ōla*, Ašk. *aulú*, Kati *al* 'big' < **āpula-* (T1211).

MAHAL (*mahā́l(l)*, محل) 'place, locality; palace'. — Pšt. ← Ar.

MAIDAN (*maydā́n*, میدان) 'public square; plain, broad valley'. — Pšt. ← Ar.

MORAH (*moṛá*, موړه) 'range (of mountains, waves); edge, lip'. — Pšt. ← IA (?). BELLEW, NEVP 52: cf. T10233 *mūta-*, **muṭtha-*[2], **mōṭha-*[1] 'basket', '*bundle' [← Drav. cf. Tam. *muṭi* 'knot, tuft, bundle' &c. DED 4030]: Lhd. *mohṛā* 'small bundle, baggage'? 'bundle' → 'hillock'?

NAWE (*nə́way*, نوی) 'new, fresh, young; anew; something new'. — Pšt. < Ir. **nawa-ka-*. NEVP 60; see also EP. 138, EVP 54, notes MORGENSTIERNE [**nawakī*]: Av. *nava-ka-*.

QALA (*qalā́*, کلا، قلا، قلعه) 'castle, kala (local kind of large two- or three-story house surrounded by a high ence); fortress, fort'. — Pšt. ← Ar.

SAR (*sar*, سر) 'top, topmost part, apex, summit'. — Pšt. < Ir. **sara-*. See EVP 69; IESOJ III 73-76; GRJUNBERG/ÈDEL'MAN 1987: 31: Av. *sarah-*, Phl. *sar*, Prth. *sar*, Khwar. *sar*, Khot. *sāra-*, Oss. *sær* 'head' < **sarah-*, Prs. Taǰ. *sar*, Kurd. *säri*, Orm. *sar*, Par. *sōr*, Išk. *sar, sur*, Sgl. *sōr*, Yγn. *sar* (IESOJ III 73-76), Wa. *sar* ← Taǰ. Prs. (STEBLIN-KAMENSKIJ 1999: 308), Šγ. Roš. Bart. *sar* (SOKOLOVA 1960: 152), Bal. *sar* 'head, chief; point, end, beginning'.

SERAI (*ceráy*, څیری) 'divided, separated, parted' → 'apportioned, assigned, allotted'. See SULTAN-I-ROME 2016: 48 ff.: "There were lands that were under permanent ownership and were not liable to reallotment or interchange in the *wesh* system. These were called *serai* and were allotted to persons of special status, i.e. Sayyads and Mullas, in the allotment of Shaikh Mali", then he quotes (pp. 49-51) Raverty, pp. 205-206:

> The portion allotted to Khas'his [Khakhai branch of the Afghans/Pukhtuns] was termed *daftar*, and that assigned to Sayyids, Mullas, and the three confederate tribes, was called *tsira'i* [*serai*], by which terms these lands are still known; and in all cases of dispute the distribution made by Shaikh Mali was referred to, and continues to be referred to this day. *Daftar* is a Persian word signifying, 'a record', 'register', 'archives', here used as an adjective for 'registered', 'recorded'; and '*tsira'i*' is Pus'hto [Pashto], signifying 'divided', 'separated', 'parted', here meaning 'apportioned', 'assigned', 'allotted'. [...] It is pertinent to mention that the *serai* lands were not always, as a rule, situated on disputed land of two communities or on the banks of streams; lands were excluded from the *dawtar* category and allotted as *serai* due to other motives and factors as well, e.g. as *nazranah* (present, tribute) and *shukranah* (gratitude, thanksgiving), to obligate, to seek pleasure and goodwill, to reward for a favour or for giving assistance, or the settlement of some dispute and the like. *Serai* were also allotted to mosques for meeting everyday costs and in some cases to the *imams*, the produce of which they were entitled to receive as long as they were *imams*. Furthermore, most of the Khans and Malaks also held *serai* lands which were excluded from the *wesh*, e.g. *da khanai serai* (*serai* of Khanship), *da malakai serai* (*serai* of Mlakship), *da daday serai* (*serai* for serving guests with maize cobs), *da melmah serai* (*serai* for serving guests), *da telu serai* (*serai* for oil for burning in the *hujrah* lamps) [...] Since these *serai* lands were by their very nature exempted from the periodic *wesh*, the Khans and Malaks enjoyed these huge tracts of land on a permanent basis in addition to their *dawtar* shares. The *serai* lands were *mundai*, namely with fixed area and boundaries and no proportionate share in other types of the land, *shamilat*, and forests [...] Besides, some professionals like a *nayi* (barber), *sarkhamar/ darzi* (tailor), *kakhay* (fields-keeper), and *ubuwaray* (water carrier) received their remuneration in kind at the time of the summer/spring and winter/ autumn harvest. But other professionals like *ingar* (blacksmith), *duruzgar* (carpenter), *nishanchi* (standard-bearer), *ghobah* (village cattleherder), and *jalawan* (ferryman) were assigned land, who sere part of the *dawtar* under the ownership of the concerned *dawtari*s and these professionals received the produce of the assigned land as long as they served the concerned *dawtari*s. They were liable to ejection by the concerned *dawtari*s at their will, but were often not ejected as long as they served them properly or as required.

— Pšt., from Pšt. *cirə́l* 'to tear, rend; to cleave, split, break' ← IA. Cf. Si. *cīraṇu* 'to split, slit, saw', Lhd. *cīraṇ* 'to split', Panj. *cīrnā* 'to rend, split, saw', Hi. *cīrnā* 'to split, tear' (T4844; see also EP. 17; EVP 18; KEWA I 392; EWAia I 545; NEVP 18).

[1]**TANGAI (*tangáy*, تنګی)** 'ravine, gorge; narrow valley; pass'. — Pšt., from Pšt. *tang* 'narrow, tight', in turn derived from Ir., cf. Prs. *tang*, etc.

[2]**TANGAI (*ṭāngáy*, ټانګی)** 'table mountain; flat-topped hill'. — Cf. prec.?

TSUKAI (*cúka*, څوکه) 'top, apex, sharp peak (of a mountain), pinnacle, crown, mountain top'. — Pšt. ← IA. (?). Cf. Khow. *ṭek* 'top, upper/elevated part; elevated platform at front of Khow house' (BASHIR 2005).

ZYARAT (*zyārát (gāh)*, زيارت) 'place of pilgrimage; shrine, holy place'. — Pšt. ← Ar.

GLOSSARY OF OLD GEONYMS INCORPORATED IN THE TOPONYMS

°ABAD (***ăbắd***, **اباد**) 'populated, settled, inhabited; cultivated'. — Pšt. < Ir. **āpāt-*.

°BAGH (***bāγar***, **رباغر**) 'garden'. — Pšt. < Ir. **bāga-*.

°BANR (***baṇ***, **بڼ**) 'garden; forest'. — Pšt. < Ir. **ham-par(ə)na-*? Not ← Hi. or Panj. *ban*, whose semantics and form are incompatible ("forest", absence of *ṇ*). Better East Ir. (?) **ham-parṇa-* (to be remarked that Av. *parəna-*, according to BARTHOLOMAE, is just 'Feder', and not 'leaf'): 'gathering of leaves'.

°DARRA (***dar(r)á***, **دره**) 'valley; gorge; ravine; mountain pass'. — Pšt. ← Prs. or IA.? See MOKRI 1997 and ÈSIJ II 344-345. Cf. T6188 *dará-* 'hole in the ground, cave': K. *dar* 'cave'; B. *dar* 'cave, hole, hollow in ground'; Guǰ. *dar* 'hole, burrow'; M. *dar* 'hole for putting a tree or stake in'; Si. *dara* 'cave, chasm'; B. *darā* 'cave, valley'; Hi. Guǰ. *darī* 'cave, valley'

°GRAM (***grām***, **گرام**) 'village'. — Dard.? Cf. T4368 *grā́ma-* 'troop, village', Dam. Kho. *gram*, Tor. *gām*, Panj. *grā̃*. See DE CHIARA 2019: 68, quoting FUSSMAN 1972.

°KOT (***koṭ***, **کوټ**) '1) small fort; 2) small village, small settlement'. "KOT [*koṭ*]: Kot is a military fort. In every day usage it is a large KALAY. Kot as a suffix to a name conveys the meaning of 'constructed by or in the era of'. For example, Jalalkot means the KOT constructed by Jalauddin or the city founded in the era of Jalaluddin" (ATAYEE 1979: 49, n. 165). — Pšt. ← IA. See RAVERTY, BELLEW, DARMESTETER 1888-1890: §8, LORIMER 1915, DOERFER 1967: 1658, ILEB-I169, NEVP 40: Hind. *kôṭ* 'fort, château', Lhd. *koṭ* 'fort; mud bank around a village', Si. *koṭu*; T3500 *kōṭṭa-*[1] 'fort': Si. *koṭu*, Lhd. *koṭ*, Panj. *koṭ* 'fort, mud bank round a village or field', Hi. *koṭ*; Bal. *koṭ*.

°PUR (***pur***, **پور**) *used in geographic names*: 'Sultanpur (settlement near Jalalabad)'. — Dard.? Cf. T8278 *púra-* 'fortress, town, gynaeceum', Pa. Pkt. *pura-* 'fortress, town' (Pkt. *purī-*, *purā-* < *púr-*); K. *pūru* 'hamlet, quarter of a town'; Panj. *purā* 'section of a city'; Ku. *puro* 'storey of a house'; B. *Pur* 'the city of Patna'; Hi. *purā* 'large village, town, ward'; G. *parũ* 'suburb'; M. *purā* 'ward of a town'; Si. *pura* 'large village, town' (*puraya*, *purē* ← Skt.). See also KEWA II 327 *pū́ḥ*, EWAia II 145 *púr-*.

°PATAI (***paṭáy***, **پټی**) 'area which has been sown, field under crops'. — Pšt. ← IA. See DARMESTETER 1888-1890: § 8; RAMSTEDT 1952: 11; NEVP 67 ["originally prob. 'leased field'"]: T7699 *paṭṭa-* 'slab, tablet': Lhd. *paṭṭā* 'lease', *paṭṭī* 'narrow strip of level (leased) ground'.

GAZETTEER

1. **ABWA ابوهه *(aboha)*** *Map 2*

Big village located in the large and fertile valley, on the left side of the Swat river, between Kotah and Goratai at the beginning of the Tehsil of Barikot, near the boundary with Malakand. The name in Google Earth is Aboha. The toponym is attested only on the Russian map, not on the Pakistani one. This village is already mentioned by RAVERTY (1888: 199) as Abū-wah.

Prs. *ābah* 'name of a village; clear, limpid' (STEINGASS): the toponym should be related to Prs. *āb* 'water'. Cf. Abu in ADAMEC V 14, "a village on the left bank of the Arghastan river about 28 miles east or east -southeast of Kandahar". To be excluded a link with Pšt. *ab-u-hawā* '(good) climate'.

2. **ACHRO-BANDA اچرو بانده *(ačro-bānḍa)*** *Map 28*

Pasture located in the Tehsil of Chabagh, near the Achro-kandao and the Achro-sar (Gadwa-sar), on the ridge separating Swat from Shangla. Both sides of the mountain are covered with trees, however not enough to form a thick forest.

Pšt. 'pasture of the silver firs *(ačar)*' (see SULTAN-I-ROME 2016: 221). However, see also MORGENSTIERNE 1973: 159: "*Ac'ūř G'ol* side valley below Rumbur; Mil. Rep. *Achholgaho-gol* nala draining into the Rumbur stream; Schomb. 179 *Acholgah*; S, XIX, 13 *Achhoagar*", and Dard. *id.* 'nut': FUSSMAN 1972, II: 239-241: "A l'Est du Kunar et en Woṭ. le mot 'noix' < *akṣoṭa-* avec traitement spécifiquement darde du groupe *-kṣ-* > *-(k)kh-* régulièrement". Cf. also T48 *akṣoṭa-* 'walnut': Waig. *ačhṓṛ* 'walnut', Bašk. *ḉhōr*, Tor. *aṣṓ*, Phal. *ačhṓṛ*, *ačhūṛī* 'the tree', Shum. *ačhṓ* 'walnut', *ačhói* 'the tree'. KEWA I 16 quotes TURNER's proposal (1931: 61a) of a loanword from a non-IA source and LAUFER (1919: 248, 255) of a loanword ← Ir. **a(ṅ)gōẓa*.

3. **ACHRO-KANDAO اچرو کنډو *(ačro-kanḍaw)*** *Map 28*

Pass south of the Achro-sar (Gadwa-sar) and the Achro-banda, in the Tehsil of Charbagh, on the ridge separating Swat from Shangla.

Pšt. 'pass of the silver firs'. Cf. prec.

4. **ADAI ادی *(adəy)*** *Map 29*

Small group of houses surrounded by fields and terraces, located in the Tehsil of Charbagh, at the spring of the Makad-khwar and near the Ramotai-loe-sar, not far from the boundary with the Tehsil of Khwazakhela. Nowadays it is called Ado.

Pšt. *adə́y/aḍə́y* 'fields or land surrounding a village'.

5. **ADRER ادریړ *(adreṛ)*** *Map 47*

Village located on the left side of the Swāt river, in the Tehsil of Bahrain, on a terrace covered with thick trees.

IA. origin: cf. Kal. *adrax* 'hillside, forest' (*adrák* 'forest, woods', without etymologic analysis in TRAIL/COOPER 1999)? See TUCCI 1977: 47: "On his way to Mássaga Alexander, as we saw, had captured Andraka (identification uncertain)" and fn. 61: "We may perhaps connect Andraka with a Kowar word, *adrakax* (< Kalaśa *adrakh* 'hillside, forest'): MORGENSTIERNE 1973, p. 332".

6. AGAL اغل (*aγal*) *Map 41*

Village in the large plain of the Harnoi-khwar, south of Barthana, Tehsil of Maṭṭa. On Google Earth this toponym is written Aghal, as confirmed also by M.A. DINAKHEL (p.c.).

Possibly Pšt. *agál* 'ditch, drainage ditch'. However, cf. also Pšt. *āγál* 'enclosure, corral (for cattle)', as suggested by the Pšt. script.

7. AGOR اګور (*agor*) *Map 37*

Group of houses in the terraced mountain; Tehsil of Khwazakhela. Only on the Russian map.

Cf. T68 *ágra-* 'top, summit': Pa. Pkt. *agga-* 'top, front, point', Gy. eur. *agor* 'end, corner, point' ("doubtful whether *-gor* < *gr-*, prob. ext. with MIA. *-ra-* or *-ḍa-*, since *kr-* > *k-*"); Panj. *aggar*, *aggā* 'front, privities'; or T52 *ăgāra-* 'house' [Prob. ← Drav., KEWA I 17 with lit.]: Pa. *ăgāra-*, *°aka-*, Pkt. *āgāra-*.

8. AHINGARO-BABA-KANDAO اهنګرو بابا کنډو (*ahingaro-bābā-kanḍaw*) *Map 10*

Pass on the frontier with Dir at the sources of the Ramogai-khwar, Tehsil of Kabal, at an altitude of about 1,640 metres. As noted by M.A. DINAKHEL (p.c.), it is pronounced *ingaro* or *engaro* (اینګرو), the /h/ disappearing in the pronunciation.

Pšt. 'pass of Ahingaro Bābā'. It takes its name from the near Zyārat of Ahingaro Bābā. Cf. also Tor. *āyingar* 'a place in Chail valley'.

9.-10. AHINGARO-DERAI اهنګرو ډېرى (*ahingaro-ḍerəy*) *Maps 18, 44*

Name of two villages: 1) in the Tehsil of Babuzai, in the periphery of Mingaora, in the wide plain on the left side of the Swat river; 2) group of houses in a lateral valley on the right bank of the Swāt river, on the slopes of the Babu-sar, Tehsil of Bahrain (only on the Russian map).

Pšt. *āhingar°ḍeré* 'quarters of the blacksmiths'. Cf. prec.

11. AIN ايين (*ayin*) *Map 45*

Village on a terrace on the left bank of the Swāt river, north of Madyan, Tehsil of Bahrain.

Cf. T586 [IIr. etymology: cf. Av. *ayō*, *ayanəm*, KEWA I 46] *áyana-* 'going, path': Pa. *ayana-* 'road, goal', Pkt. *ayaṇa-*; Panj. *aiṇ* 'exit hole in the bottom of an earthen grain bin', *àiṇ* 'hole in bottom of a polā to let grain out'; Si. *ayan* 'way, street'. Cf. Tor. *ẹ̃hẹ̃* 'Ayun, a town south of Chitral'. Cf. also 'Ainak in ADAMEC II 17, 'Aini in ADAMEC III 16, 'Ain Kala in ADAMEC IV 45 and 'Aino/'Ayno Kalay in ADAMEC V 28.

12. **AJORAI اجوړی (*aǰoṛay*)** *Map 36*

Small village in the terraced Miandam-khwar valley, Tehsil of Khwazakhela. Only on the Russian map.

Cf. T163 [IE. etymology: see KEWA I 23] **ajya* 'flock of goats': Lhd. *ajjaṛ*, Panj. *ajjaṛ*, *ijjaṛ* — Deriv. Lhd. *ājaṛī* 'shepherd', Panj. *ājṛī*.

13. **AKHUN-KALAI اخون کلی (*āxun-kalay*)** *Map 8*

Village in the plain near Kabal, on the right side of the Swāt river, Tehsil of Kabal.

RAVERTY (1888: 201) quotes this village as Ákhúnd Kalaey and adds that here "is the tomb of the Ákhúnd, Ḳásim, author of the Fawá'íd-ush-Sharí'at. His descendants still dwell there". On the other hand, see also TUCCI 1977: 41 n. 50:

> Udabhāṇḍa may also have two alternative spellings: Udakhāṇḍa and Udabhāṇḍa; the first survives in the name of the village Khunda (according to Colonel Deane in Foucher 1901, p. 367, note and Mm., p. 73). It should be added that Bhaṇḍu and Khaṇḍu are quoted in *Gaṇapāṭha* 4, 2, 77. See also Eggermont 1975, pp. 139, 176. In Udakhāṇḍa, *khāṇḍa* is a Saka word for 'town, village'.

Cf. T2680 *kanṭhá* (*d*) '*border, immediate proximity' ("Mayrhofer EWA i 146 accepts connexion with Drav. (T. Burrow BSOAS xi [1943] 133) but considers both IA. and Drav. forms to have originated in Muṇḍa (Kuiper PMWS [1948] 29). This is supported by the many forms with a varying degree of phonet. similarity not referable to a common IA. original"): Pkt. *kaṁṭha-* 'border, edge'; Lhd. *kaḍḍhā* 'bank', Panj. *kaṇḍhā* 'bank, shore', °*ḍhī* 'land bordering on a mountain', N. *kānlo*, *kā̃llo* 'boundary line of stones dividing two fields', *kā̃ṭh* 'outskirts of a town', Guǰ. *kā̃ṭhɔ* 'bank, coast, limit, margin of a well' — Lhd. Panj. *kaṇḍh* 'wall' perh. infl. in meaning by *kanthā-*. In conclusion, we can hypothesize an ancient Khunda 'village' (cf. also Khot., as in TUCCI's quotation), subsequently Pashtunized to Akhun and interpreted as Pšt. *āxund kəlay* 'Akhund' village'.

14. **ALAMGANJ عالم گنج (*ālamganǰ*)** *Map 30*

Village located on the left bank of the Swāt river, in the alluvial plain at the foot of the hills, in the Tehsil of Charbagh, at the border with the Tehsil of Khwazakhela.

Pšt. 'treasure (*ganǰ*) of the learned (*'ālám*)'.

15. **ALIGAI الیگی (*aligay*)** *Map 34*

Group of houses in the periphery of Kotanai, on the low terraced hills on the left side of the Swat river, Tehsil of Khwazakhela.

IA. 'small ridge in the field' (*ālī* + sf. dimin. *-gay*). Cf. foll. We can exclude a Pšt. formation *'place of Ali'.

16.-17. **ALIGRAM علي گرام (*aligrām*)** *Maps 9, 40*

Name of two villages: 1) in the Tehsil of Kabal, not far from Kabal itself, in the fertile plain on the right bank of the Swāt river and near the Deolai-khwar, at the foot of the first hills. Quoted already by RAVERTY (1888: 232). 2) in the Tehsil of Maṭṭa, in the terraced hills on the left bank of the Shaurai-khwar.

According to TUCCI (1977: 50), “Unfortunately, the name of the village is recent; it is now called Aligrāma ‘the village (*grām*) of Ali’”. However, the first part of the toponym can be analysed differently: in particular, it can be identified with *āḍi, āli* ‘row, line, ridge’ (T1102): Pa. *āḷi, āli* ‘line, dam’, Pkt. *ālī* ‘line, row’, N. *āli* ‘ridge in a field’; A. *āli* ‘embankment across a rice-field, road’; B. *āli, ail* ‘dividing ridge in a field’. The meaning of the toponym would then be ‘village on the ridge’, which is also supported by the physical features, at least for the second toponym, but also in the first toponym we can identify the hills behind as the ‘ridge’.

Considering the preceding observations, we can exclude the possibility of seing in *ali°* the outcome of IA. *adhi*, cf. T249: *ádhi* ‘up, above, on’: Pal. *adhi*, Pkt. *adhi, ahi*; Kho. *ahi, aih* ‘up’, with IIr. **t, *d, *dh* > Pšt. *l*, and with the meaning of ‘upper village’.

According to HAKIMZAY (1997: 7-8), the first element in all toponyms, as Aligrām, Allahābād, Allahḍhanḍ, Aligay, Allahḍher, Alāyi, Ilam, Iləy, etc., is to be analysed as < *el*, the ancient name of ‘God’, which became *Allah*, near the pronunciations *Ela*, *Alio*, *Ali* and *Ala*.

18. ALLAHABAD الاه اباد (*allah-ābād*) *Map 30*

Village north of Charbagh in the Tehsil of Charbagh, in the fertile plain on the left bank of the Swāt river. According to M.A. DINAKHEL (p.c.), “people call it as Alabad, الله اباد”.

Pšt. ‘town of Allāh’. Cf. also prec.

19. ALTANGURAI التنګوړی (*altanguṛay*) *Map 5*

Group of houses in the Tehsil of Barikot, up of the Jolagrām-khwar, on the right side of the Swat river. It is located at the foot of the hills leading from the small valley of Khazana to the boundary with Dir. According to the Russian map its name is Ananguray, ‘the small pomegranate (Pšt. *anang*)’, which seems more plausible due to the numerous crops present in the terraced configuration of the field.

Possibly Pšt. *āl-tang-uṛay* ‘small (*-uṛay*) red (*āl*) ravine/valley (*tang*)’. Or cf. Pšt. *hal* ‘handle of a plough, plough’ (RAVERTY)? Cf. ADAMEC I 18 *Altan Jalab* (*Atin Jilaō*).

20. ALWARA الوره (*alwara*) *Map 43*

Small group of houses in one of the narrow valleys formed by the Roringar Stream in the Tehsil of Maṭṭa. The average altitude is about 2,000 metres and the flanks of the mountains are covered with trees.

Pšt. *alwā́r* ‘wood, lumber, timber’.

21. AMAN-KOT امانکوټ (*amānkoṭ*) *Map 18*

Village near Mingaora, Tehsil of Babuzai. According to the residents, its ancient name was Kateləy (q.v.), but on the Pakistani maps both the villages, Aman-kot and Katelay, are noted. It is located at the entrance of the Saidu-khwar valley, towards the hills leading to the Swat valley. Probably it is a more recent quartier of Katelai.

Pšt. ‘secure (*amā́n* Ar.) fort (*koṭ*)’.

22. **AMLUK املوک (*amluk*)** *Map 44*

Group of houses in the Barwai-khwar valley, Tehsil of Maṭṭa. Only on the Russian map.

Pšt. 'the sloes (*amluk*)' (Diospyros lotus in ALAM 2011).

23. **AMLUKBANR املوک بڼ (*amluk-baṇ*)** *Map 38*

Village on north-eastern side of the Bauro-sar, Tehsil of Maṭṭa, west of the Harnoi-khwar.

Pšt. *amluk baṇ* 'wood of sloes (*amluk*)'.

24. **AMLUKDARA املوک دره (*amluk-dara*)** *Map 4*

Village located in the middle of a secondary valley of the Karakar valley, Tehsil of Barikot, surrounded by hills and mountains with sparse trees.

Pšt. 'valley of the sloes (*amluk*)'.

25. **AMLUKTAL-BANDA املوک ټل باڼډه (*amluk-ṭal-bāṇḍa*)** *Map 12*

Pasture composed of a group of houses near Komyati, Tehsil of Kabal, in a field full of plantations and terraces.

Pšt. *amluk°ṭal* 'pasture with dense (*ṭal*[4]) sloes (*amluk*)' or 'pasture of the meadow (*ṭal*[2]) of the sloes (*amluk*)'.

26. **AMLUK-TANGAI املوک تنګی (*amluk-tangay*)** *Map 10*

Group of houses on the bare western side of the Dokat-sar, in the Tehsil of Kabal.

Pšt. 'pass of the sloes (*amluk*)' (Diospyros lotus in ALAM 2011). The Amluk tree is not named in SULTAN-I-ROME 2016, notwithstanding its importance in the Swāt valley.

27. **ANISAR انسر (*anisar*)** *Map 48*

Group of houses in the narrow mountainous valley of the Daral-khwar, Tehsil of Bahrain.

Kal. *ān* 'mountain pass, boundary' + Pšt. *sar* (see Geonyms for both). See also MORGENSTIERNE 1973: 159: "*An'iš*; Schomb. 36 *Anish Gram*; S, XIX, 13 *Anizh* Kal. vill. in Bumboret — Kh. Mil. Rep. *Anjin*".

28. **ANWAR-DHERE انوار ډهېری (*anwār-ḍhere*)** *Map 20*

Group of houses near the top of the mountains, south of Salampur, Tehsil of Babuzai.

Pšt. *alwā́r*, *anwā́r* 'wood, timber': 'residences of wood' (Pšt. 'brightest (*anwar*) residences' can be excluded). Alternance between *l* and *n* in consonant cluster is common in Pashto.

29. **ARA اړه (*āṛa*)** *Map 25*

Village in the narrow mountainous Bishbanr-khwar valley, Tehsil of Babuzai. On the Russian map it is called Arkh (possibly Pšt. *aṛx* 'side; edge; slope (of a mountain)').

Pšt. *āṛa* 'screen, shelter, concealment'.

30. **ARANGELAI-GHAKHAI ارنګېلی غاښی (*arangelay-γā̌xay*)** *Map 21*

Pass on the path leading from Mingaora to Sangota in the Tehsil of Babuzai. Local name: Pšt. *māre-kanḍaw* 'pass of the serpents'.

Pšt. *γā̌xay* 'crest (of mountain); mountain pass', + Arangelai: Pšt. *har* 'every' (Pšt. *h-* is not pronounced) + *angál* 'noise, confusion' (Pashtoon), *angolā* 'howl (as of a dog at night, or of a jackal)' (Raverty), etc.? → 'pass full of howling/resounding'? Cf. also Ved. *āraṅgará-* 'a bee', attested only in RV 10, 106, 10 (MONIER-WILLIAMS and EWA I 173), which would contain a foreign prefix *ā-* and a foreign suffix *-ra-*, according to KUIPER (1991: 41 and 46).

31. **ARBUT اربوټ (*arbuṭ*)** *Map 22*

Group of houses on the terraced hills of the Jambil-khwar valley, on the opposite side of Jambil, Tehsil of Babuzai. Variant of the name: Arabut. In this place a relief with a Buddha was found: see FILIGENZI 2015: fig. 42a, b.

According to M.A. DINAKHEL (p.c.), the *-r-* is not retroflex, then we should discard connexion with Pšt. *āṛ*, *aṛ* 'shelter, etc.' and Pšt. *āṛa* 'id.' + *-buṭ* 'idol, Buddha': 'idol's protection' or 'shelter of/for the Buddha' (cf. also Ara). Possibly the first member is Pšt. *har* (cf. prec.) 'every': '(place) full of idols' (lit. 'every idol').

32. **ARCHALAI-BANDA ارچلی بانده (*arčaləy-bānḍa*)** *Map 13*

Pasture located in the lush valley of the Manrai-khwar, Tehsil of Kabal.

Pšt. 'pasture of juniper' (+ sf. *-(a)lay*): cf. Uzb. *arča* 'juniper' (see DE CHIARA 2015a: 83). See DARMESTETER 1888-1890: CXXIX for the sf. *-(a)lay*, having a "valeur purement adjectivale". Another, less convincing possibility would be Pšt. *har°čaláy* 'every kind (*har*) of ear (of corn, grain, etc.) (*čaláy*)'.

33.-34. **ARKHUNA ارخونه (*arxuna*)** *Maps 36, 44*

Name of two groups of houses: 1) in the Tehsil of Khwazakhela, in a lateral valley where the Miandam-khwar flows; 2) on a small stream springing from the slopes of the Babusar, on the valley of the Daral-khwar, Tehsil of Bahrain.

Pšt. *arāx* 'a rivulet, a brook, a linn, a sluice, a gush or rush of water', pl. *ārāxuna* (RAVERTY).

35. **ARKOT اړکوټ (*aṛkoṭ*)** *Map 38*

Village in the fertile plain of the Harnoi-khwar, Tehsil of Maṭṭa.

Pšt. *āṛ*, *aṛ* '1. hinderance, stoppage, prevention; 2. difficulty, embarrassment, perplexity, dilemma; 3. screen, shelter, concealment, protection' (RAVERTY) and Pšt. *āṛa* 'obstacle, hindrance, impediment, stop, prevention; 2. screen, shelter, concealment' (← IA: T188 **aḍḍ-* 'obstruct, stop' [← Drav.]: Hi. *āṛ* 'interruption, covering'), + Pšt. *koṭ* 'castle': 'castle of protection'. According to HAKIMZAY (1997: 112, 169), the name is derived from Harkoṭ, as "the Pashtuns cannot pronounce the *h*" [our translation from Pashto]: 'Hari fort', where Hari is "Name of vishnee. A name of Maha deva". ROSSI (p.c.) suggests connexion with the narrowing of the valley and the supply of waters in the fields.

36. **ARKOT-QILA اركوټ قلا (*arkoṭ-qila*)** *Map 14*

Group of houses in the wide and fertile Deolai-khwar valley, Tehsil of Kabal.

Pšt. 'Qila of Arkot': cf. Arkot and Dang-arkot-qala. In Qila we must see a mixture between Pšt. *kəlay* 'village' and Pšt. *qalā* 'fortress'. In the English-type transcriptions, atonic *-i-* often renders Pšt. indistinct/centralized vowels (ROSSI, p.c.).

37. **ASAGAI اساګی (*asāgay*)** *Map 47*

Group of houses in the forest on the slopes of the mountains above Bahrain, Tehsil of Bahrain.

Tor. *asāgayi* 'a summer pasture near Darolai village'. Cf. T1476 ^{2}*āsa-* '*throwing', 'ashes, light dust' [< IE, KEWA I 83, EWAia I 182-183]: Pkt. *āsa-* 'throwing', Kati *asə* 'ashes', Waig. *ásä*, Paš. *āsək*, Shum. *āsik*.

38. **ASALA اساله (*asāla*)** *Map 34*

Village lying on the left bank of the Swāt river in the fertile plain north of Khwazakhela, Tehsil of Khwazakhela. Nowadays Google Earth distinguishes between Kuza-asala, near the Swat river, and Bara-asala, towards the hills (corresponding to Khanabad).

Cf. Paš. *asəl* 'cultivated field' (IIFL III 18). According to HAKIMZAY (1997: 9-10), *āsā* in the old language means 'place (*jāy*) of shelter (*panā*)': 'shelter, stay, anchor, protection'; and he wonders if the road to the other villages in the north of the valley passed through this same Asala.

39.-42. **ASHARAI اشاړی (*ašāṛəy*)** *Maps 28, 33, 39, 39*

Name of four toponyms: 1) a small village in the Tehsil of Charbagh, on the side of the bare mountain culminating with the the Gadwa-sar; 2) a small group of houses in the Tehsil of Khwazakhela, on the terraced slopes of the Semprai-sar, not far from Shalpin; 3-4) in the Tehsil of Maṭṭa, a village on the right bank of the Swat river near Baskhela, surrounded by fields and trees, and a group of houses in a narrow lateral valley east of the Harnoi-khwar valley.

Pšt. *ašāṛáy* 'dried fruit with a bitter pit'. However, it could be connected with Ashar, then *ačar*: cf. Achro-banda.

43. **ASHARAI-BANDA اشاړی بانډه (*ašāṛəy-bānḍa*)** *Map 12*

Pasture in the hills around the upper Deolai-khwar valley, Tehsil of Kabal.

Pšt. 'pasture of the *ašāṛáy*'. Cf. prec.

44.-45. **ASHARBANR اشاربڼ (*ašārbaṇ*)** *Maps 30, 38*

Name of two villages: 1) in the Tehsil of Charbagh, in a small lateral valley near Charbagh, near one of the rare forests in this part of the valley; 2) a small group of houses in the Tehsil of Maṭṭa, under the Saso-sar.

Pšt. 'wood of silver firs (*ačar*)', cf. Achro-bānda. HAKIMZAY (1997: 39) sees in Ashār Sanskrit *asār* "hollow, not solid" and interprets it as 'garden of hollows'.

46. **ASHAR-GARAI اشر گړی (*ašar-gaṛəy*)** *Map 24*

Group of houses on the hill dominating Banjot, in the Landai-khwar valley, Tehsil of Babuzai.

Pšt. 'valley of the silver firs (*ačar*)', cf. Achro Bānda. See MORGENSTIERNE 1973: 159: "*Ashangar Pass*. Schomb. 83"?

47. **ASHARO-PAIZA اشاړو پیزه (*ašāṛo-payza*)** *Map 30*

Group of houses near Charbagh, on the slopes of the Khadang-sar, Tehsil of Charbagh.

Pšt. 'peak (*péza*) of the *ašāṛəy*' (see Asharai), or, if *ašaro-payza* (with -*aṛ*-), 'peak of the silver firs (*ačar*).

48. **ASHAROPATAI اشاړو پټی (*ašāṛo-pəṭay*)** *Map 53*

Group of houses on the right bank of the Swāt river (on the Russian map it is located on the left), in the upper part of the valley, north of Kolalai, Tehsil of Bahrain.

Pšt. 'field of the *ašāṛay* or silver firs (*ačar*)': cf. Asharai and Achro-banda. See prec.

49. **ASRIT اسرت (*asrit*)** *Map 53*

Small village located at the confluence of the Asrit-khwar in the Swāt river, on its right bank, Tehsil of Bahrain.

Cf. foll.

50. **ASRIT-KHWAR اسرت خوړ (*asrit-xwaṛ*)** *Map 53*

Asrit-khwar (Asrīt-khwar) is an intermittent stream, located in the Tehsil of Bahrain at an elevation of 2,188 meters above sea level, flowing into the Swāt river on its right side, one of the first tributaries from north.

IA: Skt. *ā-sru-*, pres. *ā-sravati* 'to flow near or towards; to flow, stream'. Cf. also many Skt. names in *-sarit* 'river'.

51. **ATERAN اټېران (*aṭerān*)** *Map 31*

Group of houses in the terraced slopes south of Khwazakhela, Tehsil of Khwazakhela.

Et. unkn.: unlikely comparison with Pšt. *aṭerān* 'a reel for winding silk, thread, cotton, etc.' (RAVERTY), or Pšt. *atrang* 'the name of a plant used in dyeing' (RAVERTY).

52. **ATIA-QALA اتیا قالا (*atyā-qālā*)** *Map 41*

Group of houses in the valley of the Roringar-khwar, Tehsil of Maṭṭa.

Pšt. 'eighty (*atyā*) castles (*qāla*)'.

53. **ATSAR اڅر (*acar*)** *Map 48*

Small group of houses in the narrow Daral-khwar valley, covered with forests, Tehsil of Bahrain.

Cf. T2445 *ṛkṣa-* 'bear': Kho. *orċ*, Bašk. *iċh*, Tor. *īṣ*, Si. *richu*, Lhd. *rich*? Doubtul the comparison with Bašk. *āṣēr* 'apricot', Pal. *aṣāṛ* (*āṣāṛī* 'apricot tree'), Pšt. LW *ašarai* 'dried apricot', ← Skt. **āṣāḍhikā* 'belonging to June/July' (MORGENSTIERNE 1940: 225) (see also Asharai), due to the presence of *-ts-*.

54. AWAI-SHAH اوی شاه (*away-šāh*) *Map 39*

Group of houses near Chupriāl, Tehsil of Maṭṭa, in one of the secondary valleys of the Harnoi-khwar.

Person's name.

55.-58. AWARAI اواری (*awāray*) *Maps 40, 41, 43, 44*

Name of four toponyms: 1-3) in the Tehsils of Maṭṭa, a group of houses on a spur in the hills on the Shaurai-khwar valley, north of the Harnoi-khwar; a group of houses on the slopes of the mountains west of the upper Harnoi-khwar valley (only in the Russian map); and a group of houses in a lateral valley of the Roringar-khwar; and 4) a village in the Tehsil of Bahrain, in the last fields at the foot of the hills on the right bank of the Swat river, on the other side of Madyan.

Probably Pšt. *hawā́r* 'even, flat, smooth; uniform', *hawā́ra* 'plain'.

59. AWI-KAS اوی کس (*away-kas*) *Map 38*

Group of houses south of Arkot, in the fertile plain of the Harnoi-khwar, Tehsil of Maṭṭa.

Pšt. 'irrigational (*awī́*) ravine/hollow (*kas*)' (cf. Awai-shah).

60. AZAD-BANDA ازاد بانده (*āzād-bānḍa*) *Map 44*

Pasture located in a lateral valley of the Barwai-khwar, north of Darmai, Tehsil of Maṭṭa.

Pšt. 'free (*āzād*) pasture'.

61. AZGHARAI ازغری (*azγaṛay*) *Map 23*

Small village located in the fields of the Landai-khwar valley, near Manglaor, Tehsil of Babuzai.

Pšt. *azγáy, aγzáy* 'prickle, thorn' + sf. *-ṛay* → 'small thorn'. See DARMESTETER 1888-1890: CXXXVIII and SHAFEEV 1964: 21 for the diminutive suffix *-ṛay*.

62. BAB باب (*bāb*) *Map 38*

Group of houses on the right bank of the Swāt river at the entry of the bridge leading to Matta, Tehsil of Maṭṭa.

Pšt. *bāb* 'door'. To be excluded a cf. with T9387 **bhabbā* 'apple': Gy. eur. *phab*, *phabái* 'apple', Waig. *babə́ŕ* 'pear (?)'; Dam. *bâbâ* 'apple', *babāi*, Gaw. *bōbái*, Bašk. *bōbäi*, Tor. *babaí*, Gau. *bàbou*, Sv. *bōbái*, Phal. *babái*.

63. **BABA-DERAI بابا ډېرۍ (*bābā-ḍerəy*)** *Map 4*

Place near Barikot, on the left bank of the Swat river, Tehsil of Barikot.

Pšt. ‘residence of Bābā’.

64. **BABAR-GHAKHAI-KANDAO ببر غاښى کنډو (*babar-γāx̌ay-kanḍaw*)** *Map 5*

Pass in the Tehsil of Barikot, leading from the Jolagram-khwar valley to Dir.

Pšt. ‘Pass of Babar’. See RAVERTY 1888: 234:

> Subsequent to the capture of the stronghold of the Gibarí Sulṭán of Bájawṛ, Bábar Bádsháh, who wanted to get Malik Aḥmad into his power, crossed the river of Panj-Korah and encamped at Dayarún and entered Suwát by Tálásh. Dayarún is situated about two kuroh from the T’ra’í Ghásh’haey or Pass. The defile by which Bábar entered Suwád was called Da Bábar Ghás’hí from that day. It lies farther north than the Káṭ-gala’h Ghás’haey, and is distant about three kuroh north-west of the Úchhún, as the two villages of Úchh are styled.

65. **BABU-SAR بابو سر (*bābu-sar*)** *Map 44*

Mountain of about 3,850 mt on the border between the Tehsils of Maṭṭa and Bahrain, east of the Barwai-khwar valley, Tehsil of Maṭṭa.

Pšt. ‘mountain of the chiefs (*bābú*)’ or ‘mountain of the goblins (*babáw*)’.

66. **BACHCHI-DERAI بچى ډېرۍ (*bači-ḍerəy*)** *Map 46*

Group of houses in the mountainous upper Olal-khwar valley, Tehsil of Bahrain.

Pšt. ‘residence of the children (*bačay*)’.

67. **BACHI-KANDAO بچى کنډو (*bači-kanḍaw*)** *Map 43*

Pass near the Jalba-sar, leading from the Barwai-khwar valley to the Roringar-khwar valley, in the Tehsil of Maṭṭa.

Pšt. ‘pass of the children (*bačáy*)’. Cf. prec.

68. **BADAI بډۍ (*baḍəy*)** *Map 51*

Small village at the confluence between the Jaba-khwar valley and the Mankial-khwar valley, Tehsil of Bahrain.

Notwithstanding according to M.A. DINAKHEL (p.c.) the right writing is with *-ḍ-*, we have here probably Pšt. *badəy* ‘bank of a canal subject to erosion’, as confirmed also by locals (IKRAM, p.c.), stating that: “in mountainous areas, the narrow fields are called Badai”. See also ADAMEC VI 48 Badai, “a village located near Bak in Paktia province”.

69. **BADDER بدېر (*bader*)** *Map 48*

Group of houses in the terraced Daral-khwar valley, Tehsil of Bahrain. Only on the Russian map.

Cf. Pšt. *badár, badáṛ* ‘name of a tree, the white poplar (RAVERTY); Euphrates poplar; cotton tree (ASLANOV)’.

70. **BADKOT بادکوټ (*bādkoṭ*)** *Map 39*

Mountain of about 1,880 mt half-way between the Harnoi-khwar valley and the valley of the Swāt river, Tehsil of Maṭṭa.

Pšt. 'wind (*bād*) castle'.

71. **BADRE بدری (*badray*)** *Map 37*

Group of houses on the slopes of the Dobar-sar, in the Paiti-khwar valley, Tehsil of Khwazakhela. It is called Shne-banda (Pšt. 'green pasture') on the Russian map.

Cf. Badder. See also RAVERTY *badrəy* 'name of a small river near Panjtār, in the Yusufzi country'.

72. **BADWAI-KANDAO بدوی کنډو (*badway-kanḍaw*)** *Map 54*

Pass leading from the Utror valley to Dir, Tehsil of Bahrain.

Pšt. 'pass of the bedouins/nomads (*badawí*)'.

73. **BAGAI-KANDAO بګی کنډو (*bagəy-kanḍaw*)** *Map 5*

Pass on the path leading to Chalera from Khazana and Gamkot, Tehsil of Barikot.

Pšt. 'pass of the carriages (*bagə́y* 'two-wheeled cart, buggy)'.

74. **BAGH باغ (*bāγ*)** *Map 21*

Group of houses in the fertile part of the Jambil-khwar valley, Tehsil of Babuzai.

Pšt. 'garden'.

75. **BAGHSAR باغ سر (*bāγ-sar*)** *Map 47*

Group of houses located in the mountains above the upper Baral-darra valley, Tehsil of Bahrain.

Pšt. 'mountain of the garden'.

76. **BAGOLAI بګولی (*bagoləy*)** *Map 30*

Group of houses in the fertile part of the Charbagh-khwar valley, Tehsil of Charbagh.

Pšt. *bāgə́ra, bāgolə́y, bāgə́wa* 'witch, hag'.

77. **BAGORIA بګوریا (*bagoryā*)** *Map 21*

Group of houses on the hills over the Landai-khwar valley, Tehsil of Babuzai.

Cf. Pšt. *bogurí* 'attack of a dog (with howling and snarling)' (PASHTOON) + sf. *-yā(ṇa)* 'place'? Or Pšt. *bagoṛā́* 'curds, cottage cheese' (ASLANOV), *bagoṛá* 'coagulated milk, a kind of cheese, the Persian *qurut* (RAVERTY)', + *-yā(ṇa)* → 'place where the *bagoṛa*-cheese is prepared'?

78. **BAHADUR-BANDA بهادر بانډه (*bahādur-bānḍa*)** *Map 41*

Pasture on the hills bordering the Harnoi-khwar valley, Tehsil of Maṭṭa. Only on the Russian map.

Pšt. ‘Pasture of Bahadur (person’s name)’ or ‘of the brave’ (*bahādur* ‘brave, valiant’ ← Mong.).

79. **BAHADUR-KHELO-CHARAI بهادر خېلو چرى (*bahādur-xelo-čaray*)** *Map 47*

Group of houses in the mountains above the upper Baral-darra valley, Tehsil of Bahrain.

Pšt. ‘*Charai* of the Bahadur Xel (tribe name)’. Cf. Pšt. *čārí, čārə́y* ‘wooden tool for making terraces used in irrigation’.

80. **BAHANDRA-GOL بهندره گول (*bahandra-gol*)** *Map 54*

Intermittent stream, whose average elevation is 2,047 metres, flowing to Kalam. One of the two sources of the Swāt river, Tehsil of Bahrain.

Cf. T11456 *vahana-* ‘carrying’, ‘flowing of water’, ‘ship’: Pa. *vahana-* ‘current’, Pkt. *vahaṇa-* ‘carriage, boat’, Lhd. *vauhaṇ* ‘mountain torrent’, Panǰ. *vahiṇ*, *vaihaṇ* ‘flowing of a stream’, *vahṇ*, *ba°* ‘flowing, surface of a roughly ploughed field’, Hi. *bahnī* ‘channel carrying juice from sugarcane mill’; T11457 *vahant-* ‘carrying, flowing’: Pkt. *vahaṃta-*, Panj. *vahīdā* ‘flowing (of water)’. Cf. also Pšt. *bahedə́l* ‘to flow’ ← IA. See also Biha-khwar.

81. **BAHNIUM بهنيوم (*bahnium*)** *Map 53*

Group of houses in the narrow valley on the left bank of the upper Swāt river, Tehsil of Bahrain.

Cf. T11452 *vaha-* (in cmpds.) ‘carrying, bearing along (of rivers); river’: Lhd. *vah*, *vāh*, *vahā* ‘watercourse, canal’; Panj. *bāhā* ‘arm of river or canal’; Mth. *bah* ‘channel conveying water into a field’; Pkt. *vahōla-* ‘small stream’. See also Biha-khwar.

82. **BAIDARRA بيدره (*baydara*)** *Map 39*

Village at the foot of the hills bordering the fertile plain on the right bank of the Swāt river, Tehsil of Maṭṭa.

Cf. T9348 *bhagín-* ‘prosperous, happy’: Paš. *bai* ‘good’ (IIFL iii 3, 27), Shum. *bäi* ‘good (of grass for pasture), well (of health)’; Gaw. *bäi* ‘good’: ‘prosperous valley’. Baidara is also the name of a town in India, Western Bengal. Cf. also Prs. *beh* ‘better’. However see also ADAMEC IV 92 Bai, “two villages in the Kachan subdivision of the-sar-i-Pul district”, and ADAMEC VI 56 Baindarra.

83. **BAKANRAN بکاڼان (*bakāṇān*)** *Map 30*

Group of houses on the hills sloping towards the left bank of the Swāt river, Tehsil of Charbagh.

Cf. Pšt. *bakāyáṇ, bakāyáṇa* ‘Indian ash-tree, Indian lilac, *melia azedarach*’; ‘Melia sempervirens’ (Hi. *bakāyan*) (RAVERTY). Cf. also Baki-banda and Baknai.

84. **BAKAR بکر (*bakar*)** *Map 20*

Group of houses in the mountainous upper Saidu-khwar valley, Tehsil of Babuzai.

Pšt. *bakə́ra, bakrə́y* 'flint', but cf. also T9153 *bárkara-* 'kid, lamb': Tir. *bakará* 'ram'; Bašk. *bákar* 'goats'; Tor. *bogho* 'sheep'; Phal. *bakāra* 'goats', *bhakar, bhāṇāl* 'goat-house'; K. *bakar* 'goat', Si. *b̲akaru, b̲akiro, b̲akirī*, Lhd. *bakkrā*, Panj. *bakkar, bakkrā*, Hi. *bakrā*. According to EWAia II 211, this IA etymon is "nicht aufgeklärt", but there is found quotation of KUIPER (1991: 57-58). See also KEWA II 410-411.

85. **BAKI-BANDA باقی بانده (*bāqi-bānḍa*)** *Map 35*

Pasture at the top of the Paiti-khwar valley, near the Kopra-sar, Tehsil of Khwazakhela. Only on the Russian map.

Cf. Bakanran.

86. **BAKNAI بکنی (*baknay*)** *Map 53*

Group of houses in the valley on the right bank of the upper Swāt river, Tehsil of Bahrain.

Tor. *bakānay* 'a type of wild tree', cf. Bakanran.

87. **BAKOR بکوړ (*bakoṛ*)** *Map 41*

Group of houses on the hills bordering the Harnoi-khwar valley, Tehsil of Maṭṭa. On the Russian map it is called Bachorai.

Cf. Bakar? or Pšt. *bay-koṛ* 'prosperous (cf. Baidarra) gurgling (*koṛ* 'gurgling of water')'?

88. **BAKRO بکرو (*bakro*)** *Map 37*

Group of houses on the slopes of the Dobar-sar towards the Swāt river, Tehsil of Khwazakhela.

Variant *bakaro*, obl. pl. from Bakar.

89. **BALA-AN بالا ان (*bālā-ān*)** *Map 54*

Pass leading from the upper Ushu-gol valley to Gilgit, Tehsil of Bahrain.

Pšt. 'higher/upper (*bālā́*) pass'.

90. **BALAGAN-BANDA بلاگان بانده (*bālāgān-bānḍa*)** *Map 12*

Pasture in the Deolai-khwar valley, on the opposite side of Dheri, Tehsil of Kabal.

Pšt. 'pasture of the witches (*balā́*)'.

91. **BALA-KOR بالا کور (*bālā kor*)** *Map 28*

Group of houses on the slopes of the Banda-sar, separating Swat from Shangla, Tehsil of Charbagh.

Pšt. 'higher/upper (*bālā́*) house'.

92. **BALALAI بالالی (*bālālay*)** *Map 30*

Group of houses on the left bank of the Swāt river, at the foot of the hills, Tehsil of Charbagh.

Pšt. 'standing above' (*bālā* + sf.-*lay*).

93. **BALASUR بالاسور (*bālāsur*)** *Map 39*

Group of houses on the slopes of the Lito-sar degrading towards the Harnoi-khwar valley, in Tehsil of Maṭṭa.

Pšt. *bālā́* + *sar* 'top': 'highest top'. However, cf. also the name of the fortress of Peshawar, Bālā Hisār. According to HAKIMZAY (1997: 96), its meaning if 'high (*bālā*) hero (*sur* ← Ur.)'. Cf. also the Ḥiṣār-i bālā of the Ṣifat-nāma (SCARCIA 1965: 128).

94. **BALAT بالات (*bālāt*)** *Map 40*

Group of houses located above the narrow terraced valley of the Shaurai-khwar, Tehsil of Maṭṭa.

Prs. *bālātar* 'higher, superior'.

95. **BALOGRAM بلوگرام (*balogrām*)** *Map 18*

Village on the road leading from Barikot to Mingaora, in the fertile valley on the left bank of the Swat river and at the foot of the hills, Tehsil of Babuzai. Already quoted by DEANE (1895).

Cf. T9161 *bála* 'power, strength; strong': 1. Pa. Pkt. NiDoc. *bala-* 'strength'; Kal. rumb. *bau* 'army', Kho. *bòl*; K. *bal* 'strength'; Lhd. (JUKES) *b̲al* 'strength, ability' (→ Si. *b̲alu*), Panj. Ku. *bal*. The final meaning would be 'stronghold'. However, cf. also Tor. *balai* 'wind', Bašk. *bālā* 'wind, heavy rain', Woṭ. *bālai* 'wind' (T11497, *vātara-* 'windy, stormy'). HAKIMZAY (1997: 26) identifies *balo-* with *bal* 'sacrifice', afterwards become *bul* 'strenght'.

96. **BALO-KALAI بلو کلی (*balo-kəlay*)** *Map 2*

Village in the Kandak-khwar valley, Tehsil of Barikot, not far from the main valley of the Swat river. It is called Bālo by STEIN (1929: 31).

Cf. prec.

97.-98. **BAN بان (*bān*)** *Maps 45, 47*

Name of two groups of houses both located in the Tehsil of Bahrain: 1) in a lateral valley on the right bank of the Swāt river; 2) in the mountains above the upper Baraldarra valley.

Tor. *bān* 'pasture in mountains' or cf. T11258 *vána-* 'single tree; forest, timber': Pa. Aś. *vana-* 'forest', Pkt. *vaṇa-*; (Waig. *bẵn* 'forest', Kt. *bən*, *ben*, Gaw. *ban* ← a *b-* dialect NTS xii 159); Dam. *ban* 'forest'; Sh. (LORIMER) *bvn* 'jungle, grazing ground'; Si. *vaṇu* 'tree, bush', Lhd. *vaṇ*; Panj. *vaṇ* 'a partic. kind of tree', *ban* 'forest'.

99.-101. **BANDA باندہ (*bāṇḍa*)** *Maps 17, 33, 46*

Name of some groups of houses: 1) on the slopes of the mountains above Kanju in the Tehsil of Kabal; 2) in the mountainous terraced upper Khwazakhela-khwar valley, Tehsil of Khwazakhela; 3) in a lateral valley of the Olal-khwar valley, Tehsil of Bahrain.

Pšt. 'small village'/'pasture'.

102. **BANDA-GHAL باندہ غل (*bāṇḍa-γal*)** *Map 24*

Group of houses in the mountainous upper Landai-khwar valley, Tehsil of Babuzai.

Pšt. 'pasture of the thief (*γal*)'.

103. **BANDAI باندی (*bānday*)** *Map 31*

Small village on the left bank of the Swāt river, at the foot of the hills, near Khwazakhela, Tehsil of Khwazakhela.

Pšt. *bāndináy* 'upper'.

104. **BANDANR باندان (*bāndāṇ*)** *Map 22*

Group of houses in the mountainous upper Jambil-khwar valley, near the boundary with Buner, Tehsil of Babuzai.

Pšt. 'pasture' + sf. of place *-(y)āṇ*.

105. **BANDA-SAR باندہ سر (*bāṇḍa-sar*)** *Map 28*

Mountain of about 2,300 mt located on the boundary between the Tehsil of Charbagh and Shangla.

Pšt. 'mountain of the pasture'.

106. **BANDI-BANDA باندي باندہ (*bāndi-bāṇḍa*)** *Map 12*

Pasture in the mountainous upper Deolai-khwar valley, Tehsil of Kabal.

Pšt. 'upper pasture'.

107. **BANG بنگ (*bang*)** *Map 34*

Group of houses on the hills near Kotanai, Tehsil of Khwazakhela.

Pšt. 'hemp (cannabis sativa)' or Pšt. *bāng* 'voice, crying out, sound, the voice of the mu'azzin calling the faithful to prayer, the crowing of the cock' (RAVERTY).

108. **BANGAI-BANDA بنگی باندہ (*bangay-bāṇḍa*)** *Map 3*

Pasture at the top of the hill dividing the Najigram-khwar valley and the Karakar-khwar valley, Tehsil of Barikot.

Pšt. 'pasture of the buzzing/whispering' or Pšt. *bangí* 'one who is in the habit of intoxicating himslef with bang' (RAVERTY)?

109. **BANGESH بنګش (*bangaš*)** *Map 45*

Group of houses in the narrow valley on the left bank of the Swāt river, Tehsil of Bahrain.

Name of the Pšt. tribe? Cf. ADAMEC V 86 Bangesh, "a village located on the Jangali Rud, about 6 miles from its junction with the Arghandab river in Ghazni province".

110. **BANGO-SAR بنګو سر (*bango-sar*)** *Map 27*

Mountain between the Tambagat-khwar valley and the Dre-khwar valley, Tehsil of Charbagh.

Pšt. 'mountain of the hemp (cannabis sativa, obl. pl.)'. See Bangai-banda.

111. **BANJ-BANDA بنج بانډه (*banǰ-bānḍa*)** *Map 38*

Pasture in the mountains of a lateral valley on the right bank of the Harnoi-khwar, Tehsil of Maṭṭa.

Pšt. 'pasture of the quercus ilex (*banǰ*)' or 'of the eggplants (*bānǰáṇ*)'. *Banj* is the 'oak' (SULTAN-I-ROME 2016: 222: "Quercus incanna, Quercus leucotricophora, Baloot").

112. **BANJOT بنجوټ (*banǰoṭ*)** *Map 24*

Village in the narrow upper Landai-khwar valley, Tehsil of Babuzai.

Pšt. 'small banǰ tree'.

113. **BANJ-SAR بنج سر (*banǰ-sar*)** *Map 22*

Mountain of about 2,351 mt located on the boundary between Buner and the Tehsil of Babuzai.

Pšt. 'mountain of the oak'.

114. **BANKARA بنکره (*bankara*)** *Map 39*

Group of houses in the hills on the right bank of the Swāt river, Tehsil of Maṭṭa. Only on the Russian map.

Cf. T11193 *vaṅkara-* '*crooked', 'bend of a river' [quoted by KUIPER 1948: 87; see KEWA III 124 and EWAia II 489]: Bhoj. *bǎkar* 'crooked'. Or cf. Bankor.

115. **BAN-KHWAR بان خوړ (*bān-xwaṛ*)** *Map 54*

Group of houses located in the Bahandra-gol valley, Tehsil of Bahrain. Only on the Russian map.

Tor. 'stream of mountain-pasture'.

116. **BANKOR بانکور (*bānkor*)** *Map 48*

Group of houses in the Daral-khwar valley, Tehsil of Bahrain.

Pšt. 'house of the forest' or 'house of the mountain-pasture' (see prec.).

117. **BANMANAI-KANDAO بانمنی کندو (*bānmənay-kanḍaw*)** *Map 13*

Pass between the Shaurai-khwar valley and the Manrai-khwar valley, connecting the two Tehsils of Kabal and Maṭṭa.

Pšt. 'pass of the autumnal (*mənay*) mountain-pasture', in reference to the transhumance.

118. **BANPAKIA بانپاکیا (*bānpākyā*)** *Map 35*

Group of houses in a lateral valley of the Paiti-khwar valley, Tehsil of Khwazakhela.

Pšt. 'cleaning (*pākyā*) of the garden'?

119. **BAN-PANGHARAI بان پاڼغاړی (*bān-pāṇγāṛay*)** *Map 42*

Group of houses on the northern slopes of the Prangman-sar, Tehsil of Maṭṭa.

The name should be corrected in Band-pangharai: Pšt. *band* 'group of trees' + *pangharai* 'where the cattles are gathered' (IKRAM, p.c.). However, cf. also Pšt. *pāṇ* 'steep or scarped bank of a river' (RAVERTY) and *γāṛa* 'shore, border, margin, coast': 'garden on the scarped bank of the river'.

120. **BAN-PUR-SAR بان پور سر (*bān-pur-sar*)** *Map 27*

Group of houses on the hill between the Makad-khwar and the Dre-khwar, Tehsil of Charbagh.

Cf. Pšt. *poṛ* 'half grown, nearly ripe (as fruit)' (RAVERTY), but probably to be corrected to Banr-pur-sar 'mountain full (*pur*) of trees' (IKRAM, p.c.).

121. **BANR بڼ (*baṇ*)** *Map 49*

Group of houses in the upper Daral-khwar valley, Tehsil of Bahrain.

Pšt. 'garden'.

122. **BANRAGAI بڼگی (*baṇagay*)** *Map 43*

Group of houses in the narrow Roringar-khwar valley, Tehsil of Maṭṭa. Only on the Russian map.

Pšt. 'small garden' (+ dimin. -*gay*).

123. **BARABARAI برابری (*barābaray*)** *Map 42*

Group of houses in the narrow mountainous Harnoi-khwar valley, Tehsil of Maṭṭa. In STEIN 1930 it is called Chatiakōt.

Pšt. *barābar* 'parallel direction; equality' → 'levelled, in plain', or 'upper garden' (cf. Barai): in many Ir. languages (Prs., etc.) it means 'flatten land' (ROSSI, p.c.).

124. **BARAGAT بارگت (*bāragat*)** *Map 16*

Group of houses in a mountainous lateral valley of the Deolai-khwar valley at the frontier with the Tehsil of Maṭṭa, Tehsil of Kabal.

Pšt. *bāra* 'fortification, defence, rampart, ditch, palisade, entrenchment, breastwork' (RAVERTY) + Pšt. *gāṭ/gaṭ* 'boulder; cliff, reef, stone'.

125.-126. BARAI باړى (bāṛəy) *Maps 51, 53*

Name of two groups of houses, both in the Tehsil of Bahrain: 1) in the narrow valley on the left bank of the upper Swāt river; 2) in the Mankial-khwar valley (Warai on the Russian map).

Possibly, cf. Phal. *bāṛ* 'goat-pen'. According to HAKIMZAY (1997: 27), *bāṛi* 'garden, orchard, enclosure' ← Skt., and these areas possibly were in old times leisure places. Cf. also Tor. *baṛi* 'a place name in Mankiyal valley'. Cf. Bararai?

127. BARAL برال (barāl) *Map 47*

Small village in the narrow Baral-darra valley, Tehsil of Bahrain. Apparently, its name is Nund (Pšt. 'submerged') on the Russian map.

Cf. foll.

128. BARAL-DARRA برال دره (barāl-dara) *Map 47*

Stream originating from the Luda-sar and flowing into the left side of the Swāt river, Tehsil of Bahrain.

Cf. Tor. *baṛāl* 'a place near Gornai village'; Shum. *buṛā́la* 'old' (T9271), but better Tor. *baṛel* 'pebble'? → 'river of the pebbles': from a semantic point of view, this etymology would be confirmed by that proposed for the Karakar-khwar (q.v.). Concerning *darra*, see FUSSMAN 1972, 2: 314-316, quoting P 1, 2 *dary'ū*, P 23 *dary'āp*, P 25 *dary'au*, Bur. *dəri.a*, Lhd. *daryā*, Panj. *daryā*, all with the meaning 'river', and precising that: "Les emprunts sont assez fréquents. Si l'on admet que *daryā* est exclusivement Pers. et *daryāp* exclusivement Psht., règle qui souffre beaucoup d'exceptions, [...]". To be excluded for semantic reasons the possibility to see in *darra* the name of the 'valley' (see MOKRI 1997).

129. BARANIAL برانيال (barāṇyāl) *Map 48*

Main village of the Tehsil of Bahrain, on the right bank of the Swāt river and at the confluence of the Daral-khwar. Quoted already by RAVERTY (1888: 236) as Birán-yál, "inhabited by the Torú Ál, or Torw Ál". Its actual name, attributed from the last Wāli of Swāt, is Bahrain (← Ar. dual from *bahar*: 'two waters').

Pšt. *baranáy* 'upper (living or located in the mountains)' + sf. *-yāl* (on this sf., cf. s.v. Mankial). HAKIMZAY (1997: 176) thinks to Dard. *barin*, variant of *baran*, meaning 'big': 'big waters'.

130. BARANWAI بارانوى (bārānway) *Map 46*

Group of houses in a lateral mountainous valley of the Swāt river valley, Tehsil of Bahrain. Only on the Russian map.

Pšt. 'upper' + sf. *-way*?

131. **BARARAI برارى (*barāray*)** *Map 31*

Group of houses on the hills sloping towards the left bank of the Swāt river, Tehsil of Khwazakhela.

Pšt. *barrai* [*barrí* Ar.] 'rectangular shaped patch of land, somewhat greater in length and width – also may have some additional advantage of having been fertile or being the best type or category of land'; Pšt. *birarrai* 'a much narrower rectangular patch of land' (SULTAN-I-ROME 2016: 476); see also *ibid.*: 485:

> *Barrai*: Basically rain fed land, but which has been irrigated by the owner by channelling in rain water or by not allowing rain water to flow out, e.g. by levelling it or by raising the boundaries etc. This land too is cropped twice a year.

132. **BAR-BAMAKHEL بر باماخېل (*bar-bāmāxel*)** *Map 38*

Village located in the fertile plain between the Harnoi-khwar and the right bank of the Swāt river, Tehsil of Maṭṭa. RAVERTY (1888: 201, 230) quotes this village as Banbá Khel.

Name of the tribe Bami Khel.

133. **BAR-BANDAI بر باڼدى (*bar-bānḍəy*)** *Map 17*

Big village in the fertile plain on the right bank of the Swāt river, Tehsil of Kabal. Already quoted by RAVERTY (1888: 230) as Bánḍí-i-Bálá.

Pšt. 'upper pasture'.

134. **BAR-BANJIR-BANDA بر بنجير بانډه (*bar-banǰir-bānḍa*)** *Map 2*

Pasture in the upper Kandak-khwar valley, Tehsil of Barikot, near the Bostani-sar.

Pšt. 'upper pasture of the oak (*banǰ*)'.

135. **BAR-BARGIN بر بارګين (*bar-bārgiṇ*)** *Map 35*

Small village in the narrow mountainous Bargin-khwar valley, Tehsil of Khwazakhela. On the Russian map only Kuz-bargin is named.

Pšt. 'upper Bargin (q.v.)'.

136. **BAR-BATAI-BANDA بر بتى بانډه (*bar-batay-bānḍa*)** *Map 3*

Pasture in the upper Najigram-khwar valley, Tehsil of Barikot, on the slopes of the mountains separating the Kandak-khwar valley from the Najigram-khwar valley.

Pšt. 'pasture of the upper fallow land (*batí*)'.

137. **BAR-BELA بر بېله (*bar-bela*)** *Map 47*

Group of houses on the mountain above the Baral-darra valley, Tehsil of Bahrain.

Pšt. 'upper Bela' (q.v.).

138. **BAR-DURSHKHEL بر درشخېل (*bar-duršxel*)** *Map 39*

Village in the fertile plain on the right bank of the Swāt river, Tehsil of Maṭṭa. Quoted already by RAVERTY (1888: 200, 233) as Darwesh Khel-i-Bálá or Bar Darwesh Khel.

Pšt. 'upper Duršxel'. Ethnic name. Cf. also the "Dushkhel country" in Dir (GODFREY 1912: 50: "it is noticeable that the Dashui Kohistanis still claim the Dushkhel country of Dir, now in possession of the Yusafzais, as part of their ancestral property").

139. **BAR-DURZGHAR-BANDA بر درزګر بانډه (*bar-durzgar-bānḍa*)** *Map 3*

Pasture in the upper Najigram-khwar valley, Tehsil of Barikot, on the slopes of the mountains separating the Kandak-khwar valley from the Najigram-khwar valley.

Pšt. 'upper pasture of the platforms', with *dəráz* 'platform; embankment (low mound of earth along the sides of a peasant house' (ASLANOV), or Pšt. *darz* 'crack, fissure', or *draz, drəz* 'thunder', + adj. sf. *-gar*.

140. **BARET بریټ (*baret*)** *Map 33*

Group of houses in the mountainous upper Khwazakhela-khwar valley on the slopes of the Semprai-sar, Tehsil of Khwazakhela.

Pšt. *bareet* 'bird cherry' (SULTAN-I-ROME 2016: 221). Cf. also Tor. *barid* 'border, demarcation'.

141. **BAR-GARAI بر ګړی (*bar-gaṛəy*)** *Map 45*

Group of houses located in the narrow valley on the left bank of the Swāt river, Tehsil of Bahrain.

Pšt. 'upper Garai (q.v.)'.

142. **BAR-GHUZAN بر غوزان (*bar-γuzān*)** *Map 24*

Group of houses in the high and narrow Lewanai-khwar valley, Tehsil of Babuzai.

Pšt. 'upper (place of the) walnuts'.

143. **BARGIN بارګيڼ (*bārgiṇ*)** *Map 35*

Stream flowing into the Swāt river on the left side, in the northern part of the Tehsil of Khwazakhela.

Probably with HAKIMZAY (1997: 28): Pšt. 'the place full (*gin*) of fruits (*bār*)', due to the *-ṇ* (Pšt. *gaṇ* 'thick, dense'). Or Pšt. *barg* 'leaf' + sf. *-iṇ/-in* (?). Cf. also Prs. *bārgin* 'cistern, sink, stagnant, fetid, or putrid water' (STEINGASS), 'sink, sewer; cistern' (HAYYIM). Bargin is also the name of a place in the region of Gilgit-Baltistan, Northern Areas of Pakistan.

144. **BAR-GORSHAI بر ګورشی (*bar-goršay*)** *Map 45*

Group of houses in a lateral valley on the right bank of the Swāt river on the slopes of the Babu-sar, Tehsil of Bahrain.

IA 'upper Goršay', cf. Goshai.

145. **BAR-GUNAGUZ بر گناگز (*bar-gunāguz*)** *Map 50*

Group of houses on the right bank of the Swāt river near the Kedam-khwar valley, Tehsil of Bahrain.

Cf. Prs. *gauzi-kunā* 'the thorn-apple' and *gūk-kunā* 'Datura' (STEINGASS), with inversion of the two members of the nominal compound? Or cf. Pšt. *gungú* 'bush having dark-yellow wood; saffron; wild safflower'?

146. **BARIAM بریم (*baryam*)** *Map 38*

Group of houses on the right bank of the Harnoi river at the foot of the hills bordering the plain, Tehsil of Maṭṭa.

Cf. T11309 *vará-* 'suitor, bridegroom, husband': Pa. *vara-* 'suitor, husband, daughter's husband', Pkt. *vara-*, *°aya-* 'suitor, husband'; Panj. *var*, *bar* 'bridegroom' + T10421 *yamá*[1] 'twin': Pa. *yama-* 'twin, pair', in the meaning of 'couple of bridegrooms'? Or cf. T11322 *varayātrā-* 'procession of suitor or bridegroom': Panj. *varāt*, *barāt* 'groom's procession', N. *bariyāt* 'suitor's procession'?

147. **BARIKOT بریکوټ (*barikoṭ*)** *Map 4*

Big village in the vast and fertile valley on the left bank of the Swat river, at the confluence between the Kandak-khwar and the Karakar-khwar, Tehsil of Barikot.

Many studies have been devoted to this toponym:

1. GODFREY 1912: 50:

> Barikot is reached in an hour from Biar. It is situated on a high cliff on the left bank of the river, spanned by the usual strong cantilever bridge. [...] Above the terrace-built village a steep path leads up a cliff to the remains of an old fort. This, the villagers state, was held by their ancestor, Baria, a Kafir or unbeliever in Islam, who came from upper Swat when his village, Barikot, there was destroyed by the invading army of the Mohammedans eight generations ago. This story is confirmed by the traditions of the Yusafzais who now hold Barikot, in upper Swat, and who gave me a similar account when I visited them. The site of this old fort, of which the trace is plainly visible, occupies an exactly similar position to that of the now deserted houses and forts on the Malakand and Digar passes which connect lower Swat and Peshawar territory. Those houses and forts the Yusafzais of Swat can only now account for by saying that they were built by 'Kafirs,' and they closely resemble the many similar ruins in the Talash and Dushkhel valleys of Dir.

2. STEIN 1930: 28-29 (see also ID. 1929: 47-48 and 1930: 27-29):

> On the philological side it is easy to prove that the name *Bīr-kōṭ*, "the castle of Bīr," preserves in its first part the direct phonetic derivative of the ancient name which the Greek form *Bazira* was intended to reproduce [...] From the restored form **Bajira*: **Bayira* it is not difficult to trace the gradual phonetic change into *Bīr* or *Bir*. In the development of all Indo-Aryan languages, as illustrated by the transition from Sanskrit into Prakrit and from this into the modern Indo-Aryan vernaculars, the elision of intervocalic mediæ *j* and *y* is a well-known rule, and this holds good also of the related Dardic languages [...] The subsequent reduction of the resultant diphthong *ai*, as in **Baira*, into *ī* or *i* is a phonetic change for which analogies are equally plentiful in the two language groups [...] Thus we can account without any difficulty for the successive change of **Bajira (Bayira)* > **Baira* > *Bīr*. The addition of the designation *kōṭ*, "castle, fort" (Sanskrit *koṭṭa*), to the name is readily understood the term *kōṭ* being generally applied to any fortified place

throughout the North-West of India, whatever the language spoken [fn. 14: The term *kōṭ* is quite common in local names of Hindukush valleys, like Darēl and Tangīr, where Dardic languages are spoken, and is also separately used in Pashtu].

3. TUCCI 1958: 296 [= TUCCI 1997: 84]:

> The place therefore for its situation had great importance from the very beginning of the history of Swat; and, as shown by Stein, it corresponds beyond doubt to the Bazira of Arrian; its name in Sanskrit was Vajīrasthāna [fn. 28: The identification Bari-kot, Bir-kot is beyond any doubt; in fact we know from a Sanskrit inscription discovered in that locality and contemporary with Jayapāladeva, 10th century A.D., that the name as was heard by the Greeks survived also at the times of that king; it is in fact called in that inscription: Vajīrasthāna, the place Vajīra. See Rai Bahadur Daya Ram Shastri, 'Six Inscriptions in the Lahore Museum', *EI* XXI, p. 301 (the editor identifies wrongly Vajīrasthāna with Waziristan)].

4. TUCCI 1963a [= TUCCI 1997: 117] (see also TUCCI 1977: 43 and 49):

> Their [of the Assakenoi] most important places were Massaga (not yet located with certainty, but which must have lain somewhere near Chakdarra), Bazira = Vajīra, Vajīrasthāna in an inscription [28] of Jayapāladeva (*EI* XXI, p. 301), now Barikot, Ora (Uḍegram), Dyrta (not located). These were the cities of the Assakenoi, Āśvāyana, Assakenoi-Āśvakāyana (Kātyāyana, VI, I, 99) and Aurdāyana, from Urdi (Ora), mentioned by Kātyāyana on IV, II, 99. The name of the last tribe cannot be separated from Oḍḍiyāna < Aurdiyāna, Audriyāna.

5. More recently, BAUMS 2019: 169-170:

> two different name forms transmitted for the city of Barikot (Bīr-koṭ-ghwaṇḍai) in the classical sources: Curtius Rufus calls the city Beira, [...] while Arrian refers to it as Bazira. [...] The latter form can be interpreted quite straightforwardly as Sanskrit *vajra* 'thunderbolt' with superficial epenthetic *i*. The compound name Vajrakūṭa 'Thunderbolt Peak' is attested not only in a Gāndhārī inscription (CKI 404: *vajrakuḍae ... thubami* 'at the Thunderbolt-Peak Stūpa), but also as the name of a fabulous city in the story collection Kathāsaritsāgara (*vajrakūṭākhyaṃ pṛṣthe himavataḥ puraṃ* 'the city behind the Himalaya called Thunderbolt Peak') and in the modern place-name Bajrakot in Orissa (Salomon 2000: 64-65). The former form, Curtius' Beira, has, however, so far remained obscure. I would like to suggest that it reflects a vernacular, Middle Indo-Aryan pronunciation of the same place-name. As written, we would expect Beira to be based on a Greek spelling *Βεῖρα with a pronunciation [ʋejira]. This then corresponds quite precisely to the Gāndhārī form of the word, spelt *vayira* in CKI 249 and 367, *vaïra* in CKI 367, and likewise pronounced [ʋejirə]. In other words, the sources of Curtius Rufus on the one hand and of Ptolemy on the other appear to have ultimately drawn from two different sociolinguistic levels among their Indian informants (one using the vernacular, the other Sanskrit) when eliciting the name of the city of Barikot.

6. IORI/OLIVIERI, forthcoming:

> During the last phases of the Soviet-Afghan war, another Barikot, a third very small border trade point in Kunar, probably founded in the 20th century, became famous as a crucial battlefield. Finally, we should not forget the once famous Barikot Cinema Theatre, still a ruined landmark in Kabul. The name, quite unattractive for a movie theatre when compared to most appealing brands like Pameer and Ariana Cinemas, derives from the neighborhood, composed mostly of families who migrated from the third Barikot". And *ibid.*: "*Vajira*, which might have had, by metonimy, the meaning of 'unconquerable' like the Greek placename 'Adamas', seems having two distinct linguistic traditions: one, Bazira-*vajra*, Sanskritic and preserved until medieval times in official records; the second,

> Beira/Baira-*va(y)ira*, vernacular and local, attested till today. Stefan Baums provided the key to contextualise the vernacular form, as the local Prakrit form of *vajra* is *vayira*, a term which is positively attested in Gāndhārī, was locally pronounced [ve(j)irə], which makes Curtius' information (and sources) on the local name of the city ('*Beira incolae vocant*', VIII, 34) very precise indeed.

7. See also MORGENSTIERNE (1973: 160) cites "*Birkot* S, XXI, 7 Afghan border vill. On the Kunar".

See the description of another Birkot or Barikot contained in ADAMEC VI 110:

> One of the five Gabar villages of the Kunar valley, on the right bank of the river, opposite to, and 1,000 yards south of, Arundu (Arnawai) as the crow flies. The houses, about 60 in number, are closely fitted together in the form of a square and surrounded by an 18 -foot wall, with a tower at each corner. The eastern face of the wall is in a dilapidated condition. The houses are built up against the wall. The centre of the village is an extremely filthy farmyard, where extremely narrow lanes converge. The entrance to the village is by a gate in the south wall. There is here a garrison of one infantry regiment and two mountain guns, whose lines, together with the married quarters, are outside the walls to the south and southwest, and not fortified in any way. The ground round Birkot is highly cultivated, chiefly with rice and a little Indian corn. The valley at Birkot, from the river to the hills on the right bank, is about 1/2 mile wide. The river banks are very high and the river flows very rapidly. From bank to bank is about 100 yards and in autumn the water is about 60 yards wide. There is no bridge or ferny here, and the river is crossed by inflated skins. The hills are wooded. One mile above Birkot are the ruins of an old bridge. The river is very narrow here and the site is a good one for a bridge.

HAKIMZAY (1997: 20) analyses Bir as 'hero, brave', but this hypothesis can be excluded.

148. BAR-JABAR بر جبر (*bar-ǰabar*) *Map 24*

Group of houses in the high and narrow Lewanai-khwar valley, Tehsil of Babuzai.

Cf. Jabrai.

149. BAR-KADAR بر کدر (*bar-kadar*) *Map 42*

Group of houses on the slopes near the boundary with Dir, Tehsil of Maṭṭa. Only on the Russian map.

Cf. Pšt. *kaḍál* 'hut or cabin made of reeds or grass'?

150. BAR-KANDAK بر کندک (*bar-kandak*) *Map 2*

Small village in the high Kandak-khwar valley, Tehsil of Barikot.

IA 'upper Kandak' (q.v.).

151.-152. BAR-KANDAO بر کنډو (*bar-kanḍaw*) *Maps 24, 42*

Name of two passes: 1) leading from the Dosara-khwar valley to Shangla, Tehsil of Babuzai; 2) leading from the upper Harnoi-khwar valley to Dir, Tehsil of Maṭṭa (only on the Russian map).

Pšt. 'upper pass'.

153. **BAR-KANDAO-BANDA بر کندو بانده (*bar-kanḍaw-bānḍa*)** *Map 24*

Pasture in the mountains above the Dosara-khwar valley, Tehsil of Babuzai.

Pšt. 'pasture of the upper pass'.

154. **BAR-KANJU بر کانجو (*bar-kānǰu*)** *Map 17*

Big village in the fertile plain on the right bank of the Swāt river, Tehsil of Kabal.

Cf. Kanju.

155. **BAR-KARINGAL بر کرنگال (*bar-karingāl*)** *Map 33*

Group of houses in the mountainous upper Khwazakhela-khwar valley, on the slopes of the Semprai-sar, Tehsil of Khwazakhela.

Cf. Karange + sf. *-āl* (on this sf., cf. s.v. Mankial).

156. **BARKHAI برخی (*barxay*)** *Map 36*

Group of houses in the mountainous upper Miandam-khwar valley, Tehsil of Khwazakhela. Only on the Russian map.

Pšt. *bar* + sf. *-xay*?

157. **BAR-LAIKOT بر لایکوټ (*bar-lāykoṭ*)** *Map 53*

Group of houses in the narrow valley on the right bank of the upper Swāt river, Tehsil of Bahrain. Quoted already by RAVERTY (1888: 237) as Iláhí-Koṭ.

Possibly Pšt. 'upper (*bar*) fort (*koṭ*) done of mud (*lāy*, RAVERTY)'. According to HAKIMZAY (1997: 115), its meaning is 'fort on the road (*lāyāla*).

158. **BAR-LALKU بر لالکو (*bar-lālku*)** *Map 44*

Village in the mountainous Barwai-khwar valley, Tehsil of Maṭṭa.

Cf. Lalku-kandao.

159. **BAR-LEWANAI بر لیونی (*bar-lewanay*)** *Map 24*

Group of houses in the high and narrow Spedar-khwar valley, Tehsil of Babuzai.

Pšt. 'upper Lewanai' (q.v.).

160. **BAR-MANASAR بر مناسر (*bar-manāsar*)** *Map 26*

Group of houses in the upper Bishbanr-khwar valley, Tehsil of Babuzai.

Cf. Manasar-sar and foll.

161. **BARMAN-SAR برمان سر (*barmān-sar*)** *Map 12*

Mountain on the border with Dir and the Deolai-khwar valley, Tehsil of Kabal.

Cf. Pšt. *barmanḍ*, *barbanḍ* 'naked, denude, bare, undressed, stripped, unclothed' (RAVERTY): it could be due to its conformation. To be excluded Pšt. *bar* + sf. *man*.

162. BARO بارو (*bāro*) *Map 39*

Group of houses on the Lito-sar, Tehsil of Maṭṭa.

Cf. Pšt. *bāra* 'fortification, defence, rampart, ditch, palisade, entrenchment, breast-work' (RAVERTY); but cf. also Urtsun *brho* 'high mountain' (MORGENSTIERNE 1973: 85). According to HAKIMZAY (1997: 26) it springs from Skt. *bāru* 'sand (= Pšt. *šəga*)'. This proposal is also possible. As the author adds: "Baro's land indeed is sandy".

163. BARONA بارونه (*bāruna*) *Map 42*

Group of houses on the slopes of the Prangman-sar towards the Harnoi-khwar valley, Tehsil of Maṭṭa. Only on the Russian map.

Pšt. *bār* 'load, burden, fruit, time, once', pl. (*bāruna*).

164. BAR-PATAI بر پټى (*bar-pəṭay*) *Map 10*

Group of houses on the western side of the Dokat-sar, in a lateral terraced valley of the Ramogai-khwar valley, Tehsil of Kabal.

Pšt. 'upper Patay' (q.v.).

165. BAR-SAMSARA بر سمسره (*bar-samsara*) *Map 3*

Group of houses in the narrow upper Najigram-khwar valley, Tehsil of Barikot, near the boundary with Buner.

Cf. Kuz-samsara.

166. BAR-SHAUR بر شور (*bar-šawr*) *Map 40*

Village in the narrow terraced valley of the Shaurai-khwar, Tehsil of Maṭṭa.

Pšt. 'upper Shaur' (cf. Shaurai-khwar).

167. BARTHANA برتهانه (*barthāna*) *Map 41*

Village on the fertile bank of the Harnoi-khwar near the confluence with the Roringar-khwar, Tehsil of Maṭṭa.

Pšt. 'upper checkpoint'.

168. BARUJ بروج (*baruǰ*) *Map 44*

Group of houses in a lateral valley on the right bank of the Swāt river on the slopes of the Babu-sar, Tehsil of Bahrain. Only on the Russian map.

Cf. Pšt. *burǰ* 'tower, turret, bastion', Ar. pl. *burúǰ*? Or cf. Pšt. *barǰ* 'the bark of a tree, which is very slight and often used as paper'.

169. **BAR-UZBUK بر ازبک (*bar-uzbuk*)** *Map 24*

Group of houses located in the high and narrow Dosara-khwar valley, Tehsil of Babuzai.

Pšt. 'upper Uzbuk (q.v.)'.

170. **BARWA بړوه (*baṛwa*)** *Map 7*

Group of houses in the mountainous region near the Landai-sar, Tehsil of Barikot, in a lateral valley towards Ghaligay. On the Pakistani map, near Barwa it is also marked Bureh, but it should be just a variant of the former.

Cf. Baurai and Burai.

171. **BARWAI بړوی (*baṛway*)** *Map 44*

Group of houses on the eastern slopes of the mountains dividing the Barwai-khwar valley from the Harnoi-khwar valley, Tehsil of Maṭṭa.

Cf. Baurai.

172. **BARWAI-KHWAR بړوی خوړ (*baṛway-xwaṛ*)** *Map 44*

Stream flowing into the right side of the Swāt river from the mountains on the border with Dir, Tehsil of Maṭṭa. Called Lālku River in STEIN 1930.

Cf. Baurai.

173. **BASESAR بسیسر (*basesar*)** *Map 47*

Group of houses on the slopes of the Baral-darra valley, Tehsil of Bahrain.

Cf. T9223 **bāṣmá-*: Ašk. *bas* 'steam', Waig. *bās*, Paš. *bāse* 'steam, sweat, mist'? → 'Mountain of mist'?

174. **BASHKAL باشکل (*bāškal*)** *Map 46*

Group of houses in the narrow valley of the Olal-khwar, Tehsil of Bahrain.

Better than 'season of rains' (cf. T11392 *varṣá-* 'rain' and ff., and DE CHIARA 2018: 106-107 for comparisons), cf. the ethnic name Bashgáli, "a tribe of the Siáh-posh Káfirs" (ROSE 1911: 69) or the ethnic name Bashkár (cf. foll.).

175. **BASHKARO-AN بشکارو ان (*baškāro-an*)** *Map 54*

Pass leading from the upper Ushu-gol valley to Gilgit, Tehsil of Bahrain.

'Pass of the Baškars'. See ROSE 1911: 69:

> Bashkár, a group of non-Paṭhán tribes which used to occupy the Panjkora Kohístán or Kohístán-i-Malízai in Dír [...] The Bashkarí languages is said to be the same as the Garhwí. According to Biddulph the Bashkárik, as he terms them, have three clans; Múlanor, Kútchkor and Joghior.

176. **BASKHELA باسخېله (*bāsxela*)** *Map 39*

Village at the foot of the Shah-dop-sar, in the plain on the right bank of the Swāt river, Tehsil of Maṭṭa. According to M.A. DINAKHEL (p.c.), a variant of this toponym is Bazkhela.

Cf. the Busa Khel tribe and the name of the chieftown of Malakand, Batkhela. Cf. also ADAMEC V 95 Basukhel, "a village located about 14 miles west-southwest of Shahjui in Zabul province". HAKIMZAY (1997: 178-179) proposes Skt. *bās* 'dwelling, habitation, residence' + *ke* (successively > *xe*).

177. **BAT-KORAN بټ کورن (*baṭ-koran*)** *Map 18*

Village in the vast plain of the Jambil-khwar valley, Tehsil of Babuzai, nowadays absorbed in the metropolitan area of Mingaora.

Cf. Phal. Tor. *bāṭ*, Bašk. *baṭ* 'stone' (cf. T11348: **varta-* 'round stone': Ash. Wg. *wāṭ*, Kt. *woṭ*, Dm. *bɔ̄'ṭ*, Tir. *baṭ*, Niṅg. *bōt*, Woṭ. *baṭ* m., Gaw. *wāṭ* 'stone, millstone'; Kal. rumb. *bat* 'stone', Kho. *bort*, Bašk. *baṭ*, Tor. *bāṭ*, etc.) + Bašk. *kōr* 'large stone' (T3018 *kāṭha-* 'rock'). But cf. also Pšt. *baṭ* 'large iron pan or cauldron for roasting grain, furnace, kiln; luck, prosperity, felicity; the bark of a tree, bark, rind, peel, husk' (RAVERTY).

178. **BATKU بټکو (*batku*)** *Map 44*

Group of houses in the mountainous Barwai-khwar valley, Tehsil of Maṭṭa.

Cf. prec. and Phal. *batak* 'pebble' (cf. T11349: *vartaka-* '*something round'). Or see MORGENSTIERNE 1930: "Tor. *batkūmā* maid. °*kūmā* < Skr. *kumārī-*, cf. Tir. *kumār* daughter &c. *bat-* = **baḍ-* < *vr̥ddha-*?".

179. **BATOL بتول (*batol*)** *Map 39*

Group of houses on the slopes of the Shah-dop-sar near Baskhela, Tehsil of Maṭṭa.

Kal. *baṭh'ula* 'fat, thick; strong' or Pšt. 'pullets (*batála*)'?

180. **BATORA باتوره (*bātora*)** *Map 18*

Village in the first hills of the upper Saidu-khwar valley, towards Marghuzar, Tehsil of Babuzai.

Pšt. *bātura* 'name of a poisonous plant, the thorn-apple' (RAVERTY).

181. **BATRA باتره (*bātra*)** *Map 23*

Group of houses in the fertile plain of the Landai-khwar valley, Tehsil of Babuzai.

Cf. prec.

182. **BATUL-BANDA بتول بنده (*batul-bānḍa*)** *Map 13*

Pasture in the high Manrai-khwar valley, towards the boundary with Dir, Tehsil of Kabal.

Cf. Batol.

183. **BAURAI باروی (*bāwṛəy*)** *Map 17*

Group of houses on the slopes of the Bauro-sar, Tehsil of Maṭṭa.

Pšt. *buṛa* 'table land, flat mountain land' (RAVERTY), cf. Bura-sar. HAKIMZAY (1997: 33) proposes a Hi. origin, from *bir* 'hero, brave', but this appears improbable.

184. **BAURO-SAR باوړو سر (*bawṛo-sar*)** *Map 17*

Mountain of about 1,800 mt on the boundary between the Tehsils of Kabal and Maṭṭa. Local name: Saso-sar.

Cf. prec.

185. **BAYAN-BANDA بایان بانډه (*bāyān-bānḍa*)** *Map 12*

Pasture in the mountains of the Deolai-khwar valley, opposide side of Dheri, Tehsil of Kabal.

Pšt. 'pasture of the colt (*biān* 'colt, foal, filly', RAVERTY)'. To be excluded Pšt. 'pasture of the declaration (*bayā́n*)'.

186. **BAZAI-DERAI بزی ډیری (*bazay-derəy*)** *Map 24*

Group of houses in the mountainous upper Landai-khwar valley, Tehsil of Babuzai.

Pšt. 'hill/residence of the falcon (*bāz*)'. Possibly also Pšt. 'hill/residence of the game (*bāzí*)'. See also ADAMEC I 45 Bāzā'ī Gunbad.

187. **BAZWANANO-DERAI بزوانانو ډیری (*bazwānāno ḍerəy*)** *Map 24*

Group of houses at the end of the upper Jambil-khwar valley, between the Unran-sar and the Guli-sar, Tehsil of Babuzai.

Pšt. 'residence of the goat keepers (*buzwān*)/of the falconers (*bāzwān*)'.

188.-189. **BEDAG بیدگ (*bedag*)** *Map 46*

Name of two groups of houses on the slopes of the Olal-khwar valley and at the confluence of the Olal-khwar valley with the Swāt river, Tehsil of Bahrain.

Cf. Kal. *bádik* 'to increase in number' (T11376 *várdhatē* 'grows, increases')? Or cf. T9621 **bhaiḍraka* 'pertaining to sheep', *bhaiṇḍaka-*? This root is linked to *meṇḍha-* 'ram' and is considered by KUIPER (1948: 109-110) a loanword ← Muṇḍa in reason of the alternation *bh-: m-*; see KEWA II 682 and EWAia III 415. HAKIMZAY (1997: 18) analyses it as Sanskrit Baidak 'A Brahman well versed in the Vedas', but this proposal seems quite improbable.

190. **BEHAR بیهار (*behār*)** *Map 32*

Small village on the hills in the Khwazakhela-khwar valley, on the road leading to Shangla, Tehsil of Khwazakhela.

IA 'abode; monastery'. Cf. T12033 *vihāra-* 'arrangement; roaming, pleasure ground; monastery': Pa. Pkt. *vihāra-* 'walking about, sojourning, monastery', Pa. °*aka-* 'hut'. Cf.

also the name of the Indian state of Bihar. See MORGENSTIERNE 1973: 159: "*Bihal*, Mil. Rep.; M °*ar* vill. in Birir".

191.-194. BELA بيله (*bela*) *Maps 11, 33, 46, 50*

Name of four villages: 1) Group of houses in the fertile part of the Spanai-khwar valley, Tehsil of Kabal; 2) village in the plain of the Khwazakhela-khwar, near Khwazakhela, Tehsil of Khwazakhela; 3) in the upper Olal-khwar valley, Tehsil of Bahrain; 4) group of houses on the right bank of the Swāt river near the Kedam-khwar valley, Tehsil of Bahrain.

Cf. Geonyms.

195. BELA-BANDA بيله بانده (*bela-bānḍa*) *Map 13*

Pasture in the upper Manrai-khwar valley, towards the boundary with Matta, Tehsil of Kabal.

Pšt. 'pasture of Bela'. Cf. Pšt. *belá* 'whistle'?

196. BERANG بيرنگ (*berang*) *Map 45*

Group of houses located in the narrow valley on the left bank of the Swāt river, Tehsil of Bahrain. Only on the Russian map.

Cf. Pšt. *bayráng*, *beráng* 'relating to additional payment' or *beránga* 'colorless'; or T12144 *vairāgya* 'indifference to the world': Pkt. *vēragga-* 'freedom from passion'; Panj.ludh. *barāg* 'homesick'?

197. BHOKA بهوكه (*bhoka*) *Map 16*

Group of houses in a mountainous lateral valley of the Deolai-khwar valley at the frontier with the Tehsil of Maṭṭa, Tehsil of Kabal.

Tor. *bhugo* 'a summer pasture in Gurnai' cf. Si. *bhūku* 'blockhead'; Hi. *bhõkas* 'wizard' (T9519 **bhukkhara-* 'defective')?

198. BIAKAND بياكند (*byākand*) *Map 38*

Group of houses in the hills of a lateral valley on the right bank of the Harnoi-khwar, Tehsil of Maṭṭa.

Possibly IA 'second/friend town': cf. T6680 *dvitīya-* 'second; foe, friend': Pkt. *biia-*, *bīa-*, *biijja-*, Tor. *bī* 'again'; Si. *b̲īo*, *b̲ījo* 'second, another'. We can exclude (ROSSI, p.c.) any connexion with IA 'prosperous town' (T9348 *bhagín-* 'prosperous, happy': Paš. *bai* 'good' (IIFL iii 3, 27), Shum. *bäi* 'good (of grass for pasture), well (of health)'; Gaw. *bäi* 'good'). Cf. also Biakor.

199. BIAKAND-KANDAO بياكند كندو (*byākand-kanḍaw*) *Map 16*

Pass leading from Kabal to Matta, Tehsil of Kabal.

IA 'pass of Biakand'.

200. **BIAKOR بیاکور (*byākor*)** *Map 16*

Group of houses in a mountainous lateral valley of the Deolai-khwar valley, Tehsil of Kabal.

IA 'second/friend town'? Cf. Biakand.

201. **BIHA بیها (*bihā*)** *Map 42*

Village in the narrow mountainous Biha-khwar valley, Tehsil of Maṭṭa.

Cf. foll.

202. **BIHA-KHWAR بیها خوړ (*bihā-xwaṛ*)** *Map 42*

Stream originating from the slopes of the Landai-sar and flowing into the Harnoi-khwar, Tehsil of Maṭṭa.

Possibly connected with Pšt. *bahedə́l* 'to flow' < IA., T11453. See s.v. Bahandra-gol for further details.

203. **BIJAI بیجی (*biǰay*)** *Map 50*

Group of houses in the narrow valley on the right bank of the upper Swāt river, Tehsil of Bahrain.

Cf. Phal. *biǰǰi* 'lightning'?

204. **BIJORA بیجوره (*biǰora*)** *Map 39*

Village in the hills bordering the plain on the right bank of the Swāt river near the road to Durshkhela, Tehsil of Maṭṭa.

Possibly < *bijour*, name of the Abies webbiana (see ALAM 2011). To be excluded Pšt. *biǰoṛé* 'incomparable, superlative, remarkable'.

205. **BIKAI بیکی (*bikay*)** *Map 22*

Group of houses in the mountainous upper Landai-khwar valley, Tehsil of Charbagh.

Cf. T9236 *biggāī 'a kind of insect': Pkt. *biggāī-*, *biggāiā-*; Guǰ. *bagāī* 'an insect found on the body of cattle'?

206. **BIKAN بیکن (*bikan*)** *Map 26*

Group of houses in the upper Bishbanr-khwar valley, Tehsil of Babuzai.

Cf. foll.

207. **BIKAN-KHWAR بیکن خوړ (*bikan-xwaṛ*)** *Map 26*

Stream flowing from the frontier with Shangla into the Bishbanr-khwar, Tehsil of Babuzai. Its estimate terrain elevation above sea level is 2277 metres, and its source there is the homonymic village of Bikan.

Cf. Kho. *bik-* 'to go' (< *ápaiti* or *vyēti* 'goes away'); N. *bagnu* 'to flow, glide; be carried away, be swept away', Hi. *bagnā* 'to move': "perh. < Sk. *válgati* springs: Pa. *vaggati*; Pkt. *vaggaï* springs, goes. — Or poss. < **vagga-*, analogical past part. to Pkt. *vajjaï* moves [...] < **vrajyati* (in Dard. Tor. *baj-* to go, Sh. úbreve; or < **vrajati*, see below) beside Sk[t]. *vrájati* moves: Pa. *vajati*, Pk[t]. *vayaï*; Sgh. *vadinu*. — A nasalized pres. stem **vrajati* in Ap. *vrācaḍa vajaï*, L[hd]. *vajaṇ*, Si. *vaaṇu*. — Similar change of stem in Pk[t]. *vajjaï* sounds (< **vadyate*, v.s.v. *bājnu*) > L[hd]. *vagaṇ* to sound, Si. *vagaṇu*, Guǰ. *vāgvũ* (beside regular *vajaṇu*, *vājvũ*). — Finally cf. Pa. *vaṅgati* walks (Sk[t]. dhātup. *vaṅgati*)" (TURNER 1931: 414).

208. **BILADRAM بلادرام (bilādrām)** *Map 32*

Village in the fertile part of the Khwazakhela-khwar valley, Tehsil of Khwazakhela.

The name has clearly an Indo-Aryan appearance. Could be T11497 *vātala-* 'windy, stormy': Woṭ. *bālái* 'wind'; Bašk. *bālā* 'wind, heavy rain'; Tor. *balai* 'wind', Hi. *bāl* + T6757 *dharman-* 'support, prop': Kal.rumb. *drāmī* → 'support against the wind'? Or a corrupted variant of Balogram?

209. **BILMAZ-SAR بلماز سر (bilmāz-sar)** *Map 27*

Mountain of about 2,750 mt near Malam-jabba, on the boundary with Shangla, Tehsil of Charbagh.

Pšt. 'profane, unholy, irreligious (*bilmāz*, RAVERTY) mountain'.

210. **BINKAT بينكټ (binkaṭ)** *Map 37*

Small village on the left bank of the Swāt river, Tehsil of Khwazakhela. It is called Nawe-kalai on the Russian map and Google Earth.

According to HAKIMZAY (1997: 31), Binkaṭ is the name of a small descent of the Gujar Chauhan Khel.

211. **BINWAR-BANDA بنور بانده (binwar-bānḍa)** *Map 12*

Pasture located on the mountain separating the the Deolai-khwar valley from the Qalagai-khwar valley, Tehsil of Kabal.

HAKIMZAY (1997: 32) analyses Binoṛəy as a derived of Skt. *beni* 'The junction of two rivers as that of Ganges and Jumna at Allahabad, India' (cf. T12094 *vēṇi* 'river confluence': N. B. *beni* 'confluence of two rivers'). In the entry *vēṇi-*, TURNER asks if it could be the same as *vēṇi-*[1] 'braided hair', seen by KUIPER (1948: 32) as a ← Muṇḍa: see KEWA III 253 and EWAia II 578. The identification of Binwar with Binoṛəy and the proposed etymology are improbable, as suggested by ROSSI, p.c., also quoting D'ERME 1972.

212. **BISHAI بشى (bišay)** *Map 53*

Group of houses in the narrow valley on the left bank of the upper Swāt river, Tehsil of Bahrain.

Tor. *biš* 'wooden beam'; Bašk. *bīš* 'main roof-beam'; Kal. *baš* 'rafter' (T11182 *váṁśya* 'crossbeam' [→ Par. *wē* 'roof beam', Psht. *bainš*, Waz. *wēša*, IIFL i 296]: Dam. *bãš*, *bā̃š* 'rafter', Paš.lauṛ. *waš*, Shum. *wā̃š*, *wāš*, Kal.rumb. *baš*, urt. *bhā̃š*, Bashk. *bīš*, Suv. *bẽš*, Phal. *bhẽš*, Sh. *bõi*. Cf. Bishgram and also Tor. *Bišā̃yi* 'a summer pasture'.

213. **BISHBANR بشبڼ (*bišbaṇ*)** *Map 25*

The most important village located in the narrow mountainous Bishbanr-khwar valley, Tehsil of Babuzai.

Pšt. 'Garden of the forest (*beša*, RAVERTY)'. Cf. also Bishgram.

214. **BISHBANR-KHWAR بشبڼ خوړ (*bišbaṇ-xwaṛ*)** *Map 25*

Stream flowing in lower Swāt, into the Ugad-khwar, Tehsil of Babuzai.

Cf. prec.

215. **BISHGRAM بشګرام (*bišgrām*)** *Map 46*

Group of houses in the narrow Olal-khwar valley, Tehsil of Bahrain. In STEIN 1930 it is called Wazirābād.

Dard. 'village of the main roof-beam', cf. Bishai. Or Dard. 'resting village': cf. T11947 *viśrama* 'rest': Pkt. *vissama*, *vīsa°* m. 'rest'; Sh. (LORIMER) *bišom* 'rest, peace, keeping still'; N. *bisā* 'rest, pause, halt (esp. of porters)'. Cf. also Bašk. *bišim-* 'to rest' (MORGENSTIERNE 1940: 228).

216. **BIZOBAN-KANDAO بزوبن کنډو (*bizoban-kaṇḍaw*)** *Map 5*

Pass leading from the Jolagram-khwar valley, Tehsil of Barikot, to the Tehsil of Kabal, near the boundary with Dir.

Pšt. 'pass of the goats'.

217. **BODIGRAM بوډیګرام (*boḍigrām*)** *Map 38*

Village in the fertile plain between the Harnoi-khwar and the right bank of the Swāt river, Tehsil of Maṭṭa.

Dard. 'village of the enlightenment (*bodhi*)'.

218. **BOLAT بولات (*bolāt*)** *Map 20*

Small village in the upper Saidu-khwar valley, Tehsil of Babuzai. We can possibly identify with this village the locality Balan, quoted by TUCCI (1958: 313).

Cf. Pšt. *buland* 'high, elevated, lofty' (RAVERTY). Cf. also Pšt. *Bālā́*?

219. **BOSTANI-SAR بوستاني سر (*bostāni-sar*)** *Map 2*

Mountain on the boundary with Buner, Tehsil of Barikot, at the end of the Kandak-khwar valley.

Cf. Pšt. *bostā́n* 'flower bed'.

220. **BUDAI بوډی (*buḍay*)** *Map 32*

Group of houses in the upper Khwazakhela-khwar valley, near Topsin, on the road to Shangla, Tehsil of Khwazakhela.

Pšt. *buḍáy* '(venerable) old man'.

221. **BUJABANR بجبڼ (*buǰabaṇ*)** *Map 47*

Group of houses located on the left side of the Swāt river, on the Baral-darra, Tehsil of Bahrain. Only on the Russian map.

IA: possibly 'garden of the birch trees': cf. T9570 *bhūrja* 'the birch tree Betula bhojpattra'; **bhaurja-* 'pertaining to the birch tree': Pa. *bhūja-* 'a kind of willow'; Pkt. *bhujja-*, *bhūja-* 'birch'; Panj. *bhoj* 'birch', Hi. Guǰ. *bhoj*. Or T9526 *bhujaṁga* 'snake': Pa. *bhujaṅga-*, *bhujaga-*, Pkt. *bhuaṁga-*; Panj. *bhuaṅg*, *bhavaṅg* 'a kind of snake': 'garden of the snakes'. However, cf. also T9525 *bhúja* 'arm' and *bhuj-* 'to enjoy': 'garden of the enjoyment'.

222. **BURAI بړی (*buṛay*)** *Map 33*

Group of houses located in the wide terraced Khwazakhela-khwar valley, Tehsil of Khwazakhela.

Pšt. *buṛáy* 'projection, protuberance, prong'. But cf. Bararai.

223. **BURA-SAR بوړا سر (*buṛā-sar*)** *Map 46*

Mountain of about 2,700 mt half-way between the Swāt river, the Olal-khwar and the Shanku stream, Tehsil of Bahrain.

Cf. prec.: Pšt. *buṛáy* 'projection, protuberance, prong'. To be excluded Pšt. *buṛa* 'table land, flat mountain land' (RAVERTY).

224. **BURJAL-KANDAO برجل کنډو (*burǰal-kanḍaw*)** *Map 15*

Pass leading from Mahak to Taghma in the mountains near the Deolai-khwar valley, Tehsil of Kabal.

Pšt. 'pass of the dwelling (*borǰál*)'. ROSSI, p.c., suggests a link with Pšt. *burǰ* 'tower'.

225. **BURJOSAR-BANDA برجوسر بانډه (*burǰosar-bānḍa*)** *Map 42*

Pasture on the slopes above the upper Biha-khwar valley, Tehsil of Maṭṭa.

Pšt. *burǰ* 'tower, turret, bastion' or *barǰ* 'the bark of a tree, which is very slight and often used as paper'.

226. **CHAKUR چاقور (*čāqur*)** *Map 39*

Village at the foot of the hills bordering the fertile plain on the right bank of the Swāt river, Tehsil of Maṭṭa.

Cf. Phal. *čukrī* 'n. of a plant, Potentilla (?)'? According to HAKIMZAY (1997: 75), it could be *čāk* 'mill-stone'.

227. **CHALERA چلیړه (*čaleṛa*)** *Map 5*

Small village on the mountain above Khazana and the Jolagram-khwar valley, at the border with Dir, Tehsil of Barikot.

Cf. Bašk. *čēl* (prob. = *čhēl*) she-goat, Tor. *čhāl*, Phal. *čhēli*. + Pšt. dimin. sf. *-ṛay*? Cf. also Pšt. *čilay* 'young male kid'.

228. **CHALIAR چالیار (*čāliār*)** *Map 31*

Village in the plain on the left side of the Swāt river, near Khwazakhela, Tehsil of Khwazakhela.

Pšt. *čāl* 'gait, moition, movement' (+ sf. *-yār*), with reference to its strategic position on the main road.

229.-234. **CHAM چم (*čam*)** *Maps 32, 32, 39, 43, 45, 50*

Name of six groups of houses: 1) in the upper Khwazakhela-khwar valley, near Topsin, on the road to Shangla, Tehsil of Khwazakhela (on the map it is indicated in the same place of the Veterinary Hospital); 2) in the terraced Khwazakhela-khwar valley, Tehsil of Khwazakhela; 3) village at the foot of the hills bordering the fertile plain on the right bank of the Swāt river, Tehsil of Maṭṭa; 4) in the narrow Roringar-khwar valley, Tehsil of Maṭṭa (only on the Russian map); 5) village in the narrow valley on the right bank of the upper Swāt river, Tehsil of Bahrain. Quoted already by RAVERTY (1888); 6) village in the narrow valley on the right bank of the Swāt river, Tehsil of Bahrain.

Pšt. *čam* 'part, branch (of a tribe), clan; quartier, district' (cf. Geonyms).

235. **CHAMBAR چمبر (*čambar*)** *Map 49*

Group of houses in the upper Daral-khwar valley, Tehsil of Bahrain.

Pšt. *čanbár* 'fence, wall (around a house, castle, etc.)' (difficult Pšt. 'high (*bar*) quartier' for syntactic reasons: the right form would have been *bar-čam*).

236. **CHAMBAR-GHAKHAI چمبر غاښی (*čambar-γāx̌ay*)** *Map 49*

Mountain of about 5,000 mt north of Chambar at the source of the Daral-khwar and of the Utror, Tehsil of Bahrain.

Pšt. 'crest (of mountain) of Chambar'.

237. **CHAM-SERAI چم سیری (*čam-seray*)** *Map 38*

Group of houses on the hills on the right bank of an affluent of the Harnoi-khwar, Tehsil of Maṭṭa.

Cf. Cham and Serai.

238. **CHAM-SHAUR چم شور (*čam-šawr*)** *Map 40*

Group of houses in the Shaurai-khwar valley near Bar-shaur, Tehsil of Maṭṭa.

Pšt. 'quartier of Shaur' (cf. Shaurai-khwar).

239. **CHAM-SINPORA چم سینپوره (*čam-sinpora*)** *Map 38*

Small village in the fertile plain on the left bank of the Harnoi-khwar, north of Matta, Tehsil of Maṭṭa.

Pšt. 'quartier of Sinpora' (q.v.).

240. **CHAMTIA چمتیا (*čamtyā*)** *Map 32*

Village in the fertile part of the Khwazakhela-khwar valley, Tehsil of Khwazakhela. It is called Chamtalay (چمتلی *čamtaləy*) in STEIN 1930, on the Russian map and on Google Earth.

Cf. Cham.

241. **CHANCHAR چنچر (*čančar*)** *Map 37*

Group of houses on the slopes of the Dobar-sar towards the Swāt river, Tehsil of Khwazakhela. Only on the Russian map.

Cf. T4566 *cañcarin* '*moving rapidly', 'bee', °*rī*-: Pkt. *caṁcarīa*- 'bee'; N. *c̃ācari* 'partic. kind of bird'; Hi. *c̃ācrī* 'water running down over rocks, partic. kind of small bird'. Cf. also T4569 *cañcu* 'beak' [← Drav. EWAia I 368 with lit.]: Pkt. *caṁcu*- 'beak', Guǰ. *c̃āc* (whence *c̃ācaṛ*, °*caṇ* 'flea'?).

242. **CHANDA-KHORA چنده خوړه (*čanda-xwaṛa*)** *Map 8*

Small village at the foot of the Parrai-ghar on the right bank of the Swāt river, Tehsil of Kabal. Quoted already by RAVERTY (1888: 232).

Possibly Pšt. 'portion (*čánḍa*) of dry stream (*xwaṛá* 'sandy bottom of a ravine or watercourse, the dry bed of a river', RAVERTY)'. For the first element, see ADAMEC II 54 Chand Gundi, "A low hill on the road from Gargarok (Baluchistan) to Khwaja Ali".

243. **CHANDAKHWARA چنده خوړه (*čandaxwaṛa*)** *Map 9*

Village near Kabbal, in the vast and fertile plain on the right bank of the Swāt river, Tehsil of Kabal.

Cf. prec.

244. **CHANGAI-DOP-SAR چنګی دوپ سر (*čangay-dop-sar*)** *Map 8*

Mountain of about 2,000 mt height, on the boundary with Dir, Tehsil of Kabal.

Cf. foll. + dop (see geonyms).

245. **CHANGLALAI چینګلالی (*činglāləy*)** *Map 41*

Small village on the right bank of the Harnoi-khwar, on the last slopes of the Prangmansar, Tehsil of Maṭṭa.

Probably Pšt. *čangúl* 'measure of land equal to fifteen *jarībs*, or quarter of a plough' (RAVERTY) + dim. sf. *-ālay* → 'little čangúl'. See also ADAMEC II 55 Changūlak, "A village in Naozad, said to contain 40 Barakzai houses" and ADAMEC V 109 Changul, "a village lying to the north of the Baba Wali Kotal on the left bank of the Arghandab".

246. **CHANKOLAI چینکولی (*činkolay*)** *Map 33*

Village located in a lateral terraced valley of the Khwazakhela-khwar valley, Tehsil of Khwazakhela.

Cf. Pšt. *čankāw* 'sprinkling water' (RAVERTY) + denominative and qualifying sf. *-(o)lay* (see DARMESTETER 1888-1890).

247. **CHANMARANG-KANDAO چانمارنګ کنډو (*čānmārang-kanḍaw*)** *Map 13*

Pass north of the Manrai-khwar valley, leading from the Tehsil of Kabal to the Tehsil of Kabal.

Cf. Pšt. *čān(d)mārə́y* 'firing (rifle, etc.); execution by shooting'.

248. **CHAPRAI چپړی (*čapṛay*)** *Map 44*

Group of houses located in a lateral valley on the right bank of the Swāt river, Tehsil of Bahrain.

Cf. T4696 *carpaṭa-* 'lying flat to the head (of ears); palm of hand, thin biscuit of flour' [according to KEWA I 377 ← Drav. (more dubitative EWAia III 182), but KUIPER 1948: 57-60 considers it a lw. ← Muṇḍa]: Pkt. *cappuḍī-*'snapping the fingers'; Ash. Waig. *čapāl* 'palm of hand'; Ash. *čapḗṛ* 'flat of hand'; Paš. *čapilū* 'slap', Kal. rumb. *čapŕéaka*; Si. *capiṛī* 'a kind of unleavened bread', *cāpoṛo* 'flat clod of dried earth'; Lhd. *capṛī* 'small flat piece of wood'; Panj. *capṛī* 'small flat piece of wood'; Hi. *cāpaṛ* 'flattened, level', *cāpṛī* 'cake of cowdung'. Cf. in particular the Lhd., Panj. and Hi. words. Probably to be excluded Pšt. *čāpṛā́x* 'open; spacious, wide'. See ADAMEC III 73 Chapri, "pass over the Band-i-Baian, crossed by a road leading from Taiwara to Daulat Yar".

249. **CHAPRAI-BANDA چپړی بانډه (*čapṛay-bānḍa*)** *Map 11*

Pasture on the boundary with Dir, at the end of the Kolalai-khwar valley, Tehsil of Kabal.

Cf. prec.

250.-251. **CHAR چړ (*čaṛ*)** *Maps 43, 47*

Name of two groups of houses: 1) in the upper Roringar-khwar valley, near the boundary with Dir, Tehsil of Maṭṭa; 2) in the mountains above the upper Baral-darra valley, Tehsil of Bahrain.

Pšt. *čaṛ* 'ford (of a river)'. Or, less probable, Pšt. *čur* 'basin, reservoir'.

252.-254. **CHARAI چړی (*čaṛay*)** *Maps 24, 27, 44*

Name of three groups of houses: 1) in the high and narrow Spedar-khwar valley, Tehsil of Babuzai; 2) on the terraced hills above the upper Ugad-khwar valley, Tehsil of Charbagh; 3) in the mountainous upper Barwai-khwar valley, Tehsil of Maṭṭa.

Pšt. *čārí*, *čārə́y* 'wooden tool for making terraces used in irrigation; shoulder blade'? Cf. Bahadur Khelo Charai.

255.-256. **CHARAI-KANDAO چړی کنډو (*čaṛay-kanḍaw*)** *Maps 46-47*

Name of two passes: 1) leading from the Olal-khwar valley to the Baral-darra valley, Tehsil of Bahrain (called Bahadur-khelo-charai-kandao on the Russian map); 2) on the boundary with Kohistan from the Baral-darra valley.

Cf. prec.

257. **CHARBAGH چارباغ (*čārbāγ*)** *Map 30*

The main village of the homonym Tehsil, on the left bank of the Swāt river, in a wide and fertile plain. Chhár-Bágh in the transcription of RAVERTY (1888: 233).

Pšt. 'garden of the ford' or 'the four gardens'.

258. **CHARBAGH-KHWAR چارباغ خوړ (*čārbāγ-xwaṛ*)** *Maps 29-30*

Stream flowing into the left bank of the Swāt river, Tehsil of Charbagh.

Cf. prec.

259. **CHARMA چارمه (*čārma*)** *Map 43*

Group of houses in the narrow Roringar-khwar valley, Tehsil of Maṭṭa.

Possibly, abbreviation of Pšt. *čārmaγz* 'walnut' (Juglans regia in ALAM 2011).

260. **CHATKARAI چتکړی (*čatkəṛay*)** *Map 43*

Group of houses located in the Roringar-khwar valley, Tehsil of Maṭṭa. Only on the Russian map.

Cf. Pšt. *čat* 'the roof of a house or room, ceiling, platform' + *kəṛay* 'done'?

261. **CHATURIA چاتوریه (*čāturya*)** *Map 40*

Group of houses in the narrow terraced valley of the Shaurai-khwar, Tehsil of Maṭṭa.

Cf. Ur. *čāturya* 'cleverness, ability, shrewdness, skilfulness, dexterity' (PLATTS)? Or a derived of 'four' (cf. Ur. *čaturtha* 'fourth part, quarter')? See ADAMEC VI 135 Chatur, Chotur, "A village on the Nuristan river, 4 miles southwest of Gadwal".

262. **CHAUTAR چوتر (*čawtar*)** *Map 15*

Group of houses in the mountainous valley of the Mahakai stream, Tehsil of Kabal.

Cf. prec.? Cf. Ur. *čūtaṛ* 'backside, bum, buttock, posteriors, rump, hip'? Cf. also Pšt. *čo(n)tará*, *čau(n)tará* 'platform, rise, elevation'?

263. **CHERE چیری (*čere*)** *Map 26*

Group of houses in the narrow mountainous Bishbanr-khwar valley, Tehsil of Babuzai.

Possibly cf. T4963 *chagalá* 'goat': Hi. *cherī*. Improbable Pšt. 'where' and T3645 Kho. (LORIMER) *čhɛr* 'bruised split grain'.

264. **CHERIPUN چېرپون (*čeripun*)** *Map 45*

Group of houses in a lateral valley on the right bank of the Swāt river on the slopes of the Babu-sar, Tehsil of Bahrain. Only on the Russian map.

Cf. prec. + T8339 *pūrṇá* 'filled, full': Hi. *pūn* 'full'.

265. **CHHERI چېرى (*čeri*)** *Map 44*

Group of houses in the mountainous Barwai-khwar valley, Tehsil of Maṭṭa.

Cf. Chere.

266. **CHIL-SHOGGAI چيل شوګى (*čil-šogay*)** *Map 18*

Village located in the Saidu-khwar valley, on the opposite side of Saidu-sharif, Tehsil of Babuzai, at the foot of the Kosa mountain.

Pšt. *šāgə́y* 'low mountain, mountain foothills, foot of a mountain' + Pšt. *čilu* 'a kind of herb or vegetable' (RAVERTY).

267. **CHINA-KANDAO چينه کنډو (*čina-kanḍaw*)** *Map 35*

Pass leading from the northern Khwazakhela valley to the Bargin-khwar valley, near the Churlak-sar, Tehsil of Khwazakhela.

Pšt. 'pass of the spring'.

268. **CHINA-KILI چينه کلى (*čina-kəlay*)** *Map 14*

Small village located in the narrow Deolai-khwar valley, between Dolai and Dheri, Tehsil of Kabal.

Pšt. 'village of the spring'.

269. **CHINA-SAR چينه سر (*čina-sar*)** *Map 46*

Mountain of about 3,300 mt at the end of a lateral narrow valley of the Olal-khwar valley, Tehsil of Bahrain.

Pšt. 'mountain of the spring'.

270. **CHINGAI چينګى (*čingay*)** *Map 5*

Village in the plain on the Jolagram-khwar on the right bank of the Swāt river, Tehsil of Barikot.

Pšt. 'small (sf. *-gay*) spring (*čina*)'. Cf. also Pšt. *čing* 'open, gaping (of a mouth, beak)'; *čungí* 'local duty, municipal tax'; *čang* 'hook (for drawing a bucket up from a well, etc.)'; etc. See ADAMEC III 80 Chingurak, "A pass over the hills in the northwest corner of Kala Nao. At the north foot of the kotal is the Chashma Chingurak, a strong spring of good water, which is said never to dry up. From this place a good easy camel track leads up to the kotal", and ADAMEC IV 165 Chingar, "The name given in Maitland's diary to some scattered khirgah villages west of the Dara-i-Suf subdistrict".

271. **CHINGAI-BANDA چینګی باندہ (*čingay-bāṇḍa*)** *Map 15*

Pasture in the slopes of the Mahakai stream valley, Tehsil of Kabal.

Pšt. 'pasture of the small spring'. Cf. prec.

272. **CHINGALAI چینګلی (*čingalay*)** *Map 30*

Group of houses on the hills sloping towards the left bank of the Swāt river, Tehsil of Charbagh.

Cf. prec. or Ur. *cangel* 'a herb which springs out of ruined buildings (the seed of which, called *k͟hubāzī*, is used in medicine)' (PLATTS). Cf. also Changlalai?

273. **CHIRAI چیری (*čiray*)** *Map 48*

Group of houses in the terraced Daral-khwar valley, Tehsil of Bahrain.

Cf. Chere.

274. **CHITOR چیتوړ (*čitoṛ*)** *Map 19*

Small village in the fields at the confluence between the Saidu-khwar and the Marghuzar-khwar, Tehsil of Babuzai.

HAKIMZAY (1997: 73) interprets it as *chet* 'consciousness' + *or* 'fire', but then he states that the meaning could be 'the place where the corpses are burned', as *chita* would identify "the place where wood is put in order to burn deads". Not fully convincing: instead, cf. Pšt. *čit* 'flat, plane' + *-or/ṛ*?

275. **CHOARO-KANDAO چورو کنډو (*čwaro-kanḍaw*)** *Map 11*

Pass near the Qalagai-banda area, leading to Dir, Tehsil of Kabal. On Google Earth it is called Chopro-kandao.

Pšt. 'pass of the ravines (*čur*, pl. obl.)'.

276. **CHOBEK چوبک (*čobek*)** *Map 47*

Group of houses in the narrow valley on the left bank of the Swāt river, Tehsil of Bahrain.

Cf. Pšt. *čobák* 'drumstick'? See ADAMEC IV 167 Chobaki, "village at the head of the Dara Gaokush in Dara-i-Suf".

277. **CHODGRAM چودګرام (*čodgrām*)** *Map 53*

Group of houses in the narrow valley on the right bank of the upper Swāt river, Tehsil of Bahrain. Quoted already by RAVERTY (1888: 237) as Chawat-Grám.

Cf. T4605 *caturdaśa-* 'fourteen': Tir. *čauda*, Paš. *čadäi*, Niṅg. *ċaudēs*, Shum. *ċäudas*, Gaw. *ċudāš*, Bašk. *čoundə*, Tor. *čattẽš*, Lhd. *côdã̄*, mult. *côḍã̄*, khet. *caudẵ*, Panj. *caudã̄* → 'fourteen villages'? Or cf. T4600 *caturtha-* 'fourth': Paš. weg. *čõṛe* 'on 4th day, i.e. three days hence', lauṛ. *čauṛak* (< **cauṭ(h)*<-> with abnormal development > **cauḍ*), Shum. *čõṛĩn* (similarly < **cauṭh*<-> > **cauḍ* → Ḍ. *cauḍé-dos*). New name Bālākoṭ (Pšt. 'upper castle'): SULTAN-I-ROME 2016: 23, 142, 197.

278. CHOHRIA چوهریه (*čohrya*) *Map 24*

Village in the mountains above the Spedar-khwar valley, Tehsil of Babuzai

Cf. Pšt. *čuhā́ṛay* 'trash-picker'? Cf. however T5070 **chōkara-* 'boy': Pkt. *chōhara-* 'boy', Si. *chuharu*, Lhd. *chohur*, awāṇ. *chòr*, Panj. *chohar*, Hi. *chohrā*? See ADAMEC V 116 Chuhara, "village located west of Kala-i-Rashid, on the Surkhab Rud in Zabul province".

279.-280. CHOKEL-BANDA چوکل بانډه (*čokel-bānḍa*) *Map 52*

Name of two pastures located on the slopes of the Mankial-khwar valley, Tehsil of Bahrain. Quoted already by RAVERTY (1888: 237).

Kal. *čõk* (**čoŋk*) 'thorn': 'thorny pasture'.

281. CHOKEL-KANDAO چوکل کنډو (*čokel-kanḍaw*) *Map 52*

High pass leading from the Mankial-khwar valley to the Swāt river valley, Tehsil of Bahrain.

Cf. prec.: 'pass of Chokel'.

282. CHONGIALA-SAR چونګیاله سر (*čongyāla-sar*) *Map 16*

Mountain bordering the Deolai-khwar valley, at the frontier with Matta, Tehsil of Kabal.

Cf. Pšt. *čangúray* 'piece, fragment (e.g., of rock)' + sf. *-yāl* (on this sf., see s.v. Mankial).

283. CHOPAL چوپال (*čopāl*) *Map 43*

Village in the cultivated fields of the Roringar-khwar valley, Tehsil of Maṭṭa. Only on the Russian map.

Pšt. *čopāṛ, čopāl* 'summer-house, temporary dwelling, pavillion, generally made of the branches of trees' ← IA. (RAVERTY).

284. CHOPALU-KANDAO چوپالو کنډو (*čopālu-kanḍaw*) *Map 12*

Pass leading to Dir from the Jarendo-bela-khwar valley, Tehsil of Kabal.

Pšt. 'Pass of the Chopalu-sar'.

285. CHOPALU-SAR چوپالو سر (*čopālu-sar*) *Map 12*

Mountain on the border with Dir, near the Jarendo-bela-khwar valley, Tehsil of Kabal.

Pšt. 'mountain of the summer-house': cf. Chopal.

286. CHOPRA-SAR چوپړه سر (*čopṛa-sar*) *Map 32*

Mountain of about 2,300 mt on the border with Shangla, Tehsil of Khwazakhela.

Cf. prec.

287. **CHORPUNARI چورپنړی (*čorpunari*)** *Map 13*

Village on the hills between the Jarendo-bela-khwar valley and the Manrai-khwar valley, Tehsil of Kabal.

Cf. Pšt. *čur* '1. powder, sawdust; 2. robbery, raid; 3. ravine, gully; 4. sharp stone (for slaughtering cattle)' (PASHTOON); RAVERTY only 'ravine, chasm, fissure, gully' + *puṇəy* 'roll of cotton for spinning from'?

288. **CHOTAR-BANDA چوتار بانډه (*čotār-bānḍa*)** *Map 12*

Pasture in the mountainous upper Deolai-khwar valley, Tehsil of Kabal, near the border with Dir.

Cf. Chautar.

289. **CHOTKAN چوتکن (*čotkan*)** *Map 50*

Group of houses in the narrow valley on the right bank of the upper Swāt river, Tehsil of Bahrain. Only on the Russian map.

Et. unkn.

290. **CHUPRIAL چپریال (*čupryāl*)** *Map 39*

Main village of the Harnoi-khwar valley surrounded by cultivated fields, Tehsil of Maṭṭa.

Cf. Chopra-sar, + sf. *-yāl*. HAKIMZAY (1997: 69-70) identifies in it Ur. *chupar* 'room' + *yāl* 'water'. The second part remains doubtful (on this sf., see Mankial).

291. **CHURARAI چوړړی (*čurṛəy*)** *Map 45*

Village in the narrow valley on the left bank of the Swāt river, Tehsil of Bahrain. Actual name Madyan. Cf. also Zara-churarai. Quoted already by RAVERTY (1888: 236).

Cf. Pšt. (← IA) *čawṛ*, *čur* 'destroyed, desolated, deserted, ruined' (RAVERTY) + dimin. sf. *-ṛay* (but cf. also Pšt. *čuṛ* 'the part of a door which revolves in a socket in the lintel and serves the purpose of a hinge', RAVERTY). Cf. also *čur* 'ravine, chasm, fissure, gully' (RAVERTY) + the same dimin. sf. According to HAKIMZAY (1997: 67-68), it is formed by Hi. *chhor* 'border, edge, end, bank, boundary' + *ṛay* 'earth, land', with the global meaning 'earth of frontier'. But cf. T5064 *chēda* 'section, piece': Si. *cheṛo* 'end'; Guǰ. *cheṛɔ* 'end, boundary', and Ur. *chor* 'Border, edge, margin, bank, shore; limit, boundary; side, end, extremity, tip, point, summit, brow (of a hill)'.

292. **CHUR-BANDA چور بانډه (*čur-bānḍa*)** *Map 12*

Pasture in the Jarendo-bela-khwar valley, Tehsil of Kabal, near the boundary with Dir.

Pšt. 'pasture of the ravine (*čur*)'.

293. **CHURKHAI چورخی (*čurxay*)** *Map 1*

Village in the Kotah-khwar valley, Tehsil of Barikot, down the Mora-sar.

Cf. prec. + sf. *-xay* (? diminutive? → 'small ravine'?).

294.-295. CHURLAK-SAR چورلک سر (*čurlak-sar*) *Maps 27, 35*

Name of two mountains: 1) near the Tambagat-khwar, Tehsil of Charbagh; 2) between the Bargin-khwar and the Khwazakhela-khwar (2,300 mt), Tehsil of Khwazakhela.

Pšt. 'turning (*čurlák*) mountain', but cf. also Pšt. *čurláka* 'wooden top'.

296. CHUWA چووه (*čuwa*) *Map 1*

Group of houses at the spring of the Kotah-khwar, Tehsil of Barikot, on the slopes on the boundary with Malakand.

Cf. Pšt. *čawá* 'small irrigation well (in a melon field)'.

297. DABARGAI ډبرګی (*ḍabargay*) *Map 46*

Group of houses in a lateral narrow valley of the Olal-khwar valley, Tehsil of Bahrain. Only on the Russian map.

Pšt. *ḍabára* 'stone, rock, pebble' and *ḍabarkə́y, ḍabargə́y* 'pebble'.

298. DABNA دبنا (*dabnā*) *Map 53*

Group of houses in a valley on the right bank of the upper Swāt river, Tehsil of Bahrain.

IA. Cf. T5561 **ḍubb-* 'to sink': Panj. *ḍubbṇā*, Hi. *ḍū̆bnā*; T9272 **buḍyati* 'sinks': Si. *b̲uḍ̲aḍu*, Lhd. *buḍḍan*; Panj. *buḍḍṇā*; cf. Pšt. *ḍub* 'sunk, submerged'. Cf. also Pšt. *doāba* 'a country between two rivers, twice irrigated land'.

299. DAD ډډ (*ḍaḍ*) *Map 32*

Group of houses located in the mountainous upper Khwazakhela-khwar valley, Tehsil of Khwazakhela.

Pšt. *ḍaḍ* 'hollow'. To be excluded Pšt. *dad* 'wild animal, beast'.

300. DADALBHO ددلبهو (*dadalbho*) *Map 54*

Mountain of about 5,850 mt on the boundary with Chitral and Gilgit, Tehsil of Bahrain.

The second part is prob. connected with T8141 **pāhāḍa* 'rock, hill': K. *pahār* 'mountain', Lhd. Panj. Ku. *pahāṛ*; etc. For the first element cf. T6137 **danḍāli* 'boundary ridge'?

301. DADARILI-AN ددريلي ان (*dadarili-an*) *Map 54*

Pass leading from the upper Ushu-gol valley to Gilgit, Tehsil of Bahrain.

Cf. T6495 *dūrá-* 'distant': Waig. *dudār* 'distant', Kho. *dudéri*.

302. DAD-BANDA ډډ بانډه (*ḍaḍ-bānḍa*) *Map 2*

Pasture in the higher narrow Kandak-khwar valley, Tehsil of Barikot.

Cf. Dad.

303. **DADHRAH** ددهره **(*ḍaḍhrah*)** *Map 8*

Village on the right bank of the Swāt river, on the Dadhrah-khwar, in a small valley, Tehsil of Kabal. = Dadahara (SULTAN-I-ROME 2016: 60).

Cf. foll.

304. **DADHRA-KHWAR** ددهره خوړ **(*ḍaḍhra-xwaṛ*)** *Map 8*

Short stream flowing into the Swāt river on the right side, near Dadhra, Tehsil of Kabal.

Cf. T6882 **dhōdda-* 'hollow, swollen': N. *dhodro, dhotro* 'hollow'; and T5577 **ḍhaḍḍhara-* 'hollow': Pkt. *ḍhaḍḍhara-* 'old'; Si. *ḍhaḍharu* 'hollow in treetrunk; belly of a vessel'.

305. **DADPANRAI** ډيډ پاڼی **(*ḍiḍpāṇəy*)** *Map 38*

Village in the fertile plain on the left bank of the Harnoi-khwar, north of Matta, Tehsil of Maṭṭa.

Pšt. *ḍuḍ* 'lotus flower' + *pāṇəy* 'leaf': 'leaf of the lotus flower'.

306.-307. **DAGAI** ډاګی **(*ḍāgəy*)** *Maps 8, 41*

Name of two villages: 1) on the right bank of the Swāt river, Tehsil of Kabal, in the wide and fertile plain of Kabal; 2) group of houses in the narrow mountainous upper Harnoi-khwar valley, Tehsil of Maṭṭa.

Pšt. *ḍāgə́y* 'low mound of earth along the walls of a peasant's house'. Differently HAKIMZAY (1997: 84), for whom it means *maydān*, 'place'.

308. **DAKKO-BANDA** ډکو بانډه **(*ḍako-bānḍa*)** *Map 12*

Pasture in the upper Deolai-khwar valley, Tehsil of Kabal, near the border with Dir.

See SULTAN-I-ROME 2016: 486: "*Dhaka chiragah*: Communal grazing land of a village, *tal* or *qaum*, etc.; non-cropped land and usually *shamilat*. *Dhaka darakhtan*: Non-cropped forestland; any non-cropped land bearing trees, either timber or scrub forests or both". Other, less probable, hypothesis: Pšt. 'pasture of the bandits (*ḍākú, ḍākamā́r*)'.

309. **DAKORAK** دکوړک **(*dakoṛak*)** *Map 30*

Village in the wide plain of Charbagh on the left bank of the Swat river, north of Charbagh, Tehsil of Charbagh. It is called Dokarak on the Russian map.

Cf. T5605 [1]**ḍhōṅga-* 'projecting part of body': Shum. *ḍuā̃lik* 'knee', *ḍuṅgurik* 'elbow', Savi *ḍuiṅgya*'elbow, ankle-bone', etc. Cf. also T5603 **ḍhōkka-* 'rock': Kho. (LORIMER) *ḍok* 'high ground, hillock, heap'; Hi. *ḍhok* 'large piece of broken stone'.

310. **DAM** ډوم **(*ḍum*)** *Map 47*

Group of houses on the left side of the Swāt river, north of the Baral-darra, Tehsil of Bahrain.

Pšt. *ḍum* 'a caste of singers and musicians, the females of which dance and sing in public'.

311. **DAMAKAL دماکال (*ḍamākāl*)** *Map 23*

Group of houses south of Manglaor, in the hills bordering the lower Ugad-khwar valley, Tehsil of Babuzai.

Pšt. *ḍuma-kəlay* 'village of the Dums'? Pšt. *dāmān* 'skirt, foot, or declivity of a mountain; plain' (RAVERTY) / *dāmān, dāmana* 'skirt, hem of a skirt; foot (of a hill, mountain); valley; summer pasture' (ASLANOV) can be excluded, as it always used for villages at the foot of mountains and not hills (ROSSI, p.c.).

312. **DAMAMA دمامه (*ḍamāma*)** *Map 39*

Group of houses in the hills on the right bank of the Swāt river, Tehsil of Maṭṭa.

Cf. prec.: Pšt. *ḍuma* 'of the Dums'? According to HAKIMZAY (1997: 85), Pšt. *ḍamāme* is a 'musical instruments', but he thinks here to *ḍumā*, a Hindu king.

313. **DAMBAR-KANDAO دمبر کنډو (*dambar-kanḍaw*)** *Map 40*

Pass north of the Manrai-khwar valley, leading from the Tehsil of Kabal to that of Maṭṭa.

Cf. foll.

314. **DAMBAR-SAR دمبر سر (*dambar-sar*)** *Map 11*

Mountain between the Deolai-khwar valley and the Qalagai-khwar valley, Tehsil of Kabal. Dambar is also the name of a mountain in Central Afghanistan

Probably a variant of Pšt. *ḍabára* 'stone, rock, pebble' (see Dabargai). However, cf. also Pšt. *ḍanbara* 'the name of a tree producing a small black berry somewhat like pepper in size and flavour; a species of the *nigella*, probably the black cumin of Scripture. In the mountain districts north of Peshāwer, where pepper is not obtainable, it is used as such' (RAVERTY).

315. **DAMGHAR دمغار (*damγār*)** *Map 17*

Village located in the fertile plain on the right bank of the Swāt river, Tehsil of Kabal. Quoted already by RAVERTY (1888: 230): "This also is a large village, close to which, on the left hand, is one branch of the river of Suwád", and (*ibid.*: 231): "Damghár is one of the most noted places in the valley, but not a word do we hear about it". Always according to RAVERTY (*ibid.*: 230), citing Akhund Darweza, Akbar was building here a fort.

Pšt. 'pit (*γār*) of the Dams'. According to the locals, the right form would be Damx̌ār: 'the town (*x̌ār*)' of the Ḍams.

316.-317. **DAND ډنډ (*ḍanḍ*)** *Maps 37, 39*

Name of two villages: 1) on the slopes of the Dandai-sar, dividing the Paiti-khwar valley from the Swat river valley, Tehsil of Khwazakhela; 2) Group of houses on the slopes of the Shah-dop-sar near Baskhela, Tehsil of Maṭṭa (only on the Russian map).

Pšt. *ḍanḍá* 'club, stick; handle; trunk': cf. T6128 *daṇḍá-* 'stick, club': Pkt. *daṁḍa-* 'stick'; Sir. *ḏanḍā*, Si. *ḍanḏō*, etc. This kind of semantics is common in mountain (ROSSI, p.c.). To be excluded Pšt. *ḍanḍ* 'lake', not present in these places.

318.-319. **DANDA** ډنډا **(*danḍā*)** *Map 46*

Name of two groups of houses in the Tehsil of Bahrain, in a lateral valley of the Olal-khwar and on the mountainous Nali-darra.

Pšt. *ḍanḍá* 'club, stick; handle; trunk', and *ḍánḍa* 'section of a field in the form of a long strip (on which rice is grown)': cf. prec.

320.-321. **DANDAI** ډنډی **(*ḍanḍay*)** *Map 40*

Name of two villages on the slopes of the Prangman-sar, Tehsil of Maṯṯa.

Cf. prec.

322. **DANDAI-SAR** ډنډی سر **(*ḍanḍay-sar*)** *Map 37*

Mountain of about 2,100 mt, Tehsil of Khwazakhela. Only on the Russian map.

Cf. prec.

323. **DANDARAI** ډنډاری **(*ḍanḍāṛay*)** *Map 41*

Group of houses in the narrow upper Harnoi-khwar valley, in Tehsil of Maṯṯa. Only on the Russian map.

Pšt. 'small stick' (cf. Dand + dim. sf. *-uṛay*). Pšt. *ḍanḍārá* 'large red wasp or hornet' and Pšt. *ḍanḍ* 'lake' + dim. sf. *-uṛay* can be excluded.

324. **DAND-BANDA** ډنډ بانډه **(*ḍanḍ-bānḍa*)** *Map 49*

Pasture in the upper Daral-khwar valley, Tehsil of Bahrain.

Cf. Dand.

325.-326. **DANDE** ډنډې **(*ḍanḍe*)** *Maps 16, 33*

Name of two groups of houses: 1) in a mountainous lateral valley of the Deolai-khwar valley at the frontier with the Tehsil of Maṯṯa, Tehsil of Kabal; 2) near the top of the Khardu-sar, Tehsil of Khwazakhela.

Cf. Danda.

327. **DAND-KANDAO** ډنډ کنډو **(*ḍanḍ-kandāw*)** *Map 44*

Pass leading to the Tehsil of Bahrain from the upper Barwai-khwar valley, Tehsil of Maṯṯa. Only on the Russian map.

Cf. Dand.

328. **DANDO** ډنډو **(*ḍanḍo*)** *Map 27*

Group of houses located in the mountainous upper Tambagat-khwar valley, Tehsil of Charbagh.

Cf. Danda.

329. **DANDUN-QALA دندون قلا (*ḍanḍun-qalā*)** *Map 18*

Village in the Tehsil of Babuzai, in the periphery of Mingaora, in the wide plain on the left side of the Swat river.

Cf. Danda. (+ sf. *-un*?) + Pšt. *qalā* 'castle'.

330. **DANG-ARKOT-QALA دنگ ارکوټ قلا (*dang-arkoṭ-qalā*)** *Map 38*

Small village in the plain on the right bank of the Harnoi-khwar, near Arkot, Tehsil of Maṭṭa.

Pšt. 'Castle of the high Arkot (q.v.)'. For *dang* cf. AKBAR *dang* 'haut, élevé, éminent' and PASHTOON 'tall, strapping' (examples: *yaw lwaṛ dang saṛay* 'tall person' and *danga māṇəy* 'tall building')

331. **DANGBANR دنگبڼ (*dangbaṇ*)** *Map 47*

Group of houses in the narrow Baral-darra valley, Tehsil of Bahrain.

Pšt. 'high (*dang*) garden'. Another possibility is Pšt. 'garden of the *ḍāngəy*': *ḍāngəy* 'name of a tree from which clubs or sticks are made, and which bears a fruit like an apple' (RAVERTY).

332. **DANGRAM دنگرام (*dangrām*)** *Map 21*

Village in the fertile part of the Jambil-khwar valley, Tehsil of Babuzai.

"Two other places can also be located with great probability: Dhānyapura and Naitarī of *Vinaya* seem to me correspond reciprocally to Dangram and to Nat-mera" (TUCCI 1997: 78). If TUCCI's proposal is correct, we can see in °*dan* a derived of Skt. *dhānyà-* 'pertaining to grain; grain, corn; rice' (T6778: Pkt. *dhaṇṇa-* 'corn, growing rice', Si. *dan* 'growing rice'; see also EDGERTON 1953, 2: s.v.): 'village of the grain'.

333. **DARAL-KHWAR درال خوړ (*darāl-xwaṛ*)** *Maps 48-49*

Stream flowing directly into the right bank of the Swat river from the mountains on the boundary with Dir, Tehsil of Bahrain.

Cf. Skt. *dhārā̆-* 'stream', in *dhāra-pūta-* (RV) 'streaming down' (T6788): Pkt. *dhāra-* 'spring water', Si. *dhāra* 'stream, current', Lhd. *dhār* 'stream (esp. of milk)', awāṇ. *dhār* 'current'; Panj. *dhār* 'stream, current'; Si. *daraya* 'torrent, heavy rain', + a sf. *-al*. Cf. also Sau *d(h)år, d(h)ār* 'mountain' (BUDDRUSS 1967: 94)? We can here also identify the sf. *-āl/ -yāl* indicating water (see also HAKIMZAY 1997: 173-174; on this sf., see s.v. Mankial).

334. **DAR-BANDA در بانډه (*dar-bānḍa*)** *Map 44*

Pasture in the mountainous upper Barwai-khwar valley, Tehsil of Maṭṭa. According to M.A. DINAKHEL (p.c.), the correct spelling of this toponym is Daral-banḍa, 'pasture of the Daral'.

Pšt. 'pasture of the valley (Pšt. *dará, darrá* 'valley; gorge, ravine, mountain pass)'.

335.-336. **DARD** درد ***(dard)*** *Maps 16, 32*

Name of two groups of houses: 1) in a mountainous lateral valley of the Deolai-khwar valley at the frontier with the Tehsil of Maṭṭa, Tehsil of Kabal; 2) in the Khwazakhela-khwar valley, Tehsil of Khwazakhela, called Dand ('pool, lake') on the Russian map.

Ethnic name.

337. **DARDIAL** دردیال ***(daryāl)*** *Map 12*

Village in the terraced Jarendo-bela-khwar valley, Tehsil of Kabal.

Ethnic name + sf. *-yāl* (on this sf., see s.v. Mankial).

338. **DARMAI** درمی ***(darmay)*** *Map 44*

Village in the wide plain of the Barwai-khwar, Tehsil of Maṭṭa.

Cf. Pšt. *darma* 'a reed from which mats are made; a shepherd's pipe' (RAVERTY). HAKIMZAY (1997: 78, 149) links this toponym to the *dharma* and to Skt. *mahi* 'earth, land' (cf. T9974 *mahī* 'the earth': Pa. Pkt. *mahī-* 'the earth'), with the resulting translation 'earth of the dharma'.

339. **DAROZGAR** دروزگر ***(darozgar)*** *Map 38*

Group of houses in a lateral valley of the Harnoi-khwar valley, at the foot of the Badkot, Tehsil of Maṭṭa.

Pšt. *daruzgar* 'carpenter, joiner' (RAVERTY).

340. **DARRA** دره ***(dara)*** *Map 29*

Group of houses in the upper Malakad-khwar valley, Tehsil of Charbagh.

Pšt. (Prs.) 'valley'. See Glossary of the Geonyms.

341. **DEDAWAR** ډېډور ***(dedawar)*** *Map 6*

Village at the foot of the hills on the right bank of the Swāt river, Tehsil of Barikot.

Cf. Pšt. *ḍiḍa* 'a bottle stopper, a piece of wood in the centre of the lower millstone on which the upper one revolves' + sf. *-war*?

342. **DELAI** ډېلی ***(ḍelay)*** *Map 17*

Village in the fertile plain, right on the right bank of the Swāt river, Tehsil of Kabal.

Cf. foll. In HAKIMZAY's opinion (1997: 77) the meaning of *deolai* in Ur. is 'small lamp', but it is not convincing.

343. **DEOLAI-KHWAR** دېولی خوړ ***(dewləy-xwaṛ)*** *Map 9*

Stream, whose terrain elevation above seal level is 885 metres, flowing from the mountains at the boundary with Dir into the right side of the Swāt river, near Kabbal, Tehsil of Kabal.

Cf. T6542 *dēvālaya-* 'temple': Pkt. *dēvālaa-*; Dm. *dēwalā́i* 'sky' (NTS xii 167); Panj. *dewālā, diw°* 'temple', A. *dewāl*, Hi. *dewālaī*? But cf. also Ur. *ḍe'olā* 'mound; high ground' (PLATTS)?

344.-353. DERAI ډېرى (*ḍerəy*) *Maps 14, 17, 34, 37, 41, 44, 45, 45, 46, 46*

Name of ten villages: 1) main village in the Deolai-khwar valley, Tehsil of Kabal; 2) in the fertile plain on the right bank of the Swāt river, Tehsil of Kabal; its actual name is Baba-derai ('the residence of Baba'); 3) on the left bank of the Swāt river in the fertile plain north of Khwazakhela, Tehsil of Khwazakhela; 4) in the upper Roringar-khwar valley, near the boundary with Dir, Tehsil of Maṭṭa (only on the Russian map); 5) group of houses on the slopes of the Prangman-sar, in a lateral valley of the upper Harnoi-khwar valley, Tehsil of Maṭṭa (apparently called Kandar, Pšt. *kándra, kándara* 'ravine, hollow, depression', on the Russian map); 6) village in the wide plain of the Barwai-khwar, Tehsil of Maṭṭa; 7) in the narrow valley on the right bank of the Swāt river, Tehsil of Bahrain (only on the Russian map); 8) in the narrow valley on the left bank of the Swāt river, Tehsil of Bahrain; 9-10) on the slopes bordering the Olal-khwar valley near the Swat river and in the upper Olal-khwar valley, in the Tehsil of Bahrain.

Pšt. 'residence'. See Glossary of the Geonyms.

354. DERANPATAI ډېرانپټى (*ḍerānpəṭay*) *Map 38*

Small village in a lateral valley of the Harnoi-khwar valley, Tehsil of Maṭṭa.

Pšt. 'field of the manure pit (*ḍerā́n*)'.

355. DESAN-KANDAO ديسن كنډو (*desan-kanḍāw*) *Map 54*

Pass on a path leading from the main Swāt valley to the Gabral valley near Utror, Tehsil of Bahrain. Only on the Russian map.

Possibly cf. T6547 *dēśá* 'point, region, part; province, country': Pa. *dēsa-* 'place, country'; NiDoc. KharI. *deśa* 'region, country'; Pkt. *dēsa-* 'part, country'; Ash. *dešī* 'village', Wg. *dēš*; Kal.rumb. *dēš*, 'country', *dēša* 'far, distant'; Phal. *dēš, dīš* 'village'; Paš. kuṛ. *deš* 'cultivated field'; Hi. *des* 'a small country'.

356.-357. DEWAN ديوان (*dewān*) *Maps 52-53*

Name of two villages on the left and on the right bank of the Swāt river, south of Kalam, near the Mankial-khwar valley, Tehsil of Bahrain.

Pšt. *diwā́n* 'demons'.

358. DHERI ډهيري (*ḍheri*) *Map 14*

Big village in the upper Deolai-khwar valley, between the foot of the mountains and the fields bordering the stream, Tehsil of Kabal. On Google Earth it is called Shahderai. On the Russian map it is called Čaču-deray.

Cf. Derai.

359. DILBAN دلبان (*dilbān*) *Map 48*

Group of houses in the terraced Daral-khwar valley, Tehsil of Bahrain.

Tor. *ḍili°bān* 'a summer pasture of Bahrain'. For *ḍili* cf. T5536 **ḍala-*, etc. 'lump': Bašk. *dil* 'clod'; Lhd. *ḍilhī̃* (pl.) 'boulder, clod', Hi. *ḍīl* 'lump, ploughed land'; Si. *dali* 'clod of clay or earth', etc.

360. DIRLAM درلام (*dirlām*) *Map 53*

Group of houses in a valley on the left bank of the upper Swāt river, Tehsil of Bahrain.

Cf. Tor. *ḍiṛil* 'a type of grass'?

361. DIRO ديرو (*diro*) *Map 47*

Group of houses in the Gurnai-khwar valley, Tehsil of Bahrain.

Cf. Pšt. *dera* 'tent, dwelling'.

362. DIWANBUT ديوانبوټ (*diwānbuṭ*) *Map 24*

Group of houses in the mountainous upper Landai-khwar valley, Tehsil of Babuzai.

Pšt. *dew* 'devil, evil spirit' + *bhut* 'evil spirit, demon'.

363. DIWANGAR ديوانګر (*diwāngar*) *Map 54*

Lake on the Ushu-gol, Tehsil of Bahrain, indicated only on the Russian map. Nowadays it seems have disappeared.

Cf. prec.

364. DOBAR-SAR ډوبر سر (*ḍobar-sar*) *Map 36*

Mountain (2,700 mt) bordering to the north the Paiti-khwar valley, Tehsil of Khwazakhela.

Pšt. *ḍabára* 'stone, rock'. Cf. also Pšt. *ḍabəhā́r* 'thunder, roar'. The shape of the mountain is represented by two peaks: a link with '2' is also possible.

365. DOB-BANDA دوب بانډه (*dob-bānḍa*) *Map 13*

Pasture in the upper Manrai-khwar valley, towards the boundary with Dir, Tehsil of Kabal.

Pšt. 'meadow (*dob*) pasture' (see also *ḍub* 'dipped' or *ḍab* 'hollow, depression', DE CHIARA 2011: 209).

366. DODA دوده (*doda*) *Map 46*

Group of houses in the mountain in a lateral valley of the upper Olal-khwar valley, Tehsil of Bahrain.

Cf. Pšt. *dudá* 'soot', better than Pšt. *ḍuḍ* 'the lotus flower'. See ADAMEC VI 161 Dodamast, "A village one mile northwest of the Band-i-Qargha, on the way from Kabul to Paghman".

367. **DODA-DERAI دوده ډېرى (*doda-ḍerəy*)** *Map 48*

Group of houses in the terraced Daral-khwar valley, Tehsil of Bahrain. Only on the Russian map.

Cf. prec.

368. **DOGHALGAI ډوغلگى (*ḍoγalgay*)** *Map 27*

Group of houses in the mountainous upper Tambagat-khwar valley, Tehsil of Charbagh.

Pšt. 'place (*-gay*) of the hole/pit/hollow (*ḍuγál*)'.

369. **DOGHALGAI-KANDAO ډوغلگى كنډو (*doγalgay-kanḍaw*)** *Map 12*

Pass leading to Dir from the Deolai-khwar valley, Tehsil of Kabal.

Cf. prec.

370. **DOGHLAI ډوغلى (*ḍoγlay*)** *Map 40*

Group of houses in the Shaurai-khwar valley, Tehsil of Maṭṭa. Doghlahay on the Russian map.

Cf. Pšt. *ḍoγal* 'cavity, hole, pit, cavern, abyss' (RAVERTY).

371. **DOKADAI ډوكډى (*ḍokaday*)** *Map 34*

Group of houses in the periphery of Kotanai, on the low terraced hills on the left side of the Swat river, Tehsil of Khwazakhela.

Cf. foll.

372. **DOKAT-SAR ډوكټ سر (*ḍokaṭ-sar*)** *Map 10*

Mountain of about 1,620 mt of height, dividing the Ramogai-khwar valley and the Kotlay-khwar valley, Tehsil of Kabal.

Kal. *ḍhok* 'high forest' or Kal. *ḍuk* 'top' + T180 ^{2}*aṭṭa-* 'high; tower, watchtower' (non-Aryan according to KEWA I 25; see KUIPER 1938: 304): Paš. *aṭ* 'rock'.

373. **DOP ډوپ (*ḍup*)** *Map 34*

Small village in the plain on the left bank of the Swāt river, north of Khwazakhela, Tehsil of Khwazakhela.

Possibly IA 'submerged': cf. foll.

374. **DOPIALO-SAR ډوپيالو سر (*ḍopyālo-sar*)** *Map 1*

Peak of about 2,050 mt on the boundary with Malakand, on the spur separating the Kotah-khwar valley from the Kandak-khwar valley, Tehsil of Barikot.

Possibly cf. T5561 **ḍubb-* 'to sink', caus. **ḍōbb-* [Metath. of MIA. *buḍḍaï* < **buḍyati*]: Paš. *ḍub-* 'to be drowned', Mai. *ḍūb-*; Phal. *ḍup* 'sinking'; Sh. (Lor.) *ḍup* 'plunged in';

Panj. *ḍubbṇā*, Hi. *ḍūbnā*; T9272 **buḍyati* 'sinks': Si. *b̲uḏaḏu*, Lhd. *buḍḍan*; Panj. *buḍḍṇā*. + sf. *-yāl* (on this sf., see s.v. Mankial). The resulting meaning would be 'peak (cause) of drowning waters'.

375. **DOP-SAR دوپ سر (*ḍup-sar*)** *Map 18*

Mountain of about 1,600 mt, near the Saidu-khwar valley, Tehsil of Babuzai.

Cf. prec., but possibly abbreviation of Pšt. *ḍupkanə́y* 'hillock, heap, mound'.

376. **DORALAI دارولی (*doralay*)** *Map 47*

Group of houses located in the narrow valley on the left bank of the Swāt river, Tehsil of Bahrain.

Cf. Kal. *dur* 'house; door'? T6423 **dúr-* 'door': Paš. *dur* 'door', etc. + sf. *-alay*?

377. **DOSARA دوسره (*dosara*)** *Map 24*

Mountain of about 3,000 mt at the end of the Dosara-khwar valley, Tehsil of Babuzai, on the boundary with Shangla. Called Dosirri by DEANE (1895).

Pšt. 'Two heads'.

378. **DOSARA-KHWAR دوسره خوړ (*dosara-xwaṛ*)** *Map 24*

Stream located at an elevation of 2,322 meters above sea level, flowing into the Spedar-khwar from the boundary with Shangla, Tehsil of Babuzai.

Pšt. 'stream of Dosara (Sar)'.

379. **DOSHAGRAM دوشاگرام (*došāgrām*)** *Map 44*

Small village in the Barwai-khwar valley, near the confluence with the Swāt river, Tehsil of Maṭṭa. Only on the Russian map.

Cf. T6466 *duścara* 'difficult to pass': Pkt. *duccara-* 'difficult to enter'. According to HAKIMZAY (1997: 126), *doši* in Ur. would mean 'guilty'.

380. **DRE-BANDAI دری باندی (*dre-bānḍay*)** *Map 21*

Pasture in a lateral mountainous valley near Sangota, Tehsil of Babuzai.

Pšt. 'three pastures'.

381. **DRE-KHWAR دری خوړ (*dre-xwaṛ*)** *Map 28*

Intermittent stream located at an elevation of 882 meters above sea level flowing into the Ugad-khwar from the mountains at the boundary with Shangla, Tehsil of Charbagh.

Not to be linked with Pšt. 'three' ('three streams'), but cf. Daral-khwar: Skt. *dhārā̆-* 'stream', in *dhāra-pūta-* (RV) 'streaming down' (T6788): Pkt. *dhāra-* 'spring water', Si. *dhāra* 'stream, current'; Si. *daraya* 'torrent, heavy rain'.

382. **DUBA دوبه (*duba*)** *Map 24*

Group of houses located in the high and narrow Lewanai-khwar valley, Tehsil of Babuzai.

Possibly 'summer(-pasture)', Pšt. *dóbay* 'summer'? According to ROSSI, p.c., Pšt. *do'āba* 'a country between two rivers, twice irrigated land' (RAVERTY) is to be excluded for semantic and phonetic reasons.

383. **DURBAK-BANDA دربک بانډه (*durbak-bānḍa*)** *Map 22*

Pasture in the mountainous upper Jambil-khwar valley, near the boundary with Buner, Tehsil of Babuzai. It is called Dubrak-banda on the Russian map.

IA 'Pasture of the flowing stream'? Cf. T6788 *dhārā̆-* 'stream': Kho. (LORIMER) *dar* 'swift water in river', and T12223 *vyēti* 'goes away': Kho. *bik* 'to go'.

384. **DURE-SHAH دوری شاه (*dure-šāh*)** *Map 22*

Group of houses in the mountainous upper Landai-khwar valley, Tehsil of Babuzai.

Person's name.

385. **DURMAN-UNRA-SAR درمن اونه سر (*durman-uṇa-sar*)** *Map 12*

Mountain of about 2,730 mt on the boundary with Dir, in the upper part of the Qalagai-banda area, Tehsil of Kabal.

Cf. Unra sar + Pšt. *darman(d)* 'smooth, even, level (ground)' (RAVERTY).

386. **DUTPANRAI دوټپاڼی (*ḍuṭpāṇəy*)** *Map 40*

Group of houses in the narrow terraced valley of the Shaurai-khwar, Tehsil of Maṭṭa.

Possibly, Pšt. 'having lotus (*ḍuḍ*) leaves'. HAKIMZAY (1997: 43-44) mentions it as Ḍiṭpāṇəy, without any etymologic proposal.

387. **EHSANABAD احسان‌اباد (*ehsānābād*)** *Map 9*

Village in the wide and fertile Deolai-khwar valley, north of Sirsanai, Tehsil of Kabal.

Pšt. 'town of grace/goodness (*ihsān* Ar.)'.

388. **FAIZABAD فیزاباد (*fayzābād*)** *Map 18*

Village near Mingaora, Tehsil of Babuzai, it is located in the Saidu-khwar valley, towards the hills leading to the Swat valley.

Pšt. 'blessed abode (*fayz* Ar.)' (see BALLAND 1999).

389. **FAIZAH فیزه (*fayzah*)** *Map 21*

Group of houses in the hills on the Jambil-khwar valley, Tehsil of Babuzai.

Pšt. 'grace/abundance/blessed (*fayz* Ar.)', also a widespread feminine name (ROSSI, p.c.).

390. **FALAK-SAR فلک سر (*falak-sar*)** *Map 54*

The highest mountain in Swāt, near the boundary with Kohistan, Tehsil of Bahrain.

Pšt. 'mountain of the heavens (*falak*)': *falak* 'heavens, sky, firmament; fate, fortune, destiny' (RAVERTY).

391. **FAQIRA فقيرا (*faqirā*)** *Map 33*

Group of houses in the terraced mountainous upper Khwazakhela-khwar valley, Tehsil of Khwazakhela. It is called Barorai (cf. Bararai) on the Russian map.

Cf. foll.

392. **FAQIRAN-BANDA فقيران بانده (*faqirān-bānḍa*)** *Map 13*

Pasture on the Manrai-khwar, Tehsil of Kabal.

Pšt. 'pasture of the Faqirs'.

393. **FAZALBEG فازل بيگ (*fāzal-beg*)** *Map 44*

Village in the mountainous narrow Barwai-khwar valley, Tehsil of Maṭṭa.

Person's name. Cf. Pšt. (Ar.) *fazl* 'excellence, virtue; gift, reward, favour, grace' + Tk. *beg*.

394. **FIZIL-BANDA فازيل بانده (*fāzil-bānḍa*)** *Map 42*

Village in the narrow mountainous Harnoi-khwar valley, Tehsil of Maṭṭa. Only on the Russian map, but already quoted by RAVERTY (1888: 230) as Fáẓil Bánḍa'h.

Person's name.

395. **GABRAL گهبرال (*ghabrāl*)** *Map 54*

Village in the Gabral river valley at the confluence with the Bahandra-gol, Tehsil of Bahrain. According to RAVERTY (1888: 238), the nome should be Gabriál and his source "should have written, 'village of the Gárwí Ál,' not 'village of Gabriál.' Both parts referred to are inhabited by Gárwí Ál or Gárwí tribe"

RAVERTY's analysis is interesting. However, cf. also foll.

396. **GABRAL RIVER گهبرال (*ghabrāl*)** *Map 54*

Main tributary of the Swat river together with the Ushu-gol, originating from the high mountains at the boundary with Dir and Chitral, Tehsil of Bahrain.

The better explanation is probably represented by HAKIMZAY's proposal (1997: 172): Hi. *gabbar* 'rich, proud' + the sf. *-āl/-yāl* indicating water (on this sf., see s.v. Mankial). The comparison with Dard. and Kaf. gives rise to many phonetic and semantic difficulties. Cf. Kal. *gha* گها *N.* 'Small valley, vale or ravine where a stream or streambed flows' (*Syn:* dará. *Variant: ga; gah; gahal* (Urtsun (Tu)), < **ghala-* 'stream' (TRAIL/COOPER 1999), T4453, **ghala* 'stream' [to root *ghṛ-* 'to drip' (see WHITNEY 1885): see KEWA I 433 *jígharti* 'besprinkles']: Ash. *gul* 'inhabited valley, country' (whence *golī* 'tribe'), Wg. *gōl* 'valley', Kt. *gul;* Pr. *gul* 'valley, country'; Dm. *gʌl* 'valley'; Tir. *gálə* 'rivulet'; Paš.

lauṛ. *ghal* 'river', weg. *gal;* Shum. *gäl* 'ravine, valley', Gaw. *g'al*, Kal. urt. *gəhal*, rumb. *ghau*, st. *ghāl*, Kho. *gól*, Bašk. *gʌl*. Cf. also (?) Kal. *bro* برو *N.* 'Mountain top or succession of peaks which make up a ridge' < *br̥hánt-* 'tall, high' T9302 (TRAIL/ COOPER 1999): Kal. urt. *brhɔ* 'high mountain'): 'stream of mountain'?

397. GABRANAI گبرنی **(*gabranay*)** *Map 44*

Group of houses in a lateral valley on the right side of the Swāt river, Tehsil of Maṭṭa.

Cf. prec.

398. GACHKOR-BANDA بانده گاچکور **(*gāčkor-bānḍa*)** *Map 12*

Pasture in the Jarendo-bela-khwar valley, Tehsil of Kabal, near the boundary with Dir.

Pšt. 'pasture of the pen-house': *gāč* 'pen (for sheep) made of thornbush'.

399.-400. GADAKOT گدکوټ **(*gaḍakoṭ*)** *Maps 22-23*

Name of two villages on the hills bordering the Landai-khwar valley, Tehsil of Babuzai.

Possibly Pšt. 'the castle of the rams (*gəḍ*)', but cf. also T4054 *gardabhá-* 'ass': Waig. Woṭ. Gaw. *gadā*, Bašk. *gʌdā*.

401. GADWA-SAR گدوه سر **(*gaḍwa-sar*)** *Map 28*

Mountain near the Dre-khwar, on the boundary with Shangla, Tehsil of Charbagh. It is also said Achro-sar, 'the mountain of the Silver firs': cf. Achro-banda and Achro-kandao, which are located not far north and south, on the same boundary with Shangla.

Cf. Pšt. 'mountain of the ewes' (Pšt. *gəḍ*). Cf. also Pšt. *gaḍ°waḍ* 'topsy-turvy, higgledy-piggledy, in confusion'?

402. GALOCH گالوچ **(*gāloč*)** *Map 14*

Village in the wide and fertile Deolai-khwar valley, north of Sirsanai, Tehsil of Kabal.

Cf. Pšt. *gal* 'large hailstones; first snow on the mountain peaks' and *ğaləy* 'hail, hoar, frost' (RAVERTY) + Pšt. *wəč* 'dry'. See ADAMEC VI 173 Galuch, "A village some 12 miles northeast of-sarobi".

403. GAMCHANA گمچنه **(*gamčana*)** *Map 42*

Group of houses on the slopes above the upper Biha-khwar valley, Tehsil of Maṭṭa. Only on the Russian map.

Cf. Gamkot?

404. GAMKAT-BANDA گمکټ بانده **(*gamkat-bānḍa*)** *Map 33*

Pasture in the mountainous upper Khwazakhela-khwar valley, on the slopes of the Semprai-sar, Tehsil of Khwazakhela, near the boundary with Shangla.

Cf. foll.

405. GAMKOT گمکټ (*gamkoṭ*) *Map 5*

Group of houses at the end of the Jolagram-khwar valley, after Khazana, Tehsil of Barikot.

Cf. Tor. Bašk. *gām*, T4368 *grāma-* 'troop, village': 'the castle of the village'.

406. GAMPORA گامپوره (*gāmpora*) *Map 14*

Village in the Deolai-khwar valley, near Deolai, Tehsil of Kabal.

Cf. prec. + tautological *-pura*.

407. GAMSAR گمسر (*gamsar*) *Map 43*

Group of houses in the narrow Roringar-khwar valley, Tehsil of Maṭṭa. Only on the Russian map.

Cf. foll.

408. GAMSIR گمسر (*gamsir*) *Map 47*

Village in the narrow valley on the left bank of the Swāt river, Tehsil of Bahrain. Only on the Russian map.

Cf. Pšt. *garmsér*, *garmsél* 'warm countries, subtropics'; name of a district in south-western Afghanistan. This and the preceding toponym remind the summery quartiers of the seasonal migrations (ROSSI, p.c.).

409. GANAJIR گناجر (*ganāǰir*) *Map 28*

Village in the upper mountainous Dre-khwar valley, Tehsil of Charbagh.

Possibly 'flock of goats': cf. T146 **ajakaṭa* 'flock of goats': Si. *ajaṛu* 'flock of goats' (< **ayyaṛu*?), Lhd. *eiyuṛ*, (Jukes) *aiyyaṛ* 'flock of sheep or goats', Panj. *ayyaṛ*; and T3988 *gaṇá* 'troop, flock': Pa. Pkt. *gaṇa-* 'troop, flock', Tor. (Biddulph) *gan* 'herd'?

410.-411. GANDERAI گنډهېرى (*ganḍherəy*) *Maps 30, 39*

Name of two groups of houses: 1) on the slopes of the Charbagh-khwar valley, Tehsil of Charbagh; 2) in the hills on the right bank of the Swāt river, Tehsil of Maṭṭa (only on the Russian map).

Cf. Pšt. *ganḍ(h)ér* 'bitter taste; *Ristolocia rodaphne*; poison' (Nerium indicum, according to ALAM 2011). According to HAKIMZAY (1997: 129), its meaning is 'village (*ḍherəy*) of the virtuous/good people (*bun*, ← Ur.)'.

412. GANTAR گنتر (*gantar*) *Map 48*

Group of houses in the terraced Daral-khwar valley, Tehsil of Bahrain. Only on the Russian map.

Cf. T3991 **gaṇadhārī* 'holding a swarm' or T4426 **ghanatara* 'thicker'? In this latter case, IA *gh-* > Pšt. *g-* is regular, cf. IA *ghaṇa-* > Pšt. *gaṇ*. However, both proposals would not really fit semantically.

413. **GANUDAI گنوډی (*ganuḍay*)** *Map 21*

Group of houses in the fertile part of the Jambil-khwar valley, Tehsil of Babuzai.

Et. unkn.

414. **GAORARBAN گورربن (*gawrarban*)** *Map 50*

Group of houses on the left bank of the upper Swāt river valley, Tehsil of Bahrain.

Possibly Pšt. 'garden of the herd of cattle (*gāhár*)'?

415.-421. **GARAI ګړی (*gaṛəy*)** *Maps 5, 8, 39, 44, 44, 45, 50*

Name of seven villages: 1) at the end of the Jolagram-khwar valley, Tehsil of Barikot. According to RAVERTY (1888: 201), this village is hidden by the Súe-galí [= Surgalai] crest; 2) on the right bank of the Swāt river, in the fertile and wide plain of Kabal, Tehsil of Kabal, to be possibly identified with the Gari of DEANE (1895: "The name of an old Ruler of Odigram is given by mentioned by Gujars as being Giria—Odigram is said to have been an important city, and it is said also by some to have borne the same name as its chief Giria. The same name is said to exist in Gari on the opposite bank of the River"); 3-4) two groups of houses in the mountainous Barwai-khwar valley, Tehsil of Maṭṭa; 5) on the right bank of the Swāt river, slightly north of the confluence with the Barwai-khwar, Tehsil of Maṭṭa; 6) on the left bank of the Harnoi-khwar, Tehsil of Maṭṭa; 7) Group of houses in the narrow valley on the right bank of the upper Swāt river, Tehsil of Bahrain.

Pšt. 'small fortress'.

422. **GARASA گراسه (*garāsa*)** *Map 21*

Group of houses in the Jambil-khwar valley, Tehsil of Babuzai.

Cf. Kal. *grāst* 'wolf', *grhās*; Phal. *grāsta*, Dam. *graċ* (T4362, *grastṛ-* 'swallower (of sun or moon)', see KUIPER 1934: 217).

423. **GARDAISAR گردیسر (*gardaysar*)** *Map 39*

Group of houses on the eastern slopes of the mountains dividing the Barwai-khwar valley from the Harnoi-khwar valley, Tehsil of Maṭṭa.

Pšt. 'round (*gərdáy*) head (*sar*)'.

424. **GARGAI-SHALKHAI ګرګی شلخی (*gargay-šalxay*)** *Map 46*

Group of houses in the upper Olal-khwar valley, Tehsil of Bahrain.

Pšt. *garga* 'log of wood, piece of unhewn timber; trunk or stem of a tree or shrub, stalk of a plant' (RAVERTY) + Pšt. *šalxay* 'name of a species of potherb' (RAVERTY).

425. **GARHI ګړهي (*gaṛhi*)** *Map 23*

Village in the fertile plain on the left bank of the Swāt river, near the Ugad-khwar, Tehsil of Babuzai.

Pšt. *gaṛ(h)ə́y* 'small fortress'.

426. **GARNAI گرنی (*garnay*)** *Map 47*

Group of houses on a terrace above the Baral-darra valley and the Swāt river valley, Tehsil of Bahrain.

Cf. Dam. *grēṇ* 'knot' (cf. T4354)?

427. **GASHKOR گاشکوړ (*gāškoṛ*)** *Map 31*

Village located on the left bank of the Swāt river, at the foot of the hills, Tehsil of Khwazakhela.

Pšt. 'fold (*gāš/gāṛá*)-house'.

428.-429. **GAT گټ (*gaṭ*)** *Maps 26, 40*

Name of two groups of houses: 1) in the mountains above the Bishbanr-khwar valley, Tehsil of Charbagh; 2) in the narrow terraced valley of the Shaurai-khwar, Tehsil of Maṭṭa.

Pšt. *gāṭ/gaṭ* 'boulder; cliff, reef, stone'.

430. **GAT-KANDAO گټ کنډو (*gaṭ-kanḍaw*)** *Map 26*

Pass leading from the Bikan-khwar valley to the Tambagat-khwar valley, Tehsil of Charbagh.

Cf. prec.

431. **GATKOTAL گټکوتل (*gaṭkotal*)** *Map 38*

Village on the right bank of the Swāt river at the foot of the hills bordering the plain, Tehsil of Maṭṭa.

Cf. Gat + Pšt. *kotal* 'pass'. See prec.

432. **GATO گټو (*gaṭo*)** *Map 25*

Village in the narrow mountainous Bishbanr-khwar valley, Tehsil of Babuzai.

Pšt. *gaṭ* 'large round stone, rock' (RAVERTY).

433. **GATO-SAR-BANDA گټو سر بانډه (*gaṭo-sar-bānḍa*)** *Map 32*

Pasture in a lateral valley of the Khwazakhela-khwar valley, Tehsil of Khwazakhela.

Pšt. 'pasture of the rocky mountain'.

434. **GATSAR گټ سر (*gaṭ-sar*)** *Map 48*

Group of houses in the terraced Daral-khwar valley, Tehsil of Bahrain. Only on the Russian map.

Cf. prec.

435. GATSAR-BANDA گټ سر بانډه (*gaṭ-sar-bānḍa*) *Map 36*

Pasture in the mountainous upper Paiti-khwar valley, Tehsil of Khwazakhela.

Cf. prec.

436. GHAKHE-BANDA غاښی بانډه (*γāx̌ay-bānḍa*) *Map 10*

Pasture in the upper Ramogai-khwar valley, Tehsil of Kabal.

Pšt. 'pasture of the crest/mountain pass' (*γā́x̌ay*)'.

437. GHALIGAY غالیګی (*γāligay*) *Map 7*

Big village on the left bank of the Swāt river, Tehsil of Barikot, in a valley between the hills where also Shingardar is located and those leading to the boundary with the Tehsil of Babuzai. Quoted by RAVERTY (1888: 199) as Ghálí-gaey.

Pšt. 'quiet (*γə́lay*) place (*-gay*)'. The quotation in DEANE (1895) as Ghaligai and Ghalizai, confirms the analysis of *-gay* as the suffix of place, as also *-jāy* means 'place' in Pashto.

438. GHAMJABA غمجبه (*γamǰaba*) *Map 9*

Village near Kabbal in the vast and fertile plain on the right bank of the Swāt river, Tehsil of Kabal.

Pšt. 'swamp (*ǰabá* 'swamp, marshy field') of sorrow (*γam*)'.

439.-440. GHARIBABAD غریباباد (*γaribābād*) *Maps 17, 30*

Name of two villages: 1) a quartier of Kanju, in the plain of the Swat river, Tehsil of Kabal; 2) on the left bank of the Swāt river, at the foot of the hills, north of Charbagh, Tehsil of Charbagh.

Pšt. 'town of the poors (*γarib*)'.

441. GHARI-BALA غریباله (*γari-bāla*) *Map 38*

Group of houses on the hills of the Saso-sar, Tehsil of Maṭṭa.

Pšt. 'mountaneous (*γari*)' + Pšt. *bālā́* 'higher/upper'? Or Pšt. 'upper bank (Pšt. *γāṛa*)'.

442. GHOJALAI غوجلی (*γoǰalay*) *Map 18*

Group of houses in the fertile valley on the left bank of the Swat river, between the Swat river and the Saidu-khwar, Tehsil of Babuzai.

Pšt. 'little (*-ay*) cowshed (*γoǰə́l*)'.

443. GHOREJAI غوربجی (*γoreǰay*) *Map 47*

Village located on the left side of the Swāt river, on the Baral-darra, on a terrace covered with thick trees, Tehsil of Bahrain.

Cf. Pšt. *γarečay* 'mountain; mountaineer, mountain dweller'.

444. **GHULKHWARO-SAR-BANDA غلخوړو سر بانډه (*γulxwaṛo-sar-bānḍa*)** *Map 31*

Pasture on the hills sloping towards the left bank of the Swāt river, Tehsil of Khwazakhela.

Pšt. 'pasture of the mountainous ravine (*xwaṛ*) of the feces (*γwul*)/of the herd (*γol*)'.

445. **GHUMBAT گمبت (*gumbat*)** *Map 22*

Group of houses in the hills bordering the Jambil-khwar valley, towards the Landai-khwar valley, Tehsil of Babuzai.

M.A. DINAKHEL, p.c., suggests the transcription gumbat. However, according to ROSSI, p.c., it could possibly be Pšt. *γumba* 'protuberance, knot' (RAVERTY): cf. Prs. *gumbad* 'dome', "borr. also in Lhd. *gōmbat* etc. 'bullock's hump'" (EVP 25; NEVP 31).

446. **GHUREJO غرېجو (*γureǰo*)** *Map 17*

Village in the fertile plain, right on the right bank of the Swāt river, Tehsil of Kabal.

Cf. Ghorejai.

447. **GHUZ غوز (*γuz*)** *Map 22*

Group of houses in the hills bordering the Jambil-khwar valley, towards the Landai-khwar valley, Tehsil of Babuzai.

Pšt. *γuz* 'walnut' (see also SULTAN-I-ROME 2016: 221).

448. **GHUZANO-BANDA غوزانو بانډه (*γuzāno-bānḍa*)** *Map 53*

Pasture located in the narrow valley on the right bank of the upper Swāt river, Tehsil of Bahrain.

Pšt. 'pasture of the walnuts'.

449.-450. **GHUZANO-CHAM غوزانو چم (*γuzāno-čam*)** *Map 38*

Name of two groups of houses at the foot of the Uchrai-sar and in the plain on the right bank of the Harnoi-khwar, Tehsil of Maṭṭa.

Pšt. 'quartier of the walnuts'.

451. **GHUZANO-SAR غوزانو سر (*γuzāno-sar*)** *Map 13*

Mountain north of the Manrai-khwar, Tehsil of Kabal, on the boundary with the Tehsil of Maṭṭa.

Pšt. 'mountain of the walnuts'.

452. **GHUZBANR غوزبڼ (*γuzbaṇ*)** *Map 31*

Group of houses on the hills sloping towards the left bank of the Swāt river, Tehsil of Khwazakhela.

Pšt. 'garden of the walnut(s)'.

453. GHUZKAS غوزكس (*γuzkas*) *Map 44*

Group of houses in the mountainous Barwai-khwar valley, Tehsil of Maṭṭa.

Pšt. 'ravine/hollow (*kas*) of the walnut(s)', better '*Kas* of the walnut' (cf. Kas, s.v.).

454. GHWAI-BANDA غوايي بانده (*γwāyi-bānḍa*) *Map 43*

Pasture in the narrow Roringar-khwar valley, Tehsil of Maṭṭa.

Pšt. 'pasture of the cows (*γwāyí*)'.

455. GIDAR ګيدړ (*gidaṛ*) *Map 46*

Group of houses in the upper mountainous Olal-khwar valley, Tehsil of Bahrain. Only on the Russian map.

Pšt. *gidáṛ* 'jackal/fox'.

456.-457. GIDAR-SAR-BANDA ګيدړ سر بانده (*gidaṛ-sar-bānḍa*) *Maps 32-33*

Name of two pastures in the Tehsil of Khwazakhela: 1) in the mountain in the upper Khwazakhela-khwar valley, near Tarogai; 2) in a lateral valley of the Khwazakhela-khwar valley, Tehsil of Khwazakhela.

Pšt. 'pasture of the jackal/fox (*gidáṛ*)-head'.

458. GIGA ګيګه (*giga*) *Map 38*

Village on the right bank of the Harnoi river at the foot of the hills bordering the plain, Tehsil of Maṭṭa.

See SULTAN-I-ROME 2016: 478: "*Gaga*: Canal type watercourse".

459. GIRA ګيره (*gira*) *Map 18*

Mountain dividing the Swat river valley from the Saidu-khwar valley, Tehsil of Babuzai. Quoted by DEANE (1895) as Giria.

Pšt. *ger* 'enclosed with a fence; surrounded'. Better Pšt. 'Mountain' cf. Raja-gira = Udigram.

460. GISHAR ګيشار (*gišāṛ*) *Map 27*

Group of houses in the mountainous narrow Tambagat-khwar valley, Tehsil of Charbagh.

Et. unkn.

461. GOAL ګوال (*gwāl*) *Map 43*

Group of houses on the eastern slopes of the mountains dividing the Barwai-khwar valley from the Harnoi-khwar valley, Tehsil of Maṭṭa.

Pšt. *gwāl* 'reach, stretch (of a river); bend (of a mountain range); gently sloping drop'. HAKIMZAY (1997: 131) indentifies this tononym with *gohāl*, corresponding to Pšt. *gohār* 'herd'. However, he states that this is also the name of a Gujar tribe.

462. **GODA-BANDA گوده بانډه (*goda-bānḍa*)** *Map 13*

Pasture in the upper Manrai-khwar valley, towards the boundary with Matta, Tehsil of Kabal.

Cf. foll.: abreviated form of *godar*? Or cf. *godá* 'cellar which is not equipped for human habitation'. According to IKRAM, p.c., *goda* means 'pulp'.

463. **GODAR گودر (*godar*)** *Map 20*

Group of houses in the mountain on the Saidu-khwar valley, Tehsil of Babuzai.

Pšt. 'ford'? Difficult for semantic reasons (ROSSI, p.c.).

464. **GODHANU-BANDA گوډنو بانډه (*goḍanu-bānḍa*)** *Map 14*

Pasture in the wide and fertile Deolai-khwar valley, Tehsil of Kabal.

Probably Pšt. 'pasture of the lambs (*gəḍ, gəḍuray*)'.

465. **GOGDARA گوگدره (*gogdara*)** *Map 18*

Village on the road leading from Barikot to Mingaora, in the fertile valley on the left bank of the Swat river and at the foot of the hills, Tehsil of Babuzai. Quoted already by RAVERTY 1888.

Cf. Pšt. *gogaṛ* 'brimstone, sulphur' → 'valley of brimstone'? Or cf. T4097 **gavāṁgūtha-* 'cowdung': Kho. *gaṅguru*? See ADAMEC VI 233 Godara, "A village located on a stream west of Doaw. Another village with this name is located on the Panjshir river, northeast of Astana". HAKIMZAY (1997: 81) thinks that the first element, *gogā*, indicates a name of a Buddhist demon.

466. **GOJALAI گوجلی (*gošalay*)** *Map 38*

Village on the right bank of the Swāt river at the foot of the hills bordering the plain, Tehsil of Maṭṭa.

Variant of Pšt. *gušaray* 'of the Gujars'?

467. **GOLRA گوړره (*golra*)** *Map 38*

Village on the right bank of the Harnoi river at the foot of the hills bordering the plain, Tehsil of Maṭṭa.

Cf. Pšt. *gulrú* 'rosy-faced'? See ADAMEC III 146-148 Gulran.

468. **GORA-DAKA گوره ډاکه (*gora-ḍāka*)** *Map 52*

Group of houses in the upper Mankial-khwar valley, Tehsil of Bahrain.

Cf. T4264 *gōcara-* 'pasture ground': Pkt. *gōara-*; Paš. *gōr* 'herd of cows' (but see ROSSI 2018). Cf. also T4345 *gaurá-* 'white, yellowish, pale red': Pa. Pkt. *gōra-* 'white'; Dam. *gōra* 'white', Kal. *gɔ̄ra*; Bašk. *gūr, gū* 'khaki-coloured, yellow'; Phal. *gūrɔ̃* 'yellow (?)'; Sh. *gūru̯* 'brown, grey, selfcoloured', (LORIMER) *gvrilo* 'yellow, withered'; Si. *goro* 'fair-complexioned'; Lhd. *gorā* 'white, pale, red (of cattle)'; Panj. *gorā* 'white, pale'.

And cf. T5603 *ḍhōkka[2] 'rock': Kho. (LORIMER) ḍok 'high ground, hillock, heap'; Hi. *ḍhok* 'large piece of broken stone'. Or cf. Pšt. *gur* 'thick, close, compact; shady, umbrageous (of a tree); misty, muggy' (RAVERTY) + Pšt. *ḍaka* 'full'?

469. **GORA-DAKA-KANDAO گوره ډاکه کنډو (*gora-ḍāka-kanḍaw*)** *Map 51*

Pass leading from the Jaba-khwar valley to Kohistan, Tehsil of Bahrain.

Cf. prec.

470. **GORAIL گوریل (*gorayl*)** *Map 53*

Group of houses in the narrow valley on the right bank of the upper Swāt river, Tehsil of Bahrain.

Cf. prec.

471. **GORATAI گورتی (*goratəy*)** *Map 2*

Village in the vast and fertile valley on the left bank of the Swat river, near Barikot, Tehsil of Barikot.

Cf. prec. HAKIMZAY (1997: 41) sees a link with *guru* 'spiritual guide'.

472. **GORI-BELA گوري بېله (*gori-bela*)** *Map 51*

Group of houses in the mountainous Jaba-khwar valley, Tehsil of Bahrain.

Cf. prec.

473. **GOSH گوش (*goš*)** *Map 53*

Group of houses in the narrow valley on the right bank of the upper Swāt river, Tehsil of Bahrain. Only on the Russian map.

Cf. T4528 *ghṓṣa* 'noise, sound of words at a distance; station of herdsmen, herdsmen': Pa. Pkt. *ghōsa-* 'shout'; Si. *gosa* 'noise, roar of thunder'; Pkt. *ghōsa-* ' cowherd's station'; Sh. koh. gur. *goṣ* 'house', pales. *gōṣ*; Hi. *ghos* 'a caste of herdsmen', *ghosī* 'herdsman'.

474. **GOSHAI گوشی (*gošay*)** *Map 50*

Group of houses on the left bank of the upper Swāt river valley, Tehsil of Bahrain.

Cf. T4335 **gōśrayaṇa-* 'cow-house': Paš. kuṛ. *gēšín* 'house', chil. *gušīn*, ar. *gəšín*; Paš. weg. *gṓšiṅg*. Cf. also prec.

475. **GUJARBANR گوجربڼ (*guǰarbaṇ*)** *Map 39*

Group of houses on the slopes of the Shah-dop-sar on the left bank of the Harnoi-khwar, Tehsil of Maṭṭa.

Pšt. 'garden of the Gujars'. See SULTAN-I-ROME 2008: 325:

> *Gujars* (*Gujran*) are an ethnic group, not Afghans but of the Jat or Rajput group. They did not possess a hereditary share in the land in the Swat State areas by virtue of their de-

scent, and remained merely vassals to the *dawtar* and-serai landowners. Generally, they possessed cattle, i.e. cows and buffaloes, and sometimes also a few goats. They were not necessarily nomads. They are now a powerful segment or group and are found in all walks of life.

476.-477. GUL-BANDA گل بانډه (*gwəl-bānḍa*) *Maps 19, 40*

Name of two pastures: 1) in the narrow Marghuzar-khwar valley, towards Marghuzar, Tehsil of Babuzai; 2) in the narrow terraced valley of the Shaurai-khwar, Tehsil of Maṭṭa.

Pšt. 'pasture of the flowers' or Kati *gul* 'valley, country' (see MORGENSTIERNE 1931: 442; TUCCI 1977: 17).

478. GUL-DERAI گل ډېرى (*gwəl-ḍerəy*) *Map 34*

Group of houses in the periphery of Kotanai, on the low terraced hills on the left side of the Swat river, Tehsil of Khwazakhela.

Pšt. 'residence of the flowers'.

479. GULIBAGH گلي باغ (*gulibāγ*) *Map 30*

Village on the left bank of the Swāt river, at the foot of the hills, north of Charbagh, Tehsil of Charbagh. Quoted already by RAVERTY (1888: 233).

Pšt. 'garden of the flowers'.

480. GULIGRAM گليګرام (*gwəligrām*) *Map 18*

Village in the last flat narrow plain of the Saidu-khwar valley, towards Marghuzar, Tehsil of Babuzai. Quoted by RAVERTY (1888: 251) as Gulaey-Grám.

Pšt. 'village of the flowers'.

481. GULI-SAR گلي سر (*gwəli-sar*) *Map 24*

Mountain of about 2,850 mt between the Jambil-khwar valley and the Lewanai-khwar valley, Tehsil of Babuzai, near the boundary with Buner.

Pšt. 'mountain of the flowers'.

482. GUL-PAIZA گل پيزه (*gul-payza*) *Map 28*

Small group of houses located on the road to Malam-jabba in the Tehsil of Charbagh at a height of about 1800 meters.

Cf. Pšt. 'flower' + Pšt. *péza* 'ledge (on a mountain); pinnacle (mountain); peak'.

483. GUMBATUNA-BANDA گومبتونه بانډه (*gumbatuna-bānḍa*) *Map 6*

Pasture at the foot of the hills on the right bank of the Swāt river, on the opposite side of Goratai, Tehsil of Barikot. Quoted also by STEIN (1929: 18).

Pšt. 'pasture of the cupolas (*gumbad*)'.

484. GUND-PATAI گوند پتی (gund-pəṭay) *Map 52*

Group of houses on the left bank of the upper Swāt river, Tehsil of Bahrain. Only on the Russian map.

Pšt. 'field (*pəṭay*) of the subdivision (*gund*)'.

485. GURNAI-KHWAR گورنی خوړ (gurnəy-xwaṛ) *Map 47*

Stream flowing on the left side of the Swāt river, Tehsil of Bahrain. Only on the Russian map.

Cf. Pšt. *gaṛandáy*, *gṛandáy* 'quick'?

486. GURTAI-ABADAN گورتی ابادن (gurtəy-abādan) *Map 23*

Village in the narrow Landai-khwar valley, Tehsil of Babuzai.

Gurtai possibly person's name.

487. GURTAI-KANDAR گودتی کندر (gurtəy-kandar) *Map 23*

Village in the narrow Landai-khwar valley, Tehsil of Babuzai.

Cf. Kandar and prec.

488. GWALERAI گوالېری (gwālerəy) *Map 41*

Village in the plain at the confluence among the Harnoi-khwar, the Roringar-khwar and the Biha-khwar, Tehsil of Maṭṭa.

Pšt. *gwāl* 'reach, stretch (of a river); bend (of a mountain range); gently sloping drop': 'small (*-eṛay*) slope'.

489. HAIUM هیوم (hayum) *Map 53*

Group of houses in the narrow valley on the left bank of the upper Swāt river, Tehsil of Bahrain.

Cf. Paš. (IIFL III 202) *yi:m* 'snow', var. *i:im* and *hi:m*. Cf. also Paš. *ye:m'a:n, hem'u:n, em'e:n* 'winter': cf. T14164 *hēmantá-* 'winter': Šum. *yéman*, Gaw. *hemánd*, Bašk. *hāman*, Tor. *himān*, etc.

490. HAJI-BABA حاجی بابا (hāji-bābā) *Map 18*

Quartier of Mingaora, at the confluence between the Jambil-khwar and the Saidu-khwar, Tehsil of Babuzai.

Person's name.

491. HAMWARAI همواری (hamwāray) *Map 30*

Group of houses on the hills on the left bank of the Swāt river, Tehsil of Charbagh.

Pšt. *hamwārí* 'plain'.

492. **HAMWARAK هموارک (*hamwārak*)** *Map 31*

Group of houses on the hills sloping towards the left bank of the Swāt river, Tehsil of Khwazakhela.

Cf. prec. + diminutive sf.

493. **HARIANAI هريانی (*haryānay*)** *Map 53*

Group of houses in the narrow valley on the left bank of the upper Swāt river, Tehsil of Bahrain. Called in STEIN 1930 Eranai, while in RAVERTY 1888: 237 Har-yání. In ID. 1862: 152 it is called Haranaey, "about twelve miles from Chúr-rra'í".

Cf. foll.

494. **HARIANAI-BAGLA هريانی بگلا (*haryānay-baglā*)** *Map 53*

Group of houses in the narrow valley on the right bank of the upper Swāt river, Tehsil of Bahrain.

Cf. Pšt. *haryānay* 'amazed' + *bagla* 'field' (IKRAM, p.c.).

495. **HARNOI-KHWAR هرنوی خوړ (*harnoy-xwaṛ*)** *Maps 38-39, 41*

Long stream, located at an elevation of 1,007 meters above sea level, flowing from the mountains at the boundary with Dir into the right side of the Swāt river, Tehsil of Maṭṭa.

See ADAMEC III 151 Hari Rud, "river formed by two chief confluents, the-sar-i-Jangal and Lal, which rise in the Dai Zangi country. [...] From the confluence, about 9 miles below Daulat Yar, the river flows west by a little south to Herat, some 210 miles".

See ESIJ III 369-371 ²**har-* ← IA. **sar-*, and VOGELSANG 2003, on the Hari Rud: "Old Iranian **Harayu* 'with velocity'; compare Sanskrit-*saráyu*".

See KEWA III 470-472 *sísarti* 'streckt aus, dehnt / stretches, extends' and comparisons, precising (pp. 471-472) that "Die ved. Sippe *sar-* bedeutet nicht 'fliessen' [...] Doch bezieht sich *sar-* 'eilen, loslaufen' sehr oft aus Gewässer; Namen von Flüssen und Bächen wie-*saráyuḥ*, RV 10, 75, 6 *Su-sártu-* f. Name eines Flusses (und *sarít*?) können daher mit *sar-* verbunden werden, nicht jedoch Bezeichnungen stehender Wasser [...] Unter dem irrigen Bedeutungsansatz 'fliessen' wird *sar-* gewöhnlich mit einer idg. Sippe **ser-* 'fliessen' verbunden (...), die aber im wesentlichen auf der Verbindbarkeit mit **sr-eu-* (...) und auf Flussnamen Europas (...) beruht". See also EWAia II 705-506. Cf. also T13250 *sárati* 'runs, flows, glides' and derived, *sáras* 'lake, pool', etc.

Cf. also T13980 *hárati* 'carries, brings; takes away': Pa. *harati* 'carries, brings, takes away, plunders'; NiDoc. *haradi* 'takes away', Pkt. *haraï*, Ḍ. *harina*; Panj. *harnā* 'to take away, steal', Ku. *harṇo*, N. *harnu*, Hi. *harnā* 'to take, seize, plunder'; Marw. *harṇo* 'to take away', OSi. dat. inf. *harnā*.

496. **HAWAI هوای (*hawāy*)** *Map 51*

Group of houses on the left bank of the upper Swāt river, Tehsil of Bahrain.

Derived form of Pšt. *hawā* 'air, atmosphere; weather; wind'.

497. **HAWAR هوار (*hawār*)** *Map 42*

Group of houses on the northern slopes of the Prangman-sar, Tehsil of Maṭṭa.

Pšt. *hawā́r* 'even, flat, smooth'.

498. **HAWARAI هوارى (*hawāray*)** *Map 33*

Group of houses on the terraced slopes of a lateral valley of the Khwazakhela-khwar valley, Tehsil of Khwazakhela.

Cf. prec. and Awarai.

499. **HAZARA هزاره (*hazāra*)** *Map 9*

Village near Kabal, in the vast and fertile plain on the right bank of the Swāt river, Tehsil of Kabal. Quoted already by RAVERTY (1888: 232) and DEANE (1895).

Pšt. *hazārá* 'Hazara'.

500. **HINDUBEG-BANDA هندوبيک بانده (*hindubeg-bānḍa*)** *Map 43*

Pasture in the narrow Roringar-khwar valley, Tehsil of Maṭṭa.

Pšt. 'pasture of the Hindu beg'. Beg is the name of a small tribe.

501. **HINDUBEG-SAR هندوبيک سر (*hindubeg-sar*)** *Map 43*

Mountain of about 3,500 mt between the Roringar-khwar valley and the Barwai-khwar valley, Tehsil of Maṭṭa. Only on the Russian map.

Cf. prec.

502. **HUNRA-SAR هونه سر (*huṇa-sar*)** *Map 16*

Mountain of about 2,400 mt located on the border with the Tehsil of Maṭṭa, Tehsil of Kabal.

Pšt. 'mountain of the snares (*hoṇā́* 'trap noose [for trapping birds])'? HAKIMZAY (1997: 170) relates it to the name of the Huns. However, better cf. Unran-sar.

503. **IGALBANR ايگلبن (*igalbaṇ*)** *Map 30*

Group of houses located on the slopes bordering the plain of Charbagh, Tehsil of Charbagh.

Cf. T1554 *iṅguda* 'the medicinal tree Terminalia catappa; its nut; the tree': Pkt. *iṁgudī-* 'the tree' and T14080 *hiṅgula* 'preparation of mercury with sulphur, vermilion' [KEWA III 593 quotes KUIPER (1948: 66, considering this word a lw. ← Mon *ngu* + Muṇḍa prefix *hi-*), but then states that "doch bleibt zu untersuchen, ob das Mon-Wort nicht aus arischer Quelle stammt": this quotation indeed has disappeared in EWAia III 538]: Pa. *hiṅguli-* 'vermilion', Pkt. *hiṁgula-*, Si. *hiṅgulū*. Cf. Pšt. *agál* 'ditch, drainage ditch' (?) + *baṇ*.

504. **ILAM ايلم (*ilam*)** *Map 19*

Mythical mountain in the Tehsil of Barikot at the frontier with Buner. Its height is about 2,800 mt. Called Ilm by DEANE (1895).

See TUCCI (1977: 54) for a description of mythology and cults and sacrality of Mount Ilam; STEIN 1930: 19: "The top of the mountain was an object of pious pilgrimage already in Buddhist times, as shown by Hsüan-tsang's description of Mount *Hi-lo* the identity of which with Ilam I was subsequently able to establish". Local name: Jogyāno-sar 'Mountain of the Yogis'. Its ancient name was Varnu, according to the Indian sources, corresponding to the district of Varna of the Avesta (see OLIVIERI 2009a: 39).

TUCCI (1977: 52-53) reconsiders the identification proposed by STEIN of the Ilam with mount Pir-sar (Unran-sar):

> Let us consider e.g. the question of the Áornos. After the conquest of Ora the inhabitants of Bazíra, discouraged, fled at the dead of night along with people of other tribes and took shelter in the *petra*, 'the rock' which Arrianus calls *Áornos* (and Curtius *Áornis*) which is = Prakrit *āvaraṇa*, a common name for any sheltered place (cf. also Pashai *war* 'wall') [note 64: ALTHEIM-STIEHL 1970, p. 166, derives *Áornos* from a *hu-varan* which does not seem to me to be acceptable; *āvaraṇa* is also in Skr. a fortified place. We find another Áornos in Bactria: Arrianus, *An.* III 29, 1]. Sir A. STEIN (1927, p. 432) considers that the Ilam was the place where the inhabitants of Barikot, Bazíra (Vajīrasthāna) took shelter when they fled from their town; but he thinks that the Áornos is not identical with the Ilam [...] The Áornos has been identified by Sir Aurel Stein with Unʳa sar, Pir sar to the north of Chakrēsar, overlooking the Indus.

According to TUCCI 1963a: 171, Ilam = Áornos. See ID. 1977: 52 ff. for the entire reasoning; see also OLIVIERI 1996: 64-70 and COLORU/OLIVIERI 2019 and bibliography.

For the etymology of Mount Aornos see Unran-sar.

505. **ILANAI ايلانى (*ilānay*)** *Map 28*

Group of houses in the mountainous Dre-khwar valley, Tehsil of Charbagh.

According to IKRAM, p.c., *ilonai* is a 'kind of plant belonging to the group of zyziphus'. Cf. also T14282 *ālīna-*: Paš.pach. *ālinūk* 'beard of maize' MORGENSTIERNE with (?).

506. **ILANI ايلاني (*ilāni*)** *Map 39*

Small village under the Lito-sar and left side of the Harnoi-khwar, in Tehsil of Maṭṭa.

Cf. prec.

507. **ILLA ايله (*illa*)** *Map 52*

Group of houses in the upper Mankial-khwar valley, Tehsil of Bahrain.

Cf. T1593 **illi* 'a kite': Si. *hila*, Lhd. *hill*, Panj. *ill* 'kite, a kind of hawk'; — semant. connexion doubtful with Pkt. *illi* 'lion, tiger', Hi. *īl* 'a wild animal'? Cf. also Ilanai.

508. **ILMAN ايلمن (*ilman*)** *Map 33*

Group of houses located in the hills of the upper Khwazakhela-khwar valley, Tehsil of Khwazakhela. It is called Xman (Pšt. *xamə́n* 'bent, crooked'?) on the Russian map.

Pšt. *ilbánd* 'summer pasture, mountain meadow'.

509. **INZARO-BANDA انځرو بانډه (*injəro-bāṇḍa*)** *Map 11*

Pasture in the mountains above the Kolalai-khwar valley, Tehsil of Kabal.

Pšt. 'pasture of the figs (*injə́r*)'.

510. **INZAR-TANGAI انځر تنګی (*injər-tangay*)** *Map 23*

Group of houses in the Landai-khwar valley, near Manglaor, Tehsil of Babuzai.

Pšt. 'gorge (*tangáy*) of the figs (*injə́r*, see ALAM 2011: Ficus carica)'.

511. **IROBAI ایروبی (*irobay*)** *Map 48*

Group of houses in the terraced Daral-khwar valley, Tehsil of Bahrain.

Cf. Pšt. *yarbá* 'slope, incline, declivity'? Or cf. the first element in *hiṛ-mánd* 'Hilmend (River)' + Pšt. *obə́* 'water'? See also and better SULTAN-I-ROME 2016: 478: "*Irab*: The water coming from springs used for irrigation — though not necessarily but also used for feeding and washing cattle, watermills, and other similar purposes — usually it flows near the village and also in the village fields", "*Irabah*: The water that flows out of a canal, *walah*, and *lakhtay*, etc. It also refers to water flowing out of a tract of land at the time of irrigation".

512. **ISLAMPUR اسلام پور (*islāmpur*)** *Map 20*

Village in the upper Saidu-khwar valley, Tehsil of Babuzai. Its actual name is Salampur (*salāmpur*, Pšt. 'town of peace'). RAVERTY 1888 provides the old name Islámpúr. This village "was the residence of Mí-án Núr, the grandson of Akhúnd Darwezah, upon whom Khushhál Khán, the renowned Khattak chief and poet, launched his bitter irony in his *kasídah* or poem on Suwát; and here also, the tomb of the Mí-án may still be seen" (RAVERTY 1862: 247).

Pšt. 'town of Islām'.

513. **JABA جبه (*ǰaba*)** *Map 51*

Group of houses in the mountainous Jaba-khwar valley, Tehsil of Bahrain.

Pšt. *ǰabá* 'swamp, marshy field' (see also SULTAN-I-ROME 2016: 478) or, better, T5128 *jamba* 'mud' [possibly ← Proto-Muṇḍa: KUIPER 1948: 60-62; KEWA I 418 and EWAia III 207]: Pa. *jambāla-* 'mud'; Pkt. *jaṁbāla-* 'mud, slime'.

514. **JABA-BANDA جبه بانډه (*ǰaba-bāṇḍa*)** *Map 51*

Pasture in the mountainous Jaba-khwar valley, Tehsil of Bahrain.

Cf. prec.

515. **JABAGAI جبګی (*ǰabagay*)** *Map 5*

Group of houses on the mountain at the border with Dir, near Rangela and the the Jolagram-khwar valley, Tehsil of Barikot. On the Russian map it is called Jabagram, attesting a pre-Pashto phase.

Derived from the old name, Jabagram, as attested on the Russian map: cf. T5128 *jamba* 'mud': Pa. *jambāla-* 'mud'; Pkt. *jaṁbāla-* 'mud, slime'. With a resulting meaning of 'town of mud'. Due to successive phonetic simplications, this name shuld have become Jabagai, subsequently interpreted as Pšt. 'small marshy field' (+ dimin. sf. *-gay*). Cf. Jaba.

516. JABA-KHWAR جبه خوړ (ǰaba-xwaṛ) *Map 51*

Stream originating from the mountains on the border with Kohistan and flowing into the Mankial, Tehsil of Bahrain.

IA 'muddy stream': cf. Jaba (or Pšt. 'river of Jaba').

517.-518. JABBA جبه (ǰaba) *Maps 22, 49*

Name of two groups of houses: 1) in the hills bordering the Jambil-khwar valley, towards the Landai-khwar valley, Tehsil of Babuzai; 2) in the upper Daral-khwar valley, Tehsil of Bahrain.

Cf. Jaba.

519.-521. JABRAI جبړی (ǰabṛəy) *Maps 33, 36, 39*

Name of three groups of houses: 1) in a lateral valley of the Khwazakhela-khwar valley, Tehsil of Khwazakhela; 2) in the mountainous Paiti-khwar valley, Tehsil of Khwazakhela; 3) in the hills on the right bank of the Swāt river, Tehsil of Maṭṭa (only on the Russian map).

Possibly with HAKIMZAY (1997: 66), a loanword from Ur. *jhābar* 'low-land on which water lies; a pool: marshy land, a marsh, fen, swamp'? Cf. also Jaba, etc.

522. JAI جی (ǰay) *Map 50*

Group of houses in the narrow valley on the left bank of the upper Swāt river, Tehsil of Bahrain.

Cf. Pšt. *ǰəy/žəy* 'edge, border, side of the road'? Cf. T5141 *jayá* 'victory': Pa. Pkt. *jaya-*, T5143 *jáyati* 'conquers': Pa. *jēti*, Pkt. *jayaï*, NiDoc. *jayaṁta*, *jey* 'victorious'? Or cf. T5227 *jiyā-*, *jyā-*, *j(i)yākā-* 'bowstring': Pa. *jiyā-*, *jyā-*, NiDoc. *jiya*, Ash. *žī*, Waig. Kt. *ǰī*, Pr. *žī*, Kal. rumb. Tor. *ǰī*?

523. JAIKOT جیکوټ (ǰaykoṭ) *Map 25*

Village in the mountain dividing the Bishbanr-khwar valley from the Tambagat-khwar valley, Tehsil of Charbagh.

Cf. prec. + Pšt. *koṭ*.

524. JALBA جلبه (ǰalba) *Map 43*

Group of houses in the narrow Roringar-khwar valley, Tehsil of Maṭṭa.

Cf. Pšt. *ǰalbang* 'a kind of plant which stings on touching it, a kind of stinging nettle, the tops and leaves of which are cooked and eaten' (RAVERTY). Cf. also T5355 **jhalla-*

‘bush’: Paš. dar. *ǰal* ‘tree’, nir. *ǰāl*, ar. *ǰōl*, kuṛ. *zal*, chil. *zol*, Gmb. *ǰalā*; Kal. *ǰəhal* ‘jungle’; Sh. *ǰēl* ‘forest’; Lhd. *jhall* ‘jungle’; Panj. *jhall* ‘reed-bed, thicket’ + *baṇ*. Cf. also the following entry.

525. **JALBAN جلبن (*ǰalban*)** *Map 54*

Village on the right bank of the upper Swāt river, south of Kalam, Tehsil of Bahrain. Only on the Russian map.

Cf. prec. However, HAKIMZAY’s proposal (1997: 42: Skt./Hi. *jala* ‘water’: cf. T5155 *jala* ‘water’ [KUIPER (1948: 138) proposes a Muṇḍa origin, but this is disputed by KEWA I 423 and EWAia I 579 (“Nicht-idg. Ursprung des schon ved. Wortes (anders Kui, PMW 138f.) ist nicht wahrscheinlich”]: Pa. Pkt. *jala-* ‘water’; Lhd. (JUKES) *ǰal*; Hi. *jal*) seems quite reliable.

526. **JALBA-SAR جالبه سر (*ǰālba-sar*)** *Map 43*

Mountain of about 3,150 mt on the Roringai-khwar valley, Tehsil of Maṭṭa.

Cf. Jalba.

527. **JALGAR-BANDA جالګر بانډه (*ǰālgar-bānḍa*)** *Map 3*

Pasture in the upper Najigram-khwar valley, Tehsil of Barikot, near the boundary with Buner.

Cf. Pšt. *ǰəlga* ‘plain, steppe; small meadow, pasture, grassplot’? Cf. also the Pinus gerardiana name jalghzai, jaghoza (ALAM 2011)? See ADAMEC V 191 Jalga, “A nala rising under the Nikah Ziarat hill, and forming the head of the Sinzala Nala, which joins the Kadanai below Dobandi”.

528. **JAMALASAR جملسر (*ǰamalasar*)** *Map 39*

Group of houses on the slopes of the Shah-dop-sar towards the Barwai-khwar valley, Tehsil of Maṭṭa. Only on the Russian map.

Cf. possibly T10426 *yamala* ‘twin, paired’: Pa. *yamala-* ‘twin’; Pkt. *jamala-* ‘pair’.

529. **JAMBIL جامبيل (*ǰāmbil*)** *Map 22*

Village in the mountainous upper Jambil-khwar valley, Tehsil of Babuzai.

Cf. foll.

530. **JAMBIL-KHWAR جامبيل خوړ (*ǰāmbil-xwaṛ*)** *Map 21, 22*

Stream, whose estimate terrain elevation above seal level is 918 metres, originating from the mountains at the boundary with Buner and flowing into the Saidu-khwar, Tehsil of Babuzai.

Cf. T5130 *jambīra-* ‘citron tree’ [← Muṇḍa, according to KUIPER 1948: 84; see KEWA I 418 and EWAia III 207]: Pkt. *jaṃbīriya*, Hi. *jā̃mbhīrī* ‘the lime Citrus acida and its fruit’.

531. **JAMPUR-DERAI جمپور ډیرى (*ǰampur-ḍerəy*)** *Map 30*

Group of houses in the lower Charbagh-khwar valley, Tehsil of Charbagh.

IA *ǰam-pur* 'city of the Jams (caste name)'. Cf. Jampur, the city and tehsil in Rajanpur District, Punjab, south of Dera Ghazi Khan.

532.-533. **JAMRAI جمړى (*ǰamṛay*)** *Maps 49, 50*

Name of two groups of houses in the Tehsil of Bahrain: 1) in the upper Daral-khwar valley; 2) on the right bank of the Swāt river, near the confluence with the Kedam-khwar.

Pšt. *ǰum* 'turf, turf used in strengthening the banks of a canal or pond, clod of earth' (RAVERTY) + dim. sf. *-ṛay*.

534. **JANA جانه (*ǰāna*)** *Map 41*

Group of houses on the hills bordering the Harnoi-khwar valley, Tehsil of Maṭṭa. Only on the Russian map.

Cf. Jano.

535. **JANDERO جنډيرو (*ǰandeṛo*)** *Map 18*

Group of houses in the fertile valley on the left bank of the Swat river and at the foot of the hills, Tehsil of Babuzai. Its actual name is Qadirabad (*qadirābād*, Pšt. 'town of the Qadir').

Pšt. *ǰandra* 'padlock; instrument for drawing wire'; cf. foll.

536. **JANDRAI جندرى (*ǰandray*)** *Map 49*

Group of houses in the upper Daral-khwar valley, Tehsil of Bahrain.

Pšt. *žandra* 'mill; padlock'.

537. **JANO جانو (*ǰāno*)** *Map 31*

Village located in the plain of the Khwazakhela-khwar, near Khwazakhela, Tehsil of Khwazakhela.

T5098 *jána* 'race, person': Pa. *jana-* 'person, people', pl. 'people'; Pkt. *jaṇa-*, Paš. lauṛ. *ǰan*, Si. *ǰaṇo*; Lhd. *jaṇā* 'person, husband', mult. *jaṇ* 'the inhabitants of a village', awāṇ. *jaṇā* 'person', Panj. *jaṇā*; Hi. *janā*, Marw. *jaṇo*. HAKIMZAY (1997: 64) compares for Jano and Jana the name Japan and derives all from Skt. *pān/ṇ* in the meaning of 'encircled by waters': this proposal is quite unlikely. However, cf. also Pšt. *ǰən* 'virgin, maiden, spinster', or Tor. *ǰān* 'snake'.

538. **JAN-PATAI جان پيټى (*ǰān-peṭəy*)** *Map 33*

Group of houses located in the mountainous upper Khwazakhela-khwar valley, Tehsil of Khwazakhela.

Cf. Pšt. *peṭəy* 'load, burden, weight'? Or Pšt. 'field of the beloved (*ǰān*)'.

539. **JARANDA-KANDAO** جرنده کندو (*ǰaranda-kandāw*) *Map 42*

Pass leading from the upper Biha-khwar valley to Dir, Tehsil of Maṭṭa. Only on the Russian map.

Cf. foll.

540. **JARENDO-BELA-KHWAR** جرندو بیله خوړ (*ǰarendo-bela-xwaṛ*) *Map 12*

Stream flowing into the Manrai-khwar from the boundary with Dir, Tehsil of Kabal.

Probably obl. pl. of Pšt. *žránda* 'water-mill', local pronunciation *ǰranda*. Cf. T5344 *jharaṇa-* in *jharaṇōdaka-* 'water from a cascade': Pkt. *jharaṇa-* 'falling, dripping'; Si. *jharṇo* 'spring of water'; Panj. *jharnā* 'grating in a waterway, cullender'.

541. **JARO** جاړو (*ǰāṛo*) *Map 37*

Village in the narrow valley on the left bank of the Swāt river, Tehsil of Bahrain.

Cf. Pšt. *ǰāṛ* 'thickets, bushes; uncultivated land'.

542. **JARUGAI** جاړوگی (*ǰāṛugay*) *Map 42*

Group of houses on the border with Dir, on the Bar-kandao, on the slopes above the upper Harnoi-khwar valley, Tehsil of Maṭṭa. Only on the Russian map.

Cf. prec. + dimin. sf. *-gay*.

543. **JASHAR** جیشاړ (*ǰišāṛ*) *Map 33*

Group of houses in the terraced mountainous upper Khwazakhela-khwar valley, Tehsil of Khwazakhela.

Cf. Pšt. *ǰišay* 'name of a prickly thorn or shrub which adheres to one's clothes' (RAVERTY)?

544. **JATKOT** جټکوټ (*ǰaṭkoṭ*) *Map 17*

Small village located on the slopes of the hills in the Sigram-khwar valley, Tehsil of Kabal.

Pšt. 'village of the Jaṭs'.

545. **JATKOT-KANDAO** جټکوټ کنډو (*ǰaṭkoṭ kanḍaw*) *Map 17*

Pass leading from Jatkot to Ningulai, Tehsil of Kabal.

Cf. prec.

546. **JAUHAR-KANDAO** جوهر کنډو (*ǰawhar-kanḍaw*) *Map 26*

Pass leading from the Bikan-khwar valley to Shangla, Tehsil of Babuzai.

Pšt. 'pass of the jewels (*ǰawhár*)'.

547.-550. JAUR-BANDA جور باندہ (ǰaur-bānḍa) *Maps 2, 41*

Name of four pastures: 1) in the Kandak-khwar valley, Tehsil of Barikot, on the slopes on the boundary with the Kotah-khwar valley, near the Kakai-kandao; 2-4) on the slopes of the Lito-sar degrading towards the Harnoi-khwar valley, in Tehsil of Maṭṭa.

Pšt. *ǰawar* 'deep, profound, not shallow' (RAVERTY).

551. JAUZAN جوزان (ǰawzān) *Map 53*

Group of houses in the narrow valley on the left bank of the upper Swāt river, Tehsil of Bahrain. Only on the Russian map.

Pšt. *ǰawz* 'walnut', pl.

552. JAUZ-KANDAO جوز کندو (ǰawz-kanḍaw) *Map 19*

Pass on the boundary between the Tehsil of Babuzai and Buner, near the Moi-kandao. Called Jaosu-kandao by STEIN 1929.

Cf. prec.

553. JAWARKAS جوارکس (ǰawārkas) *Map 53*

Group of houses in the narrow valley on the left bank of the upper Swāt river, Tehsil of Bahrain.

Cf. foll.

554. JAWAR-KAS جوارکس (ǰawār kas) *Map 45*

Group of houses in the narrow valley on the right bank of the Swāt river, Tehsil of Bahrain.

Pšt. 'corn (*ǰ(a)wār*)-Kas (v. s.v.)'.

555. JAWI جاوي (ǰāwi) *Map 42*

Group of houses in the mountains above the Harnoi-khwar valley, Tehsil of Maṭṭa.

Cf. Pšt. *ǰuy* 'irrigation shaft; small irrigation ditch or channel'.

556. JIJAL-KANDAO ججال کندو (ǰiǰāl-kanḍaw) *Map 36*

Pass leading from the Miandam-khwar valley to Shangla, Tehsil of Khwazakhela.

Cf. T9570 *bhūrja-* 'the birch tree Betula bhojpattra': Bašk. *ǰiǰ* (< **bhrujji*), Sh.gil. *ǰūṣ* 'birch', (LORIMER) *J̣ūṣ*, pl. *J̣ūJi* 'birch bark', jij. *J̣ūṣ* 'birch'? See ADAMEC II 130 Jīja, "A Nurzai settlement on the Adraskand river, here called the Sabzawar, 50 miles (by road) north of Farah".

557. JIRA جیرہ (ǰira) *Map 53*

Group of houses in the narrow valley on the right bank of the upper Swāt river, Tehsil of Bahrain. Lira on the Russian map.

Cf. T5234 *jīraka-* 'cummin-seed': Pa. *jīraka-*, Pkt. *jīraya-*; Si. *jīro* 'cummin-seed', Panj. *jīrā*, Hi. *jīrā*?

558. **JOBE-KANDAO جوبي کندو (*ǰobe-kanḍaw*)** *Map 27*

Pass leading from the Tambagat-khwar to the Dre-khwar valley, Tehsil of Charbagh.

Pšt. 'pass of the caravans (*ǰopa*)'.

559. **JOLAGRAM-KHWAR جولگرام خوړ (*ǰolagrām-xwaṛ*)** *Map 5*

Stream located at an elevation of 850 meters above sea level, flowing into the right side of the Swāt river, Tehsil of Barikot.

Cf. T5155 *jala-* 'water': Pkt. Pa. *jala-*. Or T5355 **jhalla-* 'bush': Paš. ar. *ǰōl* 'tree'.

560. **JONTAR جونتر (*ǰontar*)** *Map 37*

Village in the plain on the left bank of the Swāt river, Tehsil of Khwazakhela. Only on the Russian map.

Cf. T10412 *yantrá* 'controlling device; any implement or contrivance; handmill': Pkt. *jaṁta-* 'machine, oil mill, water machine'; Gy. pal. *ǰándir*, *ǰándri* 'mill', Dm. *žandra*, *žan*; Paš. lauṛ. *žantr* 'watermill', ar. *žã̄r*, *yȭr*, dar. *yan*, kuṛ. *yã̄l*; Kal.rumb. *žõtr*, urt. *žã̄tr* 'mill'; Lhd. *jandar* 'watermill, lever for pounding rice', *jandrā* 'large wooden rake, padlock', *jandrī* 'small mill, mule pannier', khet. *jandrā* 'mill'; Panj. *jandar*, *jand* 'watermill, wooden rake', *jand*(*r*)*ā* 'padlock, rake', *jand*(*r*)*ī* 'small lock'.

561. **JOR-BANDA جوړ بانده (*ǰoṛ-bānḍa*)** *Map 10*

Pasture on the northern side of the Changai-dop-sar, in a lateral valley of the Ramogai-khwar valley, Tehsil of Kabal, on the boundary with Dir.

Pšt. 'good (*ǰoṛ*) pasture'.

562. **JOWARI-KANDAO جواری کندو (*ǰowāri-kanḍaw*)** *Map 20*

Pass on the boundary between the Tehsil of Babuzai and Buner, near the Ranjro-sar.

Pšt. 'pass of the corn (*ǰowār*)'.

563. **JUKHMAI جوخمی (*ǰuxmay*)** *Map 37*

Group of houses in the terraced mountainous Paiti-khwar valley, Tehsil of Khwazakhela. Only on the Russian map. Probably to be read Jukhtai, as in STEIN 1929 and 1930.

Cf. Pšt. *ǰuxt* 'situated alongside, located very close to, adjoining; paired; flat, even, level, smooth'.

564. **JURA جوره (*ǰura*)** *Map 38*

Village on the right bank of the Harnoi river at the foot of the hills bordering the plain, Tehsil of Maṭṭa.

HAKIMZAY (1997: 15) sees in *-ra* a suffix for 'region, village', coming from the "old language": "*də ǰo kəlay*", 'the village of Jo', not precising what Jo is, but suggesting a person's name. At p. 64 he derives Jura from an old Hi. term meaning 'male falcon'. This second hypothesis seems more plausible. However, cf. also Pšt. *ǰóṛa* 'harmony, peace'?

565. KABAL-BANDA کبل باندہ (*kabal-bānḍa*) *Map 12*

Pasture in the upper Deolai-khwar valley, Tehsil of Kabal, near the border with Dir.

Pšt. 'pasture of the meadow (see Kabbal)'.

566. KABALKU کابلکو (*kābalku*) *Map 43*

Group of houses in the narrow Roringar-khwar valley, Tehsil of Maṭṭa.

Cf. prec.

567. KABBAL کبل (*kabal*) *Map 9*

Big village in the vast and fertile plain on the right bank of the Swāt river, main village of the Tehsil of Kabal. It is probably RAVERTY's (1888: 201) Díw-lí, thaking its name from the name of the stream.

Pšt. *kabál* 'Bermuda grass, bent grass', cf. *kabalzā́r* 'meadow, lawn'. See also SULTAN-I-ROME 2008: 326: "*Kabal.* A kind of grass; the place where Miangul Abdul Wadud was installed as Bacha of Swat State; also, the Tahsil headquarter. It now also stands for the village Chindakhwara, capital of Abdul Jabbar Shah".

568. KACHAL-BELA کاچل بیلہ (*kāčal-bela*) *Map 49*

Group of houses in the upper Daral-khwar valley, Tehsil of Bahrain.

Cf. Bašk. *kaçāl*, Tor. *kaṣāl*, Gaw. *kaċyāl*, "ext. with *-āl-* to form cmpds. with 'bottom, root' as in neighbouring Ir. lggs. [...] From the meaning 'side, edge' derive prob. some adverbs and postpositions" (T2588).

569. KACHCHA-KOR کچہ کور (*kačča-kor*) *Map 22*

Group of houses in the hills bordering the Jambil-khwar valley, towards the Landai-khwar valley, Tehsil of Babuzai.

Pšt. 'rammed-earth (*kačá*) house (*kor*)'.

570. KACHHIKHANI-AN کچھیخاني ان (*kačhixāni-an*) *Map 54*

Pass leading from the upper Bahandra-gol valley to Chitral, Tehsil of Bahrain.

Cf. prec. with *xāna* instead of *kor*.

571.-572. KAD کډ (*kaḍ*) *Map 24*

Name of two groups of houses in the Tehsil of Babuzai: 1) in the mountainous upper Landai-khwar valley; 2) in the slopes of the Spedar-khwar valley, Tehsil of Babuzai.

Pšt. *káḍa* 'family (among the nomads); nomad's camp' (cf. the example quoted by ASLANOV: *zə lə swāta dəlta pə kaḍa rāɣlay yəm* 'I moved here from Swāt' [English translation by PASHTOON]).

573. **KADARCHAKA کدرچکه (*kadarčaka*)** *Map 42*

Group of houses on the slopes of the Prangman-sar towards the Harnoi-khwar valley, Tehsil of Maṭṭa. Only on the Russian map.

Cf. Ur. *kadar* 'being turbid or muddy; turbidness, muddiness, dirtiness; perturbation, agitation (of mind), trouble, affliction, solicitude' + Ur. *ćaukā* 'a square piece of ground; a square slab of marble or other stone'? Cf. also the name of the village Kadar Chowk in Uttar Pradesh.

574. **KADIAR کډیار (*kaḍyār*)** *Map 42*

Group of houses located on the slopes above the upper Biha-khwar valley, Tehsil of Maṭṭa.

Cf. Pšt. *kaḍhə́l, kaḍəhə́l, kaḍəhál* 'land or a portion of land prepared for sowing rice in' (RAVERTY), 'pit, hole; pit filled with water; ground prepared for planting rice' (ASLANOV). Another possibility, less likely, could be Pšt. *kaḍa* 'family (such as wife, children, mother, sister, domestics, etc.) the household in general; migration, march' (RAVERTY) + sf. *-yār*. See ADAMEC V 201 Kadir (*qādir*), "A hamlet in the Kushobai valley; 6 houses of Pirakzai Nurzais".

575. **KADKHWAR کډخوړ (*kaḍxwaṛ*)** *Map 43*

Group of houses in the narrow Roringar-khwar valley, Tehsil of Maṭṭa. Only on the Russian map.

Possibly cf. T2680 *kaṇṭhá* '(*b*) narrowest part of a hole; (*d*) *border, immediate proximity' [possibly ← Muṇḍa: KUIPER 1948: 29-30; see KEWA I 146-147 and EWAia I 292]: (*b*) Bašk. *kāṇḍə*; (*d*) Pkt. *kaṁṭha-* 'border, edge'; Lhd. awāṇ. *kaḍḍhā* 'bank'; Panj. *kaṇḍhā* 'bank, shore', °*ḍhī* 'land bordering on a mountain'. And T2720 *kanthā* 'wall, town' [← Ir. EWAia I 151 with lit. coincides with *kaṇṭhá-* in meanings 'wall, border, bank']: Lhd. *kaddh, kandh* 'wall', *kaddhī, kandhī* 'river-bank', awāṇ. *kadh* 'wall', khet. *khand*; Panj. *kandh* 'wall': 'stream-bank'.

576. **KAFIR-BANDA کافر بانډه (*kāfir-bānḍa*)** *Map 46*

Pasture in the Nali-darra valley, Tehsil of Bahrain.

Pšt. 'pasture of the Kafirs'.

577.-578. **KAHAI کاهی (*kāhay*)** *Map 47*

Name of two groups of houses in the mountains above the upper Baral-darra valley, Tehsil of Bahrain.

Pšt. *kāhəy* 'ditch, trench, moat, ravine'.

579. **KAKAI کاکی (*kākay*)** *Map 1*

Group of houses on the hills of the Kotah-khwar leading to the Kandak-khwar valley, Tehsil of Barikot.

Cf. prec. or Pšt. *kakaway* 'name of a bird, about the size of a crow, which cries at night. It dwells on the banks of rivers' (RAVERTY), and T2993 *kāka* 'crow', °*kī*-: Pa. *kākī*-, Paš. *kaxī*?

580. **KAKAI-KANDAO کاکی کنډو (*kākay-kanḍaw*)** *Map 1*

Pass near Kakai, leading from the Kotah-khwar valley to the Kandak-khwar valley, Tehsil of Barikot.

Pšt. 'pass of Kakai'. See OLIVIERI/VIDALE 2002; OLIVIERI 2004; OLIVIERI 2005; OLIVIERI/VIDALE ET AL. 2006.

581. **KAKARDAM کاکړدم (*kākaṛdam*)** *Map 33*

Group of houses located in the wide terraced Khwazakhela-khwar valley, Tehsil of Khwazakhela.

Possibly, Pšt. 'pond/lake (*ḍam*) of the Kākaṛs (tribe)', but cf. also T3211 *kukkuramardaka*, °*dana*- 'a plant with fragrant leaves': Hi. *kukurõdā*, °*rū̃dā*, °*raũdhā*, *kukrõdā*, *kak*° 'the plant Celsia and its fruit'. See ADAMEC VI 370, "A village located on a stream, some six miles east of Mamai in southeastern Ghazni province".

582. **KAKHAI-DERAI کخی ډېری (*kaxay ḍerəy*)** *Map 32*

Group of houses in the plain of the Khwazakhela-khwar, near Khwazakhela, Tehsil of Khwazakhela.

Cf. Kahai.

583. **KAKOT ککوټ (*kakoṭ*)** *Map 28*

Group of houses in the narrow upper Dre-khwar valley, Tehsil of Charbagh. Only on the Russian map.

Cf. Pšt. *kakóṛa*, *kākóṛa* 'colocynth, bitter apple' (ASLANOV) and *kākutí* 'ziziphora'?

584. **KALA کاله (*kāla*)** *Map 14*

Village in the wide and fertile Deolai-khwar valley, north of Sirsanai, Tehsil of Kabal. Quoted already by RAVERTY (1888: 232). Called Kalakhela by TUCCI (1958: 319), Kalakalay in Google Earth.

= Pšt. *qalā́* 'castle'.

585. **KALAGAI قلاګی (*qalāgay*)** *Map 38*

Group of houses on the hills of the Saso-sar, Tehsil of Maṭṭa.

Pšt. 'small castle'.

586. **KALAGRAM كلكرام (*kalagrām*)** *Map 44*

Group of houses located in the last fields at the foot of the hills on the right bank of the Swat river, on the other side of Madyan, Tehsil of Bahrain. Only on the Russian map.

Cf. T3083 *kāla* 'black, dark-blue' [← Drav.: see KEWA I 203, but also EWAia I 343]: Pa. *kāḷa-*, Pkt. *kāla-*, Lhd. Panj. *kālā*: → 'black village'.

587. **KALAKOT كالاكوټ (*kālākoṭ*)** *Map 44*

Village located on the right bank of the Swāt river, at the confluence with the Barwai-khwar, Tehsil of Maṭṭa. Already quoted by RAVERTY (1888: 234) as Kálá-Koṭ. According to the same author, it is possible to reach a village called Dawárika'h, proceeding "eight kuroh north, inclining north-east": the name of this place, "which is inhabited by Kohistánís", was "known to the author of these surveys ninety years ago, like that of the Báshḳár Dara'h [...] has not hitherto been made known to Europeans, and escaped the notice of the person whom I sent into Suwát, and whose account of the Kohistán is mentioned farther on". In this village, again according to RAVERTY (*ibid.*: 242), the Ákhúnd Karím-Dád was killed while "fighting with the Spín Káfirís".

Pšt. *qalā́* + *koṭ* 'stronghold'.

588. **KALAM كالام (*kālām*)** *Map 54*

One of the most northern villages, on the Swāt river, at the confluence between the Ushu-gol, the Gabral river and the Bahandra-gol, Tehsil of Bahrain. Quoted already by RAVERTY (1888: 237) and by DEANE (1895).

Cf. T3187 *kilima* 'a kind of pine': Kho. *kelel* 'resin', Bašk. *kalál;* Phal. *kīlum* 'tar'; Sh. *kalēl* 'resin'; K. *kĕlam* 'resin of deodar or other fir'. Cf. also Kalel-kandao.

589. **KALEL-KANDAO كاليل كندو (*kālel-kanḍaw*)** *Map 22*

Pass leading to Buner from the Jambil-khwar valley, Tehsil of Kabal.

Cf. prec.

590. **KALO-BANDA كلو بانډه (*kalo-bānḍa*)** *Map 43*

Pasture in the narrow Roringar-khwar valley, Tehsil of Maṭṭa. Only on the Russian map.

Cf. Kala.

591. **KAMALI-BANDA كملي بانډه (*kamali-bānḍa*)** *Map 39*

Pasture on the slopes of the Shah-dop-sar, Tehsil of Maṭṭa.

Cf. Pšt. *kamāl* 'complete, entire, perfect, finished' (RAVERTY): 'perfect pasture', or T2764 *kamala* 'lotus' [← Drav.: KEWA I 160; see also EWAia I 305]: Pa. Pkt. *kamala-*; Panj. *kamal* 'blue gentian'?

592. **KAMARBAGH کمرباغ (*kamarbāγ*)** *Map 30*

Group of houses in the wide plain of Charbagh near Charbagh and towards the Swat river, Tehsil of Charbagh.

Pšt. 'garden of the rock'.

593. **KAMAR-BANDA کمر بانده (*kamar-bānḍa*)** *Map 17*

Pasture on the slopes of the hills in the Sigram-khwar valley, Tehsil of Kabal.

Pšt. 'pasture of the rock'.

594. **KAMARGAI کمرگی (*kamargay*)** *Map 30*

Group of houses on the hills on the left bank of the Swāt river, Tehsil of Charbagh.

Cf. prec.

595. **KAMARKHA کمرخه (*kamarxa*)** *Map 52*

Group of houses in the upper Mankial-khwar valley, Tehsil of Bahrain. Only on the Russian map.

Cf. prec. + sf. *-xa* (?).

596. **KAMBAR قمبر (*qambar*)** *Map 18*

Village on the road leading from Barikot to Mingaora, in the fertile valley on the left bank of the Swat river and at the foot of the hills, on the Saidu-khwar, Tehsil of Babuzai. Already quoted by RAVERTY 1888.

Pšt. 'precipice' (*kamár*). To be excluded a connection with the tribal name Kampar (RAVERTY 1959: 342) in the name Qal 'a-i Qanbar of the Ṣifat-nāma (SCARCIA 1965: 135). Cf. also T2770 *kambara* 'variegated', also in Bal. (ROSSI, p.c.)?

597. **KAMYARAI-BANDA کمیاری بانده (*kamyāray-bānḍa*)** *Map 12*

Pasture in the terraced Jarendo-bela-khwar valley, Tehsil of Kabal.

Pšt. 'pasture "having few (*kam*) friends (*yār*)"'?

598.-599. **KANATI کنتي (*kanati*)** *Map 42*

Name of two groups of houses in the Tehsil of Maṭṭa, one in the upper Harnoi-khwar valley, the other on the slopes above the Biha-khwar valley. Both only on the Russian map.

Cf. T2679 *kanṭin* '*thorny' ('name of various plants'): Pkt. *kaṁṭiya-* 'thorny'; Si. *kaṇḍī* 'thorn bush'?

600. **KAND كند (*kand*)** *Map 43*

Group of houses on the slopes of the narrow Roringar-khwar valley, Tehsil of Maṭṭa.

Pšt. *kand* 'ravine, gorge'. See EILERS 1987: 24: "Hoch- und Engpässe sowie darnach benannte Siedlungen mit *kand* (auch allein *Kand*; nicht zu verwechseln mit türkisiertem -*qand* 'Dorf, Stadt') sind über ganz Iran verbreitet".

601. KANDAI کندی (*kanday*) *Map 41*

Group of houses on the hills bordering the Harnoi-khwar valley, Tehsil of Maṭṭa. Only on the Russian map.

Pšt. *kandəy* 'uneven or broken ground, ground filled with ravines and chasms' (RAVERTY) or Pšt. *kanday* 'division, district, parish, ward, quarter of a town or city' (RAVERTY). Cf. also prec.

602. KANDAK کنداک (*kandāk*) *Map 2*

Main village in the Kandak-khwar valley, Tehsil of Barikot. It is called Kandag by STEIN (1929: 31), in the description of his itinerary through Goratai, Goratuna-banda, Barikot, Bālo, Kandag, Najigram, Amlukdara, Karakar-banda, Shingardar, Ghaligay, Manyar, etc.

Cf. Kandak-khwar.

603. KANDAKAI کندکی (*kandakay*) *Map 24*

Group of houses in the mountainous upper Landai-khwar valley, Tehsil of Babuzai.

See prec. 'of Kandak'.

604. KANDAK-KHWAR کندک خوړ (*kandak-xwaṛ*) *Map 2*

Stream located at an elevation of 774 meters above sea level, Tehsil of Barikot, flowing from the boundary with Buner to the Swat river, near Barikot.

Cf. the river name in Nepal Gaṇḍakī, Skt. *gaṇḍakī* 'N. of a river in the northern part of India' (MBh. ii, 1062) (MONIER-WILLIAMS). See KEWA I 317: "Name eines schnell fließenden Flusses. Wohl ein nasalisiertes Munda-Wort **gaṇḍak*' "Fluß" (ho *gaḍa* "Fluß" usw.), das möglicherweise auch im Namen der *Gáṅgā* vorliegt (s. d.!). Vgl. Pinnow, BzN 5, 3f.". See also OLIVIERI 2015 and DE CHIARA 2008: 131.

605.-607. KANDAO کنډو (*kanḍaw*) *Maps 16, 28, 37*

Name of three villages: 1) in a mountainous lateral valley of the Deolai-khwar valley at the frontier with the Tehsil of Maṭṭa, Tehsil of Kabal; 2) on the pass separating the Dre-khwar valley and the Makad-khwar valley, Tehsil of Charbagh; 3) group of houses on the slopes of the Dobar-sar towards the Swāt river, Tehsil of Khwazakhela (only on the Russian map).

Pšt. 'pass'.

608.-609. KANDAO-BANDA کنډو بانډه (*kanḍaw-bānḍa*) *Maps 26, 35*

Name of two pastures: 1) in the Bishbanr-khwar valley, Tehsil of Charbagh; 2) in a lateral valley on the left bank of the Swāt river, near Asala, Tehsil of Khwazakhela.

Pšt. 'pasture of the pass'.

610. **KANDAOGAI کندوگی (*kanḍawgay*)** *Map 40*

Group of houses in the narrow terraced valley of the Shaurai-khwar, Tehsil of Maṭṭa.

Pšt. 'small pass'/'place of the pass'.

611.-614. **KANDAR کندر (*kanḍar*)** *Maps 30, 41, 44, 50*

Name of four groups of houses: 1) on the flank of the mountains bordering the Charbagh-khwar valley, Tehsil of Charbagh; 2) in the narrow upper Harnoi-khwar valley, in Tehsil of Maṭṭa (only on the Russian map); 3) in the mountainous Barwai-khwar valley, Tehsil of Maṭṭa (only on the Russian map); 4) on the right bank of the Swāt river near the Kedam-khwar valley, Tehsil of Bahrain.

Pšt. *kándra, kándara* 'ravine, hollow, depression'.

615. **KANDIA-KANDAO کندیه کندو (*kandya-kanḍaw*)** *Map 52*

Pass leading from the Mankial-khwar valley to Kohistan, Tehsil of Bahrain.

Cf. Pšt. *kanḍyā́la* 'stall, stable; ruins'.

616. **KANDIMAR کندیمار (*kandimār*)** *Map 53*

Group of houses in the narrow valley on the right bank of the upper Swāt river, Tehsil of Bahrain.

Cf. Kand and Kandar.

617. **KANDOWALA-MORAH کندواله موره (*kanḍowāla-mora*)** *Map 22*

Group of houses in the mountainous upper Jambil-khwar valley, near Jambil, Tehsil of Babuzai.

Pšt. 'range of the ruins (*kanḍwālá*)'.

618. **KANGALAI کانګلی (*kāngalay*)** *Map 22*

Village located on the slopes of the mountains above the Jambil-khwar valley, Tehsil of Babuzai.

Pšt. *kangə́lay* 'iced, frozed'? Cf. also T2628 *kañjala* 'the bird Gracula religiosa', *kañjara-* 'peacock' [unkn. origin, according to EWAia III 45]: Kt. *kaǰuřák* 'a particular bird'; Kal. *kanǰə̄ř, °ǰəř* 'a large black bird', Kho. *kanǰóḷ* 'a biggish black bird', (LORIMER) *kanǰōl* 'a singing bird blue-black in colour and twice the size of a blackbird'?

619. **KANGAR کنګر (*kangar*)** *Map 43*

Group of houses in the Roringar-khwar valley, near the boundary with Dir, Tehsil of Maṭṭa.

Pšt. *kangrá* 'turret; merlon; wall with loopholes; summit (of a mountain)'.

620. **KANJ-KANDAO کنج کندو (*kanǰ-kanḍaw*)** *Map 26*

Pass leading from the Spedar-khwar valley to Shangla, Tehsil of Babuzai.

Pšt. *kunǰ* 'corner, confined place, grove, bower' (RAVERTY).

621. **KANJU کانجو (*kānǰu*)** *Map 9*

Big village in the fertile plain on the right bank of the Swāt river, Tehsil of Kabal. Quoted already by RAVERTY (1888: 230) as Kánjú-án. Here is the shrine of Karim-Dād, the son of Akhund Darweza.

Cf. T2605 *kaṅgu-* 'Panicum italicum' [In KEWA I 138 the hypothesis of a Proto-Muṇḍa comparison; see also EWAia III 43]: Pa. *kāṅgu-* 'millet', etc.? Cf. prec.?

622. **KANR کڼ (*kaṇ*)** *Map 48*

Group of houses in a lateral valley on the right bank of the Swāt river, Tehsil of Bahrain.

Pšt. *kāṇay* 'stone, stone for grinding condiments, muller' (RAVERTY).

623. **KANRO-SAR-BANDA کاڼو سر بانډه (*kāṇo-sar-bānḍa*)** *Map 45*

Pasture in a lateral valley on the right bank of the Swāt river on the slopes of the Babu-sar, Tehsil of Bahrain. Only on the Russian map.

Pšt. 'pasture of the rocky mountain'.

624. **KANRTIKAI کاڼټکی (*kāṇṭikay*)** *Map 48*

Group of houses in the Daral-khwar valley, Tehsil of Bahrain. Only on the Russian map.

Pšt. 'rocky (*kāṇ*) summer pasture (*ṭikay*).

625.-626. **KAR کاړ (*kāṛ*)** *Maps 44, 47*

Name of two groups of houses in the Tehsil of Bahrain: 1) in a lateral valley on the right bank of the Swāt river on the slopes of the Babu-sar; 2) in the upper Baral-darra valley.

Pšt. *kāṛ* 'pebbles; rocky terrain'. Or cf. Pšt. *kār* 'work'.

627. **KARAI کرای (*karāy*)** *Map 33*

Small village in the terraced mountainous upper Khwazakhela-khwar valley, Tehsil of Khwazakhela.

Pšt. *karāyí, karāhá* 'rented, hired'. Cf. foll.?

628. **KARAI-SAR کاړی سر (*kāṛay-sar*)** *Map 19*

Mountain of about 2,200 mt, in the Tehsil of Babuzai, on the boundary with Buner and with the Tehsil of Barikot.

Pšt. *kāṛ* 'pebbles; rocky terrain': 'rocky mountain'. Cf. prec.?

629. **KARAKAL کرکل (*karakal*)** *Map 41*

Group of houses on the slopes of the Prangman-sar, in a lateral valley of the upper Harnoi-khwar valley, Tehsil of Maṭṭa.

Cf. Pšt. *karkaṇa* 'the wild jujube and its fruit; a small thorny tree, a brier' (RAVERTY)? See ADAMEC V 272 Karam Kala, "A village located on the Jahangir river, about 1 mile from Shaikhu in Zabul province. Another village with this name is located on the Duri Rud, about 15 miles south of Takhtapul", ADAMEC VI 393 Karakul (*qara qul*), "A village located on the source of the Garmab river, southeast of the Kuh-i-Khalta. Another place with this name is located southwest of the Kuh-i-Khalta, on a tributary of the Garmab river in southern Bamian province", and *ibid.* Karamkol (*karam qol*), "A village located on a tributary of the Dara-i-Jelga, about 1 mile north of Suja in Maidan province. Another place with this name is located on a tributary of the Garmab river in southern Bamian province".

630. **KARAKAR-BANDA کرکر بانډه (*karakar-bānḍa*)** *Map 4*

Pasture on the hills borderning the Karakar-khwar valley, Tehsil of Barikot, towards the boundary with Buner.

Cf. Karakar-khwar.

631. **KARAKAR-KANDAO کرکر کنډو (*karakar-kanḍaw*)** *Map 4*

Pass at the end of the Karakar-khwar valley on the boundary with Buner.

Cf. foll.

632. **KARAKAR-KHWAR کرکر خوړ (*karakar-xwaṛ*)** *Map 4*

Stream located at an elevation of 774 meters above sea level, Tehsil of Barikot, flowing from the boundary with Buner to the Kandak-khwar near Barikot.

Cf. the account of O rgyan pa (TUCCI 1971: 397-398), where he reaches K'a rag k'ar (= Karakar). "From there (i.e. to the N) O rgyan pa sees the green and lavish valley of a River Kodambhar, which should be the ancient name of the Karakar River" (OLIVIERI 2017: 89). Cf. T2819 *karkara-*[1] 'hard, firm' (Pa. *kakkaratā-*, *°riya-* 'roughness, harshness'; Pkt. *kakkara-* 'hard, firm'; Tir. *kaṅgará*, Paš. *kaṅgarā́* 'ice' (→ Psht. *kaṅgal*, *karaṅg* 'ice' IIFL iii 3, 95); K. *trakoru* 'hard, rough' < **krak-*; Lhd. *kakkar* 'frost, raw thong'; Panj. *kakkar* 'frost') and T2820 *karkara-*[2] 'stone' ("Prob. same as KARKARA-[1]: for semant. development 'ice ~ hail ~ stone'"; cf. Pkt. *kakkara-* 'stone, pebble'; Si. *kakiro* 'stone, stone in the bladder'; Lhd. *kakrā* 'gravel'). KUIPER (1948: 121-122) proposes a Muṇḍa origin and compares Skt. *śarkarā-* 'gravel, grit', but MAYRHOFER (KEWA III 308-309 and EWAia II 618-619) does not agree and proposes instead an IE. etymology. From a semantic point of view, a meaning as 'stony stream' would indirectly also confirm the etymology of the Baral-darra (q.v.).

633. **KARAMAR کرامار (*karāmār*)** *Map 46*

Group of houses in the upper Olal-khwar valley, Tehsil of Bahrain.

Cf. the Karamar hills in the Mardan district, important in the Pashtun legend of Yusuf Khan aw Sher Bano. It possibly contains T3784 *khaḍaka* '*erect, bolt, post': Si. *kharo* 'standing erect', Panj. *khaṛā*, + Pšt. *mār* 'serpent', in the meaning of 'erect serpent'?

634. KARANDUKAI قارندوکی (*qārandukay*) *Map 53*

Group of houses in the narrow valley on the left bank of the upper Swāt river, Tehsil of Bahrain.

Cf. Pšt. *karwandá/karawndá* 'cultivated land' + sf. diminutive *-kay*.

635. KARANGE کرنګي (*karange*) *Map 32*

Group of houses on the slope of the hills north of the Shalwa-kandao, south of the Khwazakhela-khwar, Tehsil of Khwazakhela.

Cf. Pšt. *karangedə́l* 'to be covered with ice'.

636. KAR-BANDA کاړ بانډه (*kāṛ-bānḍa*) *Map 50*

Pasture in the Kedam-khwar valley, Tehsil of Bahrain.

Pšt. 'pasture of the pebbles (*kāṛ*)'.

637. KAR-BELA کاړ بېله (*kāṛ-bela*) *Map 53*

Group of houses in the narrow valley on the right bank of the upper Swāt river, Tehsil of Bahrain. Only on the Russian map.

Pšt. 'village (*bela*) of the pebbles (*kāṛ*)'.

638. KARIAL کاړیال (*kāṛyāl*) *Map 46*

Group of houses in the upper Olal-khwar valley, Tehsil of Bahrain.

Possibly Pšt. *kāṛ* 'pebbles; rocky terrain' + sf. *-yāl* (on this sf., see s.v. Mankial).

639. KARINUNA کارینونه (*kārinuna*) *Map 43*

Village in the mountainous narrow Barwai-khwar valley, Tehsil of Maṭṭa.

Pšt. *kārín* 'mountainous plot of land temporarily used for crops'. See SULTAN-I-ROME 2016: 488: "*Karin*: A plot of land situated on a hill" and *ibid.*: 538: "The terraces on hillside land that cannot be cultivated by plough and therefore are cultivated with a pickaxe. The term is sometimes used to designate land cleared in the forests but cultivated by plough".

640. KARO-BANDA کاړو بانډه (*kāṛo-bānḍa*) *Map 42*

Pasture in the upper Biha-khwar valley, Tehsil of Maṭṭa.

Pšt. *kāṛ* 'pebbles; rocky terrain'. Possible also Pšt. 'pasture of the karu (a measure of land area)'.

641. **KARORAI کاروړی (*kāroṛay*)** *Map 33*

Group of houses on the crest on the boundary with Shangla, Tehsil of Khwazakhela.

Pšt. 'blackberries (*karúṛa*)'.

642. **KARORAI-KANDAO کاروړی کنډو (*kāroṛay-kanḍaw*)** *Map 33*

Pass leading to Shangla from the upper Khwazakhela-khwar valley, Tehsil of Khwazakhela.

Pšt. 'pass of the blackberries (*karúṛa*)'.

643. **KARPO کرپو (*karpo*)** *Map 20*

Group of houses in the spur between the Saidu-khwar valley and the Jambil-khwar valley, near Jambil, Tehsil of Babuzai.

Cf. Pšt. *kṛap* 'slam, bang, swap, dab' (RAVERTY).

644.-646. **KAS کس (*kas*)** *Maps 24, 46, 53*

Name of three villages or groups of houses: 1) village in the mountains above the Spedar-khwar valley, Tehsil of Babuzai; 2) village in the Nali-darra valley, Tehsil of Bahrain; 3) group of houses in the narrow valley on the left bank of the upper Swāt river, Tehsil of Bahrain (it is called Kats on the Russian map).

Pšt. *kas* 'ravine, hollow, depression'; better SULTAN-I-ROME 2016: 479: "*Kas*: A vast patch or portion of land (synonymous with *wand*) but usually level".

647. **KASAI کسی (*kasay*)** *Map 8*

Small village on the slopes of the Kotlai-khwar valley leading to the boundary with Dir, under the Changai-dop-sar, Tehsil of Kabal.

Cf. prec.

648. **KASHALA کشاله (*kašāla*)** *Map 7*

Mountain in the Tehsils of Barikot, at the boundary with the Tehsil of Babuzai and on the main valley of the Swat river. Its height is about 1,810 mt.

Pšt. *kašāla* 'pulling or draging along, trailing along the ground' (RAVERTY).

649. **KASHANKAD کاشنکد (*kāšankad*)** *Map 46*

Group of houses in the Shanku-khwar valley and on the slopes of the Bura-sar, Tehsil of Bahrain.

Possibly IA 'dark valley': cf. T3451 *kṛṣṇá-* 'dark blue, black': Pkt. *kasiṇa-*, *°saṇa-*, Bašk. *kiṣin*, Tor. *kəṣən* + T3790 **khaḍḍa* 'hole, pit': Pkt. *khaḍḍā-* 'hole, mine, cave', Bašk. (BIDDULPH) "*kād*" (= *khaḍ*?) 'valley'; K. *khŏḍ* 'pit', Si. *khaḍa* 'pit'; Lhd. *khaḍḍ* 'pit, cavern, ravine'; Panj. *khaḍḍ* 'pit, ravine'.

650. **KASHKAR-BANDA کاشکار بانډه (*kāškār-bānḍa*)** *Map 11*

Pasture in the Qalagai-khwar valley, Tehsil of Kabal.

Pšt. 'pasture of the magpies (*kəškára*)'.

651. **KASUNA کسونه (*kasuna*)** *Map 27*

Village near the Tambagat-khwar, Tehsil of Charbagh.

Pšt. *kas* 'ravine, hollow, depression', pl.

652. **KAT-DERA کت ډېره (*kat-ḍera*)** *Map 49*

Group of houses in the upper Daral-khwar valley, Tehsil of Bahrain.

Pšt. *kat* 'heap, pile, store, supply, repository' (RAVERTY). Or Pšt. *kat* 'Catechu, terra japonica, an astringent vegetable extract from the Mimosa (Chadria)' (RAVERTY).

653. **KATELAI کاټېلی (*kāṭelay*)** *Map 18*

Village at the confluence between the Saidu-khwar and the Jambil-khwar, near Mingaora, Tehsil of Babuzai. According to the residents, Katelai is the old name of Aman-koṭ (q.v.), even if both the villages are quoted on the Pakistani map. RAVERTY (1862 and 1888: 199) gives the orthography Káṭlí. Considering the antiquity of the first mention of this village, Aman-koṭ can only be a recent quartier of Katelai.

Cf. T3018 *kāṭha* 'rock' + dim. sf. *-li*, or Ur. *kāṭ* 'passage, way, channel' and Ur. *kāṭh* 'Wood, timber; piece of wood or timber, log, stock, block' (PLATTS); cf. also T2851 *kartá-* 'hole' [cf. *kāṭá-* 'hole' — "The extensive interchange of sounds, voiced with unvoiced, retroflex with dental or *l*, inexplicable within Indo-Aryan itself, in a group of words all indicating 'digging' and 'hole' strongly supports assumption of Dravidian origin for it (T. Burrow BSOAS xii 370 [1948]) despite the early attestation of *kartá-*, *kāṭá-*, *gárta-* (EWA i 173). Beside Kan. *kaḍḍa* 'pitfall for elephants' cf. Kan. *gal̤de* (9th cent.), *gardde* (11th cent.), *gaddĕ* 'paddy field', Brah. *kaṛak* 'hole'"]. KUIPER (1955: 162) proposes proto-Muṇḍa origin (discarded by KEWA I 196); see also EWAia I 336-337. Cf. also Pšt. *kaṭeyəl* 'to cut, clip, dock' and Pšt. *katəlay* 'looked'?

654. **KATIYA کټیا (*kaṭiyā*)** *Map 14*

Small village in the narrow Deolai-khwar valley, between Dolai and Dheri, Tehsil of Kabal.

Cf. prec.? According to IKRAM, p.c., possibly Katyar: in this case, cf. Pšt. *kaṭér* 'collective work, help, assistance; cartel, peasants' cooperative, workers' cooperative'. Semantically, this would partly confirm an IA etymology: cf. Skt. *kaṭyā-* 'multitude', according to KUIPER (1948: 55, see also KEWA I 143) ← Austro-As.

655. **KATOSAR-BANDA کتوسر بانډه (*katosar-bānḍa*)** *Map 34*

Small village in the plain on the left bank of the Swāt river, south of the Bargin-khwar, Tehsil of Khwazakhela. Only on the Russian map.

Pšt. 'pasture of the top (*sar*) of the Catechu (*kat*)', cf. Kat-dera?

656. **KEDAM-BELA کېدام بېله (*kedām-belā*)** *Map 50*

Group of houses on the right bank of the Swāt river near the confluence with the Kedam-khwar valley, Tehsil of Bahrain.

Cf. foll.

657. **KEDAM-KHWAR کېدام خوړ (*kedām-xwaṛ*)** *Map 50*

Stream located at an elevation of 1,544 meters above sea level, springing from the mountain on the right bank of the Swāt river, Tehsil of Bahrain.

Cf. the village? According to Google, the name is *kedara*: cf. T3463 *kēdāra* 'field (esp. one under water)' [← Drav., see BURROW 1943: 124 and KEWA I 265]: Pa. *kēdāra-* 'irrigated field'; Pkt. *kēāra-* 'field'; Lhd. *kiārā* 'large plot in a field'; Panj. *keārā*, *kiārā* 'bed in a field or garden'. Addenda: *kēdāra-*: WPah.kṭg. *kyār* 'irrigated paddy field', etc.

658. **KETAL کېتل (*ketal*)** *Map 47*

Group of houses on the left side of the Swāt river, north of the Baral-darra, Tehsil of Bahrain.

It could be related to T3463 *kēdāra* 'field (esp. one under water)': cf. prec. However, in the north-west Prakrits intervocalic *-d-* normally disappears, as in Pkt. *kēāra-* 'field', Lhd. Panj. *kiārā* 'large plot in a field', etc., belonging to the same root.

659. **KHABIN خبين (*xabin*)** *Map 45*

Group of houses in the narrow valley on the right bank of the Swāt river, Tehsil of Bahrain. Only on the Russian map.

Possibly Pšt. 'good (*x̌a*) building (*binā*)'?

660. **KHACHAR خچر (*xačar*)** *Map 39*

Group of houses in the narrow upper Harnoi-khwar valley, in Tehsil of Maṭṭa. Only on the Russian map.

Pšt. 'mule'.

661.-662. **KHADANG خدنګ (*xadang*)** *Maps 29, 39*

Name of two groups of houses: 1) on the crest near the Khadang-sar separating the Makad-khwar from the Charbagh-khwar valley, Tehsil of Charbagh; 2) at the foot of the hills on the right bank of the Swāt river, Tehsil of Maṭṭa.

Pšt. *xadáng* 'silver poplar' (Populus canescens, according to ALAM 2011). In the opinion of HAKIMZAY (1997: 76), it is a kind of arm.

663. **KHADANG-SAR خدنګ سر (*xadang-sar*)** *Map 29*

Mountain of abouth 1,700 mt. On the border between the Makad-khwar valley and the Charbagh-khwar valley, Tehsil of Charbagh.

Cf. prec.

664. **KHADARZO-PATAI خدرزو پټی (*xadarzo-pəṭay*)** *Map 29*

Group of houses located in the mountainous Makad-khwar valley, on the slopes of the Welan-sar, Tehsil of Charbagh.

Pšt. 'field of the Khidarzais' (one of the Yusufzai tribes).

665. **KHAIRABAD خيراباد (*xayrābād*)** *Map 38*

Small village located in the plain on the right bank of the Harnoi-khwar valley, Tehsil of Maṭṭa.

Pšt. 'town of the good (*xayr*)'.

666. **KHAMAS خماس (*xamās*)** *Map 16*

Group of houses in the hills of a lateral valley on the right bank of the Harnoi-khwar, Tehsil of Maṭṭa.

Et. unkn. Pšt. *x̌a* 'good' + ?

667. **KHANABAD خاناباد (*xānābād*)** *Map 34*

Village in the wide plain on the left bank of the Swāt river, Tehsil of Khwazakhela. Called Khúna'h or Khúna'h Khela'h by RAVERTY (1888: 233, 235).

Pšt. 'town of the Xān'.

668. **KHANPATAI خانپټی (*xānpəṭay*)** *Map 38*

Group of houses in the hills of a lateral valley on the right bank of the Harnoi-khwar, Tehsil of Maṭṭa.

Pšt. 'field of the Xān'.

669. **KHARAIRAI خريړی (*xarayṛay*)** *Map 38*

Village located in the fertile plain on the left bank of the Harnoi-khwar, north of Matta, Tehsil of Maṭṭa. It is quoted by RAVERTY (1888: 201) as Khareṛa'í, but by him placed to the south of Kuz-bamakhel, between this village and Shakardarra.

According to HAKIMZAY (1997: 77), it should be derived from a source as Ur. *karari* 'hard, firm and strong', in the final meaning of 'hard earth (*ṛay*)': this opinion is quite doubtful in reason of the initial *x*-. Comparison with Pšt. *xareṛay* 'thick sour milk, or coagulated milk mixed with fresh milk; a kind of junket; buttermilk; mushroom, toad-stool' (RAVERTY) is also doubtful.

670. **KHARAIRAI-CHAM خريړی چم (*xarayṛay-čam*)** *Map 38*

A quartier of Kharairai in the fertile plain on the left bank of the Harnoi-khwar, north of Matta, Tehsil of Maṭṭa.

Cf. prec.

671. **KHARAWE خروې (*xarawe*)** *Map 33*

Group of houses in the terraced mountainous upper Khwazakhela-khwar valley, Tehsil of Khwazakhela.

Cf. Kharwe.

672. **KHAR-BANDA خر بانډه (*xar-bānḍa*)** *Map 11*

Pasture in the mountainous Loe-khwar valley, Tehsil of Kabal.

Pšt. 'pasture of the donkey (*xar*)'.

673. **KHARDU-SAR خاردو سر (*xārdu-sar*)** *Map 33*

Mountain of about 2,400 mt separating the Khwazakhela-khwar valley and the Bargin-khwar valley, Tehsil of Khwazakhela.

Cf. Pšt. *x̌āru* 'mainā (Coracias indicus)' (RAVERTY)? Or based on Pšt. *xār* 'thorn' (cf. *xārdā́r* 'thorny')?

674. **KHARESHA خرېشو (*xarešo*)** *Map 45*

Group of houses in the narrow valley on the right bank of the Swāt river, Tehsil of Bahrain.

Cf. Pšt. *xaršin* 'dung (of a horse or donkey), manure'? Or cf. T3819 *khára-* 'hard, sharp, pungent': Ext. Pkt. *kharaḍia-* 'rough'; Or. *khararā* 'slightly parched', Bašk. *khärúṣ* 'rough, rugged'?

675.-678. **KHARKAI خرکی (*xarkay*)** *Maps 42, 43, 47, 53*

Name of four groups of houses: 1) in the mountains above the Harnoi-khwar valley, Tehsil of Maṭṭa; 2) in the Barwai-khwar valley, Tehsil of Maṭṭa (only on the Russian map); 3) in the upper Baral-darra valley, Tehsil of Bahrain; 4) in the narrow valley on the left bank of the upper Swāt river, Tehsil of Bahrain.

Pšt. 'small donkey' (sf. *-kay*)?

679. **KHARKARAI خرکری (*xarkaray*)** *Map 42*

Group of houses in the narrow mountainous Harnoi-khwar valley, Tehsil of Maṭṭa. Only on the Russian map.

Cf. prec.

680. **KHARO-KANDAO خرو کنډو (*xaro-kanḍaw*)** *Map 34*

Pass on the path leading from Khwazakhela to Shalpin, Tehsil of Khwazakhela.

Pšt. 'pass of the donkeys'.

681. **KHARWE خاروې (*xārwe*)** *Map 31*

Group of houses located on the hills sloping towards the left bank of the Swāt river, Tehsil of Khwazakhela.

Pšt. *xār* 'thron, thistle, bramble; spike, splinter' (RAVERTY)? Cf. T3832 *kharvá* 'mutilated, imperfect': Pkt. *khavva-* 'hunchbacked, dwarfish', Kal. rumb. *khäuŕi*? According to IKRAM, p.c., possibly it is Kharaway, the name of a local plant.

682. KHATKOTAI ختكوټى (*xaṭkoṭəy*) *Map 9*

Village in the Deolai-khwar valley, north of Sirsanai, Tehsil of Kabal.

Pšt. 'pavilion of the hill': *xaṭ* 'hill, hillock, mound, knoll, mount; bank of clouds' (RAVERTY) + *koṭəy* 'villa, pavillon' (Akbar).

683. KHAZANA خزانه (*xazāna*) *Map 5*

Village in the fertile Jolagram-khwar valley, Tehsil of Barikot. According to RAVERTY (1888: 201), this village is hidden by the Súe-galí [= Surgalai] spur.

Pšt. *xazā́na* 'treasure'.

684. KHAZANAI-BANDA خزانى بانډه (*xazānay-bānḍa*) *Map 11*

Pasture in the Qalagai-khwar valley, Tehsil of Kabal.

Pšt. 'pasture of the treasure'.

685. KHELKHONA خېلخونه (*xelxona*) *Map 39*

Small village encircled by fields on the left bank of the Harnoi-khwar, Tehsil of Maṭṭa.

Pšt. *xelxāná* 'tribe, clan'? Or 'olive of the khel'? (cf. *khuna* 'olive', SULTAN-I-ROME 2016: 221).

686. KHEMDARRA خېمدره (*xemdara*) *Map 8*

Village on the slopes of the Dokat-sar, in a lateral valley of the Kotlai-khwar valley, Tehsil of Kabal.

Probably Pšt. 'valley of the tents', with *xaymá*, *xemá* 'tent, pavilion'.

687. KHETA خېټه (*xeṭa*) *Map 21*

Village in the spur on the left bank of the Swat river, on the road leading from Mingaora to Sangota, Tehsil of Babuzai.

Cf. Pšt. *xíta* 'line mark'? But better MIA. *khēṭa* 'village' (MBh.) < *kṣētra-* 'field' (MASICA 1991: 157): cf. T3735 *kṣḗtra-* 'land' [√*kṣi-*]: Pa. *khetta-* 'field', NiDoc. *kṣetra*, Pkt. *khetta-*, *khit°*, Kal. *ćhetr*, Kho. *ćhétur*, Phal. *ćhītru*, Sh. *ćeć*; Si. *kheṭru* 'field', Panj. *khetar*, *khet*, kgr. *khetru*, bhaṭ. *khettar*, H. *khet*; Si. *keta* 'field, house'.

688. KHOJARBORI-SAR خوجربوري سر (*xoǰarbori-sar*) *Map 15*

Mountain between the Deolai-khwar valley and the Mahakai stream valley, Tehsil of Kabal.

Cf. T3929 *khōjja 'mark, footprint': Pkt. *khojja-* 'footmark'; Lhd. *khojī* 'tracker'; Panj. *khoj* 'footprint'?

689. **KHORGARAI خوړګړی (*xwaṛgaṛəy*)** *Map 34*

Group of houses on the hills near Kotanai, Tehsil of Khwazakhela.

Pšt. *gaṛə́y* 'small fortress or bottom of a valley' + *-xwaṛ* 'ravine, gully, hollow'.

690. **KHUSHNAB-BABA خشناب بابا (*xušnāb-bābā*)** *Map 18*

Village on the road leading from Barikot to Mingaora, in the fertile valley on the left bank of the Swat river and at the foot of the hills, Tehsil of Babuzai.

Person's name.

691.-692. **KHWAR خوړ (*xwaṛ*)** *Maps 45, 53*

Name of two groups of houses in the Tehsil of Bahrain: in the narrow valley on the right bank (only on the Russian map) and on the left bank of the Swāt river.

Pšt. 'stream'.

693. **KHWAR-MANDAONA خوړ منډونه (*xwaṛ-manḍawna*)** *Map 16*

Group of houses in the mountain bordering the plain of the right bank of the Harnoi-khwar, Tehsil of Maṭṭa.

Cf. Pšt. *manḍaw* 'hut of grass or wood, shed, porch' (RAVERTY): 'huts of the stream'.

694. **KHWAZAKHELA خوازه خېله (*xwāzaxela*)** *Map 31*

Main village of the homonym Tehsil, in the plain on the left side of the Swāt river. Quoted also by RAVERTY (1888: 233).

One of the tribes of Yusufzais of Swāt (*xwaja khel*): see RAVERTY 1888: 207 (Khází Khel).

695. **KHWAZAKHELA-KHWAR خوازه خېله خوړ (*xwāzaxela-xwaṛ*)** *Map 31*

Stream flowing into the Swāt river on its left side, Tehsil of Khwazakhela.

Cf. prec.

696. **KIT کیټ (*kiṭ*)** *Map 53*

Group of houses in the narrow valley on the right bank of the upper Swāt river, Tehsil of Bahrain.

Cf. T3156 *kiṭṭa* 'secretion': Pkt. *kiṭṭa-* 'dirt, rust, lees', Si. *kiṭī* 'dregs'; Hi. *kīṭ* 'sediment, dregs of oil in a lamp'? See ADAMEC V 294 Kiti, "A village located on the western part of the Koh-i-Kurd in Oruzgan province" and ADAMEC VI 440 Kitti, "A village in Nuristan, 2 miles north of Aramtel".

697. **KOCHLA کوچله (*kočla*)** *Map 33*

Group of houses in the hills on the Khwazakhela-khwar valley, Tehsil of Khwazakhela.

Cf. Pšt. *kučlə́y* 'sheepfold, sheep pen'.

698. **KODARAI-DERAI کودری ډېرى (*kodaray-ḍerəy*)** *Map 11*

Village in the terraced and cultivated Qalagai-khwar valley, Tehsil of Kabal.

Pšt. *kawdaray* 'shard, fragment of any brittle substance'.

699. **KOGA کوگه (*koga*)** *Map 43*

Group of houses on the spur connecting the Lito-sar to the Jalba-sar, Tehsil of Maṭṭa. Only on the Russian map.

Possibly cf. T3481 *kṓka* 'wolf', *kōkaḍa-* 'fox': Pa. *kōka-* 'wolf'; Kho. *kog* 'wild dog', or cf. Pšt. *koğ*, *kog* 'hyena' (RAVERTY).

700. **KOHI کوهي (*kohi*)** *Map 49*

Group of houses in the upper Daral-khwar valley, Tehsil of Bahrain.

Ethnic name.

701. **KOHISTANI-BANDA کوهيستاني بانډه (*kohistāni-bānḍa*)** *Map 43*

Pasture located on the slopes of the Barwai-khwar valley, Tehsil of Maṭṭa. Only on the Russian map.

'Pasture of Kohistan/of the Kohistanis'.

702. **KOHISTAN-TIKAI کوهيستان ټيکى (*kohistān-ṭikay*)** *Map 50*

Group of houses in a lateral valley on the right bank of the Swāt river, Tehsil of Bahrain.

Tor. 'summer pasture (*ṭikay*) of Kohistan/of the Kohistanis'.

703. **KOKARAI کوکارى (*kokārəy*)** *Map 22*

Village in the fertile part of the Jambil-khwar valley, Tehsil of Babuzai.

Cf. Pšt. *kukaṛay* 'large round cake of bread' or *kukuray* 'puppy, cub' (cf. T3329 *kurkurá-* 'dog' [← Drav.? See BURROW 1948: 373, KEWA I 237 and EWAia I 372]: Pa. *kukkura-*, Pkt. *kukkura-*, H. *kūkar*, °*krī*)? Or T3208 *kukkuṭá* 'cock': Si. *kukuṛu*, Lhd. *kukkuṛ*, Panj. *kukkaṛ*. According to IKRAM, p.c., it is the name of a beautiful woman.

704. **KOLALAI کولالى (*kolālay*)** *Map 51*

Group of houses on the left bank of the upper Swāt river, Tehsil of Bahrain.

Cf. Tor. *kulāl* 'potter' (T3341 *kulāla-*). Cf. Kulalai-khwar.

705. **KOLAM-KHWAR کولام خوړ (*kolām-xwaṛ*)** *Map 24*

Stream located at an elevation of 1,140 meters above sea level, flowing into the Landai-khwar, Tehsil of Babuzai.

Cf. T3533 **kōla-*[4] 'curved, crooked': Dam. *kōla* 'crooked', Paš. *kōlā* 'curved, crooked', Šum. *kolāṇṭa*?

706. **KOLANDA-BANDA کولانده بانده (*kolānda-bānḍa*)** *Map 12*

Pasture in the upper Deolai-khwar valley, Tehsil of Kabal, near the border with Dir.

Pšt. 'pasture of the sticks (*kulánḍ*)'.

707. **KOLBANR کولبڼ (*kolbaṇ*)** *Map 46*

Group of houses in a lateral narrow valley of the Olal-khwar valley, Tehsil of Bahrain.

Probably Pšt. 'garden of the lake/pond (*kol*)', but cf. also Pšt. *kul* 'earth that is thrown up when digging a canal'. HAKIMZAY (1997: 38) proposes to see in *kol-* 'the family priest'.

708. **KOMYATI کوميتي (*komyati*)** *Map 12*

Group of houses at the end of the Deolai-khwar valley, Tehsil of Kabal.

Et. unkn.

709. **KONTARGAT کونترګټ (*kawntargaṭ*)** *Map 30*

Group of houses on the hills on the left bank of the Swāt river, Tehsil of Charbagh.

Pšt. 'rock/cliff/stone (*gaṭ*) of the doves (*kawntár*)'.

710. **KONTARO-BANDA کونترو بانده (*kawntaro-bānḍa*)** *Map 16*

Pasture in the mountain at the frontier with the Tehsil of Maṭṭa, Tehsil of Kabal.

Pšt. 'pasture of the doves'.

711. **KONTARO-SAR کونترو سر (*kawntaro-sar*)** *Map 16*

Mountain on the border between Matta and Kabal, Tehsil of Kabal.

Pšt. 'mountain of the doves'.

712. **KOPRA-SAR کوپره سر (*kopra-sar*)** *Map 36*

Mountain of about 3,270 mt on the boundary with Shangla, Tehsil of Khwazakhela.

Cf. T3519 **kōppara* 'coconut, skull': Bašk. *kōpar* 'top of head'; Lhd. *kōpar* 'a large head'.

713. **KORAI-BANDA کورى بانده (*koray-bānḍa*)** *Map 11*

Pasture in the Qalagai-khwar valley, Tehsil of Kabal.

Cf. Pšt. *koray* 'a kind of net for carrying grass or forage'. Cf. also Pšt. *koṛa* 'hole or pit made in the ground to fire into in a game at marbles' (RAVERTY).

714. **KORATA کوراته (*korāta*)** *Map 22*

Group of houses in the mountainous upper Jambil-khwar valley, near Jambil, Tehsil of Babuzai.

Der. of Pšt. *kor*?

715. **KORMAL کورمال (koṛmāl)** *Map 32*

Group of houses in the fertile terraced part of the Khwazakhela-khwar valley, Tehsil of Khwazakhela.

Pšt. *kwṛám* 'standing (of water); pond, deep lake' + sf. *-āl* (on this sf., see s.v. Mankial).

716. **KORUNA کورونه (koruna)** *Map 19*

Group of houses located in the upper mountainous Marghuzar-khwar valley, Tehsil of Babuzai.

Pšt. 'the houses'.

717. **KOSA کوسه (kosa)** *Map 18*

Summit of the spur separating the Saidu-khwar valley and the Swat river valley, Tehsil of Babuzai.

Cf. T3539 *kṓśa* 'bucket; case, cover; sheath; storeroom' [MAYRHOFER (KEWA I 273 and EWAia I 403-404) quotes two variants: *kóśaḥ* and *kóṣaḥ*]: Pa. *kōsa-* 'box, sheath, storeroom, cocoon, praeputium'; Pkt. *kōsa-* 'sheath, storeroom, pod'? Or T3611 *krṓśa* 'shout; a measure of distance (as far as a voice carries)': Pkt. *kōsa-* 'a distance of about two miles'? See ADAMEC V 297 Kosaka, "Two springs of good water and a powindah camping – ground at the southwest extremity of the Shah Ghar hills, on the main road from Taraki Tirwah to Ghazni".

718. **KOSAR-BANDA کوسر بانډه (kosar-bānḍa)** *Map 22*

Pasture in the mountainous upper Jambil-khwar valley, near the boundary with Buner, Tehsil of Babuzai.

Probably contraction of Koh-sar-banda: Pšt. 'pasture of the top (*sar*) of the mountain (*koh*)'.

719.-721. **KOT کوټ (koṭ)** *Maps 23, 33, 53*

Name of three villages: 1) Group of houses in the fertile plain on the left bank of the Swāt river, near the Ugad-khwar, Tehsil of Babuzai; 2) on the slopes of the Churlak-sar, Tehsil of Khwazakhela; 3) Group of houses in the narrow valley on the right bank of the upper Swāt river, Tehsil of Bahrain (only on the Russian map). Possibly this is the village quoted by RAVERTY (1888: 237) as Iláhí-Koṭ.

Pšt. 'small fort; small village, small settlement'.

722. **KOTAH کوټه (koṭa)** *Map 1*

Big village in the vast and fertile valley on the left bank of the Swat river, on the Kotah-khwar, Tehsil of Barikot. Quoted also by RAVERTY (1888: 198), who mentions also that: "to the south of which, on the very summit of the mountain, there are the extensive ruins of an ancient city", and then he provides a rough description of the still preserved buildings.

Pšt. *koṭá* 'room', or cf. Kot or Kotah-sar. Cf. also foll.

723. **KOTAH-KHWAR کوټه خوړ (*koṭa-xwaṛ*)** *Map 1*

Stream located at an elevation of 735 meters above sea level, Tehsil of Barikot, flowing from the boundary with Malakand to the Swat river, near Landakai.

Possibly Pšt. *koṭá* 'room', but cf. also T3243 **kuṭṭha-* 'knee', "Conn. KUṬ[1] 'bend' GRIERSON Tor. 162 [1929] with (?). But a long range of names for joints and limbs 'ankle — heel — foot — leg — knee wrist' are characterized by the sequence of guttural — *u/ō* — retroflex": Paš. *kōṭa*, Bašk. *kuṭ, kuṭh*, Tor. *kūṭh*.

724. **KOTAH-SAR کوټه سر (*koṭa-sar*)** *Map 2*

Mountain on the boundary with Buner, Tehsil of Barikot, at the end of the Kandak-khwar valley.

Cf. Pšt. *kwáṭa* 'hillock, hill'.

725. **KOTANAI کوټنی (*koṭanəy*)** *Map 34*

Village lying on the left bank of the Swāt river in the fertile plain north of Khwazakhela, Tehsil of Khwazakhela.

Pšt. *kwəṭanə́y* 'small heap', or *koṭanə́y* 'small house, hut, peasant's house'.

726. **KOTGAI-BANDA کوټګی بانډه (*kotgay-bānḍa*)** *Map 12*

Pasture located at the end of the Deolai-khwar valley, near Tal and the Jarendo-bela-khwar, Tehsil of Kabal.

Pšt. 'pasture of the small fort'.

727.-728. **KOTKAI کوټکی (*koṭkay*)** *Maps 30, 40*

Name of two villages: 1) on the hills sloping towards the left bank of the Swāt river, Tehsil of Charbagh; 2) in the narrow terraced valley of the Shaurai-khwar, Tehsil of Maṭṭa.

Pšt. 'small fort' (*koṭ* + dim. sf. *-kay/-gay*).

729. **KOTKILAI کوټکلی (*koṭkəlay*)** *Map 23*

Village located in the fertile plain on the left bank of the Swāt river, near the Ugad-khwar, Tehsil of Babuzai.

Pšt. 'village of the fort'.

730. **KOTLAI کوټلی (*koṭlay*)** *Map 8*

Village located at the end of the Swat river plain, on the hills of the Kotlai-khwar valley, Tehsil of Kabal.

Possibly T3232 *kuṭī-* 'hut' [← Drav., see EWAia I 222]: Pa. *kuṭī-*, Pkt. *kuḍī-* 'hut'; Si. *kiḷiya* 'hut, small house' + sf. dimin. *-lay*? Cf. also foll. or cf. *kotal* 'pass'?

731. KOTLAI-KHWAR کوټلی خوړ (*koṭlay-xwaṛ*) *Map 8*

Stream located at an elevation of 842 meters above sea level, flowing into the Swat river on its right side, Tehsil of Kabal.

Cf. T3231 *kuṭilá-* 'bent, crooked', and see the name of the village. Cf. Kotah-khwar.

732. KUAR-SAR-BANDA کور سر بانډه (*kwar-sar-bānḍa*) *Map 22*

Pasture in the mountainous upper Jambil-khwar valley, near the boundary with Buner, Tehsil of Babuzai.

Pšt. 'pasture of the mountain of the grape (*kwar*)'.

733. KUDIMAR کډیمار (*kuḍimār*) *Map 32*

Group of houses in the upper Khwazakhela-khwar valley, Tehsil of Khwazakhela.

Pšt. *kuḍəy* 'hut, shed, temporary shelter of straw, branches of trees' (RAVERTY) + sf. *-mār*.

734.-736. KUH کوه (*kuh*) *Maps 27, 35, 47*

Name of three groups of houses: 1) in the upper mountainous Tambagat-khwar valley, Tehsil of Charbagh; 2) in the narrow mountainous upper Bargin-khwar valley, Tehsil of Khwazakhela; 3) near Bahrain, on the left bank of the Swāt river, Tehsil of Bahrain.

Pšt. 'mountain'.

737. KUKRAI ککړی (*kukṛəy*) *Map 19*

Village in the narrow Saidu-khwar valley, towards Marghuzar, Tehsil of Babuzai. Already quoted by RAVERTY (1888: 252) as Kokraey.

Cf. Kokarai.

738. KULADER کلادیر (*kulāder*) *Map 18*

Group of houses in the fertile valley on the left bank of the Swat river, near Balogram, Tehsil of Babuzai.

Cf. Pšt. *kolanḍ* 'block of wood, fastened to the neck of an ox or cow to prevent their straying'?

739. KULAI کولی (*kulay*) *Map 32*

Group of houses in the plain of the Khwazakhela-khwar, near Khwazakhela, Tehsil of Khwazakhela.

Pšt. *koláy* 'earthenware bin for storing grain'.

740. KULALAI-BANDA کولالی بانډه (*kulālay-bānḍa*) *Map 11*

Pasture in the Kolalai-khwar valley, Tehsil of Kabal.

Cf. foll.

741. **KULALAI-KHWAR کولالی خوړ (*kulālay-xwaṛ*)** *Map 11*

Stream flowing into the Qalagai-khwar, Tehsil of Kabal.

T3352 *kulyā-* 'small river, canal, ditch': Pkt. *kullā-* 'stream, channel'. Cf. also T3341 *kulāla-* 'potter' (and Kolalai).

742. **KULBAN کولبن (*kulban*)** *Map 48*

Group of houses in the terraced Daral-khwar valley, Tehsil of Bahrain. Only on the Russian map.

Cf. prec. + *ban* 'garden'.

743. **KULIYA کولییه (*kuliya*)** *Map 22*

Group of houses in the hills bordering the Jambil-khwar valley, towards the Landai-khwar valley, Tehsil of Babuzai.

Cf. Pšt. *kolyāṛ* 'name of a tree (Bauhinia variegata)' (RAVERTY). Or cf. Kulai.

744. **KUN کون (*kun*)** *Map 48*

Group of houses located on the right bank of the Swāt river, south of Torwal, Tehsil of Bahrain.

Tor. *kun* 'a hamlet near Torwal'. Cf. T13627 *skandhá-* 'shoulder, upper part of back', 'trunk of tree, mass (esp. of an army)': Paš.kuṛ. *kōn* 'shoulder'; Bašk. *kān* 'shoulder, upper part of back'; Tor. *kan* 'shoulder'? Or better cf. T3023 *kāṇḍa* 'single joint of a plant', 'arrow', 'cluster, heap' [← Drav. or Austro-As.? See KUIPER 1948: 50, KEWA I 197 and EWAia I 336-337]: Ash. *kaṇ* 'arrow', Kt. *kåṇ*, Waig. *kāṇ*, Pr. *kə̃*, Dam. *kăn*; Paš. lauṛ. *kāṇḍ*, *kāṇ*, ar. *kōṇ*, kuṛ. *kõ*, dar. *kāṛ* 'arrow'; Shum. *kõṛ*, *kõ* 'arrow', Gaw. *kāṇḍ*, *kāṇ*; Kho. *kan* 'tree, large bush'; Bašk. *kā`'n* 'arrow', Tor. *kan*, Phal. *kōṇ*, Sh. gil. *kōn*, pales. *kōṇ*? See ADAMEC VI 459, "A small village on the right bank of the Kunar river, about 18 miles from Jalalabad".

745. **KUND کونډ (*kwənḍ*)** *Map 32*

Group of houses in the mountainous upper Khwazakhela-khwar valley, Tehsil of Khwazakhela.

Pšt. *kwənḍ* 'top, summit (of a mountain)'.

746. **KUND-BANDA کونډ بانډه (*kwənḍ-bānḍa*)** *Map 11*

Pasture in the Kolalai-khwar valley, Tehsil of Kabal.

Pšt. 'pasture of the summit'.

747. **KUND-KANDAO کونډ کنډو (*kwənḍ-kanḍaw*)** *Map 12*

Pass leading to Dir from the Deolai-khwar valley, Tehsil of Kabal.

Pšt. 'pass of the summit'.

748. **KUND-SAR کونډ سر (*kwənḍ-sar*)** *Map 12*

Mountain located on the border with Dir and the Deolai-khwar valley, Tehsil of Kabal.

Pšt. 'mountain of the summit'.

749. **KUNJ کونج (*kunǰ*)** *Map 17*

Group of houses located near the Sigram-khwar, in the mountains above Kanju, Tehsil of Kabal.

Pšt. *kunǰ* 'corner; end' or cf. Kanju.

750. **KUOI کوی (*kwoy*)** *Map 5*

Small village at the foot of the hills in the lateral valley of the Jolagram-khwar, Tehsil of Barikot.

Cf. T3400 *kūpa-* 'hole, hollow, cave' [← Drav., BURROW 1943: 135, KEWA I 253 and EWAia I 385]: Pkt. *kūva-*, Gaw. *kūé*; Kal. *kūi* 'valley', Kho. *kuf*, Bašk. *kōī* 'well'; Tor. *kū* 'valley', *kūī* 'well'; Sh. (LORIMER) *ku* 'nullah', *kui* 'valley, inhabited place, village'. And cf. Pšt. *kuhay* 'well' (pronounced [ku'wɛ]).

751.-752. **KURAI کوری (*kawray*)** *Maps 38, 45*

Name of two villages: 1) in the fertile plain on the left bank of the Harnoi-khwar, north of Matta, Tehsil of Maṭṭa; 2) in the narrow valley on the right bank of the Swāt river, Tehsil of Bahrain.

Pšt. *kawráy* 'hillock, knoll' or Pšt. *koṛáy* 'sloping, slanting (of a mountain)'.

753. **KURATAI-KANDAO کړتی کنډو (*kuṛaṭay-kanḍaw*)** *Map 38*

Pass south of the Shah-dop-sar leading from the Harnoi-khwar valley to the Swāt river valley, Tehsil of Maṭṭa.

Cf. Pšt. *kṛaṭay* 'wrinkle, furrow in the face or body, crease, crumple, pucker, plait, rumple'?

754. **KUZA-JABAGAI کوزه جبگی (*kuza-ǰabagay*)** *Map 23*

Small village in the hills bordering fertile plain on the left bank of the Swāt river, near the Ugad-khwar, Tehsil of Babuzai.

Pšt. 'low small (*-gay*) marshy field (*ǰabá*)'.

755. **KUZ-BAMAKHEL کوز باماخیل (*kuz-bāmāxel*)** *Map 38*

Village located in the fertile plain between the Harnoi-khwar and the right bank of the Swāt river, Tehsil of Maṭṭa. RAVERTY (1888: 201, 230) gives the form Banbá Khel.

Cf. Bar-bamakhel.

756. **KUZ-BANDAI کوز باندی (*kuz-bānḍay*)** *Map 17*

Big village in the fertile plain on the right bank of the Swāt river, Tehsil of Kabal. Quoted already by RAVERTY (1888: 230) as Bánḍí-i-Pá'ín.

Cf. Bar-bandai.

757. **KUZ-BANJIR-BANDA کوز بنجیر بانده (*kuz-banǰir-bānḍa*)** *Map 2*

Pasture in the upper Kandak-khwar valley, Tehsil of Barikot, near the Bostani-sar.

Cf. Bar-banjir-banda.

758. **KUZ-BARGIN کوز بارگین (*kuz-bārgiṇ*)** *Map 35*

Group of houses located in the narrow mountainous Bargin-khwar valley, Tehsil of Khwazakhela.

Cf. Bar-bargin.

759. **KUZ-BATAI-BANDA کوز بتی بانده (*kuz-baṭay-bānḍa*)** *Map 3*

Pasture in the upper Najigram-khwar valley, Tehsil of Barikot, on the slopes of the mountains separating the Kandak-khwar valley from the Najigram-khwar valley.

Cf. Bar-batai-banda.

760. **KUZ-BELA کوز بیله (*kuz-bela*)** *Map 47*

Village in the narrow valley on the left bank of the Swāt river, Tehsil of Bahrain. Only on the Russian map.

Cf. Bela.

761. **KUZ-DURSHKHELA کوز درشخیله (*kuz-duršxela*)** *Map 39*

Village located in the fertile plain on the right bank of the Swāt river, Tehsil of Maṭṭa. Quoted already by RAVERTY (1888: 201, 233) as Darwesh Khel-i-Pá'ín or Kúz Darwesh Khel.

Cf. Bar-durshkhel.

762. **KUZ-GARAI کوز گړی (*kuz-gaṛəy*)** *Map 45*

Group of houses located in the narrow valley on the right bank of the Swāt river, Tehsil of Bahrain.

Cf. Garai.

763. **KUZ-GHUZAN کوز غوزان (*kuz-γuzān*)** *Map 24*

Group of houses in the narrow Lewanai-khwar valley, Tehsil of Babuzai.

Pšt. 'Lower walnuts'.

764. **KUZ-GORSHAI کوز گوړشی (*kuz-goṛšay*)** *Map 45*

Group of houses on the slopes of the Babu-sar on the right bank of the Swāt river, Tehsil of Bahrain. Only on the Russian map.

Cf. Goshai.

765. **KUZ-JABAR کوز جبر (*kuz-ǰabar*)** *Map 24*

Group of houses located in the high and narrow Lewanai-khwar valley, Tehsil of Babuzai.

Cf. Bar-jabar.

766. **KUZ-KANDAO کوز کنډو (*kuz-kanḍaw*)** *Map 24*

Pass leading from the Dosara-khwar valley to Buner, Tehsil of Babuzai.

Pšt. 'Lower pass': cf. Bar-kandao.

767. **KUZ-KANDAO-BANDA کوز کنډو بانډه (*kuz-kanḍaw-bānḍa*)** *Map 24*

Pasture located in the mountain in the upper part of the Dosara-khwar valley, Tehsil of Babuzai.

Pšt. 'Pasture of the lower pass'.

768. **KUZ-KANJU کوز کانجو (*kuz-kānǰu*)** *Map 17*

Big village located in the fertile plain on the right bank of the Swāt river, Tehsil of Kabal.

Cf. Kanju.

769. **KUZ-KARINGAL کوز کرنګال (*kuz-karingāl*)** *Map 33*

Group of houses in the mountainous upper Khwazakhela-khwar valley, on the slopes of the Semprai-sar, Tehsil of Khwazakhela.

Cf. Karange.

770. **KUZ-KEDAM کوز کېدام (*kuz-kedām*)** *Map 50*

Group of houses on the right bank of the Swāt river near the Kedam-khwar valley, Tehsil of Bahrain. Also said Kedam.

Cf. Kedam-khwar.

771. **KUZ-LAIKOT کوز ليکوټ (*kuz-laykoṭ*)** *Map 53*

Group of houses in the narrow valley on the left bank of the upper Swāt river, Tehsil of Bahrain. Only on the Russian map.

Cf. Bar-kaikot.

772. **KUZ-LALKU کوز لالکو (*kuz-lālku*)** *Map 44*

Village in the mountainous narrow Barwai-khwar valley, Tehsil of Maṭṭa.

Cf. Lalku-kandao.

773. **KUZ-MANASAR کوز مناسر (*kuz-manāsar*)** *Map 26*

Group of houses in the upper Bishbanr-khwar valley, Tehsil of Babuzai.

Cf. Manasar-sar.

774. **KUZ-SAMSARA کوز سمسره (*kuz-samsara*)** *Map 3*

Group of houses in the narrow upper Najigram-khwar valley, Tehsil of Barikot.

Cf. Pšt. *samsāra* 'large lizard or iguana, land crocodile, alligator' (RAVERTY).

775. **KUZ-SHAUR کوز شور (*kuz-šawr*)** *Map 40*

Village in the narrow terraced valley of the Shaurai-khwar, Tehsil of Maṭṭa.

Cf. Shaurai-khwar.

776. **KUZ-TIKAI کوز ټیکی (*kuz-ṭikay*)** *Map 50*

Group of houses in the Kedam-khwar valley, Tehsil of Bahrain.

Tor. 'lower (*kuz*) summer pasture'.

777. **KUZ-UZBUK کوز ازبک (*kuz-uzbuk*)** *Map 24*

Group of houses in the high and narrow Dosara-khwar valley, Tehsil of Babuzai.

Pšt. 'lower Uzbuk' (q.v.).

778. **LADU لادو (*lādu*)** *Map 32*

Group of houses located in a lateral valley of the Khwazakhela-khwar valley, Tehsil of Khwazakhela.

Pšt. *lād/ḍu* 'broad mountain slope broken with ravines'.

779. **LAI لای (*lāy*)** *Map 41*

Group of houses on the slopes on the confluence among the Harnoi-khwar, the Roringar-khwar and the Biha-khwar, Tehsil of Maṭṭa.

Possibly Pšt. *lāy* 'sediment, deposition', 'mud, mire; fold, plait' (RAVERTY).

780. **LAKAI-KALAI لکی کلی (*lakay-kəlay*)** *Map 14*

Group of houses in the wide and fertile Deolai-khwar valley, at the confluence with the Loe-khwar, north of Sirsanai, Tehsil of Kabal.

Possibly ‘red village’: cf. T11003: 1. *lākṣiká* ‘dyed with lac’; 2. **lākṣaka-* ‘red’: 1. Kal. *laçhīa* ‘red’; Si. *lākhī* ‘dyed with lac’; Lhd.khet. *lākhī* ‘red’; Guǰ. *lākhī* ‘coloured like sealing wax’; M. *lākhī* ‘having the colour of lac’. 2. Dam. *lâçhâ* ‘red’; Lhd. *lākkhā* ‘red, brown, black (of cattle)’, khet. *lākhā* ‘red’; Panj. *lākkhā* ‘red, brown, black’; Hi. *lākhā* ‘lac dye’. Difficult Pšt. *lakedə́l* ‘to be established, installed, set up’: ‘village installed’?

781. LAKAI-KOTA لکی کوټه (*lakay-koṭa*) *Map 38*

Group of houses in the hills of a lateral valley on the right bank of the Harnoi-khwar, Tehsil of Maṭṭa.

Possibly ‘red hut’: cf. prec., T11003, + T3546 *kṓṣṭha* ‘pot; granary, storeroom; inner apartment’: Pa. *koṭṭha-* ‘monk’s cell, storeroom’; Pkt. *koṭṭha-* ‘granary, storeroom’; Si. *koṭho* ‘large room’; Lhd. *koṭhā* ‘hut, room, house’; Panj. *koṭṭhā*, *koṭhā* ‘house with mud roof and walls, granary’; Hi. *koṭhā* ‘granary’.

782. LAKHAR لاښار (*lāx̌ār*) *Map 35*

Group of houses on the hills bordering the left bank of the Swāt river, near the access of the Bargin-khwar valley, Tehsil of Khwazakhela.

Cf. Pšt. *lāx̌* ‘steep or scarped place in a mountain inaccessible’ (RAVERTY) + sf. *-ar* (?).

783. LALBAT لابټ (*lābaṭ*) *Map 41*

Village in the plain at the confluence among the Harnoi-khwar, the Roringar-khwar and the Biha-khwar, Tehsil of Maṭṭa.

Cf. Pšt. *lāl* ‘ruby’ + *baṭ* ‘the bark of a tree, bark, rind, peel, husk’.

784. LALKU-KANDAO لالکو کنډو (*lālku-kanḍaw*) *Map 44*

Pass leading from the right bank of the Swāt river to the Barwai-khwar valley, Tehsil of Bahrain.

Pšt. *lāl* ‘ruby’: ‘mountain (*kuh*) of the rubies’ or ‘mountain of ruby colour’.

785. LALOBANDA لالوبنډه (*lālobānḍa*) *Map 17*

Village on the slopes of the hills in the Sigram-khwar valley, Tehsil of Kabal.

Pšt. ‘pasture of the rubies’.

786.-788. LANDAI لندی (*landay*) *Maps 30, 43, 44*

Name of three villages: 1) on the left bank of the Swāt river, at the foot of the hills, north of Charbagh, Tehsil of Charbagh; 2) in the mountainous narrow Barwai-khwar valley, Tehsil of Maṭṭa (only on the Russian map); 3) on the right bank of the Swāt river, at the confluence with the Barwai-khwar, Tehsil of Maṭṭa. Quoted already by RAVERTY (1888: 230), it was the place to which the Swāt river could be crossed from the actual Naborai (Bin-waṛí of RAVERTY, but also in Google Earth). RAVERTY adds that “the breadth of the stream at this ferry being about one hundred yards, and very deep. At this point too the banks are steep. It was remarked that, where the river ran deep, the banks were scarped and high, but, where the water was shallow, the banks were more sloping and gravelly like the sea-shore".

See SULTAN-I-ROME 2016: 479: "*Lanw-dah/Lamdah/Lwandah*: After occupation of the land and devising the *wesh* system: 'Shaikh Mali first divided Suwat (Swat) for convenvience sake into two nominal parts, lying on either side of the river. To that portion lying between the right bank and the mountains bordering it on the north-west, and comprising the eight minor dara'hs [minor-valleys, i.e. On the side of a valley or branch valleys] [...] opening into it, he gave the name of *lanw-dah*, the plural form of the Pus'hto [Pashto] adjective *lund*, signifying "moist," "damp," etc. from its enjoying a greater portion of moisture than the other, for, where the river separates into several branches is part of this moist tract, hence its name [...] The bounds of the *lanw-dah* half of the valley were fixed by the Shaikh from B'rangolaey, the boundary village of Lower Suwat, nearly facing Tutakan, on the opposite bank of the river, as far as Landaey, the lowest village to the north, just opposite Pia, a tract extending in length about sixty miles' (H. G. Raverty, *Notes on Afghanistan and Baluchistan*, Vol. 1, 206)". HAKIMZAY (1997: 139-140) relates it to IA *nadi* 'river, rivulet'.

789. LANDAI-KHWAR لندی خوړ (*landay-xwaṛ*) *Map 23, 24*

Stream, located at an elevation of 1,700 meters above sea level, flowing into the Ugad-khwar, Tehsil of Babuzai.

According to RAVERTY (1888: 244-245), "the Lúnd, or Lúndaey Khwaṛ, is so called from the Pus'hto or Afghán word *lúnd* for 'wet', 'watery', 'moist', etc. [...] Its plural form, with a masculine noun, is *lánw-dah*, and with a feminine, *landa'h* and *landey* respectively. Like other adjectives of its class, in the masculine, it takes the affix *aey* [...], used to indicate diminution and to lessen the importance of a word, or to convey contempt". Note that even if the Lúndaey Khwaṛ here quoted is not this same stream, Raverty's analysis remains relevant. Cf. also Pšt. 'lower (*lānde* 'down, below') stream' and prec.

790.-791. LANDAI-SAR لاندې سر (*lānde-sar*) *Maps 19, 42*

Name of two mountains: 1) in the Tehsils of Barikot, at the boundary with the Tehsil of Babuzai. Its height is about 1,990 mt; 2) in the Tehsil of Maṭṭa, on the boundary with Dir, of about 3,680 mt.

See STEIN 1929: 132 and ID. 1930: 79: *Lānde-sar* 'the lower height' (Pšt.), or cf. prec.

792. LANDAI-SHAH لندی شاه (*landay-šāh*) *Map 28*

Village on the Dre-khwar, Tehsil of Charbagh. It is called Lodia on the Russian map.

Cf. Landai or person's name.

793. LANDAKAY لنداکی (*landākay*) *Map 1*

Village located at the beginning of the Tehsil of Barikot, where the hills of Malakand descend in the vast lower Swat valley. The village is cited by RAVERTY (1888: 197, 241), where he mentions also the Landakey mountain, the spur above-quoted, and the Lanḍakay pass, adding that "This last-named mountain [Lanḍakaey] has no connection with that of the Mora'h Ghar, but it is a spur from the great range of which the Mora'h

Ghar forms a part, which has come down close upon the river, or rather the river washes its base". See also STEIN 1929: 21.

Cf. Landai.

794. **LANDE لندی (*landay*)** *Map 19*

Village in the narrow Marghuzar-khwar valley, towards Marghuzar, Tehsil of Babuzai.

Cf. Landai, or *lanḍəy* 'broad-headed snake, small poisonous reptile found in Afghanistan, like a snak with a nob at the tail' (RAVERTY).

795. **LANDI-CHOYA لندي چويه (*landi-čoya*)** *Map 14*

Village in the wide and fertile Deolai-khwar valley, north of Sirsanai, Tehsil of Kabal.

Cf. Landai and Pšt. *čawa* 'grassy glade, hollow; small irrigation well (in a melon field)'.

796.-797. **LANGAR لنګر (*langar*)** *Maps 12, 31*

Name of two villages: 1) in the Deolai-khwar valley, Tehsil of Kabal; 2) in the plain of the Khwazakhela-khwar, Tehsil of Khwazakhela.

Pšt. *langár* 'almshouse, refuge, asylum (run by a sheikh, pir)'. Or maybe, as suggested also by HAKIMZAY (1997: 142-143), cf. T10900 **laṅga* 'tray, basket, net': Panj. *laṅgarā* 'earthen vessel used by dyers'; A. *lāṅgi* 'fishing net'. See also Talang for *lang*.

798. **LANGAR-DERAI لنګر ډیری (*langar ḍerəy*)** *Map 39*

Village at the foot of the hills bordering the fertile plain on the right bank of the Swāt river, Tehsil of Maṭṭa.

Pšt. 'residence of the almshouse'. Cf. prec.

799. **LANGONR لانګوڼ (*lāngoṇ*)** *Map 48*

Group of houses located in the Daral-khwar valley, Tehsil of Bahrain. Langanr on the Russian map.

Cf. Pšt. *lānga* 'name of a tree from the wood of which arrows are made; name of a village' (RAVERTY). HAKIMZAY (1997: 144) sees in this toponym (he refers to Lāngaṇ in the Tehsil of Kabal) *angaṇ*, *angan* 'courtyard'. However, cf. also *lang* in Talang (q.v.).

800. **LARUKA لروکه (*laruka*)** *Map 1*

Group of houses at the spring of the Kotah-khwar, Tehsil of Barikot, on the slopes on the boundary with Malakand.

Et. unkn. Cf. Pšt. *lārwrəkay* 'going astray, losing one's way; getting lost'?

801. **LETAI لېټی (*leṭay*)** *Map 36*

Group of houses in the terraced mountainous Paiti-khwar valley, Tehsil of Khwazakhela.

Pšt. *leṭáy* 'hard clay'.

802.-803. LEWANAI لېونی (*lewanay*) *Maps 24, 26*

Name of two groups of houses: 1) in the high and narrow Spedar-khwar valley, Tehsil of Babuzai; 2) in the upper Bishbanr-khwar valley, Tehsil of Charbagh.

Pšt. 'crazy'.

804. LEWANAI-KHWAR لېونی خوړ (*lewanay-xwaṛ*) *Map 24*

Stream located at an elevation of 2,205 meters above sea level, flowing into the Spedar-khwar, Tehsil of Babuzai.

Pšt. 'crazy stream'.

805. LILBANR ليلبڼ (*lilbaṇ*) *Map 26*

Group of houses in the Spedar-khwar valley, Tehsil of Babuzai.

Possibly 'blue garden', cf. T7563 *nīla* 'dark blue, dark green, black': 1. Pa. *nīla-* 'dark blue, blue-green'; Pkt. *ṇīla<->* 'blue, green'; Wg. *nyīlə*, *nīrə* 'blue', Kt. *nīlə*, *ninyílë*, Pr. *nīl*, *nyīli*, Dam. *nīla*; Tir. *nīlə* 'green blue'; Paš. *nil* 'dark blue'; Shum. *nīl* 'blue', Gaw. *nīla*, Kal.urt. *nīl*, Bašk. (BIDDULPH) *nül*, Tor. *nīlə*; Phal. *nīlo* 'green, blue', Sh. *nīlụ*; Lhd. *nīlā*, Panj. *nīlā*, *līlā*; Hi. *nīlā*, *līl*(*ā*) 'blue', Guǰ. *nīḷū*, *nīlū̃*, *līlū̃*; Lhd. *nīl* 'indigo', Panj. *nīl*, *līl*. HAKIMZAY (1997: 38) also confirms this etymology.

806. LILIBANR ليليبڼ (*lilibaṇ*) *Map 41*

Small village on the right bank of the Harnoi-khwar, on the last slopes of the Prang-man-sar, Tehsil of Maṭṭa.

Cf. prec.

807. LITO-SAR ليتو سر (*lito-sar*) *Map 41*

Mountain of about 2,300 mt between the Barwai-khwar valley and the Harnoi-Khwar valley, Tehsil of Maṭṭa.

Pšt. 'slippery/smooth (*lit*) mountain'.

808. LIZZAT-BANDA لزت بانډه (*lizat-bānḍa*) *Map 53*

Pasture located in the narrow valley on the right bank of the upper Swāt river, Tehsil of Bahrain.

Pšt. *lazzat* (Ar.) 'pleasure, enjoyment, delight, flavour, taste, savour, sweetness, deliciousness' (RAVERTY).

809. LOAR-DEOLAI لوړ دېولی (*lwaṛ-dewləy*) *Map 14*

Village on the hills of the Deolai-khwar valley, above Sam-deolai, north of Lakai-kalai, Tehsil of Kabal, where the valley begins to become narrow.

Pšt. 'high (*lwaṛ*)' + Deolai (see Deolai-khwar).

810. **LOAR-SERAI لوړ سېرى (*lwaṛ-seray*)** *Map 18*

Group of houses in the fertile valley on the left bank of the Swat river, between the Swat river and the Saidu-khwar, Tehsil of Babuzai.

Pšt. 'high (*lwaṛ*)' + *-serai* (see Glossary of Geonyms).

811. **LO-BANDA لوى بانډه (*loy-bānḍa*)** *Map 48*

Pasture in the Daral-khwar valley, Tehsil of Bahrain.

Pšt. 'big pasture'.

812. **LOE-BANR لوى بڼ (*loy-baṇ*)** *Map 21*

Village in the vast plain of the Jambil-khwar valley, Tehsil of Babuzai (in TUCCI 1958 also called Sheralai).

Pšt. 'great (*loy*) forest (*baṇ*)' (see TUCCI 1977: 22: "*Loebanr* 'great forest' is the survival, in Pashtu, of the name of the Mahāvana 'great forest'; probably it started at the head of the Jāmbīl and extended to the mountains bordering the Yūsufzai territory up to Buner (cf. Lévi, 1915 Mm. p. 72)").

813. **LOE-KHWAR لوى خوړ (*loy-xwaṛ*)** *Map 11*

Stream, located at an elevation of 2,695 meters above sea level, flowing into the Deolai-khwar, Tehsil of Kabal.

Pšt. 'great (*loy*) stream'.

814. **LOE-NAMAL لوى نمل (*loy-namal*)** *Map 40*

Group of houses in the terraced hills above the Shaurai-khwar valley, Tehsil of Maṭṭa.

Pšt. 'great Namal', with *namal* metathesis of *lamən* 'border, hem, skirt; base (of a mountain); etc.'? According to IKRAM, p.c., *namal* is 'ant, moist'.

815. **LOE-NAO لوى ناو (*loy-nāw*)** *Map 37*

Group of houses on the slopes in the narrow valley on the left bank of the Swāt river, Tehsil of Bahrain. Only on the Russian map.

Cf. Pšt. *nāw* 'hollow, depression, valley': 'big hollow'.

816. **LOE-SAR لوى سر (*loy-sar*)** *Map 22*

Mountain of about 2,570 mt, near the boundary with Buner, Tehsil of Babuzai.

Pšt. 'big (*loy*) mountain'.

817. **LUDA-SAR لوده سر (*luda-sar*)** *Map 47*

Mountain of about 4,525 mt at the source of the Baral-darra and of the Gurnay-khwar, Tehsil of Bahrain.

Cf. T11076 **luṭṭa* 'defective'. 2. **luṭṭha-*; 7. **luṇḍa-*: 1. Ash. *luṭ* 'young man'; Waig. *lūṭ* 'young bearded man'; Tor. *lūṭ* 'small'; 2. Pkt. *luṭṭha-* 'broken piece of brick'; Gaw. *luṭh*, *luṭ* 'young'; Kho. (MORGENSTIERNE) *luṭh* 'big', (LORIMER) *luṭ* 'big, senior, old'; 4. Tor. *luḍ* 'small' (or < *lūṭ* in 1); 7. Sh. (LORIMER) *lund*, *lon*, jij. (MORGENSTIERNE) *lɔṇ* 'penis'; Hi. *lū̃ḍā* 'tailless, cropped'.

818. **LUNDAI لوندی (*lunday*)** *Map 20*

Group of houses in the spur between the Saidu-khwar valley and the Jambil-khwar valley, near Jambil, Tehsil of Babuzai.

Cf. Landai. See ADAMEC VI 504 Landi or Landay, "village located some 3 miles north west of Pachire Agam and southwest of Jalalabad in Nangarhar province. Other places with this name are located a few miles south of Ghanikhel on the way north to the Kabul river [...]; in the Khairaspan area, southwest of Zurket in Paktia province [...]; about 5 miles south of Chamkani in eastern Paktia province [...]; south of Tani on the way to Matun in Paktia province" and *ibid.*: 532 Londi, "village located on a tributary of the Tagab, about 10 miles northeast of Tagab in Kapisa province".

819. **LUNDAI-KANDAO لوندی کنډو (*lunday-kanḍaw*)** *Map 12*

Pass leanding to Dir from the Jarendo-bela-khwar valley, Tehsil of Kabal.

Cf. prec. or Landai-sar.

820. **LUNDAI-SAR لوندی سر (*lunday-sar*)** *Map 12*

Mountain on the border with Dir and the Jarendo-bela-khwar valley, Tehsil of Kabal.

Cf. Lundai or Landai-sar.

821. **LUNDAKAI لونداکی (*lundākay*)** *Map 30*

Small village on the left bank of the Swāt river, at the foot of the hills, north of Charbagh, Tehsil of Charbagh.

Cf. Lundai and Landakai.

822. **MABANR مهابڼ (*mahābaṇ*)** *Map 38*

Small village in the plain on the right bank of the Harnoi-khwar valley, Tehsil of Maṭṭa. *h* is not pronounced in Pashto and *-aā-* > *-ā-*.

HAKIMZAY (1997: 161), probably rightly, derives the first part from Skt. *mahā* 'big': 'big garden'. Or an abbreviation of *maṇebaṇ* 'garden of the apples', as it is mentioned also on Google Earth? The analysis as Pšt. 'garden of the moon (*māh*)' can be excluded.

823. **MACHA مچه (*mača*)** *Map 37*

Village in the plain on the left bank of the Swāt river, Tehsil of Khwazakhela.

Pšt. *məč* 'fly, horsefly'. HAKIMZAY (1997: 148) proposes Hi. *machh* 'name of the first incarnation of Vishnu in the shape of a fish'.

824. **MADONA مدونه (*madona*)** *Map 39*

Group of houses on the slopes of the Lito-sar degrading towards the Harnoi-khwar valley, in Tehsil of Maṭṭa.

Cf. T9843 *manthānaka-* 'species of grass; Cassia fistula': Si. *mā̃dhāṇo* 'species of grass'? Or cf. Pšt. *mādún* 'lower, standing below; subordinate' (← Ar.)?

825. **MAGON مگون (*magon*)** *Map 29*

Group of houses in the narrow Malakad-khwar valley, Tehsil of Charbagh.

Pšt. *məg*, *məǧ* 'rams'?

826. **MAHAK مهک (*mahak*)** *Map 15*

Village located in a lateral valley of the Deolai-khwar valley, not far from Kala, Tehsil of Kabal.

Ethnic name: see TUCCI 1977: 42:

> Maśakāvatī mentioned in the *Bhāṣya* (IV 2, 71) must be here recorded because its name cannot be isolated from that of Mássaga; it is quoted as the name of a river though the suffix-*vatī* can be applied also to a town (Puskalāvatī). But the important fact is the presence of such a toponymy in the NW part of the subcontinent. It is also interesting that near Aligrāma there is a *khwaṛ* which is now called Mahak > Masak.

And *ibid.*: 51:

> The name of the capital of the Assakenói: Mássaga, Mássaka, Mázaka, Másoga (Strabo XV 698) reminds me forcibly of the Massagetae (see references from classical sources in *RE*, s.v. the Massagetae and the Scythians). Altheim and Stiehl 1970, p. 128 connect the name of the Massagetae with the Ossetic word *mäsig, mäsug* 'tower', Marquart with [A]v. *masyō* (exactly: *masya*, Bartholomae, p. 1155; Skr. *matsya* 'fish') (Iran II, p. 78).

827. **MAHAKAI مهکی (*mahakay*)** *Map 15*

Stream flowing into the Deolai-khwar, Tehsil of Kabal.

Cf. prec.

828. **MAHASAR مهاسر (*mahāsar*)** *Map 46*

Group of houses in the Olal-khwar valley and on the slopes of the Bura-sar, Tehsil of Bahrain. Only on the Russian map.

IA 'big mountain'.

829. **MAHO-DAND ماهوډنډ (*māho-ḍanḍ*)** *Map 54*

Lake on the Ushu-gol, Tehsil of Bahrain, indicated only on the Russian map. Nowadays it seems to have disappeared.

Pšt. 'lake of the fishes'.

830. **MAIDAR میدار (*maydār*)** *Map 46*

Group of houses in the upper Olal-khwar valley, Tehsil of Bahrain.

Variant of *maydān* 'plain, field, ground': accordingly, in IKRAM's opinion (p.c.), the correct name is Maidan.

831. **MAILAGA مایلگا (*māylagā*)** *Map 8*

Small village on the slopes of the Kotlai-khwar valley leading to the boundary with Dir, under the Changai-dop-sar, Tehsil of Kabal.

Cf. Pšt. (← Ar.) *māyil* 'inclined, bent, sloping': 'sloping place' (+ sf. *-gāh*).

832.-833. **MAIRA میره (*mayra*)** *Maps 25, 33*

Name of two villages: 1) in the narrow mountainous Bishbanr-khwar valley, Tehsil of Babuzai; 2) group of houses in the wide terraced Khwazakhela-khwar valley, Tehsil of Khwazakhela.

Pšt. *mayrá* 'steppe, plain; non-irrigated land'; Maira is also the area between Attok and Peshawar.

834. **MAIRA-BANDA میره بانده (*mayra-bānḍa*)** *Map 12*

Pasture in the mountainous Manrai-khwar valley, near Tal, Tehsil of Kabal.

Cf. prec.

835. **MAIR-BANDA میر بانده (*mayr-bānḍa*)** *Map 43*

Pasture on the mountain above the upper Roringar-khwar valley, near the boundary with Dir, Tehsil of Maṭṭa.

Cf. foll. and Maira-banda.

836. **MAKAD-KHWAR مکد خوړ (*makad-xwaṛ*)** *Map 29*

Stream, located at an elevation of 1,238 meters above sea level, flowing into the Ugad-khwar, Tehsil of Charbagh.

Cf. T9882 *markaṭa-*^{1} 'monkey' [← Drav. or Austro-As.? See BURROW 1948: 389-390; KEWA II 592-593; EWAia II 322-323] or T9883 *markaṭa-*^{2} 'spider': Pkt. *makkaḍa-*, *maṃkaḍa-*? → 'stream of the monkeys/spiders'?

837. **MAKAT-BANDA ماکت بانده (*mākat-bānḍa*)** *Map 12*

Pasture in the upper Deolai-khwar valley, Tehsil of Kabal, near the border with Dir.

Cf. prec.

838. **MALAK-ABAD ملک آباد (*malak-ābād*)** *Map 27*

Group of houses in the pass leading from the Tambagat-khwar valley to the Dre-khwar valley, near the Jobe-kandao, Tehsil of Charbagh.

Pšt. 'town of the mālik (owner, landowner)' [or *malík* 'leader, master, lord, sovereign, king']. See SULTAN-I-ROME 2008: 327: "*Malak/Malik.* A tribal chief recognized as head of the whole tribe, or of its major or minor sub-divisions, or a section or sub-section. Among the Swat Yusufzais, on the whole, Malak/Malik was the lesser tribal chief as compared to the Khan and sometimes subordinate to the respective Khan as well".

839.-840. MALALAI ملالی (*malālay*) *Maps 24, 40*

Name of two villages: 1) in the narrow Landai-khwar valley, Tehsil of Babuzai, called Malolai on the Russian map; 2) group of houses in the narrow terraced valley of the Shaurai-khwar, Tehsil of Maṭṭa.

Pšt. *malāláy* 'beautiful, handsome, pretty'.

841. MALAL-DAKORAK ملال دکورک (*malāl-dakorak*) *Map 30*

Village in the wide plain of Charbagh on the left bank of the Swat river, north of Charbagh, Tehsil of Charbagh.

Cf. Dakorak + cf. Pšt. *mala* 'kind of grass' (see Malam), or cf. Malalai.

842. MALAM ملم (*malam*) *Map 27*

Small village on a terrace in the Dre-khwar valley, Tehsil of Charbagh.

Cf. T9810 *madhyamá* 'middlemost': Bašk. *mäīm* 'middle'. Development *d/dh* > *l* is possibley both in Pashto and in Gandhārī. Or cf. Pšt. *malham* 'salve, plaster, ointment' (← Prs.), *mala* 'kind of grass' (RAVERTY)?

843. MALAM-JABBA ملم جبه (*malam-ǰabba*) *Map 27*

Small village in the mountainous upper Tambagat-khwar valley, Tehsil of Charbagh.

IA 'swamp/marshy field (*ǰabá*) of Malam'.

844. MALCHALCHARAI ملچلچری (*malčalčaray*) *Map 47*

Group of houses in the upper Baral-darra valley, Tehsil of Bahrain. Only on the Russian map.

Cf. T4719 *calācalá* 'evermoving': Pa. Pkt. *calācala-* 'in constant motion, unsteady'; Paš. *čolāl* 'belongings, property' IIFL III 3: 44 with (?) + as first element T9908 *malla* 'name of a people in NE of India' or T9907 *malla* 'wrestler by profession, athlete; member of a mixed caste': Pa. Pkt. *malla-* 'wrestler'; Panj. *mall* 'wrestler'?

845. MALIKABAD ملکاباد (*malikābād*) *Map 17*

Quartier of Kanju, located in the fertile plain on the right bank of the Swāt river, Tehsil of Kabal.

Cf. Malak-abad.

846. **MALKANA-BANDA ملکانه باڼده (*malkāna-bānḍa*)** *Map 14*

Pasture on the hills bordering on the west side the Deolai-khwar valley, Tehsil of Kabal.

Pšt. 'landowner's (*mālikāná*) pasture'.

847. **MALOCH مالوچ (*māloč*)** *Map 17*

Village in a lateral valley of the Deolai-khwar valley, Tehsil of Kabal.

Pšt. *mālúč* 'ginned cotton'.

848. **MALUKA ملوکه (*maluka*)** *Map 17*

Village in the upper Sigram-khwar valley, Tehsil of Kabal.

Probably Pšt. *malík* 'leader, master, lord, sovereign, king' (pl. Ar.), cf. foll. See ADAMEC V 324 Maluk, "village located on a stream about 6 miles southwest of Lam in Kandahar province".

849. **MALUKABAD ملوک آباد (*malukābād*)** *Map 21*

Village at the foot of the hills towards the Jambil-khwar valley, Tehsil of Babuzai, in the metropolitan area of Mingaora.

Pšt. 'town of the leaders/masters'.

850. **MAM-DERAI مام ډېرى (*mām ḍerəy*)** *Map 17*

Village in the fertile plain, right on the right bank of the Swāt river, Tehsil of Kabal.

Pšt. 'residence of the maternal uncle (*māmā*)'. According to HAKIMZAY (1997: 154), it is 'residence of the mother (← Hi.)'.

851. **MANAGO-SAR مناګو سر (*manāgo-sar*)** *Map 15*

Mountain between the Deolai-khwar and the Sigram-khwar valley, Tehsil of Kabal.

Derived from *manắ* 'hut, tower for a watchman who guards a field' [see RAVERTY 'raised stage for watching a field from']. Difficult Pšt. *mangor* 'kind of viper, very venomous'.

852. **MANALI-AN منلي ان (*manali-an*)** *Map 54*

Pass leading from the upper Gabral river valley to Dir, Tehsil of Bahrain.

Cf. T10208 **munāla* or **mōnāla-* 'pheasant': Panj. *munāl*, *manāl* 'pheasant'; Hi. *munāl* 'pheasant'? Cf. also Pšt. *manḍ* 'pathway made in the snow from one village to another' (RAVERTY)?

853. **MANASAR-SAR مناسر سر (*manāsar-sar*)** *Map 26*

Mountain of about 3,000 mt near the boundary with Shangla, Tehsil of Babuzai.

Pšt. *manắ* 'hut, tower for a watchman who guards a field' + twice *sar*.

854. **MANDUR ماندور (*māndur*)** *Map 39*

Village at the foot of the hills bordering the fertile plain on the right bank of the Swāt river, Tehsil of Maṭṭa.

Cf. Pšt. *mānda* 'the dry bed of a river, or the bed of a torrent'. HAKIMZAY (1997: 156) finds in this toponym Hi. *mān* 'son in law, honour', but this hypothesis cannot be accepted.

855. **MANGALTAN منګلتان (*mangaltān*)** *Map 30*

Group of houses in the Charbagh-khwar valley, Tehsil of Charbagh. It is called Malatan on the Russian map, Mingvalthān in STEIN 1930.

Possibly Pšt. 'place of the Mangal (tribe)'. See ADAMEC VI 550 Mangal, "A tribe which inhabits the southern and upper portion of the Kurram valley, and also part of Zurmat". Cf. Manglaor.

856. **MANGAR-KOT منګرکوټ (*mangar-koṭ*)** *Map 28*

Group of houses in the narrow upper Dre-khwar valley, Tehsil of Charbagh.

Cf. Ur. *mangarā* 'having strong joints, well-knit, strong, powerful' (PLATTS), as proposed also by HAKIMZAY (1997: 152-153). Other possibilities are Pšt. 'small fort of of the bugs' (*mangúṛ*), or Pšt. *mangráy* 'snake (small poisonous snake) and *mangṛə́y* 'gecko (lizard)'. See ADAMEC V 327 Mangur, "A village located on the stream of the same name, about 8 miles south of Kafter Khana and northeast of Bambalestan in Oruzgan province", and ID. VI 551 Mangara Toy, "A village located about 5 miles southwest of Sarobi in southern Paktia province".

857. **MANGAZAI-KANDAO منګزی کنډو (*mangazay-kanḍaw*)** *Map 36*

Pass leading from the Paiti-khwar valley to Shangla, Tehsil of Khwazakhela.

Pšt. 'place (*-zay*) of the pot/pitcher (*mangay*)/of the rats (*mənğak*)'. However, cf. also T9705 *maṅga* 'head of a boat, mast or side of a ship': Hi. *mā̃g* 'head of a boat', *mā̃grā* 'ridgepole'.

858. **MANGLAOR منګلور (*manglawər*)** *Map 23*

Village on the Ugad-khwar, Tehsil of Babuzai. Cited by RAVERTY (1888: 234) as Manglawar and by DEANE (1895) as Minglaur.

According to STEIN 1930: 47-48 (and 76), "Sanskrit **Mangalapura* of which the modern name *Manglawar* is the direct phonetic derivative". HAKIMZAY (1997: 159-160) states that in Skt. *mangal* means 'pleasure, happiness'. Cf. indeed STEIN's analysis and T9706 *maṅgalá* 'auspicious sign' (in cmpds.), 'anything auspicious; happiness': Pa. *maṅgala-* 'auspicious'; Pkt. *maṁgala-*; Panj. *maṅgal* 'gladness'; Hi. *maṅgal* 'fortunate'. HAKIMZAY (*ibid.*) identifies also a *mang* trying without any linguistic support to translate it 'water'.

859. **MANGRAL-BELA منګرل بیله (*mangral-bela*)** *Map 45*

Group of houses in a lateral valley on the right bank of the Swāt river on the slopes of the Babu-sar, Tehsil of Bahrain. It is called Lal-bela on the Russian map.

Cf. prec. with metathesis?

860. **MANIAUR منیور (*manyawr*)** *Map 8*

Small village on the right bank of the Swāt river, Tehsil of Kabal, in the wide and fertile plain of Kabal.

Pšt. *māṇə́y* 'palace, mansion; building, structure, multistory house' + sf. *yār*?

861. **MANI-PATAI منی پټی (*məni-pəṭay*)** *Map 41*

Group of houses in the narrow upper Harnoi-khwar valley, in Tehsil of Maṭṭa. Only on the Russian map.

Pšt. 'autumnal field'.

862. **MANJA منجه (*manǰa*)** *Map 11*

Village in the Qalagai-khwar valley, near Kodarai-derai and slightly north of Tutanbanda, Tehsil of Kabal. Quoted already by RAVERTY (1888: 232). Called Manjahei by TUCCI (1958: 319).

Pšt. *manǰ* 'sleeping accommodations, bed'.

863. **MANJA-KANDAO منجه کنډو (*manǰa-kanḍaw*)** *Map 11*

Pass near the Qalagai-khwar, Tehsil of Kabal.

Cf. prec.

864. **MANKAR منکر (*mankar*)** *Map 45*

Group of houses in the narrow valley on the left bank of the Swāt river, Tehsil of Bahrain. Only on the Russian map.

Cf. Tor. Manku 'Mankar, a village name'. Cf. foll.?

865. **MANKI مانکی (*mānki*)** *Map 24*

Group of houses located in the high and narrow Dosara-khwar valley, Tehsil of Babuzai.

Cf. foll.

866. **MANKIAL منکیال (*maṇkyāl*)** *Map 52*

Small village on the left bank of the upper Swāt river, Tehsil of Bahrain. Only on the Russian map.

Cf. foll. HAKIMZAY (1997: 155) quotes a doubtful *yāl* 'water' + Hi. *mānig* 'ruby' and mentions the position of this village between the Mankial-khwar and the Swāt river. On the sf. *-yāl*, cf. also T2588: "ext. with *-āl-* to form cmpds. with 'bottom, root' as in neighbouring Ir. lggs. [...] From the meaning 'side, edge' derive prob. some adverbs and postpositions". However, if HAKIMZAY's opinion is correct, this sf. *-(y)āl* would explain the meaning of many toponyms. The first part of this toponym remains very doubtful.

867. **MANKIAL منکیال (*māṇkyal*)** *Map 52*

Stream flowing into the left side of the Swāt river, Tehsil of Bahrain.

Cf. T9704 *maṅkatē* 'moves': Pkt. *maṃkia-* 'advancing by leaps'; Bhoj. *mā̃kal* 'to jump, leap'.

868. **MANKIAL-TSUKAI منکیال څوکی (*maṇkyāl-cukay*)** *Map 52*

Mountain of about 5,710 mt north of the Mankial-khwar valley and near the boundary with Kohistan, Tehsil of Bahrain.

Cf. prec.

869.-870. **MANRAI مانړی (*māṇe*)** *Maps 16, 42*

Name of two groups of houses: 1) in a mountainous lateral valley of the Deolai-khwar valley at the frontier with the Tehsil of Maṭṭa, Tehsil of Kabal; 2) in the upper Harnoi-khwar valley, Tehsil of Maṭṭa (only on the Russian map).

Pšt. 'apples'. HAKIMZAY (1997: 153) proposes Hi. *māṛi* 'upper room; balcony; shrine sacred to an inferior deity'.

871. **MANRAI-BANDA مانړی بانډه (*maṇe-bānḍa*)** *Map 13*

Pasture in the Manrai-khwar valley, towards the boundary with Matta, Tehsil of Kabal.

Pšt. 'pasture of the apples (*maṇá*)'.

872. **MANRAI-KHWAR مانړی خوړ (*māṇe-xwaṛ*)** *Map 13*

Stream (elevation is 1,290 meters) flowing into the Deolai-khwar, Tehsil of Kabal.

Pšt. 'stream of the apples (*maṇá*)'.

873. **MANR-PATAI ماڼ پټی (*maṇ-paṭay*)** *Map 34*

Village in a lateral terraced valley on the left bank of the Swāt river, near Asala, Tehsil of Khwazakhela.

Pšt. 'field of the apples (*maṇá*)'.

874. **MANYAR مانیار (*mānyār*)** *Map 7*

Last village of the Tehsil of Barikot, on the left bank of the Swāt river, in the plain at the foot of the hills. Quoted already by RAVERTY (1888: 199) as Mán-yár, "formerly known as Máni-har, probably its ancient name".

Cf. Maniaur.

875. **MANZA منزا (*manzā*)** *Map 44*

Village in the mountainous narrow Barwai-khwar valley, Tehsil of Maṭṭa.

Cf. Pšt. *manj* 'between, midst' → 'in the middle' → 'in the plain'? Or cf. foll.?

876. **MANZARAI-BANDA منزری بانده (*manzaray-bānḍa*)** *Map 12*

Pasture in the mountainous upper Deolai-khwar valley, Tehsil of Kabal.

Pšt. 'pasture of the lion/tiger (*manzaráy*)'.

877. **MANZE منزې (*manze*)** *Map 20*

Group of houses in the mountainous upper Saidu-khwar valley, Tehsil of Babuzai.

Cf. Manza.

878. **MANZGHUNDAI-BANDA منځغوندی بانده (*manjγwənḍəy-bānḍa*)** *Map 10*

Pasture located in the upper mountaneous Ramogai-khwar valley, Tehsil of Kabal.

Pšt. 'pasture of the hill (*γwənḍəy*) in the middle (*manj*)'.

879. **MARAN-SAR ماران سر (*mārān-sar*)** *Map 19*

Mountain of about 2,190 mt, located in the Tehsils of Barikot, at the boundary with the Tehsil of Babuzai.

Pšt. 'mountain of the serpents (*mār*)'.

880. **MARCHIL مارچل (*mārčil*)** *Map 44*

Village in the wide plain of the Barwai-khwar, Tehsil of Maṭṭa.

Cf. Pšt. *māṛay-hāṛay* 'exclamation of lamentation, complaint or supplication' (RAVERTY)?

881. **MARGATER مرگتېر (*margater*)** *Map 47*

Group of houses in the mountains above the upper Baral-darra valley, Tehsil of Bahrain.

Cf. Makad-khwar? Or linked to the root for 'pearl' (*marγalara*)? Sf.-*ter*? Cf. also Samter.

882. **MARGHUZAR مرغزار (*marγuzār*)** *Map 19*

Village in the narrow upper mountainous Marghuzar-khwar valley, Tehsil of Babuzai.

Pšt. *marγzā́r* 'meadow' [or 'crows/birds'?]. See MORGENSTIERNE 1931: 440 (Munǰan).

883. **MARGHUZAR-KHWAR مرغزار خوړ (*marγuzār-xwaṛ*)** *Map 19*

Stream flowing into the Saidu-khwar, Tehsil of Babuzai.

Cf. prec.

884. **MASHKUMAI مشکومی (*maškumay*)** *Map 32*

Small village in the fertile terraced Khwazakhela-khwar valley, Tehsil of Khwazakhela.

Cf. Pšt. *mašk* 'leather bag for carrying water, water bag' (RAVERTY)? According to HAKIMZAY (1997: 148-149), it is formed on Mashku, person's name, and Skt. *mahi* 'earth, land' (cf. T9974 *mahī* 'the earth': Pa. Pkt. *mahī-* 'the earth'): 'earth of Mašku'.

885.-886. **MASHKUN ماشکون (*māškun*)** *Maps 51, 53*

Name of two villages in the Tehsil of Bahrain: 1) on the slopes separating the Swāt valley from the Jaba-khwar valley (apparently, its name is Kafir-banda on the Russian map); 2) group of houses in the narrow valley on the right bank of the upper Swāt river, Tehsil of Bahrain.

Cf. Tor. *māš* 'fish' + sf. of place *-kun* (?).

887. **MATARKUN مترکون (*matarkun*)** *Map 50*

Group of houses in the narrow valley on the right bank of the upper Swāt river, Tehsil of Bahrain.

Cf. T9746 *maṇḍūka-* 'frog' [see KEWA II 561-562 and EWAia II 295]: Dam. *maṭrak*, etc.?

888. **MATLIT-AN متیلت ان (*maṭlit-an*)** *Map 54*

Pass leading from the Ushu-gol valley to Kohistan, Tehsil of Bahrain. Only on the Russian map.

Et. unkn., but probably of IA origin.

889. **MATRAPENDAI متریپنډی (*matrapeṇḍəy*)** *Map 19*

Group of houses in the upper mountainous Marghuzar-khwar valley, Tehsil of Babuzai, near the boundary with Buner.

Panj. *piṇḍ* 'village' (cf. Rawalpindi) and cf. Ur. *moṭrā* 'bundle, package, load' (PLATTS), or *moṭhṛā* 'a kind of mixed cotton and silk cloth'?

890.-892. **MATTA مته (*maṭa*)** *Maps 37, 38, 43*

Name of three villages: 1) Group of houses on the slopes of the Dobar-sar towards the Swāt river, Tehsil of Khwazakhela (only on the Russian map); 2) Main village of the homonym Tehsil, in the fertile plain between the Harnoi-khwar and the right bank of the Swāt river, Tehsil of Maṭṭa; 3) Group of houses on the hills bordering the Roringar-khwar, Tehsil of Maṭṭa (only on the Russian map).

Pšt. *máṭa* 'dust, white clay'. HAKIMZAY (1997: 151) proposes Hi. *mat* 'faith, religion', but the proposal does not appear reliable.

893. **MATTAI متی (*maṭṭay*)** *Map 28*

Group of houses in the upper terraced Dre-khwar valley, Tehsil of Charbagh.

Possibly Pšt. *muṭəy* 'instrument for cleaning cotton, also the club with which the cleaner strikes the string of the instrument; handle of a plough; part of anything which is held in the hand, as a haft, shaft, etc.' (RAVERTY)?

894. **MEGAI میږی (*meğay*)** *Map 33*

Group of houses in the wide terraced Khwazakhela-khwar valley, Tehsil of Khwazakhela.

Pšt. *meğáy* 'ant'.

895. **MEGO-DERAI میږو دېرى (*meğo-ḍerəy*)** *Map 37*

Group of houses located on the slopes of the Dobar-sar towards the Swāt river, Tehsil of Khwazakhela.

Pšt. 'residence of the ants'.

896. **MEHERGAI مېرګى (*mayragəy*)** *Map 19*

Village in the narrow upper mountainous Marghuzar-khwar valley, near Marghuzar, Tehsil of Babuzai.

Pšt. 'small steppe'.

897. **MELEGAI مېلېګى (*melegay*)** *Map 21*

Group of houses in the hills on the Jambil-khwar valley, Tehsil of Babuzai.

Pšt. 'place of the fair (*melá*)'.

898. **MENDURIA-KANDAO مېندوريه کنډو (*mendurya-kanḍaw*)** *Map 35*

Pass leading from the Bargin-khwar valley to Shangla, Tehsil of Khwazakhela.

Cf. T10310 *mēṇḍha* 'ram', *mēṇḍhra-*, *mēḍhra-*: Pa. *meṇḍa-* 'ram'; Pkt. *meḍḍha-*, Dam. Gaw. *miṇ*; Bashk. *mināl* 'ram'; Tor. *miṇḍ* 'ram', *miṇḍāl* 'markhor'; Panj. *mẽḍhā*. Or cf. T9746 *maṇḍūka-* 'frog', *maṇḍūra-*: Pkt. *maṁḍūka-*; Pkt. *maṁdūra-*. According to KUIPER (1955: 109-112), this is an Austro-As. loanword in IA (see also KEWA II 682 and EWAia III 415).

899. **MERAGAI مېرګى (*meragay*)** *Map 22*

Group of houses in the mountainous upper Jambil-khwar valley, near Jambil, Tehsil of Babuzai.

Cf. Mehergai or Maira.

900. **MIAN-BABA-BANDA ميان بابا بانده (*myān-bābā-bānḍa*)** *Map 12*

Pasture in the mountains near the Deolai-khwar valley, Tehsil of Kabal.

Pšt. origin. See SULTAN-I-ROME 2016: 540: "*Mian* (plural: *Miangan*): The descendants of saints and spiritual leaders of the past who have acquired widespread fame and reputation among many tribes". See also *ibid.*: *Miangul*: Abdul Ghafur alias Saidu Baba of Swat, was not yet ranked *Mian* so his descendants were given the courtesy title of Miangul (plural: *Miangwalan*). In a sense it is lesser of a title to *Mian*. It is also a term used for addressing the minors' of the Mians".

901. **MIAN-BELA-BANDA ميان بېله بانده (*myān-bela-bānḍa*)** *Map 12*

Pasture in the mountainous upper Deolai-khwar valley, Tehsil of Kabal.

Cf. prec. or foll.

902. **MIANDAM میاندم (*myāndam*)** *Map 36*

Village at the confluence between the Miandam-khwar valley and the Paiti-khwar valley, Tehsil of Khwazakhela.

HAKIMZAY (1997: 162-163) reads it as Myādam and proposes to see in it a Gujar root for 'middle', as this place "is located in the middle of the mountains": better 'in the middle of the two streams. According to IKRAM, p.c., "Mian" is a race of people linked with the Holy Prophet, but 'Mian' is also a great Saint and 'Dam' means 'to blow over some spiritual words'". Cf. also foll.

903. **MIANDAM میاندم (*myāndam*)** *Map 36*

Stream flowing into the Paiti-khwar, Tehsil of Khwazakhela.

Cf. prec.

904. **MIAN-KILI میان کلي (*myān-kəli*)** *Map 38*

Small village in the hills at the source of an affluent of the right side of the Harnoi-khwar, Tehsil of Maṭṭa. According to M.A. DINAKHEL (p.c.), "the actual phoneme is not /n/, but a nasalisation corresponding to Urdu ں, that does not exist in Pashto: so میان is actually میا".

Cf. prec.

905. **MIANKOTE میانکوټې (*myānkoṭe*)** *Map 30*

Group of houses in the wide plain of Charbagh near Charbagh, Tehsil of Charbagh.

Cf. Mian-baba-banda + -*koṭa* 'room', pl.

906. **MIAN-MAZRA میان مزره (*myān-mazra*)** *Map 38*

Small village located in the plain on the right bank of the Harnoi-khwar valley, Tehsil of Maṭṭa.

Cf. prec. + Pšt. *mazaray* 'kind of grass or reed from which sandals or mats are manufactured'.

907. **MIANWARA-BANDA میانواره بانډه (*myānwāra-bānḍa*)** *Map 13*

Pasture in the high Manrai-khwar valley, towards the boundary with Matta, Tehsil of Kabal.

Cf. Mian-baba-banda.

908. **MILKATLI ملکتلي (*milkatli*)** *Map 43*

Group of houses on the eastern slopes of the mountains dividing the Barwai-khwar valley from the Harnoi-khwar valley, Tehsil of Maṭṭa.

Pšt. *milk* 'possession, property, right, dominion' + sf. -*aṭ(i)*? Or Pšt. *malik* + *kaṭay* 'male buffalo-calf': 'master of the calf'?

909. **MINGAORA مينګوره (*mingawəra*)** *Map 18*

Main village of the Swāt valley, on the left bank of the Swāt river, Tehsil of Babuzai. Quoted by RAVERTY (1888) as Míngowaṛa'h and by DEANE (1895) as Mingaur. "Mingora est implantée sur la rive gauche de la rivière Swat dont le lit s'élargit ici jusqu'à plusieurs centaines de mètres. Deux cours d'eau dévalent les vallées qui prolongent l'agglomération au sud, le Saidu Khwar [...] et le Jambil Khwar, qui se rencontrent en amont du bazar et vont se jeter en aval dans la Swat. Saidu Sharif se développe parallèlement au Saidu Khwar au sud de Mingora, alors que celle-ci se développe au nord, entre le Jambil Khwar et la Swat. Les deux ponts sur le Jambil Khwar marquent la limite entre les deux ensembles urbains. La zone de plaine, fortement urbanisée dans toutes les directions, est fermée au nord par des chaînes de collines arides, de part et d'autre du Saidu Khwar et au sudouest du Jambil Khwar. Ce sont dans ces dernières qu'est exploitée la mine d'émeraudes dont la qualité est appréciée des joailliers" (VIARO/ ZIEGLER 1999: 120). See also HISAM/VIARO 2002.

TUCCI 1997: 78: "It seemed to me there could be no further doubt that [Chin.] Mêng chie li corresponds to Mingora and not to Mangalaor and that the capital mentioned by the Chinese pilgrims must have stood on this site, where all the roads met, surrounded as it was by luxuriant valleys, with a hinterland that could feed a dense population". See also TUCCI 1977: 75 n. 105. Cf. Manglaor.

910. **MIRATI-KANDAO مرتي کندو (*mirati-kanḍaw*)** *Map 5*

Pass in the Tehsil of Barikot, leading from the Jolagram-khwar valley to Dir.

Probably Pšt. *mir* 'chief, leader' + sf. *-ti* (?).

911. **MIRMI مرمي (*mirmi*)** *Map 39*

Group of houses in the hills on the right bank of the Swāt river, Tehsil of Maṭṭa.

Pšt. *mermən* 'mistress'?

912. **MOGILAI موګلی (*mogilay*)** *Map 39*

Group of houses on the slopes of the Shah-dop-sar on the left bank of the Harnoi-khwar, Tehsil of Maṭṭa.

Possibly Pšt. *moğáy* 'wooden peg or stake' (RAVERTY) + sf. *-ilay*.

913. **MOI-KANDAO موی کندو (*moy-kanḍaw*)** *Map 19*

Pass on the boundary with Buner, Tehsil of Babuzai, at the end of the Marghuzar-khwar valley.

Cf. T10104 *māsa-* 'moon, month': Paš. *mōi*, etc.: → 'pass of the moon'.

914. **MOMIN-PATAI مومين پټی (*momin-pəṭay*)** *Map 2*

Group of houses in the upper Kandak-khwar valley, Tehsil of Barikot, at the boundary with Buner.

Person's name or Pšt. 'field of the believer'.

915. **MORAGAI موړگی (*moragay*)** *Map 38*

Group of houses at the foot of the hills bordering the plain of the right bank of the Har-noi-khwar, Tehsil of Maṭṭa.

Pšt. 'small range of mountains'.

916. **MORA-SAR موره سر (*moṛa-sar*)** *Map 1*

Mountain of about 1,300 mt near the Kotah-khwar and on the boundary with Malakand, Tehsil of Barikot. This mountain is also called Mora'h Ghar by RAVERTY (1888: 195). The Mora-kandao lies some kilometers out the actual boundaries of Swat and is already cited by RAVERTY (1888: 235, 240). YOUNGHUSBAND (1895: 83 ff.) and THOMSON (1895: 158) mention this pass while relating the events concerning the Chitral campaign. DEANE (1895) quotes the village Morah Banda.

Cf. Pšt. *moṛá* 'range (of mountains), edge'.

917. **MOZRIBANR موزربین (*mozribaṇ*)** *Map 30*

Group of houses on the slopes of the Charbagh plain, Tehsil of Charbagh.

Cf. Pšt. *moz* 'plantain': 'garden of the small plantains'.

918. **MUHAMMAD-BEG محمد بیگ (*muhamad-beg*)** *Map 16*

Group of houses in the mountainous valley of the Mahakai stream, Tehsil of Kabal.

Person's name.

919. **MULLA-PATA ملا پته (*mulā-paṭa*)** *Map 16*

Group of houses in a mountainous lateral valley of the Deolai-khwar valley at the frontier with the Tehsil of Maṭṭa, Tehsil of Kabal.

Pšt. 'address (*paṭa*) of the Mullah'. However, we can also imagine a reduction of patai (*pəṭay* 'field'): 'Mullah's field'.

920. **MURAI موری (*muray*)** *Map 28*

Group of houses on a terrace in the Dre-khwar valley, Tehsil of Charbagh.

Cf. Pšt. *morəy* 'pipe or subterranean passage for water' (RAVERTY).

921. **MURDAR-BANDA مردار بانده (*murdār-bānḍa*)** *Map 10*

Pasture on the Dokat-sar, in a lateral valley of the Ramogai-khwar valley, Tehsil of Kabal.

Pšt. 'pasture of the dead/scoundrel (*murdā́r*)'.

922. **NABIPATAI نبیپتی (*nabipəṭay*)** *Map 51*

Group of houses in the mountainous Jaba-khwar valley, Tehsil of Bahrain.

Pšt. 'field of the prophet (*nabí* Ar.)'.

923. **NABORAI نبوړی (*naboṛay*)** *Map 37*

Village in the plain on the left bank of the Swāt river, Tehsil of Khwazakhela. Quoted already by RAVERTY (1888: 230) as Ban-waṛí, from where it was possible to cross the Swāt river.

Cf. prec. + dim. sf. -*ṛay*.

924. **NAGRAI نګړی (*nagṛay*)** *Map 32*

Small village in the upper Khwazakhela-khwar valley, Tehsil of Khwazakhela.

Possibly Pšt. *rangṛáy, nangṛáy* 'sparse, scattered' (*scil. koruna* 'houses'): indeed, according to IKRAM, p.c., *nagrai* means 'small village'. However, cf. also Pšt. *nigār* 'pictur, idol, effigy' and T14656 *nagará-* 'town' [← Drav.: see KEWA II 125 and EWAia II 5 for literature and discussion]: Kt. (in a myth) *niṅar* 'castle'; Kal. *Náṅgar* 'name of a village south of Drosh' → Kho. *Nagar* ~ *nogor*?

925. **NAGWA نګوه (*nagwa*)** *Map 6*

Village at the foot of the Tsapparai-sar on the right bank of the Swāt river, Tehsil of Barikot.

Cf. T6983 *náva-*, *navaka-* 'new, young': Waig. *núge*, Dam. *nū̃(w)a*, Paš.dar. *nõā*, lauṛ. *nūṅga*, weg. *nogā*, ar. *nəgṓ* (< **nõṅk-* < *navaka-* IIFL iii 3, 132), Gaw. *núṅga*? According to IKRAM, p.c. the right form of the toponym is Nagoha: *nāga* 'snake' + *gāh* 'place' = 'place of the snakes'.

926. **NAJIGRAM نجیګرام (*naǰigrām*)** *Map 3*

Village located in the last fertile plain of the Najigram-khwar valley, Tehsil of Barikot, before the confluence with the Karakar-khwar valley.

Cf. T398 *annādya-* 'food': Kat. *anǰī* 'bread, food', Lhd. *anāj*, Panj. *anāj*, *nāj*, Hi. *anāj*, *nāj* 'grain'? See ADAMEC VI 581 Naji, "A village located some 12 miles southeast of Ghazni in Ghazni province".

927. **NAJIGRAM-KHWAR نجیګرام خوړ (*naǰigrām-xwaṛ*)** *Map 3*

Stream located at an elevation of 809 meters above sea level, Tehsil of Barikot, flowing from the boundary with Buner to the Karakar-khwar, near Natmaira.

Cf. prec.

928. **NAKHTAR نښتر (*naẋtar*)** *Map 16*

Group of houses in the mountains bordering a lateral valley on the right bank of the Harnoi-khwar, Tehsil of Maṭṭa.

Pšt. *nəẋtár* 'Himalayan pine, *Pinus excelsa*' (see also SULTAN-I-ROME 2016: 221).

929. **NALI نلي (*nali*)** *Map 39*

Small village in the fertile plain on the right bank of the Swāt river north of the Harnoi-khwar, Tehsil of Maṭṭa. Called Naya on the Russian map.

Prob. cf. T7047 *nāḍī* 'tubular stalk of any plant, tubular organ, tube; windpipe': Pa. *nāḷa-*, *nāla-* 'hollow stalk (esp. of lotus)', °*ḷī-* 'id., tube'; Pkt. *ṇāḍī-*, *ṇāḷī-* 'hollow stalk'; Lhd. *nāl* 'tube', *nāḷā* 'canal'; Panj. *nāl*, °*lī* 'hollow stalk of wheat &c., tube', bhaṭ. *nāḷ* 'stream'; Hi. *nāl* 'hollow stalk, tube, throat', °*lā* 'watercourse, ravine'. Cf. also foll.

930. **NALI-DARRA نلي دره (*nali-dara*)** *Map 46*

Stream flowing into the Olal-khwar, Tehsil of Bahrain.

IA: cf. Dam. *nalī*, etc. (T6943: *nadī* 'river' RV : Pa. *nadī-* 'river', Pkt. *ṇaī-*, Si. *nāī* 'mountain torrent'; Lhd. *naī* 'natural watercourse, flood from the hills'; Panj. *naī*, *nai* 'river'. With early nasalization **nandī-* : Ash. *nẽdī*, *nẽdī*, Wg. *nădī*, Kt. *nanī*, Dm. *nalī* < **nanī* (MORGENSTIERNE 1942b: 126), Paš.lauṛ. *nandī*, ar. *nádī*, Niṅg. *nandī*, Shum. *nädī*, Woṭ. *nyed* f., Gaw. *nẽndi*, Bašk. *nʌndə*, Tor. *ned* m., Sv. *nẽelī*). Cf. prec.

931.-932. **NALKOT نلكوټ (*nālkoṭ*)** *Maps 42, 46*

Name of two villages: 1) in the plain at the confluence among the Harnoi-khwar, the Roringar-khwar and the Biha-khwar, Tehsil of Maṭṭa; 2) in the Olal-khwar valley, Tehsil of Bahrain.

Pšt. 'fort of the rivulet (*nāla* 'rivulet, brook, canal, gutter, furrow, ravine')'. According to HAKIMZAY (1997: 164), Hi. *Nal* is 'the name of a Raja, the husband of Damyanti, who lost his entire kingdom at a game of dice".

933. **NAO ناو (*nāw*)** *Map 26*

Group of houses in the upper Bishbanr-khwar valley, Tehsil of Babuzai.

Pšt. *nāw* 'hollow, depression, valley'.

934. **NAONA ناونه (*nāuna*)** *Map 40*

Group of houses in a small valley in the hills above the Shaurai-khwar, Tehsil of Maṭṭa.

Cf. prec. (pl.).

935. **NARAI-BANDA نری بانډه (*naray-bānḍa*)** *Map 3*

Pasture in the Najigram-khwar valley, Tehsil of Barikot, near the boundary with Buner.

Pšt. 'narrow (*naráy*) pasture' or cf. Pšt. 'pasture of the small green valley (*nāṛə́y*)'?

936. **NARAI-SUR-BANDA نری سور بانډه (*naray-sur-bānḍa*)** *Map 25*

Pasture in the mountain dividing the Bishbanr-khwar valley from the Tambagat-khwar valley, Tehsil of Charbagh.

Cf. prec.

937. **NARANJPURA نرنجپوره (*naranǰpura*)** *Map 15*

Group of houses in the mountainous valley of the Mahakai stream, Tehsil of Kabal.

Pšt. 'town of the oranges'.

938. **NAREDALAI نړېدلی (*naṛedəlay*)** *Map 39*

Group of houses in the hills on the right bank of the Swāt river, Tehsil of Maṭṭa.

Pšt. *naṛedə́lay* 'destroyed, ruined' (see FUSSMAN 1972, II: 315 n. 2: Ašk. *nāṛ, nā̃ṛ* 'ravin').

939. **NAROSAI نروسی (*narosay*)** *Map 43*

Group of houses on the hills bordering the Harnoi-khwar valley, Tehsil of Maṭṭa. Only on the Russian map.

Possibly Pšt. *narútskay* 'rather thin; somewhat emaciated, drawn'?

940. **NASAFAI ناسافی (*nāsāfay*)** *Map 8*

Small village on the right bank of the Swāt river, Tehsil of Kabal, in the wide and fertile plain of Kabal.

Cf. Pšt. (← Ar.) *nisf* 'half' and Ur. (← Prs.) *nasfat* نصفت 'reaching to the middle'. To be excluded Pšt. *nācā́pa, nācāpe* 'unexpected, sudden, suddenly'.

941. **NASAPAI نڅپی (*nacapay*)** *Map 44*

Small village in the wide plain of the Barwai-khwar, Tehsil of Maṭṭa.

Cf. prec.

942. **NASRAT نسرت (*nasrat*)** *Map 14*

Village in a lateral valley of the Deolai-khwar valley, near Deolai, Tehsil of Kabal.

Probably Pšt. *nasrát* نصرت (← Ar.) 'victory, triumph; help, assistance'. See ADAMEC VI 361 Nasratzai, "Of which there are two families, viz., Nasratzai and Shahinchibashi; they are a sept of the Barakzai Duranis. The title of Shahinchibashi (Chief falconer) belongs to the family of Ahmad Khan, Nasratzai, to whom the title was given by Ahmad Shah" and ID. VI 593-594 Nari [*nāṛi*] or Nasrat, Nalai, "Elevation 3,000 feet. A village on the left bank the Kunar river, lying some 150 feet above its level, 8 miles below Arnawai. It contains about 100 houses, and is built on the pattern of Birkot, except that the lanes between the houses are somewhat broader".

943. **NATAL ناتل (*nātal*)** *Map 45*

Group of houses located on the cliff of a lateral valley on the right bank of the Swāt river, Tehsil of Bahrain.

Cf. Tor. *nathar* 'cliff'?

944. **NATMAIRA نټمیره (*naṭmayra*)** *Map 3*

Village located in the narrow valley of the Karakar-khwar, Tehsil of Barikot.

Pšt. *mayrá* 'steppe, plain; non-irrigated land' as second element. Could the first element be *naṭ* 'the name of a tribe who are generally jugglers, rope-dancers, tumblers, etc.' (RAVERTY)?

945. **NAWAGAY ناواګی (*nāwāgəy*)** *Map 4*

Village located in the fertile plain at the confluence between the Najigram-khwar valley and the Karakar-khwar valley, Tehsil of Barikot.

Pšt. 'new' or 'small valley (*nāwá*)'.

946.-951. **NAWE-KALAI نوی کلی (*nəway-kəlay*)** *Maps 2, 7, 18, 23, 34, 38*

Name of six villages: 1) in the vast and fertile valley on the left bank of the Swat river, between Kotah and Abwa, Tehsil of Barikot; 2-4) in the fertile valley on the left bank of the Swat river, Tehsil of Babuzai, near Mingaora, near Pajigram on the boundary with Barikot, and near the Ugad-khwar on the boundary with Charbagh; 5) north of Kotanai, on the left side of the Swat river, Tehsil of Khwazakhela (called Farhat Abad on Google Earth, and Bedasto on the Pakistani maps and Bēdastu in STEIN 1930); 6) on the right bank of the Swāt river at the foot of the hills bordering the plain, Tehsil of Maṭṭa.

Pšt. 'new village'. According to STEIN (1929: 23), the name of the village n. 1 would be Nawē Kala, 'the new castle', but this opinion is not shared by RAVERTY (1888: 199), one of the sources of Stein, who calls it simply Nowaey Kalaey.

The village in the Tehsil of Khwazakhela (n. 5) is also called Bedasto: according to HAKIMZAY (1997: 17), it could derive from *bed/baid* or *vedā*, and could indicate many things, as a kind of gruel; or he analyses it as *ava-stha* 'state, circumstances'.

952. **NEZA-MUNDO نېزه مندو (*neza-mando*)** *Map 20*

Group of houses located in the mountainous upper Saidu-khwar valley, Tehsil of Babuzai.

Pšt. *neza* 'spear, lance, javelin, dart, pike; piece of reed from which pens are made' (RAVERTY) + Pšt. *mānda* 'the dry bed of a river, or the bed of a torrent'.

953. **NIAM نیام (*nyām*)** *Map 48*

Small village located in the narrow valley on the right bank of the Swāt river, Tehsil of Bahrain.

Cf. Pšt. *nihā́m* 'hidden; secret'.

954. **NIKO-DERAI نیکو ډېرې (*niko-ḍerəy*)** *Map 26*

Group of houses in the upper Bishbanr-khwar valley, Tehsil of Charbagh.

Pšt. 'residence of the grand-fathers (*nikə́*)'.

955. **NILGRAM نلګرام (*nilgrām*)** *Map 38*

Group of houses at the foot of the hills bordering the plain of the right bank of the Harnoi-khwar, Tehsil of Maṭṭa.

IA. 'blue village'.

956.-957. NIMAKAI نمکی (*nimakay*) *Maps 16, 37*

Name of two groups of houses: 1) in a mountainous lateral valley of the Deolai-khwar valley at the frontier with the Tehsil of Maṭṭa, Tehsil of Kabal; 2) on the slopes of the Dobar-sar towards the Swāt river, Tehsil of Khwazakhela (only on the Russian map).

Pšt. *nimakáy* 'balcony'.

958. NIMAKI نمکي (*nimaki*) *Map 35*

Group of houses located in the narrow mountainous upper Bargin-khwar valley, Tehsil of Khwazakhela.

Cf. prec.

959. NIMOGRAM نیموگرام (*nimogrām*) *Map 5*

Small village on the mountain above Khazana and the Jolagram-khwar valley, at the border with Dir, Tehsil of Barikot.

Cf. T6983 *náva-*, *navaka-* 'new, young': Woṭ. *nam*, Bashk. *nim* 'new'; Tor. *nam* 'new', *nem* 'the new moon'; Si. *nãõ* 'new': 'new town'. Less probable connection with T7247 *nimbū-* 'the lime Citrus acida' [← Austro-As.: KUIPER 1948: 84, KEWA II 166 and EWAia III 292; see also BURROW 1945: 614]: Si. *līmo* 'lime', Ku. *nimū*, etc.: → 'town of the lemons'?

960. NINGULAI ننګولی (*ningulәy*) *Map 17*

Village at the foot of the hills in the last part of the fertile plain on the right bank of the Swāt river, Tehsil of Kabal. RAVERTY (1888: 201, 230) notes it as Ním-galí. STEIN 1929 calls it Mingulai.

Cf. Pšt. *ningấnay* 'span (e.g., of land)'. HAKIMZAY (1997: 165) proposes to see in it Hi. *nim* 'religious' and *gwәli* 'flower'.

961. NINGULAI-GHUNDAI ننګولی غونډی (*ningulay-γwәnḍәy*) *Map 17*

Top of the hill of the Ningulai village, located at the foot of the hills in the last part of the fertile plain on the right bank of the Swāt river, Tehsil of Kabal. RAVERTY (1888: 201, 230) records also the Kotal ('pass').

Cf. prec. + *γwәnḍa* 'detached hill, separated from the higher range' (see ROSSI 2002).

962. NIZAM-BANDA نزام بانده (*nizām bānḍa*) *Map 20*

Pasture in the mountainous upper Saidu-khwar valley, Tehsil of Babuzai.

Cf. Neza Mundo.

963. NOCHA نوچه (*noča*) *Map 28*

Group of houses in one of the three main terraced valleys of the Dre-khwar valley, Tehsil of Charbagh.

Cf. Pšt. *nawčák* 'dew; new, fresh, just appearing' (ASLANOV)?

964. **NOKHARA نوخاره (*nowxāra*)** *Map 44*

Village in the wide plain of the Barwai-khwar, Tehsil of Maṭṭa.

Possibly Pšt. *xārá* 'undeveloped land' + Pšt. *naw* 'moisture, dampness, wetness'. Cf. also Pšt. *nauх̌ár* 'Naushera (city near Peshawar)' → possibly Pšt. 'new city'?

965. **OBO اوبو (*obo*)** *Map 28*

Small group of houses located on the road leading to Malam-jabba in the Tehsil of Čārbāγ at a height of about 1800 meters. It is called on the Russian map Spin-obo, 'white waters'.

Pšt. *obə́* 'water'.

966. **OLAL-KHWAR اولال خوړ (*olāl-xwaṛ*)** *Map 46*

Stream tributary of Swāt river on the left side in the Tehsil of Bahrain, also called Bashigrām-khwar (cf. Bishgram); its elevation is 1,594 meters.

Tor. *olāl* 'stream of Chail valley' and the verb Tor. *uluṭu-* 'to roll'. Cf. T2377 *ullāla* '*springing up or out': M. *ulāḷ*, *ullāḷ*, *ulhāḷ* m. 'a spring'; T2373 *ullalati* 'jumps out': Pkt. *ullalaï* 'jumps up, wobbles'.

967. **ONA اونا (*oṇā*)** *Map 41*

Group of houses on the slopes of the Prangman-sar, in a lateral valley of the upper Harnoi-khwar valley, Tehsil of Maṭṭa.

Cf. T2349 *úraṇa* 'ram, sheep, young ram': Pkt. *ūraṇa-*; Tir. *uráni* 'sheep'; Sh. *ŭrăṇ* 'lamb'; Lhd. khet. *ornā* 'lamb'. Less probable, Pšt. *wə́na* 'tree'. However, it could be also related to the etymology of the Unran-sar.

968. **ORMAL-KANDAO ارمال كندو (*ormāl-kanḍaw*)** *Map 28*

Pass leading from the Khwazakhela-khwar valley in Khwazakhela Tehsil to the Dre-khwar valley in Charbagh Tehsil.

Pšt. 'pass of the fig trees (*urmál*)'.

969. **PACHAABAD پاچاباد (*pāčāābād*)** *Map 37*

Village in the plain on the left bank of the Swāt river, Tehsil of Khwazakhela. It is called Badeshai ('id.') on the Russian map.

Pšt. 'town of the king (*pāčā*)'.

970.-971. **PACHA-KILI-BANDA پاچا كلي بانده (*pāčā-kəli-bānḍa*)** *Map 13*

Name of two pastures located in the high upper Manrai-khwar valley, towards the boundary with Dir, Tehsil of Kabal.

Pšt. 'pasture of the village of the king (*pāčā*)'.

972. PAINDA-SHAH-PATAI پینده شاه پټی (*paynda-šāh-pəṭay*) *Map 8*

Small village on the slopes of the Kotlai-khwar valley leading to the boundary with Dir, under the Changai-dop-sar, Tehsil of Kabal.

Person's name.

973. PAITI-KHWAR پیتي خوړ (*payti-xwaṛ*) *Map 36-37*

Stream flowing into the Swāt river, south of Madyan, Tehsil of Khwazakhela.

Probably cf. foll. However, cf. also T7732 **patta-* 'back', "as a specifically NW word it may derive from Indo-Ir. **pati* (Av. *paiti*, &c. ~ Sk. *prati*) with doubling of *-t-* as in *iyattaká-* or Pk. *itti* ~ ɪᴛɪ": Paš. *pat* 'after', Gaw. *pata* 'behind', Bašk. *pat* 'after', *patai* 'second', Tor. *pat, pad* 'behind', etc. Or cf. T7733 *pattra-* 'wing-feather': Paš. *paṭā*, Gaw. *phaṭa*, Si. *petta* (pl. *peti*) 'slice, thin piece of wood'.

974. PAITISAR پیتي سر (*payti-sar*) *Map 37*

Village in the plain on the left bank of the Swāt river, Tehsil of Khwazakhela. Its actual name is Fatehpur. It is probably the village quoted by Raverty (1888: 235) as Petaey.

According to Hakimzay (1997: 53), Hi. *payt* means 'love', but cf. also Skt. *pati* 'master, lord, governor'. This second proposal seems more convincing, as it agrees also with the modern name, Fatehpur, 'town of the conqueror'. Cf. also prec.

975. PAJA پجا (*paǰā*) *Map 52*

Group of houses in the upper Mankial-khwar valley, Tehsil of Bahrain.

Cf. Pšt. *paǰa* 'brick-kiln, furnace'. Or cf. T7778 *pádyā* 'footsteps; path, road': Pa. *pajja-* 'path'; Pkt. *pajjā-* 'flight of steps, road'; Guǰ. *pāj* 'bridge, quay'; M. *pāj* 'mountain pass'? See Adamec V 378 Paj Kotal and Id. VI 616 Paja, "A village 22 miles south of the Bajgah pass, 20 houses".

976. PAJIGRAM پجیگرام (*paǰigrām*) *Map 7*

Village in the vast and fertile valley on the left bank of the Swat river, Tehsil of Babuzai. Quoted already by Raverty (1888) and by Deane (1895: Panjigram).

A variant of the village name is Panjigram (q.v.), then the origin must be IA: *panj grām* 'five villages'. To be excluded connexion with T7990 **paśca-* 'hinder part': Tor. *pāǰi, paiž* 'behind'. However, cf. also prec.

977. PALESAR-AN پلیسر ان (*palesar-an*) *Map 54*

Pass leading from the upper Ushu-gol valley to Kohistan, Tehsil of Bahrain.

Cf. Paloga-gol for the root *pal-*.

978. PALOGA-AN پلوگه ان (*paloga-an*) *Map 54*

Pass leading from the Paloga-gol valley to Kohistan, Tehsil of Bahrain.

Cf. foll.

979. **PALOGA-GOL پلوګه ګول (*paloga-gol*)** *Map 54*

Stream, whose estimate terrain elevation above seal level is 2451 metres, flowing into the Ushu-gol, Tehsil of Bahrain.

Cf. Kal. *palargá N.* The summer village of Palarga in upper Rumbur Valley. Cf. also Kal. *paḷáik V.* To flee, run away. *Etym:* pálāyatē 'flees' T7955: *pálāyatē* 'flees'. Caus. **palāpayati*; 1. Pa. *palāyati*, *palēti* 'runs away'; NiDoc. *palayiti* absol. 'having fled'; Pkt. *palāyaï*, *palaï* 'flees', *paḍāiavva-*; Dam. *paléim* 'I flee', Tir. imper. *palḗ*, Woṭ. *pal-*, Kal. 1st sg. pres. *palāam*; Panj. *palāuṇā* 'to run away'.

980. **PANAI پنی (*panay*)** *Map 44*

Group of houses in the mountainous Barwai-khwar valley, Tehsil of Maṭṭa.

Pšt. *panay* 'a kind of grass from which brooms are made (Andropogon muricatum)' (RAVERTY). However, cf. also Pšt. *pāṇ* 'steep or scarped bank of a river' (RAVERTY): cf. Pankanai.

981. **PANJAO پنجاو (*panǯāw*)** *Map 46*

Group of houses located in a lateral narrow valley of the Olal-khwar valley, Tehsil of Bahrain.

Derived from *panǯ* 'five'.

982. **PANJGRAM پنجګرام (*panǯgrām*)** *Map 45*

Group of houses in the narrow valley on the right bank of the Swāt river, Tehsil of Bahrain.

IA. 'five villages'. See also Pajigram.

983. **PANKANAI پاڼکاڼی (*pāṇkāṇay*)** *Map 40*

Village in the narrow terraced valley of the Shaurai-khwar, Tehsil of Maṭṭa.

Probably Pšt. *pāṇ* 'steep or scarped bank of a river' (RAVERTY) + *kāṇay* 'rock'.

984. **PANR پاڼ (*pāṇ*)** *Map 21*

Village south-east of Mingaora, at the entrance of the Jambil-khwar valley, Tehsil of Babuzai.

Pšt. *pāṇ* 'precipice, abyss, steep bank'. HAKIMZAY (1997: 43) sees in this toponym Skt. *pan* 'drinking beverage, drink', but it seems quite improbable.

985. **PANRASHAI پڼاشی (*paṇāšay*)** *Map 47*

Group of houses located in the mountains above the upper Baral-darra valley, Tehsil of Bahrain.

Cf. prec.

986. PANRASHAI-KANDAO پڼاشی کندو (*paṇāšay-kanḍaw*) *Map 47*

Pass on the boundary with Kohistan, Tehsil of Bahrain.

Cf. Ashar-garai + *pāṇ*, prec.

987. PANRSAT پانساټ (*pāṇsāt*) *Map 40*

Group of houses located on the mountains in the Shaurai-khwar valley, Tehsil of Maṭṭa.

Pšt. 'protection (*sāt*) from the precipice'.

988. PAPAR پاپر (*pāpar*) *Map 23*

Village in the narrow Landai-khwar valley, Tehsil of Babuzai.

Cf. Pšt. *pāpə́ṛ* 'thin cookie made from groundpea flour and cooked in hot oil'? Or cf. T8093 *pāparddhi* 'hunting'?

989. PARANIAL-KANDAO پرنیال کندو (*paranyāl-kanḍaw*) *Map 23*

Pass on the road leading to Sangota from Mingaora, on the left bank of the Swāt river, Tehsil of Babuzai.

Cf. Baranial?

990. PARKHA پرخه (*parxa*) *Map 25*

Village in the lower Bishbanr-khwar valley, Tehsil of Babuzai.

Pšt. *pərxá* 'dew' or Pšt. *pə́rx̌a* 'mushroom'.

991. PAR-PATAI پر پټی (*par-pəṭay*) *Map 39*

Group of houses on the slopes of the Lito-sar degrading towards the Harnoi-khwar valley, in Tehsil of Maṭṭa. Only on the Russian map.

Pšt. 'upper field'.

992.-993. PARRAI پاړړی (*pāṛṛəy*) *Maps 6, 43*

1) Big village at the foot of the Tsapparai-sar and the Parrai-ghar, on the right bank of the Swāt river, Tehsil of Barikot. 2) Group of houses in the narrow Roringar-khwar valley, Tehsil of Maṭṭa (only on the Russian map).

According to Hakimzay (1997: 53-54), it is related to Skt. *par* 'the opposite bank or shore' and to *roh* and *rehar* 'barren or saline soil'. This opinion can be shared. But cf. also T8362 *pr̥dāku-* 'snake; tiger, panther' (according to Bailey 1946: 782 orig. meaning could be 'spotted', both may be same word and the latter not necessarily ← Ir. (Psht. *pṛāng*, &c.): see KEWA II 335 and EWAia II 163): Lhd. *parṛā* 'leopard' (< **praḍā-*). Or Pšt. *pāṛay* 'hog-deer (Cervus porcinus)' (Raverty) and Pšt. *paṛay* 'cord, small rope, line, thread, string in general' (Raverty).

994. **PARRAI-GHAR پاړى غر (*pārṛəy-γar*)** *Map 8*

Mountain on the right bank of the Swāt river, Tehsil of Barikot, above Parrai.

Cf. prec.

995. **PARWAN پروان (*parwān*)** *Map 17*

Group of houses in the upper Sigram-khwar valley, Tehsil of Kabal.

Cf. the Province of Parwān in Afghanistan and the related old town (actual name Jebel-us-Siraya). Cf. Prs. *parwān* 'sight, show, anything wonderful' (STEINGASS)?

996. **PASHINO-BANDA پشينو بانده (*pašino-bānḍa*)** *Map 43*

Pasture on the mountain above the upper Roringar-khwar valley, near the boundary with Dir, Tehsil of Maṭṭa.

Cf. Pšt. *pəš* 'blacksmith'.

997. **PASHMAL پشمال (*pašmāl*)** *Map 53*

Small village in the narrow valley on the right bank of the upper Swāt river, Tehsil of Bahrain. Quoted already by RAVERTY (1888: 237).

In Pšt. it could be interpreted as 'rich (*māl*) in blacksmiths (*paš*)', but here we can follow HAKIMZAY's interpretation (1997: 48) as 'necklace of flowers', from IA *puṣpa* 'flower' + *mālā* 'necklace' (cf. Peshawar).

998.-999. **PATAI پټى (*pəṭay*)** *Maps 39, 52*

Name of two groups of houses: 1) at the foot of the hills on the right bank of the Swāt river, Tehsil of Maṭṭa, quoted already by RAVERTY (1888: 235); 2) in the Jaba-khwar valley, Tehsil of Bahrain.

Pšt. 'field'.

1000. **PATA-SAR پټه سر (*pəṭa-sar*)** *Map 24*

Mountain between the Jambil-khwar valley and the Lewanai-khwar valley, Tehsil of Babuzai, near the boundary with Buner.

Pšt. 'the hidden mountain'.

1001. **PATEMAN پټېمن (*paṭeman*)** *Map 40*

Group of houses in the Shaurai-khwar, Tehsil of Maṭṭa. Only on the Russian map.

Pšt. *pəṭay* 'field' + sf. *-man* (for adj.).

1002. **PATIBAST-BANDA پټبست بانده (*patibast-bānḍa*)** *Map 15*

Village in a lateral valley of the Deolai-khwar valley, Tehsil of Kabal.

Pšt. 'pasture of the refuge (*bast*) of the field (*pəṭay*)'.

1003. **PIA پیا (*pyā*)** *Map 37*

Village in the narrow valley on the left bank of the Swāt river, Tehsil of Bahrain. RAVERTY (1888: 200) states that: "Pé'á is the most northern place in Upper Suwát belonging to the Afgháns, and at that point Upper Suwát terminates".

Et. unkn. Improbable connections with T7790 *páyas* 'any fluid (esp. milk)' (Pa. *paya-* 'milk, juice'; Pkt. *paya-* 'milk, water'; Mai. *pai* 'milk'; Si. *paya, pā* 'milk, water'; cf. also Pšt. *pəy* 'milk'), and with T8974 *priyá* 'beloved': Pa. Pkt. *piya-* 'beloved'; Lhd. *pīā* 'lover, husband'; Panj. *pī, pīā* 'friend'. See ADAMEC VI 654 Piadara, "A village located a few miles southeast of Safidab in southern Bamian province", and Piadara, "A kotal leading over the hills north of Kharwar".

1004. **PIAZ پیاز (*pyāz*)** *Map 46*

Group of houses in the Nali-darra valley and on the slopes of the Punnubat-sar, Tehsil of Bahrain.

Cf. Pšt. *pyāz* 'onion'?

1005. **PINORAI-BANDA پنوری بانده (*pinoṛay-bānḍa*)** *Map 12*

Pasture in the Jarendo-bela-khwar valley, Tehsil of Kabal, near the boundary with Dir.

Cf. Pšt. *pina* 'wooden bowl or trough for making dough in; piece, patch' + dimin. sf. *-oṛay*.

1006. **PIRANAI پیرانی (*pirānay*)** *Map 50*

Group of houses located in a lateral valley on the right bank of the Swāt river, Tehsil of Bahrain.

Pšt. 'of the Pir': see foll.

1007. **PIR-BAGLAI پیر بگلی (*pir-baglay*)** *Map 34*

Group of houses in a lateral terraced valley on the left bank of the Swāt river, near Asala, Tehsil of Khwazakhela.

Pšt. *pir* 'old man, pir' + *bagla* 'field' (IKRAM, p.c.): 'field of the pir'. See DE CHIARA, forthcoming a: "*pīr*: a master, or saint, whose descendants enjoy the consideration accorded to the descendants of a saint".

1008. **PIR-CHAM پیر چم (*pir-čam*)** *Map 14*

Village in the wide and fertile Deolai-khwar valley, Tehsil of Kabal.

Pšt. 'quartier of the Pir'. See Pir-baglai.

1009. **PIRDARRA پیردره (*pirdara*)** *Map 48*

Group of houses in the Daral-khwar valley, Tehsil of Bahrain.

Pšt. 'valley of the Pir'. See Pir-baglai.

1010. **PIR-GANDAI پير ګاندي (*pir-gānde*)** *Map 35*

Group of houses located in the narrow mountainous upper Bargin-khwar valley, Tehsil of Khwazakhela.

Person's name. See Pir-baglai.

1011. **PIRJAI پيرجى (*pirǰay*)** *Map 42*

Group of houses located in the mountainous upper Biha-khwar valley, Tehsil of Maṭṭa.

Pšt. 'Pir-ǰaṭ'. See Pir-baglai.

1012. **PIR-KALAI پير کلى (*pir-kəlay*)** *Map 38*

Village on the right bank of the Harnoi river at the foot of the hills bordering the plain, Tehsil of Maṭṭa.

Pšt. 'village of the Pir'. See Pir-baglai.

1013. **PIRKAND پيرکند (*pirkand*)** *Map 43*

Group of houses located in the narrow Roringar-khwar valley, Tehsil of Maṭṭa. Only on the Russian map.

Pšt. 'ravine/gorge/high pass (*kand*) of the Pir'. See Pir-baglai and quotation from EILERS 1987, s.v. Kand.

1014. **PIRMAN-DERAI پيرمن ډېرى (*pirman-ḍerəy*)** *Map 18*

Group of houses in the fertile valley on the left bank of the Swat river, between the Swat river and the Saidu-khwar, Tehsil of Babuzai.

Pšt. 'residence of the Pir' (+ sf. *-man*, for adj.). See Pir-baglai.

1015. **PIRODAI پيرودى (*piroday*)** *Map 39*

Group of houses in the hills on the right bank of the Swāt river, Tehsil of Maṭṭa. Only on the Russian map.

Pšt. 'bought, purchased (*pirodəlay*)'?

1016. **PIR-PATAI پير پټى (*pir-pəṭay*)** *Map 37*

Village in the plain on the left bank of the Swāt river, Tehsil of Khwazakhela. Only on the Russian map.

Pšt. 'field of the Pir'. See Pir-baglai.

1017. **PIR-PATAI-BANDA پير پټى بانډه (*pir-pəṭay-bānḍa*)** *Map 11*

Name of a pasture in the Kolalai-khwar valley, Tehsil of Kabal.

Pšt. 'pasture of the field of the Pir'. See Pir-baglai.

1018. **PORAI-MAIDAN پورى ميدان (*poray-maydān*)** *Map 53*

Group of houses in the narrow valley on the right bank of the upper Swāt river, Tehsil of Bahrain.

Pšt. 'closed (*póre* 'bordering something; closed; connected with; etc.') place'.

1019. **PRANGMAN-SAR پړانګمان سر (*pṛāngmān-sar*)** *Map 42*

Mountain of about 3,000 mt between the Shaurai-khwar valley and the Biha-khwar valley, Tehsil of Maṭṭa.

Pšt. *pṛāng* 'tiger' + sf. *-man* (for adj.).

1020. **PUKHTUNPATAI پښتونپټى (*paxtunpəṭay*)** *Map 51*

Group of houses located in the upper valley of the Swāt river, on the left bank, Tehsil of Bahrain.

Pšt. 'field of the Pashtuns'.

1021. **PUL-BELA پول بيله (*pul-bela*)** *Map 50*

Group of houses located in a lateral valley on the right bank of the Swāt river, Tehsil of Bahrain.

Pšt. 'village of the bridge (*pul*)'.

1022. **PUL-DERAI پول ډيرى (*pul-ḍerəy*)** *Map 37*

Village in the plain on the left bank of the Swāt river, Tehsil of Khwazakhela. Only on the Russian map.

Pšt. 'village of the bridge (*pul*)'.

1023. **PUNNUBAT پنبت (*punubat*)** *Map 46*

Group of houses in the Shanku-khwar valley and on the slopes of the Punnubat-sar, Tehsil of Bahrain.

Cf. T7783 *panthapāla* 'guarding the road': Phal. *panwāl* 'road-guard'?

1024. **PUNNUBAT-SAR پنبت سر (*punubat-sar*)** *Map 46*

Mountain of about 3,400 mt between the Shanku-khwar valley and the Nali-darra valley, Tehsil of Bahrain.

Cf. prec.

1025. **PUROA پوروه (*purwa*)** *Map 41*

Group of houses in the narrow upper Harnoi-khwar valley, in Tehsil of Maṭṭa.

Cf. Pšt. *parwā* 'care, anxiety, concern; quite, repose'?

1026. **PURONAI پورونی (*puronay*)** *Map 22*

Group of houses in the mountainous upper Jambil-khwar valley, near the boundary with Buner, Tehsil of Babuzai.

Cf. Pšt. *prowuna* 'selling, vending, disposing; sale, vent, disposal' (RAVERTY).

1027. **PUSHTUNAI پشتونی (*puštuṇəy*)** *Map 42*

Village in the plain at the confluence among the Harnoi-khwar, the Roringar-khwar and the Biha-khwar, Tehsil of Maṭṭa.

Pšt. 'of the Pushtuns'.

1028. **QALA قلا (*qalā*)** *Map 25*

Village in the lower Bishbanr-khwar valley, Tehsil of Babuzai.

Pšt. 'fort'.

1029.-1033. **QALAGAI-BANDA قلاگی بانده (*qalāgay-bānḍa*)** *Map 11*

Name of five pastures spread in the upper mountainous Qalagai-khwar area, Tehsil of Kabal.

Pšt. 'pasture of the small fortress'. But see SULTAN-I-ROME 2016: 541: "*Qalang/kalang*: Rent, whether in cash or in kind", and *ibid.*: 542: "*Qalangi banday*: Those *bandah*s which the owners do not use as pastures themselves but rent out to non-owners. The rent may be divided among the concerned landowners according to *riwaj* or the prevailing rules of the area".

1034. **QALAGAI-KHWAR قلاگی خوړ (*qalāgay-xwaṛ*)** *Map 11*

Stream flowing into the Deolai-khwar, Tehsil of Kabal.

Cf. prec.

1035. **QALAGAI-SAR قلاگی سر (*qalāgay-sar*)** *Map 11*

Peak of an height of about 2,880 mt, in the area of Qalagai-banda, on the boundary with Dir, Tehsil of Kabal.

Pšt. 'mountain of the small fortress'.

1036. **QANDALU-GHAKHAI قندالو غاښی (*qandālu-γāx̌ay*)** *Map 49*

Peak of about 4,750 mt near the Kedam-khwar valley, Tehsil of Bahrain.

Pšt. 'sugar (*qand*) plum (*alu*)' (?) + Pšt. *γā́x̌ay* 'crest (of mountain); mountain pass'.

1037. **RAGISTUN رگستون (*ragistun*)** *Map 44*

Group of houses on the right bank of the Swāt river, slightly north of the confluence with the Barwai-khwar, Tehsil of Maṭṭa. Only on the Russian map.

Pšt. *registā́n* 'stoney desert; Registan (various districts)'. Cf. also Pšt. *ragə́y* 'difficult road'. Among others, see ADAMEC II 246 Rēgistān-i-Siddīqī, "Also called Pushta-ha-ye Registan-i- Siddiqi is a desert area covered by sand dunes, located in southern Nimruz near the border of Baluchistan"; V 394-397 Registan, "This word means 'the country of sand', and is applied to the great desert which stretches eastward from Sistan and the Persian frontier. In common parlance, it is spoken of merely as the reg [...]"; VI 670-671 Reg-i-Rawan, "A hill 40 miles north of Kabul".

1038. RAHIMABAD رحيم آباد (*rahim-ābād*) *Map 18*

Village near Mingaora, Tehsil of Babuzai; old name Sarkanəy.

Pšt. 'gracious (*rahím*) town'.

1039. RAKYA رکيه (*rakya*) *Map 43*

Group of houses on the eastern slopes of the mountains dividing the Barwai-khwar valley from the Harnoi-khwar valley, Tehsil of Maṭṭa.

Cf. T10538 **rakka*: Lhd. *rakkaṛ* 'poor soil', Panj. *rakkaṛ* 'hard and barren (of land)'.

1040. RAMA رمه (*rama*) *Map 17*

Group of houses in the upper Sigram-khwar valley, Tehsil of Kabal.

Pšt. *ramá* 'flock (of sheep, goats), herd'.

1041. RAMA-KANDAO رمه کندو (*rama-kanḍaw*) *Map 17*

Pass leading from the Sigram-khwar valley to the Tehsil of Maṭṭa, Tehsil of Kabal.

Pšt. 'pass of the herd'.

1042. RAMBAKI رامبېکي (*rambeki*) *Map 33*

Group of houses in the terraced mountainous upper Khwazakhela-khwar valley, Tehsil of Khwazakhela.

Pšt. *rambəkáy* 'bellowing'.

1043. RAMET رامېټ (*rāmeṭ*) *Map 47*

Group of houses on a terrace in the Gurnai-khwar valley, Tehsil of Bahrain. Quoted already by RAVERTY (1888: 237).

Cf. T10627 *ramaṇī-* 'Aloe indica': Kho. *romēn* 'aspen', Kal. *rāma* 'kind of maple' + sf. *-eṭ*? HAKIMZAY (1997: 86-89) thinks to the name of the Hindu god Rāma.

1044. RAMOGAI-KHWAR رموگی خوړ (*ramogay-xwaṛ*) *Map 10*

Stream flowing into the Spanai-khwar, Tehsil of Kabal.

Pšt. *rama* 'herd, flock' + sf. *-gay*? 'Place of the herd'?

1045. RAMOTAI-LOE-SAR رموټی لوی سر (ramoṭay-loy-sar) *Map 29*

Mountain of about 2,300 at the border with the Tehsil of Charbagh, at the top of the Makad-khwar, Tehsil of Khwazakhela.

Pšt. *rama* 'flock, herd' + dimin. sf. *-oṭay*? It is possible that all the toponyms Ramet, Ramogai, Ramotai and Rampatai, are derived from the name of the god Rāma, as suggested by HAKIMZAY (1997: 86-89).

1046. RAMPATAI رمپټی (rampəṭay) *Map 40*

Group of houses on the mountains in the Shaurai-khwar valley, Tehsil of Maṭṭa.

Pšt. 'field of the flock' or 'field of Rama'.

1047. RANASAR رڼاسر (raṇāsar) *Map 37*

Group of houses on the slopes of the Dobar-sar towards the Swāt river, Tehsil of Khwazakhela. Only on the Russian map.

Cf. T1492 **āsāra* 'firm': Kho. *asár* 'high solid wall, revetment of a field terrace' (MORGENSTIERNE Belvalkar Vol [1957] 86) + T10595 *ráṇa* 'delight, battle': Pa. *raṇa-* 'intoxication, battle'; Pkt. *raṇa-* 'battle'; Si. *riṇu* 'field of battle', Lhd. *raṇ* 'battle' (or T10596 *raṇa* 'noise': Pkt. *raṇa-* 'noise'). → 'field terrace of the battle' (or 'noiy field terrace'). The whole slope is densely terraced. Or Pšt. 'mountain of the light (*raṇā*)'.

1048. RANGA-KANDAO رنګه کنډو (ranga-kanḍaw) *Map 28*

Pass in the Dre-khwar valley, leading to Ser from Shin-khad, Tehsil of Charbagh.

Pšt. 'coloured (*rangá*) pass'.

1049. RANGELA رانګېله (rāngela) *Map 5*

Small village in the hills at the end of the Jolagram-khwar valley, Tehsil of Barikot.

Cf. T10571 **raṅgita-* 'coloured'; Pšt. *rang* 'color, coloring; paint, dye; kind, type'.

1050. RANI-SAR راڼي سر (rāṇi-sar) *Map 24*

Mountain on the boundary with Shangla, Tehsil of Babuzai.

Pšt. 'mountain of the light (*raṇāí* 'illumination')' or 'of the ranee (*rāṇə́y*)'.

1051. RANJAI رنجی (ranǰay) *Map 37*

Group of houses on the slopes of the Dobar-sar, Tehsil of Khwazakhela.

Cf. T10589 *rañjita* 'coloured, dyed': Pa. *rañjita-*, Pkt. *raṁjia-*. Improbable Pšt. *ranǰ* 'grief'.

1052. RANJRO-SAR رنجرو سر (ranǰro-sar) *Map 19*

Mountain, 2,550 mt, on the boundary with Buner, on the Saidu-khwar, Tehsil of Babuzai.

See SULTAN-I-ROME 2016: 221 *ranzra* 'deodar' → 'mountain of the deodars'.

1053. **RASULIBANR رسولیبن (*rasulibaṇ*)** *Map 16*

Group of houses on the terraced slopes of the near the Harnoi-khwar valley, Tehsil of Maṭṭa.

Pšt. 'garden of the prophet (*rasúl*)'.

1054. **REMA ریمه (*rema*)** *Map 40*

Group of houses located on the mountains in the Shaurai-khwar valley, Tehsil of Maṭṭa.

Cf. T10636 *ramyà* 'to be enjoyed, beautiful'?

1055. **RORIA روړیا (*roṛyā*)** *Map 30*

Group of houses on the hills sloping towards the left bank of the Swāt river, Tehsil of Charbagh.

Cf. T10769 **rōḍa-*, **rōḍha-* 'lump': Lhd. *roṛā* 'lump, clod, pebble', *roṛī* 'small bit of road-metal'; Panj. *roṛā* 'hard clod, brickbat', *roṛī* 'lump of earth'; N. *roṛā* 'pebbles'; Hi. *roṛā* 'fragment of stone, brickbat'; Guǰ. *roṛū̃* 'clod, brickbat'. Improbable possibilities could be also T10625 *rama* 'lover': ext. *-ḍ-*: WPah. bhiḍ. khaś. *roṛo* 'good, handsome', or T10864 *rōhiṇī-* 'red cow, cow': Gaw. *ruīnī*, Kal. *rṓra*, etc.

1056. **RORINGAR روړینګار (*roṛingār*)** *Map 43*

Village in the cultivated fields of the Roringar-khwar valley, Tehsil of Maṭṭa.

Cf. foll.

1057. **RORINGAR-KHWAR روړینګار خوړ (*roṛingār-xwaṛ*)** *Map 43*

Stream flowing into the Harnoi-khwar, Tehsil of Maṭṭa.

Cf. Roria; or T10625 *rama* 'lover': ext. *-ḍ-*: WPah. bhiḍ. khaś. *roṛo* 'good, handsome'. Cf. also Skt. *rúru-* 'a species of antelope' (see KEWA III 69, EWA II 454), according to KUIPER (1955: 141, 151; 1991) ← Mu.

1058. **RUNIAL روڼیال (*ruṇyāl*)** *Map 38*

Small village located in the plain on the right bank of the Harnoi-khwar valley, Tehsil of Maṭṭa.

Derived of Pšt. *ruṇ* 'bright, luminous, shining' + sf. *-yāl* (on this sf., see s.v. Mankial). HAKIMZAY (1997: 176) thinks to Skt. *rohni* 'the fourth lunar mansion, comprising Aldebaran and four other stars in Taurus'.

1059. **RUSTAM-SAR روستم سر (*rustam-sar*)** *Map 53*

Mountain of about 4,100 mt on the right bank of the Swāt river, Tehsil of Bahrain. Only on the Russian map.

Pšt. 'peak of Rustam'.

1060. **SABAR-SHAH سبره شاه (*sabra-šāh*)** *Map 27*

Group of houses in the mountainous Dre-khwar valley, Tehsil of Charbagh.

Person's name.

1061. **SABUNAI سابوڼی (*sābuṇay*)** *Map 21*

Group of houses in the hills on the Jambil-khwar valley, Tehsil of Babuzai.

Pšt. *sabóṇay* 'leavened dough'.

1062. **SADA سده (*sada*)** *Map 16*

Group of houses in a lateral valley of the Deolai-khwar valley, near Deolai, Tehsil of Kabal.

See SULTAN-I-ROME 2016: 481: "*Sadin*: Rain fed land", and *ibid.*: 492: "*Sadin*: Rain fed land that yields only one crop a year".

1063. **SADDO-KHAN سدو خان (*sado-xān*)** *Map 1*

Group of houses at the spring of the Kotah-khwar, Tehsil of Barikot, on the slopes on the boundary with Malakand.

Person's name.

1064. **SAFASHI-BANDA سفاشي بانډه (*safāši-bānḍa*)** *Map 3*

Pasture in the upper Najigram-khwar valley, Tehsil of Barikot, near the boundary with Buner. On the Russian map the name is Safishi-banda.

Pšt. 'cleaned (*safā-šəway*) pasture'.

1065. **SAGAR سگار (*sagār*)** *Map 39*

Group of houses on the slopes of the Shah-dop-sar, Tehsil of Maṭṭa. Only on the Russian map.

Cf. T13108 *satkāra* 'hospitality, kind treatment': Lhd. *sakār* 'mud-built grain receptacle'?

1066. **SAIDA سیده (*sayda*)** *Map 37*

Group of houses in the lower Bargin-khwar valley, Tehsil of Khwazakhela.

Pšt. *sayyíd* (Ar.) 'sayyid' (see Saidu-sharif).

1067. **SAIDGI-KANDAO سیدگي کنډو (*saydgi-kanḍaw*)** *Map 43*

Pass leading to Dir from the upper Roringar-khwar valley, Tehsil of Maṭṭa.

Cf. Saida.

1068. **SAIDU-KHWAR سیدو خوړ (*saydu-xwaṛ*)** *Map 20*

Stream in Tehsil of Babuzai: according to RAVERTY (1888), it is the Islampur dara'h.

Cf. foll.

1069. SAIDU-SHARIF سیدو شریف (*saydu-šarif*) *Map 18*

Big village in the valley of the Saidu-khwar, near Mingaora, Tehsil of Babuzai. RAVERTY (1862 and 1888) calls it also Saydúgán and adds that it is hidden by the valley, as Islampur. See also s.v. Mingaora for a more analytic description of this village. Apparently, its ancient name was Baligram.

On Saidu, see SULTAN-I-ROME 2016: 542: "*Sayyads*/*Sayyids*: Descendants commonly believed to be of the line of Prophet Muhammad (PBUH) from his daughter Fatima and son-in-law Ali". Pšt. *šarif* 'noble, wellborn; Sherif (title of the governor of Mecca and of the descendants of Mohammed)'. Both terms are ← Ar.

1070. SAIYIDANO-NAWE-KALAI سیدانو نوی کلی (*saydāno-nəway-kəlay*) *Map 34*

Small village in the plain on the left bank of the Swāt river, north of Khwazakhela, Tehsil of Khwazakhela.

Pšt. 'new village of the sayyids'.

1071. SAKHI-SAR سخي سر (*saxi-sar*) *Map 7*

Mountain dividing the Swat river valley from the Saidu-khwar valley, Tehsil of Babuzai.

Cf. T13321 *sākṣin* 'witness': Pa. *sakkhi-* 'witness', Pkt. *sakkhi-*, Si. Lhd. Panj. *sākhī*; T13322 **sākṣī-*: Pkt. *sakkhijja-* 'evidence', Panj. *sākhī* 'evidence' → '*visible mountain'?

1072. SAKHRA سخره (*saxra*) *Map 44*

Village in the wide plain of the Barwai-khwar, Tehsil of Maṭṭa.

Pšt. *sáxra* 'stone, rock'. HAKIMZAY (1997: 89-90) states that *saxra* was a stone of the good luck.

1073. SALATANR سولاتڼ (*salātaṇ*) *Map 43*

Group of houses in the narrow Roringar-khwar valley, Tehsil of Maṭṭa. Only on the Russian map.

Cf. Pšt. *salā́ṭ* 'trench, entrenchment' or *səlṭá* 'fortification, breastwork, parapet'?

1074. SALIM-KHAN سلیم خان (*sulim-xān*) *Map 20*

Mountain of about 1,890 mt between the Saidu-khwar valley and the Jambil-khwar valley, Tehsil of Babuzai.

Cf. foll.

1075. SALIM-KHAN-BANDA سلیم خان بانډه (*sulim-xān-bānḍa*) *Map 20*

Pasture in the spur between the Saidu-khwar valley and the Jambil-khwar valley, near Jambil, Tehsil of Babuzai.

Pšt. 'pasture of Sulim Khan (person's name)'.

1076. SAMAI-KILI سمی کلی (*samay-kəlay*) *Map 13*

Village in the Manrai-khwar valley, north of Tal, Tehsil of Kabal.

Pšt. 'plain/smooth (*sam*) village'; cf. Pšt. *sáma* '2.3 Sama (region of the Yousufzai land between the rivers Kabul, Buner and Swat)' (PASHTOON).

1077. SAMBAT سمبت (*sambat*) *Map 38*

Village at the foot of the hills bordering the fertile plain on the right bank of the Swāt river, Tehsil of Maṭṭa. Quoted by RAVERTY (1888: 201) as Ṣaubat, but placed to the south of Kuz-bamakhel, between this village and Shakardarra.

Cf. T12955 *saṁbandha* 'connexion, kinship', 'kinsman, friend': Pa. *sambandha-* 'connexion, tie'; Si. *sabaňda* 'connected with', *sabaňdā* 'friend' and T12957 *saṁbandhin* 'connected by marriage': Pkt. *saṁbaṁdhi-* 'connected by marriage'? According to IKRAM, p.c., it is Pšt. *sam* + *bat* 'stone mansonry (the walls of a well, kahriz, etc.)'.

1078. SAM-DEOLAI سم دیولی (*sam-ḍeolay*) *Map 14*

Big village in the Deolai-khwar valley, north of Lakai-kalai, Tehsil of Kabal, where the valley begins to become narrow.

Pšt. 'plain (*sam*)' + deolai (see Deolai-khwar).

1079. SAMI سمي (*sami*) *Map 43*

Group of houses on the hills bordering the Roringar-khwar, Tehsil of Maṭṭa.

Pšt. *sam* 'plain' → *samí* 'smoothness'. According to HAKIMZAY (1997: 150), it is formed by Skt. *som* 'moon' and *mahi* 'earth, land' (cf. T9974 *mahī* 'the earth': Pa. Pkt. *mahī-* 'the earth'): 'earth of the moon'.

1080. SAMIR سامیر (*sāmir*) *Map 34*

Group of houses in a lateral terraced valley on the left bank of the Swāt river, near Asala, Tehsil of Khwazakhela.

Cf. T13186 **samayāra* 'of same age': Wg. *samayárä* 'comrade of same age'?

1081. SAMSEL-BANDA سمسیل بانده (*samsel-bānḍa*) *Map 9*

Pasture on the slopes of the Dokat-sar, in the Deolai-khwar valley, Tehsil of Kabal.

Possibly T13173 *samá*[1] 'equal, alike, level; together with': Pa. Pkt. *sama-* 'equal, like, level'; Dam. *sam* 'equal to, like'; Paš.dar. *sam* 'straight' (IIFL III 157 ← Psht. ← IA.); Bašk. *sam* 'flat' + T12459 *śilā* 'rock, crag; lower millstone': Pa. *silā-* 'rock, stone'; Aś. *silā-* 'stone'; Pkt. *silā-* 'stone slab'; Sh. (LORIMER) *šil* 'flat stone for braying things on'; Si. *sira* 'brick', Lhd.khet. *sil*; Panj. *sil* 'stone slab used for sharpening knives or grinding spices'.

1082. SAMTER سمتیر (*samter*) *Map 24*

Group of houses in the mountainous upper Landai-khwar valley, Tehsil of Babuzai.

Pšt. *sam* 'level, straight, flat, even, plane' + sf. *-ter* (?), cf. Margater.

1083. **SANDOK سندوک (*sandok*)** *Map 1*

Group of houses at the spring of the Kotah-khwar, Tehsil of Barikot, on the slopes on the boundary with Malakand.

Cf. Pšt. *canḍa* 'side, brim, edge, brink, margin, rim' (RAVERTY)? According to IKRAM, p.c., it could be Pšt. *sind* 'river' + *dok* 'high edge': in this case, it could also be Pšt. *ḍək* 'oak leaf'. See ADAMEC VI 691 Sanduq, "A village located about 2 miles north of Achin and 10 miles southwest of Ghani Khel in Nangarhar province".

1084. **SANGAR سنگر (*sangar*)** *Map 22*

Group of houses in the mountainous upper Jambil-khwar valley, near the boundary with Buner, Tehsil of Babuzai.

Cf. Pšt. *singār* 'ornament, dress, embellishment, decoration' (RAVERTY, ← Skt.).

1085. **SANGOTA سنگوټه (*sangoṭa*)** *Map 23*

Village in the fertile plain on the left bank of the Swāt river, near the Ugad-khwar, Tehsil of Babuzai.

Cf. T13346 *sāmaka* '*even, *level': Paš.lauṛ. *sāṅg* 'earth, ground' + T3546 *kṓṣṭha* 'pot', 'granary, storeroom', 'inner apartment': Pa. *koṭṭha-* 'monk's cell, storeroom'; Pkt. *koṭṭha-*, *kuṭ*°, *koṭṭhaya-* 'granary, storeroom'; Si. *koṭho* 'large room'; Lhd. *koṭhā* 'hut, room, house'; Panj. *koṭṭhā*, *koṭhā* 'house with mud roof and walls, granary', etc. (→ Pšt. *koṭa*)? HAKIMZAY (1997: 91-92) analyses this toponym as 'village of the lion' or 'village of the Sikh'. See ADAMEC VI 695, a village in the Hisarak division of the Jalalabad district, about ½ mile southwest of Marhez. Inhabitants: Shinwaris (Jenkyns).

1086. **SANGRAI سنگرى (*sangray*)** *Map 35*

Group of houses in the narrow mountainous upper Bargin-khwar valley, Tehsil of Khwazakhela. Only on the Russian map.

Cf. Sangar.

1087. **SAPRAI څپرى (*capəray*)** *Map 38*

Group of houses on the hills of the Saso-sar, Tehsil of Maṭṭa.

Pšt. *capə́ray* 'flat summit (of a mountain)'.

1088. **SAR سر (*sar*)** *Map 24*

Group of houses in the spur between the Landai-khwar valley and the Spedar-khwar valley, Tehsil of Babuzai.

Pšt. 'top of the mountain'.

1089. **SARAI سړى (*saṛay*)** *Map 47*

Group of houses on the mountain above the Baral-darra valley, Tehsil of Bahrain.

Pšt. 'man'.

1090. **SARA-SHAH سره شاه (*sara-šāh*)** *Map 24*

Group of houses on the mountain between the Spedar-khwar valley and the Bishbanr-khwar valley, Tehsil of Babuzai.

Person's name.

1091. **SARBAB سرباب (*sarbāb*)** *Map 19*

Group of houses in the Tehsil of Babuzai, on the boundary with the Tehsil of Barikot, between the mount Ilam and the Maran-sar.

Pšt. 'top (*sar*) gate (*bāb*)'?

1092. **SARBALA سرباله (*sarbāla*)** *Map 10*

Small village in the mountainous upper Ramogai-khwar valley, Tehsil of Kabal.

Pšt. *sar* 'head' + *bālā* 'upper', referring to the height of the village (see also HAKIMZAY 1997: 93-94): cf. Prs. *sar-bālā* 'hill, mountain; uphill, ascending' (STEINGASS). See ADAMEC V 413-sarbiland, "A village of 40 houses on the right bank of the Lora, distant 13 miles by road from Amin Kala, on the road leading up the valley of the Arghastan and entering that of the Lora at the village of Mir Afzal, and 12 miles below Wuchbar Ghoberak".

1093. **SARBALA-BANDA سرباله بانده (*sarbāla-bānḍa*)** *Map 10*

Pasture on the boundary with Dir, above the Ramogai-khwar valley, Tehsil of Kabal.

Cf. prec.

1094.-1099. **SAR-BANDA سر بانده (*sar-bānḍa*)** *Maps 38, 40, 44, 50, 50, 50*

Name of six pastures: 1-2) in the mountains bordering the plain of the right bank of the Harnoi-khwar, north and south of the Uchrai-sar, Tehsil of Maṭṭa; 3) in a lateral valley on the right bank of the Swāt river on the slopes of the Babu-sar, Tehsil of Bahrain; 4-5) on the slopes of the Kedam-khwar valley on the right bank of the Swāt river, Tehsil of Bahrain; 6) on the right bank of the Swāt river, south of the Asrit-khwar, Tehsil of Bahrain. Number 4, 5 or 6 is quoted also by RAVERTY (1888: 205), stating that: "from Sar-Bánḍa'h down to the boundary of Upper Suwát, there are immense numbers of trees, both along the river's banks, and in the mountains on either side to their very summits".

Pšt. 'pasture at the top'.

1100. **SARBARAI سرباری (*sarbāray*)** *Map 37*

Group of houses located on the slopes of the Dobar-sar towards the Swāt river, Tehsil of Khwazakhela. According to the locals the new name is Berarai.

Cf. Pšt. *sarbāndəy* 'piece of land or portion of a field left unploughed or uncut'?

1101. **SAR-CHINA-BANDA سر چینه بانده (*sar-čina-bānḍa*)** *Map 20*

Pasture on the boundary with Buner, near the Saidu-khwar, Tehsil of Babuzai.

Pšt. 'pasture of the mountainous spring'.

1102. SARDAN سردان (*sardān*) *Map 41*

Group of houses in the terraced hills above the Shaurai-khwar valley, Tehsil of Maṭṭa.

According to HAKIMZAY (1997: 94-95), in Urdu *dān* means 'gift, alms, charity' and *sar* 'god', with a resulting meaning of 'alms of god'. This seems quite doubful to me.

1103. SARDARI سرداري (*sardāri*) *Map 24*

Group of houses in the mountainous upper Landai-khwar valley, Tehsil of Babuzai.

Pšt. *sardará* 'upper part of a valley'.

1104. SARGAI-BANDA سرگی بانده (*sargay-bānḍa*) *Map 15*

Pasture on the slopes of the Manago-sar, Tehsil of Kabal.

Cf. foll.

1105. SARGE سرگي (*sarge*) *Map 36*

Group of houses on the slopes of the Dobar-sar, on the hills bordering the Paiti-khwar valley, Tehsil of Khwazakhela.

See OLIVIERI/VIDALE 2002; OLIVIERI 2004; 2005; OLIVIERI/VIDALE ET AL. 2006. Pšt. 'place (-*gay*) of the head (*sar*)'.

1106. SARGI سرگي (*sargi*) *Map 42*

Group of houses in the mountains above the Harnoi-khwar valley, Tehsil of Maṭṭa.

Cf. prec.

1107. SARKANDA سرکنده (*sarkanda*) *Map 36*

Group of houses on the hills bordering the Paiti-khwar valley, Tehsil of Khwazakhela.

Pšt. 'main (*sar*) division (*kanday*)'.

1108. SARKARAI سرکاری (*sarkāray*) *Map 40*

Group of houses in the narrow terraced valley of the Shaurai-khwar, Tehsil of Maṭṭa.

Pšt. *sarkārí* 'management, superintendence', *sarkar* 'government'.

1109. SARKHANAI-KANDAO سرخنی کندو (*sarxanay-kanḍaw*) *Map 5*

Pass leading from the Jolagram-khwar valley, Tehsil of Barikot, to the Tehsil of Kabal.

Pšt. 'pass of the camel stall (*sarxānə́y*)'.

1110. SARLE-BANDA سرلي بانده (*sarle-bānḍa*) *Map 34*

Pasture on the hills bordering the Bargin-khwar valley, Tehsil of Khwazakhela.

Pšt. *sar* + adj. sf. -*lay* 'of the head'.

1111. **SARMAI سرمی (sarmay)** *Map 43*

Group of houses located at an elevation of about 1,800 mt, in the narrow Roringar-khwar valley, Tehsil of Maṭṭa. Only on the Russian map.

According to HAKIMZAY (1997: 149-150), it is formed by Skt. *sar* 'god' and *mahi* 'earth, land' (cf. T9974 *mahī* 'the earth': Pa. Pkt. *mahī-* 'the earth'): 'earth of god'. ROSSI, p.c., suggests another term for the wintry seasonal migration: cf. Prs. *sarmā(y)* 'winter, cold' (STEINGASS).

1112. **SAR-TIKAI سر ټیکی (sar-ṭikay)** *Map 50*

Group of houses in the Kedam-khwar valley, Tehsil of Bahrain.

Tor. 'mountain of the summer pasture (*ṭikay*)'.

1113. **SASO-SAR ساسو سر (sāso-sar)** *Map 38*

Mountain on the border between the Tehsils of Kabal and Maṭṭa, Tehsil of Kabal.

Cf. T12646 *sōṣu-* 'drought, thirst': Ašk. *susu-būm* 'steppe', *susu-stə* 'dry'; Paš. *susuwā* 'dry'.

1114. **SATAI ستی (satay)** *Map 35*

Group of houses in the hills bordering to the north the narrow mountainous Bargin-khwar valley, Tehsil of Khwazakhela.

Cf. T13364 *sārtha* 'caravan, troop, company'; **sārthī-*; *sārthēna* 'in company with': Pa. Pkt. *sattha-* 'caravan'; Paš. *sāṭha* 'village'; Tor. *sāth*, *sāt* 'with', Sh. *sāṭi̯*.

1115. **SEKHA سیخه (sexa)** *Map 33*

Group of houses in the hills of the Khwazakhela-khwar valley, Tehsil of Khwazakhela.

Possibly Pšt. *sexa* 'straight' (IKRAM, p.c.). Cf. also Pšt. *caxa* 'at the side, near, about'?

1116. **SEKHDARRA سیخدره (sexdara)** *Map 43*

Group of houses on the hills bordering the Roringar-khwar, Tehsil of Maṭṭa. Only on the Russian map.

Possibly Pšt. 'straight (*sexa*) valley'. We can exclude Pšt. *səx* 'happiness, luck, good fortune'.

1117. **SELAI-KANDAO سیلی کندو (selay-kanḍaw)** *Map 13*

Pass leading to Dir from the Manrai-khwar valley, Tehsil of Kabal.

Pšt. 'pass of the snow storm (*siləy*)'.

1118. **SEMPRAI-SAR سیمپری سر (sempray-sar)** *Map 33*

Mountain of about 2,800 mt on the boundary with Shangla, Tehsil of Khwazakhela.

Cf. T12951 *saṁprāpta* 'having reached': Pa. *sampatta-* 'reached'; Pkt. *saṁpatta-* 'fully obtained, arrived'; Si. *sapat* 'arrived, attained'?

1119. **SENAI سېنی (*senay*)** *Map 36*

Group of houses located in the terraced mountainous Paiti-khwar valley, Tehsil of Khwazakhela.

Cf. T13602 *saín(i)ya-*, *sainika-* 'belonging to an army; soldier; army': Hi. *senā* 'general, official who collects revenue in a village'; Pkt. *seṇṇa-*, *siṇṇa-* 'army'; NiDoc. *seniya*, *seni*.

1120.-1121. **SER سېر (*ser*)** *Maps 27, 37*

Name of two villages: 1) in the mountainous Tambagat-khwar valley, Tehsil of Charbagh; 2) in the narrow valley on the left bank of the Swāt river, Tehsil of Bahrain.

Cf. glossary of geonyms.

1122.-1130. **SERAI سېری (*seray*)** *Maps 16, 18, 18, 28, 34, 37, 40, 43, 52*

Name of nine villages: 1) in a mountainous lateral valley of the Deolai-khwar valley at the frontier with the Tehsil of Maṭṭa, Tehsil of Kabal; 2-3) in the last flat narrow plain of the Saidu-khwar valley, towards Marghuzar, Tehsil of Babuzai; 4) in the narrow upper Dre-khwar valley, Tehsil of Charbagh; 5) in the plain on the left bank of the Swāt river, north of Khwazakhela, at the foot of the hills, Tehsil of Khwazakhela. It can be identified with the "Bar Sheṟn, or Upper Sheṟn, and Kúz Sheṟn, or Lower Sheṟn" mentioned by RAVERTY (1888: 235), as it stands between Khwazakhela and Khanabad (Khonah in RAVERTY); 6) in the terraced mountainous Paiti-khwar valley, Tehsil of Khwazakhela; 7) group of houses in the narrow terraced valley of the Shaurai-khwar, Tehsil of Maṭṭa; 8) on the bank of the Roringar-khwar, Tehsil of Maṭṭa; 9) group of houses in the Mankial-khwar valley, Tehsil of Bahrain.

Cf. Pšt. *seráy* 'côté ombragé' (AKBAR) and glossary of geonyms.

1131. **SERAI-BADAI سېری بدی (*seray-baday*)** *Map 51*

Group of houses in the mountainous Jaba-khwar valley, Tehsil of Bahrain.

Cf. Pšt. *seray* + Pšt. *badəy* 'bank of a canal subject to erosion'. IKRAM, p.c.: "in mountainous area, the narrow fields are called Badai".

1132. **SHABEKA شابېکه (*šābeka*)** *Map 16*

Group of houses in a mountainous lateral valley of the Deolai-khwar valley at the frontier with the Tehsil of Maṭṭa, Tehsil of Kabal.

Cf. Pšt. *šabaka* 'lattice, window of lattice work; net, reticulated veil' (RAVERTY). See ADAMEC VI 707 Shabak or Batai-kandao, "A pass leading from the neighbourhood of Manduri in Kurram to the Shama, or Kaitu, valley in Khost".

1133. **SHADHAND-BANDA شاډنډ بانډه (*šāḍanḍ-bānḍa*)** *Map 10*

Pasture in the fertile Ramogai-khwar valley, near Tutan-banda, Tehsil of Kabal.

Pšt. 'pasture of the lake (*ḍanḍ*) of the šāh'.

1134. **SHADO شادو (*šādo*)** *Map 33*

Group of houses in the mountainous upper Khwazakhela-khwar valley, on the slopes of the Semprai-sar, Tehsil of Khwazakhela.

Pšt. *šādó* 'monkey'.

1135. **SHAGAI-BANDA شگی بانده (*šagəy-bānḍa*)** *Map 10*

Pasture on the boundary with Dir, above the Ramogai-khwar valley, Tehsil of Kabal.

Pšt. 'pasture of the low mountain/mountain foothills/foot of a mountain (*šāgə́y*)'.

1136. **SHAGAR-SAR شگر سر (*šagar-sar*)** *Map 26*

Mountain of about 3,000 mt between the Bikan-khwar valley and the Tambagat-khwar valley, Tehsil of Charbagh.

Cf. Pšt. *šəglə́n* 'sandy; gravelly, granular': 'sandy mountain'?

1137.-1138. **SHAGGAI شگی (*šagay*)** *Maps 18, 27*

Name of two villages: 1) in the plain of the Saidu-khwar valley, towards Marghuzar, Tehsil of Babuzai; 2) in the mountainous narrow Dre-khwar valley, Tehsil of Charbagh.

Pšt. *šāgə́y* 'low mountain, mountain foothills, foot of a mountain'. Or cf. foll.

1139. **SHAGO-PATAI شگو پتی (*šəgo-pəṭay*)** *Map 52*

Group of houses on the left bank of the upper Swāt river, Tehsil of Bahrain. Only on the Russian map.

Pšt. 'field of the sand (*šəga*)'. On Ir. **sikā-* in the toponymy, see KIRAKOSIAN 2015.

1140. **SHAGO-SAR شگو سر (*šəgo-sar*)** *Map 43*

Mountain of about 3,980 mt on the boundary with Dir, at the end of the Roringar-khwar valley, Tehsil of Maṭṭa.

Pšt. *šəga* 'sand, gravel, small pebbles': 'mountain of the small pebbles. Cf. prec.

1141. **SHAH-DOP-SAR شاه دوپ سر (*šāh-dop-sar*)** *Map 39*

Mountain of about 2,400 mt half-way between the Harnoi-khwar valley and the valley of the Swāt river, Tehsil of Maṭṭa.

Cf. Dop geonyms.

1142. **SHAHGRAM شاگرام (*šāgrām*)** *Map 45*

Village in the narrow valley on the right bank of the Swāt river, Tehsil of Bahrain. Apparently, it is called Darab on the Russian map. Called Shá-Grám by RAVERTY (1888: 239), as *h* is not pronounced in Pashto.

IA. 'village of the šāh'.

1143. **SHAHI-BANDA شاهي بانده (*šāhi-bānḍa*)** *Map 48*

Pasture in the Daral-khwar valley, Tehsil of Bahrain. Only on the Russian map.

Pšt. 'royal pasture'.

1144. **SHAHID-BELA شاهيد بيله (*šāhid-bela*)** *Map 44*

Group of houses in the mountainous Barwai-khwar valley, Tehsil of Maṭṭa.

Pšt. *šāhíd* (Ar.) 'witness, martyr'.

1145. **SHAHID-KHPA شاهيد ښپه (*šāhid-x̌pa*)** *Map 40*

Group of houses in the narrow terraced valley of the Shaurai-khwar, Tehsil of Maṭṭa.

Pšt. *šahid* 'witness, martyr', Pšt. *x̌pa* 'foot'.

1146. **SHAHID-TAKAI شاهيد ټکی (*šāhid-takay*)** *Map 45*

Group of houses on the slopes of the Babu-sar in the Daral-khwar valley, Tehsil of Bahrain.

Cf. prec.

1147. **SHAHJAHAN-BANDA شاه جهان بانده (*šāhǰahān-bānḍa*)** *Map 12*

Pasture in the mountains near the Deolai-khwar valley, Tehsil of Kabal.

Person's name.

1148. **SHAHNUR شاهنور (*šāhnur*)** *Map 47*

Group of houses in the Gurnai-khwar valley, Tehsil of Bahrain.

Pšt. 'light (*nur*) of the Shah' or person's name.

1149. **SHAHRO شهرو (*šahro*)** *Map 40*

Group of houses in the narrow terraced valley of the Shaurai-khwar, Tehsil of Maṭṭa.

Cf. Shaurai-khwar. Cf. also Pšt. *šuhrat* 'renown, fame, celebrity, rumor' and Pšt. *šxaṛa* 'nonsense, useless talk, gibberish, twaddle, stuff'. See ADAMEC VI 710 Shahristan, "A halting place on the main Kabul-Hazarajat-Daulat Yar road, 15 miles west of Panjao-sarai".

1150. **SHAI شای (*šāy*)** *Map 47*

Group of houses in the Gurnai-khwar valley, Tehsil of Bahrain.

Cf. T12673 *śyāvíyā* 'darkness': Sh. (LORIMER) *šaiĩ* 'soot'?

1151. **SHAKARDARRA شکردره (*šakardara*)** *Map 38*

Village on the right bank of the Swāt river at the foot of the hills bordering the plain, Tehsil of Maṭṭa. Quoted already by RAVERTY as Shankar-darah (1862: 238) and as Shankar-dár (1888: 199).

Pšt. *šingrəy* 'tower, outwork to the gate of a fort; mould for casting or forming earthen vessels' (RAVERTY): RAVERTY (1862: 238) states that "Close to this latter place, there is a tower called Shankar-dár", and that "Shankar in the Sanskrit language, is one of the names of Siva". HAKIMZAY (1997: 82) proposes Buddh. Skt. *šukar* 'Friday'.

1152. SHALADAR شلدر (*šaladar*) *Map 48*

Group of houses located in the terraced Daral-khwar valley, Tehsil of Bahrain. Only on the Russian map.

Cf. foll.

1153. SHALHAND شلهن (*šalhaṇ*) *Map 16*

Village in a lateral valley of the Deolai-khwar valley, Tehsil of Kabal. According to M.A. DINAKHEL (p.c.), the correct spelling of this toponym is *šalhaṇ*.

Probably T12414 *śālā-* 'shed, stable, house': Dam. *šâl*, Waig. *šāl*, etc. Cf. also T12578 *śṛgālá* 'jackal': Sh. *šāl* 'wolf', (LORIMER) *šāl*; + T13970 **handha-* 'place, house': Kal. *han* 'house', Si. *handhu* 'place, abode, bed, bedding' (→ Bal. *hand* 'place, dwelling').

1154.-1155. SHALKHOSAR شلخوسر (*šalxosar*) *Map 44*

Name of two groups of houses in the mountainous Barwai-khwar valley, Tehsil of Maṭṭa.

Cf. prec. + *xosar* (?). Or cf. Pšt. *šalxay* 'name of a species of potherb' + Pšt. *sar* 'head'.

1156. SHALKHOSAR-BANDA شلخوسر بانڈه (*šalxosar-bānḍa*) *Map 16*

Pasture in a mountainous lateral valley of the Deolai-khwar valley at the frontier with the Tehsil of Maṭṭa, Tehsil of Kabal.

Cf. prec.

1157. SHALKHOSAR-KANDAO شلخوسر کنډو (*šalxosar-kanḍaw*) *Map 16*

Pass leading to the Tehsil of Maṭṭa from the Tehsil of Kabal.

Cf. prec.

1158. SHALPALAM شلپلم (*šalpalam*) *Map 38*

Village on the right bank of the Swāt river at the foot of the hills bordering the plain, Tehsil of Maṭṭa.

Cf. Shalpin? According to IKRAM, p.c., Shalpalam is derived from Sherspalam, 'lion or tiger of reddish colour'. HAKIMZAY (1997: 146) confirms this form of the toponym, but identifies it with a person's name: → 'rest place for travellers of Sher' (with Skt. *pauh* 'stand where water is kept for travellers').

1159. SHALPIN شالپين (*šālpin*) *Map 33*

Village located in the terraced and fertile part of the Khwazakhela-khwar valley, Tehsil of Khwazakhela.

Cf. T12414 *śālā-* 'shed, stable, house': Dam. *šâl*, Waig. *šāl*, etc. Cf. also T12578 *śr̥gālá* 'jackal': Sh. *šāl* 'wolf', (LORIMER) *šāl*. + T8168 *píṇḍa* 'lump, clod, piece': Panj. *pinn* 'ball of rice or sugar', *pinnā* 'ball of twine', *pinnī* 'mass of wet sand, calf of leg'? According to HAKIMZAY (1997: 105), *pin* indicates 'waters' in Ur.

1160. SHALTALU شلتلو (*šaltālu*) *Map 28*

Group of houses in the Dre-khwar valley, Tehsil of Charbagh.

Pšt. *šaltālú* 'peach'.

1161. SHALUN شالون (*šālun*) *Map 32*

Group of houses located in the mountainous upper Khwazakhela-khwar valley, Tehsil of Khwazakhela.

Cf. Shalpin.

1162. SHALWA-KANDAO شلوه كندو (*šalwa-kanḍaw*) *Map 30*

Pass leading from the Charbagh-khwar valley to the Khwazakhela-khwar valley, Tehsil of Charbagh.

Cf. Shalpin?

1163. SHAMELAI شامېلى (*šāmelay*) *Map 21*

Village in the spur on the left bank of the Swat river, on the road leading from Mingaora to Sangota, Tehsil of Babuzai.

Cf. foll.

1164. SHAMELAI-KANDAO شامېلى كندو (*šāmelay-kanḍaw*) *Map 21*

Pass leading from Mingaora to Manglaor, Tehsil of Babuzai. RAVERTY (1888: 234) calls it Shámelí, followed also by DEANE (1895).

TUCCI 1977: 63-64 [= TUCCI 1997: 220]:

> The story supposes that when it was introduced in the Vinaya MSV, Buddhism had already penetrated in Chitrāl, if Śyāmāka — a fervent Buddhist — was offered the kingship of the country; if Shê-mi corresponds, as it seems certain, to Chitrāl, Shê-mi is connected with Śyāmāka which meant that Śyāmāka was considered the eponym of the country. Hui-Ch'ao (Fuchs 1939, P. 447) Calls Chitrāl Śamāharāja (Fuchs: or Śāmarāja) [note 88: "Cf. the name of Shamelai, a ridge above Mingora in Swāt. (The story is at the same time an eulogium of the Country and of the royal family. For such examples of the name of a king instead of that of the people alone cf. *Br̥hatsaṃhitā*, above p. 33, note 37; p. 62, note 85)"]. Here is repeated the same pattern of the learned etymology of the name of Lampāka.

At p. 63 he states:

> The itinerary first led the arhat to Lampāka; accompanied, by Syāmāka, he went to Laghman, where Syāmāka, who flew in the air, held on to the dress of Kātyāyana. When the local people saw him flying in that manner, they said: "Lambate, lambate, he hangs down"; this was the origin of the name of Lambāka, Lampāka (also Laṅkā). All this means that the local Buddhists wanted to connect the origin of their name with a marvel-

lous event, which could warrant the antiquity of their communities, though the radical of Lampāka is Dardic; paśai: lam.

See SULTAN-I-ROME 2016: 543: "*Shamilat*: Land, hills, and forests, etc. held in common by the *dawtar* landowners on the basis of their *dawtar* shares; wasteland, hillside, etc. included in a piece of land".

1165. **SHAMI-DERAI شامي ډېرى (*šāmi-ḍerəy*)** *Map 46*

Group of houses in the upper Olal-khwar valley, Tehsil of Bahrain.

Cf. prec.

1166. **SHAMKOR-BANDA شمكور بانډه (*šamkor-bānḍa*)** *Map 47*

Pasture on a lateral valley of the Jaba-khwar valley, Tehsil of Bahrain.

Cf. Pšt. *šamkor* 'night-blind, one troubled with night-blindness' (RAVERTY).

1167. **SHANDAL شندل (*šandal*)** *Map 40*

Group of houses in the narrow terraced valley of the Shaurai-khwar, Tehsil of Maṭṭa. Only on the Russian map.

Cf. T12797 *ṣaṇḍá* 'wood, thicket': Pa. *saṇḍa-* 'cluster, grove'; Pkt. *saṁḍa-* 'thicket'?

1168. **SHANGA شنګه (*šanga*)** *Map 36*

Group of houses in the terraced mountainous Paiti-khwar valley, Tehsil of Khwazakhela. Only on the Russian map.

Cf. Shanku and Shangawatai?

1169. **SHANGARAI شانګرى (*šāngaray*)** *Map 40*

Group of houses in the terraced hills above the Shaurai-khwar valley, Tehsil of Maṭṭa.

Cf. Shangora-banda. Possibly Pšt. *šingrə́y* 'portico, turret' or Pšt. *šāngúṛay* 'protuberant; hunchbacked, bent'.

1170. **SHANGAWATAI شانګواټى (*šāngawāṭəy*)** *Map 38*

Village encircled by cultivated fields, on a lateral branch on the right bank of the Harnoi-khwar, Tehsil of Maṭṭa. Only on the Russian map.

Cf. possibly T11480 *vāṭa* 'enclosure, fence', *vāṭī-* 'enclosed land': Pa. *vāṭa-* 'enclosure, circle'; Pkt. *vāḍa-* 'fence'; Si. *vāṛo* 'cattle enclosure', *vāṛi* 'fence, hedge'; Lhd. *vāṛī* 'sheepfold, melon patch'; Panj. *vāṛī* 'garden'? According to HAKIMZAY (1997: 102), this name is formed by Ur. *haṭəy* 'shop' + *šāngu*, p.n.: → 'shop of Shangu'.

1171. **SHANGLA-KANDAO شانګله کنډو (*šāngla-kanḍaw*)** *Map 28*

Pass leading from the upper Dre-khwar valley to Shangla, Tehsil of Charbagh.

'Pass leading to Shangla'. On Shangla cf. Panj. *saṅglā* 'plank bridge in the hills' (T12260).

1172.-1173. SHANGORA-BANDA شانګوړه باندہ (*šāngoṛa-bānḍa*) *Map 13*

Name of two pastures in the upper Manrai-khwar valley, towards the boundary with Dir, Tehsil of Kabal.

Possibly Pšt. *šāngúṛay* 'protuberant; hunchbacked, bent' ← T12264 *śaṅkha* 'temporal bone or frontal bone': Bašk. *šeṅ* 'throat', Tor. *šāṅg*; Phal. *šaṅgīruṛ* 'inside of throat'; Lhd. (JUKES) *sãgh* 'throat'; WPah. *śãgī* 'throat'. Cf. also Shangarai.

1174. SHANGO-SAR شنګو سر (*šango-sar*) *Map 28*

Mountain of about 2,300 mt on the boundary between the Tehsil of Charbagh and Shangla.

Probably related to the name of Shangla, but cf. also Pšt. *šingrəy* 'tower, outwork to the gate of a fort', or T12260 *śaṅku*-[1] 'peg, spike'. Cf. Shanga.

1175. SHANKU شانکو (*šānku*) *Map 46*

Stream flowin into the Olal-khwar, Tehsil of Bahrain.

Cf. T12260 *śaṅku*-[1] 'peg, spike': Dam. *šaṅ* 'branch, twig', *šãkolī* 'small do.', Gaw. *šaṅkolī*, etc.? Or cf. T12623 *śṓṇa*[1] 'red, crimson, purple; yellow; Bignonia indica, red sugar-cane', *śṓṇaka*- 'B. indica': Pa. *sōṇa*- 'a kind of tree'; Pkt. *sōṇa*- 'red'; Paš.lauṛ. *ṣōṇāk* 'red', lagh. *šōnek*, dar. *šoṇek*, nir. *sūṇek*.

1176.-1177. SHAR شر (*šar*) *Map 47, 49*

Name of two groups of houses in the Tehsil of Bahrain: 1) near Bahrain, on the left bank of the Swāt river (apparently, its name is Nawe-banda on the Russian map); 2) in the upper Daral-khwar valley.

Cf. T12331 *śarabhá* 'a kind of deer': Kt. *šurú* 'the wild goat or markhor', Paš.lauṛ. dar. *šarṓ*, ar. *šarū*, weg. *sarṓ*; Shum. *šāru* 'ibex'; Gaw. *sārṓu* 'markhor', Kal.rumb. *šāra*, Kho. *šara*, Bašk. *šara*, Phal. *šarāi*, Sh. *šă̄ră̆*. See ADAMEC VI 723 Shar, "A village on a tributary of the Dara-i-Mur, some 7 miles north of Panjao in Bamian province".

1178. SHARARA شراره (*šarāra*) *Map 21*

Village located at the foot of the hills bordering the lower Jambil-khwar valley, Tehsil of Babuzai.

Cf. Pšt. *šarārat* (← Ar.) 'wicknedness, vice, mischief, depravity, villany'?

1179. SHAR-BANDA شر باندہ (*šar-bānḍa*) *Map 53*

Pasture in the Asrit-khwar valley, Tehsil of Bahrain.

Cf. Shar.

1180. SHARBANR شربڼ (*šarbaṇ*) *Map 16*

Group of houses located in a mountainous lateral valley of the Deolai-khwar valley, Tehsil of Kabal.

Cf. Asharbanr.

1181. SHAR-DERA شار ډېره (*šār ḍera*) *Map 49*

Group of houses in the upper Daral-khwar valley, Tehsil of Bahrain.

Pšt. 'residence of the poet' or cf. Shar.

1182. SHARGARTAN شرګرتن (*šargartan*) *Map 42*

Group of houses on the slopes above the Biha-khwar valley, Tehsil of Maṭṭa. Only on the Russian map.

Cf. Shingardar.

1183. SHARIFAI-BANDA شريفى بانډه (*šarifay-bānḍa*) *Map 10*

Pasture on the northern side of the Dokat-sar, in a lateral valley of the Ramogai-khwar valley, Tehsil of Kabal.

Pšt. 'pasture of the noble (*Šarif*)'.

1184. SHARNA شرنه (*šarəna*) *Map 23*

Village in the narrow Landai-khwar valley, Tehsil of Babuzai.

Cf. T12326 *śaraṇá* 'protecting; shelter, home': Pa. Pkt. *saraṇa-* 'protection, shelter, house'; Dm. *šaran*; Panj. *saraṇ* 'protection, asylum'.

1185. SHARORAI شروړى (*šaroṛay*) *Map 32*

Group of houses in the upper Khwazakhela-khwar valley, near Topsin, on the road to Shangla, Tehsil of Khwazakhela.

Cf. Pšt. *šāṛ* 'uncultivated (of land)' + dimin. sf. *-uṛay*.

1186.-1187. SHARSHAI شرشى (*šaršəy*) *Maps 40, 45*

Name of two villages: 1) in the narrow terraced valley of the Shaurai-khwar, Tehsil of Maṭṭa; 2) group of houses in the narrow valley on the left bank of the Swāt river, Tehsil of Bahrain.

Possibly Pšt. *šaršāyí* 'sharshai (measure of weight equal to one Indian tola, 24 grains)'. See ADAMEC VI 724 Sharshahi, "A group of villages on the left bank of the Papin river, about 21 miles southeast of Jalalaba".

1188. SHAURAI-KHWAR شورى خوړ (*šawray-xwaṛ*) *Map 40*

Stream, located at an elevation of 1,251 meters above sea level, flowing into the Harnoi-khwar from the slopes of the Prangman-sar, Tehsil of Maṭṭa.

The most plausible etymology is T12269 *śaṭati* 'goes', **śāṭayati* 'drives': Paš.lauṛ. *šāṛ-*, gul. *šār-*, dar. weg. *šǎṛ-*, kuṛ. *šoṛ-*, ar. *šuṛ-* 'to go away, wander, flow'; Paš.lauṛ. *šārai-* 'to carry off, lead away', dar. weg. *ṣaräi-* 'to herd (cattle)'. However, cf. also Pšt. 'river of the small sissoo' (SULTAN-I-ROME 2016: 221 *shawa* 'sissoo' + dimin. sf. *-ṛay*); or T12331 *śarabha-* 'a kind of deer': cf. Shar.

1189. **SHEKHAN شېخان (*šexān*)** *Map 41*

Group of houses on the eastern slopes of the mountains dividing the Barwai-khwar valley from the Harnoi-khwar valley, Tehsil of Maṭṭa.

Pšt. 'the Sheikhs'.

1190. **SHEKHORAI شېخوړی (*šexoray*)** *Map 23*

Small village in the Ugad-khwar valley, Tehsil of Babuzai.

Cf. prec. + dimin. sf. *-uṛay*.

1191. **SHERAI شېری (*šeray*)** *Map 33*

Group of houses in the terraced mountainous upper Khwazakhela-khwar valley, Tehsil of Khwazakhela.

Cf. all proposals s.v. Shaurai-khwar.

1192. **SHER-ATRAF شېر اتراف (*šer-atrāf*)** *Map 20*

Group of houses located in the mountain bordering the Saidu-khwar valley, Tehsil of Babuzai.

Person's name.

1193. **SHER-KHONE شېر خونې (*šer-xone*)** *Map 19*

Group of houses located in the upper mountainous Marghuzar-khwar valley, Tehsil of Babuzai.

Pšt. 'milk-house'.

1194. **SHEWA-GHAR شېوه غر (*šewa-γar*)** *Map 5*

Mountain of about 1,500 mt, on the boundary with Dir, Tehsil of Barikot, above the Jolagram-khwar valley.

Pšt. *šewá* 'descent, declivity, inclination, slope' (RAVERTY) + Pšt. *γar* 'mountain'. However, according to DEAN (1895), the name Shewa should be identified with the Sissoo (Shesham) tree.

1195. **SHINGARDAR شینګردار (*šingardār*)** *Map 7*

Small village on the left bank of the Swāt river, Tehsil of Barikot, at the foot of the hills. Between Barikot and Shingardar, Google Earth indicates nowadays the presence of other small inhabitated places: Gul-abad, Chinogan and Wanai, located on the road coming from Barikot to Mingaora. It is called Shankardār by DEANE (1895) and STEIN (1929: 49).

Pšt. *šingrəy* 'tower, outwork to the gate of a fort; mould for casting or forming earthen vessels' (RAVERTY). Cf. also Shargartan and Shakardarra.

1196. **SHINGRAI شینګری (*šingray*)** *Map 23*

Group of houses located on the mountain between the Landai-khwar valley and the Ugad-khwar valley, Tehsil of Babuzai.

Pšt. *šin* + Pšt. *gaṛəy* 'large pool of rain water, mere' (RAVERTY).

1197.-1198. **SHINI شیني (*šini*)** *Maps 37, 39*

Name of two villages: 1) on the left bank of the Swāt river, at the estuary of the Bargin-khwar, Tehsil of Khwazakhela, quoted already by RAVERTY (1888: 235); it is called Samshin by STEIN 1930; 2) Group of houses on the slopes of the Lito-sar degrading towards the Harnoi-khwar valley, in Tehsil of Maṭṭa.

Pšt. 'of blue/green colour'.

1199. **SHIN-KHAD شین خد (*šin-xad*)** *Map 28*

Village in the terraced upper Dre-khwar valley at a height of about 1,500 mt, Tehsil of Charbagh. The toponym is written Shin-kad in all other maps.

Pšt. 'blue/green (*šin*)' + possibly Pšt. *xāda* 'pole, piece of wood placed as a mark at the head of a grave' (RAVERTY).

1200. **SHNAI شنی (*šne*)** *Map 30*

Group of houses on the hills sloping towards the left bank of the Swāt river, Tehsil of Charbagh.

Cf. prec., pl. fem.

1201. **SHOLGRA شولګره (*šolgra*)** *Map 44*

Group of houses in the mountainous upper Barwai-khwar valley, Tehsil of Maṭṭa.

Pšt. *šolgára* 'rice paddy; field under rice cultivation'; see also SULTAN-I-ROME 2016: 482 and 493: "*Sholgara*: A kind of *abi* land, but which gives only one rice crop due to it becoming marshy afterwards".

1202. **SHUDAM شودام (*šudām*)** *Map 21*

Group of houses in the spur on the left bank of the Swat river, on the road leading from Mingaora to Sangota, Tehsil of Babuzai.

Et. unkn.

1203. **SHUKHDARRA شوخدره (*šuxdara*)** *Map 38*

Village in the fertile plain on the left bank of the Harnoi-khwar, north of Matta, Tehsil of Maṭṭa.

According to HAKIMZAY (1997: 103), the originary form of this name would have been Shawqdara, deriving from king Aśoka's name. Even if possible, this hypothesis seems to me quite unlikely.

1204. **SHUPIN شوپین (*šupin*)** *Map 40*

Group of houses in the narrow terraced valley of the Shaurai-khwar, Tehsil of Maṭṭa.

Possibly a variant of Shulpin (q.v.).

1205. **SHURO-SAR شورو سر (*šuro-sar*)** *Map 32*

Mountain dividing two valleys of the Khwazakhela-khwar bassin, Tehsil of Khwazakhela.

T12671 **śyāra* 'freezing' (cf. *śāra-* 'wind' and Wkh. *sūr* 'cold' < Ir. **sāra-* IIFL iii 3, 167): Paš.kuṛ. *šōro* 'ice', Shum. *šārä*; Kho. *šaru* 'cold'. Cf. also Shaurai-khwar.

1206. **SIAKAS-BANDA سیاکس باندہ (*syākas-bānḍa*)** *Map 42*

Pasture in the upper Biha-khwar valley, Tehsil of Maṭṭa. Only on the Russian map.

Pšt. 'pasture of the dark (*syāh*) ravine (*kas*)'.

1207. **SIGRAM سیگرام (*sigrām*)** *Map 17*

Main village of the Sigram-khwar valley, Tehsil of Kabal, in the fertile high valley.

Cf. T13585 *sētu-* 'dam, bridge': Pkt. *sēu* 'dam, bridge, seedbed, basin round tree', Ašk. Waig. *sēw*, Dam. *sēwa*, Tor. *sē*, Bašk. *sā*, etc. + IA. *grāma*.

1208. **SIGRAM-KHWAR سیگرام خوړ (*sigrām-xwaṛ*)** *Map 17*

Stream located at an elevation of 879 meters above sea level, Tehsil of Kabal, flowing into the Swāt river near Kanju.

Cf. prec.

1209. **SIJBANR سجبڼ (*siǰbaṇ*)** *Map 38*

Village in the plain on the right bank of the Harnoi-khwar valley, Tehsil of Maṭṭa.

Cf. T13574 *sūrya-* 'sun': Pa. *surya-*, Pkt. *sujja-*, Lhd.khet. *suj*; Si. *sivi* 'the sun's ray' < **suye*; Si. *sij̄u*, *siju* 'sun', Lhd. *sijjh*, (JUKES) *sijh*, mult. *sejj*: 'sun-garden'?

1210. **SIKKA-BANDA سیکہ باندہ (*sika-bānḍa*)** *Map 16*

Pasture in a mountainous lateral valley of the Deolai-khwar valley at the frontier with the Tehsil of Maṭṭa, Tehsil of Kabal.

Pšt. 'pasture of the Sikhs'.

1211. **SINPORA سینپورہ (*sinpora*)** *Map 38*

Village located in the plain on the left bank of the Harnoi-khwar, north of Matta, Tehsil of Maṭṭa.

According to HAKIMZAY (1997: 90), this toponym is derived from Skt. *senā* 'army' + *pura* 'village': 'village of the army'. This opinion is acceptable. Otherwise, we could also think to IA 'town of the river (*sind*)'.

1212. **SIPAR سیپر (*sipar*)** *Map 27*

Village in the mountainous Dre-khwar valley, Tehsil of Charbagh.

Pšt. *cápar* 'hut'.

1213. **SIPHAN سیپهن (*siphan*)** *Map 7*

Place of Ghaligay on the left bank of the Swāt river, Tehsil of Barikot. Probably just an indication of the place of the barracks and not a real toponym. The name is present only on the Pakistani map.

Cf. Pšt. *sipa* 'army, soldiers', also Ur. *sipāh* 'soldiery, soldiers, troops, forces, army'.

1214. **SIRIKAR-KANDAO سریکار کندو (*sirikār-kanḍaw*)** *Map 51*

Pass leading from the Jaba-khwar valley to Kohistan, Tehsil of Bahrain.

Cf. Pšt. *cirika* 'spot, splace, sprinkle (as of mud), gush, flow' (RAVERTY).

1215. **SIRSANAI سرسنی (*sirsaṇəy*)** *Map 9*

Village at the end of the Deolai-khwar valley, in the vast and fertile plain on the right bank of the Swāt river, Tehsil of Kabal. On the Russian map its name is Sinsanay.

According to HAKIMZAY (1997: 91), Ur. *sar* means 'a god' and *senā* 'army', with the resulting meaning of 'place of the army of god'. However, cf. also T13256 **sarasa-* 'juniper': Dam. *saras*, Kal. *sāras*. But cf. also T13254 *saras-* 'lake, pool: Kal. *sar, sāruna*? Or cf. T12449 **śiraādhāna* 'resting-place for the head': Si. *sirāṇo* 'pillow'; Lhd. *sirhāṇā*, *sar°* 'head of bed, pillow', Panj. *sarhāṇā*? And Pšt. *saṇ* 'name of a plant from which tow is made (Crotolaria juncea)' (RAVERTY, ← IA). There are many possibilities, also taking into account the Russian form of this toponym.

1216. **SMATS سمڅ (*sməc*)** *Map 46*

Group of houses in a lateral mountainous valley of the Swāt river valley, Tehsil of Bahrain. Only on the Russian map.

Pšt. *sməc* 'cavern, cave, grotto; mine, excavation, subterranean passage' (RAVERTY, ASLANOV).

1217. **SOKO-KANDAO سوکو کندو (*soko-kanḍaw*)** *Map 28*

Pass leading from the Dre-khwar valley to Shangla, Tehsil of Charbagh.

Possibly Pšt. 'pass of the peaks (*cúka*)'.

1218.-1219. **SORAI سوری (*suray*)** *Maps 8, 48*

Name of two small villages: 1) on the right bank of the Swāt river, Tehsil of Kabal, in the wide and fertile plain of Kabal; 2) Group of houses in the Daral-khwar valley, Tehsil of Bahrain (only on the Russian map).

Pšt. *suráy* 'hole' or Pšt. *sóray* 'shady spots'.

1220. **SPALMAI-BANDA سپلمی بانده (*spalmay-bānḍa*)** *Map 15*

Pasture in a lateral valley of the Deolai-khwar valley, Tehsil of Kabal.

Pšt. *spəlmáy* 'horse with a star on its forehead'.

1221. **SPANAI-KHWAR سپنی خوړ (*spanay-xwaṛ*)** *Map 10*

Stream, located at an elevation of 969 meters above sea level, flowing into the Deolai-khwar, Tehsil of Kabal.

Possibly cf. Pšt. *spaṇkay* 'spark'.

1222. **SPARGAI سپرگی (*spargay*)** *Map 27*

Group of houses located in the mountainous upper Tambagat-khwar valley, Tehsil of Charbagh.

Cf. Pšt. *sparγa* 'well'?

1223. **SPEDAR-BANDA سپېدار بانده (*spedār-bānḍa*)** *Map 26*

Pasture at the end of the Spedar-khwar valley, on the boundary with Shangla, Tehsil of Babuzai.

Pšt. 'pasture of the white poplar (*sapedā́r, spedā́r*, Populus alba, according to ALAM 2011)'.

1224. **SPEDAR-KHWAR سپېدار خوړ (*spedār-xwaṛ*)** *Map 24*

Stream, whose average elevation is 2322 meters, flowing from the mountain on the boundary with Shangla towards the Kolam-khwar, Tehsil of Babuzai.

Cf. prec.

1225. **SPERAI سپېری (*speray*)** *Map 40*

Group of houses located in the narrow terraced valley of the Shaurai-khwar, Tehsil of Maṭṭa.

Cf. Pšt. *sperə́* 'light grey; ruined, devastated; not rich (of food)'.

1226. **SPERALGOT-SAR سپېرلگوټ سر (*speralgot-sar*)** *Map 13*

Mountain located on the boundary with Dir, near the Manrai-khwar valley, Tehsil of Kabal.

According to IKRAM, p.c., possibly Speragat-sar 'top of the grey stone'.

1227. **SPERKAI سپېرکی (*sperkay*)** *Map 34*

Group of houses on the hills near Kotanai, Tehsil of Khwazakhela.

Pšt. *sperkáy* 'greyish, ash-coloured'. Another possibility is Pšt. 'scoundrel, villain' (?).

1228. **SPERKAI-BANDA سپېرکی بانډه (*sperkay-bānḍa*)** *Map 12*

Pasture in the Jarendo-bela-khwar valley, Tehsil of Kabal, near the boundary with Dir.

Cf. prec.

1229. **SPIGHOG-KANDAO سپیغوګ کنډو (*spiγog-kanḍaw*)** *Map 19*

Pass leading from the Saidu-khwar valley to Buner, Tehsil of Babuzai.

Pšt. 'pass of the cries of the dogs'.

1230. **SPINAGATTA سپینکټه (*spinagaṭa*)** *Map 39*

Village in the Harnoi-khwar valley surrounded by cultivated fields, Tehsil of Maṭṭa.

Pšt. *spina°gaṭa* 'white rock'.

1231. **SPINKOTO-BANDA سپینکوټو بانډه (*spinkoṭo-bānḍa*)** *Map 32*

Pasture in the mountainous upper Khwazakhela-khwar valley, Tehsil of Khwazakhela.

Pšt. 'pass of the white rooms'.

1232. **SULAIMAN-GHUNDAI سلیمان غونډی (*sulaymān-γunḍəy*)** *Map 34*

Group of houses in the plain on the left bank of the Swāt river, north of Khwazakhela, at the foot of the hills, Tehsil of Khwazakhela.

Person's name.

1233. **SULI-BANDA سولي بانډه (*suli-bānḍa*)** *Map 24*

Pasture in the high and narrow Lewanai-khwar valley, Tehsil of Babuzai.

Cf. T12575 *śūla* 'spike, spit; impaling stake; any sharp pain, esp. colic': Pa. *sūla-* 'stake'; Pkt. *sūla-* 'spit, trident, a partic. disease', *°lī-*, *°liyā-* 'sharp iron stake'; Paš.lauṛ. *šūl* 'thorn'; Bašk. *šūl* 'wound'; Sh. (LORIMER) *šūl*, *šūlə* 'labour pains'; Lhd. *sūl* 'colic in horses' (JUKES also 'dysentery'), awāṇ. *sūl* 'colic'; Panj. *sūl* 'spike, thorn, colic', *sūlī* 'impaling stake'?

1234. **SUND-DERA سنډ ډېره (*sund-dera*)** *Map 17*

Village in the fertile plain, right on the right bank of the Swāt river, Tehsil of Kabal.

Cf. Pšt. *sunḍ* 'green ginger' (RAVERTY), or Pšt. *sunḍ* 'hemp' (ASLANOV). Cf. also T12515 *śuṇṭhī* 'dry ginger': Pkt. *suṁṭhī-* 'dry ginger', Si. *suṇḍhi*, Lhd. (JUKES) *sũḍh*, awāṇ. *suḍh*, poṭh. *suṇḍh*, Panj. *suṇḍh*.

1235. **SUNDIMAR سنډیمار (*sunḍimār*)** *Map 34*

Group of houses in the plain on the left bank of the Swāt river, Tehsil of Khwazakhela.

Cf. prec. + sf. of agent *-mār* (see SHAFEEV 1964).

1236. **SUPAL-BANDA سپل بانده (*supal-bānḍa*)** *Map 19*

Village in the narrow Marghuzar-khwar valley, towards Marghuzar, Tehsil of Babuzai. Quoted by RAVERTY (1888: 252) as "Saif Báṇḍa'h (probably, Saifál Báṇḍa'h)".

Cf. T13477 **suparṇikā-* 'having good leaves': Paš. *suplaī̃* 'a kind of oak with leaves edible for cattle'?

1237. **SURAI-TANGAI سوری تانګی (*suray-tangay*)** *Map 27*

Group of houses located in the mountainous upper Tambagat-khwar valley, Tehsil of Charbagh.

Pšt. 'gorge (*tangáy*)-hole (*suráy*)'.

1238. **SURBANR سوربڼ (*surbaṇ*)** *Map 24*

Group of houses located in the mountainous upper Landai-khwar valley, Tehsil of Babuzai.

Pšt. 'red garden'.

1239. **SURBAT سورباټ (*surbāṭ*)** *Map 38*

Group of houses on the hills of the Saso-sar, Tehsil of Maṭṭa.

Cf. Pšt. *surbād* = *ǰawānwān* 'Amni copticum, Trachyspermum copticum (a kind of herb)', Pšt. *soṛ°bād* 'cold wind' or Pšt. *sur* 'red' + *baṭ* 'the bark of a tree, bark, rind, peel, husk' (RAVERTY, ← IA). According to HAKIMZAY (1997: 97), another possibility could be 'a hero's route' (*sur* 'hero' + *baṭ* 'way').

1240. **SUR-DERAI سور ډېرى (*sur-ḍerəy*)** *Map 28*

Group of houses in the mountainous Dre-khwar valley, Tehsil of Charbagh.

Pšt. 'red (*sur*) residence'.

1241. **SURGALAI سورګلی (*surgalay*)** *Map 8*

Village located in the mountainous region on the upper Dadhra-khwar valley, Tehsil of Kabal.

Pšt. *surgúlay* 'kind of greenery', or Pšt. 'rich in red roses'.

1242. **SURGALAI-KANDAO سورګلی کنډو (*surgalay-kanḍaw*)** *Map 8*

Pass near the Jolagram-khwar, Tehsil of Barikot. According to RAVERTY (1888: 201), "The Súe-galí Kotal is mentioned three centuries and a half ago, in the history of the conquest of Suwát", as also told at p. 234. The Surgalai spur hides part of the Jolagram-khwar valley, and in particular the villages of Khazana and Garai, mentioned by RAVERTY (*ibid.*).

Pšt. 'pass of the red roses'.

1243. **SURKAMAR سورکمر (*surkamar*)** *Map 37*

Group of houses in the lower Bargin-khwar valley, Tehsil of Khwazakhela. Only on the Russian map.

Pšt. 'red rock'.

1244. **SURKAR-KANDAO سورکر کندو (*surkar-kanḍaw*)** *Map 52*

Pass leading from the Mankial-khwar valley to Kohistan, Tehsil of Bahrain. Local name Richo-kandao.

Pšt. *sur* 'red' + *kāṛ* 'pebbles; rocky terrain': 'pass of the red pebbles'.

1245. **SURKH-PAHUT سورخ پهوت (*surx-pahut*)** *Map 19*

Group of houses in the narrow Marghuzar-khwar valley, towards Marghuzar, Tehsil of Babuzai. Apparently, in STEIN 1930 it is called Miana.

Prs. *surx* 'red' + Prs. *phūt* 'the musk melon (Cucumis momordica)' (STEINGASS): cf. T13844 *sphuṭī* 'melon' [← Muṇḍa? See KUIPER 1948: 144, KEWA III 543-544 and EWAia III 528]: MIA. **phuṭṭi-*: Hi. *phūṭ* 'melon, cucumber run to seed, Cucumis momordica'.

1246. **SWAT سوات (*swāt*)**

Main river of the Swāt valley, flowing from the mountains in the upper Swāt (its two main sources are the Ushu-gol and the Gabral river) to the Kabul river. For all details, see introduction.

For the etymological analysis of the name Swāt see also the introduction.

1247. **SWATAI-KANDAO سواتی کندو (*swātay-kanḍaw*)** *Map 42*

Pass leading from the upper Harnoi-khwar valley to Dir, Tehsil of Maṭṭa.

Pšt. 'pass of Swāt', or cf. foll.

1248. **SWATI سواتي (*swāti*)** *Map 42*

Group of houses in the narrow mountainous Harnoi-khwar valley, Tehsil of Maṭṭa. Only on the Russian map.

Ethnic name.

1249. **TAGHAN تغن (*ṭaγan*)** *Map 25*

Village in the lower Bishbanr-khwar valley, Tehsil of Babuzai.

Pšt. *ṭaγán* 'noisy'. Cf. also *taghar, takhum, tugh, tartchum* 'Celtis caucasica' in ALAM 2011?

1250. **TAGHMA تغمه (*taγma*)** *Map 16*

Group of houses in a lateral valley of the Deolai-khwar valley, Tehsil of Kabal.

Pšt. *taγmá* 'mark, welt, scar, blemish' (RAVERTY).

1251. **TAIP تیپ (*tayp*)** *Map 51*

Group of houses in the mountainous Jaba-khwar valley, Tehsil of Bahrain.

Cf. T5685 *tapyatí* 'heat': Kt. *tipī*, *tpī* 'hot', Wg. *tapḗ*, Pr. *tábe*; Paš.lauṛ. *tapē*, dar. *tapīā* 'hot', ar. *tapīk* 'sweat'; Shum. *tapik* 'sweat', Gaw. *tapī.*

1252. **TAJAR-BELA تاجر بیله (*tāǰar-bela*)** *Map 38*

Small village in the plain on the right bank of the Harnoi-khwar, near Arkot, Tehsil of Maṭṭa.

Cf. Pšt. (Ar.) *tāǰír* 'merchant'.

1253. **TAKHTABAND تخته بند (*taxta-band*)** *Map 18*

Village in the fertile valley on the left bank of the Swat river, between the Swat river and the Saidu-khwar, Tehsil of Babuzai.

Pšt. *taxtabandí* 'veneering with boards; lining, facing'. ROSSI (p.c.) highlights that *taxt* is a common term of the landscape ('mesa', as Takht-e Jamshid)

1254. **TAKHTO-BELA تختو بیله (*taxto-bela*)** *Map 49*

Group of houses in the upper Daral-khwar valley, Tehsil of Bahrain.

Cf. prec. (suggestion by A.V. ROSSI, p.c.) and Pšt. *taxta* 'plank, board, stool, bench, bier, sheet of paper' or Pšt. *taxt* 'throne'. See ADAMEC V 469 Takhta Pul, "small district on the Dori, 22 miles from Kandahar on the Quetta road. It consists of a group of eight villages".

1255. **TAL ټل (*ṭal*)** *Map 12*

Main village of the upper Deolai-khwar valley, Tehsil of Kabal.

Cf. Pšt. *ṭal* 'quarter (of a town, village); crops; meadow; the fourth part of a settlement's land'. HAKIMZAY (1997: 54) links it to Hi. *tal* 'low grounds' and (*ibid.*: 60) to Hi. *ṭhāl* 'the state of being out of employment, holiday'.

1256. **TALANG تلنګ (*talang*)** *Map 1*

Village located in the narrow valley of the Kotah-khwar, Tehsil of Barikot.

Cf. Pšt. *talā́nga* 'echo'; but cf. also Pšt. *ṭal* 'quarter (of a town, village); crops; meadow; the fourth part of a settlement's land' (ASLANOV), 'thickness or closeness of grain in a field, or of trees in a grove or forest, or hair of the head; ward or division of a town or village; large field, the fourth part of the lands of a village, a bed of flowers, etc., a plot or plat of land' (RAVERTY) and *ṭalgay*, diminutive of the preceding, 'small field, few houses close to each other' (*ibid.*). It could also contain the second element *lang*, for which cf. T11006 *lāṅgala* 'plough' [→ Ir. dial of Lar in South Persia *liṅgṓr* 'plough' (MORGENSTIERNE). Initial *n-* in all Drav. forms (DED 2368); KUIPER 1948: 127 derives both IA. and Drav. words from Mu. sources: see KEWA III 97-98 and EWAia II 477]: Pa. *naṅgala-* 'plough', Pkt. *laṁgala-*, *ṇa°*, *ṇaṁgara*<->. See ZOLFAGHARI 2017: 57-62, and in particular LUBOTSKY's suggestion quoted at p. 61. See also OLIVIERI/VIDALE ET AL. 2006; DE CHIARA 2011: 210.

1257. **TALAO-KANDAO تالاو کنډو (*tālāw-kanḍaw*)** *Map 5*

Pass in the Tehsil of Barikot, leading from the Jolagram-khwar valley to Dir.

Pšt. *tālāw* 'pond, tank, reservoir'.

1258. **TALGO-NAKHTAR تالګو نختر (*tālgo-naxtar*)** *Map 1*

Group of houses on the hills of the Kotah-khwar, Tehsil of Barikot.

SULTAN-I-ROME 2016: 221 (and ALAM 2011: Pinus excelsa) *nakhtar* 'pinus longifolia'. According to IKRAM, p.c., *talgo* means 'group or pitches'. However, cf. also *ṭalgáy* 'small farm; small cultivated field'.

1259. **TALKAR تالکار (*tālkār*)** *Map 40*

Group of houses in the Shaurai-khwar valley, Tehsil of Maṭṭa.

Probably Pšt. *talk* 'Vitis hissarica/vinifera' (ALAM 2011): cf. the various names of plants ending in *-ar* (*spedar*, *naxtar*, etc.). However, Pšt. *tālā* 'plunder, spoil, sack, booty' + *kār* 'work' could also be compared.

1260. **TALKAR-KANDAO تالکار کنډو (*tālkār-kanḍaw*)** *Map 16*

Pass north of the Manrai-khwar valley, leading from the Tehsil of Kabal to the Tehsil of Maṭṭa.

Cf. prec.

1261. **TALURAI تلوړی (*taluṛay*)** *Map 24*

Group of houses in the high and narrow Lewanai-khwar valley, Tehsil of Babuzai. Only on the Russian map.

Cf. Tal + dimin. sf. *-uṛay*.

1262.-1263. **TAMBAGAT تمبګټ (*tambagaṭ*)** *Maps 27, 42*

Name of two groups of houses: 1) in the mountainous narrow Tambagat-khwar valley, Tehsil of Charbagh; 2) in the narrow mountainous Harnoi-khwar valley, Tehsil of Maṭṭa.

Pšt. *tanba* 'copper' + *gaṭ* 'large round stone, rock'.

1264. **TAMBAGAT-KHWAR تمبګټ خوړ (*tambagaṭ-xwaṛ*)** *Map 27*

Stream, located at an elevation of 1,272 meters above sea level, flowing into the Ugad-khwar, Tehsil of Charbagh.

Cf. prec.

1265. **TANAZGAH تنازګاه (*tanāzgāh*)** *Map 53*

Group of houses in the valley on the left bank of the upper Swāt river, Tehsil of Bahrain.

Tor. 'place (*-gāh*) of the dispute (*tanāzā*)'.

1266. **TANDAR-BANDA تندر بانډه (*tandar-bānḍa*)** *Map 24*

Pasture in the high and narrow Lewanai-khwar valley, Tehsil of Babuzai.

Pšt. 'pasture of the lightning (*tandə́r*)'.

1267. **TANDORA تندوره (*tandora*)** *Map 49*

Group of houses in the upper Daral-khwar valley, Tehsil of Bahrain.

Pšt. *tan(d)úr* 'oven'. To be excluded Pšt. *tundurá* 'cascade, waterfall; steep slope'.

1268. **TANGAI تنګی (*tangay*)** *Map 28*

Group of houses in the mountainous Dre-khwar valley, Tehsil of Charbagh.

Pšt. *tangáy* 'ravine, gorge, narrow valley; pass' or Pšt. *ṭāngáy* 'table mountain; flat-topped hill'. See SULTAN-I-ROME 2016: 482: "*Taangay*: A very small patch of *taang* [a patch of land that was created due to a river or stream altering its course; it may be situated in-between the branches of the river or stream or on their sides]; the patch between the two draining-lines of tomato plants". And *ibid.*: "*Tangay*: A narrow gorge or dry ravine, but sometime having a water spring".

1269. **TANGAI-BANDA تنګی بانډه (*tangay-bānḍa*)** *Map 46*

Pasture in the upper Olal-khwar valley, Tehsil of Bahrain.

Pšt. 'pasture of the Tangai'.

1270. **TANGAI-WARA تنګی وړه (*tangay-waṛa*)** *Map 12*

Group of houses in the Deolai-khwar valley, opposide side of Dheri, Tehsil of Kabal.

Pšt. 'small Tangai'.

1271. **TANGANUN تنګنون (*tanganun*)** *Map 45*

Group of houses in the narrow valley on the right bank of the Swāt river, Tehsil of Bahrain.

Pšt. *tang* 'narrow'?

1272.-1273. **TANGAR ټانګار (*ṭāngār*)** *Maps 41, 45*

Name of two villages: 1) in the plain at the confluence of the Harnoi-khwar, the Roringar-khwar and the Biha-khwar, Tehsil of Maṭṭa; 2) in the narrow valley on the left bank of the Swāt river at the confluence with the Olal-khwar, Tehsil of Bahrain.

See SULTAN-I-ROME 2016: 482: "*Taanguray*: A small patch of *taang*", cf. Tangay. HAKIMZAY (1997: 61), attributing Tangar to the Tehsil of Maṭṭa, analyses the toponym as formed by *ṭān* 'region, village' and *gār* or *angār* 'sparks remaining in ashes, burning charcoal' and concludes that in this regions the Buddhists venered the fire as the Zoroastrians and that this was the place of the fire. This opinion, however, cannot be accepted.

1274. **TANGBANR تنګبڼ (*tangbaṇ*)** *Map 38*

Village on the last slopes of the Saso-sar, on the right bank of the Harnoi river, Tehsil of Maṭṭa.

In this same Council there are two other villages, whose name is compounded with °*baṇ* (cf. amluk-baṇ and ahar-baṇ). Pšt. 'garden of the Tang', cf. Tangai.

1275.-1276. TANGO ټانګو (*ṭāngu*) *Maps 20, 33*

Name of two groups of houses: 1) in the mountainous upper Saidu-khwar valley, Tehsil of Babuzai; 2) in the mountainous upper Khwazakhela-khwar valley, on the slopes of the Semprai-sar, Tehsil of Khwazakhela.

Cf. Tangai, or Pšt. *ṭāngú* 'wild pear (tree)'.

1277. **TANGU-BANDA ټانګو بانډه (*ṭāngu-bānḍa*)** *Map 12*

Pasture in the mountainous upper Deolai-khwar valley, Tehsil of Kabal, near the border with Dir.

Pšt. 'pasture of the wild pears (*ṭāngu* 'name of a tree bearing a fruit like the apple in appearance', RAVERTY)', but better Pšt. 'pasture of the flat-topped hill (*ṭāngáy*)': see Tangai.

1278. **TAPRA تپړی (*tapṛay*)** *Map 38*

Group of houses on the hills of the Saso-sar, on the right bank of the Harnoi river, Tehsil of Maṭṭa.

See SULTAN-I-ROME 2016: 45, quoting MCMAHON/RAMSAY: "90. On the occupation of this country by the Pathans all lands were divided between the sub-divisions of each tribe. The portion, *daftar*, of each main sub-division was called a *tappa* [*tapah*]". Tapra could then be the 'small *tappa*'.

1279. **TAQAI تاقی (*tāqay*)** *Map 7*

Group of houses located in the Tehsils of Babuzai, in a small lateral valley of the Marghuzar-khwar valley, at the boundary with Barikot.

Cf. Pšt. *ṭāq* 'discharge, report, crack' or Pšt. *ṭakay* 'spot, dot, mark, streak, stripe; drop; bullock with a spot on the forehead; appointed time or place' (RAVERTY)?

1280. **TARAGAT تاړګټ (*tāṛagaṭ*)** *Map 20*

Group of houses in the mountain on the Saidu-khwar valley, Tehsil of Babuzai.

Pšt. *tāṛa* 'ruined, spoiled, poor, wretched' + *gaṭ* 'large round stone, rock'.

1281. **TARAKAI-KANDAO ترکی کنډو (*tarakəy-kanḍaw*)** *Map 2*

Pass on the boundary of Swat leading from the Kandak-khwar valley to Malakand, Tehsil of Barikot.

Pšt. 'pass of the cluster of rocks (apart from a mountain ridge) (*tarakə́y*)'.

1282. TARANO تارانو (*tārāṇo*) *Map 16*

Group of houses in a mountainous lateral valley of the Deolai-khwar valley at the frontier with the Tehsil of Maṭṭa, Tehsil of Kabal.

Cf. T5795 *tāraṇa* 'crossing, safe passage, surmounting of difficulties': Pkt. *tāraṇa-* 'taking across'.

1283. TAREL تریل (*tarel*) *Map 50*

Group of houses on the right bank of the Swāt river near the Kedam-khwar valley, Tehsil of Bahrain.

Cf. T6060 *trihalya* 'thrice-ploughed': Lhd. *trel*, mult. *taril* 'the third ploughing'?

1284. TARIS تریس (*taris*) *Map 51*

Group of houses on the slopes of the Tikai-sar, in the mountainous Mankial-khwar valley, Tehsil of Bahrain.

Et. unkn.

1285. TARJA ترجه (*tarǰa*) *Map 44*

Group of houses in a lateral valley on the right bank of the Swāt river on the slopes of the Babu-sar, Tehsil of Bahrain.

Et. unkn.

1286.-1288. TARKANA ترکنه (*tarkana*) *Maps 50, 51, 51*

Name of three groups of houses in the Tehsil of Bahrain: 1) in the Kedam-khwar valley; 2-3) in the Jaba-khwar valley.

Cf. Pšt. *tarkā́ṇ* 'carpenter'? Better *tarkana* (*chinaranga*) 'maple' (SULTAN-I-ROME 2016: 221).

1289. TAR-KANA ترکنه (*tar-kana*) *Map 50*

Group of houses in the Kedam-khwar valley, Tehsil of Bahrain.

Cf. Tarkana.

1290. TARKANADARRA ترکندره (*tarkanadara*) *Map 49*

Group of houses in the upper Daral-khwar valley, Tehsil of Bahrain.

Pšt. 'valley of the maples'.

1291. TARKANI ترکاني (*tarkāṇi*) *Map 15*

Group of houses in the mountainous valley of the Mahakai stream, Tehsil of Kabal.

Pšt. *tarkāṇí* 'carpentry, woodwork'? Better pl. of *tarkana* (*chinaranga*) 'maple' (SULTAN-I-ROME 2016: 221).

1292. **TAROGAI تاروگی (*tārogay*)** *Map 32*

Village in the mountainous terraced part of the Khwazakhela-khwar valley, Tehsil of Khwazakhela.

Cf. Pšt. *trogáy* 'spurge, euphorbia'.

1293. **TAWAUN توان (*tawān*)** *Map 29*

Group of houses located in the upper mountainous Malakad-khwar valley, Tehsil of Charbagh.

Pšt. *tawān* 'power; armed forces'.

1294. **TAWDE-OBO تودي اوبو (*tawde-obo*)** *Map 37*

Village located at the entry of the Paiti-khwar valley, Tehsil of Khwazakhela. Only on the Russian map.

Pšt. 'hot waters'.

1295. **TENDO-DAK تیندوډاګ (*tendo-ḍāg*)** *Map 7*

Village on the road leading from Barikot to Mingaora, in the fertile valley on the left bank of the Swat river and at the foot of the hills, Tehsil of Babuzai.

The second element is Pšt. *ḍāg* 'dale, plain, flatland (as contrasted to forest or mountains)'. HAKIMZAY (1997: 59) thinks for the first element to Hi. *tendua* 'leopard, panther': the resulting meaning would be 'plain of the leopards'. However, for the first element, cf. also Pšt. *tindáka* 'stream, fountain'?

1296. **TIGHAK-BANDA تیغک بانده (*tiγak-bānḍa*)** *Map 10*

Pasture located in the Ramogai-khwar valley, Tehsil of Kabal. Quoted already by RAVERTY (1888: 232).

Possibly Pšt. 'pasture of the small (*-ak*) jay (*ṭaγ* 'coracias bengalensis')'. Cf. also Pšt. *teγ* 'young plant, sprout, shoot' (RAVERTY).

1297.-1299. **TIKAI ټیکی (*ṭikay*)** *Maps 46, 48, 51*

Name of three groups of houses located in the Tehsil of Bahrain: 1) in the mountainous Nali-darra valley; 2) in the Daral-khwar valley; 3) in the mountainous Mankial-khwar valley.

Tor. 'summer pasture'.

1300. **TIKAI-SAR تیکی سر (*tikay-sar*)** *Map 51*

Mountain of about 4,980 mt between the Mankial-khwar and the Jaba-khwar, Tehsil of Bahrain.

Tor. 'mountain of the summer pasture'.

1301. **TIKDARA تیکداری (*ṭikdārəy*)** *Map 31*

Village in the plain on the left side of the Swāt river, near Khwazakhela, Tehsil of Khwazakhela.

Cf. Tikai + *dắra* 'current (of a river); stream' (*Eastern*: ASLANOV)?

1302. **TILAI تلی (*tilay*)** *Map 39*

Group of houses in the hills on the right bank of the Swāt river, Tehsil of Maṭṭa. Only on the Russian map.

Cf. foll.

1303. **TILGRAM تیلگرام (*tilgrām*)** *Map 25*

Village at the confluence between the Ugad-khwar valley and the Makad-khwar valley, Tehsil of Charbagh.

Possibly cf. T5827 *tilá-* 'Sesamum indicum' [← Muṇḍa? See KUIPER 1955: 157; KEWA I 504-505 and EWAia I 648]: Pa. *tila-* 'sesamum plant', Pkt. *tila*<-> 'the seed', Lhd. Panj. WPah.bhiḍ. Ku. N. A. B. *til* 'the seed'; Hi. *til* 'sesamum plant and seed, a minute fragment'; OMarw. *tila* 'small particle'; and T5958 *tailá* 'sesamum oil, oil': Pa. *tēla-* 'sesamum oil, oil'; Pkt. *tēla-*; Gy. arm. *tel* 'oil, fat, butter', pers. *tell*; Paš. *tēl* 'oil', Kal. urt. *tel*, rumb. *teu*, Kho. Sh. *tel*, Lhd. *tēl*, Panj. *tel*. However, cf. also T5731 *tala-* 'base, bottom': Bašk. *til* 'palm', Tor. *tel* 'roof'; etc.

1304. **TINKA تنکه (*tinka*)** *Map 53*

Group of houses in the narrow valley on the right bank of the upper Swāt river, Tehsil of Bahrain.

Cf. T5839 *tīkṣṇá* 'sharp; hot, pungent': Pa. *tikkha-* 'sharp, clever', *tikhiṇa-* 'pointed, sharp, pungent', *tiṇha-* 'sharp (of weapons &c.)'; Pkt. *tikkha-*, *tiṇha-* 'sharp, fine, pure'; Gy. eur. *tikno* 'small'; Bašk. *tī'n* 'sharp'; Tor. *tīn* 'sharp'; Si. *tikho* 'sharp, fiery, quick'; Lhd. *tikkhā* 'quick', khet. *tikkā*; Panj. *tikkhā*, *tīkhā* 'sharp, pointed, quick'?

1305. **TIRANG تیرنگ (*tirang*)** *Map 5*

Village in the plain on the Jolagram-khwar on the right bank of the Swāt river, Tehsil of Barikot. Quoted by RAVERTY (1888: 234) as Tirhang.

Cf. T6040 **triyaṅgula-* 'three-fingered': Kho. *thriṅgul* 'pitchfork with three or four prongs'?

1306. **TIRAT تیرات (*tirāt*)** *Map 45*

Village in the narrow valley on the right bank of the Swāt river, Tehsil of Bahrain. Quoted already by RAVERTY (1862: 251 and 1888: 236) as Tírátaey.

Cf. Ur. (PLATTS) *tīrth* (Skt.), *tīrath* (Ur.) 'A bathing place, a shrine or sacred place of pilgrimage (as Benares, &c.; especially particular spots along the course of sacred streams, as the Ganges, &c.); pilgrimage'. Cf. Skt. *tīrthám* 'passage, watering-, bathing-place, ford', Prakr. *tūha-*, Dard. (Kho.) *tūrt* 'ford', IE. **tṛh_2-th$_2$ó-* (KEWA I 507;

EWAia I 650). HAKIMZAY (1997: 55) agrees with this analysis. A Tira is also attested ("Tira, attested in two inscriptions from Swat connected to the Oḍi royal house (CKI [*Corpus of Kharoṣṭhī inscriptions*] 334 and 401), appears to have been the capital or at least a major city of this dynasty", BAUMS 2019: 168): is there any possible link? The final *-t* represents a formal problem of difficult solution.

1307. TITABAT تیټابټ (*ṭiṭābaṭ*) *Map 31*

Village in the plain on the left side of the Swāt river, near Khwazakhela, Tehsil of Khwazakhela.

Cf. foll. or T5938 *tr̥ṣṭa-* 'harsch, rough': Tor. *ṭīṭ* 'bitter, gall-bladder'? HAKIMZAY (1997: 60) states that *ṭiṭ* in old Hindi means 'real, genuine and pure' (*asəl*, *xālis* and *pāk*). Doubtful.

1308. TITAIWALA ټیټواله (*titaywāla*) *Map 30*

Group of houses on the slopes bordering the plain of Charbagh, Tehsil of Charbagh.

Cf. Pšt. *ṭíṭa* 'low place, low country, depression, hollow'.

1309. TOBAI ټوبی (*ṭobay*) *Map 33*

Group of houses in the terraced Khwazakhela-khwar valley, Tehsil of Khwazakhela.

Pšt. *ṭubáy* 'sand dune overgrown with grasses'.

1310.-1311. TOPSIN ټوپسین (*ṭopsin*) *Maps 20, 32*

Name of two villages: 1) Group of houses in the spur between the Saidu-khwar valley and the Jambil-khwar valley, near Jambil, Tehsil of Babuzai; 2) in the upper Khwazakhela-khwar valley, on the road to Shangla, Tehsil of Khwazakhela.

HAKIMZAY (1997: 61-62) derives it from Skt. and translates 'temple (*ṭop*) of the army (*senā*)'. This latter opinion seems more plausible, seen also the great religious activity in the region (as also attested by the findings of the the Italian Archaeological Mission): indeed, the top of the *stūpa* appears as a sort of hat or cap. Cf. T5481 **ṭōppa* 'hat, covering': Pkt. *ṭōpiā-* 'helmet'; Dam. *ṭópai* 'peak'; Gaw. *ṭopī* 'hat, cap'; Lhd. *ṭopī*, awāṇ. *ṭōp*, Panj. *ṭop*, *ṭoppā*, *ṭoppī*, *ṭopī*; etc., in the meaning of 'covering of the temple'. And T13587 *sḗnā* 'army': Pa. *sēnā-* 'army', Dhp. *seṇa*, KharI. *sena*, Pkt. *seṇā-*, Hi. *sen*, Si. *sen*.

1312. TOP-TUT ټوپ توت (*ṭop-tut*) *Map 28*

Village in the Dre-khwar valley. Tehsil of Charbagh. Only on the Russian map.

Pšt. 'heap (*ṭop*) or temple (*ṭop*) of mulberry (*tut*)'.

1313. TORKAMAR تورکمر (*torkamar*) *Map 20*

Group of houses in the mountainous upper Saidu-khwar valley, Tehsil of Babuzai.

Pšt. 'black (*tor*) precipice/slope/rock (*kamár*)' (see DE CHIARA 2011: 210; EILERS 1954: 371 ff. ["*Kamar* 'Kreuz, Rücken' (Gürtelgegend) —> 'Berg; Terrasse, Steilhang' ~ *sar*

'Haupf, Kopf' —> 'Gipfel', auch 'Vorgebirge'"]; BARTH/ MORGENSTIERNE 1958: 125 [*kámer* 'rock/cliff']).

1314. TORUSATTA-BANDA تورسته بانده (*torusata-bānḍa*) *Map 13*

Pasture located in the high Manrai-khwar valley, towards the boundary with Dir, Tehsil of Kabal.

Cf. Pšt. *saṭ* 'block of wood on which an anvil is placed, the root or trunk of a tree remaining in the ground, log of wood' (RAVERTY) + *tor* 'black'?

1315. TORWAL توروال (*torwāl*) *Map 48*

Group of houses on the right bank of the Swāt river, Tehsil of Bahrain. Quoted already by RAVERTY (1888: 237).

Ethnic name (see Foreword for references).

1316. TOTAKAI ټوټکی (*ṭoṭakay*) *Map 30*

Group of houses on the hills sloping towards the left bank of the Swāt river, Tehsil of Charbagh.

Pšt. 'small piece (*ṭoṭá*)'.

1317.-1318. TSAPPAR څپر (*capar*) *Maps 43, 46*

Name of two groups of houses: 1) in the upper Roringar-khwar valley, near the boundary with Dir, Tehsil of Maṭṭa; 2) in a lateral narrow valley of the Olal-khwar valley, Tehsil of Bahrain.

Pšt. *capə́r* 'flat summit (of a mountain)' or Pšt. *cápar* 'hut'.

1319.-1320. TSAPPARAI څپری (*caparay*) *Maps 33, 46*

Name of two groups of houses: 1) in the mountainous upper Khwazakhela-khwar valley, Tehsil of Khwazakhela; 2) in a lateral narrow valley of the Olal-khwar valley, Tehsil of Bahrain.

Cf. Pšt. *capā́ray* 'lump, snowball', or Pšt. *capə́r* 'flat summit (of a mountain)' or Pšt. *cápar* 'hut'.

1321. TSAPPARAI-KANDAO څپری کندو (*caparay-kanḍaw*) *Map 1*

Pass in the Tehsil of Barikot on the boundary with Malakand, south of the Mora-sar.

Cf. prec.

1322. TSAPPARAI-SAR څپری سر (*caparay-sar*) *Map 6*

Mountain of about 1,480 mt, on the right bank of the Swāt river, Tehsil of Barikot, above Nagwa.

Pšt. *capā́ray* 'lump, snowball'.

1323. TSAPPARUNA څپرونه (*caparuna*) *Map 46*

Group of houses in the upper mountainous Olal-khwar valley, Tehsil of Bahrain. Only on the Russian map.

Cf. Tsappar.

1324. TSUKAI څوکی (*cukay*) *Map 50*

Group of houses on the slopes on the left bank of the upper Swāt river valley, Tehsil of Bahrain.

Pšt. 'mountain top'.

1325. TUKATAKI توتکي (*tukataki*) *Map 54*

Lake on the Ushu-gol, Tehsil of Bahrain, indicated only on the Russian map. Nowadays it seems have disappeared.

Et. unkn.

1326. TUNGOWALA-MORAH تونګواله موره (*tungowāla-morah*) *Map 20*

Group of houses in the spur between the Saidu-khwar valley and the Jambil-khwar valley, near Jambil, Tehsil of Babuzai.

Probably Pšt. *tangáy* 'ravine, gorge, narrow valley; pass' + *wyālá*, *wālá* 'canal' + *moṛá* 'saddlecloth (under the saddle); packsaddle (of a camel); range (of mountains, waves); edge, lip; lockage, long-term constipation; stool; rampart around a tent; kind of embroidery; welt from being hit with a twig'.

1327. TUTAN-BANDA توتان بانډه (*tutān-bānḍa*) *Map 10*

Main village in the last part of the fertile plain of the Spanai-khwar valley, Tehsil of Kabal. Quoted already by RAVERTY (1888: 232).

Pšt. 'pasture of the berries (*tut*)'.

1328. TUT-BANRIN توت بڼين (*tut-baṇin*) *Map 17*

Group of houses on the hills on the Deolai-khwar valley, Tehsil of Kabal.

Pšt. *tut* 'mulberry' (see SULTAN-I-ROME 2016: 221 and ALAM 2011) + *baṇ* + sf. *-in* for adjectives ('wooded'): 'densely wooded by mulberries'.

1329.-1330. TUTKAI توتکی (*tutkay*) *Maps 38-39*

Name of two villages in the Tehsil of Maṭṭa: 1) nowadays a quartier of Matta, in the fertile plain between the Harnoi-khwar and the right bank of the Swāt river; 2) Group of houses on the eastern slopes of the mountains separating the Barwai-khwar valley from the Harnoi-khwar valley.

Pšt. 'small berry'.

1331. TUTPANRAI-SAR توتپانی سر (*tutpāṇay-sar*) *Map 17*

Mountain of 1,363 mt on the plain of the Swat river, near the beginning of the Deolai-khwar valley, Tehsil of Kabal. Only on the Russian map.

Cf. Tut-banrin as kind of formation. Instead of *baṇ*, *pāṇá* 'leaf' + the equivalent adj. sf. *-ay*: 'mountain full of mulberry leaves'.

1332. TUWA توه (*təwa*) *Map 29*

Group of houses in the upper Malakad-khwar valley, Tehsil of Charbagh.

Pšt. *tə́wa* 'small bank, small earthen wall (for holding back water in a field)'.

1333. UCHRAI اوچړی (*učṛay*) *Map 40*

Small group of houses on the slopes right the Harnoi river, Tehsil of Maṭṭa.

Probably, cf. Skt. *ucca-* 'high' (see KEWA I 99) + Pšt. dimin. sf. *-ṛay*. However, cf. also Bašk. *ūč* 'spring, fountain', Kal. *uk* 'water' (T1921 *udaká-* 'water'); Kal. *uc̣hár* 'waterfall' (T1922, 735, 14248, 14315 **udakakṣāra-*, **avakṣāra-* 'waterfall'); and SULTAN-I-ROME 2016: 483: "*Wuchah/Wachah*: 'To the [...] portion of Suwat, lying between the left bank and the mountains on the south-east, and containing the other seventeen minor dara'hs, he [Shaikh Mali] gave the name of *wucha*, signifying "dry," "arid," etc. [...] The *wucha* portion extended from the village of Tutakan, in Lower Suwat, to Pi'a, the boundary village of Upper Suwat, a distance of sixty-three miles.' (H. G. Raverty, *Notes on Afghanistan and Baluchistan*, Vol. 1, 206)". Cf. also the town of Uchh, Dir and many other places, on which see ELLIOT 1867: Ossadii or Oxydracæ. See also Wuch.

1334. UCHRAI-SAR اوچړی سر (*učṛay-sar*) *Map 40*

Mountain of about 1,900 mt bordering the plain on the right bank of the Harnoi-khwar, Tehsil of Maṭṭa.

Cf. prec.

1335. UDIGRAM اوډیگرام (*uḍigrām*) *Map 18*

Village on the road leading from Barikot to Mingaora, in the fertile valley on the left bank of the Swat river and at the foot of the hills, Tehsil of Babuzai. Quoted by RAVERTY (1862: 239 and 1888: 199) as Waḍí-Grám, by DEANE (1895) as Odigram and by STEIN (1929: 49) as Uḍe-grām.

IA. See STEIN 1929: 60 (see also ID. 1930: 40):

> The first part *Uḍe-*, also heard as *Uḍi-*, is pronounced with that cerebral consonant *ḍ* which to European ears, in classical times as now, always sounded like an *r* and often undergoes that change to *r* in modern Indian and Dardic languages. Thus the temptation is great to recognize in Arrian's Ὦρα the Greek rendering of an earlier form of this name *Uḍe-*, and to derive this name itself from the ancient Sanskrit name of Swāt, *Uḍḍiyana*. The phonetic changes that such a derivation assumes in the history of the name can all be fully accounted for by well-known rules affecting the transition of Sanskrit words into later Indo-Aryan forms.

And TUCCI 1963a [= TUCCI 1997: 117]:

> Their [of the Assakenoi] most important places were Massaga (not yet located with certainty, but which must have lain somewhere near Chakdarra), Bazira = Vajīra, Vajīrasthāna in an inscription [28] of Jayapāladeva (*EI* XXI, p. 301), now Barikot, Ora (Uḍegram), Dyrta (not located). These were the cities of the Assakenoi, Āśvāyana, Assakenoi-Āśvakāyana (Kātyāyana, VI, I, 99) and Aurdāyana, from Urdi (Ora), mentioned by Kātyāyana on IV, II, 99. The name of the last tribe cannot be separated from Oḍḍiyāna < Aurdiyāna, Audriyāna.

1336. **UGAD-KHWAR اوګد خوړ (*ugad-xwaṛ*)** *Map 23*

Stream flowing into the Swāt river, on the left side near Manglaor, whose main course is in Charbagh Tehsil; it is located at an elevation of 971 meters above sea level.

Cf. Tor. *ugan* 'watery'. Cf. also Tor. *ughu* 'ugly, deformed' (s. Usho)? Or possibly Pšt. *uǧd* 'long': 'long stream'?

1337. **UGDAI اوږدی (*uǧday*)** *Map 18*

Group of houses in the fertile valley on the left bank of the Swat river, between the Swat river and the Saidu-khwar, Tehsil of Babuzai.

Cf. prec. or Pšt. *uǧd* 'long'?

1338. **UNRAN-SAR اوڼان سر (*uṇān-sar*)** *Map 24*

Mountain of about 2,850 mt between the Jambil-khwar valley and the Lewanai-khwar valley, Tehsil of Babuzai, near the boundary with Buner.

From a formal etymological point of view, it corresponds to the Mount Aornos of the classical sources: indeed, the name *uṇa* is the result of the regular phonetic development *rn* > *ṇ* in Pashto. (see DE CHIARA forthcoming b; STEIN 1929: 115 ff. and 151 ff., and ID. 1930: 75 and 89-90). STEIN (1929: 129) tried to identify it with the Pir-sar, 'the holy man's height' (see also OLIVIERI 2015c). However, the toponym (h)unran appears in the denomination of many peaks in all Swāt valley. See Ilam for the entire reasoning.

Recently ROLLINGER (2014) discussed the different proposed etymologies for Mount Aornos: STEIN's (1927: 536; 1929: 152) IA **avaraṇa-* 'colourless' and WILSON's (1841: 192; LASSEN 1861-1874, vol. II/2: 148 n. 3) Skt. *āvaraṇa-* (Pkt. *āaraṇa-*), a common name for any sheltered place (see TUCCI 1977: 52-53). ROLLINGER (2014: 627) concludes that the Greek identification with possible ἄ-ορνος 'birdless', 'without birds' belongs to the concept of the birdless mountain, which

> covers a period from the late second millennium BCE until the last third of the first millennium CE, and even further. It proves beyond any doubt that Alexander's Aornos was only one of many of sites so described through the centuries. The conception of a birdless mountain could be applied to various mountains from the Zagros ranges to the Hindu Kush. Whether of Assyrian or of local origin somewhere in the Zagros, it was reused and reshaped by western conquerors, who adapted it for their specific needs. The Assyrian kings were the first to use this literary motif which was further developed according to their own ideological concerns. The same is true for Alexander the Great. The Greek term Aornos/Aornis is a perfect translation of this concept and not a popular etymology of a presumable original Indian term.

1339. **URDAM** اردم **(*urdam*)** *Map 32*

Group of houses in the upper Khwazakhela-khwar valley, near Topsin, on the road to Shangla, Tehsil of Khwazakhela.

Cf. Kal. *uruḍí* 'Ururi village in Birir valley'?

1340. **URWANA-KOTLAI** اوروانه کوتلی **(*urwāna-koṭlay*)** *Map 8*

Group of houses on the slopes of the Kotlai-khwar valley leading to the boundary with Dir, under the Changai-dop-sar, Tehsil of Kabal. On the Russian map its name is Urgana-kotlai.

Pšt. *waṛukay kotlay*, 'small Kotlay'?

1341. **USHO** اوشو **(*ušo*)** *Map 54*

Village located in the Ushu-gol valley, Tehsil of Bahrain. It is called Matiltan on Google Earth.

Cf. foll. This village is identified by DEANE (1895) with the village of Laspur, an old toponym formed with the old toponym of possibly Dardic origin *-pur*.

1342. **USHU-GOL** اوشو گول **(*ušu-gol*)** *Map 54*

Stream flowing down to Kalam, Tehsil of Bahrain, and origin of the Swāt river.

Cf. Tor. *ušo* 'ugly' [*bad surat*] or Tor. *ušu* 'to stand up; to wake up'. Cf. Tor. *uṣā/ awaṣa*? 'a village in Daral valley'. Better, cf. Kal. *oš* 'cold; snow, ice' (T855 *avaśyā-* 'hoar-frost, dew').

1343. **USMANI-SAR** اوسماني سر **(*usmāni-sar*)** *Map 17*

Mountain (1619 mt.) located near Shakardarra, in the Tehsil of Kabal, at the frontier with the Tehsil of Maṭṭa. Its local name is also Ali-khān-dop.

Pšt. 'light-blue (*asmānī*) mountain'? Person's name? See ADAMEC V 486-487 Usmanzai.

1344. **UTROR** اترور **(*utror*)** *Map 54*

Stream located in the Tehsil of Bahrain, flowing from west down to Kalam.

Tor. *Utroṛ*. See AFTAB AHMAD 2015: 15 *utroṛ say khār* 'a stream in Utror valley'.

1345. **UTROT** اتروت **(*utrot*)** *Map 54*

Village located at the confluence of the Utror and Gabral rivers, near Kalam, Tehsil of Bahrain. Quoted already by RAVERTY (1888: 237) and DEANE (1895).

Cf. prec. According to HAKIMZAY (1997: 9), in Sanskrit *Utar* and *Uttra* mean respectively 'The North' and 'Northern', and *Or* indicates the 'region' and the 'side': the toponym would then mean → 'on the northern side'. He wonders also if northern in relation to Kalam or Tirat.

1346. **UZBUK-SAR ازبک سر (*uzbuk-sar*)** *Map 24*

Mountain (2860 mt.) located near the southern frontier of Swāt with Buner, between the Lewanai-khwar valley and the Dosara-khwar valley, Tehsil of Babuzai.

Pšt. 'mountain of the Uzbeks'? See ADAMEC V 487 Uzbak, "village located about halfway between the valleys of the Shaikhiran and the Siandara streams in Oruzgan province".

1347. **WADAN-MANDAO ودان منډو (*wadān-manḍaw*)** *Map 23*

Small village in the flat lower Ugad-khwar valley, Tehsil of Babuzai.

Pšt. *wadā́n* 'built, equipped' + *manḍaw* 'hut of grass or wood, shed, porch' (RAVERTY).

1348. **WAINAI وينى (*waynay*)** *Map 40*

Small village at the confluence of the Shaurai-khwar in the plain on the right bank of the Harnoi-khwar valley, Tehsil of Maṭṭa.

Cf. Pšt. *wayná* 'crystal; glass'.

1349. **WAKILABAD وکيلاباد (*wakilābād*)** *Map 39*

Village at the foot of the hills bordering the fertile plain on the right bank of the Swāt river, Tehsil of Maṭṭa.

Pšt. 'town of the *wakíl* ('agent/representative/deputy/official/lawyer')'.

1350. **WALIABAD ولياباد (*waliābād*)** *Map 30*

Group of houses on the left bank of the Swāt river, at the foot of the hills, Tehsil of Charbagh. RAVERTY (1888: 200) quotes a village named Kábul-Grám, which lies half-way between Charbagh and Khwazakhela, "along the river's bank": we can possibly identify Waliabad as the ancient Kabulgram.

Pšt. 'town of the Wali [the official title of the two rulers of Swat State namely Miangul Abdul Wadud and Miangul Jahanzeb, according to SULTAN-I-ROME 2016: 544]'. See also ID. 2008: 328: "*Wali.* A prince; a chief; a master; a ruler; a sovereign. It is inferior in sense and status to that of Bacha/Badshah, which means a king; an emperor".

1351. **WAR-PATAI وار پټى (*wār-pəṭay*)** *Map 16*

Group of houses in a mountainous lateral valley of the Deolai-khwar valley at the frontier with the Tehsil of Maṭṭa, Tehsil of Kabal.

Pšt. 'field of the (good) time', with Pšt. *wār* 'time, period, turn (for duty, etc.)' (← Hi.?) (RAVERTY).

1352. **WARUKAI-NAMAL وړوکى نمل (*waṛukay-namal*)** *Map 41*

Group of houses located in the narrow mountainous upper Harnoi-khwar valley, Tehsil of Maṭṭa.

Pšt. 'small (*waṛúkay*) Namal'. Cf. Loe-namal.

1353. **WELAN-SAR ویلان سر (*welān-sar*)** *Map 28*

Peak of about 1,800 mt between the Makad-khwar valley and the Dre-khwar valley, Tehsil of Charbagh.

Cf. Pšt. *welə́na* 'mint'.

1354. **WUCH ووچ (*wuč*)** *Map 44*

Group of houses in a lateral valley on the right bank of the Swāt river on the slopes of the Babu-sar, Tehsil of Bahrain. Only on the Russian map.

Cf. Skt. *ucca-* 'high' (see KEWA I 99). Cf. also Uchrai and SULTAN-I-ROME's quotation (2016: 483).

1355. **YAKABANJ-BANDA یکابنج بانده (*yakābanǰ-bānḍa*)** *Map 3*

Pasture in the upper Kandak-khwar valley, Tehsil of Barikot, near the Bostani-sar.

Cf. Pšt. *banǰ* 'oak' + Pšt. *yax* 'cold'? See ADAMEC VI 807 Yakatut, "A collection of villages lying to the east of Sherpur (Kabul district), and about 2 miles from it", and Yakawlang or Yakh Walang, "name of a woleswali in the Bamian province".

1356. **YAKH یخ (*yax*)** *Map 30*

Group of houses in the upper Charbagh-khwar valley, Tehsil of Charbagh. It is called Yakh-china-darra on the Russian map.

Pšt. *yax* 'cold'.

1357. **YAKH-KANDAO یخ کندو (*yax-kanḍaw*)** *Map 46*

Pass leading to Shangla from the upper Olal-khwar valley, Tehsil of Bahrain.

Pšt. 'cold pass'.

1358. **YAKH-TANGAI-SAR یخ ټنګی سر (*yax-ṭangay-sar*)** *Map 16*

Mountain, high about 1,720 mt, in the spur dividing the Deolai-khwar valley from the eastern lateral valley, Tehsil of Kabal.

Pšt. 'mountain of the cold gorge'.

1359. **ZAMBAK زمبک (*zambak*)** *Map 42*

Group of houses on the slopes on the narrow mountainous Harnoi-khwar valley, Tehsil of Maṭṭa.

Pšt. *zambák* 'lily; iris; yellow flag'.

1360. **ZANGAR زنګر (*zangar*)** *Map 30*

Group of houses in the Charbagh-khwar valley, Tehsil of Charbagh.

Deformation of Pšt. *zangal* 'forest, wood, wild'?

1361. **ZANGI-BANDA زنګي بانډه (*zangi-bānḍa*)** *Map 29*

Pasture in the Malakad-khwar valley, Tehsil of Charbagh.

Pšt. 'pasture of the Black (person)/of the dancer (*zangí*)'? See ADAMEC V 504 Zangiabad or Zangabad, "An important village in the doab of the Arghandab and Dori rivers, situated on the left bank of the former just below Sperwan. It consists of three hamlets containing 147 houses with 502 inhabitants".

1362. **ZANGUN زنګون (*zangun*)** *Map 38*

Village on the right bank of the Swāt river at the foot of the hills bordering the plain, Tehsil of Maṭṭa.

Pšt. *zangún* 'knee'.

1363. **ZARA-CHURRAI زړه چوړړی (*zaṛa-čurṛay*)** *Map 45*

Village in the narrow valley on the left bank of the Swāt river, Tehsil of Bahrain.

Pšt. 'old Churarai' (q.v.).

1364. **ZARIKHELA زرخېله (*zarixela*)** *Map 5*

Village in the plain on the Jolagram-khwar on the right bank of the Swāt river, Tehsil of Barikot. RAVERTY (1888: 201) calls it Zírah Khel. The village of Zarikhela is called Shamozai on Google Earth.

Zarikhel tribe. HAKIMZAY (1997: 178) thinks to *zar* 'gold' + *ke* (later on > *xe*).

1365. **ZARINAL زرينال (*zarināl*)** *Map 52*

Group of houses on the left bank of the upper Swāt river, Tehsil of Bahrain.

Pšt. 'golden (*zarin*)'?

1366. **ZEWALA زېواله (*zewāla*)** *Map 32*

Small village in the terraced Khwazakhela-khwar valley, Tehsil of Khwazakhela. It is called Zawala on the Russian map.

Pšt. *jāy*- 'place' + *wyālá*, *wālá* 'canal'.

1367. **ZHANDRAI-KANDAO ژندرى کنډو (*žandray-kanḍaw*)** *Map 54*

Pass leading from the Utror valley to Dir, Tehsil of Bahrain.

Pšt. 'pass of the lock (*žandərá*)' or 'of the wiredrawing bench (*žandrə́y*)'; or 'mill'.

1368. **ZIARAT-KHPA زيارت خپه (*zyārat-xpa*)** *Map 40*

Group of houses in the narrow terraced valley of the Shaurai-khwar, Tehsil of Maṭṭa.

Pšt. 'foot (*x̌pa*) of the sanctuary'.

1369. **ZIMDARRA زیمدره (*zimdara*)** *Map 39*

Group of houses on the eastern slopes of the mountains dividing the Barwai-khwar valley from the Harnoi-khwar valley, Tehsil of Maṭṭa.

Pšt. 'valley of the moisture (*zyam*)'? Better SULTAN-I-ROME 2016: 483: "*Zyam*: Water-logging; the water trickling or flowing out especially from cultivated land; the water flowing in a very small quantity especially used for irrigation".

1370. **ZINDWALA زیندواله (*zindwāla*)** *Map 30*

Group of houses located on the slopes bordering the Charbagh-khwar valley, Tehsil of Charbagh.

Cf. Pšt. *zindān* 'jail, prison' or Pšt. *zindəy* 'halter, noose for hanging criminals'?

1371. **ZINKHARAI زینخری (*zinxaray*)** *Map 34*

Group of houses on the hills near Kotanai, Tehsil of Khwazakhela.

Pšt. *zin* 'saddle' + *xar* 'donkey'?

1372. **ZIN-SAR زین سر (*zin-sar*)** *Map 35*

Mountain of about 2,300 mt on the Bargin-khwar valley, Tehsil of Khwazakhela.

Pšt. 'saddle (*zin*)-mountain': the geographic shape reminds indeed a saddle.

1373. **ZIZRAT ززرت (*zizrat*)** *Map 37*

Village in the plain on the left bank of the Swāt river, Tehsil of Khwazakhela. Only on the Russian map.

Et. unkn.

1374. **ZOR-CHEL زوړ چیل (*zoṛ-čel*)** *Map 46*

Group of houses in the narrow valley of the Olal-khwar, Tehsil of Bahrain. Only on the Russian map. In STEIN 1930 it is called Chahil and after this village our Olal-khwar is called Chihil-dara.

Pšt. 'old (*zoṛ*) Chel', where *čel* could be Pšt. *čilu* 'kind of herb or vegetable' or *čilay* 'young male kid'?

1375. **ZOR-SHALPIN زوړ شالپین (*zoṛ-šālpin*)** *Map 33*

Group of houses in the terraced mountainous upper Khwazakhela-khwar valley, Tehsil of Khwazakhela.

Pšt. 'old (*zoṛ*) Šalpin (q.v.)'.

A SHORT NOTE ON THE FORTUNE OF TOPONYMY STUDIES IN SWĀT AND GANDHĀRA

By Luca M. OLIVIERI

We know that the Greeks were not exact in their mode of spelling the names of the towns and countries which they invaded [...]
(COURT 1836: 395)

In the early years of the antiquarian research into Gandhara, interest of the scholars – in many cases adventurous *dilettanti* – was driven by the possibility of locating ancient toponyms whose exotic whereabouts were long coveted. For example, Bazira, Massaka, Aornos, to name just some of the locations mentioned by the Alexandrographers. To the best of my knowledge, the earliest of these studies, all conducted partly in the field, partly from second-hand information obtained from local spies, informants or agents, was the memoir published by general M. COURT in the *Journal of the Asiatic Society*, July 1836, pp. 387-395. It was soon followed by many others. The quest for the Aornos occupied many people for more than a century, for example: A. CUNNINGHAM (1848), J. ABBOTT (1854), O. BARATIERI (1879), A. STEIN (1898, 1899, 1905, 1929, 1930), O. CAROE (1958), Ph. EGGERMONT (1970, 1984), and TUCCI (1958, 1977). We hope that this endless gradus ad Aornon can be finally considered as concluded with the recent reassessment by O. COLORU (in COLORU/OLIVIERI 2019).

The search for toponyms was driven by two major questions, and by a third minor one. On one side the "quest for Alexander", which was particularly attractive for military officers, adventurers and political agents. On the other side were the descriptions of "Western world" as left by the triad of the Chinese pilgrims, the last, most productive and, therefore most studied, being Xuangzang. The tradition of that specific branch of toponymy studies reached its climax pretty early as it was initiated by a connoisseur like A. FOUCHER in 1902, whose map further elaborated in his 1942 work on the *vieille route de l'Inde* is still reproduced in many modern studies. The location of the early development of the itineraries of Xuangzang and the other Chinese sources was the Malakand Fort. We know this from the many documents discovered in 2008 and published a few years later (OLIVIERI 2015a). The office of the Political Agent H. DEANE and the guesthouse, where both A. STEIN and A. FOUCHER spent Christmas in 1896, were the *aulae* where these locations were debated, after and before hard days of walking and climbing in the wilderness. The result of those adventurous days were the cited works by STEIN, FOUCHER, and the DEANE's *Notes on Udyāna* (1896; the critical edition based on the Malakand manuscripts will soon be published by Ll. MORGAN). This approach turned out to be very lucky. In 1932, a late epigone of DEANE, E.H. COBB, Political Agent at Malakand, wrote to MARSHALL, the then don of Indian archaeology, about the discovery of a superb statue of Bodhisattva (OLIVIERI 2015a: Doc. 325). His letter is richly flavoured with identification of local villages with the *loci* found in the translations of the travelogues of 'Hinan-Tsang' and 'Sang-Yan'.

The third question (the "quest for Uḍḍiyāna") led TUCCI, before visiting Swat, to establish the itinerary of some Tibetan pilgrims who had visited Swat in late 13th century and later (TUCCI

1940). It had been the discovery of these manuscripts in Tibet that eventually led Tucci to initiate his first surveys of Swat in 1955 and 1956. TUCCI's first report (1958) is full of interpretations and identifications of modern toponyms. A few years later this approach was imitated by A.H. DANI in his pages on Dir (1967). But, with the advent of proper archaeology, toponyms became a secondary target and were slowly forgotten. It was only later, with the second phase of the excavations and fieldwork of the Italian Archaeological

Mission in Swat, around the 1990s, that these studies became more cogent, less occasional, and more fruitful. The study published on the previous page, which in my view can be considered a masterwork in its genre, was generated in that environment. For the first time in Gandhara, the study of the toponyms was taken as a systematic survey of the more or less erratic data of a linguistic stratification. In this context, important key-points, which were debated for a century, are now a *fait accompli*: Bazira (BAUMS 2019; VON HINÜBER 2020) and Ilam-Aornos (cit. above). Other research is expected soon: on the toponyms of the Oḍirāja dedicatory inscriptions, as well as on the small amount of pre-IA evidence still preserved in the toponymy of the region.

APPENDIX

MICRO-TOPONYMY OF THE KANDAK AND NEARBY VALLEYS

This appendix lists all Swāt toponyms published in archaeological and general surveys since the second half of the 19th century. In particular, data contained in the following publications have been included:

- RAVERTY 1862
- RAVERTY 1888
- STEIN 1930
- TUCCI 1958
- OLIVIERI/VIDALE ET AL. 2006
- FILIGENZI 2015
- OLIVIERI 2015a

The Italian Archaeological Mission (IAM) has been working in the Swāt valley since 1956, thanks to the impulsion of Giuseppe TUCCI. With the passing of time and especially in the more recent years, many international projects headed by the IAM have increased our knowledge of this area, which is nowadays one of the more studied in Asia.
In the most part of cases, the toponyms included in this appendix are local, and for this reason, we can speak of "micro-toponymy" (cf. DODYXUDOJEV 1975). The Kandak and nearby valleys project, led by the AMSV (Archaeological Mission in the Swāt Valley), also adopts a comparable approach.
A similar project, even if not centred on archaeology, was developed in the '90's in northern Italy and continues its publications and researches nowadays. Directed by Valerio FERRARI[1], it aimed at listing and analysing in a capillary way all toponyms of the province of Cremona (*Atlante toponomastico della provincia di Cremona*, 1994-, 15 vols.). To bring on these researches, not only authorities and researchers were implicated, but also students of all ages attending the local schools: they in particular were in charge of the collection of all micro-toponyms. The interest of this project is made explicit at p. 3 of vol. 1:

> Per chi ami addentrarsi in un più stretto rapporto di conoscenza con il proprio territorio, può costituire motivo di interesse sapere che il nome di un paese, di una cascina, di un corso d'acqua o di una semplice località campestre ha significato preciso, anche se spesso non immediatamente evidente. Diviene allora appassionante scoprire nomi scaturiti da condizioni ambientali, morfologiche, vegetazionali precise; ovvero da situazioni legate alla storia locale, al costume; conservate nel toponimo stesso, attribuitogli magari più di mille anni fa.

Similarly, all IAM projects involve not only international researchers and authorities, but also local residents, thus promoting a multiplication of efforts, interests and awareness.

---

[1] The same author also published two works on zoology and botany in the same area of Cremona (cf. FERRARI 2010 and 2016).

For all toponyms already mentioned in the Gazetteer, the reader can refer to that section. Due to their local character, to the fact that this corpus includes quite only village, locality and pasture names, and that the valleys under observation are the most southern in Swāt, i.e. in the Tehsils of Barikot and Babuzai, all the nomenclature is recent and of Pashto origin, apart some exceptions (as, for instance, Besham and Lekha-gata).
The toponyms listed in this appendix are important for their historical character, but also for the nature of the underlying project, which, while investigating places known since the first British explorations in Swāt, opens to further future inquiries.

Toponyms

ABADI	'Inhabited (place)': Pšt. *ābād* 'populated, settled, inhabited; cultivated'.
ABBASAHEB-CHINA	'Source of Saheb Abba': Pšt. (← Ar.) *sāhíb* 'gentleman, sir, mister; owner'; Pšt. (← Ar.) *abā* 'father'.
AB-CHINA	'Source of Ab' or 'source of water': Pšt. *āb* (← Prs.) 'water'.
ABWA	See Gazetteer.
ALIDAD	'Hollow of Ali': Pšt. *ḍaḍ* 'hollow'. For *Ali°* cf. Gazetteer s.v. *Aligram.*
AMLUK	See Gazetteer.
AMLUKDARA	See Gazetteer.
ARABKHAN-CHINA	'Source of Khan Arab', person's name, or 'source of the Khan of the Arabs'.
ARABUT	See Gazetteer s.v. Arbut.
ASHARAI	See Gazetteer.
ASHTARAI-GHAR	The first element of this toponym is not clear. It is probably a loanword in Pashto from Arabic (*išti-*). It could be *ištihārí* 'proclamation, announcement': 'Mountain (*γar*) of the proclamation'.
BADAMA	Cf. Pšt. *bādāmá* 'snowstorm' or Pšt. *bādā́m* 'almond tree'.
BADZE	'Bad (*bad*) place (*zay*)'.
BAGH-DERI	'Hill/residence (cf. Glossary of Geonyms) of the garden (*bāγ*)'.
BALAH-KALAI	'Upper (*bālā*) village (*kəlay*)'.
BANDU-CHINA	'Source of the pastures (*bānḍa*, pl. obl.)'.
BANG-DOGHAL	Pšt. 'hole/pit/hollow (*ḍuγál*) of the hemp (*cannabis sativa*)'.
BANG-KHAS	'Brushwood (*xas*) of hemp'.
BANJ-GHWANDAI	'Hill (*γwənḍəy*) of the oak (*banǰ*)'.
BANJOT	See Gazetteer.
BARA-JAMSARA	'Upper Jamsara (unkn.: IA origin?)'.

BARA-KAMAL-CHINA — 'Upper beautiful/perfect (*kamāl*) spring (*čina*)'.

BAR-SANDOK — 'Upper Sandok (see Gazetteer)'.

BAZAR-KHELA-KANDERAI — 'Market of the tribe (*xel*) of the ruins (Pšt. *kanḍár*, *kanḍər*)'.

BAZDRA — See Gazetteer s.v. Barikot.

BEGUM-KOT — 'Fort of the lady'.

BESHAM — Cf. the name of the main city in the Shangla District. For the etymology cf. perhaps T12124 *vēśá* 'inhabitant (of a *víś*-), neighbour' [*víś*- 'tribe, habitation']: Kho. Kal. rumb. *gram-bešu* 'neighbour'. On the base of this latter comparison, we could hypothesize a **beś-gram* > *beśam* 'neighbour village'.

BILA-TANGAI — For the first part cf. Gazetteer s.v. *Biladram*, + 'gorge'.

BILKANAI — Cf. prec. + *kāṇay* 'stone, rock'.

BOLIGRAM — Cf. foll.

BOLOGRAM — See Gazetteer s.v. Bolat? + *grām* 'village'. Or see Gazetteer s.v. Balogram.

BUTKARA — According to HAKIMZAY (1997: 31-32), its meaning is 'house (*kāṛa*) of Buddha (*buṭ*)': in this place, indeed, a sacred area with stupa has been found.

CHINA — 'Source, spring (*čina*)'.

CHINA-BARA — 'Upper (*bar*) source'.

CHIRGAI-GAT — 'Stone (*gaṭ*) of the hen (*čirgay*)'.

CHURKAI — See Gazetteer s.v. Churkhai?

CHURRAI — See Gazetteer s.v. Churarai.

CHUWA — See Gazetteer.

DAB — Pšt. *ḍab* 'hollow, depression'.

DABAGAI — Variant of Dabargai (see Gazetteer): Pšt. *ḍabára* 'stone, rock, pebble' and *ḍabarkə́y, ḍabargə́y* 'pebble'? Or cf. Pšt. *ḍabá* 'place of assembly; low mound of earth along the walls of a peasant's house; center (of a market)' + dim. sf. *-gay*.

DANDI — Cf. foll.

DANDI-SAR — See Gazetteer s.v. Dandai-sar.

DANGRAM — See Gazetteer.

DARANA — Cf. Pšt. *draná* (f. of *drund*) 'heavy'?

DAUD-BANDAI — 'Pasture of Daud (person's name)'.

DHERI — See Gazetteer.

DODEHARRA — See Gazetteer s.v. Dadhra-khwar?

DRE-BANDAI — See Gazetteer.

DUR-BANDAI — 'Distant (*dur*) pasture'.

DWAGALAI — 'Two flocks (Pšt. *gal(l)á*)'?

DWOLASMANE-PATAI	'Field (*paṭay*) worth 12 (*dwolas*) *mane*', i.e. 'a rich, productive field'; *mana* is a a weight unit; *maṇe* could also be read as 'apples'.
ELANAI-KAMAR	For *kamar* 'precipice; steep cliff', cf. Glossary of Geonyms. For Elanai cf. Pšt. *ilbánd* 'summer pasture, mountain medow' and *ilonai* 'kind of plant belonging to the group of zyziphus': see Gazetteer s.v. Ilanai.
GALIKO-DHERI	For the first element cf. Pšt. *gəlega* 'unplowed land'? + *dheri* 'hillock'.
GARAM	Possibly Pšt. *garəm* 'hot'.
GARASA	See Gazetteer.
GAT-PATAI	'Field (*pəṭay*) of the stone (*gáṭa*)'.
GHADIAR	Cf. Pšt. (← Ar.) *γadír* 'lake'? Or cf. Pšt. (← Ar.) *γadə́y* 'robbery, banditry, brigandage'?
GHAR-PATAI	'Field (*pəṭay*) of the mountain (*γar*)'.
GHOBA-KHEL	'Tribe (*xel*) of cowherds': cf. Pšt. *γobún*, *γobá* 'herdsman, cowherd, drover'.
GHWANDAI	Pšt. *γwənḍəy* 'hill'.
GIRBAN/MANAGOSAR	Possibly Pšt. *ger* 'enclosed with a fence' + *baṇ* 'garden': 'garden enclosed'.
GOGDARA	See Gazetteer.
GORATAI	See Gazetteer.
GORATAI-KANDAO	Cf. prec.
GULISAR	See Gazetteer.
GUMBAT	'Cupola (*gumbad*)'.
GUMBATKE-CHINA	'Spring of the small cupola', cf. Gumbat.
GUMBAT-PATAI	'Field of the cupola', cf. Gumbat.
GUMBATUNA	'Cupolas' (pl.), cf. Gumbat.
GURNAI	Cf. RAVERTY (1888: 237): Gurnai 'village'.
GWAREJO-PATAI	'Field of the herd of cattle' (Pšt. *guwā́r*)? Sf. *-ǰo*? See Gazetteer s.v. Ghurejo and Ghorejai.
GWEL[ANGASO]-DHERAI	To be read *gwəluna-kaso*: '*ḍheri* of the land (*kas*: see Gazetteer s.v.) of flowers (*gwəl*)'.
HAKIM/BARIKOT	See Gazetteer s.v. Barikot.
HISAR	Pšt. (← Ar.) *hisā́r* 'stronghold, fort, fortification'.
INZAR-BANDAI	See Gazetteer s.v. Inzaro-banda.
JABBRAI	See Gazetteer s.v. Jabrai.
JAHANGIR	Person's name.
JALALAI	Cf. *jalālay ow kamālay* 'the name of two hills on the Indus a little below Aṭṭak' (RAVERTY). Cf. Pšt. (← Ar.) *ǰalāl* 'dignity, grandeur, state' or Pšt. *ǰəlā́lai* 'spring'.
JAMBIL	See Gazetteer.
JAURBANDA-GHAR	'Mountain of Jaur-banda (see Gazetteer)'.

JAWAN-KOTE	'Rooms (*koṭe*, pl. of *koṭa*) of the young (*jwān*)'.
JERANDO-DAG	Pšt. *žránda* 'water-mill' + *ḍāg* 'dale, plain, flatland (as contrasted to forest or mountains)': 'plain of the water-mill'.
JOWAR-[JABAGAI]	'Small (*-gay*) marshy field (*ǰabá*) of corn (*ǰowār*)'.
JOWAR-BANDAI	'Pasture of the corn (*ǰowār*)'.
KAFIR-KOT	'Fort (*koṭ*) of the infidels'. This toponym is quoted also by DEANE (1895).
KAKAI-KANDAO	See Gazetteer.
KALKATA	To be read *Kal(ā)-koṭe* (OLIVIERI, p.c.): 'rooms of the castle (*qalā́*)'.
KAMAL-CHINA	'Beautiful/perfect (*kamāl*) spring (*čina*)'.
KANDAK	See Gazetteer.
KANDAK-DHERAI	Cf. prec. + Glossary of Geonyms s.v. Derai.
KANDARAI	Pšt. *kándra, kándara* 'ravine, hollow, depression'. Cf. also foll.
KANDERAI	Cf. prec., but also Pšt. *kanḍár*, *kanḍə́r* 'ruins' and *kanḍə́ray* 'burdock that has gotten stuck in the wool of sheep'.
KANJAR-KOTE	'Rooms (*koṭe*, pl. of *koṭa*) of the kanǰaṇ (? Cf. RAVERTY *kanǰaṇ* 'large wooden shaft or axle of a Persian wheel' or T2628 *kañjara-* 'peacock': Kati *kaǰuřák* 'a partic. bird'; Kal. *kanǰə́ř, °ǰəř* 'a large black bird'?)'.
KARAKAR-KANDAO	See Gazetteer.
KATELAI	See Gazetteer.
KAUDERE-PATAI	'Field (*pəṭay*) of the potsherds (*kawdə́ray*, *kawdə́rkay* 'shard, potsherd, fragment').
KHWAZAKHELA	See Gazetteer.
KILARANO-TANGAI	'Gorge of the villagers (?)'.
KOLAI	See Gazetteer s.v. Kulai?
KOTAH	See Gazetteer.
KUKRAI	See Gazetteer.
KULIA	See Gazetteer s.v. Kuliya.
KUZ-JAMSARA	Cf. Bara-jamsara.
KUZ-JOWAR-BANDAI	Cf. Jowar-bandai.
LEKHA-GATA	'Inscribed (Hindko *lekha*, OLIVIERI, p.c.) stone (*gáṭa*)'. For *lexa* cf. T11101 *lēkha* 'line, stroke; writing': Pa. *lēkha-* 'writing' and T11107 *lḗkhā* 'scratch, streak, line': Pa. *lēkhā-* 'scratch, line'.
LOEBANR-JURJURAI	For the first part of the name cf. Gazetteer s.v. Loe-banr.
MAISHKANO-KANDAO	According to OLIVIERI, p.c., 'pass of the beggar (*miskin*, ← Ar.)'.
MAISHKANO-MAIDAN	'Place of the sheep (*meš/meğ*) rock (*kāṇa*)'. Cf. prec.

MALAK-ZIARAT	'Sanctuary (*ziyārat*) of the angel/ owner (*malak*)'.
MANGALKOT/MINGWALTHAN	'Fort of the Mangal': cf. Gazetteer s.v. Mangaltan.
MANGLAOR	See Gazetteer.
MANICHINAR	'Autumnal (*mənay*) poplar tree (*činār*)'?
MANYAR	See Gazetteer.
MANZARE	'Tiger/lion'.
MANZARE-TANGAI	'Gorge (*tangáy*) of the tiger/lion'.
MARANO-TANGAI	'Defile (*tangáy*) of the snakes (*marāno*)'.
MASUM-SHAHID	'Child-martyr (*šāhíd* ← Ar.)' or person's name.
MATA-BARA	'Upper Mata (Pšt. *maṭa* 'clay-soil, marl': see Gazetteer s.v. Matta)'.
MENA	Pšt. 'residence, dwelling, abode'.
MERAGAI	See Gazetteer.
MIAGE	Cf. Pšt. *myā* 'title given to holy men, master, sir' (RAVERTY).
MIAGE-SAR	'Peak of Miage', cf. prec.
MIA-KOTE	See Gazetteer s.v. Miankote.
MIANDAM	See Gazetteer.
MINGAORA	See Gazetteer.
MORPANDAI	'Village (Panj. *piṇḍ*: see Gazetteer s.v. Matrapendai) of the mother/peacock/ant (*mor*)'.
MUHAMMAD-PATAI	'Field of Muhammad (person's name)'.
MULLA-HASAN	Person's name.
NAITMARA	See Gazetteer s.v. Natmaira.
NAJIGRAM	See Gazetteer.
NAKHTAR-PATAI	'Field of the pine tree'.
NARE-TANGAI	'Narrow (*nare*) gorge'.
NAWAGAI	See Gazetteer s.v. Nawagay.
NAWARALE-TANGAI	'Gorge of the small water reservoir (*nāwə́r* 'water reservoir, shallow lake' + dim. sf. *-lay*)'.
NAWE-KALAI	See Gazetteer.
NINGULAI-KOTAL	'Pass of Ningulai (see Gazetteer s.v.)'.
NIRBAZAI	To be possibly read (OLIVIERI, p.c.) Nərbaz 'male (*nər*) he-goat (*baz*)'.
NOOR-BAND-GUMBAT	'Light (*nur*) bond (*band*) cupola (*gumbad*)'.
PAKKADHERI	Possibly, among many options, Pšt. 'clean (*pāk*, f. *pāka*) hillock (*ḍheri*)'.
PALWANO-GATA	'Boulder (*gáṭa* 'rock/pebble') of the giants'.
PANR	See Gazetteer.
PARLA-BANDA-DAMAZAI	'Place of rest (*dama-jāy*, or place of the Dums?), adjoining (*pə́rla*) the pasture'.
PARRAI	See Gazetteer.

PORE-TANGAI 'Gorge on the opposite side (*pore*)'.

PRANG-TANGAI 'Gorge of the tiger/lion (*pṛāng*)'.

QALA/NANGRIAL For the first name, cf. Gazetteer. For the second one, cf. Ur. *naṅgā* 'naked, nude, bare' or T6924 *nagará-* 'town': Pa. *nagara-*, °*rī-* 'stronghold, city', Pkt. *ṇagara-*, °*rī-*; Kho. *nogór* 'fort, castle'; and T6925 *nagarīya* 'belonging to a town' + sf. *-āl* (cf. Gazetteer s.v. Mankial).

RAGAST Could it be a derivative of the root *rañj-* 'to colour' (cf. T10583 *rajyatē* 'is dyed, is coloured red')? Cf. for instance Ur. *ragat* 'blood' and *raṅgat* 'colouring; tint; complexion' (PLATTS).

RASHO-DHERAI 'Hillock of provisions (*raša* 'heap of grain, supply', pl. obl., RAVERTY)'.

REDAWAN According to ASLANOV, it could be Pšt. *redwā́n*, *rebdún* '*Tesota undulata*, a tree'.

SAFAR-KANDAO 'Pass of the journey (*safar*)'.

SAIDU SHARIF See Gazetteer.

SALAMPUR See Gazetteer s.v. Islampur.

SAMGALAI 'Plain (*sam*) flocks (Pšt. *gal(l)á*)'?

SANCHAR Probably related to T12869 *saṁcāra* 'walking about, passage, transit': Pa. *sañcāra-* 'entrance, passage, road'; Pkt. *saṁcāra-* 'going'.

SANDA-SAR 'Mountain (*sar*) of the buffalo (*sanḍa*)'?

SANDOK See Gazetteer.

SANDOK-TANGAI Cf. prec.

SARDARI See Gazetteer.

SARGAH-SAR 'Peak of the head': *sarγa* means 'the place of the head, or face', while the suffix *-sar* indicates any peak or hill top. See above *Lal-kamar*. Cf. also EILERS 1987: 25 (*saxt(e)-sar* 'difficult pass').

SHAGA-MALKIDAM 'Sandy (*šəga* 'sand') low land (*malkidam*, OLIVIERI, p.c.)'.

SHAHR-BANDA 'Pasture of the city (*šahr*)'.

SHAKHORAI Cf. Pšt. *škoray* 'flat basket with a cover like a tray, made of cane, grass or wood' (RAVERTY).

SHANKU See Gazetteer.

SHNAISHA The first part could be Pšt. *šin* 'green' or *šna* 'grass, hay' + a non attested adj. sf. *-šā* → 'greenish'?

SHORGHAR 'Mountain (*γar*) of the noise (*šor*)'.

SKA-CHINA According to OLIVIERI, p.c., the meaning of this toponym is 'dirty (*sxā* 'rotten, decayed, putrid, rank, stinking, offensive', RAVERTY) spring'. Another improbable meaning could be that of 'potable (cf. Pšt. *cx̌əl* 'to drink', in the local pronunciation *skəl*) spring (*čina*)'.

SPERKI-GUMBAT	'Grayish (*sperkáy* 'grayish, ash-colored') cupola (*gumbad*)'.
SPINUBO	'White/transparent (*spin*) waters (*obə*)'.
SUPAL-BANDAI	See Gazetteer s.v. Supal-banda.
SURAI-TANGE	See Gazetteer.
SUR-KAMAR	See Gazetteer.
TAHSILDAR[SEP]-KABIRUNA	Administrative place of the Tahsildār (the head of the Tahsil).
TALANG	See Gazetteer.
TANARE-GHARAI	Possibly to be read *tāṇaṛay-γāṛe* 'bank (*γāṛa*) of the small guard post (*tāṇa* + dim. sf. *-ṛay*)'.
TANGAI-KOTE	'Rooms (*koṭa*) of the ravine (*tangay*)' or better 'narrow (*tang*, f. pl. *tange*) rooms'.
TAPA	Possibly Pšt. *təpá* 'mountain, hill, mound; high place; region, province'.
TILGRAM	See Gazetteer.
TINDO-DAG	See Gazetteer s.v. Tendo-dak.
TOKAR-DARA	Cf. Pšt. *ṭukə́rkay* 'broken piece of pottery; fragment' and *ṭukə́r* 'piece, part' → 'valley of the pieces of pottery'?
TOK-DARA	Cf. prec.
TOP-CHINA	'Spring of the cap (*ṭop*)'. See Gazetteer s.v. Topsin for the explanation of Pšt. *ṭop* 'cap', but often → 'temple'.
TOP-DARA	'Valley of the cap (*ṭop*)'. Cf. prec.
TOP-DARA/SHANDALA	Cf. prec.
TOPE-CHINA	Cf. Top-china.
TOPIALAI	'Small cap (*ṭop* + dim. sf. *-yālay*)'. Cf. Top-china.
TOR-GUMBAT	'Black (*tor*) cupola (*gumbad*)'.
TOR-KAMAR	See Gazetteer.
TORKMARA-PATAI	Cf. prec.
UDEGRAM	See Gazetteer s.v. Udigram.
UECH-TANGAI	'Dry (*wəč*) gorge'.
ULU-TANGAI	'Gorge of the flocks (*olə́*, obl. pl.)'.
USMANI	Person's name.
WAINAI	See Gazetteer.
ZINDWALA	See Gazetteer.

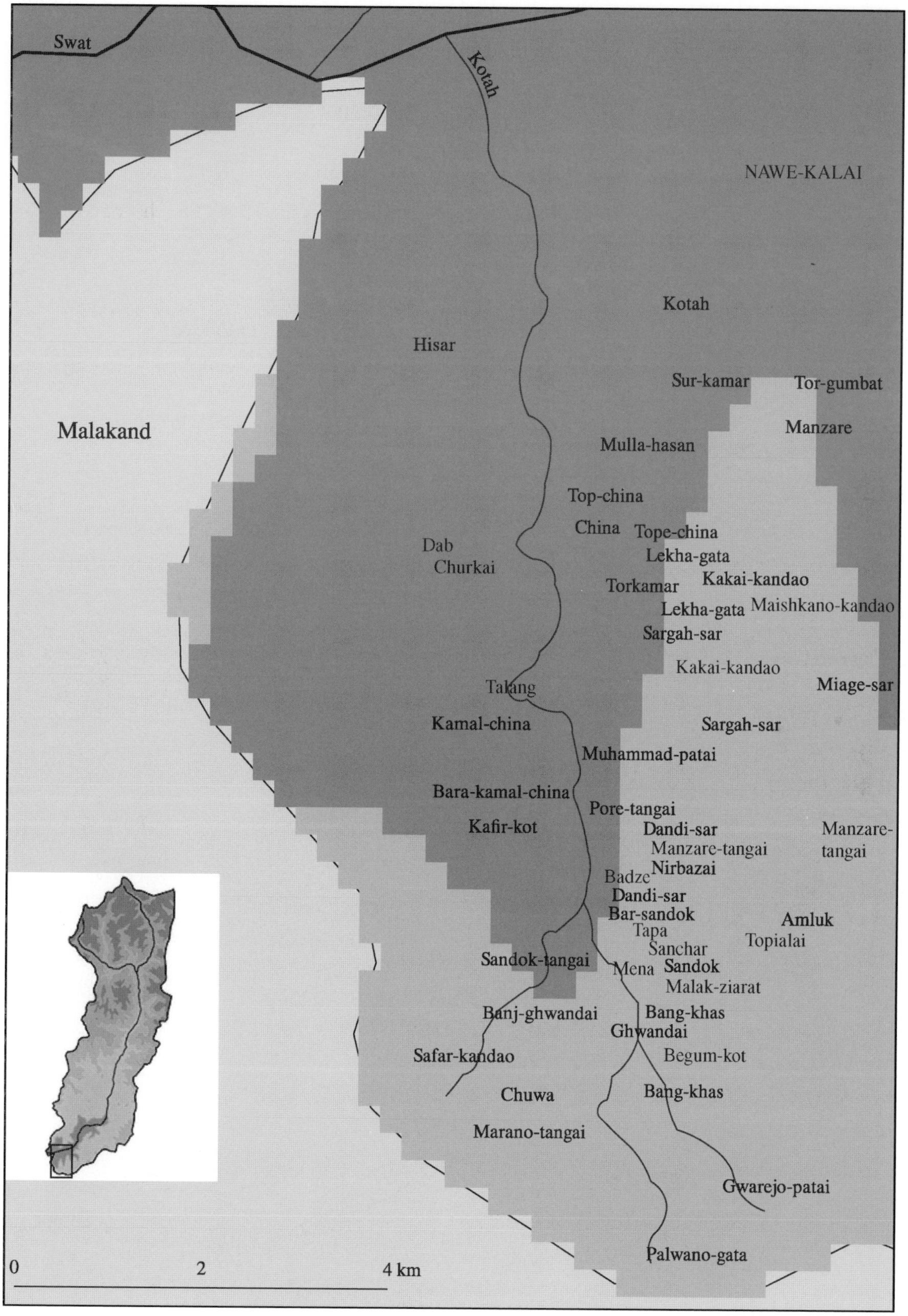

Fig. 38. Micro-toponymy of the Kotah-khwar valley.

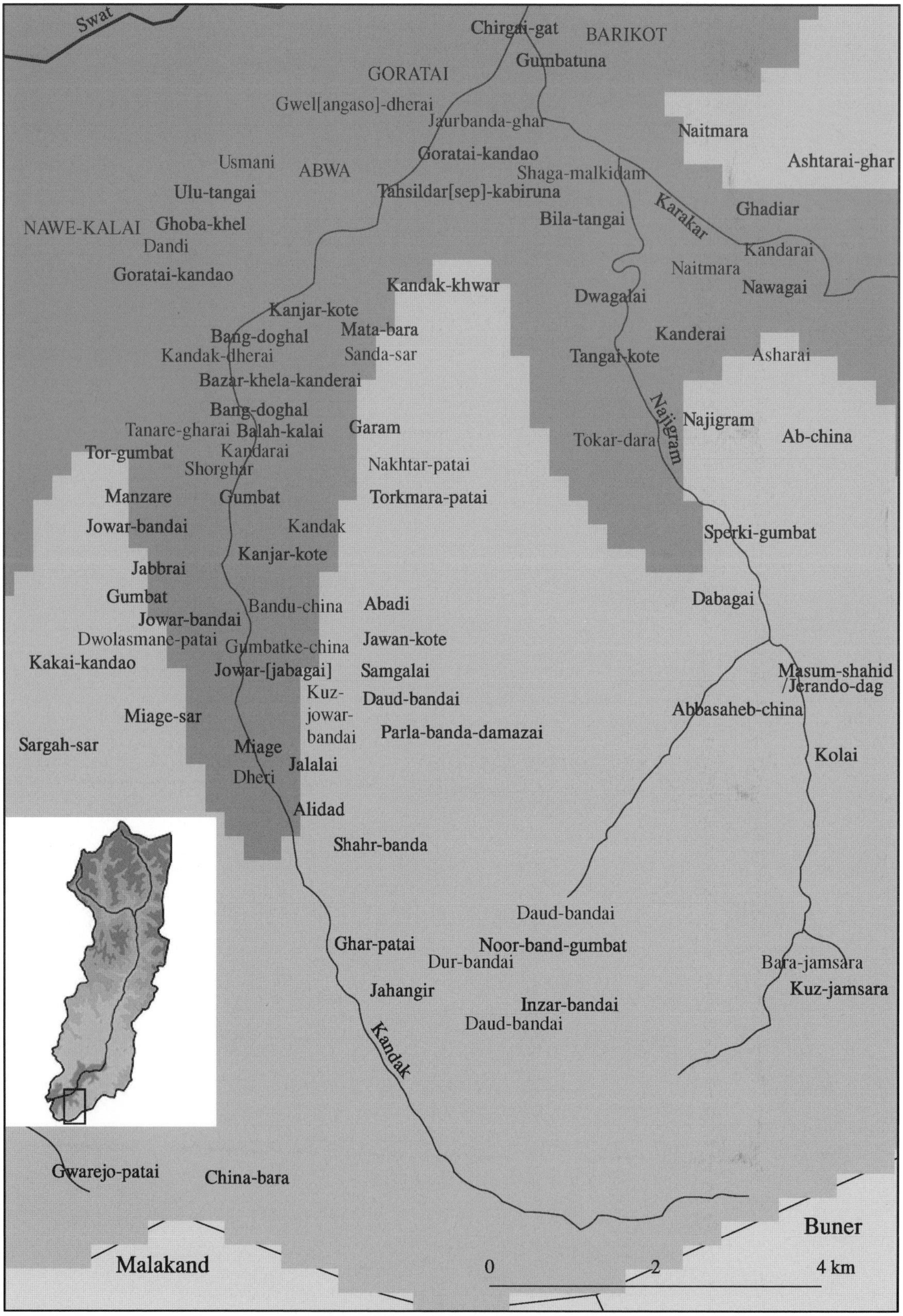

Fig. 39. Micro-toponymy of the Kandak-khwar valley.

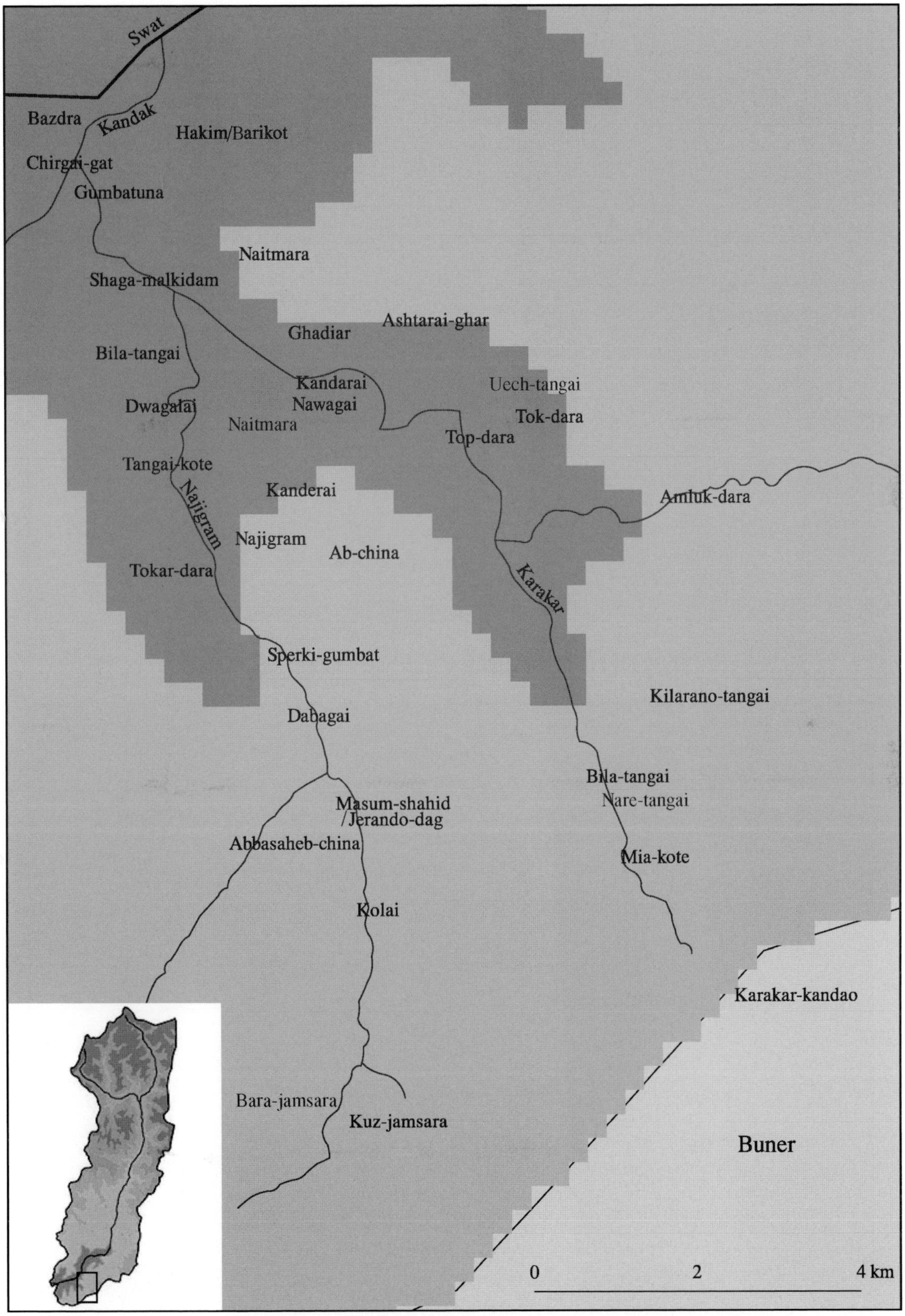

Fig. 40. Micro-toponymy of the Najigram-khwar and Karakar-khwar valleys.

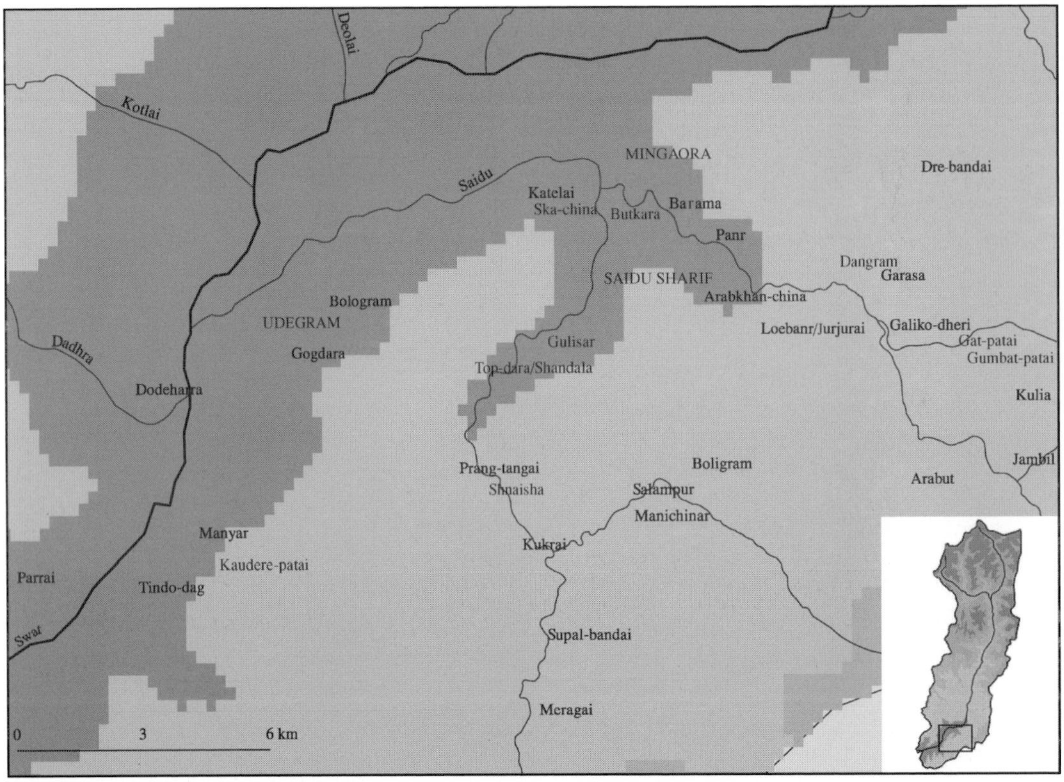

Fig. 41. Micro-toponymy of the Saidu-khwar valley.

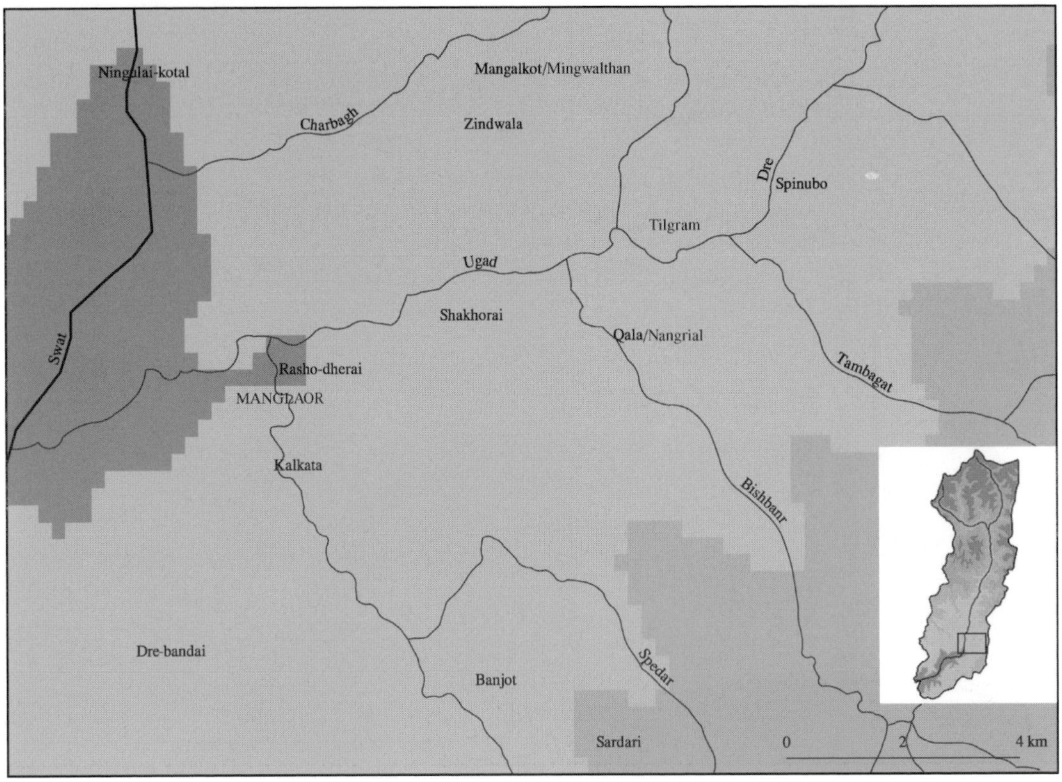

Fig. 42. Micro-toponymy of the Ugad-khwar valley.

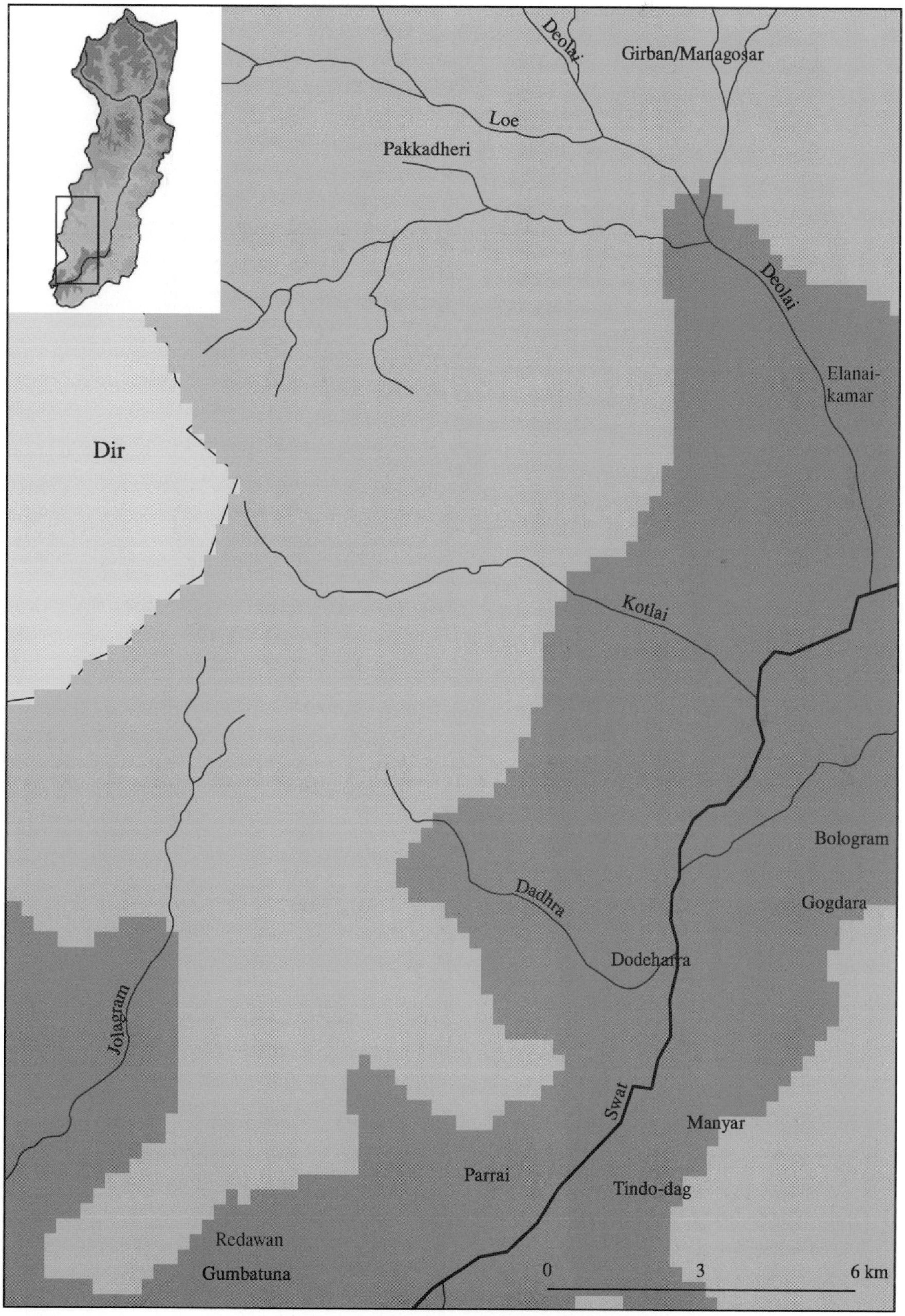

Fig. 43. Micro-toponymy in Kabal.

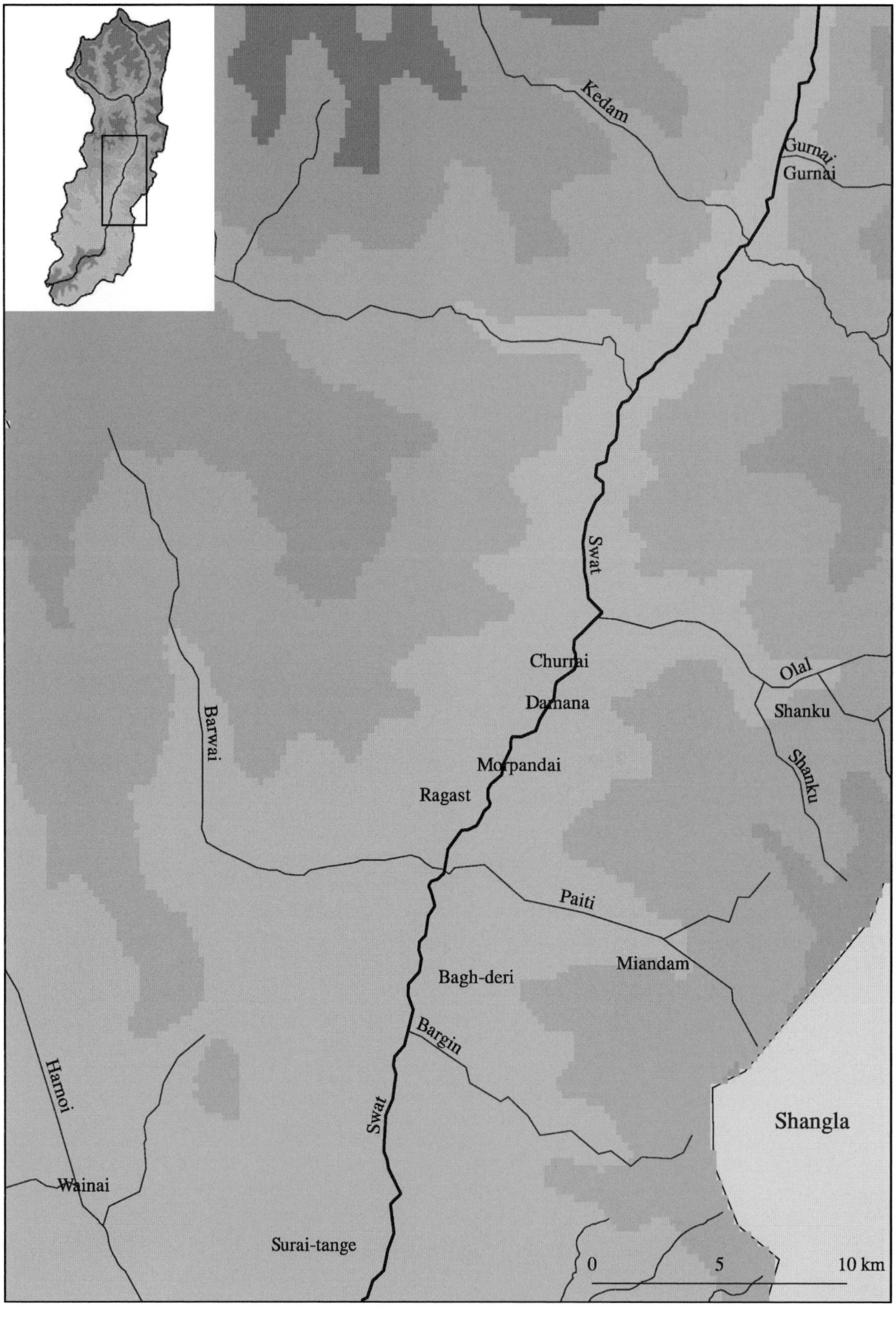

Fig. 44. Micro-toponymy in the north.

BIBLIOGRAPHY

ABBOTT, J. (1854) Gradus ad Aornon. *Journal of the Royal Asiatic Society of Bengal*, pp. 338-344.

ADAMEC, L.W., ed. (1972-1985) *Historical and political gazetteer of Afghanistan*, 6 vols. Graz.

AFTAB AHMAD (2015) *Torwali-Urdu-English Dictionary*. Bahrain, Swāt.

AGRAWALA, V.S. (1953) *India as known to Pāṇini (A Study of the Cultural Material of the Ashṭādhyāyī)*. Lucknow.

AKBAR, W. (2015) *Dictionnaire général pashto-français*. Paris.

ALAM, M. (2011) *Trees and Shrubs in Afghanistan*. Lausanne.

ALTHEIM, F. and R. STIEHL (1970) *Geschichte Mittelasiens im Altertum*. Berlin.

ANDREEV, M.S. and E.M. PEŠČEREVA (1957) *Jagnobskie Teksty*. Moscow-Leningrad.

ARRIAN (1983) *Anabasis of Alexander, Volume II: Books 5-7. Indica*. Transl. by P.A. BRUNT. Cambridge, MA.

ASLANOV, M.G. (1966) *Afgansko-russkij slovar' (pushtu)*. Moskva.

ASSADORIAN, A. (2017) On the Systematic Classification of Iranian Toponyms. *American Journal of Linguistics*, 5, pp. 51-56.

ATAYEE, Ibrahim M. (1358/1979) *A Dictionary of the Terminology of Pashtun's Tribal Customary Law and Usages*. Translated into English by A. Mohammad SHINWARY, International Centre for Pashto Studies, Academy of Sciences of Afghanistan. Kabul.

BAART, J.L. (1999) *A sketch of Kalam Kohistani grammar*. Islamabad.

BAART, J.L. and M.L. SAGAR (2004) *Kalam Kohistani texts*. Islamabad.

BAILEY, H.W. (1946) Gāndhārī. *Bulletin of the School of Oriental and African Studies*, 11, pp. 764-797.

BALALA, A.Q. (2000) *The Charming Swat*. Lahore.

BALLAND, D. (1999) Fayzābād. In *Encyclopedia Iranica*, IX, pp. 456-457.

Baluchistan District Gazetteer Series, vol. VIII - *Las Bela*. Allahabad, 1907.

BARATIERI, O. (1879), L'Afghanistan e le campagne di Alessandro nel Caucaso Indiano. *La Nuova Antologia*, XVIII 48, pp. 645-671.

BARTH, F. (1956a) *Indus and Swat Kohistan, an Ethnographic Survey*. Oslo.

BARTH, F. (1956b) Ecologic Relationships of Ethnic Groups in Swat, North Pakistan. *American Anthropologist*, 58, pp. 1079-1089.

BARTH, F. (1959) *Political Leadership among Swat Pathans*. London.

BARTH, F. (1985) *The Last Wali of Swat: an Autobiography as told to Fredrik Barth*. Bangkok.

BARTH, F. and G. MORGENSTIERNE (1958) Vocabularies and Specimens of Some S.E. Dardic Dialects. *Norsk Tidsskrift for Sprogvidenskap*, 18, pp. 118-136.

BARTHOLOMAE, C. (1904) *Altiranisches Wörterbuch*. Strassburg.

BASHAM, A.L. (1975) *Cultural Heritage of India*. Oxford.

BASHIR, E. (2005) *A digital Khowar-English dictionary with audio: 1,000 words / compiled by Elena Bashir with Maula Nigah and Rahmat Karim Baig*. Chicago.

BAUMS, S. (2019) A survey of place-names in Gāndhārī inscriptions and a new oil lamp from Malakand. In W. RIENJANG and P. STEWART, eds., *The Geography of Gandhāran Art. Proceedings of the Second International Workshop of the Gandhāra Connections Project, University of Oxford, 22nd-23rd March, 2018*. Oxford, pp. 167-174.

BELLEW, H.W. (1864) *A General Report on the Yusufzais*. London.

BELLEW, H.W. (1867) *A Vocabulary of the Pukkhto or Pukshto Language*. London.

BIDDULPH, J. (1971) *Tribes of the Hindoo Koosh*. Graz. [1st ed.: Calcutta, 1880.]

BUDDRUSS, G. (1960) *Die Sprache von Wotapur und Katarqala*. Bonn.

BUDDRUSS, G. (1967) *Die Sprache von Sau in Ostafghanistan: Beiträge zur Kenntnis des Dardischen Phalūra*. Munich.

Burrow, Th. (1943) Dravidian Studies III. *Bulletin of the School of Oriental and African Studies*, 11, pp. 122-139.

Burrow, Th. (1945) Dravidian Studies V. *Bulletin of the School of Oriental and African Studies*, 11, pp. 595-616.

Burrow, Th. (1948) Dravidian Studies VII. *Bulletin of the School of Oriental and African Studies*, 12, pp. 365-396.

Caroe, O. (1958) *The Pathans*. Oxford.

Cheung, J. (2005) Review of NEVP. *Bulletin of the School of Oriental and African Studies*, 68, pp. 127-129.

Cheung, J. (2007) *Etymological Dictionary of the Iranian Verb*. Leiden-Boston.

Coletti, A. (1980) *Lessico della lingua Pashtu afghana e pakistana*. Roma.

Coloru, O. and L.M. Olivieri (2019) Mount Aornos and the Operations of the Macedonian Army in Swat. Sources and Archaeological Data. *Pakistan Heritage*, 11, pp. 105-121.

Court, M. (1836) Conjectures on the march of Alexander. *Journal of Asiatic Society*, pp. 387-395.

Cunningham, A. (1848) Corrispondence of the Commissioners Deputed to the Tibetan Frontier. *Journal of the Asiatic Society of Bengal*, XVII, pp. 89-132.

Cunningham, A. (1871) *The Ancient Geography of India. I. The Buddhist Period, including the campaigns of Alexander, and the travels of Hwen-Thsang*. London.

Dani, A.H., ed. (1967) *Timargarha and Gandhara Grave Culture*. Special issue of *Ancient Pakistan*, 3.

Darmesteter, J. (1888-1890) *Chants populaires des Afghans*. Paris.

Daryāb 1994 = Qalandar Momand (1994) *Daryāb Dictionary*. Peshawar.

Deane, H.A. (1895) Note on Udyana and Gandhara. Document 1/4 of the *Malakand Fort documentation, Folder one (8, 9/ XX: Miscellaneous/ 1/ Archaeology of the Swat Valley (For detailed index <see written>) Rules etc./Vol. I* [3253/600 (bottom left)] (see Olivieri 2015b: 33-34).

De Chiara, M. (2008) *Studi sulla fonetica storica e sulla lessicologia della lingua pashto*. PhD, University of Naples "L'Orientale", 2008. N.p.

De Chiara, M. (2015) Swat Toponymy. In Olivieri 2015a: 209-210.

De Chiara, M. (2015a) Turkish and Mongolian loanwords in Pashto. In M. De Chiara and E. Grassi, eds., *Iranian Languages and Literatures of Central Asia (from the eighteenth century to the present). Cahiers de Studia Iranica*, 57. Paris, pp. 67-97.

De Chiara, M. (2018) Les noms des saisons, des mois et des jours de la semaine à Swāt. In M. De Chiara, A.V. Rossi and D. Septfonds, eds., *Mélanges d'ethnographie et de dialectologie irano-aryennes à la mémoire de Charles-Martin Kieffer*. Paris, pp. 99-126.

De Chiara, M. (2019) Swāt Hydronymy at the Border between Iranian and Indo-Aryan Languages. *Iran and the Caucasus*, 23, pp. 64-74.

De Chiara, M. (forthcoming a) Pashtun Religiosity and Popular Traditions. In M. Carrin, ed.-in-chief, M. Boivin, G. Toffin, P. Hockings, R. Rousseleau, T. Subba, H. Lambs-Tyche, section eds., *BERIPSA* (*Brill's Encyclopedia of the Religions of the Indigenous People of South Asia Online*).

De Chiara, M. (forthcoming b) *Pashto Historical Phonetics*.

DED = Burrow, T. and M.B. Emeneau (1961) *A Dravidian Etymological Dictionary*. Oxford.

D'Erme, G.M. (1972) In margine al Dizionario Persiano-Italiano: il "Paese dell'Ischia di Mezzo". *Annali della Facoltà di Lingue e Letterature Straniere di Ca' Foscari. Sezione orientale*, 11, pp. 173-184.

DKS = H.W. Bailey (1979) *A Dictionary of Khotan Saka*. Cambridge.

Dodyxudojev, R.X. (1975) *Pamirskaja mikrotoponimija (Issljedovanije i materialy)*. Dušanbe.

Doerfer, G. (1963-1975) *Türkische und mongolische Elemente im Neupersischen*, 4 vols. Wiesbaden.

Dörfer, G. (1967) *Türkische Lehnwörter im Tadschikischen*. Wiesbaden.

Èdel'man, D.I. (1986) *Sravnitel'naja grammatica vostočnoiranskix jazykov, fonologija*. Moskva.

Edgerton, F. (1953) *Buddhist Hybrid Sanskrit Grammar and Dictionary*. 2 vols. New Haven.

Eggermont, P.H.L. (1975) *Alexander's Campaign in Sind and Baluchistan and the Siege of the Brahmin Town of Harmatelia*. Leuven.

Eggermont, P.H.L. (1984) Ptolemy, the Geographer, and the People of the Dards: Alexander in Buner, the Aornus Problem and the Dards of Dyrta. *Journal of Central Asia*, 7, pp. 73-123.

EILERS, W. (1954) Der Name Demawend. *Archiv Orientální*, 22, pp. 267-374.
EILERS, W. (1964) Kyros. Eine namenkundliche Studie. *Beiträge zur Namenforschung*, 15, pp. 180-236.
EILERS, W. (1987) *Iranische Ortsnamenstudien*. Wien.
ELFENBEIN, J. (1989) Balōčī. In R. SCHMITT, ed., *Compendium Linguarum Iranicarum*, Wiesbaden, pp. 350-362.
ELLIOT, H.M. (1867) *The History of India, as told by its own historians*. Vol. I, *The Muhammadan period*, J. Dowson, ed., pp. 366-367.
EMMERICK, R.E. (1970) Some Chorasmian and Khotanese Etymologies. *Journal of the Royal Asiatic Society*, pp. 67-70.
EP = W. GEIGER (1897) Etymologie und Lautlehre des Afghānischen. *Abhandlungen der Bayerischen Akademie der Wissenschaften, Phil.-hist. Klasse*, 20, 1. München, pp. 167-222.
ÈSIJ = V.S. RASTORGUEVA and D.I. ÈDEL'MAN (2000-) *Ètimologičeskij slovar' iranskix jazykov*, 5 vols. Moskva.
ÈSKJ = R.L. CABOLOV (2001-2010) *Ètimologičeskij slovar' kurdskogo jazyka*, 2 vols. Moskva.
EVP = G. MORGENSTIERNE (1927) *An Etymological Vocabulary of Pashto*. Oslo.
EVShG = G. MORGENSTIERNE (1974) *Etymological Vocabulary of the Shughni Group*. Wiesbaden.
EWAia = M. MAYRHOFER (1992-2003) *Etymologisches Wörterbuch des Altindoarischen*, 3 vols. Heidelberg.
FAQIR MUHAMMAD KHAN (n.p.) *Working Plan for the Lower Indus Kohistan and Buner Forests, Swat State (1964-1978)*.
FAUTZ, B. (1963) *Sozialstruktur und Bodennutzung in der Kulturlandschaft des Swat*. Giessen.
FAZAL KHALIQ (2014) *The Uddiyana Kingdom: the Forgotten Holy Land of Swat*. Lahore.
FERRARI, V., ed. (1994-) *Atlante toponomastico della provincia di Cremona*. 15 vols. Cremona.
FERRARI, V. (2010) *Lessico zoologico popolare della provincia di Cremona dialettale, etimologico*. Cremona.
FERRARI, V. (2016) *Lessico botanico popolare della provincia di Cremona dialettale, etimologico*. Cremona.
FILIGENZI, A. (2015) *Art and Landscape. Buddhist Rock Sculptures of Late Antique Swat / Uḍḍiyāna*. With contributions by L.M. OLIVIERI and a note by P. ROCKWELL. Wien.
FOUCHER, A. (1901) Notes sur la géographie ancienne du Gandhâra (Commentaire à un chapitre de Hiuen-Tsang). *Bulletin de l'École Française d'Extrême-Orient*, 1, pp. 322-369.
FUCHS, W. (1939) *Huei ch'ao's Pilgerreise durch Nordwestindien und Zentral-Asien um 726*. Phil.-hist. Klasse, XXX. Berlin.
FUSSMAN, G. (1972) *Atlas linguistique des parlers Dardes et Kafirs*, 2 vols. Paris.
Gazetteer of Pakistan (1983^3) Prepared by W.R. GARREN and C.R. PAGE. Names approved by the United States Board on Geographic Names. Washington.
General Staff Army Headquarters (1910) *A Dictionary of the Pathan Tribes on the North-West Frontier of India*. Calcutta.
GMS = I. GERSHEVITCH (1954) *A grammar of Manichaean Sogdian*. Oxford.
GODFREY, S.H. (1912) A Summer Exploration in the Panjkora Kohistan. *Geographical Journal*, 40, pp. 45-57.
GRIERSON, G.A. (1929) *Torwali. An Account of a Dardic Language of the Swat Kohistan*. London.
GRJUNBERG, A.L. and D.I. ÈDEL'MAN (1987) Afganskij jazyk [Pashto]. In *Osnovy iranskovo jazykoznanija* IV, pp. 1-154.
HAKIMZAY, W.Kh. (1997) *Daγa zmunǧ kəlay day*. Maṯṯa, Swāt.
HALLBERG, D. (1992 [2004^2]) *Pashto, Waneci, Ormuri*. Islamabad.
HAROON, S. (2007) *Frontier of Faith. Islam in the Indo-Afghan Borderland*. London.
HAYYIM, S. (1934-1936) *New Persian-English dictionary, complete and modern, designed to give the English meanings of over 50,000 words, terms, idioms, and proverbs in the Persian language, as well as the transliteration of the words in English characters. Together with a sufficient treatment of all the grammatical features of the Persian Language*. Teheran.

HINÜBER, O. von (2020) Addendum: The name of the city. In L.M. OLIVIERI, *Ceramics from the excavations in the historic settlement at Bīr-koṭ-ghwaṇḍai (Barikot) Swat, Pakistan (1984-1992). 1. The Study*. Lahore, pp. 54-55.
HISAM, Z. and A. VIARO (2002) *Mingora, the unplanned city*. Karachi.
HOPKINS, B.D. (2013) A History of the "Hindustani Fanatics" on the Frontier. In B.D. HOPKINS and M. MARSDEN, eds., *Beyond Swat. History, Society and Economy along the Afghanistan-Pakistan Frontier*. London, pp. 39-49.
HÜBSCHMANN, H. (1895) *Persische Studien*. Strassburg.
HÜBSCHMANN, H. (1897) *Armenische Grammatik I. Armenische Etymologie*. Leipzig.
IESOJ = V.I. ABAEV (1958-1995) *Istoriko-ètimologičeskij slovar' osetinskogo jazyka*, 5 vols. Moskva-Leningrad.
IIFL = G. MORGENSTIERNE (1929-1972) *Indo-Iranian Frontier Languages*, 6 vols. Oslo.
ILEB = A.V. ROSSI (1979) *Iranian Lexical Elements in Brāhūī*. Naples.
Imperial Gazetteer of India, Provincial Series, North-West Frontier Province, Oxford, 1908.
INAM-UR-RAHIM and A. VIARO (2002) *Swat. An Afghan Society in Pakistan. Urbanisation and Change in a Tribal Environment*. Karachi.
INAYAT-UR-RAHMAN (1968-1984) *Folk Tales of Swat*, 2 vols. Rome-Peshawar.
IORI, E. and L.M. OLIVIERI (forthcoming) Before Indo-Greek Bazira. Complexity and continuity in an early-Historic urban town (Swat, Pakistan).
JENNY, M. and P. SIDWELL, eds. (2014) *The Handbook of Austroasiatic Languages*. Leiden-Boston.
JUKES, A. (1900) *Dictionary of the Jatki or western Panjábi language*. Lahore.
KABIR, H. and W. AKBAR (1999) *Dictionnaire pashto-français*. Paris.
KABIR, H. and W. AKBAR (2005) *Dictionnaire français-pashto*. Paris.
KEWA = M. MAYRHOFER (1956-1980) *Kurzgefasstes etymologisches Wörterbuch des Altindischen*, 4 vols. Heidelberg.
KHAN, M.A. (1963) *The Story of Swat, as told by the Founder Miangul Abdul Wadud Badshah Sahib to Muhammad Asif Khan*. Transl. and Preface by A.A. HUSAIN. Peshawar.
KIEFFER, Ch.M. (1974) L'établissement des cartes phonétiques: premiers resultats. In G. REDARD, Ch.M. KIEFFER and S. SANA, *L'atlas linguistique des parlers iraniens: Atlas de l'Afghanistan*, Universität Bern. Institut für Sprachwissenschaft. Arbeitspapiere, 13. Bern, pp. 21-34.
KIEFFER, Ch.M. (1975) *Dialectologie du paṣ̌tō*. Distribution et typologie des parlers *paṣ̌tō* d'après les premières cartes de l'Atlas linguistique de l'Afghanistan (ALA). In *Colloque sur l'établissement d'un Centre d'étude de la langue et de la littérature paṣ̌tō, Caboul, 22-29 novembre 1975*. N.p.
KIRAKOSIAN, H. (2015) Les traces de l'iranien ancien **sikā-* « pierre » dans la toponymie iranienne. *Iran & the Caucasus*, 19, pp. 269-276.
KRAHE, H. (1949) *Ortsnamen als Geschichtsquelle*. Heidelberg.
KUIPER, F.B.J. (1934) Zur Geschichte der indoiranischen *s*-Präsentia. *Acta Orientalia*, 16, pp. 190-306.
KUIPER, F.B.J. (1938) Indo-Iranica. *Acta Orientalia*, 16, pp. 203-220, 295-326.
KUIPER, F.B.J. (1948) *Proto-Munda Words in Sanskrit*. Amsterdam.
KUIPER, F.B.J. (1950) *An Austro-Asiatic myth in the RV*. Amsterdam.
KUIPER, F.B.J. (1955) Rigvedic loanwords. In O. SPIES, ed., *Studia Indologica: Festschrift für Willibald Kirfel zur Vollendung seines 70. Lebensjahres*. Bonn, pp. 137-185.
KUIPER, F.B.J. (1991) *Aryans in the Rigveda*. Amsterdam-Atlanta, GA.
LASSEN, Ch. (1861-1874^2) *Indische Altertumskunde*. 4 Vols. Lepzig-Bonn-London.
LAUFER, B. (1919) *Sino-Iranica. Chinese Contributions to the History of Civilization in Ancient Iran. With Special Reference to the History of Cultivated Plants and Products*. Chicago.
LEECH, R. (1839) A grammar of the Pashtoo or Afghanee language. *Journal of the Royal Asiatic Society of Bengal*, pp. 1-16.
LÉVI, S. (1915) Le Catalogue géographique des Yakṣa dans la Mahāmāyūrī. *Journal Asiatique*, 11.5, pp. 19-138.
LORIMER, D.L.R. (1915) *Pashtu, part I. Syntax of Colloquial Pashto*. Oxford.
LSI = G.A. GRIERSON (1921) *Linguistic Survey of India*, vol. X: *Eranian Languages*. Calcutta.
MACDONELL, A.A. (1929) *Practical Sanskrit dictionary with transliteration, accentuation, and etymological analysis throughout*. London.

MacKenzie, D.N. (1970) *The 'Sūtra of the causes and effects of actions' in Sogdian*. London.
Marquart, J. von (1905) *Untersuchungen zur Geschichte von Eran*, 2 vols. Leipzig.
Masica, C. (1991) *The Indo-Aryan Languages*. Cambridge.
McCrindle, J.W. (1893) *The Invasion of India by Alexander the Great: as Described by Arrian, Q. Curtius, Diodoros, Plutarch and Justin*. Westminster.
McMahon, A.H. and A.D.G. Ramsay (1916) *Report on the Tribes of the Malakand Political Agency (Exclusive of Chitral)*. Peshawar.
McMahon, A.H. and A.D.G. Ramsay (1981^2 [1901]) *Report on the Tribes of Dir, Swat and Bajour together with the Utman-Khel and Sam Ranizai*. Peshawar.
Mokri, M. (1997) *Le nom de vallée dans les toponymes iraniens*. Paris.
Monchi-Zadeh, D. (1990) *Wörter aus Xurāsān und ihre Herkunft*. Leiden.
Monier-Williams, M. (1899) *A Sanskrit-English dictionary*. Oxford.
Morgenstierne, G. (1925) Afghan *kōr* 'maison'. *Bulletin de la Société Linguistique de Paris*, 25, p. 65.
Morgenstierne, G. (1926) *Report on a Linguistic Mission to Afghanistan*. Oslo.
Morgenstierne, G. (1930a) Notes on Torwali. *Acta Orientalia*, 8, pp. 294-310.
Morgenstierne, G. (1930b) The name *Munjān* and some other names of places and peoples in the Hindu Kush. *Bulletin of the School of Oriental Studies*, 6, pp. 439-444.
Morgenstierne, G. (1931) The Story of an Afridi sepoy. In *Studia Indo-Iranica. Ehrengabe für W. Geiger*. Leipzig, pp. 289-300.
Morgenstierne, G. (1932) Supplementary notes on Ormuri. *Norsk Tidsskrift for Sprogvidenskap*, 5, pp. 5-36.
Morgenstierne, G. (1940) Notes on Bashkarīk. *Acta Orientalia*, 18, pp. 206-257.
Morgenstierne, G. (1941) *Notes on Phalūṛa. An unknown Dardic Language of Chitral*. Oslo.
Morgenstierne, G. (1942a) Additional Pashto Etymologies. *Norsk Tidsskrift for Sprogvidenskap*, 12, pp. 261-265.
Morgenstierne, G. (1942b) Notes on Dameli, a Kafir-Dardic language of Chitral. *Norsk Tidsskrift for Sprogvidenskap*, 12, pp. 115-198.
Morgenstierne, G. (1945) Notes on Shumashti, a Dardic dialect of the Gawar-Bati type. *Norsk Tidsskrift for Sprogvidenskap*, 13, pp. 239-281.
Morgenstierne, G. (1950) *Notes on Gawar-Bati*. Oslo.
Morgenstierne, G. (1954) The Waigali Language. *Norsk Tidsskrift for Sprogvidenskap*, 17, pp. 146-324.
Morgenstierne, G. (1957) Sanskritic words in Khowar. In *Felicitation Volume presented to S.K. Bevalkar*. Banaras, pp. 84-98 [= Morgenstierne 1973: 256-272]
Morgenstierne, G. (1973) *Irano-Dardica*. Wiesbaden.
Morgenstierne, G. and A. Lloyd-James (1928) Notes on the pronunciation of Pashto (dialect of the Hazara District). *Bulletin of the School of Oriental Studies*, 5, pp. 53-62.
NEVP = G. Morgenstierne (2004) *A New Etymological Vocabulary of Pashto*. Compiled and edited by J. Elfenbein, D.N. MacKenzie and N. Sims-Williams. Wiesbaden.
Olivieri, L.M. (1996) Notes on the Problematical Sequence of Alexander's Itinerary in Swat. A Geo-historical Approach. *East & West*, 46, pp. 45-78.
Olivieri, L.M. (2004) Late Protohistoric Painted Shelters from Swat Valley (North Pakistan). In E. Anati, ed., *XXI Valcamonica Symposium*. Capo di Ponte, pp. 373-375.
Olivieri, L.M. (2005) Gogdara I and Beyond. The Cultural Sequence of the Non-Buddhist Rock Art in Swat Valley. Preliminary Conclusions. In U. Franke-Vogt and H.J. Weisshaar, eds., *South Asian Archaeology 2003*, Aachen. pp. 215-222.
Olivieri, L.M. (2006a) The IsIAO Italian Archaeological Mission in Pakistan. A Selected Bibliography (1956-2006). *East and West*, 56, dedicated to the 50th Anniversary of the IsIAO Archaeological Mission in Pakistan (1956-2006), L.M. Oliveri, ed., pp. 301-318.
Olivieri, L.M. (2006b) Outline History of the IsIAO Italian Archaeological Mission in Pakistan (1956-2006). *East and West*, 56, dedicated to the 50th Anniversary of the IsIAO Archaeological Mission in Pakistan (1956-2006), L.M. Oliveri, ed., pp. 23-42.
Olivieri, L.M. (2009a) *Swat. Storia di una frontiera*. Roma.

OLIVIERI, L.M. (2009b) Archaeology in Swat: Activities and Challenges of the Italian Mission, 2000-2010. *Ancient Pakistan*, XX, pp. 97-102.

OLIVIERI, L.M. (2014) L'attività di formazione, scavo e restauro della Missione Italiana nello Swat (2011-2014). In L. CATERINA and B. GENITO, eds., *Archeologie delle 'Vie della Seta': Percorsi, Immagini e Cultura Materiale. III Ciclo di Conferenze*, 1. Naples, pp. 1-25.

OLIVIERI, L.M. (2015a) *Talking Stones. Painted Rock Shelters of the Swat Valley*. With contributions by M. DE CHIARA and M.W. MEISTER. Lahore.

OLIVIERI, L.M. (2015b) *M.A. Stein and the "Lords of the Marches". New Archival Materials*. With contributions by K. BEHRENDT, P. BRANCACCIO and M. DE CHIARA. M. DE CHIARA and A. KAMRAN, eds. Lahore.

OLIVIERI, L.M. (2015c) 'Frontier Archaeology': Sir Aurel Stein, Swat, and the Indian Aornos. *South Asian Studies*, 31, pp. 58-70.

OLIVIERI, L.M. (2016) Guru Padmasambhava in Context: Archaeological and Historical Evidence from Swat/Uddiyana (c. 8th century CE). *Journal of Bhutan Studies*, 34, pp. 20-42.

OLIVIERI, L.M. (2017) The itinerary of O rgyan pa in Swat/Uddiyana (second half of 13th Century). *Journal of Asian Civilizations*, 40/1, pp. 87-101.

OLIVIERI, L.M. (2018) Archaeology from below in Swat, Pakistan: Heritage and Social Mobilisation in a Post-Conflict Reality. In P. NEWSON and R. YOUNG, eds., *Post-Conflict Archaeology and Cultural Heritage. Rebuilding Knowledge, Memory and Community from War-Damaged Material Culture*. New-York-Oxon, pp. 217-237.

OLIVIERI, L.M. and M. VIDALE (2002) Painted Rock Shelters from Swat Valley. Further Discoveries and New Hypotheses. *East and West*, 52, pp. 173-223.

OLIVIERI, L.M., M. VIDALE ET AL. (2006) Archaeology and Settlement History in a Test Area of the Swat Valley. Preliminary Report on the AMSV Project (1st Phase). *East and West*, 56, dedicated to the 50th Anniversary of the IsIAO Archaeological Mission in Pakistan (1956-2006). L.M. OLIVERI, ed., pp. 73-150.

PASHTOON, Z. (2009) *Pashto-English Dictionary*. Hyatsville.

PENZL, H. (1955) *A Grammar of Pashto*. Washington.

PINNOW, H.-J. (1963) The position of the Munda languages within the Austroasiatic language family. In H.L. SHORTO, ed., *Linguistic Comparison in Southeast Asia and the Pacific*. London, pp. 140-152.

PINNOW, H.-J. (1966) A comparative study of the verb in the Munda languages. In N. ZIDE, ed., *Studies in Comparative Austroasiatic Linguistics*. The Hague, pp. 96-193.

PLATTS, J.T. (1884) *A Dictionary of Urdū, classical Hindī and English*. London.

QADEER M.A. KHAN (n.p.) *Working Plan for the Forests of Swat and Swat-Kohistan, Swat State (Malakand Agency, 1965-1980)*.

RAI BAHADUR DAYA RAM SHASTRI (1931) Six Inscriptions in the Lahore Museum. *Epigraphia Indica*, XXI, pp. 293-301.

RAMSTEDT, G. J. (1952) *Marginal notes on Pashto etymology*. Compiled, revised and edited by P. AALTO (Studia Orientalia, XVII). Helsinki.

RAVERTY, H.G. (1859) Notes on Káfiristán. *Journal of the Asiatic Society of Bengal*, 28, pp. 317-368.

RAVERTY, H.G. (1860) *A Vocabulary of the Pukhto, Pushto or Language of the Afghans*. London.

RAVERTY, H.G. (1862) An account of Upper and Lower Suwat, and the Kohistān, to the source of the Suwāt River; with an account of the tribes inhabiting those valleys. *Journal of the Asiatic Society of Bengal*, 31, pp. 227-281.

RAVERTY, H.G. (1888) *Notes on Afghanistan and Part of Baluchistan*. London.

RENSCH, C.R. (1992) Patterns of language use among the Kohistani of the Swat valley. In C.R. RENSCH, S.J. DECKER and D.G. HALLBERG, *Sociolinguistic Survey of Northern Pakistan, Volume 1, Languages of Kohistan*. Islamabad, pp. 3-62.

ROLLINGER, R. (2014) Aornos and the Mountains of the East: the Assyrian Kings and Alexander the Great. In S. GASPA, A. GRECO, D. MORANDI BONACOSSI, S. PONCHIA and R. ROLLINGER, eds., *From Source to History Studies on Ancient Near Eastern Worlds and Beyond* (Dedicated to Giovanni Battista Lanfranchi on the Occasion of His 65th Birthday on June 23, 2014). Münster, pp. 597-635.

ROSE, H.A. (1911) *A Glossary of the Tribes and Castes of the Punjab and North-West Frontier Province*. Lahore.

ROSSI, A.V. (1998) Ossetic and Balochi in V.I. Abaev's *Slovar'*. In *Studia Iranica et Alanica, Festschirft for Prof. Vasilij Ivanovič Abaeva on the Occasion of His 95th Birthday*. Roma, pp. 373-431.

ROSSI, A.V. (2002) Middle Iranian *gund* between Aramaic and Indo-Iranian. *Jerusalem Studies in Arabic and Islam*, 26, pp. 140-171.

ROSSI, A.V. (2018) Une note de Charles Kieffer sur le type *gōrəm* "troupeau". In M. DE CHIARA, A.V. ROSSI and D. SEPTFONDS, eds., *Mélanges d'ethnographie et de dialectologie irano-aryennes à la mémoire de Charles-Martin Kieffer*. Paris, pp. 349-359.

SCARCIA, G. (1965) *ṢIFAT-NĀMA-YI DARVĪŠ MUḤAMMAD ḪĀN-I ĠĀZĪ. Cronaca di una crociata musulmana contro i Kafiri di Laġmān nell'anno 1582*. Roma.

SEPTFONDS, D. (1994) *Le Dzadrāni. Un parler pashto du Paktyā (Afghanistan)*. Paris.

SEPTFONDS, D. (2006) review of NEVP. *Studia Iranica*, 35, pp. 109-114.

SEPTFONDS, D. and H. KABIR (2013) *Manuel de pashto*. Paris.

SGS = R.E. EMMERICK (1968) *Saka Grammatical Studies*. London.

SHAFEEV, D.A. (1964) *A Short Grammatical Outline of Pashto*. Engl. trans. H.H. PAPER. Bloomington-The Hague. [Orig. published in P.B. ZUDIN (1955) *Russko-afganskij slovar'*. Moskva.]

SIDDIQUE, A. (2014) *The Pashtuns. The Unresolved Key to the Future of Pakistan and Afghanistan*. London.

SIDWELL, P. (2009) *Classifying the Austroasiatic languages: History and state of the art*. Muenchen.

SKJÆRVØ, P.O. (1989) Pashto. In R. SCHMITT, ed., *Compendium Linguarum Iranicarum*. Wiesbaden, pp. 384-410.

SOKOLOVA, V.S. (1960) *Bartangskje teksty i slovar'*. Moskva-Leningrad.

STEBLIN-KAMENSKIJ, I.M. (1999) *Etimologičeskij slovar' vaxanskogo jazyka*. St. Petersburg.

STEIN, A. (1898) Preliminary Notes on an Archaeological Tour with the Buner Field Force. *Proceedings, Asiatic Society of Bengal*, 6, pp. 108-113.

STEIN, A. (1899) Detailed Report of an Archaeological Tour with the Buner Field Force. [*The*] *Indian Antiquary*, XXVIII, pp.14-46, 58-64.

STEIN, A. (1905) *Report of Archaeological Survey Work un the North-West Frontier Province and Baluchistan for the Period from January 2nd 1904 to March 31st 1905*. Peshawar.

STEIN, A. (1925) Notes on Tirahi: the speakers of Tirahi. *Journal of the Royal Asiatic Society*, pp. 400-404.

STEIN, A. (1927) Alexander's Campaign in the Indian North-West Frontier. *Geographical Journal*, LXX, pp. 418-440, 515-540.

STEIN, A. (1929) *On Alexander's Track to the Indus*. London.

STEIN, A. (1930) *An Archaeological tour in Upper Swat and Adjacent Hill Tracts*. Calcutta.

STEINGASS, F. (1963[5]) *A comprehensive Persian-English dictionary*. London.

STRABO (1932) *Geography of Claudius Ptolemy*. Ed. and transl. by E.L. STEVENSON. New York.

SULTAN-I-ROME (2008) *Swat State (1915-1969): from Genesis to Merges. An Analysis of Political, Administrative, Socio-Political, and Economic Developments*. Karachi.

SULTAN-I-ROME (2014) Khushal Khan Khattak and Swat. *JRSP*, 51, pp. 109-138.

SULTAN-I-ROME (2016) *Land and Forest Governance in Swat. Transition from Tribal System to State to Pakistan*. Karachi.

T.... = R.L. TURNER (1966) *A Comparative Dictionary of the Indo-Aryan Languages*. London.

TABASSUM MAJEED (2016) *Insurgency in Swat. Conflit Settlement and Peace Building (2001-2011)*. Lahore.

TARN, W.V. (1951) *The Greeks in Bactria and India*. Cambridge.

TASHRIHI 1979 = *Pashto-Pashto Descriptive Dictionary* (2005) Institute of Languages and Literature, Academy of Science of Afghanistan, Kabul, Vol. 1-4.

THOMSON, H.C. (1895) *The Chitral Campaign. A Narrative of Events in Chitral, Swat, and Bajour*. London.

TOMASCHEK, W. (1880) Centralasiatische Studien II. Die Parmir-Dialekte. *Sb. der Kaiserlichen Akademie der Wissenschaften*, phil.-hist. Kl., 96, pp. 735-900.

TRAIL, R.L. and G.R. COOPER (1999) *Kalasha Dictionary — with English and Urdu*. Islamabad.

TREMBLAY, X. (2005) review of NEVP. *Bulletin de la Société Linguistique de Paris*, 100, pp. 173-184.
TUCCI, G. (1940) *Travels of Tibetan Pilgrims in the Swat Valley*. Calcutta. [Repr. in *Opera minora*, II, Roma 1971, pp. 369-418.]
TUCCI, G. (1958) Preliminary Report on an Archaeological Survey in Swat. *East and West*, 9, pp. 279-328. [= TUCCI 1997: 59-114.]
TUCCI, G. (1963a) The Tombs of the Asvakayana-Assakenoi. *East and West*, XIV.1-2, pp. 27-28. [= TUCCI 1997: 115-118]
TUCCI, G. (1963b) *La via dello Swat*. Roma.
TUCCI, G. (1977) On Swāt. The Dards and Connected Problems. *East and West*, 27, pp. 9-103.
TUCCI, G. (1997) *On Swāt. Historical and Archaeological Notes*. P. CALLIERI and A. FILIGENZI, eds. Rome.
TURNER, R.L. (1931) *A comparative and etymological dictionary of the Nepali language*. London.
VIARO, A. and A. ZIEGLER (1999) Habitat et urbanité : Mingora et la vallée de la Swat. *Le globe, Revue genevoise de géographie*, 139, pp. 109-142.
VOGELSANG, W.J. (2003) Herat ii. History, Pre-Islamic Period. In *Encyclopedia Iranica*, XII, pp. 205-206.
WHITNEY, W.D. (1885) *The roots, verb-forms, and primary derivatives of the Sanskrit language. A supplement to his Sanskrit grammar*. Leipzig.
WILSON, H.H. (1841) *Ariana Antiqua. A Descriptive Account of the Antiquities and Coins of Afghanistan*. London.
WITCZAK, K.T. (2006) review of NEVP. *Studia Iranica*, 2006, pp. 115-123.
WITZEL, M. (1999a) Substrate Languages in Old Indo-Aryan (Ṛgvedic, Middle and Late Vedic). *Electronic Journal of Vedic Studies*, 5, pp. 1-67.
WITZEL, M. (1999b) Aryan and non-Aryan Names in Vedic India. Data for the linguistic situation, c. 1900-500 B.C. In J. BRONKHORST and M. DESHPANDE, eds. *Aryan and Non-Non-Aryan in South Asia. Evidence, Interpretation and Ideology*. Cambridge, pp. 337-404.
YOUNGHUSBAND, G.J. (1895) *The Relief of Chitral*. London.
ZOLFAGHARI, S. (2017) *The Bakhtiaris: an anthropological-linguistic lexical study of Haft Lang nomads of southwestern Iran*. PhD thesis. Leiden University. Leiden.

LANGUAGE ABBREVIATIONS

For abbreviations of other minor dialects, see TURNER 1966.

A.	Assamese
Ap.	Apabhraṃśa
Ar.	Arabic
Arm.	Armenian
Aś.	Aśokan inscriptions
Ašk.	Aškun
Austro-As.	Austro-Asiatic
Av.	Avestan
B.	Bengali
Bactr.	Bactrian
Bal.	Baluchi
Bart.	Bartangi
Bašk.	Baškarik
Bhoj.	Bhojpuri
Brah.	Brahui
Bur.	Burušaski
Dam.	Dameli
Dard.	Dardic
Drav.	Dravidian
Gaw.	Gawar-bati
Guǰ.	Guǰarati
Gy.	Gypsy
Haz.	Hazara
Hi.	Hindi
Hind.	Hindustani
IA.	Indo-Aryan
IE.	Indo-European
IIr.	Indo-Iranian
Ir.	Iranian
Išk.	Iškašmi
Jadr.	Jadrani
K.	Kaśmiri
Kaf.	Kafiri
Kal.	Kalaša
Kan.	Kanarese
Kand.	Kandahari
Kho.	Khowari
Khot.	Khotanese
Khwar.	Khwaresmian
Koh.	Kohistani
Kt.	Kati
Ku.	Kumaoni
Kurd.	Kurdish
Lhd.	Lahndi
M.	Maraṭhi
MIA.	Middle Indo-Aryan
Mnj.	Munǰi
Mong.	Mongolian
MPrs.	Middle Persian
Mu.	Muṇḍa
N.	Nepali
OInd.	Old Indian
OPrs.	Old Persian
Orm.	Ormuri
Oro.	Orošori
Oss.	Ossetian
Pa.	Pāli
Pah.	Pahari
Panj.	Panjabi
Par.	Parači
Paš.	Pašai
Phal.	Phaluṛa
Phl.	Pahlavi
Pkt.	Prakrit
Pras.	Prasun
Prs.	Persian
Prth.	Partico
Pšt.	Pašto
Roš.	Rošani
Sar.	Sariqoli
Sgh.	Singhalese
Sh.	Shina
Si.	Sindhi
Sir.	Siraiki
Skt.	Sanskrit
Sogd.	Sogdian
Shum.	Shumasti
Sv.	Savi
Taǰ.	Taǰik
Tal.	Taleši
Tir.	Tirahi
Tk.	Turkish
Tor.	Torwali
Uig.	Uigur
Ur.	Urdu
Ved.	Vedic
Wa.	Wakhi
Waig.	Waigali
Wǰ.	Wanǰi
Woṭ.	Woṭapur
WPah.	West Pahaṛi
Xu.	Xufi
Yd.	Yidγa
Yγn.	Yaγnobi
Yzg.	Yazgulami

INDEXES OF TOPONYMS

A. By typology

1. Streams

Name	Number	Map
Asrit-khwar	50	53
Bahandra-gol	80	54
Baral-darra	128	47
Bargin	143	35
Barwai-khwar	172	44
Biha-khwar	202	42
Bikan-khwar	207	26
Bishbanr-khwar	214	25
Charbagh-khwar	258	29-30
Dadhra-khwar	304	8
Daral-khwar	333	44
Deolai-khwar	343	9
Dosara-khwar	378	24
Dre-khwar	381	28
Gabral River	396	54
Gurnai-khwar	485	47
Harnoi-khwar	495	38-39, 41
Jaba-khwar	516	51
Jambil-khwar	530	21, 22
Jarendo-bela-khwar	540	12
Jolagram-khwar	559	5
Kandak-khwar	604	2
Karakar-khwar	632	4
Kedam-khwar	657	50
Khwazakhela-khwar	695	31
Kolam-khwar	705	24
Kotah-khwar	723	1
Kotlai-khwar	731	8
Kulalai-khwar	741	11
Landai-khwar	789	23, 24
Lewanai-khwar	804	24
Loe-khwar	813	11
Mahakai	827	15
Makad-khwar	836	29
Mankial	867	52
Manrai-khwar	872	13
Marghuzar-khwar	883	19
Miandam	903	36
Najigram-khwar	927	3
Nali-darra	930	46
Olal-khwar	966	46
Paiti-khwar	973	36-37
Paloga-gol	979	54
Qalagai-khwar	1034	11
Ramogai-khwar	1044	10
Roringar-khwar	1057	43
Saidu-khwar	1068	20
Shanku	1175	46
Shaurai-khwar	1188	40
Sigram-khwar	1208	17
Spanai-khwar	1221	10
Spedar-khwar	1224	24
Swat	1246	
Tambagat-khwar	1264	27
Ugad-khwar	1336	23
Ushu-gol	1342	54
Utror	1344	54

2. Lakes

Name	Number	Tehsil	Map
Diwangar	363	Bahrain	54
Maho-dand	829	Bahrain	54
Tukataki	1325	Bahrain	54

3. Peaks

Name	Number	Tehsil	Map
Babu-sar	65	Maṭṭa	44
Badkot	70	Maṭṭa	39
Banda-sar	105	Charbagh	28
Bango-sar	110	Charbagh	27
Banj-sar	113	Babuzai	22
Barman-sar	161	Kabal	12
Bauro-sar	184	Kabal	17
Bilmaz-sar	209	Charbagh	27

Bostani-sar	219	Barikot	2
Bura-sar	222	Bahrain	46
Chambar-ghakhai	236	Bahrain	49
Changai-dop-sar	244	Kabal	8
China-sar	269	Bahrain	46
Chongiala-sar	282	Kabal	16
Chopalu-sar	285	Kabal	12
Chopra-sar	286	Khwazakhela	32
Churlak-sar	294	Charbagh	27
Churlak-sar	295	Khwazakhela	35
Dadalbho	300	Bahrain	54
Dambar-sar	314	Kabal	11
Dandai-sar	322	Khwazakhela	37
Dobar-sar	364	Khwazakhela	36
Dokat-sar	372	Kabal	10
Dopialo-sar	374	Barikot	1
Dop-sar	375	Babuzai	18
Dosara	377	Babuzai	24
Durman-unra-sar	385	Kabal	12
Falak-sar	390	Bahrain	54
Gadwa-sar	401	Charbagh	28
Ghuzano-sar	451	Kabal	13
Gira	459	Babuzai	18
Guli-sar	481	Babuzai	18
Hindubeg-sar	501	Maṭṭa	43
Hunra-sar	502	Kabal	16
Ilam	504	Barikot	19
Jalba-sar	526	Maṭṭa	43
Karai-sar	628	Babuzai	19
Kashala	648	Barikot	7
Khadang-sar	663	Charbagh	29
Khardu-sar	673	Khwazakhela	33
Khojarbori-sar	688	Kabal	15
Kontaro-sar	711	Kabal	16
Kopra-sar	712	Khwazakhela	36
Kosa	717	Babuzai	18
Kotah-sar	724	Barikot	2
Kund-sar	748	Kabal	12
Landai-sar	790	Maṭṭa	19
Landai-sar	791	Barikot	42
Lito-sar	807	Maṭṭa	41
Loe-sar	816	Babuzai	22
Luda-sar	817	Bahrain	47
Lundai-sar	820	Kabal	12
Manago-sar	851	Kabal	15
Manasar-sar	853	Babuzai	26
Mankial-tsukai	868	Bahrain	52
Maran-sar	879	Barikot	19
Mora-sar	916	Barikot	1
Parrai-ghar	994	Barikot	8
Pata-sar	1000	Babuzai	24
Prangman-sar	1019	Maṭṭa	42
Punnubat-sar	1024	Bahrain	46
Qalagai-sar	1035	Kabal	11
Qandalu-ghakhai	1036	Bahrain	49
Ramotai-loe-sar	1045	Khwazakhela	29
Rani-sar	1050	Babuzai	24
Ranjro-sar	1052	Babuzai	19
Rustam-sar	1059	Bahrain	53
Sakhi-sar	1071	Babuzai	7
Salim-khan	1074	Babuzai	20
Saso-sar	1113	Kabal	38
Semprai-sar	1118	Khwazakhela	33
Shagar-sar	1136	Charbagh	26
Shago-sar	1140	Maṭṭa	43
Shah-dop-sar	1141	Maṭṭa	39
Shango-sar	1174	Charbagh	28
Shewa-ghar	1194	Barikot	5
Shuro-sar	1205	Khwazakhela	32
Speralgot-sar	1226	Kabal	13
Tikai-sar	1300	Bahrain	51
Tsapparai-sar	1322	Barikot	6
Tutpanrai-sar	1331	Kabal	17
Uchrai-sar	1334	Maṭṭa	40
Unran-sar	1338	Babuzai	24
Usmani-sar	1343	Kabal	17
Uzbuk-sar	1346	Babuzai	24
Welan-sar	1353	Charbagh	28
Yakh-tangai-sar	1358	Kabal	16
Zin-sar	1370	Khwazakhela	35

4. Passes

Name	**Number**	**Tehsil**	**Map**
Achro-kandao	3	Charbagh	28
Ahingaro-baba-kandao	8	Kabal	10
Arangelai-ghakhai	30	Babuzai	21
Babar-ghakhai-kandao	64	Barikot	5
Bachi-kandao	67	Maṭṭa	43
Badwai-kandao	72	Bahrain	54
Bagai-kandao	73	Barikot	5
Bala-an	89	Bahrain	54
Banmanai-kandao	117	Kabal	13
Bar-kandao	151	Babuzai	24
Bar-kandao	152	Maṭṭa	42
Bashkaro-an	175	Bahrain	54
Biakand-kandao	199	Kabal	16
Bizoban-kandao	216	Barikot	5
Burjal-kandao	224	Kabal	15
Chanmarang-kandao	247	Kabal	13
Charai-kandao	255	Bahrain	46
Charai-kandao	256	Bahrain	47
China-kandao	267	Khwazakhela	35
Choaro-kandao	275	Kabal	11
Chokel-kandao	281	Bahrain	52
Chopalu-kandao	284	Kabal	12
Dadarili-an	301	Bahrain	54
Dambar-kandao	313	Kabal	40
Dand-kandao	325	Maṭṭa	44
Desan-kandao	355	Bahrain	54

Doghalgai-kandao	369	Kabal	12
Gat-kandao	430	Charbagh	26
Gora-daka-kandao	469	Bahrain	51
Jaranda-kandao	539	Maṭṭa	42
Jatkot-kandao	545	Kabal	17
Jauhar-kandao	546	Babuzai	26
Jauz-kandao	552	Babuzai	19
Jijal-kandao	556	Khwazakhela	36
Jobe-kandao	558	Charbagh	27
Jowari-kandao	562	Babuzai	20
Kachhikhani-an	570	Bahrain	54
Kakai-kandao	580	Barikot	1
Kalel-kandao	589	Babuzai	22
Kandia-kandao	615	Bahrain	52
Kanj-kandao	620	Babuzai	26
Karakar-kandao	631	Barikot	4
Karorai-kandao	642	Khwazakhela	33
Kharo-kandao	680	Khwazakhela	34
Kund-kandao	747	Kabal	12
Kuratai-kandao	753	Maṭṭa	38
Kuz-kandao	766	Babuzai	24
Lalku-kandao	784	Bahrain	44
Lundai-kandao	819	Kabal	12
Manali-an	852	Bahrain	54
Mangazai-kandao	857	Khwazakhela	36
Manja-kandao	863	Kabal	11
Matlit-an	888	Bahrain	54
Menduria-kandao	898	Khwazakhela	35
Mirati-kandao	910	Barikot	5
Moi-kandao	913	Babuzai	19
Ormal-kandao	968	Khwazakhela	28
Palesar-an	977	Bahrain	54
Paloga-an	978	Bahrain	54
Panrashai-kandao	985	Bahrain	47
Paranial-kandao	989	Babuzai	23
Rama-kandao	1041	Kabal	17
Ranga-kandao	1048	Charbagh	28
Saidgi-kandao	1067	Maṭṭa	43
Sarkhanai-kandao	1109	Barikot	5
Selai-kandao	1117	Kabal	13
Shalkhosar-kandao	1157	Kabal	16
Shalwa-kandao	1162	Charbagh	30
Shamelai-kandao	1164	Babuzai	21
Shangla-kandao	1171	Charbagh	28
Sirikar-kandao	1214	Bahrain	51
Soko-kandao	1217	Charbagh	28
Spighog-kandao	1229	Babuzai	19
Surgalai-kandao	1242	Barikot	8
Surkar-kandao	1243	Bahrain	52
Swatai-kandao	1247	Maṭṭa	42
Talao-kandao	1257	Barikot	5
Talkar-kandao	1260	Kabal	16
Tarakai-kandao	1281	Barikot	2
Tsapparai-kandao	1321	Barikot	1
Yakh-kandao	1357	Bahrain	46
Zhandrai pass	1367	Bahrain	54

5. Pastures

Name	Number	Tehsil	Map
Achro-banda	2	Charbagh	28
Amluktal-banda	25	Kabal	12
Archalai-banda	32	Kabal	13
Asharai-banda	43	Kabal	12
Azad-banda	60	Maṭṭa	44
Bahadur-banda	78	Maṭṭa	41
Baki-banda	85	Khwazakhela	35
Balagan-banda	90	Kabal	12
Bandi-banda	106	Kabal	12
Bangai-banda	108	Barikot	3
Banj-banda	111	Maṭṭa	38
Bar-banjir-banda	134	Barikot	2
Bar-batai-banda	136	Barikot	3
Bar-durzghar-banda	139	Barikot	3
Bar-kandao-banda	153	Babuzai	24
Batul-banda	182	Kabal	13
Bayan-banda	185	Kabal	12
Bela-banda	195	Kabal	13
Binwar-banda	211	Kabal	12
Burjosar-banda	225	Maṭṭa	42
Chaprai-banda	249	Kabal	11
Chingai-banda	270	Kabal	15
Chokel-banda	279	Bahrain	52
Chokel-banda	280	Bahrain	52
Chotar-banda	288	Kabal	12
Chur-banda	292	Kabal	12
Dad-banda	302	Barikot	2
Dakko-banda	308	Kabal	12
Dand-banda	324	Bahrain	49
Dar-banda	334	Maṭṭa	48-49
Dob-banda	365	Kabal	13
Dre-bandai	380	Babuzai	21
Durbak-banda	383	Babuzai	22
Faqiran-banda	392	Kabal	13
Gachkor-banda	398	Kabal	12
Gamkat-banda	404	Khwazakhela	33
Gato-sar-banda	433	Khwazakhela	32
Gatsar-banda	435	Khwazakhela	36
Ghakhe-banda	436	Kabal	10
Ghulkhwaro-sar-banda	444	Khwazakhela	31
Ghuzano-banda	448	Bahrain	53
Ghwai-banda	454	Maṭṭa	43
Gidar-sar-banda	456	Khwazakhela	32
Gidar-sar-banda	457	Khwazakhela	33
Goda-banda	462	Kabal	13
Godhanu-banda	464	Kabal	14
Gul-banda	476	Babuzai	19
Gul-banda	477	Maṭṭa	40
Gumbatuna-banda	483	Barikot	6
Hindubeg-banda	500	Maṭṭa	43

Inzaro-banda	509	Kabal	11
Jaba-banda	514	Bahrain	51
Jalgar-banda	527	Barikot	3
Jaur-banda	547	Barikot	2
Jaur-banda	548	Maṭṭa	41
Jaur-banda	549	Maṭṭa	41
Jaur-banda	550	Maṭṭa	41
Jor-banda	561	Kabal	10
Kabal-banda	565	Kabal	12
Kafir-banda	576	Bahrain	46
Kalo-banda	590	Maṭṭa	43
Kamali-banda	591	Maṭṭa	39
Kamar-banda	593	Kabal	30
Kamyarai-banda	597	Kabal	12
Kandao-banda	608	Charbagh	26
Kandao-banda	609	Khwazakhela	35
Kanro-sar-banda	623	Bahrain	45
Karakar-banda	630	Barikot	4
Kar-banda	636	Bahrain	50
Karo-banda	640	Maṭṭa	42
Kashkar-banda	650	Kabal	11
Khar-banda	672	Kabal	11
Khazanai-banda	684	Kabal	11
Kohistani-banda	702	Maṭṭa	43
Kolanda-banda	706	Kabal	12
Kontaro-banda	710	Kabal	16
Korai-banda	713	Kabal	11
Kosar-banda	718	Babuzai	22
Kotgai-banda	726	Kabal	12
Kuar-sar-banda	732	Babuzai	22
Kulalai-banda	740	Kabal	11
Kund-banda	746	Kabal	11
Kuz-banjir-banda	757	Barikot	2
Kuz-batai-banda	759	Barikot	3
Kuz-kandao-banda	767	Babuzai	24
Lizzat-banda	808	Bahrain	53
Lo-banda	811	Bahrain	48
Maira-banda	834	Kabal	12
Mair-banda	835	Maṭṭa	43
Makat-banda	837	Kabal	12
Malkana-banda	846	Kabal	14
Manrai-banda	871	Kabal	13
Manzarai-banda	876	Kabal	12
Manzghundai-banda	878	Kabal	10
Mian-baba-banda	900	Kabal	12
Mian-bela-banda	901	Kabal	12
Mianwara-banda	907	Kabal	13
Murdar-banda	921	Kabal	10
Narai-banda	935	Barikot	3
Narai-sur-banda	936	Charbagh	25
Nizam-banda	962	Babuzai	20
Pacha-kili-banda	970	Kabal	13
Pacha-kili-banda	971	Kabal	13
Pashino-banda	996	Maṭṭa	43
Patibast-banda	1002	Kabal	15
Pinorai-banda	1005	Kabal	12
Pir-patai-banda	1015	Kabal	11
Qalagai-banda	1029	Kabal	11
Qalagai-banda	1030	Kabal	11
Qalagai-banda	1031	Kabal	11
Qalagai-banda	1032	Kabal	11
Qalagai-banda	1033	Kabal	11
Safashi-banda	1064	Barikot	3
Salim-khan-banda	1075	Babuzai	20
Samsel-banda	1081	Kabal	9
Sarbala-banda	1093	Kabal	10
Sar-banda	1094	Maṭṭa	38
Sar-banda	1095	Maṭṭa	40
Sar-banda	1096	Bahrain	44
Sar-banda	1097	Bahrain	50
Sar-banda	1098	Bahrain	50
Sar-banda	1099	Bahrain	50
Sar-china-banda	1101	Babuzai	20
Sargai-banda	1104	Kabal	15
Sarle-banda	1110	Khwazakhela	34
Shadhand-banda	1133	Kabal	10
Shagai-banda	1135	Kabal	10
Shahi-banda	1143	Bahrain	48
Shahjahan-banda	1147	Kabal	12
Shalkhosar-banda	1156	Kabal	16
Shamkor-banda	1166	Bahrain	47
Shangora-banda	1172	Kabal	13
Shangora-banda	1173	Kabal	13
Shar-banda	1179	Bahrain	53
Sharifai-banda	1183	Kabal	10
Siakas-banda	1206	Maṭṭa	42
Sikka-banda	1210	Kabal	16
Spalmai-banda	1220	Kabal	15
Spedar-banda	1223	Babuzai	26
Sperkai-banda	1228	Kabal	12
Spinkoto-banda	1231	Khwazakhela	32
Suli-banda	1233	Babuzai	24
Tandar-banda	1266	Babuzai	24
Tangai-banda	1269	Bahrain	46
Tangu-banda	1277	Kabal	12
Tighak-banda	1296	Kabal	10
Torusatta-banda	1314	Kabal	13
Yakabanj-banda	1355	Barikot	3
Zangi-banda	1361	Charbagh	29

6. Villages

Name	Number	Tehsil	Map
Abwa	1	Barikot	2
Adai	4	Charbagh	29
Adrer	5	Bahrain	47
Agal	6	Maṭṭa	41
Agor	7	Khwazakhela	37
Ahingaro-derai	9	Babuzai	18

Ahingaro-derai	10	Bahrain	44
Ain	11	Bahrain	45
Ajorai	12	Khwazakhela	36
Akhun-kalai	13	Kabal	8
Alamganj	14	Charbagh	30
Aligai	15	Khwazakhela	34
Aligram	16	Kabal	9
Aligram	17	Maṭṭa	40
Allahabad	18	Charbagh	30
Altangurai	19	Barikot	5
Alwara	20	Maṭṭa	43
Aman-kot	21	Babuzai	18
Amluk	22	Maṭṭa	44
Amlukbanr	23	Maṭṭa	38
Amlukdara	24	Barikot	4
Amluk-tangai	26	Kabal	10
Anisar	27	Bahrain	48
Anwar-dhere	28	Babuzai	20
Ara	29	Babuzai	25
Arbut	31	Babuzai	22
Arkhuna	33	Bahrain	36
Arkhuna	34	Khwazakhela	44
Arkot	35	Maṭṭa	38
Arkot-qila	36	Kabal	14
Asagai	37	Bahrain	47
Asala	38	Khwazakhela	34
Asharai	39	Charbagh	28
Asharai	40	Khwazakhela	33
Asharai	41	Maṭṭa	39
Asharai	42	Maṭṭa	39
Asharbanr	44	Charbagh	30
Asharbanr	45	Maṭṭa	38
Ashar-garai	46	Babuzai	24
Asharo-paiza	47	Charbagh	30
Asharopatai	48	Bahrain	53
Asrit	49	Bahrain	53
Ateran	51	Khwazakhela	31
Atia-qala	52	Maṭṭa	41
Atsar	53	Bahrain	48
Awai-shah	54	Maṭṭa	39
Awarai	55	Bahrain	40
Awarai	56	Maṭṭa	41
Awarai	57	Maṭṭa	43
Awarai	58	Maṭṭa	44
Awi-kas	59	Maṭṭa	38
Azgharai	61	Babuzai	23
Bab	62	Maṭṭa	38
Baba-derai	63	Barikot	4
Bachchi-derai	66	Bahrain	46
Badai	68	Bahrain	51
Badder	69	Bahrain	48
Badre	71	Khwazakhela	37
Bagh	74	Babuzai	21
Baghsar	75	Bahrain	47
Bagolai	76	Charbagh	30
Bagoria	77	Babuzai	21
Bahadur-khelo-charai	79	Bahrain	47
Bahnium	81	Bahrain	53
Baidarra	82	Maṭṭa	39
Bakanran	83	Charbagh	30
Bakar	84	Babuzai	20
Baknai	86	Bahrain	53
Bakor	87	Maṭṭa	41
Bakro	88	Khwazakhela	37
Bala-kor	91	Charbagh	28
Balalai	92	Charbagh	30
Balasur	93	Maṭṭa	39
Balat	94	Maṭṭa	40
Balogram	95	Babuzai	18
Balo-kalai	96	Barikot	2
Ban	97	Bahrain	45
Ban	98	Bahrain	47
Banda	99	Khwazakhela	17
Banda	100	Bahrain	33
Banda	101	Kabal	46
Banda-ghal	102	Babuzai	24
Bandai	103	Khwazakhela	31
Bandanr	104	Babuzai	22
Bang	107	Khwazakhela	34
Bangesh	109	Bahrain	45
Banjot	112	Babuzai	24
Bankara	114	Maṭṭa	39
Ban-khwar	115	Bahrain	54
Bankor	116	Bahrain	48
Banpakia	118	Khwazakhela	35
Ban-pangharai	119	Maṭṭa	42
Ban-pur-sar	120	Charbagh	27
Banr	121	Bahrain	49
Banragai	122	Maṭṭa	43
Barabarai	123	Maṭṭa	42
Baragat	124	Kabal	16
Barai	125	Bahrain	51
Barai	126	Bahrain	53
Baral	127	Bahrain	47
Baranial	129	Bahrain	48
Baranwai	130	Bahrain	46
Bararai	131	Khwazakhela	31
Bar-bamakhel	132	Maṭṭa	38
Bar-bandai	133	Kabal	17
Bar-bargin	135	Khwazakhela	35
Bar-bela	137	Bahrain	47
Bar-durshkhel	138	Maṭṭa	39
Baret	140	Khwazakhela	33
Bar-garai	141	Bahrain	45
Bar-ghuzan	142	Babuzai	24
Bar-gorshai	144	Bahrain	45
Bar-gunaguz	145	Bahrain	50
Bariam	146	Maṭṭa	38
Barikot	147	Barikot	4
Bar-jabar	148	Babuzai	24
Bar-kadar	149	Maṭṭa	42
Bar-kandak	150	Barikot	2
Bar-kanju	154	Kabal	17
Bar-karingal	155	Khwazakhela	33
Barkhai	156	Khwazakhela	36
Bar-laikot	157	Bahrain	53

Bar-lalku	158	Maṭṭa	44
Bar-lewanai	159	Babuzai	24
Bar-manasar	160	Babuzai	26
Baro	162	Maṭṭa	39
Barona	163	Maṭṭa	42
Bar-patai	164	Kabal	10
Bar-samsara	165	Barikot	3
Bar-shaur	166	Maṭṭa	40
Barthana	167	Maṭṭa	41
Bar-uzbuk	168	Babuzai	24
Baruj	169	Bahrain	44
Barwa	170	Barikot	7
Barwai	171	Maṭṭa	44
Basesar	173	Bahrain	47
Bashkal	174	Bahrain	46
Baskhela	176	Maṭṭa	39
Bat-koran	177	Babuzai	18
Batku	178	Maṭṭa	44
Batol	179	Maṭṭa	39
Batora	180	Babuzai	18
Batra	181	Babuzai	23
Baurai	183	Maṭṭa	17
Bazai-derai	186	Babuzai	24
Bazwanano-derai	187	Babuzai	24
Bedag	188	Bahrain	46
Bedag	189	Bahrain	46
Behar	190	Khwazakhela	32
Bela	191	Khwazakhela	11
Bela	192	Bahrain	33
Bela	193	Bahrain	46
Bela	194	Kabal	50
Berang	196	Bahrain	45
Bhoka	197	Kabal	16
Biakand	198	Maṭṭa	38
Biakor	200	Kabal	16
Biha	201	Maṭṭa	42
Bijai	203	Bahrain	50
Bijora	204	Maṭṭa	39
Bikai	205	Babuzai	22
Bikan	206	Charbagh	26
Biladram	208	Khwazakhela	32
Binkat	210	Khwazakhela	37
Bishai	212	Bahrain	53
Bishbanr	213	Babuzai	25
Bishgram	215	Bahrain	46
Bodigram	217	Maṭṭa	38
Bolat	218	Babuzai	20
Budai	220	Khwazakhela	32
Bujabanr	221	Bahrain	47
Burai	223	Khwazakhela	33
Chakur	226	Maṭṭa	39
Chalera	227	Barikot	5
Chaliar	228	Khwazakhela	31
Cham	229	Khwazakhela	32
Cham	230	Maṭṭa	32
Cham	231	Bahrain	39
Cham	232	Khwazakhela	43
Cham	233	Maṭṭa	45
Cham	234	Bahrain	50
Chambar	235	Bahrain	49
Cham-serai	237	Maṭṭa	38
Cham-shaur	238	Maṭṭa	40
Cham-sinpora	239	Maṭṭa	38
Chamtia	240	Khwazakhela	32
Chanchar	241	Khwazakhela	37
Chanda-khora	242	Kabal	8
Chandakhwara	243	Kabal	9
Changlalai	245	Maṭṭa	41
Chankolai	246	Khwazakhela	33
Chaprai	248	Bahrain	44
Char	250	Maṭṭa	43
Char	251	Bahrain	47
Charai	252	Babuzai	24
Charai	253	Charbagh	27
Charai	254	Maṭṭa	44
Charbagh	257	Charbagh	30
Charma	259	Maṭṭa	43
Chatkarai	260	Maṭṭa	43
Chaturia	261	Maṭṭa	40
Chautar	262	Kabal	15
Chere	263	Babuzai	26
Cheripun	264	Bahrain	45
Chheri	265	Maṭṭa	44
Chil-shoggai	266	Babuzai	18
China-kili	268	Kabal	14
Chingalai	271	Charbagh	30
Chingai	272	Barikot	5
Chirai	273	Bahrain	48
Chitor	274	Babuzai	19
Chobek	276	Bahrain	47
Chodgram	277	Bahrain	53
Chohria	278	Babuzai	24
Chopal	283	Maṭṭa	43
Chorpunari	287	Kabal	13
Chotkan	289	Bahrain	50
Chuprial	290	Maṭṭa	39
Churarai	291	Bahrain	45
Churkhai	293	Barikot	1
Chuwa	296	Barikot	1
Dabargai	297	Bahrain	46
Dabna	298	Bahrain	53
Dad	299	Khwazakhela	32
Dadhrah	303	Kabal	8
Dadpanrai	305	Maṭṭa	38
Dagai	306	Kabal	8
Dagai	307	Maṭṭa	41
Dakorak	309	Charbagh	30
Dam	310	Bahrain	47
Damakal	311	Babuzai	23
Damama	312	Maṭṭa	39
Damghar	315	Kabal	17
Dand	316	Khwazakhela	37
Dand	317	Maṭṭa	39
Danda	318	Bahrain	46
Danda	319	Bahrain	46
Dandai	320	Maṭṭa	40

Dandai	321	Maṭṭa	40
Dandarai	323	Maṭṭa	41
Dande	326	Kabal	16
Dande	327	Khwazakhela	33
Dando	328	Charbagh	27
Dandun-qala	329	Babuzai	18
Dang-arkot-qala	330	Maṭṭa	38
Dangbanr	331	Bahrain	47
Dangram	332	Babuzai	21
Dard	335	Khwazakhela	16
Dard	336	Kabal	32
Dardial	337	Kabal	12
Darmai	338	Maṭṭa	44
Darozgar	339	Maṭṭa	38
Darra	340	Charbagh	29
Dedawar	341	Barikot	6
Delai	342	Kabal	17
Derai	344	Kabal	14
Derai	345	Kabal	17
Derai	346	Maṭṭa	34
Derai	347	Maṭṭa	37
Derai	348	Maṭṭa	41
Derai	349	Bahrain	44
Derai	350	Bahrain	45
Derai	351	Bahrain	45
Derai	352	Bahrain	46
Derai	353	Khwazakhela	46
Deranpatai	354	Maṭṭa	38
Dewan	356	Bahrain	52
Dewan	357	Bahrain	53
Dheri	358	Kabal	14
Dilban	359	Bahrain	48
Dirlam	360	Bahrain	53
Diro	361	Bahrain	47
Diwanbut	362	Babuzai	24
Doda	366	Bahrain	46
Doda-derai	367	Bahrain	48
Doghalgai	368	Charbagh	27
Doghlai	370	Maṭṭa	40
Dokadai	371	Khwazakhela	34
Dop	373	Khwazakhela	34
Doralai	376	Bahrain	47
Doshagram	379	Maṭṭa	44
Duba	382	Babuzai	24
Dure-shah	384	Babuzai	22
Dutpanrai	386	Maṭṭa	40
Ehsanabad	387	Kabal	9
Faizabad	388	Babuzai	18
Faizah	389	Babuzai	21
Faqira	391	Khwazakhela	33
Fazalbeg	393	Maṭṭa	44
Fizil-banda	394	Maṭṭa	42
Gabral	395	Bahrain	54
Gabranai	397	Maṭṭa	44
Gadakot	399	Babuzai	22
Gadakot	400	Babuzai	23
Galoch	402	Kabal	14
Gamchana	403	Maṭṭa	42
Gamkot	405	Barikot	5
Gampora	406	Kabal	14
Gamsar	407	Maṭṭa	43
Gamsir	408	Bahrain	47
Ganajir	409	Charbagh	28
Ganderai	410	Charbagh	30
Ganderai	411	Maṭṭa	39
Gantar	412	Bahrain	48
Ganudai	413	Babuzai	21
Gaorarban	414	Bahrain	50
Garai	415	Barikot	5
Garai	416	Maṭṭa	8
Garai	417	Kabal	39
Garai	418	Maṭṭa	44
Garai	419	Maṭṭa	44
Garai	420	Maṭṭa	45
Garai	421	Bahrain	50
Garasa	422	Babuzai	21
Gardaisar	423	Maṭṭa	39
Gargai-shalkhai	424	Bahrain	46
Garhi	425	Babuzai	23
Garnai	426	Bahrain	47
Gashkor	427	Khwazakhela	31
Gat	428	Charbagh	26
Gat	429	Maṭṭa	40
Gatkotal	431	Maṭṭa	38
Gato	432	Babuzai	25
Gatsar	434	Bahrain	48
Ghaligay	437	Barikot	7
Ghamjaba	438	Kabal	9
Gharibabad	439	Charbagh	17
Gharibabad	440	Kabal	30
Ghari-bala	441	Maṭṭa	38
Ghojalai	442	Babuzai	18
Ghorejai	443	Bahrain	47
Ghumbat	445	Babuzai	22
Ghurejo	446	Kabal	17
Ghuz	447	Babuzai	22
Ghuzano-cham	449	Maṭṭa	38
Ghuzano-cham	450	Maṭṭa	38
Ghuzbanr	452	Khwazakhela	31
Ghuzkas	453	Maṭṭa	44
Gidar	455	Bahrain	46
Giga	458	Maṭṭa	38
Gishar	460	Charbagh	27
Goal	461	Maṭṭa	43
Godar	463	Babuzai	20
Gogdara	465	Babuzai	18
Gojalai	466	Maṭṭa	38
Golra	467	Maṭṭa	38
Gora-daka	468	Bahrain	52
Gorail	470	Bahrain	53
Goratai	471	Barikot	2
Gori-bela	472	Bahrain	51
Gosh	473	Bahrain	53
Goshai	474	Bahrain	50
Gujarbanr	475	Maṭṭa	39
Gul-derai	478	Khwazakhela	34

Gulibagh	479	Charbagh	24
Guligram	480	Babuzai	30
Gul-paiza	482	Charbagh	28
Gund-patai	484	Bahrain	52
Gurtai-abadan	486	Babuzai	23
Gurtai-kandar	487	Babuzai	23
Gwalerai	488	Maṭṭa	41
Haium	489	Bahrain	53
Haji-baba	490	Babuzai	18
Hamwarai	491	Charbagh	30
Hamwarak	492	Khwazakhela	31
Harianai	493	Bahrain	53
Harianai-bagla	494	Bahrain	53
Hawai	496	Bahrain	51
Hawar	497	Maṭṭa	42
Hawarai	498	Khwazakhela	33
Hazara	499	Kabal	9
Igalbanr	503	Charbagh	30
Ilanai	505	Charbagh	28
Ilani	506	Maṭṭa	39
Illa	507	Bahrain	52
Ilman	508	Khwazakhela	33
Inzar-tangai	510	Babuzai	23
Irobai	511	Bahrain	48
Islampur	512	Babuzai	20
Jaba	513	Bahrain	51
Jabagai	515	Barikot	5
Jabba	517	Babuzai	22
Jabba	518	Bahrain	49
Jabrai	519	Khwazakhela	33
Jabrai	520	Khwazakhela	36
Jabrai	521	Maṭṭa	39
Jai	522	Bahrain	50
Jaikot	523	Charbagh	25
Jalba	524	Maṭṭa	43
Jalban	525	Bahrain	54
Jamalasar	528	Maṭṭa	39
Jambil	529	Babuzai	22
Jampur-derai	531	Charbagh	30
Jamrai	532	Bahrain	49
Jamrai	533	Bahrain	50
Jana	534	Maṭṭa	41
Jandero	535	Babuzai	18
Jandrai	536	Bahrain	49
Jano	537	Khwazakhela	31
Jan-patai	538	Khwazakhela	33
Jaro	541	Bahrain	37
Jarugai	542	Maṭṭa	42
Jashar	543	Khwazakhela	33
Jatkot	544	Kabal	17
Jauzan	551	Bahrain	53
Jawarkas	553	Bahrain	45
Jawar-kas	554	Bahrain	53
Jawi	555	Maṭṭa	42
Jira	557	Bahrain	53
Jontar	560	Khwazakhela	37
Jukhmai	563	Khwazakhela	37
Jura	564	Maṭṭa	38
Kabalku	566	Maṭṭa	43
Kabbal	567	Kabal	9
Kachal-bela	568	Bahrain	49
Kachcha-kor	569	Babuzai	22
Kad	571	Babuzai	24
Kad	572	Babuzai	24
Kadarchaka	573	Maṭṭa	42
Kadkhwar	574	Maṭṭa	43
Kadiar	575	Maṭṭa	42
Kahai	577	Bahrain	47
Kahai	578	Bahrain	47
Kakai	579	Barikot	1
Kakardam	581	Khwazakhela	33
Kakhai-derai	582	Khwazakhela	32
Kakot	583	Charbagh	28
Kala	584	Kabal	14
Kalagai	585	Maṭṭa	38
Kalagram	586	Bahrain	44
Kalakot	587	Maṭṭa	44
Kalam	588	Bahrain	54
Kamarbagh	592	Charbagh	17
Kamargai	594	Charbagh	30
Kamarkha	595	Bahrain	52
Kambar	596	Babuzai	18
Kanati	598	Maṭṭa	42
Kanati	599	Maṭṭa	42
Kand	600	Maṭṭa	43
Kandai	601	Maṭṭa	41
Kandak	602	Barikot	2
Kandakai	603	Babuzai	24
Kandao	605	Charbagh	16
Kandao	606	Kabal	28
Kandao	607	Khwazakhela	37
Kandaogai	610	Maṭṭa	40
Kandar	611	Charbagh	30
Kandar	612	Bahrain	41
Kandar	613	Maṭṭa	44
Kandar	614	Maṭṭa	50
Kandimar	616	Bahrain	53
Kandowala-morah	617	Babuzai	22
Kangalai	618	Babuzai	22
Kangar	619	Maṭṭa	43
Kanju	621	Kabal	9
Kanr	622	Bahrain	48
Kanrtikai	624	Bahrain	48
Kar	625	Bahrain	44
Kar	626	Bahrain	47
Karai	627	Khwazakhela	33
Karakal	629	Maṭṭa	41
Karamar	633	Bahrain	46
Karandukai	634	Bahrain	53
Karange	635	Khwazakhela	32
Kar-bela	637	Bahrain	53
Karial	638	Bahrain	46
Karinuna	639	Maṭṭa	43
Karorai	641	Khwazakhela	33
Karpo	643	Babuzai	20
Kas	644	Babuzai	24

Kas	645	Bahrain 46
Kas	646	Bahrain 53
Kasai	647	Kabal 8
Kashankad	649	Bahrain 46
Kasuna	651	Charbagh 27
Kat-dera	652	Bahrain 49
Katelai	653	Babuzai 18
Katiya	654	Kabal 14
Katosar-banda	655	Khwazakhela 34
Kedam-bela	656	Bahrain 50
Ketal	658	Bahrain 47
Khabin	659	Bahrain 45
Khachar	660	Maṭṭa 39
Khadang	661	Charbagh 29
Khadang	662	Maṭṭa 39
Khadarzo-patai	664	Charbagh 29
Khairabad	665	Maṭṭa 38
Khamas	666	Maṭṭa 16
Khanabad	667	Khwazakhela 34
Khanpatai	668	Maṭṭa 38
Kharairai	669	Maṭṭa 38
Kharairai-cham	670	Maṭṭa 38
Kharawe	671	Khwazakhela 33
Kharesha	674	Bahrain 45
Kharkai	675	Maṭṭa 42
Kharkai	676	Bahrain 43
Kharkai	677	Bahrain 47
Kharkai	678	Maṭṭa 53
Kharkarai	679	Maṭṭa 42
Kharwe	681	Khwazakhela 31
Khatkotai	682	Kabal 9
Khazana	683	Barikot 5
Khelkhona	685	Maṭṭa 39
Khemdarra	686	Kabal 8
Kheta	687	Babuzai 21
Khorgarai	689	Khwazakhela 34
Khushnab-baba	690	Babuzai 18
Khwar	691	Bahrain 45
Khwar	692	Bahrain 53
Khwar-mandaona	693	Maṭṭa 16
Khwazakhela	694	Khwazakhela 31
Kit	696	Bahrain 53
Kochla	697	Khwazakhela 33
Kodarai-derai	698	Kabal 11
Koga	699	Maṭṭa 43
Kohi	700	Bahrain 49
Kohistan-tikai	701	Bahrain 50
Kokarai	703	Babuzai 22
Kolalai	704	Bahrain 51
Kolbanr	707	Bahrain 46
Komyati	708	Kabal 12
Kontargat	709	Charbagh 30
Korata	714	Babuzai 22
Kormal	715	Khwazakhela 32
Koruna	716	Babuzai 19
Kot	719	Khwazakhela 23
Kot	720	Babuzai 33
Kot	721	Bahrain 53
Kotah	722	Barikot 1
Kotanai	725	Khwazakhela 34
Kotkai	727	Maṭṭa 30
Kotkai	728	Charbagh 40
Kotkilai	729	Babuzai 23
Kotlai	730	Kabal 8
Kudimar	733	Khwazakhela 32
Kuh	734	Charbagh 27
Kuh	735	Khwazakhela 35
Kuh	736	Bahrain 47
Kukrai	737	Babuzai 19
Kulader	738	Babuzai 18
Kulai	739	Khwazakhela 32
Kulban	742	Bahrain 48
Kuliya	743	Babuzai 22
Kun	744	Bahrain 48
Kund	745	Khwazakhela 32
Kunj	749	Kabal 17
Kuoi	750	Barikot 5
Kurai	751	Maṭṭa 38
Kurai	752	Bahrain 45
Kuza-jabagai	754	Babuzai 23
Kuz-bamakhel	755	Maṭṭa 38
Kuz-bandai	756	Kabal 17
Kuz-bargin	758	Khwazakhela 35
Kuz-bela	760	Bahrain 47
Kuz-durshkhela	761	Maṭṭa 39
Kuz-garai	762	Bahrain 45
Kuz-ghuzan	763	Babuzai 24
Kuz-gorshai	764	Bahrain 45
Kuz-jabar	765	Babuzai 24
Kuz-kanju	768	Kabal 17
Kuz-karingal	769	Khwazakhela 33
Kuz-kedam	770	Bahrain 50
Kuz-laikot	771	Bahrain 53
Kuz-lalku	772	Maṭṭa 44
Kuz-manasar	773	Babuzai 26
Kuz-samsara	774	Barikot 3
Kuz-shaur	775	Maṭṭa 40
Kuz-tikai	776	Bahrain 50
Kuz-uzbuk	777	Babuzai 24
Ladu	778	Khwazakhela 32
Lai	779	Maṭṭa 41
Lakai-kalai	780	Kabal 14
Lakai-kota	781	Maṭṭa 38
Lakhar	782	Khwazakhela 35
Lalbat	783	Maṭṭa 41
Lalobanda	785	Kabal 17
Landai	786	Charbagh 30
Landai	787	Maṭṭa 43
Landai	788	Maṭṭa 44
Landai-shah	792	Charbagh 28
Landakai	793	Barikot 1
Lande	794	Babuzai 19
Landi-choya	795	Kabal 14
Langar	796	Kabal 12
Langar	797	Khwazakhela 31
Langar-derai	798	Maṭṭa 39

Langonr	799	Bahrain	48
Laruka	800	Barikot	1
Letai	801	Khwazakhela	36
Lewanai	802	Babuzai	24
Lewanai	803	Charbagh	26
Lilbanr	805	Babuzai	26
Lilibanr	806	Maṭṭa	41
Loar-deolai	809	Kabal	14
Loar-serai	810	Babuzai	18
Loe-banr	812	Babuzai	21
Loe-namal	814	Maṭṭa	40
Loe-nao	815	Bahrain	37
Lundai	818	Babuzai	20
Lundakai	821	Charbagh	30
Mabanr	822	Maṭṭa	38
Macha	823	Khwazakhela	37
Madona	824	Maṭṭa	39
Magon	825	Charbagh	29
Mahak	826	Kabal	15
Mahasar	828	Bahrain	46
Maidar	830	Bahrain	46
Mailaga	831	Kabal	8
Maira	832	Babuzai	25
Maira	833	Khwazakhela	33
Malak-abad	838	Charbagh	27
Malalai	839	Babuzai	24
Malalai	840	Maṭṭa	40
Malal-dakorak	841	Charbagh	30
Malam	842	Charbagh	27
Malam-jabba	843	Charbagh	27
Malchalcharai	844	Bahrain	47
Malikabad	845	Kabal	17
Maloch	847	Kabal	17
Maluka	848	Kabal	17
Malukabad	849	Babuzai	21
Mam-derai	850	Kabal	17
Mandur	854	Maṭṭa	39
Mangaltan	855	Charbagh	30
Mangar-kot	856	Charbagh	28
Manglaor	858	Babuzai	23
Mangral-bela	859	Bahrain	45
Maniaur	860	Kabal	8
Mani-patai	861	Maṭṭa	41
Manja	862	Kabal	11
Mankar	864	Bahrain	45
Manki	865	Babuzai	24
Mankial	866	Bahrain	52
Manrai	869	Kabal	16
Manrai	870	Maṭṭa	42
Manr-patai	873	Khwazakhela	34
Manyar	874	Barikot	7
Manza	875	Maṭṭa	44
Manze	877	Babuzai	20
Marchil	880	Maṭṭa	44
Margater	881	Bahrain	47
Marghuzar	882	Babuzai	19
Mashkumai	884	Khwazakhela	32
Mashkun	885	Bahrain	51
Mashkun	886	Bahrain	53
Matarkun	887	Bahrain	50
Matrapendai	889	Babuzai	19
Matta	890	Maṭṭa	37
Matta	891	Maṭṭa	38
Matta	892	Khwazakhela	43
Mattai	893	Charbagh	28
Megai	894	Khwazakhela	33
Mego-derai	895	Khwazakhela	37
Mehergai	896	Babuzai	19
Melegai	897	Babuzai	21
Meragai	899	Babuzai	22
Miandam	902	Khwazakhela	36
Mian-kili	904	Maṭṭa	38
Miankote	905	Charbagh	30
Mian-mazra	906	Maṭṭa	38
Milkatli	908	Maṭṭa	43
Mingaora	909	Babuzai	18
Mirmi	911	Maṭṭa	39
Mogilai	912	Maṭṭa	39
Molnin-patai	914	Barikot	2
Moragai	915	Maṭṭa	38
Mozribanr	917	Charbagh	30
Muhammad-beg	918	Kabal	16
Mulla-pata	919	Kabal	16
Murai	920	Charbagh	28
Nabipatai	922	Bahrain	51
Naborai	923	Khwazakhela	37
Nagrai	924	Khwazakhela	32
Nagwa	925	Barikot	6
Najigram	926	Barikot	3
Nakhtar	928	Maṭṭa	16
Nali	929	Maṭṭa	39
Nalkot	931	Bahrain	42
Nalkot	932	Maṭṭa	46
Nao	933	Babuzai	26
Naona	934	Maṭṭa	40
Naranjpura	937	Kabal	15
Naredalai	938	Maṭṭa	39
Narosai	939	Maṭṭa	43
Nasafai	940	Kabal	8
Nasapai	941	Maṭṭa	44
Nasrat	942	Kabal	14
Natal	943	Bahrain	45
Natmaira	944	Barikot	3
Nawagay	945	Barikot	4
Nawe-kalai	946	Barikot	2
Nawe-kalai	947	Babuzai	7
Nawe-kalai	948	Babuzai	18
Nawe-kalai	949	Maṭṭa	23
Nawe-kalai	950	Khwazakhela	34
Nawe-kalai	951	Babuzai	38
Neza-mundo	952	Babuzai	20
Niam	953	Bahrain	48
Niko-derai	954	Charbagh	26
Nilgram	955	Maṭṭa	38
Nimakai	956	Kabal	16
Nimakai	957	Khwazakhela	37

Nimaki	958	Khwazakhela	35
Nimogram	959	Barikot	5
Ningulai	960	Kabal	17
Ningulai-ghunda	961	Kabal	17
Nocha	963	Charbagh	28
Nokhara	964	Maṭṭa	44
Obo	965	Charbagh	28
Ona	967	Maṭṭa	41
Pachaabad	969	Khwazakhela	37
Painda-shah-patai	972	Kabal	8
Paitisar	974	Khwazakhela	37
Paja	975	Bahrain	52
Pajigram	976	Babuzai	7
Panai	980	Maṭṭa	44
Panjao	981	Bahrain	46
Panjgram	982	Bahrain	45
Pankanai	983	Maṭṭa	40
Panr	984	Babuzai	21
Panrashai	986	Bahrain	47
Panrsat	987	Maṭṭa	40
Papar	988	Babuzai	23
Parkha	990	Babuzai	25
Par-patai	991	Maṭṭa	39
Parrai	992	Barikot	6
Parrai	993	Maṭṭa	43
Parwan	995	Kabal	17
Pashmal	997	Bahrain	53
Patai	998	Maṭṭa	39
Patai	999	Bahrain	52
Pateman	1001	Maṭṭa	40
Pia	1003	Bahrain	37
Piaz	1004	Bahrain	46
Piranai	1006	Bahrain	50
Pir-baglai	1007	Khwazakhela	34
Pir-cham	1008	Kabal	14
Pirdarra	1009	Bahrain	48
Pir-gandai	1010	Khwazakhela	35
Pirjat	1011	Maṭṭa	42
Pir-kalai	1012	Maṭṭa	38
Pirman-derai	1013	Babuzai	18
Pir-patai	1014	Khwazakhela	37
Pirkand	1016	Maṭṭa	43
Pirodai	1017	Maṭṭa	39
Porai-maidan	1018	Bahrain	53
Pukhtunpatai	1020	Bahrain	51
Pul-bela	1021	Bahrain	50
Pul-derai	1022	Khwazakhela	37
Punnubat	1023	Bahrain	46
Puroa	1025	Maṭṭa	41
Puronai	1026	Babuzai	22
Pushtunai	1027	Maṭṭa	42
Qala	1028	Babuzai	25
Ragistun	1037	Maṭṭa	44
Rahimabad	1038	Babuzai	18
Rakya	1039	Maṭṭa	43
Rama	1040	Kabal	17
Rambaki	1042	Khwazakhela	33
Ramet	1043	Bahrain	47
Rampatai	1046	Maṭṭa	40
Ranasar	1047	Khwazakhela	37
Rangela	1049	Barikot	5
Ranjai	1051	Khwazakhela	37
Rasulibanr	1053	Maṭṭa	16
Rema	1054	Maṭṭa	40
Roria	1055	Charbagh	30
Roringar	1056	Maṭṭa	43
Runial	1058	Maṭṭa	38
Sabar-shah	1060	Charbagh	27
Sabunai	1061	Babuzai	21
Sada	1062	Kabal	16
Saddo-khan	1063	Barikot	1
Sagar	1065	Maṭṭa	39
Saida	1066	Khwazakhela	37
Saidu-sharif	1069	Babuzai	18
Saiyidano-nawe-kalai	1070	Khwazakhela	34
Sakhra	1072	Maṭṭa	44
Salatanr	1073	Maṭṭa	43
Samai-kili	1076	Kabal	13
Sambat	1077	Maṭṭa	38
Sam-deolai	1078	Kabal	14
Sami	1079	Maṭṭa	43
Samir	1080	Khwazakhela	34
Samter	1082	Babuzai	24
Sandok	1083	Barikot	1
Sangar	1084	Babuzai	22
Sangota	1085	Babuzai	23
Sangrai	1086	Khwazakhela	35
Saprai	1087	Maṭṭa	38
Sar	1088	Babuzai	24
Sarai	1089	Bahrain	47
Sara-shah	1090	Babuzai	24
Sarbab	1091	Babuzai	19
Sarbala	1092	Kabal	10
Sarbarai	1100	Khwazakhela	37
Sardan	1102	Maṭṭa	41
Sardari	1103	Babuzai	24
Sarge	1105	Khwazakhela	36
Sargi	1106	Maṭṭa	42
Sarkanda	1107	Khwazakhela	36
Sarkarai	1108	Maṭṭa	40
Sarmai	1111	Maṭṭa	43
Sar-tikai	1112	Bahrain	50
Satai	1114	Khwazakhela	35
Sekhdarra	1115	Maṭṭa	43
Sekha	1116	Khwazakhela	33
Senai	1119	Khwazakhela	36
Ser	1120	Charbagh	27
Ser	1121	Bahrain	37
Serai	1122	Babuzai	16
Serai	1123	Babuzai	18
Serai	1124	Maṭṭa	18
Serai	1125	Khwazakhela	28
Serai	1126	Khwazakhela	34
Serai	1127	Kabal	37
Serai	1128	Maṭṭa	40
Serai	1129	Bahrain	43

Serai	1130	Charbagh	52
Serai-badai	1131	Bahrain	51
Shabeka	1132	Kabal	16
Shado	1134	Khwazakhela	33
Shaggai	1137	Babuzai	18
Shaggai	1138	Charbagh	27
Shago-patai	1139	Bahrain	52
Shahgram	1142	Bahrain	45
Shahid-bela	1144	Maṭṭa	44
Shahid-khpa	1145	Maṭṭa	40
Shahid-takai	1146	Bahrain	45
Shahnur	1148	Bahrain	47
Shahro	1149	Maṭṭa	40
Shai	1150	Bahrain	47
Shakardarra	1151	Maṭṭa	38
Shaladar	1152	Bahrain	48
Shalhand	1153	Kabal	16
Shalkhosar	1154	Maṭṭa	44
Shalkhosar	1155	Maṭṭa	44
Shalpalam	1158	Maṭṭa	38
Shalpin	1159	Khwazakhela	33
Shaltalu	1160	Charbagh	28
Shalun	1161	Khwazakhela	32
Shamelai	1163	Babuzai	21
Shami-derai	1165	Bahrain	46
Shandal	1167	Maṭṭa	40
Shanga	1168	Khwazakhela	36
Shangarai	1169	Maṭṭa	40
Shangawatai	1170	Maṭṭa	38
Shar	1176	Bahrain	47
Shar	1177	Bahrain	49
Sharara	1178	Babuzai	21
Sharbanr	1180	Kabal	16
Shar-dera	1181	Bahrain	49
Shargartan	1182	Maṭṭa	42
Sharna	1184	Babuzai	23
Sharorai	1185	Khwazakhela	32
Sharshai	1186	Maṭṭa	40
Sharshai	1187	Bahrain	45
Shekhan	1189	Maṭṭa	41
Shekhorai	1190	Babuzai	23
Sherai	1191	Khwazakhela	33
Sher-atraf	1192	Babuzai	20
Sher-khone	1193	Babuzai	19
Shingardar	1195	Barikot	7
Shingrai	1196	Babuzai	23
Shini	1197	Maṭṭa	37
Shini	1198	Khwazakhela	39
Shin-khad	1199	Charbagh	28
Shnai	1200	Charbagh	30
Sholgra	1201	Maṭṭa	44
Shudam	1202	Babuzai	21
Shukhdarra	1203	Maṭṭa	38
Shupin	1204	Maṭṭa	40
Sigram	1207	Kabal	17
Sijban	1209	Maṭṭa	38
Sinpora	1211	Maṭṭa	38
Sipar	1212	Charbagh	27
Siphan	1213	Barikot	7
Sirsanai	1215	Kabal	9
Smats	1216	Bahrain	46
Sorai	1218	Kabal	8
Sorai	1219	Bahrain	48
Spargai	1222	Charbagh	27
Sperai	1225	Maṭṭa	40
Sperkai	1227	Khwazakhela	34
Spinagatta	1230	Maṭṭa	39
Sulalman-ghundai	1232	Khwazakhela	34
Sund-dera	1234	Kabal	17
Sundimar	1235	Khwazakhela	34
Supal-banda	1236	Babuzai	19
Surai-tangai	1237	Charbagh	27
Surbanr	1238	Babuzai	24
Surbat	1239	Maṭṭa	38
Sur-derai	1240	Charbagh	28
Surgalai	1241	Kabal	8
Surkamar	1244	Khwazakhela	37
Surkh-pahut	1245	Babuzai	19
Swati	1248	Maṭṭa	42
Taghan	1249	Charbagh	25
Taghma	1250	Kabal	16
Taip	1251	Bahrain	51
Tajar-bela	1252	Maṭṭa	38
Takhtaband	1253	Babuzai	18
Takhto-bela	1254	Bahrain	49
Tal	1255	Kabal	12
Talang	1256	Barikot	1
Talgo-nakhtar	1258	Barikot	1
Talkar	1259	Maṭṭa	40
Talurai	1261	Babuzai	24
Tambagat	1262	Charbagh	27
Tambagat	1263	Maṭṭa	42
Tanazgah	1265	Bahrain	53
Tandora	1267	Bahrain	49
Tangai	1268	Charbagh	28
Tangai-wara	1270	Kabal	12
Tanganun	1271	Bahrain	45
Tangar	1272	Maṭṭa	41
Tangar	1273	Bahrain	45
Tangbanr	1274	Maṭṭa	38
Tango	1275	Babuzai	20
Tango	1276	Khwazakhela	33
Tapra	1278	Maṭṭa	38
Taqai	1279	Babuzai	7
Taragat	1280	Babuzai	20
Tarano	1282	Kabal	16
Tarel	1283	Bahrain	50
Taris	1284	Bahrain	51
Tarja	1285	Bahrain	44
Tarkana	1286	Bahrain	50
Tarkana	1287	Bahrain	51
Tarkana	1288	Bahrain	51
Tar-kana	1289	Bahrain	50
Tarkanadarra	1290	Bahrain	49
Tarkani	1291	Kabal	15
Tarogai	1292	Khwazakhela	32

Tawaun	1293	Charbagh	29
Tawde-obo	1294	Khwazakhela	37
Tendo-dak	1295	Babuzai	7
Tikai	1297	Bahrain	46
Tikai	1298	Bahrain	48
Tikai	1299	Bahrain	51
Tikdara	1301	Khwazakhela	31
Tilai	1302	Maṭṭa	39
Tilgram	1303	Charbagh	25
Tinka	1304	Bahrain	53
Tirang	1305	Barikot	5
Tirat	1306	Bahrain	45
Titabat	1307	Khwazakhela	31
Titaiwala	1308	Charbagh	30
Tobai	1309	Khwazakhela	33
Topsin	1310	Babuzai	20
Topsin	1311	Khwazakhela	32
Top-tut	1312	Charbagh	28
Torkamar	1313	Babuzai	20
Torwal	1315	Bahrain	48
Totakai	1316	Charbagh	30
Tsappar	1317	Maṭṭa	43
Tsappar	1318	Bahrain	46
Tsapparai	1319	Khwazakhela	33
Tsapparai	1320	Bahrain	46
Tsapparuna	1323	Bahrain	46
Tsukai	1324	Bahrain	50
Tungowala-morah	1326	Babuzai	20
Tutan-banda	1327	Kabal	10
Tut-banrin	1328	Kabal	17
Tutkai	1329	Maṭṭa	38
Tutkai	1330	Maṭṭa	39
Tuwa	1332	Charbagh	29
Uchrai	1333	Maṭṭa	40
Udigram	1335	Babuzai	18
Ugdai	1337	Babuzai	18
Urdam	1339	Khwazakhela	32
Urwana-kotlai	1340	Kabal	8
Usho	1341	Bahrain	54
Utrot	1345	Bahrain	54
Wadan-mandao	1347	Babuzai	23
Wainai	1348	Maṭṭa	40
Wakilabad	1349	Maṭṭa	39
Waliabad	1350	Charbagh	30
War-patai	1351	Kabal	16
Warukai-namal	1352	Maṭṭa	41
Wuch	1354	Bahrain	44
Yakh	1356	Charbagh	30
Zambak	1359	Maṭṭa	42
Zangar	1360	Charbagh	30
Zangun	1362	Maṭṭa	38
Zara-churrai	1363	Bahrain	45
Zarikhela	1364	Barikot	5
Zarinal	1365	Bahrain	52
Zewala	1366	Khwazakhela	32
Ziarat-khpa	1368	Maṭṭa	40
Zimdarra	1369	Maṭṭa	39
Zindwala	1371	Charbagh	30
Zinkharai	1372	Khwazakhela	34
Zizrat	1373	Khwazakhela	37
Zor-chel	1374	Bahrain	46
Zor-shalpin	1375	Khwazakhela	33

B. By Tehsil

1. Barikot

Name	Number	Typology	Map
Abwa	1	Village	2
Altangurai	19	Village	5
Amlukdara	24	Village	4
Baba-derai	63	Village	4
Babar-ghakhai-kandao	64	Pass	5
Bagai-kandao	73	Pass	5
Balo-kalai	96	Village	2
Bangai-banda	108	Pasture	3
Bar-banjir-banda	134	Pasture	2
Bar-batai-banda	136	Pasture	3
Bar-durzghar-banda	139	Pasture	3
Barikot	147	Village	4
Bar-kandak	150	Village	2
Bar-samsara	165	Village	3
Barwa	170	Village	7
Bizoban-kandao	216	Pass	5
Bostani-sar	219	Peak	2
Chalera	227	Village	5
Chingai	272	Village	5
Churkhai	293	Village	1
Chuwa	296	Village	1
Dad-banda	302	Pasture	2
Dedawar	341	Village	6
Dopialo-sar	374	Peak	1
Gamkot	405	Village	5
Garai	415	Village	5
Ghaligay	437	Village	7
Goratai	471	Village	2
Gumbatuna-banda	483	Pasture	6
Ilam	504	Peak	19
Jabagai	515	Village	5
Jalgar-banda	527	Pasture	3
Jaur-banda	547	Pasture	2
Kakai	579	Village	1
Kakai-kandao	580	Pass	1
Kandak	602	Village	2

Karakar-banda	630	Pasture	4
Karakar-kandao	631	Pass	4
Kashala	648	Peak	7
Khazana	683	Village	5
Kotah	722	Village	1
Kotah-sar	724	Peak	2
Kuoi	750	Village	5
Kuz-banjir-banda	757	Pasture	2
Kuz-batai-banda	759	Pasture	3
Kuz-samsara	774	Village	3
Landai-sar	791	Peak	42
Landakai	793	Village	1
Laruka	800	Village	1
Manyar	874	Village	7
Maran-sar	879	Peak	19
Mirati-kandao	910	Pass	5
Molnin-patai	914	Village	2
Mora-sar	916	Peak	1
Nagwa	925	Village	6
Najigram	926	Village	3
Narai-banda	935	Pasture	3
Natmaira	944	Village	3
Nawagay	945	Village	4
Nawe-kalai	946	Village	2
Nimogram	959	Village	5
Parrai	992	Village	6
Parrai-ghar	994	Peak	8
Rangela	1049	Village	5
Saddo-khan	1063	Village	1
Safashi-banda	1064	Pasture	3
Sandok	1083	Village	1
Sarkhanai-kandao	1109	Pass	5
Shewa-ghar	1194	Peak	5
Shingardar	1195	Village	7
Siphan	1213	Village	7
Surgalai-kandao	1242	Pass	8
Talang	1256	Village	1
Talao-kandao	1257	Pass	5
Talgo-nakhtar	1258	Village	1
Tarakai-kandao	1281	Pass	2
Tirang	1305	Village	5
Tsapparai-kandao	1321	Pass	1
Tsapparai-sar	1322	Peak	6
Yakabanj-banda	1355	Pasture	3
Zarikhela	1364	Village	5

2. Babuzai

Name	Number	Typology	Map
Ahingaro-derai	9	Village	18
Aman-kot	21	Village	18
Anwar-dhere	28	Village	20
Ara	29	Village	25
Arangelai-ghakhai	30	Pass	21
Arbut	31	Village	22
Ashar-garai	46	Village	24
Azgharai	61	Village	23
Bagh	74	Village	21
Bagoria	77	Village	21
Bakar	84	Village	20
Balogram	95	Village	18
Banda-ghal	102	Village	24
Bandanr	104	Village	22
Banjot	112	Village	24
Banj-sar	113	Peak	22
Bar-ghuzan	142	Village	24
Bar-jabar	148	Village	24
Bar-kandao	151	Pass	24
Bar-kandao-banda	153	Pasture	24
Bar-lewanai	159	Village	24
Bar-manasar	160	Village	26
Bar-uzbuk	168	Village	24
Bat-koran	177	Village	18
Batora	180	Village	18
Batra	181	Village	23
Bazai-derai	186	Village	24
Bazwanano-derai	187	Village	24
Bikai	205	Village	22
Bishbanr	213	Village	25
Bolat	218	Village	20
Charai	252	Village	24
Chere	263	Village	26
Chil-shoggai	266	Village	18
Chitor	274	Village	19
Chohria	278	Village	24
Damakal	311	Village	23
Dandun-qala	329	Village	18
Dangram	332	Village	21
Diwanbut	362	Village	24
Dop-sar	375	Peak	18
Dosara	377	Peak	24
Dre-bandai	380	Pasture	21
Duba	382	Village	24
Durbak-banda	383	Pasture	22
Dure-shah	384	Village	22
Faizabad	388	Village	18
Faizah	389	Village	21
Gadakot	399	Village	22
Gadakot	400	Village	23
Ganudai	413	Village	21
Garasa	422	Village	21
Garhi	425	Village	23
Gato	432	Village	25
Ghojalai	442	Village	18
Ghumbat	445	Village	22
Ghuz	447	Village	22
Gira	459	Peak	18
Godar	463	Village	20
Gogdara	465	Village	18

Gul-banda	476	Pasture	19
Guligram	480	Village	30
Guli-sar	481	Peak	18
Gurtai-abadan	486	Village	23
Gurtai-kandar	487	Village	23
Haji-baba	490	Village	18
Inzar-tangai	510	Village	23
Islampur	512	Village	20
Jabba	517	Village	22
Jambil	529	Village	22
Jandero	535	Village	18
Jauhar-kandao	546	Pass	26
Jauz-kandao	552	Pass	19
Jowari-kandao	562	Pass	20
Kachcha-kor	569	Village	22
Kad	571	Village	24
Kad	572	Village	24
Kalel-kandao	589	Pass	22
Kambar	596	Village	18
Kandakai	603	Village	24
Kandowala-morah	617	Village	22
Kangalai	618	Village	22
Kanj-kandao	620	Pass	26
Karai-sar	628	Peak	19
Karpo	643	Village	20
Kas	644	Village	24
Katelai	653	Village	18
Kheta	687	Village	21
Khushnab-baba	690	Village	18
Kokarai	703	Village	22
Korata	714	Village	22
Koruna	716	Village	19
Kosa	717	Peak	18
Kosar-banda	718	Pasture	22
Kot	720	Village	33
Kotkilai	729	Village	23
Kuar-sar-banda	732	Pasture	22
Kukrai	737	Village	19
Kulader	738	Village	18
Kuliya	743	Village	22
Kuza-jabagai	754	Village	23
Kuz-ghuzan	763	Village	24
Kuz-jabar	765	Village	24
Kuz-kandao	766	Pass	24
Kuz-kandao-banda	767	Pasture	24
Kuz-manasar	773	Village	26
Kuz-uzbuk	777	Village	24
Lande	794	Village	19
Lewanai	802	Village	24
Lilbanr	805	Village	26
Loar-serai	810	Village	18
Loe-banr	812	Village	21
Loe-sar	816	Peak	22
Lundai	818	Village	20
Maira	832	Village	25
Malalai	839	Village	24
Malukabad	849	Village	21
Manasar-sar	853	Peak	26
Manglaor	858	Village	23
Manki	865	Village	24
Manze	877	Village	20
Marghuzar	882	Village	19
Matrapendai	889	Village	19
Mehergai	896	Village	19
Melegai	897	Village	21
Meragai	899	Village	22
Mingaora	909	Village	18
Moi-kandao	913	Pass	19
Nao	933	Village	26
Nawe-kalai	947	Village	7
Nawe-kalai	948	Village	18
Nawe-kalai	951	Village	38
Neza-mundo	952	Village	20
Nizam-banda	962	Pasture	20
Pajigram	976	Village	7
Panr	984	Village	21
Papar	988	Village	23
Paranial-kandao	989	Pass	23
Parkha	990	Village	25
Pata-sar	1000	Peak	24
Pirman-derai	1013	Village	18
Puronai	1026	Village	22
Qala	1028	Village	25
Rahimabad	1038	Village	18
Rani-sar	1050	Peak	24
Ranjro-sar	1052	Peak	19
Sabunai	1061	Village	21
Saidu-sharif	1069	Village	18
Sakhi-sar	1071	Peak	7
Salim-khan	1074	Peak	20
Salim-khan-banda	1075	Pasture	20
Samter	1082	Village	24
Sangar	1084	Village	22
Sangota	1085	Village	23
Sar	1088	Village	24
Sara-shah	1090	Village	24
Sarbab	1091	Village	19
Sar-china-banda	1101	Pasture	20
Sardari	1103	Village	24
Serai	1122	Village	16
Serai	1123	Village	18
Shaggai	1137	Village	18
Shamelai	1163	Village	21
Shamelai-kandao	1164	Pass	21
Sharara	1178	Village	21
Sharna	1184	Village	23
Shekhorai	1190	Village	23
Sher-atraf	1192	Village	20
Sher-khone	1193	Village	19
Shingrai	1196	Village	23
Shudam	1202	Village	21
Spedar-banda	1223	Pasture	26
Spighog-kandao	1229	Pass	19
Suli-banda	1233	Pasture	24
Supal-banda	1236	Village	19
Surbanr	1238	Village	24

Surkh-pahut	1245	Village	19
Takhtaband	1253	Village	18
Talurai	1261	Village	24
Tandar-banda	1266	Pasture	24
Tango	1275	Village	20
Taqai	1279	Village	7
Taragat	1280	Village	20
Tendo-dak	1295	Village	7
Topsin	1310	Village	20
Torkamar	1313	Village	20
Tungowala-morah	1326	Village	20
Udigram	1335	Village	18
Ugdai	1337	Village	18
Unran-sar	1338	Peak	24
Uzbuk-sar	1346	Peak	24
Wadan-mandao	1347	Village	23

3. Kabal

Name	Number	Typology	Map
Ahingaro-baba-kandao	8	Pass	10
Akhun-kalai	13	Village	8
Aligram	16	Village	9
Amluktal-banda	25	Pasture	12
Amluk-tangai	26	Village	10
Archalai-banda	32	Pasture	13
Arkot-qila	36	Village	14
Asharai-banda	43	Pasture	12
Balagan-banda	90	Pasture	12
Banda	101	Village	46
Bandi-banda	106	Pasture	12
Banmanai-kandao	117	Pass	13
Baragat	124	Village	16
Bar-bandai	133	Village	17
Bar-kanju	154	Village	17
Barman-sar	161	Peak	12
Bar-patai	164	Village	10
Batul-banda	182	Pasture	13
Bauro-sar	184	Peak	17
Bayan-banda	185	Pasture	12
Bela	194	Village	50
Bela-banda	195	Pasture	13
Bhoka	197	Village	16
Biakand-kandao	199	Pass	16
Biakor	200	Village	16
Binwar-banda	211	Pasture	12
Burjal-kandao	224	Pass	15
Chanda-khora	242	Village	8
Chandakhwara	243	Village	9
Changai-dop-sar	244	Peak	8
Chanmarang-kandao	247	Pass	13
Chaprai-banda	249	Pasture	11
Chautar	262	Village	15
China-kili	268	Village	14
Chingai-banda	270	Pasture	15
Choaro-kandao	275	Pass	11
Chongiala-sar	282	Peak	16
Chopalu-kandao	284	Pass	12
Chopalu-sar	285	Peak	12
Chorpunari	287	Village	13
Chotar-banda	288	Pasture	12
Chur-banda	292	Pasture	12
Dadhrah	303	Village	8
Dagai	306	Village	8
Dakko-banda	308	Pasture	12
Dambar-kandao	313	Pass	40
Dambar-sar	314	Peak	11
Damghar	315	Village	17
Dande	326	Village	16
Dard	336	Village	32
Dardial	337	Village	12
Delai	342	Village	17
Derai	344	Village	14
Derai	345	Village	17
Dheri	358	Village	14
Dob-banda	365	Pasture	13
Doghalgai-kandao	369	Pass	12
Dokat-sar	372	Peak	10
Durman-unra-sar	385	Peak	12
Ehsanabad	387	Village	9
Faqiran-banda	392	Pasture	13
Gachkor-banda	398	Pasture	12
Galoch	402	Village	14
Gampora	406	Village	14
Garai	417	Village	39
Ghakhe-banda	436	Pasture	10
Ghamjaba	438	Village	9
Gharibabad	440	Village	30
Ghurejo	446	Village	17
Ghuzano-sar	451	Peak	13
Goda-banda	462	Pasture	13
Godhanu-banda	464	Pasture	14
Hazara	499	Village	9
Hunra-sar	502	Peak	16
Inzaro-banda	509	Pasture	11
Jatkot	544	Village	17
Jatkot-kandao	545	Pass	17
Jor-banda	561	Pasture	10
Kabal-banda	565	Pasture	12
Kabbal	567	Village	9
Kala	584	Village	14
Kamar-banda	593	Pasture	30
Kamyarai-banda	597	Pasture	12
Kandao	606	Village	28
Kanju	621	Village	9
Kasai	647	Village	8
Kashkar-banda	650	Pasture	11
Katiya	654	Village	14
Khar-banda	672	Pasture	11
Khatkotai	682	Village	9

Khazanai-banda	684	Pasture	11
Khemdarra	686	Village	8
Khojarbori-sar	688	Peak	15
Kodarai-derai	698	Village	11
Kolanda-banda	706	Pasture	12
Komyati	708	Village	12
Kontaro-banda	710	Pasture	16
Kontaro-sar	711	Peak	16
Korai-banda	713	Pasture	11
Kotgai-banda	726	Pasture	12
Kotlai	730	Village	8
Kulalai-banda	740	Pasture	11
Kund-banda	746	Pasture	11
Kund-kandao	747	Pass	12
Kund-sar	748	Peak	12
Kunj	749	Village	17
Kuz-bandai	756	Village	17
Kuz-kanju	768	Village	17
Lakai-kalai	780	Village	14
Lalobanda	785	Village	17
Landi-choya	795	Village	14
Langar	796	Village	12
Loar-deolai	809	Village	14
Lundai-kandao	819	Pass	12
Lundai-sar	820	Peak	12
Mahak	826	Village	15
Mailaga	831	Village	8
Maira-banda	834	Pasture	12
Makat-banda	837	Pasture	12
Malikabad	845	Village	17
Malkana-banda	846	Pasture	14
Maloch	847	Village	17
Maluka	848	Village	17
Mam-derai	850	Village	17
Manago-sar	851	Peak	15
Maniaur	860	Village	8
Manja	862	Village	11
Manja-kandao	863	Pass	11
Manrai	869	Village	16
Manrai-banda	871	Pasture	13
Manzarai-banda	876	Pasture	12
Manzghundai-banda	878	Pasture	10
Mian-baba-banda	900	Pasture	12
Mian-bela-banda	901	Pasture	12
Mianwara-banda	907	Pasture	13
Muhammad-beg	918	Village	16
Mulla-pata	919	Village	16
Murdar-banda	921	Pasture	10
Naranjpura	937	Village	15
Nasafai	940	Village	8
Nasrat	942	Village	14
Nimakai	956	Village	16
Ningulai	960	Village	17
Ningulai-ghunda	961	Village	17
Pacha-kili-banda	970	Pasture	13
Pacha-kili-banda	971	Pasture	13
Painda-shah-patai	972	Village	8
Parwan	995	Village	17
Patibast-banda	1002	Pasture	15
Pinorai-banda	1005	Pasture	12
Pir-cham	1008	Village	14
Pir-patai-banda	1015	Pasture	11
Qalagai-banda	1029	Pasture	11
Qalagai-banda	1030	Pasture	11
Qalagai-banda	1031	Pasture	11
Qalagai-banda	1032	Pasture	11
Qalagai-banda	1033	Pasture	11
Qalagai-sar	1035	Peak	11
Rama	1040	Village	17
Rama-kandao	1041	Pass	17
Sada	1062	Village	16
Samai-kili	1076	Village	13
Sam-deolai	1078	Village	14
Samsel-banda	1081	Pasture	9
Sarbala	1092	Village	10
Sarbala-banda	1093	Pasture	10
Sargai-banda	1104	Pasture	15
Saso-sar	1113	Peak	38
Selai-kandao	1117	Pass	13
Serai	1127	Village	37
Shabeka	1132	Village	16
Shadhand-banda	1133	Pasture	10
Shagai-banda	1135	Pasture	10
Shahjahan-banda	1147	Pasture	12
Shalhand	1153	Village	16
Shalkhosar-banda	1156	Pasture	16
Shalkhosar-kandao	1157	Pass	16
Shangora-banda	1172	Pasture	13
Shangora-banda	1173	Pasture	13
Sharbanr	1180	Village	16
Sharifai-banda	1183	Pasture	10
Sigram	1207	Village	17
Sikka-banda	1210	Pasture	16
Sirsanai	1215	Village	9
Sorai	1218	Village	8
Spalmai-banda	1220	Pasture	15
Speralgot-sar	1226	Peak	13
Sperkai-banda	1228	Pasture	12
Sund-dera	1234	Village	17
Surgalai	1241	Village	8
Taghma	1250	Village	16
Tal	1255	Village	12
Talkar-kandao	1260	Pass	16
Tangai-wara	1270	Village	12
Tangu-banda	1277	Pasture	12
Tarano	1282	Village	16
Tarkani	1291	Village	15
Tighak-banda	1296	Pasture	10
Torusatta-banda	1314	Pasture	13
Tutan-banda	1327	Village	10
Tut-banrin	1328	Village	17
Tutpanrai-sar	1331	Peak	17
Urwana-kotlai	1340	Village	8
Usmani-sar	1343	Peak	17
War-patai	1351	Village	16
Yakh-tangai-sar	1358	Peak	16

4. Charbagh

Name	Number	Typology	Map
Achro-banda	2	Pasture	28
Achro-kandao	3	Pass	28
Adai	4	Village	29
Alamganj	14	Village	30
Allahabad	18	Village	30
Asharai	39	Village	28
Asharbanr	44	Village	30
Asharo-paiza	47	Village	30
Bagolai	76	Village	30
Bakanran	83	Village	30
Bala-kor	91	Village	28
Balalai	92	Village	30
Banda-sar	105	Peak	28
Bango-sar	110	Peak	27
Ban-pur-sar	120	Village	27
Bikan	206	Village	26
Bilmaz-sar	209	Peak	27
Charai	253	Village	27
Charbagh	257	Village	30
Chingalai	271	Village	30
Churlak-sar	294	Peak	27
Dakorak	309	Village	30
Dando	328	Village	27
Darra	340	Village	29
Doghalgai	368	Village	27
Gadwa-sar	401	Peak	28
Ganajir	409	Village	28
Ganderai	410	Village	30
Gat	428	Village	26
Gat-kandao	430	Pass	26
Gharibabad	439	Village	17
Gishar	460	Village	27
Gulibagh	479	Village	24
Gul-paiza	482	Village	28
Hamwarai	491	Village	30
Igalbanr	503	Village	30
Ilanai	505	Village	28
Jaikot	523	Village	25
Jampur-derai	531	Village	30
Jobe-kandao	558	Pass	27
Kakot	583	Village	28
Kamarbagh	592	Village	17
Kamargai	594	Village	30
Kandao	605	Village	16
Kandao-banda	608	Pasture	26
Kandar	611	Village	30
Kasuna	651	Village	27
Khadang	661	Village	29
Khadang-sar	663	Peak	29
Khadarzo-patai	664	Village	29
Kontargat	709	Village	30
Kotkai	728	Village	40
Kuh	734	Village	27
Landai	786	Village	30
Landai-shah	792	Village	28
Lewanai	803	Village	26
Lundakai	821	Village	30
Magon	825	Village	29
Malak-abad	838	Village	27
Malal-dakorak	841	Village	30
Malam	842	Village	27
Malam-jabba	843	Village	27
Mangaltan	855	Village	30
Mangar-kot	856	Village	28
Mattai	893	Village	28
Miankote	905	Village	30
Mozribanr	917	Village	30
Murai	920	Village	28
Narai-sur-banda	936	Pasture	25
Niko-derai	954	Village	26
Nocha	963	Village	28
Obo	965	Village	28
Ranga-kandao	1048	Pass	28
Roria	1055	Village	30
Sabar-shah	1060	Village	27
Ser	1120	Village	27
Serai	1130	Village	52
Shagar-sar	1136	Peak	26
Shaggai	1138	Village	27
Shaltalu	1160	Village	28
Shalwa-kandao	1162	Pass	30
Shangla-kandao	1171	Pass	28
Shango-sar	1174	Peak	28
Shin-khad	1199	Village	28
Shnai	1200	Village	30
Sipar	1212	Village	27
Soko-kandao	1217	Pass	28
Spargai	1222	Village	27
Surai-tangai	1237	Village	27
Sur-derai	1240	Village	28
Taghan	1249	Village	25
Tambagat	1262	Village	27
Tangai	1268	Village	28
Tawaun	1293	Village	29
Tilgram	1303	Village	25
Titaiwala	1308	Village	30
Top-tut	1312	Village	28
Totakai	1316	Village	30
Tuwa	1332	Village	29
Waliabad	1350	Village	30
Welan-sar	1353	Peak	28
Yakh	1356	Village	30
Zangar	1360	Village	30
Zangi-banda	1361	Pasture	29
Zindwala	1371	Village	30

5. Khwazakhela

Name	Number	Typology	Map
Agor	7	Village	37
Ajorai	12	Village	36
Aligai	15	Village	34
Arkhuna	34	Village	44
Asala	38	Village	34
Asharai	40	Village	33
Ateran	51	Village	31
Badre	71	Village	37
Baki-banda	85	Pasture	35
Bakro	88	Village	37
Banda	99	Village	17
Bandai	103	Village	31
Bang	107	Village	34
Banpakia	118	Village	35
Bararai	131	Village	31
Bar-bargin	135	Village	35
Baret	140	Village	33
Bar-karingal	155	Village	33
Barkhai	156	Village	36
Behar	190	Village	32
Bela	191	Village	11
Biladram	208	Village	32
Binkat	210	Village	37
Budai	220	Village	32
Burai	223	Village	33
Chaliar	228	Village	31
Cham	229	Village	32
Cham	232	Village	43
Chamtia	240	Village	32
Chanchar	241	Village	37
Chankolai	246	Village	33
China-kandao	267	Pass	35
Chopra-sar	286	Peak	32
Churlak-sar	295	Peak	35
Dad	299	Village	32
Dand	316	Village	37
Dandai-sar	322	Peak	37
Dande	327	Village	33
Dard	335	Village	16
Derai	353	Village	46
Dobar-sar	364	Peak	36
Dokadai	371	Village	34
Dop	373	Village	34
Faqira	391	Village	33
Gamkat-banda	404	Pasture	33
Gashkor	427	Village	31
Gato-sar-banda	433	Pasture	32
Gatsar-banda	435	Pasture	36
Ghulkhwaro-sar-banda	444	Pasture	31
Ghuzbanr	452	Village	31
Gidar-sar-banda	456	Pasture	32
Gidar-sar-banda	457	Pasture	33
Gul-derai	478	Village	34
Hamwarak	492	Village	31
Hawarai	498	Village	33
Ilman	508	Village	33
Jabrai	519	Village	33
Jabrai	520	Village	36
Jano	537	Village	31
Jan-patai	538	Village	33
Jashar	543	Village	33
Jijal-kandao	556	Pass	36
Jontar	560	Village	37
Jukhmai	563	Village	37
Kakardam	581	Village	33
Kakhai-derai	582	Village	32
Kandao	607	Village	37
Kandao-banda	609	Pasture	35
Karai	627	Village	33
Karange	635	Village	32
Karorai	641	Village	33
Karorai-kandao	642	Pass	33
Katosar-banda	655	Village	34
Khanabad	667	Village	34
Kharawe	671	Village	33
Khardu-sar	673	Peak	33
Kharo-kandao	680	Pass	34
Kharwe	681	Village	31
Khorgarai	689	Village	34
Khwazakhela	694	Village	31
Kochla	697	Village	33
Kopra-sar	712	Peak	36
Kormal	715	Village	32
Kot	719	Village	23
Kotanai	725	Village	34
Kudimar	733	Village	32
Kuh	735	Village	35
Kulai	739	Village	32
Kund	745	Village	32
Kuz-bargin	758	Village	35
Kuz-karingal	769	Village	33
Ladu	778	Village	32
Lakhar	782	Village	35
Langar	797	Village	31
Letai	801	Village	36
Macha	823	Village	37
Maira	833	Village	33
Mangazai-kandao	857	Pass	36
Manr-patai	873	Village	34
Mashkumai	884	Village	32
Matta	892	Village	43
Megai	894	Village	33
Mego-derai	895	Village	37
Menduria-kandao	898	Pass	35
Miandam	902	Village	36
Naborai	923	Village	37
Nagrai	924	Village	32
Nawe-kalai	950	Village	34
Nimakai	957	Village	37
Nimaki	958	Village	35

Ormal-kandao	968	Pass	28
Pachaabad	969	Village	37
Paitisar	974	Village	37
Pir-baglai	1007	Village	34
Pir-gandai	1010	Village	35
Pir-patai	1014	Village	37
Pul-derai	1022	Village	37
Rambaki	1042	Village	33
Ramotai-loe-sar	1045	Peak	29
Ranasar	1047	Village	37
Ranjai	1051	Village	37
Saida	1066	Village	37
Saiyidano-nawe-kalai	1070	Village	34
Samir	1080	Village	34
Sangrai	1086	Village	35
Sarbarai	1100	Village	37
Sarge	1105	Village	36
Sarkanda	1107	Village	36
Sarle-banda	1110	Pasture	34
Satai	1114	Village	35
Sekha	1116	Village	33
Semprai-sar	1118	Peak	33
Senai	1119	Village	36
Serai	1125	Village	28
Serai	1126	Village	34
Shado	1134	Village	33
Shalpin	1159	Village	33
Shalun	1161	Village	32
Shanga	1168	Village	36
Sharorai	1185	Village	32
Sherai	1191	Village	33
Shini	1198	Village	39
Shuro-sar	1205	Peak	32
Sperkai	1227	Village	34
Spinkoto-banda	1231	Pasture	32
Sulalman-ghundai	1232	Village	34
Sundimar	1235	Village	34
Surkamar	1244	Village	37
Tango	1276	Village	33
Tarogai	1292	Village	32
Tawde-obo	1294	Village	37
Tikdara	1301	Village	31
Titabat	1307	Village	31
Tobai	1309	Village	33
Topsin	1311	Village	32
Tsapparai	1319	Village	33
Urdam	1339	Village	32
Zewala	1366	Village	32
Zin-sar	1370	Peak	35
Zinkharai	1372	Village	34
Zizrat	1373	Village	37
Zor-shalpin	1375	Village	33

6. Maṭṭa

Name	**Number**	**Typology**	**Map**
Agal	6	Village	41
Aligram	17	Village	40
Alwara	20	Village	43
Amluk	22	Village	44
Amlukbanr	23	Village	38
Arkot	35	Village	38
Asharai	41	Village	39
Asharai	42	Village	39
Asharbanr	45	Village	38
Atia-qala	52	Village	41
Awai-shah	54	Village	39
Awarai	56	Village	41
Awarai	57	Village	43
Awarai	58	Village	44
Awi-kas	59	Village	38
Azad-banda	60	Pasture	44
Bab	62	Village	38
Babu-sar	65	Peak	44
Bachi-kandao	67	Pass	43
Badkot	70	Peak	39
Bahadur-banda	78	Pasture	41
Baidarra	82	Village	39
Bakor	87	Village	41
Balasur	93	Village	39
Balat	94	Village	40
Banj-banda	111	Pasture	38
Bankara	114	Village	39
Ban-pangharai	119	Village	42
Banragai	122	Village	43
Barabarai	123	Village	42
Bar-bamakhel	132	Village	38
Bar-durshkhel	138	Village	39
Bariam	146	Village	38
Bar-kadar	149	Village	42
Bar-kandao	152	Pass	42
Bar-lalku	158	Village	44
Baro	162	Village	39
Barona	163	Village	42
Bar-shaur	166	Village	40
Barthana	167	Village	41
Barwai	171	Village	44
Baskhela	176	Village	39
Batku	178	Village	44
Batol	179	Village	39
Baurai	183	Village	17
Biakand	198	Village	38
Biha	201	Village	42
Bijora	204	Village	39
Bodigram	217	Village	38
Burjosar-banda	225	Pasture	42
Chakur	226	Village	39
Cham	230	Village	32
Cham	233	Village	45
Cham-serai	237	Village	38

Cham-shaur	238	Village	40
Cham-sinpora	239	Village	38
Changlalai	245	Village	41
Char	250	Village	43
Charai	254	Village	44
Charma	259	Village	43
Chatkarai	260	Village	43
Chaturia	261	Village	40
Chheri	265	Village	44
Chopal	283	Village	43
Chuprial	290	Village	39
Dadpanrai	305	Village	38
Dagai	307	Village	41
Damama	312	Village	39
Dand	317	Village	39
Dandai	320	Village	40
Dandai	321	Village	40
Dandarai	323	Village	41
Dand-kandao	325	Pass	44
Dang-arkot-qala	330	Village	38
Dar-banda	334	Pasture	48-49
Darmai	338	Village	44
Darozgar	339	Village	38
Derai	346	Village	34
Derai	347	Village	37
Derai	348	Village	41
Deranpatai	354	Village	38
Doghlai	370	Village	40
Doshagram	379	Village	44
Dutpanrai	386	Village	40
Fazalbeg	393	Village	44
Fizil-banda	394	Village	42
Gabranai	397	Village	44
Gamchana	403	Village	42
Gamsar	407	Village	43
Ganderai	411	Village	39
Garai	416	Village	8
Garai	418	Village	44
Garai	419	Village	44
Garai	420	Village	45
Gardaisar	423	Village	39
Gat	429	Village	40
Gatkotal	431	Village	38
Ghari-bala	441	Village	38
Ghuzano-cham	449	Village	38
Ghuzano-cham	450	Village	38
Ghuzkas	453	Village	44
Ghwai-banda	454	Pasture	43
Giga	458	Village	38
Goal	461	Village	43
Gojalai	466	Village	38
Golra	467	Village	38
Gujarbanr	475	Village	39
Gul-banda	477	Pasture	40
Gwalerai	488	Village	41
Hawar	497	Village	42
Hindubeg-banda	500	Pasture	43
Hindubeg-sar	501	Peak	43

Ilani	506	Village	39
Jabrai	521	Village	39
Jalba	524	Village	43
Jalba-sar	526	Peak	43
Jamalasar	528	Village	39
Jana	534	Village	41
Jaranda-kandao	539	Pass	42
Jarugai	542	Village	42
Jaur-banda	548	Pasture	41
Jaur-banda	549	Pasture	41
Jaur-banda	550	Pasture	41
Jawi	555	Village	42
Jura	564	Village	38
Kabalku	566	Village	43
Kadarchaka	573	Village	42
Kadkhwar	574	Village	43
Kadiar	575	Village	42
Kalagai	585	Village	38
Kalakot	587	Village	44
Kalo-banda	590	Pasture	43
Kamali-banda	591	Pasture	39
Kanati	598	Village	42
Kanati	599	Village	42
Kand	600	Village	43
Kandai	601	Village	41
Kandaogai	610	Village	40
Kandar	613	Village	44
Kandar	614	Village	50
Kangar	619	Village	43
Karakal	629	Village	41
Karinuna	639	Village	43
Karo-banda	640	Pasture	42
Khachar	660	Village	39
Khadang	662	Village	39
Khairabad	665	Village	38
Khamas	666	Village	16
Khanpatai	668	Village	38
Kharairai	669	Village	38
Kharairai-cham	670	Village	38
Kharkai	675	Village	42
Kharkai	678	Village	53
Kharkarai	679	Village	42
Khelkhona	685	Village	39
Khwar-mandaona	693	Village	16
Koga	699	Village	43
Kohistani-banda	702	Pasture	43
Kotkai	727	Village	30
Kurai	751	Village	38
Kuratai-kandao	753	Pass	38
Kuz-bamakhel	755	Village	38
Kuz-durshkhela	761	Village	39
Kuz-lalku	772	Village	44
Kuz-shaur	775	Village	40
Lai	779	Village	41
Lakai-kota	781	Village	38
Lalbat	783	Village	41
Landai	787	Village	43
Landai	788	Village	44

Landai-sar	790	Peak	19
Langar-derai	798	Village	39
Lilibanr	806	Village	41
Lito-sar	807	Peak	41
Loe-namal	814	Village	40
Mabanr	822	Village	38
Madona	824	Village	39
Mair-banda	835	Pasture	43
Malalai	840	Village	40
Mandur	854	Village	39
Mani-patai	861	Village	41
Manrai	870	Village	42
Manza	875	Village	44
Marchil	880	Village	44
Matta	890	Village	37
Matta	891	Village	38
Mian-kili	904	Village	38
Mian-mazra	906	Village	38
Milkatli	908	Village	43
Mirmi	911	Village	39
Mogilai	912	Village	39
Moragai	915	Village	38
Nakhtar	928	Village	16
Nali	929	Village	39
Nalkot	932	Village	46
Naona	934	Village	40
Naredalai	938	Village	39
Narosai	939	Village	43
Nasapai	941	Village	44
Nawe-kalai	949	Village	23
Nilgram	955	Village	38
Nokhara	964	Village	44
Ona	967	Village	41
Panai	980	Village	44
Pankanai	983	Village	40
Panrsat	987	Village	40
Par-patai	991	Village	39
Parrai	993	Village	43
Pashino-banda	996	Pasture	43
Patai	998	Village	39
Pateman	1001	Village	40
Pirjat	1011	Village	42
Pir-kalai	1012	Village	38
Pirkand	1016	Village	43
Pirodai	1017	Village	39
Prangman-sar	1019	Peak	42
Puroa	1025	Village	41
Pushtunai	1027	Village	42
Ragistun	1037	Village	44
Rakya	1039	Village	43
Rampatai	1046	Village	40
Rasulibanr	1053	Village	16
Rema	1054	Village	40
Roringar	1056	Village	43
Runial	1058	Village	38
Sagar	1065	Village	39
Saidgi-kandao	1067	Pass	43
Sakhra	1072	Village	44
Salatanr	1073	Village	43
Sambat	1077	Village	38
Sami	1079	Village	43
Saprai	1087	Village	38
Sar-banda	1094	Pasture	38
Sar-banda	1095	Pasture	40
Sardan	1102	Village	41
Sargi	1106	Village	42
Sarkarai	1108	Village	40
Sarmai	1111	Village	43
Sekhdarra	1115	Village	43
Serai	1124	Village	18
Serai	1128	Village	40
Shago-sar	1140	Peak	43
Shah-dop-sar	1141	Peak	39
Shahid-bela	1144	Village	44
Shahid-khpa	1145	Village	40
Shahro	1149	Village	40
Shakardarra	1151	Village	38
Shalkhosar	1154	Village	44
Shalkhosar	1155	Village	44
Shalpalam	1158	Village	38
Shandal	1167	Village	40
Shangarai	1169	Village	40
Shangawatai	1170	Village	38
Shargartan	1182	Village	42
Sharshai	1186	Village	40
Shekhan	1189	Village	41
Shini	1197	Village	37
Sholgra	1201	Village	44
Shukhdarra	1203	Village	38
Shupin	1204	Village	40
Siakas-banda	1206	Pasture	42
Sijban	1209	Village	38
Sinpora	1211	Village	38
Sperai	1225	Village	40
Spinagatta	1230	Village	39
Surbat	1239	Village	38
Swatai-kandao	1247	Pass	42
Swati	1248	Village	42
Tajar-bela	1252	Village	38
Talkar	1259	Village	40
Tambagat	1263	Village	42
Tangar	1272	Village	41
Tangbanr	1274	Village	38
Tapra	1278	Village	38
Tilai	1302	Village	39
Tsappar	1317	Village	43
Tutkai	1329	Village	38
Tutkai	1330	Village	39
Uchrai	1333	Village	40
Uchrai-sar	1334	Peak	40
Wainai	1348	Village	40
Wakilabad	1349	Village	39
Warukai-namal	1352	Village	41
Zambak	1359	Village	42
Zangun	1362	Village	38
Ziarat-khpa	1368	Village	40
Zimdarra	1369	Village	39

7. Bahrain

Name	Number	Typology	Map
Adrer	5	Village	47
Ahingaro-derai	10	Village	44
Ain	11	Village	45
Anisar	27	Village	48
Arkhuna	33	Village	36
Asagai	37	Village	47
Asharopatai	48	Village	53
Asrit	49	Village	53
Atsar	53	Village	48
Awarai	55	Village	40
Bachchi-derai	66	Village	46
Badai	68	Village	51
Badder	69	Village	48
Badwai-kandao	72	Pass	54
Baghsar	75	Village	47
Bahadur-khelo-charai	79	Village	47
Bahnium	81	Village	53
Baknai	86	Village	53
Bala-an	89	Pass	54
Ban	97	Village	45
Ban	98	Village	47
Banda	100	Village	33
Bangesh	109	Village	45
Ban-khwar	115	Village	54
Bankor	116	Village	48
Banr	121	Village	49
Barai	125	Village	51
Barai	126	Village	53
Baral	127	Village	47
Baranial	129	Village	48
Baranwai	130	Village	46
Bar-bela	137	Village	47
Bar-garai	141	Village	45
Bar-gorshai	144	Village	45
Bar-gunaguz	145	Village	50
Bar-laikot	157	Village	53
Baruj	169	Village	44
Basesar	173	Village	47
Bashkal	174	Village	46
Bashkaro-an	175	Pass	54
Bedag	188	Village	46
Bedag	189	Village	46
Bela	192	Village	33
Bela	193	Village	46
Berang	196	Village	45
Bijai	203	Village	50
Bishai	212	Village	53
Bishgram	215	Village	46
Bujabanr	221	Village	47
Bura-sar	222	Peak	46
Cham	231	Village	39
Cham	234	Village	50
Chambar	235	Village	49
Chambar-ghakhai	236	Peak	49
Chaprai	248	Village	44
Char	251	Village	47
Charai-kandao	255	Pass	46
Charai-kandao	256	Pass	47
Cheripun	264	Village	45
China-sar	269	Peak	46
Chirai	273	Village	48
Chobek	276	Village	47
Chodgram	277	Village	53
Chokel-banda	279	Pasture	52
Chokel-banda	280	Pasture	52
Chokel-kandao	281	Pass	52
Chotkan	289	Village	50
Churarai	291	Village	45
Dabargai	297	Village	46
Dabna	298	Village	53
Dadalbho	300	Peak	54
Dadarili-an	301	Pass	54
Dam	310	Village	47
Danda	318	Village	46
Danda	319	Village	46
Dand-banda	324	Pasture	49
Dangbanr	331	Village	47
Derai	349	Village	44
Derai	350	Village	45
Derai	351	Village	45
Derai	352	Village	46
Desan-kandao	355	Pass	54
Dewan	356	Village	52
Dewan	357	Village	53
Diwangar	363	Lake	54
Dilban	359	Village	48
Dirlam	360	Village	53
Diro	361	Village	47
Doda	366	Village	46
Doda-derai	367	Village	48
Doralai	376	Village	47
Falak-sar	390	Peak	54
Gabral	395	Village	54
Gamsir	408	Village	47
Gantar	412	Village	48
Gaorarban	414	Village	50
Garai	421	Village	50
Gargai-shalkhai	424	Village	46
Garnai	426	Village	47
Gatsar	434	Village	48
Ghorejai	443	Village	47
Ghuzano-banda	448	Pasture	53
Gidar	455	Village	46
Gora-daka	468	Village	52
Gora-daka-kandao	469	Pass	51
Gorail	470	Village	53
Gori-bela	472	Village	51
Gosh	473	Village	53
Goshai	474	Village	50
Gund-patai	484	Village	52

Haium	489	Village	53
Harianai	493	Village	53
Harianai-bagla	494	Village	53
Hawai	496	Village	51
Illa	507	Village	52
Irobai	511	Village	48
Jaba	513	Village	51
Jaba-banda	514	Pasture	51
Jabba	518	Village	49
Jai	522	Village	50
Jalban	525	Village	54
Jamrai	532	Village	49
Jamrai	533	Village	50
Jandrai	536	Village	49
Jaro	541	Village	37
Jauzan	551	Village	53
Jawarkas	553	Village	45
Jawar-kas	554	Village	53
Jira	557	Village	53
Kachal-bela	568	Village	49
Kachhikhani-an	570	Pass	54
Kafir-banda	576	Pasture	46
Kahai	577	Village	47
Kahai	578	Village	47
Kalagram	586	Village	44
Kalam	588	Village	54
Kamarkha	595	Village	52
Kandar	612	Village	41
Kandia-kandao	615	Pass	52
Kandimar	616	Village	53
Kanr	622	Village	48
Kanro-sar-banda	623	Pasture	45
Kanrtikai	624	Village	48
Kar	625	Village	44
Kar	626	Village	47
Karamar	633	Village	46
Karandukai	634	Village	53
Kar-banda	636	Pasture	50
Kar-bela	637	Village	53
Karial	638	Village	46
Kas	645	Village	46
Kas	646	Village	53
Kashankad	649	Village	46
Kat-dera	652	Village	49
Kedam-bela	656	Village	50
Ketal	658	Village	47
Khabin	659	Village	45
Kharesha	674	Village	45
Kharkai	676	Village	43
Kharkai	677	Village	47
Khwar	691	Village	45
Khwar	692	Village	53
Kit	696	Village	53
Kohi	700	Village	49
Kohistan-tikai	701	Village	50
Kolalai	704	Village	51
Kolbanr	707	Village	46
Kot	721	Village	53

Kuh	736	Village	47
Kulban	742	Village	48
Kun	744	Village	48
Kurai	752	Village	45
Kuz-bela	760	Village	47
Kuz-garai	762	Village	45
Kuz-gorshai	764	Village	45
Kuz-kedam	770	Village	50
Kuz-laikot	771	Village	53
Kuz-tikai	776	Village	50
Lalku-kandao	784	Pass	44
Langonr	799	Village	48
Lizzat-banda	808	Pasture	53
Lo-banda	811	Pasture	48
Loe-nao	815	Village	37
Luda-sar	817	Peak	47
Mahasar	828	Village	46
Maho-dand	829	Lake	54
Maidar	830	Village	46
Malchalcharai	844	Village	47
Manali-an	852	Pass	54
Mangral-bela	859	Village	45
Mankar	864	Village	45
Mankial	866	Village	52
Mankial-tsukai	868	Peak	52
Margater	881	Village	47
Mashkun	885	Village	51
Mashkun	886	Village	53
Matarkun	887	Village	50
Matlit-an	888	Pass	54
Nabipatai	922	Village	51
Nalkot	931	Village	42
Natal	943	Village	45
Niam	953	Village	48
Paja	975	Village	52
Palesar-an	977	Pass	54
Paloga-an	978	Pass	54
Panjao	981	Village	46
Panjgram	982	Village	45
Panrashai-kandao	985	Pass	47
Panrashai	986	Village	47
Pashmal	997	Village	53
Patai	999	Village	52
Pia	1003	Village	37
Piaz	1004	Village	46
Piranai	1006	Village	50
Pirdarra	1009	Village	48
Porai-maidan	1018	Village	53
Pukhtunpatai	1020	Village	51
Pul-bela	1021	Village	50
Punnubat	1023	Village	46
Punnubat-sar	1024	Peak	46
Qandalu-ghakhai	1036	Peak	49
Ramet	1043	Village	47
Rustam-sar	1059	Peak	53
Sarai	1089	Village	47
Sar-banda	1096	Pasture	44
Sar-banda	1097	Pasture	50

Sar-banda	1098	Pasture	50
Sar-banda	1099	Pasture	50
Sar-tikai	1112	Village	50
Ser	1121	Village	37
Serai	1129	Village	43
Serai-badai	1131	Village	51
Shago-patai	1139	Village	52
Shahgram	1142	Village	45
Shahi-banda	1143	Pasture	48
Shahid-takai	1146	Village	45
Shahnur	1148	Village	47
Shai	1150	Village	47
Shaladar	1152	Village	48
Shami-derai	1165	Village	46
Shamkor-banda	1166	Pasture	47
Shar	1176	Village	47
Shar	1177	Village	49
Shar-banda	1179	Pasture	53
Shar-dera	1181	Village	49
Sharshai	1187	Village	45
Sirikar-kandao	1214	Pass	51
Smats	1216	Village	46
Sorai	1219	Village	48
Surkar-kandao	1243	Pass	52
Taip	1251	Village	51
Takhto-bela	1254	Village	49
Tanazgah	1265	Village	53
Tandora	1267	Village	49
Tangai-banda	1269	Pasture	46
Tanganun	1271	Village	45
Tangar	1273	Village	45
Tarel	1283	Village	50
Taris	1284	Village	51
Tarja	1285	Village	44
Tarkana	1286	Village	50
Tarkana	1287	Village	51
Tarkana	1288	Village	51
Tar-kana	1289	Village	50
Tarkanadarra	1290	Village	49
Tikai	1297	Village	46
Tikai	1298	Village	48
Tikai	1299	Village	51
Tikai-sar	1300	Peak	51
Tinka	1304	Village	53
Tirat	1306	Village	45
Torwal	1315	Village	48
Tsappar	1318	Village	46
Tsapparai	1320	Village	46
Tsapparuna	1323	Village	46
Tsukai	1324	Village	50
Tukataki	1325	Lake	54
Usho	1341	Village	54
Utrot	1345	Village	54
Wuch	1354	Village	44
Yakh-kandao	1357	Pass	46
Zara-churrai	1363	Village	45
Zarinal	1365	Village	52
Zhandrai pass	1367	Pass	54
Zor-chel	1374	Village	46

MAPS

The following maps contain all toponyms quoted in the Gazetteer. For practical reasons, I decided to divide the entire District of Swāt in 54 maps, being identifiable with all minor valleys. All maps are in different scales, according to editing requirements and major or minor presence of toponyms: as an instance, map 54, "Kalam", represents about one third of the entire Swāt valley, due to the scarce presence of settlements in these high mountain areas. For the same reasons of book format, some maps are horizontal, while for the sake of legibility the bulk of maps are vertical. Titles of each map are merely indicative: accordingly, the toponyms included in each map do not necessarily belong to the valley, which entitles the map itself. For the analytic description of each point, its position and geographic features, the reader will refer to the Gazetteer.

List of maps

1. Kotah
2. Kandak
3. Najigram
4. Karakar
5. Jolagram
6. Swat 1 – Dedawar
7. Swat 2 – Ghaligai
8. Dadhra-Kotlai
9. Deolai
10. Ramogai-Spanai
11. Loe-Qalagai-Kulalai
12. Jarendo-bela-Deolai
13. Manrai
14. Middle Deolai
15. Mahakai
16. Upper Deolai
17. Sigram
18. Swat 3 – Udigram
19. Marghuzar
20. Saidu
21. Jambil-Dangram
22. Jambil
23. Ugad-Landai
24. Spedar-Lewanai-Dosara
25. Bishbanr
26. Bikan
27. Tambagat
28. Dre
29. Makad
30. Charbagh
31. Khwazakhela 1
32. Khazakhela 2 – Topsin
33. Khwazakhela 3 – Shalpin
34. Swat 4 – Kotanai
35. Bargin
36. Paiti-Miandam
37. Paiti
38. Harnoi 1
39. Harnoi 2 – Chuprial-Swat
40. Shaurai
41. Harnoi 3 – Barthana
42. Biha
43. Roringar
44. Barwai
45. Swat 5 – Tirat
46. Shanku-Nali-Olal
47. Baral
48. Daral 1 – Baranial
49. Daral 2
50. Kedam
51. Jaba
52. Mankial
53. Asrit
54. Kalam

Synthetic table

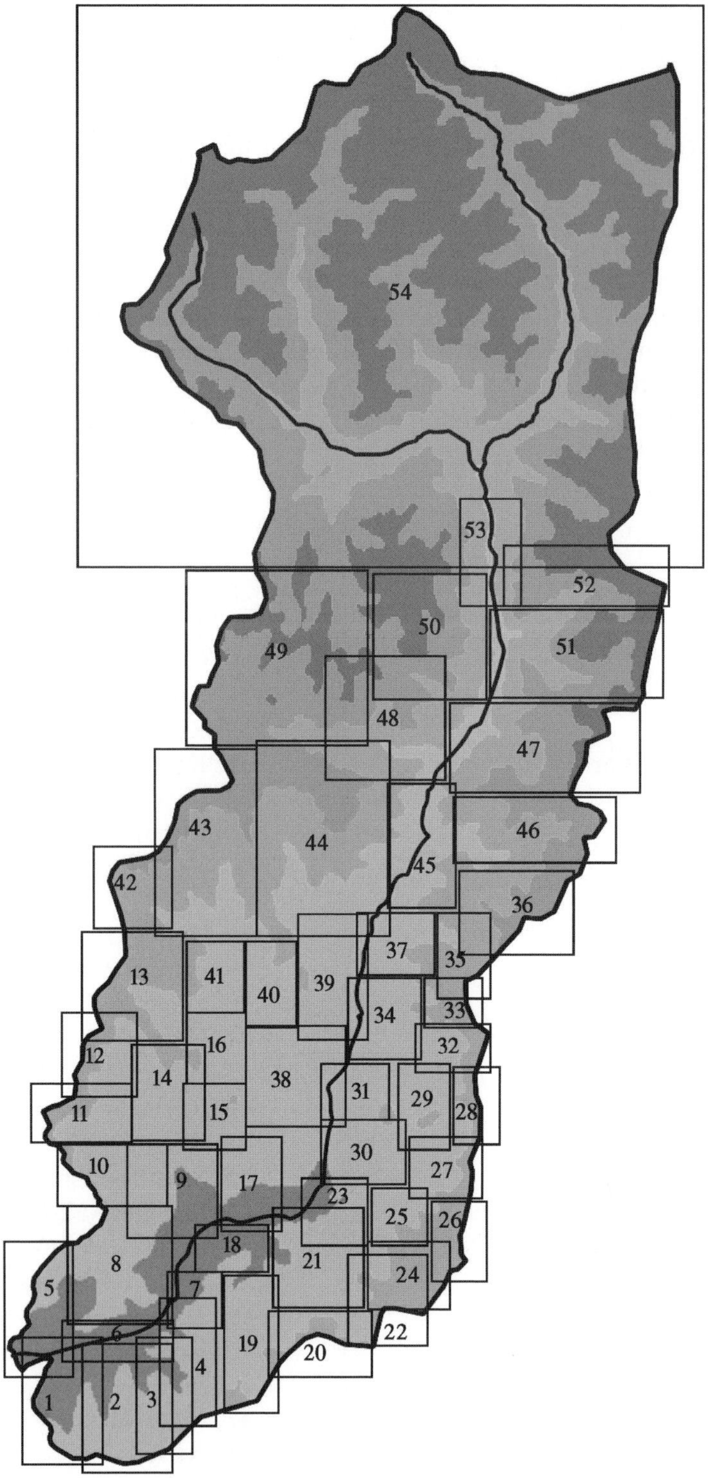

Map 1. Kotah

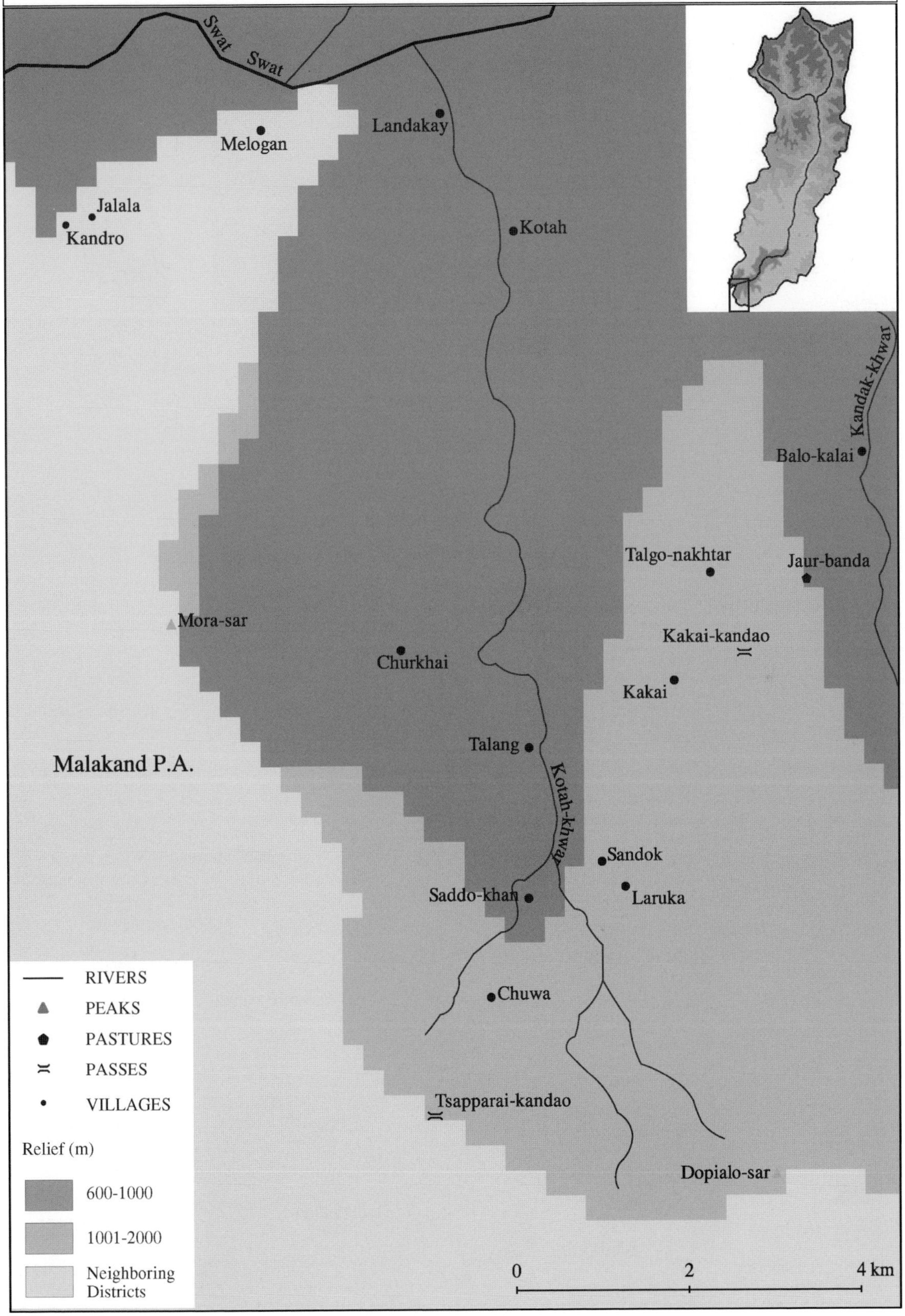

Swat
Swat
Melogan
Landakay
Jalala
Kandro
Kotah
Kandak-khwar
Balo-kalai
Talgo-nakhtar
Jaur-banda
Mora-sar
Kakai-kandao
Churkhai
Kakai
Talang
Malakand P.A.
Kotah-khwar
Sandok
Saddo-khan
Laruka
Chuwa
Tsapparai-kandao
Dopialo-sar
RIVERS
PEAKS
PASTURES
PASSES
VILLAGES
Relief (m)
600-1000
1001-2000
Neighboring Districts
0
2
4 km

Map 2. Kandak

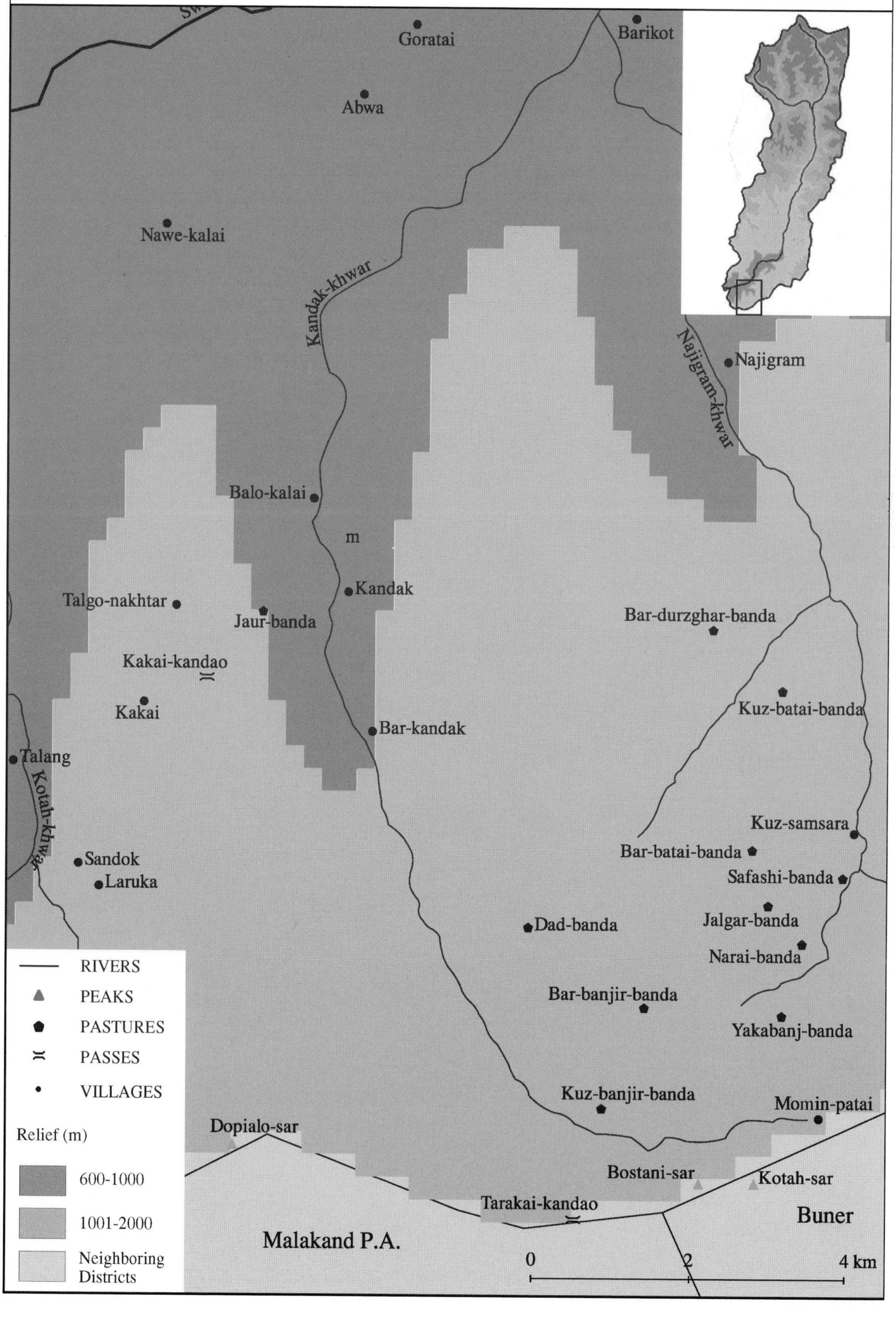
Goratai
Barikot
Abwa
Nawe-kalai
Kandak-khwar
Najigram
Najigram-khwar
Balo-kalai
m
Kandak
Talgo-nakhtar
Jaur-banda
Bar-durzghar-banda
Kakai-kandao
Kakai
Kuz-batai-banda
Bar-kandak
Talang
Kotah-khwar
Kuz-samsara
Bar-batai-banda
Sandok
Laruka
Safashi-banda
Jalgar-banda
Dad-banda
Narai-banda
Bar-banjir-banda
Yakabanj-banda
Kuz-banjir-banda
Momin-patai
Dopialo-sar
Bostani-sar
Kotah-sar
Tarakai-kandao
Buner
Malakand P.A.
0
2
4 km
RIVERS
PEAKS
PASTURES
PASSES
VILLAGES
Relief (m)
600-1000
1001-2000
Neighboring Districts

Map 3. Najigram

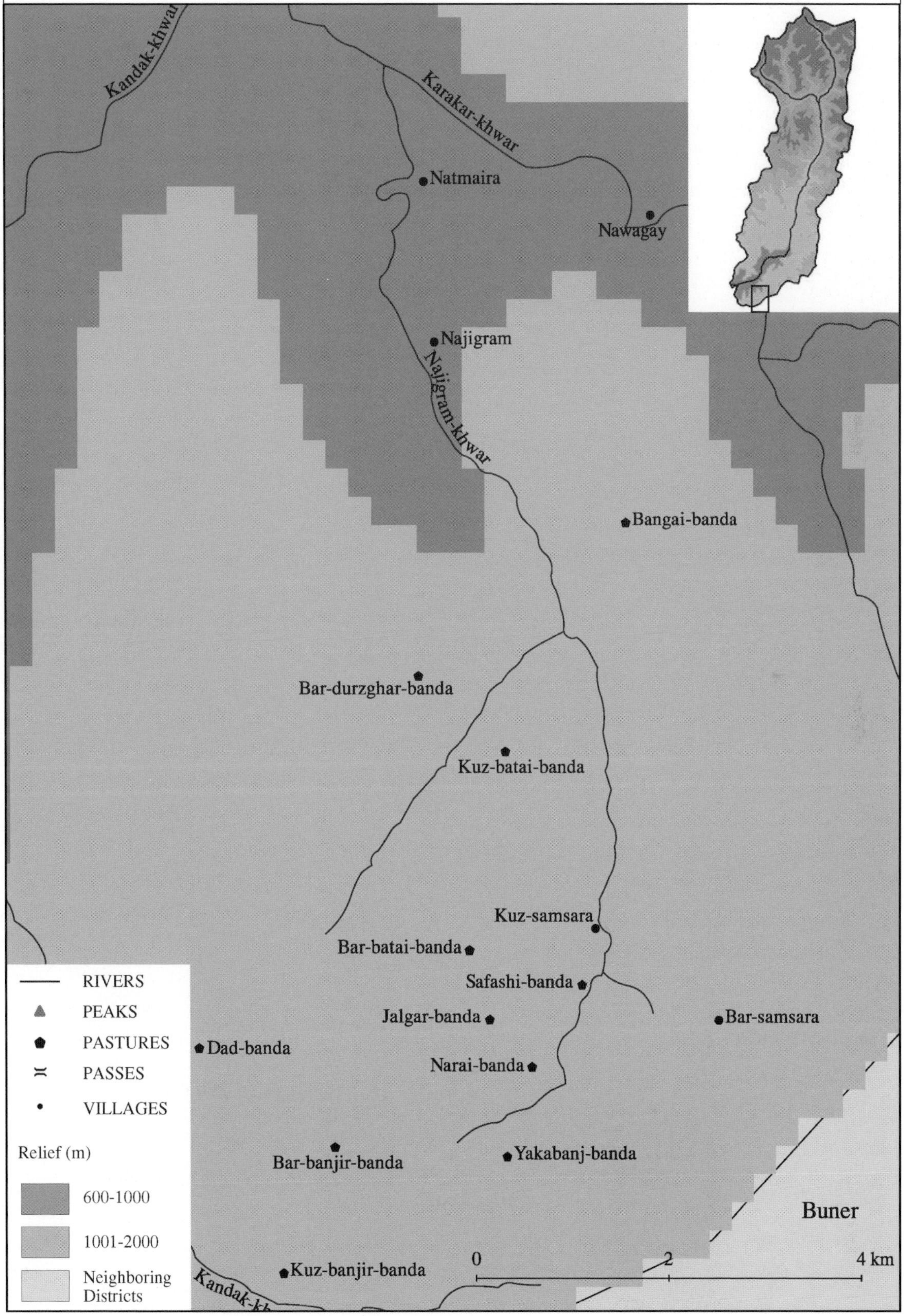
Kandak-khwar
Karakar-khwar
Natmaira
Nawagay
Najigram
Najigram-khwar
Bangai-banda
Bar-durzghar-banda
Kuz-batai-banda
Kuz-samsara
Bar-batai-banda
Safashi-banda
Jalgar-banda
Bar-samsara
Dad-banda
Narai-banda
Bar-banjir-banda
Yakabanj-banda
Buner
Kuz-banjir-banda
0
2
4 km
RIVERS
PEAKS
PASTURES
PASSES
VILLAGES
Relief (m)
600-1000
1001-2000
Neighboring Districts

Map 4. Karakar

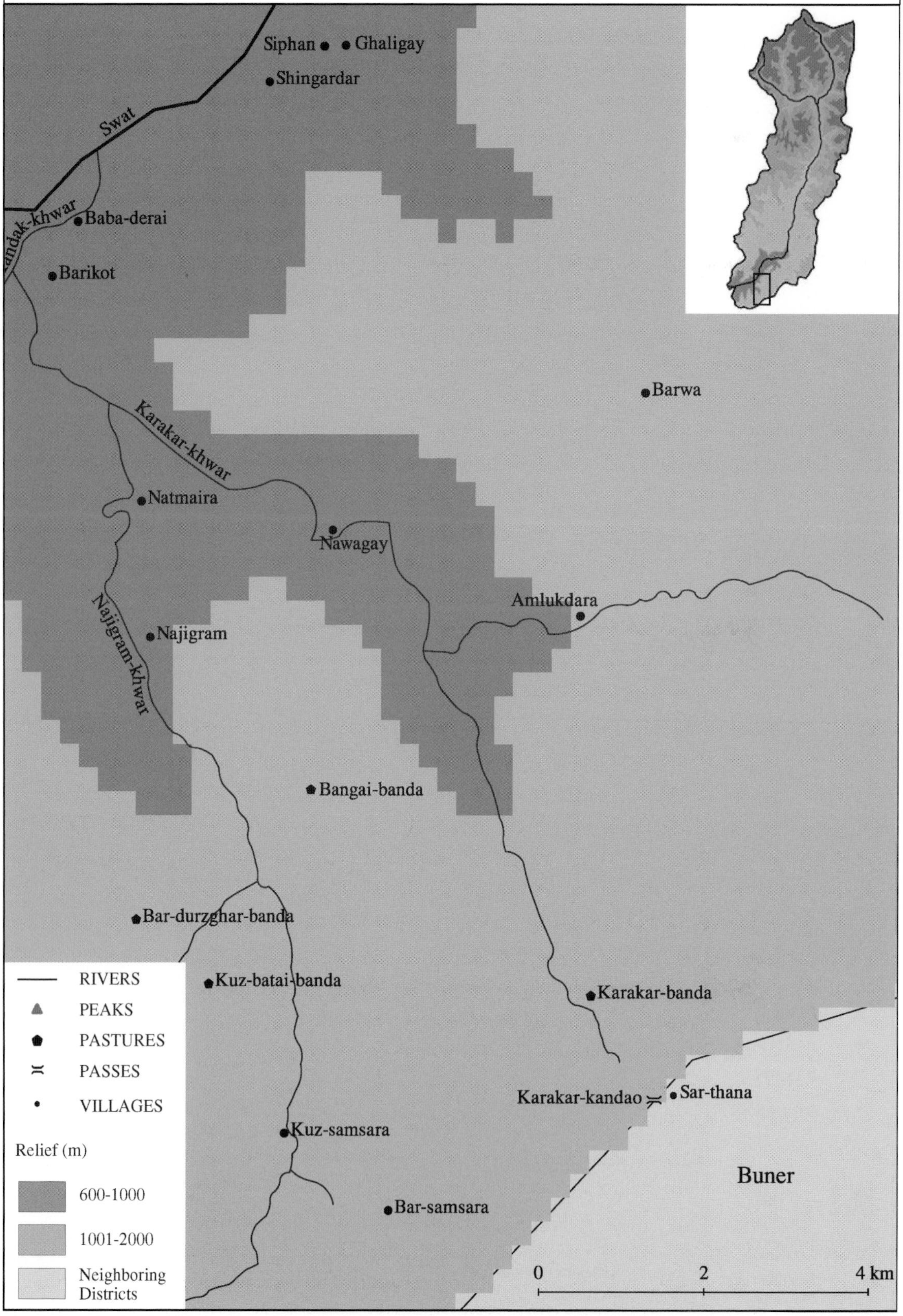

Swat
Siphan
Ghaligay
Shingardar
Kandak-khwar
Baba-derai
Barikot
Barwa
Karakar-khwar
Natmaira
Nawagay
Amlukdara
Najigram-khwar
Najigram
Bangai-banda
Bar-durzghar-banda
Kuz-batai-banda
Karakar-banda
Karakar-kandao
Sar-thana
Kuz-samsara
Bar-samsara
Buner
RIVERS
PEAKS
PASTURES
PASSES
VILLAGES
Relief (m)
600-1000
1001-2000
Neighboring Districts
0
2
4 km

Map 5. Jolagram

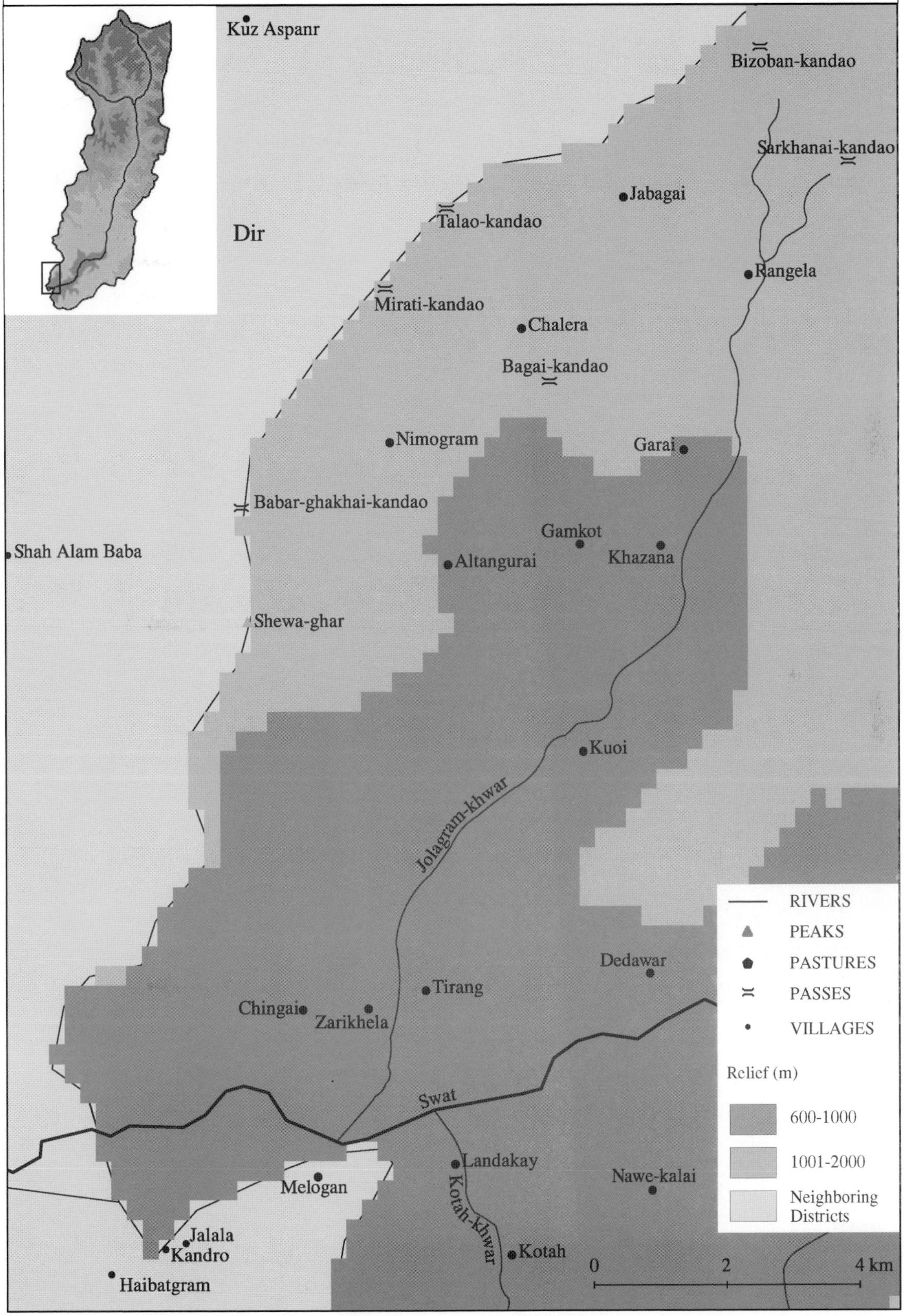
Kuz Aspanr
Bizoban-kandao
Sarkhanai-kandao
Jabagai
Talao-kandao
Dir
Rangela
Mirati-kandao
Chalera
Bagai-kandao
Nimogram
Garai
Babar-ghakhai-kandao
Gamkot
Khazana
Altangurai
Shah Alam Baba
Shewa-ghar
Kuoi
Jolagram-khwar
Dedawar
Tirang
Chingai
Zarikhela
Swat
Landakay
Melogan
Nawe-kalai
Kotah-khwar
Jalala
Kandro
Kotah
Haibatgram
0
2
4 km
RIVERS
PEAKS
PASTURES
PASSES
VILLAGES
Relief (m)
600-1000
1001-2000
Neighboring Districts

Map 6. Swat 1 – Dedawar

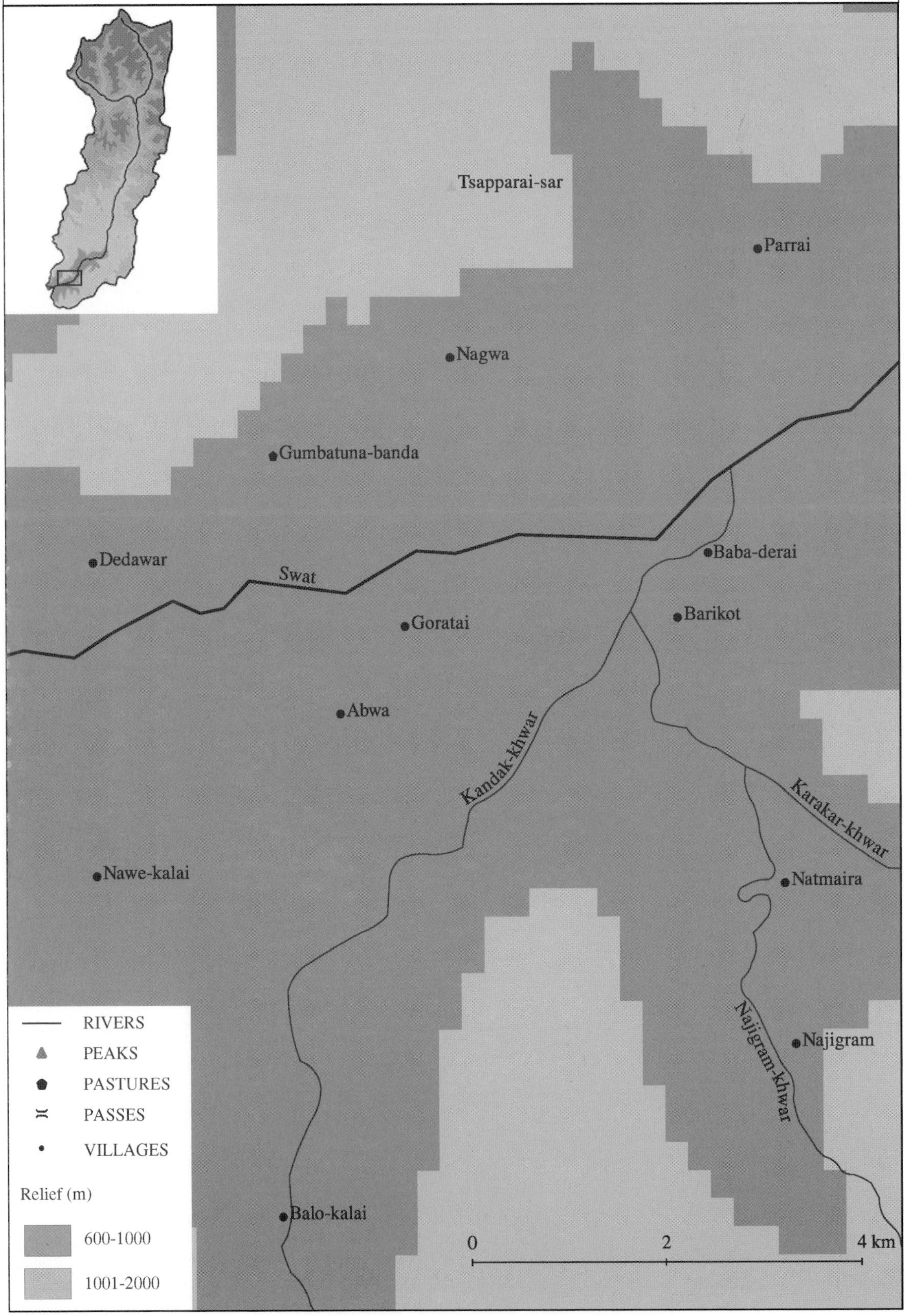
Tsapparai-sar
Parrai
Nagwa
Gumbatuna-banda
Dedawar
Swat
Baba-derai
Barikot
Goratai
Abwa
Kandak-khwar
Karakar-khwar
Nawe-kalai
Natmaira
Najigram-khwar
Najigram
Balo-kalai
RIVERS
PEAKS
PASTURES
PASSES
VILLAGES
Relief (m)
600-1000
1001-2000
0
2
4 km

Map 7. – Ghaligai

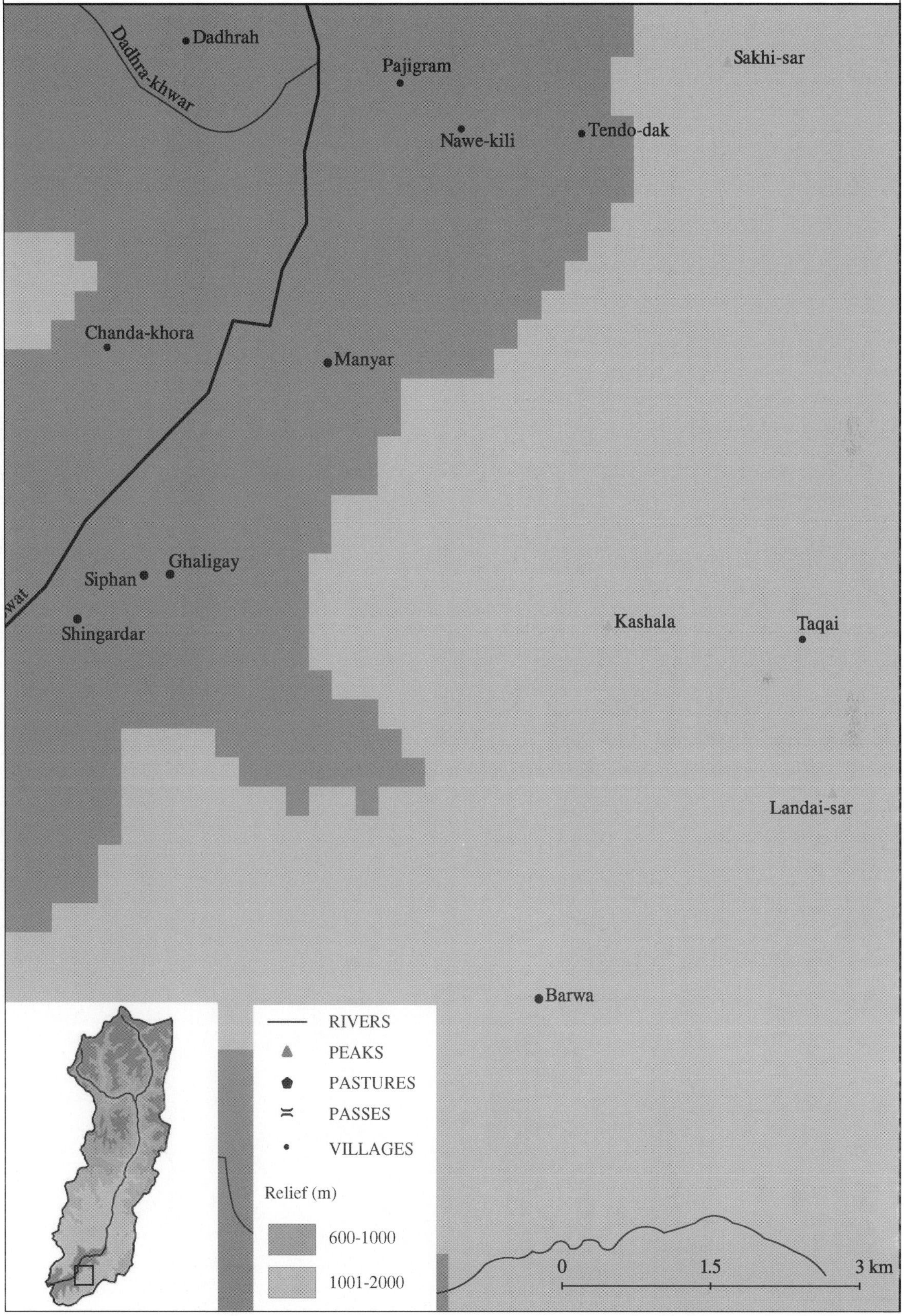
Dadhrah
Dadhra-khwar
Pajigram
Sakhi-sar
Nawe-kili
Tendo-dak
Chanda-khora
Manyar
Ghaligay
Siphan
wat
Shingardar
Kashala
Taqai
Landai-sar
Barwa
RIVERS
PEAKS
PASTURES
PASSES
VILLAGES
Relief (m)
600-1000
1001-2000
0
1.5
3 km

Map 8. Dadhra-Kotlai

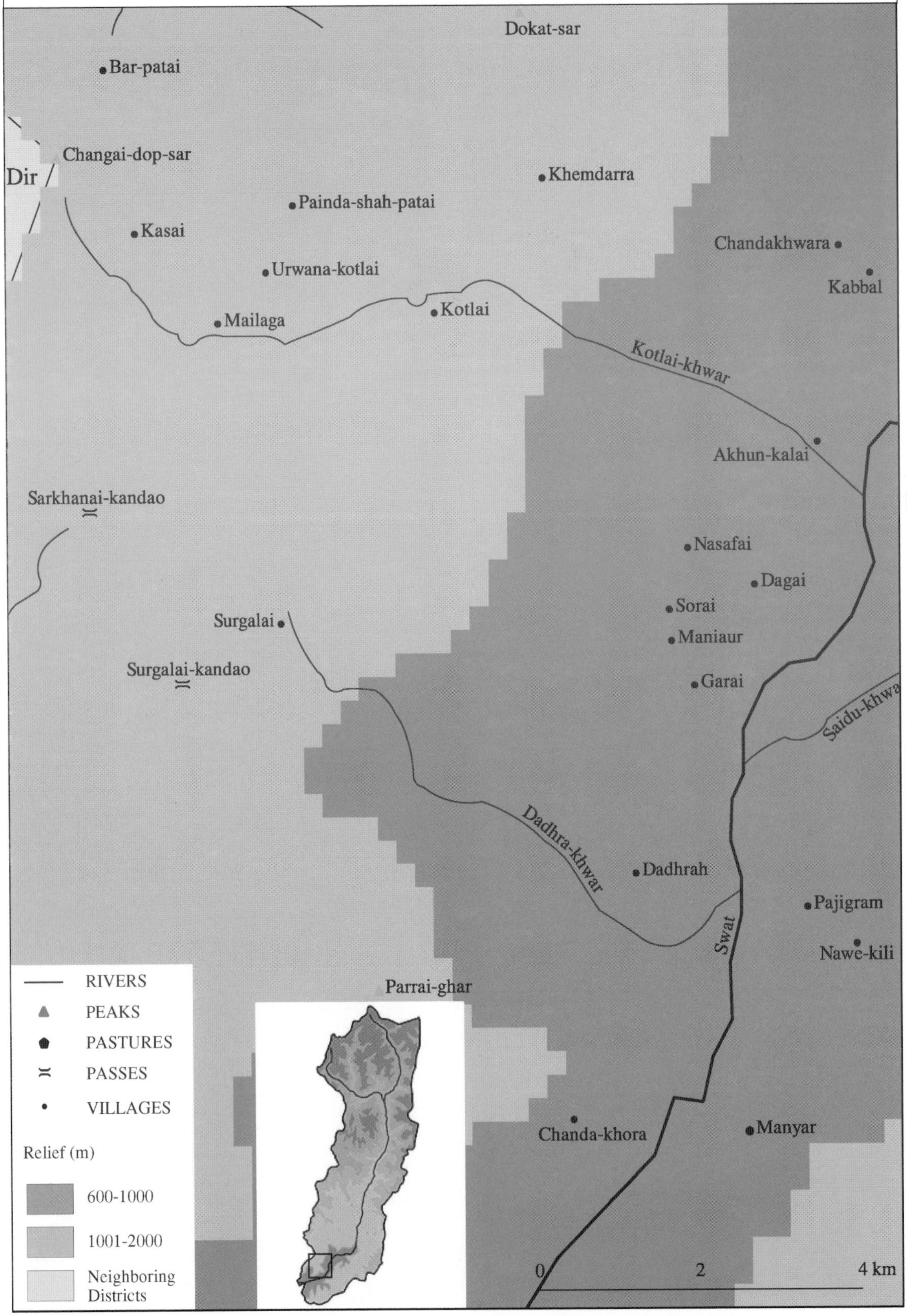

Dokat-sar
Bar-patai
Changai-dop-sar
Dir
Khemdarra
Painda-shah-patai
Kasai
Chandakhwara
Kabbal
Urwana-kotlai
Kotlai
Mailaga
Kotlai-khwar
Akhun-kalai
Sarkhanai-kandao
Nasafai
Dagai
Sorai
Surgalai
Maniaur
Surgalai-kandao
Garai
Saidu-khwa
Dadhra-khwar
Dadhrah
Pajigram
Swat
Nawe-kili
RIVERS
PEAKS
PASTURES
PASSES
VILLAGES
Relief (m)
600-1000
1001-2000
Neighboring Districts
Parrai-ghar
Chanda-khora
Manyar
0
2
4 km

Map 9. Deolai

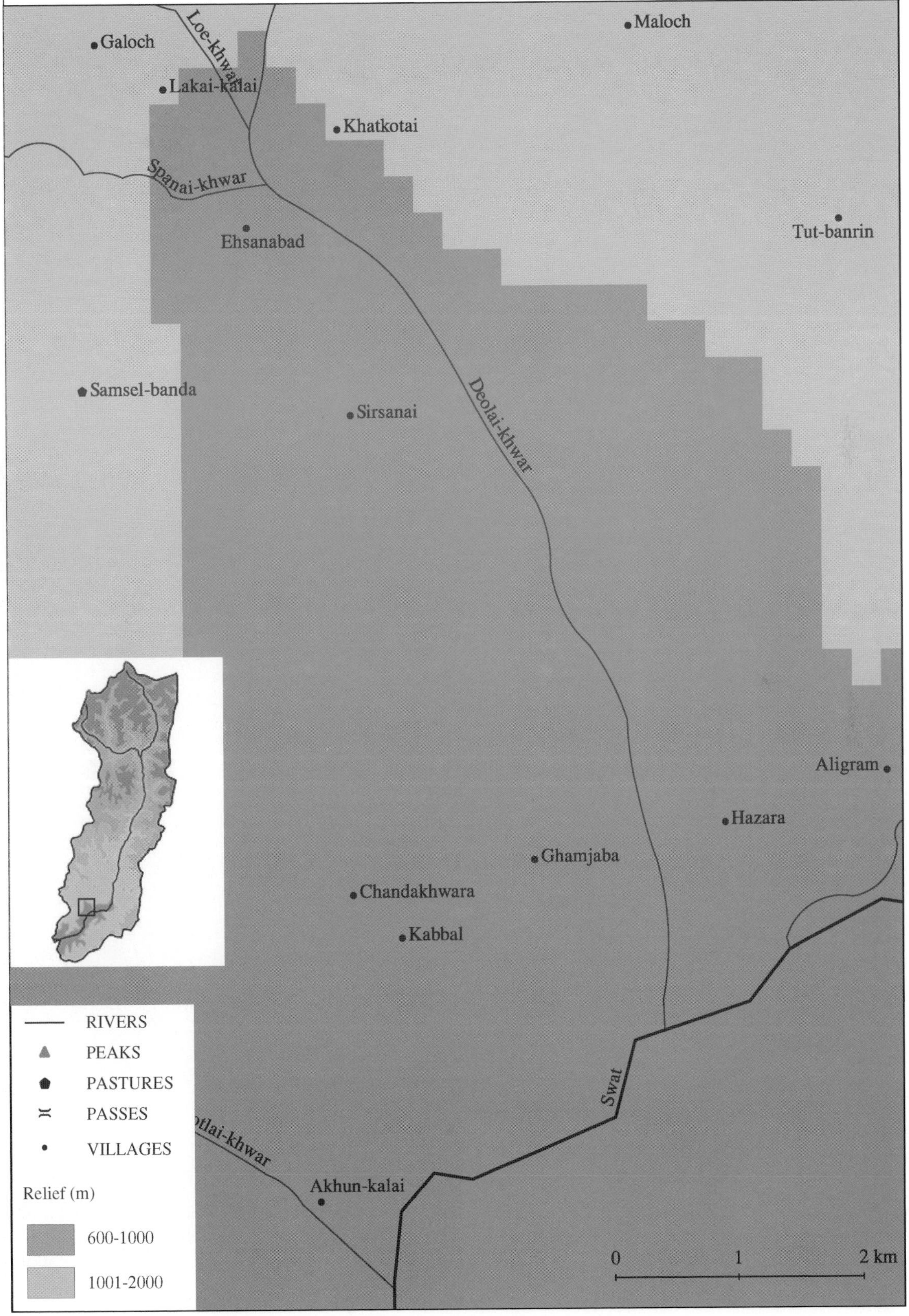
Galoch
Loe-khwar
Lakai-kalai
Maloch
Khatkotai
Spanai-khwar
Ehsanabad
Tut-banrin
Samsel-banda
Sirsanai
Deolai-khwar
Aligram
Hazara
Ghamjaba
Chandakhwara
Kabbal
Swat
Akhun-kalai
RIVERS
PEAKS
PASTURES
PASSES
VILLAGES
Relief (m)
600-1000
1001-2000
0
1
2 km

Map 10. Ramogai-Spanai

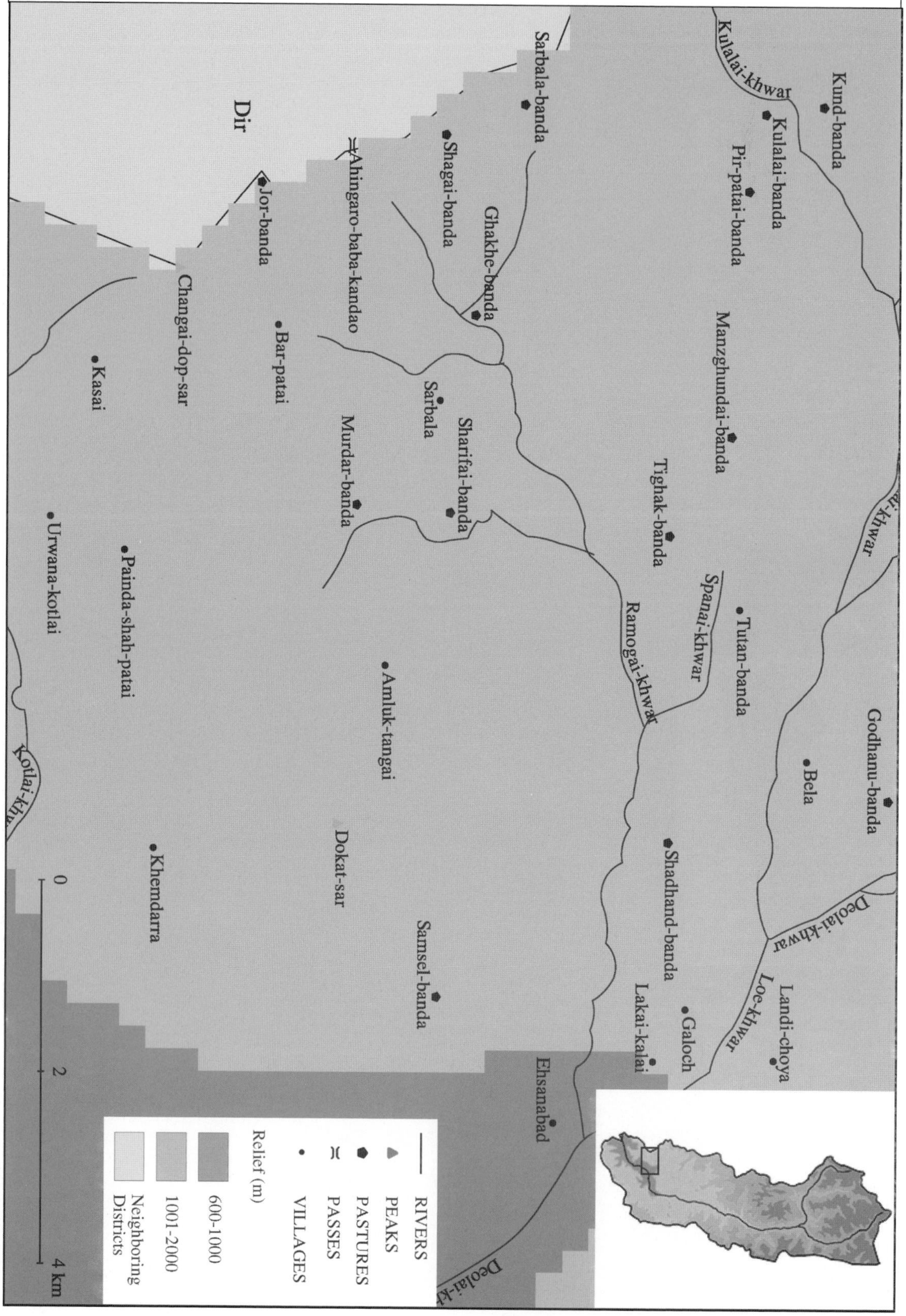
Dir
Sarbala-banda
Shagai-banda
Ahingaro-baba-kandao
Jor-banda
Ghakhe-banda
Changai-dop-sar
Bar-patai
Kasai
Sarbala
Sharifai-banda
Murdar-banda
Kund-banda
Kulalai-khwar
Kulalai-banda
Pir-patai-banda
Manzghundai-banda
Tighak-banda
Spanai-khwar
Tutan-banda
Ramogai-khwar
Khwar
Godhanu-banda
Bela
Shadhand-banda
Deolai-khwar
Loe-khwar
Landi-choya
Galoch
Lakai-kalai
Ehsanabad
Samsel-banda
Dokat-sar
Amluk-tangai
Urwana-kotlai
Painda-shah-patai
Khemdarra
Kotlai-Khw
Deolai-Kh
0
2
4 km
RIVERS
PEAKS
PASTURES
PASSES
VILLAGES
Relief (m)
600-1000
1001-2000
Neighboring Districts

Map 11. Loe-Qalagai-Kulalai

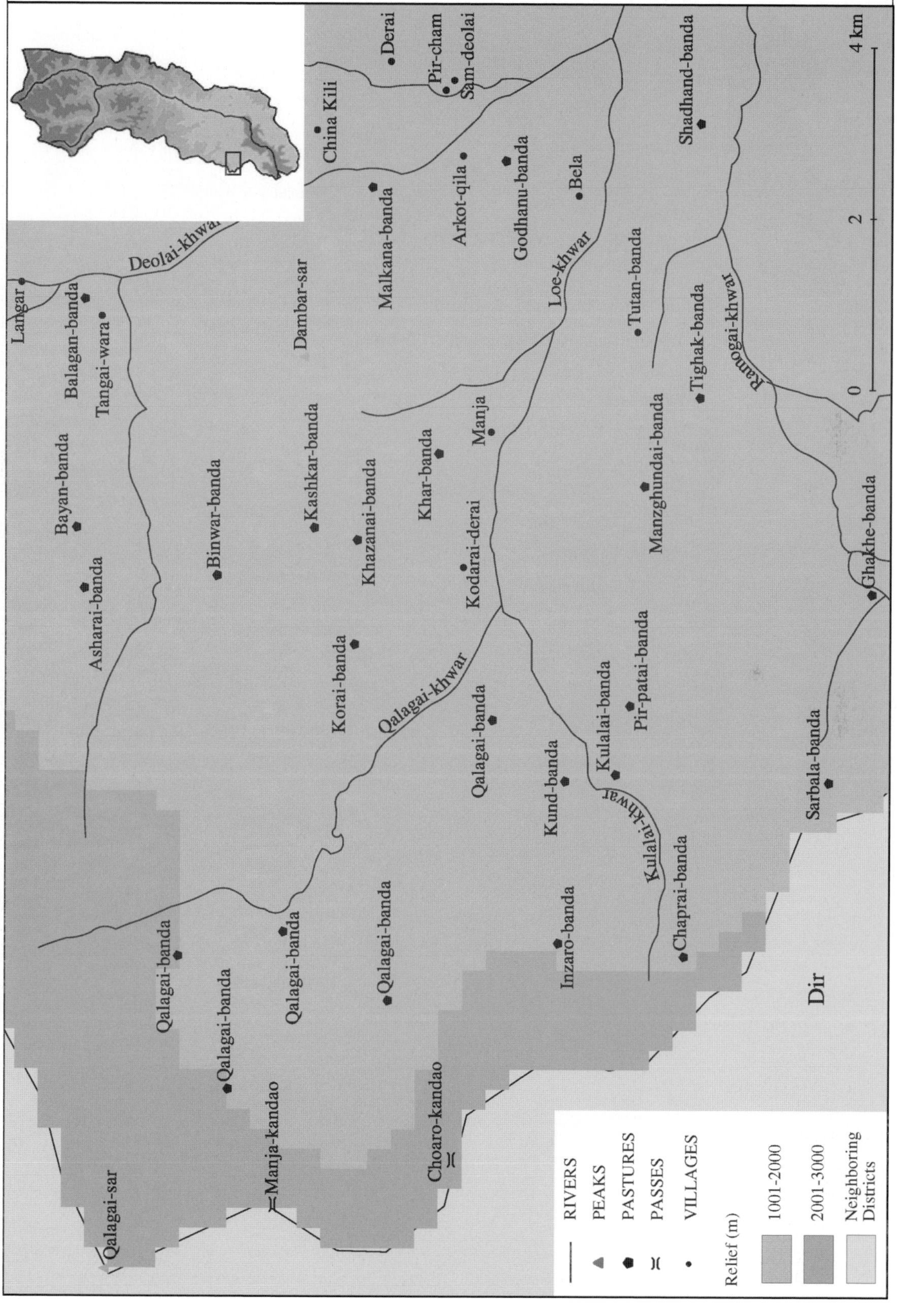

Deolai-khwar
Langar
Balagan-banda
Tangai-wara
Dambar-sar
China Kili
Derai
Pir-cham
Sam-deolai
Malkana-banda
Arkot-qila
Godhanu-banda
Bela
Shadhand-banda
Loe-khwar
Tutan-banda
Tighak-banda
Ramogai-khwar
Bayan-banda
Binwar-banda
Kashkar-banda
Khazanai-banda
Khar-banda
Manja
Kodarai-derai
Manzghundai-banda
Ghakhe-banda
Asharai-banda
Korai-banda
Qalagai-khwar
Qalagai-banda
Kulalai-banda
Pir-patai-banda
Kund-banda
Kulalai-khwar
Sarbala-banda
Chaprai-banda
Inzaro-banda
Qalagai-banda
Qalagai-banda
Qalagai-banda
Qalagai-banda
Qalagai-banda
Dir
Qalagai-sar
Manja-kandao
Choaro-kandao
0
2
4 km
RIVERS
PEAKS
PASTURES
PASSES
VILLAGES
Relief (m)
1001-2000
2001-3000
Neighboring Districts

Map 12. Jarendo-bela-Deolai

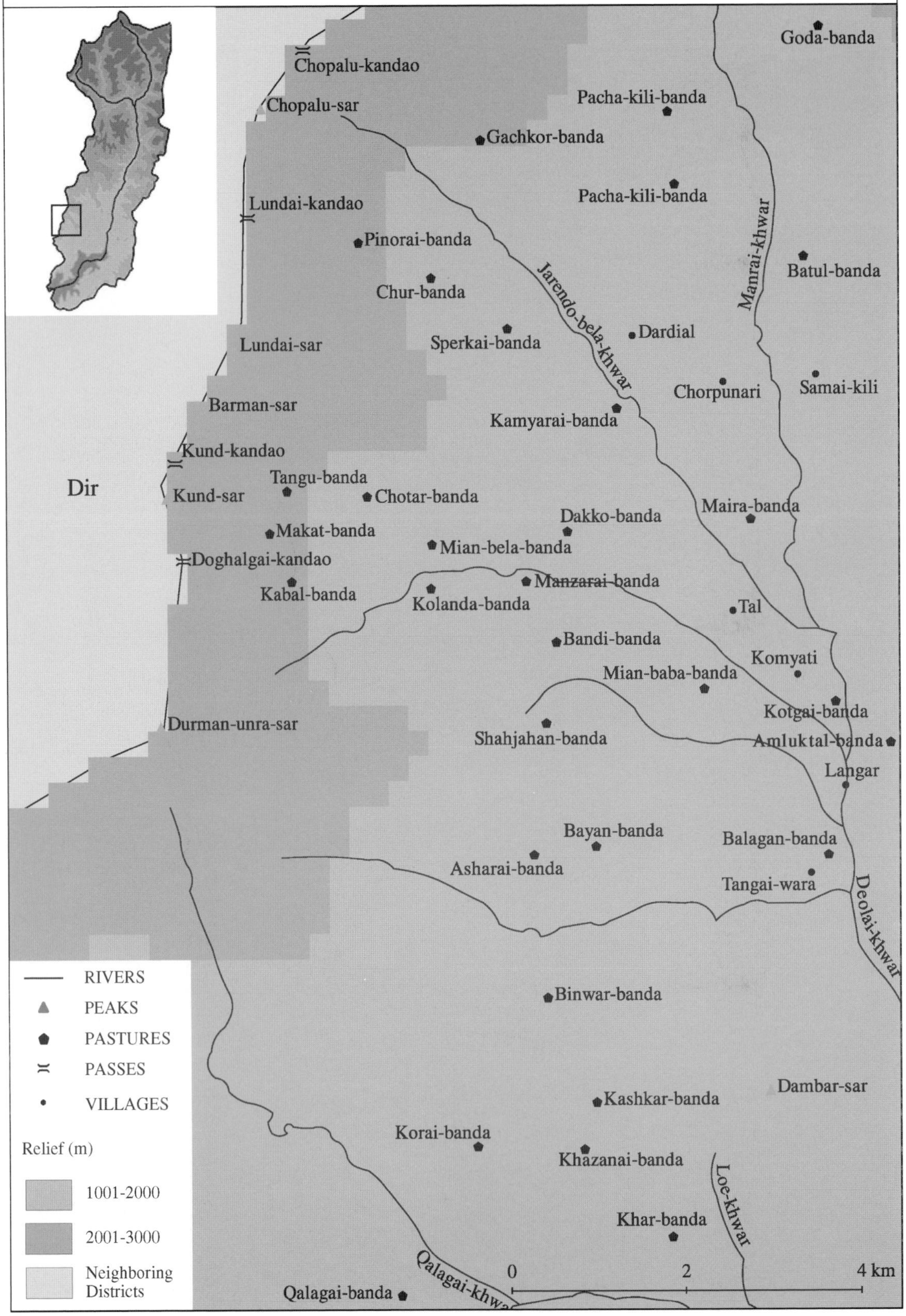

Goda-banda
Chopalu-kandao
Chopalu-sar
Pacha-kili-banda
Gachkor-banda
Pacha-kili-banda
Lundai-kandao
Pinorai-banda
Manrai-khwar
Batul-banda
Chur-banda
Jarendo-bela-khwar
Dardial
Lundai-sar
Sperkai-banda
Chorpunari
Samai-kili
Barman-sar
Kamyarai-banda
Kund-kandao
Dir
Tangu-banda
Kund-sar
Chotar-banda
Dakko-banda
Maira-banda
Makat-banda
Mian-bela-banda
Doghalgai-kandao
Manzarai-banda
Kabal-banda
Kolanda-banda
Tal
Bandi-banda
Komyati
Mian-baba-banda
Kotgai-banda
Durman-unra-sar
Shahjahan-banda
Amluktal-banda
Langar
Bayan-banda
Balagan-banda
Asharai-banda
Tangai-wara
Deolai-khwar
RIVERS
PEAKS
PASTURES
PASSES
VILLAGES
Relief (m)
1001-2000
2001-3000
Neighboring Districts
Binwar-banda
Dambar-sar
Kashkar-banda
Korai-banda
Khazanai-banda
Loe-khwar
Khar-banda
Qalagai-khwar
0
2
4 km
Qalagai-banda

Map 13. Manrai

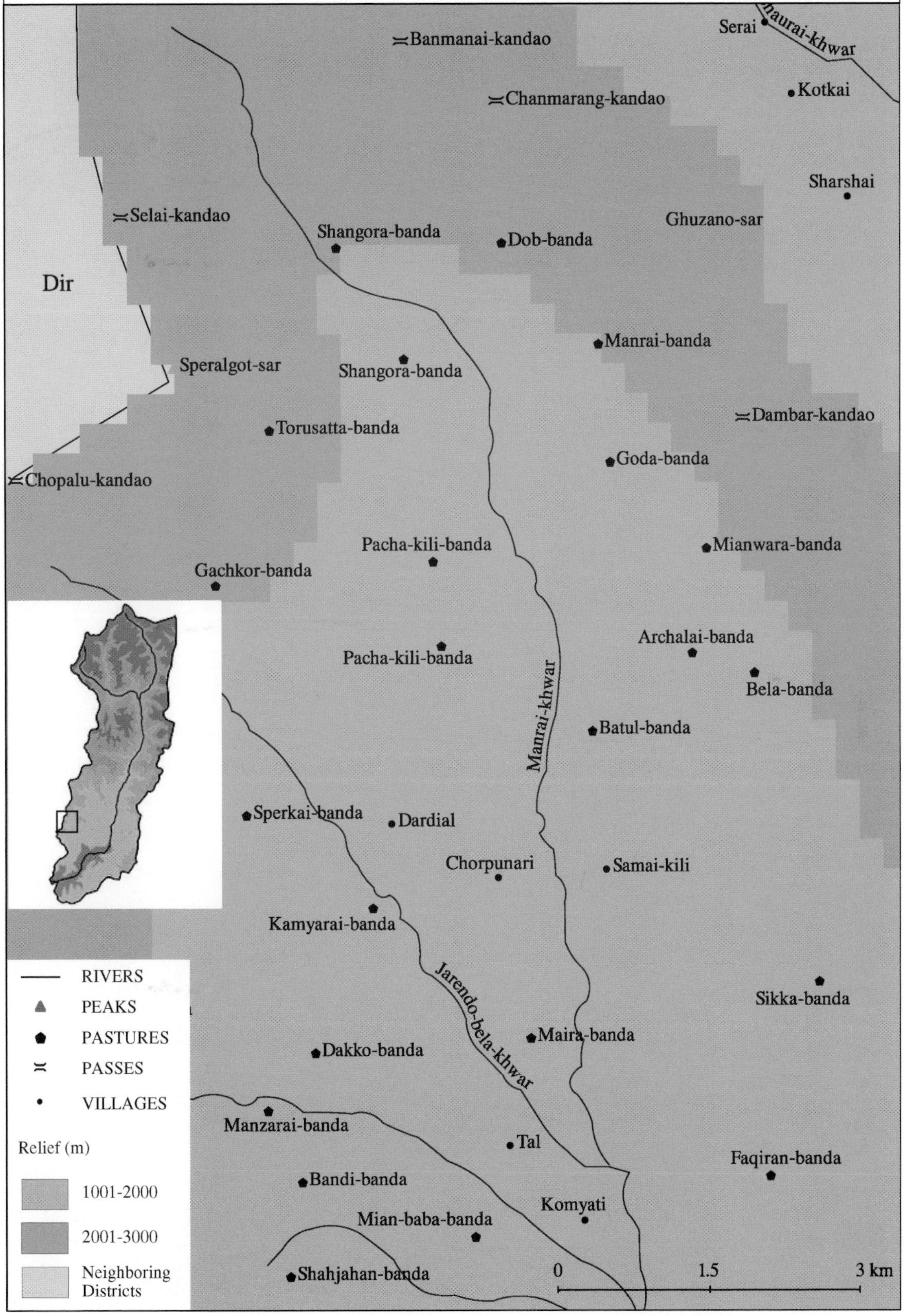
Banmanai-kandao
Serai
naurai-khwar
Kotkai
Chanmarang-kandao
Sharshai
Selai-kandao
Shangora-banda
Dob-banda
Ghuzano-sar
Dir
Manrai-banda
Speralgot-sar
Shangora-banda
Dambar-kandao
Torusatta-banda
Goda-banda
Chopalu-kandao
Pacha-kili-banda
Mianwara-banda
Gachkor-banda
Archalai-banda
Pacha-kili-banda
Bela-banda
Manrai-khwar
Batul-banda
Sperkai-banda
Dardial
Chorpunari
Samai-kili
Kamyarai-banda
Jarendo-bela-khwar
Sikka-banda
Maira-banda
Dakko-banda
Manzarai-banda
Tal
Faqiran-banda
Bandi-banda
Komyati
Mian-baba-banda
Shahjahan-banda
0
1.5
3 km
RIVERS
PEAKS
PASTURES
PASSES
VILLAGES
Relief (m)
1001-2000
2001-3000
Neighboring Districts

Map 14. Middle Deolai

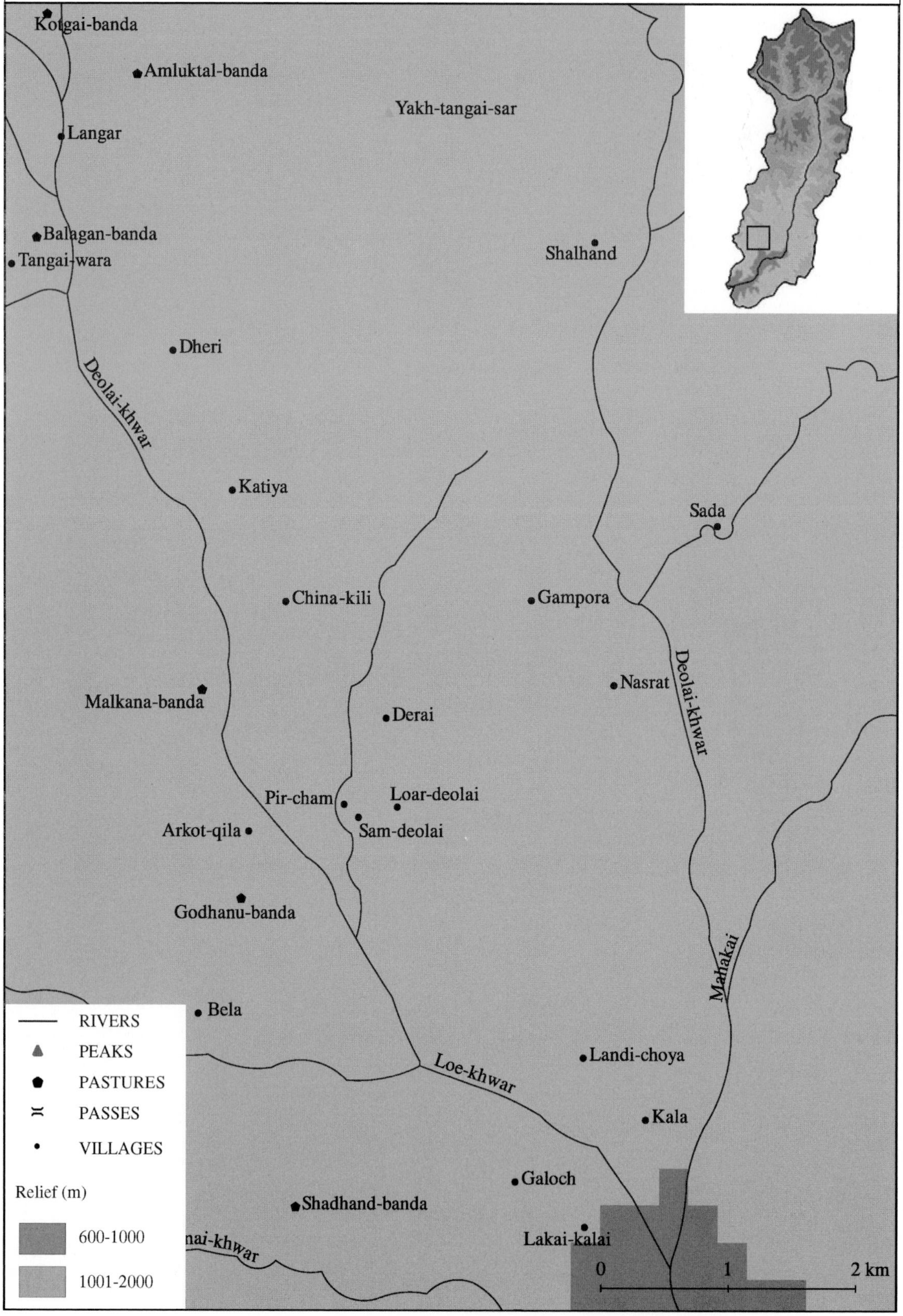

Kotgai-banda
Amluktal-banda
Yakh-tangai-sar
Langar
Balagan-banda
Tangai-wara
Shalhand
Dheri
Deolai-khwar
Katiya
Sada
China-kili
Gampora
Nasrat
Deolai-khwar
Malkana-banda
Derai
Pir-cham
Loar-deolai
Arkot-qila
Sam-deolai
Godhanu-banda
Mahakai
Bela
Loe-khwar
Landi-choya
Kala
Galoch
Shadhand-banda
Lakai-kalai
nai-khwar
RIVERS
PEAKS
PASTURES
PASSES
VILLAGES
Relief (m)
600-1000
1001-2000
0
1
2 km

Map 15. Mahakai

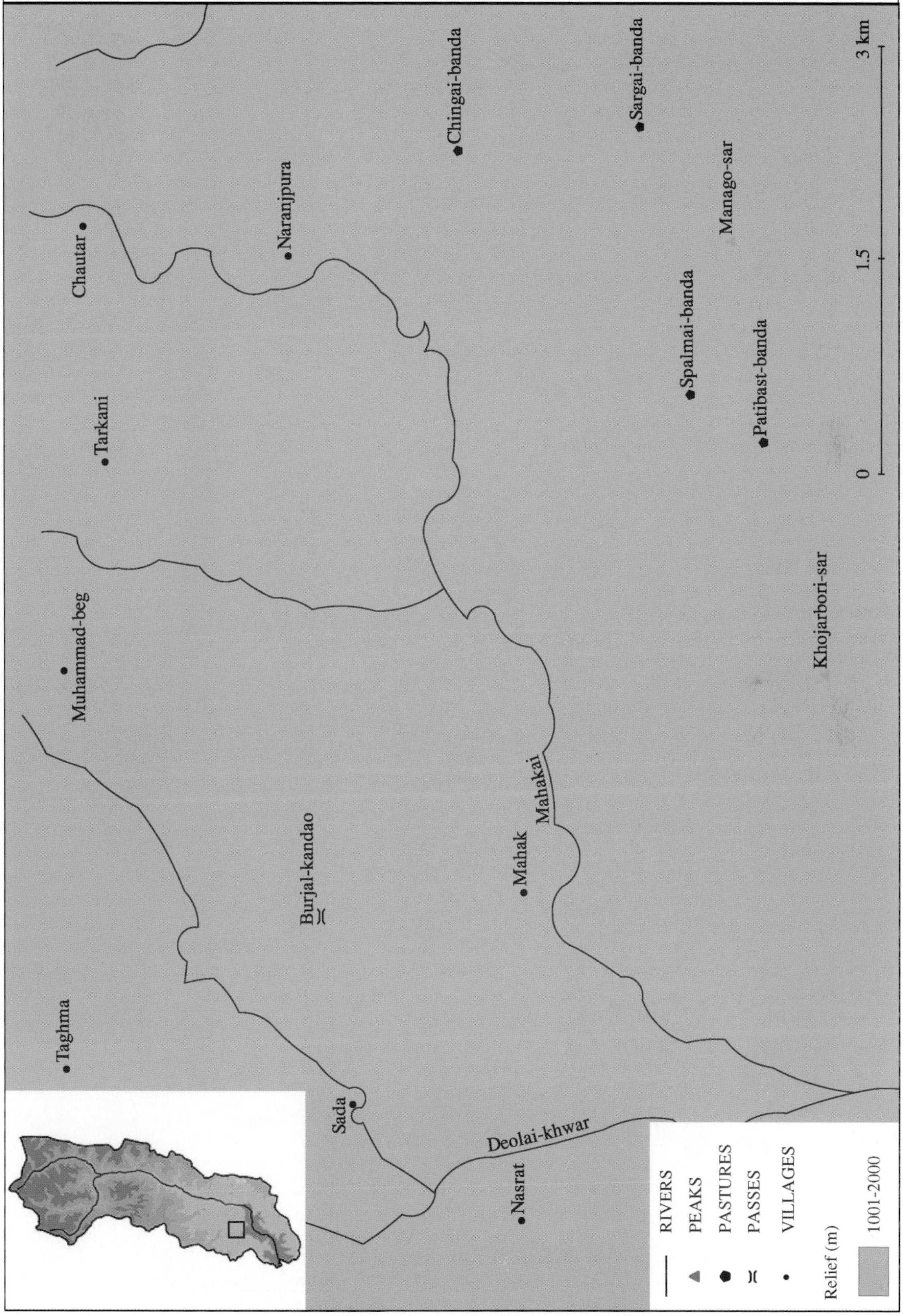

Map 16. Upper Deolai

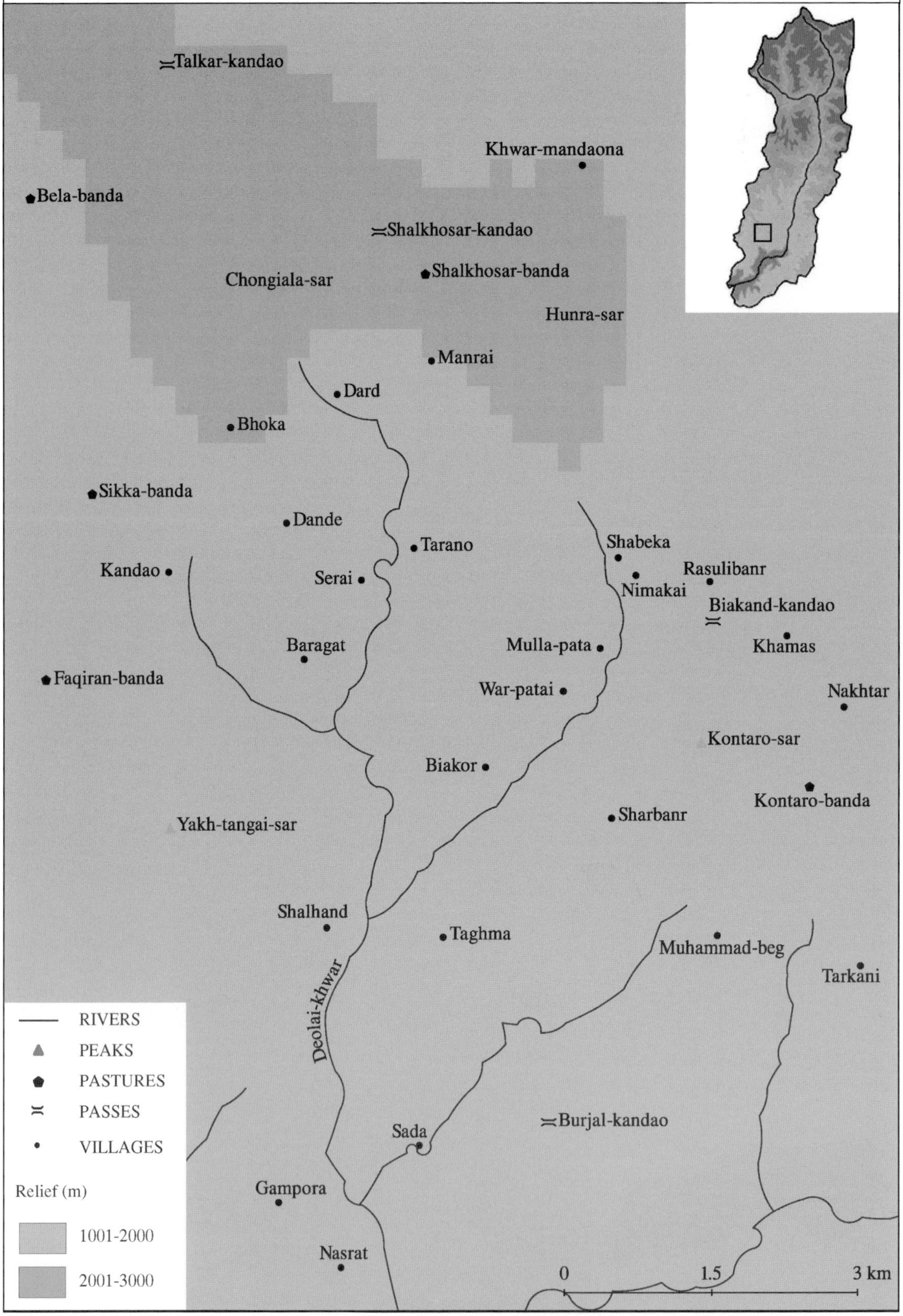
Talkar-kandao
Khwar-mandaona
Bela-banda
Shalkhosar-kandao
Chongiala-sar
Shalkhosar-banda
Hunra-sar
Manrai
Dard
Bhoka
Sikka-banda
Dande
Tarano
Kandao
Serai
Shabeka
Nimakai
Rasulibanr
Biakand-kandao
Khamas
Baragat
Mulla-pata
Faqiran-banda
War-patai
Nakhtar
Kontaro-sar
Biakor
Kontaro-banda
Sharbanr
Yakh-tangai-sar
Shalhand
Taghma
Muhammad-beg
Tarkani
Deolai-khwar
Sada
Burjal-kandao
Gampora
Nasrat
RIVERS
PEAKS
PASTURES
PASSES
VILLAGES
Relief (m)
1001-2000
2001-3000
0
1.5
3 km

Map 17. Sigram

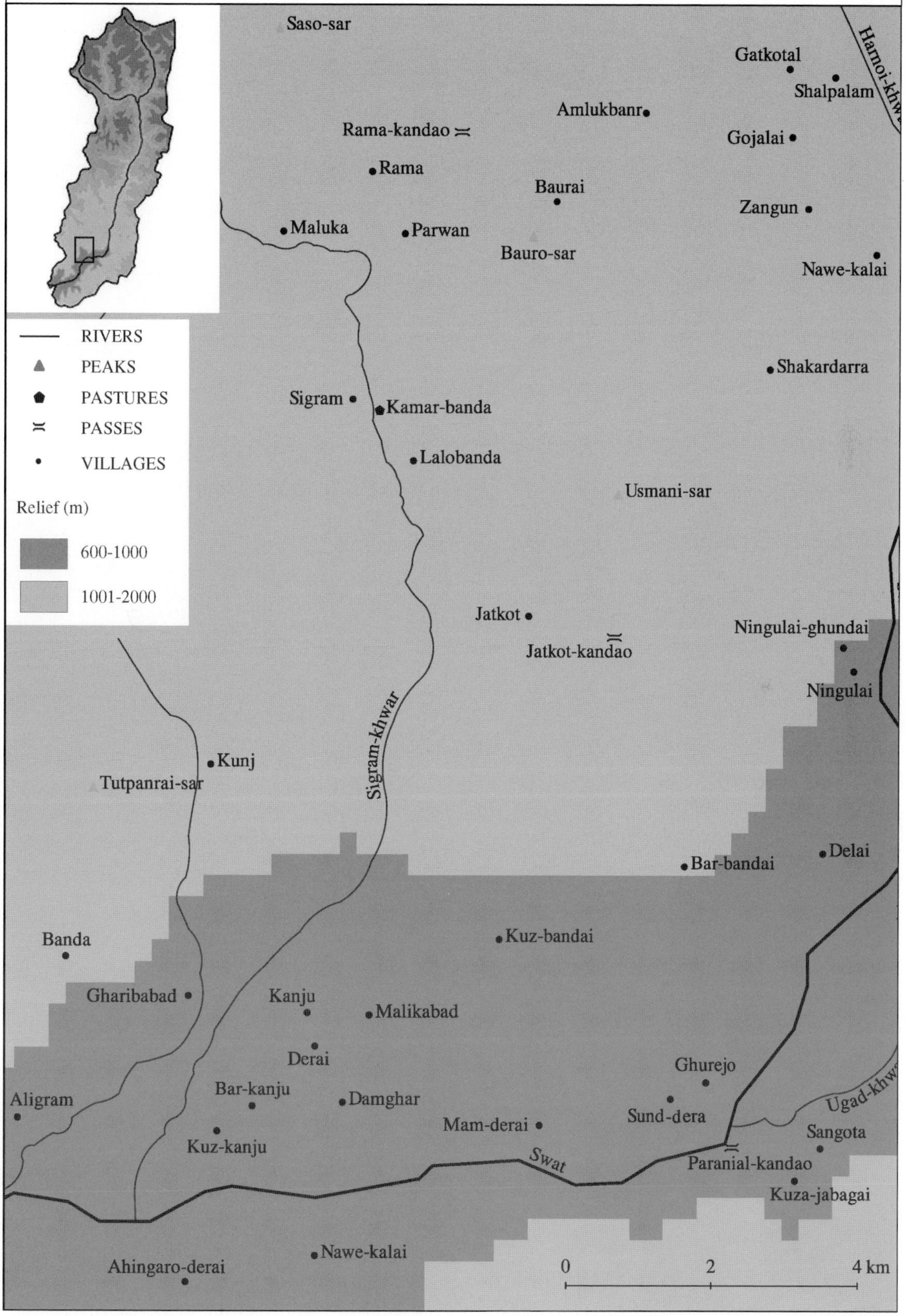
Saso-sar
Gatkotal
Shalpalam
Hamoi-khwar
Amlukbanr
Rama-kandao
Gojalai
Rama
Baurai
Zangun
Maluka
Parwan
Bauro-sar
Nawe-kalai
RIVERS
PEAKS
PASTURES
PASSES
VILLAGES
Relief (m)
600-1000
1001-2000
Shakardarra
Sigram
Kamar-banda
Lalobanda
Usmani-sar
Jatkot
Jatkot-kandao
Ningulai-ghundai
Ningulai
Sigram-khwar
Kunj
Tutpanrai-sar
Delai
Bar-bandai
Kuz-bandai
Banda
Gharibabad
Kanju
Malikabad
Derai
Ghurejo
Bar-kanju
Damghar
Aligram
Sund-dera
Ugad-khwar
Mam-derai
Sangota
Kuz-kanju
Swat
Paranial-kandao
Kuza-jabagai
Nawe-kalai
Ahingaro-derai
0
2
4 km

Map 18. Swat 3 – Udigram

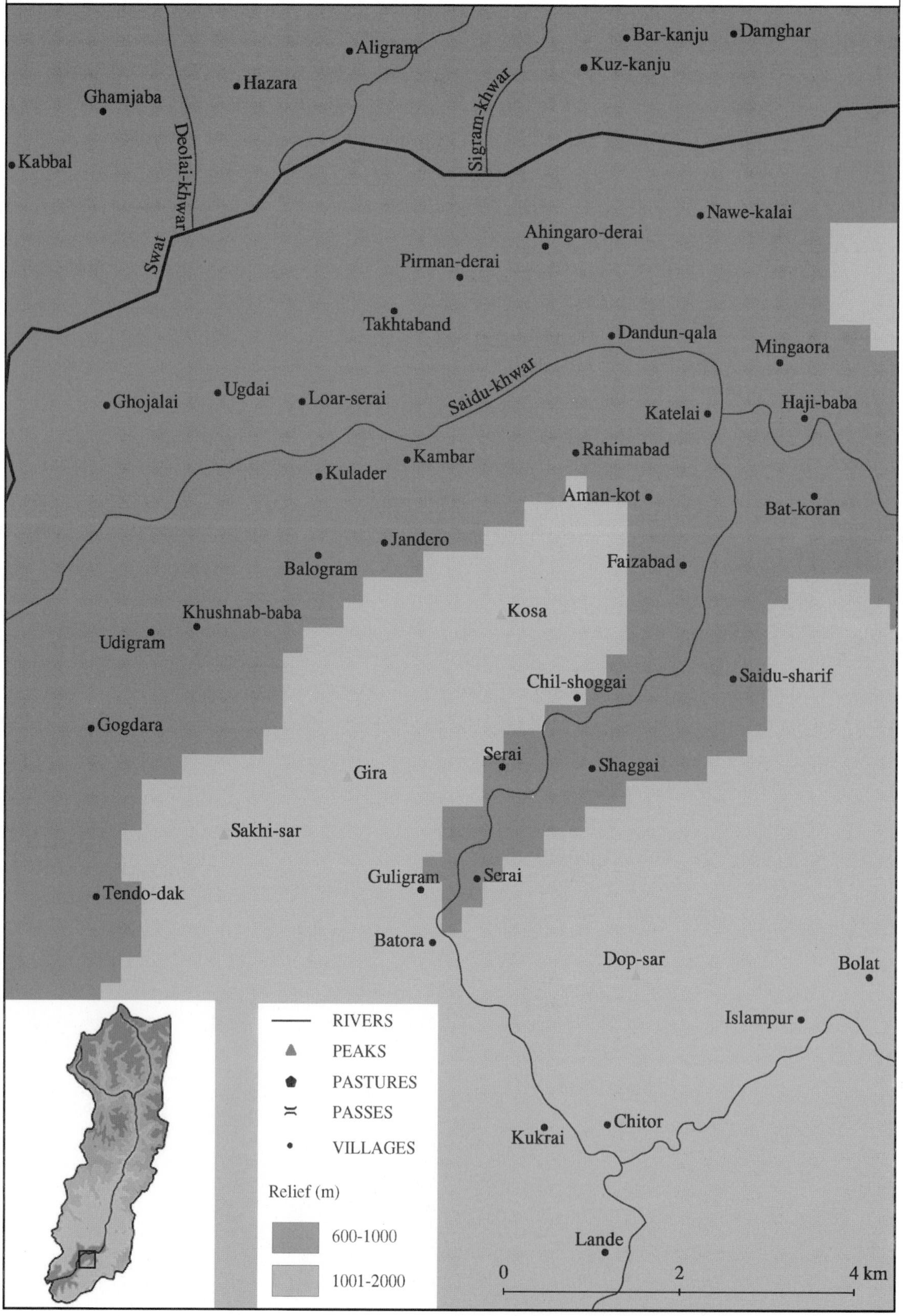
Bar-kanju
Damghar
Aligram
Kuz-kanju
Hazara
Ghamjaba
Sigram-khwar
Deolai-khwar
Kabbal
Swat
Nawe-kalai
Ahingaro-derai
Pirman-derai
Takhtaband
Dandun-qala
Mingaora
Saidu-khwar
Ghojalai
Ugdai
Loar-serai
Katelai
Haji-baba
Kambar
Rahimabad
Kulader
Aman-kot
Bat-koran
Jandero
Balogram
Faizabad
Khushnab-baba
Kosa
Udigram
Chil-shoggai
Saidu-sharif
Gogdara
Serai
Shaggai
Gira
Sakhi-sar
Guligram
Serai
Tendo-dak
Batora
Dop-sar
Bolat
Islampur
RIVERS
PEAKS
PASTURES
PASSES
VILLAGES
Relief (m)
600-1000
1001-2000
Chitor
Kukrai
Lande
0
2
4 km

Map 19. Marghuzar

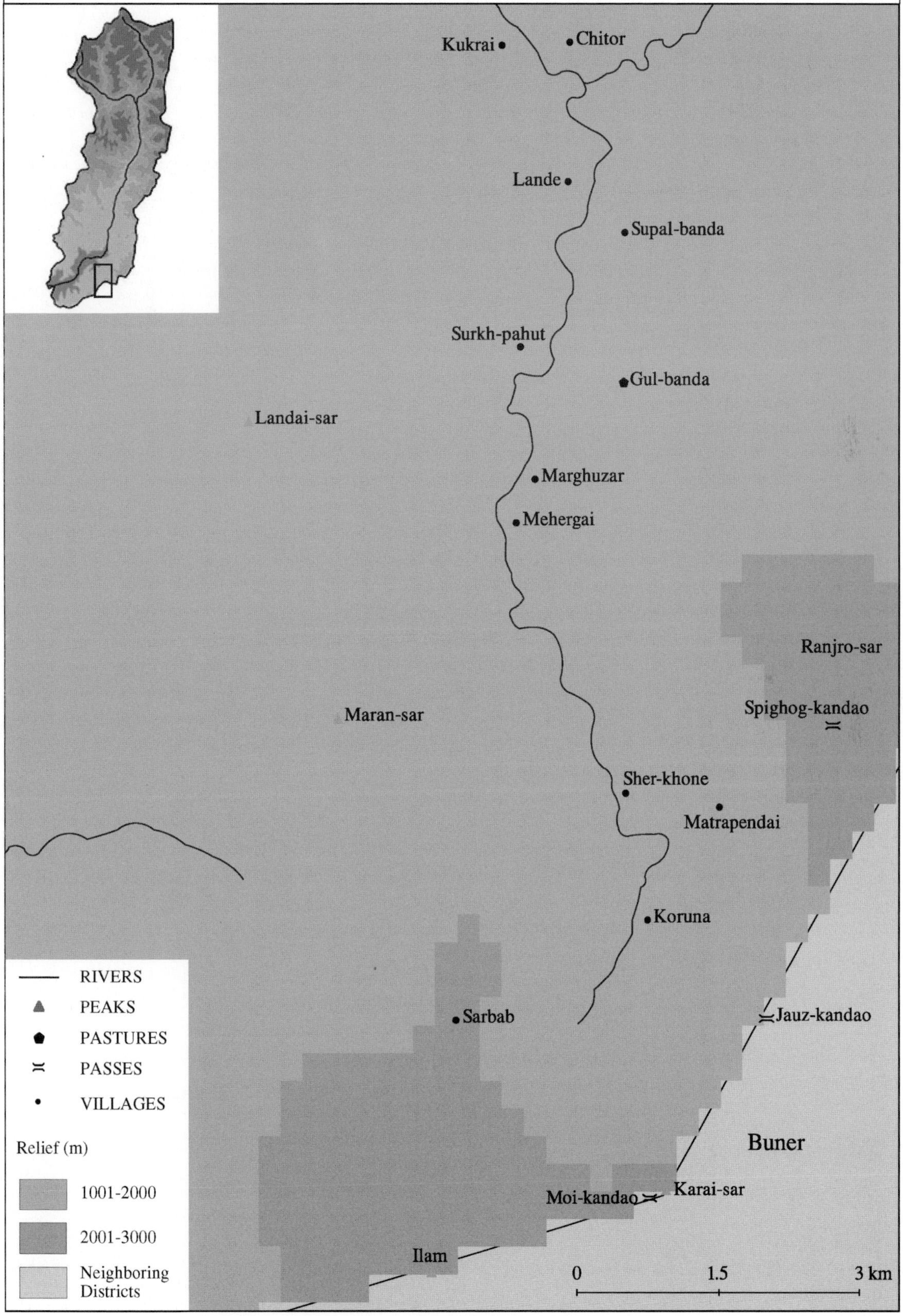
Kukrai
Chitor
Lande
Supal-banda
Surkh-pahut
Gul-banda
Landai-sar
Marghuzar
Mehergai
Ranjro-sar
Spighog-kandao
Maran-sar
Sher-khone
Matrapendai
Koruna
Sarbab
Jauz-kandao
Buner
Moi-kandao
Karai-sar
Ilam
RIVERS
PEAKS
PASTURES
PASSES
VILLAGES
Relief (m)
1001-2000
2001-3000
Neighboring Districts
0
1.5
3 km

Map 20. Saidu

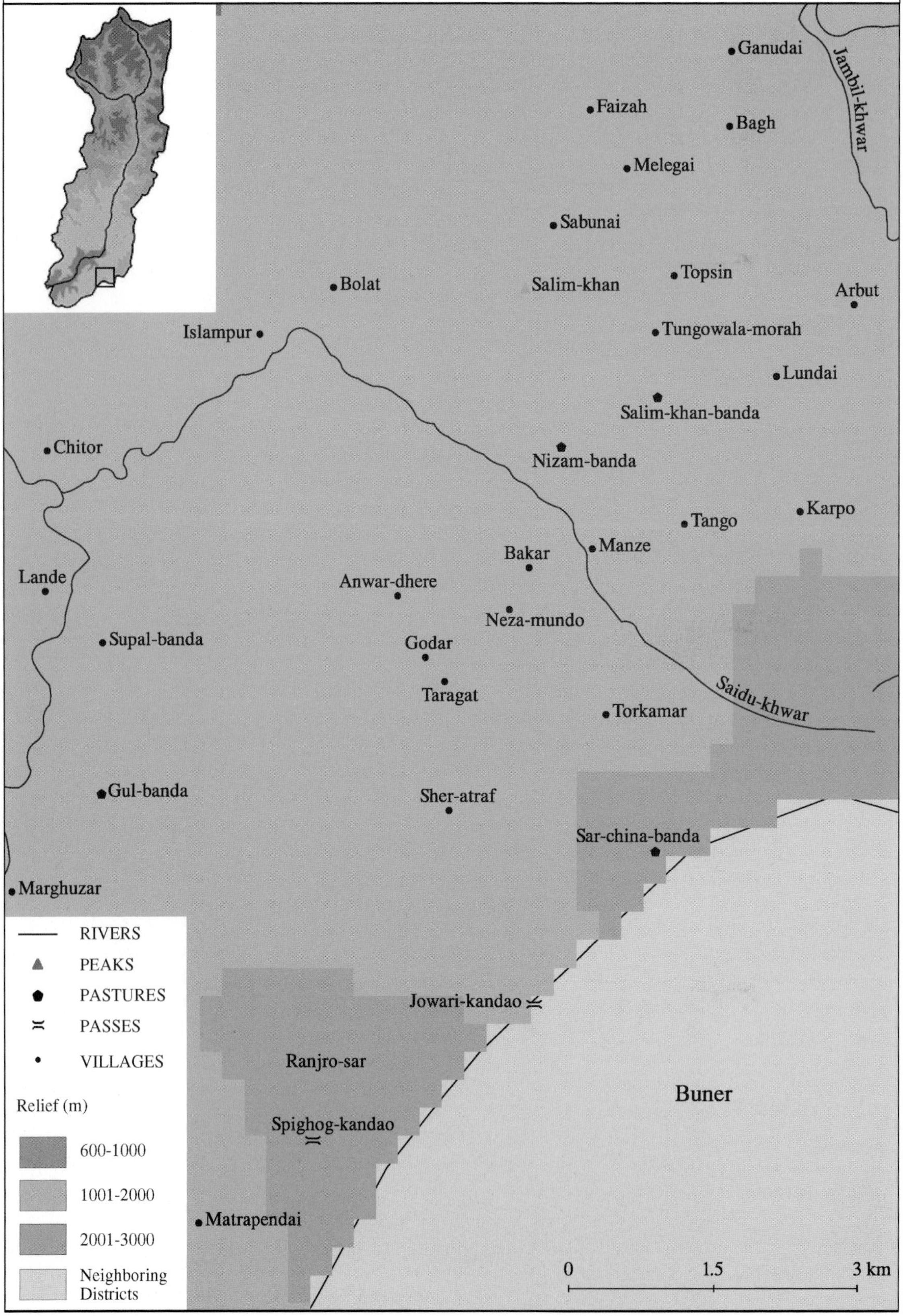
Ganudai
Jambil-khwar
Faizah
Bagh
Melegai
Sabunai
Topsin
Bolat
Salim-khan
Arbut
Islampur
Tungowala-morah
Lundai
Salim-khan-banda
Chitor
Nizam-banda
Karpo
Tango
Manze
Bakar
Lande
Anwar-dhere
Neza-mundo
Supal-banda
Godar
Taragat
Saidu-khwar
Torkamar
Gul-banda
Sher-atraf
Sar-china-banda
Marghuzar
RIVERS
PEAKS
PASTURES
PASSES
VILLAGES
Jowari-kandao
Ranjro-sar
Buner
Relief (m)
Spighog-kandao
600-1000
1001-2000
2001-3000
Matrapendai
0
1.5
3 km
Neighboring Districts

Map 21. Jambil-Dangram

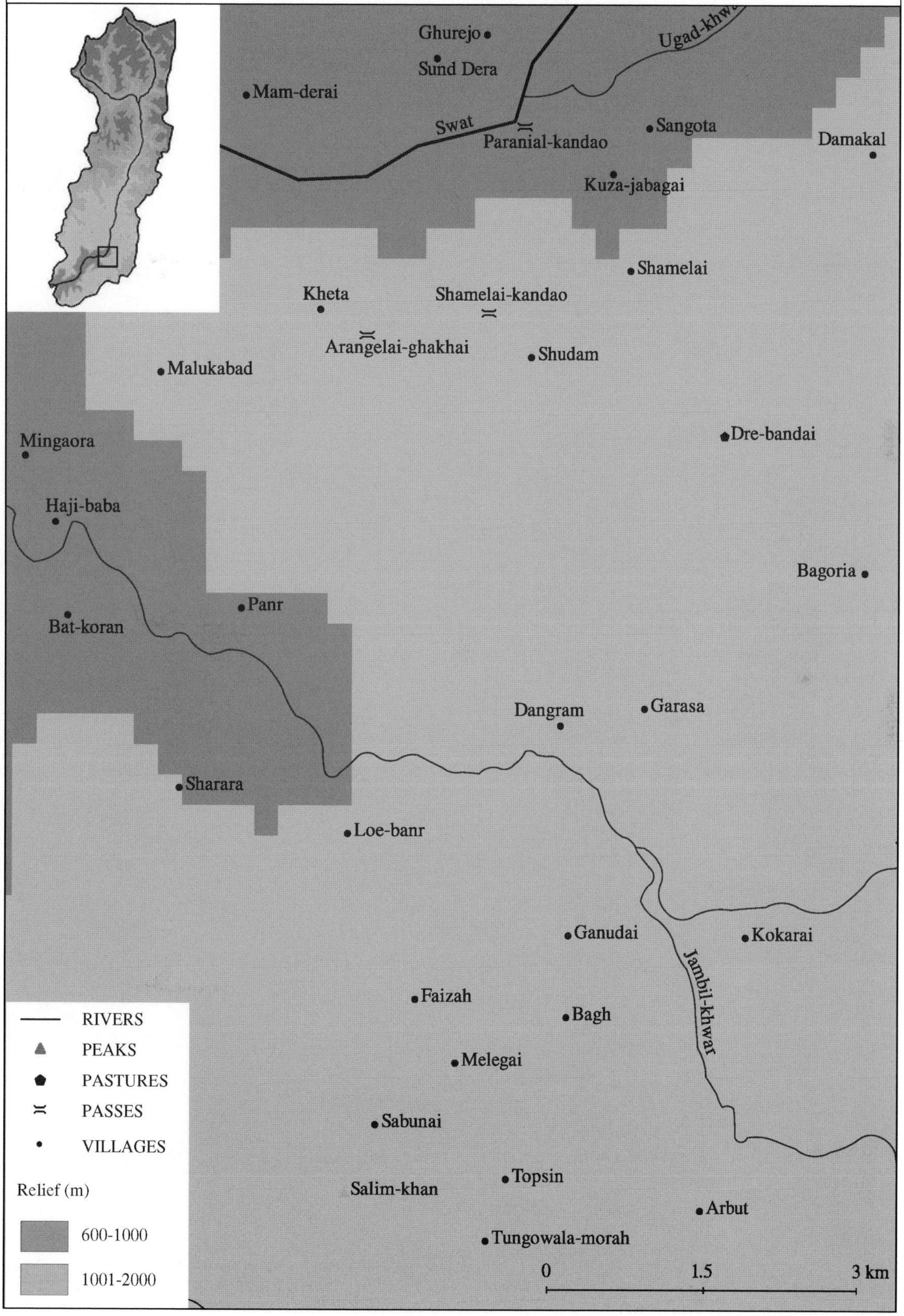

Ghurejo
Sund Dera
Ugad-khw
Mam-derai
Swat
Paranial-kandao
Sangota
Damakal
Kuza-jabagai
Shamelai
Kheta
Shamelai-kandao
Arangelai-ghakhai
Shudam
Malukabad
Dre-bandai
Mingaora
Haji-baba
Bagoria
Panr
Bat-koran
Dangram
Garasa
Sharara
Loe-banr
Ganudai
Kokarai
Jambil-khwar
Faizah
Bagh
Melegai
Sabunai
Topsin
Salim-khan
Arbut
Tungowala-morah
RIVERS
PEAKS
PASTURES
PASSES
VILLAGES
Relief (m)
600-1000
1001-2000
0
1.5
3 km

Map 22. Jambil

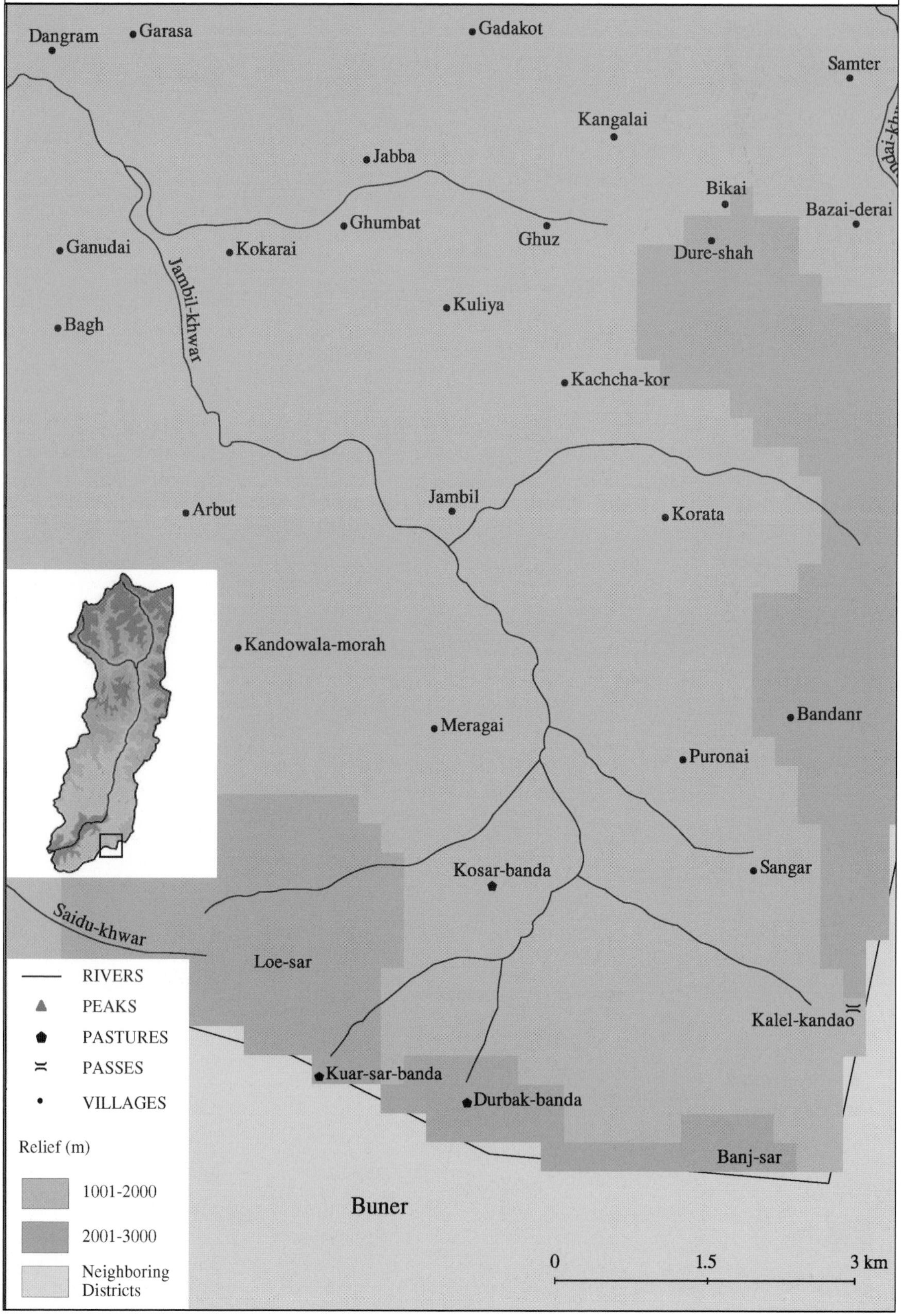

Dangram
Garasa
Gadakot
Samter
Kangalai
Jabba
Bikai
Bazai-derai
Ghumbat
Ghuz
Dure-shah
Ganudai
Kokarai
Jambil-khwar
Kuliya
Bagh
Kachcha-kor
Jambil
Arbut
Korata
Kandowala-morah
Bandanr
Meragai
Puronai
Sangar
Kosar-banda
Saidu-khwar
Loe-sar
Kalel-kandao
Kuar-sar-banda
Durbak-banda
Banj-sar
Buner
RIVERS
PEAKS
PASTURES
PASSES
VILLAGES
Relief (m)
1001-2000
2001-3000
Neighboring Districts
0
1.5
3 km

Map 23. Ugad-Landai

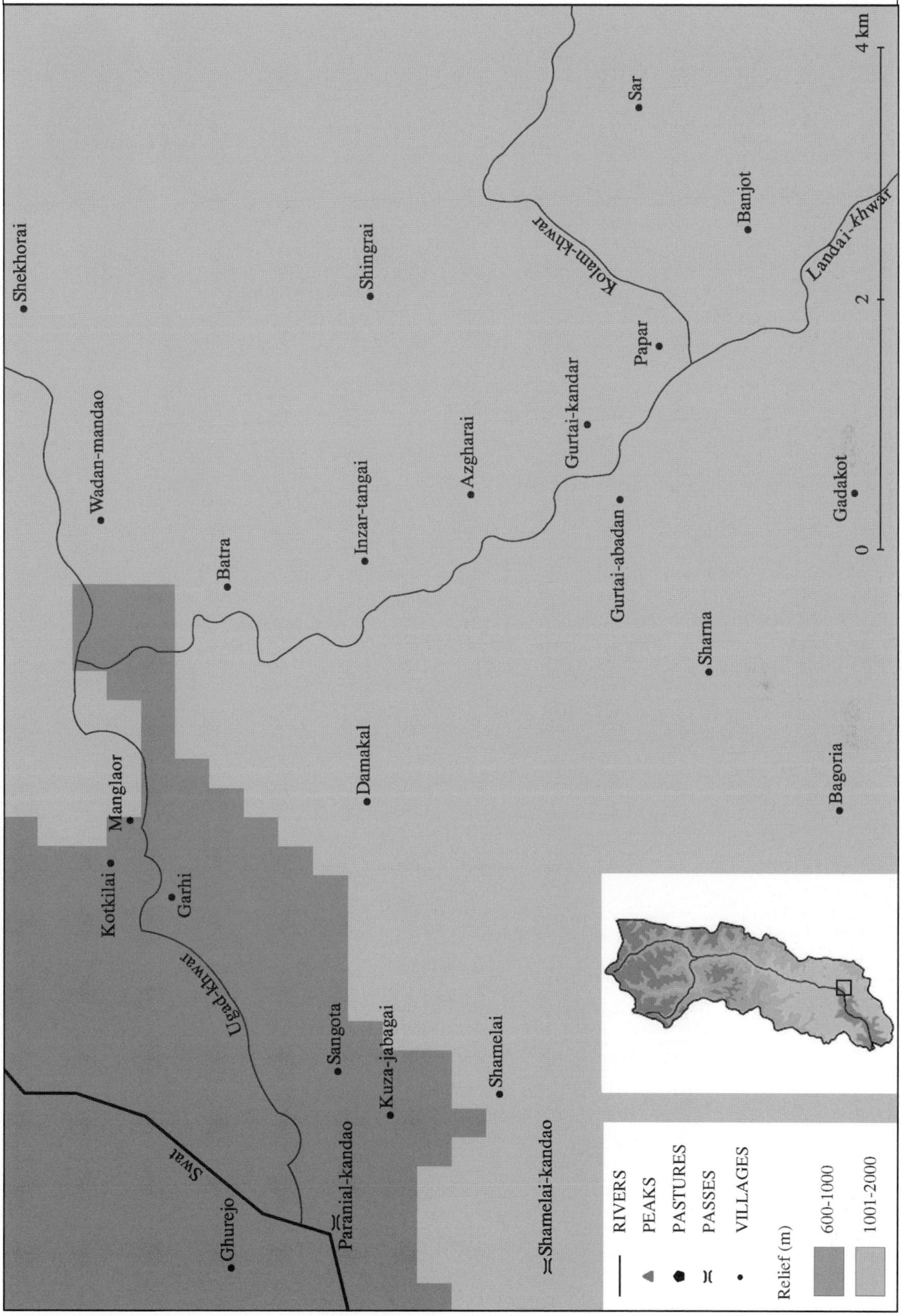

Shekhorai
Wadan-mandao
Shingrai
Batra
Inzar-tangai
Azgharai
Gurtai-kandar
Papar
Sar
Banjot
Kolam-khwar
Landai-khwar
Gurtai-abadan
Gadakot
Sharna
Damakal
Bagoria
Manglaor
Kotkilai
Garhi
Ugad-khwar
Sangota
Kuza-jabagai
Shamelai
Swat
Ghurejo
Paranial-kandao
Shamelai-kandao
0
2
4 km
RIVERS
PEAKS
PASTURES
PASSES
VILLAGES
Relief (m)
600-1000
1001-2000

Map 24. Spedar-Lewanai-Dosara

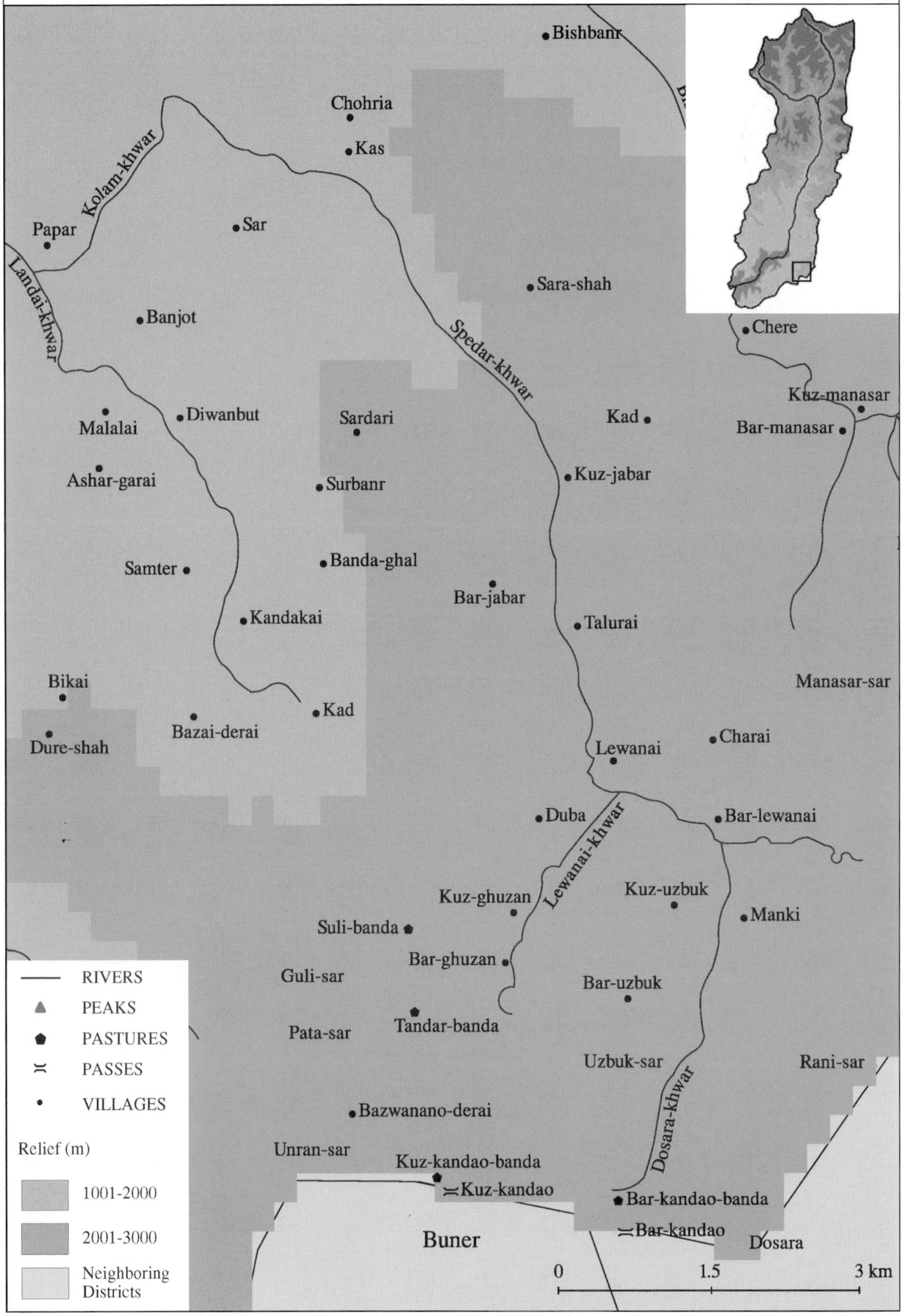
Bishbanr
Chohria
Kas
Kolam-khwar
Papar
Sar
Landai-khwar
Sara-shah
Banjot
Spedar-khwar
Chere
Kuz-manasar
Malalai
Diwanbut
Sardari
Kad
Bar-manasar
Ashar-garai
Surbanr
Kuz-jabar
Samter
Banda-ghal
Bar-jabar
Kandakai
Talurai
Bikai
Manasar-sar
Kad
Dure-shah
Bazai-derai
Lewanai
Charai
Duba
Bar-lewanai
Lewanai-khwar
Kuz-ghuzan
Kuz-uzbuk
Suli-banda
Manki
Bar-ghuzan
Guli-sar
Bar-uzbuk
Pata-sar
Tandar-banda
Uzbuk-sar
Rani-sar
Dosara-khwar
Bazwanano-derai
Unran-sar
Kuz-kandao-banda
Kuz-kandao
Bar-kandao-banda
Bar-kandao
Buner
Dosara
0
1.5
3 km
RIVERS
PEAKS
PASTURES
PASSES
VILLAGES
Relief (m)
1001-2000
2001-3000
Neighboring Districts

Map 25. Bishbanr

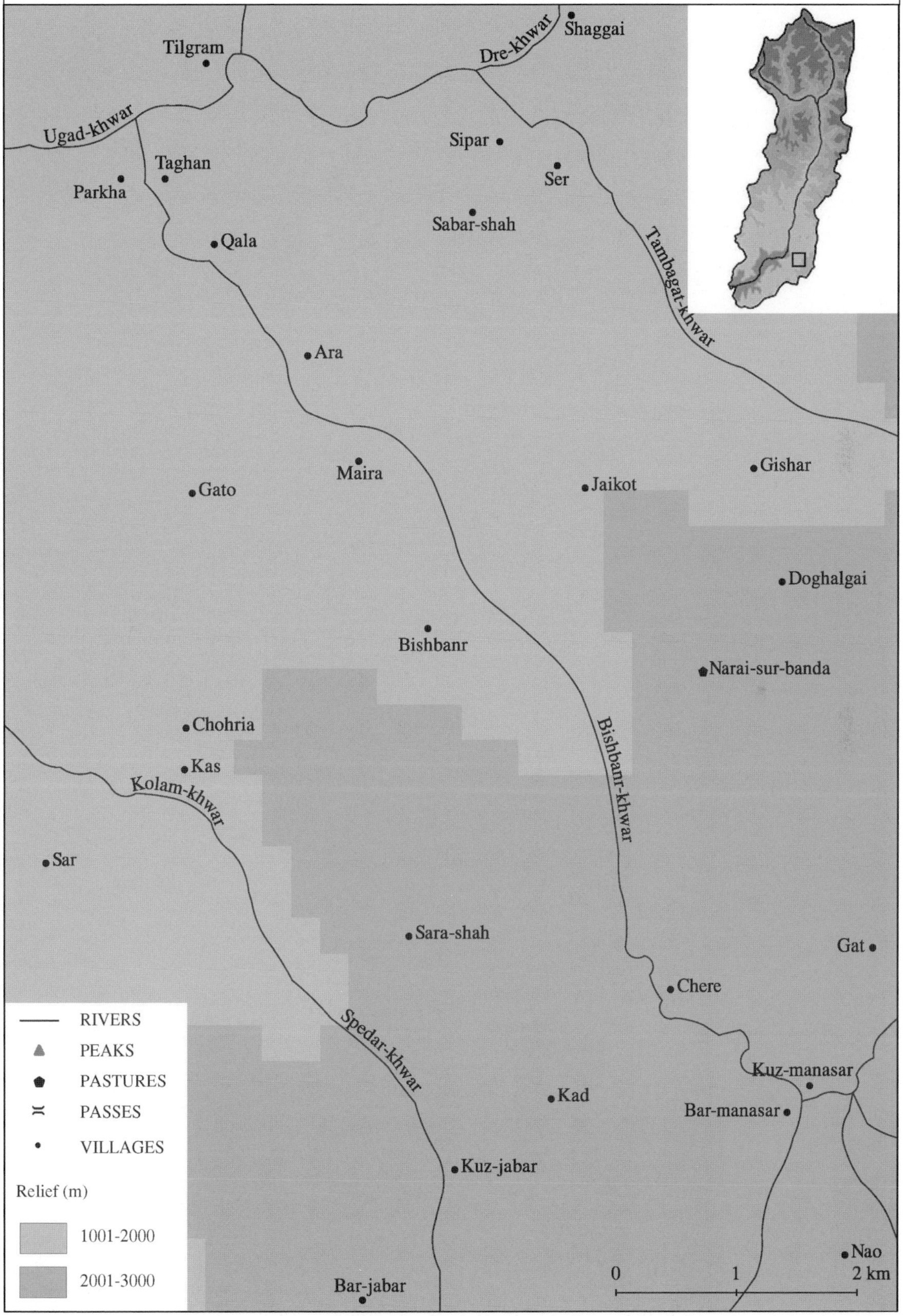

Shaggai
Tilgram
Dre-khwar
Ugad-khwar
Sipar
Taghan
Parkha
Ser
Sabar-shah
Qala
Tambagat-khwar
Ara
Gishar
Maira
Jaikot
Gato
Doghalgai
Bishbanr
Narai-sur-banda
Chohria
Bishbanr-khwar
Kas
Kolam-khwar
Sar
Sara-shah
Gat
Chere
Spedar-khwar
Kuz-manasar
Kad
Bar-manasar
Kuz-jabar
Nao
Bar-jabar
RIVERS
PEAKS
PASTURES
PASSES
VILLAGES
Relief (m)
1001-2000
2001-3000
0
1
2 km

Map 26. Bikan

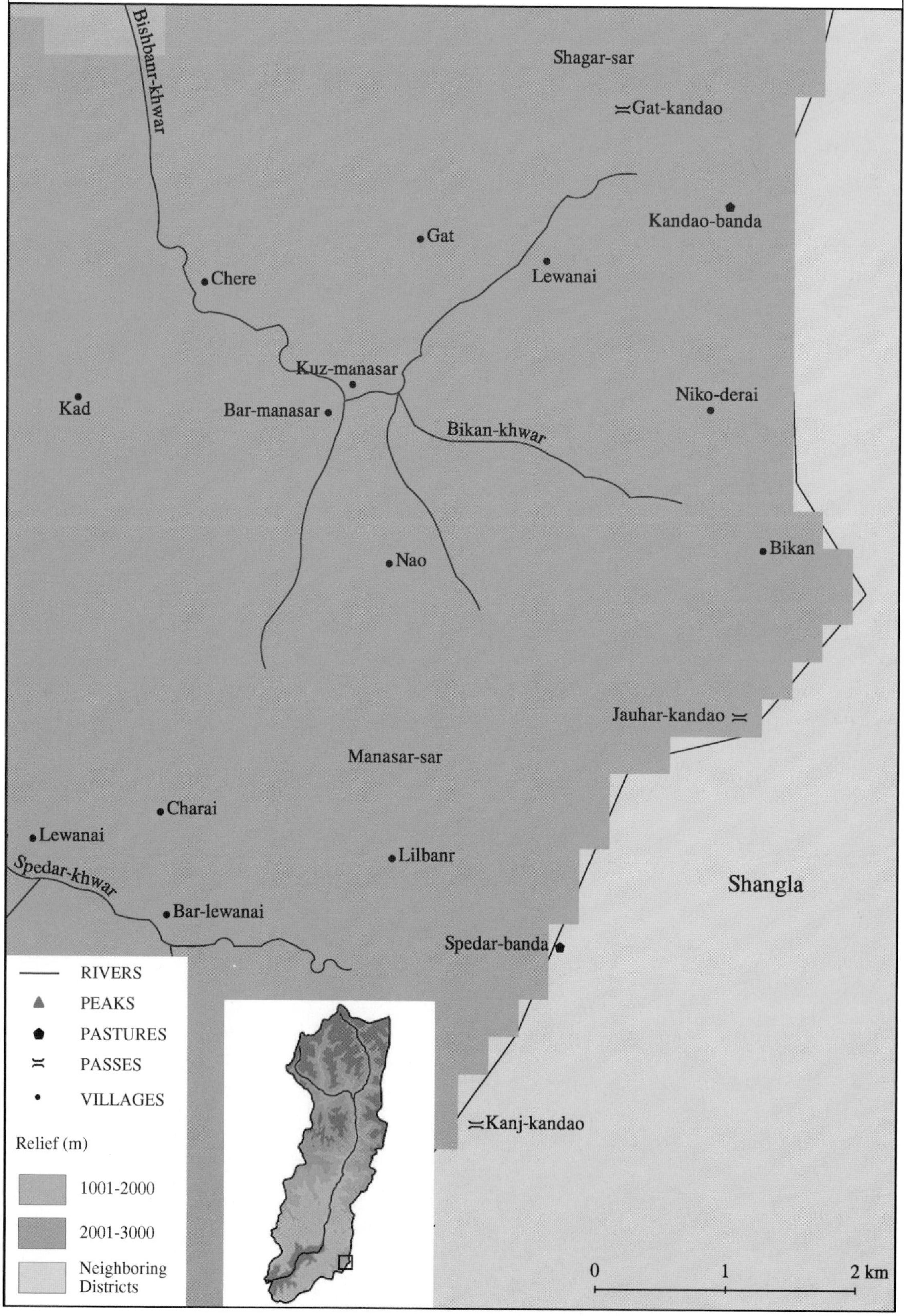

Bishbanr-khwar
Shagar-sar
Gat-kandao
Kandao-banda
Gat
Lewanai
Chere
Kuz-manasar
Kad
Bar-manasar
Niko-derai
Bikan-khwar
Nao
Bikan
Jauhar-kandao
Manasar-sar
Charai
Lewanai
Lilbanr
Shangla
Spedar-khwar
Bar-lewanai
Spedar-banda
RIVERS
PEAKS
PASTURES
PASSES
VILLAGES
Kanj-kandao
Relief (m)
1001-2000
2001-3000
Neighboring Districts
0
1
2 km

Map 27. Tambagat

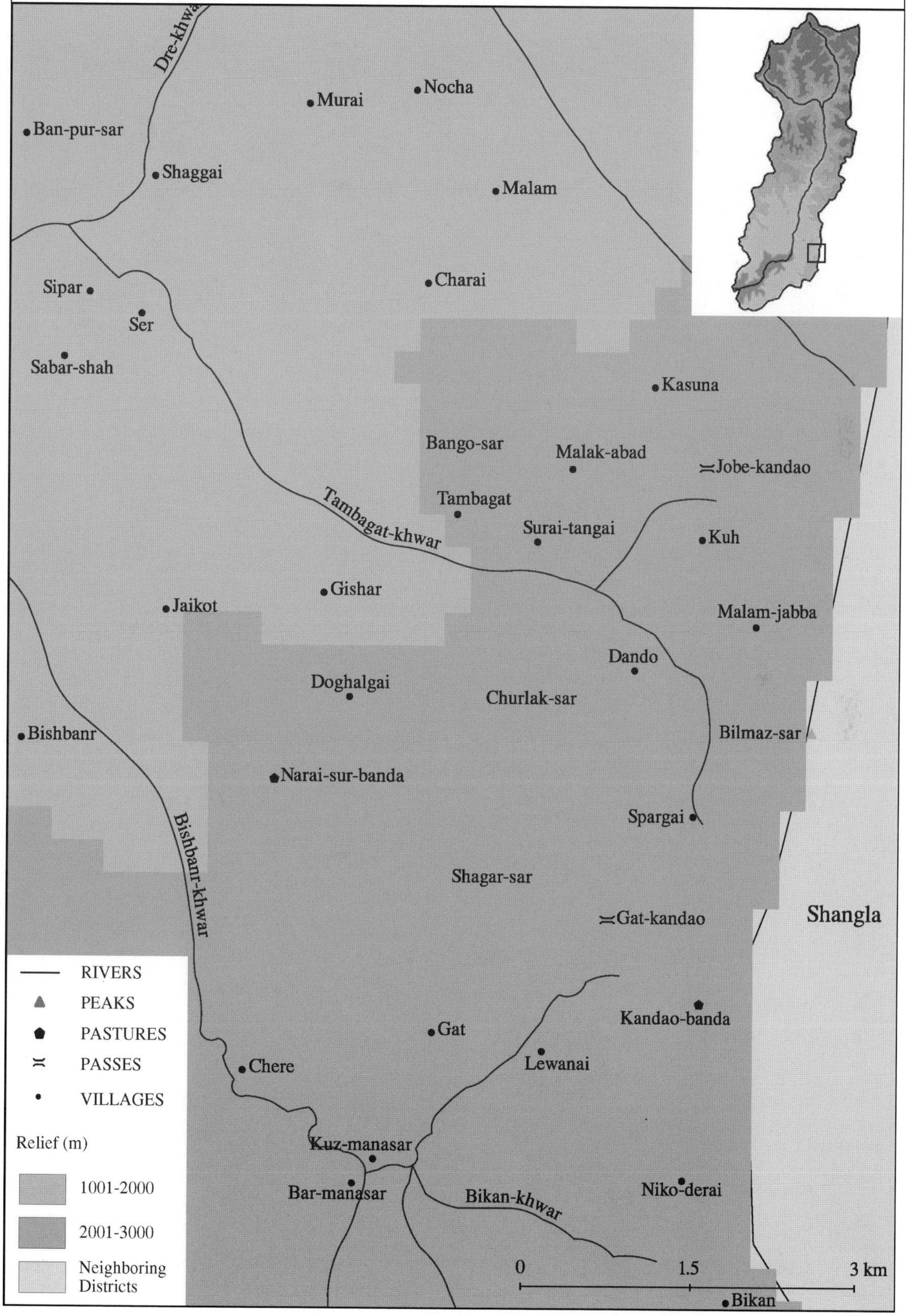
Dre-khwar
Murai
Nocha
Ban-pur-sar
Shaggai
Malam
Charai
Sipar
Ser
Sabar-shah
Kasuna
Bango-sar
Malak-abad
Jobe-kandao
Tambagat
Surai-tangai
Tambagat-khwar
Kuh
Gishar
Jaikot
Malam-jabba
Dando
Doghalgai
Churlak-sar
Bishbanr
Bilmaz-sar
Narai-sur-banda
Spargai
Bishbanr-khwar
Shagar-sar
Gat-kandao
Shangla
RIVERS
PEAKS
PASTURES
PASSES
VILLAGES
Kandao-banda
Gat
Lewanai
Chere
Relief (m)
Kuz-manasar
1001-2000
Bar-manasar
Bikan-khwar
Niko-derai
2001-3000
Neighboring Districts
0
1.5
3 km
Bikan

Map 28. Dre

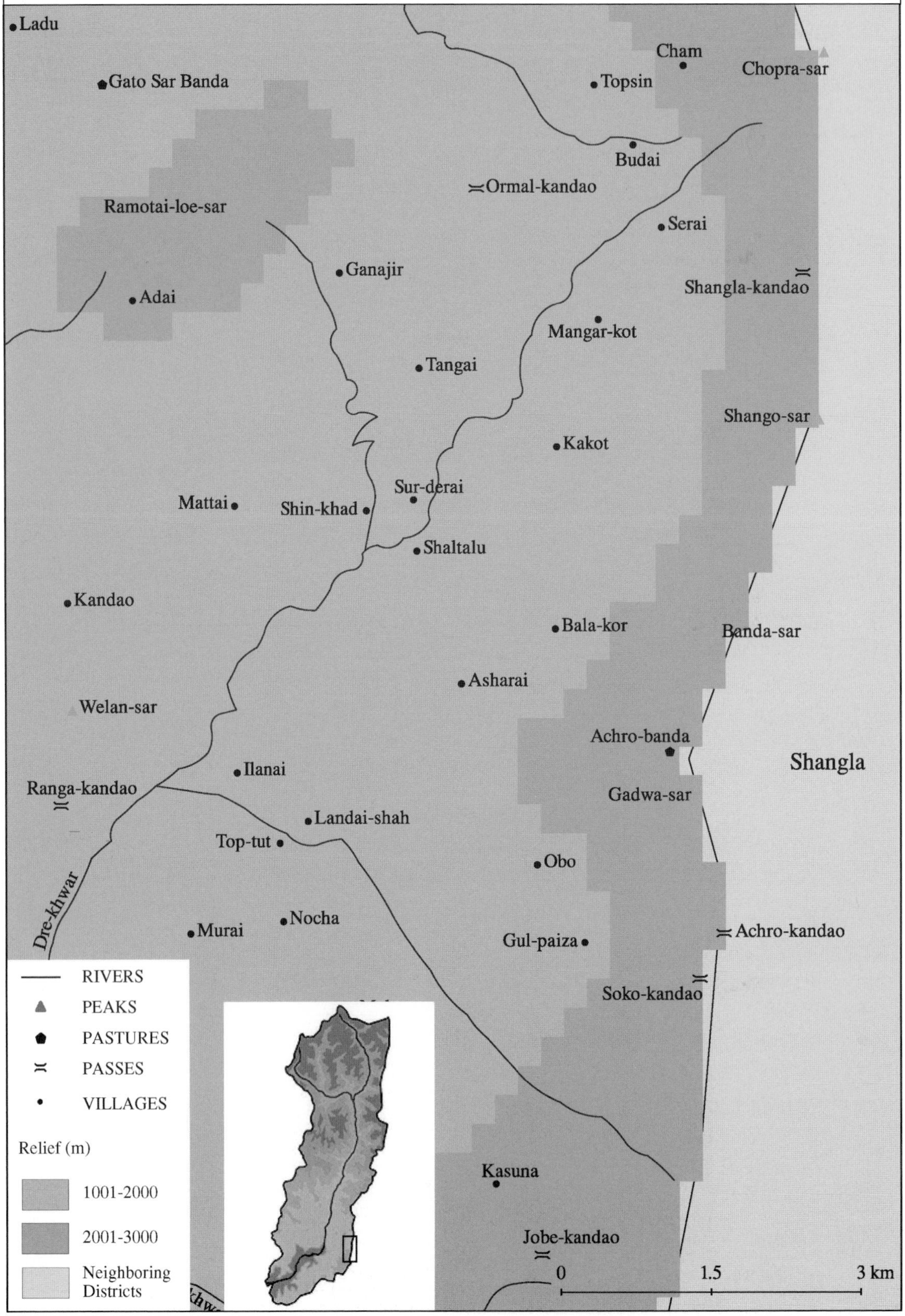

Ladu
Gato Sar Banda
Cham
Chopra-sar
Topsin
Budai
Ormal-kandao
Ramotai-loe-sar
Serai
Ganajir
Shangla-kandao
Adai
Mangar-kot
Tangai
Shango-sar
Kakot
Sur-derai
Mattai
Shin-khad
Shaltalu
Kandao
Bala-kor
Banda-sar
Asharai
Welan-sar
Achro-banda
Shangla
Ilanai
Gadwa-sar
Ranga-kandao
Landai-shah
Top-tut
Obo
Dre-khwar
Nocha
Murai
Gul-paiza
Achro-kandao
Soko-kandao
RIVERS
PEAKS
PASTURES
PASSES
VILLAGES
Relief (m)
1001-2000
2001-3000
Neighboring Districts
Kasuna
Jobe-kandao
0
1.5
3 km

Map 29. Makad

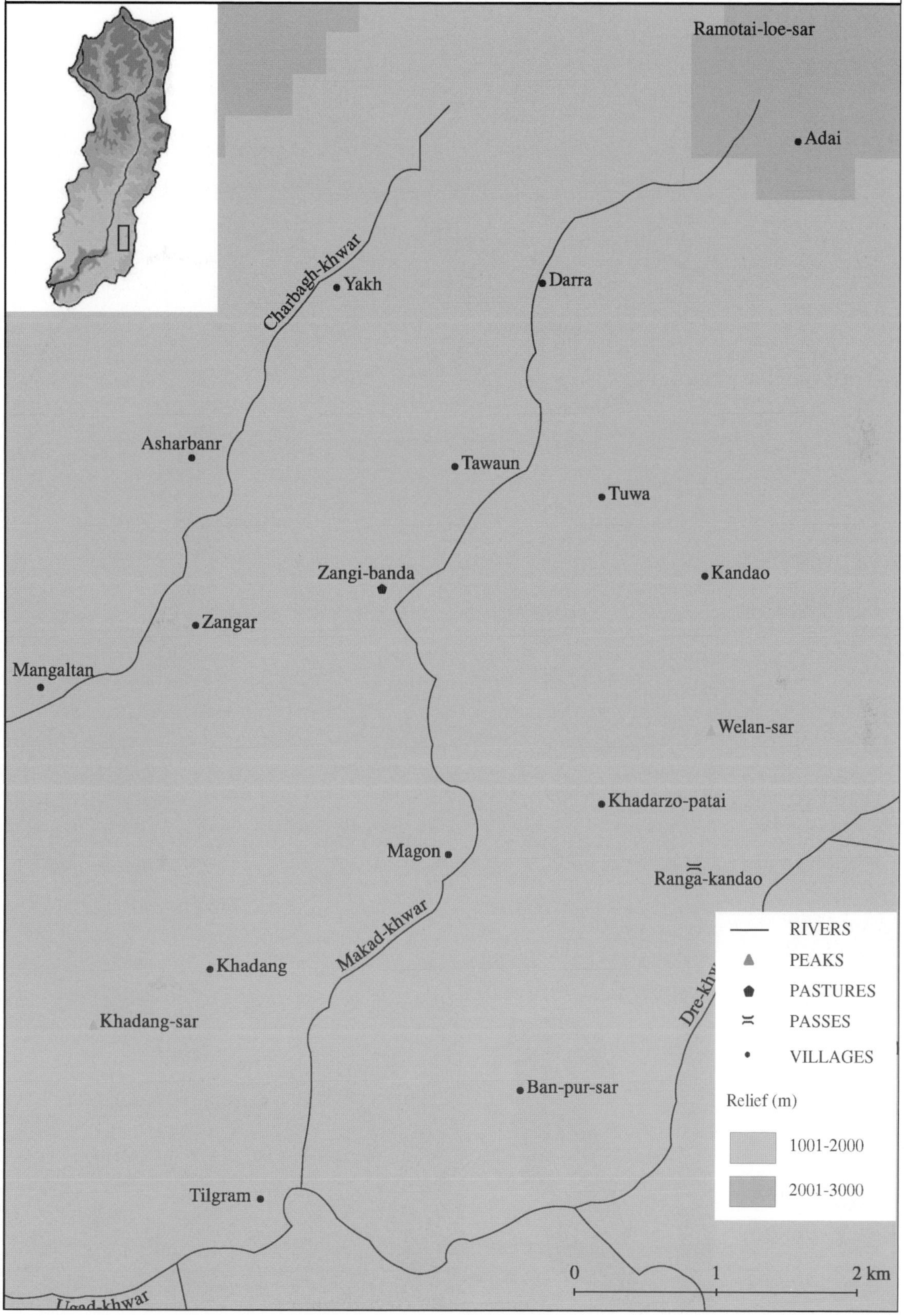
Ramotai-loe-sar
Adai
Charbagh-khwar
Yakh
Darra
Asharbanr
Tawaun
Tuwa
Zangi-banda
Kandao
Zangar
Mangaltan
Welan-sar
Khadarzo-patai
Magon
Ranga-kandao
Makad-khwar
Khadang
Khadang-sar
Ban-pur-sar
Tilgram
RIVERS
PEAKS
PASTURES
PASSES
VILLAGES
Relief (m)
1001-2000
2001-3000
0
1
2 km

Map 30. Charbagh

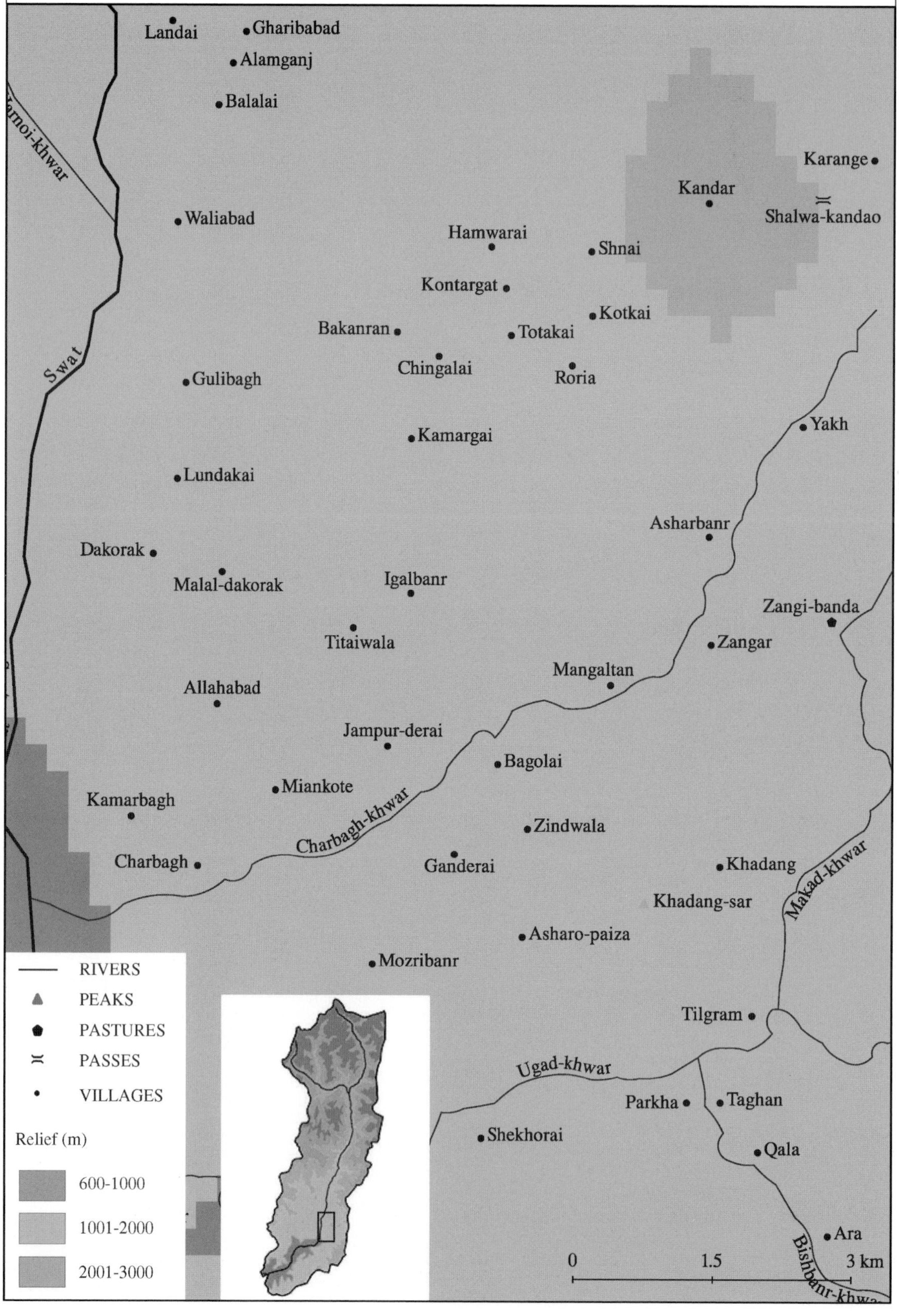
Landai
Gharibabad
Alamganj
Balalai
Swat
Waliabad
Hamwarai
Shnai
Kandar
Karange
Shalwa-kandao
Kontargat
Kotkai
Bakanran
Totakai
Chingalai
Roria
Gulibagh
Yakh
Kamargai
Lundakai
Asharbanr
Dakorak
Malal-dakorak
Igalbanr
Zangi-banda
Titaiwala
Zangar
Mangaltan
Allahabad
Jampur-derai
Bagolai
Miankote
Kamarbagh
Zindwala
Charbagh-khwar
Charbagh
Ganderai
Khadang
Makad-khwar
Khadang-sar
Asharo-paiza
Mozribanr
Tilgram
Ugad-khwar
Parkha
Taghan
Shekhorai
Qala
Ara
Bishbanr-khwar
0
1.5
3 km
RIVERS
PEAKS
PASTURES
PASSES
VILLAGES
Relief (m)
600-1000
1001-2000
2001-3000

Map 31. Khwazakhela 1

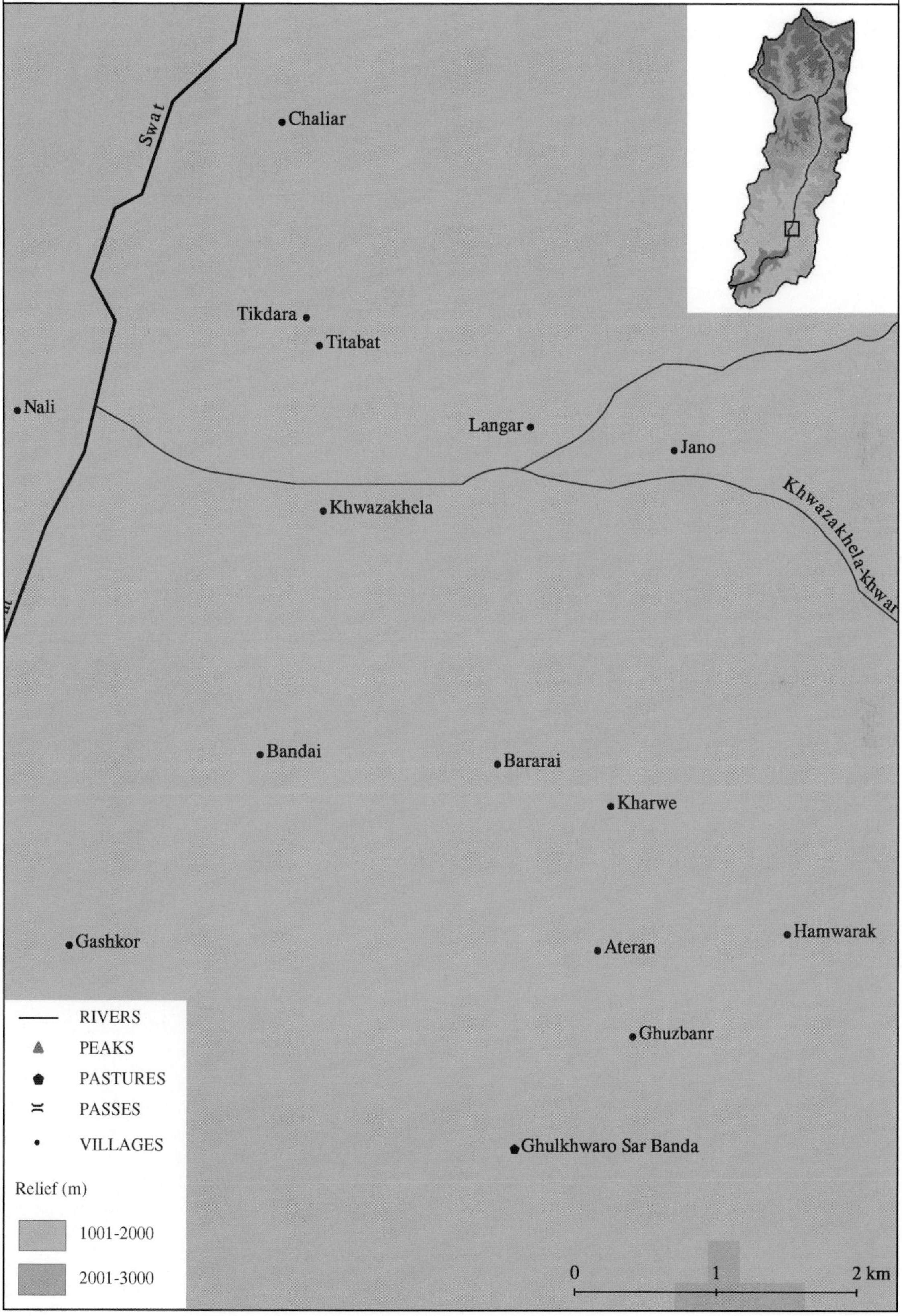
Swat
Chaliar
Tikdara
Titabat
Nali
Langar
Jano
Khwazakhela
Khwazakhela-khwar
Bandai
Bararai
Kharwe
Gashkor
Ateran
Hamwarak
Ghuzbanr
Ghulkhwaro Sar Banda
RIVERS
PEAKS
PASTURES
PASSES
VILLAGES
Relief (m)
1001-2000
2001-3000
0
1
2 km

Map 32. Khazakhela 2 – Topsin

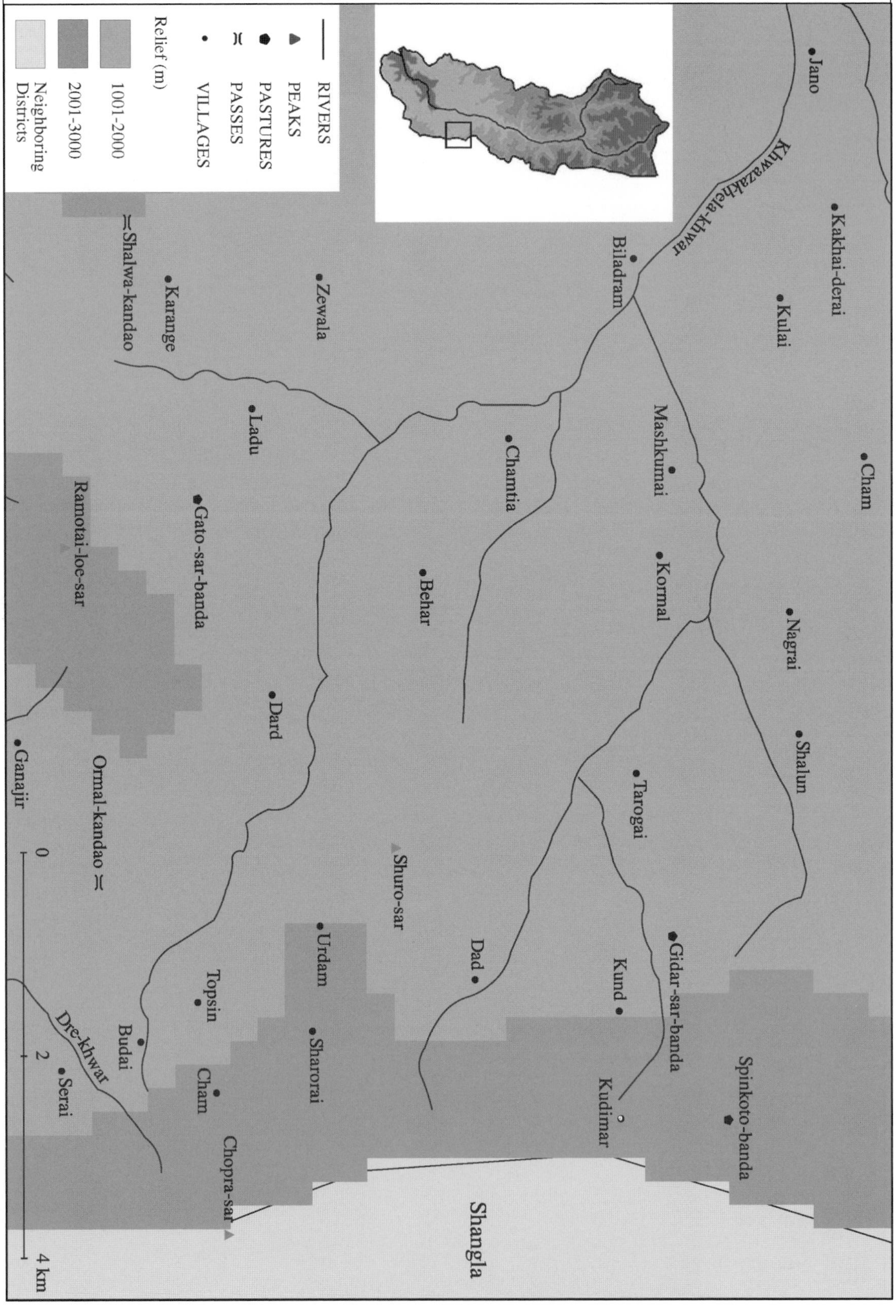

Map 33. Khwazakhela 3 – Shalpin

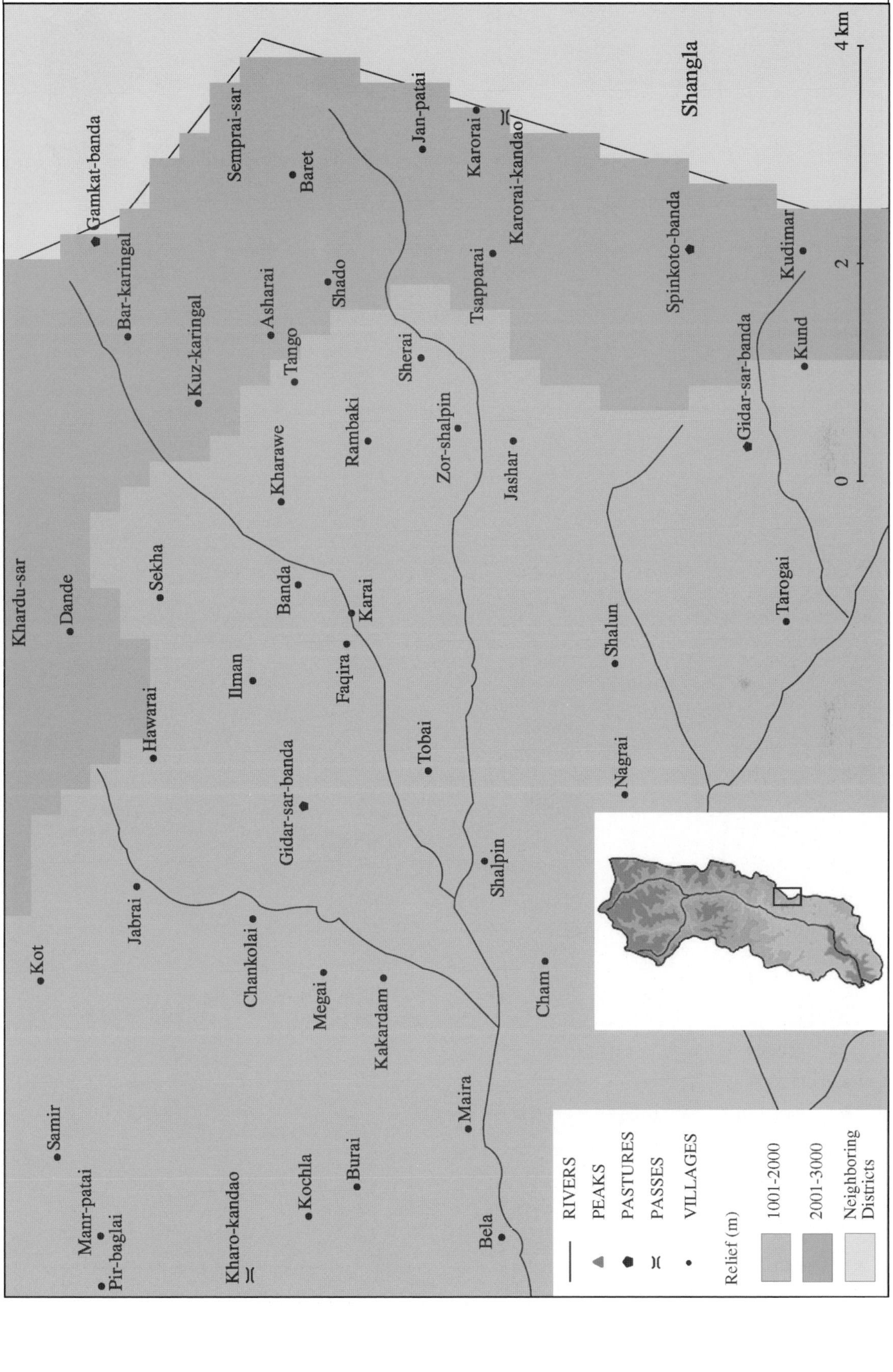
Gamkat-banda
Semprai-sar
Baret
Jan-patai
Karorai
Karorai-kandao
Shangla
Bar-karingal
Kuz-karingal
Asharai
Shado
Tsapparai
Spinkoto-banda
Kudimar
Tango
Sherai
Kund
Gidar-sar-banda
Rambaki
Zor-shalpin
Jashar
Kharawe
Khardu-sar
Dande
Sekha
Banda
Karai
Faqira
Ilman
Hawarai
Shalun
Tarogai
Tobai
Gidar-sar-banda
Nagrai
Shalpin
Jabrai
Chankolai
Kot
Megai
Kakardam
Cham
Maira
Samir
Manr-patai
Pir-baglai
Kharo-kandao
Kochla
Burai
Bela
RIVERS
PEAKS
PASTURES
PASSES
VILLAGES
Relief (m)
1001-2000
2001-3000
Neighboring Districts
0
2
4 km

Map 34. Swat 4 – Kotanai

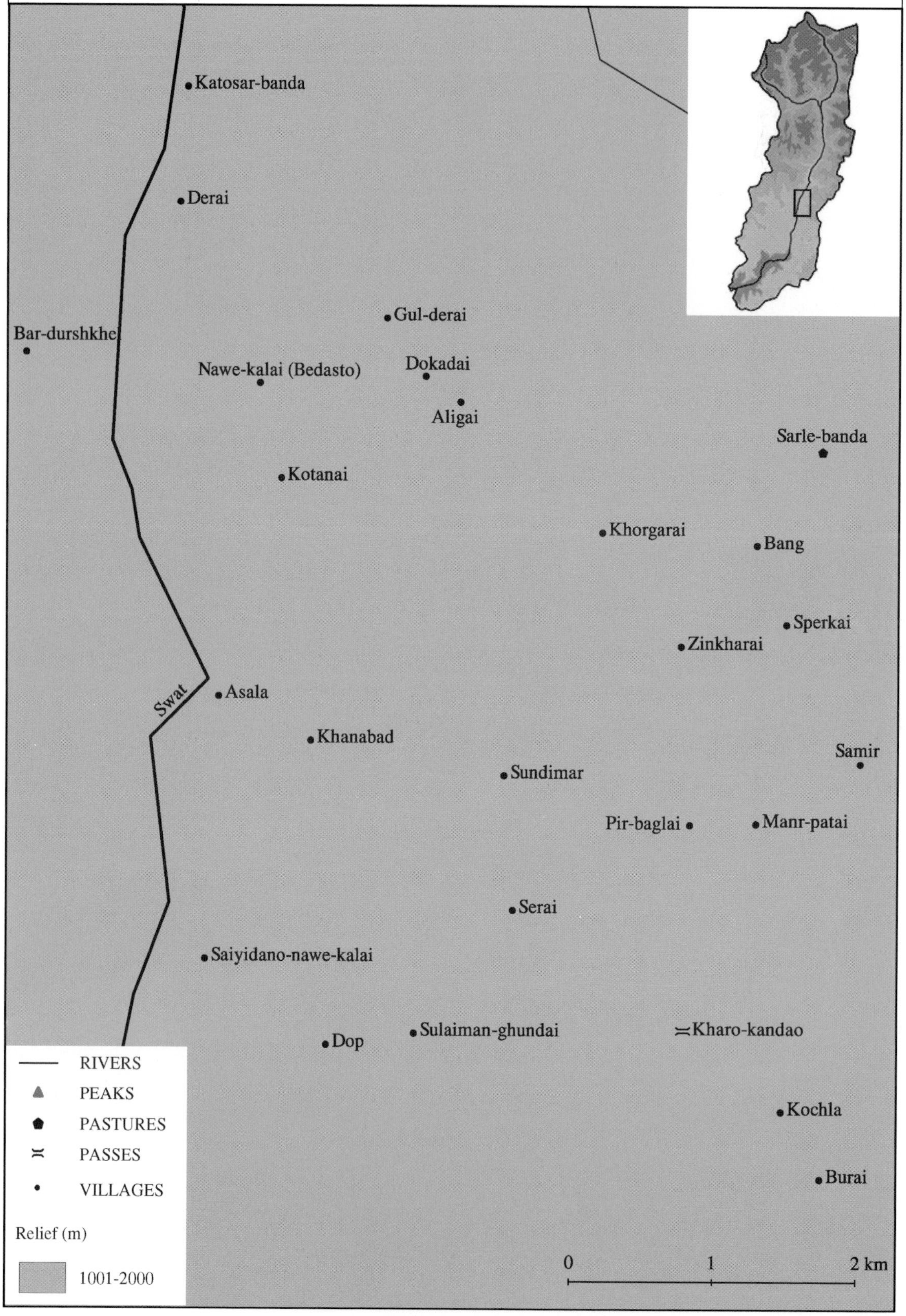
Katosar-banda
Derai
Gul-derai
Bar-durshkhe
Nawe-kalai (Bedasto)
Dokadai
Aligai
Sarle-banda
Kotanai
Khorgarai
Bang
Sperkai
Zinkharai
Swat
Asala
Khanabad
Samir
Sundimar
Pir-baglai
Manr-patai
Serai
Saiyidano-nawe-kalai
Dop
Sulaiman-ghundai
Kharo-kandao
Kochla
Burai
RIVERS
PEAKS
PASTURES
PASSES
VILLAGES
Relief (m)
1001-2000
0
1
2 km

Map 35. Bargin

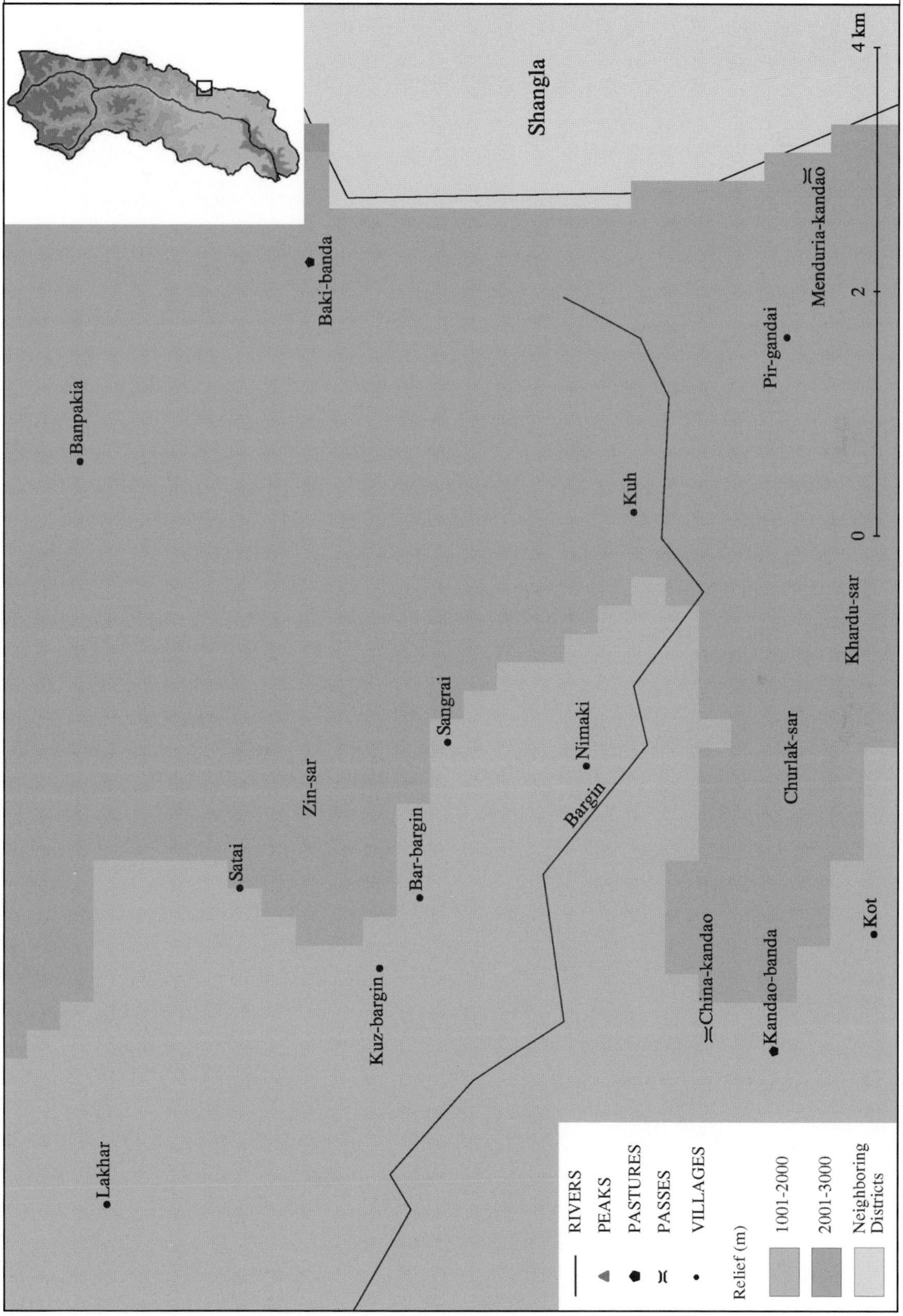
Shangla
Baki-banda
Banpakia
Menduria-kandao
Pir-gandai
Kuh
Khardu-sar
Sangrai
Nimaki
Churlak-sar
Zin-sar
Bargin
Bar-bargin
Satai
Kot
China-kandao
Kandao-banda
Kuz-bargin
Lakhar
0
2
4 km
RIVERS
PEAKS
PASTURES
PASSES
VILLAGES
Relief (m)
1001-2000
2001-3000
Neighboring Districts

Map 36. Paiti-Miandam

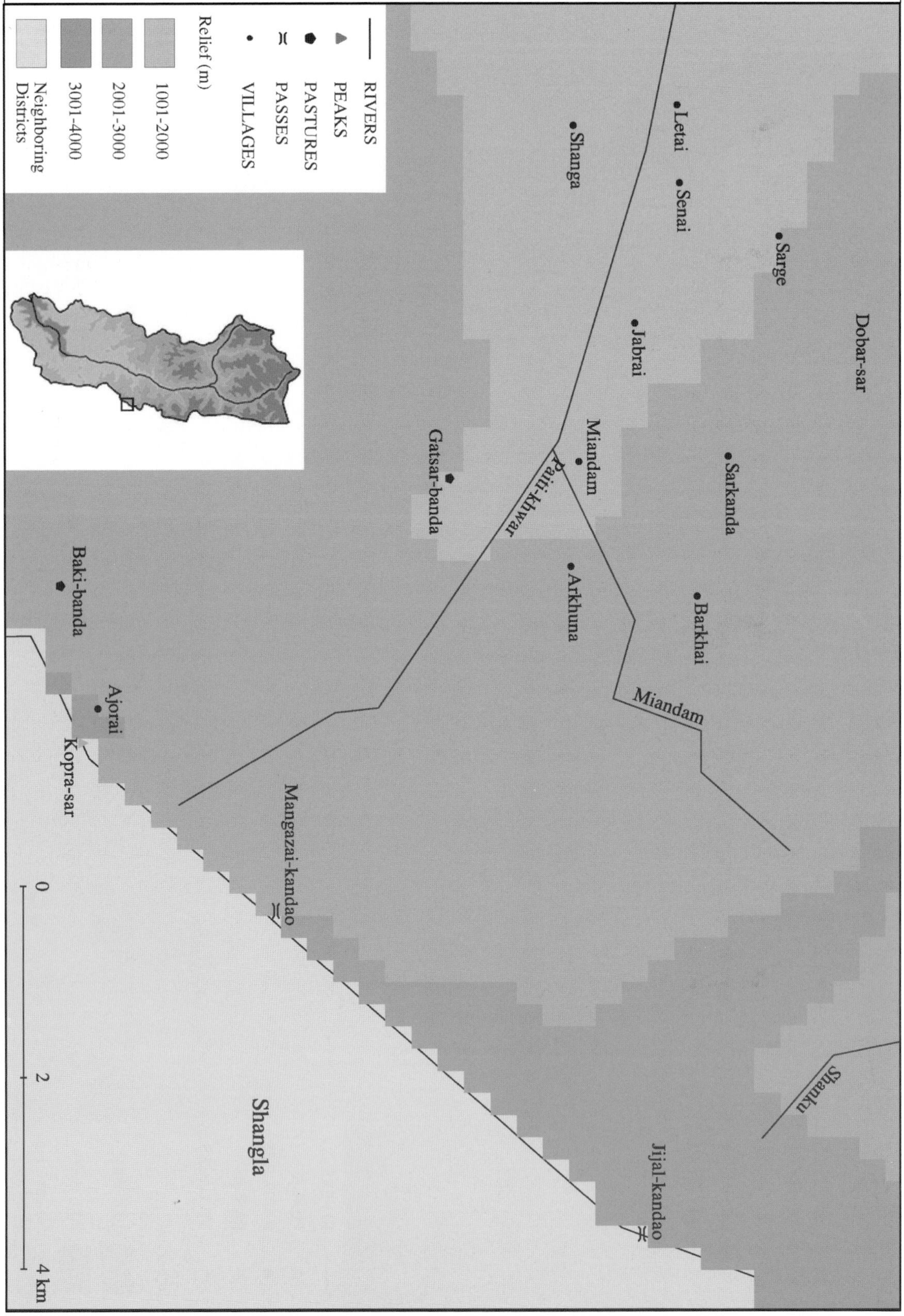
RIVERS
PEAKS
PASTURES
PASSES
VILLAGES
Relief (m)
1001-2000
2001-3000
3001-4000
Neighboring Districts
Dobar-sar
Sarge
Letai
Senai
Shanga
Jabrai
Miandam
Sarkanda
Gatsar-banda
Paiti-Khwar
Arkhuna
Barkhai
Miandam
Baki-banda
Ajorai
Kopra-sar
Mangazai-kandao
Shanku
Jijal-kandao
Shangla
0
2
4 km

Map 37. Paiti

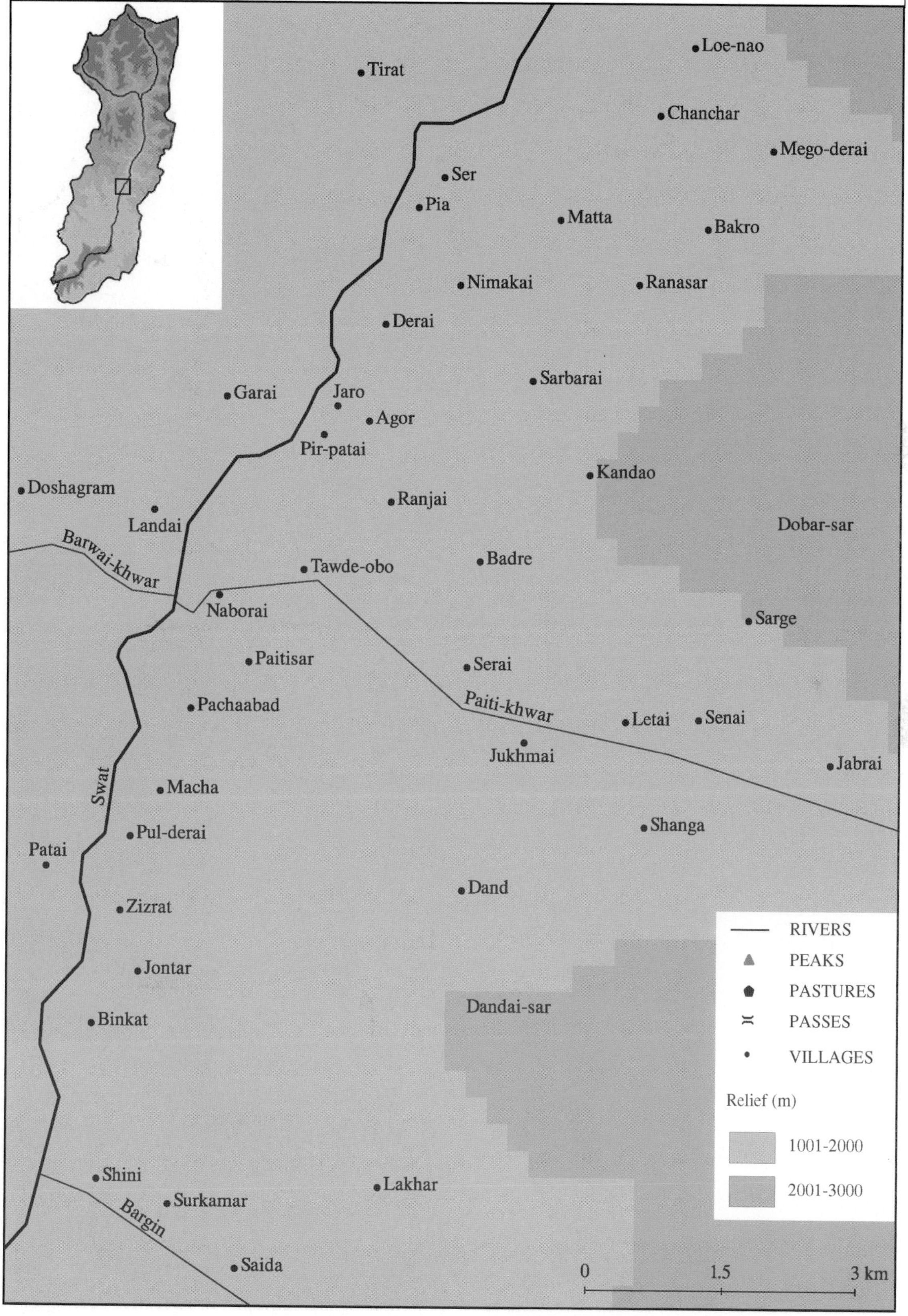

Loe-nao

Tirat

Chanchar

Mego-derai

Ser

Pia

Matta

Bakro

Nimakai

Ranasar

Derai

Sarbarai

Garai

Jaro

Agor

Pir-patai

Kandao

Dobar-sar

Doshagram

Ranjai

Landai

Barwai-khwar

Badre

Tawde-obo

Sarge

Naborai

Paitisar

Serai

Paiti-khwar

Pachaabad

Letai

Senai

Jabrai

Jukhmai

Swat

Macha

Patai

Pul-derai

Shanga

Zizrat

Dand

Jontar

Binkat

Dandai-sar

	RIVERS
▲	PEAKS
⬟	PASTURES
≍	PASSES
•	VILLAGES

Relief (m)

| | 1001-2000 |
| | 2001-3000 |

Shini

Lakhar

Bargin

Surkamar

Saida

0   1.5   3 km

Map 38. Harnoi 1

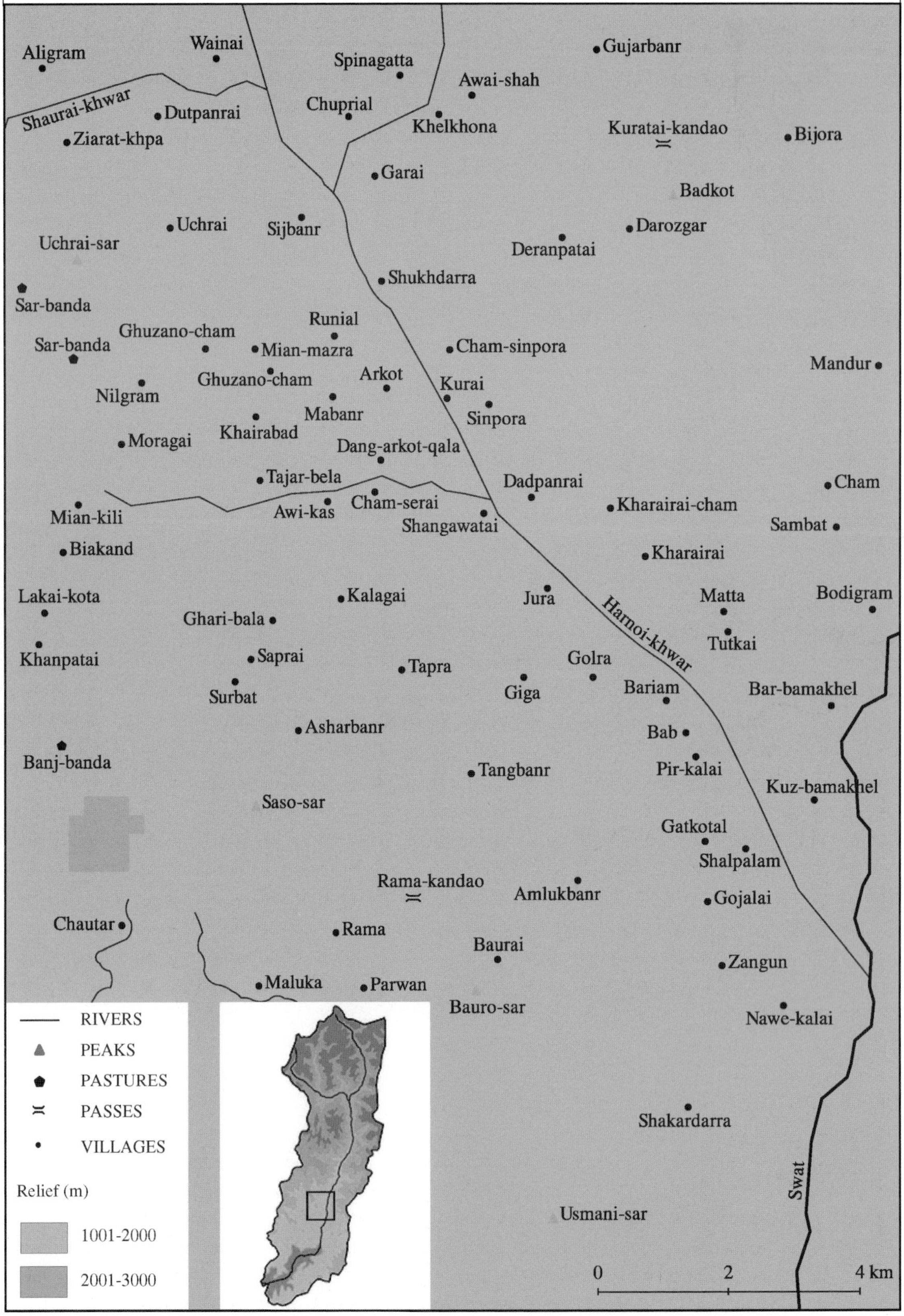
Aligram
Wainai
Spinagatta
Gujarbanr
Awai-shah
Shaurai-khwar
Dutpanrai
Chuprial
Khelkhona
Kuratai-kandao
Bijora
Ziarat-khpa
Garai
Badkot
Uchrai
Sijbanr
Darozgar
Uchrai-sar
Deranpatai
Shukhdarra
Sar-banda
Runial
Ghuzano-cham
Mian-mazra
Cham-sinpora
Sar-banda
Mandur
Ghuzano-cham
Arkot
Kurai
Nilgram
Mabanr
Sinpora
Khairabad
Moragai
Dang-arkot-qala
Tajar-bela
Dadpanrai
Cham
Cham-serai
Awi-kas
Kharairai-cham
Mian-kili
Shangawatai
Sambat
Biakand
Kharairai
Lakai-kota
Kalagai
Jura
Matta
Bodigram
Ghari-bala
Harnoi-khwar
Tutkai
Khanpatai
Saprai
Golra
Tapra
Giga
Bariam
Bar-bamakhel
Surbat
Asharbanr
Bab
Banj-banda
Tangbanr
Pir-kalai
Kuz-bamakhel
Saso-sar
Gatkotal
Shalpalam
Rama-kandao
Amlukbanr
Gojalai
Chautar
Rama
Baurai
Zangun
Maluka
Parwan
Bauro-sar
Nawe-kalai
RIVERS
PEAKS
PASTURES
PASSES
VILLAGES
Relief (m)
1001-2000
2001-3000
Shakardarra
Swat
Usmani-sar
0
2
4 km

Map 39. Harnoi 2 – Chuprial-Swat

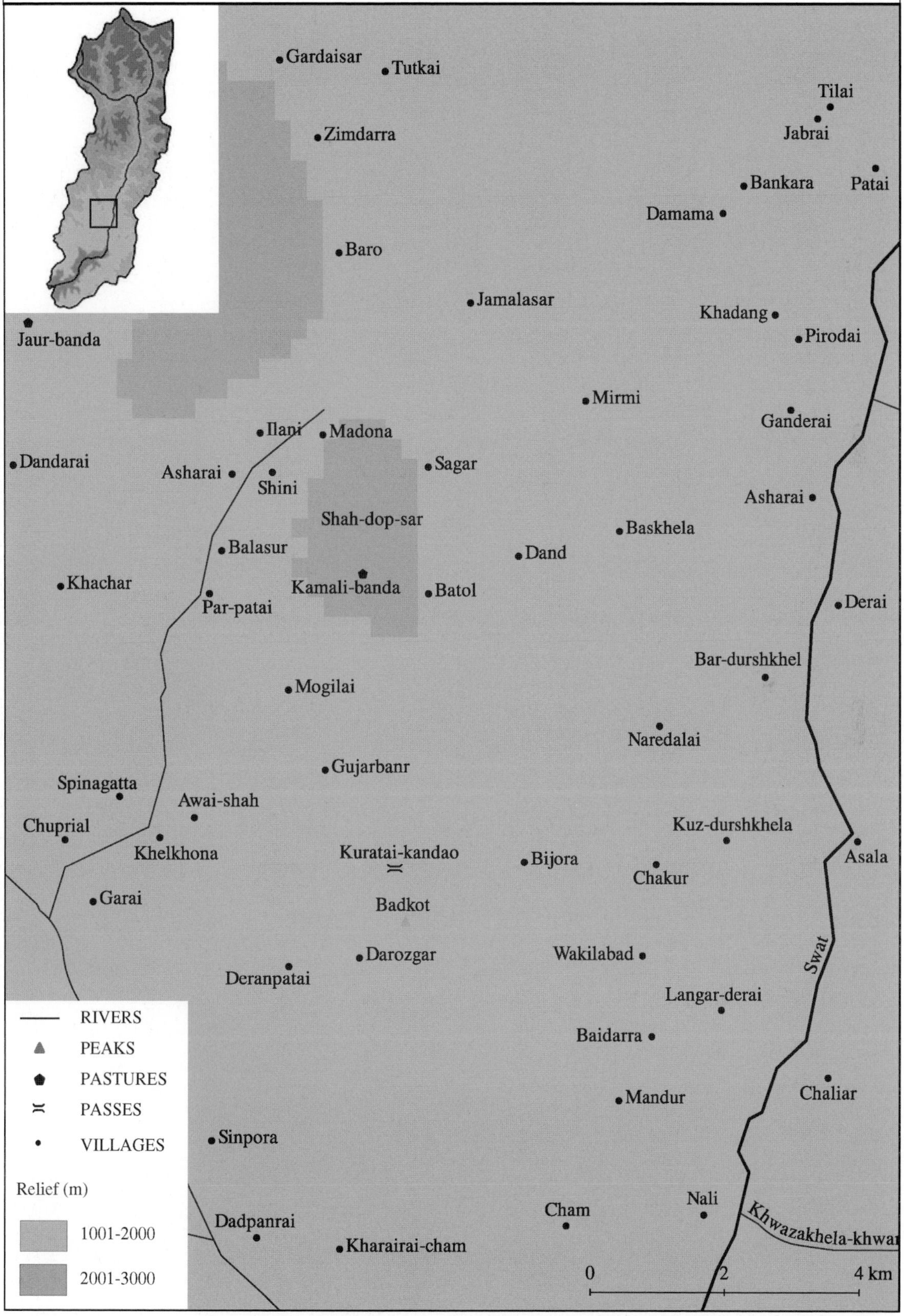
Gardaisar
Tutkai
Tilai
Jabrai
Zimdarra
Bankara
Patai
Damama
Baro
Jamalasar
Khadang
Pirodai
Jaur-banda
Mirmi
Ganderai
Ilani
Madona
Dandarai
Asharai
Shini
Sagar
Asharai
Shah-dop-sar
Baskhela
Balasur
Dand
Khachar
Kamali-banda
Batol
Par-patai
Derai
Bar-durshkhel
Mogilai
Naredalai
Gujarbanr
Spinagatta
Awai-shah
Chuprial
Kuz-durshkhela
Khelkhona
Kuratai-kandao
Bijora
Chakur
Asala
Garai
Badkot
Darozgar
Wakilabad
Deranpatai
Swat
Langar-derai
Baidarra
RIVERS
PEAKS
PASTURES
PASSES
VILLAGES
Relief (m)
1001-2000
2001-3000
Mandur
Chaliar
Sinpora
Nali
Cham
Dadpanrai
Khwazakhela-khwar
Kharairai-cham
0
2
4 km

Map 40. Shaurai

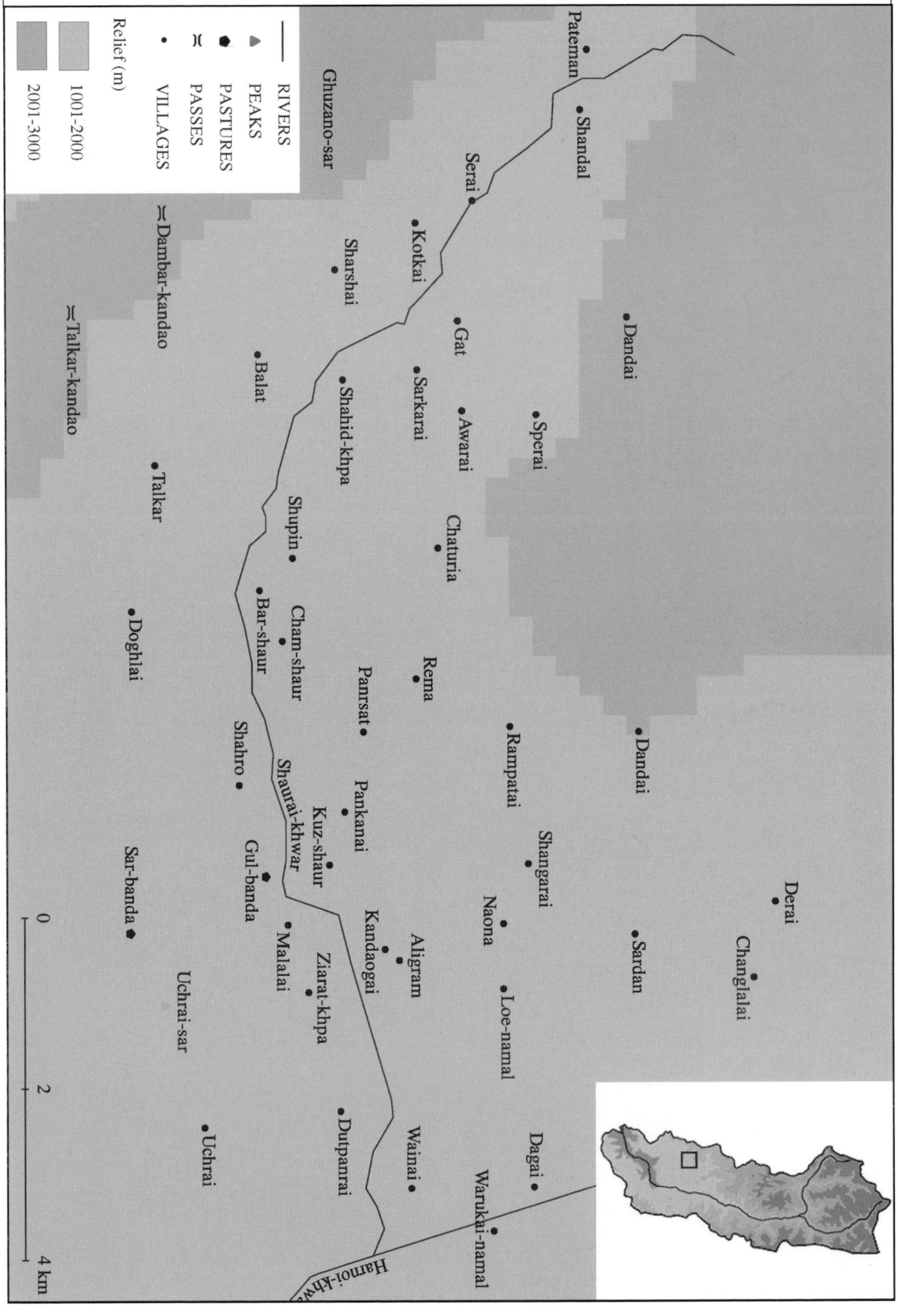

Map 41. Harnoi 3 – Barthana

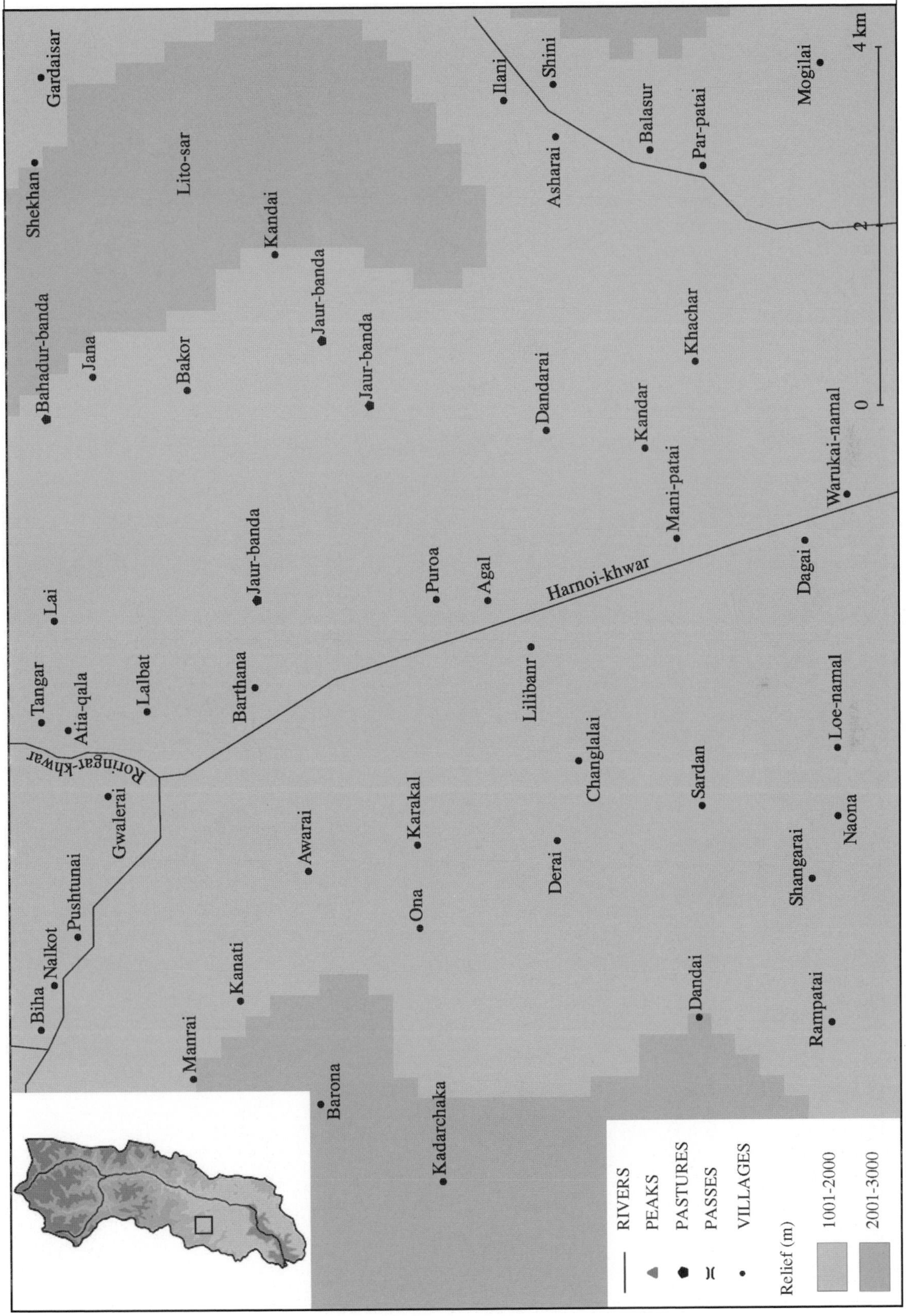

Gardaisar
Shekhan
Lito-sar
Kandai
Bahadur-banda
Jana
Bakor
Jaur-banda
Jaur-banda
Ilani
Shini
Asharai
Balasur
Par-patai
Mogilai
4 km
2
0
Dandarai
Khachar
Kandar
Warukai-namal
Mani-patai
Jaur-banda
Lai
Puroa
Agal
Harnoi-khwar
Dagai
Tangar
Atia-qala
Lalbat
Barthana
Lilibanr
Loe-namal
Roringar-khwar
Changlalai
Gwalerai
Sardan
Karakal
Awarai
Naona
Derai
Pushtunai
Shangarai
Ona
Nalkot
Biha
Kanati
Dandai
Rampatai
Manrai
Barona
Kadarchaka
RIVERS
PEAKS
PASTURES
PASSES
VILLAGES
Relief (m)
1001-2000
2001-3000

Map 42. Biha

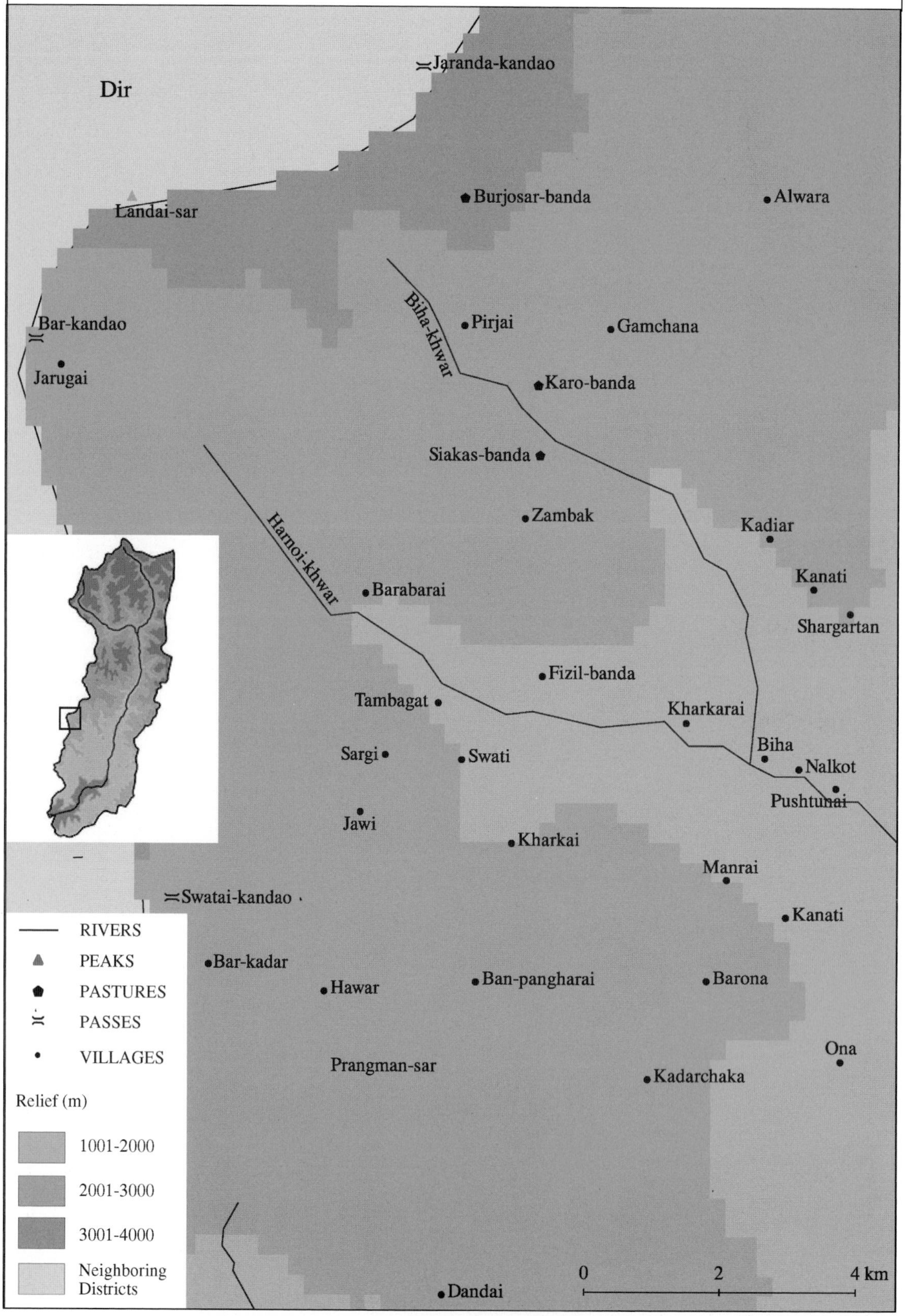

Jaranda-kandao
Dir
Burjosar-banda
Alwara
Landai-sar
Biha-khwar
Bar-kandao
Pirjai
Gamchana
Jarugai
Karo-banda
Siakas-banda
Harnoi-khwar
Zambak
Kadiar
Kanati
Barabarai
Shargartan
Fizil-banda
Tambagat
Kharkarai
Sargi
Swati
Biha
Nalkot
Pushtunai
Jawi
Kharkai
Manrai
Swatai-kandao
Kanati
RIVERS
PEAKS
PASTURES
PASSES
VILLAGES
Bar-kadar
Hawar
Ban-pangharai
Barona
Ona
Prangman-sar
Kadarchaka
Relief (m)
1001-2000
2001-3000
3001-4000
Neighboring Districts
0
2
4 km
Dandai

Map 43. Roringar

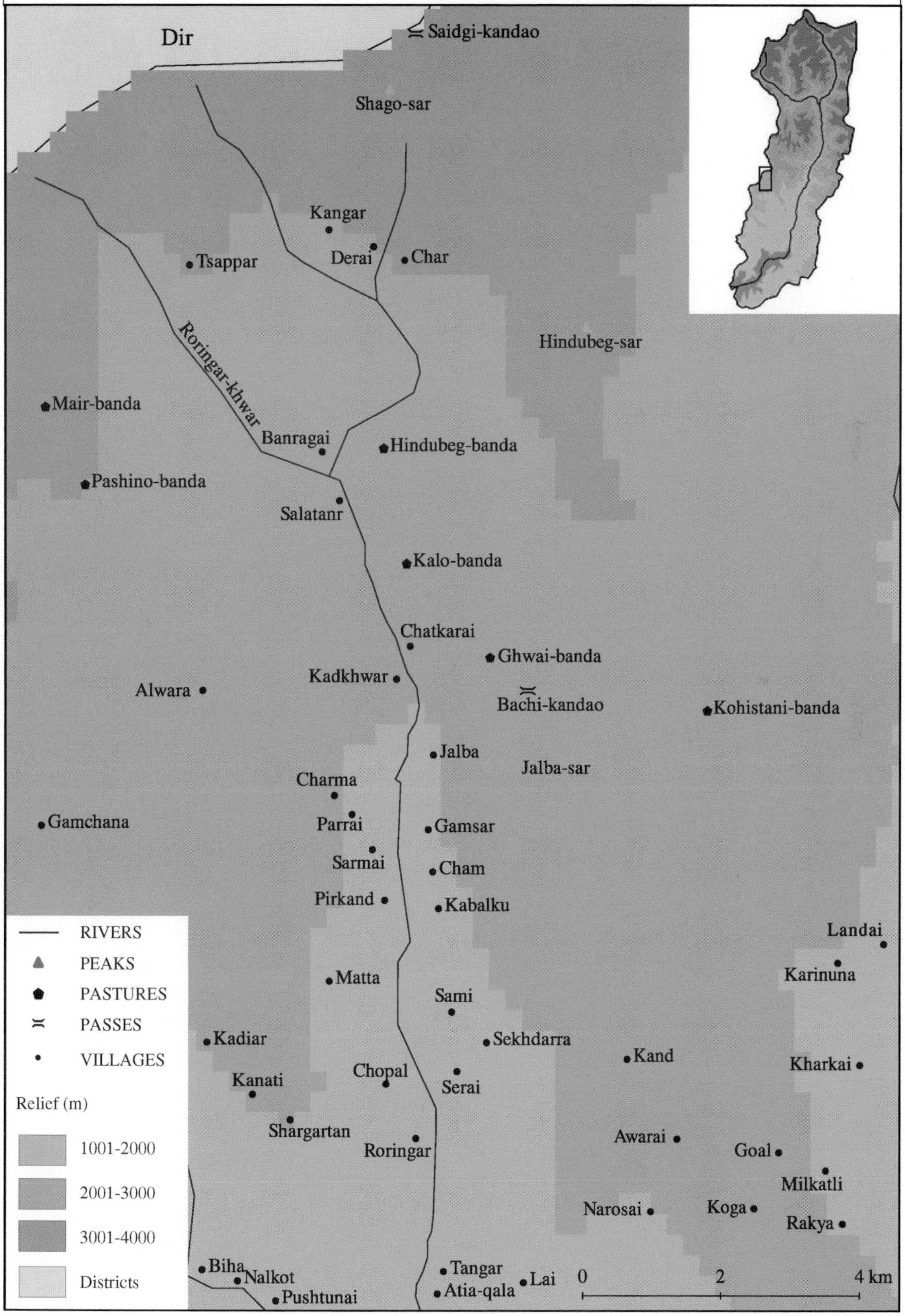

Dir
Saidgi-kandao
Shago-sar
Kangar
Derai
Char
Tsappar
Roringar-khwar
Hindubeg-sar
Mair-banda
Banragai
Hindubeg-banda
Pashino-banda
Salatanr
Kalo-banda
Chatkarai
Ghwai-banda
Kadkhwar
Alwara
Bachi-kandao
Kohistani-banda
Jalba
Jalba-sar
Charma
Gamchana
Parrai
Gamsar
Sarmai
Cham
Pirkand
Kabalku
Landai
Karinuna
Matta
Sami
Sekhdarra
Kadiar
Kand
Kharkai
Kanati
Chopal
Serai
Shargartan
Roringar
Awarai
Goal
Milkatli
Narosai
Koga
Rakya
Biha
Nalkot
Pushtunai
Tangar
Atia-qala
Lai
0
2
4 km
RIVERS
PEAKS
PASTURES
PASSES
VILLAGES
Relief (m)
1001-2000
2001-3000
3001-4000
Districts

Map 44. Barwai

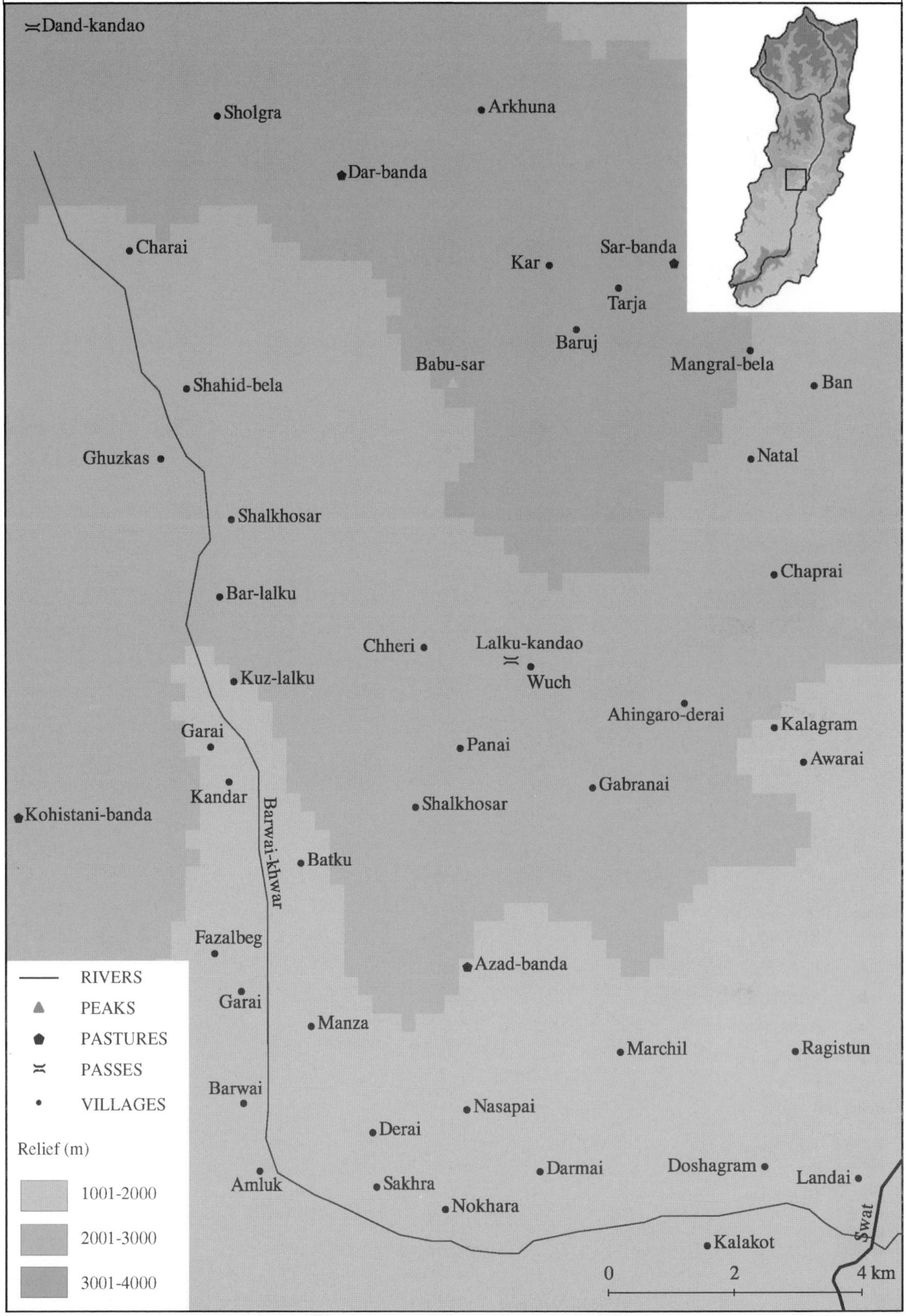
Dand-kandao
Sholgra
Arkhuna
Dar-banda
Charai
Sar-banda
Kar
Tarja
Baruj
Babu-sar
Mangral-bela
Ban
Shahid-bela
Ghuzkas
Natal
Shalkhosar
Chaprai
Bar-lalku
Chheri
Lalku-kandao
Wuch
Kuz-lalku
Ahingaro-derai
Kalagram
Garai
Panai
Awarai
Kandar
Gabranai
Shalkhosar
Kohistani-banda
Barwai-khwar
Batku
Fazalbeg
Azad-banda
Garai
Manza
Marchil
Ragistun
Barwai
Nasapai
Derai
Amluk
Sakhra
Darmai
Doshagram
Landai
Nokhara
Kalakot
Swat
0
2
4 km
RIVERS
PEAKS
PASTURES
PASSES
VILLAGES
Relief (m)
1001-2000
2001-3000
3001-4000

Map 45. Swat 5 – Tirat

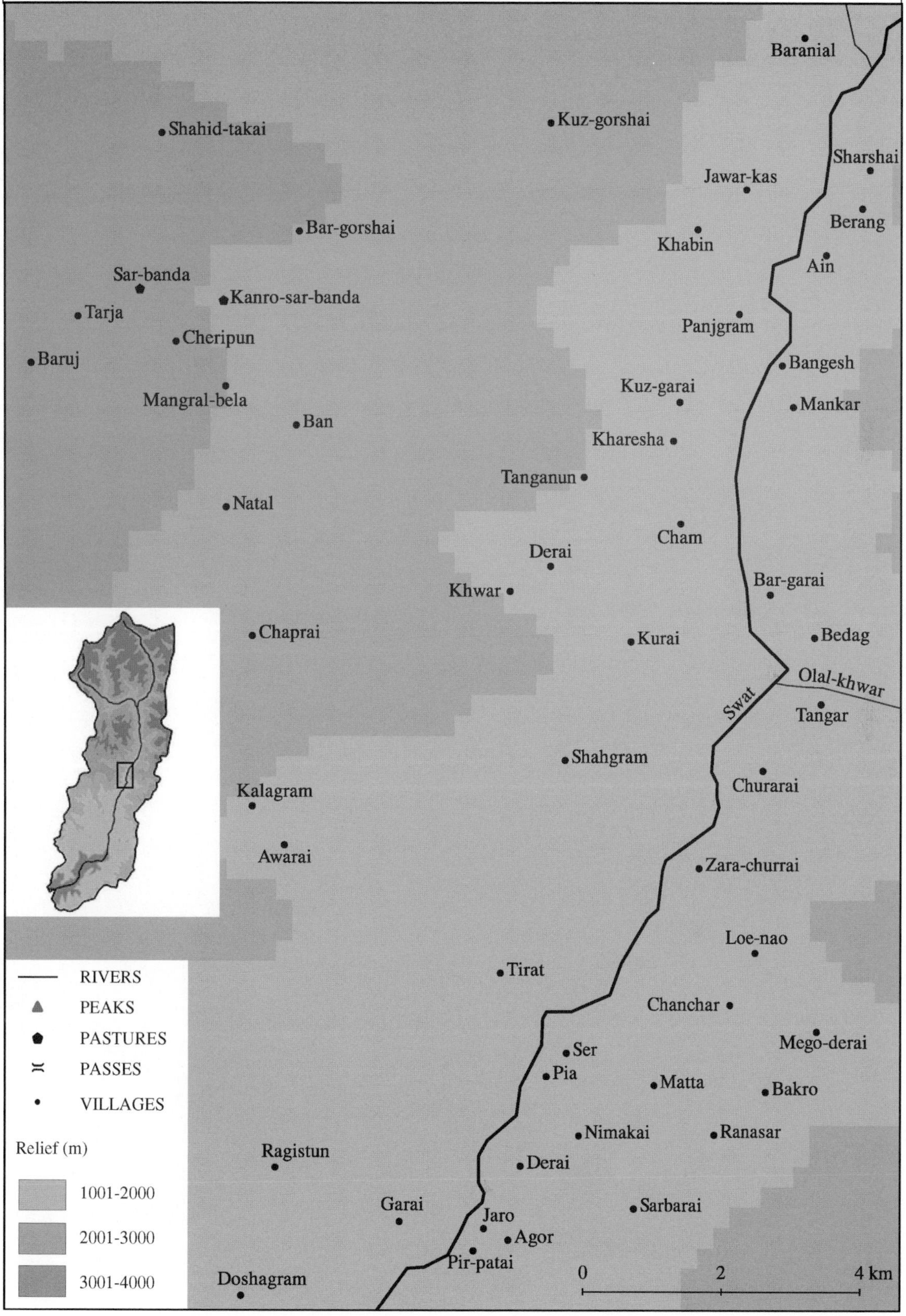
Baranial
Kuz-gorshai
Shahid-takai
Sharshai
Jawar-kas
Berang
Bar-gorshai
Khabin
Ain
Sar-banda
Kanro-sar-banda
Tarja
Panjgram
Cheripun
Baruj
Bangesh
Mangral-bela
Kuz-garai
Mankar
Ban
Kharesha
Tanganun
Natal
Cham
Derai
Bar-garai
Khwar
Chaprai
Kurai
Bedag
Olal-khwar
Swat
Tangar
Shahgram
Churarai
Kalagram
Awarai
Zara-churrai
Loe-nao
Tirat
Chanchar
Mego-derai
Ser
Pia
Matta
Bakro
Nimakai
Ranasar
Ragistun
Derai
Garai
Sarbarai
Jaro
Agor
Pir-patai
Doshagram
0
2
4 km
RIVERS
PEAKS
PASTURES
PASSES
VILLAGES
Relief (m)
1001-2000
2001-3000
3001-4000

Map 46. Shanku-Nali-Olal

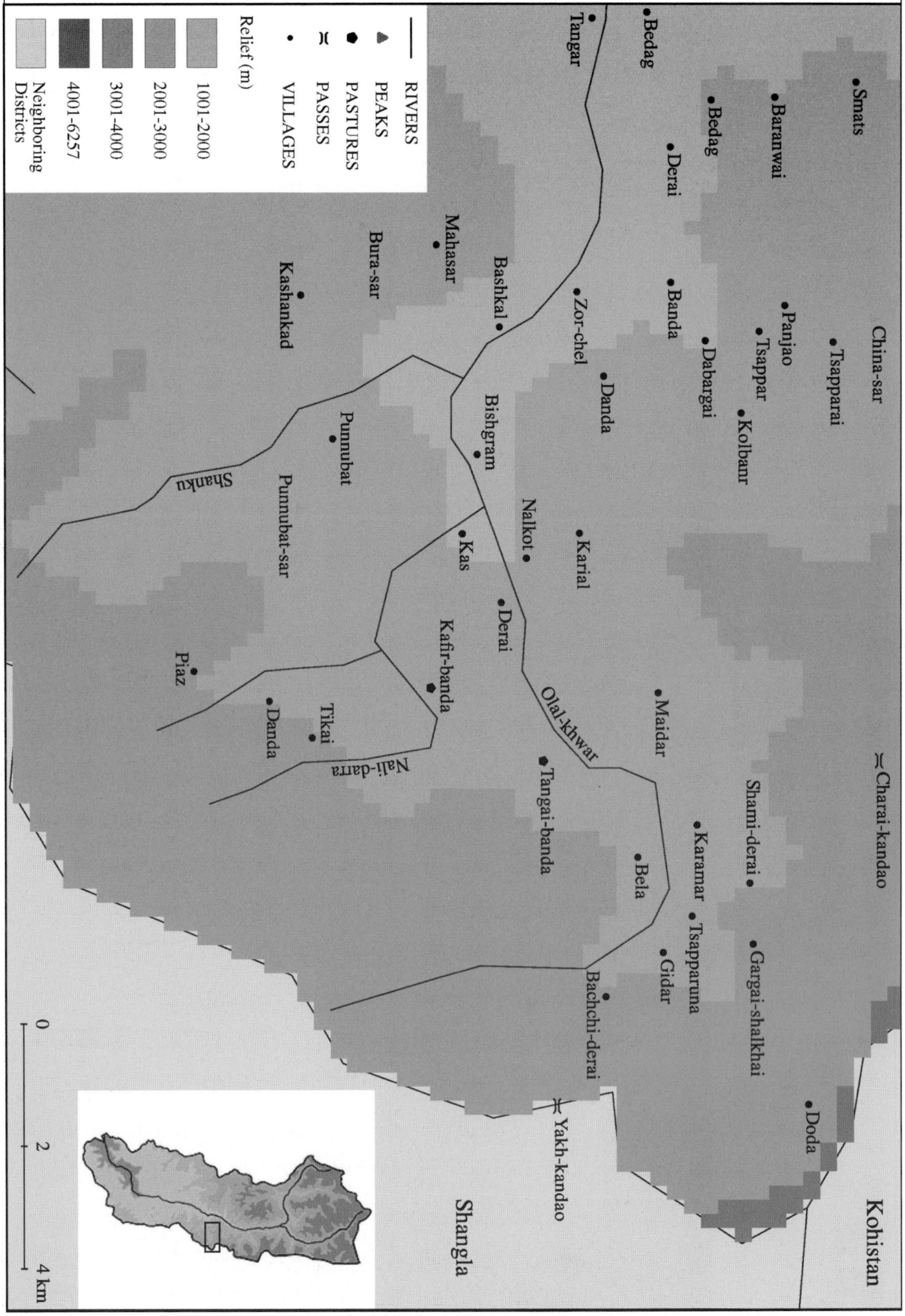
RIVERS
PEAKS
PASTURES
PASSES
VILLAGES
Relief (m)
1001-2000
2001-3000
3001-4000
4001-6257
Neighboring Districts
Smats
Baranwai
Bedag
Bedag
Tangar
Derai
China-sar
Tsapparai
Panjao
Tsappar
Dabargai
Banda
Kolbanr
Zor-chel
Danda
Bashkal
Mahasar
Bura-sar
Kashankad
Bishgram
Punnubat
Punnubat-sar
Shanku
Nalkot
Karial
Kas
Derai
Kafir-banda
Piaz
Tikai
Danda
Nali-darra
Olal-khwar
Maidar
Tangai-banda
Charai-kandao
Shami-derai
Karamar
Bela
Tsapparuna
Gidar
Gargai-shalkhai
Bachchi-derai
Doda
Yakh-kandao
Kohistan
Shangla
0
2
4 km

Map 47. Baral

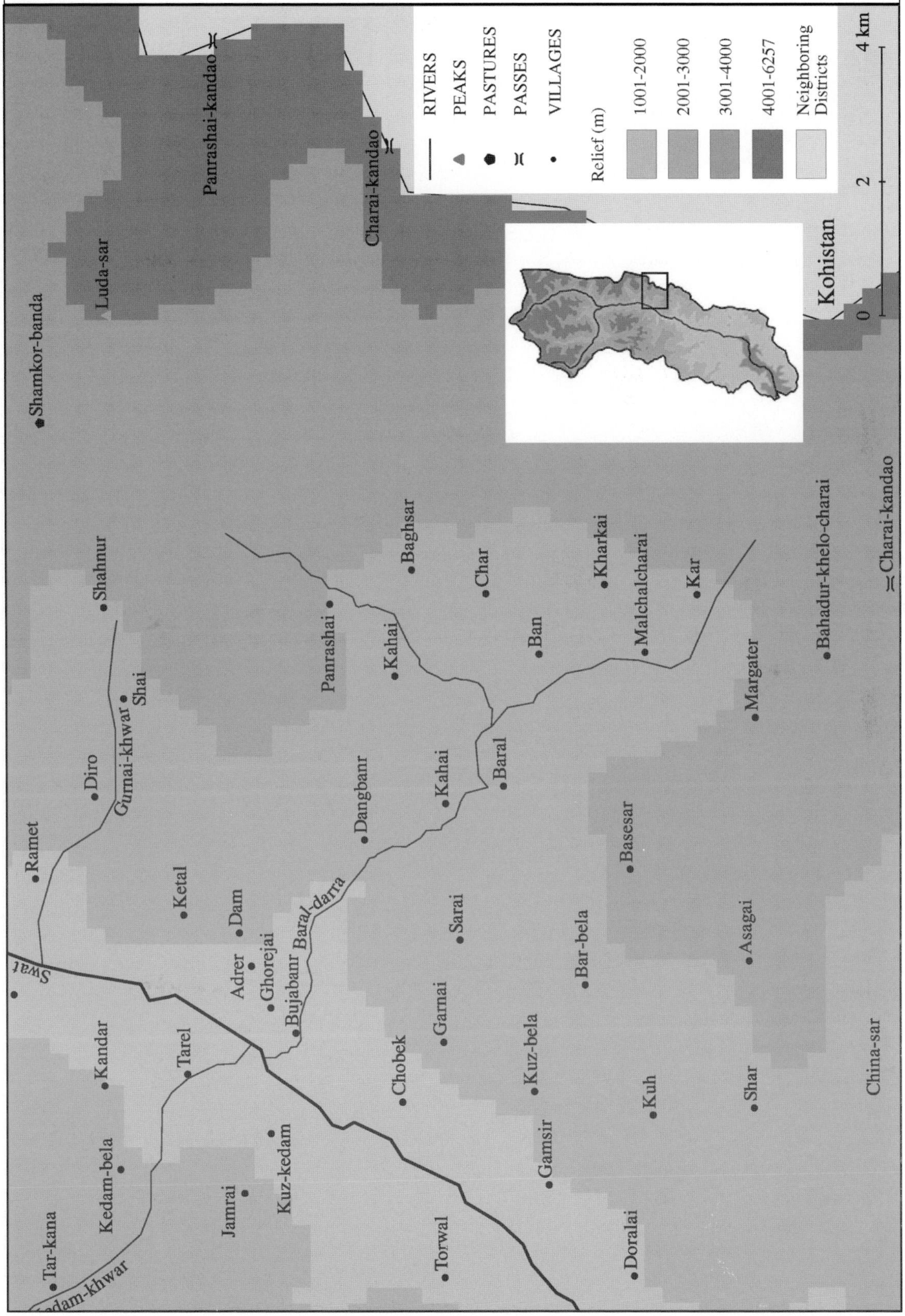
RIVERS
PEAKS
PASTURES
PASSES
VILLAGES
Relief (m)
1001-2000
2001-3000
3001-4000
4001-6257
Neighboring Districts
0
2
4 km
Kohistan
Shamkor-banda
Luda-sar
Panrashai-kandao
Charai-kandao
Charai-kandao
Bahadur-khelo-charai
Baghsar
Char
Kharkai
Malchalcharai
Kar
Shahnur
Panrashai
Kahai
Ban
Shai
Gurnai-khwar
Diro
Dangbanr
Kahai
Baral
Margater
Ramet
Ketal
Dam
Basesar
Sarai
Baral-darra
Adrer
Ghorejai
Bujabanr
Swat
Bar-bela
Asagai
Kandar
Tarel
Chobek
Garmai
Kuz-bela
China-sar
Kedam-bela
Kuz-kedam
Gamsir
Kuh
Shar
Jamrai
Tar-kana
Kedam-khwar
Torwal
Doralai

Map 48. Daral 1 – Baranial

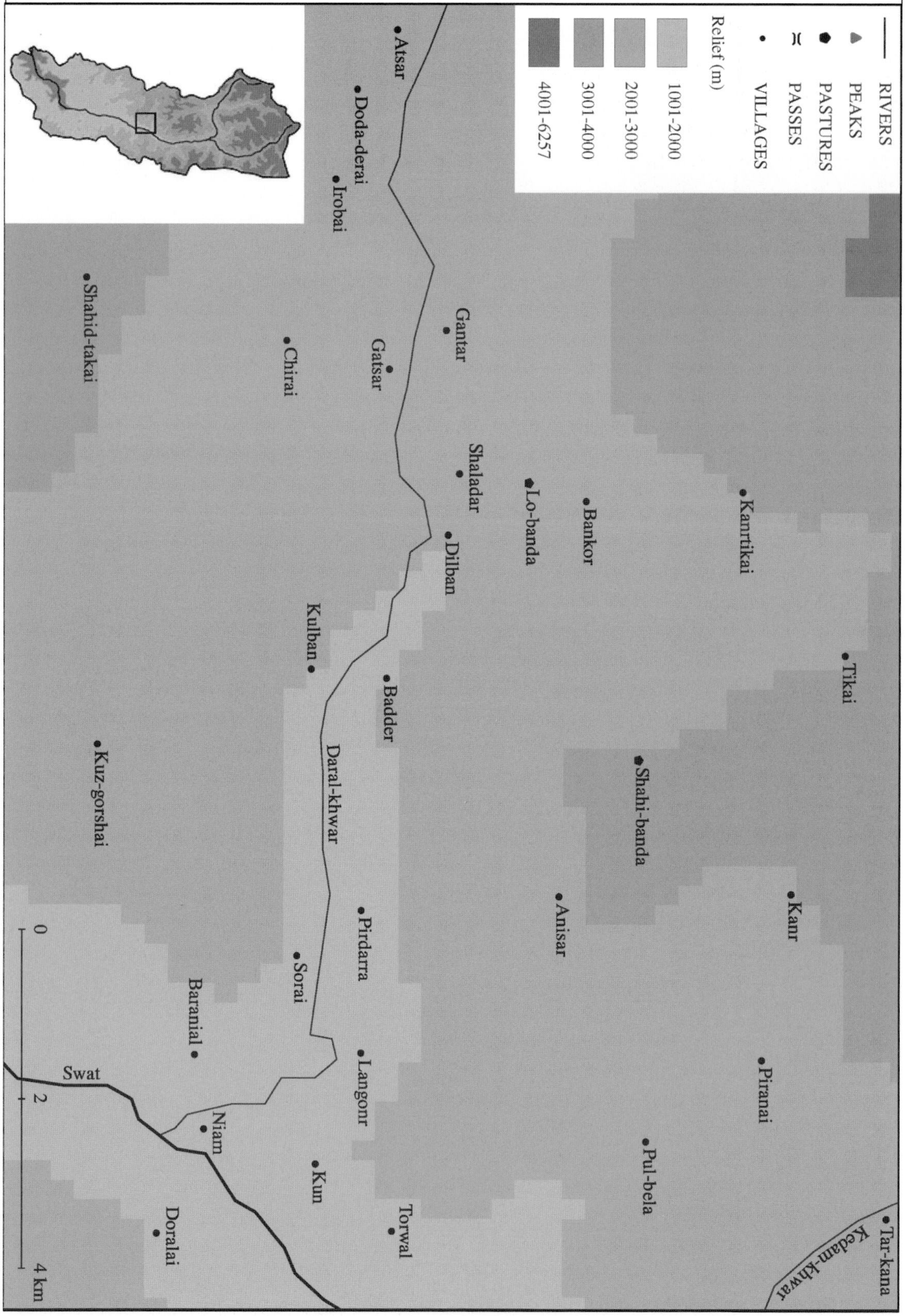

RIVERS
PEAKS
PASTURES
PASSES
VILLAGES
Relief (m)
1001-2000
2001-3000
3001-4000
4001-6257
Atsar
Doda-derai
Irobai
Shahid-takai
Gantar
Gatsar
Chirai
Shaladar
Lo-banda
Bankor
Kanrtikai
Dilban
Kulban
Badder
Tikai
Shahi-banda
Kuz-gorshai
Daral-khwar
Anisar
Kanr
Pirdarra
Sorai
Baranial
Langonr
Piranai
Swat
Niam
Pul-bela
Kun
Torwal
Doralai
Tar-kana
Kedam-khwar
0
2
4 km

Map 49. Daral 2

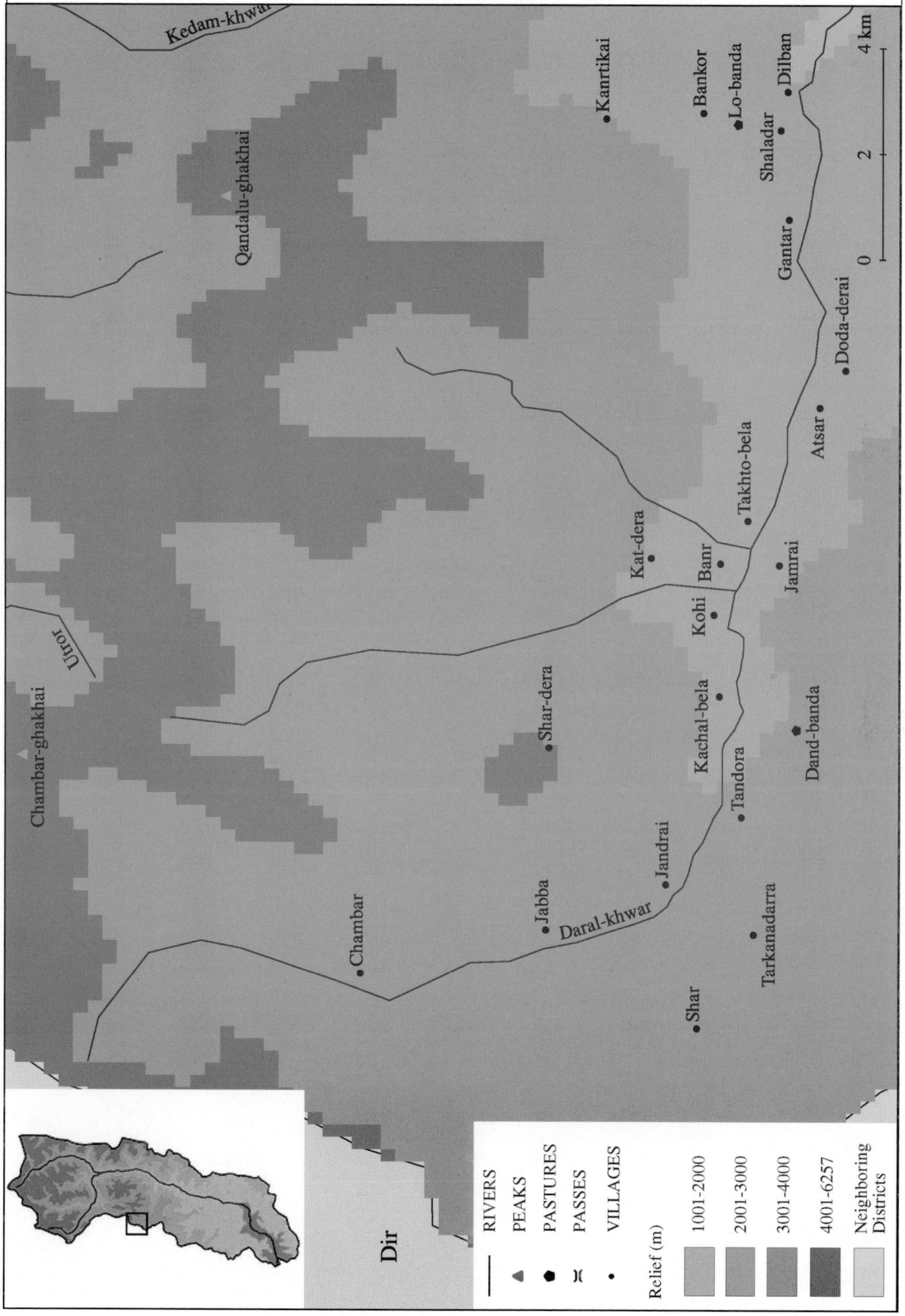

Kedam-khwar
Qandalu-ghakhai
Kanrtikai
Bankor
Lo-banda
Dilban
Shaladar
Gantar
Doda-derai
Atsar
Takhto-bela
Kat-dera
Banr
Jamrai
Kohi
Utror
Chambar-ghakhai
Shar-dera
Kachal-bela
Dand-banda
Tandora
Jandrai
Jabba
Daral-khwar
Chambar
Tarkanadarra
Shar
Dir
0
2
4 km
RIVERS
PEAKS
PASTURES
PASSES
VILLAGES
Relief (m)
1001-2000
2001-3000
3001-4000
4001-6257
Neighboring Districts

Map 50. Kedam

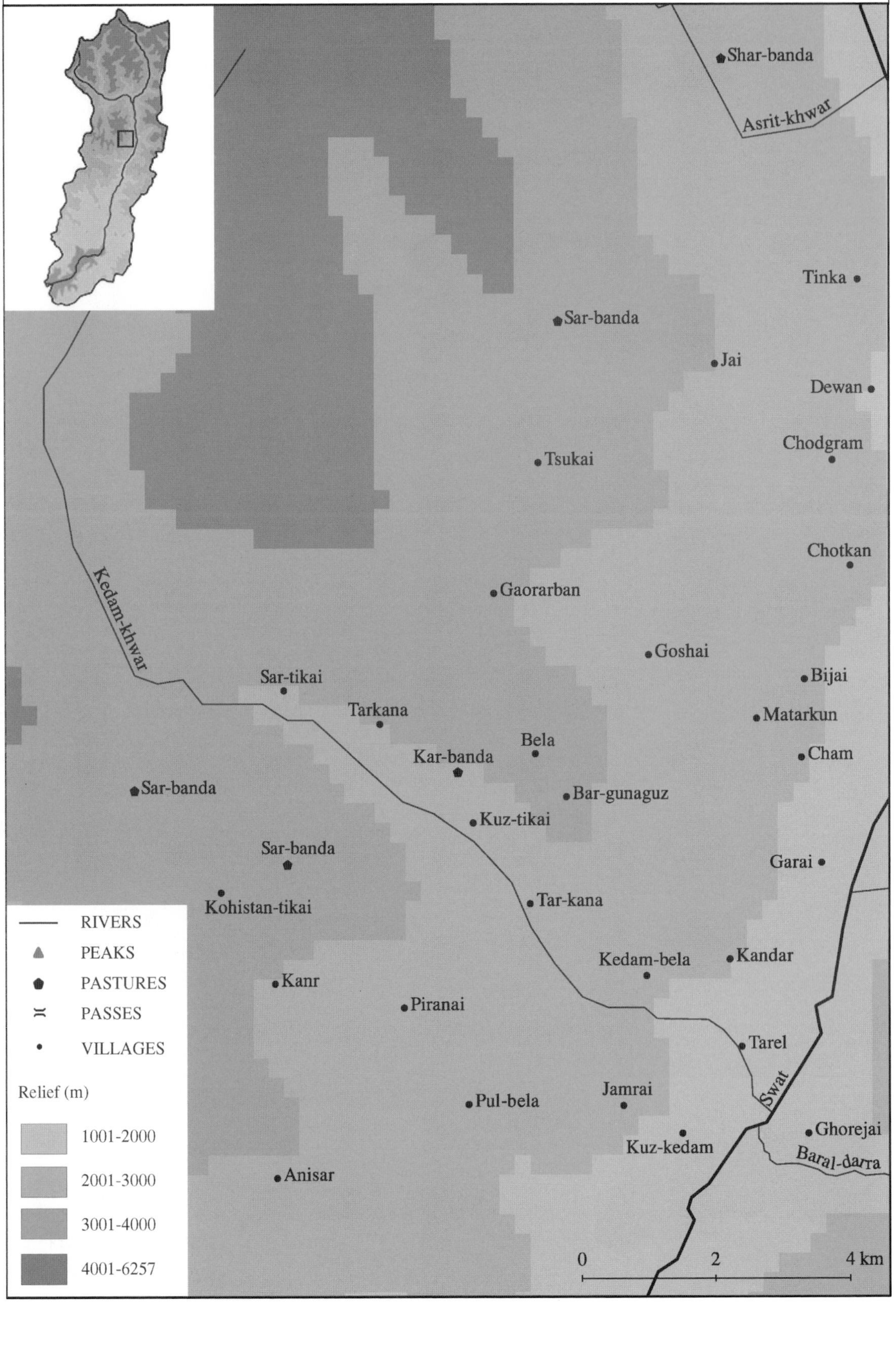

Shar-banda
Asrit-khwar
Tinka
Sar-banda
Jai
Dewan
Chodgram
Tsukai
Chotkan
Gaorarban
Kedam-khwar
Goshai
Bijai
Sar-tikai
Tarkana
Matarkun
Bela
Kar-banda
Cham
Sar-banda
Bar-gunaguz
Kuz-tikai
Sar-banda
Garai
Kohistan-tikai
Tar-kana
RIVERS
PEAKS
PASTURES
PASSES
VILLAGES
Kedam-bela
Kandar
Kanr
Piranai
Tarel
Relief (m)
Jamrai
Pul-bela
Swat
Ghorejai
1001-2000
Kuz-kedam
Baral-darra
2001-3000
Anisar
3001-4000
4001-6257
0
2
4 km

Map 51. Jaba

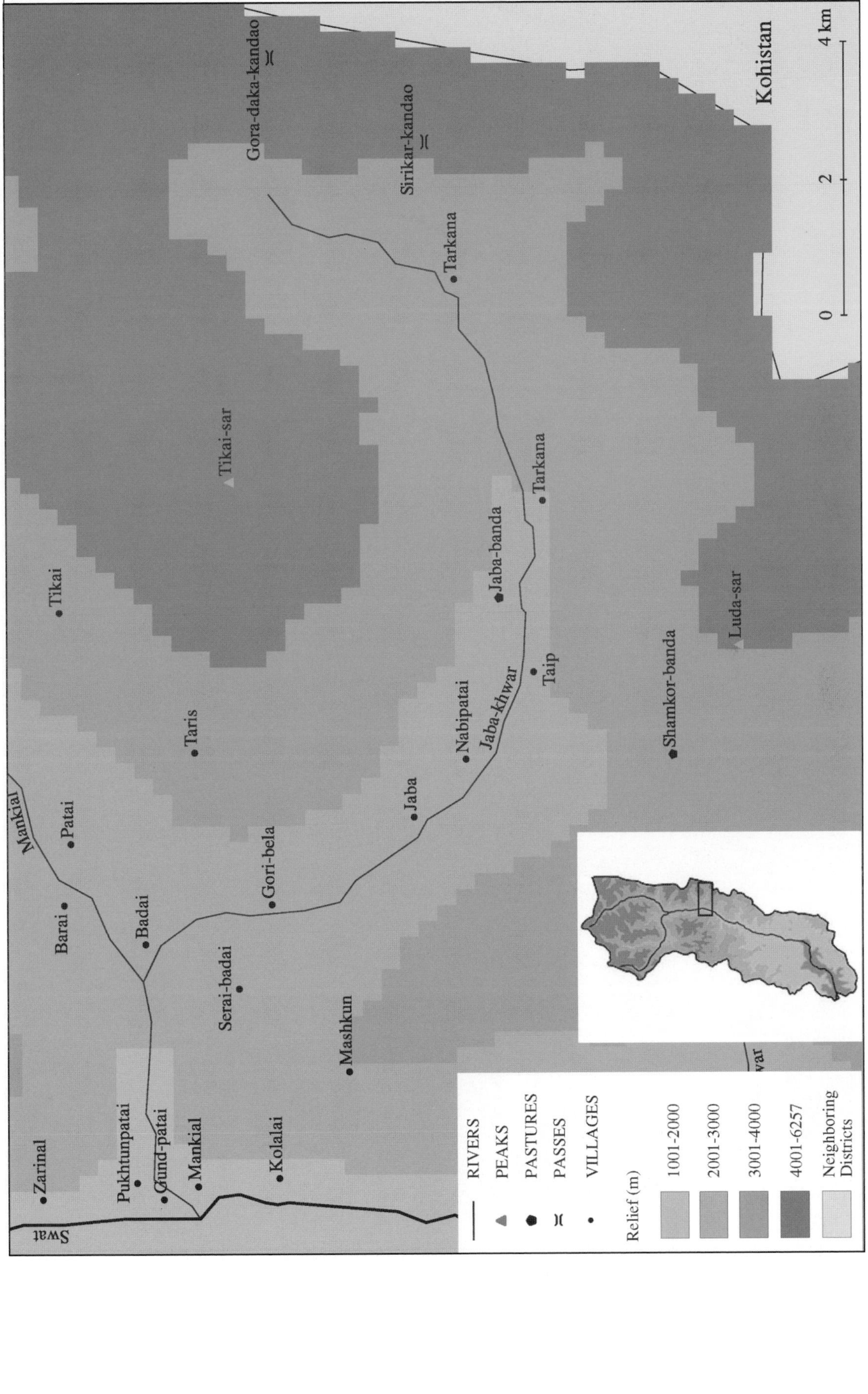

Gora-daka-kandao
Sirikar-kandao
Kohistan
0
2
4 km
Tarkana
Tikai-sar
Tarkana
Jaba-banda
Tikai
Luda-sar
Taip
Shamkor-banda
Taris
Nabipatai
Jaba-khwar
Jaba
Mankial
Patai
Gori-bela
Barai
Badai
Serai-badai
Mashkun
Zarinal
Pukhtunpatai
Gund-patai
Mankial
Kolalai
Swat
RIVERS
PEAKS
PASTURES
PASSES
VILLAGES
Relief (m)
1001-2000
2001-3000
3001-4000
4001-6257
Neighboring Districts

Map 52. Mankial

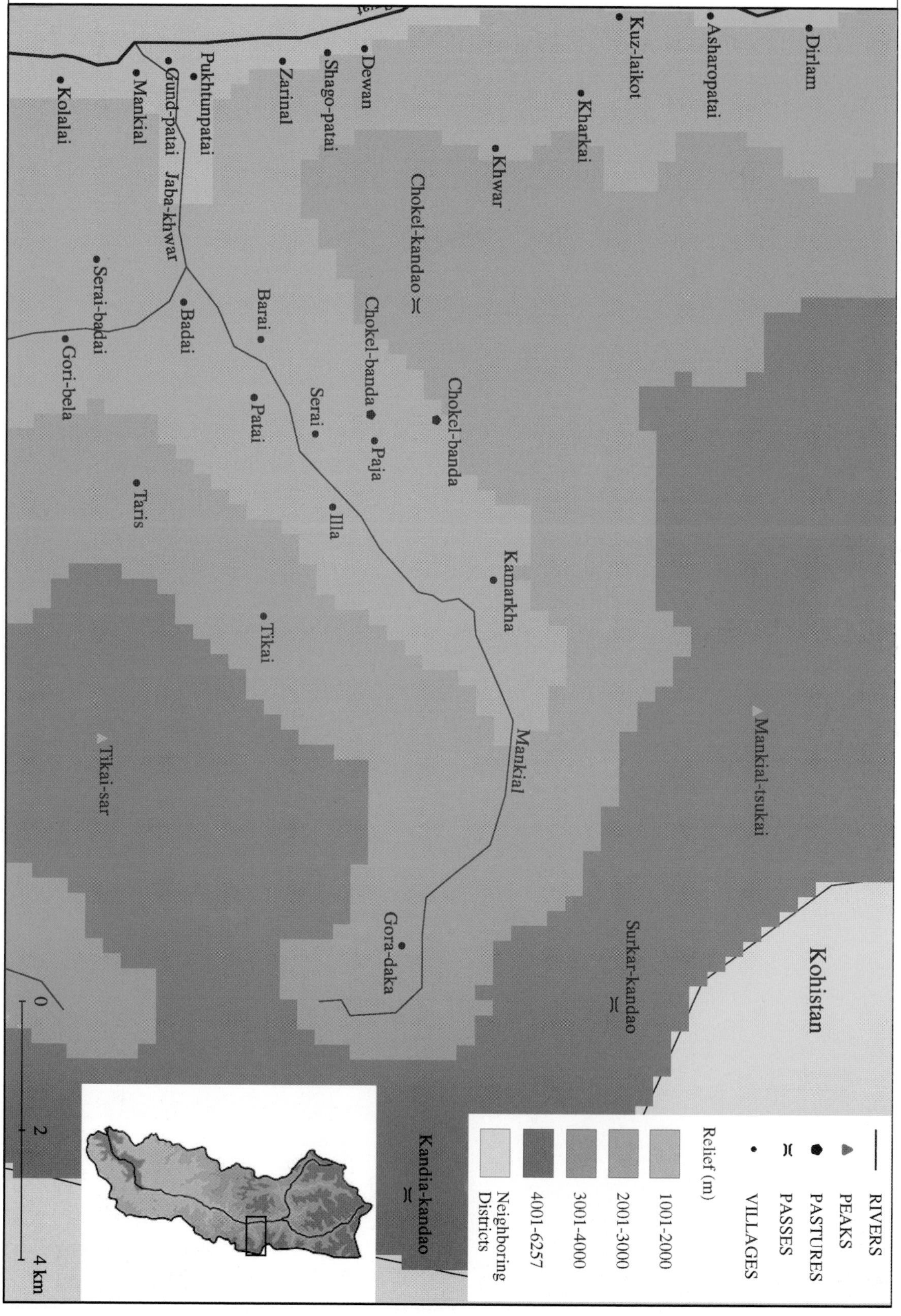

Dirlam
Asharopatai
Kuz-laikot
Kharkai
Khwar
Dewan
Shago-patai
Zarinal
Pukhtunpatai
Gund-patai
Mankial
Kolalai
Jaba-khwar
Chokel-kandao
Serai-badai
Badai
Barai
Chokel-banda
Chokel-banda
Serai
Patai
Paja
Gori-bela
Taris
Illa
Kamarkha
Tikai
Mankial
Mankial-tsukai
Tikai-sar
Gora-daka
Surkar-kandao
Kohistan
Kandia-kandao
RIVERS
PEAKS
PASTURES
PASSES
VILLAGES
Relief (m)
1001-2000
2001-3000
3001-4000
4001-6257
Neighboring Districts
0
2
4 km

Map 53. Asrit

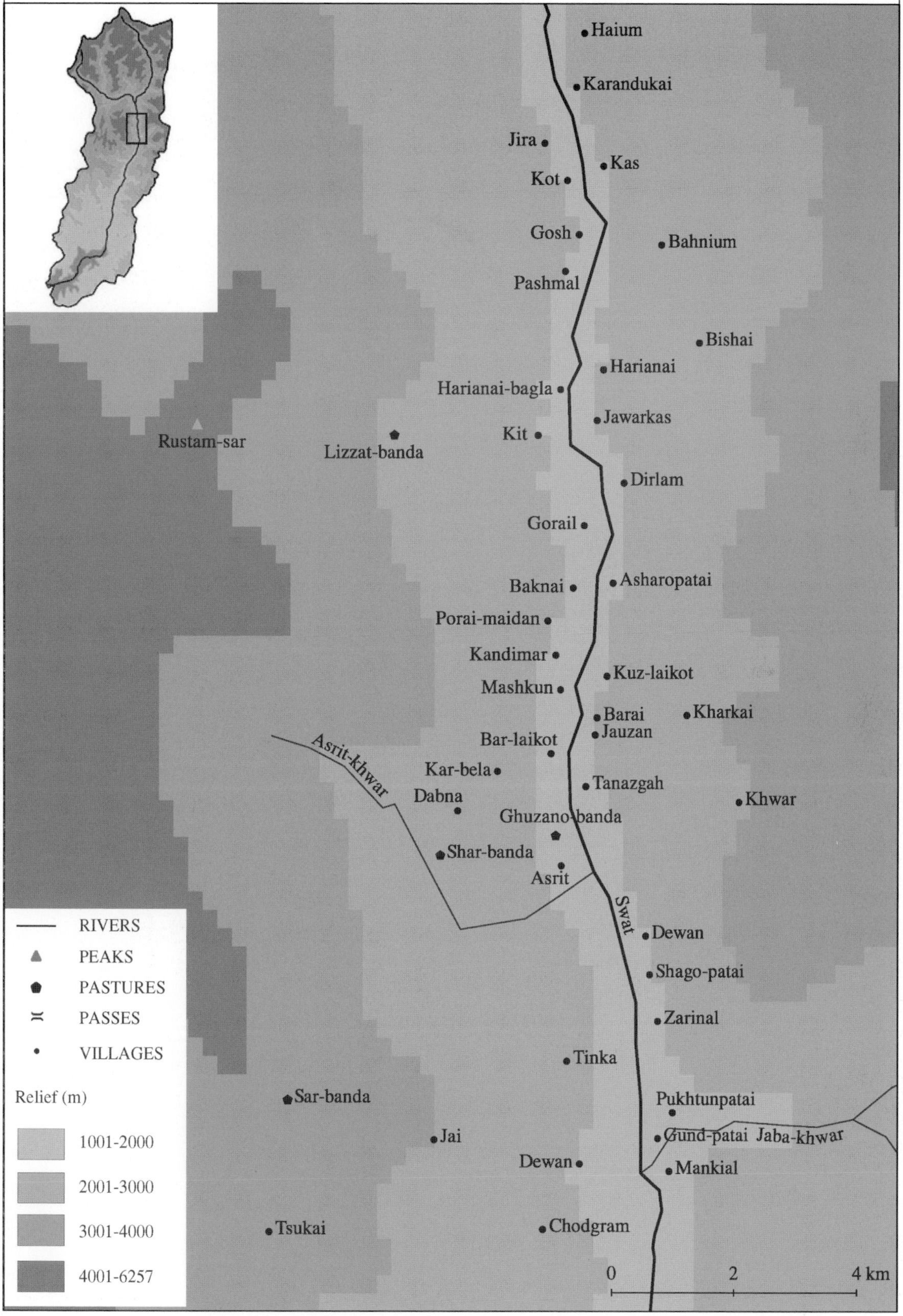

Haium
Karandukai
Jira
Kas
Kot
Gosh
Bahnium
Pashmal
Bishai
Harianai
Harianai-bagla
Jawarkas
Rustam-sar
Lizzat-banda
Kit
Dirlam
Gorail
Baknai
Asharopatai
Porai-maidan
Kandimar
Kuz-laikot
Mashkun
Barai
Kharkai
Jauzan
Bar-laikot
Asrit-khwar
Kar-bela
Tanazgah
Khwar
Dabna
Ghuzano-banda
Shar-banda
Asrit
Swat
Dewan
Shago-patai
Zarinal
Tinka
Pukhtunpatai
Sar-banda
Gund-patai
Jaba-khwar
Jai
Dewan
Mankial
Tsukai
Chodgram
RIVERS
PEAKS
PASTURES
PASSES
VILLAGES
Relief (m)
1001-2000
2001-3000
3001-4000
4001-6257
0
2
4 km

Map 54. Kalam

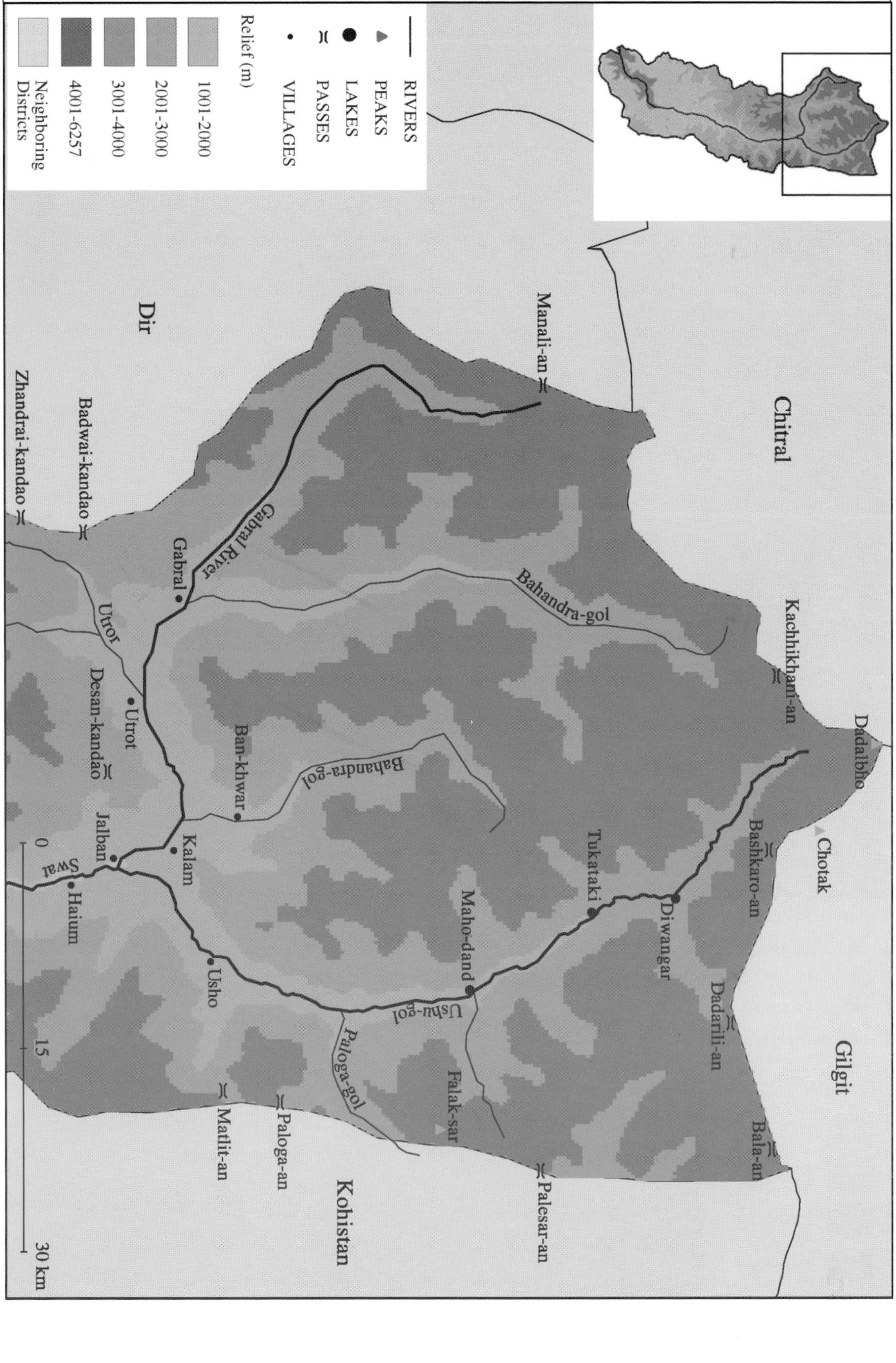

RIVERS
PEAKS
LAKES
PASSES
VILLAGES
Relief (m)
1001-2000
2001-3000
3001-4000
4001-6257
Neighboring Districts
Chitral
Gilgit
Dir
Kohistan
Manali-an
Gabral River
Gabral
Bahandra-gol
Kachhikhani-an
Dadalbho
Chotak
Bashkaro-an
Diwangar
Tukataki
Maho-dand
Ushu-gol
Dadarili-an
Bala-an
Falak-sar
Palesar-an
Paloga-gol
Paloga-an
Matlit-an
Usho
Kalam
Ban-khwar
Utrot
Desan-kandao
Jalban
Swat
Haium
Badwai-kandao
Zhandrai-kandao
0
15
30 km